SOUTHERN STARS

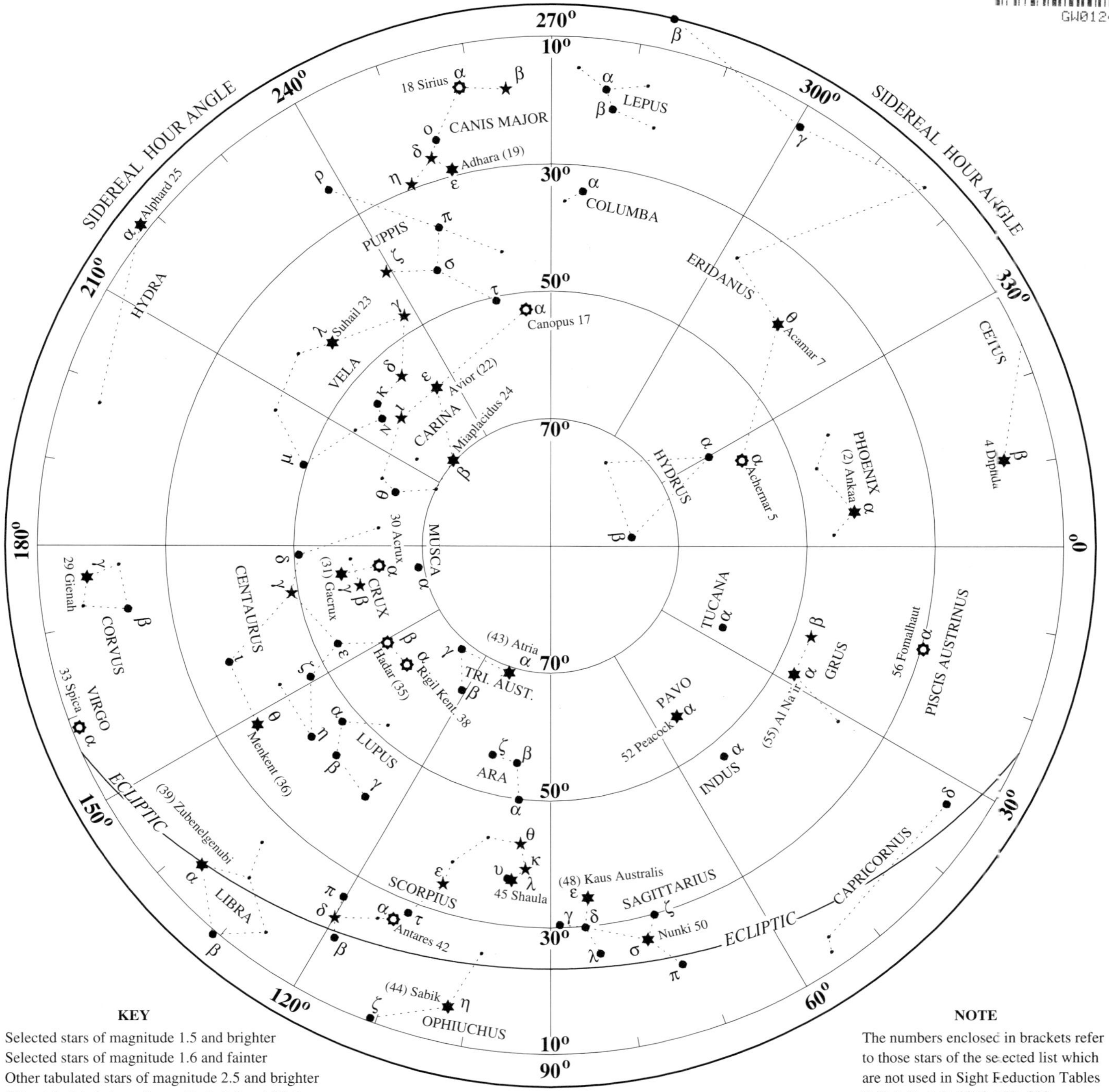

KEY

- Selected stars of magnitude 1.5 and brighter
- Selected stars of magnitude 1.6 and fainter
- Other tabulated stars of magnitude 2.5 and brighter
- Other tabulated stars of magnitude 2.6 and fainter
- Untabulated stars

NOTE

The numbers enclosed in brackets refer to those stars of the selected list which are not used in Sight Reduction Tables H.O. 249, A.P. 3270, N.P. 303.

EQUATORIAL STARS (SHA 180° to 360°)

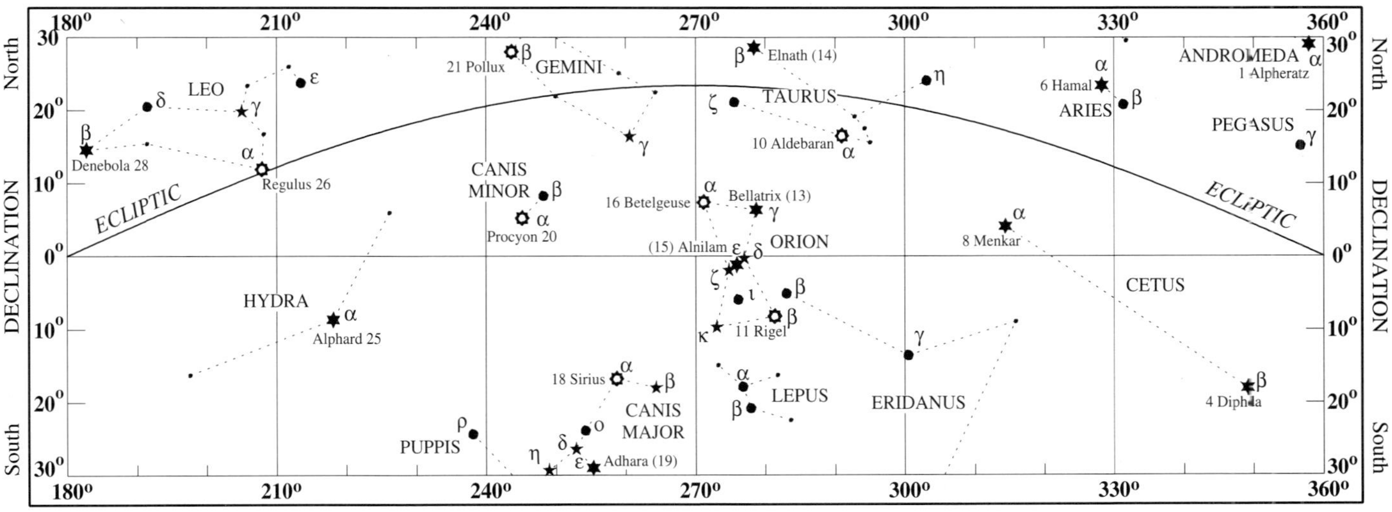

SIDEREAL HOUR ANGLE

NAVIGATIONAL STARS, EPOCH 2005·0

Alphabetical Order					Order of SHA				
Name	No.	Mag. Visual	SHA	Dec	Name	No.	Mag. Visual	SHA	Dec
			° ′	° ′				° ′	° ′
Acamar	7	3·1	315 23	S 40 17	*Markab	57	2·6	13 45	N 15 14
ACHERNAR	5	0·6	335 32	S 57 13	FOMALHAUT	56	1·3	15 31	S 29 36
ACRUX	30	1·1	173 17	S 63 08	*Al Na'ir	55	2·2	27 52	S 46 56
*Adhara	19	1·6	255 18	S 28 59	Enif	54	2·5	33 54	N 9 54
ALDEBARAN	10	1·1	290 57	N 16 31	DENEB	53	1·3	49 36	N 45 18
Alioth	32	1·7	166 26	N 55 56	Peacock	52	2·1	53 29	S 56 43
Alkaid	34	1·9	153 04	N 49 17	ALTAIR	51	0·9	62 15	N 8 53
*Al Na'ir	55	2·2	27 52	S 46 56	Nunki	50	2·1	76 06	S 26 17
*Alnilam	15	1·8	275 53	S 1 12	VEGA	49	0·1	80 43	N 38 47
Alphard	25	2·2	218 03	S 8 41	*Kaus Australis	48	2·0	83 52	S 34 23
Alphecca	41	2·3	126 17	N 26 42	*Eltanin	47	2·4	90 49	N 51 29
Alpheratz	1	2·2	357 50	N 29 07	Rasalhague	46	2·1	96 12	N 12 33
ALTAIR	51	0·9	62 15	N 8 53	Shaula	45	1·7	96 31	S 37 06
*Ankaa	2	2·4	353 22	S 42 17	*Sabik	44	2·6	102 20	S 15 44
ANTARES	42	1·2	112 34	S 26 27	*Atria	43	1·9	107 42	S 69 02
ARCTURUS	37	0·2	146 02	N 19 09	ANTARES	42	1·2	112 34	S 26 27
*Atria	43	1·9	107 42	S 69 02	Alphecca	41	2·3	126 17	N 26 42
*Avior	22	1·7	234 21	S 59 32	*Zubenelgenubi	39	2·9	137 13	S 16 04
*Bellatrix	13	1·7	278 39	N 6 21	Kochab	40	2·2	137 20	N 74 08
BETELGEUSE	16	0·1–1·2	271 08	N 7 24	RIGIL KENT.	38	0·1	140 01	S 60 51
CANOPUS	17	−0·9	263 59	S 52 42	ARCTURUS	37	0·2	146 02	N 19 09
CAPELLA	12	0·2	280 44	N 46 00	*Menkent	36	2·3	148 15	S 36 24
DENEB	53	1·3	49 36	N 45 18	*HADAR	35	0·9	148 57	S 60 24
Denebola	28	2·2	182 40	N 14 33	Alkaid	34	1·9	153 04	N 49 17
Diphda	4	2·2	349 02	S 17 58	SPICA	33	1·2	158 38	S 11 11
Dubhe	27	2·0	194 00	N 61 43	Alioth	32	1·7	166 26	N 55 56
*Elnath	14	1·8	278 21	N 28 37	*Gacrux	31	1·6	172 08	S 57 08
*Eltanin	47	2·4	90 49	N 51 29	ACRUX	30	1·1	173 17	S 63 08
Enif	54	2·5	33 54	N 9 54	Gienah	29	2·8	175 59	S 17 34
FOMALHAUT	56	1·3	15 31	S 29 36	Denebola	28	2·2	182 40	N 14 33
*Gacrux	31	1·6	172 08	S 57 08	Dubhe	27	2·0	194 00	N 61 43
Gienah	29	2·8	175 59	S 17 34	REGULUS	26	1·3	207 50	N 11 57
*HADAR	35	0·9	148 57	S 60 24	Alphard	25	2·2	218 03	S 8 41
Hamal	6	2·2	328 08	N 23 29	Miaplacidus	24	1·8	221 41	S 69 44
*Kaus Australis	48	2·0	83 52	S 34 23	Suhail	23	2·2	222 57	S 43 27
Kochab	40	2·2	137 20	N 74 08	*Avior	22	1·7	234 21	S 59 32
*Markab	57	2·6	13 45	N 15 14	POLLUX	21	1·2	243 36	N 28 01
Menkar	8	2·8	314 22	N 4 07	PROCYON	20	0·5	245 07	N 5 13
*Menkent	36	2·3	148 15	S 36 24	*Adhara	19	1·6	255 18	S 28 59
Miaplacidus	24	1·8	221 41	S 69 44	SIRIUS	18	−1·6	258 40	S 16 43
Mirfak	9	1·9	308 50	N 49 53	CANOPUS	17	−0·9	263 59	S 52 42
Nunki	50	2·1	76 06	S 26 17	BETELGEUSE	16	0·1–1·2	271 08	N 7 24
Peacock	52	2·1	53 29	S 56 43	*Alnilam	15	1·8	275 53	S 1 12
POLLUX	21	1·2	243 36	N 28 01	*Elnath	14	1·8	278 21	N 28 37
PROCYON	20	0·5	245 07	N 5 13	*Bellatrix	13	1·7	278 39	N 6 21
Rasalhague	46	2·1	96 12	N 12 33	CAPELLA	12	0·2	280 44	N 46 00
REGULUS	26	1·3	207 50	N 11 57	RIGEL	11	0·3	281 18	S 8 12
RIGEL	11	0·3	281 18	S 8 12	ALDEBARAN	10	1·1	290 57	N 16 31
RIGIL KENT.	38	0·1	140 01	S 60 51	Mirfak	9	1·9	308 50	N 49 53
*Sabik	44	2·6	102 20	S 15 44	Menkar	8	2·8	314 22	N 4 07
Schedar	3	2·5	349 48	N 56 34	Acamar	7	3·1	315 23	S 40 17
Shaula	45	1·7	96 31	S 37 06	Hamal	6	2·2	328 08	N 23 29
SIRIUS	18	−1·6	258 40	S 16 43	ACHERNAR	5	0·6	335 32	S 57 13
SPICA	33	1·2	158 38	S 11 11	Diphda	4	2·2	349 02	S 17 58
Suhail	23	2·2	222 57	S 43 27	Schedar	3	2·5	349 48	N 56 34
VEGA	49	0·1	80 43	N 38 47	*Ankaa	2	2·4	353 22	S 42 17
*Zubenelgenubi	39	2·9	137 13	S 16 04	Alpheratz	1	2·2	357 50	N 29 07

The star numbers and names are the same as in *The Nautical Almanac*.

* Not in the tabular pages of Volume **1**.

AP 3270 / NP 303

Rapid
Sight Reduction Tables for Navigation

VOLUME 3

Latitudes 39°–89°

Declinations 0°–29°

LONDON: TSO

UNITED KINGDOM EDITION

TSO
St Crispins, Duke Street, Norwich NR3 1PD
Fourth impression 2006

ISBN 978 0 11 887557 8
ISBN 0 11 887557 4

Published by TSO (The Stationery Office) and available from:

Online
www.tsoshop.co.uk

Mail, Telephone, Fax & E-mail
TSO
PO Box 29, Norwich, NR3 1GN
Telephone orders/General enquiries 0870 600 5522
Fax orders 0870 600 5533
E-mail: customer.services@tso.co.uk
Textphone 0870 240 3701

TSO Shops
123 Kingsway, London WC2B 6PQ
020 7242 6393 Fax 020 7242 6394
68-69 Bull Street, Birmingham B4 6AD
0121 236 9696 Fax 0121 236 9699
9-21 Princess Street, Manchester M60 8AS
0161 834 7201 Fax 0161 833 0634
16 Arthur Street, Belfast BT1 4GD
028 9023 8451 Fax 028 9023 5401
18-19 High Street, Cardiff CF10 1PT
029 2039 5548 Fax 029 2038 4347
71 Lothian Road, Edinburgh EH3 9AZ
0870 606 5566 Fax 0870 606 5588

TSO Accredited Agents
(see Yellow Pages)

and through good booksellers

UNITED STATES EDITION

For sale by
authorized sales agents of the
Defence Mapping Agency
Bethesda, MD 20816-5003

Printed in the United Kingdom for The Stationery Office
ID: 5392541 07/06 C5 9385 26395

CONTENTS

DEDICATION

This book is dedicated to The Royal Greenwich Observatory (RGO). It is poignant to note that the RGO was originally established in 1675 in order to "... find out the so-much-desired longitude of places for the perfecting of the art of navigation".

ACKNOWLEDGEMENTS

I am most grateful to Dr. B.D. Yallop for his continuing help and interest in preparing this edition.

I am grateful to Lieutenant Commander Royal Navy B. Norman of the Royal Navy School of Navigation and Lieutenant Commander Royal Navy A. Peacock of the Fleet Staff Authors Group, for all their advice.

I would also like to thank the members of HMNAO, in particular S.A. Bell and D.B. Taylor, and the Nautical Almanac Office of the U.S. Naval Observatory for their valuable support and assistance. Thanks are also due to J. Magraw.

Technical Support

HMNAO welcomes your comments, criticisms, suggestions, and reports of any problems that you encounter when using this book. We regret that we cannot respond directly to any telephone inquiries or correspondence sent by e-mail or FAX. We appreciate your understanding and cooperation in this regard.

Please send all correspondence concerning AP 3270 to HM Nautical Almanac Office at the address given on the following page.

C.Y. Hohenkerk
HM Nautical Almanac Office
www.nao.rl.ac.uk

2002 August

FOREWORD

Rapid Sight Reduction Tables for Navigation consist of three volumes of comprehensive tables of altitude and azimuth designed for the rapid reduction of astronomical sights. These volumes were originally entitled *Sight Reduction Tables for Air Navigation*. The modified title and change in emphasis of the explanation, examples and auxiliary tables are due to their popularity for marine navigation. However, the United States edition remains unchanged in title and content.

The present volume (Volume **3**) contains tables for integral degrees of declination, for latitudes 39°–89° north and south, and provides for sights of the Sun, Moon and planets; Volume **2** contains similar tables for latitude 0°–40°. These tables are permanent. Volume **1** contains tables for selected stars for all latitudes, calculated for a specific epoch (2005·0 in the current edition); it is intended for use for about five years, when it will be replaced by a new edition based on a later epoch.

The time argument in the examples is denoted by UT (Universal Time). It is also known as GMT (Greenwich Mean Time).

Rapid Sight Reduction Tables for Navigation are published as AP 3270 or NP 303 in the UK, and as Pub. No. 249 *Sight Reduction Tables for Air Navigation* in the USA. HM Nautical Almanac Office, the Defence Mapping Agency, and the Nautical Almanac Office of the US Naval Observatory, have co-operated in the design and preparation of these tables. The explanatory pages and auxiliary tables of the UK edition of AP 3270 (NP 303) Volume **3** have been typeset in TEX by HM Nautical Almanac Office.

RICHARD HOLDAWAY
Director

Space Science and Technology Department
Rutherford Appleton Laboratory
Chilton, Didcot, OX110QX
United Kingdom

1. INTRODUCTION

These tables, designated as Volume **3** of the three-volume series of AP 3270 / NP 303, *Rapid Sight Reduction Tables for Navigation*, together with the similar Volume 2, supplement Volume **1** containing tabulations for the stars. They together contain values of the altitude (H_c) and azimuth angle (Z) for integral degrees of declination from 29° north to 29° south, for the complete range of latitudes and for all hour angles at which the zenith distance is less than 95° (97° between latitudes 70° and the poles); provision is made for interpolation for declination. As in Volume **1**, no correction for refraction has been included in the tabulated altitudes; azimuth angle is given in contrast to the true azimuth for the selected stars. Volume **2** caters for latitudes 0°–40° and Volume **3** for latitudes 39°–89°; they are divided purely for convenience in handling, and are otherwise similar in all aspects.

The emphasis of the explanation and examples of this edition has been directed towards marine navigation, the use of *The Nautical Almanac* and the reduction of sights for the Sun, Moon, planets, and stars with declinations less than 30° north or south. There are also tables for dip, refraction, and the conversion of arc to time. There is a sight reduction form and the tables of corrections for movement of the vessel, and movement of the body when special reduction techniques are used. In addition, there are star charts to assist with identification and also a list of the positions (2005·0) of the 57 navigational stars.

For observations of the Sun, it is possible to use this volume without reference to an almanac. The GHA and declination of the Sun is tabulated, to an accuracy of about 1'.6, for 2001 – 2036, together with the relevant interpolation tables. The altitude correction table for the Sun, which combines semi-diameter, parallax and refraction, is similar to that published in *The Nautical Almanac* has also been included.

The main tables may be used to calculate an observed position to an accuracy of about 0·5 nautical miles, where an observed position is the point on the earth's surface where two or more position lines intersect. *The Nautical Almanac* and the six volume series *Sight Reduction Tables for Marine Navigation* (NP 401) can produce an observed position to between 0·2 and 0·3 nautical miles. The concise sight reduction tables in *The Nautical Almanac* produce much less accurate observed positions at 1·0 nautical mile, and in certain cases this increases to 2·0 nautical miles. On the other hand the software NavPac (or AstroNavPC) will calculate an observed position to an accuracy of 0·15 nautical miles. These errors are quoted from *The Admiralty Manual of Navigation*, volume 2 (BR 45(2)), produced by the Fleet Staff Authors Group.

This introduction and examples are aimed at illustrating how to use this volume for marine navigation. It is not a text book on astro-navigation. AP 3270 was originally designed for use in conjunction with *The Air Almanac* for air navigation. The format of the main tabulations of altitude and azimuth angle remain unchanged. It is only the explanation, examples and some of the auxiliary tables that have been updated for use by marine navigators. Air navigators use bubble sextants, fly high above the ground and at speed causing large changes in position in a very short time. Thus, those tables dealing with speed, Coriolis forces, dome refraction, and refraction at height have been removed or modified. Those who require these tables, which do not depend on time, should check our web site (www.nao.rl.ac.uk) where the relevant auxiliary tables may be downloaded.

2. THE ALTITUDE & AZIMUTH TABLES

These tables tabulate the computed altitude (H_c), the difference, *d*, between H_c and that for the next higher declination, and azimuth angle (Z). The tables are entered with three arguments, *latitude*, *declination* and *local hour angle* of the body. The resulting H_c and *d* are tabulated to the nearest minute of arc, while azimuth angle is given to the nearest degree. The rules for converting Z to Z_n (true azimuth) are given on each page.

The compact arrangement reflects the desire to include the maximum amount of data in the smallest practicable space. The range of declination, and the extension to negative altitudes, explains the necessity for arranging the tables across the page.

Tabulations are given in two volumes (Volumes **2** and **3**) for every whole degree of *latitude* from 0° to 89°; there are four pages for latitude 0°, six pages for latitudes 1° to 47°, eight pages for latitudes 48° to 69°, four pages for latitudes 70° to 74° and six pages for latitudes 75° to 89°. Volume **2** covers latitudes 39°–89° and Volume **3** latitudes 0°–40°.

The full range of *declination* is divided up into two groups of 15 values: 0° to 14° and 15° to 29°. One or other of these groups is the horizontal argument on every page. Within the section (of 4, 6 or 8 pages) corresponding to each degree of latitude, tabulations (of 2, 3 or 4 pages) for the first group of declinations, 0° to 14°, are given first; when completed they are followed by precisely similar tabulations for the second group of declinations, 15° to 29°.

The vertical argument on each page is the *local hour angle of the body* (LHA) observed. Use an almanac, such as *The Nautical Almanac* to form the LHA in the usual way (see below). The interval for LHA is 1° for latitudes 0° to 69°, but this is increased to 2° for latitudes 70° to 89°. Within each sub-section of latitude and declination group, tabulations are first given for declinations of the *same* name as the latitude with LHA *increasing* on the left-hand side from 0° to 180°, or to some smaller limit depending on the altitude; while on the right-hand side the argument decreases from 360° to 180° (or some larger limit). Tabulations for declinations of the *contrary* name to the latitude follow after a break, and the order of LHA is reversed; the left-hand side *decreases* from 180°, or generally from some smaller limit, to 0°, while the right-hand argument increases from 180° (or some larger limit).

The tabulations for *contrary* name are seen to be arranged in the reverse way from those for the *same* name; working backwards (upwards instead of downwards) from the end of the sub-section, they appear precisely as those for the *same* name when working forwards (downwards) in the normal way.

Values of LHA between 0° and 180° are always found on the left; values between 180° and 360° are always on the right. The LHA of the body is calculated from the following formula

$$\text{LHA} = \text{GHA} \begin{matrix} -\text{ west} \\ +\text{ east} \end{matrix} \text{ longitude}$$

where the GHA of the body is taken in the usual way from an almanac such as *The Nautical Almanac*, for the actual time (UT) of observation.

2.1 Interpolation for Declination

The main tables tabulate the altitude and azimuth angle for whole degrees of declination only. However, the declination of the observed body will have a value of degrees (Dec°) and minutes of arc (Dec′). Table **5** — Correction to Tabulated Altitude for Minutes of Declination (page 348), gives the change in altitude due to the fact that the main tables use only whole degrees of declination.

This table is entered with the difference *d* (tabulated with the altitude), between H_C and that for the next higher declination as the horizontal argument, and the minutes of declination (Dec′) as the vertical argument. If *d* or the minutes of declination are zero then there is no correction. The correction extracted from the table must be applied to tabulated altitude H_C in the correct *algebraic* manner. You may easily determine whether the correction is to be added or subtracted by inspecting neighbouring columns to see whether the altitude increases or decreases with declination.

3. AUXILIARY TABLES, STAR CHARTS, PLOTS AND THE SUN

This section describes the various auxiliary tables and charts that are included in this volume.

3.1 Star Charts

There are four charts that show the constellations and the relative positions and magnitudes of the 173 navigational stars that are published in *The Nautical Almanac*. This includes the 57 stars that are printed on page ii. They may be identified on the chart by name and number. Those with their number enclosed in brackets are not used in Volume **1**. A few other stars are included to make the constellation patterns recognizable.

The two polar charts, for the northern and southern stars, are centered on their respective poles with declinations from about 10° to the pole. The two equatorial charts are for the stars with declinations within 30° of the equator, and sidereal hour angle (SHA) from 0° to 180°, and from 180° to 360°. The ecliptic, the apparent path of the Sun, is shown on each chart.

3.2 The Navigational Stars

Alphabetical Order					Order of SHA				
Name	No.	Mag. Visual	SHA	Dec	Name	No.	Mag. Visual	SHA	Dec
			° ′	° ′				° ′	° ′
**Adhara*	19	1·6	255 18	S 28 59	**Markab*	57	2·6	13 45	N 15 14
ALDEBARAN	10	1·1	290 57	N 16 31	*FOMALHAUT*	56	1·3	15 31	S 29 36
**Alnilam*	15	1·8	275 53	S 1 12	*Enif*	54	2·5	33 54	N 9 54
Alphard	25	2·2	218 03	S 8 41	*ALTAIR*	51	0·9	62 15	N 8 53
Alphecca	41	2·3	126 17	N 26 42	*Nunki*	50	2·1	76 06	S 26 17
Alpheratz	1	2·2	357 50	N 29 07	*Rasalhague*	46	2·1	96 12	N 12 33
ALTAIR	51	0·9	62 15	N 8 53	**Sabik*	44	2·6	102 20	S 15 44
ANTARES	42	1·2	112 34	S 26 27	*ANTARES*	42	1·2	112 34	S 26 27
ARCTURUS	37	0·2	146 02	N 19 09	*Alphecca*	41	2·3	126 17	N 26 42
**Bellatrix*	13	1·7	278 39	N 6 21	**Zubenelgenubi*	39	2·9	137 13	S 16 04
BETELGEUSE	16	0·1–1·2	271 08	N 7 24	*ARCTURUS*	37	0·2	146 02	N 19 09
Denebola	28	2·2	182 40	N 14 33	*SPICA*	33	1·2	158 38	S 11 11
Diphda	4	2·2	349 02	S 17 58	*Gienah*	29	2·8	175 59	S 17 34
**Elnath*	14	1·8	278 21	N 28 37	*Denebola*	28	2·2	182 40	N 14 33
Enif	54	2·5	33 54	N 9 54	*REGULUS*	26	1·3	207 50	N 11 57
FOMALHAUT	56	1·3	15 31	S 29 36	*Alphard*	25	2·2	218 03	S 8 41
Gienah	29	2·8	175 59	S 17 34	*POLLUX*	21	1·2	243 36	N 28 01
Hamal	6	2·2	328 08	N 23 29	*PROCYON*	20	0·5	245 07	N 5 13
**Markab*	57	2·6	13 45	N 15 14	**Adhara*	19	1·6	255 18	S 28 59
Menkar	8	2·8	314 22	N 4 07	*SIRIUS*	18	−1·6	258 40	S 16 43
Nunki	50	2·1	76 06	S 26 17	*BETELGEUSE*	16	0·1–1·2	271 08	N 7 24
POLLUX	21	1·2	243 36	N 28 01	**Alnilam*	15	1·8	275 53	S 1 12
PROCYON	20	0·5	245 07	N 5 13	**Elnath*	14	1·8	278 21	N 28 37
Rasalhague	46	2·1	96 12	N 12 33	**Bellatrix*	13	1·7	278 39	N 6 21
REGULUS	26	1·3	207 50	N 11 57	*RIGEL*	11	0·3	281 18	S 8 12
RIGEL	11	0·3	281 18	S 8 12	*ALDEBARAN*	10	1·1	290 57	N 16 31
**Sabik*	44	2·6	102 20	S 15 44	*Menkar*	8	2·8	314 22	N 4 07
SIRIUS	18	−1·6	258 40	S 16 43	*Hamal*	6	2·2	328 08	N 23 29
SPICA	33	1·2	158 38	S 11 11	*Diphda*	4	2·2	349 02	S 17 58
**Zubenelgenubi*	39	2·9	137 13	S 16 04	*Alpheratz*	1	2·2	357 50	N 29 07

The star numbers and names are the same as in *The Nautical Almanac*.

* Not in the tabular pages of Volume **1**.

The table on the previous page lists the thirty stars, the sub-set of navigational stars, with declinations less than 30° north or south, that may be reduced using Volumes **2** or **3** and an almanac.

The 57 stars used in navigation are listed on page ii and are the same stars that are given in the daily pages of *The Nautical Almanac* and includes the 41 stars (marked with an asterisk) used in Volume **1**. The stars are listed in alphabetic and SHA order. The lists contain proper name, number (the same number that is used in *The Nautical Almanac*), visual magnitude, and SHA and declination.

If Volume **1** is unavailable, these positions may be used, however an almanac will be needed to calculate the GHA♈. The positions are also for epoch and mean equinox of 2005·0 and thus, for strict accuracy, a correction for precession and nutation may be needed (see Volume **1**).

3.3 The Sun 2001 – 2036

The Greenwich hour angle (GHA) and declination (Dec) of the Sun may be formed for any time during the period 2001 to 2036 using Table **4** and its supplementary Tables a, b, c, and d.

The main table gives E, the equation of time +5° and declination of the Sun for the argument "Orbit Time" (OT). Thus the table is tabulated so that the vernal equinox (March), when the declination of the Sun is zero occurs at 0^h OT. The 5° ensures that all values of E are positive, and this offset is removed in Table c.

Table a, entered with the year, gives the time correction from UT (the time of observation) to OT, the time argument of the table. In leap years the upper value of the correction is to be used for January and February and the lower value for the rest of the year. Thus:

		d	h	m		d	h	m
Date and UT	2016 February	29	16	31	2016 March	1	05	29
Correction UT to OT (Table **4**a)			−5				+19	
Date and OT		29	11	31		1	24	29
rounded to the nearest hour	2016 February	29	12		2016 March	2	00	

Note, that in the February example the minutes have rounded up the hours of orbit time, while in the March example the day has changed as well.

Corrections to E and declination for hours of OT are determined by entering Table b with the difference between consecutive values of *E* and of declination respectively as the horizontal argument, with the number of hours (to the nearest hour) of OT as the vertical argument. The declination differences are given in the main table while those for E may be found by inspection.

The GHA is obtained by adding to the corrected E the value of the diurnal arc obtained from Tables c, and d, the argument of which is the UT time.

The error when using the GHA and declination of the Sun calculated with these tables is always less than $2'.0$ of arc. During the period through to 2022 the differences only occasionally reach $1'.7$ when compared hourly at $37^m 53^s$ with equivalent positions from the Jet Propulsion Laboratory's DE405 ephemeris. From 2023 the number of differences greater than $1'.7$ increase, and from 2034 occasionally reach $2'.0$.

3.4 Altitude Corrections due to the Observer

These corrections are applied to the sextant altitude (H_S) in order to form the observed altitude (H_O) — the altitude that may be directly compared with the calculated (tabulated) altitude (H_C). They are sextant index error, dip, refraction, parallax and semi-diameter. Dip, refraction and parallax are all due to the observers position. The correction for semi-diameter is due to the choice of limb observed, while index error is a function of the sextant.

The corrections for sextant index error and dip are applied first, forming the apparent altitude (H_a). Usually both these are constant for a set of observations, but this need not necessarily be the case. The remaining corrections are often combined and depend on the object. Parallax and semi-diameter are not required for stars. For the Sun and Moon observations are made of a limb and not the centre of the disc, thus semi-diameter is needed. For the Moon, if an error of 0'.2 is significant, then the parallax correction should include a term for the oblateness of the earth (see the NA page 280). *The Nautical Almanac* includes a correction for the phase of Venus in its tabulated position, due to the fact that the light observed does not come from the centre of the disc.

This volume tabulates dip and refraction. For the Sun it also tabulates the combined correction for standard refraction, parallax, and semi-diameter.

3.4.1 Dip of the Horizon The visible horizon is used as a 'base' from which the altitude of the body is measured. However, where an observer sees the horizon depends on their height above the ground and the bending of the light by the atmosphere as it travels from the horizon to the observer's eye. This effect is called dip and it is always negative. The dip (D) and the sextant index error (IE) must be applied to the sextant altitude to give the apparent altitude (H_a), viz:

$$H_a = H_s + IE + D$$

Navigators using bubble sextants must set the dip to zero. The apparent altitude, the altitude of the body corrected for index error and the effect of looking towards the horizon, are required in order to calculate refraction and parallax in altitude (PA).

The dip table, Table **6**a, is a critical table, tabulated for height in metres and feet and is very similar to that given in *The Nautical Almanac*. Here the height of eye of the observer is tabulated from the ground to 50·0 m (164·7 ft) and gives dip to the nearest 0'.1. Alternatively, the following expressions may be used

$$D = -1'.76\sqrt{h} \quad \text{metres} \qquad \text{or} \qquad D = -0'.97\sqrt{h} \quad \text{feet}.$$

3.4.2 Refraction The light from objects (stars, Sun, planets, Moon) is bent as it passes through the atmosphere. This bending, refraction (R), causes the object to appear closer to the zenith. Table **6**b gives the amount of refraction, to be applied to the apparent altitude (H_a), i.e. the quantity from the table is subtracted from H_a to give the observed altitude, viz.:

$$H_o = H_a + R$$

where R is tabulated with a negative sign and H_a, the apparent altitude, is the sextant altitude corrected for index error and dip.

For the Sun and Moon, the correction for refraction is usually included with those for semi-diameter (limb observed) and parallax (see 3.4.3). Thus Table **6**b is usually only used for the stars or planets.

It is recommended to observe objects away from the horizon where the effect of refraction is unpredictable and large. Refraction is a function of the atmospheric conditions along the path of the ray of light as it travels through the atmosphere. The standard temperature and pressure specified in *The Nautical Almanac* are 10°C and 1010 mb pressure, respectively. For the record, Table **6**b is now tabulated for *The Nautical Almanac* standard atmospheric conditions which are, from 2004, a temperature of 10°C, 1010 mb pressure, 80% humidity, wavelength 0·01569 μm, latitude 45°, and temperature gradient (lapse rate) of 0·0065°Km^{-1}. Of all these parameters it is the changes in temperature and pressure that produce the most significant differences in the tabulated values of refraction.

To cater for non-standard atmospheric conditions Table **6**c gives a correction to the refraction obtained from the standard conditions (Table **6**b) for a range of temperatures (−30°C to +40°C) and pressures (970 mb to 1050 mb). Locate the zone letter (A, B, . . ., N) in the top graph where the arguments of temperature and pressure at the time of the observation intersect. Then find the entry in the table below where the column with the zone letter crosses the row with the apparent altitude. Interpolation may be necessary, however, due to the uncertainty at low altitudes this will probably not lead to a more accurate correction.

3.4.3 Parallax Almanacs usually tabulate positions assuming that the observer is at the centre of the Earth. Parallax, the effect that the observer is looking from the surface of the Earth is significant for relatively close objects, i.e. the Moon, Venus and Mars, and the Sun, and is dependent on the objects distance from the Earth, which changes with time.

The correction, when applied to the altitude is called parallax in altitude (PA) and is given by

$$\mathrm{PA} = \mathrm{HP} \cos \mathrm{H_a}$$

where HP is the horizontal parallax, and $\mathrm{H_a}$ is the apparent altitude.

The Altitude Correction Tables for the Sun (Table **6**d page 351) and Moon (see the NA pages xxxiv-xxxv) include this correction. For Venus and Mars this correction is tabulated each year on page A2 of the NA. The HP of the Moon is given hourly in the tabular pages of the NA.

3.4.4 Semi-diameter Navigators usually observe the limb, upper (UL) or lower (LL), of the Sun and Moon which appear as large discs. Almanacs on the other hand tabulate the position of their centre. Thus a correction for semi-diameter (±SD), must be applied. Use the + sign for observations of the lower limb and the − sign for the upper limb.

The altitude correction tables in *The Nautical Almanac* include this correction, which is dependent on the date. For the Sun the semi-diameter correction is for October to March or April to September. For the Moon, see the notes on page xxxiv of the NA for details. The SD is tabulated on the daily pages of the NA.

3.4.5 Altitude Correction Tables Various altitude correction tables are provided so that the navigator has the minimum number of terms to apply to the sextant altitude. The sight reduction form provided on page 353 allows for three corrections. The table below summarizes the various tables and corrections.

		Altitude Correction Tables	
Object	**Arguments**	Main Correction	Additional Corrections
Sun	$\mathrm{H_a}$, month, limb	R + PA ± SD	Non-standard refraction
Moon	$\mathrm{H_a}$	R + PA + SD	(HP + limb†) & Non-standard refraction
Venus and Mars	$\mathrm{H_a}$, date	R	PA & Non-standard refraction
Jupiter, Saturn, Stars	$\mathrm{H_a}$	R	Non-standard refraction

The Sun and Moon have their own tables that apply these corrections. For the Moon the correction is in two parts and care must be taken when the upper limb† is observed, as a constant of $-30'$ must also be applied (read the instructions in the NA carefully). Venus and Mars have two corrections (PA and R), Jupiter, Saturn and the stars just require refraction (R). All objects also need non-standard refraction (Table **6**c) if temperature and pressure at the time of observation are significantly different from the standard conditions, and the apparent altitude is less than 50°.

The altitude correction tables for the Moon are not reproduced here. They may be found on pages xxxiv-xxxv at the back of *The Nautical Almanac* and do not change from year to year, but the HP is also required which is tabulated hourly on the daily pages. For Venus and Mars the correction for parallax in altitude is given on page A2, which changes each year.

The altitude corrections for the Sun are described below.

3.4.6. Altitude Correction Tables for the Sun For the Sun, tables are included (Table **6**d) that combine the effects of refraction, parallax, and semi-diameter. The first two tables are for apparent altitudes less than 10°.

The third is a critical table, like the refraction table, for altitudes from just below 10° to the zenith. Each of these tables is divided into sections for October to March, or April to September. This division allows for the change in the Sun's semi-diameter during the year. Each period has two columns, one for observations of the lower limb the other for observations of the upper limb.

3.5 Altitude Corrections due to Changes in Position

These corrections allow for the movement of the vessel during the observations (MOO), and change in position of the body (MOB) when special techniques are used. They may be applied to the observed altitude, the tabulated altitude, or the intercept (position line). To minimize errors, always apply the corrections to the same quantities. All examples in this volume apply the corrections to the intercept.

3.5.1 Change in the Position of the Observer In practice this correction (MOO), for the change in position of the observer, is often made on the plotting chart by transferring the position line for the motion of the vessel. Table **1** tabulates this correction for every 2° of *relative* azimuth and for movement of the vessel (distance made good) between the time of the observations and the time of the fix. Care must be taken to ensure that the correct sign is used. This depends on whether the fix is **later** or **earlier** than the observation, and where the correction is applied; the observed altitude, the tabulated altitude, or the intercept (position line). A table at the bottom of the page gives these options.

In previous editions, this quantity was tabulated in terms of the speed and the change occurring in 4^{m} and 1^{m} (Alternative Table 1), rather than distance made good. For marine navigation this correction is often negligible, because speeds are relatively slow and observations, such as star observations, are made over a short time span (during nautical twilight). However, observations of the Sun are often made in the morning and afternoon (Sun-run-Sun). In adverse weather conditions it might be necessary to combine morning and evening observations. Alternatively, when there is sufficient moonlight to illuminate the horizon, it would be possible to observe bodies (star, planet, Moon) outside this period of twilight. In these circumstances, assuming the vessel is moving, this correction could be significant.

The correction, in minutes of arc, is given by

$$\text{DMG}\cos(\text{Rel.Z}_\text{n}) = \text{DMG}\cos(\text{Z}_\text{n} - C)$$

where DMG is the distance made good in nautical miles and the relative azimuth, Rel.Z_n, is the difference between the azimuth of the body (Z_n) and the vessel's true track (C). DMG may be estimated, ignoring the effects of wind, tide and variable speed, by $(\text{UT}_\text{f} - \text{UT})V$ where $(\text{UT}_\text{f} - \text{UT})$, is the time between the fix and the observation, in hours, and V is the speed in knots; Table **1** is tabulated in terms of the distance made good (DMG), and relative azimuth.

3.5.2 Change in the Position of the Body The body's position changes when special reduction techniques (see section 5.2.5) are used which first assumes that all the observations are taken at the same time (the time of the fix). Movement of the body (MOB) corrects for the movement of the body due to the rotation of earth between the time of observation and the time the tables were looked up (usually the time of fix). **Care** must be taken for the Sun, Moon and planets if the period of time is large and the object has moved. The hourly rates (v and d) in the NA will give the change in position during an hour.

Table **2** tabulates for every 5° of latitude and 3° of azimuth (Z_n), the altitude correction due to the change in position of the body during one minute of time. The arithmetic is made much simpler if one of the observations is made at the time of the fix, and the interval between the fix and the remainder of the observations are made at intervals of exact multiples of a minute. However, if required, an interpolation table for seconds of time is given below the main table. Care must be taken to ensure that the correct sign is used. This, like the correction for

MOO, depends on whether the fix is **later** or **earlier** than the observation, and where the correction is applied; the observed altitude, the tabulated altitude, or the intercept (position line). A table beneath the main table gives these options.

This correction, in minutes of arc, is given by

$$15{\cdot}0411\,(UT_f - UT)\cos Lat \sin Z_n$$

where $UT_f - UT$, the difference in time between the fix and the time of the observation is expressed in minutes of time. Table **2** is tabulated for a minute interval, $UT_f - UT = 1^m$. Strictly speaking 15·0411 is for stars. For the Sun and Planets use 15·0. It is unadvisable to use the Moon when using this method.

3.6 Rapid Sight Reduction Form

A blank sight reduction form is given at the back (page 353) of this volume. This follows the format of the examples. However, some minor modifications have been made to ensure that it fits onto an A4 page. To help the user, the example in section 3.5.1 has been repeated using this form (see page 352).

The form covers observations of three bodies. The information for each body is contained within a column. These are preceded by the column (first) that contains a summary of the instructions. Each block of this column contains the step number and main function, in bold. Subsequent lines give a reminder of the action needed, the arguments required, and the symbol for the quantity calculated or extracted from the tables. The arguments needed for entering the tables are indicated in parenthesis. In the example form the arguments are only included and/or repeated for each observation if they change or are not obvious.

The form may be freely copied and/or downloaded from our web site (www.nao.rl.ac.uk).

4. NOMENCLATURE AND TERMINOLOGY

The following is a list of symbols and their definition used in this volume.

AP — Assumed position, sometimes referred to as the chosen position. The latitude and longitude closest to the dead reckoning or estimated position (DR/EP) that have the following properties. The assumed latitude is the DR (or EP) latitude rounded to the nearest degree. Similarly, the assumed longitude is the longitude closest to the DR longitude that makes the LHA♈ a whole degree, or even degree for latitudes above 60°. This allows the tables to be entered easily without interpolation.

C — True track (or course) of the vessel. *C* is measured from true north through east, south, west and back to north. The range is from 0° to 360°.

D — Dip of the horizon see section 3.4.1.

d — The difference in altitude (H_c) between the current entry and that calculated using the next value of declination.

Dec — Declination of the body.

Dec° — The degrees portion of the declination, excluding the minutes. Dec = Dec° + Dec′

Dec′ — The minutes of arc portion of the declination, Dec = Dec° + Dec′

Date — Greenwich date, or local date.

DMG — Distance made good.

DR — Dead Reckoning position. Position based on course and speed only.

DWE — Deck Watch Error. The error in the watch used to make the observations.

EP — Estimated position. The most accurate position that can be obtained by calculation and estimation alone; including leeway and tidal effects.

Epoch	An arbitrary fixed instant, identified by date and time.
GHA♈	Greenwich hour angle of Aries. The range of GHA♈ is from 0° to 360° starting at 0° on the Greenwich meridian increasing to the west, back to 360° on the Greenwich meridian. It is a function of the Greenwich date and UT time.
GHA	Greenwich hour angle of a body. Its range, etc., is as GHA♈.
GMT	Greenwich mean time. In this context the name (GMT) is synonymous with universal time (UT).
H_a	Apparent altitude. This is the sextant altitude (H_s) corrected for sextant index error (IE) and dip (D). It is needed for calculating refraction and parallax in altitude (PA).
H_c	Calculated altitude, sometimes called the tabulated altitude. It is the altitude tabulated in the tables for a given latitude, declination and LHA.
H_o	Observed altitude, sometimes referred to as the true altitude. It is the apparent altitude (H_a) corrected for refraction (R), parallax in altitude (PA) and semi-diameter (SD), and phase-effect as appropriate.
HP	Horizontal parallax.
H_s	Sextant altitude. The altitude measured by a sextant between the visible horizon and the object on an arc towards the observer's zenith.
IE	Sextant index error. *On the arc* errors are *negative*, they reduce the sextant altitude. *Off the arc* errors are *positive*, and increase the sextant altitude.
Lat	Latitude. The sign convention is north is positive, south is negative. The range is from −90° to +90°.
LHA♈	Local hour angle of Aries is given by $$\text{LHA}♈ = \text{GHA}♈ \begin{matrix} -\text{ west} \\ +\text{ east} \end{matrix} \text{ longitude}$$ and increases to the west from 0° on the local meridian to 360°.
LHA	Local hour angle of a body. $$\text{LHA} = \text{GHA} \begin{matrix} -\text{ west} \\ +\text{ east} \end{matrix} \text{ longitude}$$ Its range, etc., is as LHA♈.
LL	Lower limb.
Long	Longitude. The sign convention is east is positive, west is negative. The range is −180° to +180°.
p	Intercept, $p = H_o - H_c$, may be *positive* or *negative*, and thus the position line should be plotted *towards*, or *away* from the direction of the body, respectively (see 5.2.1).
PA	Parallax in altitude (see 3.4.3).
R	Atmospheric refraction see section 3.4.2. The bending of the light ray as it passes through the atmosphere. The amount of refraction depends on the apparent altitude (H_a) and the atmospheric conditions, in particular the temperature and pressure. The apparent altitude is always greater than the observed altitude (H_o).
SD	Semi-diameter. The distance, usually given in minutes of arc, from the centre of the object (e.g. Sun and Moon) to the limb (edge).
SHA	Sidereal hour angle. The range is 0° to 360°.
UL	Upper limb.
UT	Universal Time, the time scale required for use in sight reduction. Radio time signals are usually based on the system of Universal Coordinated Time (UTC). A correction may be required to convert from UTC to UT (see 4.1).
Rel.Z_n	Relative azimuth, Rel.$Z_n = Z_n - C$, where C is the true course of the vessel.

Z — Azimuth angle. Convert the azimuth angle to true azimuth (Z_n) using the following rules:-

	North Latitudes	South Latitudes
LHA > 180°	$Z_n = Z$	$Z_n = 180° - Z$
LHA < 180°	$Z_n = 360° - Z$	$Z_n = 180° + Z$

These rules are given at the top and bottom of each page of both Volumes **2** and **3**. If LHA = 180° then either rule for the appropriate latitude may be used.

Zenith — Point directly above the observer. Zenith distance is 90° − altitude.

Z_n — Azimuth (true) or true bearing. Z_n is measured from true north through east, south, west and back to north. The range is from 0° to 360°.

ZT — Zone time correction. The time correction to be applied to the local time to give Universal Time (UT). Usually the ZT is added for west longitudes and subtracted for east longitudes,

$$\text{UT} = \text{local time} \begin{smallmatrix} + \\ - \end{smallmatrix} \text{ZT for} \begin{smallmatrix} \text{west} \\ \text{east} \end{smallmatrix} \text{longitude}$$

If appropriate, allow for daylight saving (or summer) time. Remember, the ZT might cause the date to change.

4.1 Time Scales, UT and UTC

It is necessary to record the time of each observation and convert it, as necessary, to UT1. UT1, usually denoted by UT, is the time argument of the tables for GHAΥ and thus for LHAΥ. The navigator relies on radio time signals to ensure that the accuracy of the deck watch used to time observations is maintained. Radio time signals, which promulgate UTC are at present kept within $0^{s}.9$ of UT1. This difference,

$$\text{DUT} = \text{UT1} - \text{UTC}$$

is at present kept small, and to the accuracy of these tables it may be ignored.

However, if UTC and UT are allowed to diverge (there are proposals for this), then navigators will probably need to adapt their procedures. A correction must then be made to the time of each observation. Alternatively, the longitude deduced from astronomical observations must be corrected by the corresponding amount. This correction, in minutes of arc, to be added to the longitude is given by

$$-15 \times \frac{\text{DUT}}{60}$$

where DUT is given in seconds of time. DUT is also promulgated by some radio time signals.

The table below gives the corrections for small values of DUT:

DUT	Correction to longitude
$2^{s}.0$	$0'.5$
$1^{s}.0$	$0'.2$
$0^{s}.5$	$0'.1$

Negative values of DUT move the longitude to the east, while positive values move the longitude to the west.

Please check our web site (www.nao.rl.ac.uk) where more information is available.

5. USE OF THESE TABLES

The tables are mainly intended for the reduction of observations. Also, they may be used to extract the tabulated altitudes and azimuths at a predetermined time for identification and setting the sextant before the observations. However, unlike Volume **1**, it does not provide a selection of objects to observe.

5.1 Planning Sextant Observations

When using this volume to plan observations some knowledge of what objects are available at the required time is needed. This volume gives the altitude and azimuth angle of each chosen object. This is dependent on the particular GHA of the object, its declination as well as the assumed position of the observer.

By calculating the positions of the chosen objects and finding their altitudes and azimuths from the tables for the time of the fix, rather than the time of each observation, reduces the amount of interpolation from the almanac that is required. It also allows presetting of the sextant and makes identification easy. If the object's H_C is not given, or negative, it will be below the horizon and not observable. However, a correction (MOB) will need to be applied to cater for this assumption (see 5.2.5).

5.1.1 Method of Planning Observations The following procedure and example illustrates the process of finding the altitude and azimuth of the selected object.

Step 1. Estimate the approximate position (latitude and longitude) at the proposed time of the fix. The zone time correction will also be needed.

Step 2. Convert the local date and proposed time of the fix to the Greenwich date and UT time using the zone time correction (ZT).

Step 3. Calculate GHA and Dec or (GHA♈ for stars) from an almanac from the Greenwich date and UT time.

Step 4. Calculate LHA of the object from the estimated longitude (east longitudes are positive, and west longitudes are negative) and GHA of the object.

Step 5. From the estimate of the latitude, the declination (Dec°), noting whether the latitude and declination are same or contrary, and LHA of the object, (latitude and LHA both rounded to the nearest degree), look up the appropriate page of the main tabulations and extract the calculated altitude (H_C), d, and azimuth angle (Z) of the object.

Step 6. Interpolate calculated altitude (H_C) for minutes of declination and convert azimuth angle (Z) to true azimuth (Z_n).

These are basically the first five steps for the reduction of an observation. See section 5.2.1 for a fuller description.

5.1.2 Example of Planning Observations The following example illustrates how a navigator will plan to make some observations.

The example highlights the simplifications that may be made. The time of fix is chosen to be on the hour, thus no interpolation in the NA is required. However, whatever the time the same minutes of time increment and correction table will be used, but remember to use the correct column for the appropriate object.

Note too, that these positions may also be used whatever the actual time of observations. In this case apply the MOB correction (see 5.2.5). If the vessel has also moved during the observations then the MOO correction (see 5.2.4) will be needed as well.

Example. The navigator requires a fix at $20^h 00^m 00^s$ UT between civil and nautical twilight on 2003 March 19. At that time the DR position is expected to be N39°, W20°, with a zone time of $+1^h$. The navigator plans to use Saturn, Jupiter and *Sirius*, objects that are known to be above the horizon at that time.

		h m s
1	DR position N 39°, W 20° at the time of fix	
2	Convert Fix time to UT:	
	Local time of Fix, 2003 March 19	19 00 00
	Zone Correction	+1
	UT of Fix	20 00 00

			Saturn		Jupiter		*Sirius*
3	Dec and GHA or (SHA and GHAϒ) from the NA 2003 March 19:	h	° ′	h	° ′	h	° ′
	Dec at UT of fix	20	N 22 12·7	20	N 19 00·6		S 16 43·3
	SHA for stars						258 40·8
	GHA body or GHAϒ at UT^h		34 47·6		345 51·0		116 57·0
	GHA body for UT of Fix = Sum	20	34 47·6	20	345 51·0	20	375 37·8
4	Calculate LHA: assumed longitude (−ve west)		−19 47·6		−19 51·0		−19 37·8
	LHA body = Sum		15		326		356
5	Extracted quantities from main tables, arguments:						
	Assumed latitude	N 39°	} Same	N 39°	} Same	N 39°	} Contrary
	Declination, degrees (Dec°)	N 22°		N 19°		S 16°	
	Declination, minutes (Dec′)	13′		01′		43′	
	LHA	15°		326°		356°	
	Tabular page	5		5		7	
	H_c, *d*, Z from main tables		° ′ 68 43 ′ +49 ° 139		° ′ 54 30 ′ +39 ° 114		° ′ 34 52 ′ −59 ° 175
6	Correction for mins. of Dec, Table **5** (Dec′, *d*)		+11		+1		−42
	Calculated altitude	H_c	68 54		54 31		34 10
	Convert Z to Z_n, North latitude and		LHA < 180° 360		LHA > 180°		LHA > 180°
	Azimuth angle	Z	139		114		175
	Azimuth, true bearing	Z_n	$Z_n = 360° - Z = 221$		Z_n = Z = 114		Z_n = Z = 175

5.2 Finding Position from Sextant Observations

The methods and examples of sight reduction given here, illustrate how to use these tables efficiently to find your position from sextant observations, by calculating the intercept and azimuth and then plotting the resulting position lines on a chart.

In general terms "sight reduction" or "reduction of sights" is the process of comparing sextant observations with the equivalent calculated data, and thus determining a position — a fix.

The navigator must first make an initial estimate of position. This may either be a dead reckoning (DR) or estimated position (EP). The techniques given here concentrate on methods that rely on paper and pencil, tables and charts. Thus for best results the navigator should use the most accurate position available. Other techniques for determining a fix from sights are given in *NavPac and Compact Data*, (*AstroNavPC and Compact Data*), or *The Nautical Almanac*.

This method then involves adopting an assumed position (AP), close to the DR/EP, from which the sight is plotted. This position may vary for each sight and may be adjusted for various assumptions. These assumptions may be corrected at this stage or applied to the position line (intercept). It is good practice to always apply these corrections in a consistent manner. In this explanation these corrections are always made to the intercept (see below).

Before the main tabulation may be used the navigator must first find, in the usual way, the GHA and declination of the observed body from *The Nautical Almanac* for the actual time (UT) of observation. The GHA is then combined with an assumed longitude, close to the DR/EP longitude, to make the LHA a whole number of degrees, or even degrees for latitudes above 69°.

The main tabulations may then be entered with (a) the adopted latitude (the DR/EP latitude rounded to the nearest whole degree), (b) the degree of declination (Dec°) numerically less than that of the body (i.e. ignoring the minutes), and (c) the value of LHA found above, taking care to choose the portion of the table corresponding to the *same* or *contrary* name, as appropriate.

The table gives the tabulated (or calculated) altitude (H_c), the difference, *d*, and the azimuth angle (Z) for the whole degree of declination chosen. Use Table **5** (page 348) to interpolate the altitude for the minutes of declination (Dec′) that have been ignored to obtain the calculated altitude for the time required. The sign of *d* determines if the correction is added (+), or subtracted (−). Take particular care where negative altitudes are tabulated as the interpolation correction must be applied algebraically (see section 3.2.1)

Convert the azimuth angle Z to true azimuth (Z_n); viz

Northern Latitudes	**Southern Latitudes**
LHA greater than 180° ... $Z_n = Z$	LHA greater than 180° ... $Z_n = 180° - Z$
LHA less than 180° ... $Z_n = 360° - Z$	LHA less than 180° ... $Z_n = 180° + Z$

These rules are repeated in the left-hand corner at the top and bottom of each page. If LHA = 180° then either rule for the latitude may be used. In general, Z need not be interpolated for declination.

In order to make a valid comparison both the calculated altitude (H_c) and the sextant altitude (H_s) must be on the same system and with respect to the same origin. Thus, when reducing observations, the sextant altitude (H_s) must be corrected for sextant index error (IE), dip (3.4.1), refraction (3.4.2), parallax and semi-diameter, as appropriate, to give the observed (H_o) altitude. These corrections cannot be made to the tabulated positions since they are functions of the following quantities; the particular sextant, height of eye of the observer above the horizon, and the atmospheric condition, such as temperature and pressure, at the time of the observations, object and limb observed.

The comparison between the observed and calculated altitudes may then be made. It is called the intercept (*p*) and is the difference between them ($H_o - H_c$).

However, depending on the practice and assumptions of the navigator, it may be necessary to apply corrections to the intercept, or the assumed position.

These corrections are for the movement of the observer (MOO), when the observations are made over an extended interval (see 5.2.4), or for movement of the body (MOB) when a fixed time is adopted (see section 5.2.5). Thus, in the first case, the position line may be advanced or retarded to another time by running it "on" or "back" along the ship's course or course made good when the tidal stream and ocean currents, etc. are included.

Finally, the intercept (*p*), adjusted as necessary, and true azimuth (Z_n), are then used to plot the position line. The intersection of two position lines determines an observed position. When position lines of three bodies are plotted, they should form a triangle, a cocked-hat, the area within which should contain the fix. The errors and uncertainties of this fix are not dealt with in this publication.

5.2.1 Sight Reduction Method The following steps give the procedure for calculating the intercept and azimuth of an observation and the resulting position line plot.

Step 1. Estimate the approximate position (DR/EP), the latitude and longitude, at the time that the fix is required. The time zone correction will also be needed.

Step 2. Convert the local date and time of the fix, and each of the observations, to their respective Greenwich date and UT time using the time zone correction (ZT), remembering to apply any errors (DWE) due to inaccuracies of the watch used to make the observation.
If the vessel has moved location significantly between observations and the time of the fix, or if special reduction techniques are used then record the difference between the time of the fix and the

time of each observation. Note too whether the time of the fix is later or earlier than each of the observations. Corrections for these assumptions are made at step 8.

Step 3. Calculate the GHA and declination (Dec) of the body using an almanac such as *The Nautical Almanac* (NA) for the time of the observation, i.e. from its Greenwich date and UT time. Add or subtract multiples of 360° to put GHA between 0° and 360° if appropriate. For stars, form the GHA by adding the SHA to GHA♈ interpolated to the UT time of observation.

Step 4. For each observation (if appropriate) adopt an assumed position (AP) such that the sum of the assumed longitude (east longitudes are positive, and west longitudes are negative) and the respective GHA gives the LHA to a whole number of degrees, or an even degree for latitudes above 69°. Ensure that LHA is between 0° and 360° by adding or subtracting multiples of 360°.

Step 5. Extract the tabulated (calculated) altitude (H_C), the difference d for correcting the altitude for minutes of declination (Dec′) and azimuth angle (Z) of the body from the main tabulations.

These are found by going to the pages for the assumed latitude (the estimated latitude rounded to the nearest degree). Then find the appropriate declination group, entering with the whole number of degrees (Dec°), and the value of LHA (Step 4), taking care to choose the portion of the table corresponding to the *same* or *contrary* name, as appropriate.

Correct the altitude for minutes part of the declination using Table **5** with arguments Dec′ and d. Ensure that the correction is applied algebraically.

Step 6. Correct the sextant altitude (H_S) by allowing for index error, dip (Table **6**a and the height of the observer's eye above the horizon), refraction (Table **6**b, d), semi-diameter and parallax, as appropriate, to give the observed altitude (H_O). An additional correction for refraction (Table **6**c) may be needed if the temperature and pressure are different from the standard conditions (see 3.4.2) and the object is low in the sky.

Step 7. Calculate the intercept $p = H_O - H_C$. The intercept will be *positive* (towards) if the observed altitude is *greater* than the tabulated altitude. On the other hand the intercept will be *negative* (away) if the observed altitude is *less* than the tabulated altitude.

Convert azimuth angle, Z, to true azimuth (Z_n).

Step 8. Apply any relevant corrections to the intercept:

(a) for movement of the observer (MOO). The vessel has changed its position considerably between the time of the observations and the time of the fix (see 5.2.4);

(b) for movement of the object (MOB). Section 5.2.5 explains the details and the advantages of adopting an assumed position at the time of the fix and then making corrections for this assumption; It is possible to apply all these corrections at other stages of the calculation.

Step 9. Plot the position lines from the intercept (p), corrected as necessary, and azimuth (Z_n) to determine the fix.

For each observation in turn mark the assumed position and then plot its position line.

Firstly establish whether the position line is *towards* or *away* from the direction of the body. If the intercept is *positive*, then the position line is plotted *towards* the direction (azimuth) of the body. On the other hand if the intercept is *negative*, then the position line is plotted in the opposite direction to (i.e. *away* from) the body.

Then draw the position line perpendicular to the direction of the body, where the direction of the body (Z_n) is measured at the assumed position (AP) used for that observation. The line is drawn at a distance given by the intercept, *towards* or *away from* the direction of the body.

Three position lines should define a small triangular area (cocked-hat) within which the fix is located. However, the fix may lie outside this area if the band of error either side of the position lines exceeds the diameter of the cocked-hat. Analysis of the accuracy of sextant observations and the resulting position lines may be found in other manuals e.g. *The Admiralty Manual of Navigation*.

Simply summarized: (1) estimate position at the time of fix, (2) convert dates and times to UT, (3) calculate GHA and declination of the body, (4) adopt an assumed position and form the LHA, (5) extract the tabulated (calculated) altitude, difference *d*, and azimuth angle; correct the altitude for minutes of declination, (6) correct sextant altitudes, remembering semi-diameter and parallax if appropriate, (7) calculate the intercept and form true azimuth (Z_n), (8) apply any corrections if appropriate, and finally (9) plot the position line on the chart.

A sight reduction form (see 3.6) giving these steps is printed at the back of this volume. It may be freely copied or downloaded from our web site (www.nao.rl.ac.uk).

5.2.2 Reduction of a Single Observation The following example follows the steps given above, but for one observation only.

Example. During the morning of 2003 August 7 in the Tasman Sea in DR position S 40° 52′, E 157° 05′, zone time of -10^h, an observation of the lower limb (LL) of the Sun was made at $09^h\ 20^m\ 45^s$ local time. The sextant reading was 24° 05′.2, with an index error of 1′.3 *on the arc* (−1′.3), and the height of the observer's eye above the horizon was 6 metres (20 feet). At the time of observation the temperature and pressure were 5°C, and 1013 mb, respectively.

1 Estimated position S 40° 52′, E 157° 05′

				h	m	s
2	Convert local date and time	d				
		2003 August 7		09	20	45
	Zone Correction	ZT	=	−10	00	00
	Greenwich Date and UT; 2003 August 6			23	20	45

				°	′	′		°	′	′
3	Use the NA to calculate GHA and Dec of the Sun 2003 Aug. 6:									
	Tabular values at 23^h UT		=	163	31·9		Dec N	16	36·5	0·7
	Increment and correction for $20^m\ 45^s$		=	5	11·3				−0·2	
	Sum:	GHA	=	168	43·2		Dec N	16	36·3	
4	Calculate LHA Sun: assumed longitude (east, add)		=	157	16·8					
	Sum, remove multiples of 360° if required	LHA	=	326						
5	Extract quantities from main tables using arguments:									
	Assumed latitude	41°S } Contrary								
	Declination of Sun, degrees only (step 3) Dec°	16°N								
	Declination of Sun, minutes only (step 3) Dec′	36′								
	LHA Sun (step 4)	326°								
	Tabular page	19								
	Extracted values (H_c, *d*, Z)			24	52	−53		144		
	Correction for minutes of Dec, Table **5**, (36′,−53′)				−32					
	Calculated altitude	H_c	=	24	20					
6	Correct the sextant altitude:			°	′					
	Sextant altitude	H_s	=	24	05·2					
	Index error	IE	=		−1·3					
	Dip, Table **6**a, height 6 m	*D*	=		−4·3					
	Apparent altitude	H_a	=	23	59·6					
	Altitude correction, Sun, Table **6**d (H_a, LL, Aug.)	R+PA+SD	=		+13·9					
	Additional refraction, Table **6**c, H_a, 5°C, 1013 mb				0·0					
	Observed altitude	H_o	=	24	13·5					
7	Intercept: calculated altitude (step 5)	H_c	=	24	20·0					
	$H_o - H_c$	*p*	=		−6·5					
	$H_o < H_c$, *p* −ve, intercept is			*away*	6·5					
	Convert Z to Z_n, South latitude, LHA > 180°							180		
	Azimuth angle (step 5)	±Z	=					−144		
	Azimuth, true bearing = 180° − Z	Z_n	=					36		

8 No correction for MOO or MOB are required.

9 The plot is centered on the assumed position (AP) at S 41°, E 157° 16·8′. The DR position is at S 40° 52′, E 157° 05′.

The position line is drawn, perpendicular to the true azimuth (36°) to the Sun, at a distance of 6′·5 from the AP on the opposite (*away*) side to the direction to the Sun.

The azimuth line is not normally drawn, but is often indicated by the small bars at each end of the position line pointing in the direction of the body.

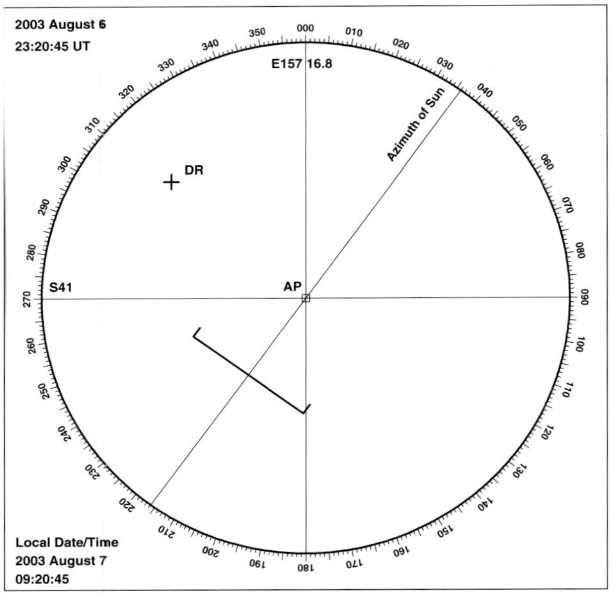

5.2.3 A 3-Body Fix The following example together with its position line plot, illustrates the use of the tables for the reduction of a typical set of observations and the determination of a fix.

The fix is usually required for some instant during, or near, the period of the observations. In the following example the observations are taken in rapid succession and any movement of the vessel during this time is negligible. No special techniques are used.

Example. On 2003 June 10 at $19^h\ 40^m\ 00^s$ local time the DR position was N 44° 49′, W 50° 05′, zone time correction $+3^h$. Determine a fix at this time from observations of *Arcturus*, the Moon and Jupiter. The observations were taken at $19^h\ 38^m\ 53^s$, $19^h\ 40^m\ 30^s$ and $19^h\ 42^m\ 15^s$ local time, and the sextant altitudes were 56° 21′·8, 31° 34′·0 and 38° 51′·5, respectively. The height of eye of the observer was 6·6 m (22ft.), and the temperature and pressure were 15°C and 990 mb, respectively. The sextant index error was 1′·6 *off the arc* (+1′·6) and there was negligible motion of the vessel between observations.

1 Estimated position N 44° 49′, W 50° 05′, 2003 June 10 at $19^h\ 40^m$ local time, the time of the fix.

	Arcturus		Moon (lower limb)		Jupiter	
2 Convert observation time to UT: 2003 June 10	h m s		h m s		h m s	
Local time	19 38 53		19 40 30		19 42 15	
Zone Correction	+3		+3		+3	
UT of observation	22 38 53		22 40 30		22 42 15	
3 Dec and GHA or (SHA and GHA♈) from the NA:		° ′		° ′		° ′
Dec 2003 June 10 at 22^h UT		N 19 10·0		S 09 08·3		N 17 18·0
Correction for *d* and minutes			(15′·4)	+10·4	(0′·1)	−0·1
Sum = Declination for given UT		N 19 10·0		S 09 18·7		N 17 17·9
SHA for stars		146 02·7				
GHA♈ or GHA body for 2003 June 10 at UT	22	228 50·4	22	19 48·7	22	91 47·3
Increment for minutes and seconds	38 53	9 44·8	40 30	9 39·8	42 15	10 33·8
Correction for *v*			(9′·7)	+6·5	(2′·1)	+1·5
Sum = GHA body for given UT	22 38 53	384 37·9	22 40 30	29 35·0	22 42 15	102 22·6
4 Calculate LHA: ±360° if appropriate				+360		
				389 35·0		
Assumed longitude, subtract because west		−49 37·9		−50 35·0		−50 22·6
LHA body = Sum		335		339		52

Step	Quantity		*Arcturus*	Moon (lower limb)	Jupiter
5	Extracted quantities from main tables, arguments:				
	Assumed latitude		N 45° } Same	N 45° } Contrary	N 45° } Same
	Declination, degrees (Dec°)		N 19°	S 09°	N 17°
	Declination, minutes (Dec′)		10′	19′	18′
	LHA		335°	339°	52°
	Tabular page		41	40	41
	Extracted H_c, d, Z		56° 44′ +50′ 133°	32° 47′ −57′ 155°	38° 32′ +42′ 106°
	Correction for mins. of Dec, Table **5** (Dec′, d)		+8	−18	+13
	Calculated altitude	H_c	56 52	32 29	38 45
6	Correct sextant altitudes:		° ′	° ′	° ′
	Sextant altitude	H_s	56 21·8	31 34·0	38 51·5
	Index error	IE	+1·6	+1·6	+1·6
	Dip, Table **6**a, height 6·6 m	D	−4·5	−4·5	−4·5
	Apparent altitude	H_a	56 18·9	31 31·1	38 48·6
	Refraction, Table **6**b, H_a	R	−0·6		−1·2
	Moon, main correction (H_a), (see 3.4.5)			58·2	
	Moon L/U correction (H_a, HP = 60′·3, LL)			7·9	
	Additional refraction (H_a, 15°C, 990 mb)		0·0	+0·1	0·0
	Observed altitude	H_o	56 18·3	32 37·3	38 47·4
7	Intercept: calculated altitude (step 5)	H_c	56 52	32 29	38 45
	$p = H_o - H_c$		−33·7	+8·3	+2·4
		p	*away* 33·7	*towards* 8·3	*towards* 2·4
	Convert Z to Z_n, North latitude and		LHA > 180°	LHA > 180°	LHA < 180° 360
	Azimuth angle (step 5)	±Z	133	155	−106
	Azimuth, true bearing	Z_n	Z_n = Z = 133	Z_n = Z = 155	Z_n = 360° − Z = 254

8 The correction (a) MOO is negligible in this example as the time of the fix is very close to the time of the observations. No special techniques have been used so correction (b) MOB is not applicable.

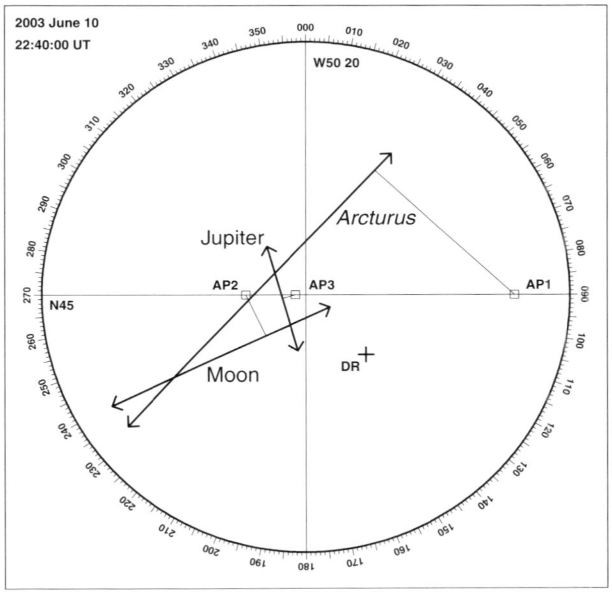

9 The plot shows the DR position at N 44° 49′, W 50° 05′ and the position lines for *Arcturus*, the Moon and Jupiter, indicated with the arrows at each end. They are plotted with respect to their assumed positions; N 45°, W 49° 37′·9 (AP1), N 45°, W 50° 35′·0 (AP2) and N 45°, W 50° 22′·6 (AP3), respectively (see step 4).

The lighter lines represent the intercepts, one for each body.

The fix is indicated by the area of the cocked-hat, but may lie outside it, if the band of error either side of the position line exceeds the diameter of the cocked-hat.

5.2.4 A Fix with Movement of the Observer The following example illustrates the case when there has been a significant change in the position of the observer between the observations.

With stars (see Volume **1**) which are observed during twilight, the movement of the vessel during this period may usually be ignored. However, in cloudy conditions it may sometimes be necessary to combine observations, from one evening with those taken the next morning, for example. It is also possible, when there is sufficient moonlight to illuminate the horizon, to make observations outside the nautical twilight period.

For the Sun there is often significant movement of the vessel between the morning and afternoon sights as shown in the following example.

Example. Sailing towards Crozet Islands in the Southern Indian Ocean During, three observations of the lower limb (LL) of the Sun were made on 2003 October 26. The observations were timed at 07ʰ 38ᵐ 47ˢ, 11ʰ 58ᵐ 59ˢ and 16ʰ 39ᵐ 40ˢ local time; 4ʰ ahead of UT. The morning altitude was recorded at 25° 32′.5, when the temperature was 9°C. The temperature rose to 17°C when the second observation was made with altitude 52° 54′.5. The sextant altitude of the last observation was 22° 17′.7, when the temperature had fallen to 15°C. The pressure remained constant at 990 mb throughout the day. The height of the navigator's eye above the horizon was 6 m (20 ft.), and the index error of the sextant was 1′.3 *on the arc* (−1′.3). A fix is required at 08ʰ UT (12ʰ local time), when the DR position was S49° 12′, E56° 20′. During the passage the course was 345°(T) and the speed varied between 8 and 10 knots. Thus the navigator estimated that during the morning run the distance made good was 30 nm, while the distance during the afternoon run was 50 nm.

1 DR position S 49° 12′, E 56° 20′, 2003 October 26 at 12ʰ 00ᵐ 00ˢ local time, the time of the fix.

2 Convert Sun observation time to UT:	h m s	h m s	h m s
Local time 2003 October 26	07 38 47	11 58 59	16 39 40
Zone Correction	−4	−4	−4
UT of the observation	03 38 47	07 58 59	12 39 40
UT of Fix	08 00 00	08 00 00	08 00 00
Time of Fix − Time of Observation	+4 21 13	+1 01	−4 39 40
The Fix is	*later*	*later*	*earlier*
than the observation by	4 21 13	1 01	4 39 40

3 Dec and GHA or (SHA and GHA♈) from the NA:		° ′		° ′		° ′
Dec 2003 October 26 at UTʰ		S 12 15·9		S 12 19·3		S 12 23·6
Correction for *d* and minutes of time	(0′.9)	+0·6	(0′.9)	+0·9	(0′.9)	+0·6
Sum = Declination for UT of observation		S 12 16·5		S 12 20·2		S 12 24·2
GHA Sun 2003 October 26 at UTʰ	03	228 59·2	07	288 59·5	12	3 59·8
Increment for minutes and seconds	38 47	9 41·8	58 59	14 44·8	39 40	9 55·0
Sum = GHA Sun given UT	03 38 47	238 41·0	07 58 59	303 44·3	12 39 40	13 54·8
4 Calculate LHA: assumed longitude, add as east		+56 19·0		+56 15·7		+56 05·2
LHA Sun = Sum		295		360		70

5 Extracted quantities from main tables, arguments:				
Assumed latitude		S 49° } Same	S 49° } Same	S 49° } Same
Declination, degrees (Dec°)		S 12°	S 12°	S 12°
Declination, minutes (Dec′)		16′	20′	24′
LHA		295°	000°	70°
Tabular page		64	64	65
Extracted H_C, *d*, Z		25° 21′ +45′ 101°	53° 00′ +60′ 180°	22° 07′ +44′ 97°
Correction for *d* and Dec′, Table **5**		+12	+20	+18
Calculated altitude	H_C	25 33	53 20	22 25
6 Correct sextant altitudes:		° ′	° ′	° ′
Sextant altitude	H_S	25 32·5	52 54·5	22 17·7
Index error	IE	−1·3	−1·3	−1·3
Dip, Table **6**a, height 6 m	*D*	−4·3	−4·3	−4·3
Apparent altitude	H_a	25 26·9	52 48·9	22 12·1
Altitude correction, Sun, Table **6**d, Oct.		+14·3	+15·5	+13·9
Additional refraction **6**c (T° C, 990 mb)		0·0	0·0	+0·1
Observed altitude	H_O	25 41·2	53 04·4	22 26·1
7 Intercept: calculated altitude, step 5	H_C	25 33·0	53 20·0	22 25·0
$H_O - H_C$	*p*	+8·2	−15·6	+1·1

Continued . . .

Continued . . . $H_o - H_c$	*p*	+8·2		−15·6		+1·1	
Convert Z to Z_n, South latitude		LHA > 180°	180	LHA < 180°	180	LHA < 180°	180
Azimuth angle	±Z		−101		+180		+97
Azimuth, true bearing	Z_n	$Z_n = 180° - Z =$	079	$Z_n = 180° + Z =$	360	$Z_n = 180° + Z =$	277
8 Correction (a) Movement of vessel:			360				360
Add or subtract 360° as appropriate			439				637
True course (track) of vessel	*C*		345		345		345
Relative bearing = $Z_n - C$	Rel.Z_n		94		15		292
Distance made good	DMG		30nm	negligible			50nm
Table **1**, DMG, Rel.Z_n			−2′.1				+18′.7
Fix is . . . than the observation			*later*				*earlier*
Thus the correction is	MOO	−2·1				−18·7	
Intercept, corrected	*p*	+6·1		−15·6		−17·6	
	p	*towards* 6·1		*away* 15·6		*away* 17·6	
Azimuth (true bearing) (step 7)	Z_n	079°		000°		277°	

Special care must be taken with the sign of MOO. In the above example, the value for the afternoon run was +18′.7. However, the rules given below Table **1** indicate that since the time of the fix was *earlier* than the time of the observation and the sign from the table was positive (+), then the correction must be *subtracted* from the intercept. Note that although the time difference is not explicitly used it will probably be needed for calculating the distance made good. The formulae for calculating this correction is given in 3.5.1, and is $(UT_f - UT)\ V \cos(\text{Rel.}Z_n)$, where the distance made good may be given by DMG = $(UT_f - UT)\ V$, (time in hours × speed (V) in knots), and ignores factors such as wind, tide and variable speed of the vessel.

9 The plot shows the position line of each observation of the Sun plotted with respect to the appropriate assumed position; latitude S 49°, E 56° 19′.0 (AP1), S 49°, E 56° 15′.7 (AP2) and S 49°, E 56° 05′.2 (AP3), respectively (see step 4). These are the lighter lines. The lines with the double arrows at each end are the position lines from the morning and afternoon observations transferred to the time that the fix is required at 08ʰ UT. The position line of the middle observation is close to the time of the fix and thus does not require to be transferred.

The fix is indicated by the tiny area of the cocked-hat, but may lie outside it, if the band of error either side of the position line exceeds the diameter of the cocked-hat.

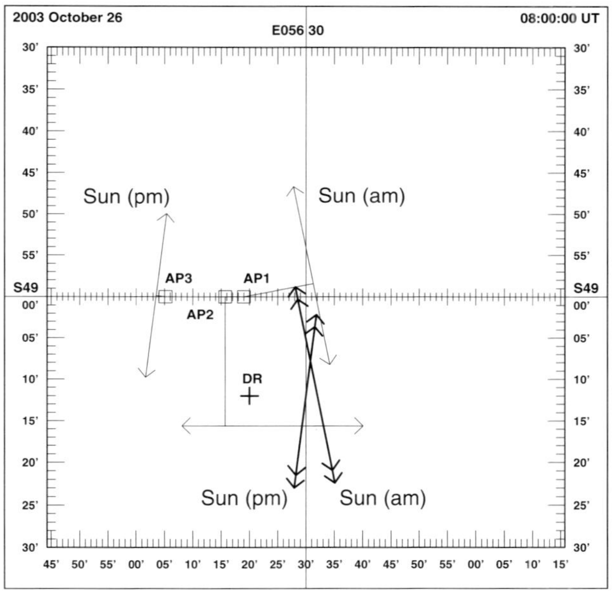

An alternative to using *The Nautical Almanac* for the ephemeris of the Sun is to use the ephemeris given in Table **4** (page 346). These positions are less accurate than the NA (see 3.3), but the table is valid from 2001 to 2036. The working below illustrates the process using data from the pervious example.

GHA and Declination of the Sun for 2003 October 26 using Table **4**

	h m s	h m s	h m s
UT of observation	03 38 47	07 58 59	12 39 40
Table **4**a UT corr. 2003	−1	−1	−1
OT of observation	02 38 47	06 58 59	11 39 40

Continued GHA and Declination of the Sun for 2003 October 26 using Table **4**

	h m s	° ′ ′	° ′ ′	h m s	° ′ ′	° ′ ′	h m s	° ′ ′	° ′ ′
Table **4**, Oct. 26		8 59 +2	S12 14 +21		8 59 +2	S12 14 +21		8 59 +2	S12 14 +21
4b, OT^h and diff.	03	0	+3	07	1	6	12	1	11
E and Dec, corrected		8 59	S12 17		9 00	S12 20		9 00	S12 25
4c: h and m of UT	03 30	227 30		07 50	292 30		12 30	2 30	
4d: m and s of UT	8 47	2 12		8 59	2 15		9 40	2 25	
GHA Sun = Sum	03 38 47	238 41		07 58 59	303 45		12 39 40	13 55	

Note that the orbit time (OT) is rounded to the nearest hour for looking up Table **4**a, while the UT time is used for Table **4**c and Table **4**d.

5.2.5 Special Techniques for Rapid Reduction This technique may be used when observations have been planned (see 5.1). The advantage being that the same assumed position and LHA, and thus H_C's and Z_n's from the planning stage are re-used in the actual reduction of the observations. This reduces the amount of calculation considerably. Thus the following example illustrates how to perform the calculation at a fixed time (the time planned, usually the time of the fix) and the correction that has to be applied to correct to the time of observation. This correction allows for the effect of the rotation of the sky between the time of fix and the time of observation and is referred to as the movement of the body (MOB).

In order to use this technique it is necessary to form the difference (see step 2) between the observations and the time of the fix (the time the GHA of the objects were calculated). Note, also, whether the fix is after the observation, when the interval is positive, or before the observation, when the interval is negative. This time interval is needed later (step 8b) for calculating the total correction (MOB), since the table (Table **2**) only gives the movement during a 1^m interval. In this example MOB is applied to the intercept.

The following example illustrates the advantages of using this special technique after planning your observations and is a continuation of the example in section 5.1.

Example. On the evening of 2003 March 19 the skies are clear and the navigator proceeds with the planned fix (see page xx). The current estimate of the position (DR) at $19^h\ 00^m$ local time is N 39° 05′, W 19° 45′, with a zone time of $+1^h$. Due to weather conditions observations of Saturn and Jupiter were made in close succession at $18^h\,55^m\,34^s$ and $18^h\,57^m\,34^s$, when the sextant readings were 69° 07′.5 and 54° 49′.5, respectively. Unfortunately the observation of *Sirius* did not occur until $19^h\,11^m\,04^s$ when the sextant reading was 34° 39′.9. The time of the observations were chosen allowing for the inaccuracy of the deck watch (fast by 4 seconds (-4^s)) and remembering that the MOB correction is easier to deal with in whole minutes.

During the period that the observations were made the distance made good (DMG) between each observation and the time of fix was estimated to be 1 nm, 0 nm, and 3 nm respectively. The navigator was at a height of 6 m (20ft.) and the temperature and pressure was 5°C and 980 mb, respectively. The error of the sextant was 1′.2 off the arc (+1′.2) and the vessel was on course of 60°T and the speed varied between about 10 and 13 knots.

	Saturn		Jupiter		*Sirius*	
	Date	h m s	Date	h m s	Date	h m s
Watch time of observations	2003 Mar. 19	18 55 34	2003 Mar. 19	18 57 34	2003 Mar. 19	19 11 04
Watch error (DWE)		−04		−04		−04
Local time of observations		18 55 30		18 57 30		19 11 00
Zone Correction		+1		+1		+1
UT of observations	2003 Mar. 19	19 55 30	2003 Mar. 19	19 57 30	2003 Mar. 19	20 11 00

Note that the current estimate of position is slightly different from that used in the planning example, but the tabulated latitude is still 39° N. The vessel may have reduced speed. The difference in the estimate of position might matter if you needed to use a different tabulated latitude (i.e. if the assumed latitude was now 40° N).

The result of this would be to change the calculated altitude (H_C) and thus reduce the size of the intercepts. The other effect would be that the object may not be in such a favourable position.

			Saturn	Jupiter	*Sirius*
1	Estimated position N 39° 05′, W 19° 45′				
			h m s	h m s	h m s
2	UT of Fix: 2003 March 19		20 00 00	20 00 00	20 00 00
	UT of observation		19 55 30	19 57 30	20 11 00
	Time of Fix − time of Observation		+4 30	+2 30	−11 00
	The Fix is		later	later	earlier
	than the observation by		4 30	2 30	11 00
3	GHA and Dec for UT of fix, see page xx		° ′	° ′	° ′
	Declination		N 22 12·7	N 19 00·6	S 16 43·3
	GHA of body		34 47·6	345 51·0	375 37·8
4	Assumed longitude, subtract because west		−19 47·6	−19 51·0	−19 37·8
	LHA of object at UT of fix		15	326	356
5	Extracted quantities, (see example page xx):	page	5	5	7
			° ′	° ′	° ′
	Calculated altitude	H_c	68 54	54 31	34 10
	Azimuth	Z_n	221	114	175
6	Correct sextant altitudes:				
	Sextant altitude	H_s	69 07·5	54 49·5	34 39·9
	Index error	IE	+1·2	+1·2	+1·2
	Dip, Table **6**a (height 6 m)	*D*	−4·3	−4·3	−4·3
	Apparent altitude	H_a	69 04·4	54 46·4	34 35·8
	Refraction Table **6**b	*R*	−0·4	−0·7	−1·4
	Additional refraction Table **6**c, 5°C, 980 mb		0·0	0·0	0·0
	Observed altitude	H_o	69 04·0	54 45·7	34 35·4
7	Intercept: calculated altitude (step 5)	H_c	68 54	54 31	34 10
	$p = H_o - H_c$		+10·0	+14·7	+25·4
8	(a) Correction: observer's motion (see below)	MOO	−0·9	0·0	+1·3
	(b) Correction: fixed LHA body (see below)	MOB	−34·7	+26·8	−11·0
	Intercept, corrected	*p*	−25·6	+41·5	+15·7
		p	*away* 25·6	*towards* 41·5	*towards* 15·7
	Azimuth (true bearing) (step 5)	Z_n	221°	114°	175°

9 The plot shows the DR position (N 39° 05′, W 19° 45′) and the position lines (lighter lines) for Saturn, Jupiter and *Sirius* plotted with respect to the appropriate assumed position N 39°, W 19° 47′·6 (AP1), N 39°, W 19° 51′·0 (AP2), and N 39°, W 19° 37′·8 (AP3) (see step 4).

The correction for MOO and MOB transfer the position lines, the darker lines, plotted with the double arrows at each end.

The fix is indicated by the area of the cocked-hat, but may lie outside it if the band of error either side of the position line exceeds the diameter of the cocked-hat.

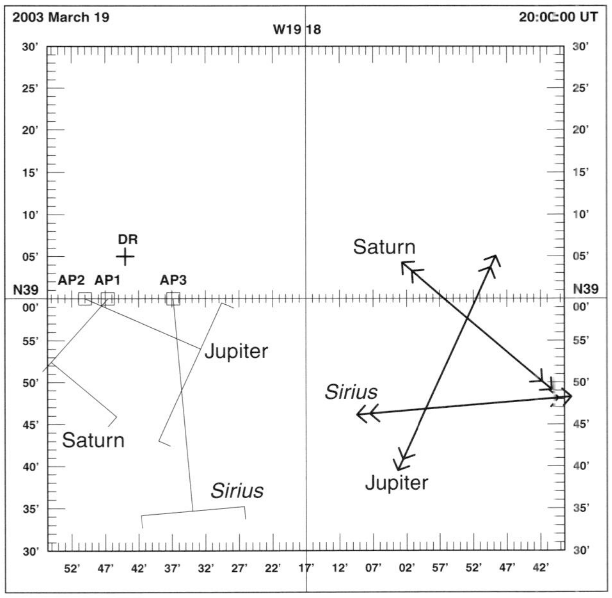

EXPLANATION

The example below illustrates how the corrections MOO and MOB, given in step 8 above, are calculated. The first correction, MOO, is described in detail in the previous example. It is required because the observer has moved between the time the observations were taken and the fix is required. The second correction, MOB, is for using a fixed value of LHA♈. A fixed value of LHA♈ was used as the positions of the bodies were obtained at the time of the fix and not at the time of observations.

In particular the total MOB correction for Saturn, for the $+4^{m}\ 30^{s}$ is calculated from $(+4{\cdot}5) \times (-7{\cdot}7) = -34'{\cdot}7$. Where the $-7'{\cdot}7$ is found by interpolating in Table **2** between latitudes 35° and 40°, and azimuths 219° and 222°. Alternatively, the correction for whole minutes may be calculated from Table **2** and the correction for the remaining fraction of a minute from the small table at the bottom of the page which also requires interpolation, as follows $(+4 \times -7{\cdot}7) - 3{\cdot}9 = -34'{\cdot}7$. The values tabulated in the table at the bottom of the page are (value from Table **2** × seconds/60). The calculation is simpler if the observations are made at multiples of whole minutes from the time of the fix. Care should be taken to ensure that the precision of the numbers is maintained.

		Saturn		Jupiter		*Sirius*	
True azimuth (bearing)	Z_n,		221°		114°		175°
Relative azimuth	Rel.$Z_n = Z_n - C$		221° − 60° = 161°		114° − 60° = 54°		175° − 60° = 115°
Distance made good	DMG		1 nm		0 nm		3 nm
Step 8a: Correction for movement of observer:			′		′		′
Table **1**, DMG, Rel.Z_n	MOO		− 0·9 *away*		0·0		+ 1·3 *towards*
Step 8b: Correction for using fixed UT:		m s	′	m s	′	m s	′
Table **2** correction; N 39°, Z_n		+1	− 7·7	+1	+10·7	+1	+ 1·0
Time Interval, see step 2	minutes	+4	−30·8	+2	+21·4	−11	−11·0
	seconds	30	− 3·9	30	+ 5·4	00	0·0
	MOB	+4 30	−34·7 *away*	+2 30	+26·8 *towards*	−11 00	−11·0 *away*

It is clear that the accuracy of this method depends on the azimuth (Z_n) of the object and how it changes between the time of the fix and the time of observation. This is shown by looking at Table **2** for MOB. For example the correction for 1^{m} of time for latitude 45° changes by 0′·0 for azimuths from 90° to 96°. However, for the same latitude and time period, but for azimuths 171° to 177° the correction changes by 1′·1.

RAPID
SIGHT REDUCTION TABLES
FOR
NAVIGATION

TABULATIONS FOR

LATITUDES 39°–89°

DECLINATIONS 0°–29°

LHA	0° Hc	0° d	0° Z	1° Hc	1° d	1° Z	2° Hc	2° d	2° Z	3° Hc	3° d	3° Z	4° Hc	4° d	4° Z
	° ′	′	°	° ′	′	°	° ′	′	°	° ′	′	°	° ′	′	°
0	51 00	+60	180	52 00	+60	180	53 00	+60	180	54 00	+60	180	55 00	+60	180
1	50 59	60	178	51 59	60	178	52 59	60	178	53 59	60	178	54 59	60	178
2	50 57	60	177	51 57	60	177	52 57	60	177	53 57	60	177	54 57	60	177
3	50 54	60	175	51 54	60	175	52 54	60	175	53 54	60	175	54 54	60	175
4	50 50	60	174	51 50	59	174	52 49	60	173	53 49	60	173	54 49	59	173
5	50 44	+60	172	51 44	+59	172	52 43	+60	172	53 43	+59	172	54 42	+60	171
6	50 37	59	171	51 36	60	170	52 36	59	170	53 35	60	170	54 35	59	170
7	50 29	59	169	51 28	59	169	52 27	59	169	53 26	60	168	54 26	59	168
8	50 19	59	167	51 18	59	167	52 17	59	167	53 16	59	167	54 15	59	166
9	50 08	59	166	51 07	59	166	52 06	59	165	53 05	59	165	54 04	58	165
10	49 56	+59	164	50 55	+58	164	51 53	+59	164	52 52	+58	163	53 50	+59	163
11	49 43	58	163	50 41	59	163	51 40	58	162	52 38	58	162	53 36	58	161
12	49 29	58	161	50 27	58	161	51 25	58	161	52 23	58	160	53 21	57	160
13	49 13	58	160	50 11	58	159	51 09	57	159	52 06	58	159	53 04	57	158
14	48 57	57	158	49 54	57	158	50 51	58	158	51 49	57	157	52 46	57	157
15	48 39	+57	157	49 36	+57	157	50 33	+57	156	51 30	+57	156	52 27	+56	155
16	48 20	57	156	49 17	56	155	50 13	57	155	51 10	56	154	52 06	56	153
17	48 00	57	154	48 57	56	154	49 53	56	153	50 49	56	153	51 45	56	152
18	47 39	56	153	48 35	56	152	49 31	56	152	50 27	55	151	51 22	56	150
19	47 17	56	151	48 13	56	151	49 09	55	150	50 04	55	150	50 59	55	149
20	46 55	+55	150	47 50	+55	149	48 45	+55	149	49 40	+54	148	50 34	+55	148
21	46 31	55	149	47 26	54	148	48 20	55	147	49 15	54	147	50 09	54	146
22	46 06	54	147	47 00	55	147	47 55	54	146	48 49	53	145	49 42	54	145
23	45 40	54	146	46 34	54	145	47 28	54	145	48 22	53	144	49 15	53	143
24	45 14	53	145	46 07	54	144	47 01	53	143	47 54	53	143	48 47	52	142
25	44 47	+53	144	45 40	+53	143	46 33	+52	142	47 25	+52	141	48 17	+52	141
26	44 18	53	142	45 11	52	142	46 03	53	141	46 56	51	140	47 47	52	139
27	43 49	53	141	44 42	52	140	45 34	51	140	46 25	52	139	47 17	51	138
28	43 20	52	140	44 12	51	139	45 03	51	138	45 54	51	138	46 45	51	137
29	42 49	52	139	43 41	51	138	44 32	51	137	45 23	50	136	46 13	50	136
30	42 18	+51	138	43 09	+51	137	44 00	+50	136	44 50	+50	135	45 40	+50	135
31	41 46	51	136	42 37	50	136	43 27	50	135	44 17	49	134	45 06	50	133
32	41 14	50	135	42 04	50	135	42 54	49	134	43 43	49	133	44 32	49	132
33	40 41	49	134	41 30	50	133	42 20	49	133	43 09	48	132	43 57	49	131
34	40 07	49	133	40 56	49	132	41 45	49	132	42 34	48	131	43 22	48	130
35	39 32	+49	132	40 21	+49	131	41 10	+48	130	41 58	+48	130	42 46	+47	129
36	38 57	49	131	39 46	48	130	40 34	48	129	41 22	47	129	42 09	47	128
37	38 22	48	130	39 10	48	129	39 58	47	128	40 45	47	128	41 32	47	127
38	37 46	47	129	38 33	48	128	39 21	47	127	40 08	46	127	40 54	47	126
39	37 09	47	128	37 56	47	127	38 43	47	126	39 30	46	126	40 16	46	125
40	36 32	+47	127	37 19	+47	126	38 06	+46	125	38 52	+46	125	39 38	+45	124
41	35 55	46	126	36 41	46	125	37 27	46	124	38 13	46	124	38 59	45	123
42	35 17	46	125	36 03	46	124	36 49	45	123	37 34	45	123	38 19	45	122
43	34 38	46	124	35 24	45	123	36 09	46	122	36 55	44	122	37 39	45	121
44	33 59	46	123	34 45	45	122	35 30	45	122	36 15	44	121	36 59	44	120
45	33 20	+45	122	34 05	+45	121	34 50	+44	121	35 34	+44	120	36 18	+44	119
46	32 40	45	121	33 25	45	121	34 10	44	120	34 54	43	119	35 37	44	118
47	32 00	45	120	32 45	44	120	33 29	44	119	34 13	43	118	34 56	43	117
48	31 20	44	120	32 04	44	119	32 48	43	118	33 31	43	117	34 14	43	116
49	30 39	44	119	31 23	43	118	32 06	44	117	32 50	42	116	33 32	43	115
50	29 58	+44	118	30 42	+43	117	31 25	+43	116	32 08	+42	115	32 50	+42	115
51	29 17	43	117	30 00	43	116	30 43	42	115	31 25	43	115	32 08	41	114
52	28 35	43	116	29 18	43	115	30 01	42	115	30 43	42	114	31 25	41	113
53	27 53	43	115	28 36	42	115	29 18	42	114	30 00	42	113	30 42	41	112
54	27 11	42	115	27 53	42	114	28 35	42	113	29 17	41	112	29 58	42	111
55	26 28	+42	114	27 10	+42	113	27 52	+42	112	28 34	+41	111	29 15	+41	111
56	25 46	41	113	26 27	42	112	27 09	41	111	27 50	41	111	28 31	41	110
57	25 02	42	112	25 44	41	111	26 25	41	111	27 06	41	110	27 47	40	109
58	24 19	42	112	25 01	41	111	25 42	40	110	26 22	41	109	27 03	40	108
59	23 36	41	111	24 17	41	110	24 58	40	109	25 38	40	108	26 18	40	108
60	22 52	+41	110	23 33	+40	109	24 13	+41	108	24 54	+40	108	25 34	+40	107
61	22 08	41	109	22 49	40	108	23 29	40	108	24 09	40	107	24 49	40	106
62	21 24	40	109	22 04	41	108	22 45	40	107	23 25	39	106	24 04	40	105
63	20 40	40	108	21 20	40	107	22 00	40	106	22 40	39	105	23 19	39	105
64	19 55	40	107	20 35	40	106	21 15	40	106	21 55	39	105	22 34	39	104
65	19 10	+40	106	19 50	+40	106	20 30	+39	105	21 09	+40	104	21 49	+39	103
66	18 26	39	106	19 05	40	105	19 45	39	104	20 24	39	103	21 03	39	102
67	17 41	39	105	18 20	40	104	19 00	39	103	19 39	39	103	20 18	38	102
68	16 56	39	104	17 35	39	104	18 14	39	103	18 53	39	102	19 32	38	101
69	16 10	40	104	16 50	39	103	17 29	38	102	18 07	39	101	18 46	39	100

LHA	5° Hc	5° d	5° Z	6° Hc	6° d	6° Z	7° Hc	7° d	7° Z	8° Hc	8° d	8° Z	9° Hc	9° d	9° Z
	° ′	′	°	° ′	′	°	° ′	′	°	° ′	′	°	° ′	′	°
0	56 00	+60	180	57 00	+60	180	58 00	+60	180	59 00	+60	180	60 00	+60	180
1	55 59	60	178	56 59	60	178	57 59	60	178	58 59	60	178	59 59	60	178
2	55 57	60	176	56 57	60	176	57 57	60	176	58 57	60	176	59 57	60	176
3	55 54	59	175	56 53	60	175	57 53	60	174	58 53	60	174	59 53	60	174
4	55 48	60	173	56 48	60	173	57 48	60	173	58 48	59	172	59 47	60	172
5	55 42	+60	171	56 42	+59	171	57 41	+60	171	58 41	+59	170	59 40	+60	170
6	55 34	59	169	56 33	60	169	57 33	59	169	58 32	59	169	59 31	60	168
7	55 25	59	168	56 24	59	167	57 23	59	167	58 22	59	167	59 21	59	166
8	55 14	59	166	56 13	59	166	57 12	59	165	58 11	58	165	59 09	59	164
9	55 02	59	164	56 01	58	164	56 59	59	163	57 58	58	163	58 56	58	163
10	54 49	+58	163	55 47	+58	162	56 45	+58	162	57 43	+58	161	58 41	+58	161
11	54 34	58	161	55 32	58	160	56 30	58	160	57 28	57	159	58 25	58	159
12	54 18	58	159	55 16	57	159	56 13	58	158	57 11	57	158	58 08	57	157
13	54 01	57	158	54 58	57	157	55 55	57	157	56 52	57	156	57 49	57	155
14	53 43	57	156	54 40	56	155	55 36	57	155	56 33	56	154	57 29	56	154
15	53 23	+57	154	54 20	+56	154	55 16	+56	153	56 12	+56	153	57 08	+55	152
16	53 02	56	153	53 58	56	152	54 54	56	152	55 50	55	151	56 45	55	150
17	52 41	55	151	53 36	55	151	54 31	55	150	55 26	55	149	56 21	55	149
18	52 18	55	150	53 13	55	149	54 08	54	148	55 02	54	148	55 56	55	147
19	51 54	54	148	52 48	55	148	53 43	54	147	54 37	54	146	55 31	53	145
20	51 29	+54	147	52 23	+54	146	53 17	+53	145	54 10	+54	145	55 04	+53	144
21	51 03	53	145	51 56	54	145	52 50	53	144	53 43	53	143	54 36	52	142
22	50 36	53	144	51 29	53	143	52 22	53	143	53 14	53	142	54 07	51	141
23	50 08	53	143	51 01	52	142	51 53	52	141	52 45	52	140	53 37	51	139
24	49 39	52	141	50 31	52	141	51 23	52	140	52 15	51	139	53 06	51	138
25	49 09	+52	140	50 01	+52	139	50 53	+51	138	51 44	+50	138	52 34	+51	137
26	48 39	51	139	49 30	51	138	50 21	51	137	51 12	50	136	52 02	50	135
27	48 08	51	137	48 59	50	137	49 49	50	136	50 39	50	135	51 29	49	134
28	47 36	50	136	48 26	50	135	49 16	50	134	50 06	49	134	50 55	48	133
29	47 03	50	135	47 53	49	134	48 42	49	133	49 31	49	132	50 20	48	131
30	46 30	+49	134	47 19	+49	133	48 08	+49	132	48 57	+48	131	49 45	+48	130
31	45 56	49	133	46 45	48	132	47 33	48	131	48 21	48	130	49 09	47	129
32	45 21	48	131	46 09	48	131	46 57	48	130	47 45	47	129	48 32	47	128
33	44 46	48	130	45 34	47	129	46 21	47	129	47 08	47	128	47 55	46	127
34	44 10	47	129	44 57	47	128	45 44	47	127	46 31	46	126	47 17	46	126
35	43 33	+47	128	44 20	+47	127	45 07	+46	126	45 53	+46	125	46 39	+46	124
36	42 56	47	127	43 43	46	126	44 29	46	125	45 15	46	124	46 01	44	123
37	42 19	46	126	43 05	46	125	43 51	45	124	44 36	45	123	45 21	45	122
38	41 41	45	125	42 26	46	124	43 12	45	123	43 57	45	122	44 42	44	121
39	41 02	46	124	41 48	45	123	42 33	44	122	43 17	45	121	44 02	43	120
40	40 23	+45	123	41 08	+45	122	41 53	+44	121	42 37	+44	120	43 21	+43	119
41	39 44	44	122	40 28	45	121	41 13	44	120	41 57	43	119	42 40	43	118
42	39 04	44	121	39 48	44	120	40 32	44	119	41 16	43	118	41 59	42	117
43	38 24	44	120	39 08	43	119	39 51	43	118	40 34	43	117	41 17	43	116
44	37 43	44	119	38 27	43	118	39 10	43	117	39 53	42	116	40 35	42	115
45	37 02	+43	118	37 45	+43	117	38 28	+43	116	39 11	+42	115	39 53	+42	114
46	36 21	43	117	37 04	42	116	37 46	43	115	38 29	41	115	39 10	42	114
47	35 39	43	116	36 22	42	115	37 04	42	115	37 46	42	114	38 28	41	113
48	34 57	42	115	35 40	42	114	36 22	41	114	37 03	41	113	37 44	41	112
49	34 15	42	115	34 57	42	114	35 39	41	113	36 20	41	112	37 01	40	111
50	33 32	+42	114	34 14	+42	113	34 56	+41	112	35 37	+40	111	36 17	+41	110
51	32 49	42	113	33 31	41	112	34 12	41	111	34 53	40	110	35 33	40	109
52	32 06	42	112	32 48	41	111	33 29	40	110	34 09	40	109	34 49	40	109
53	31 23	41	111	32 04	41	110	32 45	40	110	33 25	40	109	34 05	40	108
54	30 40	41	111	31 20	41	110	32 01	40	109	32 41	40	108	33 21	39	107
55	29 56	+40	110	30 36	+40	109	31 16	+40	108	31 56	+40	107	32 36	+39	106
56	29 12	40	109	29 52	40	108	30 32	40	107	31 12	39	106	31 51	39	105
57	28 27	41	108	29 08	39	107	29 47	40	106	30 27	39	106	31 06	39	105
58	27 43	40	107	28 23	40	107	29 03	39	106	29 42	39	105	30 21	38	104
59	26 58	40	106	27 38	40	106	28 18	39	105	28 57	38	104	29 35	39	103
60	26 14	+39	106	26 53	+39	105	27 32	+39	104	28 11	+39	103	28 50	+38	103
61	25 29	39	105	26 08	39	104	26 47	39	104	27 26	38	103	28 04	38	102
62	24 44	39	104	25 23	39	103	26 02	38	103	26 40	39	102	27 19	38	101
63	23 58	40	104	24 38	39	103	25 16	39	102	25 55	38	101	26 33	38	100
64	23 13	39	103	23 52	39	102	24 31	38	101	25 09	38	101	25 47	38	100
65	22 28	+38	102	23 06	+39	102	23 45	+38	101	24 23	+38	100	25 01	+37	99
66	21 42	39	102	22 21	38	101	22 59	38	100	23 37	38	99	24 15	37	98
67	20 56	39	101	21 35	38	100	22 13	38	99	22 51	38	98	23 29	37	98
68	20 10	39	100	20 49	38	99	21 27	38	99	22 05	37	98	22 42	38	97
69	19 25	38	100	20 03	38	99	20 41	38	98	21 19	37	97	21 56	37	96

10° Hc	10° d	10° Z	11° Hc	11° d	11° Z	12° Hc	12° d	12° Z	13° Hc	13° d	13° Z	14° Hc	14° d	14° Z	LHA
° ′	′	°	° ′	′	°	° ′	′	°	° ′	′	°	° ′	′	°	
61 00	+60	180	62 00	+60	180	63 00	+60	180	64 00	+60	180	65 00	+60	180	360
60 59	60	178	61 59	60	178	62 59	60	178	63 59	60	178	64 59	60	178	359
60 57	60	176	61 57	60	176	62 57	59	176	63 56	60	176	64 56	60	175	358
60 53	59	174	61 52	60	174	62 52	60	174	63 52	60	173	64 52	59	173	357
60 47	59	172	61 46	60	172	62 46	60	171	63 46	59	171	64 45	60	171	356
60 40	+59	170	61 39	+59	170	62 38	+60	169	63 38	+59	169	64 37	+59	169	355
60 31	59	168	61 30	59	168	62 29	59	167	63 28	59	167	64 27	59	166	354
60 20	59	166	61 19	59	166	62 18	58	165	63 16	59	165	64 15	58	164	353
60 08	58	164	61 06	59	164	62 05	58	163	63 03	58	163	64 01	58	162	352
59 54	59	162	60 53	58	162	61 51	57	161	62 48	58	161	63 46	58	160	351
59 39	+58	160	60 37	+58	160	61 35	+57	159	62 32	+57	159	63 29	+58	158	350
59 23	57	158	60 20	57	158	61 17	57	157	62 14	57	157	63 11	57	156	349
59 05	57	157	60 02	56	156	60 58	57	155	61 55	56	155	62 51	56	154	348
58 46	56	155	59 42	56	154	60 38	56	153	61 34	56	153	62 30	55	152	347
58 25	56	153	59 21	56	152	60 17	55	152	61 12	55	151	62 07	55	150	346
58 03	+56	151	58 59	+55	151	59 54	+55	150	60 49	+54	149	61 43	+54	148	345
57 40	55	150	58 35	55	149	59 30	54	148	60 24	54	147	61 18	53	146	344
57 16	54	148	58 10	54	147	59 04	54	146	59 58	53	145	60 51	53	144	343
56 51	53	146	57 44	54	145	58 38	53	145	59 31	52	144	60 23	53	143	342
56 24	53	145	57 17	53	144	58 10	53	143	59 03	52	142	59 55	51	141	341
55 57	+52	143	56 49	+52	142	57 41	+52	141	58 33	+52	140	59 25	+51	139	340
55 28	52	142	56 20	52	141	57 12	51	140	58 03	51	139	58 54	50	138	339
54 58	52	140	55 50	51	139	56 41	51	138	57 32	50	137	58 22	50	136	338
54 28	51	139	55 19	51	138	56 10	50	137	57 00	49	136	57 49	49	135	337
53 57	50	137	54 47	50	136	55 37	50	135	56 27	49	134	57 16	48	133	336
53 25	+49	136	54 14	+50	135	55 04	+49	134	55 53	+48	133	56 41	+48	132	335
52 52	49	134	53 41	49	133	54 30	48	132	55 18	48	131	56 06	47	130	334
52 18	49	133	53 07	48	132	53 55	48	131	54 43	47	130	55 30	47	129	333
51 43	49	132	52 32	47	131	53 19	48	130	54 07	46	129	54 53	46	128	332
51 08	48	131	51 56	47	130	52 43	47	129	53 30	46	127	54 16	46	126	331
50 33	+47	129	51 20	+46	128	52 06	+47	127	52 53	+45	126	53 38	+45	125	330
49 56	47	128	50 43	46	127	51 29	46	126	52 15	45	125	53 00	44	124	329
49 19	46	127	50 05	46	126	50 51	45	125	51 36	45	124	52 21	44	123	328
48 41	46	126	49 27	46	125	50 13	44	124	50 57	44	123	51 41	44	122	327
48 03	46	125	48 49	44	124	49 33	45	123	50 18	43	122	51 01	43	120	326
47 25	+45	123	48 10	+44	122	48 54	+44	121	49 38	+43	120	50 21	+43	119	325
46 45	45	122	47 30	44	121	48 14	43	120	48 57	43	119	49 40	42	118	324
46 06	44	121	46 50	43	120	47 33	43	119	48 16	43	118	48 59	42	117	323
45 26	43	120	46 09	44	119	46 53	42	118	47 35	42	117	48 17	41	116	322
44 45	44	119	45 29	42	118	46 11	42	117	46 53	42	116	47 35	41	115	321
44 04	+43	118	44 47	+43	117	45 30	+41	116	46 11	+42	115	46 53	+40	114	320
43 23	43	117	44 06	42	116	44 48	41	115	45 29	41	114	46 10	40	113	319
42 41	43	116	43 24	41	115	44 05	41	114	44 46	41	113	45 27	40	112	318
42 00	41	115	42 41	42	114	43 23	40	113	44 03	41	112	44 44	39	111	317
41 17	42	114	41 59	41	114	42 40	40	113	43 20	40	112	44 00	39	110	316
40 35	+41	114	41 16	+40	113	41 56	+41	112	42 37	+39	111	43 16	+39	110	315
39 52	41	113	40 33	40	112	41 13	40	111	41 53	39	110	42 32	39	109	314
39 09	40	112	39 49	40	111	40 29	40	110	41 09	39	109	41 48	39	108	313
38 25	40	111	39 05	40	110	39 45	40	109	40 25	38	108	41 03	39	107	312
37 41	40	110	38 21	40	109	39 01	39	108	39 40	39	107	40 19	38	106	311
36 58	+39	109	37 37	+40	108	38 17	+39	107	38 56	+38	106	39 34	+38	105	310
36 13	40	108	36 53	39	108	37 32	39	107	38 11	38	106	38 49	38	105	309
35 29	39	108	36 08	39	107	36 47	39	106	37 26	38	105	38 04	37	104	308
34 45	39	107	35 24	38	106	36 02	39	105	36 41	37	104	37 18	38	103	307
34 00	39	106	34 39	38	105	35 17	38	104	35 55	38	103	36 33	37	102	306
33 15	+39	105	33 54	+38	104	34 32	+38	103	35 10	+37	103	35 47	+37	102	305
32 30	38	105	33 08	39	104	33 47	37	103	34 24	37	102	35 01	37	101	304
31 45	38	104	32 23	38	103	33 01	37	102	33 38	38	101	34 16	36	100	303
30 59	38	103	31 37	38	102	32 15	38	101	32 53	37	100	33 30	36	99	302
30 14	38	102	30 52	37	101	31 29	38	101	32 07	37	100	32 44	36	99	301
29 28	+38	102	30 06	+38	101	30 44	+37	100	31 21	+36	99	31 57	+37	98	300
28 42	38	101	29 20	38	100	29 58	37	99	30 35	36	98	31 11	36	97	299
27 57	37	100	28 34	37	99	29 11	37	98	29 48	37	98	30 25	36	97	298
27 11	37	100	27 48	37	99	28 25	37	98	29 02	37	97	29 39	36	96	297
26 25	37	99	27 02	37	98	27 39	37	97	28 16	36	96	28 52	36	95	296
25 38	+38	98	26 16	+37	97	26 53	+36	96	27 29	+37	96	28 06	+36	95	295
24 52	37	97	25 29	37	97	26 06	37	96	26 43	36	95	27 19	36	94	294
24 06	37	97	24 43	37	96	25 20	36	95	25 56	37	94	26 33	36	93	293
23 20	37	96	23 57	36	95	24 33	37	94	25 10	36	94	25 46	36	93	292
22 33	37	95	23 10	37	95	23 47	36	94	24 23	37	93	25 00	35	92	291

N. Lat. {LHA greater than 180°....... Zn=Z / LHA less than 180°........... Zn=360−Z}

DECLINATION (0°-14°) SAME NAME AS LATITUDE

LHA	0°			1°			2°			3°			4°			5°			6°			7°			8°			9°			10°			11°			12°			13°			14°			LHA
	Hc	d	Z	Hc	d	Z	Hc	d	Z	Hc	d	Z	Hc	d	Z	Hc	d	Z	Hc	d	Z	Hc	d	Z	Hc	d	Z	Hc	d	Z	Hc	d	Z	Hc	d	Z	Hc	d	Z	Hc	d	Z	Hc	d	Z	
	° ′	′	°	° ′	′	°	° ′	′	°	° ′	′	°	° ′	′	°	° ′	′	°	° ′	′	°	° ′	′	°	° ′	′	°	° ′	′	°	° ′	′	°	° ′	′	°	° ′	′	°	° ′	′	°	° ′	′	°	
70	15 25	+39	103	16 04	+39	102	16 43	+39	101	17 22	+38	101	18 00	+39	100	18 39	+38	99	19 17	+38	98	19 55	+37	97	20 32	+38	96	21 10	+37	96	21 47	+37	95	22 24	+36	94	23 00	+37	93	23 37	+36	92	24 13	+36	91	290
71	14 39	39	102	15 18	39	101	15 57	39	101	16 36	38	100	17 14	38	99	17 52	38	98	18 30	38	97	19 08	38	97	19 46	37	96	20 23	37	95	21 00	37	94	21 37	37	93	22 14	36	92	22 50	36	92	23 26	36	91	289
72	13 54	39	102	14 33	38	101	15 11	39	100	15 50	38	99	16 28	38	98	17 06	38	98	17 44	38	97	18 22	37	96	18 59	38	95	19 37	37	94	20 14	37	94	20 51	36	93	21 27	37	92	22 04	36	91	22 40	35	90	288
73	13 08	39	101	13 47	38	100	14 25	39	99	15 04	38	99	15 42	38	98	16 20	38	97	16 58	37	96	17 35	38	95	18 13	37	95	18 50	37	94	19 27	37	93	20 04	37	92	20 41	36	91	21 17	36	90	21 53	36	89	287
74	12 22	39	100	13 01	38	99	13 39	39	99	14 18	38	98	14 56	38	97	15 34	37	96	16 11	38	96	16 49	37	95	17 26	38	94	18 04	37	93	18 41	36	92	19 17	37	91	19 54	36	91	20 30	36	90	21 06	36	89	286
75	11 36	+39	100	12 15	+38	99	12 53	+38	98	13 31	+38	97	14 09	+38	96	14 47	+38	96	15 25	+38	95	16 03	+37	94	16 40	+37	93	17 17	+37	92	17 54	+37	92	18 31	+36	91	19 07	+37	90	19 44	+36	89	20 20	+36	88	285
76	10 50	39	99	11 29	38	98	12 07	38	97	12 45	38	97	13 23	38	96	14 01	38	95	14 39	37	94	15 16	37	93	15 53	38	93	16 31	36	92	17 07	37	91	17 44	37	90	18 21	36	89	18 57	36	88	19 33	36	88	284
77	10 04	38	98	10 42	39	98	11 21	38	97	11 59	38	96	12 37	37	95	13 14	38	94	13 52	37	94	14 29	38	93	15 07	37	92	15 44	37	91	16 21	37	90	16 58	36	89	17 34	36	89	18 10	37	88	18 47	36	87	283
78	09 18	38	98	09 56	38	97	10 34	38	96	11 12	38	95	11 50	38	95	12 28	37	94	13 05	38	93	13 43	37	92	14 20	37	91	14 57	37	91	15 34	37	90	16 11	37	89	16 48	36	88	17 24	36	87	18 00	36	86	282
79	08 32	38	97	09 10	38	96	09 48	38	95	10 26	38	95	11 04	37	94	11 41	38	93	12 19	37	92	12 56	38	91	13 34	37	91	14 11	37	90	14 48	36	89	15 24	37	88	16 01	36	87	16 37	37	87	17 14	36	86	281
80	07 45	+38	96	08 23	+38	96	09 01	+38	95	09 39	+38	94	10 17	+38	93	10 55	+37	92	11 32	+38	92	12 10	+37	91	12 47	+37	90	13 24	+37	89	14 01	+37	88	14 38	+36	88	15 14	+37	87	15 51	+36	86	16 27	+36	85	280
81	06 59	38	96	07 37	38	95	08 15	38	94	08 53	37	93	09 30	38	93	10 08	38	92	10 46	37	91	11 23	37	90	12 00	37	89	12 37	37	89	13 14	37	88	13 51	37	87	14 28	36	86	15 04	37	85	15 41	36	85	279
82	06 13	38	95	06 51	37	94	07 28	38	94	08 06	38	93	08 44	38	92	09 22	37	91	09 59	37	90	10 36	38	90	11 14	37	89	11 51	37	88	12 28	37	87	13 05	36	86	13 41	37	86	14 18	36	85	14 54	36	84	278
83	05 26	38	94	06 04	38	94	06 42	38	93	07 20	37	92	07 57	38	91	08 35	37	91	09 12	38	90	09 50	37	89	10 27	37	88	11 04	37	87	11 41	37	87	12 18	37	86	12 55	36	85	13 31	37	84	14 08	36	83	277
84	04 40	37	94	05 17	38	93	05 55	38	92	06 33	38	91	07 11	37	91	07 48	38	90	08 26	37	89	09 03	37	88	09 40	38	88	10 18	37	87	10 55	37	86	11 32	36	85	12 08	37	84	12 45	37	84	13 22	36	83	276
85	03 53	+38	93	04 31	+38	92	05 09	+37	92	05 46	+38	91	06 24	+38	90	07 02	+37	89	07 39	+38	89	08 17	+37	88	08 54	+37	87	09 31	+37	86	10 08	+37	85	10 45	+37	85	11 22	+37	84	11 59	+36	83	12 35	+37	82	275
86	03 06	38	93	03 44	38	92	04 22	38	91	05 00	37	90	05 37	38	89	06 15	38	89	06 53	37	88	07 30	37	87	08 07	38	86	08 45	37	86	09 22	37	85	09 59	37	84	10 36	37	83	11 13	36	82	11 49	37	82	274
87	02 20	38	92	02 58	37	91	03 35	38	90	04 13	38	90	04 51	37	89	05 28	38	88	06 06	37	87	06 43	38	86	07 21	37	86	07 58	37	85	08 35	37	84	09 12	38	83	09 50	36	83	10 26	37	82	11 03	37	81	273
88	01 33	38	91	02 11	38	90	02 49	37	90	03 26	38	89	04 04	38	88	04 42	37	87	05 19	38	87	05 57	37	86	06 34	38	85	07 12	37	84	07 49	37	83	08 26	37	83	09 03	37	82	09 40	37	81	10 17	37	80	272
89	00 47	37	91	01 24	38	90	02 02	38	89	02 40	38	88	03 18	37	88	03 55	38	87	04 33	37	86	05 10	38	85	05 48	37	84	06 25	38	84	07 03	37	83	07 40	37	82	08 17	37	81	08 54	37	80	09 31	37	80	271
90	00 00	+38	90	00 38	+38	89	01 16	+37	88	01 53	+38	88	02 31	+38	87	03 09	+37	86	03 46	+38	85	04 24	+38	85	05 02	+37	84	05 39	+37	83	06 16	+38	82	06 54	+37	81	07 31	+37	81	08 08	+37	80	08 45	+37	79	270
91	−0 47	38	89	−0 09	38	89	00 29	38	88	01 07	37	87	01 44	38	86	02 22	38	85	03 00	38	85	03 38	37	84	04 15	38	83	04 53	37	82	05 30	38	82	06 08	37	81	06 45	38	80	07 23	37	79	08 00	37	78	269
92	−1 33	38	89	−0 55	37	88	−0 18	38	87	00 20	38	86	00 58	38	86	01 36	37	85	02 13	38	84	02 51	38	83	03 29	38	83	04 07	37	82	04 44	38	81	05 22	37	80	05 59	38	79	06 37	37	79	07 14	37	78	268
93	−2 20	38	88	−1 42	38	87	−1 04	38	87	−0 26	37	86	00 11	38	85	00 49	38	84	01 27	38	83	02 05	38	83	02 43	37	82	03 20	38	81	03 58	38	80	04 36	38	80	05 14	37	79	05 51	38	78	06 29	37	77	267
94	−3 06	37	87	−2 29	38	87	−1 51	38	86	−1 13	38	85	−0 35	38	84	00 03	38	84	00 41	38	83	01 19	38	82	01 57	37	81	02 34	38	80	03 12	38	80	03 50	38	79	04 28	38	78	05 06	37	77	05 43	38	77	266
95	−3 53	+38	87	−3 15	+38	86	−2 37	+38	85	−1 59	+38	85	−1 21	+38	84	−0 43	+38	83	−0 05	+38	82	00 33	+38	81	01 11	+37	81	01 48	+38	80	02 26	+38	79	03 04	+38	78	03 42	+38	78	04 20	+38	77	04 58	+38	76	265
96	−4 40	38	86	−4 02	38	85	−3 24	38	85	−2 46	38	84	−2 08	38	83	−1 30	38	82	−0 52	38	82	−0 14	39	81	00 25	38	80	01 03	38	79	01 41	38	78	02 19	38	78	02 57	38	77	03 35	38	76	04 13	38	75	264
97	−5 26	38	86	−4 48	38	85	−4 10	38	84	−3 32	38	83	−2 54	38	82	−2 16	38	82	−1 38	38	81	−1 00	39	80	−0 21	38	79	00 17	38	79	00 55	38	78	01 33	38	77	02 11	38	76	02 49	39	76	03 28	38	75	263
98	−6 13	38	85	−5 35	39	84	−4 56	38	83	−4 18	38	83	−3 40	38	82	−3 02	38	81	−2 24	39	80	−1 45	38	80	−1 07	38	79	−0 29	39	78	00 10	38	77	00 48	38	76	01 26	38	76	02 04	39	75	02 43	38	74	262
99				−6 21	38	84	−5 43	38	83	−5 05	39	82	−4 26	38	81	−3 48	38	80	−3 10	39	80	−2 31	38	79	−1 53	39	78	−1 14	38	77	−0 36	39	77	00 03	38	76	00 41	38	75	01 19	39	74	01 58	38	74	261
100							−6 29	+38	82	−5 51	+39	81	−5 12	+38	81	−4 34	+39	80	−3 55	+38	79	−3 17	+39	78	−2 38	+38	77	−2 00	+39	77	−1 21	+38	76	−0 43	+39	75	−0 04	+39	74	00 35	+38	74	01 13	+39	73	260
101													−5 58	38	80	−5 20	39	79	−4 41	38	78	−4 03	39	78	−3 24	39	77	−2 45	39	76	−2 06	38	75	−1 28	39	75	−0 49	39	74	−0 10	39	73	00 29	39	72	259
102																−6 06	39	78	−5 27	39	78	−4 48	39	77	−4 09	39	76	−3 30	39	75	−2 51	39	75	−2 12	38	74	−1 34	39	73	−0 55	39	72	−0 16	39	72	258
103																			−6 12	39	77	−5 33	39	76	−4 54	39	76	−4 15	39	75	−3 36	39	74	−2 57	39	73	−2 18	39	73	−1 39	39	72	−1 00	39	71	257
104																						−6 19	39	76	−5 40	40	75	−5 00	39	74	−4 21	39	73	−3 42	40	73	−3 02	39	72	−2 23	39	71	−1 44	40	70	256
105																									−6 24	+39	74	−5 45	+39	74	−5 06	+40	73	−4 26	+39	72	−3 47	+40	71	−3 07	+39	70	−2 28	+40	70	255
106																															−5 50	39	72	−5 11	40	71	−4 31	40	71	−3 51	40	70	−3 11	40	69	254
107																																		−5 55	40	71	−5 15	40	70	−4 35	40	69	−3 55	40	68	253
108																																					−5 58	40	69	−5 18	40	69	−4 38	40	68	252
109																																								−6 02	41	68	−5 21	40	67	251
110																																											−6 04	+41	66	250

DECLINATION (0°-14°) CONTRARY NAME TO LATITUDE

LHA	0°			1°			2°			3°			4°			5°			6°			7°			8°			9°			10°			11°			12°			13°			14°			LHA
98	−6 13	38	85	262																																										
97	−5 26	38	86	−6 04	38	86	263																																							
96	−4 40	37	86	−5 17	38	87	−5 55	38	88	264																																				
95	−3 53	−38	87	−4 31	−38	88	−5 09	−37	88	−5 46	−38	89	−6 24	−38	90	265																														
94	−3 06	38	87	−3 44	38	88	−4 22	38	89	−5 00	37	90	−5 37	38	91	−6 15	38	91	266																											
93	−2 20	38	88	−2 58	37	89	−3 35	38	90	−4 13	38	90	−4 51	37	91	−5 28	38	92	−6 06	37	93	267																								
92	−1 33	38	89	−2 11	38	90	−2 49	37	90	−3 26	38	91	−4 04	38	92	−4 42	37	93	−5 19	38	93	−5 57	37	94	268																					
91	−0 47	37	89	−1 24	38	90	−2 02	38	91	−2 40	38	92	−3 18	37	92	−3 55	38	93	−4 33	37	94	−5 10	38	95	−5 48	37	96	−6 25	38	96	269															
90	00 00	−38	90	−0 38	−38	91	−1 16	−37	92	−1 53	−38	92	−2 31	−38	93	−3 09	−37	94	−3 46	−38	95	−4 24	−38	95	−5 02	−37	96	−5 39	−37	97	−6 16	−38	98	270												
89	00 47	38	91	00 09	38	91	−0 29	38	92	−1 07	37	93	−1 44	38	94	−2 22	38	95	−3 00	38	95	−3 38	37	96	−4 15	38	97	−4 53	37	98	−5 30	38	98	−6 08	37	99	271									
88	01 33	38	91	00 55	37	92	00 18	38	93	−0 20	38	94	−0 58	38	94	−1 36	37	95	−2 13	38	96	−2 51	38	97	−3 29	38	97	−4 07	37	98	−4 44	38	99	−5 22	37	100	−5 59	38	101	272						
87	02 20	38	92	01 42	38	93	01 04	38	93	00 26	37	94	−0 11	38	95	−0 49	38	96	−1 27	38	97	−2 05	38	97	−2 43	37	98	−3 20	38	99	−3 58	38	100	−4 36	38	100	−5 14	37	101	−5 51	38	102	−6 29	37	103	273
86	03 06	37	93	02 29	38	93	01 51	38	94	01 13	38	95	00 35	38	96	−0 03	38	96	−0 41	38	97	−1 19	38	98	−1 57	37	99	−2 34	38	100	−3 12	38	100	−3 50	38	101	−4 28	38	102	−5 06	37	103	−5 43	38	103	274
85	03 53	−38	93	03 15	−38	94	02 37	−38	95	01 59	−38	95	01 21	−38	96	00 43	−38	97	00 05	−38	98	−0 33	−38	99	−1 11	−37	99	−1 48	−38	100	−2 26	−38	101	−3 04	−38	102	−3 42	−38	102	−4 20	−38	103	−4 58	−38	104	275
84	04 40	38	94	04 02	38	95	03 24	38	95	02 46	38	96	02 08	38	97	01 30	38	98	00 52	38	98	00 14	39	99	−0 25	38	100	−1 03	38	101	−1 41	38	102	−2 19	38	102	−2 57	38	103	−3 35	38	104	−4 13	38	105	276
83	05 26	38	94	04 48	38	95	04 10	38	96	03 32	38	97	02 54	38	98	02 16	38	98	01 38	38	99	01 00	39	100	00 21	38	101	−0 17	38	101	−0 55	38	102	−1 33	38	103	−2 11	38	104	−2 49	39	104	−3 28	38	105	277
82	06 13	38	95	05 35	39	96	04 56	38	97	04 18	38	97	03 40	38	98	03 02	38	99	02 24	39	100	01 45	38	100	01 07	38	101	00 29	39	102	−0 10	38	103	−0 48	38	104	−1 26	38	104	−2 04	39	105	−2 43	38	106	278
81	06 59	38	96	06 21	38	97	05 43	38	97	05 05	39	98	04 26	38	99	03 48	38	100	03 10	39	100	02 31	38	101	01 53	39	102	01 14	38	103	00 36	39	103	−0 03	38	104	−0 41	38	105	−1 19	39	106	−1 58	38	106	279
80	07 45	−38	96	07 07	−38	97	06 29	−38	98	05 51	−39	99	05 12	−38	99	04 34	−39	100	03 55	−38	101	03 17	−39	102	02 38	−38	103	02 00	−39	103	01 21	−38	104	00 43	−39	105	00 04	−39	106	−0 35	−38	106	−1 13	−39	107	280
79	08 32	39	97	07 53	38	98	07 15	38	99	06 37	39	99	05 58	38	100	05 20	39	101	04 41	38	102	04 03	39	102	03 24	39	103	02 45	39	104	02 06	38	105	01 28	39	105	00 49	39	106	00 10	39	107	−0 29	39	108	281
78	09 18	38	98	08 40	39	98	08 01	38	99	07 23	39	100	06 44	38	101	06 06	39	102	05 27	39	102	04 48	39	103	04 09	39	104	03 30	39	105	02 51	39	105	02 12	38	106	01 34	39	107	00 55	39	108	00 16	39	108	282
77	10 04	38	98	09 26	39	99	08 47	38	100	08 09	39	101	07 30	39	101	06 51	39	102	06 12	39	103	05 33	39	104	04 54	39	104	04 15	39	105	03 36	39	106	02 57	39	107	02 18	39	107	01 39	39	108	01 00	39	109	283
76	10 50	38	99	10 12	39	100	09 33	39	101	08 54	38	101	08 16	39	102	07 37	39	103	06 58	39	104	06 19	39	104	05 40	40	105	05 00	39	106	04 21	39	107	03 42	40	107	03 02	39	108	02 23	39	109	01 44	40	110	284
75	11 36	−38	100	10 58	−39	100	10 19	−39	101	09 40	−39	102	09 01	−39	103	08 22	−39	103	07 43	−39	104	07 04	−40	105	06 24	−39	106	05 45	−39	107	05 06	−40	107	04 26	−39	108	03 47	−40	109	03 07	−39	110	02 28	−40	110	285
74	12 22	39	100	11 43	38	101	11 05	39	102	10 26	39	103	09 47	40	103	09 07	39	104	08 28	39	105	07 49	40	106	07 09	39	106	06 30	40	107	05 50	39	108	05 11	40	109	04 31	40	109	03 51	40	110	03 11	40	111	286
73	13 08	39	101	12 29	39	102	11 50	39	102	11 11	39	103	10 32	39	104	09 53	40	105	09 13	39	106	08 34	40	106	07 54	40	107	07 14	40	108	06 34	39	109	05 55	40	109	05 15	40	110	04 35	40	111	03 55	40	112	287
72	13 54	39	102	13 15	39	102	12 36	40	103	11 56	39	104	11 17	39	105	10 38	40	105	09 58	40	106	09 18	40	107	08 38	39	108	07 59	40	109	07 19	40	109	06 39	41	110	05 58	40	111	05 18	40	112	04 38	40	112	288
71	14 39	39	102	14 00	39	103	13 21	39	104	12 42	40	105	12 02	40	105	11 22	39	106	10 43	40	107	10 03	40	108	09 23	40	108	08 43	40	109	08 03	41	110	07 22	40	111	06 42	40	111	06 02	41	112	05 21	40	113	289
70	15 25	−39	103	14 46	−40	104	14 06	−39	105	13 27	−40	105	12 47	−40	106	12 07	−40	107	11 27	−40	108	10 47	−40	108	10 07	−40	109	09 27	−41	110	08 46	−40	111	08 06	−41	111	07 25	−40	112	06 45	−41	113	06 04	−41	114	290

S. Lat. {LHA greater than 180°....... Zn=180−Z / LHA less than 180°........... Zn=180+Z}

N. Lat. {LHA greater than 180°........ Zn=Z; LHA less than 180°........... Zn=360−Z}

DECLINATION (0°-14°) CONTRARY NAME TO LATITUDE

LAT 39°

LHA	0° Hc	d	Z	1° Hc	d	Z	2° Hc	d	Z	3° Hc	d	Z	4° Hc	d	Z
	° ′	′	°	° ′	′	°	° ′	′	°	° ′	′	°	° ′	′	°
69	16 10	39	104	15 31	40	104	14 51	39	105	14 12	40	106	13 32	40	107
68	16 56	40	104	16 16	40	105	15 36	40	106	14 56	40	107	14 16	40	107
67	17 41	40	105	17 01	40	106	16 21	40	107	15 41	40	107	15 01	41	108
66	18 26	40	106	17 46	40	106	17 06	41	107	16 25	40	108	15 45	41	109
65	19 10	−40	106	18 30	−40	107	17 50	−40	108	17 10	−41	109	16 29	−41	110
64	19 55	40	107	19 15	41	108	18 34	40	109	17 54	41	109	17 13	41	110
63	20 40	41	108	19 59	40	109	19 19	41	109	18 38	41	110	17 57	42	111
62	21 24	41	109	20 43	41	109	20 02	41	110	19 21	41	111	18 40	41	112
61	22 08	41	109	21 27	41	110	20 46	41	111	20 05	42	112	19 23	41	112
60	22 52	−41	110	22 11	−41	111	21 30	−42	112	20 48	−42	112	20 06	−42	113
59	23 36	42	111	22 54	41	112	22 13	42	112	21 31	42	113	20 49	42	114
58	24 19	41	112	23 38	42	112	22 56	42	113	22 14	42	114	21 32	43	115
57	25 02	41	112	24 21	42	113	23 39	43	114	22 56	42	115	22 14	43	115
56	25 46	43	113	25 03	42	114	24 21	42	115	23 39	43	115	22 56	43	116
55	26 28	−42	114	25 46	−43	115	25 03	−42	115	24 21	−43	116	23 38	−44	117
54	27 11	43	115	26 28	43	115	25 45	43	116	25 02	43	117	24 19	43	118
53	27 53	43	115	27 10	43	116	26 27	43	117	25 44	44	118	25 00	44	119
52	28 35	43	116	27 52	43	117	27 09	44	118	26 25	44	119	25 41	44	119
51	29 17	44	117	28 33	43	118	27 50	44	119	27 06	44	119	26 22	45	120
50	29 58	−44	118	29 14	−44	119	28 30	−44	119	27 46	−44	120	27 02	−45	121
49	30 39	44	119	29 55	44	120	29 11	45	120	28 26	44	121	27 42	46	122
48	31 20	44	120	30 36	45	120	29 51	45	121	29 06	45	122	28 21	45	123
47	32 00	44	120	31 16	45	121	30 31	45	122	29 46	46	123	29 00	46	124
46	32 40	45	121	31 55	45	122	31 10	45	123	30 25	46	124	29 39	46	124
45	33 20	−45	122	32 35	−46	123	31 49	−46	124	31 03	−46	125	30 17	−46	125
44	33 59	45	123	33 14	46	124	32 28	47	125	31 41	46	125	30 55	47	126
43	34 38	46	124	33 52	46	125	33 06	47	126	32 19	47	126	31 32	47	127
42	35 17	47	125	34 30	46	126	33 44	47	127	32 57	48	127	32 09	47	128
41	35 55	47	126	35 08	47	127	34 21	47	127	33 34	48	128	32 46	48	129
40	36 32	−47	127	35 45	−47	128	34 58	−48	128	34 10	−48	129	33 22	−48	130
39	37 09	47	128	36 22	48	129	35 34	48	129	34 46	48	130	33 58	49	131
38	37 46	48	129	36 58	48	130	36 10	49	130	35 21	48	131	34 33	49	132
37	38 22	48	130	37 34	49	131	36 45	49	131	35 56	49	132	35 07	49	133
36	38 57	48	131	38 09	49	132	37 20	50	132	36 30	49	133	35 41	50	134
35	39 32	−49	132	38 43	−49	133	37 54	−50	133	37 04	−50	134	36 14	−50	135
34	40 07	50	133	39 17	50	134	38 27	50	135	37 37	50	135	36 47	50	136
33	40 41	50	134	39 51	51	135	39 00	50	136	38 10	51	136	37 19	51	137
32	41 14	51	135	40 23	50	136	39 33	51	137	38 42	51	137	37 51	51	138
31	41 46	51	136	40 55	51	137	40 04	51	138	39 13	51	138	38 22	52	139
30	42 18	−51	138	41 27	−51	138	40 36	−52	139	39 44	−52	140	38 52	−52	140
29	42 49	51	139	41 58	52	139	41 06	52	140	40 14	53	141	39 21	52	141
28	43 20	52	140	42 28	53	141	41 35	52	141	40 43	53	142	39 50	53	142
27	43 49	52	141	42 57	53	142	42 04	53	142	41 11	53	143	40 18	53	144
26	44 18	52	142	43 26	54	143	42 32	53	144	41 39	53	144	40 46	54	145
25	44 47	−54	144	43 53	−53	144	43 00	−54	145	42 06	−54	145	41 12	−54	146
24	45 14	54	145	44 20	54	145	43 26	54	146	42 32	54	147	41 38	55	147
23	45 40	54	146	44 46	54	147	43 52	55	147	42 57	54	148	42 03	55	148
22	46 06	54	147	45 12	55	148	44 17	55	149	43 22	55	149	42 27	55	150
21	46 31	55	149	45 36	55	149	44 41	56	150	43 45	55	150	42 50	56	151
20	46 55	−56	150	45 59	−55	151	45 04	−56	151	44 08	−56	152	43 12	−56	152
19	47 17	55	151	46 22	56	152	45 26	56	152	44 30	56	153	43 34	57	153
18	47 39	56	153	46 43	56	153	45 47	56	154	44 51	57	154	43 54	57	155
17	48 00	56	154	47 04	57	155	46 07	57	155	45 10	56	156	44 14	57	156
16	48 20	57	156	47 23	57	156	46 26	57	156	45 29	57	157	44 32	57	157
15	48 39	−57	157	47 42	−58	157	46 44	−57	158	45 47	−57	158	44 50	−58	159
14	48 57	58	158	47 59	58	159	47 01	57	159	46 04	58	160	45 06	58	160
13	49 13	58	160	48 15	58	160	47 17	58	161	46 19	58	161	45 21	58	161
12	49 29	58	161	48 31	59	162	47 32	58	162	46 34	58	162	45 36	59	163
11	49 43	58	163	48 45	59	163	47 46	58	164	46 48	59	164	45 49	59	164
10	49 56	−58	164	48 58	−59	165	47 59	−59	165	47 00	−59	165	46 01	−59	166
9	50 08	59	166	49 09	59	166	48 10	59	166	47 11	59	167	46 12	59	167
8	50 19	59	167	49 20	59	168	48 21	60	168	47 21	59	168	46 22	59	168
7	50 29	60	169	49 29	59	169	48 30	60	169	47 30	59	170	46 31	59	170
6	50 37	60	171	49 37	59	171	48 38	60	171	47 38	59	171	46 39	60	171
5	50 44	−60	172	49 44	−59	172	48 45	−60	172	47 45	−60	173	46 45	−59	173
4	50 50	60	174	49 50	60	174	48 50	60	174	47 50	59	174	46 51	60	174
3	50 54	60	175	49 54	60	175	48 54	59	175	47 55	60	176	46 55	60	176
2	50 57	59	177	49 58	60	177	48 58	60	177	47 58	60	177	46 58	60	177
1	50 59	60	178	49 59	60	178	48 59	60	179	47 59	60	179	46 59	60	179
0	51 00	−60	180	50 00	−60	180	49 00	−60	180	48 00	−60	180	47 00	−60	180

LHA	5° Hc	d	Z	6° Hc	d	Z	7° Hc	d	Z	8° Hc	d	Z	9° Hc	d	Z
	° ′	′	°	° ′	′	°	° ′	′	°	° ′	′	°	° ′	′	°
69	12 52	40	108	12 12	41	108	11 31	40	109	10 51	41	110	10 10	40	111
68	13 36	40	108	12 56	41	109	12 15	40	110	11 35	41	110	10 54	41	111
67	14 20	40	109	13 40	41	110	12 59	41	110	12 18	41	111	11 37	41	112
66	15 04	40	110	14 24	41	110	13 43	41	111	13 02	41	112	12 21	42	113
65	15 48	−41	110	15 07	−41	111	14 26	−41	112	13 45	−41	113	13 04	−42	113
64	16 32	41	111	15 51	42	112	15 09	41	112	14 28	42	113	13 46	41	114
63	17 15	41	112	16 34	42	112	15 52	41	113	15 11	42	114	14 29	42	115
62	17 59	42	112	17 17	42	113	16 35	42	114	15 53	42	115	15 11	42	115
61	18 42	42	113	18 00	42	114	17 18	43	115	16 35	42	115	15 53	42	116
60	19 24	−42	114	18 42	−42	115	18 00	−43	115	17 17	−42	116	16 35	−43	117
59	20 07	42	115	19 25	43	115	18 42	43	116	17 59	43	117	17 16	43	118
58	20 49	42	115	20 07	43	116	19 24	43	117	18 41	44	118	17 57	43	118
57	21 31	43	116	20 48	43	117	20 05	43	118	19 22	44	118	18 38	43	119
56	22 13	43	117	21 30	44	118	20 46	43	118	20 03	44	119	19 19	44	120
55	22 54	−43	118	22 11	−44	118	21 27	−44	119	20 43	−44	120	19 59	−44	121
54	23 36	44	118	22 52	44	119	22 08	44	120	21 24	45	121	20 39	44	121
53	24 16	44	119	23 32	44	120	22 48	44	121	22 04	45	121	21 19	45	122
52	24 57	44	120	24 13	45	121	23 28	45	122	22 43	45	122	21 58	45	123
51	25 37	45	121	24 52	44	122	24 08	46	122	23 22	45	123	22 37	45	124
50	26 17	−45	122	25 32	−45	122	24 47	−46	123	24 01	−45	124	23 16	−46	125
49	26 56	45	123	26 11	45	123	25 26	46	124	24 40	46	125	23 54	46	125
48	27 36	46	123	26 50	46	124	26 04	46	125	25 18	46	126	24 32	47	126
47	28 14	46	124	27 28	46	125	26 42	46	126	25 56	47	126	25 09	47	127
46	28 53	47	125	28 06	46	126	27 20	47	127	26 33	47	127	25 46	47	128
45	29 31	−47	126	28 44	−47	127	27 57	−47	127	27 10	−47	128	26 23	−48	129
44	30 08	47	127	29 21	47	128	28 34	47	128	27 47	48	129	26 59	48	130
43	30 45	47	128	29 58	48	129	29 10	47	129	28 23	48	130	27 35	49	131
42	31 22	48	129	30 34	48	129	29 46	48	130	28 58	48	131	28 10	49	131
41	31 58	48	130	31 10	48	130	30 22	49	131	29 33	48	132	28 45	49	132
40	32 34	−49	131	31 45	−48	131	30 57	−49	132	30 08	−49	133	29 19	−50	133
39	33 09	49	132	32 20	49	132	31 31	49	133	30 42	50	134	29 52	49	134
38	33 44	50	133	32 54	49	133	32 05	50	134	31 15	49	135	30 26	50	135
37	34 18	50	134	33 28	50	134	32 38	50	135	31 48	50	136	30 58	50	136
36	34 51	50	135	34 01	50	135	33 11	50	136	32 21	51	137	31 30	51	137
35	35 24	−50	136	34 34	−51	136	33 43	−50	137	32 53	−51	137	32 02	−51	138
34	35 57	51	137	35 06	51	137	34 15	51	138	33 24	51	139	32 33	52	139
33	36 28	51	138	35 37	51	138	34 46	52	139	33 54	51	140	33 03	52	140
32	37 00	52	139	36 08	52	139	35 16	52	140	34 24	52	141	33 32	52	141
31	37 30	52	140	36 38	52	140	35 46	52	141	34 54	53	142	34 01	52	142
30	38 00	−52	141	37 08	−53	141	36 15	−53	142	35 22	−52	143	34 30	−53	143
29	38 29	53	142	37 36	53	143	36 43	53	143	35 50	53	144	34 57	53	144
28	38 57	53	143	38 04	53	144	37 11	53	144	36 18	54	145	35 24	54	145
27	39 25	53	144	38 32	54	145	37 38	54	145	36 44	54	146	35 50	54	146
26	39 52	54	145	38 58	54	146	38 04	54	147	37 10	54	147	36 16	55	148
25	40 18	−54	147	39 24	−55	147	38 29	−54	148	37 35	−55	148	36 40	−55	149
24	40 43	54	148	39 49	55	148	38 54	55	149	37 59	55	149	37 04	55	150
23	41 08	55	149	40 13	55	149	39 18	55	150	38 23	56	150	37 27	55	151
22	41 32	56	150	40 36	55	151	39 41	56	151	38 45	56	152	37 49	55	152
21	41 54	55	151	40 59	56	152	40 03	56	152	39 07	56	153	38 11	56	153
20	42 16	−56	153	41 20	−56	153	40 24	−56	154	39 28	−57	154	38 31	−56	154
19	42 37	56	154	41 41	57	154	40 44	56	155	39 48	57	155	38 51	57	156
18	42 57	56	155	42 01	57	156	41 04	57	156	40 07	57	156	39 10	57	157
17	43 17	57	156	42 20	58	157	41 22	57	157	40 25	57	158	39 28	57	158
16	43 35	58	158	42 37	57	158	41 40	58	159	40 42	57	159	39 45	58	159
15	43 52	−58	159	42 54	−57	159	41 57	−58	160	40 59	−58	160	40 01	−58	161
14	44 08	58	160	43 10	58	161	42 12	58	161	41 14	58	161	40 16	58	162
13	44 23	58	162	43 25	58	162	42 27	59	162	41 28	58	163	40 30	58	163
12	44 37	58	163	43 39	59	163	42 40	58	164	41 42	59	164	40 43	58	164
11	44 50	58	165	43 52	59	165	42 53	59	165	41 54	59	165	40 55	58	166
10	45 02	−59	166	44 03	−59	166	43 04	−59	166	42 05	−59	167	41 06	−59	167
9	45 13	59	167	44 14	59	168	43 15	59	168	42 16	59	168	41 17	60	168
8	45 23	59	169	44 24	60	169	43 24	59	169	42 25	59	169	41 26	60	169
7	45 32	60	170	44 32	59	170	43 33	60	170	42 33	59	171	41 34	60	171
6	45 39	59	171	44 40	60	172	43 40	60	172	42 40	59	172	41 41	60	172
5	45 46	−60	173	44 46	−60	173	43 46	−60	173	42 46	−59	173	41 47	−60	173
4	45 51	60	174	44 51	60	174	43 51	60	175	42 51	60	175	41 51	59	175
3	45 55	60	176	44 55	60	176	43 55	60	176	42 55	60	176	41 55	60	176
2	45 58	60	177	44 58	60	177	43 58	60	177	42 58	60	177	41 58	60	177
1	45 59	60	179	44 59	60	179	43 59	60	179	42 59	59	179	42 00	60	179
0	46 00	−60	180	45 00	−60	180	44 00	−60	180	43 00	−60	180	42 00	−60	180

LHA	10° Hc	d	Z	11° Hc	d	Z	12° Hc	d	Z	13° Hc	d	Z	14° Hc	d	Z	LHA
	° ′	′	°	° ′	′	°	° ′	′	°	° ′	′	°	° ′	′	°	
69	09 30	41	111	08 49	41	112	08 08	40	113	07 28	41	113	06 47	41	114	291
68	10 13	41	112	09 32	41	113	08 51	41	113	08 10	41	114	07 29	41	115	292
67	10 56	41	113	10 15	41	113	09 34	41	114	08 53	42	115	08 11	41	116	293
66	11 39	41	113	10 58	42	114	10 16	41	115	09 35	42	116	08 53	42	116	294
65	12 22	−42	114	11 40	−41	115	10 59	−42	115	10 17	−42	116	09 35	−42	117	295
64	13 05	42	115	12 23	42	115	11 41	42	116	10 59	43	117	10 16	42	118	296
63	13 47	42	115	13 05	43	116	12 22	42	117	11 40	42	118	10 58	43	118	297
62	14 29	43	116	13 46	42	117	13 04	43	118	12 21	43	118	11 38	42	119	298
61	15 11	43	117	14 28	43	118	13 45	43	118	13 02	43	119	12 19	43	120	299
60	15 52	−43	118	15 09	−43	118	14 26	−43	119	13 43	−44	120	12 59	−43	120	300
59	16 33	43	118	15 50	43	119	15 07	44	120	14 23	43	120	13 40	44	121	301
58	17 14	43	119	16 31	44	120	15 47	44	121	15 03	44	121	14 19	44	122	302
57	17 55	44	120	17 11	44	121	16 27	44	121	15 43	44	122	14 59	45	123	303
56	18 35	44	121	17 51	44	121	17 07	45	122	16 22	44	123	15 38	45	123	304
55	19 15	−44	121	18 31	−45	122	17 46	−45	123	17 01	−44	123	16 17	−45	124	305
54	19 55	45	122	19 10	45	123	18 25	45	124	17 40	45	124	16 55	45	125	306
53	20 34	45	123	19 49	45	124	19 04	45	124	18 19	46	125	17 33	45	126	307
52	21 13	45	124	20 28	46	124	19 42	45	125	18 57	46	126	18 11	46	126	308
51	21 52	46	124	21 06	46	125	20 20	46	126	19 34	46	127	18 48	46	127	309
50	22 30	−46	125	21 44	−46	126	20 58	−46	127	20 12	−47	127	19 25	−46	128	310
49	23 08	46	126	22 22	47	127	21 35	47	127	20 48	46	128	20 02	47	129	311
48	23 45	46	127	22 59	47	128	22 12	47	128	21 25	47	129	20 38	47	130	312
47	24 22	47	128	23 35	47	128	22 48	47	129	22 01	47	130	21 14	48	130	313
46	24 59	47	129	24 12	48	129	23 24	47	130	22 37	48	131	21 49	48	131	314
45	25 35	−47	130	24 48	−48	130	24 00	−48	131	23 12	−48	131	22 24	−49	132	315
44	26 11	48	130	25 23	48	131	24 35	48	132	23 47	49	132	22 58	49	133	316
43	26 46	48	131	25 58	49	132	25 09	48	133	24 21	49	133	23 32	49	134	317
42	27 21	48	132	26 33	49	133	25 44	49	133	24 55	50	134	24 05	49	135	318
41	27 56	49	133	27 07	50	134	26 17	49	134	25 28	50	135	24 38	50	136	319
40	28 29	−49	134	27 40	−50	135	26 50	−49	135	26 01	−50	136	25 11	−51	136	320
39	29 03	50	135	28 13	50	136	27 23	50	136	26 33	51	137	25 42	50	137	321
38	29 36	51	136	28 45	50	136	27 55	51	137	27 04	50	138	26 14	51	138	322
37	30 08	51	137	29 17	51	137	28 26	50	138	27 36	51	139	26 45	52	139	323
36	30 39	50	138	29 49	52	138	28 57	51	139	28 06	51	140	27 15	52	140	324
35	31 11	−52	139	30 19	−51	139	29 28	−52	140	28 36	−52	141	27 44	−52	141	325
34	31 41	52	140	30 49	51	140	29 58	52	141	29 06	53	141	28 13	52	142	326
33	32 11	52	141	31 19	52	141	30 27	53	142	29 34	52	142	28 42	53	143	327
32	32 40	52	142	31 48	53	142	30 55	53	143	30 02	52	143	29 10	53	144	328
31	33 09	53	143	32 16	53	143	31 23	53	144	30 30	53	144	29 37	54	145	329
30	33 37	−54	144	32 43	−53	144	31 50	−53	145	30 57	−54	145	30 03	−53	146	330
29	34 04	54	145	33 10	53	145	32 17	54	146	31 23	54	146	30 29	54	147	331
28	34 30	54	146	33 36	54	146	32 42	54	147	31 48	54	147	30 54	54	148	332
27	34 56	54	147	34 02	54	148	33 08	55	148	32 13	55	149	31 18	54	149	333
26	35 21	54	148	34 27	55	149	33 32	55	149	32 37	55	150	31 42	55	150	334
25	35 45	−54	149	34 51	−55	150	33 56	−56	150	33 00	−55	151	32 05	−55	151	335
24	36 09	55	150	35 14	56	151	34 18	55	151	33 23	56	152	32 27	55	152	336
23	36 32	56	151	35 36	56	152	34 40	55	152	33 45	56	153	32 49	56	153	337
22	36 54	56	153	35 58	56	153	35 02	56	153	34 06	57	154	33 09	56	154	338
21	37 15	57	154	36 18	56	154	35 22	56	155	34 26	57	155	33 29	56	155	339
20	37 35	−57	155	36 38	−56	155	35 42	−57	156	34 45	−57	156	33 48	−57	157	340
19	37 54	56	156	36 58	57	156	36 01	57	157	35 04	58	157	34 06	57	158	341
18	38 13	57	157	37 16	58	158	36 18	57	158	35 21	57	158	34 24	58	159	342
17	38 31	58	158	37 33	57	159	36 36	58	159	35 38	58	160	34 40	57	160	343
16	38 47	58	160	37 49	57	160	36 52	58	160	35 54	58	161	34 56	58	161	344
15	39 03	−58	161	38 05	−58	161	37 07	−58	162	36 09	−58	162	35 11	−58	162	345
14	39 18	58	162	38 20	59	162	37 21	58	163	36 23	58	163	35 25	59	163	346
13	39 32	59	163	38 33	58	164	37 35	59	164	36 36	58	164	35 38	59	164	347
12	39 45	59	165	38 46	59	165	37 47	59	165	36 48	58	165	35 50	59	166	348
11	39 57	59	166	38 58	59	166	37 59	59	166	37 00	59	167	36 01	59	167	349
10	40 07	−59	167	39 08	−59	167	38 09	−59	168	37 10	−59	168	36 11	−59	168	350
9	40 17	59	168	39 18	59	169	38 19	59	169	37 20	60	169	36 20	59	169	351
8	40 26	59	170	39 27	60	170	38 27	59	170	37 28	59	170	36 29	60	170	352
7	40 34	59	171	39 35	60	171	38 35	60	171	37 35	59	171	36 36	60	172	353
6	40 41	60	172	39 41	59	172	38 42	60	173	37 42	60	173	36 42	59	173	354
5	40 47	−60	174	39 47	−60	174	38 47	−60	174	37 47	−59	174	36 48	−60	174	355
4	40 52	60	175	39 52	60	175	38 52	60	175	37 52	60	175	36 52	60	175	356
3	40 55	60	176	39 55	60	176	38 55	59	176	37 56	60	176	36 56	60	176	357
2	40 58	60	177	39 58	60	177	38 58	60	178	37 58	60	178	36 58	60	178	358
1	41 00	60	179	40 00	60	179	39 00	60	179	38 00	60	179	37 00	60	179	359
0	41 00	−60	180	40 00	−60	180	39 00	−60	180	38 00	−60	180	37 00	−60	180	360

S. Lat. {LHA greater than 180°........ Zn=180−Z; LHA less than 180°........... Zn=180+Z}

DECLINATION (0°-14°) CONTRARY NAME TO LATITUDE

N. Lat. {LHA greater than 180°....... Zn=Z
{LHA less than 180°.......... Zn=360−Z

DECLINATION (15°-29°) SAME NAME AS LATITUDE

LHA	15° Hc	d	Z	16° Hc	d	Z	17° Hc	d	Z	18° Hc	d	Z	19° Hc	d	Z
	° ′	′	°	° ′	′	°	° ′	′	°	° ′	′	°	° ′	′	°
0	66 00	+60	180	67 00	+60	180	68 00	+60	180	69 00	+60	180	70 00	+60	180
1	65 59	60	178	66 59	60	178	67 59	60	177	68 59	60	177	69 59	60	177
2	65 56	60	175	66 56	60	175	67 56	60	175	68 56	60	175	69 56	59	175
3	65 51	60	173	66 51	60	173	67 51	59	172	68 50	60	172	69 50	60	172
4	65 45	59	171	66 44	60	170	67 44	59	170	68 43	59	170	69 42	59	169
5	65 36	+59	168	66 35	+59	168	67 34	+59	167	68 33	+59	167	69 32	+59	166
6	65 26	58	166	66 24	59	166	67 23	59	165	68 22	58	164	69 20	59	164
7	65 13	59	164	66 12	58	163	67 10	58	163	68 08	58	162	69 06	58	161
8	64 59	58	162	65 57	58	161	66 55	58	160	67 53	57	159	68 50	57	159
9	64 44	57	159	65 41	57	159	66 38	57	158	67 35	57	157	68 32	57	156
10	64 27	+56	157	65 23	+57	156	66 20	+56	156	67 16	+56	155	68 12	+56	154
11	64 08	56	155	65 04	56	154	66 00	56	153	66 56	55	152	67 51	55	151
12	63 47	56	153	64 43	55	152	65 38	55	151	66 33	55	150	67 28	54	149
13	63 25	55	151	64 20	55	150	65 15	54	149	66 09	54	148	67 03	54	147
14	63 02	54	149	63 56	54	148	64 50	54	147	65 44	53	146	66 37	53	145
15	62 37	+54	147	63 31	+53	146	64 24	+53	145	65 17	+52	144	66 09	+52	143
16	62 11	53	145	63 04	53	144	63 57	52	143	64 49	52	142	65 41	51	141
17	61 44	52	143	62 36	52	142	63 28	52	141	64 20	50	140	65 10	51	139
18	61 16	51	142	62 07	52	141	62 59	50	139	63 49	50	138	64 39	50	137
19	60 46	51	140	61 37	51	139	62 28	50	138	63 18	49	137	64 07	48	135
20	60 16	+50	138	61 06	+50	137	61 56	+49	136	62 45	+48	135	63 33	+48	133
21	59 44	50	137	60 34	49	136	61 23	48	134	62 11	48	133	62 59	47	132
22	59 12	49	135	60 01	48	134	60 49	48	133	61 37	47	132	62 24	46	130
23	58 38	49	134	59 27	47	132	60 14	48	131	61 02	46	130	61 48	45	129
24	58 04	48	132	58 52	47	131	59 39	46	130	60 25	46	128	61 11	45	127
25	57 29	+47	131	58 16	+47	129	59 03	+45	128	59 48	+45	127	60 33	+45	126
26	56 53	47	129	57 40	46	128	58 26	45	127	59 11	44	126	59 55	44	124
27	56 17	46	128	57 03	45	127	57 48	45	125	58 33	43	124	59 16	43	123
28	55 39	46	127	56 25	45	125	57 10	44	124	57 54	43	123	58 37	42	122
29	55 02	45	125	55 47	44	124	56 31	43	123	57 14	43	122	57 57	42	120
30	54 23	+45	124	55 08	+43	123	55 51	+43	122	56 34	+42	120	57 16	+42	119
31	53 44	44	123	54 28	43	122	55 11	43	120	55 54	41	119	56 35	41	118
32	53 05	43	122	53 48	43	120	54 31	42	119	55 13	41	118	55 54	40	117
33	52 25	43	120	53 08	42	119	53 50	41	118	54 31	41	117	55 12	40	116
34	51 44	43	119	52 27	42	118	53 09	41	117	53 50	40	116	54 30	39	114
35	51 04	+42	118	51 46	+41	117	52 27	+40	116	53 07	+40	115	53 47	+39	113
36	50 22	42	117	51 04	41	116	51 45	40	115	52 25	39	114	53 04	39	112
37	49 41	41	116	50 22	40	115	51 02	40	114	51 42	39	113	52 21	38	111
38	48 58	41	115	49 39	40	114	50 19	40	113	50 59	38	112	51 37	38	110
39	48 16	40	114	48 56	40	113	49 36	39	112	50 15	38	111	50 53	38	109
40	47 33	+40	113	48 13	+40	112	48 53	+38	111	49 31	+38	110	50 09	+38	109
41	46 50	40	112	47 30	39	111	48 09	38	110	48 47	38	109	49 25	37	108
42	46 07	39	111	46 46	39	110	47 25	38	109	48 03	37	108	48 40	37	107
43	45 23	39	110	46 02	39	109	46 41	38	108	47 19	37	107	47 56	36	106
44	44 39	39	109	45 18	38	108	45 56	38	107	46 34	37	106	47 11	36	105
45	43 55	+39	109	44 34	+38	107	45 12	+37	106	45 49	+37	105	46 26	+35	104
46	43 11	38	108	43 49	38	107	44 27	37	106	45 04	36	104	45 40	36	103
47	42 27	38	107	43 05	37	106	43 42	37	105	44 19	36	104	44 55	35	103
48	41 42	38	106	42 20	37	105	42 57	36	104	43 33	36	103	44 09	35	102
49	40 57	37	105	41 34	37	104	42 11	37	103	42 48	35	102	43 23	36	101
50	40 12	+37	104	40 49	+37	103	41 26	+36	102	42 02	+36	101	42 38	+35	100
51	39 27	37	104	40 04	36	103	40 40	36	102	41 16	36	101	41 52	34	99
52	38 41	37	103	39 18	36	102	39 54	36	101	40 30	36	100	41 06	34	99
53	37 56	36	102	38 32	37	101	39 09	35	100	39 44	35	99	40 19	35	98
54	37 10	37	101	37 47	36	100	38 23	35	99	38 58	35	98	39 33	35	97
55	36 24	+37	101	37 01	+36	100	37 37	+35	99	38 12	+35	98	38 47	+34	97
56	35 38	37	100	36 15	35	99	36 50	36	98	37 26	35	97	38 01	34	96
57	34 52	36	99	35 28	36	98	36 04	35	97	36 39	35	96	37 14	34	95
58	34 06	36	98	34 42	36	97	35 18	35	97	35 53	35	96	36 28	34	94
59	33 20	36	98	33 56	36	97	34 32	35	96	35 07	34	95	35 41	34	94
60	32 34	+36	97	33 10	+35	96	33 45	+35	95	34 20	+35	94	34 55	+34	93
61	31 47	36	96	32 23	36	95	32 59	35	94	33 34	34	93	34 08	34	93
62	31 01	36	96	31 37	35	95	32 12	35	94	32 47	34	93	33 21	34	92
63	30 15	35	95	30 50	36	94	31 26	34	93	32 00	35	92	32 35	34	91
64	29 28	36	94	30 04	35	93	30 39	35	92	31 14	34	92	31 48	34	91
65	28 42	+35	94	29 17	+35	93	29 52	+35	92	30 27	+35	91	31 02	+34	90
66	27 55	36	93	28 31	35	92	29 06	35	91	29 41	34	90	30 15	34	89
67	27 09	35	92	27 44	35	91	28 19	35	91	28 54	34	90	29 28	34	89
68	26 22	35	92	26 57	36	91	27 33	34	90	28 07	35	89	28 42	34	88
69	25 35	36	91	26 11	35	90	26 46	35	89	27 21	34	88	27 55	34	87

LHA	20° Hc	d	Z	21° Hc	d	Z	22° Hc	d	Z	23° Hc	d	Z	24° Hc	d	Z
	° ′	′	°	° ′	′	°	° ′	′	°	° ′	′	°	° ′	′	°
0	71 00	+60	180	72 00	+60	180	73 00	+60	180	74 00	+60	180	75 00	+60	180
1	70 59	60	177	71 59	60	177	72 59	60	177	73 59	60	177	74 59	60	177
2	70 55	60	174	71 55	60	174	72 55	60	174	73 55	59	173	74 54	60	173
3	70 50	59	171	71 49	60	171	72 49	59	171	73 48	59	170	74 47	59	170
4	70 41	60	169	71 41	59	168	72 40	59	168	73 39	58	167	74 37	59	166
5	70 31	+59	166	71 30	+58	165	72 28	+59	164	73 27	+58	164	74 25	+58	163
6	70 19	58	163	71 17	58	162	72 15	57	162	73 12	58	161	74 10	57	160
7	70 04	57	160	71 01	58	160	71 59	57	159	72 56	56	158	73 52	56	156
8	69 47	57	158	70 44	57	157	71 41	56	156	72 37	55	155	73 32	56	153
9	69 29	56	155	70 25	55	154	71 20	56	153	72 16	54	152	73 10	55	150
10	69 08	+55	153	70 03	+55	152	70 58	+55	150	71 53	+53	149	72 46	+53	148
11	68 46	54	150	69 40	54	149	70 34	54	148	71 28	53	147	72 21	51	145
12	68 22	54	148	69 16	53	147	70 09	52	145	71 01	52	144	71 53	51	142
13	67 57	52	146	68 49	53	145	69 42	51	143	70 33	51	142	71 24	49	140
14	67 30	52	144	68 22	51	142	69 13	50	141	70 03	50	139	70 53	48	138
15	67 01	+51	142	67 52	+51	140	68 43	+49	139	69 32	+49	137	70 21	+47	135
16	66 32	50	139	67 22	49	138	68 11	49	137	69 00	47	135	69 47	47	133
17	66 01	49	138	66 50	49	136	67 39	47	135	68 26	47	133	69 13	45	131
18	65 29	48	136	66 17	48	134	67 05	46	133	67 51	46	131	68 37	45	129
19	64 55	48	134	65 43	47	132	66 30	46	131	67 16	45	129	68 01	43	127
20	64 21	+47	132	65 08	+46	131	65 54	+45	129	66 39	+44	127	67 23	+43	126
21	63 46	46	130	64 32	46	129	65 18	44	127	66 02	43	126	66 45	42	124
22	63 10	46	129	63 56	44	127	64 40	44	126	65 24	42	124	66 06	41	122
23	62 33	45	127	63 18	44	126	64 02	43	124	64 45	41	123	65 26	40	121
24	61 56	44	126	62 40	43	124	63 23	42	123	64 05	41	121	64 46	39	119
25	61 18	+43	124	62 01	+42	123	62 43	+42	121	63 25	+40	120	64 05	+39	118
26	60 39	43	123	61 22	41	121	62 03	41	120	62 44	39	118	63 23	39	117
27	59 59	42	122	60 41	42	120	61 23	40	119	62 03	39	117	62 42	37	115
28	59 19	42	120	60 01	40	119	60 41	40	117	61 21	38	116	61 59	37	114
29	58 39	41	119	59 20	40	118	60 00	39	116	60 39	37	115	61 16	37	113
30	57 58	+40	118	58 38	+39	116	59 17	+39	115	59 56	+37	113	60 33	+36	112
31	57 16	40	117	57 56	39	115	58 35	38	114	59 13	37	112	59 50	35	111
32	56 34	40	115	57 14	38	114	57 52	38	113	58 30	36	111	59 06	35	110
33	55 52	39	114	56 31	38	113	57 09	37	111	57 46	36	110	58 22	35	109
34	55 09	39	113	55 48	37	112	56 25	37	110	57 02	35	109	57 37	35	107
35	54 26	+38	112	55 04	+37	111	55 41	+37	109	56 18	+35	108	56 53	+34	107
36	53 43	37	111	54 20	37	110	54 57	36	108	55 33	35	107	56 08	34	106
37	52 59	37	110	53 36	37	109	54 13	35	107	54 48	35	106	55 23	34	105
38	52 15	37	109	52 52	36	108	53 28	36	107	54 04	34	105	54 38	33	104
39	51 31	37	108	52 08	35	107	52 43	35	106	53 18	34	104	53 52	33	103
40	50 47	+36	107	51 23	+35	106	51 58	+35	105	52 33	+34	103	53 07	+33	102
41	50 02	36	106	50 38	35	105	51 13	35	104	51 48	33	103	52 21	33	101
42	49 17	36	105	49 53	35	104	50 28	34	103	51 02	33	102	51 35	33	100
43	48 32	36	105	49 08	34	103	49 42	34	102	50 16	33	101	50 49	33	100
44	47 47	35	104	48 22	35	103	48 57	33	101	49 30	33	100	50 03	32	99
45	47 01	+36	103	47 37	+34	102	48 11	+34	101	48 45	+32	99	49 17	+32	98
46	46 16	35	102	46 51	34	101	47 25	33	100	47 58	33	99	48 31	32	97
47	45 30	35	101	46 05	34	100	46 39	33	99	47 12	33	98	47 45	31	97
48	44 44	35	101	45 19	34	99	45 53	33	98	46 26	32	97	46 58	32	96
49	43 59	34	100	44 33	34	99	45 07	33	98	45 40	32	96	46 12	31	95
50	43 13	+34	99	43 47	+33	98	44 20	+33	97	44 53	+32	96	45 25	+32	94
51	42 26	35	98	43 01	33	97	43 34	33	96	44 07	32	95	44 39	31	94
52	41 40	34	98	42 14	34	97	42 48	32	95	43 20	32	94	43 52	32	93
53	40 54	34	97	41 28	33	96	42 01	33	95	42 34	32	94	43 06	31	92
54	40 08	34	96	40 42	33	95	41 15	32	94	41 47	32	93	42 19	31	92
55	39 21	+34	95	39 55	+33	94	40 28	+33	93	41 01	+32	92	41 33	+31	91
56	38 35	34	95	39 09	33	94	39 42	32	93	40 14	32	92	40 46	31	90
57	37 48	34	94	38 22	33	93	38 55	33	92	39 28	31	91	39 59	32	90
58	37 02	33	93	37 35	33	92	38 08	33	91	38 41	32	90	39 13	31	89
59	36 15	34	93	36 49	33	92	37 22	32	91	37 54	32	90	38 26	31	89
60	35 29	+33	92	36 02	+33	91	36 35	+33	90	37 08	+32	89	37 40	+31	88
61	34 42	34	92	35 16	33	90	35 49	32	89	36 21	32	88	36 53	31	87
62	33 55	34	91	34 29	33	90	35 02	32	89	35 34	32	88	36 06	32	87
63	33 09	33	90	33 42	33	89	34 15	33	88	34 48	32	87	35 20	31	86
64	32 22	34	90	32 56	33	89	33 29	32	88	34 01	32	87	34 33	32	86
65	31 36	+33	89	32 09	+33	88	32 42	+33	87	33 15	+32	86	33 47	+31	85
66	30 49	34	88	31 23	33	87	31 56	32	86	32 28	32	85	33 00	32	84
67	30 02	34	88	30 36	33	87	31 09	33	86	31 42	32	85	32 14	32	84
68	29 16	33	87	29 49	34	86	30 23	32	85	30 55	33	84	31 28	32	83
69	28 29	34	87	29 03	33	86	29 36	33	85	30 09	32	84	30 41	32	83

LHA	25° Hc	d	Z	26° Hc	d	Z	27° Hc	d	Z	28° Hc	d	Z	29° Hc	d	Z	LHA
	° ′	′	°	° ′	′	°	° ′	′	°	° ′	′	°	° ′	′	°	
0	76 00	+60	180	77 00	+60	180	78 00	+60	180	79 00	+60	180	80 00	+60	180	360
1	75 59	59	176	76 58	60	176	77 58	60	176	78 58	60	175	79 58	60	175	359
2	75 54	60	173	76 54	59	172	77 53	60	172	78 53	59	171	79 52	59	170	358
3	75 46	60	169	76 46	59	168	77 45	58	167	78 43	59	166	79 42	58	165	357
4	75 36	58	165	76 34	59	164	77 33	58	163	78 31	57	162	79 28	57	161	356
5	75 23	+57	162	76 20	+58	161	77 18	+57	159	78 15	+56	158	79 11	+55	156	355
6	75 07	57	158	76 04	56	157	77 00	55	156	77 55	55	154	78 50	54	152	354
7	74 48	56	155	75 44	55	154	76 39	54	152	77 33	54	150	78 27	52	148	353
8	74 28	54	152	75 22	54	150	76 16	53	149	77 09	52	147	78 01	50	144	352
9	74 05	53	149	74 58	53	147	75 51	51	145	76 42	50	143	77 32	49	141	351
10	73 39	+53	146	74 32	+51	144	75 23	+50	142	76 13	+49	140	77 02	+47	137	350
11	73 12	51	143	74 03	50	141	74 53	49	139	75 42	47	137	76 29	46	134	349
12	72 44	50	141	73 34	48	139	74 22	47	137	75 09	46	134	75 55	44	132	348
13	72 13	49	138	73 02	47	136	73 49	46	134	74 35	45	132	75 20	42	129	347
14	71 41	48	136	72 29	46	134	73 15	45	132	74 00	43	129	74 43	41	127	346
15	71 08	+47	134	71 55	+45	132	72 40	+43	129	73 23	+42	127	74 05	+40	124	345
16	70 34	45	131	71 19	44	129	72 03	42	127	72 45	41	125	73 26	38	122	344
17	69 58	45	129	70 43	42	127	71 25	42	125	72 07	39	123	72 46	38	120	343
18	69 22	43	127	70 05	42	125	70 47	40	123	71 27	38	121	72 05	37	119	342
19	68 44	43	126	69 27	40	124	70 07	40	121	70 47	37	119	71 24	36	117	341
20	68 06	+41	124	68 47	+40	122	69 27	+39	120	70 06	+36	118	70 42	+35	115	340
21	67 27	40	122	68 07	39	120	68 46	38	118	69 24	36	116	70 00	34	114	339
22	66 47	40	121	67 27	38	119	68 05	37	117	68 42	35	114	69 17	33	112	338
23	66 06	40	119	66 46	37	117	67 23	36	115	67 59	34	113	68 33	33	111	337
24	65 25	39	118	66 04	37	116	66 41	35	114	67 16	34	112	67 50	31	110	336
25	64 44	+37	116	65 21	+37	114	65 58	+34	112	66 32	+34	110	67 06	+31	108	335
26	64 02	37	115	64 39	35	113	65 14	35	111	65 49	32	109	66 21	31	107	334
27	63 19	37	114	63 56	35	112	64 31	33	110	65 04	32	108	65 36	31	106	333
28	62 36	36	112	63 12	35	111	63 47	33	109	64 20	31	107	64 51	30	105	332
29	61 53	35	111	62 28	34	110	63 02	33	108	63 35	31	106	64 06	30	104	331
30	61 09	+35	110	61 44	+34	108	62 18	+32	107	62 50	+31	105	63 21	+29	103	330
31	60 25	35	109	61 00	33	107	61 33	32	106	62 05	30	104	62 35	29	102	329
32	59 41	34	108	60 15	33	106	60 48	32	105	61 20	30	103	61 50	28	101	328
33	58 57	33	107	59 30	33	105	60 03	31	104	60 34	30	102	61 04	28	100	327
34	58 12	33	106	58 45	32	104	59 17	31	103	59 48	30	101	60 18	28	99	326
35	57 27	+33	105	58 00	+32	103	58 32	+30	102	59 02	+30	100	59 32	+28	98	325
36	56 42	33	104	57 15	31	103	57 46	31	101	58 17	29	99	58 46	27	98	324
37	55 57	32	103	56 29	31	102	57 00	30	100	57 30	29	98	57 59	28	97	323
38	55 11	32	102	55 43	31	101	56 14	30	99	56 44	29	98	57 13	27	96	322
39	54 25	32	101	54 57	31	100	55 28	30	98	55 58	29	97	56 27	27	95	321
40	53 40	+31	101	54 11	+31	99	54 42	+30	98	55 12	+28	96	55 40	+27	95	320
41	52 54	31	100	53 25	31	98	53 56	29	97	54 25	29	95	54 54	27	94	319
42	52 08	31	99	52 39	31	98	53 10	29	96	53 39	28	95	54 07	27	93	318
43	51 22	31	98	51 53	30	97	52 23	29	95	52 52	29	94	53 21	27	93	317
44	50 35	32	97	51 07	30	96	51 37	29	95	52 06	28	93	52 34	27	92	316
45	49 49	+31	97	50 20	+30	95	50 50	+29	94	51 19	+28	93	51 47	+27	91	315
46	49 03	31	96	49 34	30	95	50 04	29	93	50 33	28	92	51 01	27	91	314
47	48 16	31	95	48 47	30	94	49 17	29	93	49 46	28	91	50 14	27	90	313
48	47 30	31	95	48 01	29	93	48 30	29	92	48 59	28	91	49 27	27	89	312
49	46 43	31	94	47 14	30	93	47 44	29	91	48 13	28	90	48 41	27	89	311
50	45 57	+30	93	46 27	+30	92	46 57	+29	91	47 26	+28	89	47 54	+27	88	310
51	45 10	31	93	45 41	30	91	46 11	29	90	46 40	28	89	47 08	27	87	309
52	44 24	30	92	44 54	30	91	45 24	29	89	45 53	28	88	46 21	27	87	308
53	43 37	31	91	44 08	29	90	44 37	29	89	45 06	29	88	45 35	27	86	307
54	42 50	31	91	43 21	30	89	43 51	29	88	44 20	28	87	44 48	27	86	306
55	42 04	+30	90	42 34	+30	89	43 04	+29	88	43 33	+29	86	44 02	+27	85	305
56	41 17	31	89	41 48	30	88	42 18	29	87	42 47	28	86	43 15	28	85	304
57	40 31	30	89	41 01	30	88	41 31	29	86	42 00	29	85	42 29	27	84	303
58	39 44	31	88	40 15	30	87	40 45	29	86	41 14	28	85	41 42	28	84	302
59	38 57	31	87	39 28	30	86	39 58	29	85	40 27	29	84	40 56	28	83	301
60	38 11	+31	87	38 42	+30	86	39 12	+29	85	39 41	+29	84	40 10	+28	82	300
61	37 24	31	86	37 55	30	85	38 25	30	84	38 55	29	83	39 24	28	82	299
62	36 38	31	86	37 09	30	85	37 39	29	84	38 08	29	82	38 37	29	81	298
63	35 51	31	85	36 22	31	84	36 53	29	83	37 22	29	82	37 51	29	81	297
64	35 05	31	85	35 36	30	84	36 06	30	82	36 36	29	81	37 05	29	80	296
65	34 18	+32	84	34 50	+30	83	35 20	+30	82	35 50	+30	81	36 20	+28	80	295
66	33 32	31	83	34 03	31	82	34 34	30	81	35 04	30	80	35 34	29	79	294
67	32 46	31	83	33 17	31	82	33 48	30	81	34 18	30	80	34 48	29	79	293
68	32 00	31	82	32 31	31	81	33 02	30	80	33 32	30	79	34 02	30	78	292
69	31 13	32	82	31 45	31	81	32 16	31	80	32 47	30	79	33 17	29	78	291

S. Lat. {LHA greater than 180°....... Zn=180−Z
{LHA less than 180°.......... Zn=180+Z

DECLINATION (15°-29°) SAME NAME AS LATITUDE

DECLINATION (15°-29°) SAME NAME AS LATITUDE

N. Lat. {LHA greater than 180°....... Zn=Z; LHA less than 180°.......... Zn=360−Z}

LHA	15° Hc	d	Z	16° Hc	d	Z	17° Hc	d	Z	18° Hc	d	Z	19° Hc	d	Z
	° ′	′	°	° ′	′	°	° ′	′	°	° ′	′	°	° ′	′	°
70	24 49	+35	90	25 24	+35	90	25 59	+35	89	26 34	+35	88	27 09	+34	87
71	24 02	36	90	24 38	35	89	25 13	35	88	25 48	34	87	26 22	34	86
72	23 15	36	89	23 51	35	88	24 26	35	87	25 01	35	87	25 36	34	86
73	22 29	35	89	23 04	36	88	23 40	34	87	24 14	35	86	24 49	34	85
74	21 42	36	88	22 18	35	87	22 53	35	86	23 28	35	85	24 03	34	84
75	20 56	+35	87	21 31	+36	86	22 07	+35	86	22 42	+34	85	23 16	+35	84
76	20 09	36	87	20 45	35	86	21 20	35	85	21 55	35	84	22 30	34	83
77	19 23	35	86	19 58	36	85	20 34	35	84	21 09	35	84	21 44	34	83
78	18 36	36	86	19 12	35	85	19 47	35	84	20 22	35	83	20 57	35	82
79	17 50	35	85	18 25	36	84	19 01	35	83	19 36	35	82	20 11	35	82
80	17 03	+36	84	17 39	+36	83	18 15	+35	83	18 50	+35	82	19 25	+35	81
81	16 17	36	84	16 53	35	83	17 28	36	82	18 04	35	81	18 39	35	80
82	15 30	36	83	16 06	36	82	16 42	36	81	17 18	35	81	17 53	35	80
83	14 44	36	83	15 20	36	82	15 56	36	81	16 32	35	80	17 07	36	79
84	13 58	36	82	14 34	36	81	15 10	36	80	15 46	36	79	16 22	35	79
85	13 12	+36	81	13 48	+36	80	14 24	+36	80	15 00	+36	79	15 36	+36	78
86	12 26	36	81	13 02	37	80	13 39	36	79	14 15	36	78	14 51	35	77
87	11 40	36	80	12 16	37	79	12 53	36	78	13 29	36	78	14 05	36	77
88	10 54	37	79	11 31	36	79	12 07	37	78	12 44	36	77	13 20	36	76
89	10 08	37	79	10 45	37	78	11 22	36	77	11 58	37	76	12 35	36	76
90	09 22	+37	78	09 59	+37	77	10 36	+37	77	11 13	+36	76	11 49	+37	75
91	08 37	37	78	09 14	37	77	09 51	37	76	10 28	36	75	11 04	37	74
92	07 51	38	77	08 29	37	76	09 06	37	75	09 43	37	75	10 20	36	74
93	07 06	37	76	07 43	38	76	08 21	37	75	08 58	37	74	09 35	37	73
94	06 21	37	76	06 58	38	75	07 36	37	74	08 13	37	74	08 50	37	73
95	05 36	+37	75	06 13	+38	74	06 51	+37	74	07 28	+38	73	08 06	+37	72
96	04 51	37	75	05 28	38	74	06 06	38	73	06 44	38	72	07 22	37	72
97	04 06	38	74	04 44	38	73	05 22	38	72	06 00	37	72	06 37	38	71
98	03 21	38	73	03 59	38	73	04 37	38	72	05 15	38	71	05 53	38	70
99	02 36	39	73	03 15	38	72	03 53	38	71	04 31	39	70	05 10	38	70
100	01 52	+38	72	02 30	+39	71	03 09	+38	71	03 47	+39	70	04 26	+38	69
101	01 08	38	72	01 46	39	71	02 25	39	70	03 04	39	69	03 43	38	68
102	00 23	39	71	01 02	39	70	01 41	39	69	02 20	39	69	02 59	39	68
103	-0 21	40	70	00 19	39	69	00 58	39	69	01 37	39	68	02 16	39	67
104	-1 04	39	70	-0 25	39	69	00 14	40	68	00 54	39	67	01 33	40	67
105	-1 48	+40	69	-1 08	+39	68	-0 29	+40	67	00 11	+40	67	00 51	+39	66
106	-2 31	39	68	-1 52	40	68	-1 12	40	67	-0 32	40	66	00 08	40	65
107	-3 15	40	68	-2 35	41	67	-1 54	40	66	-1 14	40	65	-0 34	40	65
108	-3 58	41	67	-3 17	40	66	-2 37	40	66	-1 57	41	65	-1 16	40	64
109	-4 41	41	66	-4 00	41	66	-3 19	40	65	-2 39	41	64	-1 58	41	63
110	-5 23	+41	66	-4 42	+41	65	-4 01	+40	64	-3 21	+41	64	-2 40	+41	63
111	-6 06	41	65	-5 25	42	64	-4 43	41	64	-4 02	41	63	-3 21	41	62
112				-6 06	41	64	-5 25	41	63	-4 44	42	62	-4 02	41	61
113							-6 06	41	62	-5 25	42	62	-4 43	42	61
114										-6 06	42	61	-5 24	43	60
115													-6 04	+42	60

LHA	20° Hc	d	Z	21° Hc	d	Z	22° Hc	d	Z	23° Hc	d	Z	24° Hc	d	Z
	° ′	′	°	° ′	′	°	° ′	′	°	° ′	′	°	° ′	′	°
70	27 43	+33	86	28 16	+34	85	28 50	+33	84	29 23	+32	83	29 55	+32	82
71	26 56	34	85	27 30	33	84	28 03	33	83	28 36	33	83	29 09	32	82
72	26 10	34	85	26 44	33	84	27 17	33	83	27 50	33	82	28 23	32	81
73	25 23	34	84	25 57	34	83	26 31	33	82	27 04	33	81	27 37	32	80
74	24 37	34	84	25 11	34	83	25 45	33	82	26 18	33	81	26 51	33	80
75	23 51	+34	83	24 25	+34	82	24 59	+33	81	25 32	+33	80	26 05	+33	79
76	23 04	35	82	23 39	34	81	24 13	33	81	24 46	33	80	25 19	33	79
77	22 18	35	82	22 53	34	81	23 27	33	80	24 00	34	79	24 34	33	78
78	21 32	35	81	22 07	34	80	22 41	34	79	23 15	33	79	23 48	33	78
79	20 46	35	81	21 21	34	80	21 55	34	79	22 29	34	78	23 03	33	77
80	20 00	+35	80	20 35	+34	79	21 09	+34	78	21 43	+34	77	22 17	+34	77
81	19 14	35	79	19 49	35	79	20 24	34	78	20 58	34	77	21 32	34	76
82	18 28	35	79	19 03	35	78	19 38	35	77	20 13	34	76	20 47	34	75
83	17 43	35	78	18 18	35	77	18 53	34	77	19 27	35	76	20 02	34	75
84	16 57	35	78	17 32	35	77	18 07	35	76	18 42	35	75	19 17	34	74
85	16 12	+35	77	16 47	+35	76	17 22	+35	75	17 57	+35	75	18 32	+35	74
86	15 26	36	77	16 02	35	76	16 37	35	75	17 12	35	74	17 47	35	73
87	14 41	36	76	15 17	35	75	15 52	36	74	16 28	35	73	17 03	35	73
88	13 56	36	75	14 32	35	75	15 07	36	74	15 43	35	73	16 18	35	72
89	13 11	36	75	13 47	36	74	14 23	35	73	14 58	36	72	15 34	35	72
90	12 26	+36	74	13 02	+36	73	13 38	+36	73	14 14	+36	72	14 50	+35	71
91	11 41	36	74	12 17	37	73	12 54	36	72	13 30	36	71	14 06	36	70
92	10 56	37	73	11 33	37	72	12 10	36	71	12 46	36	71	13 22	36	70
93	10 12	37	73	10 49	36	72	11 25	37	71	12 02	36	70	12 38	37	69
94	09 27	37	72	10 04	37	71	10 41	37	70	11 18	37	70	11 55	36	69
95	08 43	+37	71	09 20	+38	71	09 58	+37	70	10 35	+37	69	11 12	+36	68
96	07 59	38	71	08 37	37	70	09 14	37	69	09 51	37	68	10 28	37	68
97	07 15	38	70	07 53	37	69	08 30	38	69	09 08	37	68	09 45	38	67
98	06 31	38	70	07 09	38	69	07 47	38	68	08 25	38	67	09 03	37	66
99	05 48	38	69	06 26	38	68	07 04	38	67	07 42	38	67	08 20	38	66
100	05 04	+39	68	05 43	+38	68	06 21	+38	67	06 59	+39	66	07 38	+38	65
101	04 21	39	68	05 00	38	67	05 38	39	66	06 17	38	65	06 55	39	65
102	03 38	39	67	04 17	39	66	04 56	39	66	05 35	38	65	06 13	39	64
103	02 55	39	66	03 34	39	66	04 13	39	65	04 52	39	64	05 31	39	63
104	02 13	39	66	02 52	39	65	03 31	40	64	04 11	39	64	04 50	39	63
105	01 30	+40	65	02 10	+39	64	02 49	+40	64	03 29	+39	63	04 08	+40	62
106	00 48	40	65	01 28	40	64	02 08	40	63	02 48	39	62	03 27	40	62
107	00 06	40	64	00 46	40	63	01 26	40	62	02 06	40	62	02 46	41	61
108	-0 36	41	63	00 05	40	63	00 45	40	62	01 25	41	61	02 06	40	60
109	-1 17	40	63	-0 37	41	62	00 04	41	61	00 45	40	61	01 25	41	60
110	-1 59	+41	62	-1 18	+41	61	-0 37	+41	61	00 04	+41	60	00 45	+41	59
111	-2 40	41	61	-1 59	42	61	-1 17	41	60	-0 36	41	59	00 05	42	59
112	-3 21	42	61	-2 39	41	60	-1 58	42	59	-1 16	42	59	-0 34	41	58
113	-4 01	42	60	-3 19	42	59	-2 37	41	59	-1 56	42	58	-1 14	42	57
114	-4 41	42	59	-3 59	42	59	-3 17	42	58	-2 35	42	57	-1 53	42	57
115	-5 22	+43	59	-4 39	+42	58	-3 57	+43	57	-3 14	+42	57	-2 32	+43	56
116	-6 01	42	58	-5 19	43	57	-4 36	43	57	-3 53	43	56	-3 10	43	55
117				-5 58	43	57	-5 15	44	56	-4 31	43	55	-3 48	43	55
118							-5 53	43	55	-5 10	44	55	-4 26	43	54
119										-5 48	44	54	-5 04	44	53
120													-5 41	+44	53

LHA	25° Hc	d	Z	26° Hc	d	Z	27° Hc	d	Z	28° Hc	d	Z	29° Hc	d	Z	LHA
	° ′	′	°	° ′	′	°	° ′	′	°	° ′	′	°	° ′	′	°	
70	30 27	+32	81	30 59	+31	80	31 30	+31	79	32 01	+30	78	32 31	+30	77	290
71	29 41	32	81	30 13	31	80	30 44	31	79	31 15	31	78	31 46	30	77	289
72	28 55	32	80	29 27	32	79	29 59	31	78	30 30	30	77	31 00	31	76	288
73	28 09	33	79	28 42	31	79	29 13	31	78	29 44	31	77	30 15	31	76	287
74	27 24	32	79	27 56	32	78	28 28	31	77	28 59	31	76	29 30	31	75	286
75	26 38	+32	78	27 10	+32	77	27 42	+32	76	28 14	+31	76	28 45	+31	75	285
76	25 52	33	78	26 25	32	77	26 57	32	76	27 29	31	75	28 00	31	74	284
77	25 07	33	77	25 40	32	76	26 12	32	75	26 44	32	74	27 16	31	74	283
78	24 21	33	77	24 54	33	76	25 27	32	75	25 59	32	74	26 31	31	73	282
79	23 36	33	76	24 09	33	75	24 42	32	74	25 14	32	73	25 46	32	72	281
80	22 51	+33	76	23 24	+33	75	23 57	+33	74	24 30	+32	73	25 02	+32	72	280
81	22 06	33	75	22 39	33	74	23 12	33	73	23 45	33	72	24 18	32	71	279
82	21 21	33	75	21 54	34	74	22 28	33	73	23 01	33	72	23 34	32	71	278
83	20 36	34	74	21 10	33	73	21 43	34	72	22 17	33	71	22 50	32	70	277
84	19 51	34	73	20 25	34	73	20 59	34	72	21 33	33	71	22 06	33	70	276
85	19 07	+34	73	19 41	+34	72	20 15	+34	71	20 49	+33	70	21 22	+33	69	275
86	18 22	35	72	18 57	34	71	19 31	34	71	20 05	34	70	20 39	33	69	274
87	17 38	34	72	18 12	35	71	18 47	34	70	19 21	34	69	19 55	34	68	273
88	16 53	35	71	17 28	35	70	18 03	35	70	18 38	34	69	19 12	34	68	272
89	16 09	36	71	16 45	35	70	17 20	34	69	17 54	35	68	18 29	34	67	271
90	15 25	+36	70	16 01	+35	69	16 36	+35	68	17 11	+35	68	17 46	+34	67	270
91	14 42	35	70	15 17	36	69	15 53	35	68	16 28	35	67	17 03	35	66	269
92	13 58	36	69	14 34	36	68	15 10	35	67	15 45	36	67	16 21	35	66	268
93	13 15	36	68	13 51	36	68	14 27	36	67	15 03	35	66	15 38	36	65	267
94	12 31	37	68	13 08	36	67	13 44	36	66	14 20	36	65	14 56	36	65	266
95	11 48	+37	67	12 25	+36	67	13 01	+37	66	13 38	+36	65	14 14	+36	64	265
96	11 05	37	67	11 42	37	66	12 19	37	65	12 56	36	64	13 32	37	64	264
97	10 23	37	66	11 00	37	65	11 37	37	65	12 14	37	64	12 51	36	63	263
98	09 40	38	66	10 18	37	65	10 55	37	64	11 32	37	63	12 09	37	62	262
99	08 58	37	65	09 35	38	64	10 13	38	63	10 51	37	63	11 28	37	62	261
100	08 16	+38	64	08 54	+38	64	09 32	+37	63	10 09	+38	62	10 47	+38	61	260
101	07 34	38	64	08 12	38	63	08 50	38	62	09 28	38	62	10 06	38	61	259
102	06 52	38	63	07 30	39	63	08 09	38	62	08 47	39	61	09 26	38	60	258
103	06 10	39	63	06 49	39	62	07 28	39	61	08 07	38	60	08 45	39	60	257
104	05 29	39	62	06 08	39	61	06 47	39	61	07 26	39	60	08 05	39	59	256
105	04 48	+39	61	05 27	+40	61	06 07	+39	60	06 46	+39	59	07 25	+40	58	255
106	04 07	40	61	04 47	40	60	05 27	39	59	06 06	40	59	06 46	39	58	254
107	03 27	40	60	04 07	40	60	04 47	40	59	05 27	39	58	06 06	40	57	253
108	02 46	40	60	03 26	41	59	04 07	40	58	04 47	40	57	05 27	40	57	252
109	02 06	41	59	02 47	40	58	03 27	41	58	04 08	40	57	04 48	41	56	251
110	01 26	+41	58	02 07	+41	58	02 48	+41	57	03 29	+41	56	04 10	+41	55	250
111	00 47	41	58	01 28	41	57	02 09	41	56	02 50	42	56	03 32	41	55	249
112	00 07	42	57	00 49	41	56	01 30	42	56	02 12	42	55	02 54	41	54	248
113	-0 32	42	57	00 10	42	56	00 52	42	55	01 34	42	54	02 16	42	54	247
114	-1 11	43	56	-0 28	42	55	00 14	42	54	00 56	42	54	01 38	43	53	246
115	-1 49	+43	55	-1 06	+42	55	-0 24	+43	54	00 19	+42	53	01 01	+43	52	245
116	-2 27	43	55	-1 44	43	54	-1 01	43	53	-0 18	43	53	00 25	42	52	244
117	-3 05	43	54	-2 22	43	53	-1 39	44	53	-0 55	43	52	-0 12	43	51	243
118	-3 43	44	53	-2 59	44	53	-2 15	43	52	-1 32	44	51	-0 48	44	51	242
119	-4 20	44	53	-3 36	44	52	-2 52	44	51	-2 08	44	51	-1 24	44	50	241
120	-4 57	+45	52	-4 12	+44	51	-3 28	+44	51	-2 44	+45	50	-1 59	+44	49	240
121	-5 33	44	51	-4 49	45	51	-4 04	45	50	-3 19	44	49	-2 35	45	49	239
122	-6 10	45	51	-5 25	45	50	-4 40	45	49	-3 55	46	49	-3 09	45	48	238
123				-6 00	45	49	-5 15	46	49	-4 29	45	48	-3 44	46	47	237
124							-5 50	46	48	-5 04	46	47	-4 18	46	47	236
125										-5 38	+46	47	-4 52	+46	46	235
126													-5 25	47	45	234
127													-5 58	47	45	233

DECLINATION (15°-29°) CONTRARY NAME TO LATITUDE

S. Lat. {LHA greater than 180°....... Zn=180−Z; LHA less than 180°.......... Zn=180+Z}

LHA	15° Hc	d	Z	16° Hc	d	Z	17° Hc	d	Z	18° Hc	d	Z	19° Hc	d	Z
86	-6 21	37	104												
85	-5 36	-37	105	-6 13	-38	106									
84	-4 51	37	105	-5 28	38	106	-6 06	38	107						
83	-4 06	38	106	-4 44	38	107	-5 22	38	108	-6 00	37	108			
82	-3 21	38	107	-3 59	38	107	-4 37	38	108	-5 15	38	109	-5 53	38	110
81	-2 36	39	107	-3 15	38	108	-3 53	38	109	-4 31	39	110	-5 10	38	110
80	-1 52	-38	108	-2 30	-39	109	-3 09	-38	109	-3 47	-39	110	-4 26	-38	111
79	-1 08	38	108	-1 46	39	109	-2 25	39	110	-3 04	39	111	-3 43	38	112
78	-0 23	39	109	-1 02	39	110	-1 41	39	111	-2 20	39	111	-2 59	39	112
77	00 21	40	110	-0 19	39	111	-0 58	39	111	-1 37	39	112	-2 16	39	113
76	01 04	39	110	00 25	39	111	-0 14	40	112	-0 54	39	113	-1 33	40	113
75	01 48	-40	111	01 08	-39	112	00 29	-40	113	-0 11	-40	113	-0 51	-39	114
74	02 31	39	112	01 52	40	112	01 12	40	113	00 32	40	114	-0 08	40	115
73	03 15	40	112	02 35	41	113	01 54	40	114	01 14	40	115	00 34	40	115
72	03 58	41	113	03 17	40	114	02 37	40	114	01 57	41	115	01 16	40	116
71	04 41	41	114	04 00	41	114	03 19	40	115	02 39	41	116	01 58	41	117
70	05 23	-41	114	04 42	-41	115	04 01	-40	116	03 21	-41	116	02 40	-41	117

LHA	20° Hc	d	Z	21° Hc	d	Z	22° Hc	d	Z	23° Hc	d	Z	24° Hc	d	Z
81	-5 48	38	111												
80	-5 04	-39	112	-5 43	-38	112	-6 21	-38	113						
79	-4 21	39	112	-5 00	38	113	-5 38	39	114	-6 17	38	115			
78	-3 38	39	113	-4 17	39	114	-4 56	39	114	-5 35	38	115	-6 13	39	116
77	-2 55	39	114	-3 34	39	114	-4 13	39	115	-4 52	39	116	-5 31	39	117
76	-2 13	39	114	-2 52	39	115	-3 31	40	116	-4 11	39	116	-4 50	39	117
75	-1 30	-40	115	-2 10	-39	116	-2 49	-40	116	-3 29	-39	117	-4 08	-40	118
74	-0 48	40	115	-1 28	40	116	-2 08	40	117	-2 48	39	118	-3 27	40	118
73	-0 06	40	116	-0 46	40	117	-1 26	40	118	-2 06	40	118	-2 46	41	119
72	00 36	41	117	-0 05	40	117	-0 45	40	118	-1 25	41	119	-2 06	40	120
71	01 17	40	117	00 37	41	118	-0 04	41	119	-0 45	40	119	-1 25	41	120
70	01 59	-41	118	01 18	-41	119	00 37	-41	119	-0 04	-41	120	-0 45	-41	121

LHA	25° Hc	d	Z	26° Hc	d	Z	27° Hc	d	Z	28° Hc	d	Z	29° Hc	d	Z	LHA
86																274
85																275
84																276
83																277
82																278
81																279
80																280
79																281
78																282
77	-6 10	39	117													283
76	-5 29	39	118	-6 08	39	119										284
75	-4 48	-39	119	-5 27	-40	119	-6 07	-39	120							285
74	-4 07	40	119	-4 47	40	120	-5 27	39	121	-6 06	40	121				286
73	-3 27	40	120	-4 07	40	120	-4 47	40	121	-5 27	39	122	-6 06	40	123	287
72	-2 46	40	120	-3 26	41	121	-4 07	40	122	-4 47	40	123	-5 27	40	123	288
71	-2 06	41	121	-2 47	40	122	-3 27	41	122	-4 08	40	123	-4 48	41	124	289
70	-1 26	-41	122	-2 07	-41	122	-2 48	-41	123	-3 29	-41	124	-4 10	-41	125	290

N. Lat. {LHA greater than 180°....... Zn=Z; LHA less than 180°........... Zn=360−Z}

DECLINATION (15°-29°) CONTRARY NAME TO LATITUDE

LHA	15°			16°			17°			18°			19°		
	Hc	d	Z	Hc	d	Z	Hc	d	Z	Hc	d	Z	Hc	d	Z
	° ′	′	°	° ′	′	°	° ′	′	°	° ′	′	°	° ′	′	°
69	06 06	41	115	05 25	42	116	04 43	41	116	04 02	41	117	03 21	41	118
68	06 48	42	116	06 06	41	116	05 25	41	117	04 44	42	118	04 02	41	119
67	07 30	42	116	06 48	42	117	06 06	41	118	05 25	42	118	04 43	42	119
66	08 11	41	117	07 30	42	118	06 48	42	118	06 06	42	119	05 24	43	120
65	08 53	−42	118	08 11	−42	118	07 29	−43	119	06 46	−42	120	06 04	−42	121
64	09 34	42	118	08 52	43	119	08 09	42	120	07 27	43	121	06 44	43	121
63	10 15	43	119	09 32	42	120	08 50	43	120	08 07	43	121	07 24	43	122
62	10 56	43	120	10 13	43	120	09 30	44	121	08 46	43	122	08 03	43	123
61	11 36	43	120	10 53	44	121	10 09	43	122	09 26	44	123	08 42	43	123
60	12 16	−44	121	11 32	−43	122	10 49	−44	123	10 05	−44	123	09 21	−44	124
59	12 56	44	122	12 12	44	123	11 28	44	123	10 44	44	124	10 00	44	125
58	13 35	44	123	12 51	44	123	12 07	45	124	11 22	44	125	10 38	45	125
57	14 14	44	123	13 30	45	124	12 45	44	125	12 01	45	125	11 16	45	126
56	14 53	45	124	14 08	45	125	13 23	45	125	12 38	45	126	11 53	45	127
55	15 32	−45	125	14 47	−46	126	14 01	−45	126	13 16	−45	127	12 31	−46	128
54	16 10	46	126	15 24	45	126	14 39	46	127	13 53	46	128	13 07	46	128
53	16 48	46	126	16 02	46	127	15 16	46	128	14 30	46	128	13 44	46	129
52	17 25	46	127	16 39	46	128	15 53	47	128	15 06	46	129	14 20	47	130
51	18 02	47	128	17 15	46	129	16 29	47	129	15 42	46	130	14 56	47	131
50	18 39	−47	129	17 52	−47	129	17 05	−47	130	16 18	−47	131	15 31	−47	131
49	19 15	47	130	18 28	48	130	17 40	47	131	16 53	47	131	16 06	48	132
48	19 51	48	130	19 03	47	131	18 16	48	132	17 28	48	132	16 40	48	133
47	20 26	48	131	19 38	48	132	18 50	48	132	18 02	48	133	17 14	48	134
46	21 01	48	132	20 13	49	133	19 24	48	133	18 36	48	134	17 48	49	134
45	21 35	−48	133	20 47	−49	133	19 58	−49	134	19 09	−48	135	18 21	−49	135
44	22 09	49	134	21 20	48	134	20 32	50	135	19 42	49	135	18 53	49	136
43	22 43	49	134	21 54	50	135	21 04	49	136	20 15	50	136	19 25	49	137
42	23 16	50	135	22 26	49	136	21 37	50	137	20 47	50	137	19 57	50	138
41	23 48	49	136	22 59	50	137	22 09	51	137	21 18	50	138	20 28	50	139
40	24 20	−50	137	23 30	−50	138	22 40	−51	138	21 49	−50	139	20 59	−51	139
39	24 52	51	138	24 01	50	139	23 11	51	139	22 20	51	140	21 29	51	140
38	25 23	51	139	24 32	51	139	23 41	51	140	22 50	52	141	21 58	51	141
37	25 53	51	140	25 02	51	140	24 11	52	141	23 19	52	141	22 27	51	142
36	26 23	51	141	25 32	52	141	24 40	52	142	23 48	52	142	22 56	52	143
35	26 52	−52	142	26 00	−52	142	25 08	−52	143	24 16	−52	143	23 24	−53	144
34	27 21	52	143	26 29	53	143	25 36	52	144	24 44	53	144	23 51	53	145
33	27 49	53	144	26 56	52	144	26 04	53	145	25 11	53	145	24 18	54	146
32	28 17	53	145	27 24	54	145	26 30	53	146	25 37	53	146	24 44	54	147
31	28 43	53	145	27 50	54	146	26 56	53	147	26 03	54	147	25 09	54	148
30	29 10	−54	146	28 16	−54	147	27 22	−54	147	26 28	−54	148	25 34	−54	148
29	29 35	54	147	28 41	54	148	27 47	55	148	26 52	54	149	25 58	55	149
28	30 00	55	148	29 05	54	149	28 11	55	149	27 16	55	150	26 21	55	150
27	30 24	55	149	29 29	55	150	28 34	55	150	27 39	55	151	26 44	55	151
26	30 47	55	151	29 52	55	151	28 57	56	151	28 01	55	152	27 06	55	152
25	31 10	−56	152	30 14	−55	152	29 19	−56	152	28 23	−56	153	27 27	−55	153
24	31 32	56	153	30 36	56	153	29 40	56	153	28 44	56	154	27 48	56	154
23	31 53	56	154	30 57	57	154	30 00	56	154	29 04	56	155	28 08	56	155
22	32 13	56	155	31 17	57	155	30 20	56	156	29 24	57	156	28 27	57	156
21	32 33	57	156	31 36	57	156	30 39	57	157	29 42	56	157	28 46	57	157
20	32 51	−57	157	31 54	−57	157	30 57	−57	158	30 00	−57	158	29 03	−57	158
19	33 09	57	158	32 12	57	158	31 15	58	159	30 17	57	159	29 20	57	159
18	33 26	57	159	32 29	58	159	31 31	57	160	30 34	58	160	29 36	58	160
17	33 43	58	160	32 45	58	161	31 47	58	161	30 49	58	161	29 51	58	161
16	33 58	58	161	33 00	58	162	32 02	58	162	31 04	58	162	30 06	58	163
15	34 13	−59	162	33 14	−58	163	32 16	−58	163	31 18	−59	163	30 19	−58	164
14	34 26	58	164	33 28	59	164	32 29	58	164	31 31	59	164	30 32	58	165
13	34 39	59	165	33 40	58	165	32 42	59	165	31 43	59	165	30 44	59	166
12	34 51	59	166	33 52	59	166	32 53	59	166	31 54	59	167	30 55	59	167
11	35 02	59	167	34 03	59	167	33 04	59	167	32 05	59	168	31 06	60	168
10	35 12	−59	168	34 13	−60	168	33 13	−59	169	32 14	−59	169	31 15	−59	169
9	35 21	59	169	34 22	60	170	33 22	59	170	32 23	60	170	31 23	59	170
8	35 29	59	171	34 30	60	171	33 30	59	171	32 31	60	171	31 31	59	171
7	35 36	59	172	34 37	60	172	33 37	59	172	32 38	60	172	31 38	60	172
6	35 43	60	173	34 43	60	173	33 43	60	173	32 43	59	173	31 44	60	173
5	35 48	−60	174	34 48	−60	174	33 48	−59	174	32 49	−60	174	31 49	−60	174
4	35 52	60	175	34 52	59	175	33 53	60	175	32 53	60	176	31 53	60	176
3	35 56	60	176	34 56	60	177	33 56	60	177	32 56	60	177	31 56	60	177
2	35 58	60	178	34 58	60	178	33 58	60	178	32 58	60	178	31 58	60	178
1	36 00	60	179	35 00	60	179	34 00	60	179	33 00	60	179	32 00	60	179
0	36 00	−60	180	35 00	−60	180	34 00	−60	180	33 00	−60	180	32 00	−60	180
	15°			16°			17°			18°			19°		

LHA	20°			21°			22°			23°			24°		
	Hc	d	Z	Hc	d	Z	Hc	d	Z	Hc	d	Z	Hc	d	Z
	° ′	′	°	° ′	′	°	° ′	′	°	° ′	′	°	° ′	′	°
69	02 40	41	119	01 59	42	119	01 17	41	120	00 36	41	121	−0 05	42	121
68	03 21	42	119	02 39	41	120	01 58	42	121	01 16	42	121	00 34	41	122
67	04 01	42	120	03 19	42	121	02 37	41	121	01 56	42	122	01 14	42	123
66	04 41	42	121	03 59	42	121	03 17	42	122	02 35	42	123	01 53	42	123
65	05 22	−43	121	04 39	−42	122	03 57	−43	123	03 14	−42	123	02 32	−43	124
64	06 01	42	122	05 19	43	123	04 36	43	123	03 53	43	124	03 10	43	125
63	06 41	43	123	05 58	43	123	05 15	44	124	04 31	43	125	03 48	43	125
62	07 20	43	123	06 37	44	124	05 53	43	125	05 10	44	125	04 26	43	126
61	07 59	44	124	07 15	44	125	06 31	43	125	05 48	44	126	05 04	44	127
60	08 37	−44	125	07 53	−44	125	07 09	−44	126	06 25	−44	127	05 41	−44	127
59	09 16	45	125	08 31	44	126	07 47	45	127	07 02	44	127	06 18	45	128
58	09 53	44	126	09 09	45	127	08 24	45	127	07 39	45	128	06 54	44	129
57	10 31	45	127	09 46	45	127	09 01	45	128	08 16	45	129	07 31	46	129
56	11 08	45	127	10 23	46	128	09 37	45	129	08 52	45	129	08 07	46	130
55	11 45	−46	128	10 59	−45	129	10 14	−46	130	09 28	−46	130	08 42	−46	131
54	12 21	45	129	11 36	47	130	10 49	46	130	10 03	46	131	09 17	46	132
53	12 58	47	130	12 11	46	130	11 25	47	131	10 38	46	132	09 52	47	132
52	13 33	46	130	12 47	47	131	12 00	47	132	11 13	47	132	10 26	47	133
51	14 09	47	131	13 22	47	132	12 35	48	132	11 47	47	133	11 00	47	134
50	14 44	−48	132	13 56	−47	133	13 09	−48	133	12 21	−47	134	11 34	−48	134
49	15 18	48	133	14 30	47	133	13 43	48	134	12 55	48	135	12 07	48	135
48	15 52	48	133	15 04	48	134	14 16	48	135	13 28	49	135	12 39	48	136
47	16 26	49	134	15 37	48	135	14 49	49	136	14 00	48	136	13 12	49	137
46	16 59	49	135	16 10	49	136	15 21	49	136	14 32	49	137	13 43	49	137
45	17 32	−49	136	16 43	−50	136	15 53	−49	137	15 04	−49	138	14 15	−50	138
44	18 04	50	137	17 14	49	137	16 25	50	138	15 35	49	138	14 46	50	139
43	18 36	50	138	17 46	50	138	16 56	50	139	16 06	50	139	15 16	50	140
42	19 07	50	138	18 17	50	139	17 27	51	139	16 36	50	140	15 46	51	141
41	19 38	51	139	18 47	50	140	17 57	51	140	17 06	51	141	16 15	51	141
40	20 08	−51	140	19 17	−51	141	18 26	−51	141	17 35	−51	142	16 44	−51	142
39	20 38	52	141	19 46	51	141	18 55	51	142	18 04	52	143	17 12	51	143
38	21 07	52	142	20 15	51	142	19 24	52	143	18 32	52	143	17 40	52	144
37	21 36	52	143	20 44	52	143	19 52	52	144	19 00	53	144	18 07	52	145
36	22 04	53	143	21 11	52	144	20 19	52	145	19 27	53	145	18 34	53	146
35	22 31	−52	144	21 39	−53	145	20 46	−53	145	19 53	−53	146	19 00	−53	146
34	22 58	53	145	22 05	53	146	21 12	53	146	20 19	53	147	19 26	54	147
33	23 24	53	146	22 31	53	147	21 38	54	147	20 44	53	148	19 51	54	148
32	23 50	54	147	22 56	53	148	22 03	54	148	21 09	54	149	20 15	54	149
31	24 15	54	148	23 21	54	148	22 27	54	149	21 33	54	149	20 39	54	150
30	24 40	−55	149	23 45	−54	149	22 51	−55	150	21 56	−54	150	21 02	−55	151
29	25 03	54	150	24 09	55	150	23 14	55	151	22 19	55	151	21 24	54	152
28	25 26	55	151	24 31	55	151	23 36	55	152	22 41	55	152	21 46	55	153
27	25 49	55	152	24 54	56	152	23 58	55	153	23 03	56	153	22 07	55	153
26	26 11	56	153	25 15	56	153	24 19	55	154	23 24	56	154	22 28	56	154
25	26 32	−56	154	25 36	−56	154	24 40	−56	155	23 44	−56	155	22 48	−56	155
24	26 52	56	155	25 56	56	155	25 00	57	155	24 03	56	156	23 07	56	156
23	27 12	57	156	26 15	56	156	25 19	57	156	24 22	56	157	23 26	57	157
22	27 30	56	157	26 34	57	157	25 37	57	157	24 40	57	158	23 43	57	158
21	27 49	57	158	26 52	57	158	25 55	57	158	24 58	58	159	24 00	57	159
20	28 06	−57	159	27 09	−58	159	26 11	−57	159	25 14	−57	160	24 17	−58	160
19	28 23	58	160	27 25	57	160	26 28	58	160	25 30	58	161	24 32	57	161
18	28 38	57	161	27 41	58	161	26 43	58	161	25 45	58	162	24 47	58	162
17	28 53	58	162	27 55	58	162	26 57	58	162	25 59	58	163	25 01	58	163
16	29 08	59	163	28 09	58	163	27 11	58	163	26 13	58	164	25 15	59	164
15	29 21	−58	164	28 23	−59	164	27 24	−58	164	26 26	−59	165	25 27	−58	165
14	29 34	59	165	28 35	59	165	27 36	58	165	26 38	59	166	25 39	59	166
13	29 45	58	166	28 47	59	166	27 48	59	166	26 49	59	167	25 50	59	167
12	29 56	59	167	28 57	59	167	27 58	59	167	26 59	59	168	26 00	59	168
11	30 06	59	168	29 07	59	168	28 08	59	168	27 09	59	169	26 10	59	169
10	30 16	−60	169	29 16	−59	169	28 17	−59	170	27 18	−59	170	26 19	−60	170
9	30 24	59	170	29 25	60	170	28 25	59	171	27 26	60	171	26 26	59	171
8	30 32	60	171	29 32	59	171	28 33	60	172	27 33	60	172	26 33	59	172
7	30 38	59	172	29 39	60	173	28 39	60	173	27 39	59	173	26 40	60	173
6	30 44	60	173	29 44	59	174	28 45	60	174	27 45	60	174	26 45	60	174
5	30 49	−60	175	29 49	−60	175	28 49	−60	175	27 49	−59	175	26 50	−60	175
4	30 53	60	176	29 53	60	176	28 53	60	176	27 53	60	176	26 53	60	176
3	30 56	60	177	29 56	60	177	28 56	60	177	27 56	60	177	26 56	60	177
2	30 58	60	178	29 58	60	178	28 58	60	178	27 58	60	178	26 58	60	178
1	31 00	60	179	30 00	60	179	29 00	60	179	28 00	60	179	27 00	60	179
0	31 00	−60	180	30 00	−60	180	29 00	−60	180	28 00	−60	180	27 00	−60	180
	20°			21°			22°			23°			24°		

25°			26°			27°			28°			29°			LHA
Hc	d	Z	Hc	d	Z	Hc	d	Z	Hc	d	Z	Hc	d	Z	
° ′	′	°	° ′	′	°	° ′	′	°	° ′	′	°	° ′	′	°	
−0 47	41	122	−1 28	41	123	−2 09	41	124	−2 50	42	124	−3 32	41	125	291
−0 07	42	123	−0 49	41	124	−1 30	42	124	−2 12	42	125	−2 54	41	126	292
00 32	42	123	−0 10	42	124	−0 52	42	125	−1 34	42	126	−2 16	42	126	293
01 11	43	124	00 28	42	125	−0 14	42	126	−0 56	42	126	−1 38	43	127	294
01 49	−43	125	01 06	−42	125	00 24	−43	126	−0 19	−42	127	−1 01	−43	128	295
02 27	43	125	01 44	43	126	01 01	43	127	00 18	43	127	−0 25	42	128	296
03 05	43	126	02 22	43	127	01 39	44	127	00 55	43	128	00 12	43	129	297
03 43	44	127	02 59	44	127	02 15	43	128	01 32	44	129	00 48	44	129	298
04 20	44	127	03 36	44	128	02 52	44	129	02 08	44	129	01 24	44	130	299
04 57	−45	128	04 12	−44	129	03 28	−44	129	02 44	−45	130	01 59	−44	131	300
05 33	44	129	04 49	45	129	04 04	45	130	03 19	44	131	02 35	45	131	301
06 10	45	129	05 25	45	130	04 40	45	131	03 55	46	131	03 09	45	132	302
06 45	45	130	06 00	45	131	05 15	46	131	04 29	45	132	03 44	46	133	303
07 21	46	131	06 35	45	131	05 50	46	132	05 04	46	133	04 18	46	133	304
07 56	−46	131	07 10	−46	132	06 24	−46	133	05 38	−46	133	04 52	−46	134	305
08 31	47	132	07 44	46	133	06 58	46	133	06 12	47	134	05 25	47	135	306
09 05	46	133	08 19	47	134	07 32	47	134	06 45	47	135	05 58	47	135	307
09 39	47	134	08 52	47	134	08 05	47	135	07 18	47	136	06 31	48	136	308
10 13	48	134	09 25	47	135	08 38	48	136	07 50	47	136	07 03	48	137	309
10 46	−48	135	09 58	−48	136	09 10	−48	136	08 22	−48	137	07 34	−48	138	310
11 19	48	136	10 31	49	136	09 42	48	137	08 54	48	138	08 06	49	138	311
11 51	49	137	11 02	48	137	10 14	49	138	09 25	48	138	08 37	49	139	312
12 23	49	137	11 34	49	138	10 45	49	138	09 56	49	139	09 07	49	140	313
12 54	49	138	12 05	49	139	11 16	50	139	10 26	49	140	09 37	49	140	314
13 25	−49	139	12 36	−50	139	11 46	−50	140	10 56	−49	141	10 07	−50	141	315
13 56	50	140	13 06	50	140	12 16	50	141	11 26	50	141	10 36	51	142	316
14 26	51	140	13 35	50	141	12 45	50	142	11 55	51	142	11 04	50	143	317
14 55	50	141	14 05	51	142	13 14	51	142	12 23	51	143	11 32	51	143	318
15 24	51	142	14 33	51	143	13 42	51	143	12 51	51	144	12 00	51	144	319
15 53	−52	143	15 01	−51	143	14 10	−51	144	13 19	−52	144	12 27	−52	145	320
16 21	52	144	15 29	52	144	14 37	51	145	13 46	52	145	12 54	52	146	321
16 48	52	144	15 56	52	145	15 04	52	145	14 12	52	146	13 20	53	146	322
17 15	52	145	16 23	53	146	15 30	52	146	14 38	53	147	13 45	52	147	323
17 41	52	146	16 49	53	147	15 56	53	147	15 03	53	148	14 10	53	148	324
18 07	−53	147	17 14	−53	147	16 21	−53	148	15 28	−53	148	14 35	−54	149	325
18 32	53	148	17 39	53	148	16 46	54	149	15 52	53	149	14 59	54	150	326
18 57	54	149	18 03	53	149	17 10	54	150	16 16	54	150	15 22	54	150	327
19 21	54	149	18 27	54	150	17 33	54	150	16 39	54	151	15 45	55	151	328
19 45	55	150	18 50	54	151	17 56	55	151	17 01	54	152	16 07	55	152	329
20 07	−54	151	19 13	−55	152	18 18	−55	152	17 23	−55	152	16 28	−55	153	330
20 30	55	152	19 35	55	153	18 40	56	153	17 44	55	153	16 49	55	154	331
20 51	55	153	19 56	56	153	19 00	55	154	18 05	55	154	17 10	56	155	332
21 12	56	154	20 16	55	154	19 21	56	155	18 25	56	155	17 29	55	155	333
21 32	56	155	20 36	56	155	19 40	56	156	18 44	56	156	17 48	56	156	334
21 52	−56	156	20 56	−57	156	19 59	−56	156	19 03	−56	157	18 07	−56	157	335
22 11	57	157	21 14	56	157	20 18	57	157	19 21	56	158	18 25	57	158	336
22 29	57	158	21 32	57	158	20 35	56	158	19 39	57	159	18 42	57	159	337
22 46	57	158	21 49	57	159	20 52	57	159	19 55	57	159	18 58	57	160	338
23 03	57	159	22 06	57	160	21 09	57	160	20 12	58	160	19 14	57	161	339
23 19	−57	160	22 22	−58	161	21 24	−57	161	20 27	−58	161	19 29	−57	162	340
23 35	58	161	22 37	58	162	21 39	57	162	20 42	58	162	19 44	58	162	341
23 49	58	162	22 51	57	163	21 54	58	163	20 56	58	163	19 58	58	163	342
24 03	58	163	23 05	58	163	22 07	58	164	21 09	58	164	20 11	59	164	343
24 16	58	164	23 18	58	164	22 20	59	165	21 21	58	165	20 23	58	165	344
24 29	−59	165	23 30	−58	165	22 32	−59	166	21 33	−58	166	20 35	−59	166	345
24 40	58	166	23 42	59	166	22 43	59	167	21 44	58	167	20 46	59	167	346
24 51	59	167	23 52	58	167	22 54	59	167	21 55	59	168	20 56	59	168	347
25 01	59	168	24 02	59	168	23 03	59	168	22 04	59	169	21 05	59	169	348
25 11	59	169	24 12	60	169	23 12	59	169	22 13	59	170	21 14	59	170	349
25 19	−59	170	24 20	−59	170	23 21	−60	170	22 21	−59	171	21 22	−60	171	350
25 27	59	171	24 28	60	171	23 28	59	171	22 29	60	171	21 29	59	172	351
25 34	60	172	24 34	59	172	23 35	60	172	22 35	59	172	21 36	60	172	352
25 40	60	173	24 40	59	173	23 41	60	173	22 41	60	173	21 41	59	173	353
25 45	59	174	24 46	60	174	23 46	60	174	22 46	60	174	21 46	60	174	354
25 50	−60	175	24 50	−60	175	23 50	−60	175	22 50	−60	175	21 50	−59	175	355
25 53	59	176	24 54	60	176	23 54	60	176	22 54	60	176	21 54	60	176	356
25 56	60	177	24 56	60	177	23 56	59	177	22 57	60	177	21 57	60	177	357
25 58	60	178	24 58	60	178	23 58	60	178	22 58	59	178	21 59	60	178	358
26 00	60	179	25 00	60	179	24 00	60	179	23 00	60	179	22 00	60	179	359
26 00	−60	180	25 00	−60	180	24 00	−60	180	23 00	−60	180	22 00	−60	180	360
25°			26°			27°			28°			29°			

S. Lat. {LHA greater than 180°........ Zn=180−Z; LHA less than 180°............ Zn=180+Z}

DECLINATION (15°-29°) CONTRARY NAME TO LATITUDE

N. Lat. {LHA greater than 180°....... Zn=Z; LHA less than 180°........... Zn=360−Z}

DECLINATION (0°-14°) SAME NAME AS LATITUDE

LAT 40°

LHA	0° Hc	0° d	0° Z	1° Hc	1° d	1° Z	2° Hc	2° d	2° Z	3° Hc	3° d	3° Z	4° Hc	4° d	4° Z
	° ′	′	°	° ′	′	°	° ′	′	°	° ′	′	°	° ′	′	°
0	50 00	+60	180	51 00	+60	180	52 00	+60	180	53 00	+60	180	54 00	+60	180
1	49 59	60	178	50 59	60	178	51 59	60	178	52 59	60	178	53 59	60	178
2	49 58	60	177	50 58	59	177	51 57	60	177	52 57	60	177	53 57	60	177
3	49 54	60	175	50 54	60	175	51 54	60	175	52 54	60	175	53 54	60	175
4	49 50	60	174	50 50	60	174	51 50	59	174	52 49	60	173	53 49	60	173
5	49 45	+59	172	50 44	+60	172	51 44	+59	172	52 43	+60	172	53 43	+60	172
6	49 38	59	171	50 37	60	171	51 37	59	170	52 36	60	170	53 36	59	170
7	49 30	59	169	50 29	59	169	51 28	60	169	52 28	59	169	53 27	59	168
8	49 20	60	168	50 20	59	167	51 19	59	167	52 18	59	167	53 17	59	167
9	49 10	59	166	50 09	59	166	51 08	59	166	52 07	59	165	53 06	58	165
10	48 58	+59	165	49 57	+59	164	50 56	+58	164	51 54	+59	164	52 53	+59	163
11	48 46	58	163	49 44	59	163	50 43	58	163	51 41	58	162	52 39	58	162
12	48 32	58	162	49 30	58	161	50 28	58	161	51 26	58	161	52 24	58	160
13	48 17	58	160	49 15	58	160	50 13	57	159	51 10	58	159	52 08	58	159
14	48 01	57	159	48 58	58	158	49 56	57	158	50 53	58	158	51 51	57	157
15	47 44	+57	157	48 41	+57	157	49 38	+57	157	50 35	+57	156	51 32	+57	156
16	47 25	57	156	48 22	57	156	49 19	57	155	50 16	56	155	51 12	57	154
17	47 06	57	155	48 03	56	154	48 59	57	154	49 56	56	153	50 52	56	153
18	46 46	56	153	47 42	56	153	48 38	56	152	49 34	56	152	50 30	56	151
19	46 25	56	152	47 21	55	151	48 16	56	151	49 12	55	150	50 07	55	150
20	46 03	+55	151	46 58	+55	150	47 53	+55	149	48 48	+55	149	49 43	+55	148
21	45 39	56	149	46 35	54	149	47 29	55	148	48 24	55	147	49 19	54	147
22	45 15	55	148	46 10	55	147	47 05	54	147	47 59	54	146	48 53	54	145
23	44 51	54	147	45 45	54	146	46 39	54	145	47 33	53	145	48 26	54	144
24	44 25	54	145	45 19	53	145	46 12	54	144	47 06	53	143	47 59	53	143
25	43 58	+54	144	44 52	+53	143	45 45	+53	143	46 38	+53	142	47 31	+52	141
26	43 31	53	143	44 24	53	142	45 17	52	142	46 09	53	141	47 02	52	140
27	43 03	52	142	43 55	53	141	44 48	52	140	45 40	52	140	46 32	51	139
28	42 34	52	140	43 26	52	140	44 18	52	139	45 10	51	138	46 01	51	138
29	42 04	52	139	42 56	51	139	43 47	52	138	44 39	51	137	45 30	51	136
30	41 34	+51	138	42 25	+51	137	43 16	+51	137	44 07	+51	136	44 58	+50	135
31	41 03	51	137	41 54	50	136	42 44	51	136	43 35	50	135	44 25	50	134
32	40 31	51	136	41 22	50	135	42 12	50	134	43 02	50	134	43 52	49	133
33	39 59	50	135	40 49	50	134	41 39	49	133	42 28	50	133	43 18	49	132
34	39 26	49	134	40 15	50	133	41 05	49	132	41 54	49	131	42 43	49	131
35	38 52	+49	133	39 41	+50	132	40 31	+48	131	41 19	+49	130	42 08	+48	130
36	38 18	49	132	39 07	49	131	39 56	48	130	40 44	48	129	41 32	48	128
37	37 43	49	131	38 32	48	130	39 20	48	129	40 08	48	128	40 56	47	127
38	37 08	48	129	37 56	48	129	38 44	48	128	39 32	47	127	40 19	47	126
39	36 32	48	128	37 20	48	128	38 08	47	127	38 55	47	126	39 42	46	125
40	35 56	+47	128	36 43	+48	127	37 31	+47	126	38 18	+46	125	39 04	+46	124
41	35 19	47	127	36 06	47	126	36 53	47	125	37 40	46	124	38 26	46	123
42	34 42	47	126	35 29	46	125	36 15	46	124	37 01	46	123	37 47	46	122
43	34 04	47	125	34 51	46	124	35 37	46	123	36 23	45	122	37 08	45	121
44	33 26	46	124	34 12	46	123	34 58	46	122	35 44	45	121	36 29	45	121
45	32 48	+46	123	33 34	+45	122	34 19	+45	121	35 04	+45	120	35 49	+45	120
46	32 09	45	122	32 54	46	121	33 40	44	120	34 24	45	120	35 09	44	119
47	31 30	45	121	32 15	45	120	33 00	44	119	33 44	44	119	34 28	44	118
48	30 50	45	120	31 35	44	119	32 19	45	119	33 04	44	118	33 48	43	117
49	30 10	45	119	30 55	44	118	31 39	44	118	32 23	43	117	33 06	44	116
50	29 30	+44	118	30 14	+44	118	30 58	+44	117	31 42	+43	116	32 25	+43	115
51	28 49	44	118	29 33	44	117	30 17	43	116	31 00	43	115	31 43	43	114
52	28 08	44	117	28 52	43	116	29 35	43	115	30 18	43	114	31 01	43	114
53	27 27	44	116	28 11	43	115	28 54	42	114	29 36	43	114	30 19	42	113
54	26 46	43	115	27 29	43	114	28 12	42	114	28 54	42	113	29 36	42	112
55	26 04	+43	114	26 47	+42	113	27 29	+43	113	28 12	+42	112	28 54	+41	111
56	25 22	42	113	26 04	43	113	26 47	42	112	27 29	42	111	28 11	41	110
57	24 40	42	113	25 22	42	112	26 04	42	111	26 46	41	110	27 27	42	110
58	23 57	42	112	24 39	42	111	25 21	42	110	26 03	41	110	26 44	41	109
59	23 14	42	111	23 56	42	110	24 38	41	110	25 19	41	109	26 00	41	108
60	22 31	+42	110	23 13	+41	110	23 54	+42	109	24 36	+40	108	25 16	+41	107
61	21 48	42	110	22 30	41	109	23 11	41	108	23 52	40	107	24 32	41	106
62	21 05	41	109	21 46	41	108	22 27	41	107	23 08	40	107	23 48	41	106
63	20 21	41	108	21 02	41	107	21 43	41	107	22 24	40	106	23 04	40	105
64	19 37	41	107	20 18	41	107	20 59	40	106	21 39	40	105	22 19	40	104
65	18 53	+41	107	19 34	+41	106	20 15	+40	105	20 55	+40	104	21 35	+40	104
66	18 09	41	106	18 50	40	105	19 30	40	104	20 10	40	104	20 50	40	103
67	17 25	40	105	18 05	41	105	18 46	39	104	19 25	40	103	20 05	40	102
68	16 41	40	105	17 21	40	104	18 01	40	103	18 41	39	102	19 20	40	101
69	15 56	40	104	16 36	40	103	17 16	40	102	17 56	39	102	18 35	39	101

LHA	5° Hc	5° d	5° Z	6° Hc	6° d	6° Z	7° Hc	7° d	7° Z	8° Hc	8° d	8° Z	9° Hc	9° d	9° Z
	° ′	′	°	° ′	′	°	° ′	′	°	° ′	′	°	° ′	′	°
0	55 00	+60	180	56 00	+60	180	57 00	+60	180	58 00	+60	180	59 00	+60	180
1	54 59	60	178	55 59	60	178	56 59	60	178	57 59	60	178	58 59	60	178
2	54 57	60	177	55 57	60	176	56 57	60	176	57 57	60	176	58 57	60	176
3	54 54	60	175	55 54	59	175	56 53	60	175	57 53	60	174	58 53	60	174
4	54 49	60	173	55 49	59	173	56 48	60	173	57 48	60	173	58 48	59	172
5	54 43	+59	171	55 42	+60	171	56 42	+59	171	57 41	+60	171	58 41	+59	171
6	54 35	60	170	55 35	59	169	56 34	59	169	57 33	60	169	58 33	59	169
7	54 26	59	168	55 25	60	168	56 25	59	167	57 24	59	167	58 23	59	167
8	54 16	59	166	55 15	59	166	56 14	59	166	57 13	58	165	58 11	59	165
9	54 04	59	165	55 03	59	164	56 02	58	164	57 00	59	164	57 59	58	163
10	53 52	+58	163	54 50	+58	163	55 48	+59	162	56 47	+58	162	57 45	+58	161
11	53 37	59	161	54 36	58	161	55 34	57	160	56 31	58	160	57 29	58	160
12	53 22	58	160	54 20	58	159	55 18	57	159	56 15	57	158	57 12	58	158
13	53 06	57	158	54 03	57	158	55 00	57	157	55 57	57	157	56 54	57	156
14	52 48	57	157	53 45	57	156	54 42	56	156	55 38	57	155	56 35	56	154
15	52 29	+57	155	53 26	+56	154	54 22	+56	154	55 18	+57	153	56 15	+55	153
16	52 09	56	153	53 05	56	153	54 01	56	152	54 57	56	152	55 53	55	151
17	51 48	56	152	52 44	55	151	53 39	56	151	54 35	55	150	55 30	55	149
18	51 26	55	150	52 21	55	150	53 16	55	149	54 11	55	149	55 06	54	148
19	51 02	55	149	51 57	55	148	52 52	55	148	53 47	54	147	54 41	54	146
20	50 38	+55	148	51 33	+54	147	52 27	+54	146	53 21	+54	145	54 15	+53	145
21	50 13	54	146	51 07	54	145	52 01	54	145	52 55	53	144	53 48	53	143
22	49 47	54	145	50 41	53	144	51 34	53	143	52 27	53	143	53 20	52	142
23	49 20	53	143	50 13	53	143	51 06	53	142	51 59	52	141	52 51	52	140
24	48 52	53	142	49 45	52	141	50 37	52	141	51 29	52	140	52 21	51	139
25	48 23	+53	141	49 16	+51	140	50 07	+52	139	50 59	+51	138	51 50	+51	138
26	47 54	52	139	48 46	51	139	49 37	51	138	50 28	51	137	51 19	50	136
27	47 23	52	138	48 15	51	137	49 06	50	137	49 56	51	136	50 47	50	135
28	46 52	51	137	47 43	51	136	48 34	50	135	49 24	50	134	50 14	49	134
29	46 21	50	136	47 11	50	135	48 01	50	134	48 51	49	133	49 40	49	132
30	45 48	+50	134	46 38	+50	134	47 28	+49	133	48 17	+49	132	49 06	+48	131
31	45 15	49	133	46 04	50	132	46 54	48	132	47 42	49	131	48 31	48	130
32	44 41	49	132	45 30	49	131	46 19	48	130	47 07	48	130	47 55	48	129
33	44 07	48	131	44 55	49	130	45 44	48	129	46 32	47	128	47 19	47	128
34	43 32	48	130	44 20	48	129	45 08	47	128	45 55	47	127	46 42	47	126
35	42 56	+48	129	43 44	+47	128	44 31	+47	127	45 18	+47	126	46 05	+46	125
36	42 20	47	128	43 07	47	127	43 54	47	126	44 41	46	125	45 27	46	124
37	41 43	47	127	42 30	47	126	43 17	46	125	44 03	46	124	44 49	45	123
38	41 06	47	126	41 53	46	125	42 39	46	124	43 25	45	123	44 10	45	122
39	40 28	47	125	41 15	45	124	42 00	46	123	42 46	45	122	43 31	45	121
40	39 50	+46	124	40 36	+46	123	41 22	+45	122	42 07	+44	121	42 51	+45	120
41	39 12	45	123	39 57	45	122	40 42	45	121	41 27	44	120	42 11	44	119
42	38 33	45	122	39 18	45	121	40 03	44	120	40 47	44	119	41 31	44	118
43	37 53	45	121	38 38	45	120	39 23	44	119	40 07	43	118	40 50	43	117
44	37 14	44	120	37 58	44	119	38 42	44	118	39 26	43	117	40 09	43	116
45	36 34	+44	119	37 18	+43	118	38 01	+44	117	38 45	+43	116	39 28	+42	115
46	35 53	44	118	36 37	43	117	37 20	43	116	38 03	43	115	38 46	42	114
47	35 12	44	117	35 56	43	116	36 39	43	115	37 22	42	114	38 04	42	113
48	34 31	43	116	35 14	43	115	35 57	43	114	36 40	42	114	37 22	41	113
49	33 50	43	115	34 33	42	114	35 15	42	114	35 57	42	113	36 39	41	112
50	33 08	+43	114	33 51	+42	114	34 33	+42	113	35 15	+41	112	35 56	+41	111
51	32 26	42	114	33 08	42	113	33 50	42	112	34 32	41	111	35 13	41	110
52	31 44	42	113	32 26	41	112	33 07	42	111	33 49	41	110	34 30	41	109
53	31 01	42	112	31 43	41	111	32 24	42	110	33 06	40	109	33 46	41	108
54	30 18	42	111	31 00	41	110	31 41	41	109	32 22	41	109	33 03	40	108
55	29 35	+42	110	30 17	+41	109	30 58	+40	109	31 38	+41	108	32 19	+40	107
56	28 52	41	109	29 33	41	109	30 14	41	108	30 55	40	107	31 35	39	106
57	28 09	40	109	28 49	41	108	29 30	40	107	30 10	40	106	30 50	40	105
58	27 25	41	108	28 06	40	107	28 46	40	106	29 26	40	105	30 06	39	105
59	26 41	41	107	27 22	40	106	28 02	40	106	28 42	39	105	29 21	40	104
60	25 57	+40	106	26 37	+40	106	27 17	+40	105	27 57	+40	104	28 37	+39	103
61	25 13	40	106	25 53	40	105	26 33	40	104	27 13	39	103	27 52	39	102
62	24 29	40	105	25 09	39	104	25 48	40	103	26 28	39	102	27 07	39	102
63	23 44	40	104	24 24	39	103	25 03	40	103	25 43	39	102	26 22	39	101
64	22 59	40	103	23 39	40	103	24 19	39	102	24 58	39	101	25 37	38	100
65	22 15	+39	103	22 54	+39	102	23 33	+40	101	24 13	+38	100	24 51	+39	99
66	21 30	39	102	22 09	39	101	22 48	39	100	23 27	39	100	24 06	38	99
67	20 45	39	101	21 24	39	101	22 03	39	100	22 42	38	99	23 20	39	98
68	20 00	39	101	20 39	39	100	21 18	38	99	21 56	39	98	22 35	38	97
69	19 14	39	100	19 53	39	99	20 32	39	98	21 11	38	98	21 49	38	97

LHA	10° Hc	10° d	10° Z	11° Hc	11° d	11° Z	12° Hc	12° d	12° Z	13° Hc	13° d	13° Z	14° Hc	14° d	14° Z	LHA
	° ′	′	°	° ′	′	°	° ′	′	°	° ′	′	°	° ′	′	°	
0	60 00	+60	180	61 00	+60	180	62 00	+60	180	63 00	+60	180	64 00	+60	180	360
1	59 59	60	178	60 59	60	178	61 59	60	178	62 59	60	178	63 59	60	178	359
2	59 57	60	176	60 57	60	176	61 57	60	176	62 57	60	176	63 57	59	176	358
3	59 53	60	174	60 53	60	174	61 53	59	174	62 52	60	174	63 52	60	173	357
4	59 47	60	172	60 47	60	172	61 47	59	172	62 46	60	172	63 46	59	171	356
5	59 40	+60	170	60 40	+59	170	61 39	+60	170	62 39	+59	169	63 38	+59	169	355
6	59 32	59	168	60 31	59	168	61 30	59	168	62 29	59	167	63 28	59	167	354
7	59 22	59	166	60 21	59	166	61 20	58	166	62 18	59	165	63 17	59	165	353
8	59 10	59	165	60 09	58	164	61 07	59	164	62 06	58	163	63 04	59	163	352
9	58 57	58	163	59 55	59	162	60 54	58	162	61 52	58	161	62 50	58	161	351
10	58 43	+58	161	59 41	+58	160	60 39	+57	160	61 36	+58	159	62 34	+57	159	350
11	58 27	57	159	59 24	58	158	60 22	57	158	61 19	57	157	62 16	57	157	349
12	58 10	57	157	59 07	57	157	60 04	57	156	61 01	56	155	61 57	56	155	348
13	57 51	57	155	58 48	56	155	59 44	57	154	60 41	56	153	61 37	56	153	347
14	57 31	57	154	58 28	56	153	59 24	55	152	60 19	56	152	61 15	55	151	346
15	57 10	+56	152	58 06	+56	151	59 02	+55	151	59 57	+55	150	60 52	+55	149	345
16	56 48	56	150	57 44	54	150	58 38	55	149	59 33	55	148	60 28	54	147	344
17	56 25	55	149	57 20	54	148	58 14	54	147	59 08	54	146	60 02	53	145	343
18	56 00	55	147	56 55	54	146	57 49	53	145	58 42	53	145	59 35	53	144	342
19	55 35	54	145	56 29	53	145	57 22	53	144	58 15	53	143	59 08	52	142	341
20	55 08	+53	144	56 01	+53	143	56 54	+53	142	57 47	+52	141	58 39	+51	140	340
21	54 41	52	142	55 33	53	142	56 26	52	141	57 18	51	140	58 09	51	139	339
22	54 12	52	141	55 04	52	140	55 56	51	139	56 47	51	138	57 38	51	137	338
23	53 43	51	139	54 34	52	139	55 26	50	138	56 16	51	137	57 07	49	136	337
24	53 12	52	138	54 04	50	137	54 54	50	136	55 44	50	135	56 34	49	134	336
25	52 41	+51	137	53 32	+50	136	54 22	+50	135	55 12	+49	134	56 01	+48	133	335
26	52 09	50	135	52 59	50	134	53 49	49	133	54 38	49	132	55 27	48	131	334
27	51 37	49	134	52 26	49	133	53 15	49	132	54 04	48	131	54 52	47	130	333
28	51 03	49	133	51 52	49	132	52 41	48	131	53 29	47	130	54 16	47	129	332
29	50 29	49	131	51 18	48	130	52 06	47	130	52 53	47	129	53 40	47	127	331
30	49 54	+48	130	50 42	+48	129	51 30	+47	128	52 17	+46	127	53 03	+46	126	330
31	49 19	47	129	50 06	47	128	50 53	47	127	51 40	46	126	52 26	45	125	329
32	48 43	47	128	49 30	46	127	50 16	46	126	51 02	46	125	51 48	45	124	328
33	48 06	47	127	48 53	46	126	49 39	45	125	50 24	46	124	51 10	44	123	327
34	47 29	46	125	48 15	46	125	49 01	45	124	49 46	45	123	50 31	44	121	326
35	46 51	+46	124	47 37	+45	123	48 22	+45	122	49 07	+44	121	49 51	+44	120	325
36	46 13	45	123	46 58	45	122	47 43	44	121	48 27	44	120	49 11	43	119	324
37	45 34	45	122	46 19	45	121	47 04	44	120	47 48	43	119	48 31	43	118	323
38	44 55	45	121	45 40	44	120	46 24	43	119	47 07	43	118	47 50	43	117	322
39	44 16	44	120	45 00	43	119	45 43	44	118	46 27	42	117	47 09	42	116	321
40	43 36	+43	119	44 19	+44	118	45 03	+42	117	45 45	+43	116	46 28	+41	115	320
41	42 55	44	118	43 39	43	117	44 22	42	116	45 04	42	115	45 46	41	114	319
42	42 15	43	117	42 58	42	116	43 40	42	115	44 22	42	114	45 04	41	113	318
43	41 33	43	116	42 16	42	115	42 58	42	114	43 40	41	113	44 21	41	112	317
44	40 52	42	115	41 34	42	114	42 16	42	113	42 58	41	112	43 39	40	111	316
45	40 10	+42	114	40 52	+42	113	41 34	+41	112	42 15	+41	111	42 56	+40	110	315
46	39 28	42	113	40 10	41	113	40 51	41	112	41 32	41	111	42 13	39	110	314
47	38 46	41	113	39 27	41	112	40 08	41	111	40 49	40	110	41 29	40	109	313
48	38 03	42	112	38 45	40	111	39 25	41	110	40 06	40	109	40 46	39	108	312
49	37 20	41	111	38 01	41	110	38 42	40	109	39 22	40	108	40 02	39	107	311
50	36 37	+41	110	37 18	+40	109	37 58	+40	108	38 38	+40	107	39 18	+38	106	310
51	35 54	41	109	36 35	40	108	37 15	39	107	37 54	39	106	38 33	39	105	309
52	35 11	40	108	35 51	40	107	36 31	39	107	37 10	39	106	37 49	38	105	308
53	34 27	40	108	35 07	39	107	35 46	40	106	36 26	38	105	37 04	39	104	307
54	33 43	40	107	34 23	39	106	35 02	39	105	35 41	39	104	36 20	38	103	306
55	32 59	+39	106	33 38	+40	105	34 18	+38	104	34 56	+39	103	35 35	+38	102	305
56	32 14	40	105	32 54	39	104	33 33	39	103	34 12	38	102	34 50	38	102	304
57	31 30	39	104	32 09	39	104	32 48	39	103	33 27	38	102	34 05	37	101	303
58	30 45	40	104	31 25	38	103	32 03	39	102	32 42	38	101	33 20	37	100	302
59	30 01	39	103	30 40	38	102	31 18	38	101	31 56	38	100	32 34	38	99	301
60	29 16	+39	102	29 55	+38	101	30 33	+38	100	31 11	+38	100	31 49	+37	99	300
61	28 31	38	101	29 09	39	101	29 48	38	100	30 26	37	99	31 03	38	98	299
62	27 46	38	101	28 24	38	100	29 02	38	99	29 40	38	98	30 18	37	97	298
63	27 01	38	100	27 39	38	99	28 17	38	98	28 55	37	97	29 32	37	97	297
64	26 15	38	99	26 53	38	98	27 31	38	98	28 09	37	97	28 46	37	96	296
65	25 30	+38	99	26 08	+38	98	26 46	+37	97	27 23	+38	96	28 01	+37	95	295
66	24 44	38	98	25 22	38	97	26 00	38	96	26 38	37	95	27 15	37	94	294
67	23 59	38	97	24 37	37	96	25 14	38	96	25 52	37	95	26 29	37	94	293
68	23 13	38	97	23 51	38	96	24 29	37	95	25 06	37	94	25 43	37	93	292
69	22 27	38	96	23 05	38	95	23 43	37	94	24 20	37	93	24 57	37	92	291

0° 1° 2° 3° 4° 5° 6° 7° 8° 9° 10° 11° 12° 13° 14°

S. Lat. {LHA greater than 180°....... Zn=180−Z; LHA less than 180°........... Zn=180+Z}

DECLINATION (0°-14°) SAME NAME AS LATITUDE

LAT 40°

N. Lat. {LHA greater than 180°....... Zn=Z; LHA less than 180°........... Zn=360−Z}

DECLINATION (0°-14°) SAME NAME AS LATITUDE

LHA	0° Hc	d	Z	1° Hc	d	Z	2° Hc	d	Z	3° Hc	d	Z	4° Hc	d	Z	LHA
	° ′	′	°	° ′	′	°	° ′	′	°	° ′	′	°	° ′	′	°	
70	15 11	+40	103	15 51	+40	102	16 31	+40	102	17 11	+39	101	17 50	+39	100	290
71	14 27	39	103	15 06	40	102	15 46	39	101	16 25	40	100	17 05	39	99	289
72	13 42	39	102	14 21	40	101	15 01	39	100	15 40	39	100	16 19	39	99	288
73	12 57	39	101	13 36	39	100	14 15	40	100	14 55	39	99	15 34	39	98	287
74	12 11	40	100	12 51	39	100	13 30	39	99	14 09	39	98	14 48	39	97	286
75	11 26	+39	100	12 05	+40	99	12 45	+39	98	13 24	+39	97	14 03	+38	97	285
76	10 41	39	99	11 20	39	98	11 59	39	98	12 38	39	97	13 17	39	96	284
77	09 55	40	98	10 35	39	98	11 14	38	97	11 52	39	96	12 31	39	95	283
78	09 10	39	98	09 49	39	97	10 28	39	96	11 07	38	96	11 45	39	95	282
79	08 24	39	97	09 03	39	96	09 42	39	96	10 21	38	95	10 59	39	94	281
80	07 39	+39	97	08 18	+38	96	08 56	+39	95	09 35	+39	94	10 14	+38	93	280
81	06 53	39	96	07 32	39	95	08 11	38	94	08 49	39	94	09 28	38	93	279
82	06 07	39	95	06 46	39	94	07 25	38	94	08 03	39	93	08 42	38	92	278
83	05 21	39	95	06 00	39	94	06 39	38	93	07 17	39	92	07 56	38	91	277
84	04 36	38	94	05 14	39	93	05 53	38	92	06 31	39	92	07 10	38	91	276
85	03 50	+38	93	04 28	+39	92	05 07	+38	92	05 45	+39	91	06 24	+38	90	275
86	03 04	38	93	03 42	39	92	04 21	38	91	04 59	39	90	05 38	38	90	274
87	02 18	38	92	02 56	39	91	03 35	39	90	04 14	38	90	04 52	38	89	273
88	01 32	38	91	02 10	39	91	02 49	39	90	03 28	38	89	04 06	38	88	272
89	00 46	39	91	01 25	38	90	02 03	39	89	02 42	38	88	03 20	39	88	271
90	00 00	+39	90	00 39	+38	89	01 17	+39	88	01 56	+38	88	02 34	+39	87	270
91	−0 46	39	89	−0 07	38	89	00 31	39	88	01 10	38	87	01 48	39	86	269
92	−1 32	39	89	−0 53	38	88	−0 15	39	87	00 24	38	86	01 02	39	86	268
93	−2 18	39	88	−1 39	38	87	−1 01	39	87	−0 22	39	86	00 17	38	85	267
94	−3 04	39	87	−2 25	39	87	−1 46	38	86	−1 08	39	85	−0 29	39	84	266
95	−3 50	+39	87	−3 11	+39	86	−2 32	+38	85	−1 54	+39	84	−1 15	+39	84	265
96	−4 36	39	86	−3 57	39	85	−3 18	39	85	−2 39	39	84	−2 00	38	83	264
97	−5 21	38	85	−4 43	39	85	−4 04	39	84	−3 25	39	83	−2 46	39	82	263
98	−6 07	39	85	−5 28	38	84	−4 50	39	83	−4 11	39	83	−3 32	39	82	262
99				−6 14	39	83	−5 35	39	83	−4 56	39	82	−4 17	39	81	261
100							−6 21	+39	82	−5 42	+40	81	−5 02	+39	80	260
101										−6 27	39	81	−5 48	40	80	259

LHA	5° Hc	d	Z	6° Hc	d	Z	7° Hc	d	Z	8° Hc	d	Z	9° Hc	d	Z	LHA
	° ′	′	°	° ′	′	°	° ′	′	°	° ′	′	°	° ′	′	°	
70	18 29	+39	99	19 08	+39	98	19 47	+38	98	20 25	+39	97	21 04	+38	96	290
71	17 44	39	99	18 23	38	98	19 01	39	97	19 40	38	96	20 18	38	95	289
72	16 58	39	98	17 37	39	97	18 16	38	96	18 54	38	96	19 32	38	95	288
73	16 13	38	97	16 51	39	96	17 30	38	96	18 08	38	95	18 46	38	94	287
74	15 27	39	97	16 06	38	96	16 44	38	95	17 22	38	94	18 00	38	93	286
75	14 41	+39	96	15 20	+38	95	15 58	+38	94	16 36	+38	94	17 14	+38	93	285
76	13 56	38	95	14 34	38	94	15 12	39	94	15 51	38	93	16 29	37	92	284
77	13 10	38	95	13 48	38	94	14 26	39	93	15 05	38	92	15 43	37	91	283
78	12 24	38	94	13 02	39	93	13 41	38	92	14 19	38	92	14 57	37	91	282
79	11 38	38	93	12 16	39	93	12 55	38	92	13 33	38	91	14 11	37	90	281
80	10 52	+38	93	11 30	+39	92	12 09	+38	91	12 47	+38	90	13 25	+38	89	280
81	10 06	39	92	10 45	38	91	11 23	38	90	12 01	38	90	12 39	38	89	279
82	09 20	39	91	09 59	38	91	10 37	38	90	11 15	38	89	11 53	38	88	278
83	08 34	39	91	09 13	38	90	09 51	38	89	10 29	38	88	11 07	38	88	277
84	07 48	39	90	08 27	38	89	09 05	38	89	09 43	38	88	10 21	38	87	276
85	07 02	+39	89	07 41	+38	89	08 19	+38	88	08 57	+38	87	09 35	+38	86	275
86	06 16	39	89	06 55	38	88	07 33	38	87	08 11	38	86	08 49	38	86	274
87	05 30	39	88	06 09	38	87	06 47	38	87	07 25	38	86	08 03	38	85	273
88	04 44	39	87	05 23	38	87	06 01	38	86	06 39	39	85	07 18	38	84	272
89	03 59	38	87	04 37	38	86	05 15	39	85	05 54	38	85	06 32	38	84	271
90	03 13	+38	86	03 51	+39	85	04 30	+38	85	05 08	+38	84	05 46	+39	83	270
91	02 27	38	86	03 05	39	85	03 44	38	84	04 22	39	83	05 01	38	82	269
92	01 41	39	85	02 20	38	84	02 58	39	83	03 37	38	83	04 15	39	82	268
93	00 55	39	84	01 34	39	83	02 13	38	83	02 51	39	82	03 30	38	81	267
94	00 10	38	84	00 48	39	83	01 27	39	82	02 06	38	81	02 44	39	81	266
95	−0 36	+39	83	00 03	+38	82	00 41	+39	81	01 20	+39	81	01 59	+39	80	265
96	−1 22	39	82	−0 43	39	82	−0 04	39	81	00 35	39	80	01 14	39	79	264
97	−2 07	39	82	−1 28	39	81	−0 49	39	80	−0 10	39	79	00 29	39	79	263
98	−2 53	39	81	−2 14	40	80	−1 34	39	80	−0 55	39	79	−0 16	39	78	262
99	−3 38	39	80	−2 59	39	80	−2 20	40	79	−1 40	39	78	−1 01	39	77	261
100	−4 23	+39	80	−3 44	+39	79	−3 05	+40	78	−2 25	+39	77	−1 46	+39	77	260
101	−5 08	39	79	−4 29	39	78	−3 50	40	78	−3 10	39	77	−2 31	40	76	259
102	−5 54	40	78	−5 14	40	78	−4 34	39	77	−3 55	40	76	−3 15	39	75	258
103				−5 59	40	77	−5 19	40	76	−4 39	39	75	−4 00	40	75	257
104							−6 04	40	76	−5 24	40	75	−4 44	40	74	256
105										−6 08	+40	74	−5 28	+40	73	255
106													−6 12	40	73	254

LHA	10° Hc	d	Z	11° Hc	d	Z	12° Hc	d	Z	13° Hc	d	Z	14° Hc	d	Z	LHA
	° ′	′	°	° ′	′	°	° ′	′	°	° ′	′	°	° ′	′	°	
70	21 42	+37	95	22 19	+38	94	22 57	+37	94	23 34	+37	93	24 11	+37	92	290
71	20 56	38	95	21 34	37	94	22 11	37	93	22 48	37	92	23 25	37	91	289
72	20 10	38	94	20 48	37	93	21 25	37	92	22 02	37	91	22 39	37	91	288
73	19 24	38	93	20 02	37	92	20 39	37	92	21 16	37	91	21 53	37	90	287
74	18 38	38	93	19 16	37	92	19 53	38	91	20 31	36	90	21 07	37	89	286
75	17 52	+38	92	18 30	+37	91	19 07	+38	90	19 45	+37	89	20 22	+36	89	285
76	17 06	38	91	17 44	37	90	18 21	38	90	18 59	37	89	19 36	36	88	284
77	16 20	38	91	16 58	37	90	17 35	38	89	18 13	37	88	18 50	36	87	283
78	15 34	38	90	16 12	37	89	16 49	38	88	17 27	37	88	18 04	37	87	282
79	14 48	38	89	15 26	38	89	16 04	37	88	16 41	37	87	17 18	37	86	281
80	14 03	+37	89	14 40	+38	88	15 18	+37	87	15 55	+37	86	16 32	+37	85	280
81	13 17	37	88	13 54	38	87	14 32	37	86	15 09	37	86	15 46	37	85	279
82	12 31	37	87	13 08	38	87	13 46	37	86	14 23	38	85	15 01	37	84	278
83	11 45	37	87	12 22	38	86	13 00	38	85	13 38	37	84	14 15	37	84	277
84	10 59	38	86	11 37	37	85	12 14	38	85	12 52	37	84	13 29	37	83	276
85	10 13	+38	86	10 51	+38	85	11 29	+37	84	12 06	+38	83	12 44	+37	82	275
86	09 27	38	85	10 05	38	84	10 43	38	83	11 21	37	83	11 58	37	82	274
87	08 41	38	84	09 19	38	83	09 57	38	83	10 35	38	82	11 13	37	81	273
88	07 56	38	84	08 34	38	83	09 12	38	82	09 50	37	81	10 27	38	80	272
89	07 10	38	83	07 48	38	82	08 26	38	81	09 04	38	81	09 42	38	80	271
90	06 25	+38	82	07 03	+38	82	07 41	+38	81	08 19	+38	80	08 57	+38	79	270
91	05 39	38	82	06 17	39	81	06 56	38	80	07 34	38	79	08 12	38	79	269
92	04 54	38	81	05 32	38	80	06 10	39	80	06 49	38	79	07 27	38	78	268
93	04 08	39	80	04 47	38	80	05 25	39	79	06 04	38	78	06 42	38	77	267
94	03 23	39	80	04 02	38	79	04 40	39	78	05 19	38	78	05 57	38	77	266
95	02 38	+38	79	03 16	+39	78	03 55	+39	78	04 34	+38	77	05 12	+39	76	265
96	01 53	38	79	02 31	39	78	03 10	39	77	03 49	39	76	04 28	38	75	264
97	01 08	39	78	01 47	39	77	02 26	38	76	03 04	39	76	03 43	39	75	263
98	00 23	39	77	01 02	39	76	01 41	39	76	02 20	39	75	02 59	39	74	262
99	−0 22	39	77	00 17	39	76	00 56	40	75	01 36	39	74	02 15	39	74	261
100	−1 07	+40	76	−0 27	+39	75	00 12	+40	74	00 52	+39	74	01 31	+39	73	260
101	−1 51	39	75	−1 12	40	75	−0 32	39	74	00 07	40	73	00 47	40	72	259
102	−2 36	40	75	−1 56	40	74	−1 16	40	73	−0 36	39	72	00 03	40	72	258
103	−3 20	40	74	−2 40	40	73	−2 00	40	72	−1 20	40	72	−0 40	40	71	257
104	−4 04	40	73	−3 24	40	73	−2 44	40	72	−2 04	40	71	−1 24	41	70	256
105	−4 48	+40	73	−4 08	+41	72	−3 27	+40	71	−2 47	+40	70	−2 07	+41	70	255
106	−5 32	41	72	−4 51	40	71	−4 11	41	71	−3 30	40	70	−2 50	41	69	254
107	−6 15	40	71	−5 35	41	71	−4 54	41	70	−4 13	40	69	−3 33	41	68	253
108				−6 18	41	70	−5 37	41	69	−4 56	41	68	−4 15	41	68	252
109							−6 20	41	68	−5 39	41	68	−4 58	42	67	251
110										−6 21	+41	67	−5 40	+42	66	250
111													−6 22	42	66	249

DECLINATION (0°-14°) CONTRARY NAME TO LATITUDE

LHA	0° Hc	d	Z	1° Hc	d	Z	2° Hc	d	Z	3° Hc	d	Z	4° Hc	d	Z	LHA
98	−6 07	39	85													262
97	−5 21	39	85	−6 00	39	86										263
96	−4 36	38	86	−5 14	39	87	−5 53	38	88	−6 31	39	88				264
95	−3 50	−38	87	−4 28	−39	88	−5 07	−38	88	−5 45	−39	89	−6 24	−38	90	265
94	−3 04	38	87	−3 42	39	88	−4 21	38	89	−4 59	39	90	−5 38	38	90	266
93	−2 18	38	88	−2 56	39	89	−3 35	39	90	−4 14	38	90	−4 52	38	91	267
92	−1 32	38	89	−2 10	39	89	−2 49	39	90	−3 28	38	91	−4 06	38	92	268
91	−0 46	39	89	−1 25	38	90	−2 03	39	91	−2 42	38	92	−3 20	39	92	269
90	00 00	−39	90	−0 39	−38	91	−1 17	−39	92	−1 56	−38	92	−2 34	−39	93	270
89	00 46	39	91	00 07	38	91	−0 31	39	92	−1 10	38	93	−1 48	39	94	271
88	01 32	39	91	00 53	38	92	00 15	39	93	−0 24	38	94	−1 02	39	94	272
87	02 18	39	92	01 39	38	93	01 01	39	93	00 22	39	94	−0 17	38	95	273
86	03 04	39	93	02 25	39	93	01 46	38	94	01 08	39	95	00 29	39	96	274
85	03 50	−39	93	03 11	−39	94	02 32	−38	95	01 54	−39	96	01 15	−39	96	275
84	04 36	39	94	03 57	39	95	03 18	39	95	02 39	39	96	02 00	38	97	276
83	05 21	38	95	04 43	39	95	04 04	39	96	03 25	39	97	02 46	39	98	277
82	06 07	39	95	05 28	38	96	04 50	39	97	04 11	39	97	03 32	39	98	278
81	06 53	39	96	06 14	39	97	05 35	39	97	04 56	39	98	04 17	39	99	279
80	07 39	−39	97	07 00	−39	97	06 21	−39	98	05 42	−40	99	05 02	−39	100	280
79	08 24	39	97	07 45	39	98	07 06	39	99	06 27	39	99	05 48	40	100	281
78	09 10	39	98	08 31	39	99	07 52	40	99	07 12	39	100	06 33	39	101	282
77	09 55	39	98	09 16	39	99	08 37	39	100	07 58	40	101	07 18	40	102	283
76	10 41	39	99	10 02	40	100	09 22	39	101	08 43	40	101	08 03	40	102	284
75	11 26	−39	100	10 47	−40	101	10 07	−39	101	09 28	−40	102	08 48	−40	103	285
74	12 11	39	100	11 32	40	101	10 52	39	102	10 13	40	103	09 33	40	104	286
73	12 57	40	101	12 17	40	102	11 37	40	103	10 57	40	103	10 17	40	104	287
72	13 42	40	102	13 02	40	103	12 22	40	103	11 42	40	104	11 02	40	105	288
71	14 27	40	103	13 47	40	103	13 07	41	104	12 26	40	105	11 46	40	106	289
70	15 11	−40	103	14 31	−40	104	13 51	−40	105	13 11	−41	106	12 30	−40	106	290

LHA	5° Hc	d	Z	6° Hc	d	Z	7° Hc	d	Z	8° Hc	d	Z	9° Hc	d	Z	LHA
94	−6 16	39	91													266
93	−5 30	39	92	−6 09	38	93										267
92	−4 44	39	93	−5 23	38	93	−6 01	38	94							268
91	−3 59	38	93	−4 37	38	94	−5 15	39	95	−5 54	38	95				269
90	−3 13	−38	94	−3 51	−39	95	−4 30	−38	95	−5 08	−38	96	−5 46	−39	97	270
89	−2 27	38	94	−3 05	39	95	−3 44	38	96	−4 22	39	97	−5 01	38	98	271
88	−1 41	39	95	−2 20	38	96	−2 58	39	97	−3 37	38	97	−4 15	39	98	272
87	−0 55	39	96	−1 34	39	97	−2 13	38	97	−2 51	39	98	−3 30	38	99	273
86	−0 10	38	96	−0 48	39	97	−1 27	39	98	−2 06	38	99	−2 44	39	99	274
85	00 36	−39	97	−0 03	−38	98	−0 41	−39	99	−1 20	−39	99	−1 59	−39	100	275
84	01 22	39	98	00 43	39	98	00 04	39	99	−0 35	39	100	−1 14	39	101	276
83	02 07	39	98	01 28	39	99	00 49	39	100	00 10	39	101	−0 29	39	101	277
82	02 53	39	99	02 14	40	100	01 34	39	100	00 55	39	101	00 16	39	102	278
81	03 38	39	100	02 59	39	100	02 20	40	101	01 40	39	102	01 01	39	103	279
80	04 23	−39	100	03 44	−39	101	03 05	−40	102	02 25	−39	103	01 46	−39	103	280
79	05 08	39	101	04 29	39	102	03 50	40	102	03 10	39	103	02 31	40	104	281
78	05 54	40	102	05 14	40	102	04 34	39	103	03 55	40	104	03 15	39	105	282
77	06 38	39	102	05 59	40	103	05 19	40	104	04 39	39	105	04 00	40	105	283
76	07 23	39	103	06 44	40	104	06 04	40	104	05 24	40	105	04 44	40	106	284
75	08 08	−40	104	07 28	−40	104	06 48	−40	105	06 08	−40	106	05 28	−40	107	285
74	08 53	40	104	08 13	40	105	07 33	41	106	06 52	40	107	06 12	40	107	286
73	09 37	40	105	08 57	40	106	08 17	41	106	07 36	40	107	06 56	41	108	287
72	10 22	41	106	09 41	40	106	09 01	41	107	08 20	40	108	07 40	41	109	288
71	11 06	41	106	10 25	40	107	09 45	41	108	09 04	41	109	08 23	41	109	289
70	11 50	−41	107	11 09	−41	108	10 28	−41	109	09 47	−41	109	09 06	−41	110	290

LHA	10° Hc	d	Z	11° Hc	d	Z	12° Hc	d	Z	13° Hc	d	Z	14° Hc	d	Z	LHA
90	−6 25	−38	98													270
89	−5 39	38	98	−6 17	39	99										271
88	−4 54	38	99	−5 32	38	100	−6 10	39	100							272
87	−4 08	39	100	−4 47	38	100	−5 25	39	101	−6 04	38	102				273
86	−3 23	39	100	−4 02	38	101	−4 40	39	102	−5 19	38	102	−5 57	38	103	274
85	−2 38	−38	101	−3 16	−39	102	−3 55	−39	102	−4 34	−38	103	−5 12	−39	104	275
84	−1 53	38	101	−2 31	39	102	−3 10	39	103	−3 49	39	104	−4 28	38	105	276
83	−1 08	39	102	−1 47	39	103	−2 26	38	104	−3 04	39	104	−3 43	39	105	277
82	−0 23	39	103	−1 02	39	104	−1 41	39	104	−2 20	39	105	−2 59	39	106	278
81	00 22	39	103	−0 17	39	104	−0 56	40	105	−1 36	39	106	−2 15	39	106	279
80	01 07	−40	104	00 27	−39	105	−0 12	−40	106	−0 52	−39	106	−1 31	−39	107	280
79	01 51	39	105	01 12	40	105	00 32	39	106	−0 07	40	107	−0 47	40	108	281
78	02 36	40	105	01 56	40	106	01 16	40	107	00 36	39	108	−0 03	40	108	282
77	03 20	40	106	02 40	40	107	02 00	40	108	01 20	40	108	00 40	40	109	283
76	04 04	40	107	03 24	40	107	02 44	40	108	02 04	40	109	01 24	41	110	284
75	04 48	−40	107	04 08	−41	108	03 27	−40	109	02 47	−40	110	02 07	−41	110	285
74	05 32	41	108	04 51	40	109	04 11	41	109	03 30	40	110	02 50	41	111	286
73	06 15	40	109	05 35	41	109	04 54	41	110	04 13	40	111	03 33	41	112	287
72	06 59	41	109	06 18	41	110	05 37	41	111	04 56	41	112	04 15	41	112	288
71	07 42	41	110	07 01	41	111	06 20	41	112	05 39	41	112	04 58	42	113	289
70	08 25	−41	111	07 44	−41	111	07 03	−42	112	06 21	−41	113	05 40	−42	114	290

S. Lat. {LHA greater than 180°....... Zn=180−Z; LHA less than 180°........... Zn=180+Z}

N. Lat. {LHA greater than 180°....... Zn=Z; LHA less than 180°........... Zn=360−Z}

DECLINATION (0°-14°) CONTRARY NAME TO LATITUDE

LHA	0° Hc	d	Z	1° Hc	d	Z	2° Hc	d	Z	3° Hc	d	Z	4° Hc	d	Z
	° ′	′	°	° ′	′	°	° ′	′	°	° ′	′	°	° ′	′	°
69	15 56	40	104	15 16	40	105	14 36	41	105	13 55	41	106	13 14	40	107
68	16 41	41	105	16 00	40	105	15 20	41	106	14 39	41	107	13 58	41	108
67	17 25	40	105	16 45	41	106	16 04	41	107	15 23	41	108	14 42	41	108
66	18 09	40	106	17 29	41	107	16 48	41	108	16 07	41	108	15 26	42	109
65	18 53	−40	107	18 13	−41	108	17 32	−42	108	16 50	−41	109	16 09	−42	110
64	19 37	41	107	18 56	41	108	18 15	41	109	17 34	42	110	16 52	42	111
63	20 21	41	108	19 40	42	109	18 58	41	110	18 17	42	110	17 35	42	111
62	21 05	42	109	20 23	41	110	19 42	42	110	19 00	42	111	18 18	42	112
61	21 48	42	110	21 06	41	110	20 25	42	111	19 43	43	112	19 00	42	113
60	22 31	−42	110	21 49	−42	111	21 07	−42	112	20 25	−42	113	19 43	−43	113
59	23 14	42	111	22 32	42	112	21 50	43	113	21 07	42	113	20 25	43	114
58	23 57	42	112	23 15	43	113	22 32	43	113	21 49	43	114	21 06	43	115
57	24 40	43	113	23 57	43	113	23 14	43	114	22 31	43	115	21 48	43	116
56	25 22	43	113	24 39	43	114	23 56	43	115	23 13	44	116	22 29	43	117
55	26 04	−43	114	25 21	−43	115	24 38	−44	116	23 54	−44	117	23 10	−44	117
54	26 46	44	115	26 02	43	116	25 19	44	117	24 35	44	117	23 51	44	118
53	27 27	43	116	26 44	44	117	26 00	44	117	25 16	45	118	24 31	44	119
52	28 08	43	117	27 25	45	117	26 40	44	118	25 56	44	119	25 12	45	120
51	28 49	44	118	28 05	44	118	27 21	45	119	26 36	45	120	25 51	45	121
50	29 30	−44	118	28 46	−45	119	28 01	−45	120	27 16	−45	121	26 31	−46	121
49	30 10	44	119	29 26	45	120	28 41	46	121	27 55	45	122	27 10	46	122
48	30 50	45	120	30 05	45	121	29 20	46	122	28 34	46	122	27 48	46	123
47	31 30	46	121	30 44	45	122	29 59	46	122	29 13	46	123	28 27	47	124
46	32 09	46	122	31 23	46	123	30 37	46	123	29 51	46	124	29 05	47	125
45	32 48	−46	123	32 02	−46	124	31 16	−47	124	30 29	−47	125	29 42	−47	126
44	33 26	46	124	32 40	47	124	31 53	46	125	31 07	48	126	30 19	47	127
43	34 04	46	125	33 18	47	126	32 31	47	126	31 44	48	127	30 56	48	128
42	34 42	47	126	33 55	47	126	33 08	48	127	32 20	48	128	31 32	48	128
41	35 19	47	127	34 32	48	127	33 44	48	128	32 56	48	129	32 08	48	129
40	35 56	−48	128	35 08	−48	128	34 20	−48	129	33 32	−49	130	32 43	−48	130
39	36 32	48	128	35 44	48	129	34 56	49	130	34 07	49	131	33 18	49	131
38	37 08	49	129	36 19	48	130	35 31	49	131	34 42	50	132	33 52	49	132
37	37 43	49	131	36 54	49	131	36 05	49	132	35 16	50	133	34 26	50	133
36	38 18	49	132	37 29	50	132	36 39	50	133	35 49	50	134	34 59	50	134
35	38 52	−50	133	38 02	−50	133	37 12	−50	134	36 22	−50	135	35 32	−51	135
34	39 26	50	134	38 36	51	134	37 45	50	135	36 55	51	136	36 04	51	136
33	39 59	51	135	39 08	51	135	38 17	51	136	37 26	51	137	36 35	51	137
32	40 31	51	136	39 40	51	137	38 49	51	137	37 58	52	138	37 06	52	139
31	41 03	52	137	40 11	51	138	39 20	52	138	38 28	52	139	37 36	52	140
30	41 34	−52	138	40 42	−52	139	39 50	−52	139	38 58	−52	140	38 06	−53	141
29	42 04	52	139	41 12	52	140	40 20	53	141	39 27	53	141	38 34	52	142
28	42 34	53	140	41 41	52	141	40 49	53	142	39 56	53	142	39 03	54	143
27	43 03	53	142	42 10	53	142	41 17	54	143	40 23	53	144	39 30	54	144
26	43 31	53	143	42 38	54	143	41 44	54	144	40 50	53	145	39 57	55	145
25	43 58	−53	144	43 05	−54	145	42 11	−54	145	41 17	−55	146	40 22	−54	146
24	44 25	54	145	43 31	55	146	42 36	54	147	41 42	55	147	40 47	54	148
23	44 51	55	147	43 56	55	147	43 01	54	148	42 07	55	148	41 12	56	149
22	45 15	54	148	44 21	55	148	43 26	56	149	42 30	55	150	41 35	55	150
21	45 39	55	149	44 44	55	150	43 49	56	150	42 53	55	151	41 58	56	151
20	46 03	−56	151	45 07	−56	151	44 11	−56	152	43 15	−56	152	42 19	−56	153
19	46 25	56	152	45 29	56	152	44 33	57	153	43 36	56	153	42 40	57	154
18	46 46	56	153	45 50	57	154	44 53	57	154	43 56	56	155	43 00	57	155
17	47 06	57	155	46 09	56	155	45 13	57	156	44 16	57	156	43 19	57	156
16	47 25	57	156	46 28	57	156	45 31	57	157	44 34	57	157	43 37	58	158
15	47 44	−58	157	46 46	−57	158	45 49	−58	158	44 51	−57	159	43 54	−58	159
14	48 01	58	159	47 03	58	159	46 05	58	160	45 07	57	160	44 10	58	160
13	48 17	58	160	47 19	58	161	46 21	58	161	45 23	59	161	44 24	58	162
12	48 32	58	162	47 34	59	162	46 35	58	162	45 37	59	163	44 38	58	163
11	48 46	59	163	47 47	58	164	46 49	59	164	45 50	59	164	44 51	58	164
10	48 58	−58	165	48 00	−59	165	47 01	−59	165	46 02	−59	166	45 03	−59	166
9	49 10	59	166	48 11	59	166	47 12	59	167	46 13	59	167	45 14	59	167
8	49 20	59	168	48 21	59	168	47 22	59	168	46 23	60	168	45 23	59	169
7	49 30	60	169	48 30	59	169	47 31	60	170	46 31	59	170	45 32	59	170
6	49 38	60	171	48 38	59	171	47 39	60	171	46 39	60	171	45 39	59	171
5	49 45	−60	172	48 45	−60	172	47 45	−60	173	46 45	−59	173	45 46	−60	173
4	49 50	60	174	48 50	60	174	47 50	59	174	46 51	60	174	45 51	60	174
3	49 54	59	175	48 55	60	175	47 55	60	176	46 55	60	176	45 55	60	176
2	49 58	60	177	48 58	60	177	47 58	60	177	46 58	60	177	45 58	60	177
1	49 59	60	178	48 59	60	179	47 59	60	179	46 59	60	179	45 59	60	179
0	50 00	−60	180	49 00	−60	180	48 00	−60	180	47 00	−60	180	46 00	−60	180

LHA	5° Hc	d	Z	6° Hc	d	Z	7° Hc	d	Z	8° Hc	d	Z	9° Hc	d	Z
	° ′	′	°	° ′	′	°	° ′	′	°	° ′	′	°	° ′	′	°
69	12 34	41	108	11 53	41	108	11 12	41	109	10 31	42	110	09 49	41	111
68	13 17	41	108	12 36	41	109	11 55	41	110	11 14	42	111	10 32	41	111
67	14 01	41	109	13 20	42	110	12 38	41	111	11 57	42	111	11 15	42	112
66	14 44	41	110	14 03	42	111	13 21	42	111	12 39	41	112	11 58	42	113
65	15 27	−41	111	14 46	−42	111	14 04	−42	112	13 22	−42	113	12 40	−42	113
64	16 10	42	111	15 28	42	112	14 46	42	113	14 04	42	113	13 22	43	114
63	16 53	42	112	16 11	42	113	15 29	43	113	14 46	42	114	14 04	43	115
62	17 36	43	113	16 53	42	113	16 11	43	114	15 28	43	115	14 45	43	116
61	18 18	43	113	17 35	42	114	16 53	43	115	16 10	43	116	15 27	44	116
60	19 00	−43	114	18 17	−43	115	17 34	−43	116	16 51	−43	116	16 08	−44	117
59	19 42	43	115	18 59	44	116	18 15	43	116	17 32	44	117	16 48	43	118
58	20 23	43	116	19 40	44	116	18 56	43	117	18 13	44	118	17 29	44	119
57	21 05	44	116	20 21	44	117	19 37	44	118	18 53	44	119	18 09	44	119
56	21 46	44	117	21 02	44	118	20 18	45	119	19 33	44	119	18 49	45	120
55	22 26	−44	118	21 42	−44	119	20 58	−45	120	20 13	−44	120	19 29	−45	121
54	23 07	45	119	22 22	44	120	21 38	45	120	20 53	45	121	20 08	45	122
53	23 47	45	120	23 02	45	120	22 17	45	121	21 32	45	122	20 47	46	123
52	24 27	45	120	23 42	46	121	22 56	45	122	22 11	46	123	21 25	45	123
51	25 06	45	121	24 21	46	122	23 35	45	123	22 50	46	123	22 04	46	124
50	25 45	−45	122	25 00	−46	123	24 14	−46	124	23 28	−46	124	22 42	−47	125
49	26 24	46	123	25 38	46	124	24 52	46	124	24 06	47	125	23 19	47	126
48	27 02	46	124	26 16	46	125	25 30	47	125	24 43	47	126	23 56	47	127
47	27 40	46	125	26 54	47	125	26 07	47	126	25 20	47	127	24 33	47	127
46	28 18	47	126	27 31	47	126	26 44	47	127	25 57	48	128	25 09	47	128
45	28 55	−47	126	28 08	−47	127	27 21	−48	128	26 33	−48	129	25 45	−48	129
44	29 32	48	127	28 44	47	128	27 57	48	129	27 09	49	129	26 20	48	130
43	30 08	48	128	29 20	48	129	28 32	48	130	27 44	49	130	26 55	48	131
42	30 44	48	129	29 56	49	130	29 07	48	131	28 19	49	131	27 30	49	132
41	31 20	49	130	30 31	49	131	29 42	49	131	28 53	49	132	28 04	49	133
40	31 55	−49	131	31 06	−50	132	30 16	−49	132	29 27	−50	133	28 37	−49	134
39	32 29	49	132	31 40	50	133	30 50	50	133	30 00	50	134	29 10	50	135
38	33 03	50	133	32 13	50	134	31 23	50	134	30 33	50	135	29 43	51	136
37	33 36	50	134	32 46	50	135	31 56	51	135	31 05	50	136	30 15	51	137
36	34 09	50	135	33 19	51	136	32 28	51	136	31 37	51	137	30 46	51	138
35	34 41	−51	136	33 50	−51	137	32 59	−51	137	32 08	−51	138	31 17	−52	139
34	35 13	51	137	34 22	52	138	33 30	51	138	32 39	52	139	31 47	52	140
33	35 44	52	138	34 52	51	139	34 01	52	139	33 09	52	140	32 17	53	141
32	36 14	52	139	35 22	52	140	34 30	52	140	33 38	52	141	32 46	53	142
31	36 44	52	140	35 52	53	141	34 59	52	141	34 07	53	142	33 14	53	143
30	37 13	−52	141	36 21	−53	142	35 28	−53	143	34 35	−54	143	33 41	−53	144
29	37 42	53	142	36 49	54	143	35 55	53	144	35 02	54	144	34 08	53	145
28	38 09	53	144	37 16	54	144	36 22	54	145	35 28	53	145	34 35	54	146
27	38 36	54	145	37 42	54	145	36 48	54	146	35 54	54	146	35 00	54	147
26	39 02	54	146	38 08	54	146	37 14	54	147	36 20	55	147	35 25	55	148
25	39 28	−55	147	38 33	−54	148	37 39	−55	148	36 44	−55	149	35 49	−55	149
24	39 53	55	148	38 58	55	149	38 03	55	149	37 08	56	150	36 12	55	150
23	40 16	55	149	39 21	55	150	38 26	56	150	37 30	56	151	36 35	56	151
22	40 40	56	151	39 44	56	151	38 48	56	152	37 52	56	152	36 56	56	153
21	41 02	56	152	40 06	56	152	39 10	56	153	38 14	57	153	37 17	56	154
20	41 23	−56	153	40 27	−57	154	39 30	−56	154	38 34	−57	154	37 37	−56	155
19	41 43	56	154	40 47	57	155	39 50	57	155	38 53	57	156	37 56	57	156
18	42 03	57	156	41 06	57	156	40 09	57	156	39 12	57	157	38 15	57	157
17	42 22	58	157	41 24	57	157	40 27	57	158	39 30	58	158	38 32	57	158
16	42 39	57	158	41 42	58	159	40 44	58	159	39 46	57	159	38 49	58	160
15	42 56	−58	159	41 58	−58	160	41 00	−58	160	40 02	−58	160	39 04	−56	161
14	43 12	59	161	42 13	58	161	41 15	58	161	40 17	58	162	39 19	58	162
13	43 26	58	162	42 28	58	162	41 30	59	163	40 31	58	163	39 33	59	163
12	43 40	59	163	42 41	58	164	41 43	59	164	40 44	59	164	39 45	58	165
11	43 53	59	165	42 54	59	165	41 55	59	165	40 56	59	166	39 57	59	166
10	44 04	−59	166	43 05	−59	166	42 06	−59	167	41 07	−59	167	40 08	−59	167
9	44 15	59	167	43 16	60	168	42 16	59	168	41 17	59	168	40 18	59	168
8	44 24	59	169	43 25	60	169	42 25	59	169	41 26	59	169	40 27	60	170
7	44 33	60	170	43 33	59	170	42 34	60	171	41 34	60	171	40 34	59	171
6	44 40	60	172	43 40	59	172	42 41	60	172	41 41	60	172	40 41	59	172
5	44 46	−60	173	43 46	−60	173	42 46	−59	173	41 47	−60	173	40 47	−60	174
4	44 51	60	174	43 51	60	175	42 51	59	175	41 52	60	175	40 52	60	175
3	44 55	60	176	43 55	60	176	42 55	60	176	41 55	60	176	40 55	60	176
2	44 58	60	177	43 58	60	177	42 58	60	177	41 58	60	177	40 58	60	177
1	44 59	60	179	43 59	59	179	43 00	60	179	42 00	60	179	41 00	60	179
0	45 00	−60	180	44 00	−60	180	43 00	−60	180	42 00	−60	180	41 00	−60	180

LHA	10° Hc	d	Z	11° Hc	d	Z	12° Hc	d	Z	13° Hc	d	Z	14° Hc	d	Z	LHA
	° ′	′	°	° ′	′	°	° ′	′	°	° ′	′	°	° ′	′	°	
69	09 08	41	111	08 27	42	112	07 45	41	113	07 04	42	114	06 22	42	114	291
68	09 51	42	112	09 09	42	113	08 27	41	114	07 46	42	114	07 04	42	115	292
67	10 33	42	113	09 51	42	114	09 09	42	114	08 27	42	115	07 45	42	116	293
66	11 16	43	114	10 33	42	114	09 51	42	115	09 09	42	116	08 27	43	116	294
65	11 58	−43	114	11 15	−42	115	10 33	−43	116	09 50	−42	116	09 08	−43	117	295
64	12 39	42	115	11 57	43	116	11 14	43	116	10 31	43	117	09 48	42	118	296
63	13 21	43	116	12 38	43	116	11 55	43	117	11 12	43	118	10 29	43	119	297
62	14 02	43	116	13 19	43	117	12 36	43	118	11 53	44	119	11 09	43	119	298
61	14 43	43	117	14 00	43	118	13 17	44	119	12 33	44	119	11 49	43	120	299
60	15 24	−43	118	14 41	−44	119	13 57	−44	119	13 13	−44	120	12 29	−44	121	300
59	16 05	44	119	15 21	44	119	14 37	44	120	13 53	45	121	13 08	44	121	301
58	16 45	44	119	16 01	45	120	15 16	44	121	14 32	44	121	13 48	45	122	302
57	17 25	45	120	16 40	44	121	15 56	45	121	15 11	45	122	14 26	45	123	303
56	18 04	44	121	17 20	45	122	16 35	45	122	15 50	45	123	15 05	46	124	304
55	18 44	−45	122	17 59	−45	122	17 14	−46	123	16 28	−45	124	15 43	−46	124	305
54	19 23	46	122	18 37	45	123	17 52	46	124	17 06	45	124	16 21	46	125	306
53	20 01	45	123	19 16	46	124	18 30	46	125	17 44	46	125	16 58	46	126	307
52	20 40	46	124	19 54	46	125	19 08	47	125	18 21	46	126	17 35	46	127	308
51	21 18	47	125	20 31	46	126	19 45	47	126	18 58	46	127	18 12	47	128	309
50	21 55	−46	126	21 09	−47	126	20 22	−47	127	19 35	−47	128	18 48	−47	128	310
49	22 32	46	126	21 46	48	127	20 58	47	128	20 11	47	128	19 24	48	129	311
48	23 09	47	127	22 22	47	128	21 35	48	129	20 47	48	129	19 59	47	130	312
47	23 46	48	128	22 58	48	129	22 10	48	129	21 22	48	130	20 34	48	131	313
46	24 22	48	129	23 34	48	130	22 46	49	130	21 57	48	131	21 09	48	132	314
45	24 57	−48	130	24 09	−49	131	23 20	−48	131	22 32	−49	132	21 43	−49	132	315
44	25 32	48	131	24 44	49	131	23 55	49	132	23 06	49	133	22 17	49	133	316
43	26 07	49	132	25 18	49	132	24 29	49	133	23 40	50	134	22 50	49	134	317
42	26 41	49	133	25 52	50	133	25 02	49	134	24 13	50	134	23 23	50	135	318
41	27 15	50	133	26 25	50	134	25 35	50	135	24 45	50	135	23 55	50	136	319
40	27 48	−50	134	26 58	−50	135	26 08	−51	136	25 17	−50	136	24 27	−51	137	320
39	28 20	50	135	27 30	50	136	26 40	51	137	25 49	51	137	24 58	51	138	321
38	28 52	50	136	28 02	51	137	27 11	51	137	26 20	51	138	25 29	51	139	322
37	29 24	51	137	28 33	51	138	27 42	51	138	26 51	52	139	25 59	52	140	323
36	29 55	51	138	29 04	52	139	28 12	52	139	27 20	51	140	26 29	52	140	324
35	30 25	−51	139	29 34	−52	140	28 42	−52	140	27 50	−52	141	26 58	−53	141	325
34	30 55	52	140	30 03	52	141	29 11	52	141	28 19	53	142	27 26	53	142	326
33	31 24	52	141	30 32	53	142	29 39	52	142	28 47	53	143	27 54	53	143	327
32	31 53	53	142	31 00	53	143	30 07	53	143	29 14	53	144	28 21	53	144	328
31	32 21	53	143	31 28	54	144	30 34	53	144	29 41	53	145	28 48	54	145	329
30	32 48	−53	144	31 55	−54	145	31 01	−54	145	30 07	−54	146	29 13	−54	146	330
29	33 15	54	145	32 21	54	146	31 27	54	146	30 33	54	147	29 39	55	147	331
28	33 41	55	146	32 46	54	147	31 52	54	147	30 58	55	148	30 03	54	148	332
27	34 06	55	147	33 11	54	148	32 17	55	148	31 22	55	149	30 27	55	149	333
26	34 30	55	148	33 35	55	149	32 40	55	149	31 45	55	150	30 50	55	150	334
25	34 54	−55	150	33 59	−56	150	33 03	−55	150	32 08	−55	151	31 13	−56	151	335
24	35 17	56	151	34 21	55	151	33 26	56	152	32 30	56	152	31 34	56	152	336
23	35 39	56	152	34 43	56	152	33 47	56	153	32 51	56	153	31 55	56	154	337
22	36 00	56	153	35 04	56	153	34 08	56	154	33 12	57	154	32 15	56	155	338
21	36 21	57	154	35 24	56	154	34 28	57	155	33 31	56	155	32 35	57	156	339
20	36 41	−57	155	35 44	−57	156	34 47	−57	156	33 50	−57	156	32 53	−57	157	340
19	36 59	56	156	36 02	57	157	35 05	57	157	34 08	57	158	33 11	57	158	341
18	37 18	58	158	36 20	57	158	35 23	58	158	34 25	57	159	33 28	58	159	342
17	37 35	58	159	36 37	58	159	35 39	57	159	34 42	58	160	33 44	58	160	343
16	37 51	58	160	36 53	58	160	35 55	58	161	34 57	58	161	33 59	58	161	344
15	38 06	−58	161	37 08	−58	161	36 10	−58	162	35 12	−58	162	34 14	−59	162	345
14	38 21	59	162	37 22	58	163	36 24	58	163	35 26	59	163	34 27	58	164	346
13	38 34	58	164	37 36	59	164	36 37	59	164	35 38	58	164	34 40	59	165	347
12	38 47	59	165	37 48	59	165	36 49	59	165	35 50	58	166	34 52	59	166	348
11	38 58	59	166	37 59	59	166	37 00	59	167	36 01	59	167	35 02	59	167	349
10	39 09	−59	167	38 10	−59	168	37 11	−60	168	36 11	−59	168	35 12	−59	168	350
9	39 19	60	169	38 19	59	169	37 20	59	169	36 21	60	169	35 21	59	169	351
8	39 27	59	170	38 28	60	170	37 28	59	170	36 29	60	170	35 29	59	171	352
7	39 35	60	171	38 35	59	171	37 36	60	171	36 36	59	172	35 37	60	172	353
6	39 42	60	172	38 42	60	172	37 42	59	173	36 42	59	173	35 43	60	173	354
5	39 47	−60	174	38 47	−59	174	37 48	−60	174	36 48	−60	174	35 48	−60	174	355
4	39 52	60	175	38 52	60	175	37 52	60	175	36 52	60	175	35 52	60	175	356
3	39 55	60	176	38 55	59	176	37 56	60	176	36 56	60	176	35 56	60	176	357
2	39 58	60	177	38 58	60	178	37 58	60	178	36 58	60	178	35 58	60	178	358
1	40 00	60	179	39 00	60	179	38 00	60	179	37 00	60	179	36 00	60	179	359
0	40 00	−60	180	39 00	−60	180	38 00	−60	180	37 00	−60	180	36 00	−60	180	360

S. Lat. {LHA greater than 180°....... Zn=180−Z; LHA less than 180°........... Zn=180+Z}

DECLINATION (0°-14°) CONTRARY NAME TO LATITUDE

LAT 40°

N. Lat. {LHA greater than 180°........ Zn=Z
{LHA less than 180°............ Zn=360−Z

DECLINATION (15°-29°) SAME NAME AS LATITUDE

LHA	15° Hc	d	Z	16° Hc	d	Z	17° Hc	d	Z	18° Hc	d	Z	19° Hc	d	Z	LHA
	° ′	′	°	° ′	′	°	° ′	′	°	° ′	′	°	° ′	′	°	
0	65 00	+60	180	66 00	+60	180	67 00	+60	180	68 00	+60	180	69 00	+60	180	360
1	64 59	60	178	65 59	60	178	66 59	60	178	67 59	60	178	68 59	60	177	359
2	64 56	60	175	65 56	60	175	66 56	60	175	67 56	60	175	68 56	60	175	358
3	64 52	60	173	65 52	59	173	66 51	60	173	67 51	60	172	68 51	59	172	357
4	64 45	60	171	65 45	59	171	66 44	60	170	67 44	59	170	68 43	60	170	356
5	64 37	+60	169	65 37	+59	168	66 36	+59	168	67 35	+59	167	68 34	+59	167	355
6	64 27	59	167	65 26	59	166	66 25	59	166	67 24	59	165	68 23	58	164	354
7	64 16	58	164	65 14	59	164	66 13	58	163	67 11	58	163	68 09	58	162	353
8	64 03	58	162	65 01	58	162	65 59	57	161	66 56	58	160	67 54	58	160	352
9	63 48	57	160	64 45	58	159	65 43	57	159	66 40	57	158	67 37	57	157	351
10	63 31	+57	158	64 28	+57	157	65 25	+57	157	66 22	+56	156	67 18	+57	155	350
11	63 13	57	156	64 10	56	155	65 06	56	154	66 02	56	154	66 58	55	153	349
12	62 53	57	154	63 50	55	153	64 45	56	152	65 41	55	151	66 36	55	150	348
13	62 33	55	152	63 28	55	151	64 23	55	150	65 18	55	149	66 13	54	148	347
14	62 10	55	150	63 05	55	149	64 00	54	148	64 54	54	147	65 48	53	146	346
15	61 47	+54	148	62 41	+54	147	63 35	+53	146	64 28	+53	145	65 21	+53	144	345
16	61 22	53	146	62 15	54	145	63 09	52	144	64 01	53	143	64 54	51	142	344
17	60 55	54	145	61 49	52	144	62 41	52	143	63 33	52	141	64 25	51	140	343
18	60 28	53	143	61 21	52	142	62 13	51	141	63 04	51	140	63 55	50	138	342
19	60 00	52	141	60 52	51	140	61 43	51	139	62 34	50	138	63 24	49	137	341
20	59 30	+52	139	60 22	+50	138	61 12	+50	137	62 02	+50	136	62 52	+48	135	340
21	59 00	51	138	59 51	49	137	60 40	50	136	61 30	49	134	62 19	48	133	339
22	58 29	50	136	59 19	49	135	60 08	49	134	60 57	48	133	61 45	47	132	338
23	57 56	50	135	58 46	48	134	59 34	48	133	60 22	48	131	61 10	47	130	337
24	57 23	49	133	58 12	48	132	59 00	48	131	59 48	46	130	60 34	46	129	336
25	56 49	+48	132	57 37	+48	131	58 25	+47	130	59 12	+46	128	59 58	+45	127	335
26	56 15	47	130	57 02	47	129	57 49	46	128	58 35	46	127	59 21	45	126	334
27	55 39	47	129	56 26	47	128	57 13	45	127	57 58	45	126	58 43	44	124	333
28	55 03	47	128	55 50	45	127	56 35	46	125	57 21	44	124	58 05	44	123	332
29	54 27	45	126	55 12	46	125	55 58	44	124	56 42	44	123	57 26	43	122	331
30	53 49	+46	125	54 35	+44	124	55 19	+44	123	56 03	+44	122	56 47	+42	120	330
31	53 11	45	124	53 56	44	123	54 40	44	122	55 24	43	120	56 07	42	119	329
32	52 33	44	123	53 17	44	122	54 01	43	120	54 44	42	119	55 26	42	118	328
33	51 54	44	122	52 38	43	120	53 21	43	119	54 04	42	118	54 46	41	117	327
34	51 15	43	120	51 58	43	119	52 41	42	118	53 23	41	117	54 04	41	116	326
35	50 35	+43	119	51 18	+42	118	52 00	+42	117	52 42	+41	116	53 23	+40	115	325
36	49 54	43	118	50 37	42	117	51 19	41	116	52 00	41	115	52 41	40	114	324
37	49 14	42	117	49 56	41	116	50 37	41	115	51 18	40	114	51 58	40	113	323
38	48 33	41	116	49 14	42	115	49 56	40	114	50 36	40	113	51 16	39	112	322
39	47 51	42	115	48 33	40	114	49 13	41	113	49 54	39	112	50 33	39	111	321
40	47 09	+41	114	47 50	+41	113	48 31	+40	112	49 11	+39	111	49 50	+38	110	320
41	46 27	41	113	47 08	40	112	47 48	40	111	48 28	38	110	49 06	38	109	319
42	45 45	40	112	46 25	40	111	47 05	39	110	47 44	39	109	48 23	38	108	318
43	45 02	40	111	45 42	40	110	46 22	39	109	47 01	38	108	47 39	37	107	317
44	44 19	40	110	44 59	39	109	45 38	39	108	46 17	38	107	46 55	37	106	316
45	43 36	+39	109	44 15	+39	108	44 54	+39	107	45 33	+37	106	46 10	+37	105	315
46	42 52	40	109	43 32	38	108	44 10	38	106	44 48	38	105	45 26	37	104	314
47	42 09	39	108	42 48	38	107	43 26	38	106	44 04	37	105	44 41	37	103	313
48	41 25	39	107	42 04	38	106	42 42	38	105	43 20	37	104	43 57	36	103	312
49	40 41	38	106	41 19	38	105	41 57	38	104	42 35	37	103	43 12	36	102	311
50	39 56	+39	105	40 35	+38	104	41 13	+37	103	41 50	+37	102	42 27	+36	101	310
51	39 12	38	104	39 50	38	103	40 28	37	102	41 05	36	101	41 41	36	100	309
52	38 27	38	104	39 05	38	103	39 43	37	102	40 20	36	101	40 56	36	100	308
53	37 43	37	103	38 20	38	102	38 58	37	101	39 35	36	100	40 11	35	99	307
54	36 58	37	102	37 35	38	101	38 13	36	100	38 49	36	99	39 25	36	98	306
55	36 13	+37	101	36 50	+37	100	37 27	+37	99	38 04	+36	98	38 40	+35	97	305
56	35 28	37	101	36 05	37	100	36 42	36	99	37 18	36	98	37 54	35	97	304
57	34 42	38	100	35 20	36	99	35 56	37	98	36 33	35	97	37 08	36	96	303
58	33 57	37	99	34 34	37	98	35 11	36	97	35 47	36	96	36 23	35	95	302
59	33 12	37	98	33 49	36	97	34 25	36	96	35 01	36	96	35 37	35	95	301
60	32 26	+37	98	33 03	+36	97	33 39	+36	96	34 15	+36	95	34 51	+35	94	300
61	31 41	36	97	32 17	37	96	32 54	36	95	33 30	35	94	34 05	35	93	299
62	30 55	37	96	31 32	36	95	32 08	36	94	32 44	35	93	33 19	35	93	298
63	30 09	37	96	30 46	36	95	31 22	36	94	31 58	35	93	32 33	35	92	297
64	29 23	37	95	30 00	36	94	30 36	36	93	31 12	35	92	31 47	35	91	296
65	28 38	+36	94	29 14	+36	93	29 50	+36	92	30 26	+35	91	31 01	+35	91	295
66	27 52	36	94	28 28	36	93	29 04	36	92	29 40	35	91	30 15	35	90	294
67	27 06	36	93	27 42	36	92	28 18	36	91	28 54	35	90	29 29	35	89	293
68	26 20	36	92	26 56	36	91	27 32	36	90	28 08	36	90	28 44	35	89	292
69	25 34	36	92	26 10	36	91	26 46	36	90	27 22	36	89	27 58	35	88	291

LHA	20° Hc	d	Z	21° Hc	d	Z	22° Hc	d	Z	23° Hc	d	Z	24° Hc	d	Z	LHA
	° ′	′	°	° ′	′	°	° ′	′	°	° ′	′	°	° ′	′	°	
0	70 00	+60	180	71 00	+60	180	72 00	+60	180	73 00	+60	180	74 00	+60	180	360
1	69 59	60	177	70 59	60	177	71 59	60	177	72 59	60	177	73 59	60	177	359
2	69 56	59	175	70 55	60	174	71 55	60	174	72 55	60	174	73 55	59	173	358
3	69 50	60	172	70 50	59	171	71 49	60	171	72 49	59	171	73 48	59	170	357
4	69 43	59	169	70 42	59	169	71 41	59	168	72 40	59	168	73 39	59	167	356
5	69 33	+59	166	70 32	+58	166	71 30	+59	165	72 29	+58	165	73 27	+59	164	355
6	69 21	58	164	70 19	59	163	71 18	58	162	72 16	57	162	73 13	58	161	354
7	69 07	58	161	70 05	58	161	71 03	57	160	72 00	57	159	72 57	57	158	353
8	68 52	57	159	69 49	57	158	70 46	56	157	71 42	56	156	72 38	56	155	352
9	68 34	56	156	69 30	57	155	70 27	55	154	71 22	56	153	72 18	55	152	351
10	68 15	+55	154	69 10	+56	153	70 06	+55	152	71 01	+54	151	71 55	+54	149	350
11	67 53	56	152	68 49	54	151	69 43	54	149	70 37	54	148	71 31	53	147	349
12	67 31	54	149	68 25	54	148	69 19	53	147	70 12	53	146	71 05	52	144	348
13	67 07	53	147	68 00	53	146	68 53	52	145	69 45	52	143	70 37	51	142	347
14	66 41	53	145	67 34	52	144	68 26	51	142	69 17	51	141	70 08	50	139	346
15	66 14	+52	143	67 06	+51	142	67 57	+51	140	68 48	+49	139	69 37	+49	137	345
16	65 45	52	141	66 37	50	140	67 27	50	138	68 17	49	137	69 06	47	135	344
17	65 16	50	139	66 06	50	138	66 56	49	136	67 45	48	135	68 33	46	133	343
18	64 45	50	137	65 35	48	136	66 23	48	134	67 11	47	133	67 58	46	131	342
19	64 13	49	135	65 02	48	134	65 50	47	133	66 37	46	131	67 23	45	129	341
20	63 40	+48	134	64 28	+48	132	65 16	+46	131	66 02	+45	129	66 47	+45	128	340
21	63 07	47	132	63 54	46	131	64 40	46	129	65 26	45	128	66 11	43	126	339
22	62 32	47	130	63 19	45	129	64 04	45	127	64 49	44	126	65 33	43	124	338
23	61 57	45	129	62 42	45	127	63 27	44	126	64 11	44	124	64 55	41	123	337
24	61 20	45	127	62 05	45	126	62 50	43	124	63 33	43	123	64 16	41	121	336
25	60 43	+45	126	61 28	+44	124	62 12	+42	123	62 54	+42	121	63 36	+40	120	335
26	60 06	44	124	60 50	43	123	61 33	42	122	62 15	41	120	62 56	40	118	334
27	59 27	44	123	60 11	42	122	60 53	42	120	61 35	40	119	62 15	39	117	333
28	58 49	42	122	59 31	42	120	60 13	41	119	60 54	40	117	61 34	39	116	332
29	58 09	42	120	58 51	42	119	59 33	40	118	60 13	39	116	60 52	38	115	331
30	57 29	+42	119	58 11	+41	118	58 52	+39	116	59 31	+39	115	60 10	+38	113	330
31	56 49	41	118	57 30	40	117	58 10	40	115	58 50	38	114	59 28	37	112	329
32	56 08	41	117	56 49	39	115	57 28	39	114	58 07	38	113	58 45	37	111	328
33	55 27	40	116	56 07	39	114	56 46	39	113	57 25	37	111	58 02	36	110	327
34	54 45	40	114	55 25	39	113	56 04	38	112	56 42	37	110	57 19	36	109	326
35	54 03	+39	113	54 42	+39	112	55 21	+37	111	55 58	+37	109	56 35	+36	108	325
36	53 21	39	112	54 00	38	111	54 38	37	110	55 15	36	108	55 51	36	107	324
37	52 38	39	111	53 17	37	110	53 54	37	109	54 31	36	107	55 07	35	106	323
38	51 55	38	110	52 33	38	109	53 11	36	108	53 47	36	106	54 23	35	105	322
39	51 12	38	109	51 50	37	108	52 27	36	107	53 03	35	106	53 38	35	104	321
40	50 28	+38	108	51 06	+37	107	51 43	+36	106	52 19	+35	105	52 54	+34	103	320
41	49 44	38	108	50 22	36	106	50 58	36	105	51 34	35	104	52 09	34	102	319
42	49 01	37	107	49 38	36	105	50 14	35	104	50 49	35	103	51 24	34	102	318
43	48 16	37	106	48 53	36	105	49 29	35	103	50 04	35	102	50 39	33	101	317
44	47 32	37	105	48 09	35	104	48 44	35	102	49 19	35	101	49 54	33	100	316
45	46 47	+37	104	47 24	+35	103	47 59	+35	102	48 34	+34	100	49 08	+34	99	315
46	46 03	36	103	46 39	35	102	47 14	35	101	47 49	34	100	48 23	33	98	314
47	45 18	36	102	45 54	35	101	46 29	35	100	47 04	33	99	47 37	33	98	313
48	44 33	36	102	45 09	35	100	45 44	34	99	46 18	34	98	46 52	33	97	312
49	43 48	35	101	44 23	35	100	44 58	35	99	45 33	33	97	46 06	33	96	311
50	43 03	+35	100	43 38	+35	99	44 13	+34	98	44 47	+33	97	45 20	+33	95	310
51	42 17	36	99	42 53	34	98	43 27	34	97	44 01	34	96	44 35	32	95	309
52	41 32	35	98	42 07	35	97	42 42	34	96	43 16	33	95	43 49	32	94	308
53	40 46	35	98	41 21	35	97	41 56	34	96	42 30	33	94	43 03	32	93	307
54	40 01	35	97	40 36	34	96	41 10	34	95	41 44	33	94	42 17	32	93	306
55	39 15	+35	96	39 50	+34	95	40 24	+34	94	40 58	+33	93	41 31	+32	92	305
56	38 29	35	96	39 04	34	95	39 38	34	93	40 12	33	92	40 45	33	91	304
57	37 44	34	95	38 18	35	94	38 53	33	93	39 26	33	92	39 59	33	91	303
58	36 58	35	94	37 33	34	93	38 07	33	92	38 40	33	91	39 13	33	90	302
59	36 12	35	94	36 47	34	93	37 21	33	91	37 54	33	90	38 27	33	89	301
60	35 26	+35	93	36 01	+34	92	36 35	+33	91	37 08	+33	90	37 41	+33	89	300
61	34 40	35	92	35 15	34	91	35 49	33	90	36 22	33	89	36 55	33	88	299
62	33 54	35	92	34 29	34	91	35 03	33	90	35 36	33	89	36 09	33	88	298
63	33 08	35	91	33 43	34	90	34 17	33	89	34 50	34	88	35 24	32	87	297
64	32 22	35	90	32 57	34	89	33 31	34	88	34 05	33	87	34 38	32	86	296
65	31 36	+35	90	32 11	+34	89	32 45	+34	88	33 19	+33	87	33 52	+32	86	295
66	30 50	35	89	31 25	34	88	31 59	34	87	32 33	33	86	33 06	33	85	294
67	30 04	35	88	30 39	34	87	31 13	34	86	31 47	33	85	32 20	33	84	293
68	29 19	34	88	29 53	34	87	30 27	34	86	31 01	33	85	31 34	33	84	292
69	28 33	34	87	29 07	35	86	29 42	33	85	30 15	34	84	30 49	33	83	291

LHA	25° Hc	d	Z	26° Hc	d	Z	27° Hc	d	Z	28° Hc	d	Z	29° Hc	d	Z	LHA
	° ′	′	°	° ′	′	°	° ′	′	°	° ′	′	°	° ′	′	°	
0	75 00	+60	180	76 00	+60	180	77 00	+60	180	78 00	+60	180	79 00	+60	180	360
1	74 59	60	177	75 59	59	176	76 58	60	176	77 58	60	176	78 58	60	176	359
2	74 54	60	173	75 54	60	173	76 54	59	172	77 53	60	172	78 53	59	171	358
3	74 47	60	170	75 47	59	169	76 46	59	168	77 45	59	167	78 44	58	167	357
4	74 38	59	166	75 37	58	165	76 35	58	165	77 33	58	163	78 31	58	162	356
5	74 26	+58	163	75 24	+57	162	76 21	+58	161	77 19	+57	160	78 16	+56	158	355
6	74 11	57	160	75 08	57	159	76 05	56	157	77 01	56	156	77 57	55	154	354
7	73 54	56	157	74 50	56	155	75 46	55	154	76 41	54	152	77 35	54	150	353
8	73 34	56	154	74 30	54	152	75 24	54	151	76 18	53	149	77 11	52	147	352
9	73 13	54	151	74 07	54	149	75 01	52	147	75 53	52	146	76 45	51	143	351
10	72 49	+53	148	73 42	+53	146	74 35	+51	144	75 26	+51	142	76 17	+49	140	350
11	72 24	52	145	73 16	51	143	74 07	50	142	74 57	49	140	75 46	48	138	349
12	71 57	51	143	72 48	50	141	73 38	49	139	74 27	47	137	75 14	46	135	348
13	71 28	50	140	72 18	49	138	73 07	47	136	73 54	47	134	74 41	44	132	347
14	70 58	49	138	71 47	47	136	72 34	47	134	73 21	45	132	74 06	43	130	346
15	70 26	+48	136	71 14	+47	134	72 01	+45	132	72 46	+44	130	73 30	+42	127	345
16	69 53	47	133	70 40	46	132	71 26	44	130	72 10	43	127	72 53	41	125	344
17	69 19	46	131	70 05	45	130	70 50	43	128	71 33	42	125	72 15	39	123	343
18	68 44	45	129	69 29	44	128	70 13	42	126	70 55	41	123	71 36	38	121	342
19	68 08	44	128	68 52	43	126	69 35	41	124	70 16	40	122	70 56	38	119	341
20	67 32	+43	126	68 15	+41	124	68 56	+41	122	69 37	+39	120	70 16	+36	118	340
21	66 54	42	124	67 36	41	122	68 17	40	120	68 57	38	118	69 35	36	116	339
22	66 16	41	123	66 57	40	121	67 37	39	119	68 16	37	117	68 53	35	115	338
23	65 36	41	121	66 17	40	119	66 57	38	117	67 35	36	115	68 11	35	113	337
24	64 57	40	120	65 37	38	118	66 15	38	116	66 53	35	114	67 28	35	112	336
25	64 16	+40	118	64 56	+38	116	65 34	+36	115	66 10	+36	113	66 46	+33	111	335
26	63 36	38	117	64 14	38	115	64 52	36	113	65 28	34	111	66 02	33	109	334
27	62 54	38	115	63 32	37	114	64 09	36	112	64 45	34	110	65 19	32	108	333
28	62 13	37	114	62 50	37	112	63 27	34	111	64 01	34	109	64 35	32	107	332
29	61 30	38	113	62 08	35	111	62 43	35	110	63 18	33	108	63 51	31	106	331
30	60 48	+37	112	61 25	+35	110	62 00	+34	108	62 34	+33	107	63 07	+31	105	330
31	60 05	36	111	60 41	35	109	61 16	34	107	61 50	32	106	62 22	31	104	329
32	59 22	36	110	59 58	34	108	60 32	33	106	61 05	32	105	61 37	31	103	328
33	58 38	36	109	59 14	34	107	59 48	33	105	60 21	31	104	60 52	31	102	327
34	57 55	35	107	58 30	33	106	59 03	33	104	59 36	31	103	60 07	30	101	326
35	57 11	+34	106	57 45	+34	105	58 19	+32	103	58 51	+31	102	59 22	+30	100	325
36	56 27	34	106	57 01	33	104	57 34	32	102	58 06	31	101	58 37	29	99	324
37	55 42	34	105	56 16	33	103	56 49	32	102	57 21	30	100	57 51	30	98	323
38	54 58	33	104	55 31	33	102	56 04	32	101	56 36	30	99	57 06	29	98	322
39	54 13	33	103	54 46	33	101	55 19	31	100	55 50	30	98	56 20	29	97	321
40	53 28	+33	102	54 01	+32	101	54 33	+32	99	55 05	+30	98	55 35	+28	96	320
41	52 43	33	101	53 16	32	100	53 48	31	98	54 19	30	97	54 49	29	95	319
42	51 58	33	100	52 31	31	99	53 02	31	97	53 33	30	96	54 03	29	95	318
43	51 12	33	99	51 45	32	98	52 17	31	97	52 48	29	95	53 17	29	94	317
44	50 27	33	99	51 00	31	97	51 31	31	96	52 02	29	95	52 31	29	93	316
45	49 42	+32	98	50 14	+31	97	50 45	+31	95	51 16	+29	94	51 45	+29	92	315
46	48 56	32	97	49 28	32	96	50 00	30	95	50 30	30	93	51 00	28	92	314
47	48 10	32	96	48 42	32	95	49 14	30	94	49 44	30	92	50 14	28	91	313
48	47 25	32	96	47 57	31	94	48 28	30	93	48 58	30	92	49 28	28	90	312
49	46 39	32	95	47 11	31	94	47 42	30	92	48 12	30	91	48 42	28	90	311
50	45 53	+32	94	46 25	+31	93	46 56	+30	92	47 26	+30	90	47 56	+28	89	310
51	45 07	32	94	45 39	31	92	46 10	30	91	46 40	30	90	47 10	28	89	309
52	44 21	32	93	44 53	31	92	45 24	30	90	45 54	30	89	46 24	28	88	308
53	43 35	32	92	44 07	31	91	44 38	30	90	45 08	30	89	45 38	29	87	307
54	42 49	32	92	43 21	31	90	43 52	30	89	44 22	30	88	44 52	29	87	306
55	42 03	+32	91	42 35	+31	90	43 06	+31	89	43 37	+29	87	44 06	+29	86	305
56	41 18	31	90	41 49	31	89	42 20	31	88	42 51	29	87	43 20	29	86	304
57	40 32	31	90	41 03	31	88	41 34	31	87	42 05	29	86	42 34	29	85	303
58	39 46	31	89	40 17	31	88	40 48	31	87	41 19	30	86	41 49	29	84	302
59	39 00	31	88	39 31	32	87	40 03	30	86	40 33	30	85	41 03	29	84	301
60	38 14	+32	88	38 46	+31	87	39 17	+30	85	39 47	+30	84	40 17	+30	83	300
61	37 28	32	87	38 00	31	86	38 31	31	85	39 02	30	84	39 32	29	83	299
62	36 42	32	86	37 14	31	85	37 45	31	84	38 16	30	83	38 46	30	82	298
63	35 56	32	86	36 28	32	85	37 00	30	84	37 30	31	83	38 01	29	82	297
64	35 10	32	85	35 42	32	84	36 14	31	83	36 45	30	82	37 15	30	81	296
65	34 24	+33	85	34 57	+31	84	35 28	+31	83	35 59	+31	82	36 30	+30	80	295
66	33 39	32	84	34 11	32	83	34 43	31	82	35 14	31	81	35 45	30	80	294
67	32 53	32	83	33 25	32	82	33 57	32	81	34 29	30	80	34 59	31	79	293
68	32 07	33	83	32 40	32	82	33 12	31	81	33 43	31	80	34 14	31	79	292
69	31 22	32	82	31 54	32	81	32 26	32	80	32 58	31	79	33 29	31	78	291

S. Lat. {LHA greater than 180°........ Zn=180−Z
{LHA less than 180°............ Zn=180+Z

DECLINATION (15°-29°) SAME NAME AS LATITUDE

LAT 40°

N. Lat. {LHA greater than 180° .... Zn=Z; LHA less than 180° .... Zn=360−Z}

DECLINATION (15°-29°) SAME NAME AS LATITUDE

Each cell gives Hc (° ′), d (′), Z (°).

LHA	15°	16°	17°	18°	19°	20°	21°	22°	23°	24°	25°	26°	27°	28°	29°	LHA
70	24 48 +36 91	25 24 +36 90	26 00 +36 89	26 36 +36 88	27 12 +35 87	27 47 +34 86	28 21 +35 86	28 56 +34 85	29 30 +33 84	30 03 +33 83	30 36 +33 82	31 09 +32 81	31 41 +32 80	32 13 +31 79	32 44 +31 78	290
71	24 02 36 90	24 38 37 89	25 15 35 89	25 50 36 88	26 26 35 87	27 01 35 86	27 36 34 85	28 10 34 84	28 44 34 83	29 18 33 82	29 51 33 81	30 24 32 80	30 56 32 79	31 28 31 78	31 59 31 77	289
72	23 16 36 90	23 52 37 89	24 29 35 88	25 04 36 87	25 40 35 86	26 15 35 85	26 50 34 84	27 24 34 83	27 58 34 82	28 32 34 82	29 06 32 81	29 38 33 80	30 11 32 79	30 43 32 78	31 15 31 77	288
73	22 30 37 89	23 07 36 88	23 43 36 87	24 19 35 86	24 54 35 86	25 29 35 85	26 04 35 84	26 39 34 83	27 13 34 82	27 47 33 81	28 20 33 80	28 53 33 79	29 26 32 78	29 58 32 77	30 30 31 76	287
74	21 44 37 88	22 21 36 88	22 57 36 87	23 33 35 86	24 08 36 85	24 44 35 84	25 19 34 83	25 53 34 82	26 27 34 81	27 01 34 80	27 35 33 79	28 08 33 78	28 41 32 78	29 13 32 77	29 45 32 76	286
75	20 58 +37 88	21 35 +36 87	22 11 +36 86	22 47 +36 85	23 23 +35 84	23 58 +35 83	24 33 +35 83	25 08 +34 82	25 42 +34 81	26 16 +34 80	26 50 +33 79	27 23 +33 78	27 56 +33 77	28 29 +32 76	29 01 +32 75	285
76	20 12 37 87	20 49 36 86	21 25 36 85	22 01 36 85	22 37 35 84	23 12 35 83	23 47 35 82	24 22 35 81	24 57 34 80	25 31 34 79	26 05 33 78	26 38 33 77	27 11 33 76	27 44 33 76	28 17 32 75	284
77	19 26 37 86	20 03 36 86	20 39 36 85	21 15 36 84	21 51 36 83	22 27 35 82	23 02 35 81	23 37 35 80	24 12 34 80	24 46 34 79	25 20 34 78	25 54 33 77	26 27 33 76	27 00 32 75	27 32 33 74	283
78	18 41 36 86	19 17 37 85	19 54 36 84	20 30 36 83	21 06 35 82	21 41 36 82	22 17 35 81	22 52 34 80	23 26 35 79	24 01 34 78	24 35 34 77	25 09 33 76	25 42 33 75	26 15 33 74	26 48 33 73	282
79	17 55 36 85	18 31 37 84	19 08 36 84	19 44 36 83	20 20 36 82	20 56 35 81	21 31 35 80	22 06 35 79	22 41 35 78	23 16 34 78	23 50 34 77	24 24 34 76	24 58 33 75	25 31 33 74	26 04 33 73	281
80	17 09 +37 85	17 46 +36 84	18 22 +37 83	18 59 +36 82	19 35 +35 81	20 10 +36 80	20 46 +35 80	21 21 +35 79	21 56 +35 78	22 31 +35 77	23 06 +34 76	23 40 +34 75	24 14 +33 74	24 47 +33 73	25 20 +33 72	280
81	16 23 37 84	17 00 37 83	17 37 36 82	18 13 36 82	18 49 36 81	19 25 36 80	20 01 35 79	20 36 35 78	21 11 35 77	21 46 35 76	22 21 34 75	22 55 34 75	23 29 34 74	24 03 34 73	24 37 33 72	279
82	15 38 36 83	16 14 37 83	16 51 37 82	17 28 36 81	18 04 36 80	18 40 36 79	19 16 35 78	19 51 36 78	20 27 35 77	21 02 35 76	21 37 34 75	22 11 34 74	22 45 34 73	23 19 34 72	23 53 33 71	278
83	14 52 37 83	15 29 37 82	16 06 36 81	16 42 37 80	17 19 36 79	17 55 36 79	18 31 36 78	19 07 35 77	19 42 35 76	20 17 35 75	20 52 35 74	21 27 35 73	22 02 34 73	22 36 34 72	23 10 33 71	277
84	14 06 37 82	14 43 37 81	15 20 37 81	15 57 37 80	16 34 36 79	17 10 36 78	17 46 36 77	18 22 35 76	18 57 36 76	19 33 35 75	20 08 35 74	20 43 35 73	21 18 34 72	21 52 34 71	22 26 34 70	276
85	13 21 +37 82	13 58 +37 81	14 35 +37 80	15 12 +36 79	15 48 +37 78	16 25 +36 77	17 01 +36 77	17 37 +36 76	18 13 +36 75	18 49 +35 74	19 24 +35 73	19 59 +35 72	20 34 +35 71	21 09 +34 71	21 43 +34 70	275
86	12 35 38 81	13 13 37 80	13 50 37 79	14 27 37 78	15 04 36 78	15 40 37 77	16 17 36 76	16 53 36 75	17 29 36 74	18 05 35 74	18 40 35 73	19 15 36 72	19 51 34 71	20 25 35 70	21 00 34 69	274
87	11 50 37 80	12 27 38 79	13 05 37 79	13 42 37 78	14 19 36 77	14 55 37 76	15 32 36 75	16 08 37 75	16 45 36 74	17 21 35 73	17 56 36 72	18 32 35 71	19 07 35 70	19 42 35 70	20 17 35 69	273
88	11 05 37 80	11 42 38 79	12 20 37 78	12 57 37 77	13 34 37 76	14 11 37 76	14 48 36 75	15 24 37 74	16 01 36 73	16 37 36 72	17 13 35 72	17 48 36 71	18 24 35 70	18 59 35 69	19 34 35 68	272
89	10 20 37 79	10 57 38 78	11 35 37 77	12 12 37 77	12 49 37 76	13 26 37 75	14 03 37 74	14 40 37 73	15 17 36 73	15 53 36 72	16 29 36 71	17 05 36 70	17 41 36 69	18 17 35 68	18 52 35 68	271
90	09 35 +37 78	10 12 +38 78	10 50 +37 77	11 27 +38 76	12 05 +37 75	12 42 +37 74	13 19 +37 74	13 56 +37 73	14 33 +36 72	15 09 +37 71	15 46 +36 70	16 22 +36 70	16 58 +36 69	17 34 +35 68	18 09 +36 67	270
91	08 50 38 78	09 28 37 77	10 05 38 76	10 43 37 75	11 20 38 75	11 58 37 74	12 35 37 73	13 12 37 72	13 49 37 71	14 26 37 71	15 03 36 70	15 39 36 69	16 15 36 68	16 51 36 67	17 27 36 66	269
92	08 05 38 77	08 43 38 76	09 21 38 76	09 59 37 75	10 36 38 74	11 14 37 73	11 51 38 72	12 29 37 72	13 06 37 71	13 43 37 70	14 20 36 69	14 56 37 68	15 33 36 68	16 09 36 67	16 45 36 66	268
93	07 20 38 77	07 58 38 76	08 36 38 75	09 14 38 74	09 52 38 73	10 30 37 73	11 07 38 72	11 45 37 71	12 22 38 70	13 00 37 69	13 37 37 69	14 14 36 68	14 50 37 67	15 27 36 66	16 03 37 65	267
94	06 35 39 76	07 14 38 75	07 52 38 74	08 30 38 74	09 08 38 73	09 46 38 72	10 24 38 71	11 02 37 70	11 39 38 70	12 17 37 69	12 54 37 68	13 31 37 67	14 08 37 66	14 45 37 66	15 22 36 65	266
95	05 51 +38 75	06 29 +39 75	07 08 +38 74	07 46 +38 73	08 24 +38 72	09 02 +38 71	09 40 +38 71	10 18 +38 70	10 56 +38 69	11 34 +37 68	12 11 +38 68	12 49 +37 67	13 26 +37 66	14 03 +37 65	14 40 +37 64	265
96	05 06 39 75	05 45 39 74	06 24 38 73	07 02 39 72	07 41 38 72	08 19 38 71	08 57 38 70	09 35 38 69	10 13 38 69	10 51 38 68	11 29 38 67	12 07 37 66	12 44 38 65	13 22 37 65	13 59 37 64	264
97	04 22 39 74	05 01 39 73	05 40 38 73	06 18 39 72	06 57 39 71	07 36 38 70	08 14 38 69	08 52 39 69	09 31 38 68	10 09 38 67	10 47 38 66	11 25 38 66	12 03 37 65	12 40 38 64	13 18 37 63	263
98	03 38 39 73	04 17 39 73	04 56 39 72	05 35 39 71	06 14 38 70	06 52 39 70	07 31 39 69	08 10 38 68	08 48 39 67	09 27 38 67	10 05 38 66	10 43 38 65	11 21 38 64	11 59 38 63	12 37 38 63	262
99	02 54 39 73	03 33 39 72	04 12 39 71	04 51 39 71	05 30 39 70	06 09 39 69	06 48 39 68	07 27 39 68	08 06 39 67	08 45 38 66	09 23 39 65	10 02 38 64	10 40 38 64	11 18 38 63	11 56 38 62	261
100	02 10 +40 72	02 50 +39 71	03 29 +39 71	04 08 +39 70	04 47 +40 69	05 27 +39 68	06 06 +39 68	06 45 +39 67	07 24 +39 66	08 03 +38 65	08 41 +39 65	09 20 +39 64	09 59 +38 63	10 37 +39 62	11 16 +38 61	260
101	01 27 39 72	02 06 40 71	02 46 39 70	03 25 40 69	04 05 39 69	04 44 39 68	05 23 40 67	06 03 39 66	06 42 39 66	07 21 39 65	08 00 39 64	08 39 39 63	09 18 39 62	09 57 38 62	10 35 39 61	259
102	00 43 40 71	01 23 39 70	02 02 40 69	02 42 40 69	03 22 39 68	04 01 40 67	04 41 40 66	05 21 39 66	06 00 40 65	06 40 39 64	07 19 39 63	07 58 39 63	08 37 39 62	09 16 39 61	09 55 39 60	258
103	00 00 40 70	00 40 40 70	01 20 39 69	01 59 40 68	02 39 40 67	03 19 40 67	03 59 40 66	04 39 40 65	05 19 39 64	05 58 40 64	06 38 39 63	07 17 40 62	07 57 39 61	08 36 40 61	09 16 39 60	257
104	−0 43 40 70	−0 03 40 69	00 37 40 68	01 17 40 67	01 57 40 67	02 37 40 66	03 17 40 65	03 57 40 64	04 37 40 64	05 17 40 63	05 57 40 62	06 37 40 61	07 17 39 61	07 56 40 60	08 36 40 59	256
105	−1 26 +40 69	−0 46 +40 68	−0 06 +41 67	00 35 +40 67	01 15 +40 66	01 55 +41 65	02 36 +40 65	03 16 +40 64	03 56 +40 63	04 36 +41 62	05 17 +40 62	05 57 +40 61	06 37 +40 60	07 17 +40 59	07 57 +40 59	255
106	−2 09 40 68	−1 29 41 68	−0 48 40 67	−0 08 41 66	00 33 41 65	01 14 40 65	01 54 41 64	02 35 40 63	03 15 41 62	03 56 40 62	04 36 41 61	05 17 40 60	05 57 40 59	06 37 41 59	07 18 40 58	254
107	−2 52 41 68	−2 11 41 67	−1 30 41 66	−0 49 40 65	−0 09 41 65	00 32 41 64	01 13 41 63	01 54 41 63	02 35 41 62	03 16 40 61	03 56 41 60	04 37 41 60	05 18 40 59	05 58 41 58	06 39 40 57	253
108	−3 34 41 67	−2 53 41 66	−2 12 41 66	−1 31 41 65	−0 50 41 64	−0 09 41 63	00 32 41 63	01 13 41 62	01 54 41 61	02 35 41 60	03 16 41 60	03 57 41 59	04 38 41 58	05 19 41 58	06 00 41 57	252
109	−4 16 41 66	−3 35 41 66	−2 54 41 65	−2 13 42 64	−1 31 41 63	−0 50 41 63	−0 09 42 62	00 33 41 61	01 14 42 61	01 56 41 60	02 37 41 59	03 18 41 58	03 59 42 58	04 41 41 57	05 22 41 56	251
110	−4 58 +41 66	−4 17 +42 65	−3 35 +41 64	−2 54 +42 63	−2 12 +41 63	−1 31 +42 62	−0 49 +42 61	−0 07 +41 61	00 34 +42 60	01 16 +42 59	01 58 +41 58	02 39 +42 58	03 21 +41 57	04 02 +42 56	04 44 +41 56	250
111	−5 40 42 65	−4 58 41 64	−4 17 42 64	−3 35 42 63	−2 53 42 62	−2 11 42 61	−1 29 42 61	−0 47 42 60	−0 05 42 59	00 37 42 59	01 19 41 58	02 00 42 57	02 42 42 56	03 24 42 56	04 06 42 55	249
112	−6 22 42 64	−5 40 42 64	−4 58 42 63	−4 16 43 62	−3 33 42 61	−2 51 42 61	−2 09 42 60	−1 27 42 59	−0 45 43 59	−0 02 42 58	00 40 42 57	01 22 42 56	02 04 42 56	02 46 43 55	03 29 42 54	248
113		−6 21 42 63	−5 39 43 62	−4 56 42 61	−4 14 43 61	−3 31 42 60	−2 49 43 59	−2 06 42 59	−1 24 43 58	−0 41 42 57	00 01 43 57	00 44 42 56	01 26 43 55	02 09 42 54	02 51 43 54	247
114			−6 19 43 61	−5 36 42 61	−4 54 43 60	−4 11 43 59	−3 28 43 59	−2 45 42 58	−2 03 43 57	−1 20 43 57	−0 37 43 56	00 06 43 55	00 49 43 54	01 32 43 54	02 15 42 53	246
115				−6 16 +43 60	−5 33 +43 59	−4 50 +43 59	−4 07 +43 58	−3 24 +43 57	−2 41 +43 57	−1 58 +43 56	−1 15 +43 55	−0 32 +44 55	00 12 +43 54	00 55 +43 53	01 38 +43 53	245
116					−6 13 43 59	−5 30 44 58	−4 46 43 57	−4 03 44 57	−3 19 43 56	−2 36 44 55	−1 52 43 55	−1 09 44 54	−0 25 43 53	00 18 44 53	01 02 43 52	244
117						−6 08 43 57	−5 25 44 57	−4 41 44 56	−3 57 43 55	−3 14 44 55	−2 30 44 54	−1 46 44 53	−1 02 44 53	−0 18 44 52	00 26 44 51	243
118							−6 03 44 56	−5 19 44 55	−4 35 44 55	−3 51 44 54	−3 07 44 53	−2 23 45 53	−1 38 44 52	−0 54 44 51	−0 10 44 51	242
119								−5 57 45 55	−5 12 44 54	−4 28 45 53	−3 43 44 53	−2 59 45 52	−2 14 44 51	−1 30 45 51	−0 45 44 50	241
120									−5 49 +44 53	−5 05 +45 53	−4 20 +45 52	−3 35 +45 51	−2 50 +45 51	−2 05 +45 50	−1 20 +45 49	240
121										−5 41 45 52	−4 56 45 51	−4 11 46 51	−3 25 45 50	−2 40 45 49	−1 55 45 49	239
122											−5 31 45 51	−4 46 46 50	−4 00 45 49	−3 15 46 49	−2 29 45 48	238
123											−6 07 46 50	−5 21 46 49	−4 35 46 49	−3 49 46 48	−3 03 46 47	237
124												−5 56 47 48	−5 09 46 48	−4 23 46 47	−3 37 47 47	236
125													−5 43 +46 47	−4 57 +47 47	−4 10 +47 46	235
126														−5 30 47 46	−4 43 47 45	234
127														−6 03 48 45	−5 15 47 44	233
128															−5 47 47 44	232

DECLINATION (15°-29°) CONTRARY NAME TO LATITUDE

LHA	15°	16°	17°	18°	19°	20°	21°	22°	23°	24°	25°	26°	27°	28°	29°	LHA
85	−5 51 −38 105															275
84	−5 06 39 105	−5 45 39 106	−6 24 38 107													276
83	−4 22 39 106	−5 01 39 107	−5 40 38 107	−6 18 39 108												277
82	−3 38 39 107	−4 17 39 107	−4 56 39 108	−5 35 39 109	−6 14 38 110											278
81	−2 54 39 107	−3 33 39 108	−4 12 39 109	−4 51 39 109	−5 30 39 110	−6 09 39 111										279
80	−2 10 −40 108	−2 50 −39 109	−3 29 −39 109	−4 08 −39 110	−4 47 −40 111	−5 27 −39 112	−6 06 −39 112									280
79	−1 27 39 108	−2 06 40 109	−2 46 39 110	−3 25 40 111	−4 05 39 111	−4 44 39 112	−5 23 40 113	−6 03 39 114								281
78	−0 43 40 109	−1 23 39 110	−2 02 40 111	−2 42 40 111	−3 22 39 112	−4 01 40 113	−4 41 40 114	−5 21 39 114	−6 00 40 115							282
77	00 00 40 110	−0 40 40 110	−1 20 39 111	−1 59 40 112	−2 39 40 113	−3 19 40 113	−3 59 40 114	−4 39 40 115	−5 19 39 116	−5 58 40 116						283
76	00 43 40 110	00 03 40 111	−0 37 40 112	−1 17 40 113	−1 57 40 113	−2 37 40 114	−3 17 40 115	−3 57 40 116	−4 37 40 116	−5 17 40 117	−5 57 40 118					284
75	01 26 −40 111	00 46 −40 112	00 06 −41 113	−0 35 −40 113	−1 15 −40 114	−1 55 −41 115	−2 36 −40 115	−3 16 −40 116	−3 56 −40 117	−4 36 −41 118	−5 17 −40 118	−5 57 −40 119				285
74	02 09 40 112	01 29 41 112	00 48 40 113	00 08 41 114	−0 33 41 115	−1 14 40 115	−1 54 41 116	−2 35 40 117	−3 15 41 118	−3 56 40 118	−4 36 41 119	−5 17 40 120	−5 57 40 121			286
73	02 52 41 112	02 11 41 113	01 30 41 114	00 49 40 115	00 09 41 115	−0 32 41 116	−1 13 41 117	−1 54 41 117	−2 35 41 118	−3 16 40 119	−3 56 41 120	−4 37 41 120	−5 18 40 121	−5 58 41 122		287
72	03 34 41 113	02 53 41 114	02 12 41 114	01 31 41 115	00 50 41 116	00 09 41 117	−0 32 41 117	−1 13 41 118	−1 54 41 119	−2 35 41 120	−3 16 41 120	−3 57 41 121	−4 38 41 122	−5 19 41 122	−6 00 41 123	288
71	04 16 41 114	03 35 41 114	02 54 41 115	02 13 42 116	01 31 41 117	00 50 41 117	00 09 42 118	−0 33 41 119	−1 14 42 119	−1 56 41 120	−2 37 41 121	−3 18 41 122	−3 59 42 122	−4 41 41 123	−5 22 41 124	289
70	04 58 −41 114	04 17 −42 115	03 35 −41 116	02 54 −42 117	02 12 −41 117	01 31 −42 118	00 49 −42 119	00 07 −41 119	−0 34 −42 120	−1 16 −42 121	−1 58 −41 122	−2 39 −42 122	−3 21 −41 123	−4 02 −42 124	−4 44 −41 124	290

S. Lat. {LHA greater than 180° .... Zn=180−Z; LHA less than 180° .... Zn=180+Z}

N. Lat. {LHA greater than 180°........ Zn=Z
{LHA less than 180°........... Zn=360−Z

DECLINATION (15°-29°) CONTRARY NAME TO LATITUDE

LHA	15° Hc	d	Z	16° Hc	d	Z	17° Hc	d	Z	18° Hc	d	Z	19° Hc	d	Z	LHA
	° ′	′	°	° ′	′	°	° ′	′	°	° ′	′	°	° ′	′	°	
69	05 40	42	115	04 58	41	116	04 17	42	116	03 35	42	117	02 53	42	118	291
68	06 22	42	116	05 40	42	116	04 58	42	117	04 16	43	118	03 33	42	119	292
67	07 03	42	116	06 21	42	117	05 39	43	118	04 56	42	119	04 14	43	119	293
66	07 44	42	117	07 02	43	118	06 19	43	119	05 36	42	119	04 54	43	120	294
65	08 25	-43	118	07 42	-43	119	06 59	-43	119	06 16	-43	120	05 33	-43	121	295
64	09 06	44	119	08 22	43	119	07 39	43	120	06 56	43	121	06 13	43	121	296
63	09 46	44	119	09 02	43	120	08 19	43	121	07 36	44	121	06 52	44	122	297
62	10 26	44	120	09 42	44	121	08 58	43	121	08 15	44	122	07 31	44	123	298
61	11 06	44	121	10 22	44	121	09 38	44	122	08 54	45	123	08 09	44	123	299
60	11 45	-44	121	11 01	-45	122	10 16	-44	123	09 32	-44	123	08 48	-45	124	300
59	12 24	44	122	11 40	45	123	10 55	45	123	10 10	44	124	09 26	45	125	301
58	13 03	45	123	12 18	45	124	11 33	45	124	10 48	45	125	10 03	45	126	302
57	13 41	45	124	12 56	45	124	12 11	45	125	11 26	46	126	10 40	45	126	303
56	14 19	45	124	13 34	45	125	12 49	46	126	12 03	46	126	11 17	45	127	304
55	14 57	-45	125	14 12	-46	126	13 26	-46	126	12 40	-46	127	11 54	-46	128	305
54	15 35	46	126	14 49	46	126	14 03	47	127	13 16	46	128	12 30	46	128	306
53	16 12	46	127	15 26	47	127	14 39	46	128	13 53	47	129	13 06	47	129	307
52	16 49	47	127	16 02	47	128	15 15	47	129	14 28	47	129	13 41	47	130	308
51	17 25	47	128	16 38	47	129	15 51	47	129	15 04	48	130	14 16	47	131	309
50	18 01	-47	129	17 14	-48	130	16 26	-47	130	15 39	-48	131	14 51	-48	132	310
49	18 36	47	130	17 49	48	130	17 01	48	131	16 13	48	132	15 25	48	132	311
48	19 12	48	131	18 24	48	131	17 36	49	132	16 47	48	132	15 59	48	133	312
47	19 46	48	131	18 58	48	132	18 10	49	133	17 21	48	133	16 33	49	134	313
46	20 21	49	132	19 32	49	133	18 43	49	133	17 54	49	134	17 05	49	135	314
45	20 54	-48	133	20 06	-50	134	19 16	-49	134	18 27	-49	135	17 38	-49	135	315
44	21 28	49	134	20 39	50	135	19 49	49	135	19 00	50	136	18 10	50	136	316
43	22 01	50	135	21 11	50	135	20 21	50	136	19 31	50	137	18 41	50	137	317
42	22 33	50	136	21 43	50	136	20 53	50	137	20 03	50	137	19 13	51	138	318
41	23 05	50	137	22 15	51	137	21 24	50	138	20 34	51	138	19 43	51	139	319
40	23 36	-50	137	22 46	-51	138	21 55	-51	139	21 04	-51	139	20 13	-51	140	320
39	24 07	51	138	23 16	51	139	22 25	51	139	21 34	51	140	20 43	52	141	321
38	24 38	52	139	23 46	51	140	22 55	52	140	22 03	51	141	21 12	52	141	322
37	25 07	51	140	24 16	52	141	23 24	52	141	22 32	52	142	21 40	52	142	323
36	25 37	52	141	24 45	52	142	23 53	53	142	23 00	52	143	22 08	53	143	324
35	26 05	-52	142	25 13	-53	143	24 20	-52	143	23 28	-53	144	22 35	-53	144	325
34	26 33	52	143	25 41	53	143	24 48	53	144	23 55	53	144	23 02	53	145	326
33	27 01	53	144	26 08	53	144	25 15	54	145	24 21	53	145	23 28	54	146	327
32	27 28	54	145	26 34	53	145	25 41	54	146	24 47	54	146	23 53	53	147	328
31	27 54	54	146	27 00	54	146	26 06	54	147	25 12	54	147	24 18	54	148	329
30	28 19	-54	147	27 25	-54	147	26 31	-54	148	25 37	-54	148	24 43	-55	149	330
29	28 44	54	148	27 50	55	148	26 55	54	149	26 01	55	149	25 06	55	150	331
28	29 09	55	149	28 14	55	149	27 19	55	150	26 24	55	150	25 29	55	151	332
27	29 32	55	150	28 37	55	150	27 42	55	151	26 47	56	151	25 51	55	152	333
26	29 55	56	151	28 59	55	151	28 04	55	152	27 09	56	152	26 13	56	153	334
25	30 17	-56	152	29 21	-55	152	28 26	-56	153	27 30	-56	153	26 34	-56	154	335
24	30 38	56	153	29 42	56	153	28 46	56	154	27 50	56	154	26 54	56	155	336
23	30 59	56	154	30 03	57	154	29 06	56	155	28 10	57	155	27 13	56	156	337
22	31 19	57	155	30 22	56	155	29 26	57	156	28 29	57	156	27 32	57	157	338
21	31 38	57	156	30 41	57	156	29 44	57	157	28 47	57	157	27 50	57	158	339
20	31 56	-57	157	30 59	-57	157	30 02	-57	158	29 05	-58	158	28 07	-57	159	340
19	32 14	58	158	31 16	57	159	30 19	58	159	29 21	57	159	28 24	58	160	341
18	32 30	57	159	31 33	58	160	30 35	58	160	29 37	57	160	28 40	58	161	342
17	32 46	58	160	31 48	58	161	30 50	58	161	29 52	58	161	28 54	58	162	343
16	33 01	58	162	32 03	58	162	31 05	58	162	30 07	58	162	29 09	59	163	344
15	33 15	-58	163	32 17	-58	163	31 19	-59	163	30 20	-58	163	29 22	-59	164	345
14	33 29	59	164	32 30	58	164	31 32	59	165	30 33	59	165	29 34	58	165	346
13	33 41	59	165	32 42	58	165	31 44	59	165	30 45	59	166	29 46	59	166	347
12	33 53	59	166	32 54	59	166	31 55	59	167	30 56	59	167	29 57	59	167	348
11	34 03	59	167	33 04	59	167	32 05	59	168	31 06	59	168	30 07	59	168	349
10	34 13	-59	168	33 14	-59	169	32 15	-60	169	31 15	-59	169	30 16	-59	169	350
9	34 22	59	170	33 23	60	170	32 23	59	170	31 24	60	170	30 24	59	170	351
8	34 30	60	171	33 30	59	171	32 31	60	171	31 31	59	171	30 32	60	171	352
7	34 37	60	172	33 37	59	172	32 38	60	172	31 38	60	172	30 38	59	172	353
6	34 43	60	173	33 43	59	173	32 44	60	173	31 44	60	173	30 44	60	173	354
5	34 48	-60	174	33 48	-59	174	32 49	-60	174	31 49	-60	174	30 49	-60	175	355
4	34 52	59	175	33 53	60	175	32 53	60	175	31 53	60	176	30 53	60	176	356
3	34 56	60	177	33 56	60	177	32 56	60	177	31 56	60	177	30 56	60	177	357
2	34 58	60	178	33 58	60	178	32 58	60	178	31 58	60	178	30 58	60	178	358
1	35 00	60	179	34 00	60	179	33 00	60	179	32 00	60	179	31 00	60	179	359
0	35 00	-60	180	34 00	-60	180	33 00	-60	180	32 00	-60	180	31 00	-60	180	360
	15°			16°			17°			18°			19°			

LHA	20° Hc	d	Z	21° Hc	d	Z	22° Hc	d	Z	23° Hc	d	Z	24° Hc	d	Z	LHA
	° ′	′	°	° ′	′	°	° ′	′	°	° ′	′	°	° ′	′	°	
69	02 11	42	119	01 29	42	119	00 47	42	120	00 05	42	121	-0 37	42	121	291
68	02 51	42	119	02 09	42	120	01 27	42	121	00 45	43	121	00 02	42	122	292
67	03 31	42	120	02 49	43	121	02 06	42	121	01 24	43	122	00 41	42	123	293
66	04 11	43	121	03 28	43	121	02 45	42	122	02 03	43	123	01 20	43	123	294
65	04 50	-43	121	04 07	-43	122	03 24	-43	123	02 41	-43	123	01 58	-43	124	295
64	05 30	44	122	04 46	43	123	04 03	44	123	03 19	43	124	02 36	44	125	296
63	06 08	43	123	05 25	44	123	04 41	44	124	03 57	43	125	03 14	44	125	297
62	06 47	44	123	06 03	44	124	05 19	44	125	04 35	44	125	03 51	44	126	298
61	07 25	44	124	06 41	44	125	05 57	45	125	05 12	44	126	04 28	45	127	299
60	08 03	-44	125	07 19	-45	125	06 34	-45	126	05 49	-44	127	05 05	-45	127	300
59	08 41	45	125	07 56	45	126	07 11	45	127	06 26	45	127	05 41	45	128	301
58	09 18	45	126	08 33	45	127	07 48	46	128	07 02	45	128	06 17	46	129	302
57	09 55	45	127	09 10	46	128	08 24	46	128	07 38	45	129	06 53	46	130	303
56	10 32	46	128	09 46	46	128	09 00	46	129	08 14	46	130	07 28	46	130	304
55	11 08	-46	128	10 22	-47	129	09 35	-46	130	08 49	-46	130	08 03	-47	131	305
54	11 44	47	129	10 57	46	130	10 11	47	130	09 24	47	131	08 37	46	132	306
53	12 19	47	130	11 32	46	130	10 46	47	131	09 59	48	132	09 11	47	132	307
52	12 54	47	131	12 07	47	131	11 20	47	132	10 33	48	133	09 45	47	133	308
51	13 29	47	131	12 42	48	132	11 54	48	133	11 06	47	133	10 19	48	134	309
50	14 03	-47	132	13 16	-48	133	12 28	-48	133	11 40	-48	134	10 52	-49	135	310
49	14 37	48	133	13 49	48	134	13 01	48	134	12 13	49	135	11 24	48	135	311
48	15 11	49	134	14 22	48	134	13 34	49	135	12 45	49	136	11 56	49	136	312
47	15 44	49	134	14 55	49	135	14 06	49	136	13 17	49	136	12 28	49	137	313
46	16 16	49	135	15 27	49	136	14 38	49	136	13 49	50	137	12 59	49	138	314
45	16 49	-50	136	15 59	-50	137	15 09	-49	137	14 20	-50	138	13 30	-50	138	315
44	17 20	50	137	16 30	50	137	15 40	50	138	14 50	50	139	14 00	50	139	316
43	17 51	50	138	17 01	50	138	16 11	51	139	15 20	50	139	14 30	51	140	317
42	18 22	50	139	17 32	51	139	16 41	51	140	15 50	51	140	14 59	51	141	318
41	18 52	51	139	18 01	51	140	17 10	51	141	16 19	51	141	15 28	51	142	319
40	19 22	-51	140	18 31	-52	141	17 39	-51	141	16 48	-51	142	15 57	-52	142	320
39	19 51	51	141	19 00	52	142	18 08	52	142	17 16	52	143	16 24	52	143	321
38	20 20	52	142	19 28	52	142	18 36	52	143	17 44	52	143	16 52	53	144	322
37	20 48	52	143	19 56	53	143	19 03	52	144	18 11	53	144	17 18	52	145	323
36	21 15	52	144	20 23	53	144	19 30	53	145	18 37	52	145	17 45	53	146	324
35	21 42	-53	145	20 49	-53	145	19 56	-53	146	19 03	-53	146	18 10	-53	147	325
34	22 09	54	145	21 15	53	146	20 22	53	146	19 29	54	147	18 35	53	147	326
33	22 34	53	146	21 41	54	147	20 47	53	147	19 54	54	148	19 00	54	148	327
32	23 00	54	147	22 06	54	148	21 12	54	148	20 18	54	149	19 24	55	149	328
31	23 24	54	148	22 30	54	149	21 36	55	149	20 41	54	150	19 47	55	150	329
30	23 48	-54	149	22 54	-55	150	21 59	-55	150	21 04	-54	150	20 10	-55	151	330
29	24 11	54	150	23 17	55	151	22 22	55	151	21 27	55	151	20 32	56	152	331
28	24 34	55	151	23 39	55	151	22 44	56	152	21 48	55	152	20 53	55	153	332
27	24 56	55	152	24 01	56	152	23 05	56	153	22 09	55	153	21 14	56	154	333
26	25 17	55	153	24 22	56	153	23 26	56	154	22 30	56	154	21 34	56	155	334
25	25 38	-56	154	24 42	-56	154	23 46	-56	155	22 50	-57	155	21 53	-56	155	335
24	25 58	57	155	25 01	56	155	24 05	56	156	23 09	57	156	22 12	56	156	336
23	26 17	57	156	25 20	56	156	24 24	57	157	23 27	57	157	22 30	57	157	337
22	26 35	56	157	25 39	57	157	24 42	57	158	23 45	57	158	22 48	57	158	338
21	26 53	57	158	25 56	57	158	24 59	57	159	24 02	58	159	23 04	57	159	339
20	27 10	-57	159	26 13	-58	159	25 15	-57	160	24 18	-58	160	23 20	-57	160	340
19	27 26	57	160	26 29	58	160	25 31	58	161	24 33	57	161	23 36	58	161	341
18	27 42	58	161	26 44	58	161	25 46	58	161	24 48	58	162	23 50	58	162	342
17	27 56	58	162	26 58	58	162	26 00	58	162	25 02	58	163	24 04	58	163	343
16	28 10	58	163	27 12	58	163	26 14	59	163	25 15	58	164	24 17	58	164	344
15	28 23	-58	164	27 25	-59	164	26 26	-58	165	25 28	-59	165	24 29	-58	165	345
14	28 36	59	165	27 37	59	165	26 38	58	166	25 40	59	166	24 41	59	166	346
13	28 47	59	166	27 48	58	166	26 50	59	167	25 51	59	167	24 52	59	167	347
12	28 58	59	167	27 59	59	167	27 00	59	168	26 01	59	168	25 02	59	168	348
11	29 08	59	168	28 09	60	168	27 09	59	169	26 10	59	169	25 11	59	169	349
10	29 17	-60	169	28 17	-59	169	27 18	-59	170	26 19	-59	170	25 20	-60	170	350
9	29 25	59	170	28 26	60	170	27 26	59	171	26 27	60	171	25 27	59	171	351
8	29 32	59	171	28 33	60	172	27 33	59	172	26 34	60	172	25 34	60	172	352
7	29 39	60	172	28 39	60	173	27 39	59	173	26 40	60	173	25 40	60	173	353
6	29 44	59	174	28 45	60	174	27 45	60	174	26 45	60	174	25 45	59	174	354
5	29 49	-60	175	28 49	-59	175	27 50	-60	175	26 50	-60	175	25 50	-60	175	355
4	29 53	60	176	28 53	60	176	27 53	60	176	26 53	59	176	25 54	60	176	356
3	29 56	60	177	28 56	60	177	27 56	60	177	26 56	60	177	25 56	60	177	357
2	29 58	60	178	28 58	60	178	27 58	60	178	26 58	60	178	25 58	60	178	358
1	30 00	60	179	29 00	60	179	28 00	60	179	27 00	60	179	26 00	60	179	359
0	30 00	-60	180	29 00	-60	180	28 00	-60	180	27 00	-60	180	26 00	-60	180	360
	20°			21°			22°			23°			24°			

LHA	25° Hc	d	Z	26° Hc	d	Z	27° Hc	d	Z	28° Hc	d	Z	29° Hc	d	Z	LHA
	° ′	′	°	° ′	′	°	° ′	′	°	° ′	′	°	° ′	′	°	
69	-1 19	41	122	-2 00	42	123	-2 42	42	124	-3 24	42	124	-4 06	42	125	291
68	-0 40	42	123	-1 22	42	124	-2 04	42	124	-2 46	43	125	-3 29	42	126	292
67	-0 01	43	123	-0 44	42	124	-1 26	43	125	-2 09	42	126	-2 51	43	126	293
66	00 37	43	124	-0 06	43	125	-0 49	43	126	-1 32	43	126	-2 15	42	127	294
65	01 15	-43	125	00 32	-44	125	-0 12	-43	126	-0 55	-43	127	-1 38	-43	127	295
64	01 52	43	125	01 09	44	126	00 25	43	127	-0 18	44	127	-1 02	43	128	296
63	02 30	44	126	01 46	44	127	01 02	44	127	00 18	44	128	-0 26	44	129	297
62	03 07	44	127	02 23	45	127	01 38	44	128	00 54	44	129	00 10	44	129	298
61	03 43	44	127	02 59	45	128	02 14	44	129	01 30	45	129	00 45	44	130	299
60	04 20	-45	128	03 35	-45	129	02 50	-45	129	02 05	-45	130	01 20	-45	131	300
59	04 56	45	129	04 11	46	129	03 25	45	130	02 40	45	131	01 55	45	131	301
58	05 31	45	129	04 46	46	130	04 00	45	131	03 15	46	131	02 29	45	132	302
57	06 07	46	130	05 21	46	131	04 35	46	131	03 49	46	132	03 03	46	133	303
56	06 42	46	131	05 56	47	132	05 09	46	132	04 23	46	133	03 37	47	133	304
55	07 16	-46	132	06 30	-47	132	05 43	-46	133	04 57	-47	133	04 10	-47	134	305
54	07 51	47	132	07 04	47	133	06 17	47	134	05 30	47	134	04 43	47	135	306
53	08 24	47	133	07 37	47	134	06 50	47	134	06 03	48	135	05 15	47	136	307
52	08 58	48	134	08 10	47	134	07 23	48	135	06 35	48	136	05 47	47	136	308
51	09 31	48	134	08 43	48	135	07 55	48	136	07 07	48	136	06 19	48	137	309
50	10 03	-48	135	09 15	-48	136	08 27	-48	136	07 39	-49	137	06 50	-48	138	310
49	10 36	49	136	09 47	49	137	08 58	48	137	08 10	49	138	07 21	49	138	311
48	11 07	49	137	10 18	49	137	09 30	50	138	08 40	49	138	07 51	49	139	312
47	11 39	50	137	10 49	49	138	10 00	49	139	09 11	50	139	08 21	49	140	313
46	12 10	50	138	11 20	50	139	10 30	49	139	09 41	50	140	08 51	50	141	314
45	12 40	-50	139	11 50	-50	140	11 00	-50	140	10 10	-50	141	09 20	-50	141	315
44	13 10	50	140	12 20	51	140	11 29	50	141	10 39	51	141	09 48	50	142	316
43	13 39	50	141	12 49	51	141	11 58	51	142	11 07	50	142	10 17	51	143	317
42	14 08	51	141	13 17	51	142	12 26	51	142	11 35	51	143	10 44	51	143	318
41	14 37	51	142	13 46	52	143	12 54	51	143	12 03	52	144	11 11	51	144	319
40	15 05	-52	143	14 13	-51	143	13 22	-52	144	12 30	-52	145	11 38	-52	145	320
39	15 32	52	144	14 40	52	144	13 48	52	145	12 56	52	145	12 04	52	146	321
38	15 59	52	145	15 07	52	145	14 15	53	146	13 22	52	146	12 30	53	147	322
37	16 26	53	145	15 33	53	146	14 40	52	146	13 48	53	147	12 55	53	147	323
36	16 52	53	146	15 59	53	147	15 06	54	147	14 12	53	148	13 19	53	148	324
35	17 17	-53	147	16 24	-54	148	15 30	-53	148	14 37	-54	148	13 43	-53	149	325
34	17 42	54	148	16 48	54	148	15 54	53	149	15 01	54	149	14 07	54	150	326
33	18 06	54	149	17 12	54	149	16 18	54	150	15 24	54	150	14 30	54	151	327
32	18 29	54	150	17 35	54	150	16 41	55	151	15 46	54	151	14 52	54	151	328
31	18 52	54	150	17 58	55	151	17 03	55	151	16 08	54	152	15 14	55	152	329
30	19 15	-55	151	18 20	-55	152	17 25	-55	152	16 30	-55	153	15 35	-55	153	330
29	19 36	55	152	18 41	55	153	17 46	55	153	16 51	56	153	15 55	55	154	331
28	19 58	56	153	19 02	55	154	18 07	56	154	17 11	56	154	16 15	55	155	332
27	20 18	56	154	19 22	55	154	18 27	56	155	17 31	56	155	16 35	56	156	333
26	20 38	56	155	19 42	56	155	18 46	56	156	17 50	56	156	16 54	57	156	334
25	20 57	-56	156	20 01	-57	156	19 04	-56	157	18 08	-56	157	17 12	-57	157	335
24	21 16	57	157	20 19	57	157	19 22	56	157	18 26	57	158	17 29	57	158	336
23	21 33	56	158	20 37	57	158	19 40	57	158	18 43	57	159	17 46	57	159	337
22	21 51	57	159	20 54	58	159	19 56	57	159	18 59	57	160	18 02	57	160	338
21	22 07	57	160	21 10	58	160	20 12	57	160	19 15	57	160	18 18	58	161	339
20	22 23	-58	160	21 25	-57	161	20 28	-58	161	19 30	-58	161	18 32	-57	162	340
19	22 38	58	161	21 40	58	162	20 42	58	162	19 44	57	162	18 47	58	163	341
18	22 52	58	162	21 54	58	163	20 56	58	163	19 58	58	163	19 00	58	163	342
17	23 06	58	163	22 08	59	164	21 09	58	164	20 11	58	164	19 13	58	164	343
16	23 19	59	164	22 20	58	165	21 22	59	165	20 23	58	165	19 25	59	165	344
15	23 31	-59	165	22 32	-58	165	21 34	-59	166	20 35	-59	166	19 36	-58	166	345
14	23 42	59	166	22 43	58	166	21 45	59	167	20 46	59	167	19 47	59	167	346
13	23 53	59	167	22 54	59	167	21 55	59	168	20 56	59	168	19 57	59	168	347
12	24 03	59	168	23 04	59	168	22 05	60	169	21 05	59	169	20 06	59	169	348
11	24 12	59	169	23 13	60	169	22 13	59	169	21 14	59	170	20 15	59	170	349
10	24 20	-59	170	23 21	-60	170	22 21	-59	170	21 22	-59	171	20 23	-60	171	350
9	24 28	60	171	23 28	59	171	22 29	60	171	21 29	59	172	20 30	60	172	351
8	24 34	59	172	23 35	60	172	22 35	59	172	21 36	60	172	20 36	60	173	352
7	24 40	59	173	23 41	60	173	22 41	60	173	21 41	59	173	20 42	60	174	353
6	24 46	60	174	23 46	60	174	22 46	60	174	21 46	59	174	20 47	60	174	354
5	24 50	-60	175	23 50	-60	175	22 50	-59	175	21 51	-60	175	20 51	-60	175	355
4	24 54	60	176	23 54	60	176	22 54	60	176	21 54	60	176	20 54	60	176	356
3	24 56	59	177	23 57	60	177	22 57	60	177	21 57	60	177	20 57	60	177	357
2	24 58	60	178	23 58	60	178	22 58	59	178	21 59	60	178	20 59	60	178	358
1	25 00	60	179	24 00	60	179	23 00	60	179	22 00	60	179	21 00	60	179	359
0	25 00	-60	180	24 00	-60	180	23 00	-60	180	22 00	-60	180	21 00	-60	180	360
	25°			26°			27°			28°			29°			

S. Lat. {LHA greater than 180°....... Zn=180−Z
{LHA less than 180°............ Zn=180+Z

DECLINATION (15°-29°) CONTRARY NAME TO LATITUDE

N. Lat. {LHA greater than 180°....... Zn=Z; LHA less than 180°........... Zn=360−Z}

DECLINATION (0°-14°) SAME NAME AS LATITUDE

LHA	0° Hc	d	Z	1° Hc	d	Z	2° Hc	d	Z	3° Hc	d	Z	4° Hc	d	Z
	° ′	′	°	° ′	′	°	° ′	′	°	° ′	′	°	° ′	′	°
0	49 00	+60	180	50 00	+60	180	51 00	+60	180	52 00	+60	180	53 00	+60	180
1	48 59	60	179	49 59	60	178	50 59	60	178	51 59	60	178	52 59	60	178
2	48 58	60	177	49 58	60	177	50 58	59	177	51 57	60	177	52 57	60	177
3	48 55	60	175	49 55	59	175	50 54	60	175	51 54	60	175	52 54	60	175
4	48 50	60	174	49 50	60	174	50 50	60	174	51 50	60	174	52 50	59	173
5	48 45	+60	172	49 45	+59	172	50 44	+60	172	51 44	+60	172	52 44	+59	172
6	48 38	60	171	49 38	60	171	50 38	59	171	51 37	60	170	52 37	59	170
7	48 31	59	169	49 30	60	169	50 30	59	169	51 29	59	169	52 28	59	169
8	48 22	59	168	49 21	59	168	50 20	59	167	51 19	60	167	52 19	59	166
9	48 12	59	166	49 11	59	166	50 10	59	166	51 09	59	166	52 08	58	165
10	48 01	+58	165	48 59	+59	165	49 58	+59	164	50 57	+59	164	51 56	+58	164
11	47 48	59	164	48 47	58	163	49 45	59	163	50 44	58	163	51 42	59	162
12	47 35	58	162	48 33	58	162	49 31	59	161	50 30	58	161	51 28	58	161
13	47 20	58	161	48 18	58	160	49 16	58	160	50 14	58	159	51 12	58	159
14	47 05	58	159	48 03	57	159	49 00	58	158	49 58	57	158	50 55	58	158
15	46 48	+58	158	47 46	+57	157	48 43	+57	157	49 40	+57	157	50 37	+57	156
16	46 31	57	156	47 28	57	156	48 25	57	156	49 22	56	155	50 18	57	155
17	46 12	57	155	47 09	56	155	48 05	57	154	49 02	56	154	49 58	57	153
18	45 52	57	154	46 49	56	153	47 45	56	153	48 41	56	152	49 37	56	152
19	45 32	56	152	46 28	56	152	47 24	56	151	48 20	55	151	49 15	56	150
20	45 10	+56	151	46 06	+56	151	47 02	+55	150	47 57	+55	149	48 52	+55	149
21	44 48	55	150	45 43	55	149	46 38	55	149	47 33	55	148	48 28	55	147
22	44 24	56	148	45 20	54	148	46 14	55	147	47 09	54	147	48 03	55	146
23	44 00	55	147	44 55	54	147	45 49	55	146	46 44	54	145	47 38	54	145
24	43 35	55	146	44 30	54	145	45 24	53	145	46 17	54	144	47 11	54	143
25	43 09	+54	145	44 03	+54	144	44 57	+53	143	45 50	+54	143	46 44	+53	142
26	42 43	53	143	43 36	54	143	44 30	53	142	45 23	52	141	46 15	53	141
27	42 15	54	142	43 09	52	142	44 01	53	141	44 54	52	140	45 46	53	140
28	41 47	53	141	42 40	52	140	43 32	53	140	44 25	52	139	45 17	51	138
29	41 18	53	140	42 11	52	139	43 03	52	139	43 55	51	138	44 46	51	137
30	40 49	+52	139	41 41	+51	138	42 32	+52	137	43 24	+51	137	44 15	+51	136
31	40 19	51	138	41 10	51	137	42 01	51	136	42 52	51	135	43 43	51	135
32	39 48	51	136	40 39	51	136	41 30	50	135	42 20	51	134	43 11	50	134
33	39 16	51	135	40 07	50	135	40 57	51	134	41 48	49	133	42 37	50	132
34	38 44	50	134	39 34	50	134	40 24	50	133	41 14	50	132	42 04	49	131
35	38 11	+50	133	39 01	+50	132	39 51	+49	132	40 40	+49	131	41 29	+49	130
36	37 38	49	132	38 27	50	131	39 17	49	131	40 06	49	130	40 55	48	129
37	37 04	49	131	37 53	49	130	38 42	49	130	39 31	48	129	40 19	48	128
38	36 30	48	130	37 18	49	129	38 07	48	129	38 55	48	128	39 43	48	127
39	35 55	48	129	36 43	48	128	37 31	48	128	38 19	48	127	39 07	47	126
40	35 19	+48	128	36 07	+48	127	36 55	+48	127	37 43	+47	126	38 30	+47	125
41	34 43	48	127	35 31	48	126	36 19	47	126	37 06	47	125	37 53	46	124
42	34 07	47	126	34 54	48	125	35 42	46	125	36 28	47	124	37 15	46	123
43	33 30	47	125	34 17	47	124	35 04	47	124	35 51	46	123	36 37	46	122
44	32 53	47	124	33 40	46	123	34 26	46	123	35 12	46	122	35 58	46	121
45	32 15	+47	123	33 02	+46	122	33 48	+46	122	34 34	+45	121	35 19	+45	120
46	31 37	46	122	32 23	46	122	33 09	46	121	33 55	45	120	34 40	45	119
47	30 59	46	122	31 45	45	121	32 30	45	120	33 15	45	119	34 00	45	118
48	30 20	45	121	31 05	46	120	31 51	45	119	32 36	44	118	33 20	44	118
49	29 41	45	120	30 26	45	119	31 11	44	118	31 55	45	117	32 40	44	117
50	29 01	+45	119	29 46	+45	118	30 31	+44	117	31 15	+44	117	31 59	+44	116
51	28 21	45	118	29 06	44	117	29 50	44	116	30 34	44	116	31 18	44	115
52	27 41	45	117	28 26	44	116	29 10	43	116	29 53	44	115	30 37	43	114
53	27 01	44	116	27 45	44	116	28 29	43	114	29 12	43	114	29 55	43	113
54	26 20	44	116	27 04	43	115	27 47	44	114	28 31	43	113	29 14	42	112
55	25 39	+44	115	26 23	+43	114	27 06	+43	113	27 49	+43	112	28 32	+42	112
56	24 58	43	114	25 41	43	113	26 24	43	112	27 07	43	112	27 50	42	111
57	24 16	43	113	24 59	43	112	25 42	43	112	26 25	42	111	27 07	42	110
58	23 34	43	112	24 17	43	112	25 00	42	111	25 42	42	110	26 24	42	109
59	22 52	43	112	23 35	42	111	24 17	43	110	25 00	42	109	25 42	41	108
60	22 10	+43	111	22 53	+42	110	23 35	+42	109	24 17	+41	108	24 58	+42	108
61	21 28	42	110	22 10	42	109	22 52	42	108	23 34	41	108	24 15	41	107
62	20 45	42	109	21 27	42	109	22 09	41	108	22 50	41	107	23 32	41	106
63	20 02	42	109	20 44	42	108	21 26	41	107	22 07	41	106	22 48	41	105
64	19 19	42	108	20 01	41	107	20 42	41	106	21 23	41	105	22 04	41	105
65	18 36	+41	107	19 17	+42	106	19 59	+41	106	20 40	+41	105	21 21	+40	104
66	17 53	41	106	18 34	41	106	19 15	41	105	19 56	41	104	20 37	40	103
67	17 09	41	106	17 50	41	105	18 31	41	104	19 12	40	103	19 52	41	103
68	16 25	41	105	17 06	41	104	17 47	41	103	18 28	40	103	19 08	40	102
69	15 42	40	104	16 22	41	103	17 03	40	103	17 43	41	102	18 24	40	101

LHA	5° Hc	d	Z	6° Hc	d	Z	7° Hc	d	Z	8° Hc	d	Z	9° Hc	d	Z
	° ′	′	°	° ′	′	°	° ′	′	°	° ′	′	°	° ′	′	°
0	54 00	+60	180	55 00	+60	180	56 00	+60	180	57 00	+60	180	58 00	+60	180
1	53 59	60	178	54 59	60	178	55 59	60	178	56 59	60	178	57 59	60	178
2	53 57	60	177	54 57	60	177	55 57	60	177	56 57	60	176	57 57	60	176
3	53 54	60	175	54 54	60	175	55 54	60	175	56 54	59	175	57 53	60	174
4	53 49	60	173	54 49	60	173	55 49	60	173	56 49	59	173	57 48	60	173
5	53 43	+60	172	54 43	+60	171	55 43	+59	171	56 42	+60	171	57 42	+59	171
6	53 36	60	170	54 36	59	170	55 35	59	169	56 34	60	169	57 34	59	169
7	53 27	60	168	54 27	59	168	55 26	59	168	56 25	59	167	57 24	59	167
8	53 18	59	167	54 17	59	166	55 16	59	166	56 15	58	166	57 13	59	165
9	53 06	59	165	54 05	59	165	55 04	59	164	56 03	58	164	57 01	59	164
10	52 54	+59	163	53 53	+58	163	54 51	+58	163	55 49	+59	162	56 48	+58	162
11	52 41	58	162	53 39	58	161	54 37	58	161	55 35	58	161	56 33	58	160
12	52 26	58	160	53 24	57	160	54 21	58	159	55 19	58	159	56 17	57	158
13	52 10	57	159	53 07	58	158	54 05	57	158	55 02	58	157	55 59	58	157
14	51 53	57	157	52 50	57	157	53 47	57	156	54 44	57	156	55 41	57	155
15	51 34	+57	156	52 31	+57	155	53 28	+57	154	54 25	+56	154	55 21	+56	153
16	51 15	57	154	52 12	56	153	53 08	56	153	54 04	56	152	55 00	56	152
17	50 55	56	153	51 51	56	152	52 47	56	151	53 43	55	151	54 38	55	150
18	50 33	56	151	51 29	56	150	52 25	55	150	53 20	55	149	54 15	55	149
19	50 11	55	150	51 06	55	148	52 01	55	148	52 56	55	148	53 51	54	147
20	49 47	+55	148	50 42	+55	148	51 37	+54	147	52 31	+55	146	53 26	+54	146
21	49 23	55	147	50 18	54	146	51 12	54	145	52 06	53	145	52 59	54	144
22	48 58	54	145	49 52	54	145	50 46	53	144	51 39	53	143	52 32	53	143
23	48 32	53	144	49 25	54	143	50 19	53	143	51 12	52	142	52 04	53	141
24	48 05	53	143	48 58	53	142	49 51	52	141	50 43	53	141	51 36	52	140
25	47 37	+52	141	48 29	+53	141	49 22	+52	140	50 14	+52	139	51 06	+51	138
26	47 08	52	140	48 00	52	139	48 52	52	139	49 44	51	138	50 35	51	137
27	46 39	51	139	47 30	52	138	48 22	51	137	49 13	51	137	50 04	51	136
28	46 08	52	138	47 00	51	137	47 51	51	136	48 42	50	135	49 32	50	134
29	45 37	51	136	46 28	51	136	47 19	50	135	48 09	50	134	48 59	50	133
30	45 06	+50	135	45 56	+51	134	46 47	+49	134	47 36	+50	133	48 26	+49	132
31	44 34	50	134	45 24	49	133	46 13	50	132	47 03	49	132	47 52	49	131
32	44 01	49	133	44 50	50	132	45 40	49	131	46 29	48	130	47 17	49	130
33	43 27	49	132	44 16	49	131	45 05	49	130	45 54	48	129	46 42	48	128
34	42 53	49	131	43 42	48	130	44 30	49	129	45 19	47	128	46 06	48	127
35	42 18	+49	129	43 07	+48	129	43 55	+48	128	44 43	+47	127	45 30	+47	126
36	41 43	48	128	42 31	48	128	43 19	47	127	44 06	47	126	44 53	47	125
37	41 07	48	127	41 55	47	127	42 42	47	126	43 29	47	125	44 16	46	124
38	40 31	47	126	41 18	47	125	42 05	47	125	42 52	46	124	43 38	46	123
39	39 54	47	125	40 41	47	124	41 28	46	124	42 14	46	123	43 00	45	122
40	39 17	+46	124	40 03	+47	123	40 50	+46	123	41 36	+45	122	42 21	+45	121
41	38 39	46	123	39 25	46	122	40 11	46	122	40 57	45	121	41 42	45	120
42	38 01	46	122	38 47	46	121	39 33	45	121	40 18	44	120	41 02	45	119
43	37 23	45	121	38 08	45	120	38 53	45	120	39 38	45	119	40 23	44	118
44	36 43	45	120	37 29	45	120	38 14	44	119	38 58	44	118	39 42	44	117
45	36 04	+45	119	36 49	+45	119	37 34	+44	118	38 18	+44	117	39 02	+43	116
46	35 25	44	118	36 09	45	118	36 54	43	117	37 37	44	116	38 21	43	115
47	34 45	44	118	35 29	44	117	36 13	44	116	36 57	43	115	37 40	43	114
48	34 04	44	117	34 48	44	116	35 32	43	115	36 15	43	114	36 58	43	113
49	33 24	44	116	34 08	43	115	34 51	43	114	35 34	43	113	36 17	42	112
50	32 43	+43	115	33 26	+43	114	34 09	+43	113	34 52	+43	112	35 35	+42	112
51	32 02	43	114	32 45	43	113	33 28	42	112	34 10	42	112	34 52	42	111
52	31 20	43	113	32 03	43	112	32 46	42	112	33 28	42	111	34 10	41	110
53	30 38	43	112	31 21	42	112	32 03	42	111	32 45	42	110	33 27	41	109
54	29 56	43	112	30 39	42	111	31 21	42	110	32 03	41	109	32 44	41	108
55	29 14	+42	111	29 56	+42	110	30 38	+42	109	31 20	+41	108	32 01	+41	107
56	28 32	42	110	29 14	41	109	29 55	42	108	30 37	41	108	31 18	41	107
57	27 49	42	109	28 31	41	108	29 12	42	108	29 54	40	107	30 34	41	106
58	27 06	42	108	27 48	41	108	28 29	41	107	29 10	41	106	29 51	40	105
59	26 23	42	108	27 05	41	107	27 46	40	106	28 26	41	105	29 07	40	104
60	25 40	+41	107	26 21	+41	106	27 02	+41	105	27 43	+40	104	28 23	+40	104
61	24 56	41	106	25 37	41	105	26 18	41	104	26 59	40	104	27 39	40	103
62	24 13	41	105	24 54	40	105	25 34	41	104	26 15	40	103	26 55	39	102
63	23 29	41	105	24 10	40	104	24 50	40	103	25 30	40	102	26 10	40	101
64	22 45	41	104	23 26	40	103	24 06	40	102	24 46	40	101	25 26	39	101
65	22 01	+41	103	22 42	+40	102	23 22	+40	102	24 02	+39	101	24 41	+40	100
66	21 17	40	102	21 57	40	102	22 37	40	101	23 17	40	100	23 57	39	99
67	20 33	40	102	21 13	40	101	21 53	39	100	22 32	40	99	23 12	39	99
68	19 48	40	101	20 28	40	100	21 08	40	99	21 48	39	99	22 27	39	98
69	19 04	40	100	19 44	39	100	20 23	40	99	21 03	39	98	21 42	39	97

LHA	10° Hc	d	Z	11° Hc	d	Z	12° Hc	d	Z	13° Hc	d	Z	14° Hc	d	Z	LHA
	° ′	′	°	° ′	′	°	° ′	′	°	° ′	′	°	° ′	′	°	
0	59 00	+60	180	60 00	+60	180	61 00	+60	180	62 00	+60	180	63 00	+60	180	360
1	58 59	60	178	59 59	60	178	60 59	60	178	61 59	60	178	62 59	60	178	359
2	58 57	60	176	59 57	60	176	60 57	60	176	61 57	60	176	62 57	60	176	358
3	58 53	60	174	59 53	60	174	60 53	60	174	61 53	59	174	62 52	60	174	357
4	58 48	60	172	59 48	59	172	60 47	60	172	61 47	60	172	62 47	59	172	356
5	58 41	+60	171	59 41	+59	170	60 40	+60	170	61 40	+59	170	62 39	+59	169	355
6	58 33	59	169	59 32	60	168	60 32	59	168	61 31	59	168	62 30	59	167	354
7	58 23	59	167	59 22	59	166	60 21	59	166	61 20	59	166	62 19	59	165	353
8	58 12	59	165	59 11	59	165	60 10	58	164	61 08	59	164	62 07	58	163	352
9	58 00	58	163	58 58	59	163	59 57	58	162	60 55	58	162	61 53	58	161	351
10	57 46	+58	161	58 44	+58	161	59 42	+58	160	60 40	+58	160	61 38	+57	159	350
11	57 31	58	160	58 29	57	159	59 26	58	159	60 24	57	158	61 21	57	157	349
12	57 14	58	158	58 12	57	157	59 09	57	157	60 06	57	156	61 03	56	155	348
13	56 57	57	156	57 54	56	156	58 50	57	155	59 47	56	154	60 43	56	154	347
14	56 38	56	154	57 34	56	154	58 30	56	153	59 26	56	152	60 22	56	152	346
15	56 17	+56	153	57 13	+56	152	58 09	+56	151	59 05	+55	151	60 00	+55	150	345
16	55 56	56	151	56 52	55	150	57 47	55	150	58 42	55	149	59 37	54	148	344
17	55 33	56	149	56 29	54	149	57 23	55	148	58 18	54	147	59 12	54	146	343
18	55 10	55	148	56 05	54	147	56 59	54	146	57 53	54	146	58 47	53	145	342
19	54 45	54	146	55 39	54	146	56 33	54	145	57 27	53	144	58 20	53	143	341
20	54 20	+53	145	55 13	+54	144	56 07	+53	143	57 00	+52	142	57 52	+53	141	340
21	53 53	53	143	54 46	53	142	55 39	52	142	56 31	53	141	57 24	51	140	339
22	53 25	53	142	54 18	52	141	55 10	52	140	56 02	52	139	56 54	51	138	338
23	52 57	52	140	53 49	52	140	54 41	51	139	55 32	51	138	56 23	51	137	337
24	52 28	51	139	53 19	51	138	54 10	51	137	55 01	51	136	55 52	50	135	336
25	51 57	+52	138	52 49	+50	137	53 39	+51	136	54 30	+50	135	55 20	+49	134	335
26	51 26	51	136	52 17	50	135	53 07	50	134	53 57	50	134	54 47	48	133	334
27	50 55	50	135	51 45	50	134	52 35	49	133	53 24	49	132	54 13	48	131	333
28	50 22	50	134	51 12	49	133	52 01	49	132	52 50	48	131	53 38	48	130	332
29	49 49	49	132	50 38	49	131	51 27	48	131	52 15	48	130	53 03	48	129	331
30	49 15	+49	131	50 04	+48	130	50 52	+48	129	51 40	+47	128	52 27	+47	127	330
31	48 41	48	130	49 29	48	129	50 17	47	128	51 04	47	127	51 51	46	126	329
32	48 06	47	129	48 53	48	128	49 41	47	127	50 28	46	126	51 14	46	125	328
33	47 30	47	127	48 17	47	127	49 04	47	126	49 51	46	125	50 37	45	124	327
34	46 54	47	126	47 41	46	125	48 27	46	124	49 13	46	124	49 59	45	123	326
35	46 17	+47	125	47 04	+46	124	47 50	+45	123	48 35	+45	122	49 20	+45	121	325
36	45 40	46	124	46 26	46	123	47 12	45	122	47 57	44	121	48 41	45	120	324
37	45 02	46	123	45 48	45	122	46 33	45	121	47 18	44	120	48 02	44	119	323
38	44 24	45	122	45 09	45	121	45 54	44	120	46 38	44	119	47 22	44	118	322
39	43 45	45	121	44 30	45	120	45 15	44	119	45 59	43	118	46 42	43	117	321
40	43 06	+45	120	43 51	+44	119	44 35	+44	118	45 19	+43	117	46 02	+42	116	320
41	42 27	44	119	43 11	44	118	43 55	43	117	44 38	43	116	45 21	42	115	319
42	41 47	44	118	42 31	43	117	43 14	43	116	43 57	43	115	44 40	42	114	318
43	41 07	43	117	41 50	43	116	42 33	43	115	43 16	42	114	43 58	42	113	317
44	40 26	43	116	41 09	43	115	41 52	43	114	42 35	41	113	43 16	42	112	316
45	39 45	+43	115	40 28	+43	114	41 11	+42	113	41 53	+41	112	42 34	+41	111	315
46	39 04	43	114	39 47	42	113	40 29	42	112	41 11	41	111	41 52	41	110	314
47	38 23	42	113	39 05	42	112	39 47	41	111	40 28	41	111	41 10	40	110	313
48	37 41	42	112	38 23	42	112	39 05	41	111	39 46	41	110	40 27	40	109	312
49	36 59	42	112	37 41	41	111	38 22	41	110	39 03	41	109	39 44	40	108	311
50	36 17	+41	111	36 58	+41	110	37 39	+41	109	38 20	+41	108	39 01	+39	107	310
51	35 34	41	110	36 15	41	109	36 56	41	108	37 37	40	107	38 17	40	106	309
52	34 51	42	109	35 33	40	108	36 13	41	107	36 54	40	106	37 34	39	105	308
53	34 08	41	108	34 49	41	107	35 30	40	106	36 10	40	105	36 50	39	105	307
54	33 25	41	107	34 06	40	107	34 46	40	106	35 26	40	105	36 06	39	104	306
55	32 42	+41	107	33 23	+40	106	34 03	+39	105	34 42	+40	104	35 22	+39	103	305
56	31 59	40	106	32 39	40	105	33 19	39	104	33 58	40	103	34 38	38	102	304
57	31 15	40	105	31 55	40	104	32 35	39	103	33 14	39	102	33 53	39	101	303
58	30 31	40	104	31 11	40	103	31 51	39	103	32 30	39	102	33 09	38	101	302
59	29 47	40	103	30 27	39	103	31 06	39	102	31 45	39	101	32 24	39	100	301
60	29 03	+40	103	29 43	+39	102	30 22	+39	101	31 01	+39	100	31 40	+38	99	300
61	28 19	39	102	28 58	39	101	29 37	39	100	30 16	39	99	30 55	38	98	299
62	27 34	40	101	28 14	39	100	28 53	39	100	29 32	38	99	30 10	38	98	298
63	26 50	39	101	27 29	39	100	28 08	39	99	28 47	38	98	29 25	38	97	297
64	26 05	39	100	26 44	39	99	27 23	39	98	28 02	38	97	28 40	38	96	296
65	25 21	+39	99	26 00	+38	98	26 38	+39	97	27 17	+38	97	27 55	+38	96	295
66	24 36	39	98	25 15	39	98	25 54	38	97	26 32	38	96	27 10	38	95	294
67	23 51	39	98	24 30	39	97	25 09	38	96	25 47	38	95	26 25	38	94	293
68	23 06	39	97	23 45	38	96	24 23	39	95	25 02	38	94	25 40	37	94	292
69	22 21	39	96	23 00	38	95	23 38	39	95	24 17	37	94	24 54	38	93	291

S. Lat. {LHA greater than 180°....... Zn=180−Z; LHA less than 180°........... Zn=180+Z}

DECLINATION (0°-14°) SAME NAME AS LATITUDE

N. Lat. {LHA greater than 180°....... Zn=Z; LHA less than 180°.......... Zn=360−Z}

DECLINATION (0°-14°) SAME NAME AS LATITUDE

LHA	0°			1°			2°			3°			4°			5°			6°			7°			8°			9°			10°			11°			12°			13°			14°			LHA
	Hc	d	Z	Hc	d	Z	Hc	d	Z	Hc	d	Z	Hc	d	Z	Hc	d	Z	Hc	d	Z	Hc	d	Z	Hc	d	Z	Hc	d	Z	Hc	d	Z	Hc	d	Z	Hc	d	Z	Hc	d	Z	Hc	d	Z	
	° ′	′	°	° ′	′	°	° ′	′	°	° ′	′	°	° ′	′	°	° ′	′	°	° ′	′	°	° ′	′	°	° ′	′	°	° ′	′	°	° ′	′	°	° ′	′	°	° ′	′	°	° ′	′	°	° ′	′	°	
70	14 58	+40	103	15 38	+41	103	16 19	+40	102	16 59	+40	101	17 39	+40	100	18 19	+40	100	18 59	+40	99	19 39	+39	98	20 18	+39	97	20 57	+39	96	21 36	+39	96	22 15	+38	95	22 53	+38	94	23 31	+38	93	24 09	+38	92	290
71	14 13	41	103	14 54	40	102	15 34	41	101	16 15	40	100	16 55	40	100	17 35	39	99	18 14	40	98	18 54	39	97	19 33	39	97	20 12	39	96	20 51	39	95	21 30	38	94	22 08	38	93	22 46	38	92	23 24	38	92	289
72	13 29	41	102	14 10	40	101	14 50	40	101	15 30	40	100	16 10	40	99	16 50	39	98	17 29	40	97	18 09	39	97	18 48	39	96	19 27	39	95	20 06	38	94	20 44	39	93	21 23	38	93	22 01	38	92	22 39	37	91	288
73	12 45	40	101	13 25	40	101	14 05	40	100	14 45	40	99	15 25	40	98	16 05	39	98	16 44	40	97	17 24	39	96	18 03	39	95	18 42	39	94	19 21	38	94	19 59	38	93	20 37	39	92	21 16	37	91	21 53	38	90	287
74	12 00	41	101	12 41	40	100	13 21	40	99	14 01	39	98	14 40	40	98	15 20	39	97	15 59	40	96	16 39	39	95	17 18	39	94	17 57	38	94	18 35	39	93	19 14	38	92	19 52	38	91	20 30	38	90	21 08	38	90	286
75	11 16	+40	100	11 56	+40	99	12 36	+40	98	13 16	+39	98	13 55	+40	97	14 35	+39	96	15 14	+40	95	15 54	+39	95	16 33	+39	94	17 12	+38	93	17 50	+39	92	18 29	+38	91	19 07	+38	91	19 45	+38	90	20 23	+37	89	285
76	10 31	40	99	11 11	40	99	11 51	40	98	12 31	39	97	13 10	40	96	13 50	39	96	14 29	39	95	15 08	39	94	15 47	39	93	16 26	39	92	17 05	38	92	17 43	39	91	18 22	38	90	19 00	38	89	19 38	37	88	284
77	09 47	39	99	10 26	40	98	11 06	40	97	11 46	39	96	12 25	40	96	13 05	39	95	13 44	39	94	14 23	39	93	15 02	39	92	15 41	39	92	16 20	38	91	16 58	38	90	17 36	38	89	18 14	38	88	18 52	38	88	283
78	09 02	40	98	09 42	39	97	10 21	40	96	11 01	39	96	11 40	40	95	12 20	39	94	12 59	39	93	13 38	39	93	14 17	39	92	14 56	38	91	15 34	39	90	16 13	38	89	16 51	38	89	17 29	38	88	18 07	38	87	282
79	08 17	40	97	08 57	39	97	09 36	40	96	10 16	39	95	10 55	40	94	11 35	39	93	12 14	39	93	12 53	39	92	13 32	38	91	14 10	39	90	14 49	39	90	15 28	38	89	16 06	38	88	16 44	38	87	17 22	38	86	281
80	07 32	+40	97	08 12	+39	96	08 51	+40	95	09 31	+39	94	10 10	+39	94	10 49	+39	93	11 28	+39	92	12 07	+39	91	12 46	+39	91	13 25	+39	90	14 04	+38	89	14 42	+39	88	15 21	+38	87	15 59	+38	87	16 37	+38	86	280
81	06 47	39	96	07 26	40	95	08 06	39	94	08 45	40	94	09 25	39	93	10 04	39	92	10 43	39	91	11 22	39	91	12 01	39	90	12 40	39	89	13 19	38	88	13 57	38	87	14 35	39	87	15 14	38	86	15 52	37	85	279
82	06 02	39	95	06 41	40	95	07 21	39	94	08 00	40	93	08 40	39	92	09 19	39	92	09 58	39	91	10 37	39	90	11 16	39	89	11 55	38	88	12 33	39	88	13 12	38	87	13 50	38	86	14 28	38	85	15 06	38	84	278
83	05 17	39	95	05 56	40	94	06 36	39	93	07 15	39	92	07 54	40	92	08 34	39	91	09 13	39	90	09 52	39	89	10 31	38	89	11 09	39	88	11 48	39	87	12 27	38	86	13 05	38	85	13 43	38	85	14 21	38	84	277
84	04 31	40	94	05 11	39	93	05 50	40	92	06 30	39	92	07 09	39	91	07 48	39	90	08 27	39	89	09 06	39	89	09 45	39	88	10 24	39	87	11 03	38	86	11 41	39	86	12 20	38	85	12 58	38	84	13 36	39	83	276
85	03 46	+40	93	04 26	+39	93	05 05	+39	92	05 44	+40	91	06 24	+39	90	07 03	+39	90	07 42	+39	89	08 21	+39	88	09 00	+39	87	09 39	+39	86	10 18	+38	86	10 56	+39	85	11 35	+38	84	12 13	+39	83	12 52	+38	83	275
86	03 01	39	93	03 40	40	92	04 20	39	91	04 59	39	90	05 38	40	90	06 18	39	89	06 57	39	88	07 36	39	87	08 15	39	87	08 54	39	86	09 33	38	85	10 11	39	84	10 50	38	83	11 28	39	83	12 07	38	82	274
87	02 16	39	92	02 55	40	91	03 35	39	90	04 14	39	90	04 53	39	89	05 32	40	88	06 12	39	87	06 51	39	87	07 30	39	86	08 09	38	85	08 47	39	84	09 26	39	84	10 05	38	83	10 43	39	82	11 22	38	81	273
88	01 31	39	91	02 10	39	91	02 49	40	90	03 29	39	89	04 08	39	88	04 47	39	88	05 26	39	87	06 05	40	86	06 45	39	85	07 24	38	85	08 02	39	84	08 41	39	83	09 20	39	82	09 59	38	81	10 37	39	81	272
89	00 45	40	91	01 25	39	90	02 04	39	89	02 43	40	88	03 23	39	88	04 02	39	87	04 41	39	86	05 20	39	85	05 59	39	85	06 38	39	84	07 17	39	83	07 56	39	82	08 35	39	82	09 14	39	81	09 53	38	80	271
90	00 00	+39	90	00 39	+40	89	01 19	+39	88	01 58	+39	88	02 37	+40	87	03 17	+39	86	03 56	+39	85	04 35	+39	85	05 14	+39	84	05 53	+40	83	06 33	+39	82	07 12	+38	82	07 50	+39	81	08 29	+39	80	09 08	+39	79	270
91	−0 45	39	89	−0 06	39	89	00 33	40	88	01 13	39	87	01 52	40	86	02 32	39	86	03 11	39	85	03 50	39	84	04 29	40	83	05 09	39	83	05 48	39	82	06 27	39	81	07 06	39	80	07 45	39	80	08 24	38	79	269
92	−1 31	40	89	−0 51	39	88	−0 12	40	87	00 28	39	86	01 07	39	86	01 46	40	85	02 26	39	84	03 05	39	83	03 44	40	83	04 24	39	82	05 03	39	81	05 42	39	80	06 21	39	80	07 00	39	79	07 39	39	78	268
93	−2 16	40	88	−1 36	39	87	−0 57	39	87	−0 18	40	86	00 22	39	85	01 01	40	84	01 41	39	84	02 20	40	83	03 00	39	82	03 39	39	81	04 18	39	80	04 57	40	80	05 37	39	79	06 16	39	78	06 55	39	77	267
94	−3 01	39	87	−2 22	40	87	−1 42	39	86	−1 03	40	85	−0 23	39	84	00 16	40	84	00 56	39	83	01 35	40	82	02 15	39	81	02 54	40	81	03 34	39	80	04 13	39	79	04 52	40	78	05 32	39	78	06 11	39	77	266
95	−3 46	+39	87	−3 07	+40	86	−2 27	+39	85	−1 48	+40	84	−1 08	+39	84	−0 29	+40	83	00 11	+39	82	00 50	+40	81	01 30	+40	81	02 10	+39	80	02 49	+40	79	03 29	+39	78	04 08	+39	78	04 47	+40	77	05 27	+39	76	265
96	−4 31	39	86	−3 52	40	85	−3 12	39	85	−2 33	40	84	−1 53	39	83	−1 14	40	82	−0 34	40	82	00 06	39	81	00 45	40	80	01 25	40	79	02 05	39	79	02 44	40	78	03 24	39	77	04 03	40	76	04 43	39	76	264
97	−5 17	40	85	−4 37	40	85	−3 57	39	84	−3 18	40	83	−2 38	40	82	−1 58	39	82	−1 19	40	81	−0 39	40	80	00 01	40	79	00 41	39	79	01 20	40	78	02 00	40	77	02 40	39	76	03 19	40	76	03 59	40	75	263
98	−6 02	40	85	−5 22	40	84	−4 42	39	83	−4 03	40	82	−3 23	40	82	−2 43	40	81	−2 03	39	80	−1 24	40	79	−0 44	40	79	−0 04	40	78	00 36	40	77	01 16	40	76	01 56	40	76	02 36	39	75	03 15	40	74	262
99				−6 07	40	83	−5 27	39	83	−4 48	40	82	−4 08	40	81	−3 28	40	80	−2 48	40	80	−2 08	40	79	−1 28	40	78	−0 48	40	77	−0 08	40	77	00 32	40	76	01 12	40	75	01 52	40	74	02 32	40	74	261
100							−6 12	+40	82	−5 32	+40	81	−4 52	+40	80	−4 12	+40	80	−3 32	+40	79	−2 52	+40	78	−2 12	+40	77	−1 32	+40	77	−0 52	+40	76	−0 12	+40	75	00 28	+40	74	01 08	+40	74	01 48	+41	73	260
101										−6 17	40	80	−5 37	40	80	−4 57	40	79	−4 17	40	78	−3 37	41	77	−2 56	40	77	−2 16	40	76	−1 36	40	75	−0 56	41	75	−0 15	40	74	00 25	40	73	01 05	41	72	259
102													−6 22	41	79	−5 41	40	78	−5 01	40	78	−4 21	41	77	−3 40	40	76	−3 00	40	75	−2 20	41	75	−1 39	40	74	−0 59	41	73	−0 18	40	72	00 22	41	72	258
103																−6 26	41	78	−5 45	40	77	−5 05	41	76	−4 24	40	75	−3 44	41	75	−3 03	40	74	−2 23	41	73	−1 42	41	72	−1 01	40	72	−0 21	41	71	257
104																						−5 49	41	75	−5 08	41	75	−4 27	40	74	−3 47	41	73	−3 06	41	73	−2 25	41	72	−1 44	41	71	−1 03	40	70	256
105																									−5 52	+41	74	−5 11	+41	73	−4 30	+41	73	−3 49	+41	72	−3 08	+41	71	−2 27	+41	70	−1 46	+41	70	255
106																												−5 54	41	73	−5 13	41	72	−4 32	41	71	−3 51	41	70	−3 10	42	70	−2 28	41	69	254
107																															−5 56	41	71	−5 15	42	70	−4 33	41	70	−3 52	41	69	−3 11	42	68	253
108																																		−5 57	41	70	−5 16	42	69	−4 34	42	68	−3 52	41	68	252
109																																					−5 58	42	68	−5 16	42	68	−4 34	42	67	251
110																																								−5 58	+42	67	−5 16	+42	66	250
111																																											−5 57	42	66	249

LHA	0°			1°			2°			3°			4°			5°			6°			7°			8°			9°			10°			11°			12°			13°			14°			LHA
98	−6 02	39	85	262																																										
97	−5 17	39	85	−5 56	40	86	263																																							
96	−4 31	40	86	−5 11	39	87	−5 50	40	88	−6 30	39	88	264																																	
95	−3 46	−40	87	−4 26	−39	87	−5 05	−39	88	−5 44	−40	89	−6 24	−39	90	265																														
94	−3 01	39	87	−3 40	40	88	−4 20	39	89	−4 59	39	90	−5 38	40	90	−6 18	39	91	266																											
93	−2 16	39	88	−2 55	40	89	−3 35	39	90	−4 14	39	90	−4 53	39	91	−5 32	40	92	−6 12	39	93	267																								
92	−1 31	39	89	−2 10	39	89	−2 49	40	90	−3 29	39	91	−4 08	39	92	−4 47	39	92	−5 26	39	93	−6 05	40	94	268																					
91	−0 45	40	89	−1 25	39	90	−2 04	39	91	−2 43	40	92	−3 23	39	92	−4 02	39	93	−4 41	39	94	−5 20	39	95	−5 59	39	95	269																		
90	00 00	−39	90	−0 39	−40	91	−1 19	−39	92	−1 58	−39	92	−2 37	−40	93	−3 17	−39	94	−3 56	−39	95	−4 35	−39	95	−5 14	−39	96	−5 53	−40	97	270															
89	00 45	39	91	00 06	39	91	−0 33	40	92	−1 13	39	93	−1 52	40	94	−2 32	39	94	−3 11	39	95	−3 50	39	96	−4 29	40	97	−5 09	39	97	−5 48	39	98	−6 27	39	99	271									
88	01 31	40	91	00 51	39	92	00 12	40	93	−0 28	39	94	−1 07	39	94	−1 46	40	95	−2 26	39	96	−3 05	39	97	−3 44	40	97	−4 24	39	98	−5 03	39	99	−5 42	39	100	−6 21	39	100	272						
87	02 16	40	92	01 36	39	93	00 57	39	93	00 18	40	94	−0 22	39	95	−1 01	40	96	−1 41	39	96	−2 20	40	97	−3 00	39	98	−3 39	39	99	−4 18	39	100	−4 57	40	100	−5 37	39	101	−6 16	39	102	273			
86	03 01	39	93	02 22	40	93	01 42	39	94	01 03	40	95	00 23	39	96	−0 16	40	96	−0 56	39	97	−1 35	40	98	−2 15	39	99	−2 54	40	99	−3 34	39	100	−4 13	39	101	−4 52	40	102	−5 32	39	102	−6 11	39	103	274
85	03 46	−39	93	03 07	−40	94	02 27	−39	95	01 48	−40	96	01 08	−39	96	00 29	−40	97	−0 11	−39	98	−0 50	−40	99	−1 30	−40	99	−2 10	−39	100	−2 49	−40	101	−3 29	−39	102	−4 08	−39	102	−4 47	−40	103	−5 27	−39	104	275
84	04 31	39	94	03 52	40	95	03 12	39	95	02 33	40	96	01 53	39	97	01 14	40	98	00 34	40	98	−0 06	39	99	−0 45	40	100	−1 25	40	101	−2 05	39	101	−2 44	40	102	−3 24	39	103	−4 03	40	104	−4 43	39	104	276
83	05 17	40	95	04 37	40	95	03 57	39	96	03 18	40	97	02 38	40	98	01 58	39	98	01 19	40	99	00 39	40	100	−0 01	40	101	−0 41	39	101	−1 20	40	102	−2 00	40	103	−2 40	39	104	−3 19	40	104	−3 59	40	105	277
82	06 02	40	95	05 22	40	96	04 42	39	97	04 03	40	98	03 23	40	98	02 43	40	99	02 03	39	100	01 24	40	101	00 44	40	101	00 04	40	102	−0 36	40	103	−1 16	40	104	−1 56	40	104	−2 36	39	105	−3 15	40	106	278
81	06 47	40	96	06 07	40	97	05 27	39	97	04 48	40	98	04 08	40	99	03 28	40	100	02 48	40	100	02 08	40	101	01 28	40	102	00 48	40	103	00 08	40	103	−0 32	40	104	−1 12	40	105	−1 52	40	106	−2 32	40	106	279
80	07 32	−40	97	06 52	−40	97	06 12	−40	98	05 32	−40	99	04 52	−40	100	04 12	−40	100	03 32	−40	101	02 52	−40	102	02 12	−40	103	01 32	−40	103	00 52	−40	104	00 12	−40	105	−0 28	−40	106	−1 08	−40	106	−1 48	−41	107	280
79	08 17	40	97	07 37	40	98	06 57	40	99	06 17	40	100	05 37	40	100	04 57	40	101	04 17	40	102	03 37	41	103	02 56	40	103	02 16	40	104	01 36	40	105	00 56	41	105	00 15	40	106	−0 25	40	107	−1 05	41	108	281
78	09 02	40	98	08 22	40	99	07 42	40	99	07 02	40	100	06 22	41	101	05 41	40	102	05 01	40	102	04 21	41	103	03 40	40	104	03 00	40	105	02 20	41	105	01 39	40	106	00 59	41	107	00 18	40	108	−0 22	41	108	282
77	09 47	40	99	09 07	41	99	08 26	40	100	07 46	40	101	07 06	40	102	06 26	41	102	05 45	40	103	05 05	41	104	04 24	40	105	03 44	41	105	03 03	40	106	02 23	41	107	01 42	41	108	01 01	40	108	00 21	41	109	283
76	10 31	40	99	09 51	40	100	09 11	40	101	08 31	41	102	07 50	40	102	07 10	41	103	06 29	40	104	05 49	41	105	05 08	41	105	04 27	40	106	03 47	41	107	03 06	41	107	02 25	41	108	01 44	41	109	01 03	40	110	284
75	11 16	−40	100	10 36	−41	101	09 55	−40	102	09 15	−40	102	08 35	−41	103	07 54	−41	104	07 13	−40	105	06 33	−41	105	05 52	−41	106	05 11	−41	107	04 30	−41	107	03 49	−41	108	03 08	−41	109	02 27	−41	110	01 46	−41	110	285
74	12 00	40	101	11 20	40	101	10 40	41	102	09 59	40	103	09 19	41	104	08 38	41	104	07 57	41	105	07 16	41	106	06 35	41	107	05 54	41	107	05 13	41	108	04 32	41	109	03 51	41	110	03 10	42	110	02 28	41	111	286
73	12 45	41	101	12 04	40	102	11 24	41	103	10 43	40	104	10 03	41	104	09 22	41	105	08 41	41	106	08 00	41	107	07 19	42	107	06 37	41	108	05 56	41	109	05 15	42	110	04 33	41	110	03 52	41	111	03 11	42	112	287
72	13 29	40	102	12 49	41	103	12 08	41	104	11 27	41	104	10 46	41	105	10 05	41	106	09 24	41	107	08 43	41	107	08 02	42	108	07 20	41	109	06 39	42	109	05 57	41	110	05 16	42	111	04 34	42	112	03 52	41	112	288
71	14 13	40	103	13 33	41	104	12 52	41	104	12 11	41	105	11 30	41	106	10 49	41	107	10 08	42	107	09 26	41	108	08 45	42	109	08 03	42	109	07 21	41	110	06 40	42	111	05 58	42	112	05 16	42	112	04 34	42	113	289
70	14 58	−41	103	14 17	−41	104	13 36	−41	105	12 55	−42	106	12 13	−41	106	11 32	−41	107	10 51	−42	108	10 09	−42	109	09 27	−41	109	08 46	−42	110	08 04	−42	111	07 22	−42	112	06 40	−42	112	05 58	−42	113	05 16	−42	114	290
	0°			1°			2°			3°			4°			5°			6°			7°			8°			9°			10°			11°			12°			13°			14°			

S. Lat. {LHA greater than 180°....... Zn=180−Z; LHA less than 180°.......... Zn=180+Z}

DECLINATION (0°-14°) CONTRARY NAME TO LATITUDE

LAT 41°

N. Lat. {LHA greater than 180°...... Zn=Z; LHA less than 180°.......... Zn=360−Z}

DECLINATION (0°-14°) CONTRARY NAME TO LATITUDE

LHA	0° Hc	0° d	0° Z	1° Hc	1° d	1° Z	2° Hc	2° d	2° Z	3° Hc	3° d	3° Z	4° Hc	4° d	4° Z
	° ′	′	°	° ′	′	°	° ′	′	°	° ′	′	°	° ′	′	°
69	15 42	41	104	15 01	42	105	14 19	41	106	13 38	41	106	12 57	42	107
68	16 25	41	105	15 44	41	106	15 03	41	106	14 22	42	107	13 40	42	108
67	17 09	41	106	16 28	42	106	15 46	41	107	15 05	42	108	14 23	42	109
66	17 53	42	106	17 11	41	107	16 30	42	108	15 48	42	109	15 06	42	109
65	18 36	−42	107	17 54	−41	108	17 13	−42	109	16 31	−42	109	15 49	−43	110
64	19 19	42	108	18 37	42	109	17 55	42	109	17 13	42	110	16 31	43	111
63	20 02	42	109	19 20	42	109	18 38	42	110	17 56	43	111	17 13	42	112
62	20 45	42	109	20 03	42	110	19 21	43	111	18 38	43	112	17 55	43	112
61	21 28	43	110	20 45	42	111	20 03	42	112	19 20	43	112	18 37	43	113
60	22 10	−42	111	21 28	−43	112	20 45	−43	112	20 02	−43	113	19 19	−44	114
59	22 52	42	112	22 10	43	112	21 27	44	113	20 43	43	114	20 00	44	115
58	23 34	43	112	22 51	43	113	22 08	43	114	21 25	44	115	20 41	44	115
57	24 16	43	113	23 33	44	114	22 49	43	115	22 06	44	115	21 22	44	116
56	24 58	44	114	24 14	43	115	23 31	44	115	22 47	45	116	22 02	44	117
55	25 39	−44	115	24 55	−44	115	24 11	−44	116	23 27	−44	117	22 43	−45	118
54	26 20	44	116	25 36	44	116	24 52	45	117	24 07	44	118	23 23	45	119
53	27 01	44	116	26 17	45	117	25 32	45	118	24 47	45	119	24 02	45	119
52	27 41	44	117	26 57	45	118	26 12	45	119	25 27	45	119	24 42	46	120
51	28 21	44	118	27 37	46	119	26 51	45	120	26 06	45	120	25 21	46	121
50	29 01	−45	119	28 16	−45	120	27 31	−46	120	26 45	−46	121	25 59	−46	122
49	29 41	46	120	28 55	45	120	28 10	46	121	27 24	46	122	26 38	47	123
48	30 20	46	121	29 34	46	121	28 48	46	122	28 02	46	123	27 16	47	124
47	30 59	46	122	30 13	47	122	29 26	46	123	28 40	47	124	27 53	47	124
46	31 37	46	122	30 51	47	123	30 04	47	124	29 17	47	125	28 30	47	125
45	32 15	−46	123	31 29	−47	124	30 42	−48	125	29 54	−47	126	29 07	−48	126
44	32 53	47	124	32 06	47	125	31 19	48	126	30 31	48	126	29 43	48	127
43	33 30	47	125	32 43	48	126	31 55	48	127	31 07	48	127	30 19	48	128
42	34 07	48	126	33 19	48	127	32 31	48	128	31 43	48	128	30 55	49	129
41	34 43	48	127	33 55	48	128	33 07	48	128	32 19	49	129	31 30	49	130
40	35 19	−48	128	34 31	−49	129	33 42	−49	129	32 53	−49	130	32 04	−49	131
39	35 55	49	129	35 06	49	130	34 17	49	130	33 28	50	131	32 38	49	132
38	36 30	49	130	35 41	50	131	34 51	49	131	34 02	50	132	33 12	50	133
37	37 04	49	131	36 15	50	132	35 25	50	132	34 35	50	133	33 45	51	134
36	37 38	50	132	36 48	50	133	35 58	50	134	35 08	51	134	34 17	51	135
35	38 11	−50	133	37 21	−50	134	36 31	−51	135	35 40	−51	135	34 49	−51	136
34	38 44	51	134	37 53	50	135	37 03	51	136	36 12	52	136	35 20	51	137
33	39 16	51	135	38 25	51	136	37 34	51	137	36 43	52	137	35 51	52	138
32	39 48	52	136	38 56	51	137	38 05	52	138	37 13	52	138	36 21	52	139
31	40 19	52	138	39 27	52	138	38 35	52	139	37 43	53	139	36 50	52	140
30	40 49	−52	139	39 57	−53	139	39 04	−52	140	38 12	−53	141	37 19	−53	141
29	41 18	52	140	40 26	53	140	39 33	53	141	38 40	53	142	37 47	53	142
28	41 47	53	141	40 54	53	142	40 01	53	142	39 08	53	143	38 15	54	143
27	42 15	53	142	41 22	53	143	40 29	54	143	39 35	54	144	38 41	54	145
26	42 43	54	143	41 49	54	144	40 55	54	145	40 01	54	145	39 07	54	146
25	43 09	−54	145	42 15	−54	145	41 21	−54	146	40 27	−55	146	39 32	−54	147
24	43 35	54	146	42 41	55	146	41 46	54	147	40 52	55	148	39 57	55	148
23	44 00	54	147	43 06	55	148	42 11	56	148	41 15	55	149	40 20	55	149
22	44 24	55	148	43 29	55	149	42 34	55	149	41 39	56	150	40 43	56	151
21	44 48	56	150	43 52	55	150	42 57	56	151	42 01	56	151	41 05	56	152
20	45 10	−56	151	44 14	−56	152	43 18	−56	152	42 22	−56	153	41 26	−57	153
19	45 32	57	152	44 35	56	153	43 39	56	153	42 43	57	154	41 46	57	154
18	45 52	56	154	44 56	57	154	43 59	57	155	43 02	57	155	42 05	57	156
17	46 12	57	155	45 15	57	156	44 18	57	156	43 21	57	156	42 24	58	157
16	46 31	58	156	45 33	57	157	44 36	57	157	43 39	58	158	42 41	58	158
15	46 48	−57	158	45 51	−58	158	44 53	−58	159	43 55	−58	159	42 57	−57	159
14	47 05	58	159	46 07	58	160	45 09	58	160	44 11	58	160	43 13	58	161
13	47 20	58	161	46 22	58	161	45 24	58	161	44 26	59	162	43 27	58	162
12	47 35	59	162	46 36	58	162	45 38	58	163	44 40	59	163	43 41	59	163
11	47 48	58	164	46 50	59	164	45 51	59	164	44 52	59	164	43 53	58	165
10	48 01	−59	165	47 02	−59	165	46 03	−59	166	45 04	−59	166	44 05	−59	166
9	48 12	59	166	47 13	59	167	46 14	60	167	45 14	59	167	44 15	59	167
8	48 22	59	168	47 23	60	168	46 23	59	168	45 24	59	169	44 25	60	169
7	48 31	60	169	47 31	59	170	46 32	60	170	45 32	59	170	44 33	60	170
6	48 38	59	171	47 39	60	171	46 39	59	171	45 40	60	171	44 40	60	172
5	48 45	−60	172	47 45	−59	173	46 46	−60	173	45 46	−60	173	44 46	−60	173
4	48 50	59	174	47 51	60	174	46 51	60	174	45 51	60	174	44 51	60	174
3	48 55	60	175	47 55	60	176	46 55	60	176	45 55	60	176	44 55	60	176
2	48 58	60	177	47 58	60	177	46 58	60	177	45 58	60	177	44 58	60	177
1	48 59	60	179	47 59	60	179	46 59	60	179	45 59	60	179	44 59	59	179
0	49 00	−60	180	48 00	−60	180	47 00	−60	180	46 00	−60	180	45 00	−60	180

LHA	5° Hc	5° d	5° Z	6° Hc	6° d	6° Z	7° Hc	7° d	7° Z	8° Hc	8° d	8° Z	9° Hc	9° d	9° Z
	° ′	′	°	° ′	′	°	° ′	′	°	° ′	′	°	° ′	′	°
69	12 15	41	108	11 34	42	109	10 52	42	109	10 10	42	110	09 28	42	111
68	12 58	41	109	12 17	42	109	11 35	42	110	10 53	43	111	10 10	42	112
67	13 41	42	109	12 59	42	110	12 17	42	111	11 35	43	112	10 52	42	112
66	14 24	42	110	13 42	43	111	12 59	42	112	12 17	43	112	11 34	42	113
65	15 06	−42	111	14 24	−43	112	13 41	−42	112	12 59	−43	113	12 16	−43	114
64	15 48	42	112	15 06	43	112	14 23	43	113	13 40	43	114	12 57	43	114
63	16 31	43	112	15 48	43	113	15 05	43	114	14 22	44	114	13 38	43	115
62	17 12	43	113	16 29	43	114	15 46	43	114	15 03	44	115	14 19	43	116
61	17 54	43	114	17 11	44	114	16 27	43	115	15 44	44	116	15 00	44	117
60	18 35	−43	115	17 52	−44	115	17 08	−44	116	16 24	−44	117	15 40	−44	117
59	19 16	43	115	18 33	44	116	17 49	44	117	17 05	45	117	16 20	44	118
58	19 57	44	116	19 13	44	117	18 29	44	117	17 45	45	118	17 00	45	119
57	20 38	45	117	19 53	44	118	19 09	45	118	18 24	44	119	17 40	45	120
56	21 18	45	118	20 33	44	118	19 49	45	119	19 04	45	120	18 19	45	120
55	21 58	−45	118	21 13	−45	119	20 28	−45	120	19 43	−45	121	18 58	−46	121
54	22 38	45	119	21 53	46	120	21 07	45	121	20 22	46	121	19 36	45	122
53	23 17	45	120	22 32	46	121	21 46	46	121	21 00	45	122	20 15	47	123
52	23 56	46	121	23 10	45	122	22 25	46	122	21 39	47	123	20 52	46	124
51	24 35	46	122	23 49	46	122	23 03	47	123	22 16	46	124	21 30	47	124
50	25 13	−46	123	24 27	−46	123	23 41	−47	124	22 54	−47	125	22 07	−47	125
49	25 51	46	123	25 05	47	124	24 18	47	125	23 31	47	125	22 44	47	126
48	26 29	47	124	25 42	47	125	24 55	47	126	24 08	48	126	23 20	47	127
47	27 06	47	125	26 19	47	126	25 32	48	126	24 44	48	127	23 56	48	128
46	27 43	47	126	26 56	48	127	26 08	48	127	25 20	48	128	24 32	48	129
45	28 19	−47	127	27 32	−48	128	26 44	−49	128	25 55	−48	129	25 07	−49	130
44	28 55	48	128	28 07	48	128	27 19	49	129	26 30	48	130	25 42	49	130
43	29 31	48	129	28 43	49	129	27 54	49	130	27 05	49	131	26 16	49	131
42	30 06	49	130	29 17	49	130	28 28	49	131	27 39	49	132	26 50	50	132
41	30 41	49	131	29 52	50	131	29 02	49	132	28 13	50	133	27 23	50	133
40	31 15	−50	132	30 25	−49	132	29 36	−50	133	28 46	−50	133	27 56	−50	134
39	31 49	50	133	30 59	50	133	30 09	50	134	29 19	51	134	28 28	50	135
38	32 22	50	133	31 32	51	134	30 41	50	135	29 51	51	135	29 00	51	136
37	32 54	50	134	32 04	51	135	31 13	51	136	30 22	51	136	29 31	51	137
36	33 26	50	135	32 36	52	136	31 44	51	137	30 53	51	137	30 02	52	138
35	33 58	−51	137	33 07	−52	137	32 15	−51	138	31 24	−52	138	30 32	−52	139
34	34 29	52	138	33 37	52	138	32 45	52	139	31 53	52	139	31 01	52	140
33	34 59	52	139	34 07	52	139	33 15	52	140	32 23	53	140	31 30	52	141
32	35 29	53	140	34 36	52	140	33 44	53	141	32 51	53	141	31 58	53	142
31	35 58	53	141	35 05	53	141	34 12	53	142	33 19	53	142	32 26	53	143
30	36 26	−53	142	35 33	−53	142	34 40	−53	143	33 47	−54	143	32 53	−54	144
29	36 54	54	143	36 00	53	143	35 07	54	144	34 13	54	145	33 19	54	145
28	37 21	54	144	36 27	54	145	35 33	54	145	34 39	54	146	33 45	54	146
27	37 47	54	145	36 53	54	146	35 59	55	146	35 04	54	147	34 10	55	147
26	38 13	55	146	37 18	54	147	36 24	55	147	35 29	55	148	34 34	55	148
25	38 38	−55	147	37 43	−55	148	36 48	−55	148	35 53	−56	149	34 57	−55	149
24	39 02	56	149	38 06	55	149	37 11	55	150	36 16	56	150	35 20	56	151
23	39 25	56	150	38 29	55	150	37 34	56	151	36 38	56	151	35 42	56	152
22	39 47	56	151	38 51	56	151	37 55	56	152	36 59	56	152	36 03	56	153
21	40 09	56	152	39 13	57	153	38 16	56	153	37 20	57	154	36 23	56	154
20	40 29	−56	153	39 33	−57	154	38 36	−56	154	37 40	−57	155	36 43	−57	155
19	40 49	56	155	39 53	57	155	38 56	57	156	37 59	57	156	37 02	58	156
18	41 08	57	156	40 11	57	156	39 14	57	157	38 17	58	157	37 19	57	157
17	41 26	57	157	40 29	58	158	39 31	57	158	38 34	58	158	37 36	57	159
16	41 43	57	158	40 46	58	159	39 48	58	159	38 50	58	160	37 52	57	160
15	42 00	−58	160	41 02	−58	160	40 04	−58	160	39 06	−58	161	38 08	−59	161
14	42 15	58	161	41 17	59	161	40 18	58	162	39 20	58	162	38 22	59	162
13	42 29	58	162	41 31	59	163	40 32	58	163	39 34	59	163	38 35	58	164
12	42 42	58	164	41 44	59	164	40 45	59	164	39 46	58	165	38 48	59	165
11	42 55	59	165	41 56	59	165	40 57	59	166	39 58	59	166	38 59	59	166
10	43 06	−59	166	42 07	−59	167	41 08	−59	167	40 09	−59	167	39 10	−60	167
9	43 16	59	168	42 17	59	168	41 18	60	168	40 18	59	168	39 19	59	169
8	43 25	59	169	42 26	60	169	41 26	59	169	40 27	59	170	39 28	60	170
7	43 33	59	170	42 34	60	171	41 34	59	171	40 35	60	171	39 35	59	171
6	43 40	59	172	42 41	60	172	41 41	60	172	40 41	59	172	39 42	60	172
5	43 46	−59	173	42 47	−60	173	41 47	−60	173	40 47	−60	174	39 47	−59	174
4	43 51	60	175	42 51	59	175	41 52	60	175	40 52	60	175	39 52	60	175
3	43 55	60	176	42 55	60	176	41 55	60	176	40 55	60	176	39 55	59	176
2	43 58	60	177	42 58	60	177	41 58	60	177	40 58	60	177	39 58	60	177
1	44 00	60	179	43 00	60	179	42 00	60	179	41 00	60	179	40 00	60	179
0	44 00	−60	180	43 00	−60	180	42 00	−60	180	41 00	−60	180	40 00	−60	180

LHA	10° Hc	10° d	10° Z	11° Hc	11° d	11° Z	12° Hc	12° d	12° Z	13° Hc	13° d	13° Z	14° Hc	14° d	14° Z	LHA
	° ′	′	°	° ′	′	°	° ′	′	°	° ′	′	°	° ′	′	°	
69	08 46	42	112	08 04	42	112	07 22	42	113	06 40	43	114	05 57	42	114	291
68	09 28	42	112	08 46	43	113	08 03	42	114	07 21	43	114	06 38	42	115	292
67	10 10	43	113	09 27	42	114	08 45	43	114	08 02	43	115	07 19	43	116	293
66	10 52	43	114	10 09	43	114	09 26	43	115	08 43	43	116	08 00	43	117	294
65	11 33	−43	114	10 50	−43	115	10 07	−43	116	09 24	−44	117	08 40	−43	117	295
64	12 14	43	115	11 31	44	116	10 47	43	117	10 04	44	117	09 20	43	118	296
63	12 55	44	116	12 11	43	117	11 28	44	117	10 44	44	118	10 00	44	119	297
62	13 36	44	117	12 52	44	117	12 08	44	118	11 24	44	119	10 40	44	119	298
61	14 16	44	117	13 32	44	118	12 48	44	119	12 04	45	119	11 19	44	120	299
60	14 56	−44	118	14 12	−45	119	13 27	−44	119	12 43	−45	120	11 58	−44	121	300
59	15 36	45	119	14 51	44	120	14 07	45	120	13 22	45	121	12 37	45	122	301
58	16 15	44	120	15 31	45	120	14 46	45	121	14 01	45	122	13 16	46	122	302
57	16 55	45	120	16 10	46	121	15 24	45	122	14 39	45	122	13 54	46	123	303
56	17 34	46	121	16 48	45	122	16 03	46	123	15 17	46	123	14 31	45	124	304
55	18 12	−45	122	17 27	−46	123	16 41	−46	123	15 55	−46	124	15 09	−46	125	305
54	18 51	46	123	18 05	46	123	17 19	47	124	16 32	46	125	15 46	46	125	306
53	19 28	46	124	18 42	46	124	17 56	47	125	17 09	46	126	16 23	47	126	307
52	20 06	46	124	19 20	47	125	18 33	47	126	17 46	47	126	16 59	47	127	308
51	20 43	47	125	19 56	46	126	19 10	48	126	18 22	47	127	17 35	47	128	309
50	21 20	−47	126	20 33	−47	127	19 46	−48	127	18 58	−47	128	18 11	−48	129	310
49	21 57	48	127	21 09	47	127	20 22	48	128	19 34	48	129	18 46	48	129	311
48	22 33	48	128	21 45	48	128	20 57	48	129	20 09	48	130	19 21	48	130	312
47	23 08	48	128	22 20	48	129	21 32	48	130	20 44	49	130	19 55	48	131	313
46	23 44	49	129	22 55	48	130	22 07	49	131	21 18	49	131	20 29	49	132	314
45	24 18	−48	130	23 30	−49	131	22 41	−49	131	21 52	−49	132	21 03	−50	133	315
44	24 53	49	131	24 04	49	132	23 15	50	132	22 25	49	133	21 36	50	134	316
43	25 27	50	132	24 37	49	133	23 48	50	133	22 58	50	134	22 08	50	134	317
42	26 00	49	133	25 11	50	134	24 21	50	134	23 31	51	135	22 40	50	135	318
41	26 33	50	134	25 43	50	134	24 53	50	135	24 03	51	136	23 12	51	136	319
40	27 06	−51	135	26 15	−50	135	25 25	−51	136	24 34	−51	137	23 43	−51	137	320
39	27 38	51	136	26 47	51	136	25 56	51	137	25 05	51	137	24 14	52	138	321
38	28 09	51	137	27 18	51	137	26 27	52	138	25 35	51	138	24 44	52	139	322
37	28 40	52	138	27 48	51	138	26 57	52	139	26 05	52	139	25 13	52	140	323
36	29 10	52	139	28 18	52	139	27 26	52	140	26 34	52	140	25 42	52	141	324
35	29 40	−52	140	28 48	−52	140	27 56	−53	141	27 03	−52	141	26 11	−53	142	325
34	30 09	52	140	29 17	53	141	28 24	53	142	27 31	53	142	26 38	53	143	326
33	30 38	53	141	29 45	53	142	28 52	53	143	27 59	53	143	27 06	54	144	327
32	31 05	53	143	30 12	53	143	29 19	53	144	28 26	54	144	27 32	53	145	328
31	31 33	54	144	30 39	53	144	29 46	54	145	28 52	54	145	27 58	54	146	329
30	31 59	−53	145	31 06	−54	145	30 12	−54	146	29 18	−55	146	28 23	−54	147	330
29	32 25	54	146	31 31	54	146	30 37	54	147	29 43	55	147	28 48	54	148	331
28	32 51	55	147	31 56	54	147	31 02	55	148	30 07	55	148	29 12	55	149	332
27	33 15	55	148	32 20	55	148	31 25	55	149	30 30	55	149	29 35	55	150	333
26	33 39	55	149	32 44	55	149	31 49	56	150	30 53	55	150	29 58	56	151	334
25	34 02	−55	150	33 07	−56	150	32 11	−55	151	31 16	−56	151	30 20	−56	152	335
24	34 24	55	151	33 29	56	151	32 33	56	152	31 37	56	152	30 41	56	153	336
23	34 46	56	152	33 50	56	153	32 54	56	153	31 58	57	153	31 01	56	154	337
22	35 07	56	153	34 11	57	154	33 14	56	154	32 18	57	154	31 21	57	155	338
21	35 27	57	154	34 30	56	155	33 34	57	155	32 37	57	156	31 40	57	156	339
20	35 46	−57	156	34 49	−57	156	33 52	−57	156	32 55	−57	157	31 58	−57	157	340
19	36 04	57	157	35 07	57	157	34 10	57	157	33 13	58	158	32 15	57	158	341
18	36 22	57	158	35 25	58	158	34 27	58	159	33 29	57	159	32 32	58	159	342
17	36 39	58	159	35 41	58	159	34 43	58	160	33 45	57	160	32 48	58	160	343
16	36 55	58	160	35 57	58	161	34 59	59	161	34 00	58	161	33 02	58	161	344
15	37 09	−58	161	36 11	−58	162	35 13	−58	162	34 15	−59	162	33 16	−58	163	345
14	37 23	58	163	36 25	58	163	35 27	59	163	34 28	58	163	33 30	59	164	346
13	37 37	59	164	36 38	59	164	35 39	58	164	34 41	59	165	33 42	59	165	347
12	37 49	59	165	36 50	59	165	35 51	59	166	34 52	59	166	33 53	59	166	348
11	38 00	59	166	37 01	59	166	36 02	59	167	35 03	59	167	34 04	59	167	349
10	38 10	−59	167	37 11	−59	168	36 12	−59	168	35 13	−59	168	34 14	−60	168	350
9	38 20	60	169	37 20	59	169	36 21	59	169	35 22	60	169	34 22	59	169	351
8	38 28	59	170	37 29	60	170	36 29	59	170	35 30	60	170	34 30	59	171	352
7	38 36	60	171	37 36	60	171	36 36	59	172	35 37	60	172	34 37	59	172	353
6	38 42	60	172	37 42	59	173	36 43	60	173	35 43	60	173	34 43	59	173	354
5	38 48	−60	174	37 48	−60	174	36 48	−60	174	35 48	−60	174	34 48	−59	174	355
4	38 52	60	175	37 52	60	175	36 52	60	175	35 52	59	175	34 53	60	175	356
3	38 56	60	176	37 56	60	176	36 56	60	176	35 56	60	176	34 56	60	176	357
2	38 58	60	178	37 58	60	178	36 58	60	178	35 58	60	178	34 58	60	178	358
1	39 00	60	179	38 00	60	179	37 00	60	179	36 00	60	179	35 00	60	179	359
0	39 00	−60	180	38 00	−60	180	37 00	−60	180	36 00	−60	180	35 00	−60	180	360

S. Lat. {LHA greater than 180°....... Zn=180−Z; LHA less than 180°........... Zn=180+Z}

DECLINATION (0°-14°) CONTRARY NAME TO LATITUDE

LAT 41°

N. Lat. {LHA greater than 180° .... Zn=Z / LHA less than 180° .... Zn=360−Z}

DECLINATION (15°-29°) SAME NAME AS LATITUDE

LHA	15° Hc	d	Z	16° Hc	d	Z	17° Hc	d	Z	18° Hc	d	Z	19° Hc	d	Z	LHA
	° ′	′	°	° ′	′	°	° ′	′	°	° ′	′	°	° ′	′	°	
0	64 00	+60	180	65 00	+60	180	66 00	+60	180	67 00	+60	180	68 00	+60	180	360
1	63 59	60	178	64 59	60	178	65 59	60	178	66 59	60	178	67 59	60	178	359
2	63 57	59	176	64 56	60	176	65 56	60	175	66 56	60	175	67 56	60	175	358
3	63 52	60	173	64 52	60	173	65 52	59	173	66 51	60	173	67 51	60	173	357
4	63 46	60	171	64 46	59	171	65 45	60	171	66 45	59	170	67 44	60	170	356
5	63 38	+60	169	64 38	+59	169	65 37	+59	168	66 36	+59	168	67 35	+59	168	355
6	63 29	59	167	64 28	59	167	65 27	59	166	66 26	59	166	67 25	58	165	354
7	63 18	59	165	64 17	58	164	65 15	59	164	66 14	58	163	67 12	58	163	353
8	63 05	59	163	64 04	58	162	65 02	58	162	66 00	58	161	66 58	57	160	352
9	62 51	58	161	63 49	58	160	64 47	57	159	65 44	58	159	66 42	57	158	351
10	62 35	+58	159	63 33	+57	158	64 30	+57	157	65 27	+57	157	66 24	+56	156	350
11	62 18	57	157	63 15	57	156	64 12	56	155	65 08	57	155	66 05	55	154	349
12	61 59	57	155	62 56	56	154	63 52	56	153	64 48	56	152	65 44	55	151	348
13	61 39	56	153	62 35	56	152	63 31	55	151	64 26	55	150	65 21	55	149	347
14	61 18	55	151	62 13	55	150	63 08	55	149	64 03	54	148	64 57	54	147	346
15	60 55	+55	149	61 50	+55	148	62 45	+54	147	63 39	+53	146	64 32	+54	145	345
16	60 31	55	147	61 26	53	146	62 19	54	145	63 13	53	144	64 06	52	143	344
17	60 06	54	146	61 00	53	145	61 53	53	144	62 46	52	143	63 38	52	142	343
18	59 40	53	144	60 33	53	143	61 26	52	142	62 18	52	141	63 10	51	140	342
19	59 13	52	142	60 05	52	141	60 57	52	140	61 49	51	139	62 40	50	138	341
20	58 45	+51	141	59 36	+52	140	60 28	+51	138	61 19	+50	137	62 09	+50	136	340
21	58 15	51	139	59 06	51	138	59 57	50	137	60 47	50	136	61 37	49	135	339
22	57 45	51	137	58 36	50	136	59 26	49	135	60 15	49	134	61 04	49	133	338
23	57 14	50	136	58 04	49	135	58 53	49	133	59 42	49	133	60 31	47	131	337
24	56 42	49	134	57 31	49	133	58 20	49	132	59 09	47	131	59 56	47	130	336
25	56 09	+49	133	56 58	+48	132	57 46	+48	131	58 34	+47	130	59 21	+47	128	335
26	55 35	49	132	56 24	48	130	57 12	47	129	57 59	46	128	58 45	46	127	334
27	55 01	48	130	55 49	47	129	56 36	47	128	57 23	46	127	58 09	45	126	333
28	54 26	47	129	55 13	47	128	56 00	46	127	56 46	46	125	57 32	44	124	332
29	53 51	46	128	54 37	47	126	55 24	45	125	56 09	45	124	56 54	44	123	331
30	53 14	+47	126	54 01	+45	125	54 46	+45	124	55 31	+45	123	56 16	+43	122	330
31	52 37	46	125	53 23	45	124	54 08	45	123	54 53	44	122	55 37	43	120	329
32	52 00	45	124	52 45	45	123	53 30	44	122	54 14	44	120	54 58	42	119	328
33	51 22	45	123	52 07	44	122	52 51	44	120	53 35	43	119	54 18	42	118	327
34	50 44	44	121	51 28	44	120	52 12	43	119	52 55	43	118	53 38	42	117	326
35	50 05	+44	120	50 49	+43	119	51 32	+43	118	52 15	+42	117	52 57	+42	116	325
36	49 26	43	119	50 09	43	118	50 52	43	117	51 35	41	116	52 16	41	115	324
37	48 46	43	118	49 29	43	117	50 12	42	116	50 54	41	115	51 35	41	114	323
38	48 06	43	117	48 49	42	116	49 31	41	115	50 12	41	114	50 53	41	113	322
39	47 25	43	116	48 08	42	115	48 50	41	114	49 31	40	113	50 11	40	112	321
40	46 44	+42	115	47 26	+42	114	48 08	+41	113	48 49	+40	112	49 29	+40	111	320
41	46 03	42	114	46 45	41	113	47 26	41	112	48 07	40	111	48 47	39	110	319
42	45 22	41	113	46 03	41	112	46 44	40	111	47 24	40	110	48 04	39	109	318
43	44 40	41	112	45 21	41	111	46 02	40	110	46 42	39	109	47 21	39	108	317
44	43 58	41	111	44 39	40	110	45 19	40	109	45 59	39	108	46 38	38	107	316
45	43 15	+41	110	43 56	+40	109	44 36	+39	108	45 15	+39	107	45 54	+38	106	315
46	42 33	40	109	43 13	40	108	43 53	39	107	44 32	39	106	45 11	38	105	314
47	41 50	40	109	42 30	40	108	43 10	39	107	43 49	38	106	44 27	38	104	313
48	41 07	40	108	41 47	39	107	42 26	39	106	43 05	38	105	43 43	38	104	312
49	40 24	39	107	41 03	39	106	41 42	39	105	42 21	38	104	42 59	37	103	311
50	39 40	+40	106	40 20	+39	105	40 59	+38	104	41 37	+38	103	42 15	+37	102	310
51	38 57	39	105	39 36	39	104	40 15	38	103	40 53	37	102	41 30	37	101	309
52	38 13	39	104	38 52	38	103	39 30	38	102	40 08	38	101	40 46	37	100	308
53	37 29	39	104	38 08	38	103	38 46	38	102	39 24	37	101	40 01	37	100	307
54	36 45	39	103	37 24	38	102	38 02	37	101	38 39	37	100	39 16	37	99	306
55	36 01	+38	102	36 39	+38	101	37 17	+38	100	37 55	+37	99	38 32	+36	98	305
56	35 16	39	101	35 55	38	100	36 33	37	99	37 10	37	98	37 47	36	98	304
57	34 32	38	101	35 10	38	100	35 48	37	99	36 25	37	98	37 02	36	97	303
58	33 47	38	100	34 25	38	99	35 03	37	98	35 40	37	97	36 17	36	96	302
59	33 03	38	99	33 41	37	98	34 18	37	97	34 55	37	96	35 32	36	95	301
60	32 18	+38	98	32 56	+37	97	33 33	+37	96	34 10	+37	96	34 47	+36	95	300
61	31 33	38	98	32 11	37	97	32 48	37	96	33 25	37	95	34 02	36	94	299
62	30 48	38	97	31 26	37	96	32 03	37	95	32 40	36	94	33 16	36	93	298
63	30 03	38	96	30 41	37	95	31 18	37	94	31 55	36	93	32 31	36	92	297
64	29 18	38	95	29 56	37	95	30 33	36	94	31 09	37	93	31 46	36	92	296
65	28 33	+37	95	29 10	+37	94	29 47	+37	93	30 24	+37	92	31 01	+36	91	295
66	27 48	37	94	28 25	37	93	29 02	37	92	29 39	36	91	30 15	36	90	294
67	27 03	37	93	27 40	37	93	28 17	37	92	28 54	36	91	29 30	36	90	293
68	26 17	38	93	26 55	37	92	27 32	36	91	28 08	37	90	28 45	36	89	292
69	25 32	37	92	26 09	37	91	26 46	37	90	27 23	36	90	27 59	36	89	291

LHA	20° Hc	d	Z	21° Hc	d	Z	22° Hc	d	Z	23° Hc	d	Z	24° Hc	d	Z	LHA
	° ′	′	°	° ′	′	°	° ′	′	°	° ′	′	°	° ′	′	°	
0	69 00	+60	180	70 00	+60	180	71 00	+60	180	72 00	+60	180	73 00	+60	180	360
1	68 59	60	177	69 59	60	177	70 59	60	177	71 59	60	177	72 59	60	177	359
2	68 56	60	175	69 56	60	175	70 56	59	174	71 55	60	174	72 55	60	174	358
3	68 51	59	172	69 50	60	172	70 50	60	172	71 50	59	171	72 49	59	171	357
4	68 44	59	170	69 43	59	169	70 42	59	169	71 41	59	168	72 40	59	168	356
5	68 34	+59	167	69 33	+59	167	70 32	+59	166	71 31	+59	165	72 30	+55	165	355
6	68 23	59	165	69 22	58	164	70 20	58	163	71 18	59	163	72 17	57	162	354
7	68 10	58	162	69 08	58	161	70 06	58	161	71 04	57	160	72 01	57	159	353
8	67 55	58	160	68 53	57	159	69 50	57	158	70 47	57	157	71 44	56	156	352
9	67 39	57	157	68 36	56	156	69 32	57	156	70 29	56	155	71 25	55	153	351
10	67 20	+57	155	68 17	+56	154	69 13	+55	153	70 08	+55	152	71 03	+55	151	350
11	67 00	56	153	67 56	55	152	68 51	55	151	69 46	54	150	70 40	54	148	349
12	66 39	55	151	67 34	54	149	68 28	54	148	69 22	54	147	70 16	52	146	348
13	66 16	54	148	67 10	54	147	68 04	53	146	68 57	52	145	69 49	52	143	347
14	65 51	54	146	66 45	53	145	67 38	52	144	68 30	52	143	69 22	51	141	346
15	65 26	+52	144	66 18	+52	143	67 10	+52	142	68 02	+51	140	68 53	+50	139	345
16	64 58	52	142	65 50	52	141	66 42	50	140	67 32	50	138	68 22	49	137	344
17	64 30	51	140	65 21	51	139	66 12	50	138	67 02	49	136	67 51	48	135	343
18	64 01	50	139	64 51	50	137	65 41	49	136	66 30	48	135	67 18	48	133	342
19	63 30	50	137	64 20	49	135	65 09	48	134	65 57	48	133	66 45	46	131	341
20	62 59	+49	135	63 48	+48	134	64 36	+47	132	65 23	+47	131	66 10	+46	129	340
21	62 26	48	133	63 14	48	132	64 02	47	131	64 49	46	129	65 35	44	128	339
22	61 53	47	132	62 40	47	130	63 27	46	129	64 13	45	128	64 58	44	126	338
23	61 18	47	130	62 05	47	129	62 52	45	127	63 37	44	126	64 21	44	124	337
24	60 43	47	129	61 30	45	127	62 15	45	126	63 00	44	124	63 44	42	123	336
25	60 08	+45	127	60 53	+45	126	61 38	+44	124	62 22	+43	123	63 05	+42	122	335
26	59 31	45	126	60 16	45	124	61 01	43	123	61 44	42	122	62 26	42	120	334
27	58 54	45	124	59 39	43	123	60 22	43	122	61 05	42	120	61 47	41	119	333
28	58 16	44	123	59 00	44	122	59 44	42	120	60 26	41	119	61 07	40	117	332
29	57 38	44	122	58 22	42	120	59 04	42	119	59 46	41	118	60 27	39	116	331
30	56 59	+43	120	57 42	+42	119	58 24	+41	118	59 05	+41	116	59 46	+39	115	330
31	56 20	42	119	57 02	42	118	57 44	41	117	58 25	39	115	59 04	39	114	329
32	55 40	42	118	56 22	41	117	57 03	41	115	57 44	39	114	58 23	38	113	328
33	55 00	42	117	55 42	40	116	56 22	40	114	57 02	39	113	57 41	38	112	327
34	54 20	41	116	55 01	40	114	55 41	39	113	56 20	39	112	56 59	37	110	326
35	53 39	+40	115	54 19	+40	113	54 59	+39	112	55 38	+38	111	56 16	+37	109	325
36	52 57	40	114	53 37	40	112	54 17	38	111	54 55	38	110	55 33	37	108	324
37	52 16	39	113	52 55	39	111	53 34	39	110	54 13	37	109	54 50	36	107	323
38	51 34	39	112	52 13	39	110	52 52	38	109	53 30	37	108	54 07	36	106	322
39	50 51	39	111	51 30	39	109	52 09	37	108	52 46	37	107	53 23	36	105	321
40	50 09	+39	110	50 48	+38	108	51 26	+37	107	52 03	+36	106	52 39	+36	105	320
41	49 26	38	109	50 04	38	107	50 42	37	106	51 19	36	105	51 55	36	104	319
42	48 43	38	108	49 21	38	107	49 59	36	105	50 35	36	104	51 11	35	103	318
43	48 00	38	107	48 38	37	106	49 15	36	104	49 51	36	103	50 27	35	102	317
44	47 16	38	106	47 54	37	105	48 31	36	104	49 07	36	102	49 43	34	101	316
45	46 32	+38	105	47 10	+37	104	47 47	+36	103	48 23	+35	102	48 58	+35	100	315
46	45 49	37	104	46 26	37	103	47 03	35	102	47 38	36	101	48 14	34	99	314
47	45 05	37	103	45 42	36	102	46 18	36	101	46 54	35	100	47 29	34	99	313
48	44 21	36	103	44 57	37	101	45 34	35	100	46 09	35	99	46 44	34	98	312
49	43 36	37	102	44 13	36	101	44 49	35	99	45 24	35	98	45 59	34	97	311
50	42 52	+36	101	43 28	+36	100	44 04	+36	99	44 40	+34	98	45 14	+34	96	310
51	42 07	37	100	42 44	36	99	43 20	35	98	43 55	34	97	44 29	34	96	309
52	41 23	36	99	41 59	36	98	42 35	35	97	43 10	34	96	43 44	34	95	308
53	40 38	36	99	41 14	36	98	41 50	35	96	42 25	34	95	42 59	34	94	307
54	39 53	36	98	40 29	36	97	41 05	35	96	41 40	34	95	42 14	33	94	306
55	39 08	+36	97	39 44	+36	96	40 20	+34	95	40 54	+35	94	41 29	+33	93	305
56	38 23	36	96	38 59	35	95	39 34	35	94	40 09	34	93	40 43	34	92	304
57	37 38	36	96	38 14	35	95	38 49	35	94	39 24	34	93	39 58	34	92	303
58	36 53	36	95	37 29	35	94	38 04	35	93	38 39	34	92	39 13	33	91	302
59	36 08	36	94	36 44	35	93	37 19	34	92	37 53	35	91	38 28	33	90	301
60	35 23	+35	94	35 58	+36	93	36 34	+34	92	37 08	+34	91	37 42	+34	90	300
61	34 38	35	93	35 13	35	92	35 48	35	91	36 23	34	90	36 57	34	89	299
62	33 52	36	92	34 28	35	91	35 03	35	90	35 38	34	89	36 12	33	88	298
63	33 07	36	92	33 43	35	91	34 18	34	90	34 52	35	89	35 26	34	88	297
64	32 22	35	91	32 57	35	90	33 32	35	89	34 07	34	88	34 41	34	87	296
65	31 37	+35	90	32 12	+35	89	32 47	+35	88	33 22	+34	87	33 56	+34	86	295
66	30 51	36	90	31 27	35	89	32 02	35	88	32 37	34	87	33 11	34	86	294
67	30 06	36	89	30 42	35	88	31 17	34	87	31 51	35	86	32 26	34	85	293
68	29 21	35	88	29 56	35	87	30 31	35	86	31 06	35	85	31 41	34	84	292
69	28 35	36	88	29 11	35	87	29 46	35	86	30 21	35	85	30 56	34	84	291

LHA	25° Hc	d	Z	26° Hc	d	Z	27° Hc	d	Z	28° Hc	d	Z	29° Hc	d	Z	LHA
	° ′	′	°	° ′	′	°	° ′	′	°	° ′	′	°	° ′	′	°	
0	74 00	+60	180	75 00	+60	180	76 00	+60	180	77 00	+60	180	78 00	+60	180	360
1	73 59	60	177	74 59	60	177	75 59	59	176	76 58	60	176	77 58	60	176	359
2	73 55	60	173	74 55	59	173	75 54	60	173	76 54	59	172	77 53	60	172	358
3	73 48	60	170	74 48	59	170	75 47	59	169	76 46	59	168	77 45	59	168	357
4	73 39	59	167	74 38	59	166	75 37	59	166	76 36	58	165	77 34	58	164	356
5	73 28	+58	164	74 26	+58	163	75 24	+58	162	76 22	+58	161	77 20	+57	160	355
6	73 14	58	161	74 12	57	160	75 09	57	159	76 06	57	157	77 03	55	156	354
7	72 58	57	158	73 55	57	157	74 52	55	155	75 47	56	154	76 43	54	152	353
8	72 40	56	155	73 36	56	154	74 32	54	152	75 26	55	151	76 21	53	149	352
9	72 20	55	152	73 15	55	151	74 10	53	149	75 03	53	148	75 56	52	146	351
10	71 58	+54	149	72 52	+53	148	73 45	+53	146	74 38	+52	145	75 30	+50	143	350
11	71 34	53	147	72 27	52	145	73 19	52	144	74 11	50	142	75 01	49	140	349
12	71 08	53	144	72 01	51	143	72 52	50	141	73 42	49	139	74 31	48	137	348
13	70 41	51	142	71 32	51	140	72 23	49	139	73 12	48	137	74 00	46	135	347
14	70 13	50	140	71 03	49	138	71 52	48	136	72 40	47	134	73 27	45	132	346
15	69 43	+49	137	70 32	+48	136	71 20	+47	134	72 07	+45	132	72 52	+45	130	345
16	69 11	49	135	70 00	47	134	70 47	46	132	71 33	44	130	72 17	43	128	344
17	68 39	47	133	69 26	46	132	70 12	45	130	70 57	44	128	71 41	42	126	343
18	68 06	46	131	68 52	45	130	69 37	44	128	70 21	42	126	71 03	41	124	342
19	67 31	46	130	68 17	44	128	69 01	43	126	69 44	41	124	70 25	40	122	341
20	66 56	+44	128	67 40	+44	126	68 24	+42	124	69 06	+41	122	69 47	+39	120	340
21	66 19	44	126	67 03	43	124	67 46	41	123	68 27	40	121	69 07	38	118	339
22	65 42	44	124	66 26	41	123	67 07	41	121	67 48	39	119	68 27	37	117	338
23	65 05	42	123	65 47	41	121	66 28	40	119	67 08	38	117	67 46	37	115	337
24	64 26	42	121	65 08	40	120	65 48	39	118	66 27	38	116	67 05	36	114	336
25	63 47	+41	120	64 28	+40	118	65 08	+39	116	65 47	+37	115	66 24	+35	113	335
26	63 08	40	119	63 48	39	117	64 27	38	115	65 05	37	113	65 42	34	111	334
27	62 28	40	117	63 08	38	116	63 46	37	114	64 23	36	112	64 59	35	110	333
28	61 47	39	116	62 26	38	114	63 04	37	113	63 41	36	111	64 17	33	109	332
29	61 06	39	115	61 45	37	113	62 22	37	111	62 59	35	110	63 34	33	108	331
30	60 25	+38	113	61 03	+37	112	61 40	+36	110	62 16	+34	109	62 50	+33	107	330
31	59 43	38	112	60 21	36	111	60 57	36	109	61 33	34	107	62 07	32	106	329
32	59 01	37	111	59 38	36	110	60 14	35	108	60 49	34	106	61 23	32	105	328
33	58 19	37	110	58 56	35	109	59 31	35	107	60 06	33	105	60 39	32	104	327
34	57 36	36	109	58 12	36	108	58 48	34	106	59 22	33	104	59 55	32	103	326
35	56 53	+36	108	57 29	+35	106	58 04	+34	105	58 38	+33	103	59 11	+31	102	325
36	56 10	36	107	56 46	34	106	57 20	34	104	57 54	32	102	58 26	32	101	324
37	55 26	36	106	56 02	34	105	56 36	34	103	57 10	32	102	57 42	31	100	323
38	54 43	35	105	55 18	34	104	55 52	33	102	56 25	32	101	56 57	31	99	322
39	53 59	35	104	54 34	34	103	55 08	33	101	55 41	31	100	56 12	31	98	321
40	53 15	+35	103	53 50	+33	102	54 23	+33	100	54 56	+32	99	55 28	+30	98	320
41	52 31	34	102	53 05	34	101	53 39	32	100	54 11	32	98	54 43	30	97	319
42	51 46	35	102	52 21	33	100	52 54	32	99	53 26	32	97	53 58	30	96	318
43	51 02	34	101	51 36	33	99	52 09	32	98	52 41	31	97	53 13	30	95	317
44	50 17	34	100	50 51	33	99	51 24	32	97	51 56	31	96	52 27	30	94	316
45	49 33	+33	99	50 06	+33	98	50 39	+32	96	51 11	+31	95	51 42	+30	94	315
46	48 48	34	98	49 22	32	97	49 54	32	96	50 26	31	94	50 57	30	93	314
47	48 03	34	97	48 37	32	96	49 09	32	95	49 41	31	94	50 12	30	92	313
48	47 18	34	97	47 52	32	95	48 24	32	94	48 56	31	93	49 27	29	92	312
49	46 33	33	96	47 06	33	95	47 39	32	94	48 11	30	92	48 41	30	91	311
50	45 48	+33	95	46 21	+33	94	46 54	+31	93	47 25	+31	92	47 56	+30	90	310
51	45 03	33	95	45 36	32	93	46 08	32	92	46 40	31	91	47 11	30	90	309
52	44 18	33	94	44 51	32	93	45 23	32	91	45 55	30	90	46 25	30	89	308
53	43 33	33	93	44 06	32	92	44 38	31	91	45 09	31	90	45 40	30	88	307
54	42 47	33	92	43 20	33	91	43 53	31	90	44 24	31	89	44 55	30	88	306
55	42 02	+33	92	42 35	+32	91	43 07	+32	89	43 39	+31	88	44 10	+30	87	305
56	41 17	33	91	41 50	32	90	42 22	32	89	42 54	30	88	43 24	31	86	304
57	40 32	33	90	41 05	32	89	41 37	31	88	42 08	31	87	42 39	30	86	303
58	39 46	33	90	40 19	33	89	40 52	31	87	41 23	31	86	41 54	30	85	302
59	39 01	33	89	39 34	32	88	40 06	32	87	40 38	31	86	41 09	30	85	301
60	38 16	+33	88	38 49	+32	87	39 21	+32	86	39 53	+31	85	40 24	+30	84	300
61	37 31	33	88	38 04	32	87	38 36	32	86	39 08	31	85	39 39	31	84	299
62	36 45	33	87	37 18	33	86	37 51	32	85	38 23	31	84	38 54	31	83	298
63	36 00	33	87	36 33	33	86	37 06	32	84	37 38	31	83	38 09	31	82	297
64	35 15	33	86	35 48	33	85	36 21	32	84	36 53	31	83	37 24	31	82	296
65	34 30	+33	85	35 03	+33	84	35 36	+32	83	36 08	+31	82	36 39	+32	81	295
66	33 45	33	85	34 18	33	84	34 51	32	83	35 23	32	82	35 55	31	81	294
67	33 00	33	84	33 33	33	83	34 06	32	82	34 38	32	81	35 10	31	80	293
68	32 15	33	84	32 48	33	83	33 21	33	81	33 54	32	81	34 26	31	80	292
69	31 30	33	83	32 03	33	82	32 36	33	81	33 09	32	80	33 41	32	79	291

S. Lat. {LHA greater than 180° .... Zn=180−Z / LHA less than 180° .... Zn=180+Z}

DECLINATION (15°-29°) SAME NAME AS LATITUDE

LAT 41°

LAT 41°

N. Lat. {LHA greater than 180°....... Zn=Z; LHA less than 180°........... Zn=360−Z}

DECLINATION (15°-29°) SAME NAME AS LATITUDE

LHA	15° Hc	15° d	15° Z	16° Hc	16° d	16° Z	17° Hc	17° d	17° Z	18° Hc	18° d	18° Z	19° Hc	19° d	19° Z	20° Hc	20° d	20° Z	21° Hc	21° d	21° Z	22° Hc	22° d	22° Z	23° Hc	23° d	23° Z	24° Hc	24° d	24° Z	25° Hc	25° d	25° Z	26° Hc	26° d	26° Z	27° Hc	27° d	27° Z	28° Hc	28° d	28° Z	29° Hc	29° d	29° Z	LHA
	° ′	′	°	° ′	′	°	° ′	′	°	° ′	′	°	° ′	′	°	° ′	′	°	° ′	′	°	° ′	′	°	° ′	′	°	° ′	′	°	° ′	′	°	° ′	′	°	° ′	′	°	° ′	′	°	° ′	′	°	
70	24 47	+37	91	25 24	+37	91	26 01	+37	90	26 38	+36	89	27 14	+36	88	27 50	+36	87	28 26	+35	86	29 01	+35	85	29 36	+35	84	30 11	+34	83	30 45	+33	82	31 18	+34	81	31 52	+32	80	32 24	+33	79	32 57	+32	78	290
71	24 02	37	91	24 39	37	90	25 16	37	89	25 53	36	88	26 29	36	87	27 05	36	86	27 41	35	85	28 16	35	85	28 51	35	84	29 26	34	83	30 00	34	82	30 34	33	81	31 07	33	80	31 40	32	79	32 12	32	78	289
72	23 16	38	90	23 54	37	89	24 31	36	88	25 07	37	87	25 44	36	87	26 20	36	86	26 56	35	85	27 31	35	84	28 06	35	83	28 41	34	82	29 15	34	81	29 49	33	80	30 22	34	79	30 56	32	78	31 28	32	77	288
73	22 31	37	89	23 08	37	89	23 45	37	88	24 22	37	87	24 59	36	86	25 35	36	85	26 11	35	84	26 46	35	83	27 21	35	82	27 56	34	81	28 30	34	81	29 04	34	80	29 38	33	79	30 11	33	78	30 44	32	77	287
74	21 46	37	89	22 23	37	88	23 00	37	87	23 37	36	86	24 13	37	85	24 50	36	84	25 26	35	84	26 01	35	83	26 36	35	82	27 11	35	81	27 46	34	80	28 20	34	79	28 54	33	78	29 27	33	77	30 00	33	76	286
75	21 00	+38	88	21 38	+37	87	22 15	+37	86	22 52	+36	86	23 28	+37	85	24 05	+36	84	24 41	+35	83	25 16	+36	82	25 52	+35	81	26 27	+34	80	27 01	+35	79	27 36	+33	78	28 09	+34	78	28 43	+33	77	29 16	+33	76	285
76	20 15	38	87	20 53	37	87	21 30	37	86	22 07	36	85	22 43	37	84	23 20	36	83	23 56	35	82	24 31	36	81	25 07	35	81	25 42	35	80	26 17	34	79	26 51	34	78	27 25	34	77	27 59	33	76	28 32	33	75	284
77	19 30	37	87	20 07	38	86	20 45	37	85	21 22	36	84	21 58	37	83	22 35	36	83	23 11	36	82	23 47	35	81	24 22	35	80	24 57	35	79	25 32	35	78	26 07	34	77	26 41	34	76	27 15	34	75	27 49	33	75	283
78	18 45	37	86	19 22	37	85	19 59	38	85	20 37	36	84	21 13	37	83	21 50	36	82	22 26	36	81	23 02	36	80	23 38	35	79	24 13	35	79	24 48	35	78	25 23	34	77	25 57	34	76	26 31	34	75	27 05	33	74	282
79	18 00	37	86	18 37	37	85	19 14	38	84	19 52	36	83	20 28	37	82	21 05	36	81	21 41	36	81	22 17	36	80	22 53	36	79	23 29	35	78	24 04	35	77	24 39	34	76	25 13	35	75	25 48	34	74	26 22	33	73	281
80	17 15	+37	85	17 52	+37	84	18 29	+38	83	19 07	+37	82	19 44	+36	82	20 20	+37	81	20 57	+36	80	21 33	+36	79	22 09	+36	78	22 45	+35	77	23 20	+35	76	23 55	+35	76	24 30	+34	75	25 04	+34	74	25 38	+34	73	280
81	16 29	38	84	17 07	38	83	17 45	37	83	18 22	37	82	18 59	37	81	19 36	36	80	20 12	37	79	20 49	36	78	21 25	35	78	22 00	36	77	22 36	35	76	23 11	35	75	23 46	35	74	24 21	34	73	24 55	34	72	279
82	15 44	38	84	16 22	38	83	17 00	37	82	17 37	37	81	18 14	37	80	18 51	37	80	19 28	36	79	20 04	36	78	20 40	36	77	21 16	36	76	21 52	36	75	22 28	35	74	23 03	35	74	23 38	34	73	24 12	34	72	278
83	14 59	38	83	15 37	38	82	16 15	37	81	16 52	38	81	17 30	37	80	18 07	36	79	18 43	37	78	19 20	36	77	19 56	36	76	20 32	36	76	21 08	36	75	21 44	35	74	22 19	35	73	22 54	35	72	23 29	35	71	277
84	14 15	37	82	14 52	38	82	15 30	38	81	16 08	37	80	16 45	37	79	17 22	37	78	17 59	37	78	18 36	36	77	19 12	37	76	19 49	36	75	20 25	36	74	21 01	35	73	21 36	35	72	22 11	35	72	22 46	35	71	276
85	13 30	+38	82	14 08	+37	81	14 45	+38	80	15 23	+38	79	16 01	+37	79	16 38	+37	78	17 15	+37	77	17 52	+37	76	18 29	+36	75	19 05	+36	74	19 41	+36	74	20 17	+36	73	20 53	+35	72	21 28	+36	71	22 04	+35	70	275
86	12 45	38	81	13 23	38	80	14 01	38	80	14 39	37	79	15 16	38	78	15 54	37	77	16 31	37	76	17 08	37	75	17 45	36	75	18 21	37	74	18 58	36	73	19 34	36	72	20 10	36	71	20 46	35	70	21 21	35	70	274
87	12 00	38	81	12 38	38	80	13 16	38	79	13 54	38	78	14 32	38	77	15 10	37	77	15 47	37	76	16 24	37	75	17 01	37	74	17 38	37	73	18 15	36	72	18 51	36	72	19 27	36	71	20 03	36	70	20 39	35	69	273
88	11 16	38	80	11 54	38	79	12 32	38	78	13 10	38	78	13 48	38	77	14 26	37	76	15 03	38	75	15 41	37	74	16 18	37	73	16 55	37	73	17 32	36	72	18 08	37	71	18 45	36	70	19 21	36	69	19 57	35	68	272
89	10 31	38	79	11 09	39	78	11 48	38	78	12 26	38	77	13 04	38	76	13 42	37	75	14 19	38	74	14 57	37	74	15 34	38	73	16 12	37	72	16 49	36	71	17 25	37	70	18 02	36	70	18 38	37	69	19 15	36	68	271
90	09 47	+38	79	10 25	+39	78	11 04	+38	77	11 42	+38	76	12 20	+38	75	12 58	+38	75	13 36	+38	74	14 14	+37	73	14 51	+38	72	15 29	+37	71	16 06	+37	71	16 43	+37	70	17 20	+36	69	17 56	+37	68	18 33	+36	67	270
91	09 02	39	78	09 41	38	77	10 19	39	76	10 58	38	76	11 36	38	75	12 14	39	74	12 53	37	73	13 30	38	72	14 08	38	72	14 46	37	71	15 23	37	70	16 00	38	69	16 38	36	68	17 14	37	68	17 51	37	67	269
92	08 18	39	77	08 57	39	77	09 36	38	76	10 14	39	75	10 53	38	74	11 31	38	73	12 09	38	73	12 47	38	72	13 25	38	71	14 03	38	70	14 41	37	69	15 18	38	69	15 56	37	68	16 33	37	67	17 10	36	66	268
93	07 34	39	77	08 13	39	76	08 52	38	75	09 30	39	74	10 09	39	74	10 48	38	73	11 26	38	72	12 04	39	71	12 43	38	70	13 21	37	70	13 58	38	69	14 36	38	68	15 14	37	67	15 51	37	66	16 28	37	66	267
94	06 50	39	76	07 29	39	75	08 08	39	75	08 47	39	74	09 26	38	73	10 04	39	72	10 43	39	71	11 22	38	71	12 00	38	70	12 38	38	69	13 16	38	68	13 54	38	68	14 32	38	67	15 10	37	66	15 47	37	65	266
95	06 06	+39	75	06 45	+39	75	07 24	+40	74	08 04	+39	73	08 43	+38	72	09 21	+39	72	10 00	+39	71	10 39	+39	70	11 18	+38	69	11 56	+38	69	12 34	+38	68	13 12	+39	67	13 51	+37	66	14 28	+38	65	15 06	+38	65	265
96	05 22	40	75	06 02	39	74	06 41	39	73	07 20	39	73	07 59	40	72	08 39	39	71	09 18	38	70	09 56	39	69	10 35	39	69	11 14	39	68	11 53	38	67	12 31	38	66	13 09	38	66	13 47	38	65	14 25	38	64	264
97	04 39	39	74	05 18	40	73	05 58	39	73	06 37	40	72	07 17	39	71	07 56	39	70	08 35	39	70	09 14	39	69	09 53	39	68	10 32	39	67	11 11	39	67	11 50	38	66	12 28	39	65	13 07	38	64	13 45	38	63	263
98	03 55	40	73	04 35	40	73	05 15	39	72	05 54	40	71	06 34	39	71	07 13	40	70	07 53	39	69	08 32	39	68	09 11	39	67	09 50	39	67	10 29	39	66	11 08	39	65	11 47	39	64	12 26	38	64	13 04	39	63	262
99	03 12	40	73	03 52	40	72	04 32	39	71	05 11	40	71	05 51	40	70	06 31	40	69	07 11	39	68	07 50	40	68	08 30	39	67	09 09	39	66	09 48	39	65	10 27	39	65	11 06	39	64	11 45	39	63	12 24	39	62	261
100	02 29	+40	72	03 09	+40	71	03 49	+40	71	04 29	+40	70	05 09	+40	69	05 49	+40	69	06 29	+39	68	07 08	+40	67	07 48	+40	66	08 28	+39	65	09 07	+40	65	09 47	+39	64	10 26	+39	63	11 05	+39	62	11 44	+39	62	260
101	01 46	40	72	02 26	40	71	03 06	40	70	03 46	40	69	04 26	41	69	05 07	40	68	05 47	40	67	06 27	40	66	07 07	40	66	07 47	39	65	08 26	40	64	09 06	40	63	09 46	39	63	10 25	40	62	11 05	39	61	259
102	01 03	40	71	01 43	41	70	02 24	40	69	03 04	40	69	03 44	41	68	04 25	40	67	05 05	40	67	05 45	41	66	06 26	40	65	07 06	40	64	07 46	40	64	08 26	40	63	09 06	39	62	09 45	40	61	10 25	40	60	258
103	00 20	41	70	01 01	40	70	01 41	41	69	02 22	41	68	03 03	40	67	03 43	41	67	04 24	40	66	05 04	41	65	05 45	40	64	06 25	40	64	07 05	41	63	07 46	40	62	08 26	40	61	09 06	40	61	09 46	40	60	257
104	−0 23	41	70	00 18	41	69	00 59	41	68	01 40	41	67	02 21	41	67	03 02	40	66	03 42	41	65	04 23	41	64	05 04	41	64	05 45	40	63	06 25	41	62	07 06	40	62	07 46	41	61	08 27	40	60	09 07	40	59	256
105	−1 05	+41	69	−0 24	+41	68	00 17	+41	67	00 58	+41	67	01 39	+41	66	02 20	+41	65	03 01	+41	65	03 42	+41	64	04 23	+41	63	05 04	+41	62	05 45	+41	62	06 26	+41	61	07 07	+40	60	07 47	+41	59	08 28	+41	59	255
106	−1 47	41	68	−1 06	42	68	−0 24	41	67	00 17	41	66	00 58	41	65	01 39	42	65	02 21	41	64	03 02	41	63	03 43	41	62	04 24	41	62	05 05	42	61	05 47	41	60	06 28	41	60	07 09	40	59	07 49	41	58	254
107	−2 29	41	68	−1 48	42	67	−1 06	42	66	−0 24	41	65	00 17	42	65	00 59	41	64	01 40	42	63	02 22	41	63	03 03	42	62	03 45	41	61	04 26	41	60	05 07	42	60	05 49	41	59	06 30	41	58	07 11	41	58	253
108	−3 11	42	67	−2 29	42	66	−1 47	41	66	−1 06	42	65	−0 24	42	64	00 18	42	63	01 00	42	63	01 42	41	62	02 23	42	61	03 05	42	60	03 47	41	60	04 28	42	59	05 10	42	58	05 52	41	58	06 33	42	57	252
109	−3 52	42	66	−3 10	42	66	−2 28	42	65	−1 46	42	64	−1 04	42	63	−0 22	42	63	00 20	42	62	01 02	42	61	01 44	42	61	02 26	42	60	03 08	42	59	03 50	42	58	04 32	42	58	05 14	41	57	05 55	42	56	251
110	−4 34	+42	66	−3 52	+43	65	−3 09	+42	64	−2 27	+42	63	−1 45	+43	63	−1 02	+42	62	−0 20	+42	61	00 22	+42	61	01 04	+43	60	01 47	+42	59	02 29	+42	58	03 11	+42	58	03 53	+43	57	04 36	+42	56	05 18	+42	56	250
111	−5 15	43	65	−4 32	42	64	−3 50	43	63	−3 07	42	63	−2 25	43	62	−1 42	42	61	−1 00	43	61	−0 17	42	60	00 25	43	59	01 08	43	59	01 51	42	58	02 33	43	57	03 16	42	56	03 58	43	56	04 41	42	55	249
112	−5 56	43	64	−5 13	43	63	−4 30	42	63	−3 48	43	62	−3 05	43	61	−2 22	43	61	−1 39	43	60	−0 56	43	59	−0 13	42	59	00 29	43	58	01 12	43	57	01 55	43	56	02 38	43	56	03 21	43	55	04 04	42	54	248
113				−5 53	42	63	−5 11	44	62	−4 27	43	61	−3 44	43	61	−3 01	43	60	−2 18	43	59	−1 35	43	59	−0 52	43	58	−0 09	43	57	00 34	44	57	01 18	43	56	02 01	43	55	02 44	43	54	03 27	43	54	247
114							−5 50	43	61	−5 07	43	61	−4 24	44	60	−3 40	43	59	−2 57	43	59	−2 14	44	58	−1 30	43	57	−0 47	44	57	−0 03	43	56	00 40	44	55	01 24	43	55	02 07	44	54	02 51	43	53	246
115										−5 47	+44	60	−5 03	+44	59	−4 19	+43	59	−3 36	+44	58	−2 52	+44	57	−2 08	+44	57	−1 24	+43	56	−0 41	+44	55	00 03	+44	55	00 47	+44	54	01 31	+43	53	02 14	+44	53	245
116													−5 42	44	59	−4 58	44	58	−4 14	44	57	−3 30	44	57	−2 46	44	56	−2 02	44	55	−1 18	44	55	−0 34	45	54	00 11	44	53	00 55	44	53	01 39	44	52	244
117																−5 36	44	57	−4 52	45	57	−4 07	44	56	−3 23	44	55	−2 39	45	55	−1 54	44	54	−1 10	44	53	−0 26	45	53	00 19	44	52	01 03	45	51	243
118																−6 14	45	57	−5 29	44	56	−4 45	45	55	−4 00	44	55	−3 16	45	54	−2 31	45	53	−1 46	45	53	−1 01	44	52	−0 17	45	51	00 28	45	51	242
119																			−6 07	45	55	−5 22	45	54	−4 37	45	54	−3 52	45	53	−3 07	45	53	−2 22	45	52	−1 37	45	51	−0 52	45	51	−0 07	45	50	241
120																						−5 59	+46	54	−5 13	+45	53	−4 28	+45	53	−3 43	+46	52	−2 57	+45	51	−2 12	+45	51	−1 27	+46	50	−0 41	+45	49	240
121																									−5 49	45	52	−5 04	46	52	−4 18	46	51	−3 32	45	51	−2 47	46	50	−2 01	46	49	−1 15	45	49	239
122																												−5 39	46	51	−4 53	46	50	−4 07	46	50	−3 21	46	49	−2 35	46	49	−1 49	46	48	238
123																															−5 28	46	50	−4 42	47	49	−3 55	46	48	−3 09	46	48	−2 23	47	47	237
124																															−6 02	46	49	−5 16	47	48	−4 29	47	48	−3 42	46	47	−2 56	47	47	236
125																																		−5 49	+47	48	−5 02	+47	47	−4 15	+47	46	−3 28	+47	46	235
126																																					−5 35	47	46	−4 48	47	46	−4 01	48	45	234
127																																								−5 20	47	45	−4 33	48	44	233
128																																								−5 52	48	44	−5 04	48	44	232
129																																											−5 35	48	43	231

DECLINATION (15°-29°) CONTRARY NAME TO LATITUDE

LHA	15° Hc	15° d	15° Z	16° Hc	16° d	16° Z	17° Hc	17° d	17° Z	18° Hc	18° d	18° Z	19° Hc	19° d	19° Z	20° Hc	20° d	20° Z	21° Hc	21° d	21° Z	22° Hc	22° d	22° Z	23° Hc	23° d	23° Z	24° Hc	24° d	24° Z	25° Hc	25° d	25° Z	26° Hc	26° d	26° Z	27° Hc	27° d	27° Z	28° Hc	28° d	28° Z	29° Hc	29° d	29° Z	LHA
85	−6 06	−39	105																																											275
84	−5 22	40	105	−6 02	39	106																																								276
83	−4 39	39	106	−5 18	40	107	−5 58	39	107																																					277
82	−3 55	40	107	−4 35	40	107	−5 15	39	108	−5 54	40	109																																		278
81	−3 12	40	107	−3 52	40	108	−4 32	39	109	−5 11	40	109	−5 51	40	110																															279
80	−2 29	−40	108	−3 09	−40	109	−3 49	−40	109	−4 29	−40	110	−5 09	−40	111	−5 49	−40	111																												280
79	−1 46	40	108	−2 26	40	109	−3 06	40	110	−3 46	40	111	−4 26	41	111	−5 07	40	112	−5 47	40	113																									281
78	−1 03	40	109	−1 43	41	110	−2 24	40	111	−3 04	40	111	−3 44	41	112	−4 25	40	113	−5 05	40	113	−5 45	41	114																						282
77	−0 20	41	110	−1 01	40	110	−1 41	41	111	−2 22	41	112	−3 03	40	113	−3 43	41	113	−4 24	40	114	−5 04	41	115	−5 45	40	116																			283
76	00 23	41	110	−0 18	41	111	−0 59	41	112	−1 40	41	113	−2 21	41	113	−3 02	40	114	−3 42	41	115	−4 23	41	116	−5 04	41	116	−5 45	40	117																284
75	01 05	−41	111	00 24	−41	112	−0 17	−41	113	−0 58	−41	113	−1 39	−41	114	−2 20	−41	115	−3 01	−41	115	−3 42	−41	116	−4 23	−41	117	−5 04	−41	118	−5 45	−41	118													285
74	01 47	41	112	01 06	42	112	00 24	41	113	−0 17	41	114	−0 58	41	115	−1 39	42	115	−2 21	41	116	−3 02	41	117	−3 43	41	118	−4 24	41	118	−5 05	42	119	−5 47	41	120										286
73	02 29	41	112	01 48	42	113	01 06	42	114	00 24	41	115	−0 17	42	115	−0 59	41	116	−1 40	42	117	−2 22	41	117	−3 03	42	118	−3 45	41	119	−4 26	41	120	−5 07	42	120	−5 49	41	121							287
72	03 11	42	113	02 29	42	114	01 47	41	114	01 06	42	115	00 24	42	116	−0 18	42	117	−1 00	42	117	−1 42	41	118	−2 23	42	119	−3 05	42	120	−3 47	41	120	−4 28	42	121	−5 10	42	122	−5 52	41	122				288
71	03 52	42	114	03 10	42	114	02 28	42	115	01 46	42	116	01 04	42	117	00 22	42	117	−0 20	42	118	−1 02	42	119	−1 44	42	119	−2 26	42	120	−3 08	42	121	−3 50	42	122	−4 32	42	122	−5 14	41	123	−5 55	42	124	289
70	04 34	−42	114	03 52	−43	115	03 09	−42	116	02 27	−42	117	01 45	−43	117	01 02	−42	118	00 20	−42	119	−0 22	−42	119	−1 04	−43	120	−1 47	−42	121	−2 29	−42	122	−3 11	−42	122	−3 53	−43	123	−4 36	−42	124	−5 18	−42	124	290

S. Lat. {LHA greater than 180°....... Zn=180−Z; LHA less than 180°........... Zn=180+Z}

N. Lat. {LHA greater than 180°....... Zn=Z
{LHA less than 180°........... Zn=360−Z

DECLINATION (15°-29°) CONTRARY NAME TO LATITUDE

LHA	15° Hc	15° d	15° Z	16° Hc	16° d	16° Z	17° Hc	17° d	17° Z	18° Hc	18° d	18° Z	19° Hc	19° d	19° Z
	° ′	′	°	° ′	′	°	° ′	′	°	° ′	′	°	° ′	′	°
69	05 15	43	115	04 32	42	116	03 50	43	117	03 07	42	117	02 25	43	118
68	05 56	43	116	05 13	43	117	04 30	42	117	03 48	43	118	03 05	43	119
67	06 36	43	117	05 53	42	117	05 11	44	118	04 27	43	119	03 44	43	119
66	07 17	43	117	06 34	44	118	05 50	43	119	05 07	43	119	04 24	44	120
65	07 57	−43	118	07 14	−44	119	06 30	−43	119	05 47	−44	120	05 03	−44	121
64	08 37	44	119	07 53	44	119	07 09	43	120	06 26	44	121	05 42	44	121
63	09 16	43	119	08 33	44	120	07 49	45	121	07 04	44	121	06 20	44	122
62	09 56	44	120	09 12	45	121	08 27	44	121	07 43	45	122	06 58	44	123
61	10 35	45	121	09 50	44	121	09 06	45	122	08 21	45	123	07 36	44	124
60	11 14	−45	122	10 29	−45	122	09 44	−45	123	08 59	−45	124	08 14	−45	124
59	11 52	45	122	11 07	45	123	10 22	45	124	09 37	46	124	08 51	45	125
58	12 30	45	123	11 45	46	124	10 59	45	124	10 14	46	125	09 28	45	126
57	13 08	46	124	12 22	45	124	11 37	46	125	10 51	46	126	10 05	46	126
56	13 46	46	125	13 00	46	125	12 14	47	126	11 27	46	126	10 41	46	127
55	14 23	−46	125	13 37	−47	126	12 50	−46	127	12 04	−47	127	11 17	−46	128
54	15 00	47	126	14 13	47	127	13 26	46	127	12 40	47	128	11 53	47	129
53	15 36	47	127	14 49	47	127	14 02	47	128	13 15	47	129	12 28	47	129
52	16 12	47	128	15 25	47	128	14 38	48	129	13 50	47	130	13 03	48	130
51	16 48	48	128	16 00	47	129	15 13	48	130	14 25	48	130	13 37	48	131
50	17 23	−48	129	16 35	−48	130	15 47	−48	130	14 59	−48	131	14 11	−48	132
49	17 58	48	130	17 10	48	131	16 22	49	131	15 33	48	132	14 45	49	132
48	18 33	49	131	17 44	48	131	16 56	49	132	16 07	49	133	15 18	49	133
47	19 07	49	132	18 18	49	132	17 29	49	133	16 40	49	133	15 51	49	134
46	19 40	49	132	18 51	49	133	18 02	49	134	17 13	50	134	16 23	49	135
45	20 13	−49	133	19 24	−50	134	18 34	−49	135	17 45	−50	135	16 55	−50	136
44	20 46	50	134	19 56	49	135	19 07	50	135	18 17	50	136	17 27	51	137
43	21 18	50	135	20 28	50	136	19 38	50	136	18 48	51	137	17 57	50	137
42	21 50	50	136	21 00	51	137	20 09	50	137	19 19	51	138	18 28	51	138
41	22 21	50	137	21 31	51	137	20 40	51	138	19 49	51	139	18 58	51	139
40	22 52	−51	138	22 01	−51	138	21 10	−51	139	20 19	−52	139	19 27	−51	140
39	23 22	51	139	22 31	51	139	21 40	52	140	20 48	52	140	19 56	52	141
38	23 52	52	139	23 00	51	140	22 09	52	141	21 17	52	141	20 25	53	142
37	24 21	52	140	23 29	52	141	22 37	52	141	21 45	53	142	20 52	52	143
36	24 50	52	141	23 58	53	142	23 05	53	142	22 12	52	143	21 20	53	143
35	25 18	−53	142	24 25	−53	143	23 32	−52	143	22 40	−54	144	21 46	−53	144
34	25 45	53	143	24 52	53	144	23 59	53	144	23 06	53	145	22 13	54	145
33	26 12	53	144	25 19	54	145	24 25	53	145	23 32	54	146	22 38	54	146
32	26 39	54	145	25 45	54	146	24 51	54	146	23 57	54	147	23 03	54	147
31	27 04	54	146	26 10	54	147	25 16	54	147	24 22	54	148	23 28	55	148
30	27 29	−54	147	26 35	−55	148	25 40	−54	148	24 46	−55	148	23 51	−54	149
29	27 54	55	148	26 59	55	149	26 04	55	149	25 09	55	149	24 14	55	150
28	28 17	55	149	27 22	55	150	26 27	55	150	25 32	55	150	24 37	56	151
27	28 40	55	150	27 45	55	151	26 50	56	151	25 54	55	151	24 59	56	152
26	29 02	55	151	28 07	56	152	27 11	56	152	26 15	55	152	25 20	56	153
25	29 24	−56	152	28 28	−56	153	27 32	−56	153	26 36	−56	153	25 40	−56	154
24	29 45	56	153	28 49	57	154	27 52	56	154	26 56	56	154	26 00	57	155
23	30 05	56	154	29 09	57	155	28 12	57	155	27 15	56	155	26 19	57	156
22	30 24	56	155	29 28	57	156	28 31	57	156	27 34	57	156	26 37	57	157
21	30 43	57	156	29 46	57	157	28 49	57	157	27 52	57	157	26 55	57	158
20	31 01	−57	157	30 04	−58	158	29 06	−57	158	28 09	−57	158	27 12	−58	159
19	31 18	58	158	30 20	57	159	29 23	58	159	28 25	57	159	27 28	58	160
18	31 34	58	160	30 36	57	160	29 39	58	160	28 41	58	160	27 43	58	161
17	31 50	58	161	30 52	58	161	29 54	58	161	28 56	58	162	27 58	59	162
16	32 04	58	162	31 06	58	162	30 08	58	162	29 10	59	163	28 11	58	163
15	32 18	−58	163	31 20	−59	163	30 21	−58	163	29 23	−59	164	28 24	−58	164
14	32 31	59	164	31 32	58	164	30 34	59	164	29 35	59	165	28 36	58	165
13	32 43	59	165	31 44	58	165	30 46	59	166	29 47	59	166	28 48	59	166
12	32 54	59	166	31 55	59	166	30 56	59	167	29 57	59	167	28 58	59	167
11	33 05	59	167	32 06	59	168	31 07	60	168	30 07	59	168	29 08	59	168
10	33 14	−59	168	32 15	−59	169	31 16	−60	169	30 16	−59	169	29 17	−59	169
9	33 23	59	170	32 24	60	170	31 24	59	170	30 25	60	170	29 25	59	170
8	33 31	60	171	32 31	59	171	31 32	60	171	30 32	59	171	29 33	60	171
7	33 38	60	172	32 38	60	172	31 38	59	172	30 39	60	172	29 39	60	172
6	33 44	60	173	32 44	60	173	31 44	60	173	30 44	59	173	29 45	60	174
5	33 49	−60	174	32 49	−60	174	31 49	−60	174	30 49	−60	175	29 49	−60	175
4	33 53	60	175	32 53	60	175	31 53	60	176	30 53	60	176	29 53	60	176
3	33 56	60	177	32 56	60	177	31 56	60	177	30 56	60	177	29 56	60	177
2	33 58	60	178	32 58	60	178	31 58	60	178	30 58	60	178	29 58	60	178
1	34 00	60	179	33 00	60	179	32 00	60	179	31 00	60	179	30 00	60	179
0	34 00	−60	180	33 00	−60	180	32 00	−60	180	31 00	−60	180	30 00	−60	180

LHA	20° Hc	20° d	20° Z	21° Hc	21° d	21° Z	22° Hc	22° d	22° Z	23° Hc	23° d	23° Z	24° Hc	24° d	24° Z
	° ′	′	°	° ′	′	°	° ′	′	°	° ′	′	°	° ′	′	°
69	01 42	42	119	01 00	43	119	00 17	42	120	−0 25	43	121	−1 08	43	121
68	02 22	43	119	01 39	43	120	00 56	43	121	00 13	42	121	−0 29	43	122
67	03 01	43	120	02 18	43	121	01 35	43	121	00 52	43	122	00 09	43	123
66	03 40	43	121	02 57	43	121	02 14	44	122	01 30	43	123	00 47	44	123
65	04 19	−43	121	03 36	−44	122	02 52	−44	123	02 08	−44	123	01 24	−43	124
64	04 58	44	122	04 14	44	123	03 30	44	123	02 46	44	124	02 02	44	125
63	05 36	44	123	04 52	45	123	04 07	44	124	03 23	44	125	02 39	45	125
62	06 14	45	123	05 29	44	124	04 45	45	125	04 00	44	125	03 16	45	126
61	06 52	45	124	06 07	45	125	05 22	45	126	04 37	45	126	03 52	45	127
60	07 29	−45	125	06 44	−45	126	05 59	−46	126	05 13	−45	127	04 28	−45	127
59	08 06	45	126	07 21	46	126	06 35	46	127	05 49	45	128	05 04	46	128
58	08 43	46	126	07 57	46	127	07 11	46	128	06 25	46	128	05 39	46	129
57	09 19	46	127	08 33	46	128	07 47	46	128	07 01	47	129	06 14	46	130
56	09 55	46	128	09 09	47	128	08 22	46	129	07 36	47	130	06 49	47	130
55	10 31	−47	129	09 44	−47	129	08 57	−47	130	08 10	−47	130	07 23	−47	131
54	11 06	47	129	10 19	47	130	09 32	47	131	08 45	48	131	07 57	47	132
53	11 41	48	130	10 53	47	131	10 06	47	131	09 19	48	132	08 31	48	133
52	12 15	47	131	11 28	48	131	10 40	48	132	09 52	48	133	09 04	48	133
51	12 49	48	132	12 01	48	132	11 13	48	133	10 25	48	133	09 37	48	134
50	13 23	−48	132	12 35	−49	133	11 46	−48	134	10 58	−49	134	10 09	−48	135
49	13 56	48	133	13 08	49	134	12 19	49	134	11 30	49	135	10 41	49	135
48	14 29	49	134	13 40	49	134	12 51	49	135	12 02	49	136	11 13	49	136
47	15 02	50	135	14 12	49	135	13 23	49	136	12 34	50	136	11 44	50	137
46	15 34	50	135	14 44	50	136	13 54	49	137	13 05	50	137	12 15	50	138
45	16 05	−50	136	15 15	−50	137	14 25	−50	137	13 35	−50	138	12 45	−50	139
44	16 36	50	137	15 46	50	138	14 56	51	138	14 05	50	139	13 15	51	139
43	17 07	51	138	16 16	50	139	15 26	51	139	14 35	51	140	13 44	51	140
42	17 37	51	139	16 46	51	139	15 55	51	140	15 04	51	140	14 13	51	141
41	18 07	52	140	17 15	51	140	16 24	51	141	15 33	52	141	14 41	51	142
40	18 36	−52	140	17 44	−51	141	16 53	−52	142	16 01	−52	142	15 09	−52	143
39	19 04	52	141	18 12	52	142	17 20	52	142	16 28	52	143	15 36	52	143
38	19 32	52	142	18 40	52	143	17 48	53	143	16 55	52	144	16 03	53	144
37	20 00	53	143	19 07	52	144	18 15	53	144	17 22	53	145	16 29	53	145
36	20 27	53	144	19 34	53	144	18 41	53	145	17 48	53	145	16 55	53	146
35	20 53	−53	145	20 00	−53	145	19 07	−54	146	18 13	−53	146	17 20	−53	147
34	21 19	53	146	20 26	54	146	19 32	54	147	18 38	53	147	17 45	54	148
33	21 44	53	147	20 51	54	147	19 57	54	148	19 03	54	148	18 09	55	148
32	22 09	54	148	21 15	54	148	20 21	55	148	19 26	54	149	18 32	54	149
31	22 33	54	148	21 39	55	149	20 44	54	149	19 50	55	150	18 55	55	150
30	22 57	−55	149	22 02	−55	150	21 07	−55	150	20 12	−55	151	19 17	−55	151
29	23 19	55	150	22 24	55	151	21 29	55	151	20 34	55	152	19 39	56	152
28	23 41	55	151	22 46	55	152	21 51	56	152	20 55	55	152	20 00	56	153
27	24 03	56	152	23 07	55	153	22 12	56	153	21 16	56	153	20 20	56	154
26	24 24	56	153	23 28	56	154	22 32	56	154	21 36	56	154	20 40	56	155
25	24 44	−56	154	23 48	−57	155	22 51	−56	155	21 55	−56	155	20 59	−57	156
24	25 03	56	155	24 07	57	155	23 10	56	156	22 14	57	156	21 17	57	157
23	25 22	57	156	24 25	56	156	23 29	57	157	22 32	57	157	21 35	57	157
22	25 40	57	157	24 43	57	157	23 46	57	158	22 49	57	158	21 52	57	158
21	25 58	58	158	25 00	57	158	24 03	57	159	23 06	58	159	22 08	57	159
20	26 14	−57	159	25 17	−58	159	24 19	−57	160	23 22	−58	160	22 24	−58	160
19	26 30	58	160	25 32	58	160	24 34	57	161	23 37	58	161	22 39	58	161
18	26 45	58	161	25 47	58	161	24 49	58	162	23 51	58	162	22 53	58	162
17	26 59	58	162	26 01	58	162	25 03	58	163	24 05	58	163	23 07	59	163
16	27 13	58	163	26 15	59	163	25 16	58	164	24 18	59	164	23 19	58	164
15	27 26	−59	164	26 27	−58	164	25 29	−59	165	24 30	−59	165	23 31	−58	165
14	27 38	59	165	26 39	59	165	25 40	58	166	24 42	59	166	23 43	59	166
13	27 49	59	166	26 50	59	166	25 51	59	167	24 52	59	167	23 53	59	167
12	27 59	59	167	27 00	59	167	26 01	59	168	25 02	59	168	24 03	59	168
11	28 09	59	168	27 10	59	169	26 11	60	169	25 11	59	169	24 12	59	169
10	28 18	−59	169	27 19	−60	170	26 19	−59	170	25 20	−60	170	24 20	−59	170
9	28 26	60	170	27 26	59	171	26 27	60	171	25 27	59	171	24 28	60	171
8	28 33	60	171	27 33	59	172	26 34	60	172	25 34	59	172	24 35	60	172
7	28 39	59	173	27 40	60	173	26 40	60	173	25 40	59	173	24 41	60	173
6	28 45	60	174	27 45	60	174	26 45	59	174	25 46	60	174	24 46	60	174
5	28 49	−59	175	27 50	−60	175	26 50	−60	175	25 50	−60	175	24 50	−60	175
4	28 53	60	176	27 53	60	176	26 53	59	176	25 54	60	176	24 54	60	176
3	28 56	60	177	27 56	60	177	26 56	60	177	25 56	60	177	24 56	59	177
2	28 58	60	178	27 58	60	178	26 58	60	178	25 58	60	178	24 58	60	178
1	29 00	60	179	28 00	60	179	27 00	60	179	26 00	60	179	25 00	60	179
0	29 00	−60	180	28 00	−60	180	27 00	−60	180	26 00	−60	180	25 00	−60	180

LHA	25° Hc	25° d	25° Z	26° Hc	26° d	26° Z	27° Hc	27° d	27° Z	28° Hc	28° d	28° Z	29° Hc	29° d	29° Z	LHA
	° ′	′	°	° ′	′	°	° ′	′	°	° ′	′	°	° ′	′	°	
69	−1 51	42	122	−2 33	43	123	−3 16	42	124	−3 58	43	124	−4 41	42	125	291
68	−1 12	43	123	−1 55	43	124	−2 38	43	124	−3 21	43	125	−4 04	42	126	292
67	−0 34	44	123	−1 18	43	124	−2 01	43	125	−2 44	43	126	−3 27	43	126	293
66	00 03	43	124	−0 40	44	125	−1 24	43	125	−2 07	44	126	−2 51	43	127	294
65	00 41	−44	125	−0 03	−44	125	−0 47	−44	126	−1 31	−43	127	−2 14	−44	127	295
64	01 18	44	125	00 34	45	126	−0 11	44	127	−0 55	44	127	−1 39	44	128	296
63	01 54	44	126	01 10	44	127	00 26	45	127	−0 19	44	128	−1 03	45	129	297
62	02 31	45	127	01 46	45	127	01 01	44	128	00 17	45	129	−0 28	45	129	298
61	03 07	45	127	02 22	45	128	01 37	45	129	00 52	45	129	00 07	45	130	299
60	03 43	−46	128	02 57	−45	129	02 12	−45	129	01 27	−46	130	00 41	−45	131	300
59	04 18	46	129	03 32	45	129	02 47	46	130	02 01	46	131	01 15	45	131	301
58	04 53	46	130	04 07	46	130	03 21	46	131	02 35	46	131	01 49	46	132	302
57	05 28	46	130	04 42	47	131	03 55	46	132	03 09	46	132	02 23	47	133	303
56	06 02	46	131	05 16	47	132	04 29	47	132	03 42	46	133	02 56	47	133	304
55	06 36	−47	132	05 49	−47	132	05 02	−47	133	04 15	−47	134	03 28	−47	134	305
54	07 10	47	132	06 23	48	133	05 35	47	134	04 48	47	134	04 01	48	135	306
53	07 43	47	133	06 56	48	134	06 08	48	134	05 20	47	135	04 33	48	136	307
52	08 16	48	134	07 28	48	134	06 40	48	135	05 52	48	136	05 04	48	136	308
51	08 49	49	135	08 00	48	135	07 12	48	136	06 24	49	136	05 35	48	137	309
50	09 21	−49	135	08 32	−49	136	07 43	−48	137	06 55	−49	137	06 06	−49	138	310
49	09 52	48	136	09 04	50	137	08 14	49	137	07 25	49	138	06 36	49	138	311
48	10 24	50	137	09 34	49	137	08 45	49	138	07 56	50	139	07 06	49	139	312
47	10 54	49	138	10 05	50	138	09 15	50	139	08 25	49	139	07 36	50	140	313
46	11 25	50	138	10 35	50	139	09 45	50	139	08 55	50	140	08 05	51	141	314
45	11 55	−51	139	11 04	−50	140	10 14	−50	140	09 24	−51	141	08 33	−50	141	315
44	12 24	51	140	11 33	50	140	10 43	51	141	09 52	51	142	09 01	51	142	316
43	12 53	51	141	12 02	51	141	11 11	51	142	10 20	51	142	09 29	51	143	317
42	13 22	52	141	12 30	51	142	11 39	52	143	10 47	51	143	09 56	52	144	318
41	13 50	52	142	12 58	52	143	12 06	52	143	11 14	51	144	10 23	52	144	319
40	14 17	−52	143	13 25	−52	144	12 33	−52	144	11 41	−52	145	10 49	−52	145	320
39	14 44	52	144	13 52	53	144	12 59	52	145	12 07	53	145	11 14	52	146	321
38	15 10	52	145	14 18	53	145	13 25	53	146	12 32	52	146	11 40	53	147	322
37	15 36	53	146	14 43	53	146	13 50	53	147	12 57	53	147	12 04	53	147	323
36	16 02	54	146	15 08	53	147	14 15	53	147	13 22	54	148	12 28	53	148	324
35	16 27	−54	147	15 33	−54	148	14 39	−53	148	13 46	−54	149	12 52	−54	149	325
34	16 51	54	148	15 57	54	149	15 03	54	149	14 09	54	149	13 15	54	150	326
33	17 14	54	149	16 20	54	149	15 26	54	150	14 32	55	150	13 37	54	151	327
32	17 38	55	150	16 43	54	150	15 49	55	151	14 54	55	151	13 59	54	152	328
31	18 00	55	151	17 05	54	151	16 11	55	152	15 16	55	152	14 21	55	152	329
30	18 22	−55	152	17 27	−55	152	16 32	−55	152	15 37	−56	153	14 41	−55	153	330
29	18 43	55	152	17 48	55	153	16 53	56	153	15 57	55	154	15 02	56	154	331
28	19 04	56	153	18 08	55	154	17 13	56	154	16 17	56	154	15 21	56	155	332
27	19 24	56	154	18 28	56	155	17 32	56	155	16 36	56	155	15 40	56	156	333
26	19 44	57	155	18 47	56	155	17 51	56	156	16 55	56	156	15 59	57	157	334
25	20 02	−56	156	19 06	−57	156	18 09	−56	157	17 13	−57	157	16 16	−56	157	335
24	20 20	56	157	19 24	57	157	18 27	57	158	17 30	57	158	16 33	56	158	336
23	20 38	57	158	19 41	57	158	18 44	57	158	17 47	57	159	16 50	57	159	337
22	20 55	57	159	19 58	58	159	19 00	57	159	18 03	57	160	17 06	58	160	338
21	21 11	58	160	20 13	57	160	19 16	58	160	18 18	57	161	17 21	58	161	339
20	21 26	−57	161	20 29	−58	161	19 31	−58	161	18 33	−58	161	17 35	−57	162	340
19	21 41	58	162	20 43	58	162	19 45	58	162	18 47	58	162	17 49	58	163	341
18	21 55	58	162	20 57	58	163	19 59	58	163	19 01	58	163	18 03	59	164	342
17	22 08	58	163	21 10	58	164	20 12	59	164	19 13	58	164	18 15	58	164	343
16	22 21	59	164	21 22	58	165	20 24	59	165	19 25	58	165	18 27	59	165	344
15	22 33	−59	165	21 34	−58	166	20 36	−59	166	19 37	−59	166	18 38	−59	166	345
14	22 44	59	166	21 45	59	167	20 46	59	167	19 47	58	167	18 49	59	167	346
13	22 54	59	167	21 55	59	167	20 56	59	168	19 57	59	168	18 58	59	168	347
12	23 04	59	168	22 05	59	168	21 06	59	169	20 07	60	169	19 07	59	169	348
11	23 13	59	169	22 14	60	169	21 14	59	170	20 15	59	170	19 16	60	170	349
10	23 21	−59	170	22 22	−60	170	21 22	−59	170	20 23	−60	171	19 23	−59	171	350
9	23 28	59	171	22 29	60	171	21 29	59	171	20 30	60	172	19 30	59	172	351
8	23 35	60	172	22 35	59	172	21 36	60	172	20 36	59	173	19 37	60	173	352
7	23 41	60	173	22 41	60	173	21 41	59	173	20 42	60	173	19 42	60	174	353
6	23 46	60	174	22 46	60	174	21 46	59	174	20 47	60	174	19 47	60	174	354
5	23 50	−60	175	22 50	−59	175	21 51	−60	175	20 51	−60	175	19 51	−60	175	355
4	23 54	60	176	22 54	60	176	21 54	60	176	20 54	60	176	19 54	60	176	356
3	23 57	60	177	22 57	60	177	21 57	60	177	20 57	60	177	19 57	60	177	357
2	23 58	59	178	22 59	60	178	21 59	60	178	20 59	60	178	19 59	60	178	358
1	24 00	60	179	23 00	60	179	22 00	60	179	21 00	60	179	20 00	60	179	359
0	24 00	−60	180	23 00	−60	180	22 00	−60	180	21 00	−60	180	20 00	−60	180	360

15°	16°	17°	18°	19°	20°	21°	22°	23°	24°	25°	26°	27°	28°	29°

S. Lat. {LHA greater than 180°....... Zn=180−Z
{LHA less than 180°........... Zn=180+Z

DECLINATION (15°-29°) CONTRARY NAME TO LATITUDE

LAT 41°

N. Lat. {LHA greater than 180°....... Zn=Z; LHA less than 180°........... Zn=360−Z}

DECLINATION (0°-14°) SAME NAME AS LATITUDE

LAT 42°

LHA	0° Hc	0° d	0° Z	1° Hc	1° d	1° Z	2° Hc	2° d	2° Z	3° Hc	3° d	3° Z	4° Hc	4° d	4° Z
	° ′	′	°	° ′	′	°	° ′	′	°	° ′	′	°	° ′	′	°
0	48 00	+60	180	49 00	+60	180	50 00	+60	180	51 00	+60	180	52 00	+60	180
1	47 59	60	179	48 59	60	179	49 59	60	178	50 59	60	178	51 59	60	178
2	47 58	60	177	48 58	60	177	49 58	60	177	50 58	60	177	51 58	59	177
3	47 55	60	176	48 55	60	175	49 55	59	175	50 54	60	175	51 54	60	175
4	47 51	60	174	48 51	59	174	49 50	60	174	50 50	60	174	51 50	60	174
5	47 46	+59	173	48 45	+60	172	49 45	+60	172	50 45	+59	172	51 44	+60	172
6	47 39	60	171	48 39	59	171	49 38	60	171	50 38	59	171	51 37	60	170
7	47 32	59	170	48 31	60	169	49 31	59	169	50 30	59	169	51 29	60	169
8	47 23	59	168	48 22	60	168	49 22	59	168	50 21	59	167	51 20	59	167
9	47 13	59	167	48 12	60	166	49 12	59	166	50 11	59	166	51 10	58	166
10	47 03	+58	165	48 01	+59	165	49 00	+59	165	49 59	+59	164	50 58	+59	164
11	46 51	58	164	47 49	59	164	48 48	59	163	49 47	58	163	50 45	58	163
12	46 38	58	162	47 36	59	162	48 35	58	162	49 33	58	161	50 31	58	161
13	46 24	58	161	47 22	58	161	48 20	58	160	49 18	58	160	50 16	58	159
14	46 09	58	160	47 07	57	159	48 04	58	159	49 02	58	158	50 00	57	158
15	45 53	+57	158	46 50	+58	158	47 48	+57	157	48 45	+57	157	49 42	+58	157
16	45 35	58	157	46 33	57	156	47 30	57	156	48 27	57	156	49 24	57	155
17	45 17	57	155	46 14	57	155	47 11	57	155	48 08	57	154	49 05	56	154
18	44 58	57	154	45 55	57	154	46 52	56	153	47 48	56	153	48 44	57	152
19	44 38	57	153	45 35	56	152	46 31	56	152	47 27	56	151	48 23	56	151
20	44 18	+56	152	45 14	+56	151	46 10	+55	150	47 05	+56	150	48 01	+55	149
21	43 56	56	150	44 52	55	150	45 47	55	149	46 42	56	149	47 38	55	148
22	43 33	56	149	44 29	55	148	45 24	55	148	46 19	55	147	47 14	54	147
23	43 10	55	148	44 05	55	147	45 00	54	147	45 54	55	146	46 49	54	145
24	42 45	55	146	43 40	55	146	44 35	54	145	45 29	54	145	46 23	54	144
25	42 20	+55	145	43 15	+54	145	44 09	+54	144	45 03	+53	143	45 56	+54	143
26	41 55	53	144	42 48	54	143	43 42	53	143	44 35	54	142	45 29	53	141
27	41 28	53	143	42 21	54	142	43 15	53	142	44 08	53	141	45 01	52	140
28	41 00	54	142	41 54	52	141	42 46	53	140	43 39	53	140	44 32	52	139
29	40 32	53	140	41 25	53	140	42 18	52	139	43 10	52	138	44 02	52	138
30	40 04	+52	139	40 56	+52	139	41 48	+52	138	42 40	+52	137	43 32	+51	137
31	39 34	52	138	40 26	52	137	41 18	51	137	42 09	52	136	43 01	51	135
32	39 04	52	137	39 56	51	136	40 47	51	136	41 38	51	135	42 29	51	134
33	38 33	52	136	39 25	51	135	40 16	50	135	41 06	51	134	41 57	50	133
34	38 02	51	135	38 53	50	134	39 43	51	133	40 34	50	133	41 24	50	132
35	37 30	+50	134	38 20	+51	133	39 11	+50	132	40 01	+49	132	40 50	+50	131
36	36 57	51	133	37 48	49	132	38 37	50	131	39 27	49	131	40 16	49	130
37	36 24	50	132	37 14	50	131	38 04	49	130	38 53	49	130	39 42	49	129
38	35 51	49	131	36 40	49	130	37 29	49	129	38 18	49	128	39 07	48	128
39	35 17	49	130	36 06	49	129	36 55	48	128	37 43	48	127	38 31	48	127
40	34 42	+49	129	35 31	+48	128	36 19	+48	127	37 07	+48	126	37 55	+48	126
41	34 07	48	128	34 55	48	127	35 43	48	126	36 31	48	125	37 19	47	125
42	33 31	48	127	34 19	48	126	35 07	48	125	35 55	47	124	36 42	47	124
43	32 55	48	126	33 43	48	125	34 31	47	124	35 18	47	123	36 05	46	123
44	32 19	47	125	33 06	47	124	33 53	47	123	34 40	47	123	35 27	46	122
45	31 42	+47	124	32 29	+47	123	33 16	+46	122	34 02	+47	122	34 49	+46	121
46	31 05	47	123	31 52	46	122	32 38	46	121	33 24	46	121	34 10	46	120
47	30 27	47	122	31 14	46	121	32 00	46	121	32 46	45	120	33 31	46	119
48	29 49	46	121	30 35	46	120	31 21	46	120	32 07	45	119	32 52	45	118
49	29 11	46	120	29 57	45	119	30 42	46	119	31 28	45	118	32 13	44	117
50	28 32	+46	119	29 18	+45	119	30 03	+45	118	30 48	+45	117	31 33	+44	116
51	27 53	45	119	28 38	45	118	29 23	45	117	30 08	45	116	30 53	44	115
52	27 14	45	118	27 59	45	117	28 44	44	116	29 28	44	115	30 12	44	115
53	26 34	45	117	27 19	44	116	28 03	45	115	28 48	44	115	29 32	43	114
54	25 54	45	116	26 39	44	115	27 23	44	114	28 07	44	114	28 51	43	113
55	25 14	+44	115	25 58	+44	114	26 42	+44	114	27 26	+43	113	28 09	+44	112
56	24 33	44	114	25 17	44	114	26 01	44	113	26 45	43	112	27 28	43	111
57	23 53	43	114	24 36	44	113	25 20	43	112	26 03	43	111	26 46	43	110
58	23 12	43	113	23 55	43	112	24 38	44	111	25 22	42	110	26 04	43	110
59	22 30	44	112	23 14	43	111	23 57	43	110	24 40	42	110	25 22	43	109
60	21 49	+43	111	22 32	+43	110	23 15	+43	110	23 58	+42	109	24 40	+42	108
61	21 07	43	110	21 50	43	110	22 33	42	109	23 15	43	108	23 58	42	107
62	20 25	43	110	21 08	42	109	21 50	43	108	22 33	42	107	23 15	42	107
63	19 43	43	109	20 26	42	108	21 08	42	107	21 50	42	107	22 32	42	106
64	19 01	42	108	19 43	42	107	20 25	42	107	21 07	42	106	21 49	42	105
65	18 18	+43	107	19 01	+42	107	19 43	+41	106	20 24	+42	105	21 06	+41	104
66	17 36	42	107	18 18	42	106	19 00	41	105	19 41	42	104	20 23	41	104
67	16 53	42	106	17 35	41	105	18 16	42	104	18 58	41	104	19 39	41	103
68	16 10	42	105	16 52	41	104	17 33	42	104	18 15	41	103	18 56	41	102
69	15 27	41	104	16 08	42	104	16 50	41	103	17 31	41	102	18 12	41	101

LHA	5° Hc	5° d	5° Z	6° Hc	6° d	6° Z	7° Hc	7° d	7° Z	8° Hc	8° d	8° Z	9° Hc	9° d	9° Z
	° ′	′	°	° ′	′	°	° ′	′	°	° ′	′	°	° ′	′	°
0	53 00	+60	180	54 00	+60	180	55 00	+60	180	56 00	+60	180	57 00	+60	180
1	52 59	60	178	53 59	60	178	54 59	60	178	55 59	60	178	56 59	60	178
2	52 57	60	177	53 57	60	177	54 57	60	177	55 57	60	177	56 57	60	176
3	52 54	60	175	53 54	60	175	54 54	60	175	55 54	60	175	56 54	60	175
4	52 50	60	173	53 50	59	173	54 49	60	173	55 49	60	173	56 49	60	173
5	52 44	+60	172	53 44	+59	172	54 43	+60	171	55 43	+59	171	56 42	+60	171
6	52 37	59	170	53 36	60	170	54 36	59	170	55 35	60	169	56 35	59	169
7	52 29	59	169	53 28	59	168	54 27	60	168	55 27	59	168	56 26	59	167
8	52 19	59	167	53 18	59	167	54 17	59	166	55 16	59	166	56 15	59	166
9	52 08	59	165	53 07	59	165	54 06	59	165	55 05	59	164	56 04	58	164
10	51 57	+58	164	52 55	+59	163	53 54	+58	163	54 52	+59	163	55 51	+58	162
11	51 43	59	162	52 42	58	162	53 40	58	161	54 38	58	161	55 36	59	161
12	51 29	58	161	52 27	58	160	53 25	58	160	54 23	58	159	55 21	58	159
13	51 14	58	159	52 12	57	159	53 09	58	158	54 07	57	158	55 04	58	157
14	50 57	58	158	51 55	57	157	52 52	57	157	53 49	57	156	54 46	57	156
15	50 40	+57	156	51 37	+57	156	52 34	+57	155	53 31	+56	155	54 27	+57	154
16	50 21	57	155	51 18	56	154	52 14	57	154	53 11	56	153	54 07	56	152
17	50 01	57	153	50 58	56	153	51 54	56	152	52 50	56	151	53 46	56	151
18	49 41	56	152	50 37	55	151	51 32	56	151	52 28	56	150	53 24	55	149
19	49 19	56	150	50 15	55	150	51 10	55	149	52 05	55	148	53 00	55	148
20	48 56	+56	149	49 52	+55	148	50 47	+54	148	51 41	+55	147	52 36	+54	146
21	48 33	55	147	49 28	54	147	50 22	55	146	51 17	54	145	52 11	54	145
22	48 08	55	146	49 03	54	145	49 57	54	145	50 51	54	144	51 45	53	143
23	47 43	54	145	48 37	54	144	49 31	53	143	50 24	53	143	51 17	53	142
24	47 17	53	143	48 10	54	143	49 04	53	142	49 57	53	141	50 50	52	141
25	46 50	+53	142	47 43	+53	141	48 36	+52	141	49 28	+53	140	50 21	+52	139
26	46 22	53	141	47 15	52	140	48 07	52	139	48 59	52	139	49 51	52	138
27	45 53	53	140	46 46	52	139	47 38	51	138	48 29	52	137	49 21	51	137
28	45 24	52	138	46 16	51	138	47 07	52	137	47 59	51	136	48 50	51	135
29	44 54	51	137	45 45	52	136	46 37	50	136	47 27	51	135	48 18	50	134
30	44 23	+51	136	45 14	+51	135	46 05	+50	134	46 55	+51	134	47 46	+49	133
31	43 52	50	135	44 42	51	134	45 33	50	133	46 23	50	132	47 13	49	132
32	43 20	50	134	44 10	50	133	45 00	50	132	45 50	49	131	46 39	49	130
33	42 47	50	132	43 37	49	132	44 26	50	131	45 16	49	130	46 05	48	129
34	42 14	49	131	43 03	49	130	43 52	49	130	44 41	49	129	45 30	48	128
35	41 40	+49	130	42 29	+49	129	43 18	+48	129	44 06	+48	128	44 54	+48	127
36	41 05	49	129	41 54	49	128	42 43	48	127	43 31	47	127	44 18	48	126
37	40 31	48	128	41 19	48	127	42 07	48	126	42 55	47	126	43 42	47	125
38	39 55	48	127	40 43	48	126	41 31	47	125	42 18	47	125	43 05	47	124
39	39 19	48	126	40 07	47	125	40 54	47	124	41 41	47	123	42 28	46	123
40	38 43	+47	125	39 30	+47	124	40 17	+47	123	41 04	+46	122	41 50	+46	122
41	38 06	47	124	38 53	47	123	39 40	46	122	40 26	46	121	41 12	45	121
42	37 29	46	123	38 15	47	122	39 02	46	121	39 48	45	120	40 33	45	120
43	36 51	46	122	37 37	46	121	38 23	46	120	39 09	45	119	39 54	45	119
44	36 13	46	121	36 59	46	120	37 45	45	119	38 30	45	119	39 15	44	118
45	35 35	+45	120	36 20	+46	119	37 06	+45	118	37 51	+44	118	38 35	+44	117
46	34 56	45	119	35 41	45	118	36 26	45	117	37 11	44	117	37 55	44	116
47	34 17	45	118	35 02	45	117	35 47	44	117	36 31	44	116	37 15	44	115
48	33 37	45	117	34 22	44	116	35 06	45	116	35 51	43	115	36 34	44	114
49	32 57	45	116	33 42	44	116	34 26	44	115	35 10	43	114	35 53	44	113
50	32 17	+45	116	33 02	+43	115	33 45	+44	114	34 29	+43	113	35 12	+43	112
51	31 37	44	115	32 21	44	114	33 05	43	113	33 48	43	112	34 31	42	111
52	30 56	44	114	31 40	43	113	32 23	43	112	33 06	43	111	33 49	43	111
53	30 15	44	113	30 59	43	112	31 42	43	111	32 25	42	111	33 07	42	110
54	29 34	43	112	30 17	43	111	31 00	43	111	31 43	42	110	32 25	42	109
55	28 53	+43	111	29 36	+42	111	30 18	+43	110	31 01	+42	109	31 43	+42	108
56	28 11	43	111	28 54	42	110	29 36	43	109	30 19	41	108	31 00	42	107
57	27 29	43	110	28 12	42	109	28 54	42	108	29 36	42	107	30 18	41	106
58	26 47	42	109	27 29	43	108	28 12	41	107	28 53	42	106	29 35	41	106
59	26 05	42	108	26 47	42	107	27 29	41	107	28 10	42	106	28 52	41	105
60	25 22	+42	107	26 04	+42	107	26 46	+41	106	27 27	+42	105	28 09	+40	104
61	24 40	41	107	25 21	42	106	26 03	41	105	26 44	41	104	27 25	41	103
62	23 57	41	106	24 38	42	105	25 20	41	104	26 01	41	103	26 42	40	103
63	23 14	41	105	23 55	42	104	24 37	41	103	25 18	40	103	25 58	41	102
64	22 31	41	104	23 12	41	104	23 53	41	103	24 34	41	102	25 15	40	101
65	21 47	+42	104	22 29	+41	103	23 10	+40	102	23 50	+41	101	24 31	+40	100
66	21 04	41	103	21 45	41	102	22 26	40	101	23 06	41	100	23 47	40	100
67	20 20	41	102	21 01	41	101	21 42	41	101	22 23	40	100	23 03	40	99
68	19 37	41	101	20 18	40	101	20 58	41	100	21 39	40	99	22 19	40	98
69	18 53	41	101	19 34	40	100	20 14	40	99	20 54	41	98	21 35	39	98

LHA	10° Hc	10° d	10° Z	11° Hc	11° d	11° Z	12° Hc	12° d	12° Z	13° Hc	13° d	13° Z	14° Hc	14° d	14° Z	LHA
	° ′	′	°	° ′	′	°	° ′	′	°	° ′	′	°	° ′	′	°	
0	58 00	+60	180	59 00	+60	180	60 00	+60	180	61 00	+60	180	62 00	+60	180	360
1	57 59	60	178	58 59	60	178	59 59	60	178	60 59	60	178	61 59	60	178	359
2	57 57	60	176	58 57	60	176	59 57	60	176	60 57	60	176	61 57	60	176	358
3	57 54	59	174	58 53	60	174	59 53	60	174	60 53	60	174	61 53	60	174	357
4	57 49	59	173	58 48	60	172	59 48	60	172	60 48	59	172	61 47	60	172	356
5	57 42	+60	171	58 42	+59	171	59 41	+60	170	60 41	+59	170	61 40	+59	170	355
6	57 34	60	169	58 34	59	169	59 33	59	168	60 32	59	168	61 31	60	168	354
7	57 25	59	167	58 24	59	167	59 23	59	167	60 22	59	166	61 21	59	166	353
8	57 14	59	165	58 13	59	165	59 12	59	165	60 11	58	164	61 09	59	164	352
9	57 02	59	164	58 01	58	163	58 59	59	163	59 58	58	162	60 56	58	162	351
10	56 49	+58	162	57 47	+59	161	58 46	+58	161	59 44	+58	160	60 42	+57	160	350
11	56 35	57	160	57 32	58	160	58 30	58	159	59 28	57	159	60 25	58	158	349
12	56 19	57	158	57 16	58	158	58 14	57	157	59 11	57	157	60 08	57	156	348
13	56 02	57	157	56 59	57	156	57 56	57	156	58 53	56	155	59 49	57	154	347
14	55 43	57	155	56 40	57	154	57 37	56	154	58 33	56	153	59 29	56	153	346
15	55 24	+56	153	56 20	+56	153	57 16	+56	152	58 12	+56	151	59 08	+56	151	345
16	55 03	56	152	55 59	56	151	56 55	55	150	57 50	56	150	58 46	55	149	344
17	54 42	55	150	55 37	55	150	56 32	55	149	57 27	55	148	58 22	55	147	343
18	54 19	55	149	55 14	55	148	56 09	54	147	57 03	55	146	57 58	53	146	342
19	53 55	55	147	54 50	54	146	55 44	54	146	56 38	54	145	57 32	53	144	341
20	53 30	+54	146	54 24	+54	145	55 18	+54	144	56 12	+53	143	57 05	+53	142	340
21	53 05	53	144	53 58	54	143	54 52	53	143	55 45	52	142	56 37	53	141	339
22	52 38	53	143	53 31	53	142	54 24	53	141	55 17	52	140	56 09	51	139	338
23	52 10	53	141	53 03	53	140	53 56	52	140	54 48	51	139	55 39	51	138	337
24	51 42	52	140	52 34	52	139	53 26	52	138	54 18	51	137	55 09	50	136	336
25	51 13	+52	138	52 05	+51	138	52 56	+51	137	53 47	+51	136	54 38	+50	135	335
26	50 43	51	137	51 34	51	136	52 25	51	135	53 16	50	134	54 06	49	134	334
27	50 12	51	136	51 03	50	135	51 53	50	134	52 43	50	133	53 33	49	132	333
28	49 41	50	134	50 31	50	134	51 21	49	133	52 10	50	132	53 00	48	131	332
29	49 08	50	133	49 58	50	132	50 48	49	131	51 37	48	131	52 25	49	130	331
30	48 35	+50	132	49 25	+49	131	50 14	+49	130	51 03	+48	129	51 51	+47	128	330
31	48 02	49	131	48 51	49	130	49 40	48	129	50 28	47	128	51 15	48	127	329
32	47 28	48	130	48 16	49	129	49 05	47	128	49 52	48	127	50 40	46	126	328
33	46 53	48	128	47 41	48	127	48 29	47	127	49 16	47	126	50 03	46	125	327
34	46 18	48	127	47 06	47	126	47 53	47	125	48 40	46	124	49 26	46	124	326
35	45 42	+47	126	46 29	+47	125	47 16	+47	124	48 03	+46	123	48 49	+45	122	325
36	45 06	47	125	45 53	46	124	46 39	46	123	47 25	46	122	48 11	45	121	324
37	44 29	46	124	45 15	47	123	46 02	45	122	46 47	45	121	47 32	45	120	323
38	43 52	46	123	44 38	46	122	45 24	45	121	46 09	45	120	46 54	44	119	322
39	43 14	46	122	44 00	45	121	44 45	45	120	45 30	45	119	46 15	43	118	321
40	42 36	+45	121	43 21	+45	120	44 06	+45	119	44 51	+44	118	45 35	+44	117	320
41	41 57	45	120	42 42	45	119	43 27	44	118	44 11	44	117	44 55	43	116	319
42	41 18	45	119	42 03	34	118	42 47	44	117	43 31	44	116	44 15	43	115	318
43	40 39	45	118	41 24	44	117	42 08	43	116	42 51	43	115	43 34	43	114	317
44	39 59	45	117	40 44	43	116	41 27	44	115	42 11	42	114	42 53	43	113	316
45	39 19	+44	116	40 03	+44	115	40 47	+43	114	41 30	+42	113	42 12	+42	112	315
46	38 39	44	115	39 23	43	114	40 06	43	113	40 49	42	112	41 31	42	111	314
47	37 59	43	114	38 42	43	113	39 25	42	112	40 07	42	111	40 49	42	110	313
48	37 18	43	113	38 01	42	112	38 43	42	111	39 25	42	110	40 07	41	110	312
49	36 37	42	112	37 19	43	111	38 02	42	110	38 44	41	110	39 25	41	109	311
50	35 55	+43	111	36 38	+42	111	37 20	+41	110	38 01	+42	109	38 43	+40	108	310
51	35 13	43	111	35 56	42	110	36 38	41	109	37 19	41	108	38 00	41	107	309
52	34 32	42	110	35 14	41	109	35 55	41	108	36 36	41	107	37 17	41	106	308
53	33 49	42	109	34 31	42	108	35 13	41	107	35 54	40	106	36 34	41	105	307
54	33 07	42	108	33 49	41	107	34 30	41	106	35 11	40	105	35 51	40	104	306
55	32 25	+41	107	33 06	+41	106	33 47	+41	105	34 28	+40	105	35 08	+40	104	305
56	31 42	41	106	32 23	41	106	33 04	40	105	33 44	41	104	34 25	39	103	304
57	30 59	41	106	31 40	41	105	32 21	40	104	33 01	40	103	33 41	40	102	303
58	30 16	41	105	30 57	40	104	31 37	41	103	32 18	39	102	32 57	40	101	302
59	29 33	41	104	30 14	40	103	30 54	40	102	31 34	40	101	32 14	39	101	301
60	28 49	+41	103	29 30	+40	102	30 10	+40	102	30 50	+40	101	31 30	+39	100	300
61	28 06	40	103	28 46	41	102	29 27	39	101	30 06	40	100	30 46	39	99	299
62	27 22	41	102	28 03	40	101	28 43	39	100	29 22	40	99	30 02	39	98	298
63	26 39	40	101	27 19	40	100	27 59	39	99	28 38	39	98	29 17	39	98	297
64	25 55	40	100	26 35	40	99	27 15	39	99	27 54	39	98	28 33	39	97	296
65	25 11	+40	100	25 51	+40	99	26 31	+39	98	27 10	+39	97	27 49	+39	96	295
66	24 27	40	99	25 07	39	98	25 46	40	97	26 26	39	96	27 05	38	95	294
67	23 43	40	98	24 23	39	97	25 02	39	96	25 41	39	96	26 20	39	95	293
68	22 59	39	97	23 38	40	97	24 18	39	96	24 57	39	95	25 36	38	94	292
69	22 14	40	97	22 54	39	96	23 33	39	95	24 12	39	94	24 51	39	93	291

S. Lat. {LHA greater than 180°....... Zn=180−Z; LHA less than 180°........... Zn=180+Z}

DECLINATION (0°-14°) SAME NAME AS LATITUDE

LAT 42°

N. Lat. {LHA greater than 180°....... Zn=Z; LHA less than 180°........... Zn=360−Z}

DECLINATION (0°-14°) SAME NAME AS LATITUDE

Each cell: Hc (° ′) d (′) Z (°)

LHA	0°	1°	2°	3°	4°	5°	6°	7°	8°	9°	10°	11°	12°	13°	14°	LHA
70	14 44 +41 104	15 25 +41 103	16 06 +41 102	16 47 +41 101	17 28 +41 101	18 09 +41 100	18 50 +40 99	19 30 +40 98	20 10 +40 98	20 50 +40 97	21 30 +40 96	22 10 +39 95	22 49 +39 94	23 28 +39 94	24 07 +38 93	290
71	14 00 41 103	14 41 42 102	15 23 41 102	16 04 40 101	16 44 41 100	17 25 41 99	18 06 40 98	18 46 40 98	19 26 40 97	20 06 40 96	20 46 39 95	21 25 39 94	22 04 39 94	22 43 39 93	23 22 39 92	289
72	13 17 41 102	13 58 41 102	14 39 41 101	15 20 40 100	16 00 41 99	16 41 40 99	17 21 41 98	18 02 40 97	18 42 40 96	19 22 39 95	20 01 40 95	20 41 39 94	21 20 39 93	21 59 39 92	22 38 38 91	288
73	12 33 41 102	13 14 41 101	13 55 41 100	14 36 40 99	15 16 41 99	15 57 40 98	16 37 40 97	17 17 40 96	17 57 40 95	18 37 40 95	19 17 39 94	19 56 39 93	20 35 39 92	21 14 39 91	21 53 38 91	287
74	11 49 41 101	12 30 41 100	13 11 41 99	13 52 40 99	14 32 41 98	15 13 40 97	15 53 40 96	16 33 40 96	17 13 40 95	17 53 39 94	18 32 40 93	19 12 39 92	19 51 39 92	20 30 38 91	21 08 39 90	286
75	11 05 +41 100	11 46 +41 99	12 27 +41 99	13 08 +40 98	13 48 +40 97	14 28 +41 96	15 09 +40 96	15 49 +40 95	16 29 +39 94	17 08 +40 93	17 48 +39 93	18 27 +39 92	19 06 +39 91	19 45 +39 90	20 24 +38 89	285
76	10 21 41 100	11 02 41 99	11 43 40 98	12 23 41 97	13 04 40 97	13 44 40 96	14 24 40 95	15 04 40 94	15 44 40 93	16 24 39 93	17 03 39 92	17 42 40 91	18 22 39 90	19 01 38 89	19 39 39 89	284
77	09 37 41 99	10 18 41 98	10 59 40 97	11 39 40 97	12 19 41 96	13 00 40 95	13 40 40 94	14 20 40 94	15 00 39 93	15 39 40 92	16 19 39 91	16 58 39 90	17 37 39 90	18 16 39 89	18 55 38 88	283
78	08 53 41 98	09 34 40 97	10 14 41 97	10 55 40 96	11 35 40 95	12 15 40 94	12 55 40 94	13 35 40 93	14 15 40 92	14 55 39 91	15 34 39 91	16 13 39 90	16 52 39 89	17 31 39 88	18 10 39 87	282
79	08 09 41 97	08 50 40 97	09 30 40 96	10 10 41 95	10 51 40 94	11 31 40 94	12 11 40 93	12 51 39 92	13 30 40 91	14 10 39 91	14 49 40 90	15 29 39 89	16 08 39 88	16 47 39 87	17 26 38 87	281
80	07 25 +40 97	08 05 +41 96	08 46 +40 95	09 26 +40 95	10 06 +40 94	10 46 +40 93	11 26 +40 92	12 06 +40 92	12 46 +39 91	13 25 +40 90	14 05 +39 89	14 44 +39 88	15 23 +39 88	16 02 +39 87	16 41 +39 86	280
81	06 41 40 96	07 21 40 95	08 01 41 95	08 42 40 94	09 22 40 93	10 02 40 92	10 42 40 92	11 22 39 91	12 01 40 90	12 41 39 89	13 20 40 89	14 00 39 88	14 39 39 87	15 18 39 86	15 57 38 85	279
82	05 56 41 95	06 37 40 95	07 17 40 94	07 57 40 93	08 37 40 92	09 17 40 92	09 57 40 91	10 37 40 90	11 17 39 89	11 56 40 89	12 36 39 88	13 15 39 87	13 54 39 86	14 33 39 86	15 12 39 85	278
83	05 12 40 95	05 52 40 94	06 32 40 93	07 12 41 93	07 53 40 92	08 33 40 91	09 13 39 90	09 52 40 89	10 32 40 89	11 12 39 88	11 51 40 87	12 31 39 86	13 10 39 86	13 49 39 85	14 28 39 84	277
84	04 27 41 94	05 08 40 93	05 48 40 93	06 28 40 92	07 08 40 91	07 48 40 90	08 28 40 90	09 08 39 89	09 47 40 88	10 27 40 87	11 07 39 87	11 46 39 86	12 25 39 85	13 04 40 84	13 44 38 83	276
85	03 43 +40 93	04 23 +40 93	05 03 +40 92	05 43 +40 91	06 23 +40 90	07 03 +40 90	07 43 +40 89	08 23 +40 88	09 03 +40 87	09 43 +39 87	10 22 +40 86	11 02 +39 85	11 41 +39 84	12 20 +39 84	12 59 +39 83	275
86	02 58 40 93	03 38 41 92	04 19 40 91	04 59 40 90	05 39 40 90	06 19 40 89	06 59 40 88	07 39 39 87	08 18 40 87	08 58 40 86	09 38 39 85	10 17 40 84	10 57 39 84	11 36 39 83	12 15 39 82	274
87	02 14 40 92	02 54 40 91	03 34 40 91	04 14 40 90	04 54 40 89	05 34 40 88	06 14 40 88	06 54 40 87	07 34 40 86	08 14 39 85	08 53 40 85	09 33 39 84	10 12 40 83	10 52 39 82	11 31 39 81	273
88	01 29 40 91	02 09 40 91	02 49 41 90	03 30 40 89	04 10 40 88	04 50 40 88	05 30 40 87	06 10 39 86	06 49 40 85	07 29 40 85	08 09 40 84	08 49 39 83	09 28 40 82	10 08 39 82	10 47 39 81	272
89	00 45 40 91	01 25 40 90	02 05 40 89	02 45 40 88	03 25 40 88	04 05 40 87	04 45 40 86	05 25 40 86	06 05 40 85	06 45 40 84	07 25 39 83	08 04 40 82	08 44 39 82	09 23 40 81	10 03 39 80	271
90	00 00 +40 90	00 40 +40 89	01 20 +40 89	02 00 +41 88	02 41 +40 87	03 21 +40 86	04 01 +40 86	04 41 +40 85	05 21 +40 84	06 01 +39 83	06 40 +40 83	07 20 +40 82	08 00 +39 81	08 39 +40 80	09 19 +39 80	270
91	−0 45 41 89	−0 04 40 89	00 36 40 88	01 16 40 87	01 56 40 86	02 36 40 86	03 16 40 85	03 56 40 84	04 36 40 83	05 16 40 83	05 56 40 82	06 36 40 81	07 16 40 80	07 56 39 80	08 35 40 79	269
92	−1 29 40 89	−0 49 40 88	−0 09 40 87	00 31 41 86	01 12 40 86	01 52 40 85	02 32 40 84	03 12 40 83	03 52 40 83	04 32 40 82	05 12 40 81	05 52 40 81	06 32 40 80	07 12 40 79	07 52 39 78	268
93	−2 14 40 88	−1 34 41 87	−0 53 40 86	−0 13 40 86	00 27 40 85	01 07 40 84	01 47 41 84	02 28 40 83	03 08 40 82	03 48 40 81	04 28 40 81	05 08 40 80	05 48 40 79	06 28 40 78	07 08 40 78	267
94	−2 58 40 87	−2 18 40 87	−1 38 40 86	−0 58 41 85	−0 17 40 84	00 23 40 84	01 03 40 83	01 43 41 82	02 24 40 81	03 04 40 81	03 44 40 80	04 24 40 79	05 04 40 78	05 44 40 78	06 24 40 77	266
95	−3 43 +40 87	−3 03 +41 86	−2 22 +40 85	−1 42 +40 84	−1 02 +41 84	−0 21 +40 83	00 19 +40 82	00 59 +41 81	01 40 +40 81	02 20 +40 80	03 00 +40 79	03 40 +41 79	04 21 +40 78	05 01 +40 77	05 41 +40 76	265
96	−4 27 40 86	−3 47 40 85	−3 07 41 84	−2 26 40 84	−1 46 40 83	−1 06 41 82	−0 25 40 82	00 15 41 81	00 56 40 80	01 36 40 79	02 16 41 79	02 57 40 78	03 37 40 77	04 17 41 76	04 58 40 76	264
97	−5 12 41 85	−4 31 40 85	−3 51 40 84	−3 11 41 83	−2 30 40 82	−1 50 41 82	−1 09 40 81	−0 29 41 80	00 12 40 79	00 52 41 79	01 33 40 78	02 13 41 77	02 54 40 76	03 34 41 76	04 15 40 75	263
98	−5 56 40 85	−5 16 41 84	−4 35 40 83	−3 55 41 82	−3 14 40 82	−2 34 41 81	−1 53 40 80	−1 13 41 79	−0 32 41 79	00 09 40 78	00 49 41 77	01 30 41 77	02 11 40 76	02 51 41 75	03 32 40 74	262
99		−6 00 40 83	−5 20 41 82	−4 39 41 82	−3 58 40 81	−3 18 41 80	−2 37 41 80	−1 56 40 79	−1 16 41 78	−0 35 41 77	00 06 41 77	00 47 40 76	01 27 41 75	02 08 41 74	02 49 40 74	261
100			−6 04 +41 82	−5 23 +41 81	−4 42 +40 80	−4 02 +41 80	−3 21 +41 79	−2 40 +41 78	−1 59 +41 77	−1 18 +41 77	−0 37 +40 76	00 03 +41 75	00 44 +41 74	01 25 +41 74	02 06 +41 73	260
101				−6 07 41 80	−5 26 41 80	−4 45 40 79	−4 05 41 78	−3 24 41 77	−2 43 41 77	−2 02 41 76	−1 21 41 75	−0 40 41 75	00 01 41 74	00 42 42 73	01 24 41 72	259
102					−6 10 41 79	−5 29 41 78	−4 48 41 77	−4 07 41 77	−3 26 41 76	−2 45 41 75	−2 04 42 75	−1 22 41 74	−0 41 40 73	−0 01 42 72	00 41 41 72	258
103						−6 13 41 77	−5 32 42 77	−4 50 41 76	−4 09 41 75	−3 28 41 75	−2 47 42 74	−2 05 41 73	−1 24 41 72	−0 43 42 72	−0 01 41 71	257
104							−6 15 41 76	−5 34 42 75	−4 52 41 75	−4 11 42 74	−3 29 41 73	−2 48 42 72	−2 06 41 72	−1 25 42 71	−0 43 41 70	256
105								−6 17 +42 75	−5 35 +41 74	−4 54 +43 73	−4 11 +41 73	−3 30 +41 72	−2 49 +42 71	−2 07 +42 70	−1 25 +42 70	255
106									−6 18 42 73	−5 36 42 73	−4 54 41 72	−4 13 42 71	−3 31 42 70	−2 49 42 70	−2 07 42 69	254
107										−6 19 42 72	−5 37 42 71	−4 55 42 70	−4 13 43 70	−3 30 42 69	−2 48 42 68	253
108											−6 19 42 70	−5 37 43 70	−4 54 42 69	−4 12 42 68	−3 30 43 68	252
109												−6 18 42 69	−5 36 43 68	−4 53 42 68	−4 11 43 67	251
110													−6 17 +42 68	−5 35 +43 67	−4 52 +43 66	250
111														−6 15 43 66	−5 32 43 65	249
112															−6 13 43 65	248

DECLINATION (0°-14°) CONTRARY NAME TO LATITUDE

S. Lat. {LHA greater than 180°....... Zn=180−Z; LHA less than 180°........... Zn=180+Z}

LHA	0°	1°	2°	3°	4°	5°	6°	7°	8°	9°	10°	11°	12°	13°	14°	LHA
98	−5 56 41 85															262
97	−5 12 40 85	−5 52 40 86														263
96	−4 27 41 86	−5 08 40 87	−5 48 40 87	−6 28 40 88												264
95	−3 43 −40 87	−4 23 −40 87	−5 03 −40 88	−5 43 −40 89	−6 23 −40 90											265
94	−2 58 40 87	−3 38 41 88	−4 19 40 89	−4 59 40 90	−5 39 40 90	−6 19 40 91										266
93	−2 14 40 88	−2 54 40 89	−3 34 40 89	−4 14 40 90	−4 54 40 91	−5 34 40 92	−6 14 40 92									267
92	−1 29 40 89	−2 09 40 89	−2 49 41 90	−3 30 40 91	−4 10 40 92	−4 50 40 92	−5 30 40 93	−6 10 39 94								268
91	−0 45 40 89	−1 25 40 90	−2 05 40 91	−2 45 40 92	−3 25 40 92	−4 05 40 93	−4 45 40 94	−5 25 40 94	−6 05 40 95							269
90	00 00 −40 90	−0 40 −40 91	−1 20 −40 91	−2 00 −41 92	−2 41 −40 93	−3 21 −40 94	−4 01 −40 94	−4 41 −40 95	−5 21 −40 96	−6 01 −39 97						270
89	00 45 41 91	00 04 40 91	−0 36 40 92	−1 16 40 93	−1 56 40 94	−2 36 40 94	−3 16 40 95	−3 56 40 96	−4 36 40 97	−5 16 40 97	−5 56 40 98					271
88	01 29 40 91	00 49 40 92	00 09 40 93	−0 31 41 94	−1 12 40 94	−1 52 40 95	−2 32 40 96	−3 12 40 97	−3 52 40 97	−4 32 40 98	−5 12 40 99	−5 52 40 99				272
87	02 14 40 92	01 34 41 93	00 53 40 94	00 13 40 94	−0 27 40 95	−1 07 40 96	−1 47 41 96	−2 28 40 97	−3 08 40 98	−3 48 40 99	−4 28 40 99	−5 08 40 100	−5 48 40 101			273
86	02 58 40 93	02 18 40 93	01 38 40 94	00 58 41 95	00 17 40 96	−0 23 40 96	−1 03 40 97	−1 43 41 98	−2 24 40 99	−3 04 40 99	−3 44 40 100	−4 24 40 101	−5 04 40 102	−5 44 40 102	−6 24 40 103	274
85	03 43 −40 93	03 03 −41 94	02 22 −40 95	01 42 −40 96	01 02 −41 96	00 21 −40 97	−0 19 −40 98	−0 59 −41 99	−1 40 −40 99	−2 20 −40 100	−3 00 −40 101	−3 40 −41 101	−4 21 −40 102	−5 01 −40 103	−5 41 −40 104	275
84	04 27 40 94	03 47 40 95	03 07 41 96	02 26 40 96	01 46 40 97	01 06 41 98	00 25 40 98	−0 15 41 99	−0 56 40 100	−1 36 40 101	−2 16 41 101	−2 57 40 102	−3 37 40 103	−4 17 41 104	−4 58 40 104	276
83	05 12 41 95	04 31 40 95	03 51 40 96	03 11 41 97	02 30 40 98	01 50 41 98	01 09 40 99	00 29 41 100	−0 12 40 101	−0 52 41 101	−1 33 40 102	−2 13 41 103	−2 54 40 104	−3 34 41 104	−4 15 40 105	277
82	05 56 40 95	05 16 41 96	04 35 40 97	03 55 41 98	03 14 40 98	02 34 41 99	01 53 40 100	01 13 41 101	00 32 41 101	−0 09 40 102	−0 49 41 103	−1 30 41 103	−2 11 40 104	−2 51 41 105	−3 32 40 106	278
81	06 41 41 96	06 00 40 97	05 20 41 98	04 39 41 98	03 58 40 99	03 18 41 100	02 37 41 100	01 56 40 101	01 16 41 102	00 35 41 103	−0 06 41 103	−0 47 40 104	−1 27 41 105	−2 08 41 106	−2 49 40 106	279
80	07 25 −41 97	06 44 −40 98	06 04 −41 98	05 23 −41 99	04 42 −40 100	04 02 −41 100	03 21 −41 101	02 40 −41 102	01 59 −41 103	01 18 −41 103	00 37 −40 104	−0 03 −41 105	−0 44 −41 106	−1 25 −41 106	−2 06 −41 107	280
79	08 09 40 97	07 29 41 98	06 48 41 99	06 07 41 100	05 26 41 100	04 45 40 101	04 05 41 102	03 24 41 103	02 43 41 103	02 02 41 104	01 21 41 105	00 40 41 105	−0 01 41 106	−0 42 42 107	−1 24 41 108	281
78	08 53 40 98	08 13 41 99	07 32 41 100	06 51 41 100	06 10 41 101	05 29 41 102	04 48 41 103	04 07 41 103	03 26 41 104	02 45 41 105	02 04 42 105	01 22 41 106	00 41 40 107	00 01 42 108	−0 41 41 108	282
77	09 37 40 99	08 57 41 100	08 16 41 100	07 35 41 101	06 54 41 102	06 13 41 103	05 32 42 103	04 50 41 104	04 09 41 105	03 28 41 105	02 47 42 106	02 05 41 107	01 24 41 108	00 43 42 108	00 01 41 109	283
76	10 21 40 100	09 41 41 100	09 00 41 101	08 19 42 102	07 37 41 102	06 56 41 103	06 15 41 104	05 34 42 105	04 52 41 105	04 11 42 106	03 29 41 107	02 48 42 108	02 06 41 108	01 25 42 109	00 43 41 110	284
75	11 05 −41 100	10 24 −41 101	09 43 −41 102	09 02 −41 102	08 21 −41 103	07 40 −42 104	06 58 −41 105	06 17 −42 105	05 35 −41 106	04 54 −43 107	04 11 −41 107	03 30 −41 108	02 49 −42 109	02 07 −42 110	01 25 −42 110	285
74	11 49 41 101	11 08 41 102	10 27 41 102	09 46 42 103	09 04 41 104	08 23 42 105	07 41 41 105	07 00 42 106	06 18 42 107	05 36 42 107	04 54 41 108	04 13 42 109	03 31 42 110	02 49 42 110	02 07 42 111	286
73	12 33 41 102	11 52 42 102	11 10 41 103	10 29 41 104	09 48 42 105	09 06 42 105	08 24 42 106	07 42 41 107	07 01 42 107	06 19 42 108	05 37 42 109	04 55 42 110	04 13 43 110	03 30 42 111	02 48 42 112	287
72	13 17 [illegible] 102	12 35 41 103	11 54 42 104	11 12 41 105	10 31 42 105	09 49 42 106	09 07 42 107	08 25 42 107	07 43 42 108	07 01 42 109	06 19 42 110	05 37 43 110	04 54 42 111	04 12 42 112	03 30 43 112	288
71	14 00 41 103	13 19 42 104	12 37 42 105	11 55 41 105	11 14 42 106	10 32 42 107	09 50 42 107	09 08 43 108	08 25 42 109	07 43 42 110	07 01 43 110	06 18 42 111	05 36 43 112	04 53 42 112	04 11 43 113	289
70	14 44 −42 104	14 02 −42 104	13 20 −42 105	12 38 −42 106	11 56 −42 107	11 14 −42 107	10 32 −42 108	09 50 −43 109	09 07 −42 110	08 25 −42 110	07 43 −43 111	07 00 −43 112	06 17 −42 112	05 35 −43 113	04 52 −43 114	290

N. Lat. {LHA greater than 180°....... Zn=Z; LHA less than 180°........... Zn=360−Z}

DECLINATION (0°-14°) CONTRARY NAME TO LATITUDE

LHA	0° Hc	0° d	0° Z	1° Hc	1° d	1° Z	2° Hc	2° d	2° Z	3° Hc	3° d	3° Z	4° Hc	4° d	4° Z
	° ′	′	°	° ′	′	°	° ′	′	°	° ′	′	°	° ′	′	°
69	15 27	42	104	14 45	42	105	14 03	42	106	13 21	42	107	12 39	42	107
68	16 10	42	105	15 28	42	106	14 46	42	107	14 04	42	107	13 22	43	108
67	16 53	42	106	16 11	42	107	15 29	43	107	14 46	42	108	14 04	43	109
66	17 36	43	107	16 53	42	107	16 11	42	108	15 29	43	109	14 46	43	110
65	18 18	-42	107	17 36	-43	108	16 53	-42	109	16 11	-43	110	15 28	-43	110
64	19 01	43	108	18 18	42	109	17 36	43	110	16 53	43	110	16 10	44	111
63	19 43	43	109	19 00	43	110	18 17	43	110	17 34	43	111	16 51	43	112
62	20 25	43	110	19 42	43	110	18 59	43	111	18 16	44	112	17 32	43	113
61	21 07	43	110	20 24	43	111	19 41	44	112	18 57	44	113	18 13	43	113
60	21 49	-44	111	21 05	-43	112	20 22	-44	113	19 38	-44	113	18 54	-44	114
59	22 30	43	112	21 47	44	113	21 03	44	113	20 19	44	114	19 35	44	115
58	23 12	44	113	22 28	44	113	21 44	44	114	21 00	45	115	20 15	44	116
57	23 53	44	114	23 09	45	114	22 24	44	115	21 40	45	116	20 55	44	116
56	24 33	44	114	23 49	44	115	23 05	45	116	22 20	45	117	21 35	45	117
55	25 14	-45	115	24 29	-44	116	23 45	-45	117	23 00	-45	117	22 15	-46	118
54	25 54	45	116	25 09	45	117	24 24	45	117	23 39	45	118	22 54	46	119
53	26 34	45	117	25 49	45	118	25 04	46	118	24 18	45	119	23 33	46	120
52	27 14	46	118	26 28	45	118	25 43	46	119	24 57	46	120	24 11	46	121
51	27 53	45	119	27 08	46	119	26 22	46	120	25 36	46	121	24 50	47	121
50	28 32	-46	119	27 46	-46	120	27 00	-46	121	26 14	-46	122	25 28	-47	122
49	29 11	46	120	28 25	47	121	27 38	46	122	26 52	47	122	26 05	47	123
48	29 49	46	121	29 03	47	122	28 16	47	123	27 29	47	123	26 42	47	124
47	30 27	46	122	29 41	47	123	28 54	48	123	28 06	47	124	27 19	47	125
46	31 05	47	123	30 18	47	124	29 31	48	124	28 43	48	125	27 55	47	126
45	31 42	-47	124	30 55	-48	125	30 07	-48	125	29 19	-48	126	28 31	-48	127
44	32 19	48	125	31 31	48	125	30 43	48	126	29 55	48	127	29 07	48	128
43	32 55	48	126	32 07	48	126	31 19	48	127	30 31	49	128	29 42	49	128
42	33 31	48	127	32 43	48	127	31 55	49	128	31 06	49	129	30 17	49	129
41	34 07	49	128	33 18	48	128	32 30	50	129	31 40	49	130	30 51	49	130
40	34 42	-49	129	33 53	-49	129	33 04	-49	130	32 15	-50	131	31 25	-50	131
39	35 17	50	130	34 27	49	130	33 38	50	131	32 48	50	132	31 58	50	132
38	35 51	50	131	35 01	50	131	34 11	50	132	33 21	50	133	32 31	51	133
37	36 24	50	132	35 34	50	132	34 44	50	133	33 54	51	134	33 03	51	134
36	36 57	51	133	36 07	50	133	35 17	51	134	34 26	51	135	33 35	51	135
35	37 30	-51	134	36 39	-51	134	35 48	-51	135	34 57	-51	136	34 06	-52	136
34	38 02	51	135	37 11	51	135	36 20	52	136	35 28	52	137	34 36	52	137
33	38 33	51	136	37 42	52	137	36 50	52	137	35 58	52	138	35 06	52	138
32	39 04	52	137	38 12	52	138	37 20	52	138	36 28	52	139	35 36	53	140
31	39 34	52	138	38 42	52	139	37 50	53	139	36 57	53	140	36 04	53	141
30	40 04	-53	139	39 11	-53	140	38 18	-53	140	37 25	-53	141	36 32	-53	142
29	40 32	53	140	39 39	53	141	38 46	53	141	37 53	53	142	37 00	54	143
28	41 00	53	142	40 07	53	142	39 14	54	143	38 20	54	143	37 26	54	144
27	41 28	54	143	40 34	54	143	39 40	54	144	38 46	54	144	37 52	54	145
26	41 55	55	144	41 00	54	145	40 06	54	145	39 12	55	146	38 17	54	146
25	42 20	-54	145	41 26	-55	146	40 31	-54	146	39 37	-55	147	38 42	-55	147
24	42 45	54	146	41 51	55	147	40 56	55	148	40 01	55	148	39 06	56	149
23	43 10	55	148	42 15	56	148	41 19	55	149	40 24	56	149	39 28	55	150
22	43 33	55	149	42 38	56	149	41 42	56	150	40 46	55	150	39 51	56	151
21	43 56	56	150	43 00	56	151	42 04	56	151	41 08	56	152	40 12	56	152
20	44 18	-57	152	43 21	-56	152	42 25	-56	152	41 29	-57	153	40 32	-56	153
19	44 38	56	153	43 42	57	153	42 45	56	154	41 49	57	154	40 52	57	155
18	44 58	56	154	44 02	57	155	43 05	57	155	42 08	57	155	41 11	58	156
17	45 17	57	155	44 20	57	156	43 23	57	156	42 26	58	157	41 28	57	157
16	45 35	57	157	44 38	57	157	43 41	58	158	42 43	58	158	41 45	57	158
15	45 53	-58	158	44 55	-58	159	43 57	-58	159	42 59	-58	159	42 01	-58	160
14	46 09	58	160	45 11	58	160	44 13	59	160	43 14	58	161	42 16	58	161
13	46 24	59	161	45 25	58	161	44 27	58	162	43 29	59	162	42 30	58	162
12	46 38	59	162	45 39	58	163	44 41	59	163	43 42	59	163	42 43	58	164
11	46 51	59	164	45 52	59	164	44 53	59	164	43 54	58	165	42 56	59	165
10	47 03	-59	165	46 04	-59	166	45 05	-59	166	44 06	-59	166	43 07	-59	166
9	47 13	59	167	46 14	59	167	45 15	59	167	44 16	59	167	43 17	60	168
8	47 23	59	168	46 24	60	168	45 24	59	169	44 25	59	169	43 26	60	169
7	47 32	60	170	46 32	59	170	45 33	60	170	44 33	59	170	43 34	60	170
6	47 39	59	171	46 40	60	171	45 40	60	171	44 40	59	172	43 41	60	172
5	47 46	-60	173	46 46	-60	173	45 46	-60	173	44 46	-59	173	43 47	-60	173
4	47 51	60	174	46 51	60	174	45 51	60	174	44 51	60	174	43 51	59	175
3	47 55	60	176	46 55	60	176	45 55	60	176	44 55	60	176	43 55	60	176
2	47 58	60	177	46 58	60	177	45 58	60	177	44 58	60	177	43 58	60	177
1	47 59	60	179	46 59	60	179	45 59	59	179	45 00	60	179	44 00	60	179
0	48 00	-60	180	47 00	-60	180	46 00	-60	180	45 00	-60	180	44 00	-60	180

LHA	5° Hc	5° d	5° Z	6° Hc	6° d	6° Z	7° Hc	7° d	7° Z	8° Hc	8° d	8° Z	9° Hc	9° d	9° Z
	° ′	′	°	° ′	′	°	° ′	′	°	° ′	′	°	° ′	′	°
69	11 57	43	108	11 14	43	109	10 32	43	110	09 49	42	110	09 07	43	111
68	12 39	42	109	11 57	43	110	11 14	43	110	10 31	43	111	09 48	43	112
67	13 21	43	110	12 38	42	110	11 56	43	111	11 13	43	112	10 30	44	112
66	14 03	43	110	13 20	43	111	12 37	43	112	11 54	43	112	11 11	44	113
65	14 45	-43	111	14 02	-43	112	13 19	-44	112	12 35	-43	113	11 52	-44	114
64	15 26	43	112	14 43	43	113	14 00	44	113	13 16	44	114	12 32	43	115
63	16 08	44	113	15 24	44	113	14 40	43	114	13 57	44	115	13 13	44	115
62	16 49	44	113	16 05	44	114	15 21	44	115	14 37	44	115	13 53	44	116
61	17 30	44	114	16 46	44	115	16 02	45	115	15 17	44	116	14 33	45	117
60	18 10	-44	115	17 26	-44	116	16 42	-45	116	15 57	-44	117	15 13	-45	118
59	18 51	45	116	18 06	44	116	17 22	45	117	16 37	45	118	15 52	45	118
58	19 31	45	116	18 46	45	117	18 01	45	118	17 16	45	118	16 31	45	119
57	20 11	45	117	19 26	46	118	18 40	45	119	17 55	45	119	17 10	46	120
56	20 50	45	118	20 05	45	119	19 20	46	119	18 34	46	120	17 48	45	121
55	21 29	-45	119	20 44	-46	119	19 58	-46	120	19 12	-45	121	18 27	-47	122
54	22 08	45	120	21 23	46	120	20 37	46	121	19 51	47	122	19 04	46	122
53	22 47	46	120	22 01	46	121	21 15	47	122	20 28	46	122	19 42	47	123
52	23 25	46	121	22 39	47	122	21 52	46	123	21 06	47	123	20 19	47	124
51	24 03	46	122	23 17	47	123	22 30	47	123	21 43	47	124	20 56	47	125
50	24 41	-47	123	23 54	-47	124	23 07	-47	124	22 20	-48	125	21 32	-47	126
49	25 18	47	124	24 31	47	124	23 44	48	125	22 56	48	126	22 08	47	126
48	25 55	47	125	25 08	48	125	24 20	48	126	23 32	48	127	22 44	48	127
47	26 32	48	126	25 44	48	126	24 56	48	127	24 08	49	128	23 19	48	128
46	27 08	48	126	26 20	49	127	25 31	48	128	24 43	49	128	23 54	48	129
45	27 43	-48	127	26 55	-49	128	26 06	-48	129	25 18	-49	129	24 29	-49	130
44	28 19	49	128	27 30	49	129	26 41	49	130	25 52	49	130	25 03	50	131
43	28 53	49	129	28 04	49	130	27 15	49	130	26 26	50	131	25 36	49	132
42	29 28	50	130	28 38	49	131	27 49	50	131	26 59	50	132	26 09	50	133
41	30 02	50	131	29 12	50	132	28 22	50	132	27 32	50	133	26 42	50	134
40	30 35	-50	132	29 45	-50	133	28 55	-50	133	28 05	-51	134	27 14	-51	134
39	31 08	50	133	30 18	51	134	29 27	51	134	28 36	50	135	27 46	51	135
38	31 40	50	134	30 50	51	135	29 59	51	135	29 08	51	136	28 17	52	136
37	32 12	51	135	31 21	51	136	30 30	51	136	29 39	52	137	28 47	52	137
36	32 44	52	136	31 52	51	137	31 01	52	137	30 09	52	138	29 17	52	138
35	33 14	-51	137	32 23	-52	138	31 31	-52	138	30 39	-53	139	29 46	-52	139
34	33 44	52	138	32 52	52	139	32 00	52	139	31 08	53	140	30 15	52	140
33	34 14	52	139	33 22	53	140	32 29	53	140	31 36	53	141	30 43	53	141
32	34 43	53	140	33 50	53	141	32 57	53	141	32 04	53	142	31 11	53	142
31	35 11	53	141	34 18	53	142	33 25	53	142	32 32	54	143	31 38	54	143
30	35 39	-53	142	34 46	-54	143	33 52	-54	143	32 58	-54	144	32 04	-54	144
29	36 06	54	143	35 12	54	144	34 18	54	144	33 24	54	145	32 30	54	145
28	36 32	54	144	35 38	54	145	34 44	54	146	33 50	55	146	32 55	55	147
27	36 58	55	146	36 03	54	146	35 09	55	147	34 14	55	147	33 19	55	148
26	37 23	55	147	36 28	55	147	35 33	55	148	34 38	55	148	33 43	55	149
25	37 47	-55	148	36 52	-55	148	35 57	-56	149	35 01	-55	149	34 06	-56	150
24	38 10	55	149	37 15	56	150	36 19	55	150	35 24	56	150	34 28	56	151
23	38 33	56	150	37 37	56	151	36 41	56	151	35 45	56	152	34 49	56	152
22	38 55	56	151	37 59	57	152	37 02	56	152	36 06	56	153	35 10	57	153
21	39 16	57	153	38 19	56	153	37 23	57	153	36 26	57	154	35 29	56	154
20	39 36	-57	154	38 39	-57	154	37 42	-57	155	36 45	-57	155	35 48	-57	155
19	39 55	57	155	38 58	57	155	38 01	57	156	37 04	57	156	36 07	58	157
18	40 13	57	156	39 16	57	157	38 19	58	157	37 21	57	157	36 24	58	158
17	40 31	58	158	39 33	57	158	38 36	58	158	37 38	58	159	36 40	57	159
16	40 48	58	159	39 50	58	159	38 52	58	159	37 54	58	160	36 56	58	160
15	41 03	-58	160	40 05	-58	160	39 07	-58	161	38 09	-58	161	37 11	-58	161
14	41 18	58	161	40 20	59	162	39 21	58	162	38 23	58	162	37 25	59	163
13	41 32	59	163	40 33	58	163	39 35	59	163	38 36	58	163	37 38	59	164
12	41 45	59	164	40 46	59	164	39 47	58	164	38 49	59	165	37 50	59	165
11	41 57	59	165	40 58	59	165	39 59	59	166	39 00	59	166	38 01	59	166
10	42 08	-60	167	41 08	-59	167	40 09	-59	167	39 10	-59	167	38 11	-59	167
9	42 17	59	168	41 18	59	168	40 19	59	168	39 20	60	168	38 20	59	169
8	42 26	59	169	41 27	60	169	40 27	59	170	39 28	59	170	38 29	60	170
7	42 34	59	171	41 35	60	171	40 35	59	171	39 36	60	171	38 36	60	171
6	42 41	60	172	41 41	59	172	40 42	60	172	39 42	60	172	38 42	59	172
5	42 47	-60	173	41 47	-60	173	40 47	-59	173	39 48	-60	174	38 48	-60	174
4	42 52	60	175	41 52	60	175	40 52	60	175	39 52	60	175	38 52	60	175
3	42 55	60	176	41 55	60	176	40 55	59	176	39 56	60	176	38 56	60	176
2	42 58	60	177	41 58	60	177	40 58	60	177	39 58	60	177	38 58	60	177
1	43 00	60	179	42 00	60	179	41 00	60	179	40 00	60	179	39 00	60	179
0	43 00	-60	180	42 00	-60	180	41 00	-60	180	40 00	-60	180	39 00	-60	180

LHA	10° Hc	10° d	10° Z	11° Hc	11° d	11° Z	12° Hc	12° d	12° Z	13° Hc	13° d	13° Z	14° Hc	14° d	14° Z	LHA
	° ′	′	°	° ′	′	°	° ′	′	°	° ′	′	°	° ′	′	°	
69	08 24	43	112	07 41	43	112	06 58	43	113	06 15	43	114	05 32	43	115	291
68	09 05	43	112	08 22	43	113	07 39	43	114	06 56	43	115	06 13	43	115	292
67	09 46	43	113	09 03	43	114	08 20	43	115	07 37	44	115	06 53	43	116	293
66	10 27	43	114	09 44	44	115	09 00	43	115	08 17	44	116	07 33	44	117	294
65	11 08	-44	115	10 24	-43	115	09 41	-44	116	08 57	-44	117	08 13	-44	117	295
64	11 49	44	115	11 05	44	116	10 21	44	117	09 37	45	117	08 52	44	118	296
63	12 29	44	116	11 45	45	117	11 00	44	117	10 16	44	118	09 32	45	119	297
62	13 09	45	117	12 24	44	117	11 40	45	118	10 55	44	119	10 11	45	120	298
61	13 48	44	118	13 04	45	118	12 19	45	119	11 34	45	120	10 49	45	120	299
60	14 28	-45	118	13 43	-45	119	12 58	-45	120	12 13	-45	120	11 28	-46	121	300
59	15 07	45	119	14 22	46	120	13 36	45	120	12 51	45	121	12 06	46	122	301
58	15 46	46	120	15 00	45	121	14 15	46	121	13 29	46	122	12 43	45	123	302
57	16 24	45	121	15 39	46	121	14 53	46	122	14 07	46	123	13 21	46	123	303
56	17 03	46	121	16 17	47	122	15 30	46	123	14 44	46	123	13 58	46	124	304
55	17 40	-46	122	16 54	-46	123	16 08	-47	124	15 21	-46	124	14 35	-47	125	305
54	18 18	46	123	17 32	47	124	16 45	47	124	15 58	47	125	15 11	47	126	306
53	18 55	47	124	18 08	46	124	17 22	48	125	16 34	47	126	15 47	47	126	307
52	19 32	47	125	18 45	47	125	17 58	47	126	17 11	48	127	16 23	48	127	308
51	20 09	48	125	19 21	47	126	18 34	48	127	17 46	48	127	16 58	48	128	309
50	20 45	-48	126	19 57	-48	127	19 09	-48	128	18 21	-48	128	17 33	-48	129	310
49	21 21	48	127	20 33	48	128	19 45	49	128	18 56	48	129	18 08	49	130	311
48	21 56	48	128	21 08	49	129	20 19	48	129	19 31	49	130	18 42	49	130	312
47	22 31	49	129	21 42	48	129	20 54	49	130	20 05	49	131	19 16	49	131	313
46	23 06	49	130	22 17	49	130	21 28	50	131	20 38	49	132	19 49	49	132	314
45	23 40	-50	131	22 50	-49	131	22 01	-49	132	21 12	-50	132	20 22	-50	133	315
44	24 13	49	131	23 24	50	132	22 34	50	133	21 44	50	133	20 54	50	134	316
43	24 47	50	132	23 57	50	133	23 07	50	134	22 17	51	134	21 26	50	135	317
42	25 19	50	133	24 29	50	134	23 39	51	134	22 48	50	135	21 58	51	136	318
41	25 52	51	134	25 01	51	135	24 10	50	135	23 20	51	136	22 29	51	137	319
40	26 23	-51	135	25 32	-51	136	24 41	-51	136	23 50	-51	137	22 59	-51	137	320
39	26 55	52	136	26 03	51	137	25 12	51	137	24 21	52	138	23 29	52	138	321
38	27 25	51	137	26 34	52	138	25 42	52	138	24 50	51	139	23 59	52	139	322
37	27 55	51	138	27 04	52	138	26 12	52	139	25 20	53	140	24 27	52	140	323
36	28 25	52	139	27 33	52	139	26 41	53	140	25 48	52	141	24 56	53	141	324
35	28 54	-52	140	28 02	-53	140	27 09	-53	141	26 16	-53	141	25 23	-52	142	325
34	29 23	53	141	28 30	53	141	27 37	53	142	26 44	53	142	25 51	54	143	326
33	29 50	53	142	28 57	53	142	28 04	53	143	27 11	54	143	26 17	53	144	327
32	30 18	54	143	29 24	53	143	28 31	54	144	27 37	54	144	26 43	54	145	328
31	30 44	53	144	29 51	54	144	28 57	54	145	28 03	54	145	27 09	55	146	329
30	31 10	-54	145	30 16	-54	145	29 22	-54	146	28 28	-55	146	27 33	-54	147	330
29	31 36	55	146	30 41	54	146	29 47	55	147	28 52	55	147	27 57	54	148	331
28	32 00	54	147	31 06	55	147	30 11	55	148	29 16	55	148	28 21	55	149	332
27	32 24	55	148	31 29	55	148	30 34	55	149	29 39	55	149	28 44	56	150	333
26	32 48	56	149	31 52	55	150	30 57	56	150	30 01	55	150	29 06	56	151	334
25	33 10	-56	150	32 14	-55	151	31 19	-56	151	30 23	-56	152	29 27	-56	152	335
24	33 32	56	151	32 36	56	152	31 40	56	152	30 44	56	153	29 48	57	153	336
23	33 53	56	152	32 57	57	153	32 00	56	153	31 04	57	154	30 07	56	154	337
22	34 13	56	154	33 17	57	154	32 20	57	154	31 23	56	155	30 27	57	155	338
21	34 33	57	155	33 36	57	155	32 39	57	155	31 42	57	156	30 45	57	156	339
20	34 51	-57	156	33 54	-57	156	32 57	-57	157	32 00	-57	157	31 03	-58	157	340
19	35 09	57	157	34 12	57	157	33 15	58	158	32 17	57	158	31 20	58	158	341
18	35 26	57	158	34 29	58	158	33 31	58	159	32 33	57	159	31 36	58	159	342
17	35 43	58	159	34 45	58	160	33 47	58	160	32 49	58	160	31 51	58	161	343
16	35 58	58	160	35 00	58	161	34 02	58	161	33 04	59	161	32 05	58	162	344
15	36 13	-59	162	35 14	-58	162	34 16	-58	162	33 18	-59	162	32 19	-58	163	345
14	36 26	58	163	35 28	59	163	34 29	58	163	33 31	59	164	32 32	59	164	346
13	36 39	59	164	35 40	58	164	34 42	59	165	33 43	59	165	32 44	59	165	347
12	36 51	59	165	35 52	59	165	34 53	59	166	33 54	59	166	32 55	59	166	348
11	37 02	59	166	36 03	59	167	35 04	59	167	34 05	60	167	33 05	59	167	349
10	37 12	-59	168	36 13	-60	168	35 13	-59	168	34 14	-59	168	33 15	-59	168	350
9	37 21	59	169	36 22	60	169	35 22	59	169	34 23	60	169	33 23	59	170	351
8	37 29	59	170	36 30	60	170	35 30	59	170	34 31	60	171	33 31	60	171	352
7	37 36	59	171	36 37	60	171	35 37	60	172	34 37	59	172	33 38	60	172	353
6	37 43	60	173	36 43	60	173	35 43	60	173	34 43	59	173	33 44	60	173	354
5	37 48	-60	174	36 48	-60	174	35 48	-60	174	34 48	-59	174	33 49	-60	174	355
4	37 52	60	175	36 52	59	175	35 53	60	175	34 53	60	175	33 53	60	175	356
3	37 56	60	176	36 56	60	176	35 56	60	176	34 56	60	176	33 56	60	177	357
2	37 58	60	178	36 58	60	178	35 58	60	178	34 58	60	178	33 58	60	178	358
1	38 00	60	179	37 00	60	179	36 00	60	179	35 00	60	179	34 00	60	179	359
0	38 00	-60	180	37 00	-60	180	36 00	-60	180	35 00	-60	180	34 00	-60	180	360

S. Lat. {LHA greater than 180°....... Zn=180−Z; LHA less than 180°........... Zn=180+Z}

DECLINATION (0°-14°) CONTRARY NAME TO LATITUDE

N. Lat. {LHA greater than 180°....... Zn=Z
{LHA less than 180°........... Zn=360−Z

DECLINATION (15°-29°) SAME NAME AS LATITUDE

LHA	15° Hc	15° d	15° Z	16° Hc	16° d	16° Z	17° Hc	17° d	17° Z	18° Hc	18° d	18° Z	19° Hc	19° d	19° Z
	° ′	′	°	° ′	′	°	° ′	′	°	° ′	′	°	° ′	′	°
0	63 00	+60	180	64 00	+60	180	65 00	+60	180	66 00	+60	180	67 00	+60	180
1	62 59	60	178	63 59	60	178	64 59	60	178	65 59	60	178	66 59	60	178
2	62 57	60	176	63 57	60	176	64 57	59	176	65 56	60	175	66 56	60	175
3	62 53	59	174	63 52	60	173	64 52	60	173	65 52	60	173	66 52	59	173
4	62 47	59	172	63 46	60	171	64 46	60	171	65 46	59	171	66 45	60	170
5	62 39	+60	169	63 39	+59	169	64 38	+59	169	65 37	+60	168	66 37	+59	168
6	62 31	59	167	63 30	59	167	64 29	59	167	65 28	59	166	66 27	58	166
7	62 20	59	165	63 19	59	165	64 18	58	164	65 16	59	164	66 15	58	163
8	62 08	58	163	63 06	59	163	64 05	58	162	65 03	58	162	66 01	58	161
9	61 54	58	161	62 52	58	161	63 50	58	160	64 48	58	160	65 46	57	159
10	61 39	+58	159	62 37	+57	159	63 34	+58	158	64 32	+57	157	65 29	+57	157
11	61 23	57	157	62 20	57	157	63 17	57	156	64 14	57	155	65 11	56	155
12	61 05	57	156	62 02	56	155	62 58	57	154	63 55	56	153	64 51	55	153
13	60 46	56	154	61 42	56	153	62 38	56	152	63 34	55	151	64 29	55	150
14	60 25	56	152	61 21	56	151	62 17	55	150	63 12	55	149	64 07	54	148
15	60 04	+55	150	60 59	+55	149	61 54	+54	148	62 48	+55	147	63 43	+53	147
16	59 41	54	148	60 35	55	147	61 30	54	147	62 24	53	146	63 17	54	145
17	59 17	54	146	60 11	54	146	61 05	53	145	61 58	53	144	62 51	52	143
18	58 51	54	145	59 45	53	144	60 38	53	143	61 31	52	142	62 23	52	141
19	58 25	53	143	59 18	53	142	60 11	52	141	61 03	52	140	61 55	51	139
20	57 58	+52	142	58 50	+52	141	59 42	+52	140	60 34	+51	139	61 25	+51	138
21	57 30	52	140	58 22	51	139	59 13	51	138	60 04	50	137	60 54	50	136
22	57 00	52	138	57 52	51	137	58 43	50	136	59 33	50	135	60 23	49	134
23	56 30	51	137	57 21	51	136	58 12	49	135	59 01	50	134	59 51	48	133
24	55 59	51	135	56 50	50	134	57 40	49	133	58 29	48	132	59 17	48	131
25	55 28	+49	134	56 17	+50	133	57 07	+48	132	57 55	+48	131	58 43	+48	130
26	54 55	49	133	55 44	49	132	56 33	48	131	57 21	48	129	58 09	47	128
27	54 22	49	131	55 11	48	130	55 59	47	129	56 46	47	128	57 33	47	127
28	53 48	48	130	54 36	48	129	55 24	47	128	56 11	46	127	56 57	46	126
29	53 14	47	129	54 01	47	128	54 48	47	126	55 35	46	125	56 21	45	124
30	52 38	+48	127	53 26	+46	126	54 12	+46	125	54 58	+46	124	55 44	+44	123
31	52 03	46	126	52 49	47	125	53 36	45	124	54 21	45	123	55 06	44	122
32	51 26	47	125	52 13	45	124	52 58	45	123	53 43	45	122	54 28	44	121
33	50 49	46	124	51 35	45	123	52 20	45	122	53 05	44	120	53 49	43	119
34	50 12	45	123	50 57	45	121	51 42	44	120	52 26	44	119	53 10	43	118
35	49 34	+45	121	50 19	+45	120	51 04	+43	119	51 47	+43	118	52 30	+43	117
36	48 56	44	120	49 40	44	119	50 24	44	118	51 08	43	117	51 51	42	116
37	48 17	44	119	49 01	44	118	49 45	43	117	50 28	42	116	51 10	42	115
38	47 38	44	118	48 22	43	117	49 05	43	116	49 48	42	115	50 30	41	114
39	46 58	44	117	47 42	43	116	48 25	42	115	49 07	42	114	49 49	41	113
40	46 19	+43	116	47 02	+42	115	47 44	+42	114	48 26	+41	113	49 07	+41	112
41	45 38	43	115	46 21	42	114	47 03	42	113	47 45	41	112	48 26	40	111
42	44 58	42	114	45 40	42	113	46 22	41	112	47 03	41	111	47 44	40	110
43	44 17	42	113	44 59	42	112	45 41	41	111	46 22	40	110	47 02	40	109
44	43 36	42	112	44 18	41	111	44 59	41	110	45 40	40	109	46 20	39	108
45	42 54	+42	111	43 36	+41	110	44 17	+40	109	44 57	+40	108	45 37	+39	107
46	42 13	41	110	42 54	41	109	43 35	40	108	44 15	39	107	44 54	40	106
47	41 31	41	109	42 12	40	108	42 52	40	107	43 32	40	106	44 12	38	105
48	40 48	41	109	41 29	40	108	42 09	40	107	42 49	39	106	43 28	39	105
49	40 06	41	108	40 47	40	107	41 27	39	106	42 06	39	105	42 45	39	104
50	39 23	+41	107	40 04	+40	106	40 44	+39	105	41 23	+39	104	42 02	+38	103
51	38 41	40	106	39 21	39	105	40 00	40	104	40 40	38	103	41 18	38	102
52	37 58	40	105	38 38	39	104	39 17	39	103	39 56	39	102	40 35	38	101
53	37 15	39	104	37 54	40	103	38 34	38	102	39 12	39	101	39 51	38	100
54	36 31	40	104	37 11	39	103	37 50	39	102	38 29	38	101	39 07	38	100
55	35 48	+39	103	36 27	+39	102	37 06	+39	101	37 45	+38	100	38 23	+37	99
56	35 04	40	102	35 44	38	101	36 22	39	100	37 01	38	99	37 39	37	98
57	34 21	39	101	35 00	38	100	35 38	39	99	36 17	38	98	36 55	37	97
58	33 37	39	100	34 16	38	100	34 54	39	99	35 33	37	98	36 10	38	97
59	32 53	39	100	33 32	38	99	34 10	38	98	34 48	38	97	35 26	37	96
60	32 09	+39	99	32 48	+38	98	33 26	+38	97	34 04	+38	96	34 42	+37	95
61	31 25	38	98	32 03	39	97	32 42	38	96	33 20	37	95	33 57	37	95
62	30 41	38	97	31 19	38	97	31 57	38	96	32 35	38	95	33 13	37	94
63	29 56	39	97	30 35	38	96	31 13	38	95	31 51	37	94	32 28	37	93
64	29 12	38	96	29 50	39	95	30 29	37	94	31 06	38	93	31 44	37	92
65	28 28	+38	95	29 06	+38	94	29 44	+38	94	30 22	+37	93	30 59	+37	92
66	27 43	39	95	28 22	38	94	29 00	37	93	29 37	38	92	30 15	36	91
67	26 59	38	94	27 37	38	93	28 15	38	92	28 53	37	91	29 30	37	90
68	26 14	39	93	26 53	37	92	27 30	38	91	28 08	37	91	28 45	37	90
69	25 30	38	93	26 08	38	92	26 46	37	91	27 23	38	90	28 01	37	89

LHA	20° Hc	20° d	20° Z	21° Hc	21° d	21° Z	22° Hc	22° d	22° Z	23° Hc	23° d	23° Z	24° Hc	24° d	24° Z
	° ′	′	°	° ′	′	°	° ′	′	°	° ′	′	°	° ′	′	°
0	68 00	+60	180	69 00	+60	180	70 00	+60	180	71 00	+60	180	72 00	+60	180
1	67 59	60	178	68 59	60	177	69 59	60	177	70 59	60	177	71 59	60	177
2	67 56	60	175	68 56	60	175	69 56	60	175	70 56	59	174	71 55	60	174
3	67 51	60	173	68 51	60	172	69 51	59	172	70 50	60	172	71 50	59	171
4	67 45	59	170	68 44	59	170	69 43	60	169	70 43	59	169	71 42	59	168
5	67 36	+59	168	68 35	+59	167	69 34	+59	167	70 33	+59	166	71 32	+58	165
6	67 25	59	165	68 24	59	165	69 23	58	164	70 21	58	163	71 19	59	163
7	67 13	58	163	68 11	58	162	69 09	58	162	70 07	58	161	71 05	58	160
8	66 59	58	161	67 57	57	160	68 54	58	159	69 52	57	158	70 49	57	157
9	66 43	58	158	67 41	56	157	68 37	57	157	69 34	57	156	70 31	56	155
10	66 26	+57	156	67 23	+56	155	68 19	+56	154	69 15	+56	153	70 11	+55	152
11	66 07	56	154	67 03	56	153	67 59	55	152	68 54	55	151	69 49	54	150
12	65 46	56	152	66 42	55	151	67 37	54	150	68 31	55	149	69 26	53	147
13	65 24	55	150	66 19	55	149	67 14	53	147	68 07	54	146	69 01	53	145
14	65 01	54	147	65 55	54	146	66 49	53	145	67 42	52	144	68 34	52	143
15	64 36	+54	145	65 30	+53	144	66 23	+52	143	67 15	+52	142	68 07	+51	141
16	64 11	52	144	65 03	52	142	65 55	52	141	66 47	51	140	67 38	50	139
17	63 43	52	142	64 35	52	141	65 27	51	139	66 18	50	138	67 08	49	137
18	63 15	52	140	64 07	50	139	64 57	50	137	65 47	50	136	66 37	48	135
19	62 46	51	138	63 37	50	137	64 27	49	136	65 16	48	134	66 04	48	133
20	62 16	+50	136	63 06	+49	135	63 55	+49	134	64 44	+47	133	65 31	+47	131
21	61 44	50	135	62 34	48	133	63 22	48	132	64 10	47	131	64 57	46	129
22	61 12	49	133	62 01	48	132	62 49	47	131	63 36	46	129	64 22	46	128
23	60 39	48	132	61 27	48	130	62 15	46	129	63 01	46	128	63 47	44	126
24	60 05	48	130	60 53	46	129	61 39	46	127	62 25	45	126	63 10	44	125
25	59 31	+47	129	60 18	+46	127	61 04	+45	126	61 49	+44	125	62 33	+44	123
26	58 56	46	127	59 42	45	126	60 27	45	125	61 12	44	123	61 56	42	122
27	58 20	45	126	59 05	45	124	59 50	44	123	60 34	43	122	61 17	43	120
28	57 43	45	124	58 28	45	123	59 13	43	122	59 56	43	120	60 39	41	119
29	57 06	45	123	57 51	43	122	58 34	43	120	59 17	42	119	59 59	42	118
30	56 28	+44	122	57 12	+44	121	57 56	+42	119	58 38	+42	118	59 20	+40	116
31	55 50	44	121	56 34	43	119	57 17	42	118	57 59	41	117	58 40	40	115
32	55 12	43	119	55 55	42	118	56 37	41	117	57 18	41	115	57 59	40	114
33	54 32	43	118	55 15	42	117	55 57	41	116	56 38	40	114	57 18	39	113
34	53 53	42	117	54 35	42	116	55 17	40	115	55 57	40	113	56 37	39	112
35	53 13	+42	116	53 55	+41	115	54 36	+40	113	55 16	+39	112	55 55	+39	111
36	52 33	41	115	53 14	41	114	53 55	40	112	54 35	39	111	55 14	38	110
37	51 52	41	114	52 33	40	113	53 13	40	111	53 53	38	110	54 31	38	109
38	51 11	41	113	51 52	40	112	52 32	39	110	53 11	38	109	53 49	38	108
39	50 30	40	112	51 10	40	111	51 50	38	109	52 28	38	108	53 06	38	107
40	49 48	+40	111	50 28	+39	110	51 07	+39	108	51 46	+38	107	52 24	+37	106
41	49 06	40	110	49 46	39	109	50 25	38	107	51 03	38	106	51 41	36	105
42	48 24	40	109	49 04	38	108	49 42	38	106	50 20	37	105	50 57	37	104
43	47 42	39	108	48 21	38	107	48 59	38	106	49 37	37	104	50 14	36	103
44	46 59	39	107	47 38	38	106	48 16	38	105	48 54	37	103	49 31	36	102
45	46 16	+39	106	46 55	+38	105	47 33	+37	104	48 10	+37	103	48 47	+36	101
46	45 34	38	105	46 12	38	104	46 50	37	103	47 27	36	102	48 03	36	101
47	44 50	39	104	45 29	37	103	46 06	37	102	46 43	36	101	47 19	36	100
48	44 07	38	103	44 45	38	102	45 23	36	101	45 59	36	100	46 35	36	99
49	43 24	37	103	44 01	38	102	44 39	36	100	45 15	36	99	45 51	35	98
50	42 40	+38	102	43 18	+37	101	43 55	+36	100	44 31	+36	99	45 07	+35	97
51	41 56	38	101	42 34	37	100	43 11	36	99	43 47	36	98	44 23	35	97
52	41 13	37	100	41 50	37	99	42 27	36	98	43 03	35	97	43 38	35	96
53	40 29	37	99	41 06	37	98	41 43	36	97	42 19	35	96	42 54	35	95
54	39 45	37	99	40 22	36	98	40 58	36	97	41 34	36	96	42 10	34	94
55	39 00	+37	98	39 37	+37	97	40 14	+36	96	40 50	+35	95	41 25	+35	94
56	38 16	37	97	38 53	37	96	39 30	35	95	40 05	36	94	40 41	34	93
57	37 32	37	96	38 09	36	95	38 45	36	94	39 21	35	93	39 56	35	92
58	36 48	36	96	37 24	37	95	38 01	35	94	38 36	36	93	39 12	34	92
59	36 03	37	95	36 40	36	94	37 16	36	93	37 52	35	92	38 27	35	91
60	35 19	+36	94	35 55	+37	93	36 32	+35	92	37 07	+35	91	37 42	+35	90
61	34 34	37	94	35 11	36	93	35 47	36	92	36 23	35	91	36 58	34	90
62	33 50	36	93	34 26	36	92	35 02	36	91	35 38	35	90	36 13	35	89
63	33 05	37	92	33 42	36	91	34 18	35	90	34 53	36	89	35 29	34	88
64	32 21	36	92	32 57	36	91	33 33	36	90	34 09	35	89	34 44	35	88
65	31 36	+37	91	32 13	+36	90	32 49	+35	89	33 24	+36	88	34 00	+34	87
66	30 51	37	90	31 28	36	89	32 04	36	88	32 40	35	87	33 15	35	86
67	30 07	36	89	30 43	37	89	31 20	35	00	31 55	36	87	32 31	34	86
68	29 22	37	89	29 59	36	88	30 35	36	87	31 11	35	86	31 46	35	85
69	28 38	36	88	29 14	36	87	29 50	36	86	30 26	36	85	31 02	35	84

25° Hc	25° d	25° Z	26° Hc	26° d	26° Z	27° Hc	27° d	27° Z	28° Hc	28° d	28° Z	29° Hc	29° d	29° Z	LHA
° ′	′	°	° ′	′	°	° ′	′	°	° ′	′	°	° ′	′	°	
73 00	+60	180	74 00	+60	180	75 00	+60	180	76 00	+60	180	77 00	+60	180	360
72 59	60	177	73 59	60	177	74 59	60	177	75 59	60	176	76 59	59	176	359
72 55	60	174	73 55	60	174	74 55	59	173	75 54	60	173	76 54	60	172	358
72 49	60	171	73 49	59	170	74 48	59	170	75 47	60	169	76 47	59	169	357
72 41	59	168	73 40	59	167	74 39	59	166	75 38	58	166	76 36	59	165	356
72 30	+59	165	73 29	+58	164	74 27	+58	163	75 25	+58	162	76 23	+58	161	355
72 18	57	162	73 15	58	161	74 13	57	160	75 10	57	159	76 07	57	158	354
72 03	57	159	73 00	57	158	73 57	56	157	74 53	56	156	75 49	56	154	353
71 46	56	156	72 42	56	155	73 38	56	154	74 34	55	153	75 29	54	151	352
71 27	55	154	72 22	55	152	73 17	55	151	74 12	54	150	75 06	53	148	351
71 06	+55	151	72 01	+54	150	72 55	+53	148	73 48	+53	147	74 41	+52	145	350
70 43	54	148	71 37	54	147	72 31	52	146	73 23	52	144	74 15	50	142	349
70 19	53	146	71 12	53	145	72 05	51	143	72 56	50	141	73 46	50	139	348
69 54	52	144	70 46	51	142	71 37	50	141	72 27	50	139	73 17	48	137	347
69 26	52	141	70 18	50	140	71 08	49	138	71 57	49	136	72 46	47	134	346
68 58	+50	139	69 48	+50	138	70 38	+48	136	71 26	+47	134	72 13	+46	132	345
68 28	49	137	69 17	49	136	70 06	47	134	70 53	46	132	71 39	45	130	344
67 57	49	135	68 46	47	134	69 33	47	132	70 20	45	130	71 05	44	128	343
67 25	48	133	68 13	46	132	68 59	46	130	69 45	44	128	70 29	43	126	342
66 52	47	131	67 39	46	130	68 25	44	128	69 09	44	126	69 53	42	124	341
66 18	+46	130	67 04	+45	128	67 49	+44	126	68 33	+42	124	69 15	+41	122	340
65 43	46	128	66 29	44	126	67 13	43	125	67 56	41	123	68 37	41	121	339
65 08	44	126	65 52	44	125	66 36	42	123	67 18	41	121	67 59	39	119	338
64 31	44	125	65 15	43	123	65 58	41	121	66 39	40	120	67 19	39	118	337
63 54	43	123	64 37	42	122	65 19	41	120	66 00	40	118	66 40	38	116	336
63 17	+42	122	63 59	+41	120	64 40	+41	118	65 21	+38	117	65 59	+38	115	335
62 38	42	120	63 20	41	119	64 01	39	117	64 40	39	115	65 19	37	113	334
62 00	41	119	62 41	40	117	63 21	39	116	64 00	38	114	64 38	36	112	333
61 20	41	118	62 01	40	116	62 41	38	114	63 19	37	113	63 56	36	111	332
60 41	40	116	61 21	39	115	62 00	38	113	62 38	36	111	63 14	36	110	331
60 00	+40	115	60 40	+39	114	61 19	+37	112	61 56	+36	110	62 32	+35	109	330
59 20	39	114	59 59	38	112	60 37	37	111	61 14	36	109	61 50	34	107	329
58 39	38	113	59 17	38	111	59 55	37	110	60 32	35	108	61 07	34	106	328
57 57	39	112	58 36	37	110	59 13	36	109	59 49	35	107	60 24	34	105	327
57 16	38	110	57 54	37	109	58 31	35	108	59 06	35	106	59 41	33	104	326
56 34	+37	109	57 11	+37	108	57 48	+35	107	58 23	+35	105	58 58	+33	103	325
55 52	37	108	56 29	36	107	57 05	35	106	57 40	34	104	58 14	33	102	324
55 09	37	107	55 46	36	106	56 22	35	105	56 57	34	103	57 31	32	102	323
54 27	36	106	55 03	36	105	55 39	34	104	56 13	34	102	56 47	32	101	322
53 44	36	105	54 20	35	104	54 55	35	103	55 30	33	101	56 03	32	100	321
53 01	+36	105	53 37	+35	103	54 12	+34	102	54 46	+33	100	55 19	+32	99	320
52 17	36	104	52 53	35	102	53 28	34	101	54 02	33	100	54 35	32	98	319
51 34	35	103	52 09	35	101	52 44	34	100	53 18	33	99	53 51	32	97	318
50 50	36	102	51 26	34	101	52 00	34	99	52 34	32	98	53 06	32	97	317
50 07	35	101	50 42	34	100	51 16	34	98	51 50	32	97	52 22	32	96	316
49 23	+35	100	49 58	+34	99	50 32	+33	98	51 05	+33	96	51 38	+31	95	315
48 39	35	99	49 14	34	98	49 48	33	97	50 21	32	96	50 53	32	94	314
47 55	35	99	48 30	33	97	49 03	34	96	49 37	32	95	50 09	31	94	313
47 11	34	98	47 45	34	97	48 19	33	95	48 52	32	94	49 24	32	93	312
46 26	35	97	47 01	34	96	47 35	33	95	48 08	32	93	48 40	31	92	311
45 42	+35	96	46 17	+33	95	46 50	+33	94	47 23	+32	93	47 55	+31	91	310
44 58	34	96	45 32	34	94	46 06	33	93	46 39	32	92	47 11	31	91	309
44 13	35	95	44 48	33	94	45 21	33	92	45 54	32	91	46 26	31	90	308
43 29	34	94	44 03	34	93	44 37	32	92	45 09	32	91	45 41	32	89	307
42 44	35	93	43 19	33	92	43 52	33	91	44 25	32	90	44 57	31	89	306
42 00	+34	93	42 34	+33	92	43 07	+33	90	43 40	+32	89	44 12	+32	88	305
41 15	34	92	41 49	34	91	42 23	33	90	42 56	32	89	43 28	31	87	304
40 31	34	91	41 05	33	90	41 38	33	89	42 11	32	88	42 43	32	87	303
39 46	34	91	40 20	34	90	40 54	33	88	41 27	32	87	41 59	31	86	302
39 02	34	90	39 36	33	89	40 09	33	88	40 42	32	87	41 14	32	86	301
38 17	+34	89	38 51	+34	88	39 25	+32	87	39 57	+33	86	40 30	+31	85	300
37 32	35	89	38 07	33	88	38 40	33	87	39 13	32	85	39 45	32	84	299
36 48	34	88	37 22	34	87	37 56	33	86	38 29	32	85	39 01	32	84	298
36 03	34	87	36 37	34	86	37 11	33	85	37 44	33	84	38 17	32	83	297
35 19	34	87	35 53	34	86	36 27	33	85	37 00	33	84	37 33	32	83	296
34 34	+35	86	35 09	+33	85	35 42	+34	84	36 16	+32	83	36 48	+32	82	295
33 50	34	85	34 24	34	84	34 58	33	83	35 31	33	82	36 04	33	81	294
33 05	35	85	33 40	34	84	34 14	33	83	34 47	33	82	35 20	33	81	293
32 21	35	84	32 56	34	83	33 30	33	82	34 03	33	81	34 36	33	80	292
31 37	34	84	32 11	34	83	32 45	34	82	33 19	33	81	33 52	33	80	291

S. Lat. {LHA greater than 180°....... Zn=180−Z
{LHA less than 180°........... Zn=180+Z

DECLINATION (15°-29°) SAME NAME AS LATITUDE

LAT 42°

N. Lat. {LHA greater than 180°....... Zn=Z; LHA less than 180°........... Zn=360−Z}

DECLINATION (15°-29°) SAME NAME AS LATITUDE

LAT 42°

LHA	15° Hc	15° d	15° Z	16° Hc	16° d	16° Z	17° Hc	17° d	17° Z	18° Hc	18° d	18° Z	19° Hc	19° d	19° Z	LHA
	° ′	′	°	° ′	′	°	° ′	′	°	° ′	′	°	° ′	′	°	
70	24 45	+38	92	25 23	+38	91	26 01	+38	90	26 39	+37	89	27 16	+37	88	290
71	24 01	38	91	24 39	38	90	25 17	37	89	25 54	38	89	26 32	37	88	289
72	23 16	38	91	23 54	38	90	24 32	38	89	25 10	37	88	25 47	37	87	288
73	22 31	39	90	23 10	38	89	23 48	37	88	24 25	38	87	25 03	37	86	287
74	21 47	38	89	22 25	38	88	23 03	38	88	23 41	37	87	24 18	37	86	286
75	21 02	+38	89	21 40	+38	88	22 18	+38	87	22 56	+38	86	23 34	+37	85	285
76	20 18	38	88	20 56	38	87	21 34	38	86	22 12	37	85	22 49	37	85	284
77	19 33	38	87	20 11	39	86	20 50	37	86	21 27	38	85	22 05	37	84	283
78	18 49	38	87	19 27	38	86	20 05	38	85	20 43	38	84	21 21	37	83	282
79	18 04	39	86	18 43	38	85	19 21	38	84	19 59	37	83	20 36	38	83	281
80	17 20	+38	85	17 58	+38	84	18 36	+38	84	19 14	+38	83	19 52	+38	82	280
81	16 35	39	85	17 14	38	84	17 52	38	83	18 30	38	82	19 08	38	81	279
82	15 51	38	84	16 29	39	83	17 08	38	82	17 46	38	82	18 24	38	81	278
83	15 07	38	83	15 45	39	83	16 24	38	82	17 02	38	81	17 40	38	80	277
84	14 22	39	83	15 01	39	82	15 40	38	81	16 18	38	80	16 56	38	79	276
85	13 38	+39	82	14 17	+39	81	14 56	+38	80	15 34	+38	80	16 12	+39	79	275
86	12 54	39	81	13 33	39	81	14 12	38	80	14 50	39	79	15 29	38	78	274
87	12 10	39	81	12 49	39	80	13 28	39	79	14 07	38	78	14 45	39	78	273
88	11 26	39	80	12 05	39	79	12 44	39	79	13 23	39	78	14 02	38	77	272
89	10 42	39	79	11 21	39	79	12 00	39	78	12 39	39	77	13 18	39	76	271
90	09 58	+40	79	10 38	+39	78	11 17	+39	77	11 56	+39	76	12 35	+39	76	270
91	09 15	39	78	09 54	40	77	10 34	39	77	11 13	39	76	11 52	39	75	269
92	08 31	40	78	09 11	39	77	09 50	40	76	10 30	39	75	11 09	39	74	268
93	07 48	39	77	08 27	40	76	09 07	40	75	09 47	39	75	10 26	39	74	267
94	07 04	40	76	07 44	40	75	08 24	40	75	09 04	39	74	09 43	40	73	266
95	06 21	+40	76	07 01	+40	75	07 41	+40	74	08 21	+40	73	09 01	+39	73	265
96	05 38	40	75	06 18	40	74	06 58	40	73	07 38	40	73	08 18	40	72	264
97	04 55	40	74	05 35	41	74	06 16	40	73	06 56	40	72	07 36	40	71	263
98	04 12	41	74	04 53	40	73	05 33	40	72	06 13	41	71	06 54	40	71	262
99	03 29	41	73	04 10	41	72	04 51	40	71	05 31	41	71	06 12	40	70	261
100	02 47	+41	72	03 28	+41	72	04 09	+40	71	04 49	+41	70	05 30	+41	69	260
101	02 05	41	72	02 46	40	71	03 26	41	70	04 07	41	69	04 48	41	69	259
102	01 22	41	71	02 03	42	70	02 45	41	69	03 26	41	69	04 07	41	68	258
103	00 40	42	70	01 22	41	70	02 03	41	69	02 44	42	68	03 26	41	67	257
104	-0 02	42	70	00 40	42	69	01 22	41	68	02 03	42	67	02 45	41	67	256
105	-0 43	+41	69	-0 02	+42	68	00 40	+42	67	01 22	+42	67	02 04	+41	66	255
106	-1 25	42	68	-0 43	42	68	-0 01	42	67	00 41	42	66	01 23	42	65	254
107	-2 06	42	68	-1 24	42	67	-0 42	42	66	00 00	43	65	00 43	42	65	253
108	-2 47	42	67	-2 05	43	66	-1 22	42	65	-0 40	42	65	00 02	43	64	252
109	-3 28	42	66	-2 46	43	66	-2 03	43	65	-1 20	42	64	-0 38	43	63	251
110	-4 09	+43	66	-3 26	+43	65	-2 43	+43	64	-2 00	+43	63	-1 17	+43	63	250
111	-4 49	43	65	-4 06	43	64	-3 23	43	63	-2 40	43	63	-1 57	43	62	249
112	-5 30	44	64	-4 46	43	63	-4 03	44	63	-3 19	43	62	-2 36	43	61	248
113	-6 10	44	63	-5 26	44	63	-4 42	43	62	-3 59	44	61	-3 15	44	61	247
114				-6 06	44	62	-5 22	44	61	-4 38	44	61	-3 54	44	60	246
115							-6 01	+44	61	-5 17	+45	60	-4 32	+44	59	245
116										-5 55	45	59	-5 10	44	59	244
117													-5 48	44	58	243

LHA	20° Hc	20° d	20° Z	21° Hc	21° d	21° Z	22° Hc	22° d	22° Z	23° Hc	23° d	23° Z	24° Hc	24° d	24° Z	LHA
	° ′	′	°	° ′	′	°	° ′	′	°	° ′	′	°	° ′	′	°	
70	27 53	+37	88	28 30	+36	87	29 06	+36	86	29 42	+35	85	30 17	+35	84	290
71	27 09	36	87	27 45	37	86	28 22	36	85	28 58	35	84	29 33	35	83	289
72	26 24	37	86	27 01	36	85	27 37	36	84	28 13	36	84	28 49	35	83	288
73	25 40	36	86	26 16	37	85	26 53	36	84	27 29	36	83	28 05	35	82	287
74	24 55	37	85	25 32	37	84	26 09	36	83	26 45	36	82	27 21	35	81	286
75	24 11	+37	84	24 48	+36	83	25 24	+37	83	26 01	+35	82	26 36	+36	81	285
76	23 26	37	84	24 03	37	83	24 40	36	82	25 16	37	81	25 53	35	80	284
77	22 42	37	83	23 19	37	82	23 56	36	81	24 32	37	80	25 09	35	80	283
78	21 58	37	82	22 35	37	82	23 12	37	81	23 49	36	80	24 25	36	79	282
79	21 14	37	82	21 51	37	81	22 28	37	80	23 05	36	79	23 41	36	78	281
80	20 30	+37	81	21 07	+37	80	21 44	+37	79	22 21	+37	79	22 58	+36	78	280
81	19 46	37	81	20 23	37	80	21 00	37	79	21 37	37	78	22 14	36	77	279
82	19 02	37	80	19 39	38	79	20 17	37	78	20 54	37	77	21 31	36	77	278
83	18 18	38	79	18 56	37	78	19 33	37	78	20 10	37	77	20 47	37	76	277
84	17 34	38	79	18 12	38	78	18 50	37	77	19 27	37	76	20 04	37	75	276
85	16 51	+37	78	17 28	+38	77	18 06	+38	76	18 44	+37	76	19 21	+37	75	275
86	16 07	38	77	16 45	38	77	17 23	38	76	18 01	37	75	18 38	37	74	274
87	15 24	38	77	16 02	38	76	16 40	38	75	17 18	37	74	17 55	38	74	273
88	14 40	39	76	15 19	38	75	15 57	38	75	16 35	38	74	17 13	37	73	272
89	13 57	38	76	14 35	39	75	15 14	38	74	15 52	38	73	16 30	38	72	271
90	13 14	+39	75	13 53	+38	74	14 31	+38	73	15 09	+39	73	15 48	+38	72	270
91	12 31	39	74	13 10	38	74	13 48	39	73	14 27	38	72	15 05	39	71	269
92	11 48	39	74	12 27	39	73	13 06	39	72	13 45	38	71	14 23	39	71	268
93	11 05	39	73	11 44	40	72	12 24	39	71	13 03	38	71	13 41	39	70	267
94	10 23	39	72	11 02	39	72	11 41	40	71	12 21	39	70	13 00	38	69	266
95	09 40	+40	72	10 20	+39	71	10 59	+40	70	11 39	+39	69	12 18	+39	69	265
96	08 58	40	71	09 38	39	70	10 17	40	70	10 57	39	69	11 36	40	68	264
97	08 16	40	71	08 56	40	70	09 36	40	69	10 16	39	68	10 55	40	67	263
98	07 34	40	70	08 14	40	69	08 54	40	68	09 34	40	68	10 14	40	67	262
99	06 52	41	69	07 33	40	69	08 13	40	68	08 53	40	67	09 33	40	66	261
100	06 11	+40	69	06 51	+41	68	07 32	+40	67	08 12	+41	66	08 53	+40	66	260
101	05 29	41	68	06 10	41	67	06 51	40	66	07 31	41	66	08 12	41	65	259
102	04 48	41	67	05 29	41	67	06 10	41	66	06 51	41	65	07 32	40	64	258
103	04 07	41	67	04 48	41	66	05 29	42	65	06 11	41	64	06 52	41	64	257
104	03 26	42	66	04 08	41	65	04 49	41	65	05 30	42	64	06 12	41	63	256
105	02 45	+42	65	03 27	+42	65	04 09	+41	64	04 50	+42	63	05 32	+42	62	255
106	02 05	42	65	02 47	42	64	03 29	42	63	04 11	42	63	04 53	42	62	254
107	01 25	42	64	02 07	42	63	02 49	42	63	03 31	42	62	04 13	43	61	253
108	00 45	42	63	01 27	43	63	02 10	42	62	02 52	43	61	03 35	42	61	252
109	00 05	43	63	00 48	43	62	01 31	42	61	02 13	43	61	02 56	42	60	251
110	-0 34	+43	62	00 09	+43	61	00 52	+42	61	01 34	+43	60	02 17	+43	59	250
111	-1 14	44	61	-0 30	43	61	00 13	43	60	00 56	43	59	01 39	43	59	249
112	-1 53	44	61	-1 09	43	60	-0 26	44	59	00 18	43	59	01 01	44	58	248
113	-2 31	43	60	-1 48	44	59	-1 04	44	59	-0 20	44	58	00 24	43	57	247
114	-3 10	44	59	-2 26	44	59	-1 42	44	58	-0 58	44	57	-0 14	44	57	246
115	-3 48	+44	59	-3 04	+45	58	-2 19	+44	57	-1 35	+44	57	-0 51	+45	56	245
116	-4 26	45	58	-3 41	44	57	-2 57	45	57	-2 12	45	56	-1 27	44	55	244
117	-5 04	45	57	-4 19	45	57	-3 34	45	56	-2 49	45	55	-2 04	45	55	243
118	-5 41	45	56	-4 56	45	56	-4 11	46	55	-3 25	45	55	-2 40	45	54	242
119				-5 33	46	55	-4 47	45	54	-4 02	46	54	-3 16	46	53	241
120				-6 09	+46	54	-5 23	+46	54	-4 37	+46	53	-3 51	+45	52	240
121							-5 59	46	53	-5 13	46	52	-4 27	46	52	239
122										-5 48	46	52	-5 02	47	51	238
123													-5 36	47	50	237

LHA	25° Hc	25° d	25° Z	26° Hc	26° d	26° Z	27° Hc	27° d	27° Z	28° Hc	28° d	28° Z	29° Hc	29° d	29° Z	LHA
	° ′	′	°	° ′	′	°	° ′	′	°	° ′	′	°	° ′	′	°	
70	30 52	+35	83	31 27	+34	82	32 01	+34	81	32 35	+34	80	33 09	+32	79	290
71	30 08	35	82	30 43	34	81	31 17	34	80	31 51	34	79	32 25	33	78	289
72	29 24	35	82	29 59	34	81	30 33	35	80	31 08	33	79	31 41	33	78	288
73	28 40	35	81	29 15	35	80	29 50	34	79	30 24	34	78	30 58	33	77	287
74	27 56	35	80	28 31	35	80	29 06	34	79	29 40	34	78	30 14	34	77	286
75	27 12	+35	80	27 47	+35	79	28 22	+35	78	28 57	+34	77	29 31	+34	76	285
76	26 28	36	79	27 04	35	78	27 39	34	77	28 13	35	77	28 48	34	76	284
77	25 44	36	79	26 20	35	78	26 55	35	77	27 30	34	76	28 04	35	75	283
78	25 01	35	78	25 36	36	77	26 12	35	76	26 47	34	75	27 21	35	74	282
79	24 17	36	77	24 53	36	77	25 29	35	76	26 04	35	75	26 39	34	74	281
80	23 34	+36	77	24 10	+35	76	24 45	+36	75	25 21	+35	74	25 56	+35	73	280
81	22 50	37	76	23 27	35	75	24 02	36	75	24 38	35	74	25 13	35	73	279
82	22 07	36	76	22 43	36	75	23 19	36	74	23 55	36	73	24 31	35	72	278
83	21 24	37	75	22 01	36	74	22 37	36	73	23 13	35	73	23 48	36	72	277
84	20 41	37	75	21 18	36	74	21 54	36	73	22 30	36	72	23 06	36	71	276
85	19 58	+37	74	20 35	+37	73	21 12	+36	72	21 48	+36	71	22 24	+36	71	275
86	19 15	37	73	19 52	37	72	20 29	37	72	21 06	36	71	21 42	36	70	274
87	18 33	37	73	19 10	37	72	19 47	37	71	20 24	36	70	21 00	37	69	273
88	17 50	38	72	18 28	37	71	19 05	37	70	19 42	37	70	20 19	36	69	272
89	17 08	37	72	17 45	38	71	18 23	37	70	19 00	37	69	19 37	37	68	271
90	16 26	+37	71	17 03	+38	70	17 41	+38	69	18 19	+37	68	18 56	+37	68	270
91	15 44	38	70	16 22	38	70	17 00	37	69	17 37	38	68	18 15	37	67	269
92	15 02	38	70	15 40	38	69	16 18	38	68	16 56	38	67	17 34	37	67	268
93	14 20	38	69	14 58	39	68	15 37	38	68	16 15	38	67	16 53	38	66	267
94	13 38	39	69	14 17	39	68	14 56	38	67	15 34	38	66	16 12	38	65	266
95	12 57	+39	68	13 36	+39	67	14 15	+38	66	14 53	+39	66	15 32	+38	65	265
96	12 16	39	67	12 55	39	67	13 34	39	66	14 13	39	65	14 52	38	64	264
97	11 35	39	67	12 14	39	66	12 53	40	65	13 33	39	64	14 12	38	64	263
98	10 54	40	66	11 34	39	65	12 13	40	65	12 53	39	64	13 32	39	63	262
99	10 13	40	65	10 53	40	65	11 33	40	64	12 13	39	63	12 52	40	62	261
100	09 33	+40	65	10 13	+40	64	10 53	+40	63	11 33	+40	63	12 13	+39	62	260
101	08 53	40	64	09 33	40	64	10 13	40	63	10 53	41	62	11 34	40	61	259
102	08 12	41	64	08 53	41	63	09 34	40	62	10 14	41	61	10 55	40	61	258
103	07 33	41	63	08 14	40	62	08 54	41	62	09 35	41	61	10 16	40	60	257
104	06 53	41	62	07 34	41	62	08 15	41	61	08 56	41	60	09 37	41	59	256
105	06 14	+41	62	06 55	+42	61	07 37	+41	60	08 18	+41	60	08 59	+41	59	255
106	05 35	41	61	06 16	42	60	06 58	42	60	07 40	41	59	08 21	42	58	254
107	04 56	42	60	05 38	42	60	06 20	42	59	07 02	41	58	07 43	42	58	253
108	04 17	42	60	04 59	43	59	05 42	42	58	06 24	42	58	07 06	42	57	252
109	03 38	43	59	04 21	43	58	05 04	42	58	05 46	43	57	06 29	42	56	251
110	03 00	+43	59	03 43	+43	58	04 26	+43	57	05 09	+43	56	05 52	+42	56	250
111	02 22	44	58	03 06	43	57	03 49	43	56	04 32	43	56	05 15	43	55	249
112	01 45	43	57	02 28	44	57	03 12	43	56	03 55	43	55	04 38	44	54	248
113	01 07	44	57	01 51	44	56	02 35	44	55	03 19	43	55	04 02	44	54	247
114	00 30	44	56	01 14	44	55	01 58	45	55	02 43	44	54	03 27	43	53	246
115	-0 06	+44	55	00 38	+44	55	01 22	+45	54	02 07	+44	53	02 51	+44	53	245
116	-0 43	45	55	00 02	44	54	00 46	45	53	01 31	45	53	02 16	44	52	244
117	-1 19	45	54	-0 34	45	53	00 11	45	53	00 56	45	52	01 41	45	51	243
118	-1 55	45	53	-1 10	46	53	-0 24	45	52	00 21	45	51	01 06	45	51	242
119	-2 30	45	53	-1 45	46	52	-0 59	45	51	-0 14	46	51	00 32	46	50	241
120	-3 06	+46	52	-2 20	+46	51	-1 34	+46	51	-0 48	+46	50	-0 02	+46	49	240
121	-3 41	47	51	-2 54	46	50	-2 08	46	50	-1 22	46	49	-0 36	47	49	239
122	-4 15	46	50	-3 29	47	50	-2 42	47	49	-1 55	46	49	-1 09	47	48	238
123	-4 49	47	50	-4 02	46	49	-3 16	47	48	-2 29	47	48	-1 42	47	47	237
124	-5 23	47	49	-4 36	47	48	-3 49	47	48	-3 02	48	47	-2 14	47	47	236
125	-5 57	+48	48	-5 09	+47	48	-4 22	+48	47	-3 34	+48	46	-2 46	+47	46	235
126				-5 42	48	47	-4 54	48	46	-4 06	48	46	-3 18	48	45	234
127							-5 26	48	46	-4 38	48	45	-3 50	49	44	233
128							-5 58	49	45	-5 09	48	44	-4 21	49	44	232
129										-5 40	49	44	-4 51	49	43	231
130													-5 22	+50	42	230
131													-5 51	49	42	229

DECLINATION (15°-29°) CONTRARY NAME TO LATITUDE

LHA	15° Hc	15° d	15° Z	16° Hc	16° d	16° Z	17° Hc	17° d	17° Z	18° Hc	18° d	18° Z	19° Hc	19° d	19° Z	LHA
85	-6 21	-40	104													275
84	-5 38	40	105	-6 18	40	106										276
83	-4 55	40	106	-5 35	41	106	-6 16	40	107							277
82	-4 12	41	106	-4 53	40	107	-5 33	40	108	-6 13	41	109				278
81	-3 29	41	107	-4 10	41	108	-4 51	40	109	-5 31	41	109	-6 12	40	110	279
80	-2 47	-41	108	-3 28	-41	108	-4 09	-40	109	-4 49	-41	110	-5 30	-41	111	280
79	-2 05	41	108	-2 46	40	109	-3 26	41	110	-4 07	41	111	-4 48	41	111	281
78	-1 22	41	109	-2 03	42	110	-2 45	41	111	-3 26	41	111	-4 07	41	112	282
77	-0 40	42	110	-1 22	41	110	-2 03	41	111	-2 44	42	112	-3 26	41	113	283
76	00 02	42	110	-0 40	42	111	-1 22	41	112	-2 03	42	113	-2 45	41	113	284
75	00 43	-41	111	00 02	-42	112	-0 40	-42	113	-1 22	-42	113	-2 04	-41	114	285
74	01 25	42	112	00 43	42	112	00 01	42	113	-0 41	42	114	-1 23	42	115	286
73	02 06	42	112	01 24	42	113	00 42	42	114	00 00	43	115	-0 43	42	115	287
72	02 47	42	113	02 05	43	114	01 22	42	115	00 40	42	115	-0 02	43	116	288
71	03 28	42	114	02 46	43	114	02 03	43	115	01 20	42	116	00 38	43	117	289
70	04 09	-43	114	03 26	-43	115	02 43	-43	116	02 00	-43	117	01 17	-43	117	290

LHA	20° Hc	20° d	20° Z	21° Hc	21° d	21° Z	22° Hc	22° d	22° Z	23° Hc	23° d	23° Z	24° Hc	24° d	24° Z	LHA
80	-6 11	-40	111													280
79	-5 29	41	112	-6 10	41	113										281
78	-4 48	41	113	-5 29	41	113	-6 10	41	114							282
77	-4 07	41	113	-4 48	41	114	-5 29	42	115	-6 11	41	116				283
76	-3 26	42	114	-4 08	41	115	-4 49	41	115	-5 30	42	116	-6 12	41	117	284
75	-2 45	-42	115	-3 27	-42	115	-4 09	-41	116	-4 50	-42	117	-5 32	-42	118	285
74	-2 05	42	115	-2 47	42	116	-3 29	42	117	-4 11	42	117	-4 53	42	118	286
73	-1 25	42	116	-2 07	42	117	-2 49	42	117	-3 31	42	118	-4 13	43	119	287
72	-0 45	42	117	-1 27	43	117	-2 10	42	118	-2 52	43	119	-3 35	42	119	288
71	-0 05	43	117	-0 48	43	118	-1 31	42	119	-2 13	43	119	-2 56	42	120	289
70	00 34	-43	118	-0 09	-43	119	-0 52	-42	119	-1 34	-43	120	-2 17	-43	121	290

LHA	25° Hc	25° d	25° Z	26° Hc	26° d	26° Z	27° Hc	27° d	27° Z	28° Hc	28° d	28° Z	29° Hc	29° d	29° Z	LHA
75	-6 14	-41	118													285
74	-5 35	41	119	-6 16	42	120										286
73	-4 56	42	120	-5 38	42	120										287
72	-4 17	42	120	-4 59	43	121	-5 42	42	122							288
71	-3 38	43	121	-4 21	43	122	-5 04	42	122	-5 46	43	123				289
70	-3 00	-43	121	-3 43	-43	122	-4 26	-43	123	-5 09	-43	124	-5 52	-42	124	290

S. Lat. {LHA greater than 180°........ Zn=180−Z; LHA less than 180°........... Zn=180+Z}

LAT 42°

DECLINATION (15°-29°) CONTRARY NAME TO LATITUDE

N. Lat. {LHA greater than 180°....... Zn=Z; LHA less than 180°.......... Zn=360−Z}

LHA	15° Hc	d	Z	16° Hc	d	Z	17° Hc	d	Z	18° Hc	d	Z	19° Hc	d	Z
	° ′	′	°	° ′	′	°	° ′	′	°	° ′	′	°	° ′	′	°
69	04 49	43	115	04 06	43	116	03 23	43	117	02 40	43	117	01 57	43	118
68	05 30	44	116	04 46	43	117	04 03	44	117	03 19	43	118	02 36	43	119
67	06 10	44	117	05 26	44	117	04 42	43	118	03 59	44	119	03 15	44	119
66	06 49	43	117	06 06	44	118	05 22	44	119	04 38	44	119	03 54	44	120
65	07 29	−44	118	06 45	−44	119	06 01	−44	119	05 17	−45	120	04 32	−44	121
64	08 08	44	119	07 24	45	119	06 39	44	120	05 55	45	121	05 10	44	121
63	08 47	45	119	08 02	44	120	07 18	45	121	06 33	45	122	05 48	44	122
62	09 26	45	120	08 41	45	121	07 56	45	122	07 11	45	122	06 26	45	123
61	10 04	45	121	09 19	45	122	08 34	45	122	07 49	46	123	07 03	45	124
60	10 42	−45	122	09 57	−46	122	09 11	−45	123	08 26	−46	124	07 40	−45	124
59	11 20	46	122	10 34	45	123	09 49	46	124	09 03	46	124	08 17	46	125
58	11 58	46	123	11 12	46	124	10 26	46	125	09 40	47	125	08 53	46	126
57	12 35	46	124	11 49	47	125	11 02	46	125	10 16	47	126	09 29	46	127
56	13 12	47	125	12 25	47	125	11 38	46	126	10 52	47	127	10 05	47	127
55	13 48	−47	125	13 01	−47	126	12 14	−47	127	11 27	−47	127	10 40	−47	128
54	14 24	47	126	13 37	47	127	12 50	47	128	12 03	48	128	11 15	47	129
53	15 00	47	127	14 13	48	128	13 25	47	128	12 38	48	129	11 50	48	130
52	15 35	47	128	14 48	48	128	14 00	48	129	13 12	48	130	12 24	48	130
51	16 10	47	129	15 23	49	129	14 34	48	130	13 46	48	130	12 58	48	131
50	16 45	−48	129	15 57	−49	130	15 08	−48	131	14 20	−49	131	13 31	−48	132
49	17 19	48	130	16 31	49	131	15 42	49	131	14 53	49	132	14 04	49	133
48	17 53	49	131	17 04	49	132	16 15	49	132	15 26	49	133	14 37	49	133
47	18 27	50	132	17 37	49	133	16 48	49	133	15 59	50	134	15 09	50	134
46	19 00	50	133	18 10	50	133	17 20	49	134	16 31	50	135	15 41	50	135
45	19 32	−50	134	18 42	−50	134	17 52	−50	135	17 02	−50	135	16 12	−50	136
44	20 04	50	134	19 14	50	135	18 24	51	136	17 33	50	136	16 43	51	137
43	20 36	51	135	19 45	50	136	18 55	51	136	18 04	51	137	17 13	51	138
42	21 07	51	136	20 16	51	137	19 25	51	137	18 34	51	138	17 43	51	138
41	21 38	51	137	20 47	52	138	19 55	51	138	19 04	52	139	18 12	51	139
40	22 08	−52	138	21 16	−51	139	20 25	−52	139	19 33	−52	140	18 41	−52	140
39	22 37	51	139	21 46	52	139	20 54	52	140	20 02	52	140	19 10	52	141
38	23 07	53	140	22 14	52	140	21 22	52	141	20 30	52	141	19 38	53	142
37	23 35	52	141	22 43	53	141	21 50	52	142	20 58	53	142	20 05	53	143
36	24 03	53	142	23 10	52	142	22 18	53	143	21 25	53	143	20 32	54	144
35	24 31	−54	143	23 37	−53	143	22 44	−53	144	21 51	−53	144	20 58	−54	145
34	24 57	53	143	24 04	53	144	23 11	54	144	22 17	54	145	21 23	53	145
33	25 24	54	144	24 30	54	145	23 36	54	145	22 42	54	146	21 48	54	146
32	25 49	54	145	24 55	54	146	24 01	54	146	23 07	54	147	22 13	55	147
31	26 14	54	146	25 20	54	147	24 26	55	147	23 31	54	148	22 37	55	148
30	26 39	−55	147	25 44	−55	148	24 49	−54	148	23 55	−55	149	23 00	−55	149
29	27 03	55	148	26 08	55	149	25 13	55	149	24 18	56	150	23 22	55	150
28	27 26	56	149	26 30	55	150	25 35	55	150	24 40	56	151	23 44	55	151
27	27 48	55	150	26 53	56	151	25 57	56	151	25 01	55	152	24 06	56	152
26	28 10	56	151	27 14	56	152	26 18	56	152	25 22	56	153	24 26	56	153
25	28 31	−56	152	27 35	−56	153	26 39	−56	153	25 43	−57	154	24 46	−56	154
24	28 51	56	153	27 55	56	154	26 59	57	154	26 02	56	155	25 06	57	155
23	29 11	57	154	28 14	56	155	27 18	57	155	26 21	57	156	25 24	57	156
22	29 30	57	155	28 33	57	156	27 36	57	156	26 39	57	157	25 42	57	157
21	29 48	57	157	28 51	57	157	27 54	58	157	26 56	57	158	25 59	57	158
20	30 05	−57	158	29 08	−57	158	28 11	−58	158	27 13	−57	159	26 16	−58	159
19	30 22	58	159	29 24	57	159	28 27	58	159	27 29	58	160	26 31	57	160
18	30 38	58	160	29 40	58	160	28 42	58	160	27 44	58	161	26 46	58	161
17	30 53	58	161	29 55	58	161	28 57	58	161	27 59	59	162	27 00	58	162
16	31 07	58	162	30 09	58	162	29 11	59	162	28 12	58	163	27 14	58	163
15	31 21	−59	163	30 22	−58	163	29 24	−59	164	28 25	−58	164	27 27	−59	164
14	31 33	58	164	30 35	59	164	29 36	59	165	28 37	58	165	27 39	59	165
13	31 45	59	165	30 46	59	165	29 47	58	166	28 49	59	166	27 50	59	166
12	31 56	59	166	30 57	59	167	29 58	59	167	28 59	59	167	28 00	59	167
11	32 06	59	167	31 07	59	168	30 08	59	168	29 09	59	168	28 10	60	168
10	32 16	−60	169	31 16	−59	169	30 17	−59	169	29 18	−60	169	28 18	−59	169
9	32 24	59	170	31 25	60	170	30 25	59	170	29 26	60	170	28 26	59	170
8	32 31	59	171	31 32	60	171	30 32	59	171	29 33	60	171	28 33	59	171
7	32 38	59	172	31 39	60	172	30 39	60	172	29 39	60	172	28 39	59	173
6	32 44	60	173	31 44	60	173	30 44	59	173	29 45	60	173	28 45	60	174
5	32 49	−60	174	31 49	−60	174	30 49	−60	174	29 49	−59	175	28 50	−60	175
4	32 53	60	175	31 53	60	176	30 53	60	176	29 53	60	176	28 53	60	176
3	32 56	60	177	31 56	60	177	30 56	60	177	29 56	60	177	28 56	60	177
2	32 58	60	178	31 58	60	178	30 58	60	178	29 58	60	178	28 58	60	178
1	33 00	60	179	32 00	60	179	31 00	60	179	30 00	60	179	29 00	60	179
0	33 00	−60	180	32 00	−60	180	31 00	−60	180	30 00	−60	180	29 00	−60	180

LHA	20° Hc	d	Z	21° Hc	d	Z	22° Hc	d	Z	23° Hc	d	Z	24° Hc	d	Z
	° ′	′	°	° ′	′	°	° ′	′	°	° ′	′	°	° ′	′	°
69	01 14	44	119	00 30	43	119	−0 13	43	120	−0 56	43	121	−1 39	43	121
68	01 53	44	119	01 09	43	120	00 26	44	121	−0 18	43	121	−1 01	44	122
67	02 31	43	120	01 48	44	121	01 04	44	121	00 20	44	122	−0 24	43	123
66	03 10	44	121	02 26	44	121	01 42	44	122	00 58	44	123	00 14	44	123
65	03 48	−44	121	03 04	−45	122	02 19	−44	123	01 35	−44	123	00 51	−45	124
64	04 26	45	122	03 41	44	123	02 57	45	123	02 12	45	124	01 27	44	125
63	05 04	45	123	04 19	45	123	03 34	45	124	02 49	45	125	02 04	45	125
62	05 41	45	124	04 56	45	124	04 11	46	125	03 25	45	125	02 40	45	126
61	06 18	45	124	05 33	46	125	04 47	45	126	04 02	46	126	03 16	46	127
60	06 55	−46	125	06 09	−46	126	05 23	−46	126	04 37	−46	127	03 51	−45	128
59	07 31	46	126	06 45	46	126	05 59	46	127	05 13	46	128	04 27	46	128
58	08 07	46	126	07 21	47	127	06 34	46	128	05 48	46	128	05 02	47	129
57	08 43	47	127	07 56	46	128	07 10	47	128	06 23	47	129	05 36	47	130
56	09 18	47	128	08 31	47	129	07 44	47	129	06 57	47	130	06 10	47	130
55	09 53	−47	129	09 06	−47	129	08 19	−48	130	07 31	−47	131	06 44	−47	131
54	10 28	48	129	09 40	47	130	08 53	48	131	08 05	48	131	07 17	47	132
53	11 02	48	130	10 14	48	131	09 26	48	131	08 38	48	132	07 50	48	133
52	11 36	48	131	10 48	48	132	10 00	49	132	09 11	48	133	08 23	48	133
51	12 10	49	132	11 21	48	132	10 33	49	133	09 44	49	134	08 55	48	134
50	12 43	−49	132	11 54	−49	133	11 05	−49	134	10 16	−49	134	09 27	−49	135
49	13 15	49	133	12 26	49	134	11 37	49	134	10 48	49	135	09 59	50	136
48	13 48	50	134	12 58	49	135	12 09	50	135	11 19	49	136	10 30	50	136
47	14 19	49	135	13 30	50	135	12 40	50	136	11 50	50	137	11 00	50	137
46	14 51	50	136	14 01	50	136	13 11	50	137	12 21	51	137	11 30	50	138
45	15 22	−51	136	14 31	−50	137	13 41	−50	138	12 51	−51	138	12 00	−51	139
44	15 52	50	137	15 02	51	138	14 11	51	138	13 20	51	139	12 29	51	140
43	16 22	51	138	15 31	51	139	14 40	51	139	13 49	51	140	12 58	51	140
42	16 52	51	139	16 01	52	140	15 09	51	140	14 18	52	141	13 26	51	141
41	17 21	52	140	16 29	51	140	15 38	52	141	14 46	52	141	13 54	52	142
40	17 49	−51	141	16 58	−52	141	16 06	−53	142	15 13	−52	142	14 21	−52	143
39	18 18	53	142	17 25	52	142	16 33	52	143	15 41	53	143	14 48	53	144
38	18 45	53	142	17 52	52	143	17 00	53	143	16 07	53	144	15 14	53	144
37	19 12	53	143	18 19	53	144	17 26	53	144	16 33	53	145	15 40	53	145
36	19 38	53	144	18 45	53	145	17 52	53	145	16 59	54	146	16 05	53	146
35	20 04	−53	145	19 11	−54	146	18 17	−53	146	17 24	−54	146	16 30	−54	147
34	20 30	54	146	19 36	54	146	18 42	54	147	17 48	54	147	16 54	54	148
33	20 54	54	147	20 00	54	147	19 06	54	148	18 12	55	148	17 17	54	149
32	21 18	54	148	20 24	54	148	19 30	55	149	18 35	55	149	17 40	54	150
31	21 42	55	149	20 47	55	149	19 52	54	150	18 58	55	150	18 03	55	150
30	22 05	−55	150	21 10	−55	150	20 15	−55	150	19 20	−55	151	18 25	−56	151
29	22 27	55	151	21 32	55	151	20 37	56	151	19 41	55	152	18 46	56	152
28	22 49	56	151	21 53	55	152	20 58	56	152	20 02	56	153	19 06	56	153
27	23 10	56	152	22 14	56	153	21 18	56	153	20 22	56	154	19 26	56	154
26	23 30	56	153	22 34	56	154	21 38	56	154	20 42	57	154	19 45	56	155
25	23 50	−56	154	22 54	−57	155	21 57	−56	155	21 01	−57	155	20 04	−56	156
24	24 09	57	155	23 12	56	156	22 16	57	156	21 19	57	156	20 22	57	157
23	24 27	57	156	23 30	57	157	22 33	57	157	21 36	57	157	20 39	57	158
22	24 45	57	157	23 48	57	158	22 51	58	158	21 53	57	158	20 56	57	159
21	25 02	58	158	24 04	57	159	23 07	57	159	22 10	58	159	21 12	57	159
20	25 18	−58	159	24 20	−57	160	23 23	−58	160	22 25	−58	160	21 27	−57	160
19	25 34	58	160	24 36	58	161	23 38	58	161	22 40	58	161	21 42	58	161
18	25 48	58	161	24 50	58	162	23 52	58	162	22 54	58	162	21 56	58	162
17	26 02	58	162	25 04	58	163	24 06	58	163	23 08	59	163	22 09	58	163
16	26 16	59	163	25 17	58	164	24 19	59	164	23 20	58	164	22 22	59	164
15	26 28	−59	164	25 29	−58	165	24 31	−59	165	23 32	−59	165	22 33	−58	165
14	26 40	59	165	25 41	59	166	24 42	59	166	23 43	58	166	22 45	59	166
13	26 51	59	166	25 52	59	167	24 53	59	167	23 54	59	167	22 55	59	167
12	27 01	59	167	26 02	59	168	25 03	59	168	24 04	60	168	23 04	59	168
11	27 10	59	168	26 11	59	169	25 12	59	169	24 13	60	169	23 13	59	169
10	27 19	−59	169	26 20	−60	170	25 20	−59	170	24 21	−60	170	23 21	−59	170
9	27 27	60	171	26 27	59	171	25 28	60	171	24 28	59	171	23 29	60	171
8	27 34	60	172	26 34	60	172	25 34	59	172	24 35	60	172	23 35	59	172
7	27 40	60	173	26 40	60	173	25 40	59	173	24 41	60	173	23 41	60	173
6	27 45	60	174	26 45	59	174	25 46	60	174	24 46	60	174	23 46	60	174
5	27 50	−60	175	26 50	−60	175	25 50	−60	175	24 50	−60	175	23 50	−60	175
4	27 53	59	176	26 54	60	176	25 54	60	176	24 54	60	176	23 54	60	176
3	27 56	60	177	26 56	60	177	25 56	60	177	24 56	59	177	23 57	60	177
2	27 58	60	178	26 58	60	178	25 58	60	178	24 58	60	170	23 50	59	170
1	28 00	60	179	27 00	60	179	26 00	60	179	25 00	60	179	24 00	60	179
0	28 00	−60	180	27 00	−60	180	26 00	−60	180	25 00	−60	180	24 00	−60	180

25° Hc	d	Z	26° Hc	d	Z	27° Hc	d	Z	28° Hc	d	Z	29° Hc	d	Z	LHA
° ′	′	°	° ′	′	°	° ′	′	°	° ′	′	°	° ′	′	°	
−2 22	44	122	−3 06	43	123	−3 49	43	124	−4 32	43	124	−5 15	43	125	291
−1 45	43	123	−2 28	44	123	−3 12	43	124	−3 55	43	125	−4 38	44	126	292
−1 07	44	123	−1 51	44	124	−2 35	44	125	−3 19	43	125	−4 02	44	126	293
−0 30	44	124	−1 14	44	125	−1 58	45	125	−2 43	44	126	−3 27	43	127	294
00 06	−44	125	−0 38	−44	125	−1 22	−45	126	−2 07	−44	127	−2 51	−44	127	295
00 43	45	125	−0 02	44	126	−0 46	45	127	−1 31	45	127	−2 16	44	128	296
01 19	45	126	00 34	45	127	−0 11	45	127	−0 56	45	128	−1 41	45	129	297
01 55	45	127	01 10	46	127	00 24	45	128	−0 21	45	129	−1 06	45	129	298
02 30	45	127	01 45	46	128	00 59	45	129	00 14	46	129	−0 32	46	130	299
03 06	−46	128	02 20	−46	129	01 34	−46	129	00 48	−46	130	00 02	−46	131	300
03 41	47	129	02 54	46	130	02 08	46	130	01 22	46	131	00 36	47	131	301
04 15	46	130	03 29	47	130	02 42	47	131	01 55	46	131	01 09	47	132	302
04 49	47	130	04 02	46	131	03 16	47	132	02 29	47	132	01 42	47	133	303
05 23	47	131	04 36	47	132	03 49	47	132	03 02	48	133	02 14	47	133	304
05 57	−48	132	05 09	−47	132	04 22	−48	133	03 34	−48	134	02 46	−47	134	305
06 30	48	132	05 42	48	133	04 54	48	134	04 06	48	134	03 18	48	135	306
07 02	48	133	06 14	48	134	05 26	48	134	04 38	48	135	03 50	49	136	307
07 35	49	134	06 46	48	135	05 58	49	135	05 09	48	136	04 21	49	136	308
08 07	49	135	07 18	49	135	06 29	49	136	05 40	49	136	04 51	49	137	309
08 38	−49	135	07 49	−49	136	07 00	−49	137	06 11	−49	137	05 22	−50	138	310
09 09	49	136	08 20	50	137	07 30	49	137	06 41	50	138	05 51	49	138	311
09 40	50	137	08 50	50	138	08 00	49	138	07 11	50	139	06 21	50	139	312
10 10	50	138	09 20	50	138	08 30	50	139	07 40	50	139	06 50	51	140	313
10 40	50	138	09 50	51	139	08 59	50	140	08 09	51	140	07 18	50	141	314
11 09	−50	139	10 19	−51	140	09 28	−51	140	08 37	−51	141	07 46	−51	141	315
11 38	51	140	10 47	51	141	09 56	51	141	09 05	51	142	08 14	51	142	316
12 07	52	141	11 15	51	141	10 24	52	142	09 32	51	142	08 41	52	143	317
12 35	52	142	11 43	52	142	10 51	52	143	09 59	51	143	09 08	52	144	318
13 02	52	142	12 10	52	143	11 18	52	143	10 26	52	144	09 34	52	144	319
13 29	−52	143	12 37	−53	144	11 44	−52	144	10 52	−52	145	10 00	−53	145	320
13 55	52	144	13 03	53	145	12 10	52	145	11 18	53	146	10 25	53	146	321
14 21	52	145	13 29	53	145	12 36	53	146	11 43	54	146	10 49	53	147	322
14 47	53	146	13 54	54	146	13 00	53	147	12 07	53	147	11 14	54	148	323
15 12	54	147	14 18	53	147	13 25	54	147	12 31	54	148	11 37	53	148	324
15 36	−54	147	14 42	−54	148	13 48	−54	148	12 54	−54	149	12 00	−54	149	325
16 00	54	148	15 06	54	149	14 12	55	149	13 17	54	150	12 23	54	150	326
16 23	54	149	15 29	55	150	14 34	54	150	13 40	55	150	12 45	55	151	327
16 46	55	150	15 51	55	150	14 56	55	151	14 01	54	151	13 07	55	152	328
17 08	55	151	16 13	55	151	15 18	55	152	14 23	55	152	13 28	56	152	329
17 29	−55	152	16 34	−55	152	15 39	−56	152	14 43	−55	153	13 48	−56	153	330
17 50	55	153	16 55	56	153	15 59	56	153	15 03	55	154	14 08	56	154	331
18 10	55	153	17 15	56	154	16 19	56	154	15 23	56	155	14 27	56	155	332
18 30	56	154	17 34	56	155	16 38	56	155	15 42	57	155	14 45	56	156	333
18 49	56	155	17 53	57	156	16 56	56	156	16 00	57	156	15 03	56	157	334
19 08	−57	156	18 11	−57	156	17 14	−56	157	16 18	−57	157	15 21	−57	158	335
19 25	57	157	18 28	56	157	17 32	57	158	16 35	57	158	15 38	57	158	336
19 42	57	158	18 45	57	158	17 48	57	159	16 51	57	159	15 54	57	159	337
19 59	57	159	19 02	58	159	18 04	57	159	17 07	58	160	16 09	57	160	338
20 15	58	160	19 17	58	160	18 19	57	160	17 22	58	161	16 24	57	161	339
20 30	−58	161	19 32	−58	161	18 34	−58	161	17 36	−58	162	16 38	−57	162	340
20 44	58	162	19 46	58	162	18 48	58	162	17 50	58	162	16 52	58	163	341
20 58	58	163	20 00	59	163	19 01	58	163	18 03	58	163	17 05	58	164	342
21 11	59	164	20 12	58	164	19 14	58	164	18 16	59	164	17 17	58	165	343
21 23	58	164	20 25	59	165	19 26	58	165	18 28	59	165	17 29	59	165	344
21 35	−59	165	20 36	−59	166	19 37	−58	166	18 39	−59	166	17 40	−59	166	345
21 46	59	166	20 47	59	167	19 48	59	167	18 49	59	167	17 50	59	167	346
21 56	59	167	20 57	59	168	19 58	59	168	18 59	59	168	18 00	59	168	347
22 05	59	168	21 06	59	168	20 07	59	169	19 08	59	169	18 09	60	169	348
22 14	59	169	21 15	60	169	20 15	59	170	19 16	59	170	18 17	60	170	349
22 22	−59	170	21 23	−60	170	20 23	−59	171	19 24	−60	171	18 24	−59	171	350
22 29	59	171	21 30	60	171	20 30	59	171	19 31	60	172	18 31	60	172	351
22 36	60	172	21 36	60	172	20 36	59	172	19 37	60	173	18 37	60	173	352
22 41	59	173	21 42	60	173	20 42	60	173	19 42	60	173	18 42	59	174	353
22 46	60	174	21 46	59	174	20 47	60	174	19 47	60	174	18 47	60	175	354
22 50	−59	175	21 51	−60	175	20 51	−60	175	19 51	−60	175	18 51	−60	175	355
22 54	60	176	21 54	60	176	20 54	60	176	19 54	60	176	18 54	60	176	356
22 57	60	177	21 57	60	177	20 57	60	177	19 57	60	177	18 57	60	177	357
22 59	60	178	21 59	60	178	20 59	60	178	19 59	60	178	18 59	60	178	358
23 00	60	179	22 00	60	179	21 00	60	179	20 00	60	179	19 00	60	179	359
23 00	−60	180	22 00	−60	180	21 00	−60	180	20 00	−60	180	19 00	−60	180	360

15° 16° 17° 18° 19° 20° 21° 22° 23° 24° 25° 26° 27° 28° 29°

S. Lat. {LHA greater than 180°........ Zn=180−Z; LHA less than 180°.......... Zn=180+Z}

DECLINATION (15°-29°) CONTRARY NAME TO LATITUDE

LAT 42°

N. Lat. {LHA greater than 180°....... Zn=Z
{LHA less than 180°.......... Zn=360−Z

DECLINATION (0°-14°) **SAME** NAME AS LATITUDE

LAT 43°

LHA	0° Hc	0° d	0° Z	1° Hc	1° d	1° Z	2° Hc	2° d	2° Z	3° Hc	3° d	3° Z	4° Hc	4° d	4° Z
	° ′	′	°	° ′	′	°	° ′	′	°	° ′	′	°	° ′	′	°
0	47 00	+60	180	48 00	+60	180	49 00	+60	180	50 00	+60	180	51 00	+60	180
1	46 59	60	179	47 59	60	179	48 59	60	179	49 59	60	178	50 59	60	178
2	46 58	60	177	47 58	60	177	48 58	60	177	49 58	60	177	50 58	60	177
3	46 55	60	176	47 55	60	176	48 55	60	175	49 55	60	175	50 55	59	175
4	46 51	60	174	47 51	60	174	48 51	60	174	49 51	59	174	50 50	60	174
5	46 46	+60	173	47 46	+60	173	48 46	+59	172	49 45	+60	172	50 45	+60	172
6	46 40	60	171	47 40	59	171	48 39	60	171	49 39	59	171	50 38	60	171
7	46 33	59	170	47 32	60	170	48 32	59	169	49 31	59	169	50 30	60	169
8	46 24	60	168	47 24	59	168	48 23	59	168	49 22	60	168	50 22	59	167
9	46 15	59	167	47 14	59	167	48 13	59	166	49 12	59	166	50 11	59	166
10	46 05	+58	166	47 03	+59	165	48 02	+59	165	49 01	+59	165	50 00	+59	164
11	45 53	59	164	46 52	58	164	47 50	59	164	48 49	59	163	49 48	58	163
12	45 40	59	163	46 39	58	162	47 37	59	162	48 36	58	162	49 34	59	161
13	45 27	58	161	46 25	58	161	47 23	59	161	48 22	58	160	49 20	58	160
14	45 12	58	160	46 10	58	160	47 08	58	159	48 06	58	159	49 04	58	158
15	44 57	+58	159	45 55	+57	158	46 52	+58	158	47 50	+57	157	48 47	+58	157
16	44 40	58	157	45 38	57	157	46 35	57	156	47 32	58	156	48 30	57	156
17	44 23	57	156	45 20	57	155	46 17	57	155	47 14	57	155	48 11	57	154
18	44 04	57	155	45 01	57	154	45 58	57	154	46 55	56	153	47 51	57	153
19	43 45	57	153	44 42	56	153	45 38	56	152	46 34	57	152	47 31	56	151
20	43 25	+56	152	44 21	+56	151	45 17	+56	151	46 13	+56	150	47 09	+56	150
21	43 04	56	151	44 00	55	150	44 55	56	150	45 51	56	149	46 47	55	149
22	42 42	55	149	43 37	56	149	44 33	55	148	45 28	55	148	46 23	55	147
23	42 19	55	148	43 14	55	148	44 09	55	147	45 04	55	147	45 59	55	146
24	41 55	55	147	42 50	55	146	43 45	55	146	44 40	54	145	45 34	54	145
25	41 31	+55	146	42 26	+54	145	43 20	+54	145	44 14	+54	144	45 08	+54	143
26	41 06	54	144	42 00	54	144	42 54	54	143	43 48	54	143	44 42	53	142
27	40 40	54	143	41 34	54	143	42 28	53	142	43 21	53	141	44 14	53	141
28	40 13	54	142	41 07	53	142	42 00	53	141	42 53	53	140	43 46	53	140
29	39 46	53	141	40 39	53	140	41 32	53	140	42 25	52	139	43 17	53	138
30	39 18	+53	140	40 11	+52	139	41 03	+53	139	41 56	+52	138	42 48	+52	137
31	38 49	53	139	39 42	52	138	40 34	52	137	41 26	52	137	42 18	51	136
32	38 20	52	138	39 12	52	137	40 04	52	136	40 56	51	136	41 47	51	135
33	37 50	52	136	38 42	51	136	39 33	51	135	40 24	52	134	41 16	50	134
34	37 19	52	135	38 11	51	135	39 02	51	134	39 53	50	133	40 43	51	133
35	36 48	+51	134	37 39	+51	134	38 30	+51	133	39 21	+50	132	40 11	+50	132
36	36 17	50	133	37 07	51	133	37 58	50	132	38 48	50	131	39 38	49	130
37	35 44	51	132	36 35	50	132	37 25	50	131	38 15	49	130	39 04	49	129
38	35 12	50	131	36 02	49	130	36 51	50	130	37 41	49	129	38 30	49	128
39	34 38	50	130	35 28	49	129	36 17	49	129	37 06	49	128	37 55	49	127
40	34 04	+50	129	34 54	+49	128	35 43	+49	128	36 32	+48	127	37 20	+48	126
41	33 30	49	128	34 19	49	127	35 08	48	127	35 56	48	126	36 44	48	125
42	32 55	49	127	33 44	48	126	34 32	49	126	35 21	47	125	36 08	48	124
43	32 20	49	126	33 09	48	126	33 57	47	125	34 44	48	124	35 32	47	123
44	31 45	48	125	32 33	47	125	33 20	48	124	34 08	47	123	34 55	47	122
45	31 09	+47	124	31 56	+48	124	32 44	+47	123	33 31	+47	122	34 18	+46	121
46	30 32	47	123	31 19	48	123	32 07	46	122	32 53	47	121	33 40	46	120
47	29 55	47	123	30 42	47	122	31 29	47	121	32 16	46	120	33 02	46	120
48	29 18	47	122	30 05	46	121	30 51	47	120	31 38	46	119	32 24	46	119
49	28 40	47	121	29 27	46	120	30 13	46	119	30 59	46	119	31 45	46	118
50	28 03	+46	120	28 49	+46	119	29 35	+46	118	30 21	+45	118	31 06	+45	117
51	27 24	46	119	28 10	46	118	28 56	45	117	29 41	46	117	30 27	45	116
52	26 46	45	118	27 31	46	117	28 17	45	117	29 02	45	116	29 47	45	115
53	26 07	45	117	26 52	46	117	27 38	45	116	28 23	44	115	29 07	45	114
54	25 28	45	116	26 13	45	116	26 58	45	115	27 43	44	114	28 27	44	113
55	24 48	+45	116	25 33	+45	115	26 18	+44	114	27 02	+45	113	27 47	+44	113
56	24 08	45	115	24 53	45	114	25 38	44	113	26 22	44	113	27 06	44	112
57	23 28	45	114	24 13	44	113	24 57	44	112	25 41	44	112	26 25	44	111
58	22 48	44	113	23 32	45	112	24 17	43	112	25 00	44	111	25 44	43	110
59	22 08	44	112	22 52	44	112	23 36	43	111	24 19	44	110	25 03	43	109
60	21 27	+44	112	22 11	+44	111	22 55	+43	110	23 38	+43	109	24 21	+43	109
61	20 46	44	111	21 30	43	110	22 13	43	109	22 56	44	109	23 40	42	108
62	20 05	43	110	20 48	44	109	21 32	43	109	22 15	43	108	22 58	42	107
63	19 24	43	109	20 07	43	108	20 50	43	108	21 33	43	107	22 16	42	106
64	18 42	43	108	19 25	43	108	20 08	43	107	20 51	42	106	21 33	43	105
65	18 00	+43	108	18 43	+43	107	19 26	+43	106	20 09	+42	105	20 51	+42	105
66	17 18	43	107	18 01	43	106	18 44	42	105	19 26	42	105	20 08	43	104
67	16 36	43	106	17 19	42	105	18 01	43	105	18 44	42	104	19 26	42	103
68	15 54	43	105	16 37	42	105	17 19	42	104	18 01	42	103	18 43	42	102
69	15 12	42	105	15 54	42	104	16 36	42	103	17 18	42	102	18 00	42	102

LHA	5° Hc	5° d	5° Z	6° Hc	6° d	6° Z	7° Hc	7° d	7° Z	8° Hc	8° d	8° Z	9° Hc	9° d	9° Z
	° ′	′	°	° ′	′	°	° ′	′	°	° ′	′	°	° ′	′	°
0	52 00	+60	180	53 00	+60	180	54 00	+60	180	55 00	+60	180	56 00	+60	180
1	51 59	60	178	52 59	60	178	53 59	60	178	54 59	60	178	55 59	60	178
2	51 58	60	177	52 58	59	177	53 57	60	177	54 57	60	177	55 57	60	177
3	51 54	60	175	52 54	60	175	53 54	60	175	54 54	60	175	55 54	60	175
4	51 50	60	174	52 50	60	173	53 50	59	173	54 49	60	173	55 49	60	173
5	51 45	+59	172	52 44	+60	172	53 44	+60	172	54 44	+59	171	55 43	+60	171
6	51 38	59	170	52 37	60	170	53 37	59	170	54 36	60	170	55 36	59	170
7	51 30	59	169	52 29	60	169	53 29	59	168	54 28	59	168	55 27	59	168
8	51 21	59	167	52 20	59	167	53 19	59	167	54 18	59	166	55 17	59	166
9	51 10	59	166	52 09	59	165	53 08	59	165	54 07	59	165	55 06	59	164
10	50 59	+59	164	51 58	+58	164	52 56	+59	163	53 55	+59	163	54 54	+58	163
11	50 46	59	163	51 45	58	162	52 43	59	162	53 42	58	161	54 40	58	161
12	50 33	58	161	51 31	58	161	52 29	58	160	53 27	58	160	54 25	58	159
13	50 18	58	160	51 16	57	159	52 13	58	159	53 11	58	158	54 09	57	158
14	50 02	57	158	50 59	58	158	51 57	57	157	52 54	58	157	53 52	57	156
15	49 45	+57	157	50 42	+57	156	51 39	+57	156	52 36	+57	155	53 33	+57	155
16	49 27	57	155	50 24	57	155	51 21	56	154	52 17	57	154	53 14	56	153
17	49 08	56	154	50 04	57	153	51 01	56	153	51 57	56	152	52 53	56	151
18	48 48	56	152	49 44	56	152	50 40	56	151	51 36	56	151	52 32	56	150
19	48 27	56	151	49 23	55	150	50 18	56	150	51 14	55	149	52 09	56	148
20	48 05	+55	149	49 00	+56	149	49 56	+55	148	50 51	+55	148	51 46	+55	147
21	47 42	55	148	48 37	55	147	49 32	55	147	50 27	55	146	51 22	54	146
22	47 18	55	147	48 13	55	146	49 08	54	145	50 02	54	145	50 56	54	144
23	46 54	54	145	47 48	54	145	48 42	54	144	49 36	54	143	50 30	53	143
24	46 28	54	144	47 22	54	143	48 16	54	143	49 10	53	142	50 03	53	141
25	46 02	+54	143	46 56	+53	142	47 49	+53	141	48 42	+53	141	49 35	+53	140
26	45 35	53	141	46 28	53	141	47 21	53	140	48 14	52	139	49 06	53	139
27	45 07	53	140	46 00	53	140	46 53	52	139	47 45	52	138	48 37	52	137
28	44 39	52	139	45 31	52	138	46 23	52	138	47 15	52	137	48 07	51	136
29	44 10	52	138	45 02	51	137	45 53	52	136	46 45	51	136	47 36	51	135
30	43 40	+51	137	44 31	+52	136	45 23	+51	135	46 14	+51	134	47 05	+50	134
31	43 09	51	135	44 00	51	135	44 51	51	134	45 42	50	133	46 32	51	132
32	42 38	51	134	43 29	50	133	44 19	51	133	45 10	50	132	46 00	49	131
33	42 06	51	133	42 57	50	132	43 47	50	132	44 37	49	131	45 26	50	130
34	41 34	50	132	42 24	50	131	43 14	49	130	44 03	49	130	44 52	49	129
35	41 01	+50	131	41 51	+49	130	42 40	+49	129	43 29	+49	129	44 18	+48	128
36	40 27	50	130	41 17	49	129	42 06	49	128	42 55	48	127	43 43	48	127
37	39 53	49	129	40 42	49	128	41 31	48	127	42 19	49	126	43 08	47	126
38	39 19	48	128	40 07	49	127	40 56	48	126	41 44	48	125	42 32	47	124
39	38 44	48	127	39 32	48	126	40 20	48	125	41 08	47	124	41 55	47	123
40	38 08	+48	126	38 56	+48	125	39 44	+47	124	40 31	+47	123	41 18	+47	122
41	37 32	48	125	38 20	47	124	39 07	47	123	39 54	47	122	40 41	46	121
42	36 56	47	124	37 43	47	123	38 30	47	122	39 17	46	121	40 03	46	120
43	36 19	47	123	37 06	47	122	37 53	46	121	38 39	46	120	39 25	46	119
44	35 42	47	122	36 29	46	121	37 15	46	120	38 01	46	119	38 47	45	118
45	35 04	+47	121	35 51	+46	120	36 37	+46	119	37 23	+45	118	38 08	+45	117
46	34 26	47	120	35 13	45	119	35 58	46	118	36 44	45	117	37 29	45	117
47	33 48	46	119	34 34	45	118	35 19	46	117	36 05	44	116	36 49	45	116
48	33 10	45	118	33 55	45	117	34 40	45	116	35 25	45	115	36 10	44	115
49	32 31	45	117	33 16	45	116	34 01	44	115	34 45	45	115	35 30	44	114
50	31 51	+45	116	32 36	+45	115	33 21	+44	115	34 05	+44	114	34 49	+44	113
51	31 12	44	115	31 56	45	114	32 41	44	114	33 25	44	113	34 09	43	112
52	30 32	44	114	31 16	44	114	32 00	44	113	32 44	44	112	33 28	43	111
53	29 52	44	114	30 36	44	113	31 20	44	112	32 04	43	111	32 47	43	110
54	29 11	44	113	29 55	44	112	30 39	43	111	31 22	44	110	32 06	42	109
55	28 31	+43	112	29 14	+44	111	29 58	+43	110	30 41	+43	109	31 24	+43	109
56	27 50	43	111	28 33	44	110	29 17	43	109	30 00	42	109	30 42	43	108
57	27 09	43	110	27 52	43	109	28 35	43	109	29 18	42	108	30 00	43	107
58	26 27	44	109	27 11	42	109	27 53	43	108	28 36	42	107	29 18	42	106
59	25 46	43	109	26 29	43	108	27 12	42	107	27 54	42	106	28 36	42	105
60	25 04	+43	108	25 47	+43	107	26 30	+42	106	27 12	+42	105	27 54	+41	105
61	24 22	43	107	25 05	42	106	25 47	42	105	26 29	42	105	27 11	42	104
62	23 40	43	106	24 23	42	105	25 05	42	105	25 47	42	104	26 29	41	103
63	22 58	42	105	23 40	42	105	24 22	42	104	25 04	42	103	25 46	41	102
64	22 16	42	105	22 58	42	104	23 40	41	103	24 21	42	102	25 03	41	102
65	21 33	+42	104	22 15	+42	103	22 57	+41	102	23 38	+42	102	24 20	+41	101
66	20 51	41	103	21 32	42	102	22 14	41	102	22 55	42	101	23 37	41	100
67	20 08	41	102	20 49	42	102	21 31	41	101	22 12	41	100	22 53	41	99
68	19 25	41	102	20 06	42	101	20 48	41	100	21 29	41	99	22 10	41	99
69	18 42	41	101	19 23	42	100	20 05	41	99	20 46	41	99	21 27	40	98

10° Hc	10° d	10° Z	11° Hc	11° d	11° Z	12° Hc	12° d	12° Z	13° Hc	13° d	13° Z	14° Hc	14° d	14° Z	LHA
° ′	′	°	° ′	′	°	° ′	′	°	° ′	′	°	° ′	′	°	
57 00	+60	180	58 00	+60	180	59 00	+60	180	60 00	+60	180	61 00	+60	180	360
56 59	60	178	57 59	60	178	58 59	60	178	59 59	60	178	60 59	60	178	359
56 57	60	176	57 57	60	176	58 57	60	176	59 57	60	176	60 57	60	176	358
56 54	60	175	57 54	60	175	58 54	59	174	59 53	60	174	60 53	60	174	357
56 49	60	173	57 49	59	173	58 48	60	172	59 48	60	172	60 48	59	172	356
56 43	+59	171	57 42	+60	171	58 42	+59	171	59 41	+60	170	60 41	+59	170	355
56 35	60	169	57 35	59	169	58 34	59	169	59 33	60	168	60 33	59	168	354
56 26	60	168	57 26	59	167	58 25	59	167	59 24	59	167	60 23	59	166	353
56 16	59	166	57 15	59	165	58 14	59	165	59 13	59	165	60 12	58	164	352
56 05	58	164	57 03	59	164	58 02	59	163	59 01	58	163	59 59	58	162	351
55 52	+58	162	56 50	+59	162	57 49	+58	161	58 47	+58	161	59 45	+58	161	350
55 38	58	161	56 36	58	160	57 34	58	160	58 32	58	159	59 30	57	159	349
55 23	58	159	56 21	57	158	57 18	58	158	58 16	57	157	59 13	57	157	348
55 06	58	157	56 04	57	157	57 01	57	156	57 58	57	156	58 55	57	155	347
54 49	57	156	55 46	57	155	56 43	56	155	57 39	57	154	58 36	56	153	346
54 30	+57	154	55 27	+56	153	56 23	+57	153	57 20	+56	152	58 16	+55	152	345
54 10	57	152	55 07	56	152	56 03	55	151	56 58	56	151	57 54	55	150	344
53 49	56	151	54 45	56	150	55 41	55	150	56 36	55	149	57 31	55	148	343
53 28	55	149	54 23	55	149	55 18	55	148	56 13	55	147	57 08	54	147	342
53 05	55	148	54 00	54	147	54 54	55	146	55 49	54	146	56 43	54	145	341
52 41	+54	146	53 35	+55	146	54 30	+54	145	55 24	+53	144	56 17	+54	143	340
52 16	54	145	53 10	54	144	54 04	53	143	54 57	54	143	55 51	52	142	339
51 50	54	143	52 44	53	143	53 37	53	142	54 30	53	141	55 23	52	140	338
51 23	54	142	52 17	53	141	53 10	52	140	54 02	52	140	54 54	52	139	337
50 56	53	141	51 49	52	140	52 41	52	139	53 33	52	138	54 25	51	137	336
50 28	+52	139	51 20	+52	138	52 12	+52	138	53 04	+51	137	53 55	+51	136	335
49 59	51	138	50 50	52	137	51 42	51	136	52 33	51	135	53 24	50	135	334
49 29	51	137	50 20	51	136	51 11	51	135	52 02	50	134	52 52	50	133	333
48 58	51	135	49 49	51	134	50 40	50	134	51 30	50	133	52 20	49	132	332
48 27	51	134	49 18	50	133	50 08	49	132	50 57	50	131	51 47	49	131	331
47 55	+50	133	48 45	+50	132	49 35	+49	131	50 24	+49	130	51 13	+49	129	330
47 23	49	132	48 12	50	131	49 02	48	130	49 50	49	129	50 39	48	128	329
46 49	50	130	47 39	49	130	48 28	48	129	49 16	48	128	50 04	48	127	328
46 16	48	129	47 04	49	128	47 53	48	127	48 41	48	127	49 29	47	126	327
45 41	49	128	46 30	48	127	47 18	47	126	48 05	48	125	48 53	46	124	326
45 06	+48	127	45 54	+48	126	46 42	+47	125	47 29	+47	124	48 16	+47	123	325
44 31	48	126	45 19	47	125	46 06	47	124	46 53	46	123	47 39	46	122	324
43 55	47	125	44 42	47	124	45 29	47	123	46 16	46	122	47 02	45	121	323
43 19	47	124	44 06	46	123	44 52	46	122	45 38	46	121	46 24	45	120	322
42 42	47	123	43 29	46	122	44 15	46	121	45 01	45	120	45 46	45	119	321
42 05	+46	122	42 51	+46	121	43 37	+45	120	44 22	+45	119	45 07	+45	118	320
41 27	46	121	42 13	46	120	42 59	45	119	43 44	44	118	44 28	45	117	319
40 49	46	120	41 35	45	119	42 20	45	118	43 05	44	117	43 49	44	116	318
40 11	45	119	40 56	45	118	41 41	44	117	42 25	44	116	43 09	44	115	317
39 32	45	118	40 17	45	117	41 02	44	116	41 46	43	115	42 29	44	114	316
38 53	+45	117	39 38	+44	116	40 22	+44	115	41 06	+43	114	41 49	+43	113	315
38 14	44	116	38 58	44	115	39 42	43	114	40 25	44	113	41 09	42	112	314
37 34	44	115	38 18	44	114	39 02	43	113	39 45	43	112	40 28	42	111	313
36 54	44	114	37 38	43	113	38 21	43	112	39 04	43	111	39 47	42	110	312
36 14	43	113	36 57	43	112	37 40	43	111	38 23	42	110	39 05	42	109	311
35 33	+43	112	36 16	+43	111	36 59	+43	110	37 42	+42	109	38 24	+42	109	310
34 52	43	111	35 35	43	110	36 18	42	109	37 00	42	109	37 42	42	108	309
34 11	43	110	34 54	42	109	35 36	43	109	36 19	41	108	37 00	42	107	308
33 30	42	109	34 12	43	109	34 55	42	108	35 37	41	107	36 18	41	106	307
32 48	43	109	33 31	42	108	34 13	42	107	34 55	41	106	35 36	41	105	306
32 07	+42	108	32 49	+42	107	33 31	+41	106	34 12	+42	105	34 54	+40	104	305
31 25	42	107	32 07	42	106	32 49	41	105	33 30	41	104	34 11	41	104	304
30 43	42	106	31 25	41	105	32 06	41	104	32 47	41	104	33 28	41	103	303
30 00	42	105	30 42	42	105	31 24	41	104	32 05	40	103	32 45	41	102	302
29 18	42	105	30 00	41	104	30 41	41	103	31 22	40	102	32 02	41	101	301
28 35	+42	104	29 17	+41	103	29 58	+41	102	30 39	+40	101	31 19	+40	100	300
27 53	41	103	28 34	41	102	29 15	41	101	29 56	40	101	30 36	40	100	299
27 10	41	102	27 51	41	101	28 32	40	101	29 12	41	100	29 53	40	99	298
26 27	41	102	27 08	41	101	27 49	40	100	28 29	40	99	29 09	40	98	297
25 44	41	101	26 25	40	100	27 05	41	99	27 46	40	98	28 26	39	97	296
25 01	+41	100	25 42	+40	99	26 22	+40	98	27 02	+40	98	27 42	+40	97	295
24 18	40	99	24 58	41	98	25 39	40	98	26 19	40	97	26 59	39	96	294
23 34	41	99	24 15	40	98	24 55	40	97	25 35	40	96	26 15	39	95	293
22 51	40	98	23 31	41	97	24 12	40	96	24 52	39	95	25 31	40	95	292
22 07	41	97	22 48	40	96	23 28	40	95	24 08	39	95	24 47	40	94	291

S. Lat. {LHA greater than 180°....... Zn=180−Z
{LHA less than 180°.......... Zn=180+Z

DECLINATION (0°-14°) **SAME** NAME AS LATITUDE

DECLINATION (0°-14°) SAME NAME AS LATITUDE

N. Lat. {LHA greater than 180°....... Zn=Z; LHA less than 180°........... Zn=360−Z}

LHA	0°			1°			2°			3°			4°			5°			6°			7°			8°			9°			10°			11°			12°			13°			14°			LHA
	Hc	d	Z	Hc	d	Z	Hc	d	Z	Hc	d	Z	Hc	d	Z	Hc	d	Z	Hc	d	Z	Hc	d	Z	Hc	d	Z	Hc	d	Z	Hc	d	Z	Hc	d	Z	Hc	d	Z	Hc	d	Z	Hc	d	Z	LHA
	° ′	′	°	° ′	′	°	° ′	′	°	° ′	′	°	° ′	′	°	° ′	′	°	° ′	′	°	° ′	′	°	° ′	′	°	° ′	′	°	° ′	′	°	° ′	′	°	° ′	′	°	° ′	′	°	° ′	′	°	
70	14 29	+42	104	15 11	+42	103	15 53	+42	103	16 35	+42	102	17 17	+42	101	17 59	+41	100	18 40	+41	99	19 21	+41	99	20 02	+41	98	20 43	+41	97	21 24	+40	96	22 04	+40	96	22 44	+40	95	23 24	+40	94	24 04	+39	93	290
71	13 47	42	103	14 29	42	103	15 11	41	102	15 52	42	101	16 34	41	100	17 15	42	100	17 57	41	99	18 38	41	98	19 19	40	97	19 59	41	96	20 40	40	96	21 20	40	95	22 00	40	94	22 40	40	93	23 20	39	92	289
72	13 04	42	103	13 46	42	102	14 28	41	101	15 09	42	100	15 51	41	100	16 32	41	99	17 13	41	98	17 54	41	97	18 35	41	97	19 16	40	96	19 56	41	95	20 37	40	94	21 17	39	93	21 56	40	93	22 36	39	92	288
73	12 21	42	102	13 03	41	101	13 44	42	100	14 26	41	100	15 07	42	99	15 49	41	98	16 30	41	97	17 11	41	97	17 52	40	96	18 32	41	95	19 13	40	94	19 53	40	93	20 33	40	93	21 13	39	92	21 52	39	91	287
74	11 38	42	101	12 20	41	100	13 01	42	100	13 43	41	99	14 24	41	98	15 05	41	97	15 46	41	97	16 27	41	96	17 08	40	95	17 48	41	94	18 29	40	94	19 09	40	93	19 49	40	92	20 29	39	91	21 08	40	90	286
75	10 55	+41	100	11 36	+42	100	12 18	+41	99	12 59	+42	98	13 41	+41	97	14 22	+41	97	15 03	+40	96	15 43	+41	95	16 24	+41	94	17 05	+40	94	17 45	+40	93	18 25	+40	92	19 05	+40	91	19 45	+39	91	20 24	+40	90	285
76	10 12	41	100	10 53	41	99	11 34	42	98	12 16	41	97	12 57	41	97	13 38	41	96	14 19	41	95	15 00	40	94	15 40	41	94	16 21	40	93	17 01	40	92	17 41	40	91	18 21	40	91	19 01	39	90	19 40	40	89	284
77	09 28	42	99	10 10	41	98	10 51	41	98	11 32	41	97	12 13	41	96	12 54	41	95	13 35	41	95	14 16	41	94	14 57	40	93	15 37	40	92	16 17	40	91	16 57	40	91	17 37	40	90	18 17	40	89	18 57	39	88	283
78	08 45	41	98	09 26	41	98	10 07	42	97	10 49	41	96	11 30	41	95	12 11	40	95	12 51	41	94	13 32	41	93	14 13	40	92	14 53	40	92	15 33	40	91	16 13	40	90	16 53	40	89	17 33	40	88	18 13	39	88	282
79	08 01	42	98	08 43	41	97	09 24	41	96	10 05	41	95	10 46	41	95	11 27	41	94	12 08	40	93	12 48	41	92	13 29	40	92	14 09	41	91	14 50	40	90	15 30	40	89	16 10	39	89	16 49	40	88	17 29	39	87	281
80	07 18	+41	97	07 59	+41	96	08 40	+41	95	09 21	+41	95	10 02	+41	94	10 43	+41	93	11 24	+40	92	12 04	+41	92	12 45	+40	91	13 25	+41	90	14 06	+40	89	14 46	+40	89	15 26	+39	88	16 05	+40	87	16 45	+40	86	280
81	06 34	41	96	07 15	41	95	07 56	41	95	08 37	41	94	09 18	41	93	09 59	41	93	10 40	41	92	11 21	40	91	12 01	40	90	12 41	41	90	13 22	40	89	14 02	40	88	14 42	40	87	15 22	39	86	16 01	40	86	279
82	05 51	41	96	06 32	41	95	07 13	41	94	07 54	41	93	08 35	40	93	09 15	41	92	09 56	41	91	10 37	40	90	11 17	41	90	11 58	40	89	12 38	40	88	13 18	40	87	13 58	40	87	14 38	40	86	15 18	39	85	278
83	05 07	41	95	05 48	41	94	06 29	41	93	07 10	41	93	07 51	41	92	08 32	40	91	09 12	41	90	09 53	40	90	10 33	41	89	11 14	40	88	11 54	40	87	12 34	40	87	13 14	40	86	13 54	40	85	14 34	40	84	277
84	04 23	41	94	05 04	41	93	05 45	41	93	06 26	41	92	07 07	41	91	07 48	40	90	08 28	41	90	09 09	40	89	09 49	41	88	10 30	40	87	11 10	40	87	11 50	41	86	12 31	39	85	13 10	40	84	13 50	40	84	276
85	03 39	+41	93	04 20	+41	93	05 01	+41	92	05 42	+41	91	06 23	+41	91	07 04	+40	90	07 44	+41	89	08 25	+41	88	09 06	+40	88	09 46	+40	87	10 26	+41	86	11 07	+40	85	11 47	+40	85	12 27	+40	84	13 07	+39	83	275
86	02 55	41	93	03 36	41	92	04 17	41	91	04 58	41	91	05 39	41	90	06 20	41	89	07 01	40	88	07 41	41	88	08 22	40	87	09 02	41	86	09 43	40	85	10 23	40	85	11 03	40	84	11 43	40	83	12 23	40	82	274
87	02 12	41	92	02 53	40	91	03 33	41	91	04 14	41	90	04 55	41	89	05 36	41	88	06 17	40	88	06 57	41	87	07 38	41	86	08 19	40	85	08 59	40	85	09 39	41	84	10 20	40	83	11 00	40	82	11 40	40	82	273
88	01 28	41	91	02 09	41	91	02 50	40	90	03 30	41	89	04 11	41	88	04 52	41	88	05 33	41	87	06 14	40	86	06 54	41	86	07 35	40	85	08 15	41	84	08 56	40	83	09 36	40	83	10 16	40	82	10 56	40	81	272
89	00 44	41	91	01 25	41	90	02 06	41	89	02 47	40	88	03 27	41	88	04 08	41	87	04 49	41	86	05 30	41	86	06 11	40	85	06 51	41	84	07 32	40	83	08 12	41	83	08 53	40	82	09 33	40	81	10 13	40	80	271
90	00 00	+41	90	00 41	+41	89	01 22	+41	89	02 03	+41	88	02 44	+40	87	03 24	+41	86	04 05	+41	86	04 46	+41	85	05 27	+41	84	06 08	+40	83	06 48	+41	83	07 29	+40	82	08 09	+41	81	08 50	+40	80	09 30	+40	80	270
91	−0 44	41	89	−0 03	41	89	00 38	41	88	01 19	41	87	02 00	41	86	02 41	41	86	03 22	40	85	04 02	41	84	04 43	41	83	05 24	41	83	06 05	40	82	06 45	41	81	07 26	40	81	08 06	41	80	08 47	40	79	269
92	−1 28	41	89	−0 47	41	88	−0 06	41	87	00 35	41	86	01 16	41	86	01 57	41	85	02 38	41	84	03 19	41	84	04 00	40	83	04 40	41	82	05 21	41	81	06 02	41	81	06 43	40	80	07 23	41	79	08 04	40	78	268
93	−2 12	41	88	−1 31	41	87	−0 50	41	86	−0 09	41	86	00 32	41	85	01 13	41	84	01 54	41	84	02 35	41	83	03 16	41	82	03 57	41	81	04 38	41	81	05 19	40	80	05 59	41	79	06 40	41	78	07 21	40	78	267
94	−2 55	41	87	−2 14	41	87	−1 33	41	86	−0 52	41	85	−0 11	41	84	00 30	41	84	01 11	41	83	01 52	41	82	02 33	41	81	03 14	41	81	03 55	40	80	04 35	41	79	05 16	41	79	05 57	41	78	06 38	41	77	266
95	−3 39	+41	87	−2 58	+41	86	−2 17	+41	85	−1 36	+41	84	−0 55	+41	84	−0 14	+41	83	00 27	+41	82	01 08	+41	81	01 49	+41	81	02 30	+41	80	03 11	+41	79	03 52	+41	79	04 33	+41	78	05 14	+41	77	05 55	+41	76	265
96	−4 23	41	86	−3 42	41	85	−3 01	41	84	−2 20	41	84	−1 39	42	83	−0 57	41	82	−0 16	41	82	00 25	41	81	01 06	41	80	01 47	41	79	02 28	41	79	03 09	42	78	03 51	41	77	04 32	41	76	05 13	41	76	264
97	−5 07	41	85	−4 26	41	84	−3 45	42	84	−3 03	41	83	−2 22	41	82	−1 41	41	82	−1 00	42	81	−0 18	41	80	00 23	41	79	01 04	41	79	01 45	42	78	02 27	41	77	03 08	41	76	03 49	41	76	04 30	41	75	263
98	−5 51	42	84	−5 09	41	84	−4 28	41	83	−3 47	41	82	−3 06	42	82	−2 24	41	81	−1 43	41	80	−1 02	42	79	−0 20	41	79	00 21	42	78	01 03	41	77	01 44	41	77	02 25	42	76	03 07	41	75	03 48	41	74	262
			99	−5 53	41	83	−5 12	42	82	−4 30	41	82	−3 49	41	81	−3 08	42	80	−2 26	41	79	−1 45	42	79	−1 03	41	78	−0 22	42	77	00 20	41	77	01 01	42	76	01 43	41	75	02 24	42	74	03 06	41	74	261
						100	−5 55	+41	82	−5 14	+42	81	−4 32	+41	80	−3 51	+42	80	−3 09	+41	79	−2 28	+42	78	−1 46	+42	77	−1 04	+41	77	−0 23	+42	76	00 19	+41	75	01 00	+42	74	01 42	+42	74	02 24	+41	73	260
									101	−5 57	41	80	−5 16	42	79	−4 34	42	79	−3 52	41	78	−3 11	42	77	−2 29	42	77	−1 47	42	76	−1 05	41	75	−0 24	42	74	00 18	42	74	01 00	42	73	01 42	41	72	259
												102	−5 59	42	79	−5 17	42	78	−4 35	42	77	−3 53	42	77	−3 11	41	76	−2 30	42	75	−1 48	42	75	−1 06	42	74	−0 24	42	73	00 18	42	72	01 00	42	72	258
															103	−6 00	42	77	−5 18	42	77	−4 36	42	76	−3 54	42	75	−3 12	42	75	−2 30	42	74	−1 48	42	73	−1 06	42	72	−0 24	42	72	00 18	43	71	257
																		104	−6 01	43	76	−5 18	42	75	−4 36	42	75	−3 54	42	74	−3 12	42	73	−2 30	42	72	−1 48	43	72	−1 05	42	71	−0 23	42	70	256
																					105	−6 01	+42	75	−5 19	+43	74	−4 36	+42	73	−3 54	+42	72	−3 12	+43	72	−2 29	+42	71	−1 47	+43	70	−1 04	+42	70	255
																								106	−6 01	43	73	−5 18	42	72	−4 36	43	72	−3 53	42	71	−3 11	43	70	−2 28	43	70	−1 45	42	69	254
																											107	−6 00	43	72	−5 17	42	71	−4 35	43	70	−3 52	43	70	−3 09	43	69	−2 26	43	68	253
																														108	−5 59	43	70	−5 16	43	70	−4 33	43	69	−3 50	43	68	−3 07	43	68	252
																																	109	−5 57	43	69	−5 14	44	68	−4 30	43	68	−3 47	43	67	251
																																				110	−5 54	+43	67	−5 11	+44	67	−4 27	+43	66	250
																																							111	−5 51	43	66	−5 08	44	65	249
																																										112	−5 47	44	65	248

DECLINATION (0°-14°) CONTRARY NAME TO LATITUDE

S. Lat. {LHA greater than 180°....... Zn=180−Z; LHA less than 180°........... Zn=180+Z}

LHA	0°			1°			2°			3°			4°			5°			6°			7°			8°			9°			10°			11°			12°			13°			14°			LHA
98	−5 51	41	84	262																																										
97	−5 07	41	85	−5 48	41	86	263																																							
96	−4 23	41	86	−5 04	41	87	−5 45	41	87	−6 26	41	88	264																																	
95	−3 39	−41	87	−4 20	−41	87	−5 01	−41	88	−5 42	−41	89	−6 23	−41	89	265																														
94	−2 55	41	87	−3 36	41	88	−4 17	41	89	−4 58	41	89	−5 39	41	90	−6 20	41	91	266																											
93	−2 12	41	88	−2 53	40	89	−3 33	41	89	−4 14	41	90	−4 55	41	91	−5 36	41	92	−6 17	40	92	267																								
92	−1 28	41	89	−2 09	41	89	−2 50	40	90	−3 30	41	91	−4 11	41	92	−4 52	41	92	−5 33	41	93	−6 14	40	94	268																					
91	−0 44	41	89	−1 25	41	90	−2 06	41	91	−2 47	40	92	−3 27	41	92	−4 08	41	93	−4 49	41	94	−5 30	41	94	−6 11	40	95	269																		
90	00 00	−41	90	−0 41	−41	91	−1 22	−41	91	−2 03	−41	92	−2 44	−40	93	−3 24	−41	94	−4 05	−41	94	−4 46	−41	95	−5 27	−41	96	−6 08	−40	97	270															
89	00 44	41	91	00 03	41	91	−0 38	41	92	−1 19	41	93	−2 00	41	94	−2 41	41	94	−3 22	40	95	−4 02	41	96	−4 43	41	97	−5 24	41	97	−6 05	40	98	271												
88	01 28	41	91	00 47	41	92	00 06	41	93	−0 35	41	94	−1 16	41	94	−1 57	41	95	−2 38	41	96	−3 19	41	96	−4 00	40	97	−4 40	41	98	−5 21	41	99	−6 02	41	99	272									
87	02 12	41	92	01 31	41	93	00 50	41	94	00 09	41	94	−0 32	41	95	−1 13	41	96	−1 54	41	96	−2 35	41	97	−3 16	41	98	−3 57	41	99	−4 38	41	99	−5 19	40	100	−5 59	41	101	273						
86	02 55	41	93	02 14	41	93	01 33	41	94	00 52	41	95	00 11	41	96	−0 30	41	96	−1 11	41	97	−1 52	41	98	−2 33	41	99	−3 14	41	99	−3 55	40	100	−4 35	41	101	−5 16	41	101	−5 57	41	102	274			
85	03 39	−41	93	02 58	−41	94	02 17	−41	95	01 36	−41	96	00 55	−41	96	00 14	−41	97	−0 27	−41	98	−1 08	−41	99	−1 49	−41	99	−2 30	−41	100	−3 11	−41	101	−3 52	−41	101	−4 33	−41	102	−5 14	−41	103	−5 55	−41	104	275
84	04 23	41	94	03 42	41	95	03 01	41	96	02 20	41	96	01 39	42	97	00 57	41	98	00 16	41	98	−0 25	41	99	−1 06	41	100	−1 47	41	101	−2 28	41	101	−3 09	42	102	−3 51	41	103	−4 32	41	104	−5 13	41	104	276
83	05 07	41	95	04 26	41	96	03 45	42	96	03 03	41	97	02 22	41	98	01 41	41	98	01 00	42	99	00 18	41	100	−0 23	41	101	−1 04	41	101	−1 45	42	102	−2 27	41	103	−3 08	41	104	−3 49	41	104	−4 30	41	105	277
82	05 51	42	96	05 09	41	96	04 28	41	97	03 47	41	98	03 06	42	98	02 24	41	99	01 43	41	100	01 02	42	101	00 20	41	101	−0 21	42	102	−1 03	41	103	−1 44	41	103	−2 25	42	104	−3 07	41	105	−3 48	41	106	278
81	06 34	41	96	05 53	41	97	05 12	42	98	04 30	41	98	03 49	41	99	03 08	42	100	02 26	41	101	01 45	42	101	01 03	41	102	00 22	42	103	−0 20	41	103	−1 01	42	104	−1 43	41	105	−2 24	42	106	−3 06	41	106	279
80	07 18	−41	97	06 37	−42	98	05 55	−41	98	05 14	−42	99	04 32	−41	100	03 51	−42	100	03 09	−41	101	02 28	−42	102	01 46	−42	103	01 04	−41	103	00 23	−42	104	−0 19	−41	105	−1 00	−42	106	−1 42	−42	106	−2 24	−41	107	280
79	08 01	41	98	07 20	41	98	06 39	42	99	05 57	41	100	05 16	42	101	04 34	42	101	03 52	41	102	03 11	42	103	02 29	42	103	01 47	42	104	01 05	41	105	00 24	42	106	−0 18	42	106	−1 00	42	107	−1 42	41	108	281
78	08 45	42	98	08 03	41	99	07 22	42	100	06 40	41	100	05 59	42	101	05 17	42	102	04 35	42	103	03 53	42	103	03 11	41	104	02 30	42	105	01 48	42	105	01 06	42	106	00 24	42	107	−0 18	42	108	−1 00	42	108	282
77	09 28	41	99	08 47	42	100	08 05	42	100	07 23	41	101	06 42	42	102	06 00	42	103	05 18	42	103	04 36	42	104	03 54	42	105	03 12	42	105	02 30	42	106	01 48	42	107	01 06	42	108	00 24	42	108	−0 18	43	109	283
76	10 12	42	100	09 30	42	100	08 48	42	101	08 06	41	102	07 25	42	103	06 43	42	103	06 01	43	104	05 18	42	105	04 36	42	105	03 54	42	106	03 12	42	107	02 30	42	108	01 48	43	108	01 05	42	109	00 23	42	110	284
75	10 55	−42	100	10 13	−42	101	09 31	−42	102	08 49	−42	103	08 07	−42	103	07 25	−42	104	06 43	−42	105	06 01	−42	105	05 19	−43	106	04 36	−42	107	03 54	−42	108	03 12	−43	108	02 29	−42	109	01 47	−43	110	01 04	−42	110	285
74	11 38	42	101	10 56	42	102	10 14	42	103	09 32	42	103	08 50	42	104	08 08	43	105	07 25	42	105	06 43	42	106	06 01	43	107	05 18	42	108	04 36	43	108	03 53	42	109	03 11	43	110	02 28	43	110	01 45	42	111	286
73	12 21	42	102	11 39	42	103	10 57	42	103	10 15	43	104	09 32	42	105	08 50	42	105	08 08	43	106	07 25	42	107	06 43	43	108	06 00	43	108	05 17	42	109	04 35	43	110	03 52	43	110	03 09	43	111	02 26	43	112	287
72	13 04	42	103	12 22	42	103	11 40	43	104	10 57	42	105	10 15	43	105	09 32	42	106	08 50	43	107	08 07	43	108	07 24	42	108	06 42	43	109	05 59	43	110	05 16	43	110	04 33	43	111	03 50	43	112	03 07	43	112	288
71	13 47	43	103	13 04	42	104	12 22	42	105	11 40	43	105	10 57	43	106	10 14	42	107	09 32	43	108	08 49	43	108	08 06	43	109	07 23	43	110	06 40	43	110	05 57	43	111	05 14	44	112	04 30	43	112	03 47	43	113	289
70	14 29	−42	104	13 47	−43	105	13 04	−42	105	12 22	−43	106	11 39	−43	107	10 56	−43	108	10 13	−43	108	09 30	−43	109	08 47	−43	110	08 04	−43	110	07 21	−43	111	06 38	−44	112	05 54	−43	113	05 11	−44	113	04 27	−43	114	290
	0°			1°			2°			3°			4°			5°			6°			7°			8°			9°			10°			11°			12°			13°			14°			

LAT 43°

LAT 43°

N. Lat. {LHA greater than 180°....... Zn=Z; LHA less than 180°........... Zn=360−Z}

DECLINATION (0°-14°) CONTRARY NAME TO LATITUDE

LAT 43°

LHA	0° Hc	0° d	0° Z	1° Hc	1° d	1° Z	2° Hc	2° d	2° Z	3° Hc	3° d	3° Z	4° Hc	4° d	4° Z	LHA
	° ′	′	°	° ′	′	°	° ′	′	°	° ′	′	°	° ′	′	°	
69	15 12	43	105	14 29	42	105	13 47	43	106	13 04	43	107	12 21	43	108	291
68	15 54	43	105	15 11	42	106	14 29	43	107	13 46	43	108	13 03	43	108	292
67	16 36	42	106	15 54	43	107	15 11	43	108	14 28	44	108	13 44	43	109	293
66	17 18	43	107	16 35	43	108	15 52	43	108	15 09	43	109	14 26	44	110	294
65	18 00	−43	108	17 17	−43	108	16 34	−43	109	15 51	−44	110	15 07	−44	111	295
64	18 42	43	108	17 59	44	109	17 15	43	110	16 32	44	111	15 48	44	111	296
63	19 24	44	109	18 40	44	110	17 56	43	111	17 13	44	111	16 29	44	112	297
62	20 05	44	110	19 21	44	111	18 37	44	111	17 53	44	112	17 09	44	113	298
61	20 46	44	111	20 02	44	111	19 18	44	112	18 34	44	113	17 50	45	114	299
60	21 27	−44	112	20 43	−44	112	19 59	−45	113	19 14	−44	114	18 30	−45	114	300
59	22 08	45	112	21 23	44	113	20 39	45	114	19 54	44	114	19 10	45	115	301
58	22 48	44	113	22 04	45	114	21 19	45	115	20 34	45	115	19 49	45	116	302
57	23 28	44	114	22 44	45	115	21 59	45	115	21 14	46	116	20 28	45	117	303
56	24 08	44	115	23 24	46	115	22 38	45	116	21 53	45	117	21 08	46	118	304
55	24 48	−45	116	24 03	−45	116	23 18	−46	117	22 32	−46	118	21 46	−46	118	305
54	25 28	46	116	24 42	45	117	23 57	46	118	23 11	46	119	22 25	46	119	306
53	26 07	46	117	25 21	46	118	24 35	46	119	23 49	46	119	23 03	47	120	307
52	26 46	46	118	26 00	46	119	25 14	47	120	24 27	46	120	23 41	47	121	308
51	27 24	46	119	26 38	46	120	25 52	47	120	25 05	47	121	24 18	47	122	309
50	28 03	−47	120	27 16	−47	121	26 29	−47	121	25 42	−47	122	24 55	−47	123	310
49	28 40	46	121	27 54	47	121	27 07	47	122	26 20	48	123	25 32	47	123	311
48	29 18	47	122	28 31	47	122	27 44	48	123	26 56	47	124	26 09	48	124	312
47	29 55	47	123	29 08	48	123	28 20	47	124	27 33	48	125	26 45	48	125	313
46	30 32	48	123	29 44	47	124	28 57	48	125	28 09	49	125	27 20	48	126	314
45	31 09	−48	124	30 21	−49	125	29 32	−48	126	28 44	−48	126	27 56	−49	127	315
44	31 45	49	125	30 56	48	126	30 08	49	127	29 19	49	127	28 30	49	128	316
43	32 20	48	126	31 32	49	127	30 43	49	128	29 54	49	128	29 05	50	129	317
42	32 55	48	127	32 07	50	128	31 17	49	129	30 28	49	129	29 39	50	130	318
41	33 30	49	128	32 41	49	129	31 52	50	130	31 02	50	130	30 12	50	131	319
40	34 04	−49	129	33 15	−50	130	32 25	−50	130	31 35	−50	131	30 45	−50	132	320
39	34 38	50	130	33 48	50	131	32 58	50	131	32 08	50	132	31 18	51	133	321
38	35 12	51	131	34 21	50	132	33 31	51	132	32 40	50	133	31 50	51	134	322
37	35 44	50	132	34 54	51	133	34 03	51	134	33 12	51	134	32 21	51	135	323
36	36 17	51	133	35 26	51	134	34 35	52	135	33 43	51	135	32 52	52	136	324
35	36 48	−51	134	35 57	−51	135	35 06	−52	136	34 14	−52	136	33 22	−52	137	325
34	37 19	51	135	36 28	52	136	35 36	52	137	34 44	52	137	33 52	52	138	326
33	37 50	52	136	36 58	52	137	36 06	52	138	35 14	53	138	34 21	52	139	327
32	38 20	52	138	37 28	53	138	36 35	52	139	35 43	53	139	34 50	53	140	328
31	38 49	52	139	37 57	53	139	37 04	53	140	36 11	53	140	35 18	54	141	329
30	39 18	−53	140	38 25	−53	140	37 32	−53	141	36 39	−54	142	35 45	−54	142	330
29	39 46	53	141	38 53	54	142	37 59	53	142	37 06	54	143	36 12	54	143	331
28	40 13	53	142	39 20	54	143	38 26	54	143	37 32	54	144	36 38	55	144	332
27	40 40	54	143	39 46	54	144	38 52	55	144	37 57	54	145	37 03	55	145	333
26	41 06	55	144	40 11	54	145	39 17	55	146	38 22	55	146	37 27	55	147	334
25	41 31	−55	146	40 36	−55	146	39 41	−55	147	38 46	−55	147	37 51	−55	148	335
24	41 55	55	147	41 00	55	147	40 05	55	148	39 10	56	148	38 14	55	149	336
23	42 19	55	148	41 24	56	149	40 28	56	149	39 32	55	150	38 37	56	150	337
22	42 42	56	149	41 46	56	150	40 50	56	150	39 54	56	151	38 58	56	151	338
21	43 04	56	151	42 08	57	151	41 11	56	152	40 15	56	152	39 19	57	153	339
20	43 25	−57	152	42 28	−56	152	41 32	−57	153	40 35	−56	153	39 39	−57	154	340
19	43 45	57	153	42 48	56	154	41 52	57	154	40 55	57	155	39 58	57	155	341
18	44 04	57	155	43 07	57	155	42 10	57	155	41 13	57	156	40 16	58	156	342
17	44 23	58	156	43 25	57	156	42 28	57	157	41 31	58	157	40 33	58	157	343
16	44 40	57	157	43 43	58	158	42 45	58	158	41 47	58	158	40 49	57	159	344
15	44 57	−58	159	43 59	−58	159	43 01	−58	159	42 03	−58	160	41 05	−58	160	345
14	45 12	58	160	44 14	58	160	43 16	58	161	42 18	58	161	41 20	59	161	346
13	45 27	58	161	44 29	59	162	43 30	58	162	42 32	59	162	41 33	58	163	347
12	45 40	58	163	44 42	59	163	43 43	58	163	42 45	59	164	41 46	59	164	348
11	45 53	59	164	44 54	59	164	43 55	59	165	42 56	58	165	41 58	59	165	349
10	46 05	−59	166	45 06	−60	166	44 06	−59	166	43 07	−59	166	42 08	−59	167	350
9	46 15	59	167	45 16	59	167	44 17	60	167	43 17	59	168	42 18	59	168	351
8	46 24	59	168	45 25	59	169	44 26	60	169	43 26	59	169	42 27	60	169	352
7	46 33	60	170	45 33	59	170	44 34	60	170	43 34	59	170	42 35	60	171	353
6	46 40	60	171	45 40	59	171	44 41	60	172	43 41	60	172	42 41	59	172	354
5	46 46	−60	173	45 46	−59	173	44 47	−60	173	43 47	−60	173	42 47	−60	173	355
4	46 51	60	174	45 51	60	174	44 51	59	174	43 52	60	175	42 52	60	175	356
3	46 55	60	176	45 55	60	176	44 55	60	176	43 55	60	176	42 55	60	176	357
2	46 58	60	177	45 58	60	177	44 58	60	177	43 58	60	177	42 58	60	177	358
1	46 59	60	179	45 59	59	179	45 00	60	179	44 00	60	179	43 00	60	179	359
0	47 00	−60	180	46 00	−60	180	45 00	−60	180	44 00	−60	180	43 00	−60	180	360

LHA	5° Hc	5° d	5° Z	6° Hc	6° d	6° Z	7° Hc	7° d	7° Z	8° Hc	8° d	8° Z	9° Hc	9° d	9° Z	LHA
	° ′	′	°	° ′	′	°	° ′	′	°	° ′	′	°	° ′	′	°	
69	11 38	43	108	10 55	43	109	10 12	43	110	09 29	44	110	08 45	43	111	291
68	12 20	44	109	11 36	43	110	10 53	43	110	10 10	44	111	09 26	44	112	292
67	13 01	43	110	12 18	44	111	11 34	44	111	10 50	43	112	10 07	44	113	293
66	13 42	43	111	12 59	44	111	12 15	44	112	11 31	44	113	10 47	44	113	294
65	14 23	−44	111	13 39	−43	112	12 56	−45	113	12 11	−44	113	11 27	−44	114	295
64	15 04	44	112	14 20	44	113	13 36	44	113	12 52	45	114	12 07	44	115	296
63	15 45	45	113	15 00	44	113	14 16	44	114	13 32	45	115	12 47	45	116	297
62	16 25	44	114	15 41	45	114	14 56	45	115	14 11	45	116	13 26	44	116	298
61	17 05	45	114	16 20	44	115	15 36	45	116	14 51	45	116	14 06	45	117	299
60	17 45	−45	115	17 00	−45	116	16 15	−45	116	15 30	−45	117	14 45	−46	118	300
59	18 25	46	116	17 39	45	117	16 54	45	117	16 09	46	118	15 23	45	119	301
58	19 04	45	117	18 19	46	117	17 33	46	118	16 47	45	119	16 02	46	120	302
57	19 43	46	117	18 57	45	118	18 12	46	119	17 26	46	120	16 40	46	120	303
56	20 22	46	118	19 36	46	119	18 50	46	119	18 04	46	120	17 18	47	121	304
55	21 00	−46	119	20 14	−46	120	19 28	−46	120	18 42	−47	121	17 55	−47	122	305
54	21 39	47	120	20 52	46	121	20 06	47	121	19 19	47	122	18 32	47	123	306
53	22 16	46	121	21 30	47	121	20 43	47	122	19 56	47	123	19 09	47	123	307
52	22 54	47	122	22 07	47	122	21 20	47	123	20 33	48	124	19 45	47	124	308
51	23 31	47	122	22 44	47	123	21 57	48	124	21 09	47	124	20 22	48	125	309
50	24 08	−47	123	23 21	−48	124	22 33	−48	125	21 45	−48	125	20 57	−48	126	310
49	24 45	48	124	23 57	48	125	23 09	48	125	22 21	48	126	21 33	49	127	311
48	25 21	48	125	24 33	48	126	23 45	49	126	22 56	48	127	22 08	49	128	312
47	25 57	49	126	25 08	48	127	24 20	49	127	23 31	49	128	22 42	49	129	313
46	26 32	49	127	25 43	49	127	24 54	49	128	24 05	49	129	23 16	49	129	314
45	27 07	−49	128	26 18	−49	128	25 29	−49	129	24 40	−50	130	23 50	−49	130	315
44	27 41	49	129	26 52	49	129	26 03	50	130	25 13	50	131	24 23	49	131	316
43	28 15	49	130	27 26	50	130	26 36	50	131	25 46	50	131	24 56	50	132	317
42	28 49	50	131	27 59	50	131	27 09	50	132	26 19	50	132	25 29	51	133	318
41	29 22	50	131	28 32	50	132	27 42	51	133	26 51	51	133	26 00	50	134	319
40	29 55	−51	132	29 04	−50	133	28 14	−51	134	27 23	−51	134	26 32	−51	135	320
39	30 27	51	133	29 36	51	134	28 45	51	135	27 54	51	135	27 03	52	136	321
38	30 59	52	134	30 07	51	135	29 16	51	136	28 25	52	136	27 33	52	137	322
37	31 30	52	135	30 38	51	136	29 47	52	137	28 55	52	137	28 03	52	138	323
36	32 00	51	136	31 09	52	137	30 17	53	138	29 24	52	138	28 32	52	139	324
35	32 30	−52	137	31 38	−52	138	30 46	−53	139	29 53	−52	139	29 01	−53	140	325
34	33 00	53	138	32 07	52	139	31 15	53	140	30 22	53	140	29 29	53	141	326
33	33 29	53	139	32 36	53	140	31 43	53	141	30 50	53	141	29 57	54	142	327
32	33 57	53	141	33 04	54	141	32 10	53	142	31 17	53	142	30 24	54	143	328
31	34 24	53	142	33 31	54	142	32 37	53	143	31 44	54	143	30 50	54	144	329
30	34 51	−53	143	33 58	−54	143	33 04	−54	144	32 10	−55	144	31 15	−54	145	330
29	35 18	54	144	34 24	55	144	33 29	54	145	32 35	54	145	31 41	55	146	331
28	35 43	54	145	34 49	55	145	33 54	54	146	33 00	55	146	32 05	55	147	332
27	36 08	54	146	35 14	55	146	34 19	55	147	33 24	55	147	32 29	56	148	333
26	36 32	55	147	35 37	55	148	34 42	55	148	33 47	55	149	32 52	56	149	334
25	36 56	−55	148	36 01	−56	149	35 05	−56	149	34 09	−55	150	33 14	−56	150	335
24	37 19	56	149	36 23	56	150	35 27	56	150	34 31	56	151	33 35	56	151	336
23	37 41	56	151	36 45	56	151	35 49	57	151	34 52	56	152	33 56	56	152	337
22	38 02	56	152	37 06	57	152	36 09	56	153	35 13	57	153	34 16	57	153	338
21	38 22	56	153	37 26	57	153	36 29	57	154	35 32	57	154	34 35	57	155	339
20	38 42	−57	154	37 45	−57	155	36 48	−57	155	35 51	−57	155	34 54	−57	156	340
19	39 01	58	155	38 03	57	156	37 06	57	156	36 09	57	157	35 12	58	157	341
18	39 18	57	157	38 21	57	157	37 24	58	157	36 26	58	158	35 28	57	158	342
17	39 35	57	158	38 38	58	158	37 40	58	159	36 42	58	159	35 44	57	159	343
16	39 52	58	159	38 54	58	159	37 56	58	160	36 58	58	160	36 00	59	160	344
15	40 07	−58	160	39 09	−59	161	38 10	−58	161	37 12	−58	161	36 14	−58	162	345
14	40 21	58	162	39 23	59	162	38 24	58	162	37 26	59	162	36 27	58	163	346
13	40 35	59	163	39 36	59	163	38 37	58	163	37 39	59	164	36 40	59	164	347
12	40 47	59	164	39 48	59	164	38 49	58	165	37 51	59	165	36 52	59	165	348
11	40 59	59	165	40 00	59	166	39 01	59	166	38 02	59	166	37 03	60	166	349
10	41 09	−59	167	40 10	−59	167	39 11	−59	167	38 12	−60	167	37 12	−59	168	350
9	41 19	60	168	40 19	59	168	39 20	59	168	38 21	60	169	37 21	59	169	351
8	41 27	59	169	40 28	60	170	39 28	59	170	38 29	60	170	37 29	59	170	352
7	41 35	60	171	40 35	59	171	39 36	60	171	38 36	59	171	37 37	60	171	353
6	41 42	60	172	40 42	60	172	39 42	59	172	38 43	60	172	37 43	60	173	354
5	41 47	−60	173	40 47	−59	173	39 48	−60	174	38 48	−60	174	37 48	−60	174	355
4	41 52	60	175	40 52	60	175	39 52	60	175	38 52	60	175	37 52	59	175	356
3	41 55	59	176	40 56	60	176	39 56	60	176	38 56	60	176	37 56	60	176	357
2	41 58	60	177	40 58	60	177	39 58	60	177	38 58	60	178	37 58	60	178	358
1	42 00	60	179	41 00	60	179	40 00	60	179	39 00	60	179	38 00	60	179	359
0	42 00	−60	180	41 00	−60	180	40 00	−60	180	39 00	−60	180	38 00	−60	180	360

LHA	10° Hc	10° d	10° Z	11° Hc	11° d	11° Z	12° Hc	12° d	12° Z	13° Hc	13° d	13° Z	14° Hc	14° d	14° Z	LHA
	° ′	′	°	° ′	′	°	° ′	′	°	° ′	′	°	° ′	′	°	
69	08 02	44	112	07 18	43	113	06 35	44	113	05 51	43	114	05 08	44	115	291
68	08 42	43	113	07 59	44	113	07 15	44	114	06 31	44	115	05 47	44	115	292
67	09 23	44	113	08 39	44	114	07 55	44	115	07 11	44	115	06 27	44	116	293
66	10 03	44	114	09 19	44	115	08 35	44	115	07 51	45	116	07 06	44	117	294
65	10 43	−44	115	09 59	−45	115	09 14	−44	116	08 30	−45	117	07 45	−44	117	295
64	11 23	45	116	10 38	44	116	09 54	45	117	09 09	45	118	08 24	45	118	296
63	12 02	44	116	11 18	45	117	10 33	45	118	09 48	45	118	09 03	45	119	297
62	12 42	45	117	11 57	46	118	11 11	45	118	10 26	45	119	09 41	45	120	298
61	13 21	46	118	12 35	45	118	11 50	46	119	11 04	45	120	10 19	46	120	299
60	13 59	−45	119	13 14	−46	119	12 28	−46	120	11 42	−45	121	10 57	−46	121	300
59	14 38	46	119	13 52	46	120	13 06	46	121	12 20	46	121	11 34	46	122	301
58	15 16	46	120	14 30	46	121	13 44	47	121	12 57	46	122	12 11	46	123	302
57	15 54	47	121	15 07	46	122	14 21	47	122	13 34	46	123	12 48	47	123	303
56	16 31	46	122	15 45	47	122	14 58	47	123	14 11	47	124	13 24	47	124	304
55	17 08	−46	122	16 22	−47	123	15 35	−47	124	14 48	−48	124	14 00	−47	125	305
54	17 45	47	123	16 58	47	124	16 11	47	125	15 24	48	125	14 36	47	126	306
53	18 22	48	124	17 34	47	125	16 47	48	125	15 59	47	126	15 12	48	127	307
52	18 58	48	125	18 10	47	126	17 23	48	126	16 35	48	127	15 47	48	127	308
51	19 34	48	126	18 46	48	126	17 58	48	127	17 10	49	128	16 21	48	128	309
50	20 09	−48	127	19 21	−48	127	18 33	−49	128	17 44	−48	128	16 56	−49	129	310
49	20 44	48	127	19 56	49	128	19 07	49	129	18 18	48	129	17 30	49	130	311
48	21 19	49	128	20 30	49	129	19 41	49	130	18 52	49	130	18 03	49	131	312
47	21 53	49	129	21 04	49	130	20 15	49	130	19 26	50	131	18 36	49	132	313
46	22 27	49	130	21 38	50	131	20 48	49	131	19 59	50	132	19 09	50	132	314
45	23 01	−50	131	22 11	−50	131	21 21	−50	132	20 31	−50	133	19 41	−50	133	315
44	23 34	51	132	22 43	50	132	21 53	50	133	21 03	50	134	20 13	51	134	316
43	24 06	50	133	23 16	51	133	22 25	50	134	21 35	51	134	20 44	51	135	317
42	24 38	51	134	23 47	50	134	22 57	51	135	22 06	51	135	21 15	51	136	318
41	25 10	51	135	24 19	51	135	23 28	52	136	22 36	51	136	21 45	51	137	319
40	25 41	−52	135	24 49	−51	136	23 58	−51	137	23 07	−52	137	22 15	−52	138	320
39	26 11	51	136	25 20	52	137	24 28	52	137	23 36	52	138	22 44	52	139	321
38	26 41	52	137	25 49	52	138	24 57	52	138	24 05	52	139	23 13	52	140	322
37	27 11	52	138	26 19	53	139	25 26	52	139	24 34	53	140	23 41	52	140	323
36	27 40	53	139	26 47	52	140	25 55	53	140	25 02	53	141	24 09	53	141	324
35	28 08	−53	140	27 15	−53	141	26 22	−53	141	25 29	−53	142	24 36	−53	142	325
34	28 36	53	141	27 43	53	142	26 50	54	142	25 56	53	143	25 03	54	143	326
33	29 03	53	142	28 10	54	143	27 16	54	143	26 22	53	144	25 29	54	144	327
32	29 30	54	143	28 36	54	144	27 42	54	144	26 48	54	145	25 54	54	145	328
31	29 56	54	144	29 02	54	145	28 08	55	145	27 13	54	146	26 19	55	146	329
30	30 21	−54	145	29 27	−55	146	28 32	−54	146	27 38	−55	147	26 43	−55	147	330
29	30 46	55	146	29 51	55	147	28 56	54	147	28 02	55	148	27 07	56	148	331
28	31 10	55	147	30 15	55	148	29 20	55	148	28 25	56	149	27 29	55	149	332
27	31 33	55	148	30 38	55	149	29 43	56	149	28 47	55	150	27 52	56	150	333
26	31 56	56	149	31 00	55	150	30 05	56	150	29 09	56	151	28 13	56	151	334
25	32 18	−56	151	31 22	−56	151	30 26	−56	151	29 30	−56	152	28 34	−56	152	335
24	32 39	56	152	31 43	56	152	30 47	57	152	29 50	56	153	28 54	56	153	336
23	33 00	57	153	32 03	56	153	31 07	57	154	30 10	56	154	29 13	56	154	337
22	33 19	56	154	32 23	57	154	31 26	57	155	30 29	57	155	29 32	57	155	338
21	33 38	57	155	32 41	57	155	31 44	58	156	30 47	57	156	29 50	57	156	339
20	33 57	−58	156	32 59	−57	156	32 02	−57	157	31 05	−58	157	30 07	−57	157	340
19	34 14	57	157	33 17	58	158	32 19	58	158	31 21	57	158	30 24	58	159	341
18	34 31	58	158	33 33	58	159	32 35	58	159	31 37	57	159	30 40	58	160	342
17	34 47	58	160	33 49	58	160	32 51	59	160	31 52	58	160	30 54	58	161	343
16	35 01	58	161	34 03	58	161	33 05	58	161	32 07	58	162	31 09	59	162	344
15	35 16	−59	162	34 17	−58	162	33 19	−59	162	32 20	−58	163	31 22	−59	163	345
14	35 29	59	163	34 30	58	163	33 32	59	164	32 33	59	164	31 34	58	164	346
13	35 41	59	164	34 42	58	164	33 44	59	165	32 45	59	165	31 46	59	165	347
12	35 53	59	165	34 54	59	166	33 55	59	166	32 56	59	166	31 57	59	166	348
11	36 03	59	167	35 04	59	167	34 05	59	167	33 06	59	167	32 07	59	167	349
10	36 13	−59	168	35 14	−59	168	34 15	−60	168	33 15	−59	168	32 16	−59	169	350
9	36 22	59	169	35 23	60	169	34 23	59	169	33 24	60	170	32 24	59	170	351
8	36 30	60	170	35 30	59	170	34 31	60	171	33 31	59	171	32 32	60	171	352
7	36 37	60	171	35 37	59	172	34 38	60	172	33 38	60	172	32 38	59	172	353
6	36 43	60	173	35 43	59	173	34 44	60	173	33 44	60	173	32 44	60	173	354
5	36 48	−60	174	35 48	−59	174	34 49	−60	174	33 49	−60	174	32 49	−60	174	355
4	36 53	60	175	35 53	60	175	34 53	60	175	33 53	60	175	32 53	60	175	356
3	36 56	60	176	35 56	60	176	34 56	60	176	33 56	60	177	32 56	60	177	357
2	36 58	60	178	35 58	60	178	34 58	60	178	33 58	60	178	32 58	60	178	358
1	37 00	60	179	36 00	60	179	35 00	60	179	34 00	60	179	33 00	60	179	359
0	37 00	−60	180	36 00	−60	180	35 00	−60	180	34 00	−60	180	33 00	−60	180	360

S. Lat. {LHA greater than 180°....... Zn=180−Z; LHA less than 180°........... Zn=180+Z}

DECLINATION (0°-14°) CONTRARY NAME TO LATITUDE

LAT 43°

N. Lat. {LHA greater than 180°........ Zn=Z
{LHA less than 180°.......... Zn=360−Z

DECLINATION (15°-29°) SAME NAME AS LATITUDE

LHA	15° Hc	d	Z	16° Hc	d	Z	17° Hc	d	Z	18° Hc	d	Z	19° Hc	d	Z
	° ′	′	°	° ′	′	°	° ′	′	°	° ′	′	°	° ′	′	°
0	62 00	+60	180	63 00	+60	180	64 00	+60	180	65 00	+60	180	66 00	+60	180
1	61 59	60	178	62 59	60	178	63 59	60	178	64 59	60	178	65 59	60	178
2	61 57	60	176	62 57	60	176	63 57	60	176	64 57	59	176	65 56	60	175
3	61 53	60	174	62 53	60	174	63 53	59	174	64 52	60	173	65 52	60	173
4	61 47	60	172	62 47	60	172	63 47	59	171	64 46	60	171	65 46	59	171
5	61 40	+60	170	62 40	+59	170	63 39	+60	169	64 39	+59	169	65 38	+59	169
6	61 32	59	168	62 31	59	167	63 30	59	167	64 29	59	167	65 28	59	166
7	61 22	59	166	62 21	59	165	63 20	58	165	64 18	59	165	65 17	59	164
8	61 10	59	164	62 09	58	163	63 07	59	163	64 06	58	162	65 04	58	162
9	60 57	59	162	61 56	58	161	62 54	58	161	63 52	58	160	64 50	57	160
10	60 43	+58	160	61 41	+58	159	62 39	+57	159	63 36	+58	158	64 34	+57	158
11	60 27	58	158	61 25	57	158	62 22	57	157	63 19	57	156	64 16	57	155
12	60 10	57	156	61 07	57	156	62 04	57	155	63 01	56	154	63 57	56	153
13	59 52	57	154	60 49	56	154	61 45	56	153	62 41	56	152	63 37	55	151
14	59 32	56	153	60 28	56	152	61 24	56	151	62 20	55	150	63 15	55	150
15	59 11	+56	151	60 07	+55	150	61 02	+56	149	61 58	+54	148	62 52	+55	148
16	58 49	56	149	59 45	54	148	60 39	55	148	61 34	54	147	62 28	54	146
17	58 26	55	147	59 21	54	147	60 15	54	146	61 09	54	145	62 03	53	144
18	58 02	54	146	58 56	54	145	59 50	53	144	60 43	53	143	61 36	53	142
19	57 37	53	144	58 30	54	143	59 24	53	142	60 17	52	141	61 09	52	140
20	57 11	+53	143	58 04	+52	142	58 56	+53	141	59 49	+51	140	60 40	+52	139
21	56 43	53	141	57 36	52	140	58 28	52	139	59 20	51	138	60 11	51	137
22	56 15	52	139	57 07	52	138	57 59	51	138	58 50	51	137	59 41	50	135
23	55 46	52	138	56 38	51	137	57 29	50	136	58 19	50	135	59 09	50	134
24	55 16	51	136	56 07	51	136	56 58	50	135	57 48	49	134	58 37	49	132
25	54 46	+50	135	55 36	+50	134	56 26	+50	133	57 16	+49	132	58 05	+48	131
26	54 14	50	134	55 04	50	133	55 54	49	132	56 43	48	131	57 31	48	130
27	53 42	50	132	54 32	49	131	55 21	48	130	56 09	48	129	56 57	47	128
28	53 09	49	131	53 58	49	130	54 47	48	129	55 35	47	128	56 22	47	127
29	52 36	48	130	53 24	48	129	54 12	48	128	55 00	47	127	55 47	46	125
30	52 02	+48	128	52 50	+47	127	53 37	+47	126	54 24	+47	125	55 11	+45	124
31	51 27	48	127	52 15	47	126	53 02	46	125	53 48	46	124	54 34	45	123
32	50 52	47	126	51 39	46	125	52 25	46	124	53 11	46	123	53 57	45	122
33	50 16	46	125	51 02	47	124	51 49	45	123	52 34	45	122	53 19	45	120
34	49 39	47	124	50 26	45	123	51 11	46	121	51 57	44	120	52 41	44	119
35	49 03	+45	122	49 48	+46	121	50 34	+45	120	51 19	+44	119	52 03	+43	118
36	48 25	46	121	49 11	45	120	49 56	44	119	50 40	44	118	51 24	43	117
37	47 47	46	120	48 33	44	119	49 17	44	118	50 01	44	117	50 45	42	116
38	47 09	45	119	47 54	44	118	48 38	44	117	49 22	43	116	50 05	42	115
39	46 31	44	118	47 15	44	117	47 59	43	116	48 42	43	115	49 25	42	114
40	45 52	+44	117	46 36	+43	116	47 19	+43	115	48 02	+43	114	48 45	+41	113
41	45 13	43	116	45 56	43	115	46 39	43	114	47 22	42	113	48 04	42	112
42	44 33	43	115	45 16	43	114	45 59	42	113	46 41	42	112	47 23	41	111
43	43 53	43	114	44 36	43	113	45 19	42	112	46 01	41	111	46 42	41	110
44	43 13	42	113	43 55	43	112	44 38	41	111	45 19	42	110	46 01	40	109
45	42 32	+43	112	43 15	+42	111	43 57	+41	110	44 38	+41	109	45 19	+40	108
46	41 51	43	111	42 34	41	110	43 15	42	109	43 57	40	108	44 37	40	107
47	41 10	42	110	41 52	42	109	42 34	41	108	43 15	40	107	43 55	40	106
48	40 29	42	109	41 11	41	108	41 52	41	107	42 33	40	106	43 13	40	105
49	39 47	42	108	40 29	41	108	41 10	41	107	41 51	40	106	42 31	39	105
50	39 06	+41	108	39 47	+41	107	40 28	+40	106	41 08	+40	105	41 48	+39	104
51	38 24	41	107	39 05	41	106	39 46	40	105	40 26	39	104	41 05	39	103
52	37 42	41	106	38 23	40	105	39 03	40	104	39 43	39	103	40 22	39	102
53	36 59	41	105	37 40	40	104	38 20	40	103	39 00	40	102	39 40	38	101
54	36 17	40	104	36 57	41	103	37 38	39	102	38 17	39	101	38 56	39	100
55	35 34	+41	103	36 15	+40	103	36 55	+39	102	37 34	+39	101	38 13	+39	100
56	34 52	40	103	35 32	40	102	36 12	39	101	36 51	39	100	37 30	38	99
57	34 09	40	102	34 49	39	101	35 28	40	100	36 08	38	99	36 46	39	98
58	33 26	40	101	34 06	39	100	34 45	39	99	35 24	39	98	36 03	38	97
59	32 43	39	100	33 22	40	99	34 02	39	99	34 41	38	98	35 19	39	97
60	31 59	+40	100	32 39	+39	99	33 18	+39	98	33 57	+39	97	34 36	+38	96
61	31 16	40	99	31 56	39	98	32 35	39	97	33 14	38	96	33 52	38	95
62	30 33	39	98	31 12	39	97	31 51	39	96	32 30	38	95	33 08	38	94
63	29 49	39	97	30 28	40	96	31 08	38	96	31 46	39	95	32 25	38	94
64	29 05	40	97	29 45	39	96	30 24	39	95	31 03	38	94	31 41	38	93
65	28 22	+39	96	29 01	+39	95	29 40	+39	94	30 19	+38	93	30 57	+38	92
66	27 38	39	95	28 17	39	94	28 56	39	93	29 35	38	93	30 13	38	92
67	26 54	40	94	27 34	39	94	28 13	38	93	28 51	38	92	29 29	38	91
68	26 11	39	94	26 50	39	93	27 29	38	92	28 07	38	91	28 45	38	90
69	25 27	39	93	26 06	39	92	26 45	38	91	27 23	39	90	28 02	37	90

LHA	20° Hc	d	Z	21° Hc	d	Z	22° Hc	d	Z	23° Hc	d	Z	24° Hc	d	Z
	° ′	′	°	° ′	′	°	° ′	′	°	° ′	′	°	° ′	′	°
0	67 00	+60	180	68 00	+60	180	69 00	+60	180	70 00	+60	180	71 00	+60	180
1	66 59	60	178	67 59	60	178	68 59	60	177	69 59	60	177	70 59	60	177
2	66 56	60	175	67 56	60	175	68 56	60	175	69 56	60	175	70 56	60	174
3	66 52	59	173	67 51	60	173	68 51	60	172	69 51	59	172	70 50	60	172
4	66 45	60	170	67 45	59	170	68 44	60	170	69 44	59	169	70 43	59	169
5	66 37	+59	168	67 36	+60	168	68 36	+59	167	69 35	+59	167	70 34	+58	166
6	66 27	59	166	67 26	59	165	68 25	59	165	69 24	58	164	70 22	58	164
7	66 16	58	164	67 14	58	163	68 12	59	162	69 11	58	162	70 09	57	161
8	66 02	58	161	67 00	58	161	67 58	58	160	68 56	57	159	69 53	57	158
9	65 47	58	159	66 45	57	158	67 42	57	158	68 39	57	157	69 36	57	156
10	65 31	+57	157	66 28	+57	156	67 25	+56	155	68 21	+56	154	69 17	+56	153
11	65 13	56	155	66 09	56	154	67 05	56	153	68 01	56	152	68 57	55	151
12	64 53	56	153	65 49	56	152	66 45	55	151	67 40	55	150	68 35	54	149
13	64 32	56	151	65 28	55	150	66 23	54	149	67 17	54	148	68 11	54	146
14	64 10	55	149	65 05	54	148	65 59	54	147	66 53	53	145	67 46	53	144
15	63 47	+54	147	64 41	+53	146	65 34	+53	145	66 27	+53	143	67 20	+52	142
16	63 22	53	145	64 15	53	144	65 08	53	143	66 01	51	141	66 52	52	140
17	62 56	53	143	63 49	52	142	64 41	52	141	65 33	51	140	66 24	50	138
18	62 29	52	141	63 21	52	140	64 13	51	139	65 04	50	138	65 54	50	136
19	62 01	51	139	62 52	51	138	63 43	50	137	64 33	50	136	65 23	49	134
20	61 32	+51	138	62 23	+50	137	63 13	+49	135	64 02	+49	134	64 51	+48	133
21	61 02	50	136	61 52	49	135	62 41	49	134	63 30	49	132	64 19	47	131
22	60 31	49	134	61 20	49	133	62 09	49	132	62 58	47	131	63 45	47	129
23	59 59	49	133	60 48	48	132	61 36	48	130	62 24	47	129	63 11	46	128
24	59 26	49	131	60 15	47	130	61 02	47	129	61 49	47	128	62 36	45	126
25	58 53	+48	130	59 41	+47	129	60 28	+46	127	61 14	+46	126	62 00	+45	125
26	58 19	47	128	59 06	47	127	59 53	45	126	60 38	45	125	61 23	45	123
27	57 44	47	127	58 31	46	126	59 17	45	125	60 02	44	123	60 46	44	122
28	57 09	46	126	57 55	45	124	58 40	45	123	59 25	44	122	60 09	43	121
29	56 33	45	124	57 18	45	123	58 03	45	122	58 48	43	121	59 31	42	119
30	55 56	+45	123	56 41	+45	122	57 26	+43	121	58 09	+43	119	58 52	+42	118
31	55 19	45	122	56 04	44	121	56 48	43	119	57 31	42	118	58 13	42	117
32	54 42	44	121	55 26	43	119	56 09	43	118	56 52	42	117	57 34	41	116
33	54 04	43	119	54 47	43	118	55 30	43	117	56 13	41	116	56 54	41	114
34	53 25	43	118	54 08	43	117	54 51	42	116	55 33	41	115	56 14	40	113
35	52 46	+43	117	53 29	+42	116	54 11	+42	115	54 53	+40	113	55 33	+40	112
36	52 07	42	116	52 49	42	115	53 31	41	114	54 12	41	112	54 53	39	111
37	51 27	42	115	52 09	42	114	52 51	41	113	53 32	40	111	54 12	39	110
38	50 47	42	114	51 29	41	113	52 10	41	112	52 51	39	110	53 30	39	109
39	50 07	41	113	50 48	41	112	51 29	40	110	52 09	40	109	52 49	38	108
40	49 26	+42	112	50 08	+40	111	50 48	+40	109	51 28	+39	108	52 07	+38	107
41	48 46	40	111	49 26	40	110	50 06	40	109	50 46	39	107	51 25	38	106
42	48 04	41	110	48 45	40	109	49 25	39	108	50 04	38	106	50 42	38	105
43	47 23	40	109	48 03	40	108	48 43	39	107	49 22	38	105	50 00	37	104
44	46 41	40	108	47 21	40	107	48 01	38	106	48 39	38	105	49 17	38	103
45	45 59	+40	107	46 39	+39	106	47 18	+39	105	47 57	+38	104	48 35	+37	103
46	45 17	40	106	45 57	39	105	46 36	38	104	47 14	38	103	47 52	37	102
47	44 35	39	105	45 14	39	104	45 53	38	103	46 31	38	102	47 09	36	101
48	43 53	39	104	44 32	38	103	45 10	38	102	45 48	37	101	46 25	37	100
49	43 10	39	104	43 49	38	103	44 27	38	101	45 05	37	100	45 42	37	99
50	42 27	+39	103	43 06	+38	102	43 44	+38	101	44 22	+37	100	44 59	+36	98
51	41 44	39	102	42 23	38	101	43 01	38	100	43 39	36	99	44 15	37	98
52	41 01	39	101	41 40	38	100	42 18	37	99	42 55	37	98	43 32	36	97
53	40 18	39	100	40 57	37	99	41 34	38	98	42 12	36	97	42 48	36	96
54	39 35	38	100	40 13	38	98	40 51	37	97	41 28	37	96	42 05	35	95
55	38 52	+38	99	39 30	+37	98	40 07	+37	97	40 44	+37	96	41 21	+36	95
56	38 08	38	98	38 46	38	97	39 24	37	96	40 01	36	95	40 37	36	94
57	37 25	38	97	38 03	37	96	38 40	37	95	39 17	36	94	39 53	36	93
58	36 41	38	96	37 19	37	95	37 56	37	94	38 33	36	93	39 09	36	92
59	35 58	37	96	36 35	38	95	37 13	36	94	37 49	37	93	38 26	35	92
60	35 14	+38	95	35 52	+37	94	36 29	+37	93	37 06	+36	92	37 42	+35	91
61	34 30	38	94	35 08	37	93	35 45	37	92	36 22	36	91	36 58	36	90
62	33 46	38	94	34 24	37	93	35 01	37	92	35 38	36	91	36 14	36	90
63	33 03	37	93	33 40	37	92	34 17	37	91	34 54	36	90	35 30	36	89
64	32 19	37	92	32 56	37	91	33 33	37	90	34 10	36	89	34 46	36	88
65	31 35	+37	91	32 12	+37	91	32 49	+37	90	33 26	+36	89	34 02	+36	88
66	30 51	38	91	31 29	37	90	32 06	36	89	32 42	37	88	33 19	35	87
67	30 07	38	90	30 45	37	89	31 22	36	88	31 58	37	87	32 35	36	86
68	29 23	38	89	30 01	37	88	30 38	37	88	31 15	36	87	31 51	36	86
69	28 39	38	89	29 17	37	88	29 54	37	87	30 31	36	86	31 07	36	85

LHA	25° Hc	d	Z	26° Hc	d	Z	27° Hc	d	Z	28° Hc	d	Z	29° Hc	d	Z	LHA
	° ′	′	°	° ′	′	°	° ′	′	°	° ′	′	°	° ′	′	°	
0	72 00	+60	180	73 00	+60	180	74 00	+60	180	75 00	+60	180	76 00	+60	180	360
1	71 59	60	177	72 59	60	177	73 59	60	177	74 59	60	177	75 59	60	176	359
2	71 56	59	174	72 55	60	174	73 55	60	174	74 55	60	173	75 55	59	173	358
3	71 50	60	171	72 50	59	171	73 49	59	170	74 48	60	170	75 48	59	169	357
4	71 42	59	168	72 41	59	168	73 40	59	167	74 39	59	167	75 38	59	166	356
5	71 32	+59	166	72 31	+59	165	73 30	+58	164	74 28	+58	163	75 26	+58	162	355
6	71 20	59	163	72 19	57	162	73 16	58	161	74 14	58	160	75 12	57	159	354
7	71 06	58	160	72 04	57	159	73 01	57	158	73 58	57	157	74 55	56	156	353
8	70 50	57	157	71 47	57	156	72 44	56	155	73 40	56	154	74 36	55	153	352
9	70 33	56	155	71 29	56	154	72 25	55	153	73 20	55	151	74 15	54	150	351
10	70 13	+56	152	71 09	+54	151	72 03	+55	150	72 58	+54	148	73 52	+53	147	350
11	69 52	54	150	70 46	55	149	71 41	53	147	72 34	53	146	73 27	52	144	349
12	69 29	54	148	70 23	53	146	71 16	53	145	72 09	51	143	73 00	51	142	348
13	69 05	53	145	69 58	52	144	70 50	52	142	71 42	50	141	72 32	50	139	347
14	68 39	52	143	69 31	51	142	70 22	51	140	71 13	50	138	72 03	48	137	346
15	68 12	+51	141	69 03	+51	139	69 54	+49	138	70 43	+49	136	71 32	+47	134	345
16	67 44	50	139	68 34	50	137	69 24	48	136	70 12	48	134	71 00	47	132	344
17	67 14	50	137	68 04	48	135	68 52	48	134	69 40	47	132	70 27	46	130	343
18	66 44	48	135	67 32	48	133	68 20	47	132	69 07	46	130	69 53	45	128	342
19	66 12	48	133	67 00	47	132	67 47	46	130	68 33	45	128	69 18	44	126	341
20	65 39	+48	131	66 27	+46	130	67 13	+45	128	67 58	+44	126	68 42	+43	125	340
21	65 06	46	130	65 52	46	128	66 38	44	126	67 22	44	125	68 06	42	123	339
22	64 32	45	128	65 17	45	126	66 02	44	125	66 46	43	123	67 29	41	121	338
23	63 57	45	126	64 42	44	125	65 26	43	123	66 09	42	121	66 51	40	120	337
24	63 21	44	125	64 05	44	123	64 49	42	122	65 31	41	120	66 12	40	118	336
25	62 45	+43	123	63 28	+43	122	64 11	+42	120	64 53	+40	119	65 33	+40	117	335
26	62 08	43	122	62 51	42	120	63 33	41	119	64 14	40	117	64 54	39	115	334
27	61 30	43	120	62 13	41	119	62 54	41	117	63 35	39	116	64 14	38	114	333
28	60 52	42	119	61 34	41	118	62 15	40	116	62 55	39	114	63 34	37	113	332
29	60 13	42	118	60 55	40	116	61 35	40	115	62 15	38	113	62 53	37	112	331
30	59 34	+41	117	60 15	+40	115	60 55	+39	114	61 34	+38	112	62 12	+37	110	330
31	58 55	40	115	59 35	40	114	60 15	38	112	60 53	38	111	61 31	36	109	329
32	58 15	40	114	58 55	39	113	59 34	38	111	60 12	37	110	60 49	36	108	328
33	57 35	39	113	58 14	39	112	58 53	38	110	59 31	36	109	60 07	36	107	327
34	56 54	39	112	57 33	39	111	58 12	37	109	58 49	36	108	59 25	35	106	326
35	56 13	+39	111	56 52	+38	109	57 30	+37	108	58 07	+36	107	58 43	+35	105	325
36	55 32	39	110	56 11	37	108	56 48	37	107	57 25	36	106	58 01	34	104	324
37	54 51	38	109	55 29	37	107	56 06	37	106	56 43	35	105	57 18	34	103	323
38	54 09	38	108	54 47	37	106	55 24	36	105	56 00	35	104	56 35	34	102	322
39	53 27	38	107	54 05	36	105	54 41	36	104	55 17	35	103	55 52	34	101	321
40	52 45	+37	106	53 22	+37	105	53 59	+35	103	54 34	+35	102	55 09	+34	100	320
41	52 03	37	105	52 40	36	104	53 16	35	102	53 51	35	101	54 26	33	100	319
42	51 20	37	104	51 57	36	103	52 33	35	101	53 08	34	100	53 42	34	99	318
43	50 37	37	103	51 14	36	102	51 50	35	101	52 25	34	99	52 59	33	98	317
44	49 55	36	102	50 31	36	101	51 07	35	100	51 42	33	98	52 15	33	97	316
45	49 12	+36	101	49 48	+35	100	50 23	+35	99	50 58	+34	98	51 32	+33	96	315
46	48 29	36	101	49 05	35	99	49 40	35	98	50 15	33	97	50 48	33	95	314
47	47 45	36	100	48 21	36	98	48 57	34	97	49 31	34	96	50 05	32	95	313
48	47 02	36	99	47 38	35	98	48 13	34	96	48 47	34	95	49 21	32	94	312
49	46 19	35	98	46 54	35	97	47 29	35	96	48 04	33	94	48 37	33	93	311
50	45 35	+36	97	46 11	+35	96	46 46	+34	95	47 20	+33	94	47 53	+33	93	310
51	44 52	35	97	45 27	35	95	46 02	34	94	46 36	33	93	47 09	33	92	309
52	44 08	35	96	44 43	35	95	45 18	34	93	45 52	33	92	46 25	33	91	308
53	43 24	36	95	44 00	34	94	44 34	34	93	45 08	34	92	45 42	32	90	307
54	42 40	36	94	43 16	34	93	43 50	34	92	44 24	34	91	44 58	32	90	306
55	41 57	+35	94	42 32	+35	92	43 07	+34	91	43 41	+33	90	44 14	+32	89	305
56	41 13	35	93	41 48	35	92	42 23	34	91	42 57	33	90	43 30	33	88	304
57	40 29	35	92	41 04	35	91	41 39	34	90	42 13	33	89	42 46	33	88	303
58	39 45	35	91	40 20	35	90	40 55	34	89	41 29	33	88	42 02	33	87	302
59	39 01	35	91	39 36	35	90	40 11	34	89	40 45	33	88	41 18	33	86	301
60	38 17	+36	90	38 53	+34	89	39 27	+34	88	40 01	+34	87	40 35	+32	86	300
61	37 34	35	89	38 09	34	88	38 43	34	87	39 17	34	86	39 51	33	85	299
62	36 50	35	89	37 25	35	88	38 00	34	87	38 34	33	86	39 07	33	85	298
63	36 06	35	88	36 41	35	87	37 16	34	86	37 50	34	85	38 24	33	84	297
64	35 22	35	87	35 57	35	86	36 32	34	85	37 06	34	84	37 40	33	83	296
65	34 38	+35	87	35 13	+35	86	35 48	+35	85	36 23	+33	84	36 56	+34	83	295
66	33 54	36	86	34 30	35	85	35 05	34	84	35 39	34	83	36 13	33	82	294
67	33 11	35	85	33 46	35	84	34 21	35	83	34 56	34	82	35 30	33	81	293
68	32 27	35	85	33 02	35	84	33 37	35	83	34 12	34	82	34 46	34	81	292
69	31 43	36	84	32 19	35	83	32 54	35	82	33 29	34	81	34 03	34	80	291

S. Lat. {LHA greater than 180°....... Zn=180−Z
{LHA less than 180°........... Zn=180+Z

DECLINATION (15°-29°) SAME NAME AS LATITUDE

LAT 43°

N. Lat. {LHA greater than 180°....... Zn=Z; LHA less than 180°........... Zn=360−Z}

DECLINATION (15°-29°) SAME NAME AS LATITUDE

LAT 43°

LHA	15° Hc d Z	16° Hc d Z	17° Hc d Z	18° Hc d Z	19° Hc d Z	20° Hc d Z	21° Hc d Z	22° Hc d Z	23° Hc d Z	24° Hc d Z	25° Hc d Z	26° Hc d Z	27° Hc d Z	28° Hc d Z	29° Hc d Z	LHA
	° ′ ′ °	° ′ ′ °	° ′ ′ °	° ′ ′ °	° ′ ′ °	° ′ ′ °	° ′ ′ °	° ′ ′ °	° ′ ′ °	° ′ ′ °	° ′ ′ °	° ′ ′ °	° ′ ′ °	° ′ ′ °	° ′ ′ °	
70	24 43 +39 92	25 22 +39 91	26 01 +38 91	26 39 +39 90	27 18 +38 89	27 56 +37 88	28 33 +37 87	29 10 +37 86	29 47 +37 85	30 24 +36 84	31 00 +35 84	31 35 +36 83	32 11 +34 82	32 45 +35 81	33 20 +34 80	290
71	23 59 39 92	24 38 39 91	25 17 39 90	25 56 38 89	26 34 38 89	27 12 37 87	27 49 37 86	28 26 37 86	29 03 37 85	29 40 36 84	30 16 36 83	30 52 35 82	31 27 35 81	32 02 35 80	32 37 34 79	289
72	23 15 39 91	23 54 39 90	24 33 39 89	25 12 38 88	25 50 38 88	26 28 37 87	27 05 38 86	27 43 37 85	28 20 36 84	28 56 37 83	29 33 35 82	30 08 36 81	30 44 35 80	31 19 35 79	31 54 34 78	288
73	22 31 40 90	23 11 38 89	23 49 39 89	24 28 38 88	25 06 38 87	25 44 38 86	26 22 37 85	26 59 37 84	27 36 37 83	28 13 36 83	28 49 36 82	29 25 36 81	30 01 35 80	30 36 35 79	31 11 34 78	287
74	21 48 39 90	22 27 38 89	23 05 39 88	23 44 38 87	24 22 38 86	25 00 38 85	25 38 37 85	26 15 38 84	26 53 36 83	27 29 37 82	28 06 36 81	28 42 35 80	29 17 36 79	29 53 35 78	30 28 34 77	286
75	21 04 +39 89	21 43 +39 88	22 22 +38 87	23 00 +39 86	23 39 +38 86	24 17 +37 85	24 54 +38 84	25 32 +37 83	26 09 +37 82	26 46 +36 81	27 22 +37 80	27 59 +35 79	28 34 +36 79	29 10 +35 78	29 45 +35 77	285
76	20 20 39 88	20 59 39 87	21 38 38 87	22 16 39 86	22 55 38 85	23 33 38 84	24 11 37 83	24 48 38 82	25 26 37 82	26 03 36 81	26 39 37 80	27 16 35 79	27 51 36 78	28 27 35 77	29 02 35 76	284
77	19 36 39 88	20 15 39 87	20 54 39 86	21 33 38 85	22 11 38 84	22 49 38 83	23 27 38 83	24 05 37 82	24 42 37 81	25 19 37 80	25 56 37 79	26 33 36 78	27 09 35 77	27 44 36 76	28 20 35 76	283
78	18 52 39 87	19 31 39 86	20 10 39 85	20 49 38 84	21 27 39 84	22 06 38 83	22 44 37 82	23 21 38 81	23 59 37 80	24 36 37 79	25 13 37 79	25 50 36 78	26 26 36 77	27 02 35 76	27 37 36 75	282
79	18 08 40 86	18 48 39 85	19 27 38 85	20 05 39 84	20 44 38 83	21 22 38 82	22 00 38 81	22 38 38 80	23 16 37 80	23 53 37 79	24 30 37 78	25 07 36 77	25 43 36 76	26 19 36 75	26 55 35 74	281
80	17 25 +39 86	18 04 +39 85	18 43 +39 84	19 22 +38 83	20 00 +39 82	20 39 +38 82	21 17 +38 81	21 55 +38 80	22 33 +37 79	23 10 +37 78	23 47 +37 77	24 24 +37 76	25 01 +36 76	25 37 +36 75	26 13 +35 74	280
81	16 41 39 85	17 20 39 84	17 59 39 83	18 38 39 82	19 17 38 82	19 55 39 81	20 34 38 80	21 12 38 79	21 50 37 78	22 27 37 78	23 04 37 77	23 41 37 76	24 18 37 75	24 55 36 74	25 31 36 73	279
82	15 57 40 84	16 37 39 83	17 16 39 83	17 55 39 82	18 34 38 81	19 12 39 80	19 51 38 79	20 29 38 79	21 07 37 78	21 44 38 77	22 22 37 76	22 59 37 75	23 36 37 74	24 13 36 74	24 49 36 73	278
83	15 14 39 84	15 53 39 83	16 32 39 82	17 11 39 81	17 50 39 80	18 29 38 80	19 07 39 79	19 46 38 78	20 24 38 77	21 02 37 76	21 39 38 75	22 17 37 75	22 54 37 74	23 31 36 73	24 07 36 72	277
84	14 30 39 83	15 09 40 82	15 49 39 81	16 28 39 81	17 07 39 80	17 46 39 79	18 25 38 78	19 03 38 77	19 41 38 77	20 19 38 76	20 57 37 75	21 34 38 74	22 12 37 73	22 49 36 72	23 25 37 71	276
85	13 46 +40 82	14 26 +40 81	15 06 +39 81	15 45 +39 80	16 24 +39 79	17 03 +39 78	17 42 +38 78	18 20 +39 77	18 59 +38 76	19 37 +38 75	20 15 +37 74	20 52 +38 73	21 30 +37 73	22 07 +37 72	22 44 +37 71	275
86	13 03 40 82	13 43 39 81	14 22 40 80	15 02 39 79	15 41 39 78	16 20 39 78	16 59 39 77	17 38 38 76	18 16 38 75	18 54 38 74	19 32 38 74	20 10 38 73	20 48 37 72	21 25 37 71	22 02 37 70	274
87	12 20 39 81	12 59 40 80	13 39 40 79	14 19 39 79	14 58 39 78	15 37 39 77	16 16 39 76	16 55 39 75	17 34 38 75	18 12 38 74	18 50 38 73	19 28 38 72	20 06 38 71	20 44 37 71	21 21 37 70	273
88	11 36 40 80	12 16 40 80	12 56 40 79	13 36 39 78	14 15 39 77	14 54 40 76	15 34 39 76	16 13 38 75	16 51 39 74	17 30 39 73	18 09 38 72	18 47 38 72	19 25 38 71	20 03 37 70	20 40 38 69	272
89	10 53 40 80	11 33 40 79	12 13 40 78	12 53 39 77	13 32 40 77	14 12 39 76	14 51 39 75	15 30 39 74	16 09 39 73	16 48 39 73	17 27 38 72	18 05 38 71	18 43 38 70	19 21 38 69	19 59 38 69	271
90	10 10 +40 79	10 50 +40 78	11 30 +40 77	12 10 +40 77	12 50 +39 76	13 29 +40 75	14 09 +39 74	14 48 +39 74	15 27 +39 73	16 06 +39 72	16 45 +39 71	17 24 +38 70	18 02 +38 70	18 40 +39 69	19 19 +37 68	270
91	09 27 40 78	10 07 40 78	10 47 40 77	11 27 40 76	12 07 40 75	12 47 40 75	13 27 39 74	14 06 40 73	14 46 39 72	15 25 39 71	16 04 39 71	16 43 38 70	17 21 39 69	18 00 38 68	18 38 38 67	269
92	08 44 40 78	09 24 41 77	10 05 40 76	10 45 40 75	11 25 40 75	12 05 40 74	12 45 39 73	13 24 40 72	14 04 39 72	14 43 39 71	15 22 39 70	16 01 39 69	16 40 39 68	17 19 39 68	17 58 38 67	268
93	08 01 41 77	08 42 40 76	09 22 40 75	10 02 41 75	10 43 40 74	11 23 40 73	12 03 40 72	12 43 39 72	13 22 40 71	14 02 39 70	14 41 40 69	15 21 39 69	16 00 39 68	16 39 38 67	17 17 39 66	267
94	07 19 40 76	07 59 41 76	08 40 40 75	09 20 41 74	10 01 40 73	10 41 40 73	11 21 40 72	12 01 40 71	12 41 40 70	13 21 39 70	14 00 40 69	14 40 39 68	15 19 39 67	15 58 39 66	16 37 39 66	266
95	06 36 +41 76	07 17 +41 75	07 58 +40 74	08 38 +41 73	09 19 +40 73	09 59 +40 72	10 39 +41 71	11 20 +40 70	12 00 +40 70	12 40 +39 69	13 19 +40 68	13 59 +40 67	14 39 +39 67	15 18 +39 66	15 57 +39 65	265
96	05 54 41 75	06 35 40 74	07 15 41 74	07 56 41 73	08 37 40 72	09 17 41 71	09 58 40 71	10 38 41 70	11 19 40 69	11 59 40 68	12 39 40 68	13 19 40 67	13 59 39 66	14 38 40 65	15 18 39 64	264
97	05 11 41 74	05 52 41 74	06 33 41 73	07 14 41 72	07 55 41 71	08 36 41 71	09 17 40 70	09 57 41 69	10 38 40 68	11 18 40 68	11 58 41 67	12 39 40 66	13 19 39 65	13 58 40 65	14 38 40 64	263
98	04 29 41 74	05 10 42 73	05 52 41 72	06 33 41 71	07 14 41 71	07 55 41 70	08 36 40 69	09 16 41 69	09 57 41 68	10 38 40 67	11 18 41 66	11 59 40 66	12 39 40 65	13 19 40 64	13 59 40 63	262
99	03 47 41 73	04 28 42 72	05 10 41 72	05 51 41 71	06 32 41 70	07 13 42 69	07 55 41 69	08 36 41 68	09 17 40 67	09 57 41 66	10 38 41 66	11 19 40 65	11 59 41 64	12 40 40 63	13 20 40 63	261
100	03 05 +42 72	03 47 +41 72	04 28 +42 71	05 10 +41 70	05 51 +42 69	06 33 +41 69	07 14 +41 68	07 55 +41 67	08 36 +41 67	09 17 +41 66	09 58 +41 65	10 39 +41 64	11 20 +41 64	12 01 +40 63	12 41 +40 62	260
101	02 23 42 72	03 05 42 71	03 47 42 70	04 29 41 69	05 10 42 69	05 52 41 68	06 33 42 67	07 15 41 67	07 56 41 66	08 37 42 65	09 19 41 65	10 00 41 64	10 41 41 63	11 22 40 62	12 02 41 61	259
102	01 42 42 71	02 24 42 70	03 06 42 70	03 48 41 69	04 29 42 68	05 11 42 67	05 53 42 67	06 35 41 66	07 16 42 65	07 58 41 65	08 39 41 64	09 20 42 63	10 02 41 62	10 43 41 62	11 24 41 61	258
103	01 01 42 70	01 43 42 70	02 25 42 69	03 07 42 68	03 49 42 67	04 31 42 67	05 13 42 66	05 55 41 65	06 36 42 65	07 18 42 64	08 00 41 63	08 41 42 62	09 23 41 62	10 04 42 61	10 46 41 60	257
104	00 19 43 70	01 02 42 69	01 44 42 68	02 26 42 67	03 08 42 67	03 50 43 66	04 33 42 65	05 15 42 65	05 57 42 64	06 39 42 63	07 21 42 63	08 03 42 62	08 45 41 61	09 26 42 60	10 08 41 60	256
105	−0 22 +43 69	00 21 +42 68	01 03 +43 68	01 46 +42 67	02 28 +42 66	03 10 +43 65	03 53 +42 65	04 35 +43 64	05 18 +42 63	06 00 +42 63	06 42 +42 62	07 24 +42 61	08 06 +42 60	08 48 +42 60	09 30 +42 59	255
106	−1 03 43 68	−0 20 43 68	00 23 42 67	01 05 43 66	01 48 43 65	02 31 42 65	03 13 43 64	03 56 42 63	04 38 43 63	05 21 42 62	06 03 43 61	06 46 42 61	07 28 43 60	08 11 42 59	08 53 42 58	254
107	−1 43 43 68	−1 00 43 67	−0 17 42 66	00 25 43 65	01 08 43 65	01 51 43 64	02 34 43 63	03 17 43 63	04 00 42 62	04 42 43 61	05 25 43 61	06 08 42 60	06 50 43 59	07 33 42 58	08 15 43 58	253
108	−2 24 43 67	−1 41 43 66	−0 58 44 65	−0 14 43 65	00 29 43 64	01 12 43 63	01 55 43 63	02 38 43 62	03 21 43 61	04 04 43 61	04 47 43 60	05 30 43 59	06 13 43 59	06 56 43 58	07 39 42 57	252
109	−3 04 43 66	−2 21 44 65	−1 37 43 65	−0 54 43 64	−0 11 44 63	00 33 43 63	01 16 43 62	01 59 44 61	02 43 43 61	03 26 43 60	04 09 43 59	04 52 44 59	05 36 43 58	06 19 43 57	07 02 43 56	251
110	−3 44 +44 65	−3 00 +43 65	−2 17 +44 64	−1 33 +43 63	−0 50 +44 63	−0 06 +43 62	00 37 +44 61	01 21 +44 61	02 05 +43 60	02 48 +44 59	03 32 +43 59	04 15 +44 58	04 59 +43 57	05 42 +43 57	06 25 +44 56	250
111	−4 24 44 65	−3 40 44 64	−2 56 44 63	−2 12 43 63	−1 29 44 62	−0 45 44 61	−0 01 44 61	00 43 44 60	01 27 44 59	02 11 43 59	02 54 44 58	03 38 44 57	04 22 44 57	05 06 43 56	05 49 44 55	249
112	−5 03 44 64	−4 19 44 63	−3 35 44 63	−2 51 44 62	−2 07 44 61	−1 23 44 61	−0 39 44 60	00 05 44 59	00 49 44 58	01 33 44 58	02 17 44 57	03 01 44 57	03 45 44 56	04 29 44 55	05 13 44 55	248
113	−5 43 45 63	−4 58 44 63	−4 14 44 62	−3 30 44 61	−2 46 45 61	−2 01 44 60	−1 17 44 59	−0 33 45 59	00 12 44 58	00 56 45 57	01 41 44 57	02 25 44 56	03 09 44 55	03 53 45 55	04 38 44 54	247
114		−5 37 44 62	−4 53 45 61	−4 08 44 61	−3 24 45 60	−2 39 44 59	−1 55 45 59	−1 10 45 58	−0 25 44 57	00 19 45 57	01 04 45 56	01 49 44 56	02 33 45 55	03 18 44 54	04 02 45 53	246
115		−6 16 +45 61	−5 31 +45 60	−4 46 +44 60	−4 02 +45 59	−3 17 +45 59	−2 32 +45 58	−1 47 +45 57	−1 02 +45 57	−0 17 +45 56	00 28 +45 55	01 13 +45 55	01 58 +45 54	02 43 +44 53	03 27 +45 53	245
116			−6 09 45 60	−5 24 45 59	−4 39 45 58	−3 54 45 58	−3 09 45 57	−2 24 46 57	−1 38 45 56	−0 53 45 55	−0 08 45 55	00 37 45 54	01 22 46 53	02 08 45 53	02 53 45 52	244
117				−6 02 46 58	−5 16 45 58	−4 31 45 57	−3 46 46 56	−3 00 45 56	−2 15 46 55	−1 29 45 55	−0 44 46 54	00 02 45 53	00 47 46 53	01 33 45 52	02 18 46 51	243
118					−5 53 45 57	−5 08 46 56	−4 22 46 56	−3 36 45 55	−2 51 46 54	−2 05 46 54	−1 19 46 53	−0 33 46 53	00 13 46 52	00 59 45 51	01 44 46 50	242
119						−5 44 46 56	−4 58 46 55	−4 12 46 54	−3 26 46 54	−2 40 46 53	−1 54 46 52	−1 08 46 52	−0 22 46 51	00 24 47 51	01 11 46 50	241
120							−5 34 +46 54	−4 48 +47 54	−4 01 +46 53	−3 15 +46 52	−2 29 +47 52	−1 42 +46 51	−0 56 +47 51	−0 09 +46 50	00 37 +47 49	240
121							−6 09 46 54	−5 23 47 53	−4 36 46 52	−3 50 47 52	−3 03 47 51	−2 16 47 50	−1 29 46 50	−0 43 47 49	00 04 47 49	239
122								−5 58 47 52	−5 11 47 52	−4 24 47 51	−3 37 47 50	−2 50 47 49	−2 03 47 49	−1 16 47 48	−0 29 47 48	238
123									−5 45 47 51	−4 58 48 50	−4 10 47 50	−3 23 47 49	−2 36 48 48	−1 48 47 48	−1 01 47 47	237
124										−5 31 47 49	−4 44 48 49	−3 56 48 48	−3 08 47 48	−2 21 48 47	−1 33 48 47	236
125										−6 05 +48 49	−5 17 +48 48	−4 29 +48 48	−3 41 +48 47	−2 53 +48 46	−2 05 +48 46	235
126											−5 49 48 47	−5 01 48 47	−4 13 49 46	−3 24 48 46	−2 36 48 45	234
127												−5 33 49 46	−4 44 49 46	−3 55 48 45	−3 07 49 44	233
128													−5 15 49 45	−4 26 49 44	−3 37 49 44	232
129													−5 46 49 44	−4 57 50 44	−4 07 49 43	231
130														−5 27 +50 43	−4 37 +50 42	230
131														−5 56 50 42	−5 06 50 41	229
132															−5 35 50 41	228
84	−5 54 41 105	276														
83	−5 11 41 106	−5 52 41 106	277													
82	−4 29 41 106	−5 10 42 107	−5 52 41 108	278												
81	−3 47 41 107	−4 28 42 108	−5 10 41 108	−5 51 41 109	279											
80	−3 05 −42 108	−3 47 −41 108	−4 28 −42 109	−5 10 −41 110	−5 51 −42 111	280										
79	−2 23 42 108	−3 05 42 109	−3 47 42 110	−4 29 41 111	−5 10 42 111	−5 52 41 112	281									
78	−1 42 42 109	−2 24 42 110	−3 06 42 110	−3 48 41 111	−4 29 42 112	−5 11 42 113	−5 53 42 113	282								
77	−1 01 42 110	−1 43 42 110	−2 25 42 111	−3 07 42 112	−3 49 42 112	−4 31 42 113	−5 13 42 114	−5 55 41 115	283							
76	−0 19 43 110	−1 02 42 111	−1 44 42 112	−2 26 42 113	−3 08 42 113	−3 50 43 114	−4 33 42 115	−5 15 42 115	−5 57 42 116	284						
75	00 22 −43 111	−0 21 −42 112	−1 03 −43 112	−1 46 −42 113	−2 28 −42 114	−3 10 −43 115	−3 53 −42 115	−4 35 −43 116	−5 18 −42 117	−6 00 −42 117	285					
74	01 03 43 112	00 20 43 112	−0 23 42 113	−1 05 43 114	−1 48 43 115	−2 31 42 115	−3 13 43 116	−3 56 42 117	−4 38 43 117	−5 21 42 118	−6 03 43 119	286				
73	01 43 43 112	01 00 43 113	00 17 42 114	−0 25 43 115	−1 08 43 115	−1 51 43 116	−2 34 43 117	−3 17 43 117	−4 00 42 118	−4 42 43 119	−5 25 43 119	−6 08 42 120	287			
72	02 24 43 113	01 41 43 114	00 58 44 115	00 14 43 115	−0 29 43 116	−1 12 43 117	−1 55 43 117	−2 38 43 118	−3 21 43 119	−4 04 43 119	−4 47 43 120	−5 30 43 121	−6 13 43 121	288		
71	03 04 43 114	02 21 44 115	01 37 43 115	00 54 43 116	00 11 44 117	−0 33 43 117	−1 16 43 118	−1 59 44 119	−2 43 43 119	−3 26 43 120	−4 09 43 121	−4 52 44 121	−5 36 43 122	289		
70	03 44 −44 115	03 00 −43 115	02 17 −44 116	01 33 −43 117	00 50 −44 117	00 06 −43 118	−0 37 −44 119	−1 21 −44 119	−2 05 −43 120	−2 48 −44 121	−3 32 −43 121	−4 15 −44 122	−4 59 −43 123	−5 42 −43 123	290	
	15°	16°	17°	18°	19°	20°	21°	22°	23°	24°	25°	26°	27°	28°	29°	

S. Lat. {LHA greater than 180°....... Zn=180−Z; LHA less than 180°........... Zn=180+Z}

DECLINATION (15°-29°) CONTRARY NAME TO LATITUDE

N. Lat. {LHA greater than 180°....... Zn=Z; LHA less than 180°........... Zn=360−Z}

DECLINATION (15°-29°) CONTRARY NAME TO LATITUDE

LHA	15° Hc	d	Z	16° Hc	d	Z	17° Hc	d	Z	18° Hc	d	Z	19° Hc	d	Z
	° ′	′	°	° ′	′	°	° ′	′	°	° ′	′	°	° ′	′	°
69	04 24	44	115	03 40	44	116	02 56	44	117	02 12	43	117	01 29	44	118
68	05 03	44	116	04 19	44	117	03 35	44	118	02 51	44	118	02 07	44	119
67	05 43	45	117	04 58	44	117	04 14	44	118	03 30	44	119	02 46	45	119
66	06 22	45	117	05 37	44	118	04 53	45	119	04 08	44	119	03 24	45	120
65	07 01	-45	118	06 16	-45	119	05 31	-45	120	04 46	-44	120	04 02	-45	121
64	07 39	45	119	06 54	45	120	06 09	45	120	05 24	45	121	04 39	45	122
63	08 18	46	120	07 32	45	120	06 47	45	121	06 02	46	122	05 16	45	122
62	08 56	46	120	08 10	45	121	07 25	46	122	06 39	46	122	05 53	45	123
61	09 33	45	121	08 48	46	122	08 02	46	122	07 16	46	123	06 30	46	124
60	10 11	-46	122	09 25	-46	123	08 39	-46	123	07 53	-47	124	07 06	-46	124
59	10 48	46	123	10 02	47	123	09 15	46	124	08 29	46	125	07 43	47	125
58	11 25	47	123	10 38	46	124	09 52	47	125	09 05	47	125	08 18	47	126
57	12 01	47	124	11 14	46	125	10 28	47	125	09 41	47	126	08 54	47	127
56	12 37	47	125	11 50	47	126	11 03	47	126	10 16	47	127	09 29	48	127
55	13 13	-47	126	12 26	-48	126	11 38	-47	127	10 51	-48	128	10 03	-47	128
54	13 49	48	126	13 01	48	127	12 13	47	128	11 26	48	128	10 38	48	129
53	14 24	48	127	13 36	48	128	12 48	48	128	12 00	48	129	11 12	49	130
52	14 59	49	128	14 10	48	129	13 22	48	129	12 34	49	130	11 45	48	130
51	15 33	49	129	14 44	48	129	13 56	49	130	13 07	49	131	12 18	48	131
50	16 07	-49	130	15 18	-49	130	14 29	-49	131	13 40	-49	131	12 51	-49	132
49	16 41	50	130	15 51	49	131	15 02	49	132	14 13	49	132	13 24	50	133
48	17 14	50	131	16 24	49	132	15 35	50	133	14 45	49	133	13 56	50	134
47	17 47	50	132	16 57	50	133	16 07	50	133	15 17	50	134	14 27	50	134
46	18 19	50	133	17 29	50	134	16 39	50	134	15 49	51	135	14 58	50	135
45	18 51	-51	134	18 00	-50	134	17 10	-50	135	16 20	-51	136	15 29	-51	136
44	19 22	50	135	18 32	51	135	17 41	51	136	16 50	51	136	15 59	51	137
43	19 53	51	136	19 02	51	136	18 11	51	137	17 20	51	137	16 29	51	138
42	20 24	52	136	19 32	51	137	18 41	51	138	17 50	52	138	16 58	51	139
41	20 54	52	137	20 02	51	138	19 11	52	138	18 19	52	139	17 27	52	139
40	21 23	-52	138	20 31	-52	139	19 39	-52	139	18 47	-52	140	17 55	-52	140
39	21 52	52	139	21 00	52	140	20 08	53	140	19 15	52	141	18 23	52	141
38	22 21	53	140	21 28	52	141	20 36	53	141	19 43	53	142	18 50	53	142
37	22 49	53	141	21 56	53	141	21 03	53	142	20 10	53	142	19 17	53	143
36	23 16	53	142	22 23	53	142	21 30	53	143	20 37	54	143	19 43	53	144
35	23 43	-54	143	22 49	-53	143	21 56	-54	144	21 02	-53	144	20 09	-54	145
34	24 09	54	144	23 15	53	144	22 22	54	145	21 28	54	145	20 34	54	146
33	24 35	54	145	23 41	54	145	22 47	54	146	21 53	55	146	20 58	54	147
32	25 00	54	146	24 06	55	146	23 11	54	147	22 17	55	147	21 22	54	147
31	25 24	54	147	24 30	55	147	23 35	55	148	22 40	54	148	21 46	55	148
30	25 48	-55	148	24 53	-55	148	23 58	-55	148	23 03	-55	149	22 08	-55	149
29	26 11	55	149	25 16	55	149	24 21	55	149	23 26	56	150	22 30	55	150
28	26 34	55	150	25 39	56	150	24 43	56	150	23 47	55	151	22 52	56	151
27	26 56	56	151	26 00	56	151	25 04	55	151	24 09	56	152	23 13	56	152
26	27 17	56	152	26 21	56	152	25 25	56	152	24 29	56	153	23 33	56	153
25	27 38	-57	153	26 41	-56	153	25 45	-56	153	24 49	-57	154	23 52	-56	154
24	27 58	57	154	27 01	57	154	26 04	56	154	25 08	57	155	24 11	57	155
23	28 17	57	155	27 20	57	155	26 23	57	155	25 26	57	156	24 29	57	156
22	28 35	57	156	27 38	57	156	26 41	57	156	25 44	57	157	24 47	57	157
21	28 53	57	157	27 56	58	157	26 58	57	157	26 01	57	158	25 04	58	158
20	29 10	-58	158	28 12	-57	158	27 15	-58	158	26 17	-57	159	25 20	-58	159
19	29 26	58	159	28 28	57	159	27 31	58	159	26 33	58	160	25 35	58	160
18	29 42	58	160	28 44	58	160	27 46	58	161	26 48	58	161	25 50	59	161
17	29 56	58	161	28 58	58	161	28 00	58	162	27 02	59	162	26 03	58	162
16	30 10	58	162	29 12	59	162	28 13	58	163	27 15	58	163	26 17	59	163
15	30 23	-58	163	29 25	-59	163	28 26	-58	164	27 28	-59	164	26 29	-59	164
14	30 36	59	164	29 37	59	165	28 38	59	165	27 39	58	165	26 41	59	165
13	30 47	59	165	29 48	59	166	28 49	59	166	27 50	59	166	26 51	59	166
12	30 58	59	167	29 59	59	167	29 00	59	167	28 01	60	167	27 01	59	167
11	31 08	60	168	30 08	59	168	29 09	59	168	28 10	59	168	27 11	59	168
10	31 17	-60	169	30 17	-59	169	29 18	-59	169	28 19	-60	169	27 19	-59	169
9	31 25	60	170	30 25	59	170	29 26	60	170	28 26	59	170	27 27	60	170
8	31 32	59	171	30 33	60	171	29 33	59	171	28 33	59	171	27 34	60	172
7	31 39	60	172	30 39	60	172	29 39	59	172	28 40	60	172	27 40	60	173
6	31 44	59	173	30 45	60	173	29 45	60	173	28 45	60	174	27 45	59	174
5	31 49	-60	174	30 49	-60	174	29 49	-59	175	28 50	-60	175	27 50	-60	175
4	31 53	60	175	30 53	60	176	29 53	60	176	28 53	60	176	27 53	59	176
3	31 56	60	177	30 56	60	177	29 56	60	177	28 56	60	177	27 56	60	177
2	31 58	60	178	30 58	60	178	29 58	60	178	28 58	60	178	27 58	60	178
1	32 00	60	179	31 00	60	179	30 00	60	179	29 00	60	179	28 00	60	179
0	32 00	-60	180	31 00	-60	180	30 00	-60	180	29 00	-60	180	28 00	-60	180

LHA	20° Hc	d	Z	21° Hc	d	Z	22° Hc	d	Z	23° Hc	d	Z	24° Hc	d	Z
	° ′	′	°	° ′	′	°	° ′	′	°	° ′	′	°	° ′	′	°
69	00 45	44	119	00 01	44	119	-0 43	44	120	-1 27	44	121	-2 11	43	121
68	01 23	44	119	00 39	44	120	-0 05	44	121	-0 49	44	121	-1 33	44	122
67	02 01	44	120	01 17	44	121	00 33	45	121	-0 12	44	122	-0 56	45	123
66	02 39	44	121	01 55	45	121	01 10	45	122	00 25	44	123	-0 19	45	123
65	03 17	-45	121	02 32	-45	122	01 47	-45	123	01 02	-45	123	00 17	-45	124
64	03 54	45	122	03 09	45	123	02 24	46	123	01 38	45	124	00 53	45	125
63	04 31	45	123	03 46	46	124	03 00	45	124	02 15	46	125	01 29	45	125
62	05 08	46	124	04 22	46	124	03 36	45	125	02 51	46	126	02 05	46	126
61	05 44	46	124	04 58	46	125	04 12	46	126	03 26	46	126	02 40	46	127
60	06 20	-46	125	05 34	-46	126	04 48	-47	126	04 01	-46	127	03 15	-46	128
59	06 56	47	126	06 09	46	126	05 23	47	127	04 36	46	128	03 50	47	128
58	07 31	46	127	06 45	47	127	05 58	47	128	05 11	47	128	04 24	47	129
57	08 07	48	127	07 19	47	128	06 32	47	129	05 45	47	129	04 58	48	130
56	08 41	47	128	07 54	48	129	07 06	47	129	06 19	48	130	05 31	47	131
55	09 16	-48	129	08 28	-48	129	07 40	-48	130	06 52	-47	131	06 05	-48	131
54	09 50	48	130	09 02	48	130	08 14	48	131	07 26	49	131	06 37	48	132
53	10 23	48	130	09 35	48	131	08 47	49	132	07 58	48	132	07 10	49	133
52	10 57	49	131	10 08	49	132	09 19	48	132	08 31	49	133	07 42	49	133
51	11 30	49	132	10 41	49	132	09 52	49	133	09 03	49	134	08 14	50	134
50	12 02	-49	133	11 13	-49	133	10 24	-50	134	09 34	-49	134	08 45	-50	135
49	12 34	49	133	11 45	50	134	10 55	50	135	10 05	49	135	09 16	50	136
48	13 06	50	134	12 16	50	135	11 26	50	135	10 36	50	136	09 46	50	137
47	13 37	50	135	12 47	50	136	11 57	50	136	11 07	51	137	10 16	50	137
46	14 08	51	136	13 17	50	136	12 27	51	137	11 36	50	138	10 46	51	138
45	14 38	-50	137	13 48	-51	137	12 57	-51	138	12 06	-51	138	11 15	-51	139
44	15 08	51	138	14 17	51	138	13 26	51	139	12 35	51	139	11 44	52	140
43	15 38	52	138	14 46	51	139	13 55	52	139	13 03	51	140	12 12	52	140
42	16 07	52	139	15 15	52	140	14 23	52	140	13 31	52	141	12 39	51	141
41	16 35	52	140	15 43	52	141	14 51	52	141	13 59	52	142	13 07	53	142
40	17 03	-52	141	16 11	-53	141	15 18	-52	142	14 26	-53	142	13 33	-52	143
39	17 31	53	142	16 38	53	142	15 45	52	143	14 53	53	143	14 00	53	144
38	17 57	52	143	17 05	53	143	16 12	53	144	15 19	54	144	14 25	53	145
37	18 24	53	143	17 31	54	144	16 37	53	144	15 44	53	145	14 51	54	145
36	18 50	54	144	17 56	53	145	17 03	54	145	16 09	54	146	15 15	53	146
35	19 15	-54	145	18 21	-54	146	17 27	-53	146	16 34	-54	147	15 40	-54	147
34	19 40	54	146	18 46	54	147	17 52	55	147	16 57	54	147	16 03	54	148
33	20 04	54	147	19 10	55	147	18 15	54	148	17 21	55	148	16 26	54	149
32	20 28	55	148	19 33	55	148	18 38	54	149	17 44	55	149	16 49	55	150
31	20 51	55	149	19 56	55	149	19 01	55	150	18 06	55	150	17 11	56	151
30	21 13	-55	150	20 18	-55	150	19 23	-56	151	18 27	-55	151	17 32	-56	151
29	21 35	56	151	20 39	55	151	19 44	56	152	18 48	55	152	17 53	56	152
28	21 56	56	152	21 00	55	152	20 05	56	152	19 09	56	153	18 13	56	153
27	22 17	56	153	21 21	56	153	20 25	57	153	19 28	56	154	18 32	56	154
26	22 37	57	154	21 40	56	154	20 44	56	154	19 48	57	155	18 51	56	155
25	22 56	-57	155	21 59	-56	155	21 03	-57	155	20 06	-57	156	19 09	-56	156
24	23 14	56	155	22 18	57	156	21 21	57	156	20 24	57	157	19 27	57	157
23	23 32	57	156	22 35	57	157	21 38	57	157	20 41	57	157	19 44	57	158
22	23 50	58	157	22 52	57	158	21 55	57	158	20 58	58	158	20 00	57	159
21	24 06	57	158	23 09	58	159	22 11	57	159	21 14	58	159	20 16	58	160
20	24 22	-58	159	23 24	-58	160	22 26	-57	160	21 29	-58	160	20 31	-58	161
19	24 37	58	160	23 39	58	161	22 41	58	161	21 43	58	161	20 45	58	162
18	24 51	58	161	23 53	58	162	22 55	58	162	21 57	58	162	20 59	58	162
17	25 05	58	162	24 07	59	163	23 08	58	163	22 10	58	163	21 12	59	163
16	25 18	58	163	24 20	59	164	23 21	58	164	22 23	59	164	21 24	59	164
15	25 30	-58	164	24 32	-59	165	23 33	-59	165	22 34	-59	165	21 35	-58	165
14	25 42	59	165	24 43	59	166	23 44	59	166	22 45	59	166	21 46	59	166
13	25 52	59	166	24 53	59	167	23 54	59	167	22 55	59	167	21 56	59	167
12	26 02	59	167	25 03	59	168	24 04	59	168	23 05	59	168	22 06	59	168
11	26 12	60	169	25 12	59	169	24 13	59	169	23 14	60	169	22 14	59	169
10	26 20	-60	170	25 20	-59	170	24 21	-59	170	23 22	-60	170	22 22	-59	170
9	26 27	59	171	25 28	60	171	24 28	59	171	23 29	60	171	22 29	59	171
8	26 34	59	172	25 35	60	172	24 35	59	172	23 35	59	172	22 36	59	172
7	26 40	59	173	25 41	60	173	24 41	60	173	23 41	60	173	22 41	59	173
6	26 46	60	174	25 46	60	174	24 46	60	174	23 46	60	174	22 46	59	174
5	26 50	-60	175	25 50	-60	175	24 50	-60	175	23 50	-59	175	22 51	-60	175
4	26 54	60	176	25 54	60	176	24 54	60	176	23 54	60	176	22 54	60	176
3	26 56	60	177	25 56	59	177	24 57	60	177	23 57	60	177	22 57	60	177
2	26 58	60	178	25 58	60	178	24 58	59	178	23 59	60	178	22 59	60	178
1	27 00	60	179	26 00	60	179	25 00	60	179	24 00	60	179	23 00	60	179
0	27 00	-60	180	26 00	-60	180	25 00	-60	180	24 00	-60	180	23 00	-60	180

LHA	25° Hc	d	Z	26° Hc	d	Z	27° Hc	d	Z	28° Hc	d	Z	29° Hc	d	Z	LHA
	° ′	′	°	° ′	′	°	° ′	′	°	° ′	′	°	° ′	′	°	
69	-2 54	44	122	-3 38	44	123	-4 22	44	123	-5 06	43	124	-5 49	44	125	291
68	-2 17	44	123	-3 01	44	123	-3 45	44	124	-4 29	44	125	-5 13	44	125	292
67	-1 41	44	123	-2 25	44	124	-3 09	44	125	-3 53	45	125	-4 38	44	126	293
66	-1 04	45	124	-1 49	44	125	-2 33	45	125	-3 18	44	126	-4 02	45	127	294
65	-0 28	-45	125	-1 13	-45	125	-1 58	-45	126	-2 43	-44	127	-3 27	-45	127	295
64	00 08	45	125	-0 37	45	126	-1 22	46	127	-2 08	45	127	-2 53	45	128	296
63	00 44	46	126	-0 02	45	127	-0 47	46	127	-1 33	45	128	-2 18	46	129	297
62	01 19	46	127	00 33	46	127	-0 13	46	128	-0 59	45	129	-1 44	46	129	298
61	01 54	46	128	01 08	46	128	00 22	46	129	-0 24	47	129	-1 11	46	130	299
60	02 29	-47	128	01 42	-46	129	00 56	-47	129	00 09	-46	130	-0 37	-47	131	300
59	03 03	47	129	02 16	47	130	01 29	46	130	00 43	47	131	-0 04	47	131	301
58	03 37	47	130	02 50	47	130	02 03	47	131	01 16	47	132	00 29	47	132	302
57	04 10	47	130	03 23	47	131	02 36	48	132	01 48	47	132	01 01	47	133	303
56	04 44	48	131	03 56	48	132	03 08	47	132	02 21	48	133	01 33	48	133	304
55	05 17	-48	132	04 29	-48	132	03 41	-48	133	02 53	-48	134	02 05	-48	134	305
54	05 49	48	133	05 01	48	133	04 13	49	134	03 24	48	134	02 36	48	135	306
53	06 21	48	133	05 33	49	134	04 44	49	134	03 55	48	135	03 07	49	136	307
52	06 53	49	134	06 04	49	135	05 15	49	135	04 26	49	136	03 37	49	136	308
51	07 24	49	135	06 35	49	135	05 46	49	136	04 57	50	136	04 07	49	137	309
50	07 55	-49	136	07 06	-50	136	06 16	-49	137	05 27	-50	137	04 37	-50	138	310
49	08 26	50	136	07 36	50	137	06 46	50	137	05 56	50	138	05 06	50	139	311
48	08 56	50	137	08 06	50	138	07 16	50	138	06 26	51	139	05 35	50	139	312
47	09 26	51	138	08 35	50	138	07 45	51	139	06 54	50	139	06 04	51	140	313
46	09 55	51	139	09 04	50	139	08 14	51	140	07 23	50	140	06 32	51	141	314
45	10 24	-51	139	09 33	-51	140	08 42	-51	140	07 51	-52	141	06 59	-51	142	315
44	10 52	51	140	10 01	52	141	09 09	51	141	08 18	52	142	07 26	51	142	316
43	11 20	52	141	10 28	51	141	09 37	52	142	08 45	52	143	07 53	52	143	317
42	11 48	52	142	10 56	52	142	10 04	53	143	09 11	52	143	08 19	52	144	318
41	12 14	52	143	11 22	52	143	10 30	53	144	09 37	52	144	08 45	52	145	319
40	12 41	-53	143	11 48	-52	144	10 56	-53	144	10 03	-53	145	09 10	-53	145	320
39	13 07	53	144	12 14	53	145	11 21	53	145	10 28	53	146	09 35	53	146	321
38	13 32	53	145	12 39	53	146	11 46	53	146	10 53	54	146	09 59	53	147	322
37	13 57	53	146	13 04	54	146	12 10	53	147	11 17	54	147	10 23	54	148	323
36	14 22	54	147	13 28	54	147	12 34	54	148	11 40	54	148	10 46	54	148	324
35	14 46	-55	148	13 51	-54	148	12 57	-54	148	12 03	-54	149	11 09	-54	149	325
34	15 09	55	148	14 14	54	149	13 20	54	149	12 26	55	150	11 31	54	150	326
33	15 32	55	149	14 37	55	150	13 42	55	150	12 47	54	151	11 53	55	151	327
32	15 54	55	150	14 59	55	151	14 04	55	151	13 09	55	151	12 14	55	152	328
31	16 15	55	151	15 20	55	151	14 25	55	152	13 30	56	152	12 34	55	153	329
30	16 36	-55	152	15 41	-56	152	14 45	-55	153	13 50	-56	153	12 54	-55	153	330
29	16 57	56	153	16 01	56	153	15 05	55	153	14 10	56	154	13 14	56	154	331
28	17 17	56	154	16 21	56	154	15 25	56	154	14 29	56	155	13 33	57	155	332
27	17 36	56	155	16 40	57	155	15 43	56	155	14 47	56	156	13 51	57	156	333
26	17 55	57	155	16 58	56	156	16 02	57	156	15 05	57	156	14 08	56	157	334
25	18 13	-57	156	17 16	-57	157	16 19	-57	157	15 22	-57	157	14 25	-56	158	335
24	18 30	57	157	17 33	57	158	16 36	57	158	15 39	57	158	14 42	57	158	336
23	18 47	57	158	17 50	58	158	16 52	57	159	15 55	57	159	14 58	58	159	337
22	19 03	58	159	18 05	57	159	17 08	58	160	16 10	57	160	15 13	58	160	338
21	19 18	57	160	18 21	58	160	17 23	58	161	16 25	57	161	15 28	58	161	339
20	19 33	-58	161	18 35	-58	161	17 37	-58	161	16 39	-58	162	15 41	-57	162	340
19	19 47	58	162	18 49	58	162	17 51	58	162	16 53	58	163	15 55	58	163	341
18	20 01	59	163	19 02	58	163	18 04	58	163	17 06	59	163	16 07	58	164	342
17	20 13	58	164	19 15	59	164	18 16	58	164	17 18	59	164	16 19	58	165	343
16	20 25	58	165	19 27	59	165	18 28	59	165	17 29	58	165	16 31	59	165	344
15	20 37	-59	166	19 38	-59	166	18 39	-59	166	17 40	-58	166	16 42	-59	166	345
14	20 47	59	166	19 48	59	167	18 49	58	167	17 51	59	167	16 52	59	167	346
13	20 57	59	167	19 58	59	168	18 59	59	168	18 00	59	168	17 01	59	168	347
12	21 07	60	168	20 07	59	169	19 08	59	169	18 09	59	169	17 10	60	169	348
11	21 15	59	169	20 16	60	170	19 16	59	170	18 17	59	170	17 18	60	170	349
10	21 23	-60	170	20 23	-59	170	19 24	-60	171	18 24	-59	171	17 25	-59	171	350
9	21 30	60	171	20 30	59	171	19 31	60	172	18 31	59	172	17 32	60	172	351
8	21 36	59	172	20 37	60	172	19 37	60	172	18 37	59	173	17 38	60	173	352
7	21 42	60	173	20 42	60	173	19 42	59	173	18 43	60	174	17 43	60	174	353
6	21 47	60	174	20 47	60	174	19 47	60	174	18 47	60	174	17 47	59	175	354
5	21 51	-60	175	20 51	-60	175	19 51	-60	175	18 51	-60	175	17 51	-60	175	355
4	21 54	60	176	20 54	60	176	19 54	60	176	18 54	60	176	17 54	59	176	356
3	21 57	60	177	20 57	60	177	19 57	60	177	18 57	60	177	17 57	60	177	357
2	21 59	60	178	20 59	60	178	19 59	60	178	18 59	60	178	17 59	60	178	358
1	22 00	60	179	21 00	60	179	20 00	60	179	19 00	60	179	18 00	60	179	359
0	22 00	-60	180	21 00	-60	180	20 00	-60	180	19 00	-60	180	18 00	-60	180	360

S. Lat. {LHA greater than 180°....... Zn=180−Z; LHA less than 180°........... Zn=180+Z}

DECLINATION (15°-29°) CONTRARY NAME TO LATITUDE

LAT 43°

LHA	0°			1°			2°			3°			4°		
	Hc	d	Z	Hc	d	Z	Hc	d	Z	Hc	d	Z	Hc	d	Z
	° ′	′	°	° ′	′	°	° ′	′	°	° ′	′	°	° ′	′	°
0	46 00	+60	180	47 00	+60	180	48 00	+60	180	49 00	+60	180	50 00	+60	180
1	46 00	59	179	46 59	60	179	47 59	60	179	48 59	60	179	49 59	60	178
2	45 58	60	177	46 58	60	177	47 58	60	177	48 58	60	177	49 58	60	177
3	45 55	60	176	46 55	60	176	47 55	60	176	48 55	60	175	49 55	60	175
4	45 51	60	174	46 51	60	174	47 51	60	174	48 51	60	174	49 51	60	174
5	45 47	+59	173	46 46	+60	173	47 46	+60	173	48 46	+59	172	49 45	+60	172
6	45 41	59	171	46 40	60	171	47 40	59	171	48 39	60	171	49 39	60	171
7	45 34	59	170	46 33	60	170	47 33	59	170	48 32	60	169	49 32	59	169
8	45 26	59	169	46 25	59	168	47 24	60	168	48 24	59	168	49 23	59	168
9	45 17	59	167	46 16	59	167	47 15	59	167	48 14	59	166	49 13	59	166
10	45 06	+59	166	46 05	+59	166	47 04	+59	165	48 03	+59	165	49 02	+59	165
11	44 55	59	164	45 54	59	164	46 53	59	164	47 52	58	164	48 50	59	163
12	44 43	59	163	45 42	58	163	46 40	59	162	47 39	58	162	48 37	59	162
13	44 30	58	162	45 28	59	161	46 27	58	161	47 25	58	161	48 23	58	160
14	44 16	58	160	45 14	58	160	46 12	58	160	47 10	58	159	48 08	58	159
15	44 01	+58	159	44 59	+58	159	45 57	+57	158	46 54	+58	158	47 52	+58	157
16	43 45	58	158	44 43	57	157	45 40	58	157	46 38	57	156	47 35	57	156
17	43 28	57	156	44 25	58	156	45 23	57	155	46 20	57	155	47 17	57	155
18	43 10	57	155	44 07	57	155	45 04	57	154	46 01	57	154	46 58	57	153
19	42 51	57	154	43 48	57	153	44 45	56	153	45 41	57	152	46 38	56	152
20	42 32	+56	152	43 28	+57	152	44 25	+56	151	45 21	+56	151	46 17	+56	150
21	42 11	57	151	43 08	56	151	44 04	56	150	45 00	55	150	45 55	56	149
22	41 50	56	150	42 46	56	149	43 42	55	149	44 37	56	148	45 33	55	148
23	41 28	55	149	42 23	56	148	43 19	55	148	44 14	55	147	45 09	55	146
24	41 05	55	147	42 00	55	147	42 55	55	146	43 50	55	146	44 45	55	145
25	40 41	+55	146	41 36	+55	146	42 31	+55	145	43 26	+54	145	44 20	+54	144
26	40 17	54	145	41 11	55	144	42 06	54	144	43 00	54	143	43 54	54	143
27	39 52	54	144	40 46	54	143	41 40	54	143	42 34	54	142	43 28	53	141
28	39 26	54	143	40 20	53	142	41 13	54	141	42 07	53	141	43 00	53	140
29	38 59	54	141	39 53	53	141	40 46	53	140	41 39	53	140	42 32	53	139
30	38 32	+53	140	39 25	+53	140	40 18	+53	139	41 11	+53	138	42 04	+52	138
31	38 04	53	139	38 57	53	139	39 50	52	138	40 42	52	137	41 34	52	137
32	37 36	52	138	38 28	52	137	39 20	52	137	40 12	52	136	41 04	52	136
33	37 06	53	137	37 59	52	136	38 51	51	136	39 42	52	135	40 34	51	134
34	36 37	51	136	37 28	52	135	38 20	51	135	39 11	52	134	40 03	51	133
35	36 06	+52	135	36 58	+51	134	37 49	+51	134	38 40	+51	133	39 31	+50	132
36	35 35	52	134	36 27	50	133	37 17	51	132	38 08	51	132	38 59	50	131
37	35 04	51	133	35 55	50	132	36 45	51	131	37 36	50	131	38 26	50	130
38	34 32	50	132	35 22	51	131	36 13	50	130	37 03	49	130	37 52	50	129
39	33 59	51	131	34 50	49	130	35 39	50	129	36 29	50	129	37 19	49	128
40	33 26	+50	130	34 16	+50	129	35 06	+49	128	35 55	+49	128	36 44	+49	127
41	32 53	49	129	33 42	50	128	34 32	49	127	35 21	49	127	36 10	48	126
42	32 19	49	128	33 08	49	127	33 57	49	126	34 46	48	126	35 34	49	125
43	31 45	48	127	32 33	49	126	33 22	49	125	34 11	48	125	34 59	48	124
44	31 10	48	126	31 58	49	125	32 47	48	124	33 35	48	124	34 23	47	123
45	30 34	+49	125	31 23	+48	124	32 11	+48	123	32 59	+47	123	33 46	+48	122
46	29 59	48	124	30 47	48	123	31 35	47	123	32 22	47	122	33 09	48	121
47	29 23	48	123	30 11	47	122	30 58	47	122	31 45	47	121	32 32	47	120
48	28 46	48	122	29 34	47	121	30 21	47	121	31 08	47	120	31 55	46	119
49	28 10	47	121	28 57	47	120	29 44	46	120	30 30	47	119	31 17	46	118
50	27 33	+46	120	28 19	+47	120	29 06	+47	119	29 53	+46	118	30 39	+46	117
51	26 55	47	119	27 42	46	119	28 28	46	118	29 14	46	117	30 00	46	117
52	26 17	47	119	27 04	46	118	27 50	46	117	28 36	45	116	29 21	46	116
53	25 39	46	118	26 25	46	117	27 11	46	116	27 57	45	116	28 42	46	115
54	25 01	46	117	25 47	45	116	26 32	46	115	27 18	45	115	28 03	45	114
55	24 22	+46	116	25 08	+45	115	25 53	+45	115	26 38	+45	114	27 23	+45	113
56	23 43	46	115	24 29	45	114	25 14	45	114	25 59	45	113	26 44	44	112
57	23 04	45	114	23 49	45	114	24 34	45	113	25 19	45	112	26 04	44	111
58	22 25	44	114	23 09	45	113	23 54	45	112	24 39	44	111	25 23	44	111
59	21 45	45	113	22 30	44	112	23 14	45	111	23 59	44	111	24 43	44	110
60	21 05	+44	112	21 49	+45	111	22 34	+44	110	23 18	+44	110	24 02	+44	109
61	20 25	44	111	21 09	44	110	21 53	44	110	22 37	44	109	23 21	44	108
62	19 44	44	110	20 28	45	110	21 13	43	109	21 56	44	108	22 40	43	107
63	19 04	44	110	19 48	44	109	20 32	43	108	21 15	44	107	21 59	43	107
64	18 23	44	109	19 07	43	108	19 50	44	107	20 34	43	107	21 17	43	106
65	17 42	+44	108	18 26	+43	107	19 09	+43	107	19 52	+44	106	20 36	+43	105
66	17 01	43	107	17 44	44	107	18 28	43	106	19 11	43	105	19 54	43	104
67	16 19	44	106	17 03	43	106	17 46	43	105	18 29	43	104	19 12	43	104
68	15 38	43	106	16 21	43	105	17 04	43	104	17 47	43	104	18 30	42	103
69	14 56	43	105	15 39	43	104	16 22	43	104	17 05	43	103	17 48	42	102

LHA	5°			6°			7°			8°			9°		
	Hc	d	Z	Hc	d	Z	Hc	d	Z	Hc	d	Z	Hc	d	Z
	° ′	′	°	° ′	′	°	° ′	′	°	° ′	′	°	° ′	′	°
0	51 00	+60	180	52 00	+60	180	53 00	+60	180	54 00	+60	180	55 00	+60	180
1	50 59	60	178	51 59	60	178	52 59	60	178	53 59	60	178	54 59	60	178
2	50 58	60	177	51 58	60	177	52 58	60	177	53 58	59	177	54 57	60	177
3	50 55	60	175	51 55	59	175	52 54	60	175	53 54	60	175	54 54	60	175
4	50 51	59	174	51 50	60	174	52 50	60	173	53 50	60	173	54 50	59	173
5	50 45	+60	172	51 45	+60	172	52 45	+59	172	53 44	+60	172	54 44	+60	171
6	50 39	59	171	51 38	60	170	52 38	59	170	53 37	60	170	54 37	59	170
7	50 31	59	169	51 30	60	169	52 30	59	169	53 29	60	168	54 29	59	168
8	50 22	59	167	51 21	60	167	52 21	59	167	53 20	59	167	54 19	59	166
9	50 12	59	166	51 11	59	166	52 10	59	165	53 09	59	165	54 08	59	165
10	50 01	+59	164	51 00	+59	164	51 59	+59	164	52 58	+58	163	53 56	+59	163
11	49 49	59	163	50 48	58	163	51 46	59	162	52 45	58	162	53 43	58	161
12	49 36	58	161	50 34	58	161	51 32	59	161	52 31	58	160	53 29	58	160
13	49 21	59	160	50 20	58	160	51 18	57	159	52 15	58	159	53 13	58	158
14	49 06	58	158	50 04	58	158	51 02	57	158	51 59	58	157	52 57	57	157
15	48 50	+57	157	49 47	+58	157	50 45	+57	156	51 42	+57	156	52 39	+57	155
16	48 32	57	156	49 29	58	155	50 27	57	155	51 24	56	154	52 20	57	154
17	48 14	57	154	49 11	57	154	50 08	56	153	51 04	57	153	52 01	56	152
18	47 55	56	153	48 51	56	152	49 47	57	152	50 44	56	151	51 40	56	151
19	47 34	56	151	48 30	57	151	49 27	55	150	50 22	56	150	51 18	56	149
20	47 13	+56	150	48 09	+56	149	49 05	+55	149	50 00	+55	148	50 55	+56	148
21	46 51	55	149	47 46	56	148	48 42	55	147	49 37	55	147	50 32	55	146
22	46 28	55	147	47 23	55	147	48 18	55	146	49 13	54	145	50 07	55	145
23	46 04	55	146	46 59	55	145	47 54	54	145	48 48	54	144	49 42	54	143
24	45 40	54	145	46 34	54	144	47 28	54	143	48 22	54	143	49 16	53	142
25	45 14	+54	143	46 08	+54	143	47 02	+54	142	47 56	+53	141	48 49	+53	141
26	44 48	54	142	45 42	53	141	46 35	53	141	47 28	53	140	48 21	53	139
27	44 21	53	141	45 14	53	140	46 07	53	140	47 00	53	139	47 53	52	138
28	43 53	53	140	44 46	53	139	45 39	52	138	46 31	52	138	47 23	52	137
29	43 25	53	138	44 18	52	138	45 10	52	137	46 02	52	136	46 54	51	136
30	42 56	+52	137	43 48	+52	137	44 40	+52	136	45 32	+51	135	46 23	+51	134
31	42 26	52	136	43 18	52	135	44 10	51	135	45 01	51	134	45 52	50	133
32	41 56	51	135	42 47	52	134	43 39	50	133	44 29	51	133	45 20	50	132
33	41 25	51	134	42 16	51	133	43 07	50	132	43 57	51	132	44 48	49	131
34	40 54	50	133	41 44	51	132	42 35	50	131	43 25	50	130	44 15	49	130
35	40 21	+51	131	41 12	+50	131	42 02	+50	130	42 52	+49	129	43 41	+49	128
36	39 49	50	130	40 39	49	130	41 28	50	129	42 18	49	128	43 07	49	127
37	39 16	49	129	40 05	50	129	40 55	49	128	41 44	48	127	42 32	49	126
38	38 42	49	128	39 31	49	128	40 20	49	127	41 09	48	126	41 57	48	125
39	38 08	49	127	38 57	48	126	39 45	49	126	40 34	48	125	41 22	47	124
40	37 33	+49	126	38 22	+48	125	39 10	+48	125	39 58	+48	124	40 46	+47	123
41	36 58	48	125	37 46	48	124	38 34	48	124	39 22	47	123	40 09	47	122
42	36 23	48	124	37 11	47	123	37 58	48	123	38 46	47	122	39 33	46	121
43	35 47	47	123	36 34	48	122	37 22	47	122	38 09	46	121	38 55	47	120
44	35 10	48	122	35 58	47	121	36 45	46	121	37 31	47	120	38 18	46	119
45	34 34	+47	121	35 21	+46	120	36 07	+47	120	36 54	+46	119	37 40	+46	118
46	33 57	46	120	34 43	47	120	35 30	46	119	36 16	46	118	37 02	45	117
47	33 19	47	119	34 06	46	119	34 52	46	118	35 38	45	117	36 23	45	116
48	32 41	46	118	33 27	46	118	34 13	46	117	34 59	45	116	35 44	45	115
49	32 03	46	118	32 49	46	117	33 35	45	116	34 20	45	115	35 05	45	114
50	31 25	+45	117	32 10	+46	116	32 56	+45	115	33 41	+45	114	34 26	+44	114
51	30 46	45	116	31 31	46	115	32 17	44	114	33 01	45	113	33 46	44	113
52	30 07	45	115	30 52	45	114	31 37	45	113	32 22	44	113	33 06	44	112
53	29 28	45	114	30 13	44	113	30 57	45	112	31 42	44	112	32 26	44	111
54	28 48	45	113	29 33	44	112	30 17	44	112	31 01	44	111	31 45	44	110
55	28 08	+45	112	28 53	+44	112	29 37	+44	111	30 21	+44	110	31 05	+43	109
56	27 28	44	111	28 12	45	111	28 57	43	110	29 40	44	109	30 24	43	108
57	26 48	44	111	27 32	44	110	28 16	43	109	28 59	44	108	29 43	43	108
58	26 07	44	110	26 51	44	109	27 35	43	108	28 18	43	108	29 01	43	107
59	25 27	43	109	26 10	44	108	26 54	43	108	27 37	43	107	28 20	43	106
60	24 46	+43	108	25 29	+44	107	26 13	+43	107	26 56	+42	106	27 38	+43	105
61	24 05	43	107	24 48	43	107	25 31	43	106	26 14	43	105	26 57	42	104
62	23 23	44	107	24 07	43	106	24 50	42	105	25 32	43	104	26 15	42	104
63	22 42	43	106	23 25	43	105	24 08	42	104	24 50	43	104	25 33	42	103
64	22 00	43	105	22 43	43	104	23 26	42	104	24 08	43	103	24 51	42	102
65	21 19	+42	104	22 01	+43	104	22 44	+42	103	23 26	+42	102	24 08	+42	101
66	20 37	42	104	21 19	43	103	22 02	42	102	22 44	42	101	23 26	42	101
67	19 55	42	103	20 37	42	102	21 19	43	101	22 02	41	101	22 43	42	100
68	19 12	43	102	19 55	42	101	20 37	42	101	21 19	42	100	22 01	41	99
69	18 30	42	101	19 12	43	101	19 55	41	100	20 36	42	99	21 18	42	98

LHA	10°			11°			12°			13°			14°			LHA
	Hc	d	Z	Hc	d	Z	Hc	d	Z	Hc	d	Z	Hc	d	Z	
	° ′	′	°	° ′	′	°	° ′	′	°	° ′	′	°	° ′	′	°	
0	56 00	+60	180	57 00	+60	180	58 00	+60	180	59 00	+60	180	60 00	+60	180	360
1	55 59	60	178	56 59	60	178	57 59	60	178	58 59	60	178	59 59	60	178	359
2	55 57	60	177	56 57	60	176	57 57	60	176	58 57	60	176	59 57	60	176	358
3	55 54	60	175	56 54	60	175	57 54	60	175	58 54	59	174	59 53	60	174	357
4	55 49	60	173	56 49	60	173	57 49	60	173	58 49	59	173	59 48	60	172	356
5	55 44	+59	171	56 43	+60	171	57 43	+59	171	58 42	+60	171	59 42	+59	170	355
6	55 36	60	170	56 36	59	169	57 35	60	169	58 35	59	169	59 34	59	169	354
7	55 28	59	168	56 27	59	168	57 26	59	167	58 25	60	167	59 25	59	167	353
8	55 18	59	166	56 17	59	166	57 16	59	165	58 15	59	165	59 14	59	165	352
9	55 07	59	164	56 06	59	164	57 05	58	164	58 03	59	163	59 02	58	163	351
10	54 55	+58	163	55 53	+59	162	56 52	+58	162	57 50	+58	162	58 48	+59	161	350
11	54 41	59	161	55 40	58	161	56 38	58	160	57 36	58	160	58 34	58	159	349
12	54 27	58	159	55 25	58	159	56 23	57	159	57 20	58	158	58 18	57	157	348
13	54 11	58	158	55 09	57	157	56 06	57	157	57 03	58	156	58 01	57	156	347
14	53 54	57	156	54 51	57	156	55 48	57	155	56 45	57	155	57 42	57	154	346
15	53 36	+57	155	54 33	+57	154	55 30	+56	154	56 26	+57	153	57 23	+56	152	345
16	53 17	57	153	54 14	56	152	55 10	56	152	56 06	56	151	57 02	56	151	344
17	52 57	56	152	53 53	56	151	54 49	56	150	55 45	55	150	56 40	56	149	343
18	52 36	56	150	53 32	55	149	54 27	55	149	55 22	55	148	56 17	55	147	342
19	52 14	55	148	53 09	55	148	54 04	55	147	54 59	55	146	55 54	54	146	341
20	51 51	+55	147	52 46	+54	146	53 40	+55	146	54 35	+54	145	55 29	+54	144	340
21	51 27	54	146	52 21	54	145	53 15	54	144	54 09	54	143	55 03	54	143	339
22	51 02	54	144	51 56	54	143	52 50	53	143	53 43	53	142	54 36	53	141	338
23	50 36	54	143	51 30	53	142	52 23	53	141	53 16	53	141	54 09	52	140	337
24	50 09	54	141	51 03	53	141	51 56	52	140	52 48	53	139	53 41	52	138	336
25	49 42	+53	140	50 35	+52	139	51 27	+53	138	52 20	+51	138	53 11	+52	137	335
26	49 14	52	139	50 06	52	138	50 58	52	137	51 50	52	136	52 42	51	135	334
27	48 45	52	137	49 37	52	137	50 29	51	136	51 20	51	135	52 11	50	134	333
28	48 15	52	136	49 07	51	135	49 58	51	134	50 49	51	134	51 40	50	133	332
29	47 45	51	135	48 36	51	134	49 27	50	133	50 17	51	132	51 08	49	132	331
30	47 14	+51	134	48 05	+50	133	48 55	+50	132	49 45	+50	131	50 35	+49	130	330
31	46 42	51	132	47 33	50	132	48 23	49	131	49 12	50	130	50 02	48	129	329
32	46 10	50	131	47 00	50	130	47 50	49	130	48 39	49	129	49 28	48	128	328
33	45 37	50	130	46 27	49	129	47 16	49	128	48 05	48	127	48 53	48	127	327
34	45 04	49	129	45 53	49	128	46 42	48	127	47 30	48	126	48 18	48	125	326
35	44 30	+49	128	45 19	+48	127	46 07	+48	126	46 55	+48	125	47 43	+47	124	325
36	43 56	48	127	44 44	48	126	45 32	48	125	46 20	47	124	47 07	47	123	324
37	43 21	48	125	44 09	47	125	44 56	48	124	45 44	47	123	46 31	46	122	323
38	42 45	48	124	43 33	47	124	44 20	47	123	45 07	47	122	45 54	46	121	322
39	42 09	48	123	42 57	47	122	43 44	46	122	44 30	46	121	45 16	46	120	321
40	41 33	+47	122	42 20	+47	121	43 07	+46	121	43 53	+46	120	44 39	+45	119	320
41	40 56	47	121	41 43	46	120	42 29	46	120	43 15	46	119	44 01	45	118	319
42	40 19	47	120	41 06	46	119	41 52	45	119	42 37	45	118	43 22	45	117	318
43	39 42	46	119	40 28	46	118	41 14	45	118	41 59	45	117	42 44	44	116	317
44	39 04	46	118	39 50	45	117	40 35	45	117	41 20	45	116	42 05	44	115	316
45	38 26	+45	117	39 11	+45	116	39 56	+45	116	40 41	+44	115	41 25	+44	114	315
46	37 47	45	116	38 32	45	116	39 17	45	115	40 02	44	114	40 46	43	113	314
47	37 08	45	115	37 53	45	115	38 38	44	114	39 22	44	113	40 06	43	112	313
48	36 29	45	115	37 14	44	114	37 58	44	113	38 42	44	112	39 26	43	111	312
49	35 50	44	114	36 34	44	113	37 18	44	112	38 02	43	111	38 45	43	110	311
50	35 10	+44	113	35 54	+44	112	36 38	+44	111	37 22	+43	110	38 05	+42	109	310
51	34 30	44	112	35 14	44	111	35 58	43	110	36 41	43	109	37 24	42	108	309
52	33 50	44	111	34 34	43	110	35 17	43	109	36 00	43	108	36 43	42	108	308
53	33 10	43	110	33 53	43	109	34 36	43	108	35 19	42	108	36 01	42	107	307
54	32 29	43	109	33 12	43	108	33 55	43	108	34 38	42	107	35 20	42	106	306
55	31 48	+43	108	32 31	+43	108	33 14	+42	107	33 56	+42	106	34 38	+42	105	305
56	31 07	43	108	31 50	42	107	32 32	43	106	33 15	42	105	33 57	41	104	304
57	30 26	42	107	31 08	43	106	31 51	42	105	32 33	42	104	33 15	41	103	303
58	29 44	43	106	30 27	42	105	31 09	42	104	31 51	42	103	32 33	41	103	302
59	29 03	42	105	29 45	42	104	30 27	42	103	31 09	41	103	31 50	41	102	301
60	28 21	+42	104	29 03	+42	104	29 45	+42	103	30 27	+41	102	31 08	+41	101	300
61	27 39	42	104	28 21	42	103	29 03	41	102	29 44	42	101	30 26	41	100	299
62	26 57	42	103	27 39	42	102	28 21	41	101	29 02	41	100	29 43	41	99	298
63	26 15	42	102	26 57	41	101	27 38	42	100	28 20	41	100	29 01	40	99	297
64	25 33	41	101	26 14	42	100	26 56	41	100	27 37	41	99	28 18	40	98	296
65	24 50	+42	100	25 32	+41	100	26 13	+41	99	26 54	+41	98	27 35	+41	97	295
66	24 08	41	100	24 49	41	99	25 30	41	98	26 11	41	97	26 52	41	96	294
67	23 25	42	99	24 07	41	98	24 48	41	97	25 29	40	97	26 09	41	96	293
68	22 42	42	98	23 24	41	97	24 05	41	97	24 46	40	96	25 26	41	95	292
69	22 00	41	98	22 41	41	97	23 22	41	96	24 03	40	95	24 43	41	94	291

0° 1° 2° 3° 4° 5° 6° 7° 8° 9° 10° 11° 12° 13° 14°

S. Lat. {LHA greater than 180°....... Zn=180−Z
{LHA less than 180°........... Zn=180+Z

DECLINATION (0°-14°) **SAME** NAME AS LATITUDE

LAT 44°

N. Lat. {LHA greater than 180°....... Zn=Z
{LHA less than 180°.......... Zn=360−Z

DECLINATION (0°-14°) SAME NAME AS LATITUDE

LHA	0° Hc d Z	1° Hc d Z	2° Hc d Z	3° Hc d Z	4° Hc d Z	5° Hc d Z	6° Hc d Z	7° Hc d Z
	° ′ ′ °	° ′ ′ °	° ′ ′ °	° ′ ′ °	° ′ ′ °	° ′ ′ °	° ′ ′ °	° ′ ′ °
70	14 15 +43 104	14 58 +42 104	15 40 +43 103	16 23 +42 102	17 05 +43 101	17 48 +42 101	18 30 +42 100	19 12 +42 99
71	13 33 43 104	14 16 42 103	14 58 43 102	15 41 42 101	16 23 42 101	17 05 42 100	17 47 42 99	18 29 42 98
72	12 51 42 103	13 33 43 102	14 16 42 101	14 58 43 101	15 41 42 100	16 23 42 99	17 05 42 98	17 47 41 98
73	12 08 43 102	12 51 43 101	13 34 42 101	14 16 42 100	14 58 42 99	15 40 42 98	16 22 42 98	17 04 41 97
74	11 26 43 101	12 09 42 101	12 51 42 100	13 33 42 99	14 15 42 98	14 57 42 98	15 39 42 97	16 21 41 96
75	10 44 +42 101	11 26 +42 100	12 08 +43 99	12 51 +42 98	13 33 +42 98	14 15 +41 97	14 56 +42 96	15 38 +41 95
76	10 01 43 100	10 44 42 99	11 26 42 98	12 08 42 98	12 50 42 97	13 32 41 96	14 13 42 95	14 55 41 95
77	09 19 42 99	10 01 42 98	10 43 42 98	11 25 42 97	12 07 42 96	12 49 41 96	13 30 42 95	14 12 41 94
78	08 36 42 98	09 18 42 98	10 00 42 97	10 42 42 96	11 24 42 96	12 06 41 95	12 47 42 94	13 29 41 93
79	07 53 42 98	08 35 42 97	09 17 42 96	09 59 42 96	10 41 42 95	11 23 41 94	12 04 42 93	12 46 41 93
80	07 11 +42 97	07 53 +41 96	08 34 +42 96	09 16 +42 95	09 58 +42 94	10 40 +41 93	11 21 +42 93	12 03 +41 92
81	06 28 42 96	07 10 41 96	07 51 42 95	08 33 42 94	09 15 42 93	09 57 41 93	10 38 41 92	11 19 42 91
82	05 45 42 96	06 27 41 95	07 08 42 94	07 50 42 93	08 32 41 93	09 13 42 92	09 55 41 91	10 36 42 91
83	05 02 42 95	05 44 41 94	06 25 42 93	07 07 42 93	07 49 41 92	08 30 42 91	09 12 41 91	09 53 41 90
84	04 19 42 94	05 01 41 94	05 42 42 93	06 24 42 92	07 06 41 91	07 47 42 91	08 29 41 90	09 10 41 89
85	03 36 +41 93	04 17 +42 93	04 59 +42 92	05 41 +41 91	06 22 +42 91	07 04 +41 90	07 45 +42 89	08 27 +41 88
86	02 53 41 93	03 34 42 92	04 16 42 91	04 58 41 91	05 39 42 90	06 21 41 89	07 02 42 88	07 44 41 88
87	02 09 42 92	02 51 42 91	03 33 41 91	04 14 42 90	04 56 42 89	05 38 41 89	06 19 42 88	07 01 41 87
88	01 26 42 91	02 08 42 91	02 50 41 90	03 31 42 89	04 13 41 89	04 54 42 88	05 36 41 87	06 17 42 86
89	00 43 42 91	01 25 42 90	02 07 41 89	02 48 42 89	03 30 41 88	04 11 42 87	04 53 41 86	05 34 42 86
90	00 00 +42 90	00 42 +41 89	01 23 +42 89	02 05 +42 88	02 47 +41 87	03 28 +42 86	04 10 +41 86	04 51 +42 85
91	−0 43 42 89	−0 01 41 89	00 40 42 88	01 22 42 87	02 04 41 86	02 45 42 86	03 27 41 85	04 08 42 84
92	−1 26 41 89	−0 45 42 88	−0 03 42 87	00 39 41 86	01 20 42 86	02 02 42 85	02 44 41 84	03 25 42 84
93	−2 09 41 88	−1 28 42 87	−0 46 42 86	−0 04 41 86	00 37 42 85	01 19 42 84	02 01 42 84	02 43 41 83
94	−2 53 42 87	−2 11 42 86	−1 29 42 86	−0 47 42 85	−0 05 41 84	00 36 42 84	01 18 42 83	02 00 42 82
95	−3 36 +42 87	−2 54 +42 86	−2 12 +42 85	−1 30 +42 84	−0 48 +41 84	−0 07 +42 83	00 35 +42 82	01 17 +42 82
96	−4 19 42 86	−3 37 42 85	−2 55 42 84	−2 13 42 84	−1 31 42 83	−0 49 42 82	−0 07 41 82	00 34 42 81
97	−5 02 42 85	−4 20 42 84	−3 38 42 84	−2 56 42 83	−2 14 42 82	−1 32 42 82	−0 50 42 81	−0 08 42 80
98	−5 45 42 84	−5 03 42 84	−4 21 42 83	−3 39 42 82	−2 57 42 82	−2 15 42 81	−1 33 42 80	−0 51 43 79
	99	−5 46 42 83	−5 04 42 82	−4 22 43 82	−3 39 42 81	−2 57 42 80	−2 15 42 79	−1 33 42 79
		100	−5 46 +42 82	−5 04 +42 81	−4 22 +42 80	−3 40 +42 79	−2 58 +43 79	−2 15 +42 78
			101	−5 47 42 80	−5 05 43 79	−4 22 42 79	−3 40 43 78	−2 57 42 77
				102	−5 47 42 79	−5 05 43 78	−4 22 43 77	−3 39 42 77
					103	−5 47 43 77	−5 04 43 77	−4 21 42 76
						104	−5 46 43 76	−5 03 43 75
							105	−5 45 +43 74
								106

8° Hc d Z	9° Hc d Z	10° Hc d Z	11° Hc d Z	12° Hc d Z	13° Hc d Z	14° Hc d Z	LHA
° ′ ′ °	° ′ ′ °	° ′ ′ °	° ′ ′ °	° ′ ′ °	° ′ ′ °	° ′ ′ °	
19 54 +41 98	20 35 +42 98	21 17 +41 97	21 58 +41 96	22 39 +41 95	23 20 +40 94	24 00 +40 94	290
19 11 42 98	19 53 41 97	20 34 41 96	21 15 41 95	21 56 41 94	22 37 40 94	23 17 40 93	289
18 28 42 97	19 10 41 96	19 51 41 95	20 32 41 95	21 13 41 94	21 54 40 93	22 34 40 92	288
17 45 42 96	18 27 41 95	19 08 41 95	19 49 41 94	20 30 40 93	21 10 41 92	21 51 40 91	287
17 02 42 95	17 44 41 95	18 25 41 94	19 06 41 93	19 47 40 92	20 27 41 92	21 08 40 91	286
16 19 +42 95	17 01 +41 94	17 42 +41 93	18 23 +41 92	19 04 +40 92	19 44 +41 91	20 25 +40 90	285
15 36 42 94	16 18 41 93	16 59 41 92	17 40 40 92	18 20 41 91	19 01 40 90	19 41 41 89	284
14 53 42 93	15 35 41 93	16 16 41 92	16 57 40 91	17 37 41 90	18 18 40 89	18 58 40 89	283
14 10 41 93	14 51 41 92	15 32 41 91	16 13 41 90	16 54 41 90	17 35 40 89	18 15 40 88	282
13 27 41 92	14 08 41 91	14 49 41 90	15 30 41 90	16 11 41 89	16 52 40 88	17 32 40 87	281
12 44 +41 91	13 25 +41 90	14 06 +41 90	14 47 +41 89	15 28 +40 88	16 08 +41 87	16 49 +40 87	280
12 01 41 90	12 42 41 90	13 23 41 89	14 04 41 88	14 45 40 87	15 25 41 87	16 06 40 86	279
11 18 41 90	11 59 41 89	12 40 41 88	13 21 41 88	14 02 40 87	14 42 41 86	15 23 40 85	278
10 34 42 89	11 16 41 88	11 57 41 88	12 38 41 87	13 19 40 86	13 59 41 85	14 40 40 85	277
09 51 41 88	10 32 42 88	11 14 41 87	11 55 40 86	12 35 41 85	13 16 41 85	13 57 40 84	276
09 08 +41 88	09 49 +42 87	10 31 +41 86	11 12 +40 85	11 52 +41 85	12 33 +41 84	13 14 +40 83	275
08 25 41 87	09 06 41 86	09 47 42 86	10 29 41 85	11 10 40 84	11 50 41 83	12 31 41 83	274
07 42 41 86	08 23 41 86	09 04 42 85	09 46 41 84	10 27 41 83	11 08 40 83	11 48 41 82	273
06 59 41 86	07 40 42 85	08 22 41 84	09 03 41 83	09 44 41 83	10 25 41 82	11 06 40 81	272
06 16 41 85	06 57 42 84	07 39 41 84	08 20 41 83	09 01 41 82	09 42 41 81	10 23 41 81	271
05 33 +41 84	06 14 +42 84	06 56 +41 83	07 37 +41 82	08 18 +41 81	08 59 +42 81	09 41 +41 80	270
04 50 42 84	05 32 41 83	06 13 41 82	06 54 42 81	07 36 41 81	08 17 41 80	08 58 41 79	269
04 07 42 83	04 49 41 82	05 30 42 81	06 12 41 81	06 53 41 80	07 34 42 79	08 16 41 79	268
03 24 42 82	04 06 42 81	04 48 41 81	05 29 42 80	06 11 41 79	06 52 42 79	07 34 41 78	267
02 42 41 81	03 23 42 81	04 05 42 80	04 47 41 79	05 28 42 79	06 10 41 78	06 51 42 77	266
01 59 +42 81	02 41 +42 80	03 23 +41 79	04 04 +42 79	04 46 +42 78	05 28 +41 77	06 09 +42 77	265
01 16 42 80	01 58 42 79	02 40 42 79	03 22 42 78	04 04 42 77	04 46 41 77	05 27 42 76	264
00 34 42 79	01 16 42 79	01 58 42 78	02 40 42 77	03 22 42 77	04 04 42 76	04 46 42 75	263
−0 08 42 79	00 34 42 78	01 16 42 77	01 58 42 77	02 40 42 76	03 22 42 75	04 04 42 74	262
−0 51 42 78	−0 09 43 77	00 34 42 77	01 16 42 76	01 58 42 75	02 40 42 74	03 22 43 74	261
−1 33 +42 77	−0 51 +43 77	−0 08 +42 76	00 34 +42 75	01 16 +43 74	01 59 +42 74	02 41 +42 73	260
−2 15 43 77	−1 32 42 76	−0 50 42 75	−0 08 43 74	00 35 42 74	01 17 43 73	02 00 42 72	259
−2 57 43 76	−2 14 42 75	−1 32 43 74	−0 49 43 74	−0 06 42 73	00 36 43 72	01 19 42 72	258
−3 39 43 75	−2 56 43 74	−2 13 43 74	−1 30 42 73	−0 48 43 72	−0 05 43 72	00 38 43 71	257
−4 20 43 74	−3 37 42 74	−2 55 43 73	−2 12 43 72	−1 29 43 72	−0 46 43 71	−0 03 43 70	256
−5 02 +43 74	−4 19 +43 73	−3 36 +43 72	−2 53 +43 72	−2 10 +44 71	−1 26 +43 70	−0 43 +43 70	255
−5 43 43 73	−5 00 43 72	−4 17 43 72	−3 34 44 71	−2 50 43 70	−2 07 43 70	−1 24 44 69	254
107	−5 41 43 72	−4 58 44 71	−4 14 43 70	−3 31 44 70	−2 47 43 69	−2 04 44 68	253
	108	−5 38 43 70	−4 55 44 70	−4 11 43 69	−3 28 44 68	−2 44 44 67	252
	109	−6 19 44 69	−5 35 44 69	−4 51 44 68	−4 07 43 67	−3 24 44 67	251
		110	−6 15 +44 68	−5 31 +44 67	−4 47 +44 67	−4 03 +44 66	250
			111	−6 11 44 67	−5 27 45 66	−4 42 44 65	249
				112	−6 06 44 65	−5 22 45 65	248
					113	−6 01 45 64	247

DECLINATION (0°-14°) CONTRARY NAME TO LATITUDE

LHA	0° Hc d Z	1° Hc d Z	2° Hc d Z	3° Hc d Z	4° Hc d Z	5° Hc d Z	6° Hc d Z	7° Hc d Z
98	−5 45 42 84	262						
97	−5 02 42 85	−5 44 41 86	−6 25 42 87	263				
96	−4 19 42 86	−5 01 41 86	−5 42 42 87	−6 24 42 88	264			
95	−3 36 −41 87	−4 17 −42 87	−4 59 −42 88	−5 41 −41 89	−6 22 −41 89	265		
94	−2 53 41 87	−3 34 42 88	−4 16 42 89	−4 58 41 89	−5 39 42 90	−6 21 41 91	266	
93	−2 09 42 88	−2 51 42 89	−3 33 41 89	−4 14 42 90	−4 56 42 91	−5 38 41 91	−6 19 42 92	267
92	−1 26 42 89	−2 08 42 89	−2 50 41 90	−3 31 42 91	−4 13 41 91	−4 54 42 92	−5 36 41 93	−6 17 42 94
91	−0 43 42 89	−1 25 42 90	−2 07 41 91	−2 48 42 91	−3 30 41 92	−4 11 42 93	−4 53 41 94	−5 34 42 94
90	00 00 −42 90	−0 42 −41 91	−1 23 −42 91	−2 05 −42 92	−2 47 −41 93	−3 28 −42 94	−4 10 −41 94	−4 51 −42 95
89	00 43 42 91	00 01 41 91	−0 40 42 92	−1 22 42 93	−2 04 41 94	−2 45 42 94	−3 27 41 95	−4 08 42 96
88	01 26 41 91	00 45 42 92	00 03 42 93	−0 39 41 94	−1 20 42 94	−2 02 42 95	−2 44 41 96	−3 25 42 96
87	02 09 41 92	01 28 42 93	00 46 42 94	00 04 41 94	−0 37 42 95	−1 19 42 96	−2 01 42 96	−2 43 41 97
86	02 53 42 93	02 11 42 94	01 29 42 94	00 47 42 95	00 05 41 96	−0 36 42 96	−1 18 42 97	−2 00 42 98
85	03 36 −42 93	02 54 −42 94	02 12 −42 95	01 30 −42 96	00 48 −41 96	00 07 −42 97	−0 35 −42 98	−1 17 −42 98
84	04 19 42 94	03 37 42 95	02 55 42 96	02 13 42 96	01 31 42 97	00 49 42 98	00 07 41 98	−0 34 42 99
83	05 02 42 95	04 20 42 96	03 38 42 96	02 56 42 97	02 14 42 98	01 32 42 98	00 50 42 99	00 08 42 100
82	05 45 42 96	05 03 42 96	04 21 42 97	03 39 42 98	02 57 42 98	02 15 42 99	01 33 42 100	00 51 43 101
81	06 28 42 96	05 46 42 97	05 04 42 98	04 22 43 98	03 39 42 99	02 57 42 100	02 15 42 101	01 33 42 101
80	07 11 −42 97	06 29 −43 98	05 46 −42 98	05 04 −42 99	04 22 −42 100	03 40 −42 101	02 58 −43 101	02 15 −42 102
79	07 53 42 98	07 11 42 98	06 29 42 99	05 47 42 100	05 05 43 101	04 22 42 101	03 40 43 102	02 57 42 103
78	08 36 42 98	07 54 42 99	07 12 43 100	06 29 42 101	05 47 42 101	05 05 43 102	04 22 43 103	03 39 42 103
77	09 19 42 99	08 37 43 100	07 54 42 101	07 12 43 101	06 29 42 102	05 47 43 103	05 04 43 103	04 21 42 104
76	10 01 42 100	09 19 42 101	08 37 43 101	07 54 43 102	07 11 42 103	06 29 43 103	05 46 43 104	05 03 43 105
75	10 44 −43 101	10 01 −42 101	09 19 −43 102	08 36 −43 103	07 53 −42 103	07 11 −43 104	06 28 −43 105	05 45 −43 106
74	11 26 42 101	10 44 43 102	10 01 43 103	09 18 43 103	08 35 43 104	07 52 43 105	07 09 43 106	06 26 43 106
73	12 08 42 102	11 26 43 103	10 43 43 103	10 00 43 104	09 17 43 105	08 34 43 106	07 51 43 106	07 08 44 107
72	12 51 43 103	12 08 43 103	11 25 43 104	10 42 43 105	09 59 43 106	09 16 44 106	08 32 43 107	07 49 43 108
71	13 33 43 104	12 50 43 104	12 07 43 105	11 24 44 106	10 40 43 106	09 57 43 107	09 14 44 108	08 30 44 108
70	14 15 −43 104	13 32 −44 105	12 48 −43 106	12 05 −43 106	11 22 −44 107	10 38 −43 108	09 55 −44 108	09 11 −44 109

LHA	8° Hc d Z	9° Hc d Z	10° Hc d Z	11° Hc d Z	12° Hc d Z	13° Hc d Z	14° Hc d Z	LHA
92	268							
91	−6 16 41 95	269						
90	−5 33 −41 96	−6 14 −42 96	270					
89	−4 50 42 96	−5 32 41 97	−6 13 41 98	271				
88	−4 07 42 97	−4 49 41 98	−5 30 42 99	−6 12 41 99	272			
87	−3 24 42 98	−4 06 42 99	−4 48 41 99	−5 29 42 100	−6 11 41 101	273		
86	−2 42 41 99	−3 23 42 99	−4 05 42 100	−4 47 41 101	−5 28 42 101	−6 10 41 102	274	
85	−1 59 −42 99	−2 41 −42 100	−3 23 −41 101	−4 04 −42 101	−4 46 −42 102	−5 28 −41 103	−6 09 −42 103	275
84	−1 16 42 100	−1 58 42 101	−2 40 42 101	−3 22 42 102	−4 04 42 103	−4 46 41 103	−5 27 42 104	276
83	−0 34 42 101	−1 16 42 101	−1 58 42 102	−2 40 42 103	−3 22 42 103	−4 04 42 104	−4 46 42 105	277
82	00 08 42 101	−0 34 42 102	−1 16 42 103	−1 58 42 103	−2 40 42 104	−3 22 42 105	−4 04 42 106	278
81	00 51 42 102	00 09 43 103	−0 34 42 103	−1 16 42 104	−1 58 42 105	−2 40 42 106	−3 22 43 106	279
80	01 33 −42 103	00 51 −43 103	00 08 −42 104	−0 34 −42 105	−1 16 −43 106	−1 59 −42 106	−2 41 −42 107	280
79	02 15 43 103	01 32 42 104	00 50 42 105	00 08 43 106	−0 35 42 106	−1 17 43 107	−2 00 42 108	281
78	02 57 43 104	02 14 42 105	01 32 43 106	00 49 43 106	00 06 42 107	−0 36 43 108	−1 19 42 108	282
77	03 39 43 105	02 56 43 106	02 13 43 106	01 30 42 107	00 48 43 108	00 05 43 108	−0 38 43 109	283
76	04 20 43 106	03 37 42 106	02 55 43 107	02 12 43 108	01 29 43 108	00 46 43 109	00 03 43 110	284
75	05 02 −43 106	04 19 −43 107	03 36 −43 108	02 53 −43 108	02 10 −44 109	01 26 −43 110	00 43 −43 110	285
74	05 43 43 107	05 00 43 108	04 17 43 108	03 34 44 109	02 50 43 110	02 07 43 110	01 24 44 111	286
73	06 24 43 108	05 41 43 108	04 58 44 109	04 14 43 110	03 31 44 110	02 47 43 111	02 04 44 112	287
72	07 06 44 108	06 22 44 109	05 38 43 110	04 55 44 110	04 11 43 111	03 20 44 112	02 44 44 113	288
71	07 46 43 109	07 03 44 110	06 19 44 111	05 35 44 111	04 51 44 112	04 07 43 113	03 24 44 113	289
70	08 27 −44 110	07 43 −44 111	06 59 −44 111	06 15 −44 112	05 31 −44 113	04 47 −44 113	04 03 −44 114	290

S. Lat. {LHA greater than 180°........ Zn=180−Z
{LHA less than 180°........... Zn=180+Z

N. Lat. {LHA greater than 180°……. Zn=Z; LHA less than 180°………. Zn=360−Z}

DECLINATION (0°-14°) CONTRARY NAME TO LATITUDE

LHA	0° Hc	0° d	0° Z	1° Hc	1° d	1° Z	2° Hc	2° d	2° Z	3° Hc	3° d	3° Z	4° Hc	4° d	4° Z
	° ′	′	°	° ′	′	°	° ′	′	°	° ′	′	°	° ′	′	°
69	14 56	43	105	14 13	43	106	13 30	44	106	12 46	43	107	12 03	44	108
68	15 38	43	106	14 55	44	106	14 11	43	107	13 28	44	108	12 44	44	109
67	16 19	43	106	15 36	44	107	14 52	43	108	14 09	44	109	13 25	44	109
66	17 01	44	107	16 17	44	108	15 33	44	109	14 49	44	109	14 05	44	110
65	17 42	−44	108	16 58	−44	109	16 14	−44	109	15 30	−44	110	14 46	−45	111
64	18 23	44	109	17 39	44	109	16 55	45	110	16 10	44	111	15 26	45	112
63	19 04	44	110	18 20	45	110	17 35	44	111	16 51	45	112	16 06	45	112
62	19 44	44	110	19 00	45	111	18 15	44	112	17 31	45	112	16 46	45	113
61	20 25	45	111	19 40	45	112	18 55	44	113	18 11	46	113	17 25	45	114
60	21 05	−45	112	20 20	−45	113	19 35	−45	113	18 50	−45	114	18 05	−46	115
59	21 45	45	113	21 00	45	113	20 15	46	114	19 29	45	115	18 44	46	116
58	22 25	46	114	21 39	45	114	20 54	46	115	20 08	45	116	19 23	46	116
57	23 04	45	114	22 19	46	115	21 33	46	116	20 47	46	116	20 01	46	117
56	23 43	45	115	22 58	46	116	22 12	46	117	21 26	46	117	20 40	47	118
55	24 22	−46	116	23 36	−46	117	22 50	−46	117	22 04	−46	118	21 18	−47	119
54	25 01	46	117	24 15	47	118	23 28	46	118	22 42	47	119	21 55	46	120
53	25 39	46	118	24 53	47	118	24 06	46	119	23 20	47	120	22 33	47	120
52	26 17	46	119	25 31	47	119	24 44	47	120	23 57	47	121	23 10	48	121
51	26 55	47	119	26 08	47	120	25 21	47	121	24 34	47	121	23 47	48	122
50	27 33	−48	120	26 45	−47	121	25 58	−47	122	25 11	−48	122	24 23	−48	123
49	28 10	48	121	27 22	47	122	26 35	48	123	25 47	48	123	24 59	48	124
48	28 46	47	122	27 59	48	123	27 11	48	123	26 23	48	124	25 35	49	125
47	29 23	48	123	28 35	48	124	27 47	49	124	26 58	48	125	26 10	49	126
46	29 59	48	124	29 11	49	125	28 22	48	125	27 34	49	126	26 45	49	127
45	30 34	−48	125	29 46	−49	126	28 57	−49	126	28 08	−49	127	27 19	−49	127
44	31 10	49	126	30 21	49	126	29 32	49	127	28 43	50	128	27 53	49	128
43	31 45	50	127	30 55	49	127	30 06	49	128	29 17	50	129	28 27	50	129
42	32 19	49	128	31 30	50	128	30 40	50	129	29 50	50	130	29 00	50	130
41	32 53	50	129	32 03	50	129	31 13	50	130	30 23	50	131	29 33	51	131
40	33 26	−50	130	32 36	−50	130	31 46	−50	131	30 56	−51	132	30 05	−51	132
39	33 59	50	131	33 09	51	131	32 18	50	132	31 28	51	133	30 37	51	133
38	34 32	51	132	33 41	51	132	32 50	51	133	31 59	51	134	31 08	51	134
37	35 04	51	133	34 13	51	133	33 22	52	134	32 30	51	135	31 39	52	135
36	35 35	51	134	34 44	52	134	33 52	51	135	33 01	52	136	32 09	52	136
35	36 06	−51	135	35 15	−52	135	34 23	−52	136	33 31	−53	137	32 38	−52	137
34	36 37	52	136	35 45	53	137	34 52	52	137	34 00	53	138	33 07	52	138
33	37 06	52	137	36 14	52	138	35 22	53	138	34 29	53	139	33 36	53	139
32	37 36	53	138	36 43	53	139	35 50	53	139	34 57	53	140	34 04	54	140
31	38 04	53	139	37 11	53	140	36 18	53	140	35 25	54	141	34 31	54	141
30	38 32	−53	140	37 39	−54	141	36 45	−54	141	35 51	−53	142	34 58	−54	143
29	38 59	53	141	38 06	54	142	37 12	54	143	36 18	54	143	35 24	55	144
28	39 26	54	143	38 32	54	143	37 38	55	144	36 43	54	144	35 49	55	145
27	39 52	55	144	38 57	54	144	38 03	55	145	37 08	55	145	36 13	55	146
26	40 17	55	145	39 22	55	146	38 27	55	146	37 32	55	147	36 37	55	147
25	40 41	−55	146	39 46	−55	147	38 51	−55	147	37 56	−56	148	37 00	−55	148
24	41 05	55	147	40 10	56	148	39 14	55	148	38 19	56	149	37 23	56	149
23	41 28	56	149	40 32	56	149	39 36	55	150	38 41	57	150	37 44	56	151
22	41 50	56	150	40 54	56	150	39 58	56	151	39 02	57	151	38 05	56	152
21	42 11	56	151	41 15	56	152	40 19	57	152	39 22	57	152	38 25	56	153
20	42 32	−57	152	41 35	−57	153	40 38	−56	153	39 42	−57	154	38 45	−57	154
19	42 51	57	154	41 54	57	154	40 57	57	155	40 00	57	155	39 03	57	155
18	43 10	57	155	42 13	57	155	41 16	58	156	40 18	57	156	39 21	58	157
17	43 28	58	156	42 30	57	157	41 33	58	157	40 35	57	157	39 38	58	158
16	43 45	58	158	42 47	58	158	41 49	58	158	40 51	57	159	39 54	58	159
15	44 01	−58	159	43 03	−58	159	42 05	−58	160	41 07	−58	160	40 09	−59	160
14	44 16	58	160	43 18	59	161	42 19	58	161	41 21	58	161	40 23	59	162
13	44 30	58	162	43 32	59	162	42 33	59	162	41 34	58	163	40 36	59	163
12	44 43	59	163	43 44	58	163	42 46	59	164	41 47	59	164	40 48	59	164
11	44 55	59	164	43 56	59	165	42 57	58	165	41 59	59	165	41 00	59	165
10	45 06	−59	166	44 07	−59	166	43 08	−59	166	42 09	−59	167	41 10	−59	167
9	45 17	60	167	44 17	59	167	43 18	59	168	42 19	60	168	41 19	59	168
8	45 26	60	169	44 26	59	169	43 27	60	169	42 27	59	169	41 28	60	169
7	45 34	60	170	44 34	59	170	43 35	60	170	42 35	60	171	41 35	59	171
6	45 41	60	171	44 41	60	172	43 41	59	172	42 42	60	172	41 42	60	172
5	45 47	−60	173	44 47	−60	173	43 47	−60	173	42 47	−60	173	41 47	−59	173
4	45 51	59	174	44 52	60	174	43 52	60	175	42 52	60	175	41 52	60	175
3	45 55	60	176	44 55	60	176	43 55	60	176	42 55	59	176	41 56	60	176
2	45 58	60	177	44 58	60	177	43 58	60	177	42 58	60	177	41 58	60	177
1	46 00	60	179	45 00	60	179	44 00	60	179	43 00	60	179	42 00	60	179
0	46 00	−60	180	45 00	−60	180	44 00	−60	180	43 00	−60	180	42 00	−60	180

LHA	5° Hc	5° d	5° Z	6° Hc	6° d	6° Z	7° Hc	7° d	7° Z	8° Hc	8° d	8° Z	9° Hc	9° d	9° Z
	° ′	′	°	° ′	′	°	° ′	′	°	° ′	′	°	° ′	′	°
69	11 19	44	109	10 35	43	109	09 52	44	110	09 08	44	111	08 24	45	111
68	12 00	44	109	11 16	44	110	10 32	44	111	09 48	44	111	09 04	45	112
67	12 41	44	110	11 57	45	111	11 12	44	111	10 28	44	112	09 44	45	113
66	13 21	44	111	12 37	45	111	11 52	44	112	11 08	45	113	10 23	44	114
65	14 01	−44	112	13 17	−45	112	12 32	−44	113	11 48	−45	114	11 03	−45	114
64	14 41	44	112	13 57	45	113	13 12	45	114	12 27	45	114	11 42	45	115
63	15 21	45	113	14 36	45	114	13 51	45	114	13 06	45	115	12 21	45	116
62	16 01	45	114	15 16	45	114	14 31	46	115	13 45	45	116	13 00	46	117
61	16 40	45	115	15 55	45	115	15 10	46	116	14 24	46	117	13 38	45	117
60	17 19	−45	115	16 34	−46	116	15 48	−46	117	15 02	−45	117	14 17	−46	118
59	17 58	45	116	17 13	46	117	16 27	46	118	15 41	47	118	14 54	46	119
58	18 37	46	117	17 51	46	118	17 05	46	118	16 19	47	119	15 32	46	120
57	19 15	46	118	18 29	46	118	17 43	47	119	16 56	46	120	16 10	47	120
56	19 53	46	119	19 07	47	119	18 20	47	120	17 33	46	121	16 47	47	121
55	20 31	−47	119	19 44	−47	120	18 57	−47	121	18 10	−47	121	17 23	−47	122
54	21 09	47	120	20 22	48	121	19 34	47	122	18 47	47	122	18 00	48	123
53	21 46	48	121	20 58	47	122	20 11	47	122	19 24	48	123	18 36	48	124
52	22 22	47	122	21 35	48	123	20 47	47	123	20 00	48	124	19 12	48	125
51	22 59	48	123	22 11	48	123	21 23	48	124	20 35	48	125	19 47	48	125
50	23 35	−48	124	22 47	−48	124	21 59	−48	125	21 11	−49	126	20 22	−49	126
49	24 11	49	125	23 22	48	125	22 34	49	126	21 45	48	126	20 57	49	127
48	24 46	48	125	23 58	49	126	23 09	49	127	22 20	49	127	21 31	49	128
47	25 21	49	126	24 32	49	127	23 43	49	128	22 54	49	128	22 05	50	129
46	25 56	49	127	25 07	50	128	24 17	49	128	23 28	50	129	22 38	50	130
45	26 30	−50	128	25 40	−49	129	24 51	−50	129	24 01	−50	130	23 11	−50	131
44	27 04	50	129	26 14	50	130	25 24	50	130	24 34	50	131	23 44	51	132
43	27 37	50	130	26 47	50	131	25 57	51	131	25 06	50	132	24 16	51	132
42	28 10	50	131	27 20	51	132	26 29	51	132	25 38	50	133	24 48	51	133
41	28 42	50	132	27 52	51	132	27 01	51	133	26 10	51	134	25 19	51	134
40	29 14	−51	133	28 23	−51	133	27 32	−51	134	26 41	−52	135	25 49	−51	135
39	29 46	52	134	28 54	51	134	28 03	52	135	27 11	51	136	26 20	52	136
38	30 17	52	135	29 25	52	135	28 33	52	136	27 41	52	137	26 49	52	137
37	30 47	52	136	29 55	52	136	29 03	52	137	28 11	53	138	27 18	52	138
36	31 17	52	137	30 25	53	137	29 32	52	138	28 40	53	138	27 47	53	139
35	31 46	−52	138	30 54	−53	138	30 01	−53	139	29 08	−53	139	28 15	−53	140
34	32 15	53	139	31 22	53	139	30 29	53	140	29 36	53	140	28 43	54	141
33	32 43	53	140	31 50	54	140	30 56	53	141	30 03	54	142	29 09	53	142
32	33 10	53	141	32 17	54	141	31 23	53	142	30 30	54	143	29 36	54	143
31	33 37	53	142	32 44	54	143	31 50	54	143	30 56	55	144	30 01	54	144
30	34 04	−55	143	33 09	−54	144	32 15	−54	144	31 21	−55	145	30 26	−54	145
29	34 29	54	144	33 35	55	145	32 40	54	145	31 46	55	146	30 51	55	146
28	34 54	55	145	33 59	54	146	33 05	55	146	32 10	55	147	31 15	56	147
27	35 18	55	146	34 23	55	147	33 28	55	147	32 33	55	148	31 38	56	148
26	35 42	55	148	34 47	56	148	33 51	55	148	32 56	56	149	32 00	56	149
25	36 05	−56	149	35 09	−56	149	34 13	−55	150	33 18	−56	150	32 22	−56	150
24	36 27	56	150	35 31	56	150	34 35	56	151	33 39	56	151	32 43	57	152
23	36 48	56	151	35 52	56	151	34 56	57	152	33 59	56	152	33 03	57	153
22	37 09	57	152	36 12	56	153	35 16	57	153	34 19	57	153	33 22	56	154
21	37 29	57	153	36 32	57	154	35 35	57	154	34 38	57	154	33 41	57	155
20	37 48	−57	155	36 51	−57	155	35 54	−58	155	34 56	−57	156	33 59	−57	156
19	38 06	57	156	37 09	58	156	36 11	57	156	35 14	58	157	34 16	57	157
18	38 23	57	157	37 26	58	157	36 28	58	158	35 30	57	158	34 33	58	158
17	38 40	58	158	37 42	58	158	36 44	58	159	35 46	58	159	34 48	58	159
16	38 56	59	159	37 57	58	160	36 59	58	160	36 01	58	160	35 03	58	161
15	39 10	−58	161	38 12	−58	161	37 14	−59	161	36 15	−58	162	35 17	−58	162
14	39 24	58	162	38 26	59	162	37 27	58	162	36 29	59	163	35 30	59	163
13	39 37	58	163	38 39	59	163	37 40	59	164	36 41	59	164	35 42	58	164
12	39 49	59	164	38 50	58	165	37 52	59	165	36 53	59	165	35 54	59	165
11	40 01	60	166	39 01	59	166	38 02	59	166	37 03	59	166	36 04	59	167
10	40 11	−59	167	39 12	−60	167	38 12	−59	167	37 13	−59	168	36 14	−59	168
9	40 20	59	168	39 21	60	168	38 21	59	169	37 22	59	169	36 23	60	169
8	40 28	59	170	39 29	60	170	38 29	59	170	37 30	60	170	36 30	59	170
7	40 36	60	171	39 36	59	171	38 37	60	171	37 37	60	171	36 37	59	171
6	40 42	59	172	39 43	60	172	38 43	60	172	37 43	60	173	36 43	59	173
5	40 48	−60	173	39 48	−60	174	38 48	−60	174	37 48	−60	174	36 48	−59	174
4	40 52	60	175	39 52	60	175	38 52	60	175	37 52	59	175	36 53	60	175
3	40 56	60	176	39 56	60	176	38 56	60	176	37 56	60	176	36 56	60	176
2	40 58	60	177	39 58	60	177	38 58	60	177	37 58	60	178	36 58	60	178
1	41 00	60	179	40 00	60	179	39 00	60	179	38 00	60	179	37 00	60	179
0	41 00	−60	180	40 00	−60	180	39 00	−60	180	38 00	−60	180	37 00	−60	180

LHA	10° Hc	10° d	10° Z	11° Hc	11° d	11° Z	12° Hc	12° d	12° Z	13° Hc	13° d	13° Z	14° Hc	14° d	14° Z	LHA
	° ′	′	°	° ′	′	°	° ′	′	°	° ′	′	°	° ′	′	°	
69	07 39	44	112	06 55	44	113	06 11	44	113	05 27	45	114	04 42	44	115	291
68	08 19	44	113	07 35	44	113	06 51	45	114	06 06	44	115	05 22	45	115	292
67	08 59	44	113	08 15	45	114	07 30	45	115	06 45	44	115	06 01	45	116	293
66	09 39	45	114	08 54	45	115	08 09	45	116	07 24	45	116	06 39	45	117	294
65	10 18	−45	115	09 33	−45	116	08 48	−45	116	08 03	−45	117	07 18	−46	118	295
64	10 57	45	116	10 12	46	116	09 26	45	117	08 41	45	118	07 56	46	118	296
63	11 36	46	116	10 50	45	117	10 05	46	118	09 19	45	118	08 34	46	119	297
62	12 14	45	117	11 29	46	118	10 43	46	119	09 57	46	119	09 11	46	120	298
61	12 53	46	118	12 07	46	119	11 21	46	119	10 35	47	120	09 48	46	121	299
60	13 31	−47	119	12 44	−46	119	11 58	−46	120	11 12	−47	121	10 25	−46	121	300
59	14 08	46	120	13 22	47	120	12 35	46	121	11 49	47	121	11 02	46	122	301
58	14 46	47	120	13 59	47	121	13 12	46	122	12 26	47	122	11 39	47	123	302
57	15 23	47	121	14 36	47	122	13 49	47	122	13 02	47	123	12 15	48	124	303
56	16 00	48	122	15 12	47	123	14 25	47	123	13 38	47	124	12 51	48	124	304
55	16 36	−47	123	15 49	−48	123	15 01	−47	124	14 14	−48	125	13 26	−48	125	305
54	17 12	47	124	16 25	48	124	15 37	48	125	14 49	48	125	14 01	48	126	306
53	17 48	48	124	17 00	48	125	16 12	48	126	15 24	48	126	14 36	49	127	307
52	18 24	49	125	17 35	48	126	16 47	48	126	15 59	49	127	15 10	48	128	308
51	18 59	49	126	18 10	48	127	17 22	49	127	16 33	49	128	15 44	49	128	309
50	19 33	−48	127	18 45	−49	127	17 56	−49	128	17 07	−49	129	16 18	−49	129	310
49	20 08	49	128	19 19	49	128	18 30	50	129	17 40	49	130	16 51	49	130	311
48	20 42	50	129	19 52	49	129	19 03	50	130	18 13	49	130	17 24	50	131	312
47	21 15	49	129	20 26	50	130	19 36	50	131	18 46	50	131	17 56	50	132	313
46	21 48	49	130	20 59	50	131	20 09	51	132	19 18	50	132	18 28	50	133	314
45	22 21	−50	131	21 31	−50	132	20 41	−51	132	19 50	−50	133	19 00	−51	134	315
44	22 53	50	132	22 03	51	133	21 12	50	133	20 22	51	134	19 31	51	134	316
43	23 25	51	133	22 34	50	134	21 44	51	134	20 53	52	135	20 01	51	135	317
42	23 57	51	134	23 06	52	134	22 14	51	135	21 23	51	136	20 32	52	136	318
41	24 28	52	135	23 36	51	135	22 45	52	136	21 53	52	137	21 01	51	137	319
40	24 58	−52	136	24 06	−52	136	23 14	−51	137	22 23	−52	137	21 31	−53	138	320
39	25 28	52	137	24 36	52	137	23 44	53	138	22 51	52	138	21 59	52	139	321
38	25 57	52	138	25 05	53	138	24 12	52	139	23 20	53	139	22 27	52	140	322
37	26 26	53	139	25 33	52	139	24 41	53	140	23 48	53	140	22 55	53	141	323
36	26 54	53	140	26 01	53	140	25 08	53	141	24 15	53	141	23 22	53	142	324
35	27 22	−53	141	26 29	−53	141	25 36	−54	142	24 42	−53	142	23 49	−54	143	325
34	27 49	53	142	26 56	54	142	26 02	54	143	25 08	53	143	24 15	54	144	326
33	28 16	54	143	27 22	54	143	26 28	54	144	25 34	54	144	24 40	54	144	327
32	28 42	54	144	27 48	55	144	26 53	54	145	25 59	54	145	25 05	55	145	328
31	29 07	54	145	28 13	55	145	27 18	54	146	26 24	55	146	25 29	55	146	329
30	29 32	−55	146	28 37	−55	146	27 42	−54	147	26 48	−55	147	25 53	−55	147	330
29	29 56	55	147	29 01	55	147	28 06	55	148	27 11	55	148	26 16	56	148	331
28	30 19	55	148	29 24	55	148	28 29	56	149	27 33	55	149	26 38	56	149	332
27	30 42	55	149	29 47	56	149	28 51	56	150	27 55	56	150	26 59	56	150	333
26	31 04	56	150	30 08	55	150	29 13	56	151	28 17	57	151	27 20	56	151	334
25	31 26	−56	151	30 30	−57	151	29 33	−56	152	28 37	−56	152	27 41	−57	152	335
24	31 46	56	152	30 50	56	152	29 54	57	153	28 57	57	153	28 00	56	153	336
23	32 06	56	153	31 10	57	153	30 13	57	154	29 16	57	154	28 19	56	155	337
22	32 26	57	154	31 29	57	155	30 32	57	155	29 35	57	155	28 38	57	156	338
21	32 44	57	155	31 47	57	156	30 50	58	156	29 52	57	156	28 55	57	157	339
20	33 02	−58	156	32 04	−57	157	31 07	−58	157	30 09	−57	157	29 12	−58	158	340
19	33 19	58	157	32 21	58	158	31 23	57	158	30 26	58	158	29 28	58	159	341
18	33 35	58	159	32 37	58	159	31 39	58	159	30 41	58	160	29 43	58	160	342
17	33 50	58	160	32 52	58	160	31 54	58	160	30 56	58	161	29 58	58	161	343
16	34 05	58	161	33 07	59	161	32 08	58	161	31 10	59	162	30 11	58	162	344
15	34 19	−59	162	33 20	−58	162	32 22	−59	163	31 23	−59	163	30 24	−58	163	345
14	34 31	58	163	33 33	59	163	32 34	59	164	31 35	58	164	30 37	59	164	346
13	34 44	59	164	33 45	59	165	32 46	59	165	31 47	59	165	30 48	59	165	347
12	34 55	59	166	33 56	59	166	32 57	59	166	31 58	59	166	30 59	60	166	348
11	35 05	59	167	34 06	59	167	33 07	59	167	32 08	60	167	31 08	59	168	349
10	35 15	−60	168	34 15	−59	168	33 16	−59	168	32 17	−60	169	31 17	−59	169	350
9	35 23	59	169	34 24	60	169	33 24	59	169	32 25	60	170	31 25	59	170	351
8	35 31	60	170	34 31	59	171	33 32	60	171	32 32	59	171	31 33	60	171	352
7	35 38	60	171	34 38	60	172	33 38	59	172	32 39	60	172	31 39	60	172	353
6	35 44	60	173	34 44	60	173	33 44	60	173	32 44	59	173	31 45	60	173	354
5	35 49	−60	174	34 49	−60	174	33 49	−60	174	32 49	−60	174	31 49	−60	174	355
4	35 53	60	175	34 53	60	175	33 53	60	175	32 53	60	175	31 53	60	175	356
3	35 56	60	176	34 56	60	176	33 56	60	177	32 56	60	177	31 56	60	177	357
2	35 58	60	178	34 58	60	178	33 58	60	178	32 58	60	178	31 58	60	178	358
1	36 00	60	179	35 00	60	179	34 00	60	179	33 00	60	179	32 00	60	179	359
0	36 00	−60	180	35 00	−60	180	34 00	−60	180	33 00	−60	180	32 00	−60	180	360

S. Lat. {LHA greater than 180°……. Zn=180−Z; LHA less than 180°………. Zn=180+Z}

DECLINATION (0°-14°) CONTRARY NAME TO LATITUDE

LAT 44°

N. Lat. {LHA greater than 180°....... Zn=Z
{LHA less than 180°........... Zn=360−Z

DECLINATION (15°-29°) SAME NAME AS LATITUDE

LHA	15° Hc	15° d	15° Z	16° Hc	16° d	16° Z	17° Hc	17° d	17° Z	18° Hc	18° d	18° Z	19° Hc	19° d	19° Z
	° ′	′	°	° ′	′	°	° ′	′	°	° ′	′	°	° ′	′	°
0	61 00	+60	180	62 00	+60	180	63 00	+60	180	64 00	+60	180	65 00	+60	180
1	60 59	60	178	61 59	60	178	62 59	60	178	63 59	60	178	64 59	60	178
2	60 57	60	176	61 57	60	176	62 57	60	176	63 57	60	176	64 57	60	176
3	60 53	60	174	61 53	60	174	62 53	60	174	63 53	59	174	64 52	60	173
4	60 48	60	172	61 48	59	172	62 47	60	172	63 47	60	171	64 47	59	171
5	60 41	+60	170	61 41	+59	170	62 40	+60	170	63 40	+59	169	64 39	+59	169
6	60 33	60	168	61 33	59	168	62 32	59	168	63 31	59	167	64 30	59	167
7	60 24	59	166	61 23	59	166	62 22	59	165	63 21	58	165	64 19	59	165
8	60 13	58	164	61 11	59	164	62 10	59	163	63 09	58	163	64 07	58	163
9	60 00	59	162	60 59	58	162	61 57	58	162	62 55	58	161	63 53	58	160
10	59 47	+58	161	60 45	+58	160	61 43	+57	160	62 40	+58	159	63 38	+58	158
11	59 32	57	159	60 29	58	158	61 27	57	158	62 24	57	157	63 21	57	156
12	59 15	58	157	60 13	57	156	61 10	57	156	62 07	56	155	63 03	57	154
13	58 58	57	155	59 55	56	155	60 51	57	154	61 48	56	153	62 44	56	152
14	58 39	56	153	59 35	57	153	60 32	56	152	61 28	55	151	62 23	56	150
15	58 19	+56	152	59 15	+56	151	60 11	+55	150	61 06	+55	149	62 01	+55	149
16	57 58	55	150	58 53	56	149	59 49	55	148	60 44	54	148	61 38	55	147
17	57 36	55	148	58 31	54	147	59 25	55	147	60 20	54	146	61 14	54	145
18	57 12	55	147	58 07	54	146	59 01	54	145	59 55	54	144	60 49	53	143
19	56 48	54	145	57 42	54	144	58 36	53	143	59 29	53	142	60 22	53	142
20	56 23	+53	143	57 16	+54	143	58 10	+53	142	59 03	+52	141	59 55	+52	140
21	55 57	53	142	56 50	52	141	57 42	53	140	58 35	52	139	59 27	51	138
22	55 29	53	140	56 22	52	139	57 14	52	139	58 06	51	138	58 57	51	137
23	55 01	53	139	55 54	51	138	56 45	52	137	57 37	50	136	58 27	51	135
24	54 33	51	137	55 24	51	137	56 15	51	136	57 06	51	135	57 57	49	134
25	54 03	+51	136	54 54	+51	135	55 45	+50	134	56 35	+50	133	57 25	+49	132
26	53 33	50	135	54 23	50	134	55 13	50	133	56 03	50	132	56 53	48	131
27	53 01	51	133	53 52	49	132	54 41	50	131	55 31	48	130	56 19	49	129
28	52 30	49	132	53 19	50	131	54 09	48	130	54 57	49	129	55 46	47	128
29	51 57	49	131	52 46	49	130	53 35	49	129	54 24	47	128	55 11	48	127
30	51 24	+49	129	52 13	+48	128	53 01	+48	127	53 49	+47	126	54 36	+47	125
31	50 50	49	128	51 39	48	127	52 27	47	126	53 14	47	125	54 01	46	124
32	50 16	48	127	51 04	48	126	51 52	46	125	52 38	47	124	53 25	46	123
33	49 41	48	126	50 29	47	125	51 16	46	124	52 02	46	123	52 48	46	122
34	49 06	47	124	49 53	47	124	50 40	46	123	51 26	45	122	52 11	45	120
35	48 30	+47	123	49 17	+46	122	50 03	+46	121	50 49	+45	120	51 34	+44	119
36	47 54	46	122	48 40	46	121	49 26	45	120	50 11	45	119	50 56	44	118
37	47 17	46	121	48 03	45	120	48 48	45	119	49 33	45	118	50 18	44	117
38	46 40	45	120	47 25	46	119	48 11	44	118	48 55	44	117	49 39	44	116
39	46 02	45	119	46 47	45	118	47 32	44	117	48 16	44	116	49 00	43	115
40	45 24	+45	118	46 09	+45	117	46 54	+43	116	47 37	+44	115	48 21	+43	114
41	44 46	44	117	45 30	45	116	46 15	43	115	46 58	43	114	47 41	43	113
42	44 07	44	116	44 51	44	115	45 35	44	114	46 19	42	113	47 01	43	112
43	43 28	44	115	44 12	44	114	44 56	43	113	45 39	42	112	46 21	42	111
44	42 49	44	114	43 33	43	113	44 16	42	112	44 58	43	111	45 41	41	110
45	42 09	+44	113	42 53	+43	112	43 36	+42	111	44 18	+42	110	45 00	+41	109
46	41 29	43	112	42 12	43	111	42 55	42	110	43 37	42	109	44 19	41	108
47	40 49	43	111	41 32	43	110	42 15	41	109	42 56	42	108	43 38	41	107
48	40 09	42	110	40 51	43	109	41 34	41	108	42 15	42	107	42 57	40	106
49	39 28	43	109	40 11	42	108	40 53	41	107	41 34	41	106	42 15	41	105
50	38 47	+42	108	39 29	+42	107	40 11	+42	107	40 53	+40	106	41 33	+41	105
51	38 06	42	108	38 48	42	107	39 30	41	106	40 11	41	105	40 52	40	104
52	37 25	42	107	38 07	41	106	38 48	41	105	39 29	41	104	40 10	40	103
53	36 43	42	106	37 25	41	105	38 06	41	104	38 47	40	103	39 27	40	102
54	36 02	41	105	36 43	41	104	37 24	41	103	38 05	40	102	38 45	40	101
55	35 20	+41	104	36 01	+41	103	36 42	+41	102	37 23	+40	101	38 03	+39	100
56	34 38	41	103	35 19	41	102	36 00	40	102	36 40	40	101	37 20	40	100
57	33 56	41	103	34 37	41	102	35 18	40	101	35 58	40	100	36 38	39	99
58	33 14	41	102	33 55	40	101	34 35	40	100	35 15	40	99	35 55	39	98
59	32 31	41	101	33 12	41	100	33 53	40	99	34 33	39	98	35 12	39	97
60	31 49	+41	100	32 30	+40	99	33 10	+40	98	33 50	+39	98	34 29	+39	97
61	31 07	40	99	31 47	40	99	32 27	40	98	33 07	39	97	33 46	39	96
62	30 24	40	99	31 04	40	98	31 44	40	97	32 24	39	96	33 03	39	95
63	29 41	41	98	30 22	40	97	31 02	39	96	31 41	39	95	32 20	39	94
64	28 58	41	97	29 39	40	96	30 19	39	95	30 58	39	95	31 37	39	94
65	28 16	+40	96	28 56	+40	96	29 36	+39	95	30 15	+39	94	30 54	+39	93
66	27 33	40	96	28 13	40	95	28 53	39	94	29 32	39	93	30 11	39	92
67	26 50	40	95	27 30	39	94	28 09	40	93	28 49	39	92	29 28	39	92
68	26 07	40	94	26 47	39	93	27 26	40	93	28 06	39	92	28 45	39	91
69	25 24	40	93	26 04	39	93	26 43	40	92	27 23	39	91	28 02	39	90

LHA	20° Hc	20° d	20° Z	21° Hc	21° d	21° Z	22° Hc	22° d	22° Z	23° Hc	23° d	23° Z	24° Hc	24° d	24° Z
	° ′	′	°	° ′	′	°	° ′	′	°	° ′	′	°	° ′	′	°
0	66 00	+60	180	67 00	+60	180	68 00	+60	180	69 00	+60	180	70 00	+60	180
1	65 59	60	178	66 59	60	178	67 59	60	178	68 59	60	177	69 59	60	177
2	65 57	59	175	66 56	60	175	67 56	60	175	68 56	60	175	69 56	60	175
3	65 52	60	173	66 52	60	173	67 52	59	173	68 51	60	172	69 51	60	172
4	65 46	60	171	66 46	59	171	67 45	60	170	68 45	59	170	69 44	59	169
5	65 38	+60	169	66 38	+59	168	67 37	+59	168	68 36	+59	167	69 35	+59	167
6	65 29	59	166	66 28	59	166	67 27	59	165	68 26	58	165	69 24	59	164
7	65 18	59	164	66 17	58	164	67 15	59	163	68 14	58	162	69 12	58	162
8	65 05	59	162	66 04	58	161	67 02	58	161	68 00	57	160	68 57	58	159
9	64 51	58	160	65 49	58	159	66 47	57	158	67 44	57	158	68 41	57	157
10	64 36	+57	158	65 33	+57	157	66 30	+57	156	67 27	+56	155	68 23	+57	155
11	64 18	57	156	65 15	57	155	66 12	56	154	67 08	56	153	68 04	56	152
12	64 00	56	154	64 56	56	153	65 52	56	152	66 48	55	151	67 43	55	150
13	63 40	56	152	64 36	55	151	65 31	55	150	66 26	55	149	67 21	54	148
14	63 19	55	150	64 14	55	149	65 09	54	148	66 03	54	147	66 57	54	146
15	62 56	+55	148	63 51	+54	147	64 45	+54	146	65 39	+53	145	66 32	+53	144
16	62 33	54	146	63 27	53	145	64 20	53	144	65 13	53	143	66 06	52	142
17	62 08	53	144	63 01	53	143	63 54	53	142	64 47	52	141	65 39	51	140
18	61 42	53	142	62 35	52	141	63 27	52	140	64 19	51	139	65 10	51	138
19	61 15	52	141	62 07	52	140	62 59	51	138	63 50	51	137	64 41	49	136
20	60 47	+52	139	61 39	+51	138	62 30	+50	137	63 20	+50	135	64 10	+49	134
21	60 18	51	137	61 09	51	136	62 00	49	135	62 49	50	134	63 39	48	133
22	59 48	51	136	60 39	50	135	61 29	49	133	62 18	48	132	63 06	48	131
23	59 18	50	134	60 08	49	133	60 57	48	132	61 45	48	131	62 33	48	129
24	58 46	50	133	59 36	48	131	60 24	48	130	61 12	48	129	62 00	46	128
25	58 14	+49	131	59 03	+48	130	59 51	+47	129	60 38	+47	128	61 25	+46	126
26	57 41	48	130	58 29	48	129	59 17	47	127	60 04	46	126	60 50	45	125
27	57 08	47	128	57 55	47	127	58 42	47	126	59 29	45	125	60 14	45	123
28	56 33	48	127	57 21	46	126	58 07	46	125	58 53	45	123	59 38	44	122
29	55 59	46	126	56 45	46	124	57 31	45	123	58 16	45	122	59 01	44	121
30	55 23	+46	124	56 09	+46	123	56 55	+45	122	57 40	+44	121	58 24	+43	119
31	54 47	46	123	55 33	45	122	56 18	44	121	57 02	44	119	57 46	42	118
32	54 11	45	122	54 56	44	121	55 40	44	119	56 24	43	118	57 07	43	117
33	53 34	45	121	54 19	44	119	55 03	43	118	55 46	43	117	56 29	42	116
34	52 56	45	119	53 41	43	118	54 24	43	117	55 07	43	116	55 50	41	115
35	52 18	+44	118	53 02	+44	117	53 46	+42	116	54 28	+42	115	55 10	+41	113
36	51 40	44	117	52 24	43	116	53 07	42	115	53 49	41	114	54 30	41	112
37	51 02	43	116	51 45	42	115	52 27	42	114	53 09	41	113	53 50	41	111
38	50 23	42	115	51 05	43	114	51 48	41	113	52 29	41	112	53 10	40	110
39	49 43	43	114	50 26	42	113	51 08	41	112	51 49	40	110	52 29	40	109
40	49 04	+42	113	49 46	+41	112	50 27	+41	111	51 08	+41	109	51 49	+39	108
41	48 24	42	112	49 06	41	111	49 47	41	110	50 28	39	109	51 07	40	107
42	47 44	41	111	48 25	41	110	49 06	40	109	49 46	40	108	50 26	39	106
43	47 03	41	110	47 44	41	109	48 25	40	108	49 05	40	107	49 45	38	105
44	46 22	41	109	47 03	41	108	47 44	40	107	48 24	39	106	49 03	38	105
45	45 41	+41	108	46 22	+40	107	47 02	+40	106	47 42	+39	105	48 21	+38	104
46	45 00	41	107	45 41	40	106	46 21	39	105	47 00	39	104	47 39	38	103
47	44 19	40	106	44 59	40	105	45 39	39	104	46 18	39	103	46 57	38	102
48	43 37	41	105	44 18	39	104	44 57	39	103	45 36	39	102	46 15	37	101
49	42 56	40	104	43 36	39	103	44 15	39	102	44 54	38	101	45 32	38	100
50	42 14	+40	104	42 54	+39	103	43 33	+38	102	44 11	+39	100	44 50	+37	99
51	41 32	39	103	42 11	39	102	42 50	39	101	43 29	38	100	44 07	37	99
52	40 50	39	102	41 29	39	101	42 08	38	100	42 46	38	99	43 24	37	98
53	40 07	40	101	40 47	38	100	41 25	39	99	42 04	37	98	42 41	38	97
54	39 25	39	100	40 04	39	99	40 43	38	98	41 21	38	97	41 59	37	96
55	38 42	+39	100	39 21	+39	99	40 00	+38	98	40 38	+38	97	41 16	+37	96
56	38 00	39	99	38 39	38	98	39 17	38	97	39 55	38	96	40 33	37	95
57	37 17	39	98	37 56	38	97	38 34	38	96	39 12	38	95	39 50	36	94
58	36 34	39	97	37 13	38	96	37 51	38	95	38 29	38	94	39 07	36	93
59	35 51	39	96	36 30	38	95	37 08	38	95	37 46	37	94	38 23	37	93
60	35 08	+39	96	35 47	+38	95	36 25	+38	94	37 03	+37	93	37 40	+37	92
61	34 25	39	95	35 04	38	94	35 42	38	93	36 20	37	92	36 57	37	91
62	33 42	39	94	34 21	38	93	34 59	38	92	35 37	37	91	36 14	37	90
63	32 59	39	93	33 38	38	93	34 16	38	92	34 54	37	91	35 31	37	90
64	32 16	39	93	32 55	38	92	33 33	37	91	34 10	38	90	34 48	36	89
65	31 33	+39	92	32 12	+38	91	32 50	+37	90	33 27	+38	89	34 05	+36	88
66	30 50	38	91	31 28	38	90	32 06	38	90	32 44	37	89	33 21	37	88
67	30 07	38	91	30 45	38	90	31 23	38	89	32 01	37	88	32 38	37	87
68	29 24	38	90	30 02	38	89	30 40	38	88	31 18	37	87	31 55	37	86
69	28 41	38	89	29 19	38	88	29 57	38	87	30 35	37	87	31 12	37	86

LHA	25° Hc	25° d	25° Z	26° Hc	26° d	26° Z	27° Hc	27° d	27° Z	28° Hc	28° d	28° Z	29° Hc	29° d	29° Z	LHA
	° ′	′	°	° ′	′	°	° ′	′	°	° ′	′	°	° ′	′	°	
0	71 00	+60	180	72 00	+60	180	73 00	+60	180	74 00	+60	180	75 00	+60	180	360
1	70 59	60	177	71 59	60	177	72 59	60	177	73 59	60	177	74 59	60	177	359
2	70 56	60	174	71 56	59	174	72 55	60	174	73 55	60	174	74 55	60	173	358
3	70 51	59	172	71 50	60	171	72 50	59	171	73 49	60	171	74 49	59	170	357
4	70 43	60	169	71 43	59	169	72 42	59	168	73 41	59	167	74 40	59	167	356
5	70 34	+59	166	71 33	+59	166	72 32	+58	165	73 30	+59	164	74 29	+58	163	355
6	70 23	58	164	71 21	59	163	72 20	58	162	73 18	57	161	74 15	58	160	354
7	70 10	58	161	71 08	57	160	72 05	58	159	73 03	57	158	74 00	56	157	353
8	69 55	57	159	70 52	57	158	71 49	57	157	72 46	56	156	73 42	56	154	352
9	69 38	57	156	70 35	56	155	71 31	56	154	72 27	55	153	73 22	55	151	351
10	69 20	+56	154	70 16	+55	153	71 11	+55	151	72 06	+55	150	73 01	+54	149	350
11	69 00	55	151	69 55	55	150	70 50	54	149	71 44	54	148	72 38	52	146	349
12	68 38	55	149	69 33	54	148	70 27	53	146	71 20	53	145	72 13	51	144	348
13	68 15	54	147	69 09	53	145	70 02	52	144	70 54	52	143	71 46	51	141	347
14	67 51	53	145	68 44	52	143	69 36	52	142	70 28	50	140	71 18	50	139	346
15	67 25	+52	142	68 17	+52	141	69 09	+50	140	69 59	+50	138	70 49	+49	136	345
16	66 58	51	140	67 49	51	139	68 40	50	138	69 30	49	136	70 19	48	134	344
17	66 30	50	138	67 20	50	137	68 10	49	136	68 59	48	134	69 47	48	132	343
18	66 01	49	137	66 50	50	135	67 40	48	134	68 28	47	132	69 15	46	130	342
19	65 30	50	135	66 20	48	133	67 08	47	132	67 55	47	130	68 42	45	128	341
20	64 59	+49	133	65 48	+47	131	66 35	+47	130	67 22	+45	128	68 07	+45	127	340
21	64 27	48	131	65 15	47	130	66 02	46	128	66 48	44	127	67 32	44	125	339
22	63 54	47	130	64 41	46	128	65 27	46	127	66 13	44	125	66 57	43	123	338
23	63 21	46	128	64 07	45	126	64 52	45	125	65 37	43	123	66 20	42	122	337
24	62 46	46	126	63 32	45	125	64 17	43	123	65 00	43	122	65 43	42	120	336
25	62 11	+45	125	62 56	+44	123	63 40	+43	122	64 23	+43	120	65 06	+40	119	335
26	61 35	45	123	62 20	43	122	63 03	43	121	63 46	41	119	64 27	41	117	334
27	60 59	44	122	61 43	43	121	62 26	42	119	63 08	41	118	63 49	40	116	333
28	60 22	43	121	61 05	43	119	61 48	41	118	62 29	41	116	63 10	39	115	332
29	59 45	43	119	60 28	41	118	61 09	41	116	61 50	40	115	62 30	39	113	331
30	59 07	+42	118	59 49	+42	117	60 31	+40	115	61 11	+39	114	61 50	+39	112	330
31	58 28	42	117	59 10	41	115	59 51	40	114	60 31	39	113	61 10	38	111	329
32	57 50	41	116	58 31	41	114	59 12	39	113	59 51	39	111	60 30	37	110	328
33	57 11	41	114	57 52	40	113	58 32	39	112	59 11	38	110	59 49	37	109	327
34	56 31	41	113	57 12	40	112	57 52	38	111	58 30	38	109	59 08	37	108	326
35	55 51	+41	112	56 32	+39	111	57 11	+38	109	57 49	+38	108	58 27	+36	107	325
36	55 11	40	111	55 51	39	110	56 30	38	108	57 08	37	107	57 45	36	106	324
37	54 31	39	110	55 10	39	109	55 49	38	107	56 27	37	106	57 04	35	105	323
38	53 50	39	109	54 29	39	108	55 08	37	106	55 45	37	105	56 22	35	104	322
39	53 09	39	108	53 48	38	107	54 26	37	105	55 03	37	104	55 40	35	103	321
40	52 28	+39	107	53 07	+38	106	53 45	+36	104	54 21	+37	103	54 58	+35	102	320
41	51 47	38	106	52 25	38	105	53 03	36	104	53 39	36	102	54 15	35	101	319
42	51 05	38	105	51 43	38	104	52 21	36	103	52 57	36	101	53 33	34	100	318
43	50 23	38	104	51 01	37	103	51 38	37	102	52 15	35	100	52 50	35	99	317
44	49 41	38	103	50 19	37	102	50 56	36	101	51 32	36	100	52 08	34	98	316
45	48 59	+38	102	49 37	+37	101	50 14	+36	100	50 50	+35	99	51 25	+34	97	315
46	48 17	37	102	48 54	37	100	49 31	36	99	50 07	35	98	50 42	34	97	314
47	47 35	37	101	48 12	36	100	48 48	36	98	49 24	35	97	49 59	34	96	313
48	46 52	37	100	47 29	37	99	48 06	35	98	48 41	35	96	49 16	34	95	312
49	46 10	37	99	46 47	36	98	47 23	35	97	47 58	35	96	48 33	34	94	311
50	45 27	+37	98	46 04	+36	97	46 40	+35	96	47 15	+35	95	47 50	+34	94	310
51	44 44	37	98	45 21	36	96	45 57	35	95	46 32	35	94	47 07	34	93	309
52	44 01	37	97	44 38	36	96	45 14	35	94	45 49	35	93	46 24	34	92	308
53	43 19	36	96	43 55	36	95	44 31	35	94	45 06	35	93	45 41	33	91	307
54	42 36	36	95	43 12	36	94	43 48	35	93	44 23	34	92	44 57	34	91	306
55	41 53	+36	94	42 29	+36	93	43 05	+35	92	43 40	+34	91	44 14	+34	90	305
56	41 10	36	94	41 46	36	93	42 22	35	92	42 57	34	90	43 31	34	89	304
57	40 26	37	93	41 03	35	92	41 38	36	91	42 14	34	90	42 48	34	89	303
58	39 43	37	92	40 20	35	91	40 55	35	90	41 30	35	89	42 05	34	88	302
59	39 00	36	92	39 36	36	91	40 12	35	89	40 47	35	88	41 22	34	87	301
60	38 17	+36	91	38 53	+36	90	39 29	+35	89	40 04	+35	88	40 39	+34	87	300
61	37 34	36	90	38 10	36	89	38 46	35	88	39 21	35	87	39 56	34	86	299
62	36 51	36	89	37 27	36	88	38 03	35	87	38 38	35	86	39 13	34	85	298
63	36 08	36	89	36 44	36	88	37 20	35	87	37 55	35	86	38 30	34	85	297
64	35 24	37	88	36 01	36	87	36 37	35	86	37 12	35	85	37 47	34	84	296
65	34 41	+37	87	35 18	+35	86	35 53	+36	85	36 29	+35	84	37 04	+34	83	295
66	33 58	37	87	34 35	35	86	35 10	36	85	35 46	35	84	36 21	34	83	294
67	33 15	37	86	33 52	36	85	34 28	35	84	35 03	35	83	35 38	35	82	293
68	32 32	37	85	33 09	36	84	33 45	35	84	34 20	35	83	34 55	35	82	292
69	31 49	37	85	32 26	36	84	33 02	35	83	33 37	36	82	34 13	34	81	291

S. Lat. {LHA greater than 180°....... Zn=180−Z
{LHA less than 180°........... Zn=180+Z

DECLINATION (15°-29°) SAME NAME AS LATITUDE

N. Lat. {LHA greater than 180°...... Zn=Z
{LHA less than 180°.......... Zn=360−Z

DECLINATION (15°-29°) SAME NAME AS LATITUDE

LHA	15° Hc	d	Z	16° Hc	d	Z	17° Hc	d	Z	18° Hc	d	Z	19° Hc	d	Z
	° ′	′	°	° ′	′	°	° ′	′	°	° ′	′	°	° ′	′	°
70	24 40	+40	93	25 20	+40	92	26 00	+39	91	26 39	+40	90	27 19	+38	89
71	23 57	40	92	24 37	40	91	25 17	39	90	25 56	39	90	26 35	39	89
72	23 14	40	91	23 54	40	91	24 34	39	90	25 13	39	89	25 52	39	88
73	22 31	40	91	23 11	40	90	23 51	39	89	24 30	39	88	25 09	39	87
74	21 48	40	90	22 28	39	89	23 07	40	88	23 47	39	88	24 26	39	87
75	21 05	+40	89	21 45	+39	88	22 24	+40	88	23 04	+39	87	23 43	+39	86
76	20 22	39	89	21 01	40	88	21 41	40	87	22 21	39	86	23 00	39	85
77	19 38	40	88	20 18	40	87	20 58	40	86	21 38	39	86	22 17	39	85
78	18 55	40	87	19 35	40	86	20 15	40	86	20 55	39	85	21 34	39	84
79	18 12	40	87	18 52	40	86	19 32	40	85	20 12	39	84	20 51	39	83
80	17 29	+40	86	18 09	+40	85	18 49	+40	84	19 29	+39	83	20 08	+40	83
81	16 46	40	85	17 26	40	84	18 06	40	84	18 46	39	83	19 25	40	82
82	16 03	40	85	16 43	40	84	17 23	40	83	18 03	40	82	18 43	39	81
83	15 20	40	84	16 00	41	83	16 41	39	82	17 20	40	82	18 00	40	81
84	14 37	41	83	15 18	40	82	15 58	40	82	16 38	40	81	17 18	39	80
85	13 54	+41	82	14 35	+40	82	15 15	+40	81	15 55	+40	80	16 35	+40	79
86	13 12	40	82	13 52	41	81	14 33	40	80	15 13	40	80	15 53	40	79
87	12 29	41	81	13 10	40	80	13 50	40	80	14 30	41	79	15 11	39	78
88	11 46	41	80	12 27	41	80	13 08	40	79	13 48	40	78	14 28	40	77
89	11 04	41	80	11 45	40	79	12 25	41	78	13 06	40	78	13 46	41	77
90	10 22	+40	79	11 02	+41	78	11 43	+41	78	12 24	+40	77	13 04	+41	76
91	09 39	41	78	10 20	41	78	11 01	41	77	11 42	40	76	12 22	41	75
92	08 57	41	78	09 38	41	77	10 19	41	76	11 00	41	76	11 41	40	75
93	08 15	41	77	08 56	41	76	09 37	41	76	10 18	41	75	10 59	41	74
94	07 33	41	76	08 14	41	76	08 55	42	75	09 37	41	74	10 18	41	74
95	06 51	+41	76	07 32	+42	75	08 14	+41	74	08 55	+41	74	09 36	+42	73
96	06 09	42	75	06 51	41	74	07 32	42	74	08 14	41	73	08 55	42	72
97	05 28	41	74	06 09	42	74	06 51	42	73	07 33	41	72	08 14	42	72
98	04 46	42	74	05 28	42	73	06 10	42	72	06 52	41	72	07 33	42	71
99	04 05	42	73	04 47	42	72	05 29	42	72	06 11	42	71	06 53	42	70
100	03 23	+43	72	04 06	+42	72	04 48	+42	71	05 30	+42	70	06 12	+42	70
101	02 42	43	72	03 25	42	71	04 07	43	70	04 50	42	70	05 32	42	69
102	02 01	43	71	02 44	43	70	03 27	42	70	04 09	43	69	04 52	42	68
103	01 21	43	70	02 04	42	70	02 46	43	69	03 29	43	68	04 12	42	67
104	00 40	43	70	01 23	43	69	02 06	43	68	02 49	43	68	03 32	43	67
105	00 00	+43	69	00 43	+43	68	01 26	+43	68	02 09	+43	67	02 52	+43	66
106	−0 40	43	68	00 03	43	68	00 46	44	67	01 30	43	66	02 13	43	65
107	−1 20	43	68	−0 37	44	67	00 07	43	66	00 50	44	65	01 34	43	65
108	−2 00	44	67	−1 16	43	66	−0 33	44	65	00 11	44	65	00 55	44	64
109	−2 40	44	66	−1 56	44	65	−1 12	44	65	−0 28	44	64	00 16	44	63
110	−3 19	+44	65	−2 35	+44	65	−1 51	+45	64	−1 06	+44	63	−0 22	+44	63
111	−3 58	44	65	−3 14	45	64	−2 29	44	63	−1 45	45	63	−1 00	44	62
112	−4 37	45	64	−3 52	44	63	−3 08	45	63	−2 23	45	62	−1 38	44	61
113	−5 16	45	63	−4 31	45	63	−3 46	45	62	−3 01	45	61	−2 16	45	61
114	−5 54	45	62	−5 09	45	62	−4 24	45	61	−3 39	45	61	−2 54	46	60
115				−5 47	+45	61	−5 02	+46	60	−4 16	+45	60	−3 31	+46	59
116							−5 39	46	60	−4 53	45	59	−4 08	46	58
117										−5 30	46	58	−4 44	46	58
118										−6 07	46	58	−5 21	47	57
119													−5 57	47	56

LHA	20° Hc	d	Z	21° Hc	d	Z	22° Hc	d	Z	23° Hc	d	Z	24° Hc	d	Z
	° ′	′	°	° ′	′	°	° ′	′	°	° ′	′	°	° ′	′	°
70	27 57	+39	89	28 36	+38	88	29 14	+38	87	29 52	+37	86	30 29	+37	85
71	27 14	39	88	27 53	38	87	28 31	38	86	29 09	37	85	29 46	37	84
72	26 31	39	87	27 10	38	86	27 48	38	85	28 26	37	85	29 03	37	84
73	25 48	39	87	26 27	38	86	27 05	38	85	27 43	37	84	28 20	38	83
74	25 05	39	86	25 44	38	85	26 22	38	84	27 00	38	83	27 38	37	82
75	24 22	+39	85	25 01	+38	84	25 39	+38	84	26 17	+38	83	26 55	+37	82
76	23 39	39	85	24 18	38	84	24 56	38	83	25 34	38	82	26 12	38	81
77	22 56	39	84	23 35	38	83	24 13	39	82	24 52	38	81	25 30	37	80
78	22 13	39	83	22 52	39	82	23 31	38	82	24 09	38	81	24 47	38	80
79	21 30	39	83	22 09	39	82	22 48	38	81	23 26	39	80	24 05	37	79
80	20 48	+39	82	21 27	+38	81	22 05	+39	80	22 44	+38	79	23 22	+38	79
81	20 05	39	81	20 44	39	80	21 23	39	80	22 02	38	79	22 40	38	78
82	19 22	39	81	20 01	39	80	20 40	39	79	21 19	39	78	21 58	38	77
83	18 40	39	80	19 19	39	79	19 58	39	78	20 37	39	78	21 16	38	77
84	17 57	40	79	18 37	39	78	19 16	39	78	19 55	39	77	20 34	38	76
85	17 15	+39	79	17 54	+40	78	18 34	+39	77	19 13	+39	76	19 52	+39	75
86	16 33	39	78	17 12	40	77	17 52	39	76	18 31	39	76	19 10	39	75
87	15 50	40	77	16 30	40	77	17 10	39	76	17 49	40	75	18 29	39	74
88	15 08	40	77	15 48	40	76	16 28	40	75	17 08	39	74	17 47	40	74
89	14 27	40	76	15 07	40	75	15 47	39	74	16 26	40	74	17 06	39	73
90	13 45	+40	75	14 25	+40	75	15 05	+40	74	15 45	+40	73	16 25	+39	72
91	13 03	40	75	13 43	41	74	14 24	40	73	15 04	40	72	15 44	40	72
92	12 21	41	74	13 02	40	73	13 42	41	73	14 23	40	72	15 03	40	71
93	11 40	41	73	12 21	40	73	13 01	41	72	13 42	40	71	14 22	40	70
94	10 59	41	73	11 40	40	72	12 20	41	71	13 01	41	71	13 42	40	70
95	10 18	+41	72	10 59	+41	71	11 40	+40	71	12 20	+41	70	13 01	+41	69
96	09 37	41	71	10 18	41	71	10 59	41	70	11 40	41	69	12 21	41	68
97	08 56	41	71	09 37	42	70	10 19	41	69	11 00	41	69	11 41	41	68
98	08 15	42	70	08 57	41	69	09 38	42	69	10 20	41	68	11 01	41	67
99	07 35	41	69	08 16	42	69	08 58	42	68	09 40	41	67	10 21	42	67
100	06 54	+42	69	07 36	+42	68	08 18	+42	67	09 00	+42	67	09 42	+42	66
101	06 14	42	68	06 56	42	67	07 38	43	67	08 21	42	66	09 03	41	65
102	05 34	43	67	06 17	42	67	06 59	42	66	07 41	42	65	08 23	43	65
103	04 54	43	67	05 37	43	66	06 20	42	65	07 02	43	65	07 45	42	64
104	04 15	43	66	04 58	43	65	05 41	42	65	06 23	43	64	07 06	43	63
105	03 35	+44	65	04 19	+43	65	05 02	+43	64	05 45	+42	63	06 27	+43	63
106	02 56	44	65	03 40	43	64	04 23	43	63	05 06	43	63	05 49	43	62
107	02 17	44	64	03 01	43	63	03 44	44	63	04 28	43	62	05 11	44	61
108	01 39	43	63	02 22	44	63	03 06	44	62	03 50	43	61	04 33	44	61
109	01 00	44	63	01 44	44	62	02 28	44	61	03 12	44	61	03 56	44	60
110	00 22	+44	62	01 06	+44	61	01 50	+45	61	02 35	+44	60	03 19	+44	59
111	−0 16	44	61	00 28	45	61	01 13	44	60	01 57	45	59	02 42	44	59
112	−0 54	45	61	−0 09	45	60	00 36	44	59	01 20	45	59	02 05	45	58
113	−1 31	45	60	−0 46	45	59	−0 01	45	59	00 44	45	58	01 29	45	57
114	−2 08	45	59	−1 23	45	59	−0 38	45	58	00 07	45	57	00 52	46	57
115	−2 45	+45	58	−2 00	+46	58	−1 14	+45	57	−0 29	+46	57	00 17	+45	56
116	−3 22	46	58	−2 36	45	57	−1 51	46	56	−1 05	46	56	−0 19	46	55
117	−3 58	46	57	−3 12	46	56	−2 26	46	56	−1 40	46	55	−0 54	46	54
118	−4 34	46	56	−3 48	46	56	−3 02	46	55	−2 16	47	54	−1 29	46	54
119	−5 10	46	56	−4 24	47	55	−3 37	46	54	−2 51	47	54	−2 04	47	53
120	−5 46	+47	55	−4 59	+47	54	−4 12	+47	54	−3 25	+47	53	−2 38	+47	52
121				−5 34	47	53	−4 47	48	53	−3 59	47	52	−3 12	47	52
122				−6 08	47	53	−5 21	48	52	−4 33	47	52	−3 46	47	51
123							−5 55	48	51	−5 07	48	51	−4 19	47	50
124										−5 40	48	50	−4 52	48	49
125													−5 25	+48	49
126													−5 57	48	48

LHA	25° Hc	d	Z	26° Hc	d	Z	27° Hc	d	Z	28° Hc	d	Z	29° Hc	d	Z	LHA
	° ′	′	°	° ′	′	°	° ′	′	°	° ′	′	°	° ′	′	°	
70	31 06	+37	84	31 43	+36	83	32 19	+36	82	32 55	+35	81	33 30	+35	80	290
71	30 23	37	83	31 00	36	83	31 36	36	82	32 12	36	81	32 48	35	80	289
72	29 40	37	83	30 17	37	82	30 54	36	81	31 30	35	80	32 05	35	79	288
73	28 58	36	82	29 34	37	81	30 11	36	80	30 47	36	79	31 23	35	78	287
74	28 15	37	82	28 52	37	81	29 29	36	80	30 05	36	79	30 41	35	78	286
75	27 32	+37	81	28 09	+37	80	28 46	+36	79	29 22	+37	78	29 59	+35	77	285
76	26 50	37	80	27 27	37	79	28 04	36	78	28 40	36	78	29 16	36	77	284
77	26 07	38	80	26 45	37	79	27 22	36	78	27 58	37	77	28 35	35	76	283
78	25 25	37	79	26 02	37	78	26 39	37	77	27 16	37	76	27 53	36	75	282
79	24 42	38	78	25 20	37	78	25 57	37	77	26 34	37	76	27 11	36	75	281
80	24 00	+38	78	24 38	+37	77	25 15	+38	76	25 53	+36	75	26 29	+37	74	280
81	23 18	38	77	23 56	38	76	24 34	37	75	25 11	37	75	25 48	37	74	279
82	22 36	38	76	23 14	38	76	23 52	37	75	24 29	38	74	25 07	36	73	278
83	21 54	38	76	22 32	38	75	23 10	38	74	23 48	37	73	24 25	37	72	277
84	21 12	39	75	21 51	38	74	22 29	38	74	23 07	37	73	23 44	38	72	276
85	20 31	+38	75	21 09	+39	74	21 48	+38	73	22 26	+37	72	23 03	+38	71	275
86	19 49	39	74	20 28	38	73	21 06	39	72	21 45	38	72	22 23	37	71	274
87	19 08	39	73	19 47	38	73	20 25	39	72	21 04	38	71	21 42	38	70	273
88	18 27	39	73	19 06	38	72	19 44	39	71	20 23	38	70	21 01	39	70	272
89	17 45	40	72	18 25	39	71	19 04	38	71	19 42	39	70	20 21	38	69	271
90	17 04	+40	72	17 44	+39	71	18 23	+39	70	19 02	+39	69	19 41	+38	68	270
91	16 24	39	71	17 03	40	70	17 43	39	69	18 22	39	69	19 01	39	68	269
92	15 43	40	70	16 23	39	69	17 02	40	69	17 42	39	68	18 21	39	67	268
93	15 02	40	70	15 42	40	69	16 22	40	68	17 02	39	67	17 41	40	67	267
94	14 22	40	69	15 02	40	68	15 42	40	67	16 22	40	67	17 02	39	66	266
95	13 42	+40	68	14 22	+40	68	15 02	+41	67	15 43	+40	66	16 23	+39	65	265
96	13 02	40	68	13 42	41	67	14 23	40	66	15 03	41	65	15 44	40	65	264
97	12 22	41	67	13 03	41	66	13 44	40	66	14 24	41	65	15 05	40	64	263
98	11 42	41	66	12 23	41	66	13 04	41	65	13 45	41	64	14 26	40	63	262
99	11 03	41	66	11 44	41	65	12 25	41	64	13 06	41	64	13 47	41	63	261
100	10 24	+41	65	11 05	+42	64	11 47	+41	64	12 28	+41	63	13 09	+41	62	260
101	09 44	42	65	10 26	42	64	11 08	42	63	11 50	41	62	12 31	41	62	259
102	09 06	42	64	09 48	42	63	10 30	41	62	11 11	42	62	11 53	42	61	258
103	08 27	42	63	09 09	42	63	09 51	43	62	10 34	42	61	11 16	42	60	257
104	07 49	42	63	08 31	43	62	09 14	42	61	09 56	42	60	10 38	42	60	256
105	07 10	+43	62	07 53	+43	61	08 36	+43	61	09 19	+42	60	10 01	+43	59	255
106	06 32	43	61	07 15	43	61	07 58	43	60	08 41	43	59	09 24	43	58	254
107	05 55	43	61	06 38	43	60	07 21	43	59	08 04	44	59	08 48	43	58	253
108	05 17	44	60	06 01	43	59	06 44	44	59	07 28	43	58	08 11	43	57	252
109	04 40	44	59	05 24	44	59	06 08	43	58	06 51	44	57	07 35	44	57	251
110	04 03	+44	59	04 47	+44	58	05 31	+44	57	06 15	+44	57	06 59	+44	56	250
111	03 26	45	58	04 11	44	57	04 55	44	57	05 39	45	56	06 24	44	55	249
112	02 50	44	57	03 34	45	57	04 19	45	56	05 04	44	55	05 48	45	55	248
113	02 14	44	57	02 58	45	56	03 43	45	55	04 28	45	55	05 13	45	54	247
114	01 38	45	56	02 23	45	55	03 08	45	55	03 53	45	54	04 38	45	53	246
115	01 02	+46	55	01 48	+45	55	02 33	+45	54	03 18	+46	53	04 04	+45	53	245
116	00 27	46	55	01 13	45	54	01 58	46	53	02 44	46	53	03 30	45	52	244
117	−0 08	46	54	00 38	46	53	01 24	46	53	02 10	46	52	02 56	46	51	243
118	−0 43	46	53	00 03	47	53	00 50	46	52	01 36	46	51	02 22	47	51	242
119	−1 17	46	52	−0 31	47	52	00 16	47	51	01 03	46	51	01 49	47	50	241
120	−1 51	+47	52	−1 04	+46	51	−0 18	+47	51	00 29	+47	50	01 16	+47	49	240
121	−2 25	47	51	−1 38	47	50	−0 51	48	50	−0 03	47	49	00 44	47	49	239
122	−2 59	48	50	−2 11	48	50	−1 23	47	49	−0 36	48	48	00 12	47	48	238
123	−3 32	48	50	−2 44	48	49	−1 56	48	48	−1 08	48	48	−0 20	48	47	237
124	−4 04	48	49	−3 16	48	48	−2 28	48	48	−1 40	48	47	−0 52	48	46	236
125	−4 37	+49	48	−3 48	+48	48	−3 00	+49	47	−2 11	+48	46	−1 23	+49	46	235
126	−5 09	49	47	−4 20	49	47	−3 31	49	46	−2 42	48	46	−1 54	49	45	234
127	−5 40	49	47	−4 51	49	46	−4 02	49	46	−3 13	49	45	−2 24	49	44	233
128				−5 22	49	45	−4 33	50	45	−3 43	49	44	−2 54	50	44	232
129				−5 53	50	45	−5 03	50	44	−4 13	50	43	−3 23	49	43	231
130							−5 33	+50	43	−4 43	+50	43	−3 53	+50	42	230
131										−5 12	51	42	−4 21	50	41	229
132										−5 40	50	41	−4 50	51	41	228
133													−5 18	51	40	227
134													−5 45	51	39	226

DECLINATION (15°-29°) CONTRARY NAME TO LATITUDE

LHA	15° Hc	d	Z	16° Hc	d	Z	17° Hc	d	Z	18° Hc	d	Z	19° Hc	d	Z
84	−6 09	42	105	276											
83	−5 28	41	106	−6 09	42	106	277								
82	−4 46	42	106	−5 28	42	107	−6 10	42	108	278					
81	−4 05	42	107	−4 47	42	108	−5 29	42	108	−6 11	42	109	279		
80	−3 23	−43	108	−4 06	−42	108	−4 48	−42	109	−5 30	−42	110	−6 12	−42	110
79	−2 42	43	108	−3 25	42	109	−4 07	43	110	−4 50	42	110	−5 32	42	111
78	−2 01	43	109	−2 44	43	110	−3 27	42	110	−4 09	43	111	−4 52	42	112
77	−1 21	43	110	−2 04	42	110	−2 46	43	111	−3 29	43	112	−4 12	42	113
76	−0 40	43	110	−1 23	43	111	−2 06	43	112	−2 49	43	112	−3 32	43	113
75	00 00	−43	111	−0 43	−43	112	−1 26	−43	112	−2 09	−43	113	−2 52	−43	114
74	00 40	43	112	−0 03	43	112	−0 46	44	113	−1 30	43	114	−2 13	43	115
73	01 20	43	112	00 37	44	113	−0 07	43	114	−0 50	44	115	−1 34	43	115
72	02 00	44	113	01 16	43	114	00 33	44	115	−0 11	44	115	−0 55	44	116
71	02 40	44	114	01 56	44	115	01 12	44	115	00 28	44	116	−0 16	44	117
70	03 19	−44	115	02 35	−44	115	01 51	−45	116	01 06	−44	117	00 22	−44	117

LHA	20° Hc	d	Z	21° Hc	d	Z	22° Hc	d	Z	23° Hc	d	Z	24° Hc	d	Z
80	280														
79	−6 14	42	112	281											
78	−5 34	43	113	−6 17	42	113	282								
77	−4 54	43	113	−5 37	43	114	283								
76	−4 15	43	114	−4 58	43	115	−5 41	42	115	284					
75	−3 35	−44	115	−4 19	−43	115	−5 02	−43	116	−5 45	−42	117	285		
74	−2 56	44	115	−3 40	43	116	−4 23	43	117	−5 06	43	117	−5 49	43	118
73	−2 17	44	116	−3 01	43	117	−3 44	44	117	−4 28	43	118	−5 11	44	119
72	−1 39	43	117	−2 22	44	117	−3 06	44	118	−3 50	43	119	−4 33	44	119
71	−1 00	44	117	−1 44	44	118	−2 28	44	119	−3 12	44	119	−3 56	44	120
70	−0 22	−44	118	−1 06	−44	119	−1 50	−45	119	−2 35	−44	120	−3 19	−44	121

LHA	25° Hc	d	Z	26° Hc	d	Z	27° Hc	d	Z	28° Hc	d	Z	29° Hc	d	Z
74	286														
73	−5 55	43	119	287											
72	−5 17	44	120	−6 01	43	121	288								
71	−4 40	44	121	−5 24	44	121	−6 08	43	122	289					
70	−4 03	−44	121	−4 47	−44	122	−5 31	−44	123	290					

S. Lat. {LHA greater than 180°........ Zn=180−Z
{LHA less than 180°........... Zn=180+Z

N. Lat. {LHA greater than 180°....... Zn=Z / LHA less than 180°........... Zn=360−Z}

DECLINATION (15°-29°) CONTRARY NAME TO LATITUDE

LHA	15° Hc	d	Z	16° Hc	d	Z	17° Hc	d	Z	18° Hc	d	Z	19° Hc	d	Z
	° ′	′	°	° ′	′	°	° ′	′	°	° ′	′	°	° ′	′	°
69	03 58	44	115	03 14	45	116	02 29	44	117	01 45	45	117	01 00	44	118
68	04 37	45	116	03 52	44	117	03 08	45	117	02 23	45	118	01 38	44	119
67	05 16	45	117	04 31	45	117	03 46	45	118	03 01	45	119	02 16	45	119
66	05 54	45	118	05 09	45	118	04 24	45	119	03 39	45	119	02 54	46	120
65	06 32	−45	118	05 47	−45	119	05 02	−46	120	04 16	−45	120	03 31	−46	121
64	07 10	45	119	06 25	46	120	05 39	46	120	04 53	45	121	04 08	46	122
63	07 48	46	120	07 02	46	120	06 16	46	121	05 30	46	122	04 44	46	122
62	08 25	46	120	07 39	46	121	06 53	46	122	06 07	46	122	05 21	47	123
61	09 02	46	121	08 16	46	122	07 30	47	123	06 43	46	123	05 57	47	124
60	09 39	−47	122	08 52	−46	123	08 06	−47	123	07 19	−46	124	06 33	−47	125
59	10 16	47	123	09 29	47	123	08 42	47	124	07 55	47	125	07 08	47	125
58	10 52	47	124	10 05	48	124	09 17	47	125	08 30	47	125	07 43	47	126
57	11 27	47	124	10 40	47	125	09 53	48	126	09 05	47	126	08 18	48	127
56	12 03	48	125	11 15	47	126	10 28	48	126	09 40	48	127	08 52	48	128
55	12 38	−48	126	11 50	−48	126	11 02	−48	127	10 14	−48	128	09 26	−48	128
54	13 13	48	127	12 25	48	127	11 37	49	128	10 48	48	128	10 00	48	129
53	13 47	48	127	12 59	48	128	12 11	49	129	11 22	49	129	10 33	48	130
52	14 22	49	128	13 33	49	129	12 44	49	129	11 55	49	130	11 06	49	131
51	14 55	49	129	14 06	49	130	13 17	49	130	12 28	49	131	11 39	49	131
50	15 29	−50	130	14 39	−49	130	13 50	−49	131	13 01	−50	132	12 11	−50	132
49	16 02	50	131	15 12	50	131	14 22	49	132	13 33	50	132	12 43	50	133
48	16 34	50	132	15 44	50	132	14 54	50	133	14 04	50	133	13 14	50	134
47	17 06	50	132	16 16	50	133	15 26	50	134	14 36	51	134	13 45	50	135
46	17 38	51	133	16 47	50	134	15 57	51	134	15 06	50	135	14 16	51	135
45	18 09	−51	134	17 18	−50	135	16 28	−51	135	15 37	−51	136	14 46	−51	136
44	18 40	51	135	17 49	51	136	16 58	51	136	16 07	52	137	15 15	51	137
43	19 10	51	136	18 19	51	136	17 28	52	137	16 36	52	137	15 44	51	138
42	19 40	51	137	18 49	52	137	17 57	52	138	17 05	52	138	16 13	52	139
41	20 10	52	138	19 18	52	138	18 26	53	139	17 33	52	139	16 41	52	140
40	20 38	−52	138	19 46	−52	139	18 54	−53	140	18 01	−52	140	17 09	−53	141
39	21 07	53	139	20 14	52	140	19 22	53	140	18 29	53	141	17 36	53	141
38	21 35	53	140	20 42	53	141	19 49	53	141	18 56	53	142	18 03	53	142
37	22 02	53	141	21 09	53	142	20 16	54	142	19 22	53	143	18 29	53	143
36	22 29	54	142	21 35	53	143	20 42	54	143	19 48	53	144	18 55	54	144
35	22 55	−54	143	22 01	−53	144	21 08	−54	144	20 14	−54	145	19 20	−54	145
34	23 21	54	144	22 27	54	144	21 33	54	145	20 39	55	145	19 44	54	146
33	23 46	54	145	22 52	55	145	21 57	54	146	21 03	55	146	20 08	54	147
32	24 10	54	146	23 16	55	146	22 21	55	147	21 26	54	147	20 32	55	148
31	24 34	55	147	23 39	55	147	22 44	55	148	21 49	55	148	20 54	55	149
30	24 58	−56	148	24 02	−55	148	23 07	−55	149	22 12	−55	149	21 17	−56	150
29	25 20	55	149	24 25	56	149	23 29	55	150	22 34	56	150	21 38	55	151
28	25 42	55	150	24 47	56	150	23 51	56	151	22 55	56	151	21 59	56	151
27	26 04	56	151	25 08	56	151	24 12	56	152	23 16	56	152	22 20	57	152
26	26 24	56	152	25 28	56	152	24 32	56	153	23 36	57	153	22 39	56	153
25	26 44	−56	153	25 48	−57	153	24 51	−56	154	23 55	−57	154	22 58	−56	154
24	27 04	57	154	26 07	57	154	25 10	56	155	24 14	57	155	23 17	57	155
23	27 23	57	155	26 26	57	155	25 29	57	156	24 32	58	156	23 34	57	156
22	27 41	58	156	26 43	57	156	25 46	57	157	24 49	57	157	23 52	58	157
21	27 58	58	157	27 00	57	157	26 03	58	158	25 05	57	158	24 08	58	158
20	28 14	−57	158	27 17	−58	158	26 19	−58	159	25 21	−57	159	24 24	−58	159
19	28 30	58	159	27 32	58	159	26 34	58	160	25 36	57	160	24 39	58	160
18	28 45	58	160	27 47	58	160	26 49	58	161	25 51	58	161	24 53	58	161
17	29 00	59	161	28 01	58	161	27 03	58	162	26 05	59	162	25 06	58	162
16	29 13	58	162	28 15	59	163	27 16	58	163	26 18	59	163	25 19	58	163
15	29 26	−59	163	28 27	−58	164	27 29	−59	164	26 30	−59	164	25 31	−59	164
14	29 38	59	164	28 39	59	165	27 40	59	165	26 41	58	165	25 43	59	165
13	29 49	59	166	28 50	59	166	27 51	59	166	26 52	59	166	25 53	59	166
12	29 59	59	167	29 00	59	167	28 01	59	167	27 02	59	167	26 03	59	167
11	30 09	59	168	29 10	59	168	28 11	60	168	27 11	59	168	26 12	59	168
10	30 18	−60	169	29 18	−59	169	28 19	−59	169	27 20	−60	169	26 20	−59	169
9	30 26	60	170	29 26	59	170	28 27	60	170	27 27	59	170	26 28	60	171
8	30 33	60	171	29 33	59	171	28 34	60	171	27 34	59	171	26 35	60	172
7	30 39	59	172	29 40	60	172	28 40	60	172	27 40	59	173	26 41	60	173
6	30 45	60	173	29 45	60	173	28 45	60	174	27 45	59	174	26 46	60	174
5	30 49	−59	174	29 50	−60	175	28 50	−60	175	27 50	−60	175	26 50	−60	175
4	30 53	60	176	29 53	60	176	28 53	59	176	27 54	60	176	26 54	60	176
3	30 56	60	177	29 56	60	177	28 56	60	177	27 56	60	177	26 56	59	177
2	30 58	60	178	29 58	60	178	28 58	60	178	27 58	60	178	26 58	60	178
1	31 00	60	179	30 00	60	179	29 00	60	179	28 00	60	179	27 00	60	179
0	31 00	−60	180	30 00	−60	180	29 00	−60	180	28 00	−60	180	27 00	−60	180

LHA	20° Hc	d	Z	21° Hc	d	Z	22° Hc	d	Z	23° Hc	d	Z	24° Hc	d	Z
	° ′	′	°	° ′	′	°	° ′	′	°	° ′	′	°	° ′	′	°
69	00 16	44	119	−0 28	45	119	−1 13	44	120	−1 57	45	121	−2 42	44	121
68	00 54	45	119	00 09	45	120	−0 36	44	121	−1 20	45	121	−2 05	45	122
67	01 31	45	120	00 46	45	121	00 01	45	121	−0 44	45	122	−1 29	45	123
66	02 08	45	121	01 23	45	121	00 38	45	122	−0 07	45	123	−0 52	46	123
65	02 45	−45	122	02 00	−46	122	01 14	−45	123	00 29	−46	123	−0 17	−45	124
64	03 22	46	122	02 36	45	123	01 51	46	124	01 05	46	124	00 19	46	125
63	03 58	46	123	03 12	46	124	02 26	46	124	01 40	46	125	00 54	46	126
62	04 34	46	124	03 48	46	124	03 02	46	125	02 16	47	126	01 29	46	126
61	05 10	46	124	04 24	47	125	03 37	46	126	02 51	47	126	02 04	47	127
60	05 46	−47	125	04 59	−47	126	04 12	−47	126	03 25	−47	127	02 38	−47	128
59	06 21	47	126	05 34	47	127	04 47	48	127	03 59	47	128	03 12	47	128
58	06 56	48	127	06 08	47	127	05 21	48	128	04 33	47	128	03 46	47	129
57	07 30	47	127	06 43	48	128	05 55	48	129	05 07	48	129	04 19	47	130
56	08 04	48	128	07 16	48	129	06 28	48	129	05 40	48	130	04 52	48	131
55	08 38	−48	129	07 50	−48	130	07 02	−49	130	06 13	−48	131	05 25	−48	131
54	09 12	49	130	08 23	49	130	07 34	48	131	06 46	49	131	05 57	48	132
53	09 45	49	130	08 56	49	131	08 07	49	132	07 18	49	132	06 29	49	133
52	10 17	49	131	09 28	49	132	08 39	49	132	07 50	49	133	07 01	50	134
51	10 50	50	132	10 00	49	133	09 11	50	133	08 21	49	134	07 32	50	134
50	11 21	−49	133	10 32	−50	133	09 42	−50	134	08 52	−50	135	08 02	−49	135
49	11 53	50	134	11 03	50	134	10 13	50	135	09 23	50	135	08 33	50	136
48	12 24	50	134	11 34	51	135	10 43	50	136	09 53	50	136	09 03	51	137
47	12 55	51	135	12 04	51	136	11 13	50	136	10 23	51	137	09 32	51	137
46	13 25	51	136	12 34	51	137	11 43	51	137	10 52	51	138	10 01	51	138
45	13 55	−52	137	13 03	−51	137	12 12	−51	138	11 21	−51	138	10 30	−52	139
44	14 24	52	138	13 32	51	138	12 41	52	139	11 49	51	139	10 58	52	140
43	14 53	52	139	14 01	52	139	13 09	52	140	12 17	52	140	11 25	51	141
42	15 21	52	139	14 29	52	140	13 37	52	140	12 45	52	141	11 53	53	141
41	15 49	52	140	14 57	53	141	14 04	52	141	13 12	53	142	12 19	52	142
40	16 16	−52	141	15 24	−53	142	14 31	−53	142	13 38	−52	143	12 46	−53	143
39	16 43	53	142	15 50	53	142	14 57	53	143	14 04	53	143	13 11	53	144
38	17 10	53	143	16 17	54	143	15 23	53	144	14 30	53	144	13 37	54	145
37	17 36	54	144	16 42	53	144	15 49	54	144	14 55	54	145	14 01	53	146
36	18 01	54	145	17 07	54	145	16 13	54	145	15 19	53	146	14 26	54	146
35	18 26	−54	145	17 32	−54	146	16 38	−55	146	15 43	−54	147	14 49	−54	147
34	18 50	54	146	17 56	55	147	17 01	54	147	16 07	55	148	15 12	54	148
33	19 14	55	147	18 19	55	148	17 24	54	148	16 30	55	149	15 35	55	149
32	19 37	55	148	18 42	55	149	17 47	55	149	16 52	55	149	15 57	55	150
31	19 59	55	149	19 04	55	149	18 09	55	150	17 14	56	150	16 18	55	151
30	20 21	−55	150	19 26	−56	150	18 30	−55	151	17 35	−56	151	16 39	−55	152
29	20 43	56	151	19 47	56	151	18 51	56	152	17 55	56	152	16 59	56	152
28	21 03	56	152	20 07	56	152	19 11	56	153	18 15	56	153	17 19	56	153
27	21 23	56	153	20 27	56	153	19 31	56	154	18 35	57	154	17 38	56	154
26	21 43	57	154	20 46	56	154	19 50	57	154	18 53	56	155	17 57	57	155
25	22 02	−57	155	21 05	−57	155	20 08	−57	155	19 11	−56	156	18 15	−57	156
24	22 20	57	156	21 23	57	156	20 26	57	156	19 29	57	157	18 32	57	157
23	22 37	57	157	21 40	57	157	20 43	57	157	19 46	58	158	18 48	57	158
22	22 54	57	158	21 57	58	158	20 59	57	158	20 02	58	159	19 04	57	159
21	23 10	57	159	22 13	58	159	21 15	58	159	20 17	57	159	19 20	58	160
20	23 26	−58	160	22 28	−58	160	21 30	−58	160	20 32	−58	160	19 34	−58	161
19	23 41	58	161	22 43	59	161	21 44	58	161	20 46	58	161	19 48	58	162
18	23 55	59	162	22 56	58	162	21 58	58	162	21 00	58	162	20 02	59	163
17	24 08	58	163	23 10	59	163	22 11	58	163	21 13	59	163	20 14	58	164
16	24 21	59	164	23 22	59	164	22 23	58	164	21 25	59	164	20 26	58	164
15	24 32	−58	165	23 34	−59	165	22 35	−59	165	21 36	−59	165	20 37	−58	165
14	24 44	59	166	23 45	59	166	22 46	59	166	21 47	59	166	20 48	59	166
13	24 54	59	167	23 55	59	167	22 56	59	167	21 57	59	167	20 58	59	167
12	25 04	59	168	24 05	60	168	23 05	59	168	22 06	59	168	21 07	59	168
11	25 13	60	169	24 13	59	169	23 14	59	169	22 15	60	169	21 15	59	169
10	25 21	−60	170	24 21	−59	170	23 22	−59	170	22 23	−60	170	21 23	−59	170
9	25 28	59	171	24 29	60	171	23 29	59	171	22 30	60	171	21 30	59	171
8	25 35	60	172	24 35	59	172	23 36	60	172	22 36	60	172	21 36	59	172
7	25 41	60	173	24 41	60	173	23 41	59	173	22 42	60	173	21 42	60	173
6	25 46	60	174	24 46	60	174	23 46	59	174	22 47	60	174	21 47	60	174
5	25 50	−60	175	24 50	−59	175	23 51	−60	175	22 51	−60	175	21 51	−60	175
4	25 54	60	176	24 54	60	176	23 54	60	176	22 54	60	176	21 54	60	176
3	25 57	60	177	24 57	60	177	23 57	60	177	22 57	60	177	21 57	60	177
2	25 58	60	178	24 58	59	178	23 59	60	178	22 59	60	178	21 59	60	178
1	26 00	60	179	25 00	60	179	24 00	60	179	23 00	60	179	22 00	60	179
0	26 00	−60	180	25 00	−60	180	24 00	−60	180	23 00	−60	180	22 00	−60	180

LHA	25° Hc	d	Z	26° Hc	d	Z	27° Hc	d	Z	28° Hc	d	Z	29° Hc	d	Z	LHA
	° ′	′	°	° ′	′	°	° ′	′	°	° ′	′	°	° ′	′	°	
69	−3 26	45	122	−4 11	44	123	−4 55	44	123	−5 39	45	124				291
68	−2 50	44	123	−3 34	45	123	−4 19	45	124	−5 04	44	125	−5 48	45	125	292
67	−2 14	44	123	−2 58	45	124	−3 43	45	125	−4 28	45	125	−5 13	45	126	293
66	−1 38	45	124	−2 23	45	125	−3 08	45	125	−3 53	45	126	−4 38	45	127	294
65	−1 02	−46	125	−1 48	−45	125	−2 33	−45	126	−3 18	−46	127	−4 04	−45	127	295
64	−0 27	46	125	−1 13	46	126	−1 58	46	127	−2 44	46	127	−3 30	45	128	296
63	00 08	46	126	−0 38	46	127	−1 24	46	127	−2 10	46	128	−2 56	46	129	297
62	00 43	46	127	−0 03	47	127	−0 50	46	128	−1 36	46	129	−2 22	47	129	298
61	01 17	46	128	00 31	47	128	−0 16	47	129	−1 03	46	129	−1 49	47	130	299
60	01 51	−47	128	01 04	−46	129	00 18	−47	129	−0 29	−47	130	−1 16	−47	131	300
59	02 25	47	129	01 38	47	130	00 51	48	130	00 03	47	131	−0 44	47	131	301
58	02 59	48	130	02 11	48	130	01 23	47	131	00 36	48	132	−0 12	47	132	302
57	03 32	48	130	02 44	48	131	01 56	48	132	01 08	48	132	00 20	48	133	303
56	04 04	48	131	03 16	48	132	02 28	48	132	01 40	48	133	00 52	48	134	304
55	04 37	−49	132	03 48	−48	132	03 00	−49	133	02 11	−48	134	01 23	−49	134	305
54	05 09	49	133	04 20	49	133	03 31	49	134	02 42	48	134	01 54	49	135	306
53	05 40	49	133	04 51	49	134	04 02	49	134	03 13	49	135	02 24	49	136	307
52	06 11	49	134	05 22	49	135	04 33	50	135	03 43	49	136	02 54	50	136	308
51	06 42	49	135	05 53	50	135	05 03	50	136	04 13	50	137	03 23	49	137	309
50	07 13	−50	136	06 23	−50	136	05 33	−50	137	04 43	−50	137	03 53	−50	138	310
49	07 43	51	136	06 52	50	137	06 02	50	138	05 12	51	138	04 21	50	139	311
48	08 12	50	137	07 22	51	138	06 31	51	138	05 40	50	139	04 50	51	139	312
47	08 41	51	138	07 50	50	138	07 00	51	139	06 09	51	140	05 18	51	140	313
46	09 10	51	139	08 19	51	139	07 28	51	140	06 37	52	140	05 45	51	141	314
45	09 38	−51	140	08 47	−52	140	07 55	−51	141	07 04	−52	141	06 12	−51	142	315
44	10 06	52	140	09 14	51	141	08 23	52	141	07 31	52	142	06 39	52	142	316
43	10 34	53	141	09 41	52	142	08 49	52	142	07 57	52	143	07 05	52	143	317
42	11 00	52	142	10 08	52	142	09 16	53	143	08 23	52	143	07 31	53	144	318
41	11 27	53	143	10 34	52	143	09 42	53	144	08 49	53	144	07 56	53	145	319
40	11 53	−53	144	11 00	−53	144	10 07	−53	144	09 14	−53	145	08 21	−53	145	320
39	12 18	53	144	11 25	53	145	10 32	53	145	09 39	54	146	08 45	53	146	321
38	12 43	53	145	11 50	54	146	10 56	53	146	10 03	54	147	09 09	54	147	322
37	13 08	54	146	12 14	54	146	11 20	54	147	10 26	54	147	09 32	54	148	323
36	13 32	55	147	12 37	54	147	11 43	54	148	10 49	54	148	09 55	54	149	324
35	13 55	−54	148	13 01	−55	148	12 06	−54	149	11 12	−55	149	10 17	−54	149	325
34	14 18	55	149	13 23	55	149	12 28	54	149	11 34	55	150	10 39	55	150	326
33	14 40	55	149	13 45	55	150	12 50	55	150	11 55	55	151	11 00	55	151	327
32	15 02	55	150	14 07	56	151	13 11	55	151	12 16	55	151	11 21	55	152	328
31	15 23	55	151	14 28	56	151	13 32	55	152	12 37	56	152	11 41	55	153	329
30	15 44	−56	152	14 48	−56	152	13 52	−56	153	12 56	−55	153	12 01	−56	153	330
29	16 04	56	153	15 08	56	153	14 12	56	154	13 16	56	154	12 20	56	154	331
28	16 23	56	154	15 27	56	154	14 31	57	154	13 34	56	155	12 38	56	155	332
27	16 42	57	155	15 45	56	155	14 49	56	155	13 53	57	156	12 56	57	156	333
26	17 00	57	156	16 03	56	156	15 07	57	156	14 10	57	157	13 13	57	157	334
25	17 18	−57	156	16 21	−57	157	15 24	−57	157	14 27	−57	157	13 30	−57	158	335
24	17 35	57	157	16 38	58	158	15 40	57	158	14 43	57	158	13 46	57	159	336
23	17 51	57	158	16 54	58	159	15 56	57	159	14 59	57	159	14 02	58	159	337
22	18 07	58	159	17 09	57	159	16 12	58	160	15 14	58	160	14 16	57	160	338
21	18 22	58	160	17 24	58	160	16 26	57	161	15 29	58	161	14 31	58	161	339
20	18 36	−58	161	17 38	−58	161	16 40	−58	162	15 42	−58	162	14 44	−58	162	340
19	18 50	58	162	17 52	58	162	16 54	58	162	15 56	59	163	14 57	58	163	341
18	19 03	58	163	18 05	58	163	17 07	59	163	16 08	58	164	15 10	59	164	342
17	19 16	59	164	18 17	58	164	17 19	59	164	16 20	58	164	15 22	59	165	343
16	19 28	59	165	18 29	59	165	17 30	59	165	16 31	58	165	15 33	59	166	344
15	19 39	−59	166	18 40	−59	166	17 41	−59	166	16 42	−59	166	15 43	−59	166	345
14	19 49	59	167	18 50	59	167	17 51	59	167	16 52	59	167	15 53	59	167	346
13	19 59	59	168	19 00	60	168	18 00	59	168	17 01	59	168	16 02	59	168	347
12	20 08	59	168	19 09	60	169	18 09	59	169	17 10	59	169	16 11	60	169	348
11	20 16	59	169	19 17	60	170	18 17	59	170	17 18	59	170	16 19	60	170	349
10	20 24	−60	170	19 24	−59	171	18 25	−60	171	17 25	−59	171	16 26	−60	171	350
9	20 31	60	171	19 31	60	171	18 31	59	172	17 32	60	172	16 32	59	172	351
8	20 37	60	172	19 37	60	172	18 37	59	173	17 38	60	173	16 38	60	173	352
7	20 42	60	173	19 42	59	173	18 43	60	173	17 43	60	174	16 43	60	174	353
6	20 47	60	174	19 47	60	174	18 47	60	174	17 47	59	174	16 48	60	175	354
5	20 51	−60	175	19 51	−60	175	18 51	−60	175	17 51	−60	175	16 51	−59	175	355
4	20 54	60	176	19 54	60	176	18 54	60	176	17 54	59	176	16 55	60	176	356
3	20 57	60	177	19 57	60	177	18 57	60	177	17 57	60	177	16 57	60	177	357
2	20 59	60	178	19 59	60	178	18 59	60	178	17 59	60	178	16 59	60	178	358
1	21 00	60	179	20 00	60	179	19 00	60	179	18 00	60	179	17 00	60	179	359
0	21 00	−60	180	20 00	−60	180	19 00	−60	180	18 00	−60	180	17 00	−60	180	360

S. Lat. {LHA greater than 180°....... Zn=180−Z / LHA less than 180°........... Zn=180+Z}

DECLINATION (15°-29°) CONTRARY NAME TO LATITUDE

N. Lat. {LHA greater than 180°....... Zn=Z; LHA less than 180°.......... Zn=360−Z}

DECLINATION (0°-14°) SAME NAME AS LATITUDE

LAT 45°

LHA	0° Hc	d	Z	1° Hc	d	Z	2° Hc	d	Z	3° Hc	d	Z	4° Hc	d	Z
	° ′	′	°	° ′	′	°	° ′	′	°	° ′	′	°	° ′	′	°
0	45 00	+60	180	46 00	+60	180	47 00	+60	180	48 00	+60	180	49 00	+60	180
1	45 00	60	179	46 00	60	179	47 00	59	179	47 59	60	179	48 59	60	179
2	44 58	60	177	45 58	60	177	46 58	60	177	47 58	60	177	48 58	60	177
3	44 55	60	176	45 55	60	176	46 55	60	176	47 55	60	176	48 55	60	175
4	44 52	60	174	45 52	59	174	46 51	60	174	47 51	60	174	48 51	60	174
5	44 47	+60	173	45 47	+60	173	46 47	+59	173	47 46	+60	173	48 46	+60	172
6	44 41	60	172	45 41	60	171	46 41	59	171	47 40	60	171	48 40	59	171
7	44 35	59	170	45 34	60	170	46 34	59	170	47 33	60	170	48 33	59	169
8	44 27	59	169	45 26	60	169	46 26	59	168	47 25	59	168	48 24	60	168
9	44 18	59	167	45 17	59	167	46 16	60	167	47 16	59	167	48 15	59	166
10	44 08	+59	166	45 07	+59	166	46 06	+59	166	47 05	+59	165	48 04	+59	165
11	43 57	59	165	44 56	59	164	45 55	59	164	46 54	59	164	47 53	59	164
12	43 46	58	163	44 44	59	163	45 43	59	163	46 42	58	162	47 40	59	162
13	43 33	59	162	44 32	58	162	45 30	58	161	46 28	59	161	47 27	58	161
14	43 19	59	161	44 18	58	160	45 16	58	160	46 14	58	160	47 12	58	159
15	43 05	+58	159	44 03	+58	159	45 01	+58	159	45 59	+58	158	46 57	+57	158
16	42 49	58	158	43 47	58	158	44 45	58	157	45 43	57	157	46 40	58	156
17	42 33	57	157	43 30	58	156	44 28	57	156	45 25	58	155	46 23	57	155
18	42 16	57	155	43 13	57	155	44 10	57	155	45 07	57	154	46 04	57	154
19	41 58	57	154	42 55	56	154	43 51	57	153	44 48	57	153	45 45	57	152
20	41 39	+56	153	42 35	+57	152	43 32	+56	152	44 28	+57	151	45 25	+56	151
21	41 19	55	152	42 15	56	151	43 11	57	151	44 08	56	150	45 04	56	150
22	40 58	56	150	41 54	56	150	42 50	56	149	43 46	56	149	44 42	55	148
23	40 37	55	149	41 32	56	148	42 28	56	148	43 24	55	148	44 19	55	147
24	40 14	56	148	41 10	55	147	42 05	56	147	43 01	55	146	43 56	55	146
25	39 51	+56	147	40 47	+55	146	41 42	+55	146	42 37	+54	145	43 31	+55	145
26	39 28	55	145	40 23	54	145	41 17	55	144	42 12	54	144	43 06	55	143
27	39 03	55	144	39 58	54	144	40 52	54	143	41 46	54	143	42 40	54	142
28	38 38	54	143	39 32	54	143	40 26	54	142	41 20	54	141	42 14	54	141
29	38 12	54	142	39 06	54	141	40 00	53	141	40 53	54	140	41 47	53	140
30	37 46	+53	141	38 39	+54	140	39 33	+53	140	40 26	+53	139	41 19	+53	138
31	37 19	53	140	38 12	53	139	39 05	53	139	39 58	52	138	40 50	53	137
32	36 51	53	139	37 44	52	138	38 36	53	137	39 29	52	137	40 21	53	136
33	36 22	53	137	37 15	52	137	38 07	53	136	39 00	52	136	39 52	51	135
34	35 53	53	136	36 46	52	136	37 38	52	135	38 30	51	135	39 21	52	134
35	35 24	+52	135	36 16	+52	135	37 08	+51	134	37 59	+51	133	38 50	+52	133
36	34 54	51	134	35 45	52	134	36 37	51	133	37 28	51	132	38 19	51	132
37	34 23	51	133	35 14	51	133	36 05	51	132	36 56	51	131	37 47	50	131
38	33 52	51	132	34 43	51	132	35 34	50	131	36 24	51	130	37 15	50	130
39	33 20	51	131	34 11	50	131	35 01	51	130	35 52	50	129	36 42	49	129
40	32 48	+50	130	33 38	+50	130	34 28	+50	129	35 18	+50	128	36 08	+50	127
41	32 15	50	129	33 05	50	129	33 55	50	128	34 45	49	127	35 34	49	126
42	31 42	50	128	32 32	49	128	33 21	50	127	34 11	49	126	35 00	49	125
43	31 09	49	127	31 58	49	127	32 47	49	126	33 36	49	125	34 25	49	124
44	30 34	50	126	31 24	49	126	32 13	48	125	33 01	49	124	33 50	48	124
45	30 00	+49	125	30 49	+49	125	31 38	+48	124	32 26	+48	123	33 14	+48	123
46	29 25	49	124	30 14	48	124	31 02	48	123	31 50	48	122	32 38	48	122
47	28 50	48	123	29 38	48	123	30 26	48	122	31 14	48	121	32 02	47	121
48	28 14	48	123	29 02	48	122	29 50	48	121	30 38	47	120	31 25	47	120
49	27 38	48	122	28 26	48	121	29 14	47	120	30 01	47	120	30 48	47	119
50	27 02	+48	121	27 50	+47	120	28 37	+47	119	29 24	+47	119	30 11	+47	118
51	26 25	48	120	27 13	47	119	28 00	47	118	28 47	46	118	29 33	47	117
52	25 48	47	119	26 35	47	118	27 22	47	118	28 09	46	117	28 55	47	116
53	25 11	47	118	25 58	47	117	26 45	46	117	27 31	46	116	28 17	46	115
54	24 34	46	117	25 20	46	117	26 06	47	116	26 53	46	115	27 39	45	114
55	23 56	+46	116	24 42	+46	116	25 28	+46	115	26 14	+46	114	27 00	+45	114
56	23 18	46	116	24 04	46	115	24 50	45	114	25 35	46	113	26 21	45	113
57	22 39	46	115	23 25	46	114	24 11	45	113	24 56	45	113	25 41	46	112
58	22 00	46	114	22 46	46	113	23 32	45	112	24 17	45	112	25 02	45	111
59	21 22	45	113	22 07	45	112	22 52	45	112	23 37	45	111	24 22	45	110
60	20 42	+46	112	21 28	+45	112	22 13	+45	111	22 58	+44	110	23 42	+45	109
61	20 03	45	111	20 48	45	111	21 33	45	110	22 18	44	109	23 02	45	109
62	19 23	45	111	20 08	45	110	20 53	45	109	21 38	44	108	22 22	44	108
63	18 44	44	110	19 28	45	109	20 13	44	108	20 57	44	108	21 41	44	107
64	18 04	44	109	18 48	44	108	19 32	45	108	20 17	44	107	21 01	44	106
65	17 23	+45	108	18 08	+44	108	18 52	+44	107	19 36	+44	106	20 20	+44	105
66	16 43	44	108	17 27	44	107	18 11	44	106	18 55	44	105	19 39	43	105
67	16 02	44	107	16 46	44	106	17 30	44	105	18 14	44	105	18 58	43	104
68	15 22	44	106	16 06	43	105	16 49	44	105	17 33	44	104	18 17	43	103
69	14 41	44	105	15 25	43	105	16 08	44	104	16 52	43	103	17 35	43	102

LHA	5° Hc	d	Z	6° Hc	d	Z	7° Hc	d	Z	8° Hc	d	Z	9° Hc	d	Z
	° ′	′	°	° ′	′	°	° ′	′	°	° ′	′	°	° ′	′	°
0	50 00	+60	180	51 00	+60	180	52 00	+60	180	53 00	+60	180	54 00	+60	180
1	49 59	60	179	50 59	60	178	51 59	60	178	52 59	60	178	53 59	60	178
2	49 58	60	177	50 58	60	177	51 58	60	177	52 58	60	177	53 58	60	177
3	49 55	60	175	50 55	60	175	51 55	60	175	52 55	59	175	53 54	60	175
4	49 51	60	174	50 51	60	174	51 51	59	174	52 50	60	173	53 50	60	173
5	49 46	+59	172	50 45	+60	172	51 45	+60	172	52 45	+60	172	53 45	+59	172
6	49 39	60	171	50 39	60	171	51 39	59	170	52 38	60	170	53 38	59	170
7	49 32	60	169	50 32	59	169	51 31	59	169	52 30	60	169	53 30	59	168
8	49 24	59	168	50 23	59	168	51 22	59	167	52 21	60	167	53 21	59	167
9	49 14	59	166	50 13	59	166	51 12	59	166	52 11	59	165	53 10	59	165
10	49 03	+59	165	50 02	+59	164	51 01	+59	164	52 00	+59	164	52 59	+58	164
11	48 52	58	163	49 50	59	163	50 49	59	163	51 48	58	162	52 46	59	162
12	48 39	58	162	49 37	59	161	50 36	58	161	51 34	58	161	52 32	59	160
13	48 25	58	160	49 23	58	160	50 21	58	160	51 19	58	159	52 17	58	159
14	48 10	58	159	49 08	58	158	50 06	58	158	51 04	58	158	52 02	57	157
15	47 54	+58	157	48 52	+58	157	49 50	+57	157	50 47	+58	156	51 45	+57	156
16	47 38	57	156	48 35	57	156	49 32	57	155	50 29	57	155	51 26	57	154
17	47 20	57	155	48 17	57	154	49 14	57	154	50 11	56	153	51 07	57	153
18	47 01	57	153	47 58	57	153	48 55	56	152	49 51	56	152	50 47	57	151
19	46 42	56	152	47 38	56	151	48 34	56	151	49 30	56	150	50 26	56	150
20	46 21	+56	150	47 17	+56	150	48 13	+56	149	49 09	+56	149	50 05	+55	148
21	46 00	55	149	46 55	56	148	47 51	56	148	48 47	55	147	49 42	55	146
22	45 37	56	148	46 33	55	147	47 28	55	147	48 23	55	146	49 18	55	145
23	45 14	55	146	46 09	55	146	47 04	55	145	47 59	55	145	48 54	54	144
24	44 51	54	145	45 45	55	145	46 40	54	144	47 34	54	143	48 28	54	143
25	44 26	+54	144	45 20	+55	143	46 15	+54	143	47 09	+53	142	48 02	+54	141
26	44 01	54	143	44 55	53	142	45 48	54	141	46 42	53	141	47 35	54	140
27	43 34	54	141	44 28	54	141	45 22	53	140	46 15	53	140	47 08	53	139
28	43 08	53	140	44 01	53	140	44 54	53	139	45 47	53	138	46 40	52	138
29	42 40	53	139	43 33	53	138	44 26	52	138	45 18	53	137	46 11	52	136
30	42 12	+52	138	43 04	+53	137	43 57	+52	136	44 49	+52	136	45 41	+51	135
31	41 43	52	137	42 35	52	136	43 27	52	135	44 19	52	135	45 11	51	134
32	41 14	51	135	42 05	52	135	42 57	51	134	43 48	52	133	44 40	50	133
33	40 43	52	134	41 35	51	134	42 26	51	133	43 17	51	132	44 08	51	132
34	40 13	51	133	41 04	51	133	41 55	51	132	42 46	50	131	43 36	50	130
35	39 42	+50	132	40 32	+51	131	41 23	+50	131	42 13	+50	130	43 03	+50	129
36	39 10	50	131	40 00	51	130	40 51	50	130	41 41	49	129	42 30	50	128
37	38 37	51	130	39 28	50	129	40 18	49	129	41 07	50	128	41 57	49	127
38	38 05	50	129	38 55	49	128	39 44	49	127	40 33	49	127	41 22	49	126
39	37 31	50	128	38 21	49	127	39 10	49	126	39 59	49	126	40 48	48	125
40	36 58	+49	127	37 47	+49	126	38 36	+48	125	39 24	+49	125	40 13	+48	124
41	36 23	49	126	37 12	49	125	38 01	48	124	38 49	48	124	39 37	48	123
42	35 49	48	125	36 37	49	124	37 26	48	123	38 14	47	123	39 01	48	122
43	35 14	48	124	36 02	48	123	36 50	48	122	37 38	47	122	38 25	47	121
44	34 38	48	123	35 26	48	122	36 14	47	121	37 01	47	121	37 48	47	120
45	34 02	+48	122	34 50	+47	121	35 37	+48	120	36 25	+46	120	37 11	+47	119
46	33 26	47	121	34 13	48	120	35 01	46	119	35 47	47	119	36 34	46	118
47	32 49	48	120	33 37	46	119	34 23	47	118	35 10	46	118	35 56	46	117
48	32 12	47	119	32 59	47	118	33 46	46	118	34 32	46	117	35 18	46	116
49	31 35	47	118	32 22	46	117	33 08	46	117	33 54	46	116	34 40	46	115
50	30 58	+46	117	31 44	+46	116	32 30	+46	116	33 16	+45	115	34 01	+46	114
51	30 20	46	116	31 06	46	116	31 52	45	115	32 37	46	114	33 23	45	113
52	29 41	46	115	30 27	46	115	31 13	45	114	31 58	45	113	32 43	45	112
53	29 03	46	115	29 49	45	114	30 34	45	113	31 19	45	112	32 04	45	111
54	28 24	46	114	29 10	45	113	29 55	45	112	30 40	45	111	31 25	44	111
55	27 45	+45	113	28 30	+45	112	29 15	+45	111	30 00	+45	111	30 45	+44	110
56	27 06	45	112	27 51	45	111	28 36	44	110	29 20	45	110	30 05	44	109
57	26 27	44	111	27 11	45	110	27 56	44	110	28 40	44	109	29 24	44	108
58	25 47	44	110	26 31	45	110	27 16	44	109	28 00	44	108	28 44	44	107
59	25 07	44	109	25 51	45	109	26 36	44	108	27 20	43	107	28 03	44	106
60	24 27	+44	109	25 11	+44	108	25 55	+44	107	26 39	+44	106	27 23	+43	106
61	23 47	44	108	24 31	44	107	25 15	43	106	25 58	44	106	26 42	43	105
62	23 06	44	107	23 50	44	106	24 34	43	106	25 17	44	105	26 01	43	104
63	22 25	44	106	23 09	44	106	23 53	43	105	24 36	43	104	25 19	43	103
64	21 45	43	105	22 28	44	105	23 12	43	104	23 55	43	103	24 38	43	102
65	21 04	+43	105	21 47	+43	104	22 30	+44	103	23 14	+42	102	23 56	+43	102
66	20 22	44	104	21 06	43	103	21 49	43	102	22 32	43	102	23 15	42	101
67	19 41	43	103	20 24	44	102	21 08	42	102	21 50	43	101	22 33	43	100
68	19 00	43	102	19 43	43	102	20 26	43	101	21 09	42	100	21 51	43	99
69	18 18	43	102	19 01	43	101	19 44	43	100	20 27	42	99	21 09	43	99

LHA	10° Hc	d	Z	11° Hc	d	Z	12° Hc	d	Z	13° Hc	d	Z	14° Hc	d	Z	LHA
	° ′	′	°	° ′	′	°	° ′	′	°	° ′	′	°	° ′	′	°	
0	55 00	+60	180	56 00	+60	180	57 00	+60	180	58 00	+60	180	59 00	+60	180	360
1	54 59	60	178	55 59	60	178	56 59	60	178	57 59	60	178	58 59	60	178	359
2	54 58	59	177	55 57	60	177	56 57	60	176	57 57	60	176	58 57	60	176	358
3	54 54	60	175	55 54	60	175	56 54	60	175	57 54	60	175	58 54	60	174	357
4	54 50	60	173	55 50	59	173	56 49	60	173	57 49	60	173	58 49	60	173	356
5	54 44	+60	172	55 44	+59	171	56 43	+60	171	57 43	+60	171	58 43	+59	171	355
6	54 37	60	170	55 37	59	170	56 36	60	169	57 36	59	169	58 35	59	169	354
7	54 29	59	168	55 28	60	168	56 28	59	168	57 27	59	167	58 26	59	167	353
8	54 20	59	166	55 19	59	166	56 18	59	166	57 17	59	166	58 16	59	165	352
9	54 09	59	165	55 08	59	164	56 07	59	164	57 06	58	164	58 04	59	163	351
10	53 57	+59	163	54 56	+59	163	55 55	+58	162	56 53	+59	162	57 52	+58	162	350
11	53 45	58	162	54 43	58	161	55 41	58	161	56 39	59	160	57 38	58	160	349
12	53 31	58	160	54 29	58	159	55 27	57	159	56 24	58	159	57 22	58	158	348
13	53 15	58	158	54 13	58	158	55 11	57	157	56 08	58	157	57 06	57	156	347
14	52 59	58	157	53 57	57	156	54 54	57	156	55 51	57	155	56 48	57	155	346
15	52 42	+57	155	53 39	+57	155	54 36	+57	154	55 33	+56	154	56 29	+57	153	345
16	52 23	57	154	53 20	57	153	54 17	56	153	55 13	57	152	56 10	56	151	344
17	52 04	56	152	53 00	57	152	53 57	56	151	54 53	56	150	55 49	55	150	343
18	51 44	56	151	52 40	56	150	53 36	55	149	54 31	56	149	55 27	55	148	342
19	51 22	56	149	52 18	56	149	53 14	55	148	54 09	55	147	55 04	55	147	341
20	51 00	+55	148	51 55	+55	147	52 50	+55	146	53 45	+55	146	54 40	+54	145	340
21	50 37	55	146	51 32	55	146	52 27	54	145	53 21	54	144	54 15	54	144	339
22	50 13	54	145	51 07	55	144	52 02	54	143	52 56	53	143	53 49	54	142	338
23	49 48	54	143	50 42	54	143	51 36	54	142	52 30	53	141	53 23	53	141	337
24	49 22	54	142	50 16	54	141	51 10	53	141	52 03	53	140	52 56	52	139	336
25	48 56	+53	141	49 49	+53	140	50 42	+53	139	51 35	+52	139	52 27	+53	138	335
26	48 29	53	139	49 22	52	139	50 14	52	138	51 06	52	137	51 58	52	136	334
27	48 01	52	138	48 53	52	137	49 45	52	137	50 37	52	136	51 29	51	135	333
28	47 32	52	137	48 24	52	136	49 16	51	135	50 07	51	135	50 58	51	134	332
29	47 03	51	136	47 54	52	135	48 46	51	134	49 37	50	133	50 27	51	132	331
30	46 32	+52	134	47 24	+51	134	48 15	+50	133	49 05	+51	132	49 56	+50	131	330
31	46 02	51	133	46 53	50	132	47 43	51	132	48 34	50	131	49 24	49	130	329
32	45 30	51	132	46 21	50	131	47 11	50	130	48 01	50	130	48 51	49	129	328
33	44 59	50	131	45 49	50	130	46 39	49	129	47 28	49	128	48 17	49	127	327
34	44 26	50	130	45 16	49	129	46 05	50	128	46 55	48	127	47 43	49	126	326
35	43 53	+50	128	44 43	+49	128	45 32	+48	127	46 20	+49	126	47 09	+48	125	325
36	43 20	49	127	44 09	48	127	44 57	49	126	45 46	48	125	46 34	47	124	324
37	42 46	48	126	43 34	49	125	44 23	48	125	45 11	47	124	45 58	48	123	323
38	42 11	49	125	43 00	48	124	43 48	47	124	44 35	48	123	45 23	46	122	322
39	41 36	48	124	42 24	48	123	43 12	47	122	43 59	47	122	44 46	47	121	321
40	41 01	+48	123	41 49	+47	122	42 36	+47	121	43 23	+47	121	44 10	+46	120	320
41	40 25	47	122	41 12	48	121	42 00	46	120	42 46	47	119	43 33	45	119	319
42	39 49	47	121	40 36	47	120	41 23	46	119	42 09	46	118	42 55	46	118	318
43	39 12	47	120	39 59	47	119	40 46	46	118	41 32	45	117	42 17	46	117	317
44	38 35	47	119	39 22	46	118	40 08	46	117	40 54	45	116	41 39	45	116	316
45	37 58	+46	118	38 44	+46	117	39 30	+46	116	40 16	+45	116	41 01	+44	115	315
46	37 20	46	117	38 06	46	116	38 52	45	115	39 37	45	115	40 22	44	114	314
47	36 42	46	116	37 28	45	115	38 13	45	114	38 58	45	114	39 43	44	113	313
48	36 04	46	115	36 50	45	114	37 35	44	114	38 19	45	113	39 04	44	112	312
49	35 26	45	114	36 11	45	113	36 56	44	113	37 40	44	112	38 24	44	111	311
50	34 47	+45	113	35 32	+44	113	36 16	+45	112	37 01	+43	111	37 44	+44	110	310
51	34 08	44	112	34 52	45	112	35 37	44	111	36 21	43	110	37 04	44	109	309
52	33 28	45	112	34 13	44	111	34 57	44	110	35 41	43	109	36 24	43	108	308
53	32 49	44	111	33 33	44	110	34 17	44	109	35 01	43	108	35 44	43	107	307
54	32 09	44	110	32 53	44	109	33 37	43	108	34 20	43	107	35 03	43	107	306
55	31 29	+44	109	32 13	+43	108	32 56	+44	107	33 40	+43	107	34 23	+42	106	305
56	30 49	43	108	31 32	44	107	32 16	43	107	32 59	43	106	33 42	42	105	304
57	30 08	44	107	30 52	43	107	31 35	43	106	32 18	42	105	33 00	43	104	303
58	29 28	43	106	30 11	43	106	30 54	43	105	31 37	42	104	32 19	42	103	302
59	28 47	43	106	29 30	43	105	30 13	43	104	30 56	42	103	31 38	42	102	301
60	28 06	+43	105	28 49	+43	104	29 32	+42	103	30 14	+42	102	30 56	+42	102	300
61	27 25	43	104	28 08	42	103	28 50	43	102	29 33	42	102	30 15	41	101	299
62	26 44	42	103	27 26	43	102	28 09	42	102	28 51	42	101	29 33	42	100	298
63	26 02	43	102	26 45	42	102	27 27	42	101	28 09	42	100	28 51	42	99	297
64	25 21	42	102	26 03	43	101	26 46	42	100	27 28	41	99	28 09	42	99	296
65	24 39	+43	101	25 22	+42	100	26 04	+42	99	26 46	+41	99	27 27	+42	98	295
66	23 57	43	100	24 40	42	99	25 22	42	99	26 04	41	98	26 45	41	97	294
67	23 16	42	99	23 58	42	99	24 40	42	98	25 22	41	97	26 03	41	96	293
68	22 34	42	98	23 16	42	98	23 58	41	97	24 39	42	96	25 21	41	96	292
69	21 52	42	98	22 34	42	97	23 16	41	96	23 57	42	96	24 39	41	95	291

S. Lat. {LHA greater than 180°....... Zn=180−Z; LHA less than 180°.......... Zn=180+Z}

DECLINATION (0°-14°) SAME NAME AS LATITUDE

LAT 45°

N. Lat. {LHA greater than 180°....... Zn=Z; LHA less than 180°........... Zn=360−Z}

DECLINATION (0°-14°) SAME NAME AS LATITUDE

LHA	0° Hc	d	Z	1° Hc	d	Z	2° Hc	d	Z	3° Hc	d	Z	4° Hc	d	Z	LHA
	° ′	′	°	° ′	′	°	° ′	′	°	° ′	′	°	° ′	′	°	
70	14 00	+43	104	14 43	+44	104	15 27	+43	103	16 10	+44	102	16 54	+43	102	290
71	13 19	43	104	14 02	44	103	14 46	43	102	15 29	43	102	16 12	43	101	289
72	12 37	44	103	13 21	43	102	14 04	43	102	14 47	43	101	15 30	43	100	288
73	11 56	43	102	12 39	43	102	13 22	44	101	14 06	42	100	14 48	43	99	287
74	11 14	44	102	11 58	43	101	12 41	43	100	13 24	43	99	14 07	42	99	286
75	10 33	+43	101	11 16	+43	100	11 59	+43	99	12 42	+43	99	13 25	+42	98	285
76	09 51	43	100	10 34	43	99	11 17	43	99	12 00	42	98	12 42	43	97	284
77	09 09	43	99	09 52	43	99	10 35	43	98	11 18	42	97	12 00	43	96	283
78	08 27	43	99	09 10	43	98	09 53	43	97	10 36	42	96	11 18	43	96	282
79	07 45	43	98	08 28	43	97	09 11	42	96	09 53	43	96	10 36	42	95	281
80	07 03	+43	97	07 46	+43	96	08 29	+42	96	09 11	+43	95	09 54	+42	94	280
81	06 21	43	96	07 04	42	96	07 46	43	95	08 29	42	94	09 11	43	94	279
82	05 39	43	96	06 22	42	95	07 04	43	94	07 47	42	94	08 29	42	93	278
83	04 57	42	95	05 39	43	94	06 22	42	94	07 04	43	93	07 47	42	92	277
84	04 14	43	94	04 57	42	94	05 39	43	93	06 22	42	92	07 04	42	91	276
85	03 32	+42	94	04 14	+43	93	04 57	+42	92	05 39	+43	91	06 22	+42	91	275
86	02 50	42	93	03 32	43	92	04 15	42	91	04 57	42	91	05 39	43	90	274
87	02 07	43	92	02 50	42	91	03 32	43	91	04 15	42	90	04 57	42	89	273
88	01 25	42	91	02 07	43	91	02 50	42	90	03 32	42	89	04 14	43	89	272
89	00 42	43	91	01 25	42	90	02 07	43	89	02 50	42	89	03 32	42	88	271
90	00 00	+42	90	00 42	+43	89	01 25	+42	89	02 07	+43	88	02 50	+42	87	270
91	−0 42	42	89	00 00	42	89	00 42	43	88	01 25	42	87	02 07	43	86	269
92	−1 25	43	89	−0 42	42	88	00 00	42	87	00 42	43	86	01 25	42	86	268
93	−2 07	42	88	−1 25	43	87	−0 42	42	86	00 00	43	86	00 43	42	85	267
94	−2 50	43	87	−2 07	42	86	−1 25	43	86	−0 42	42	85	00 00	43	84	266
95	−3 32	+43	86	−2 49	+42	86	−2 07	+43	85	−1 24	+42	84	−0 42	+43	84	265
96	−4 14	42	86	−3 32	43	85	−2 49	42	84	−2 07	43	84	−1 24	43	83	264
97	−4 57	43	85	−4 14	43	84	−3 31	42	84	−2 49	43	83	−2 06	43	82	263
98	−5 39	43	84	−4 56	43	84	−4 13	42	83	−3 31	43	82	−2 48	43	82	262
99	−6 21	43	84	−5 38	42	83	−4 56	43	82	−4 13	43	81	−3 30	43	81	261
100				−6 20	+42	82	−5 38	+43	81	−4 55	+43	81	−4 12	+43	80	260
101							−6 20	43	81	−5 37	44	80	−4 53	43	79	259
102										−6 18	43	79	−5 35	43	79	258
103													−6 17	44	78	257

LHA	5° Hc	d	Z	6° Hc	d	Z	7° Hc	d	Z	8° Hc	d	Z	9° Hc	d	Z	LHA
	° ′	′	°	° ′	′	°	° ′	′	°	° ′	′	°	° ′	′	°	
70	17 37	+43	101	18 20	+42	100	19 02	+43	99	19 45	+42	99	20 27	+43	98	290
71	16 55	43	100	17 38	43	99	18 21	42	99	19 03	42	98	19 45	42	97	289
72	16 13	43	99	16 56	43	99	17 39	42	98	18 21	42	97	19 03	42	96	288
73	15 31	43	99	16 14	42	98	16 56	43	97	17 39	42	96	18 21	42	96	287
74	14 49	43	98	15 32	42	97	16 14	43	96	16 57	42	96	17 39	42	95	286
75	14 07	+43	97	14 50	+42	96	15 32	+42	96	16 14	+42	95	16 56	+42	94	285
76	13 25	43	96	14 08	42	96	14 50	42	95	15 32	42	94	16 14	42	94	284
77	12 43	42	96	13 25	43	95	14 08	42	94	14 50	42	94	15 32	42	93	283
78	12 01	42	95	12 43	42	94	13 25	42	94	14 07	42	93	14 49	42	92	282
79	11 18	43	94	12 01	42	94	12 43	42	93	13 25	42	92	14 07	42	91	281
80	10 36	+42	94	11 18	+43	93	12 01	+42	92	12 43	+42	91	13 25	+41	91	280
81	09 54	42	93	10 36	42	92	11 18	42	91	12 00	42	91	12 42	42	90	279
82	09 11	43	92	09 54	42	91	10 36	42	91	11 18	42	90	12 00	42	89	278
83	08 29	42	91	09 11	42	91	09 53	42	90	10 35	42	89	11 17	42	89	277
84	07 46	43	91	08 29	42	90	09 11	42	89	09 53	42	89	10 35	42	88	276
85	07 04	+42	90	07 46	+42	89	08 28	+43	89	09 11	+42	88	09 53	+41	87	275
86	06 22	42	89	07 04	42	89	07 46	42	88	08 28	42	87	09 10	42	86	274
87	05 39	42	89	06 21	43	88	07 04	42	87	07 46	42	86	08 28	42	86	273
88	04 57	42	88	05 39	42	87	06 21	42	86	07 03	43	86	07 46	42	85	272
89	04 14	43	87	04 57	42	86	05 39	42	86	06 21	42	85	07 03	42	84	271
90	03 32	+42	86	04 14	+43	86	04 57	+42	85	05 39	+42	84	06 21	+42	84	270
91	02 50	42	86	03 32	42	85	04 14	43	84	04 57	42	84	05 39	42	83	269
92	02 07	43	85	02 50	42	84	03 32	43	84	04 15	42	83	04 57	42	82	268
93	01 25	43	84	02 08	42	84	02 50	42	83	03 32	43	82	04 15	42	82	267
94	00 43	42	84	01 25	43	83	02 08	42	82	02 50	43	82	03 33	42	81	266
95	00 01	+42	83	00 43	+43	82	01 26	+43	82	02 09	+42	81	02 51	+43	80	265
96	−0 41	42	82	00 01	43	82	00 44	43	81	01 27	42	80	02 09	43	79	264
97	−1 23	42	82	−0 41	43	81	00 02	43	80	00 45	43	79	01 28	42	79	263
98	−2 05	43	81	−1 22	42	80	−0 40	43	79	00 03	43	79	00 46	43	78	262
99	−2 47	43	80	−2 04	43	79	−1 21	43	79	−0 38	43	78	00 05	42	77	261
100	−3 29	+43	79	−2 46	+43	79	−2 03	+43	78	−1 20	+43	77	−0 37	+43	77	260
101	−4 10	43	79	−3 27	43	78	−2 44	43	77	−2 01	43	77	−1 18	43	76	259
102	−4 52	43	78	−4 09	43	77	−3 26	44	77	−2 42	43	76	−1 59	43	75	258
103	−5 33	43	77	−4 50	43	77	−4 07	44	76	−3 23	43	75	−2 40	44	74	257
104	−6 15	44	76	−5 31	43	76	−4 48	44	75	−4 04	43	74	−3 21	44	74	256
105				−6 12	+43	75	−5 29	+44	74	−4 45	+44	74	−4 01	+43	73	255
106							−6 10	44	74	−5 26	44	73	−4 42	44	72	254
107										−6 06	44	72	−5 22	44	72	253
108													−6 02	44	71	252

LHA	10° Hc	d	Z	11° Hc	d	Z	12° Hc	d	Z	13° Hc	d	Z	14° Hc	d	Z	LHA
	° ′	′	°	° ′	′	°	° ′	′	°	° ′	′	°	° ′	′	°	
70	21 10	+42	97	21 52	+41	96	22 33	+42	96	23 15	+41	95	23 56	+41	94	290
71	20 27	42	96	21 09	42	96	21 51	42	95	22 33	41	94	23 14	41	93	289
72	19 45	42	96	20 27	42	95	21 09	41	94	21 50	42	93	22 32	41	93	288
73	19 03	42	95	19 45	41	94	20 26	42	93	21 08	41	93	21 49	41	92	287
74	18 21	42	94	19 03	41	93	19 44	42	93	20 26	41	92	21 07	41	91	286
75	17 38	+42	94	18 20	+42	93	19 02	+41	92	19 43	+41	91	20 24	+41	90	285
76	16 56	42	93	17 38	41	92	18 19	42	91	19 01	41	91	19 42	41	90	284
77	16 14	41	92	16 55	42	91	17 37	41	91	18 18	41	90	18 59	41	89	283
78	15 31	42	91	16 13	41	91	16 54	42	90	17 36	41	89	18 17	41	88	282
79	14 49	42	91	15 31	41	90	16 12	41	89	16 53	42	88	17 35	41	88	281
80	14 06	+42	90	14 48	+42	89	15 30	+41	88	16 11	+41	88	16 52	+41	87	280
81	13 24	42	89	14 06	41	88	14 47	42	88	15 29	41	87	16 10	41	86	279
82	12 42	41	89	13 23	42	88	14 05	41	87	14 46	42	86	15 28	41	86	278
83	11 59	42	88	12 41	41	87	13 22	42	86	14 04	41	86	14 45	42	85	277
84	11 17	42	87	11 59	41	86	12 40	42	86	13 22	41	85	14 03	41	84	276
85	10 34	+42	86	11 16	+42	86	11 58	+41	85	12 39	+42	84	13 21	+41	83	275
86	09 52	42	86	10 34	42	85	11 16	41	84	11 57	42	84	12 39	41	83	274
87	09 10	42	85	09 52	41	84	10 33	42	84	11 15	42	83	11 57	41	82	273
88	08 28	41	84	09 09	42	84	09 51	42	83	10 33	42	82	11 15	41	81	272
89	07 45	42	84	08 27	42	83	09 09	42	82	09 51	42	81	10 33	41	81	271
90	07 03	+42	83	07 45	+42	82	08 27	+42	82	09 09	+42	81	09 51	+42	80	270
91	06 21	42	82	07 03	42	82	07 45	42	81	08 27	42	80	09 09	42	79	269
92	05 39	42	82	06 21	43	81	07 04	42	80	07 46	42	79	08 28	42	79	268
93	04 57	43	81	05 40	42	80	06 22	42	79	07 04	42	79	07 46	42	78	267
94	04 15	43	80	04 58	42	79	05 40	42	79	06 22	43	78	07 05	42	77	266
95	03 34	+42	79	04 16	+43	79	04 59	+42	78	05 41	+42	77	06 23	+43	77	265
96	02 52	43	79	03 35	42	78	04 17	43	77	05 00	42	77	05 42	43	76	264
97	02 10	43	78	02 53	43	77	03 36	42	77	04 18	43	76	05 01	43	75	263
98	01 29	43	77	02 12	43	77	02 55	42	76	03 37	43	75	04 20	43	75	262
99	00 47	44	77	01 31	42	76	02 13	43	75	02 56	43	75	03 39	43	74	261
100	00 06	+43	76	00 49	+44	75	01 33	+43	75	02 16	+43	74	02 59	+43	73	260
101	−0 35	44	75	00 09	43	74	00 52	43	74	01 35	43	73	02 18	43	72	259
102	−1 16	44	74	−0 32	43	74	00 11	43	73	00 54	44	72	01 38	43	72	258
103	−1 56	43	74	−1 13	44	73	−0 29	43	72	00 14	43	72	00 57	44	71	257
104	−2 37	44	73	−1 53	43	72	−1 10	44	72	−0 26	43	71	00 17	44	70	256
105	−3 18	+44	72	−2 34	+44	72	−1 50	+44	71	−1 06	+44	70	−0 22	+43	70	255
106	−3 58	44	72	−3 14	44	71	−2 30	44	70	−1 46	44	70	−1 02	44	69	254
107	−4 38	44	71	−3 54	44	70	−3 10	44	70	−2 26	44	69	−1 42	45	68	253
108	−5 18	44	70	−4 34	44	69	−3 50	45	69	−3 05	44	68	−2 21	45	67	252
109	−5 58	44	69	−5 14	45	69	−4 29	45	68	−3 44	44	67	−3 00	45	67	251
110				−5 53	+45	68	−5 08	+44	67	−4 24	+45	67	−3 39	+45	66	250
111							−5 47	45	67	−5 02	45	66	−4 17	45	65	249
112										−5 41	45	65	−4 56	45	65	248
113													−5 34	45	64	247
114													−6 12	46	63	246

DECLINATION (0°-14°) CONTRARY NAME TO LATITUDE

LHA	0° Hc	d	Z	1° Hc	d	Z	2° Hc	d	Z	3° Hc	d	Z	4° Hc	d	Z	LHA
99	−6 21	43	84	261												
98	−5 39	43	84	−6 22	42	85	262									
97	−4 57	42	85	−5 39	43	86	−6 22	42	86	263						
96	−4 14	43	86	−4 57	42	86	−5 39	43	87	−6 22	42	88	264			
95	−3 32	−42	86	−4 14	−43	87	−4 57	−42	88	−5 39	−43	89	−6 22	−42	89	
94	−2 50	42	87	−3 32	43	88	−4 15	42	89	−4 57	42	89	−5 39	43	90	
93	−2 07	43	88	−2 50	42	89	−3 32	43	89	−4 15	42	90	−4 57	42	91	
92	−1 25	42	89	−2 07	43	89	−2 50	42	90	−3 32	42	91	−4 14	43	91	
91	−0 42	43	89	−1 25	42	90	−2 07	43	91	−2 50	42	91	−3 32	42	92	
90	00 00	−42	90	−0 42	−43	91	−1 25	−42	91	−2 07	−43	92	−2 50	−42	93	
89	00 42	42	91	00 00	42	91	−0 42	43	92	−1 25	42	93	−2 07	43	94	
88	01 25	43	91	00 42	42	92	00 00	42	93	−0 42	43	94	−1 25	42	94	
87	02 07	42	92	01 25	43	93	00 42	42	94	00 00	43	94	−0 43	42	95	
86	02 50	43	93	02 07	42	94	01 25	43	94	00 42	42	95	00 00	43	96	
85	03 32	−43	94	02 49	−42	94	02 07	−43	95	01 24	−42	96	00 42	−43	96	
84	04 14	42	94	03 32	43	95	02 49	42	96	02 07	43	96	01 24	43	97	276
83	04 57	43	95	04 14	43	96	03 31	42	96	02 49	43	97	02 06	43	98	277
82	05 39	43	96	04 56	43	96	04 13	42	97	03 31	43	98	02 48	43	98	278
81	06 21	43	96	05 38	42	97	04 56	43	98	04 13	43	99	03 30	43	99	279
80	07 03	−43	97	06 20	−42	98	05 38	−43	99	04 55	−43	99	04 12	−43	100	280
79	07 45	43	98	07 02	42	99	06 20	43	99	05 37	44	100	04 53	43	101	281
78	08 27	43	99	07 44	43	99	07 01	43	100	06 18	43	101	05 35	43	101	282
77	09 09	43	99	08 26	43	100	07 43	43	101	07 00	43	101	06 17	44	102	283
76	09 51	43	100	09 08	43	101	08 25	44	101	07 41	43	102	06 58	43	103	284
75	10 33	−43	101	09 50	−44	101	09 06	−43	102	08 23	−44	103	07 39	−43	104	285
74	11 14	43	102	10 31	43	102	09 48	44	103	09 04	43	104	08 21	44	104	286
73	11 56	43	102	11 13	44	103	10 29	44	104	09 45	43	104	09 02	44	105	287
72	12 37	43	103	11 54	44	104	11 10	44	104	10 26	43	105	09 43	44	106	288
71	13 19	44	104	12 35	44	104	11 51	44	105	11 07	44	106	10 23	44	107	289
70	14 00	−44	104	13 16	−44	105	12 32	−44	106	11 48	−44	107	11 04	−44	107	290
	0°			1°			2°			3°			4°			

LHA	5° Hc	d	Z	6° Hc	d	Z	7° Hc	d	Z	8° Hc	d	Z	9° Hc	d	Z	LHA
95	265															
94	−6 22	42	91	266												
93	−5 39	42	91	−6 21	43	92	267									
92	−4 57	42	92	−5 39	42	93	−6 21	42	94	268						
91	−4 14	43	93	−4 57	42	94	−5 39	42	94	−6 21	42	95	269			
90	−3 32	−42	94	−4 14	−43	94	−4 57	−42	95	−5 39	−42	96	−6 21	−42	96	
89	−2 50	42	94	−3 32	42	95	−4 14	43	96	−4 57	42	96	−5 39	42	97	
88	−2 07	43	95	−2 50	42	96	−3 32	43	96	−4 15	42	97	−4 57	42	98	
87	−1 25	43	96	−2 08	42	96	−2 50	42	97	−3 32	43	98	−4 15	42	98	
86	−0 43	42	96	−1 25	43	97	−2 08	42	98	−2 50	43	98	−3 33	42	99	
85	−0 01	−42	97	−0 43	−43	98	−1 26	−43	98	−2 09	−42	99	−2 51	−43	100	
84	00 41	42	98	−0 01	43	98	−0 44	43	99	−1 27	42	100	−2 09	43	101	276
83	01 23	42	98	00 41	43	99	−0 02	43	100	−0 45	43	101	−1 28	42	101	277
82	02 05	43	99	01 22	42	100	00 40	43	101	−0 03	43	101	−0 46	43	102	278
81	02 47	43	100	02 04	43	101	01 21	43	101	00 38	43	102	−0 05	42	103	279
80	03 29	−43	101	02 46	−43	101	02 03	−43	102	01 20	−43	103	00 37	−43	103	280
79	04 10	43	101	03 27	43	102	02 44	43	103	02 01	43	103	01 18	43	104	281
78	04 52	43	102	04 09	43	103	03 26	44	103	02 42	43	104	01 59	43	105	282
77	05 33	43	103	04 50	43	103	04 07	44	104	03 23	43	105	02 40	44	106	283
76	06 15	44	104	05 31	43	104	04 48	44	105	04 04	43	106	03 21	44	106	284
75	06 56	−44	104	06 12	−43	105	05 29	−44	106	04 45	−44	106	04 01	−43	107	285
74	07 37	44	105	06 53	43	106	06 10	44	106	05 26	44	107	04 42	44	108	286
73	08 18	44	106	07 34	44	106	06 50	44	107	06 06	44	108	05 22	44	108	287
72	08 59	44	106	08 15	44	107	07 31	44	108	06 47	45	109	06 02	44	109	288
71	09 39	44	107	08 55	44	108	08 11	44	109	07 27	45	109	06 42	44	110	289
70	10 20	−45	108	09 35	−44	109	08 51	−44	109	08 07	−45	110	07 22	−44	111	290
	5°			6°			7°			8°			9°			

LHA	10° Hc	d	Z	11° Hc	d	Z	12° Hc	d	Z	13° Hc	d	Z	14° Hc	d	Z	LHA
90	270															
89	−6 21	42	98	271												
88	−5 39	42	98	−6 21	43	99	272									
87	−4 57	43	99	−5 40	42	100	−6 22	42	101	273						
86	−4 15	43	100	−4 58	42	101	−5 40	42	101	−6 22	43	102	274			
85	−3 34	−42	101	−4 16	−43	101	−4 59	−42	102	−5 41	−42	103	275			
84	−2 52	43	101	−3 35	42	102	−4 17	43	103	−5 00	42	103	−5 42	43	104	276
83	−2 10	43	102	−2 53	43	103	−3 36	42	103	−4 18	43	104	−5 01	43	105	277
82	−1 29	43	103	−2 12	43	103	−2 55	42	104	−3 37	43	105	−4 20	43	105	278
81	−0 47	44	103	−1 31	42	104	−2 13	43	105	−2 56	43	105	−3 39	43	106	279
80	−0 06	−43	104	−0 49	−44	105	−1 33	−43	105	−2 16	−43	106	−2 59	−43	107	280
79	00 35	44	105	−0 09	43	106	−0 52	43	106	−1 35	43	107	−2 18	43	108	281
78	01 16	44	106	00 32	43	106	−0 11	43	107	−0 54	44	108	−1 38	43	108	282
77	01 56	43	106	01 13	44	107	00 29	43	108	−0 14	43	108	−0 57	44	109	283
76	02 37	44	107	01 53	43	108	01 10	44	108	00 26	43	109	−0 17	44	110	284
75	03 18	−44	108	02 34	−44	108	01 50	−44	109	01 06	−44	110	00 22	−43	110	285
74	03 58	44	108	03 14	44	109	02 30	44	110	01 46	44	110	01 02	44	111	286
73	04 38	44	109	03 54	44	110	03 10	44	110	02 26	44	111	01 42	45	112	287
72	05 18	44	110	04 34	44	111	03 50	45	111	03 05	44	112	02 21	45	113	288
71	05 58	44	111	05 14	45	111	04 29	45	112	03 44	44	113	03 00	45	113	289
70	06 38	−45	111	05 53	−45	112	05 08	−44	113	04 24	−45	113	03 39	−45	114	290
	10°			11°			12°			13°			14°			

S. Lat. {LHA greater than 180°....... Zn=180−Z; LHA less than 180°........... Zn=180+Z}

DECLINATION (0°-14°) CONTRARY NAME TO LATITUDE

LAT 45°

N. Lat. {LHA greater than 180°....... Zn=Z; LHA less than 180°.......... Zn=360−Z}

DECLINATION (0°-14°) CONTRARY NAME TO LATITUDE

LHA	0° Hc	d	Z	1° Hc	d	Z	2° Hc	d	Z	3° Hc	d	Z	4° Hc	d	Z
	° ′	′	°	° ′	′	°	° ′	′	°	° ′	′	°	° ′	′	°
69	14 41	44	105	13 57	44	106	13 13	44	107	12 29	45	107	11 44	44	108
68	15 22	44	106	14 38	45	107	13 53	44	107	13 09	44	108	12 25	45	109
67	16 02	44	107	15 18	44	107	14 34	45	108	13 49	44	109	13 05	45	110
66	16 43	44	108	15 59	45	108	15 14	45	109	14 29	44	110	13 45	45	110
65	17 23	−44	108	16 39	−45	109	15 54	−45	110	15 09	−45	110	14 24	−45	111
64	18 04	45	109	17 19	45	110	16 34	45	110	15 49	45	111	15 04	45	112
63	18 44	45	110	17 59	45	111	17 14	46	111	16 28	45	112	15 43	45	113
62	19 23	45	111	18 38	45	111	17 53	45	112	17 08	46	113	16 22	45	113
61	20 03	45	111	19 18	46	112	18 32	45	113	17 47	46	114	17 01	46	114
60	20 42	−45	112	19 57	−46	113	19 11	−45	114	18 26	−46	114	17 40	−46	115
59	21 22	46	113	20 36	46	114	19 50	46	114	19 04	46	115	18 18	46	116
58	22 00	45	114	21 15	46	115	20 29	47	115	19 42	46	116	18 56	46	117
57	22 39	46	115	21 53	46	115	21 07	47	116	20 20	46	117	19 34	47	117
56	23 18	47	116	22 31	46	116	21 45	47	117	20 58	47	118	20 11	47	118
55	23 56	−47	116	23 09	−46	117	22 23	−47	118	21 36	−47	118	20 49	−48	119
54	24 34	47	117	23 47	47	118	23 00	47	119	22 13	47	119	21 26	48	120
53	25 11	47	118	24 24	47	119	23 37	47	119	22 50	48	120	22 02	47	121
52	25 48	47	119	25 01	47	120	24 14	48	120	23 26	48	121	22 38	47	122
51	26 25	47	120	25 38	48	121	24 50	48	121	24 02	48	122	23 14	48	123
50	27 02	−48	121	26 14	−48	121	25 26	−48	122	24 38	−48	123	23 50	−48	123
49	27 38	48	122	26 50	48	122	26 02	48	123	25 14	49	124	24 25	48	124
48	28 14	48	123	27 26	48	123	26 38	49	124	25 49	49	125	25 00	49	125
47	28 50	49	123	28 01	48	124	27 13	49	125	26 24	49	125	25 35	49	126
46	29 25	49	124	28 36	49	125	27 47	49	126	26 58	49	126	26 09	50	127
45	30 00	−49	125	29 11	−49	126	28 22	−50	127	27 32	−49	127	26 43	−50	128
44	30 34	49	126	29 45	49	127	28 56	50	128	28 06	50	128	27 16	50	129
43	31 09	50	127	30 19	50	128	29 29	50	129	28 39	50	129	27 49	51	130
42	31 42	50	128	30 52	50	129	30 02	50	129	29 12	51	130	28 21	51	131
41	32 15	50	129	31 25	50	130	30 35	51	130	29 44	51	131	28 53	51	132
40	32 48	−51	130	31 57	−50	131	31 07	−51	131	30 16	−51	132	29 25	−52	133
39	33 20	51	131	32 29	51	132	31 38	51	132	30 47	51	133	29 56	52	134
38	33 52	51	132	33 01	52	133	32 09	51	133	31 18	52	134	30 26	52	135
37	34 23	51	133	33 32	52	134	32 40	52	134	31 48	52	135	30 56	52	136
36	34 54	52	134	34 02	52	135	33 10	52	135	32 18	53	136	31 25	52	137
35	35 24	−52	135	34 32	−53	136	33 39	−52	137	32 47	−53	137	31 54	−53	138
34	35 53	52	136	35 01	53	137	34 08	52	138	33 16	53	138	32 23	54	139
33	36 22	52	137	35 30	53	138	34 37	53	139	33 44	54	139	32 50	53	140
32	36 51	53	139	35 58	54	139	35 04	53	140	34 11	54	140	33 17	53	141
31	37 19	54	140	36 25	53	140	35 32	54	141	34 38	54	141	33 44	54	142
30	37 46	−54	141	36 52	−54	141	35 58	−54	142	35 04	−54	142	34 10	−54	143
29	38 12	54	142	37 18	54	143	36 24	54	143	35 30	55	144	34 35	55	144
28	38 38	54	143	37 44	55	144	36 49	55	144	35 54	54	145	35 00	55	145
27	39 03	54	144	38 09	55	145	37 14	55	145	36 19	55	146	35 24	56	146
26	39 28	55	145	38 33	56	146	37 37	55	146	36 42	55	147	35 47	56	147
25	39 51	−55	147	38 56	−55	147	38 01	−56	148	37 05	−56	148	36 09	−55	149
24	40 14	55	148	39 19	56	148	38 23	56	149	37 27	56	149	36 31	56	150
23	40 37	56	149	39 41	56	150	38 45	57	150	37 48	56	150	36 52	56	151
22	40 58	56	150	40 02	57	151	39 05	56	151	38 09	57	152	37 12	56	152
21	41 19	57	152	40 22	56	152	39 26	57	152	38 29	57	153	37 32	57	153
20	41 39	−57	153	40 42	−57	153	39 45	−57	154	38 48	−57	154	37 51	−57	154
19	41 58	58	154	41 00	57	154	40 03	57	155	39 06	57	155	38 09	58	156
18	42 16	58	155	41 18	57	156	40 21	58	156	39 23	57	157	38 26	58	157
17	42 33	58	157	41 35	57	157	40 38	58	157	39 40	58	158	38 42	58	158
16	42 49	58	158	41 51	57	158	40 54	58	159	39 56	59	159	38 57	58	159
15	43 05	−58	159	42 07	−58	160	41 09	−59	160	40 10	−58	160	39 12	−58	161
14	43 19	58	161	42 21	58	161	41 23	59	161	40 24	58	162	39 26	59	162
13	43 33	59	162	42 34	58	162	41 36	59	163	40 37	58	163	39 39	59	163
12	43 46	59	163	42 47	59	164	41 48	59	164	40 49	59	164	39 50	58	164
11	43 57	58	165	42 59	59	165	42 00	60	165	41 00	59	165	40 01	59	166
10	44 08	−59	166	43 09	−59	166	42 10	−59	167	41 11	−59	167	40 12	−60	167
9	44 18	59	167	43 19	60	168	42 19	59	168	41 20	59	168	40 21	60	168
8	44 27	60	169	43 27	59	169	42 28	60	169	41 28	59	169	40 29	60	170
7	44 35	60	170	43 35	60	170	42 35	59	171	41 36	60	171	40 36	59	171
6	44 41	59	172	43 42	60	172	42 42	60	172	41 42	60	172	40 42	59	172
5	44 47	−60	173	43 47	−60	173	42 47	−59	173	41 48	−60	173	40 48	−60	173
4	44 52	60	174	43 52	60	174	42 52	60	175	41 52	60	175	40 52	60	175
3	44 55	60	176	43 55	59	176	42 56	60	176	41 56	60	176	40 56	60	176
2	44 58	60	177	43 58	60	177	42 58	60	177	41 58	60	177	40 58	60	177
1	45 00	60	179	44 00	60	179	43 00	60	179	42 00	60	179	41 00	60	179
0	45 00	−60	180	44 00	−60	180	43 00	−60	180	42 00	−60	180	41 00	−60	180

LHA	5° Hc	d	Z	6° Hc	d	Z	7° Hc	d	Z	8° Hc	d	Z	9° Hc	d	Z
	° ′	′	°	° ′	′	°	° ′	′	°	° ′	′	°	° ′	′	°
69	11 00	44	109	10 16	45	109	09 31	45	110	08 46	44	111	08 02	45	111
68	11 40	44	109	10 56	45	110	10 11	45	111	09 26	45	111	08 41	45	112
67	12 20	45	110	11 35	45	111	10 50	45	112	10 05	45	112	09 20	45	113
66	13 00	45	111	12 15	45	112	11 30	45	112	10 45	46	113	09 59	45	114
65	13 39	−45	112	12 54	−45	112	12 09	−45	113	11 24	−46	114	10 38	−45	114
64	14 19	46	113	13 33	45	113	12 48	46	114	12 02	45	115	11 17	46	115
63	14 58	46	113	14 12	45	114	13 27	46	115	12 41	46	115	11 55	46	116
62	15 37	46	114	14 51	46	115	14 05	46	115	13 19	46	116	12 33	46	117
61	16 15	46	115	15 29	46	116	14 43	46	116	13 57	46	117	13 11	47	118
60	16 54	−47	116	16 07	−46	116	15 21	−46	117	14 35	−47	118	13 48	−46	118
59	17 32	47	116	16 45	46	117	15 59	47	118	15 12	47	118	14 25	46	119
58	18 10	47	117	17 23	47	118	16 36	47	119	15 49	47	119	15 02	47	120
57	18 47	47	118	18 00	47	119	17 13	47	119	16 26	47	120	15 39	47	121
56	19 24	47	119	18 37	47	120	17 50	47	120	17 03	48	121	16 15	47	122
55	20 01	−47	120	19 14	−47	120	18 27	−48	121	17 39	−48	122	16 51	−47	122
54	20 38	47	121	19 51	48	121	19 03	48	122	18 15	48	123	17 27	48	123
53	21 15	48	121	20 27	48	122	19 39	48	123	18 51	49	123	18 02	48	124
52	21 51	48	122	21 03	49	123	20 14	48	124	19 26	48	124	18 38	49	125
51	22 26	48	123	21 38	48	124	20 50	49	124	20 01	49	125	19 12	49	126
50	23 02	−49	124	22 13	−49	125	21 24	−49	125	20 35	−49	126	19 46	−49	127
49	23 37	49	125	22 48	49	126	21 59	49	126	21 10	50	127	20 20	49	127
48	24 11	49	126	23 22	49	126	22 33	50	127	21 43	49	128	20 54	50	128
47	24 46	50	127	23 56	49	127	23 07	50	128	22 17	50	129	21 27	50	129
46	25 19	49	128	24 30	50	128	23 40	50	129	22 50	50	129	22 00	50	130
45	25 53	−50	129	25 03	−50	129	24 13	−51	130	23 22	−50	130	22 32	−50	131
44	26 26	50	129	25 36	51	130	24 45	50	131	23 55	51	131	23 04	51	132
43	26 58	50	130	26 08	51	131	25 17	51	132	24 26	51	132	23 35	51	133
42	27 30	50	131	26 40	51	132	25 49	51	133	24 58	52	133	24 06	51	134
41	28 02	51	132	27 11	51	133	26 20	52	133	25 28	51	134	24 37	52	135
40	28 33	−51	133	27 42	−52	134	26 50	−51	134	25 59	−52	135	25 07	−52	136
39	29 04	52	134	28 12	52	135	27 20	52	135	26 28	52	136	25 36	52	136
38	29 34	52	135	28 42	52	136	27 50	52	136	26 58	53	137	26 05	52	137
37	30 04	53	136	29 11	52	137	28 19	53	137	27 26	52	138	26 34	53	138
36	30 33	53	137	29 40	52	138	28 48	53	138	27 55	53	139	27 02	53	139
35	31 01	−52	138	30 09	−53	139	29 16	−54	139	28 22	−53	140	27 29	−53	140
34	31 29	53	139	30 36	53	140	29 43	54	140	28 49	53	141	27 56	54	141
33	31 57	54	140	31 03	53	141	30 10	54	141	29 16	54	142	28 22	54	142
32	32 24	54	141	31 30	54	142	30 36	54	142	29 42	54	143	28 48	55	143
31	32 50	54	142	31 56	54	143	31 02	55	143	30 07	54	144	29 13	55	144
30	33 16	−55	143	32 21	−54	144	31 27	−55	144	30 32	−55	145	29 37	−55	145
29	33 40	54	145	32 46	55	145	31 51	55	146	30 56	55	146	30 01	55	146
28	34 05	55	146	33 10	55	146	32 15	56	147	31 19	55	147	30 24	55	148
27	34 28	55	147	33 33	55	147	32 38	56	148	31 42	55	148	30 47	56	149
26	34 51	55	148	33 56	56	148	33 00	56	149	32 04	56	149	31 08	56	150
25	35 14	−56	149	34 18	−56	149	33 22	−56	150	32 26	−57	150	31 29	−56	151
24	35 35	56	150	34 39	56	151	33 43	57	151	32 46	56	151	31 50	57	152
23	35 56	57	151	34 59	56	152	34 03	57	152	33 06	56	153	32 10	57	153
22	36 16	57	152	35 19	57	153	34 22	57	153	33 25	56	154	32 29	57	154
21	36 35	57	154	35 38	57	154	34 41	57	154	33 44	57	155	32 47	57	155
20	36 54	−58	155	35 56	−57	155	34 59	−57	156	34 02	−58	156	33 04	−57	156
19	37 11	57	156	36 14	58	156	35 16	57	157	34 19	58	157	33 21	58	157
18	37 28	58	157	36 30	57	158	35 33	58	158	34 35	58	158	33 37	58	159
17	37 44	58	158	36 46	58	159	35 48	58	159	34 50	58	159	33 52	58	160
16	37 59	58	160	37 01	58	160	36 03	58	160	35 05	59	161	34 06	58	161
15	38 14	−59	161	37 15	−58	161	36 17	−59	161	35 18	−58	162	34 20	−59	162
14	38 27	58	162	37 29	59	162	36 30	59	163	35 31	58	163	34 33	59	163
13	38 40	59	163	37 41	59	164	36 42	59	164	35 43	58	164	34 45	59	164
12	38 52	59	165	37 53	59	165	36 54	59	165	35 55	59	165	34 56	59	166
11	39 02	59	166	38 03	59	166	37 04	59	166	36 05	59	167	35 06	59	167
10	39 12	−59	167	38 13	−59	167	37 14	−60	168	36 14	−59	168	35 15	−59	168
9	39 21	59	168	38 22	59	169	37 23	60	169	36 23	59	169	35 24	60	169
8	39 29	59	170	38 30	60	170	37 30	59	170	36 31	60	170	35 31	59	170
7	39 37	60	171	38 37	60	171	37 37	59	171	36 38	60	171	35 38	60	172
6	39 43	60	172	38 43	60	172	37 43	59	173	36 44	60	173	35 44	60	173
5	39 48	−60	174	38 48	−60	174	37 48	−59	174	36 49	−60	174	35 49	−60	174
4	39 52	60	175	38 52	59	175	37 53	60	175	36 53	60	175	35 53	60	175
3	39 56	60	176	38 56	60	176	37 56	60	176	36 56	60	176	35 56	60	176
2	39 58	60	177	38 58	60	177	37 58	60	178	36 58	60	178	35 58	60	178
1	40 00	60	179	39 00	60	179	38 00	60	179	37 00	60	179	36 00	60	179
0	40 00	−60	180	39 00	−60	180	38 00	−60	180	37 00	−60	180	36 00	−60	180

LHA	10° Hc	d	Z	11° Hc	d	Z	12° Hc	d	Z	13° Hc	d	Z	14° Hc	d	Z	LHA
	° ′	′	°	° ′	′	°	° ′	′	°	° ′	′	°	° ′	′	°	
69	07 17	45	112	06 32	45	113	05 47	45	113	05 02	45	114	04 17	45	115	291
68	07 56	45	113	07 11	45	114	06 26	45	114	05 41	45	115	04 56	45	115	292
67	08 35	45	114	07 50	45	114	07 05	46	115	06 19	45	116	05 34	45	116	293
66	09 14	45	114	08 29	46	115	07 43	45	116	06 58	46	116	06 12	46	117	294
65	09 53	−46	115	09 07	−46	116	08 21	−45	116	07 36	−46	117	06 50	−46	118	295
64	10 31	46	116	09 45	46	117	08 59	46	117	08 13	46	118	07 27	46	118	296
63	11 09	46	117	10 23	46	117	09 37	46	118	08 51	47	119	08 04	46	119	297
62	11 47	46	117	11 01	47	118	10 14	46	119	09 28	47	119	08 41	46	120	298
61	12 24	46	118	11 38	47	119	10 51	46	119	10 05	47	120	09 18	47	121	299
60	13 02	−47	119	12 15	−47	120	11 28	−47	120	10 41	−47	121	09 54	−47	122	300
59	13 39	47	120	12 52	47	120	12 05	48	121	11 17	47	122	10 30	47	122	301
58	14 15	47	121	13 28	47	121	12 41	48	122	11 53	47	122	11 06	48	123	302
57	14 52	48	121	14 04	47	122	13 17	48	123	12 29	48	123	11 41	47	124	303
56	15 28	48	122	14 40	48	123	13 52	48	123	13 04	47	124	12 17	49	125	304
55	16 04	−48	123	15 16	−48	124	14 28	−48	124	13 40	−49	125	12 51	−48	125	305
54	16 39	48	124	15 51	48	124	15 03	49	125	14 14	48	126	13 26	49	126	306
53	17 14	48	125	16 26	49	125	15 37	48	126	14 49	49	126	14 00	49	127	307
52	17 49	49	125	17 00	49	126	16 11	49	127	15 22	49	127	14 33	49	128	308
51	18 23	49	126	17 34	49	127	16 45	49	128	15 56	49	128	15 07	50	129	309
50	18 57	−49	127	18 08	−49	128	17 19	−50	128	16 29	−49	129	15 40	−50	130	310
49	19 31	50	128	18 41	49	129	17 52	50	129	17 02	50	130	16 12	50	130	311
48	20 04	50	129	19 14	49	129	18 25	50	130	17 35	51	131	16 44	50	131	312
47	20 37	50	130	19 47	50	130	18 57	50	131	18 07	51	131	17 16	50	132	313
46	21 10	51	131	20 19	50	131	19 29	51	132	18 38	51	132	17 47	50	133	314
45	21 42	−51	132	20 51	−51	132	20 00	−51	133	19 09	−51	133	18 18	−51	134	315
44	22 13	51	132	21 22	51	133	20 31	51	134	19 40	51	134	18 49	52	135	316
43	22 44	51	133	21 53	51	134	21 02	52	134	20 10	51	135	19 19	52	136	317
42	23 15	52	134	22 23	51	135	21 32	52	135	20 40	52	136	19 48	52	136	318
41	23 45	52	135	22 53	52	136	22 01	52	136	21 09	52	137	20 17	52	137	319
40	24 15	−52	136	23 23	−52	137	22 31	−53	137	21 38	−52	138	20 46	−53	138	320
39	24 44	52	137	23 52	53	138	22 59	52	138	22 07	53	139	21 14	53	139	321
38	25 13	53	138	24 20	53	138	23 27	53	139	22 34	53	140	21 41	53	140	322
37	25 41	53	139	24 48	53	139	23 55	53	140	23 02	54	140	22 08	53	141	323
36	26 09	54	140	25 15	53	140	24 22	54	141	23 28	53	141	22 35	54	142	324
35	26 36	−54	141	25 42	−54	141	24 48	−53	142	23 55	−54	142	23 01	−54	143	325
34	27 02	54	142	26 08	54	142	25 14	54	143	24 20	54	143	23 26	54	144	326
33	27 28	54	143	26 34	54	143	25 40	55	144	24 45	54	144	23 51	54	145	327
32	27 53	54	144	26 59	54	144	26 05	55	145	25 10	55	145	24 15	54	146	328
31	28 18	55	145	27 23	54	145	26 29	55	146	25 34	55	146	24 39	55	147	329
30	28 42	−55	146	27 47	−55	146	26 52	−55	147	25 57	−55	147	25 02	−55	148	330
29	29 06	55	147	28 11	56	147	27 15	55	148	26 20	56	148	25 24	55	149	331
28	29 29	56	148	28 33	55	148	27 38	56	149	26 42	56	149	25 46	56	150	332
27	29 51	56	149	28 55	56	149	27 59	56	150	27 03	56	150	26 07	56	151	333
26	30 12	56	150	29 16	56	150	28 20	56	151	27 24	56	151	26 28	57	152	334
25	30 33	−56	151	29 37	−56	152	28 41	−57	152	27 44	−56	152	26 48	−57	153	335
24	30 53	56	152	29 57	57	153	29 00	57	153	28 03	56	153	27 07	57	154	336
23	31 13	57	153	30 16	57	154	29 19	57	154	28 22	57	154	27 25	57	155	337
22	31 32	58	154	30 34	57	155	29 37	57	155	28 40	57	155	27 43	57	156	338
21	31 50	58	156	30 52	57	156	29 55	58	156	28 57	57	157	28 00	57	157	339
20	32 07	−58	157	31 09	−57	157	30 12	−58	157	29 14	−58	158	28 16	−57	158	340
19	32 23	57	158	31 26	58	158	30 28	58	158	29 30	58	159	28 32	58	159	341
18	32 39	58	159	31 41	58	159	30 43	58	159	29 45	58	160	28 47	58	160	342
17	32 54	58	160	31 56	58	160	30 58	59	161	29 59	58	161	29 01	58	161	343
16	33 08	58	161	32 10	59	161	31 11	58	162	30 13	59	162	29 14	58	162	344
15	33 21	−58	162	32 23	−59	163	31 24	−58	163	30 26	−59	163	29 27	−59	163	345
14	33 34	59	163	32 35	59	164	31 36	58	164	30 38	59	164	29 39	59	164	346
13	33 46	59	165	32 47	59	165	31 48	59	165	30 49	59	165	29 50	59	165	347
12	33 57	59	166	32 58	60	166	31 58	59	166	30 59	59	166	30 00	59	167	348
11	34 07	60	167	33 07	59	167	32 08	59	167	31 09	59	168	30 10	60	168	349
10	34 16	−59	168	33 17	−60	168	32 17	−59	168	31 18	−60	169	30 18	−59	169	350
9	34 24	59	169	33 25	60	169	32 25	59	170	31 26	60	170	30 26	59	170	351
8	34 32	60	170	33 32	59	171	32 33	60	171	31 33	60	171	30 33	59	171	352
7	34 38	59	172	33 39	60	172	32 39	60	172	31 39	59	172	30 40	60	172	353
6	34 44	60	173	33 44	59	173	32 45	60	173	31 45	60	173	30 45	60	173	354
5	34 49	−60	174	33 49	−60	174	32 49	−60	174	31 49	−59	174	30 50	−60	174	355
4	34 53	60	175	33 53	60	175	32 53	60	175	31 53	60	175	30 53	60	176	356
3	34 56	60	176	33 56	60	176	32 56	60	177	31 56	60	177	30 56	60	177	357
2	34 58	60	178	33 58	60	178	32 58	60	178	31 58	60	178	30 58	60	178	358
1	35 00	60	179	34 00	60	179	33 00	60	179	32 00	60	179	31 00	60	179	359
0	35 00	−60	180	34 00	−60	180	33 00	−60	180	32 00	−60	180	31 00	−60	180	360

S. Lat. {LHA greater than 180°....... Zn=180−Z; LHA less than 180°.......... Zn=180+Z}

DECLINATION (0°-14°) CONTRARY NAME TO LATITUDE

LAT 45°

N. Lat. {LHA greater than 180°....... Zn=Z; LHA less than 180°........... Zn=360−Z}

DECLINATION (15°-29°) SAME NAME AS LATITUDE

LHA	15° Hc	d	Z	16° Hc	d	Z	17° Hc	d	Z	18° Hc	d	Z	19° Hc	d	Z
	° ′	′	°	° ′	′	°	° ′	′	°	° ′	′	°	° ′	′	°
0	60 00	+60	180	61 00	+60	180	62 00	+60	180	63 00	+60	180	64 00	+60	180
1	59 59	60	178	60 59	60	178	61 59	60	178	62 59	60	178	63 59	60	178
2	59 57	60	176	60 57	60	176	61 57	60	176	62 57	60	176	63 57	60	176
3	59 54	59	174	60 53	60	174	61 53	60	174	62 53	60	174	63 53	60	174
4	59 49	59	172	60 48	60	172	61 48	60	172	62 48	59	172	63 47	60	171
5	59 42	+60	170	60 42	+59	170	61 41	+60	170	62 41	+59	170	63 40	+60	169
6	59 34	60	169	60 34	59	168	61 33	59	168	62 32	60	168	63 32	59	167
7	59 25	59	167	60 24	60	166	61 24	58	166	62 22	59	166	63 21	59	165
8	59 15	59	165	60 14	58	164	61 12	59	164	62 11	59	164	63 10	58	163
9	59 03	59	163	60 02	58	163	61 00	58	162	61 58	59	162	62 57	58	161
10	58 50	+58	161	59 48	+58	161	60 46	+58	160	61 44	+58	160	62 42	+58	159
11	58 36	57	159	59 33	58	159	60 31	58	158	61 29	57	158	62 26	58	157
12	58 20	57	158	59 17	58	157	60 15	57	156	61 12	57	156	62 09	57	155
13	58 03	57	156	59 00	57	155	59 57	57	155	60 54	57	154	61 51	56	153
14	57 45	57	154	58 42	56	153	59 38	57	153	60 35	56	152	61 31	56	151
15	57 26	+56	152	58 22	+56	152	59 18	+56	151	60 14	+56	150	61 10	+55	150
16	57 06	56	151	58 02	55	150	58 57	56	149	59 53	55	149	60 48	55	148
17	56 44	56	149	57 40	55	148	58 35	55	148	59 30	55	147	60 25	54	146
18	56 22	55	147	57 17	55	147	58 12	54	146	59 06	54	145	60 00	54	144
19	55 59	54	146	56 53	54	145	57 47	54	144	58 41	54	143	59 35	53	143
20	55 34	+54	144	56 28	+54	144	57 22	+54	143	58 16	+53	142	59 09	+52	141
21	55 09	54	143	56 03	53	142	56 56	53	141	57 49	53	140	58 42	52	139
22	54 43	53	141	55 36	53	140	56 29	52	140	57 21	52	139	58 13	52	138
23	54 16	53	140	55 09	52	139	56 01	52	138	56 53	52	137	57 45	51	136
24	53 48	52	138	54 40	52	138	55 32	52	137	56 24	51	136	57 15	50	135
25	53 20	+51	137	54 11	+52	136	55 03	+51	135	55 54	+50	134	56 44	+50	133
26	52 50	51	136	53 41	51	135	54 32	51	134	55 23	50	133	56 13	50	132
27	52 20	51	134	53 11	50	133	54 01	50	132	54 51	50	131	55 41	49	130
28	51 49	51	133	52 40	50	132	53 30	49	131	54 19	49	130	55 08	49	129
29	51 18	50	132	52 08	49	131	52 57	49	130	53 46	49	129	54 35	48	128
30	50 46	+49	130	51 35	+49	129	52 24	+49	128	53 13	+48	127	54 01	+48	126
31	50 13	49	129	51 02	49	128	51 51	48	127	52 39	48	126	53 27	47	125
32	49 40	48	128	50 28	49	127	51 17	48	126	52 05	47	125	52 52	47	124
33	49 06	48	127	49 54	48	126	50 42	48	125	51 30	46	124	52 16	47	123
34	48 32	48	125	49 20	47	124	50 07	47	124	50 54	46	123	51 40	46	122
35	47 57	+47	124	48 44	+47	123	49 31	+47	122	50 18	+46	121	51 04	+46	120
36	47 21	48	123	48 09	46	122	48 55	47	121	49 42	45	120	50 27	45	119
37	46 46	46	122	47 32	47	121	48 19	46	120	49 05	45	119	49 50	45	118
38	46 09	47	121	46 56	46	120	47 42	45	119	48 27	45	118	49 12	45	117
39	45 33	46	120	46 19	46	119	47 05	45	118	47 50	44	117	48 34	45	116
40	44 56	+46	119	45 42	+45	118	46 27	+45	117	47 12	+44	116	47 56	+44	115
41	44 18	46	118	45 04	45	117	45 49	44	116	46 33	44	115	47 17	44	114
42	43 41	45	117	44 26	45	116	45 11	44	115	45 55	44	114	46 39	43	113
43	43 03	44	116	43 47	45	115	44 32	44	114	45 16	43	113	45 59	43	112
44	42 24	45	115	43 09	44	114	43 53	44	113	44 37	43	112	45 20	42	111
45	41 45	+45	114	42 30	+44	113	43 14	+43	112	43 57	+43	111	44 40	+42	110
46	41 06	45	113	41 51	43	112	42 34	43	111	43 17	43	110	44 00	42	109
47	40 27	44	112	41 11	43	111	41 54	43	110	42 37	43	109	43 20	42	108
48	39 48	43	111	40 31	43	110	41 14	43	109	41 57	42	108	42 39	42	107
49	39 08	43	110	39 51	43	109	40 34	43	108	41 17	42	107	41 59	41	106
50	38 28	+43	109	39 11	+43	108	39 54	+42	107	40 36	+42	106	41 18	+41	105
51	37 48	43	108	38 31	42	107	39 13	42	106	39 55	42	106	40 37	41	105
52	37 07	43	107	37 50	42	106	38 32	42	106	39 14	42	105	39 56	41	104
53	36 27	42	107	37 09	42	106	37 51	42	105	38 33	41	104	39 14	41	103
54	35 46	42	106	36 28	42	105	37 10	42	104	37 52	41	103	38 33	41	102
55	35 05	+42	105	35 47	+42	104	36 29	+41	103	37 10	+41	102	37 51	+41	101
56	34 24	42	104	35 06	42	103	35 48	41	102	36 29	41	101	37 10	40	100
57	33 43	42	103	34 25	41	102	35 06	41	101	35 47	41	101	36 28	40	100
58	33 01	42	102	33 43	41	102	34 24	42	101	35 06	40	100	35 46	40	99
59	32 20	41	102	33 01	42	101	33 43	41	100	34 24	40	99	35 04	40	98
60	31 38	+42	101	32 20	+41	100	33 01	+41	99	33 42	+40	98	34 22	+40	97
61	30 56	42	100	31 38	41	99	32 19	41	98	33 00	40	97	33 40	40	97
62	30 15	41	99	30 56	41	98	31 37	41	98	32 18	40	97	32 58	40	96
63	29 33	41	98	30 14	41	98	30 55	40	97	31 35	41	96	32 16	39	95
64	28 51	41	98	29 32	41	97	30 13	40	96	30 53	40	95	31 33	40	94
65	28 09	+41	97	28 50	+40	96	29 30	+41	95	30 11	+40	94	30 51	+40	94
66	27 26	41	96	28 07	41	95	28 48	41	95	29 29	40	94	30 09	39	93
67	26 44	41	95	27 25	41	95	28 06	40	94	28 46	40	93	29 26	40	92
68	26 02	41	95	26 43	40	94	27 23	41	93	28 04	40	92	28 44	39	91
69	25 20	41	94	26 01	40	93	26 41	40	92	27 21	40	92	28 01	40	91

LHA	20° Hc	d	Z	21° Hc	d	Z	22° Hc	d	Z	23° Hc	d	Z	24° Hc	d	Z
	° ′	′	°	° ′	′	°	° ′	′	°	° ′	′	°	° ′	′	°
0	65 00	+60	180	66 00	+60	180	67 00	+60	180	68 00	+60	180	69 00	+60	180
1	64 59	60	178	65 59	60	178	66 59	60	178	67 59	60	178	68 59	60	178
2	64 57	60	176	65 57	60	175	66 57	59	175	67 56	60	175	68 56	60	175
3	64 53	59	173	65 52	60	173	66 52	60	173	67 52	60	173	68 52	59	172
4	64 47	60	171	65 47	59	171	66 46	60	171	67 46	59	170	68 45	59	170
5	64 40	+59	169	65 39	+59	169	66 38	+60	168	67 38	+59	168	68 37	+59	167
6	64 31	59	167	65 30	59	166	66 29	59	166	67 28	59	166	68 27	58	165
7	64 20	59	165	65 19	59	164	66 18	58	164	67 16	59	163	68 15	58	163
8	64 08	59	163	65 07	58	162	66 05	58	161	67 03	58	161	68 01	58	160
9	63 55	58	161	64 53	58	160	65 51	57	159	66 48	58	159	67 46	57	158
10	63 40	+58	158	64 38	+57	158	65 35	+57	157	66 32	+57	156	67 29	+57	156
11	63 24	57	156	64 21	57	156	65 18	56	155	66 14	57	154	67 11	56	153
12	63 06	57	154	64 03	56	154	64 59	56	153	65 55	56	152	66 51	55	151
13	62 47	56	153	63 43	56	152	64 39	56	151	65 35	55	150	66 30	55	149
14	62 27	55	151	63 22	56	150	64 18	55	149	65 13	54	148	66 07	54	147
15	62 05	+55	149	63 00	+55	148	63 55	+54	147	64 49	+54	146	65 43	+54	145
16	61 43	54	147	62 37	54	146	63 31	54	145	64 25	53	144	65 18	53	143
17	61 19	54	145	62 13	54	144	63 07	53	143	64 00	52	142	64 52	52	141
18	60 54	54	143	61 48	53	142	62 41	52	141	63 33	52	140	64 25	52	139
19	60 28	53	142	61 21	53	141	62 14	51	140	63 05	52	139	63 57	51	137
20	60 01	+53	140	60 54	+52	139	61 46	+51	138	62 37	+51	137	63 28	+50	136
21	59 34	51	138	60 25	52	137	61 17	50	136	62 07	51	135	62 58	49	134
22	59 05	51	137	59 56	51	136	60 47	50	135	61 37	50	134	62 27	48	132
23	58 36	50	135	59 26	50	134	60 16	50	133	61 06	49	132	61 55	48	131
24	58 05	50	134	58 55	50	133	59 45	49	132	60 34	48	130	61 22	48	129
25	57 34	+50	132	58 24	+49	131	59 13	+48	130	60 01	+48	129	60 49	+47	128
26	57 03	49	131	57 52	48	130	58 40	48	129	59 28	47	127	60 15	47	126
27	56 30	49	129	57 19	48	128	58 07	47	127	58 54	47	126	59 41	45	125
28	55 57	48	128	56 45	47	127	57 32	47	126	58 19	46	125	59 05	46	123
29	55 23	48	127	56 11	47	126	56 58	46	125	57 44	46	123	58 30	45	122
30	54 49	+47	125	55 36	+46	124	56 22	+46	123	57 08	+45	122	57 53	+45	121
31	54 14	47	124	55 01	46	123	55 47	45	122	56 32	45	121	57 17	44	120
32	53 39	46	123	54 25	45	122	55 10	45	121	55 55	45	120	56 40	43	118
33	53 03	46	122	53 49	45	121	54 34	44	119	55 18	44	118	56 02	43	117
34	52 26	46	121	53 12	45	119	53 57	44	118	54 41	43	117	55 24	43	116
35	51 50	+45	119	52 35	+44	118	53 19	+44	117	54 03	+43	116	54 46	+42	115
36	51 12	45	118	51 57	44	117	52 41	43	116	53 24	43	115	54 07	42	114
37	50 35	44	117	51 19	44	116	52 03	43	115	52 46	42	114	53 28	42	113
38	49 57	44	116	50 41	43	115	51 24	43	114	52 07	42	113	52 49	41	112
39	49 19	43	115	50 02	43	114	50 45	42	113	51 27	42	112	52 09	41	111
40	48 40	+43	114	49 23	+43	113	50 06	+42	112	50 48	+41	111	51 29	+41	109
41	48 01	43	113	48 44	42	112	49 26	42	111	50 08	41	110	50 49	40	108
42	47 22	42	112	48 04	42	111	48 46	42	110	49 28	41	109	50 09	40	108
43	46 42	43	111	47 25	41	110	48 06	42	109	48 48	40	108	49 28	40	107
44	46 02	43	110	46 45	41	109	47 26	41	108	48 07	40	107	48 47	40	106
45	45 22	+42	109	46 04	+42	108	46 46	+40	107	47 26	+40	106	48 06	+40	105
46	44 42	42	108	45 24	41	107	46 05	40	106	46 45	40	105	47 25	40	104
47	44 02	41	107	44 43	41	106	45 24	40	105	46 04	40	104	46 44	39	103
48	43 21	41	106	44 02	41	105	44 43	40	104	45 23	40	103	46 03	38	102
49	42 40	41	105	43 21	41	104	44 02	40	103	44 42	39	102	45 21	39	101
50	41 59	+41	104	42 40	+40	103	43 20	+40	102	44 00	+39	101	44 39	+39	100
51	41 18	41	104	41 59	40	103	42 39	39	102	43 18	40	101	43 58	38	100
52	40 37	40	103	41 17	40	102	41 57	40	101	42 37	39	100	43 16	38	99
53	39 55	41	102	40 36	40	101	41 16	39	100	41 55	39	99	42 34	38	98
54	39 14	40	101	39 54	40	100	40 34	39	99	41 13	39	98	41 52	38	97
55	38 32	+40	100	39 12	+40	99	39 52	+39	98	40 31	+38	97	41 09	+39	96
56	37 50	40	100	38 30	40	99	39 10	39	98	39 49	38	97	40 27	38	96
57	37 08	40	99	37 48	40	98	38 28	39	97	39 07	38	96	39 45	38	95
58	36 26	40	98	37 06	39	97	37 45	39	96	38 24	39	95	39 03	38	94
59	35 44	40	97	36 24	39	96	37 03	39	95	37 42	38	94	38 20	38	93
60	35 02	+40	96	35 42	+39	95	36 21	+39	95	37 00	+38	94	37 38	+38	93
61	34 20	40	96	35 00	39	95	35 39	38	94	36 17	39	93	36 56	37	92
62	33 38	39	95	34 17	39	94	34 56	39	93	35 35	38	92	36 13	38	91
63	32 55	40	94	33 35	39	93	34 14	39	92	34 53	38	91	35 31	38	90
64	32 13	39	93	32 52	40	93	33 32	38	92	34 10	38	91	34 48	38	90
65	31 31	+39	93	32 10	+39	92	32 49	+39	91	33 28	+38	90	34 06	+38	89
66	30 48	40	92	31 28	39	91	32 07	38	90	32 45	39	89	33 24	37	88
67	30 06	39	91	30 45	39	90	31 24	39	89	32 03	38	89	32 41	38	88
68	29 23	40	91	30 03	39	90	30 42	38	89	31 20	39	88	31 59	38	87
69	28 41	39	90	29 20	39	89	29 59	39	88	30 38	38	87	31 16	38	86

LHA	25° Hc	d	Z	26° Hc	d	Z	27° Hc	d	Z	28° Hc	d	Z	29° Hc	d	Z	LHA
	° ′	′	°	° ′	′	°	° ′	′	°	° ′	′	°	° ′	′	°	
0	70 00	+60	180	71 00	+60	180	72 00	+60	180	73 00	+60	180	74 00	+60	180	360
1	69 59	60	177	70 59	60	177	71 59	60	177	72 59	60	177	73 59	60	177	359
2	69 56	60	175	70 56	60	175	71 56	60	174	72 56	59	174	73 55	60	174	358
3	69 51	60	172	70 51	59	172	71 50	60	171	72 50	60	171	73 50	59	171	357
4	69 44	60	170	70 44	59	169	71 43	59	169	72 42	59	168	73 41	59	168	356
5	69 36	+59	167	70 35	+59	166	71 34	+58	166	72 32	+59	165	73 31	+59	164	355
6	69 25	59	164	70 24	58	164	71 22	59	163	72 21	58	162	73 19	58	161	354
7	69 13	58	162	70 11	58	161	71 09	58	160	72 07	57	160	73 04	57	159	353
8	68 59	57	159	69 56	58	159	70 54	57	158	71 51	57	157	72 48	56	156	352
9	68 43	57	157	69 40	57	156	70 37	56	155	71 33	56	154	72 29	56	153	351
10	68 26	+56	155	69 22	+56	154	70 18	+56	153	71 14	+55	152	72 09	+55	150	350
11	68 07	56	152	69 03	55	151	69 58	55	150	70 53	54	149	71 47	54	148	349
12	67 46	55	150	68 41	55	149	69 36	54	148	70 30	54	147	71 24	53	145	348
13	67 25	54	148	68 19	54	147	69 13	53	146	70 06	53	144	70 59	52	143	347
14	67 01	54	146	67 55	53	145	68 48	53	143	69 41	52	142	70 33	51	141	346
15	66 37	+53	144	67 30	+52	143	68 22	+52	141	69 14	+51	140	70 05	+50	138	345
16	66 11	53	142	67 04	51	141	67 55	51	139	68 46	50	138	69 36	50	136	344
17	65 44	52	140	66 36	51	139	67 27	50	137	68 17	49	136	69 06	49	134	343
18	65 17	50	138	66 07	51	137	66 58	49	135	67 47	48	134	68 35	48	132	342
19	64 48	50	136	65 38	49	135	66 27	49	133	67 16	48	132	68 04	46	130	341
20	64 18	+49	134	65 07	+49	133	65 56	+48	132	66 44	+47	130	67 31	+46	129	340
21	63 47	49	133	64 36	48	131	65 24	47	130	66 11	46	128	66 57	45	127	339
22	63 15	49	131	64 04	47	130	64 51	46	128	65 37	46	127	66 23	44	125	338
23	62 43	48	129	63 31	46	128	64 17	46	127	65 03	45	125	65 48	44	124	337
24	62 10	47	128	62 57	46	127	63 43	45	125	64 28	44	124	65 12	43	122	336
25	61 36	+46	126	62 22	+46	125	63 08	+44	124	63 52	+44	122	64 36	+42	121	335
26	61 02	45	125	61 47	45	124	62 32	44	122	63 16	43	121	63 59	42	119	334
27	60 26	46	124	61 12	44	122	61 56	43	121	62 39	43	119	63 22	41	118	333
28	59 51	44	122	60 35	44	121	61 19	43	119	62 02	42	118	62 44	41	116	332
29	59 15	44	121	59 59	43	119	60 42	42	118	61 24	42	117	62 06	40	115	331
30	58 38	+44	120	59 22	+42	118	60 04	+42	117	60 46	+41	115	61 27	+40	114	330
31	58 01	43	118	58 44	42	117	59 26	42	116	60 08	40	114	60 48	39	113	329
32	57 23	43	117	58 06	42	116	58 48	41	114	59 29	40	113	60 09	39	111	328
33	56 45	42	116	57 27	42	115	58 09	40	113	58 49	40	112	59 29	39	110	327
34	56 07	42	115	56 49	41	113	57 30	40	112	58 10	39	111	58 49	38	109	326
35	55 28	+42	114	56 10	+40	112	56 50	+40	111	57 30	+39	110	58 09	+38	108	325
36	54 49	41	112	55 30	40	111	56 10	40	110	56 50	38	108	57 28	38	107	324
37	54 10	40	111	54 50	40	110	55 30	40	109	56 10	38	107	56 48	37	106	323
38	53 30	40	110	54 10	40	109	54 50	39	108	55 29	38	106	56 07	37	105	322
39	52 50	40	109	53 30	40	108	54 10	38	107	54 48	38	105	55 26	37	104	321
40	52 10	+40	108	52 50	+39	107	53 29	+38	106	54 07	+38	105	54 45	+36	103	320
41	51 29	40	107	52 09	39	106	52 48	38	105	53 26	37	104	54 03	37	102	319
42	50 49	39	106	51 28	39	105	52 07	38	104	52 45	37	103	53 22	36	101	318
43	50 08	39	105	50 47	39	104	51 26	37	103	52 03	37	102	52 40	36	100	317
44	49 27	39	104	50 06	38	103	50 44	38	102	51 22	36	101	51 58	36	100	316
45	48 46	+39	104	49 25	+38	102	50 03	+37	101	50 40	+36	100	51 16	+36	99	315
46	48 05	38	103	48 43	38	102	49 21	37	100	49 58	36	99	50 34	36	98	314
47	47 23	38	102	48 01	38	101	48 39	37	100	49 16	36	98	49 52	36	97	313
48	46 41	39	101	47 20	37	100	47 57	37	99	48 34	36	97	49 10	35	96	312
49	46 00	38	100	46 38	37	99	47 15	37	98	47 52	36	97	48 28	35	95	311
50	45 18	+38	99	45 56	+37	98	46 33	+37	97	47 10	+36	96	47 46	+35	95	310
51	44 36	38	98	45 14	37	97	45 51	37	96	46 28	35	95	47 03	35	94	309
52	43 54	38	98	44 32	37	97	45 09	36	95	45 45	36	94	46 21	35	93	308
53	43 12	38	97	43 50	37	96	44 27	36	95	45 03	36	94	45 39	35	92	307
54	42 30	37	96	43 07	37	95	43 44	37	94	44 21	35	93	44 56	35	92	306
55	41 48	+37	95	42 25	+37	94	43 02	+36	93	43 38	+36	92	44 14	+35	91	305
56	41 05	38	95	41 43	37	94	42 20	36	92	42 56	35	91	43 31	35	90	304
57	40 23	37	94	41 00	37	93	41 37	36	92	42 13	36	91	42 49	35	90	303
58	39 41	37	93	40 18	37	92	40 55	36	91	41 31	36	90	42 07	35	89	302
59	38 58	38	92	39 36	36	91	40 12	37	90	40 49	35	89	41 24	35	88	301
60	38 16	+37	92	38 53	+37	91	39 30	+36	90	40 06	+36	89	40 42	+35	88	300
61	37 33	38	91	38 11	36	90	38 47	37	89	39 24	35	88	39 59	36	87	299
62	36 51	37	90	37 28	37	89	38 05	36	88	38 41	36	87	39 17	35	86	298
63	36 09	37	89	36 46	37	89	37 23	36	88	37 59	36	87	38 35	35	85	297
64	35 26	37	89	36 03	37	88	36 40	37	87	37 17	35	86	37 52	36	85	296
65	34 44	+37	88	35 21	+37	87	35 58	+36	86	36 34	+36	85	37 10	+36	84	295
66	34 01	38	87	34 39	37	86	35 16	36	86	35 52	36	85	36 28	36	84	294
67	33 19	37	87	33 56	37	86	34 33	37	85	35 10	36	84	35 46	36	83	293
68	32 37	37	86	33 14	37	85	33 51	37	84	34 28	36	83	35 04	36	82	292
69	31 54	38	85	32 32	37	84	33 09	37	84	33 46	36	83	34 22	36	82	291

S. Lat. {LHA greater than 180°....... Zn=180−Z; LHA less than 180°........... Zn=180+Z}

DECLINATION (15°-29°) SAME NAME AS LATITUDE

N. Lat. {LHA greater than 180°....... Zn=Z / LHA less than 180°........... Zn=360−Z}

DECLINATION (15°-29°) SAME NAME AS LATITUDE

LAT 45°

	15°			16°			17°			18°			19°			20°			21°			22°			23°			24°			25°			26°			27°			28°			29°			
LHA	Hc	d	Z	Hc	d	Z	Hc	d	Z	Hc	d	Z	Hc	d	Z	Hc	d	Z	Hc	d	Z	Hc	d	Z	Hc	d	Z	Hc	d	Z	Hc	d	Z	Hc	d	Z	Hc	d	Z	Hc	d	Z	Hc	d	Z	LHA
	° ′	′	°	° ′	′	°	° ′	′	°	° ′	′	°	° ′	′	°	° ′	′	°	° ′	′	°	° ′	′	°	° ′	′	°	° ′	′	°	° ′	′	°	° ′	′	°	° ′	′	°	° ′	′	°	° ′	′	°	
70	24 37	+41	93	25 18	+41	92	25 59	+40	92	26 39	+40	91	27 19	+40	90	27 59	+39	89	28 38	+39	88	29 17	+39	87	29 56	+38	87	30 34	+38	86	31 12	+38	85	31 50	+37	84	32 27	+37	83	33 04	+36	82	33 40	+36	81	290
71	23 55	41	93	24 36	40	92	25 16	41	91	25 57	40	90	26 37	39	89	27 16	40	88	27 56	39	88	28 35	38	87	29 13	39	86	29 52	38	85	30 30	37	84	31 07	38	83	31 45	37	82	32 22	36	81	32 58	36	80	289
72	23 13	40	92	23 53	41	91	24 34	40	90	25 14	40	89	25 54	40	89	26 34	39	88	27 13	39	87	27 52	39	86	28 31	39	85	29 10	38	84	29 48	37	83	30 25	38	82	31 03	37	82	31 40	36	81	32 16	36	80	288
73	22 30	41	91	23 11	40	90	23 51	41	89	24 32	40	89	25 12	39	88	25 51	40	87	26 31	39	86	27 10	39	85	27 49	38	84	28 27	39	84	29 06	37	83	29 43	38	82	30 21	37	81	30 58	37	80	31 35	36	79	287
74	21 48	40	90	22 28	41	90	23 09	40	89	23 49	40	88	24 29	40	87	25 09	40	86	25 49	39	85	26 28	39	85	27 07	38	84	27 45	38	83	28 23	38	82	29 01	38	81	29 39	37	80	30 16	37	79	30 53	36	78	286
75	21 05	+41	90	21 46	+41	89	22 27	+40	88	23 07	+40	87	23 47	+40	86	24 27	+39	86	25 06	+40	85	25 46	+39	84	26 25	+38	83	27 03	+39	82	27 42	+38	81	28 20	+37	81	28 57	+38	80	29 35	+36	79	30 11	+37	78	285
76	20 23	41	89	21 04	40	88	21 44	41	87	22 25	40	87	23 05	39	86	23 44	40	85	24 24	39	84	25 03	39	83	25 42	39	82	26 21	39	82	27 00	38	81	27 38	38	80	28 16	37	79	28 53	37	78	29 30	37	77	284
77	19 40	41	88	20 21	41	87	21 02	40	87	21 42	40	86	22 22	40	85	23 02	40	84	23 42	39	83	24 21	39	83	25 00	39	82	25 39	39	81	26 18	38	80	26 56	38	79	27 34	38	78	28 12	37	77	28 49	37	77	283
78	18 58	41	88	19 39	40	87	20 19	41	86	21 00	40	85	21 40	40	84	22 20	40	84	23 00	39	83	23 39	39	82	24 18	39	81	24 57	39	80	25 36	38	79	26 14	38	79	26 52	38	78	27 30	38	77	28 08	37	76	282
79	18 16	41	87	18 57	40	86	19 37	41	85	20 18	40	85	20 58	40	84	21 38	40	83	22 18	39	82	22 57	40	81	23 37	39	80	24 16	38	80	24 54	39	79	25 33	38	78	26 11	38	77	26 49	37	76	27 26	38	75	281
80	17 33	+41	86	18 14	+41	85	18 55	+40	85	19 35	+41	84	20 16	+40	83	20 56	+40	82	21 36	+39	81	22 15	+40	81	22 55	+39	80	23 34	+39	79	24 13	+38	78	24 51	+39	77	25 30	+38	76	26 08	+37	76	26 45	+38	75	280
81	16 51	41	85	17 32	41	85	18 13	40	84	18 53	41	83	19 34	40	82	20 14	40	82	20 54	40	81	21 34	39	80	22 13	39	79	22 52	39	78	23 31	39	78	24 10	39	77	24 49	38	76	25 27	38	75	26 05	37	74	279
82	16 09	41	85	16 50	41	84	17 31	40	83	18 11	41	82	18 52	40	82	19 32	40	81	20 12	40	80	20 52	39	79	21 31	40	79	22 11	39	78	22 50	39	77	23 29	38	76	24 07	39	75	24 46	38	74	25 24	38	74	278
83	15 27	41	84	16 08	40	83	16 48	41	83	17 29	41	82	18 10	40	81	18 50	40	80	19 30	40	79	20 10	40	79	20 50	39	78	21 29	40	77	22 09	39	76	22 48	39	75	23 27	38	75	24 05	38	74	24 43	38	73	277
84	14 44	41	83	15 25	41	83	16 06	41	82	16 47	41	81	17 28	40	80	18 08	41	80	18 49	40	79	19 29	39	78	20 08	40	77	20 48	40	76	21 28	39	76	22 07	39	75	22 46	38	74	23 24	39	73	24 03	38	72	276
85	14 02	+41	83	14 43	+41	82	15 24	+41	81	16 05	+41	80	16 46	+41	80	17 27	+40	79	18 07	+40	78	18 47	+40	77	19 27	+40	77	20 07	+40	76	20 47	+39	75	21 26	+39	74	22 05	+39	73	22 44	+38	73	23 22	+39	72	275
86	13 20	41	82	14 01	42	81	14 43	41	81	15 24	40	80	16 04	41	79	16 45	41	78	17 26	40	77	18 06	40	77	18 46	40	76	19 26	40	75	20 06	39	74	20 45	39	74	21 24	39	73	22 03	39	72	22 42	39	71	274
87	12 38	42	81	13 20	41	81	14 01	41	80	14 42	41	79	15 23	41	78	16 04	40	78	16 44	41	77	17 25	40	76	18 05	40	75	18 45	40	75	19 25	40	74	20 05	39	73	20 44	39	72	21 23	39	71	22 02	39	70	273
88	11 56	42	81	12 38	41	80	13 19	41	79	14 00	41	78	14 41	41	78	15 22	41	77	16 03	41	76	16 44	40	75	17 24	40	75	18 04	40	74	18 44	40	73	19 24	40	72	20 04	39	71	20 43	39	71	21 22	39	70	272
89	11 14	42	80	11 56	41	79	12 37	42	79	13 19	41	78	14 00	41	77	14 41	41	76	15 22	41	76	16 03	40	75	16 43	40	74	17 23	41	73	18 04	40	72	18 44	40	72	19 24	39	71	20 03	40	70	20 43	39	69	271
90	10 33	+41	79	11 14	+42	79	11 56	+41	78	12 37	+42	77	13 19	+41	76	14 00	+41	76	14 41	+41	75	15 22	+40	74	16 02	+41	73	16 43	+40	73	17 23	+41	72	18 04	+40	71	18 44	+39	70	19 23	+40	69	20 03	+39	69	270
91	09 51	42	79	10 33	42	78	11 15	41	77	11 56	41	76	12 37	42	76	13 19	41	75	14 00	41	74	14 41	41	73	15 22	41	73	16 03	40	72	16 43	40	71	17 23	41	70	18 04	40	70	18 44	40	69	19 24	39	68	269
92	09 10	41	78	09 51	42	77	10 33	42	76	11 15	41	76	11 56	42	75	12 38	41	74	13 19	41	74	14 00	41	73	14 41	41	72	15 22	41	71	16 03	41	71	16 44	40	70	17 24	40	69	18 04	40	68	18 44	40	67	268
93	08 28	42	77	09 10	42	77	09 52	42	76	10 34	42	75	11 16	41	74	11 57	42	74	12 39	41	73	13 20	41	72	14 01	41	71	14 42	41	71	15 23	41	70	16 04	41	69	16 45	40	68	17 25	40	68	18 05	40	67	267
94	07 47	42	77	08 29	42	76	09 11	42	75	09 53	42	74	10 35	41	74	11 16	42	73	11 58	42	72	12 40	41	71	13 21	41	71	14 02	41	70	14 43	41	69	15 24	41	68	16 05	41	68	16 46	40	67	17 26	41	66	266
95	07 06	+42	76	07 48	+42	75	08 30	+42	74	09 12	+42	74	09 54	+42	73	10 36	+42	72	11 18	+41	72	11 59	+42	71	12 41	+41	70	13 22	+42	69	14 04	+41	69	14 45	+41	68	15 26	+41	67	16 07	+41	66	16 48	+40	66	265
96	06 25	42	75	07 07	42	75	07 49	42	74	08 31	43	73	09 14	42	72	09 56	42	72	10 38	41	71	11 19	42	70	12 01	42	69	12 43	41	69	13 24	42	68	14 06	41	67	14 47	41	66	15 28	41	66	16 09	41	65	264
97	05 44	42	75	06 26	43	74	07 09	42	73	07 51	42	72	08 33	42	72	09 15	43	71	09 58	42	70	10 40	42	70	11 22	41	69	12 03	42	68	12 45	42	67	13 27	41	67	14 08	42	66	14 50	41	65	15 31	41	64	263
98	05 03	42	74	05 45	43	73	06 28	43	72	07 11	42	72	07 53	42	71	08 35	43	70	09 18	42	70	10 00	42	69	10 42	42	68	11 24	42	67	12 06	42	67	12 48	42	66	13 30	41	65	14 11	42	64	14 53	41	64	262
99	04 22	43	73	05 05	43	72	05 48	42	72	06 30	43	71	07 13	43	70	07 56	42	70	08 38	43	69	09 21	42	68	10 03	42	67	10 45	42	67	11 27	42	66	12 09	42	65	12 51	42	65	13 33	42	64	14 15	41	63	261
100	03 42	+43	72	04 25	+43	72	05 08	+42	71	05 50	+43	70	06 33	+43	70	07 16	+43	69	07 59	+42	68	08 41	+43	68	09 24	+42	67	10 06	+43	66	10 49	+42	65	11 31	+42	65	12 13	+42	64	12 55	+42	63	13 37	+42	62	260
101	03 01	43	72	03 44	43	71	04 27	44	70	05 11	43	70	05 54	42	69	06 36	43	68	07 19	43	68	08 02	43	67	08 45	43	66	09 28	42	65	10 10	43	65	10 53	42	64	11 35	42	63	12 17	43	63	13 00	42	62	259
102	02 21	43	71	03 04	44	70	03 48	43	70	04 31	43	69	05 14	43	68	05 57	43	68	06 40	43	67	07 23	43	66	08 06	43	65	08 49	43	65	09 32	43	64	10 15	42	63	10 57	43	63	11 40	42	62	12 22	43	61	258
103	01 41	43	70	02 24	44	70	03 08	43	69	03 51	44	68	04 35	43	68	05 18	43	67	06 01	44	66	06 45	43	66	07 28	43	65	08 11	43	65	08 54	43	64	09 37	43	63	10 20	43	62	11 03	42	61	11 45	43	61	257
104	01 01	44	70	01 45	43	69	02 28	44	68	03 12	44	68	03 56	43	67	04 39	44	66	05 23	43	66	06 06	43	65	06 49	44	64	07 33	43	63	08 16	43	63	08 59	43	62	09 42	43	61	10 25	43	61	11 08	43	60	256
105	00 21	+44	69	01 05	+44	68	01 49	+44	68	02 33	+44	67	03 17	+43	66	04 00	+44	65	04 44	+44	65	05 28	+43	64	06 11	+44	63	06 55	+44	63	07 39	+43	62	08 22	+43	61	09 05	+44	61	09 49	+43	60	10 32	+43	59	255
106	−0 18	44	68	00 26	44	68	01 10	44	67	01 54	44	66	02 38	44	65	03 22	44	65	04 06	44	64	04 50	44	63	05 34	43	63	06 17	44	62	07 01	44	61	07 45	43	61	08 28	44	60	09 12	43	59	09 55	44	59	254
107	−0 57	44	68	−0 13	44	67	00 31	44	66	01 15	44	65	01 59	45	65	02 44	44	64	03 28	44	63	04 12	44	63	04 56	44	62	05 40	44	61	06 24	44	61	07 08	44	60	07 52	44	59	08 36	43	59	09 19	44	58	253
108	−1 36	44	67	−0 52	44	66	−0 08	45	65	00 37	44	65	01 21	45	64	02 06	44	63	02 50	44	63	03 34	45	62	04 19	44	61	05 03	44	61	05 47	44	60	06 31	44	59	07 15	45	59	08 00	44	58	08 44	44	57	252
109	−2 15	44	66	−1 31	45	65	−0 46	45	65	−0 01	44	64	00 43	45	63	01 28	44	63	02 12	45	62	02 57	44	61	03 41	45	61	04 26	45	60	05 11	44	59	05 55	44	59	06 39	45	58	07 24	44	57	08 08	44	57	251
110	−2 54	+45	65	−2 09	+45	65	−1 24	+44	64	−0 40	+45	63	00 05	+45	63	00 50	+45	62	01 35	+45	61	02 20	+45	61	03 05	+44	60	03 49	+45	59	04 34	+45	59	05 19	+45	58	06 04	+44	57	06 48	+45	57	07 33	+44	56	250
111	−3 32	45	65	−2 47	45	64	−2 02	45	63	−1 17	45	63	−0 32	45	62	00 13	45	61	00 58	45	61	01 43	45	60	02 28	45	59	03 13	45	59	03 58	45	58	04 43	45	57	05 28	45	57	06 13	45	56	06 58	44	55	249
112	−4 11	46	64	−3 25	45	63	−2 40	45	63	−1 55	45	62	−1 10	46	61	−0 24	45	61	00 21	45	60	01 06	46	59	01 52	45	59	02 37	45	58	03 22	45	57	04 07	46	57	04 53	45	56	05 38	45	55	06 23	45	55	248
113	−4 49	46	63	−4 03	45	63	−3 18	46	62	−2 32	45	61	−1 47	46	61	−1 01	45	60	−0 16	46	59	00 30	46	59	01 16	45	58	02 01	46	57	02 47	45	57	03 32	46	56	04 18	45	55	05 03	45	55	05 48	46	54	247
114	−5 26	45	62	−4 41	46	62	−3 55	46	61	−3 09	46	60	−2 23	45	60	−1 38	46	59	−0 52	46	59	−0 06	46	58	00 40	45	57	01 25	46	57	02 11	46	56	02 57	46	55	03 43	46	55	04 29	45	54	05 14	46	53	246
115	−6 04	+46	62	−5 18	+46	61	−4 32	+46	60	−3 46	+46	60	−3 00	+46	59	−2 14	+46	58	−1 28	+46	58	−0 42	+46	57	00 04	+46	57	00 50	+46	56	01 36	+46	55	02 22	+46	55	03 08	+46	54	03 54	+46	53	04 40	+46	53	245
			116	−5 55	46	60	−5 09	46	60	−4 23	47	59	−3 36	46	58	−2 50	46	58	−2 04	47	57	−1 17	46	56	−0 31	46	56	00 15	47	55	01 02	46	55	01 48	46	54	02 34	46	53	03 20	47	53	04 07	46	52	244
						117	−5 45	46	59	−4 59	47	58	−4 12	46	58	−3 26	47	57	−2 39	46	56	−1 53	47	56	−1 06	47	55	−0 19	46	54	00 27	47	54	01 14	46	53	02 00	47	53	02 47	46	52	03 33	47	51	243
									118	−5 35	47	57	−4 48	47	57	−4 01	47	56	−3 14	46	56	−2 28	47	55	−1 41	47	54	−0 54	47	54	−0 07	47	53	00 40	47	53	01 27	47	52	02 14	46	51	03 00	47	51	242
									119	−6 10	47	57	−5 23	47	56	−4 36	47	56	−3 49	47	55	−3 02	47	54	−2 15	47	54	−1 28	47	53	−0 41	47	52	00 06	48	52	00 54	47	51	01 41	47	51	02 28	47	50	241
												120	−5 58	+47	55	−5 11	+47	55	−4 24	+48	54	−3 36	+47	54	−2 49	+47	53	−2 02	+48	52	−1 14	+47	52	−0 27	+48	51	00 21	+47	51	01 08	+47	50	01 55	+48	49	240
															121	−5 46	48	54	−4 58	48	53	−4 10	47	53	−3 23	48	52	−2 35	48	52	−1 47	47	51	−1 00	48	50	−0 12	48	50	00 36	48	49	01 24	47	49	239
																		122	−5 32	48	53	−4 44	48	52	−3 56	48	52	−3 08	48	51	−2 20	48	50	−1 32	48	50	−0 44	48	49	00 04	48	48	00 52	48	48	238
																		123	−6 06	49	52	−5 17	48	51	−4 29	48	51	−3 41	48	50	−2 53	49	50	−2 04	48	49	−1 16	48	48	−0 28	49	48	00 21	48	47	237
																					124	−5 50	48	51	−5 02	49	50	−4 13	48	49	−3 25	49	49	−2 36	48	48	−1 48	49	48	−0 59	49	47	−0 10	48	46	236
																								125	−5 34	+49	49	−4 45	+48	49	−3 57	+49	48	−3 08	+49	47	−2 19	+49	47	−1 30	+49	46	−0 41	+49	46	235
83	−5 44	42	105	277																							126	−5 17	49	48	−4 28	49	47	−3 39	49	47	−2 50	50	46	−2 00	49	46	−1 11	49	45	234
82	−5 03	42	106	−5 45	43	107	278																				127	−5 48	49	47	−4 59	50	47	−4 09	49	46	−3 20	49	45	−2 31	50	45	−1 41	49	44	233
81	−4 22	43	107	−5 05	43	108	−5 48	42	108	279																				128	−5 30	50	46	−4 40	50	45	−3 50	50	45	−3 00	50	44	−2 10	49	44	232
80	−3 42	−43	108	−4 25	−43	108	−5 08	−42	109	−5 50	−43	110	280																	129	−6 00	50	45	−5 10	50	44	−4 20	50	44	−3 30	50	43	−2 40	51	43	231
79	−3 01	43	108	−3 44	43	109	−4 27	44	110	−5 11	43	110	−5 54	42	111	281																	130	−5 39	+50	44	−4 49	+50	43	−3 59	+51	43	−3 08	+50	42	230
78	−2 21	43	109	−3 04	44	110	−3 48	43	110	−4 31	43	111	−5 14	43	112	−5 57	43	112	282																131	−5 18	51	42	−4 27	51	42	−3 36	50	41	229
77	−1 41	43	110	−2 24	44	110	−3 08	43	111	−3 51	44	112	−4 35	43	112	−5 18	43	113	−6 01	44	114	283													132	−5 46	51	42	−4 55	51	41	−4 04	51	41	228
76	−1 01	44	110	−1 45	43	111	−2 28	44	112	−3 12	44	112	−3 56	43	113	−4 39	44	114	−5 23	43	114	−6 06	43	115	284												133	−5 23	51	40	−4 32	52	40	227
75	−0 21	−44	111	−1 05	−44	112	−1 49	−44	112	−2 33	−44	113	−3 17	−43	114	−4 00	−44	115	−4 44	−44	115	−5 28	−43	116	−6 11	−44	117	285											134	−5 50	51	40	−4 59	52	39	226
74	00 18	44	112	−0 26	44	112	−1 10	44	113	−1 54	44	114	−2 38	44	115	−3 22	44	115	−4 06	44	116	−4 50	44	117	−5 34	43	117	286														135	−5 25	+52	38	225
73	00 57	44	112	00 13	44	113	−0 31	44	114	−1 15	44	115	−1 59	45	115	−2 44	44	116	−3 28	44	117	−4 12	44	117	−4 56	44	118	−5 40	44	119	287											136	−5 52	53	38	224
72	01 36	44	113	00 52	44	114	00 08	45	115	−0 37	44	115	−1 21	45	116	−2 06	44	117	−2 50	44	117	−3 34	45	118	−4 19	44	119	−5 03	44	119	−5 47	44	120	288													
71	02 15	44	114	01 31	45	115	00 46	45	115	00 01	44	116	−0 43	45	117	−1 28	44	117	−2 12	45	118	−2 57	44	119	−3 41	45	119	−4 26	45	120	−5 11	44	121	−5 55	44	121	289									
70	02 54	−45	115	02 09	−45	115	01 24	−44	116	00 40	−45	117	−0 05	−45	117	−0 50	−45	118	−1 35	−45	119	−2 20	−45	119	−3 05	−44	120	−3 49	−45	121	−4 34	−45	121	−5 19	−45	122	−6 04	−44	123	290						
	15°			16°			17°			18°			19°			20°			21°			22°			23°			24°			25°			26°			27°			28°			29°			

S. Lat. {LHA greater than 180°....... Zn=180−Z / LHA less than 180°........... Zn=180+Z}

DECLINATION (15°-29°) CONTRARY NAME TO LATITUDE

N. Lat. {LHA greater than 180°....... Zn=Z; LHA less than 180°........... Zn=360−Z}

DECLINATION (15°-29°) CONTRARY NAME TO LATITUDE

LHA	15° Hc	d	Z	16° Hc	d	Z	17° Hc	d	Z	18° Hc	d	Z	19° Hc	d	Z	20° Hc	d	Z	21° Hc	d	Z	22° Hc	d	Z	23° Hc	d	Z	24° Hc	d	Z	25° Hc	d	Z	26° Hc	d	Z	27° Hc	d	Z	28° Hc	d	Z	29° Hc	d	Z	LHA
	° ′	′	°	° ′	′	°	° ′	′	°	° ′	′	°	° ′	′	°	° ′	′	°	° ′	′	°	° ′	′	°	° ′	′	°	° ′	′	°	° ′	′	°	° ′	′	°	° ′	′	°	° ′	′	°	° ′	′	°	
69	03 32	45	115	02 47	45	116	02 02	45	117	01 17	45	117	00 32	45	118	−0 13	45	119	−0 58	45	119	−1 43	45	120	−2 26	45	121	−3 13	45	121	−3 58	45	122	−4 43	45	123	−5 28	45	123	291						
68	04 11	46	116	03 25	45	117	02 40	45	117	01 55	45	118	01 10	46	119	00 24	45	119	−0 21	45	120	−1 06	46	121	−1 52	45	121	−2 37	45	122	−3 22	45	123	−4 07	46	123	−4 53	45	124	−5 38	45	125	292			
67	04 49	46	117	04 03	45	117	03 18	46	118	02 32	45	119	01 47	46	119	01 01	45	120	00 16	46	121	−0 30	46	121	−1 16	45	122	−2 01	46	123	−2 47	45	123	−3 32	46	124	−4 18	45	125	−5 03	45	125	−5 48	46	126	293
66	05 26	45	118	04 41	46	118	03 55	46	119	03 09	46	120	02 23	45	120	01 38	46	121	00 52	46	121	00 06	46	122	−0 40	45	123	−1 25	46	123	−2 11	46	124	−2 57	46	125	−3 43	46	125	−4 29	45	126	−5 14	46	127	294
65	06 04	−46	118	05 18	−46	119	04 32	−46	120	03 46	−46	120	03 00	−46	121	02 14	−46	122	01 28	−46	122	00 42	−46	123	−0 04	−46	123	−0 50	−46	124	−1 36	−46	125	−2 22	−46	125	−3 08	−46	126	−3 54	−46	127	−4 40	−46	127	295
64	06 41	46	119	05 55	46	120	05 09	46	120	04 23	47	121	03 36	46	122	02 50	46	122	02 04	47	123	01 17	46	124	00 31	46	124	−0 15	47	125	−1 02	46	125	−1 48	46	126	−2 34	46	127	−3 20	47	127	−4 07	46	128	296
63	07 18	46	120	06 32	47	120	05 45	46	121	04 59	47	122	04 12	46	122	03 26	47	123	02 39	46	124	01 53	47	124	01 06	47	125	00 19	46	126	−0 27	47	126	−1 14	46	127	−2 00	47	127	−2 47	46	128	−3 33	47	129	297
62	07 55	47	121	07 08	47	121	06 21	46	122	05 35	47	123	04 48	47	123	04 01	47	124	03 14	46	124	02 28	47	125	01 41	47	126	00 54	47	126	00 07	47	127	−0 40	47	127	−1 27	47	128	−2 14	46	129	−3 00	47	129	298
61	08 31	47	121	07 44	47	122	06 57	47	123	06 10	47	123	05 23	47	124	04 36	47	124	03 49	47	125	03 02	47	126	02 15	47	126	01 28	47	127	00 41	47	128	−0 06	48	128	−0 54	47	129	−1 41	47	129	−2 28	47	130	299
60	09 07	−47	122	08 20	−47	123	07 33	−47	123	06 46	−48	124	05 58	−47	125	05 11	−47	125	04 24	−48	126	03 36	−47	126	02 49	−47	127	02 02	−48	128	01 14	−47	128	00 27	−48	129	−0 21	−47	129	−1 08	−47	130	−1 55	−48	131	300
59	09 43	47	123	08 56	48	124	08 08	47	124	07 21	48	125	06 33	47	125	05 46	48	126	04 58	48	127	04 10	47	127	03 23	48	128	02 35	48	128	01 47	47	129	01 00	48	130	00 12	48	130	−0 36	48	131	−1 24	47	131	301
58	10 18	47	124	09 31	48	124	08 43	48	125	07 55	47	126	07 08	48	126	06 20	48	127	05 32	48	127	04 44	48	128	03 56	48	128	03 08	48	129	02 20	48	130	01 32	48	130	00 44	48	131	−0 04	48	132	−0 52	48	132	302
57	10 54	48	124	10 06	48	125	09 18	48	126	08 30	48	126	07 42	48	127	06 54	48	128	06 06	49	128	05 17	48	129	04 29	48	129	03 41	48	130	02 53	49	130	02 04	48	131	01 16	48	132	00 28	49	132	−0 21	48	133	303
56	11 28	48	125	10 40	48	126	09 52	48	126	09 04	48	127	08 16	49	128	07 27	48	128	06 39	49	129	05 50	48	129	05 02	49	130	04 13	48	131	03 25	49	131	02 36	48	132	01 48	49	132	00 59	49	133	00 10	48	134	304
55	12 03	−48	126	11 15	−49	127	10 26	−48	127	09 38	−49	128	08 49	−49	128	08 00	−48	129	07 12	−49	130	06 23	−49	130	05 34	−49	131	04 45	−48	131	03 57	−49	132	03 08	−49	133	02 19	−49	133	01 30	−49	134	00 41	−49	134	305
54	12 37	49	127	11 48	48	127	11 00	49	128	10 11	49	129	09 22	49	129	08 33	49	130	07 44	49	130	06 55	49	131	06 06	49	132	05 17	49	132	04 28	49	133	03 39	49	133	02 50	50	134	02 00	49	134	01 11	49	135	306
53	13 11	49	128	12 22	49	128	11 33	49	129	10 44	49	129	09 55	49	130	09 06	50	131	08 16	49	131	07 27	49	132	06 38	50	132	05 48	49	133	04 59	50	133	04 09	49	134	03 20	49	135	02 31	50	135	01 41	49	136	307
52	13 44	49	128	12 55	49	129	12 06	49	130	11 17	50	130	10 27	49	131	09 38	50	131	08 48	49	132	07 59	50	133	07 09	50	133	06 19	49	134	05 30	50	134	04 40	50	135	03 50	50	135	03 00	50	136	02 10	49	136	308
51	14 17	49	129	13 28	50	130	12 38	49	130	11 49	50	131	10 59	50	132	10 09	49	132	09 20	50	133	08 30	50	133	07 40	50	134	06 50	50	134	06 00	50	135	05 10	50	136	04 20	50	136	03 30	50	137	02 40	51	137	309
50	14 50	−50	130	14 00	−49	131	13 11	−50	131	12 21	−50	132	11 31	−50	132	10 41	−50	133	09 51	−51	134	09 00	−50	134	08 10	−50	135	07 20	−50	135	06 30	−51	136	05 39	−50	136	04 49	−50	137	03 59	−51	137	03 08	−50	138	310
49	15 22	50	131	14 32	50	132	13 42	50	132	12 52	50	133	12 02	50	133	11 12	51	134	10 21	50	134	09 31	51	135	08 40	50	135	07 50	51	136	06 59	50	136	06 09	51	137	05 18	51	138	04 27	51	138	03 36	50	139	311
48	15 54	50	132	15 04	50	132	14 14	51	133	13 23	50	133	12 33	51	134	11 42	51	135	10 51	50	135	10 01	51	136	09 10	51	136	08 19	51	137	07 28	51	137	06 37	51	138	05 46	51	138	04 55	51	139	04 04	51	139	312
47	16 26	51	133	15 35	51	133	14 44	50	134	13 54	51	134	13 03	51	135	12 12	51	135	11 21	51	136	10 30	51	136	09 39	51	137	08 48	51	138	07 57	51	138	07 06	52	139	06 14	51	139	05 23	51	140	04 32	52	140	313
46	16 57	51	133	16 06	51	134	15 15	51	135	14 24	51	135	13 33	51	136	12 42	52	136	11 50	51	137	10 59	51	137	10 08	52	138	09 16	51	138	08 25	52	139	07 33	51	139	06 42	52	140	05 50	51	140	04 59	52	141	314
45	17 27	−51	134	16 36	−51	135	15 45	−51	135	14 54	−52	136	14 02	−51	136	13 11	−52	137	12 19	−51	138	11 28	−52	138	10 36	−52	139	09 44	−51	139	08 53	−52	140	08 01	−52	140	07 09	−52	141	06 17	−52	141	05 25	−52	142	315
44	17 57	51	135	17 06	51	136	16 15	52	136	15 23	52	137	14 31	51	137	13 40	52	138	12 48	52	138	11 56	52	139	11 04	52	139	10 12	52	140	09 20	52	140	08 28	52	141	07 36	52	141	06 44	52	142	05 52	53	142	316
43	18 27	52	136	17 35	51	137	16 44	52	137	15 52	52	138	15 00	52	138	14 08	52	139	13 16	52	139	12 24	53	140	11 31	52	140	10 39	52	141	09 47	53	141	08 54	52	142	08 02	52	142	07 10	53	143	06 17	52	143	317
42	18 56	52	137	18 04	52	137	17 12	52	138	16 20	52	138	15 28	52	139	14 36	53	140	13 43	52	140	12 51	53	141	11 58	52	141	11 06	53	142	10 13	52	142	09 21	53	142	08 28	53	143	07 35	53	143	06 42	52	144	318
41	19 25	52	138	18 33	52	138	17 41	53	139	16 48	52	139	15 56	53	140	15 03	53	140	14 10	52	141	13 18	53	141	12 25	53	142	11 32	53	142	10 39	53	143	09 46	53	143	08 53	53	144	08 00	53	144	07 07	53	145	319
40	19 53	−52	139	19 01	−53	139	18 08	−53	140	17 15	−52	140	16 23	−53	141	15 30	−53	141	14 37	−53	142	13 44	−53	142	12 51	−53	143	11 58	−53	143	11 05	−54	144	10 11	−53	144	09 18	−53	145	08 25	−53	145	07 32	−54	146	320
39	20 21	53	140	19 28	53	140	18 35	53	141	17 42	53	141	16 49	53	142	15 56	53	142	15 03	53	143	14 10	54	143	13 16	53	144	12 23	54	144	11 29	53	144	10 36	54	145	09 42	53	145	08 49	54	146	07 55	53	146	321
38	20 48	53	141	19 55	53	141	19 02	53	142	18 09	54	142	17 15	53	142	16 22	54	143	15 28	53	143	14 35	54	144	13 41	53	144	12 48	54	145	11 54	54	145	11 00	54	146	10 06	53	146	09 13	54	147	08 19	54	147	322
37	21 15	53	141	20 22	54	142	19 28	53	142	18 35	54	143	17 41	54	143	16 47	53	144	15 54	54	144	15 00	54	145	14 06	54	145	13 12	54	146	12 18	54	146	11 24	54	147	10 30	54	147	09 36	54	147	08 42	55	148	323
36	21 41	53	142	20 48	54	143	19 54	54	143	19 00	54	144	18 06	54	144	17 12	54	145	16 18	54	145	15 24	54	146	14 30	54	146	13 36	55	147	12 41	54	147	11 47	54	147	10 53	55	148	09 58	54	148	09 04	55	149	324
35	22 07	−54	143	21 13	−54	144	20 19	−54	144	19 25	−54	145	18 31	−55	145	17 36	−54	146	16 42	−54	146	15 48	−55	146	14 53	−54	147	13 59	−55	147	13 04	−54	148	12 10	−55	148	11 15	−55	149	10 20	−54	149	09 26	−55	149	325
34	22 32	54	144	21 38	55	145	20 43	54	145	19 49	54	146	18 55	55	146	18 00	54	147	17 05	54	147	16 11	55	147	15 16	55	148	14 21	54	148	13 27	55	149	12 32	55	149	11 37	55	149	10 42	55	150	09 47	55	150	326
33	22 57	55	145	22 02	55	146	21 07	54	146	20 13	55	147	19 18	55	147	18 23	55	148	17 28	55	148	16 33	55	148	15 38	55	149	14 43	55	149	13 48	55	149	12 53	55	150	11 58	55	150	11 03	55	151	10 08	55	151	327
32	23 21	55	146	22 26	55	147	21 31	55	147	20 36	55	147	19 41	55	148	18 46	55	148	17 51	55	149	16 56	56	149	16 00	55	150	15 05	55	150	14 10	56	150	13 14	55	151	12 19	55	151	11 24	56	152	10 28	55	152	328
31	23 44	55	147	22 49	55	148	21 54	56	148	20 58	55	148	20 03	55	149	19 08	56	149	18 12	55	150	17 17	55	150	16 22	56	150	15 26	56	151	14 30	55	151	13 35	56	152	12 39	56	152	11 43	55	152	10 48	56	153	329
30	24 07	−56	148	23 11	−55	149	22 16	−56	149	21 20	−55	149	20 25	−56	150	19 29	−55	150	18 34	−56	151	17 38	−56	151	16 42	−56	151	15 46	−55	152	14 51	−56	152	13 55	−56	152	12 59	−56	153	12 03	−56	153	11 07	−56	154	330
29	24 29	56	149	23 33	55	149	22 38	56	150	21 42	56	150	20 46	56	151	19 50	56	151	18 54	56	151	17 58	56	152	17 02	56	152	16 06	56	153	15 10	56	153	14 14	56	153	13 18	56	154	12 22	56	154	11 26	57	154	331
28	24 50	56	150	23 54	55	150	22 59	56	151	22 03	57	151	21 06	56	152	20 10	56	152	19 14	56	152	18 18	56	153	17 22	56	153	16 26	57	153	15 29	56	154	14 33	56	154	13 37	57	155	12 40	56	155	11 44	57	155	332
27	25 11	56	151	24 15	56	151	23 19	56	152	22 23	57	152	21 26	56	153	20 30	56	153	19 34	57	153	18 37	56	154	17 41	57	154	16 44	56	154	15 48	57	155	14 51	57	155	13 54	56	155	12 58	57	156	12 01	57	156	333
26	25 31	56	152	24 35	56	152	23 39	57	153	22 42	56	153	21 46	57	154	20 49	57	154	19 52	56	154	18 56	57	155	17 59	57	155	17 02	56	155	16 06	57	156	15 09	57	156	14 12	57	156	13 15	57	157	12 18	57	157	334
25	25 51	−57	153	24 54	−56	153	23 58	−57	154	23 01	−57	154	22 04	−57	155	21 07	−56	155	20 11	−57	155	19 14	−57	156	18 17	−57	156	17 20	−57	156	16 23	−57	157	15 26	−57	157	14 29	−57	157	13 32	−58	157	12 34	−57	158	335
24	26 10	57	154	25 13	57	154	24 16	57	155	23 19	57	155	22 22	57	155	21 25	57	156	20 28	57	156	19 31	57	156	18 34	57	157	17 37	58	157	16 39	57	157	15 42	57	158	14 45	57	158	13 48	58	158	12 50	57	159	336
23	26 28	57	155	25 31	57	155	24 34	57	156	23 37	57	156	22 40	58	156	21 42	57	157	20 45	57	157	19 48	58	157	18 50	57	158	17 53	58	158	16 55	57	158	15 58	58	159	15 00	57	159	14 03	58	159	13 05	57	160	337
22	26 46	58	156	25 48	57	156	24 51	57	157	23 54	58	157	22 56	57	157	21 59	58	158	21 01	57	158	20 04	58	158	19 06	58	159	18 08	57	159	17 11	58	159	16 13	58	160	15 15	57	160	14 18	58	160	13 20	58	160	338
21	27 03	58	157	26 05	58	157	25 07	57	158	24 10	58	158	23 12	58	158	22 14	57	159	21 17	58	159	20 19	58	159	19 21	58	160	18 23	57	160	17 26	58	160	16 28	58	160	15 30	58	161	14 32	58	161	13 34	58	161	339
20	27 19	−58	158	26 21	−58	159	25 23	−58	159	24 25	−58	159	23 27	−57	159	22 30	−58	160	21 32	−58	160	20 34	−58	160	19 36	−58	161	18 38	−58	161	17 40	−58	161	16 42	−58	161	15 44	−59	162	14 45	−58	162	13 47	−58	162	340
19	27 34	58	159	26 36	58	160	25 38	58	160	24 40	58	160	23 42	58	160	22 44	58	161	21 46	58	161	20 48	58	161	19 50	59	161	18 51	58	162	17 53	58	162	16 55	58	162	15 57	59	162	14 58	58	163	14 00	58	163	341
18	27 49	58	160	26 51	59	161	25 52	58	161	24 54	58	161	23 56	58	161	22 58	59	162	21 59	58	162	21 01	58	162	20 03	59	162	19 04	58	163	18 06	58	163	17 08	59	163	16 09	58	163	15 11	59	164	14 12	58	164	342
17	28 03	59	161	27 04	58	162	26 06	58	162	25 08	59	162	24 09	58	162	23 11	59	163	22 12	58	163	21 14	59	163	20 15	58	163	19 17	59	164	18 18	58	164	17 20	59	164	16 21	59	164	15 22	58	165	14 24	59	165	343
16	28 16	59	162	27 17	58	163	26 19	59	163	25 20	58	163	24 22	59	163	23 23	59	164	22 24	58	164	21 26	59	164	20 27	59	164	19 28	58	165	18 30	59	165	17 31	59	165	16 32	59	165	15 33	58	165	14 35	59	166	344
15	28 28	−58	164	27 30	−59	164	26 31	−59	164	25 32	−59	164	24 33	−58	164	23 35	−59	165	22 36	−59	165	21 37	−59	165	20 38	−59	165	19 39	−59	166	18 40	−58	166	17 42	−59	166	16 43	−59	166	15 44	−59	166	14 45	−59	167	345
14	28 40	59	165	27 41	59	165	26 42	59	165	25 43	59	165	24 44	58	165	23 46	59	166	22 47	59	166	21 48	59	166	20 49	59	166	19 50	59	166	18 51	59	167	17 52	59	167	16 53	59	167	15 54	59	167	14 55	60	167	346
13	28 51	59	166	27 52	59	166	26 53	59	166	25 54	59	166	24 55	59	166	23 56	59	167	22 57	59	167	21 58	60	167	20 58	59	167	19 59	59	167	19 00	59	168	18 01	59	168	17 02	59	168	16 03	60	168	15 03	59	168	347
12	29 01	59	167	28 02	59	167	27 03	59	167	26 04	60	167	25 04	59	168	24 05	59	168	23 06	59	168	22 07	60	168	21 07	59	168	20 08	59	168	19 09	59	169	18 10	60	169	17 10	59	169	16 11	59	169	15 12	59	169	348
11	29 10	59	168	28 11	59	168	27 12	59	168	26 13	60	168	25 13	59	169	24 14	59	169	23 15	60	169	22 15	59	169	21 16	60	169	20 16	59	169	19 17	59	169	18 18	60	170	17 18	59	170	16 19	60	170	15 19	59	170	349
10	29 19	−59	169	28 20	−60	169	27 20	−59	169	26 21	−60	169	25 21	−59	170	24 22	−60	170	23 22	−59	170	22 23	−60	170	21 23	−59	170	20 24	−60	170	19 24	−59	170	18 25	−59	171	17 26	−60	171	16 26	−60	171	15 26	−59	171	350
9	29 27	60	170	28 27	59	170	27 28	60	170	26 28	59	170	25 29	60	171	24 29	59	171	23 30	60	171	22 30	60	171	21 30	59	171	20 31	60	171	19 31	59	171	18 32	60	172	17 32	60	172	16 32	59	172	15 33	60	172	351
8	29 34	60	171	28 34	60	171	27 34	59	171	26 35	60	172	25 35	59	172	24 36	60	172	23 36	60	172	22 36	59	172	21 37	60	172	20 37	60	172	19 37	59	172	18 38	60	172	17 38	60	173	16 38	59	173	15 39	60	173	352
7	29 40	60	172	28 40	60	172	27 40	59	172	26 41	60	173	25 41	60	173	24 41	59	173	23 42	60	173	22 42	60	173	21 42	60	173	20 42	59	173	19 43	60	173	18 43	60	173	17 43	60	174	16 43	59	174	15 44	60	174	353
6	29 45	60	173	28 45	59	173	27 46	60	174	26 46	60	174	25 46	60	174	24 46	60	174	23 46	59	174	22 47	60	174	21 47	60	174	20 47	60	174	19 47	60	174	18 47	59	174	17 48	60	174	16 48	60	175	15 48	60	175	354
5	29 50	−60	174	28 50	−60	175	27 50	−60	175	26 50	−60	175	25 50	−60	175	24 50	−59	175	23 51	−60	175	22 51	−60	175	21 51	−60	175	20 51	−60	175	19 51	−60	175	18 51	−60	175	17 51	−59	175	16 52	−60	175	15 52	−60	176	355
4	29 53	59	176	28 54	60	176	27 54	60	176	26 54	60	176	25 54	60	176	24 54	60	176	23 54	60	176	22 54	60	176	21 54	60	176	20 54	60	176	19 54	60	176	18 54	59	176	17 55	60	176	16 55	60	176	15 55	60	176	356
3	29 56	60	177	28 56	60	177	27 56	60	177	26 56	59	177	25 57	60	177	24 57	60	177	23 57	60	177	22 57	60	177	21 57	60	177	20 57	60	177	19 57	60	177	18 57	60	177	17 57	60	177	16 57	60	177	15 57	60	177	357
2	29 58	60	178	28 58	60	178	27 58	60	178	26 58	60	178	25 58	59	178	24 59	60	178	23 59	60	178	22 59	60	178	21 59	60	178	20 59	60	178	19 59	60	178	18 59	60	178	17 59	60	178	16 59	60	178	15 59	60	178	358
1	30 00	60	179	29 00	60	179	28 00	60	179	27 00	60	179	26 00	60	179	25 00	60	179	24 00	60	179	23 00	60	179	22 00	60	179	21 00	60	179	20 00	60	179	19 00	60	179	18 00	60	179	17 00	60	179	16 00	60	179	359
0	30 00	−60	180	29 00	−60	180	28 00	−60	180	27 00	−60	180	26 00	−60	180	25 00	−60	180	24 00	−60	180	23 00	−60	180	22 00	−60	180	21 00	−60	180	20 00	−60	180	19 00	−60	180	18 00	−60	180	17 00	−60	180	16 00	−60	180	360
	15°			16°			17°			18°			19°			20°			21°			22°			23°			24°			25°			26°			27°			28°			29°			

S. Lat. {LHA greater than 180°....... Zn=180−Z; LHA less than 180°........... Zn=180+Z}

DECLINATION (15°-29°) CONTRARY NAME TO LATITUDE

LAT 45°

N. Lat. {LHA greater than 180°....... Zn=Z; LHA less than 180°........... Zn=360−Z}

DECLINATION (0°-14°) SAME NAME AS LATITUDE

LHA	0° Hc	d	Z	1° Hc	d	Z	2° Hc	d	Z	3° Hc	d	Z	4° Hc	d	Z
	° ′	′	°	° ′	′	°	° ′	′	°	° ′	′	°	° ′	′	°
0	44 00	+60	180	45 00	+60	180	46 00	+60	180	47 00	+60	180	48 00	+60	180
1	44 00	60	179	45 00	60	179	46 00	60	179	47 00	60	179	48 00	59	179
2	43 58	60	177	44 58	60	177	45 58	60	177	46 58	60	177	47 58	60	177
3	43 56	59	176	44 55	60	176	45 55	60	176	46 55	60	176	47 55	60	176
4	43 52	60	174	44 52	60	174	45 52	60	174	46 52	59	174	47 51	60	174
5	43 47	+60	173	44 47	+60	173	45 47	+60	173	46 47	+60	173	47 47	+59	173
6	43 42	60	172	44 42	59	172	45 41	60	171	46 41	60	171	47 41	59	171
7	43 35	60	170	44 35	60	170	45 35	59	170	46 34	60	170	47 34	59	170
8	43 28	59	169	44 27	60	169	45 27	59	169	46 26	60	168	47 26	59	168
9	43 19	60	168	44 19	59	167	45 18	59	167	46 17	60	167	47 17	59	167
10	43 10	+59	166	44 09	+59	166	45 08	+59	166	46 07	+59	166	47 06	+59	165
11	43 00	59	165	43 59	59	165	44 58	58	164	45 56	59	164	46 55	59	164
12	42 48	59	164	43 47	59	163	44 46	59	163	45 45	58	163	46 43	59	162
13	42 36	59	162	43 35	58	162	44 33	59	162	45 32	58	161	46 30	59	161
14	42 23	58	161	43 21	59	161	44 20	58	160	45 18	58	160	46 16	58	160
15	42 09	+58	160	43 07	+58	159	44 05	+58	159	45 03	+58	159	46 01	+58	158
16	41 54	58	158	42 52	57	158	43 49	58	158	44 47	58	157	45 45	58	157
17	41 38	57	157	42 35	58	157	43 33	58	156	44 31	57	156	45 28	58	155
18	41 21	58	156	42 19	57	155	43 16	57	155	44 13	57	155	45 10	57	154
19	41 03	58	154	42 01	57	154	42 58	57	154	43 55	57	153	44 52	57	153
20	40 45	+57	153	41 42	+57	153	42 39	+57	152	43 36	+56	152	44 32	+57	151
21	40 26	57	152	41 23	56	152	42 19	56	151	43 15	57	151	44 12	56	150
22	40 06	56	151	41 02	56	150	41 58	57	150	42 55	56	149	43 51	56	149
23	39 45	56	150	40 41	56	149	41 37	56	149	42 33	56	148	43 29	55	148
24	39 23	56	148	40 19	56	148	41 15	55	147	42 10	56	147	43 06	55	146
25	39 01	+56	147	39 57	+55	147	40 52	+55	146	41 47	+55	146	42 42	+55	145
26	38 38	55	146	39 33	55	145	40 28	55	145	41 23	55	144	42 18	55	144
27	38 14	55	145	39 09	55	144	40 04	55	144	40 59	54	143	41 53	54	143
28	37 50	55	144	38 45	54	143	39 39	54	143	40 33	54	142	41 27	54	141
29	37 25	54	142	38 19	54	142	39 13	54	141	40 07	54	141	41 01	54	140
30	36 59	+54	141	37 53	+54	141	38 47	+53	140	39 40	+54	140	40 34	+53	139
31	36 33	53	140	37 26	54	140	38 20	53	139	39 13	53	138	40 06	53	138
32	36 06	53	139	36 59	53	138	37 52	53	138	38 45	53	137	39 38	53	137
33	35 38	53	138	36 31	53	137	37 24	53	137	38 17	52	136	39 09	52	136
34	35 10	53	137	36 03	52	136	36 55	52	136	37 47	53	135	38 40	51	134
35	34 41	+52	136	35 33	+53	135	36 26	+52	135	37 18	+51	134	38 09	+52	133
36	34 12	52	135	35 04	52	134	35 56	51	134	36 47	52	133	37 39	51	132
37	33 42	52	134	34 34	51	133	35 25	52	132	36 17	51	132	37 08	51	131
38	33 11	52	133	34 03	51	132	34 54	51	131	35 45	51	131	36 36	51	130
39	32 40	52	132	33 32	51	131	34 23	50	130	35 13	51	130	36 04	50	129
40	32 09	+51	131	33 00	+51	130	33 51	+50	129	34 41	+50	129	35 31	+50	128
41	31 37	51	130	32 28	50	129	33 18	50	128	34 08	50	128	34 58	50	127
42	31 05	50	129	31 55	50	128	32 45	50	127	33 35	50	127	34 25	49	126
43	30 32	50	128	31 22	50	127	32 12	49	126	33 01	50	126	33 51	49	125
44	29 59	50	127	30 49	49	126	31 38	49	125	32 27	50	125	33 17	48	124
45	29 25	+50	126	30 15	+49	125	31 04	+49	124	31 53	+49	124	32 42	+48	123
46	28 51	49	125	29 40	49	124	30 29	49	124	31 18	49	123	32 07	48	122
47	28 17	49	124	29 06	48	123	29 54	49	123	30 43	48	122	31 31	48	121
48	27 42	49	123	28 31	48	122	29 19	48	122	30 07	48	121	30 55	48	120
49	27 07	48	122	27 55	48	121	28 43	48	121	29 31	48	120	30 19	48	119
50	26 31	+48	121	27 19	+48	120	28 07	+48	120	28 55	+48	119	29 43	+47	118
51	25 55	48	120	26 43	48	120	27 31	48	119	28 19	47	118	29 06	47	118
52	25 19	48	119	26 07	47	119	26 54	48	118	27 42	47	117	28 29	47	117
53	24 43	47	119	25 30	47	118	26 17	47	117	27 04	47	116	27 51	47	116
54	24 06	47	118	24 53	47	117	25 40	47	116	26 27	47	116	27 14	46	115
55	23 29	+47	117	24 16	+47	116	25 03	+46	115	25 49	+47	115	26 36	+46	114
56	22 52	46	116	23 38	47	115	24 25	46	115	25 11	46	114	25 57	46	113
57	22 14	46	115	23 00	47	114	23 47	46	114	24 33	46	113	25 19	46	112
58	21 36	46	114	22 22	47	114	23 09	45	113	23 54	46	112	24 40	46	111
59	20 58	46	113	21 44	46	113	22 30	46	112	23 16	45	111	24 01	46	111
60	20 19	+46	113	21 05	+46	112	21 51	+46	111	22 37	+45	111	23 22	+45	110
61	19 41	46	112	20 27	45	111	21 12	46	110	21 58	45	110	22 43	45	109
62	19 02	46	111	19 48	45	110	20 33	45	110	21 18	45	109	22 03	45	108
63	18 23	45	110	19 08	46	109	19 54	45	109	20 39	45	108	21 24	44	107
64	17 44	45	109	18 29	45	109	19 14	45	108	19 59	45	107	20 44	44	107
65	17 04	+45	109	17 49	+45	108	18 34	+45	107	19 19	+45	106	20 04	+44	106
66	16 25	45	108	17 10	44	107	17 54	45	106	18 39	45	106	19 24	44	105
67	15 45	45	107	16 30	44	106	17 14	45	106	17 59	44	105	18 43	44	104
68	15 05	45	106	15 50	44	106	16 34	45	105	17 19	44	104	18 03	44	103
69	14 25	44	105	15 09	45	105	15 54	44	104	16 38	44	103	17 22	44	103

LHA	5° Hc	d	Z	6° Hc	d	Z	7° Hc	d	Z	8° Hc	d	Z	9° Hc	d	Z
	° ′	′	°	° ′	′	°	° ′	′	°	° ′	′	°	° ′	′	°
0	49 00	+60	180	50 00	+60	180	51 00	+60	180	52 00	+60	180	53 00	+60	180
1	48 59	60	179	49 59	60	179	50 59	60	178	51 59	60	178	52 59	60	178
2	48 58	60	177	49 58	60	177	50 58	60	177	51 58	60	177	52 58	60	177
3	48 55	60	175	49 55	60	175	50 55	60	175	51 55	60	175	52 55	60	175
4	48 51	60	174	49 51	60	174	50 51	60	174	51 51	60	174	52 51	59	174
5	48 46	+60	172	49 46	+60	172	50 46	+59	172	51 45	+60	172	52 45	+60	172
6	48 40	60	171	49 40	59	171	50 39	60	171	51 39	60	170	52 39	59	170
7	48 33	60	169	49 33	59	169	50 32	60	169	51 32	59	169	52 31	59	169
8	48 25	59	168	49 24	60	168	50 24	59	168	51 23	59	167	52 22	59	167
9	48 16	59	167	49 15	59	166	50 14	59	166	51 13	59	166	52 12	59	165
10	48 05	+59	165	49 04	+59	165	50 03	+59	164	51 02	+59	164	52 01	+59	164
11	47 54	59	164	48 53	59	163	49 52	58	163	50 50	59	163	51 49	59	162
12	47 42	58	162	48 40	59	162	49 39	58	161	50 37	59	161	51 36	58	161
13	47 29	58	161	48 27	58	160	49 25	58	160	50 23	58	160	51 21	59	159
14	47 14	58	159	48 12	58	159	49 10	58	159	50 08	58	158	51 06	58	158
15	46 59	+58	158	47 57	+58	157	48 55	+57	157	49 52	+58	157	50 50	+57	156
16	46 43	57	156	47 40	58	156	48 38	57	156	49 35	57	155	50 32	58	155
17	46 26	57	155	47 23	57	155	48 20	57	154	49 17	57	154	50 14	57	153
18	46 07	57	154	47 04	57	153	48 01	57	153	48 58	57	152	49 55	56	152
19	45 49	56	152	46 45	57	152	47 42	56	151	48 38	57	151	49 35	56	150
20	45 29	+56	151	46 25	+56	150	47 21	+56	150	48 17	+56	149	49 13	+56	149
21	45 08	56	150	46 04	56	149	47 00	56	149	47 56	55	148	48 51	56	148
22	44 47	55	148	45 42	56	148	46 38	55	147	47 33	56	147	48 29	55	146
23	44 24	56	147	45 20	55	146	46 15	55	146	47 10	55	145	48 05	55	145
24	44 01	55	146	44 56	55	145	45 51	55	145	46 46	54	144	47 40	55	143
25	43 37	+55	144	44 32	+55	144	45 27	+54	143	46 21	+54	143	47 15	+54	142
26	43 13	54	143	44 07	54	143	45 01	54	142	45 55	54	141	46 49	54	141
27	42 47	54	142	43 41	54	141	44 35	54	141	45 29	53	140	46 22	54	140
28	42 21	54	141	43 15	54	140	44 09	53	140	45 02	53	139	45 55	53	138
29	41 55	53	140	42 48	53	139	43 41	53	138	44 34	53	138	45 27	52	137
30	41 27	+53	138	42 20	+53	138	43 13	+53	137	44 06	+52	136	44 58	+52	136
31	40 59	53	137	41 52	52	137	42 44	53	136	43 37	52	135	44 29	52	135
32	40 31	52	136	41 23	52	135	42 15	52	135	43 07	52	134	43 59	51	133
33	40 01	52	135	40 53	52	134	41 45	52	134	42 37	51	133	43 28	51	132
34	39 31	52	134	40 23	52	133	41 15	51	132	42 06	51	132	42 57	51	131
35	39 01	+52	133	39 53	+51	132	40 44	+51	131	41 35	+50	131	42 25	+51	130
36	38 30	51	132	39 21	51	131	40 12	51	130	41 03	50	130	41 53	50	129
37	37 59	50	131	38 49	51	130	39 40	50	129	40 30	50	128	41 20	50	128
38	37 27	50	129	38 17	50	129	39 07	50	128	39 57	50	127	40 47	49	127
39	36 54	50	128	37 44	50	128	38 34	50	127	39 24	49	126	40 13	49	126
40	36 21	+50	127	37 11	+50	127	38 01	+49	126	38 50	+49	125	39 39	+49	125
41	35 48	50	126	36 38	49	126	37 27	49	125	38 16	49	124	39 05	48	123
42	35 14	49	125	36 03	49	125	36 52	49	124	37 41	49	123	38 30	48	122
43	34 40	49	124	35 29	49	124	36 18	48	123	37 06	48	122	37 54	48	121
44	34 05	49	123	34 54	48	123	35 42	49	122	36 31	47	121	37 18	48	120
45	33 30	+49	122	34 19	+48	122	35 07	+48	121	35 55	+47	120	36 42	+48	119
46	32 55	48	121	33 43	48	121	34 31	48	120	35 19	47	119	36 06	47	118
47	32 19	48	120	33 07	48	120	33 55	47	119	34 42	47	118	35 29	47	118
48	31 43	48	120	32 31	47	119	33 18	47	118	34 05	47	117	34 52	46	117
49	31 07	47	119	31 54	47	118	32 41	47	117	33 28	46	116	34 14	47	116
50	30 30	+47	118	31 17	+47	117	32 04	+46	116	32 50	+47	116	33 37	+46	115
51	29 53	47	117	30 40	46	116	31 26	47	115	32 13	46	115	32 59	45	114
52	29 16	46	116	30 02	46	115	30 48	47	114	31 35	45	114	32 20	46	113
53	28 38	46	115	29 24	46	114	30 10	46	114	30 56	46	113	31 42	45	112
54	28 00	46	114	28 46	46	113	29 32	46	113	30 18	45	112	31 03	45	111
55	27 22	+46	113	28 08	+45	113	28 53	+46	112	29 39	+45	111	30 24	+45	110
56	26 43	46	112	27 29	46	112	28 15	45	111	29 00	45	110	29 45	45	109
57	26 05	45	112	26 50	46	111	27 36	45	110	28 21	45	109	29 06	44	109
58	25 26	45	111	26 11	45	110	26 56	45	109	27 41	45	109	28 26	44	108
59	24 47	45	110	25 32	45	109	26 17	45	108	27 02	44	108	27 46	44	107
60	24 07	+45	109	24 52	+45	108	25 37	+45	108	26 22	+44	107	27 06	+44	106
61	23 28	45	108	24 13	44	108	24 57	45	107	25 42	44	106	26 26	44	105
62	22 48	45	107	23 33	44	107	24 17	45	106	25 02	44	105	25 46	44	105
63	22 08	45	107	22 53	44	106	23 37	44	105	24 21	44	104	25 05	44	104
64	21 28	45	106	22 13	44	105	22 57	44	104	23 41	44	104	24 25	43	103
65	20 48	+44	105	21 32	+45	104	22 17	+43	104	23 00	+44	103	23 44	+44	102
66	20 08	44	104	20 52	44	104	21 36	44	103	22 20	43	102	23 03	44	101
67	19 27	44	104	20 11	44	103	20 55	44	102	21 39	43	101	22 22	44	101
68	18 47	44	103	19 31	43	102	20 14	44	101	20 58	43	101	21 41	43	100
69	18 06	44	102	18 50	44	101	19 34	43	101	20 17	43	100	21 00	43	99

LHA	10° Hc	d	Z	11° Hc	d	Z	12° Hc	d	Z	13° Hc	d	Z	14° Hc	d	Z	LHA
	° ′	′	°	° ′	′	°	° ′	′	°	° ′	′	°	° ′	′	°	
0	54 00	+60	180	55 00	+60	180	56 00	+60	180	57 00	+60	180	58 00	+60	180	360
1	53 59	60	178	54 59	60	178	55 59	60	178	56 59	60	178	57 59	60	178	359
2	53 58	60	177	54 58	60	177	55 58	59	177	56 57	60	176	57 57	60	176	358
3	53 55	59	175	54 54	60	175	55 54	60	175	56 54	60	175	57 54	60	175	357
4	53 50	60	173	54 50	60	173	55 50	60	173	56 50	59	173	57 49	60	173	356
5	53 45	+60	172	54 45	+59	172	55 44	+60	171	56 44	+59	171	57 43	+60	171	355
6	53 38	60	170	54 38	59	170	55 37	60	170	56 37	59	169	57 36	60	169	354
7	53 30	60	168	54 30	59	168	55 29	59	168	56 28	60	168	57 28	59	167	353
8	53 21	60	167	54 21	59	166	55 20	59	166	56 19	59	166	57 18	59	166	352
9	53 11	59	165	54 10	59	165	55 09	59	165	56 08	59	164	57 07	59	164	351
10	53 00	+59	164	53 59	+58	163	54 57	+59	163	55 56	+59	162	56 55	+58	162	350
11	52 48	58	162	53 46	59	162	54 45	58	161	55 43	58	161	56 41	58	160	349
12	52 34	58	160	53 32	58	160	54 30	59	160	55 29	58	159	56 27	57	159	348
13	52 20	57	159	53 17	58	158	54 15	58	158	55 13	58	157	56 11	57	157	347
14	52 04	58	157	53 02	57	157	53 59	58	156	54 57	57	156	55 54	57	155	346
15	51 47	+58	156	52 45	+57	155	53 42	+57	155	54 39	+57	154	55 36	+57	154	345
16	51 30	57	154	52 27	56	154	53 23	57	153	54 20	57	153	55 17	56	152	344
17	51 11	57	153	52 08	56	152	53 04	57	152	54 01	56	151	54 57	56	150	343
18	50 51	57	151	51 48	56	151	52 44	56	150	53 40	56	150	54 36	55	149	342
19	50 31	56	150	51 27	56	149	52 23	55	149	53 18	56	148	54 14	55	147	341
20	50 09	+56	148	51 05	+55	148	52 00	+56	147	52 56	+55	146	53 51	+54	146	340
21	49 47	55	147	50 42	55	146	51 37	55	146	52 32	55	145	53 27	54	144	339
22	49 24	55	146	50 19	54	145	51 13	55	144	52 08	54	144	53 02	54	143	338
23	49 00	54	144	49 54	54	144	50 48	55	143	51 43	53	142	52 36	54	141	337
24	48 35	54	143	49 29	54	142	50 23	54	141	51 17	53	141	52 10	53	140	336
25	48 09	+54	141	49 03	+53	141	49 56	+54	140	50 50	+53	139	51 43	+52	139	335
26	47 43	53	140	48 36	53	139	49 29	53	139	50 22	53	138	51 15	52	137	334
27	47 16	53	139	48 09	52	138	49 01	53	137	49 54	52	137	50 46	52	136	333
28	46 48	53	138	47 41	52	137	48 33	52	136	49 25	52	135	50 17	51	135	332
29	46 19	53	136	47 12	52	136	48 04	51	135	48 55	52	134	49 47	51	133	331
30	45 50	+52	135	46 42	+52	134	47 34	+51	134	48 25	+51	133	49 16	+51	132	330
31	45 21	51	134	46 12	51	133	47 03	51	132	47 54	51	132	48 45	50	131	329
32	44 50	51	133	45 41	51	132	46 32	51	131	47 23	50	130	48 13	50	130	328
33	44 19	51	131	45 10	50	131	46 00	51	130	46 51	49	129	47 40	50	128	327
34	43 48	50	130	44 38	50	130	45 28	50	129	46 18	49	128	47 07	50	127	326
35	43 16	+50	129	44 06	+49	128	44 55	+50	128	45 45	+49	127	46 34	+49	126	325
36	42 43	50	128	43 33	49	127	44 22	49	127	45 11	49	126	46 00	48	125	324
37	42 10	49	127	42 59	49	126	43 48	49	125	44 37	49	125	45 26	48	124	323
38	41 36	49	126	42 25	49	125	43 14	49	124	44 03	48	123	44 51	47	123	322
39	41 02	49	125	41 51	48	124	42 39	49	123	43 28	47	122	44 15	48	122	321
40	40 28	+48	124	41 16	+48	123	42 04	+48	122	42 52	+48	121	43 40	+47	120	320
41	39 53	48	123	40 41	48	122	41 29	47	121	42 16	47	120	43 03	47	119	319
42	39 18	48	122	40 06	47	121	40 53	47	120	41 40	47	119	42 27	46	118	318
43	38 42	48	121	39 30	47	120	40 17	47	119	41 04	46	118	41 50	46	117	317
44	38 06	47	120	38 53	47	119	39 40	47	118	40 27	46	117	41 13	46	116	316
45	37 30	+47	119	38 17	+46	118	39 03	+46	117	39 49	+46	116	40 35	+46	115	315
46	36 53	47	118	37 40	46	117	38 26	46	116	39 12	46	115	39 58	45	114	314
47	36 16	46	117	37 02	46	116	37 48	46	115	38 34	45	114	39 19	46	114	313
48	35 38	47	116	36 25	45	115	37 10	46	114	37 56	45	113	38 41	45	113	312
49	35 01	46	115	35 47	45	114	36 32	46	113	37 18	45	112	38 03	44	112	311
50	34 23	+45	114	35 08	+46	113	35 54	+45	112	36 39	+45	112	37 24	+44	111	310
51	33 44	46	113	34 30	45	112	35 15	45	111	36 00	45	111	36 45	44	110	309
52	33 06	45	112	33 51	45	111	34 36	45	111	35 21	44	110	36 05	44	109	308
53	32 27	45	111	33 12	45	111	33 57	45	110	34 42	44	109	35 26	43	108	307
54	31 48	45	110	32 33	45	110	33 18	44	109	34 02	44	108	34 46	44	107	306
55	31 09	+45	110	31 54	+44	109	32 38	+44	108	33 22	+44	107	34 06	+43	106	305
56	30 30	44	109	31 14	44	108	31 58	44	107	32 42	44	106	33 26	43	105	304
57	29 50	44	108	30 34	44	107	31 18	44	106	32 02	44	105	32 46	43	105	303
58	29 10	45	107	29 55	43	106	30 38	44	105	31 22	43	105	32 05	43	104	302
59	28 30	44	106	29 14	44	105	29 58	44	105	30 42	43	104	31 25	43	103	301
60	27 50	+44	105	28 34	+44	105	29 18	+43	104	30 01	+43	103	30 44	+43	102	300
61	27 10	44	105	27 54	43	104	28 37	43	103	29 20	43	102	30 03	43	101	299
62	26 30	43	104	27 13	43	103	27 56	44	102	28 40	42	101	29 22	43	101	298
63	25 49	43	103	26 32	44	102	27 16	43	101	27 59	42	101	28 41	43	100	297
64	25 08	44	102	25 52	43	101	26 35	43	101	27 18	42	100	28 00	42	99	296
65	24 28	+43	101	25 11	+43	101	25 54	+42	100	26 36	+43	99	27 19	+42	98	295
66	23 47	43	101	24 30	43	100	25 13	42	99	25 55	43	98	26 38	42	97	294
67	23 06	43	100	23 49	42	99	24 31	43	98	25 14	42	98	25 56	42	97	293
68	22 24	43	99	23 07	43	98	23 50	43	98	24 33	42	97	25 15	42	96	292
69	21 43	43	98	22 26	43	98	23 09	42	97	23 51	42	96	24 33	42	95	291

S. Lat. {LHA greater than 180°....... Zn=180−Z; LHA less than 180°........... Zn=180+Z}

DECLINATION (0°-14°) SAME NAME AS LATITUDE

N. Lat. {LHA greater than 180°....... Zn=Z; LHA less than 180°........... Zn=360−Z}

DECLINATION (0°-14°) SAME NAME AS LATITUDE

	0°			1°			2°			3°			4°			5°			6°			7°			8°			9°			10°			11°			12°			13°			14°			
LHA	Hc	d	Z	Hc	d	Z	Hc	d	Z	Hc	d	Z	Hc	d	Z	Hc	d	Z	Hc	d	Z	Hc	d	Z	Hc	d	Z	Hc	d	Z	Hc	d	Z	Hc	d	Z	Hc	d	Z	Hc	d	Z	Hc	d	Z	LHA
	° ′	′	°	° ′	′	°	° ′	′	°	° ′	′	°	° ′	′	°	° ′	′	°	° ′	′	°	° ′	′	°	° ′	′	°	° ′	′	°	° ′	′	°	° ′	′	°	° ′	′	°	° ′	′	°	° ′	′	°	
70	13 45	+44	105	14 29	+44	104	15 13	+44	103	15 57	+44	103	16 41	+44	102	17 25	+44	101	18 09	+43	100	18 52	+44	100	19 36	+43	99	20 19	+43	98	21 02	+43	98	21 45	+42	97	22 27	+43	96	23 10	+42	95	23 52	+42	94	290
71	13 04	45	104	13 49	44	103	14 33	44	103	15 17	44	102	16 01	43	101	16 44	44	100	17 28	43	100	18 11	44	99	18 55	43	98	19 38	43	98	20 21	42	97	21 03	43	96	21 46	42	95	22 28	42	95	23 10	42	94	289
72	12 24	44	103	13 08	44	103	13 52	44	102	14 36	44	101	15 20	43	100	16 03	44	100	16 47	43	99	17 30	43	98	18 13	43	98	18 56	43	97	19 39	43	96	20 22	42	95	21 04	43	95	21 47	42	94	22 29	41	93	288
73	11 43	44	102	12 27	44	102	13 11	44	101	13 55	44	100	14 39	43	100	15 22	44	99	16 06	43	98	16 49	43	97	17 32	43	97	18 15	43	96	18 58	42	95	19 40	43	95	20 23	42	94	21 05	42	93	21 47	42	92	287
74	11 02	44	102	11 46	44	101	12 30	44	100	13 14	43	100	13 57	44	99	14 41	43	98	15 24	43	97	16 07	44	97	16 51	42	96	17 33	43	95	18 16	43	95	18 59	42	94	19 41	42	93	20 23	42	92	21 05	42	92	286
75	10 22	+43	101	11 05	+44	100	11 49	+44	100	12 33	+43	99	13 16	+44	98	14 00	+43	97	14 43	+43	97	15 26	+43	96	16 09	+43	95	16 52	+43	95	17 35	+42	94	18 17	+43	93	19 00	+42	92	19 42	+42	92	20 24	+41	91	285
76	09 41	43	100	10 24	44	100	11 08	43	99	11 51	44	98	12 35	43	97	13 18	43	97	14 01	44	96	14 45	43	95	15 28	42	95	16 10	43	94	16 53	43	93	17 36	42	92	18 18	42	92	19 00	42	91	19 42	42	90	284
77	08 59	44	99	09 43	44	99	10 27	43	98	11 10	44	97	11 54	43	97	12 37	43	96	13 20	43	95	14 03	43	95	14 46	43	94	15 29	42	93	16 11	43	92	16 54	42	92	17 36	42	91	18 18	42	90	19 00	42	89	283
78	08 18	44	99	09 02	43	98	09 45	44	97	10 29	43	97	11 12	43	96	11 55	43	95	12 38	43	95	13 21	43	94	14 04	43	93	14 47	43	92	15 30	42	92	16 12	43	91	16 55	42	90	17 37	42	89	18 19	41	89	282
79	07 37	44	98	08 21	43	97	09 04	43	97	09 47	44	96	10 31	43	95	11 14	43	95	11 57	43	94	12 40	43	93	13 23	42	92	14 05	43	92	14 48	43	91	15 31	42	90	16 13	42	89	16 55	42	89	17 37	42	88	281
80	06 56	+43	97	07 39	+44	97	08 23	+43	96	09 06	+43	95	09 49	+43	94	10 32	+43	94	11 15	+43	93	11 58	+43	92	12 41	+43	92	13 24	+42	91	14 06	+43	90	14 49	+42	89	15 31	+42	89	16 13	+42	88	16 55	+42	87	280
81	06 14	44	97	06 58	43	96	07 41	43	95	08 24	44	94	09 08	43	94	09 51	43	93	10 34	43	92	11 17	42	92	11 59	43	91	12 42	43	90	13 25	42	89	14 07	42	89	14 49	43	88	15 32	42	87	16 14	42	87	279
82	05 33	43	96	06 16	44	95	07 00	43	94	07 43	43	94	08 26	43	93	09 09	43	92	09 52	43	92	10 35	43	91	11 18	42	90	12 00	43	89	12 43	42	89	13 25	43	88	14 08	42	87	14 50	42	87	15 32	42	86	278
83	04 51	44	95	05 35	43	94	06 18	43	94	07 01	43	93	07 44	43	92	08 27	43	92	09 10	43	91	09 53	43	90	10 36	43	89	11 19	42	89	12 01	43	88	12 44	42	87	13 26	42	87	14 08	43	86	14 51	42	85	277
84	04 10	43	94	04 53	43	94	05 36	44	93	06 20	43	92	07 03	43	92	07 46	43	91	08 29	43	90	09 12	42	89	09 54	43	89	10 37	43	88	11 20	42	87	12 02	43	87	12 45	42	86	13 27	42	85	14 09	42	84	276
85	03 28	+43	94	04 11	+44	93	04 55	+43	92	05 38	+43	92	06 21	+43	91	07 04	+43	90	07 47	+43	89	08 30	+43	89	09 13	+42	88	09 55	+43	87	10 38	+43	87	11 21	+42	86	12 03	+42	85	12 45	+43	84	13 28	+42	84	275
86	02 47	43	93	03 30	43	92	04 13	43	91	04 56	43	91	05 39	43	90	06 22	43	89	07 05	43	89	07 48	43	88	08 31	43	87	09 14	43	87	09 57	42	86	10 39	43	85	11 22	42	84	12 04	42	84	12 46	42	83	274
87	02 05	43	92	02 48	43	91	03 31	43	91	04 14	44	90	04 58	43	89	05 41	43	89	06 24	43	88	07 07	42	87	07 49	43	87	08 32	43	86	09 15	43	85	09 58	42	84	10 40	43	84	11 23	42	83	12 05	42	82	273
88	01 23	44	91	02 07	43	91	02 50	43	90	03 33	43	89	04 16	43	89	04 59	43	88	05 42	43	87	06 25	43	87	07 08	43	86	07 51	42	85	08 33	43	84	09 16	43	84	09 59	42	83	10 41	43	82	11 24	42	82	272
89	00 42	43	91	01 25	43	90	02 08	43	89	02 51	43	89	03 34	43	88	04 17	43	87	05 00	43	87	05 43	43	86	06 26	43	85	07 09	43	84	07 52	43	84	08 35	42	83	09 17	43	82	10 00	42	82	10 42	43	81	271
90	00 00	+43	90	00 43	+43	89	01 26	+43	89	02 09	+44	88	02 53	+43	87	03 36	+43	87	04 19	+43	86	05 02	+43	85	05 45	+43	84	06 28	+43	84	07 11	+42	83	07 53	+43	82	08 36	+43	82	09 19	+42	81	10 01	+43	80	270
91	−0 42	43	89	00 01	44	89	00 45	43	88	01 28	43	87	02 11	43	86	02 54	43	86	03 37	43	85	04 20	43	84	05 03	43	84	05 46	43	83	06 29	43	82	07 12	43	82	07 55	43	81	08 38	42	80	09 20	43	80	269
92	−1 23	43	89	−0 40	43	88	00 03	43	87	00 46	43	86	01 29	44	86	02 13	43	85	02 56	43	84	03 39	43	84	04 22	43	83	05 05	43	82	05 48	43	82	06 31	43	81	07 14	43	80	07 57	42	80	08 39	43	79	268
93	−2 05	43	88	−1 22	43	87	−0 39	44	86	00 05	43	86	00 48	43	85	01 31	43	84	02 14	43	84	02 57	44	83	03 41	43	82	04 24	43	82	05 07	43	81	05 50	43	80	06 33	43	80	07 16	43	79	07 59	42	78	267
94	−2 47	44	87	−2 03	43	86	−1 20	43	86	−0 37	43	85	00 06	44	84	00 50	43	84	01 33	43	83	02 16	43	82	02 59	43	82	03 42	44	81	04 26	43	80	05 09	43	80	05 52	43	79	06 35	43	78	07 18	43	77	266
95	−3 28	+43	86	−2 45	+43	86	−2 02	+44	85	−1 18	+43	84	−0 35	+43	84	00 08	+43	83	00 51	+44	82	01 35	+43	82	02 18	+43	81	03 01	+44	80	03 45	+43	79	04 28	+43	79	05 11	+43	78	05 54	+43	77	06 37	+43	77	265
96	−4 10	43	86	−3 27	44	85	−2 43	43	84	−2 00	43	84	−1 17	44	83	−0 33	43	82	00 10	44	82	00 54	43	81	01 37	43	80	02 20	44	79	03 04	43	79	03 47	43	78	04 30	44	77	05 14	43	77	05 57	43	76	264
97	−4 51	43	85	−4 08	43	84	−3 25	44	84	−2 41	43	83	−1 58	44	82	−1 14	43	81	−0 31	44	81	00 13	43	80	00 56	43	79	01 39	44	79	02 23	43	78	03 06	44	77	03 50	43	77	04 33	43	76	05 16	44	75	263
98	−5 33	44	84	−4 49	43	84	−4 06	43	83	−3 23	44	82	−2 39	43	81	−1 56	44	81	−1 12	43	80	−0 29	44	79	00 15	44	79	00 59	43	78	01 42	44	77	02 26	43	77	03 09	44	76	03 53	43	75	04 36	44	75	262
99	−6 14	43	83	−5 31	44	83	−4 47	43	82	−4 04	44	81	−3 20	43	81	−2 37	44	80	−1 53	44	79	−1 09	43	79	−0 26	44	78	00 18	44	77	01 02	43	77	01 45	44	76	02 29	43	75	03 12	44	75	03 56	43	74	261
100				−6 12	+43	82	−5 29	+44	81	−4 45	+44	81	−4 01	+43	80	−3 18	+44	79	−2 34	+44	79	−1 50	+44	78	−1 06	+43	77	−0 23	+44	77	00 21	+44	76	01 05	+44	75	01 49	+43	75	02 32	+44	74	03 16	+44	73	260
101							−6 10	44	81	−5 26	44	80	−4 42	43	79	−3 59	44	79	−3 15	44	78	−2 31	44	77	−1 47	44	77	−1 03	44	76	−0 19	44	75	00 25	43	74	01 08	44	74	01 52	44	73	02 36	44	72	259
102										−6 07	44	79	−5 23	44	78	−4 39	44	78	−3 55	43	77	−3 12	44	76	−2 28	44	76	−1 44	44	75	−1 00	44	74	−0 16	44	74	00 28	45	73	01 13	44	72	01 57	44	72	258
103													−6 04	44	78	−5 20	44	77	−4 36	44	76	−3 52	44	76	−3 08	44	75	−2 24	44	74	−1 40	45	74	−0 55	44	73	−0 11	44	72	00 33	44	72	01 17	44	71	257
104																−6 01	44	76	−5 17	45	76	−4 32	44	75	−3 48	44	74	−3 04	44	74	−2 20	45	73	−1 35	44	72	−0 51	44	72	−0 07	45	71	00 38	44	70	256
105																			−5 57	+44	75	−5 13	+45	74	−4 28	+44	74	−3 44	+45	73	−2 59	+44	72	−2 15	+45	72	−1 30	+44	71	−0 46	+45	70	−0 01	+44	70	255
106																						−5 53	45	74	−5 08	44	73	−4 24	45	72	−3 39	45	72	−2 54	44	71	−2 10	45	70	−1 25	45	70	−0 40	44	69	254
107																									−5 48	45	72	−5 03	45	71	−4 18	44	71	−3 34	45	70	−2 49	45	69	−2 04	45	69	−1 19	45	68	253
108																												−5 43	45	71	−4 58	45	70	−4 13	45	69	−3 28	45	69	−2 43	45	68	−1 58	45	67	252
109																															−5 37	45	69	−4 52	45	69	−4 07	46	68	−3 21	45	67	−2 36	45	67	251
110																															−6 16	+46	69	−5 30	+45	68	−4 45	+45	67	−4 00	+46	67	−3 14	+45	66	250
111																																		−6 09	46	67	−5 23	45	66	−4 38	46	66	−3 52	45	65	249
112																																					−6 02	46	66	−5 16	46	65	−4 30	46	64	248
113																																								−5 54	46	64	−5 08	46	64	247
114																																											−5 45	46	63	246

DECLINATION (0°-14°) CONTRARY NAME TO LATITUDE

LHA	Hc	d	Z	Hc	d	Z	Hc	d	Z	Hc	d	Z	Hc	d	Z	Hc	d	Z	Hc	d	Z	Hc	d	Z	Hc	d	Z	Hc	d	Z	Hc	d	Z	Hc	d	Z	Hc	d	Z	Hc	d	Z	Hc	d	Z	LHA
99	−6 14	44	83																																											261
98	−5 33	43	84	−6 16	44	85																																								262
97	−4 51	44	85	−5 35	43	86	−6 18	43	86																																					263
96	−4 10	43	86	−4 53	43	86	−5 36	44	87	−6 20	43	88																																		264
95	−3 28	−43	86	−4 11	−44	87	−4 55	−43	88	−5 38	−43	88	−6 21	−43	89																															265
94	−2 47	43	87	−3 30	43	88	−4 13	43	89	−4 56	43	89	−5 39	43	90	−6 22	43	91																												266
93	−2 05	43	88	−2 48	43	89	−3 31	43	89	−4 14	44	90	−4 58	43	91	−5 41	43	91																												267
92	−1 23	44	89	−2 07	43	89	−2 50	43	90	−3 33	43	91	−4 16	43	91	−4 59	43	92	−5 42	43	93																									268
91	−0 42	43	89	−1 25	43	90	−2 08	43	91	−2 51	43	91	−3 34	43	92	−4 17	43	93	−5 00	43	93	−5 43	43	94																						269
90	00 00	−43	90	−0 43	−43	91	−1 26	−43	91	−2 09	−44	92	−2 53	−43	93	−3 36	−43	93	−4 19	−43	94	−5 02	−43	95	−5 45	−43	96																			270
89	00 42	43	91	−0 01	44	91	−0 45	43	92	−1 28	43	93	−2 11	43	94	−2 54	43	94	−3 37	43	95	−4 20	43	96	−5 03	43	96	−5 46	43	97																271
88	01 23	43	91	00 40	43	92	−0 03	43	93	−0 46	43	94	−1 29	44	94	−2 13	43	95	−2 56	43	96	−3 39	43	96	−4 22	43	97	−5 05	43	98	−5 48	43	98													272
87	02 05	43	92	01 22	43	93	00 39	44	94	−0 05	43	94	−0 48	43	95	−1 31	43	96	−2 14	43	96	−2 57	44	97	−3 41	43	98	−4 24	43	98	−5 07	43	99	−5 50	43	100										273
86	02 47	44	93	02 03	43	94	01 20	43	94	00 37	43	95	−0 06	44	96	−0 50	43	96	−1 33	43	97	−2 16	43	98	−2 59	43	98	−3 42	44	99	−4 26	43	100	−5 09	43	100	−5 52	43	101							274
85	03 28	−43	94	02 45	−43	94	02 02	−44	95	01 18	−43	96	00 35	−43	96	−0 08	−43	97	−0 51	−44	98	−1 35	−43	98	−2 18	−43	99	−3 01	−44	100	−3 45	−43	101	−4 28	−43	101	−5 11	−43	102	−5 54	−43	103				275
84	04 10	43	94	03 27	44	95	02 43	43	96	02 00	43	96	01 17	44	97	00 33	43	98	−0 10	44	98	−0 54	43	99	−1 37	43	100	−2 20	44	101	−3 04	43	101	−3 47	43	102	−4 30	44	103	−5 14	43	103	−5 57	43	104	276
83	04 51	43	95	04 08	43	96	03 25	44	96	02 41	43	97	01 58	44	98	01 14	43	99	00 31	44	99	−0 13	43	100	−0 56	43	101	−1 39	44	101	−2 23	43	102	−3 06	44	103	−3 50	43	103	−4 33	43	104	−5 16	44	105	277
82	05 33	44	96	04 49	43	96	04 06	43	97	03 23	44	98	02 39	43	99	01 56	44	99	01 12	43	100	00 29	44	101	−0 15	44	101	−0 59	43	102	−1 42	44	103	−2 26	43	103	−3 09	44	104	−3 53	43	105	−4 36	44	105	278
81	06 14	43	97	05 31	44	97	04 47	43	98	04 04	44	99	03 20	43	99	02 37	44	100	01 53	44	101	01 09	43	101	00 26	44	102	−0 18	44	103	−1 02	43	103	−1 45	44	104	−2 29	43	105	−3 12	44	105	−3 56	43	106	279
80	06 56	−44	97	06 12	−43	98	05 29	−44	99	04 45	−44	99	04 01	−43	100	03 18	−44	101	02 34	−44	101	01 50	−44	102	01 06	−43	103	00 23	−44	103	−0 21	−44	104	−1 05	−44	105	−1 49	−43	105	−2 32	−44	106	−3 16	−44	107	280
79	07 37	44	98	06 53	43	99	06 10	44	99	05 26	44	100	04 42	43	101	03 59	44	101	03 15	44	102	02 31	44	103	01 47	44	103	01 03	44	104	00 19	44	105	−0 25	43	106	−1 08	44	106	−1 52	44	107	−2 36	44	108	281
78	08 18	43	99	07 35	44	99	06 51	44	100	06 07	44	101	05 23	44	102	04 39	44	102	03 55	43	103	03 12	44	104	02 28	44	104	01 44	44	105	01 00	44	106	00 16	44	106	−0 28	45	107	−1 13	44	108	−1 57	44	108	282
77	08 59	43	99	08 16	44	100	07 32	44	101	06 48	44	102	06 04	44	102	05 20	44	103	04 36	44	104	03 52	44	104	03 08	44	105	02 24	44	106	01 40	45	106	00 55	44	107	00 11	44	108	−0 33	44	108	−1 17	44	109	283
76	09 41	44	100	08 57	44	101	08 13	44	102	07 29	44	102	06 45	44	103	06 01	44	104	05 17	45	104	04 32	44	105	03 48	44	106	03 04	44	106	02 20	45	107	01 35	44	108	00 51	44	108	00 07	45	109	−0 38	44	110	284
75	10 22	−44	101	09 38	−44	102	08 54	−44	102	08 10	−45	103	07 25	−44	104	06 41	−44	104	05 57	−44	105	05 13	−45	106	04 28	−44	106	03 44	−45	107	02 59	−44	108	02 15	−45	108	01 30	−44	109	00 46	−45	110	00 01	−44	110	285
74	11 02	44	102	10 18	44	102	09 34	44	103	08 50	44	104	08 06	45	104	07 21	44	105	06 37	44	106	05 53	45	106	05 08	44	107	04 24	45	108	03 39	45	108	02 54	44	109	02 10	45	110	01 25	45	110	00 40	44	111	286
73	11 43	44	102	10 59	44	103	10 15	45	104	09 30	44	105	08 46	44	105	08 02	45	106	07 17	44	107	06 33	45	107	05 48	45	108	05 03	45	109	04 18	44	109	03 34	45	110	02 49	45	111	02 04	45	111	01 19	45	112	287
72	12 24	44	103	11 40	45	104	10 55	44	105	10 11	45	105	09 26	44	106	08 42	45	107	07 57	45	107	07 12	45	108	06 27	44	109	05 43	45	109	04 58	45	110	04 13	45	111	03 28	45	111	02 43	45	112	01 58	45	113	288
71	13 04	44	104	12 20	45	105	11 35	44	105	10 51	45	106	10 06	44	107	09 22	45	107	08 37	45	108	07 52	45	109	07 07	45	109	06 22	45	110	05 37	45	111	04 52	45	111	04 07	46	112	03 21	45	113	02 36	45	113	289
70	13 45	−45	105	13 00	−44	105	12 16	−45	106	11 31	−45	107	10 46	−45	107	10 01	−45	108	09 16	−45	109	08 31	−45	109	07 46	−45	110	07 01	−45	111	06 16	−46	111	05 30	−45	112	04 45	−45	113	04 00	−46	113	03 14	−45	114	290
	0°			1°			2°			3°			4°			5°			6°			7°			8°			9°			10°			11°			12°			13°			14°			

S. Lat. {LHA greater than 180°....... Zn=180−Z; LHA less than 180°........... Zn=180+Z}

LAT 46°

N. Lat. {LHA greater than 180°....... Zn=Z
LHA less than 180°........... Zn=360−Z}

DECLINATION (0°-14°) CONTRARY NAME TO LATITUDE

LHA	0°			1°			2°			3°			4°		
	Hc	d	Z	Hc	d	Z	Hc	d	Z	Hc	d	Z	Hc	d	Z
	° ′	′	°	° ′	′	°	° ′	′	°	° ′	′	°	° ′	′	°
69	14 25	45	105	13 40	44	106	12 56	45	107	12 11	45	108	11 26	45	108
68	15 05	45	106	14 20	45	107	13 35	45	108	12 50	45	108	12 05	45	109
67	15 45	45	107	15 00	45	108	14 15	45	108	13 30	45	109	12 45	46	110
66	16 25	45	108	15 40	45	108	14 55	46	109	14 09	45	110	13 24	46	111
65	17 04	-45	109	16 19	-45	109	15 34	-46	110	14 48	-45	111	14 03	-46	111
64	17 44	46	109	16 58	45	110	16 13	46	111	15 27	46	111	14 41	45	112
63	18 23	46	110	17 37	45	111	16 52	46	112	16 06	46	112	15 20	46	113
62	19 02	46	111	18 16	46	112	17 30	46	112	16 44	46	113	15 58	46	114
61	19 41	46	112	18 55	46	112	18 09	46	113	17 23	47	114	16 36	46	114
60	20 19	-46	113	19 33	-46	113	18 47	-46	114	18 01	-47	115	17 14	-46	115
59	20 58	46	113	20 12	47	114	19 25	46	115	18 39	47	115	17 52	47	116
58	21 36	46	114	20 50	47	115	20 03	47	116	19 16	47	116	18 29	47	117
57	22 14	47	115	21 27	47	116	20 40	47	116	19 53	47	117	19 06	47	118
56	22 52	47	116	22 05	47	117	21 18	48	117	20 30	47	118	19 43	48	119
55	23 29	-47	117	22 42	-48	117	21 54	-47	118	21 07	-48	119	20 19	-47	119
54	24 06	47	118	23 19	48	118	22 31	48	119	21 43	47	120	20 56	48	120
53	24 43	48	119	23 55	48	119	23 07	48	120	22 19	48	120	21 31	48	121
52	25 19	48	119	24 31	48	120	23 43	48	121	22 55	48	121	22 07	49	122
51	25 55	48	120	25 07	48	121	24 19	48	122	23 31	49	122	22 42	49	123
50	26 31	-48	121	25 43	-49	122	24 54	-48	122	24 06	-49	123	23 17	-49	124
49	27 07	49	122	26 18	49	123	25 29	48	123	24 41	50	124	23 51	49	125
48	27 42	49	123	26 53	49	124	26 04	49	124	25 15	49	125	24 26	50	126
47	28 17	49	124	27 28	50	125	26 38	49	125	25 49	50	126	24 59	49	126
46	28 51	49	125	28 02	50	125	27 12	49	126	26 23	50	127	25 33	50	127
45	29 25	-49	126	28 36	-50	126	27 46	-50	127	26 56	-50	128	26 06	-51	128
44	29 59	50	127	29 09	50	127	28 19	50	128	27 29	51	129	26 38	50	129
43	30 32	50	128	29 42	51	128	28 51	50	129	28 01	51	130	27 10	51	130
42	31 05	51	129	30 14	50	129	29 24	51	130	28 33	51	131	27 42	51	131
41	31 37	51	130	30 46	51	130	29 55	51	131	29 04	51	131	28 13	51	132
40	32 09	-51	131	31 18	-51	131	30 27	-52	132	29 35	-51	132	28 44	-52	133
39	32 40	51	132	31 49	51	132	30 58	52	133	30 06	52	133	29 14	52	134
38	33 11	51	133	32 20	52	133	31 28	52	134	30 36	52	134	29 44	53	135
37	33 42	52	134	32 50	52	134	31 58	53	135	31 05	52	135	30 13	53	136
36	34 12	53	135	33 19	52	135	32 27	53	136	31 34	52	137	30 42	53	137
35	34 41	-53	136	33 48	-52	136	32 56	-53	137	32 03	-53	138	31 10	-53	138
34	35 10	53	137	34 17	53	137	33 24	53	138	32 31	54	139	31 37	53	139
33	35 38	53	138	34 45	53	139	33 52	54	139	32 58	54	140	32 04	53	140
32	36 06	54	139	35 12	53	140	34 19	54	140	33 25	54	141	32 31	54	141
31	36 33	54	140	35 39	54	141	34 45	54	141	33 51	54	142	32 57	55	142
30	36 59	-54	141	36 05	-54	142	35 11	-55	142	34 16	-54	143	33 22	-55	143
29	37 25	55	142	36 30	54	143	35 36	55	143	34 41	55	144	33 46	54	144
28	37 50	55	144	36 55	55	144	36 00	55	145	35 05	55	145	34 10	55	146
27	38 14	55	145	37 19	55	145	36 24	55	146	35 29	55	146	34 34	56	147
26	38 38	55	146	37 43	56	146	36 47	55	147	35 52	56	147	34 56	56	148
25	39 01	-55	147	38 06	-56	148	37 10	-56	148	36 14	-56	149	35 18	-56	149
24	39 23	55	148	38 28	56	149	37 32	57	149	36 35	56	150	35 39	56	150
23	39 45	56	150	38 49	56	150	37 53	57	150	36 56	56	151	36 00	57	151
22	40 06	57	151	39 09	56	151	38 13	57	152	37 16	57	152	36 19	56	152
21	40 26	57	152	39 29	57	152	38 32	57	153	37 35	57	153	36 38	57	154
20	40 45	-57	153	39 48	-57	154	38 51	-57	154	37 54	-57	154	36 57	-58	155
19	41 03	57	154	40 06	57	155	39 09	58	155	38 11	57	156	37 14	58	156
18	41 21	57	156	40 24	58	156	39 26	58	156	38 28	57	157	37 31	58	157
17	41 38	58	157	40 40	58	157	39 42	58	158	38 44	58	158	37 46	58	158
16	41 54	58	158	40 56	58	159	39 58	59	159	38 59	58	159	38 01	58	160
15	42 09	-59	160	41 10	-58	160	40 12	-58	160	39 14	-59	161	38 15	-58	161
14	42 23	59	161	41 24	58	161	40 26	59	162	39 27	58	162	38 29	59	162
13	42 36	59	162	41 37	58	163	40 39	59	163	39 40	59	163	38 41	59	163
12	42 48	59	164	41 49	59	164	40 50	58	164	39 52	59	164	38 53	59	165
11	43 00	59	165	42 01	60	165	41 01	59	165	40 02	59	166	39 03	59	166
10	43 10	-59	166	42 11	-59	167	41 12	-60	167	40 12	-59	167	39 13	-59	167
9	43 19	59	168	42 20	59	168	41 21	60	168	40 21	59	168	39 22	59	168
8	43 28	60	169	42 28	59	169	41 29	60	169	40 29	59	170	39 30	60	170
7	43 35	59	170	42 36	60	171	41 36	59	171	40 37	60	171	39 37	60	171
6	43 42	60	172	42 42	60	172	41 42	59	172	40 43	60	172	39 43	60	172
5	43 47	-59	173	42 48	-60	173	41 48	-60	173	40 48	-60	173	39 48	-60	174
4	43 52	60	174	42 52	60	175	41 52	60	175	40 52	60	175	39 52	59	175
3	43 56	60	176	42 56	60	176	41 56	60	176	40 56	60	176	39 56	60	176
2	43 58	60	177	42 58	60	177	41 58	60	177	40 58	60	177	39 58	60	177
1	44 00	60	179	43 00	60	179	42 00	60	179	41 00	60	179	40 00	60	179
0	44 00	-60	180	43 00	-60	180	42 00	-60	180	41 00	-60	180	40 00	-60	180
	0°			1°			2°			3°			4°		

LHA	5°			6°			7°			8°			9°		
	Hc	d	Z	Hc	d	Z	Hc	d	Z	Hc	d	Z	Hc	d	Z
	° ′	′	°	° ′	′	°	° ′	′	°	° ′	′	°	° ′	′	°
69	10 41	45	109	09 56	46	110	09 10	45	110	08 25	45	111	07 40	46	112
68	11 20	45	110	10 35	46	110	09 49	45	111	09 04	45	112	08 19	46	112
67	11 59	45	110	11 14	46	111	10 28	45	112	09 43	46	112	08 57	46	113
66	12 38	45	111	11 53	46	112	11 07	46	113	10 21	46	113	09 35	46	114
65	13 17	-46	112	12 31	-46	113	11 45	-46	113	10 59	-46	114	10 13	-46	115
64	13 56	46	113	13 10	46	113	12 24	47	114	11 37	46	115	10 51	46	115
63	14 34	46	114	13 48	47	114	13 01	46	115	12 15	46	116	11 29	47	116
62	15 12	46	114	14 26	47	115	13 39	46	116	12 53	47	116	12 06	47	117
61	15 50	47	115	15 03	46	116	14 17	47	116	13 30	47	117	12 43	47	118
60	16 28	-47	116	15 41	-47	117	14 54	-47	117	14 07	-47	118	13 20	-47	119
59	17 05	47	117	16 18	47	117	15 31	47	118	14 44	48	119	13 56	47	119
58	17 42	47	118	16 55	48	118	16 07	47	119	15 20	48	120	14 32	47	120
57	18 19	48	118	17 31	47	119	16 44	48	120	15 56	48	120	15 08	48	121
56	18 55	47	119	18 08	48	120	17 20	48	121	16 32	48	121	15 44	48	122
55	19 32	-48	120	18 44	-48	121	17 56	-48	121	17 08	-49	122	16 19	-48	123
54	20 08	49	121	19 19	48	122	18 31	48	122	17 43	49	123	16 54	48	123
53	20 43	48	122	19 55	49	122	19 06	48	123	18 18	49	124	17 29	49	124
52	21 18	48	123	20 30	49	123	19 41	49	124	18 52	49	124	18 03	49	125
51	21 53	48	124	21 05	50	124	20 15	49	125	19 26	49	125	18 37	49	126
50	22 28	-49	124	21 39	-49	125	20 50	-50	126	20 00	-49	126	19 11	-50	127
49	23 02	49	125	22 13	50	126	21 23	49	126	20 34	50	127	19 44	50	128
48	23 36	50	126	22 46	49	127	21 57	50	127	21 07	50	128	20 17	50	129
47	24 10	50	127	23 20	50	128	22 30	51	128	21 39	50	129	20 49	50	129
46	24 43	51	128	23 52	50	129	23 02	50	129	22 12	51	130	21 21	51	130
45	25 15	-50	129	24 25	-51	129	23 34	-50	130	22 44	-51	131	21 53	-51	131
44	25 48	51	130	24 57	51	130	24 06	51	131	23 15	51	132	22 24	51	132
43	26 19	51	131	25 28	51	131	24 37	51	132	23 46	51	132	22 55	52	133
42	26 51	52	132	25 59	51	132	25 08	52	133	24 16	51	133	23 25	52	134
41	27 22	52	133	26 30	52	133	25 38	51	134	24 47	52	134	23 55	52	135
40	27 52	-52	134	27 00	-52	134	26 08	-52	135	25 16	-52	135	24 24	-52	136
39	28 22	52	135	27 30	52	135	26 38	53	136	25 45	52	136	24 53	53	137
38	28 51	52	136	27 59	53	136	27 06	52	137	26 14	53	137	25 21	53	138
37	29 20	52	137	28 28	53	137	27 35	53	138	26 42	53	138	25 49	53	139
36	29 49	53	138	28 56	53	138	28 03	54	139	27 09	53	139	26 16	53	140
35	30 17	-54	139	29 23	-53	139	28 30	-54	140	27 36	-53	140	26 43	-54	141
34	30 44	54	140	29 50	53	140	28 57	54	141	28 03	54	141	27 09	54	142
33	31 11	54	141	30 17	54	141	29 23	54	142	28 29	55	142	27 34	54	143
32	31 37	54	142	30 43	55	142	29 48	54	143	28 54	55	143	27 59	54	144
31	32 02	54	143	31 08	55	143	30 13	54	144	29 19	55	144	28 24	55	145
30	32 27	-55	144	31 32	-54	144	30 38	-55	145	29 43	-55	145	28 48	-55	146
29	32 52	56	145	31 56	55	145	31 01	55	146	30 06	55	146	29 11	56	147
28	33 15	55	146	32 20	56	147	31 24	55	147	30 29	56	147	29 33	55	148
27	33 38	55	147	32 43	56	148	31 47	56	148	30 51	56	148	29 55	56	149
26	34 00	55	148	33 05	56	149	32 09	56	149	31 13	56	150	30 17	57	150
25	34 22	-56	149	33 26	-56	150	32 30	-57	150	31 33	-56	151	30 37	-56	151
24	34 43	56	151	33 47	57	151	32 50	56	151	31 54	57	152	30 57	57	152
23	35 03	57	152	34 06	56	152	33 10	57	152	32 13	57	153	31 16	57	153
22	35 23	57	153	34 26	57	153	33 29	57	154	32 32	57	154	31 35	58	154
21	35 41	57	154	34 44	57	154	33 47	57	155	32 50	58	155	31 52	57	155
20	35 59	-57	155	35 02	-58	156	34 04	-57	156	33 07	-58	156	32 09	-57	157
19	36 16	57	156	35 19	58	157	34 21	58	157	33 23	57	157	32 26	58	158
18	36 33	58	158	35 35	58	158	34 37	58	158	33 39	58	158	32 41	58	159
17	36 48	58	159	35 50	58	159	34 52	58	159	33 54	58	160	32 56	58	160
16	37 03	58	160	36 05	59	160	35 06	58	161	34 08	58	161	33 10	59	161
15	37 17	-58	161	36 19	-59	161	35 20	-59	162	34 21	-58	162	33 23	-59	162
14	37 30	59	162	36 31	58	163	35 33	59	163	34 34	59	163	33 35	59	163
13	37 42	59	164	36 43	58	164	35 45	59	164	34 46	59	164	33 47	59	165
12	37 54	59	165	36 55	59	165	35 56	59	165	34 57	59	166	33 58	60	166
11	38 04	59	166	37 05	59	166	36 06	59	166	35 07	60	167	34 07	59	167
10	38 14	-60	167	37 14	-59	168	36 15	-59	168	35 16	-60	168	34 16	-59	168
9	38 23	60	169	37 23	59	169	36 24	60	169	35 24	59	169	34 25	60	169
8	38 30	59	170	37 31	60	170	36 31	59	170	35 32	60	170	34 32	59	170
7	38 37	59	171	37 38	60	171	36 38	60	171	35 38	59	172	34 39	60	172
6	38 43	59	172	37 44	60	172	36 44	60	173	35 44	60	173	34 44	59	173
5	38 48	-59	174	37 49	-60	174	36 49	-60	174	35 49	-60	174	34 49	-60	174
4	38 53	60	175	37 53	60	175	36 53	60	175	35 53	60	175	34 53	60	175
3	38 56	60	176	37 56	60	176	36 56	60	176	35 56	60	176	34 56	60	176
2	38 58	60	177	37 58	60	178	36 58	60	178	35 58	60	178	34 58	60	178
1	39 00	60	179	38 00	60	179	37 00	60	179	36 00	60	179	35 00	60	179
0	39 00	-60	180	38 00	-60	180	37 00	-60	180	36 00	-60	180	35 00	-60	180
	5°			6°			7°			8°			9°		

LHA	10°			11°			12°			13°			14°			LHA
	Hc	d	Z	Hc	d	Z	Hc	d	Z	Hc	d	Z	Hc	d	Z	
	° ′	′	°	° ′	′	°	° ′	′	°	° ′	′	°	° ′	′	°	
69	06 54	45	112	06 09	46	113	05 23	45	114	04 38	46	114	03 52	45	115	291
68	07 33	46	113	06 47	45	114	06 02	46	114	05 16	46	115	04 30	46	116	292
67	08 11	46	114	07 25	45	114	06 40	46	115	05 54	46	116	05 08	46	116	293
66	08 49	46	114	08 03	46	115	07 17	46	116	06 31	46	116	05 45	46	117	294
65	09 27	-46	115	08 41	-46	116	07 55	-47	117	07 08	-46	117	06 22	-47	118	295
64	10 05	47	116	09 18	46	117	08 32	47	117	07 45	46	118	06 59	47	119	296
63	10 42	47	117	09 55	46	117	09 09	47	118	08 22	47	119	07 35	47	119	297
62	11 19	47	118	10 32	47	118	09 45	47	119	08 58	47	119	08 11	47	120	298
61	11 56	47	118	11 09	47	119	10 22	47	120	09 35	48	120	08 47	47	121	299
60	12 33	-48	119	11 45	-47	120	10 58	-48	120	10 10	-47	121	09 23	-48	122	300
59	13 09	48	120	12 21	47	121	11 34	48	121	10 46	48	122	09 58	48	122	301
58	13 45	48	121	12 57	48	121	12 09	48	122	11 21	48	123	10 33	48	123	302
57	14 20	48	122	13 32	48	122	12 44	48	123	11 56	48	123	11 08	48	124	303
56	14 56	48	122	14 08	49	123	13 19	48	124	12 31	49	124	11 42	48	125	304
55	15 31	-49	123	14 42	-48	124	13 54	-49	124	13 05	-49	125	12 16	-48	126	305
54	16 06	49	124	15 17	49	125	14 28	49	125	13 39	49	126	12 50	49	126	306
53	16 40	49	125	15 51	49	125	15 02	49	126	14 13	49	127	13 24	50	127	307
52	17 14	49	126	16 25	49	126	15 36	50	127	14 46	49	127	13 57	50	128	308
51	17 48	50	127	16 58	49	127	16 09	50	128	15 19	50	128	14 29	50	129	309
50	18 21	-50	127	17 31	-50	128	16 41	-49	129	15 52	-50	129	15 02	-51	130	310
49	18 54	50	128	18 04	50	129	17 14	50	129	16 24	51	130	15 33	50	131	311
48	19 27	51	129	18 36	50	130	17 46	51	130	16 55	50	131	16 05	51	131	312
47	19 59	51	130	19 08	50	131	18 18	51	131	17 27	51	132	16 36	51	132	313
46	20 30	50	131	19 40	51	131	18 49	51	132	17 58	51	133	17 07	52	133	314
45	21 02	-51	132	20 11	-52	132	19 19	-51	133	18 28	-51	133	17 37	-52	134	315
44	21 33	52	133	20 41	51	133	19 50	52	134	18 58	51	134	18 07	52	135	316
43	22 03	52	134	21 11	51	134	20 20	52	135	19 28	52	135	18 36	52	136	317
42	22 33	52	135	21 41	52	135	20 49	52	136	19 57	52	136	19 05	52	137	318
41	23 03	53	135	22 10	52	136	21 18	52	137	20 26	53	137	19 33	52	138	319
40	23 32	-53	136	22 39	-52	137	21 47	-53	137	20 54	-53	138	20 01	-53	138	320
39	24 00	53	137	23 07	53	138	22 14	52	138	21 22	53	139	20 29	54	139	321
38	24 28	53	138	23 35	53	139	22 42	53	139	21 49	54	140	20 55	53	140	322
37	24 56	54	139	24 02	53	140	23 09	54	140	22 15	53	141	21 22	54	141	323
36	25 23	54	140	24 29	54	141	23 35	53	141	22 42	54	142	21 48	54	142	324
35	25 49	-54	141	24 55	-54	142	24 01	-54	142	23 07	-54	143	22 13	-54	143	325
34	26 15	54	142	25 21	54	143	24 27	55	143	23 32	54	144	22 38	55	144	326
33	26 40	54	143	25 46	55	144	24 51	54	144	23 57	55	145	23 02	55	145	327
32	27 05	55	144	26 10	55	145	25 15	54	145	24 21	55	146	23 26	55	146	328
31	27 29	55	145	26 34	55	146	25 39	55	146	24 44	55	147	23 49	56	147	329
30	27 53	-56	146	26 57	-55	147	26 02	-55	147	25 07	-56	148	24 11	-55	148	330
29	28 15	55	147	27 20	56	148	26 24	55	148	25 29	56	148	24 33	56	149	331
28	28 38	56	148	27 42	56	149	26 46	56	149	25 50	56	150	24 54	56	150	332
27	28 59	56	149	28 03	56	150	27 07	56	150	26 11	56	151	25 15	56	151	333
26	29 20	56	150	28 24	56	151	27 28	57	151	26 31	56	152	25 35	57	152	334
25	29 41	-57	151	28 44	-56	152	27 48	-57	152	26 51	-57	153	25 54	-57	153	335
24	30 00	57	152	29 03	56	153	28 07	57	153	27 10	57	154	26 13	57	154	336
23	30 19	57	154	29 22	57	154	28 25	57	154	27 28	57	155	26 31	57	155	337
22	30 37	57	155	29 40	57	155	28 43	57	155	27 46	58	156	26 48	57	156	338
21	30 55	58	156	29 57	57	156	29 00	58	156	28 02	57	157	27 05	58	157	339
20	31 12	-58	157	30 14	-58	157	29 16	-57	157	28 19	-58	158	27 21	-58	158	340
19	31 28	58	158	30 30	58	158	29 32	58	159	28 34	58	159	27 36	58	159	341
18	31 43	58	159	30 45	58	159	29 47	58	160	28 49	59	160	27 50	58	160	342
17	31 58	59	160	30 59	58	160	30 01	58	161	29 03	59	161	28 04	58	161	343
16	32 11	58	161	31 13	59	162	30 14	58	162	29 16	59	162	28 17	58	162	344
15	32 24	-58	162	31 26	-59	163	30 27	-59	163	29 28	-58	163	28 30	-59	163	345
14	32 36	58	164	31 38	59	164	30 39	59	164	29 40	59	164	28 41	59	165	346
13	32 48	59	165	31 49	59	165	30 50	59	165	29 51	59	165	28 52	59	166	347
12	32 58	59	166	31 59	59	166	31 00	59	166	30 01	59	167	29 02	59	167	348
11	33 08	59	167	32 09	59	167	31 10	60	167	30 10	59	168	29 11	59	168	349
10	33 17	-59	168	32 18	-60	168	31 18	-59	169	30 19	-59	169	29 20	-60	169	350
9	33 25	59	169	32 26	60	170	31 26	59	170	30 27	60	170	29 27	59	170	351
8	33 33	60	171	32 33	60	171	31 33	59	171	30 34	60	171	29 34	60	171	352
7	33 39	60	172	32 39	59	172	31 40	60	172	30 40	60	172	29 40	60	172	353
6	33 45	60	173	32 45	60	173	31 45	60	173	30 45	60	173	29 45	59	173	354
5	33 49	-60	174	32 49	-59	174	31 50	-60	174	30 50	-60	174	29 50	-60	174	355
4	33 53	60	175	32 53	60	175	31 53	60	175	30 53	59	176	29 54	60	176	356
3	33 56	60	176	32 56	60	177	31 56	60	177	30 56	60	177	29 56	60	177	357
2	33 58	60	178	32 58	60	178	31 58	60	178	30 58	60	178	29 58	60	178	358
1	34 00	60	179	33 00	60	179	32 00	60	179	31 00	60	179	30 00	60	179	359
0	34 00	-60	180	33 00	-60	180	32 00	-60	180	31 00	-60	180	30 00	-60	180	360
	10°			11°			12°			13°			14°			

S. Lat. {LHA greater than 180°....... Zn=180−Z
LHA less than 180°........... Zn=180+Z}

DECLINATION (0°-14°) CONTRARY NAME TO LATITUDE

N. Lat. {LHA greater than 180°....... Zn=Z
{LHA less than 180°........... Zn=360−Z

DECLINATION (15°-29°) **SAME** NAME AS LATITUDE

LHA	15° Hc	d	Z	16° Hc	d	Z	17° Hc	d	Z	18° Hc	d	Z	19° Hc	d	Z
	° ′	′	°	° ′	′	°	° ′	′	°	° ′	′	°	° ′	′	°
0	59 00	+60	180	60 00	+60	180	61 00	+60	180	62 00	+60	180	63 00	+60	180
1	58 59	60	178	59 59	60	178	60 59	60	178	61 59	60	178	62 59	60	178
2	58 57	60	176	59 57	60	176	60 57	60	176	61 57	60	176	62 57	60	176
3	58 54	60	174	59 54	60	174	60 54	59	174	61 53	60	174	62 53	60	174
4	58 49	60	173	59 49	60	172	60 49	59	172	61 48	60	172	62 48	60	172
5	58 43	+60	171	59 43	+59	170	60 42	+60	170	61 42	+59	170	62 41	+60	170
6	58 36	59	169	59 35	59	169	60 34	60	168	61 34	59	168	62 33	59	168
7	58 27	59	167	59 26	59	167	60 25	59	166	61 24	59	166	62 23	59	166
8	58 17	59	165	59 16	59	165	60 15	59	164	61 14	58	164	62 12	59	164
9	58 06	58	163	59 04	59	163	60 03	58	163	61 01	59	162	62 00	58	162
10	57 53	+58	162	58 51	+59	161	59 50	+58	161	60 48	+58	160	61 46	+58	160
11	57 39	58	160	58 37	58	159	59 35	58	159	60 33	58	158	61 31	57	158
12	57 24	58	158	58 22	58	158	59 20	57	157	60 17	58	157	61 15	57	156
13	57 08	58	156	58 06	57	156	59 03	57	155	60 00	57	155	60 57	57	154
14	56 51	57	155	57 48	57	154	58 45	57	154	59 42	56	153	60 38	56	152
15	56 33	+56	153	57 29	+57	152	58 26	+56	152	59 22	+56	151	60 18	+56	150
16	56 13	56	151	57 09	56	151	58 05	56	150	59 01	56	149	59 57	55	149
17	55 53	56	150	56 49	55	149	57 44	56	148	58 40	55	148	59 35	54	147
18	55 31	56	148	56 27	55	148	57 22	55	147	58 17	54	146	59 11	55	145
19	55 09	55	147	56 04	55	146	56 59	54	145	57 53	54	144	58 47	54	144
20	54 45	+55	145	55 40	+54	144	56 34	+54	144	57 28	+54	143	58 22	+53	142
21	54 21	54	144	55 15	54	143	56 09	54	142	57 03	53	141	57 56	53	140
22	53 56	54	142	54 50	53	141	55 43	53	141	56 36	53	140	57 29	52	139
23	53 30	53	141	54 23	53	140	55 16	53	139	56 09	52	138	57 01	52	137
24	53 03	53	139	53 56	52	138	54 48	52	138	55 40	52	137	56 32	51	136
25	52 35	+53	138	53 28	+52	137	54 20	+51	136	55 11	+52	135	56 03	+51	134
26	52 07	52	136	52 59	52	136	53 51	51	135	54 42	51	134	55 33	50	133
27	51 38	51	135	52 29	52	134	53 21	50	133	54 11	51	132	55 02	50	132
28	51 08	51	134	51 59	51	133	52 50	50	132	53 40	50	131	54 30	50	130
29	50 38	50	132	51 28	51	132	52 19	50	131	53 09	49	130	53 58	49	129
30	50 07	+50	131	50 57	+50	130	51 47	+49	129	52 36	+49	129	53 25	+49	128
31	49 35	50	130	50 25	49	129	51 14	49	128	52 03	49	127	52 52	48	126
32	49 03	49	129	49 52	49	128	50 41	49	127	51 30	48	126	52 18	48	125
33	48 30	49	127	49 19	49	127	50 08	48	126	50 56	48	125	51 44	47	124
34	47 57	48	126	48 45	48	125	49 33	48	125	50 21	48	124	51 09	47	123
35	47 23	+48	125	48 11	+48	124	48 59	+47	123	49 46	+47	122	50 33	+47	121
36	46 48	48	124	47 36	48	123	48 24	47	122	49 11	46	121	49 57	47	120
37	46 14	47	123	47 01	47	122	47 48	47	121	48 35	46	120	49 21	46	119
38	45 38	48	122	46 26	46	121	47 12	47	120	47 59	46	119	48 45	45	118
39	45 03	47	121	45 50	46	120	46 36	46	119	47 22	46	118	48 08	45	117
40	44 27	+46	120	45 13	+46	119	45 59	+46	118	46 45	+45	117	47 30	+45	116
41	43 50	46	119	44 36	46	118	45 22	46	117	46 08	45	116	46 53	44	115
42	43 13	46	118	43 59	46	117	44 45	45	116	45 30	45	115	46 15	44	114
43	42 36	46	117	43 22	45	116	44 07	45	115	44 52	44	114	45 36	44	113
44	41 59	45	116	42 44	45	115	43 29	45	114	44 14	44	113	44 58	44	112
45	41 21	+45	115	42 06	+45	114	42 51	+44	113	43 35	+44	112	44 19	+43	111
46	40 43	45	114	41 28	44	113	42 12	44	112	42 56	44	111	43 40	43	110
47	40 05	44	113	40 49	44	112	41 33	44	111	42 17	44	110	43 01	43	109
48	39 26	44	112	40 10	44	111	40 54	44	110	41 38	43	109	42 21	43	108
49	38 47	44	111	39 31	44	110	40 15	44	109	40 59	42	108	41 41	43	107
50	38 08	+44	110	38 52	+44	109	39 36	+43	108	40 19	+43	107	41 02	+42	106
51	37 29	43	109	38 12	44	108	38 56	43	107	39 39	42	106	40 21	43	105
52	36 49	44	108	37 33	43	107	38 16	43	106	38 59	42	105	39 41	42	105
53	36 09	44	107	36 53	43	106	37 36	43	105	38 19	42	105	39 01	42	104
54	35 30	43	106	36 13	43	106	36 56	42	105	37 38	42	104	38 20	42	103
55	34 49	+43	106	35 32	+43	105	36 15	+43	104	36 58	+41	103	37 39	+42	102
56	34 09	43	105	34 52	43	104	35 35	42	103	36 17	42	102	36 59	41	101
57	33 29	43	104	34 12	42	103	34 54	42	102	35 36	42	101	36 18	41	100
58	32 48	43	103	33 31	42	102	34 13	42	101	34 55	42	100	35 37	41	100
59	32 08	42	102	32 50	42	101	33 32	42	101	34 14	41	100	34 55	41	99
60	31 27	+42	101	32 09	+42	101	32 51	+42	100	33 33	+41	99	34 14	+41	98
61	30 46	42	101	31 28	42	100	32 10	42	99	32 52	41	98	33 33	41	97
62	30 05	42	100	30 47	42	99	31 29	41	98	32 10	41	97	32 51	41	96
63	29 24	42	99	30 06	41	98	30 47	42	97	31 29	41	97	32 10	41	96
64	28 42	42	98	29 24	42	97	30 06	41	97	30 47	42	96	31 29	40	95
65	28 01	+42	97	28 43	+42	97	29 25	+41	96	30 06	+41	95	30 47	+41	94
66	27 20	42	97	28 02	41	96	28 13	41	95	29 24	41	94	30 05	41	93
67	26 38	42	96	27 20	42	95	28 02	41	94	28 43	41	93	29 24	40	93
68	25 57	42	95	26 39	41	94	27 20	41	94	28 01	41	93	28 42	41	92
69	25 15	42	94	25 57	41	94	26 38	42	93	27 20	40	92	28 00	41	91

LHA	20° Hc	d	Z	21° Hc	d	Z	22° Hc	d	Z	23° Hc	d	Z	24° Hc	d	Z
	° ′	′	°	° ′	′	°	° ′	′	°	° ′	′	°	° ′	′	°
0	64 00	+60	180	65 00	+60	180	66 00	+60	180	67 00	+60	180	68 00	+60	180
1	63 59	60	178	64 59	60	178	65 59	60	178	66 59	60	178	67 59	60	178
2	63 57	60	176	64 57	60	176	65 57	60	175	66 57	60	175	67 57	59	175
3	63 53	60	174	64 53	60	173	65 53	59	173	66 52	60	173	67 52	60	173
4	63 48	59	172	64 47	60	171	65 47	59	171	66 46	60	171	67 46	59	170
5	63 41	+59	169	64 40	+59	169	65 39	+60	169	66 39	+59	168	67 38	+59	168
6	63 32	59	167	64 31	60	167	65 31	59	167	66 30	59	166	67 29	58	166
7	63 22	59	165	64 21	59	165	65 20	59	164	66 19	58	164	67 17	59	163
8	63 11	59	163	64 10	58	163	65 08	56	162	66 06	58	162	67 04	59	161
9	62 58	58	161	63 56	58	161	64 54	58	160	65 52	58	159	66 50	58	159
10	62 44	+58	159	63 42	+57	159	64 39	+58	158	65 37	+57	157	66 34	+57	157
11	62 28	58	157	63 26	57	157	64 23	57	156	65 20	57	155	66 17	56	154
12	62 12	57	155	63 09	56	155	64 05	57	154	65 02	56	153	65 58	56	152
13	61 54	56	153	62 50	56	153	63 46	56	152	64 42	56	151	65 38	55	150
14	61 34	56	152	62 30	56	151	63 26	55	150	64 21	56	149	65 17	54	148
15	61 14	+55	150	62 09	+56	149	63 05	+54	148	63 59	+55	147	64 54	+54	146
16	60 52	55	148	61 47	55	147	62 42	54	146	63 36	54	145	64 30	54	144
17	60 29	55	146	61 24	54	145	62 18	54	144	63 12	53	143	64 05	53	142
18	60 06	54	144	61 00	53	144	61 53	53	143	62 46	53	142	63 39	52	141
19	59 41	53	143	60 34	53	142	61 27	53	141	62 20	52	140	63 12	52	139
20	59 15	+53	141	60 08	+53	140	61 01	+52	139	61 53	+51	138	62 44	+51	137
21	58 49	52	139	59 41	52	139	60 33	51	138	61 24	51	136	62 15	51	135
22	58 21	52	138	59 13	51	137	60 04	51	136	60 55	51	135	61 46	49	134
23	57 53	51	136	58 44	51	135	59 35	50	134	60 25	50	133	61 15	49	132
24	57 23	51	135	58 14	51	134	59 05	50	133	59 55	49	132	60 44	48	131
25	56 54	+50	133	57 44	+50	132	58 34	+49	131	59 23	+49	130	60 12	+48	129
26	56 23	50	132	57 13	49	131	58 02	49	130	58 51	48	129	59 39	48	128
27	55 52	49	131	56 41	49	130	57 30	48	128	58 18	48	127	59 06	47	126
28	55 20	48	129	56 08	49	128	56 57	48	127	57 45	47	126	58 32	46	125
29	54 47	48	128	55 35	48	127	56 23	48	126	57 11	46	125	57 57	46	123
30	54 14	+48	127	55 02	+47	126	55 49	+47	124	56 36	+46	123	57 22	+46	122
31	53 40	47	125	54 27	47	124	55 14	47	123	56 01	46	122	56 47	45	121
32	53 06	47	124	53 53	46	123	54 39	46	122	55 25	46	121	56 11	44	120
33	52 31	47	123	53 18	46	122	54 04	45	121	54 49	45	120	55 34	44	118
34	51 56	46	122	52 42	46	121	53 28	45	119	54 13	44	118	54 57	44	117
35	51 20	+46	120	52 06	+45	119	52 51	+45	118	53 36	+44	117	54 20	+43	116
36	50 44	45	119	51 29	45	118	52 14	45	117	52 59	43	116	53 42	43	115
37	50 07	45	118	50 52	45	117	51 37	44	116	52 21	43	115	53 04	43	114
38	49 30	45	117	50 15	44	116	50 59	44	115	51 43	43	114	52 26	43	113
39	48 53	44	116	49 37	44	115	50 21	44	114	51 05	43	113	51 48	42	112
40	48 15	+44	115	48 59	+44	114	49 43	+43	113	50 26	+43	112	51 09	+41	111
41	47 37	44	114	48 21	44	113	49 05	42	112	49 47	42	111	50 29	42	110
42	46 59	44	113	47 43	43	112	48 26	42	111	49 08	42	110	49 50	41	109
43	46 20	44	112	47 04	43	111	47 47	42	110	48 29	42	109	49 11	41	108
44	45 42	43	111	46 25	42	110	47 07	42	109	47 49	42	108	48 31	40	107
45	45 02	+43	110	45 45	+43	109	46 28	+41	108	47 09	+42	107	47 51	+40	106
46	44 23	43	109	45 06	42	108	45 48	41	107	46 29	41	106	47 10	41	105
47	43 44	42	108	44 26	42	107	45 08	41	106	45 49	41	105	46 30	40	104
48	43 04	42	107	43 46	42	106	44 28	41	105	45 09	41	104	45 50	40	103
49	42 24	42	106	43 06	41	105	43 47	41	104	44 28	41	103	45 09	40	102
50	41 44	+42	105	42 26	+41	104	43 07	+41	103	43 48	+40	102	44 28	+40	101
51	41 04	41	104	41 45	41	104	42 26	41	103	43 07	40	102	43 47	40	101
52	40 23	42	104	41 05	41	103	41 46	40	102	42 26	40	101	43 06	40	100
53	39 43	41	103	40 24	41	102	41 05	40	101	41 45	40	100	42 25	39	99
54	39 02	41	102	39 43	41	101	40 24	40	100	41 04	40	99	41 44	39	98
55	38 21	+41	101	39 02	+41	100	39 43	+40	99	40 23	+39	98	41 02	+40	97
56	37 40	41	100	38 21	40	99	39 01	40	98	39 41	40	97	40 21	39	96
57	36 59	41	99	37 40	40	99	38 20	40	98	39 00	40	97	39 40	39	96
58	36 18	40	99	36 58	41	98	37 39	40	97	38 19	39	96	38 58	39	95
59	35 36	41	98	36 17	40	97	36 57	40	96	37 37	40	95	38 17	38	94
60	34 55	+41	97	35 36	+40	96	36 16	+40	95	36 56	+39	94	37 35	+39	93
61	34 14	40	96	34 54	40	95	35 34	40	95	36 14	39	94	36 53	39	93
62	33 32	41	96	34 13	40	95	34 53	39	94	35 32	40	93	36 12	38	92
63	32 51	40	95	33 31	40	94	34 11	40	93	34 51	39	92	35 30	39	91
64	32 09	41	94	32 50	40	93	33 30	39	92	34 09	39	91	34 48	39	90
65	31 28	+40	93	32 08	+40	92	32 48	+39	92	33 27	+40	91	34 07	+38	90
66	30 46	40	93	31 26	40	92	32 06	40	91	32 46	39	90	33 25	39	89
67	30 04	41	92	30 45	40	91	31 25	39	90	32 04	39	89	32 43	39	88
68	29 23	40	91	30 03	40	90	30 43	39	89	31 22	40	88	32 02	38	88
69	28 41	40	90	29 21	40	90	30 01	40	89	30 41	39	88	31 20	39	87

25° Hc	d	Z	26° Hc	d	Z	27° Hc	d	Z	28° Hc	d	Z	29° Hc	d	Z	LHA
° ′	′	°	° ′	′	°	° ′	′	°	° ′	′	°	° ′	′	°	
69 00	+60	180	70 00	+60	180	71 00	+60	180	72 00	+60	180	73 00	+60	180	360
68 59	60	178	69 59	60	177	70 59	60	177	71 59	60	177	72 59	60	177	359
68 56	60	175	69 56	60	175	70 56	60	175	71 56	60	174	72 56	59	174	358
68 52	59	172	69 51	60	172	70 51	60	172	71 51	59	172	72 50	60	171	357
68 45	60	170	69 45	59	170	70 44	60	169	71 44	59	169	72 43	59	168	356
68 37	+59	168	69 36	+59	167	70 35	+59	167	71 34	+59	166	72 33	+59	165	355
68 27	59	165	69 26	59	165	70 25	58	164	71 23	59	163	72 22	58	162	354
68 16	58	163	69 14	58	162	70 12	58	161	71 10	58	161	72 08	58	160	353
68 03	57	160	69 00	58	160	69 58	58	159	70 56	57	158	71 53	57	157	352
67 48	57	158	68 45	57	157	69 42	57	156	70 39	56	155	71 35	57	154	351
67 31	+57	156	68 28	+57	155	69 25	+56	154	70 21	+56	153	71 17	+55	152	350
67 13	57	154	68 10	55	153	69 05	56	152	70 01	55	151	70 56	55	149	349
66 54	56	151	67 50	55	150	68 45	55	149	69 40	54	148	70 34	54	147	348
66 33	55	149	67 28	55	148	68 23	54	147	69 17	54	146	70 11	52	145	347
66 11	55	147	67 06	54	146	68 00	53	145	68 53	53	144	69 46	52	142	346
65 48	+54	145	66 42	+53	144	67 35	+53	143	68 28	+52	142	69 20	+51	140	345
65 24	53	143	66 17	52	142	67 09	52	141	68 01	51	139	68 52	51	138	344
64 58	52	141	65 50	52	140	66 42	51	139	67 33	51	138	68 24	49	136	343
64 31	52	139	65 23	51	138	66 14	51	137	67 05	49	136	67 54	49	134	342
64 04	51	138	64 55	50	136	65 45	50	135	66 35	49	134	67 24	48	132	341
63 35	+51	136	64 26	+49	135	65 15	+49	133	66 04	+49	132	66 53	+47	130	340
63 06	50	134	63 56	49	133	64 45	48	132	65 33	48	130	66 21	46	129	339
62 35	50	133	63 25	48	131	64 13	48	130	65 01	47	129	65 48	45	127	338
62 04	49	131	62 53	48	130	63 41	47	128	64 28	46	127	65 14	45	125	337
61 32	48	129	62 20	48	128	63 08	46	127	63 54	46	125	64 40	44	124	336
61 00	+47	128	61 47	+47	127	62 34	+46	125	63 20	+45	124	64 05	+44	122	335
60 27	46	126	61 13	47	125	62 00	45	124	62 45	44	122	63 29	44	121	334
59 53	46	125	60 39	46	124	61 25	44	122	62 09	44	121	62 53	43	119	333
59 18	46	124	60 04	45	122	60 49	44	121	61 33	44	120	62 17	42	118	332
58 43	46	122	59 29	44	121	60 13	44	120	60 57	43	118	61 40	41	117	331
58 08	+45	121	58 53	+44	120	59 37	+43	118	60 20	+42	117	61 02	+41	115	330
57 32	44	120	58 16	44	118	59 00	42	117	59 42	42	116	60 24	41	114	329
56 55	44	118	57 39	43	117	58 22	43	116	59 05	41	114	59 46	41	113	328
56 18	44	117	57 02	43	116	57 45	42	115	58 27	41	113	59 08	40	112	327
55 41	43	116	56 24	43	115	57 07	41	113	57 48	41	112	58 29	39	111	326
55 03	+43	115	55 46	+42	114	56 28	+41	112	57 09	+41	111	57 50	+39	110	325
54 25	43	114	55 08	41	113	55 49	41	111	56 30	40	110	57 10	39	109	324
53 47	42	113	54 29	41	111	55 10	41	110	55 51	40	109	56 31	38	108	323
53 09	41	112	53 50	41	110	54 31	40	109	55 11	40	108	55 51	38	107	322
52 30	41	111	53 11	41	109	53 52	40	108	54 32	39	107	55 11	38	106	321
51 50	+42	110	52 32	+40	108	53 12	+40	107	53 52	+38	106	54 30	+38	105	320
51 11	41	109	51 52	40	107	52 32	39	106	53 11	39	105	53 50	38	104	319
50 31	41	108	51 12	40	106	51 52	39	105	52 31	38	104	53 09	38	103	318
49 52	40	107	50 32	40	105	51 12	38	104	51 50	39	103	52 29	37	102	317
49 11	41	106	49 52	39	104	50 31	39	103	51 10	38	102	51 48	37	101	316
48 31	+40	105	49 11	+39	104	49 50	+39	102	50 29	+38	101	51 07	+37	100	315
47 51	40	104	48 31	39	103	49 10	38	102	49 48	38	100	50 26	36	99	314
47 10	40	103	47 50	39	102	48 29	38	101	49 07	37	99	49 44	37	98	313
46 30	39	102	47 09	39	101	47 48	38	100	48 26	37	99	49 03	37	97	312
45 49	39	101	46 28	39	100	47 07	37	99	47 44	38	98	48 22	36	97	311
45 08	+39	100	45 47	+38	99	46 25	+38	98	47 03	+37	97	47 40	+37	96	310
44 27	39	99	45 06	38	98	45 44	38	97	46 22	37	96	46 59	36	95	309
43 46	38	99	44 24	39	98	45 03	37	96	45 40	37	95	46 17	36	94	308
43 04	39	98	43 43	38	97	44 21	38	96	44 59	37	95	45 36	36	93	307
42 23	39	97	43 02	38	96	43 40	37	95	44 17	37	94	44 54	36	93	306
41 42	+38	96	42 20	+38	95	42 58	+38	94	43 36	+36	93	44 12	+37	92	305
41 00	39	95	41 39	38	94	42 17	37	93	42 54	37	92	43 31	36	91	304
40 19	38	95	40 57	38	94	41 35	37	93	42 12	37	92	42 49	36	91	303
39 37	38	94	40 15	38	93	40 53	38	92	41 31	36	91	42 07	36	90	302
38 55	39	93	39 34	38	92	40 12	37	91	40 49	37	90	41 26	36	89	301
38 14	+38	92	38 52	+38	91	39 30	+37	90	40 07	+37	89	40 44	+36	88	300
37 32	38	92	38 10	38	91	38 48	38	90	39 26	36	89	40 02	37	88	299
36 50	39	91	37 29	38	90	38 07	37	89	38 44	37	88	39 21	36	87	298
36 09	38	90	36 47	38	89	37 25	37	88	38 02	37	87	38 39	36	86	297
35 27	38	90	36 05	38	89	36 43	38	88	37 21	37	87	37 58	36	86	296
34 45	+39	89	35 24	+38	88	36 02	+37	87	36 39	+37	86	37 16	+36	85	295
34 04	38	88	34 42	38	87	35 20	37	86	35 57	37	85	36 34	37	84	294
33 22	38	87	34 00	38	86	34 38	38	86	35 16	37	85	35 53	37	84	293
32 40	39	87	33 19	38	86	33 57	38	85	34 35	37	84	35 12	36	83	292
31 59	38	86	32 37	38	85	33 15	38	84	33 53	37	83	34 30	37	82	291

S. Lat. {LHA greater than 180°....... Zn=180−Z
{LHA less than 180°........... Zn=180+Z

DECLINATION (15°-29°) SAME NAME AS LATITUDE

LAT 46°

LAT 46°

N. Lat. {LHA greater than 180°....... Zn=Z; LHA less than 180°........... Zn=360–Z}

DECLINATION (15°-29°) SAME NAME AS LATITUDE

LHA	15° Hc	d	Z	16° Hc	d	Z	17° Hc	d	Z	18° Hc	d	Z	19° Hc	d	Z	LHA
	° ′	′	°	° ′	′	°	° ′	′	°	° ′	′	°	° ′	′	°	
70	24 34	+41	94	25 15	+42	93	25 57	+41	92	26 38	+41	91	27 19	+40	90	290
71	23 52	42	93	24 34	41	92	25 15	41	91	25 56	41	91	26 37	41	90	289
72	23 10	42	92	23 52	41	91	24 33	42	91	25 15	40	90	25 55	41	89	288
73	22 29	41	91	23 10	42	91	23 52	41	90	24 33	41	89	25 14	40	88	287
74	21 47	42	91	22 29	41	90	23 10	41	89	23 51	41	88	24 32	41	88	286
75	21 05	+42	90	21 47	+41	89	22 28	+42	88	23 10	+40	88	23 50	+41	87	285
76	20 24	41	89	21 05	42	89	21 47	41	88	22 28	41	87	23 09	41	86	284
77	19 42	42	89	20 24	41	88	21 05	41	87	21 46	41	86	22 27	41	86	283
78	19 00	42	88	19 42	42	87	20 24	41	86	21 05	41	86	21 46	41	85	282
79	18 19	41	87	19 00	42	86	19 42	41	86	20 23	41	85	21 04	41	84	281
80	17 37	+42	86	18 19	+41	86	19 00	+42	85	19 42	+41	84	20 23	+41	83	280
81	16 56	41	86	17 37	42	85	18 19	41	84	19 00	41	84	19 41	41	83	279
82	16 14	42	85	16 56	41	84	17 37	42	84	18 19	41	83	19 00	41	82	278
83	15 33	41	84	16 14	42	84	16 56	42	83	17 38	41	82	18 19	41	81	277
84	14 51	42	84	15 33	42	83	16 15	41	82	16 56	42	81	17 38	41	81	276
85	14 10	+42	83	14 52	+42	82	15 34	+41	82	16 15	+42	81	16 57	+41	80	275
86	13 28	42	82	14 10	42	82	14 52	42	81	15 34	42	80	16 16	41	79	274
87	12 47	42	82	13 29	42	81	14 11	42	80	14 53	42	79	15 35	41	79	273
88	12 06	42	81	12 48	42	80	13 30	42	79	14 12	42	79	14 54	42	78	272
89	11 25	42	80	12 07	42	79	12 49	42	79	13 31	42	78	14 13	42	77	271
90	10 44	+42	80	11 26	+42	79	12 08	+43	78	12 51	+42	77	13 33	+42	77	270
91	10 03	42	79	10 45	43	78	11 28	42	77	12 10	42	77	12 52	42	76	269
92	09 22	43	78	10 05	42	77	10 47	43	77	11 30	42	76	12 12	42	75	268
93	08 41	43	77	09 24	43	77	10 07	42	76	10 49	43	75	11 32	42	75	267
94	08 01	43	77	08 44	42	76	09 26	43	75	10 09	43	75	10 52	42	74	266
95	07 20	+43	76	08 03	+43	75	08 46	+43	75	09 29	+43	74	10 12	+42	73	265
96	06 40	43	75	07 23	43	75	08 06	43	74	08 49	43	73	09 32	43	73	264
97	06 00	43	75	06 43	43	74	07 26	43	73	08 09	43	73	08 52	43	72	263
98	05 20	43	74	06 03	43	73	06 46	43	73	07 29	44	72	08 13	43	71	262
99	04 39	44	73	05 23	44	73	06 07	43	72	06 50	43	71	07 33	44	70	261
100	04 00	+43	72	04 43	+44	72	05 27	+44	71	06 11	+43	70	06 54	+44	70	260
101	03 20	44	72	04 04	44	71	04 48	43	70	05 31	44	70	06 15	44	69	259
102	02 41	43	71	03 24	44	70	04 08	44	70	04 52	44	69	05 36	44	68	258
103	02 01	44	70	02 45	44	70	03 29	44	69	04 13	45	68	04 58	44	68	257
104	01 22	44	70	02 06	45	69	02 51	44	68	03 35	44	68	04 19	44	67	256
105	00 43	+45	69	01 28	+44	68	02 12	+44	68	02 56	+45	67	03 41	+44	66	255
106	00 04	45	68	00 49	45	68	01 34	44	67	02 18	45	66	03 03	44	66	254
107	–0 34	44	67	00 10	45	67	00 55	45	66	01 40	45	65	02 25	45	65	253
108	–1 13	45	67	–0 28	45	66	00 17	45	65	01 02	45	65	01 47	45	64	252
109	–1 51	45	66	–1 06	46	65	–0 20	45	65	00 25	45	64	01 10	45	63	251
110	–2 29	+45	65	–1 44	+46	65	–0 58	+45	64	–0 13	+46	63	00 33	+45	63	250
111	–3 07	46	65	–2 21	46	64	–1 35	45	63	–0 50	46	63	–0 04	46	62	249
112	–3 44	46	64	–2 58	45	63	–2 13	46	63	–1 27	46	62	–0 41	46	61	248
113	–4 22	47	63	–3 35	46	62	–2 49	46	62	–2 03	46	61	–1 17	46	61	247
114	–4 59	47	62	–4 12	46	62	–3 26	46	61	–2 40	47	60	–1 53	46	60	246
115	–5 35	+46	62	–4 49	+47	61	–4 02	+46	60	–3 16	+47	60	–2 29	+46	59	245
116	–6 12	47	61	–5 25	47	60	–4 38	46	60	–3 52	47	59	–3 05	47	58	244
117				–6 01	47	59	–5 14	47	59	–4 27	47	58	–3 40	47	58	243
118							–5 50	47	58	–5 03	48	57	–4 15	47	57	242
119										–5 38	48	57	–4 50	48	56	241
120													–5 24	+47	55	240
121													–5 59	49	55	239

LHA	20° Hc	d	Z	21° Hc	d	Z	22° Hc	d	Z	23° Hc	d	Z	24° Hc	d	Z	LHA
	° ′	′	°	° ′	′	°	° ′	′	°	° ′	′	°	° ′	′	°	
70	27 59	+41	90	28 40	+40	89	29 20	+39	88	29 59	+39	87	30 38	+39	86	290
71	27 18	40	89	27 58	40	88	28 38	40	87	29 18	39	86	29 57	39	86	289
72	26 36	40	88	27 16	40	87	27 56	40	87	28 36	39	86	29 15	39	85	288
73	25 54	41	88	26 35	40	87	27 15	39	86	27 54	40	85	28 34	39	84	287
74	25 13	40	87	25 53	40	86	26 33	40	85	27 13	39	84	27 52	40	83	286
75	24 31	+41	86	25 12	+40	85	25 52	+39	84	26 31	+40	84	27 11	+39	83	285
76	23 50	40	85	24 30	40	85	25 10	40	84	25 50	40	83	26 30	39	82	284
77	23 08	41	85	23 49	40	84	24 29	40	83	25 09	39	82	25 48	40	81	283
78	22 27	40	84	23 07	40	83	23 47	40	82	24 27	40	82	25 07	40	81	282
79	21 45	41	83	22 26	40	83	23 06	40	82	23 46	40	81	24 26	40	80	281
80	21 04	+40	83	21 44	+41	82	22 25	+40	81	23 05	+40	80	23 45	+40	79	280
81	20 22	41	82	21 03	41	81	21 44	40	80	22 24	40	80	23 04	40	79	279
82	19 41	41	81	20 22	41	81	21 03	40	80	21 43	40	79	22 23	40	78	278
83	19 00	41	81	19 41	41	80	20 22	40	79	21 02	41	78	21 43	40	77	277
84	18 19	41	80	19 00	41	79	19 41	41	78	20 22	40	78	21 02	40	77	276
85	17 38	+41	79	18 19	+41	78	19 00	+41	78	19 41	+41	77	20 22	+40	76	275
86	16 57	41	79	17 38	42	78	18 20	40	77	19 00	41	76	19 41	41	75	274
87	16 16	42	78	16 58	41	77	17 39	41	76	18 20	41	76	19 01	41	75	273
88	15 36	41	77	16 17	42	76	16 59	41	76	17 40	41	75	18 21	41	74	272
89	14 55	42	77	15 37	41	76	16 18	42	75	17 00	41	74	17 41	41	74	271
90	14 15	+41	76	14 56	+42	75	15 38	+41	74	16 19	+42	74	17 01	+41	73	270
91	13 34	42	75	14 16	42	74	14 58	42	74	15 40	41	73	16 21	41	72	269
92	12 54	42	75	13 36	42	74	14 18	42	73	15 00	41	72	15 41	42	72	268
93	12 14	42	74	12 56	42	73	13 38	42	72	14 20	42	72	15 02	42	71	267
94	11 34	42	73	12 16	43	72	12 59	42	72	13 41	42	71	14 23	42	70	266
95	10 54	+43	72	11 37	+42	72	12 19	+42	71	13 01	+43	70	13 44	+42	70	265
96	10 15	42	72	10 57	43	71	11 40	42	70	12 22	43	70	13 05	42	69	264
97	09 35	43	71	10 18	43	70	11 01	42	70	11 43	43	69	12 26	42	68	263
98	08 56	43	70	09 39	43	70	10 22	42	69	11 04	43	68	11 47	43	68	262
99	08 17	43	70	09 00	43	69	09 43	43	68	10 26	43	68	11 09	43	67	261
100	07 38	+43	69	08 21	+43	68	09 04	+43	68	09 47	+44	67	10 31	+43	66	260
101	06 59	43	68	07 42	44	68	08 26	43	67	09 09	44	66	09 53	43	66	259
102	06 20	44	68	07 04	44	67	07 48	43	66	08 31	44	66	09 15	43	65	258
103	05 42	44	67	06 26	43	66	07 09	44	66	07 53	44	65	08 37	44	64	257
104	05 03	45	66	05 48	44	66	06 32	44	65	07 16	44	64	08 00	44	64	256
105	04 25	+45	66	05 10	+44	65	05 54	+44	64	06 38	+44	64	07 22	+45	63	255
106	03 47	45	65	04 32	45	64	05 17	44	64	06 01	44	63	06 45	45	62	254
107	03 10	45	64	03 55	44	63	04 39	45	63	05 24	45	62	06 09	44	62	253
108	02 32	45	63	03 17	45	63	04 02	45	62	04 47	45	61	05 32	45	61	252
109	01 55	45	63	02 40	46	62	03 26	45	61	04 11	45	61	04 56	45	60	251
110	01 18	+46	62	02 04	+45	61	02 49	+46	61	03 35	+45	60	04 20	+45	59	250
111	00 42	45	61	01 27	46	61	02 13	46	60	02 59	45	59	03 44	46	59	249
112	00 05	46	61	00 51	46	60	01 37	46	59	02 23	46	59	03 09	46	58	248
113	–0 31	46	60	00 15	46	59	01 01	46	59	01 47	46	58	02 33	47	57	247
114	–1 07	46	59	–0 21	47	59	00 26	46	58	01 12	47	57	01 59	46	57	246
115	–1 43	+47	58	–0 56	+47	58	–0 09	+46	57	00 37	+47	57	01 24	+46	56	245
116	–2 18	47	58	–1 31	47	57	–0 44	47	56	00 03	46	56	00 49	47	55	244
117	–2 53	47	57	–2 06	47	56	–1 19	47	56	–0 32	47	55	00 15	48	54	243
118	–3 28	47	56	–2 41	48	56	–1 53	47	55	–1 06	48	54	–0 18	47	54	242
119	–4 02	47	55	–3 15	48	55	–2 27	48	54	–1 39	47	54	–0 52	48	53	241
120	–4 37	+48	55	–3 49	+48	54	–3 01	+48	54	–2 13	+48	53	–1 25	+48	52	240
121	–5 10	48	54	–4 22	48	53	–3 34	48	53	–2 46	48	52	–1 58	48	52	239
122	–5 44	48	53	–4 56	49	53	–4 07	48	52	–3 19	49	51	–2 30	48	51	238
123				–5 29	49	52	–4 40	49	51	–3 51	49	51	–3 02	48	50	237
124				–6 01	49	51	–5 12	49	50	–4 23	49	50	–3 34	49	49	236
125							–5 44	+49	50	–4 55	+49	49	–4 06	+50	49	235
126										–5 26	49	48	–4 37	50	48	234
127										–5 57	49	48	–5 08	50	47	233
128													–5 38	50	46	232

LHA	25° Hc	d	Z	26° Hc	d	Z	27° Hc	d	Z	28° Hc	d	Z	29° Hc	d	Z	LHA
	° ′	′	°	° ′	′	°	° ′	′	°	° ′	′	°	° ′	′	°	
70	31 17	+39	85	31 56	+38	84	32 34	+38	83	33 12	+37	83	33 49	+37	82	290
71	30 36	38	85	31 14	39	84	31 53	37	83	32 30	38	82	33 08	37	81	289
72	29 54	39	84	30 33	38	83	31 11	38	82	31 49	38	81	32 27	37	80	288
73	29 13	39	83	29 52	38	82	30 30	38	82	31 08	38	81	31 46	37	80	287
74	28 32	38	83	29 10	39	82	29 49	38	81	30 27	38	80	31 05	37	79	286
75	27 50	+39	82	28 29	+39	81	29 08	+38	80	29 46	+38	79	30 24	+37	78	285
76	27 09	39	81	27 48	39	80	28 27	38	80	29 05	38	79	29 43	38	78	284
77	26 28	39	81	27 07	39	80	27 46	38	79	28 24	38	78	29 02	38	77	283
78	25 47	39	80	26 26	39	79	27 05	39	78	27 44	38	77	28 22	38	77	282
79	25 06	39	79	25 45	39	78	26 24	39	78	27 03	38	77	27 41	38	76	281
80	24 25	+39	79	25 04	+40	78	25 44	+38	77	26 22	+39	76	27 01	+38	75	280
81	23 44	40	78	24 24	39	77	25 03	39	76	25 42	39	75	26 21	38	75	279
82	23 03	40	77	23 43	40	76	24 23	39	76	25 02	39	75	25 41	38	74	278
83	22 23	40	77	23 03	39	76	23 42	40	75	24 22	39	74	25 01	38	73	277
84	21 42	40	76	22 22	40	75	23 02	40	74	23 42	39	74	24 21	39	73	276
85	21 02	+40	75	21 42	+40	75	22 22	+40	74	23 02	+39	73	23 41	+39	72	275
86	20 22	40	75	21 02	40	74	21 42	40	73	22 22	40	72	23 02	39	71	274
87	19 42	40	74	20 22	40	73	21 02	40	72	21 42	40	72	22 22	40	71	273
88	19 02	40	73	19 42	41	73	20 23	40	72	21 03	40	71	21 43	40	70	272
89	18 22	40	73	19 02	41	72	19 43	40	71	20 23	41	70	21 04	40	70	271
90	17 42	+41	72	18 23	+41	71	19 04	+40	71	19 44	+41	70	20 25	+40	69	270
91	17 02	42	71	17 44	40	71	18 24	41	70	19 05	41	69	19 46	40	68	269
92	16 23	41	71	17 04	41	70	17 45	41	69	18 26	41	69	19 07	41	68	268
93	15 44	41	70	16 25	42	69	17 07	41	69	17 48	41	68	18 29	41	67	267
94	15 05	41	69	15 46	42	69	16 28	41	68	17 09	41	67	17 50	42	66	266
95	14 26	+42	69	15 08	+41	68	15 49	+42	67	16 31	+41	67	17 12	+42	66	265
96	13 47	42	68	14 29	42	67	15 11	42	67	15 53	41	66	16 34	42	65	264
97	13 08	43	68	13 51	42	67	14 33	42	66	15 15	42	65	15 57	41	65	263
98	12 30	42	67	13 12	43	66	13 55	42	65	14 37	42	65	15 19	42	64	262
99	11 52	42	66	12 34	43	65	13 17	42	65	13 59	43	64	14 42	42	63	261
100	11 14	+43	66	11 57	+42	65	12 39	+43	64	13 22	+43	63	14 05	+42	63	260
101	10 36	43	65	11 19	43	64	12 02	43	63	12 45	43	63	13 28	43	62	259
102	09 58	44	64	10 42	43	64	11 25	43	63	12 08	43	62	12 51	43	61	258
103	09 21	43	64	10 04	44	63	10 48	43	62	11 31	44	61	12 15	43	61	257
104	08 44	43	63	09 27	44	62	10 11	44	61	10 55	43	61	11 38	44	60	256
105	08 07	+44	62	08 51	+44	62	09 35	+44	61	10 19	+43	60	11 02	+44	59	255
106	07 30	44	62	08 14	44	61	08 58	45	60	09 43	44	59	10 27	44	59	254
107	06 53	45	61	07 38	44	60	08 22	45	60	09 07	44	59	09 51	44	58	253
108	06 17	45	60	07 02	45	60	07 47	44	59	08 31	45	58	09 16	44	57	252
109	05 41	45	59	06 26	45	59	07 11	45	58	07 56	45	57	08 41	45	57	251
110	05 05	+46	59	05 51	+45	58	06 36	+45	57	07 21	+45	57	08 06	+45	56	250
111	04 30	45	58	05 15	46	57	06 01	45	57	06 46	46	56	07 32	45	55	249
112	03 55	45	57	04 40	46	57	05 26	46	56	06 12	46	55	06 58	45	55	248
113	03 20	46	57	04 06	46	56	04 52	46	55	05 38	46	55	06 24	46	54	247
114	02 45	46	56	03 31	46	55	04 17	47	55	05 04	46	54	05 50	46	53	246
115	02 10	+47	55	02 57	+47	55	03 44	+46	54	04 30	+47	53	05 17	+46	53	245
116	01 36	47	55	02 23	47	54	03 10	47	53	03 57	47	53	04 44	46	52	244
117	01 03	47	54	01 50	47	53	02 37	47	53	03 24	47	52	04 11	47	51	243
118	00 29	47	53	01 16	48	53	02 04	47	52	02 51	47	51	03 38	48	51	242
119	–0 04	47	52	00 43	48	52	01 31	48	51	02 19	47	51	03 06	48	50	241
120	–0 37	+48	52	00 11	+48	51	00 59	+48	51	01 47	+48	50	02 35	+47	49	240
121	–1 10	49	51	–0 21	48	50	00 27	48	50	01 15	48	49	02 03	48	49	239
122	–1 42	49	50	–0 53	48	50	–0 05	49	49	00 44	48	48	01 32	49	48	238
123	–2 14	49	50	–1 25	49	49	–0 36	49	48	00 13	48	48	01 01	50	47	237
124	–2 45	49	49	–1 56	49	48	–1 07	49	48	–0 18	49	47	00 31	49	46	236
125	–3 16	+49	48	–2 27	+49	47	–1 38	+50	47	–0 48	+49	46	00 01	+49	46	235
126	–3 47	49	47	–2 58	50	47	–2 08	50	46	–1 18	49	46	–0 29	50	45	234
127	–4 18	50	47	–3 28	50	46	–2 38	50	45	–1 48	50	45	–0 58	50	44	233
128	–4 48	50	46	–3 58	51	45	–3 07	50	45	–2 17	50	44	–1 27	50	44	232
129	–5 17	50	45	–4 27	50	44	–3 37	51	44	–2 46	50	43	–1 56	51	43	231
130	–5 47	+51	44	–4 56	+51	44	–4 05	+51	43	–3 14	+50	43	–2 24	+51	42	230
131				–5 25	51	43	–4 34	51	42	–3 43	52	42	–2 51	51	41	229
132				–5 53	51	42	–5 02	52	42	–4 10	51	41	–3 19	52	41	228
133							–5 29	52	41	–4 37	51	40	–3 46	52	40	227
134										–5 04	52	40	–4 12	52	39	226
135										–5 31	+53	39	–4 38	+52	38	225
136													–5 04	53	38	224
137													–5 29	53	37	223

DECLINATION (15°-29°) CONTRARY NAME TO LATITUDE

S. Lat. {LHA greater than 180°....... Zn=180–Z; LHA less than 180°........... Zn=180+Z}

LHA	15° Hc	d	Z	16° Hc	d	Z	17° Hc	d	Z	18° Hc	d	Z	19° Hc	d	Z	20° Hc	d	Z
83	–6 00	43	105	277														
82	–5 20	43	106	–6 03	43	107	278											
81	–4 39	44	107	–5 23	44	107	–6 07	43	108	279								
80	–4 00	–43	108	–4 43	–44	108	–5 27	–44	109	–6 11	–43	110	280					
79	–3 20	44	108	–4 04	44	109	–4 48	43	110	–5 31	44	110	–6 15	44	111	281		
78	–2 41	43	109	–3 24	44	110	–4 08	44	110	–4 52	44	111	–5 36	44	112	282		
77	–2 01	44	110	–2 45	44	110	–3 29	44	111	–4 13	45	112	–4 58	44	112	–5 42	44	113
76	–1 22	44	110	–2 06	45	111	–2 51	44	112	–3 35	44	112	–4 19	44	113	–5 03	45	114
75	–0 43	–45	111	–1 28	–44	112	–2 12	–44	112	–2 56	–45	113	–3 41	–44	114	–4 25	–45	114
74	–0 04	45	112	–0 49	45	112	–1 34	44	113	–2 18	45	114	–3 03	44	114	–3 47	45	115
73	00 34	44	113	–0 10	45	113	–0 55	45	114	–1 40	45	115	–2 25	45	115	–3 10	45	116
72	01 13	45	113	00 28	45	114	–0 17	45	115	–1 02	45	115	–1 47	45	116	–2 32	45	117
71	01 51	45	114	01 06	46	115	00 20	45	115	–0 25	45	116	–1 10	45	117	–1 55	45	117
70	02 29	–45	115	01 44	–46	115	00 58	–45	116	00 13	–46	117	–0 33	–45	117	–1 18	–46	118

LHA	21° Hc	d	Z	22° Hc	d	Z	23° Hc	d	Z	24° Hc	d	Z	25° Hc	d	Z	26° Hc	d	Z	27°
77	283																		
76	–5 48	44	114	284															
75	–5 10	–44	115	–5 54	–44	116	285												
74	–4 32	45	116	–5 17	44	116	–6 01	44	117	286									
73	–3 55	44	117	–4 39	45	117	–5 24	45	118	–6 09	44	118	287						
72	–3 17	45	117	–4 02	45	118	–4 47	45	119	–5 32	45	119	288						
71	–2 40	46	118	–3 26	45	119	–4 11	45	119	–4 56	45	120	–5 41	45	121	289			
70	–2 04	–45	119	–2 49	–46	119	–3 35	–45	120	–4 20	–45	121	–5 05	–46	121	–5 51	–45	122	290

N. Lat. {LHA greater than 180°....... Zn=Z
{LHA less than 180°.......... Zn=360−Z

DECLINATION (15°-29°) CONTRARY NAME TO LATITUDE

LHA	15° Hc	d	Z	16° Hc	d	Z	17° Hc	d	Z	18° Hc	d	Z	19° Hc	d	Z
	° ′	′	°	° ′	′	°	° ′	′	°	° ′	′	°	° ′	′	°
69	03 07	46	115	02 21	46	116	01 35	45	117	00 50	46	117	00 04	46	118
68	03 44	46	116	02 58	45	117	02 13	46	117	01 27	46	118	00 41	46	119
67	04 22	47	117	03 35	46	118	02 49	46	118	02 03	46	119	01 17	46	119
66	04 59	47	118	04 12	46	118	03 26	46	119	02 40	47	120	01 53	46	120
65	05 35	−46	118	04 49	−47	119	04 02	−46	120	03 16	−47	120	02 29	−46	121
64	06 12	47	119	05 25	47	120	04 38	46	120	03 52	47	121	03 05	47	122
63	06 48	47	120	06 01	47	121	05 14	47	121	04 27	47	122	03 40	47	122
62	07 24	47	121	06 37	47	121	05 50	47	122	05 03	48	123	04 15	47	123
61	08 00	48	121	07 12	47	122	06 25	47	123	05 38	48	123	04 50	48	124
60	08 35	−47	122	07 48	−48	123	07 00	−48	123	06 12	−48	124	05 24	−47	125
59	09 10	47	123	08 23	48	124	07 35	48	124	06 47	48	125	05 59	49	125
58	09 45	48	124	08 57	48	124	08 09	48	125	07 21	49	126	06 32	48	126
57	10 20	49	125	09 31	48	125	08 43	49	126	07 54	48	126	07 06	49	127
56	10 54	49	125	10 05	48	126	09 17	49	127	08 28	49	127	07 39	49	128
55	11 28	−49	126	10 39	−49	127	09 50	−49	127	09 01	−49	128	08 12	−49	129
54	12 01	49	127	11 12	49	128	10 23	49	128	09 34	50	129	08 44	49	129
53	12 34	49	128	11 45	50	128	10 55	49	129	10 06	50	130	09 16	49	130
52	13 07	50	129	12 17	49	129	11 28	50	130	10 38	50	130	09 48	50	131
51	13 39	50	129	12 49	50	130	11 59	50	131	11 09	50	131	10 19	50	132
50	14 11	−50	130	13 21	−50	131	12 31	−50	131	11 41	−51	132	10 50	−50	133
49	14 43	50	131	13 53	51	132	13 02	51	132	12 11	50	133	11 21	51	133
48	15 14	51	132	14 23	50	133	13 33	51	133	12 42	51	134	11 51	51	134
47	15 45	51	133	14 54	51	133	14 03	51	134	13 12	51	134	12 21	52	135
46	16 15	51	134	15 24	51	134	14 33	52	135	13 41	51	135	12 50	52	136
45	16 45	−51	135	15 54	−52	135	15 02	−52	136	14 10	−51	136	13 19	−52	137
44	17 15	52	135	16 23	52	136	15 31	52	136	14 39	52	137	13 47	52	137
43	17 44	52	136	16 52	52	137	16 00	53	137	15 07	52	138	14 15	52	138
42	18 13	53	137	17 20	52	138	16 28	53	138	15 35	52	139	14 43	53	139
41	18 41	53	138	17 48	53	139	16 55	53	139	16 02	52	140	15 10	53	140
40	19 08	−53	139	18 15	−53	139	17 22	−53	140	16 29	−53	140	15 36	−53	141
39	19 35	53	140	18 42	53	140	17 49	53	141	16 56	54	141	16 02	53	142
38	20 02	53	141	19 09	54	141	18 15	54	142	17 21	53	142	16 28	54	143
37	20 28	54	142	19 34	53	142	18 41	54	143	17 47	54	143	16 53	54	144
36	20 54	54	143	20 00	54	143	19 06	54	144	18 12	55	144	17 17	54	144
35	21 19	−54	144	20 25	−55	144	19 30	−54	144	18 36	−55	145	17 41	−54	145
34	21 43	54	144	20 49	55	145	19 54	54	145	19 00	55	146	18 05	55	146
33	22 07	55	145	21 12	54	146	20 18	55	146	19 23	55	147	18 28	55	147
32	22 31	55	146	21 36	56	147	20 40	55	147	19 45	55	148	18 50	55	148
31	22 53	55	147	21 58	55	148	21 03	56	148	20 07	55	149	19 12	56	149
30	23 16	−56	148	22 20	−56	149	21 24	−55	149	20 29	−56	150	19 33	−56	150
29	23 37	56	149	22 41	55	150	21 46	56	150	20 50	56	150	19 54	56	151
28	23 58	56	150	23 02	56	151	22 06	56	151	21 10	56	151	20 14	57	152
27	24 19	57	151	23 22	56	152	22 26	56	152	21 30	57	152	20 33	56	153
26	24 38	56	152	23 42	57	153	22 45	56	153	21 49	57	153	20 52	57	154
25	24 57	−56	153	24 01	−57	154	23 04	−57	154	22 07	−57	154	21 10	−57	155
24	25 16	57	154	24 19	57	155	23 22	57	155	22 25	57	155	21 28	58	156
23	25 34	58	155	24 36	57	156	23 39	57	156	22 42	58	156	21 44	57	157
22	25 51	58	156	24 53	57	157	23 56	58	157	22 58	57	157	22 01	58	158
21	26 07	57	157	25 10	58	158	24 12	58	158	23 14	58	158	22 16	57	159
20	26 23	−58	158	25 25	−58	159	24 27	−58	159	23 29	−58	159	22 31	−58	160
19	26 38	58	159	25 40	58	160	24 42	58	160	23 44	58	160	22 46	59	161
18	26 52	58	161	25 54	58	161	24 56	59	161	23 57	58	161	22 59	58	162
17	27 06	59	162	26 07	58	162	25 09	59	162	24 10	58	162	23 12	59	163
16	27 19	59	163	26 20	59	163	25 21	58	163	24 23	59	163	23 24	59	164
15	27 31	−59	164	26 32	−59	164	25 33	−59	164	24 34	−58	164	23 36	−59	165
14	27 42	59	165	26 43	59	165	25 44	59	165	24 45	59	165	23 46	59	166
13	27 53	59	166	26 54	59	166	25 55	59	166	24 56	60	166	23 56	59	167
12	28 03	60	167	27 03	59	167	26 04	59	167	25 05	59	167	24 06	59	168
11	28 12	60	168	27 12	59	168	26 13	59	168	25 14	60	168	24 14	59	169
10	28 20	−59	169	27 21	−60	169	26 21	−59	169	25 22	−60	170	24 22	−59	170
9	28 28	60	170	27 28	59	170	26 29	60	170	25 29	60	171	24 29	59	171
8	28 34	59	171	27 35	60	171	26 35	59	171	25 36	60	172	24 36	60	172
7	28 40	59	172	27 41	60	172	26 41	60	173	25 41	59	173	24 42	60	173
6	28 46	60	173	27 46	60	174	26 46	60	174	25 46	60	174	24 46	59	174
5	28 50	−60	175	27 50	−60	175	26 50	−60	175	25 50	−59	175	24 51	−60	175
4	28 54	60	176	27 54	60	176	26 54	60	176	25 54	60	176	24 54	60	176
3	28 56	60	177	27 56	59	177	26 57	60	177	25 57	60	177	24 57	60	177
2	28 58	60	178	27 58	60	178	26 58	59	178	25 59	60	178	24 59	60	178
1	29 00	60	179	28 00	60	179	27 00	60	179	26 00	60	179	25 00	60	179
0	29 00	−60	180	28 00	−60	180	27 00	−60	180	26 00	−60	180	25 00	−60	180

LHA	20° Hc	d	Z	21° Hc	d	Z	22° Hc	d	Z	23° Hc	d	Z	24° Hc	d	Z
	° ′	′	°	° ′	′	°	° ′	′	°	° ′	′	°	° ′	′	°
69	−0 42	45	119	−1 27	46	119	−2 13	46	120	−2 59	45	121	−3 44	46	121
68	−0 05	46	119	−0 51	46	120	−1 37	46	121	−2 23	46	121	−3 09	46	122
67	00 31	46	120	−0 15	46	121	−1 01	46	121	−1 47	46	122	−2 33	47	123
66	01 07	46	121	00 21	47	121	−0 26	46	122	−1 12	47	123	−1 59	46	123
65	01 43	−47	122	00 56	−47	122	00 09	−46	123	−0 37	−47	123	−1 24	−46	124
64	02 18	47	122	01 31	47	123	00 44	47	124	−0 03	46	124	−0 49	47	125
63	02 53	47	123	02 06	47	124	01 19	47	124	00 32	47	125	−0 15	48	126
62	03 28	47	124	02 41	48	124	01 53	47	125	01 06	48	126	00 18	47	126
61	04 02	47	125	03 15	48	125	02 27	48	126	01 39	47	126	00 52	48	127
60	04 37	−48	125	03 49	−48	126	03 01	−48	126	02 13	−48	127	01 25	−48	128
59	05 10	48	126	04 22	48	127	03 34	48	127	02 46	48	128	01 58	48	128
58	05 44	48	127	04 56	49	127	04 07	48	128	03 19	49	129	02 30	48	129
57	06 17	48	128	05 29	49	128	04 40	49	129	03 51	49	129	03 02	48	130
56	06 50	49	128	06 01	49	129	05 12	49	130	04 23	49	130	03 34	49	131
55	07 23	−50	129	06 33	−49	130	05 44	−49	130	04 55	−49	131	04 06	−50	131
54	07 55	50	130	07 05	49	130	06 16	50	131	05 26	49	132	04 37	50	132
53	08 27	50	131	07 37	50	131	06 47	50	132	05 57	49	132	05 08	50	133
52	08 58	50	131	08 08	50	132	07 18	50	133	06 28	50	133	05 38	50	134
51	09 29	50	132	08 39	50	133	07 49	51	133	06 58	50	134	06 08	51	134
50	10 00	−51	133	09 09	−50	134	08 19	−51	134	07 28	−51	135	06 37	−50	135
49	10 30	51	134	09 39	51	134	08 48	50	135	07 58	51	136	07 07	51	136
48	11 00	51	135	10 09	51	135	09 18	51	136	08 27	52	136	07 35	51	137
47	11 29	51	136	10 38	51	136	09 47	52	137	08 55	51	137	08 04	52	138
46	11 58	51	136	11 07	52	137	10 15	52	137	09 23	51	138	08 32	52	138
45	12 27	−52	137	11 35	−52	138	10 43	−52	138	09 51	−52	139	08 59	−52	139
44	12 55	52	138	12 03	52	139	11 11	53	139	10 18	52	140	09 26	52	140
43	13 23	53	139	12 30	52	139	11 38	53	140	10 45	52	140	09 53	53	141
42	13 50	53	140	12 57	53	140	12 04	52	141	11 12	53	141	10 19	53	142
41	14 17	53	141	13 24	53	141	12 31	53	142	11 38	54	142	10 44	53	142
40	14 43	−53	141	13 50	−54	142	12 56	−53	142	12 03	−53	143	11 10	−54	143
39	15 09	54	142	14 15	53	143	13 22	54	143	12 28	54	144	11 34	53	144
38	15 34	54	143	14 40	54	144	13 46	53	144	12 53	54	145	11 59	54	145
37	15 59	54	144	15 05	54	144	14 11	55	145	13 16	54	145	12 22	54	146
36	16 23	54	145	15 29	55	145	14 34	54	146	13 40	55	146	12 45	54	147
35	16 47	−55	146	15 52	−54	146	14 58	−55	147	14 03	−55	147	13 08	−55	147
34	17 10	55	147	16 15	55	147	15 20	55	148	14 25	55	148	13 30	55	148
33	17 33	55	148	16 38	56	148	15 42	55	148	14 47	55	149	13 52	55	149
32	17 55	56	148	16 59	55	149	16 04	55	149	15 09	56	150	14 13	55	150
31	18 16	55	149	17 21	56	150	16 25	56	150	15 29	55	151	14 34	56	151
30	18 37	−56	150	17 41	−56	151	16 45	−55	151	15 50	−56	151	14 54	−56	152
29	18 58	56	151	18 02	57	152	17 05	56	152	16 09	56	152	15 13	56	153
28	19 17	56	152	18 21	56	153	17 25	57	153	16 28	56	153	15 32	57	154
27	19 37	57	153	18 40	57	153	17 43	56	154	16 47	57	154	15 50	57	155
26	19 55	57	154	18 58	56	154	18 02	57	155	17 05	57	155	16 08	57	155
25	20 13	−57	155	19 16	−57	155	18 19	−57	156	17 22	−57	156	16 25	−57	156
24	20 30	57	156	19 33	57	156	18 36	57	157	17 39	58	157	16 41	57	157
23	20 47	57	157	19 50	58	157	18 52	57	158	17 55	58	158	16 57	57	158
22	21 03	58	158	20 05	57	158	19 08	58	158	18 10	58	159	17 12	57	159
21	21 19	58	159	20 21	58	159	19 23	58	159	18 25	58	160	17 27	58	160
20	21 33	−58	160	20 35	−58	160	19 37	−58	160	18 39	−58	161	17 41	−58	161
19	21 47	58	161	20 49	58	161	19 51	58	161	18 53	59	162	17 54	58	162
18	22 01	59	162	21 02	58	162	20 04	58	162	19 06	59	163	18 07	58	163
17	22 13	58	163	21 15	59	163	20 16	58	163	19 18	59	163	18 19	58	164
16	22 25	58	164	21 27	59	164	20 28	59	164	19 29	58	164	18 31	59	165
15	22 37	−59	165	21 38	−59	165	20 39	−59	165	19 40	−59	165	18 41	−59	166
14	22 47	59	166	21 48	59	166	20 49	59	166	19 50	59	166	18 51	59	167
13	22 57	59	167	21 58	59	167	20 59	59	167	20 00	59	167	19 01	59	167
12	23 07	60	168	22 07	59	168	21 08	59	168	20 09	60	168	19 09	59	168
11	23 15	59	169	22 16	60	169	21 16	59	169	20 17	60	169	19 17	59	169
10	23 23	−60	170	22 23	−59	170	21 24	−60	170	20 24	−59	170	19 25	−60	170
9	23 30	60	171	22 30	59	171	21 31	60	171	20 31	59	171	19 32	60	171
8	23 36	59	172	22 37	60	172	21 37	60	172	20 37	60	172	19 37	59	172
7	23 42	60	173	22 42	60	173	21 42	59	173	20 43	60	173	19 43	60	173
6	23 47	60	174	22 47	60	174	21 47	60	174	20 47	60	174	19 47	59	174
5	23 51	−60	175	22 51	−60	175	21 51	−60	175	20 51	−60	175	19 51	−60	175
4	23 54	60	176	22 54	60	176	21 54	60	176	20 54	60	176	19 54	60	176
3	23 57	60	177	22 57	60	177	21 57	60	177	20 57	60	177	19 57	60	177
2	23 59	60	178	22 59	60	178	21 59	60	178	20 59	60	178	19 59	60	178
1	24 00	60	179	23 00	60	179	22 00	60	179	21 00	60	179	20 00	60	179
0	24 00	−60	180	23 00	−60	180	22 00	−60	180	21 00	−60	180	20 00	−60	180

LHA	25° Hc	d	Z	26° Hc	d	Z	27° Hc	d	Z	28° Hc	d	Z	29° Hc	d	Z	LHA
	° ′	′	°	° ′	′	°	° ′	′	°	° ′	′	°	° ′	′	°	
69	−4 30	45	122	−5 15	46	123	−6 01	45	123							291
68	−3 55	45	123	−4 40	46	123	−5 26	46	124							292
67	−3 20	46	123	−4 06	46	124	−4 52	46	125	−5 38	46	125				293
66	−2 45	46	124	−3 31	46	125	−4 17	47	125	−5 04	46	126	−5 50	46	127	294
65	−2 10	−47	125	−2 57	−47	125	−3 44	−46	126	−4 30	−47	127	−5 17	−46	127	295
64	−1 36	47	125	−2 23	47	126	−3 10	47	127	−3 57	47	127	−4 44	46	128	296
63	−1 03	47	126	−1 50	47	127	−2 37	47	127	−3 24	47	128	−4 11	47	129	297
62	−0 29	47	127	−1 16	48	127	−2 04	47	128	−2 51	47	129	−3 38	48	129	298
61	00 04	47	128	−0 43	48	128	−1 31	48	129	−2 19	47	129	−3 06	48	130	299
60	00 37	−48	128	−0 11	−48	129	−0 59	−48	129	−1 47	−48	130	−2 35	−47	131	300
59	01 10	49	129	00 21	48	130	−0 27	48	130	−1 15	48	131	−2 03	48	131	301
58	01 42	49	130	00 53	48	130	00 05	49	131	−0 44	48	132	−1 32	49	132	302
57	02 14	49	130	01 25	49	131	00 36	49	132	−0 13	48	132	−1 01	50	133	303
56	02 45	49	131	01 56	49	132	01 07	49	132	00 18	49	133	−0 31	49	134	304
55	03 16	−49	132	02 27	−49	133	01 38	−50	133	00 48	−49	134	−0 01	−49	134	305
54	03 47	49	133	02 58	50	133	02 08	50	134	01 18	49	134	00 29	50	135	306
53	04 18	50	133	03 28	50	134	02 38	50	135	01 48	50	135	00 58	50	136	307
52	04 48	50	134	03 58	51	135	03 07	50	135	02 17	50	136	01 27	50	136	308
51	05 17	50	135	04 27	50	136	03 37	51	136	02 46	50	137	01 56	51	137	309
50	05 47	−51	136	04 56	−51	136	04 05	−51	137	03 14	−50	137	02 24	−51	138	310
49	06 16	51	137	05 25	51	137	04 34	51	138	03 43	52	138	02 51	51	139	311
48	06 44	51	137	05 53	51	138	05 02	52	138	04 10	51	139	03 19	52	139	312
47	07 12	51	138	06 21	52	139	05 29	52	139	04 37	51	140	03 46	52	140	313
46	07 40	52	139	06 48	52	139	05 56	52	140	05 04	52	140	04 12	52	141	314
45	08 07	−52	140	07 15	−52	140	06 23	−52	141	05 31	−53	141	04 38	−52	142	315
44	08 34	53	141	07 41	52	141	06 49	53	141	05 56	52	142	05 04	53	142	316
43	09 00	53	141	08 07	52	142	07 15	53	142	06 22	53	143	05 29	53	143	317
42	09 26	53	142	08 33	53	143	07 40	53	143	06 47	53	144	05 54	53	144	318
41	09 51	53	143	08 58	53	143	08 05	53	144	07 12	54	144	06 18	53	145	319
40	10 16	−53	144	09 23	−54	144	08 29	−53	145	07 36	−54	145	06 42	−54	146	320
39	10 41	54	145	09 47	54	145	08 53	54	145	07 59	54	146	07 05	53	146	321
38	11 05	54	145	10 11	54	146	09 17	55	146	08 22	54	147	07 28	54	147	322
37	11 28	54	146	10 34	55	147	09 39	54	147	08 45	54	148	07 51	55	148	323
36	11 51	55	147	10 56	54	147	10 02	55	148	09 07	54	148	08 13	55	149	324
35	12 13	−54	148	11 19	−55	148	10 24	−55	149	09 29	−55	149	08 34	−55	150	325
34	12 35	55	149	11 40	55	149	10 45	55	150	09 50	55	150	08 55	55	150	326
33	12 57	56	150	12 01	55	150	11 06	55	150	10 11	56	151	09 15	55	151	327
32	13 18	56	150	12 22	56	151	11 26	55	151	10 31	56	152	09 35	56	152	328
31	13 38	56	151	12 42	56	152	11 46	56	152	10 50	56	152	09 54	55	153	329
30	13 58	−56	152	13 02	−57	153	12 05	−56	153	11 09	−56	153	10 13	−56	154	330
29	14 17	57	153	13 20	56	153	12 24	56	154	11 28	57	154	10 31	56	155	331
28	14 35	56	154	13 39	57	154	12 42	56	155	11 46	57	155	10 49	56	155	332
27	14 53	56	155	13 57	57	155	13 00	57	156	12 03	57	156	11 06	57	156	333
26	15 11	57	156	14 14	57	156	13 17	57	156	12 20	57	157	11 23	57	157	334
25	15 28	−57	157	14 31	−58	157	13 33	−57	157	12 36	−57	158	11 39	−57	158	335
24	15 44	57	158	14 47	58	158	13 49	57	158	12 52	58	158	11 54	57	159	336
23	16 00	58	158	15 02	58	159	14 04	57	159	13 07	58	159	12 09	57	160	337
22	16 15	58	159	15 17	58	160	14 19	58	160	13 21	58	160	12 23	57	160	338
21	16 29	58	160	15 31	58	161	14 33	58	161	13 35	58	161	12 37	58	161	339
20	16 43	−58	161	15 45	−58	161	14 47	−59	162	13 48	−58	162	12 50	−58	162	340
19	16 56	58	162	15 58	59	162	14 59	58	163	14 01	58	163	13 03	59	163	341
18	17 09	59	163	16 10	58	163	15 12	59	163	14 13	58	164	13 15	59	164	342
17	17 21	59	164	16 22	59	164	15 23	58	164	14 25	59	165	13 26	59	165	343
16	17 32	59	165	16 33	59	165	15 34	59	165	14 35	58	165	13 37	59	166	344
15	17 42	−59	166	16 43	−59	166	15 44	−58	166	14 46	−59	166	13 47	−59	167	345
14	17 52	59	167	16 53	59	167	15 54	59	167	14 55	59	167	13 56	59	167	346
13	18 02	60	168	17 02	59	168	16 03	59	168	15 04	59	168	14 05	59	168	347
12	18 10	59	169	17 11	59	169	16 12	60	169	15 12	59	169	14 13	59	169	348
11	18 18	59	170	17 19	60	170	16 19	59	170	15 20	60	170	14 20	59	170	349
10	18 25	−59	171	17 26	−60	171	16 26	−59	171	15 27	−60	171	14 27	−59	171	350
9	18 32	60	171	17 32	59	172	16 33	60	172	15 33	60	172	14 33	59	172	351
8	18 38	60	172	17 38	60	173	16 38	59	173	15 39	60	173	14 39	60	173	352
7	18 43	60	173	17 43	60	173	16 43	59	174	15 44	60	174	14 44	60	174	353
6	18 48	60	174	17 48	60	174	16 48	60	174	15 48	60	175	14 48	60	175	354
5	18 51	−60	175	17 51	−59	175	16 52	−60	175	15 52	−60	175	14 52	−60	176	355
4	18 54	59	176	17 55	60	176	16 55	60	176	15 55	60	176	14 55	60	176	356
3	18 57	60	177	17 57	60	177	16 57	60	177	15 57	60	177	14 57	60	177	357
2	18 59	60	178	17 59	60	178	16 59	60	178	15 59	60	178	14 59	60	178	358
1	19 00	60	179	18 00	60	179	17 00	60	179	16 00	60	179	15 00	60	179	359
0	19 00	−60	180	18 00	−60	180	17 00	−60	180	16 00	−60	180	15 00	−60	180	360

S. Lat. {LHA greater than 180°....... Zn=180−Z
{LHA less than 180°.......... Zn=180+Z

LAT 47°

N. Lat. {LHA greater than 180°....... Zn=Z / LHA less than 180°.......... Zn=360−Z}

DECLINATION (0°-14°) SAME NAME AS LATITUDE

LHA	0° Hc	d	Z	1° Hc	d	Z	2° Hc	d	Z	3° Hc	d	Z	4° Hc	d	Z
	° ′	′	°	° ′	′	°	° ′	′	°	° ′	′	°	° ′	′	°
0	43 00	+60	180	44 00	+60	180	45 00	+60	180	46 00	+60	180	47 00	+60	180
1	43 00	60	179	44 00	60	179	45 00	60	179	46 00	60	179	47 00	60	179
2	42 58	60	177	43 58	60	177	44 58	60	177	45 58	60	177	46 58	60	177
3	42 56	60	176	43 56	60	176	44 56	59	176	45 55	60	176	46 55	60	176
4	42 52	60	175	43 52	60	174	44 52	60	174	45 52	60	174	46 52	60	174
5	42 48	+60	173	43 48	+59	173	44 47	+60	173	45 47	+60	173	46 47	+60	173
6	42 43	59	172	43 42	60	172	44 42	60	172	45 42	59	171	46 41	60	171
7	42 36	60	171	43 36	59	170	44 35	60	170	45 35	60	170	46 35	59	170
8	42 29	59	169	43 28	60	169	44 28	59	169	45 27	60	169	46 27	59	168
9	42 21	59	168	43 20	59	168	44 19	60	167	45 19	59	167	46 18	59	167
10	42 12	+59	166	43 11	+59	166	44 10	+59	166	45 09	+59	166	46 08	+59	166
11	42 02	59	165	43 01	59	165	44 00	59	165	44 59	59	164	45 58	59	164
12	41 51	59	164	42 50	58	164	43 48	59	163	44 47	59	163	45 46	59	163
13	41 39	58	163	42 37	59	162	43 36	59	162	44 35	58	162	45 33	59	161
14	41 26	59	161	42 25	58	161	43 23	58	161	44 21	59	160	45 20	58	160
15	41 12	+59	160	42 11	+58	160	43 09	+58	159	44 07	+58	159	45 05	+58	159
16	40 58	58	159	41 56	58	158	42 54	58	158	43 52	58	158	44 50	58	157
17	40 43	57	157	41 40	58	157	42 38	58	157	43 36	58	156	44 34	57	156
18	40 26	58	156	41 24	57	156	42 21	58	155	43 19	57	155	44 16	58	155
19	40 09	58	155	41 07	57	154	42 04	57	154	43 01	57	154	43 58	57	153
20	39 51	+58	154	40 49	+57	153	41 46	+57	153	42 43	+56	152	43 39	+57	152
21	39 33	57	152	40 30	56	152	41 26	57	152	42 23	57	151	43 20	56	151
22	39 13	57	151	40 10	57	151	41 07	56	150	42 03	56	150	42 59	56	149
23	38 53	57	150	39 50	56	149	40 46	56	149	41 42	56	149	42 38	56	148
24	38 32	56	149	39 28	56	148	40 24	56	148	41 20	56	147	42 16	55	147
25	38 11	+55	148	39 06	+56	147	40 02	+56	147	40 58	+55	146	41 53	+55	146
26	37 48	56	146	38 44	55	146	39 39	55	145	40 34	55	145	41 29	55	144
27	37 25	55	145	38 20	56	145	39 16	54	144	40 10	54	144	41 05	55	143
28	37 02	54	144	37 56	55	144	38 51	55	143	39 46	54	142	40 40	55	142
29	36 37	55	143	37 32	54	142	38 26	55	142	39 21	54	141	40 15	54	141
30	36 12	+54	142	37 06	+55	141	38 01	+54	141	38 55	+53	140	39 48	+54	140
31	35 46	54	141	36 40	54	140	37 34	54	140	38 28	54	139	39 22	53	139
32	35 20	54	140	36 14	53	139	37 07	54	138	38 01	53	138	38 54	53	137
33	34 53	54	138	35 47	53	138	36 40	53	137	37 33	53	137	38 26	53	136
34	34 26	53	137	35 19	53	137	36 12	53	136	37 05	52	136	37 57	53	135
35	33 58	+53	136	34 51	+52	136	35 43	+53	135	36 36	+52	135	37 28	+52	134
36	33 29	53	135	34 22	52	135	35 14	52	134	36 06	52	133	36 58	52	133
37	33 00	52	134	33 52	52	134	34 44	52	133	35 36	52	132	36 28	52	132
38	32 31	51	133	33 22	52	133	34 14	52	132	35 06	51	131	35 57	51	131
39	32 00	52	132	32 52	52	132	33 44	51	131	34 35	51	130	35 26	51	130
40	31 30	+51	131	32 21	+51	131	33 12	+51	130	34 03	+51	129	34 54	+51	129
41	30 59	51	130	31 50	51	130	32 41	50	129	33 31	51	128	34 22	50	128
42	30 27	51	129	31 18	51	129	32 09	50	128	32 59	50	127	33 49	50	127
43	29 55	51	128	30 46	50	128	31 36	50	127	32 26	50	126	33 16	50	126
44	29 23	50	127	30 13	50	127	31 03	50	126	31 53	50	125	32 43	49	125
45	28 50	+50	126	29 40	+50	126	30 30	+49	125	31 19	+50	124	32 09	+49	124
46	28 17	49	125	29 06	50	125	29 56	49	124	30 45	50	123	31 35	49	123
47	27 43	50	124	28 33	49	124	29 22	49	123	30 11	49	122	31 00	49	122
48	27 09	49	123	27 58	49	123	28 47	49	122	29 36	49	121	30 25	48	121
49	26 35	49	122	27 24	49	122	28 13	48	121	29 01	49	121	29 50	48	120
50	26 00	+49	122	26 49	+48	121	27 37	+49	120	28 26	+48	120	29 14	+48	119
51	25 25	49	121	26 14	48	120	27 02	48	119	27 50	48	119	28 38	48	118
52	24 50	48	120	25 38	48	119	26 26	48	118	27 14	48	118	28 02	47	117
53	24 14	48	119	25 02	48	118	25 50	48	118	26 38	47	117	27 25	47	116
54	23 38	48	118	24 26	47	117	25 13	48	117	26 01	47	116	26 48	47	115
55	23 02	+47	117	23 49	+48	117	24 37	+47	116	25 24	+47	115	26 11	+47	114
56	22 25	48	116	23 13	47	116	24 00	47	115	24 47	47	114	25 34	46	114
57	21 48	48	115	22 36	47	115	23 23	46	114	24 09	47	113	24 56	46	113
58	21 11	47	115	21 58	47	114	22 45	47	113	23 32	46	113	24 18	46	112
59	20 34	47	114	21 21	46	113	22 07	47	112	22 54	46	112	23 40	46	111
60	19 56	+47	113	20 43	+46	112	21 29	+47	112	22 16	+46	111	23 02	+46	110
61	19 19	46	112	20 05	46	111	20 51	46	111	21 37	46	110	22 23	46	109
62	18 40	47	111	19 27	46	111	20 13	46	110	20 59	46	109	21 45	45	109
63	18 02	46	110	18 48	46	110	19 34	46	109	20 20	46	108	21 06	45	108
64	17 24	46	110	18 10	45	109	18 55	46	108	19 41	46	108	20 27	45	107
65	16 45	+46	109	17 31	+46	108	18 17	+45	108	19 02	+45	107	19 47	+45	106
66	16 06	46	108	16 52	45	107	17 37	46	107	18 23	45	106	19 08	45	105
67	15 27	46	107	16 13	45	107	16 58	45	106	17 43	45	105	18 28	45	105
68	14 48	46	107	15 34	45	106	16 19	45	105	17 04	45	104	17 49	44	104
69	14 09	45	106	14 54	45	105	15 39	45	104	16 24	45	104	17 09	45	103

LHA	5° Hc	d	Z	6° Hc	d	Z	7° Hc	d	Z	8° Hc	d	Z	9° Hc	d	Z
	° ′	′	°	° ′	′	°	° ′	′	°	° ′	′	°	° ′	′	°
0	48 00	+60	180	49 00	+60	180	50 00	+60	180	51 00	+60	180	52 00	+60	180
1	48 00	60	179	49 00	59	179	49 59	60	179	50 59	60	178	51 59	60	178
2	47 58	60	177	48 58	60	177	49 58	60	177	50 58	60	177	51 58	60	177
3	47 55	60	176	48 55	60	176	49 55	60	175	50 55	60	175	51 55	60	175
4	47 52	59	174	48 51	60	174	49 51	60	174	50 51	60	174	51 51	60	174
5	47 47	+60	173	48 47	+59	172	49 46	+60	172	50 46	+60	172	51 46	+59	172
6	47 41	60	171	48 41	59	171	49 40	60	171	50 40	60	171	51 40	59	170
7	47 34	60	170	48 34	59	169	49 33	60	169	50 33	59	169	51 32	60	169
8	47 26	60	168	48 26	59	168	49 25	59	168	50 24	60	168	51 24	59	167
9	47 17	60	167	48 17	59	167	49 16	59	166	50 15	59	166	51 14	59	166
10	47 07	+60	165	48 07	+59	165	49 06	+59	165	50 05	+58	165	51 03	+59	164
11	46 57	58	164	47 55	59	164	48 54	59	163	49 53	59	163	50 52	58	163
12	46 45	58	163	47 43	59	162	48 42	59	162	49 41	58	161	50 39	59	161
13	46 32	58	161	47 30	59	161	48 29	58	160	49 27	58	160	50 25	59	160
14	46 18	58	160	47 16	58	159	48 14	59	159	49 13	58	159	50 11	57	158
15	46 03	+58	158	47 01	+58	158	47 59	+58	157	48 57	+58	157	49 55	+57	157
16	45 48	57	157	46 45	58	156	47 43	58	156	48 41	57	156	49 38	57	155
17	45 31	58	155	46 29	57	155	47 26	57	155	48 23	57	154	49 20	57	154
18	45 14	57	154	46 11	57	154	47 08	57	153	48 05	57	153	49 02	57	152
19	44 55	57	153	45 52	57	152	46 49	57	152	47 46	56	151	48 42	57	151
20	44 36	+57	151	45 33	+56	151	46 29	+57	151	47 26	+56	150	48 22	+56	149
21	44 16	56	150	45 12	57	150	46 09	56	149	47 05	56	149	48 01	55	148
22	43 55	56	149	44 51	56	148	45 47	56	148	46 43	56	147	47 39	55	147
23	43 34	55	148	44 29	56	147	45 25	56	147	46 20	56	146	47 16	55	145
24	43 11	56	146	44 07	55	146	45 02	55	145	45 57	55	145	46 52	55	144
25	42 48	+55	145	43 43	+55	144	44 38	+55	144	45 33	+55	143	46 28	+54	143
26	42 24	55	144	43 19	55	143	44 14	54	143	45 08	55	142	46 03	54	141
27	42 00	54	143	42 54	55	142	43 49	54	141	44 43	54	141	45 37	53	140
28	41 35	54	141	42 29	54	141	43 23	54	140	44 17	53	140	45 10	53	139
29	41 09	54	140	42 03	53	140	42 56	54	139	43 50	53	138	44 43	53	138
30	40 42	+54	139	41 36	+53	138	42 29	+53	138	43 22	+53	137	44 15	+53	136
31	40 15	53	138	41 08	53	137	42 01	53	137	42 54	52	136	43 46	53	135
32	39 47	53	137	40 40	53	136	41 33	52	135	42 25	52	135	43 17	52	134
33	39 19	52	136	40 11	53	135	41 04	52	134	41 56	52	134	42 48	51	133
34	38 50	52	134	39 42	52	134	40 34	52	133	41 26	51	132	42 17	52	132
35	38 20	+52	133	39 12	+52	133	40 04	+51	132	40 55	+51	131	41 46	+51	131
36	37 50	52	132	38 42	51	132	39 33	51	131	40 24	51	130	41 15	51	129
37	37 20	51	131	38 11	51	130	39 02	51	130	39 53	50	129	40 43	51	128
38	36 48	51	130	37 39	51	129	38 30	51	129	39 21	50	128	40 11	50	127
39	36 17	51	129	37 08	50	128	37 58	50	128	38 48	50	127	39 38	50	126
40	35 45	+50	128	36 35	+50	127	37 25	+50	127	38 15	+50	126	39 05	+49	125
41	35 12	50	127	36 02	50	126	36 52	50	126	37 42	49	125	38 31	49	124
42	34 39	50	126	35 29	50	125	36 19	49	125	37 08	49	124	37 57	49	123
43	34 06	50	125	34 56	49	124	35 45	49	124	36 34	49	123	37 23	48	122
44	33 32	49	124	34 21	49	123	35 10	49	123	35 59	49	122	36 48	48	121
45	32 58	+49	123	33 47	+49	122	34 36	+48	122	35 24	+49	121	36 13	+47	120
46	32 24	48	122	33 12	49	121	34 01	48	121	34 49	48	120	35 37	48	119
47	31 49	48	121	32 37	48	120	33 25	48	120	34 13	48	119	35 01	47	118
48	31 13	49	120	32 02	48	119	32 50	47	119	33 37	48	118	34 25	47	117
49	30 38	48	119	31 26	47	118	32 13	48	118	33 01	47	117	33 48	46	116
50	30 02	+48	118	30 50	+47	118	31 37	+47	117	32 24	+47	116	33 11	+47	115
51	29 26	47	117	30 13	47	117	31 00	47	116	31 47	47	115	32 34	47	114
52	28 49	47	116	29 36	47	116	30 23	47	115	31 10	47	114	31 57	46	114
53	28 12	47	116	28 59	47	115	29 46	47	114	30 33	46	113	31 19	46	113
54	27 35	47	115	28 22	47	114	29 09	46	113	29 55	46	112	30 41	46	112
55	26 58	+47	114	27 45	+46	113	28 31	+46	112	29 17	+46	112	30 03	+46	111
56	26 20	47	113	27 07	46	112	27 53	46	111	28 39	46	111	29 25	45	110
57	25 42	47	112	26 29	46	111	27 15	46	111	28 01	45	110	28 46	46	109
58	25 04	46	111	25 50	46	110	26 36	46	110	27 22	45	109	28 07	46	108
59	24 26	46	110	25 12	46	110	25 58	45	109	26 43	45	108	27 28	45	107
60	23 48	+45	110	24 33	+46	109	25 19	+45	108	26 04	+45	107	26 49	+45	107
61	23 09	46	109	23 55	45	108	24 40	45	107	25 25	45	107	26 10	45	106
62	22 30	46	108	23 16	45	107	24 01	45	106	24 46	45	106	25 31	44	105
63	21 51	45	107	22 36	45	106	23 21	45	106	24 06	45	105	24 51	44	104
64	21 12	45	106	21 57	45	106	22 42	45	105	23 27	44	104	24 11	45	103
65	20 32	+45	105	21 17	+45	105	22 02	+45	104	22 47	+44	103	23 31	+45	103
66	19 53	45	105	20 38	44	104	21 22	45	103	22 07	44	102	22 51	44	102
67	19 13	45	104	19 58	45	103	20 43	44	102	21 27	44	102	22 11	44	101
68	18 33	45	103	19 18	45	102	20 03	44	102	20 47	44	101	21 31	44	100
69	17 54	44	102	18 38	44	102	19 22	45	101	20 07	44	100	20 51	43	99

10° Hc	d	Z	11° Hc	d	Z	12° Hc	d	Z	13° Hc	d	Z	14° Hc	d	Z	LHA
° ′	′	°	° ′	′	°	° ′	′	°	° ′	′	°	° ′	′	°	
53 00	+60	180	54 00	+60	180	55 00	+60	180	56 00	+60	180	57 00	+60	180	360
52 59	60	178	53 59	60	178	54 59	60	178	55 59	60	178	56 59	60	178	359
52 58	60	177	53 58	60	177	54 58	60	177	55 58	60	177	56 58	59	176	358
52 55	60	175	53 55	60	175	54 55	59	175	55 54	60	175	56 54	60	175	357
52 51	60	174	53 51	59	173	54 50	60	173	55 50	60	173	56 50	60	173	356
52 45	+60	172	53 45	+60	172	54 45	+60	172	55 45	+59	171	56 44	+60	171	355
52 39	60	170	53 39	59	170	54 38	60	170	55 38	59	170	56 37	60	169	354
52 32	59	169	53 31	59	168	54 30	60	168	55 30	59	168	56 29	59	168	353
52 23	59	167	53 22	59	167	54 21	60	167	55 21	59	166	56 20	59	166	352
52 13	59	165	53 12	59	165	54 11	59	165	55 10	59	165	56 09	59	164	351
52 02	+59	164	53 01	+59	164	54 00	+59	163	54 59	+58	163	55 57	+59	163	350
51 50	59	162	52 49	59	162	53 48	58	162	54 46	59	161	55 45	58	161	349
51 38	58	161	52 36	58	160	53 34	58	160	54 32	59	160	55 31	58	159	348
51 24	58	159	52 22	58	159	53 20	58	158	54 18	57	158	55 15	58	158	347
51 08	58	158	52 06	58	157	53 04	58	157	54 02	57	156	54 59	58	156	346
50 52	+58	156	51 50	+57	156	52 47	+58	155	53 45	+57	155	54 42	+57	154	345
50 35	58	155	51 33	57	154	52 30	57	154	53 27	57	153	54 24	56	153	344
50 17	57	153	51 14	57	153	52 11	57	152	53 08	56	152	54 04	57	151	343
49 59	56	152	50 55	57	151	51 52	56	151	52 48	56	150	53 44	56	150	342
49 39	56	150	50 35	56	150	51 31	56	149	52 27	56	149	53 23	55	148	341
49 18	+56	149	50 14	+56	148	51 10	+55	148	52 05	+56	147	53 01	+55	147	340
48 56	56	148	49 52	56	147	50 48	55	146	51 43	55	146	52 38	55	145	339
48 34	55	146	49 29	55	146	50 24	55	145	51 19	55	144	52 14	54	144	338
48 11	55	145	49 06	54	144	50 00	55	144	50 55	54	143	51 49	54	142	337
47 47	54	143	48 41	55	143	49 36	54	142	50 30	54	142	51 24	53	141	336
47 22	+54	142	48 16	+54	141	49 10	+54	141	50 04	+53	140	50 57	+54	139	335
46 57	53	141	47 50	54	140	48 44	53	140	49 37	53	139	50 30	53	138	334
46 30	54	140	47 24	53	139	48 17	53	138	49 10	53	137	50 03	52	137	333
46 03	54	138	46 57	52	138	47 49	53	137	48 42	52	136	49 34	52	135	332
45 36	53	137	46 29	52	136	47 21	52	136	48 13	52	135	49 05	52	134	331
45 08	+52	136	46 00	+52	135	46 52	+52	134	47 44	+52	134	48 36	+51	133	330
44 39	52	135	45 31	52	134	46 23	51	133	47 14	51	132	48 05	51	132	329
44 09	52	133	45 01	51	133	45 52	52	132	46 44	50	131	47 34	51	130	328
43 39	52	132	44 31	51	131	45 22	50	131	46 12	51	130	47 03	50	129	327
43 09	51	131	44 00	50	130	44 50	51	130	45 41	50	129	46 31	50	128	326
42 37	+51	130	43 28	+51	129	44 19	+50	128	45 09	+49	128	45 58	+50	127	325
42 06	50	129	42 56	50	128	43 46	50	127	44 36	49	127	45 25	49	126	324
41 34	50	128	42 24	49	127	43 13	50	126	44 03	49	125	44 52	49	125	323
41 01	50	127	41 51	49	126	42 40	49	125	43 29	49	124	44 18	48	123	322
40 28	49	126	41 17	49	125	42 06	49	124	42 55	49	123	43 44	48	122	321
39 54	+49	124	40 43	+49	124	41 32	+49	123	42 21	+48	122	43 09	+48	121	320
39 20	49	123	40 09	49	123	40 58	48	122	41 46	48	121	42 34	47	120	319
38 46	48	122	39 34	49	122	40 23	48	121	41 11	47	120	41 58	47	119	318
38 11	48	121	38 59	48	121	39 47	48	120	40 35	47	119	41 22	47	118	317
37 36	48	120	38 24	48	120	39 12	47	119	39 59	47	118	40 46	47	117	316
37 00	+48	119	37 48	+48	119	38 36	+47	118	39 23	+46	117	40 09	+47	116	315
36 25	47	118	37 12	47	118	37 59	47	117	38 46	46	116	39 32	46	115	314
35 48	48	117	36 36	46	117	37 22	47	116	38 09	46	115	38 55	46	114	313
35 12	47	116	35 59	46	116	36 46	46	115	37 32	46	114	38 18	45	113	312
34 35	47	116	35 22	46	115	36 08	46	114	36 54	46	113	37 40	45	112	311
33 58	+47	115	34 45	+46	114	35 31	+46	113	36 17	+45	112	37 02	+45	111	310
33 21	46	114	34 07	46	113	34 53	46	112	35 39	45	111	36 24	45	111	309
32 43	46	113	33 29	46	112	34 15	45	111	35 00	45	110	35 45	45	110	308
32 05	46	112	32 51	46	111	33 37	45	110	34 22	45	110	35 07	44	109	307
31 27	46	111	32 13	45	110	32 58	45	109	33 43	45	109	34 28	44	108	306
30 49	+45	110	31 34	+45	109	32 19	+45	109	33 04	+45	108	33 49	+44	107	305
30 10	46	109	30 56	45	108	31 41	44	108	32 25	45	107	33 10	44	106	304
29 32	45	108	30 17	44	108	31 01	45	107	31 46	44	106	32 30	44	105	303
28 53	45	108	29 38	44	107	30 22	45	106	31 07	44	105	31 51	43	104	302
28 13	45	107	28 58	45	106	29 43	44	105	30 27	44	104	31 11	43	104	301
27 34	+45	106	28 19	+44	105	29 03	+44	104	29 47	+44	104	30 31	+44	103	300
26 55	44	105	27 39	44	104	28 23	44	104	29 07	44	103	29 51	44	102	299
26 15	44	104	26 59	44	103	27 44	43	103	28 27	44	102	29 11	43	101	298
25 35	45	103	26 20	44	103	27 04	43	102	27 47	44	101	28 31	43	100	297
24 56	44	103	25 40	44	102	26 24	43	101	27 07	44	100	27 51	43	100	296
24 16	+44	102	25 00	+43	101	25 43	+44	100	26 27	+43	100	27 10	+43	99	295
23 35	44	101	24 19	44	100	25 03	43	100	25 46	44	99	26 30	43	98	294
22 55	44	100	23 39	44	99	24 23	43	99	25 06	43	98	25 49	43	97	293
22 15	44	99	22 59	44	99	23 42	43	98	24 25	43	97	25 08	43	96	292
21 34	44	99	22 18	44	98	23 02	43	97	23 45	43	96	24 28	42	96	291

S. Lat. {LHA greater than 180°....... Zn=180−Z / LHA less than 180°.......... Zn=180+Z}

DECLINATION (0°-14°) SAME NAME AS LATITUDE

N. Lat. {LHA greater than 180°....... Zn=Z; LHA less than 180°........... Zn=360−Z}

DECLINATION (0°-14°) SAME NAME AS LATITUDE

LHA	0° Hc	d	Z	1° Hc	d	Z	2° Hc	d	Z	3° Hc	d	Z	4° Hc	d	Z	LHA
	° ′	′	°	° ′	′	°	° ′	′	°	° ′	′	°	° ′	′	°	
70	13 29	+45	105	14 14	+45	104	14 59	+45	104	15 44	+45	103	16 29	+45	102	290
71	12 50	45	104	13 35	45	104	14 20	44	103	15 04	45	102	15 49	44	101	289
72	12 10	45	103	12 55	45	103	13 40	44	102	14 24	45	101	15 09	44	101	288
73	11 30	45	103	12 15	45	102	13 00	44	101	13 44	44	101	14 28	45	100	287
74	10 50	45	102	11 35	44	101	12 19	45	101	13 04	44	100	13 48	44	99	286
75	10 10	+45	101	10 55	+44	100	11 39	+44	100	12 23	+45	99	13 08	+44	98	285
76	09 30	44	100	10 14	45	100	10 59	44	99	11 43	44	98	12 27	44	98	284
77	08 50	44	100	09 34	44	99	10 18	44	98	11 02	45	98	11 47	44	97	283
78	08 09	44	99	08 53	45	98	09 38	44	98	10 22	44	97	11 06	44	96	282
79	07 29	44	98	08 13	44	97	08 57	44	97	09 41	44	96	10 25	44	95	281
80	06 48	+44	97	07 32	+44	97	08 16	+44	96	09 00	+44	95	09 44	+44	95	280
81	06 08	44	97	06 52	44	96	07 36	44	95	08 20	44	95	09 04	43	94	279
82	05 27	44	96	06 11	44	95	06 55	44	95	07 39	44	94	08 23	44	93	278
83	04 46	44	95	05 30	44	94	06 14	44	94	06 58	44	93	07 42	44	92	277
84	04 05	44	94	04 49	44	94	05 33	44	93	06 17	44	92	07 01	44	92	276
85	03 24	+44	94	04 08	+44	93	04 52	+44	92	05 36	+44	92	06 20	+44	91	275
86	02 44	44	93	03 28	43	92	04 11	44	92	04 55	44	91	05 39	44	90	274
87	02 03	44	92	02 47	44	92	03 31	43	91	04 14	44	90	04 58	44	89	273
88	01 22	44	91	02 06	44	91	02 50	43	90	03 33	44	89	04 17	44	89	272
89	00 41	44	91	01 25	44	90	02 09	44	89	02 53	43	89	03 36	44	88	271
90	00 00	+44	90	00 44	+44	89	01 28	+44	89	02 12	+43	88	02 55	+44	87	270
91	−0 41	44	89	00 03	44	89	00 47	44	88	01 31	44	87	02 15	43	87	269
92	−1 22	44	89	−0 38	44	88	00 06	44	87	00 50	44	86	01 34	44	86	268
93	−2 03	44	88	−1 19	44	87	−0 35	44	86	00 09	44	86	00 53	44	85	267
94	−2 44	44	87	−2 00	44	86	−1 16	44	86	−0 32	44	85	00 12	44	84	266
95	−3 24	+44	86	−2 40	+44	86	−1 56	+44	85	−1 12	+44	84	−0 28	+44	84	265
96	−4 05	44	86	−3 21	44	85	−2 37	44	84	−1 53	44	84	−1 09	44	83	264
97	−4 46	44	85	−4 02	44	84	−3 18	44	84	−2 34	44	83	−1 50	44	82	263
98	−5 27	44	84	−4 43	44	83	−3 59	45	83	−3 14	44	82	−2 30	44	81	262
99	−6 08	45	83	−5 23	44	83	−4 39	44	82	−3 55	44	81	−3 11	45	81	261
100				−6 04	+44	82	−5 20	+45	81	−4 35	+44	81	−3 51	+44	80	260
101							−6 00	44	81	−5 16	45	80	−4 31	44	79	259
102										−5 56	45	79	−5 11	44	78	258
103													−5 51	44	78	257

LHA	5° Hc	d	Z	6° Hc	d	Z	7° Hc	d	Z	8° Hc	d	Z	9° Hc	d	Z	LHA
	° ′	′	°	° ′	′	°	° ′	′	°	° ′	′	°	° ′	′	°	
70	17 14	+44	102	17 58	+44	101	18 42	+44	100	19 26	+44	99	20 10	+44	99	290
71	16 33	45	101	17 18	44	100	18 02	44	99	18 46	44	99	19 30	43	98	289
72	15 53	44	100	16 37	44	99	17 21	44	99	18 05	44	98	18 49	44	97	288
73	15 13	44	99	15 57	44	99	16 41	44	98	17 25	43	97	18 08	44	96	287
74	14 32	44	98	15 16	44	98	16 00	44	97	16 44	44	96	17 28	43	96	286
75	13 52	+44	98	14 36	+44	97	15 20	+43	96	16 03	+44	96	16 47	+44	95	285
76	13 11	44	97	13 55	44	96	14 39	44	96	15 23	43	95	16 06	44	94	284
77	12 31	43	96	13 14	44	95	13 58	44	95	14 42	43	94	15 25	44	93	283
78	11 50	44	95	12 34	43	95	13 17	44	94	14 01	44	93	14 45	43	93	282
79	11 09	44	95	11 53	44	94	12 37	43	93	13 20	44	93	14 04	43	92	281
80	10 28	+44	94	11 12	+44	93	11 56	+43	93	12 39	+44	92	13 23	+43	91	280
81	09 47	44	93	10 31	44	93	11 15	43	92	11 58	44	91	12 42	43	90	279
82	09 07	43	92	09 50	44	92	10 34	43	91	11 17	44	90	12 01	43	90	278
83	08 26	43	92	09 09	44	91	09 53	44	90	10 37	43	90	11 20	43	89	277
84	07 45	43	91	08 28	44	90	09 12	44	90	09 56	43	89	10 39	43	88	276
85	07 04	+44	90	07 48	+43	90	08 31	+44	89	09 15	+43	88	09 58	+44	88	275
86	06 23	44	90	07 07	43	89	07 50	44	88	08 34	43	87	09 17	44	87	274
87	05 42	44	89	06 26	43	88	07 09	44	87	07 53	43	87	08 36	44	86	273
88	05 01	44	88	05 45	43	87	06 28	44	87	07 12	44	86	07 56	43	85	272
89	04 20	44	87	05 04	44	87	05 48	43	86	06 31	44	85	07 15	43	85	271
90	03 39	+44	87	04 23	+44	86	05 07	+44	85	05 51	+43	85	06 34	+44	84	270
91	02 58	44	86	03 42	44	85	04 26	44	84	05 10	44	84	05 54	43	83	269
92	02 18	44	85	03 02	43	84	03 45	44	84	04 29	44	83	05 13	44	82	268
93	01 37	44	84	02 21	44	84	03 05	44	83	03 49	43	82	04 32	44	82	267
94	00 56	44	84	01 40	44	83	02 24	44	82	03 08	44	82	03 52	44	81	266
95	00 16	+44	83	01 00	+44	82	01 44	+44	82	02 28	+44	81	03 12	+44	80	265
96	−0 25	44	82	00 19	44	82	01 03	44	81	01 47	44	80	02 31	44	80	264
97	−1 06	45	81	−0 21	44	81	00 23	44	80	01 07	44	79	01 51	44	79	263
98	−1 46	44	81	−1 02	45	80	−0 17	44	79	00 27	44	79	01 11	44	78	262
99	−2 26	44	80	−1 42	44	79	−0 58	45	79	−0 13	44	78	00 31	44	77	261
100	−3 07	+45	79	−2 22	+44	79	−1 38	+45	78	−0 53	+44	77	−0 09	+45	77	260
101	−3 47	45	79	−3 02	44	78	−2 18	45	77	−1 33	44	77	−0 49	45	76	259
102	−4 27	45	78	−3 42	45	77	−2 57	44	76	−2 13	45	76	−1 28	45	75	258
103	−5 07	45	77	−4 22	45	76	−3 37	45	76	−2 52	44	75	−2 08	45	74	257
104	−5 47	45	76	−5 02	45	76	−4 17	45	75	−3 32	45	74	−2 47	45	74	256
105				−5 41	+45	75	−4 56	+45	74	−4 11	+45	74	−3 26	+45	73	255
106							−5 36	46	73	−4 50	45	73	−4 05	45	72	254
107							−6 15	46	73	−5 29	45	72	−4 44	45	71	253
108										−6 08	45	71	−5 23	46	71	252
109													−6 01	45	70	251

LHA	10° Hc	d	Z	11° Hc	d	Z	12° Hc	d	Z	13° Hc	d	Z	14° Hc	d	Z	LHA
	° ′	′	°	° ′	′	°	° ′	′	°	° ′	′	°	° ′	′	°	
70	20 54	+44	98	21 38	+43	97	22 21	+43	96	23 04	+43	96	23 47	+43	95	290
71	20 13	44	97	20 57	43	96	21 40	43	96	22 23	43	95	23 06	43	94	289
72	19 33	43	96	20 16	43	96	20 59	43	95	21 42	43	94	22 25	43	93	288
73	18 52	43	96	19 35	44	95	20 19	43	94	21 02	42	93	21 44	43	93	287
74	18 11	44	95	18 55	43	94	19 38	43	93	20 21	43	93	21 04	42	92	286
75	17 31	+43	94	18 14	+43	93	18 57	+43	93	19 40	+43	92	20 23	+42	91	285
76	16 50	43	93	17 33	43	93	18 16	43	92	18 59	43	91	19 42	42	90	284
77	16 09	43	93	16 52	43	92	17 35	43	91	18 18	43	90	19 01	42	90	283
78	15 28	43	92	16 11	43	91	16 54	43	90	17 37	43	90	18 20	43	89	282
79	14 47	43	91	15 30	43	90	16 13	43	90	16 56	43	89	17 39	43	88	281
80	14 06	+43	90	14 49	+43	90	15 32	+43	89	16 15	+43	88	16 58	+43	88	280
81	13 25	43	90	14 08	43	89	14 51	43	88	15 34	43	88	16 17	43	87	279
82	12 44	43	89	13 27	44	88	14 11	43	88	14 54	42	87	15 36	43	86	278
83	12 03	44	88	12 47	43	88	13 30	43	87	14 13	43	86	14 56	42	85	277
84	11 22	44	88	12 06	43	87	12 49	43	86	13 32	43	85	14 15	43	85	276
85	10 42	+43	87	11 25	+43	86	12 08	+43	85	12 51	+43	85	13 34	+43	84	275
86	10 01	43	86	10 44	43	85	11 27	43	85	12 10	43	84	12 53	43	83	274
87	09 20	43	85	10 03	44	85	10 47	43	84	11 30	43	83	12 13	43	83	273
88	08 39	44	85	09 23	43	84	10 06	43	83	10 49	43	83	11 32	43	82	272
89	07 58	44	84	08 42	43	83	09 25	44	83	10 09	43	82	10 52	43	81	271
90	07 18	+43	83	08 01	+44	82	08 45	+43	82	09 28	+44	81	10 12	+43	80	270
91	06 37	44	82	07 21	43	82	08 04	44	81	08 48	43	80	09 31	44	80	269
92	05 57	43	82	06 40	44	81	07 24	44	80	08 08	43	80	08 51	43	79	268
93	05 16	44	81	06 00	44	80	06 44	43	80	07 27	44	79	08 11	43	78	267
94	04 36	44	80	05 20	43	80	06 03	44	79	06 47	44	78	07 31	44	78	266
95	03 56	+43	80	04 39	+44	79	05 23	+44	78	06 07	+44	78	06 51	+44	77	265
96	03 15	44	79	03 59	44	78	04 43	44	77	05 27	44	77	06 11	44	76	264
97	02 35	44	78	03 19	44	77	04 03	45	77	04 48	44	76	05 32	44	75	263
98	01 55	44	77	02 39	45	77	03 24	44	76	04 08	44	75	04 52	44	75	262
99	01 15	45	77	02 00	44	76	02 44	44	75	03 28	45	75	04 13	44	74	261
100	00 36	+44	76	01 20	+45	75	02 05	+44	75	02 49	+44	74	03 33	+45	73	260
101	−0 04	45	75	00 41	44	74	01 25	45	74	02 10	44	73	02 54	45	73	259
102	−0 43	44	74	00 01	45	74	00 46	45	73	01 31	44	72	02 15	45	72	258
103	−1 23	45	74	−0 38	45	73	00 07	45	72	00 52	45	72	01 37	44	71	257
104	−2 02	45	73	−1 17	45	72	−0 32	45	72	00 13	45	71	00 58	45	70	256
105	−2 41	+45	72	−1 56	+45	72	−1 11	+45	71	−0 26	+45	70	00 19	+46	70	255
106	−3 20	45	71	−2 35	46	71	−1 49	45	70	−1 04	45	70	−0 19	46	69	254
107	−3 59	46	71	−3 13	45	70	−2 28	46	69	−1 42	45	69	−0 57	46	68	253
108	−4 37	45	70	−3 52	46	69	−3 06	46	69	−2 20	45	68	−1 35	46	67	252
109	−5 16	46	69	−4 30	46	69	−3 44	46	68	−2 58	46	67	−2 12	45	67	251
110	−5 54	+46	68	−5 08	+46	68	−4 22	+46	67	−3 36	+46	67	−2 50	+46	66	250
111				−5 46	47	67	−4 59	46	66	−4 13	46	66	−3 27	46	65	249
112							−5 37	46	66	−4 51	47	65	−4 04	46	64	248
113							−6 14	46	65	−5 28	47	64	−4 41	47	64	247
114										−6 04	46	63	−5 18	47	63	246
115													−5 54	+47	62	245

DECLINATION (0°-14°) CONTRARY NAME TO LATITUDE

S. Lat. {LHA greater than 180°....... Zn=180−Z; LHA less than 180°........... Zn=180+Z}

LHA	0° Hc	d	Z	1° Hc	d	Z	2° Hc	d	Z	3° Hc	d	Z	4° Hc	d	Z	LHA
99	−6 08	44	83													261
98	−5 27	44	84	−6 11	44	85										262
97	−4 46	44	85	−5 30	44	86	−6 14	44	86							263
96	−4 05	44	86	−4 49	44	86	−5 33	44	87	−6 17	44	88				264
95	−3 24	−44	86	−4 08	−44	87	−4 52	−44	88	−5 36	−44	88	−6 20	−44	89	265
94	−2 44	44	87	−3 28	43	88	−4 11	44	88	−4 55	44	89	−5 39	44	90	266
93	−2 03	44	88	−2 47	44	88	−3 31	43	89	−4 14	44	90	−4 58	44	91	267
92	−1 22	44	89	−2 06	44	89	−2 50	43	90	−3 33	44	91	−4 17	44	91	268
91	−0 41	44	89	−1 25	44	90	−2 09	44	91	−2 53	43	91	−3 36	44	92	269
90	00 00	−44	90	−0 44	−44	91	−1 28	−44	91	−2 12	−43	92	−2 55	−44	93	270
89	00 41	44	91	−0 03	44	91	−0 47	44	92	−1 31	44	93	−2 15	43	93	271
88	01 22	44	91	00 38	44	92	−0 06	44	93	−0 50	44	94	−1 34	44	94	272
87	02 03	44	92	01 19	44	93	00 35	44	94	−0 09	44	94	−0 53	44	95	273
86	02 44	44	93	02 00	44	94	01 16	44	94	00 32	44	95	−0 12	44	96	274
85	03 24	−44	94	02 40	−44	94	01 56	−44	95	01 12	−44	96	00 28	−44	96	275
84	04 05	44	94	03 21	44	95	02 37	44	96	01 53	44	96	01 09	44	97	276
83	04 46	44	95	04 02	44	96	03 18	44	96	02 34	44	97	01 50	44	98	277
82	05 27	44	96	04 43	44	97	03 59	45	97	03 14	44	98	02 30	44	99	278
81	06 08	45	97	05 23	44	97	04 39	44	98	03 55	44	99	03 11	45	99	279
80	06 48	−44	97	06 04	−44	98	05 20	−45	99	04 35	−44	99	03 51	−44	100	280
79	07 29	45	98	06 44	44	99	06 00	44	99	05 16	45	100	04 31	44	101	281
78	08 09	44	99	07 25	45	100	06 40	44	100	05 56	45	101	05 11	44	102	282
77	08 50	45	100	08 05	44	100	07 21	45	101	06 36	45	102	05 51	44	102	283
76	09 30	45	100	08 45	44	101	08 01	45	102	07 16	45	102	06 31	44	103	284
75	10 10	−45	101	09 25	−44	102	08 41	−45	102	07 56	−45	103	07 11	−45	104	285
74	10 50	45	102	10 05	44	103	09 21	45	103	08 36	45	104	07 51	45	105	286
73	11 30	45	103	10 45	45	103	10 00	45	104	09 15	45	105	08 30	45	105	287
72	12 10	45	103	11 25	45	104	10 40	45	105	09 55	45	105	09 10	46	106	288
71	12 50	45	104	12 05	45	105	11 20	46	106	10 34	45	106	09 49	45	107	289
70	13 29	−45	105	12 44	−45	106	11 59	−45	106	11 14	−46	107	10 28	−45	108	290

LHA	5° Hc	d	Z	6° Hc	d	Z	7° Hc	d	Z	8° Hc	d	Z	9° Hc	d	Z	LHA
93	−5 42	44	91													267
92	−5 01	44	92	−5 45	43	93										268
91	−4 20	44	93	−5 04	44	93	−5 48	43	94							269
90	−3 39	−44	93	−4 23	−44	94	−5 07	−44	95	−5 51	−43	95				270
89	−2 58	44	94	−3 42	44	95	−4 26	44	96	−5 10	44	96	−5 54	43	97	271
88	−2 18	44	95	−3 02	43	96	−3 45	44	96	−4 29	44	97	−5 13	44	98	272
87	−1 37	44	96	−2 21	44	96	−3 05	44	97	−3 49	43	98	−4 32	44	98	273
86	−0 56	44	96	−1 40	44	97	−2 24	44	98	−3 08	44	98	−3 52	44	99	274
85	−0 16	−44	97	−1 00	−44	98	−1 44	−44	98	−2 28	−44	99	−3 12	−44	100	275
84	00 25	44	98	−0 19	44	98	−1 03	44	99	−1 47	44	100	−2 31	44	100	276
83	01 06	45	99	00 21	44	99	−0 23	44	100	−1 07	44	101	−1 51	44	101	277
82	01 46	44	99	01 02	45	100	00 17	44	101	−0 27	44	101	−1 11	44	102	278
81	02 26	44	100	01 42	44	101	00 58	45	101	00 13	44	102	−0 31	44	103	279
80	03 07	−45	101	02 22	−44	101	01 38	−45	102	00 53	−44	103	00 09	−45	103	280
79	03 47	45	101	03 02	44	102	02 18	45	103	01 33	44	103	00 49	45	104	281
78	04 27	45	102	03 42	45	103	02 57	44	104	02 13	45	104	01 28	45	105	282
77	05 07	45	103	04 22	45	104	03 37	45	104	02 52	44	105	02 08	45	106	283
76	05 47	45	104	05 02	45	104	04 17	45	105	03 32	45	106	02 47	45	106	284
75	06 26	−45	105	05 41	−45	105	04 56	−45	106	04 11	−45	106	03 26	−45	107	285
74	07 06	45	105	06 21	45	106	05 36	46	107	04 50	45	107	04 05	45	108	286
73	07 45	45	106	07 00	45	107	06 15	46	107	05 29	45	108	04 44	45	109	287
72	08 24	45	107	07 39	45	107	06 54	46	108	06 08	45	109	05 23	46	109	288
71	09 04	46	108	08 18	45	108	07 33	46	109	06 47	46	110	06 01	45	110	289
70	09 43	−46	108	08 57	−46	109	08 11	−46	110	07 25	−45	110	06 40	−46	111	290

LHA	10° Hc	d	Z	11° Hc	d	Z	12° Hc	d	Z	13° Hc	d	Z	14° Hc	d	Z	LHA
88	−5 57	43	98													272
87	−5 16	44	99	−6 00	44	100										273
86	−4 36	44	100	−5 20	43	100	−6 03	44	101							274
85	−3 56	−43	100	−4 39	−44	101	−5 23	−44	102	−6 07	−44	102				275
84	−3 15	44	101	−3 59	44	102	−4 43	44	103	−5 27	44	103	−6 11	44	104	276
83	−2 35	44	102	−3 19	44	103	−4 03	45	103	−4 48	44	104	−5 32	44	105	277
82	−1 55	44	103	−2 39	45	103	−3 24	44	104	−4 08	44	105	−4 52	44	105	278
81	−1 15	45	103	−2 00	44	104	−2 44	44	105	−3 28	45	105	−4 13	44	106	279
80	−0 36	−44	104	−1 20	−45	105	−2 05	−44	105	−2 49	−44	106	−3 33	−45	107	280
79	00 04	45	105	−0 41	44	106	−1 25	45	106	−2 10	44	107	−2 54	45	107	281
78	00 43	44	106	−0 01	45	106	−0 46	45	107	−1 31	44	108	−2 15	45	108	282
77	01 23	45	106	00 38	45	107	−0 07	45	108	−0 52	45	108	−1 37	44	109	283
76	02 02	45	107	01 17	45	108	00 32	45	108	−0 13	45	109	−0 58	45	110	284
75	02 41	−45	108	01 56	−45	108	01 11	−45	109	00 26	−45	110	−0 19	−46	110	285
74	03 20	45	109	02 35	46	109	01 49	45	110	01 04	45	110	00 19	46	111	286
73	03 59	46	109	03 13	45	110	02 28	46	111	01 42	45	111	00 57	46	112	287
72	04 37	45	110	03 52	46	111	03 06	46	111	02 20	45	112	01 35	46	113	288
71	05 16	46	111	04 30	46	111	03 44	46	112	02 58	46	113	02 12	45	113	289
70	05 54	−46	112	05 08	−46	112	04 22	−46	113	03 36	−46	113	02 50	−46	114	290

LAT 47°

N. Lat. {LHA greater than 180°........ Zn=Z / LHA less than 180°........... Zn=360−Z

DECLINATION (0°-14°) CONTRARY NAME TO LATITUDE

LHA	0° Hc	0° d	0° Z	1° Hc	1° d	1° Z	2° Hc	2° d	2° Z	3° Hc	3° d	3° Z	4° Hc	4° d	4° Z
	° ′	′	°	° ′	′	°	° ′	′	°	° ′	′	°	° ′	′	°
69	14 09	45	106	13 24	46	106	12 38	45	107	11 53	46	108	11 07	46	108
68	14 48	45	107	14 03	46	107	13 17	45	108	12 32	46	109	11 46	46	109
67	15 27	45	107	14 42	46	108	13 56	46	109	13 10	46	109	12 24	46	110
66	16 06	45	108	15 21	46	109	14 35	46	109	13 49	46	110	13 03	46	111
65	16 45	−46	109	15 59	−46	110	15 13	−46	110	14 27	−46	111	13 41	−46	112
64	17 24	46	110	16 38	46	110	15 52	47	111	15 05	46	112	14 19	47	112
63	18 02	46	110	17 16	46	111	16 30	47	112	15 43	46	112	14 57	47	113
62	18 40	46	111	17 54	46	112	17 08	47	113	16 21	47	113	15 34	47	114
61	19 19	47	112	18 32	47	113	17 45	47	113	16 58	47	114	16 11	47	115
60	19 56	−46	113	19 10	−47	114	18 23	−47	114	17 36	−48	115	16 48	−47	116
59	20 34	47	114	19 47	47	114	19 00	47	115	18 13	48	116	17 25	47	116
58	21 11	47	115	20 24	47	115	19 37	48	116	18 49	47	117	18 02	48	117
57	21 48	47	115	21 01	48	116	20 13	47	117	19 26	48	117	18 38	48	118
56	22 25	47	116	21 38	48	117	20 50	48	118	20 02	48	118	19 14	48	119
55	23 02	−48	117	22 14	−48	118	21 26	−48	118	20 38	−48	119	19 50	−49	120
54	23 38	48	118	22 50	48	119	22 02	48	119	21 14	49	120	20 25	48	121
53	24 14	48	119	23 26	49	120	22 37	48	120	21 49	49	121	21 00	49	121
52	24 50	49	120	24 01	48	120	23 13	49	121	22 24	49	122	21 35	49	122
51	25 25	49	121	24 36	48	121	23 48	49	122	22 59	50	123	22 09	49	123
50	26 00	−49	122	25 11	−49	122	24 22	−49	123	23 33	−49	123	22 44	−50	124
49	26 35	49	122	25 46	50	123	24 56	49	124	24 07	50	124	23 17	50	125
48	27 09	49	123	26 20	50	124	25 30	50	125	24 40	49	125	23 51	50	126
47	27 43	50	124	26 53	49	125	26 04	50	126	25 14	50	126	24 24	51	127
46	28 17	50	125	27 27	50	126	26 37	50	127	25 47	51	127	24 56	50	128
45	28 50	−50	126	28 00	−51	127	27 09	−50	127	26 19	−51	128	25 28	−50	129
44	29 23	51	127	28 32	50	128	27 42	51	128	26 51	51	129	26 00	51	130
43	29 55	50	128	29 05	51	129	28 14	51	129	27 23	52	130	26 31	51	131
42	30 27	51	129	29 36	51	130	28 45	51	130	27 54	52	131	27 02	51	132
41	30 59	52	130	30 07	51	131	29 16	52	131	28 24	51	132	27 33	52	132
40	31 30	−52	131	30 38	−51	132	29 47	−52	132	28 55	−52	133	28 03	−52	133
39	32 00	51	132	31 09	52	133	30 17	53	133	29 24	52	134	28 32	52	134
38	32 31	53	133	31 38	52	134	30 46	52	134	29 54	53	135	29 01	53	135
37	33 00	52	134	32 08	53	135	31 15	52	135	30 23	53	136	29 30	53	136
36	33 29	52	135	32 37	53	136	31 44	53	136	30 51	53	137	29 58	54	137
35	33 58	−53	136	33 05	−53	137	32 12	−54	137	31 18	−53	138	30 25	−53	138
34	34 26	53	137	33 33	54	138	32 39	53	138	31 46	54	139	30 52	54	140
33	34 53	53	138	34 00	54	139	33 06	54	140	32 12	54	140	31 18	54	141
32	35 20	54	140	34 26	54	140	33 32	54	141	32 38	54	141	31 44	54	142
31	35 46	54	141	34 52	54	141	33 58	54	142	33 04	55	142	32 09	55	143
30	36 12	−54	142	35 18	−55	142	34 23	−55	143	33 28	−54	143	32 34	−55	144
29	36 37	55	143	35 42	54	143	34 48	55	144	33 53	55	144	32 58	56	145
28	37 02	55	144	36 07	56	145	35 11	55	145	34 16	55	145	33 21	56	146
27	37 25	55	145	36 30	55	146	35 35	56	146	34 39	56	147	33 43	55	147
26	37 48	55	146	36 53	56	147	35 57	56	147	35 01	56	148	34 05	56	148
25	38 11	−56	148	37 15	−56	148	36 19	−56	148	35 23	−56	149	34 27	−57	149
24	38 32	56	149	37 36	56	149	36 40	56	150	35 44	57	150	34 47	56	150
23	38 53	56	150	37 57	57	150	37 00	56	151	36 04	57	151	35 07	57	152
22	39 13	56	151	38 17	57	152	37 20	57	152	36 23	57	152	35 26	57	153
21	39 33	57	152	38 36	57	153	37 39	57	153	36 42	57	154	35 45	58	154
20	39 51	−57	154	38 54	−57	154	37 57	−57	154	37 00	−58	155	36 02	−57	155
19	40 09	57	155	39 12	58	155	38 14	57	156	37 17	58	156	36 19	58	156
18	40 26	57	156	39 29	58	156	38 31	58	157	37 33	58	157	36 35	58	157
17	40 43	58	157	39 45	58	158	38 47	58	158	37 49	59	158	36 50	58	159
16	40 58	58	159	40 00	58	159	39 02	59	159	38 03	58	160	37 05	58	160
15	41 12	−58	160	40 14	−58	160	39 16	−59	161	38 17	−58	161	37 19	−59	161
14	41 26	59	161	40 27	58	162	39 29	59	162	38 30	58	162	37 32	59	162
13	41 39	59	163	40 40	59	163	39 41	59	163	38 42	58	163	37 44	59	164
12	41 51	59	164	40 52	59	164	39 53	59	164	38 54	59	165	37 55	59	165
11	42 02	59	165	41 03	60	165	40 03	59	166	39 04	59	166	38 05	59	166
10	42 12	−60	166	41 12	−59	167	40 13	−59	167	39 14	−59	167	38 15	−60	167
9	42 21	60	168	41 21	59	168	40 22	59	168	39 23	60	168	38 23	59	169
8	42 29	60	169	41 29	59	169	40 30	60	170	39 30	59	170	38 31	60	170
7	42 36	59	171	41 37	60	171	40 37	60	171	39 37	59	171	38 38	60	171
6	42 43	60	172	41 43	60	172	40 43	60	172	39 43	59	172	38 44	60	172
5	42 48	−60	173	41 48	−60	173	40 48	−60	173	39 48	−59	174	38 49	−60	174
4	42 52	60	175	41 52	60	175	40 52	59	175	39 53	60	175	38 53	60	175
3	42 56	60	176	41 56	60	176	40 56	60	176	39 56	60	176	38 56	60	176
2	42 58	60	177	41 58	60	177	40 58	60	177	39 58	60	177	38 58	60	177
1	43 00	60	179	42 00	60	179	41 00	60	179	40 00	60	179	39 00	60	179
0	43 00	−60	180	42 00	−60	180	41 00	−60	180	40 00	−60	180	39 00	−60	180

LHA	5° Hc	5° d	5° Z	6° Hc	6° d	6° Z	7° Hc	7° d	7° Z	8° Hc	8° d	8° Z	9° Hc	9° d	9° Z
	° ′	′	°	° ′	′	°	° ′	′	°	° ′	′	°	° ′	′	°
69	10 21	45	109	09 36	46	110	08 50	46	110	08 04	46	111	07 18	46	112
68	11 00	46	110	10 14	46	110	09 28	46	111	08 42	46	112	07 56	46	112
67	11 38	46	111	10 52	46	111	10 06	46	112	09 20	47	113	08 33	46	113
66	12 17	47	111	11 30	46	112	10 44	47	113	09 57	46	113	09 11	47	114
65	12 55	−47	112	12 08	−46	113	11 22	−47	113	10 35	−47	114	09 48	−47	115
64	13 32	46	113	12 46	47	114	11 59	47	114	11 12	47	115	10 25	47	116
63	14 10	47	114	13 23	47	114	12 36	47	115	11 49	47	116	11 02	47	116
62	14 47	47	115	14 00	47	115	13 13	47	116	12 26	47	116	11 39	48	117
61	15 24	47	115	14 37	47	116	13 50	48	117	13 02	47	117	12 15	48	118
60	16 01	−47	116	15 14	−48	117	14 26	−47	117	13 39	−48	118	12 51	−48	119
59	16 38	48	117	15 50	48	118	15 02	47	118	14 15	48	119	13 27	48	120
58	17 14	48	118	16 26	48	118	15 38	48	119	14 50	48	120	14 02	48	120
57	17 50	48	119	17 02	48	119	16 14	48	120	15 26	49	121	14 37	48	121
56	18 26	48	120	17 38	49	120	16 49	48	121	16 01	49	121	15 12	48	122
55	19 01	−48	120	18 13	−49	121	17 24	−48	122	16 36	−49	122	15 47	−49	123
54	19 37	49	121	18 48	49	122	17 59	49	122	17 10	49	123	16 21	49	124
53	20 11	48	122	19 23	50	123	18 33	49	123	17 44	49	124	16 55	49	125
52	20 46	49	123	19 57	49	124	19 08	50	124	18 18	49	125	17 29	50	125
51	21 20	49	124	20 31	50	124	19 41	49	125	18 52	50	126	18 02	50	126
50	21 54	−50	125	21 04	−49	125	20 15	−50	126	19 25	−50	127	18 35	−50	127
49	22 27	49	126	21 38	50	126	20 48	51	127	19 57	50	127	19 07	50	128
48	23 01	51	127	22 10	50	127	21 20	50	128	20 30	51	128	19 39	50	129
47	23 33	50	127	22 43	51	128	21 52	50	129	21 02	51	129	20 11	51	130
46	24 06	51	128	23 15	51	129	22 24	51	129	21 33	51	130	20 42	51	131
45	24 38	−51	129	23 47	−51	130	22 56	−52	130	22 04	−51	131	21 13	−51	132
44	25 09	51	130	24 18	51	131	23 27	52	131	22 35	51	132	21 44	52	132
43	25 40	51	131	24 49	52	132	23 57	52	132	23 05	51	133	22 14	52	133
42	26 11	52	132	25 19	52	133	24 27	52	133	23 35	52	134	22 43	52	134
41	26 41	52	133	25 49	52	134	24 57	53	134	24 04	52	135	23 12	52	135
40	27 11	−53	134	26 18	−52	135	25 26	−53	135	24 33	−52	136	23 41	−53	136
39	27 40	53	135	26 47	52	136	25 55	53	136	25 02	53	137	24 09	53	137
38	28 08	52	136	27 16	53	137	26 23	53	137	25 30	54	138	24 36	53	138
37	28 37	53	137	27 44	54	138	26 50	53	138	25 57	53	139	25 04	54	139
36	29 04	53	138	28 11	54	139	27 17	53	139	26 24	54	140	25 30	54	140
35	29 32	−54	139	28 38	−54	140	27 44	−54	140	26 50	−54	141	25 56	−54	141
34	29 58	54	140	29 04	54	141	28 10	54	141	27 16	54	142	26 22	55	142
33	30 24	54	141	29 30	54	142	28 36	55	142	27 41	54	143	26 47	55	143
32	30 50	55	142	29 55	54	143	29 01	55	143	28 06	55	144	27 11	55	144
31	31 14	54	143	30 20	55	144	29 25	55	144	28 30	55	145	27 35	55	145
30	31 39	−55	144	30 44	−55	145	29 49	−56	145	28 53	−55	146	27 58	−55	146
29	32 02	55	145	31 07	55	146	30 12	56	146	29 16	55	147	28 21	56	147
28	32 25	55	146	31 30	56	147	30 34	56	147	29 38	55	148	28 43	56	148
27	32 48	56	148	31 52	56	148	30 56	56	148	30 00	56	149	29 04	56	149
26	33 09	56	149	32 13	56	149	31 17	56	149	30 21	56	150	29 25	57	150
25	33 30	−56	150	32 34	−56	150	31 38	−57	151	30 41	−56	151	29 45	−57	151
24	33 51	57	151	32 54	57	151	31 57	56	152	31 01	57	152	30 04	57	152
23	34 10	57	152	33 13	56	152	32 17	57	153	31 20	58	153	30 22	57	153
22	34 29	57	153	33 32	57	154	32 35	57	154	31 38	58	154	30 40	57	155
21	34 47	57	154	33 50	57	155	32 53	58	155	31 55	57	155	30 58	58	156
20	35 05	−58	155	34 07	−57	156	33 10	−58	156	32 12	−58	156	31 14	−58	157
19	35 21	57	157	34 24	58	157	33 26	58	157	32 28	58	158	31 30	58	158
18	35 37	58	158	34 39	58	158	33 41	58	158	32 43	58	159	31 45	58	159
17	35 52	58	159	34 54	58	159	33 56	58	160	32 58	59	160	31 59	58	160
16	36 07	59	160	35 08	58	160	34 10	59	161	33 11	58	161	32 13	59	161
15	36 20	−58	161	35 22	−59	162	34 23	−59	162	33 24	−58	162	32 26	−59	162
14	36 33	59	163	35 34	59	163	34 35	58	163	33 37	59	163	32 38	59	164
13	36 45	59	164	35 46	59	164	34 47	59	164	33 48	59	165	32 49	59	165
12	36 56	59	165	35 57	59	165	34 58	60	165	33 58	59	166	32 59	59	166
11	37 06	59	166	36 07	60	166	35 07	59	167	34 08	59	167	33 09	59	167
10	37 15	−59	167	36 16	−59	168	35 17	−60	168	34 17	−59	168	33 18	−60	168
9	37 24	60	169	36 24	59	169	35 25	60	169	34 25	59	169	33 26	60	169
8	37 31	59	170	36 32	60	170	35 32	60	170	34 33	60	170	33 33	60	171
7	37 38	60	171	36 38	59	171	35 39	60	171	34 39	60	172	33 39	59	172
6	37 44	60	172	36 44	60	173	35 44	60	173	34 45	60	173	33 45	60	173
5	37 49	−60	174	36 49	−60	174	35 49	−60	174	34 49	−60	174	33 49	−59	174
4	37 53	60	175	36 53	60	175	35 53	60	175	34 53	60	175	33 53	60	175
3	37 56	60	176	36 56	60	176	35 56	60	176	34 56	60	176	33 56	60	176
2	37 58	60	178	36 58	60	178	35 58	60	178	34 58	60	178	33 58	60	178
1	38 00	60	179	37 00	60	179	36 00	60	179	35 00	60	179	34 00	60	179
0	38 00	−60	180	37 00	−60	180	36 00	−60	180	35 00	−60	180	34 00	−60	180

LHA	10° Hc	10° d	10° Z	11° Hc	11° d	11° Z	12° Hc	12° d	12° Z	13° Hc	13° d	13° Z	14° Hc	14° d	14° Z	LHA
	° ′	′	°	° ′	′	°	° ′	′	°	° ′	′	°	° ′	′	°	
69	06 32	46	112	05 46	47	113	04 59	46	114	04 13	46	114	03 27	46	115	291
68	07 10	47	113	06 23	46	114	05 37	46	114	04 51	47	115	04 04	46	116	292
67	07 47	46	114	07 01	47	114	06 14	46	115	05 28	47	116	04 41	47	116	293
66	08 24	46	115	07 38	47	115	06 51	46	116	06 04	46	117	05 18	47	117	294
65	09 01	−46	115	08 15	−47	116	07 28	−47	117	06 41	−47	117	05 54	−47	118	295
64	09 38	47	116	08 51	47	117	08 04	47	117	07 17	47	118	06 30	47	119	296
63	10 15	47	117	09 28	48	118	08 40	47	118	07 53	47	119	07 06	48	119	297
62	10 51	47	118	10 04	48	118	09 16	47	119	08 29	48	120	07 41	47	120	298
61	11 27	47	119	10 40	48	119	09 52	48	120	09 04	48	120	08 16	47	121	299
60	12 03	−48	119	11 15	−48	120	10 27	−48	121	09 39	−48	121	08 51	−48	122	300
59	12 39	48	120	11 51	48	121	11 03	49	121	10 14	48	122	09 26	48	123	301
58	13 14	48	121	12 26	49	122	11 37	48	122	10 49	49	123	10 00	48	123	302
57	13 49	49	122	13 00	48	122	12 12	49	123	11 23	49	124	10 34	48	124	303
56	14 24	49	123	13 35	49	123	12 46	49	124	11 57	49	124	11 08	49	125	304
55	14 58	−49	123	14 09	−49	124	13 20	−49	125	12 31	−50	125	11 41	−49	126	305
54	15 32	49	124	14 43	50	125	13 53	49	125	13 04	49	126	12 15	50	127	306
53	16 06	50	125	15 16	49	126	14 27	50	126	13 37	50	127	12 47	50	127	307
52	16 39	50	126	15 49	50	127	14 59	49	127	14 10	50	128	13 20	50	128	308
51	17 12	50	127	16 22	50	127	15 32	50	128	14 42	50	129	13 52	51	129	309
50	17 45	−51	128	16 54	−50	128	16 04	−50	129	15 14	−51	129	14 23	−50	130	310
49	18 17	51	129	17 26	50	129	16 36	51	130	15 45	51	130	14 54	50	131	311
48	18 49	51	129	17 58	51	130	17 07	51	131	16 16	51	131	15 25	51	132	312
47	19 20	51	130	18 29	51	131	17 38	51	131	16 47	51	132	15 56	52	132	313
46	19 51	51	131	19 00	52	132	18 08	51	132	17 17	51	133	16 26	52	133	314
45	20 22	−52	132	19 30	−51	133	18 39	−52	133	17 47	−52	134	16 55	−52	134	315
44	20 52	52	133	20 00	52	134	19 08	52	134	18 16	52	135	17 24	52	135	316
43	21 22	52	134	20 30	53	134	19 37	52	135	18 45	52	135	17 53	52	136	317
42	21 51	52	135	20 59	53	135	20 06	52	136	19 14	53	136	18 21	53	137	318
41	22 20	53	136	21 27	53	136	20 34	52	137	19 42	53	137	18 49	53	138	319
40	22 48	−53	137	21 55	−53	137	21 02	−53	138	20 09	−53	138	19 16	−53	139	320
39	23 16	53	138	22 23	53	138	21 30	54	139	20 36	53	139	19 43	54	140	321
38	23 43	53	139	22 50	54	139	21 56	53	140	21 03	54	140	20 09	53	141	322
37	24 10	54	140	23 16	53	140	22 23	54	141	21 29	54	141	20 35	54	141	323
36	24 36	54	141	23 42	54	141	22 48	54	141	21 54	54	142	21 00	54	142	324
35	25 02	−54	141	24 08	−54	142	23 14	−55	142	22 19	−54	143	21 25	−54	143	325
34	25 27	54	142	24 33	55	143	23 38	54	143	22 44	55	144	21 49	55	144	326
33	25 52	55	144	24 57	54	144	24 03	55	144	23 08	55	145	22 13	55	145	327
32	26 16	55	144	25 21	55	145	24 26	55	145	23 31	55	146	22 36	55	146	328
31	26 40	56	145	25 44	55	146	24 49	55	146	23 54	56	147	22 58	55	147	329
30	27 03	−56	146	26 07	−55	147	25 12	−56	147	24 16	−56	148	23 20	−55	148	330
29	27 25	56	148	26 29	56	148	25 33	55	148	24 38	56	149	23 42	56	149	331
28	27 47	56	149	26 51	56	149	25 55	56	149	24 59	57	150	24 02	56	150	332
27	28 08	57	150	27 11	56	150	26 15	56	150	25 19	57	151	24 22	56	151	333
26	28 28	56	151	27 32	57	151	26 35	56	151	25 39	57	152	24 42	57	152	334
25	28 48	−57	152	27 51	−57	152	26 54	−56	152	25 58	−57	153	25 01	−57	153	335
24	29 07	57	153	28 10	57	153	27 13	57	153	26 16	57	154	25 19	57	154	336
23	29 25	57	154	28 28	57	154	27 31	57	155	26 34	57	155	25 37	58	155	337
22	29 43	57	155	28 46	58	155	27 48	57	156	26 51	58	156	25 53	57	156	338
21	30 00	57	156	29 03	58	156	28 05	58	157	27 07	57	157	26 10	58	157	339
20	30 16	−57	157	29 19	−58	157	28 21	−58	158	27 23	−58	158	26 25	−58	158	340
19	30 32	58	158	29 34	58	158	28 36	58	159	27 38	58	159	26 40	58	159	341
18	30 47	58	159	29 49	58	160	28 51	59	160	27 52	58	160	26 54	58	160	342
17	31 01	58	160	30 03	59	161	29 04	58	161	28 06	59	161	27 07	58	161	343
16	31 14	58	162	30 16	59	162	29 17	58	162	28 19	59	162	27 20	59	163	344
15	31 27	−59	163	30 28	−58	163	29 30	−59	163	28 31	−59	163	27 32	−59	164	345
14	31 39	59	164	30 40	59	164	29 41	59	164	28 42	59	164	27 43	59	165	346
13	31 50	59	165	30 51	59	165	29 52	59	165	28 53	59	166	27 54	59	166	347
12	32 00	59	166	31 01	59	166	30 02	59	166	29 03	60	167	28 03	59	167	348
11	32 10	60	167	31 10	59	167	30 11	59	168	29 12	60	168	28 12	59	168	349
10	32 18	−59	168	31 19	−59	169	30 20	−60	169	29 20	−59	169	28 21	−60	169	350
9	32 26	59	170	31 27	60	170	30 27	59	170	29 28	60	170	28 28	59	170	351
8	32 33	59	171	31 34	60	171	30 34	60	171	29 34	59	171	28 35	60	171	352
7	32 40	60	172	31 40	60	172	30 40	60	172	29 40	59	172	28 41	60	172	353
6	32 45	60	173	31 45	60	173	30 45	59	173	29 46	60	173	28 46	60	173	354
5	32 50	−60	174	31 50	−60	174	30 50	−60	174	29 50	−60	174	28 50	−60	175	355
4	32 53	60	175	31 53	59	175	30 54	60	175	29 54	60	176	28 54	60	176	356
3	32 56	60	177	31 56	60	177	30 56	60	177	29 56	60	177	28 56	59	177	357
2	32 58	60	178	31 58	60	178	30 58	60	178	29 58	60	178	28 58	60	178	358
1	33 00	60	179	32 00	60	179	31 00	60	179	30 00	60	179	29 00	60	179	359
0	33 00	−60	180	32 00	−60	180	31 00	−60	180	30 00	−60	180	29 00	−60	180	360

S. Lat. {LHA greater than 180°....... Zn=180−Z / LHA less than 180°........... Zn=180+Z

DECLINATION (0°-14°) CONTRARY NAME TO LATITUDE

LAT 47°

N. Lat. {LHA greater than 180°....... Zn=Z
LHA less than 180°........... Zn=360−Z}

DECLINATION (15°-29°) SAME NAME AS LATITUDE

LHA	15°			16°			17°			18°			19°		
	Hc	d	Z	Hc	d	Z	Hc	d	Z	Hc	d	Z	Hc	d	Z
	° ′	′	°	° ′	′	°	° ′	′	°	° ′	′	°	° ′	′	°
0	58 00	+60	180	59 00	+60	180	60 00	+60	180	61 00	+60	180	62 00	+60	180
1	57 59	60	178	58 59	60	178	59 59	60	178	60 59	60	178	61 59	60	178
2	57 57	60	176	58 57	60	176	59 57	60	176	60 57	60	176	61 57	60	176
3	57 54	60	175	58 54	60	174	59 54	60	174	60 54	60	174	61 54	59	174
4	57 50	59	173	58 49	60	173	59 49	60	172	60 49	60	172	61 49	59	172
5	57 44	+59	171	58 43	+60	171	59 43	+60	171	60 43	+59	170	61 42	+60	170
6	57 37	59	169	58 36	60	169	59 36	59	169	60 35	59	168	61 34	60	168
7	57 28	60	167	58 28	59	167	59 27	59	167	60 26	59	166	61 25	59	166
8	57 19	59	166	58 18	59	165	59 17	59	165	60 16	59	165	61 15	58	164
9	57 08	59	164	58 07	59	164	59 06	58	163	60 04	59	163	61 03	58	162
10	56 56	+59	162	57 55	+58	162	58 53	+58	161	59 51	+59	161	60 50	+58	160
11	56 43	58	160	57 41	58	160	58 39	58	160	59 37	58	159	60 35	58	158
12	56 29	58	159	57 27	57	158	58 24	58	158	59 22	58	157	60 20	57	157
13	56 13	58	157	57 11	57	157	58 08	58	156	59 06	57	155	60 03	57	155
14	55 57	57	155	56 54	57	155	57 51	57	154	58 48	57	154	59 45	56	153
15	55 39	+57	154	56 36	+57	153	57 33	+56	153	58 29	+57	152	59 26	+56	151
16	55 20	57	152	56 17	56	152	57 13	56	151	58 09	56	150	59 05	56	150
17	55 01	56	151	55 57	56	150	56 53	56	149	57 49	55	149	58 44	55	148
18	54 40	56	149	55 36	55	148	56 31	56	148	57 27	55	147	58 22	55	146
19	54 18	56	147	55 14	55	147	56 09	55	146	57 04	55	145	57 59	54	145
20	53 56	+55	146	54 51	+55	145	55 46	+54	145	56 40	+54	144	57 34	+54	143
21	53 33	54	144	54 27	54	144	55 21	54	143	56 15	54	142	57 09	54	141
22	53 08	54	143	54 02	54	142	54 56	54	141	55 50	53	141	56 43	53	140
23	52 43	54	142	53 37	53	141	54 30	54	140	55 24	52	139	56 16	53	138
24	52 17	54	140	53 11	53	139	54 04	52	139	54 56	53	138	55 49	52	137
25	51 51	+53	139	52 44	+52	138	53 36	+52	137	54 28	+52	136	55 20	+52	135
26	51 23	53	137	52 16	52	137	53 08	52	136	54 00	51	135	54 51	51	134
27	50 55	52	136	51 47	52	135	52 39	51	134	53 30	51	133	54 21	51	133
28	50 26	52	135	51 18	51	134	52 09	51	133	53 00	51	132	53 51	50	131
29	49 57	51	133	50 48	51	133	51 39	51	132	52 30	50	131	53 20	50	130
30	49 27	+51	132	50 18	+50	131	51 08	+50	130	51 58	+50	130	52 48	+50	129
31	48 56	51	131	49 47	50	130	50 37	50	129	51 27	49	128	52 16	49	127
32	48 25	50	130	49 15	50	129	50 05	49	128	50 54	49	127	51 43	49	126
33	47 53	50	128	48 43	49	128	49 32	49	127	50 21	49	126	51 10	48	125
34	47 21	49	127	48 10	49	126	48 59	49	125	49 48	48	125	50 36	48	124
35	46 48	+49	126	47 37	+48	125	48 25	+49	124	49 14	+48	123	50 02	+47	122
36	46 14	49	125	47 03	48	124	47 51	48	123	48 39	48	122	49 27	47	121
37	45 41	48	124	46 29	48	123	47 17	48	122	48 05	47	121	48 52	46	120
38	45 06	48	123	45 54	48	122	46 42	47	121	47 29	47	120	48 16	46	119
39	44 32	47	122	45 19	48	121	46 07	47	120	46 54	46	119	47 40	46	118
40	43 57	+47	120	44 44	+47	120	45 31	+47	119	46 18	+46	118	47 04	+45	117
41	43 21	47	119	44 08	47	119	44 55	46	118	45 41	46	117	46 27	45	116
42	42 45	47	118	43 32	46	118	44 18	46	117	45 04	46	116	45 50	45	115
43	42 09	47	117	42 56	46	117	43 42	45	116	44 27	46	115	45 13	45	114
44	41 33	46	116	42 19	46	115	43 05	45	115	43 50	45	114	44 35	45	113
45	40 56	+46	115	41 42	+45	115	42 27	+46	114	43 13	+44	113	43 57	+45	112
46	40 19	45	114	41 04	46	114	41 50	45	113	42 35	44	112	43 19	44	111
47	39 41	46	113	40 27	45	113	41 12	44	112	41 56	45	111	42 41	44	110
48	39 03	46	112	39 49	45	112	40 34	44	111	41 18	44	110	42 02	44	109
49	38 25	46	112	39 11	44	111	39 55	44	110	40 39	44	109	41 23	44	108
50	37 47	+45	111	38 32	+45	110	39 17	+44	109	40 01	+43	108	40 44	+44	107
51	37 09	44	110	37 53	45	109	38 38	44	108	39 22	43	107	40 05	43	106
52	36 30	45	109	37 15	44	108	37 59	43	107	38 42	44	106	39 26	43	105
53	35 51	45	108	36 36	44	107	37 20	43	106	38 03	43	105	38 46	43	104
54	35 12	44	107	35 56	44	106	36 40	44	105	37 24	42	104	38 06	43	104
55	34 33	+44	106	35 17	+44	105	36 01	+43	104	36 44	+43	104	37 27	+42	103
56	33 54	43	105	34 37	44	104	35 21	43	104	36 04	43	103	36 47	42	102
57	33 14	44	104	33 58	43	104	34 41	43	103	35 24	43	102	36 07	42	101
58	32 34	44	104	33 18	43	103	34 01	43	102	34 44	42	101	35 26	42	100
59	31 55	43	103	32 38	43	102	33 21	43	101	34 04	42	100	34 46	42	99
60	31 15	+43	102	31 58	+43	101	32 41	+42	100	33 23	+43	99	34 06	+41	99
61	30 35	43	101	31 18	42	100	32 00	43	100	32 43	42	99	33 25	42	98
62	29 54	43	100	30 37	43	100	31 20	42	99	32 02	43	98	32 45	41	97
63	29 14	43	100	29 57	43	99	30 40	42	98	31 22	42	97	32 04	42	96
64	28 34	42	99	29 16	43	98	29 59	42	97	30 41	42	96	31 23	42	96
65	27 53	+43	98	28 36	+42	97	29 18	+43	96	30 01	+41	96	30 42	+42	95
66	27 13	42	97	27 55	43	96	28 38	42	96	29 20	42	95	30 02	41	94
67	26 32	43	96	27 15	42	96	27 57	42	95	28 39	42	94	29 21	41	93
68	25 51	43	96	26 34	42	95	27 16	42	94	27 58	42	93	28 40	41	92
69	25 10	43	95	25 53	42	94	26 35	42	93	27 17	42	93	27 59	41	92

LHA	20°			21°			22°			23°			24°		
	Hc	d	Z	Hc	d	Z	Hc	d	Z	Hc	d	Z	Hc	d	Z
	° ′	′	°	° ′	′	°	° ′	′	°	° ′	′	°	° ′	′	°
0	63 00	+60	180	64 00	+60	180	65 00	+60	180	66 00	+60	180	67 00	+60	180
1	62 59	60	178	63 59	60	178	64 59	60	178	65 59	60	178	66 59	60	178
2	62 57	60	176	63 57	60	176	64 57	60	176	65 57	60	176	66 57	60	175
3	62 53	60	174	63 53	60	174	64 53	60	173	65 53	60	173	66 53	59	173
4	62 48	60	172	63 48	60	172	64 48	59	171	65 47	60	171	66 47	59	171
5	62 42	+59	170	63 41	+60	169	64 41	+59	169	65 40	+59	169	66 39	+60	168
6	62 34	59	168	63 33	59	167	64 32	59	167	65 31	59	167	66 30	59	166
7	62 24	59	166	63 23	59	165	64 22	59	165	65 21	59	164	66 20	58	164
8	62 13	59	164	63 12	59	163	64 11	58	163	65 09	59	162	66 08	58	162
9	62 01	59	162	63 00	58	161	63 58	58	161	64 56	58	160	65 54	58	160
10	61 48	+58	160	62 46	+58	159	63 44	+57	159	64 41	+58	158	65 39	+57	157
11	61 33	58	158	62 31	57	157	63 28	57	157	64 25	58	156	65 23	56	155
12	61 17	57	156	62 14	57	155	63 11	57	155	64 08	57	154	65 05	56	153
13	61 00	57	154	61 57	56	154	62 53	57	153	63 50	56	152	64 46	56	151
14	60 41	57	152	61 38	56	152	62 34	56	151	63 30	55	150	64 25	56	149
15	60 22	+56	151	61 18	+55	150	62 13	+56	149	63 09	+55	148	64 04	+55	147
16	60 01	56	149	60 57	55	148	61 52	55	147	62 47	54	146	63 41	54	145
17	59 39	55	147	60 34	55	146	61 29	54	145	62 23	54	145	63 17	54	144
18	59 17	54	145	60 11	54	145	61 05	54	144	61 59	54	143	62 53	53	142
19	58 53	54	144	59 47	54	143	60 41	53	142	61 34	53	141	62 27	52	140
20	58 28	+54	142	59 22	+53	141	60 15	+53	140	61 08	+52	139	62 00	+52	138
21	58 03	53	141	58 56	52	140	59 48	52	139	60 40	52	138	61 32	52	137
22	57 36	53	139	58 29	52	138	59 21	52	137	60 13	51	136	61 04	50	135
23	57 09	52	137	58 01	52	137	58 53	51	136	59 44	50	135	60 34	51	133
24	56 41	51	136	57 32	51	135	58 23	51	134	59 14	50	133	60 04	50	132
25	56 12	+51	135	57 03	+51	134	57 54	+50	133	58 44	+49	132	59 33	+50	130
26	55 42	51	133	56 33	50	132	57 23	50	131	58 13	49	130	59 02	48	129
27	55 12	50	132	56 02	50	131	56 52	49	130	57 41	49	129	58 30	48	128
28	54 41	50	130	55 31	49	129	56 20	49	128	57 09	48	127	57 57	48	126
29	54 10	49	129	54 59	49	128	55 48	48	127	56 36	48	126	57 24	47	125
30	53 38	+48	128	54 26	+49	127	55 15	+48	126	56 03	+47	125	56 50	+46	123
31	53 05	48	126	53 53	48	125	54 41	48	124	55 29	46	123	56 15	46	122
32	52 32	48	125	53 20	47	124	54 07	47	123	54 54	46	122	55 40	46	121
33	51 58	47	124	52 45	48	123	53 33	46	122	54 19	46	121	55 05	45	120
34	51 24	47	123	52 11	47	122	52 58	46	121	53 44	45	120	54 29	45	118
35	50 49	+47	122	51 36	+46	121	52 22	+46	119	53 08	+45	118	53 53	+45	117
36	50 14	46	120	51 00	46	119	51 46	46	118	52 32	45	117	53 17	44	116
37	49 38	46	119	50 24	46	118	51 10	45	117	51 55	45	116	52 40	43	115
38	49 02	46	118	49 48	45	117	50 33	45	116	51 18	44	115	52 02	44	114
39	48 26	46	117	49 12	45	116	49 57	44	115	50 41	44	114	51 25	43	113
40	47 49	+46	116	48 35	+44	115	49 19	+44	114	50 03	+44	113	50 47	+43	112
41	47 12	45	115	47 57	45	114	48 42	44	113	49 26	43	112	50 09	42	111
42	46 35	45	114	47 20	44	113	48 04	43	112	48 47	43	111	49 30	43	110
43	45 58	44	113	46 42	44	112	47 26	43	111	48 09	43	110	48 52	42	109
44	45 20	44	112	46 04	43	111	46 47	43	110	47 30	43	109	48 13	42	108
45	44 42	+43	111	45 25	+44	110	46 09	+43	109	46 52	+42	108	47 34	+42	107
46	44 03	44	110	44 47	43	109	45 30	43	108	46 13	42	107	46 55	41	106
47	43 25	43	109	44 08	43	108	44 51	42	107	45 33	42	106	46 15	41	105
48	42 46	43	108	43 29	43	107	44 12	42	106	44 54	42	105	45 36	41	104
49	42 07	43	107	42 50	42	106	43 32	42	105	44 14	42	104	44 56	41	103
50	41 28	+42	106	42 10	+43	105	42 53	+42	104	43 35	+41	103	44 16	+41	102
51	40 48	43	105	41 31	42	104	42 13	42	103	42 55	41	102	43 36	40	101
52	40 09	42	104	40 51	42	104	41 33	42	103	42 15	41	102	42 56	40	101
53	39 29	42	104	40 11	42	103	40 53	41	102	41 34	41	101	42 15	41	100
54	38 49	42	103	39 31	42	102	40 13	41	101	40 54	41	100	41 35	40	99
55	38 09	+42	102	38 51	+42	101	39 33	+41	100	40 14	+40	99	40 54	+41	98
56	37 29	42	101	38 11	41	100	38 52	41	99	39 33	41	98	40 14	40	97
57	36 49	42	100	37 31	41	99	38 12	41	98	38 53	40	97	39 33	40	96
58	36 08	42	99	36 50	41	98	37 31	41	98	38 12	41	97	38 53	39	96
59	35 28	42	99	36 10	41	98	36 51	40	97	37 31	41	96	38 12	40	95
60	34 47	+42	98	35 29	+41	97	36 10	+41	96	36 51	+40	95	37 31	+40	94
61	34 07	41	97	34 48	41	96	35 29	41	95	36 10	40	94	36 50	40	93
62	33 26	42	96	34 08	41	95	34 49	40	94	35 29	40	94	36 09	40	93
63	32 46	41	95	33 27	41	95	34 08	40	94	34 48	40	93	35 28	40	92
64	32 05	41	95	32 46	41	94	33 27	40	93	34 07	41	92	34 48	39	91
65	31 24	+41	94	32 05	+41	93	32 46	+40	92	33 26	+41	91	34 07	+39	90
66	30 43	41	93	31 24	41	92	32 05	41	91	32 46	40	91	33 26	39	90
67	30 02	41	92	30 43	41	92	31 24	41	91	32 05	40	90	32 45	40	89
68	29 21	41	92	30 02	41	91	30 43	41	90	31 24	40	89	32 04	40	88
69	28 40	42	91	29 22	40	90	30 02	41	89	30 43	40	88	31 23	40	88

LHA	25°			26°			27°			28°			29°			LHA
	Hc	d	Z	Hc	d	Z	Hc	d	Z	Hc	d	Z	Hc	d	Z	
	° ′	′	°	° ′	′	°	° ′	′	°	° ′	′	°	° ′	′	°	
0	68 00	+60	180	69 00	+60	180	70 00	+60	180	71 00	+60	180	72 00	+60	180	360
1	67 59	60	178	68 59	60	178	69 59	60	177	70 59	60	177	71 59	60	177	359
2	67 57	59	175	68 56	60	175	69 56	60	175	70 56	60	175	71 56	60	174	358
3	67 52	60	173	68 52	60	173	69 52	59	172	70 51	60	172	71 51	60	172	357
4	67 46	60	170	68 46	59	170	69 45	60	170	70 45	59	169	71 44	59	169	356
5	67 39	+59	168	68 38	+59	168	69 37	+59	167	70 36	+59	167	71 35	+59	166	355
6	67 29	59	166	68 28	59	165	69 27	59	165	70 26	58	164	71 24	59	163	354
7	67 18	59	163	68 17	58	163	69 15	59	162	70 14	58	162	71 12	57	161	353
8	67 06	58	161	68 04	58	160	69 02	58	160	70 00	57	159	70 57	58	158	352
9	66 52	58	159	67 50	57	158	68 47	57	157	69 44	57	157	70 41	57	156	351
10	66 36	+58	157	67 34	+56	156	68 30	+57	155	69 27	+56	154	70 23	+56	153	350
11	66 19	57	155	67 16	56	154	68 12	56	153	69 08	56	152	70 04	55	151	349
12	66 01	56	152	66 57	56	152	67 53	55	151	68 48	55	150	69 43	55	148	348
13	65 42	55	150	66 37	55	149	67 32	55	148	68 27	54	147	69 21	54	146	347
14	65 21	55	148	66 16	54	147	67 10	54	146	68 04	54	145	68 58	53	144	346
15	64 59	+54	146	65 53	+54	145	66 47	+53	144	67 40	+53	143	68 33	+52	142	345
16	64 35	54	144	65 29	53	143	66 22	53	142	67 15	52	141	68 07	52	140	344
17	64 11	53	143	65 04	53	141	65 57	52	140	66 49	51	139	67 40	51	138	343
18	63 46	52	141	64 38	52	140	65 30	51	138	66 21	51	137	67 12	50	136	342
19	63 19	52	139	64 11	51	138	65 02	51	137	65 53	50	135	66 43	49	134	341
20	62 52	+51	137	63 43	+51	136	64 34	+50	135	65 24	+49	134	66 13	+49	132	340
21	62 24	50	136	63 14	50	134	64 04	50	133	64 54	48	132	65 42	48	130	339
22	61 54	51	134	62 45	49	133	63 34	49	131	64 23	48	130	65 11	47	129	338
23	61 25	49	132	62 14	49	131	63 03	48	130	63 51	47	129	64 38	47	127	337
24	60 54	49	131	61 43	48	130	62 31	48	128	63 19	46	127	64 05	46	126	336
25	60 23	+48	129	61 11	+48	128	61 59	+47	127	62 46	+46	125	63 32	+45	124	335
26	59 50	48	128	60 38	48	127	61 26	46	125	62 12	46	124	62 58	44	123	334
27	59 18	47	126	60 05	47	125	60 52	46	124	61 38	45	123	62 23	44	121	333
28	58 45	46	125	59 31	47	124	60 18	45	122	61 03	45	121	61 48	43	120	332
29	58 11	46	124	58 57	46	122	59 43	45	121	60 28	44	120	61 12	43	118	331
30	57 36	+46	122	58 22	+45	121	59 07	+45	120	59 52	+44	118	60 36	+42	117	330
31	57 01	46	121	57 47	45	120	58 32	44	119	59 16	43	117	59 59	42	116	329
32	56 26	45	120	57 11	45	119	57 56	43	117	58 39	43	116	59 22	42	115	328
33	55 50	45	119	56 35	44	117	57 19	43	116	58 02	42	115	58 44	42	113	327
34	55 14	44	117	55 58	44	116	56 42	43	115	57 25	42	114	58 07	41	112	326
35	54 38	+44	116	55 22	+43	115	56 05	+42	114	56 47	+42	112	57 29	+40	111	325
36	54 01	43	115	54 44	43	114	55 27	42	113	56 09	41	111	56 50	41	110	324
37	53 23	44	114	54 07	42	113	54 49	42	112	55 31	41	110	56 12	40	109	323
38	52 46	43	113	53 29	42	112	54 11	41	110	54 52	41	109	55 33	40	108	322
39	52 08	43	112	52 51	41	111	53 32	42	109	54 14	40	108	54 54	39	107	321
40	51 30	+42	111	52 12	+42	110	52 54	+41	108	53 35	+40	107	54 15	+39	106	320
41	50 51	42	110	51 33	42	109	52 15	40	107	52 55	40	106	53 35	39	105	319
42	50 13	42	109	50 55	41	108	51 36	40	106	52 16	40	105	52 56	38	104	318
43	49 34	41	108	50 15	41	107	50 56	40	105	51 36	40	104	52 16	38	103	317
44	48 55	41	107	49 36	41	106	50 17	40	104	50 57	39	103	51 36	38	102	316
45	48 16	+41	106	48 57	+40	105	49 37	+40	104	50 17	+39	102	50 56	+38	101	315
46	47 36	41	105	48 17	40	104	48 57	40	103	49 37	38	101	50 15	39	100	314
47	46 56	41	104	47 37	40	103	48 17	39	102	48 56	39	101	49 35	38	99	313
48	46 17	40	103	46 57	40	102	47 37	39	101	48 16	39	100	48 55	38	99	312
49	45 37	40	102	46 17	40	101	46 57	39	100	47 36	38	99	48 14	38	98	311
50	44 57	+40	101	45 37	+39	100	46 16	+39	99	46 55	+39	98	47 34	+37	97	310
51	44 16	40	100	44 56	40	99	45 36	39	98	46 15	38	97	46 53	38	96	309
52	43 36	40	100	44 16	39	99	44 55	39	97	45 34	38	96	46 12	38	95	308
53	42 56	39	99	43 35	40	98	44 15	38	97	44 53	38	96	45 31	38	94	307
54	42 15	40	98	42 55	39	97	43 34	39	96	44 13	38	95	44 51	37	94	306
55	41 35	+39	97	42 14	+39	96	42 53	+39	95	43 32	+38	94	44 10	+37	93	305
56	40 54	40	96	41 34	39	95	42 13	38	94	42 51	38	93	43 29	37	92	304
57	40 13	40	96	40 53	39	95	41 32	38	94	42 10	38	92	42 48	37	91	303
58	39 32	40	95	40 12	39	94	40 51	38	93	41 29	38	92	42 07	37	91	302
59	38 52	39	94	39 31	39	93	40 10	38	92	40 48	38	91	41 26	37	90	301
60	38 11	+39	93	38 50	+39	92	39 29	+38	91	40 07	+38	90	40 45	+38	89	300
61	37 30	39	92	38 09	39	91	38 48	39	91	39 27	37	90	40 04	38	89	299
62	36 49	39	92	37 28	39	91	38 07	39	90	38 46	37	89	39 23	38	88	298
63	36 08	39	91	36 47	39	90	37 26	39	89	38 05	38	88	38 43	37	87	297
64	35 27	40	90	36 07	38	89	36 45	39	88	37 24	38	87	38 02	37	86	296
65	34 46	+40	89	35 26	+39	89	36 05	+38	88	36 43	+38	87	37 21	+37	86	295
66	34 05	40	89	34 45	39	88	35 24	38	87	36 02	38	86	36 40	38	85	294
67	33 25	39	88	34 04	39	87	34 43	38	86	35 21	38	85	35 59	38	84	293
68	32 44	39	87	33 23	39	86	34 02	39	86	34 41	38	85	35 19	37	84	292
69	32 03	39	87	32 42	39	86	33 21	39	85	34 00	38	84	34 38	38	83	291
	25°			26°			27°			28°			29°			

S. Lat. {LHA greater than 180°....... Zn=180−Z
LHA less than 180°........... Zn=180+Z}

DECLINATION (15°-29°) SAME NAME AS LATITUDE

LAT 47°

N. Lat. {LHA greater than 180°....... Zn=Z
{LHA less than 180°.......... Zn=360−Z

DECLINATION (15°-29°) SAME NAME AS LATITUDE

LHA	15° Hc	d	Z	16° Hc	d	Z	17° Hc	d	Z	18° Hc	d	Z	19° Hc	d	Z	20° Hc	d	Z	21° Hc	d	Z	22° Hc	d	Z	23° Hc	d	Z	24° Hc	d	Z	25° Hc	d	Z	26° Hc	d	Z	27° Hc	d	Z	28° Hc	d	Z	29° Hc	d	Z	LHA
	° ′	′	°	° ′	′	°	° ′	′	°	° ′	′	°	° ′	′	°	° ′	′	°	° ′	′	°	° ′	′	°	° ′	′	°	° ′	′	°	° ′	′	°	° ′	′	°	° ′	′	°	° ′	′	°	° ′	′	°	
70	24 30	+42	94	25 12	+42	93	25 54	+42	93	26 36	+42	92	27 18	+41	91	27 59	+42	90	28 41	+40	89	29 21	+41	89	30 02	+40	88	30 42	+40	87	31 22	+39	86	32 01	+40	85	32 41	+38	84	33 19	+39	83	33 58	+37	82	290
71	23 49	42	93	24 31	43	93	25 14	41	92	25 55	42	91	26 37	42	90	27 19	41	89	28 00	41	89	28 41	40	88	29 21	40	87	30 01	40	86	30 41	40	85	31 21	39	84	32 00	39	83	32 39	38	83	33 17	38	82	289
72	23 08	42	93	23 50	43	92	24 33	42	91	25 15	41	90	25 56	42	90	26 38	41	89	27 19	41	88	28 00	40	87	28 40	40	86	29 20	40	85	30 00	40	85	30 40	39	84	31 19	39	83	31 58	39	82	32 37	38	81	288
73	22 27	43	92	23 10	42	91	23 52	42	90	24 34	41	90	25 15	42	89	25 57	41	88	26 38	41	87	27 19	40	86	27 59	41	86	28 40	40	85	29 20	39	84	29 59	40	83	30 39	39	82	31 18	38	81	31 56	38	80	287
74	21 46	43	91	22 29	42	90	23 11	42	90	23 53	41	89	24 34	42	88	25 16	41	87	25 57	41	86	26 38	41	86	27 19	40	85	27 59	40	84	28 39	40	83	29 19	39	82	29 58	39	81	30 37	39	81	31 16	38	80	286
75	21 05	+43	90	21 48	+42	90	22 30	+42	89	23 12	+42	88	23 54	+41	87	24 35	+41	87	25 16	+41	86	25 57	+41	85	26 38	+40	84	27 18	+40	83	27 58	+40	82	28 38	+40	82	29 18	+39	81	29 57	+39	80	30 36	+38	79	285
76	20 24	43	90	21 07	42	89	21 49	42	88	22 31	42	87	23 13	41	87	23 54	41	86	24 35	41	85	25 16	41	84	25 57	41	83	26 38	40	83	27 18	40	82	27 58	39	81	28 37	40	80	29 17	39	79	29 56	38	78	284
77	19 43	43	89	20 26	42	88	21 08	42	87	21 50	42	87	22 32	41	86	23 13	42	85	23 55	41	84	24 36	41	84	25 17	40	83	25 57	40	82	26 37	40	81	27 17	40	80	27 57	40	79	28 37	39	79	29 16	38	78	283
78	19 03	42	88	19 45	42	88	20 27	42	87	21 09	42	86	21 51	42	85	22 33	41	84	23 14	41	84	23 55	41	83	24 36	41	82	25 17	40	81	25 57	40	80	26 37	40	80	27 17	39	79	27 56	40	78	28 36	38	77	282
79	18 22	42	88	19 04	42	87	19 46	42	86	20 28	42	85	21 10	42	85	21 52	41	84	22 33	42	83	23 15	41	82	23 56	40	81	24 36	41	81	25 17	40	80	25 57	40	79	26 37	40	78	27 17	39	77	27 56	39	76	281
80	17 41	+42	87	18 23	+43	86	19 06	+42	85	19 48	+42	85	20 30	+41	84	21 11	+42	83	21 53	+41	82	22 34	+41	81	23 15	+41	81	23 56	+41	80	24 37	+40	79	25 17	+40	78	25 57	+40	77	26 37	+39	77	27 16	+39	76	280
81	17 00	42	86	17 42	43	85	18 25	42	85	19 07	42	84	19 49	42	83	20 31	41	82	21 12	42	82	21 54	41	81	22 35	41	80	23 16	40	79	23 56	41	78	24 37	40	78	25 17	40	77	25 57	40	76	26 37	39	75	279
82	16 19	43	85	17 02	42	85	17 44	42	84	18 26	42	83	19 08	42	82	19 50	42	82	20 32	41	81	21 13	42	80	21 55	41	79	22 36	40	79	23 16	41	78	23 57	40	77	24 37	40	76	25 17	40	75	25 57	40	74	278
83	15 38	43	85	16 21	42	84	17 03	43	83	17 46	42	82	18 28	42	82	19 10	42	81	19 52	41	80	20 33	41	79	21 14	42	79	21 56	40	78	22 36	41	77	23 17	41	76	23 58	40	75	24 38	40	75	25 18	39	74	277
84	14 58	42	84	15 40	43	83	16 23	42	82	17 05	42	82	17 47	42	81	18 29	42	80	19 11	42	79	19 53	41	79	20 34	42	78	21 16	41	77	21 57	40	76	22 37	41	76	23 18	40	75	23 58	40	74	24 38	40	73	276
85	14 17	+43	83	15 00	+42	83	15 42	+43	82	16 25	+42	81	17 07	+42	80	17 49	+42	80	18 31	+42	79	19 13	+41	78	19 54	+42	77	20 36	+41	77	21 17	+41	76	21 58	+41	75	22 39	+40	74	23 19	+40	73	23 59	+40	73	275
86	13 36	43	83	14 19	43	82	15 02	42	81	15 44	43	80	16 27	42	80	17 09	42	79	17 51	42	78	18 33	42	77	19 15	41	77	19 56	41	76	20 37	41	75	21 18	41	74	21 59	41	73	22 40	40	73	23 20	41	72	274
87	12 56	43	82	13 39	42	81	14 21	43	80	15 04	43	80	15 47	42	79	16 29	42	78	17 11	42	77	17 53	42	77	18 35	41	76	19 16	42	75	19 58	41	74	20 39	41	74	21 20	41	73	22 01	41	72	22 42	40	71	273
88	12 15	43	81	12 58	43	80	13 41	43	80	14 24	42	79	15 06	43	78	15 49	42	77	16 31	42	77	17 13	42	76	17 55	42	75	18 37	42	74	19 19	41	74	20 00	41	73	20 41	41	72	21 22	41	71	22 03	40	71	272
89	11 35	43	80	12 18	43	80	13 01	43	79	13 44	42	78	14 26	43	78	15 09	42	77	15 51	43	76	16 34	42	75	17 16	42	75	17 58	41	74	18 39	42	73	19 21	41	72	20 02	41	72	20 43	41	71	21 24	41	70	271
90	10 55	+43	80	11 38	+43	79	12 21	+43	78	13 04	+43	78	13 47	+42	77	14 29	+43	76	15 12	+42	75	15 54	+42	75	16 36	+42	74	17 18	+42	73	18 00	+42	72	18 42	+42	72	19 24	+41	71	20 05	+41	70	20 46	+41	69	270
91	10 15	43	79	10 58	43	78	11 41	43	78	12 24	43	77	13 07	43	76	13 50	42	75	14 32	43	75	15 15	42	74	15 57	42	73	16 39	42	72	17 21	42	72	18 03	42	71	18 45	42	70	19 27	41	69	20 08	41	69	269
92	09 34	44	78	10 18	43	78	11 01	43	77	11 44	43	76	12 27	43	75	13 10	43	75	13 53	42	74	14 35	43	73	15 18	42	73	16 00	43	72	16 43	42	71	17 25	42	70	18 07	41	70	18 48	42	69	19 30	41	68	268
93	08 54	44	78	09 38	43	77	10 21	43	76	11 04	44	75	11 48	43	75	12 31	43	74	13 14	42	73	13 56	43	73	14 39	43	72	15 22	42	71	16 04	42	70	16 46	42	70	17 28	42	69	18 10	42	68	18 52	42	67	267
94	08 15	43	77	08 58	44	76	09 42	43	75	10 25	43	75	11 08	43	74	11 51	43	73	12 34	43	73	13 17	43	72	14 00	43	71	14 43	43	70	15 26	42	70	16 08	42	69	16 50	42	68	17 32	42	68	18 14	42	67	266
95	07 35	+43	76	08 18	+44	75	09 02	+43	75	09 45	+44	74	10 29	+43	73	11 12	+43	73	11 55	+44	72	12 39	+43	71	13 22	+42	71	14 04	+43	70	14 47	+43	69	15 30	+42	68	16 12	+43	68	16 55	+42	67	17 37	+42	66	265
96	06 55	44	75	07 39	44	75	08 23	43	74	09 06	44	73	09 50	43	73	10 33	44	72	11 17	43	71	12 00	43	71	12 43	43	70	13 26	43	69	14 09	43	68	14 52	43	68	15 35	42	67	16 17	42	66	16 59	43	65	264
97	06 16	43	75	06 59	44	74	07 43	44	73	08 27	44	73	09 11	43	72	09 54	44	71	10 38	43	71	11 21	44	70	12 05	43	69	12 48	43	68	13 31	43	68	14 14	43	67	14 57	43	66	15 40	42	66	16 22	43	65	263
98	05 36	44	74	06 20	44	73	07 04	44	73	07 48	44	72	08 32	44	71	09 16	43	71	09 59	44	70	10 43	44	69	11 27	43	68	12 10	43	68	12 53	44	67	13 37	43	66	14 20	43	66	15 03	42	65	15 45	43	64	262
99	04 57	44	73	05 41	44	73	06 25	44	72	07 09	44	71	07 53	44	71	08 37	44	70	09 21	44	69	10 05	44	69	10 49	43	68	11 32	44	67	12 16	43	66	12 59	44	66	13 43	43	65	14 26	43	64	15 09	43	64	261
100	04 18	+44	73	05 02	+44	72	05 46	+45	71	06 31	+44	71	07 15	+44	70	07 59	+44	69	08 43	+44	69	09 27	+44	68	10 11	+44	67	10 55	+43	66	11 38	+44	66	12 22	+44	65	13 06	+43	64	13 49	+43	64	14 32	+43	63	260
101	03 39	44	72	04 23	45	71	05 08	44	71	05 52	44	70	06 36	45	69	07 21	44	68	08 05	44	68	08 49	44	67	09 33	44	66	10 17	44	66	11 01	44	65	11 45	44	64	12 29	43	64	13 12	44	63	13 56	43	62	259
102	03 00	45	71	03 45	44	70	04 29	45	70	05 14	44	69	05 58	45	68	06 43	44	68	07 27	45	67	08 12	44	66	08 56	44	66	09 40	44	65	10 24	44	64	11 08	44	64	11 52	44	63	12 36	44	62	13 20	43	62	258
103	02 21	45	70	03 06	45	70	03 51	45	69	04 36	44	68	05 20	45	68	06 05	45	67	06 50	44	66	07 34	45	66	08 19	44	65	09 03	44	64	09 47	45	64	10 32	44	63	11 16	44	62	12 00	44	62	12 44	44	61	257
104	01 43	45	70	02 28	45	69	03 13	45	68	03 58	45	68	04 43	44	67	05 27	45	66	06 12	45	66	06 57	45	65	07 42	44	64	08 26	45	64	09 11	44	63	09 55	45	62	10 40	44	62	11 24	44	61	12 08	44	60	256
105	01 05	+45	69	01 50	+45	68	02 35	+46	68	03 21	+44	67	04 05	+45	66	04 50	+45	66	05 35	+45	65	06 20	+45	64	07 05	+45	64	07 50	+45	63	08 35	+44	62	09 19	+45	62	10 04	+44	61	10 48	+45	60	11 33	+44	60	255
106	00 27	45	68	01 12	45	68	01 57	45	67	02 42	46	66	03 28	45	66	04 13	45	65	04 58	45	64	05 43	45	64	06 28	45	63	07 13	45	62	07 58	45	62	08 43	45	61	09 28	45	60	10 13	45	60	10 58	44	59	254
107	−0 11	45	67	00 34	46	67	01 20	45	66	02 05	45	66	02 50	46	65	03 36	45	64	04 21	46	64	05 07	45	63	05 52	45	62	06 37	46	62	07 23	45	61	08 08	45	60	08 53	45	60	09 38	45	59	10 23	45	58	253
108	−0 49	46	67	−0 03	45	66	00 42	46	65	01 28	46	65	02 14	45	64	02 59	46	64	03 45	45	63	04 30	46	62	05 16	45	62	06 01	46	61	06 47	45	60	07 32	46	60	08 18	45	59	09 03	45	58	09 48	45	58	252
109	−1 27	46	66	−0 41	46	65	00 05	46	65	00 51	46	64	01 37	46	63	02 23	45	63	03 08	46	62	03 54	46	61	04 40	46	61	05 26	46	60	06 12	45	60	06 57	46	59	07 43	45	58	08 28	46	58	09 14	45	57	251
110	−2 04	+46	65	−1 18	+46	65	−0 32	+46	64	00 14	+46	63	01 00	+46	63	01 46	+46	62	02 32	+46	61	03 18	+46	61	04 04	+46	60	04 50	+46	59	05 36	+46	59	06 22	+46	58	07 08	+46	58	07 54	+46	57	08 40	+45	56	250
111	−2 41	46	65	−1 55	47	64	−1 08	46	63	−0 22	46	63	00 24	46	62	01 10	47	61	01 57	46	61	02 43	46	60	03 29	46	59	04 15	47	59	05 02	46	58	05 48	46	58	06 34	46	57	07 20	46	56	08 06	46	56	249
112	−3 18	47	64	−2 31	46	63	−1 45	47	62	−0 58	46	62	−0 12	47	61	00 35	46	61	01 21	47	60	02 08	46	59	02 54	46	59	03 40	47	58	04 27	46	57	05 13	47	57	06 00	46	56	06 46	46	56	07 32	46	55	248
113	−3 54	46	63	−3 08	47	62	−2 21	47	62	−1 34	46	61	−0 48	47	61	−0 01	47	60	00 46	46	59	01 32	47	59	02 19	47	58	03 06	46	57	03 52	47	57	04 39	47	56	05 26	46	56	06 12	47	55	06 59	46	54	247
114	−4 31	47	62	−3 44	47	62	−2 57	47	61	−2 10	47	60	−1 23	47	60	−0 36	47	59	00 11	47	59	00 58	47	58	01 45	47	57	02 32	46	57	03 18	47	56	04 05	47	55	04 52	47	55	05 39	47	54	06 26	46	54	246
115	−5 07	+47	61	−4 20	+47	61	−3 33	+48	60	−2 45	+47	60	−1 58	+47	59	−1 11	+47	58	−0 24	+47	58	00 23	+47	57	01 10	+47	57	01 57	+48	56	02 45	+47	55	03 32	+47	55	04 19	+47	54	05 06	+47	54	05 53	+47	53	245
116	−5 43	48	61	−4 55	47	60	−4 08	47	60	−3 21	48	59	−2 33	47	58	−1 46	47	58	−0 59	48	57	−0 11	47	56	00 36	48	56	01 24	47	55	02 11	47	55	02 58	48	54	03 46	47	53	04 33	48	53	05 21	47	52	244
117				−5 31	48	59	−4 43	47	59	−3 56	48	58	−3 08	48	58	−2 20	47	57	−1 33	48	56	−0 45	48	56	00 03	47	55	00 50	48	55	01 38	48	54	02 26	47	53	03 13	48	53	04 01	47	52	04 48	48	51	243
118				−6 06	48	59	−5 18	48	58	−4 30	48	57	−3 42	48	57	−2 54	47	56	−2 07	48	55	−1 19	48	55	−0 31	48	54	00 17	48	54	01 05	48	53	01 53	48	53	02 41	48	52	03 29	47	51	04 16	48	51	242
119							−5 53	48	57	−5 05	49	56	−4 16	48	56	−3 28	48	55	−2 40	48	55	−1 52	48	54	−1 04	48	54	−0 16	48	53	00 32	49	53	01 21	48	52	02 09	48	51	02 57	48	51	03 45	48	50	241
120										−5 39	+49	56	−4 50	+48	55	−4 02	+49	55	−3 13	+48	54	−2 25	+48	53	−1 37	+49	53	−0 48	+48	52	00 00	+49	52	00 49	+48	51	01 37	+48	51	02 25	+49	50	03 14	+48	49	240
121													−5 24	49	54	−4 35	49	54	−3 46	48	53	−2 58	49	53	−2 09	48	52	−1 21	49	52	−0 32	49	51	00 17	49	50	01 06	48	50	01 54	49	49	02 43	48	49	239
122													−5 57	49	54	−5 08	49	53	−4 19	49	53	−3 30	49	52	−2 41	49	51	−1 52	49	51	−1 03	48	50	−0 15	49	50	00 34	49	49	01 23	49	49	02 12	49	48	238
123																−5 41	50	52	−4 51	49	52	−4 02	49	51	−3 13	49	51	−2 24	49	50	−1 35	49	49	−0 46	50	49	00 04	49	48	00 53	49	48	01 42	49	47	237
124																			−5 23	49	51	−4 34	49	50	−3 45	50	50	−2 55	49	49	−2 06	50	49	−1 16	49	48	−0 27	50	48	00 23	49	47	01 12	50	46	236
125																			−5 55	+50	50	−5 05	+49	50	−4 16	+50	49	−3 26	+50	49	−2 36	+49	48	−1 47	+50	47	−0 57	+50	47	−0 07	+50	46	00 43	+50	46	235
126																						−5 36	50	49	−4 46	49	48	−3 57	50	48	−3 07	51	47	−2 16	50	47	−1 26	50	46	−0 36	50	46	00 14	50	45	234
127																									−5 17	50	48	−4 27	51	47	−3 36	50	46	−2 46	50	46	−1 56	51	45	−1 05	50	45	−0 15	50	44	233
128																									−5 47	51	47	−4 56	50	46	−4 06	51	46	−3 15	50	45	−2 25	51	45	−1 34	50	44	−0 44	51	44	232
129																												−5 26	51	45	−4 35	51	45	−3 44	51	44	−2 53	51	44	−2 02	50	43	−1 12	51	43	231
130																												−5 55	+51	45	−5 04	+51	44	−4 13	+52	44	−3 21	+51	43	−2 30	+51	43	−1 39	+51	42	230
131																															−5 32	51	43	−4 41	52	43	−3 49	51	42	−2 58	52	42	−2 06	51	41	229
132																																		−5 08	51	42	−4 17	52	42	−3 25	52	41	−2 33	51	41	228
133																																		−5 36	52	41	−4 44	52	41	−3 52	52	40	−3 00	52	40	227
134																																					−5 10	52	40	−4 18	52	40	−3 26	53	39	226
135																																					−5 36	+52	39	−4 44	+53	39	−3 51	+53	38	225
136																																								−5 09	53	38	−4 16	53	38	224
137																																								−5 34	53	37	−4 41	53	37	223
138																																											−5 05	53	36	222
139																																											−5 29	53	35	221

LHA	15° Hc	d	Z	16° Hc	d	Z	17° Hc	d	Z	18° Hc	d	Z	19° Hc	d	Z	20° Hc	d	Z	21° Hc	d	Z	22° Hc	d	Z	23° Hc	d	Z	24° Hc	d	Z	25° Hc	d	Z	26° Hc	d	Z
83	−6 16	43	105	277																																
82	−5 36	44	106	278																																
81	−4 57	44	107	−5 41	44	107	279																													
80	−4 18	−44	107	−5 02	−44	108	−5 46	−45	109	280																										
79	−3 39	44	108	−4 23	45	109	−5 08	44	109	−5 52	44	110	281																							
78	−3 00	45	109	−3 45	44	110	−4 29	45	110	−5 14	44	111	−5 58	45	112	282																				
77	−2 21	45	110	−3 06	45	110	−3 51	45	111	−4 36	44	112	−5 20	45	112	−6 05	45	113	283																	
76	−1 43	45	110	−2 28	45	111	−3 13	45	112	−3 58	45	112	−4 43	44	113	−5 27	45	114	−6 12	45	114	284														
75	−1 05	−45	111	−1 50	−45	112	−2 35	−46	112	−3 21	−44	113	−4 05	−45	114	−4 50	−45	114	−5 35	−45	115	285														
74	−0 27	45	112	−1 12	45	112	−1 57	45	113	−2 42	46	114	−3 28	45	114	−4 13	45	115	−4 58	45	116	−5 43	45	116	286											
73	00 11	45	113	−0 34	46	113	−1 20	45	114	−2 05	45	114	−2 50	46	115	−3 36	45	116	−4 21	46	116	−5 07	45	117	−5 52	45	118	287								
72	00 49	46	113	00 03	45	114	−0 42	46	115	−1 28	46	115	−2 14	45	116	−2 59	46	116	−3 45	45	117	−4 30	46	118	−5 16	45	118	−6 01	46	119	288					
71	01 27	46	114	00 41	46	115	−0 05	46	115	−0 51	46	116	−1 37	46	117	−2 23	45	117	−3 08	46	118	−3 54	46	119	−4 40	46	119	−5 26	46	120	289					
70	02 04	−46	115	01 18	−46	115	00 32	−46	116	−0 14	−46	117	−1 00	−46	117	−1 46	−46	118	−2 32	−46	119	−3 18	−46	119	−4 04	−46	120	−4 50	−46	121	−5 36	−46	121	290		

S. Lat. {LHA greater than 180°........ Zn=180−Z
{LHA less than 180°.............. Zn=180+Z

DECLINATION (15°-29°) CONTRARY NAME TO LATITUDE

N. Lat. {LHA greater than 180°....... Zn=Z; LHA less than 180°.......... Zn=360−Z}

DECLINATION (15°-29°) CONTRARY NAME TO LATITUDE

LHA	15° Hc	15° d	15° Z	16° Hc	16° d	16° Z	17° Hc	17° d	17° Z	18° Hc	18° d	18° Z	19° Hc	19° d	19° Z
	° ′	′	°	° ′	′	°	° ′	′	°	° ′	′	°	° ′	′	°
69	02 41	46	115	01 55	47	116	01 08	46	117	00 22	46	117	−0 24	46	118
68	03 18	47	116	02 31	46	117	01 45	47	118	00 58	46	118	00 12	47	119
67	03 54	46	117	03 08	47	118	02 21	47	118	01 34	46	119	00 48	47	119
66	04 31	47	118	03 44	47	118	02 57	47	119	02 10	47	120	01 23	47	120
65	05 07	−47	119	04 20	−47	119	03 33	−48	120	02 45	−47	120	01 58	−47	121
64	05 43	48	119	04 55	47	120	04 08	47	120	03 21	48	121	02 33	47	122
63	06 18	47	120	05 31	48	121	04 43	47	121	03 56	48	122	03 08	48	122
62	06 54	48	121	06 06	48	121	05 18	48	122	04 30	48	123	03 42	48	123
61	07 29	48	122	06 41	48	122	05 53	48	123	05 05	49	124	04 16	48	124
60	08 03	−48	122	07 15	−48	123	06 27	−48	124	05 39	−49	124	04 50	−48	125
59	08 38	49	123	07 49	48	124	07 01	49	124	06 12	48	125	05 24	49	126
58	09 12	49	124	08 23	49	125	07 34	48	125	06 46	49	126	05 57	49	126
57	09 46	49	125	08 57	49	125	08 08	49	126	07 19	49	127	06 30	49	127
56	10 19	49	126	09 30	49	126	08 41	50	127	07 51	49	127	07 02	49	128
55	10 52	−49	126	10 03	−50	127	09 13	−49	128	08 24	−50	128	07 34	−49	129
54	11 25	50	127	10 35	49	128	09 46	50	128	08 56	50	129	08 06	50	129
53	11 57	49	128	11 08	50	129	10 18	50	129	09 28	50	130	08 38	51	130
52	12 30	51	129	11 39	50	129	10 49	50	130	09 59	50	131	09 09	51	131
51	13 01	50	130	12 11	51	130	11 20	50	131	10 30	51	131	09 39	50	132
50	13 33	−51	130	12 42	−51	131	11 51	−51	132	11 00	−50	132	10 10	−51	133
49	14 04	51	131	13 13	51	132	12 22	51	132	11 31	51	133	10 40	52	133
48	14 34	51	132	13 43	51	133	12 52	52	133	12 00	51	134	11 09	51	134
47	15 04	51	133	14 13	52	134	13 21	51	134	12 30	52	135	11 38	52	135
46	15 34	52	134	14 42	51	134	13 51	52	135	12 59	52	135	12 07	52	136
45	16 03	−52	135	15 11	−52	135	14 19	−52	136	13 27	−52	136	12 35	−52	137
44	16 32	52	136	15 40	52	136	14 48	53	137	13 55	52	137	13 03	53	138
43	17 01	53	137	16 08	52	137	15 16	53	138	14 23	53	138	13 30	52	139
42	17 28	52	137	16 36	53	138	15 43	53	138	14 50	53	139	13 57	53	139
41	17 56	53	138	17 03	53	139	16 10	53	139	15 17	53	140	14 24	54	140
40	18 23	−53	139	17 30	−54	140	16 36	−53	140	15 43	−53	141	14 50	−54	141
39	18 49	53	140	17 56	54	141	17 02	53	141	16 09	54	142	15 15	54	142
38	19 16	54	141	18 22	54	141	17 28	54	142	16 34	54	142	15 40	54	143
37	19 41	54	142	18 47	54	142	17 53	54	143	16 59	54	143	16 05	55	144
36	20 06	54	143	19 12	55	143	18 17	54	144	17 23	55	144	16 28	54	145
35	20 31	−55	144	19 36	−55	144	18 41	−54	145	17 47	−55	145	16 52	−55	146
34	20 54	54	145	20 00	55	145	19 05	55	146	18 10	55	146	17 15	55	146
33	21 18	55	146	20 23	55	146	19 28	56	147	18 32	55	147	17 37	55	147
32	21 41	56	147	20 45	55	147	19 50	55	147	18 55	56	148	17 59	55	148
31	22 03	56	148	21 07	55	148	20 12	56	148	19 16	56	149	18 20	55	149
30	22 25	−56	149	21 29	−56	149	20 33	−56	149	19 37	−56	150	18 41	−56	150
29	22 46	56	150	21 50	56	150	20 54	57	150	19 57	56	151	19 01	56	151
28	23 06	56	151	22 10	56	151	21 14	57	151	20 17	56	152	19 21	57	152
27	23 26	56	151	22 30	57	152	21 33	57	152	20 36	56	153	19 40	57	153
26	23 45	56	152	22 49	57	153	21 52	57	153	20 55	57	154	19 58	57	154
25	24 04	−57	153	23 07	−57	154	22 10	−57	154	21 13	−57	155	20 16	−57	155
24	24 22	57	155	23 25	58	155	22 27	57	155	21 30	57	155	20 33	57	156
23	24 39	57	156	23 42	58	156	22 44	57	156	21 47	58	156	20 49	57	157
22	24 56	58	157	23 58	57	157	23 01	58	157	22 03	58	157	21 05	57	158
21	25 12	58	158	24 14	58	158	23 16	58	158	22 18	58	158	21 20	57	159
20	25 27	−58	159	24 29	−58	159	23 31	−58	159	22 33	−58	159	21 35	−58	160
19	25 42	58	160	24 44	59	160	23 45	58	160	22 47	58	160	21 49	58	161
18	25 56	59	161	24 57	58	161	23 59	58	161	23 01	59	161	22 02	58	162
17	26 09	59	162	25 10	58	162	24 12	59	162	23 13	58	162	22 15	59	163
16	26 21	58	163	25 23	59	163	24 24	59	163	23 25	58	163	22 27	59	164
15	26 33	−59	164	25 34	−58	164	24 36	−59	164	23 37	−59	164	22 38	−59	165
14	26 44	59	165	25 45	59	165	24 46	59	165	23 47	59	165	22 48	59	166
13	26 55	59	166	25 56	60	166	24 56	59	166	23 57	59	167	22 58	59	167
12	27 04	59	167	26 05	59	167	25 06	60	167	24 06	59	168	23 07	59	168
11	27 13	59	168	26 14	60	168	25 14	59	168	24 15	59	169	23 16	60	169
10	27 21	−59	169	26 22	−60	169	25 22	−59	169	24 23	−60	170	23 23	−59	170
9	27 29	60	170	26 29	60	170	25 29	59	171	24 30	60	171	23 30	59	171
8	27 35	60	171	26 35	59	171	25 36	60	172	24 36	60	172	23 36	59	172
7	27 41	60	172	26 41	60	173	25 41	59	173	24 42	60	173	23 42	60	173
6	27 46	60	173	26 46	60	174	25 46	59	174	24 47	60	174	23 47	60	174
5	27 50	−60	175	26 50	−59	175	25 51	−60	175	24 51	−60	175	23 51	−60	175
4	27 54	60	176	26 54	60	176	25 54	60	176	24 54	60	176	23 54	60	176
3	27 57	60	177	26 57	60	177	25 57	60	177	24 57	60	177	23 57	60	177
2	27 58	59	178	26 59	60	178	25 59	60	178	24 59	60	178	23 59	60	178
1	28 00	60	179	27 00	60	179	26 00	60	179	25 00	60	179	24 00	60	179
0	28 00	−60	180	27 00	−60	180	26 00	−60	180	25 00	−60	180	24 00	−60	180

LHA	20° Hc	20° d	20° Z	21° Hc	21° d	21° Z	22° Hc	22° d	22° Z	23° Hc	23° d	23° Z	24° Hc	24° d	24° Z
	° ′	′	°	° ′	′	°	° ′	′	°	° ′	′	°	° ′	′	°
69	−1 10	47	119	−1 57	46	119	−2 43	46	120	−3 29	46	121	−4 15	47	121
68	−0 35	46	119	−1 21	47	120	−2 08	46	121	−2 54	46	121	−3 40	47	122
67	00 01	47	120	−0 46	46	121	−1 32	47	121	−2 19	47	122	−3 06	46	123
66	00 36	47	121	−0 11	47	121	−0 58	47	122	−1 45	47	123	−2 32	46	123
65	01 11	−47	122	00 24	−47	122	−0 23	−47	123	−1 10	−47	123	−1 57	−48	124
64	01 46	47	122	00 59	48	123	00 11	47	124	−0 36	48	124	−1 24	47	125
63	02 20	47	123	01 33	48	124	00 45	48	124	−0 03	47	125	−0 50	48	125
62	02 54	47	124	02 07	48	124	01 19	48	125	00 31	48	126	−0 17	48	126
61	03 28	48	125	02 40	48	125	01 52	48	126	01 04	48	126	00 16	48	127
60	04 02	−49	125	03 13	−48	126	02 25	−48	127	01 37	−49	127	00 48	−48	128
59	04 35	49	126	03 46	48	127	02 58	49	127	02 09	48	128	01 21	49	128
58	05 08	49	127	04 19	49	127	03 30	49	128	02 41	49	129	01 52	49	129
57	05 41	50	128	04 51	49	128	04 02	49	129	03 13	49	129	02 24	49	130
56	06 13	50	128	05 23	49	129	04 34	49	130	03 45	50	130	02 55	49	131
55	06 45	−50	129	05 55	−50	130	05 05	−49	130	04 16	−50	131	03 26	−50	131
54	07 16	50	130	06 26	50	131	05 36	50	131	04 46	49	132	03 57	50	132
53	07 47	50	131	06 57	50	131	06 07	50	132	05 17	50	132	04 27	51	133
52	08 18	50	132	07 28	51	132	06 37	50	133	05 47	51	133	04 56	50	134
51	08 49	51	132	07 58	51	133	07 07	50	133	06 17	51	134	05 26	51	135
50	09 19	−51	133	08 28	−51	134	07 37	−51	134	06 46	−51	135	05 55	−51	135
49	09 48	51	134	08 57	51	135	08 06	51	135	07 15	52	136	06 23	51	136
48	10 18	52	135	09 26	51	135	08 35	52	136	07 43	51	136	06 52	52	137
47	10 46	51	136	09 55	52	136	09 03	52	137	08 11	52	137	07 19	52	138
46	11 15	52	136	10 23	52	137	09 31	52	137	08 39	52	138	07 47	52	139
45	11 43	−52	137	10 51	−53	138	09 58	−52	138	09 06	−52	139	08 14	−53	139
44	12 10	52	138	11 18	53	139	10 25	52	139	09 33	53	140	08 40	53	140
43	12 38	53	139	11 45	53	139	10 52	53	140	09 59	53	140	09 06	53	141
42	13 04	53	140	12 11	53	140	11 18	53	141	10 25	53	141	09 32	53	142
41	13 30	53	141	12 37	53	141	11 44	54	142	10 50	53	142	09 57	54	143
40	13 56	−53	142	13 03	−54	142	12 09	−54	142	11 15	−53	143	10 22	−54	143
39	14 21	54	142	13 27	53	143	12 34	54	143	11 40	54	144	10 46	54	144
38	14 46	54	143	13 52	54	144	12 58	54	144	12 04	55	145	11 09	54	145
37	15 10	54	144	14 16	54	145	13 22	55	145	12 27	54	145	11 33	55	146
36	15 34	55	145	14 39	54	145	13 45	55	146	12 50	55	146	11 55	54	147
35	15 57	−55	146	15 02	−55	146	14 07	−54	147	13 13	−55	147	12 18	−55	148
34	16 20	55	147	15 25	55	147	14 30	56	148	13 34	55	148	12 39	55	148
33	16 42	55	148	15 47	56	148	14 51	55	149	13 56	56	149	13 00	55	149
32	17 04	56	149	16 08	56	149	15 12	55	149	14 17	56	150	13 21	56	150
31	17 25	56	150	16 29	56	150	15 33	56	150	14 37	56	151	13 41	56	151
30	17 45	−56	150	16 49	−56	151	15 53	−56	151	14 57	−56	152	14 01	−57	152
29	18 05	56	151	17 09	57	152	16 12	56	152	15 16	56	152	14 20	57	153
28	18 24	56	152	17 28	57	153	16 31	56	153	15 35	57	153	14 38	57	154
27	18 43	57	153	17 46	56	154	16 50	57	154	15 53	57	154	14 56	57	155
26	19 01	57	154	18 04	57	155	17 07	57	155	16 10	57	155	15 13	57	156
25	19 19	−57	155	18 22	−58	155	17 24	−57	156	16 27	−57	156	15 30	−57	156
24	19 36	58	156	18 38	57	156	17 41	58	157	16 43	57	157	15 46	57	157
23	19 52	58	157	18 54	57	157	17 57	58	158	16 59	58	158	16 01	57	158
22	20 08	58	158	19 10	58	158	18 12	58	159	17 14	58	159	16 16	57	159
21	20 23	58	159	19 25	58	159	18 27	58	160	17 29	58	160	16 31	58	160
20	20 37	−58	160	19 39	−58	160	18 41	−58	160	17 43	−59	161	16 44	−58	161
19	20 51	59	161	19 52	58	161	18 54	58	161	17 56	59	162	16 57	58	162
18	21 04	59	162	20 05	58	162	19 07	59	162	18 08	58	163	17 10	59	163
17	21 16	58	163	20 18	59	163	19 19	59	163	18 20	58	164	17 22	59	164
16	21 28	59	164	20 29	59	164	19 30	59	164	18 31	58	165	17 33	59	165
15	21 39	−59	165	20 40	−59	165	19 41	−59	165	18 42	−59	165	17 43	−59	166
14	21 49	59	166	20 50	59	166	19 51	59	166	18 52	59	166	17 53	59	167
13	21 59	59	167	21 00	59	167	20 01	60	167	19 01	59	167	18 02	59	168
12	22 08	59	168	21 09	60	168	20 09	59	168	19 10	59	168	18 11	60	169
11	22 16	59	169	21 17	60	169	20 17	59	169	19 18	59	169	18 19	60	169
10	22 24	−60	170	21 24	−59	170	20 25	−60	170	19 25	−59	170	18 26	−60	170
9	22 31	60	171	21 31	60	171	20 31	59	171	19 32	60	171	18 32	59	171
8	22 37	60	172	21 37	60	172	20 37	59	172	19 38	60	172	18 38	60	172
7	22 42	60	173	21 42	59	173	20 43	60	173	19 43	60	173	18 43	60	173
6	22 47	60	174	21 47	60	174	20 47	60	174	19 47	59	174	18 48	60	174
5	22 51	−60	175	21 51	−60	175	20 51	−60	175	19 51	−60	175	18 51	−59	175
4	22 54	60	176	21 54	60	176	20 54	60	176	19 54	59	176	18 55	60	176
3	22 57	60	177	21 57	60	177	20 57	60	177	19 57	60	177	18 57	60	177
2	22 59	60	178	21 59	60	178	20 59	60	178	19 59	60	178	18 59	60	178
1	23 00	60	179	22 00	60	179	21 00	60	179	20 00	60	179	19 00	60	179
0	23 00	−60	180	22 00	−60	180	21 00	−60	180	20 00	−60	180	19 00	−60	180

LHA	25° Hc	25° d	25° Z	26° Hc	26° d	26° Z	27° Hc	27° d	27° Z	28° Hc	28° d	28° Z	29° Hc	29° d	29° Z	LHA
	° ′	′	°	° ′	′	°	° ′	′	°	° ′	′	°	° ′	′	°	
69	−5 02	46	122	−5 48	46	122	291									
68	−4 27	46	123	−5 13	47	123	−6 00	46	124	292						
67	−3 52	47	123	−4 39	47	124	−5 26	46	124	293						
66	−3 18	47	124	−4 05	47	125	−4 52	47	125	−5 39	47	126	294			
65	−2 45	−47	125	−3 32	−47	125	−4 19	−47	126	−5 06	−47	126	−5 53	−47	127	295
64	−2 11	47	125	−2 58	48	126	−3 46	47	127	−4 33	48	127	−5 21	47	128	296
63	−1 38	48	126	−2 26	47	127	−3 13	48	127	−4 01	47	128	−4 48	48	129	297
62	−1 05	48	127	−1 53	48	127	−2 41	48	128	−3 29	47	129	−4 16	48	129	298
61	−0 32	49	128	−1 21	48	128	−2 09	48	129	−2 57	48	129	−3 45	48	130	299
60	00 00	−49	128	−0 49	−48	129	−1 37	−48	129	−2 25	−49	130	−3 14	−48	131	300
59	00 32	49	129	−0 17	49	130	−1 06	48	130	−1 54	49	131	−2 43	48	131	301
58	01 03	48	130	00 15	49	130	−0 34	49	131	−1 23	49	131	−2 12	49	132	302
57	01 35	49	131	00 46	50	131	−0 04	49	132	−0 53	49	132	−1 42	49	133	303
56	02 06	50	131	01 16	49	132	00 27	50	132	−0 23	49	133	−1 12	50	134	304
55	02 36	−49	132	01 47	−50	133	00 57	−50	133	00 07	−50	134	−0 43	−50	134	305
54	03 07	51	133	02 16	50	133	01 26	50	134	00 36	50	134	−0 14	50	135	306
53	03 36	50	134	02 46	50	134	01 56	51	135	01 05	50	135	00 15	50	136	307
52	04 06	51	134	03 15	50	135	02 25	51	135	01 34	50	136	00 44	51	136	308
51	04 35	51	135	03 44	51	136	02 53	51	136	02 02	50	137	01 12	51	137	309
50	05 04	−51	136	04 13	−52	136	03 21	−51	137	02 30	−51	137	01 39	−51	138	310
49	05 32	51	137	04 41	52	137	03 49	51	138	02 58	52	138	02 06	51	139	311
48	06 00	52	137	05 08	51	138	04 17	52	138	03 25	52	139	02 33	51	139	312
47	06 27	51	138	05 36	52	139	04 44	52	139	03 52	52	140	03 00	52	140	313
46	06 55	53	139	06 02	52	139	05 10	52	140	04 18	52	140	03 26	53	141	314
45	07 21	−52	140	06 29	−53	140	05 36	−52	141	04 44	−53	141	03 51	−53	142	315
44	07 47	52	141	06 55	53	141	06 02	53	142	05 09	53	142	04 16	53	142	316
43	08 13	53	141	07 20	53	142	06 27	53	142	05 34	53	143	04 41	53	143	317
42	08 39	54	142	07 45	53	143	06 52	53	143	05 59	54	144	05 05	53	144	318
41	09 03	53	143	08 10	54	143	07 16	53	144	06 23	54	144	05 29	53	145	319
40	09 28	−54	144	08 34	−54	144	07 40	−54	145	06 46	−53	145	05 53	−54	146	320
39	09 52	54	145	08 58	54	145	08 04	54	146	07 10	55	146	06 15	54	146	321
38	10 15	54	146	09 21	54	146	08 27	55	146	07 32	54	147	06 38	54	147	322
37	10 38	54	146	09 44	55	147	08 49	55	147	07 54	54	148	07 00	55	148	323
36	11 01	55	147	10 06	55	148	09 11	55	148	08 16	55	148	07 21	55	149	324
35	11 23	−55	148	10 28	−56	148	09 32	−55	149	08 37	−55	149	07 42	−55	150	325
34	11 44	55	149	10 49	56	149	09 53	55	150	08 58	55	150	08 03	56	150	326
33	12 05	56	150	11 09	55	150	10 14	56	151	09 18	55	151	08 23	56	151	327
32	12 25	55	151	11 30	56	151	10 34	56	151	09 38	56	152	08 42	56	152	328
31	12 45	56	151	11 49	56	152	10 53	56	152	09 57	56	153	09 01	56	153	329
30	13 04	−56	152	12 08	−56	153	11 12	−56	153	10 16	−57	153	09 19	−56	154	330
29	13 23	56	153	12 27	57	154	11 30	56	154	10 34	57	154	09 37	56	155	331
28	13 41	56	154	12 45	57	154	11 48	57	155	10 51	56	155	09 55	57	155	332
27	13 59	57	155	13 02	57	155	12 05	57	156	11 08	57	156	10 11	57	156	333
26	14 16	57	156	13 19	57	156	12 22	57	156	11 25	57	157	10 28	58	157	334
25	14 33	−58	157	13 35	−57	157	12 38	−57	157	11 41	−58	158	10 43	−57	158	335
24	14 49	58	158	13 51	57	158	12 54	58	158	11 56	58	159	10 58	57	159	336
23	15 04	58	159	14 06	58	159	13 08	57	159	12 11	58	159	11 13	58	160	337
22	15 19	58	159	14 21	58	160	13 23	58	160	12 25	58	160	11 27	58	161	338
21	15 33	58	160	14 35	58	161	13 37	59	161	12 38	58	161	11 40	58	161	339
20	15 46	−58	161	14 48	−58	162	13 50	−59	162	12 51	−58	162	11 53	−58	162	340
19	15 59	58	162	15 01	59	162	14 02	58	163	13 04	59	163	12 05	58	163	341
18	16 11	58	163	15 13	59	163	14 14	58	164	13 16	59	164	12 17	59	164	342
17	16 23	59	164	15 24	59	164	14 25	58	164	13 27	59	165	12 28	59	165	343
16	16 34	59	165	15 35	59	165	14 36	59	165	13 37	59	166	12 38	58	166	344
15	16 44	−59	166	15 45	−59	166	14 46	−59	166	13 47	−59	166	12 48	−59	167	345
14	16 54	59	167	15 55	59	167	14 56	59	167	13 57	60	167	12 57	59	168	346
13	17 03	59	168	16 04	60	168	15 04	59	168	14 05	59	168	13 06	59	168	347
12	17 11	59	169	16 12	59	169	15 13	60	169	14 13	59	169	13 14	59	169	348
11	17 19	59	170	16 20	60	170	15 20	59	170	14 21	60	170	13 21	59	170	349
10	17 26	−59	171	16 27	−60	171	15 27	−59	171	14 28	−60	171	13 28	−60	171	350
9	17 33	60	171	16 33	60	172	15 33	59	172	14 34	60	172	13 34	60	172	351
8	17 38	59	172	16 39	60	173	15 39	60	173	14 39	60	173	13 39	59	173	352
7	17 43	59	173	16 44	60	173	15 44	60	174	14 44	60	174	13 44	59	174	353
6	17 48	60	174	16 48	60	174	15 48	60	174	14 48	60	175	13 48	59	175	354
5	17 52	−60	175	16 52	−60	175	15 52	−60	175	14 52	−60	175	13 52	−60	176	355
4	17 55	60	176	16 55	60	176	15 55	60	176	14 55	60	176	13 55	60	176	356
3	17 57	60	177	16 57	60	177	15 57	60	177	14 57	60	177	13 57	60	177	357
2	17 59	60	178	16 59	60	178	15 59	60	178	14 59	60	178	13 59	60	178	358
1	18 00	60	179	17 00	60	179	16 00	60	179	15 00	60	179	14 00	60	179	359
0	18 00	−60	180	17 00	−60	180	16 00	−60	180	15 00	−60	180	14 00	−60	180	360

S. Lat. {LHA greater than 180°....... Zn=180−Z; LHA less than 180°.......... Zn=180+Z}

DECLINATION (15°-29°) CONTRARY NAME TO LATITUDE

N. Lat. {LHA greater than 180°....... Zn=Z; LHA less than 180°........... Zn=360−Z}

DECLINATION (0°-14°) SAME NAME AS LATITUDE

LAT 48°

LHA	0° Hc	0° d	0° Z	1° Hc	1° d	1° Z	2° Hc	2° d	2° Z	3° Hc	3° d	3° Z	4° Hc	4° d	4° Z	LHA
	° ′	′	°	° ′	′	°	° ′	′	°	° ′	′	°	° ′	′	°	
0	42 00	+60	180	43 00	+60	180	44 00	+60	180	45 00	+60	180	46 00	+60	180	360
1	42 00	60	179	43 00	60	179	44 00	60	179	45 00	60	179	46 00	60	179	359
2	41 58	60	177	42 58	60	177	43 58	60	177	44 58	60	177	45 58	60	177	358
3	41 56	60	176	42 56	60	176	43 56	60	176	44 56	60	176	45 56	59	176	357
4	41 53	59	175	42 52	60	175	43 52	60	175	44 52	60	174	45 52	60	174	356
5	41 48	+60	173	42 48	+60	173	43 48	+60	173	44 48	+60	173	45 48	+59	173	355
6	41 43	60	172	42 43	60	172	43 43	59	172	44 42	60	172	45 42	60	171	354
7	41 37	60	171	42 37	59	171	43 36	60	170	44 36	60	170	45 36	59	170	353
8	41 30	60	169	42 30	59	169	43 29	60	169	44 29	59	169	45 28	60	169	352
9	41 22	60	168	42 22	59	168	43 21	59	168	44 20	60	167	45 20	59	167	351
10	41 13	+60	167	42 13	+59	166	43 12	+59	166	44 11	+59	166	45 10	+59	166	350
11	41 04	59	165	42 03	59	165	43 02	59	165	44 01	59	165	45 00	59	164	349
12	40 53	59	164	41 52	59	164	42 51	59	164	43 50	59	163	44 49	58	163	348
13	40 42	58	163	41 40	59	163	42 39	59	162	43 38	58	162	44 36	59	162	347
14	40 29	59	162	41 28	58	161	42 26	59	161	43 25	58	161	44 23	59	160	346
15	40 16	+58	160	41 14	+59	160	42 13	+58	160	43 11	+58	159	44 09	+59	159	345
16	40 02	58	159	41 00	58	159	41 58	58	158	42 56	58	158	43 54	58	158	344
17	39 47	58	158	40 45	58	157	41 43	58	157	42 41	58	157	43 39	57	156	343
18	39 31	58	156	40 29	58	156	41 27	58	156	42 25	57	155	43 22	58	155	342
19	39 15	57	155	40 12	58	155	41 10	57	154	42 07	58	154	43 05	57	154	341
20	38 58	+57	154	39 55	+57	154	40 52	+57	153	41 49	+57	153	42 46	+57	152	340
21	38 40	57	153	39 37	57	152	40 34	57	152	41 31	56	152	42 27	57	151	339
22	38 21	57	152	39 18	56	151	40 14	57	151	41 11	56	150	42 07	57	150	338
23	38 01	57	150	38 58	56	150	39 54	57	149	40 51	56	149	41 47	56	149	337
24	37 41	56	149	38 37	56	149	39 33	57	148	40 30	56	148	41 26	55	147	336
25	37 20	+56	148	38 16	+56	147	39 12	+56	147	40 08	+55	147	41 03	+56	146	335
26	36 58	56	147	37 54	56	146	38 50	55	146	39 45	56	145	40 41	55	145	334
27	36 36	55	146	37 31	56	145	38 27	55	145	39 22	55	144	40 17	55	144	333
28	36 13	55	144	37 08	55	144	38 03	55	143	38 58	55	143	39 53	55	142	332
29	35 49	55	143	36 44	55	143	37 39	55	142	38 34	54	142	39 28	55	141	331
30	35 25	+55	142	36 20	+54	142	37 14	+54	141	38 08	+55	141	39 03	+54	140	330
31	35 00	54	141	35 54	55	141	36 49	54	140	37 43	54	139	38 37	53	139	329
32	34 34	55	140	35 29	53	139	36 22	54	139	37 16	54	138	38 10	53	138	328
33	34 08	54	139	35 02	54	138	35 56	53	138	36 49	54	137	37 43	53	137	327
34	33 42	53	138	34 35	53	137	35 28	54	137	36 22	53	136	37 15	53	136	326
35	33 14	+54	137	34 08	+53	136	35 01	+53	136	35 54	+52	135	36 46	+53	134	325
36	32 47	52	136	33 39	53	135	34 32	53	135	35 25	52	134	36 17	53	133	324
37	32 18	53	135	33 11	52	134	34 03	53	134	34 56	52	133	35 48	52	132	323
38	31 49	53	134	32 42	52	133	33 34	52	132	34 26	52	132	35 18	52	131	322
39	31 20	52	133	32 12	52	132	33 04	52	131	33 56	52	131	34 48	51	130	321
40	30 50	+52	132	31 42	+52	131	32 34	+51	130	33 25	+52	130	34 17	+51	129	320
41	30 20	52	131	31 12	51	130	32 03	51	129	32 54	51	129	33 45	51	128	319
42	29 49	51	130	30 40	52	129	31 32	51	128	32 23	50	128	33 13	51	127	318
43	29 18	51	129	30 09	51	128	31 00	51	127	31 51	50	127	32 41	50	126	317
44	28 46	51	128	29 37	51	127	30 28	50	126	31 18	50	126	32 08	51	125	316
45	28 14	+51	127	29 05	+50	126	29 55	+50	125	30 45	+50	125	31 35	+50	124	315
46	27 42	50	126	28 32	50	125	29 22	50	124	30 12	50	124	31 02	50	123	314
47	27 09	50	125	27 59	50	124	28 49	50	124	29 39	49	123	30 28	49	122	313
48	26 36	50	124	27 26	49	123	28 15	50	123	29 05	49	122	29 54	49	121	312
49	26 02	50	123	26 52	49	122	27 41	50	122	28 31	49	121	29 20	48	120	311
50	25 29	+49	122	26 18	+49	121	27 07	+49	121	27 56	+49	120	28 45	+48	119	310
51	24 54	49	121	25 43	49	120	26 32	49	120	27 21	49	119	28 10	48	118	309
52	24 20	49	120	25 09	48	120	25 57	49	119	26 46	48	118	27 34	48	118	308
53	23 45	48	119	24 33	49	119	25 22	48	118	26 10	48	117	26 58	48	117	307
54	23 10	48	118	23 58	48	118	24 46	48	117	25 34	48	116	26 22	48	116	306
55	22 34	+48	118	23 22	+48	117	24 10	+48	116	24 58	+48	116	25 46	+48	115	305
56	21 58	48	117	22 46	48	116	23 34	48	115	24 22	47	115	25 09	48	114	304
57	21 22	48	116	22 10	48	115	22 58	47	115	23 45	48	114	24 33	47	113	303
58	20 46	48	115	21 34	47	114	22 21	47	114	23 08	48	113	23 56	47	112	302
59	20 10	47	114	20 57	47	113	21 44	47	113	22 31	47	112	23 18	47	111	301
60	19 33	+47	113	20 20	+47	113	21 07	+47	112	21 54	+47	111	22 41	+46	111	300
61	18 56	47	112	19 43	47	112	20 30	47	111	21 17	46	110	22 03	47	110	299
62	18 19	46	112	19 05	47	111	19 52	47	110	20 39	46	110	21 25	47	109	298
63	17 41	47	111	18 28	46	110	19 14	47	109	20 01	46	109	20 47	46	108	297
64	17 03	47	110	17 50	47	109	18 37	46	109	19 23	46	108	20 09	46	107	296
65	16 26	+46	109	17 12	+46	109	17 58	+47	108	18 45	+46	107	19 31	+45	106	295
66	15 48	46	108	16 34	46	108	17 20	46	107	18 06	46	106	18 52	46	106	294
67	15 09	47	108	15 56	46	107	16 42	45	106	17 27	46	106	18 13	46	105	293
68	14 31	46	107	15 17	46	106	16 03	46	105	16 49	45	105	17 34	46	104	292
69	13 53	45	106	14 38	46	105	15 24	46	105	16 10	45	104	16 55	46	103	291

LHA	5° Hc	5° d	5° Z	6° Hc	6° d	6° Z	7° Hc	7° d	7° Z	8° Hc	8° d	8° Z	9° Hc	9° d	9° Z	LHA
	° ′	′	°	° ′	′	°	° ′	′	°	° ′	′	°	° ′	′	°	
0	47 00	+60	180	48 00	+60	180	49 00	+60	180	50 00	+60	180	51 00	+60	180	360
1	47 00	60	179	48 00	60	179	49 00	60	179	50 00	60	179	51 00	59	178	359
2	46 58	60	177	47 58	60	177	48 58	60	177	49 58	60	177	50 58	60	177	358
3	46 55	60	176	47 55	60	176	48 55	60	176	49 55	60	175	50 55	60	175	357
4	46 52	60	174	47 52	60	174	48 52	59	174	49 51	60	174	50 51	60	174	356
5	46 47	+60	173	47 47	+60	173	48 47	+60	173	49 47	+59	172	50 46	+60	172	355
6	46 42	59	171	47 41	60	171	48 41	60	171	49 41	59	171	50 40	60	171	354
7	46 35	60	170	47 35	59	170	48 34	60	170	49 34	59	169	50 33	60	169	353
8	46 28	59	168	47 27	59	168	48 26	60	168	49 26	59	168	50 25	59	168	352
9	46 19	59	167	47 18	60	167	48 18	59	167	49 17	59	166	50 16	59	166	351
10	46 09	+60	166	47 09	+59	165	48 08	+59	165	49 07	+59	165	50 06	+59	165	350
11	45 59	59	164	46 58	59	164	47 57	59	164	48 56	58	163	49 54	59	163	349
12	45 47	59	163	46 46	59	162	47 45	59	162	48 44	58	162	49 42	59	162	348
13	45 35	59	161	46 34	58	161	47 32	59	161	48 31	58	160	49 29	58	160	347
14	45 22	58	160	46 20	58	160	47 18	59	159	48 17	58	159	49 15	58	159	346
15	45 08	+58	159	46 06	+58	158	47 04	+58	158	48 02	+58	158	49 00	+57	157	345
16	44 52	58	157	45 50	58	157	46 48	58	156	47 46	58	156	48 44	57	156	344
17	44 36	58	156	45 34	58	156	46 32	57	155	47 29	57	155	48 26	58	154	343
18	44 20	57	155	45 17	57	154	46 14	57	154	47 11	58	153	48 09	57	153	342
19	44 02	57	153	44 59	57	153	45 56	57	152	46 53	57	152	47 50	56	151	341
20	43 43	+57	152	44 40	+57	151	45 37	+57	151	46 34	+56	151	47 30	+56	150	340
21	43 24	57	151	44 21	56	150	45 17	56	150	46 13	57	149	47 10	56	149	339
22	43 04	56	149	44 00	56	149	44 56	56	148	45 52	56	148	46 48	56	147	338
23	42 43	56	148	43 39	56	148	44 35	56	147	45 31	55	147	46 26	56	146	337
24	42 21	56	147	43 17	56	146	44 13	55	146	45 08	55	145	46 03	55	145	336
25	41 59	+55	146	42 54	+56	145	43 50	+55	144	44 45	+55	144	45 40	+55	143	335
26	41 36	55	144	42 31	55	144	43 26	55	143	44 21	54	143	45 15	55	142	334
27	41 12	55	143	42 07	55	143	43 02	54	142	43 56	54	141	44 50	54	140	333
28	40 48	54	142	41 42	54	141	42 36	55	141	43 31	54	140	44 25	53	140	332
29	40 23	54	141	41 17	54	140	42 11	54	140	43 05	53	139	43 58	54	138	331
30	39 57	+54	140	40 51	+53	139	41 44	+54	138	42 38	+53	138	43 31	+53	137	330
31	39 30	54	138	40 24	53	138	41 17	54	137	42 11	53	137	43 04	52	136	329
32	39 03	54	137	39 57	53	137	40 50	53	136	41 43	52	135	42 35	53	135	328
33	38 36	53	136	39 29	53	135	40 22	52	135	41 14	53	134	42 07	52	134	327
34	38 08	52	135	39 00	53	134	39 53	52	134	40 45	52	133	41 37	52	132	326
35	37 39	+52	134	38 31	+52	133	39 23	+52	133	40 15	+52	132	41 07	+52	131	325
36	37 10	52	133	38 02	52	132	38 54	51	131	39 45	52	131	40 37	51	130	324
37	36 40	52	132	37 32	51	131	38 23	52	130	39 15	51	130	40 06	51	129	323
38	36 10	51	131	37 01	51	130	37 52	52	129	38 44	50	129	39 34	51	128	322
39	35 39	51	130	36 30	51	129	37 21	51	128	38 12	50	128	39 02	51	127	321
40	35 08	+51	129	35 59	+50	128	36 49	+51	127	37 40	+50	127	38 30	+50	126	320
41	34 36	51	127	35 27	50	127	36 17	50	126	37 07	50	125	37 57	50	125	319
42	34 04	50	126	34 54	51	126	35 45	49	125	36 34	50	124	37 24	50	124	318
43	33 31	51	125	34 22	49	125	35 11	50	124	36 01	50	123	36 51	49	123	317
44	32 59	49	124	33 48	50	124	34 38	49	123	35 27	50	122	36 17	48	122	316
45	32 25	+50	123	33 15	+49	123	34 04	+49	122	34 53	+49	121	35 42	+49	121	315
46	31 52	49	123	32 41	49	122	33 30	49	121	34 19	48	120	35 07	49	120	314
47	31 17	50	122	32 07	48	121	32 55	49	120	33 44	48	119	34 32	49	119	313
48	30 43	49	121	31 32	49	120	32 21	48	119	33 09	48	119	33 57	48	118	312
49	30 08	49	120	30 57	48	119	31 45	48	118	32 33	48	118	33 21	48	117	311
50	29 33	+49	119	30 22	+48	118	31 10	+48	117	31 58	+47	117	32 45	+48	116	310
51	28 58	48	118	29 46	48	117	30 34	48	116	31 22	47	116	32 09	47	115	309
52	28 22	48	117	29 10	48	116	29 58	47	116	30 45	48	115	31 33	47	114	308
53	27 46	48	116	28 34	48	115	29 22	47	115	30 09	47	114	30 56	47	113	307
54	27 10	48	115	27 58	47	114	28 45	47	114	29 32	47	113	30 19	47	112	306
55	26 34	+47	114	27 21	+47	114	28 08	+47	113	28 55	+47	112	29 42	+46	111	305
56	25 57	47	113	26 44	47	113	27 31	47	112	28 18	46	111	29 04	46	111	304
57	25 20	47	112	26 07	46	112	26 53	47	111	27 40	46	110	28 26	46	110	303
58	24 43	46	112	25 29	47	111	26 16	46	110	27 02	46	110	27 48	46	109	302
59	24 05	47	111	24 52	46	110	25 38	46	109	26 24	46	109	27 10	46	108	301
60	23 27	+47	110	24 14	+46	109	25 00	+46	109	25 46	+46	108	26 32	+46	107	300
61	22 50	46	109	23 36	46	108	24 22	46	108	25 08	46	107	25 54	45	106	299
62	22 12	46	108	22 58	46	108	23 44	46	107	24 29	46	106	25 15	45	105	298
63	21 33	46	107	22 19	46	107	23 05	46	106	23 51	45	105	24 36	45	105	297
64	20 55	46	107	21 41	45	106	22 26	46	105	23 12	45	105	23 57	45	104	296
65	20 16	+46	106	21 02	+46	105	21 48	+45	104	22 33	+45	104	23 18	+45	103	295
66	19 38	45	105	20 23	46	104	21 09	45	104	21 54	45	103	22 39	45	102	294
67	18 59	45	104	19 44	46	103	20 30	45	103	21 15	45	102	22 00	44	101	293
68	18 20	45	103	19 05	45	103	19 50	45	102	20 35	45	101	21 20	45	101	292
69	17 41	45	103	18 26	45	102	19 11	45	101	19 56	45	101	20 41	44	100	291

LHA	10° Hc	10° d	10° Z	11° Hc	11° d	11° Z	12° Hc	12° d	12° Z	13° Hc	13° d	13° Z	14° Hc	14° d	14° Z	LHA
	° ′	′	°	° ′	′	°	° ′	′	°	° ′	′	°	° ′	′	°	
0	52 00	+60	180	53 00	+60	180	54 00	+60	180	55 00	+60	180	56 00	+60	180	360
1	51 59	60	178	52 59	60	178	53 59	60	178	54 59	60	178	55 59	60	178	359
2	51 58	60	177	52 58	60	177	53 58	60	177	54 58	60	177	55 58	60	177	358
3	51 55	60	175	52 55	60	175	53 55	60	175	54 55	60	175	55 55	59	175	357
4	51 51	60	174	52 51	60	174	53 51	60	173	54 51	59	173	55 50	60	173	356
5	51 46	+60	172	52 46	+60	172	53 46	+59	172	54 45	+60	172	55 45	+60	171	355
6	51 40	60	170	52 40	59	170	53 39	60	170	54 39	59	170	55 38	60	170	354
7	51 33	59	169	52 32	60	169	53 32	59	168	54 31	59	168	55 30	60	168	353
8	51 24	60	168	52 24	59	167	53 23	59	167	54 22	60	167	55 22	59	166	352
9	51 15	59	166	52 14	59	166	53 13	59	165	54 12	59	165	55 11	59	165	351
10	51 05	+59	164	52 04	+59	164	53 03	+58	164	54 01	+59	163	55 00	+59	163	350
11	50 53	59	163	51 52	59	162	52 51	58	162	53 49	59	162	54 48	58	161	349
12	50 41	58	161	51 39	59	161	52 38	58	160	53 36	58	160	54 34	59	160	348
13	50 27	59	160	51 26	58	159	52 24	58	159	53 22	58	158	54 20	58	158	347
14	50 13	58	158	51 11	58	158	52 09	58	157	53 07	57	157	54 04	58	156	346
15	49 57	+58	157	50 55	+58	156	51 53	+57	156	52 50	+58	155	53 48	+57	155	345
16	49 41	58	155	50 39	57	155	51 36	57	154	52 33	57	154	53 30	57	153	344
17	49 24	57	154	50 21	57	153	51 18	57	153	52 15	57	152	53 12	56	152	343
18	49 06	56	152	50 02	57	152	50 59	57	151	51 56	56	151	52 52	56	150	342
19	48 46	57	151	49 43	56	150	50 39	57	150	51 36	56	149	52 32	56	149	341
20	48 26	+57	150	49 23	+56	149	50 19	+56	148	51 15	+56	148	52 11	+55	147	340
21	48 06	56	148	49 02	55	148	49 57	56	147	50 53	55	146	51 48	56	146	339
22	47 44	56	147	48 40	55	146	49 35	55	146	50 30	55	145	51 25	55	144	338
23	47 22	55	145	48 17	55	145	49 12	55	144	50 07	55	144	51 02	54	143	337
24	46 58	55	144	47 53	55	144	48 48	55	143	49 43	54	142	50 37	54	142	336
25	46 35	+54	143	47 29	+55	142	48 24	+54	142	49 18	+54	141	50 12	+53	140	335
26	46 10	54	141	47 04	54	141	47 58	54	140	48 52	54	140	49 46	53	139	334
27	45 44	54	140	46 38	54	140	47 32	54	139	48 26	53	138	49 19	53	138	333
28	45 18	54	139	46 12	53	138	47 05	53	138	47 58	53	137	48 51	53	136	332
29	44 52	53	138	45 45	53	137	46 38	53	136	47 31	52	136	48 23	52	135	331
30	44 24	+53	136	45 17	+53	136	46 10	+52	135	47 02	+52	134	47 54	+52	134	330
31	43 56	53	135	44 49	52	135	45 41	52	134	46 33	52	133	47 25	52	132	329
32	43 28	52	134	44 20	52	133	45 12	52	133	46 04	51	132	46 55	51	131	328
33	42 59	52	133	43 51	51	132	44 42	52	132	45 34	51	131	46 25	50	130	327
34	42 29	52	132	43 21	51	131	44 12	51	130	45 03	51	130	45 54	50	129	326
35	41 59	+51	131	42 50	+51	130	43 41	+51	129	44 32	+50	128	45 22	+50	128	325
36	41 28	51	129	42 19	51	129	43 10	50	128	44 00	50	127	44 50	50	127	324
37	40 57	50	128	41 47	51	128	42 38	50	127	43 28	49	126	44 17	50	125	323
38	40 25	50	127	41 15	50	127	42 05	50	126	42 55	50	125	43 45	49	124	322
39	39 53	50	126	40 43	50	125	41 33	49	125	42 22	49	124	43 11	49	123	321
40	39 20	+50	125	40 10	+49	124	40 59	+49	124	41 48	+49	123	42 37	+49	122	320
41	38 47	49	124	39 36	50	123	40 26	49	123	41 15	48	122	42 03	48	121	319
42	38 14	49	123	39 03	49	122	39 52	48	122	40 40	48	121	41 28	48	120	318
43	37 40	49	122	38 29	48	121	39 17	48	121	40 05	48	120	40 53	48	119	317
44	37 05	49	121	37 54	48	120	38 42	48	120	39 30	48	119	40 18	48	118	316
45	36 31	+48	120	37 19	+48	119	38 07	+48	119	38 55	+48	118	39 43	+47	117	315
46	35 56	48	119	36 44	48	118	37 32	47	118	38 19	48	117	39 07	46	116	314
47	35 21	47	118	36 08	48	117	36 56	47	117	37 43	47	116	38 30	47	115	313
48	34 45	48	117	35 33	47	116	36 20	47	116	37 07	47	115	37 54	46	114	312
49	34 09	47	116	34 56	48	115	35 44	46	115	36 30	47	114	37 17	46	113	311
50	33 33	+47	115	34 20	+47	114	35 07	+47	114	35 54	+46	113	36 40	+46	112	310
51	32 56	47	114	33 43	47	114	34 30	46	113	35 16	47	112	36 03	45	111	309
52	32 20	46	113	33 06	47	113	33 53	46	112	34 39	46	111	35 25	46	110	308
53	31 43	46	113	32 29	46	112	33 15	47	111	34 02	45	110	34 47	46	109	307
54	31 05	47	112	31 52	46	111	32 38	46	110	33 24	45	109	34 09	45	109	306
55	30 28	+46	111	31 14	+46	110	32 00	+46	109	32 46	+45	108	33 31	+45	108	305
56	29 50	46	110	30 36	46	109	31 22	45	108	32 07	46	108	32 53	45	107	304
57	29 12	46	109	29 58	46	108	30 44	45	107	31 29	45	107	32 14	45	106	303
58	28 34	46	108	29 20	45	107	30 05	46	107	30 51	44	106	31 35	45	105	302
59	27 56	46	107	28 42	45	106	29 27	45	106	30 12	45	105	30 57	44	104	301
60	27 18	+45	106	28 03	+45	106	28 48	+45	105	29 33	+45	104	30 18	+44	103	300
61	26 39	45	106	27 24	45	105	28 09	45	104	28 54	44	103	29 38	45	103	299
62	26 00	45	105	26 45	45	104	27 30	45	103	28 15	44	102	28 59	44	102	298
63	25 21	45	104	26 06	45	103	26 51	45	102	27 36	44	102	28 20	44	101	297
64	24 42	45	103	25 27	45	102	26 12	44	102	26 56	44	101	27 40	44	100	296
65	24 03	+45	102	24 48	+44	102	25 32	+45	101	26 17	+44	100	27 01	+44	99	295
66	23 24	44	101	24 08	45	101	24 53	44	100	25 37	44	99	26 21	44	98	294
67	22 44	45	101	23 29	44	100	24 13	44	99	24 57	44	98	25 41	44	98	293
68	22 05	44	100	22 49	45	99	23 34	44	98	24 18	43	98	25 01	44	97	292
69	21 25	45	99	22 10	44	98	22 54	44	98	23 38	44	97	24 22	43	96	291

S. Lat. {LHA greater than 180°....... Zn=180−Z; LHA less than 180°........... Zn=180+Z}

DECLINATION (0°-14°) SAME NAME AS LATITUDE

N. Lat. {LHA greater than 180°……. Zn=Z; LHA less than 180°………. Zn=360−Z}

DECLINATION (0°-14°) SAME NAME AS LATITUDE

LHA	0° Hc	0° d	0° Z	1° Hc	1° d	1° Z	2° Hc	2° d	2° Z	3° Hc	3° d	3° Z	4° Hc	4° d	4° Z	5° Hc	5° d	5° Z	6° Hc	6° d	6° Z	7° Hc	7° d	7° Z
	° ′	′	°	° ′	′	°	° ′	′	°	° ′	′	°	° ′	′	°	° ′	′	°	° ′	′	°	° ′	′	°
70	13 14	+46	105	14 00	+45	105	14 45	+46	104	15 31	+45	103	16 16	+45	102	17 01	+46	102	17 47	+45	101	18 32	+44	100
71	12 35	46	104	13 21	45	104	14 06	46	103	14 52	45	102	15 37	45	102	16 22	45	101	17 07	45	100	17 52	45	100
72	11 56	46	104	12 42	45	103	13 27	45	102	14 12	46	102	14 58	45	101	15 43	45	100	16 28	44	100	17 12	45	99
73	11 17	45	103	12 02	46	102	12 48	45	102	13 33	45	101	14 18	45	100	15 03	45	99	15 48	45	99	16 33	44	98
74	10 38	45	102	11 23	45	101	12 08	45	101	12 53	45	100	13 38	45	99	14 23	45	99	15 08	45	98	15 53	44	97
75	09 58	+46	101	10 44	+45	101	11 29	+45	100	12 14	+45	99	12 59	+45	99	13 44	+44	98	14 28	+45	97	15 13	+44	97
76	09 19	45	101	10 04	45	100	10 49	45	99	11 34	45	99	12 19	45	98	13 04	45	97	13 49	44	96	14 33	45	96
77	08 39	46	100	09 25	45	99	10 10	44	98	10 54	45	98	11 39	45	97	12 24	45	96	13 09	44	96	13 53	45	95
78	08 00	45	99	08 45	45	98	09 30	45	98	10 15	44	97	10 59	45	96	11 44	45	96	12 29	44	95	13 13	44	94
79	07 20	45	98	08 05	45	98	08 50	45	97	09 35	44	96	10 19	45	96	11 04	45	95	11 49	44	94	12 33	44	94
80	06 40	+45	98	07 25	+45	97	08 10	+45	96	08 55	+44	96	09 39	+45	95	10 24	+45	94	11 09	+44	93	11 53	+44	93
81	06 01	44	97	06 45	45	96	07 30	45	95	08 15	44	95	08 59	45	94	09 44	44	93	10 28	45	93	11 13	44	92
82	05 21	44	96	06 05	45	95	06 50	45	95	07 35	44	94	08 19	45	93	09 04	44	93	09 48	45	92	10 33	44	91
83	04 41	44	95	05 25	45	95	06 10	45	94	06 55	44	93	07 39	45	93	08 24	44	92	09 08	45	91	09 53	44	91
84	04 01	44	94	04 45	45	94	05 30	45	93	06 15	44	93	06 59	45	92	07 44	44	91	08 28	44	90	09 12	45	90
85	03 21	+44	94	04 05	+45	93	04 50	+44	92	05 34	+45	92	06 19	+45	91	07 04	+44	90	07 48	+44	90	08 32	+45	89
86	02 41	44	93	03 25	45	92	04 10	44	92	04 54	45	91	05 39	44	90	06 23	45	90	07 08	44	89	07 52	44	88
87	02 00	45	92	02 45	45	92	03 30	44	91	04 14	45	90	04 59	44	90	05 43	45	89	06 28	44	88	07 12	44	88
88	01 20	45	91	02 05	44	91	02 49	45	90	03 34	45	89	04 19	44	89	05 03	45	88	05 48	44	88	06 32	44	87
89	00 40	45	91	01 25	44	90	02 09	45	89	02 54	44	89	03 38	45	88	04 23	44	87	05 07	45	87	05 52	44	86
90	00 00	+45	90	00 45	+44	89	01 29	+45	89	02 14	+44	88	02 58	+45	87	03 43	+44	87	04 27	+45	86	05 12	+44	85
91	−0 40	44	89	00 04	45	89	00 49	45	88	01 34	44	87	02 18	45	87	03 03	44	86	03 47	45	85	04 32	44	85
92	−1 20	44	89	−0 36	45	88	00 09	45	87	00 54	44	87	01 38	45	86	02 23	44	85	03 07	45	85	03 52	44	84
93	−2 00	44	88	−1 16	45	87	−0 31	44	86	00 13	45	86	00 58	45	85	01 43	44	84	02 27	45	84	03 12	45	83
94	−2 41	45	87	−1 56	45	86	−1 11	44	86	−0 27	45	85	00 18	45	84	01 03	44	84	01 47	45	83	02 32	45	82
95	−3 21	+45	86	−2 36	+45	86	−1 51	+44	85	−1 07	+45	84	−0 22	+45	84	00 23	+45	83	01 08	+44	82	01 52	+45	82
96	−4 01	45	86	−3 16	45	85	−2 31	45	84	−1 46	44	84	−1 02	45	83	−0 17	45	82	00 28	45	82	01 13	44	81
97	−4 41	45	85	−3 56	45	84	−3 11	45	83	−2 26	45	83	−1 41	44	82	−0 57	45	81	−0 12	45	81	00 33	45	80
98	−5 21	45	84	−4 36	45	83	−3 51	45	83	−3 06	45	82	−2 21	45	81	−1 36	45	81	−0 51	45	80	−0 06	45	79
99	−6 01	45	83	−5 16	45	83	−4 31	45	82	−3 46	45	81	−3 01	45	81	−2 16	45	80	−1 31	45	79	−0 46	45	79
100				−5 55	+44	82	−5 11	+46	81	−4 25	+45	81	−3 40	+45	80	−2 55	+45	79	−2 10	+45	79	−1 25	+45	78
101							−5 50	45	80	−5 05	45	80	−4 20	45	79	−3 35	45	78	−2 50	46	78	−2 04	45	77
102										−5 45	46	79	−4 59	45	78	−4 14	45	78	−3 29	46	77	−2 43	45	76
103													−5 39	46	78	−4 53	45	77	−4 08	46	76	−3 22	45	76
104													−6 18	46	77	−5 32	45	76	−4 47	46	76	−4 01	45	75
105																−6 11	+45	75	−5 26	+46	75	−4 40	+46	74
106																			−6 04	46	74	−5 18	45	73
107																						−5 57	46	73

LHA	8° Hc	8° d	8° Z	9° Hc	9° d	9° Z	10° Hc	10° d	10° Z	11° Hc	11° d	11° Z	12° Hc	12° d	12° Z	13° Hc	13° d	13° Z	14° Hc	14° d	14° Z	LHA
	° ′	′	°	° ′	′	°	° ′	′	°	° ′	′	°	° ′	′	°	° ′	′	°	° ′	′	°	
70	19 16	+45	100	20 01	+45	99	20 46	+44	98	21 30	+44	98	22 14	+44	97	22 58	+44	96	23 42	+43	95	290
71	18 37	44	99	19 21	45	98	20 06	44	98	20 50	44	97	21 34	44	96	22 18	44	95	23 02	43	95	289
72	17 57	45	98	18 42	44	97	19 26	44	97	20 10	44	96	20 54	44	95	21 38	44	95	22 22	43	94	288
73	17 17	45	97	18 02	44	97	18 46	44	96	19 30	44	95	20 14	44	95	20 58	44	94	21 42	43	93	287
74	16 37	45	97	17 22	44	96	18 06	44	95	18 50	44	94	19 34	44	94	20 18	43	93	21 01	44	92	286
75	15 57	+45	96	16 42	+44	95	17 26	+44	94	18 10	+44	94	18 54	+44	93	19 38	+43	92	20 21	+44	92	285
76	15 18	44	95	16 02	44	94	16 46	44	94	17 30	44	93	18 14	44	92	18 58	43	92	19 41	44	91	284
77	14 38	44	94	15 22	44	94	16 06	44	93	16 50	44	92	17 34	43	92	18 17	44	91	19 01	43	90	283
78	13 57	45	94	14 42	44	93	15 26	44	92	16 10	44	91	16 54	43	91	17 37	44	90	18 21	43	89	282
79	13 17	45	93	14 02	44	92	14 46	44	91	15 30	43	91	16 13	44	90	16 57	44	89	17 41	43	89	281
80	12 37	+44	92	13 21	+45	91	14 06	+44	91	14 50	+43	90	15 33	+44	89	16 17	+44	89	17 01	+43	88	280
81	11 57	44	91	12 41	44	91	13 25	44	90	14 09	44	89	14 53	44	89	15 37	43	88	16 20	44	87	279
82	11 17	44	91	12 01	44	90	12 45	44	89	13 29	44	89	14 13	44	88	14 57	43	87	15 40	44	86	278
83	10 37	44	90	11 21	44	89	12 05	44	88	12 49	44	88	13 33	44	87	14 17	43	86	15 00	44	86	277
84	09 57	44	89	10 41	44	88	11 25	44	88	12 09	44	87	12 53	44	86	13 37	43	86	14 20	44	85	276
85	09 17	+44	88	10 01	+44	88	10 45	+44	87	11 29	+44	86	12 13	+44	86	12 57	+43	85	13 40	+44	84	275
86	08 36	45	88	09 21	44	87	10 05	44	86	10 49	44	86	11 33	44	85	12 17	43	84	13 00	44	83	274
87	07 56	45	87	08 41	44	86	09 25	44	86	10 09	44	85	10 53	44	84	11 37	44	83	12 21	43	83	273
88	07 16	45	86	08 01	44	85	08 45	44	85	09 29	44	84	10 13	44	83	10 57	44	83	11 41	44	82	272
89	06 36	45	85	07 21	44	85	08 05	44	84	08 49	44	83	09 33	44	83	10 17	44	82	11 01	44	81	271
90	05 56	+45	85	06 41	+44	84	07 25	+44	83	08 09	+44	83	08 53	+44	82	09 37	+44	81	10 21	+44	81	270
91	05 16	45	84	06 01	44	83	06 45	44	83	07 29	45	82	08 14	44	81	08 58	44	81	09 42	44	80	269
92	04 36	45	83	05 21	44	83	06 05	45	82	06 50	44	81	07 34	44	80	08 18	44	80	09 02	45	79	268
93	03 57	44	82	04 41	45	82	05 26	44	81	06 10	44	80	06 54	45	80	07 39	44	79	08 23	44	78	267
94	03 17	44	82	04 01	45	81	04 46	45	80	05 31	44	80	06 15	44	79	06 59	45	78	07 44	44	78	266
95	02 37	+45	81	03 22	+44	80	04 06	+45	80	04 51	+45	79	05 36	+44	78	06 20	+45	78	07 05	+44	77	265
96	01 57	45	80	02 42	45	80	03 27	45	79	04 12	44	78	04 56	45	78	05 41	45	77	06 26	44	76	264
97	01 18	45	79	02 03	45	79	02 48	44	78	03 32	45	77	04 17	45	77	05 02	45	76	05 47	44	76	263
98	00 39	44	79	01 23	45	78	02 08	45	77	02 53	45	77	03 38	45	76	04 23	45	75	05 08	45	75	262
99	−0 01	45	78	00 44	45	77	01 29	45	77	02 14	45	76	02 59	45	75	03 44	45	75	04 29	45	74	261
100	−0 40	+45	77	00 05	+45	77	00 50	+45	76	01 35	+45	75	02 20	+46	75	03 06	+45	74	03 51	+45	73	260
101	−1 19	45	76	−0 34	45	76	00 11	46	75	00 57	45	75	01 42	45	74	02 27	45	73	03 12	45	73	259
102	−1 58	45	76	−1 13	46	75	−0 27	45	74	00 18	45	74	01 03	46	73	01 49	45	72	02 34	45	72	258
103	−2 37	46	75	−1 51	45	74	−1 06	46	74	−0 20	45	73	00 25	46	72	01 11	45	72	01 56	45	71	257
104	−3 16	46	74	−2 30	46	74	−1 44	45	73	−0 59	46	72	−0 13	45	72	00 32	46	71	01 18	46	70	256
105	−3 54	+46	73	−3 08	+45	73	−2 23	+46	72	−1 37	+46	72	−0 51	+46	71	−0 05	+45	70	00 40	+46	70	255
106	−4 33	46	73	−3 47	46	72	−3 01	46	71	−2 15	46	71	−1 29	46	70	−0 43	46	70	00 03	46	69	254
107	−5 11	46	72	−4 25	46	71	−3 39	46	71	−2 53	46	70	−2 07	46	69	−1 21	46	69	−0 35	47	68	253
108	−5 49	46	71	−5 03	46	71	−4 17	47	70	−3 30	46	69	−2 44	46	69	−1 58	46	68	−1 12	47	67	252
109				−5 41	47	70	−4 54	46	69	−4 08	47	69	−3 21	46	68	−2 35	46	67	−1 49	47	67	251
110							−5 32	+47	68	−4 45	+46	68	−3 59	+47	67	−3 12	+47	66	−2 25	+46	66	250
111							−6 09	47	68	−5 22	47	67	−4 35	46	66	−3 49	48	66	−3 01	46	65	249
112										−5 59	47	66	−5 12	47	66	−4 25	47	65	−3 38	47	64	248
113													−5 49	47	65	−5 02	48	64	−4 14	47	64	247
114																−5 38	48	63	−4 50	47	63	246
115																			−5 26	+48	62	245
116																			−6 01	48	61	244

0°	1°	2°	3°	4°	5°	6°	7°	8°	9°	10°	11°	12°	13°	14°

S. Lat. {LHA greater than 180°……. Zn=180−Z; LHA less than 180°………. Zn=180+Z}

DECLINATION (0°-14°) SAME NAME AS LATITUDE

LAT 48°

LAT 48°

N. Lat. {LHA greater than 180°....... Zn=Z; LHA less than 180°.......... Zn=360−Z}

DECLINATION (0°-14°) CONTRARY NAME TO LATITUDE

LHA	0° Hc	d	Z	1° Hc	d	Z	2° Hc	d	Z	3° Hc	d	Z	4° Hc	d	Z	5° Hc	d	Z	6° Hc	d	Z	7° Hc	d	Z
	° ′	′	°	° ′	′	°	° ′	′	°	° ′	′	°	° ′	′	°	° ′	′	°	° ′	′	°	° ′	′	°
99	-6 01	44	83																					
98	-5 21	44	84	-6 05	45	85																		
97	-4 41	44	85	-5 25	45	85	-6 10	45	86															
96	-4 01	44	86	-4 45	45	86	-5 30	45	87	-6 15	44	87												
95	-3 21	-44	86	-4 05	-45	87	-4 50	-44	88	-5 34	-45	88	-6 19	-45	89									
94	-2 41	44	87	-3 25	45	88	-4 10	44	88	-4 54	45	89	-5 39	44	90									
93	-2 00	45	88	-2 45	45	88	-3 30	44	89	-4 14	45	90	-4 59	44	90	-5 43	45	91						
92	-1 20	45	89	-2 05	44	89	-2 49	45	90	-3 34	45	91	-4 19	44	91	-5 03	45	92	-5 48	44	92			
91	-0 40	45	89	-1 25	44	90	-2 09	45	91	-2 54	44	91	-3 38	45	92	-4 23	44	93	-5 07	45	93	-5 52	44	94
90	00 00	-45	90	-0 45	-44	91	-1 29	-45	91	-2 14	-44	92	-2 58	-45	93	-3 43	-44	93	-4 27	-45	94	-5 12	-44	95
89	00 40	44	91	-0 04	45	91	-0 49	45	92	-1 34	44	93	-2 18	45	93	-3 03	44	94	-3 47	45	95	-4 32	44	95
88	01 20	44	91	00 36	45	92	-0 09	45	93	-0 54	44	93	-1 38	45	94	-2 23	44	95	-3 07	45	95	-3 52	44	96
87	02 00	44	92	01 16	45	93	00 31	44	94	-0 13	45	94	-0 58	45	95	-1 43	44	96	-2 27	45	96	-3 12	45	97
86	02 41	45	93	01 56	45	94	01 11	44	94	00 27	45	95	-0 18	45	96	-1 03	44	96	-1 47	45	97	-2 32	45	98
85	03 21	-45	94	02 36	-45	94	01 51	-44	95	01 07	-45	96	00 22	-45	96	-0 23	-45	97	-1 08	-44	98	-1 52	-45	98
84	04 01	45	94	03 16	45	95	02 31	45	96	01 46	44	96	01 02	45	97	00 17	45	98	-0 28	45	98	-1 13	44	99
83	04 41	45	95	03 56	45	96	03 11	45	97	02 26	45	97	01 41	44	98	00 57	45	99	00 12	45	99	-0 33	45	100
82	05 21	45	96	04 36	45	97	03 51	45	97	03 06	45	98	02 21	45	99	01 36	45	99	00 51	45	100	00 06	45	101
81	06 01	45	97	05 16	45	97	04 31	45	98	03 46	45	99	03 01	45	99	02 16	45	100	01 31	45	101	00 46	45	101
80	06 40	-45	98	05 55	-44	98	05 11	-46	99	04 25	-45	99	03 40	-45	100	02 55	-45	101	02 10	-45	101	01 25	-45	102
79	07 20	45	98	06 35	45	99	05 50	45	100	05 05	45	100	04 20	45	101	03 35	45	102	02 50	46	102	02 04	45	103
78	08 00	45	99	07 15	45	100	06 30	45	100	05 45	46	101	04 59	45	102	04 14	45	102	03 29	46	103	02 43	45	104
77	08 39	45	100	07 54	45	100	07 09	45	101	06 24	45	102	05 39	46	102	04 53	45	103	04 08	46	104	03 22	45	104
76	09 19	45	101	08 34	46	101	07 48	45	102	07 03	45	103	06 18	46	103	05 32	45	104	04 47	46	104	04 01	45	105
75	09 58	-45	101	09 13	-45	102	08 28	-46	103	07 42	-45	103	06 57	-46	104	06 11	-45	105	05 26	-46	105	04 40	-46	106
74	10 38	46	102	09 52	45	103	09 07	46	103	08 21	45	104	07 36	46	105	06 50	46	105	06 04	46	106	05 18	45	107
73	11 17	46	103	10 31	45	104	09 46	46	104	09 00	46	105	08 14	45	105	07 29	46	106	06 43	46	107	05 57	46	107
72	11 56	46	104	11 10	45	104	10 25	46	105	09 39	46	106	08 53	46	106	08 07	46	107	07 21	46	108	06 35	46	108
71	12 35	46	104	11 49	46	105	11 03	45	106	10 18	46	106	09 32	47	107	08 45	46	108	07 59	46	108	07 13	46	109
70	13 14	-46	105	12 28	-46	106	11 42	-46	107	10 56	-46	107	10 10	-46	108	09 24	-47	108	08 37	-46	109	07 51	-46	110

LHA	8° Hc	d	Z	9° Hc	d	Z	10° Hc	d	Z	11° Hc	d	Z	12° Hc	d	Z	13° Hc	d	Z	14° Hc	d	Z	LHA
	° ′	′	°	° ′	′	°	° ′	′	°	° ′	′	°	° ′	′	°	° ′	′	°	° ′	′	°	
99																						261
98																						262
97																						263
96																						264
95																						265
94																						266
93																						267
92																						268
91																						269
90	-5 56	-45	95																			270
89	-5 16	45	96	-6 01	44	97																271
88	-4 36	45	97	-5 21	44	97	-6 05	45	98													272
87	-3 57	44	98	-4 41	45	98	-5 26	44	99	-6 10	44	100										273
86	-3 17	44	98	-4 01	45	99	-4 46	45	100	-5 31	44	100	-6 15	44	101							274
85	-2 37	-45	99	-3 22	-44	100	-4 06	-45	100	-4 51	-45	101	-5 36	-44	102							275
84	-1 57	45	100	-2 42	45	100	-3 27	45	101	-4 12	44	102	-4 56	45	102	-5 41	45	103				276
83	-1 18	45	101	-2 03	45	101	-2 48	44	102	-3 32	45	103	-4 17	45	103	-5 02	45	104	-5 47	44	104	277
82	-0 39	44	101	-1 23	45	102	-2 08	45	103	-2 53	45	103	-3 38	45	104	-4 23	45	105	-5 08	45	105	278
81	00 01	45	102	-0 44	45	103	-1 29	45	103	-2 14	45	104	-2 59	45	105	-3 44	45	105	-4 29	45	106	279
80	00 40	-45	103	-0 05	-45	103	-0 50	-45	104	-1 35	-45	105	-2 20	-46	105	-3 06	-45	106	-3 51	-45	107	280
79	01 19	45	104	00 34	45	104	-0 11	46	105	-0 57	45	105	-1 42	45	106	-2 27	45	107	-3 12	45	107	281
78	01 58	45	104	01 13	46	105	00 27	45	106	-0 18	45	106	-1 03	46	107	-1 49	45	108	-2 34	45	108	282
77	02 37	46	105	01 51	45	106	01 06	46	106	00 20	45	107	-0 25	46	108	-1 11	45	108	-1 56	45	109	283
76	03 16	46	106	02 30	46	106	01 44	45	107	00 59	46	108	00 13	45	108	-0 32	46	109	-1 18	46	110	284
75	03 54	-46	107	03 08	-45	107	02 23	-46	108	01 37	-46	108	00 51	-46	109	00 05	-45	110	-0 40	-46	110	285
74	04 33	46	107	03 47	46	108	03 01	46	109	02 15	46	109	01 29	46	110	00 43	46	110	-0 03	46	111	286
73	05 11	46	108	04 25	46	109	03 39	46	109	02 53	46	110	02 07	46	111	01 21	46	111	00 35	47	112	287
72	05 49	46	109	05 03	46	109	04 17	47	110	03 30	46	111	02 44	46	111	01 58	46	112	01 12	47	113	288
71	06 27	46	110	05 41	47	110	04 54	46	111	04 08	47	111	03 21	46	112	02 35	46	113	01 49	47	113	289
70	07 05	-47	110	06 18	-46	111	05 32	-47	112	04 45	-46	112	03 59	-47	113	03 12	-47	114	02 25	-46	114	290

S. Lat. {LHA greater than 180°....... Zn=180−Z; LHA less than 180°.......... Zn=180+Z}

DECLINATION (0°-14°) CONTRARY NAME TO LATITUDE

N. Lat. {LHA greater than 180°........ Zn=Z; LHA less than 180°........ Zn=360−Z}

DECLINATION (0°-14°) CONTRARY NAME TO LATITUDE

LHA	0° Hc	0° d	0° Z	1° Hc	1° d	1° Z	2° Hc	2° d	2° Z	3° Hc	3° d	3° Z	4° Hc	4° d	4° Z
	° ′	′	°	° ′	′	°	° ′	′	°	° ′	′	°	° ′	′	°
69	13 53	46	106	13 07	47	107	12 20	46	107	11 34	46	108	10 48	46	109
68	14 31	46	107	13 45	46	107	12 59	47	108	12 12	46	109	11 26	47	109
67	15 09	46	108	14 23	46	108	13 37	47	109	12 50	46	110	12 04	47	110
66	15 48	47	108	15 01	46	109	14 15	47	110	13 28	47	110	12 41	46	111
65	16 26	−47	109	15 39	−47	110	14 52	−46	110	14 06	−47	111	13 19	−47	112
64	17 03	46	110	16 17	47	111	15 30	47	111	14 43	47	112	13 56	47	113
63	17 41	47	111	16 54	47	111	16 07	47	112	15 20	47	113	14 33	47	113
62	18 19	47	112	17 32	48	112	16 44	47	113	15 57	47	114	15 10	48	114
61	18 56	47	112	18 09	48	113	17 21	47	114	16 34	48	114	15 46	47	115
60	19 33	−48	113	18 45	−47	114	17 58	−48	115	17 10	−47	115	16 23	−48	116
59	20 10	48	114	19 22	48	115	18 34	48	115	17 46	47	116	16 59	49	117
58	20 46	48	115	19 58	48	116	19 10	48	116	18 22	48	117	17 34	48	118
57	21 22	48	116	20 34	48	116	19 46	48	117	18 58	48	118	18 10	49	118
56	21 58	48	117	21 10	48	117	20 22	48	118	19 34	49	119	18 45	49	119
55	22 34	−48	118	21 46	−49	118	20 57	−48	119	20 09	−49	119	19 20	−49	120
54	23 10	49	118	22 21	49	119	21 32	48	120	20 44	49	120	19 55	50	121
53	23 45	49	119	22 56	49	120	22 07	49	121	21 18	49	121	20 29	50	122
52	24 20	49	120	23 31	49	121	22 42	50	121	21 52	49	122	21 03	50	123
51	24 54	49	121	24 05	49	122	23 16	50	122	22 26	50	123	21 36	49	124
50	25 29	−50	122	24 39	−50	123	23 49	−49	123	23 00	−50	124	22 10	−50	124
49	26 02	49	123	25 13	50	124	24 23	50	124	23 33	50	125	22 43	51	125
48	26 36	50	124	25 46	50	124	24 56	50	125	24 06	51	126	23 15	50	126
47	27 09	50	125	26 19	50	125	25 29	51	126	24 38	51	127	23 47	50	127
46	27 42	50	126	26 52	51	126	26 01	51	127	25 10	51	128	24 19	51	128
45	28 14	−50	127	27 24	−51	127	26 33	−51	128	25 42	−51	128	24 51	−52	129
44	28 46	51	128	27 55	51	128	27 04	51	129	26 13	51	129	25 22	52	130
43	29 18	51	129	28 27	52	129	27 35	51	130	26 44	52	130	25 52	51	131
42	29 49	51	130	28 58	52	130	28 06	52	131	27 14	52	131	26 22	52	132
41	30 20	52	131	29 28	52	131	28 36	52	132	27 44	52	132	26 52	52	133
40	30 50	−52	132	29 58	−52	132	29 06	−52	133	28 14	−53	133	27 21	−52	134
39	31 20	52	133	30 28	53	133	29 35	52	134	28 43	53	134	27 50	53	135
38	31 49	52	134	30 57	53	134	30 04	53	135	29 11	53	135	28 18	53	136
37	32 18	53	135	31 25	53	135	30 32	53	136	29 39	53	136	28 46	53	137
36	32 47	54	136	31 53	53	136	31 00	53	137	30 07	54	137	29 13	53	138
35	33 14	−53	137	32 21	−54	137	31 27	−53	138	30 34	−54	138	29 40	−54	139
34	33 42	54	138	32 48	54	138	31 54	54	139	31 00	54	139	30 06	54	140
33	34 08	54	139	33 14	54	139	32 20	54	140	31 26	54	140	30 32	55	141
32	34 34	54	140	33 40	54	141	32 46	55	141	31 51	54	142	30 57	55	142
31	35 00	55	141	34 05	54	142	33 11	55	142	32 16	55	143	31 21	55	143
30	35 25	−55	142	34 30	−55	143	33 35	−55	143	32 40	−55	144	31 45	−55	144
29	35 49	55	143	34 54	55	144	33 59	55	144	33 04	56	145	32 08	55	145
28	36 13	55	144	35 18	56	145	34 22	55	145	33 27	56	146	32 31	56	146
27	36 36	56	146	35 40	55	146	34 45	56	147	33 49	56	147	32 53	56	147
26	36 58	56	147	36 02	56	147	35 06	56	148	34 10	56	148	33 14	56	149
25	37 20	−56	148	36 24	−56	148	35 28	−57	149	34 31	−56	149	33 35	−57	150
24	37 41	56	149	36 45	57	150	35 48	56	150	34 52	57	150	33 55	57	151
23	38 01	56	150	37 05	57	151	36 08	57	151	35 11	57	152	34 14	57	152
22	38 21	57	152	37 24	57	152	36 27	57	152	35 30	57	153	34 33	57	153
21	38 40	58	153	37 42	57	153	36 45	57	153	35 48	57	154	34 51	58	154
20	38 58	−58	154	38 00	−57	154	37 03	−58	155	36 05	−57	155	35 08	−58	155
19	39 15	58	155	38 17	57	156	37 20	58	156	36 22	58	156	35 24	58	157
18	39 31	57	156	38 34	58	157	37 36	58	157	36 38	58	157	35 40	58	158
17	39 47	58	158	38 49	58	158	37 51	58	158	36 53	58	159	35 55	59	159
16	40 02	58	159	39 04	59	159	38 05	58	160	37 07	58	160	36 09	59	160
15	40 16	−58	160	39 18	−59	161	38 19	−59	161	37 20	−58	161	36 22	−59	161
14	40 29	58	162	39 31	59	162	38 32	59	162	37 33	59	162	36 34	58	163
13	40 42	59	163	39 43	59	163	38 44	59	163	37 45	59	164	36 46	59	164
12	40 53	59	164	39 54	59	164	38 55	59	165	37 56	59	165	36 57	59	165
11	41 04	60	165	40 04	59	166	39 05	59	166	38 06	59	166	37 07	59	166
10	41 13	−59	167	40 14	−59	167	39 15	−60	167	38 15	−59	167	37 16	−59	167
9	41 22	59	168	40 23	60	168	39 23	59	168	38 24	60	169	37 24	59	169
8	41 30	59	169	40 31	60	170	39 31	60	170	38 31	59	170	37 32	60	170
7	41 37	60	171	40 37	59	171	39 38	60	171	38 38	60	171	37 38	59	171
6	41 43	60	172	40 43	59	172	39 44	60	172	38 44	60	172	37 44	60	172
5	41 48	−60	173	40 48	−59	173	39 49	−60	174	38 49	−60	174	37 49	−60	174
4	41 53	60	175	40 53	60	175	39 53	60	175	38 53	60	175	37 53	60	175
3	41 56	60	176	40 56	60	176	39 56	60	176	38 56	60	176	37 56	60	176
2	41 58	60	177	40 58	60	177	39 58	60	177	38 58	60	177	37 58	60	178
1	42 00	60	179	41 00	60	179	40 00	60	179	39 00	60	179	38 00	60	179
0	42 00	−60	180	41 00	−60	180	40 00	−60	180	39 00	−60	180	38 00	−60	180

LHA	5° Hc	5° d	5° Z	6° Hc	6° d	6° Z	7° Hc	7° d	7° Z	8° Hc	8° d	8° Z	9° Hc	9° d	9° Z
	° ′	′	°	° ′	′	°	° ′	′	°	° ′	′	°	° ′	′	°
69	10 02	47	109	09 15	46	110	08 29	47	111	07 42	46	111	06 56	47	112
68	10 39	46	110	09 53	47	111	09 06	46	111	08 20	47	112	07 33	47	113
67	11 17	47	111	10 30	46	111	09 44	47	112	08 57	47	113	08 10	47	113
66	11 55	47	112	11 08	47	112	10 21	47	113	09 34	47	114	08 47	48	114
65	12 32	−47	112	11 45	−47	113	10 58	−48	114	10 10	−47	114	09 23	−47	115
64	13 09	47	113	12 22	48	114	11 34	47	114	10 47	48	115	09 59	47	116
63	13 46	48	114	12 58	47	115	12 11	48	115	11 23	48	116	10 35	47	117
62	14 22	47	115	13 35	48	115	12 47	48	116	11 59	48	117	11 11	48	117
61	14 59	48	116	14 11	48	116	13 23	48	117	12 35	48	117	11 47	48	118
60	15 35	−48	116	14 47	−48	117	13 59	−49	118	13 10	−48	118	12 22	−48	119
59	16 10	48	117	15 22	48	118	14 34	48	119	13 46	49	119	12 57	48	120
58	16 46	48	118	15 58	49	119	15 09	48	119	14 21	49	120	13 32	49	121
57	17 21	48	119	16 33	49	120	15 44	49	120	14 55	49	121	14 06	49	121
56	17 56	49	120	17 07	48	120	16 19	49	121	15 30	50	122	14 40	49	122
55	18 31	−49	121	17 42	−49	121	16 53	−49	122	16 04	−50	122	15 14	−49	123
54	19 05	49	122	18 16	49	122	17 27	50	123	16 37	49	123	15 48	50	124
53	19 39	49	122	18 50	50	123	18 00	49	124	17 11	50	124	16 21	50	125
52	20 13	49	123	19 24	50	124	18 34	50	124	17 44	50	125	16 54	50	126
51	20 47	50	124	19 57	50	125	19 07	50	125	18 17	51	126	17 26	50	126
50	21 20	−50	125	20 30	−51	126	19 39	−50	126	18 49	−51	127	17 58	−50	127
49	21 52	50	126	21 02	50	127	20 12	51	127	19 21	51	128	18 30	51	128
48	22 25	51	127	21 34	51	127	20 43	51	128	19 52	50	129	19 02	52	129
47	22 57	51	128	22 06	51	128	21 15	51	129	20 24	52	129	19 32	51	130
46	23 28	51	129	22 37	51	129	21 46	51	130	20 55	52	130	20 03	52	131
45	23 59	−51	130	23 08	−51	130	22 17	−52	131	21 25	−52	131	20 33	−52	132
44	24 30	51	131	23 39	52	131	22 47	52	132	21 55	52	132	21 03	52	133
43	25 01	52	131	24 09	52	132	23 17	53	133	22 24	52	133	21 32	52	134
42	25 30	52	132	24 38	52	133	23 46	52	134	22 54	53	134	22 01	53	135
41	26 00	53	133	25 07	52	134	24 15	53	134	23 22	53	135	22 29	52	136
40	26 29	−53	134	25 36	−53	135	24 43	−53	135	23 50	−53	136	22 57	−53	136
39	26 57	53	135	26 04	53	136	25 11	53	136	24 18	53	137	23 25	54	137
38	27 25	53	136	26 32	53	137	25 39	54	137	24 45	53	138	23 52	54	138
37	27 53	54	137	26 59	53	138	26 06	54	138	25 12	54	139	24 18	54	139
36	28 20	54	138	27 26	54	139	26 32	54	139	25 38	54	140	24 44	54	140
35	28 46	−54	139	27 52	−54	140	26 58	−54	140	26 04	−54	141	25 10	−55	141
34	29 12	54	140	28 18	55	141	27 23	54	141	26 29	55	142	25 34	54	142
33	29 37	54	141	28 43	55	142	27 48	54	142	26 54	55	143	25 59	55	143
32	30 02	55	142	29 07	55	143	28 12	55	143	27 17	55	144	26 22	55	144
31	30 26	55	144	29 31	55	144	28 36	55	144	27 41	55	145	26 46	56	145
30	30 50	−55	145	29 55	−56	145	28 59	−55	145	28 04	−56	146	27 08	−55	146
29	31 13	56	146	30 17	55	146	29 22	56	147	28 26	56	147	27 30	56	147
28	31 35	56	147	30 39	55	147	29 44	56	148	28 48	56	148	27 52	57	148
27	31 57	56	148	31 01	56	148	30 05	56	149	29 09	57	149	28 12	56	149
26	32 18	56	149	31 22	57	149	30 25	56	150	29 29	57	150	28 32	56	151
25	32 38	−56	150	31 42	−57	150	30 45	−56	151	29 49	−57	151	28 52	−57	152
24	32 58	57	151	32 01	56	152	31 05	57	152	30 08	57	152	29 11	57	153
23	33 17	57	152	32 20	57	153	31 23	57	153	30 26	57	153	29 29	57	154
22	33 36	58	153	32 38	57	154	31 41	57	154	30 44	58	154	29 46	57	155
21	33 53	57	155	32 56	58	155	31 58	57	155	31 01	58	156	30 03	58	156
20	34 10	−58	156	33 12	−57	156	32 15	−58	156	31 17	−58	157	30 19	−58	157
19	34 26	58	157	33 28	58	157	32 30	58	158	31 32	58	158	30 34	58	158
18	34 42	58	158	33 44	59	158	32 45	58	159	31 47	58	159	30 49	58	159
17	34 56	58	159	33 58	58	160	33 00	59	160	32 01	58	160	31 03	58	160
16	35 10	58	160	34 12	59	161	33 13	58	161	32 15	59	161	31 16	58	161
15	35 23	−58	162	34 25	−59	162	33 26	−59	162	32 27	−58	162	31 29	−59	163
14	35 36	59	163	34 37	59	163	33 38	59	163	32 39	59	164	31 40	59	164
13	35 47	59	164	34 48	59	164	33 49	59	164	32 50	59	165	31 51	59	165
12	35 58	59	165	34 59	59	165	34 00	60	166	33 00	59	166	32 01	59	166
11	36 08	60	166	35 08	59	167	34 09	59	167	33 10	59	167	32 11	60	167
10	36 17	−60	168	35 17	−59	168	34 18	−60	168	33 18	−59	168	32 19	−59	168
9	36 25	60	169	35 25	59	169	34 26	60	169	33 26	59	169	32 27	60	170
8	36 32	59	170	35 33	60	170	34 33	60	170	33 33	59	171	32 34	60	171
7	36 39	60	171	35 39	60	171	34 39	59	172	33 40	60	172	32 40	60	172
6	36 44	59	173	35 45	60	173	34 45	60	173	33 45	60	173	32 45	60	173
5	36 49	−60	174	35 49	−60	174	34 49	−59	174	33 50	−60	174	32 50	−60	174
4	36 53	60	175	35 53	60	175	34 53	60	175	33 53	60	175	32 53	59	175
3	36 56	60	176	35 56	60	176	34 56	60	176	33 56	60	176	32 56	60	177
2	36 58	60	178	35 58	60	178	34 58	60	178	33 58	60	178	32 58	60	178
1	37 00	60	179	36 00	60	179	35 00	60	179	34 00	60	179	33 00	60	179
0	37 00	−60	180	36 00	−60	180	35 00	−60	180	34 00	−60	180	33 00	−60	180

LHA	10° Hc	10° d	10° Z	11° Hc	11° d	11° Z	12° Hc	12° d	12° Z	13° Hc	13° d	13° Z	14° Hc	14° d	14° Z	LHA
	° ′	′	°	° ′	′	°	° ′	′	°	° ′	′	°	° ′	′	°	
69	06 09	47	112	05 22	47	113	04 35	46	114	03 49	48	114	03 01	46	115	291
68	06 46	47	113	05 59	47	114	05 12	47	114	04 25	47	115	03 38	47	116	292
67	07 23	47	114	06 36	47	115	05 49	47	115	05 02	48	116	04 14	47	116	293
66	07 59	47	115	07 12	47	115	06 25	47	116	05 38	48	117	04 50	47	117	294
65	08 36	−48	116	07 48	−47	116	07 01	−48	117	06 13	−47	117	05 26	−48	118	295
64	09 12	48	116	08 24	47	117	07 37	48	118	06 49	48	118	06 01	48	119	296
63	09 48	48	117	09 00	48	118	08 12	48	118	07 24	48	119	06 36	48	120	297
62	10 23	48	118	09 35	48	119	08 47	48	119	07 59	48	120	07 11	48	120	298
61	10 59	48	119	10 11	49	119	09 22	48	120	08 34	48	121	07 46	49	121	299
60	11 34	−49	120	10 45	−48	120	09 57	−49	121	09 08	−48	121	08 20	−49	122	300
59	12 09	49	120	11 20	49	121	10 31	48	122	09 43	49	122	08 54	49	123	301
58	12 43	49	121	11 54	49	122	11 05	49	122	10 16	49	123	09 27	49	124	302
57	13 17	49	122	12 28	49	123	11 39	49	123	10 50	49	124	10 01	50	124	303
56	13 51	49	123	13 02	49	123	12 13	50	124	11 23	49	125	10 34	50	125	304
55	14 25	−50	124	13 35	−49	124	12 46	−50	125	11 56	−50	125	11 06	−49	126	305
54	14 58	50	124	14 08	49	125	13 19	50	126	12 29	50	126	11 39	50	127	306
53	15 31	50	125	14 41	50	126	13 51	50	126	13 01	50	127	12 11	51	128	307
52	16 04	51	126	15 13	50	127	14 23	50	127	13 33	51	128	12 42	50	128	308
51	16 36	51	127	15 45	50	128	14 55	51	128	14 04	50	129	13 14	51	129	309
50	17 08	−51	128	16 17	−51	128	15 26	−51	129	14 35	−50	130	13 45	−51	130	310
49	17 39	51	129	16 48	51	129	15 57	51	130	15 06	51	130	14 15	51	131	311
48	18 10	51	130	17 19	51	130	16 28	51	131	15 37	52	131	14 45	51	132	312
47	18 41	51	131	17 50	52	131	16 58	51	132	16 07	52	132	15 15	52	133	313
46	19 11	51	131	18 20	52	132	17 28	52	133	16 36	52	133	15 44	52	134	314
45	19 41	−52	132	18 49	−52	133	17 57	−52	133	17 05	−52	134	16 13	−52	134	315
44	20 11	52	133	19 19	53	134	18 26	52	134	17 34	52	135	16 42	53	135	316
43	20 40	53	134	19 47	52	135	18 55	53	135	18 02	52	136	17 10	53	136	317
42	21 08	52	135	20 16	53	136	19 23	53	136	18 30	53	137	17 37	53	137	318
41	21 37	53	136	20 44	53	137	19 51	53	137	18 58	54	138	18 04	53	138	319
40	22 04	−53	137	21 11	−53	137	20 18	−54	138	19 24	−53	138	18 31	−53	139	320
39	22 31	53	138	21 38	54	138	20 44	53	139	19 51	54	139	18 57	54	140	321
38	22 58	54	139	22 04	53	139	21 11	54	140	20 17	54	140	19 23	54	141	322
37	23 24	54	140	22 30	54	140	21 36	54	141	20 42	54	141	19 48	54	142	323
36	23 50	54	141	22 56	54	141	22 02	55	142	21 07	54	142	20 13	55	143	324
35	24 15	−54	142	23 21	−55	142	22 26	−54	143	21 32	−55	143	20 37	−55	144	325
34	24 40	55	143	23 45	55	143	22 50	55	144	21 55	55	144	21 00	55	145	326
33	25 04	55	144	24 09	55	144	23 14	55	145	22 19	56	145	21 23	55	145	327
32	25 27	55	145	24 32	55	145	23 37	56	146	22 41	55	146	21 46	55	146	328
31	25 50	55	146	24 55	56	146	23 59	55	147	23 04	56	147	22 08	56	147	329
30	26 13	−56	147	25 17	−56	147	24 21	−56	148	23 25	−56	148	22 29	−56	148	330
29	26 34	56	148	25 38	56	148	24 42	56	149	23 46	56	149	22 50	56	149	331
28	26 55	56	149	25 59	56	149	25 03	56	150	24 07	57	150	23 10	56	150	332
27	27 16	57	150	26 19	56	150	25 23	57	151	24 26	56	151	23 30	57	151	333
26	27 36	57	151	26 39	57	151	25 42	56	152	24 46	57	152	23 49	57	152	334
25	27 55	−57	152	26 58	−57	152	26 01	−57	153	25 04	−57	153	24 07	−57	153	335
24	28 14	57	153	27 17	58	153	26 19	57	154	25 22	57	154	24 25	57	154	336
23	28 32	58	154	27 34	57	154	26 37	58	155	25 39	57	155	24 42	57	155	337
22	28 49	58	155	27 51	57	155	26 54	58	156	25 56	58	156	24 58	57	156	338
21	29 05	57	156	28 08	58	157	27 10	58	157	26 12	58	157	25 14	58	157	339
20	29 21	−58	157	28 23	−58	158	27 25	−58	158	26 27	−58	158	25 29	−58	158	340
19	29 36	58	158	28 38	58	159	27 40	58	159	26 42	58	159	25 44	59	160	341
18	29 51	58	160	28 53	59	160	27 54	58	160	26 56	59	160	25 57	58	161	342
17	30 05	59	161	29 06	58	161	28 08	59	161	27 09	58	161	26 11	59	162	343
16	30 18	59	162	29 19	59	162	28 20	58	162	27 22	59	162	26 23	59	163	344
15	30 30	−59	163	29 31	−59	163	28 32	−59	163	27 33	−59	164	26 34	−58	164	345
14	30 41	59	164	29 42	59	164	28 43	59	164	27 44	59	165	26 45	59	165	346
13	30 52	59	165	29 53	59	165	28 54	59	165	27 55	59	166	26 56	60	166	347
12	31 02	59	166	30 03	59	166	29 04	60	167	28 04	59	167	27 05	59	167	348
11	31 11	59	167	30 12	59	168	29 13	60	168	28 13	59	168	27 14	60	168	349
10	31 20	−60	169	30 20	−59	169	29 21	−60	169	28 21	−59	169	27 22	−60	169	350
9	31 27	59	170	30 28	60	170	29 28	59	170	28 29	60	170	27 29	60	170	351
8	31 34	60	171	30 34	59	171	29 35	60	171	28 35	60	171	27 35	59	171	352
7	31 40	60	172	30 40	59	172	29 41	60	172	28 41	60	172	27 41	60	172	353
6	31 45	59	173	30 46	60	173	29 46	60	173	28 46	60	173	27 46	60	173	354
5	31 50	−60	174	30 50	−60	174	29 50	−60	174	28 50	−60	174	27 50	−59	175	355
4	31 54	60	175	30 54	60	175	29 54	60	176	28 54	60	176	27 54	60	176	356
3	31 56	60	177	30 56	60	177	29 56	59	177	28 57	60	177	27 57	60	177	357
2	31 58	60	178	30 58	60	178	29 58	60	178	28 58	59	178	27 59	60	178	358
1	32 00	60	179	31 00	60	179	30 00	60	179	29 00	60	179	28 00	60	179	359
0	32 00	−60	180	31 00	−60	180	30 00	−60	180	29 00	−60	180	28 00	−60	180	360

S. Lat. {LHA greater than 180°........ Zn=180−Z; LHA less than 180°........ Zn=180+Z}

DECLINATION (0°-14°) CONTRARY NAME TO LATITUDE

N. Lat. {LHA greater than 180°........ Zn=Z; LHA less than 180°........ Zn=360−Z}

DECLINATION (15°-29°) SAME NAME AS LATITUDE

LAT 48°

LHA	15° Hc	15° d	15° Z	16° Hc	16° d	16° Z	17° Hc	17° d	17° Z	18° Hc	18° d	18° Z	19° Hc	19° d	19° Z
	° ′	′	°	° ′	′	°	° ′	′	°	° ′	′	°	° ′	′	°
0	57 00	+60	180	58 00	+60	180	59 00	+60	180	60 00	+60	180	61 00	+60	180
1	56 59	60	178	57 59	60	178	58 59	60	178	59 59	60	178	60 59	60	178
2	56 58	60	177	57 58	59	176	58 57	60	176	59 57	60	176	60 57	60	176
3	56 54	60	175	57 54	60	175	58 54	60	174	59 54	60	174	60 54	60	174
4	56 50	60	173	57 50	60	173	58 50	59	173	59 49	60	172	60 49	60	172
5	56 45	+59	171	57 44	+60	171	58 44	+59	171	59 43	+60	171	60 43	+60	170
6	56 38	59	169	57 37	60	169	58 37	59	169	59 36	60	169	60 36	59	168
7	56 30	59	168	57 29	59	167	58 28	60	167	59 28	59	167	60 27	59	167
8	56 21	59	166	57 20	59	166	58 19	59	165	59 18	59	165	60 17	59	165
9	56 10	59	164	57 09	59	164	58 08	59	164	59 07	59	163	60 06	58	163
10	55 59	+59	163	56 58	+58	162	57 56	+59	162	58 55	+58	161	59 53	+58	161
11	55 46	59	161	56 45	58	161	57 43	58	160	58 41	58	160	59 39	58	159
12	55 33	58	159	56 31	58	159	57 29	58	158	58 27	57	158	59 24	58	157
13	55 18	58	158	56 16	57	157	57 13	58	157	58 11	57	156	59 08	58	156
14	55 02	57	156	55 59	58	155	56 57	57	155	57 54	57	154	58 51	57	154
15	54 45	+57	154	55 42	+57	154	56 39	+57	153	57 36	+57	153	58 33	+56	152
16	54 27	57	153	55 24	57	152	56 21	56	152	57 17	56	151	58 13	57	150
17	54 08	57	151	55 05	56	151	56 01	56	150	56 57	56	149	57 53	56	149
18	53 48	57	150	54 45	56	149	55 41	55	148	56 36	56	148	57 32	55	147
19	53 28	55	148	54 23	56	148	55 19	55	147	56 14	55	146	57 09	55	145
20	53 06	+55	147	54 01	+56	146	54 57	+55	145	55 52	+54	145	56 46	+55	144
21	52 44	55	145	53 39	54	145	54 33	55	144	55 28	54	143	56 22	54	142
22	52 20	55	144	53 15	54	143	54 09	54	142	55 03	54	142	55 57	54	141
23	51 56	54	142	52 50	54	142	53 44	54	141	54 38	53	140	55 31	53	139
24	51 31	54	141	52 25	53	140	53 18	54	139	54 12	53	139	55 05	52	138
25	51 05	+54	140	51 59	+53	139	52 52	+53	138	53 45	+52	137	54 37	+53	136
26	50 39	53	138	51 32	53	137	52 25	52	137	53 17	52	136	54 09	52	135
27	50 12	52	137	51 04	53	136	51 57	52	135	52 49	52	134	53 41	51	134
28	49 44	52	135	50 36	52	135	51 28	52	134	52 20	51	133	53 11	51	132
29	49 15	52	134	50 07	52	133	50 59	51	133	51 50	51	132	52 41	51	131
30	48 46	+52	133	49 38	+51	132	50 29	+51	131	51 20	+50	130	52 10	+50	130
31	48 17	51	132	49 08	51	131	49 59	50	130	50 49	50	129	51 39	50	128
32	47 46	51	130	48 37	51	130	49 28	50	129	50 18	49	128	51 07	50	127
33	47 15	51	129	48 06	50	128	48 56	50	128	49 46	49	127	50 35	49	126
34	46 44	50	128	47 34	50	127	48 24	49	126	49 13	49	126	50 02	49	125
35	46 12	+50	127	47 02	+49	126	47 51	+49	125	48 40	+49	124	49 29	+48	123
36	45 40	49	126	46 29	49	125	47 18	49	124	48 07	48	123	48 55	48	122
37	45 07	49	125	45 56	49	124	46 45	48	123	47 33	48	122	48 21	48	121
38	44 34	48	123	45 22	49	123	46 11	48	122	46 59	47	121	47 46	48	120
39	44 00	48	122	44 48	49	122	45 37	47	121	46 24	48	120	47 12	46	119
40	43 26	+48	121	44 14	+48	120	45 02	+47	120	45 49	+47	119	46 36	+47	118
41	42 51	48	120	43 39	48	119	44 27	47	119	45 14	46	118	46 00	47	117
42	42 16	48	119	43 04	47	118	43 51	47	118	44 38	46	117	45 24	46	116
43	41 41	47	118	42 28	47	117	43 15	47	116	44 02	46	116	44 48	46	115
44	41 06	47	117	41 53	46	116	42 39	47	115	43 26	46	115	44 12	45	114
45	40 30	+46	116	41 16	+47	115	42 03	+46	114	42 49	+46	114	43 35	+45	113
46	39 53	47	115	40 40	46	114	41 26	46	113	42 12	45	113	42 57	45	112
47	39 17	46	114	40 03	46	113	40 49	46	113	41 35	45	112	42 20	45	111
48	38 40	46	113	39 26	46	112	40 12	45	112	40 57	45	111	41 42	45	110
49	38 03	46	112	38 49	46	111	39 35	45	111	40 20	44	110	41 04	45	109
50	37 26	+46	111	38 12	+45	111	38 57	+45	110	39 42	+44	109	40 26	+44	108
51	36 48	46	110	37 34	45	110	38 19	45	109	39 04	44	108	39 48	44	107
52	36 11	45	109	36 56	45	109	37 41	44	108	38 25	45	107	39 10	43	106
53	35 33	45	109	36 18	44	108	37 02	45	107	37 47	44	106	38 31	43	105
54	34 54	45	108	35 39	45	107	36 24	44	106	37 08	44	105	37 52	44	104
55	34 16	+45	107	35 01	+44	106	35 45	+44	105	36 29	+44	104	37 13	+43	103
56	33 38	44	106	34 22	44	105	35 06	44	104	35 50	44	103	36 34	43	103
57	32 59	44	105	33 43	44	104	34 27	44	103	35 11	44	103	35 55	43	102
58	32 20	44	104	33 04	44	103	33 48	44	103	34 32	43	102	35 15	43	101
59	31 41	44	103	32 25	44	103	33 09	44	102	33 53	43	101	34 36	43	100
60	31 02	+44	103	31 46	+44	102	32 30	+43	101	33 13	+43	100	33 56	+43	99
61	30 23	44	102	31 07	43	101	31 50	44	100	32 34	43	99	33 17	42	98
62	29 43	44	101	30 27	44	100	31 11	43	99	31 54	43	99	32 37	42	98
63	29 04	44	100	29 48	43	99	30 31	43	99	31 14	43	98	31 57	43	97
64	28 24	44	99	29 08	43	99	29 51	43	98	30 34	43	97	31 17	43	96
65	27 45	+43	99	28 28	+43	98	29 11	+43	97	29 54	+43	96	30 37	+43	95
66	27 05	43	98	27 48	44	97	28 32	43	96	29 15	42	95	29 57	43	95
67	26 25	43	97	27 08	44	96	27 52	43	95	28 35	42	95	29 17	42	94
68	25 45	43	96	26 28	44	95	27 12	42	95	27 54	43	94	28 37	42	93
69	25 05	43	95	25 48	44	95	26 32	42	94	27 14	43	93	27 57	42	92

LHA	20° Hc	20° d	20° Z	21° Hc	21° d	21° Z	22° Hc	22° d	22° Z	23° Hc	23° d	23° Z	24° Hc	24° d	24° Z
	° ′	′	°	° ′	′	°	° ′	′	°	° ′	′	°	° ′	′	°
0	62 00	+60	180	63 00	+60	180	64 00	+60	180	65 00	+60	180	66 00	+60	180
1	61 59	60	178	62 59	60	178	63 59	60	178	64 59	60	178	65 59	60	178
2	61 57	60	176	62 57	60	176	63 57	60	176	64 57	60	176	65 57	60	176
3	61 54	60	174	62 54	59	174	63 53	60	174	64 53	60	174	65 53	60	173
4	61 49	60	172	62 49	59	172	63 48	60	172	64 48	60	171	65 48	59	171
5	61 43	+59	170	62 42	+60	170	63 42	+59	170	64 41	+60	169	65 41	+59	169
6	61 35	59	168	62 34	60	168	63 34	59	167	64 33	59	167	65 32	59	167
7	61 26	59	166	62 25	59	166	63 24	59	165	64 23	59	165	65 22	59	165
8	61 16	59	164	62 15	58	164	63 13	59	163	64 12	59	163	65 11	58	162
9	61 04	59	162	62 03	58	162	63 01	59	161	64 00	58	161	64 58	58	160
10	60 51	+59	160	61 50	+58	160	62 48	+58	159	63 46	+57	159	64 43	+58	158
11	60 37	58	159	61 35	58	158	62 33	57	157	63 30	58	157	64 28	57	156
12	60 22	58	157	61 20	57	156	62 17	57	156	63 14	57	155	64 11	57	154
13	60 06	57	155	61 03	57	154	62 00	56	154	62 56	57	153	63 53	56	152
14	59 48	57	153	60 45	56	153	61 41	57	152	62 38	56	151	63 34	55	150
15	59 29	+57	151	60 26	+56	151	61 22	+56	150	62 18	+55	149	63 13	+55	148
16	59 10	55	150	60 05	56	149	61 01	55	148	61 56	55	147	62 51	55	147
17	58 49	55	148	59 44	55	147	60 39	55	146	61 34	55	146	62 29	54	145
18	58 27	55	146	59 22	55	146	60 17	54	145	61 11	54	144	62 05	54	143
19	58 04	55	145	58 59	54	144	59 53	54	143	60 47	53	142	61 40	53	141
20	57 41	+54	143	58 35	+53	142	59 28	+54	141	60 22	+53	141	61 15	+52	140
21	57 16	54	141	58 10	53	141	59 03	53	140	59 56	52	139	60 48	52	138
22	56 51	53	140	57 44	52	139	58 36	53	138	59 29	52	137	60 21	51	136
23	56 24	53	138	57 17	52	138	58 09	52	137	59 01	52	136	59 53	51	135
24	55 57	52	137	56 50	51	136	57 41	52	135	58 33	51	134	59 24	50	133
25	55 30	+51	136	56 21	+52	135	57 13	+51	134	58 04	+50	133	58 54	+50	132
26	55 01	51	134	55 52	51	133	56 43	51	132	57 34	50	131	58 24	49	130
27	54 32	51	133	55 23	50	132	56 13	50	131	57 03	50	130	57 53	49	129
28	54 02	50	131	54 52	51	130	55 43	49	129	56 32	49	128	57 21	49	127
29	53 32	50	130	54 22	49	129	55 11	49	128	56 00	49	127	56 49	48	126
30	53 00	+50	129	53 50	+49	128	54 39	+49	127	55 28	+48	126	56 16	+48	125
31	52 29	49	127	53 18	49	126	54 07	48	125	54 55	48	124	55 43	47	123
32	51 57	49	126	52 46	48	125	53 34	48	124	54 22	47	123	55 09	47	122
33	51 24	48	125	52 12	48	124	53 00	48	123	53 48	47	122	54 35	46	121
34	50 51	48	124	51 39	48	123	52 27	47	122	53 14	46	121	54 00	46	120
35	50 17	+48	123	51 05	+47	122	51 52	+47	121	52 39	+46	120	53 25	+46	119
36	49 43	47	121	50 30	47	120	51 17	47	119	52 04	46	118	52 50	45	117
37	49 09	47	120	49 56	46	119	50 42	46	118	51 28	46	117	52 14	45	116
38	48 34	46	119	49 20	47	118	50 07	45	117	50 52	46	116	51 38	44	115
39	47 58	47	118	48 45	46	117	49 31	45	116	50 16	45	115	51 01	44	114
40	47 23	+46	117	48 09	+45	116	48 54	+46	115	49 40	+44	114	50 24	+44	113
41	46 47	46	116	47 33	45	115	48 18	45	114	49 03	44	113	49 47	44	112
42	46 10	46	115	46 56	45	114	47 41	45	113	48 26	44	112	49 10	43	111
43	45 34	45	114	46 19	45	113	47 04	44	112	47 48	44	111	48 32	43	110
44	44 57	45	113	45 42	45	112	46 27	44	111	47 11	43	110	47 54	43	109
45	44 20	+45	112	45 05	+44	111	45 49	+44	110	46 33	+43	109	47 16	+43	108
46	43 42	45	111	44 27	44	110	45 11	44	109	45 55	43	108	46 38	42	107
47	43 05	44	110	43 49	44	109	44 33	43	108	45 16	43	107	45 59	42	106
48	42 27	44	109	43 11	44	108	43 55	43	107	44 38	42	106	45 20	43	105
49	41 49	44	108	42 33	43	107	43 16	43	106	43 59	43	105	44 42	42	104
50	41 10	+44	107	41 54	+43	106	42 37	+43	105	43 20	+43	103	44 03	+41	103
51	40 32	44	106	41 16	43	105	41 59	42	104	42 41	42	103	43 23	42	102
52	39 53	44	105	40 37	43	104	41 20	42	103	42 02	42	102	42 44	42	101
53	39 14	44	104	39 58	43	103	40 41	42	103	41 23	42	102	42 05	41	101
54	38 36	43	103	39 19	42	103	40 01	42	102	40 43	42	101	41 25	41	100
55	37 56	+43	103	38 39	+43	102	39 22	+42	101	40 04	+42	100	40 46	+41	99
56	37 17	43	102	38 00	42	101	38 42	42	100	39 24	42	99	40 06	41	98
57	36 38	42	101	37 20	43	100	38 03	42	99	38 45	41	98	39 26	41	97
58	35 58	43	100	36 41	42	99	37 23	42	98	38 05	41	97	38 46	41	97
59	35 19	42	99	36 01	42	98	36 43	42	98	37 25	41	97	38 06	41	96
60	34 39	+42	98	35 21	+42	98	36 03	+42	97	36 45	+41	96	37 26	+41	95
61	33 59	43	98	34 42	42	97	35 24	41	96	36 05	41	95	36 46	41	94
62	33 19	43	97	34 02	42	96	34 44	41	95	35 25	41	94	36 06	41	93
63	32 40	42	96	33 22	42	95	34 04	41	94	34 45	41	93	35 26	41	93
64	32 00	42	95	32 42	42	94	33 24	41	94	34 05	41	93	34 46	41	92
65	31 20	+42	94	32 02	+41	94	32 43	+42	93	33 25	+41	92	34 06	+41	91
66	30 40	42	94	31 22	41	93	32 03	42	92	32 45	41	91	33 26	40	90
67	29 59	42	93	30 41	42	92	31 23	42	91	32 05	41	90	32 46	40	90
68	29 19	42	92	30 01	42	91	30 43	41	91	31 24	41	90	32 05	41	89
69	28 39	42	91	29 21	42	91	30 03	41	90	30 44	41	89	31 25	41	88

LHA	25° Hc	25° d	25° Z	26° Hc	26° d	26° Z	27° Hc	27° d	27° Z	28° Hc	28° d	28° Z	29° Hc	29° d	29° Z	LHA
	° ′	′	°	° ′	′	°	° ′	′	°	° ′	′	°	° ′	′	°	
0	67 00	+60	180	68 00	+60	180	69 00	+60	180	70 00	+60	180	71 00	+60	180	360
1	66 59	60	178	67 59	60	178	68 59	60	178	69 59	60	177	70 59	60	177	359
2	66 57	60	175	67 57	60	175	68 57	59	175	69 56	60	175	70 56	60	175	358
3	66 53	60	173	67 53	59	173	68 52	60	173	69 52	60	172	70 52	59	172	357
4	66 47	60	171	67 47	59	171	68 46	60	170	69 46	59	170	70 45	59	169	356
5	66 40	+59	169	67 39	+59	168	68 38	+60	168	69 38	+59	167	70 37	+59	167	355
6	66 31	59	166	67 30	59	166	68 29	59	165	69 28	59	165	70 27	58	164	354
7	66 21	59	164	67 20	58	164	68 18	59	163	69 17	58	162	70 15	58	162	353
8	66 09	58	162	67 07	59	161	68 06	58	161	69 04	57	160	70 01	58	159	352
9	65 56	58	160	66 54	57	159	67 51	58	158	68 49	57	158	69 46	57	157	351
10	65 41	+58	158	66 39	+57	157	67 36	+57	156	68 33	+57	155	69 30	+56	154	350
11	65 25	57	155	66 22	57	155	67 19	56	154	68 15	56	153	69 11	56	152	349
12	65 08	56	153	66 04	56	153	67 00	56	152	67 56	56	151	68 52	55	150	348
13	64 49	56	151	65 45	56	151	66 41	55	150	67 36	55	149	68 31	54	148	347
14	64 29	56	149	65 25	55	149	66 20	55	148	67 15	54	147	68 09	54	145	346
15	64 08	+55	148	65 03	+55	147	65 58	+54	146	66 52	+53	144	67 45	+53	143	345
16	63 46	54	146	64 40	54	145	65 34	54	144	66 28	53	143	67 21	52	141	344
17	63 23	54	144	64 17	53	143	65 10	53	142	66 03	52	141	66 55	52	139	343
18	62 59	53	142	63 52	53	141	64 45	52	140	65 37	51	139	66 28	51	137	342
19	62 33	53	140	63 26	52	139	64 18	52	138	65 10	51	137	66 01	50	136	341
20	62 07	+52	139	62 59	+52	137	63 51	+51	136	64 42	+50	135	65 32	+50	134	340
21	61 40	52	137	62 32	51	136	63 23	50	135	64 13	50	133	65 03	49	132	339
22	61 12	51	135	62 03	51	134	62 54	49	133	63 43	50	132	64 33	48	130	338
23	60 44	50	134	61 34	50	133	62 24	49	131	63 13	49	130	64 02	47	129	337
24	60 14	50	132	61 04	49	131	61 53	49	130	62 42	48	129	63 30	47	127	336
25	59 44	+49	131	60 33	+49	129	61 22	+48	128	62 10	+48	127	62 58	+46	126	335
26	59 13	49	129	60 02	48	128	60 50	48	127	61 38	47	126	62 25	46	124	334
27	58 42	48	128	59 30	48	127	60 18	47	125	61 05	46	124	61 51	46	123	333
28	58 10	48	126	58 58	47	125	59 45	46	124	60 31	46	123	61 17	45	121	332
29	57 37	47	125	58 24	47	124	59 11	46	123	59 57	46	121	60 43	44	120	331
30	57 04	+47	124	57 51	+46	122	58 37	+46	121	59 23	+45	120	60 08	+44	119	330
31	56 30	47	122	57 17	45	121	58 02	46	120	58 48	44	119	59 32	44	117	329
32	55 56	46	121	56 42	45	120	57 27	45	119	58 12	44	117	58 56	43	116	328
33	55 21	46	120	56 07	45	119	56 52	44	117	57 36	44	116	58 20	43	115	327
34	54 46	46	119	55 32	44	117	56 16	44	116	57 00	43	115	57 43	43	114	326
35	54 11	+45	117	54 56	+44	116	55 40	+44	115	56 24	+42	114	57 06	+42	113	325
36	53 35	44	116	54 19	44	115	55 03	44	114	55 47	42	113	56 29	42	111	324
37	52 59	44	115	53 43	44	114	54 27	42	113	55 09	43	112	55 52	41	110	323
38	52 22	44	114	53 06	43	113	53 49	43	112	54 32	42	111	55 14	41	109	322
39	51 45	44	113	52 29	43	112	53 12	42	111	53 54	42	109	54 36	41	108	321
40	51 08	+44	112	51 52	+42	111	52 34	+42	110	53 16	+42	108	53 58	+40	107	320
41	50 31	43	111	51 14	42	110	51 56	42	109	52 38	41	107	53 19	40	106	319
42	49 53	43	110	50 36	42	109	51 18	42	108	52 00	40	106	52 40	41	105	318
43	49 15	43	109	49 58	42	108	50 40	41	107	51 21	41	105	52 02	40	104	317
44	48 37	42	108	49 19	42	107	50 01	41	106	50 42	41	104	51 23	39	103	316
45	47 59	+42	107	48 41	+41	106	49 22	+41	105	50 03	+40	104	50 43	+40	102	315
46	47 20	42	106	48 02	41	105	48 43	41	104	49 24	40	103	50 04	40	101	314
47	46 41	42	105	47 23	41	104	48 04	41	103	48 45	40	102	49 25	39	101	313
48	46 03	41	104	46 44	41	103	47 25	41	102	48 06	39	101	48 45	39	100	312
49	45 24	41	103	46 05	41	102	46 46	40	101	47 26	40	100	48 06	39	99	311
50	44 44	+42	102	45 26	+40	101	46 06	+40	100	46 46	+40	99	47 26	+39	98	310
51	44 05	41	101	44 46	41	100	45 27	40	99	46 07	39	98	46 46	39	97	309
52	43 26	41	101	44 07	40	100	44 47	40	98	45 27	39	97	46 06	39	96	308
53	42 46	41	100	43 27	40	99	44 07	40	98	44 47	39	97	45 26	39	96	307
54	42 06	41	99	42 47	41	98	43 28	39	97	44 07	39	96	44 46	39	95	306
55	41 27	+40	98	42 07	+41	97	42 48	+39	96	43 27	+39	95	44 06	+39	94	305
56	40 47	41	97	41 28	40	96	42 08	39	95	42 47	39	94	43 26	39	93	304
57	40 07	41	96	40 48	40	95	41 28	39	94	42 07	39	93	42 46	38	92	303
58	39 27	41	96	40 08	40	95	40 48	39	94	41 27	39	93	42 06	38	92	302
59	38 47	41	95	39 28	39	94	40 07	40	93	40 47	39	92	41 26	38	91	301
60	38 07	+40	94	38 47	+40	93	39 27	+40	92	40 07	+39	91	40 46	+38	90	300
61	37 27	40	93	38 07	40	92	38 47	40	91	39 27	39	90	40 06	38	89	299
62	36 47	40	92	37 27	40	92	38 07	40	91	38 47	38	90	39 25	39	89	298
63	36 07	40	92	36 47	40	91	37 27	39	90	38 06	39	89	38 45	39	88	297
64	35 27	40	91	36 07	40	90	36 47	39	89	37 26	39	88	38 05	39	87	296
65	34 47	+40	90	35 27	+40	89	36 07	+39	88	36 46	+39	87	37 25	+39	86	295
66	34 06	41	89	34 47	40	89	35 27	39	88	36 06	39	87	36 45	39	86	294
67	33 26	41	89	34 07	39	88	34 46	40	87	35 26	39	86	36 05	39	85	293
68	32 46	40	88	33 26	40	87	34 06	40	86	34 46	39	85	35 25	39	84	292
69	32 06	40	87	32 46	40	86	33 26	40	85	34 06	39	85	34 45	39	84	291

S. Lat. {LHA greater than 180°........ Zn=180−Z; LHA less than 180°........ Zn=180+Z}

DECLINATION (15°-29°) SAME NAME AS LATITUDE

N. Lat. {LHA greater than 180°....... Zn=Z
{LHA less than 180°........... Zn=360−Z

DECLINATION (15°-29°) SAME NAME AS LATITUDE

LHA	15° Hc	15° d	15° Z	16° Hc	16° d	16° Z	17° Hc	17° d	17° Z	18° Hc	18° d	18° Z	19° Hc	19° d	19° Z	LHA
	° ′	′	°	° ′	′	°	° ′	′	°	° ′	′	°	° ′	′	°	
70	24 25	+43	95	25 08	+43	94	25 51	+43	93	26 34	+43	92	27 17	+42	91	290
71	23 45	43	94	24 28	43	93	25 11	43	92	25 54	43	92	26 37	42	91	289
72	23 05	43	93	23 48	43	92	24 31	43	92	25 14	43	91	25 57	42	90	288
73	22 25	43	92	23 08	43	92	23 51	43	91	24 34	42	90	25 16	43	89	287
74	21 45	43	92	22 28	43	91	23 11	43	90	23 54	42	89	24 36	43	89	286
75	21 05	+43	91	21 48	+43	90	22 31	+43	89	23 14	+42	89	23 56	+42	88	285
76	20 25	43	90	21 08	43	89	21 51	42	89	22 33	43	88	23 16	42	87	284
77	19 44	44	89	20 28	43	89	21 11	42	88	21 53	43	87	22 36	42	86	283
78	19 04	43	89	19 47	43	88	20 30	43	87	21 13	43	86	21 56	42	86	282
79	18 24	43	88	19 07	43	87	19 50	43	86	20 33	43	86	21 16	42	85	281
80	17 44	+43	87	18 27	+43	86	19 10	+43	86	19 53	+43	85	20 36	+42	84	280
81	17 04	43	86	17 47	43	86	18 30	43	85	19 13	43	84	19 56	43	83	279
82	16 24	43	86	17 07	43	85	17 50	43	84	18 33	43	83	19 16	43	83	278
83	15 44	43	85	16 27	43	84	17 10	43	83	17 53	43	83	18 36	43	82	277
84	15 04	43	84	15 47	44	83	16 31	43	83	17 14	43	82	17 57	42	81	276
85	14 24	+43	83	15 07	+44	83	15 51	+43	82	16 34	+43	81	17 17	+43	81	275
86	13 44	44	83	14 28	43	82	15 11	43	81	15 54	43	81	16 37	43	80	274
87	13 04	44	82	13 48	43	81	14 31	44	81	15 15	43	80	15 58	43	79	273
88	12 25	43	81	13 08	44	81	13 52	43	80	14 35	44	79	15 19	43	78	272
89	11 45	44	81	12 29	43	80	13 12	44	79	13 56	43	78	14 39	44	78	271
90	11 05	+44	80	11 49	+44	79	12 33	+44	78	13 17	+43	78	14 00	+44	77	270
91	10 26	44	79	11 10	44	78	11 54	43	78	12 37	44	77	13 21	44	76	269
92	09 47	44	78	10 31	44	78	11 15	43	77	11 58	44	76	12 42	44	76	268
93	09 07	44	78	09 51	44	77	10 35	44	76	11 19	44	76	12 03	44	75	267
94	08 28	44	77	09 12	45	76	09 57	44	76	10 41	44	75	11 25	43	74	266
95	07 49	+44	76	08 33	+45	76	09 18	+44	75	10 02	+44	74	10 46	+44	74	265
96	07 10	45	76	07 55	44	75	08 39	44	74	09 23	45	74	10 08	44	73	264
97	06 31	45	75	07 16	44	74	08 00	45	73	08 45	44	73	09 29	45	72	263
98	05 53	44	74	06 37	45	73	07 22	45	73	08 07	44	72	08 51	45	71	262
99	05 14	45	73	05 59	45	73	06 44	45	72	07 29	44	71	08 13	45	71	261
100	04 36	+45	73	05 21	+45	72	06 06	+45	71	06 51	+44	71	07 35	+45	70	260
101	03 57	46	72	04 43	45	71	05 28	45	71	06 13	45	70	06 58	45	69	259
102	03 19	46	71	04 05	45	71	04 50	45	70	05 35	45	69	06 20	45	69	258
103	02 41	46	70	03 27	45	70	04 12	46	69	04 58	45	68	05 43	45	68	257
104	02 04	45	70	02 49	46	69	03 35	45	68	04 20	46	68	05 06	46	67	256
105	01 26	+46	69	02 12	+46	68	02 58	+45	68	03 43	+46	67	04 29	+46	66	255
106	00 49	46	68	01 35	46	68	02 21	46	67	03 07	45	66	03 52	46	66	254
107	00 12	46	67	00 58	46	67	01 44	46	66	02 30	46	66	03 16	46	65	253
108	-0 25	46	67	00 21	46	66	01 07	46	65	01 53	47	65	02 40	46	64	252
109	-1 02	46	66	-0 16	47	65	00 31	46	65	01 17	47	64	02 04	46	63	251
110	-1 39	+47	65	-0 52	+47	65	-0 05	+46	64	00 41	+47	63	01 28	+47	63	250
111	-2 15	47	64	-1 28	47	64	-0 41	46	63	00 05	47	63	00 52	47	62	249
112	-2 51	47	64	-2 04	47	63	-1 17	47	62	-0 30	47	62	00 17	47	61	248
113	-3 27	47	63	-2 40	47	62	-1 53	48	62	-1 05	47	61	-0 18	47	60	247
114	-4 03	48	62	-3 15	47	62	-2 28	48	61	-1 40	47	60	-0 53	48	60	246
115	-4 38	+48	61	-3 50	+47	61	-3 03	+48	60	-2 15	+48	60	-1 27	+47	59	245
116	-5 13	48	61	-4 25	47	60	-3 38	48	59	-2 50	48	59	-2 02	48	58	244
117	-5 48	48	60	-5 00	48	59	-4 12	48	59	-3 24	48	58	-2 36	48	57	243
118				-5 34	48	58	-4 46	48	58	-3 58	49	57	-3 09	48	57	242
119							-5 20	49	57	-4 31	48	57	-3 43	49	56	241
120							-5 54	+49	56	-5 05	+49	56	-4 16	+49	55	240
121										-5 38	49	55	-4 49	49	54	239
122													-5 21	49	54	238
123													-5 54	50	53	237

LHA	20° Hc	20° d	20° Z	21° Hc	21° d	21° Z	22° Hc	22° d	22° Z	23° Hc	23° d	23° Z	24° Hc	24° d	24° Z	LHA
	° ′	′	°	° ′	′	°	° ′	′	°	° ′	′	°	° ′	′	°	
70	27 59	+42	91	28 41	+42	90	29 23	+41	89	30 04	+41	88	30 45	+41	87	290
71	27 19	42	90	28 01	42	89	28 43	41	88	29 24	41	88	30 05	41	87	289
72	26 39	42	89	27 21	42	88	28 03	41	88	28 44	41	87	29 25	41	86	288
73	25 59	42	88	26 41	41	88	27 22	42	87	28 04	41	86	28 45	41	85	287
74	25 19	42	88	26 01	41	87	26 42	42	86	27 24	41	85	28 05	41	85	286
75	24 38	+42	87	25 20	+42	86	26 02	+42	85	26 44	+41	85	27 25	+41	84	285
76	23 58	42	86	24 40	42	86	25 22	42	85	26 04	41	84	26 45	41	83	284
77	23 18	42	86	24 00	42	85	24 42	42	84	25 24	41	83	26 05	42	82	283
78	22 38	42	85	23 20	42	84	24 02	42	83	24 44	42	83	25 26	41	82	282
79	21 58	43	84	22 41	42	83	23 23	41	83	24 04	42	82	24 46	41	81	281
80	21 18	+43	83	22 01	+42	83	22 43	+42	82	23 25	+41	81	24 06	+42	80	280
81	20 39	42	83	21 21	42	82	22 03	42	81	22 45	42	80	23 27	41	80	279
82	19 59	42	82	20 41	43	81	21 24	42	80	22 06	41	80	22 47	42	79	278
83	19 19	43	81	20 02	42	81	20 44	42	80	21 26	42	79	22 08	42	78	277
84	18 39	43	81	19 22	43	80	20 05	42	79	20 47	42	78	21 29	42	78	276
85	18 00	+43	80	18 43	+42	79	19 25	+42	78	20 07	+43	78	20 50	+42	77	275
86	17 20	43	79	18 03	43	78	18 46	42	78	19 28	43	77	20 11	42	76	274
87	16 41	43	78	17 24	43	78	18 07	42	77	18 49	43	76	19 32	42	76	273
88	16 02	43	78	16 45	43	77	17 28	42	76	18 10	43	76	18 53	42	75	272
89	15 23	43	77	16 06	43	76	16 49	43	76	17 32	42	75	18 14	43	74	271
90	14 44	+43	76	15 27	+43	76	16 10	+43	75	16 53	+43	74	17 36	+42	73	270
91	14 05	43	76	14 48	43	75	15 31	43	74	16 14	43	74	16 57	43	73	269
92	13 26	43	75	14 09	44	74	14 53	43	74	15 36	43	73	16 19	43	72	268
93	12 47	44	74	13 31	43	74	14 14	44	73	14 58	43	72	15 41	43	71	267
94	12 08	44	74	12 52	44	73	13 36	43	72	14 19	44	71	15 03	43	71	266
95	11 30	+44	73	12 14	+44	72	12 58	+44	71	13 42	+43	71	14 25	+44	70	265
96	10 52	44	72	11 36	44	71	12 20	44	71	13 04	43	70	13 47	44	69	264
97	10 14	44	71	10 58	44	71	11 42	44	70	12 26	44	69	13 10	44	69	263
98	09 36	44	71	10 20	44	70	11 04	45	69	11 49	44	69	12 33	44	68	262
99	08 58	44	70	09 42	45	69	10 27	44	69	11 11	45	68	11 56	44	67	261
100	08 20	+45	69	09 05	+45	69	09 50	+44	68	10 34	+45	67	11 19	+44	67	260
101	07 43	45	69	08 28	44	68	09 12	45	67	09 57	45	67	10 42	44	66	259
102	07 05	46	68	07 51	45	67	08 36	45	67	09 21	44	66	10 05	45	65	258
103	06 28	46	67	07 14	45	67	07 59	45	66	08 44	45	65	09 29	45	65	257
104	05 52	45	66	06 37	45	66	07 22	46	65	08 08	45	65	08 53	45	64	256
105	05 15	+45	66	06 00	+46	65	06 46	+46	64	07 32	+45	64	08 17	+45	63	255
106	04 38	46	65	05 24	46	64	06 10	46	64	06 56	45	63	07 41	46	62	254
107	04 02	46	64	04 48	46	64	05 34	46	63	06 20	46	62	07 06	46	62	253
108	03 26	46	64	04 12	46	63	04 58	47	62	05 45	46	62	06 31	46	61	252
109	02 50	47	63	03 37	46	62	04 23	46	62	05 09	47	61	05 56	46	60	251
110	02 15	+46	62	03 01	+47	61	03 48	+46	61	04 34	+47	60	05 21	+46	60	250
111	01 39	47	61	02 26	47	61	03 13	47	60	04 00	46	59	04 46	47	59	249
112	01 04	47	61	01 51	47	60	02 38	47	59	03 25	47	59	04 12	47	58	248
113	00 29	47	60	01 16	48	59	02 04	47	59	02 51	47	58	03 38	47	57	247
114	-0 05	47	59	00 42	48	59	01 30	47	58	02 17	47	57	03 04	48	57	246
115	-0 40	+48	58	00 08	+48	58	00 56	+47	57	01 43	+48	57	02 31	+48	56	245
116	-1 14	48	58	-0 26	48	57	00 22	48	56	01 10	48	56	01 58	48	55	244
117	-1 48	49	57	-0 59	48	56	-0 11	48	56	00 37	48	55	01 25	48	55	243
118	-2 21	48	56	-1 33	49	56	-0 44	48	55	00 04	49	54	00 53	48	54	242
119	-2 54	48	55	-2 06	49	55	-1 17	49	54	-0 28	48	54	00 20	49	53	241
120	-3 27	+49	55	-2 38	+49	54	-1 49	+48	53	-1 01	+49	53	-0 12	+49	52	240
121	-4 00	49	54	-3 11	50	53	-2 21	49	53	-1 32	49	52	-0 43	49	52	239
122	-4 32	49	53	-3 43	50	52	-2 53	49	52	-2 04	50	51	-1 14	49	51	238
123	-5 04	50	52	-4 14	49	52	-3 25	50	51	-2 35	50	51	-1 45	49	50	237
124	-5 36	50	51	-4 46	50	51	-3 56	50	50	-3 06	50	50	-2 16	50	49	236
125				-5 17	+50	50	-4 27	+51	50	-3 36	+50	49	-2 46	+50	49	235
126				-5 47	50	49	-4 57	50	49	-4 07	51	48	-3 16	50	48	234
127							-5 27	51	48	-4 36	50	48	-3 46	51	47	233
128							-5 57	51	47	-5 06	51	47	-4 15	51	46	232
129										-5 35	51	46	-4 44	52	45	231
130													-5 12	+51	45	230
131													-5 40	52	44	229

LHA	25° Hc	25° d	25° Z	26° Hc	26° d	26° Z	27° Hc	27° d	27° Z	28° Hc	28° d	28° Z	29° Hc	29° d	29° Z	LHA
	° ′	′	°	° ′	′	°	° ′	′	°	° ′	′	°	° ′	′	°	
70	31 26	+40	87	32 06	+40	86	32 46	+40	85	33 26	+39	84	34 05	+39	83	290
71	30 46	40	86	31 26	40	85	32 06	40	84	32 46	39	83	33 25	39	82	289
72	30 06	40	85	30 46	40	84	31 26	40	83	32 06	40	82	32 46	39	82	288
73	29 26	40	84	30 06	41	84	30 47	40	83	31 27	39	82	32 06	39	81	287
74	28 46	41	84	29 27	40	83	30 07	40	82	30 47	39	81	31 26	40	80	286
75	28 06	+41	83	28 47	+40	82	29 27	+40	81	30 07	+40	80	30 47	+39	80	285
76	27 26	41	82	28 07	41	81	28 48	40	81	29 28	39	80	30 07	40	79	284
77	26 47	40	82	27 27	41	81	28 08	40	80	28 48	40	79	29 28	40	78	283
78	26 07	41	81	26 48	40	80	27 28	41	79	28 09	40	78	28 49	40	78	282
79	25 27	41	80	26 08	41	79	26 49	41	79	27 30	40	78	28 10	40	77	281
80	24 48	+41	80	25 29	+41	79	26 10	+40	78	26 50	+41	77	27 31	+40	76	280
81	24 08	42	79	24 50	41	78	25 31	40	77	26 11	41	76	26 52	40	76	279
82	23 29	41	78	24 10	41	77	24 51	41	77	25 32	41	76	26 13	40	75	278
83	22 50	41	77	23 31	41	77	24 12	41	76	24 53	41	75	25 34	41	74	277
84	22 11	41	77	22 52	42	76	23 34	41	75	24 15	41	74	24 56	40	74	276
85	21 32	+41	76	22 13	+42	75	22 55	+41	75	23 36	+41	74	24 17	+41	73	275
86	20 53	42	75	21 35	41	75	22 16	42	74	22 58	41	73	23 39	41	72	274
87	20 14	42	75	20 56	42	74	21 38	41	73	22 19	42	72	23 01	41	72	273
88	19 35	42	74	20 17	42	73	20 59	42	73	21 41	42	72	22 23	41	71	272
89	18 57	42	73	19 39	42	73	20 21	42	72	21 03	42	71	21 45	41	70	271
90	18 18	+43	73	19 01	+42	72	19 43	+42	71	20 25	+42	70	21 07	+42	70	270
91	17 40	43	72	18 23	42	71	19 05	42	71	19 47	43	70	20 30	41	69	269
92	17 02	43	71	17 45	42	71	18 27	43	70	19 10	42	69	19 52	42	68	268
93	16 24	43	71	17 07	43	70	17 50	42	69	18 32	43	68	19 15	42	68	267
94	15 46	43	70	16 29	43	69	17 12	43	69	17 55	43	68	18 38	42	67	266
95	15 09	+43	69	15 52	+43	69	16 35	+43	68	17 18	+43	67	18 01	+43	66	265
96	14 31	44	69	15 15	43	68	15 58	43	67	16 41	43	67	17 24	43	66	264
97	13 54	44	68	14 38	43	67	15 21	44	67	16 05	43	66	16 48	43	65	263
98	13 17	44	67	14 01	43	67	14 44	44	66	15 28	43	65	16 11	44	64	262
99	12 40	44	67	13 24	44	66	14 08	44	65	14 52	43	65	15 35	44	64	261
100	12 03	+44	66	12 47	+44	65	13 31	+45	65	14 16	+43	64	14 59	+44	63	260
101	11 26	45	65	12 11	44	65	12 55	45	64	13 40	44	63	14 24	44	62	259
102	10 50	45	65	11 35	44	64	12 19	45	63	13 04	44	62	13 48	45	62	258
103	10 14	45	64	10 59	45	63	11 44	44	63	12 28	45	62	13 13	45	61	257
104	09 38	45	63	10 23	45	63	11 08	45	62	11 53	45	61	12 38	45	60	256
105	09 02	+46	62	09 48	+45	62	10 33	+45	61	11 18	+45	60	12 03	+45	60	255
106	08 27	45	62	09 12	46	61	09 58	45	60	10 43	46	60	11 29	45	59	254
107	07 52	45	61	08 37	46	60	09 23	46	60	10 09	45	59	10 54	46	58	253
108	07 17	46	60	08 03	46	60	08 49	45	59	09 34	46	58	10 20	46	58	252
109	06 42	46	60	07 28	46	59	08 14	46	58	09 00	46	58	09 46	46	57	251
110	06 07	+47	59	06 54	+46	58	07 40	+47	58	08 27	+46	57	09 13	+46	56	250
111	05 33	47	58	06 20	46	58	07 06	47	57	07 53	47	56	08 40	46	56	249
112	04 59	47	58	05 46	47	57	06 33	47	56	07 20	47	56	08 07	46	55	248
113	04 25	48	57	05 13	47	56	06 00	47	56	06 47	47	55	07 34	47	54	247
114	03 52	47	56	04 39	48	55	05 27	47	55	06 14	47	54	07 01	48	54	246
115	03 19	+47	55	04 06	+48	55	04 54	+48	54	05 42	+47	54	06 29	+48	53	245
116	02 46	48	55	03 34	48	54	04 22	47	53	05 09	48	53	05 57	48	52	244
117	02 13	48	54	03 01	49	53	03 50	48	53	04 38	48	52	05 26	48	52	243
118	01 41	48	53	02 29	49	53	03 18	48	52	04 06	48	51	04 54	49	51	242
119	01 09	49	52	01 58	48	52	02 46	49	51	03 35	48	51	04 23	49	50	241
120	00 37	+49	51	01 26	+49	51	02 15	+49	51	03 04	+49	50	03 53	+48	49	240
121	00 06	49	51	00 55	49	50	01 44	49	50	02 33	49	49	03 22	49	49	239
122	-0 25	49	50	00 24	50	50	01 14	49	49	02 03	49	49	02 52	50	48	238
123	-0 56	50	49	-0 06	50	49	00 44	49	48	01 33	50	48	02 23	49	47	237
124	-1 26	50	49	-0 36	50	48	00 14	50	48	01 04	50	47	01 54	49	46	236
125	-1 56	+50	48	-1 06	+50	47	-0 16	+50	47	00 34	+51	46	01 25	+50	46	235
126	-2 26	51	47	-1 35	50	47	-0 45	51	46	00 06	50	46	00 56	50	45	234
127	-2 55	51	46	-2 04	50	46	-1 14	51	45	-0 23	51	45	00 28	50	44	233
128	-3 24	51	46	-2 33	51	45	-1 42	51	45	-0 51	51	44	00 00	51	44	232
129	-3 52	51	45	-3 01	51	44	-2 10	51	44	-1 19	51	43	-0 28	52	43	231
130	-4 21	+52	44	-3 29	+51	44	-2 38	+52	43	-1 46	+51	43	-0 55	+52	42	230
131	-4 48	51	43	-3 57	52	43	-3 05	52	42	-2 13	52	42	-1 21	51	41	229
132	-5 16	52	43	-4 24	52	42	-3 32	52	42	-2 40	52	41	-1 48	52	41	228
133	-5 43	53	42	-4 50	52	41	-3 58	52	41	-3 06	52	40	-2 14	53	40	227
134				-5 17	53	40	-4 24	52	40	-3 32	53	40	-2 39	53	39	226
135				-5 43	+53	40	-4 50	+53	39	-3 57	+53	39	-3 04	+53	38	225
136							-5 15	53	38	-4 22	53	38	-3 29	53	37	224
137							-5 40	54	38	-4 46	53	37	-3 53	53	37	223
138										-5 10	53	36	-4 17	54	36	222
139										-5 34	54	36	-4 40	54	35	221

S. Lat. {LHA greater than 180°....... Zn=180−Z
{LHA less than 180°........... Zn=180+Z

DECLINATION (15°-29°) SAME NAME AS LATITUDE

N. Lat. {LHA greater than 180°....... Zn=Z; LHA less than 180°........... Zn=360−Z}

DECLINATION (15°-29°) SAME NAME AS LATITUDE

LHA	28° (Hc d Z)	29° Hc	29° d	29° Z	LHA
	°	° ′	′	°	
	140	−5 03	+54	34	220
	141	−5 26	55	34	219

DECLINATION (15°-29°) CONTRARY NAME TO LATITUDE

(Each cell gives Hc d Z.)

LHA	15°	16°	17°	18°	19°	20°	21°	22°	23°	24°	25°	26°	27°	28°	29°
82	−5 53 44 106	278													
81	−5 14 45 107	−5 59 45 107	279												
80	−4 36 −45 107	−5 21 −45 108	−6 06 −45 109	280											
79	−3 57 46 108	−4 43 45 109	−5 28 45 109	−6 13 45 110	281										
78	−3 19 46 109	−4 05 45 109	−4 50 45 110	−5 35 45 111	282										
77	−2 41 46 110	−3 27 45 110	−4 12 46 111	−4 58 45 112	−5 43 45 112	283									
76	−2 04 45 110	−2 49 46 111	−3 35 45 112	−4 20 46 112	−5 06 46 113	−5 52 45 114	284								
75	−1 26 −46 111	−2 12 −46 112	−2 58 −45 112	−3 43 −46 113	−4 29 −46 114	−5 15 −45 114	−6 00 −46 115	285							
74	−0 49 46 112	−1 35 46 112	−2 21 46 113	−3 07 45 114	−3 52 46 114	−4 38 46 115	−5 24 46 116	−6 10 46 116	286						
73	−0 12 46 113	−0 58 46 113	−1 44 46 114	−2 30 46 114	−3 16 46 115	−4 02 46 116	−4 48 46 116	−5 34 46 117	287						
72	00 25 46 113	−0 21 46 114	−1 07 46 115	−1 53 47 115	−2 40 46 116	−3 26 46 116	−4 12 46 117	−4 58 47 118	−5 45 46 118	288					
71	01 02 46 114	00 16 47 115	−0 31 46 115	−1 17 47 116	−2 04 46 117	−2 50 47 117	−3 37 46 118	−4 23 46 118	−5 09 47 119	−5 56 46 120	289				
70	01 39 −47 115	00 52 −47 115	00 05 −46 116	−0 41 −47 117	−1 28 −47 117	−2 15 −46 118	−3 01 −47 119	−3 48 −46 119	−4 34 −47 120	−5 21 −46 120	−6 07 −47 121	290			

S. Lat. {LHA greater than 180°....... Zn=180−Z; LHA less than 180°........... Zn=180+Z}

N. Lat. {LHA greater than 180°....... Zn=Z; LHA less than 180°........... Zn=360−Z}

DECLINATION (15°-29°) CONTRARY NAME TO LATITUDE

LHA	15° Hc	d	Z	16° Hc	d	Z	17° Hc	d	Z	18° Hc	d	Z	19° Hc	d	Z	20° Hc	d	Z	21° Hc	d	Z	22° Hc	d	Z
	° ′	′	°	° ′	′	°	° ′	′	°	° ′	′	°	° ′	′	°	° ′	′	°	° ′	′	°	° ′	′	°
69	02 15	47	116	01 28	47	116	00 41	46	117	−0 05	47	117	−0 52	47	118	−1 39	47	119	−2 26	47	119	−3 13	47	120
68	02 51	47	116	02 04	47	117	01 17	47	118	00 30	47	118	−0 17	47	119	−1 04	47	119	−1 51	47	120	−2 38	47	121
67	03 27	47	117	02 40	47	118	01 53	48	118	01 05	47	119	00 18	47	120	−0 29	47	120	−1 16	48	121	−2 04	47	121
66	04 03	48	118	03 15	47	118	02 28	48	119	01 40	47	120	00 53	48	120	00 05	47	121	−0 42	48	121	−1 30	47	122
65	04 38	−48	119	03 50	−47	119	03 03	−48	120	02 15	−48	120	01 27	−47	121	00 40	−48	122	−0 08	−48	122	−0 56	−47	123
64	05 13	48	119	04 25	47	120	03 38	48	121	02 50	48	121	02 02	48	122	01 14	48	122	00 26	48	123	−0 22	48	124
63	05 48	48	120	05 00	48	121	04 12	48	121	03 24	48	122	02 36	48	123	01 48	49	123	00 59	48	124	00 11	48	124
62	06 23	49	121	05 34	48	122	04 46	48	122	03 58	49	123	03 09	48	123	02 21	48	124	01 33	49	124	00 44	48	125
61	06 57	48	122	06 09	49	122	05 20	49	123	04 31	48	123	03 43	49	124	02 54	48	125	02 06	49	125	01 17	49	126
60	07 31	−49	123	06 42	−48	123	05 54	−49	124	05 05	−49	124	04 16	−49	125	03 27	−49	125	02 38	−49	126	01 49	−48	127
59	08 05	49	123	07 16	49	124	06 27	49	124	05 38	49	125	04 49	49	126	04 00	49	126	03 11	50	127	02 21	49	127
58	08 38	49	124	07 49	49	125	07 00	49	125	06 11	50	126	05 21	49	126	04 32	49	127	03 43	50	128	02 53	49	128
57	09 11	49	125	08 22	49	125	07 33	50	126	06 43	49	127	05 54	50	127	05 04	50	128	04 14	49	128	03 25	50	129
56	09 44	50	126	08 54	49	126	08 05	50	127	07 15	50	127	06 25	49	128	05 36	50	129	04 46	50	129	03 56	50	130
55	10 17	−50	127	09 27	−50	127	08 37	−50	128	07 47	−50	128	06 57	−50	129	06 07	−50	129	05 17	−50	130	04 27	−51	130
54	10 49	50	127	09 59	51	128	09 08	50	128	08 18	50	129	07 28	50	130	06 38	51	130	05 47	50	131	04 57	50	131
53	11 20	50	128	10 30	50	129	09 40	51	129	08 49	50	130	07 59	51	130	07 08	50	131	06 18	51	131	05 27	51	132
52	11 52	51	129	11 01	50	130	10 11	51	130	09 20	51	131	08 29	51	131	07 38	50	132	06 48	51	132	05 57	51	133
51	12 23	51	130	11 32	51	130	10 41	51	131	09 50	51	131	08 59	51	132	08 08	51	133	07 17	51	133	06 26	51	134
50	12 54	−51	131	12 03	−52	131	11 11	−51	132	10 20	−51	132	09 29	−51	133	08 38	−52	133	07 46	−51	134	06 55	−51	134
49	13 24	51	132	12 33	52	132	11 41	51	133	10 50	52	133	09 58	51	134	09 07	52	134	08 15	52	135	07 23	51	135
48	13 54	52	132	13 02	51	133	12 11	52	133	11 19	52	134	10 27	52	134	09 35	51	135	08 44	52	135	07 52	52	136
47	14 23	52	133	13 31	51	134	12 40	52	134	11 48	52	135	10 56	52	135	10 04	53	136	09 11	52	136	08 19	52	137
46	14 52	52	134	14 00	52	135	13 08	52	135	12 16	52	136	11 24	53	136	10 31	52	137	09 39	52	137	08 47	53	138
45	15 21	−52	135	14 29	−53	135	13 36	−52	136	12 44	−53	136	11 51	−52	137	10 59	−53	137	10 06	−52	138	09 14	−53	138
44	15 49	52	136	14 57	53	136	14 04	53	137	13 11	52	137	12 19	53	138	11 26	53	138	10 33	53	139	09 40	53	139
43	16 17	53	137	15 24	53	137	14 31	53	138	13 38	53	138	12 45	53	139	11 52	53	139	10 59	53	140	10 06	53	140
42	16 44	53	138	15 51	53	138	14 58	53	139	14 05	53	139	13 12	54	140	12 18	53	140	11 25	53	140	10 32	54	141
41	17 11	53	138	16 18	54	139	15 24	53	139	14 31	54	140	13 37	53	140	12 44	54	141	11 50	53	141	10 57	54	142
40	17 38	−54	139	16 44	−54	140	15 50	−53	140	14 57	−54	141	14 03	−54	141	13 09	−54	142	12 15	−54	142	11 21	−54	143
39	18 03	53	140	17 10	54	141	16 16	54	141	15 22	54	142	14 28	54	142	13 34	54	143	12 40	55	143	11 45	54	143
38	18 29	54	141	17 35	54	142	16 41	55	142	15 46	54	143	14 52	54	143	13 58	54	143	13 04	55	144	12 09	54	144
37	18 54	55	142	17 59	54	143	17 05	54	143	16 11	55	143	15 16	54	144	14 22	55	144	13 27	55	145	12 32	54	145
36	19 18	54	143	18 24	55	144	17 29	55	144	16 34	54	144	15 40	55	145	14 45	55	145	13 50	55	146	12 55	55	146
35	19 42	−55	144	18 47	−55	144	17 52	−55	145	16 57	−55	145	16 02	−55	146	15 07	−55	146	14 12	−55	147	13 17	−55	147
34	20 05	55	145	19 10	55	145	18 15	55	146	17 20	55	146	16 25	55	147	15 30	56	147	14 34	55	147	13 39	55	148
33	20 28	55	146	19 33	55	146	18 38	56	147	17 42	55	147	16 47	56	148	15 51	55	148	14 56	56	148	14 00	56	149
32	20 51	56	147	19 55	56	147	18 59	55	148	18 04	56	148	17 08	56	148	16 12	55	149	15 17	56	149	14 21	56	150
31	21 12	56	148	20 16	55	148	19 21	56	149	18 25	56	149	17 29	56	149	16 33	56	150	15 37	56	150	14 41	56	150
30	21 33	−56	149	20 37	−56	149	19 41	−56	150	18 45	−56	150	17 49	−56	150	16 53	−56	151	15 57	−57	151	15 00	−56	151
29	21 54	56	150	20 58	57	150	20 01	56	150	19 05	56	151	18 09	57	151	17 12	56	152	16 16	57	152	15 19	56	152
28	22 14	57	151	21 17	56	151	20 21	57	151	19 24	56	152	18 28	57	152	17 31	57	152	16 34	56	153	15 38	57	153
27	22 33	56	152	21 37	57	152	20 40	57	152	19 43	57	153	18 46	57	153	17 49	56	153	16 53	57	154	15 56	57	154
26	22 52	57	153	21 55	57	153	20 58	57	153	20 01	57	154	19 04	57	154	18 07	57	154	17 10	57	155	16 13	57	155
25	23 10	−57	154	22 13	−57	154	21 16	−57	154	20 19	−58	155	19 21	−57	155	18 24	−57	155	17 27	−57	156	16 30	−58	156
24	23 28	58	155	22 30	57	155	21 33	57	155	20 36	58	156	19 38	57	156	18 41	58	156	17 43	57	157	16 46	58	157
23	23 45	58	156	22 47	58	156	21 49	57	156	20 52	58	157	19 54	57	157	18 57	58	157	17 59	58	157	17 01	57	158
22	24 01	58	157	23 03	58	157	22 05	57	157	21 08	58	158	20 10	58	158	19 12	58	158	18 14	58	158	17 16	58	159
21	24 16	58	158	23 18	57	158	22 21	58	158	21 23	58	159	20 25	58	159	19 27	59	159	18 28	58	159	17 30	58	160
20	24 31	−58	159	23 33	−58	159	22 35	−58	159	21 37	−58	160	20 39	−58	160	19 41	−59	160	18 42	−58	160	17 44	−58	161
19	24 45	58	160	23 47	58	160	22 49	58	160	21 51	59	161	20 52	58	161	19 54	58	161	18 56	59	161	17 57	58	162
18	24 59	58	161	24 01	59	161	23 02	58	161	22 04	59	162	21 05	58	162	20 07	59	162	19 08	58	162	18 10	59	163
17	25 12	59	162	24 13	58	162	23 15	59	162	22 16	59	163	21 17	58	163	20 19	59	163	19 20	59	163	18 21	58	163
16	25 24	59	163	24 25	58	163	23 27	59	163	22 28	59	164	21 29	59	164	20 30	59	164	19 31	58	164	18 33	59	164
15	25 36	−59	164	24 37	−59	164	23 38	−59	164	22 39	−59	165	21 40	−59	165	20 41	−59	165	19 42	−59	165	18 43	−59	165
14	25 46	59	165	24 47	59	165	23 48	59	165	22 49	59	166	21 50	59	166	20 51	59	166	19 52	59	166	18 53	59	166
13	25 56	59	166	24 57	59	166	23 58	59	166	22 59	59	167	22 00	59	167	21 01	60	167	20 01	59	167	19 02	59	167
12	26 06	60	167	25 06	59	167	24 07	59	167	23 08	59	168	22 09	60	168	21 09	59	168	20 10	59	168	19 11	60	168
11	26 14	59	168	25 15	59	168	24 16	60	169	23 16	59	169	22 17	60	169	21 17	59	169	20 18	60	169	19 18	59	169
10	26 22	−59	169	25 23	−60	169	24 23	−59	170	23 24	−60	170	22 24	−59	170	21 25	−60	170	20 25	−59	170	19 26	−60	170
9	26 29	59	170	25 30	60	170	24 30	59	171	23 31	60	171	22 31	60	171	21 31	59	171	20 32	60	171	19 32	59	171
8	26 36	60	171	25 36	60	172	24 36	59	172	23 37	60	172	22 37	60	172	21 37	59	172	20 38	60	172	19 38	60	172
7	26 41	59	172	25 42	60	173	24 42	60	173	23 42	60	173	22 42	59	173	21 43	60	173	20 43	60	173	19 43	60	173
6	26 46	59	174	25 47	60	174	24 47	60	174	23 47	60	174	22 47	60	174	21 47	60	174	20 47	59	174	19 48	60	174
5	26 51	−60	175	25 51	−60	175	24 51	−60	175	23 51	−60	175	22 51	−60	175	21 51	−60	175	20 51	−60	175	19 51	−59	175
4	26 54	60	176	25 54	60	176	24 54	60	176	23 54	60	176	22 54	60	176	21 54	60	176	20 54	59	176	19 55	60	176
3	26 57	60	177	25 57	60	177	24 57	60	177	23 57	60	177	22 57	60	177	21 57	60	177	20 57	60	177	19 57	60	177
2	26 59	60	178	25 59	60	178	24 59	60	178	23 59	60	178	22 59	60	178	21 59	60	178	20 59	60	178	19 59	60	178
1	27 00	60	179	26 00	60	179	25 00	60	179	24 00	60	179	23 00	60	179	22 00	60	179	21 00	60	179	20 00	60	179
0	27 00	−60	180	26 00	−60	180	25 00	−60	180	24 00	−60	180	23 00	−60	180	22 00	−60	180	21 00	−60	180	20 00	−60	180

LHA	23° Hc	d	Z	24° Hc	d	Z	25° Hc	d	Z	26° Hc	d	Z	27° Hc	d	Z	28° Hc	d	Z	29° Hc	d	Z	LHA
	° ′	′	°	° ′	′	°	° ′	′	°	° ′	′	°	° ′	′	°	° ′	′	°	° ′	′	°	
69	−4 00	46	121	−4 46	47	121	−5 33	47	122	291												
68	−3 25	47	121	−4 12	47	122	−4 59	47	122	−5 46	47	123	292									
67	−2 51	47	122	−3 38	47	123	−4 25	48	123	−5 13	47	124	−6 00	47	124	293						
66	−2 17	47	123	−3 04	48	123	−3 52	47	124	−4 39	48	125	−5 27	47	125	294						
65	−1 43	−48	123	−2 31	−48	124	−3 19	−47	125	−4 06	−48	125	−4 54	−48	126	−5 42	−47	126	295			
64	−1 10	48	124	−1 58	48	125	−2 46	48	125	−3 34	48	126	−4 22	47	127	−5 09	48	127	−5 57	48	128	296
63	−0 37	48	125	−1 25	48	125	−2 13	48	126	−3 01	49	127	−3 50	48	127	−4 38	48	128	−5 26	48	128	297
62	−0 04	49	126	−0 53	48	126	−1 41	48	127	−2 29	49	127	−3 18	48	128	−4 06	48	129	−4 54	49	129	298
61	00 28	48	126	−0 20	49	127	−1 09	49	128	−1 58	48	128	−2 46	49	129	−3 35	48	129	−4 23	49	130	299
60	01 01	−49	127	00 12	−49	128	−0 37	−49	129	−1 26	−49	129	−2 15	−49	129	−3 04	−49	130	−3 53	−48	131	300
59	01 32	49	128	00 43	49	128	−0 06	49	129	−0 55	49	130	−1 44	49	130	−2 33	49	131	−3 22	49	131	301
58	02 04	50	129	01 14	49	129	00 25	49	130	−0 24	50	130	−1 14	49	131	−2 03	49	131	−2 52	50	132	302
57	02 35	50	129	01 45	49	130	00 56	50	131	00 06	50	131	−0 44	49	132	−1 33	50	132	−2 23	49	133	303
56	03 06	50	130	02 16	50	131	01 26	50	131	00 36	50	132	−0 14	50	132	−1 04	50	133	−1 54	49	134	304
55	03 36	−50	131	02 46	−50	131	01 56	−50	132	01 06	−50	133	00 16	−50	133	−0 34	−51	134	−1 25	−50	134	305
54	04 07	51	132	03 16	50	132	02 26	51	133	01 35	50	133	00 45	51	134	−0 06	50	134	−0 56	50	135	306
53	04 36	50	132	03 46	51	133	02 55	51	134	02 04	50	134	01 14	51	135	00 23	51	135	−0 28	50	136	307
52	05 06	51	133	04 15	51	134	03 24	51	134	02 33	51	135	01 42	51	136	00 51	51	136	00 00	51	136	308
51	05 35	51	134	04 44	52	135	03 52	51	135	03 01	51	136	02 10	51	136	01 19	51	137	00 28	52	137	309
50	06 04	−52	135	05 12	−51	135	04 21	−52	136	03 29	−51	136	02 38	−52	137	01 46	−51	137	00 55	−52	138	310
49	06 32	52	136	05 40	52	136	04 48	51	137	03 57	52	137	03 05	52	138	02 13	52	138	01 21	51	139	311
48	07 00	52	136	06 08	52	137	05 16	52	137	04 24	52	138	03 32	52	138	02 40	52	139	01 48	52	139	312
47	07 27	52	137	06 35	52	138	05 43	53	138	04 50	52	139	03 58	52	139	03 06	52	140	02 14	53	140	313
46	07 54	52	138	07 02	53	139	06 09	52	139	05 17	53	140	04 24	52	140	03 32	53	140	02 39	53	141	314
45	08 21	−53	139	07 28	−53	139	06 35	−52	140	05 43	−53	140	04 50	−53	141	03 57	−53	141	03 04	−53	142	315
44	08 47	53	140	07 54	53	140	07 01	53	141	06 08	53	141	05 15	53	142	04 22	53	142	03 29	53	143	316
43	09 13	53	141	08 20	54	141	07 26	53	141	06 33	53	142	05 40	54	142	04 46	53	143	03 53	53	143	317
42	09 38	53	141	08 45	54	142	07 51	53	142	06 58	54	143	06 04	53	143	05 10	53	144	04 17	54	144	318
41	10 03	54	142	09 09	54	143	08 15	53	143	07 22	54	144	06 28	54	144	05 34	54	144	04 40	54	145	319
40	10 27	−54	143	09 33	−54	144	08 39	−54	144	07 45	−54	144	06 51	−54	145	05 57	−54	145	05 03	−54	146	320
39	10 51	54	144	09 57	54	144	09 03	54	145	08 09	55	145	07 14	54	146	06 20	54	146	05 26	55	146	321
38	11 15	55	145	10 20	54	145	09 26	55	146	08 31	54	146	07 37	55	146	06 42	55	147	05 47	54	147	322
37	11 38	55	146	10 43	55	146	09 48	55	146	08 53	54	147	07 59	55	147	07 04	55	148	06 09	55	148	323
36	12 00	55	146	11 05	55	147	10 10	55	147	09 15	55	148	08 20	55	148	07 25	55	148	06 30	55	149	324
35	12 22	−55	147	11 27	−55	148	10 32	−56	148	09 36	−55	149	08 41	−55	149	07 46	−55	149	06 51	−56	150	325
34	12 44	56	148	11 48	55	149	10 53	56	149	09 57	55	149	09 02	56	150	08 06	55	150	07 11	56	151	326
33	13 04	55	149	12 09	56	149	11 13	56	150	10 17	55	150	09 22	56	151	08 26	56	151	07 30	56	151	327
32	13 25	56	150	12 29	56	150	11 33	56	151	10 37	56	151	09 41	56	151	08 45	56	152	07 49	56	152	328
31	13 45	56	151	12 49	57	151	11 52	56	152	10 56	56	152	10 00	56	152	09 04	56	153	08 08	56	153	329
30	14 04	−56	152	13 08	−57	152	12 11	−56	152	11 15	−56	153	10 19	−57	153	09 22	−56	153	08 26	−57	154	330
29	14 23	57	153	13 26	56	153	12 30	57	153	11 33	57	154	10 36	56	154	09 40	57	154	08 43	57	155	331
28	14 41	57	154	13 44	57	154	12 47	56	154	11 51	57	155	10 54	57	155	09 57	57	155	09 00	57	155	332
27	14 59	57	154	14 02	57	155	13 05	57	155	12 08	57	155	11 11	57	156	10 14	57	156	09 17	58	156	333
26	15 16	57	155	14 19	58	156	13 21	57	156	12 24	57	156	11 27	57	157	10 30	58	157	09 32	57	157	334
25	15 32	−57	156	14 35	−57	157	13 38	−58	157	12 40	−57	157	11 43	−58	157	10 45	−57	158	09 48	−58	158	335
24	15 48	57	157	14 51	58	157	13 53	58	158	12 55	57	158	11 58	58	158	11 00	57	159	10 03	58	159	336
23	16 04	58	158	15 06	58	158	14 08	58	159	13 10	58	159	12 12	57	159	11 15	58	159	10 17	58	160	337
22	16 18	58	159	15 20	58	159	14 22	58	160	13 24	58	160	12 26	58	160	11 28	58	160	10 30	58	161	338
21	16 32	58	160	15 34	58	160	14 36	58	160	13 38	58	161	12 40	58	161	11 42	59	161	10 43	58	161	339
20	16 46	−58	161	15 48	−59	161	14 49	−58	161	13 51	−58	162	12 53	−59	162	11 54	−58	162	10 56	−58	162	340
19	16 59	59	162	16 00	58	162	15 02	59	162	14 03	58	162	13 05	59	163	12 06	58	163	11 08	59	163	341
18	17 11	59	163	16 12	58	163	15 14	59	163	14 15	58	163	13 17	59	164	12 18	59	164	11 19	58	164	342
17	17 23	59	164	16 24	59	164	15 25	59	164	14 26	58	164	13 28	59	165	12 29	59	165	11 30	59	165	343
16	17 34	59	165	16 35	59	165	15 36	59	165	14 37	59	165	13 38	59	165	12 39	59	166	11 40	59	166	344
15	17 44	−59	166	16 45	−59	166	15 46	−59	166	14 47	−59	166	13 48	−59	166	12 49	−59	166	11 50	−59	167	345
14	17 54	59	167	16 55	60	167	15 55	59	167	14 56	59	167	13 57	59	167	12 58	59	167	11 59	59	168	346
13	18 03	59	167	17 04	60	168	16 04	59	168	15 05	59	168	14 06	59	168	13 07	60	168	12 07	59	168	347
12	18 11	59	168	17 12	59	169	16 13	60	169	15 13	59	169	14 14	60	169	13 14	59	169	12 15	59	169	348
11	18 19	59	169	17 20	60	170	16 20	59	170	15 21	60	170	14 21	59	170	13 22	60	170	12 22	59	170	349
10	18 26	−59	170	17 27	−60	170	16 27	−60	171	15 27	−59	171	14 28	−60	171	13 28	−59	171	12 29	−60	171	350
9	18 33	60	171	17 33	60	171	16 33	59	172	15 34	60	172	14 34	60	172	13 34	59	172	12 35	60	172	351
8	18 38	59	172	17 39	60	172	16 39	60	172	15 39	60	173	14 39	59	173	13 40	60	173	12 40	60	173	352
7	18 43	59	173	17 44	60	173	16 44	60	173	15 44	60	174	14 44	60	174	13 44	59	174	12 45	60	174	353
6	18 48	60	174	17 48	60	174	16 48	60	174	15 48	60	174	14 48	59	175	13 49	60	175	12 49	60	175	354
5	18 52	−60	175	17 52	−60	175	16 52	−60	175	15 52	−60	175	14 52	−60	175	13 52	−60	176	12 52	−60	176	355
4	18 55	60	176	17 55	60	176	16 55	60	176	15 55	60	176	14 55	60	176	13 55	60	176	12 55	60	176	356
3	18 57	60	177	17 57	60	177	16 57	60	177	15 57	60	177	14 57	60	177	13 57	60	177	12 57	60	177	357
2	18 59	60	178	17 59	60	178	16 59	60	178	15 59	60	178	14 59	60	178	13 59	60	178	12 59	60	178	358
1	19 00	60	179	18 00	60	179	17 00	60	179	16 00	60	179	15 00	60	179	14 00	60	179	13 00	60	179	359
0	19 00	−60	180	18 00	−60	180	17 00	−60	180	16 00	−60	180	15 00	−60	180	14 00	−60	180	13 00	−60	180	360

15°	16°	17°	18°	19°	20°	21°	22°	23°	24°	25°	26°	27°	28°	29°

S. Lat. {LHA greater than 180°....... Zn=180−Z; LHA less than 180°........... Zn=180+Z}

DECLINATION (15°-29°) CONTRARY NAME TO LATITUDE

LAT 48°

N. Lat. {LHA greater than 180°....... Zn=Z
{LHA less than 180°.......... Zn=360−Z

DECLINATION (0°-14°) SAME NAME AS LATITUDE

LHA	0° Hc	d	Z	1° Hc	d	Z	2° Hc	d	Z	3° Hc	d	Z	4° Hc	d	Z
	° ′	′	°	° ′	′	°	° ′	′	°	° ′	′	°	° ′	′	°
0	41 00	+60	180	42 00	+60	180	43 00	+60	180	44 00	+60	180	45 00	+60	180
1	41 00	60	179	42 00	60	179	43 00	60	179	44 00	60	179	45 00	60	179
2	40 58	60	177	41 58	60	177	42 58	60	177	43 58	60	177	44 58	60	177
3	40 56	60	176	41 56	60	176	42 56	60	176	43 56	60	176	44 56	60	176
4	40 53	60	175	41 53	60	175	42 53	59	175	43 52	60	175	44 52	60	174
5	40 49	+60	173	41 49	+59	173	42 48	+60	173	43 48	+60	173	44 48	+60	173
6	40 44	59	172	41 43	60	172	42 43	60	172	43 43	60	172	44 43	59	172
7	40 38	59	171	41 37	60	171	42 37	60	171	43 37	59	170	44 36	60	170
8	40 31	60	170	41 31	59	169	42 30	60	169	43 30	59	169	44 29	60	169
9	40 23	60	168	41 23	59	168	42 22	60	168	43 22	59	168	44 21	59	167
10	40 15	+59	167	41 14	+60	167	42 14	+59	166	43 13	+59	166	44 12	+59	166
11	40 06	59	166	41 05	59	165	42 04	59	165	43 03	59	165	44 02	59	165
12	39 55	59	164	40 54	59	164	41 53	59	164	42 52	59	164	43 51	59	163
13	39 44	59	163	40 43	59	163	41 42	59	163	42 41	58	162	43 39	59	162
14	39 32	59	162	40 31	59	161	41 30	58	161	42 28	59	161	43 27	58	161
15	39 19	+59	161	40 18	+58	160	41 16	+59	160	42 15	+58	160	43 13	+59	159
16	39 06	58	159	40 04	59	159	41 03	58	159	42 01	58	158	42 59	58	158
17	38 52	58	158	39 50	58	158	40 48	58	157	41 46	58	157	42 44	58	157
18	38 36	58	157	39 34	58	156	40 32	58	156	41 30	58	156	42 28	57	155
19	38 20	58	156	39 18	58	155	40 16	57	155	41 13	58	154	42 11	57	154
20	38 04	+57	154	39 01	+58	154	39 59	+57	154	40 56	+57	153	41 53	+57	153
21	37 46	57	153	38 43	58	153	39 41	57	152	40 38	57	152	41 35	57	152
22	37 28	57	152	38 25	57	151	39 22	57	151	40 19	57	151	41 16	56	150
23	37 09	57	151	38 06	57	150	39 03	56	150	39 59	57	149	40 56	56	149
24	36 49	57	150	37 46	56	149	38 42	57	149	39 39	56	148	40 35	56	148
25	36 29	+56	148	37 25	+57	148	38 22	+56	147	39 18	+56	147	40 14	+55	147
26	36 08	56	147	37 04	56	147	38 00	56	146	38 56	55	146	39 51	56	145
27	35 46	56	146	36 42	56	146	37 38	55	145	38 33	56	145	39 29	55	144
28	35 24	55	145	36 19	56	144	37 15	55	144	38 10	55	143	39 05	55	143
29	35 01	55	144	35 56	55	143	36 51	55	143	37 46	55	142	38 41	55	142
30	34 37	+55	143	35 32	+55	142	36 27	+55	142	37 22	+55	141	38 17	+54	141
31	34 13	55	142	35 08	54	141	36 02	55	141	36 57	54	140	37 51	54	139
32	33 48	55	140	34 43	54	140	35 37	54	139	36 31	54	139	37 25	54	138
33	33 23	54	139	34 17	54	139	35 11	54	138	36 05	54	138	36 59	53	137
34	32 57	54	138	33 51	54	138	34 45	53	137	35 38	54	137	36 32	53	136
35	32 31	+53	137	33 24	+54	137	34 18	+53	136	35 11	+53	136	36 04	+53	135
36	32 03	54	136	32 57	53	136	33 50	53	135	34 43	53	134	35 36	53	134
37	31 36	53	135	32 29	53	135	33 22	53	134	34 15	52	133	35 07	53	133
38	31 08	53	134	32 01	52	134	32 53	53	133	33 46	52	132	34 38	52	132
39	30 39	53	133	31 32	52	132	32 24	53	132	33 17	52	131	34 09	52	131
40	30 10	+53	132	31 03	+52	131	31 55	+52	131	32 47	+52	130	33 39	+51	130
41	29 41	52	131	30 33	52	130	31 25	51	130	32 16	52	129	33 08	51	129
42	29 11	52	130	30 03	51	129	30 54	52	129	31 46	51	128	32 37	51	128
43	28 40	52	129	29 32	51	128	30 23	52	128	31 15	51	127	32 06	50	127
44	28 10	51	128	29 01	51	127	29 52	51	127	30 43	51	126	31 34	50	126
45	27 38	+51	127	28 29	+51	126	29 20	+51	126	30 11	+51	125	31 02	+50	125
46	27 07	51	126	27 58	50	126	28 48	51	125	29 39	50	124	30 29	50	124
47	26 35	50	125	27 25	51	125	28 16	50	124	29 06	50	123	29 56	50	123
48	26 02	51	124	26 53	50	124	27 43	50	123	28 33	50	122	29 23	49	122
49	25 30	50	123	26 20	50	123	27 10	49	122	27 59	50	121	28 49	49	121
50	24 57	+49	122	25 46	+50	122	26 36	+50	121	27 26	+49	121	28 15	+49	120
51	24 23	50	121	25 13	49	121	26 02	50	120	26 52	49	120	27 41	49	119
52	23 49	50	121	24 39	49	120	25 28	49	119	26 17	49	119	27 06	49	118
53	23 15	50	120	24 05	49	119	24 54	49	118	25 43	48	118	26 31	49	117
54	22 41	49	119	23 30	49	118	24 19	49	118	25 08	48	117	25 56	48	116
55	22 06	+49	118	22 55	+49	117	23 44	+48	117	24 32	+49	116	25 21	+48	115
56	21 31	49	117	22 20	48	116	23 08	49	116	23 57	48	115	24 45	48	114
57	20 56	49	116	21 45	48	116	22 33	48	115	23 21	48	114	24 09	48	114
58	20 21	48	115	21 09	48	115	21 57	48	114	22 45	48	113	23 33	47	113
59	19 45	48	114	20 33	48	114	21 21	48	113	22 09	47	113	22 56	48	112
60	19 09	+48	114	19 57	+48	113	20 45	+47	112	21 32	+48	112	22 20	+47	111
61	18 33	47	113	19 20	48	112	20 08	47	111	20 55	48	111	21 43	47	110
62	17 56	48	112	18 44	47	111	19 31	48	111	20 19	47	110	21 06	47	109
63	17 20	47	111	18 07	47	110	18 54	47	110	19 41	47	109	20 28	47	108
64	16 43	47	110	17 30	47	110	18 17	47	109	19 04	47	108	19 51	47	108
65	16 06	+47	109	16 53	+47	109	17 40	+47	108	18 27	+46	107	19 13	+47	107
66	15 29	47	109	16 16	46	108	17 02	47	107	17 49	47	107	18 36	46	106
67	14 51	47	108	15 38	47	107	16 25	46	107	17 11	47	106	17 58	46	105
68	14 14	46	107	15 00	47	106	15 47	46	106	16 33	47	105	17 20	46	104
69	13 36	46	106	14 22	47	106	15 09	46	105	15 55	46	104	16 41	46	104

LHA	5° Hc	d	Z	6° Hc	d	Z	7° Hc	d	Z	8° Hc	d	Z	9° Hc	d	Z
	° ′	′	°	° ′	′	°	° ′	′	°	° ′	′	°	° ′	′	°
0	46 00	+60	180	47 00	+60	180	48 00	+60	180	49 00	+60	180	50 00	+60	180
1	46 00	60	179	47 00	60	179	48 00	60	179	49 00	60	179	50 00	60	179
2	45 58	60	177	46 58	60	177	47 58	60	177	48 58	60	177	49 58	60	177
3	45 56	60	176	46 56	59	176	47 55	60	176	48 55	60	176	49 55	60	175
4	45 52	60	174	46 52	60	174	47 52	60	174	48 52	60	174	49 52	59	174
5	45 48	+60	173	46 48	+59	173	47 47	+60	173	48 47	+60	173	49 47	+60	172
6	45 42	60	171	46 42	60	171	47 42	59	171	48 41	60	171	49 41	60	171
7	45 36	60	170	46 36	59	170	47 35	60	170	48 35	59	170	49 34	60	169
8	45 29	59	169	46 28	60	168	47 28	59	168	48 27	60	168	49 27	59	168
9	45 20	60	167	46 20	59	167	47 19	59	167	48 18	60	167	49 18	59	166
10	45 11	+59	166	46 10	+60	166	47 10	+59	165	48 09	+59	165	49 08	+59	165
11	45 01	59	164	46 00	59	164	46 59	59	164	47 58	59	164	48 57	59	163
12	44 50	59	163	45 49	59	163	46 48	59	163	47 47	58	162	48 45	59	162
13	44 38	59	162	45 37	58	161	46 35	59	161	47 34	59	161	48 33	58	160
14	44 25	59	160	45 24	58	160	46 22	59	160	47 21	58	159	48 19	58	159
15	44 12	+58	159	45 10	+58	159	46 08	+58	158	47 06	+58	158	48 04	+58	158
16	43 57	58	158	44 55	58	157	45 53	58	157	46 51	58	157	47 49	57	156
17	43 42	57	156	44 39	58	156	45 37	58	156	46 35	57	155	47 32	58	155
18	43 25	58	155	44 23	57	155	45 20	58	154	46 18	57	154	47 15	57	153
19	43 08	58	154	44 06	57	153	45 03	57	153	46 00	57	152	46 57	57	152
20	42 50	+57	152	43 47	+57	152	44 44	+57	152	45 41	+57	151	46 38	+57	151
21	42 32	56	151	43 28	57	151	44 25	57	150	45 22	56	150	46 18	57	149
22	42 12	57	150	43 09	56	149	44 05	56	149	45 01	57	148	45 58	56	148
23	41 52	56	149	42 48	56	148	43 44	56	148	44 40	56	147	45 36	56	147
24	41 31	56	147	42 27	56	147	43 23	56	146	44 19	55	146	45 14	56	145
25	41 09	+56	146	42 05	+56	146	43 01	+55	145	43 56	+55	145	44 51	+56	144
26	40 47	55	145	41 42	56	144	42 38	55	144	43 33	55	143	44 28	55	143
27	40 24	55	144	41 19	55	143	42 14	55	143	43 09	55	142	44 04	54	141
28	40 00	55	142	40 55	55	142	41 50	54	141	42 44	55	141	43 39	54	140
29	39 36	54	141	40 30	55	141	41 25	54	140	42 19	54	140	43 13	54	139
30	39 11	+54	140	40 05	+54	140	40 59	+54	139	41 53	+54	138	42 47	+54	138
31	38 45	54	139	39 39	54	138	40 33	54	138	41 27	53	137	42 20	54	137
32	38 19	54	138	39 13	53	137	40 06	54	137	41 00	53	136	41 53	53	135
33	37 52	54	137	38 46	53	136	39 39	53	135	40 32	53	135	41 25	53	134
34	37 25	53	136	38 18	53	135	39 11	53	134	40 04	52	134	40 56	53	133
35	36 57	+53	134	37 50	+53	134	38 43	+52	133	39 35	+52	133	40 27	+52	132
36	36 29	52	133	37 21	53	133	38 14	52	132	39 06	52	131	39 58	52	131
37	36 00	52	132	36 52	52	132	37 44	52	131	38 36	52	130	39 28	51	130
38	35 30	52	131	36 22	52	131	37 14	52	130	38 06	51	129	38 57	51	129
39	35 01	51	130	35 52	52	129	36 44	51	129	37 35	51	128	38 26	51	128
40	34 30	+52	129	35 22	+51	128	36 13	+51	128	37 04	+51	127	37 55	+50	126
41	33 59	52	128	34 51	51	127	35 42	50	127	36 32	51	126	37 23	50	125
42	33 28	51	127	34 19	51	126	35 10	50	126	36 00	51	125	36 51	50	124
43	32 56	51	126	33 47	51	125	34 38	50	125	35 28	50	124	36 18	50	123
44	32 24	51	125	33 15	50	124	34 05	50	124	34 55	50	123	35 45	49	122
45	31 52	+50	124	32 42	+50	123	33 32	+50	123	34 22	+49	122	35 11	+50	121
46	31 19	50	123	32 09	50	122	32 59	49	122	33 48	49	121	34 37	50	120
47	30 46	50	122	31 36	49	121	32 25	49	121	33 14	49	120	34 03	49	119
48	30 12	50	121	31 02	49	120	31 51	49	120	32 40	49	119	33 29	48	118
49	29 38	50	120	30 28	49	120	31 17	48	119	32 05	49	118	32 54	48	117
50	29 04	+49	119	29 53	+49	119	30 42	+49	118	31 31	+48	117	32 19	+48	117
51	28 30	49	118	29 19	48	118	30 07	48	117	30 55	49	116	31 44	47	116
52	27 55	48	117	28 43	49	117	29 32	48	116	30 20	48	115	31 08	48	115
53	27 20	48	116	28 08	48	116	28 56	48	115	29 44	48	114	30 32	48	114
54	26 44	49	116	27 33	48	115	28 21	47	114	29 08	48	114	29 56	47	113
55	26 09	+48	115	26 57	+47	114	27 44	+48	113	28 32	+47	113	29 19	+48	112
56	25 33	48	114	26 21	47	113	27 08	48	112	27 56	47	112	28 43	47	111
57	24 57	47	113	25 44	48	112	26 32	47	112	27 19	47	111	28 06	47	110
58	24 20	48	112	25 08	47	111	25 55	47	111	26 42	47	110	27 29	46	109
59	23 44	47	111	24 31	47	111	25 18	47	110	26 05	47	109	26 52	46	108
60	23 07	+47	110	23 54	+47	110	24 41	+47	109	25 28	+46	108	26 14	+46	108
61	22 30	47	109	23 17	47	109	24 04	46	108	24 50	47	107	25 37	46	107
62	21 53	46	109	22 39	47	108	23 26	46	107	24 12	47	107	24 59	46	106
63	21 15	47	108	22 02	46	107	22 48	47	106	23 35	46	106	24 21	46	105
64	20 38	46	107	21 24	47	106	22 11	46	106	22 57	46	105	23 43	45	104
65	20 00	+46	106	20 46	+47	105	21 33	+46	105	22 19	+45	104	23 04	+46	103
66	19 22	46	105	20 08	46	105	20 54	46	104	21 40	46	103	22 26	46	103
67	18 44	46	105	19 30	46	104	20 16	46	103	21 02	46	102	21 48	45	102
68	18 06	46	104	18 52	46	103	19 38	45	102	20 23	46	102	21 09	45	101
69	17 27	46	103	18 13	46	102	18 59	46	102	19 45	45	101	20 30	46	100

10° Hc	d	Z	11° Hc	d	Z	12° Hc	d	Z	13° Hc	d	Z	14° Hc	d	Z	LHA
° ′	′	°	° ′	′	°	° ′	′	°	° ′	′	°	° ′	′	°	
51 00	+60	180	52 00	+60	180	53 00	+60	180	54 00	+60	180	55 00	+60	180	360
51 00	60	178	52 00	59	178	52 59	60	178	53 59	60	178	54 59	60	178	359
50 58	60	177	51 58	60	177	52 58	60	177	53 58	60	177	54 58	60	177	358
50 55	60	175	51 55	60	175	52 55	60	175	53 55	60	175	54 55	60	175	357
50 51	60	174	51 51	60	174	52 51	60	174	53 51	60	173	54 51	60	173	356
50 47	+59	172	51 46	+60	172	52 46	+60	172	53 46	+60	172	54 46	+59	172	355
50 41	59	171	51 40	60	171	52 40	60	170	53 40	59	170	54 39	60	170	354
50 34	59	169	51 33	60	169	52 33	59	169	53 32	60	169	54 32	59	168	353
50 26	59	168	51 25	60	167	52 25	59	167	53 24	59	167	54 23	59	167	352
50 17	59	166	51 16	59	166	52 15	59	166	53 14	60	165	54 14	59	165	351
50 07	+59	165	51 06	+59	164	52 05	+59	164	53 04	+59	164	54 03	+59	163	350
49 56	59	163	50 55	59	163	51 54	58	162	52 52	59	162	53 51	59	162	349
49 44	59	162	50 43	58	161	51 41	59	161	52 40	58	161	53 38	58	160	348
49 31	58	160	50 29	59	160	51 28	58	159	52 26	58	159	53 24	58	159	347
49 17	58	159	50 15	58	158	51 13	58	158	52 11	58	157	53 09	58	157	346
49 02	+58	157	50 00	+58	157	50 58	+58	156	51 56	+57	156	52 53	+58	155	345
48 46	58	156	49 44	58	155	50 42	57	155	51 39	57	154	52 36	58	154	344
48 30	57	154	49 27	57	154	50 24	58	153	51 22	57	153	52 19	57	152	343
48 12	57	153	49 09	57	152	50 06	57	152	51 03	57	151	52 00	57	151	342
47 54	57	151	48 51	56	151	49 47	57	150	50 44	56	150	51 40	57	149	341
47 35	+56	150	48 31	+57	150	49 28	+56	149	50 24	+56	149	51 20	+56	148	340
47 15	56	149	48 11	56	148	49 07	56	148	50 03	56	147	50 59	55	147	339
46 54	56	147	47 50	55	147	48 45	56	146	49 41	55	146	50 36	56	145	338
46 32	56	146	47 28	55	145	48 23	55	145	49 18	55	144	50 13	55	144	337
46 10	55	145	47 05	55	144	48 00	55	144	48 55	55	143	49 50	54	142	336
45 47	+55	143	46 42	+54	143	47 36	+55	142	48 31	+54	142	49 25	+54	141	335
45 23	54	142	46 17	55	142	47 12	54	141	48 06	54	140	49 00	54	140	334
44 58	55	141	45 53	54	140	46 47	54	140	47 41	53	139	48 34	54	138	333
44 33	54	140	45 27	54	139	46 21	53	138	47 14	54	138	48 08	53	137	332
44 07	54	138	45 01	53	138	45 54	54	137	46 48	53	136	47 41	52	136	331
43 41	+53	137	44 34	+53	137	45 27	+53	136	46 20	+53	135	47 13	+52	134	330
43 14	53	136	44 07	52	135	44 59	53	135	45 52	52	134	46 44	52	133	329
42 46	53	135	43 39	52	134	44 31	52	133	45 23	52	133	46 15	52	132	328
42 18	52	134	43 10	52	133	44 02	52	132	44 54	52	132	45 46	51	131	327
41 49	52	132	42 41	52	132	43 33	51	131	44 24	52	130	45 16	51	130	326
41 19	+52	131	42 11	+52	131	43 03	+51	130	43 54	+51	129	44 45	+51	128	325
40 50	51	130	41 41	51	129	42 32	51	129	43 23	51	128	44 14	50	127	324
40 19	51	129	41 10	51	128	42 01	51	128	42 52	50	127	43 42	51	126	323
39 48	51	128	40 39	51	127	41 30	50	127	42 20	50	126	43 10	50	125	322
39 17	51	127	40 08	50	126	40 58	50	125	41 48	50	125	42 38	49	124	321
38 45	+51	126	39 36	+50	125	40 26	+50	124	41 16	+49	124	42 05	+49	123	320
38 13	50	125	39 03	50	124	39 53	50	123	40 43	49	123	41 32	49	122	319
37 41	49	124	38 30	50	123	39 20	49	122	40 09	49	122	40 58	49	121	318
37 08	49	123	37 57	49	122	38 46	49	121	39 35	49	120	40 24	49	120	317
36 34	50	122	37 24	49	121	38 13	48	120	39 01	49	119	39 50	48	119	316
36 01	+49	121	36 50	+48	120	37 38	+49	119	38 27	+48	118	39 15	+48	118	315
35 27	48	120	36 15	49	119	37 04	48	118	37 52	48	117	38 40	48	117	314
34 52	49	119	35 41	48	118	36 29	48	117	37 17	48	116	38 05	47	116	313
34 17	49	118	35 06	48	117	35 54	48	116	36 42	47	115	37 29	47	115	312
33 42	48	117	34 30	48	116	35 18	48	115	36 06	47	115	36 53	47	114	311
33 07	+48	116	33 55	+48	115	34 43	+47	114	35 30	+47	114	36 17	+47	113	310
32 31	48	115	33 19	48	114	34 07	47	113	34 54	47	113	35 41	46	112	309
31 56	47	114	32 43	47	113	33 30	47	112	34 17	47	112	35 04	46	111	308
31 20	47	113	32 07	47	112	32 54	47	112	33 41	46	111	34 27	46	110	307
30 43	47	112	31 30	47	111	32 17	47	111	33 04	46	110	33 50	46	109	306
30 07	+46	111	30 53	+47	110	31 40	+46	110	32 26	+47	109	33 13	+45	108	305
29 30	46	110	30 16	47	110	31 03	46	109	31 49	46	108	32 35	46	107	304
28 53	46	109	29 39	47	109	30 26	46	108	31 12	45	107	31 57	46	106	303
28 15	47	109	29 02	46	108	29 48	46	107	30 34	46	106	31 20	45	106	302
27 38	46	108	28 24	46	107	29 10	46	106	29 56	46	106	30 42	45	105	301
27 00	+47	107	27 47	+45	106	28 32	+46	105	29 18	+45	105	30 03	+46	104	300
26 23	46	106	27 09	45	105	27 54	46	105	28 40	45	104	29 25	45	103	299
25 45	46	105	26 31	45	104	27 16	46	104	28 02	45	103	28 47	45	102	298
25 07	45	104	25 52	46	104	26 38	45	103	27 23	45	102	28 08	45	101	297
24 28	46	104	25 14	45	103	25 59	46	102	26 45	45	101	27 30	44	101	296
23 50	+46	103	24 36	+45	102	25 21	+45	101	26 06	+45	101	26 51	+44	100	295
23 12	45	102	23 57	45	101	24 42	45	100	25 27	45	100	26 12	45	99	294
22 33	45	101	23 18	46	100	24 04	44	100	24 48	45	99	25 33	45	98	293
21 54	46	100	22 40	45	100	23 25	44	99	24 09	45	98	24 54	44	97	292
21 16	45	99	22 01	45	99	22 46	44	98	23 30	45	97	24 15	44	97	291

S. Lat. {LHA greater than 180°....... Zn=180−Z
{LHA less than 180°.......... Zn=180+Z

DECLINATION (0°-14°) SAME NAME AS LATITUDE

N. Lat. {LHA greater than 180°....... Zn=Z
LHA less than 180°........... Zn=360−Z}

DECLINATION (0°-14°) SAME NAME AS LATITUDE

LHA	0°			1°			2°			3°			4°		
	Hc	d	Z	Hc	d	Z	Hc	d	Z	Hc	d	Z	Hc	d	Z
	° ′	′	°	° ′	′	°	° ′	′	°	° ′	′	°	° ′	′	°
70	12 58	+46	105	13 44	+47	105	14 31	+46	104	15 17	+46	103	16 03	+46	103
71	12 20	46	105	13 06	47	104	13 53	46	103	14 39	46	103	15 25	45	102
72	11 42	46	104	12 28	46	103	13 14	46	103	14 00	46	102	14 46	46	101
73	11 04	46	103	11 50	46	102	12 36	46	102	13 22	45	101	14 07	46	100
74	10 25	46	102	11 11	46	102	11 57	46	101	12 43	46	100	13 29	45	100
75	09 47	+46	101	10 33	+45	101	11 18	+46	100	12 04	+46	100	12 50	+45	99
76	09 08	46	101	09 54	46	100	10 40	45	99	11 25	46	99	12 11	45	98
77	08 29	46	100	09 15	46	99	10 01	45	99	10 46	46	98	11 32	45	97
78	07 50	46	99	08 36	46	99	09 22	45	98	10 07	46	97	10 53	45	97
79	07 12	45	98	07 57	46	98	08 43	45	97	09 28	46	96	10 14	45	96
80	06 33	+45	98	07 18	+46	97	08 04	+45	96	08 49	+45	96	09 34	+46	95
81	05 53	46	97	06 39	45	96	07 24	46	96	08 10	45	95	08 55	45	94
82	05 14	46	96	06 00	45	95	06 45	46	95	07 31	45	94	08 16	45	93
83	04 35	46	95	05 21	45	95	06 06	45	94	06 51	46	93	07 37	45	93
84	03 56	45	95	04 41	46	94	05 27	45	93	06 12	45	93	06 57	45	92
85	03 17	+45	94	04 02	+45	93	04 47	+46	92	05 33	+45	92	06 18	+45	91
86	02 37	46	93	03 23	45	92	04 08	45	92	04 53	46	91	05 39	45	90
87	01 58	45	92	02 43	46	92	03 29	45	91	04 14	45	90	04 59	45	90
88	01 19	45	92	02 04	45	91	02 49	46	90	03 35	45	90	04 20	45	89
89	00 39	46	91	01 25	45	90	02 10	45	89	02 55	45	89	03 40	46	88
90	00 00	+45	90	00 45	+46	89	01 31	+45	89	02 16	+45	88	03 01	+45	87
91	−0 39	45	89	00 06	45	89	00 51	45	88	01 36	46	87	02 22	45	87
92	−1 19	46	88	−0 33	45	88	00 12	45	87	00 57	45	87	01 42	46	86
93	−1 58	45	88	−1 13	46	87	−0 27	45	86	00 18	45	86	01 03	46	85
94	−2 37	45	87	−1 52	45	86	−1 07	46	86	−0 21	45	85	00 24	45	84
95	−3 17	+46	86	−2 31	+45	86	−1 46	+45	85	−1 01	+46	84	−0 15	+45	84
96	−3 56	45	85	−3 11	46	85	−2 25	45	84	−1 40	46	83	−0 54	45	83
97	−4 35	45	85	−3 50	46	84	−3 04	45	83	−2 19	46	83	−1 33	45	82
98	−5 14	45	84	−4 29	46	83	−3 43	45	83	−2 58	46	82	−2 12	45	81
99	−5 53	45	83	−5 08	46	82	−4 22	45	82	−3 37	46	81	−2 51	46	81
100				−5 47	+46	82	−5 01	+45	81	−4 16	+46	80	−3 30	+46	80
101							−5 40	46	80	−4 54	45	80	−4 09	46	79
102										−5 33	46	79	−4 47	46	78
103										−6 12	46	78	−5 26	46	77
104													−6 04	46	77

LHA	5°			6°			7°			8°			9°		
	Hc	d	Z	Hc	d	Z	Hc	d	Z	Hc	d	Z	Hc	d	Z
	° ′	′	°	° ′	′	°	° ′	′	°	° ′	′	°	° ′	′	°
70	16 49	+46	102	17 35	+46	101	18 21	+45	101	19 06	+46	100	19 52	+45	99
71	16 10	46	101	16 56	46	101	17 42	45	100	18 27	46	99	19 13	45	99
72	15 32	45	101	16 17	46	100	17 03	45	99	17 48	46	98	18 34	45	98
73	14 53	46	100	15 39	45	99	16 24	45	98	17 09	46	98	17 55	45	97
74	14 14	46	99	15 00	45	98	15 45	45	98	16 30	46	97	17 16	44	96
75	13 35	+46	98	14 21	+45	98	15 06	+45	97	15 51	+45	96	16 36	+45	95
76	12 56	46	97	13 42	45	97	14 27	45	96	15 12	45	95	15 57	45	95
77	12 17	46	97	13 03	45	96	13 48	45	95	14 33	45	95	15 18	45	94
78	11 38	45	96	12 23	46	95	13 09	45	95	13 54	45	94	14 39	44	93
79	10 59	45	95	11 44	45	94	12 29	45	94	13 14	45	93	13 59	45	92
80	10 20	+45	94	11 05	+45	94	11 50	+45	93	12 35	+45	92	13 20	+45	92
81	09 40	46	94	10 26	45	93	11 11	45	92	11 56	45	92	12 41	44	91
82	09 01	45	93	09 46	45	92	10 31	45	91	11 16	45	91	12 01	45	90
83	08 22	45	92	09 07	45	91	09 52	45	91	10 37	45	90	11 22	45	89
84	07 42	46	91	08 28	45	91	09 13	45	90	09 58	44	89	10 42	45	89
85	07 03	+45	91	07 48	+45	90	08 33	+45	89	09 18	+45	89	10 03	+45	88
86	06 24	45	90	07 09	45	89	07 54	45	88	08 39	45	88	09 24	45	87
87	05 44	45	89	06 29	46	88	07 15	45	88	08 00	45	87	08 45	44	86
88	05 05	45	88	05 50	45	88	06 35	45	87	07 20	45	86	08 05	45	86
89	04 26	45	87	05 11	45	87	05 56	45	86	06 41	45	86	07 26	45	85
90	03 46	+45	87	04 31	+46	86	05 17	+45	85	06 02	+45	85	06 47	+45	84
91	03 07	45	86	03 52	45	85	04 37	46	85	05 23	45	84	06 08	45	83
92	02 28	45	85	03 13	45	85	03 58	45	84	04 43	46	83	05 29	45	83
93	01 49	45	84	02 34	45	84	03 19	45	83	04 04	46	82	04 50	45	82
94	01 09	46	84	01 55	45	83	02 40	45	82	03 25	46	82	04 11	45	81
95	00 30	+46	83	01 16	+45	82	02 01	+45	82	02 46	+46	81	03 32	+45	80
96	−0 09	46	82	00 37	45	82	01 22	46	81	02 08	45	80	02 53	46	80
97	−0 48	46	81	−0 02	45	81	00 43	46	80	01 29	45	79	02 14	46	79
98	−1 27	46	81	−0 41	46	80	00 05	45	79	00 50	46	79	01 36	45	78
99	−2 05	45	80	−1 20	46	79	−0 34	46	79	00 12	45	78	00 57	46	77
100	−2 44	+46	79	−1 58	+45	79	−1 13	+46	78	−0 27	+46	77	00 19	+46	77
101	−3 23	46	78	−2 37	46	78	−1 51	46	77	−1 05	46	76	−0 19	46	76
102	−4 01	46	78	−3 15	46	77	−2 29	46	76	−1 43	46	76	−0 57	46	75
103	−4 40	46	77	−3 54	47	76	−3 07	46	76	−2 21	46	75	−1 35	46	74
104	−5 18	46	76	−4 32	46	75	−3 46	47	75	−2 59	46	74	−2 13	46	74
105	−5 56	+46	75	−5 10	+47	75	−4 23	+46	74	−3 37	+46	73	−2 51	+47	73
106				−5 48	47	74	−5 01	46	73	−4 15	47	73	−3 28	46	72
107							−5 39	47	72	−4 52	46	72	−4 06	47	71
108										−5 30	47	71	−4 43	47	70
109										−6 07	47	70	−5 20	47	70
110													−5 57	+47	69

LHA	10°			11°			12°			13°			14°			LHA
	Hc	d	Z	Hc	d	Z	Hc	d	Z	Hc	d	Z	Hc	d	Z	
	° ′	′	°	° ′	′	°	° ′	′	°	° ′	′	°	° ′	′	°	
70	20 37	+45	99	21 22	+45	98	22 07	+44	97	22 51	+45	97	23 36	+44	96	290
71	19 58	45	98	20 43	45	97	21 28	44	96	22 12	45	96	22 57	44	95	289
72	19 19	45	97	20 04	44	96	20 48	45	96	21 33	44	95	22 17	45	94	288
73	18 40	45	96	19 25	44	96	20 09	45	95	20 54	44	94	21 38	44	93	287
74	18 00	45	96	18 45	45	95	19 30	45	94	20 15	44	93	20 59	44	93	286
75	17 21	+45	95	18 06	+45	94	18 51	+44	93	19 35	+45	93	20 20	+44	92	285
76	16 42	45	94	17 27	44	93	18 11	45	93	18 56	44	92	19 40	44	91	284
77	16 03	44	93	16 47	45	93	17 32	45	92	18 17	44	91	19 01	44	90	283
78	15 23	45	92	16 08	45	92	16 53	44	91	17 37	44	90	18 21	45	90	282
79	14 44	45	92	15 29	44	91	16 13	45	90	16 58	44	90	17 42	44	89	281
80	14 05	+44	91	14 49	+45	90	15 34	+44	90	16 18	+45	89	17 03	+44	88	280
81	13 25	45	90	14 10	45	90	14 55	44	89	15 39	44	88	16 23	45	87	279
82	12 46	45	89	13 31	44	89	14 15	45	88	15 00	44	87	15 44	44	87	278
83	12 07	44	89	12 51	45	88	13 36	44	87	14 20	45	87	15 05	44	86	277
84	11 27	45	88	12 12	45	87	12 57	44	87	13 41	45	86	14 26	44	85	276
85	10 48	+45	87	11 33	+44	87	12 17	+45	86	13 02	+44	85	13 46	+45	84	275
86	10 09	44	86	10 53	45	86	11 38	45	85	12 23	44	84	13 07	45	84	274
87	09 29	45	86	10 14	45	85	10 59	45	84	11 44	44	84	12 28	45	83	273
88	08 50	45	85	09 35	45	84	10 20	45	84	11 05	44	83	11 49	45	82	272
89	08 11	45	84	08 56	45	84	09 41	44	83	10 25	45	82	11 10	45	81	271
90	07 32	+45	83	08 17	+45	83	09 02	+45	82	09 47	+44	81	10 31	+45	81	270
91	06 53	45	83	07 38	45	82	08 23	45	81	09 08	44	81	09 52	45	80	269
92	06 14	45	82	06 59	45	81	07 44	45	81	08 29	45	80	09 14	45	79	268
93	05 35	45	81	06 20	45	81	07 05	45	80	07 50	45	79	08 35	45	79	267
94	04 56	45	80	05 41	45	80	06 26	46	79	07 12	45	78	07 57	45	78	266
95	04 17	+46	80	05 03	+45	79	05 48	+45	78	06 33	+45	78	07 18	+45	77	265
96	03 39	45	79	04 24	45	78	05 09	46	78	05 55	45	77	06 40	45	76	264
97	03 00	45	78	03 45	46	78	04 31	45	77	05 16	46	76	06 02	45	76	263
98	02 21	46	77	03 07	46	77	03 53	45	76	04 38	46	75	05 24	45	75	262
99	01 43	46	77	02 29	45	76	03 14	46	75	04 00	46	75	04 46	45	74	261
100	01 05	+46	76	01 51	+45	75	02 36	+46	75	03 22	+46	74	04 08	+46	73	260
101	00 27	46	75	01 13	46	75	01 59	45	74	02 44	46	73	03 30	46	73	259
102	−0 11	46	74	00 35	46	74	01 21	46	73	02 07	46	72	02 53	46	72	258
103	−0 49	46	74	−0 03	46	73	00 43	46	72	01 29	46	72	02 15	47	71	257
104	−1 27	46	73	−0 41	47	72	00 06	46	72	00 52	46	71	01 38	47	70	256
105	−2 04	+46	72	−1 18	+46	72	−0 32	+47	71	00 15	+46	70	01 01	+47	70	255
106	−2 42	47	71	−1 55	46	71	−1 09	47	70	−0 22	46	69	00 24	47	69	254
107	−3 19	47	71	−2 32	46	70	−1 46	47	69	−0 59	47	69	−0 12	47	68	253
108	−3 56	47	70	−3 09	47	69	−2 22	47	69	−1 35	46	68	−0 49	47	67	252
109	−4 33	47	69	−3 46	47	68	−2 59	47	68	−2 12	47	67	−1 25	47	67	251
110	−5 10	+48	68	−4 22	+47	68	−3 35	+47	67	−2 48	+47	66	−2 01	+47	66	250
111	−5 46	47	67	−4 59	48	67	−4 11	47	66	−3 24	47	66	−2 37	48	65	249
112				−5 35	48	66	−4 47	47	66	−4 00	48	65	−3 12	47	64	248
113				−6 11	48	65	−5 23	48	65	−4 35	47	64	−3 48	48	64	247
114							−5 59	48	64	−5 11	48	63	−4 23	48	63	246
115										−5 46	+48	63	−4 58	+49	62	245
116													−5 32	48	61	244
117													−6 07	49	60	243

S. Lat. {LHA greater than 180°....... Zn=180−Z
LHA less than 180°........... Zn=180+Z}

DECLINATION (0°-14°) SAME NAME AS LATITUDE

LAT 49°

LHA	0°			1°			2°			3°			4°			5°			6°			7°			8°			9°			10°			11°			12°			13°			14°			LHA
	Hc	d	Z	Hc	d	Z	Hc	d	Z	Hc	d	Z	Hc	d	Z	Hc	d	Z	Hc	d	Z	Hc	d	Z	Hc	d	Z	Hc	d	Z	Hc	d	Z	Hc	d	Z	Hc	d	Z	Hc	d	Z	Hc	d	Z	
	° ′	′	°	° ′	′	°	° ′	′	°	° ′	′	°	° ′	′	°	° ′	′	°	° ′	′	°	° ′	′	°	° ′	′	°	° ′	′	°	° ′	′	°	° ′	′	°	° ′	′	°	° ′	′	°	° ′	′	°	
99	−5 53	46	83	261																																										
98	−5 14	46	84	−6 00	45	85	262																																							
97	−4 35	46	85	−5 21	45	85	−6 06	45	86	263																																				
96	−3 56	45	85	−4 41	46	86	−5 27	45	87	−6 12	45	87	264																																	
95	−3 17	−45	86	−4 02	−45	87	−4 47	−46	88	−5 33	−45	88	−6 18	−45	89	265																														
94	−2 37	46	87	−3 23	45	88	−4 08	45	88	−4 53	46	89	−5 39	45	90	266																														
93	−1 58	45	88	−2 43	46	88	−3 29	45	89	−4 14	45	90	−4 59	45	90	−5 44	45	91	267																											
92	−1 19	45	88	−2 04	45	89	−2 49	46	90	−3 35	45	90	−4 20	45	91	−5 05	45	92	−5 50	45	92	268																								
91	−0 39	46	89	−1 25	45	90	−2 10	45	91	−2 55	45	91	−3 40	46	92	−4 26	45	93	−5 11	45	93	−5 56	45	94	269																					
90	00 00	−45	90	−0 45	−46	91	−1 31	−45	91	−2 16	−45	92	−3 01	−45	93	−3 46	−45	93	−4 31	−46	94	−5 17	−45	95	−6 02	−45	95	270																		
89	00 39	45	91	−0 06	45	91	−0 51	45	92	−1 36	46	93	−2 22	45	93	−3 07	45	94	−3 52	45	95	−4 37	46	95	−5 23	45	96	−6 08	45	97	271															
88	01 19	46	92	00 33	45	92	−0 12	45	93	−0 57	45	93	−1 42	46	94	−2 28	45	95	−3 13	45	95	−3 58	45	96	−4 43	46	97	−5 29	45	97	−6 14	45	98	272												
87	01 58	45	92	01 13	46	93	00 27	45	94	−0 18	45	94	−1 03	46	95	−1 49	45	96	−2 34	45	96	−3 19	45	97	−4 04	46	98	−4 50	45	98	−5 35	45	99	273												
86	02 37	45	93	01 52	45	94	01 07	46	94	00 21	45	95	−0 24	45	96	−1 09	46	96	−1 55	45	97	−2 40	45	98	−3 25	46	98	−4 11	45	99	−4 56	45	100	−5 41	45	100	274									
85	03 17	−46	94	02 31	−45	94	01 46	−45	95	01 01	−46	96	00 15	−45	96	−0 30	−46	97	−1 16	−45	98	−2 01	−45	98	−2 46	−46	99	−3 32	−45	100	−4 17	−46	100	−5 03	−45	101	−5 48	−45	102	275						
84	03 56	45	95	03 11	46	95	02 25	45	96	01 40	46	97	00 54	45	97	00 09	46	98	−0 37	45	98	−1 22	46	99	−2 08	45	100	−2 53	46	100	−3 39	45	101	−4 24	45	102	−5 09	46	102	−5 55	45	103	276			
83	04 35	45	95	03 50	46	96	03 04	45	97	02 19	46	97	01 33	45	98	00 48	46	99	00 02	45	99	−0 43	46	100	−1 29	45	101	−2 14	46	101	−3 00	45	102	−3 45	46	102	−4 31	45	103	−5 16	46	104	−6 02	45	104	277
82	05 14	45	96	04 29	46	97	03 43	45	97	02 58	46	98	02 12	45	99	01 27	46	99	00 41	46	100	−0 05	45	101	−0 50	46	101	−1 36	45	102	−2 21	46	103	−3 07	46	103	−3 53	45	104	−4 38	46	105	−5 24	45	105	278
81	05 53	45	97	05 08	46	98	04 22	45	98	03 37	46	99	02 51	46	99	02 05	45	100	01 20	46	101	00 34	46	101	−0 12	45	102	−0 57	46	103	−1 43	46	103	−2 29	45	104	−3 14	46	105	−4 00	46	105	−4 46	45	106	279
80	06 33	−46	98	05 47	−46	98	05 01	−45	99	04 16	−46	100	03 30	−46	100	02 44	−46	101	01 58	−45	101	01 13	−46	102	00 27	−46	103	−0 19	−46	103	−1 05	−46	104	−1 51	−45	105	−2 36	−46	105	−3 22	−46	106	−4 08	−46	107	280
79	07 12	46	98	06 26	46	99	05 40	46	100	04 54	45	100	04 09	46	101	03 23	46	102	02 37	46	102	01 51	46	103	01 05	46	104	00 19	46	104	−0 27	46	105	−1 13	46	105	−1 59	45	106	−2 44	46	107	−3 30	46	107	281
78	07 50	45	99	07 05	46	100	06 19	46	100	05 33	46	101	04 47	46	102	04 01	46	102	03 15	46	103	02 29	46	104	01 43	46	104	00 57	46	105	00 11	46	106	−0 35	46	106	−1 21	46	107	−2 07	46	108	−2 53	46	108	282
77	08 29	46	100	07 43	45	101	06 58	46	101	06 12	46	102	05 26	46	103	04 40	46	103	03 54	47	104	03 07	46	104	02 21	46	105	01 35	46	106	00 49	46	106	00 03	46	107	−0 43	46	108	−1 29	46	108	−2 15	47	109	283
76	09 08	46	101	08 22	46	101	07 36	46	102	06 50	46	103	06 04	46	103	05 18	46	104	04 32	46	105	03 46	47	105	02 59	46	106	02 13	46	106	01 27	46	107	00 41	47	108	−0 06	46	108	−0 52	46	109	−1 38	47	110	284
75	09 47	−46	101	09 01	−46	102	08 15	−47	103	07 28	−46	103	06 42	−46	104	05 56	−46	105	05 10	−47	105	04 23	−46	106	03 37	−46	107	02 51	−47	107	02 04	−46	108	01 18	−46	108	00 32	−47	109	−0 15	−46	110	−1 01	−47	110	285
74	10 25	46	102	09 39	46	103	08 53	46	104	08 07	47	104	07 20	46	105	06 34	46	105	05 48	47	106	05 01	46	107	04 15	47	107	03 28	46	108	02 42	47	109	01 55	46	109	01 09	47	110	00 22	46	111	−0 24	47	111	286
73	11 04	47	103	10 17	46	104	09 31	46	104	08 45	47	105	07 58	46	106	07 12	47	106	06 25	46	107	05 39	47	108	04 52	46	108	04 06	47	109	03 19	47	109	02 32	46	110	01 46	47	111	00 59	47	111	00 12	47	112	287
72	11 42	46	104	10 56	47	104	10 09	46	105	09 23	47	106	08 36	46	106	07 50	47	107	07 03	47	108	06 16	46	108	05 30	47	109	04 43	47	110	03 56	47	110	03 09	47	111	02 22	47	111	01 35	46	112	00 49	47	113	288
71	12 20	46	105	11 34	47	105	10 47	46	106	10 01	47	107	09 14	47	107	08 27	47	108	07 40	46	108	06 54	47	109	06 07	47	110	05 20	47	110	04 33	47	111	03 46	47	112	02 59	47	112	02 12	47	113	01 25	47	113	289
70	12 58	−46	105	12 12	−47	106	11 25	−47	107	10 38	−47	107	09 51	−46	108	09 05	−47	109	08 18	−47	109	07 31	−47	110	06 44	−47	110	05 57	−47	111	05 10	−48	112	04 22	−47	112	03 35	−47	113	02 48	−47	114	02 01	−47	114	290
	0°			1°			2°			3°			4°			5°			6°			7°			8°			9°			10°			11°			12°			13°			14°			

N. Lat. {LHA greater than 180°....... Zn=Z
LHA less than 180°.......... Zn=360−Z}

DECLINATION (0°-14°) CONTRARY NAME TO LATITUDE

LHA	0° Hc	0° d	0° Z	1° Hc	1° d	1° Z	2° Hc	2° d	2° Z	3° Hc	3° d	3° Z	4° Hc	4° d	4° Z	5° Hc	5° d	5° Z	6° Hc	6° d	6° Z	7° Hc	7° d	7° Z
	° ′	′	°	° ′	′	°	° ′	′	°	° ′	′	°	° ′	′	°	° ′	′	°	° ′	′	°	° ′	′	°
69	13 36	47	106	12 49	46	107	12 03	47	107	11 16	47	108	10 29	47	109	09 42	47	109	08 55	47	110	08 08	47	111
68	14 14	47	107	13 27	47	108	12 40	47	108	11 53	47	109	11 06	47	110	10 19	47	110	09 32	48	111	08 44	47	111
67	14 51	47	108	14 04	47	108	13 17	47	109	12 30	47	110	11 43	47	110	10 56	48	111	10 08	47	112	09 21	47	112
66	15 29	47	109	14 42	48	109	13 54	47	110	13 07	47	111	12 20	48	111	11 32	47	112	10 45	48	112	09 57	47	113
65	16 06	−47	109	15 19	−48	110	14 31	−47	111	13 44	−48	111	12 56	−47	112	12 09	−48	113	11 21	−48	113	10 33	−47	114
64	16 43	47	110	15 56	48	111	15 08	47	112	14 21	48	112	13 33	48	113	12 45	48	113	11 57	48	114	11 09	48	115
63	17 20	48	111	16 32	47	112	15 45	48	112	14 57	48	113	14 09	48	114	13 21	48	114	12 33	48	115	11 45	48	115
62	17 56	47	112	17 09	48	113	16 21	48	113	15 33	48	114	14 45	48	114	13 57	48	115	13 09	48	116	12 21	49	116
61	18 33	48	113	17 45	48	113	16 57	48	114	16 09	48	115	15 21	48	115	14 33	49	116	13 44	48	116	12 56	49	117
60	19 09	−48	114	18 21	−48	114	17 33	−48	115	16 45	−49	115	15 56	−48	116	15 08	−49	117	14 19	−48	117	13 31	−49	118
59	19 45	48	114	18 57	49	115	18 08	48	116	17 20	48	116	16 32	49	117	15 43	49	118	14 54	48	118	14 05	49	119
58	20 21	49	115	19 32	48	116	18 44	49	117	17 55	48	117	17 07	49	118	16 18	49	118	15 29	49	119	14 40	49	120
57	20 56	48	116	20 08	49	117	19 19	49	117	18 30	49	118	17 41	49	119	16 52	49	119	16 03	49	120	15 14	50	120
56	21 31	48	117	20 43	49	118	19 54	49	118	19 05	49	119	18 16	50	119	17 26	49	120	16 37	49	121	15 48	50	121
55	22 06	−49	118	21 17	−49	119	20 28	−49	119	19 39	−49	120	18 50	−50	120	18 00	−49	121	17 11	−50	122	16 21	−50	122
54	22 41	49	119	21 52	49	119	21 03	50	120	20 13	49	121	19 24	50	121	18 34	50	122	17 44	50	122	16 54	50	123
53	23 15	49	120	22 26	49	120	21 37	50	121	20 47	50	122	19 57	50	122	19 07	50	123	18 17	50	123	17 27	50	124
52	23 49	49	121	23 00	50	121	22 10	50	122	21 20	50	122	20 30	50	123	19 40	50	124	18 50	50	124	18 00	51	125
51	24 23	50	121	23 33	50	122	22 43	50	123	21 53	50	123	21 03	50	124	20 13	51	124	19 22	50	125	18 32	51	126
50	24 57	−50	122	24 07	−51	123	23 16	−50	124	22 26	−50	124	21 36	−51	125	20 45	−50	125	19 55	−51	126	19 04	−51	126
49	25 30	51	123	24 39	50	124	23 49	50	125	22 59	51	125	22 08	51	126	21 17	51	126	20 26	51	127	19 35	51	127
48	26 02	50	124	25 12	51	125	24 21	50	125	23 31	51	126	22 40	51	127	21 49	51	127	20 58	52	128	20 06	51	128
47	26 35	51	125	25 44	51	126	24 53	51	126	24 02	51	127	23 11	51	128	22 20	51	128	21 29	52	129	20 37	51	129
46	27 07	51	126	26 16	51	127	25 25	51	127	24 34	52	128	23 42	51	128	22 51	52	129	21 59	52	130	21 07	51	130
45	27 38	−51	127	26 47	−51	128	25 56	−52	128	25 04	−51	129	24 13	−52	129	23 21	−52	130	22 29	−52	130	21 37	−52	131
44	28 10	52	128	27 18	51	129	26 27	52	129	25 35	52	130	24 43	52	130	23 51	52	131	22 59	52	131	22 07	52	132
43	28 40	51	129	27 49	52	130	26 57	52	130	26 05	52	131	25 13	52	131	24 21	53	132	23 28	52	132	22 36	53	133
42	29 11	52	130	28 19	52	131	27 27	52	131	26 35	53	132	25 42	52	132	24 50	53	133	23 57	52	133	23 05	53	134
41	29 41	52	131	28 49	53	132	27 56	52	132	27 04	53	133	26 11	53	133	25 18	52	134	24 26	53	134	23 33	53	135
40	30 10	−52	132	29 18	−53	133	28 25	−52	133	27 33	−53	134	26 40	−53	134	25 47	−53	135	24 54	−54	135	24 00	−53	136
39	30 39	52	133	29 47	53	134	28 54	53	134	28 01	53	135	27 08	54	135	26 14	53	136	25 21	53	136	24 28	54	137
38	31 08	53	134	30 15	53	135	29 22	53	135	28 29	54	136	27 35	53	136	26 42	54	137	25 48	54	137	24 54	53	138
37	31 36	53	135	30 43	54	136	29 49	53	136	28 56	54	137	28 02	53	137	27 09	54	138	26 15	54	138	25 21	54	139
36	32 03	53	136	31 10	54	137	30 16	53	137	29 23	54	138	28 29	54	138	27 35	54	139	26 41	54	139	25 47	55	140
35	32 31	−54	137	31 37	−54	138	30 43	−54	138	29 49	−54	139	28 55	−54	139	28 01	−55	140	27 06	−54	140	26 12	−55	141
34	32 57	54	138	32 03	54	139	31 09	54	139	30 15	55	140	29 20	54	140	28 26	55	141	27 31	55	141	26 36	54	142
33	33 23	54	139	32 29	55	140	31 34	54	140	30 40	55	141	29 45	55	141	28 50	54	142	27 56	55	142	27 01	55	143
32	33 48	54	140	32 54	55	141	31 59	55	141	31 04	55	142	30 09	55	142	29 14	55	143	28 19	55	143	27 24	55	144
31	34 13	55	142	33 18	55	142	32 23	55	142	31 28	55	143	30 33	55	143	29 38	55	144	28 43	56	144	27 47	55	145
30	34 37	−55	143	33 42	−55	143	32 47	−55	144	31 52	−56	144	30 56	−55	144	30 01	−56	145	29 05	−55	145	28 10	−56	146
29	35 01	55	144	34 06	56	144	33 10	55	145	32 15	56	145	31 19	56	146	30 23	56	146	29 27	55	146	28 32	56	147
28	35 24	56	145	34 28	55	145	33 33	56	146	32 37	56	146	31 41	56	147	30 45	56	147	29 49	56	147	28 53	56	148
27	35 46	56	146	34 50	55	146	33 55	57	147	32 58	56	147	32 02	56	148	31 06	56	148	30 10	57	149	29 13	56	149
26	36 08	56	147	35 12	56	148	34 16	57	148	33 19	56	148	32 23	56	149	31 27	57	149	30 30	57	150	29 33	56	150
25	36 29	−56	148	35 33	−57	149	34 36	−56	149	33 40	−57	150	32 43	−57	150	31 46	−56	150	30 50	−57	151	29 53	−57	151
24	36 49	56	150	35 53	57	150	34 56	57	150	33 59	57	151	33 02	56	151	32 06	57	151	31 09	57	152	30 12	58	152
23	37 09	57	151	36 12	57	151	35 15	57	151	34 18	57	152	33 21	57	152	32 24	57	153	31 27	57	153	30 30	58	153
22	37 28	57	152	36 31	57	152	35 34	57	153	34 37	58	153	33 39	57	153	32 42	58	154	31 44	57	154	30 47	58	154
21	37 46	57	153	36 49	57	153	35 52	58	154	34 54	57	154	33 57	58	155	32 59	58	155	32 01	57	155	31 04	58	156
20	38 04	−58	154	37 06	−57	155	36 09	−58	155	35 11	−58	155	34 13	−58	156	33 15	−57	156	32 18	−58	156	31 20	−58	157
19	38 20	57	156	37 23	58	156	36 25	58	156	35 27	58	157	34 29	58	157	33 31	58	157	32 33	58	157	31 35	58	158
18	38 36	58	157	37 38	58	157	36 40	58	157	35 42	58	158	34 44	58	158	33 46	58	158	32 48	58	159	31 50	59	159
17	38 52	59	158	37 53	58	158	36 55	58	159	35 57	58	159	34 59	59	159	34 00	58	159	33 02	59	160	32 03	58	160
16	39 06	58	159	38 08	59	160	37 09	58	160	36 11	59	160	35 12	58	160	34 14	59	161	33 15	59	161	32 16	58	161
15	39 19	−58	161	38 21	−59	161	37 22	−58	161	36 24	−59	161	35 25	−59	162	34 26	−58	162	33 28	−59	162	32 29	−59	162
14	39 32	58	162	38 34	59	162	37 35	59	162	36 36	59	163	35 37	59	163	34 38	59	163	33 39	59	163	32 40	58	163
13	39 44	59	163	38 45	59	163	37 46	59	164	36 47	59	164	35 48	59	164	34 49	59	164	33 50	59	164	32 51	59	165
12	39 55	59	164	38 56	59	165	37 57	59	165	36 58	59	165	35 59	59	165	35 00	59	165	34 01	60	166	33 01	59	166
11	40 06	60	166	39 06	59	166	38 07	59	166	37 08	59	166	36 09	60	166	35 09	59	167	34 10	59	167	33 11	60	167
10	40 15	−59	167	39 16	−60	167	38 16	−59	167	37 17	−60	167	36 17	−59	168	35 18	−59	168	34 19	−60	168	33 19	−59	168
9	40 23	59	168	39 24	60	168	38 24	59	169	37 25	60	169	36 25	59	169	35 26	60	169	34 26	59	169	33 27	60	169
8	40 31	59	170	39 32	60	170	38 32	60	170	37 32	59	170	36 33	60	170	35 33	60	170	34 33	59	170	33 34	60	171
7	40 38	60	171	39 38	60	171	38 38	59	171	37 39	60	171	36 39	60	171	35 39	59	171	34 40	60	172	33 40	60	172
6	40 44	60	172	39 44	60	172	38 44	60	172	37 44	59	172	36 45	60	173	35 45	60	173	34 45	60	173	33 45	60	173
5	40 49	−60	173	39 49	−60	174	38 49	−60	174	37 49	−60	174	36 49	−60	174	35 49	−59	174	34 50	−60	174	33 50	−60	174
4	40 53	60	175	39 53	60	175	38 53	60	175	37 53	60	175	36 53	60	175	35 53	60	175	34 53	60	175	33 53	59	175
3	40 56	60	176	39 56	60	176	38 56	60	176	37 56	60	176	36 56	60	176	35 56	60	176	34 56	60	176	33 56	60	176
2	40 58	60	177	39 58	60	177	38 58	60	177	37 58	60	178	36 58	60	178	35 58	60	178	34 58	60	178	33 58	60	178
1	41 00	60	179	40 00	60	179	39 00	60	179	38 00	60	179	37 00	60	179	36 00	60	179	35 00	60	179	34 00	60	179
0	41 00	−60	180	40 00	−60	180	39 00	−60	180	38 00	−60	180	37 00	−60	180	36 00	−60	180	35 00	−60	180	34 00	−60	180

LHA	8° Hc	8° d	8° Z	9° Hc	9° d	9° Z	10° Hc	10° d	10° Z	11° Hc	11° d	11° Z	12° Hc	12° d	12° Z	13° Hc	13° d	13° Z	14° Hc	14° d	14° Z	LHA
	° ′	′	°	° ′	′	°	° ′	′	°	° ′	′	°	° ′	′	°	° ′	′	°	° ′	′	°	
69	07 21	48	111	06 33	47	112	05 46	47	113	04 59	48	113	04 11	47	114	03 24	47	114	02 37	48	115	291
68	07 57	47	112	07 10	48	113	06 22	47	113	05 35	48	114	04 47	47	114	04 00	48	115	03 12	47	116	292
67	08 34	48	113	07 46	48	113	06 58	47	114	06 11	48	115	05 23	48	115	04 35	47	116	03 48	48	116	293
66	09 10	48	114	08 22	48	114	07 34	48	115	06 46	47	115	05 59	48	116	05 11	48	117	04 23	48	117	294
65	09 46	−48	114	08 58	−48	115	08 10	−48	116	07 22	−48	116	06 34	−48	117	05 46	−48	117	04 58	−49	118	295
64	10 21	48	115	09 33	48	116	08 45	48	116	07 57	48	117	07 09	48	118	06 21	49	118	05 32	48	119	296
63	10 57	48	116	10 09	49	117	09 20	48	117	08 32	48	118	07 44	49	118	06 55	48	119	06 07	49	120	297
62	11 32	48	117	10 44	49	117	09 55	48	118	09 07	49	119	08 18	49	119	07 29	48	120	06 41	49	120	298
61	12 07	48	118	11 19	49	118	10 30	49	119	09 41	49	119	08 52	49	120	08 03	49	121	07 14	48	121	299
60	12 42	−49	119	11 53	−49	119	11 04	−49	120	10 15	−49	120	09 26	−49	121	08 37	−49	121	07 48	−49	122	300
59	13 16	49	119	12 27	49	120	11 38	49	121	10 49	49	121	10 00	49	122	09 11	50	122	08 21	49	123	301
58	13 51	50	120	13 01	49	121	12 12	49	121	11 23	50	122	10 33	49	123	09 44	50	123	08 54	49	124	302
57	14 24	49	121	13 35	49	122	12 46	50	122	11 56	50	123	11 06	49	123	10 17	50	124	09 27	50	124	303
56	14 58	50	122	14 08	49	122	13 19	50	123	12 29	50	124	11 39	50	124	10 49	50	125	09 59	50	125	304
55	15 31	−49	123	14 42	−50	123	13 52	−50	124	13 02	−51	124	12 11	−50	125	11 21	−50	126	10 31	−50	126	305
54	16 04	50	124	15 14	50	124	14 24	50	125	13 34	50	125	12 44	51	126	11 53	50	126	11 03	51	127	306
53	16 37	50	124	15 47	51	125	14 56	50	126	14 06	51	126	13 15	50	127	12 25	51	127	11 34	51	128	307
52	17 09	50	125	16 19	51	126	15 28	50	126	14 38	51	127	13 47	51	128	12 56	51	128	12 05	51	129	308
51	17 41	50	126	16 51	51	127	16 00	51	127	15 09	51	128	14 18	51	128	13 27	51	129	12 36	52	129	309
50	18 13	−51	127	17 22	−51	128	16 31	−51	128	15 40	−51	129	14 49	−52	129	13 57	−51	130	13 06	−52	130	310
49	18 44	51	128	17 53	51	128	17 02	52	129	16 10	51	130	15 19	52	130	14 27	51	131	13 36	52	131	311
48	19 15	51	129	18 24	52	129	17 32	52	130	16 40	51	130	15 49	52	131	14 57	52	132	14 05	52	132	312
47	19 46	52	130	18 54	52	130	18 02	52	131	17 10	52	131	16 18	52	132	15 26	52	132	14 34	52	133	313
46	20 16	52	131	19 24	52	131	18 32	52	132	17 40	53	132	16 47	52	133	15 55	52	133	15 03	52	134	314
45	20 45	−52	132	19 53	−52	132	19 01	−52	133	18 09	−53	133	17 16	−52	134	16 24	−53	134	15 31	−52	135	315
44	21 15	53	132	20 22	52	133	19 30	53	134	18 37	53	134	17 44	52	135	16 52	53	135	15 59	53	136	316
43	21 43	52	133	20 51	53	134	19 58	53	134	19 05	53	135	18 12	53	135	17 19	53	136	16 26	53	136	317
42	22 12	53	134	21 19	53	135	20 26	53	135	19 33	53	136	18 40	53	136	17 47	54	137	16 53	53	137	318
41	22 40	53	135	21 47	54	136	20 53	53	136	20 00	53	137	19 07	54	137	18 13	53	138	17 20	54	138	319
40	23 07	−53	136	22 14	−54	137	21 20	−53	137	20 27	−54	138	19 33	−53	138	18 40	−54	139	17 46	−54	139	320
39	23 34	53	137	22 41	54	138	21 47	54	138	20 53	54	139	19 59	54	139	19 05	54	140	18 11	54	140	321
38	24 01	54	138	23 07	54	139	22 13	54	139	21 19	54	140	20 25	54	140	19 31	55	141	18 36	54	141	322
37	24 27	54	139	23 33	55	140	22 38	54	140	21 44	54	141	20 50	55	141	19 55	54	141	19 01	55	142	323
36	24 52	54	140	23 58	55	141	23 03	54	141	22 09	55	142	21 14	54	142	20 20	55	142	19 25	55	143	324
35	25 17	−54	141	24 23	−55	142	23 28	−55	142	22 33	−55	142	21 38	−55	143	20 43	−54	143	19 49	−55	144	325
34	25 42	55	142	24 47	55	143	23 52	55	143	22 57	55	143	22 02	55	144	21 07	55	144	20 12	56	145	326
33	26 06	55	143	25 11	56	144	24 15	55	144	23 20	55	144	22 25	56	145	21 29	55	145	20 34	56	146	327
32	26 29	55	144	25 34	56	145	24 38	55	145	23 43	56	145	22 47	55	146	21 52	56	146	20 56	56	147	328
31	26 52	56	145	25 56	55	146	25 01	56	146	24 05	56	146	23 09	56	147	22 13	56	147	21 17	56	148	329
30	27 14	−56	146	26 18	−56	147	25 22	−56	147	24 26	−56	147	23 30	−56	148	22 34	−56	148	21 38	−56	149	330
29	27 36	56	147	26 40	57	148	25 43	56	148	24 47	56	148	23 51	56	149	22 55	57	149	21 58	56	150	331
28	27 57	57	148	27 00	56	149	26 04	56	149	25 08	57	149	24 11	56	150	23 15	57	150	22 18	56	151	332
27	28 17	56	149	27 21	57	150	26 24	57	150	25 27	56	150	24 31	57	151	23 34	57	151	22 37	57	152	333
26	28 37	57	150	27 40	57	151	26 43	57	151	25 46	56	152	24 50	57	152	23 53	57	152	22 56	57	153	334
25	28 56	−57	151	27 59	−57	152	27 02	−57	152	26 05	−57	153	25 08	−57	153	24 11	−57	153	23 14	−58	154	335
24	29 14	57	153	28 17	57	153	27 20	57	153	26 23	57	154	25 26	58	154	24 28	57	154	23 31	58	155	336
23	29 32	57	154	28 35	57	154	27 38	58	154	26 40	57	155	25 43	58	155	24 45	58	155	23 47	57	156	337
22	29 49	57	155	28 52	58	155	27 54	57	155	26 57	58	156	25 59	58	156	25 01	58	156	24 03	57	157	338
21	30 06	58	156	29 08	58	156	28 10	57	156	27 13	58	157	26 15	58	157	25 17	58	157	24 19	58	158	339
20	30 22	−58	157	29 24	−58	157	28 26	−58	158	27 28	−58	158	26 30	−58	158	25 32	−59	158	24 33	−58	159	340
19	30 37	58	158	29 39	58	158	28 41	59	159	27 42	58	159	26 44	58	159	25 46	58	159	24 48	59	160	341
18	30 51	58	159	29 53	58	159	28 55	59	160	27 56	58	160	26 58	59	160	25 59	58	160	25 01	59	161	342
17	31 05	59	160	30 06	58	161	29 08	59	161	28 09	58	161	27 11	59	161	26 12	58	162	25 14	59	162	343
16	31 18	59	161	30 19	58	162	29 21	59	162	28 22	59	162	27 23	59	162	26 24	58	163	25 26	59	163	344
15	31 30	−59	163	30 31	−59	163	29 32	−58	163	28 34	−59	163	27 35	−59	163	26 36	−59	164	25 37	−59	164	345
14	31 42	59	164	30 43	59	164	29 44	59	164	28 45	59	164	27 46	59	165	26 47	60	165	25 47	59	165	346
13	31 52	59	165	30 53	59	165	29 54	59	165	28 55	59	165	27 56	59	166	26 57	60	166	25 57	59	166	347
12	32 02	59	166	31 03	59	166	30 04	60	166	29 04	59	167	28 05	59	167	27 06	59	167	26 07	60	167	348
11	32 11	59	167	31 12	59	167	30 13	60	167	29 13	59	168	28 14	60	168	27 14	59	168	26 15	59	168	349
10	32 20	−60	168	31 20	−59	168	30 21	−60	169	29 21	−59	169	28 22	−60	169	27 22	−59	169	26 23	−60	169	350
9	32 27	59	169	31 28	60	170	30 28	59	170	29 29	60	170	28 29	60	170	27 29	59	170	26 30	60	170	351
8	32 34	59	171	31 35	60	171	30 35	60	171	29 35	59	171	28 36	60	171	27 36	60	171	26 36	59	171	352
7	32 40	59	172	31 41	60	172	30 41	60	172	29 41	60	172	28 41	59	172	27 42	60	172	26 42	60	172	353
6	32 45	59	173	31 46	60	173	30 46	60	173	29 46	60	173	28 46	60	173	27 46	59	173	26 47	60	174	354
5	32 50	−60	174	31 50	−60	174	30 50	−60	174	29 50	−60	174	28 50	−59	174	27 51	−60	175	26 51	−60	175	355
4	32 54	60	175	31 54	60	175	30 54	60	175	29 54	60	176	28 54	60	176	27 54	60	176	26 54	60	176	356
3	32 56	60	177	31 56	59	177	30 57	60	177	29 57	60	177	28 57	60	177	27 57	60	177	26 57	60	177	357
2	32 58	60	178	31 58	60	178	30 58	60	178	29 58	59	178	28 59	60	178	27 59	60	178	26 59	60	178	358
1	33 00	60	179	32 00	60	179	31 00	60	179	30 00	60	179	29 00	60	179	28 00	60	179	27 00	60	179	359
0	33 00	−60	180	32 00	−60	180	31 00	−60	180	30 00	−60	180	29 00	−60	180	28 00	−60	180	27 00	−60	180	360

0° 1° 2° 3° 4° 5° 6° 7° 8° 9° 10° 11° 12° 13° 14°

S. Lat. {LHA greater than 180°....... Zn=180−Z
LHA less than 180°.......... Zn=180+Z}

DECLINATION (0°-14°) CONTRARY NAME TO LATITUDE

N. Lat. {LHA greater than 180°..... Zn=Z; LHA less than 180°.......... Zn=360−Z}

DECLINATION (15°-29°) SAME NAME AS LATITUDE

LHA	15° Hc	15° d	15° Z	16° Hc	16° d	16° Z	17° Hc	17° d	17° Z	18° Hc	18° d	18° Z	19° Hc	19° d	19° Z
	° ′	′	°	° ′	′	°	° ′	′	°	° ′	′	°	° ′	′	°
0	56 00	+60	180	57 00	+60	180	58 00	+60	180	59 00	+60	180	60 00	+60	180
1	55 59	60	178	56 59	60	178	57 59	60	178	58 59	60	178	59 59	60	178
2	55 58	60	177	56 58	60	177	57 58	60	176	58 58	59	176	59 57	60	176
3	55 55	60	175	56 55	59	175	57 54	60	175	58 54	60	175	59 54	60	174
4	55 51	59	173	56 50	60	173	57 50	60	173	58 50	60	173	59 50	59	173
5	55 45	+60	171	56 45	+60	171	57 45	+59	171	58 44	+60	171	59 44	+59	171
6	55 39	59	170	56 38	60	170	57 38	59	169	58 37	60	169	59 37	59	169
7	55 31	60	168	56 31	59	168	57 30	59	168	58 29	60	167	59 29	59	167
8	55 22	60	166	56 22	59	166	57 21	59	166	58 20	59	165	59 19	59	165
9	55 13	59	165	56 12	59	164	57 11	58	164	58 09	59	164	59 08	59	163
10	55 02	+58	163	56 00	+59	163	56 59	+59	162	57 58	+58	162	58 56	+59	161
11	54 50	58	161	55 48	59	161	56 47	58	161	57 45	58	160	58 43	58	160
12	54 36	59	160	55 35	58	159	56 33	58	159	57 31	58	158	58 29	58	158
13	54 22	58	158	55 20	58	158	56 18	58	157	57 16	58	157	58 14	57	156
14	54 07	58	157	55 05	57	156	56 02	58	156	57 00	57	155	57 57	57	155
15	53 51	+57	155	54 48	+58	154	55 46	+57	154	56 43	+57	153	57 40	+56	153
16	53 34	57	153	54 31	57	153	55 28	57	152	56 25	56	152	57 21	57	151
17	53 16	56	152	54 12	57	151	55 09	56	151	56 05	57	150	57 02	56	150
18	52 57	56	150	53 53	56	150	54 49	56	149	55 45	56	149	56 41	56	148
19	52 37	56	149	53 33	56	148	54 29	55	148	55 24	56	147	56 20	55	146
20	52 16	+56	147	53 12	+55	147	54 07	+55	146	55 02	+55	145	55 57	+55	145
21	51 54	55	146	52 49	56	145	53 45	55	145	54 40	54	144	55 34	55	143
22	51 32	55	144	52 27	54	144	53 21	55	143	54 16	54	142	55 10	54	142
23	51 08	55	143	52 03	54	142	52 57	55	142	53 52	53	141	54 45	54	140
24	50 44	55	142	51 39	54	141	52 33	53	140	53 26	54	140	54 20	53	139
25	50 19	+54	140	51 13	+54	140	52 07	+53	139	53 00	+54	138	53 54	+52	137
26	49 54	54	139	50 48	53	138	51 41	53	138	52 34	53	137	53 27	52	136
27	49 28	53	138	50 21	53	137	51 14	52	136	52 06	53	135	52 59	52	135
28	49 01	53	136	49 54	52	136	50 46	52	135	51 38	52	134	52 30	52	133
29	48 33	53	135	49 26	52	134	50 18	52	134	51 10	51	133	52 01	52	132
30	48 05	+52	134	48 57	+52	133	49 49	+52	132	50 41	+51	131	51 32	+51	131
31	47 36	52	133	48 28	52	132	49 20	51	131	50 11	51	130	51 02	50	129
32	47 07	51	131	47 58	52	131	48 50	50	130	49 40	51	129	50 31	50	128
33	46 37	51	130	47 28	51	129	48 19	50	128	49 09	51	128	50 00	49	127
34	46 07	51	129	46 58	50	128	47 48	50	127	48 38	50	126	49 28	49	126
35	45 36	+50	128	46 26	+50	127	47 16	+50	126	48 06	+50	125	48 56	+48	124
36	45 04	51	127	45 55	49	126	46 44	50	125	47 34	49	124	48 23	48	123
37	44 33	49	125	45 22	50	125	46 12	49	124	47 01	49	123	47 50	48	122
38	44 00	50	124	44 50	49	123	45 39	49	123	46 28	48	122	47 16	48	121
39	43 27	50	123	44 17	49	122	45 06	48	122	45 54	48	121	46 42	48	120
40	42 54	+49	122	43 43	+49	121	44 32	+48	120	45 20	+48	120	46 08	+47	119
41	42 21	48	121	43 09	49	120	43 58	48	119	44 46	47	119	45 33	47	118
42	41 47	48	120	42 35	48	119	43 23	48	118	44 11	47	118	44 58	47	117
43	41 13	48	119	42 01	47	118	42 48	48	117	43 36	47	116	44 23	46	116
44	40 38	48	118	41 26	47	117	42 13	47	116	43 00	47	115	43 47	46	115
45	40 03	+47	117	40 50	+48	116	41 38	+47	115	42 25	+46	114	43 11	+46	114
46	39 28	47	116	40 15	47	115	41 02	47	114	41 49	46	113	42 35	46	113
47	38 52	47	115	39 39	47	114	40 26	46	113	41 12	46	112	41 58	46	112
48	38 16	47	114	39 03	47	113	39 50	46	112	40 36	46	111	41 22	45	111
49	37 40	47	113	38 27	46	112	39 13	46	111	39 59	46	111	40 45	45	110
50	37 04	+46	112	37 50	+46	111	38 36	+46	110	39 22	+45	110	40 07	+46	109
51	36 27	46	111	37 13	46	110	37 59	46	109	38 45	45	109	39 30	45	108
52	35 50	46	110	36 36	46	109	37 22	45	109	38 07	46	108	38 53	44	107
53	35 13	46	109	35 59	46	108	36 45	45	108	37 30	45	107	38 15	44	106
54	34 36	46	108	35 22	45	107	36 07	45	107	36 52	45	106	37 37	44	105
55	33 58	+46	107	34 44	+45	107	35 29	+45	106	36 14	+45	105	36 59	+44	104
56	33 21	45	107	34 06	45	106	34 51	45	105	35 36	44	104	36 20	45	103
57	32 43	45	106	33 28	45	105	34 13	45	104	34 58	44	103	35 42	44	102
58	32 05	45	105	32 50	45	104	33 35	44	103	34 19	45	102	35 04	43	102
59	31 27	45	104	32 12	45	103	32 57	44	102	33 41	44	102	34 25	44	101
60	30 49	+44	103	31 33	+45	102	32 18	+44	102	33 02	+44	101	33 46	+44	100
61	30 10	45	102	30 55	44	102	31 39	45	101	32 24	43	100	33 07	44	99
62	29 32	44	101	30 16	45	101	31 01	44	100	31 45	44	99	32 29	43	98
63	28 53	45	101	29 38	44	100	30 22	44	99	31 06	44	98	31 50	43	98
64	28 14	45	100	28 59	44	99	29 43	44	98	30 27	43	98	31 10	44	97
65	27 35	+45	99	28 20	+44	98	29 04	+44	97	29 48	+43	97	30 31	+44	96
66	26 57	44	98	27 41	44	97	28 25	44	97	29 09	43	96	29 52	43	95
67	26 18	44	97	27 02	44	97	27 46	43	96	28 29	44	95	29 13	43	94
68	25 38	45	97	26 23	44	96	27 07	43	95	27 50	44	94	28 34	43	94
69	24 59	44	96	25 43	44	95	26 27	44	94	27 11	43	94	27 54	43	93

LHA	20° Hc	20° d	20° Z	21° Hc	21° d	21° Z	22° Hc	22° d	22° Z	23° Hc	23° d	23° Z	24° Hc	24° d	24° Z
	° ′	′	°	° ′	′	°	° ′	′	°	° ′	′	°	° ′	′	°
0	61 00	+60	180	62 00	+60	180	63 00	+60	180	64 00	+60	180	65 00	+60	180
1	60 59	60	178	61 59	60	178	62 59	60	178	63 59	60	178	64 59	60	178
2	60 57	60	176	61 57	60	176	62 57	60	176	63 57	60	176	64 57	60	176
3	60 54	60	174	61 54	60	174	62 54	60	174	63 54	59	174	64 53	60	174
4	60 49	60	172	61 49	60	172	62 49	60	172	63 49	59	172	64 48	60	171
5	60 43	+60	170	61 43	+60	170	62 43	+59	170	63 42	+60	170	64 42	+59	169
6	60 36	60	169	61 36	59	168	62 35	59	168	63 34	60	168	64 34	59	167
7	60 28	59	167	61 27	59	166	62 26	59	166	63 25	59	166	64 24	59	165
8	60 18	59	165	61 17	59	164	62 16	59	164	63 15	58	164	64 13	59	163
9	60 07	59	163	61 06	58	162	62 04	59	162	63 03	58	162	64 01	58	161
10	59 55	+58	161	60 53	+58	161	61 51	+59	160	62 50	+58	160	63 48	+58	159
11	59 41	58	159	60 39	58	159	61 37	58	158	62 35	58	158	63 33	57	157
12	59 27	58	157	60 25	57	157	61 22	58	156	62 20	57	156	63 17	57	155
13	59 11	57	156	60 08	58	155	61 06	57	154	62 03	57	154	63 00	56	153
14	58 54	57	154	59 51	57	153	60 48	57	153	61 45	56	152	62 41	56	151
15	58 36	+57	152	59 33	+57	152	60 30	+56	151	61 26	+56	150	62 22	+55	149
16	58 18	56	151	59 14	56	150	60 10	56	149	61 06	55	148	62 01	55	148
17	57 58	56	149	58 54	55	148	59 49	55	147	60 44	55	147	61 39	55	146
18	57 37	55	147	58 32	55	146	59 27	55	146	60 22	55	145	61 17	54	144
19	57 15	55	146	58 10	55	145	59 05	54	144	59 59	54	143	60 53	54	142
20	56 52	+55	144	57 47	+54	143	58 41	+54	142	59 35	+54	142	60 29	+53	141
21	56 29	54	142	57 23	54	142	58 17	53	141	59 10	53	140	60 03	53	139
22	56 04	54	141	56 58	53	140	57 51	53	139	58 44	53	138	59 37	52	137
23	55 39	53	139	56 32	53	139	57 25	53	138	58 18	52	137	59 10	52	136
24	55 13	53	138	56 06	52	137	56 58	53	136	57 51	51	135	58 42	52	134
25	54 46	+53	137	55 39	+52	136	56 31	+52	135	57 23	+51	134	58 14	+51	133
26	54 19	52	135	55 11	52	134	56 03	51	133	56 54	51	132	57 45	50	131
27	53 51	51	134	54 42	52	133	55 34	50	132	56 24	51	131	57 15	50	130
28	53 22	51	132	54 13	51	131	55 04	50	131	55 54	50	130	56 44	50	129
29	52 53	50	131	53 43	51	130	54 34	50	129	55 24	49	129	56 13	49	127
30	52 23	+50	130	53 13	+50	129	54 03	+49	128	54 52	+50	127	55 42	+48	126
31	51 52	50	128	52 42	50	128	53 32	49	127	54 21	48	126	55 09	48	125
32	51 21	50	127	52 11	49	126	53 00	48	125	53 48	49	124	54 37	47	123
33	50 49	49	126	51 38	49	125	52 27	49	124	53 16	48	123	54 04	47	122
34	50 17	49	125	51 06	48	124	51 54	48	123	52 42	48	122	53 30	47	121
35	49 44	+49	124	50 33	+48	123	51 21	+48	122	52 09	+47	121	52 56	+47	120
36	49 11	49	122	50 00	47	121	50 47	48	120	51 35	47	119	52 22	46	118
37	48 38	48	121	49 26	47	120	50 13	47	119	51 00	47	118	51 47	46	117
38	48 04	48	120	48 52	47	119	49 39	46	118	50 25	47	117	51 12	45	116
39	47 30	47	119	48 17	47	118	49 04	46	117	49 50	46	116	50 36	45	115
40	46 55	+47	118	47 42	+47	117	48 29	+46	116	49 15	+45	115	50 00	+45	114
41	46 20	47	117	47 07	46	116	47 53	46	115	48 39	45	114	49 24	45	113
42	45 45	46	116	46 31	46	115	47 17	46	114	48 03	45	113	48 48	44	112
43	45 09	46	115	45 55	46	114	46 41	45	113	47 26	45	112	48 11	44	111
44	44 33	46	114	45 19	46	113	46 05	45	112	46 50	44	111	47 34	44	110
45	43 57	+46	113	44 43	+45	112	45 28	+45	111	46 13	+44	110	46 57	+44	109
46	43 21	45	112	44 06	45	111	44 51	45	110	45 36	44	109	46 20	43	108
47	42 44	45	111	43 29	45	110	44 14	44	109	44 58	44	108	45 42	44	107
48	42 07	45	110	42 52	45	109	43 37	44	108	44 21	43	107	45 04	44	106
49	41 30	45	109	42 15	44	108	42 59	44	107	43 43	43	106	44 26	43	105
50	40 53	+44	108	41 37	+44	107	42 21	+44	106	43 05	+43	105	43 48	+43	104
51	40 15	44	107	40 59	44	106	41 43	44	105	42 27	43	104	43 10	43	103
52	39 37	44	106	40 21	44	105	41 05	44	104	41 49	43	103	42 32	42	102
53	38 59	44	105	39 43	44	104	40 27	43	103	41 10	43	102	41 53	43	102
54	38 21	44	104	39 05	44	103	39 49	43	102	40 32	43	102	41 15	42	101
55	37 43	+44	103	38 27	+43	103	39 10	+43	102	39 53	+43	101	40 36	+42	100
56	37 05	43	103	37 48	44	102	38 32	43	101	39 15	42	100	39 57	42	99
57	36 26	44	102	37 10	43	101	37 53	43	100	38 36	42	99	39 18	42	98
58	35 47	44	101	36 31	43	100	37 14	43	99	37 57	42	98	38 39	42	97
59	35 09	43	100	35 52	43	99	36 35	43	98	37 18	42	97	38 00	42	96
60	34 30	+43	99	35 13	+43	98	35 56	+43	97	36 39	+42	97	37 21	+42	96
61	33 51	43	98	34 34	43	97	35 17	43	97	36 00	42	96	36 42	41	95
62	33 12	43	98	33 55	43	97	34 38	42	96	35 20	42	95	36 02	42	94
63	32 33	43	97	33 16	43	96	33 59	42	95	34 41	42	94	35 23	42	93
64	31 54	43	96	32 37	42	95	33 19	43	94	34 02	42	93	34 44	41	93
65	31 15	+43	95	31 58	+42	94	32 40	+43	93	33 23	+41	93	34 04	+42	92
66	30 35	43	94	31 18	43	94	32 01	42	93	32 43	42	92	33 25	42	91
67	29 56	43	94	30 39	43	93	31 22	42	92	32 04	42	91	32 46	41	90
68	29 17	43	93	30 00	42	92	30 42	42	91	31 24	42	90	32 06	42	89
69	28 37	43	92	29 20	43	91	30 03	42	90	30 45	42	90	31 27	42	89

LHA	25° Hc	25° d	25° Z	26° Hc	26° d	26° Z	27° Hc	27° d	27° Z	28° Hc	28° d	28° Z	29° Hc	29° d	29° Z	LHA
	° ′	′	°	° ′	′	°	° ′	′	°	° ′	′	°	° ′	′	°	
0	66 00	+60	180	67 00	+60	180	68 00	+60	180	69 00	+60	180	70 00	+60	180	360
1	65 59	60	178	66 59	60	178	67 59	60	178	68 59	60	178	69 59	60	177	359
2	65 57	60	176	66 57	60	175	67 57	60	175	68 57	60	175	69 57	59	175	358
3	65 53	60	173	66 53	60	173	67 53	59	173	68 52	60	173	69 52	60	172	357
4	65 48	59	171	66 47	60	171	67 47	60	171	68 47	59	170	69 46	60	170	356
5	65 41	+59	169	66 40	+60	169	67 40	+59	168	68 39	+59	168	69 38	+59	167	355
6	65 33	59	167	66 32	59	166	67 31	59	166	68 30	59	165	69 29	59	165	354
7	65 23	59	165	66 22	59	164	67 21	58	164	68 19	59	163	69 18	58	163	353
8	65 12	58	163	66 10	59	162	67 09	58	161	68 07	58	161	69 05	58	160	352
9	64 59	59	160	65 58	58	160	66 56	57	159	67 53	58	159	68 51	57	158	351
10	64 46	+57	158	65 43	+58	158	66 41	+57	157	67 38	+57	156	68 35	+57	155	350
11	64 30	58	156	65 28	57	156	66 25	57	155	67 22	56	154	68 18	57	153	349
12	64 14	57	154	65 11	56	154	66 07	57	153	67 04	56	152	68 00	55	151	348
13	63 56	57	152	64 53	56	152	65 49	56	151	66 45	55	150	67 40	55	149	347
14	63 37	56	150	64 33	56	150	65 29	55	149	66 24	55	148	67 19	54	147	346
15	63 17	+56	149	64 13	+55	148	65 08	+55	147	66 03	+54	146	66 57	+54	145	345
16	62 56	55	147	63 51	55	146	64 46	54	145	65 40	54	144	66 34	53	143	344
17	62 34	55	145	63 29	54	144	64 23	53	143	65 16	53	142	66 09	53	141	343
18	62 11	54	143	63 05	53	142	63 58	53	141	64 51	53	140	65 44	52	139	342
19	61 47	53	141	62 40	53	140	63 33	53	139	64 26	51	138	65 17	52	137	341
20	61 22	+53	140	62 15	+52	139	63 07	+52	138	63 59	+51	137	64 50	+51	135	340
21	60 56	52	138	61 48	52	137	62 40	51	136	63 31	51	135	64 22	50	134	339
22	60 29	52	136	61 21	51	135	62 12	51	134	63 03	50	133	63 53	50	132	338
23	60 02	51	135	60 53	51	134	61 44	50	133	62 34	49	132	63 23	49	130	337
24	59 34	50	133	60 24	50	132	61 14	50	131	62 04	49	130	62 53	48	129	336
25	59 05	+50	132	59 55	+49	131	60 44	+50	130	61 34	+48	128	62 22	+48	127	335
26	58 35	50	130	59 25	49	129	60 14	48	128	61 02	48	127	61 50	48	126	334
27	58 05	49	129	58 54	49	128	59 43	48	127	60 31	47	126	61 18	47	124	333
28	57 34	48	128	58 22	49	126	59 11	47	125	59 58	47	124	60 45	46	123	332
29	57 02	48	126	57 50	48	125	58 38	47	124	59 25	47	123	60 12	46	121	331
30	56 30	+48	125	57 18	+47	124	58 05	+47	123	58 52	+46	121	59 38	+45	120	330
31	55 57	48	124	56 45	47	122	57 32	46	121	58 18	46	120	59 04	45	119	329
32	55 24	48	122	56 12	46	121	56 58	46	120	57 44	45	119	58 29	45	118	328
33	54 51	47	121	55 38	46	120	56 24	45	119	57 09	45	118	57 54	44	116	327
34	54 17	46	120	55 03	46	119	55 49	45	118	56 34	45	116	57 19	43	115	326
35	53 43	+46	119	54 29	+45	118	55 14	+45	116	55 59	+44	115	56 43	+43	114	325
36	53 08	45	117	53 53	46	116	54 39	44	115	55 23	44	114	56 07	43	113	324
37	52 33	45	116	53 18	45	115	54 03	44	114	54 47	43	113	55 30	43	112	323
38	51 57	45	115	52 42	45	114	53 27	43	113	54 10	43	112	54 53	43	111	322
39	51 21	45	114	52 06	44	113	52 50	44	112	53 34	42	111	54 16	43	110	321
40	50 45	+45	113	51 30	+44	112	52 14	+43	111	52 57	+42	110	53 39	+42	109	320
41	50 09	44	112	50 53	44	111	51 37	43	110	52 20	42	109	53 02	41	107	319
42	49 32	44	111	50 16	43	110	50 59	43	109	51 42	42	108	52 24	41	106	318
43	48 55	44	110	49 39	43	109	50 22	43	108	51 05	41	107	51 46	41	105	317
44	48 18	44	109	49 02	42	108	49 44	43	107	50 27	41	106	51 08	41	105	316
45	47 41	+43	108	48 24	+43	107	49 07	+42	106	49 49	+41	105	50 30	+41	104	315
46	47 03	43	107	47 46	43	106	48 29	42	105	49 11	41	104	49 52	40	103	314
47	46 26	42	106	47 08	43	105	47 51	41	104	48 32	41	103	49 13	41	102	313
48	45 48	42	105	46 30	42	104	47 12	42	103	47 54	41	102	48 35	40	101	312
49	45 09	43	104	45 52	42	103	46 34	41	102	47 15	41	101	47 56	40	100	311
50	44 31	+43	103	45 14	+41	102	45 55	+41	101	46 36	+41	100	47 17	+40	99	310
51	43 53	42	102	44 35	42	101	45 17	41	100	45 58	40	99	46 38	40	98	309
52	43 14	42	101	43 56	42	100	44 38	41	99	45 19	40	98	45 59	40	97	308
53	42 36	42	101	43 18	41	100	43 59	41	99	44 40	40	98	45 20	40	97	307
54	41 57	42	100	42 39	41	99	43 20	41	98	44 01	40	97	44 41	40	96	306
55	41 18	+42	99	42 00	+41	98	42 41	+41	97	43 22	+40	96	44 02	+39	95	305
56	40 39	42	98	41 21	41	97	42 02	40	96	42 42	40	95	43 22	40	94	304
57	40 00	42	97	40 42	41	96	41 23	40	95	42 03	40	94	42 43	40	93	303
58	39 21	41	96	40 02	41	95	40 43	41	94	41 24	40	93	42 04	39	92	302
59	38 42	41	96	39 23	41	95	40 04	41	94	40 45	40	93	41 25	39	92	301
60	38 03	+41	95	38 44	+41	94	39 25	+40	93	40 05	+40	92	40 45	+40	91	300
61	37 23	42	94	38 05	41	93	38 46	40	92	39 26	40	91	40 06	39	90	299
62	36 44	41	93	37 25	41	92	38 06	41	91	38 47	39	90	39 26	40	89	298
63	36 05	41	92	36 46	41	92	37 27	40	91	38 07	40	90	38 47	40	89	297
64	35 25	42	92	36 07	40	91	36 47	41	90	37 28	40	89	38 08	39	88	296
65	34 46	+41	91	35 27	+41	90	36 08	+40	89	36 48	+40	88	37 28	+40	87	295
66	34 07	41	90	34 48	41	89	35 29	40	88	36 09	40	87	36 49	40	86	294
67	33 27	41	89	34 09	40	88	34 49	41	88	35 30	40	87	36 10	39	86	293
68	32 48	41	89	33 29	41	88	34 10	41	87	34 51	40	86	35 31	39	85	292
69	32 09	41	88	32 50	41	87	33 31	40	86	34 11	40	85	34 51	40	84	291

15° 16° 17° 18° 19° 20° 21° 22° 23° 24° 25° 26° 27° 28° 29°

S. Lat. {LHA greater than 180°........ Zn=180−Z; LHA less than 180°........... Zn=180+Z}

DECLINATION (15°-29°) SAME NAME AS LATITUDE

LAT 49°

LHA	15° Hc	d	Z	16° Hc	d	Z	17° Hc	d	Z	18° Hc	d	Z	19° Hc	d	Z
	° ′	′	°	° ′	′	°	° ′	′	°	° ′	′	°	° ′	′	°
70	24 20	+44	95	25 04	+44	94	25 48	+44	94	26 32	+43	93	27 15	+43	92
71	23 41	44	94	24 25	44	94	25 09	43	93	25 52	44	92	26 36	43	91
72	23 02	44	94	23 46	43	93	24 29	44	92	25 13	43	91	25 56	43	90
73	22 22	44	93	23 06	44	92	23 50	44	91	24 34	43	90	25 17	43	90
74	21 43	44	92	22 27	44	91	23 11	43	90	23 54	44	90	24 38	43	89
75	21 04	+44	91	21 48	+43	90	22 31	+44	90	23 15	+43	89	23 58	+43	88
76	20 24	44	90	21 08	44	90	21 52	44	89	22 36	43	88	23 19	43	87
77	19 45	44	90	20 29	44	89	21 13	43	88	21 56	44	87	22 40	43	87
78	19 06	44	89	19 50	43	88	20 33	44	87	21 17	43	87	22 00	44	86
79	18 26	44	88	19 10	44	87	19 54	44	87	20 38	43	86	21 21	43	85
80	17 47	+44	87	18 31	+44	87	19 15	+43	86	19 58	+44	85	20 42	+43	85
81	17 08	44	87	17 52	43	86	18 35	44	85	19 19	44	85	20 03	43	84
82	16 28	44	86	17 12	44	85	17 56	44	85	18 40	44	84	19 24	43	83
83	15 49	44	85	16 33	44	85	17 17	44	84	18 01	44	83	18 45	43	82
84	15 10	44	84	15 54	44	84	16 38	44	83	17 22	44	82	18 06	43	82
85	14 31	+44	84	15 15	+44	83	15 59	+44	82	16 43	+44	82	17 27	+43	81
86	13 52	44	83	14 36	44	82	15 20	44	82	16 04	44	81	16 48	44	80
87	13 13	44	82	13 57	44	82	14 41	44	81	15 25	44	80	16 09	44	79
88	12 34	44	82	13 18	44	81	14 02	44	80	14 46	44	79	15 30	44	79
89	11 55	44	81	12 39	45	80	13 24	44	79	14 08	44	79	14 52	44	78
90	11 16	+44	80	12 00	+45	79	12 45	+44	79	13 29	+44	78	14 13	+45	77
91	10 37	45	79	11 22	44	79	12 06	45	78	12 51	44	77	13 35	44	77
92	09 59	44	79	10 43	45	78	11 28	44	77	12 12	45	77	12 57	44	76
93	09 20	45	78	10 05	45	77	10 50	44	77	11 34	45	76	12 19	44	75
94	08 42	45	77	09 27	14	76	10 11	45	76	10 56	45	75	11 41	44	74
95	08 03	+45	76	08 48	+45	76	09 33	+45	75	10 18	+45	74	11 03	+45	74
96	07 25	45	76	08 10	45	75	08 55	45	74	09 40	45	74	10 25	45	73
97	06 47	45	75	07 32	45	74	08 17	46	74	09 03	45	73	09 48	45	72
98	06 09	45	74	06 54	46	74	07 40	45	73	08 25	45	72	09 10	45	72
99	05 31	46	73	06 17	45	73	07 02	46	72	07 48	45	72	08 33	45	71
100	04 54	+45	73	05 39	+46	72	06 25	+45	71	07 10	+46	71	07 56	+45	70
101	04 16	46	72	05 02	46	71	05 48	45	71	06 33	46	70	07 19	46	69
102	03 39	46	71	04 25	45	71	05 11	45	70	05 56	46	69	06 42	46	69
103	03 02	46	70	03 48	46	70	04 34	46	69	05 20	46	69	06 06	46	68
104	02 25	46	70	03 11	46	69	03 57	46	68	04 43	46	68	05 29	46	67
105	01 48	+46	69	02 34	+46	68	03 20	+47	68	04 07	+46	67	04 53	+46	66
106	01 11	47	68	01 58	46	68	02 44	47	67	03 31	46	66	04 17	47	66
107	00 35	46	67	01 21	47	67	02 08	47	66	02 55	46	66	03 41	47	65
108	−0 02	47	67	00 45	47	66	01 32	47	65	02 19	47	65	03 06	47	64
109	−0 38	47	66	00 09	47	65	00 56	47	65	01 43	47	64	02 30	47	63
110	−1 14	+48	65	−0 26	+47	65	00 21	+47	64	01 08	+47	63	01 55	+48	63
111	−1 49	47	64	−1 02	48	64	−0 14	47	63	00 33	47	63	01 20	48	62
112	−2 25	48	64	−1 37	48	63	−0 49	47	62	−0 02	48	62	00 46	47	61
113	−3 00	48	63	−2 12	48	62	−1 24	48	62	−0 36	47	61	00 11	48	60
114	−3 35	48	62	−2 47	48	62	−1 59	48	61	−1 11	48	60	−0 23	48	60
115	−4 09	+48	61	−3 21	+48	61	−2 33	+48	60	−1 45	+48	60	−0 57	+49	59
116	−4 44	49	61	−3 55	48	60	−3 07	48	59	−2 19	49	59	−1 30	48	58
117	−5 18	49	60	−4 29	48	59	−3 41	49	59	−2 52	49	58	−2 03	48	57
118	−5 52	49	59	−5 03	49	58	−4 14	49	58	−3 25	48	57	−2 37	49	57
119				−5 37	50	58	−4 47	49	57	−3 58	49	56	−3 09	49	56
120							−5 20	+49	56	−4 31	+49	56	−3 42	+50	55
121							−5 53	50	55	−5 03	49	55	−4 14	50	54
122										−5 36	50	54	−4 46	50	54
123													−5 17	50	53
124													−5 48	50	52

LHA	20° Hc	d	Z	21° Hc	d	Z	22° Hc	d	Z	23° Hc	d	Z	24° Hc	d	Z
	° ′	′	°	° ′	′	°	° ′	′	°	° ′	′	°	° ′	′	°
70	27 58	+43	91	28 41	+43	90	29 24	+42	90	30 06	+42	89	30 48	+41	88
71	27 19	43	90	28 02	42	90	28 44	42	89	29 26	42	88	30 08	42	87
72	26 39	43	90	27 22	43	89	28 05	42	88	28 47	42	87	29 29	42	87
73	26 00	43	89	26 43	42	88	27 25	43	87	28 08	42	87	28 50	42	86
74	25 21	43	88	26 04	42	87	26 46	42	87	27 28	43	86	28 11	41	85
75	24 41	+43	87	25 24	+43	87	26 07	+42	86	26 49	+42	85	27 31	+42	84
76	24 02	43	87	24 45	43	86	25 28	42	85	26 10	42	84	26 52	42	84
77	23 23	43	86	24 06	42	85	24 48	43	84	25 31	42	84	26 13	42	83
78	22 44	43	85	23 27	42	85	24 09	43	84	24 52	42	83	25 34	42	82
79	22 04	43	85	22 47	43	84	23 30	43	83	24 13	42	82	24 55	42	81
80	21 25	+43	84	22 08	+43	83	22 51	+43	82	23 34	+42	82	24 16	+42	81
81	20 46	43	83	21 29	43	82	22 12	43	82	22 55	42	81	23 37	43	80
82	20 07	43	82	20 50	43	82	21 33	43	81	22 16	43	80	22 59	42	79
83	19 28	43	82	20 11	43	81	20 54	43	80	21 37	43	79	22 20	43	79
84	18 49	44	81	19 33	43	80	20 16	43	79	20 59	43	79	21 42	42	78
85	18 10	+44	80	18 54	+43	79	19 37	+43	79	20 20	+43	78	21 03	+43	77
86	17 32	43	79	18 15	44	79	18 59	43	78	19 42	43	77	20 25	43	77
87	16 53	44	79	17 37	43	78	18 20	43	77	19 03	44	77	19 47	43	76
88	16 14	44	78	16 58	44	77	17 42	43	77	18 25	43	76	19 08	44	75
89	15 36	44	77	16 20	44	77	17 04	43	76	17 47	43	75	18 30	44	74
90	14 58	+44	77	15 42	+43	76	16 25	+44	75	17 09	+44	74	17 53	+43	74
91	14 19	44	76	15 03	44	75	15 47	44	74	16 31	44	74	17 15	43	73
92	13 41	44	75	14 25	45	74	15 10	44	74	15 54	43	73	16 37	44	72
93	13 03	45	74	13 48	44	74	14 32	44	73	15 16	44	72	16 00	44	72
94	12 25	45	74	13 10	44	73	13 54	45	72	14 39	44	72	15 23	44	71
95	11 48	+44	73	12 32	+45	72	13 17	+44	72	14 01	+45	71	14 46	+44	70
96	11 10	45	72	11 55	45	72	12 40	44	71	13 24	45	70	14 09	44	70
97	10 33	45	72	11 18	44	71	12 02	45	70	12 47	45	70	13 32	44	69
98	09 55	45	71	10 40	45	70	11 25	45	70	12 10	45	69	12 55	45	68
99	09 18	46	70	10 04	45	70	10 49	45	69	11 34	45	68	12 19	45	67
100	08 41	+46	69	09 27	+45	69	10 12	+45	68	10 57	+45	67	11 42	+45	67
101	08 05	45	69	08 50	46	68	09 36	45	67	10 21	45	67	11 06	46	66
102	07 28	46	68	08 14	45	67	08 59	46	67	09 45	45	66	10 30	46	65
103	06 52	46	67	07 38	45	67	08 23	46	66	09 09	46	65	09 55	45	65
104	06 15	47	67	07 02	46	66	07 48	45	65	08 33	46	65	09 19	46	64
105	05 39	+47	66	06 26	+46	65	07 12	+46	65	07 58	+46	64	08 44	+46	63
106	05 04	46	65	05 50	46	64	06 36	47	64	07 23	46	63	08 09	46	63
107	04 28	47	64	05 15	46	64	06 01	47	63	06 48	46	62	07 34	47	62
108	03 53	46	64	04 39	47	63	05 26	47	62	06 13	47	62	07 00	46	61
109	03 17	47	63	04 04	47	62	04 51	47	62	05 38	47	61	06 25	47	60
110	02 43	+47	62	03 30	+47	62	04 17	+47	61	05 04	+47	60	05 51	+47	60
111	02 08	47	61	02 55	48	61	03 43	47	60	04 30	47	60	05 17	48	59
112	01 33	48	61	02 21	48	60	03 09	47	59	03 56	48	59	04 44	47	58
113	00 59	48	60	01 47	48	59	02 35	48	59	03 23	47	58	04 10	48	57
114	00 25	48	59	01 13	48	59	02 01	48	58	02 49	48	57	03 37	48	57
115	−0 08	+48	58	00 40	+48	58	01 28	+48	57	02 16	+49	57	03 05	+48	56
116	−0 42	49	58	00 07	48	57	00 55	49	56	01 44	48	56	02 32	49	55
117	−1 15	49	57	−0 26	49	56	00 23	48	56	01 11	49	55	02 00	49	55
118	−1 48	49	56	−0 59	49	56	−0 10	49	55	00 39	49	54	01 28	49	54
119	−2 20	49	55	−1 31	49	55	−0 42	49	54	00 07	49	54	00 56	50	53
120	−2 52	+49	55	−2 03	+49	54	−1 14	+50	53	−0 24	+49	53	00 25	+49	52
121	−3 24	49	54	−2 35	50	53	−1 45	49	53	−0 56	50	52	−0 06	50	52
122	−3 56	50	53	−3 06	50	52	−2 16	50	52	−1 26	49	51	−0 37	50	51
123	−4 27	50	52	−3 37	50	52	−2 47	50	51	−1 57	50	51	−1 07	50	50
124	−4 58	50	51	−4 08	50	51	−3 18	51	50	−2 27	50	50	−1 37	51	49
125	−5 29	+51	51	−4 38	+50	50	−3 48	+51	50	−2 57	+50	49	−2 07	+51	48
126	−5 59	51	50	−5 08	51	49	−4 17	50	49	−3 27	51	48	−2 36	51	48
127				−5 38	51	48	−4 47	51	48	−3 56	51	47	−3 05	51	47
128							−5 16	51	47	−4 25	52	47	−3 33	51	46
129							−5 45	52	46	−4 53	51	46	−4 02	52	45
130										−5 21	+52	45	−4 29	+51	45
131										−5 49	52	44	−4 57	52	44
132													−5 24	52	43
133													−5 51	53	42

LHA	25° Hc	d	Z	26° Hc	d	Z	27° Hc	d	Z	28° Hc	d	Z	29° Hc	d	Z	LHA
	° ′	′	°	° ′	′	°	° ′	′	°	° ′	′	°	° ′	′	°	
70	31 29	+42	87	32 11	+41	86	32 52	+40	85	33 32	+40	85	34 12	+40	84	290
71	30 50	41	86	31 31	41	86	32 12	41	85	32 53	40	84	33 33	40	83	289
72	30 11	41	86	30 52	41	85	31 33	41	84	32 14	40	83	32 54	40	82	288
73	29 32	41	85	30 13	41	84	30 54	41	83	31 35	40	82	32 15	40	82	287
74	28 52	42	84	29 34	41	83	30 15	41	83	30 56	40	82	31 36	40	81	286
75	28 13	+42	84	28 55	+41	83	29 36	+41	82	30 17	+40	81	30 57	+41	80	285
76	27 34	42	83	28 16	41	82	28 57	41	81	29 38	41	80	30 19	40	79	284
77	26 55	42	82	27 37	41	81	28 18	41	80	28 59	41	80	29 40	41	79	283
78	26 16	42	81	26 58	41	81	27 39	42	80	28 21	41	79	29 02	40	78	282
79	25 37	42	81	26 19	42	80	27 01	41	79	27 42	41	78	28 23	41	77	281
80	24 58	+42	80	25 40	+42	79	26 22	+42	78	27 04	+41	78	27 45	+41	77	280
81	24 20	42	79	25 02	42	78	25 44	41	78	26 25	41	77	27 06	41	76	279
82	23 41	42	79	24 23	42	78	25 05	42	77	25 47	41	76	26 28	41	75	278
83	23 03	42	78	23 45	42	77	24 27	42	76	25 09	41	76	25 50	42	75	277
84	22 24	43	77	23 07	42	76	23 49	42	76	24 31	41	75	25 12	42	74	276
85	21 46	+42	76	22 28	+43	76	23 11	+42	75	23 53	+42	74	24 35	+41	73	275
86	21 08	42	76	21 50	43	75	22 33	42	74	23 15	42	74	23 57	42	73	274
87	20 30	42	75	21 12	43	74	21 55	42	74	22 37	42	73	23 19	42	72	273
88	19 52	43	74	20 35	42	74	21 17	43	73	22 00	42	72	22 42	42	71	272
89	19 14	43	74	19 57	43	73	20 40	42	72	21 22	43	71	22 05	42	71	271
90	18 36	+43	73	19 19	+43	72	20 02	+43	72	20 45	+43	71	21 28	+42	70	270
91	17 58	44	72	18 42	43	72	19 25	43	71	20 08	43	70	20 51	43	69	269
92	17 21	44	72	18 05	43	71	18 48	43	70	19 31	43	69	20 14	43	69	268
93	16 44	43	71	17 27	44	70	18 11	43	70	18 54	44	69	19 38	43	68	267
94	16 07	43	70	16 50	44	70	17 34	44	69	18 18	43	68	19 01	43	67	266
95	15 30	+44	70	16 14	+44	69	16 58	+43	68	17 41	+44	67	18 25	+43	67	265
96	14 53	44	69	15 37	44	68	16 21	44	67	17 05	44	67	17 49	43	66	264
97	14 16	45	68	15 01	44	68	15 45	44	67	16 29	44	66	17 13	44	65	263
98	13 40	44	68	14 24	45	67	15 09	44	66	15 53	44	65	16 37	44	65	262
99	13 04	44	67	13 48	45	66	14 33	44	65	15 17	45	65	16 02	44	64	261
100	12 27	+45	66	13 12	+45	65	13 57	+45	65	14 42	+45	64	15 27	+44	63	260
101	11 52	45	65	12 37	45	65	13 22	45	64	14 07	44	63	14 51	45	63	259
102	11 16	45	65	12 01	45	64	12 46	46	63	13 32	45	63	14 17	45	62	258
103	10 40	46	64	11 26	45	63	12 11	46	63	12 57	45	62	13 42	45	61	257
104	10 05	46	63	10 51	46	63	11 37	45	62	12 22	46	61	13 08	45	61	256
105	09 30	+46	63	10 16	+46	62	11 02	+46	61	11 48	+45	61	12 33	+46	60	255
106	08 55	46	62	09 41	47	61	10 28	45	61	11 13	46	60	11 59	46	59	254
107	08 21	46	61	09 07	46	61	09 53	47	60	10 40	46	59	11 26	46	59	253
108	07 46	47	61	08 33	46	60	09 19	47	59	10 06	46	59	10 52	47	58	252
109	07 12	47	60	07 59	47	59	08 46	46	59	09 32	47	58	10 19	47	57	251
110	06 38	+47	59	07 25	+47	58	08 12	+47	58	08 59	+47	57	09 46	+47	57	250
111	06 05	47	58	06 52	47	58	07 39	47	57	08 26	47	56	09 13	47	56	249
112	05 31	48	58	06 19	47	57	07 06	48	56	07 54	47	56	08 41	47	55	248
113	04 58	48	57	05 46	48	56	06 34	47	56	07 21	48	55	08 09	47	54	247
114	04 25	48	56	05 13	48	56	06 01	48	55	06 49	48	54	07 37	48	54	246
115	03 53	+48	55	04 41	+48	55	05 29	+48	54	06 17	+48	54	07 05	+48	53	245
116	03 21	48	55	04 09	48	54	04 57	49	54	05 46	48	53	06 34	48	52	244
117	02 49	48	54	03 37	49	53	04 26	48	53	05 14	49	52	06 03	49	52	243
118	02 17	49	53	03 06	49	53	03 55	48	52	04 43	49	51	05 32	49	51	242
119	01 46	49	52	02 35	49	52	03 24	49	51	04 13	49	51	05 02	49	50	241
120	01 14	+50	52	02 04	+49	51	02 53	+50	51	03 43	+49	50	04 32	+49	49	240
121	00 44	49	51	01 33	50	50	02 23	50	50	03 13	49	49	04 02	50	49	239
122	00 13	50	50	01 03	50	50	01 53	50	49	02 43	50	49	03 33	50	48	238
123	−0 17	50	49	00 33	50	49	01 23	51	48	02 14	50	48	03 04	50	47	237
124	−0 46	50	49	00 04	50	48	00 54	51	48	01 45	50	47	02 35	50	47	236
125	−1 16	+51	48	−0 25	+50	47	00 25	+51	47	01 16	+50	46	02 06	+51	46	235
126	−1 45	51	47	−0 54	51	47	−0 03	51	46	00 48	50	46	01 38	51	45	234
127	−2 14	51	46	−1 23	52	46	−0 31	51	45	00 20	51	45	01 11	51	44	233
128	−2 42	51	46	−1 51	52	45	−0 59	51	45	−0 08	51	44	00 43	52	44	232
129	−3 10	52	45	−2 18	51	44	−1 27	52	44	−0 35	51	43	00 16	52	43	231
130	−3 38	+52	44	−2 46	+52	44	−1 54	+52	43	−1 02	+52	43	−0 10	+52	42	230
131	−4 05	52	43	−3 13	52	43	−2 21	53	42	−1 28	53	42	−0 35	51	41	229
132	−4 32	53	42	−3 39	52	42	−2 47	53	42	−1 54	52	41	−1 02	52	41	228
133	−4 58	53	42	−4 05	52	41	−3 13	53	41	−2 20	53	40	−1 27	52	40	227
134	−5 24	53	41	−4 31	53	40	−3 38	53	40	−2 45	53	39	−1 52	52	39	226
135	−5 50	+54	40	−4 56	+53	40	−4 03	+53	39	−3 10	+53	39	−2 17	+53	38	225
136				−5 21	53	39	−4 28	53	38	−3 35	54	38	−2 41	53	37	224
137				−5 46	54	38	−4 52	53	38	−3 59	54	37	−3 05	54	37	223
138							−5 16	54	37	−4 22	54	36	−3 28	54	36	222
139							−5 39	54	36	−4 45	54	36	−3 51	54	35	221

N. Lat. {LHA greater than 180°....... Zn=Z; LHA less than 180°........... Zn=360−Z}

DECLINATION (15°-29°) SAME NAME AS LATITUDE

LAT 49°

LHA	28° Hc	d	Z	29° Hc	d	Z	LHA
	° ′	′	°	° ′	′	°	
140	−5 08	+55	35	−4 13	+54	34	220
141	−5 30	55	34	−4 35	54	34	219
142				−4 57	55	33	218
143				−5 18	55	32	217
144				−5 39	56	31	216

LHA	15° Hc	d	Z	16° Hc	d	Z	17° Hc	d	Z	18° Hc	d	Z	19° Hc	d	Z	20° Hc	d	Z	21° Hc	d	Z	22° Hc	d	Z	23° Hc	d	Z	24° Hc	d	Z	25°
82	−6 09	45	106	278																											
81	−5 31	46	107	279																											
80	−4 54	−45	107	−5 39	−46	108	280																								
79	−4 16	46	108	−5 02	46	109	−5 48	45	109	281																					
78	−3 39	46	109	−4 25	46	109	−5 11	45	110	−5 56	46	111	282																		
77	−3 02	46	110	−3 48	46	110	−4 34	46	111	−5 20	46	111	−6 06	46	112	283															
76	−2 25	46	110	−3 11	46	111	−3 57	46	112	−4 43	46	112	−5 29	46	113	284															
75	−1 48	−46	111	−2 34	−46	112	−3 20	−47	112	−4 07	−46	113	−4 53	−46	114	−5 39	−47	114	285												
74	−1 11	47	112	−1 58	46	112	−2 44	47	113	−3 31	46	114	−4 17	47	114	−5 04	46	115	−5 50	46	116	286									
73	−0 35	46	113	−1 21	47	113	−2 08	47	114	−2 55	46	114	−3 41	47	115	−4 28	47	116	−5 15	46	116	−6 01	47	117	287						
72	00 02	47	113	−0 45	47	114	−1 32	47	115	−2 19	47	115	−3 06	47	116	−3 53	46	116	−4 39	47	117	−5 26	47	118	288						
71	00 38	47	114	−0 09	47	115	−0 56	47	115	−1 43	47	116	−2 30	47	117	−3 17	47	117	−4 04	47	118	−4 51	47	118	−5 38	47	119	289			
70	01 14	−48	115	00 26	−47	115	−0 21	−47	116	−1 08	−47	117	−1 55	−48	117	−2 43	−47	118	−3 30	−47	118	−4 17	−47	119	−5 04	−47	120	−5 51	−47	120	290

15° 16° 17° 18° 19° 20° 21° 22° 23° 24° 25° 26° 27° 28° 29°

S. Lat. {LHA greater than 180°....... Zn=180−Z; LHA less than 180°........... Zn=180+Z}

DECLINATION (15°-29°) CONTRARY NAME TO LATITUDE

N. Lat. {LHA greater than 180°……. Zn=Z; LHA less than 180°………. Zn=360−Z}

DECLINATION (15°-29°) CONTRARY NAME TO LATITUDE

LHA	15° Hc	15° d	15° Z	16° Hc	16° d	16° Z	17° Hc	17° d	17° Z	18° Hc	18° d	18° Z	19° Hc	19° d	19° Z
	° ′	′	°	° ′	′	°	° ′	′	°	° ′	′	°	° ′	′	°
69	01 49	47	116	01 02	48	116	00 14	47	117	-0 33	47	117	-1 20	48	118
68	02 25	48	116	01 37	48	117	00 49	47	118	00 02	48	118	-0 46	47	119
67	03 00	48	117	02 12	48	118	01 24	48	118	00 36	47	119	-0 11	48	120
66	03 35	48	118	02 47	48	118	01 59	48	119	01 11	48	120	00 23	48	120
65	04 09	-48	119	03 21	-48	119	02 33	-48	120	01 45	-48	120	00 57	-49	121
64	04 44	49	119	03 55	48	120	03 07	48	121	02 19	49	121	01 30	48	122
63	05 18	49	120	04 29	48	121	03 41	49	121	02 52	49	122	02 03	48	123
62	05 52	49	121	05 03	49	122	04 14	49	122	03 25	48	123	02 37	49	123
61	06 26	49	122	05 37	50	122	04 47	49	123	03 58	49	124	03 09	49	124
60	06 59	-49	123	06 10	-50	123	05 20	-49	124	04 31	-49	124	03 42	-50	125
59	07 32	50	123	06 42	49	124	05 53	50	125	05 03	49	125	04 14	50	126
58	08 05	50	124	07 15	50	125	06 25	49	125	05 36	50	126	04 46	50	126
57	08 37	50	125	07 47	50	126	06 57	50	126	06 07	50	127	05 17	50	127
56	09 09	50	126	08 19	50	126	07 29	50	127	06 39	51	128	05 48	50	128
55	09 41	-50	127	08 51	-51	127	08 00	-50	128	07 10	-51	128	06 19	-50	129
54	10 12	50	127	09 22	51	128	08 31	51	129	07 40	50	129	06 50	51	130
53	10 43	50	128	09 53	51	129	09 02	51	129	08 11	51	130	07 20	51	130
52	11 14	51	129	10 23	51	130	09 32	51	130	08 41	51	131	07 50	51	131
51	11 44	51	130	10 53	51	131	10 02	51	131	09 11	52	132	08 19	51	132
50	12 14	-51	131	11 23	-52	131	10 31	-51	132	09 40	-52	132	08 48	-52	133
49	12 44	52	132	11 52	51	132	11 01	52	133	10 09	52	133	09 17	52	134
48	13 13	52	133	12 21	52	133	11 29	52	134	10 37	52	134	09 45	52	135
47	13 42	52	133	12 50	52	134	11 58	53	134	11 05	52	135	10 13	52	135
46	14 11	53	134	13 18	52	135	12 26	53	135	11 33	53	136	10 40	52	136
45	14 39	-53	135	13 46	-53	136	12 53	-53	136	12 00	-53	137	11 07	-52	137
44	15 06	53	136	14 13	53	137	13 20	53	137	12 27	53	137	11 34	53	138
43	15 33	53	137	14 40	53	137	13 47	53	138	12 54	54	138	12 00	53	139
42	16 00	53	138	15 07	54	138	14 13	53	139	13 20	54	139	12 26	54	140
41	16 26	53	139	15 33	54	139	14 39	53	140	13 45	54	140	12 51	54	141
40	16 52	-54	140	15 58	-54	140	15 04	-54	141	14 10	-54	141	13 16	-54	141
39	17 17	54	141	16 23	54	141	15 29	54	141	14 35	55	142	13 40	54	142
38	17 42	54	141	16 48	55	142	15 53	54	142	14 59	55	143	14 04	54	143
37	18 06	54	142	17 12	55	143	16 17	55	143	15 22	54	144	14 28	55	144
36	18 30	55	143	17 35	55	144	16 40	54	144	15 46	55	145	14 51	56	145
35	18 54	-56	144	17 58	-55	145	17 03	-55	145	16 08	-55	145	15 13	-55	146
34	19 16	55	145	18 21	55	146	17 26	56	146	16 30	55	146	15 35	56	147
33	19 39	56	146	18 43	56	146	17 47	55	147	16 52	56	147	15 56	56	148
32	20 00	56	147	19 04	55	147	18 09	56	148	17 13	56	148	16 17	56	149
31	20 21	56	148	19 25	56	148	18 29	56	149	17 33	56	149	16 37	56	150
30	20 42	-56	149	19 46	-56	149	18 50	-57	150	17 53	-56	150	16 57	-56	150
29	21 02	56	150	20 06	57	150	19 09	56	151	18 13	57	151	17 16	56	151
28	21 22	57	151	20 25	57	151	19 28	57	152	18 31	56	152	17 35	57	152
27	21 40	56	152	20 44	57	152	19 47	57	153	18 50	57	153	17 53	57	153
26	21 59	57	153	21 02	57	153	20 05	58	154	19 07	57	154	18 10	57	154
25	22 16	-57	154	21 19	-57	154	20 22	-58	155	19 24	-57	155	18 27	-57	155
24	22 33	57	155	21 36	58	155	20 38	57	155	19 41	58	156	18 43	57	156
23	22 50	58	156	21 52	57	156	20 55	58	156	19 57	58	157	18 59	58	157
22	23 06	58	157	22 08	58	157	21 10	58	157	20 12	58	158	19 14	58	158
21	23 21	58	158	22 23	58	158	21 25	58	158	20 27	58	159	19 29	59	159
20	23 35	-58	159	22 37	-58	159	21 39	-58	159	20 41	-59	160	19 42	-58	160
19	23 49	58	160	22 51	59	160	21 52	58	160	20 54	58	161	19 56	59	161
18	24 02	58	161	23 04	59	161	22 05	58	161	21 07	59	162	20 08	58	162
17	24 15	59	162	23 16	58	162	22 18	59	162	21 19	59	163	20 20	59	163
16	24 27	59	163	23 28	59	163	22 29	59	163	21 30	59	164	20 31	58	164
15	24 38	-59	164	23 39	-59	164	22 40	-59	164	21 41	-59	165	20 42	-59	165
14	24 48	59	165	23 49	59	165	22 50	59	166	21 51	59	166	20 52	59	166
13	24 58	59	166	23 59	59	166	23 00	59	167	22 01	60	167	21 01	59	167
12	25 07	59	167	24 08	59	167	23 09	60	168	22 09	59	168	21 10	59	168
11	25 16	60	168	24 16	59	168	23 17	60	169	22 17	59	169	21 18	60	169
10	25 23	-59	169	24 24	-60	169	23 24	-59	170	22 25	-60	170	21 25	-59	170
9	25 30	59	170	24 31	60	171	23 31	60	171	22 31	59	171	21 32	60	171
8	25 37	60	171	24 37	60	172	23 37	60	172	22 37	59	172	21 38	60	172
7	25 42	60	173	24 42	60	173	23 42	59	173	22 43	60	173	21 43	60	173
6	25 47	60	174	24 47	60	174	23 47	60	174	22 47	60	174	21 47	59	174
5	25 51	-60	175	24 51	-60	175	23 51	60	175	22 51	-60	175	21 51	-60	175
4	25 54	60	176	24 54	60	176	23 54	60	176	22 54	60	176	21 54	59	176
3	25 57	60	177	24 57	60	177	23 57	60	177	22 57	60	177	21 57	60	177
2	25 59	60	178	24 59	60	178	23 59	60	178	22 59	60	178	21 59	60	178
1	26 00	60	179	25 00	60	179	24 00	60	179	23 00	60	179	22 00	60	179
0	26 00	-60	180	25 00	-60	180	24 00	-60	180	23 00	-60	180	22 00	-60	180

LHA	20° Hc	20° d	20° Z	21° Hc	21° d	21° Z	22° Hc	22° d	22° Z	23° Hc	23° d	23° Z	24° Hc	24° d	24° Z
	° ′	′	°	° ′	′	°	° ′	′	°	° ′	′	°	° ′	′	°
69	-2 08	47	119	-2 55	48	119	-3 43	47	120	-4 30	47	120	-5 17	48	121
68	-1 33	48	119	-2 21	48	120	-3 09	47	121	-3 56	48	121	-4 44	47	122
67	-0 59	48	120	-1 47	48	121	-2 35	48	121	-3 23	47	122	-4 10	48	123
66	-0 25	48	121	-1 13	48	121	-2 01	48	122	-2 49	48	123	-3 37	48	123
65	00 08	-48	122	-0 40	-48	122	-1 28	-48	123	-2 16	-49	123	-3 05	-48	124
64	00 42	49	122	-0 07	48	123	-0 55	49	124	-1 44	48	124	-2 32	49	125
63	01 15	49	123	00 26	49	124	-0 23	48	124	-1 11	49	125	-2 00	49	125
62	01 48	49	124	00 59	49	124	00 10	49	125	-0 39	49	126	-1 28	49	126
61	02 20	49	125	01 31	49	125	00 42	49	126	-0 07	49	126	-0 56	50	127
60	02 52	-49	125	02 03	-49	126	01 14	-50	127	00 24	-49	127	-0 25	-49	128
59	03 24	49	126	02 35	50	127	01 45	49	127	00 56	50	128	00 06	50	128
58	03 56	50	127	03 06	50	128	02 16	50	128	01 26	49	129	00 37	50	129
57	04 27	50	128	03 37	50	128	02 47	50	129	01 57	50	129	01 07	50	130
56	04 58	50	129	04 08	50	129	03 18	51	130	02 27	50	130	01 37	51	131
55	05 29	-51	129	04 38	-50	130	03 48	-51	130	02 57	-50	131	02 07	-51	132
54	05 59	51	130	05 08	51	131	04 17	50	131	03 27	51	132	02 36	51	132
53	06 29	51	131	05 38	51	132	04 47	51	132	03 56	51	133	03 05	51	133
52	06 59	52	132	06 07	51	132	05 16	51	133	04 25	52	133	03 33	51	134
51	07 28	52	133	06 36	51	133	05 45	52	134	04 53	51	134	04 02	52	135
50	07 56	-51	133	07 05	-52	134	06 13	-52	134	05 21	-52	135	04 29	-51	135
49	08 25	52	134	07 33	52	135	06 41	52	135	05 49	52	136	04 57	52	136
48	08 53	52	135	08 01	53	136	07 08	52	136	06 16	52	137	05 24	52	137
47	09 21	53	136	08 28	52	136	07 36	53	137	06 43	52	137	05 51	53	138
46	09 48	53	137	08 55	53	137	08 02	52	138	07 10	53	138	06 17	53	139
45	10 15	-53	138	09 22	-53	138	08 29	-53	139	07 36	-53	139	06 43	-53	139
44	10 41	53	138	09 48	53	139	08 55	54	139	08 01	53	140	07 08	53	140
43	11 07	54	139	10 13	53	140	09 20	54	140	08 26	53	141	07 33	54	141
42	11 32	53	140	10 39	54	141	09 45	54	141	08 51	54	141	07 57	53	142
41	11 57	54	141	11 03	53	141	10 10	54	142	09 16	54	142	08 22	55	143
40	12 22	-54	142	11 28	-54	142	10 34	-55	143	09 39	-54	143	08 45	-54	144
39	12 46	54	143	11 52	55	143	10 57	54	144	10 03	55	144	09 08	54	144
38	13 10	55	144	12 15	55	144	11 20	54	144	10 26	55	145	09 31	55	145
37	13 33	55	144	12 38	55	145	11 43	55	145	10 48	55	146	09 53	55	146
36	13 55	55	145	13 00	55	146	12 05	55	146	11 10	55	147	10 15	55	147
35	14 18	-56	146	13 22	-55	147	12 27	-55	147	11 32	-56	147	10 36	-55	148
34	14 39	55	147	13 44	56	148	12 48	55	148	11 53	56	148	10 57	56	149
33	15 00	55	148	14 05	56	148	13 09	56	149	12 13	56	149	11 17	56	150
32	15 21	56	149	14 25	56	149	13 29	56	150	12 33	56	150	11 37	56	150
31	15 41	56	150	14 45	56	150	13 49	57	151	12 52	56	151	11 56	56	151
30	16 01	-57	151	15 04	-56	151	14 08	-57	151	13 11	-56	152	12 15	-57	152
29	16 20	57	152	15 23	57	152	14 26	56	152	13 30	57	153	12 33	57	153
28	16 38	56	153	15 41	57	153	14 44	57	153	13 47	57	154	12 50	57	154
27	16 56	57	154	15 59	57	154	15 02	57	154	14 05	58	155	13 07	57	155
26	17 13	57	155	16 16	57	155	15 19	58	155	14 21	57	155	13 24	57	156
25	17 30	-58	155	16 32	-57	156	15 35	-58	156	14 37	-57	156	13 40	-58	157
24	17 46	58	156	16 48	57	157	15 51	58	157	14 53	58	158	13 55	57	158
23	18 01	58	157	17 03	57	158	16 06	58	158	15 08	58	158	14 10	58	158
22	18 16	58	158	17 18	58	159	16 20	58	159	15 22	58	159	14 24	58	159
21	18 30	58	159	17 32	58	160	16 34	58	160	15 36	58	160	14 38	58	160
20	18 44	-58	160	17 46	-58	160	16 48	-59	161	15 49	-58	161	14 51	-59	161
19	18 57	58	161	17 59	59	161	17 00	58	162	16 02	59	162	15 03	58	162
18	19 10	59	162	18 11	59	162	17 12	58	163	16 14	59	163	15 15	59	163
17	19 21	58	163	18 23	59	163	17 24	59	164	16 25	59	164	15 26	59	164
16	19 33	59	164	18 34	59	164	17 35	59	164	16 36	59	165	15 37	59	165
15	19 43	-59	165	18 44	-59	165	17 45	-59	165	16 46	-59	166	15 47	-59	166
14	19 53	59	166	18 54	59	166	17 55	60	166	16 55	59	167	15 56	59	167
13	20 02	59	167	19 03	59	167	18 04	60	167	17 04	59	168	16 05	59	168
12	20 11	60	168	19 11	59	168	18 12	60	168	17 12	59	168	16 13	59	169
11	20 18	59	169	19 19	60	169	18 19	59	169	17 20	59	169	16 21	60	170
10	20 26	-60	170	19 26	-59	170	18 27	-60	170	17 27	-60	170	16 27	-59	171
9	20 32	59	171	19 33	60	171	18 33	60	171	17 33	59	171	16 34	60	171
8	20 38	60	172	19 38	59	172	18 39	60	172	17 39	60	172	16 39	60	172
7	20 43	60	173	19 43	59	173	18 44	60	173	17 44	60	173	16 44	60	173
6	20 48	60	174	19 48	60	174	18 48	60	174	17 48	60	174	16 48	60	174
5	20 51	-59	175	19 52	-60	175	18 52	-60	175	17 52	-60	175	16 52	-60	175
4	20 55	60	176	19 55	60	176	18 55	60	176	17 55	60	176	16 55	60	176
3	20 57	60	177	19 57	60	177	18 57	60	177	17 57	60	177	16 57	60	177
2	20 59	60	178	19 59	60	178	18 59	60	178	17 59	60	178	16 59	60	178
1	21 00	60	179	20 00	60	179	19 00	60	179	18 00	60	179	17 00	60	179
0	21 00	-60	180	20 00	-60	180	19 00	-60	180	18 00	-60	180	17 00	-60	180

LHA	25° Hc	25° d	25° Z	26° Hc	26° d	26° Z	27° Hc	27° d	27° Z	28° Hc	28° d	28° Z	29° Hc	29° d	29° Z	LHA
	° ′	′	°	° ′	′	°	° ′	′	°	° ′	′	°	° ′	′	°	
69	-6 05	47	122	291												
68	-5 31	48	122	292												
67	-4 58	48	123	-5 46	48	124	293									
66	-4 25	48	124	-5 13	48	124	-6 01	48	125	294						
65	-3 53	-48	125	-4 41	-48	125	-5 29	-48	126	295						
64	-3 21	48	125	-4 09	48	126	-4 57	49	126	-5 46	48	127	296			
63	-2 49	48	126	-3 37	49	127	-4 26	48	127	-5 14	49	128	297			
62	-2 17	49	127	-3 06	49	127	-3 55	48	128	-4 43	49	129	-5 32	49	129	298
61	-1 46	49	128	-2 35	49	128	-3 24	49	129	-4 13	49	129	-5 02	49	130	299
60	-1 14	-50	128	-2 04	-49	129	-2 53	-50	129	-3 43	-49	130	-4 32	-49	131	300
59	-0 44	49	129	-1 33	50	130	-2 23	50	130	-3 13	49	131	-4 02	50	131	301
58	-0 13	50	130	-1 03	50	130	-1 53	50	131	-2 43	50	131	-3 33	50	132	302
57	00 17	50	131	-0 33	50	131	-1 23	51	132	-2 14	50	132	-3 04	50	133	303
56	00 46	50	131	-0 04	50	132	-0 54	51	132	-1 45	50	133	-2 35	50	133	304
55	01 16	-51	132	00 25	-50	133	-0 25	-51	133	-1 16	-50	134	-2 06	-51	134	305
54	01 45	51	133	00 54	51	133	00 03	51	134	-0 48	50	134	-1 38	51	135	306
53	02 14	51	134	01 23	52	134	00 31	51	135	-0 20	51	135	-1 11	51	136	307
52	02 42	51	134	01 51	52	135	00 59	51	135	00 08	51	136	-0 43	52	136	308
51	03 10	52	135	02 18	51	136	01 27	52	136	00 35	51	137	-0 16	52	137	309
50	03 38	-52	136	02 46	-52	136	01 54	-52	137	01 02	-52	137	00 10	-52	138	310
49	04 05	52	137	03 13	52	137	02 21	53	138	01 28	53	138	00 35	51	139	311
48	04 32	53	138	03 39	52	138	02 47	53	138	01 54	52	139	01 02	52	139	312
47	04 58	53	138	04 05	52	139	03 13	53	139	02 20	53	140	01 27	52	140	313
46	05 24	53	139	04 31	53	140	03 38	53	140	02 45	53	141	01 52	52	141	314
45	05 50	-54	140	04 56	-53	140	04 03	-53	141	03 10	-53	141	02 17	-53	142	315
44	06 15	54	141	05 21	53	141	04 28	53	142	03 35	54	142	02 41	53	143	316
43	06 39	53	142	05 46	54	142	04 52	53	142	03 59	54	143	03 05	54	143	317
42	07 04	54	142	06 10	54	143	05 16	54	143	04 22	54	144	03 28	54	144	318
41	07 27	54	143	06 33	54	144	05 39	54	144	04 45	54	144	03 51	54	145	319
40	07 51	-54	144	06 57	-55	144	06 02	-54	145	05 08	-55	145	04 13	-54	146	320
39	08 14	55	145	07 19	54	145	06 25	55	146	05 30	55	146	04 35	54	146	321
38	08 36	55	146	07 41	54	146	06 47	55	147	05 52	55	147	04 57	55	147	322
37	08 58	55	147	08 03	55	147	07 08	55	147	06 13	55	148	05 18	55	148	323
36	09 20	56	147	08 24	55	148	07 29	55	148	06 34	55	149	05 39	56	149	324
35	09 41	-56	148	08 45	-55	149	07 50	-56	149	06 54	-55	149	05 59	-56	150	325
34	10 01	55	149	09 06	56	149	08 10	56	150	07 14	56	150	06 18	55	151	326
33	10 21	56	150	09 25	56	150	08 29	56	151	07 33	56	151	06 37	56	151	327
32	10 41	56	151	09 45	57	151	08 48	56	152	07 52	56	152	06 56	56	152	328
31	11 00	57	152	10 03	56	152	09 07	56	152	08 11	57	153	07 14	56	153	329
30	11 18	-56	153	10 22	-57	153	09 25	-57	153	08 28	-56	154	07 32	-57	154	330
29	11 36	57	153	10 39	56	154	09 43	57	154	08 46	57	154	07 49	57	155	331
28	11 53	56	154	10 57	57	155	10 00	57	155	09 03	57	155	08 06	58	156	332
27	12 10	57	155	11 13	57	155	10 16	57	156	09 19	57	156	08 22	58	156	333
26	12 27	58	156	11 29	57	156	10 32	57	157	09 35	58	157	08 37	57	157	334
25	12 42	-57	157	11 45	-58	157	10 47	-57	158	09 50	-58	158	08 52	-57	158	335
24	12 58	58	158	12 00	58	158	11 02	58	158	10 04	57	159	09 07	58	159	336
23	13 12	58	158	12 14	58	159	11 16	58	159	10 18	58	160	09 20	57	160	337
22	13 26	58	160	12 28	58	160	11 30	58	160	10 32	58	160	09 34	58	161	338
21	13 40	59	161	12 41	58	161	11 43	58	161	10 45	58	161	09 47	59	162	339
20	13 52	-58	161	12 54	-58	162	11 56	-59	162	10 57	-58	162	09 59	-59	162	340
19	14 05	59	162	13 06	58	163	12 08	59	163	11 09	58	163	10 11	59	163	341
18	14 16	58	163	13 18	59	163	12 19	59	164	11 20	58	164	10 22	59	164	342
17	14 27	58	164	13 29	59	164	12 30	59	165	11 31	59	165	10 32	59	165	343
16	14 38	59	165	13 39	59	165	12 40	59	165	11 41	59	166	10 42	59	166	344
15	14 48	-59	166	13 49	-59	166	12 50	-59	166	11 51	-60	167	10 51	-59	167	345
14	14 57	59	167	13 58	59	167	12 59	60	167	11 59	59	167	11 00	59	168	346
13	15 06	59	168	14 06	59	168	13 07	59	168	12 08	60	168	11 08	59	168	347
12	15 14	60	169	14 14	59	169	13 15	60	169	12 15	59	169	11 16	59	169	348
11	15 21	59	170	14 22	60	170	13 22	59	170	12 23	60	170	11 23	59	170	349
10	15 28	-60	171	14 28	-59	171	13 29	-60	171	12 29	-60	171	11 29	-59	171	350
9	15 34	60	172	14 34	59	172	13 35	60	172	12 35	60	172	11 35	59	172	351
8	15 39	59	173	14 40	60	173	13 40	60	173	12 40	60	173	11 40	59	173	352
7	15 44	60	173	14 44	59	174	13 45	60	174	12 45	60	174	11 45	60	174	353
6	15 48	59	174	14 49	60	174	13 49	60	175	12 49	60	175	11 49	60	175	354
5	15 52	-60	175	14 52	-60	175	13 52	-60	175	12 52	-60	176	11 52	-60	176	355
4	15 55	60	176	14 55	60	176	13 55	60	176	12 55	60	176	11 55	60	176	356
3	15 57	60	177	14 57	60	177	13 57	60	177	12 57	60	177	11 57	60	177	357
2	15 59	60	178	14 59	60	178	13 59	60	178	12 59	60	178	11 59	60	178	358
1	16 00	60	179	15 00	60	179	14 00	60	179	13 00	60	179	12 00	60	179	359
0	16 00	-60	180	15 00	-60	180	14 00	-60	180	13 00	-60	180	12 00	-60	180	360

S. Lat. {LHA greater than 180°……. Zn=180−Z; LHA less than 180°………. Zn=180+Z}

DECLINATION (15°-29°) CONTRARY NAME TO LATITUDE

N. Lat. {LHA greater than 180°....... Zn=Z
{LHA less than 180°........... Zn=360−Z

DECLINATION (0°-14°) SAME NAME AS LATITUDE

LHA	0° Hc	0° d	0° Z	1° Hc	1° d	1° Z	2° Hc	2° d	2° Z	3° Hc	3° d	3° Z	4° Hc	4° d	4° Z	5° Hc	5° d	5° Z	6° Hc	6° d	6° Z	7° Hc	7° d	7° Z
	° ′	′	°	° ′	′	°	° ′	′	°	° ′	′	°	° ′	′	°	° ′	′	°	° ′	′	°	° ′	′	°
0	40 00	+60	180	41 00	+60	180	42 00	+60	180	43 00	+60	180	44 00	+60	180	45 00	+60	180	46 00	+60	180	47 00	+60	180
1	40 00	60	179	41 00	60	179	42 00	60	179	43 00	60	179	44 00	60	179	45 00	60	179	46 00	60	179	47 00	60	179
2	39 58	60	177	40 58	60	177	41 58	60	177	42 58	60	177	43 58	60	177	44 58	60	177	45 58	60	177	46 58	60	177
3	39 56	60	176	40 56	60	176	41 56	60	176	42 56	60	176	43 56	60	176	44 56	60	176	45 56	60	176	46 56	60	176
4	39 53	60	175	40 53	60	175	41 53	60	175	42 53	60	175	43 53	59	175	44 52	60	174	45 52	60	174	46 52	60	174
5	39 49	+60	174	40 49	+60	173	41 49	+60	173	42 49	+59	173	43 48	+60	173	44 48	+60	173	45 48	+60	173	46 48	+60	173
6	39 44	60	172	40 44	60	172	41 44	60	172	42 44	59	172	43 43	60	172	44 43	60	172	45 43	59	171	46 42	60	171
7	39 39	59	171	40 38	60	171	41 38	60	171	42 38	59	171	43 37	60	170	44 37	60	170	45 37	59	170	46 36	60	170
8	39 32	60	170	40 32	59	170	41 31	60	169	42 31	59	169	43 30	60	169	44 30	59	169	45 29	60	169	46 29	59	168
9	39 25	59	168	40 24	60	168	41 24	59	168	42 23	60	168	43 23	59	168	44 22	59	167	45 21	60	167	46 21	59	167
10	39 16	+60	167	40 16	+59	167	41 15	+59	167	42 14	+60	167	43 14	+59	166	44 13	+59	166	45 12	+60	166	46 12	+59	166
11	39 07	60	166	40 07	59	166	41 06	59	165	42 05	59	165	43 04	59	165	44 03	59	165	45 02	59	164	46 01	60	164
12	38 57	60	165	39 57	59	164	40 56	59	164	41 55	59	164	42 54	59	164	43 53	59	163	44 52	59	163	45 51	58	163
13	38 47	59	163	39 46	59	163	40 45	59	163	41 44	58	163	42 42	59	162	43 41	59	162	44 40	59	162	45 39	58	161
14	38 35	59	162	39 34	59	162	40 33	58	161	41 31	59	161	42 30	59	161	43 29	58	161	44 27	59	160	45 26	58	160
15	38 23	+59	161	39 22	+58	160	40 20	+59	160	41 19	+58	160	42 17	+59	160	43 16	+58	159	44 14	+58	159	45 12	+59	159
16	38 10	58	160	39 08	59	159	40 07	58	159	41 05	58	159	42 03	58	158	43 01	59	158	44 00	58	158	44 58	58	157
17	37 56	58	158	38 54	58	158	39 52	58	158	40 50	59	157	41 49	58	157	42 47	58	157	43 45	57	156	44 42	58	156
18	37 41	58	157	38 39	58	157	39 37	58	156	40 35	58	156	41 33	58	156	42 31	58	155	43 29	57	155	44 26	58	155
19	37 26	58	156	38 24	57	156	39 21	58	155	40 19	58	155	41 17	57	154	42 14	58	154	43 12	57	154	44 09	58	153
20	37 10	+57	155	38 07	+58	154	39 05	+57	154	40 02	+58	154	41 00	+57	153	41 57	+57	153	42 54	+58	152	43 52	+57	152
21	36 53	57	153	37 50	57	153	38 47	58	153	39 45	57	152	40 42	57	152	41 39	57	152	42 36	57	151	43 33	57	151
22	36 35	57	152	37 32	57	152	38 29	57	151	39 26	57	151	40 23	57	151	41 20	57	150	42 17	57	150	43 14	56	149
23	36 17	57	151	37 14	57	151	38 11	56	150	39 07	57	150	40 04	57	149	41 01	56	149	41 57	57	149	42 54	56	148
24	35 58	56	150	36 54	57	149	37 51	57	149	38 48	56	149	39 44	56	148	40 40	57	148	41 37	56	147	42 33	56	147
25	35 38	+56	149	36 34	+57	148	37 31	+56	148	38 27	+56	147	39 23	+57	147	40 20	+56	147	41 16	+55	146	42 11	+56	146
26	35 18	56	148	36 14	56	147	37 10	56	147	38 06	56	146	39 02	56	146	39 58	56	145	40 54	55	145	41 49	56	144
27	34 56	57	146	35 53	55	146	36 48	56	146	37 44	56	145	38 40	56	145	39 36	55	144	40 31	55	144	41 26	56	143
28	34 35	56	145	35 31	55	145	36 26	56	144	37 22	55	144	38 17	56	143	39 13	55	143	40 08	55	142	41 03	55	142
29	34 13	55	144	35 08	55	144	36 03	56	143	36 59	55	143	37 54	55	142	38 49	55	142	39 44	55	141	40 39	54	141
30	33 50	+55	143	34 45	+55	143	35 40	+55	142	36 35	+55	142	37 30	+55	141	38 25	+54	141	39 19	+55	140	40 14	+54	140
31	33 26	55	142	34 21	55	141	35 16	55	141	36 11	54	140	37 05	55	140	38 00	54	139	38 54	55	139	39 49	54	138
32	33 02	55	141	33 57	54	140	34 51	55	140	35 46	54	139	36 40	55	139	37 35	54	138	38 29	54	138	39 23	53	137
33	32 37	55	140	33 32	54	139	34 26	55	139	35 21	54	138	36 15	54	138	37 09	53	137	38 02	54	137	38 56	54	136
34	32 12	54	139	33 06	55	138	34 01	54	138	34 55	53	137	35 48	54	137	36 42	54	136	37 36	53	135	38 29	53	135
35	31 46	+54	138	32 40	+54	137	33 34	+54	137	34 28	+54	136	35 22	+53	135	36 15	+53	135	37 08	+53	134	38 01	+53	134
36	31 20	54	137	32 14	53	136	33 07	54	136	34 01	53	135	34 54	53	134	35 47	53	134	36 40	53	133	37 33	53	133
37	30 53	54	136	31 47	53	135	32 40	53	134	33 33	53	134	34 26	53	133	35 19	53	133	36 12	53	132	37 05	52	132
38	30 26	53	134	31 19	53	134	32 12	53	133	33 05	53	133	33 58	53	132	34 51	52	132	35 43	53	131	36 36	52	130
39	29 58	53	133	30 51	53	133	31 44	53	132	32 37	52	132	33 29	53	131	34 22	52	131	35 14	52	130	36 06	52	129
40	29 30	+53	132	30 23	+52	132	31 15	+53	131	32 08	+52	131	33 00	+52	130	33 52	+52	130	34 44	+52	129	35 36	+51	128
41	29 01	53	131	29 54	52	131	30 46	52	130	31 38	52	130	32 30	52	129	33 22	52	129	34 14	51	128	35 05	52	127
42	28 32	52	130	29 24	52	130	30 16	52	129	31 08	52	129	32 00	52	128	32 52	51	128	33 43	52	127	34 35	51	126
43	28 03	52	129	28 55	51	129	29 46	52	128	30 38	52	128	31 30	51	127	32 21	51	127	33 12	51	126	34 03	51	125
44	27 33	51	128	28 24	52	128	29 16	51	127	30 07	52	127	30 59	51	126	31 50	51	126	32 41	51	125	33 32	50	124
45	27 02	+52	128	27 54	+51	127	28 45	+51	126	29 36	+51	126	30 27	+51	125	31 18	+51	125	32 09	+50	124	32 59	+51	123
46	26 31	52	127	27 23	51	126	28 14	51	125	29 05	51	125	29 56	50	124	30 46	51	124	31 37	50	123	32 27	50	122
47	26 00	51	126	26 51	51	125	27 42	51	124	28 33	50	124	29 23	51	123	30 14	50	123	31 04	50	122	31 54	50	121
48	25 29	50	125	26 19	51	124	27 10	51	123	28 01	50	123	28 51	50	122	29 41	50	122	30 31	50	121	31 21	50	120
49	24 57	50	124	25 47	51	123	26 38	50	123	27 28	50	122	28 18	50	121	29 08	50	121	29 58	50	120	30 48	49	119
50	24 24	+51	123	25 15	+50	122	26 05	+50	122	26 55	+50	121	27 45	+50	120	28 35	+49	120	29 24	+50	119	30 14	+49	118
51	23 52	50	122	24 42	50	121	25 32	50	121	26 22	50	120	27 12	49	119	28 01	49	119	28 50	50	118	29 40	49	117
52	23 19	50	121	24 09	50	120	24 59	49	120	25 48	50	119	26 38	49	118	27 27	49	118	28 16	49	117	29 05	49	117
53	22 46	49	120	23 35	50	119	24 25	49	119	25 14	50	118	26 04	49	118	26 53	49	117	27 42	49	116	28 31	48	116
54	22 12	50	119	23 02	49	119	23 51	49	118	24 40	49	117	25 29	49	117	26 18	49	116	27 07	49	115	27 56	48	115
55	21 38	+50	118	22 28	+49	118	23 17	+49	117	24 06	+49	116	24 55	+49	116	25 44	+48	115	26 32	+49	114	27 21	+48	114
56	21 04	49	117	21 53	49	117	22 42	49	116	23 31	49	116	24 20	48	115	25 08	49	114	25 57	48	114	26 45	48	113
57	20 30	49	116	21 19	48	116	22 07	49	115	22 56	49	115	23 45	48	114	24 33	48	113	25 21	48	113	26 09	48	112
58	19 55	49	116	20 44	48	115	21 32	49	114	22 21	48	114	23 09	49	113	23 58	48	112	24 46	48	112	25 34	47	111
59	19 20	49	115	20 09	48	114	20 57	49	114	21 46	48	113	22 34	48	112	23 22	48	112	24 10	48	111	24 58	47	110
60	18 45	+48	114	19 33	+49	113	20 22	+48	113	21 10	+48	112	21 58	+48	111	22 46	+48	111	23 34	+47	110	24 21	+48	109
61	18 09	49	113	18 58	48	112	19 46	48	112	20 34	48	111	21 22	48	111	22 10	47	110	22 57	48	109	23 45	47	109
62	17 34	48	112	18 22	48	112	19 10	48	111	19 58	48	110	20 46	47	110	21 33	48	109	22 21	47	108	23 08	47	108
63	16 58	48	111	17 46	48	111	18 34	48	110	19 22	47	109	20 09	48	109	20 57	47	108	21 44	47	108	22 31	47	107
64	16 22	48	111	17 10	48	110	17 58	47	109	18 45	48	109	19 33	47	108	20 20	47	107	21 07	47	107	21 54	47	106
65	15 46	+48	110	16 34	+47	109	17 21	+48	108	18 09	+47	108	18 56	+47	107	19 43	+47	106	20 30	+47	106	21 17	+47	105
66	15 09	48	109	15 57	47	108	16 44	48	108	17 32	47	107	18 19	47	106	19 06	47	106	19 53	47	105	20 40	46	104
67	14 33	47	108	15 20	48	107	16 08	47	107	16 55	47	106	17 42	47	105	18 29	47	105	19 16	46	104	20 02	47	104
68	13 56	47	107	14 43	48	107	15 31	47	106	16 18	47	105	17 05	46	105	17 51	47	104	18 38	47	103	19 25	46	103
69	13 19	47	106	14 06	47	106	14 53	47	105	15 40	47	105	16 27	47	104	17 14	47	103	18 01	46	103	18 47	46	102

8° Hc	8° d	8° Z	9° Hc	9° d	9° Z	10° Hc	10° d	10° Z	11° Hc	11° d	11° Z	12° Hc	12° d	12° Z	13° Hc	13° d	13° Z	14° Hc	14° d	14° Z	LHA
° ′	′	°	° ′	′	°	° ′	′	°	° ′	′	°	° ′	′	°	° ′	′	°	° ′	′	°	
48 00	+60	180	49 00	+60	180	50 00	+60	180	51 00	+60	180	52 00	+60	180	53 00	+60	180	54 00	+60	180	360
48 00	60	179	49 00	60	179	50 00	60	179	51 00	60	178	52 00	60	178	53 00	59	178	53 59	60	178	359
47 58	60	177	48 58	60	177	49 58	60	177	50 58	60	177	51 58	60	177	52 58	60	177	53 58	60	177	358
47 56	59	176	48 55	60	176	49 55	60	175	50 55	60	175	51 55	60	175	52 55	60	175	53 55	60	175	357
47 52	60	174	48 52	60	174	49 52	60	174	50 52	60	174	51 52	59	174	52 51	60	174	53 51	60	173	356
47 48	+59	173	48 47	+60	173	49 47	+60	172	50 47	+60	172	51 47	+59	172	52 46	+60	172	53 46	+60	172	355
47 42	60	171	48 42	60	171	49 42	59	171	50 41	60	171	51 41	60	171	52 41	59	170	53 40	60	170	354
47 36	59	170	48 35	60	170	49 35	59	169	50 34	60	169	51 34	60	169	52 34	59	169	53 33	59	169	353
47 28	60	168	48 28	59	168	49 27	60	168	50 27	59	168	51 26	59	167	52 25	60	167	53 25	59	167	352
47 20	59	167	48 19	60	167	49 19	59	166	50 18	59	166	51 17	59	166	52 16	60	166	53 16	59	165	351
47 11	+59	165	48 10	+59	165	49 09	+59	165	50 08	+59	165	51 07	+59	164	52 06	+59	164	53 05	+59	164	350
47 01	59	164	48 00	59	164	48 59	58	163	49 57	59	163	50 56	59	163	51 55	59	163	52 54	59	162	349
46 49	59	163	47 48	59	162	48 47	59	162	49 46	58	162	50 44	59	161	51 43	59	161	52 42	58	161	348
46 37	59	161	47 36	59	161	48 35	58	160	49 33	59	160	50 32	58	160	51 30	58	159	52 28	58	159	347
46 24	59	160	47 23	58	159	48 21	58	159	49 19	59	159	50 18	58	158	51 16	58	158	52 14	58	158	346
46 11	+58	158	47 09	+58	158	48 07	+58	158	49 05	+58	157	50 03	+58	157	51 01	+58	156	51 59	+57	156	345
45 56	58	157	46 54	58	157	47 52	58	156	48 50	57	156	49 47	58	155	50 45	57	155	51 42	58	154	344
45 40	58	156	46 38	58	155	47 36	57	155	48 33	58	154	49 31	57	154	50 28	57	153	51 25	58	153	343
45 24	57	154	46 21	58	154	47 19	57	153	48 16	57	153	49 13	57	152	50 10	57	152	51 07	57	152	342
45 07	57	153	46 04	57	152	47 01	57	152	47 58	57	152	48 55	57	151	49 52	57	151	50 49	56	150	341
44 49	+57	152	45 46	+57	151	46 43	+56	151	47 39	+57	150	48 36	+56	150	49 32	+57	149	50 29	+56	149	340
44 30	57	150	45 27	56	150	46 23	57	149	47 20	56	149	48 16	56	148	49 12	56	148	50 08	56	147	339
44 10	57	149	45 07	56	148	46 03	56	148	46 59	56	147	47 55	56	147	48 51	56	146	49 47	56	146	338
43 50	56	148	44 46	56	147	45 42	56	147	46 38	56	146	47 34	55	146	48 29	56	145	49 25	55	144	337
43 29	56	146	44 25	56	146	45 21	55	145	46 16	56	145	47 12	55	144	48 07	55	144	49 02	55	143	336
43 07	+56	145	44 03	+55	145	44 58	+56	144	45 54	+55	143	46 49	+55	143	47 44	+54	142	48 38	+55	142	335
42 45	55	144	43 40	55	143	44 35	55	143	45 30	55	142	46 25	55	142	47 20	54	141	48 14	54	140	334
42 22	55	143	43 17	54	142	44 11	55	141	45 06	55	141	46 01	54	140	46 55	54	140	47 49	54	139	333
41 58	55	141	42 53	54	141	43 47	55	140	44 42	54	140	45 36	54	139	46 30	54	138	47 24	53	138	332
41 33	55	140	42 28	54	140	43 22	54	139	44 16	54	138	45 10	54	138	46 04	53	137	46 57	54	136	331
41 08	+54	139	42 02	+54	138	42 56	+54	138	43 50	+54	137	44 44	+53	137	45 37	+53	136	46 30	+53	135	330
40 43	54	138	41 37	53	137	42 30	54	137	43 24	53	136	44 17	53	135	45 10	53	135	46 03	53	134	329
40 16	54	137	41 10	53	136	42 03	54	135	42 57	53	135	43 50	52	134	44 42	53	133	45 35	52	133	328
39 50	53	135	40 43	53	135	41 36	53	134	42 29	53	134	43 22	52	133	44 14	52	132	45 06	52	132	327
39 22	53	134	40 15	53	134	41 08	53	133	42 01	52	132	42 53	52	132	43 45	52	131	44 37	52	130	326
38 54	+53	133	39 47	+53	133	40 40	+52	132	41 32	+52	131	42 24	+52	131	43 16	+52	130	44 08	+51	129	325
38 26	52	132	39 18	53	131	40 11	52	131	41 03	52	130	41 55	51	129	42 46	51	129	43 37	51	128	324
37 57	52	131	38 49	52	130	39 41	52	130	40 33	51	129	41 24	52	128	42 16	51	128	43 07	51	127	323
37 28	52	130	38 20	51	129	39 11	52	129	40 03	51	128	40 54	51	127	41 45	51	127	42 36	50	126	322
36 58	51	129	37 49	52	128	38 41	51	127	39 32	51	127	40 23	51	126	41 14	50	125	42 04	50	125	321
36 27	+52	128	37 19	+51	127	38 10	+51	126	39 01	+51	126	39 52	+50	125	40 42	+50	124	41 32	+50	124	320
35 57	51	127	36 48	51	126	37 39	50	125	38 29	51	125	39 20	50	124	40 10	50	123	41 00	50	123	319
35 26	50	126	36 16	51	125	37 07	50	124	37 57	51	124	38 48	50	123	39 38	49	122	40 27	50	121	318
34 54	51	125	35 45	50	124	36 35	50	123	37 25	50	123	38 15	50	122	39 05	49	121	39 54	49	120	317
34 22	50	124	35 12	51	123	36 03	49	122	36 52	50	122	37 42	50	121	38 32	49	120	39 21	49	119	316
33 50	+50	123	34 40	+50	122	35 30	+49	121	36 19	+50	121	37 09	+49	120	37 58	+49	119	38 47	+48	118	315
33 17	50	122	34 07	50	121	34 57	49	120	35 46	49	120	36 35	49	119	37 24	49	118	38 13	48	117	314
32 44	50	121	33 34	49	120	34 23	49	119	35 12	49	119	36 01	49	118	36 50	48	117	37 38	49	116	313
32 11	49	120	33 00	49	119	33 49	49	118	34 38	49	118	35 27	48	117	36 15	49	116	37 04	48	115	312
31 37	49	119	32 26	49	118	33 15	49	117	34 04	48	117	34 52	49	116	35 41	48	115	36 29	47	114	311
31 03	+49	118	31 52	+49	117	32 41	+48	116	33 29	+49	116	34 18	+48	115	35 06	+47	114	35 53	+48	113	310
30 29	48	117	31 17	49	116	32 06	48	115	32 54	48	115	33 42	48	114	34 30	48	113	35 18	47	113	309
29 54	49	116	30 43	48	115	31 31	48	115	32 19	48	114	33 07	48	113	33 55	47	112	34 42	47	112	308
29 19	49	115	30 08	48	114	30 56	48	114	31 44	48	113	32 32	47	112	33 19	47	111	34 06	47	111	307
28 44	48	114	29 32	48	113	30 20	48	113	31 08	48	112	31 56	47	111	32 43	47	111	33 30	47	110	306
28 09	+48	113	28 57	+48	112	29 45	+47	112	30 32	+48	111	31 20	+47	110	32 07	+47	110	32 54	+46	109	305
27 33	48	112	28 21	48	112	29 09	47	111	29 56	47	110	30 43	47	109	31 30	47	109	32 17	46	108	304
26 57	48	111	27 45	48	111	28 33	47	110	29 20	47	109	30 07	47	109	30 54	46	108	31 40	46	107	303
26 21	48	110	27 09	47	110	27 56	47	109	28 43	47	108	29 30	47	108	30 17	46	107	31 03	46	106	302
25 45	47	110	26 32	48	109	27 20	47	108	28 07	46	108	28 53	47	107	29 40	46	106	30 26	46	105	301
25 09	+47	109	25 56	+47	108	26 43	+47	107	27 30	+46	107	28 16	+47	106	29 03	+46	105	29 49	+46	104	300
24 32	47	108	25 19	47	107	26 06	47	106	26 53	46	106	27 39	46	105	28 25	46	104	29 11	46	104	299
23 55	47	107	24 42	47	106	25 29	46	106	26 15	47	105	27 02	46	104	27 48	46	104	28 34	46	103	298
23 18	47	106	24 05	47	105	24 52	46	105	25 38	46	104	26 24	46	103	27 10	46	103	27 56	46	102	297
22 41	47	105	23 28	46	105	24 14	47	104	25 01	46	103	25 47	46	103	26 33	45	102	27 18	46	101	296
22 04	+46	104	22 50	+47	104	23 37	+46	103	24 23	+46	102	25 09	+46	102	25 55	+45	101	26 40	+46	100	295
21 26	47	104	22 13	46	103	22 59	46	102	23 45	46	102	24 31	46	101	25 17	45	100	26 02	46	99	294
20 49	46	103	21 35	46	102	22 21	46	101	23 07	46	101	23 53	46	100	24 39	45	99	25 24	46	99	293
20 11	46	102	20 57	47	101	21 44	46	101	22 30	45	100	23 15	46	99	24 01	45	99	24 46	45	98	292
19 33	47	101	20 20	46	101	21 06	45	100	21 51	46	99	22 37	46	98	23 23	45	98	24 08	45	97	291

S. Lat. {LHA greater than 180°....... Zn=180−Z
{LHA less than 180°........... Zn=180+Z

DECLINATION (0°-14°) SAME NAME AS LATITUDE

N. Lat. {LHA greater than 180°....... Zn=Z; LHA less than 180°........... Zn=360−Z}

DECLINATION (0°-14°) SAME NAME AS LATITUDE

LHA	0° Hc	d	Z	1° Hc	d	Z	2° Hc	d	Z	3° Hc	d	Z	4° Hc	d	Z	LHA
	° ′	′	°	° ′	′	°	° ′	′	°	° ′	′	°	° ′	′	°	
70	12 42	+47	106	13 29	+47	105	14 16	+47	104	15 03	+47	104	15 50	+46	103	290
71	12 05	47	105	12 52	47	104	13 39	46	104	14 25	47	103	15 12	47	102	289
72	11 27	47	104	12 14	47	103	13 01	47	103	13 48	46	102	14 34	47	101	288
73	10 50	47	103	11 37	46	103	12 23	47	102	13 10	46	101	13 56	47	101	287
74	10 12	47	102	10 59	47	102	11 46	46	101	12 32	47	101	13 19	46	100	286
75	09 35	+46	102	10 21	+47	101	11 08	+46	100	11 54	+46	100	12 40	+47	99	285
76	08 57	46	101	09 43	47	100	10 30	46	100	11 16	46	99	12 02	47	98	284
77	08 19	46	100	09 05	47	99	09 52	46	99	10 38	46	98	11 24	46	97	283
78	07 41	46	99	08 27	46	99	09 13	47	98	10 00	46	97	10 46	46	97	282
79	07 03	46	99	07 49	46	98	08 35	46	97	09 21	47	97	10 08	46	96	281
80	06 25	+46	98	07 11	+46	97	07 57	+46	96	08 43	+46	96	09 29	+46	95	280
81	05 46	46	97	06 32	47	96	07 19	46	96	08 05	46	95	08 51	46	94	279
82	05 08	46	96	05 54	46	96	06 40	46	95	07 26	46	94	08 12	46	94	278
83	04 30	46	95	05 16	46	95	06 02	46	94	06 48	46	93	07 34	46	93	277
84	03 51	46	95	04 37	46	94	05 23	46	93	06 09	46	93	06 55	46	92	276
85	03 13	+46	94	03 59	+46	93	04 45	+46	93	05 31	+46	92	06 17	+45	91	275
86	02 34	46	93	03 20	46	92	04 06	46	92	04 52	46	91	05 38	46	91	274
87	01 56	46	92	02 42	46	92	03 28	46	91	04 14	45	90	04 59	46	90	273
88	01 17	46	92	02 03	46	91	02 49	46	90	03 35	46	90	04 21	46	89	272
89	00 39	46	91	01 25	45	90	02 10	46	89	02 56	46	89	03 42	46	88	271
90	00 00	+46	90	00 46	+46	89	01 32	+46	89	02 18	+46	88	03 04	+46	87	270
91	−0 39	46	89	00 07	46	89	00 53	46	88	01 39	46	87	02 25	46	87	269
92	−1 17	46	88	−0 31	46	88	00 15	46	87	01 01	46	87	01 47	46	86	268
93	−1 56	46	88	−1 10	46	87	−0 24	46	86	00 22	46	86	01 08	46	85	267
94	−2 34	46	87	−1 48	46	86	−1 02	46	86	−0 16	46	85	00 30	46	84	266
95	−3 13	+46	86	−2 27	+46	86	−1 41	+46	85	−0 55	+47	84	−0 08	+46	84	265
96	−3 51	46	85	−3 05	46	85	−2 19	46	84	−1 33	46	83	−0 47	46	83	264
97	−4 30	47	85	−3 43	46	84	−2 57	46	83	−2 11	46	83	−1 25	46	82	263
98	−5 08	46	84	−4 22	46	83	−3 36	47	83	−2 49	46	82	−2 03	46	81	262
99	−5 46	46	83	−5 00	46	82	−4 14	46	82	−3 28	47	81	−2 41	46	81	261
100				−5 38	+46	82	−4 52	+46	81	−4 06	+47	80	−3 19	+46	80	260
101							−5 30	46	80	−4 44	47	80	−3 57	46	79	259
102							−6 08	47	79	−5 21	46	79	−4 35	47	78	258
103										−5 59	46	78	−5 13	47	77	257
104													−5 50	47	77	256

LHA	5° Hc	d	Z	6° Hc	d	Z	7° Hc	d	Z	8° Hc	d	Z	9° Hc	d	Z	LHA
	° ′	′	°	° ′	′	°	° ′	′	°	° ′	′	°	° ′	′	°	
70	16 36	+47	102	17 23	+46	102	18 09	+47	101	18 56	+46	100	19 42	+46	100	290
71	15 59	46	102	16 45	46	101	17 31	47	100	18 18	46	100	19 04	45	99	289
72	15 21	46	101	16 07	46	100	16 53	46	99	17 39	46	99	18 25	46	98	288
73	14 43	46	100	15 29	46	99	16 15	46	99	17 01	46	98	17 47	46	97	287
74	14 05	46	99	14 51	46	99	15 37	46	98	16 23	46	97	17 09	46	97	286
75	13 27	+46	98	14 13	+46	98	14 59	+46	97	15 45	+46	96	16 31	+45	96	285
76	12 49	46	98	13 35	46	97	14 21	45	96	15 06	46	96	15 52	46	95	284
77	12 10	46	97	12 56	46	96	13 42	46	96	14 28	46	95	15 14	45	94	283
78	11 32	46	96	12 18	46	95	13 04	46	95	13 50	45	94	14 35	46	93	282
79	10 54	45	95	11 39	46	95	12 25	46	94	13 11	46	93	13 57	45	93	281
80	10 15	+46	95	11 01	+46	94	11 47	+46	93	12 33	+45	93	13 18	+46	92	280
81	09 37	46	94	10 23	45	93	11 08	46	92	11 54	46	92	12 40	45	91	279
82	08 58	46	93	09 44	46	92	10 30	45	92	11 15	46	91	12 01	46	90	278
83	08 20	45	92	09 05	46	92	09 51	46	91	10 37	45	90	11 22	46	90	277
84	07 41	46	91	08 27	46	91	09 13	45	90	09 58	46	89	10 44	45	89	276
85	07 02	+46	91	07 48	+46	90	08 34	+46	89	09 20	+45	89	10 05	+46	88	275
86	06 24	46	90	07 10	45	89	07 55	46	89	08 41	46	88	09 27	45	87	274
87	05 45	46	89	06 31	46	88	07 17	46	88	08 03	45	87	08 48	46	87	273
88	05 07	46	88	05 53	45	88	06 38	46	87	07 24	46	86	08 10	45	86	272
89	04 28	46	88	05 14	46	87	06 00	46	86	06 46	45	86	07 31	46	85	271
90	03 50	+46	87	04 36	+45	86	05 21	+46	86	06 07	+46	85	06 53	+46	84	270
91	03 11	46	86	03 57	46	85	04 43	46	85	05 29	46	84	06 15	45	83	269
92	02 33	46	85	03 19	46	85	04 05	45	84	04 50	46	83	05 36	46	83	268
93	01 54	46	84	02 40	46	84	03 26	46	83	04 12	46	83	04 58	46	82	267
94	01 16	46	84	02 02	46	83	02 48	46	82	03 34	46	82	04 20	46	81	266
95	00 38	+46	83	01 24	+46	82	02 10	+47	82	02 57	+45	81	03 42	+46	80	265
96	−0 01	47	82	00 46	46	82	01 32	46	81	02 18	46	80	03 04	46	80	264
97	−0 39	46	81	00 07	47	81	00 54	46	80	01 40	46	80	02 26	46	79	263
98	−1 17	46	81	−0 31	47	80	00 16	46	79	01 02	46	79	01 48	46	78	262
99	−1 55	46	80	−1 09	47	79	−0 22	46	79	00 24	47	78	01 11	46	77	261
100	−2 33	+47	79	−1 46	+46	78	−1 00	+47	78	−0 13	+46	77	00 33	+46	77	260
101	−3 11	47	78	−2 24	46	78	−1 38	47	77	−0 51	47	76	−0 04	46	76	259
102	−3 48	46	78	−3 02	47	77	−2 15	47	76	−1 28	46	76	−0 42	47	75	258
103	−4 26	47	77	−3 39	46	76	−2 53	47	76	−2 06	47	75	−1 19	47	74	257
104	−5 03	46	76	−4 17	47	75	−3 30	47	75	−2 43	47	74	−1 56	47	74	256
105	−5 41	+47	75	−4 54	+47	75	−4 07	+47	74	−3 20	+47	73	−2 33	+47	73	255
106				−5 31	47	74	−4 44	47	73	−3 57	47	73	−3 10	47	72	254
107				−6 08	47	73	−5 21	47	72	−4 34	48	72	−3 46	47	71	253
108							−5 58	48	72	−5 10	47	71	−4 23	48	70	252
109										−5 47	48	70	−4 59	48	70	251
110													−5 35	+48	69	250
111													−6 11	48	68	249

LHA	10° Hc	d	Z	11° Hc	d	Z	12° Hc	d	Z	13° Hc	d	Z	14° Hc	d	Z	LHA
	° ′	′	°	° ′	′	°	° ′	′	°	° ′	′	°	° ′	′	°	
70	20 28	+45	99	21 13	+46	98	21 59	+45	98	22 44	+46	97	23 30	+45	96	290
71	19 49	46	98	20 35	46	98	21 21	45	97	22 06	45	96	22 51	45	95	289
72	19 11	46	97	19 57	45	97	20 42	46	96	21 28	45	95	22 13	45	95	288
73	18 33	46	97	19 19	45	96	20 04	45	95	20 49	45	95	21 34	45	94	287
74	17 55	45	96	18 40	46	95	19 26	45	94	20 11	45	94	20 56	45	93	286
75	17 16	+46	95	18 02	+45	94	18 47	+45	94	19 32	+45	93	20 17	+45	92	285
76	16 38	45	94	17 23	46	94	18 09	45	93	18 54	45	92	19 39	45	92	284
77	15 59	46	94	16 45	45	93	17 30	45	92	18 15	45	91	19 00	45	91	283
78	15 21	45	93	16 06	45	92	16 51	46	91	17 37	45	91	18 22	45	90	282
79	14 42	46	92	15 28	45	91	16 13	45	91	16 58	45	90	17 43	45	89	281
80	14 04	+45	91	14 49	+45	91	15 34	+46	90	16 20	+45	89	17 05	+44	88	280
81	13 25	46	90	14 11	45	90	14 56	45	89	15 41	45	88	16 26	45	88	279
82	12 47	45	90	13 32	45	89	14 17	45	88	15 02	45	88	15 47	45	87	278
83	12 08	45	89	12 53	46	88	13 39	45	88	14 24	45	87	15 09	45	86	277
84	11 29	46	88	12 15	45	87	13 00	45	87	13 45	46	86	14 31	45	85	276
85	10 51	+45	87	11 36	+46	87	12 22	+45	86	13 07	+45	85	13 52	+45	85	275
86	10 12	46	87	10 58	45	86	11 43	46	85	12 29	45	85	13 14	45	84	274
87	09 34	45	86	10 19	46	85	11 05	45	85	11 50	45	84	12 35	46	83	273
88	08 55	46	85	09 41	45	84	10 26	46	84	11 12	45	83	11 57	45	82	272
89	08 17	46	84	09 03	45	84	09 48	46	83	10 34	45	82	11 19	45	82	271
90	07 39	+45	84	08 24	+46	83	09 10	+45	82	09 55	+46	82	10 41	+45	81	270
91	07 00	46	83	07 46	46	82	08 32	45	82	09 17	46	81	10 03	45	80	269
92	06 22	46	82	07 08	46	81	07 54	45	81	08 39	46	80	09 25	45	79	268
93	05 44	46	81	06 30	46	81	07 16	45	80	08 01	46	79	08 47	46	79	267
94	05 06	46	81	05 52	46	80	06 38	45	79	07 23	46	79	08 09	46	78	266
95	04 28	+46	80	05 14	+46	79	06 00	+46	79	06 46	+46	78	07 32	+45	77	265
96	03 50	46	79	04 36	46	78	05 22	46	78	06 08	46	77	06 54	46	76	264
97	03 12	46	78	03 58	46	78	04 44	47	77	05 31	46	76	06 17	46	76	263
98	02 34	47	77	03 21	46	77	04 07	46	76	04 53	46	76	05 39	46	75	262
99	01 57	46	77	02 43	47	76	03 30	46	76	04 16	46	75	05 02	46	74	261
100	01 19	+47	76	02 06	+46	75	02 52	+47	75	03 39	+46	74	04 25	+46	73	260
101	00 42	47	75	01 29	46	75	02 15	47	74	03 02	46	73	03 48	47	73	259
102	00 05	47	74	00 52	46	74	01 38	47	73	02 25	46	73	03 11	47	72	258
103	−0 32	47	74	00 15	46	73	01 01	47	72	01 48	47	72	02 35	47	71	257
104	−1 09	47	73	−0 22	47	72	00 25	47	72	01 12	46	71	01 58	47	70	256
105	−1 46	+47	72	−0 59	+47	71	−0 12	+47	71	00 35	+47	70	01 22	+47	70	255
106	−2 23	48	71	−1 35	47	71	−0 48	47	70	−0 01	47	69	00 46	47	69	254
107	−2 59	47	71	−2 12	48	70	−1 24	47	69	−0 37	47	69	00 10	48	68	253
108	−3 35	47	70	−2 48	48	69	−2 00	47	69	−1 13	48	68	−0 25	47	67	252
109	−4 11	47	69	−3 24	48	68	−2 36	47	68	−1 49	48	67	−1 01	48	67	251
110	−4 47	+47	68	−4 00	+48	68	−3 12	+48	67	−2 24	+48	66	−1 36	+48	66	250
111	−5 23	48	67	−4 35	48	67	−3 47	48	66	−2 59	48	66	−2 11	48	65	249
112	−5 59	48	67	−5 11	49	66	−4 22	48	65	−3 34	48	65	−2 46	48	64	248
113				−5 46	49	65	−4 57	48	65	−4 09	48	64	−3 21	49	63	247
114							−5 32	48	64	−4 44	49	63	−3 55	48	63	246
115							−6 07	+49	63	−5 18	+49	62	−4 29	+48	62	245
116										−5 52	49	62	−5 03	49	61	244
117													−5 37	49	60	243

0°	1°	2°	3°	4°	5°	6°	7°	8°	9°	10°	11°	12°	13°	14°

S. Lat. {LHA greater than 180°....... Zn=180−Z; LHA less than 180°........... Zn=180+Z}

DECLINATION (0°-14°) SAME NAME AS LATITUDE

N. Lat. {LHA greater than 180°....... Zn=Z; LHA less than 180°........... Zn=360−Z}

DECLINATION (0°-14°) CONTRARY NAME TO LATITUDE

LHA	0°			1°			2°			3°			4°		
	Hc	d	Z	Hc	d	Z	Hc	d	Z	Hc	d	Z	Hc	d	Z
	° ′	′	°	° ′	′	°	° ′	′	°	° ′	′	°	° ′	′	°
99	−5 46	46	83	261											
98	−5 08	46	84	−5 54	46	84	262								
97	−4 30	46	85	−5 16	46	85	−6 02	46	86	263					
96	−3 51	46	85	−4 37	46	86	−5 23	46	87	−6 09	46	87	264		
95	−3 13	−46	86	−3 59	−46	87	−4 45	−46	87	−5 31	−46	88	−6 17	−45	89
94	−2 34	46	87	−3 20	46	88	−4 06	46	88	−4 52	46	89	−5 38	46	89
93	−1 56	46	88	−2 42	46	88	−3 28	46	89	−4 14	45	90	−4 59	46	90
92	−1 17	46	88	−2 03	46	89	−2 49	46	90	−3 35	46	90	−4 21	46	91
91	−0 39	46	89	−1 25	45	90	−2 10	46	91	−2 56	46	91	−3 42	46	92
90	00 00	−46	90	−0 46	−46	91	−1 32	−46	91	−2 18	−46	92	−3 04	−46	93
89	00 39	46	91	−0 07	46	91	−0 53	46	92	−1 39	46	93	−2 25	46	93
88	01 17	46	92	00 31	46	92	−0 15	46	93	−1 01	46	93	−1 47	46	94
87	01 56	46	92	01 10	46	93	00 24	46	94	−0 22	46	94	−1 08	46	95
86	02 34	46	93	01 48	46	94	01 02	46	94	00 16	46	95	−0 30	46	96
85	03 13	−46	94	02 27	−46	94	01 41	−46	95	00 55	−47	96	00 08	−46	96
84	03 51	46	95	03 05	46	95	02 19	46	96	01 33	46	97	00 47	46	97
83	04 30	47	95	03 43	46	96	02 57	46	97	02 11	46	97	01 25	46	98
82	05 08	46	96	04 22	46	97	03 36	47	97	02 49	46	98	02 03	46	99
81	05 46	46	97	05 00	46	98	04 14	46	98	03 28	47	99	02 41	46	99
80	06 25	−47	98	05 38	−46	98	04 52	−46	99	04 06	−47	100	03 19	−46	100
79	07 03	47	99	06 16	46	99	05 30	46	100	04 44	47	100	03 57	46	101
78	07 41	47	99	06 54	46	100	06 08	47	101	05 21	46	101	04 35	47	102
77	08 19	47	100	07 32	46	101	06 46	47	101	05 59	46	102	05 13	47	103
76	08 57	47	101	08 10	46	102	07 24	47	102	06 37	47	103	05 50	47	103
75	09 35	−47	102	08 48	−47	102	08 01	−46	103	07 15	−47	104	06 28	−47	104
74	10 12	46	102	09 26	47	103	08 39	47	104	07 52	47	104	07 05	47	105
73	10 50	47	103	10 03	47	104	09 16	47	104	08 29	47	105	07 42	47	106
72	11 27	46	104	10 41	47	105	09 54	48	105	09 06	47	106	08 19	47	107
71	12 05	47	105	11 18	47	105	10 31	48	106	09 43	47	107	08 56	47	107
70	12 42	−47	106	11 55	−47	106	11 08	−48	107	10 20	−47	108	09 33	−48	108

LHA	5°			6°			7°			8°			9°		
	Hc	d	Z	Hc	d	Z	Hc	d	Z	Hc	d	Z	Hc	d	Z
	° ′	′	°	° ′	′	°	° ′	′	°	° ′	′	°	° ′	′	°
95	265														
94	266														
93	−5 45	46	91	267											
92	−5 07	46	92	−5 53	45	92	268								
91	−4 28	46	92	−5 14	46	93	−6 00	46	94	269					
90	−3 50	−46	93	−4 36	−45	94	−5 21	−46	94	−6 07	−46	95	270		
89	−3 11	46	94	−3 57	46	95	−4 43	46	95	−5 29	46	96	−6 15	45	97
88	−2 33	46	95	−3 19	46	95	−4 05	45	96	−4 50	46	97	−5 36	46	97
87	−1 54	46	96	−2 40	46	96	−3 26	46	97	−4 12	46	97	−4 58	46	98
86	−1 16	46	96	−2 02	46	97	−2 48	46	98	−3 34	46	98	−4 20	46	99
85	−0 38	−46	97	−1 24	−46	98	−2 10	−47	98	−2 57	−45	99	−3 42	−46	100
84	00 01	47	98	−0 46	46	98	−1 32	46	99	−2 18	46	100	−3 04	46	100
83	00 39	46	99	−0 07	47	99	−0 54	46	100	−1 40	46	100	−2 26	46	101
82	01 17	46	99	00 31	47	100	−0 16	46	101	−1 02	46	101	−1 48	46	102
81	01 55	46	100	01 09	47	101	00 22	46	101	−0 24	47	102	−1 11	46	103
80	02 33	−47	101	01 46	−46	102	01 00	−47	102	00 13	−46	103	−0 33	−46	103
79	03 11	47	102	02 24	46	102	01 38	47	103	00 51	47	104	00 04	46	104
78	03 48	46	102	03 02	47	103	02 15	47	104	01 28	46	104	00 42	47	105
77	04 26	47	103	03 39	46	104	02 53	47	104	02 06	47	105	01 19	47	106
76	05 03	46	104	04 17	47	105	03 30	47	105	02 43	47	106	01 56	47	106
75	05 41	−47	105	04 54	−47	105	04 07	−47	106	03 20	−47	107	02 33	−47	107
74	06 18	47	106	05 31	47	106	04 44	47	107	03 57	47	107	03 10	47	108
73	06 55	47	106	06 08	47	107	05 21	47	108	04 34	48	108	03 46	47	109
72	07 32	47	107	06 45	47	108	05 58	48	108	05 10	47	109	04 23	48	110
71	08 09	48	108	07 21	47	109	06 34	47	109	05 47	48	110	04 59	48	110
70	08 45	−47	109	07 58	−48	109	07 10	−47	110	06 23	−48	111	05 35	−48	111

LHA	10°			11°			12°			13°			14°			LHA
	Hc	d	Z	Hc	d	Z	Hc	d	Z	Hc	d	Z	Hc	d	Z	
	° ′	′	°	° ′	′	°	° ′	′	°	° ′	′	°	° ′	′	°	
89	271															
88	272															
87	−5 44	46	99	273												
86	−5 06	46	99	−5 52	46	100	274									
85	−4 28	−46	100	−5 14	−46	101	−6 00	−46	101	275						
84	−3 50	46	101	−4 36	46	102	−5 22	46	102	−6 08	46	103	276			
83	−3 12	46	102	−3 58	46	102	−4 44	47	103	−5 31	46	104	277			
82	−2 34	47	103	−3 21	46	103	−4 07	46	104	−4 53	46	104	−5 39	46	105	278
81	−1 57	46	103	−2 43	47	104	−3 30	46	104	−4 16	46	105	−5 02	46	106	279
80	−1 19	−47	104	−2 06	−46	105	−2 52	−47	105	−3 39	−46	106	−4 25	−46	107	280
79	−0 42	47	105	−1 29	46	105	−2 15	47	106	−3 02	46	107	−3 48	47	107	281
78	−0 05	47	106	−0 52	46	106	−1 38	47	107	−2 25	46	107	−3 11	47	108	282
77	00 32	47	106	−0 15	46	107	−1 01	47	108	−1 48	47	108	−2 35	47	109	283
76	01 09	47	107	00 22	47	108	−0 25	47	108	−1 12	46	109	−1 58	47	110	284
75	01 46	−47	108	00 59	−47	109	00 12	−47	109	−0 35	−47	110	−1 22	−47	110	285
74	02 23	48	109	01 35	47	109	00 48	47	110	00 01	47	111	−0 46	47	111	286
73	02 59	47	109	02 12	48	110	01 24	47	111	00 37	47	111	−0 10	48	112	287
72	03 35	47	110	02 48	48	111	02 00	47	111	01 13	48	112	00 25	47	113	288
71	04 11	47	111	03 24	48	112	02 36	47	112	01 49	48	113	01 01	48	113	289
70	04 47	−47	112	04 00	−48	112	03 12	−48	113	02 24	−48	114	01 36	−48	114	290

S. Lat. {LHA greater than 180°....... Zn=180−Z; LHA less than 180°........... Zn=180+Z}

DECLINATION (0°-14°) CONTRARY NAME TO LATITUDE

LAT 50°

N. Lat. {LHA greater than 180°........ Zn=Z; LHA less than 180°........... Zn=360−Z}

DECLINATION (0°-14°) CONTRARY NAME TO LATITUDE

	0°			1°			2°			3°			4°		
LHA	Hc	d	Z	Hc	d	Z	Hc	d	Z	Hc	d	Z	Hc	d	Z
	° ′	′	°	° ′	′	°	° ′	′	°	° ′	′	°	° ′	′	°
69	13 19	47	106	12 32	48	107	11 44	47	108	10 57	47	108	10 10	48	109
68	13 56	47	107	13 09	48	108	12 21	47	109	11 34	48	109	10 46	48	110
67	14 33	48	108	13 45	47	109	12 58	48	109	12 10	48	110	11 22	48	111
66	15 09	47	109	14 22	48	110	13 34	48	110	12 46	48	111	11 58	48	111
65	15 46	−48	110	14 58	−48	110	14 10	−48	111	13 22	−48	112	12 34	−48	112
64	16 22	48	111	15 34	48	111	14 46	48	112	13 58	48	112	13 10	49	113
63	16 58	48	111	16 10	48	112	15 22	49	113	14 33	48	113	13 45	49	114
62	17 34	48	112	16 46	49	113	15 57	48	113	15 09	49	114	14 20	48	115
61	18 09	48	113	17 21	48	114	16 33	49	114	15 44	49	115	14 55	49	116
60	18 45	−49	114	17 56	−48	115	17 08	−49	115	16 19	−49	116	15 30	−49	116
59	19 20	49	115	18 31	49	115	17 42	49	116	16 53	49	117	16 04	49	117
58	19 55	49	116	19 06	49	116	18 17	49	117	17 28	50	117	16 38	49	118
57	20 30	50	116	19 40	49	117	18 51	49	118	18 02	50	118	17 12	49	119
56	21 04	49	117	20 15	50	118	19 25	49	119	18 36	50	119	17 46	50	120
55	21 38	−49	118	20 49	−50	119	19 59	−50	119	19 09	−50	120	18 19	−50	121
54	22 12	50	119	21 22	50	120	20 32	50	120	19 42	50	121	18 52	50	122
53	22 46	50	120	21 56	50	121	21 06	51	121	20 15	50	122	19 25	50	122
52	23 19	50	121	22 29	51	122	21 38	50	122	20 48	50	123	19 58	51	123
51	23 52	51	122	23 01	50	122	22 11	51	123	21 20	50	124	20 30	51	124
50	24 24	−50	123	23 34	−51	123	22 43	−51	124	21 52	−51	125	21 01	−51	125
49	24 57	51	124	24 06	51	124	23 15	51	125	22 24	51	125	21 33	51	126
48	25 29	51	125	24 38	52	125	23 46	51	126	22 55	51	126	22 04	52	127
47	26 00	51	126	25 09	51	126	24 18	52	127	23 26	52	127	22 34	51	128
46	26 31	51	127	25 40	52	127	24 48	51	128	23 57	52	128	23 05	52	129
45	27 02	−52	128	26 10	−51	128	25 19	−52	129	24 27	−52	129	23 35	−53	130
44	27 33	52	128	26 41	52	129	25 49	53	130	24 56	52	130	24 04	52	131
43	28 03	53	129	27 10	52	130	26 18	52	131	25 26	53	131	24 33	52	132
42	28 32	52	130	27 40	53	131	26 47	52	132	25 55	53	132	25 02	53	133
41	29 01	52	131	28 09	53	132	27 16	53	133	26 23	53	133	25 30	53	134
40	29 30	−53	132	28 37	−53	133	27 44	−53	134	26 51	−53	134	25 58	−54	135
39	29 58	53	133	29 05	53	134	28 12	54	135	27 18	53	135	26 25	54	136
38	30 26	53	134	29 33	54	135	28 39	53	136	27 46	54	136	26 52	54	137
37	30 53	53	136	30 00	54	136	29 06	54	137	28 12	54	137	27 18	54	138
36	31 20	54	137	30 26	54	137	29 32	54	138	28 38	54	138	27 44	54	139
35	31 46	−54	138	30 52	−54	138	29 58	−54	139	29 04	−55	139	28 09	−54	140
34	32 12	54	139	31 18	55	139	30 23	54	140	29 29	55	140	28 34	55	141
33	32 37	54	140	31 43	55	140	30 48	55	141	29 53	55	141	28 58	55	142
32	33 02	55	141	32 07	55	141	31 12	55	142	30 17	55	142	29 22	55	143
31	33 26	55	142	32 31	55	142	31 36	56	143	30 40	55	143	29 45	56	144
30	33 50	−56	143	32 54	−55	144	31 59	−56	144	31 03	−55	144	30 08	−56	145
29	34 13	56	144	33 17	56	145	32 21	56	145	31 25	56	145	30 29	56	146
28	34 35	56	145	33 39	56	146	32 43	56	146	31 47	56	147	30 51	56	147
27	34 56	56	146	34 00	56	147	33 04	56	147	32 08	56	148	31 12	57	148
26	35 18	57	148	34 21	56	148	33 25	57	148	32 28	56	149	31 32	57	149
25	35 38	−57	149	34 41	−56	149	33 45	−57	150	32 48	−57	150	31 51	−57	150
24	35 58	57	150	35 01	57	150	34 04	57	151	33 07	57	151	32 10	57	151
23	36 17	57	151	35 20	58	151	34 22	57	152	33 25	57	152	32 28	57	153
22	36 35	57	152	35 38	58	153	34 40	57	153	33 43	57	153	32 46	58	154
21	36 53	58	153	35 55	57	154	34 58	58	154	34 00	58	154	33 02	57	155
20	37 10	−58	155	36 12	−58	155	35 14	−58	155	34 16	−58	156	33 18	−57	156
19	37 26	58	156	36 28	58	156	35 30	58	156	34 32	58	157	33 34	58	157
18	37 41	58	157	36 43	58	157	35 45	58	158	34 47	59	158	33 48	58	158
17	37 56	58	158	36 58	59	159	35 59	58	159	35 01	59	159	34 02	58	159
16	38 10	59	160	37 11	58	160	36 13	59	160	35 14	58	160	34 16	59	161
15	38 23	−59	161	37 24	−58	161	36 26	−59	161	35 27	−59	162	34 28	−59	162
14	38 35	59	162	37 36	58	162	36 38	59	163	35 39	59	163	34 40	59	163
13	38 47	59	163	37 48	59	164	36 49	59	164	35 50	59	164	34 51	59	164
12	38 57	59	165	37 58	59	165	36 59	59	165	36 00	59	165	35 01	59	165
11	39 07	59	166	38 08	59	166	37 09	59	166	36 10	60	166	35 10	59	167
10	39 16	−59	167	38 17	−59	167	37 18	−60	167	36 18	−59	168	35 19	−60	168
9	39 25	60	168	38 25	59	169	37 26	60	169	36 26	59	169	35 27	60	169
8	39 32	60	170	38 32	59	170	37 33	60	170	36 33	59	170	35 34	60	170
7	39 39	60	171	38 39	60	171	37 39	59	171	36 40	60	171	35 40	60	171
6	39 44	59	172	38 45	60	172	37 45	60	172	36 45	60	173	35 45	60	173
5	39 49	−60	174	38 49	−60	174	37 49	−59	174	36 50	−60	174	35 50	60	174
4	39 53	60	175	38 53	60	175	37 53	60	175	36 53	60	175	35 53	59	175
3	39 56	60	176	38 56	60	176	37 56	60	176	36 56	60	176	35 56	60	176
2	39 58	60	177	38 58	60	177	37 58	60	178	36 58	60	178	35 58	60	178
1	40 00	60	179	39 00	60	179	38 00	60	179	37 00	60	179	36 00	60	179
0	40 00	−60	180	39 00	−60	180	38 00	−60	180	37 00	−60	180	36 00	−60	180

	5°			6°			7°			8°			9°		
LHA	Hc	d	Z	Hc	d	Z	Hc	d	Z	Hc	d	Z	Hc	d	Z
	° ′	′	°	° ′	′	°	° ′	′	°	° ′	′	°	° ′	′	°
69	09 22	48	110	08 34	47	110	07 47	48	111	06 59	48	111	06 11	48	112
68	09 58	48	110	09 10	47	111	08 23	48	112	07 35	48	112	06 47	48	113
67	10 34	48	111	09 46	48	112	08 58	48	112	08 10	48	113	07 22	48	114
66	11 10	48	112	10 22	48	113	09 34	48	113	08 46	49	114	07 57	48	114
65	11 46	−48	113	10 58	−49	113	10 09	−48	114	09 21	−49	115	08 32	−48	115
64	12 21	48	114	11 33	49	114	10 44	48	115	09 56	49	115	09 07	49	116
63	12 56	48	114	12 08	49	115	11 19	48	116	10 31	49	116	09 42	49	117
62	13 32	49	115	12 43	49	116	11 54	49	116	11 05	49	117	10 16	49	118
61	14 06	49	116	13 17	49	117	12 28	49	117	11 39	49	118	10 50	49	118
60	14 41	−49	117	13 52	−50	118	13 02	−49	118	12 13	−49	119	11 24	−50	119
59	15 15	49	118	14 26	50	118	13 36	49	119	12 47	50	120	11 57	49	120
58	15 49	49	119	15 00	50	119	14 10	50	120	13 20	49	120	12 31	50	121
57	16 23	50	119	15 33	50	120	14 43	50	121	13 53	49	121	13 04	50	122
56	16 56	50	120	16 06	50	121	15 16	50	122	14 26	50	122	13 36	50	123
55	17 29	−50	121	16 39	−50	122	15 49	−50	122	14 59	−50	123	14 09	−51	124
54	18 02	50	122	17 12	50	123	16 22	51	123	15 31	50	124	14 41	51	124
53	18 35	51	123	17 44	50	124	16 54	51	124	16 03	51	125	15 12	51	125
52	19 07	51	124	18 16	51	124	17 25	50	125	16 35	51	126	15 44	51	126
51	19 39	51	125	18 48	51	125	17 57	51	126	17 06	51	126	16 15	52	127
50	20 10	−51	126	19 19	−51	126	18 28	−51	127	17 37	−52	127	16 45	−51	128
49	20 42	52	127	19 50	51	127	18 59	52	128	18 07	51	128	17 16	52	129
48	21 12	51	127	20 21	52	128	19 29	52	129	18 37	52	129	17 45	51	130
47	21 43	52	128	20 51	52	129	19 59	52	129	19 07	52	130	18 15	52	131
46	22 13	52	129	21 21	52	130	20 29	53	130	19 36	52	131	18 44	52	131
45	22 42	−52	130	21 50	−52	131	20 58	−53	131	20 05	−52	132	19 13	−53	132
44	23 12	53	131	22 19	52	132	21 27	53	132	20 34	53	133	19 41	53	133
43	23 41	53	132	22 48	53	133	21 55	53	133	21 02	53	134	20 09	53	134
42	24 09	53	133	23 16	53	134	22 23	53	134	21 30	53	135	20 37	54	135
41	24 37	53	134	23 44	54	135	22 50	53	135	21 57	53	136	21 04	54	136
40	25 04	−53	135	24 11	−54	136	23 17	−53	136	22 24	−54	137	21 30	−54	137
39	25 31	53	136	24 38	54	137	23 44	54	137	22 50	54	138	21 56	54	138
38	25 58	54	137	25 04	54	138	24 10	54	138	23 16	54	138	22 22	55	139
37	26 24	54	138	25 30	54	139	24 36	55	139	23 41	54	139	22 47	55	140
36	26 50	55	139	25 55	54	140	25 01	55	140	24 06	55	140	23 11	54	141
35	27 15	−55	140	26 20	−55	141	25 25	−55	141	24 30	−54	141	23 36	−55	142
34	27 39	55	141	26 44	55	142	25 49	55	142	24 54	55	142	23 59	55	143
33	28 03	55	142	27 08	55	143	26 13	55	143	25 18	56	143	24 22	55	144
32	28 27	56	143	27 31	55	144	26 36	56	144	25 40	55	144	24 45	56	145
31	28 49	55	144	27 54	56	145	26 58	56	145	26 02	55	145	25 07	56	146
30	29 12	−56	145	28 16	−56	146	27 20	−56	146	26 24	−56	146	25 28	−56	147
29	29 33	56	146	28 37	56	147	27 41	56	147	26 45	56	148	25 49	56	148
28	29 55	57	147	28 58	56	148	28 02	56	148	27 06	57	149	26 09	56	149
27	30 15	56	148	29 19	57	149	28 22	57	149	27 25	56	150	26 29	57	150
26	30 35	57	150	29 38	57	150	28 41	56	150	27 45	57	151	26 48	57	151
25	30 54	−57	151	29 57	−57	151	29 00	−57	151	28 03	−57	152	27 06	−57	152
24	31 13	57	152	30 16	58	152	29 18	57	152	28 21	57	153	27 24	58	153
23	31 31	58	153	30 33	57	153	29 36	57	154	28 39	58	154	27 41	58	154
22	31 48	58	154	30 50	57	154	29 53	58	155	28 55	58	155	27 57	57	155
21	32 05	58	155	31 07	58	155	30 09	58	156	29 11	58	156	28 13	58	156
20	32 21	−58	156	31 23	−58	157	30 25	−58	157	29 27	−59	157	28 28	−58	157
19	32 36	58	157	31 38	59	158	30 39	58	158	29 41	58	158	28 43	58	159
18	32 50	58	159	31 52	58	159	30 54	59	159	29 55	58	159	28 57	59	160
17	33 04	59	160	32 05	58	160	31 07	59	160	30 08	58	160	29 10	59	161
16	33 17	59	161	32 18	58	161	31 20	59	161	30 21	59	162	29 22	59	162
15	33 29	−58	162	32 31	−59	162	31 32	−59	163	30 33	−59	163	29 34	−59	163
14	33 41	59	163	32 42	59	163	31 43	59	164	30 44	59	164	29 45	59	164
13	33 52	59	164	32 53	60	165	31 53	59	165	30 54	59	165	29 55	59	165
12	34 02	60	166	33 02	59	166	32 03	59	166	31 04	59	166	30 05	60	166
11	34 11	59	167	33 12	60	167	32 12	59	167	31 13	60	167	30 13	59	167
10	34 19	−59	168	33 20	−60	168	32 20	−59	168	31 21	−60	168	30 21	−59	169
9	34 27	59	169	33 28	60	169	32 28	60	169	31 28	59	170	30 29	60	170
8	34 34	60	170	33 34	59	170	32 35	60	171	31 35	60	171	30 35	59	171
7	34 40	60	172	33 40	59	172	32 41	60	172	31 41	60	172	30 41	60	172
6	34 45	59	173	33 46	60	173	32 46	60	173	31 46	60	173	30 46	60	173
5	34 50	−60	174	33 50	−60	174	32 50	−60	174	31 50	−60	174	30 50	−60	174
4	34 54	60	175	33 54	60	175	32 54	60	175	31 54	60	175	30 54	60	175
3	34 56	60	176	33 56	60	176	32 56	59	177	31 57	60	177	30 57	60	177
2	34 58	60	178	33 58	60	178	32 58	60	178	31 58	60	178	30 58	59	178
1	35 00	60	179	34 00	60	179	33 00	60	179	32 00	60	179	31 00	60	179
0	35 00	−60	180	34 00	−60	180	33 00	−60	180	32 00	−60	180	31 00	−60	180

	10°			11°			12°			13°			14°			
LHA	Hc	d	Z	Hc	d	Z	Hc	d	Z	Hc	d	Z	Hc	d	Z	LHA
	° ′	′	°	° ′	′	°	° ′	′	°	° ′	′	°	° ′	′	°	
69	05 23	48	113	04 35	48	113	03 47	48	114	02 59	48	114	02 11	48	115	291
68	05 59	48	113	05 11	49	114	04 22	48	115	03 34	48	115	02 46	48	116	292
67	06 34	48	114	05 46	49	115	04 57	48	115	04 09	48	116	03 21	49	117	293
66	07 09	48	115	06 21	49	116	05 32	48	116	04 44	49	117	03 55	48	117	294
65	07 44	−49	116	06 55	−48	116	06 07	−49	117	05 18	−49	118	04 29	−48	118	295
64	08 18	48	117	07 30	49	117	06 41	49	118	05 52	49	118	05 03	49	119	296
63	08 53	49	117	08 04	49	118	07 15	49	119	06 26	49	119	05 37	49	120	297
62	09 27	49	118	08 38	49	119	07 49	49	119	07 00	50	120	06 10	49	121	298
61	10 01	49	119	09 12	50	120	08 22	49	120	07 33	50	121	06 43	49	121	299
60	10 34	−49	120	09 45	−50	120	08 55	−49	121	08 06	−50	122	07 16	−50	122	300
59	11 08	50	121	10 18	50	121	09 28	49	122	08 39	50	122	07 49	50	123	301
58	11 41	50	122	10 51	50	122	10 01	50	123	09 11	50	123	08 21	50	124	302
57	12 14	51	122	11 23	50	123	10 33	50	123	09 43	50	124	08 53	50	125	303
56	12 46	50	123	11 56	51	124	11 05	50	124	10 15	51	125	09 24	50	125	304
55	13 18	−50	124	12 28	−51	125	11 37	−51	125	10 46	−50	126	09 56	−51	126	305
54	13 50	51	125	12 59	51	125	12 08	50	126	11 18	51	127	10 27	51	127	306
53	14 21	51	126	13 30	51	126	12 39	51	127	11 48	51	127	10 57	51	128	307
52	14 53	52	127	14 01	51	127	13 10	51	128	12 19	51	128	11 28	52	129	308
51	15 23	51	128	14 32	51	128	13 41	52	129	12 49	52	129	11 57	51	130	309
50	15 54	−52	128	15 02	−51	129	14 11	−52	129	13 19	−52	130	12 27	−52	130	310
49	16 24	52	129	15 32	52	130	14 40	52	130	13 48	52	131	12 56	52	131	311
48	16 54	53	130	16 01	52	131	15 09	52	131	14 17	52	132	13 25	52	132	312
47	17 23	52	131	16 31	53	132	15 38	52	132	14 46	53	133	13 53	52	133	313
46	17 52	53	132	16 59	52	132	16 07	53	133	15 14	53	133	14 21	52	134	314
45	18 20	−52	133	17 28	−53	133	16 35	−53	134	15 42	−53	134	14 49	−53	135	315
44	18 48	53	134	17 55	53	134	17 02	53	135	16 09	53	135	15 16	53	136	316
43	19 16	53	135	18 23	53	135	17 30	54	136	16 36	53	136	15 43	54	137	317
42	19 43	53	136	18 50	54	136	17 56	53	137	17 03	54	137	16 09	54	138	318
41	20 10	54	137	19 16	53	137	18 23	54	138	17 29	54	138	16 35	54	138	319
40	20 36	−54	137	19 42	−54	138	18 48	−54	138	17 54	−54	139	17 00	−54	139	320
39	21 02	54	138	20 08	54	139	19 14	54	139	18 20	55	140	17 25	54	140	321
38	21 27	54	139	20 33	54	140	19 39	55	140	18 44	54	141	17 50	55	141	322
37	21 52	54	140	20 58	55	141	20 03	55	141	19 08	54	142	18 14	55	142	323
36	22 17	55	141	21 22	55	142	20 27	55	142	19 32	55	143	18 37	55	143	324
35	22 41	−55	142	21 46	−56	143	20 50	−55	143	19 55	−55	144	19 00	−55	144	325
34	23 04	55	143	22 09	56	144	21 13	55	144	20 18	55	145	19 23	56	145	326
33	23 27	56	144	22 31	55	145	21 36	56	145	20 40	56	145	19 44	55	146	327
32	23 49	56	145	22 53	55	146	21 58	56	146	21 02	56	146	20 06	56	147	328
31	24 11	56	146	23 15	56	147	22 19	56	147	21 23	56	147	20 27	56	148	329
30	24 32	−56	147	23 36	−56	148	22 40	−57	148	21 43	−56	148	20 47	−56	149	330
29	24 53	57	148	23 56	56	149	23 00	57	149	22 03	56	149	21 07	57	150	331
28	25 13	57	149	24 16	57	150	23 19	56	150	22 23	57	150	21 26	57	151	332
27	25 32	57	150	24 35	57	151	23 38	57	151	22 41	57	151	21 44	57	152	333
26	25 51	57	151	24 54	57	152	23 57	57	152	23 00	58	152	22 02	57	153	334
25	26 09	−57	152	25 12	−58	153	24 14	−57	153	23 17	−57	153	22 20	−58	154	335
24	26 26	57	153	25 29	57	154	24 32	58	154	23 34	57	154	22 37	58	155	336
23	26 43	57	155	25 46	58	155	24 48	57	155	23 51	58	155	22 53	58	156	337
22	27 00	58	156	26 02	58	156	25 04	58	156	24 06	58	156	23 08	58	157	338
21	27 15	58	157	26 17	58	157	25 19	58	157	24 21	58	158	23 23	58	158	339
20	27 30	−58	158	26 32	−58	158	25 34	−58	158	24 36	−58	159	23 38	−59	159	340
19	27 45	59	159	26 46	58	159	25 48	58	159	24 50	59	160	23 51	58	160	341
18	27 58	58	160	27 00	59	160	26 01	58	160	25 03	59	161	24 04	58	161	342
17	28 11	58	161	27 13	59	161	26 14	59	161	25 15	58	162	24 17	59	162	343
16	28 23	58	162	27 25	59	162	26 26	59	163	25 27	59	163	24 28	59	163	344
15	28 35	−59	163	27 36	−59	163	26 37	−59	164	25 38	−59	164	24 39	−59	164	345
14	28 46	59	164	27 47	59	164	26 48	59	165	25 49	59	165	24 50	60	165	346
13	28 56	59	165	27 57	59	166	26 58	60	166	25 58	59	166	24 59	59	166	347
12	29 05	59	166	28 06	59	167	27 07	60	167	26 07	59	167	25 08	59	167	348
11	29 14	59	168	28 15	60	168	27 15	59	168	26 16	60	168	25 16	59	168	349
10	29 22	−60	169	28 22	−59	169	27 23	−60	169	26 23	−59	169	25 24	−60	169	350
9	29 29	59	170	28 30	60	170	27 30	60	170	26 30	59	170	25 31	60	170	351
8	29 36	60	171	28 36	60	171	27 36	59	171	26 37	60	171	25 37	60	171	352
7	29 41	59	172	28 42	60	172	27 42	60	172	26 42	60	172	25 42	59	173	353
6	29 46	60	173	28 46	59	173	27 47	60	173	26 47	60	173	25 47	60	174	354
5	29 50	−59	174	28 51	−60	174	27 51	−60	175	26 51	−60	175	25 51	−60	175	355
4	29 54	60	176	28 54	60	176	27 54	60	176	26 54	60	176	25 54	60	176	356
3	29 57	60	177	28 57	60	177	27 57	60	177	26 57	60	177	25 57	60	177	357
2	29 59	60	178	28 59	60	178	27 59	60	178	26 59	60	178	25 59	60	178	358
1	30 00	60	179	29 00	60	179	28 00	60	179	27 00	60	179	26 00	60	179	359
0	30 00	−60	180	29 00	−60	180	28 00	−60	180	27 00	−60	180	26 00	−60	180	360

0° 1° 2° 3° 4° 5° 6° 7° 8° 9° 10° 11° 12° 13° 14°

S. Lat. {LHA greater than 180°........ Zn=180−Z; LHA less than 180°........... Zn=180+Z}

DECLINATION (0°-14°) CONTRARY NAME TO LATITUDE

LAT 50°

N. Lat. {LHA greater than 180°....... Zn=Z; LHA less than 180°.......... Zn=360−Z}

DECLINATION (15°-29°) SAME NAME AS LATITUDE

LAT 50°

LAT 50°

LHA	15° Hc	d	Z	16° Hc	d	Z	17° Hc	d	Z	18° Hc	d	Z	19° Hc	d	Z	LHA
	° ′	′	°	° ′	′	°	° ′	′	°	° ′	′	°	° ′	′	°	
0	55 00	+60	180	56 00	+60	180	57 00	+60	180	58 00	+60	180	59 00	+60	180	360
1	54 59	60	178	55 59	60	178	56 59	60	178	57 59	60	178	58 59	60	178	359
2	54 58	60	177	55 58	60	177	56 58	60	177	57 58	60	176	58 58	60	176	358
3	54 55	60	175	55 55	60	175	56 55	60	175	57 55	59	175	58 54	60	175	357
4	54 51	60	173	55 51	60	173	56 51	59	173	57 50	60	173	58 50	60	173	356
5	54 46	+60	172	55 46	+59	171	56 45	+60	171	57 45	+60	171	58 45	+59	171	355
6	54 40	59	170	55 39	60	170	56 39	59	170	57 38	60	169	58 38	59	169	354
7	54 32	60	168	55 32	59	168	56 31	60	168	57 31	59	168	58 30	59	167	353
8	54 24	59	167	55 23	60	166	56 23	59	166	57 22	59	166	58 21	59	166	352
9	54 15	59	165	55 14	59	165	56 13	59	164	57 12	59	164	58 11	59	164	351
10	54 04	+59	163	55 03	+59	163	56 02	+59	163	57 01	+58	162	57 59	+59	162	350
11	53 53	58	162	54 51	59	161	55 50	58	161	56 48	59	161	57 47	58	160	349
12	53 40	58	160	54 38	59	160	55 37	58	159	56 35	58	159	57 33	58	159	348
13	53 26	59	159	54 25	58	158	55 23	58	158	56 21	58	157	57 19	57	157	347
14	53 12	58	157	54 10	58	157	55 08	57	156	56 05	58	156	57 03	57	155	346
15	52 56	+58	156	53 54	+58	155	54 52	+57	155	55 49	+57	154	56 46	+57	154	345
16	52 40	57	154	53 37	57	154	54 34	58	153	55 32	56	152	56 28	57	152	344
17	52 23	57	152	53 20	56	152	54 16	57	151	55 13	57	151	56 10	56	150	343
18	52 04	57	151	53 01	57	150	53 58	56	150	54 54	56	149	55 50	56	149	342
19	51 45	56	150	52 41	57	149	53 38	56	148	54 34	56	148	55 30	55	147	341
20	51 25	+56	148	52 21	+56	147	53 17	+56	147	54 13	+55	146	55 08	+56	146	340
21	51 04	56	147	52 00	56	146	52 56	55	145	53 51	55	145	54 46	55	144	339
22	50 43	55	145	51 38	55	145	52 33	55	144	53 28	55	143	54 23	54	143	338
23	50 20	55	144	51 15	55	143	52 10	55	143	53 05	54	142	53 59	54	141	337
24	49 57	55	142	50 52	54	142	51 46	54	141	52 40	54	140	53 34	54	140	336
25	49 33	+54	141	50 27	+55	140	51 22	+54	140	52 16	+53	139	53 09	+53	138	335
26	49 08	55	140	50 03	53	139	50 56	54	138	51 50	53	138	52 43	53	137	334
27	48 43	54	138	49 37	53	138	50 30	53	137	51 23	53	136	52 16	53	136	333
28	48 17	54	137	49 11	53	136	50 04	52	136	50 56	53	135	51 49	52	134	332
29	47 51	53	136	48 44	52	135	49 36	53	134	50 29	52	134	51 21	52	133	331
30	47 23	+53	135	48 16	+52	134	49 08	+53	133	50 01	+51	132	50 52	+52	132	330
31	46 56	52	133	47 48	52	133	48 40	52	132	49 32	51	131	50 23	51	130	329
32	46 27	52	132	47 19	52	131	48 11	51	131	49 02	51	130	49 53	51	129	328
33	45 58	52	131	46 50	51	130	47 41	51	129	48 32	51	129	49 23	51	128	327
34	45 29	51	130	46 20	51	129	47 11	51	128	48 02	50	127	48 52	51	127	326
35	44 59	+51	128	45 50	+51	128	46 41	+50	127	47 31	+50	126	48 21	+50	125	325
36	44 28	51	127	45 19	51	127	46 10	50	126	47 00	50	125	47 50	49	124	324
37	43 58	50	126	44 48	50	126	45 38	50	125	46 28	49	124	47 17	49	123	323
38	43 26	50	125	44 16	50	124	45 06	50	124	45 56	49	123	46 45	49	122	322
39	42 54	50	124	43 44	50	123	44 34	49	122	45 23	49	122	46 12	48	121	321
40	42 22	+50	123	43 12	+49	122	44 01	+49	121	44 50	+49	121	45 39	+48	120	320
41	41 50	49	122	42 39	49	121	43 28	49	120	44 17	48	119	45 05	48	119	319
42	41 17	49	121	42 06	48	120	42 54	49	119	43 43	48	118	44 31	47	118	318
43	40 43	49	120	41 32	48	119	42 20	49	118	43 09	47	117	43 56	48	116	317
44	40 10	48	119	40 58	48	118	41 46	48	117	42 34	48	116	43 22	47	115	316
45	39 35	+49	118	40 24	+48	117	41 12	+47	116	41 59	+48	115	42 47	+47	114	315
46	39 01	48	117	39 49	48	116	40 37	47	115	41 24	47	114	42 11	47	113	314
47	38 27	47	116	39 14	48	115	40 02	47	114	40 49	47	113	41 36	46	112	313
48	37 52	47	115	38 39	48	114	39 27	46	113	40 13	47	112	41 00	46	111	312
49	37 16	48	114	38 04	47	113	38 51	47	112	39 38	46	111	40 24	46	110	311
50	36 41	+47	113	37 28	+47	112	38 15	+47	111	39 02	+46	110	39 48	+46	110	310
51	36 05	47	112	36 52	47	111	37 39	46	110	38 25	46	109	39 11	46	109	309
52	35 29	47	111	36 16	47	110	37 03	46	109	37 49	46	108	38 35	45	108	308
53	34 53	47	110	35 40	46	109	36 26	46	108	37 12	46	108	37 58	45	107	307
54	34 17	46	109	35 03	46	108	35 49	46	107	36 35	46	107	37 21	45	106	306
55	33 40	+47	108	34 27	+46	107	35 13	+45	107	35 58	+46	106	36 44	+45	105	305
56	33 03	47	107	33 50	45	106	34 35	46	106	35 21	45	105	36 06	45	104	304
57	32 26	47	106	33 13	45	106	33 58	46	105	34 44	45	104	35 29	45	103	303
58	31 49	46	105	32 35	46	105	33 21	45	104	34 06	45	103	34 51	45	102	302
59	31 12	46	105	31 58	45	104	32 43	46	103	33 29	44	102	34 13	45	101	301
60	30 35	+45	104	31 20	+46	103	32 06	+45	102	32 51	+45	101	33 36	+44	101	300
61	29 57	46	103	30 43	45	102	31 28	45	101	32 13	45	101	32 58	44	100	299
62	29 20	45	102	30 05	45	101	30 50	45	101	31 35	45	100	32 20	44	99	298
63	28 42	45	101	29 27	45	100	30 12	45	100	30 57	44	99	31 41	45	98	297
64	28 04	45	100	28 49	45	100	29 34	45	99	30 19	44	98	31 03	44	97	296
65	27 26	+45	100	28 11	+45	99	28 56	+45	98	29 41	+44	97	30 25	+44	96	295
66	26 48	45	99	27 33	45	98	28 18	44	97	29 02	45	97	29 47	44	96	294
67	26 10	45	98	26 55	44	97	27 39	45	96	28 24	44	96	29 08	44	95	293
68	25 31	45	97	26 16	45	96	27 01	44	96	27 45	45	95	28 30	44	94	292
69	24 53	45	96	25 38	45	96	26 23	44	95	27 07	44	94	27 51	44	93	291

LHA	20° Hc	d	Z	21° Hc	d	Z	22° Hc	d	Z	23° Hc	d	Z	24° Hc	d	Z	LHA
	° ′	′	°	° ′	′	°	° ′	′	°	° ′	′	°	° ′	′	°	
0	60 00	+60	180	61 00	+60	180	62 00	+60	180	63 00	+60	180	64 00	+60	180	360
1	59 59	60	178	60 59	60	178	61 59	60	178	62 59	60	178	63 59	60	178	359
2	59 58	59	176	60 57	60	176	61 57	60	176	62 57	60	176	63 57	60	176	358
3	59 54	60	174	60 54	60	174	61 54	60	174	62 54	60	174	63 54	60	174	357
4	59 50	60	173	60 50	59	172	61 49	60	172	62 49	60	172	63 49	60	172	356
5	59 44	+60	171	60 44	+60	170	61 44	+59	170	62 43	+60	170	63 43	+59	170	355
6	59 37	60	169	60 37	59	169	61 36	60	168	62 36	59	168	63 35	59	168	354
7	59 29	60	167	60 29	59	167	61 28	59	166	62 27	59	166	63 26	59	166	353
8	59 20	59	165	60 19	59	165	61 18	59	164	62 17	59	164	63 16	59	164	352
9	59 10	58	163	60 08	59	163	61 07	59	163	62 06	58	162	63 04	59	162	351
10	58 58	+58	162	59 56	+59	161	60 55	+58	161	61 53	+58	160	62 51	+59	160	350
11	58 45	58	160	59 43	59	159	60 42	58	159	61 40	57	158	62 37	58	158	349
12	58 31	58	158	59 29	58	158	60 27	58	157	61 25	57	156	62 22	58	156	348
13	58 16	58	156	59 14	57	156	60 11	58	155	61 09	57	155	62 06	57	154	347
14	58 00	58	155	58 58	57	154	59 55	57	153	60 52	56	153	61 48	57	152	346
15	57 43	+57	153	58 40	+57	152	59 37	+56	152	60 33	+57	151	61 30	+56	150	345
16	57 25	57	151	58 22	56	151	59 18	56	150	60 14	56	149	61 10	56	149	344
17	57 06	56	150	58 02	56	149	58 58	56	148	59 54	56	148	60 50	55	147	343
18	56 46	56	148	57 42	56	147	58 38	55	147	59 33	55	146	60 28	55	145	342
19	56 25	56	146	57 21	55	146	58 16	55	145	59 11	54	144	60 05	55	143	341
20	56 04	+55	145	56 59	+54	144	57 53	+55	143	58 48	+54	143	59 42	+54	142	340
21	55 41	55	143	56 36	54	143	57 30	54	142	58 24	54	141	59 18	53	140	339
22	55 17	55	142	56 12	54	141	57 06	53	140	57 59	54	139	58 53	52	139	338
23	54 53	54	140	55 47	54	140	56 41	53	139	57 34	53	138	58 27	52	137	337
24	54 28	54	139	55 22	53	138	56 15	53	137	57 08	52	136	58 00	52	136	336
25	54 02	+54	137	54 56	+52	137	55 48	+53	136	56 41	+52	135	57 33	+51	134	335
26	53 36	53	136	54 29	52	135	55 21	52	134	56 13	51	134	57 04	52	133	334
27	53 09	52	135	54 01	52	134	54 53	52	133	55 45	51	132	56 36	50	131	333
28	52 41	52	133	53 33	52	133	54 25	51	132	55 16	50	131	56 06	51	130	332
29	52 13	51	132	53 04	51	131	53 55	51	130	54 46	50	129	55 36	50	128	331
30	51 44	+51	131	52 35	+51	130	53 26	+50	129	54 16	+50	128	55 06	+49	127	330
31	51 14	51	129	52 05	50	129	52 55	50	128	53 45	50	127	54 35	49	126	329
32	50 44	51	128	51 35	50	127	52 25	49	126	53 14	49	125	54 03	49	124	328
33	50 14	50	127	51 04	49	126	51 53	49	125	52 42	49	124	53 31	48	123	327
34	49 43	49	126	50 32	49	125	51 21	49	124	52 10	49	123	52 59	48	122	326
35	49 11	+49	125	50 00	+49	124	50 49	+49	123	51 38	+48	122	52 26	+47	121	325
36	48 39	49	123	49 28	49	122	50 17	48	122	51 05	47	121	51 52	48	120	324
37	48 06	49	122	48 55	48	121	49 43	48	120	50 31	48	119	51 19	47	118	323
38	47 34	48	121	48 22	48	120	49 10	48	119	49 58	47	118	50 45	46	117	322
39	47 00	48	120	47 48	48	119	48 36	47	118	49 23	47	117	50 10	46	116	321
40	46 27	+48	119	47 15	+47	118	48 02	+47	117	48 49	+46	116	49 35	+46	115	320
41	45 53	47	118	46 40	47	117	47 27	47	116	48 14	46	115	49 00	46	114	319
42	45 18	48	117	46 06	47	116	46 53	46	115	47 39	46	114	48 25	45	113	318
43	44 44	47	116	45 31	46	115	46 17	47	114	47 04	45	113	47 49	45	112	317
44	44 09	47	115	44 56	46	114	45 42	46	113	46 28	45	112	47 13	45	111	316
45	43 34	+46	114	44 20	+46	113	45 06	+46	112	45 52	+45	111	46 37	+45	110	315
46	42 58	46	113	43 44	46	112	44 30	46	111	45 16	45	110	46 01	44	109	314
47	42 22	46	112	43 08	46	111	43 54	45	110	44 39	45	109	45 24	45	108	313
48	41 46	46	111	42 32	46	110	43 18	45	109	44 03	44	108	44 47	45	107	312
49	41 10	46	110	41 56	45	109	42 41	45	108	43 26	44	107	44 10	44	106	311
50	40 34	+45	109	41 19	+45	108	42 04	+45	107	42 49	+44	106	43 33	+44	105	310
51	39 57	45	108	40 42	45	107	41 27	45	106	42 12	44	105	42 56	44	104	309
52	39 20	45	107	40 05	45	106	40 50	45	105	41 35	44	104	42 18	44	103	308
53	38 43	45	106	39 28	45	105	40 13	44	104	40 57	44	103	41 41	43	102	307
54	38 06	45	105	38 51	44	104	39 35	44	103	40 19	44	102	41 03	43	102	306
55	37 29	+44	104	38 13	+45	103	38 58	+44	102	39 42	+43	102	40 25	+43	101	305
56	36 51	45	103	37 36	44	102	38 20	44	102	39 04	43	101	39 47	43	100	304
57	36 14	44	102	36 58	44	102	37 42	44	101	38 26	43	100	39 09	43	99	303
58	35 36	44	102	36 20	44	101	37 04	44	100	37 48	43	99	38 31	43	98	302
59	34 58	44	101	35 42	44	100	36 26	44	99	37 10	43	98	37 53	43	97	301
60	34 20	+44	100	35 04	+44	99	35 48	+44	98	36 32	+43	97	37 15	+42	96	300
61	33 42	44	99	34 26	44	98	35 10	43	97	35 53	43	96	36 36	43	96	299
62	33 04	44	98	33 48	44	97	34 32	43	97	35 15	43	96	35 58	43	95	298
63	32 26	44	97	33 10	43	97	33 53	43	96	34 36	43	95	35 19	43	94	297
64	31 47	44	96	32 31	44	96	33 15	43	95	33 58	43	94	34 41	42	93	296
65	31 09	+44	96	31 53	+43	95	32 36	+44	94	33 20	+42	93	34 02	+43	92	295
66	30 31	43	95	31 14	44	94	31 58	43	93	32 41	43	92	33 24	42	92	294
67	29 52	44	94	30 36	43	93	31 19	43	93	32 02	43	92	32 45	43	91	293
68	29 14	43	93	29 57	43	93	30 41	43	92	31 24	43	91	32 07	42	90	292
69	28 35	44	93	29 19	43	92	30 02	43	91	30 45	43	90	31 28	43	89	291

LHA	25° Hc	d	Z	26° Hc	d	Z	27° Hc	d	Z	28° Hc	d	Z	29° Hc	d	Z	LHA
	° ′	′	°	° ′	′	°	° ′	′	°	° ′	′	°	° ′	′	°	
0	65 00	+60	180	66 00	+60	180	67 00	+60	180	68 00	+60	180	69 00	+60	180	360
1	64 59	60	178	65 59	60	178	66 59	60	178	67 59	60	178	68 59	60	178	359
2	64 57	60	176	65 57	60	176	66 57	60	176	67 57	60	175	68 57	60	175	358
3	64 54	59	174	65 53	60	173	66 53	60	173	67 53	60	173	68 53	59	173	357
4	64 49	59	172	65 48	60	171	66 48	59	171	67 47	60	171	68 47	59	170	356
5	64 42	+60	169	65 42	+59	169	66 41	+59	169	67 40	+60	168	68 40	+59	168	355
6	64 34	60	167	65 34	59	167	66 33	59	167	67 32	59	166	68 31	59	166	354
7	64 25	59	165	65 24	59	165	66 23	59	164	67 22	58	164	68 20	59	163	353
8	64 15	58	163	65 13	59	163	66 12	58	162	67 10	59	162	68 09	58	161	352
9	64 03	58	161	65 01	58	161	65 59	58	160	66 57	58	159	67 55	58	159	351
10	63 50	+58	159	64 48	+57	159	65 45	+58	158	66 43	+58	157	67 41	+57	156	350
11	63 35	58	157	64 33	57	157	65 30	57	156	66 27	57	155	67 24	57	154	349
12	63 20	57	155	64 17	57	155	65 14	57	154	66 11	56	153	67 07	56	152	348
13	63 03	57	153	64 00	56	153	64 56	56	152	65 52	56	151	66 48	56	150	347
14	62 45	56	151	63 41	56	151	64 37	56	150	65 33	56	149	66 29	55	148	346
15	62 26	+56	150	63 22	+55	149	64 17	+56	148	65 13	+54	147	66 07	+55	146	345
16	62 06	55	148	63 01	55	147	63 56	55	146	64 51	54	145	65 45	54	144	344
17	61 45	55	146	62 40	54	145	63 34	54	144	64 28	54	143	65 22	54	142	343
18	61 23	54	144	62 17	54	143	63 11	54	142	64 05	53	141	64 58	53	140	342
19	61 00	54	143	61 54	53	142	62 47	53	141	63 40	53	140	64 33	52	139	341
20	60 36	+53	141	61 29	+53	140	62 22	+53	139	63 15	+52	138	64 07	+52	137	340
21	60 11	53	139	61 04	53	138	61 57	52	137	62 49	51	136	63 40	51	135	339
22	59 45	53	138	60 38	52	137	61 30	51	136	62 21	51	135	63 12	51	133	338
23	59 19	52	136	60 11	52	135	61 03	51	134	61 54	50	133	62 44	50	132	337
24	58 52	51	135	59 43	51	134	60 34	51	133	61 25	50	131	62 15	49	130	336
25	58 24	+51	133	59 15	+51	132	60 06	+50	131	60 56	+49	130	61 45	+49	129	335
26	57 56	50	132	58 46	50	131	59 36	50	130	60 26	49	128	61 15	48	127	334
27	57 26	51	130	58 17	49	129	59 06	49	129	59 55	49	127	60 44	48	126	333
28	56 57	49	129	57 46	49	128	58 35	49	127	59 24	48	126	60 12	47	124	332
29	56 26	49	127	57 15	49	126	58 04	48	125	58 52	48	124	59 40	47	123	331
30	55 55	+49	126	56 44	+48	125	57 32	+48	124	58 20	+47	123	59 07	+47	122	330
31	55 24	48	125	56 12	48	124	57 00	48	123	57 48	46	121	58 34	46	120	329
32	54 52	48	123	55 40	48	122	56 28	46	121	57 14	47	120	58 01	45	119	328
33	54 19	48	122	55 07	47	121	55 54	47	120	56 41	46	119	57 27	45	118	327
34	53 47	47	121	54 34	47	120	55 21	46	119	56 07	45	118	56 52	45	117	326
35	53 13	+47	120	54 00	+47	119	54 47	+46	118	55 33	+45	117	56 18	+44	115	325
36	52 40	46	119	53 26	46	118	54 12	46	116	54 58	45	115	55 43	44	114	324
37	52 06	46	117	52 52	46	116	53 38	45	115	54 23	44	114	55 07	44	113	323
38	51 31	46	116	52 17	46	115	53 03	45	114	53 48	44	113	54 32	43	112	322
39	50 56	46	115	51 42	45	114	52 27	45	113	53 12	44	112	53 56	43	111	321
40	50 21	+46	114	51 07	+45	113	51 52	+44	112	52 36	+44	111	53 20	+43	110	320
41	49 46	45	113	50 31	45	112	51 16	44	111	52 00	43	110	52 43	43	109	319
42	49 10	45	112	49 55	45	111	50 40	43	110	51 23	44	109	52 07	42	108	318
43	48 34	45	111	49 19	44	110	50 03	44	109	50 47	43	108	51 30	42	107	317
44	47 58	45	110	48 43	44	109	49 27	43	108	50 10	43	107	50 53	42	106	316
45	47 22	+44	109	48 06	+44	108	48 50	+43	107	49 33	+42	106	50 15	+42	105	315
46	46 45	44	108	47 29	44	107	48 13	43	106	48 56	42	105	49 38	42	104	314
47	46 09	43	107	46 52	44	106	47 36	42	105	48 18	43	104	49 01	41	103	313
48	45 32	43	106	46 15	43	105	46 58	43	104	47 41	42	103	48 23	41	102	312
49	44 54	44	105	45 38	43	104	46 21	42	103	47 03	42	102	47 45	41	101	311
50	44 17	+43	104	45 00	+43	103	45 43	+42	102	46 25	+42	101	47 07	+41	100	310
51	43 40	43	103	44 23	42	102	45 05	43	101	45 48	41	100	46 29	41	99	309
52	43 02	43	102	43 45	43	101	44 28	42	100	45 10	41	99	45 51	41	98	308
53	42 24	43	101	43 07	43	101	43 50	41	100	44 31	42	99	45 13	41	98	307
54	41 46	43	101	42 29	42	100	43 11	42	99	43 53	42	98	44 35	40	97	306
55	41 08	+43	100	41 51	+42	99	42 33	+42	98	43 15	+41	97	43 56	+41	96	305
56	40 30	43	99	41 13	42	98	41 55	42	97	42 37	41	96	43 18	40	95	304
57	39 52	43	98	40 35	42	97	41 17	41	96	41 58	41	95	42 39	41	94	303
58	39 14	42	97	39 56	42	96	40 38	42	95	41 20	41	94	42 01	40	93	302
59	38 36	42	96	39 18	42	95	40 00	41	95	40 41	41	94	41 22	41	93	301
60	37 57	+43	96	38 40	+41	95	39 21	+42	94	40 03	+41	93	40 44	+40	92	300
61	37 19	42	95	38 01	42	94	38 43	41	93	39 24	41	92	40 05	41	91	299
62	36 40	43	94	37 23	41	93	38 04	42	92	38 46	41	91	39 27	40	90	298
63	36 02	42	93	36 44	42	92	37 26	41	91	38 07	41	90	38 48	41	90	297
64	35 23	42	92	36 06	41	91	36 47	42	91	37 29	41	90	38 10	40	89	296
65	34 45	+42	92	35 27	+42	91	36 09	+41	90	36 50	+41	89	37 31	+40	88	295
66	34 06	42	91	34 48	42	90	35 30	42	89	36 12	40	88	36 52	41	87	294
67	33 28	42	90	34 10	42	89	34 52	41	88	35 33	41	87	36 14	41	87	293
68	32 49	42	89	33 31	42	88	34 13	41	88	34 54	41	87	35 35	41	86	292
69	32 11	42	89	32 53	42	88	33 35	41	87	34 16	41	86	34 57	41	85	291

S. Lat. {LHA greater than 180°....... Zn=180−Z; LHA less than 180°.......... Zn=180+Z}

DECLINATION (15°-29°) SAME NAME AS LATITUDE

LAT 50°

N. Lat. {LHA greater than 180°....... Zn=Z; LHA less than 180°........... Zn=360−Z}

DECLINATION (15°-29°) SAME NAME AS LATITUDE

LHA	15° Hc	d	Z	16° Hc	d	Z	17° Hc	d	Z	18° Hc	d	Z	19° Hc	d	Z	LHA
	° ′	′	°	° ′	′	°	° ′	′	°	° ′	′	°	° ′	′	°	
70	24 15	+45	96	25 00	+44	95	25 44	+45	94	26 29	+44	93	27 13	+44	93	290
71	23 36	45	95	24 21	45	94	25 06	44	93	25 50	44	93	26 34	44	92	289
72	22 58	45	94	23 43	44	93	24 27	44	92	25 11	45	92	25 56	43	91	288
73	22 19	45	93	23 04	45	92	23 49	44	92	24 33	44	91	25 17	44	90	287
74	21 41	45	92	22 26	44	92	23 10	44	91	23 54	44	90	24 38	44	89	286
75	21 02	+45	92	21 47	+44	91	22 31	+45	90	23 16	+44	89	24 00	+44	89	285
76	20 24	44	91	21 08	45	90	21 53	44	89	22 37	44	89	23 21	44	88	284
77	19 45	45	90	20 30	44	89	21 14	45	89	21 59	44	88	22 43	44	87	283
78	19 07	44	89	19 51	45	89	20 36	44	88	21 20	44	87	22 04	44	86	282
79	18 28	45	89	19 13	44	88	19 57	45	87	20 42	44	86	21 26	44	86	281
80	17 49	+45	88	18 34	+45	87	19 19	+44	86	20 03	+44	86	20 47	+44	85	280
81	17 11	45	87	17 56	44	86	18 40	45	86	19 25	44	85	20 09	44	84	279
82	16 32	45	86	17 17	45	86	18 02	44	85	18 46	45	84	19 31	44	83	278
83	15 54	45	86	16 39	44	85	17 23	45	84	18 08	44	83	18 52	45	83	277
84	15 16	44	85	16 00	45	84	16 45	45	83	17 30	44	83	18 14	44	82	276
85	14 37	+45	84	15 22	+45	83	16 07	+45	83	16 52	+44	82	17 36	+44	81	275
86	13 59	45	83	14 44	45	83	15 29	44	82	16 13	45	81	16 58	44	80	274
87	13 21	45	83	14 06	45	82	14 51	44	81	15 35	45	80	16 20	45	80	273
88	12 42	45	82	13 27	45	81	14 12	45	80	14 57	45	80	15 42	45	79	272
89	12 04	45	81	12 49	45	80	13 34	45	80	14 19	45	79	15 04	45	78	271
90	11 26	+45	80	12 11	+46	80	12 57	+45	79	13 42	+45	78	14 27	+44	78	270
91	10 48	46	80	11 34	45	79	12 19	45	78	13 04	45	78	13 49	45	77	269
92	10 10	46	79	10 56	45	78	11 41	45	77	12 26	45	77	13 11	46	76	268
93	09 33	45	78	10 18	46	77	11 04	45	77	11 49	45	76	12 34	45	75	267
94	08 55	46	77	09 41	45	77	10 26	45	76	11 11	46	75	11 57	45	75	266
95	08 17	+46	77	09 03	+46	76	09 49	+45	75	10 34	+46	75	11 20	+45	74	265
96	07 40	46	76	08 26	45	75	09 11	46	75	09 57	46	74	10 43	45	73	264
97	07 03	46	75	07 49	45	74	08 34	46	74	09 20	46	73	10 06	46	72	263
98	06 25	46	74	07 11	46	74	07 57	46	73	08 43	46	72	09 29	46	72	262
99	05 48	47	74	06 35	46	73	07 21	46	72	08 07	46	72	08 53	46	71	261
100	05 11	+47	73	05 58	+46	72	06 44	+46	72	07 30	+46	71	08 16	+46	70	260
101	04 35	46	72	05 21	46	71	06 07	47	71	06 54	46	70	07 40	46	70	259
102	03 58	47	71	04 45	46	71	05 31	47	70	06 18	46	69	07 04	46	69	258
103	03 22	46	71	04 08	47	70	04 55	47	69	05 42	46	69	06 28	47	68	257
104	02 45	47	70	03 32	47	69	04 19	47	69	05 06	47	68	05 53	46	67	256
105	02 09	+47	69	02 56	+47	68	03 43	+47	68	04 30	+47	67	05 17	+47	67	255
106	01 33	47	68	02 20	48	68	03 08	47	67	03 55	47	66	04 42	47	66	254
107	00 58	47	68	01 45	47	67	02 32	47	66	03 19	48	66	04 07	47	65	253
108	00 22	47	67	01 09	48	66	01 57	47	66	02 44	48	65	03 32	47	64	252
109	-0 13	47	66	00 34	48	65	01 22	48	65	02 10	47	64	02 57	48	64	251
110	-0 48	+47	65	-0 01	+48	65	00 47	+48	64	01 35	+48	63	02 23	+48	63	250
111	-1 23	48	64	-0 35	48	64	00 13	48	63	01 01	48	63	01 49	48	62	249
112	-1 58	48	64	-1 10	48	63	-0 22	49	62	00 27	48	62	01 15	48	61	248
113	-2 32	48	63	-1 44	48	62	-0 56	49	62	-0 07	48	61	00 41	48	61	247
114	-3 07	49	62	-2 18	48	62	-1 30	49	61	-0 41	49	60	00 08	48	60	246
115	-3 41	+49	61	-2 52	+49	61	-2 03	+49	60	-1 14	+48	60	-0 26	+49	59	245
116	-4 14	49	61	-3 25	49	60	-2 36	48	59	-1 48	49	59	-0 59	49	58	244
117	-4 48	49	60	-3 59	49	59	-3 10	50	59	-2 20	49	58	-1 31	49	57	243
118	-5 21	49	59	-4 32	50	58	-3 42	49	58	-2 53	49	57	-2 04	50	57	242
119	-5 54	50	58	-5 04	49	58	-4 15	50	57	-3 25	49	56	-2 36	50	56	241
120				-5 37	+50	57	-4 47	+50	56	-3 57	+50	56	-3 07	+49	55	240
121							-5 19	50	55	-4 29	50	55	-3 39	50	54	239
122							-5 51	51	55	-5 00	50	54	-4 10	50	54	238
123										-5 31	50	53	-4 41	51	53	237
124													-5 11	50	52	236
125													-5 42	+51	51	235

LHA	20° Hc	d	Z	21° Hc	d	Z	22° Hc	d	Z	23° Hc	d	Z	24° Hc	d	Z	LHA
	° ′	′	°	° ′	′	°	° ′	′	°	° ′	′	°	° ′	′	°	
70	27 57	+43	92	28 40	+44	91	29 24	+43	90	30 07	+43	89	30 50	+42	89	290
71	27 18	44	91	28 02	43	90	28 45	43	89	29 28	43	89	30 11	43	88	289
72	26 39	44	90	27 23	44	89	28 07	43	89	28 50	42	88	29 32	43	87	288
73	26 01	44	89	26 45	43	89	27 28	43	88	28 11	43	87	28 54	43	86	287
74	25 22	44	89	26 06	43	88	26 49	44	87	27 33	43	86	28 16	42	86	286
75	24 44	+44	88	25 28	+43	87	26 11	+43	86	26 54	+43	86	27 37	+43	85	285
76	24 05	44	87	24 49	43	86	25 32	44	86	26 16	43	85	26 59	42	84	284
77	23 27	44	86	24 11	43	86	24 54	43	85	25 37	43	84	26 20	43	83	283
78	22 48	44	86	23 32	44	85	24 16	43	84	24 59	43	83	25 42	43	83	282
79	22 10	44	85	22 54	43	84	23 37	44	83	24 21	43	83	25 04	43	82	281
80	21 31	+44	84	22 15	+44	83	22 59	+43	83	23 42	+44	82	24 26	+43	81	280
81	20 53	44	83	21 37	44	83	22 21	43	82	23 04	44	81	23 48	43	80	279
82	20 15	44	83	20 59	44	82	21 43	43	81	22 26	44	81	23 10	43	80	278
83	19 37	44	82	20 21	44	81	21 05	43	81	21 48	44	80	22 32	43	79	277
84	18 58	45	81	19 43	44	81	20 27	43	80	21 10	44	79	21 54	43	78	276
85	18 20	+45	81	19 05	+44	80	19 49	+44	79	20 33	+43	78	21 16	+44	78	275
86	17 42	45	80	18 27	44	79	19 11	44	78	19 55	44	78	20 39	43	77	274
87	17 05	44	79	17 49	44	78	18 33	44	78	19 17	44	77	20 01	44	76	273
88	16 27	44	78	17 11	45	78	17 56	44	77	18 40	44	76	19 24	44	75	272
89	15 49	45	78	16 34	44	77	17 18	44	76	18 02	44	76	18 46	44	75	271
90	15 11	+45	77	15 56	+45	76	16 41	+44	75	17 25	+44	75	18 09	+44	74	270
91	14 34	45	76	15 19	44	75	16 03	45	75	16 48	44	74	17 32	45	73	269
92	13 57	44	75	14 41	45	75	15 26	45	74	16 11	44	73	16 55	45	73	268
93	13 19	45	75	14 04	45	74	14 49	45	73	15 34	45	73	16 19	44	72	267
94	12 42	45	74	13 27	45	73	14 12	45	73	14 57	45	72	15 42	45	71	266
95	12 05	+45	73	12 50	+46	73	13 36	+45	72	14 21	+45	71	15 06	+45	71	265
96	11 28	46	73	12 14	45	72	12 59	45	71	13 44	45	71	14 29	45	70	264
97	10 52	45	72	11 37	46	71	12 23	45	70	13 08	45	70	13 53	45	69	263
98	10 15	46	71	11 01	45	70	11 46	46	70	12 32	45	69	13 17	46	68	262
99	09 39	46	70	10 25	45	70	11 10	46	69	11 56	46	68	12 42	45	68	261
100	09 02	+46	70	09 48	+46	69	10 34	+46	68	11 20	+46	68	12 06	+46	67	260
101	08 26	47	69	09 13	46	68	09 59	46	68	10 45	46	67	11 31	45	66	259
102	07 50	47	68	08 37	46	68	09 23	46	67	10 09	46	66	10 55	46	66	258
103	07 15	46	67	08 01	47	67	08 48	46	66	09 34	46	65	10 20	47	65	257
104	06 39	47	67	07 26	47	66	08 13	46	65	08 59	47	65	09 46	46	64	256
105	06 04	+47	66	06 51	+47	65	07 38	+46	65	08 24	+47	64	09 11	+47	63	255
106	05 29	47	65	06 16	47	65	07 03	47	64	07 50	47	63	08 37	47	63	254
107	04 54	47	64	05 41	47	64	06 28	47	63	07 15	48	63	08 03	47	62	253
108	04 19	48	64	05 07	47	63	05 54	47	62	06 41	48	62	07 29	47	61	252
109	03 45	47	63	04 32	48	62	05 20	47	62	06 07	48	61	06 55	47	61	251
110	03 11	+47	62	03 58	+48	62	04 46	+48	61	05 34	+48	60	06 22	+47	60	250
111	02 37	48	61	03 25	48	61	04 13	47	60	05 00	48	60	05 48	48	59	249
112	02 03	48	61	02 51	48	60	03 39	48	59	04 27	48	59	05 15	48	58	248
113	01 29	49	60	02 18	48	59	03 06	48	59	03 54	49	58	04 43	48	58	247
114	00 56	49	59	01 45	48	59	02 33	49	58	03 22	48	57	04 10	49	57	246
115	00 23	+49	58	01 12	+49	58	02 01	+48	57	02 49	+49	57	03 38	+49	56	245
116	-0 10	49	58	00 39	49	57	01 28	49	56	02 17	49	56	03 06	49	55	244
117	-0 42	49	57	00 07	49	56	00 56	50	56	01 46	49	55	02 35	49	55	243
118	-1 14	49	56	-0 25	50	56	00 25	49	55	01 14	49	54	02 03	50	54	242
119	-1 46	50	55	-0 56	49	55	-0 07	50	54	00 43	49	54	01 32	50	53	241
120	-2 18	+50	55	-1 28	+50	54	-0 38	+50	53	00 12	+50	53	01 02	+50	52	240
121	-2 49	50	54	-1 59	50	53	-1 09	50	53	-0 19	50	52	00 31	50	52	239
122	-3 20	50	53	-2 30	51	52	-1 39	50	52	-0 49	50	51	00 01	51	51	238
123	-3 50	50	52	-3 00	51	52	-2 09	50	51	-1 19	51	51	-0 28	50	50	237
124	-4 21	51	51	-3 30	51	51	-2 39	51	50	-1 48	50	50	-0 58	51	49	236
125	-4 51	+51	51	-4 00	+51	50	-3 09	+51	50	-2 18	+51	49	-1 27	+51	48	235
126	-5 20	51	50	-4 29	51	49	-3 38	51	49	-2 47	52	48	-1 55	51	48	234
127	-5 50	52	49	-4 58	51	48	-4 07	52	48	-3 15	51	47	-2 24	52	47	233
128				-5 27	52	48	-4 35	52	47	-3 43	51	47	-2 52	52	46	232
129				-5 55	52	47	-5 03	52	46	-4 11	52	46	-3 19	52	45	231
130							-5 31	+52	45	-4 39	+52	45	-3 47	+53	45	230
131										-5 06	53	44	-4 13	52	44	229
132										-5 33	53	43	-4 40	53	43	228
133													-5 06	53	42	227
134													-5 32	53	41	226

LHA	25° Hc	d	Z	26° Hc	d	Z	27° Hc	d	Z	28° Hc	d	Z	29° Hc	d	Z	LHA
	° ′	′	°	° ′	′	°	° ′	′	°	° ′	′	°	° ′	′	°	
70	31 32	+42	88	32 14	+42	87	32 56	+42	86	33 38	+41	85	34 19	+40	84	290
71	30 54	42	87	31 36	42	86	32 18	41	85	32 59	41	84	33 40	41	84	289
72	30 15	42	86	30 57	42	85	31 39	42	85	32 21	41	84	33 02	41	83	288
73	29 37	42	86	30 19	42	85	31 01	41	84	31 42	42	83	32 24	41	82	287
74	28 58	42	85	29 40	42	84	30 22	42	83	31 04	42	82	31 46	41	81	286
75	28 20	+42	84	29 02	+42	83	29 44	+42	82	30 26	+41	82	31 07	+42	81	285
76	27 41	43	83	28 24	42	83	29 06	42	82	29 48	41	81	30 29	42	80	284
77	27 03	43	83	27 46	42	82	28 28	42	81	29 10	42	80	29 52	41	79	283
78	26 25	43	82	27 08	42	81	27 50	42	80	28 32	42	79	29 14	41	79	282
79	25 47	42	81	26 29	43	80	27 12	42	80	27 54	42	79	28 36	41	78	281
80	25 09	+42	80	25 51	+43	80	26 34	+42	79	27 16	+42	78	27 58	+42	77	280
81	24 31	43	80	25 14	42	79	25 56	43	78	26 39	42	77	27 21	42	77	279
82	23 53	43	79	24 36	43	78	25 19	42	77	26 01	42	77	26 43	42	76	278
83	23 15	43	78	23 58	43	78	24 41	43	77	25 24	42	76	26 06	42	75	277
84	22 37	44	78	23 21	42	77	24 03	43	76	24 46	43	75	25 29	42	75	276
85	22 00	+43	77	22 43	+43	76	23 26	+43	75	24 09	+43	75	24 52	+42	74	275
86	21 22	44	76	22 06	43	75	22 49	43	75	23 32	43	74	24 15	42	73	274
87	20 45	43	75	21 28	44	75	22 12	43	74	22 55	43	73	23 38	42	72	273
88	20 08	43	75	20 51	44	74	21 35	43	73	22 18	43	73	23 01	43	72	272
89	19 30	44	74	20 14	44	73	20 58	43	73	21 41	44	72	22 25	43	71	271
90	18 53	+44	73	19 37	+44	73	20 21	+44	72	21 05	+43	71	21 48	+43	70	270
91	18 17	44	73	19 01	44	72	19 45	43	71	20 28	44	70	21 12	43	70	269
92	17 40	44	72	18 24	44	71	19 08	44	71	19 52	44	70	20 36	43	69	268
93	17 03	45	71	17 48	44	71	18 32	44	70	19 16	44	69	20 00	44	68	267
94	16 27	44	71	17 11	45	70	17 56	44	69	18 40	44	68	19 24	44	68	266
95	15 51	+44	70	16 35	+45	69	17 20	+44	68	18 04	+44	68	18 48	+45	67	265
96	15 14	45	69	15 59	45	68	16 44	45	68	17 29	44	67	18 13	44	66	264
97	14 38	46	68	15 24	44	68	16 08	45	67	16 53	45	66	17 38	44	66	263
98	14 03	45	68	14 48	45	67	15 33	45	66	16 18	45	66	17 03	45	65	262
99	13 27	46	67	14 13	45	66	14 58	45	66	15 43	45	65	16 28	45	64	261
100	12 52	+45	66	13 37	+46	66	14 23	+45	65	15 08	+45	64	15 53	+45	64	260
101	12 16	46	66	13 02	46	65	13 48	45	64	14 33	46	64	15 19	45	63	259
102	11 41	46	65	12 27	46	64	13 13	46	64	13 59	46	63	14 45	45	62	258
103	11 07	46	64	11 53	46	64	12 39	46	63	13 25	46	62	14 11	45	62	257
104	10 32	46	63	11 18	47	63	12 05	46	62	12 51	46	62	13 37	46	61	256
105	09 58	+46	63	10 44	+47	62	11 31	+46	61	12 17	+46	61	13 03	+47	60	255
106	09 24	46	62	10 10	47	61	10 57	46	61	11 43	47	60	12 30	46	59	254
107	08 50	47	61	09 37	46	61	10 23	47	60	11 10	47	59	11 57	47	59	253
108	08 16	47	61	09 03	47	60	09 50	47	59	10 37	47	59	11 24	47	58	252
109	07 42	48	60	08 30	47	59	09 17	47	59	10 04	47	58	10 51	48	57	251
110	07 09	+48	59	07 57	+47	59	08 44	+48	58	09 32	+47	57	10 19	+47	57	250
111	06 36	48	58	07 24	48	58	08 12	47	57	08 59	48	57	09 47	48	56	249
112	06 03	48	58	06 51	48	57	07 39	48	57	08 27	48	56	09 15	48	55	248
113	05 31	48	57	06 19	48	56	07 07	49	56	07 56	48	55	08 44	48	55	247
114	04 59	48	56	05 47	49	56	06 36	48	55	07 24	48	54	08 12	49	54	246
115	04 27	+49	55	05 16	+48	55	06 04	+49	54	06 53	+48	54	07 41	+49	53	245
116	03 55	49	55	04 44	49	54	05 33	49	54	06 22	49	53	07 11	48	52	244
117	03 24	49	54	04 13	49	53	05 02	49	53	05 51	49	52	06 40	49	52	243
118	02 53	49	53	03 42	50	53	04 32	49	52	05 21	49	52	06 10	49	51	242
119	02 22	50	53	03 12	49	52	04 01	50	51	04 51	49	51	05 40	50	50	241
120	01 52	+49	52	02 41	+50	51	03 31	+50	51	04 21	+50	50	05 11	+50	50	240
121	01 21	51	51	02 12	50	50	03 02	50	50	03 52	50	49	04 42	50	49	239
122	00 52	50	50	01 42	50	50	02 32	51	49	03 23	50	49	04 13	50	48	238
123	00 22	51	49	01 13	50	49	02 03	51	48	02 54	50	48	03 44	51	47	237
124	-0 07	51	49	00 44	51	48	01 35	50	48	02 25	51	47	03 16	51	47	236
125	-0 36	+51	48	00 15	+51	47	01 06	+51	47	01 57	+51	46	02 48	+51	46	235
126	-1 04	51	47	-0 13	51	47	00 38	52	46	01 30	51	46	02 21	51	45	234
127	-1 32	51	46	-0 41	52	46	00 11	51	45	01 02	52	45	01 54	51	44	233
128	-2 00	52	46	-1 08	51	45	-0 17	52	45	00 35	52	44	01 27	52	44	232
129	-2 27	52	45	-1 35	52	44	-0 43	51	44	00 08	52	43	01 00	53	43	231
130	-2 54	+52	44	-2 02	+52	44	-1 10	+52	43	-0 18	+52	43	00 34	+53	42	230
131	-3 21	52	43	-2 29	53	43	-1 36	52	42	-0 44	53	42	00 09	52	41	229
132	-3 47	52	42	-2 55	53	42	-2 02	53	41	-1 09	53	41	-0 16	52	41	228
133	-4 13	53	42	-3 20	53	41	-2 27	53	41	-1 34	53	40	-0 41	52	40	227
134	-4 39	54	41	-3 45	53	40	-2 52	53	40	-1 59	53	39	-1 06	53	39	226
135	-5 04	+54	40	-4 10	+53	40	-3 17	+54	39	-2 23	+53	39	-1 30	+53	38	225
136	-5 28	53	39	-4 35	54	39	-3 41	54	38	-2 47	53	38	-1 54	54	37	224
137				-4 58	53	38	-4 05	54	38	-3 11	54	37	-2 17	54	37	223
138				-5 22	54	37	-4 28	54	37	-3 34	54	36	-2 40	54	36	222
139				-5 45	54	36	-4 51	55	36	-3 56	54	35	-3 02	54	35	221

S. Lat. {LHA greater than 180°....... Zn=180−Z; LHA less than 180°........... Zn=180+Z}

DECLINATION (15°-29°) SAME NAME AS LATITUDE

LAT 50°

N. Lat. {LHA greater than 180°....... Zn=Z; LHA less than 180°........... Zn=360−Z}

DECLINATION (15°-29°) SAME NAME AS LATITUDE

LAT 50°

LHA	15° Hc d Z	16° Hc d Z	17° Hc d Z	18° Hc d Z	19° Hc d Z	20° Hc d Z	21° Hc d Z	22° Hc d Z	23° Hc d Z	24° Hc d Z	25° Hc d Z	26° Hc d Z	27° Hc d Z	28° Hc d Z	29° Hc d Z	LHA
	° ′ ′ °	° ′ ′ °	° ′ ′ °	° ′ ′ °	° ′ ′ °	° ′ ′ °	° ′ ′ °	° ′ ′ °	° ′ ′ °	° ′ ′ °	° ′ ′ °	° ′ ′ °	° ′ ′ °	° ′ ′ °	° ′ ′ °	
												140	−5 13 +54 35	−4 19 +55 35	−3 24 +55 34	220
												141	−5 35 55 34	−4 40 55 34	−3 45 55 33	219
													142	−5 02 56 33	−4 06 55 33	218
													143	−5 22 55 32	−4 27 55 32	217
														144	−4 47 55 31	216
														145	−5 07 +56 30	215
														146	−5 26 56 29	214
81	−5 48 47 106	279														
80	−5 11 −47 107	−5 58 −46 108	280													
79	−4 35 46 108	−5 21 46 109	−6 07 47 109	281												
78	−3 58 47 109	−4 45 46 109	−5 31 47 110	282												
77	−3 22 46 109	−4 08 47 110	−4 55 47 111	−5 42 46 111	283											
76	−2 45 47 110	−3 32 47 111	−4 19 47 111	−5 06 47 112	−5 53 46 113	284										
75	−2 09 −47 111	−2 56 −47 112	−3 43 −47 112	−4 30 −47 113	−5 17 −47 113	−6 04 −47 114	285									
74	−1 33 47 112	−2 20 48 112	−3 08 47 113	−3 55 47 114	−4 42 47 114	−5 29 47 115	286									
73	−0 58 47 112	−1 45 47 113	−2 32 47 114	−3 19 48 114	−4 07 47 115	−4 54 47 116	−5 41 47 116	287								
72	−0 22 47 113	−1 09 48 114	−1 57 47 114	−2 44 48 115	−3 32 47 116	−4 19 48 116	−5 07 47 117	−5 54 47 118	288							
71	00 13 47 114	−0 34 48 115	−1 22 48 115	−2 10 47 116	−2 57 48 116	−3 45 47 117	−4 32 48 118	−5 20 47 118	289							
70	00 48 −47 115	00 01 −48 115	−0 47 −48 116	−1 35 −48 117	−2 23 −48 117	−3 11 −47 118	−3 58 −48 118	−4 46 −48 119	−5 34 −48 120	290						
	15°	16°	17°	18°	19°	20°	21°	22°	23°	24°	25°	26°	27°	28°	29°	

S. Lat. {LHA greater than 180°....... Zn=180−Z; LHA less than 180°........... Zn=180+Z}

DECLINATION (15°-29°) CONTRARY NAME TO LATITUDE

N. Lat. {LHA greater than 180°........Zn=Z
{LHA less than 180°...........Zn=360−Z

DECLINATION (15°-29°) CONTRARY NAME TO LATITUDE

LHA	15° Hc	15° d	15° Z	16° Hc	16° d	16° Z	17° Hc	17° d	17° Z	18° Hc	18° d	18° Z	19° Hc	19° d	19° Z
	° ′	′	°	° ′	′	°	° ′	′	°	° ′	′	°	° ′	′	°
69	01 23	48	116	00 35	48	116	−0 13	48	117	−1 01	48	117	−1 49	48	118
68	01 58	48	116	01 10	48	117	00 22	49	118	−0 27	48	118	−1 15	48	119
67	02 32	48	117	01 44	48	118	00 56	49	118	00 07	48	119	−0 41	48	119
66	03 07	49	118	02 18	48	118	01 30	49	119	00 41	49	120	−0 08	48	120
65	03 41	−49	119	02 52	−49	119	02 03	−49	120	01 14	−48	120	00 26	−49	121
64	04 14	49	119	03 25	49	120	02 36	48	121	01 48	49	121	00 59	49	122
63	04 48	49	120	03 59	49	121	03 10	50	121	02 20	49	122	01 31	49	123
62	05 21	49	121	04 32	50	122	03 42	49	122	02 53	49	123	02 04	50	123
61	05 54	50	122	05 04	49	122	04 15	50	123	03 25	49	124	02 36	50	124
60	06 26	−49	123	05 37	−50	123	04 47	−50	124	03 57	−50	124	03 07	−49	125
59	06 59	50	124	06 09	50	124	05 19	50	125	04 29	50	125	03 39	50	126
58	07 31	50	124	06 41	50	125	05 51	51	125	05 00	50	126	04 10	50	126
57	08 03	51	125	07 12	50	126	06 22	51	126	05 31	50	127	04 41	51	127
56	08 34	51	126	07 43	50	127	06 53	51	127	06 02	51	128	05 11	50	128
55	09 05	−51	127	08 14	−51	127	07 23	−50	128	06 33	−51	128	05 42	−51	129
54	09 36	51	128	08 45	51	128	07 54	51	129	07 03	52	129	06 11	51	130
53	10 06	51	128	09 15	51	129	08 24	52	130	07 32	51	130	06 41	51	131
52	10 36	51	129	09 45	52	130	08 53	51	130	08 02	52	131	07 10	51	131
51	11 06	52	130	10 14	52	131	09 22	51	131	08 31	52	132	07 39	52	132
50	11 35	−52	131	10 43	−52	132	09 51	−52	132	08 59	−52	133	08 07	−52	133
49	12 04	52	132	11 12	52	132	10 20	52	133	09 28	53	133	08 35	52	134
48	12 33	53	133	11 40	52	133	10 48	53	134	09 55	52	134	09 03	53	135
47	13 01	53	134	12 08	52	134	11 16	53	135	10 23	53	135	09 30	53	136
46	13 29	53	134	12 36	53	135	11 43	53	135	10 50	53	136	09 57	53	136
45	13 56	−53	135	13 03	−53	136	12 10	−53	136	11 17	−54	137	10 23	−53	137
44	14 23	53	136	13 30	54	137	12 36	53	137	11 43	54	138	10 49	53	138
43	14 49	53	137	13 56	54	138	13 02	53	138	12 09	54	138	11 15	54	139
42	15 15	53	138	14 22	54	138	13 28	54	139	12 34	54	139	11 40	54	140
41	15 41	54	139	14 47	54	139	13 53	54	140	12 59	54	140	12 05	54	141
40	16 06	−54	140	15 12	−54	140	14 18	−55	141	13 23	−54	141	12 29	−54	142
39	16 31	55	141	15 36	54	141	14 42	55	142	13 47	54	142	12 53	55	142
38	16 55	55	142	16 00	54	142	15 06	55	142	14 11	55	143	13 16	55	143
37	17 19	55	143	16 24	55	143	15 29	55	143	14 34	55	144	13 39	55	144
36	17 42	55	143	16 47	55	144	15 52	55	144	14 57	56	145	14 01	55	145
35	18 05	−56	144	17 09	−55	145	16 14	−55	145	15 19	−56	146	14 23	−55	146
34	18 27	56	145	17 31	55	146	16 36	56	146	15 40	55	147	14 45	56	147
33	18 49	56	146	17 53	56	147	16 57	56	147	16 01	56	147	15 05	56	148
32	19 10	56	147	18 14	56	148	17 18	56	148	16 22	56	148	15 26	56	149
31	19 31	57	148	18 34	56	149	17 38	56	149	16 42	57	149	15 45	56	150
30	19 51	−57	149	18 54	−56	150	17 58	−57	150	17 01	−56	150	16 05	−57	151
29	20 10	56	150	19 14	57	150	18 17	57	151	17 20	57	151	16 23	56	152
28	20 29	57	151	19 32	57	151	18 35	56	152	17 39	57	152	16 42	57	152
27	20 47	57	152	19 50	57	152	18 53	57	153	17 56	57	153	16 59	57	153
26	21 05	57	153	20 08	57	153	19 11	57	154	18 14	58	154	17 16	57	154
25	21 22	−57	154	20 25	−57	154	19 28	−58	155	18 30	−57	155	17 33	−58	155
24	21 39	58	155	20 41	57	155	19 44	58	156	18 46	57	156	17 49	58	156
23	21 55	58	156	20 57	58	156	19 59	57	157	19 02	58	157	18 04	58	157
22	22 10	58	157	21 12	57	157	20 15	58	158	19 17	59	158	18 18	58	158
21	22 25	58	158	21 27	58	158	20 29	58	159	19 31	58	159	18 33	59	159
20	22 39	−58	159	21 41	−58	159	20 43	−59	160	19 44	−58	160	18 46	−58	160
19	22 53	59	160	21 54	58	160	20 56	59	161	19 57	58	161	18 59	59	161
18	23 06	59	161	22 07	59	161	21 08	58	162	20 10	59	162	19 11	59	162
17	23 18	59	162	22 19	59	162	21 20	58	163	20 22	59	163	19 23	59	163
16	23 29	59	163	22 30	58	163	21 32	59	164	20 33	59	164	19 34	59	164
15	23 40	−59	164	22 41	−59	164	21 42	−59	165	20 43	−59	165	19 44	−59	165
14	23 50	59	165	22 51	59	165	21 52	59	166	20 53	59	166	19 54	59	166
13	24 00	59	166	23 01	60	166	22 01	59	167	21 02	59	167	20 03	59	167
12	24 09	60	167	23 09	59	167	22 10	59	168	21 11	60	168	20 11	59	168
11	24 17	60	168	23 17	59	169	22 18	59	169	21 19	60	169	20 19	59	169
10	24 24	−59	169	23 25	−60	170	22 25	−59	170	21 26	−60	170	20 26	−59	170
9	24 31	60	170	23 31	59	171	22 32	60	171	21 32	59	171	20 33	60	171
8	24 37	60	172	23 37	59	172	22 38	60	172	21 38	60	172	20 38	59	172
7	24 43	60	173	23 43	60	173	22 43	60	173	21 43	60	173	20 43	59	173
6	24 47	60	174	23 47	60	174	22 47	59	174	21 48	60	174	20 48	60	174
5	24 51	−60	175	23 51	−60	175	22 51	−60	175	21 51	−59	175	20 52	−60	175
4	24 54	60	176	23 54	60	176	22 54	59	176	21 55	60	176	20 55	60	176
3	24 57	60	177	23 57	60	177	22 57	60	177	21 57	60	177	20 57	60	177
2	24 59	60	178	23 59	60	178	22 59	60	178	21 59	60	178	20 59	60	178
1	25 00	60	179	24 00	60	179	23 00	60	179	22 00	60	179	21 00	60	179
0	25 00	−60	180	24 00	−60	180	23 00	−60	180	22 00	−60	180	21 00	−60	180

LHA	20° Hc	20° d	20° Z	21° Hc	21° d	21° Z	22° Hc	22° d	22° Z	23° Hc	23° d	23° Z	24° Hc	24° d	24° Z
	° ′	′	°	° ′	′	°	° ′	′	°	° ′	′	°	° ′	′	°
69	−2 37	48	119	−3 25	48	119	−4 13	47	120	−5 00	48	120	−5 48	48	121
68	−2 03	48	119	−2 51	48	120	−3 39	48	121	−4 27	48	121	−5 15	48	122
67	−1 29	49	120	−2 18	48	121	−3 06	48	121	−3 54	49	122	−4 43	48	122
66	−0 56	49	121	−1 45	48	121	−2 33	49	122	−3 22	48	123	−4 10	49	123
65	−0 23	−49	122	−1 12	−49	122	−2 01	−48	123	−2 49	−49	123	−3 38	−49	124
64	00 10	49	122	−0 39	49	123	−1 28	49	124	−2 17	49	124	−3 06	49	125
63	00 42	49	123	−0 07	49	124	−0 56	50	124	−1 46	49	125	−2 35	49	125
62	01 14	49	124	00 25	50	124	−0 25	49	125	−1 14	49	126	−2 03	50	126
61	01 46	50	125	00 56	49	125	00 07	50	126	−0 43	49	126	−1 32	50	127
60	02 18	−50	125	01 28	−50	126	00 38	−50	127	−0 12	−50	127	−1 02	−50	128
59	02 49	50	126	01 59	50	127	01 09	50	127	00 19	50	128	−0 31	50	128
58	03 20	50	127	02 30	51	128	01 39	50	128	00 49	50	129	−0 01	51	129
57	03 50	50	128	03 00	51	128	02 09	50	129	01 19	51	129	00 28	50	130
56	04 21	51	129	03 30	51	129	02 39	51	130	01 48	50	130	00 58	51	131
55	04 51	−51	129	04 00	−51	130	03 09	−51	130	02 18	−51	131	01 27	−51	132
54	05 20	51	130	04 29	51	131	03 38	51	131	02 47	52	132	01 55	51	132
53	05 50	52	131	04 58	51	132	04 07	52	132	03 15	51	133	02 24	52	133
52	06 19	52	132	05 27	52	132	04 35	52	133	03 43	51	133	02 52	52	134
51	06 47	52	133	05 55	52	133	05 03	52	134	04 11	52	134	03 19	52	135
50	07 15	−52	134	06 23	−52	134	05 31	−52	135	04 39	−52	135	03 47	−53	135
49	07 43	52	134	06 51	53	135	05 58	52	135	05 06	53	136	04 13	52	136
48	08 10	52	135	07 18	53	136	06 25	52	136	05 33	53	137	04 40	53	137
47	08 37	52	136	07 45	53	136	06 52	53	137	05 59	53	137	05 06	53	138
46	09 04	53	137	08 11	53	137	07 18	53	138	06 25	53	138	05 32	53	139
45	09 30	−53	138	08 37	−53	138	07 44	−54	139	06 50	−53	139	05 57	−53	140
44	09 56	53	139	09 03	54	139	08 09	54	139	07 15	53	140	06 22	54	140
43	10 21	53	139	09 28	54	140	08 34	54	140	07 40	54	141	06 46	54	141
42	10 46	54	140	09 52	54	141	08 58	54	141	08 04	54	142	07 10	54	142
41	11 11	54	141	10 17	55	142	09 22	54	142	08 28	54	142	07 34	55	143
40	11 35	−55	142	10 40	−54	142	09 46	−55	143	08 51	−54	143	07 57	−55	144
39	11 58	54	143	11 04	55	143	10 09	55	144	09 14	54	144	08 20	55	145
38	12 21	55	144	11 26	54	144	10 32	55	145	09 37	55	145	08 42	55	145
37	12 44	55	145	11 49	55	145	10 54	55	145	09 59	56	146	09 03	55	146
36	13 06	55	146	12 11	56	146	11 15	55	146	10 20	55	147	09 25	56	147
35	13 28	−56	146	12 32	−55	147	11 37	−56	147	10 41	−56	148	09 45	−55	148
34	13 49	56	147	12 53	56	148	11 57	56	148	11 01	55	148	10 06	56	149
33	14 09	56	148	13 13	56	149	12 17	56	149	11 21	56	149	10 25	56	150
32	14 30	57	149	13 33	56	149	12 37	56	150	11 41	56	150	10 45	57	151
31	14 49	56	150	13 53	57	150	12 56	56	151	12 00	57	151	11 03	56	151
30	15 08	−56	151	14 12	−57	151	13 15	−57	152	12 18	−56	152	11 22	−57	152
29	15 27	57	152	14 30	57	152	13 33	57	153	12 36	57	153	11 39	57	153
28	15 45	57	153	14 48	57	153	13 51	57	153	12 54	57	154	11 57	58	154
27	16 02	57	154	15 05	57	154	14 08	58	154	13 10	57	155	12 13	57	155
26	16 19	58	155	15 21	57	155	14 24	57	155	13 27	58	156	12 29	57	156
25	16 35	−57	156	15 38	−58	156	14 40	−58	156	13 42	−57	156	12 45	−58	157
24	16 51	58	157	15 53	58	157	14 55	57	157	13 58	58	157	13 00	58	158
23	17 06	58	157	16 08	58	158	15 10	58	158	14 12	58	158	13 14	58	159
22	17 20	58	158	16 22	58	159	15 24	58	159	14 26	58	159	13 28	58	159
21	17 34	58	159	16 36	58	160	15 38	58	160	14 40	59	160	13 41	58	160
20	17 48	−59	160	16 49	−58	161	15 51	−59	161	14 52	−58	161	13 54	−58	161
19	18 00	58	161	17 02	59	162	16 03	58	162	15 05	59	162	14 06	58	162
18	18 12	58	162	17 14	59	162	16 15	59	163	15 16	58	163	14 18	59	163
17	18 24	59	163	17 25	59	163	16 26	59	164	15 27	58	164	14 29	59	164
16	18 35	59	164	17 36	59	164	16 37	59	165	15 38	59	165	14 39	59	165
15	18 45	−59	165	17 46	−59	165	16 47	−59	166	15 48	−59	166	14 49	−59	166
14	18 55	60	166	17 55	59	166	16 56	59	166	15 57	59	167	14 58	59	167
13	19 04	60	167	18 04	59	167	17 05	59	167	16 06	60	168	15 06	59	168
12	19 12	60	168	18 12	59	168	17 13	59	168	16 14	60	169	15 14	59	169
11	19 20	60	169	18 20	59	169	17 21	60	169	16 21	59	170	15 22	60	170
10	19 27	−60	170	18 27	−60	170	17 27	−59	170	16 28	−60	170	15 28	−59	171
9	19 33	60	171	18 33	59	171	17 34	60	171	16 34	60	171	15 34	59	172
8	19 39	60	172	18 39	60	172	17 39	60	172	16 39	59	172	15 40	60	172
7	19 44	60	173	18 44	60	173	17 44	60	173	16 44	60	173	15 44	59	173
6	19 48	60	174	18 48	60	174	17 48	60	174	16 48	59	174	15 49	60	174
5	19 52	−60	175	18 52	−60	175	17 52	−60	175	16 52	−60	175	15 52	−60	175
4	19 55	60	176	18 55	60	176	17 55	60	176	16 55	60	176	15 55	60	176
3	19 57	60	177	18 57	60	177	17 57	60	177	16 57	60	177	15 57	60	177
2	19 59	60	178	18 59	60	178	17 59	60	178	16 59	60	178	15 59	60	178
1	20 00	60	179	19 00	60	179	18 00	60	179	17 00	60	179	16 00	60	179
0	20 00	−60	180	19 00	−60	180	18 00	−60	180	17 00	−60	180	16 00	−60	180

LHA	25° Hc	25° d	25° Z	26° Hc	26° d	26° Z	27° Hc	27° d	27° Z	28° Hc	28° d	28° Z	29° Hc	29° d	29° Z	LHA
	° ′	′	°	° ′	′	°	° ′	′	°	° ′	′	°	° ′	′	°	
69	291															
68	−6 03	48	122	292												
67	−5 31	48	123	293												
66	−4 59	48	124	−5 47	49	124	294									
65	−4 27	−49	125	−5 16	−48	125	295									
64	−3 55	49	125	−4 44	49	126	−5 33	49	126	296						
63	−3 24	49	126	−4 13	49	127	−5 02	49	127	−5 51	49	128	297			
62	−2 53	49	127	−3 42	50	127	−4 32	49	128	−5 21	49	128	298			
61	−2 22	50	127	−3 12	49	128	−4 01	50	129	−4 51	49	129	−5 40	50	130	299
60	−1 52	−49	128	−2 41	−50	129	−3 31	−50	129	−4 21	−50	130	−5 11	−50	130	300
59	−1 21	51	129	−2 12	50	130	−3 02	50	130	−3 52	50	131	−4 42	50	131	301
58	−0 52	50	130	−1 42	50	130	−2 32	51	131	−3 23	50	131	−4 13	50	132	302
57	−0 22	51	131	−1 13	50	131	−2 03	51	132	−2 54	50	132	−3 44	51	133	303
56	00 07	51	131	−0 44	51	132	−1 35	50	132	−2 25	51	133	−3 16	51	133	304
55	00 36	−51	132	−0 15	−51	133	−1 06	−51	133	−1 57	−51	134	−2 48	−51	134	305
54	01 04	51	133	00 13	51	133	−0 38	52	134	−1 30	51	134	−2 21	51	135	306
53	01 32	51	134	00 41	52	134	−0 11	51	135	−1 02	52	135	−1 54	51	136	307
52	02 00	52	134	01 08	51	135	00 17	52	135	−0 35	52	136	−1 27	52	136	308
51	02 27	52	135	01 35	52	136	00 43	51	136	−0 08	52	137	−1 00	53	137	309
50	02 54	−52	136	02 02	−52	136	01 10	−52	137	00 18	−52	137	−0 34	−53	138	310
49	03 21	52	137	02 29	53	137	01 36	52	138	00 44	53	138	−0 09	52	139	311
48	03 47	52	138	02 55	53	138	02 02	53	139	01 09	53	139	00 16	52	139	312
47	04 13	53	138	03 20	53	139	02 27	53	139	01 34	53	140	00 41	52	140	313
46	04 39	54	139	03 45	53	140	02 52	53	140	01 59	53	141	01 06	53	141	314
45	05 04	−54	140	04 10	−53	140	03 17	−54	141	02 23	−53	141	01 30	−53	142	315
44	05 28	53	141	04 35	54	141	03 41	54	142	02 47	53	142	01 54	54	143	316
43	05 52	54	142	04 58	53	142	04 05	54	142	03 11	54	143	02 17	54	143	317
42	06 16	54	142	05 22	54	143	04 28	54	143	03 34	54	144	02 40	54	144	318
41	06 39	54	143	05 45	54	144	04 51	55	144	03 56	54	145	03 02	54	145	319
40	07 02	−54	144	06 08	−55	145	05 13	−54	145	04 19	−55	145	03 24	−55	146	320
39	07 25	55	145	06 30	55	145	05 35	55	146	04 40	55	146	03 45	55	147	321
38	07 47	55	146	06 52	55	146	05 57	55	147	05 02	56	147	04 06	55	147	322
37	08 08	55	147	07 13	55	147	06 18	56	147	05 22	55	148	04 27	55	148	323
36	08 29	55	147	07 34	56	148	06 38	55	148	05 43	56	149	04 47	55	149	324
35	08 50	−56	148	07 54	−56	149	06 58	−55	149	06 03	−56	149	05 07	−56	150	325
34	09 10	56	149	08 14	56	150	07 18	56	150	06 22	56	150	05 26	56	151	326
33	09 29	56	150	08 33	56	150	07 37	56	151	06 41	56	151	05 45	56	151	327
32	09 48	56	151	08 52	56	151	07 56	57	152	06 59	56	152	06 03	56	152	328
31	10 07	57	152	09 10	56	152	08 14	57	152	07 17	56	153	06 21	57	153	329
30	10 25	−57	153	09 28	−57	153	08 31	−56	153	07 35	−57	154	06 38	−57	154	330
29	10 42	56	153	09 46	57	154	08 49	57	154	07 52	57	154	06 55	57	155	331
28	10 59	57	154	10 02	57	155	09 05	57	155	08 08	57	155	07 11	57	156	332
27	11 16	57	155	10 19	58	156	09 21	57	156	08 24	57	156	07 27	58	156	333
26	11 32	58	156	10 34	57	156	09 37	58	157	08 39	57	157	07 42	58	157	334
25	11 47	−58	157	10 49	−57	157	09 52	−58	158	08 54	−58	158	07 56	−57	158	335
24	12 02	58	158	11 04	58	158	10 06	58	158	09 08	57	159	08 11	58	159	336
23	12 16	58	159	11 18	58	159	10 20	58	159	09 22	58	160	08 24	58	160	337
22	12 30	58	160	11 32	58	160	10 34	59	160	09 35	58	160	08 37	58	161	338
21	12 43	58	161	11 45	59	161	10 46	58	161	09 48	58	161	08 50	59	162	339
20	12 56	−59	162	11 57	−58	162	10 59	−59	162	10 00	−58	162	09 02	−59	162	340
19	13 08	59	162	12 09	59	163	11 10	58	163	10 12	59	163	09 13	59	163	341
18	13 19	59	163	12 20	59	164	11 21	58	164	10 23	59	164	09 24	59	164	342
17	13 30	59	164	12 31	59	164	11 32	59	165	10 33	59	165	09 34	59	165	343
16	13 40	59	165	12 41	59	165	11 42	59	166	10 43	59	166	09 44	59	166	344
15	13 50	−60	166	12 50	−59	166	11 51	−59	166	10 52	−59	167	09 53	−59	167	345
14	13 59	60	167	12 59	59	167	12 00	59	167	11 01	59	167	10 02	60	168	346
13	14 07	59	168	13 08	60	168	12 08	59	168	11 09	59	168	10 10	60	169	347
12	14 15	60	169	13 15	59	169	12 16	59	169	11 17	60	169	10 17	59	169	348
11	14 22	60	170	13 22	59	170	12 23	60	170	11 23	59	170	10 24	60	170	349
10	14 29	−60	171	13 29	−60	171	12 29	−59	171	11 30	−60	171	10 30	−59	171	350
9	14 35	60	172	13 35	60	172	12 35	59	172	11 36	60	172	10 36	60	172	351
8	14 40	60	173	13 40	60	173	12 40	59	173	11 41	60	173	10 41	60	173	352
7	14 45	60	173	13 45	60	174	12 45	60	174	11 45	60	174	10 45	59	174	353
6	14 49	60	174	13 49	60	174	12 49	60	175	11 49	60	175	10 49	60	175	354
5	14 52	−60	175	13 52	−60	175	12 52	−60	175	11 52	−59	176	10 53	−60	176	355
4	14 55	60	176	13 55	60	176	12 55	60	176	11 55	60	176	10 55	60	176	356
3	14 57	60	177	13 57	60	177	12 57	60	177	11 57	60	177	10 57	60	177	357
2	14 59	60	178	13 59	60	178	12 59	60	178	11 59	60	178	10 59	60	178	358
1	15 00	60	179	14 00	60	179	13 00	60	179	12 00	60	179	11 00	60	179	359
0	15 00	−60	180	14 00	−60	180	13 00	−60	180	12 00	−60	180	11 00	−60	180	360

S. Lat. {LHA greater than 180°.......Zn=180−Z
{LHA less than 180°...........Zn=180+Z

DECLINATION (15°-29°) CONTRARY NAME TO LATITUDE

LAT 50°

N. Lat. {LHA greater than 180°........ Zn=Z; LHA less than 180°........... Zn=360–Z}

DECLINATION (0°-14°) SAME NAME AS LATITUDE

LHA	0°			1°			2°			3°			4°		
	Hc	d	Z	Hc	d	Z	Hc	d	Z	Hc	d	Z	Hc	d	Z
	° ′	′	°	° ′	′	°	° ′	′	°	° ′	′	°	° ′	′	°
0	39 00	+60	180	40 00	+60	180	41 00	+60	180	42 00	+60	180	43 00	+60	180
1	39 00	60	179	40 00	60	179	41 00	60	179	42 00	60	179	43 00	60	179
2	38 58	60	177	39 58	60	177	40 58	60	177	41 58	60	177	42 58	60	177
3	38 56	60	176	39 56	60	176	40 56	60	176	41 56	60	176	42 56	60	176
4	38 53	60	175	39 53	60	175	40 53	60	175	41 53	60	175	42 53	60	175
5	38 49	+60	174	39 49	+60	174	40 49	+60	173	41 49	+60	173	42 49	+60	173
6	38 45	60	172	39 45	59	172	40 44	60	172	41 44	60	172	42 44	60	172
7	38 39	60	171	39 39	60	171	40 39	59	171	41 38	60	171	42 38	60	171
8	38 33	60	170	39 33	59	170	40 32	60	170	41 32	59	169	42 31	60	169
9	38 26	59	169	39 25	60	168	40 25	59	168	41 24	60	168	42 24	59	168
10	38 18	+59	167	39 17	+60	167	40 17	+59	167	41 16	+59	167	42 15	+60	167
11	38 09	59	166	39 08	60	166	40 08	59	166	41 07	59	165	42 06	59	165
12	38 00	59	165	38 59	59	165	39 58	59	164	40 57	59	164	41 56	59	164
13	37 49	59	164	38 48	59	163	39 47	59	163	40 46	59	163	41 45	59	163
14	37 38	59	162	38 37	59	162	39 36	59	162	40 35	58	162	41 33	59	161
15	37 26	+59	161	38 25	+59	161	39 24	+58	160	40 22	+59	160	41 21	+58	160
16	37 14	58	160	38 12	59	160	39 11	58	159	40 09	58	159	41 07	59	159
17	37 00	58	159	37 58	59	158	38 57	58	158	39 55	58	158	40 53	58	157
18	36 46	58	157	37 44	58	157	38 42	58	157	39 40	58	156	40 38	58	156
19	36 31	58	156	37 29	58	156	38 27	58	156	39 25	58	155	40 23	57	155
20	36 15	+58	155	37 13	+58	155	38 11	+58	154	39 09	+57	154	40 06	+58	154
21	35 59	58	154	36 57	57	153	37 54	58	153	38 52	57	153	39 49	57	152
22	35 42	57	153	36 39	58	152	37 37	57	152	38 34	57	151	39 31	57	151
23	35 24	57	151	36 21	57	151	37 18	57	151	38 15	57	150	39 12	57	150
24	35 06	57	150	36 03	56	150	36 59	57	149	37 56	57	149	38 53	57	149
25	34 47	+56	149	35 43	+57	149	36 40	+57	148	37 37	+56	148	38 33	+56	147
26	34 27	56	148	35 23	57	148	36 20	56	147	37 16	56	147	38 12	56	146
27	34 06	57	147	35 03	56	146	35 59	56	146	36 55	56	146	37 51	56	145
28	33 45	56	146	34 41	56	145	35 37	56	145	36 33	56	144	37 29	56	144
29	33 24	56	145	34 20	55	144	35 15	56	144	36 11	55	143	37 06	56	143
30	33 02	+55	143	33 57	+56	143	34 53	+55	143	35 48	+55	142	36 43	+55	142
31	32 39	55	142	33 34	55	142	34 29	55	141	35 24	55	141	36 19	55	140
32	32 15	55	141	33 10	55	141	34 05	55	140	35 00	55	140	35 55	55	139
33	31 51	55	140	32 46	55	140	33 41	55	139	34 36	54	139	35 30	54	138
34	31 27	55	139	32 22	54	139	33 16	54	138	34 10	55	138	35 05	54	137
35	31 02	+54	138	31 56	+55	138	32 51	+54	137	33 45	+54	137	34 39	+53	136
36	30 36	55	137	31 31	54	136	32 25	53	136	33 18	54	135	34 12	54	135
37	30 10	54	136	31 04	54	135	31 58	54	135	32 52	53	134	33 45	53	134
38	29 44	53	135	30 37	54	134	31 31	53	134	32 24	54	133	33 18	53	133
39	29 17	53	134	30 10	53	133	31 03	54	133	31 57	53	132	32 50	52	132
40	28 49	+54	133	29 43	+53	132	30 36	+52	132	31 28	+53	131	32 21	+53	131
41	28 21	53	132	29 14	53	131	30 07	53	131	31 00	52	130	31 52	53	130
42	27 53	53	131	28 46	52	130	29 38	53	130	30 31	52	129	31 23	52	129
43	27 24	53	130	28 17	52	129	29 09	52	129	30 01	52	128	30 53	52	128
44	26 55	52	129	27 47	52	128	28 39	52	128	29 31	52	127	30 23	52	127
45	26 25	+52	128	27 17	+52	127	28 09	+52	127	29 01	+52	126	29 53	+51	126
46	25 55	52	127	26 47	52	126	27 39	51	126	28 30	52	125	29 22	51	125
47	25 25	52	126	26 17	51	125	27 08	51	125	27 59	51	124	28 50	51	124
48	24 54	52	125	25 46	51	124	26 37	51	124	27 28	51	123	28 19	51	123
49	24 23	51	124	25 14	51	124	26 05	51	123	26 56	51	122	27 47	50	122
50	23 52	+51	123	24 43	+50	123	25 33	+51	122	26 24	+51	121	27 15	+50	121
51	23 20	51	122	24 11	50	122	25 01	51	121	25 52	50	120	26 42	50	120
52	22 48	50	121	23 38	51	121	24 29	50	120	25 19	50	120	26 09	50	119
53	22 15	51	120	23 06	50	120	23 56	50	119	24 46	50	119	25 36	50	118
54	21 43	50	119	22 33	50	119	23 23	50	118	24 13	49	118	25 02	50	117
55	21 10	+50	119	22 00	+49	118	22 49	+50	117	23 39	+50	117	24 29	+49	116
56	20 36	50	118	21 26	50	117	22 16	49	117	23 05	50	116	23 55	49	115
57	20 03	49	117	20 52	50	116	21 42	49	116	22 31	49	115	23 20	49	114
58	19 29	49	116	20 18	50	115	21 08	49	115	21 57	49	114	22 46	49	113
59	18 55	49	115	19 44	49	114	20 33	49	114	21 22	49	113	22 11	49	113
60	18 20	+50	114	19 10	+48	114	19 58	+49	113	20 47	+49	112	21 36	+49	112
61	17 46	49	113	18 35	49	113	19 24	48	112	20 12	49	112	21 01	48	111
62	17 11	49	113	18 00	49	112	18 49	48	111	19 37	48	111	20 25	49	110
63	16 36	49	112	17 25	48	111	18 13	49	110	19 02	48	110	19 50	48	109
64	16 01	48	111	16 49	49	110	17 38	48	110	18 26	48	109	19 14	48	108
65	15 25	+49	110	16 14	+48	109	17 02	+48	109	17 50	+48	108	18 38	+48	107
66	14 50	48	109	15 38	48	109	16 26	48	108	17 14	48	107	18 02	48	107
67	14 14	48	108	15 02	48	108	15 50	48	107	16 38	48	106	17 26	47	106
68	13 38	48	107	14 26	48	107	15 14	48	106	16 02	47	106	16 49	48	105
69	13 02	48	107	13 50	48	106	14 38	47	105	15 25	48	105	16 13	47	104

LHA	5°			6°			7°			8°			9°		
	Hc	d	Z	Hc	d	Z	Hc	d	Z	Hc	d	Z	Hc	d	Z
	° ′	′	°	° ′	′	°	° ′	′	°	° ′	′	°	° ′	′	°
0	44 00	+60	180	45 00	+60	180	46 00	+60	180	47 00	+60	180	48 00	+60	180
1	44 00	60	179	45 00	60	179	46 00	60	179	47 00	60	179	48 00	60	179
2	43 58	60	177	44 58	60	177	45 58	60	177	46 58	60	177	47 58	60	177
3	43 56	60	176	44 56	60	176	45 56	60	176	46 56	60	176	47 56	60	176
4	43 53	60	175	44 53	60	174	45 53	59	174	46 52	60	174	47 52	60	174
5	43 49	+59	173	44 48	+60	173	45 48	+60	173	46 48	+60	173	47 48	+60	173
6	43 44	59	172	44 43	60	172	45 43	60	172	46 43	60	171	47 43	59	171
7	43 38	59	170	44 37	60	170	45 37	60	170	46 37	59	170	47 36	60	170
8	43 31	60	169	44 31	59	169	45 30	60	169	46 30	59	169	47 29	60	168
9	43 23	60	168	44 23	59	167	45 22	60	167	46 22	59	167	47 21	59	167
10	43 15	+59	166	44 14	+59	166	45 13	+60	166	46 13	+59	166	47 12	+59	165
11	43 05	60	165	44 05	59	165	45 04	59	164	46 03	59	164	47 02	59	164
12	42 55	59	164	43 54	59	163	44 53	59	163	45 52	59	163	46 51	59	163
13	42 44	59	162	43 43	59	162	44 42	59	162	45 41	58	161	46 39	59	161
14	42 32	59	161	43 31	58	161	44 29	59	160	45 28	59	160	46 27	58	160
15	42 19	+59	160	43 18	+58	159	44 16	+59	159	45 15	+58	159	46 13	+58	158
16	42 06	58	158	43 04	58	158	44 02	59	158	45 01	58	157	45 59	58	157
17	41 51	59	157	42 50	58	157	43 48	58	156	44 46	57	156	45 43	58	156
18	41 36	58	156	42 34	58	155	43 32	58	155	44 30	57	155	45 27	58	154
19	41 20	58	154	42 18	58	154	43 16	57	154	44 13	58	153	45 11	57	153
20	41 04	+57	153	42 01	+58	153	42 59	+57	152	43 56	+57	152	44 53	+57	152
21	40 46	57	152	41 43	58	152	42 41	57	151	43 38	57	151	44 35	56	150
22	40 28	57	151	41 25	57	150	42 22	57	150	43 19	57	149	44 16	56	149
23	40 09	57	149	41 06	57	149	42 03	56	149	42 59	57	148	43 56	56	148
24	39 50	56	148	40 46	57	148	41 43	56	147	42 39	56	147	43 35	56	146
25	39 29	+57	147	40 26	+56	147	41 22	+56	146	42 18	+56	146	43 14	+56	145
26	39 08	56	146	40 04	56	145	41 00	56	145	41 56	56	144	42 52	55	144
27	38 47	56	145	39 43	55	144	40 38	56	144	41 34	55	143	42 29	55	143
28	38 25	55	143	39 20	56	143	40 16	55	142	41 11	55	142	42 06	55	141
29	38 02	55	142	38 57	55	142	39 52	55	141	40 47	55	141	41 42	55	140
30	37 38	+55	141	38 33	+55	141	39 28	+55	140	40 23	+54	140	41 17	+55	139
31	37 14	55	140	38 09	55	139	39 04	54	139	39 58	54	138	40 52	54	138
32	36 50	54	139	37 44	54	138	38 38	55	138	39 33	54	137	40 27	53	137
33	36 24	55	138	37 19	54	137	38 13	54	137	39 07	53	136	40 00	54	135
34	35 59	54	137	36 53	54	136	37 47	53	135	38 40	54	135	39 34	53	134
35	35 32	+54	135	36 26	+54	135	37 20	+53	134	38 13	+53	134	39 06	+53	133
36	35 06	53	134	35 59	53	134	36 52	54	133	37 46	52	133	38 38	53	132
37	34 38	54	133	35 32	53	133	36 25	53	132	37 18	52	132	38 10	53	131
38	34 11	53	132	35 04	52	132	35 56	53	131	36 49	52	130	37 41	53	130
39	33 42	53	131	34 35	53	131	35 28	52	130	36 20	52	129	37 12	52	129
40	33 14	+52	130	34 06	+52	130	34 58	+53	129	35 51	+51	128	36 42	+52	128
41	32 45	52	129	33 37	52	128	34 29	52	128	35 21	51	127	36 12	52	127
42	32 15	52	128	33 07	52	127	33 59	51	127	34 50	52	126	35 42	51	126
43	31 45	52	127	32 37	51	126	33 28	52	126	34 20	51	125	35 11	51	125
44	31 15	51	126	32 06	52	125	32 58	51	125	33 49	51	124	34 40	50	124
45	30 44	+51	125	31 35	+51	124	32 26	+51	124	33 17	+51	123	34 08	+50	123
46	30 13	51	124	31 04	51	123	31 55	50	123	32 45	51	122	33 36	50	122
47	29 41	51	123	30 32	51	122	31 23	50	122	32 13	51	121	33 04	50	121
48	29 10	50	122	30 00	51	121	30 51	50	121	31 41	50	120	32 31	50	120
49	28 37	51	121	29 28	50	121	30 18	50	120	31 08	50	119	31 58	49	119
50	28 05	+50	120	28 55	+50	120	29 45	+50	119	30 35	+49	118	31 24	+50	118
51	27 32	50	119	28 22	50	119	29 12	49	118	30 01	50	117	30 51	49	117
52	26 59	50	118	27 49	49	118	28 38	50	117	29 28	49	116	30 17	49	116
53	26 26	49	117	27 15	50	117	28 05	49	116	28 54	49	115	29 43	49	115
54	25 52	49	116	26 41	49	116	27 30	50	115	28 20	48	115	29 08	49	114
55	25 18	+49	116	26 07	+49	115	26 56	+49	114	27 45	+49	114	28 34	+48	113
56	24 44	49	115	25 33	49	114	26 22	48	113	27 10	49	113	27 59	48	112
57	24 09	49	114	24 58	49	113	25 47	48	112	26 35	49	112	27 24	48	111
58	23 35	48	113	24 23	49	112	25 12	48	112	26 00	48	111	26 48	48	110
59	23 00	48	112	23 48	49	111	24 37	48	111	25 25	48	110	26 13	48	109
60	22 25	+48	111	23 13	+48	110	24 01	+48	110	24 49	+48	109	25 37	+48	108
61	21 49	48	110	22 37	49	110	23 26	47	109	24 13	48	108	25 01	48	108
62	21 14	48	109	22 02	48	109	22 50	47	108	23 37	48	107	24 25	48	107
63	20 38	48	109	21 26	48	108	22 14	47	107	23 01	48	107	23 49	47	106
64	20 02	48	108	20 50	48	107	21 38	47	106	22 25	47	106	23 12	48	105
65	19 26	+48	107	20 14	+47	106	21 01	+48	106	21 49	+47	105	22 36	+47	104
66	18 50	47	106	19 37	48	105	20 25	47	105	21 12	47	104	21 59	47	103
67	18 13	48	105	19 01	47	105	19 48	47	104	20 35	47	103	21 22	47	103
68	17 37	47	104	18 24	47	104	19 11	48	103	19 59	47	102	20 46	46	102
69	17 00	47	104	17 47	48	103	18 35	47	102	19 22	46	102	20 08	47	101

LHA	10°			11°			12°			13°			14°			LHA
	Hc	d	Z	Hc	d	Z	Hc	d	Z	Hc	d	Z	Hc	d	Z	
	° ′	′	°	° ′	′	°	° ′	′	°	° ′	′	°	° ′	′	°	
0	49 00	+60	180	50 00	+60	180	51 00	+60	180	52 00	+60	180	53 00	+60	180	360
1	49 00	60	179	50 00	60	179	51 00	60	178	52 00	60	178	53 00	60	178	359
2	48 58	60	177	49 58	60	177	50 58	60	177	51 58	60	177	52 58	60	177	358
3	48 56	60	176	49 56	59	175	50 55	60	175	51 55	60	175	52 55	60	175	357
4	48 52	60	174	49 52	60	174	50 52	60	174	51 52	60	174	52 52	59	174	356
5	48 48	+60	173	49 48	+59	172	50 47	+60	172	51 47	+60	172	52 47	+60	172	355
6	48 42	60	171	49 42	60	171	50 42	59	171	51 41	60	171	52 41	60	170	354
7	48 36	60	170	49 36	59	169	50 35	60	169	51 35	59	169	52 34	60	169	353
8	48 29	59	168	49 28	60	168	50 28	59	168	51 27	59	167	52 26	60	167	352
9	48 20	60	167	49 20	59	166	50 19	59	166	51 18	59	166	52 17	60	166	351
10	48 11	+59	165	49 10	+59	165	50 09	+60	165	51 09	+59	164	52 08	+59	164	350
11	48 01	59	164	49 00	59	163	49 59	59	163	50 58	59	163	51 57	59	163	349
12	47 50	59	162	48 49	59	162	49 48	58	162	50 46	59	161	51 45	59	161	348
13	47 38	59	161	48 37	58	161	49 35	59	160	50 34	58	160	51 32	59	160	347
14	47 25	59	159	48 24	58	159	49 22	58	159	50 20	58	158	51 18	59	158	346
15	47 11	+59	158	48 10	+58	158	49 08	+58	157	50 06	+58	157	51 04	+58	156	345
16	46 57	58	157	47 55	58	156	48 53	58	156	49 51	57	155	50 48	58	155	344
17	46 41	58	155	47 39	58	155	48 37	57	154	49 34	58	154	50 32	57	154	343
18	46 25	58	154	47 23	57	153	48 20	57	153	49 17	58	153	50 15	57	152	342
19	46 08	57	152	47 05	57	152	48 02	57	152	48 59	57	151	49 56	57	151	341
20	45 50	+57	151	46 47	+57	151	47 44	+57	150	48 41	+56	150	49 37	+57	149	340
21	45 31	57	150	46 28	57	149	47 25	56	149	48 21	57	148	49 18	56	148	339
22	45 12	57	148	46 09	56	148	47 05	56	147	48 01	56	147	48 57	56	146	338
23	44 52	56	147	45 48	56	147	46 44	56	146	47 40	56	146	48 36	56	145	337
24	44 31	56	146	45 27	56	145	46 23	55	145	47 18	56	144	48 14	55	144	336
25	44 10	+55	145	45 05	+56	144	46 01	+55	144	46 56	+55	143	47 51	+55	142	335
26	43 47	56	143	44 43	55	143	45 38	55	142	46 33	55	142	47 28	54	141	334
27	43 24	55	142	44 19	55	142	45 14	55	141	46 09	55	140	47 04	54	140	333
28	43 01	55	141	43 56	54	140	44 50	55	140	45 45	54	139	46 39	54	138	332
29	42 37	54	140	43 31	55	139	44 26	54	138	45 20	54	138	46 14	53	137	331
30	42 12	+54	138	43 06	+54	138	44 00	+54	137	44 54	+54	137	45 48	+53	136	330
31	41 46	54	137	42 40	54	137	43 34	54	136	44 28	53	135	45 21	53	135	329
32	41 20	54	136	42 14	54	135	43 08	53	135	44 01	53	134	44 54	53	134	328
33	40 54	53	135	41 47	54	134	42 41	53	134	43 34	52	133	44 26	53	132	327
34	40 27	53	134	41 20	53	133	42 13	53	132	43 06	52	132	43 58	52	131	326
35	39 59	+53	133	40 52	+53	132	41 45	+52	131	42 37	+52	131	43 29	+52	130	325
36	39 31	53	131	40 24	52	131	41 16	52	130	42 08	52	129	43 00	52	129	324
37	39 03	52	130	39 55	52	130	40 47	52	129	41 39	51	128	42 30	52	128	323
38	38 34	52	129	39 26	51	129	40 17	52	128	41 09	51	127	42 00	51	127	322
39	38 04	52	128	38 56	51	127	39 47	52	127	40 39	51	126	41 30	51	125	321
40	37 34	+52	127	38 26	+51	126	39 17	+51	126	40 08	+51	125	40 59	+50	124	320
41	37 04	51	126	37 55	51	125	38 46	51	125	39 37	50	124	40 27	51	123	319
42	36 33	51	125	37 24	51	124	38 15	50	124	39 05	51	123	39 56	50	122	318
43	36 02	51	124	36 53	50	123	37 43	50	123	38 33	50	122	39 23	50	121	317
44	35 30	51	123	36 21	50	122	37 11	50	122	38 01	50	121	38 51	49	120	316
45	34 58	+51	122	35 49	+50	121	36 39	+50	121	37 29	+49	120	38 18	+49	119	315
46	34 26	50	121	35 16	50	120	36 06	50	119	36 56	49	119	37 45	49	118	314
47	33 54	49	120	34 43	50	119	35 33	49	118	36 22	49	118	37 11	49	117	313
48	33 21	49	119	34 10	50	118	35 00	49	118	35 49	49	117	36 38	48	116	312
49	32 47	50	118	33 37	49	117	34 26	49	117	35 15	49	116	36 04	48	115	311
50	32 14	+49	117	33 03	+49	116	33 52	+49	116	34 41	+48	115	35 29	+48	114	310
51	31 40	49	116	32 29	49	115	33 18	48	115	34 06	49	114	34 55	48	113	309
52	31 06	49	115	31 55	48	114	32 43	49	114	33 32	48	113	34 20	48	112	308
53	30 32	48	114	31 20	49	113	32 09	48	113	32 57	48	112	33 45	47	111	307
54	29 57	48	113	30 45	49	113	31 34	48	112	32 22	47	111	33 09	48	110	306
55	29 22	+48	112	30 10	+49	112	30 59	+47	111	31 46	+48	110	32 34	+47	109	305
56	28 47	48	111	29 35	48	111	30 23	48	110	31 11	47	109	31 58	47	109	304
57	28 12	48	110	29 00	48	110	29 48	47	109	30 35	47	108	31 22	47	108	303
58	27 36	48	110	28 24	48	109	29 12	47	108	29 59	47	107	30 46	47	107	302
59	27 01	47	109	27 48	48	108	28 36	47	107	29 23	47	107	30 10	47	106	301
60	26 25	+47	108	27 12	+48	107	28 00	+47	106	28 47	+47	106	29 34	+46	105	300
61	25 49	47	107	26 36	47	106	27 23	47	106	28 10	47	105	28 57	47	104	299
62	25 13	47	106	26 00	47	105	26 47	47	105	27 34	46	104	28 20	47	103	298
63	24 36	47	105	25 23	47	105	26 10	47	104	26 57	47	103	27 44	46	102	297
64	24 00	47	104	24 47	47	104	25 34	46	103	26 20	47	102	27 07	46	102	296
65	23 23	+47	104	24 10	+47	103	24 57	+46	102	25 43	+47	101	26 30	+46	101	295
66	22 46	47	103	23 33	47	102	24 20	46	101	25 06	46	101	25 52	46	100	294
67	22 09	47	102	22 56	47	101	23 43	46	101	24 29	46	100	25 15	46	99	293
68	21 32	47	101	22 19	46	100	23 05	47	100	23 52	46	99	24 38	46	98	292
69	20 55	47	100	21 42	46	100	22 28	46	99	23 14	46	98	24 00	46	97	291

S. Lat. {LHA greater than 180°....... Zn=180–Z; LHA less than 180°.......... Zn=180+Z}

DECLINATION (0°-14°) SAME NAME AS LATITUDE

LAT 51°

N. Lat. {LHA greater than 180°........ Zn=Z; LHA less than 180°........... Zn=360−Z}

DECLINATION (0°-14°) SAME NAME AS LATITUDE

LHA	0° Hc	d	Z	1° Hc	d	Z	2° Hc	d	Z	3° Hc	d	Z	4° Hc	d	Z
	° ′	′	°	° ′	′	°	° ′	′	°	° ′	′	°	° ′	′	°
70	12 26	+48	106	13 14	+47	105	14 01	+48	105	14 49	+47	104	15 36	+47	103
71	11 49	48	105	12 37	48	104	13 25	47	104	14 12	47	103	14 59	47	103
72	11 13	47	104	12 00	48	104	12 48	47	103	13 35	47	102	14 22	47	102
73	10 36	48	103	11 24	47	103	12 11	47	102	12 58	47	102	13 45	47	101
74	09 59	48	103	10 47	47	102	11 34	47	101	12 21	47	101	13 08	47	100
75	09 22	+48	102	10 10	+47	101	10 57	+47	101	11 44	+47	100	12 31	+47	99
76	08 45	48	101	09 33	47	100	10 20	47	100	11 07	47	99	11 54	46	98
77	08 08	47	100	08 55	47	100	09 42	47	99	10 29	47	98	11 16	47	98
78	07 31	47	99	08 18	47	99	09 05	47	98	09 52	47	98	10 39	47	97
79	06 54	47	99	07 41	47	98	08 28	47	97	09 15	46	97	10 01	47	96
80	06 16	+47	98	07 03	+47	97	07 50	+47	97	08 37	+47	96	09 24	+46	95
81	05 39	47	97	06 26	47	96	07 13	46	96	07 59	47	95	08 46	47	95
82	05 02	46	96	05 48	47	96	06 35	47	95	07 22	46	94	08 08	47	94
83	04 24	47	95	05 11	46	95	05 57	47	94	06 44	47	94	07 31	46	93
84	03 46	47	95	04 33	47	94	05 20	46	93	06 06	47	93	06 53	47	92
85	03 09	+46	94	03 55	+47	93	04 42	+47	93	05 29	+46	92	06 15	+47	91
86	02 31	47	93	03 18	46	92	04 04	47	92	04 51	47	91	05 38	46	91
87	01 53	47	92	02 40	47	92	03 27	46	91	04 13	47	90	05 00	46	90
88	01 16	46	92	02 02	47	91	02 49	46	90	03 35	47	90	04 22	47	89
89	00 38	46	91	01 24	47	90	02 11	47	90	02 58	46	89	03 44	47	88
90	00 00	+47	90	00 47	+46	89	01 33	+47	89	02 20	+46	88	03 06	+47	87
91	-0 38	47	89	00 09	46	89	00 55	47	88	01 42	47	87	02 29	46	87
92	-1 16	47	88	-0 29	46	88	00 17	47	87	01 04	47	87	01 51	47	86
93	-1 53	46	88	-1 07	47	87	-0 20	47	86	00 27	46	86	01 13	47	85
94	-2 31	47	87	-1 44	46	86	-0 58	47	86	-0 11	47	85	00 36	47	84
95	-3 09	+47	86	-2 22	+47	85	-1 35	+47	85	-0 48	+46	84	-0 02	+47	84
96	-3 46	46	85	-3 00	47	85	-2 13	47	84	-1 26	47	83	-0 39	47	83
97	-4 24	47	85	-3 37	47	84	-2 50	46	83	-2 04	47	83	-1 17	47	82
98	-5 02	47	84	-4 15	47	83	-3 28	47	83	-2 41	47	82	-1 54	47	81
99	-5 39	47	83	-4 52	47	82	-4 05	47	82	-3 18	47	81	-2 31	47	80
100				-5 30	+47	82	-4 43	+47	81	-3 56	+48	80	-3 08	+47	80
101				-6 07	47	81	-5 20	47	80	-4 33	47	80	-3 46	48	79
102							-5 57	47	79	-5 10	47	79	-4 23	48	78
103										-5 47	48	78	-4 59	47	77
104													-5 36	47	77
105													-6 13	+48	76

LHA	5° Hc	d	Z	6° Hc	d	Z	7° Hc	d	Z	8° Hc	d	Z	9° Hc	d	Z
	° ′	′	°	° ′	′	°	° ′	′	°	° ′	′	°	° ′	′	°
70	16 23	+48	103	17 11	+47	102	17 58	+47	101	18 45	+46	101	19 31	+47	100
71	15 46	48	102	16 34	47	101	17 21	46	101	18 07	47	100	18 54	47	99
72	15 09	47	101	15 56	47	100	16 43	47	100	17 30	47	99	18 17	46	98
73	14 32	47	100	15 19	47	100	16 06	47	99	16 53	46	98	17 39	47	98
74	13 55	47	99	14 42	47	99	15 29	46	98	16 15	47	98	17 02	46	97
75	13 18	+47	99	14 05	+46	98	14 51	+47	97	15 38	+46	97	16 24	+47	96
76	12 40	47	98	13 27	47	97	14 14	46	97	15 00	47	96	15 47	46	95
77	12 03	47	97	12 50	46	96	13 36	47	96	14 23	46	95	15 09	47	94
78	11 26	46	96	12 12	47	96	12 59	46	95	13 45	47	94	14 32	46	94
79	10 48	47	95	11 35	46	95	12 21	47	94	13 08	46	94	13 54	46	93
80	10 10	+47	95	10 57	+46	94	11 43	+47	93	12 30	+46	93	13 16	+46	92
81	09 33	46	94	10 19	47	93	11 06	46	93	11 52	46	92	12 38	47	91
82	08 55	47	93	09 42	46	92	10 28	46	92	11 14	47	91	12 01	46	91
83	08 17	47	92	09 04	46	92	09 50	47	91	10 37	46	90	11 23	46	90
84	07 40	46	92	08 26	46	91	09 12	47	90	09 59	46	90	10 45	46	89
85	07 02	+46	91	07 48	+47	90	08 35	+46	90	09 21	+46	89	10 07	+47	88
86	06 24	47	90	07 11	46	89	07 57	46	89	08 43	47	88	09 30	46	87
87	05 46	47	89	06 33	46	89	07 19	47	88	08 06	46	87	08 52	46	87
88	05 09	46	88	05 55	46	88	06 41	47	87	07 28	46	87	08 14	47	86
89	04 31	46	88	05 17	47	87	06 04	46	86	06 50	47	86	07 37	46	85
90	03 53	+47	87	04 40	+46	86	05 26	+47	86	06 13	+46	85	06 59	+46	84
91	03 15	47	86	04 02	46	85	04 48	47	85	05 35	46	84	06 21	47	84
92	02 38	46	85	03 24	47	85	04 11	46	84	04 57	47	83	05 44	46	83
93	02 00	47	84	02 47	46	84	03 33	47	83	04 20	47	83	05 07	46	82
94	01 23	46	84	02 09	47	83	02 56	47	82	03 43	46	82	04 29	47	81
95	00 45	+47	83	01 32	+46	82	02 18	+47	82	03 05	+47	81	03 52	+47	80
96	00 08	46	82	00 54	47	82	01 41	47	81	02 28	47	80	03 15	46	80
97	-0 30	47	81	00 17	47	81	01 04	47	80	01 51	47	80	02 38	46	79
98	-1 07	47	81	-0 20	47	80	00 27	47	79	01 14	47	79	02 01	46	78
99	-1 44	47	80	-0 57	47	79	-0 10	47	79	00 37	47	78	01 24	47	77
100	-2 21	+47	79	-1 34	+47	78	-0 47	+47	78	00 00	+47	77	00 47	+47	77
101	-2 58	47	78	-2 11	47	78	-1 24	47	77	-0 37	47	76	00 10	47	76
102	-3 35	47	77	-2 48	47	77	-2 01	47	76	-1 14	48	76	-0 26	47	75
103	-4 12	47	77	-3 25	47	76	-2 38	48	75	-1 50	47	75	-1 03	48	74
104	-4 49	48	76	-4 01	47	75	-3 14	47	75	-2 27	48	74	-1 39	47	73
105	-5 25	+47	75	-4 38	+48	74	-3 50	+47	74	-3 03	+48	73	-2 15	+47	73
106	-6 02	48	74	-5 14	47	74	-4 27	48	73	-3 39	48	72	-2 51	48	72
107				-5 50	47	73	-5 03	48	72	-4 15	48	72	-3 27	48	71
108							-5 39	48	71	-4 51	48	71	-4 03	48	70
109										-5 26	48	70	-4 38	48	69
110										-6 02	+49	69	-5 13	+48	69
111													-5 48	48	68

LHA	10° Hc	d	Z	11° Hc	d	Z	12° Hc	d	Z	13° Hc	d	Z	14° Hc	d	Z	LHA
	° ′	′	°	° ′	′	°	° ′	′	°	° ′	′	°	° ′	′	°	
70	20 18	+46	99	21 04	+47	99	21 51	+46	98	22 37	+46	97	23 23	+46	97	290
71	19 41	46	99	20 27	46	98	21 13	46	97	21 59	46	97	22 45	46	96	289
72	19 03	47	98	19 50	46	97	20 36	46	96	21 22	46	96	22 08	46	95	288
73	18 26	46	97	19 12	46	96	19 58	46	96	20 44	46	95	21 30	46	94	287
74	17 48	47	96	18 35	46	96	19 21	46	95	20 07	46	94	20 53	45	93	286
75	17 11	+46	95	17 57	+46	95	18 43	+46	94	19 29	+46	93	20 15	+45	93	285
76	16 33	46	95	17 19	46	94	18 05	46	93	18 51	46	93	19 37	46	92	284
77	15 56	46	94	16 42	46	93	17 28	46	92	18 14	45	92	18 59	46	91	283
78	15 18	46	93	16 04	46	92	16 50	46	92	17 36	46	91	18 22	45	90	282
79	14 40	46	92	15 26	46	92	16 12	46	91	16 58	46	90	17 44	45	90	281
80	14 02	+46	91	14 48	+46	91	15 34	+46	90	16 20	+46	89	17 06	+46	89	280
81	13 25	46	91	14 11	46	90	14 57	46	89	15 43	45	89	16 28	46	88	279
82	12 47	46	90	13 33	46	89	14 19	46	89	15 05	46	88	15 51	45	87	278
83	12 09	46	89	12 55	46	88	13 41	46	88	14 27	46	87	15 13	46	86	277
84	11 31	46	88	12 17	46	88	13 03	46	87	13 49	46	86	14 35	46	86	276
85	10 54	+46	88	11 40	+46	87	12 26	+46	86	13 12	+46	86	13 58	+45	85	275
86	10 16	46	87	11 02	46	86	11 48	46	85	12 34	46	85	13 20	46	84	274
87	09 38	46	86	10 24	47	85	11 11	46	85	11 57	45	84	12 42	46	83	273
88	09 01	46	85	09 47	46	85	10 33	46	84	11 19	46	83	12 05	46	83	272
89	08 23	46	84	09 09	46	84	09 55	47	83	10 42	46	83	11 28	46	82	271
90	07 45	+47	84	08 32	+46	83	09 18	+46	82	10 04	+46	82	10 50	+46	81	270
91	07 08	46	83	07 54	47	82	08 41	46	82	09 27	46	81	10 13	46	80	269
92	06 30	47	82	07 17	46	82	08 03	47	81	08 50	46	80	09 36	46	80	268
93	05 53	47	81	06 40	46	81	07 26	46	80	08 12	47	80	08 59	46	79	267
94	05 16	46	81	06 02	47	80	06 49	46	79	07 35	47	79	08 22	46	78	266
95	04 39	+46	80	05 25	+47	79	06 12	+46	79	06 58	+47	78	07 45	+46	77	265
96	04 01	47	79	04 48	47	78	05 35	46	78	06 21	47	77	07 08	47	77	264
97	03 24	47	78	04 11	47	78	04 58	47	77	05 45	46	76	06 31	47	76	263
98	02 47	47	77	03 34	47	77	04 21	47	76	05 08	47	76	05 55	47	75	262
99	02 11	47	77	02 58	47	76	03 45	47	75	04 32	46	75	05 18	47	74	261
100	01 34	+47	76	02 21	+47	75	03 08	+47	75	03 55	+47	74	04 42	+47	74	260
101	00 57	48	75	01 45	47	75	02 32	47	74	03 19	47	73	04 06	47	73	259
102	00 21	47	74	01 08	48	74	01 56	47	73	02 43	47	72	03 30	47	72	258
103	-0 15	47	74	00 32	48	73	01 20	47	72	02 07	47	72	02 54	48	71	257
104	-0 52	48	73	-0 04	48	72	00 44	47	72	01 31	48	71	02 19	47	70	256
105	-1 28	+48	72	-0 40	+48	71	00 08	+47	71	00 55	+48	70	01 43	+48	70	255
106	-2 03	47	71	-1 16	48	71	-0 28	48	70	00 20	48	69	01 08	47	69	254
107	-2 39	48	71	-1 51	48	70	-1 03	48	69	-0 15	48	69	00 33	47	68	253
108	-3 15	48	70	-2 27	49	69	-1 38	48	68	-0 50	48	68	-0 02	48	67	252
109	-3 50	48	69	-3 02	48	68	-2 14	49	68	-1 25	48	67	-0 37	48	66	251
110	-4 25	+48	68	-3 37	+49	68	-2 48	+48	67	-2 00	+48	66	-1 12	+49	66	250
111	-5 00	48	67	-4 12	49	67	-3 23	48	66	-2 35	49	65	-1 46	49	65	249
112	-5 35	49	67	-4 46	49	66	-3 57	48	65	-3 09	49	65	-2 20	49	64	248
113				-5 21	49	65	-4 32	49	65	-3 43	49	64	-2 54	49	63	247
114				-5 55	49	64	-5 06	49	64	-4 17	49	63	-3 28	49	63	246
115							-5 39	+49	63	-4 50	+49	62	-4 01	+49	62	245
116										-5 24	50	62	-4 34	49	61	244
117										-5 57	50	61	-5 07	50	60	243
118													-5 40	50	59	242

S. Lat. {LHA greater than 180°........ Zn=180−Z; LHA less than 180°........... Zn=180+Z}

DECLINATION (0°-14°) SAME NAME AS LATITUDE

LAT 51°

N. Lat. {LHA greater than 180°....... Zn=Z; LHA less than 180°........... Zn=360−Z}

DECLINATION (0°-14°) CONTRARY NAME TO LATITUDE

LHA	0° Hc	0° d	0° Z	1° Hc	1° d	1° Z	2° Hc	2° d	2° Z	3° Hc	3° d	3° Z	4° Hc	4° d	4° Z
	° ′	′	°	° ′	′	°	° ′	′	°	° ′	′	°	° ′	′	°
99	-5 39	47	83	261											
98	-5 02	46	84	-5 48	47	84	262								
97	-4 24	47	85	-5 11	46	85	-5 57	47	86	263					
96	-3 46	47	85	-4 33	47	86	-5 20	46	87	-6 06	47	87	264		
95	-3 09	-46	86	-3 55	-47	87	-4 42	-47	87	-5 29	-46	88	265		
94	-2 31	47	87	-3 18	46	88	-4 04	47	88	-4 51	47	89	-5 38	46	89
93	-1 53	47	88	-2 40	47	88	-3 27	46	89	-4 13	47	90	-5 00	46	90
92	-1 16	46	88	-2 02	47	89	-2 49	46	90	-3 35	47	90	-4 22	47	91
91	-0 38	46	89	-1 24	47	90	-2 11	47	90	-2 58	46	91	-3 44	47	92
90	00 00	-47	90	-0 47	-46	91	-1 33	-47	91	-2 20	-46	92	-3 06	-47	93
89	00 38	47	91	-0 09	46	91	-0 55	47	92	-1 42	47	93	-2 29	46	93
88	01 16	47	92	00 29	46	92	-0 17	47	93	-1 04	47	93	-1 51	47	94
87	01 53	46	92	01 07	47	93	00 20	47	94	-0 27	46	94	-1 13	47	95
86	02 31	47	93	01 44	46	94	00 58	47	94	00 11	47	95	-0 36	47	96
85	03 09	-47	94	02 22	-47	95	01 35	-47	95	00 48	-46	96	00 02	-47	96
84	03 46	46	95	03 00	47	95	02 13	47	96	01 26	47	97	00 39	47	97
83	04 24	47	95	03 37	47	96	02 50	46	97	02 04	47	97	01 17	47	98
82	05 02	47	96	04 15	47	97	03 28	47	97	02 41	47	98	01 54	47	99
81	05 39	47	97	04 52	47	98	04 05	47	98	03 18	47	99	02 31	47	100
80	06 16	-46	98	05 30	-47	98	04 43	-47	99	03 56	-48	100	03 08	-47	100
79	06 54	47	99	06 07	47	99	05 20	47	100	04 33	47	100	03 46	48	101
78	07 31	47	99	06 44	47	100	05 57	47	101	05 10	47	101	04 23	48	102
77	08 08	47	100	07 21	47	101	06 34	47	101	05 47	48	102	04 59	47	103
76	08 45	47	101	07 58	47	102	07 11	47	102	06 24	48	103	05 36	47	103
75	09 22	-47	102	08 35	-47	102	07 48	-48	103	07 00	-47	104	06 13	-48	104
74	09 59	47	103	09 12	47	103	08 25	48	104	07 37	47	104	06 50	48	105
73	10 36	47	103	09 49	48	104	09 01	47	105	08 14	48	105	07 26	48	106
72	11 13	48	104	10 25	47	105	09 38	48	105	08 50	48	106	08 02	48	107
71	11 49	47	105	11 02	48	106	10 14	48	106	09 26	48	107	08 38	48	107
70	12 26	-48	106	11 38	-48	106	10 50	-48	107	10 02	-48	108	09 14	-48	108

LHA	5° Hc	5° d	5° Z	6° Hc	6° d	6° Z	7° Hc	7° d	7° Z	8° Hc	8° d	8° Z	9° Hc	9° d	9° Z
	° ′	′	°	° ′	′	°	° ′	′	°	° ′	′	°	° ′	′	°
94	266														
93	-5 46	47	91	267											
92	-5 09	46	92	-5 55	46	92	268								
91	-4 31	46	92	-5 17	47	93	-6 04	46	94	269					
90	-3 53	-47	93	-4 40	-46	94	-5 26	-47	94	-6 13	-46	95	270		
89	-3 15	47	94	-4 02	46	95	-4 48	47	95	-5 35	46	96	271		
88	-2 38	46	95	-3 24	47	95	-4 11	46	96	-4 57	47	97	-5 44	46	97
87	-2 00	47	96	-2 47	46	96	-3 33	47	97	-4 20	47	97	-5 07	46	98
86	-1 23	46	96	-2 09	47	97	-2 56	47	98	-3 43	46	98	-4 29	47	99
85	-0 45	-47	97	-1 32	-46	98	-2 18	-47	98	-3 05	-47	99	-3 52	-47	100
84	-0 08	46	98	-0 54	47	98	-1 41	47	99	-2 28	47	100	-3 15	46	100
83	00 30	47	99	-0 17	47	99	-1 04	47	100	-1 51	47	100	-2 38	46	101
82	01 07	47	99	00 20	47	100	-0 27	47	101	-1 14	47	101	-2 01	46	102
81	01 44	47	100	00 57	47	101	00 10	47	101	-0 37	47	102	-1 24	47	103
80	02 21	-47	101	01 34	-47	102	00 47	-47	102	00 00	-47	103	-0 47	-47	103
79	02 58	47	102	02 11	47	102	01 24	47	103	00 37	47	104	-0 10	47	104
78	03 35	47	103	02 48	47	103	02 01	47	104	01 14	48	104	00 26	47	105
77	04 12	47	103	03 25	47	104	02 38	48	105	01 50	47	105	01 03	48	106
76	04 49	48	104	04 01	47	105	03 14	47	105	02 27	48	106	01 39	47	107
75	05 25	-47	105	04 38	-48	106	03 50	-47	106	03 03	-48	107	02 15	-47	107
74	06 02	48	106	05 14	47	106	04 27	48	107	03 39	48	108	02 51	48	108
73	06 38	48	106	05 50	47	107	05 03	48	108	04 15	48	108	03 27	48	109
72	07 14	48	107	06 26	47	108	05 39	48	109	04 51	48	109	04 03	48	110
71	07 50	48	108	07 02	48	109	06 14	48	109	05 26	48	110	04 38	48	111
70	08 26	-48	109	07 38	-48	110	06 50	-48	110	06 02	-49	111	05 13	-48	111

LHA	10° Hc	10° d	10° Z	11° Hc	11° d	11° Z	12° Hc	12° d	12° Z	13° Hc	13° d	13° Z	14° Hc	14° d	14° Z	LHA
	° ′	′	°	° ′	′	°	° ′	′	°	° ′	′	°	° ′	′	°	
88	272															
87	-5 53	47	99	273												
86	-5 16	46	99	-6 02	47	100	274									
85	-4 39	-46	100	-5 25	-47	101	-6 12	-46	101	275						
84	-4 01	47	101	-4 48	47	102	-5 35	46	102	276						
83	-3 24	47	102	-4 11	47	102	-4 58	47	103	-5 45	46	104	277			
82	-2 47	47	103	-3 34	47	103	-4 21	47	104	-5 08	47	104	-5 55	47	105	278
81	-2 11	47	103	-2 58	47	104	-3 45	47	105	-4 32	46	105	-5 18	47	106	279
80	-1 34	-47	104	-2 21	-47	105	-3 08	-47	105	-3 55	-47	106	-4 42	-47	106	280
79	-0 57	48	105	-1 45	47	105	-2 32	47	106	-3 19	47	107	-4 06	47	107	281
78	-0 21	47	106	-1 08	48	106	-1 56	47	107	-2 43	47	108	-3 30	47	108	282
77	00 15	47	106	-0 32	48	107	-1 20	47	108	-2 07	47	108	-2 54	48	109	283
76	00 52	48	107	00 04	48	108	-0 44	47	108	-1 31	48	109	-2 19	47	110	284
75	01 28	-48	108	00 40	-48	109	-0 08	-47	109	-0 55	-48	110	-1 43	-48	110	285
74	02 03	47	109	01 16	48	109	00 28	48	110	-0 20	48	111	-1 08	47	111	286
73	02 39	48	109	01 51	48	110	01 03	48	111	00 15	48	111	-0 33	47	112	287
72	03 15	48	110	02 27	49	111	01 38	48	112	00 50	48	112	00 02	48	113	288
71	03 50	48	111	03 02	48	112	02 14	49	112	01 25	48	113	00 37	48	114	289
70	04 25	-48	112	03 37	-49	112	02 48	-48	113	02 00	-48	114	01 12	-49	114	290

S. Lat. {LHA greater than 180°....... Zn=180−Z; LHA less than 180°........... Zn=180+Z}

DECLINATION (0°-14°) CONTRARY NAME TO LATITUDE

N. Lat. {LHA greater than 180°....... Zn=Z; LHA less than 180°........... Zn=360−Z}

DECLINATION (0°-14°) CONTRARY NAME TO LATITUDE

LHA	0° Hc	d	Z	1° Hc	d	Z	2° Hc	d	Z	3° Hc	d	Z	4° Hc	d	Z
	° ′	′	°	° ′	′	°	° ′	′	°	° ′	′	°	° ′	′	°
69	13 02	48	107	12 14	48	107	11 26	48	108	10 38	48	109	09 50	48	109
68	13 38	48	107	12 50	48	108	12 02	48	109	11 14	48	109	10 26	49	110
67	14 14	48	108	13 26	48	109	12 38	49	110	11 49	48	110	11 01	48	111
66	14 50	48	109	14 02	49	110	13 13	48	110	12 25	49	111	11 36	48	112
65	15 25	−48	110	14 37	−48	111	13 49	−49	111	13 00	−49	112	12 11	−48	112
64	16 01	49	111	15 12	48	111	14 24	49	112	13 35	49	113	12 46	49	113
63	16 36	49	112	15 47	48	112	14 59	49	113	14 10	49	113	13 21	49	114
62	17 11	49	113	16 22	49	113	15 33	49	114	14 44	49	114	13 55	49	115
61	17 46	49	113	16 57	49	114	16 08	49	115	15 19	50	115	14 29	49	116
60	18 20	−49	114	17 31	−49	115	16 42	−49	115	15 53	−50	116	15 03	−49	117
59	18 55	50	115	18 05	49	116	17 16	50	116	16 26	49	117	15 37	50	117
58	19 29	50	116	18 39	49	117	17 50	50	117	17 00	50	118	16 10	50	118
57	20 03	50	117	19 13	50	117	18 23	50	118	17 33	50	119	16 43	50	119
56	20 36	50	118	19 46	50	118	18 56	50	119	18 06	50	119	17 16	50	120
55	21 10	−50	119	20 20	−51	119	19 29	−50	120	18 39	−50	120	17 49	−51	121
54	21 43	51	119	20 52	50	120	20 02	50	121	19 12	51	121	18 21	51	122
53	22 15	50	120	21 25	51	121	20 34	50	122	19 44	51	122	18 53	51	123
52	22 48	51	121	21 57	51	122	21 06	50	122	20 16	51	123	19 25	52	124
51	23 20	51	122	22 29	51	123	21 38	51	123	20 47	51	124	19 56	51	124
50	23 52	−51	123	23 01	−52	124	22 09	−51	124	21 18	−51	125	20 27	−52	125
49	24 23	51	124	23 32	51	125	22 41	52	125	21 49	52	126	20 57	51	126
48	24 54	51	125	24 03	52	126	23 11	51	126	22 20	52	127	21 28	52	127
47	25 25	52	126	24 33	51	127	23 42	52	127	22 50	52	128	21 58	53	128
46	25 55	51	127	25 04	53	127	24 11	52	128	23 19	52	129	22 27	52	129
45	26 25	−52	128	25 33	−52	128	24 41	−52	129	23 49	−53	130	22 56	−52	130
44	26 55	52	129	26 03	53	129	25 10	52	130	24 18	53	130	23 25	53	131
43	27 24	52	130	26 32	53	130	25 39	53	131	24 46	53	131	23 53	53	132
42	27 53	53	131	27 00	53	131	26 07	53	132	25 14	53	132	24 21	53	133
41	28 21	53	132	27 28	53	132	26 35	53	133	25 42	53	133	24 49	54	134
40	28 49	−53	133	27 56	−53	133	27 03	−54	134	26 09	−53	134	25 16	−54	135
39	29 17	54	134	28 23	53	134	27 30	54	135	26 36	54	135	25 42	54	136
38	29 44	54	135	28 50	54	135	27 56	54	136	27 02	54	136	26 08	54	137
37	30 10	54	136	29 16	54	136	28 22	54	137	27 28	54	137	26 34	55	138
36	30 36	54	137	29 42	54	137	28 48	55	138	27 53	54	138	26 59	55	139
35	31 02	−55	138	30 07	−54	139	29 13	−55	139	28 18	−55	139	27 23	−54	140
34	31 27	55	139	30 32	55	140	29 37	54	140	28 43	55	141	27 48	56	141
33	31 51	55	140	30 56	55	141	30 01	55	141	29 06	55	142	28 11	55	142
32	32 15	55	141	31 20	55	142	30 25	55	142	29 30	56	143	28 34	55	143
31	32 39	56	142	31 43	55	143	30 48	56	143	29 52	55	144	28 57	56	144
30	33 02	−56	143	32 06	−56	144	31 10	−56	144	30 14	−56	145	29 18	−56	145
29	33 24	56	145	32 28	56	145	31 32	56	145	30 36	56	146	29 40	57	146
28	33 45	56	146	32 49	56	146	31 53	56	147	30 57	57	147	30 00	56	147
27	34 06	56	147	33 10	56	147	32 14	57	148	31 17	56	148	30 21	57	148
26	34 27	57	148	33 30	56	148	32 34	57	149	31 37	57	149	30 40	57	149
25	34 47	−57	149	33 50	−57	149	32 53	−57	150	31 56	−57	150	30 59	−57	151
24	35 06	57	150	34 09	57	151	33 12	58	151	32 14	57	151	31 17	57	152
23	35 24	57	151	34 27	57	152	33 30	58	152	32 32	57	152	31 35	58	153
22	35 42	58	153	34 44	57	153	33 47	58	153	32 49	57	154	31 52	58	154
21	35 59	58	154	35 01	57	154	34 04	58	154	33 06	58	155	32 08	58	155
20	36 15	−58	155	35 17	−57	155	34 20	−58	156	33 22	−58	156	32 24	−58	156
19	36 31	58	156	35 33	58	156	34 35	58	157	33 37	58	157	32 39	59	157
18	36 46	58	157	35 48	59	158	34 49	58	158	33 51	58	158	32 53	59	159
17	37 00	58	159	36 02	59	159	35 03	58	159	34 05	59	159	33 06	58	160
16	37 14	59	160	36 15	59	160	35 16	58	160	34 18	59	161	33 19	59	161
15	37 26	−59	161	36 27	−58	161	35 29	−59	162	34 30	−59	162	33 31	−59	162
14	37 38	59	162	36 39	59	163	35 40	59	163	34 41	59	163	33 42	59	163
13	37 49	59	164	36 50	59	164	35 51	59	164	34 52	59	164	33 53	59	164
12	38 00	60	165	37 00	59	165	36 01	59	165	35 02	59	165	34 03	59	166
11	38 09	59	166	37 10	59	166	36 11	60	166	35 11	59	167	34 12	59	167
10	38 18	−59	167	37 19	−60	167	36 19	−59	168	35 20	−60	168	34 20	−59	168
9	38 26	60	169	37 26	59	169	36 27	60	169	35 27	59	169	34 28	60	169
8	38 33	60	170	37 33	59	170	36 34	60	170	35 34	60	170	34 34	59	170
7	38 39	59	171	37 40	60	171	36 40	60	171	35 40	60	171	34 40	59	172
6	38 45	60	172	37 45	60	172	36 45	60	173	35 45	59	173	34 46	60	173
5	38 49	−59	174	37 50	−60	174	36 50	−60	174	35 50	−60	174	34 50	−60	174
4	38 53	60	175	37 53	60	175	36 53	59	175	35 54	60	175	34 54	60	175
3	38 56	60	176	37 56	60	176	36 56	60	176	35 56	60	176	34 56	60	176
2	38 58	60	177	37 58	60	178	36 58	60	178	35 58	60	178	34 58	60	178
1	39 00	60	179	38 00	60	179	37 00	60	179	36 00	60	179	35 00	60	179
0	39 00	−60	180	38 00	−60	180	37 00	−60	180	36 00	−60	180	35 00	−60	180

LHA	5° Hc	d	Z	6° Hc	d	Z	7° Hc	d	Z	8° Hc	d	Z	9° Hc	d	Z
	° ′	′	°	° ′	′	°	° ′	′	°	° ′	′	°	° ′	′	°
69	09 02	48	110	08 14	49	110	07 25	48	111	06 37	49	112	05 48	48	112
68	09 37	48	111	08 49	49	111	08 00	48	112	07 12	49	112	06 23	48	113
67	10 13	49	111	09 24	49	112	08 35	48	113	07 47	49	113	06 58	49	114
66	10 48	49	112	09 59	49	113	09 10	49	113	08 21	48	114	07 33	49	115
65	11 23	−49	113	10 34	−49	114	09 45	−49	114	08 56	−49	115	08 07	−49	115
64	11 57	49	114	11 08	49	114	10 19	49	115	09 30	49	116	08 41	49	116
63	12 32	50	115	11 42	49	115	10 53	49	116	10 04	49	116	09 15	50	117
62	13 06	49	115	12 17	50	116	11 27	49	117	10 38	50	117	09 48	49	118
61	13 40	50	116	12 50	49	117	12 01	50	117	11 11	50	118	10 21	49	119
60	14 14	−50	117	13 24	−50	118	12 34	−50	118	11 44	−50	119	10 54	−49	119
59	14 47	50	118	13 57	50	119	13 07	50	119	12 17	50	120	11 27	50	120
58	15 20	50	119	14 30	50	119	13 40	50	120	12 50	50	121	12 00	51	121
57	15 53	50	120	15 03	50	120	14 13	51	121	13 22	50	121	12 32	51	122
56	16 26	51	121	15 35	50	121	14 45	51	122	13 54	50	122	13 04	51	123
55	16 58	−50	121	16 08	−51	122	15 17	−51	123	14 26	−51	123	13 35	−51	124
54	17 30	51	122	16 39	50	123	15 49	51	123	14 58	51	124	14 07	51	125
53	18 02	51	123	17 11	51	124	16 20	51	124	15 29	51	125	14 38	52	125
52	18 33	51	124	17 42	51	125	16 51	51	125	16 00	52	126	15 08	51	126
51	19 05	52	125	18 13	51	126	17 22	52	126	16 30	52	127	15 38	51	127
50	19 35	−51	126	18 44	−52	126	17 52	−52	127	17 00	−52	128	16 08	−52	128
49	20 06	52	127	19 14	52	127	18 22	52	128	17 30	52	128	16 38	52	129
48	20 36	52	128	19 44	52	128	18 52	53	129	17 59	52	129	17 07	52	130
47	21 05	52	129	20 13	52	129	19 21	53	130	18 28	52	130	17 36	53	131
46	21 35	53	130	20 42	52	130	19 50	53	131	18 57	53	131	18 04	52	132
45	22 04	−53	131	21 11	−53	131	20 18	−53	132	19 25	−53	132	18 32	−53	133
44	22 32	53	132	21 39	53	132	20 46	53	133	19 53	53	133	19 00	53	134
43	23 00	53	132	22 07	53	133	21 14	53	133	20 21	54	134	19 27	53	134
42	23 28	53	133	22 35	54	134	21 41	53	134	20 48	54	135	19 54	54	135
41	23 55	54	134	23 01	53	135	22 08	54	135	21 14	54	136	20 20	54	136
40	24 22	−54	135	23 28	−54	136	22 34	−54	136	21 40	−54	137	20 46	−54	137
39	24 48	54	136	23 54	54	137	23 00	54	137	22 06	54	138	21 12	55	138
38	25 14	54	137	24 20	55	138	23 25	54	138	22 31	55	139	21 36	54	139
37	25 39	54	138	24 45	55	139	23 50	54	139	22 56	55	140	22 01	55	140
36	26 04	55	139	25 09	54	140	24 15	55	140	23 20	55	141	22 25	55	141
35	26 29	−55	140	25 34	−55	141	24 39	−55	141	23 44	−56	142	22 48	−55	142
34	26 52	55	141	25 57	55	142	25 02	55	142	24 07	56	143	23 11	55	143
33	27 16	56	142	26 20	55	143	25 25	56	143	24 29	55	144	23 34	56	144
32	27 39	56	143	26 43	56	144	25 47	56	144	24 51	55	145	23 56	56	145
31	28 01	56	145	27 05	56	145	26 09	56	145	25 13	56	146	24 17	56	146
30	28 22	−56	146	27 26	−56	146	26 30	−56	146	25 34	−56	147	24 38	−57	147
29	28 43	56	147	27 47	56	147	26 51	57	147	25 54	56	148	24 58	57	148
28	29 04	57	148	28 07	56	148	27 11	57	148	26 14	56	149	25 18	57	149
27	29 24	57	149	28 27	57	149	27 30	56	150	26 34	57	150	25 37	57	150
26	29 43	57	150	28 46	57	150	27 49	57	151	26 52	57	151	25 55	57	151
25	30 02	−57	151	29 05	−57	151	28 08	−58	152	27 10	−57	152	26 13	−57	152
24	30 20	57	152	29 23	58	152	28 25	57	153	27 28	58	153	26 30	57	153
23	30 37	57	153	29 40	58	153	28 42	57	154	27 45	58	154	26 47	58	154
22	30 54	58	154	29 56	57	155	28 59	58	155	28 01	58	155	27 03	58	156
21	31 10	58	155	30 12	58	156	29 14	58	156	28 16	58	156	27 18	58	157
20	31 26	−59	157	30 27	−58	157	29 29	−58	157	28 31	−58	157	27 33	−58	158
19	31 40	58	158	30 42	58	158	29 44	59	158	28 45	58	158	27 47	58	159
18	31 54	58	159	30 56	59	159	29 57	58	159	28 59	59	160	28 00	58	160
17	32 08	59	160	31 09	59	160	30 10	58	160	29 12	59	161	28 13	59	161
16	32 20	58	161	31 22	59	161	30 23	59	162	29 24	59	162	28 25	59	162
15	32 32	−59	162	31 33	−59	162	30 34	−58	163	29 36	−59	163	28 37	−59	163
14	32 43	59	163	31 44	59	164	30 45	59	164	29 46	59	164	28 47	59	164
13	32 54	59	165	31 55	59	165	30 56	60	165	29 56	59	165	28 57	59	165
12	33 04	60	166	32 04	59	166	31 05	59	166	30 06	60	166	29 06	59	166
11	33 13	60	167	32 13	59	167	31 14	60	167	30 14	59	167	29 15	60	168
10	33 21	−60	168	32 21	−59	168	31 22	−60	168	30 22	−59	169	29 23	−60	169
9	33 28	59	169	32 29	60	169	31 29	60	170	30 29	59	170	29 30	60	170
8	33 35	60	170	32 35	60	171	31 35	59	171	30 36	60	171	29 36	60	171
7	33 41	60	172	32 41	60	172	31 41	60	172	30 41	59	172	29 42	60	172
6	33 46	60	173	32 46	60	173	31 46	60	173	30 46	59	173	29 47	60	173
5	33 50	−60	174	32 50	−60	174	31 50	−59	174	30 51	−60	174	29 51	−60	174
4	33 54	60	175	32 54	60	175	31 54	60	175	30 54	60	175	29 54	60	175
3	33 56	59	176	32 57	60	176	31 57	60	177	30 57	60	177	29 57	60	177
2	33 58	60	178	32 58	59	178	31 59	60	178	30 59	60	178	29 59	60	178
1	34 00	60	179	33 00	60	179	32 00	60	179	31 00	60	179	30 00	60	179
0	34 00	−60	180	33 00	−60	180	32 00	−60	180	31 00	−60	180	30 00	−60	180

10° Hc	d	Z	11° Hc	d	Z	12° Hc	d	Z	13° Hc	d	Z	14° Hc	d	Z	LHA
° ′	′	°	° ′	′	°	° ′	′	°	° ′	′	°	° ′	′	°	
05 00	48	113	04 12	49	113	03 23	48	114	02 35	49	115	01 46	49	115	291
05 35	49	113	04 46	49	114	03 57	48	115	03 09	49	115	02 20	49	116	292
06 09	48	114	05 21	49	115	04 32	49	115	03 43	49	116	02 54	49	117	293
06 44	49	115	05 55	49	116	05 06	49	116	04 17	49	117	03 28	49	117	294
07 18	−49	116	06 29	−50	116	05 39	−49	117	04 50	−49	118	04 01	−49	118	295
07 52	50	117	07 02	49	117	06 13	49	118	05 24	50	118	04 34	49	119	296
08 25	49	118	07 36	50	118	06 46	49	119	05 57	50	119	05 07	50	120	297
08 59	50	118	08 09	50	119	07 19	49	120	06 30	50	120	05 40	50	121	298
09 32	50	119	08 42	50	120	07 52	50	120	07 02	50	121	06 12	50	121	299
10 05	−50	120	09 15	−51	121	08 24	−50	121	07 34	−50	122	06 44	−50	122	300
10 37	50	121	09 47	50	121	08 57	51	122	08 06	50	123	07 16	50	123	301
11 09	50	122	10 19	50	122	09 29	51	123	08 38	50	123	07 48	51	124	302
11 41	50	123	10 51	51	123	10 00	51	124	09 09	50	124	08 19	51	125	303
12 13	51	123	11 22	51	124	10 31	50	124	09 41	51	125	08 50	51	126	304
12 44	−51	124	11 53	−51	125	11 02	−51	125	10 11	−51	126	09 20	−51	126	305
13 16	52	125	12 24	51	126	11 33	51	126	10 42	52	127	09 50	51	127	306
13 46	51	126	12 55	52	127	12 03	51	127	11 12	52	128	10 20	51	128	307
14 17	52	127	13 25	52	127	12 33	51	128	11 42	52	128	10 50	52	129	308
14 47	52	128	13 55	52	128	13 03	52	129	12 11	52	129	11 19	52	130	309
15 16	−52	129	14 24	−52	129	13 32	−52	130	12 40	−52	130	11 48	−52	131	310
15 46	52	129	14 54	53	130	14 01	52	131	13 09	52	131	12 17	53	132	311
16 15	53	130	15 22	52	131	14 30	53	131	13 37	52	132	12 45	53	132	312
16 43	52	131	15 51	53	132	14 58	53	132	14 05	53	133	13 12	53	133	313
17 12	53	132	16 19	53	133	15 26	53	133	14 33	53	134	13 40	53	134	314
17 39	−53	133	16 46	−53	134	15 53	−53	134	15 00	−53	135	14 07	−54	135	315
18 07	54	134	17 13	53	134	16 20	53	135	15 27	54	135	14 33	53	136	316
18 34	54	135	17 40	53	135	16 47	54	136	15 53	54	136	14 59	54	137	317
19 00	54	136	18 06	53	136	17 13	54	137	16 19	54	137	15 25	54	138	318
19 26	54	137	18 32	54	137	17 38	54	138	16 44	54	138	15 50	54	139	319
19 52	−54	138	18 58	−54	138	18 04	−55	139	17 09	−54	139	16 15	−55	140	320
20 17	54	139	19 23	55	139	18 28	54	140	17 34	55	140	16 39	55	140	321
20 42	55	140	19 47	54	140	18 53	55	141	17 58	55	141	17 03	55	141	322
21 06	55	141	20 11	55	141	19 16	55	141	18 21	55	142	17 26	55	142	323
21 30	55	142	20 35	55	142	19 40	56	142	18 44	55	143	17 49	55	143	324
21 53	−55	143	20 58	−56	143	20 02	−55	143	19 07	−55	144	18 12	−56	144	325
22 16	56	144	21 20	55	144	20 25	56	144	19 29	56	145	18 33	55	145	326
22 38	56	145	21 42	56	145	20 46	55	145	19 51	56	146	18 55	56	146	327
23 00	56	146	22 04	56	146	21 08	56	146	20 12	56	147	19 16	57	147	328
23 21	56	147	22 25	57	147	21 28	56	147	20 32	56	148	19 36	56	148	329
23 41	−56	148	22 45	−56	148	21 49	−57	148	20 52	−56	149	19 56	−57	149	330
24 01	56	149	23 05	57	149	22 08	56	149	21 12	57	150	20 15	57	150	331
24 21	57	150	23 24	57	150	22 27	57	150	21 30	57	151	20 33	56	151	332
24 40	57	151	23 43	57	151	22 46	57	151	21 49	57	152	20 52	58	152	333
24 58	57	152	24 01	57	152	23 04	58	152	22 06	57	153	21 09	57	153	334
25 16	−58	153	24 18	−57	153	23 21	−58	153	22 23	−57	154	21 26	−58	154	335
25 33	58	154	24 35	57	154	23 38	58	154	22 40	58	155	21 42	57	155	336
25 49	58	155	24 51	57	155	23 54	58	155	22 56	58	156	21 58	58	156	337
26 05	58	156	25 07	58	156	24 09	58	156	23 11	58	157	22 13	58	157	338
26 20	58	157	25 22	58	157	24 24	58	157	23 26	58	158	22 28	58	158	339
26 35	−58	158	25 37	−59	158	24 38	−58	158	23 40	−58	159	22 42	−59	159	340
26 49	59	159	25 50	58	159	24 52	59	160	23 53	58	160	22 55	59	160	341
27 02	59	160	26 03	58	160	25 05	59	161	24 06	58	161	23 08	59	161	342
27 14	58	161	26 16	59	161	25 17	59	162	24 18	58	162	23 20	59	162	343
27 26	58	162	26 28	59	162	25 29	59	163	24 30	59	163	23 31	59	163	344
27 38	−59	163	26 39	−59	164	25 40	−59	164	24 41	−59	164	23 42	−60	164	345
27 48	59	164	26 49	59	165	25 50	59	165	24 51	59	165	23 52	60	165	346
27 58	59	166	26 59	60	166	25 59	59	166	25 00	59	166	24 01	59	166	347
28 07	59	167	27 08	60	167	26 08	59	167	25 09	59	167	24 10	60	167	348
28 15	59	168	27 16	59	168	26 17	60	168	25 17	59	168	24 18	60	168	349
28 23	−59	169	27 24	−60	169	26 24	−59	169	25 25	−60	169	24 25	−60	169	350
28 30	59	170	27 31	60	170	26 31	60	170	25 31	59	170	24 32	60	170	351
28 36	59	171	27 37	60	171	26 37	60	171	25 37	59	171	24 38	60	172	352
28 42	60	172	27 42	60	172	26 42	59	172	25 43	60	172	24 43	60	173	353
28 47	60	173	27 47	60	173	26 47	60	173	25 47	60	174	24 47	59	174	354
28 51	−60	174	27 51	−60	174	26 51	−60	175	25 51	−60	175	24 51	−60	175	355
28 54	60	176	27 54	60	176	26 54	60	176	25 54	60	176	24 54	60	176	356
28 57	60	177	27 57	60	177	26 57	60	177	25 57	60	177	24 57	60	177	357
28 59	60	178	27 59	60	178	26 59	60	178	25 59	60	178	24 59	60	178	358
29 00	60	179	28 00	60	179	27 00	60	179	26 00	60	179	25 00	60	179	359
29 00	−60	180	28 00	−60	180	27 00	−60	180	26 00	−60	180	25 00	−60	180	360

S. Lat. {LHA greater than 180°........ Zn=180−Z; LHA less than 180°........... Zn=180+Z}

DECLINATION (0°-14°) CONTRARY NAME TO LATITUDE

N. Lat. {LHA greater than 180°....... Zn=Z; LHA less than 180°.......... Zn=360−Z}

DECLINATION (15°-29°) SAME NAME AS LATITUDE

LAT 51°

LHA	15°			16°			17°			18°			19°			LHA
	Hc	d	Z	Hc	d	Z	Hc	d	Z	Hc	d	Z	Hc	d	Z	
	° ′	′	°	° ′	′	°	° ′	′	°	° ′	′	°	° ′	′	°	
0	54 00	+60	180	55 00	+60	180	56 00	+60	180	57 00	+60	180	58 00	+60	180	360
1	54 00	59	178	54 59	60	178	55 59	60	178	56 59	60	178	57 59	60	178	359
2	53 58	60	177	54 58	60	177	55 58	60	177	56 58	60	177	57 58	60	176	358
3	53 55	60	175	54 55	60	175	55 55	60	175	56 55	60	175	57 55	60	175	357
4	53 51	60	173	54 51	60	173	55 51	60	173	56 51	60	173	57 51	59	173	356
5	53 47	+59	172	54 46	+60	172	55 46	+60	172	56 46	+59	171	57 45	+60	171	355
6	53 41	59	170	54 40	60	170	55 40	59	170	56 39	60	170	57 39	60	169	354
7	53 34	59	169	54 33	60	168	55 33	59	168	56 32	59	168	57 31	60	168	353
8	53 26	59	167	54 25	59	167	55 24	60	166	56 24	59	166	57 23	59	166	352
9	53 17	59	165	54 16	59	165	55 15	59	165	56 14	59	165	57 13	59	164	351
10	53 07	+59	164	54 06	+59	164	55 05	+58	163	56 03	+59	163	57 02	+59	162	350
11	52 56	58	162	53 54	59	162	54 53	59	162	55 52	58	161	56 50	59	161	349
12	52 44	58	161	53 42	59	160	54 41	58	160	55 39	58	160	56 37	59	159	348
13	52 31	58	159	53 29	58	159	54 27	58	158	55 25	58	158	56 23	58	157	347
14	52 17	58	158	53 15	58	157	54 13	58	157	55 11	57	156	56 08	58	156	346
15	52 02	+58	156	53 00	+57	156	53 57	+58	155	54 55	+57	155	55 52	+58	154	345
16	51 46	57	155	52 43	58	154	53 41	57	154	54 38	57	153	55 35	57	153	344
17	51 29	57	153	52 26	58	153	53 24	57	152	54 21	56	152	55 17	57	151	343
18	51 12	57	152	52 09	56	151	53 05	57	151	54 02	57	150	54 59	56	149	342
19	50 53	57	150	51 50	56	150	52 46	57	149	53 43	56	149	54 39	56	148	341
20	50 34	+56	149	51 30	+57	148	52 27	+56	148	53 23	+56	147	54 19	+55	146	340
21	50 14	56	147	51 10	56	147	52 06	56	146	53 02	55	146	53 57	55	145	339
22	49 53	56	146	50 49	55	145	51 44	56	145	52 40	55	144	53 35	55	143	338
23	49 32	55	144	50 27	55	144	51 22	55	143	52 17	55	143	53 12	55	142	337
24	49 09	55	143	50 04	55	143	50 59	55	142	51 54	54	141	52 48	55	141	336
25	48 46	+55	142	49 41	+55	141	50 36	+54	141	51 30	+54	140	52 24	+54	139	335
26	48 22	55	140	49 17	54	140	50 11	54	139	51 05	54	138	51 59	54	138	334
27	47 58	54	139	48 52	54	138	49 46	54	138	50 40	53	137	51 33	53	136	333
28	47 33	54	138	48 27	53	137	49 20	54	136	50 14	53	136	51 07	53	135	332
29	47 07	54	137	48 01	53	136	48 54	53	135	49 47	53	134	50 40	52	134	331
30	46 41	+53	135	47 34	+53	135	48 27	+53	134	49 20	+52	133	50 12	+52	132	330
31	46 14	53	134	47 07	53	133	48 00	52	133	48 52	52	132	49 44	52	131	329
32	45 47	52	133	46 39	53	132	47 32	52	131	48 24	51	131	49 15	52	130	328
33	45 19	52	132	46 11	52	131	47 03	52	130	47 55	51	129	48 46	51	129	327
34	44 50	52	130	45 42	52	130	46 34	51	129	47 25	51	128	48 16	51	127	326
35	44 21	+52	129	45 13	+51	129	46 04	+51	128	46 55	+51	127	47 46	+51	126	325
36	43 52	51	128	44 43	51	127	45 34	51	127	46 25	50	126	47 15	51	125	324
37	43 22	51	127	44 13	51	126	45 04	50	125	45 54	50	125	46 44	50	124	323
38	42 51	51	126	43 42	51	125	44 33	50	124	45 23	50	124	46 13	49	123	322
39	42 21	50	125	43 11	50	124	44 01	50	123	44 51	50	122	45 41	49	122	321
40	41 49	+51	124	42 40	+49	123	43 29	+50	122	44 19	+49	121	45 08	+49	121	320
41	41 18	50	123	42 08	49	122	42 57	50	121	43 47	49	120	44 36	48	119	319
42	40 46	49	121	41 35	50	121	42 25	49	120	43 14	49	119	44 03	48	118	318
43	40 13	50	120	41 03	49	120	41 52	49	119	42 41	48	118	43 29	48	117	317
44	39 40	50	119	40 30	49	119	41 19	48	118	42 07	49	117	42 56	48	116	316
45	39 07	+49	118	39 56	+49	118	40 45	+48	117	41 33	+49	116	42 22	+47	115	315
46	38 34	49	117	39 23	48	117	40 11	48	116	40 59	48	115	41 47	48	114	314
47	38 00	49	116	38 49	48	116	39 37	48	115	40 25	48	114	41 13	47	113	313
48	37 26	49	115	38 15	48	115	39 03	47	114	39 50	48	113	40 38	47	112	312
49	36 52	48	114	37 40	48	114	38 28	48	113	39 16	47	112	40 03	47	111	311
50	36 17	+48	113	37 05	+48	113	37 53	+47	112	38 40	+47	111	39 27	+47	110	310
51	35 43	47	112	36 30	48	112	37 18	47	111	38 05	47	110	38 52	46	109	309
52	35 08	47	112	35 55	48	111	36 43	47	110	37 30	46	109	38 16	47	108	308
53	34 32	48	111	35 20	47	110	36 07	47	109	36 54	46	108	37 40	46	107	307
54	33 57	47	110	34 44	47	109	35 31	47	108	36 18	46	107	37 04	46	107	306
55	33 21	+47	109	34 08	+47	108	34 55	+47	107	35 42	+46	106	36 28	+46	106	305
56	32 45	47	108	33 32	47	107	34 19	46	106	35 05	46	105	35 51	46	105	304
57	32 09	47	107	32 56	47	106	33 43	46	105	34 29	46	105	35 15	45	104	303
58	31 33	47	106	32 20	46	105	33 06	46	105	33 52	46	104	34 38	46	103	302
59	30 57	46	105	31 43	47	104	32 30	46	104	33 16	45	103	34 01	46	102	301
60	30 20	+47	104	31 07	+46	104	31 53	+46	103	32 39	+45	102	33 24	+46	101	300
61	29 44	46	103	30 30	46	103	31 16	46	102	32 02	45	101	32 47	45	100	299
62	29 07	46	103	29 53	46	102	30 39	46	101	31 25	45	100	32 10	45	100	298
63	28 30	46	102	29 16	46	101	30 02	45	100	30 47	45	100	31 33	45	99	297
64	27 53	46	101	28 39	46	100	29 25	45	99	30 10	45	99	30 55	45	98	296
65	27 16	+46	100	28 02	+45	99	28 47	+46	99	29 33	+45	98	30 18	+45	97	295
66	26 38	46	99	27 24	46	98	28 10	45	98	28 55	45	97	29 40	45	96	294
67	26 01	46	98	26 47	45	98	27 32	46	97	28 18	45	96	29 03	45	95	293
68	25 24	45	98	26 09	46	97	26 55	45	96	27 40	45	95	28 25	45	95	292
69	24 46	46	97	25 32	45	96	26 17	46	95	27 03	45	95	27 48	44	94	291

LHA	20°			21°			22°			23°			24°			LHA
	Hc	d	Z	Hc	d	Z	Hc	d	Z	Hc	d	Z	Hc	d	Z	
	° ′	′	°	° ′	′	°	° ′	′	°	° ′	′	°	° ′	′	°	
0	59 00	+60	180	60 00	+60	180	61 00	+60	180	62 00	+60	180	63 00	+60	180	360
1	58 59	60	178	59 59	60	178	60 59	60	178	61 59	60	178	62 59	60	178	359
2	58 58	60	176	59 58	60	176	60 58	59	176	61 57	60	176	62 57	60	176	358
3	58 55	60	175	59 55	59	174	60 54	60	174	61 54	60	174	62 54	60	174	357
4	58 50	60	173	59 50	60	173	60 50	60	172	61 50	59	172	62 49	60	172	356
5	58 45	+60	171	59 45	+59	171	60 44	+60	171	61 44	+60	170	62 44	+59	170	355
6	58 39	59	169	59 38	60	169	60 38	59	169	61 37	59	168	62 36	60	168	354
7	58 31	59	167	59 30	59	167	60 29	60	167	61 29	59	166	62 28	59	166	353
8	58 22	59	166	59 21	59	165	60 20	59	165	61 19	59	165	62 18	59	164	352
9	58 12	59	164	59 11	59	163	60 10	59	163	61 09	58	163	62 07	59	162	351
10	58 01	+59	162	59 00	+58	162	59 58	+59	161	60 57	+58	161	61 55	+58	160	350
11	57 49	58	160	58 47	58	160	59 45	59	159	60 44	58	159	61 42	58	159	349
12	57 36	58	159	58 34	58	158	59 32	58	158	60 30	58	157	61 27	58	157	348
13	57 21	58	157	58 19	58	156	59 17	57	156	60 14	58	155	61 12	57	155	347
14	57 06	57	155	58 03	58	155	59 01	57	154	59 58	57	154	60 55	57	153	346
15	56 50	+57	154	57 47	+57	153	58 44	+57	153	59 41	+56	152	60 37	+57	151	345
16	56 32	57	152	57 29	57	151	58 26	56	151	59 22	57	150	60 19	56	149	344
17	56 14	57	150	57 11	56	150	58 07	56	149	59 03	56	148	59 59	56	148	343
18	55 55	56	149	56 51	56	148	57 47	56	148	58 43	55	147	59 38	56	146	342
19	55 35	56	147	56 31	55	147	57 26	56	146	58 22	55	145	59 17	55	144	341
20	55 14	+56	146	56 10	+55	145	57 05	+55	144	58 00	+55	144	58 55	+54	143	340
21	54 52	56	144	55 48	54	144	56 42	55	143	57 37	54	142	58 31	54	141	339
22	54 30	55	143	55 25	54	142	56 19	54	141	57 13	54	140	58 07	54	140	338
23	54 07	54	141	55 01	54	141	55 55	54	140	56 49	53	139	57 42	53	138	337
24	53 43	54	140	54 37	53	139	55 30	54	138	56 24	53	137	57 17	52	137	336
25	53 18	+54	138	54 12	+53	138	55 05	+53	137	55 58	+52	136	56 50	+53	135	335
26	52 53	53	137	53 46	53	136	54 39	52	135	55 31	52	135	56 23	52	134	334
27	52 26	53	136	53 19	53	135	54 12	52	134	55 04	52	133	55 56	51	132	333
28	52 00	52	134	52 52	52	133	53 44	52	133	54 36	52	132	55 28	51	131	332
29	51 32	52	133	52 24	52	132	53 16	52	131	54 08	51	130	54 59	50	130	331
30	51 04	+52	132	51 56	+52	131	52 48	+51	130	53 39	+50	129	54 29	+50	128	330
31	50 36	51	130	51 27	51	130	52 18	51	129	53 09	50	128	53 59	50	127	329
32	50 07	51	129	50 58	51	128	51 49	50	127	52 39	50	127	53 29	49	126	328
33	49 37	51	128	50 28	50	127	51 18	50	126	52 08	50	125	52 58	49	124	327
34	49 07	51	127	49 58	50	126	50 48	49	125	51 37	49	124	52 26	49	123	326
35	48 37	+50	125	49 27	+49	125	50 16	+50	124	51 06	+49	123	51 55	+48	122	325
36	48 06	49	124	48 55	50	123	49 45	49	123	50 34	48	122	51 22	48	121	324
37	47 34	50	123	48 24	49	122	49 13	48	121	50 01	49	120	50 50	47	120	323
38	47 02	49	122	47 51	49	121	48 40	49	120	49 29	48	119	50 17	47	118	322
39	46 30	49	121	47 19	48	120	48 07	49	119	48 56	47	118	49 43	47	117	321
40	45 57	+49	120	46 46	+48	119	47 34	+48	118	48 22	+47	117	49 09	+47	116	320
41	45 24	49	119	46 13	48	118	47 01	47	117	47 48	47	116	48 35	47	115	319
42	44 51	48	118	45 39	48	117	46 27	47	116	47 14	47	115	48 01	46	114	318
43	44 17	48	117	45 05	48	116	45 53	47	115	46 40	46	114	47 26	47	113	317
44	43 44	47	115	44 31	47	115	45 18	47	114	46 05	46	113	46 51	46	112	316
45	43 09	+48	114	43 57	+47	114	44 44	+46	113	45 30	+46	112	46 16	+46	111	315
46	42 35	47	113	43 22	47	113	44 09	46	112	44 55	46	111	45 41	45	110	314
47	42 00	47	112	42 47	46	112	43 33	47	111	44 20	45	110	45 05	46	109	313
48	41 25	47	111	42 12	46	111	42 58	46	110	43 44	45	109	44 29	46	108	312
49	40 50	46	110	41 36	46	110	42 22	46	109	43 08	45	108	43 53	45	107	311
50	40 14	+46	109	41 00	+46	109	41 46	+46	108	42 32	+45	107	43 17	+45	106	310
51	39 38	47	109	40 25	45	108	41 10	46	107	41 56	45	106	42 41	44	105	309
52	39 03	46	108	39 49	45	107	40 34	45	106	41 19	45	105	42 04	45	104	308
53	38 26	46	107	39 12	46	106	39 58	45	105	40 43	45	104	41 28	44	103	307
54	37 50	46	106	38 36	45	105	39 21	45	104	40 06	45	103	40 51	44	102	306
55	37 14	+45	105	37 59	+45	104	38 45	+44	103	39 29	+45	102	40 14	+44	101	305
56	36 37	46	104	37 23	45	103	38 08	44	102	38 52	45	101	39 37	44	101	304
57	36 00	46	103	36 46	45	102	37 31	44	101	38 15	45	101	39 00	43	100	303
58	35 24	45	102	36 09	45	101	36 54	44	101	37 38	44	100	38 22	44	99	302
59	34 47	45	101	35 32	44	101	36 16	45	100	37 01	44	99	37 45	44	98	301
60	34 10	+45	101	34 55	+44	100	35 39	+45	99	36 24	+44	98	37 08	+43	97	300
61	33 32	45	100	34 17	45	99	35 02	44	98	35 46	44	97	36 30	44	96	299
62	32 55	45	99	33 40	44	98	34 24	45	97	35 09	43	96	35 52	44	96	298
63	32 18	44	98	33 02	45	97	33 47	44	96	34 31	44	96	35 15	43	95	297
64	31 40	45	97	32 25	44	96	33 09	44	96	33 53	44	95	34 37	44	94	296
65	31 03	+44	96	31 47	+45	96	32 32	+44	95	33 16	+44	94	34 00	+43	93	295
66	30 25	45	95	31 10	44	95	31 54	44	94	32 38	44	93	33 22	43	92	294
67	29 48	44	94	30 32	44	94	31 16	44	93	32 00	44	92	32 44	43	91	293
68	29 10	44	94	29 54	45	93	30 39	44	92	31 23	43	92	32 06	44	91	292
69	28 32	45	93	29 17	44	92	30 01	44	92	30 45	44	91	31 29	43	90	291

LHA	25°			26°			27°			28°			29°			LHA
	Hc	d	Z	Hc	d	Z	Hc	d	Z	Hc	d	Z	Hc	d	Z	
	° ′	′	°	° ′	′	°	° ′	′	°	° ′	′	°	° ′	′	°	
0	64 00	+60	180	65 00	+60	180	66 00	+60	180	67 00	+60	180	68 00	+60	180	360
1	63 59	60	178	64 59	60	178	65 59	60	178	66 59	60	178	67 59	60	178	359
2	63 57	60	176	64 57	60	176	65 57	60	176	66 57	60	176	67 57	60	175	358
3	63 54	60	174	64 54	60	174	65 54	59	173	66 53	60	173	67 53	60	173	357
4	63 49	60	172	64 49	60	172	65 49	59	171	66 48	60	171	67 48	59	171	356
5	63 43	+60	170	64 43	+59	169	65 42	+60	169	66 42	+59	169	67 41	+59	168	355
6	63 36	59	168	64 35	59	167	65 34	60	167	66 34	59	167	67 33	59	166	354
7	63 27	59	166	64 26	59	165	65 25	59	165	66 24	59	164	67 23	59	164	353
8	63 17	59	164	64 16	59	163	65 15	58	163	66 13	59	162	67 12	58	162	352
9	63 06	58	162	64 04	59	161	65 03	58	161	66 01	58	160	66 59	58	160	351
10	62 53	+59	160	63 52	+58	159	64 50	+58	159	65 48	+57	158	66 45	+58	157	350
11	62 40	58	158	63 38	57	157	64 35	58	157	65 33	57	156	66 30	57	155	349
12	62 25	57	156	63 22	58	155	64 20	57	155	65 17	57	154	66 14	56	153	348
13	62 09	57	154	63 06	57	154	64 03	57	153	65 00	56	152	65 56	56	151	347
14	61 52	57	152	62 49	56	152	63 45	56	151	64 41	56	150	65 37	56	149	346
15	61 34	+56	151	62 30	+56	150	63 26	+56	149	64 22	+55	148	65 17	+55	147	345
16	61 15	56	149	62 11	55	148	63 06	56	147	64 02	54	146	64 56	55	145	344
17	60 55	55	147	61 50	55	146	62 45	55	145	63 40	54	144	64 34	54	143	343
18	60 34	55	145	61 29	54	144	62 23	55	144	63 18	53	143	64 11	54	142	342
19	60 12	54	144	61 06	54	143	62 00	54	142	62 54	54	141	63 48	52	140	341
20	59 49	+54	142	60 43	+54	141	61 37	+53	140	62 30	+53	139	63 23	+52	138	340
21	59 25	54	140	60 19	53	139	61 12	53	139	62 05	52	138	62 57	52	136	339
22	59 01	53	139	59 54	53	138	60 47	52	137	61 39	52	136	62 31	51	135	338
23	58 35	53	137	59 28	52	136	60 20	52	135	61 12	52	134	62 04	50	133	337
24	58 09	53	136	59 02	51	135	59 53	52	134	60 45	51	133	61 36	50	132	336
25	57 43	+51	134	58 34	+52	133	59 26	+51	132	60 17	+50	131	61 07	+50	130	335
26	57 15	52	133	58 07	51	132	58 58	50	131	59 48	50	130	60 38	49	129	334
27	56 47	51	131	57 38	51	130	58 29	50	129	59 19	49	128	60 08	49	127	333
28	56 19	50	130	57 09	50	129	57 59	50	128	58 49	49	127	59 38	48	126	332
29	55 49	50	129	56 39	50	128	57 29	49	127	58 18	49	125	59 07	48	124	331
30	55 19	+50	127	56 09	+49	126	56 58	+49	125	57 47	+48	124	58 35	+48	123	330
31	54 49	50	126	55 39	48	125	56 27	49	124	57 16	47	123	58 03	48	122	329
32	54 18	49	125	55 07	49	124	55 56	48	123	56 44	47	122	57 31	47	120	328
33	53 47	49	123	54 36	48	122	55 24	47	121	56 11	47	120	56 58	47	119	327
34	53 15	48	122	54 03	48	121	54 51	47	120	55 38	47	119	56 25	46	118	326
35	52 43	+48	121	53 31	+47	120	54 18	+47	119	55 05	+46	118	55 51	+46	117	325
36	52 10	48	120	52 58	47	119	53 45	47	118	54 32	46	117	55 18	45	116	324
37	51 37	48	119	52 25	46	118	53 11	47	117	53 58	45	115	54 43	45	114	323
38	51 04	47	117	51 51	47	116	52 38	45	115	53 23	46	114	54 09	44	113	322
39	50 30	47	116	51 17	46	115	52 03	46	114	52 49	45	113	53 34	44	112	321
40	49 56	+47	115	50 43	+46	114	51 29	+45	113	52 14	+45	112	52 59	+44	111	320
41	49 22	46	114	50 08	46	113	50 54	45	112	51 39	44	111	52 23	44	110	319
42	48 47	46	113	49 33	46	112	50 19	45	111	51 04	44	110	51 48	43	109	318
43	48 13	45	112	48 58	45	111	49 43	45	110	50 28	44	109	51 12	43	108	317
44	47 37	46	111	48 23	45	110	49 08	44	109	49 52	44	108	50 36	43	107	316
45	47 02	+45	110	47 47	+45	109	48 32	+44	108	49 16	+44	107	50 00	+43	106	315
46	46 26	45	109	47 11	45	108	47 56	44	107	48 40	43	106	49 23	43	105	314
47	45 51	45	108	46 35	45	107	47 20	43	106	48 03	44	105	48 47	42	104	313
48	45 15	44	107	45 59	44	106	46 43	44	105	47 27	43	104	48 10	42	103	312
49	44 38	45	106	45 23	44	105	46 07	43	104	46 50	43	103	47 33	42	102	311
50	44 02	+44	105	44 46	+44	104	45 30	+43	103	46 13	+43	102	46 56	+42	101	310
51	43 25	45	104	44 10	43	103	44 53	43	102	45 36	43	101	46 19	42	100	309
52	42 49	44	103	43 33	43	102	44 16	43	101	44 59	43	100	45 42	42	99	308
53	42 12	44	102	42 56	43	101	43 39	43	100	44 22	42	100	45 04	42	99	307
54	41 35	44	101	42 19	43	101	43 02	43	100	43 45	42	99	44 27	42	98	306
55	40 58	+43	101	41 41	+44	100	42 25	+42	99	43 07	+43	98	43 50	+41	97	305
56	40 21	43	100	41 04	43	99	41 47	43	98	42 30	42	97	43 12	42	96	304
57	39 43	44	99	40 27	43	98	41 10	42	97	41 52	43	96	42 35	41	95	303
58	39 06	43	98	39 49	43	97	40 32	43	96	41 15	42	95	41 57	41	94	302
59	38 29	43	98	39 12	43	96	39 55	42	95	40 37	42	94	41 19	42	93	301
60	37 51	+43	96	38 34	+43	95	39 17	+43	95	40 00	+41	94	40 41	+42	93	300
61	37 14	43	95	37 57	42	95	38 39	43	94	39 22	42	93	40 04	41	92	299
62	36 36	43	95	37 19	43	94	38 02	42	93	38 44	42	92	39 26	41	91	298
63	35 58	43	94	36 41	43	93	37 24	42	92	38 06	42	91	38 48	42	90	297
64	35 21	43	93	36 04	42	92	36 46	43	91	37 29	42	90	38 11	41	90	296
65	34 43	+43	92	35 26	+43	91	36 09	+42	91	36 51	+42	90	37 33	+41	89	295
66	34 05	43	91	34 48	43	91	35 31	42	90	36 13	42	89	36 55	41	88	294
67	33 27	43	91	34 10	43	90	34 53	42	89	35 35	42	88	36 17	42	87	293
68	32 50	43	90	33 33	42	89	34 15	43	88	34 58	42	87	35 40	41	86	292
69	32 12	43	89	32 55	43	88	33 38	42	87	34 20	42	87	35 02	42	86	291

S. Lat. {LHA greater than 180°....... Zn=180−Z; LHA less than 180°.......... Zn=180+Z}

DECLINATION (15°-29°) SAME NAME AS LATITUDE

N. Lat. {LHA greater than 180°........Zn=Z; LHA less than 180°...........Zn=360−Z}

DECLINATION (15°-29°) SAME NAME AS LATITUDE

LHA	15° Hc	d	Z	16° Hc	d	Z	17° Hc	d	Z	18° Hc	d	Z	19° Hc	d	Z	LHA
	° ′	′	°	° ′	′	°	° ′	′	°	° ′	′	°	° ′	′	°	
70	24 09	+45	96	24 54	+46	95	25 40	+45	95	26 25	+45	94	27 10	+45	93	290
71	23 31	46	95	24 17	45	94	25 02	45	94	25 47	45	93	26 32	45	92	289
72	22 54	45	94	23 39	45	94	24 24	45	93	25 09	45	92	25 54	45	91	288
73	22 16	45	94	23 01	46	93	23 47	45	92	24 32	45	91	25 17	44	91	287
74	21 38	46	93	22 24	45	92	23 09	45	91	23 54	45	91	24 39	45	90	286
75	21 00	+46	92	21 46	+45	91	22 31	+45	91	23 16	+45	90	24 01	+45	89	285
76	20 23	45	91	21 08	45	90	21 53	45	90	22 38	45	89	23 23	45	88	284
77	19 45	45	90	20 30	46	90	21 16	45	89	22 01	45	88	22 46	44	88	283
78	19 07	46	90	19 53	45	89	20 38	45	88	21 23	45	88	22 08	45	87	282
79	18 29	46	89	19 15	45	88	20 00	45	87	20 45	45	87	21 30	45	86	281
80	17 52	+45	88	18 37	+45	87	19 22	+46	87	20 08	+45	86	20 53	+44	85	280
81	17 14	45	87	17 59	46	87	18 45	45	86	19 30	45	85	20 15	45	85	279
82	16 36	46	87	17 22	45	86	18 07	45	85	18 52	45	84	19 37	45	84	278
83	15 59	45	86	16 44	46	85	17 30	45	84	18 15	45	84	19 00	45	83	277
84	15 21	46	85	16 07	45	84	16 52	45	84	17 37	45	83	18 22	45	82	276
85	14 43	+46	84	15 29	+45	84	16 14	+46	83	17 00	+45	82	17 45	+45	82	275
86	14 06	45	84	14 51	46	83	15 37	45	82	16 22	46	81	17 08	45	81	274
87	13 28	46	83	14 14	46	82	15 00	45	81	15 45	46	81	16 31	45	80	273
88	12 51	46	82	13 37	45	81	14 22	46	81	15 08	45	80	15 53	46	79	272
89	12 14	45	81	12 59	46	81	13 45	46	80	14 31	45	79	15 16	46	79	271
90	11 36	+46	80	12 22	+46	80	13 08	+46	79	13 54	+45	78	14 39	+46	78	270
91	10 59	46	80	11 45	46	79	12 31	46	78	13 17	46	78	14 03	45	77	269
92	10 22	46	79	11 08	46	78	11 54	46	78	12 40	46	77	13 26	46	76	268
93	09 45	46	78	10 31	46	78	11 17	46	77	12 03	46	76	12 49	46	76	267
94	09 08	46	77	09 54	47	77	10 41	46	76	11 27	46	76	12 13	46	75	266
95	08 31	+47	77	09 18	+46	76	10 04	+46	75	10 50	+46	75	11 36	+46	74	265
96	07 55	46	76	08 41	46	75	09 27	47	75	10 14	46	74	11 00	46	73	264
97	07 18	47	75	08 05	46	75	08 51	47	74	09 38	46	73	10 24	46	73	263
98	06 42	46	74	07 28	47	74	08 15	47	73	09 02	46	73	09 48	46	72	262
99	06 05	47	74	06 52	47	73	07 39	47	72	08 26	46	72	09 12	47	71	261
100	05 29	+47	73	06 16	+47	72	07 03	+47	72	07 50	+47	71	08 37	+46	70	260
101	04 53	47	72	05 40	47	72	06 27	47	71	07 14	47	70	08 01	47	70	259
102	04 17	47	71	05 04	48	71	05 52	47	70	06 39	47	70	07 26	47	69	258
103	03 42	47	71	04 29	47	70	05 16	47	69	06 03	48	69	06 51	47	68	257
104	03 06	47	70	03 53	48	69	04 41	47	69	05 28	48	68	06 16	47	67	256
105	02 31	+47	69	03 18	+48	68	04 06	+47	68	04 53	+48	67	05 41	+47	67	255
106	01 55	48	68	02 43	48	68	03 31	48	67	04 19	47	66	05 06	48	66	254
107	01 20	48	68	02 08	48	67	02 56	48	66	03 44	48	66	04 32	48	65	253
108	00 46	48	67	01 34	48	66	02 22	48	66	03 10	48	65	03 58	48	64	252
109	00 11	48	66	00 59	49	65	01 48	48	65	02 36	48	64	03 24	48	64	251
110	−0 23	+48	65	00 25	+49	65	01 14	+48	64	02 02	+48	63	02 50	+49	63	250
111	−0 57	48	64	−0 09	49	64	00 40	48	63	01 28	49	63	02 17	48	62	249
112	−1 31	48	64	−0 43	49	63	00 06	49	62	00 55	49	62	01 44	48	61	248
113	−2 05	49	63	−1 16	49	62	−0 27	49	62	00 22	49	61	01 11	48	61	247
114	−2 39	50	62	−1 49	49	61	−1 00	49	61	−0 11	49	60	00 38	49	60	246
115	−3 12	+49	61	−2 23	+50	61	−1 33	+49	60	−0 44	+49	60	00 05	+50	59	245
116	−3 45	50	60	−2 55	49	60	−2 06	50	59	−1 16	49	59	−0 27	50	58	244
117	−4 17	49	60	−3 28	50	59	−2 38	49	59	−1 49	50	58	−0 59	50	57	243
118	−4 50	50	59	−4 00	50	58	−3 10	50	58	−2 20	49	57	−1 31	50	57	242
119	−5 22	50	58	−4 32	50	57	−3 42	50	57	−2 52	50	56	−2 02	50	56	241
120	−5 54	+50	57	−5 04	+50	57	−4 14	+51	56	−3 23	+50	56	−2 33	+50	55	240
121				−5 35	50	56	−4 45	51	55	−3 54	50	55	−3 04	51	54	239
122							−5 16	51	54	−4 25	51	54	−3 34	50	53	238
123							−5 46	51	54	−4 55	50	53	−4 05	51	53	237
124										−5 26	52	52	−4 34	51	52	236
125										−5 55	+51	52	−5 04	+51	51	235
126													−5 33	51	50	234

LHA	20° Hc	d	Z	21° Hc	d	Z	22° Hc	d	Z	23° Hc	d	Z	24° Hc	d	Z	LHA
	° ′	′	°	° ′	′	°	° ′	′	°	° ′	′	°	° ′	′	°	
70	27 55	+44	92	28 39	+44	92	29 23	+44	91	30 07	+44	90	30 51	+43	89	290
71	27 17	44	92	28 01	44	91	28 45	44	90	29 29	44	89	30 13	43	88	289
72	26 39	45	91	27 24	44	90	28 08	44	89	28 52	43	88	29 35	44	88	288
73	26 01	45	90	26 46	44	89	27 30	44	88	28 14	44	88	28 58	43	87	287
74	25 24	44	89	26 08	44	88	26 52	44	88	27 36	44	87	28 20	43	86	286
75	24 46	+44	88	25 30	+44	88	26 14	+44	87	26 58	+44	86	27 42	+44	85	285
76	24 08	45	88	24 53	44	87	25 37	44	86	26 21	44	85	27 05	43	85	284
77	23 30	45	87	24 15	44	86	24 59	44	85	25 43	44	85	26 27	44	84	283
78	22 53	44	86	23 37	45	85	24 22	44	85	25 06	44	84	25 50	43	83	282
79	22 15	45	85	23 00	44	85	23 44	44	84	24 28	44	83	25 12	44	82	281
80	21 37	+45	85	22 22	+44	84	23 06	+45	83	23 51	+44	82	24 35	+44	82	280
81	21 00	45	84	21 45	44	83	22 29	44	82	23 13	44	82	23 57	44	81	279
82	20 22	45	83	21 07	45	82	21 52	44	82	22 36	44	81	23 20	44	80	278
83	19 45	45	82	20 30	44	82	21 14	45	81	21 59	44	80	22 43	44	79	277
84	19 07	45	82	19 52	45	81	20 37	45	80	21 22	44	79	22 06	44	79	276
85	18 30	+45	81	19 15	+45	80	20 00	+45	79	20 45	+44	79	21 29	+44	78	275
86	17 53	45	80	18 38	45	79	19 23	45	79	20 08	44	78	20 52	44	77	274
87	17 16	45	79	18 01	45	79	18 46	45	78	19 31	44	77	20 15	45	77	273
88	16 39	45	79	17 24	45	78	18 09	45	77	18 54	45	77	19 39	44	76	272
89	16 02	45	78	16 47	45	77	17 32	45	77	18 17	45	76	19 02	45	75	271
90	15 25	+45	77	16 10	+46	76	16 56	+45	76	17 41	+45	75	18 26	+44	74	270
91	14 48	46	76	15 34	45	76	16 19	45	75	17 04	45	74	17 49	45	74	269
92	14 12	45	76	14 57	46	75	15 43	45	74	16 28	45	74	17 13	45	73	268
93	13 35	46	75	14 21	45	74	15 06	46	74	15 52	45	73	16 37	45	72	267
94	12 59	45	74	13 44	46	74	14 30	46	73	15 16	45	72	16 01	46	72	266
95	12 22	+46	73	13 08	+46	73	13 54	+46	72	14 40	+46	71	15 26	+45	71	265
96	11 46	46	73	12 32	46	72	13 18	46	71	14 04	46	71	14 50	46	70	264
97	11 10	47	72	11 57	46	71	12 43	46	71	13 29	46	70	14 15	45	69	263
98	10 34	47	71	11 21	46	71	12 07	46	70	12 53	46	69	13 39	46	69	262
99	09 59	46	71	10 45	47	70	11 32	46	69	12 18	46	69	13 04	46	68	261
100	09 23	+47	70	10 10	+47	69	10 57	+46	68	11 43	+46	68	12 29	+47	67	260
101	08 48	47	69	09 35	46	68	10 21	47	68	11 08	47	67	11 55	46	66	259
102	08 13	47	68	09 00	47	68	09 47	46	67	10 33	47	66	11 20	47	66	258
103	07 38	47	68	08 25	47	67	09 12	47	66	09 59	47	66	10 46	47	65	257
104	07 03	47	67	07 50	48	66	08 38	47	66	09 25	47	65	10 12	47	64	256
105	06 28	+48	66	07 16	+47	65	08 03	+48	65	08 51	+47	64	09 38	+47	64	255
106	05 54	48	65	06 42	47	65	07 29	48	64	08 17	47	63	09 04	48	63	254
107	05 20	48	65	06 08	47	64	06 55	48	63	07 43	48	63	08 31	47	62	253
108	04 46	48	64	05 34	48	63	06 22	48	63	07 10	47	62	07 57	48	61	252
109	04 12	48	63	05 00	48	62	05 48	48	62	06 36	48	61	07 24	48	61	251
110	03 39	+48	62	04 27	+48	62	05 15	+48	61	06 03	+49	60	06 52	+48	60	250
111	03 05	49	61	03 54	48	61	04 42	49	60	05 31	48	60	06 19	49	59	249
112	02 32	49	61	03 21	49	60	04 10	48	60	04 58	49	59	05 47	48	58	248
113	01 59	49	60	02 48	49	59	03 37	49	59	04 26	49	59	05 15	49	58	247
114	01 27	49	59	02 16	49	59	03 05	49	58	03 54	49	58	04 43	49	57	246
115	00 55	+49	58	01 44	+49	58	02 33	+49	57	03 22	+50	57	04 12	+49	56	245
116	00 23	49	58	01 12	50	57	02 02	49	57	02 51	49	57	03 40	50	56	244
117	−0 09	49	57	00 40	50	56	01 30	50	56	02 20	49	56	03 09	50	55	243
118	−0 41	50	56	00 09	50	56	00 59	50	55	01 49	50	55	02 39	50	54	242
119	−1 12	50	55	−0 22	50	55	00 28	50	54	01 18	51	54	02 09	50	53	241
120	−1 43	+51	54	−0 52	+50	54	−0 02	+50	53	00 48	+50	53	01 38	+51	52	240
121	−2 13	50	54	−1 23	51	53	−0 32	50	53	00 18	51	52	01 09	50	52	239
122	−2 44	51	53	−1 53	51	52	−1 02	51	52	−0 11	50	51	00 39	51	51	238
123	−3 14	51	52	−2 23	51	52	−1 32	51	51	−0 41	51	51	00 10	51	50	237
124	−3 43	51	51	−2 52	51	51	−2 01	51	50	−1 10	51	50	−0 19	52	49	236
125	−4 13	+52	51	−3 21	+51	50	−2 30	+52	49	−1 38	+51	49	−0 47	+51	48	235
126	−4 42	52	50	−3 50	52	49	−2 58	51	49	−2 07	52	48	−1 15	52	47	234
127	−5 10	52	49	−4 18	51	48	−3 27	52	48	−2 35	52	47	−1 43	52	47	233
128	−5 38	52	48	−4 46	52	48	−3 54	52	47	−3 02	52	47	−2 10	52	46	232
129				−5 14	52	47	−4 22	52	46	−3 30	53	46	−2 37	52	45	231
130				−5 41	+52	46	−4 49	+53	45	−3 56	+52	45	−3 04	+53	44	230
131							−5 16	53	45	−4 23	53	44	−3 30	53	44	229
132							−5 42	53	44	−4 49	53	43	−3 56	53	43	228
133										−5 15	53	42	−4 22	54	42	227
134										−5 40	53	42	−4 47	54	41	226
135													−5 11	+53	40	225
136													−5 36	54	40	224

LHA	25° Hc	d	Z	26° Hc	d	Z	27° Hc	d	Z	28° Hc	d	Z	29° Hc	d	Z	LHA
	° ′	′	°	° ′	′	°	° ′	′	°	° ′	′	°	° ′	′	°	
70	31 34	+43	88	32 17	+43	88	33 00	+42	87	33 42	+42	86	34 24	+42	85	290
71	30 56	43	88	31 39	43	87	32 22	43	86	33 05	42	85	33 47	41	84	289
72	30 19	43	87	31 02	43	86	31 45	42	85	32 27	42	84	33 09	42	84	288
73	29 41	43	86	30 24	43	85	31 07	42	84	31 49	43	84	32 32	42	83	287
74	29 03	44	85	29 47	42	85	30 29	43	84	31 12	42	83	31 54	42	82	286
75	28 26	+43	85	29 09	+43	84	29 52	+43	83	30 35	+42	82	31 17	+42	81	285
76	27 48	43	84	28 31	43	83	29 14	43	82	29 57	43	81	30 40	42	81	284
77	27 11	43	83	27 54	43	82	28 37	43	82	29 20	42	81	30 02	43	80	283
78	26 33	44	82	27 17	43	82	28 00	43	81	28 43	42	80	29 25	43	79	282
79	25 56	43	82	26 39	44	81	27 23	43	80	28 06	42	79	28 48	43	79	281
80	25 19	+43	81	26 02	+43	80	26 45	+43	79	27 28	+43	79	28 11	+43	78	280
81	24 41	44	80	25 25	43	79	26 08	43	79	26 51	43	78	27 34	43	77	279
82	24 04	44	79	24 48	43	79	25 31	44	78	26 15	43	77	26 58	42	76	278
83	23 27	44	79	24 11	43	78	24 54	44	77	25 38	43	76	26 21	43	76	277
84	22 50	44	78	23 34	44	77	24 18	43	77	25 01	44	76	25 45	43	75	276
85	22 13	+44	77	22 57	+44	77	23 41	+44	76	24 25	+43	75	25 08	+43	74	275
86	21 36	45	77	22 21	44	76	23 05	43	75	23 48	44	74	24 32	43	74	274
87	21 00	44	76	21 44	44	75	22 28	44	74	23 12	44	74	23 56	43	73	273
88	20 23	45	75	21 08	44	74	21 52	44	74	22 36	44	73	23 20	43	72	272
89	19 47	44	74	20 31	45	74	21 16	44	73	22 00	44	72	22 44	44	72	271
90	19 10	+45	74	19 55	+45	73	20 40	+44	72	21 24	+44	72	22 08	+44	71	270
91	18 34	45	73	19 19	45	72	20 04	44	72	20 48	44	71	21 32	45	70	269
92	17 58	45	72	18 43	45	72	19 28	45	71	20 13	44	70	20 57	44	69	268
93	17 22	45	72	18 07	45	71	18 52	45	70	19 37	45	69	20 22	44	69	267
94	16 47	45	71	17 32	45	70	18 17	45	69	19 02	45	69	19 47	44	68	266
95	16 11	+45	70	16 56	+46	69	17 42	+45	69	18 27	+45	68	19 12	+45	67	265
96	15 36	45	69	16 21	46	69	17 07	45	68	17 52	45	67	18 37	45	67	264
97	15 00	46	69	15 46	46	68	16 32	45	67	17 17	45	67	18 02	46	66	263
98	14 25	46	68	15 11	46	67	15 57	46	67	16 43	45	66	17 28	45	65	262
99	13 50	46	67	14 36	46	67	15 22	46	66	16 08	46	65	16 54	45	65	261
100	13 16	+46	67	14 02	+46	66	14 48	+46	65	15 34	+46	65	16 20	+46	64	260
101	12 41	47	66	13 28	46	65	14 14	46	65	15 00	46	64	15 46	46	63	259
102	12 07	46	65	12 53	47	64	13 40	46	64	14 26	47	63	15 13	46	62	258
103	11 33	46	64	12 19	47	64	13 06	47	63	13 53	46	62	14 39	47	62	257
104	10 59	47	64	11 46	47	63	12 33	46	62	13 19	47	62	14 06	47	61	256
105	10 25	+47	63	11 12	+47	62	11 59	+47	62	12 46	+47	61	13 33	+47	60	255
106	09 52	47	62	10 39	47	62	11 26	47	61	12 13	47	60	13 00	47	60	254
107	09 18	48	61	10 06	47	61	10 53	48	60	11 41	47	60	12 28	47	59	253
108	08 45	48	61	09 33	48	60	10 21	47	60	11 08	48	59	11 56	47	58	252
109	08 12	48	60	09 00	48	59	09 48	48	59	10 36	48	58	11 24	47	58	251
110	07 40	+48	59	08 28	+48	59	09 16	+48	58	10 04	+48	57	10 52	+48	57	250
111	07 08	48	59	07 56	48	58	08 44	48	57	09 32	49	57	10 21	48	56	249
112	06 35	49	58	07 24	49	57	08 13	48	57	09 01	48	56	09 49	49	55	248
113	06 04	48	57	06 52	49	56	07 41	49	56	08 30	48	55	09 18	49	55	247
114	05 32	49	56	06 21	49	56	07 10	49	55	07 59	49	55	08 48	49	54	246
115	05 01	+49	56	05 50	+49	55	06 39	+49	54	07 28	+49	54	08 17	+49	53	245
116	04 30	49	55	05 19	50	54	06 09	49	54	06 58	49	53	07 47	49	53	244
117	03 59	50	54	04 49	49	54	05 38	50	53	06 28	49	52	07 17	50	52	243
118	03 29	50	53	04 19	49	53	05 08	50	52	05 58	50	52	06 48	50	51	242
119	02 59	50	53	03 49	50	52	04 39	50	51	05 29	50	51	06 19	50	50	241
120	02 29	+50	52	03 19	+50	51	04 09	+51	51	05 00	+50	50	05 50	+50	50	240
121	01 59	51	51	02 50	50	50	03 40	51	50	04 31	50	49	05 21	51	49	239
122	01 30	51	50	02 21	50	50	03 11	51	49	04 02	51	49	04 53	51	48	238
123	01 01	51	50	01 52	51	49	02 43	51	48	03 34	51	48	04 25	51	47	237
124	00 33	51	49	01 24	51	48	02 15	51	48	03 06	51	47	03 57	51	47	236
125	00 04	+52	48	00 56	+51	47	01 47	+52	47	02 39	+51	46	03 30	+51	46	235
126	−0 23	51	47	00 28	52	47	01 20	51	46	02 11	52	46	03 03	52	45	234
127	−0 51	52	46	00 01	52	46	00 53	52	45	01 45	52	45	02 37	51	44	233
128	−1 18	52	46	−0 26	52	45	00 26	53	45	01 19	51	44	02 10	52	44	232
129	−1 45	52	45	−0 53	53	44	00 00	52	44	00 52	52	43	01 44	53	43	231
130	−2 11	+52	44	−1 19	+53	44	−0 26	+52	43	00 26	+53	43	01 19	+53	42	230
131	−2 37	52	43	−1 45	53	43	−0 52	53	42	00 01	53	42	00 54	53	41	229
132	−3 03	53	42	−2 10	53	42	−1 17	53	42	−0 24	53	41	00 29	53	41	228
133	−3 28	53	42	−2 35	53	41	−1 42	53	41	−0 49	54	40	00 05	53	40	227
134	−3 53	53	41	−3 00	54	40	−2 06	53	40	−1 13	54	39	−0 19	53	39	226
135	−4 18	+54	40	−3 24	+54	39	−2 30	+54	39	−1 36	+53	39	−0 43	+54	38	225
136	−4 42	54	39	−3 48	54	39	−2 54	54	38	−2 00	54	38	−1 06	54	37	224
137	−5 05	54	38	−4 11	54	38	−3 17	54	38	−2 23	54	37	−1 29	55	37	223
138	−5 29	55	37	−4 34	54	37	−3 40	55	37	−2 45	54	36	−1 51	54	36	222
139				−4 57	55	36	−4 02	55	36	−3 07	54	35	−2 13	55	35	221

15°	16°	17°	18°	19°	20°	21°	22°	23°	24°	25°	26°	27°	28°	29°

S. Lat. {LHA greater than 180°........Zn=180−Z; LHA less than 180°...........Zn=180+Z}

DECLINATION (15°-29°) SAME NAME AS LATITUDE

LAT 51°

N. Lat. {LHA greater than 180°....... Zn=Z; LHA less than 180°........... Zn=360−Z}

DECLINATION (15°-29°) SAME NAME AS LATITUDE

LHA	15° Hc d Z	16° Hc d Z	17° Hc d Z	18° Hc d Z	19° Hc d Z	20° Hc d Z	21° Hc d Z	22° Hc d Z	23° Hc d Z	24° Hc d Z	25° Hc d Z		26° Hc d Z	27° Hc d Z	28° Hc d Z	29° Hc d Z	LHA
	° ′ ′ °	° ′ ′ °	° ′ ′ °	° ′ ′ °	° ′ ′ °	° ′ ′ °	° ′ ′ °	° ′ ′ °	° ′ ′ °	° ′ ′ °	° ′ ′ °		° ′ ′ °	° ′ ′ °	° ′ ′ °	° ′ ′ °	
												140	−5 19 +55 35	−4 24 +55 35	−3 29 +55 35	−2 34 +55 34	220
												141	−5 41 56 35	−4 45 55 34	−3 50 55 34	−2 55 55 33	219
													142	−5 07 56 33	−4 11 55 33	−3 16 55 33	218
													143	−5 27 55 33	−4 32 56 32	−3 36 55 32	217
														144	−4 51 55 31	−3 56 56 31	216
														145	−5 11 +56 31	−4 15 +56 30	215
														146	−5 30 56 30	−4 34 56 29	214
															147	−4 52 56 29	213
															148	−5 10 57 28	212
															149	−5 27 57 27	211

LHA	15° Hc d Z	16° Hc d Z	17° Hc d Z	18° Hc d Z	19° Hc d Z	20° Hc d Z	21° Hc d Z	22° Hc d Z	23° Hc d Z	24°	25°	26°	27°	28°	29°
81	−6 05 47 106	279													
80	−5 29 −47 107	280													
79	−4 53 47 108	−5 40 47 108	281												
78	−4 17 47 109	−5 04 48 109	−5 52 47 110	282											
77	−3 42 47 109	−4 29 47 110	−5 16 47 111	−6 03 48 111	283										
76	−3 06 47 110	−3 53 48 111	−4 41 47 111	−5 28 48 112	284										
75	−2 31 −47 111	−3 18 −48 112	−4 06 −47 112	−4 53 −48 113	−5 41 −47 113	285									
74	−1 55 48 112	−2 43 48 112	−3 31 48 113	−4 19 47 114	−5 06 48 114	−5 54 48 115	286								
73	−1 20 48 112	−2 08 48 113	−2 56 48 114	−3 44 48 114	−4 32 48 115	−5 20 48 115	287								
72	−0 46 48 113	−1 34 48 114	−2 22 48 114	−3 10 48 115	−3 58 48 116	−4 46 48 116	−5 34 48 117	288							
71	−0 11 48 114	−0 59 49 115	−1 48 48 115	−2 36 48 116	−3 24 48 116	−4 12 48 117	−5 00 48 118	−5 48 48 118	289						
70	00 23 −48 115	−0 25 −49 115	−1 14 −48 116	−2 02 −48 117	−2 50 −49 117	−3 39 −48 118	−4 27 −48 118	−5 15 −48 119	−6 03 −49 120	290					
	15°	16°	17°	18°	19°	20°	21°	22°	23°	24°	25°	26°	27°	28°	29°

S. Lat. {LHA greater than 180°....... Zn=180−Z; LHA less than 180°........... Zn=180+Z}

DECLINATION (15°-29°) CONTRARY NAME TO LATITUDE

LHA	15° Hc	15° d	15° Z	16° Hc	16° d	16° Z	17° Hc	17° d	17° Z	18° Hc	18° d	18° Z	19° Hc	19° d	19° Z
	° ′	′	°	° ′	′	°	° ′	′	°	° ′	′	°	° ′	′	°
69	00 57	48	116	00 09	49	116	−0 40	48	117	−1 28	49	117	−2 17	48	118
68	01 31	48	116	00 43	49	117	−0 06	49	118	−0 55	49	118	−1 44	48	119
67	02 05	49	117	01 16	49	118	00 27	49	118	−0 22	49	119	−1 11	48	119
66	02 39	50	118	01 49	49	119	01 00	49	119	00 11	49	120	−0 38	49	120
65	03 12	−49	119	02 23	−50	119	01 33	−49	120	00 44	−49	120	−0 05	−50	121
64	03 45	50	120	02 55	49	120	02 06	50	121	01 16	49	121	00 27	50	122
63	04 17	49	120	03 28	50	121	02 38	49	121	01 49	50	122	00 59	50	123
62	04 50	50	121	04 00	50	122	03 10	50	122	02 20	49	123	01 31	50	123
61	05 22	50	122	04 32	50	123	03 42	50	123	02 52	50	124	02 02	50	124
60	05 54	−50	123	05 04	−50	123	04 14	−51	124	03 23	−50	124	02 33	−50	125
59	06 26	51	124	05 35	50	124	04 45	51	125	03 54	50	125	03 04	51	126
58	06 57	51	124	06 06	50	125	05 16	51	126	04 25	51	126	03 34	50	127
57	07 28	51	125	06 37	51	126	05 46	51	126	04 55	50	127	04 05	51	127
56	07 59	51	126	07 08	51	127	06 17	51	127	05 26	52	128	04 34	51	128
55	08 29	−51	127	07 38	−51	127	06 47	−52	128	05 55	−51	128	05 04	−51	129
54	08 59	51	128	08 08	52	128	07 16	51	129	06 25	52	129	05 33	51	130
53	09 29	52	129	08 37	52	129	07 45	51	130	06 54	52	130	06 02	52	131
52	09 58	52	129	09 06	52	130	08 14	52	130	07 22	52	131	06 30	52	131
51	10 27	52	130	09 35	52	131	08 43	52	131	07 51	52	132	06 59	53	132
50	10 56	−52	131	10 04	−53	132	09 11	−52	132	08 19	−53	133	07 26	−52	133
49	11 24	52	132	10 32	53	132	09 39	53	133	08 46	52	133	07 54	53	134
48	11 52	53	133	10 59	53	133	10 06	52	134	09 14	53	134	08 21	53	135
47	12 19	52	134	11 27	53	134	10 34	54	135	09 40	53	135	08 47	53	136
46	12 47	54	135	11 53	53	135	11 00	53	136	10 07	53	136	09 14	54	136
45	13 13	−53	135	12 20	−54	136	11 26	−53	136	10 33	−54	137	09 39	−53	137
44	13 40	54	136	12 46	54	137	11 52	53	137	10 59	54	138	10 05	54	138
43	14 05	53	137	13 12	54	138	12 18	54	138	11 24	54	139	10 30	54	139
42	14 31	54	138	13 37	54	139	12 43	54	139	11 49	55	139	10 54	54	140
41	14 56	54	139	14 02	55	140	13 07	54	140	12 13	55	140	11 18	54	141
40	15 20	−54	140	14 26	−55	140	13 31	−54	141	12 37	−55	141	11 42	−55	142
39	15 44	54	141	14 50	55	141	13 55	55	142	13 00	55	142	12 05	55	143
38	16 08	55	142	15 13	55	142	14 18	55	143	13 23	55	143	12 28	55	143
37	16 31	55	143	15 36	55	143	14 41	55	144	13 46	56	144	12 50	55	144
36	16 54	56	144	15 58	55	144	15 03	55	144	14 08	56	145	13 12	55	145
35	17 16	−56	145	16 20	−55	145	15 25	−56	145	14 29	−56	146	13 33	−55	146
34	17 38	56	146	16 42	56	146	15 46	56	146	14 50	56	147	13 54	56	147
33	17 59	56	146	17 03	56	147	16 07	56	147	15 11	56	148	14 15	57	148
32	18 19	56	147	17 23	56	148	16 27	56	148	15 31	57	149	14 34	56	149
31	18 40	57	148	17 43	56	149	16 47	57	149	15 50	56	149	14 54	57	150
30	18 59	−57	149	18 02	−56	150	17 06	−57	150	16 09	−57	150	15 12	−56	151
29	19 18	57	150	18 21	57	151	17 24	56	151	16 28	57	151	15 31	57	152
28	19 37	57	151	18 40	57	152	17 43	58	152	16 45	57	152	15 48	57	153
27	19 54	57	152	18 57	57	153	18 00	57	153	17 03	57	153	16 06	58	154
26	20 12	58	153	19 14	57	154	18 17	57	154	17 20	58	154	16 22	57	154
25	20 28	−57	154	19 31	−58	155	18 33	−57	155	17 36	−58	155	16 38	−58	155
24	20 45	58	155	19 47	58	155	18 49	58	156	17 51	57	156	16 54	58	156
23	21 00	58	156	20 02	58	156	19 04	58	157	18 06	58	157	17 08	58	157
22	21 15	58	157	20 17	58	157	19 19	58	158	18 21	58	158	17 23	58	158
21	21 30	59	158	20 31	58	158	19 33	58	159	18 35	58	159	17 37	59	159
20	21 43	−58	159	20 45	−59	159	19 46	−58	160	18 48	−58	160	17 50	−59	160
19	21 56	58	160	20 58	59	160	19 59	58	161	19 01	59	161	18 02	58	161
18	22 09	59	161	21 10	58	161	20 12	59	162	19 13	59	162	18 14	59	162
17	22 21	59	162	21 22	59	162	20 23	59	163	19 24	59	163	18 25	58	163
16	22 32	59	163	21 33	59	163	20 34	59	164	19 35	59	164	18 36	59	164
15	22 42	−59	164	21 43	−59	165	20 44	−59	165	19 45	−59	165	18 46	−59	165
14	22 52	59	165	21 53	59	166	20 54	59	166	19 55	59	166	18 56	60	166
13	23 02	60	166	22 02	59	167	21 03	59	167	20 04	60	167	19 04	59	167
12	23 10	59	167	22 11	60	168	21 11	59	168	20 12	59	168	19 13	60	168
11	23 18	59	168	22 19	60	169	21 19	59	169	20 20	60	169	19 20	59	169
10	23 25	−59	170	22 26	−60	170	21 26	−59	170	20 27	−60	170	19 27	−60	170
9	23 32	60	171	22 32	59	171	21 33	60	171	20 33	60	171	19 33	59	171
8	23 38	60	172	22 38	60	172	21 38	59	172	20 39	60	172	19 39	60	172
7	23 43	60	173	22 43	60	173	21 43	59	173	20 44	60	173	19 44	60	173
6	23 48	60	174	22 48	60	174	21 48	60	174	20 48	60	174	19 48	60	174
5	23 51	−60	175	22 51	−59	175	21 52	−60	175	20 52	−60	175	19 52	−60	175
4	23 54	59	176	22 55	60	176	21 55	60	176	20 55	60	176	19 55	60	176
3	23 57	60	177	22 57	60	177	21 57	60	177	20 57	60	177	19 57	60	177
2	23 59	60	178	22 59	60	178	21 59	60	178	20 59	60	178	19 59	60	178
1	24 00	60	179	23 00	60	179	22 00	60	179	21 00	60	179	20 00	60	179
0	24 00	−60	180	23 00	−60	180	22 00	−60	180	21 00	−60	180	20 00	−60	180

LHA	20° Hc	20° d	20° Z	21° Hc	21° d	21° Z	22° Hc	22° d	22° Z	23° Hc	23° d	23° Z	24° Hc	24° d	24° Z
	° ′	′	°	° ′	′	°	° ′	′	°	° ′	′	°	° ′	′	°
69	−3 05	49	119	−3 54	48	119	−4 42	49	120	−5 31	48	120	291		
68	−2 32	49	119	−3 21	49	120	−4 10	48	120	−4 58	49	121	−5 47	48	122
67	−1 59	49	120	−2 48	49	121	−3 37	49	121	−4 26	49	121	−5 15	49	122
66	−1 27	49	121	−2 16	49	121	−3 05	49	122	−3 54	49	122	−4 43	49	123
65	−0 55	−49	122	−1 44	−49	122	−2 33	−49	123	−3 22	−50	123	−4 12	−49	124
64	−0 23	49	122	−1 12	50	123	−2 02	49	123	−2 51	49	123	−3 40	50	124
63	00 09	49	123	−0 40	50	124	−1 30	50	124	−2 20	49	124	−3 09	50	125
62	00 41	50	124	−0 09	50	124	−0 59	50	125	−1 49	50	125	−2 39	50	126
61	01 12	50	125	00 22	50	125	−0 28	50	126	−1 18	51	126	−2 09	50	127
60	01 43	−51	126	00 52	−50	126	00 02	−50	127	−0 48	−50	127	−1 38	−51	128
59	02 13	50	126	01 23	51	127	00 32	50	127	−0 18	51	128	−1 09	50	128
58	02 44	51	127	01 53	51	128	01 02	51	128	00 11	50	129	−0 39	51	129
57	03 14	51	128	02 23	51	128	01 32	51	129	00 41	50	129	−0 10	51	130
56	03 43	51	129	02 52	51	129	02 01	51	130	01 10	51	130	00 19	52	131
55	04 13	−52	129	03 21	−51	130	02 30	−52	131	01 38	−51	131	00 47	−51	132
54	04 42	52	130	03 50	52	131	02 58	51	131	02 07	52	132	01 15	52	133
53	05 10	52	131	04 18	51	132	03 27	52	132	02 35	52	133	01 43	52	133
52	05 38	52	132	04 46	52	132	03 54	52	133	03 02	52	133	02 10	52	134
51	06 06	52	133	05 14	52	133	04 22	52	134	03 30	53	134	02 37	52	135
50	06 34	−53	134	05 41	−52	134	04 49	−53	135	03 56	−52	135	03 04	−53	136
49	07 01	53	134	06 08	52	135	05 16	53	135	04 23	53	136	03 30	53	136
48	07 28	53	135	06 35	53	136	05 42	53	136	04 49	53	137	03 56	53	137
47	07 54	53	136	07 01	53	137	06 08	53	137	05 15	53	138	04 22	54	138
46	08 20	53	137	07 27	53	137	06 34	54	138	05 40	53	138	04 47	54	139
45	08 46	−53	138	07 52	−53	138	06 59	−54	139	06 05	−54	139	05 11	−53	140
44	09 11	54	139	08 17	54	139	07 23	53	140	06 30	54	140	05 36	54	140
43	09 36	54	140	08 42	54	140	07 48	54	140	06 54	54	141	06 00	55	141
42	10 00	54	140	09 06	54	141	08 12	55	141	07 17	54	142	06 23	54	142
41	10 24	54	141	09 30	55	142	08 35	54	142	07 41	55	143	06 46	55	143
40	10 47	−54	142	09 53	−55	143	08 58	−55	143	08 03	−54	143	07 09	−55	144
39	11 10	54	143	10 16	55	143	09 21	55	144	08 26	55	144	07 31	55	145
38	11 33	55	144	10 38	55	144	09 43	55	145	08 48	56	145	07 52	55	145
37	11 55	55	145	11 00	56	145	10 04	55	146	09 09	55	146	08 14	56	146
36	12 17	56	146	11 21	56	146	10 25	55	146	09 30	56	147	08 34	55	147
35	12 38	−56	147	11 42	−56	147	10 46	−56	147	09 50	−55	148	08 55	−56	148
34	12 58	56	147	12 02	56	148	11 06	56	148	10 10	56	149	09 14	56	149
33	13 18	56	148	12 22	56	149	11 26	56	149	10 30	56	149	09 34	57	150
32	13 38	56	149	12 42	57	150	11 45	56	150	10 49	57	150	09 52	56	151
31	13 57	56	150	13 01	57	150	12 04	57	151	11 07	56	151	10 11	57	151
30	14 16	−57	151	13 19	−57	151	12 22	−57	152	11 25	−56	152	10 29	−57	152
29	14 34	57	152	13 37	57	152	12 40	57	153	11 43	57	153	10 46	57	153
28	14 51	57	153	13 54	57	153	12 57	57	154	12 00	57	154	11 03	58	154
27	15 08	57	154	14 11	57	154	13 14	58	154	12 16	57	155	11 19	58	155
26	15 25	58	155	14 27	57	155	13 30	58	155	12 32	58	156	11 34	57	156
25	15 40	−57	156	14 43	−58	156	13 45	−58	156	12 47	−57	157	11 50	−58	157
24	15 56	58	157	14 58	58	157	14 00	58	157	13 02	58	157	12 04	58	158
23	16 10	58	158	15 12	58	158	14 14	58	158	13 16	58	158	12 18	58	159
22	16 25	59	159	15 26	58	159	14 28	58	159	13 30	58	159	12 32	58	160
21	16 38	58	159	15 40	58	160	14 42	59	160	13 43	58	160	12 45	59	160
20	16 51	−58	160	15 53	−59	161	14 54	−58	161	13 56	−59	161	12 57	−58	161
19	17 04	59	161	16 05	59	162	15 06	58	162	14 08	59	162	13 09	59	162
18	17 15	58	162	16 17	59	163	15 18	59	163	14 19	59	163	13 20	59	163
17	17 27	59	163	16 28	59	164	15 29	59	164	14 30	59	164	13 31	59	164
16	17 37	59	164	16 38	59	164	15 39	59	165	14 40	59	165	13 41	59	165
15	17 47	−59	165	16 48	−59	165	15 49	−59	166	14 50	−59	166	13 51	−60	166
14	17 56	59	166	16 57	59	166	15 58	59	167	14 59	60	167	13 59	59	167
13	18 05	59	167	17 06	60	167	16 06	59	168	15 07	59	168	14 08	60	168
12	18 13	59	168	17 14	60	168	16 14	59	168	15 15	60	169	14 15	59	169
11	18 21	60	169	17 21	59	169	16 22	60	169	15 22	59	170	14 23	60	170
10	18 27	−59	170	17 28	−60	170	16 28	−59	170	15 29	−60	171	14 29	−60	171
9	18 34	60	171	17 34	60	171	16 34	59	171	15 35	60	171	14 35	60	172
8	18 39	60	172	17 39	59	172	16 40	60	172	15 40	60	172	14 40	60	172
7	18 44	60	173	17 44	60	173	16 44	59	173	15 45	60	173	14 45	60	173
6	18 48	60	174	17 48	59	174	16 49	60	174	15 49	60	174	14 49	60	174
5	18 52	−60	175	17 52	−60	175	16 52	−60	175	15 52	−60	175	14 52	−60	175
4	18 55	60	176	17 55	60	176	16 55	60	176	15 55	60	176	14 55	60	176
3	18 57	60	177	17 57	60	177	16 57	60	177	15 57	60	177	14 57	60	177
2	18 59	60	178	17 59	60	178	16 59	60	178	15 59	60	178	14 59	60	178
1	19 00	60	179	18 00	60	179	17 00	60	179	16 00	60	179	15 00	60	179
0	19 00	−60	180	18 00	−60	180	17 00	−60	180	16 00	−60	180	15 00	−60	180

LHA	25° Hc	25° d	25° Z	26° Hc	26° d	26° Z	27° Hc	27° d	27° Z	28° Hc	28° d	28° Z	29° Hc	29° d	29° Z	LHA
	° ′	′	°	° ′	′	°	° ′	′	°	° ′	′	°	° ′	′	°	
69																
68	292															
67	293															
66	−5 32	49	124	294												
65	−5 01	−49	124	−5 50	−49	125	295									
64	−4 30	49	125	−5 19	50	126	296									
63	−3 59	50	126	−4 49	49	126	−5 38	50	127	297						
62	−3 29	50	127	−4 19	49	127	−5 08	50	128	298						
61	−2 59	50	127	−3 49	50	128	−4 39	50	129	−5 29	50	129	299			
60	−2 29	−50	128	−3 19	−50	129	−4 09	−51	129	−5 00	−50	130	−5 50	−50	130	300
59	−1 59	51	129	−2 50	50	130	−3 40	51	130	−4 31	50	131	−5 21	51	131	301
58	−1 30	51	130	−2 21	50	130	−3 11	51	131	−4 02	51	131	−4 53	51	132	302
57	−1 01	51	130	−1 52	51	131	−2 43	51	132	−3 34	51	132	−4 25	51	133	303
56	−0 33	51	131	−1 24	51	132	−2 15	51	132	−3 06	51	133	−3 57	51	133	304
55	−0 04	−52	132	−0 56	−51	133	−1 47	−52	133	−2 39	−51	134	−3 30	−51	134	305
54	00 23	51	133	−0 28	52	133	−1 20	51	134	−2 11	52	134	−3 03	52	135	306
53	00 51	52	134	−0 01	52	134	−0 53	52	135	−1 45	52	135	−2 37	51	136	307
52	01 18	52	134	00 26	52	135	−0 26	53	135	−1 19	51	136	−2 10	52	136	308
51	01 45	52	135	00 53	53	136	00 00	52	136	−0 52	52	137	−1 44	53	137	309
50	02 11	−52	136	01 19	−53	136	00 26	−52	137	−0 26	−53	137	−1 19	−53	138	310
49	02 37	52	137	01 45	53	137	00 52	53	138	−0 01	53	138	−0 54	53	139	311
48	03 03	53	138	02 10	53	138	01 17	53	138	00 24	53	139	−0 29	53	139	312
47	03 28	53	138	02 35	53	139	01 42	53	139	00 49	54	140	−0 05	53	140	313
46	03 53	53	139	03 00	54	140	02 06	53	140	01 13	54	141	00 19	53	141	314
45	04 18	−54	140	03 24	−54	141	02 30	−54	141	01 36	−53	141	00 43	−54	142	315
44	04 42	54	141	03 48	54	141	02 54	54	142	02 00	54	142	01 06	54	143	316
43	05 05	54	142	04 11	54	142	03 17	54	142	02 23	54	143	01 29	55	143	317
42	05 29	55	143	04 34	54	143	03 40	55	143	02 45	54	144	01 51	54	144	318
41	05 51	54	143	04 57	55	144	04 02	55	144	03 07	54	145	02 13	55	145	319
40	06 14	−55	144	05 19	−55	145	04 24	−55	145	03 29	−55	145	02 34	−55	146	320
39	06 36	55	145	05 41	56	145	04 45	55	146	03 50	55	146	02 55	55	147	321
38	06 57	55	146	06 02	56	146	05 07	56	147	04 11	55	147	03 16	55	147	322
37	07 18	55	147	06 23	56	147	05 27	55	147	04 32	56	148	03 36	55	148	323
36	07 39	56	148	06 43	56	148	05 47	56	148	04 51	55	149	03 56	56	149	324
35	07 59	−56	148	07 03	−56	149	06 07	−56	149	05 11	−56	149	04 15	−56	150	325
34	08 18	56	149	07 22	56	150	06 26	56	150	05 30	56	150	04 34	56	151	326
33	08 37	56	150	07 41	56	150	06 45	57	151	05 48	56	151	04 52	56	151	327
32	08 56	57	151	07 59	56	151	07 03	57	152	06 06	56	152	05 10	57	152	328
31	09 14	57	152	08 17	56	152	07 21	57	152	06 24	56	153	05 27	56	153	329
30	09 32	−57	153	08 35	−57	153	07 38	−57	153	06 41	−57	154	05 44	−57	154	330
29	09 49	57	154	08 52	57	154	07 55	57	154	06 58	58	155	06 00	57	155	331
28	10 05	57	154	09 08	57	155	08 11	57	155	07 14	58	155	06 16	57	156	332
27	10 21	57	155	09 24	57	156	08 27	58	156	07 29	57	156	06 32	58	156	333
26	10 37	58	156	09 39	57	156	08 42	58	157	07 44	58	157	06 46	57	157	334
25	10 52	−58	157	09 54	−58	157	08 56	−57	158	07 59	−58	158	07 01	−58	158	335
24	11 06	58	158	10 08	58	158	09 10	57	159	08 13	58	159	07 15	58	159	336
23	11 20	58	159	10 22	58	159	09 24	58	159	08 26	58	160	07 28	58	160	337
22	11 34	59	160	10 35	58	160	09 37	58	160	08 39	58	161	07 41	59	161	338
21	11 46	58	161	10 48	58	161	09 50	58	161	08 51	58	161	07 53	59	162	339
20	11 59	−59	162	11 00	−58	162	10 02	−59	162	09 03	−59	162	08 04	−58	162	340
19	12 10	58	162	11 12	59	163	10 13	59	163	09 14	58	163	08 16	59	163	341
18	12 21	58	163	11 23	59	164	10 24	59	164	09 25	59	164	08 26	59	164	342
17	12 32	59	164	11 33	59	164	10 34	59	165	09 35	59	165	08 36	59	165	343
16	12 42	59	165	11 43	59	165	10 44	59	166	09 45	59	166	08 46	59	166	344
15	12 51	−59	166	11 52	−59	166	10 53	−59	166	09 54	−59	167	08 55	−59	167	345
14	13 00	59	167	12 01	59	167	11 02	60	167	10 02	59	168	09 03	59	168	346
13	13 08	59	168	12 09	59	168	11 10	60	168	10 10	59	168	09 11	60	169	347
12	13 16	59	169	12 17	60	169	11 17	59	169	10 18	60	169	09 18	59	169	348
11	13 23	60	170	12 23	59	170	11 24	60	170	10 24	59	170	09 25	60	170	349
10	13 29	−59	171	12 30	−60	171	11 30	−59	171	10 31	−60	171	09 31	−60	171	350
9	13 35	60	172	12 35	59	172	11 36	60	172	10 36	60	172	09 36	59	172	351
8	13 40	59	173	12 41	60	173	11 41	60	173	10 41	60	173	09 41	59	173	352
7	13 45	60	174	12 45	60	174	11 45	59	174	10 46	60	174	09 46	60	174	353
6	13 49	60	174	12 49	60	175	11 49	60	175	10 49	59	175	09 50	60	175	354
5	13 52	−60	175	12 52	−59	175	11 53	−60	175	10 53	−60	176	09 53	−60	176	355
4	13 55	60	176	12 55	60	176	11 55	60	176	10 55	60	176	09 55	60	176	356
3	13 57	60	177	12 57	60	177	11 57	60	177	10 57	60	177	09 57	60	177	357
2	13 59	60	178	12 59	60	178	11 59	60	178	10 59	60	178	09 59	60	178	358
1	14 00	60	179	13 00	60	179	12 00	60	179	11 00	60	179	10 00	60	179	359
0	14 00	−60	180	13 00	−60	180	12 00	−60	180	11 00	−60	180	10 00	−60	180	360

N. Lat. {LHA greater than 180°....... Zn=Z; LHA less than 180°........... Zn=360−Z}

DECLINATION (0°-14°) SAME NAME AS LATITUDE

LHA	0° Hc	d	Z	1° Hc	d	Z	2° Hc	d	Z	3° Hc	d	Z	4° Hc	d	Z
	° ′	′	°	° ′	′	°	° ′	′	°	° ′	′	°	° ′	′	°
0	38 00	+60	180	39 00	+60	180	40 00	+60	180	41 00	+60	180	42 00	+60	180
1	38 00	60	179	39 00	60	179	40 00	60	179	41 00	60	179	42 00	60	179
2	37 58	60	178	38 58	60	177	39 58	60	177	40 58	60	177	41 58	60	177
3	37 56	60	176	38 56	60	176	39 56	60	176	40 56	60	176	41 56	60	176
4	37 54	59	175	38 53	60	175	39 53	60	175	40 53	60	175	41 53	60	175
5	37 50	+60	174	38 50	+60	174	39 50	+59	174	40 49	+60	173	41 49	+60	173
6	37 45	60	172	38 45	60	172	39 45	60	172	40 45	60	172	41 45	59	172
7	37 40	60	171	38 40	60	171	39 40	59	171	40 39	60	171	41 39	60	171
8	37 34	60	170	38 34	59	170	39 33	60	170	40 33	59	170	41 32	60	169
9	37 27	60	169	38 27	59	169	39 26	60	168	40 26	59	168	41 25	60	168
10	37 19	+60	167	38 19	+59	167	39 18	+60	167	40 18	+59	167	41 17	+60	167
11	37 11	59	166	38 10	60	166	39 10	59	166	40 09	59	166	41 08	59	165
12	37 02	59	165	38 01	59	165	39 00	59	165	39 59	59	164	40 58	60	164
13	36 52	59	164	37 51	59	164	38 50	59	163	39 49	59	163	40 48	59	163
14	36 41	59	162	37 40	59	162	38 39	59	162	39 38	59	162	40 37	58	162
15	36 29	+59	161	37 28	+59	161	38 27	+59	161	39 26	+58	161	40 24	+59	160
16	36 17	59	160	37 16	58	160	38 14	59	160	39 13	59	159	40 12	58	159
17	36 04	59	159	37 03	58	159	38 01	58	158	38 59	59	158	39 58	58	158
18	35 50	59	158	36 49	58	157	37 47	58	157	38 45	58	157	39 43	59	156
19	35 36	58	156	36 34	58	156	37 32	58	156	38 30	58	156	39 28	58	155
20	35 21	+58	155	36 19	+58	155	37 17	+58	155	38 15	+57	154	39 12	+58	154
21	35 05	58	154	36 03	58	154	37 01	57	153	37 58	58	153	38 56	57	153
22	34 49	57	153	35 46	58	153	36 44	57	152	37 41	57	152	38 38	58	151
23	34 31	58	152	35 29	57	151	36 26	57	151	37 23	57	151	38 20	57	150
24	34 14	57	151	35 11	57	150	36 08	57	150	37 05	57	149	38 02	57	149
25	33 55	+57	149	34 52	+57	149	35 49	+57	149	36 46	+56	148	37 42	+57	148
26	33 36	57	148	34 33	56	148	35 29	57	147	36 26	56	147	37 22	57	147
27	33 16	57	147	34 13	56	147	35 09	56	146	36 05	57	146	37 02	56	145
28	32 56	56	146	33 52	56	146	34 48	56	145	35 44	56	145	36 40	56	144
29	32 35	56	145	33 31	56	145	34 27	56	144	35 23	56	144	36 19	55	143
30	32 13	+56	144	33 09	+56	143	34 05	+56	143	35 01	+55	142	35 56	+56	142
31	31 51	56	143	32 47	55	142	33 42	56	142	34 38	55	141	35 33	55	141
32	31 28	56	142	32 24	55	141	33 19	55	141	34 14	55	140	35 09	55	140
33	31 05	55	141	32 00	55	140	32 55	55	140	33 50	55	139	34 45	55	139
34	30 42	54	139	31 36	55	139	32 31	55	139	33 26	55	138	34 21	54	138
35	30 17	+55	138	31 12	+55	138	32 07	+54	137	33 01	+54	137	33 55	+55	136
36	29 52	55	137	30 47	54	137	31 41	55	136	32 36	54	136	33 30	54	135
37	29 27	54	136	30 21	55	136	31 16	54	135	32 10	53	135	33 03	54	134
38	29 01	54	135	29 55	54	135	30 49	54	134	31 43	54	134	32 37	53	133
39	28 35	54	134	29 29	54	134	30 23	53	133	31 16	54	133	32 10	53	132
40	28 08	+54	133	29 02	+53	133	29 55	+54	132	30 49	+53	132	31 42	+53	131
41	27 41	54	132	28 35	53	132	29 28	53	131	30 21	53	131	31 14	53	130
42	27 14	53	131	28 07	53	131	29 00	53	130	29 53	52	130	30 45	53	129
43	26 46	53	130	27 39	52	130	28 31	53	129	29 24	52	129	30 16	53	128
44	26 17	53	129	27 10	53	129	28 03	52	128	28 55	52	128	29 47	52	127
45	25 48	+53	128	26 41	+52	128	27 33	+52	127	28 25	+53	127	29 18	+51	126
46	25 19	52	127	26 11	53	127	27 04	52	126	27 56	51	126	28 47	52	125
47	24 50	52	126	25 42	52	126	26 34	51	125	27 25	52	125	28 17	52	124
48	24 20	52	125	25 12	51	125	26 03	52	124	26 55	51	124	27 46	52	123
49	23 49	52	124	24 41	52	124	25 33	51	123	26 24	51	123	27 15	51	122
50	23 19	+51	124	24 10	+51	123	25 01	+52	122	25 53	+51	122	26 44	+51	121
51	22 48	51	123	23 39	51	122	24 30	51	121	25 21	51	121	26 12	51	120
52	22 17	51	122	23 08	50	121	23 58	51	121	24 49	51	120	25 40	50	119
53	21 45	51	121	22 36	50	120	23 26	51	120	24 17	50	119	25 07	51	118
54	21 13	51	120	22 04	50	119	22 54	51	119	23 45	50	118	24 35	50	117
55	20 41	+50	119	21 31	+51	118	22 22	+50	118	23 12	+50	117	24 02	+50	117
56	20 08	51	118	20 59	50	117	21 49	50	117	22 39	50	116	23 29	50	116
57	19 36	50	117	20 26	50	117	21 16	50	116	22 06	49	115	22 55	50	115
58	19 03	49	116	19 52	50	116	20 42	50	115	21 32	50	114	22 22	49	114
59	18 29	50	115	19 19	50	115	20 09	49	114	20 58	50	114	21 48	49	113
60	17 56	+49	115	18 45	+50	114	19 35	+49	113	20 24	+50	113	21 14	+49	112
61	17 22	50	114	18 12	49	113	19 01	49	112	19 50	49	112	20 39	49	111
62	16 48	49	113	17 37	50	112	18 27	49	112	19 16	49	111	20 05	49	110
63	16 14	49	112	17 03	49	111	17 52	49	111	18 41	49	110	19 30	49	110
64	15 40	49	111	16 29	49	110	17 18	48	110	18 06	49	109	18 55	49	109
65	15 05	+49	110	15 54	+49	110	16 43	+48	109	17 31	+49	108	18 20	+48	108
66	14 30	49	109	15 19	49	109	16 08	48	108	16 56	49	108	17 45	48	107
67	13 55	49	109	14 44	48	108	15 32	49	107	16 21	48	107	17 09	49	106
68	13 20	49	108	14 09	48	107	14 57	48	106	15 45	49	106	16 34	48	105
69	12 45	48	107	13 33	49	106	14 22	48	106	15 10	48	105	15 58	48	104

LHA	5° Hc	d	Z	6° Hc	d	Z	7° Hc	d	Z	8° Hc	d	Z	9° Hc	d	Z
	° ′	′	°	° ′	′	°	° ′	′	°	° ′	′	°	° ′	′	°
0	43 00	+60	180	44 00	+60	180	45 00	+60	180	46 00	+60	180	47 00	+60	180
1	43 00	60	179	44 00	60	179	45 00	60	179	46 00	60	179	47 00	60	179
2	42 58	60	177	43 58	60	177	44 58	60	177	45 58	60	177	46 58	60	177
3	42 56	60	176	43 56	60	176	44 56	60	176	45 56	60	176	46 56	60	176
4	42 53	60	175	43 53	60	175	44 53	60	174	45 53	59	174	46 53	59	174
5	42 49	+60	173	43 49	+60	173	44 49	+60	173	45 49	+59	173	46 48	+60	173
6	42 44	60	172	43 44	60	172	44 44	60	172	45 44	59	172	46 43	60	171
7	42 39	59	171	43 38	60	170	44 38	60	170	45 38	59	170	46 37	60	170
8	42 32	60	169	43 32	59	169	44 31	60	169	45 31	59	169	46 30	60	169
9	42 25	59	168	43 24	60	168	44 24	59	167	45 23	60	167	46 23	59	167
10	42 17	+59	167	43 16	+59	166	44 15	+60	166	45 15	+59	166	46 14	+59	166
11	42 07	60	165	43 07	59	165	44 06	59	165	45 05	59	164	46 04	59	164
12	41 58	59	164	42 57	59	164	43 56	59	163	44 55	59	163	45 54	59	163
13	41 47	59	163	42 46	59	162	43 45	59	162	44 44	58	162	45 42	59	161
14	41 35	59	161	42 34	59	161	43 33	59	161	44 32	58	160	45 30	59	160
15	41 23	+59	160	42 22	+58	160	43 20	+59	159	44 19	+58	159	45 17	+59	159
16	41 10	58	159	42 08	59	158	43 07	58	158	44 05	58	158	45 03	59	157
17	40 56	58	157	41 54	59	157	42 53	58	157	43 51	58	156	44 49	58	156
18	40 42	58	156	41 40	58	156	42 38	57	155	43 35	58	155	44 33	58	155
19	40 26	58	155	41 24	58	154	42 22	57	154	43 19	58	154	44 17	58	153
20	40 10	+58	154	41 08	+57	153	42 05	+58	153	43 03	+57	152	44 00	+57	152
21	39 53	58	152	40 51	57	152	41 48	57	152	42 45	57	151	43 42	58	151
22	39 36	57	151	40 33	57	151	41 30	57	150	42 27	57	150	43 24	57	149
23	39 17	57	150	40 14	57	149	41 11	57	149	42 08	57	149	43 05	56	148
24	38 59	56	149	39 55	57	148	40 52	57	148	41 49	56	147	42 45	56	147
25	38 39	+56	147	39 35	+57	147	40 32	+56	147	41 28	+56	146	42 24	+57	146
26	38 19	56	146	39 15	56	146	40 11	56	145	41 07	56	145	42 03	56	144
27	37 58	56	145	38 54	56	145	39 50	56	144	40 46	55	144	41 41	56	143
28	37 36	56	144	38 32	56	143	39 28	55	143	40 23	56	142	41 19	55	142
29	37 14	56	143	38 10	55	142	39 05	56	142	40 01	55	141	40 56	55	141
30	36 52	+55	142	37 47	+55	141	38 42	+55	141	39 37	+55	140	40 32	+55	140
31	36 28	55	140	37 23	55	140	38 18	55	139	39 13	55	139	40 08	54	138
32	36 04	55	139	36 59	55	139	37 54	54	138	38 48	55	138	39 43	54	137
33	35 40	55	138	36 35	54	138	37 29	54	137	38 23	54	137	39 17	54	136
34	35 15	54	137	36 09	55	137	37 04	54	136	37 58	54	135	38 52	53	135
35	34 50	+54	136	35 44	+54	135	36 38	+53	135	37 31	+54	134	38 25	+54	134
36	34 24	53	135	35 17	54	134	36 11	54	134	37 05	53	133	37 58	53	133
37	33 57	54	134	34 51	53	133	35 44	54	133	36 38	53	132	37 31	53	132
38	33 30	54	133	34 24	53	132	35 17	53	132	36 10	53	131	37 03	52	130
39	33 03	53	132	33 56	53	131	34 49	53	131	35 42	52	130	36 34	53	129
40	32 35	+53	131	33 28	+53	130	34 21	+52	129	35 13	+53	129	36 06	+52	128
41	32 07	52	130	32 59	53	129	33 52	52	128	34 44	52	128	35 36	52	127
42	31 38	52	129	32 30	53	128	33 23	52	127	34 15	52	127	35 07	51	126
43	31 09	52	128	32 01	52	127	32 53	52	126	33 45	52	126	34 37	51	125
44	30 39	52	126	31 31	52	126	32 23	52	125	33 15	51	125	34 06	52	124
45	30 09	+52	125	31 01	+52	125	31 53	+51	124	32 44	+51	124	33 35	+52	123
46	29 39	52	125	30 31	51	124	31 22	51	123	32 13	51	123	33 04	51	122
47	29 09	51	124	30 00	51	123	30 51	51	122	31 42	51	122	32 33	50	121
48	28 38	51	123	29 29	51	122	30 20	50	121	31 10	51	121	32 01	50	120
49	28 06	51	121	28 57	51	121	29 48	50	120	30 38	51	120	31 29	50	119
50	27 35	+50	121	28 25	+51	120	29 16	+50	119	30 06	+50	119	30 56	+50	118
51	27 03	50	120	27 53	51	119	28 44	50	118	29 34	50	118	30 24	50	117
52	26 30	51	119	27 21	50	118	28 11	50	118	29 01	50	117	29 51	49	116
53	25 58	50	118	26 48	50	117	27 38	50	117	28 28	49	116	29 17	50	115
54	25 25	50	117	26 15	50	116	27 05	49	116	27 54	50	115	28 44	49	114
55	24 52	+50	116	25 42	+49	115	26 31	+50	115	27 21	+49	114	28 10	+49	113
56	24 19	49	115	25 08	50	114	25 58	49	114	26 47	49	113	27 36	49	113
57	23 45	49	114	24 34	50	114	25 24	49	113	26 13	49	112	27 02	49	112
58	23 11	49	113	24 00	50	113	24 50	49	112	25 39	48	111	26 27	49	111
59	22 37	49	112	23 26	49	112	24 15	49	111	25 04	49	110	25 53	48	110
60	22 03	+49	111	22 52	+49	111	23 41	+48	110	24 29	+49	110	25 18	+48	109
61	21 28	49	111	22 17	49	110	23 06	48	109	23 54	49	109	24 43	48	108
62	20 54	48	110	21 42	49	109	22 31	48	108	23 19	49	108	24 08	48	107
63	20 19	48	109	21 07	49	108	21 56	48	108	22 44	48	107	23 32	48	106
64	19 44	48	108	20 32	48	107	21 20	49	107	22 09	48	106	22 57	48	105
65	19 08	+49	107	19 57	+48	107	20 45	+48	106	21 33	+48	105	22 21	+48	105
66	18 33	48	106	19 21	48	106	20 09	48	105	20 57	48	104	21 45	48	104
67	17 58	48	105	18 46	48	105	19 34	48	104	20 22	47	104	21 09	48	103
68	17 22	48	105	18 10	48	104	18 58	48	103	19 46	47	103	20 33	48	102
69	16 46	48	104	17 34	48	103	18 22	47	103	19 09	48	102	19 57	47	101

LHA	10° Hc	d	Z	11° Hc	d	Z	12° Hc	d	Z	13° Hc	d	Z	14° Hc	d	Z	LHA
	° ′	′	°	° ′	′	°	° ′	′	°	° ′	′	°	° ′	′	°	
0	48 00	+60	180	49 00	+60	180	50 00	+60	180	51 00	+60	180	52 00	+60	180	360
1	48 00	60	179	49 00	60	179	50 00	60	179	51 00	60	179	52 00	60	178	359
2	47 58	60	177	48 58	60	177	49 58	60	177	50 58	60	177	51 58	60	177	358
3	47 56	60	176	48 56	60	176	49 56	60	175	50 56	59	175	51 55	60	175	357
4	47 52	60	174	48 52	60	174	49 52	60	174	50 52	60	174	51 52	60	174	356
5	47 48	+60	173	48 48	+60	173	49 48	+60	172	50 48	+59	172	51 47	+60	172	355
6	47 43	60	171	48 43	59	171	49 42	60	171	50 42	60	171	51 42	60	171	354
7	47 37	60	170	48 37	59	170	49 36	60	169	50 36	59	169	51 35	60	169	353
8	47 30	59	168	48 29	60	168	49 29	59	168	50 28	60	168	51 28	59	168	352
9	47 22	59	167	48 21	60	167	49 21	59	166	50 20	59	166	51 19	60	166	351
10	47 13	+59	165	48 12	+60	165	49 12	+59	165	50 11	+59	165	51 10	+59	164	350
11	47 03	59	164	48 02	59	164	49 01	59	164	50 00	59	163	50 59	59	163	349
12	46 53	59	163	47 52	59	162	48 51	58	162	49 49	59	162	50 48	59	161	348
13	46 41	59	161	47 40	59	161	48 39	58	161	49 37	59	160	50 36	58	160	347
14	46 29	58	160	47 27	59	159	48 26	58	159	49 24	59	159	50 23	58	158	346
15	46 16	+58	158	47 14	+58	158	48 12	+59	158	49 11	+58	157	50 09	+58	157	345
16	46 02	58	157	47 00	58	157	47 58	58	156	48 56	58	156	49 54	58	156	344
17	45 47	58	156	46 45	58	156	47 43	57	155	48 40	58	154	49 38	58	154	343
18	45 31	58	154	46 29	57	154	47 26	58	154	48 24	57	153	49 21	58	153	342
19	45 15	57	153	46 12	58	153	47 10	57	152	48 07	57	152	49 04	57	151	341
20	44 57	+58	152	45 55	+57	151	46 52	+57	151	47 49	+57	150	48 46	+57	150	340
21	44 40	57	150	45 37	56	150	46 33	57	149	47 30	57	149	48 27	56	148	339
22	44 21	57	149	45 18	56	149	46 14	57	148	47 11	56	148	48 07	56	147	338
23	44 01	57	148	44 58	56	147	45 54	57	147	46 51	56	146	47 47	56	146	337
24	43 41	57	146	44 38	56	146	45 34	56	145	46 30	55	145	47 25	56	144	336
25	43 21	+55	145	44 16	+56	145	45 12	+56	144	46 08	+56	144	47 04	+55	143	335
26	42 59	56	144	43 55	55	143	44 50	56	143	45 46	55	142	46 41	55	142	334
27	42 37	55	143	43 32	56	142	44 28	55	142	45 23	55	141	46 18	55	140	333
28	42 14	55	141	43 09	55	141	44 04	55	140	44 59	55	140	45 54	54	139	332
29	41 51	55	140	42 46	54	140	43 40	55	139	44 35	54	139	45 29	55	138	331
30	41 27	+54	139	42 21	+55	138	43 16	+54	138	44 10	+54	137	45 04	+54	137	330
31	41 02	55	138	41 57	54	137	42 51	54	137	43 45	54	136	44 39	53	135	329
32	40 37	54	137	41 31	54	136	42 25	54	135	43 19	53	135	44 12	54	134	328
33	40 11	54	135	41 05	54	135	41 59	53	134	42 52	54	134	43 46	53	133	327
34	39 45	54	134	40 39	53	134	41 32	53	133	42 25	53	132	43 18	53	132	326
35	39 19	+53	133	40 12	+53	133	41 05	+53	132	41 58	+53	131	42 51	+52	131	325
36	38 51	53	132	39 44	53	131	40 37	53	131	41 30	52	130	42 22	52	130	324
37	38 24	52	131	39 16	53	130	40 09	52	130	41 01	53	129	41 54	51	128	323
38	37 55	53	130	38 48	52	129	39 40	52	129	40 32	52	128	41 24	52	127	322
39	37 27	52	129	38 19	52	128	39 11	52	127	40 03	52	127	40 55	51	126	321
40	36 58	+52	128	37 50	+52	127	38 42	+51	126	39 33	+52	126	40 25	+51	125	320
41	36 28	52	127	37 20	52	126	38 12	51	125	39 03	51	125	39 54	51	124	319
42	35 58	52	126	36 50	51	125	37 41	51	124	38 32	51	124	39 23	51	123	318
43	35 28	52	124	36 20	51	124	37 11	50	123	38 01	51	123	38 52	51	122	317
44	34 58	51	123	35 49	50	123	36 39	51	122	37 30	51	121	38 21	50	121	316
45	34 27	+50	122	35 17	+51	122	36 08	+50	121	36 58	+51	120	37 49	+50	120	315
46	33 55	51	121	34 46	50	121	35 36	50	120	36 26	50	119	37 16	50	119	314
47	33 23	51	120	34 14	50	120	35 04	50	119	35 54	50	118	36 44	49	118	313
48	32 51	51	119	33 42	50	119	34 32	49	118	35 21	50	117	36 11	49	117	312
49	32 19	50	118	33 09	50	118	33 59	50	117	34 49	49	116	35 38	49	116	311
50	31 46	+50	118	32 36	+50	117	33 26	+49	116	34 15	+49	115	35 04	+49	115	310
51	31 14	49	117	32 03	50	116	32 53	49	115	33 42	49	115	34 31	48	114	309
52	30 40	50	116	31 30	49	115	32 19	49	114	33 08	49	114	33 57	48	113	308
53	30 07	49	115	30 56	49	114	31 45	49	113	32 34	49	113	33 23	48	112	307
54	29 33	49	114	30 22	49	113	31 11	49	112	32 00	48	112	32 48	48	111	306
55	28 59	+49	113	29 48	+49	112	30 37	+48	111	31 25	+49	111	32 14	+48	110	305
56	28 25	49	112	29 14	48	111	30 02	48	111	30 51	48	110	31 39	48	109	304
57	27 51	48	111	28 39	49	110	29 28	48	110	30 16	48	109	31 04	48	108	303
58	27 16	49	110	28 05	48	109	28 53	48	109	29 41	48	108	30 29	47	107	302
59	26 41	49	109	27 30	48	109	28 18	48	108	29 06	47	107	29 53	48	106	301
60	26 06	+48	108	26 54	+48	108	27 42	+48	107	28 30	+48	106	29 18	+47	106	300
61	25 31	48	107	26 19	48	107	27 07	48	106	27 55	47	105	28 42	47	105	299
62	24 56	48	107	25 44	47	106	26 31	48	105	27 19	47	105	28 06	47	104	298
63	24 20	48	106	25 08	48	105	25 56	47	104	26 43	47	103	27 30	47	103	297
64	23 45	47	105	24 32	48	104	25 20	47	103	26 07	47	103	26 54	47	102	296
65	23 09	+47	104	23 56	+48	103	24 44	+47	103	25 31	+47	102	26 18	+47	101	295
66	22 33	47	103	23 20	48	102	24 08	47	102	24 55	47	101	25 42	47	100	294
67	21 57	47	102	22 44	48	102	23 32	47	101	24 19	46	100	25 05	47	100	293
68	21 21	47	101	22 08	47	101	22 55	47	100	23 42	47	99	24 29	47	99	292
69	20 44	48	101	21 32	47	100	22 19	47	99	23 06	46	99	23 52	47	98	291

S. Lat. {LHA greater than 180°....... Zn=180−Z; LHA less than 180°........... Zn=180+Z}

DECLINATION (0°-14°) SAME NAME AS LATITUDE

LAT 52°

N. Lat. {LHA greater than 180°....... Zn=Z
LHA less than 180°........... Zn=360−Z}

DECLINATION (0°-14°) SAME NAME AS LATITUDE

LHA	0° Hc	0° d	0° Z	1° Hc	1° d	1° Z	2° Hc	2° d	2° Z	3° Hc	3° d	3° Z	4° Hc	4° d	4° Z
	° ′	′	°	° ′	′	°	° ′	′	°	° ′	′	°	° ′	′	°
70	12 09	+49	106	12 58	+48	105	13 46	+48	105	14 34	+48	104	15 22	+48	104
71	11 34	48	105	12 22	48	105	13 10	48	104	13 58	48	103	14 46	48	103
72	10 58	48	104	11 46	48	104	12 34	48	103	13 22	48	103	14 10	48	102
73	10 22	48	104	11 10	48	103	11 58	48	102	12 46	48	102	13 34	48	101
74	09 46	48	103	10 34	46	102	11 22	48	102	12 10	48	101	12 58	47	100
75	09 10	+48	102	09 58	+48	101	10 46	+48	101	11 34	+47	100	12 21	+48	100
76	08 34	48	101	09 22	47	101	10 09	48	100	10 57	48	99	11 45	47	99
77	07 58	47	100	08 45	48	100	09 33	48	99	10 21	47	99	11 08	48	98
78	07 21	48	100	08 09	48	99	08 57	47	98	09 44	48	98	10 32	47	97
79	06 45	47	99	07 32	48	98	08 20	47	98	09 07	48	97	09 55	47	96
80	06 08	+48	98	06 56	+47	97	07 43	+48	97	08 31	+47	96	09 18	+47	95
81	05 32	47	97	06 19	48	97	07 07	47	96	07 54	47	95	08 41	48	95
82	04 55	47	96	05 42	48	96	06 30	47	95	07 17	47	95	08 04	48	94
83	04 18	48	96	05 06	47	95	05 53	47	94	06 40	48	94	07 28	47	93
84	03 41	48	95	04 29	47	94	05 16	47	94	06 03	48	93	06 51	47	92
85	03 05	+47	94	03 52	+47	93	04 39	+48	93	05 27	+47	92	06 14	+47	92
86	02 28	47	93	03 15	47	93	04 02	48	92	04 50	47	91	05 37	47	91
87	01 51	47	92	02 38	47	92	03 25	48	91	04 13	47	91	05 00	47	90
88	01 14	47	92	02 01	47	91	02 48	48	90	03 36	47	90	04 23	47	89
89	00 37	47	91	01 24	47	90	02 11	48	90	02 59	47	89	03 46	47	88
90	00 00	+47	90	00 47	+48	89	01 35	+47	89	02 22	+47	88	03 09	+47	88
91	−0 37	47	89	00 10	48	89	00 58	47	88	01 45	47	87	02 32	47	87
92	−1 14	47	88	−0 27	48	88	00 21	47	87	01 08	47	87	01 55	48	86
93	−1 51	48	88	−1 03	47	87	−0 16	47	86	00 31	47	86	01 18	48	85
94	−2 28	48	87	−1 40	47	86	−0 53	47	86	−0 06	48	85	00 42	47	84
95	−3 05	+48	86	−2 17	+47	85	−1 30	+48	85	−0 42	+47	84	00 05	+47	84
96	−3 41	47	85	−2 54	47	85	−2 07	48	84	−1 19	47	83	−0 32	48	83
97	−4 18	47	84	−3 31	48	84	−2 43	47	83	−1 56	48	83	−1 08	47	82
98	−4 55	48	84	−4 07	47	83	−3 20	48	82	−2 32	47	82	−1 45	48	81
99	−5 32	48	83	−4 44	47	82	−3 57	48	82	−3 09	48	81	−2 21	47	80
100	−6 08	+47	82	−5 21	+48	81	−4 33	+48	81	−3 45	+47	80	−2 58	+48	80
101				−5 57	47	81	−5 10	48	80	−4 22	48	79	−3 34	48	79
102							−5 46	48	79	−4 58	48	79	−4 10	48	78
103										−5 34	48	78	−4 46	48	77
104										−6 10	48	77	−5 22	48	76
105													−5 58	+48	76

LHA	5° Hc	5° d	5° Z	6° Hc	6° d	6° Z	7° Hc	7° d	7° Z	8° Hc	8° d	8° Z	9° Hc	9° d	9° Z
	° ′	′	°	° ′	′	°	° ′	′	°	° ′	′	°	° ′	′	°
70	16 10	+48	103	16 58	+48	102	17 46	+47	102	18 33	+48	101	19 21	+47	100
71	15 34	48	102	16 22	47	102	17 09	48	101	17 57	47	100	18 44	48	100
72	14 58	48	101	15 46	47	101	16 33	48	100	17 21	47	99	18 08	47	99
73	14 22	47	101	15 09	48	100	15 57	47	99	16 44	47	99	17 31	47	98
74	13 45	48	100	14 33	47	99	15 20	47	98	16 07	48	98	16 55	47	97
75	13 09	+47	99	13 56	+48	98	14 44	+47	98	15 31	+47	97	16 18	+47	96
76	12 32	48	98	13 20	47	97	14 07	47	97	14 54	47	96	15 41	47	96
77	11 56	47	97	12 43	47	97	13 30	47	96	14 17	47	95	15 04	47	95
78	11 19	47	96	12 06	47	96	12 53	48	95	13 41	47	95	14 28	47	94
79	10 42	47	96	11 29	48	95	12 17	47	94	13 04	47	94	13 51	47	93
80	10 05	+48	95	10 53	+47	94	11 40	+47	94	12 27	+47	93	13 14	+47	92
81	09 29	47	94	10 16	47	93	11 03	47	93	11 50	47	92	12 37	47	92
82	08 52	47	93	09 39	47	93	10 26	47	92	11 13	47	91	12 00	47	91
83	08 15	47	92	09 02	47	92	09 49	47	91	10 36	47	91	11 23	47	90
84	07 38	47	92	08 25	47	91	09 12	47	90	09 59	47	90	10 46	47	89
85	07 01	+47	91	07 48	+47	90	08 35	+47	90	09 22	+47	89	10 09	+47	88
86	06 24	47	90	07 11	47	89	07 58	47	89	08 45	47	88	09 32	47	88
87	05 47	47	89	06 34	47	89	07 21	47	88	08 08	47	87	08 55	47	87
88	05 10	47	89	05 57	47	88	06 44	48	87	07 32	47	87	08 19	46	86
89	04 33	47	88	05 20	48	87	06 08	47	87	06 55	47	86	07 42	47	85
90	03 56	+47	87	04 43	+48	86	05 31	+47	86	06 18	+47	85	07 05	+47	84
91	03 19	48	86	04 07	47	86	04 54	47	85	05 41	47	84	06 28	47	84
92	02 43	47	85	03 30	47	85	04 17	47	84	05 04	47	84	05 51	48	83
93	02 06	47	85	02 53	47	84	03 40	48	83	04 28	47	83	05 15	47	82
94	01 29	47	84	02 16	48	83	03 04	47	83	03 51	47	82	04 38	48	81
95	00 52	+48	83	01 40	+47	82	02 27	+47	82	03 14	+48	81	04 02	+47	81
96	00 16	47	82	01 03	48	82	01 51	47	81	02 38	47	80	03 25	48	80
97	−0 21	48	81	00 27	47	81	01 14	48	80	02 02	47	80	02 49	48	79
98	−0 57	47	81	−0 10	48	80	00 38	47	79	01 25	48	79	02 13	47	78
99	−1 34	48	80	−0 46	48	79	00 02	47	79	00 49	48	78	01 37	47	77
100	−2 10	+48	79	−1 22	+47	78	−0 35	+48	78	00 13	+48	77	01 01	+47	77
101	−2 46	48	78	−1 58	47	78	−1 11	48	77	−0 23	48	76	00 25	48	76
102	−3 22	48	77	−2 34	47	77	−1 47	48	76	−0 59	48	76	−0 11	48	75
103	−3 58	48	77	−3 10	48	76	−2 22	48	75	−1 34	48	75	−0 46	48	74
104	−4 34	48	76	−3 46	48	75	−2 58	48	75	−2 10	48	74	−1 22	48	73
105	−5 10	+48	75	−4 22	+48	74	−3 34	+48	74	−2 46	+49	73	−1 57	+48	73
106	−5 46	49	74	−4 57	48	74	−4 09	48	73	−3 21	49	72	−2 32	48	72
107				−5 33	49	73	−4 44	48	72	−3 56	49	72	−3 07	48	71
108				−6 08	48	72	−5 20	49	71	−4 31	49	71	−3 42	48	70
109							−5 54	48	71	−5 06	49	70	−4 17	49	69
110										−5 40	+48	69	−4 52	+49	69
111													−5 26	49	68
112													−6 00	49	67

LHA	10° Hc	10° d	10° Z	11° Hc	11° d	11° Z	12° Hc	12° d	12° Z	13° Hc	13° d	13° Z	14° Hc	14° d	14° Z	LHA
	° ′	′	°	° ′	′	°	° ′	′	°	° ′	′	°	° ′	′	°	
70	20 08	+47	100	20 55	+47	99	21 42	+47	98	22 29	+47	98	23 16	+46	97	290
71	19 32	47	99	20 19	47	98	21 06	46	98	21 52	47	97	22 39	47	96	289
72	18 55	47	98	19 42	47	97	20 29	47	97	21 16	46	96	22 02	47	95	288
73	18 18	47	97	19 05	47	97	19 52	47	96	20 39	47	95	21 26	46	95	287
74	17 42	47	96	18 29	47	96	19 16	46	95	20 02	47	95	20 49	46	94	286
75	17 05	+47	96	17 52	+47	95	18 39	+46	94	19 25	+47	94	20 12	+46	93	285
76	16 28	47	95	17 15	47	94	18 02	46	94	18 48	47	93	19 35	46	92	284
77	15 51	47	94	16 38	47	93	17 25	47	93	18 12	46	92	18 58	46	91	283
78	15 15	46	93	16 01	47	93	16 48	47	92	17 35	46	91	18 21	46	91	282
79	14 38	46	92	15 24	47	92	16 11	47	91	16 58	46	91	17 44	46	90	281
80	14 01	+47	92	14 48	+46	91	15 34	+47	90	16 21	+46	90	17 07	+47	89	280
81	13 24	47	91	14 11	46	90	14 57	47	90	15 44	46	89	16 30	47	88	279
82	12 47	47	90	13 34	46	89	14 20	47	89	15 07	46	88	15 53	47	88	278
83	12 10	47	89	12 57	46	89	13 43	47	88	14 30	47	87	15 17	46	87	277
84	11 33	47	89	12 20	47	88	13 07	46	87	13 53	47	87	14 40	46	86	276
85	10 56	+47	88	11 43	+47	87	12 30	+46	86	13 16	+47	86	14 03	+46	85	275
86	10 19	47	87	11 06	47	86	11 53	46	86	12 39	47	85	13 26	47	84	274
87	09 42	47	86	10 29	47	86	11 16	47	85	12 03	46	84	12 49	47	84	273
88	09 05	47	85	09 52	47	85	10 39	47	84	11 26	47	84	12 13	46	83	272
89	08 29	47	85	09 16	46	84	10 02	47	83	10 49	47	83	11 36	47	82	271
90	07 52	+47	84	08 39	+47	83	09 26	+47	83	10 13	+46	82	10 59	+47	81	270
91	07 15	47	83	08 02	47	82	08 49	47	82	09 36	47	81	10 23	47	81	269
92	06 39	47	82	07 26	47	82	08 13	47	81	09 00	47	80	09 47	46	80	268
93	06 02	47	82	06 49	47	81	07 36	47	80	08 23	47	80	09 10	47	79	267
94	05 26	47	81	06 13	47	80	07 00	47	79	07 47	47	79	08 34	47	78	266
95	04 49	+47	80	05 36	+48	79	06 24	+47	79	07 11	+47	78	07 58	+47	77	265
96	04 13	47	79	05 00	47	79	05 47	48	78	06 35	47	77	07 22	47	77	264
97	03 37	47	78	04 24	47	78	05 11	48	77	05 59	47	77	06 46	47	76	263
98	03 00	48	78	03 48	47	77	04 35	48	76	05 23	47	76	06 10	48	75	262
99	02 24	48	77	03 12	48	76	04 00	47	76	04 47	48	75	05 35	47	74	261
100	01 48	+48	76	02 36	+48	75	03 24	+48	75	04 12	+47	74	04 59	+48	74	260
101	01 13	47	75	02 00	48	75	02 48	48	74	03 36	48	73	04 24	48	73	259
102	00 37	48	74	01 25	48	74	02 13	48	73	03 01	48	73	03 49	47	72	258
103	00 02	48	74	00 50	48	73	01 38	48	72	02 26	48	72	03 14	47	71	257
104	−0 34	48	73	00 14	48	72	01 02	49	72	01 51	48	71	02 39	48	70	256
105	−1 09	+48	72	−0 21	+48	71	00 27	+49	71	01 16	+48	70	02 04	+48	70	255
106	−1 44	48	71	−0 56	49	71	−0 07	48	70	00 41	48	69	01 29	49	69	254
107	−2 19	48	70	−1 31	49	70	−0 42	48	69	00 06	49	69	00 55	48	68	253
108	−2 54	49	70	−2 05	48	69	−1 17	49	69	−0 28	49	68	00 21	48	67	252
109	−3 28	48	69	−2 40	49	68	−1 51	49	68	−1 02	49	67	−0 13	49	67	251
110	−4 03	+49	68	−3 14	+49	67	−2 25	+49	67	−1 36	+49	66	−0 47	+49	66	250
111	−4 37	49	67	−3 48	49	67	−2 59	49	66	−2 10	49	66	−1 21	49	65	249
112	−5 11	49	66	−4 22	50	66	−3 32	49	65	−2 43	49	65	−1 54	49	64	248
113	−5 45	50	66	−4 55	49	65	−4 06	49	65	−3 17	50	64	−2 27	49	63	247
114				−5 29	50	64	−4 39	49	64	−3 50	50	63	−3 00	50	63	246
115				−6 02	+50	63	−5 12	+50	63	−4 22	+49	62	−3 33	+50	62	245
116							−5 45	50	62	−4 55	50	62	−4 05	50	61	244
117										−5 27	50	61	−4 37	50	60	243
118										−5 59	50	60	−5 09	50	59	242
119													−5 41	51	58	241

0°	1°	2°	3°	4°	5°	6°	7°	8°	9°	10°	11°	12°	13°	14°

S. Lat. {LHA greater than 180°....... Zn=180−Z
LHA less than 180°........... Zn=180+Z}

DECLINATION (0°-14°) SAME NAME AS LATITUDE

N. Lat. {LHA greater than 180°....... Zn=Z; LHA less than 180°........... Zn=360−Z}

DECLINATION (0°-14°) CONTRARY NAME TO LATITUDE

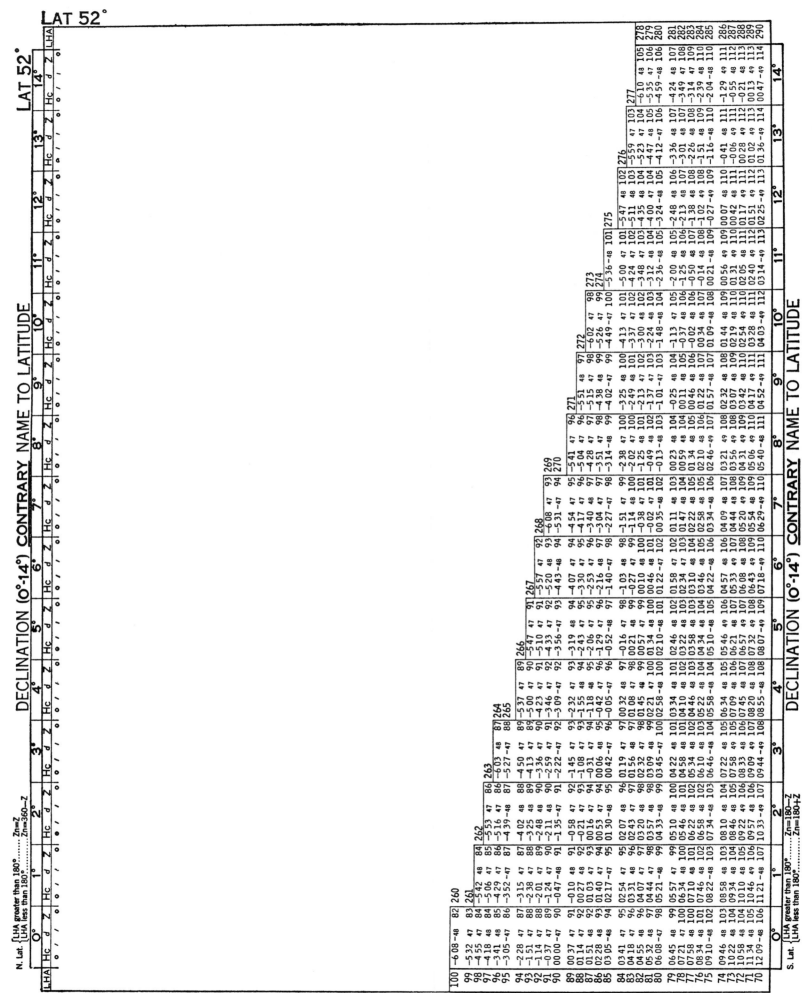

LHA	0° Hc d Z	1° Hc d Z	2° Hc d Z	3° Hc d Z	4° Hc d Z	5° Hc d Z	6° Hc d Z	7° Hc d Z	8° Hc d Z	9° Hc d Z	10° Hc d Z	11° Hc d Z	12° Hc d Z	13° Hc d Z	14° Hc d Z	LHA
	° ′ ′ °	° ′ ′ °	° ′ ′ °	° ′ ′ °	° ′ ′ °	° ′ ′ °	° ′ ′ °	° ′ ′ °	° ′ ′ °	° ′ ′ °	° ′ ′ °	° ′ ′ °	° ′ ′ °	° ′ ′ °	° ′ ′ °	
100	−6 08 −48 82	260														
99	−5 32 47 83	261														
98	−4 55 47 84	−5 42 48 84	262													
97	−4 18 48 84	−5 06 47 85	−5 53 47 86	263												
96	−3 41 48 85	−4 29 47 86	−5 16 47 86	−6 03 48 87	264											
95	−3 05 −47 86	−3 52 −47 87	−4 39 −48 87	−5 27 −47 88	265											
94	−2 28 47 87	−3 15 47 87	−4 02 48 88	−4 50 47 89	−5 37 47 89	266										
93	−1 51 47 88	−2 38 47 88	−3 25 48 89	−4 13 47 89	−5 00 47 90	−5 47 47 91	267									
92	−1 14 47 88	−2 01 47 89	−2 48 48 90	−3 36 47 90	−4 23 47 91	−5 10 47 91	−5 57 47 92	268								
91	−0 37 47 89	−1 24 47 90	−2 11 48 90	−2 59 47 91	−3 46 47 92	−4 33 47 92	−5 20 48 93	−6 08 47 93	269							
90	00 00 −47 90	−0 47 −48 91	−1 35 −47 91	−2 22 −47 92	−3 09 −47 92	−3 56 −47 93	−4 43 −48 94	−5 31 −47 94	270							
89	00 37 47 91	−0 10 48 91	−0 58 47 92	−1 45 47 93	−2 32 47 93	−3 19 48 94	−4 07 47 94	−4 54 47 95	−5 41 47 96	271						
88	01 14 47 92	00 27 48 92	−0 21 47 93	−1 08 47 93	−1 55 48 94	−2 43 47 95	−3 30 47 95	−4 17 47 96	−5 04 47 96	−5 51 48 97	272					
87	01 51 48 92	01 03 47 93	00 16 47 94	−0 31 47 94	−1 18 48 95	−2 06 47 95	−2 53 47 96	−3 40 48 97	−4 28 47 97	−5 15 47 98	−6 02 47 98	273				
86	02 28 48 93	01 40 47 94	00 53 47 94	00 06 48 95	−0 42 47 96	−1 29 47 96	−2 16 48 97	−3 04 47 97	−3 51 47 98	−4 38 48 99	−5 26 47 99	274				
85	03 05 −48 94	02 17 −47 95	01 30 −48 95	00 42 −47 96	−0 05 −47 96	−0 52 −48 97	−1 40 −47 98	−2 27 −47 98	−3 14 −48 99	−4 02 −47 99	−4 49 −47 100	−5 36 −48 101	275			
84	03 41 47 95	02 54 47 95	02 07 48 96	01 19 47 97	00 32 48 97	−0 16 47 98	−1 03 48 98	−1 51 47 99	−2 38 47 100	−3 25 48 100	−4 13 47 101	−5 00 47 101	−5 47 48 102	276		
83	04 18 47 96	03 31 48 96	02 43 47 97	01 56 48 97	01 08 47 98	00 21 48 99	−0 27 47 99	−1 14 48 100	−2 02 47 100	−2 49 48 101	−3 37 47 102	−4 24 47 102	−5 11 48 103	−5 59 47 103	277	
82	04 55 48 96	04 07 47 97	03 20 48 98	02 32 47 98	01 45 48 99	00 57 47 99	00 10 48 100	−0 38 47 101	−1 25 48 101	−2 13 47 102	−3 00 48 102	−3 48 47 103	−4 35 48 104	−5 23 47 104	−6 10 48 105	278
81	05 32 48 97	04 44 47 98	03 57 48 98	03 09 48 99	02 21 47 100	01 34 48 100	00 46 48 101	−0 02 47 101	−0 49 48 102	−1 37 47 103	−2 24 48 103	−3 12 48 104	−4 00 47 104	−4 47 48 105	−5 35 47 106	279
80	06 08 −47 98	05 21 −48 99	04 33 −48 99	03 45 −47 100	02 58 −48 100	02 10 −48 101	01 22 −47 102	00 35 −48 102	−0 13 −48 103	−1 01 −47 103	−1 48 −48 104	−2 36 −48 105	−3 24 −48 105	−4 12 −47 106	−4 59 −48 106	280
79	06 45 48 99	05 57 47 99	05 10 48 100	04 22 48 101	03 34 48 101	02 46 48 102	01 58 47 102	01 11 48 103	00 23 48 104	−0 25 48 104	−1 13 47 105	−2 00 48 105	−2 48 48 106	−3 36 48 107	−4 24 48 107	281
78	07 21 47 100	06 34 48 100	05 46 48 101	04 58 48 101	04 10 48 102	03 22 48 103	02 34 47 103	01 47 48 104	00 59 48 104	00 11 48 105	−0 37 48 106	−1 25 48 106	−2 13 48 107	−3 01 48 107	−3 49 47 108	282
77	07 58 48 100	07 10 48 101	06 22 48 102	05 34 48 102	04 46 48 103	03 58 48 103	03 10 48 104	02 22 48 105	01 34 48 105	00 46 48 106	−0 02 48 106	−0 50 48 107	−1 38 48 108	−2 26 48 108	−3 14 47 109	283
76	08 34 48 101	07 46 48 102	06 58 48 102	06 10 48 103	05 22 48 104	04 34 48 104	03 46 48 105	02 58 48 105	02 10 48 106	01 22 48 107	00 34 48 107	−0 14 48 108	−1 02 49 108	−1 51 48 109	−2 39 48 110	284
75	09 10 −48 102	08 22 −48 103	07 34 −48 103	06 46 −48 104	05 58 −48 104	05 10 −48 105	04 22 −48 106	03 34 −48 106	02 46 −49 107	01 57 −48 107	01 09 −48 108	00 21 −48 109	−0 27 −49 109	−1 16 −48 110	−2 04 −48 110	285
74	09 46 48 103	08 58 48 103	08 10 48 104	07 22 48 105	06 34 48 105	05 46 49 106	04 57 48 106	04 09 48 107	03 21 49 108	02 32 48 108	01 44 48 109	00 56 49 109	00 07 48 110	−0 41 48 111	−1 29 49 111	286
73	10 22 48 104	09 34 48 104	08 46 48 105	07 58 49 105	07 09 48 106	06 21 48 107	05 33 49 107	04 44 48 108	03 56 49 108	03 07 48 109	02 19 48 110	01 31 49 110	00 42 48 111	−0 06 49 111	−0 55 48 112	287
72	10 58 48 104	10 10 48 105	09 22 49 106	08 33 48 106	07 45 48 107	06 57 49 107	06 08 48 108	05 20 49 109	04 31 49 109	03 42 48 110	02 54 49 110	02 05 48 111	01 17 49 111	00 28 49 112	−0 21 48 113	288
71	11 34 48 105	10 46 49 106	09 57 48 106	09 09 49 107	08 20 48 108	07 32 49 108	06 43 49 109	05 54 48 109	05 06 49 110	04 17 49 111	03 28 48 111	02 40 49 112	01 51 49 112	01 02 49 113	00 13 49 113	289
70	12 09 −48 106	11 21 −48 107	10 33 −49 107	09 44 −49 108	08 55 −48 108	08 07 −49 109	07 18 −49 110	06 29 −49 110	05 40 −48 111	04 52 −49 111	04 03 −49 112	03 14 −49 113	02 25 −49 113	01 36 −49 114	00 47 −49 114	290
	0°	1°	2°	3°	4°	5°	6°	7°	8°	9°	10°	11°	12°	13°	14°	

S. Lat. {LHA greater than 180°....... Zn=180−Z; LHA less than 180°........... Zn=180+Z}

DECLINATION (0°-14°) CONTRARY NAME TO LATITUDE

LAT 52°

N. Lat. {LHA greater than 180°....... Zn=Z / LHA less than 180°.......... Zn=360−Z}

DECLINATION (0°-14°) CONTRARY NAME TO LATITUDE

LHA	0° Hc	0° d	0° Z	1° Hc	1° d	1° Z	2° Hc	2° d	2° Z	3° Hc	3° d	3° Z	4° Hc	4° d	4° Z
	° ′	′	°	° ′	′	°	° ′	′	°	° ′	′	°	° ′	′	°
69	12 45	49	107	11 56	48	107	11 08	49	108	10 19	49	109	09 30	48	109
68	13 20	49	108	12 31	48	108	11 43	49	109	10 54	49	110	10 05	49	110
67	13 55	49	109	13 06	48	109	12 18	49	110	11 29	49	110	10 40	49	111
66	14 30	49	109	13 41	49	110	12 52	49	111	12 03	49	111	11 14	49	112
65	15 05	−49	110	14 16	−49	111	13 27	−49	111	12 38	−50	112	11 48	−49	113
64	15 40	50	111	14 50	49	112	14 01	49	112	13 12	50	113	12 22	49	113
63	16 14	49	112	15 25	50	113	14 35	49	113	13 46	50	114	12 56	49	114
62	16 48	49	113	15 59	50	113	15 09	50	114	14 19	49	115	13 30	50	115
61	17 22	50	114	16 32	49	114	15 43	50	115	14 53	50	115	14 03	50	116
60	17 56	−50	115	17 06	−50	115	16 16	−50	116	15 26	−50	116	14 36	−50	117
59	18 29	50	115	17 39	50	116	16 49	50	117	15 59	50	117	15 09	50	118
58	19 03	51	116	18 12	50	117	17 22	50	117	16 32	50	118	15 42	51	119
57	19 36	51	117	18 45	50	118	17 55	50	118	17 05	51	119	16 14	51	119
56	20 08	50	118	19 18	51	119	18 27	50	119	17 37	51	120	16 46	51	120
55	20 41	−51	119	19 50	−51	120	18 59	−50	120	18 09	−51	121	17 18	−51	121
54	21 13	51	120	20 22	51	120	19 31	51	121	18 40	51	122	17 49	51	122
53	21 45	51	121	20 54	51	121	20 03	51	122	19 12	52	122	18 20	51	123
52	22 17	52	122	21 25	51	122	20 34	51	123	19 43	52	123	18 51	51	124
51	22 48	52	123	21 56	51	123	21 05	52	124	20 13	51	124	19 22	52	125
50	23 19	−52	124	22 27	−51	124	21 36	−52	125	20 44	−52	125	19 52	−52	126
49	23 49	51	124	22 58	52	125	22 06	52	126	21 14	52	126	20 22	52	127
48	24 20	52	125	23 28	52	126	22 36	52	126	21 44	53	127	20 51	52	128
47	24 50	52	126	23 58	53	127	23 05	52	127	22 13	53	128	21 20	52	128
46	25 19	52	127	24 27	53	128	23 34	52	128	22 42	53	129	21 49	53	129
45	25 48	−52	128	24 56	−53	129	24 03	−53	129	23 10	−52	130	22 18	−53	130
44	26 17	53	129	25 24	52	130	24 32	53	130	23 39	54	131	22 45	53	131
43	26 46	53	130	25 53	53	131	25 00	54	131	24 06	53	132	23 13	53	132
42	27 14	54	131	26 20	53	132	25 27	53	132	24 34	54	133	23 40	53	133
41	27 41	53	132	26 48	54	133	25 54	53	133	25 01	54	134	24 07	54	134
40	28 08	−53	133	27 15	−54	134	26 21	−54	134	25 27	−54	135	24 33	−54	135
39	28 35	54	134	27 41	54	135	26 47	54	135	25 53	54	136	24 59	54	136
38	29 01	54	135	28 07	54	136	27 13	54	136	26 19	55	137	25 24	54	137
37	29 27	54	136	28 33	55	137	27 38	54	137	26 44	55	138	25 49	55	138
36	29 52	54	137	28 58	55	138	28 03	55	138	27 08	54	139	26 14	55	139
35	30 17	−55	138	29 22	−54	139	28 28	−55	139	27 33	−56	140	26 37	−55	140
34	30 42	56	139	29 46	55	140	28 51	55	140	27 56	55	141	27 01	56	141
33	31 05	55	141	30 10	55	141	29 15	56	141	28 19	55	142	27 24	56	142
32	31 28	55	142	30 33	56	142	29 37	55	143	28 42	56	143	27 46	56	143
31	31 51	56	143	30 55	55	143	30 00	56	144	29 04	56	144	28 08	56	144
30	32 13	−56	144	31 17	−56	144	30 21	−56	145	29 25	−56	145	28 29	−56	145
29	32 35	56	145	31 39	57	145	30 42	56	146	29 46	56	146	28 50	57	147
28	32 56	57	146	31 59	56	146	31 03	57	147	30 06	56	147	29 10	57	148
27	33 16	56	147	32 20	57	148	31 23	57	148	30 26	57	148	29 29	56	149
26	33 36	57	148	32 39	57	149	31 42	57	149	30 45	57	149	29 48	57	150
25	33 55	−57	149	32 58	−57	150	32 01	−57	150	31 04	−57	151	30 07	−58	151
24	34 14	58	151	33 16	57	151	32 19	57	151	31 22	58	152	30 24	57	152
23	34 31	57	152	33 34	58	152	32 36	57	152	31 39	58	153	30 41	57	153
22	34 49	58	153	33 51	58	153	32 53	57	154	31 56	58	154	30 58	58	154
21	35 05	58	154	34 07	58	154	33 09	58	155	32 11	57	155	31 14	58	155
20	35 21	−58	155	34 23	−58	156	33 25	−58	156	32 27	−58	156	31 29	−58	156
19	35 36	58	156	34 38	58	157	33 40	59	157	32 41	58	157	31 43	58	158
18	35 50	58	158	34 52	58	158	33 54	59	158	32 55	58	158	31 57	59	159
17	36 04	58	159	35 06	59	159	34 07	58	159	33 09	59	160	32 10	59	160
16	36 17	58	160	35 19	59	160	34 20	59	161	33 21	59	161	32 22	58	161
15	36 29	−58	161	35 31	−59	162	34 32	−59	162	33 33	−59	162	32 34	−59	162
14	36 41	59	162	35 42	59	163	34 43	59	163	33 44	59	163	32 45	59	163
13	36 52	59	164	35 53	59	164	34 54	60	164	33 54	59	164	32 55	59	165
12	37 02	59	165	36 03	60	165	35 03	59	165	34 04	59	166	33 05	60	166
11	37 11	59	166	36 12	60	166	35 12	59	167	34 13	60	167	33 13	59	167
10	37 19	−59	167	36 20	−60	168	35 20	−59	168	34 21	−59	168	33 22	−60	168
9	37 27	59	169	36 28	60	169	35 28	60	169	34 28	59	169	33 29	60	169
8	37 34	60	170	36 34	59	170	35 35	60	170	34 35	60	170	33 35	59	170
7	37 40	60	171	36 40	59	171	35 41	60	171	34 41	60	172	33 41	60	172
6	37 45	59	172	36 46	60	173	35 46	60	173	34 46	60	173	33 46	60	173
5	37 50	−60	174	36 50	−60	174	35 50	−60	174	34 50	−60	174	33 50	−60	174
4	37 54	60	175	36 54	60	175	35 54	60	175	34 54	60	175	33 54	60	175
3	37 56	60	176	36 56	60	176	35 56	59	176	34 57	60	176	33 57	60	176
2	37 58	60	178	36 58	60	178	35 58	60	178	34 58	60	178	33 58	59	178
1	38 00	60	179	37 00	60	179	36 00	60	179	35 00	60	179	34 00	60	179
0	38 00	−60	180	37 00	−60	180	36 00	−60	180	35 00	−60	180	34 00	−60	180

LHA	5° Hc	5° d	5° Z	6° Hc	6° d	6° Z	7° Hc	7° d	7° Z	8° Hc	8° d	8° Z	9° Hc	9° d	9° Z
	° ′	′	°	° ′	′	°	° ′	′	°	° ′	′	°	° ′	′	°
69	08 42	49	110	07 53	49	110	07 04	49	111	06 15	49	112	05 26	49	112
68	09 16	49	111	08 27	49	111	07 38	49	112	06 49	49	112	06 00	49	113
67	09 51	49	112	09 02	50	112	08 12	49	113	07 23	49	113	06 34	49	114
66	10 25	49	112	09 36	50	113	08 46	49	113	07 57	49	114	07 08	50	115
65	10 59	−49	113	10 10	−50	114	09 20	−49	114	08 31	−50	115	07 41	−50	115
64	11 33	50	114	10 43	49	115	09 54	50	115	09 04	50	116	08 14	49	116
63	12 07	50	115	11 17	50	115	10 27	50	116	09 37	50	117	08 47	50	117
62	12 40	50	116	11 50	50	116	11 00	50	117	10 10	50	117	09 20	50	118
61	13 13	50	117	12 23	50	117	11 33	50	118	10 43	50	118	09 53	51	119
60	13 46	−50	117	12 56	−50	118	12 06	−51	119	11 15	−50	119	10 25	−51	120
59	14 19	51	118	13 28	50	119	12 38	51	119	11 47	50	120	10 57	51	120
58	14 51	50	119	14 01	51	120	13 10	51	120	12 19	50	121	11 29	51	121
57	15 23	50	120	14 33	51	121	13 42	51	121	12 51	51	122	12 00	51	122
56	15 55	51	121	15 04	51	121	14 13	51	122	13 22	51	123	12 31	51	123
55	16 27	−51	122	15 36	−51	122	14 45	−52	123	13 53	−51	123	13 02	−51	124
54	16 58	51	123	16 07	52	123	15 15	51	124	14 24	51	124	13 33	52	125
53	17 29	51	124	16 38	52	124	15 46	52	125	14 54	51	125	14 03	52	126
52	18 00	52	124	17 08	52	125	16 16	52	125	15 24	51	126	14 33	52	127
51	18 30	52	125	17 38	52	126	16 46	52	126	15 54	52	127	15 02	52	127
50	19 00	−52	126	18 08	−52	127	17 16	−52	127	16 24	−53	128	15 31	−52	128
49	19 30	53	127	18 37	52	128	17 45	52	128	16 53	53	129	16 00	52	129
48	19 59	53	128	19 06	52	129	18 14	53	129	17 21	52	130	16 29	53	130
47	20 28	53	129	19 35	53	130	18 42	52	130	17 50	53	131	16 57	53	131
46	20 56	53	130	20 03	52	130	19 11	53	131	18 18	54	131	17 24	53	132
45	21 25	−54	131	20 31	−53	131	19 38	−53	132	18 45	−53	132	17 52	−54	133
44	21 52	53	132	20 59	53	132	20 06	54	133	19 12	53	133	18 19	54	134
43	22 20	54	133	21 26	53	133	20 33	54	134	19 39	54	134	18 45	54	135
42	22 47	54	134	21 53	54	134	20 59	54	135	20 05	54	135	19 11	54	136
41	23 13	54	135	22 19	54	135	21 25	54	136	20 31	54	136	19 37	54	137
40	23 39	−54	136	22 45	−54	136	21 51	−55	137	20 56	−54	137	20 02	−54	138
39	24 05	55	137	23 10	54	137	22 16	55	138	21 21	54	138	20 27	55	138
38	24 30	55	138	23 35	54	138	22 41	55	139	21 46	55	139	20 51	55	139
37	24 54	54	139	24 00	55	139	23 05	55	140	22 10	55	140	21 15	55	140
36	25 19	55	140	24 24	56	140	23 28	55	141	22 33	55	141	21 38	55	141
35	25 42	−55	141	24 47	−55	141	23 52	−56	142	22 56	−55	142	22 01	−56	142
34	26 05	55	142	25 10	56	142	24 14	55	143	23 19	56	143	22 23	55	143
33	26 28	56	143	25 32	55	143	24 37	56	144	23 41	56	144	22 45	56	144
32	26 50	56	144	25 54	56	144	24 58	56	145	24 02	56	145	23 06	56	145
31	27 12	56	145	26 16	56	145	25 20	57	146	24 23	56	146	23 27	56	146
30	27 33	−56	146	26 37	−57	146	25 40	−56	147	24 44	−57	147	23 47	−56	147
29	27 53	56	147	26 57	57	147	26 00	56	148	25 04	57	148	24 07	57	148
28	28 13	56	148	27 17	57	148	26 20	57	149	25 23	57	149	24 26	57	149
27	28 33	57	149	27 36	57	149	26 39	57	150	25 42	57	150	24 45	58	150
26	28 51	57	150	27 54	57	150	26 57	57	151	26 00	58	151	25 02	57	152
25	29 09	−57	151	28 12	−57	152	27 15	−58	152	26 17	−57	152	25 20	−58	153
24	29 27	58	152	28 29	57	153	27 32	58	153	26 34	57	153	25 37	58	154
23	29 44	58	153	28 46	58	154	27 48	57	154	26 51	58	154	25 53	58	155
22	30 00	58	155	29 02	58	155	28 04	58	155	27 06	58	155	26 08	58	156
21	30 16	58	156	29 18	59	156	28 19	58	156	27 21	58	156	26 23	58	157
20	30 31	−59	157	29 32	−58	157	28 34	−58	157	27 36	−58	158	26 38	−59	158
19	30 45	59	158	29 46	58	158	28 48	58	158	27 50	59	159	26 51	58	159
18	30 58	58	159	30 00	59	159	29 01	58	160	28 03	59	160	27 04	58	160
17	31 11	58	160	30 13	59	160	29 14	59	161	28 15	59	161	27 16	58	161
16	31 24	59	161	30 25	59	162	29 26	59	162	28 27	59	162	27 28	59	162
15	31 35	−59	162	30 36	−59	163	29 37	−59	163	28 38	−59	163	27 39	−59	163
14	31 46	59	164	30 47	59	164	29 48	59	164	28 49	60	164	27 49	59	164
13	31 56	59	165	30 57	59	165	29 58	60	165	28 58	59	165	27 59	59	165
12	32 05	59	166	31 06	59	166	30 07	60	166	29 07	59	166	28 08	59	167
11	32 14	59	167	31 15	60	167	30 15	59	167	29 16	60	168	28 16	59	168
10	32 22	−60	168	31 22	−59	168	30 23	−60	169	29 23	−59	169	28 24	−60	169
9	32 29	59	169	31 30	60	170	30 30	60	170	29 30	59	170	28 31	60	170
8	32 36	60	171	31 36	60	171	30 36	59	171	29 37	60	171	28 37	60	171
7	32 41	59	172	31 42	60	172	30 42	60	172	29 42	60	172	28 42	60	172
6	32 46	60	173	31 46	59	173	30 47	60	173	29 47	60	173	28 47	60	173
5	32 50	−59	174	31 51	−60	174	30 51	−60	174	29 51	−60	174	28 51	−60	174
4	32 54	60	175	31 54	60	175	30 54	60	175	29 54	60	175	28 54	60	176
3	32 57	60	176	31 57	60	177	30 57	60	177	29 57	60	177	28 57	60	177
2	32 59	60	178	31 59	60	178	30 59	60	178	29 59	60	178	28 59	60	178
1	33 00	60	179	32 00	60	179	31 00	60	179	30 00	60	179	29 00	60	179
0	33 00	−60	180	32 00	−60	180	31 00	−60	130	30 00	−60	180	29 00	−60	180

LHA	10° Hc	10° d	10° Z	11° Hc	11° d	11° Z	12° Hc	12° d	12° Z	13° Hc	13° d	13° Z	14° Hc	14° d	14° Z	LHA
	° ′	′	°	° ′	′	°	° ′	′	°	° ′	′	°	° ′	′	°	
69	04 37	49	113	03 48	49	113	02 59	49	114	02 10	49	114	01 21	49	115	291
68	05 11	49	114	04 22	50	114	03 32	49	115	02 43	49	115	01 54	49	116	292
67	05 45	50	114	04 55	49	115	04 06	49	115	03 17	50	116	02 27	49	117	293
66	06 18	49	115	05 29	50	116	04 39	49	116	03 50	50	117	03 00	50	117	294
65	06 51	−49	116	06 02	−50	117	05 12	−50	117	04 22	−49	118	03 33	−50	118	295
64	07 25	50	117	06 35	50	117	05 45	50	118	04 55	50	118	04 05	50	119	296
63	07 57	50	118	07 07	50	118	06 17	50	119	05 27	50	119	04 37	50	120	297
62	08 30	50	119	07 40	50	119	06 50	51	120	05 59	50	120	05 09	50	121	298
61	09 02	50	119	08 12	50	120	07 22	51	120	06 31	50	121	05 41	51	122	299
60	09 34	−50	120	08 44	−51	121	07 53	−50	121	07 03	−51	122	06 12	−50	122	300
59	10 06	50	121	09 16	51	122	08 25	51	122	07 34	51	123	06 43	51	123	301
58	10 38	51	122	09 47	51	122	08 56	51	123	08 05	51	123	07 14	51	124	302
57	11 09	51	123	10 18	51	123	09 27	51	124	08 36	51	124	07 45	52	125	303
56	11 40	51	124	10 49	52	124	09 57	51	125	09 06	51	125	08 15	52	126	304
55	12 11	−52	124	11 19	−51	125	10 28	−52	125	09 36	−51	126	08 45	−52	127	305
54	12 41	52	125	11 49	51	126	10 58	52	126	10 06	52	127	09 14	52	127	306
53	13 11	52	126	12 19	52	127	11 27	52	127	10 35	52	128	09 43	52	128	307
52	13 41	52	127	12 49	52	128	11 57	53	128	11 04	52	129	10 12	52	129	308
51	14 10	52	128	13 18	53	128	12 25	52	129	11 33	52	129	10 41	53	130	309
50	14 39	−52	129	13 47	−53	129	12 54	−52	130	12 02	−53	130	11 09	−53	131	310
49	15 08	53	130	14 15	53	130	13 22	52	131	12 30	53	131	11 37	53	132	311
48	15 36	53	131	14 43	53	131	13 50	53	132	12 57	53	132	12 04	53	133	312
47	16 04	53	132	15 11	53	132	14 18	54	132	13 24	53	133	12 31	53	133	313
46	16 31	53	132	15 38	53	133	14 45	54	133	13 51	53	134	12 58	54	134	314
45	16 58	−53	133	16 05	−54	134	15 11	−53	134	14 18	−54	135	13 24	−54	135	315
44	17 25	54	134	16 31	53	135	15 38	54	135	14 44	54	136	13 50	54	136	316
43	17 51	54	135	16 57	54	136	16 03	54	136	15 09	54	137	14 15	54	137	317
42	18 17	54	136	17 23	54	137	16 29	54	137	15 35	55	137	14 40	54	138	318
41	18 43	55	137	17 48	54	137	16 54	55	138	15 59	54	138	15 05	55	139	319
40	19 08	−55	138	18 13	−55	138	17 18	−54	139	16 24	−55	139	15 29	−55	140	320
39	19 32	55	139	18 37	54	139	17 43	55	140	16 48	55	140	15 53	55	141	321
38	19 56	55	140	19 01	55	140	18 06	55	141	17 11	55	141	16 16	55	142	322
37	20 20	55	141	19 25	56	141	18 29	55	142	17 34	55	142	16 39	56	142	323
36	20 43	56	142	19 47	55	142	18 52	55	143	17 57	56	143	17 01	56	143	324
35	21 05	−55	143	20 10	−56	143	19 14	−55	144	18 19	−56	144	17 23	−56	144	325
34	21 28	56	144	20 32	56	144	19 36	56	145	18 40	56	145	17 44	56	145	326
33	21 49	56	145	20 53	56	145	19 57	56	146	19 01	56	146	18 05	56	146	327
32	22 10	56	146	21 14	56	146	20 18	56	147	19 22	57	147	18 25	56	147	328
31	22 31	57	147	21 34	56	147	20 38	57	147	19 41	56	148	18 45	57	148	329
30	22 51	−57	148	21 54	−56	148	20 58	−57	148	20 01	−57	149	19 04	−57	149	330
29	23 10	57	149	22 13	56	149	21 17	57	149	20 20	57	150	19 23	57	150	331
28	23 29	57	150	22 32	57	150	21 35	57	150	20 38	57	151	19 41	57	151	332
27	23 47	57	151	22 50	57	151	21 53	57	151	20 56	57	152	19 59	58	152	333
26	24 05	57	152	23 08	57	152	22 11	58	152	21 13	57	153	20 16	58	153	334
25	24 22	−57	153	23 25	−58	153	22 27	−57	153	21 30	−58	154	20 32	−58	154	335
24	24 39	58	154	23 41	57	154	22 44	58	154	21 46	58	155	20 48	58	155	336
23	24 55	58	155	23 57	58	155	22 59	58	156	22 01	58	156	21 03	58	156	337
22	25 10	58	156	24 12	58	156	23 14	58	157	22 16	58	157	21 18	58	157	338
21	25 25	58	157	24 27	58	157	23 29	59	158	22 30	58	158	21 32	58	158	339
20	25 39	−58	158	24 41	−59	158	23 42	−58	159	22 44	−58	159	21 46	−59	159	340
19	25 53	59	159	24 54	58	159	23 56	59	160	22 57	58	160	21 59	59	160	341
18	26 06	59	160	25 07	59	160	24 08	59	161	23 09	58	161	22 11	59	161	342
17	26 18	59	161	25 19	59	162	24 20	59	162	23 21	59	162	22 22	58	162	343
16	26 29	59	162	25 30	59	163	24 31	59	163	23 32	59	163	22 33	59	163	344
15	26 40	−59	163	25 41	−59	164	24 42	−59	164	23 43	−59	164	22 44	−59	164	345
14	26 50	59	165	25 51	59	165	24 52	59	165	23 53	59	165	22 54	60	165	346
13	27 00	59	166	26 01	60	166	25 01	59	166	24 02	59	166	23 03	60	166	347
12	27 09	60	167	26 09	59	167	25 10	60	167	24 10	59	167	23 11	59	167	348
11	27 17	60	168	26 17	59	168	25 18	60	168	24 18	59	168	23 19	60	168	349
10	27 24	−59	169	26 25	−60	169	25 25	−59	169	24 26	−60	169	23 26	−60	169	350
9	27 31	60	170	26 31	59	170	25 32	60	170	24 32	60	170	23 32	59	171	351
8	27 37	60	171	26 37	59	171	25 38	60	171	24 38	60	171	23 38	60	172	352
7	27 42	59	172	26 43	60	172	25 43	60	172	24 43	60	173	23 43	59	173	353
6	27 47	60	173	26 47	60	173	25 47	59	174	24 48	60	174	23 48	60	174	354
5	27 51	−60	174	26 51	−60	175	25 51	−60	175	24 51	−59	175	23 52	−60	175	355
4	27 54	60	176	26 54	60	176	25 54	59	176	24 55	60	176	23 55	60	176	356
3	27 57	60	177	26 57	60	177	25 57	60	177	24 57	60	177	23 57	60	177	357
2	27 59	60	178	26 59	60	178	25 59	60	178	24 59	60	178	23 59	60	178	358
1	28 00	60	179	27 00	60	179	26 00	60	179	25 00	60	179	24 00	60	179	359
0	28 00	−60	180	27 00	−60	180	26 00	−60	180	25 00	−60	180	24 00	−60	180	360

S. Lat. {LHA greater than 180°....... Zn=180−Z / LHA less than 180°.......... Zn=180+Z}

DECLINATION (0°-14°) CONTRARY NAME TO LATITUDE

LAT 52°

N. Lat. {LHA greater than 180°....... Zn=Z
{LHA less than 180°........... Zn=360−Z

DECLINATION (15°-29°) SAME NAME AS LATITUDE

LHA	15° Hc	15° d	15° Z	16° Hc	16° d	16° Z	17° Hc	17° d	17° Z	18° Hc	18° d	18° Z	19° Hc	19° d	19° Z
	° ′	′	°	° ′	′	°	° ′	′	°	° ′	′	°	° ′	′	°
0	53 00	+60	180	54 00	+60	180	55 00	+60	180	56 00	+60	180	57 00	+60	180
1	53 00	60	178	54 00	60	178	55 00	60	178	56 00	59	178	56 59	60	178
2	52 58	60	177	53 58	60	177	54 58	60	177	55 58	60	177	56 58	60	177
3	52 55	60	175	53 55	60	175	54 55	60	175	55 55	60	175	56 55	60	175
4	52 52	60	174	53 52	59	174	54 51	60	173	55 51	60	173	56 51	60	173
5	52 47	+60	172	53 47	+60	172	54 47	+59	172	55 46	+60	172	56 46	+60	171
6	52 42	59	170	53 41	60	170	54 41	59	170	55 40	60	170	56 40	60	170
7	52 35	59	169	53 34	60	169	54 34	59	168	55 33	60	168	56 33	59	168
8	52 27	60	167	53 27	59	167	54 26	59	167	55 25	60	167	56 25	59	166
9	52 19	59	166	53 18	59	165	54 17	59	165	55 16	59	165	56 15	59	165
10	52 09	+59	164	53 08	+59	164	54 07	+59	164	55 06	+59	163	56 05	+59	163
11	51 58	59	163	52 57	59	162	53 56	59	162	54 55	59	162	55 54	58	161
12	51 47	59	161	52 46	58	161	53 44	59	160	54 43	58	160	55 41	59	160
13	51 34	59	160	52 33	58	159	53 31	59	159	54 30	58	158	55 28	58	158
14	51 21	58	158	52 19	58	158	53 17	58	157	54 15	58	157	55 13	58	156
15	51 07	+58	157	52 05	+58	156	53 03	+57	156	54 00	+58	155	54 58	+58	155
16	50 52	57	155	51 49	58	155	52 47	58	154	53 45	57	154	54 42	57	153
17	50 36	57	154	51 33	57	153	52 30	58	153	53 28	57	152	54 25	57	152
18	50 19	57	152	51 16	57	152	52 13	57	151	53 10	57	151	54 07	57	150
19	50 01	57	151	50 58	57	150	51 55	57	150	52 52	56	149	53 48	56	149
20	49 43	+56	149	50 39	+57	149	51 36	+56	148	52 32	+56	148	53 28	+56	147
21	49 23	57	148	50 20	56	147	51 16	56	147	52 12	56	146	53 08	56	146
22	49 03	56	147	49 59	56	146	50 55	56	145	51 51	56	145	52 47	55	144
23	48 43	55	145	49 38	56	145	50 34	55	144	51 29	56	143	52 25	55	143
24	48 21	56	144	49 17	55	143	50 12	55	143	51 07	55	142	52 02	55	141
25	47 59	+55	142	48 54	+55	142	49 49	+55	141	50 44	+54	141	51 38	+55	140
26	47 36	55	141	48 31	55	141	49 26	54	140	50 20	54	139	51 14	54	139
27	47 13	54	140	48 07	54	139	49 01	55	139	49 56	54	138	50 50	53	137
28	46 48	55	139	47 43	54	138	48 37	54	137	49 31	53	137	50 24	53	136
29	46 24	54	137	47 18	53	137	48 11	54	136	49 05	53	135	49 58	53	135
30	45 58	+54	136	46 52	+53	135	47 45	+54	135	48 39	+53	134	49 32	+52	133
31	45 32	54	135	46 26	53	134	47 19	53	133	48 12	52	133	49 04	53	132
32	45 06	53	134	45 59	53	133	46 52	52	132	47 44	53	132	48 37	52	131
33	44 39	52	132	45 31	53	132	46 24	52	131	47 16	52	130	48 08	52	130
34	44 11	53	131	45 04	52	131	45 56	52	130	46 48	52	129	47 40	51	128
35	43 43	+52	130	44 35	+52	129	45 27	+52	129	46 19	+51	128	47 10	+51	127
36	43 14	52	129	44 06	52	128	44 58	52	127	45 50	51	127	46 41	50	126
37	42 45	52	128	43 37	52	127	44 29	51	126	45 20	51	126	46 11	50	125
38	42 16	51	127	43 07	52	126	43 59	50	125	44 49	51	124	45 40	50	124
39	41 46	51	125	42 37	51	125	43 28	51	124	44 19	50	123	45 09	50	123
40	41 16	+51	124	42 07	+50	124	42 57	+51	123	43 48	+50	122	44 38	+49	121
41	40 45	51	123	41 36	50	123	42 26	50	122	43 16	50	121	44 06	49	120
42	40 14	50	122	41 04	50	121	41 54	50	121	42 44	50	120	43 34	49	119
43	39 43	50	121	40 33	50	120	41 23	49	120	42 12	49	119	43 01	49	118
44	39 11	50	120	40 01	49	119	40 50	50	119	41 40	49	118	42 29	48	117
45	38 39	+49	119	39 28	+50	118	40 18	+49	118	41 07	+49	117	41 56	+48	116
46	38 06	50	118	38 56	49	117	39 45	49	117	40 34	48	116	41 22	49	115
47	37 33	50	117	38 23	49	116	39 12	48	116	40 00	49	115	40 49	48	114
48	37 00	49	116	37 49	49	115	38 38	49	115	39 27	48	114	40 15	48	113
49	36 27	49	115	37 16	48	114	38 04	49	114	38 53	48	113	39 41	47	112
50	35 53	+49	114	36 42	+48	113	37 30	+48	113	38 18	+48	112	39 06	+48	111
51	35 19	49	113	36 08	48	112	36 56	48	112	37 44	48	111	38 32	47	110
52	34 45	49	112	35 34	48	111	36 22	47	111	37 09	48	110	37 57	47	109
53	34 11	48	111	34 59	48	110	35 47	48	110	36 35	47	109	37 22	47	108
54	33 36	48	110	34 24	48	110	35 12	48	109	36 00	47	108	36 47	47	107
55	33 02	+48	109	33 50	+47	109	34 37	+47	108	35 24	+47	107	36 11	+47	106
56	32 27	47	108	33 14	48	108	34 02	47	107	34 49	47	106	35 36	46	105
57	31 52	47	108	32 39	47	107	33 26	47	106	34 13	47	105	35 00	47	105
58	31 16	48	107	32 04	47	106	32 51	47	105	33 38	46	104	34 24	47	104
59	30 41	47	106	31 28	47	105	32 15	47	104	33 02	46	104	33 48	47	103
60	30 05	+47	105	30 52	+47	104	31 39	+47	103	32 26	+46	103	33 12	+46	102
61	29 29	47	104	30 16	47	103	31 03	47	103	31 50	46	102	32 36	46	101
62	28 53	47	103	29 40	47	102	30 27	47	102	31 14	46	101	32 00	46	100
63	28 17	47	102	29 04	47	102	29 51	46	101	30 37	46	100	31 23	46	99
64	27 41	47	101	28 28	47	101	29 15	46	100	30 01	46	99	30 47	46	98
65	27 05	+47	101	27 52	+46	100	28 38	+46	99	29 24	+46	98	30 10	+46	98
66	26 29	46	100	27 15	47	99	28 02	46	98	28 48	46	98	29 34	45	97
67	25 52	47	99	26 39	46	98	27 25	46	97	28 11	46	97	28 57	45	96
68	25 16	46	98	26 02	46	97	26 48	46	97	27 34	46	96	28 20	46	95
69	24 39	46	97	25 25	47	97	26 12	46	96	26 58	45	95	27 43	46	94

LHA	20° Hc	20° d	20° Z	21° Hc	21° d	21° Z	22° Hc	22° d	22° Z	23° Hc	23° d	23° Z	24° Hc	24° d	24° Z
	° ′	′	°	° ′	′	°	° ′	′	°	° ′	′	°	° ′	′	°
0	58 00	+60	180	59 00	+60	180	60 00	+60	180	61 00	+60	180	62 00	+60	180
1	57 59	60	178	58 59	60	178	59 59	60	178	60 59	60	178	61 59	60	178
2	57 58	60	177	58 58	60	176	59 58	60	176	60 58	60	176	61 58	59	176
3	57 55	60	175	58 55	60	175	59 55	60	174	60 55	59	174	61 54	60	174
4	57 51	60	173	58 51	60	173	59 51	59	173	60 50	60	172	61 50	60	172
5	57 46	+60	171	58 46	+59	171	59 45	+60	171	60 45	+59	171	61 44	+60	170
6	57 40	59	169	58 39	60	169	59 39	59	169	60 38	60	169	61 38	59	168
7	57 32	60	168	58 32	59	167	59 31	59	167	60 30	60	167	61 30	59	167
8	57 24	59	166	58 23	59	166	59 22	59	165	60 21	59	165	61 20	59	165
9	57 14	59	164	58 13	59	164	59 12	59	164	60 11	59	163	61 10	59	163
10	57 04	+59	163	58 03	+58	162	59 01	+59	162	60 00	+59	161	60 59	+58	161
11	56 52	59	161	57 51	58	160	58 49	59	160	59 48	58	160	60 46	58	159
12	56 40	58	159	57 38	58	159	58 36	58	158	59 34	58	158	60 32	58	157
13	56 26	58	158	57 24	58	157	58 22	58	157	59 20	57	156	60 17	58	156
14	56 11	58	156	57 09	58	155	58 07	57	155	59 04	58	154	60 02	57	154
15	55 56	+57	154	56 53	+58	154	57 51	+57	153	58 48	+57	153	59 45	+57	152
16	55 39	57	153	56 36	57	152	57 33	57	152	58 30	57	151	59 27	56	150
17	55 22	57	151	56 19	56	151	57 15	57	150	58 12	56	149	59 08	56	149
18	55 04	56	150	56 00	56	149	56 56	57	148	57 53	55	148	58 48	56	147
19	54 44	57	148	55 41	56	147	56 37	55	147	57 32	56	146	58 28	55	145
20	54 24	+56	147	55 20	+56	146	56 16	+55	145	57 11	+55	145	58 06	+55	144
21	54 04	55	145	54 59	55	144	55 54	55	144	56 49	55	143	57 44	55	142
22	53 42	55	144	54 37	55	143	55 32	55	142	56 27	54	141	57 21	54	141
23	53 20	54	142	54 14	55	141	55 09	54	141	56 03	54	140	56 57	54	139
24	52 57	54	141	53 51	54	140	54 45	54	139	55 39	54	138	56 33	53	138
25	52 33	+54	139	53 27	+54	139	54 21	+53	138	55 14	+54	137	56 08	+52	136
26	52 08	54	138	53 02	54	137	53 56	53	136	54 49	53	136	55 42	52	135
27	51 43	54	137	52 37	53	136	53 30	53	135	54 23	52	134	55 15	52	133
28	51 17	54	135	52 11	52	134	53 03	53	134	53 56	52	133	54 48	52	132
29	50 51	53	134	51 44	52	133	52 36	52	132	53 28	52	131	54 20	51	131
30	50 24	+53	133	51 17	+52	132	52 09	+51	131	53 00	+52	130	53 52	+51	129
31	49 57	52	131	50 49	51	131	51 40	52	130	52 32	51	129	53 23	50	128
32	49 29	51	130	50 20	52	129	51 12	51	128	52 03	50	128	52 53	51	127
33	49 00	51	129	49 51	52	128	50 43	50	127	51 33	51	126	52 24	50	125
34	48 31	51	128	49 22	51	127	50 13	50	126	51 03	50	125	51 53	50	124
35	48 01	+51	126	48 52	+51	126	49 43	+50	125	50 33	+49	124	51 22	+50	123
36	47 31	51	125	48 22	50	124	49 12	50	124	50 02	49	123	50 51	49	122
37	47 01	50	124	47 51	50	123	48 41	50	122	49 31	49	121	50 20	48	121
38	46 30	50	123	47 20	50	122	48 10	49	121	48 59	49	120	49 48	48	119
39	45 59	50	122	46 49	49	121	47 38	49	120	48 27	48	119	49 15	48	118
40	45 27	+50	121	46 17	+49	120	47 06	+48	119	47 54	+49	118	48 43	+47	117
41	44 55	49	120	45 44	49	119	46 33	49	118	47 22	48	117	48 10	47	116
42	44 23	49	118	45 12	48	118	46 00	48	117	46 48	48	116	47 36	47	115
43	43 50	49	117	44 39	48	117	45 27	48	116	46 15	48	115	47 03	47	114
44	43 17	49	116	44 06	48	115	44 54	47	115	45 41	48	114	46 29	46	113
45	42 44	+48	115	43 32	+48	114	44 20	+47	114	45 07	+47	113	45 54	+47	112
46	42 11	47	114	42 58	48	113	43 46	47	113	44 33	47	112	45 20	46	111
47	41 37	47	113	42 24	48	112	43 12	47	112	43 59	46	111	44 45	47	110
48	41 03	47	112	41 50	47	111	42 37	47	111	43 24	47	110	44 11	46	109
49	40 28	48	111	41 16	47	110	42 03	46	110	42 49	46	109	43 35	46	108
50	39 54	+47	110	40 41	+47	109	41 28	+46	109	42 14	+46	108	43 00	+46	107
51	39 19	47	109	40 06	47	109	40 53	46	108	41 39	46	107	42 25	45	106
52	38 44	47	108	39 31	46	108	40 17	46	107	41 03	46	106	41 49	46	105
53	38 09	47	107	38 56	46	107	39 42	46	106	40 28	45	105	41 13	46	104
54	37 34	46	107	38 20	46	106	39 06	46	105	39 52	46	104	40 38	45	103
55	36 58	+46	106	37 44	+46	105	38 30	+46	104	39 16	+46	103	40 02	+44	102
56	36 22	47	105	37 09	46	104	37 55	45	103	38 40	45	102	39 25	45	101
57	35 47	46	104	36 33	45	103	37 18	46	102	38 04	45	101	38 49	45	101
58	35 11	46	103	35 57	45	102	36 42	46	101	37 28	45	100	38 13	44	100
59	34 35	45	102	35 20	46	101	36 06	45	100	36 51	45	100	37 36	45	99
60	33 58	+46	101	34 44	+46	100	35 30	+45	100	36 15	+45	99	37 00	+44	98
61	33 22	46	100	34 08	45	100	34 53	45	99	35 38	45	98	36 23	44	97
62	32 46	45	99	33 31	46	99	34 17	45	98	35 02	44	97	35 46	45	96
63	32 09	46	99	32 55	45	98	33 40	45	97	34 25	45	96	35 10	44	95
64	31 33	45	98	32 18	45	97	33 03	45	96	33 48	45	95	34 33	44	95
65	30 56	+45	97	31 41	+46	96	32 27	+44	95	33 11	+45	95	33 56	+44	94
66	30 19	46	96	31 05	45	95	31 50	45	95	32 35	44	94	33 19	44	93
67	29 42	46	95	30 28	45	94	31 13	45	94	31 58	44	93	32 42	44	92
68	29 06	45	94	29 51	45	94	30 36	45	93	31 21	44	92	32 05	44	91
69	28 29	45	94	29 14	45	93	29 59	45	92	30 44	44	91	31 28	45	91

LHA	25° Hc	25° d	25° Z	26° Hc	26° d	26° Z	27° Hc	27° d	27° Z	28° Hc	28° d	28° Z	29° Hc	29° d	29° Z	LHA
	° ′	′	°	° ′	′	°	° ′	′	°	° ′	′	°	° ′	′	°	
0	63 00	+60	180	64 00	+60	180	65 00	+60	180	66 00	+60	180	67 00	+60	180	360
1	62 59	60	178	63 59	60	178	64 59	60	178	65 59	60	178	66 59	60	178	359
2	62 57	60	176	63 57	60	176	64 57	60	176	65 57	60	176	66 57	60	176	358
3	62 54	60	174	63 54	60	174	64 54	60	174	65 54	60	174	66 54	59	173	357
4	62 50	60	172	63 50	59	172	64 49	60	172	65 49	60	171	66 49	59	171	356
5	62 44	+60	170	63 44	+59	170	64 43	+60	170	65 43	+59	169	66 42	+60	169	355
6	62 37	59	168	63 36	60	168	64 36	59	168	65 35	59	167	66 34	59	167	354
7	62 29	59	166	63 28	59	166	64 27	59	165	65 26	59	165	66 25	59	165	353
8	62 19	59	164	63 18	59	164	64 17	59	163	65 16	59	163	66 15	58	162	352
9	62 09	58	162	63 07	59	162	64 06	58	161	65 04	59	161	66 03	58	160	351
10	61 57	+58	160	62 55	+59	160	63 54	+58	159	64 52	+58	159	65 50	+58	158	350
11	61 44	58	159	62 42	58	158	63 40	58	158	64 38	57	157	65 35	58	156	349
12	61 30	58	157	62 28	57	156	63 25	58	156	64 23	57	155	65 20	57	154	348
13	61 15	57	155	62 12	57	154	63 09	57	154	64 06	57	153	65 03	57	152	347
14	60 59	57	153	61 56	57	153	62 53	56	152	63 49	56	151	64 45	57	150	346
15	60 42	+56	151	61 38	+57	151	62 35	+56	150	63 31	+56	149	64 27	+55	148	345
16	60 23	57	150	61 20	56	149	62 16	55	148	63 11	56	147	64 07	55	147	344
17	60 04	56	148	61 00	56	147	61 56	55	146	62 51	55	146	63 46	54	145	343
18	59 44	56	146	60 40	55	146	61 35	55	145	62 30	54	144	63 24	54	143	342
19	59 23	55	145	60 18	55	144	61 13	54	143	62 07	54	142	63 01	54	141	341
20	59 01	+55	143	59 56	+54	142	60 50	+54	141	61 44	+54	140	62 38	+53	139	340
21	58 39	54	141	59 33	54	141	60 27	53	140	61 20	53	139	62 13	53	138	339
22	58 15	54	140	59 09	53	139	60 02	53	138	60 55	53	137	61 48	52	136	338
23	57 51	53	138	58 44	53	137	59 37	53	137	60 30	52	136	61 22	52	135	337
24	57 26	53	137	58 19	53	136	59 12	52	135	60 04	51	134	60 55	51	133	336
25	57 00	+53	135	57 53	+52	134	58 45	+52	134	59 37	+51	133	60 28	+51	131	335
26	56 34	52	134	57 26	52	133	58 18	51	132	59 09	51	131	60 00	50	130	334
27	56 07	52	132	56 59	51	132	57 50	51	131	58 41	50	130	59 31	50	129	333
28	55 40	51	131	56 31	51	130	57 22	50	129	58 12	50	128	59 02	49	127	332
29	55 11	51	130	56 02	51	129	56 53	50	128	57 43	49	127	58 32	49	126	331
30	54 43	+50	128	55 33	+50	127	56 23	+50	126	57 13	+49	125	58 02	+49	124	330
31	54 13	51	127	55 04	49	126	55 53	50	125	56 43	48	124	57 31	48	123	329
32	53 44	50	126	54 34	49	125	55 23	49	124	56 12	48	123	57 00	48	122	328
33	53 14	49	125	54 03	49	124	54 52	49	123	55 41	47	122	56 28	48	120	327
34	52 43	49	123	53 32	49	122	54 21	48	121	55 09	47	120	55 56	47	119	326
35	52 12	+49	122	53 01	+48	121	53 49	+48	120	54 37	+47	119	55 24	+47	118	325
36	51 40	49	121	52 29	48	120	53 17	47	119	54 04	47	118	54 51	47	117	324
37	51 08	48	120	51 56	48	119	52 44	47	118	53 31	47	117	54 18	46	116	323
38	50 36	48	119	51 24	47	118	52 11	47	117	52 58	47	116	53 45	45	114	322
39	50 03	48	117	50 51	47	116	51 38	47	115	52 25	46	114	53 11	45	113	321
40	49 30	+48	116	50 18	+47	115	51 05	+46	114	51 51	+46	113	52 37	+45	112	320
41	48 57	47	115	49 44	47	114	50 31	46	113	51 17	45	112	52 02	45	111	319
42	48 23	47	114	49 10	47	113	49 57	45	112	50 42	46	111	51 28	44	110	318
43	47 50	46	113	48 36	46	112	49 22	46	111	50 08	45	110	50 53	44	109	317
44	47 15	47	112	48 02	46	111	48 48	45	110	49 33	45	109	50 18	44	108	316
45	46 41	+46	111	47 27	+46	110	48 13	+45	109	48 58	+45	108	49 43	+44	107	315
46	46 06	46	110	46 52	46	109	47 38	45	108	48 23	44	107	49 07	44	106	314
47	45 32	45	109	46 17	46	108	47 03	44	107	47 47	45	106	48 32	43	105	313
48	44 57	45	108	45 42	45	107	46 27	45	106	47 12	44	105	47 56	43	104	312
49	44 21	46	107	45 07	45	106	45 52	44	105	46 36	44	104	47 20	43	103	311
50	43 46	+45	106	44 31	+45	105	45 16	+44	104	46 00	+44	103	46 44	+43	102	310
51	43 10	45	105	43 55	45	104	44 40	44	103	45 24	44	102	46 08	43	101	309
52	42 35	44	104	43 19	45	103	44 04	44	102	44 48	44	101	45 32	43	100	308
53	41 59	44	103	42 43	45	102	43 28	44	101	44 12	43	100	44 55	43	100	307
54	41 23	44	102	42 07	45	101	42 52	43	101	43 35	44	100	44 19	42	99	306
55	40 46	+45	101	41 31	+44	101	42 15	+44	100	42 59	+43	99	43 42	+43	98	305
56	40 10	45	101	40 55	44	100	41 39	43	99	42 22	43	98	43 05	43	97	304
57	39 34	44	100	40 18	44	99	41 02	44	98	41 46	43	97	42 29	42	96	303
58	38 57	45	99	39 42	43	98	40 25	44	97	41 09	43	96	41 52	43	95	302
59	38 21	44	98	39 05	44	97	39 49	43	96	40 32	43	95	41 15	43	94	301
60	37 44	+44	97	38 28	+44	96	39 12	+43	95	39 55	+43	94	40 38	+43	94	300
61	37 07	45	96	37 52	43	95	38 35	44	95	39 19	42	94	40 01	43	93	299
62	36 31	44	95	37 15	43	95	37 58	44	94	38 42	42	93	39 24	43	92	298
63	35 54	44	95	36 38	44	94	37 22	43	93	38 05	43	92	38 48	42	91	297
64	35 17	44	94	36 01	44	93	36 45	43	92	37 28	43	91	38 11	42	90	296
65	34 40	+44	93	35 24	+44	92	36 08	+43	91	36 51	+43	90	37 34	+42	90	295
66	34 03	44	92	34 47	44	91	35 31	43	90	36 14	43	90	36 57	42	89	294
67	33 26	44	91	34 10	44	91	34 54	43	90	35 37	43	89	36 20	42	88	293
68	32 49	44	91	33 33	44	90	34 17	43	89	35 00	43	88	35 43	42	87	292
69	32 13	43	90	32 56	44	89	33 40	43	88	34 23	43	87	35 06	43	86	291

S. Lat. {LHA greater than 180°....... Zn=180−Z
{LHA less than 180°........... Zn=180+Z

DECLINATION (15°-29°) SAME NAME AS LATITUDE

N. Lat. {LHA greater than 180°....... Zn=Z; LHA less than 180°........... Zn=360−Z}

DECLINATION (15°-29°) SAME NAME AS LATITUDE

LHA	15° Hc	15° d	15° Z	16° Hc	16° d	16° Z	17° Hc	17° d	17° Z	18° Hc	18° d	18° Z	19° Hc	19° d	19° Z	LHA
	° ′	′	°	° ′	′	°	° ′	′	°	° ′	′	°	° ′	′	°	
70	24 02	+47	96	24 49	+46	96	25 35	+46	95	26 21	+45	94	27 06	+46	94	290
71	23 26	46	96	24 12	46	95	24 58	46	94	25 44	46	93	26 30	45	93	289
72	22 49	46	95	23 35	46	94	24 21	46	93	25 07	46	93	25 53	45	92	288
73	22 12	46	94	22 58	46	93	23 44	46	93	24 30	46	92	25 16	45	91	287
74	21 35	46	93	22 21	46	92	23 07	46	92	23 53	46	91	24 39	45	90	286
75	20 58	+46	92	21 44	+46	92	22 30	+46	91	23 16	+46	90	24 02	+45	90	285
76	20 21	46	92	21 07	46	91	21 53	46	90	22 39	46	89	23 25	45	89	284
77	19 44	47	91	20 31	46	90	21 17	45	89	22 02	46	89	22 48	45	88	283
78	19 07	47	90	19 54	46	89	20 40	45	89	21 25	46	88	22 11	46	87	282
79	18 30	47	89	19 17	46	89	20 03	46	88	20 49	45	87	21 34	46	86	281
80	17 54	+46	88	18 40	+46	88	19 26	+46	87	20 12	+45	86	20 57	+46	86	280
81	17 17	46	88	18 03	46	87	18 49	46	86	19 35	46	86	20 21	45	85	279
82	16 40	46	87	17 26	46	86	18 12	46	86	18 58	46	85	19 44	45	84	278
83	16 03	46	86	16 49	46	85	17 35	46	85	18 21	46	84	19 07	46	83	277
84	15 26	46	85	16 12	46	85	16 58	47	84	17 45	45	83	18 30	46	83	276
85	14 49	+47	85	15 36	+46	84	16 22	+46	83	17 08	+46	83	17 54	+46	82	275
86	14 13	46	84	14 59	46	83	15 45	46	82	16 31	46	82	17 17	46	81	274
87	13 36	46	83	14 22	47	82	15 09	46	82	15 55	46	81	16 41	46	80	273
88	12 59	47	82	13 46	46	82	14 32	46	81	15 18	46	80	16 04	46	80	272
89	12 23	46	81	13 09	47	81	13 56	46	80	14 42	46	79	15 28	46	79	271
90	11 46	+47	81	12 33	+46	80	13 19	+47	79	14 06	+46	79	14 52	+46	78	270
91	11 10	46	80	11 56	47	79	12 43	47	79	13 30	46	78	14 16	46	77	269
92	10 33	47	79	11 20	47	79	12 07	46	78	12 53	47	77	13 40	46	77	268
93	09 57	47	78	10 44	47	78	11 31	46	77	12 17	47	76	13 04	47	76	267
94	09 21	47	78	10 08	47	77	10 55	47	76	11 42	46	76	12 28	47	75	266
95	08 45	+47	77	09 32	+47	76	10 19	+47	76	11 06	+47	75	11 53	+46	74	265
96	08 09	47	76	08 56	47	75	09 43	47	75	10 30	47	74	11 17	47	74	264
97	07 33	48	75	08 21	47	75	09 08	47	74	09 55	47	73	10 42	47	73	263
98	06 58	47	75	07 45	47	74	08 32	47	73	09 19	48	73	10 07	47	72	262
99	06 22	48	74	07 10	47	73	07 57	47	73	08 44	48	72	09 32	47	71	261
100	05 47	+47	73	06 34	+48	72	07 22	+47	72	08 09	+48	71	08 57	+47	71	260
101	05 12	47	72	05 59	48	72	06 47	47	71	07 34	48	70	08 22	47	70	259
102	04 36	48	71	05 24	48	71	06 12	48	70	07 00	47	70	07 47	48	69	258
103	04 01	48	71	04 49	48	70	05 37	48	69	06 25	48	69	07 13	48	68	257
104	03 27	48	70	04 15	48	69	05 03	48	69	05 51	48	68	06 39	48	68	256
105	02 52	+48	69	03 40	+48	69	04 28	+49	68	05 17	+48	67	06 05	+48	67	255
106	02 18	48	68	03 06	48	68	03 54	49	67	04 43	48	67	05 31	48	66	254
107	01 43	49	68	02 32	48	67	03 20	49	66	04 09	48	66	04 57	49	65	253
108	01 09	49	67	01 58	49	66	02 47	48	66	03 35	49	65	04 24	48	64	252
109	00 36	48	66	01 24	49	65	02 13	49	65	03 02	49	64	03 51	48	64	251
110	00 02	+49	65	00 51	+49	65	01 40	+49	64	02 29	+49	63	03 18	+49	63	250
111	−0 32	50	64	00 18	49	64	01 07	49	63	01 56	49	63	02 45	49	62	249
112	−1 05	50	64	−0 15	49	63	00 34	49	62	01 23	49	62	02 12	50	61	248
113	−1 38	50	63	−0 48	49	62	00 01	50	62	00 51	49	61	01 40	49	61	247
114	−2 10	49	62	−1 21	50	61	−0 31	49	61	00 18	50	60	01 08	50	60	246
115	−2 43	+50	61	−1 53	+50	61	−1 03	+49	60	−0 14	+50	60	00 36	+50	59	245
116	−3 15	50	60	−2 25	50	60	−1 35	50	59	−0 45	50	59	00 05	50	58	244
117	−3 47	50	60	−2 57	50	59	−2 07	50	59	−1 17	50	58	−0 27	51	57	243
118	−4 19	50	59	−3 29	51	58	−2 38	50	58	−1 48	50	57	−0 58	51	57	242
119	−4 50	50	58	−4 00	51	57	−3 09	50	57	−2 19	51	56	−1 28	50	56	241
120	−5 22	+51	57	−4 31	+51	57	−3 40	+51	56	−2 49	+50	56	−1 59	+51	55	240
121	−5 52	50	56	−5 02	51	56	−4 11	51	55	−3 20	51	55	−2 29	51	54	239
122				−5 32	51	55	−4 41	51	54	−3 50	51	54	−2 59	52	53	238
123							−5 11	52	54	−4 19	51	53	−3 28	51	53	237
124							−5 40	51	53	−4 49	52	52	−3 57	51	52	236
125										−5 18	+52	51	−4 26	+52	51	235
126										−5 47	52	51	−4 55	52	50	234
127													−5 23	52	49	233
128													−5 51	53	48	232

LHA	20° Hc	20° d	20° Z	21° Hc	21° d	21° Z	22° Hc	22° d	22° Z	23° Hc	23° d	23° Z	24° Hc	24° d	24° Z	LHA
	° ′	′	°	° ′	′	°	° ′	′	°	° ′	′	°	° ′	′	°	
70	27 52	+45	93	28 37	+45	92	29 22	+45	91	30 07	+44	91	30 51	+45	90	290
71	27 15	45	92	28 00	45	91	28 45	45	91	29 30	44	90	30 14	45	89	289
72	26 38	45	91	27 23	45	90	28 08	45	90	28 53	45	89	29 38	44	88	288
73	26 01	45	90	26 46	45	90	27 31	45	89	28 16	45	88	29 01	44	87	287
74	25 24	45	90	26 09	45	89	26 54	45	88	27 39	45	87	28 24	44	87	286
75	24 47	+46	89	25 33	+45	88	26 18	+44	87	27 02	+45	87	27 47	+44	86	285
76	24 10	46	88	24 56	45	87	25 41	44	87	26 25	45	86	27 10	44	85	284
77	23 33	46	87	24 19	45	87	25 04	45	86	25 49	44	85	26 33	45	84	283
78	22 57	45	87	23 42	45	86	24 27	45	85	25 12	45	84	25 57	44	84	282
79	22 20	45	86	23 05	45	85	23 50	45	84	24 35	45	84	25 20	44	83	281
80	21 43	+45	85	22 28	+45	84	23 13	+45	84	23 58	+45	83	24 43	+45	82	280
81	21 06	46	84	21 52	45	84	22 37	45	83	23 22	45	82	24 07	44	81	279
82	20 29	46	83	21 15	45	83	22 00	45	82	22 45	45	81	23 30	45	81	278
83	19 53	45	83	20 38	46	82	21 24	45	81	22 09	45	81	22 54	45	80	277
84	19 16	46	82	20 02	45	81	20 47	45	81	21 32	45	80	22 17	45	79	276
85	18 40	+45	81	19 25	+46	80	20 11	+45	80	20 56	+45	79	21 41	+45	78	275
86	18 03	46	80	18 49	45	80	19 34	46	79	20 20	45	78	21 05	45	78	274
87	17 27	46	80	18 13	45	79	18 58	46	78	19 44	45	78	20 29	45	77	273
88	16 50	46	79	17 36	46	78	18 22	46	78	19 08	45	77	19 53	45	76	272
89	16 14	46	78	17 00	46	77	17 46	46	77	18 32	45	76	19 17	46	75	271
90	15 38	+46	77	16 24	+46	77	17 10	+46	76	17 56	+46	75	18 42	+45	75	270
91	15 02	46	77	15 48	46	76	16 34	46	75	17 20	46	75	18 06	46	74	269
92	14 26	47	76	15 13	46	75	15 59	46	75	16 45	46	74	17 31	45	73	268
93	13 51	46	75	14 37	46	75	15 23	46	74	16 09	46	73	16 55	46	73	267
94	13 15	46	74	14 01	47	74	14 48	46	73	15 34	46	72	16 20	46	72	266
95	12 39	+47	74	13 26	+47	73	14 13	+46	72	14 59	+46	72	15 45	+46	71	265
96	12 04	47	73	12 51	46	72	13 37	47	72	14 24	46	71	15 10	47	70	264
97	11 29	47	72	12 16	46	72	13 02	47	71	13 49	47	70	14 36	46	70	263
98	10 54	47	71	11 41	47	71	12 28	46	70	13 14	47	70	14 01	47	69	262
99	10 19	47	71	11 06	47	70	11 53	47	69	12 40	47	69	13 27	47	68	261
100	09 44	+47	70	10 31	+47	69	11 18	+48	69	12 06	+47	68	12 53	+47	67	260
101	09 09	48	69	09 57	47	69	10 44	47	68	11 31	48	67	12 19	47	67	259
102	08 35	48	68	09 23	47	68	10 10	47	67	10 57	48	67	11 45	47	66	258
103	08 01	47	68	08 48	48	67	09 36	48	66	10 24	47	66	11 11	48	65	257
104	07 27	48	67	08 15	47	66	09 02	48	66	09 50	48	65	10 38	47	64	256
105	06 53	+48	66	07 41	+48	66	08 29	+48	65	09 17	+48	64	10 05	+47	64	255
106	06 19	48	65	07 07	48	65	07 55	49	64	08 44	48	64	09 32	48	63	254
107	05 46	48	65	06 34	48	64	07 22	49	63	08 11	48	63	08 59	48	62	253
108	05 12	49	64	06 01	48	63	06 49	49	63	07 38	48	62	08 26	49	61	252
109	04 39	49	63	05 28	49	63	06 17	48	62	07 05	49	61	07 54	48	61	251
110	04 07	+48	62	04 55	+49	62	05 44	+49	61	06 33	+49	61	07 22	+49	60	250
111	03 34	49	62	04 23	49	61	05 12	49	60	06 01	49	60	06 50	49	59	249
112	03 02	49	61	03 51	49	60	04 40	49	60	05 29	49	59	06 18	49	58	248
113	02 29	50	60	03 19	49	59	04 08	50	59	04 58	49	58	05 47	49	58	247
114	01 58	49	59	02 47	50	59	03 37	49	58	04 26	50	58	05 16	49	57	246
115	01 26	+50	58	02 16	+50	58	03 06	+49	57	03 55	+50	57	04 45	+50	56	245
116	00 55	50	58	01 45	50	57	02 35	50	57	03 25	49	56	04 14	50	55	244
117	00 24	50	57	01 14	50	56	02 04	50	56	02 54	50	55	03 44	50	55	243
118	−0 07	50	56	00 43	51	56	01 34	50	55	02 24	50	54	03 14	51	54	242
119	−0 38	51	55	00 13	50	55	01 03	51	54	01 54	51	54	02 45	50	53	241
120	−1 08	+51	54	−0 17	+51	54	00 34	+50	53	01 24	+51	53	02 15	+51	52	240
121	−1 38	51	54	−0 47	51	53	00 04	51	53	00 55	51	52	01 46	51	52	239
122	−2 07	51	53	−1 16	51	52	−0 25	51	52	00 26	51	51	01 17	51	51	238
123	−2 37	52	52	−1 45	51	52	−0 54	51	51	−0 03	52	51	00 49	51	50	237
124	−3 06	52	51	−2 14	51	51	−1 23	52	50	−0 31	52	50	00 21	51	49	236
125	−3 34	+51	50	−2 43	+52	50	−1 51	+52	49	−0 59	+52	49	−0 07	+52	48	235
126	−4 03	52	50	−3 11	52	49	−2 19	52	49	−1 27	52	48	−0 35	52	48	234
127	−4 31	53	49	−3 38	52	48	−2 46	52	48	−1 54	52	47	−1 02	52	47	233
128	−4 58	52	48	−4 06	53	48	−3 13	52	47	−2 21	52	47	−1 29	53	46	232
129	−5 26	53	47	−4 33	53	47	−3 40	52	46	−2 48	53	46	−1 55	53	45	231
130	−5 53	+53	46	−5 00	+53	46	−4 07	+53	45	−3 14	+53	45	−2 21	+53	44	230
131				−5 26	53	45	−4 33	53	45	−3 40	53	44	−2 47	53	44	229
132				−5 52	53	44	−4 59	54	44	−4 05	53	43	−3 12	53	43	228
133							−5 24	54	43	−4 30	53	42	−3 37	54	42	227
134							−5 49	54	42	−4 55	54	42	−4 01	53	41	226
135										−5 20	+54	41	−4 26	+54	40	225
136										−5 44	55	40	−4 49	54	40	224
137													−5 13	55	39	223
138													−5 36	55	38	222

LHA	25° Hc	25° d	25° Z	26° Hc	26° d	26° Z	27° Hc	27° d	27° Z	28° Hc	28° d	28° Z	29° Hc	29° d	29° Z	LHA
	° ′	′	°	° ′	′	°	° ′	′	°	° ′	′	°	° ′	′	°	
70	31 36	+43	89	32 19	+44	88	33 03	+43	87	33 46	+43	87	34 29	+43	86	290
71	30 59	44	88	31 43	43	87	32 26	43	87	33 09	43	86	33 52	43	85	289
72	30 22	44	87	31 06	43	87	31 49	44	86	32 33	43	85	33 16	42	84	288
73	29 45	44	87	30 29	43	86	31 12	44	85	31 56	43	84	32 39	43	83	287
74	29 08	44	86	29 52	44	85	30 36	43	84	31 19	43	84	32 02	43	83	286
75	28 31	+44	85	29 15	+44	84	29 59	+43	84	30 42	+44	83	31 26	+42	82	285
76	27 54	44	84	28 38	44	84	29 22	44	83	30 06	43	82	30 49	43	81	284
77	27 18	44	84	28 02	44	83	28 46	43	82	29 29	44	81	30 13	43	80	283
78	26 41	44	83	27 25	44	82	28 09	44	81	28 53	43	81	29 36	43	80	282
79	26 04	45	82	26 49	44	81	27 33	43	81	28 16	44	80	29 00	43	79	281
80	25 28	+44	81	26 12	+44	81	26 56	+44	80	27 40	+44	79	28 24	+43	78	280
81	24 51	45	81	25 36	44	80	26 20	44	79	27 04	44	78	27 48	43	78	279
82	24 15	44	80	24 59	45	79	25 44	44	78	26 28	44	78	27 12	43	77	278
83	23 39	44	79	24 23	45	78	25 08	44	78	25 52	44	77	26 36	43	76	277
84	23 02	45	78	23 47	45	78	24 32	44	77	25 16	44	76	26 00	44	75	276
85	22 26	+45	78	23 11	+45	77	23 56	+44	76	24 40	+44	75	25 24	+44	75	275
86	21 50	45	77	22 35	45	76	23 20	44	76	24 04	45	75	24 49	44	74	274
87	21 14	45	76	21 59	45	76	22 44	45	75	23 29	44	74	24 13	44	73	273
88	20 38	46	75	21 24	45	75	22 09	44	74	22 53	45	73	23 38	44	73	272
89	20 03	45	75	20 48	45	74	21 33	45	73	22 18	45	73	23 03	44	72	271
90	19 27	+46	74	20 13	+45	73	20 58	+45	73	21 43	+45	72	22 28	+44	71	270
91	18 52	45	73	19 37	46	73	20 23	45	72	21 08	45	71	21 53	45	71	269
92	18 16	46	73	19 02	46	72	19 48	45	71	20 33	45	71	21 18	45	70	268
93	17 41	46	72	18 27	46	71	19 13	45	70	19 58	45	70	20 43	46	69	267
94	17 06	46	71	17 52	46	70	18 38	46	70	19 24	45	69	20 09	45	68	266
95	16 31	+46	70	17 17	+46	70	18 03	+46	69	18 49	+46	68	19 35	+45	68	265
96	15 57	46	70	16 43	46	69	17 29	46	68	18 15	46	68	19 01	45	67	264
97	15 22	47	69	16 09	46	68	16 55	46	68	17 41	46	67	18 27	46	66	263
98	14 48	46	68	15 34	47	68	16 21	46	67	17 07	46	66	17 53	46	66	262
99	14 14	46	67	15 00	47	67	15 47	46	66	16 33	47	66	17 20	46	65	261
100	13 40	+46	67	14 26	+47	66	15 13	+47	65	16 00	+46	65	16 46	+47	64	260
101	13 06	47	66	13 53	47	65	14 40	46	65	15 26	47	64	16 13	47	63	259
102	12 32	47	65	13 19	47	65	14 06	47	64	14 53	47	63	15 40	47	63	258
103	11 59	47	65	12 46	47	64	13 33	47	63	14 20	47	63	15 07	47	62	257
104	11 25	48	64	12 13	47	63	13 00	48	63	13 48	47	62	14 35	47	61	256
105	10 52	+48	63	11 40	+48	62	12 28	+47	62	13 15	+48	61	14 03	+47	61	255
106	10 20	47	62	11 07	48	62	11 55	48	61	12 43	48	61	13 31	47	60	254
107	09 47	48	62	10 35	48	61	11 23	48	60	12 11	48	60	12 59	48	59	253
108	09 15	48	61	10 03	48	60	10 51	48	60	11 39	48	59	12 27	48	58	252
109	08 42	49	60	09 31	48	60	10 19	49	59	11 08	48	58	11 56	48	58	251
110	08 11	+48	59	08 59	+49	59	09 48	+48	58	10 36	+49	58	11 25	+48	57	250
111	07 39	49	59	08 28	49	58	09 17	48	57	10 05	49	57	10 54	49	56	249
112	07 07	50	58	07 57	49	57	08 46	48	57	09 34	49	56	10 23	49	56	248
113	06 36	50	57	07 26	49	57	08 15	49	56	09 04	49	55	09 53	49	55	247
114	06 05	50	56	06 55	49	56	07 44	50	55	08 34	49	55	09 23	49	54	246
115	05 35	+49	56	06 24	+50	55	07 14	+50	55	08 04	+49	54	08 53	+50	53	245
116	05 04	50	55	05 54	50	54	06 44	50	54	07 34	50	53	08 24	49	53	244
117	04 34	50	54	05 24	51	54	06 15	50	53	07 05	50	52	07 55	49	52	243
118	04 05	50	53	04 55	50	53	05 45	50	52	06 35	51	52	07 26	50	51	242
119	03 35	51	53	04 26	50	52	05 16	51	52	06 07	50	51	06 57	50	50	241
120	03 06	+51	52	03 57	+50	51	04 47	+51	51	05 38	+51	50	06 29	+50	50	240
121	02 37	51	51	03 28	51	51	04 19	51	50	05 10	51	50	06 01	50	49	239
122	02 08	52	50	03 00	51	50	03 51	51	49	04 42	51	49	05 33	51	48	238
123	01 40	52	49	02 32	51	49	03 23	51	48	04 14	52	48	05 06	51	47	237
124	01 12	52	49	02 04	51	48	02 55	52	48	03 47	52	47	04 39	51	47	236
125	00 45	+51	48	01 36	+52	47	02 28	+52	47	03 20	+52	46	04 12	+52	46	235
126	00 17	52	47	01 09	52	47	02 01	52	46	02 53	52	46	03 45	52	45	234
127	−0 10	53	46	00 43	52	46	01 35	52	45	02 27	52	45	03 19	52	44	233
128	−0 36	52	46	00 16	53	45	01 09	52	45	02 01	53	44	02 54	52	44	232
129	−1 02	52	45	−0 10	53	44	00 43	53	44	01 36	52	43	02 28	53	43	231
130	−1 28	+53	44	−0 35	+53	44	00 18	+53	43	01 11	+52	43	02 03	+53	42	230
131	−1 54	54	43	−1 00	53	43	−0 07	53	42	00 46	53	42	01 39	53	41	229
132	−2 19	54	42	−1 25	53	42	−0 32	53	41	00 21	54	41	01 15	53	41	228
133	−2 43	53	42	−1 50	54	41	−0 56	53	41	−0 03	54	40	00 51	53	40	227
134	−3 00	54	41	−2 14	54	40	−1 20	54	40	−0 26	53	39	00 27	54	39	226
135	−3 32	+54	40	−2 38	+54	40	−1 44	+54	39	−0 50	+54	39	00 04	+54	38	225
136	−3 55	54	39	−3 01	54	39	−2 07	55	38	−1 12	54	38	−0 18	54	37	224
137	−4 18	54	38	−3 24	55	38	−2 29	54	37	−1 35	55	37	−0 40	54	37	223
138	−4 41	55	37	−3 46	54	37	−2 52	55	37	−1 57	55	36	−1 02	54	36	222
139	−5 03	55	37	−4 08	55	36	−3 13	54	36	−2 19	55	35	−1 24	55	35	221

S. Lat. {LHA greater than 180°....... Zn=180−Z; LHA less than 180°........... Zn=180+Z}

DECLINATION (15°-29°) SAME NAME AS LATITUDE

N. Lat. {LHA greater than 180°....... Zn=Z; LHA less than 180°.......... Zn=360−Z}

DECLINATION (15°-29°) SAME NAME AS LATITUDE

LHA	15°			16°			17°			18°			19°			20°			21°			22°			23°			24°			25°			26°			27°			28°			29°			LHA
	Hc	d	Z	Hc	d	Z	Hc	d	Z	Hc	d	Z	Hc	d	Z	Hc	d	Z	Hc	d	Z	Hc	d	Z	Hc	d	Z	Hc	d	Z	Hc	d	Z	Hc	d	Z	Hc	d	Z	Hc	d	Z	Hc	d	Z	
	° ′	′	°	° ′	′	°	° ′	′	°	° ′	′	°	° ′	′	°	° ′	′	°	° ′	′	°	° ′	′	°	° ′	′	°	° ′	′	°	° ′	′	°	° ′	′	°	° ′	′	°	° ′	′	°	° ′	′	°	
140																															−5 25	+55	36	−4 30	+55	35	−3 35	+55	35	−2 40	+55	35	−1 45	+55	34	220
141																																		−4 51	55	35	−3 56	55	34	−3 01	56	34	−2 05	55	33	219
142																																		−5 12	56	34	−4 16	55	33	−3 21	56	33	−2 25	55	33	218
143																																		−5 32	55	33	−4 37	56	33	−3 41	56	32	−2 45	56	32	217
144																																					−4 56	56	32	−4 00	56	31	−3 04	56	31	216
145																																					−5 15	+56	31	−4 19	+56	31	−3 23	+56	30	215
146																																					−5 34	56	30	−4 38	57	30	−3 41	56	29	214
147																																								−4 56	57	29	−3 59	56	29	213
148																																								−5 13	56	28	−4 17	57	28	212
149																																								−5 31	57	27	−4 34	57	27	211
150																																											−4 50	+57	26	210
151																																											−5 06	57	25	209
152																																											−5 22	58	24	208

LHA	15°			16°			17°			18°			19°			20°			21°			22°			23°			24°			25°			26°			27°			28°			29°			LHA
80	−5 47	−47	107																																											280
79	−5 12	47	108	−5 59	48	108																																								281
78	−4 36	48	109	−5 24	48	109																																								282
77	−4 01	48	109	−4 49	48	110	−5 37	48	111																																					283
76	−3 27	48	110	−4 15	48	111	−5 03	48	111	−5 51	48	112																																		284
75	−2 52	−48	111	−3 40	−48	111	−4 28	−49	112	−5 17	−48	113	−6 05	−48	113																															285
74	−2 18	48	112	−3 06	48	112	−3 54	49	113	−4 43	48	113	−5 31	48	114																															286
73	−1 43	49	112	−2 32	48	113	−3 20	49	114	−4 09	48	114	−4 57	49	115	−5 46	48	115																												287
72	−1 09	49	113	−1 58	49	114	−2 47	48	114	−3 35	49	115	−4 24	48	116	−5 12	49	116	−6 01	48	117																									288
71	−0 36	48	114	−1 24	49	115	−2 13	49	115	−3 02	49	116	−3 51	48	116	−4 39	49	117	−5 28	49	117																									289
70	−0 02	−49	115	−0 51	−49	115	−1 40	−49	116	−2 29	−49	117	−3 18	−49	117	−4 07	−48	118	−4 55	−49	118	−5 44	−49	119																					290

S. Lat. {LHA greater than 180°....... Zn=180−Z; LHA less than 180°.......... Zn=180+Z}

DECLINATION (15°-29°) CONTRARY NAME TO LATITUDE

N. Lat. {LHA greater than 180°....... Zn=Z
{LHA less than 180°........... Zn=360−Z

DECLINATION (15°-29°) CONTRARY NAME TO LATITUDE

LHA	15°			16°			17°			18°			19°		
	Hc	d	Z	Hc	d	Z	Hc	d	Z	Hc	d	Z	Hc	d	Z
	° ′	′	°	° ′	′	°	° ′	′	°	° ′	′	°	° ′	′	°
69	00 32	50	116	-0 18	49	116	-1 07	49	117	-1 56	49	117	-2 45	49	118
68	01 05	50	116	00 15	49	117	-0 34	49	118	-1 23	49	118	-2 12	50	119
67	01 38	50	117	00 48	49	118	-0 01	50	118	-0 51	49	119	-1 40	49	119
66	02 10	49	118	01 21	50	119	00 31	49	119	-0 18	50	120	-1 08	50	120
65	02 43	-50	119	01 53	-50	119	01 03	49	120	00 14	-50	120	-0 36	-50	121
64	03 15	50	120	02 25	50	120	01 35	50	121	00 45	50	121	-0 05	50	122
63	03 47	50	120	02 57	50	121	02 07	50	121	01 17	50	122	00 27	51	123
62	04 19	50	121	03 29	51	122	02 38	50	122	01 48	50	123	00 58	51	123
61	04 50	50	122	04 00	51	123	03 09	50	123	02 19	51	124	01 28	50	124
60	05 22	-51	123	04 31	-51	123	03 40	-51	124	02 49	-50	124	01 59	-51	125
59	05 52	50	124	05 02	51	124	04 11	51	125	03 20	51	125	02 29	51	126
58	06 23	51	125	05 32	51	125	04 41	51	126	03 50	51	126	02 59	52	127
57	06 53	51	125	06 02	51	126	05 11	52	126	04 19	51	127	03 28	51	127
56	07 23	51	126	06 32	52	127	05 40	51	127	04 49	52	128	03 57	51	128
55	07 53	-52	127	07 01	-51	128	06 10	-52	128	05 18	-52	129	04 26	-52	129
54	08 22	52	128	07 30	51	128	06 39	52	129	05 47	52	129	04 55	52	130
53	08 51	52	129	07 59	52	129	07 07	52	130	06 15	52	130	05 23	52	131
52	09 20	52	130	08 28	53	130	07 35	52	131	06 43	52	131	05 51	53	132
51	09 48	52	130	08 56	53	131	08 03	52	131	07 11	53	132	06 18	52	132
50	10 16	-52	131	09 24	-53	132	08 31	-53	132	07 38	-53	133	06 45	-52	133
49	10 44	53	132	09 51	53	133	08 58	53	133	08 05	53	134	07 12	53	134
48	11 11	53	133	10 18	53	133	09 25	53	134	08 32	53	134	07 39	54	135
47	11 38	53	134	10 45	54	134	09 51	53	135	08 58	54	135	08 04	53	136
46	12 04	53	135	11 11	54	135	10 17	53	136	09 24	54	136	08 30	54	137
45	12 30	-53	136	11 37	-54	136	10 43	-54	137	09 49	-54	137	08 55	-54	137
44	12 56	54	137	12 02	54	137	11 08	54	137	10 14	54	138	09 20	54	138
43	13 21	54	137	12 27	54	138	11 33	54	138	10 39	55	139	09 44	54	139
42	13 46	54	138	12 52	55	139	11 57	54	139	11 03	55	140	10 08	54	140
41	14 10	54	139	13 16	55	140	12 21	54	140	11 27	55	141	10 32	55	141
40	14 34	-54	140	13 40	-55	141	12 45	-55	141	11 50	-55	141	10 55	-55	142
39	14 58	55	141	14 03	55	141	13 08	55	142	12 13	55	142	11 18	55	143
38	15 21	55	142	14 26	56	142	13 30	55	143	12 35	55	143	11 40	55	144
37	15 43	55	143	14 48	55	143	13 53	56	144	12 57	55	144	12 02	56	144
36	16 05	55	144	15 10	56	144	14 14	55	145	13 19	56	145	12 23	56	145
35	16 27	-56	145	15 31	-56	145	14 35	-55	146	13 40	-56	146	12 44	-56	146
34	16 48	56	146	15 52	56	146	14 56	56	146	14 00	56	147	13 04	56	147
33	17 09	56	147	16 13	57	147	15 16	56	147	14 20	56	148	13 24	57	148
32	17 29	57	148	16 32	56	148	15 36	56	148	14 40	57	149	13 43	57	149
31	17 48	56	149	16 52	57	149	15 55	56	149	14 59	57	150	14 02	57	150
30	18 07	-56	150	17 11	-57	150	16 14	-57	150	15 17	-57	151	14 20	-57	151
29	18 26	57	150	17 29	57	151	16 32	57	151	15 35	57	151	14 38	57	152
28	18 44	57	151	17 47	57	152	16 50	58	152	15 52	57	152	14 55	57	153
27	19 01	57	152	18 04	57	153	17 07	58	153	16 09	57	153	15 12	58	154
26	19 18	57	153	18 21	58	154	17 23	57	154	16 26	58	154	15 28	58	155
25	19 34	-57	154	18 37	-58	155	17 39	-58	155	16 41	-57	155	15 44	-58	156
24	19 50	58	155	18 52	58	156	17 54	57	156	16 57	58	156	15 59	58	156
23	20 05	58	156	19 07	58	157	18 09	58	157	17 11	58	157	16 13	58	157
22	20 20	58	157	19 22	59	158	18 23	58	158	17 25	58	158	16 27	58	158
21	20 34	59	158	19 35	58	159	18 37	58	159	17 39	59	159	16 40	58	159
20	20 47	-58	159	19 49	-59	160	18 50	-58	160	17 52	-59	160	16 53	-58	160
19	21 00	59	160	20 01	58	161	19 03	59	161	18 04	59	161	17 05	58	161
18	21 12	59	161	20 13	58	162	19 15	59	162	18 16	59	162	17 17	59	162
17	21 24	59	162	20 25	59	163	19 26	59	163	18 27	59	163	17 28	59	163
16	21 34	59	163	20 35	59	164	19 36	59	164	18 37	59	164	17 38	59	164
15	21 45	-59	164	20 46	-60	165	19 46	-59	165	18 47	-59	165	17 48	-59	165
14	21 54	59	165	20 55	59	166	19 56	59	166	18 57	60	166	17 57	59	166
13	22 03	59	166	21 04	59	167	20 05	60	167	19 05	59	167	18 06	59	167
12	22 12	60	168	21 12	59	168	20 13	60	168	19 13	59	168	18 14	60	168
11	22 19	59	169	21 20	60	169	20 20	59	169	19 21	60	169	18 21	59	169
10	22 26	-59	170	21 27	-60	170	20 27	-59	170	19 28	-60	170	18 28	-60	170
9	22 33	60	171	21 33	60	171	20 33	59	171	19 34	60	171	18 34	60	171
8	22 38	59	172	21 39	60	172	20 39	60	172	19 39	60	172	18 39	59	172
7	22 44	60	173	21 44	60	173	20 44	60	173	19 44	60	173	18 44	60	173
6	22 48	60	174	21 48	60	174	20 48	60	174	19 48	60	174	18 48	59	174
5	22 52	-60	175	21 52	-60	175	20 52	-60	175	19 52	-60	175	18 52	-60	175
4	22 55	60	176	21 55	60	176	20 55	60	176	19 55	60	176	18 55	60	176
3	22 57	60	177	21 57	60	177	20 57	60	177	19 57	60	177	18 57	60	177
2	22 59	60	178	21 59	60	178	20 59	60	178	19 59	60	178	18 59	60	178
1	23 00	60	179	22 00	60	179	21 00	60	179	20 00	60	179	19 00	60	179
0	23 00	-60	180	22 00	-60	180	21 00	-60	180	20 00	-60	180	19 00	-60	180

LHA	20°			21°			22°			23°			24°		
	Hc	d	Z	Hc	d	Z	Hc	d	Z	Hc	d	Z	Hc	d	Z
	° ′	′	°	° ′	′	°	° ′	′	°	° ′	′	°	° ′	′	°
69	-3 34	49	118	-4 23	49	119	-5 12	49	120	-6 01	49	120			
68	-3 02	49	119	-3 51	49	120	-4 40	49	120	-5 29	49	121			
67	-2 29	50	120	-3 19	49	121	-4 08	50	121	-4 58	49	122	-5 47	49	122
66	-1 58	49	121	-2 47	50	121	-3 37	49	122	-4 26	50	122	-5 16	49	123
65	-1 26	-50	122	-2 16	-50	122	-3 06	-49	123	-3 55	-50	123	-4 45	-50	124
64	-0 55	50	122	-1 45	50	123	-2 35	50	123	-3 25	49	124	-4 14	50	125
63	-0 24	50	123	-1 14	50	124	-2 04	50	124	-2 54	50	125	-3 44	50	125
62	00 07	50	124	-0 43	51	124	-1 34	50	125	-2 24	50	126	-3 14	51	126
61	00 38	51	125	-0 13	50	125	-1 03	51	126	-1 54	51	126	-2 45	50	127
60	01 08	-51	126	00 17	-51	126	-0 34	-50	127	-1 24	-51	127	-2 15	-51	128
59	01 38	51	126	00 47	51	127	-0 04	51	127	-0 55	51	128	-1 46	51	128
58	02 07	51	127	01 16	51	128	00 25	51	128	-0 26	51	129	-1 17	51	129
57	02 37	52	128	01 45	51	128	00 54	51	129	00 03	52	129	-0 49	51	130
56	03 06	52	129	02 14	51	129	01 23	52	130	00 31	52	130	-0 21	51	131
55	03 34	-51	130	02 43	-52	130	01 51	-52	131	00 59	-52	131	00 07	-52	132
54	04 03	52	130	03 11	52	131	02 19	52	131	01 27	52	132	00 35	52	132
53	04 31	53	131	03 38	52	132	02 46	52	132	01 54	52	133	01 02	52	133
52	04 58	52	132	04 06	53	132	03 13	52	133	02 21	52	133	01 29	53	134
51	05 26	53	133	04 33	53	133	03 40	52	134	02 48	53	134	01 55	53	135
50	05 53	-53	134	05 00	-53	134	04 07	-53	135	03 14	-53	135	02 21	-53	136
49	06 19	53	135	05 26	53	135	04 33	53	135	03 40	53	136	02 47	53	136
48	06 45	53	135	05 52	53	136	04 59	54	136	04 05	53	137	03 12	53	137
47	07 11	53	136	06 18	54	137	05 24	54	137	04 30	53	138	03 37	54	138
46	07 36	53	137	06 43	54	138	05 49	54	138	04 55	54	138	04 01	53	139
45	08 01	-53	138	07 08	-54	138	06 14	-54	139	05 20	-54	139	04 26	-54	140
44	08 26	54	139	07 32	54	139	06 38	54	140	05 44	55	140	04 49	54	140
43	08 50	54	140	07 56	55	140	07 01	54	140	06 07	54	141	05 13	55	141
42	09 14	55	140	08 19	54	141	07 25	55	141	06 30	54	142	05 36	55	142
41	09 37	55	141	08 42	54	142	07 48	55	142	06 53	55	143	05 58	55	143
40	10 00	-55	142	09 05	-55	143	08 10	-55	143	07 15	-55	143	06 20	-55	144
39	10 23	56	143	09 27	55	143	08 32	55	144	07 37	55	144	06 42	56	145
38	10 45	56	144	09 49	55	144	08 54	56	145	07 58	55	145	07 03	56	146
37	11 06	56	145	10 10	55	145	09 15	56	146	08 19	55	146	07 24	56	146
36	11 27	56	146	10 31	55	146	09 36	56	146	08 40	56	147	07 44	56	147
35	11 48	-56	147	10 52	-56	147	09 56	-56	147	09 00	-56	148	08 04	-56	148
34	12 08	56	148	11 12	57	148	10 15	56	148	09 19	56	149	08 23	56	149
33	12 27	56	148	11 31	56	149	10 35	57	149	09 38	56	149	08 42	57	150
32	12 46	56	149	11 50	57	150	10 53	56	150	09 57	57	150	09 00	57	151
31	13 05	57	150	12 08	56	151	11 12	57	151	10 15	57	151	09 18	57	152
30	13 23	-57	151	12 26	-57	151	11 29	-57	152	10 32	-57	152	09 35	-57	152
29	13 41	57	152	12 44	57	152	11 47	58	153	10 49	57	153	09 52	57	153
28	13 58	57	153	13 01	58	153	12 03	57	154	11 06	57	154	10 09	58	154
27	14 14	57	154	13 17	58	154	12 19	57	155	11 22	58	155	10 24	57	155
26	14 30	57	155	13 33	58	155	12 35	58	155	11 37	57	156	10 40	58	156
25	14 46	-58	156	13 48	-58	156	12 50	-58	156	11 52	-57	157	10 55	-58	157
24	15 01	58	157	14 03	58	157	13 05	58	157	12 07	58	158	11 09	58	158
23	15 15	58	158	14 17	58	158	13 19	58	158	12 21	59	158	11 22	58	159
22	15 29	58	159	14 31	59	159	13 32	58	159	12 34	58	159	11 36	59	160
21	15 42	58	160	14 44	59	160	13 45	58	160	12 47	59	160	11 48	58	161
20	15 55	-59	161	14 56	-58	161	13 58	-59	161	12 59	-59	161	12 00	-58	161
19	16 07	59	161	15 08	59	162	14 09	58	162	13 11	59	162	12 12	59	162
18	16 18	59	162	15 19	58	163	14 21	59	163	13 22	59	163	12 23	59	163
17	16 29	59	163	15 30	59	164	14 31	59	164	13 32	59	164	12 33	59	164
16	16 39	59	164	15 40	59	165	14 41	59	165	13 42	59	165	12 43	59	165
15	16 49	-59	165	15 50	-59	166	14 51	-59	166	13 52	-60	166	12 52	-59	166
14	16 58	59	166	15 59	59	166	15 00	60	167	14 00	59	167	13 01	59	167
13	17 07	60	167	16 07	59	167	15 08	60	168	14 08	59	168	13 09	59	168
12	17 14	59	168	16 15	59	168	15 16	60	169	14 16	59	169	13 17	60	169
11	17 22	60	169	16 22	59	169	15 23	60	169	14 23	60	170	13 23	59	170
10	17 28	-59	170	16 29	-60	170	15 29	-60	170	14 29	-59	171	13 30	-60	171
9	17 34	59	171	16 35	60	171	15 35	60	171	14 35	59	171	13 36	60	172
8	17 40	60	172	16 40	60	172	15 40	60	172	14 40	59	172	13 41	60	173
7	17 44	59	173	16 45	60	173	15 45	60	173	14 45	60	173	13 45	60	173
6	17 49	60	174	16 49	60	174	15 49	60	174	14 49	60	174	13 49	60	174
5	17 52	-60	175	16 52	-60	175	15 52	-60	175	14 52	-60	175	13 52	-59	175
4	17 55	60	176	16 55	60	176	15 55	60	176	14 55	60	176	13 55	60	176
3	17 57	60	177	16 57	60	177	15 57	60	177	14 57	60	177	13 57	60	177
2	17 59	60	178	16 59	60	178	15 59	60	178	14 59	60	178	13 59	60	178
1	18 00	60	179	17 00	60	179	16 00	60	179	15 00	60	179	14 00	60	179
0	18 00	-60	180	17 00	-60	180	16 00	-60	180	15 00	-60	180	14 00	-60	180

LHA	25°			26°			27°			28°			29°			LHA
	Hc	d	Z	Hc	d	Z	Hc	d	Z	Hc	d	Z	Hc	d	Z	
	° ′	′	°	° ′	′	°	° ′	′	°	° ′	′	°	° ′	′	°	
69																291
68																292
67																293
66																294
65	-5 35	-49	124													295
64	-5 04	50	125	-5 54	50	126										296
63	-4 34	50	126	-5 24	51	126										297
62	-4 05	50	127	-4 55	50	127	-5 45	50	128							298
61	-3 35	51	127	-4 26	50	128	-5 16	51	128							299
60	-3 06	-51	128	-3 57	-50	129	-4 47	-51	129	-5 38	-51	130				300
59	-2 37	51	129	-3 28	51	129	-4 19	51	130	-5 10	51	130				301
58	-2 08	52	130	-3 00	51	130	-3 51	51	131	-4 42	51	131	-5 33	51	132	302
57	-1 40	52	131	-2 32	51	131	-3 23	51	132	-4 14	52	132	-5 06	51	133	303
56	-1 12	52	131	-2 04	51	132	-2 55	52	132	-3 47	52	133	-4 39	51	133	304
55	-0 45	-51	132	-1 36	-52	133	-2 28	-52	133	-3 20	-52	134	-4 12	-52	134	305
54	-0 17	52	133	-1 09	52	133	-2 01	52	134	-2 53	52	134	-3 45	52	135	306
53	00 10	53	134	-0 43	52	134	-1 35	52	135	-2 27	52	135	-3 19	52	136	307
52	00 36	52	134	-0 16	53	135	-1 09	52	135	-2 01	53	136	-2 54	52	136	308
51	01 02	52	135	00 10	53	136	-0 43	53	136	-1 36	52	137	-2 28	53	137	309
50	01 28	-53	136	00 35	-53	136	-0 18	-53	137	-1 11	-52	137	-2 03	-53	138	310
49	01 54	54	137	01 00	53	137	00 07	53	138	-0 46	53	138	-1 39	53	139	311
48	02 19	54	138	01 25	53	138	00 32	53	139	-0 21	54	139	-1 15	53	139	312
47	02 43	53	138	01 50	54	139	00 56	53	139	00 03	54	140	-0 51	53	140	313
46	03 08	54	139	02 14	54	140	01 20	54	140	00 26	53	141	-0 27	54	141	314
45	03 32	-54	140	02 38	-54	140	01 44	-54	141	00 50	-54	141	-0 04	-54	142	315
44	03 55	54	141	03 01	54	141	02 07	55	142	01 12	54	142	00 18	54	143	316
43	04 18	54	142	03 24	55	142	02 29	54	143	01 35	55	143	00 40	54	143	317
42	04 41	55	143	03 46	54	143	02 52	55	143	01 57	55	144	01 02	54	144	318
41	05 03	55	143	04 08	55	144	03 13	54	144	02 19	55	145	01 24	55	145	319
40	05 25	-55	144	04 30	-55	145	03 35	-55	145	02 40	-55	145	01 45	-55	146	320
39	05 46	55	145	04 51	55	145	03 56	55	146	03 01	56	146	02 05	55	147	321
38	06 07	55	146	05 12	56	146	04 16	55	147	03 21	56	147	02 25	55	147	322
37	06 28	56	147	05 32	55	147	04 37	56	147	03 41	56	148	02 45	56	148	323
36	06 48	56	148	05 52	56	148	04 56	56	148	04 00	56	149	03 04	56	149	324
35	07 08	-57	148	06 11	-56	149	05 15	-56	149	04 19	-56	149	03 23	-56	150	325
34	07 27	57	149	06 30	56	150	05 34	56	150	04 38	57	150	03 41	56	151	326
33	07 45	56	150	06 49	57	151	05 52	56	151	04 56	57	151	03 59	56	151	327
32	08 03	56	151	07 07	57	151	06 10	57	152	05 13	56	152	04 17	57	152	328
31	08 21	57	152	07 24	57	152	06 27	56	153	05 31	57	153	04 34	57	153	329
30	08 38	-57	153	07 41	-57	153	06 44	-57	153	05 47	-57	154	04 50	-57	154	330
29	08 55	57	154	07 58	57	154	07 01	58	154	06 03	57	155	05 06	57	155	331
28	09 11	57	155	08 14	58	155	07 16	57	155	06 19	57	155	05 22	58	156	332
27	09 27	58	155	08 29	57	156	07 32	58	156	06 34	57	156	05 37	58	157	333
26	09 42	58	156	08 44	57	157	07 47	58	157	06 49	58	157	05 51	58	157	334
25	09 57	-58	157	08 59	-58	157	08 01	-58	158	07 03	-58	158	06 05	-58	158	335
24	10 11	58	158	09 13	58	158	08 15	58	159	07 17	58	159	06 19	59	159	336
23	10 24	58	159	09 26	58	159	08 28	58	159	07 30	58	160	06 32	59	160	337
22	10 37	58	160	09 39	58	160	08 41	59	160	07 42	58	161	06 44	58	161	338
21	10 50	59	161	09 51	58	161	08 53	59	161	07 54	58	161	06 56	59	162	339
20	11 02	-59	162	10 03	-58	162	09 05	-59	162	08 06	-59	162	07 07	-58	163	340
19	11 13	59	163	10 14	58	163	09 16	59	163	08 17	59	163	07 18	59	163	341
18	11 24	59	163	10 25	59	164	09 26	59	164	08 27	58	164	07 29	59	164	342
17	11 34	59	164	10 35	59	165	09 36	59	165	08 37	59	165	07 38	59	165	343
16	11 44	59	165	10 45	59	165	09 46	59	166	08 47	59	166	07 48	60	166	344
15	11 53	-59	166	10 54	-59	166	09 55	-60	167	08 55	-59	167	07 56	-59	167	345
14	12 02	60	167	11 02	59	167	10 03	59	167	09 04	60	168	08 04	59	168	346
13	12 10	60	168	11 10	59	168	10 11	60	168	09 11	59	168	08 12	59	169	347
12	12 17	59	169	11 18	60	169	10 18	59	169	09 19	60	169	08 19	59	169	348
11	12 24	60	170	11 24	59	170	10 25	60	170	09 25	59	170	08 26	60	170	349
10	12 30	-59	171	11 31	-60	171	10 31	-60	171	09 31	-59	171	08 32	-60	171	350
9	12 36	60	172	11 36	60	172	10 36	59	172	09 37	60	172	08 37	60	172	351
8	12 41	60	173	11 41	60	173	10 41	59	173	09 42	60	173	08 42	60	173	352
7	12 45	59	174	11 46	60	174	10 46	60	174	09 46	60	174	08 46	60	174	353
6	12 49	60	174	11 49	59	175	10 50	60	175	09 50	60	175	08 50	60	175	354
5	12 53	-60	175	11 53	-60	175	10 53	-60	176	09 53	-60	176	08 53	-60	176	355
4	12 55	60	176	11 55	60	176	10 55	60	176	09 55	60	176	08 55	59	177	356
3	12 57	60	177	11 57	60	177	10 57	60	177	09 57	60	177	08 57	59	177	357
2	12 59	60	178	11 59	60	178	10 59	60	178	09 59	60	178	08 59	60	178	358
1	13 00	60	179	12 00	60	179	11 00	60	179	10 00	60	179	09 00	60	179	359
0	13 00	-60	180	12 00	-60	180	11 00	-60	180	10 00	-60	180	09 00	-60	180	360

15° 16° 17° 18° 19° 20° 21° 22° 23° 24° 25° 26° 27° 28° 29°

S. Lat. {LHA greater than 180°....... Zn=180−Z
{LHA less than 180°........... Zn=180+Z

DECLINATION (15°-29°) CONTRARY NAME TO LATITUDE

LAT 52°

N. Lat. {LHA greater than 180°……. Zn=Z; LHA less than 180°………. Zn=360−Z}

DECLINATION (0°-14°) SAME NAME AS LATITUDE

LHA	0° Hc	d	Z	1° Hc	d	Z	2° Hc	d	Z	3° Hc	d	Z	4° Hc	d	Z
	° ′	′	°	° ′	′	°	° ′	′	°	° ′	′	°	° ′	′	°
0	37 00	+60	180	38 00	+60	180	39 00	+60	180	40 00	+60	180	41 00	+60	180
1	37 00	60	179	38 00	60	179	39 00	60	179	40 00	60	179	41 00	60	179
2	36 58	60	178	37 58	60	178	38 58	60	177	39 58	60	177	40 58	60	177
3	36 57	59	176	37 56	60	176	38 56	60	176	39 56	60	176	40 56	60	176
4	36 54	60	175	37 54	60	175	38 54	59	175	39 53	60	175	40 53	60	175
5	36 50	+60	174	37 50	+60	174	38 50	+60	174	39 50	+60	174	40 50	+60	173
6	36 46	60	173	37 46	59	172	38 45	60	172	39 45	60	172	40 45	60	172
7	36 41	60	171	37 41	59	171	38 40	60	171	39 40	60	171	40 40	59	171
8	36 35	60	170	37 35	59	170	38 34	60	170	39 34	60	170	40 34	59	170
9	36 28	60	169	37 28	59	169	38 27	60	169	39 27	60	168	40 27	59	168
10	36 21	+59	168	37 20	+60	167	38 20	+59	167	39 19	+60	167	40 19	+59	167
11	36 13	59	166	37 12	59	166	38 11	60	166	39 11	59	166	40 10	59	166
12	36 04	59	165	37 03	59	165	38 02	60	165	39 02	59	165	40 01	59	164
13	35 54	59	164	36 53	59	164	37 52	59	164	38 51	60	163	39 51	59	163
14	35 44	59	163	36 43	59	162	37 42	59	162	38 41	59	162	39 40	59	162
15	35 33	+58	162	36 31	+59	161	37 30	+59	161	38 29	+59	161	39 28	+59	161
16	35 21	58	160	36 19	59	160	37 18	59	160	38 17	58	160	39 15	59	159
17	35 08	59	159	36 07	58	159	37 05	59	159	38 04	58	158	39 02	59	158
18	34 55	58	158	35 53	59	158	36 52	58	157	37 50	58	157	38 48	59	157
19	34 41	58	157	35 39	58	156	36 37	59	156	37 36	58	156	38 34	58	156
20	34 26	+58	156	35 24	+58	155	36 22	+58	155	37 20	+58	155	38 18	+58	154
21	34 11	58	154	35 09	58	154	36 07	58	154	37 05	57	153	38 02	58	153
22	33 55	58	153	34 53	57	153	35 50	58	153	36 48	58	152	37 46	57	152
23	33 38	58	152	34 36	57	152	35 33	58	151	36 31	57	151	37 28	57	151
24	33 21	58	151	34 19	57	151	35 16	57	150	36 13	57	150	37 10	57	149
25	33 03	+57	150	34 00	+58	149	34 58	+57	149	35 55	+56	149	36 51	+57	148
26	32 45	57	149	33 42	57	148	34 39	56	148	35 35	57	147	36 32	57	147
27	32 26	56	148	33 22	57	147	34 19	57	147	35 16	56	146	36 12	57	146
28	32 06	56	146	33 02	57	146	33 59	56	146	34 55	57	145	35 52	56	145
29	31 46	56	145	32 42	56	145	33 38	56	144	34 34	56	144	35 30	56	144
30	31 25	+56	144	32 21	+56	144	33 17	+56	143	34 13	+56	143	35 09	+55	142
31	31 03	56	143	31 59	56	143	32 55	56	142	33 51	55	142	34 46	56	141
32	30 41	56	142	31 37	56	142	32 33	55	141	33 28	55	141	34 23	56	140
33	30 19	55	141	31 14	56	140	32 10	55	140	33 05	55	140	34 00	55	139
34	29 56	55	140	30 51	55	139	31 46	55	139	32 41	55	138	33 36	55	138
35	29 32	+55	139	30 27	+55	138	31 22	+55	138	32 17	+55	137	33 12	+54	137
36	29 08	55	138	30 03	55	137	30 58	54	137	31 52	55	136	32 47	54	136
37	28 44	54	137	29 38	55	136	30 33	54	136	31 27	54	135	32 21	55	135
38	28 19	54	136	29 13	54	135	30 07	54	135	31 01	54	134	31 55	54	134
39	27 53	54	135	28 47	54	134	29 41	54	134	30 35	54	133	31 29	54	133
40	27 27	+54	134	28 21	+54	133	29 15	+54	133	30 09	+53	132	31 02	+54	132
41	27 01	54	133	27 55	53	132	28 48	54	132	29 42	53	131	30 35	53	131
42	26 34	54	132	27 28	53	131	28 21	53	131	29 14	53	130	30 07	53	130
43	26 07	53	131	27 00	53	130	27 53	53	130	28 46	53	129	29 39	53	129
44	25 39	53	130	26 32	53	129	27 25	53	129	28 18	53	128	29 11	52	128
45	25 11	+53	129	26 04	+53	128	26 57	+53	128	27 50	+52	127	28 42	+52	127
46	24 43	52	128	25 35	53	127	26 28	52	127	27 20	53	126	28 13	52	126
47	24 14	52	127	25 06	53	126	25 59	52	126	26 51	52	125	27 43	52	125
48	23 45	52	126	24 37	52	125	25 29	52	125	26 21	52	124	27 13	52	124
49	23 15	52	125	24 07	52	124	24 59	52	124	25 51	52	123	26 43	52	123
50	22 46	+51	124	23 37	+52	123	24 29	+52	123	25 21	+51	122	26 12	+52	122
51	22 15	52	123	23 07	52	122	23 59	51	122	24 50	52	121	25 42	51	121
52	21 45	51	122	22 36	52	121	23 28	51	121	24 19	51	120	25 10	51	120
53	21 14	51	121	22 05	52	121	22 57	51	120	23 48	51	119	24 39	51	119
54	20 43	51	120	21 34	51	120	22 25	51	119	23 16	51	118	24 07	51	118
55	20 12	+51	119	21 03	+51	119	21 54	+50	118	22 44	+51	118	23 35	+50	117
56	19 40	51	118	20 31	51	118	21 22	50	117	22 12	51	117	23 03	50	116
57	19 08	51	117	19 59	50	117	20 49	51	116	21 40	50	116	22 30	50	115
58	18 36	50	117	19 26	51	116	20 17	50	115	21 07	50	115	21 57	50	114
59	18 03	51	116	18 54	50	115	19 44	50	115	20 34	50	114	21 24	50	113
60	17 31	+50	115	18 21	+50	114	19 11	+50	114	20 01	+50	113	20 51	+50	112
61	16 58	50	114	17 48	50	113	18 38	50	113	19 28	49	112	20 17	50	112
62	16 25	50	113	17 15	49	112	18 04	50	112	18 54	50	111	19 44	49	111
63	15 51	50	112	16 41	50	112	17 31	49	111	18 20	50	110	19 10	49	110
64	15 18	49	111	16 07	50	111	16 57	49	110	17 46	50	110	18 36	49	109
65	14 44	+50	110	15 34	+49	110	16 23	+49	109	17 12	+50	109	18 02	+49	108
66	14 10	50	110	15 00	49	109	15 49	49	108	16 38	49	108	17 27	49	107
67	13 36	49	109	14 25	49	108	15 14	50	108	16 04	49	107	16 53	48	106
68	13 02	49	108	13 51	49	107	14 40	49	107	15 29	49	106	16 18	49	106
69	12 27	49	107	13 16	49	107	14 05	49	106	14 54	49	105	15 43	49	105

LHA	5° Hc	d	Z	6° Hc	d	Z	7° Hc	d	Z	8° Hc	d	Z	9° Hc	d	Z
	° ′	′	°	° ′	′	°	° ′	′	°	° ′	′	°	° ′	′	°
0	42 00	+60	180	43 00	+60	180	44 00	+60	180	45 00	+60	180	46 00	+60	180
1	42 00	60	179	43 00	60	179	44 00	60	179	45 00	60	179	46 00	60	179
2	41 58	60	177	42 58	60	177	43 58	60	177	44 58	60	177	45 58	60	177
3	41 56	60	176	42 56	60	176	43 56	60	176	44 56	60	176	45 56	60	176
4	41 53	60	175	42 53	60	175	43 53	60	175	44 53	60	174	45 53	60	174
5	41 50	+59	173	42 49	+60	173	43 49	+60	173	44 49	+60	173	45 49	+60	173
6	41 45	60	172	42 45	59	172	43 44	60	172	44 44	60	172	45 44	60	172
7	41 39	60	171	42 39	60	171	43 39	60	170	44 39	59	170	45 38	60	170
8	41 33	60	169	42 33	59	169	43 32	60	169	44 32	60	169	45 32	59	169
9	41 26	60	168	42 26	59	168	43 25	60	168	44 25	59	168	45 24	59	167
10	41 18	+60	167	42 18	+59	167	43 17	+59	166	44 16	+60	166	45 16	+59	166
11	41 09	60	165	42 09	59	165	43 08	59	165	44 07	59	165	45 06	60	165
12	41 00	59	164	41 59	59	164	42 58	59	164	43 57	59	163	44 56	59	163
13	40 50	59	163	41 49	59	163	42 48	59	162	43 47	58	162	44 45	59	162
14	40 39	58	162	41 37	59	161	42 36	59	161	43 35	59	161	44 34	58	160
15	40 27	+58	160	41 25	+59	160	42 24	+59	160	43 23	+58	159	44 21	+59	159
16	40 14	59	159	41 13	58	159	42 11	59	158	43 10	58	158	44 08	58	158
17	40 01	58	158	40 59	58	157	41 57	59	157	42 56	58	157	43 54	58	156
18	39 47	58	156	40 45	58	156	41 43	58	156	42 41	58	155	43 39	58	155
19	39 32	58	155	40 30	58	155	41 28	58	155	42 26	57	154	43 23	58	154
20	39 16	+58	154	40 14	+58	154	41 12	+57	153	42 09	+58	153	43 07	+58	152
21	39 00	58	153	39 58	57	152	40 55	58	152	41 53	57	152	42 50	57	151
22	38 43	57	151	39 40	58	151	40 38	57	151	41 35	57	150	42 32	57	150
23	38 25	58	150	39 23	57	150	40 20	57	149	41 17	57	149	42 14	57	149
24	38 07	57	149	39 04	57	149	40 01	57	148	40 58	57	148	41 55	56	147
25	37 48	+57	148	38 45	+57	147	39 42	+56	147	40 38	+57	147	41 35	+56	146
26	37 29	56	147	38 25	57	146	39 22	56	146	40 18	56	145	41 14	56	145
27	37 09	56	145	38 05	56	145	39 01	56	145	39 57	56	144	40 53	56	144
28	36 48	56	144	37 44	56	144	38 40	56	143	39 36	56	143	40 31	56	142
29	36 26	56	143	37 22	56	143	38 18	56	142	39 14	55	142	40 09	56	141
30	36 04	+56	142	37 00	+56	142	37 56	+55	141	38 51	+55	141	39 46	+55	140
31	35 42	55	141	36 37	56	140	37 33	55	140	38 28	55	139	39 23	55	139
32	35 19	55	140	36 14	55	139	37 09	55	139	38 04	55	138	38 59	54	138
33	34 55	55	139	35 50	55	138	36 45	55	138	37 40	54	137	38 34	55	137
34	34 31	55	138	35 26	54	137	36 20	55	136	37 15	54	136	38 09	54	135
35	34 06	+55	136	35 01	+54	136	35 55	+54	135	36 49	+54	135	37 43	+54	134
36	33 41	54	135	34 35	55	135	35 30	53	134	36 23	54	134	37 17	54	133
37	33 16	54	134	34 10	53	134	35 03	54	133	35 57	54	133	36 51	53	132
38	32 49	54	133	33 43	54	133	34 37	53	132	35 30	54	132	36 24	53	131
39	32 23	53	132	33 16	54	132	34 10	53	131	35 03	53	130	35 56	53	130
40	31 56	+53	131	32 49	+53	131	33 42	+53	130	34 35	+53	129	35 28	+53	129
41	31 28	53	130	32 21	53	129	33 14	53	129	34 07	53	128	35 00	52	128
42	31 00	53	129	31 53	53	128	32 46	53	128	33 39	52	127	34 31	52	127
43	30 32	53	128	31 25	52	127	32 17	53	127	33 10	52	126	34 02	52	126
44	30 03	53	127	30 56	52	126	31 48	52	126	32 40	52	125	33 32	52	125
45	29 34	+53	126	30 27	+52	125	31 19	+52	125	32 11	+52	124	33 03	+51	124
46	29 05	52	125	29 57	52	124	30 49	52	124	31 41	51	123	32 32	52	123
47	28 35	52	124	29 27	52	123	30 19	51	123	31 10	52	122	32 02	51	122
48	28 05	52	123	28 57	51	122	29 48	52	122	30 40	51	121	31 31	51	121
49	27 35	51	122	28 26	51	121	29 17	52	121	30 09	50	120	30 59	51	120
50	27 04	+51	121	27 55	+51	120	28 46	+51	120	29 37	+51	119	30 28	+51	119
51	26 33	51	120	27 24	51	120	28 15	51	119	29 06	50	118	29 56	51	118
52	26 01	51	119	26 52	51	119	27 43	51	118	28 34	50	117	29 24	50	117
53	25 30	50	118	26 20	51	118	27 11	50	117	28 01	51	116	28 52	50	116
54	24 58	50	117	25 48	51	117	26 39	50	116	27 29	50	115	28 19	50	115
55	24 25	+51	116	25 16	+50	116	26 06	+50	115	26 56	+50	115	27 46	+50	114
56	23 53	50	115	24 43	50	115	25 33	50	114	26 23	50	114	27 13	49	113
57	23 20	50	114	24 10	50	114	25 00	50	113	25 50	50	113	26 40	49	112
58	22 47	50	114	23 37	50	113	24 27	50	112	25 17	49	112	26 06	49	111
59	22 14	50	113	23 04	49	112	23 53	50	112	24 43	49	111	25 32	49	110
60	21 41	+49	112	22 30	+50	111	23 20	+49	111	24 09	+49	110	24 58	+49	109
61	21 07	49	111	21 56	50	110	22 46	49	110	23 35	49	109	24 24	49	109
62	20 33	50	110	21 23	49	109	22 12	49	109	23 01	49	108	23 50	48	108
63	19 59	49	109	20 48	49	109	21 37	49	108	22 26	49	107	23 15	49	107
64	19 25	49	108	20 14	49	108	21 03	49	107	21 52	49	107	22 41	48	106
65	18 51	+49	107	19 40	+48	107	20 28	+49	106	21 17	+49	106	22 06	+48	105
66	18 16	49	107	19 05	49	106	19 54	48	105	20 42	49	105	21 31	48	104
67	17 41	49	106	18 30	49	105	19 19	48	105	20 07	49	104	20 56	48	103
68	17 07	48	105	17 55	49	104	18 44	48	104	19 32	48	103	20 20	49	102
69	16 32	48	104	17 20	49	103	18 09	48	103	18 57	48	102	19 45	48	102

LHA	10° Hc	d	Z	11° Hc	d	Z	12° Hc	d	Z	13° Hc	d	Z	14° Hc	d	Z	LHA
	° ′	′	°	° ′	′	°	° ′	′	°	° ′	′	°	° ′	′	°	
0	47 00	+60	180	48 00	+60	180	49 00	+60	180	50 00	+60	180	51 00	+60	180	360
1	47 00	60	179	48 00	60	179	49 00	60	179	50 00	60	179	51 00	60	179	359
2	46 58	60	177	47 58	60	177	48 58	60	177	49 58	60	177	50 58	60	177	358
3	46 56	60	176	47 56	60	176	48 56	60	176	49 56	60	176	50 56	60	175	357
4	46 53	60	174	47 53	60	174	48 53	59	174	49 52	60	174	50 52	60	174	356
5	46 49	+60	173	47 49	+59	173	48 48	+60	173	49 48	+60	172	50 48	+60	172	355
6	46 44	59	171	47 43	60	171	48 43	60	171	49 43	60	171	50 43	59	171	354
7	46 38	60	170	47 38	59	170	48 37	60	170	49 37	59	169	50 36	60	169	353
8	46 31	60	169	47 31	59	168	48 30	60	168	49 30	59	168	50 29	60	168	352
9	46 23	60	167	47 23	59	167	48 22	60	167	49 22	59	167	50 21	59	166	351
10	46 15	+59	166	47 14	+60	166	48 14	+59	165	49 13	+59	165	50 12	+59	165	350
11	46 06	59	164	47 05	59	164	48 04	59	164	49 03	59	164	50 02	59	163	349
12	45 55	59	163	46 54	59	163	47 53	59	162	48 52	59	162	49 51	59	162	348
13	45 44	59	162	46 43	59	161	47 42	59	161	48 41	58	161	49 39	59	160	347
14	45 32	59	160	46 31	59	160	47 30	58	160	48 28	59	159	49 27	58	159	346
15	45 20	+58	159	46 18	+59	158	47 17	+58	158	48 15	+58	158	49 13	+59	157	345
16	45 06	59	157	46 05	58	157	47 03	58	157	48 01	58	156	48 59	58	156	344
17	44 52	58	156	45 50	58	156	46 48	58	155	47 46	58	155	48 44	58	155	343
18	44 37	58	155	45 35	58	154	46 33	57	154	47 30	58	154	48 28	58	153	342
19	44 21	58	154	45 19	57	153	46 16	58	153	47 14	57	152	48 11	58	152	341
20	44 05	+57	152	45 02	+57	152	45 59	+58	151	46 57	+57	151	47 54	+57	150	340
21	43 47	58	151	44 45	57	150	45 42	57	150	46 39	57	149	47 36	56	149	339
22	43 29	57	149	44 26	57	149	45 23	57	149	46 20	57	148	47 17	56	148	338
23	43 11	56	148	44 07	57	148	45 04	56	147	46 00	57	147	46 57	56	146	337
24	42 51	57	147	43 48	56	146	44 44	56	146	45 40	56	145	46 36	56	145	336
25	42 31	+56	146	43 27	+57	145	44 24	+56	145	45 20	+55	144	46 15	+56	144	335
26	42 10	56	144	43 06	56	144	44 02	56	143	44 58	56	143	45 54	55	142	334
27	41 49	56	143	42 45	55	143	43 40	56	142	44 36	55	142	45 31	55	141	333
28	41 27	56	142	42 23	55	141	43 18	55	141	44 13	55	140	45 08	55	140	332
29	41 05	55	141	42 00	55	140	42 55	55	140	43 50	55	139	44 45	54	139	331
30	40 41	+55	140	41 36	+55	139	42 31	+55	138	43 26	+54	138	44 20	+55	137	330
31	40 18	54	138	41 12	55	138	42 07	54	137	43 01	55	137	43 56	54	136	329
32	39 53	55	137	40 48	54	137	41 42	54	136	42 36	54	136	43 30	54	135	328
33	39 29	54	136	40 23	54	135	41 17	54	135	42 11	53	134	43 04	54	134	327
34	39 03	54	135	39 57	54	134	40 51	54	134	41 45	53	133	42 38	53	133	326
35	38 37	+54	134	39 31	+54	133	40 25	+53	133	41 18	+53	132	42 11	+53	131	325
36	38 11	53	133	39 04	54	132	39 58	53	131	40 51	53	131	41 44	53	130	324
37	37 44	53	132	38 37	53	131	39 30	53	130	40 23	53	130	41 16	53	129	323
38	37 17	53	130	38 10	53	130	39 03	52	129	39 55	53	129	40 48	52	128	322
39	36 49	53	129	37 42	52	129	38 34	53	128	39 27	52	127	40 19	52	127	321
40	36 21	+52	128	37 13	+53	128	38 06	+52	127	38 58	+52	126	39 50	+52	126	320
41	35 52	53	127	36 45	52	127	37 37	52	126	38 29	51	125	39 20	52	125	319
42	35 23	52	126	36 15	52	126	37 07	52	125	37 59	51	124	38 50	52	124	318
43	34 54	52	125	35 46	52	124	36 38	51	124	37 29	51	123	38 20	51	123	317
44	34 24	52	124	35 16	51	123	36 07	52	123	36 59	51	122	37 50	50	121	316
45	33 54	+52	123	34 46	+51	122	35 37	+51	122	36 28	+51	121	37 19	+50	120	315
46	33 24	51	122	34 15	51	121	35 06	51	121	35 57	50	120	36 47	51	119	314
47	32 53	51	121	33 44	51	120	34 35	50	120	35 25	51	119	36 16	50	118	313
48	32 22	51	120	33 13	50	119	34 03	51	119	34 54	50	118	35 44	50	118	312
49	31 50	51	119	32 41	50	118	33 31	51	118	34 22	50	117	35 12	49	116	311
50	31 19	+50	118	32 09	+50	117	32 59	+50	117	33 49	+50	116	34 39	+50	115	310
51	30 47	50	117	31 37	50	116	32 27	50	116	33 17	49	115	34 06	50	114	309
52	30 14	50	116	31 04	50	115	31 54	50	115	32 44	49	114	33 33	49	113	308
53	29 42	50	115	30 32	49	115	31 21	50	114	32 11	49	113	33 00	49	113	307
54	29 09	50	114	29 59	49	114	30 48	49	113	31 37	50	112	32 27	48	112	306
55	28 36	+49	113	29 25	+50	113	30 15	+49	112	31 04	+49	111	31 53	+49	111	305
56	28 02	50	112	28 52	49	112	29 41	49	111	30 30	49	110	31 19	49	110	304
57	27 29	49	111	28 18	49	111	29 07	49	110	29 56	49	109	30 45	48	109	303
58	26 55	49	111	27 44	49	110	28 33	49	109	29 22	49	109	30 11	48	108	302
59	26 21	49	110	27 10	49	109	27 59	49	108	28 48	48	108	29 36	48	107	301
60	25 47	+49	109	26 36	+49	108	27 25	+48	107	28 13	+48	107	29 01	+49	106	300
61	25 13	49	108	26 02	48	107	26 50	49	107	27 39	48	106	28 27	48	105	299
62	24 38	49	107	25 27	49	106	26 16	48	106	27 04	48	105	27 52	48	104	298
63	24 04	48	106	24 52	49	105	25 41	48	105	26 29	48	104	27 17	47	103	297
64	23 29	48	105	24 17	49	105	25 06	48	104	25 54	48	103	26 42	47	103	296
65	22 54	+48	104	23 42	+49	104	24 31	+47	103	25 18	+48	102	26 06	+48	102	295
66	22 19	48	104	23 07	48	103	23 55	48	102	24 43	48	102	25 31	47	101	294
67	21 44	48	103	22 32	48	102	23 20	48	101	24 08	47	101	24 55	48	100	293
68	21 09	48	102	21 57	47	101	22 44	48	101	23 32	48	100	24 20	47	99	292
69	20 33	48	101	21 21	48	100	22 09	48	100	22 57	47	99	23 44	47	98	291

S. Lat. {LHA greater than 180°……. Zn=180−Z; LHA less than 180°………. Zn=180+Z}

DECLINATION (0°-14°) SAME NAME AS LATITUDE

LAT 53°

N. Lat. {LHA greater than 180°....... Zn=Z
{LHA less than 180°.......... Zn=360−Z

DECLINATION (0°-14°) SAME NAME AS LATITUDE

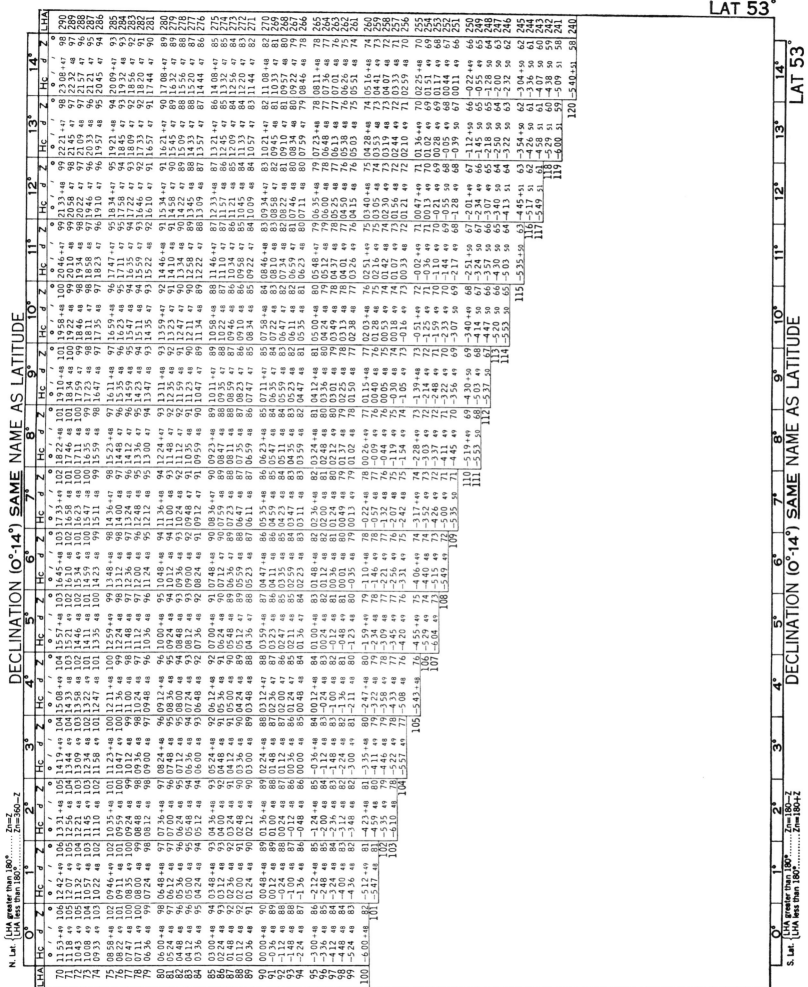

LHA	0° Hc	d	Z	1° Hc	d	Z	2° Hc	d	Z	3° Hc	d	Z	4° Hc	d	Z
	° ′	′	°	° ′	′	°	° ′	′	°	° ′	′	°	° ′	′	°
70	11 53	+49	106	12 42	+49	106	13 31	+48	105	14 19	+49	104	15 08	+49	104
71	11 18	49	105	12 07	49	105	12 56	48	104	13 44	49	104	14 33	48	103
72	10 43	49	105	11 32	49	104	12 21	48	103	13 09	49	103	13 58	48	102
73	10 08	49	104	10 57	48	103	11 45	49	103	12 34	48	102	13 22	49	101
74	09 33	49	103	10 22	48	102	11 10	48	102	11 58	49	101	12 47	48	101
75	08 58	+48	102	09 46	+49	102	10 35	+48	101	11 23	+48	100	12 11	+48	100
76	08 22	49	101	09 11	48	101	09 59	48	100	10 47	49	100	11 36	48	99
77	07 47	48	100	08 35	49	100	09 24	48	99	10 12	48	99	11 00	48	98
78	07 11	49	100	08 00	48	99	08 48	48	98	09 36	48	98	10 24	48	97
79	06 36	48	99	07 24	48	98	08 12	48	98	09 00	48	97	09 48	48	96
80	06 00	+48	98	06 48	+48	97	07 36	+48	97	08 24	+48	96	09 12	+48	96
81	05 24	48	97	06 12	48	97	07 00	48	96	07 48	48	95	08 36	48	95
82	04 48	48	96	05 36	48	96	06 24	48	95	07 12	48	95	08 00	48	94
83	04 12	48	96	05 00	48	95	05 48	48	94	06 36	48	94	07 24	48	93
84	03 36	48	95	04 24	48	94	05 12	48	94	06 00	48	93	06 48	48	92
85	03 00	+48	94	03 48	+48	93	04 36	+48	93	05 24	+48	92	06 12	+48	92
86	02 24	48	93	03 12	48	93	04 00	48	92	04 48	48	91	05 36	48	91
87	01 48	48	92	02 36	48	92	03 24	48	91	04 12	48	91	05 00	48	90
88	01 12	48	92	02 00	48	91	02 48	48	90	03 36	48	90	04 24	48	89
89	00 36	48	91	01 24	48	90	02 12	48	90	03 00	48	89	03 48	48	88
90	00 00	+48	90	00 48	+48	89	01 36	+48	89	02 24	+48	88	03 12	+47	88
91	-0 36	48	89	00 12	48	89	01 00	48	88	01 48	48	87	02 36	47	87
92	-1 12	48	88	-0 24	48	88	00 24	48	87	01 12	48	87	02 00	47	86
93	-1 48	48	88	-1 00	48	87	-0 12	48	86	00 36	48	86	01 24	47	85
94	-2 24	48	87	-1 36	48	86	-0 48	48	86	00 00	48	85	00 48	48	84
95	-3 00	+48	86	-2 12	+48	85	-1 24	+48	85	-0 36	+48	84	00 12	+48	84
96	-3 36	48	85	-2 48	48	85	-2 00	48	84	-1 12	48	83	-0 24	48	83
97	-4 12	48	84	-3 24	48	84	-2 36	48	83	-1 48	48	83	-1 00	48	82
98	-4 48	48	84	-4 00	48	83	-3 12	48	82	-2 24	48	82	-1 36	48	81
99	-5 24	48	83	-4 36	48	82	-3 48	48	82	-3 00	49	81	-2 11	48	80
100	-6 00	+48	82	-5 12	+49	81	-4 23	+48	81	-3 35	+48	80	-2 47	+48	80
101				-5 47	48	81	-4 59	48	80	-4 11	49	79	-3 22	48	79
102							-5 35	49	79	-4 46	48	79	-3 58	49	78
103							-6 10	48	78	-5 22	49	78	-4 33	48	77
104										-5 57	49	77	-5 08	48	76
105													-5 43	+48	76

LHA	5° Hc	d	Z	6° Hc	d	Z	7° Hc	d	Z	8° Hc	d	Z	9° Hc	d	Z
	° ′	′	°	° ′	′	°	° ′	′	°	° ′	′	°	° ′	′	°
70	15 57	+48	103	16 45	+48	103	17 33	+49	102	18 22	+48	101	19 10	+48	101
71	15 21	49	102	16 10	48	102	16 58	48	101	17 46	48	101	18 34	48	100
72	14 46	48	102	15 34	49	101	16 23	48	100	17 11	48	100	17 59	47	99
73	14 11	48	101	14 59	48	100	15 47	48	100	16 35	48	99	17 23	48	98
74	13 35	48	100	14 23	48	99	15 11	48	99	15 59	48	98	16 47	48	97
75	12 59	+49	99	13 48	+48	98	14 36	+47	98	15 23	+48	97	16 11	+48	97
76	12 24	48	98	13 12	48	98	14 00	48	97	14 48	47	96	15 35	48	96
77	11 48	48	97	12 36	48	97	13 24	48	96	14 12	47	96	14 59	48	95
78	11 12	48	97	12 00	48	96	12 48	48	95	13 36	47	95	14 23	48	94
79	10 36	48	96	11 24	48	95	12 12	48	95	13 00	47	94	13 47	48	93
80	10 00	+48	95	10 48	+48	94	11 36	+48	94	12 24	+47	93	13 11	+48	93
81	09 24	48	94	10 12	48	94	11 00	48	93	11 48	47	92	12 35	48	92
82	08 48	48	93	09 36	48	93	10 24	48	92	11 12	47	92	11 59	48	91
83	08 12	48	93	09 00	48	92	09 48	47	91	10 35	48	91	11 23	48	90
84	07 36	48	92	08 24	48	91	09 12	47	91	09 59	48	90	10 47	47	89
85	07 00	+48	91	07 48	+48	90	08 36	+47	90	09 23	+48	89	10 11	+47	89
86	06 24	48	90	07 12	47	90	07 59	48	89	08 47	48	88	09 35	47	88
87	05 48	48	89	06 36	47	89	07 23	48	88	08 11	48	88	08 59	47	87
88	05 12	47	89	05 59	48	88	06 47	48	87	07 35	48	87	08 23	47	86
89	04 36	47	88	05 23	48	87	06 11	48	87	06 59	48	86	07 47	47	85
90	03 59	+48	87	04 47	+48	86	05 35	+48	86	06 23	+48	85	07 11	+47	85
91	03 23	48	86	04 11	48	86	04 59	48	85	05 47	48	84	06 35	47	84
92	02 47	48	85	03 35	48	85	04 23	48	84	05 11	48	84	05 59	48	83
93	02 11	48	85	02 59	48	84	03 47	48	83	04 35	48	83	05 23	48	82
94	01 36	47	84	02 23	48	83	03 11	48	83	03 59	48	82	04 47	48	81
95	01 00	+48	83	01 48	+48	82	02 36	+48	82	03 24	+48	81	04 12	+48	81
96	00 24	48	82	01 12	48	82	02 00	48	81	02 48	48	80	03 36	48	80
97	-0 12	48	81	00 36	48	81	01 24	48	80	02 12	49	80	03 01	48	79
98	-0 48	49	81	00 01	48	80	00 49	48	79	01 37	48	79	02 25	48	78
99	-1 23	48	80	-0 35	48	79	00 13	49	79	01 02	48	78	01 50	48	77
100	-1 59	+49	79	-1 10	+48	78	-0 22	+48	78	00 26	+49	77	01 15	+48	77
101	-2 34	48	78	-1 46	49	78	-0 57	48	77	-0 09	49	76	00 40	48	76
102	-3 09	48	77	-2 21	49	77	-1 32	48	76	-0 44	49	76	00 05	48	75
103	-3 45	49	77	-2 56	49	76	-2 07	48	75	-1 19	49	75	-0 30	48	74
104	-4 20	49	76	-3 31	49	75	-2 42	48	75	-1 54	49	74	-1 05	49	73
105	-4 55	+49	75	-4 06	+49	74	-3 17	+49	74	-2 28	+49	73	-1 39	+48	73
106	-5 29	49	74	-4 40	48	74	-3 52	49	73	-3 03	49	72	-2 14	49	72
107	-6 04	49	73	-5 15	49	73	-4 26	49	72	-3 37	49	72	-2 48	49	71
108				-5 49	49	72	-5 00	49	71	-4 11	49	71	-3 22	49	70
109							-5 35	50	71	-4 45	49	70	-3 56	49	69
110										-5 19	+49	69	-4 30	+50	69
111										-5 53	50	68	-5 03	49	68
112													-5 37	50	67

LHA	10° Hc	d	Z	11° Hc	d	Z	12° Hc	d	Z	13° Hc	d	Z	14° Hc	d	Z	LHA
	° ′	′	°	° ′	′	°	° ′	′	°	° ′	′	°	° ′	′	°	
70	19 58	+48	100	20 46	+47	99	21 33	+48	99	22 21	+47	98	23 08	+47	98	290
71	19 22	48	99	20 10	48	99	20 58	47	98	21 45	47	97	22 32	48	97	289
72	18 46	48	98	19 34	48	98	20 22	47	97	21 09	48	97	21 57	47	96	288
73	18 11	47	98	18 58	48	97	19 46	47	96	20 33	48	96	21 21	47	95	287
74	17 35	48	97	18 23	47	96	19 10	47	96	19 57	48	95	20 45	47	94	286
75	16 59	+48	96	17 47	+47	95	18 34	+47	95	19 21	+48	94	20 09	+47	93	285
76	16 23	48	95	17 11	47	95	17 58	47	94	18 45	47	93	19 32	48	93	284
77	15 47	48	94	16 35	47	94	17 22	47	93	18 09	47	92	18 56	47	92	283
78	15 11	48	94	15 59	47	93	16 46	47	92	17 33	47	92	18 20	47	91	282
79	14 35	47	93	15 22	48	92	16 10	47	91	16 57	47	91	17 44	47	90	281
80	13 59	+47	92	14 46	+48	91	15 34	+47	91	16 21	+47	90	17 08	+47	89	280
81	13 23	47	91	14 10	48	91	14 58	47	90	15 45	47	89	16 32	47	89	279
82	12 47	47	90	13 34	48	90	14 22	47	89	15 09	47	88	15 56	47	88	278
83	12 11	47	90	12 58	47	89	13 45	48	88	14 33	47	88	15 20	47	87	277
84	11 34	48	89	12 22	47	88	13 09	48	87	13 57	47	87	14 44	47	86	276
85	10 58	+48	88	11 46	+47	87	12 33	+48	87	13 21	+47	86	14 08	+47	85	275
86	10 22	48	87	11 10	47	87	11 57	48	86	12 45	47	85	13 32	47	85	274
87	09 46	48	86	10 34	47	86	11 21	48	85	12 09	47	84	12 56	47	84	273
88	09 10	48	86	09 58	47	85	10 45	48	84	11 33	47	84	12 20	47	83	272
89	08 34	48	85	09 22	47	84	10 09	48	84	10 57	47	83	11 44	47	82	271
90	07 58	+48	84	08 46	+48	83	09 34	+47	83	10 21	+47	82	11 08	+48	82	270
91	07 22	48	83	08 10	48	83	08 58	47	82	09 45	48	81	10 33	47	81	269
92	06 47	47	82	07 34	48	82	08 22	48	81	09 10	47	81	09 57	48	80	268
93	06 11	48	82	06 59	47	81	07 46	48	80	08 34	48	80	09 22	47	79	267
94	05 35	48	81	06 23	48	80	07 11	48	80	07 59	47	79	08 46	48	78	266
95	05 00	+48	80	05 48	+47	79	06 35	+48	79	07 23	+48	78	08 11	+48	78	265
96	04 24	48	79	05 12	48	79	06 00	48	78	06 48	48	77	07 36	48	77	264
97	03 49	48	78	04 37	48	78	05 25	48	77	06 13	48	77	07 01	48	76	263
98	03 13	48	78	04 01	49	77	04 50	48	76	05 38	48	76	06 26	48	75	262
99	02 38	48	77	03 26	49	76	04 15	48	76	05 03	48	75	05 51	48	74	261
100	02 03	+48	76	02 51	+49	75	03 40	+48	75	04 28	+48	74	05 16	+48	74	260
101	01 28	48	75	02 16	49	75	03 05	48	74	03 53	48	73	04 41	49	73	259
102	00 53	49	74	01 42	48	74	02 30	49	73	03 19	48	73	04 07	48	72	258
103	00 18	49	74	01 07	49	73	01 56	48	72	02 44	49	72	03 33	48	71	257
104	-0 16	49	73	00 33	48	72	01 21	49	72	02 10	49	71	02 59	48	70	256
105	-0 51	+49	72	-0 02	+49	71	00 47	+49	71	01 36	+49	70	02 25	+48	70	255
106	-1 25	49	71	-0 36	49	71	00 13	49	70	01 02	49	69	01 51	49	69	254
107	-1 59	49	70	-1 10	49	70	-0 21	49	69	00 28	49	69	01 17	49	68	253
108	-2 33	49	70	-1 44	49	69	-0 55	50	68	-0 05	49	68	00 44	49	67	252
109	-3 07	50	69	-2 17	49	68	-1 28	49	68	-0 39	50	67	00 11	49	66	251
110	-3 40	+49	68	-2 51	+50	67	-2 01	+49	67	-1 12	+50	66	-0 22	+49	66	250
111	-4 14	50	67	-3 24	50	67	-2 34	49	66	-1 45	50	65	-0 55	49	65	249
112	-4 47	50	66	-3 57	50	66	-3 07	49	65	-2 18	50	65	-1 28	50	64	248
113	-5 20	50	66	-4 30	50	65	-3 40	50	64	-2 50	50	64	-2 00	50	63	247
114	-5 53	50	65	-5 03	50	64	-4 13	51	64	-3 22	50	63	-2 32	50	62	246
115				-5 35	+50	63	-4 45	+51	63	-3 54	+50	62	-3 04	+50	62	245
116							-5 17	51	62	-4 26	50	61	-3 36	50	61	244
117							-5 49	51	61	-4 58	51	61	-4 07	50	60	243
118										-5 29	51	60	-4 38	50	59	242
119										-6 00	51	59	-5 09	51	58	241
120													-5 40	+51	58	240

0°	1°	2°	3°	4°	5°	6°	7°	8°	9°	10°	11°	12°	13°	14°

S. Lat. {LHA greater than 180°....... Zn=180−Z
{LHA less than 180°.......... Zn=180+Z

DECLINATION (0°-14°) SAME NAME AS LATITUDE

LHA	0° Hc	0° d	0° Z	1° Hc	1° d	1° Z	2° Hc	2° d	2° Z	3° Hc	3° d	3° Z	4° Hc	4° d	4° Z
	° ′	′	°	° ′	′	°	° ′	′	°	° ′	′	°	° ′	′	°
100	−6 00	−48	82	260											
99	−5 24	48	83	261											
98	−4 48	48	84	−5 36	48	84	262								
97	−4 12	48	84	−5 00	48	85	−5 48	48	86	263					
96	−3 36	48	85	−4 24	48	86	−5 12	48	86	−6 00	48	87	264		
95	−3 00	−48	86	−3 48	−48	87	−4 36	−48	87	−5 24	−48	88	265		
94	−2 24	48	87	−3 12	48	87	−4 00	48	88	−4 48	48	89	−5 36	48	89
93	−1 48	48	88	−2 36	48	88	−3 24	48	89	−4 12	48	89	−5 00	48	90
92	−1 12	48	88	−2 00	48	89	−2 48	48	90	−3 36	48	90	−4 24	48	91
91	−0 36	48	89	−1 24	48	90	−2 12	48	90	−3 00	48	91	−3 48	48	92
90	00 00	−48	90	−0 48	−48	91	−1 36	−48	91	−2 24	−48	92	−3 12	−47	92
89	00 36	48	91	−0 12	48	91	−1 00	48	92	−1 48	48	93	−2 36	47	93
88	01 12	48	92	00 24	48	92	−0 24	48	93	−1 12	48	93	−2 00	47	94
87	01 48	48	92	01 00	48	93	00 12	48	94	−0 36	48	94	−1 24	47	95
86	02 24	48	93	01 36	48	94	00 48	48	94	00 00	48	95	−0 48	48	96
85	03 00	−48	94	02 12	−48	95	01 24	−48	95	00 36	−48	96	−0 12	−48	96
84	03 36	48	95	02 48	48	95	02 00	48	96	01 12	48	97	00 24	48	97
83	04 12	48	96	03 24	48	96	02 36	48	97	01 48	48	97	01 00	48	98
82	04 48	48	96	04 00	48	97	03 12	48	98	02 24	48	98	01 36	48	99
81	05 24	48	97	04 36	48	98	03 48	48	98	03 00	49	99	02 11	48	100
80	06 00	−48	98	05 12	−49	99	04 23	−48	99	03 35	−48	100	02 47	−48	100
79	06 36	49	99	05 47	48	99	04 59	48	100	04 11	49	101	03 22	48	101
78	07 11	48	100	06 23	48	100	05 35	49	101	04 46	48	101	03 58	49	102
77	07 47	49	100	06 58	48	101	06 10	48	102	05 22	49	102	04 33	48	103
76	08 22	48	101	07 34	49	102	06 45	48	103	05 57	49	103	05 08	48	104
75	08 58	−49	102	08 09	−48	103	07 21	−49	103	06 32	−49	104	05 43	−48	104
74	09 33	49	103	08 44	48	104	07 56	49	104	07 07	49	105	06 18	49	105
73	10 08	49	104	09 19	48	104	08 31	49	105	07 42	49	106	06 53	49	106
72	10 43	49	105	09 54	49	105	09 05	48	106	08 17	49	106	07 28	49	107
71	11 18	49	105	10 29	49	106	09 40	49	107	08 51	49	107	08 02	49	108
70	11 53	−49	106	11 04	−49	107	10 15	−49	107	09 26	−50	108	08 36	−49	109

LHA	5° Hc	5° d	5° Z	6° Hc	6° d	6° Z	7° Hc	7° d	7° Z	8° Hc	8° d	8° Z	9° Hc	9° d	9° Z
	° ′	′	°	° ′	′	°	° ′	′	°	° ′	′	°	° ′	′	°
94	266														
93	−5 48	48	91	267											
92	−5 12	47	91	−5 59	48	92	268								
91	−4 36	47	92	−5 23	48	93	−6 11	48	93	269					
90	−3 59	−48	93	−4 47	−48	94	−5 35	−48	94	270					
89	−3 23	48	94	−4 11	48	94	−4 59	48	95	−5 47	48	96	271		
88	−2 47	48	95	−3 35	48	95	−4 23	48	96	−5 11	48	96	−5 59	48	97
87	−2 11	48	95	−2 59	48	96	−3 47	48	97	−4 35	48	97	−5 23	48	98
86	−1 36	47	96	−2 23	48	97	−3 11	48	97	−3 59	48	98	−4 47	48	99
85	−1 00	−48	97	−1 48	−48	98	−2 36	−48	98	−3 24	−48	99	−4 12	−48	99
84	−0 24	48	98	−1 12	48	98	−2 00	48	99	−2 48	48	100	−3 36	48	100
83	00 12	48	99	−0 36	48	99	−1 24	48	100	−2 12	49	100	−3 01	48	101
82	00 48	49	99	−0 01	48	100	−0 49	48	101	−1 37	48	101	−2 25	48	102
81	01 23	48	100	00 35	48	101	−0 13	49	101	−1 02	48	102	−1 50	48	103
80	01 59	−49	101	01 10	−48	102	00 22	−48	102	−0 26	−49	103	−1 15	−48	103
79	02 34	48	102	01 46	49	102	00 57	48	103	00 09	49	104	−0 40	48	104
78	03 09	48	103	02 21	49	103	01 32	48	104	00 44	49	104	−0 05	48	105
77	03 45	49	103	02 56	49	104	02 07	48	105	01 19	49	105	00 30	48	106
76	04 20	49	104	03 31	49	105	02 42	48	105	01 54	49	106	01 05	49	107
75	04 55	−49	105	04 06	−49	106	03 17	−49	106	02 28	−49	107	01 39	−48	107
74	05 29	49	106	04 40	48	106	03 52	49	107	03 03	49	108	02 14	49	108
73	06 04	49	107	05 15	49	107	04 26	49	108	03 37	49	108	02 48	49	109
72	06 39	50	108	05 49	49	108	05 00	49	109	04 11	49	109	03 22	49	110
71	07 13	49	108	06 24	49	109	05 35	50	109	04 45	49	110	03 56	49	111
70	07 47	−49	109	06 58	−50	110	06 08	−49	110	05 19	−49	111	04 30	−50	111

LHA	10° Hc	10° d	10° Z	11° Hc	11° d	11° Z	12° Hc	12° d	12° Z	13° Hc	13° d	13° Z	14° Hc	14° d	14° Z	LHA
	° ′	′	°	° ′	′	°	° ′	′	°	° ′	′	°	° ′	′	°	
88	272															
87	273															
86	−5 35	48	99	274												
85	−5 00	−48	100	−5 48	−47	101	275									
84	−4 24	48	101	−5 12	48	101	−6 00	48	102	276						
83	−3 49	48	102	−4 37	48	102	−5 25	48	103	277						
82	−3 13	48	102	−4 01	49	103	−4 50	48	104	−5 38	48	104	278			
81	−2 38	48	103	−3 26	49	104	−4 15	48	104	−5 03	48	105	−5 51	48	106	279
80	−2 03	−48	104	−2 51	−49	105	−3 40	−48	105	−4 28	−48	106	−5 16	−48	106	280
79	−1 28	48	105	−2 16	49	105	−3 05	48	106	−3 53	48	107	−4 41	49	107	281
78	−0 53	49	106	−1 42	48	106	−2 30	49	107	−3 19	48	107	−4 07	48	108	282
77	−0 18	49	106	−1 07	49	107	−1 56	48	108	−2 44	49	108	−3 33	48	109	283
76	00 16	49	107	−0 33	48	108	−1 21	49	108	−2 10	49	109	−2 59	48	110	284
75	00 51	−49	108	00 02	−49	109	−0 47	−49	109	−1 36	−49	110	−2 25	−48	110	285
74	01 25	49	109	00 36	49	109	−0 13	49	110	−1 02	49	111	−1 51	49	111	286
73	01 59	49	110	01 10	49	110	00 21	49	111	−0 28	49	111	−1 17	49	112	287
72	02 33	49	110	01 44	49	111	00 55	50	112	00 05	49	112	−0 44	49	113	288
71	03 07	50	111	02 17	49	112	01 28	49	112	00 39	50	113	−0 11	49	114	289
70	03 40	−49	112	02 51	−50	113	02 01	−49	113	01 12	−50	114	00 22	−49	114	290

DECLINATION (0°-14°) CONTRARY NAME TO LATITUDE

N. Lat. {LHA greater than 180°....... Zn=Z / LHA less than 180°.......... Zn=360−Z}

DECLINATION (0°-14°) CONTRARY NAME TO LATITUDE

LHA	0° Hc	d	Z	1° Hc	d	Z	2° Hc	d	Z	3° Hc	d	Z	4° Hc	d	Z	LHA
	° ′	′	°	° ′	′	°	° ′	′	°	° ′	′	°	° ′	′	°	
69	12 27	49	107	11 38	49	108	10 49	49	108	10 00	50	109	09 10	49	109	291
68	13 02	49	108	12 13	50	109	11 23	49	109	10 34	50	110	09 44	49	110	292
67	13 36	49	109	12 47	50	109	11 57	49	110	11 08	50	111	10 18	49	111	293
66	14 10	49	110	13 21	50	110	12 31	49	111	11 42	50	111	10 52	50	112	294
65	14 44	−49	110	13 55	−50	111	13 05	−50	112	12 15	−50	112	11 25	−50	113	295
64	15 18	50	111	14 28	50	112	13 38	50	112	12 48	50	113	11 58	50	114	296
63	15 51	49	112	15 02	50	113	14 12	50	113	13 22	51	114	12 31	50	114	297
62	16 25	50	113	15 35	50	114	14 45	51	114	13 54	50	115	13 04	50	115	298
61	16 58	50	114	16 08	51	115	15 17	50	115	14 27	50	116	13 37	51	116	299
60	17 31	−51	115	16 40	−50	115	15 50	−50	116	15 00	−51	117	14 09	−51	117	300
59	18 03	50	116	17 13	51	116	16 22	50	117	15 32	51	117	14 41	51	118	301
58	18 36	51	117	17 45	50	117	16 55	51	118	16 04	51	118	15 13	51	119	302
57	19 08	51	117	18 17	51	118	17 26	51	119	16 35	51	119	15 44	51	120	303
56	19 40	51	118	18 49	51	119	17 58	51	119	17 07	51	120	16 16	52	121	304
55	20 12	−51	119	19 21	−52	120	18 29	−51	120	17 38	−51	121	16 47	−52	121	305
54	20 43	51	120	19 52	52	121	19 00	51	121	18 09	52	122	17 17	51	122	306
53	21 14	51	121	20 23	52	122	19 31	52	122	18 39	51	123	17 48	52	123	307
52	21 45	52	122	20 53	51	123	20 02	52	123	19 10	52	124	18 18	52	124	308
51	22 15	51	123	21 24	52	123	20 32	52	124	19 40	53	125	18 47	52	125	309
50	22 46	−52	124	21 54	−53	124	21 01	−52	125	20 09	−52	125	19 17	−53	126	310
49	23 15	52	125	22 23	52	125	21 31	53	126	20 38	52	126	19 46	53	127	311
48	23 45	53	126	22 52	52	126	22 00	53	127	21 07	52	127	20 15	53	128	312
47	24 14	53	127	23 21	52	127	22 29	53	128	21 36	53	128	20 43	53	129	313
46	24 43	53	128	23 50	53	128	22 57	53	129	22 04	53	129	21 11	53	130	314
45	25 11	−53	129	24 18	−53	129	23 25	−53	130	22 32	−53	130	21 39	−54	131	315
44	25 39	53	130	24 46	53	130	23 53	54	131	22 59	53	131	22 06	54	132	316
43	26 07	54	131	25 13	53	131	24 20	54	132	23 26	53	132	22 33	54	133	317
42	26 34	54	132	25 40	53	132	24 47	54	133	23 53	54	133	22 59	54	134	318
41	27 01	54	133	26 07	54	133	25 13	54	134	24 19	54	134	23 25	54	135	319
40	27 27	−54	134	26 33	−54	134	25 39	−54	135	24 45	−55	135	23 50	−54	136	320
39	27 53	54	135	26 59	54	135	26 05	55	136	25 10	54	136	24 16	55	137	321
38	28 19	55	136	27 24	54	136	26 30	55	137	25 35	55	137	24 40	55	138	322
37	28 44	55	137	27 49	55	137	26 54	55	138	25 59	55	138	25 04	55	139	323
36	29 08	55	138	28 13	55	138	27 18	55	139	26 23	55	139	25 28	55	140	324
35	29 32	−55	139	28 37	−55	139	27 42	−55	140	26 47	−56	140	25 51	−55	141	325
34	29 56	56	140	29 00	55	140	28 05	55	141	27 10	56	141	26 14	56	142	326
33	30 19	56	141	29 23	55	141	28 28	56	142	27 32	56	142	26 36	56	143	327
32	30 41	55	142	29 46	56	142	28 50	56	143	27 54	56	143	26 58	56	144	328
31	31 03	56	143	30 07	56	144	29 11	56	144	28 15	56	144	27 19	56	145	329
30	31 25	−56	144	30 29	−57	145	29 32	−56	145	28 36	−56	145	27 40	−57	146	330
29	31 46	57	145	30 49	56	146	29 53	57	146	28 56	56	146	28 00	57	147	331
28	32 06	57	146	31 09	56	147	30 13	57	147	29 16	57	148	28 19	57	148	332
27	32 26	57	148	31 29	57	148	30 32	57	148	29 35	57	149	28 38	57	149	333
26	32 45	57	149	31 48	57	149	30 51	57	149	29 54	58	150	28 56	57	150	334
25	33 03	−57	150	32 06	−57	150	31 09	−57	150	30 12	−58	151	29 14	−57	151	335
24	33 21	57	151	32 24	58	151	31 26	57	152	30 29	58	152	29 31	57	152	336
23	33 38	57	152	32 41	58	152	31 43	57	153	30 46	58	153	29 48	58	153	337
22	33 55	58	153	32 57	58	154	31 59	57	154	31 02	58	154	30 04	58	154	338
21	34 11	58	154	33 13	58	155	32 15	58	155	31 17	58	155	30 19	58	156	339
20	34 26	−58	156	33 28	−58	156	32 30	−58	156	31 32	−58	156	30 34	−59	157	340
19	34 41	58	157	33 43	59	157	32 44	58	157	31 46	58	158	30 48	59	158	341
18	34 55	59	158	33 56	58	158	32 58	59	158	31 59	58	159	31 01	59	159	342
17	35 08	58	159	34 10	59	159	33 11	59	160	32 12	58	160	31 14	59	160	343
16	35 21	59	160	34 22	59	161	33 23	59	161	32 24	58	161	31 26	59	161	344
15	35 33	−59	162	34 34	−59	162	33 35	−59	162	32 36	−59	162	31 37	−59	162	345
14	35 44	59	163	34 45	59	163	33 46	59	163	32 47	60	163	31 47	59	164	346
13	35 54	59	164	34 55	59	164	33 56	59	164	32 57	60	165	31 57	59	165	347
12	36 04	60	165	35 04	59	165	34 05	59	166	33 06	59	166	32 07	60	166	348
11	36 13	60	166	35 13	59	167	34 14	60	167	33 14	59	167	32 15	59	167	349
10	36 21	−60	168	35 21	−59	168	34 22	−60	168	33 22	−59	168	32 23	−60	168	350
9	36 28	59	169	35 29	60	169	34 29	60	169	33 29	59	169	32 30	60	169	351
8	36 35	60	170	35 35	59	170	34 36	60	170	33 36	60	170	32 36	60	171	352
7	36 41	60	171	35 41	60	171	34 41	59	172	33 42	60	172	32 42	60	172	353
6	36 46	60	173	35 46	60	173	34 46	60	173	33 46	59	173	32 47	60	173	354
5	36 50	−60	174	35 50	−60	174	34 50	−59	174	33 51	−60	174	32 51	−60	174	355
4	36 54	60	175	35 54	60	175	34 54	60	175	33 54	60	175	32 54	60	175	356
3	36 57	60	176	35 57	60	176	34 57	60	176	33 57	60	176	32 57	60	176	357
2	36 58	60	178	35 58	59	178	34 59	60	178	33 59	60	178	32 59	60	178	358
1	37 00	60	179	36 00	60	179	35 00	60	179	34 00	60	179	33 00	60	179	359
0	37 00	−60	180	36 00	−60	180	35 00	−60	180	34 00	−60	180	33 00	−60	180	360

LHA	5° Hc	d	Z	6° Hc	d	Z	7° Hc	d	Z	8° Hc	d	Z	9° Hc	d	Z	LHA
	° ′	′	°	° ′	′	°	° ′	′	°	° ′	′	°	° ′	′	°	
69	08 21	49	110	07 32	50	111	06 42	49	111	05 53	50	112	05 03	49	112	291
68	08 55	50	111	08 05	49	111	07 16	50	112	06 26	49	113	05 37	50	113	292
67	09 29	50	112	08 39	50	112	07 49	49	113	07 00	50	113	06 10	50	114	293
66	10 02	50	113	09 12	50	113	08 22	49	114	07 33	50	114	06 43	50	115	294
65	10 35	−50	113	09 45	−50	114	08 55	−50	114	08 05	−50	115	07 15	−50	116	295
64	11 08	50	114	10 18	50	115	09 28	50	115	08 38	50	116	07 48	51	116	296
63	11 41	50	115	10 51	50	116	10 01	51	116	09 10	50	117	08 20	50	117	297
62	12 14	50	116	11 24	51	116	10 33	50	117	09 43	51	118	08 52	51	118	298
61	12 46	50	117	11 56	51	117	11 05	51	118	10 14	50	118	09 24	51	119	299
60	13 18	−50	118	12 28	−51	118	11 37	−51	119	10 46	−51	119	09 55	−51	120	300
59	13 50	51	118	12 59	50	119	12 09	51	120	11 18	52	120	10 26	51	121	301
58	14 22	51	119	13 31	51	120	12 40	51	120	11 49	52	121	10 57	51	121	302
57	14 53	51	120	14 02	51	121	13 11	52	121	12 19	51	122	11 28	51	122	303
56	15 24	51	121	14 33	51	122	13 42	52	122	12 50	52	122	11 58	51	123	304
55	15 55	−51	122	15 04	−52	123	14 12	−52	123	13 20	−51	124	12 29	−52	124	305
54	16 26	52	123	15 34	52	123	14 42	52	124	13 50	52	124	12 58	52	125	306
53	16 56	52	124	16 04	52	124	15 12	52	125	14 20	52	125	13 28	52	126	307
52	17 26	52	125	16 34	53	125	15 41	52	126	14 49	52	126	13 57	53	127	308
51	17 55	52	126	17 03	52	126	16 11	53	127	15 18	52	127	14 26	53	128	309
50	18 24	−52	127	17 32	−53	127	16 39	−52	128	15 47	−53	128	14 54	−53	129	310
49	18 53	52	127	18 01	53	128	17 08	53	128	16 15	53	129	15 22	53	129	311
48	19 22	53	128	18 29	53	129	17 36	53	129	16 43	53	130	15 50	53	130	312
47	19 50	53	129	18 57	53	130	18 04	53	130	17 11	54	131	16 17	53	131	313
46	20 18	53	130	19 25	54	131	18 31	53	131	17 38	54	132	16 44	53	132	314
45	20 45	−53	131	19 52	−54	132	18 58	−53	132	18 05	−54	133	17 11	−54	133	315
44	21 12	54	132	20 18	53	133	19 25	54	133	18 31	54	134	17 37	54	134	316
43	21 39	54	133	20 45	54	134	19 51	54	134	18 57	54	134	18 03	54	135	317
42	22 05	54	134	21 11	54	135	20 17	55	135	19 22	54	135	18 28	54	136	318
41	22 31	55	135	21 36	54	135	20 42	54	136	19 48	55	136	18 53	54	137	319
40	22 56	−54	136	22 02	−55	136	21 07	−55	137	20 12	−54	137	19 18	−55	138	320
39	23 21	55	137	22 26	55	137	21 31	54	138	20 37	55	138	19 42	55	139	321
38	23 45	55	138	22 50	55	138	21 55	55	139	21 00	55	139	20 05	55	140	322
37	24 09	55	139	23 14	55	139	22 19	55	140	21 24	56	140	20 28	55	141	323
36	24 33	56	140	23 37	55	140	22 42	55	141	21 47	56	141	20 51	55	142	324
35	24 56	−56	141	24 00	−55	141	23 05	−56	142	22 09	−56	142	21 13	−55	143	325
34	25 18	55	142	24 23	56	142	23 27	56	143	22 31	56	143	21 35	56	144	326
33	25 40	56	143	24 44	56	143	23 48	56	144	22 52	56	144	21 56	56	145	327
32	26 02	56	144	25 06	57	144	24 09	56	145	23 13	56	145	22 17	56	146	328
31	26 23	57	145	25 26	56	145	24 30	56	146	23 34	57	146	22 37	56	147	329
30	26 43	−56	146	25 47	−57	147	24 50	−57	147	23 53	−56	147	22 57	−57	148	330
29	27 03	57	147	26 06	57	148	25 09	56	148	24 13	57	148	23 16	57	149	331
28	27 22	57	148	26 25	57	149	25 28	57	149	24 31	57	149	23 34	57	150	332
27	27 41	57	149	26 44	57	150	25 47	57	150	24 50	58	150	23 52	57	151	333
26	27 59	57	150	27 02	57	151	26 05	58	151	25 07	57	151	24 10	58	152	334
25	28 17	−58	151	27 19	−57	152	26 22	−58	152	25 24	−57	152	24 27	−58	153	335
24	28 34	58	153	27 36	58	153	26 38	57	153	25 41	58	154	24 43	58	154	336
23	28 50	58	154	27 52	58	154	26 54	58	154	25 56	57	155	24 59	58	155	337
22	29 06	58	155	28 08	58	155	27 10	58	155	26 12	58	156	25 14	59	156	338
21	29 21	58	156	28 23	58	156	27 25	59	156	26 26	58	157	25 28	58	157	339
20	29 35	−58	157	28 37	−58	157	27 39	−59	158	26 40	−58	158	25 42	−59	158	340
19	29 49	58	158	28 51	59	158	27 52	58	159	26 54	59	159	25 55	58	159	341
18	30 02	58	159	29 04	59	159	28 05	59	160	27 06	58	160	26 08	59	160	342
17	30 15	59	160	29 16	59	161	28 17	58	161	27 19	59	161	26 20	59	161	343
16	30 27	59	161	29 28	59	162	28 29	59	162	27 30	59	162	26 31	59	162	344
15	30 38	−59	163	29 39	−59	163	28 40	−59	163	27 41	−59	163	26 42	−59	163	345
14	30 48	59	164	29 49	59	164	28 50	59	164	27 51	59	164	26 52	60	165	346
13	30 58	59	165	29 59	59	165	29 00	60	165	28 00	59	165	27 01	59	166	347
12	31 07	59	166	30 08	60	166	29 08	59	166	28 09	59	167	27 10	60	167	348
11	31 16	60	167	30 16	59	167	29 17	60	168	28 17	59	168	27 18	60	168	349
10	31 23	−59	168	30 24	−60	169	29 24	−59	169	28 25	−60	169	27 25	−60	169	350
9	31 30	59	170	30 31	60	170	29 31	60	170	28 31	59	170	27 32	60	170	351
8	31 36	59	171	30 37	60	171	29 37	60	171	28 37	59	171	27 38	60	171	352
7	31 42	60	172	30 42	60	172	29 42	59	172	28 43	60	172	27 43	60	172	353
6	31 47	60	173	30 47	60	173	29 47	60	173	28 47	60	173	27 47	59	173	354
5	31 51	−60	174	30 51	−60	174	29 51	−60	174	28 51	−60	174	27 51	−60	174	355
4	31 54	60	175	30 54	60	175	29 54	60	175	28 54	60	176	27 54	60	176	356
3	31 57	60	177	30 57	60	177	29 57	60	177	28 57	60	177	27 57	60	177	357
2	31 59	60	178	30 59	60	178	29 59	60	178	28 59	60	178	27 59	60	178	358
1	32 00	60	179	31 00	60	179	30 00	60	179	29 00	60	179	28 00	60	179	359
0	32 00	−60	180	31 00	−60	180	30 00	−60	180	29 00	−60	180	28 00	−60	180	360

LHA	10° Hc	d	Z	11° Hc	d	Z	12° Hc	d	Z	13° Hc	d	Z	14° Hc	d	Z	LHA
	° ′	′	°	° ′	′	°	° ′	′	°	° ′	′	°	° ′	′	°	
69	04 14	50	113	03 24	50	113	02 34	49	114	01 45	50	115	00 55	49	115	291
68	04 47	50	114	03 57	50	114	03 07	49	115	02 18	50	115	01 28	50	116	292
67	05 20	50	114	04 30	50	115	03 40	50	116	02 50	50	116	02 00	50	117	293
66	05 53	50	115	05 03	50	116	04 13	51	116	03 22	50	117	02 32	50	118	294
65	06 25	−50	116	05 35	−50	117	04 45	−51	117	03 54	−50	118	03 04	−50	118	295
64	06 57	50	117	06 07	50	118	05 17	51	118	04 26	50	119	03 36	50	119	296
63	07 30	51	118	06 39	50	118	05 49	51	119	04 58	51	119	04 07	50	120	297
62	08 01	50	119	07 11	51	119	06 20	51	120	05 29	51	120	04 38	50	121	298
61	08 33	51	119	07 42	51	120	06 51	51	121	06 00	51	121	05 09	51	122	299
60	09 04	−51	120	08 13	−51	121	07 22	−51	121	06 31	−51	122	05 40	−51	122	300
59	09 35	51	121	08 44	51	122	07 53	51	122	07 02	52	123	06 10	51	123	301
58	10 06	51	122	09 15	52	123	08 23	51	123	07 32	51	124	06 41	52	124	302
57	10 37	52	123	09 45	51	123	08 54	52	124	08 02	52	124	07 10	51	125	303
56	11 07	52	124	10 15	52	124	09 23	51	125	08 32	52	125	07 40	52	126	304
55	11 37	−52	125	10 45	−52	125	09 53	−52	126	09 01	−52	126	08 09	−52	127	305
54	12 06	52	125	11 14	52	126	10 22	52	126	09 30	52	127	08 38	52	127	306
53	12 36	53	126	11 43	52	127	10 51	52	127	09 59	53	128	09 06	52	128	307
52	13 04	52	127	12 12	52	128	11 20	53	128	10 27	53	129	09 34	52	129	308
51	13 33	53	128	12 40	52	129	11 48	53	129	10 55	53	130	10 02	53	130	309
50	14 01	−53	129	13 08	−52	129	12 16	−53	130	11 23	−53	130	10 30	−53	131	310
49	14 29	53	130	13 36	53	130	12 43	53	131	11 50	53	131	10 57	53	132	311
48	14 57	53	131	14 04	54	131	13 10	53	132	12 17	53	132	11 24	54	133	312
47	15 24	53	132	14 31	54	132	13 37	53	133	12 44	54	133	11 50	54	134	313
46	15 51	54	133	14 57	54	133	14 03	53	134	13 10	54	134	12 16	54	134	314
45	16 17	−54	134	15 23	−54	134	14 29	−53	134	13 36	−54	135	12 42	−54	135	315
44	16 43	54	134	15 49	54	135	14 55	54	135	14 01	54	136	13 07	54	136	316
43	17 09	55	135	16 14	54	136	15 20	54	136	14 26	54	137	13 32	55	137	317
42	17 34	55	136	16 39	54	137	15 45	55	137	14 50	54	138	13 56	55	138	318
41	17 59	55	137	17 04	55	138	16 09	54	138	15 15	55	139	14 20	55	139	319
40	18 23	−55	138	17 28	−55	139	16 33	−55	139	15 38	−55	139	14 43	−55	140	320
39	18 47	55	139	17 52	55	140	16 57	55	140	16 02	56	140	15 06	55	141	321
38	19 10	55	140	18 15	55	141	17 20	56	141	16 24	55	141	15 29	55	142	322
37	19 33	55	141	18 38	56	141	17 42	55	142	16 47	56	142	15 51	55	143	323
36	19 56	56	142	19 00	56	142	18 04	55	143	17 09	56	143	16 13	56	144	324
35	20 18	−56	143	19 22	−56	143	18 26	−56	144	17 30	−56	144	16 34	−56	145	325
34	20 39	56	144	19 43	56	144	18 47	56	145	17 51	56	145	16 55	56	146	326
33	21 00	56	145	20 04	56	145	19 08	57	146	18 11	56	146	17 15	56	147	327
32	21 21	57	146	20 24	56	146	19 28	57	147	18 31	56	147	17 35	57	147	328
31	21 41	57	147	20 44	57	147	19 47	56	148	18 51	57	148	17 54	57	148	329
30	22 00	−57	148	21 03	−57	148	20 06	−56	149	19 10	−57	149	18 13	−57	149	330
29	22 19	57	149	21 22	57	149	20 25	57	150	19 28	57	150	18 31	57	150	331
28	22 37	57	150	21 40	57	150	20 43	57	151	19 46	58	151	18 48	57	151	332
27	22 55	57	151	21 58	58	151	21 00	57	152	20 03	57	152	19 06	58	152	333
26	23 12	57	152	22 15	58	152	21 17	57	153	20 20	58	153	19 22	57	153	334
25	23 29	−58	153	22 31	−57	153	21 34	−58	154	20 36	−58	154	19 38	−58	154	335
24	23 45	58	154	22 47	58	154	21 49	58	155	20 51	57	155	19 54	58	155	336
23	24 01	58	155	23 03	58	155	22 05	58	156	21 07	59	156	20 08	58	156	337
22	24 15	58	156	23 17	58	156	22 19	58	157	21 21	58	157	20 23	59	157	338
21	24 30	59	157	23 31	58	157	22 33	58	158	21 35	59	158	20 36	58	158	339
20	24 43	−58	158	23 45	−58	159	22 47	−59	159	21 48	−58	159	20 50	−59	159	340
19	24 57	59	159	23 58	59	160	22 59	58	160	22 01	59	160	21 02	59	160	341
18	25 09	59	160	24 10	58	161	23 12	59	161	22 13	59	161	21 14	59	161	342
17	25 21	59	161	24 22	59	162	23 23	59	162	22 24	59	162	21 25	59	162	343
16	25 32	59	163	24 33	59	163	23 34	59	163	22 35	59	163	21 36	59	163	344
15	25 43	−60	164	24 43	−59	164	23 44	−59	164	22 45	−59	164	21 46	−59	164	345
14	25 52	59	165	24 53	59	165	23 54	59	165	22 55	59	165	21 56	60	165	346
13	26 02	60	166	25 02	59	166	24 03	59	166	23 04	60	166	22 04	59	166	347
12	26 10	59	167	25 11	60	167	24 11	59	167	23 12	59	167	22 13	60	167	348
11	26 18	59	168	25 19	60	168	24 19	59	168	23 20	60	168	22 20	59	169	349
10	26 25	−59	169	25 26	−60	169	24 26	−59	169	23 27	−60	169	22 27	−60	170	350
9	26 32	60	170	25 32	59	170	24 33	60	170	23 33	60	170	22 33	59	171	351
8	26 38	60	171	25 38	60	171	24 38	59	171	23 39	60	172	22 39	60	172	352
7	26 43	60	172	25 43	60	172	24 43	59	173	23 44	60	173	22 44	60	173	353
6	26 48	60	173	25 48	60	174	24 48	60	174	23 48	60	174	22 48	60	174	354
5	26 51	−60	175	25 51	−59	175	24 52	−60	175	23 52	−60	175	22 52	−60	175	355
4	26 54	59	176	25 55	60	176	24 55	60	176	23 55	60	176	22 55	60	176	356
3	26 57	60	177	25 57	60	177	24 57	60	177	23 57	60	177	22 57	60	177	357
2	26 59	60	178	25 59	60	178	24 59	60	178	23 59	60	178	22 59	60	178	358
1	27 00	60	179	26 00	60	179	25 00	60	179	24 00	60	179	23 00	60	179	359
0	27 00	−60	180	26 00	−60	180	25 00	−60	180	24 00	−60	180	23 00	−60	180	360

S. Lat. {LHA greater than 180°....... Zn=180−Z / LHA less than 180°.......... Zn=180+Z}

DECLINATION (0°-14°) CONTRARY NAME TO LATITUDE

LHA	15° Hc	d	Z	16° Hc	d	Z	17° Hc	d	Z	18° Hc	d	Z	19° Hc	d	Z
	° ′	′	°	° ′	′	°	° ′	′	°	° ′	′	°	° ′	′	°
0	52 00	+60	180	53 00	+60	180	54 00	+60	180	55 00	+60	180	56 00	+60	180
1	52 00	60	178	53 00	60	178	54 00	60	178	55 00	60	178	56 00	60	178
2	51 58	60	177	52 58	60	177	53 58	60	177	54 58	60	177	55 58	60	177
3	51 56	60	175	52 56	59	175	53 55	60	175	54 55	60	175	55 55	60	175
4	51 52	60	174	52 52	60	174	53 52	60	173	54 52	60	173	55 52	59	173
5	51 48	+60	172	52 48	+59	172	53 47	+60	172	54 47	+60	172	55 47	+60	172
6	51 42	60	171	52 42	60	171	53 42	59	170	54 41	60	170	55 41	60	170
7	51 36	60	169	52 36	59	169	53 35	60	169	54 35	59	169	55 34	60	168
8	51 29	59	168	52 28	60	167	53 28	59	167	54 27	59	167	55 26	60	167
9	51 20	60	166	52 20	59	166	53 19	59	166	54 18	59	165	55 17	60	165
10	51 11	+59	165	52 10	+59	164	53 09	+59	164	54 08	+59	164	55 07	+59	163
11	51 01	59	163	52 00	59	163	52 59	59	162	53 58	59	162	54 57	58	162
12	50 50	59	162	51 49	59	161	52 48	58	161	53 46	59	161	54 45	58	160
13	50 38	59	160	51 37	58	160	52 35	59	159	53 34	58	159	54 32	58	159
14	50 25	59	159	51 24	58	158	52 22	58	158	53 20	58	157	54 18	58	157
15	50 12	+58	157	51 10	+58	157	52 08	+58	156	53 06	+58	156	54 04	+58	155
16	49 57	58	156	50 55	58	155	51 53	58	155	52 51	57	154	53 48	58	154
17	49 42	57	154	50 39	58	154	51 37	58	153	52 35	57	153	53 32	57	152
18	49 26	57	153	50 23	57	152	51 20	58	152	52 18	57	151	53 15	57	151
19	49 09	57	151	50 06	57	151	51 03	57	150	52 00	57	150	52 57	56	149
20	48 51	+57	150	49 48	+57	149	50 45	+56	149	51 41	+57	148	52 38	+56	148
21	48 32	57	149	49 29	57	148	50 26	56	148	51 22	56	147	52 18	56	146
22	48 13	57	147	49 10	56	147	50 06	56	146	51 02	56	146	51 58	56	145
23	47 53	56	146	48 49	56	145	49 45	56	145	50 41	56	144	51 37	55	144
24	47 32	56	144	48 28	56	144	49 24	55	143	50 19	56	143	51 15	55	142
25	47 11	+56	143	48 07	+55	143	49 02	+55	142	49 57	+55	141	50 52	+55	141
26	46 49	55	142	47 44	55	141	48 39	55	141	49 34	55	140	50 29	55	139
27	46 26	55	141	47 21	55	140	48 16	55	139	49 11	54	139	50 05	54	138
28	46 03	55	139	46 58	54	139	47 52	55	138	48 47	54	137	49 41	54	137
29	45 39	55	138	46 34	54	137	47 28	54	137	48 22	54	136	49 16	53	135
30	45 15	+54	137	46 09	+54	136	47 03	+54	135	47 57	+53	135	48 50	+53	134
31	44 50	54	136	45 44	53	135	46 37	54	134	47 31	53	134	48 24	53	133
32	44 24	54	134	45 18	53	134	46 11	53	133	47 04	53	132	47 57	53	132
33	43 58	53	133	44 51	53	132	45 44	53	132	46 37	53	131	47 30	52	130
34	43 31	53	132	44 24	53	131	45 17	53	131	46 10	52	130	47 02	52	129
35	43 04	+53	131	43 57	+53	130	44 50	+52	129	45 42	+52	129	46 34	+52	128
36	42 37	52	130	43 29	52	129	44 21	52	128	45 13	52	128	46 05	52	127
37	42 09	52	128	43 01	52	128	43 53	51	127	44 44	52	126	45 36	51	126
38	41 40	52	127	42 32	52	127	43 24	51	126	44 15	51	125	45 06	51	124
39	41 11	52	126	42 03	51	126	42 54	51	125	43 45	51	124	44 36	51	123
40	40 42	+51	125	41 33	+51	124	42 24	+51	124	43 15	+51	123	44 06	+50	122
41	40 12	51	124	41 03	51	123	41 54	51	123	42 45	50	122	43 35	50	121
42	39 42	51	123	40 33	51	122	41 24	50	122	42 14	50	121	43 04	50	120
43	39 11	51	122	40 02	51	121	40 53	50	120	41 43	50	120	42 33	49	119
44	38 40	51	121	39 31	50	120	40 21	50	119	41 11	50	119	42 01	49	118
45	38 09	+51	120	39 00	+50	119	39 50	+49	118	40 39	+50	118	41 29	+49	117
46	37 38	50	119	38 28	50	118	39 18	49	117	40 07	50	117	40 57	49	116
47	37 06	50	118	37 56	49	117	38 45	50	116	39 35	49	116	40 24	49	115
48	36 34	49	117	37 23	50	116	38 13	49	115	39 02	49	115	39 51	49	114
49	36 01	50	116	36 51	49	115	37 40	49	114	38 29	49	114	39 18	48	113
50	35 29	+49	115	36 18	+49	114	37 07	+49	113	37 56	+48	113	38 44	+49	112
51	34 56	49	114	35 45	49	113	36 34	48	112	37 22	49	112	38 11	48	111
52	34 22	49	113	35 11	49	112	36 00	49	111	36 49	48	111	37 37	48	110
53	33 49	49	112	34 38	48	111	35 26	49	110	36 15	48	110	37 03	48	109
54	33 15	49	111	34 04	49	110	34 53	48	109	35 41	48	109	36 29	47	108
55	32 42	+48	110	33 30	+48	109	34 18	+48	109	35 06	+48	108	35 54	+48	107
56	32 08	48	109	32 56	48	108	33 44	48	108	34 32	48	107	35 20	47	106
57	31 33	49	108	32 22	48	107	33 10	47	107	33 57	48	106	34 45	47	105
58	30 59	48	107	31 47	48	107	32 35	47	106	33 22	48	105	34 10	47	104
59	30 24	48	106	31 12	48	106	32 00	48	105	32 48	47	104	33 35	47	103
60	29 50	+47	105	30 37	+48	105	31 25	+47	104	32 12	+48	103	33 00	+46	103
61	29 15	47	105	30 02	48	104	30 50	47	103	31 37	47	102	32 24	47	102
62	28 40	47	104	29 27	48	103	30 15	47	102	31 02	47	102	31 49	47	101
63	28 04	48	103	28 52	47	102	29 39	47	101	30 26	47	101	31 13	47	100
64	27 29	48	102	28 17	47	101	29 04	47	101	29 51	47	100	30 38	46	99
65	26 54	+47	101	27 41	+47	100	28 28	+47	100	29 15	+47	99	30 02	+46	98
66	26 18	48	100	27 06	47	100	27 53	47	99	28 40	46	98	29 26	47	97
67	25 43	47	99	26 30	47	99	27 17	47	98	28 04	46	97	28 50	47	97
68	25 07	47	99	25 54	47	98	26 41	47	97	27 28	46	96	28 14	47	96
69	24 31	47	98	25 18	47	97	26 05	47	96	26 52	47	96	27 39	46	95

LHA	20° Hc	d	Z	21° Hc	d	Z	22° Hc	d	Z	23° Hc	d	Z	24° Hc	d	Z
	° ′	′	°	° ′	′	°	° ′	′	°	° ′	′	°	° ′	′	°
0	57 00	+60	180	58 00	+60	180	59 00	+60	180	60 00	+60	180	61 00	+60	180
1	57 00	59	178	57 59	60	178	58 59	60	178	59 59	60	178	60 59	60	178
2	56 58	60	177	57 58	60	177	58 58	60	176	59 58	60	176	60 58	60	176
3	56 55	60	175	57 55	60	175	58 55	60	175	59 55	60	175	60 55	60	174
4	56 51	60	173	57 51	60	173	58 51	60	173	59 51	60	173	60 51	59	173
5	56 47	+59	171	57 46	+60	171	58 46	+60	171	59 46	+59	171	60 45	+60	171
6	56 41	59	170	57 40	60	170	58 40	59	169	59 39	60	169	60 39	59	169
7	56 34	59	168	57 33	59	168	58 32	60	168	59 32	59	167	60 31	60	167
8	56 26	59	166	57 25	59	166	58 24	59	166	59 23	59	165	60 22	60	165
9	56 17	59	165	57 16	59	164	58 15	59	164	59 14	59	164	60 13	59	163
10	56 06	+59	163	57 05	+59	163	58 04	+59	162	59 03	+59	162	60 02	+58	162
11	55 55	59	161	56 54	59	161	57 53	58	161	58 51	59	160	59 50	58	160
12	55 43	59	160	56 42	58	159	57 40	58	159	58 38	59	158	59 37	58	158
13	55 30	59	158	56 29	58	158	57 27	58	157	58 25	58	157	59 23	57	156
14	55 16	58	157	56 14	58	156	57 12	58	156	58 10	58	155	59 08	57	155
15	55 02	+57	155	55 59	+58	154	56 57	+57	154	57 54	+58	153	58 52	+57	153
16	54 46	57	153	55 43	57	153	56 40	58	152	57 38	57	152	58 35	56	151
17	54 29	57	152	55 26	57	151	56 23	57	151	57 20	57	150	58 17	56	150
18	54 12	56	150	55 08	57	150	56 05	57	149	57 02	56	149	57 58	56	148
19	53 53	57	149	54 50	56	148	55 46	56	148	56 42	56	147	57 38	56	146
20	53 34	+56	147	54 30	+56	147	55 26	+56	146	56 22	+56	145	57 18	+55	145
21	53 14	56	146	54 10	56	145	55 06	55	145	56 01	55	144	56 56	55	143
22	52 54	55	144	53 49	55	144	54 44	56	143	55 40	54	142	56 34	55	142
23	52 32	55	143	53 27	55	142	54 22	55	142	55 17	55	141	56 12	54	140
24	52 10	55	142	53 05	55	141	54 00	54	140	54 54	54	139	55 48	54	139
25	51 47	+55	140	52 42	+54	139	53 36	+54	139	54 30	+54	138	55 24	+53	137
26	51 24	54	139	52 18	54	138	53 12	54	137	54 06	53	137	54 59	53	136
27	50 59	54	137	51 53	54	137	52 47	53	136	53 40	53	135	54 33	53	134
28	50 35	53	136	51 28	54	135	52 22	53	135	53 15	52	134	54 07	53	133
29	50 09	54	135	51 03	53	134	51 56	52	133	52 48	53	132	53 41	52	132
30	49 43	+53	133	50 36	+53	133	51 29	+52	132	52 21	+52	131	53 13	+52	130
31	49 17	52	132	50 09	53	131	51 02	52	131	51 54	52	130	52 46	51	129
32	48 50	52	131	49 42	52	130	50 34	52	129	51 26	51	129	52 17	51	128
33	48 22	52	130	49 14	52	129	50 06	51	128	50 57	51	127	51 48	51	126
34	47 54	52	128	48 46	51	128	49 37	51	127	50 28	51	126	51 19	50	125
35	47 26	+51	127	48 17	+51	126	49 08	+51	126	49 59	+50	125	50 49	+50	124
36	46 57	51	126	47 48	51	125	48 39	50	124	49 29	50	124	50 19	50	123
37	46 27	51	125	47 18	51	124	48 09	50	123	48 59	50	122	49 49	49	122
38	45 57	51	124	46 48	50	123	47 38	50	122	48 28	50	121	49 18	49	120
39	45 27	50	123	46 17	50	122	47 07	50	121	47 57	49	120	48 46	49	119
40	44 56	+51	121	45 47	+49	121	46 36	+50	120	47 26	+49	119	48 15	+48	118
41	44 25	50	120	45 15	50	120	46 05	49	119	46 54	49	118	47 43	48	117
42	43 54	50	119	44 44	49	118	45 33	49	118	46 22	48	117	47 10	49	116
43	43 22	50	118	44 12	49	117	45 01	48	117	45 49	49	116	46 38	48	115
44	42 50	50	117	43 40	48	116	44 28	49	116	45 17	48	115	46 05	48	114
45	42 18	+49	116	43 07	+49	115	43 56	+48	115	44 44	+48	114	45 32	+47	113
46	41 46	48	115	42 34	49	114	43 23	48	113	44 11	47	113	44 58	48	112
47	41 13	48	114	42 01	48	113	42 49	48	112	43 37	48	112	44 25	47	111
48	40 40	48	113	41 28	48	112	42 16	48	111	43 04	47	111	43 51	47	110
49	40 06	48	112	40 54	48	111	41 42	48	110	42 30	47	110	43 17	46	109
50	39 33	+48	111	40 21	+47	110	41 08	+47	109	41 55	+47	109	42 42	+47	108
51	38 59	48	110	39 47	47	109	40 34	47	109	41 21	47	108	42 08	46	107
52	38 25	47	109	39 12	48	108	40 00	47	108	40 47	46	107	41 33	46	106
53	37 51	47	108	38 38	47	107	39 25	47	107	40 12	46	106	40 58	47	105
54	37 16	47	107	38 03	47	106	38 50	47	106	39 37	46	105	40 23	46	104
55	36 42	+47	106	37 29	+47	106	38 16	+46	105	39 02	+46	104	39 48	+46	103
56	36 07	47	105	36 54	47	105	37 41	46	104	38 27	46	103	39 13	46	102
57	35 32	47	104	36 19	46	104	37 05	47	103	37 52	46	102	38 38	45	101
58	34 57	47	104	35 44	46	103	36 30	46	102	37 16	46	101	38 02	46	100
59	34 22	46	103	35 08	47	102	35 55	46	101	36 41	46	100	37 27	45	100
60	33 46	+47	102	34 33	+46	101	35 19	+46	100	36 05	+46	99	36 51	+45	99
61	33 11	47	101	33 58	46	100	34 44	46	99	35 30	45	99	36 15	46	98
62	32 36	46	100	33 22	46	99	34 08	46	99	34 54	46	98	35 40	45	97
63	32 00	46	99	32 46	46	98	33 32	46	98	34 18	46	97	35 04	45	96
64	31 24	47	98	32 11	46	98	32 57	45	97	33 42	46	96	34 28	45	95
65	30 48	+47	97	31 35	+46	97	32 21	+45	96	33 06	+46	95	33 52	+45	94
66	30 13	46	97	30 59	46	96	31 45	45	95	32 30	46	94	33 16	45	94
67	29 37	46	96	30 23	46	95	31 09	45	94	31 54	46	94	32 40	45	93
68	29 01	46	95	29 47	46	94	30 33	45	94	31 18	46	93	32 04	45	92
69	28 25	46	94	29 11	46	93	29 57	45	93	30 42	45	92	31 27	45	91

25° Hc	d	Z	26° Hc	d	Z	27° Hc	d	Z	28° Hc	d	Z	29° Hc	d	Z	LHA
° ′	′	°	° ′	′	°	° ′	′	°	° ′	′	°	° ′	′	°	
62 00	+60	180	63 00	+60	180	64 00	+60	180	65 00	+60	180	66 00	+60	180	360
61 59	60	178	62 59	60	178	63 59	60	178	64 59	60	178	65 59	60	178	359
61 58	60	176	62 58	59	176	63 57	60	176	64 57	60	176	65 57	60	176	358
61 55	59	174	62 54	60	174	63 54	60	174	64 54	60	174	65 54	60	174	357
61 50	60	172	62 50	60	172	63 50	60	172	64 50	59	172	65 49	60	171	356
61 45	+60	170	62 45	+59	170	63 44	+60	170	64 44	+59	170	65 43	+60	169	355
61 38	60	169	62 38	59	168	63 37	60	168	64 37	59	168	65 36	59	167	354
61 31	59	167	62 30	59	166	63 29	59	166	64 28	59	166	65 27	59	165	353
61 22	59	165	62 21	59	164	63 20	59	164	64 19	58	164	65 17	59	163	352
61 12	58	163	62 10	59	163	63 09	59	162	64 08	58	162	65 06	59	161	351
61 00	+59	161	61 59	+58	161	62 57	+59	160	63 56	+58	160	64 54	+58	159	350
60 48	58	160	61 46	58	159	62 44	59	158	63 43	57	158	64 40	58	157	349
60 35	58	157	61 33	58	157	62 31	57	156	63 28	58	156	64 26	57	155	348
60 20	58	156	61 18	58	155	62 16	57	155	63 13	57	154	64 10	57	153	347
60 05	57	154	61 02	57	153	61 59	57	153	62 56	57	152	63 53	57	151	346
59 49	+57	152	60 46	+56	152	61 42	+57	151	62 39	+56	150	63 35	+56	149	345
59 31	57	151	60 28	56	150	61 24	56	149	62 20	56	148	63 16	56	148	344
59 13	56	149	60 09	56	148	61 05	56	147	62 01	56	147	62 57	55	146	343
58 54	56	147	59 50	55	147	60 45	56	146	61 41	55	145	62 36	55	144	342
58 34	55	146	59 29	56	145	60 25	55	144	61 20	54	143	62 14	54	142	341
58 13	+55	144	59 08	+55	143	60 03	+55	142	60 58	+54	142	61 52	+53	141	340
57 51	55	142	58 46	55	142	59 41	54	141	60 35	53	140	61 28	54	139	339
57 29	54	141	58 23	54	140	59 17	54	139	60 11	53	138	61 04	53	137	338
57 06	54	140	58 00	53	139	58 53	54	138	59 47	52	137	60 39	53	136	337
56 42	54	138	57 36	53	137	58 29	53	136	59 22	52	135	60 14	52	134	336
56 17	+54	136	57 11	+52	136	58 03	+53	135	58 56	+52	134	59 48	+51	133	335
55 52	53	135	56 45	52	134	57 37	52	133	58 29	52	132	59 21	51	131	334
55 26	53	134	56 19	52	133	57 11	51	132	58 02	51	131	58 53	51	130	333
55 00	52	132	55 52	51	131	56 43	52	130	57 35	50	129	58 25	51	128	332
54 33	51	131	55 24	52	130	56 16	50	129	57 06	51	128	57 57	50	127	331
54 05	+51	129	54 56	+51	129	55 47	+51	128	56 38	+50	127	57 28	+49	126	330
53 37	51	128	54 28	50	127	55 18	51	126	56 09	49	125	56 58	49	124	329
53 08	51	127	53 59	50	126	54 49	50	125	55 39	49	124	56 28	49	123	328
52 39	50	126	53 29	50	125	54 19	50	124	55 09	49	123	55 58	48	122	327
52 09	50	124	52 59	50	123	53 49	49	122	54 38	49	121	55 27	48	120	326
51 39	+50	123	52 29	+49	122	53 18	+49	121	54 07	+48	120	54 55	+48	119	325
51 09	49	122	51 58	49	121	52 47	49	120	53 36	48	119	54 24	47	118	324
50 38	49	121	51 27	49	120	52 16	48	119	53 04	48	118	53 52	47	117	323
50 07	49	120	50 56	48	119	51 44	48	118	52 32	47	117	53 19	47	116	322
49 35	49	118	50 24	48	118	51 12	47	117	51 59	47	116	52 46	47	115	321
49 03	+49	117	49 52	+47	116	50 39	+48	115	51 27	+46	114	52 13	+47	113	320
48 31	48	116	49 19	48	115	50 07	47	114	50 54	46	113	51 40	46	112	319
47 59	47	115	48 46	48	114	49 34	46	113	50 20	47	112	51 07	45	111	318
47 26	47	114	48 13	47	113	49 00	47	112	49 47	46	111	50 33	45	110	317
46 53	47	113	47 40	47	112	48 27	46	111	49 13	46	110	49 59	45	109	316
46 19	+47	112	47 06	+47	111	47 53	+46	110	48 39	+46	109	49 25	+45	108	315
45 46	46	111	46 32	47	110	47 19	46	109	48 05	45	108	48 50	45	107	314
45 12	46	110	45 58	47	109	46 45	45	108	47 30	46	107	48 16	44	106	313
44 38	46	109	45 24	46	108	46 10	46	107	46 56	45	106	47 41	44	105	312
44 03	47	108	44 50	46	107	45 36	45	106	46 21	45	105	47 06	44	104	311
43 29	+46	107	44 15	+46	106	45 01	+45	105	45 46	+45	104	46 31	+44	103	310
42 54	46	106	43 40	46	105	44 26	45	104	45 11	45	103	45 56	44	102	309
42 19	46	105	43 05	46	104	43 51	45	103	44 36	44	102	45 20	44	101	308
41 45	45	104	42 30	46	103	43 16	44	102	44 00	45	101	44 45	44	100	307
41 09	46	103	41 55	45	102	42 40	45	101	43 25	44	101	44 09	44	100	306
40 34	+46	102	41 20	+45	101	42 05	+44	101	42 49	+45	100	43 34	+43	99	305
39 59	45	101	40 44	45	101	41 29	45	100	42 14	44	99	42 58	43	98	304
39 23	46	100	40 09	44	100	40 53	45	99	41 38	44	98	42 22	44	97	303
38 48	45	99	39 33	45	99	40 18	44	98	41 02	44	97	41 46	44	96	302
38 12	45	99	38 57	45	98	39 42	44	97	40 26	44	96	41 10	44	95	301
37 36	+45	98	38 21	+45	97	39 06	+44	96	39 50	+44	95	40 34	+44	94	300
37 01	45	97	37 46	44	96	38 30	44	95	39 14	44	94	39 58	44	94	299
36 25	45	96	37 10	44	95	37 54	44	94	38 38	44	94	39 22	43	93	298
35 49	45	95	36 34	44	94	37 18	44	94	38 02	44	93	38 46	43	92	297
35 13	45	94	35 58	44	94	36 42	44	93	37 26	44	92	38 10	43	91	296
34 37	+45	93	35 22	+44	93	36 06	+44	92	36 50	+44	91	37 34	+43	90	295
34 01	45	93	34 46	44	92	35 30	44	91	36 14	44	90	36 58	43	90	294
33 25	44	92	34 09	45	91	34 54	44	90	35 38	44	90	36 22	43	89	293
32 49	44	91	33 33	45	90	34 18	44	90	35 02	44	89	35 46	43	88	292
32 12	45	90	32 57	45	90	33 42	44	89	34 26	43	88	35 09	44	87	291

N. Lat. {LHA greater than 180°....... Zn=Z
{LHA less than 180°........... Zn=360−Z

DECLINATION (15°-29°) SAME NAME AS LATITUDE

	15°			16°			17°			18°			19°			
LHA	Hc	d	Z	Hc	d	Z	Hc	d	Z	Hc	d	Z	Hc	d	Z	LHA
	° ′	′	°	° ′	′	°	° ′	′	°	° ′	′	°	° ′	′	°	
70	23 55	+48	97	24 43	+46	96	25 29	+47	95	26 16	+47	95	27 03	+46	94	290
71	23 20	47	96	24 07	46	95	24 53	47	95	25 40	46	94	26 26	47	93	289
72	22 44	47	95	23 31	46	95	24 17	47	94	25 04	46	93	25 50	47	92	288
73	22 08	47	94	22 55	46	94	23 41	47	93	24 28	46	92	25 14	47	92	287
74	21 32	47	94	22 19	46	93	23 05	47	92	23 52	46	92	24 38	46	91	286
75	20 56	+46	93	21 42	+47	92	22 29	+47	91	23 16	+46	91	24 02	+46	90	285
76	20 20	46	92	21 06	47	91	21 53	47	91	22 40	46	90	23 26	46	89	284
77	19 43	47	91	20 30	47	90	21 17	47	90	22 04	46	89	22 50	46	88	283
78	19 07	47	90	19 54	47	90	20 41	46	89	21 27	47	88	22 14	46	88	282
79	18 31	47	90	19 18	47	89	20 05	46	88	20 51	47	88	21 38	46	87	281
80	17 55	+47	89	18 42	+47	88	19 29	+46	87	20 15	+47	87	21 02	+46	86	280
81	17 19	47	88	18 06	47	87	18 53	46	87	19 39	47	86	20 26	46	85	279
82	16 43	47	87	17 30	47	87	18 17	46	86	19 03	47	85	19 50	46	85	278
83	16 07	47	86	16 54	47	86	17 41	46	85	18 27	47	84	19 14	46	84	277
84	15 31	47	86	16 18	47	85	17 05	46	84	17 51	47	84	18 38	46	83	276
85	14 55	+47	85	15 42	+47	84	16 29	+47	84	17 16	+46	83	18 02	+47	82	275
86	14 19	47	84	15 06	47	83	15 53	47	83	16 40	46	82	17 26	47	81	274
87	13 43	47	83	14 30	47	83	15 17	47	82	16 04	47	81	16 51	46	81	273
88	13 07	47	82	13 54	47	82	14 41	47	81	15 28	47	81	16 15	47	80	272
89	12 31	48	82	13 19	47	81	14 06	47	80	14 53	47	80	15 40	46	79	271
90	11 56	+47	81	12 43	+47	80	13 30	+47	80	14 17	+47	79	15 04	+47	78	270
91	11 20	48	80	12 08	47	79	12 55	47	79	13 42	47	78	14 29	47	78	269
92	10 45	47	79	11 32	47	79	12 19	48	78	13 07	47	77	13 54	47	77	268
93	10 09	48	79	10 57	47	78	11 44	47	77	12 31	48	77	13 19	47	76	267
94	09 34	47	78	10 21	48	77	11 09	47	77	11 56	48	76	12 44	47	75	266
95	08 59	+47	77	09 46	+48	76	10 34	+47	76	11 21	+48	75	12 09	+47	75	265
96	08 24	47	76	09 11	48	76	09 59	48	75	10 47	47	74	11 34	48	74	264
97	07 49	47	75	08 36	48	75	09 24	48	74	10 12	48	74	11 00	47	73	263
98	07 14	48	75	08 02	47	74	08 49	48	73	09 37	48	73	10 25	48	72	262
99	06 39	48	74	07 27	48	73	08 15	48	73	09 03	48	72	09 51	48	71	261
100	06 04	+48	73	06 52	+49	73	07 41	+48	72	08 29	+48	71	09 17	+48	71	260
101	05 30	48	72	06 18	48	72	07 06	49	71	07 55	48	71	08 43	48	70	259
102	04 55	49	72	05 44	48	71	06 32	49	70	07 21	48	70	08 09	48	69	258
103	04 21	49	71	05 10	48	70	05 58	49	70	06 47	48	69	07 35	49	68	257
104	03 47	49	70	04 36	49	69	05 25	48	69	06 13	49	68	07 02	48	68	256
105	03 13	+49	69	04 02	+49	69	04 51	+49	68	05 40	+48	67	06 28	+49	67	255
106	02 40	49	68	03 29	49	68	04 18	49	67	05 07	48	67	05 55	49	66	254
107	02 06	49	68	02 55	49	67	03 44	49	66	04 33	49	66	05 22	49	65	253
108	01 33	49	67	02 22	49	66	03 11	50	66	04 01	49	65	04 50	49	64	252
109	01 00	49	66	01 49	50	65	02 39	49	65	03 28	49	64	04 17	50	64	251
110	00 27	+50	65	01 17	+49	65	02 06	+50	64	02 56	+49	63	03 45	+49	63	250
111	−0 06	50	64	00 44	50	64	01 34	49	63	02 23	50	63	03 13	50	62	249
112	−0 38	50	64	00 12	50	63	01 02	49	62	01 51	50	62	02 41	50	61	248
113	−1 10	50	63	−0 20	50	62	00 30	50	62	01 20	50	61	02 10	49	61	247
114	−1 42	50	62	−0 52	50	61	−0 02	50	61	00 48	50	60	01 38	50	60	246
115	−2 14	+50	61	−1 24	+51	61	−0 33	+50	61	00 17	+50	60	01 07	+50	59	245
116	−2 46	51	60	−1 55	50	60	−1 05	51	60	−0 14	50	59	00 36	51	58	244
117	−3 17	51	60	−2 26	50	59	−1 36	51	59	−0 45	51	58	00 06	50	57	243
118	−3 48	51	59	−2 57	51	58	−2 06	51	58	−1 15	50	57	−0 25	51	57	242
119	−4 18	50	58	−3 28	51	57	−2 37	51	57	−1 46	51	56	−0 55	51	56	241
120	−4 49	+51	57	−3 58	+51	57	−3 07	+52	57	−2 15	+51	56	−1 24	+51	55	240
121	−5 19	51	56	−4 28	52	56	−3 36	51	56	−2 45	51	55	−1 54	52	54	239
122	−5 49	52	55	−4 57	51	55	−4 06	52	55	−3 14	51	54	−2 23	52	53	238
123				−5 27	52	54	−4 35	52	54	−3 43	51	53	−2 52	52	53	237
124				−5 56	52	53	−5 04	52	53	−4 12	52	52	−3 20	52	52	236
125							−5 33	+53	52	−4 40	+52	51	−3 48	+52	51	235
126										−5 09	53	51	−4 16	52	50	234
127										−5 36	52	50	−4 44	53	49	233
128													−5 11	53	48	232
129													−5 38	53	48	231

	20°			21°			22°			23°			24°			
LHA	Hc	d	Z	Hc	d	Z	Hc	d	Z	Hc	d	Z	Hc	d	Z	LHA
	° ′	′	°	° ′	′	°	° ′	′	°	° ′	′	°	° ′	′	°	
70	27 49	+46	93	28 35	+46	93	29 21	+45	92	30 06	+45	91	30 51	+45	90	290
71	27 13	46	93	27 59	45	92	28 44	46	91	29 30	45	90	30 15	45	90	289
72	26 37	46	92	27 23	45	91	28 08	46	90	28 54	45	90	29 39	45	89	288
73	26 01	45	91	26 46	46	90	27 32	46	89	28 18	45	89	29 03	45	88	287
74	25 24	46	90	26 10	46	89	26 56	46	89	27 42	45	88	28 27	45	87	286
75	24 48	+46	89	25 34	+46	89	26 20	+46	88	27 06	+45	87	27 51	+45	86	285
76	24 12	46	89	24 58	46	88	25 44	46	87	26 30	45	86	27 15	45	86	284
77	23 36	46	88	24 22	46	87	25 08	46	86	25 54	45	86	26 39	45	85	283
78	23 00	46	87	23 46	46	86	24 32	46	86	25 18	45	85	26 03	45	84	282
79	22 24	46	86	23 10	46	85	23 56	46	85	24 42	45	84	25 27	45	83	281
80	21 48	+46	85	22 34	+46	85	23 20	+46	84	24 06	+45	83	24 51	+46	83	280
81	21 12	46	85	21 58	46	84	22 44	46	83	23 30	46	83	24 16	45	82	279
82	20 36	46	84	21 22	46	83	22 08	46	82	22 54	46	82	23 40	45	81	278
83	20 00	46	83	20 46	47	82	21 33	45	82	22 18	46	81	23 04	46	80	277
84	19 24	47	82	20 11	46	82	20 57	46	81	21 43	46	80	22 29	45	80	276
85	18 49	+46	82	19 35	+46	81	20 21	+46	80	21 07	+46	79	21 53	+46	79	275
86	18 13	46	81	18 59	47	80	19 46	46	79	20 32	46	79	21 18	46	78	274
87	17 37	47	80	18 24	46	79	19 10	46	79	19 56	47	78	20 43	45	77	273
88	17 02	46	79	17 48	47	79	18 35	46	78	19 21	46	77	20 07	46	77	272
89	16 26	47	78	17 13	47	78	18 00	46	77	18 46	46	76	19 32	46	76	271
90	15 51	+47	78	16 38	+47	77	17 25	+46	76	18 11	+46	76	18 57	+47	75	270
91	15 16	47	77	16 03	47	76	16 50	46	76	17 36	47	75	18 23	46	74	269
92	14 41	47	76	15 28	47	76	16 15	46	75	17 01	47	74	17 48	46	74	268
93	14 06	47	75	14 53	47	75	15 40	47	74	16 27	46	73	17 13	47	73	267
94	13 31	47	75	14 18	47	74	15 05	47	73	15 52	47	73	16 39	47	72	266
95	12 56	+47	74	13 43	+48	73	14 31	+47	73	15 18	+47	72	16 05	+46	71	265
96	12 22	47	73	13 09	47	73	13 56	47	72	14 43	48	71	15 31	46	71	264
97	11 47	48	72	12 35	47	72	13 22	47	71	14 09	48	70	14 57	47	70	263
98	11 13	47	72	12 00	48	71	12 48	47	70	13 35	48	70	14 23	47	69	262
99	10 39	47	71	11 26	48	70	12 14	48	70	13 02	47	69	13 49	47	68	261
100	10 05	+47	70	10 52	+48	69	11 40	+48	69	12 28	+48	68	13 16	+47	68	260
101	09 31	48	69	10 19	48	69	11 07	48	68	11 55	47	67	12 42	48	67	259
102	08 57	48	69	09 45	48	68	10 33	48	67	11 21	48	67	12 09	48	66	258
103	08 24	48	68	09 12	48	67	10 00	48	67	10 48	48	66	11 36	48	65	257
104	07 50	49	67	08 39	48	66	09 27	48	66	10 15	49	65	11 04	48	65	256
105	07 17	+49	66	08 06	+48	66	08 54	+49	65	09 43	+48	64	10 31	+48	64	255
106	06 44	49	65	07 33	49	65	08 22	48	64	09 10	49	64	09 59	48	63	254
107	06 11	49	65	07 00	49	64	07 49	49	64	08 38	49	63	09 27	48	62	253
108	05 39	49	64	06 28	49	63	07 17	49	63	08 06	49	62	08 55	49	62	252
109	05 07	49	63	05 56	49	63	06 45	49	62	07 34	49	61	08 23	49	61	251
110	04 34	+50	62	05 24	+49	62	06 13	+50	61	07 03	+49	61	07 52	+49	60	250
111	04 03	49	62	04 52	50	61	05 42	49	60	06 31	50	60	07 21	49	59	249
112	03 31	50	61	04 21	49	60	05 10	50	60	06 00	50	59	06 50	49	59	248
113	02 59	50	60	03 49	50	59	04 39	50	59	05 29	50	58	06 19	50	58	247
114	02 28	50	59	03 18	50	59	04 08	51	58	04 59	50	58	05 49	50	57	246
115	01 57	+51	58	02 48	+50	58	03 38	+50	57	04 28	+50	57	05 18	+51	56	245
116	01 27	50	58	02 17	51	57	03 08	50	57	03 58	51	56	04 49	50	56	244
117	00 56	51	57	01 47	51	56	02 38	50	56	03 28	51	55	04 19	51	55	243
118	00 26	51	56	01 17	51	56	02 08	51	55	02 59	51	54	03 50	50	54	242
119	−0 04	52	55	00 48	51	55	01 39	51	54	02 30	51	54	03 21	50	53	241
120	−0 33	+51	54	00 18	+51	54	01 09	+52	53	02 01	+51	53	02 52	+51	52	240
121	−1 02	51	54	−0 11	52	53	00 41	51	53	01 32	51	52	02 23	52	52	239
122	−1 31	51	53	−0 40	52	52	00 12	52	52	01 04	51	51	01 55	52	51	238
123	−2 00	52	52	−1 08	52	52	−0 16	52	51	00 36	51	51	01 27	52	50	237
124	−2 28	52	51	−1 36	52	51	−0 44	52	50	00 08	52	50	01 00	52	49	236
125	−2 56	+52	50	−2 04	+52	50	−1 12	+52	49	−0 20	+53	49	00 33	+52	48	235
126	−3 24	53	50	−2 31	52	49	−1 39	52	49	−0 47	53	48	00 06	52	48	234
127	−3 51	52	49	−2 59	53	48	−2 06	53	48	−1 13	52	47	−0 21	53	47	233
128	−4 18	53	48	−3 25	52	47	−2 33	53	47	−1 40	53	47	−0 47	53	46	232
129	−4 45	53	47	−3 52	53	47	−2 59	53	46	−2 06	53	46	−1 13	53	45	231
130	−5 11	+53	46	−4 18	+53	46	−3 25	+54	45	−2 31	+53	45	−1 38	+53	45	230
131	−5 37	53	45	−4 44	54	45	−3 50	53	45	−2 57	54	44	−2 03	53	44	229
132				−5 09	54	44	−4 15	53	44	−3 22	54	43	−2 28	54	43	228
133				−5 34	54	43	−4 40	54	43	−3 46	54	42	−2 52	53	42	227
134							−5 04	54	42	−4 10	54	42	−3 16	54	41	226
135							−5 28	+54	41	−4 34	+54	41	−3 40	+54	40	225
136										−4 58	55	40	−4 03	54	40	224
137										−5 21	55	39	−4 26	55	39	223
138										−5 43	55	38	−4 48	55	38	222
139													−5 10	55	37	221

	25°			26°			27°			28°			29°			
LHA	Hc	d	Z	Hc	d	Z	Hc	d	Z	Hc	d	Z	Hc	d	Z	LHA
	° ′	′	°	° ′	′	°	° ′	′	°	° ′	′	°	° ′	′	°	
70	31 36	+45	90	32 21	+45	89	33 06	+44	88	33 50	+43	87	34 33	+44	86	290
71	31 00	45	89	31 45	44	88	32 29	45	87	33 14	43	86	33 57	44	86	289
72	30 24	45	88	31 09	44	87	31 53	45	86	32 38	43	86	33 21	44	85	288
73	29 48	45	87	30 33	44	86	31 17	45	86	32 02	43	85	32 45	44	84	287
74	29 12	45	86	29 57	44	86	30 41	45	85	31 26	44	84	32 10	43	83	286
75	28 36	+45	86	29 21	+44	85	30 05	+45	84	30 50	+44	83	31 34	+43	83	285
76	28 00	45	85	28 45	45	84	29 30	44	83	30 14	44	83	30 58	44	82	284
77	27 24	45	84	28 09	45	83	28 54	44	83	29 38	44	82	30 22	44	81	283
78	26 48	45	83	27 33	45	83	28 18	44	82	29 02	45	81	29 47	44	80	282
79	26 12	45	83	26 57	45	82	27 42	45	81	28 27	44	80	29 11	44	80	281
80	25 37	+45	82	26 22	+45	81	27 07	+44	80	27 51	+45	80	28 36	+44	79	280
81	25 01	45	81	25 46	45	80	26 31	45	80	27 16	44	79	28 00	45	78	279
82	24 25	46	80	25 11	45	80	25 56	44	79	26 40	45	78	27 25	44	77	278
83	23 50	45	80	24 35	45	79	25 20	45	78	26 05	45	77	26 50	44	77	277
84	23 14	46	79	24 00	45	78	24 45	45	77	25 30	45	77	26 15	44	76	276
85	22 39	+45	78	23 24	+46	77	24 10	+45	77	24 55	+45	76	25 40	+44	75	275
86	22 04	45	77	22 49	46	77	23 35	45	76	24 20	45	75	25 05	45	74	274
87	21 28	46	77	22 14	46	76	23 00	45	75	23 45	45	74	24 30	45	74	273
88	20 53	46	76	21 39	46	75	22 25	45	74	23 10	46	74	23 56	45	73	272
89	20 18	46	75	21 04	46	74	21 50	46	74	22 36	45	73	23 21	45	72	271
90	19 44	+46	74	20 30	+46	74	21 16	+45	73	22 01	+46	72	22 47	+45	72	270
91	19 09	46	74	19 55	46	73	20 41	46	72	21 27	46	72	22 13	45	71	269
92	18 34	47	73	19 21	46	72	20 07	46	72	20 53	46	71	21 39	45	70	268
93	18 00	46	72	18 46	47	71	19 33	46	71	20 19	46	70	21 05	46	69	267
94	17 26	46	71	18 12	47	71	18 59	46	70	19 45	46	69	20 31	46	69	266
95	16 51	+47	71	17 38	+47	70	18 25	+46	69	19 11	+46	69	19 57	+47	68	265
96	16 17	47	70	17 04	47	69	17 51	47	69	18 38	46	68	19 24	46	67	264
97	15 44	47	69	16 31	47	69	17 18	46	68	18 04	47	67	18 51	46	67	263
98	15 10	47	68	15 57	47	68	16 44	47	67	17 31	47	67	18 18	46	66	262
99	14 36	48	68	15 24	47	67	16 11	47	66	16 58	47	66	17 45	47	65	261
100	14 03	+48	67	14 51	+47	66	15 38	+47	66	16 25	+47	65	17 12	+47	64	260
101	13 30	48	66	14 18	47	66	15 05	48	65	15 53	47	64	16 40	47	64	259
102	12 57	48	66	13 45	48	65	14 33	47	64	15 20	48	64	16 08	47	63	258
103	12 24	48	65	13 12	48	64	14 00	48	64	14 48	48	63	15 36	47	62	257
104	11 52	48	64	12 40	48	63	13 28	48	63	14 16	48	62	15 04	47	62	256
105	11 19	+49	63	12 08	+48	63	12 56	+48	62	13 44	+48	61	14 32	+48	61	255
106	10 47	49	63	11 36	48	62	12 24	48	61	13 12	49	61	14 01	48	60	254
107	10 15	49	62	11 04	49	61	11 53	48	61	12 41	49	60	13 30	48	59	253
108	09 44	49	61	10 33	48	60	11 21	49	60	12 10	49	59	12 59	48	59	252
109	09 12	49	60	10 01	49	60	10 50	49	59	11 39	49	59	12 28	49	58	251
110	08 41	+49	60	09 30	+49	59	10 19	+49	58	11 08	+49	58	11 57	+49	57	250
111	08 10	49	59	08 59	50	58	09 49	49	58	10 38	49	57	11 27	49	56	249
112	07 39	50	58	08 29	49	57	09 18	50	57	10 08	49	56	10 57	50	56	248
113	07 09	50	57	07 59	49	57	08 48	50	56	09 38	50	56	10 28	49	55	247
114	06 39	50	57	07 29	49	56	08 18	50	55	09 08	50	55	09 58	50	54	246
115	06 09	+50	56	06 59	+50	55	07 49	+50	55	08 39	+50	54	09 29	+50	54	245
116	05 39	50	55	06 29	51	54	07 20	50	54	08 10	50	53	09 00	50	53	244
117	05 10	50	54	06 00	51	54	06 51	50	53	07 41	50	53	08 31	51	52	243
118	04 40	51	53	05 31	51	53	06 22	51	52	07 13	50	52	08 03	51	51	242
119	04 11	51	53	05 02	51	52	05 53	51	52	06 44	51	51	07 35	51	51	241
120	03 43	+51	52	04 34	+51	51	05 25	+51	51	06 16	+51	50	07 07	+51	50	240
121	03 15	51	51	04 06	51	51	04 57	52	50	05 49	51	50	06 40	51	49	239
122	02 47	51	50	03 38	52	50	04 30	51	49	05 21	52	49	06 13	51	48	238
123	02 19	52	49	03 11	52	49	04 03	51	49	04 54	52	48	05 46	52	48	237
124	01 52	52	48	02 44	52	48	03 36	52	48	04 28	52	47	05 20	52	47	236
125	01 25	+52	48	02 17	+52	48	03 09	+52	47	04 01	+53	47	04 54	+52	46	235
126	00 58	53	47	01 51	52	47	02 43	52	46	03 35	53	46	04 28	52	45	234
127	00 32	52	46	01 24	53	46	02 17	53	45	03 10	52	45	04 02	53	44	233
128	00 06	53	46	00 59	53	45	01 52	52	45	02 44	53	44	03 37	53	44	232
129	−0 20	53	45	00 33	53	44	01 26	53	44	02 19	53	43	03 12	53	43	231
130	−0 45	+53	44	00 08	+54	44	01 02	+53	43	01 55	+53	43	02 48	+53	42	230
131	−1 10	54	43	−0 16	53	43	00 37	54	42	01 31	53	42	02 24	53	41	229
132	−1 34	53	42	−0 41	54	42	00 13	54	42	01 07	53	41	02 00	54	41	228
133	−1 59	54	42	−1 05	54	41	−0 11	54	41	00 43	54	40	01 37	54	40	227
134	−2 22	54	41	−1 28	54	40	−0 34	54	40	00 20	54	39	01 14	54	39	226
135	−2 46	+55	40	−1 51	+54	40	−0 57	+54	39	−0 03	+55	39	00 52	+54	38	225
136	−3 09	55	39	−2 14	54	39	−1 20	55	38	−0 25	55	38	00 30	54	37	224
137	−3 31	55	38	−2 36	54	38	−1 42	55	37	−0 47	55	37	00 00	54	37	223
138	−3 53	55	38	−2 58	54	37	−2 04	55	37	−1 09	55	36	−0 14	55	36	222
139	−4 15	55	37	−3 20	55	36	−2 25	55	36	−1 30	55	35	−0 35	55	35	221

LAT 53°

15°	16°	17°	18°	19°	20°	21°	22°	23°	24°	25°	26°	27°	28°	29°

S. Lat. {LHA greater than 180°........ Zn=180−Z
{LHA less than 180°........... Zn=180+Z

DECLINATION (15°-29°) SAME NAME AS LATITUDE

N. Lat. {LHA greater than 180°....... Zn=Z; LHA less than 180°.......... Zn=360−Z}

DECLINATION (15°-29°) SAME NAME AS LATITUDE

LAT 53°

LHA	15° Hc d Z	16° Hc d Z	17° Hc d Z	18° Hc d Z	19° Hc d Z	20° Hc d Z	21° Hc d Z	22° Hc d Z	23° Hc d Z	24° Hc d Z	25° Hc d Z	26° Hc d Z	27° Hc d Z	28° Hc d Z	29° Hc d Z	LHA
	° ′ ′ °	° ′ ′ °	° ′ ′ °	° ′ ′ °	° ′ ′ °	° ′ ′ °	° ′ ′ °	° ′ ′ °	° ′ ′ °	° ′ ′ °	° ′ ′ °	° ′ ′ °	° ′ ′ °	° ′ ′ °	° ′ ′ °	
140										−5 32 +56 36	−4 36 +55 36	−3 41 +55 35	−2 46 +56 35	−1 50 +55 35	−0 55 +55 34	220
141											−4 57 55 35	−4 02 56 35	−3 06 55 34	−2 11 56 34	−1 15 55 33	219
142											−5 18 56 34	−4 22 56 34	−3 26 55 33	−2 31 56 33	−1 35 56 33	218
143											−5 38 56 33	−4 42 56 33	−3 46 56 33	−2 50 56 32	−1 54 56 32	217
144												−5 01 56 32	−4 05 56 32	−3 09 56 31	−2 13 56 31	216
145												−5 20 +56 31	−4 24 +56 31	−3 28 +57 31	−2 31 +56 30	215
146													−4 42 56 30	−3 46 57 30	−2 49 56 29	214
147													−5 00 57 29	−4 03 56 29	−3 07 57 29	213
148													−5 17 57 28	−4 20 56 28	−3 24 57 28	212
149														−4 37 57 27	−3 40 57 27	211
150														−4 53 +57 26	−3 56 +57 26	210
151														−5 09 57 25	−4 12 58 25	209
152														−5 24 57 25	−4 27 58 24	208
153															−4 42 58 23	207
154															−4 56 58 23	206
155															−5 09 +58 22	205
156															−5 23 59 21	204

LHA	15° Hc d Z	16° Hc d Z	17° Hc d Z	18° Hc d Z	19° Hc d Z	20° Hc d Z	21° Hc d Z	22°	23°	24°	25°	26°	27°	28°	29°	LHA
80	−6 04 −49 107															280
79	−5 30 48 108															281
78	−4 55 49 108	−5 44 48 109														282
77	−4 21 49 109	−5 10 48 110	−5 58 49 110													283
76	−3 47 49 110	−4 36 49 111	−5 25 48 111													284
75	−3 13 −49 111	−4 02 −49 111	−4 51 −49 112	−5 40 −48 113												285
74	−2 40 49 112	−3 29 49 112	−4 18 49 113	−5 07 48 113	−5 55 49 114											286
73	−2 06 49 112	−2 55 49 113	−3 44 49 114	−4 33 49 114	−5 22 49 115											287
72	−1 33 49 113	−2 22 49 114	−3 11 50 114	−4 01 49 115	−4 50 49 116	−5 39 49 116										288
71	−1 00 49 114	−1 49 50 115	−2 39 49 115	−3 28 49 116	−4 17 50 116	−5 07 49 117	−5 56 49 117									289
70	−0 27 −50 115	−1 17 −49 115	−2 06 −50 116	−2 56 −49 117	−3 45 −49 117	−4 34 −50 118	−5 24 −49 118									290

S. Lat. {LHA greater than 180°....... Zn=180−Z; LHA less than 180°.......... Zn=180+Z}

DECLINATION (15°-29°) CONTRARY NAME TO LATITUDE

N. Lat. {LHA greater than 180°....... Zn=Z; LHA less than 180°.......... Zn=360−Z}

DECLINATION (15°-29°) CONTRARY NAME TO LATITUDE

LHA	15°			16°			17°			18°			19°			20°			21°			22°		
	Hc	d	Z	Hc	d	Z	Hc	d	Z	Hc	d	Z	Hc	d	Z	Hc	d	Z	Hc	d	Z	Hc	d	Z
	° ′	′	°	° ′	′	°	° ′	′	°	° ′	′	°	° ′	′	°	° ′	′	°	° ′	′	°	° ′	′	°
69	00 06	50	116	-0 44	50	116	-1 34	49	117	-2 23	50	117	-3 13	50	118	-4 03	49	118	-4 52	50	119	-5 42	49	120
68	00 38	50	116	-0 12	50	117	-1 02	49	118	-1 51	50	118	-2 41	50	119	-3 31	50	119	-4 21	49	120	-5 10	50	120
67	01 10	50	117	00 20	50	118	-0 30	50	118	-1 20	50	119	-2 10	49	119	-2 59	50	120	-3 49	50	121	-4 39	50	121
66	01 42	50	118	00 52	50	119	00 02	50	119	-0 48	50	120	-1 38	50	120	-2 28	50	121	-3 18	50	121	-4 08	51	122
65	02 14	-50	119	01 24	-51	119	00 33	-50	119	-0 17	-50	120	-1 07	-50	121	-1 57	-51	122	-2 48	-50	122	-3 38	-50	123
64	02 46	51	120	01 55	50	120	01 05	51	120	00 14	50	121	-0 36	51	122	-1 27	50	122	-2 17	51	123	-3 08	50	123
63	03 17	51	120	02 26	50	121	01 36	51	121	00 45	51	122	-0 06	50	123	-0 56	51	123	-1 47	51	124	-2 38	50	124
62	03 48	51	121	02 57	51	122	02 06	51	122	01 15	50	123	00 25	51	123	-0 26	51	124	-1 17	51	124	-2 08	51	125
61	04 18	50	122	03 28	51	123	02 37	51	123	01 46	51	124	00 55	51	124	00 04	52	125	-0 48	51	125	-1 39	51	126
60	04 49	-51	123	03 58	-51	123	03 07	-52	123	02 15	-51	124	01 24	-51	125	00 33	-51	126	-0 18	-51	126	-1 09	-52	127
59	05 19	51	124	04 28	52	124	03 36	51	124	02 45	51	125	01 54	52	126	01 02	51	126	00 11	52	127	-0 41	51	127
58	05 49	52	125	04 57	51	125	04 06	52	125	03 14	51	126	02 23	52	127	01 31	51	127	00 40	52	128	-0 12	52	128
57	06 19	52	125	05 27	52	126	04 35	52	126	03 43	51	127	02 52	52	127	02 00	52	128	01 08	52	128	00 16	52	129
56	06 48	52	126	05 56	52	127	05 04	52	127	04 12	52	128	03 20	52	128	02 28	52	129	01 36	52	129	00 44	52	130
55	07 17	-52	127	06 25	-52	128	05 33	-53	128	04 40	-52	129	03 48	-52	129	02 56	-52	130	02 04	-52	130	01 12	-52	131
54	07 46	53	128	06 53	52	128	06 01	52	129	05 09	53	129	04 16	52	130	03 24	53	130	02 31	52	131	01 39	52	131
53	08 14	53	129	07 21	52	129	06 29	53	130	05 36	52	130	04 44	53	131	03 51	52	131	02 59	53	132	02 06	53	132
52	08 42	53	130	07 49	53	130	06 56	52	131	06 04	53	131	05 11	53	132	04 18	53	132	03 25	52	133	02 33	53	133
51	09 09	52	131	08 17	53	131	07 24	53	132	06 31	53	132	05 38	53	132	04 45	53	133	03 52	53	133	02 59	53	134
50	09 37	-53	131	08 44	-53	132	07 51	-54	132	06 57	-53	133	06 04	-53	133	05 11	-53	134	04 18	-53	134	03 25	-54	135
49	10 04	54	132	09 10	53	133	08 17	53	133	07 24	54	134	06 30	53	134	05 37	53	135	04 44	54	135	03 50	53	135
48	10 30	53	133	09 37	54	134	08 43	53	134	07 50	54	135	06 56	53	135	06 03	54	135	05 09	54	136	04 15	53	136
47	10 56	53	134	10 03	54	134	09 09	54	135	08 15	53	135	07 22	54	136	06 28	54	136	05 34	54	137	04 40	54	137
46	11 22	54	135	10 28	54	135	09 34	54	136	08 40	53	136	07 47	54	137	06 53	54	137	05 59	55	138	05 04	54	138
45	11 48	-55	136	10 53	-54	136	09 59	-54	137	09 05	-54	137	08 11	-54	138	07 17	-54	138	06 23	-55	138	05 28	-54	139
44	12 13	55	137	11 18	54	137	10 24	54	138	09 30	55	138	08 35	54	138	07 41	55	139	06 46	54	139	05 52	54	140
43	12 37	54	138	11 43	55	138	10 48	54	138	09 54	55	139	08 59	55	139	08 04	54	140	07 10	55	140	06 15	54	141
42	13 01	54	138	12 07	55	139	11 12	55	139	10 17	55	140	09 22	54	140	08 28	55	141	07 33	55	141	06 38	55	141
41	13 25	55	139	12 30	55	140	11 35	55	140	10 40	55	141	09 45	55	141	08 50	55	141	07 55	55	142	07 00	55	142
40	13 48	-55	140	12 53	-55	141	11 58	-55	141	11 03	-55	142	10 08	-55	142	09 13	-56	142	08 17	-55	143	07 22	-55	143
39	14 11	55	141	13 16	55	142	12 21	56	142	11 25	55	142	10 30	55	143	09 35	56	143	08 39	55	144	07 44	56	144
38	14 34	56	142	13 38	55	143	12 43	56	143	11 47	55	143	10 52	56	144	09 56	56	144	09 00	55	144	08 05	56	145
37	14 56	56	143	14 00	56	143	13 04	56	144	12 08	55	144	11 13	56	145	10 17	56	145	09 21	56	145	08 25	55	146
36	15 17	56	144	14 21	56	144	13 25	56	145	12 29	56	145	11 33	55	145	10 38	56	146	09 42	57	146	08 45	56	147
35	15 38	-56	145	14 42	-56	145	13 46	-56	146	12 50	-56	146	11 54	-56	146	10 58	-57	147	10 01	-56	147	09 05	-56	147
34	15 59	57	146	15 02	56	146	14 06	56	147	13 10	57	147	12 13	56	147	11 17	56	148	10 21	57	148	09 24	56	148
33	16 19	57	147	15 22	56	147	14 26	57	148	13 29	56	148	12 33	57	148	11 36	56	149	10 40	57	149	09 43	56	149
32	16 38	56	148	15 42	57	148	14 45	57	148	13 48	56	149	12 52	57	149	11 55	57	149	10 58	57	150	10 01	56	150
31	16 57	57	149	16 00	56	149	15 04	57	149	14 07	57	150	13 10	57	150	12 13	57	150	11 16	57	151	10 19	57	151
30	17 16	-57	150	16 19	-57	150	15 22	-57	150	14 25	-57	151	13 28	-57	151	12 31	-57	151	11 34	-58	152	10 36	-57	152
29	17 34	57	151	16 37	58	151	15 39	57	151	14 42	57	152	13 45	57	152	12 48	58	152	11 50	57	153	10 53	57	153
28	17 51	57	152	16 54	57	152	15 57	58	152	14 59	57	153	14 02	58	153	13 04	57	153	12 07	58	153	11 09	57	154
27	18 08	57	153	17 11	58	153	16 13	57	153	15 16	58	153	14 18	58	154	13 20	57	154	12 23	58	154	11 25	57	155
26	18 25	58	154	17 27	58	154	16 29	58	154	15 31	57	154	14 34	58	155	13 36	58	155	12 38	57	155	11 41	58	156
25	18 40	-57	155	17 43	-58	155	16 45	-58	155	15 47	-58	155	14 49	-58	156	13 51	-58	156	12 53	-58	156	11 55	-58	156
24	18 56	58	156	17 58	58	156	17 00	58	156	16 02	58	156	15 04	58	157	14 06	58	157	13 08	59	157	12 09	58	157
23	19 10	58	156	18 12	58	157	17 14	58	157	16 16	58	157	15 18	58	158	14 20	59	158	13 21	58	158	12 23	58	158
22	19 24	58	157	18 26	58	158	17 28	58	158	16 30	59	158	15 31	58	158	14 33	58	159	13 35	59	159	12 36	58	159
21	19 38	58	158	18 40	59	159	17 41	58	159	16 43	59	159	15 44	58	159	14 46	59	160	13 47	58	160	12 49	59	160
20	19 51	-59	159	18 52	-58	160	17 54	-59	160	16 55	-58	160	15 57	-59	160	14 58	-59	161	13 59	-58	161	13 01	-59	161
19	20 03	58	160	19 05	59	161	18 06	59	161	17 07	58	161	16 09	59	161	15 10	59	162	14 11	59	162	13 12	58	162
18	20 15	59	161	19 16	58	162	18 18	59	162	17 19	59	162	16 20	59	162	15 21	59	163	14 22	59	163	13 23	59	163
17	20 26	59	163	19 27	59	163	18 28	58	163	17 30	59	163	16 31	59	163	15 32	59	163	14 33	59	164	13 34	59	164
16	20 37	59	164	19 38	59	164	18 39	59	164	17 40	59	164	16 41	59	164	15 42	60	164	14 42	59	165	13 43	59	165
15	20 47	-59	165	19 48	-59	165	18 49	-60	165	17 49	-59	165	16 50	-59	165	15 51	-59	165	14 52	-59	166	13 53	-60	166
14	20 56	59	166	19 57	59	166	18 58	60	166	17 58	59	166	16 59	59	166	16 00	59	166	15 01	60	167	14 01	59	167
13	21 05	59	167	20 06	60	167	19 06	59	167	18 07	60	167	17 07	59	167	16 08	59	167	15 09	60	167	14 09	59	168
12	21 13	59	168	20 14	60	168	19 14	59	168	18 15	60	168	17 15	59	168	16 16	60	168	15 16	59	168	14 17	60	169
11	21 21	60	169	20 21	60	169	19 21	59	169	18 22	60	169	17 22	59	169	16 23	60	169	15 23	59	169	14 24	60	170
10	21 27	-59	170	20 28	-60	170	19 28	-60	170	18 28	-59	170	17 29	-60	170	16 29	-59	170	15 30	-60	170	14 30	-60	170
9	21 34	60	171	20 34	60	171	19 34	60	171	18 34	59	171	17 35	60	171	16 35	60	171	15 35	59	171	14 36	60	171
8	21 39	60	172	20 39	59	172	19 40	60	172	18 40	60	172	17 40	60	172	16 40	59	172	15 41	60	172	14 41	60	172
7	21 44	60	173	20 44	60	173	19 44	59	173	18 45	60	173	17 45	60	173	16 45	60	173	15 45	60	173	14 45	60	173
6	21 48	60	174	20 48	59	174	19 49	60	174	18 49	60	174	17 49	60	174	16 49	60	174	15 49	60	174	14 49	60	174
5	21 52	-60	175	20 52	-60	175	19 52	-60	175	18 52	-60	175	17 52	-60	175	16 52	-60	175	15 52	-60	175	14 52	-59	175
4	21 55	60	176	20 55	60	176	19 55	60	176	18 55	60	176	17 55	60	176	16 55	60	176	15 55	60	176	14 55	60	176
3	21 57	60	177	20 57	60	177	19 57	60	177	18 57	60	177	17 57	60	177	16 57	60	177	15 57	60	177	14 57	60	177
2	21 59	60	178	20 59	60	178	19 59	60	178	18 59	60	178	17 59	60	178	16 59	60	178	15 59	60	178	14 59	60	178
1	22 00	60	179	21 00	60	179	20 00	60	179	19 00	60	179	18 00	60	179	17 00	60	179	16 00	60	179	15 00	60	179
0	22 00	-60	180	21 00	-60	180	20 00	-60	180	19 00	-60	180	18 00	-60	180	17 00	-60	180	16 00	-60	180	15 00	-60	180
	15°			16°			17°			18°			19°			20°			21°			22°		

LHA	23°			24°			25°			26°			27°			28°			29°			LHA
	Hc	d	Z	Hc	d	Z	Hc	d	Z	Hc	d	Z	Hc	d	Z	Hc	d	Z	Hc	d	Z	
	° ′	′	°	° ′	′	°	° ′	′	°	° ′	′	°	° ′	′	°	° ′	′	°	° ′	′	°	
69	291																					
68	-6 00	50	121	292																		
67	-5 29	50	122	293																		
66	-4 59	50	122	-5 49	50	123	294															
65	-4 28	-50	123	-5 18	-51	124	295															
64	-3 58	51	124	-4 49	50	124	-5 39	50	125	296												
63	-3 28	51	125	-4 19	51	125	-5 10	50	126	297												
62	-2 59	51	126	-3 50	50	126	-4 40	51	127	-5 31	51	127	298									
61	-2 30	51	126	-3 21	50	127	-4 11	51	127	-5 02	51	128	-5 53	51	128	299						
60	-2 01	-51	127	-2 52	-51	128	-3 43	-51	128	-4 34	-51	129	-5 25	-51	129	300						
59	-1 32	51	128	-2 23	52	128	-3 15	51	129	-4 06	51	129	-4 57	52	130	-5 49	51	130	301			
58	-1 04	51	129	-1 55	52	129	-2 47	51	130	-3 38	52	130	-4 30	51	131	-5 21	52	131	302			
57	-0 36	51	129	-1 27	52	130	-2 19	52	131	-3 11	52	131	-4 03	51	131	-4 54	52	132	-5 46	52	132	303
56	-0 08	52	130	-1 00	52	131	-1 52	52	132	-2 44	52	132	-3 36	52	132	-4 28	52	133	-5 20	52	133	304
55	00 20	-53	131	-0 33	-52	132	-1 25	-52	132	-2 17	-52	132	-3 09	-52	133	-4 01	-53	133	-4 54	-52	134	305
54	00 47	53	132	-0 06	52	132	-0 58	53	133	-1 51	52	133	-2 43	52	134	-3 35	53	134	-4 28	52	135	306
53	01 13	52	133	00 21	53	133	-0 32	52	134	-1 24	53	134	-2 17	53	135	-3 10	52	135	-4 02	53	136	307
52	01 40	53	133	00 47	53	134	-0 06	53	134	-0 59	53	135	-1 52	52	135	-2 44	53	136	-3 37	53	136	308
51	02 06	53	134	01 13	53	135	00 20	53	135	-0 33	53	136	-1 26	53	136	-2 19	53	137	-3 12	53	137	309
50	02 31	-53	135	01 38	-53	135	00 45	-53	136	-0 08	-54	136	-1 02	-53	137	-1 55	-53	137	-2 48	-53	138	310
49	02 57	54	136	02 03	53	136	01 10	54	137	00 16	53	137	-0 37	54	138	-1 31	53	138	-2 24	53	139	311
48	03 22	54	137	02 28	54	137	01 34	53	138	00 41	54	138	-0 13	54	138	-1 07	53	139	-2 00	54	139	312
47	03 46	54	138	02 52	53	138	01 59	54	138	01 05	54	139	00 11	54	139	-0 43	54	140	-1 37	54	140	313
46	04 10	54	138	03 16	54	139	02 22	54	139	01 28	54	140	00 34	54	140	-0 20	54	141	-1 14	54	141	314
45	04 34	-54	139	03 40	-54	140	02 46	-55	140	01 51	-54	140	00 57	-54	141	00 03	-55	141	-0 52	-54	142	315
44	04 58	55	140	04 03	54	140	03 09	55	141	02 14	54	141	01 20	55	142	00 25	55	142	-0 30	54	143	316
43	05 21	55	141	04 26	55	141	03 31	55	142	02 36	54	142	01 42	55	143	00 47	55	143	-0 08	54	143	317
42	05 43	55	142	04 48	55	142	03 53	55	142	02 58	54	143	02 04	55	143	01 09	55	144	00 14	55	144	318
41	06 05	55	143	05 10	55	143	04 15	55	143	03 20	55	144	02 25	55	144	01 30	55	145	00 35	55	145	319
40	06 27	-55	144	05 32	-56	144	04 36	-55	144	03 41	-55	145	02 46	-56	145	01 50	-55	145	00 55	-55	146	320
39	06 48	55	144	05 53	56	145	04 57	55	145	04 02	56	145	03 06	55	146	02 11	56	146	01 15	55	147	321
38	07 09	56	145	06 13	55	146	05 18	56	146	04 22	56	146	03 26	55	147	02 31	56	147	01 35	56	147	322
37	07 30	56	146	06 34	56	146	05 38	56	147	04 42	56	147	03 46	56	147	02 50	56	148	01 54	56	148	323
36	07 49	56	147	06 53	56	147	05 57	56	148	05 01	56	148	04 05	56	148	03 09	56	149	02 13	56	149	324
35	08 09	-56	148	07 13	-57	148	06 16	-56	149	05 20	-56	149	04 24	-56	149	03 28	-57	149	02 31	-56	150	325
34	08 28	56	149	07 32	57	149	06 35	56	149	05 39	57	150	04 42	56	150	03 46	57	150	02 49	56	151	326
33	08 47	57	150	07 50	57	150	06 53	56	150	05 57	57	151	05 00	57	151	04 03	56	151	03 07	57	151	327
32	09 05	57	150	08 08	57	151	07 11	57	151	06 14	57	151	05 17	57	152	04 20	56	152	03 24	57	152	328
31	09 22	57	151	08 25	57	152	07 28	57	152	06 31	57	152	05 34	57	153	04 37	57	153	03 40	57	153	329
30	09 39	-57	152	08 42	-57	153	07 45	-57	153	06 48	-57	153	05 51	-58	153	04 53	-57	154	03 56	-57	154	330
29	09 56	57	153	08 59	58	153	08 01	57	154	07 04	57	154	06 07	58	154	05 09	57	155	04 12	58	155	331
28	10 12	57	154	09 15	58	154	08 17	57	155	07 20	58	155	06 22	58	155	05 24	57	155	04 27	58	156	332
27	10 28	58	155	09 30	58	155	08 32	57	155	07 35	58	156	06 37	58	156	05 39	57	156	04 42	58	157	333
26	10 43	58	156	09 45	58	156	08 47	58	156	07 49	58	157	06 51	57	157	05 54	58	157	04 56	58	157	334
25	10 57	-58	157	09 59	-58	157	09 01	-58	157	08 03	-58	157	07 05	-58	158	06 07	-58	158	05 09	-58	158	335
24	11 11	58	158	10 13	58	158	09 15	58	158	08 17	58	158	07 19	58	159	06 21	58	159	05 23	59	159	336
23	11 25	58	159	10 27	59	159	09 28	58	159	08 30	58	159	07 32	59	159	06 33	58	160	05 35	58	160	337
22	11 38	59	159	10 39	58	160	09 41	58	160	08 43	59	160	07 44	58	160	06 46	59	161	05 47	58	161	338
21	11 50	58	160	10 52	59	161	09 53	58	161	08 55	59	161	07 56	58	161	06 58	59	161	05 59	59	162	339
20	12 02	-58	161	11 04	-59	161	10 05	-59	162	09 06	-59	162	08 07	-58	162	07 09	-59	162	06 10	-59	163	340
19	12 14	59	162	11 15	59	162	10 16	59	163	09 17	59	163	08 18	58	163	07 20	59	163	06 21	59	163	341
18	12 24	59	163	11 25	59	163	10 26	58	164	09 28	59	164	08 29	59	164	07 30	59	164	06 31	59	164	342
17	12 35	59	164	11 36	60	164	10 36	59	164	09 37	59	165	08 38	59	165	07 39	59	165	06 40	59	165	343
16	12 44	59	165	11 45	59	165	10 46	59	165	09 47	59	165	08 48	59	166	07 49	60	166	06 49	59	166	344
15	12 53	-59	166	11 54	-59	166	10 55	-59	166	09 56	-60	166	08 56	-59	167	07 57	-59	167	06 58	-59	167	345
14	13 02	59	167	12 03	60	167	11 03	59	167	10 04	59	167	09 05	60	167	08 05	59	168	07 06	60	168	346
13	13 10	60	168	12 10	59	168	11 11	59	168	10 12	60	168	09 12	59	168	08 13	60	168	07 13	59	169	347
12	13 17	59	169	12 18	60	169	11 18	59	169	10 19	60	169	09 19	59	169	08 20	60	169	07 20	59	169	348
11	13 24	60	170	12 24	59	170	11 25	60	170	10 25	59	170	09 26	60	170	08 26	59	170	07 27	60	170	349
10	13 30	-59	171	12 31	-60	171	11 31	-60	171	10 31	-59	171	09 32	-60	171	08 32	-60	171	07 32	-59	171	350
9	13 36	60	172	12 36	60	172	11 36	59	172	10 37	60	172	09 37	60	172	08 37	59	172	07 38	60	172	351
8	13 41	60	172	12 41	60	173	11 41	59	173	10 42	60	173	09 42	60	173	08 42	60	173	07 42	60	173	352
7	13 45	59	173	12 46	60	173	11 46	60	174	10 46	60	174	09 46	60	174	08 46	60	174	07 46	59	174	353
6	13 49	60	174	12 49	59	174	11 50	60	174	10 50	60	175	09 50	60	175	08 50	60	175	07 50	60	175	354
5	13 53	-60	175	12 53	-60	175	11 53	-60	175	10 53	-60	175	09 53	-60	176	08 53	-60	176	07 53	-60	176	355
4	13 55	60	176	12 55	60	176	11 55	60	176	10 55	60	176	09 55	59	176	08 56	60	176	07 56	60	177	356
3	13 57	60	177	12 57	60	177	11 57	60	177	10 57	60	177	09 57	59	177	08 58	60	177	07 58	60	177	357
2	13 59	60	178	12 59	60	178	11 59	60	178	10 59	60	178	09 59	60	178	08 59	60	178	07 59	60	178	358
1	14 00	60	179	13 00	60	179	12 00	60	179	11 00	60	179	10 00	60	179	09 00	60	179	08 00	60	179	359
0	14 00	-60	180	13 00	-60	180	12 00	-60	180	11 00	-60	180	10 00	-60	180	09 00	-60	180	08 00	-60	180	360
	23°			24°			25°			26°			27°			28°			29°			

S. Lat. {LHA greater than 180°....... Zn=180−Z; LHA less than 180°.......... Zn=180+Z}

DECLINATION (15°-29°) CONTRARY NAME TO LATITUDE

LAT 53°

N. Lat. {LHA greater than 180°....... Zn=Z; LHA less than 180°........... Zn=360−Z}

DECLINATION (0°-14°) SAME NAME AS LATITUDE

LHA	0° Hc	0° d	0° Z	1° Hc	1° d	1° Z	2° Hc	2° d	2° Z	3° Hc	3° d	3° Z	4° Hc	4° d	4° Z
	° ′	′	°	° ′	′	°	° ′	′	°	° ′	′	°	° ′	′	°
0	36 00	+60	180	37 00	+60	180	38 00	+60	180	39 00	+60	180	40 00	+60	180
1	36 00	60	179	37 00	60	179	38 00	60	179	39 00	60	179	40 00	60	179
2	35 59	60	178	36 59	59	178	37 58	60	178	38 58	60	177	39 58	60	177
3	35 57	60	176	36 57	60	176	37 57	59	176	38 56	60	176	39 56	60	176
4	35 54	60	175	36 54	60	175	37 54	60	175	38 54	60	175	39 54	60	175
5	35 51	+59	174	36 50	+60	174	37 50	+60	174	38 50	+60	174	39 50	+60	174
6	35 46	60	173	36 46	60	173	37 46	60	172	38 46	60	172	39 46	59	172
7	35 41	60	171	36 41	60	171	37 41	60	171	38 41	59	171	39 40	60	171
8	35 36	59	170	36 35	60	170	37 35	60	170	38 35	60	170	39 35	59	170
9	35 29	60	169	36 29	60	169	37 29	59	169	38 28	60	169	39 28	59	168
10	35 22	+60	168	36 22	+59	168	37 21	+60	167	38 21	+59	167	39 20	+60	167
11	35 14	60	167	36 14	59	166	37 13	60	166	38 13	59	166	39 12	59	166
12	35 06	59	165	36 05	59	165	37 04	60	165	38 04	59	165	39 03	59	165
13	34 56	60	164	35 56	59	164	36 55	59	164	37 54	59	164	38 53	59	163
14	34 46	60	163	35 46	59	163	36 45	59	162	37 44	59	162	38 43	59	162
15	34 36	+59	162	35 35	+59	161	36 34	+58	161	37 32	+59	161	38 31	+59	161
16	34 24	59	161	35 23	59	160	36 22	59	160	37 21	58	160	38 19	59	160
17	34 12	59	159	35 11	58	159	36 09	59	159	37 08	59	159	38 07	58	158
18	33 59	59	158	34 58	58	158	35 56	59	158	36 55	58	157	37 53	59	157
19	33 46	58	157	34 44	59	157	35 43	58	156	36 41	58	156	37 39	58	156
20	33 32	+58	156	34 30	+58	156	35 28	+58	155	36 26	+58	155	37 24	+58	155
21	33 17	58	155	34 15	58	154	35 13	58	154	36 11	58	154	37 09	58	153
22	33 01	58	154	33 59	58	153	34 57	58	153	35 55	58	153	36 53	57	152
23	32 45	58	152	33 43	58	152	34 41	57	152	35 38	58	151	36 36	57	151
24	32 29	57	151	33 26	58	151	34 24	57	151	35 21	57	150	36 18	58	150
25	32 11	+58	150	33 09	+57	150	34 06	+57	149	35 03	+57	149	36 00	+57	149
26	31 53	58	149	32 51	57	149	33 48	57	148	34 45	57	148	35 42	57	147
27	31 35	57	148	32 32	57	147	33 29	57	147	34 26	56	147	35 22	57	146
28	31 16	57	147	32 13	56	146	33 09	57	146	34 06	56	146	35 02	57	145
29	30 56	57	146	31 53	56	145	32 49	57	145	33 46	56	144	34 42	56	144
30	30 36	+56	145	31 32	+57	144	32 29	+56	144	33 25	+56	143	34 21	+56	143
31	30 15	56	143	31 11	57	143	32 08	56	143	33 04	55	142	33 59	56	142
32	29 54	56	142	30 50	56	142	31 46	56	142	32 42	55	141	33 37	56	141
33	29 32	56	141	30 28	56	141	31 24	55	140	32 19	56	140	33 15	55	140
34	29 10	55	140	30 05	56	140	31 01	55	139	31 56	55	139	32 51	56	138
35	28 47	+55	139	29 42	+56	139	30 38	+55	138	31 33	+55	138	32 28	+55	137
36	28 24	55	138	29 19	55	138	30 14	55	137	31 09	55	137	32 04	54	136
37	28 00	55	137	28 55	55	137	29 50	54	136	30 44	55	136	31 39	55	135
38	27 36	54	136	28 30	55	136	29 25	54	135	30 19	55	135	31 14	54	134
39	27 11	54	135	28 05	55	135	29 00	54	134	29 54	54	134	30 48	54	133
40	26 46	+54	134	27 40	+54	134	28 34	+54	133	29 28	+54	133	30 22	+54	132
41	26 20	54	133	27 14	54	133	28 08	54	132	29 02	54	132	29 56	54	131
42	25 54	54	132	26 48	54	131	27 42	54	131	28 36	53	130	29 29	54	130
43	25 28	53	131	26 21	54	130	27 15	53	130	28 08	54	129	29 02	53	129
44	25 01	53	130	25 54	54	130	26 48	53	129	27 41	53	128	28 34	53	128
45	24 34	+53	129	25 27	+53	129	26 20	+53	128	27 13	+53	127	28 06	+53	127
46	24 06	53	128	24 59	53	128	25 52	53	127	26 45	53	126	27 38	52	126
47	23 38	53	127	24 31	53	127	25 24	52	126	26 16	53	126	27 09	53	125
48	23 10	52	126	24 02	53	126	24 55	53	125	25 48	52	125	26 40	52	124
49	22 41	53	125	23 34	52	125	24 26	52	124	25 18	53	124	26 11	52	123
50	22 12	+52	124	23 04	+53	124	23 57	+52	123	24 49	+52	123	25 41	+52	122
51	21 43	52	123	22 35	52	123	23 27	52	122	24 19	52	122	25 11	51	121
52	21 13	52	122	22 05	52	122	22 57	52	121	23 49	51	121	24 40	52	120
53	20 43	52	121	21 35	52	121	22 27	51	120	23 18	52	120	24 10	51	119
54	20 13	51	120	21 04	52	120	21 56	51	119	22 47	52	119	23 39	51	118
55	19 42	+52	120	20 34	+51	119	21 25	+51	118	22 16	+52	118	23 08	+51	117
56	19 11	52	119	20 03	51	118	20 54	51	118	21 45	51	117	22 36	51	116
57	18 40	51	118	19 31	52	117	20 23	51	117	21 14	50	116	22 04	51	116
58	18 09	51	117	19 00	51	116	19 51	51	116	20 42	50	115	21 32	51	115
59	17 37	51	116	18 28	51	115	19 19	51	115	20 10	50	114	21 00	51	114
60	17 06	+50	115	17 56	+51	115	18 47	+50	114	19 37	+51	113	20 28	+50	113
61	16 33	51	114	17 24	51	114	18 15	50	113	19 05	50	113	19 55	50	112
62	16 01	51	113	16 52	50	113	17 42	50	112	18 32	50	112	19 22	50	111
63	15 29	50	112	16 19	50	112	17 09	50	111	17 59	50	111	18 49	50	110
64	14 56	50	112	15 46	50	111	16 36	50	110	17 26	50	110	18 16	50	109
65	14 23	+50	111	15 13	+50	110	16 03	+50	110	16 53	+50	109	17 43	+49	108
66	13 50	50	110	14 40	50	109	15 30	50	109	16 20	49	108	17 09	50	108
67	13 17	50	109	14 07	49	108	14 56	50	108	15 46	50	107	16 36	49	107
68	12 43	50	108	13 33	50	108	14 23	49	107	15 12	50	106	16 02	49	106
69	12 10	49	107	12 59	50	107	13 49	49	106	14 38	50	106	15 28	49	105

LHA	5° Hc	5° d	5° Z	6° Hc	6° d	6° Z	7° Hc	7° d	7° Z	8° Hc	8° d	8° Z	9° Hc	9° d	9° Z
	° ′	′	°	° ′	′	°	° ′	′	°	° ′	′	°	° ′	′	°
0	41 00	+60	180	42 00	+60	180	43 00	+60	180	44 00	+60	180	45 00	+60	180
1	41 00	60	179	42 00	60	179	43 00	60	179	44 00	60	179	45 00	60	179
2	40 58	60	177	41 58	60	177	42 58	60	177	43 58	60	177	44 58	60	177
3	40 56	60	176	41 56	60	176	42 56	60	176	43 56	60	176	44 56	60	176
4	40 54	59	175	41 53	60	175	42 53	60	175	43 53	60	175	44 53	60	174
5	40 50	+60	173	41 50	+60	173	42 50	+59	173	43 49	+60	173	44 49	+60	173
6	40 45	60	172	41 45	60	172	42 45	60	172	43 45	60	172	44 45	59	172
7	40 40	60	171	41 40	60	171	42 40	59	171	43 39	60	170	44 39	60	170
8	40 34	60	170	41 34	59	169	42 33	60	169	43 33	60	169	44 33	59	169
9	40 27	60	168	41 27	59	168	42 26	60	168	43 26	59	168	44 25	60	168
10	40 20	+59	167	41 19	+60	167	42 19	+59	167	43 18	+59	166	44 17	+60	166
11	40 11	60	166	41 11	59	165	42 10	59	165	43 09	60	165	44 09	59	165
12	40 02	59	164	41 01	60	164	42 01	59	164	43 00	59	164	43 59	59	163
13	39 52	59	163	40 51	59	163	41 50	59	163	42 49	59	162	43 48	59	162
14	39 42	59	162	40 41	58	162	41 39	59	161	42 38	59	161	43 37	59	161
15	39 30	+59	161	40 29	+59	160	41 28	+58	160	42 26	+59	160	43 25	+59	159
16	39 18	59	159	40 17	58	159	41 15	59	159	42 14	58	158	43 12	59	158
17	39 05	59	158	40 04	58	158	41 02	58	157	42 00	59	157	42 59	58	157
18	38 52	58	157	39 50	58	156	40 48	58	156	41 46	59	156	42 45	58	155
19	38 37	58	156	39 35	59	155	40 34	58	155	41 32	58	155	42 30	57	154
20	38 22	+58	154	39 20	+58	154	40 18	+58	154	41 16	+58	153	42 14	+58	153
21	38 07	57	153	39 04	58	153	40 02	58	152	41 00	57	152	41 57	58	152
22	37 50	58	152	38 48	57	151	39 45	58	151	40 43	57	151	41 40	58	150
23	37 33	58	151	38 31	57	150	39 28	57	150	40 25	57	150	41 22	57	149
24	37 16	57	149	38 13	57	149	39 10	57	149	40 07	57	148	41 04	57	148
25	36 57	+57	148	37 54	+57	148	38 51	+57	147	39 48	+57	147	40 45	+56	147
26	36 39	56	147	37 35	57	147	38 32	57	146	39 29	56	146	40 25	57	145
27	36 19	57	146	37 16	56	145	38 12	56	145	39 08	57	145	40 05	56	144
28	35 59	56	145	36 55	57	144	37 52	56	144	38 48	56	143	39 44	56	143
29	35 38	56	144	36 34	56	143	37 30	56	143	38 26	56	142	39 22	56	142
30	35 17	+56	142	36 13	+56	142	37 09	+55	142	38 04	+56	141	39 00	+56	141
31	34 55	56	141	35 51	56	141	36 47	55	140	37 42	55	140	38 37	56	139
32	34 33	55	140	35 28	56	140	36 24	55	139	37 19	55	139	38 14	55	138
33	34 10	55	139	35 05	55	139	36 00	55	138	36 55	55	138	37 50	55	137
34	33 47	55	138	34 42	55	137	35 37	54	137	36 31	55	136	37 26	55	136
35	33 23	+55	137	34 18	+54	136	35 12	+55	136	36 07	+54	135	37 01	+55	135
36	32 58	55	136	33 53	54	135	34 47	55	135	35 42	54	134	36 36	54	134
37	32 34	54	135	33 28	54	134	34 22	54	134	35 16	54	133	36 10	54	133
38	32 08	54	134	33 02	54	133	33 56	54	133	34 50	54	132	35 44	54	132
39	31 42	54	133	32 36	54	132	33 30	54	132	34 24	54	131	35 18	53	130
40	31 16	+54	132	32 10	+54	131	33 04	+53	130	33 57	+53	130	34 50	+54	129
41	30 50	53	130	31 43	54	130	32 37	53	129	33 30	53	129	34 23	53	128
42	30 23	53	129	31 16	53	129	32 09	53	128	33 02	53	128	33 55	53	127
43	29 55	53	128	30 48	53	128	31 41	53	127	32 34	53	127	33 27	52	126
44	29 27	53	127	30 20	53	127	31 13	53	126	32 06	52	126	32 58	52	125
45	28 59	+53	126	29 52	+52	126	30 44	+53	125	31 37	+52	125	32 29	+52	124
46	28 30	53	125	29 23	52	125	30 15	53	124	31 08	52	124	32 00	52	123
47	28 02	52	124	28 54	52	124	29 46	52	123	30 38	52	123	31 30	52	122
48	27 32	52	123	28 24	52	123	29 16	52	122	30 08	52	122	31 00	52	121
49	27 03	52	122	27 55	51	122	28 46	52	121	29 38	52	121	30 30	51	120
50	26 33	+52	122	27 25	+51	121	28 16	+52	120	29 08	+51	120	29 59	+51	119
51	26 02	52	121	26 54	52	120	27 46	51	119	28 37	51	119	29 28	51	118
52	25 32	51	120	26 23	52	119	27 15	51	118	28 06	51	118	28 57	51	117
53	25 01	51	119	25 52	51	118	26 43	51	117	27 34	51	117	28 25	51	116
54	24 30	51	118	25 21	51	117	26 12	51	117	27 03	51	116	27 54	50	115
55	23 59	+51	117	24 50	+50	116	25 40	+51	116	26 31	+51	115	27 22	+50	114
56	23 27	51	116	24 18	50	115	25 08	51	115	25 59	50	114	26 49	50	113
57	22 55	51	115	23 46	50	114	24 36	51	114	25 27	50	113	26 17	50	113
58	22 23	51	114	23 14	50	113	24 04	50	113	24 54	50	112	25 44	50	112
59	21 51	50	113	22 41	50	113	23 31	50	112	24 21	50	111	25 11	50	111
60	21 18	+50	112	22 08	+50	112	22 58	+50	111	23 48	+50	110	24 38	+50	110
61	20 45	50	111	21 35	50	111	22 25	50	110	23 15	50	110	24 05	49	109
62	20 12	50	110	21 02	50	110	21 52	50	109	22 42	49	109	23 31	50	108
63	19 39	50	110	20 29	50	109	21 19	49	108	22 08	50	108	22 58	49	107
64	19 06	50	109	19 56	49	108	20 45	50	107	21 35	49	107	22 24	49	106
65	18 32	+50	108	19 22	+50	107	20 12	+49	107	21 01	+49	106	21 50	+49	105
66	17 59	49	107	18 48	50	106	19 38	49	106	20 27	49	105	21 16	49	105
67	17 25	49	106	18 14	50	105	19 04	49	105	19 53	49	104	20 42	49	104
68	16 51	49	105	17 40	49	105	18 29	50	104	19 19	48	103	20 07	49	103
69	16 17	49	104	17 06	49	104	17 55	49	103	18 44	49	103	19 33	49	102

LHA	10° Hc	10° d	10° Z	11° Hc	11° d	11° Z	12° Hc	12° d	12° Z	13° Hc	13° d	13° Z	14° Hc	14° d	14° Z	LHA
	° ′	′	°	° ′	′	°	° ′	′	°	° ′	′	°	° ′	′	°	
0	46 00	+60	180	47 00	+60	180	48 00	+60	180	49 00	+60	180	50 00	+60	180	360
1	46 00	60	179	47 00	60	179	48 00	60	179	49 00	60	179	50 00	60	179	359
2	45 58	60	177	46 58	60	177	47 58	60	177	48 58	60	177	49 58	60	177	358
3	45 56	60	176	46 56	60	176	47 56	60	176	48 56	60	176	49 56	60	176	357
4	45 53	60	174	46 53	60	174	47 53	60	174	48 53	60	174	49 53	60	174	356
5	45 49	+60	173	46 49	+60	173	47 49	+60	173	48 49	+59	173	49 48	+60	173	355
6	45 44	60	172	46 44	60	171	47 44	60	171	48 44	59	171	49 43	60	171	354
7	45 39	59	170	46 38	60	170	47 38	60	170	48 38	59	170	49 37	60	170	353
8	45 32	60	169	46 32	59	169	47 31	60	168	48 31	60	168	49 31	59	168	352
9	45 25	59	167	46 24	60	167	47 24	59	167	48 23	60	167	49 23	59	167	351
10	45 17	+59	166	46 16	+59	166	47 15	+60	166	48 15	+59	165	49 14	+59	165	350
11	45 08	59	165	46 07	59	164	47 06	59	164	48 05	60	164	49 05	59	164	349
12	44 58	59	163	45 57	59	163	46 56	59	163	47 55	59	162	48 54	59	162	348
13	44 47	59	162	45 46	59	162	46 45	59	161	47 44	59	161	48 43	59	161	347
14	44 36	59	161	45 35	59	160	46 34	58	160	47 32	59	160	48 31	58	159	346
15	44 24	+58	159	45 22	+59	159	46 21	+58	159	47 19	+59	158	48 18	+58	158	345
16	44 11	58	158	45 09	59	157	46 08	58	157	47 06	58	157	48 04	58	156	344
17	43 57	58	156	44 55	59	156	45 54	58	156	46 52	58	155	47 50	58	155	343
18	43 43	58	155	44 41	58	155	45 39	58	154	46 37	57	154	47 34	58	154	342
19	43 27	58	154	44 25	58	153	45 23	58	153	46 21	57	153	47 18	58	152	341
20	43 12	+57	153	44 09	+58	152	45 07	+57	152	46 04	+58	151	47 02	+57	151	340
21	42 55	57	151	43 52	58	151	44 50	57	150	45 47	57	150	46 44	57	150	339
22	42 38	57	150	43 35	57	150	44 32	57	149	45 29	57	149	46 26	57	148	338
23	42 19	57	149	43 16	57	148	44 13	57	148	45 10	57	147	46 07	56	147	337
24	42 01	57	147	42 58	56	147	43 54	57	147	44 51	56	146	45 47	56	146	336
25	41 41	+57	146	42 38	+56	146	43 34	+57	145	44 31	+56	145	45 27	+56	144	335
26	41 22	56	145	42 18	56	144	43 14	56	144	44 10	56	144	45 06	56	143	334
27	41 01	56	144	41 57	56	143	42 53	56	143	43 49	55	142	44 44	56	142	333
28	40 40	56	142	41 36	55	142	42 31	56	142	43 27	55	141	44 22	56	140	332
29	40 18	56	141	41 14	55	141	42 09	55	140	43 04	55	140	43 59	55	139	331
30	39 56	+55	140	40 51	+55	140	41 46	+55	139	42 41	+55	139	43 36	+55	138	330
31	39 33	55	139	40 28	55	138	41 23	55	138	42 18	54	137	43 12	55	137	329
32	39 09	55	138	40 04	55	137	40 59	54	137	41 53	55	136	42 48	54	136	328
33	38 45	55	137	39 40	54	136	40 34	55	136	41 29	54	135	42 23	54	134	327
34	38 21	54	135	39 15	54	135	40 09	54	134	41 03	54	134	41 57	54	133	326
35	37 56	+54	134	38 50	+54	134	39 44	+54	133	40 38	+53	133	41 31	+54	132	325
36	37 30	54	133	38 24	54	133	39 18	53	132	40 11	54	131	41 05	53	131	324
37	37 04	54	132	37 58	53	132	38 51	54	131	39 45	53	130	40 38	53	130	323
38	36 38	53	131	37 31	54	130	38 25	53	130	39 18	53	129	40 11	52	129	322
39	36 11	53	130	37 04	53	129	37 57	53	129	38 50	53	128	39 43	52	128	321
40	35 44	+53	129	36 37	+52	128	37 29	+53	128	38 22	+53	127	39 15	+52	126	320
41	35 16	53	128	36 09	52	127	37 01	53	127	37 54	52	126	38 46	52	125	319
42	34 48	52	127	35 40	53	126	36 33	52	125	37 25	52	125	38 17	52	124	318
43	34 19	53	126	35 12	52	125	36 04	52	124	36 56	52	124	37 48	51	123	317
44	33 50	53	125	34 43	52	124	35 35	51	123	36 26	52	123	37 18	51	122	316
45	33 21	+52	124	34 13	+52	123	35 05	+52	122	35 57	+51	122	36 48	+51	121	315
46	32 52	51	123	33 43	52	122	34 35	51	121	35 26	52	121	36 18	51	120	314
47	32 22	51	122	33 13	52	121	34 05	51	120	34 56	51	120	35 47	51	119	313
48	31 52	51	121	32 43	51	120	33 34	51	119	34 25	51	119	35 16	50	118	312
49	31 21	51	120	32 12	51	119	33 03	51	118	33 54	51	118	34 45	50	117	311
50	30 50	+51	119	31 41	+51	118	32 32	+51	117	33 23	+50	117	34 13	+50	116	310
51	30 19	51	118	31 10	50	117	32 00	51	116	32 51	50	116	33 41	50	115	309
52	29 48	50	117	30 38	51	116	31 29	50	115	32 19	50	115	33 09	50	114	308
53	29 16	50	116	30 06	51	115	30 57	50	114	31 47	50	114	32 37	49	113	307
54	28 44	50	115	29 34	50	114	30 24	50	113	31 14	50	113	32 04	50	112	306
55	28 12	+50	114	29 02	+50	113	29 52	+50	113	30 42	+49	112	31 31	+50	111	305
56	27 39	50	113	28 29	50	112	29 19	50	112	30 09	49	111	30 58	50	110	304
57	27 07	50	112	27 57	49	111	28 46	50	111	29 36	49	110	30 25	49	109	303
58	26 34	50	111	27 24	49	110	28 13	50	110	29 03	49	109	29 52	49	108	302
59	26 01	50	110	26 51	49	109	27 40	49	109	28 29	49	108	29 18	49	108	301
60	25 28	+49	109	26 17	+50	109	27 07	+49	108	27 56	+49	107	28 45	+48	107	300
61	24 54	50	108	25 44	49	108	26 33	49	107	27 22	49	106	28 11	48	106	299
62	24 21	49	107	25 10	49	107	25 59	49	106	26 48	49	106	27 37	49	105	298
63	23 47	49	107	24 36	49	106	25 25	49	105	26 14	49	105	27 03	48	104	297
64	23 13	49	106	24 02	49	105	24 51	49	104	25 40	48	104	26 28	49	103	296
65	22 39	+49	105	23 28	+49	104	24 17	+48	104	25 05	+49	103	25 54	+48	102	295
66	22 05	49	104	22 54	48	103	23 42	49	103	24 31	48	102	25 19	48	101	294
67	21 31	48	103	22 19	49	102	23 08	48	102	23 56	49	101	24 45	48	100	293
68	20 56	49	102	21 45	48	102	22 33	49	101	23 22	48	100	24 10	48	100	292
69	20 22	48	101	21 10	49	101	21 59	48	100	22 47	48	99	23 35	48	99	291

S. Lat. {LHA greater than 180°....... Zn=180−Z; LHA less than 180°........... Zn=180+Z}

DECLINATION (0°-14°) SAME NAME AS LATITUDE

LAT 54°

N. Lat. {LHA greater than 180°....... Zn=Z
{LHA less than 180°.......... Zn=360−Z

DECLINATION (0°-14°) SAME NAME AS LATITUDE

LHA	0° Hc	0° d	0° Z	1° Hc	1° d	1° Z	2° Hc	2° d	2° Z	3° Hc	3° d	3° Z	4° Hc	4° d	4° Z
	° ′	′	°	° ′	′	°	° ′	′	°	° ′	′	°	° ′	′	°
70	11 36	+49	106	12 25	+50	106	13 15	+49	105	14 04	+50	105	14 54	+49	104
71	11 02	49	106	11 51	50	105	12 41	49	104	13 30	49	104	14 19	49	103
72	10 28	49	105	11 17	50	104	12 07	49	104	12 56	49	103	13 45	49	102
73	09 54	49	104	10 43	49	103	11 32	49	103	12 21	49	102	13 10	49	102
74	09 19	50	103	10 09	49	103	10 58	49	102	11 47	49	101	12 36	49	101
75	08 45	+49	102	09 34	+49	102	10 23	+49	101	11 12	+49	101	12 01	+49	100
76	08 11	49	101	09 00	49	101	09 49	48	100	10 37	49	100	11 26	49	99
77	07 36	49	101	08 25	49	100	09 14	49	99	10 03	48	99	10 51	49	98
78	07 01	49	100	07 50	49	99	08 39	49	99	09 28	48	98	10 16	49	97
79	06 26	49	99	07 15	49	98	08 04	49	98	08 53	48	97	09 41	49	97
80	05 52	+48	98	06 40	+49	98	07 29	+49	97	08 18	+48	96	09 06	+49	96
81	05 17	48	97	06 05	49	97	06 54	49	96	07 43	48	96	08 31	49	95
82	04 42	48	96	05 30	49	96	06 19	49	95	07 08	48	95	07 56	49	94
83	04 06	49	96	04 55	49	95	05 44	48	95	06 32	49	94	07 21	48	93
84	03 31	49	95	04 20	49	94	05 09	48	94	05 57	49	93	06 46	48	93
85	02 56	+49	94	03 45	+48	93	04 33	+49	93	05 22	+48	92	06 10	+49	92
86	02 21	49	93	03 10	48	93	03 58	49	92	04 47	48	91	05 35	49	91
87	01 46	48	92	02 34	49	92	03 23	48	91	04 11	49	91	05 00	48	90
88	01 11	48	92	01 59	49	91	02 48	48	90	03 36	49	90	04 25	48	89
89	00 35	49	91	01 24	48	90	02 12	49	90	03 01	48	89	03 49	49	88
90	00 00	+49	90	00 49	+48	89	01 37	+49	89	02 26	+48	88	03 14	+49	88
91	−0 35	48	89	00 13	49	89	01 02	48	88	01 50	49	87	02 39	48	87
92	−1 11	49	88	−0 22	49	88	00 27	48	87	01 15	49	87	02 04	48	86
93	−1 46	49	88	−0 57	48	87	−0 09	49	86	00 40	49	86	01 29	48	85
94	−2 21	49	87	−1 32	48	86	−0 44	49	86	00 05	48	85	00 53	49	84
95	−2 56	+48	86	−2 08	+49	85	−1 19	+49	85	−0 30	+48	84	00 18	+49	84
96	−3 31	48	85	−2 43	49	85	−1 54	49	84	−1 05	48	83	−0 17	49	83
97	−4 06	48	84	−3 18	49	84	−2 29	49	83	−1 40	48	83	−0 52	49	82
98	−4 42	49	84	−3 53	49	83	−3 04	49	82	−2 15	48	82	−1 27	49	81
99	−5 17	49	83	−4 28	49	82	−3 39	49	82	−2 50	49	81	−2 01	48	80
100	−5 52	+49	82	−5 03	+49	81	−4 14	+49	81	−3 25	+49	80	−2 36	+49	80
101				−5 38	49	80	−4 49	49	80	−4 00	49	79	−3 11	49	79
102							−5 23	49	79	−4 34	49	78	−3 45	49	78
103							−5 58	49	78	−5 09	49	78	−4 20	49	77
104										−5 43	49	77	−4 54	49	76
105													−5 28	+49	75
106													−6 02	49	75

LHA	5° Hc	5° d	5° Z	6° Hc	6° d	6° Z	7° Hc	7° d	7° Z	8° Hc	8° d	8° Z	9° Hc	9° d	9° Z
	° ′	′	°	° ′	′	°	° ′	′	°	° ′	′	°	° ′	′	°
70	15 43	+49	104	16 32	+49	103	17 21	+49	102	18 10	+48	102	18 58	+49	101
71	15 08	49	103	15 57	49	102	16 46	49	101	17 35	49	101	18 24	48	100
72	14 34	49	102	15 23	49	101	16 12	48	101	17 00	49	100	17 49	49	99
73	13 59	49	101	14 48	49	100	15 37	49	100	16 26	48	99	17 14	49	99
74	13 25	48	100	14 13	49	100	15 02	49	99	15 51	48	98	16 39	49	98
75	12 50	+49	99	13 39	+48	99	14 27	+49	98	15 16	+48	98	16 04	+49	97
76	12 15	49	99	13 04	48	98	13 52	49	97	14 41	48	97	15 29	49	96
77	11 40	49	98	12 29	48	97	13 17	49	96	14 06	48	96	14 54	48	95
78	11 05	49	97	11 54	48	96	12 42	49	96	13 31	48	95	14 19	48	94
79	10 30	49	96	11 19	48	95	12 07	48	95	12 55	49	94	13 44	48	94
80	09 55	+48	95	10 43	+49	95	11 32	+48	94	12 20	+49	93	13 09	+48	93
81	09 20	48	94	10 08	49	94	10 57	48	93	11 45	48	93	12 33	49	92
82	08 45	48	94	09 33	48	93	10 21	49	92	11 10	48	92	11 58	48	91
83	08 09	49	93	08 58	48	92	09 46	49	92	10 35	48	91	11 23	48	90
84	07 34	49	92	08 23	48	91	09 11	48	91	09 59	49	90	10 48	48	90
85	06 59	+48	91	07 47	+49	91	08 36	+48	90	09 24	+48	89	10 12	+48	89
86	06 24	48	90	07 12	48	90	08 00	49	89	08 49	48	89	09 37	48	88
87	05 48	49	90	06 37	48	89	07 25	49	88	08 14	48	88	09 02	48	87
88	05 13	49	89	06 02	48	88	06 50	48	88	07 38	49	87	08 27	48	86
89	04 38	48	88	05 26	49	87	06 15	48	87	07 03	48	86	07 51	49	86
90	04 03	+48	87	04 51	+49	86	05 40	+48	86	06 28	+48	85	07 16	+49	85
91	03 27	49	86	04 16	48	86	05 04	49	85	05 53	48	85	06 41	49	84
92	02 52	49	85	03 41	48	85	04 29	49	84	05 18	48	84	06 06	49	83
93	02 17	49	85	03 06	48	84	03 54	49	83	04 43	48	83	05 31	49	82
94	01 42	49	84	02 31	48	83	03 19	49	83	04 08	48	82	04 56	49	81
95	01 07	+49	83	01 56	+48	82	02 44	+49	82	03 33	+48	81	04 21	+49	81
96	00 32	49	82	01 21	48	82	02 09	49	81	02 58	49	80	03 47	48	80
97	−0 03	49	81	00 46	49	81	01 35	48	80	02 23	49	80	03 12	49	79
98	−0 38	49	81	00 11	49	80	01 00	49	79	01 49	48	79	02 37	49	78
99	−1 13	49	80	−0 24	49	79	00 25	49	79	01 14	49	78	02 03	49	77
100	−1 47	+49	79	−0 58	+49	78	−0 09	+49	78	00 40	+49	77	01 29	+48	77
101	−2 22	49	78	−1 33	49	78	−0 44	49	77	00 05	49	76	00 54	49	76
102	−2 56	49	77	−2 07	49	77	−1 18	49	76	−0 29	49	76	00 20	49	75
103	−3 31	50	77	−2 41	49	76	−1 52	49	75	−1 03	49	75	−0 14	49	74
104	−4 05	49	76	−3 16	50	75	−2 26	49	75	−1 37	49	74	−0 48	50	73
105	−4 39	+49	75	−3 50	+50	74	−3 00	+49	74	−2 11	+50	73	−1 21	+49	73
106	−5 13	50	74	−4 23	49	73	−3 34	49	73	−2 45	50	72	−1 55	49	72
107	−5 47	50	73	−4 57	49	73	−4 08	50	72	−3 18	50	72	−2 28	49	71
108				−5 31	50	72	−4 41	50	71	−3 51	49	71	−3 02	50	70
109				−6 04	49	71	−5 15	50	70	−4 25	50	70	−3 35	50	69
110							−5 48	+50	70	−4 58	+50	69	−4 08	+50	69
111										−5 31	51	68	−4 40	50	68
112										−6 03	50	67	−5 13	50	67
113													−5 45	50	66

LHA	10° Hc	10° d	10° Z	11° Hc	11° d	11° Z	12° Hc	12° d	12° Z	13° Hc	13° d	13° Z	14° Hc	14° d	14° Z	LHA
	° ′	′	°	° ′	′	°	° ′	′	°	° ′	′	°	° ′	′	°	
70	19 47	+49	100	20 36	+48	100	21 24	+48	99	22 12	+48	99	23 00	+48	98	290
71	19 12	49	100	20 01	48	99	20 49	48	98	21 37	48	98	22 25	48	97	289
72	18 38	48	99	19 26	48	98	20 14	48	98	21 02	48	97	21 50	48	96	288
73	18 03	48	98	18 51	48	97	19 39	48	97	20 27	48	96	21 15	48	95	287
74	17 28	48	97	18 16	48	97	19 04	48	96	19 52	48	95	20 40	48	95	286
75	16 53	+48	96	17 41	+48	96	18 29	+48	95	19 17	+48	94	20 05	+48	94	285
76	16 18	48	95	17 06	48	95	17 54	48	94	18 42	48	94	19 30	47	93	284
77	15 42	49	95	16 31	48	94	17 19	48	93	18 07	47	93	18 54	48	92	283
78	15 07	48	94	15 55	48	93	16 43	48	93	17 31	48	92	18 19	48	91	282
79	14 32	48	93	15 20	48	92	16 08	48	92	16 56	48	91	17 44	48	91	281
80	13 57	+48	92	14 45	+48	92	15 33	+48	91	16 21	+48	90	17 09	+47	90	280
81	13 22	48	91	14 10	48	91	14 58	48	90	15 46	47	90	16 33	48	89	279
82	12 46	48	91	13 34	48	90	14 22	48	89	15 10	48	89	15 58	48	88	278
83	12 11	48	90	12 59	48	89	13 47	48	89	14 35	48	88	15 23	48	87	277
84	11 36	48	89	12 24	48	88	13 12	48	88	14 00	48	87	14 48	47	86	276
85	11 00	+49	88	11 49	+48	88	12 37	+48	87	13 25	+47	86	14 12	+48	86	275
86	10 25	48	87	11 13	48	87	12 01	48	86	12 49	48	86	13 37	48	85	274
87	09 50	48	87	10 38	48	86	11 26	48	85	12 14	48	85	13 02	48	84	273
88	09 15	48	86	10 03	48	85	10 51	48	85	11 39	48	84	12 27	48	83	272
89	08 40	48	85	09 28	48	84	10 16	48	84	11 04	48	83	11 52	48	83	271
90	08 05	+48	84	08 53	+48	84	09 41	+48	83	10 29	+48	82	11 17	+48	82	270
91	07 30	48	83	08 18	48	83	09 06	48	82	09 54	48	82	10 42	48	81	269
92	06 55	48	83	07 43	48	82	08 31	48	81	09 19	49	81	10 08	48	80	268
93	06 20	48	82	07 08	48	81	07 56	49	81	08 45	48	80	09 33	48	79	267
94	05 45	48	81	06 33	49	80	07 22	48	80	08 10	48	79	08 58	49	79	266
95	05 10	+48	80	05 58	+49	80	06 47	+48	79	07 35	+49	78	08 24	+48	78	265
96	04 35	49	79	05 24	48	79	06 12	49	78	07 01	48	78	07 49	49	77	264
97	04 01	48	78	04 49	49	78	05 38	49	77	06 27	48	77	07 15	49	76	263
98	03 26	49	78	04 15	49	77	05 04	48	77	05 52	49	76	06 41	49	75	262
99	02 52	49	77	03 41	48	76	04 29	49	76	05 18	49	75	06 07	49	75	261
100	02 17	+49	76	03 06	+49	75	03 55	+49	75	04 44	+49	74	05 33	+49	74	260
101	01 43	49	75	02 32	49	75	03 21	49	74	04 10	49	74	04 59	49	73	259
102	01 09	49	74	01 58	49	74	02 47	49	73	03 36	49	73	04 25	50	72	258
103	00 35	49	74	01 24	50	73	02 14	49	73	03 03	49	72	03 52	49	71	257
104	00 02	49	73	00 51	49	72	01 40	49	72	02 29	50	71	03 19	49	71	256
105	−0 32	+49	72	00 17	+50	71	01 07	+49	71	01 56	+49	70	02 45	+50	70	255
106	−1 06	50	71	−0 16	49	71	00 33	50	70	01 23	49	70	02 12	50	69	254
107	−1 39	50	70	−0 49	49	70	00 00	50	69	00 50	50	69	01 40	49	68	253
108	−2 12	50	70	−1 22	49	69	−0 33	50	68	00 17	50	68	01 07	50	67	252
109	−2 45	50	69	−1 55	50	68	−1 05	50	68	−0 15	50	67	00 35	49	67	251
110	−3 18	+50	68	−2 28	+50	67	−1 38	+50	67	−0 48	+50	66	00 02	+50	66	250
111	−3 50	50	67	−3 00	50	67	−2 10	50	66	−1 20	50	65	−0 30	50	65	249
112	−4 23	50	66	−3 33	51	66	−2 42	50	65	−1 52	50	65	−1 02	51	64	248
113	−4 55	50	65	−4 05	51	65	−3 14	50	64	−2 24	51	64	−1 33	50	63	247
114	−5 27	51	65	−4 36	50	64	−3 46	51	64	−2 55	50	63	−2 05	51	63	246
115	−5 59	+51	64	−5 08	+51	63	−4 17	+50	63	−3 27	+51	62	−2 36	+51	62	245
116				−5 39	50	62	−4 49	51	62	−3 58	51	61	−3 07	51	61	244
117							−5 20	52	61	−4 28	51	61	−3 37	51	60	243
118							−5 50	51	60	−4 59	51	60	−4 08	51	59	242
119										−5 29	51	59	−4 38	51	58	241
120										−6 00	+52	58	−5 08	+52	58	240
121													−5 38	52	57	239

0°	1°	2°	3°	4°	5°	6°	7°	8°	9°	10°	11°	12°	13°	14°

S. Lat. {LHA greater than 180°....... Zn=180−Z
{LHA less than 180°.......... Zn=180+Z

DECLINATION (0°-14°) SAME NAME AS LATITUDE

LAT 54°

LHA	0°			1°			2°			3°			4°		
	Hc	d	Z	Hc	d	Z	Hc	d	Z	Hc	d	Z	Hc	d	Z
	° ′	′	°	° ′	′	°	° ′	′	°	° ′	′	°	° ′	′	°
100	-5 52	-48	82	260											
99	-5 17	48	83	-6 05	49	83	261								
98	-4 42	48	84	-5 30	49	84	262								
97	-4 06	49	84	-4 55	49	85	-5 44	48	85	263					
96	-3 31	49	85	-4 20	49	86	-5 09	48	86	-5 57	49	87	264		
95	-2 56	-49	86	-3 45	-48	87	-4 33	-49	87	-5 22	-48	88	-6 10	-49	88
94	-2 21	49	87	-3 10	48	87	-3 58	49	88	-4 47	48	89	-5 35	49	89
93	-1 46	48	88	-2 34	49	88	-3 23	48	89	-4 11	49	89	-5 00	48	90
92	-1 11	48	88	-1 59	49	89	-2 48	48	90	-3 36	49	90	-4 25	48	91
91	-0 35	49	89	-1 24	48	90	-2 12	49	90	-3 01	48	91	-3 49	49	92
90	00 00	-49	90	-0 49	-48	91	-1 37	-49	91	-2 26	-48	92	-3 14	-49	92
89	00 35	48	91	-0 13	49	91	-1 02	48	92	-1 50	49	93	-2 39	48	93
88	01 11	49	92	00 22	49	92	-0 27	48	93	-1 15	49	93	-2 04	48	94
87	01 46	49	92	00 57	48	93	00 09	49	94	-0 40	49	94	-1 29	48	95
86	02 21	49	93	01 32	48	94	00 44	49	94	-0 05	48	95	-0 53	49	96
85	02 56	-48	94	02 08	-49	95	01 19	-49	95	00 30	-48	96	-0 18	-49	96
84	03 31	48	95	02 43	49	95	01 54	49	96	01 05	48	97	00 17	49	97
83	04 06	48	96	03 18	49	96	02 29	49	97	01 40	48	97	00 52	49	98
82	04 42	49	96	03 53	49	97	03 04	49	98	02 15	48	98	01 27	49	99
81	05 17	49	97	04 28	49	98	03 39	49	98	02 50	49	99	02 01	48	100
80	05 52	-49	98	05 03	-49	99	04 14	-49	99	03 25	-49	100	02 36	-49	100
79	06 26	48	99	05 38	49	100	04 49	49	100	04 00	49	101	03 11	49	101
78	07 01	49	100	06 12	49	100	05 23	49	101	04 34	49	102	03 45	49	102
77	07 36	49	101	06 47	49	101	05 58	49	102	05 09	49	102	04 20	49	103
76	08 11	50	101	07 21	49	102	06 32	49	103	05 43	49	103	04 54	49	104
75	08 45	-49	102	07 56	-49	103	07 07	-49	103	06 18	-50	104	05 28	-49	105
74	09 19	49	103	08 30	49	104	07 41	49	104	06 52	50	105	06 02	49	105
73	09 54	50	104	09 04	49	105	08 15	49	105	07 26	50	106	06 36	49	106
72	10 28	49	105	09 39	50	105	08 49	49	106	08 00	50	106	07 10	50	107
71	11 02	49	106	10 13	50	106	09 23	50	107	08 33	49	107	07 44	50	108
70	11 36	-50	106	10 46	-49	107	09 57	-50	108	09 07	-50	108	08 17	-50	109
	0°			1°			2°			3°			4°		

LHA	5°			6°			7°			8°			9°		
	Hc	d	Z	Hc	d	Z	Hc	d	Z	Hc	d	Z	Hc	d	Z
	° ′	′	°	° ′	′	°	° ′	′	°	° ′	′	°	° ′	′	°
95	265														
94	266														
93	-5 48	49	90	267											
92	-5 13	49	91	-6 02	48	92	268								
91	-4 38	48	92	-5 26	49	93	269								
90	-4 03	-48	93	-4 51	-49	94	-5 40	-48	94	270					
89	-3 27	49	94	-4 16	48	94	-5 04	49	95	-5 53	48	95	271		
88	-2 52	49	95	-3 41	48	95	-4 29	49	96	-5 18	48	96	-6 06	49	97
87	-2 17	49	95	-3 06	48	96	-3 54	49	97	-4 43	48	97	-5 31	49	98
86	-1 42	49	96	-2 31	48	97	-3 19	49	97	-4 08	48	98	-4 56	49	99
85	-1 07	-49	97	-1 56	-48	98	-2 44	-49	98	-3 33	-48	99	-4 21	-49	99
84	-0 32	49	98	-1 21	48	98	-2 09	49	99	-2 58	49	100	-3 47	48	100
83	00 03	49	99	-0 46	49	99	-1 35	48	100	-2 23	49	100	-3 12	49	101
82	00 38	49	99	-0 11	49	100	-1 00	49	101	-1 49	48	101	-2 37	49	102
81	01 13	49	100	00 24	49	101	-0 25	49	101	-1 14	49	102	-2 03	49	103
80	01 47	-49	101	00 58	-49	102	00 09	-49	102	-0 40	-49	103	-1 29	-48	103
79	02 22	49	102	01 33	49	102	00 44	49	103	-0 05	49	104	-0 54	49	104
78	02 56	49	103	02 07	49	103	01 18	49	104	00 29	49	104	-0 20	49	105
77	03 31	50	103	02 41	49	104	01 52	49	105	01 03	49	105	00 14	49	106
76	04 05	49	104	03 16	50	105	02 26	49	105	01 37	49	106	00 48	50	107
75	04 39	-49	105	03 50	-50	106	03 00	-49	106	02 11	-50	107	01 21	-49	107
74	05 13	50	106	04 23	49	107	03 34	49	107	02 45	50	108	01 55	49	108
73	05 47	50	107	04 57	49	107	04 08	50	108	03 18	50	108	02 28	49	109
72	06 20	49	108	05 31	50	108	04 41	50	109	03 51	49	109	03 02	50	110
71	06 54	50	108	06 04	49	109	05 15	50	110	04 25	50	110	03 35	50	111
70	07 27	-49	109	06 38	-50	110	05 48	-50	110	04 58	-50	111	04 08	-50	111
	5°			6°			7°			8°			9°		

LHA	10°			11°			12°			13°			14°			LHA
	Hc	d	Z	Hc	d	Z	Hc	d	Z	Hc	d	Z	Hc	d	Z	
	° ′	′	°	° ′	′	°	° ′	′	°	° ′	′	°	° ′	′	°	
88	272															
87	273															
86	-5 45	48	99	274												
85	-5 10	-48	100	-5 58	-49	100	275									
84	-4 35	49	101	-5 24	48	101	276									
83	-4 01	48	102	-4 49	49	102	-5 38	49	103	277						
82	-3 26	49	102	-4 15	49	103	-5 04	48	103	-5 52	49	104	278			
81	-2 52	49	103	-3 41	48	104	-4 29	49	104	-5 18	49	105	-6 07	49	105	279
80	-2 17	-49	104	-3 06	-49	105	-3 55	-49	105	-4 44	-49	106	-5 33	-49	106	280
79	-1 43	49	105	-2 32	49	105	-3 21	49	106	-4 10	49	106	-4 59	49	107	281
78	-1 09	49	106	-1 58	49	106	-2 47	49	107	-3 36	49	107	-4 25	50	108	282
77	-0 35	49	106	-1 24	50	107	-2 14	49	107	-3 03	49	108	-3 52	49	109	283
76	-0 02	49	107	-0 51	49	108	-1 40	49	108	-2 29	50	109	-3 19	49	109	284
75	00 32	-49	108	-0 17	-50	109	-1 07	-49	109	-1 56	-49	110	-2 45	-50	110	285
74	01 06	50	109	00 16	49	109	-0 33	50	110	-1 23	49	110	-2 12	50	111	286
73	01 39	50	110	00 49	49	110	00 00	50	111	-0 50	50	111	-1 40	49	112	287
72	02 12	50	110	01 22	49	111	00 33	50	112	-0 17	50	112	-1 07	50	113	288
71	02 45	50	111	01 55	50	112	01 05	50	112	00 15	50	113	-0 35	49	113	289
70	03 18	-50	112	02 28	-50	113	01 38	-50	113	00 48	-50	114	-0 02	-50	114	290
	10°			11°			12°			13°			14°			

S. Lat. {LHA greater than 180°……. Zn=180−Z
{LHA less than 180°………. Zn=180+Z

LAT 54°

N. Lat. {LHA greater than 180°....... Zn=Z
{LHA less than 180°........... Zn=360−Z

DECLINATION (0°-14°) CONTRARY NAME TO LATITUDE

LHA	0° Hc	d	Z	1° Hc	d	Z	2° Hc	d	Z	3° Hc	d	Z	4° Hc	d	Z
	° ′	′	°	° ′	′	°	° ′	′	°	° ′	′	°	° ′	′	°
69	12 10	50	107	11 20	50	108	10 30	50	108	09 40	49	109	08 51	50	110
68	12 43	50	108	11 53	49	109	11 04	50	109	10 14	50	110	09 24	50	110
67	13 17	50	109	12 27	50	110	11 37	50	110	10 47	50	111	09 57	51	111
66	13 50	50	110	13 00	50	110	12 10	50	111	11 20	51	112	10 29	50	112
65	14 23	−50	111	13 33	−50	111	12 43	−51	112	11 52	−50	112	11 02	−50	113
64	14 56	50	112	14 06	51	112	13 15	50	113	12 25	51	113	11 34	50	114
63	15 29	51	112	14 38	50	113	13 48	51	114	12 57	50	114	12 07	51	115
62	16 01	50	113	15 11	51	114	14 20	51	114	13 29	50	115	12 39	51	116
61	16 33	50	114	15 43	51	115	14 52	51	115	14 01	51	116	13 10	51	116
60	17 06	−51	115	16 15	−51	116	15 24	−51	116	14 33	−51	117	13 42	−51	117
59	17 37	51	116	16 46	51	117	15 55	51	117	15 04	51	118	14 13	51	118
58	18 09	51	117	17 18	51	117	16 27	52	118	15 35	51	119	14 44	52	119
57	18 40	51	118	17 49	51	118	16 58	52	119	16 06	51	119	15 15	52	120
56	19 11	51	119	18 20	52	119	17 28	51	120	16 37	52	120	15 45	52	121
55	19 42	−51	120	18 51	−52	120	17 59	−52	121	17 07	−52	121	16 15	−52	122
54	20 13	52	120	19 21	52	121	18 29	52	122	17 37	52	122	16 45	52	123
53	20 43	52	121	19 51	52	122	18 59	52	122	18 07	52	123	17 15	53	124
52	21 13	52	122	20 21	52	123	19 29	53	123	18 36	52	124	17 44	53	124
51	21 43	53	123	20 50	52	124	19 58	53	124	19 05	52	125	18 13	53	125
50	22 12	−52	124	21 20	−53	125	20 27	−53	125	19 34	−52	126	18 42	−53	126
49	22 41	53	125	21 48	52	126	20 56	53	126	20 03	53	127	19 10	53	127
48	23 10	53	126	22 17	53	127	21 24	53	127	20 31	53	128	19 38	53	128
47	23 38	53	127	22 45	53	128	21 52	53	128	20 59	54	129	20 05	53	129
46	24 06	53	128	23 13	54	129	22 19	53	129	21 26	53	130	20 33	54	130
45	24 34	−54	129	23 40	−53	130	22 47	−54	130	21 53	−54	131	20 59	−53	131
44	25 01	54	130	24 07	54	130	23 13	53	131	22 20	54	131	21 26	54	132
43	25 28	54	131	24 34	54	131	23 40	54	132	22 46	54	132	21 52	54	133
42	25 54	54	132	25 00	54	132	24 06	54	133	23 12	54	133	22 18	55	134
41	26 20	54	133	25 26	54	133	24 32	55	134	23 37	54	134	22 43	55	135
40	26 46	−55	134	25 51	−54	134	24 57	−55	135	24 02	−54	135	23 08	−55	136
39	27 11	55	135	26 16	54	135	25 22	55	136	24 27	55	136	23 32	55	137
38	27 36	55	136	26 41	55	137	25 46	55	137	24 51	55	137	23 56	55	138
37	28 00	55	137	27 05	55	138	26 10	55	138	25 15	56	138	24 19	55	139
36	28 24	56	138	27 28	55	139	26 33	55	139	25 38	56	139	24 42	55	140
35	28 47	−55	139	27 52	−56	140	26 56	−56	140	26 00	−55	140	25 05	−56	141
34	29 10	56	140	28 14	56	141	27 18	55	141	26 23	56	141	25 27	56	142
33	29 32	56	141	28 36	56	142	27 40	56	142	26 44	56	143	25 48	56	143
32	29 54	56	142	28 58	56	143	28 02	56	143	27 06	57	144	26 09	56	144
31	30 15	56	143	29 19	56	144	28 23	57	144	27 26	56	145	26 30	57	145
30	30 36	−56	145	29 40	−57	145	28 43	−56	145	27 47	−57	146	26 50	−57	146
29	30 56	56	146	30 00	57	146	29 03	57	146	28 06	57	147	27 09	57	147
28	31 16	57	147	30 19	57	147	29 22	57	147	28 25	57	148	27 28	57	148
27	31 35	57	148	30 38	57	148	29 41	57	149	28 44	57	149	27 47	58	149
26	31 53	57	149	30 56	57	149	29 59	57	150	29 02	58	150	28 04	57	150
25	32 11	−57	150	31 14	−57	150	30 17	−58	151	29 19	−57	151	28 22	−58	151
24	32 29	58	151	31 31	57	152	30 34	58	152	29 36	58	152	28 38	58	153
23	32 45	57	152	31 48	58	153	30 50	58	153	29 52	58	153	28 54	58	154
22	33 01	57	154	32 04	58	154	31 06	58	154	30 08	58	154	29 10	59	155
21	33 17	58	155	32 19	58	155	31 21	58	155	30 23	59	156	29 24	58	156
20	33 32	−59	156	32 33	−58	156	31 35	−58	156	30 37	−59	157	29 38	−58	157
19	33 46	59	157	32 47	58	157	31 49	58	158	30 51	59	158	29 52	59	158
18	33 59	58	158	33 01	59	158	32 02	58	159	31 04	59	159	30 05	59	159
17	34 12	59	159	33 13	58	160	32 15	59	160	31 16	59	160	30 17	59	160
16	34 24	59	161	33 25	58	161	32 27	59	161	31 28	59	161	30 29	59	161
15	34 36	−59	162	33 37	−59	162	32 38	−59	162	31 39	−59	162	30 40	−59	163
14	34 46	59	163	33 47	59	163	32 48	59	163	31 49	59	164	30 50	59	164
13	34 56	59	164	33 57	59	164	32 58	59	165	31 59	60	165	30 59	59	165
12	35 06	60	165	34 06	59	166	33 07	59	166	32 08	60	166	31 08	59	166
11	35 14	59	167	34 15	60	167	33 15	59	167	32 16	59	167	31 17	60	167
10	35 22	−59	168	34 23	−60	168	33 23	−59	168	32 24	−60	168	31 24	−60	168
9	35 29	59	169	34 30	60	169	33 30	59	169	32 31	60	169	31 31	60	170
8	35 36	60	170	34 36	60	170	33 36	59	170	32 37	60	171	31 37	60	171
7	35 41	59	171	34 42	60	172	33 42	60	172	32 42	60	172	31 42	59	172
6	35 46	59	173	34 47	60	173	33 47	60	173	32 47	60	173	31 47	60	173
5	35 51	−60	174	34 51	−60	174	33 51	−60	174	32 51	−60	174	31 51	−60	174
4	35 54	60	175	34 54	60	175	33 54	60	175	32 54	60	175	31 54	60	175
3	35 57	60	176	34 57	60	176	33 57	60	176	32 57	60	176	31 57	60	177
2	35 59	60	178	34 59	60	178	33 59	60	178	32 59	60	178	31 59	60	178
1	36 00	60	179	35 00	60	179	34 00	60	179	33 00	60	179	32 00	60	179
0	36 00	−60	180	35 00	−60	180	34 00	−60	180	33 00	−60	180	32 00	−60	180

LHA	5° Hc	d	Z	6° Hc	d	Z	7° Hc	d	Z	8° Hc	d	Z	9° Hc	d	Z
	° ′	′	°	° ′	′	°	° ′	′	°	° ′	′	°	° ′	′	°
69	08 01	50	110	07 11	50	111	06 21	50	111	05 31	51	112	04 40	50	112
68	08 34	50	111	07 44	51	112	06 53	50	112	06 03	50	113	05 13	50	113
67	09 06	50	112	08 16	50	112	07 26	50	113	06 36	51	113	05 45	50	114
66	09 39	50	113	08 49	51	113	07 58	50	114	07 08	51	114	06 17	50	115
65	10 12	−51	114	09 21	−50	114	08 31	−51	115	07 40	−51	115	06 49	−50	116
64	10 44	51	114	09 53	50	115	09 03	51	115	08 12	51	116	07 21	51	117
63	11 16	51	115	10 25	51	116	09 34	51	116	08 43	50	117	07 53	51	117
62	11 48	51	116	10 57	51	117	10 06	51	117	09 15	51	118	08 24	51	118
61	12 19	51	117	11 28	51	117	10 37	51	118	09 46	51	119	08 55	52	119
60	12 51	−52	118	11 59	−51	118	11 08	−51	119	10 17	−52	119	09 25	−51	120
59	13 22	52	119	12 30	51	119	11 39	52	120	10 47	51	120	09 56	52	121
58	13 52	51	120	13 01	52	120	12 09	51	121	11 18	52	121	10 26	52	122
57	14 23	52	120	13 31	51	121	12 40	52	121	11 48	52	122	10 56	52	123
56	14 53	52	121	14 01	51	122	13 10	52	122	12 18	52	123	11 26	53	123
55	15 23	−52	122	14 31	−52	123	13 39	−52	123	12 47	−52	124	11 55	−52	124
54	15 53	52	123	15 01	52	124	14 09	53	124	13 16	52	125	12 24	53	125
53	16 22	52	124	15 30	52	125	14 38	53	125	13 45	52	126	12 53	53	126
52	16 51	52	125	15 59	53	125	15 06	52	126	14 14	53	126	13 21	53	127
51	17 20	52	126	16 28	53	126	15 35	53	127	14 42	53	127	13 49	53	128
50	17 49	−53	127	16 56	−53	127	16 03	−53	128	15 10	−53	128	14 17	−53	129
49	18 17	53	128	17 24	53	128	16 31	54	129	15 37	53	129	14 44	53	130
48	18 45	54	129	17 51	53	129	16 58	53	130	16 05	54	130	15 11	53	131
47	19 12	54	130	18 18	53	130	17 25	54	131	16 31	53	131	15 38	54	131
46	19 39	54	131	18 45	53	131	17 52	54	131	16 58	54	132	16 04	54	132
45	20 06	−54	131	19 12	−54	132	18 18	−54	132	17 24	−54	133	16 30	−54	133
44	20 32	54	132	19 38	54	133	18 44	54	133	17 50	55	134	16 55	54	134
43	20 58	55	133	20 03	54	134	19 09	54	134	18 15	55	135	17 20	54	135
42	21 23	54	134	20 29	55	135	19 34	54	135	18 40	55	136	17 45	55	136
41	21 48	54	135	20 54	55	136	19 59	55	136	19 04	55	137	18 09	55	137
40	22 13	−55	136	21 18	−55	137	20 23	−55	137	19 28	−55	138	18 33	−55	138
39	22 37	55	137	21 42	55	138	20 47	55	138	19 52	55	139	18 57	56	139
38	23 01	55	138	22 06	56	139	21 10	55	139	20 15	55	140	19 20	56	140
37	23 24	55	139	22 29	56	140	21 33	55	140	20 38	56	140	19 42	56	141
36	23 47	56	140	22 51	55	141	21 56	56	141	21 00	56	141	20 04	56	142
35	24 09	−56	141	23 13	−56	142	22 17	−55	142	21 22	−56	142	20 26	−56	143
34	24 31	56	142	23 35	56	143	22 39	56	143	21 43	56	143	20 47	56	144
33	24 52	56	143	23 56	56	144	23 00	56	144	22 04	57	144	21 07	56	145
32	25 13	56	144	24 17	57	145	23 20	56	145	22 24	57	145	21 27	56	146
31	25 33	56	145	24 37	57	146	23 40	56	146	22 44	57	146	21 47	57	147
30	25 53	−56	146	24 57	−57	147	24 00	−57	147	23 03	−57	147	22 06	−57	148
29	26 12	56	147	25 16	57	148	24 19	57	148	23 22	57	149	22 25	58	149
28	26 31	57	149	25 34	57	149	24 37	57	149	23 40	57	150	22 43	58	150
27	26 49	57	150	25 52	57	150	24 55	58	150	23 57	57	151	23 00	57	151
26	27 07	58	151	26 09	57	151	25 12	58	151	24 14	57	152	23 17	58	152
25	27 24	−58	152	26 26	−57	152	25 29	−58	152	24 31	−58	153	23 33	−58	153
24	27 40	57	153	26 43	58	153	25 45	58	153	24 47	58	154	23 49	58	154
23	27 56	58	154	26 58	58	154	26 00	58	154	25 02	58	155	24 04	58	155
22	28 11	58	155	27 13	58	155	26 15	58	156	25 17	58	156	24 19	58	156
21	28 26	58	156	27 28	58	156	26 30	59	157	25 31	58	157	24 33	59	157
20	28 40	−58	157	27 42	−59	157	26 43	−58	158	25 45	−59	158	24 46	−58	158
19	28 53	58	158	27 55	59	159	26 56	58	159	25 58	59	159	24 59	59	159
18	29 06	58	159	28 08	59	160	27 09	59	160	26 10	59	160	25 11	59	160
17	29 18	59	161	28 19	58	161	27 21	59	161	26 22	59	161	25 23	59	161
16	29 30	59	162	28 31	59	162	27 32	59	162	26 33	59	162	25 34	59	162
15	29 41	−60	163	28 41	−59	163	27 42	−59	163	26 43	−59	163	25 44	−59	164
14	29 51	59	164	28 52	60	164	27 52	59	164	26 53	59	164	25 54	59	165
13	30 00	59	165	29 01	59	165	28 02	60	165	27 02	59	166	26 03	59	166
12	30 09	59	166	29 10	60	166	28 10	59	167	27 11	60	167	26 11	59	167
11	30 17	59	167	29 18	60	167	28 18	59	168	27 19	60	168	26 19	60	168
10	30 24	−59	168	29 25	−60	169	28 25	−59	169	27 26	−60	169	26 26	−60	169
9	30 31	59	170	29 32	60	170	28 32	60	170	27 32	59	170	26 33	60	170
8	30 37	59	171	29 38	60	171	28 38	60	171	27 38	60	171	26 38	59	171
7	30 43	60	172	29 43	60	172	28 43	60	172	27 43	60	172	26 43	59	172
6	30 47	60	173	29 47	59	173	28 48	60	173	27 48	60	173	26 48	60	173
5	30 51	−60	174	29 51	−60	174	28 51	−60	174	27 51	−59	174	26 52	−60	175
4	30 54	60	175	29 54	60	175	28 54	59	176	27 55	60	176	26 55	60	176
3	30 57	60	177	29 57	60	177	28 57	60	177	27 57	60	177	26 57	60	177
2	30 59	60	178	29 59	60	178	28 59	60	178	27 59	60	178	26 59	60	178
1	31 00	60	179	30 00	60	179	29 00	60	179	28 00	60	179	27 00	60	179
0	31 00	−60	180	30 00	−60	180	29 00	−60	180	28 00	−60	180	27 00	−60	180

LHA	10° Hc	d	Z	11° Hc	d	Z	12° Hc	d	Z	13° Hc	d	Z	14° Hc	d	Z	LHA
	° ′	′	°	° ′	′	°	° ′	′	°	° ′	′	°	° ′	′	°	
69	03 50	50	113	03 00	50	113	02 10	50	114	01 20	50	115	00 30	50	115	291
68	04 23	50	114	03 33	51	114	02 42	50	115	01 52	50	115	01 02	51	116	292
67	04 55	50	115	04 05	51	115	03 14	50	116	02 24	51	116	01 33	50	117	293
66	05 27	51	115	04 36	50	116	03 46	51	116	02 55	50	117	02 05	51	117	294
65	05 59	−51	116	05 08	−51	117	04 17	−50	117	03 27	−51	118	02 36	−51	118	295
64	06 30	51	117	05 39	50	118	04 49	51	118	03 58	51	119	03 07	51	119	296
63	07 02	51	118	06 11	51	118	05 20	52	119	04 28	51	119	03 37	51	120	297
62	07 33	52	119	06 41	51	119	05 50	51	120	04 59	51	120	04 08	51	121	298
61	08 03	51	120	07 12	51	120	06 21	52	121	05 29	51	121	04 38	51	122	299
60	08 34	−51	120	07 43	−52	121	06 51	−51	121	06 00	−52	122	05 08	−52	122	300
59	09 04	51	121	08 13	52	122	07 21	52	122	06 29	51	123	05 38	52	123	301
58	09 34	52	122	08 42	51	123	07 51	52	123	06 59	52	124	06 07	52	124	302
57	10 04	52	123	09 12	52	124	08 20	52	124	07 28	52	125	06 36	52	125	303
56	10 33	52	124	09 41	52	124	08 49	52	125	07 57	52	125	07 05	53	126	304
55	11 03	−53	125	10 10	−52	125	09 18	−52	126	08 26	−53	126	07 33	−52	127	305
54	11 31	52	126	10 39	53	126	09 46	52	127	08 54	53	127	08 01	52	128	306
53	12 00	53	127	11 07	52	127	10 15	53	128	09 22	53	128	08 29	53	128	307
52	12 28	53	127	11 35	53	128	10 42	53	128	09 49	53	129	08 56	53	129	308
51	12 56	53	128	12 03	53	129	11 10	53	129	10 17	53	130	09 24	54	130	309
50	13 24	−54	129	12 30	−53	130	11 37	−53	130	10 44	−54	131	09 50	−53	131	310
49	13 51	54	130	12 57	53	131	12 04	54	131	11 10	53	131	10 17	54	132	311
48	14 18	54	131	13 24	54	131	12 30	53	132	11 37	54	132	10 43	54	133	312
47	14 44	54	132	13 50	54	132	12 56	54	133	12 02	53	133	11 09	54	134	313
46	15 10	54	133	14 16	54	133	13 22	54	134	12 28	54	134	11 34	54	135	314
45	15 36	−54	134	14 42	−55	134	13 47	−54	135	12 53	−54	135	11 59	−55	136	315
44	16 01	54	135	15 07	55	135	14 12	54	136	13 18	55	136	12 23	54	136	316
43	16 26	55	136	15 31	54	136	14 37	55	136	13 42	55	137	12 47	54	137	317
42	16 50	54	137	15 56	55	137	15 01	55	137	14 06	55	138	13 11	55	138	318
41	17 14	54	137	16 20	55	138	15 25	55	138	14 30	55	139	13 35	56	139	319
40	17 38	−55	138	16 43	−55	139	15 48	−55	139	14 53	−56	140	13 57	−55	140	320
39	18 01	55	139	17 06	55	140	16 11	56	140	15 15	55	141	14 20	56	141	321
38	18 24	55	140	17 29	56	141	16 33	56	141	15 37	55	142	14 42	56	142	322
37	18 46	55	141	17 51	56	142	16 55	56	142	15 59	56	142	15 03	55	143	323
36	19 08	56	142	18 12	56	143	17 16	55	143	16 21	56	143	15 25	57	144	324
35	19 30	−56	143	18 34	−57	144	17 37	−56	144	16 41	−56	144	15 45	−56	145	325
34	19 51	57	144	18 54	56	145	17 58	56	145	17 02	57	145	16 05	56	146	326
33	20 11	57	145	19 14	56	146	18 18	56	146	17 22	57	146	16 25	57	147	327
32	20 31	57	146	19 34	56	147	18 38	57	147	17 41	57	147	16 44	57	148	328
31	20 50	57	147	19 53	56	148	18 57	57	148	18 00	57	148	17 03	57	149	329
30	21 09	−57	148	20 12	−57	149	19 15	−57	149	18 18	−57	149	17 21	−57	150	330
29	21 27	57	149	20 30	57	150	19 33	57	150	18 36	57	150	17 39	58	150	331
28	21 45	57	150	20 48	57	151	19 51	58	151	18 53	57	151	17 56	58	151	332
27	22 03	58	151	21 05	57	152	20 08	58	152	19 10	58	152	18 12	57	152	333
26	22 19	57	152	21 22	58	153	20 24	58	153	19 26	57	153	18 29	58	153	334
25	22 35	−57	153	21 38	−58	154	20 40	−58	154	19 42	−58	154	18 44	−58	154	335
24	22 51	58	154	21 53	58	155	20 55	58	155	19 57	58	155	18 59	58	155	336
23	23 06	58	155	22 08	58	156	21 10	58	156	20 12	58	156	19 14	59	156	337
22	23 21	59	156	22 22	58	157	21 24	58	157	20 26	59	157	19 27	58	157	338
21	23 34	58	157	22 36	58	158	21 38	59	158	20 39	58	158	19 41	59	158	339
20	23 48	−59	158	22 49	−58	159	21 51	−59	159	20 52	−59	159	19 53	−58	159	340
19	24 00	58	160	23 02	59	160	22 03	59	160	21 04	58	160	20 06	59	160	341
18	24 12	58	161	23 14	59	161	22 15	59	161	21 16	59	161	20 17	59	161	342
17	24 24	59	162	23 25	59	162	22 26	59	162	21 27	59	162	20 28	59	162	343
16	24 35	59	163	23 36	59	163	22 37	59	163	21 38	59	163	20 39	60	163	344
15	24 45	−59	164	23 46	−59	164	22 47	−60	164	21 47	−59	164	20 48	−59	164	345
14	24 55	60	165	23 55	59	165	22 56	59	165	21 57	60	165	20 57	59	165	346
13	25 04	60	166	24 04	59	166	23 05	60	166	22 05	59	166	21 06	59	167	347
12	25 12	60	167	24 12	59	167	23 13	60	167	22 13	59	167	21 14	60	168	348
11	25 19	59	168	24 20	60	168	23 20	59	168	22 21	60	168	21 21	59	169	349
10	25 26	−59	169	24 27	−60	169	23 27	−59	169	22 28	−60	170	21 28	−60	170	350
9	25 33	60	170	24 33	60	170	23 33	59	170	22 34	60	171	21 34	60	171	351
8	25 39	60	171	24 39	60	171	23 39	60	172	22 39	60	172	21 39	59	172	352
7	25 44	60	172	24 44	60	172	23 44	60	173	22 44	60	173	21 44	60	173	353
6	25 48	60	173	24 48	60	174	23 48	60	174	22 48	60	174	21 48	59	174	354
5	25 52	−60	175	24 52	−60	175	23 52	−60	175	22 52	−60	175	21 52	−60	175	355
4	25 55	60	176	24 55	60	176	23 55	60	176	22 55	60	176	21 55	60	176	356
3	25 57	60	177	24 57	60	177	23 57	60	177	22 57	60	177	21 57	60	177	357
2	25 59	60	178	24 59	60	178	23 59	60	178	22 59	60	178	21 59	60	178	358
1	26 00	60	179	25 00	60	179	24 00	60	179	23 00	60	179	22 00	60	179	359
0	26 00	−60	180	25 00	−60	180	24 00	−60	180	23 00	−60	180	22 00	−60	180	360

S. Lat. {LHA greater than 180°........ Zn=180−Z
{LHA less than 180°........... Zn=180+Z

DECLINATION (0°-14°) CONTRARY NAME TO LATITUDE

LAT 54°

N. Lat. {LHA greater than 180°....... Zn=Z; LHA less than 180°........... Zn=360−Z}

DECLINATION (15°-29°) SAME NAME AS LATITUDE

LHA	15° Hc	d	Z	16° Hc	d	Z	17° Hc	d	Z	18° Hc	d	Z	19° Hc	d	Z
	° ′	′	°	° ′	′	°	° ′	′	°	° ′	′	°	° ′	′	°
0	51 00	+60	180	52 00	+60	180	53 00	+60	180	54 00	+60	180	55 00	+60	180
1	51 00	60	179	52 00	60	178	53 00	60	178	54 00	60	178	55 00	60	178
2	50 58	60	177	51 58	60	177	52 58	60	177	53 58	60	177	54 58	60	177
3	50 56	60	175	51 56	60	175	52 56	60	175	53 56	59	175	54 55	60	175
4	50 53	59	174	51 52	60	174	52 52	60	174	53 52	60	174	54 52	60	173
5	50 48	+60	172	51 48	+60	172	52 48	+60	172	53 48	+59	172	54 47	+60	172
6	50 43	60	171	51 43	60	171	52 43	59	171	53 42	60	170	54 42	60	170
7	50 37	60	169	51 37	59	169	52 36	60	169	53 36	59	169	54 35	60	169
8	50 30	60	168	51 30	59	168	52 29	59	167	53 28	60	167	54 28	59	167
9	50 22	59	166	51 21	60	166	52 21	59	166	53 20	59	166	54 19	60	165
10	50 13	+60	165	51 13	+59	165	52 12	+59	164	53 11	+59	164	54 10	+59	164
11	50 04	59	163	51 03	59	163	52 02	59	163	53 01	59	162	54 00	58	162
12	49 53	59	162	50 52	59	162	51 51	59	161	52 50	58	161	53 48	59	161
13	49 42	58	160	50 40	59	160	51 39	59	160	52 38	58	159	53 36	59	159
14	49 29	59	159	50 28	58	159	51 26	59	158	52 25	58	158	53 23	58	157
15	49 16	+59	158	50 15	+58	157	51 13	+58	157	52 11	+58	156	53 09	+58	156
16	49 02	58	156	50 00	58	156	50 58	58	155	51 56	58	155	52 54	58	154
17	48 48	58	155	49 46	57	154	50 43	58	154	51 41	58	153	52 39	57	153
18	48 32	58	153	49 30	57	153	50 27	58	152	51 25	57	152	52 22	57	151
19	48 16	57	152	49 13	58	151	50 11	57	151	51 08	57	150	52 05	57	150
20	47 59	+57	150	48 56	+57	150	49 53	+57	150	50 50	+57	149	51 47	+56	149
21	47 41	57	149	48 38	57	149	49 35	56	148	50 31	57	148	51 28	56	147
22	47 23	56	148	48 19	57	147	49 16	56	147	50 12	56	146	51 08	57	146
23	47 03	57	146	48 00	56	146	48 56	56	145	49 52	56	145	50 48	56	144
24	46 43	57	145	47 40	56	145	48 36	56	144	49 32	55	143	50 27	56	143
25	46 23	+56	144	47 19	+56	143	48 15	+55	143	49 10	+56	142	50 06	+55	142
26	46 02	55	142	46 57	56	142	47 53	55	141	48 48	55	141	49 43	55	140
27	45 40	55	141	46 35	56	141	47 31	55	140	48 26	54	139	49 20	55	139
28	45 18	55	140	46 13	55	139	47 08	54	139	48 02	55	138	48 57	54	138
29	44 54	55	139	45 49	55	138	46 44	54	137	47 38	55	137	48 33	54	136
30	44 31	+54	137	45 25	+55	137	46 20	+54	136	47 14	+54	136	48 08	+54	135
31	44 07	54	136	45 01	54	136	45 55	54	135	46 49	54	134	47 43	53	134
32	43 42	54	135	44 36	54	134	45 30	54	134	46 24	53	133	47 17	53	132
33	43 17	54	134	44 11	53	133	45 04	54	133	45 58	53	132	46 51	53	131
34	42 51	54	133	43 45	53	132	44 38	53	131	45 31	53	131	46 24	52	130
35	42 25	+53	131	43 18	+53	131	44 11	+53	130	45 04	+53	129	45 57	+52	129
36	41 58	53	130	42 51	53	130	43 44	53	129	44 37	52	128	45 29	52	128
37	41 31	53	129	42 24	52	128	43 16	53	128	44 09	52	127	45 01	52	126
38	41 03	53	128	41 56	52	127	42 48	52	127	43 40	52	126	44 32	52	125
39	40 35	53	127	41 28	52	126	42 20	52	126	43 12	51	125	44 03	51	124
40	40 07	+52	126	40 59	+52	125	41 51	+51	124	42 42	+52	124	43 34	+51	123
41	39 38	52	125	40 30	52	124	41 22	51	123	42 13	51	123	43 04	51	122
42	39 09	51	124	40 00	52	123	40 52	51	122	41 43	51	122	42 34	50	121
43	38 39	52	123	39 31	51	122	40 22	51	121	41 13	50	120	42 03	51	120
44	38 09	52	121	39 01	50	121	39 51	51	120	40 42	51	119	41 33	50	119
45	37 39	+51	120	38 30	+51	120	39 21	+50	119	40 11	+50	118	41 01	+50	118
46	37 09	50	119	37 59	51	119	38 50	50	118	39 40	50	117	40 30	50	117
47	36 38	50	118	37 28	51	118	38 19	50	117	39 09	49	116	39 58	50	116
48	36 06	51	117	36 57	50	117	37 47	50	116	38 37	49	115	39 26	50	115
49	35 35	50	116	36 25	50	116	37 15	50	115	38 05	49	114	38 54	49	114
50	35 03	+50	115	35 53	+50	115	36 43	+50	114	37 33	+49	113	38 22	+49	113
51	34 31	50	114	35 21	50	114	36 11	49	113	37 00	49	112	37 49	49	112
52	33 59	50	113	34 49	49	113	35 38	49	112	36 27	49	111	37 16	49	111
53	33 26	50	112	34 16	49	112	35 05	49	111	35 54	49	110	36 43	49	110
54	32 54	49	112	33 43	49	111	34 32	49	110	35 21	49	109	36 10	48	109
55	32 21	+49	111	33 10	+49	110	33 59	+49	109	34 48	+48	108	35 36	+48	108
56	31 48	49	110	32 37	49	109	33 26	48	108	34 14	49	108	35 03	48	107
57	31 14	49	109	32 03	49	108	32 52	48	107	33 40	49	107	34 29	48	106
58	30 41	49	108	31 30	48	107	32 18	49	106	33 07	48	106	33 55	48	105
59	30 07	49	107	30 56	48	106	31 44	49	106	32 33	48	105	33 21	47	104
60	29 33	+49	106	30 22	+48	105	31 10	+48	105	31 58	+48	104	32 46	+48	103
61	28 59	49	105	29 48	48	104	30 36	48	104	31 24	48	103	32 12	47	102
62	28 25	49	104	29 14	48	104	30 02	48	103	30 50	47	102	31 37	48	101
63	27 51	48	103	28 39	48	103	29 27	48	102	30 15	48	101	31 03	47	101
64	27 17	48	102	28 05	48	102	28 53	47	101	29 40	48	100	30 28	47	100
65	26 42	+48	102	27 30	+48	101	28 18	+48	100	29 06	+47	100	29 53	+47	99
66	26 07	48	101	26 55	48	100	27 43	48	99	28 31	47	99	29 18	47	98
67	25 33	48	100	26 21	47	99	27 08	48	98	27 56	47	98	28 43	47	97
68	24 58	48	99	25 46	48	98	26 34	47	98	27 21	47	97	28 08	47	96
69	24 23	48	98	25 11	48	97	25 59	47	97	26 46	47	96	27 33	47	95

LHA	20° Hc	d	Z	21° Hc	d	Z	22° Hc	d	Z	23° Hc	d	Z	24° Hc	d	Z
	° ′	′	°	° ′	′	°	° ′	′	°	° ′	′	°	° ′	′	°
0	56 00	+60	180	57 00	+60	180	58 00	+60	180	59 00	+60	180	60 00	+60	180
1	56 00	60	178	57 00	60	178	58 00	60	178	59 00	59	178	59 59	60	178
2	55 58	60	177	56 58	60	177	57 58	60	177	58 58	60	176	59 58	60	176
3	55 55	60	175	56 55	60	175	57 55	60	175	58 55	60	175	59 55	60	175
4	55 52	60	173	56 52	59	173	57 51	60	173	58 51	60	173	59 51	60	173
5	55 47	+60	172	56 47	+60	172	57 47	+59	171	58 46	+60	171	59 46	+60	171
6	55 42	59	170	56 41	60	170	57 41	59	170	58 40	60	169	59 40	59	169
7	55 35	59	168	56 34	60	168	57 34	59	168	58 33	60	168	59 33	59	167
8	55 27	60	167	56 27	59	166	57 26	59	166	58 25	59	166	59 24	60	166
9	55 19	59	165	56 18	59	165	57 17	59	164	58 16	59	164	59 15	59	164
10	55 09	+59	163	56 08	+59	163	57 07	+59	163	58 06	+59	162	59 05	+58	162
11	54 58	59	162	55 57	59	161	56 56	59	161	57 55	58	161	58 53	59	160
12	54 47	59	160	55 46	58	160	56 44	59	159	57 43	58	159	58 41	58	159
13	54 35	58	159	55 33	58	158	56 31	58	158	57 29	59	157	58 28	58	157
14	54 21	58	157	55 19	58	157	56 17	58	156	57 15	58	156	58 13	58	155
15	54 07	+58	156	55 05	+58	155	56 03	+57	155	57 00	+58	154	57 58	+57	154
16	53 52	58	154	54 50	57	154	55 47	58	153	56 45	57	152	57 42	57	152
17	53 36	57	152	54 33	58	152	55 31	57	151	56 28	57	151	57 25	57	150
18	53 19	57	151	54 16	57	150	55 13	57	150	56 10	57	149	57 07	56	149
19	53 02	57	149	53 59	56	149	54 55	57	148	55 52	56	148	56 48	56	147
20	52 43	+57	148	53 40	+56	147	54 36	+57	147	55 33	+56	146	56 29	+55	146
21	52 24	57	147	53 21	56	146	54 17	56	145	55 13	55	145	56 08	56	144
22	52 05	55	145	53 00	56	145	53 56	56	144	54 52	55	143	55 47	55	143
23	51 44	56	144	52 40	55	143	53 35	55	142	54 30	55	142	55 25	55	141
24	51 23	55	142	52 18	55	142	53 13	55	141	54 08	55	140	55 03	54	140
25	51 01	+55	141	51 56	+55	140	52 51	+54	140	53 45	+55	139	54 40	+54	138
26	50 38	55	140	51 33	54	139	52 27	55	138	53 22	54	138	54 16	53	137
27	50 15	54	138	51 09	55	138	52 04	54	137	52 58	53	136	53 51	54	135
28	49 51	54	137	50 45	54	136	51 39	54	135	52 33	53	135	53 26	53	134
29	49 27	54	136	50 21	53	135	51 14	53	134	52 07	53	133	53 00	53	133
30	49 02	+53	134	49 55	+54	134	50 49	+53	133	51 42	+52	132	52 34	+53	131
31	48 36	53	133	49 29	53	132	50 22	53	132	51 15	52	131	52 07	52	130
32	48 10	53	132	49 03	53	131	49 56	52	130	50 48	52	130	51 40	52	129
33	47 44	52	131	48 36	53	130	49 29	52	129	50 21	51	128	51 12	52	127
34	47 16	53	129	48 09	52	129	49 01	52	128	49 53	51	127	50 44	51	126
35	46 49	+52	128	47 41	+52	127	48 33	+51	127	49 24	+51	126	50 15	+51	125
36	46 21	52	127	47 13	51	126	48 04	51	125	48 55	51	125	49 46	51	124
37	45 53	51	126	46 44	51	125	47 35	51	124	48 26	51	123	49 17	50	123
38	45 24	51	125	46 15	51	124	47 06	51	123	47 57	50	122	48 47	50	121
39	44 54	51	123	45 45	51	123	46 36	51	122	47 27	50	121	48 17	49	120
40	44 25	+51	122	45 16	+50	122	46 06	+50	121	46 56	+50	120	47 46	+49	119
41	43 55	50	121	44 45	51	120	45 36	49	120	46 25	50	119	47 15	49	118
42	43 24	51	120	44 15	50	119	45 05	49	119	45 54	50	118	46 44	49	117
43	42 54	50	119	43 44	50	118	44 34	49	117	45 23	49	117	46 12	49	116
44	42 23	50	118	43 13	49	117	44 02	49	116	44 51	49	116	45 40	49	115
45	41 51	+50	117	42 41	+49	116	43 30	+49	115	44 19	+49	115	45 08	+48	114
46	41 20	49	116	42 09	49	115	42 58	49	114	43 47	49	114	44 36	48	113
47	40 48	49	115	41 37	49	114	42 26	49	113	43 15	48	113	44 03	48	112
48	40 16	49	114	41 05	49	113	41 54	48	112	42 42	48	111	43 30	48	111
49	39 43	49	113	40 32	49	112	41 21	48	111	42 09	48	110	42 57	47	110
50	39 11	+48	112	39 59	+49	111	40 48	+48	110	41 36	+48	110	42 24	+47	109
51	38 38	48	111	39 26	49	110	40 15	48	109	41 03	47	109	41 50	47	108
52	38 05	48	110	38 53	48	109	39 41	48	108	40 29	47	108	41 16	48	107
53	37 32	48	109	38 20	48	108	39 08	47	107	39 55	48	107	40 43	47	106
54	36 58	48	108	37 46	48	107	38 34	47	106	39 21	48	106	40 09	46	105
55	36 24	+48	107	37 12	+48	106	38 00	+47	106	38 47	+47	105	39 34	+47	104
56	35 51	47	106	36 38	48	105	37 26	47	105	38 13	47	104	39 00	47	103
57	35 17	47	105	36 04	48	104	36 52	47	104	37 39	47	103	38 26	46	102
58	34 43	47	104	35 30	47	104	36 17	47	103	37 04	47	102	37 51	46	101
59	34 08	48	103	34 56	47	103	35 43	47	102	36 30	46	101	37 16	47	100
60	33 34	+47	102	34 21	+47	102	35 08	+47	101	35 55	+47	100	36 42	+46	99
61	32 59	48	102	33 47	47	101	34 34	46	100	35 20	47	99	36 07	46	99
62	32 25	47	101	33 12	47	100	33 59	47	99	34 46	46	98	35 32	46	98
63	31 50	47	100	32 37	47	99	33 24	47	98	34 11	46	98	34 57	46	97
64	31 15	47	99	32 02	47	98	32 49	47	97	33 36	46	97	34 22	46	96
65	30 40	+47	98	31 27	+47	97	32 14	+47	97	33 01	+46	96	33 47	+46	95
66	30 05	47	97	30 52	47	97	31 39	46	96	32 25	47	95	33 12	46	94
67	29 30	47	96	30 17	47	96	31 04	46	95	31 50	46	94	32 36	46	93
68	28 55	47	96	29 42	47	95	30 29	46	94	31 15	46	93	32 01	46	93
69	28 20	47	95	29 07	47	94	29 54	46	93	30 40	46	93	31 26	46	92

LHA	25° Hc	d	Z	26° Hc	d	Z	27° Hc	d	Z	28° Hc	d	Z	29° Hc	d	Z	LHA
	° ′	′	°	° ′	′	°	° ′	′	°	° ′	′	°	° ′	′	°	
0	61 00	+60	180	62 00	+60	180	63 00	+60	180	64 00	+60	180	65 00	+60	180	360
1	60 59	60	178	61 59	60	178	62 59	60	178	63 59	60	178	64 59	60	178	359
2	60 58	60	176	61 58	60	176	62 58	60	176	63 58	60	176	64 58	59	176	358
3	60 55	60	174	61 55	60	174	62 55	59	174	63 54	60	174	64 54	60	174	357
4	60 51	60	173	61 51	59	172	62 50	60	172	63 50	60	172	64 50	60	172	356
5	60 46	+59	171	61 45	+60	171	62 45	+60	170	63 45	+59	170	64 44	+60	170	355
6	60 39	60	169	61 39	59	169	62 38	60	168	63 38	59	168	64 37	60	168	354
7	60 32	59	167	61 31	60	167	62 31	59	166	63 30	59	166	64 29	59	166	353
8	60 24	59	165	61 23	59	165	62 22	59	165	63 21	59	164	64 20	59	164	352
9	60 14	59	163	61 13	59	163	62 12	59	163	63 11	58	162	64 09	59	162	351
10	60 03	+59	162	61 02	+59	161	62 01	+58	161	62 59	+59	160	63 58	+58	160	350
11	59 52	58	160	60 50	59	159	61 49	58	159	62 47	58	158	63 45	58	158	349
12	59 39	58	158	60 37	58	158	61 35	58	157	62 33	58	157	63 31	58	156	348
13	59 26	57	156	60 23	58	156	61 21	58	155	62 19	57	155	63 16	57	154	347
14	59 11	58	155	60 09	57	154	61 06	57	154	62 03	57	153	63 00	57	152	346
15	58 55	+58	153	59 53	+57	152	60 50	+57	152	61 47	+56	151	62 43	+57	150	345
16	58 39	57	151	59 36	57	151	60 33	56	150	61 29	56	149	62 25	57	149	344
17	58 22	56	150	59 18	57	149	60 15	56	148	61 11	56	148	62 07	55	147	343
18	58 03	57	148	59 00	56	147	59 56	55	147	60 51	56	146	61 47	55	145	342
19	57 44	56	146	58 40	56	146	59 36	55	145	60 31	55	144	61 26	55	143	341
20	57 24	+56	145	58 20	+55	144	59 15	+55	143	60 10	+55	143	61 05	+54	142	340
21	57 04	55	143	57 59	55	143	58 54	54	142	59 48	55	141	60 43	54	140	339
22	56 42	55	142	57 37	55	141	58 32	54	140	59 26	54	139	60 20	53	139	338
23	56 20	54	140	57 14	55	140	58 09	54	139	59 03	53	138	59 56	53	137	337
24	55 57	54	139	56 51	54	138	57 45	54	137	58 39	53	136	59 32	52	136	336
25	55 34	+53	137	56 27	+54	137	57 21	+53	136	58 14	+53	135	59 07	+52	134	335
26	55 09	54	136	56 03	53	135	56 56	53	134	57 49	52	133	58 41	52	133	334
27	54 45	53	135	55 38	52	134	56 30	53	133	57 23	52	132	58 15	51	131	333
28	54 19	53	133	55 12	52	132	56 04	52	132	56 56	52	131	57 48	51	130	332
29	53 53	52	132	54 45	52	131	55 37	52	130	56 29	51	129	57 20	51	128	331
30	53 27	+52	131	54 19	+51	130	55 10	+51	129	56 01	+51	128	56 52	+51	127	330
31	52 59	52	129	53 51	51	128	54 42	51	127	55 33	51	127	56 24	50	126	329
32	52 32	51	128	53 23	51	127	54 14	51	126	55 05	50	125	55 55	49	124	328
33	52 04	51	127	52 55	50	126	53 45	51	125	54 36	49	124	55 25	50	123	327
34	51 35	51	125	52 26	50	125	53 16	50	124	54 06	50	123	54 56	49	122	326
35	51 06	+51	124	51 57	+50	123	52 47	+49	122	53 36	+49	121	54 25	+49	120	325
36	50 37	50	123	51 27	50	122	52 17	49	121	53 06	49	120	53 55	48	119	324
37	50 07	50	122	50 57	49	121	51 46	49	120	52 35	49	119	53 24	48	118	323
38	49 37	49	121	50 26	50	120	51 16	48	119	52 04	49	118	52 53	47	117	322
39	49 06	50	119	49 56	49	119	50 45	48	118	51 33	48	117	52 21	47	116	321
40	48 35	+49	118	49 24	+49	117	50 13	+48	117	51 01	+48	116	51 49	+47	115	320
41	48 04	49	117	48 53	48	116	49 41	48	115	50 29	48	114	51 17	47	114	319
42	47 33	48	116	48 21	48	115	49 09	48	114	49 57	47	113	50 44	47	112	318
43	47 01	48	115	47 49	48	114	48 37	48	113	49 25	47	112	50 12	46	111	317
44	46 29	48	114	47 17	48	113	48 05	47	112	48 52	47	111	49 39	46	110	316
45	45 56	+48	113	46 44	+48	112	47 32	+47	111	48 19	+46	110	49 05	+47	109	315
46	45 24	47	112	46 11	48	111	46 59	47	110	47 46	46	109	48 32	46	108	314
47	44 51	47	111	45 38	47	110	46 25	47	109	47 12	46	108	47 58	46	107	313
48	44 18	47	110	45 05	47	109	45 52	47	108	46 39	46	107	47 25	45	106	312
49	43 44	48	109	44 32	46	108	45 18	47	107	46 05	46	106	46 51	45	105	311
50	43 11	+47	108	43 58	+47	107	44 45	+46	106	45 31	+46	105	46 17	+45	104	310
51	42 37	47	107	43 24	47	106	44 11	46	105	44 57	45	104	45 42	45	103	309
52	42 04	46	106	42 50	47	105	43 37	45	104	44 22	46	103	45 08	45	102	308
53	41 30	46	105	42 16	46	104	43 02	46	103	43 48	45	102	44 33	45	101	307
54	40 55	47	104	41 42	46	103	42 28	46	102	43 14	45	101	43 59	45	101	306
55	40 21	+46	103	41 07	+46	102	41 53	+46	101	42 39	+45	101	43 24	+45	100	305
56	39 47	46	102	40 33	46	101	41 19	45	101	42 04	45	100	42 49	45	99	304
57	39 12	46	101	39 58	46	100	40 44	45	100	41 29	45	99	42 14	45	98	303
58	38 37	46	100	39 23	46	100	40 09	45	99	40 54	45	98	41 39	45	97	302
59	38 03	46	99	38 49	45	99	39 34	45	98	40 19	45	97	41 04	45	96	301
60	37 28	+46	99	38 14	+45	98	38 59	+45	97	39 44	+45	96	40 29	+45	95	300
61	36 53	46	98	37 39	45	97	38 24	45	96	39 09	45	95	39 54	44	94	299
62	36 18	46	97	37 04	45	96	37 49	45	95	38 34	45	94	39 19	44	94	298
63	35 43	46	96	36 29	45	95	37 14	45	94	37 59	45	94	38 44	44	93	297
64	35 08	45	95	35 53	46	94	36 39	45	94	37 24	44	93	38 08	45	92	296
65	34 33	+45	94	35 18	+46	94	36 04	+45	93	36 49	+44	92	37 33	+44	91	295
66	33 58	45	93	34 43	45	93	35 28	45	92	36 13	45	91	36 58	44	90	294
67	33 22	46	93	34 08	45	92	34 53	45	91	35 38	45	90	36 23	44	89	293
68	32 47	46	92	33 33	45	91	34 18	45	90	35 03	44	89	35 47	45	89	292
69	32 12	45	91	32 57	46	90	33 43	45	89	34 28	44	89	35 12	44	88	291

S. Lat. {LHA greater than 180°....... Zn=180−Z; LHA less than 180°........... Zn=180+Z}

N. Lat. {LHA greater than 180°....... Zn=Z; LHA less than 180°........... Zn=360−Z}

DECLINATION (15°-29°) SAME NAME AS LATITUDE

LHA	15° Hc	15° d	15° Z	16° Hc	16° d	16° Z	17° Hc	17° d	17° Z	18° Hc	18° d	18° Z	19° Hc	19° d	19° Z
	° ′	′	°	° ′	′	°	° ′	′	°	° ′	′	°	° ′	′	°
70	23 48	+48	97	24 36	+47	97	25 23	+48	96	26 11	+47	95	26 58	+47	95
71	23 13	48	96	24 01	47	96	24 48	48	95	25 36	47	94	26 23	47	94
72	22 38	48	96	23 26	47	95	24 13	48	94	25 01	47	94	25 48	47	93
73	22 03	48	95	22 51	47	94	23 38	47	93	24 25	47	93	25 12	47	92
74	21 28	47	94	22 15	48	93	23 03	47	93	23 50	47	92	24 37	47	91
75	20 53	+47	93	21 40	+48	92	22 28	+47	92	23 15	+47	91	24 02	+47	90
76	20 17	48	92	21 05	47	92	21 52	48	91	22 40	47	90	23 27	47	90
77	19 42	48	91	20 30	47	91	21 17	47	90	22 04	47	90	22 51	47	89
78	19 07	47	91	19 54	48	90	20 42	47	89	21 29	47	89	22 16	47	88
79	18 32	47	90	19 19	48	89	20 07	47	89	20 54	47	88	21 41	47	87
80	17 56	+48	89	18 44	+47	88	19 31	+48	88	20 19	+47	87	21 06	+47	86
81	17 21	48	88	18 09	47	88	18 56	47	87	19 43	48	86	20 31	47	86
82	16 46	47	87	17 33	48	87	18 21	47	86	19 08	47	86	19 55	47	85
83	16 11	47	87	16 58	48	86	17 46	47	85	18 33	47	85	19 20	47	84
84	15 35	48	86	16 23	48	85	17 11	47	85	17 58	47	84	18 45	47	83
85	15 00	+48	85	15 48	+47	84	16 35	+48	84	17 23	+47	83	18 10	+47	83
86	14 25	48	84	15 13	47	84	16 00	48	83	16 48	47	82	17 35	48	82
87	13 50	48	83	14 38	47	83	15 25	48	82	16 13	47	82	17 00	48	81
88	13 15	48	83	14 03	48	82	14 51	47	81	15 38	48	81	16 26	47	80
89	12 40	48	82	13 28	48	81	14 16	47	81	15 03	48	80	15 51	47	79
90	12 05	+48	81	12 53	+48	80	13 41	+48	80	14 29	+47	79	15 16	+48	79
91	11 30	48	80	12 18	48	80	13 06	48	79	13 54	48	78	14 42	47	78
92	10 56	48	80	11 44	48	79	12 32	48	78	13 20	47	78	14 07	48	77
93	10 21	48	79	11 09	48	78	11 57	48	78	12 45	48	77	13 33	48	76
94	09 47	48	78	10 35	48	77	11 23	48	77	12 11	48	76	12 59	48	76
95	09 12	+48	77	10 00	+49	77	10 49	+48	76	11 37	+48	75	12 25	+48	75
96	08 38	48	76	09 26	48	76	10 14	49	75	11 03	48	75	11 51	48	74
97	08 04	48	76	08 52	48	75	09 40	49	74	10 29	48	74	11 17	48	73
98	07 30	48	75	08 18	49	74	09 07	48	74	09 55	48	73	10 43	49	72
99	06 56	48	74	07 44	49	73	08 33	48	73	09 21	49	72	10 10	48	72
100	06 22	+48	73	07 10	+49	73	07 59	+49	72	08 48	+48	71	09 36	+49	71
101	05 48	49	72	06 37	49	72	07 26	49	71	08 15	48	71	09 03	49	70
102	05 15	48	72	06 03	49	71	06 52	49	70	07 41	49	70	08 30	49	69
103	04 41	49	71	05 30	49	70	06 19	49	70	07 08	49	69	07 57	49	69
104	04 08	49	70	04 57	49	69	05 46	49	69	06 35	50	68	07 25	49	68
105	03 35	+49	69	04 24	+49	69	05 13	+50	68	06 03	+49	68	06 52	+49	67
106	03 02	49	68	03 51	50	68	04 41	49	67	05 30	50	67	06 20	49	66
107	02 29	50	68	03 19	49	67	04 08	51	66	04 59	49	66	05 48	49	65
108	01 57	49	67	02 46	50	66	03 36	50	66	04 26	50	65	05 16	49	65
109	01 24	50	66	02 14	50	65	03 04	50	65	03 54	50	64	04 44	50	64
110	00 52	+50	65	01 42	+50	65	02 32	+50	64	03 22	+50	64	04 12	+50	63
111	00 20	51	64	01 11	50	64	02 01	50	63	02 51	50	63	03 41	50	62
112	−0 11	50	64	00 39	50	63	01 29	51	62	02 20	50	62	03 10	50	61
113	−0 43	51	63	00 08	50	62	00 58	51	62	01 49	50	61	02 39	50	61
114	−1 14	51	62	−0 23	50	61	00 27	51	61	01 18	50	60	02 08	51	60
115	−1 45	+51	61	−0 54	+50	61	−0 04	+51	60	00 47	+51	60	01 38	+51	59
116	−2 16	51	60	−1 25	51	60	−0 34	51	59	00 17	51	59	01 08	51	58
117	−2 46	51	60	−1 55	51	59	−1 04	51	58	−0 13	51	58	00 38	51	57
118	−3 17	52	59	−2 25	51	58	−1 34	51	58	−0 43	52	57	00 09	51	57
119	−3 47	52	58	−2 55	51	57	−2 04	52	57	−1 12	51	56	−0 21	52	56
120	−4 16	+51	57	−3 25	+52	57	−2 33	+52	56	−1 41	+51	55	−0 50	+52	55
121	−4 46	52	56	−3 54	52	56	−3 02	52	55	−2 10	51	55	−1 19	52	54
122	−5 15	52	55	−4 23	52	55	−3 31	52	54	−2 39	52	54	−1 47	52	53
123	−5 44	52	54	−4 52	53	54	−3 59	52	54	−3 07	52	53	−2 15	52	53
124				−5 20	52	53	−4 28	53	53	−3 35	52	52	−2 43	52	52
125				−5 48	+52	52	−4 56	+53	52	−4 03	+53	51	−3 10	+52	51
126							−5 23	53	51	−4 30	52	51	−3 38	53	50
127							−5 50	53	50	−4 57	52	50	−4 05	53	49
128										−5 24	53	49	−4 31	53	48
129										−5 51	54	48	−4 57	53	48
130													−5 23	+53	47
131													−5 49	54	46

LHA	20° Hc	20° d	20° Z	21° Hc	21° d	21° Z	22° Hc	22° d	22° Z	23° Hc	23° d	23° Z	24° Hc	24° d	24° Z
	° ′	′	°	° ′	′	°	° ′	′	°	° ′	′	°	° ′	′	°
70	27 45	+47	94	28 32	+46	93	29 18	+47	92	30 05	+46	92	30 51	+46	91
71	27 10	47	93	27 57	46	92	28 43	46	92	29 29	46	91	30 15	46	90
72	26 35	46	92	27 21	47	92	28 08	46	91	28 54	46	90	29 40	46	89
73	25 59	47	91	26 46	47	91	27 33	46	90	28 19	46	89	29 05	46	89
74	25 24	47	91	26 11	46	90	26 57	47	89	27 44	46	88	28 30	46	88
75	24 49	+47	90	25 36	+46	89	26 22	+46	88	27 08	+46	88	27 54	+46	87
76	24 14	46	89	25 00	47	88	25 47	46	88	26 33	46	87	27 19	46	86
77	23 38	47	88	24 25	47	87	25 12	46	87	25 58	46	86	26 44	46	85
78	23 03	47	87	23 50	46	87	24 36	47	86	25 23	46	85	26 09	46	85
79	22 28	47	87	23 15	46	86	24 01	47	85	24 48	46	85	25 34	46	84
80	21 53	+46	86	22 39	+47	85	23 26	+47	84	24 13	+46	84	24 59	+46	83
81	21 18	46	85	22 04	47	84	22 51	47	84	23 38	46	83	24 24	46	82
82	20 42	47	84	21 29	47	84	22 16	47	83	23 03	46	82	23 49	46	81
83	20 07	47	83	20 54	47	83	21 41	47	82	22 28	46	81	23 14	46	81
84	19 32	47	83	20 19	47	82	21 06	47	81	21 53	46	81	22 39	47	80
85	18 57	+47	82	19 44	+47	81	20 31	+47	81	21 18	+47	80	22 05	+46	79
86	18 23	47	81	19 10	47	80	19 57	46	80	20 43	47	79	21 30	47	78
87	17 48	47	80	18 35	47	80	19 22	47	79	20 09	47	78	20 56	46	78
88	17 13	47	80	18 00	47	79	18 47	47	78	19 34	47	78	20 21	47	77
89	16 38	48	79	17 26	47	78	18 13	47	77	19 00	47	77	19 47	47	76
90	16 04	+47	78	16 51	+48	77	17 39	+47	77	18 26	+47	76	19 13	+47	75
91	15 29	48	77	16 17	47	77	17 04	48	76	17 52	47	75	18 39	47	75
92	14 55	48	76	15 43	47	76	16 30	48	75	17 18	47	75	18 05	47	74
93	14 21	48	76	15 09	47	75	15 56	48	74	16 44	47	74	17 31	47	73
94	13 47	48	75	14 35	47	74	15 22	48	74	16 10	47	73	16 57	48	72
95	13 13	+48	74	14 01	+47	73	14 48	+48	73	15 36	+48	72	16 24	+47	72
96	12 39	48	73	13 27	48	73	14 15	48	72	15 03	47	71	15 50	48	71
97	12 05	48	73	12 53	48	72	13 41	48	71	14 29	48	71	15 17	48	70
98	11 32	48	72	12 20	48	71	13 08	48	71	13 56	48	70	14 44	48	69
99	10 58	49	71	11 47	48	70	12 35	48	70	13 23	48	69	14 11	48	69
100	10 25	+48	70	11 13	+49	70	12 02	+48	69	12 50	+48	68	13 38	+49	68
101	09 52	48	69	10 40	49	69	11 29	48	68	12 17	49	68	13 06	48	67
102	09 19	49	69	10 08	48	68	10 56	49	68	11 45	48	67	12 33	49	66
103	08 46	49	68	09 35	49	67	10 24	49	67	11 13	48	66	12 01	49	66
104	08 14	49	67	09 03	49	67	09 52	48	66	10 40	49	65	11 29	49	65
105	07 41	+49	66	08 30	+49	66	09 19	+50	65	10 09	+48	65	10 57	+49	64
106	07 09	49	66	07 58	50	65	08 48	49	64	09 37	49	64	10 26	49	63
107	06 37	49	65	07 26	50	64	08 16	49	64	09 05	50	63	09 55	49	63
108	06 05	50	64	06 55	49	63	07 44	50	63	08 34	49	62	09 23	50	62
109	05 34	49	63	06 23	50	63	07 13	50	62	08 03	49	62	08 52	50	61
110	05 02	+50	62	05 52	+50	62	06 42	+50	61	07 32	+50	61	08 22	+49	60
111	04 31	50	62	05 21	50	61	06 11	50	61	07 01	50	60	07 51	50	59
112	04 00	50	61	04 50	51	60	05 41	50	60	06 31	50	59	07 21	50	59
113	03 29	51	60	04 20	50	60	05 10	51	59	06 01	50	58	06 51	50	58
114	02 59	51	59	03 50	50	59	04 40	51	58	05 31	50	58	06 21	51	57
115	02 29	+51	58	03 20	+50	58	04 10	+51	57	05 01	+51	57	05 52	+50	56
116	01 59	51	58	02 50	51	57	03 41	51	57	04 32	51	56	05 23	50	56
117	01 29	51	57	02 20	51	56	03 11	51	56	04 02	52	55	04 54	51	55
118	01 00	51	56	01 51	51	56	02 42	52	55	03 34	51	55	04 25	51	54
119	00 31	51	55	01 22	52	55	02 14	51	54	03 05	51	54	03 56	52	53
120	00 02	+51	54	00 53	+52	54	01 45	+52	53	02 37	+51	53	03 28	+52	52
121	−0 27	52	54	00 25	52	53	01 17	52	53	02 09	51	52	03 00	52	52
122	−0 55	52	53	−0 03	52	52	00 49	52	52	01 41	52	51	02 33	52	51
123	−1 23	52	52	−0 31	52	52	00 21	53	51	01 14	52	51	02 06	52	50
124	−1 51	53	51	−0 58	52	51	−0 06	53	50	00 47	52	50	01 39	52	49
125	−2 18	+53	50	−1 25	+52	50	−0 33	+53	49	00 20	+52	49	01 12	+53	48
126	−2 45	53	50	−1 52	53	49	−0 59	52	49	−0 07	53	48	00 46	53	48
127	−3 12	53	49	−2 19	53	48	−1 26	53	48	−0 33	53	47	00 20	53	47
128	−3 38	53	48	−2 45	53	47	−1 52	54	47	−0 58	53	47	−0 05	53	46
129	−4 04	53	47	−3 11	54	47	−2 17	53	46	−1 24	54	46	−0 30	53	45
130	−4 30	+54	46	−3 36	+54	46	−2 42	+53	45	−1 49	+54	45	−0 55	+53	44
131	−4 55	54	45	−4 01	54	45	−3 07	53	44	−2 14	54	44	−1 20	54	44
132	−5 20	54	44	−4 26	54	44	−3 32	54	44	−2 38	54	43	−1 44	54	43
133	−5 44	54	44	−4 50	54	43	−3 56	54	43	−3 02	54	42	−2 08	54	42
134				−5 14	54	42	−4 20	54	42	−3 26	55	42	2 31	54	41
135				−5 38	+55	42	−4 43	+54	41	−3 49	+55	41	−2 54	+54	40
136							5 06	51	40	−4 12	55	40	−3 17	55	39
137							−5 29	55	39	−4 34	55	39	−3 39	55	39
138										−4 56	55	38	−4 01	55	38
139										−5 18	56	37	−4 22	55	37

25° Hc	25° d	25° Z	26° Hc	26° d	26° Z	27° Hc	27° d	27° Z	28° Hc	28° d	28° Z	29° Hc	29° d	29° Z	LHA
° ′	′	°	° ′	′	°	° ′	′	°	° ′	′	°	° ′	′	°	
31 37	+45	90	32 22	+45	89	33 07	+45	89	33 52	+45	88	34 37	+44	87	290
31 01	46	89	31 47	45	89	32 32	45	88	33 17	45	87	34 02	44	86	289
30 26	46	89	31 12	45	88	31 57	45	87	32 42	45	86	33 27	44	85	288
29 51	45	88	30 36	46	87	31 22	45	86	32 07	44	86	32 51	45	85	287
29 16	45	87	30 01	45	86	30 46	46	86	31 32	44	85	32 16	45	84	286
28 40	+46	86	29 26	+45	85	30 11	+45	85	30 56	+45	84	31 41	+45	83	285
28 05	46	85	28 51	45	85	29 36	45	84	30 21	45	83	31 06	45	82	284
27 30	46	85	28 16	45	84	29 01	45	83	29 46	45	82	30 31	45	82	283
26 55	46	84	27 41	45	83	28 26	45	82	29 11	45	82	29 56	45	81	282
26 20	46	83	27 06	45	82	27 51	46	82	28 37	45	81	29 22	45	80	281
25 45	+46	82	26 31	+45	82	27 16	+46	81	28 02	+45	80	28 47	+45	79	280
25 10	46	82	25 56	46	81	26 42	45	80	27 27	45	79	28 12	45	79	279
24 35	46	81	25 21	46	80	26 07	46	79	26 53	45	79	27 38	45	78	278
24 00	46	80	24 46	46	79	25 32	46	79	26 18	45	78	27 03	46	77	277
23 26	46	79	24 12	46	79	24 58	46	78	25 44	45	77	26 29	45	76	276
22 51	+46	79	23 37	+46	78	24 23	+46	77	25 09	+46	76	25 55	+45	76	275
22 17	46	78	23 03	46	77	23 49	46	76	24 35	46	76	25 21	45	75	274
21 42	47	77	22 29	46	76	23 15	46	76	24 01	46	75	24 47	45	74	273
21 08	46	76	21 54	47	76	22 41	46	75	23 27	46	74	24 13	46	73	272
20 34	46	75	21 20	47	75	22 07	46	74	22 53	46	73	23 39	46	73	271
20 00	+46	75	20 46	+47	74	21 33	+46	73	22 19	+47	73	23 06	+46	72	270
19 26	47	74	20 13	46	73	20 59	47	73	21 46	46	72	22 32	46	71	269
18 52	47	73	19 39	47	73	20 26	46	72	21 12	47	71	21 59	46	71	268
18 18	47	72	19 05	47	72	19 52	47	71	20 39	47	70	21 26	46	70	267
17 45	47	72	18 32	47	71	19 19	47	70	20 06	47	70	20 53	46	69	266
17 11	+48	71	17 59	+47	70	18 46	+47	70	19 33	+47	69	20 20	+47	68	265
16 38	47	70	17 25	48	70	18 13	47	69	19 00	47	68	19 47	47	68	264
16 05	47	69	16 52	48	69	17 40	47	68	18 27	48	68	19 15	47	67	263
15 32	48	69	16 20	47	68	17 07	48	67	17 55	47	67	18 42	48	66	262
14 59	48	68	15 47	48	67	16 35	48	67	17 23	47	66	18 10	48	65	261
14 27	+48	67	15 15	+48	67	16 03	+47	66	16 50	+48	65	17 38	+48	65	260
13 54	48	66	14 42	48	66	15 30	48	65	16 18	48	65	17 06	48	64	259
13 22	48	66	14 10	49	65	14 59	48	64	15 47	48	64	16 35	48	63	258
12 50	48	65	13 38	49	64	14 27	48	64	15 15	48	63	16 03	49	63	257
12 18	49	64	13 07	48	64	13 55	49	63	14 44	48	62	15 32	49	62	256
11 46	+49	63	12 35	+49	63	13 24	+49	62	14 13	+48	62	15 01	+49	61	255
11 15	49	63	12 04	49	62	12 53	49	62	13 42	49	61	14 31	48	60	254
10 44	49	62	11 33	49	61	12 22	49	61	13 11	49	60	14 00	49	60	253
10 13	49	61	11 02	49	61	11 51	50	60	12 41	49	59	13 30	49	59	252
09 42	50	60	10 32	49	60	11 21	49	59	12 10	50	59	13 00	49	58	251
09 11	+50	60	10 01	+50	59	10 51	+49	59	11 40	+50	58	12 30	+49	57	250
08 41	50	59	09 31	50	58	10 21	50	58	11 11	49	57	12 00	50	57	249
08 11	50	58	09 01	50	58	09 51	50	57	10 41	50	56	11 31	50	56	248
07 41	51	57	08 32	50	57	09 22	50	56	10 12	50	56	11 02	50	55	247
07 12	50	57	08 02	51	56	08 53	50	56	09 43	50	55	10 33	50	54	246
06 42	+51	56	07 33	+51	55	08 24	+50	55	09 14	+51	54	10 05	+50	54	245
06 13	51	55	07 04	51	55	07 55	51	54	08 46	50	53	09 36	51	53	244
05 45	51	54	06 36	51	54	07 27	50	53	08 17	51	53	09 08	51	52	243
05 16	51	54	06 07	51	53	06 58	52	52	07 50	51	52	08 41	51	51	242
04 48	51	53	05 39	52	52	06 31	51	52	07 22	51	51	08 13	52	51	241
04 20	+52	52	05 12	+51	51	06 03	+52	51	06 55	+51	50	07 46	+52	50	240
03 52	52	51	04 44	52	51	05 36	52	50	06 28	51	50	07 19	52	49	239
03 25	52	50	04 17	52	50	05 09	52	49	06 01	52	49	06 53	52	48	238
02 58	52	50	03 50	52	49	04 42	53	49	05 35	52	48	06 27	52	48	237
02 31	53	49	03 24	52	48	04 16	52	48	05 08	53	47	06 01	52	47	236
02 05	+53	48	02 58	+52	47	03 50	+53	47	04 43	+52	47	05 35	+53	46	235
01 39	53	47	02 32	52	47	03 24	53	46	04 17	53	46	05 10	53	45	234
01 13	53	46	02 06	53	46	02 59	53	45	03 52	53	45	04 45	53	45	233
00 48	53	46	01 41	53	45	02 34	53	45	03 27	54	44	04 21	53	44	232
00 23	53	45	01 16	54	44	02 10	53	44	03 03	53	43	03 56	54	43	231
−0 02	+54	44	00 52	+53	44	01 45	+54	43	02 39	+53	43	03 32	+54	42	230
−0 26	54	43	00 28	53	43	01 21	54	42	02 15	54	42	03 09	54	41	229
−0 50	54	42	00 04	54	42	00 58	54	41	01 52	54	41	02 46	54	41	228
−1 14	55	42	−0 19	54	41	00 35	54	41	01 29	54	40	02 23	54	40	227
1 37	55	41	−0 42	54	40	00 12	54	40	01 06	55	39	02 01	54	39	226
−2 00	+55	40	−1 05	+55	39	−0 10	+54	39	00 44	+55	39	01 39	+54	38	225
−2 22	55	39	−1 27	55	39	−0 32	54	38	00 22	55	38	01 17	55	37	224
−2 44	55	38	−1 49	55	38	−0 54	55	37	00 01	55	37	00 56	55	37	223
−3 06	55	37	−2 11	56	37	−1 15	55	37	−0 20	55	36	00 35	55	36	222
−3 27	55	37	−2 32	56	36	−1 36	55	36	−0 41	56	35	00 15	55	35	221

| 15° | 16° | 17° | 18° | 19° | 20° | 21° | 22° | 23° | 24° | 25° | 26° | 27° | 28° | 29° |

S. Lat. {LHA greater than 180°....... Zn=180−Z; LHA less than 180°........... Zn=180+Z}

DECLINATION (15°-29°) SAME NAME AS LATITUDE

LAT 54°

N. Lat. {LHA greater than 180°....... Zn=Z / LHA less than 180°.......... Zn=360−Z

DECLINATION (15°-29°) SAME NAME AS LATITUDE

LAT 54°

LHA	23° Hc	23° d	23° Z	24° Hc	24° d	24° Z	25° Hc	25° d	25° Z	26° Hc	26° d	26° Z	27° Hc	27° d	27° Z	28° Hc	28° d	28° Z	29° Hc	29° d	29° Z	LHA
	° ′	′	°	° ′	′	°	° ′	′	°	° ′	′	°	° ′	′	°	° ′	′	°	° ′	′	°	
140	−5 39	+56	36	−4 43	+55	36	−3 48	+56	36	−2 52	+55	35	−1 57	+56	35	−1 01	+56	35	−0 05	+55	34	220
141				−5 04	56	35	−4 08	56	35	−3 12	55	35	−2 17	56	34	−1 21	56	34	−0 25	56	33	219
142				−5 24	56	34	−4 28	56	34	−3 32	56	34	−2 36	56	33	−1 40	56	33	−0 44	56	33	218
143							−4 48	57	33	−3 51	56	33	−2 55	56	32	−1 59	56	32	−1 03	56	32	217
144							−5 07	57	32	−4 10	56	32	−3 14	56	32	−2 18	57	31	−1 21	56	31	216
145							−5 25	+56	31	−4 29	+57	31	−3 32	+56	31	−2 36	+57	30	−1 39	+56	30	215
146										−4 47	57	30	−3 50	57	30	−2 53	56	30	−1 57	57	29	214
147										−5 04	56	29	−4 08	57	29	−3 11	57	29	−2 14	57	28	213
148										−5 22	58	29	−4 24	57	28	−3 27	57	28	−2 30	57	28	212
149													−4 41	57	27	−3 44	57	27	−2 47	58	27	211
150													−4 57	+57	27	−4 00	+58	26	−3 02	+57	26	210
151													−5 13	58	26	−4 15	58	25	−3 17	57	25	209
152													−5 28	58	25	−4 30	58	25	−3 32	57	24	208
153																−4 44	58	24	−3 46	57	23	207
154																−4 58	58	23	−4 00	58	23	206
155																−5 12	+58	22	−4 14	+59	22	205
156																−5 25	59	21	−4 26	58	21	204
157																			−4 39	59	20	203
158																			−4 51	59	19	202
159																			−5 02	59	18	201
160																			−5 13	+59	17	200

LHA	15° Hc	15° d	15° Z	16° Hc	16° d	16° Z	17° Hc	17° d	17° Z	18° Hc	18° d	18° Z	19° Hc	19° d	19° Z	20° Hc	20° d	20° Z	21° Hc	21° d	21° Z	LHA
79	−5 48	49	108																			281
78	−5 15	48	108	−6 03	49	109																282
77	−4 41	49	109	−5 30	49	110																283
76	−4 08	49	110	−4 57	49	111	−5 46	49	111													284
75	−3 35	−49	111	−4 24	−49	111	−5 13	−50	112	−6 03	−49	112										285
74	−3 02	49	112	−3 51	50	112	−4 41	49	113	−5 30	50	113										286
73	−2 29	50	112	−3 19	49	113	−4 08	51	114	−4 59	49	114	−5 48	49	115							287
72	−1 57	49	113	−2 46	50	114	−3 36	50	114	−4 26	50	115	−5 16	49	115							288
71	−1 24	50	114	−2 14	50	115	−3 04	50	115	−3 54	50	116	−4 44	50	116	−5 34	49	117				289
70	−0 52	−50	115	−1 42	−50	115	−2 32	−50	116	−3 22	−50	116	−4 12	−50	117	−5 02	−50	118	−5 52	−50	118	290

15° 16° 17° 18° 19° 20° 21° 22° 23° 24° 25° 26° 27° 28° 29°

S. Lat. {LHA greater than 180°....... Zn=180−Z / LHA less than 180°.......... Zn=180+Z

DECLINATION (15°-29°) CONTRARY NAME TO LATITUDE

N. Lat. {LHA greater than 180°....... Zn=Z; LHA less than 180°........... Zn=360−Z}

DECLINATION (15°-29°) CONTRARY NAME TO LATITUDE

LHA	15° Hc	15° d	15° Z	16° Hc	16° d	16° Z	17° Hc	17° d	17° Z	18° Hc	18° d	18° Z	19° Hc	19° d	19° Z
	° ′	′	°	° ′	′	°	° ′	′	°	° ′	′	°	° ′	′	°
69	−0 20	51	116	−1 11	50	116	−2 01	50	117	−2 51	50	117	−3 41	50	118
68	00 11	50	116	−0 39	50	117	−1 29	51	118	−2 20	50	118	−3 10	50	119
67	00 43	51	117	−0 08	50	118	−0 58	51	118	−1 49	50	119	−2 39	50	119
66	01 14	51	118	00 23	50	119	−0 27	51	119	−1 18	50	120	−2 08	51	120
65	01 45	−51	119	00 54	−50	119	00 04	−51	120	−0 47	−51	120	−1 38	−51	121
64	02 16	51	120	01 25	51	120	00 34	51	121	−0 17	51	121	−1 08	51	122
63	02 46	51	120	01 55	51	121	01 04	51	122	00 13	51	122	−0 38	51	123
62	03 17	52	121	02 25	51	122	01 34	51	122	00 43	52	123	−0 09	51	123
61	03 47	52	122	02 55	51	123	02 04	52	123	01 12	51	124	00 21	52	124
60	04 16	−51	123	03 25	−52	123	02 33	−52	124	01 41	−51	125	00 50	−52	125
59	04 46	52	124	03 54	52	124	03 02	52	125	02 10	51	125	01 19	52	126
58	05 15	52	125	04 23	52	125	03 31	52	126	02 39	52	126	01 47	52	127
57	05 44	52	126	04 52	53	126	03 59	52	126	03 07	52	127	02 15	52	127
56	06 12	52	126	05 20	52	127	04 28	53	127	03 35	52	128	02 43	52	128
55	06 41	−53	127	05 48	−52	128	04 56	−53	128	04 03	−53	129	03 10	−52	129
54	07 09	53	128	06 16	53	129	05 23	53	129	04 30	52	129	03 38	53	130
53	07 36	53	129	06 43	53	129	05 50	53	130	04 57	52	130	04 05	53	131
52	08 03	53	130	07 10	53	130	06 17	53	131	05 24	53	131	04 31	53	132
51	08 30	53	131	07 37	53	131	06 44	53	132	05 51	54	132	04 57	53	132
50	08 57	−53	132	08 04	−54	132	07 10	−53	132	06 17	−54	133	05 23	−53	133
49	09 23	53	132	08 30	54	133	07 36	54	133	06 42	53	134	05 49	54	134
48	09 49	54	133	08 55	54	134	08 01	53	134	07 08	54	135	06 14	54	135
47	10 15	54	134	09 21	54	135	08 27	54	135	07 33	55	135	06 38	54	136
46	10 40	54	135	09 46	55	135	08 51	54	136	07 57	54	136	07 03	54	137
45	11 04	−54	136	10 10	−54	136	09 16	−55	137	08 21	−54	137	07 27	−55	138
44	11 29	55	137	10 34	54	137	09 40	55	138	08 45	55	138	07 50	54	139
43	11 53	55	138	10 58	55	138	10 03	55	139	09 08	54	139	08 14	55	139
42	12 16	55	139	11 21	55	139	10 26	55	139	09 31	55	140	08 36	55	140
41	12 39	55	140	11 44	55	140	10 49	55	140	09 54	55	141	08 59	56	141
40	13 02	−55	140	12 07	−56	141	11 11	−55	141	10 16	−55	142	09 21	−56	142
39	13 24	55	141	12 29	56	142	11 33	55	142	10 38	56	143	09 42	55	143
38	13 46	56	142	12 50	55	143	11 55	56	143	10 59	56	143	10 03	56	144
37	14 08	56	143	13 12	56	144	12 16	56	144	11 20	56	144	10 24	56	145
36	14 28	56	144	13 32	56	145	12 36	56	145	11 40	56	145	10 44	56	146
35	14 49	−56	145	13 53	−57	145	12 56	−56	146	12 00	−56	146	11 04	−57	147
34	15 09	57	146	14 12	56	146	13 16	56	147	12 20	57	147	11 23	57	147
33	15 28	56	147	14 32	57	147	13 35	57	148	12 38	56	148	11 42	57	148
32	15 47	56	148	14 51	57	148	13 54	57	149	12 57	57	149	12 00	57	149
31	16 06	57	149	15 09	57	149	14 12	57	150	13 15	57	150	12 18	57	150
30	16 24	−57	150	15 27	−57	150	14 30	−58	150	13 32	−57	151	12 35	−57	151
29	16 41	57	151	15 44	57	151	14 47	58	151	13 49	57	152	12 52	57	152
28	16 58	57	152	16 01	58	152	15 03	57	152	14 06	58	153	13 08	57	153
27	17 15	58	153	16 17	57	153	15 20	58	153	14 22	58	154	13 24	57	154
26	17 31	58	154	16 33	58	154	15 35	58	154	14 37	57	155	13 40	58	155
25	17 46	−58	155	16 48	−58	155	15 50	−58	155	14 52	−58	155	13 54	−58	156
24	18 01	58	156	17 03	58	156	16 05	58	156	15 07	58	156	14 09	59	157
23	18 15	58	157	17 17	58	157	16 19	58	157	15 21	59	157	14 22	58	158
22	18 29	58	158	17 31	59	158	16 32	58	158	15 34	59	158	14 35	58	159
21	18 42	58	159	17 44	59	159	16 45	58	159	15 47	59	159	14 48	58	160
20	18 55	−59	160	17 56	−58	160	16 58	−59	160	15 59	−59	160	15 00	−59	160
19	19 07	59	161	18 08	59	161	17 09	58	161	16 11	59	161	15 12	59	161
18	19 18	59	162	18 19	58	162	17 21	59	162	16 22	59	162	15 23	59	162
17	19 29	59	163	18 30	59	163	17 31	59	163	16 32	59	163	15 33	59	163
16	19 39	59	164	18 40	59	164	17 41	59	164	16 42	59	164	15 43	59	164
15	19 49	−59	165	18 50	−59	165	17 51	−60	165	16 51	−59	165	15 52	−59	165
14	19 58	59	166	18 59	59	166	18 00	60	166	17 00	59	166	16 01	59	166
13	20 07	60	167	19 07	59	167	18 08	60	167	17 08	59	167	16 09	59	167
12	20 14	59	168	19 15	60	168	18 15	59	168	17 16	60	168	16 16	59	168
11	20 22	60	169	19 22	59	169	18 23	60	169	17 23	60	169	16 23	59	169
10	20 28	−59	170	19 29	−60	170	18 29	−60	170	17 29	−59	170	16 30	−60	170
9	20 34	59	171	19 35	60	171	18 35	60	171	17 35	60	171	16 35	59	171
8	20 40	60	172	19 40	60	172	18 40	60	172	17 40	59	172	16 41	60	172
7	20 44	59	173	19 45	60	173	18 45	60	173	17 45	60	173	16 45	60	173
6	20 49	60	174	19 49	60	174	18 49	60	174	17 49	60	174	16 49	60	174
5	20 52	−60	175	19 52	−60	175	18 52	−60	175	17 52	−60	175	16 52	−59	175
4	20 55	60	176	19 55	60	176	18 55	60	176	17 55	60	176	16 55	60	176
3	20 57	60	177	19 57	60	177	18 57	60	177	17 57	60	177	16 57	60	177
2	20 59	60	178	19 59	60	178	18 59	60	178	17 59	60	178	16 59	60	178
1	21 00	60	179	20 00	60	179	19 00	60	179	18 00	60	179	17 00	60	179
0	21 00	−60	180	20 00	−60	180	19 00	−60	180	18 00	−60	180	17 00	−60	180

LHA	20° Hc	20° d	20° Z	21° Hc	21° d	21° Z	22° Hc	22° d	22° Z	23° Hc	23° d	23° Z	24° Hc	24° d	24° Z
	° ′	′	°	° ′	′	°	° ′	′	°	° ′	′	°	° ′	′	°
69	−4 31	50	118	−5 21	50	119	291								
68	−4 00	50	119	−4 50	51	120	−5 41	50	120	292					
67	−3 29	51	120	−4 20	50	120	−5 10	51	121	293					
66	−2 59	51	121	−3 50	50	121	−4 40	51	122	−5 31	50	122	294		
65	−2 29	−51	122	−3 20	−50	122	−4 10	−51	123	−5 01	−51	123	−5 52	−50	124
64	−1 59	51	122	−2 50	51	123	−3 41	51	123	−4 32	51	124	−5 23	50	124
63	−1 29	51	123	−2 20	51	124	−3 11	51	124	−4 02	52	125	−4 54	51	125
62	−1 00	51	124	−1 51	51	124	−2 42	52	125	−3 34	51	125	−4 25	51	126
61	−0 31	51	125	−1 22	52	125	−2 14	51	126	−3 05	51	126	−3 56	52	127
60	−0 02	−51	126	−0 53	−52	126	−1 45	−52	127	−2 37	−51	127	−3 28	−52	128
59	00 27	52	126	−0 25	52	127	−1 17	52	127	−2 09	51	128	−3 00	52	128
58	00 55	52	127	00 03	52	128	−0 49	52	128	−1 41	52	129	−2 33	52	129
57	01 23	52	128	00 31	52	128	−0 21	53	129	−1 14	52	129	−2 06	52	130
56	01 51	53	129	00 58	52	129	00 06	53	130	−0 47	52	130	−1 39	52	131
55	02 18	−53	130	01 25	−52	130	00 33	−53	131	−0 20	−52	131	−1 12	−53	132
54	02 45	53	130	01 52	53	131	00 59	52	131	00 07	53	132	−0 46	53	132
53	03 12	53	131	02 19	53	132	01 26	53	132	00 33	53	133	−0 20	53	133
52	03 38	53	132	02 45	53	133	01 52	54	133	00 58	53	133	00 05	53	134
51	04 04	53	133	03 11	54	133	02 17	53	134	01 24	54	134	00 30	53	135
50	04 30	−54	134	03 36	−54	134	02 42	−53	135	01 49	−54	135	00 55	−53	136
49	04 55	54	135	04 01	54	135	03 07	53	136	02 14	54	136	01 20	54	136
48	05 20	54	136	04 26	54	136	03 32	54	136	02 38	54	137	01 44	54	137
47	05 44	54	136	04 50	54	137	03 56	54	137	03 02	54	138	02 08	54	138
46	06 09	55	137	05 14	54	138	04 20	54	138	03 26	55	138	02 31	54	139
45	06 32	−54	138	05 38	−55	138	04 43	−54	139	03 49	−55	139	02 54	−54	140
44	06 56	55	139	06 01	55	139	05 06	54	140	04 12	55	140	03 17	55	141
43	07 19	55	140	06 24	55	140	05 29	55	141	04 34	55	141	03 39	55	141
42	07 41	55	141	06 46	55	141	05 51	55	141	04 56	55	142	04 01	55	142
41	08 03	55	142	07 08	55	142	06 13	55	142	05 18	56	143	04 22	55	143
40	08 25	−55	142	07 30	−56	143	06 34	−55	143	05 39	−56	144	04 43	−55	144
39	08 47	56	143	07 51	56	144	06 55	55	144	06 00	56	144	05 04	56	145
38	09 07	55	144	08 12	56	145	07 16	56	145	06 20	56	145	05 24	56	146
37	09 28	56	145	08 32	56	145	07 36	56	146	06 40	56	146	05 44	56	147
36	09 48	56	146	08 52	57	146	07 55	56	147	06 59	56	147	06 03	56	147
35	10 07	−56	147	09 11	−56	147	08 15	−57	148	07 18	−56	148	06 22	−57	148
34	10 26	56	148	09 30	57	148	08 33	56	148	07 37	57	149	06 40	57	149
33	10 45	57	149	09 48	56	149	08 52	57	149	07 55	57	150	06 58	57	150
32	11 03	57	150	10 06	57	150	09 09	57	150	08 12	57	151	07 15	57	151
31	11 21	57	150	10 24	57	151	09 27	57	151	08 30	58	151	07 32	57	152
30	11 38	−57	151	10 41	−57	152	09 44	−58	152	08 46	−57	152	07 49	−57	153
29	11 55	58	152	10 57	57	153	10 00	58	153	09 02	57	153	08 05	58	153
28	12 11	58	153	11 13	57	154	10 16	58	154	09 18	58	154	08 20	57	154
27	12 27	58	154	11 29	58	154	10 31	58	155	09 33	57	155	08 36	58	155
26	12 42	58	155	11 44	58	155	10 46	58	156	09 48	58	156	08 50	58	156
25	12 56	−58	156	11 58	−58	156	11 00	−58	157	10 02	−58	157	09 04	−58	157
24	13 10	58	157	12 12	58	157	11 14	58	157	10 16	58	158	09 18	59	158
23	13 24	58	158	12 26	59	158	11 27	58	158	10 29	58	159	09 31	59	159
22	13 37	58	159	12 39	59	159	11 40	58	159	10 42	59	160	09 43	58	160
21	13 50	59	160	12 51	59	160	11 52	58	160	10 54	59	160	09 55	58	161
20	14 01	−58	161	13 03	−59	161	12 04	−59	161	11 05	−58	161	10 07	−59	162
19	14 13	59	162	13 14	59	162	12 15	59	162	11 16	58	162	10 18	59	162
18	14 24	59	163	13 25	59	163	12 26	59	163	11 27	59	163	10 28	59	163
17	14 34	59	164	13 35	59	164	12 36	59	164	11 37	59	164	10 38	59	164
16	14 44	59	165	13 45	60	165	12 45	59	165	11 46	59	165	10 47	59	165
15	14 53	−59	165	13 54	−60	166	12 54	−59	166	11 55	−59	166	10 56	−59	166
14	15 02	60	166	14 02	59	167	13 03	60	167	12 03	59	167	11 04	59	167
13	15 10	60	167	14 10	59	168	13 11	60	168	12 11	59	168	11 12	60	168
12	15 17	60	168	14 17	59	168	13 18	60	169	12 18	59	169	11 19	60	169
11	15 24	60	169	14 24	59	169	13 25	60	170	12 25	60	170	11 25	59	170
10	15 30	−60	170	14 30	−59	170	13 31	−60	171	12 31	−60	171	11 31	−59	171
9	15 36	60	171	14 36	60	171	13 36	59	171	12 37	60	172	11 37	60	172
8	15 41	60	172	14 41	60	172	13 41	60	172	12 41	59	173	11 42	60	173
7	15 45	59	173	14 46	60	173	13 46	60	173	12 46	60	173	11 46	60	174
6	15 49	60	174	14 49	60	174	13 49	59	174	12 50	60	174	11 50	60	174
5	15 53	−60	175	14 53	−60	175	13 53	−60	175	12 53	−60	175	11 53	−60	175
4	15 55	60	176	14 55	60	176	13 55	60	176	12 55	60	176	11 55	59	176
3	15 57	60	177	14 57	60	177	13 57	60	177	12 57	60	177	11 57	60	177
2	15 59	60	178	14 59	60	178	13 59	60	178	12 59	60	178	11 59	60	178
1	16 00	60	179	15 00	60	179	14 00	60	179	13 00	60	179	12 00	60	179
0	16 00	−60	180	15 00	−60	180	14 00	−60	180	13 00	−60	180	12 00	−60	180

LHA	25° Hc	25° d	25° Z	26° Hc	26° d	26° Z	27° Hc	27° d	27° Z	28° Hc	28° d	28° Z	29° Hc	29° d	29° Z	LHA
	° ′	′	°	° ′	′	°	° ′	′	°	° ′	′	°	° ′	′	°	
69																
68																
67																
66																
65	295															
64	296															
63	−5 45	51	126	297												
62	−5 16	51	126	298												
61	−4 48	51	127	−5 39	52	128	299									
60	−4 20	−52	128	−5 12	−51	129	300									
59	−3 52	52	129	−4 44	52	129	−5 36	52	130	301						
58	−3 25	52	130	−4 17	52	130	−5 09	52	131	302						
57	−2 58	52	130	−3 50	52	131	−4 42	53	131	−5 35	52	132	303			
56	−2 31	53	131	−3 24	52	132	−4 16	52	132	−5 08	53	133	304			
55	−2 05	−53	132	−2 58	−52	133	−3 50	−53	133	−4 43	−52	133	−5 35	−53	134	305
54	−1 39	53	133	−2 32	52	133	−3 24	53	134	−4 17	53	134	−5 10	53	135	306
53	−1 13	53	134	−2 06	53	134	−2 59	53	135	−3 52	53	135	−4 45	53	135	307
52	−0 48	53	134	−1 41	53	135	−2 34	53	135	−3 27	54	136	−4 21	53	136	308
51	−0 23	53	135	−1 16	54	136	−2 10	53	136	−3 03	53	137	−3 56	54	137	309
50	00 02	−54	136	−0 52	−53	136	−1 45	−54	137	−2 39	−53	137	−3 32	−54	138	310
49	00 26	54	137	−0 28	53	137	−1 21	54	138	−2 15	54	138	−3 09	54	139	311
48	00 50	54	138	−0 04	54	138	−0 58	54	139	−1 52	54	139	−2 46	54	139	312
47	01 14	55	138	00 19	54	139	−0 35	54	139	−1 29	54	140	−2 23	54	140	313
46	01 37	55	139	00 42	54	140	−0 12	54	140	−1 06	55	141	−2 01	54	141	314
45	02 00	−55	140	01 05	−55	141	00 10	−54	141	−0 44	−55	141	−1 39	−54	142	315
44	02 22	55	141	01 27	55	141	00 32	54	142	−0 22	55	142	−1 17	55	143	316
43	02 44	55	142	01 49	55	142	00 54	55	143	−0 01	55	143	−0 56	55	143	317
42	03 06	55	143	02 11	56	143	01 15	55	143	00 20	55	144	−0 35	55	144	318
41	03 27	55	143	02 32	56	144	01 36	55	144	00 41	56	145	−0 15	55	145	319
40	03 48	−56	144	02 52	−55	145	01 57	−56	145	01 01	−56	145	00 05	−55	146	320
39	04 08	56	145	03 12	55	145	02 17	56	146	01 21	56	146	00 25	56	147	321
38	04 28	56	146	03 32	56	146	02 36	56	147	01 40	56	147	00 44	56	147	322
37	04 48	57	147	03 51	56	147	02 55	56	148	01 59	56	148	01 03	56	148	323
36	05 07	57	148	04 10	56	148	03 14	56	148	02 18	57	149	01 21	56	149	324
35	05 25	−56	149	04 29	−57	149	03 32	−56	149	02 36	−57	150	01 39	−56	150	325
34	05 43	56	149	04 47	57	150	03 50	57	150	02 53	56	150	01 57	57	151	326
33	06 01	57	150	05 04	56	151	04 08	57	151	03 11	57	151	02 14	57	152	327
32	06 18	56	151	05 22	58	151	04 24	57	152	03 27	57	152	02 30	57	152	328
31	06 35	57	152	05 38	57	152	04 41	57	153	03 44	57	153	02 47	58	153	329
30	06 52	−58	153	05 54	−57	153	04 57	−57	153	04 00	−58	154	03 02	−57	154	330
29	07 07	57	154	06 10	57	154	05 13	58	154	04 15	58	155	03 17	57	155	331
28	07 23	58	155	06 25	57	155	05 28	58	155	04 30	58	155	03 32	57	156	332
27	07 38	58	156	06 40	58	156	05 42	58	156	04 44	58	156	03 46	57	157	333
26	07 52	58	156	06 54	58	157	05 56	58	157	04 58	58	157	04 00	58	157	334
25	08 06	−58	157	07 08	−58	158	06 10	−58	158	05 12	−58	158	04 14	−59	158	335
24	08 19	58	158	07 21	58	158	06 23	58	159	05 25	59	159	04 26	58	159	336
23	08 32	58	159	07 34	58	159	06 36	59	160	05 37	58	160	04 39	59	160	337
22	08 45	59	160	07 46	58	160	06 48	59	160	05 49	58	161	04 51	59	161	338
21	08 57	59	161	07 58	59	161	06 59	58	161	06 01	59	161	05 02	59	162	339
20	09 08	−59	162	08 09	−59	162	07 10	−58	162	06 12	−59	162	05 13	−59	163	340
19	09 19	59	163	08 20	59	163	07 21	59	163	06 22	59	163	05 23	59	163	341
18	09 29	59	164	08 30	59	164	07 31	59	164	06 32	59	164	05 33	59	164	342
17	09 39	59	164	08 40	59	165	07 41	60	165	06 41	59	165	05 42	59	165	343
16	09 48	59	165	08 49	59	166	07 50	60	166	06 50	59	166	05 51	59	166	344
15	09 57	−60	166	08 57	−59	166	07 58	−59	167	06 59	−60	167	05 59	−59	167	345
14	10 05	60	167	09 05	59	167	08 06	59	167	07 07	60	168	06 07	59	168	346
13	10 12	59	168	09 13	60	168	08 13	59	168	07 14	60	169	06 14	59	169	347
12	10 19	59	169	09 20	60	169	08 20	59	169	07 21	60	169	06 21	59	170	348
11	10 26	60	170	09 26	59	170	08 27	60	170	07 27	60	170	06 27	59	170	349
10	10 32	−60	171	09 32	−60	171	08 32	−59	171	07 33	−60	171	06 33	−60	171	350
9	10 37	60	172	09 37	59	172	08 38	60	172	07 38	60	172	06 38	60	172	351
8	10 42	60	173	09 42	60	173	08 42	59	173	07 43	60	173	06 43	60	173	352
7	10 46	60	174	09 46	60	174	08 46	59	174	07 47	60	174	06 47	60	174	353
6	10 50	60	175	09 50	60	175	08 50	60	175	07 50	60	175	06 50	60	175	354
5	10 53	−60	175	09 53	−60	175	08 53	−60	176	07 53	−60	176	06 53	−60	176	355
4	10 56	60	176	09 56	60	176	08 56	60	176	07 56	60	176	06 56	60	177	356
3	10 57	59	177	09 58	60	177	08 58	60	177	07 58	60	177	06 58	60	177	357
2	10 59	60	178	09 59	60	178	08 59	60	178	07 59	60	178	06 59	60	178	358
1	11 00	60	179	10 00	60	179	09 00	60	179	08 00	60	179	07 00	60	179	359
0	11 00	−60	180	10 00	−60	180	09 00	−60	180	08 00	−60	180	07 00	−60	180	360

S. Lat. {LHA greater than 180°....... Zn=180−Z; LHA less than 180°........... Zn=180+Z}

DECLINATION (15°-29°) CONTRARY NAME TO LATITUDE

LAT 54°

N. Lat. {LHA greater than 180°....... Zn=Z; LHA less than 180°........... Zn=360−Z}

DECLINATION (0°-14°) SAME NAME AS LATITUDE

LHA	0° Hc	0° d	0° Z	1° Hc	1° d	1° Z	2° Hc	2° d	2° Z	3° Hc	3° d	3° Z	4° Hc	4° d	4° Z
	° ′	′	°	° ′	′	°	° ′	′	°	° ′	′	°	° ′	′	°
0	35 00	+60	180	36 00	+60	180	37 00	+60	180	38 00	+60	180	39 00	+60	180
1	35 00	60	179	36 00	60	179	37 00	60	179	38 00	60	179	39 00	60	179
2	34 59	60	178	35 59	60	178	36 59	60	178	37 59	60	178	38 59	59	177
3	34 57	60	176	35 57	60	176	36 57	60	176	37 57	60	176	38 57	60	176
4	34 54	60	175	35 54	60	175	36 54	60	175	37 54	60	175	38 54	60	175
5	34 51	+60	174	35 51	+60	174	36 51	+60	174	37 51	+59	174	38 50	+60	174
6	34 47	60	173	35 47	60	173	36 47	59	173	37 46	60	172	38 46	60	172
7	34 42	60	172	35 42	60	171	36 42	59	171	37 41	60	171	38 41	60	171
8	34 37	59	170	35 36	60	170	36 36	60	170	37 36	59	170	38 35	60	170
9	34 31	59	169	35 30	60	169	36 30	59	169	37 29	60	169	38 29	60	169
10	34 24	+59	168	35 23	+60	168	36 23	+59	168	37 22	+60	167	38 22	+59	167
11	34 16	59	167	35 15	60	167	36 15	59	166	37 14	60	166	38 14	59	166
12	34 08	59	166	35 07	59	165	36 06	60	165	37 06	59	165	38 05	59	165
13	33 59	59	164	34 58	59	164	35 57	59	164	36 56	60	164	37 56	59	164
14	33 49	59	163	34 48	59	163	35 47	59	163	36 46	60	162	37 46	59	162
15	33 39	+59	162	34 38	+59	162	35 37	+59	161	36 36	+59	161	37 35	+59	161
16	33 28	59	161	34 27	58	161	35 25	59	160	36 24	59	160	37 23	59	160
17	33 16	59	160	34 15	58	159	35 13	59	159	36 12	59	159	37 11	58	159
18	33 04	58	158	34 02	59	158	35 01	58	158	35 59	59	158	36 58	58	157
19	32 51	58	157	33 49	59	157	34 48	58	157	35 46	58	156	36 44	59	156
20	32 37	+58	156	33 35	+59	156	34 34	+58	156	35 32	+58	155	36 30	+58	155
21	32 23	58	155	33 21	58	155	34 19	58	154	35 17	58	154	36 15	58	154
22	32 08	58	154	33 06	58	153	34 04	58	153	35 02	58	153	36 00	57	153
23	31 52	58	153	32 50	58	152	33 48	58	152	34 46	57	152	35 43	58	151
24	31 36	58	152	32 34	57	151	33 31	58	151	34 29	57	151	35 26	58	150
25	31 19	+58	150	32 17	+57	150	33 14	+58	150	34 12	+57	149	35 09	+57	149
26	31 02	57	149	31 59	58	149	32 57	57	149	33 54	57	148	34 51	57	148
27	30 44	57	148	31 41	57	148	32 38	57	147	33 35	57	147	34 32	57	147
28	30 26	57	147	31 23	57	147	32 20	56	146	33 16	57	146	34 13	57	146
29	30 07	56	146	31 03	57	146	32 00	57	145	32 57	56	145	33 53	57	144
30	29 47	+57	145	30 44	+56	144	31 40	+57	144	32 37	+56	144	33 33	+56	143
31	29 27	56	144	30 23	57	143	31 20	56	143	32 16	56	143	33 12	56	142
32	29 06	57	143	30 03	56	142	30 59	56	142	31 55	55	141	32 51	56	141
33	28 45	56	142	29 41	56	141	30 37	56	141	31 33	56	140	32 29	56	140
34	28 24	55	141	29 19	56	140	30 15	56	140	31 11	55	139	32 06	56	139
35	28 02	+55	140	28 57	+56	139	29 53	+55	139	30 48	+56	138	31 44	+55	138
36	27 39	55	138	28 34	56	138	29 30	55	138	30 25	55	137	31 20	55	137
37	27 16	55	137	28 11	55	137	29 06	55	137	30 01	55	136	30 56	55	136
38	26 52	55	136	27 47	55	136	28 42	55	136	29 37	55	135	30 32	55	135
39	26 28	55	135	27 23	55	135	28 18	55	134	29 13	54	134	30 07	55	134
40	26 04	+55	134	26 59	+54	134	27 53	+55	133	28 48	+54	133	29 42	+54	132
41	25 39	55	133	26 34	54	133	27 28	54	132	28 22	54	132	29 16	54	131
42	25 14	54	132	26 08	54	132	27 02	54	131	27 56	54	131	28 50	54	130
43	24 48	54	131	25 42	54	131	26 36	54	130	27 30	54	130	28 24	54	129
44	24 22	54	130	25 16	54	130	26 10	54	129	27 04	53	129	27 57	54	128
45	23 56	+53	129	24 49	+54	129	25 43	+54	128	26 37	+53	128	27 30	+53	127
46	23 29	53	128	24 22	54	128	25 16	53	127	26 09	53	127	27 02	54	126
47	23 02	53	127	23 55	53	127	24 48	53	126	25 41	54	126	26 35	52	125
48	22 34	53	126	23 27	53	126	24 20	53	125	25 13	53	125	26 06	53	124
49	22 06	53	126	22 59	53	125	23 52	53	124	24 45	53	124	25 38	52	123
50	21 38	+53	125	22 31	+53	124	23 24	+52	124	24 16	+53	123	25 09	+52	122
51	21 10	52	124	22 02	53	123	22 55	52	123	23 47	53	122	24 40	52	122
52	20 41	52	123	21 33	53	122	22 26	52	122	23 18	52	121	24 10	52	121
53	20 12	52	122	21 04	52	121	21 56	52	121	22 48	52	120	23 40	52	120
54	19 42	52	121	20 34	52	120	21 26	52	120	22 18	52	119	23 10	52	119
55	19 12	+52	120	20 04	+52	119	20 56	+52	119	21 48	+52	118	22 40	+51	118
56	18 43	51	119	19 34	52	118	20 26	52	118	21 18	51	117	22 09	52	117
57	18 12	52	118	19 04	52	118	19 56	51	117	20 47	51	116	21 38	52	116
58	17 42	51	117	18 33	52	117	19 25	51	116	20 16	51	116	21 07	51	115
59	17 11	51	116	18 02	52	116	18 54	51	115	19 45	51	115	20 36	51	114
60	16 40	+51	115	17 31	+51	115	18 22	+52	114	19 14	+50	114	20 04	+51	113
61	16 09	51	114	17 00	51	114	17 51	51	113	18 42	51	113	19 33	50	112
62	15 37	51	114	16 28	51	113	17 19	51	112	18 10	51	112	19 01	50	111
63	15 06	51	113	15 57	50	112	16 47	51	112	17 38	51	111	18 29	50	110
64	14 34	51	112	15 25	50	111	16 15	51	111	17 06	50	110	17 56	51	110
65	14 02	+50	111	14 52	+51	110	15 43	+50	110	16 33	+51	109	17 24	+50	109
66	13 30	50	110	14 20	50	110	15 10	51	109	16 01	50	108	16 51	50	108
67	12 57	50	109	13 47	51	109	14 38	50	108	15 28	50	108	16 18	50	107
68	12 25	50	108	13 15	50	108	14 05	50	107	14 55	50	107	15 45	50	106
69	11 52	50	108	12 42	50	107	13 32	50	106	14 22	50	106	15 12	50	105

LHA	5° Hc	5° d	5° Z	6° Hc	6° d	6° Z	7° Hc	7° d	7° Z	8° Hc	8° d	8° Z	9° Hc	9° d	9° Z
	° ′	′	°	° ′	′	°	° ′	′	°	° ′	′	°	° ′	′	°
0	40 00	+60	180	41 00	+60	180	42 00	+60	180	43 00	+60	180	44 00	+60	180
1	40 00	60	179	41 00	60	179	42 00	60	179	43 00	60	179	44 00	60	179
2	39 58	60	177	40 58	60	177	41 58	60	177	42 58	60	177	43 58	60	177
3	39 57	59	176	40 56	60	176	41 56	60	176	42 56	60	176	43 56	60	176
4	39 54	60	175	40 54	60	175	41 54	60	175	42 54	59	175	43 53	60	175
5	39 50	+60	174	40 50	+60	173	41 50	+60	173	42 50	+60	173	43 50	+60	173
6	39 46	60	172	40 46	60	172	41 46	59	172	42 45	60	172	43 45	60	172
7	39 41	60	171	40 41	59	171	41 40	60	171	42 40	60	171	43 40	60	170
8	39 35	60	170	40 35	60	170	41 35	59	169	42 34	60	169	43 34	59	169
9	39 29	59	168	40 28	60	168	41 28	59	168	42 27	60	168	43 27	59	168
10	39 21	+60	167	40 21	+59	167	41 20	+60	167	42 20	+59	167	43 19	+60	166
11	39 13	60	166	40 13	59	166	41 12	59	165	42 11	60	165	43 11	59	165
12	39 04	60	165	40 04	59	164	41 03	59	164	42 02	59	164	43 01	60	164
13	38 55	59	163	39 54	59	163	40 53	59	163	41 52	59	163	42 51	59	162
14	38 45	59	162	39 44	59	162	40 43	59	162	41 42	59	161	42 41	58	161
15	38 34	+58	161	39 32	+59	161	40 31	+59	160	41 30	+59	160	42 29	+59	160
16	38 22	59	160	39 21	58	159	40 19	59	159	41 18	59	159	42 17	58	158
17	38 09	59	158	39 08	59	158	40 07	58	158	41 05	59	157	42 04	58	157
18	37 56	59	157	38 55	58	157	39 53	59	156	40 52	58	156	41 50	58	156
19	37 43	58	156	38 41	58	156	39 39	58	155	40 37	58	155	41 35	59	155
20	37 28	+58	155	38 26	+58	154	39 24	+58	154	40 22	+58	154	41 20	+58	153
21	37 13	58	153	38 11	58	153	39 09	58	153	40 07	57	152	41 04	58	152
22	36 57	58	152	37 55	58	152	38 53	57	152	39 50	58	151	40 48	57	151
23	36 41	58	151	37 39	57	151	38 36	57	150	39 33	58	150	40 31	57	150
24	36 24	57	150	37 21	58	149	38 19	57	149	39 16	57	149	40 13	57	148
25	36 06	+57	149	37 03	+58	148	38 01	+57	148	38 58	+57	147	39 55	+57	147
26	35 48	57	147	36 45	57	147	37 42	57	147	38 39	57	146	39 36	56	146
27	35 29	57	146	36 26	57	146	37 23	56	146	38 19	57	145	39 16	56	145
28	35 10	56	145	36 06	57	145	37 03	56	144	37 59	57	144	38 56	56	143
29	34 50	56	144	35 46	57	144	36 43	56	143	37 39	56	143	38 35	56	142
30	34 29	+57	143	35 26	+56	142	36 22	+56	142	37 18	+56	142	38 14	+55	141
31	34 08	56	142	35 04	56	141	36 00	56	141	36 56	56	140	37 52	55	140
32	33 47	55	141	34 42	56	140	35 38	56	140	36 34	55	139	37 29	56	139
33	33 25	55	140	34 20	56	139	35 16	55	139	36 11	55	138	37 06	55	138
34	33 02	55	138	33 57	56	138	34 53	55	137	35 48	55	137	36 43	55	137
35	32 39	+55	137	33 34	+55	137	34 29	+55	136	35 24	+55	136	36 19	+55	135
36	32 15	55	136	33 10	55	136	34 05	55	135	35 00	54	135	35 54	55	134
37	31 51	55	135	32 46	55	135	33 41	54	134	34 35	55	134	35 30	54	133
38	31 27	54	134	32 21	55	134	33 16	54	133	34 10	54	133	35 04	54	132
39	31 02	54	133	31 56	54	133	32 50	54	132	33 44	54	132	34 38	54	131
40	30 36	+54	132	31 30	+55	131	32 25	+53	131	33 18	+54	130	34 12	+54	130
41	30 10	54	131	31 04	54	130	31 58	54	130	32 52	54	129	33 46	53	129
42	29 44	54	130	30 38	54	129	31 32	53	129	32 25	54	128	33 19	53	128
43	29 18	53	129	30 11	54	128	31 05	53	128	31 58	53	127	32 51	53	127
44	28 51	53	128	29 44	53	127	30 37	53	127	31 30	53	126	32 23	53	126
45	28 23	+53	127	29 16	+54	126	30 10	+52	126	31 02	+53	125	31 55	+53	125
46	27 56	53	126	28 49	52	125	29 41	53	125	30 34	53	124	31 27	52	124
47	27 27	53	125	28 20	53	124	29 13	53	124	30 06	52	123	30 58	52	123
48	26 59	53	124	27 52	52	123	28 44	53	123	29 37	52	122	30 29	52	122
49	26 30	53	123	27 23	52	122	28 15	52	122	29 07	52	121	29 59	52	121
50	26 01	+53	122	26 54	+52	121	27 46	+52	121	28 38	+52	120	29 30	+51	120
51	25 32	52	121	26 24	52	120	27 16	52	120	28 08	51	119	28 59	52	119
52	25 02	52	120	25 54	52	119	26 46	52	119	27 38	51	118	28 29	52	118
53	24 32	52	119	25 24	52	118	26 16	51	118	27 07	52	117	27 59	51	117
54	24 02	52	118	24 54	51	118	25 45	51	117	26 36	52	116	27 28	51	116
55	23 31	+52	117	24 23	+51	117	25 14	+51	116	26 05	+52	115	26 57	+50	115
56	23 01	51	116	23 52	51	116	24 43	51	115	25 34	51	115	26 25	51	114
57	22 30	51	115	23 21	51	115	24 12	51	114	25 03	51	114	25 54	50	113
58	21 58	52	114	22 50	50	114	23 40	51	113	24 31	51	113	25 22	50	112
59	21 27	51	113	22 18	51	113	23 09	50	112	23 59	51	112	24 50	50	111
60	20 55	+51	113	21 46	+51	112	22 37	+50	111	23 27	+51	111	24 18	+50	110
61	20 23	51	112	21 14	51	111	22 05	50	111	22 55	50	110	23 45	50	109
62	19 51	51	111	20 42	50	110	21 32	51	110	22 23	50	109	23 13	50	108
63	19 19	50	110	20 09	51	109	21 00	50	109	21 50	50	108	22 40	50	108
64	18 47	50	109	19 37	50	108	20 27	50	108	21 17	50	107	22 07	50	107
65	18 14	+50	108	19 04	+50	108	19 54	+50	107	20 44	+50	106	21 34	+50	106
66	17 41	50	107	18 31	50	107	19 21	50	106	20 11	50	106	21 01	49	105
67	17 08	50	106	17 58	50	106	18 48	50	105	19 38	49	105	20 27	50	104
68	16 35	50	106	17 25	50	105	18 15	49	104	19 04	50	104	19 54	49	103
69	16 02	50	105	16 52	49	104	17 41	50	103	18 31	49	103	19 20	50	102

LHA	10° Hc	10° d	10° Z	11° Hc	11° d	11° Z	12° Hc	12° d	12° Z	13° Hc	13° d	13° Z	14° Hc	14° d	14° Z	LHA
	° ′	′	°	° ′	′	°	° ′	′	°	° ′	′	°	° ′	′	°	
0	45 00	+60	180	46 00	+60	180	47 00	+60	180	48 00	+60	180	49 00	+60	180	360
1	45 00	60	179	46 00	60	179	47 00	60	179	48 00	60	179	49 00	60	179	359
2	44 58	60	177	45 58	60	177	46 58	60	177	47 58	60	177	48 58	60	177	358
3	44 56	60	176	45 56	60	176	46 56	60	176	47 56	60	176	48 56	60	176	357
4	44 53	60	174	45 53	60	174	46 53	60	174	47 53	60	174	48 53	60	174	356
5	44 50	+59	173	45 49	+60	173	46 49	+60	173	47 49	+60	173	48 49	+60	173	355
6	44 45	60	172	45 45	60	172	46 45	59	171	47 44	60	171	48 44	60	171	354
7	44 40	59	170	45 39	60	170	46 39	60	170	47 39	59	170	48 38	60	170	353
8	44 33	60	169	45 33	60	169	46 33	59	169	47 32	60	168	48 32	59	168	352
9	44 26	60	168	45 26	59	167	46 25	60	167	47 25	59	167	48 24	60	167	351
10	44 19	+59	166	45 18	+59	166	46 17	+60	166	47 17	+59	166	48 16	+59	165	350
11	44 10	59	165	45 09	60	165	46 09	59	164	47 08	59	164	48 07	59	164	349
12	44 01	59	164	45 00	59	163	45 59	59	163	46 58	59	163	47 57	59	163	348
13	43 50	59	162	44 49	59	162	45 48	59	162	46 47	59	161	47 46	59	161	347
14	43 39	59	161	44 38	59	161	45 37	59	160	46 36	59	160	47 35	58	160	346
15	43 28	+58	159	44 26	+59	159	45 25	+59	159	46 24	+58	159	47 22	+59	158	345
16	43 15	59	158	44 14	58	158	45 12	59	158	46 11	58	157	47 09	58	157	344
17	43 02	58	157	44 00	59	157	44 59	58	156	45 57	58	156	46 55	58	156	343
18	42 48	58	156	43 46	58	155	44 44	59	155	45 43	58	155	46 41	57	154	342
19	42 34	58	154	43 32	57	154	44 29	58	154	45 27	58	153	46 25	58	153	341
20	42 18	+58	153	43 16	+58	153	44 14	+57	152	45 11	+58	152	46 09	+58	151	340
21	42 02	58	152	43 00	57	151	43 57	58	151	44 55	57	151	45 52	57	150	339
22	41 45	58	150	42 43	57	150	43 40	57	150	44 37	58	149	45 35	57	149	338
23	41 28	57	149	42 25	57	149	43 22	57	148	44 19	57	148	45 16	57	147	337
24	41 10	57	148	42 07	57	147	43 04	57	147	44 01	57	147	44 58	56	146	336
25	40 52	+56	147	41 48	+57	146	42 45	+57	146	43 42	+56	145	44 38	+56	145	335
26	40 32	57	145	41 29	56	145	42 25	57	145	43 22	56	144	44 18	56	144	334
27	40 12	57	144	41 09	56	144	42 05	56	143	43 01	56	143	43 57	56	142	333
28	39 52	56	143	40 48	56	143	41 44	56	142	42 40	56	142	43 36	55	141	332
29	39 31	56	142	40 27	56	141	41 23	55	141	42 18	56	140	43 14	55	140	331
30	39 09	+56	141	40 05	+56	140	41 01	+55	140	41 56	+55	139	42 51	+56	139	330
31	38 47	56	139	39 43	55	139	40 38	55	138	41 33	55	138	42 28	55	137	329
32	38 25	55	138	39 20	55	138	40 15	55	137	41 10	55	137	42 05	54	136	328
33	38 01	55	137	38 56	55	137	39 51	55	136	40 46	55	136	41 41	54	135	327
34	37 38	55	136	38 33	54	135	39 27	55	135	40 22	54	134	41 16	54	134	326
35	37 14	+54	135	38 08	+55	134	39 03	+54	134	39 57	+54	133	40 51	+54	133	325
36	36 49	54	134	37 43	54	133	38 37	55	133	39 32	53	132	40 25	54	132	324
37	36 24	54	133	37 18	54	132	38 12	54	132	39 06	53	131	39 59	54	130	323
38	35 58	54	132	36 52	54	131	37 46	54	130	38 40	53	130	39 33	53	129	322
39	35 32	54	130	36 26	53	130	37 19	54	129	38 13	53	129	39 06	53	128	321
40	35 06	+53	129	35 59	+54	129	36 53	+53	128	37 46	+53	128	38 39	+53	127	320
41	34 39	53	128	35 32	53	128	36 25	53	127	37 18	53	127	38 11	53	126	319
42	34 12	53	127	35 05	53	127	35 58	53	126	36 51	52	125	37 43	52	125	318
43	33 44	53	126	34 37	53	126	35 30	52	125	36 22	53	124	37 15	52	124	317
44	33 16	53	125	34 09	52	125	35 01	53	124	35 54	52	123	36 46	52	123	316
45	32 48	+52	124	33 40	+53	124	34 33	+52	123	35 25	+52	122	36 17	+51	122	315
46	32 19	52	123	33 11	53	123	34 04	52	122	34 56	51	121	35 47	52	121	314
47	31 50	52	122	32 42	52	121	33 34	52	121	34 26	52	120	35 18	51	120	313
48	31 21	52	121	32 13	51	120	33 04	52	120	33 56	51	119	34 47	52	119	312
49	30 51	52	120	31 43	51	119	32 34	52	119	33 26	51	118	34 17	51	118	311
50	30 21	+52	119	31 13	+51	118	32 04	+51	118	32 55	+51	117	33 46	+51	117	310
51	29 51	51	118	30 42	52	118	31 34	51	117	32 25	51	116	33 16	50	116	309
52	29 21	51	117	30 12	51	117	31 03	51	116	31 54	50	115	32 44	51	115	308
53	28 50	51	116	29 41	51	116	30 32	50	115	31 22	51	114	32 13	50	114	307
54	28 19	51	115	29 10	50	115	30 00	51	114	30 51	50	113	31 41	51	113	306
55	27 47	+51	114	28 38	+51	114	29 29	+50	113	30 19	+50	112	31 09	+51	112	305
56	27 16	51	113	28 07	50	113	28 57	50	112	29 47	50	111	30 37	50	111	304
57	26 44	51	112	27 35	50	112	28 25	50	111	29 15	50	111	30 05	50	110	303
58	26 12	51	111	27 03	50	111	27 53	50	110	28 43	50	110	29 33	49	109	302
59	25 40	50	111	26 30	50	110	27 20	50	109	28 10	50	109	29 00	50	108	301
60	25 08	+50	110	25 58	+50	109	26 48	+50	108	27 38	+49	108	28 27	+50	107	300
61	24 35	50	109	25 25	50	108	26 15	50	108	27 05	49	107	27 54	50	106	299
62	24 03	50	108	24 53	49	107	25 42	50	107	26 32	49	106	27 21	49	105	298
63	23 30	50	107	24 20	49	106	25 09	50	106	25 59	49	105	26 48	49	104	297
64	22 57	49	106	23 46	50	105	24 36	49	105	25 25	49	104	26 14	49	104	296
65	22 24	+49	105	23 13	+50	105	24 03	+49	104	24 52	+49	103	25 41	+49	103	295
66	21 50	50	104	22 40	49	104	23 29	49	103	24 18	49	102	25 07	49	102	294
67	21 17	49	103	22 06	50	103	22 56	49	102	23 45	49	102	24 34	48	101	293
68	20 43	50	103	21 33	49	102	22 22	49	101	23 11	49	101	24 00	48	100	292
69	20 10	49	102	20 59	49	101	21 48	49	100	22 37	49	100	23 26	48	99	291

S. Lat. {LHA greater than 180°....... Zn=180−Z; LHA less than 180°........... Zn=180+Z}

DECLINATION (0°-14°) SAME NAME AS LATITUDE

LAT 55°

N. Lat. {LHA greater than 180°....... Zn=Z; LHA less than 180°........... Zn=360−Z}

DECLINATION (0°-14°) SAME NAME AS LATITUDE

LHA	0°			1°			2°			3°			4°			5°			6°			7°		
	Hc	d	Z	Hc	d	Z	Hc	d	Z	Hc	d	Z	Hc	d	Z	Hc	d	Z	Hc	d	Z	Hc	d	Z
	° ′	′	°	° ′	′	°	° ′	′	°	° ′	′	°	° ′	′	°	° ′	′	°	° ′	′	°	° ′	′	°
70	11 19	+50	107	12 09	+50	106	12 59	+50	106	13 49	+50	105	14 39	+50	104	15 29	+49	104	16 18	+50	103	17 08	+49	103
71	10 46	50	106	11 36	50	105	12 26	50	105	13 16	49	104	14 05	50	104	14 55	50	103	15 45	49	102	16 34	50	102
72	10 13	50	105	11 03	49	104	11 52	50	104	12 42	50	103	13 32	49	103	14 21	50	102	15 11	49	102	16 00	50	101
73	09 39	50	104	10 29	50	104	11 19	50	103	12 09	49	102	12 58	50	102	13 48	49	101	14 37	50	101	15 27	49	100
74	09 06	50	103	09 56	49	103	10 45	50	102	11 35	49	102	12 24	50	101	13 14	49	100	14 03	50	100	14 53	49	99
75	08 32	+50	102	09 22	+50	102	10 12	+49	101	11 01	+50	101	11 51	+49	100	12 40	+49	100	13 29	+50	99	14 19	+49	98
76	07 59	49	102	08 48	50	101	09 38	49	100	10 27	50	100	11 17	49	99	12 06	49	99	12 55	50	98	13 45	49	98
77	07 25	49	101	08 14	50	100	09 04	49	100	09 53	50	99	10 43	49	98	11 32	49	98	12 21	49	97	13 10	50	97
78	06 51	49	100	07 40	50	99	08 30	49	99	09 19	50	98	10 09	49	98	10 58	49	97	11 47	49	96	12 36	49	96
79	06 17	49	99	07 06	50	99	07 56	49	98	08 45	49	97	09 34	50	97	10 24	49	96	11 13	49	96	12 02	49	95
80	05 43	+49	98	06 32	+50	98	07 22	+49	97	08 11	+49	97	09 00	+49	96	09 49	+50	95	10 39	+49	95	11 28	+49	94
81	05 09	49	97	05 58	50	97	06 48	49	96	07 37	49	96	08 26	49	95	09 15	49	95	10 04	49	94	10 53	49	93
82	04 35	49	97	05 24	49	96	06 13	50	95	07 03	49	95	07 52	49	94	08 41	49	94	09 30	49	93	10 19	49	93
83	04 00	50	96	04 50	49	95	05 39	49	95	06 28	49	94	07 17	49	93	08 06	50	93	08 56	49	92	09 45	49	92
84	03 26	49	95	04 15	50	94	05 05	49	94	05 54	49	93	06 43	49	93	07 32	49	92	08 21	49	92	09 10	49	91
85	02 52	+49	94	03 41	+49	94	04 30	+50	93	05 20	+49	92	06 09	+49	92	06 58	+49	91	07 47	+49	91	08 36	+49	90
86	02 18	49	93	03 07	49	93	03 56	49	92	04 45	49	92	05 34	49	91	06 23	49	90	07 12	49	90	08 01	49	89
87	01 43	49	92	02 32	50	92	03 22	49	91	04 11	49	91	05 00	49	90	05 49	49	90	06 38	49	89	07 27	49	88
88	01 09	49	92	01 58	49	91	02 47	49	90	03 36	49	90	04 25	49	89	05 14	50	89	06 04	49	88	06 53	48	88
89	00 34	50	91	01 24	49	90	02 13	49	90	03 02	49	89	03 51	49	89	04 40	49	88	05 29	49	87	06 18	49	87
90	00 00	+49	90	00 49	+49	89	01 38	+49	89	02 27	+50	88	03 17	+49	88	04 06	+49	87	04 55	+49	87	05 44	+49	86
91	−0 34	49	89	00 15	49	89	01 04	49	88	01 53	49	87	02 42	49	87	03 31	49	86	04 20	50	86	05 10	49	85
92	−1 09	49	88	−0 20	50	88	00 30	49	87	01 19	49	87	02 08	49	86	02 57	49	85	03 46	49	85	04 35	49	84
93	−1 43	49	88	−0 54	49	87	−0 05	49	86	00 44	50	86	01 34	49	85	02 23	49	85	03 12	49	84	04 01	49	84
94	−2 18	50	87	−1 28	49	86	−0 39	49	86	00 10	49	85	00 59	49	84	01 48	50	84	02 38	49	83	03 27	49	83
95	−2 52	+49	86	−2 03	+50	85	−1 13	+49	85	−0 24	+49	84	00 25	+49	84	01 14	+49	83	02 03	+50	82	02 53	+49	82
96	−3 26	49	85	−2 37	49	85	−1 48	50	84	−0 58	49	83	−0 09	49	83	00 40	49	82	01 29	50	82	02 19	49	81
97	−4 00	49	84	−3 11	49	84	−2 22	49	83	−1 33	50	83	−0 43	49	82	00 06	49	81	00 55	50	81	01 45	49	80
98	−4 35	50	83	−3 45	49	83	−2 56	49	82	−2 07	50	82	−1 17	49	81	−0 28	49	81	00 21	50	80	01 11	49	79
99	−5 09	49	83	−4 20	50	82	−3 30	49	81	−2 41	50	81	−1 51	49	80	−1 02	50	80	−0 12	49	79	00 37	49	79
100	−5 43	+49	82	−4 54	+50	81	−4 04	+49	81	−3 15	+50	80	−2 25	+49	80	−1 36	+50	79	−0 46	+49	78	00 03	+50	78
101				−5 28	50	80	−4 38	49	80	−3 49	50	79	−2 59	50	79	−2 09	49	78	−1 20	50	78	−0 30	49	77
102				−6 01	49	80	−5 12	50	79	−4 22	49	78	−3 33	50	78	−2 43	50	77	−1 53	49	77	−1 04	50	76
103							−5 46	50	78	−4 56	50	78	−4 06	49	77	−3 17	50	76	−2 27	50	76	−1 37	50	75
104										−5 30	50	77	−4 40	50	76	−3 50	50	76	−3 00	50	75	−2 10	50	75
105										−6 03	+50	76	−5 13	+50	75	−4 23	+50	75	−3 33	+50	74	−2 43	+50	74
106													−5 46	50	74	−4 56	50	74	−4 06	50	73	−3 16	50	73
107																−5 29	50	73	−4 39	50	73	−3 49	50	72
108																−6 02	50	72	−5 12	50	72	−4 22	50	71
109																			−5 45	51	71	−4 54	50	70
110																						−5 27	+51	69
111																						−5 59	51	69

LHA	8°			9°			10°			11°			12°			13°			14°			LHA
	Hc	d	Z	Hc	d	Z	Hc	d	Z	Hc	d	Z	Hc	d	Z	Hc	d	Z	Hc	d	Z	
	° ′	′	°	° ′	′	°	° ′	′	°	° ′	′	°	° ′	′	°	° ′	′	°	° ′	′	°	
70	17 57	+50	102	18 47	+49	101	19 36	+49	101	20 25	+49	100	21 14	+49	100	22 03	+49	99	22 52	+48	98	290
71	17 24	49	101	18 13	49	101	19 02	49	100	19 51	49	99	20 40	49	99	21 29	49	98	22 18	48	98	289
72	16 50	49	100	17 39	49	100	18 28	49	99	19 17	49	99	20 06	49	98	20 55	49	97	21 44	48	97	288
73	16 16	49	99	17 05	49	99	17 54	49	98	18 43	49	98	19 32	49	97	20 21	48	96	21 09	49	96	287
74	15 42	49	99	16 31	49	98	17 20	49	97	18 09	49	97	18 58	49	96	19 47	48	96	20 35	48	95	286
75	15 08	+49	98	15 57	+49	97	16 46	+49	97	17 35	+49	96	18 24	+48	95	19 12	+49	95	20 01	+48	94	285
76	14 34	49	97	15 23	49	96	16 12	49	96	17 01	48	95	17 49	49	95	18 38	48	94	19 26	49	93	284
77	14 00	49	96	14 49	48	96	15 37	49	95	16 26	49	94	17 15	49	94	18 04	48	93	18 52	48	92	283
78	13 25	49	95	14 14	49	95	15 03	49	94	15 52	49	93	16 41	48	93	17 29	49	92	18 18	48	92	282
79	12 51	49	94	13 40	49	94	14 29	49	93	15 18	48	93	16 06	49	92	16 55	48	91	17 43	49	91	281
80	12 17	+49	94	13 06	+48	93	13 54	+49	92	14 43	+49	92	15 32	+48	91	16 20	+49	91	17 09	+48	90	280
81	11 42	49	93	12 31	49	92	13 20	49	92	14 09	48	91	14 57	49	90	15 46	48	90	16 34	49	89	279
82	11 08	49	92	11 57	49	91	12 46	48	91	13 34	49	90	14 23	49	90	15 12	48	89	16 00	48	88	278
83	10 34	48	91	11 22	49	91	12 11	49	90	13 00	49	89	13 49	48	89	14 37	49	88	15 26	48	88	277
84	09 59	49	90	10 48	49	90	11 37	49	89	12 26	48	89	13 14	49	88	14 03	48	87	14 51	49	87	276
85	09 25	+49	90	10 14	+48	89	11 02	+49	88	11 51	+49	88	12 40	+48	87	13 28	+49	87	14 17	+48	86	275
86	08 50	49	89	09 39	49	88	10 28	49	88	11 17	48	87	12 05	49	86	12 54	49	86	13 43	48	85	274
87	08 16	49	88	09 05	49	87	09 54	48	87	10 42	49	86	11 31	49	86	12 20	48	85	13 08	49	84	273
88	07 41	49	87	08 30	49	86	09 19	49	86	10 08	49	85	10 57	49	85	11 46	48	84	12 34	49	84	272
89	07 07	49	86	07 56	49	86	08 45	49	85	09 34	49	84	10 23	48	84	11 11	49	83	12 00	49	83	271
90	06 33	+49	85	07 22	+49	85	08 11	+49	84	09 00	+48	84	09 48	+49	83	10 37	+49	83	11 26	+48	82	270
91	05 59	49	85	06 48	48	84	07 36	49	83	08 25	49	83	09 14	49	82	10 03	49	82	10 52	48	81	269
92	05 24	49	84	06 13	49	83	07 02	49	83	07 51	49	82	08 40	49	81	09 29	49	81	10 18	49	80	268
93	04 50	49	83	05 39	49	82	06 28	49	82	07 17	49	81	08 06	49	81	08 55	49	80	09 44	49	80	267
94	04 16	49	82	05 05	49	82	05 54	49	81	06 43	49	80	07 32	49	80	08 21	49	79	09 10	49	79	266
95	03 42	+49	81	04 31	+49	81	05 20	+49	80	06 09	+49	80	06 58	+50	79	07 48	+49	78	08 37	+48	78	265
96	03 08	49	81	03 57	49	80	04 46	50	79	05 36	49	79	06 25	49	78	07 14	49	78	08 03	49	77	264
97	02 34	49	80	03 23	50	79	04 13	49	79	05 02	49	78	05 51	49	77	06 40	49	77	07 29	50	76	263
98	02 00	50	79	02 50	49	78	03 39	49	78	04 28	50	77	05 18	49	77	06 07	49	76	06 56	49	76	262
99	01 26	50	78	02 16	49	77	03 05	50	77	03 55	49	76	04 44	49	76	05 33	50	75	06 23	49	75	261
100	00 53	+49	77	01 42	+50	77	02 32	+49	76	03 21	+50	76	04 11	+49	75	05 00	+50	74	05 50	+49	74	260
101	00 19	50	76	01 09	49	76	01 58	50	75	02 48	50	75	03 38	49	74	04 27	50	74	05 17	49	73	259
102	−0 14	50	76	00 36	49	75	01 25	50	74	02 15	50	74	03 05	49	73	03 54	50	73	04 44	49	72	258
103	−0 47	49	75	00 02	50	74	00 52	50	74	01 42	50	73	02 32	49	73	03 21	50	72	04 11	50	71	257
104	−1 20	49	74	−0 31	50	73	00 19	50	73	01 09	50	72	01 59	50	72	02 49	50	71	03 39	49	71	256
105	−1 53	+49	73	−1 04	+50	73	−0 14	+50	72	00 36	+50	71	01 26	+50	71	02 16	+50	70	03 06	+50	70	255
106	−2 26	50	72	−1 36	50	72	−0 46	50	71	00 04	50	71	00 54	50	70	01 44	50	70	02 34	50	69	254
107	−2 59	50	71	−2 09	50	71	−1 19	50	70	−0 29	51	70	00 22	50	69	01 12	50	69	02 02	50	68	253
108	−3 32	51	71	−2 41	50	70	−1 51	50	70	−1 01	50	69	−0 11	51	68	00 40	50	68	01 30	50	67	252
109	−4 04	50	70	−3 14	51	69	−2 23	50	69	−1 33	51	68	−0 42	50	68	00 08	50	67	00 58	51	67	251
110	−4 36	+50	69	−3 46	+51	68	−2 55	+50	68	−2 05	+51	67	−1 14	+50	67	−0 24	+51	66	00 27	+50	66	250
111	−5 08	50	68	−4 18	51	68	−3 27	51	67	−2 36	50	67	−1 46	51	66	−0 55	51	65	−0 04	50	65	249
112	−5 40	51	67	−4 49	50	67	−3 59	51	66	−3 08	51	66	−2 17	51	65	−1 26	51	65	−0 35	50	64	248
113				−5 21	51	66	−4 30	51	65	−3 39	51	65	−2 48	51	64	−1 57	51	64	−1 06	51	63	247
114				−5 52	51	65	−5 01	51	65	−4 10	51	64	−3 19	51	64	−2 28	51	63	−1 37	51	62	246
115							−5 32	+51	64	−4 41	+51	63	−3 50	+51	63	−2 59	+52	62	−2 07	+51	62	245
116										−5 12	52	62	−4 20	51	62	−3 29	51	61	−2 38	52	61	244
117										−5 42	52	61	−4 50	51	61	−3 59	52	60	−3 07	51	60	243
118													−5 21	52	60	−4 29	52	60	−3 37	52	59	242
119													−5 50	52	59	−4 58	51	59	−4 07	52	58	241
120																−5 28	+52	58	−4 36	+52	57	240
121																−5 57	52	57	−5 05	53	57	239
122																			−5 33	52	56	238

0°	1°	2°	3°	4°	5°	6°	7°	8°	9°	10°	11°	12°	13°	14°

S. Lat. {LHA greater than 180°.......... Zn=180−Z; LHA less than 180°........... Zn=180+Z}

DECLINATION (0°-14°) SAME NAME AS LATITUDE

N. Lat. {LHA greater than 180°....... Zn=Z
{LHA less than 180°.......... Zn=360−Z

DECLINATION (0°-14°) CONTRARY NAME TO LATITUDE

LHA	0° Hc	d	Z	1° Hc	d	Z	2° Hc	d	Z	3° Hc	d	Z	4° Hc	d	Z
	° ′	′	°	° ′	′	°	° ′	′	°	° ′	′	°	° ′	′	°
100	−5 43	−49	82	260											
99	−5 09	49	83	−5 58	50	83	261								
98	−4 35	49	83	−5 24	49	84	262								
97	−4 00	50	84	−4 50	49	85	−5 39	49	85	263					
96	−3 26	49	85	−4 15	50	86	−5 05	49	86	−5 54	49	87	264		
95	−2 52	−49	86	−3 41	−49	86	−4 30	−50	87	−5 20	−49	88	265		
94	−2 18	49	87	−3 07	49	87	−3 56	49	88	−4 45	49	88	−5 34	49	89
93	−1 43	49	88	−2 32	50	88	−3 22	49	89	−4 11	49	89	−5 00	49	90
92	−1 09	49	88	−1 58	49	89	−2 47	49	90	−3 36	49	90	−4 25	49	91
91	−0 34	50	89	−1 24	49	90	−2 13	49	90	−3 02	49	91	−3 51	49	91
90	00 00	−49	90	−0 49	−49	91	−1 38	−49	91	−2 27	−50	92	−3 17	−49	92
89	00 34	49	91	−0 15	49	91	−1 04	49	92	−1 53	49	93	−2 42	49	93
88	01 09	49	92	00 20	50	92	−0 30	49	93	−1 19	49	93	−2 08	49	94
87	01 43	49	92	00 54	49	93	00 05	49	94	−0 44	50	94	−1 34	49	95
86	02 18	50	93	01 28	49	94	00 39	49	94	−0 10	49	95	−0 59	49	96
85	02 52	−49	94	02 03	−50	95	01 13	−49	95	00 24	−49	96	−0 25	−49	96
84	03 26	49	95	02 37	49	95	01 48	50	96	00 58	49	97	00 09	49	97
83	04 00	49	96	03 11	49	96	02 22	49	97	01 33	50	97	00 43	49	98
82	04 35	50	97	03 45	49	97	02 56	49	98	02 07	50	98	01 17	49	99
81	05 09	49	97	04 20	50	98	03 30	49	99	02 41	50	99	01 51	49	100
80	05 43	−49	98	04 54	−50	99	04 04	−49	99	03 15	−50	100	02 25	−49	100
79	06 17	49	99	05 28	50	100	04 38	49	100	03 49	50	101	02 59	50	101
78	06 51	50	100	06 01	49	100	05 12	50	101	04 22	49	102	03 33	50	102
77	07 25	50	101	06 35	49	101	05 46	50	102	04 56	50	102	04 06	49	103
76	07 59	50	102	07 09	50	102	06 19	49	103	05 30	50	103	04 40	50	104
75	08 32	−49	102	07 43	−50	103	06 53	−50	104	06 03	−50	104	05 13	−50	105
74	09 06	50	103	08 16	50	104	07 26	50	104	06 36	50	105	05 46	50	106
73	09 39	50	104	08 49	50	105	07 59	50	105	07 09	50	106	06 19	50	106
72	10 13	50	105	09 23	50	106	08 33	50	106	07 43	51	107	06 52	50	107
71	10 46	50	106	09 56	50	106	09 06	51	107	08 15	50	107	07 25	50	108
70	11 19	−50	107	10 29	−51	107	09 38	−50	108	08 48	−50	108	07 58	−50	109

LHA	5° Hc	d	Z	6° Hc	d	Z	7° Hc	d	Z	8° Hc	d	Z	9° Hc	d	Z
	° ′	′	°	° ′	′	°	° ′	′	°	° ′	′	°	° ′	′	°
100															
99															
98															
97															
96															
95															
94	266														
93	−5 49	49	90	267											
92	−5 14	50	91	−6 04	49	92	268								
91	−4 40	49	92	−5 29	49	93	269								
90	−4 06	−49	93	−4 55	−49	93	−5 44	−49	94	270					
89	−3 31	49	94	−4 20	50	94	−5 10	49	95	−5 59	49	95	271		
88	−2 57	49	95	−3 46	49	95	−4 35	49	96	−5 24	49	96	272		
87	−2 23	49	95	−3 12	49	96	−4 01	49	96	−4 50	49	97	−5 39	49	98
86	−1 48	50	96	−2 38	49	97	−3 27	49	97	−4 16	49	98	−5 05	49	98
85	−1 14	−49	97	−2 03	−50	98	−2 53	−49	98	−3 42	−49	99	−4 31	−49	99
84	−0 40	49	98	−1 29	50	98	−2 19	49	99	−3 08	49	99	−3 57	49	100
83	−0 06	49	99	−0 55	50	99	−1 45	49	100	−2 34	49	100	−3 23	50	101
82	00 28	49	99	−0 21	50	100	−1 11	49	101	−2 00	50	101	−2 50	49	102
81	01 02	50	100	00 12	49	101	−0 37	49	101	−1 26	50	102	−2 16	49	103
80	01 36	−50	101	00 46	−49	102	−0 03	−50	102	−0 53	−49	103	−1 42	−50	103
79	02 09	49	102	01 20	50	102	00 30	49	103	−0 19	50	104	−1 09	49	104
78	02 43	50	103	01 53	49	103	01 04	50	104	00 14	50	104	−0 36	49	105
77	03 17	50	104	02 27	50	104	01 37	50	105	00 47	49	105	−0 02	50	106
76	03 50	50	104	03 00	50	105	02 10	50	105	01 20	49	106	00 31	50	107
75	04 23	−50	105	03 33	−50	106	02 43	−50	106	01 53	−49	107	01 04	−50	107
74	04 56	50	106	04 06	50	107	03 16	50	107	02 26	50	108	01 36	50	108
73	05 29	50	107	04 39	50	107	03 49	50	108	02 59	50	109	02 09	50	109
72	06 02	50	108	05 12	50	108	04 22	50	109	03 32	51	109	02 41	50	110
71	06 35	50	109	05 45	51	109	04 54	50	110	04 04	50	110	03 14	51	111
70	07 08	−51	109	06 17	−50	110	05 27	−51	111	04 36	−50	111	03 46	−51	112

LHA	10° Hc	d	Z	11° Hc	d	Z	12° Hc	d	Z	13° Hc	d	Z	14° Hc	d	Z	LHA
	° ′	′	°	° ′	′	°	° ′	′	°	° ′	′	°	° ′	′	°	
100																
99																
98																
97																
96																
95																
94																
93																
92																
91																
90																
89																
88																
87	273															
86	−5 54	49	99	274												
85	−5 20	−49	100	275												
84	−4 46	50	101	−5 36	49	101	276									
83	−4 13	49	101	−5 02	49	102	−5 51	49	103	277						
82	−3 39	49	102	−4 28	50	103	−5 18	49	103	278						
81	−3 05	50	103	−3 55	49	104	−4 44	49	104	−5 33	50	105	279			
80	−2 32	−49	104	−3 21	−50	104	−4 11	−49	105	−5 00	−50	106	−5 50	−49	106	280
79	−1 58	50	105	−2 48	50	105	−3 38	49	106	−4 27	50	106	−5 17	49	107	281
78	−1 25	50	106	−2 15	50	106	−3 05	49	107	−3 54	50	107	−4 44	49	108	282
77	−0 52	50	106	−1 42	50	107	−2 32	49	107	−3 21	50	108	−4 11	50	109	283
76	−0 19	50	107	−1 09	50	108	−1 59	50	108	−2 49	50	109	−3 39	49	109	284
75	00 14	−50	108	−0 36	−50	109	−1 26	−50	109	−2 16	−50	110	−3 06	−50	110	285
74	00 46	50	109	−0 04	50	109	−0 54	50	110	−1 44	50	110	−2 34	50	111	286
73	01 19	50	110	00 29	51	110	−0 22	50	111	−1 12	50	111	−2 02	50	112	287
72	01 51	50	110	01 01	50	111	00 11	51	112	−0 40	50	112	−1 30	50	113	288
71	02 23	50	111	01 33	51	112	00 42	50	112	−0 08	50	113	−0 58	51	113	289
70	02 55	−50	112	02 05	−51	113	01 14	−50	113	00 24	−51	114	−0 27	−50	114	290

S. Lat. {LHA greater than 180°....... Zn=180−Z
{LHA less than 180°.......... Zn=180+Z

DECLINATION (0°-14°) CONTRARY NAME TO LATITUDE

N. Lat. {LHA greater than 180°....... Zn=Z
{LHA less than 180°........... Zn=360−Z

DECLINATION (0°-14°) CONTRARY NAME TO LATITUDE

	0°			1°			2°			3°			4°		
LHA	Hc	d	Z	Hc	d	Z	Hc	d	Z	Hc	d	Z	Hc	d	Z
	° ′	′	°	° ′	′	°	° ′	′	°	° ′	′	°	° ′	′	°
69	11 52	50	108	11 02	51	108	10 11	50	109	09 21	51	109	08 30	50	110
68	12 25	51	108	11 34	50	109	10 44	51	109	09 53	50	110	09 03	51	111
67	12 57	50	109	12 07	51	110	11 16	50	110	10 26	51	111	09 35	51	111
66	13 30	51	110	12 39	51	111	11 48	50	111	10 58	51	112	10 07	51	112
65	14 02	−51	111	13 11	−51	112	12 20	−51	112	11 29	−50	113	10 39	−51	113
64	14 34	51	112	13 43	51	112	12 52	51	113	12 01	51	113	11 10	51	114
63	15 06	51	113	14 15	51	113	13 24	51	114	12 33	52	114	11 41	51	115
62	15 37	51	114	14 46	51	114	13 55	51	115	13 04	51	115	12 13	52	116
61	16 09	51	114	15 18	52	115	14 26	51	116	13 35	52	116	12 43	51	117
60	16 40	−51	115	15 49	−52	116	14 57	−51	116	14 06	−52	117	13 14	−51	117
59	17 11	51	116	16 20	52	117	15 28	52	117	14 36	51	118	13 45	52	118
58	17 42	52	117	16 50	52	118	15 58	51	118	15 07	52	119	14 15	52	119
57	18 12	52	118	17 20	51	119	16 29	52	119	15 37	52	120	14 45	52	120
56	18 43	52	119	17 51	52	119	16 59	53	120	16 06	52	121	15 14	52	121
55	19 12	−52	120	18 20	−52	120	17 28	−52	121	16 36	−52	121	15 44	−53	122
54	19 42	52	121	18 50	52	121	17 58	53	122	17 05	52	122	16 13	53	123
53	20 12	53	122	19 19	52	122	18 27	53	123	17 34	53	123	16 41	52	124
52	20 41	53	123	19 48	52	123	18 56	53	124	18 03	53	124	17 10	53	125
51	21 10	53	124	20 17	53	124	19 24	53	125	18 31	53	125	17 38	53	126
50	21 38	−53	125	20 45	−53	125	19 52	−53	126	18 59	−53	126	18 06	−53	127
49	22 06	53	126	21 13	53	126	20 20	53	127	19 27	54	127	18 33	53	127
48	22 34	53	126	21 41	53	127	20 48	54	127	19 54	53	128	19 01	54	128
47	23 02	54	127	22 08	53	128	21 15	54	128	20 21	54	129	19 27	53	129
46	23 29	54	128	22 35	53	129	21 42	54	129	20 48	54	130	19 54	54	130
45	23 56	−54	129	23 02	−54	130	22 08	−54	130	21 14	−54	131	20 20	−54	131
44	24 22	54	130	23 28	54	131	22 34	54	131	21 40	54	132	20 46	55	132
43	24 48	54	131	23 54	54	132	23 00	55	132	22 05	54	133	21 11	55	133
42	25 14	55	132	24 19	54	133	23 25	55	133	22 30	54	134	21 36	55	134
41	25 39	54	133	24 45	55	134	23 50	55	134	22 55	55	135	22 00	55	135
40	26 04	−55	134	25 09	−55	135	24 14	−55	135	23 19	−55	136	22 24	−55	136
39	26 28	55	135	25 33	55	136	24 38	55	136	23 43	55	137	22 48	55	137
38	26 52	55	136	25 57	55	137	25 02	55	137	24 07	56	138	23 11	55	138
37	27 16	55	137	26 21	56	138	25 25	55	138	24 30	56	139	23 34	56	139
36	27 39	56	138	26 43	55	139	25 48	56	139	24 52	56	140	23 56	55	140
35	28 02	−56	140	27 06	−56	140	26 10	−56	140	25 14	−56	141	24 18	−56	141
34	28 24	56	141	27 28	56	141	26 32	56	141	25 36	56	142	24 40	57	142
33	28 45	56	142	27 49	56	142	26 53	56	142	25 57	57	143	25 00	56	143
32	29 06	56	143	28 10	56	143	27 14	57	143	26 17	56	144	25 21	57	144
31	29 27	56	144	28 31	57	144	27 34	57	145	26 37	56	145	25 41	57	145
30	29 47	−57	145	28 50	−56	145	27 54	−57	146	26 57	−57	146	26 00	−57	146
29	30 07	57	146	29 10	57	146	28 13	57	147	27 16	57	147	26 19	57	147
28	30 26	57	147	29 29	57	147	28 32	58	148	27 34	57	148	26 37	57	148
27	30 44	57	148	29 47	57	149	28 50	58	149	27 52	57	149	26 55	57	150
26	31 02	57	149	30 05	58	150	29 07	57	150	28 10	58	150	27 12	57	151
25	31 19	−57	150	30 22	−58	151	29 24	−57	151	28 27	−58	151	27 29	−58	152
24	31 36	58	152	30 38	57	152	29 41	58	152	28 43	58	152	27 45	58	153
23	31 52	58	153	30 54	58	153	29 56	58	153	28 58	58	154	28 00	58	154
22	32 08	58	154	31 10	58	154	30 12	59	154	29 13	58	155	28 15	58	155
21	32 23	59	155	31 24	58	155	30 26	58	156	29 28	58	156	28 30	59	156
20	32 37	−58	156	31 39	−59	156	30 40	−58	157	29 42	−59	157	28 43	−58	157
19	32 51	59	157	31 52	58	158	30 54	59	158	29 55	59	158	28 56	58	158
18	33 04	59	158	32 05	59	159	31 06	58	159	30 08	59	159	29 09	59	159
17	33 16	59	160	32 17	59	160	31 18	59	160	30 19	58	160	29 21	59	161
16	33 28	59	161	32 29	59	161	31 30	59	161	30 31	59	161	29 32	59	162
15	33 39	−59	162	32 40	−59	162	31 41	−60	162	30 41	−59	163	29 42	−59	163
14	33 49	59	163	32 50	59	163	31 51	59	164	30 52	60	164	29 52	59	164
13	33 59	60	164	32 59	59	164	32 00	59	165	31 01	59	165	30 02	60	165
12	34 08	60	166	33 08	59	166	32 09	59	166	31 10	60	166	30 10	59	166
11	34 16	59	167	33 17	60	167	32 17	59	167	31 18	60	167	30 18	59	167
10	34 24	−60	168	33 24	−60	168	32 24	−59	168	31 25	−60	168	30 25	−59	168
9	34 31	60	169	33 31	60	169	32 31	59	169	31 32	60	169	30 32	60	170
8	34 37	60	170	33 37	60	170	32 37	60	171	31 37	59	171	30 38	60	171
7	34 42	60	172	33 42	59	172	32 43	60	172	31 43	60	172	30 43	60	172
6	34 47	60	173	33 47	60	173	32 47	60	173	31 47	60	173	30 47	59	173
5	34 51	−60	174	33 51	−60	174	32 51	−60	174	31 51	−60	174	30 51	−60	174
4	34 54	60	175	33 54	60	175	32 54	60	175	31 54	60	175	30 54	59	175
3	34 57	60	176	33 57	60	176	32 57	60	176	31 57	60	177	30 57	60	177
2	34 59	60	178	33 59	60	178	32 59	60	178	31 59	60	178	30 59	60	178
1	35 00	60	179	34 00	60	179	33 00	60	179	32 00	60	179	31 00	60	179
0	35 00	−60	180	34 00	−60	180	33 00	−60	180	32 00	−60	180	31 00	−60	180

	5°			6°			7°			8°			9°		
LHA	Hc	d	Z	Hc	d	Z	Hc	d	Z	Hc	d	Z	Hc	d	Z
	° ′	′	°	° ′	′	°	° ′	′	°	° ′	′	°	° ′	′	°
69	07 40	51	110	06 49	50	111	05 59	51	111	05 08	50	112	04 18	51	112
68	08 12	50	111	07 22	51	112	06 31	51	112	05 40	51	113	04 49	50	113
67	08 44	51	112	07 53	50	113	07 03	51	113	06 12	51	114	05 21	51	114
66	09 16	51	113	08 25	51	113	07 34	51	114	06 43	51	114	05 52	51	115
65	09 48	−51	114	08 57	−51	114	08 06	−51	115	07 15	−52	115	06 23	−51	116
64	10 19	51	115	09 28	51	115	08 37	51	116	07 46	52	116	06 54	51	117
63	10 50	51	115	09 59	51	116	09 08	52	116	08 16	51	117	07 25	52	117
62	11 21	51	116	10 30	52	117	09 38	51	117	08 47	52	118	07 55	51	118
61	11 52	52	117	11 00	51	118	10 09	52	118	09 17	51	119	08 26	52	119
60	12 23	−52	118	11 31	−52	119	10 39	−52	119	09 47	−52	120	08 55	−51	120
59	12 53	52	119	12 01	52	119	11 09	52	120	10 17	52	120	09 25	52	121
58	13 23	52	120	12 31	52	120	11 39	52	121	10 47	52	121	09 55	53	122
57	13 53	53	121	13 00	52	121	12 08	52	122	11 16	52	122	10 24	53	123
56	14 22	52	122	13 30	53	122	12 37	52	123	11 45	53	123	10 52	52	124
55	14 51	−52	122	13 59	−53	123	13 06	−52	123	12 14	−53	124	11 21	−53	124
54	15 20	52	123	14 28	53	124	13 35	53	124	12 42	53	125	11 49	53	125
53	15 49	53	124	14 56	53	125	14 03	53	125	13 10	53	126	12 17	53	126
52	16 17	53	125	15 24	53	126	14 31	53	126	13 38	53	127	12 45	53	127
51	16 45	53	126	15 52	53	127	14 59	54	127	14 05	53	128	13 12	53	128
50	17 13	−54	127	16 19	−53	128	15 26	−53	128	14 33	−54	128	13 39	−53	129
49	17 40	53	128	16 47	54	128	15 53	54	129	14 59	53	129	14 06	54	130
48	18 07	54	129	17 13	53	129	16 20	54	130	15 26	54	130	14 32	54	131
47	18 34	54	130	17 40	54	130	16 46	54	131	15 52	54	131	14 58	54	132
46	19 00	54	131	18 06	54	131	17 12	54	132	16 18	55	132	15 23	54	133
45	19 26	−54	132	18 32	−55	132	17 37	−54	133	16 43	−54	133	15 49	−55	134
44	19 51	54	133	18 57	55	133	18 02	54	134	17 08	55	134	16 13	54	134
43	20 16	54	134	19 22	55	134	18 27	54	135	17 33	55	135	16 38	55	135
42	20 41	55	135	19 46	54	135	18 52	55	135	17 57	55	136	17 02	55	136
41	21 05	54	136	20 11	55	136	19 16	55	136	18 20	55	137	17 25	55	137
40	21 29	−55	137	20 34	−55	137	19 39	−55	137	18 44	−55	138	17 49	−56	138
39	21 53	55	138	20 58	56	138	20 02	55	138	19 07	56	139	18 11	55	139
38	22 16	56	139	21 20	55	139	20 25	56	139	19 29	55	140	18 34	56	140
37	22 38	55	140	21 43	56	140	20 47	56	140	19 51	56	141	18 55	55	141
36	23 01	56	141	22 05	56	141	21 09	56	141	20 13	56	142	19 17	56	142
35	23 22	−56	142	22 26	−56	142	21 30	−56	142	20 34	−56	143	19 38	−56	143
34	23 43	56	143	22 47	56	143	21 51	56	143	20 55	57	144	19 58	56	144
33	24 04	56	144	23 08	57	144	22 11	56	144	21 15	57	145	20 18	56	145
32	24 24	56	145	23 28	57	145	22 31	57	145	21 34	56	146	20 38	57	146
31	24 44	57	146	23 47	57	146	22 50	56	146	21 54	57	147	20 57	57	147
30	25 03	−57	147	24 06	−57	147	23 09	−57	147	22 12	−57	148	21 15	−57	148
29	25 22	57	148	24 25	57	148	23 28	58	148	22 30	57	149	21 33	57	149
28	25 40	57	149	24 43	58	149	23 45	57	149	22 48	57	150	21 51	58	150
27	25 58	58	150	25 00	57	150	24 03	58	150	23 05	57	151	22 08	58	151
26	26 15	58	151	25 17	58	151	24 19	57	152	23 22	58	152	22 24	58	152
25	26 31	−58	152	25 33	−58	152	24 35	−57	153	23 38	−58	153	22 40	−58	153
24	26 47	58	153	25 49	58	153	24 51	58	154	23 53	58	154	22 55	58	154
23	27 02	58	154	26 04	58	154	25 06	58	155	24 08	58	155	23 10	58	155
22	27 17	58	155	26 19	58	155	25 21	59	156	24 22	58	156	23 24	58	156
21	27 31	58	156	26 33	59	157	25 34	58	157	24 36	58	157	23 38	59	157
20	27 45	−59	157	26 46	−58	158	25 48	−59	158	24 49	−58	158	23 51	−59	158
19	27 58	59	159	26 59	59	159	26 00	58	159	25 02	59	159	24 03	59	159
18	28 10	59	160	27 11	59	160	26 12	58	160	25 14	59	160	24 15	59	160
17	28 22	59	161	27 23	59	161	26 24	59	161	25 25	59	161	24 26	59	161
16	28 33	59	162	27 34	59	162	26 35	59	162	25 36	59	162	24 37	59	163
15	28 43	−59	163	27 44	−59	163	26 45	−59	163	25 46	−59	164	24 47	−60	164
14	28 53	59	164	27 54	59	164	26 55	60	164	25 55	59	165	24 56	59	165
13	29 02	59	165	28 03	60	165	27 03	59	166	26 04	59	166	25 05	60	166
12	29 11	60	166	28 11	59	166	27 12	60	167	26 12	59	167	25 13	60	167
11	29 19	60	167	28 19	60	168	27 19	59	168	26 20	60	168	25 20	59	168
10	29 26	−60	169	28 26	−60	169	27 26	−59	169	26 27	−60	169	25 27	−59	169
9	29 32	59	170	28 33	60	170	27 33	60	170	26 33	60	170	25 33	59	170
8	29 38	60	171	28 38	59	171	27 39	60	171	26 39	60	171	25 39	60	171
7	29 43	60	172	28 43	59	172	27 44	60	172	26 44	60	172	25 44	60	172
6	29 48	60	173	28 48	60	173	27 48	60	173	26 48	60	173	25 48	60	173
5	29 51	−59	174	28 52	−60	174	27 52	−60	174	26 52	−60	174	25 52	−60	175
4	29 55	60	175	28 55	60	176	27 55	60	176	26 55	60	176	25 55	60	176
3	29 57	60	177	28 57	60	177	27 57	60	177	26 57	60	177	25 57	60	177
2	29 59	60	178	28 59	60	178	27 59	60	178	26 59	60	178	25 59	60	178
1	30 00	60	179	29 00	60	179	28 00	60	179	27 00	60	179	26 00	60	179
0	30 00	−60	180	29 00	−60	180	28 00	−60	180	27 00	−60	180	26 00	−60	180

	10°			11°			12°			13°			14°			
LHA	Hc	d	Z	Hc	d	Z	Hc	d	Z	Hc	d	Z	Hc	d	Z	LHA
	° ′	′	°	° ′	′	°	° ′	′	°	° ′	′	°	° ′	′	°	
69	03 27	51	113	02 36	50	113	01 46	51	114	00 55	51	115	00 04	50	115	291
68	03 59	51	114	03 08	51	114	02 17	51	115	01 26	51	115	00 35	50	116	292
67	04 30	51	115	03 39	51	115	02 48	51	116	01 57	51	116	01 06	51	117	293
66	05 01	51	115	04 10	51	116	03 19	51	116	02 28	51	117	01 37	51	118	294
65	05 32	−51	116	04 41	−51	117	03 50	−51	117	02 59	−52	118	02 07	−51	118	295
64	06 03	51	117	05 12	52	118	04 20	51	118	03 29	51	119	02 38	52	119	296
63	06 33	51	118	05 42	52	119	04 50	51	119	03 59	52	120	03 07	51	120	297
62	07 04	52	119	06 12	51	119	05 21	52	120	04 29	52	120	03 37	52	121	298
61	07 34	52	120	06 42	52	120	05 50	52	121	04 58	51	121	04 07	52	122	299
60	08 04	−52	121	07 12	−52	121	06 20	−52	122	05 28	−52	122	04 36	−52	123	300
59	08 33	52	121	07 41	52	122	06 49	52	122	05 57	52	123	05 05	53	123	301
58	09 02	52	122	08 10	52	123	07 18	52	123	06 26	53	124	05 33	52	124	302
57	09 31	52	123	08 39	53	124	07 46	52	124	06 54	53	125	06 01	52	125	303
56	10 00	53	124	09 07	52	125	08 15	53	125	07 22	53	126	06 29	52	126	304
55	10 28	−52	125	09 36	−53	125	08 43	−53	126	07 50	−53	126	06 57	−53	127	305
54	10 56	52	126	10 04	53	126	09 11	53	127	08 18	53	127	07 25	53	128	306
53	11 24	53	127	10 31	53	127	09 38	53	128	08 45	53	128	07 52	54	129	307
52	11 52	54	128	10 58	53	128	10 05	53	129	09 12	54	129	08 18	53	129	308
51	12 19	54	128	11 25	53	129	10 32	54	129	09 38	53	130	08 45	54	130	309
50	12 46	−54	129	11 52	−54	130	10 58	−53	130	10 05	−54	131	09 11	−54	131	310
49	13 12	54	130	12 18	54	131	11 24	53	131	10 31	54	132	09 37	54	132	311
48	13 38	54	131	12 44	54	132	11 50	54	132	10 56	54	133	10 02	54	133	312
47	14 04	54	132	13 10	54	133	12 16	55	133	11 21	54	133	10 27	54	134	313
46	14 29	54	133	13 35	54	133	12 41	55	134	11 46	54	134	10 52	55	135	314
45	14 54	−54	134	14 00	−55	134	13 05	−54	135	12 11	−55	135	11 16	−55	136	315
44	15 19	55	135	14 24	55	135	13 29	54	136	12 35	55	136	11 40	55	137	316
43	15 43	55	136	14 48	55	136	13 53	55	137	12 58	55	137	12 03	55	137	317
42	16 07	55	137	15 12	55	137	14 17	55	138	13 22	56	138	12 26	55	138	318
41	16 30	55	138	15 35	55	138	14 40	56	138	13 44	55	139	12 49	55	139	319
40	16 53	−55	139	15 58	−56	139	15 02	−55	139	14 07	−56	140	13 11	−55	140	320
39	17 16	56	140	16 20	55	140	15 25	56	140	14 29	56	141	13 33	56	141	321
38	17 38	56	141	16 42	56	141	15 46	56	141	14 50	55	142	13 55	56	142	322
37	18 00	56	142	17 04	56	142	16 08	56	142	15 12	56	143	14 16	57	143	323
36	18 21	56	142	17 25	57	143	16 28	56	143	15 32	56	144	14 36	56	144	324
35	18 42	−57	143	17 45	−56	144	16 49	−56	144	15 53	−57	145	14 56	−56	145	325
34	19 02	57	144	18 05	56	145	17 09	57	145	16 12	56	145	15 16	57	146	326
33	19 22	57	145	18 25	57	146	17 28	56	146	16 32	57	146	15 35	57	147	327
32	19 41	57	146	18 44	57	147	17 47	57	147	16 50	57	147	15 53	56	148	328
31	20 00	57	147	19 03	57	148	18 06	57	148	17 09	57	148	16 12	57	149	329
30	20 18	−57	148	19 21	−57	149	18 24	−57	149	17 27	−58	149	16 29	−57	150	330
29	20 36	57	149	19 39	58	150	18 41	57	150	17 44	58	150	16 46	57	151	331
28	20 53	57	150	19 56	58	151	18 58	57	151	18 01	58	151	17 03	57	152	332
27	21 10	58	151	20 12	57	152	19 15	58	152	18 17	58	152	17 19	57	153	333
26	21 26	58	152	20 28	57	153	19 31	58	153	18 33	58	153	17 35	58	154	334
25	21 42	−58	153	20 44	−58	154	19 46	−58	154	18 48	−58	154	17 50	−58	155	335
24	21 57	58	154	20 59	58	155	20 01	58	155	19 03	58	155	18 05	59	156	336
23	22 12	59	155	21 13	58	156	20 15	58	156	19 17	58	156	18 19	59	157	337
22	22 26	59	157	21 27	58	157	20 29	59	157	19 30	58	157	18 32	58	158	338
21	22 39	58	158	21 41	59	158	20 42	58	158	19 43	58	158	18 45	59	159	339
20	22 52	−59	159	21 53	−58	159	20 55	−59	159	19 56	−59	159	18 57	−58	160	340
19	23 04	59	160	22 05	58	160	21 07	59	160	20 08	59	160	19 09	59	161	341
18	23 16	59	161	22 17	59	161	21 18	59	161	20 19	59	161	19 20	59	162	342
17	23 27	59	162	22 28	59	162	21 29	59	162	20 30	59	162	19 31	59	163	343
16	23 38	60	163	22 38	59	163	21 39	59	163	20 40	59	163	19 41	59	164	344
15	23 47	−59	164	22 48	−59	164	21 49	−59	164	20 50	−60	164	19 50	−59	165	345
14	23 57	60	165	22 57	59	165	21 58	59	165	20 59	60	165	19 59	59	166	346
13	24 05	59	166	23 06	59	166	22 07	60	166	21 07	59	166	20 08	60	167	347
12	24 13	59	167	23 14	60	167	22 14	59	167	21 15	60	167	20 15	59	168	348
11	24 21	60	168	23 21	59	168	22 22	60	168	21 22	60	169	20 22	59	169	349
10	24 28	−60	169	23 28	−60	169	22 28	−59	169	21 29	−60	170	20 29	−60	170	350
9	24 34	60	170	23 34	60	170	22 34	59	171	21 35	60	171	20 35	60	171	351
8	24 39	60	171	23 39	60	171	22 40	60	172	21 40	60	172	20 40	60	172	352
7	24 44	60	172	23 44	60	173	22 44	59	173	21 45	60	173	20 45	60	173	353
6	24 48	60	174	23 48	59	174	22 49	60	174	21 49	60	174	20 49	60	174	354
5	24 52	−60	175	23 52	−60	175	22 52	−60	175	21 52	−60	175	20 52	−60	175	355
4	24 55	60	176	23 55	60	176	22 55	60	176	21 55	60	176	20 55	60	176	356
3	24 57	60	177	23 57	60	177	22 57	60	177	21 57	60	177	20 57	60	177	357
2	24 59	60	178	23 59	60	178	22 59	60	178	21 59	60	178	20 59	60	178	358
1	25 00	60	179	24 00	60	179	23 00	60	179	22 00	60	179	21 00	60	179	359
0	25 00	−60	180	24 00	−60	180	23 00	−60	180	22 00	−60	180	21 00	−60	180	360

S. Lat. {LHA greater than 180°....... Zn=180−Z
{LHA less than 180°........... Zn=180+Z

N. Lat. {LHA greater than 180°....... Zn=Z; LHA less than 180°........... Zn=360−Z}

DECLINATION (15°-29°) SAME NAME AS LATITUDE

LHA	15° Hc	15° d	15° Z	16° Hc	16° d	16° Z	17° Hc	17° d	17° Z	18° Hc	18° d	18° Z	19° Hc	19° d	19° Z
	° ′	′	°	° ′	′	°	° ′	′	°	° ′	′	°	° ′	′	°
0	50 00	+60	180	51 00	+60	180	52 00	+60	180	53 00	+60	180	54 00	+60	180
1	50 00	60	179	51 00	60	179	52 00	60	178	53 00	60	178	54 00	60	178
2	49 58	60	177	50 58	60	177	51 58	60	177	52 58	60	177	53 58	60	177
3	49 56	60	176	50 56	60	175	51 56	60	175	52 56	60	175	53 56	60	175
4	49 53	60	174	50 53	60	174	51 53	59	174	52 52	60	174	53 52	60	174
5	49 49	+60	173	50 49	+59	172	51 48	+60	172	52 48	+60	172	53 48	+60	172
6	49 44	60	171	50 44	59	171	51 43	60	171	52 43	60	171	53 43	59	170
7	49 38	60	170	50 38	59	169	51 37	60	169	52 37	60	169	53 37	59	169
8	49 31	60	168	50 31	59	168	51 30	60	168	52 30	59	167	53 29	60	167
9	49 24	59	167	50 23	60	166	51 23	59	166	52 22	59	166	53 21	60	166
10	49 15	+60	165	50 15	+59	165	51 14	+59	165	52 13	+59	164	53 12	+59	164
11	49 06	59	164	50 05	59	163	51 04	59	163	52 03	59	163	53 02	59	163
12	48 56	59	162	49 55	59	162	50 54	59	162	51 53	59	161	52 52	58	161
13	48 45	59	161	49 44	59	161	50 43	58	160	51 41	59	160	52 40	59	160
14	48 33	59	159	49 32	59	159	50 31	58	159	51 29	59	158	52 28	58	158
15	48 21	+58	158	49 19	+59	158	50 18	+58	157	51 16	+58	157	52 14	+58	156
16	48 07	59	157	49 06	58	156	50 04	58	156	51 02	58	155	52 00	58	155
17	47 53	58	155	48 51	58	155	49 49	58	154	50 47	58	154	51 45	58	154
18	47 38	58	154	48 36	58	153	49 34	58	153	50 32	57	153	51 29	58	152
19	47 23	57	152	48 20	58	152	49 18	57	152	50 15	58	151	51 13	57	151
20	47 07	+57	151	48 04	+57	151	49 01	+57	150	49 58	+57	150	50 55	+57	149
21	46 49	58	150	47 47	57	149	48 44	57	149	49 41	56	148	50 37	57	148
22	46 32	57	148	47 29	56	148	48 25	57	147	49 22	57	147	50 19	56	146
23	46 13	57	147	47 10	57	147	48 07	56	146	49 03	56	146	49 59	56	145
24	45 54	57	146	46 51	56	145	47 47	56	145	48 43	56	144	49 39	56	144
25	45 34	+57	144	46 31	+56	144	47 27	+56	143	48 23	+55	143	49 18	+56	142
26	45 14	56	143	46 10	56	143	47 06	56	142	48 02	55	141	48 57	55	141
27	44 53	56	142	45 49	55	141	46 44	56	141	47 40	55	140	48 35	55	140
28	44 31	56	141	45 27	55	140	46 22	55	139	47 17	55	139	48 12	55	138
29	44 09	55	139	45 04	56	139	46 00	54	138	46 54	55	138	47 49	55	137
30	43 47	+54	138	44 41	+55	138	45 36	+55	137	46 31	+54	136	47 25	+55	136
31	43 23	55	137	44 18	55	136	45 13	54	136	46 07	54	135	47 01	54	134
32	42 59	55	136	43 54	54	135	44 48	54	134	45 42	54	134	46 36	54	133
33	42 35	54	134	43 29	54	134	44 23	54	133	45 17	54	133	46 11	53	132
34	42 10	54	133	43 04	54	133	43 58	54	132	44 52	53	131	45 45	53	131
35	41 45	+54	132	42 39	+53	131	43 32	+54	131	44 26	+53	130	45 19	+53	130
36	41 19	54	131	42 13	53	130	43 06	53	130	43 59	53	129	44 52	53	128
37	40 53	53	130	41 46	53	129	42 39	53	129	43 32	53	128	44 25	52	127
38	40 26	53	129	41 19	53	128	42 12	53	127	43 05	52	127	43 57	52	126
39	39 59	53	128	40 52	53	127	41 45	52	126	42 37	52	126	43 29	52	125
40	39 32	+52	126	40 24	+53	126	41 17	+52	125	42 09	+52	125	43 01	+51	124
41	39 04	52	125	39 56	52	125	40 48	52	124	41 40	52	123	42 32	51	123
42	38 35	53	124	39 28	52	124	40 20	51	123	41 11	52	122	42 03	51	122
43	38 07	52	123	38 59	51	123	39 50	52	122	40 42	51	121	41 33	51	121
44	37 38	52	122	38 30	51	121	39 21	51	121	40 12	51	120	41 03	51	119
45	37 08	+52	121	38 00	+51	120	38 51	+51	120	39 42	+51	119	40 33	+51	118
46	36 39	51	120	37 30	51	119	38 21	51	119	39 12	51	118	40 03	50	117
47	36 09	51	119	37 00	51	118	37 51	51	118	38 42	50	117	39 32	50	116
48	35 39	51	118	36 30	50	117	37 20	51	117	38 11	50	116	39 01	50	115
49	35 08	51	117	35 59	50	116	36 49	51	116	37 40	50	115	38 30	50	114
50	34 37	+51	116	35 28	+50	115	36 18	+50	115	37 08	+50	114	37 58	+50	113
51	34 06	51	115	34 57	50	114	35 47	50	114	36 37	50	113	37 27	49	112
52	33 35	50	114	34 25	50	113	35 15	50	113	36 05	50	112	36 55	49	111
53	33 03	50	113	33 53	50	112	34 43	50	112	35 33	50	111	36 23	49	110
54	32 32	50	112	33 22	49	111	34 11	50	111	35 01	49	110	35 50	49	109
55	32 00	+49	111	32 49	+50	110	33 39	+49	110	34 28	+50	109	35 18	+49	108
56	31 27	50	110	32 17	50	110	33 07	49	109	33 56	49	108	34 45	49	107
57	30 55	50	109	31 45	49	109	32 34	49	108	33 23	49	107	34 12	49	107
58	30 22	50	108	31 12	49	108	32 01	49	107	32 50	49	106	33 39	48	106
59	29 50	49	107	30 39	49	107	31 28	49	106	32 17	49	105	33 06	48	105
60	29 17	+49	107	30 06	+49	106	30 55	+49	105	31 44	+48	105	32 32	+49	104
61	28 44	49	106	29 33	49	105	30 22	48	104	31 10	49	104	31 59	48	103
62	28 10	49	105	28 59	49	104	29 48	49	103	30 37	48	103	31 25	48	102
63	27 37	49	104	28 26	49	103	29 15	48	102	30 03	48	102	30 51	49	101
64	27 03	49	103	27 52	49	102	28 41	48	102	29 29	49	101	30 18	48	100
65	26 30	+49	102	27 19	+48	101	28 07	+49	101	28 56	+48	100	29 44	+48	99
66	25 56	49	101	26 45	48	101	27 33	49	100	28 22	48	99	29 10	48	98
67	25 22	49	100	26 11	48	100	26 59	49	99	27 48	48	98	28 36	48	98
68	24 48	49	99	25 37	48	99	26 25	49	98	27 14	48	98	28 02	47	97
69	24 14	49	99	25 03	48	98	25 51	48	97	26 39	48	97	27 27	48	96

LHA	20° Hc	20° d	20° Z	21° Hc	21° d	21° Z	22° Hc	22° d	22° Z	23° Hc	23° d	23° Z	24° Hc	24° d	24° Z
	° ′	′	°	° ′	′	°	° ′	′	°	° ′	′	°	° ′	′	°
0	55 00	+60	180	56 00	+60	180	57 00	+60	180	58 00	+60	180	59 00	+60	180
1	55 00	60	178	56 00	60	178	57 00	60	178	58 00	60	178	59 00	60	178
2	54 58	60	177	55 58	60	177	56 58	60	177	57 58	60	177	58 58	60	177
3	54 56	60	175	55 56	59	175	56 55	60	175	57 55	60	175	58 55	60	175
4	54 52	60	174	55 52	60	173	56 52	60	173	57 52	60	173	58 52	59	173
5	54 48	+60	172	55 48	+59	172	56 47	+60	172	57 47	+60	171	58 47	+59	171
6	54 42	60	170	55 42	60	170	56 42	59	170	57 41	60	170	58 41	60	169
7	54 36	60	169	55 36	59	168	56 35	60	168	57 35	59	168	58 34	60	168
8	54 29	60	167	55 28	60	167	56 28	59	167	57 27	59	166	58 26	60	166
9	54 21	59	165	55 20	59	165	56 19	59	165	57 18	59	165	58 17	60	164
10	54 11	+60	164	55 11	+59	164	56 10	+59	163	57 09	+59	163	58 08	+58	163
11	54 01	59	162	55 00	59	162	55 59	59	162	56 58	59	161	57 57	58	161
12	53 50	59	161	54 49	59	160	55 48	58	160	56 46	59	160	57 45	58	159
13	53 39	58	159	54 37	59	159	55 36	58	158	56 34	58	158	57 32	58	158
14	53 26	58	158	54 24	58	157	55 22	59	157	56 21	58	156	57 19	58	156
15	53 12	+58	156	54 10	+58	156	55 08	+58	155	56 06	+58	155	57 04	+58	154
16	52 58	58	155	53 56	58	154	54 54	57	154	55 51	58	153	56 49	57	153
17	52 43	57	153	53 40	58	153	54 38	57	152	55 35	57	152	56 32	58	151
18	52 27	57	152	53 24	57	151	54 21	57	151	55 18	57	150	56 15	57	150
19	52 10	57	150	53 07	57	150	54 04	57	149	55 01	56	149	55 57	57	148
20	51 52	+57	149	52 49	+57	148	53 46	+56	148	54 42	+57	147	55 39	+56	146
21	51 34	57	147	52 31	56	147	53 27	56	146	54 23	56	146	55 19	56	145
22	51 15	56	146	52 11	57	145	53 08	55	145	54 03	56	144	54 59	56	143
23	50 55	56	144	51 51	56	144	52 47	56	143	53 43	55	143	54 38	56	142
24	50 35	56	143	51 31	55	142	52 26	56	142	53 22	55	141	54 17	55	141
25	50 14	+55	142	51 09	+56	141	52 05	+55	140	53 00	+55	140	53 55	+54	139
26	49 52	56	140	50 48	54	140	51 42	55	139	52 37	55	138	53 32	54	138
27	49 30	55	139	50 25	55	138	51 20	54	138	52 14	54	137	53 08	54	136
28	49 07	55	138	50 02	54	137	50 56	54	136	51 50	54	136	52 44	54	135
29	48 44	54	136	49 38	54	136	50 32	54	135	51 26	53	134	52 19	54	134
30	48 20	+54	135	49 14	+53	134	50 07	+54	134	51 01	+53	133	51 54	+53	132
31	47 55	54	134	48 49	53	133	49 42	54	132	50 36	52	132	51 28	53	131
32	47 30	53	133	48 23	54	132	49 17	53	131	50 10	52	130	51 02	53	130
33	47 04	54	131	47 58	52	131	48 50	53	130	49 43	53	129	50 36	52	128
34	46 38	53	130	47 31	53	129	48 24	52	129	49 16	52	128	50 08	52	127
35	46 12	+52	129	47 04	+53	128	47 57	+52	127	48 49	+52	127	49 41	+51	126
36	45 45	52	128	46 37	52	127	47 29	52	126	48 21	52	126	49 13	51	125
37	45 17	52	127	46 09	52	126	47 01	52	125	47 53	51	124	48 44	51	124
38	44 49	52	125	45 41	52	125	46 33	51	124	47 24	51	123	48 15	51	122
39	44 21	52	124	45 13	51	124	46 04	51	123	46 55	51	122	47 46	50	121
40	43 52	+52	123	44 44	+51	122	45 35	+51	122	46 26	+50	121	47 16	+51	120
41	43 23	52	122	44 15	50	121	45 05	51	121	45 56	50	120	46 46	50	119
42	42 54	51	121	43 45	51	120	44 36	50	119	45 26	50	119	46 16	50	118
43	42 24	51	120	43 15	51	119	44 06	50	118	44 56	50	118	45 46	49	117
44	41 54	51	119	42 45	50	118	43 35	50	117	44 25	50	117	45 15	49	116
45	41 24	+50	118	42 14	+50	117	43 04	+50	116	43 54	+50	115	44 44	+49	115
46	40 53	50	117	41 43	50	116	42 33	50	115	43 23	49	114	44 12	49	114
47	40 22	50	116	41 12	50	115	42 02	49	114	42 51	49	113	43 40	49	113
48	39 51	50	115	40 41	49	114	41 30	50	113	42 20	49	112	43 09	48	112
49	39 20	49	114	40 09	50	113	40 59	49	112	41 48	48	111	42 36	49	111
50	38 48	+50	113	39 38	+49	112	40 27	+49	111	41 16	+48	110	42 04	+48	110
51	38 16	49	112	39 05	49	111	39 54	49	110	40 43	48	109	41 31	49	109
52	37 44	49	111	38 33	49	110	39 22	49	109	40 11	48	108	40 59	48	108
53	37 12	49	110	38 01	48	109	38 49	49	108	39 38	48	107	40 26	48	107
54	36 39	49	109	37 28	49	108	38 17	48	107	39 05	48	106	39 53	47	106
55	36 07	+48	108	36 55	+49	107	37 44	+48	106	38 32	+48	105	39 20	+47	105
56	35 34	48	107	36 22	49	106	37 11	48	105	37 59	47	105	38 46	48	104
57	35 01	48	106	35 49	48	105	36 37	48	104	37 25	48	104	38 13	47	103
58	34 27	49	105	35 16	48	104	36 04	48	103	36 52	47	103	37 39	47	102
59	33 54	48	104	34 42	48	103	35 30	48	103	36 18	47	102	37 05	47	101
60	33 21	+48	103	34 09	+48	102	34 57	+47	102	35 44	+48	101	36 32	+47	100
61	32 47	48	102	33 35	48	101	34 23	47	101	35 10	48	100	35 58	47	99
62	32 13	48	101	33 01	48	101	33 49	47	100	34 36	48	99	35 24	46	98
63	31 40	47	100	32 27	48	100	33 15	47	99	34 02	48	98	34 50	46	97
64	31 06	47	100	31 53	48	99	32 41	47	98	33 28	47	97	34 15	47	97
65	30 32	+47	99	31 19	+48	98	32 07	+47	97	32 54	+47	97	33 41	+47	96
66	29 58	47	98	30 45	48	97	31 33	47	96	32 20	47	96	33 07	47	95
67	29 24	47	97	30 11	48	96	30 59	47	96	31 46	47	95	32 33	46	94
68	28 49	48	96	29 37	47	95	30 24	47	95	31 11	47	94	31 58	47	93
69	28 15	48	95	29 03	47	95	29 50	47	94	30 37	47	93	31 24	46	92

LHA	25° Hc	25° d	25° Z	26° Hc	26° d	26° Z	27° Hc	27° d	27° Z	28° Hc	28° d	28° Z	29° Hc	29° d	29° Z	LHA
	° ′	′	°	° ′	′	°	° ′	′	°	° ′	′	°	° ′	′	°	
0	60 00	+60	180	61 00	+60	180	62 00	+60	180	63 00	+60	180	64 00	+60	180	360
1	60 00	59	178	60 59	60	178	61 59	60	178	62 59	60	178	63 59	60	178	359
2	59 58	60	176	60 58	60	176	61 58	60	176	62 58	60	176	63 58	60	176	358
3	59 55	60	175	60 55	60	174	61 55	60	174	62 55	60	174	63 55	60	174	357
4	59 51	60	173	60 51	60	173	61 51	60	172	62 51	59	172	63 50	60	172	356
5	59 46	+60	171	60 46	+60	171	61 46	+60	171	62 46	+59	170	63 45	+60	170	355
6	59 41	59	169	60 40	60	169	61 40	59	169	62 39	60	168	63 39	59	168	354
7	59 34	59	167	60 33	59	167	61 32	60	167	62 32	59	167	63 31	59	166	353
8	59 26	59	166	60 25	59	165	61 24	59	165	62 23	59	165	63 22	59	164	352
9	59 17	59	164	60 16	59	164	61 15	58	163	62 13	59	163	63 12	59	162	351
10	59 06	+59	162	60 05	+59	162	61 04	+59	161	62 03	+58	161	63 01	+59	160	350
11	58 55	59	160	59 54	59	160	60 53	58	160	61 51	58	159	62 49	58	159	349
12	58 43	59	159	59 42	58	158	60 40	58	158	61 38	58	157	62 36	58	157	348
13	58 30	59	157	59 29	58	157	60 27	57	156	61 24	58	156	62 22	58	155	347
14	58 17	57	155	59 14	58	155	60 12	58	154	61 10	57	154	62 07	57	153	346
15	58 02	+57	154	58 59	+58	153	59 57	+57	153	60 54	+57	152	61 51	+57	151	345
16	57 46	57	152	58 43	57	152	59 40	57	151	60 37	57	150	61 34	56	150	344
17	57 30	56	151	58 26	57	150	59 23	57	149	60 20	56	149	61 16	56	148	343
18	57 12	57	149	58 09	56	148	59 05	56	148	60 01	56	147	60 57	56	146	342
19	56 54	56	147	57 50	56	147	58 46	56	146	59 42	56	145	60 38	55	145	341
20	56 35	+56	146	57 31	+56	145	58 27	+55	144	59 22	+55	144	60 17	+55	143	340
21	56 15	56	144	57 11	55	144	58 06	55	143	59 01	55	142	59 56	55	141	339
22	55 55	55	143	56 50	55	142	57 45	55	141	58 40	54	141	59 34	55	140	338
23	55 34	55	141	56 29	54	141	57 23	55	140	58 18	54	139	59 12	54	138	337
24	55 12	54	140	56 06	55	139	57 01	54	138	57 55	53	138	58 48	54	137	336
25	54 49	+54	138	55 43	+54	138	56 37	+54	137	57 31	+53	136	58 24	+53	135	335
26	54 26	54	137	55 20	54	136	56 14	53	135	57 07	53	135	58 00	53	134	334
27	54 02	54	136	54 56	53	135	55 49	53	134	56 42	53	133	57 35	52	132	333
28	53 38	53	134	54 31	53	133	55 24	53	133	56 17	52	132	57 09	52	131	332
29	53 13	53	133	54 06	52	132	54 58	53	131	55 51	52	130	56 43	51	129	331
30	52 47	+53	132	53 40	+52	131	54 32	+52	130	55 24	+52	129	56 16	+51	128	330
31	52 21	53	130	53 14	52	129	54 06	51	129	54 57	51	128	55 48	51	127	329
32	51 55	52	129	52 47	51	128	53 38	52	127	54 30	51	126	55 21	50	125	328
33	51 28	51	128	52 19	52	127	53 11	51	126	54 02	50	125	54 52	50	124	327
34	51 00	52	126	51 52	51	126	52 43	50	125	53 33	51	124	54 24	49	123	326
35	50 32	+51	125	51 23	+51	124	52 14	+51	123	53 05	+50	123	53 55	+49	122	325
36	50 04	51	124	50 55	50	123	51 45	50	122	52 35	50	121	53 25	49	120	324
37	49 35	51	123	50 26	50	122	51 16	50	121	52 06	49	120	52 55	49	119	323
38	49 06	50	122	49 56	50	121	50 46	50	120	51 36	49	119	52 25	49	118	322
39	48 36	50	120	49 26	50	120	50 16	50	119	51 06	48	118	51 54	49	117	321
40	48 07	+49	119	48 56	+50	118	49 46	+49	118	50 35	+49	117	51 24	+48	116	320
41	47 36	50	118	48 26	49	117	49 15	49	116	50 04	48	116	50 52	48	115	319
42	47 06	49	117	47 55	49	116	48 44	49	115	49 33	48	114	50 21	48	114	318
43	46 35	49	116	47 24	49	115	48 13	48	114	49 01	48	113	49 49	48	112	317
44	46 04	49	115	46 53	48	114	47 41	49	113	48 30	47	112	49 17	48	111	316
45	45 33	+48	114	46 21	+49	113	47 10	+48	112	47 58	+47	111	48 45	+47	110	315
46	45 01	49	113	45 50	48	112	46 38	47	111	47 25	48	110	48 13	47	109	314
47	44 29	48	112	45 17	48	111	46 05	48	110	46 53	47	109	47 40	47	108	313
48	43 57	48	111	44 45	48	110	45 33	47	109	46 20	47	108	47 07	47	107	312
49	43 25	48	110	44 13	47	109	45 00	48	108	45 48	46	107	46 34	47	106	311
50	42 52	+48	109	43 40	+48	108	44 28	+47	107	45 15	+46	106	46 01	+47	105	310
51	42 20	47	108	43 07	48	107	43 55	46	106	44 41	47	105	45 28	46	104	309
52	41 47	47	107	42 34	47	106	43 21	47	105	44 08	47	104	44 55	46	103	308
53	41 14	47	106	42 01	47	105	42 48	47	104	43 35	46	103	44 21	46	102	307
54	40 40	48	105	41 28	47	104	42 15	46	103	43 01	46	102	43 47	46	101	306
55	40 07	+47	104	40 54	+47	103	41 41	+47	102	42 28	+46	101	43 14	+45	101	305
56	39 34	47	103	40 21	46	102	41 07	47	101	41 54	46	101	42 40	45	100	304
57	39 00	47	102	39 47	47	101	40 34	46	100	41 20	46	100	42 06	45	99	303
58	38 26	47	101	39 13	47	100	40 00	46	100	40 46	46	99	41 32	45	98	302
59	37 52	47	100	38 39	47	99	39 26	46	99	40 12	46	98	40 58	45	97	301
60	37 19	+46	99	38 05	+47	99	38 52	+46	98	39 38	+45	97	40 23	+46	96	300
61	36 45	46	98	37 31	47	98	38 18	45	97	39 03	46	96	39 49	45	95	299
62	36 10	47	97	36 57	46	97	37 43	46	96	38 29	46	95	39 15	45	94	298
63	35 36	47	97	36 23	46	96	37 09	46	95	37 55	45	94	38 40	46	94	297
64	35 02	47	96	35 49	46	95	36 35	46	94	37 21	45	93	38 06	45	93	296
65	34 28	+46	95	35 14	+46	94	36 00	+46	93	36 46	+46	93	37 32	+45	92	295
66	33 54	46	94	34 40	46	93	35 26	46	93	36 12	45	92	36 57	45	91	294
67	33 19	47	93	34 06	46	93	34 52	45	92	35 37	46	91	36 23	45	90	293
68	32 45	46	92	33 31	46	92	34 17	46	91	35 03	45	90	35 48	46	89	292
69	32 10	47	92	32 57	46	91	33 43	46	90	34 29	45	89	35 14	45	89	291

15° 16° 17° 18° 19° 20° 21° 22° 23° 24° 25° 26° 27° 28° 29°

S. Lat. {LHA greater than 180°....... Zn=180−Z; LHA less than 180°........... Zn=180+Z}

DECLINATION (15°-29°) SAME NAME AS LATITUDE

LHA	15° Hc	d	Z	16° Hc	d	Z	17° Hc	d	Z	18° Hc	d	Z	19° Hc	d	Z
	° ′	′	°	° ′	′	°	° ′	′	°	° ′	′	°	° ′	′	°
70	23 40	+49	98	24 29	+48	97	25 17	+48	96	26 05	+48	96	26 53	+48	95
71	23 06	49	97	23 55	48	96	24 43	48	96	25 31	48	95	26 19	47	94
72	22 32	48	96	23 20	49	95	24 09	48	95	24 57	47	94	25 44	48	93
73	21 58	48	95	22 46	48	95	23 34	48	94	24 22	48	93	25 10	48	93
74	21 23	49	94	22 12	48	94	23 00	48	93	23 48	48	92	24 36	47	92
75	20 49	+48	94	21 37	+49	93	22 26	+47	92	23 13	+48	92	24 01	+48	91
76	20 15	48	93	21 03	48	92	21 51	48	91	22 39	48	91	23 27	47	90
77	19 40	49	92	20 29	48	91	21 17	48	91	22 05	47	90	22 52	48	89
78	19 06	48	91	19 54	48	90	20 42	48	90	21 30	48	89	22 18	48	88
79	18 32	48	90	19 20	48	90	20 08	48	89	20 56	48	88	21 44	47	88
80	17 57	+48	89	18 45	+48	89	19 33	+48	88	20 21	+48	87	21 09	+48	87
81	17 23	48	89	18 11	48	88	18 59	48	87	19 47	48	87	20 35	48	86
82	16 48	49	88	17 37	48	87	18 25	48	87	19 13	48	86	20 01	47	85
83	16 14	48	87	17 02	48	86	17 50	48	86	18 38	48	85	19 26	48	84
84	15 40	48	86	16 28	48	86	17 16	48	85	18 04	48	84	18 52	48	84
85	15 05	+49	85	15 54	+48	85	16 42	+48	84	17 30	+48	83	18 18	+48	83
86	14 31	48	85	15 19	49	84	16 08	48	83	16 56	48	83	17 44	48	82
87	13 57	48	84	14 45	48	83	15 33	49	82	16 22	48	82	17 10	48	81
88	13 23	48	83	14 11	48	82	14 59	49	82	15 48	48	81	16 36	48	80
89	12 49	48	82	13 37	48	82	14 25	49	81	15 14	48	80	16 02	48	80
90	12 14	+49	81	13 03	+48	81	13 51	+49	80	14 40	+48	79	15 28	+48	79
91	11 40	49	81	12 29	49	80	13 18	48	79	14 06	48	79	14 54	49	78
92	11 07	48	80	11 55	49	79	12 44	48	79	13 32	49	78	14 21	48	77
93	10 33	49	79	11 22	48	78	12 10	49	78	12 59	48	77	13 47	49	77
94	09 59	49	78	10 48	49	78	11 37	48	77	12 25	49	76	13 14	48	76
95	09 25	+49	77	10 14	+49	77	11 03	+49	76	11 52	+49	76	12 41	+48	75
96	08 52	49	77	09 41	49	76	10 30	49	75	11 19	48	75	12 07	49	74
97	08 19	49	76	09 08	49	75	09 57	48	75	10 45	49	74	11 34	49	73
98	07 45	49	75	08 34	49	74	09 23	49	74	10 12	49	73	11 01	49	73
99	07 12	49	74	08 01	50	74	08 51	49	73	09 40	49	72	10 29	49	72
100	06 39	+49	73	07 28	+50	73	08 18	+49	72	09 07	+49	72	09 56	+49	71
101	06 06	50	73	06 56	49	72	07 45	49	71	08 34	50	71	09 24	49	70
102	05 33	50	72	06 23	49	71	07 12	50	71	08 02	49	70	08 51	50	69
103	05 01	49	71	05 50	50	70	06 40	50	70	07 30	49	69	08 19	50	69
104	04 28	50	70	05 18	50	70	06 08	50	69	06 58	49	68	07 47	50	68
105	03 56	+50	69	04 46	+50	69	05 36	+50	68	06 26	+49	68	07 15	+50	67
106	03 24	50	68	04 14	50	68	05 04	50	67	05 54	50	67	06 44	50	66
107	02 52	50	68	03 42	50	67	04 32	50	67	05 22	50	66	06 12	51	65
108	02 20	51	67	03 11	50	66	04 01	50	66	04 51	50	65	05 41	50	65
109	01 49	50	66	02 39	51	65	03 30	50	65	04 20	50	64	05 10	51	64
110	01 17	+51	65	02 08	+50	65	02 58	+51	64	03 49	+50	64	04 39	+51	63
111	00 46	51	64	01 37	51	64	02 28	50	63	03 18	51	63	04 09	51	62
112	00 15	51	64	01 06	51	63	01 57	51	63	02 48	51	62	03 39	50	61
113	−0 15	51	63	00 36	51	62	01 27	51	62	02 18	50	61	03 08	51	61
114	−0 46	51	62	00 05	51	61	00 56	51	61	01 47	52	60	02 39	51	60
115	−1 16	+51	61	−0 25	+51	61	00 26	+52	60	01 18	+51	60	02 09	+51	59
116	−1 46	51	60	−0 55	52	60	−0 03	51	59	00 48	52	59	01 40	51	58
117	−2 16	52	59	−1 24	51	59	−0 33	52	58	00 19	51	58	01 10	52	57
118	−2 45	51	59	−1 54	52	58	−1 02	52	58	−0 10	52	57	00 42	51	57
119	−3 15	52	58	−2 23	52	57	−1 31	52	57	−0 39	52	56	00 13	52	56
120	−3 44	+52	57	−2 52	+52	56	−2 00	+53	56	−1 07	+52	55	−0 15	+52	55
121	−4 12	52	56	−3 20	52	56	−2 28	52	55	−1 36	53	55	−0 43	52	54
122	−4 41	53	55	−3 48	52	55	−2 56	52	54	−2 04	53	54	−1 11	52	53
123	−5 09	53	54	−4 16	52	54	−3 24	53	53	−2 31	52	53	−1 39	53	52
124	−5 37	53	54	−4 44	53	53	−3 51	52	53	−2 59	53	52	−2 06	53	52
125				−5 11	+53	52	−4 18	+52	52	−3 26	+53	51	−2 33	+53	51
126				−5 38	53	51	−4 45	53	51	−3 52	53	50	−2 59	53	50
127							−5 12	53	50	−4 19	54	50	−3 25	53	49
128							−5 38	53	49	−4 45	54	49	−3 51	53	48
129										−5 10	53	48	−4 17	54	47
130										−5 36	+54	47	−4 42	+54	47
131													−5 07	54	46
132													−5 31	54	45

LHA	20° Hc	d	Z	21° Hc	d	Z	22° Hc	d	Z	23° Hc	d	Z	24° Hc	d	Z
	° ′	′	°	° ′	′	°	° ′	′	°	° ′	′	°	° ′	′	°
70	27 41	+47	94	28 28	+48	94	29 16	+47	93	30 03	+46	92	30 49	+47	92
71	27 06	48	94	27 54	47	93	28 41	47	92	29 28	47	91	30 15	47	91
72	26 32	48	93	27 20	47	92	28 07	47	91	28 54	47	91	29 41	46	90
73	25 58	47	92	26 45	47	91	27 32	47	91	28 19	47	90	29 06	47	89
74	25 23	48	91	26 11	47	90	26 58	47	90	27 45	47	89	28 32	46	88
75	24 49	+47	90	25 36	+48	90	26 24	+47	89	27 11	+46	88	27 57	+47	87
76	24 14	48	89	25 02	47	89	25 49	47	88	26 36	47	87	27 23	47	87
77	23 40	47	89	24 27	48	88	25 15	47	87	26 02	47	87	26 49	46	86
78	23 06	47	88	23 53	47	87	24 40	47	86	25 27	47	86	26 14	47	85
79	22 31	48	87	23 19	47	86	24 06	47	86	24 53	47	85	25 40	47	84
80	21 57	+47	86	22 44	+48	86	23 32	+47	85	24 19	+47	84	25 06	+47	83
81	21 23	47	85	22 10	48	85	22 58	47	84	23 45	47	83	24 32	47	83
82	20 48	48	85	21 36	47	84	22 23	48	83	23 11	47	83	23 58	47	82
83	20 14	48	84	21 02	47	83	21 49	47	82	22 36	48	82	23 24	47	81
84	19 40	48	83	20 28	47	82	21 15	47	82	22 02	48	81	22 50	47	80
85	19 06	+47	82	19 53	+48	82	20 41	+48	81	21 29	+47	80	22 16	+47	80
86	18 32	47	81	19 19	48	81	20 07	48	80	20 55	47	79	21 42	47	79
87	17 58	48	81	18 46	47	80	19 33	48	79	20 21	47	79	21 08	48	78
88	17 24	48	80	18 12	48	79	19 00	47	79	19 47	48	78	20 35	47	77
89	16 50	48	79	17 38	48	78	18 26	48	78	19 14	47	77	20 01	48	76
90	16 16	+48	78	17 04	+48	78	17 52	+48	77	18 40	+48	76	19 28	+47	76
91	15 43	48	77	16 31	48	77	17 19	48	76	18 07	47	76	18 54	48	75
92	15 09	48	77	15 57	48	76	16 45	48	75	17 33	48	75	18 21	48	74
93	14 36	48	76	15 24	48	75	16 12	48	75	17 00	48	74	17 48	48	73
94	14 02	49	75	14 51	48	75	15 39	48	74	16 27	48	73	17 15	48	73
95	13 29	+49	74	14 18	+48	74	15 06	+48	73	15 54	+49	73	16 43	+48	72
96	12 56	49	74	13 45	48	73	14 33	49	72	15 22	48	72	16 10	48	71
97	12 23	49	73	13 12	48	72	14 00	49	72	14 49	48	71	15 37	49	70
98	11 50	49	72	12 39	49	71	13 28	49	71	14 17	48	70	15 05	49	70
99	11 18	49	71	12 07	49	71	12 56	48	70	13 44	49	69	14 33	49	69
100	10 45	+49	70	11 34	+49	70	12 23	+49	69	13 12	+49	69	14 01	+49	68
101	10 13	49	70	11 02	49	69	11 51	49	68	12 40	49	68	13 29	49	67
102	09 41	49	69	10 30	49	68	11 19	49	68	12 08	50	67	12 58	49	67
103	09 09	49	68	09 58	50	68	10 48	49	67	11 37	49	66	12 26	49	66
104	08 37	49	67	09 26	50	67	10 16	49	66	11 05	50	66	11 55	49	65
105	08 05	+50	67	08 55	+50	66	09 45	+49	65	10 34	+50	65	11 24	+49	64
106	07 34	50	66	08 24	49	65	09 13	50	65	10 03	50	64	10 53	49	63
107	07 03	50	65	07 53	49	64	08 42	50	64	09 32	50	63	10 22	50	63
108	06 31	51	64	07 22	50	64	08 12	50	63	09 02	50	62	09 52	50	62
109	06 01	50	63	06 51	50	63	07 41	50	62	08 31	50	62	09 21	51	61
110	05 30	+50	63	06 20	+51	62	07 11	+50	61	08 01	+50	61	08 51	+51	60
111	05 00	50	62	05 50	51	61	06 41	50	61	07 31	51	60	08 22	50	60
112	04 29	51	61	05 20	51	60	06 11	50	60	07 01	51	59	07 52	51	59
113	03 59	51	60	04 50	51	60	05 41	51	59	06 32	51	59	07 23	51	58
114	03 30	51	59	04 21	51	59	05 12	51	58	06 03	51	58	06 54	51	57
115	03 00	+51	59	03 51	+52	58	04 43	+51	57	05 34	+51	57	06 25	+51	56
116	02 31	51	58	03 22	52	57	04 14	51	57	05 05	51	56	05 56	52	56
117	02 02	52	57	02 54	51	56	03 45	52	56	04 37	51	55	05 28	52	55
118	01 33	52	56	02 25	52	56	03 17	51	55	04 08	52	55	05 00	52	54
119	01 05	52	55	01 57	52	55	02 49	52	54	03 41	51	54	04 32	52	53
120	00 37	+52	54	01 29	+52	54	02 21	+52	53	03 13	+52	53	04 05	+52	52
121	00 09	52	54	01 01	52	53	01 53	53	53	02 46	52	52	03 38	52	52
122	−0 19	53	53	00 34	52	52	01 26	53	52	02 19	52	51	03 11	52	51
123	−0 46	53	52	00 07	52	52	00 59	53	51	01 52	52	51	02 44	53	50
124	−1 13	53	51	−0 20	53	51	00 33	52	50	01 25	53	50	02 18	53	49
125	−1 40	+53	50	−0 47	+53	50	00 06	+53	49	00 59	+53	49	01 52	+53	48
126	−2 06	53	50	−1 13	53	49	−0 20	53	49	00 33	54	48	01 27	53	48
127	−2 32	53	49	−1 39	54	48	−0 45	53	48	00 08	53	47	01 01	54	47
128	−2 58	54	48	−2 04	53	47	−1 11	54	47	−0 17	53	46	00 36	54	46
129	−3 23	54	47	−2 29	53	47	−1 36	54	46	−0 42	54	46	00 12	53	45
130	−3 48	+54	46	−2 54	+54	46	−2 00	+54	45	−1 06	+54	45	−0 12	+53	44
131	−4 13	54	45	−3 19	54	45	−2 25	55	44	−1 30	54	44	−0 36	54	44
132	−4 37	54	44	−3 43	55	44	−2 48	54	44	−1 54	54	43	−1 00	54	43
133	−5 01	55	44	−4 06	54	43	−3 12	54	43	−2 18	55	42	−1 23	54	42
134	−5 25	55	43	−4 30	55	42	−3 35	54	42	−2 41	55	42	−1 46	55	41
135				−4 53	+55	41	−3 58	+55	41	−3 03	+55	41	−2 08	+54	40
136				−5 16	56	41	−4 20	55	40	−3 25	55	40	−2 30	55	39
137				−5 38	56	40	−4 42	55	39	−3 47	55	39	−2 52	55	39
138							−5 04	55	38	−4 09	56	38	−3 13	55	38
139							−5 25	55	38	−4 30	56	37	−3 34	55	37

LHA	25° Hc	d	Z	26° Hc	d	Z	27° Hc	d	Z	28° Hc	d	Z	29° Hc	d	Z	LHA
	° ′	′	°	° ′	′	°	° ′	′	°	° ′	′	°	° ′	′	°	
70	31 36	+46	91	32 22	+46	90	33 08	+46	89	33 54	+46	89	34 40	+45	88	290
71	31 02	46	90	31 48	46	89	32 34	46	89	33 20	45	88	34 05	45	87	289
72	30 27	47	89	31 14	46	88	32 00	45	88	32 45	46	87	33 31	45	86	288
73	29 53	46	88	30 39	46	88	31 25	46	87	32 11	46	86	32 57	45	85	287
74	29 18	47	88	30 05	46	87	30 51	46	86	31 37	45	85	32 22	46	85	286
75	28 44	+46	87	29 30	+47	86	30 17	+45	85	31 02	+46	85	31 48	+45	84	285
76	28 10	46	86	28 56	46	85	29 42	46	85	30 28	46	84	31 14	45	83	284
77	27 35	47	85	28 22	46	84	29 08	46	84	29 54	46	83	30 40	45	82	283
78	27 01	47	84	27 48	46	84	28 34	46	83	29 20	46	82	30 06	45	81	282
79	26 27	46	84	27 13	47	83	28 00	46	82	28 46	46	81	29 32	45	81	281
80	25 53	+46	83	26 39	+47	82	27 26	+46	81	28 12	+46	81	28 58	+46	80	280
81	25 19	46	82	26 05	47	81	26 52	46	81	27 38	46	80	28 24	46	79	279
82	24 45	46	81	25 31	47	81	26 18	46	80	27 04	46	79	27 50	46	78	278
83	24 11	46	80	24 57	47	80	25 44	46	79	26 30	47	78	27 17	46	78	277
84	23 37	47	80	24 24	46	79	25 10	47	78	25 57	46	78	26 43	46	77	276
85	23 03	+47	79	23 50	+47	78	24 37	+46	78	25 23	+47	77	26 10	+46	76	275
86	22 29	47	78	23 16	47	77	24 03	47	77	24 50	46	76	25 36	46	75	274
87	21 56	47	77	22 43	47	77	23 30	46	76	24 16	47	75	25 03	46	75	273
88	21 22	47	77	22 09	47	76	22 56	47	75	23 43	47	75	24 30	46	74	272
89	20 49	47	76	21 36	47	75	22 23	47	75	23 10	47	74	23 57	46	73	271
90	20 15	+48	75	21 03	+47	74	21 50	+47	74	22 37	+47	73	23 24	+47	72	270
91	19 42	48	74	20 30	47	74	21 17	47	73	22 04	47	72	22 51	47	72	269
92	19 09	48	74	19 57	47	73	20 44	48	72	21 32	47	72	22 19	47	71	268
93	18 36	48	73	19 24	47	72	20 11	48	71	20 59	47	71	21 46	47	70	267
94	18 03	48	72	18 51	48	71	19 39	48	71	20 27	47	70	21 14	47	69	266
95	17 31	+48	71	18 19	+48	71	19 07	+47	70	19 54	+48	69	20 42	+47	69	265
96	16 58	48	71	17 46	48	70	18 34	48	69	19 22	48	69	20 10	47	68	264
97	16 26	48	70	17 14	48	69	18 02	48	68	18 50	48	68	19 38	48	67	263
98	15 54	48	69	16 42	48	68	17 30	48	68	18 18	48	67	19 06	48	66	262
99	15 22	48	68	16 10	48	68	16 58	49	67	17 47	48	66	18 35	48	66	261
100	14 50	+48	67	15 38	+49	67	16 27	+48	66	17 15	+49	66	18 04	+48	65	260
101	14 18	49	67	15 07	49	66	15 56	48	65	16 44	49	65	17 33	48	64	259
102	13 47	48	66	14 35	49	65	15 24	49	65	16 13	49	64	17 02	48	64	258
103	13 15	49	65	14 04	49	65	14 53	49	64	15 42	49	63	16 31	49	63	257
104	12 44	49	64	13 33	49	64	14 22	50	63	15 12	49	63	16 01	48	62	256
105	12 13	+50	64	13 03	+49	63	13 52	+49	62	14 41	+49	62	15 30	+49	61	255
106	11 42	50	63	12 32	49	62	13 21	50	62	14 11	49	61	15 00	49	61	254
107	11 12	50	62	12 02	49	62	12 51	50	61	13 41	49	60	14 30	50	60	253
108	10 42	50	61	11 32	49	61	12 21	50	60	13 11	50	60	14 01	49	59	252
109	10 12	50	61	11 02	50	60	11 52	49	59	12 41	50	59	13 31	50	58	251
110	09 42	+50	60	10 32	+50	59	11 22	+50	59	12 12	+50	58	13 02	+50	58	250
111	09 12	50	59	10 02	51	58	10 53	50	58	11 43	50	57	12 33	50	57	249
112	08 43	50	58	09 33	51	58	10 24	50	57	11 14	51	57	12 05	50	56	248
113	08 14	50	58	09 04	51	57	09 55	51	56	10 46	50	56	11 36	51	55	247
114	07 45	51	57	08 36	50	56	09 26	51	56	10 17	51	55	11 08	51	55	246
115	07 16	+51	56	08 07	+51	55	08 58	+51	55	09 49	+51	54	10 40	+51	54	245
116	06 48	51	55	07 39	51	55	08 30	51	54	09 21	52	54	10 13	51	53	244
117	06 20	51	54	07 11	51	54	08 02	52	53	08 54	51	53	09 45	51	52	243
118	05 52	51	54	06 43	52	53	07 35	52	53	08 27	51	52	09 18	52	52	242
119	05 24	52	53	06 16	52	52	07 08	52	52	08 00	51	51	08 51	52	51	241
120	04 57	+52	52	05 49	+52	52	06 41	+52	51	07 33	+52	51	08 25	+52	50	240
121	04 30	52	51	05 22	52	51	06 14	53	50	07 07	52	50	07 59	52	49	239
122	04 03	53	50	04 56	52	50	05 48	52	49	06 40	53	49	07 33	52	48	238
123	03 37	53	50	04 30	52	49	05 22	53	49	06 15	52	48	07 07	53	48	237
124	03 11	53	49	04 04	52	48	04 56	53	48	05 49	53	47	06 42	52	47	236
125	02 45	+53	48	03 38	+53	48	04 31	+53	47	05 24	+53	47	06 17	+53	46	235
126	02 20	53	47	03 13	53	47	04 06	53	46	04 59	53	46	05 52	53	45	234
127	01 55	53	46	02 48	53	46	03 41	54	45	04 35	53	45	05 28	53	45	233
128	01 30	53	46	02 23	54	45	03 17	53	45	04 10	54	44	05 04	53	44	232
129	01 05	54	45	01 59	54	44	02 53	54	44	03 47	53	43	04 40	54	43	231
130	00 41	+54	44	01 35	+54	44	02 29	+54	43	03 23	+54	43	04 17	+54	42	230
131	00 18	54	43	01 12	54	43	02 06	54	42	03 00	54	42	03 54	54	41	229
132	−0 06	55	42	00 49	54	42	01 43	54	41	02 37	54	41	03 31	55	41	228
133	−0 29	55	42	00 26	54	41	01 20	55	41	02 15	54	40	03 09	55	40	227
134	−0 51	54	41	00 03	55	40	00 58	55	40	01 53	54	39	02 47	55	39	226
135	−1 14	+55	40	−0 19	+55	39	00 36	+55	39	01 31	+55	39	02 26	+55	38	225
136	−1 35	55	39	−0 40	55	39	00 15	55	38	01 10	55	38	02 05	55	37	224
137	−1 57	55	38	−1 02	56	38	−0 06	55	37	00 49	55	37	01 44	55	37	223
138	−2 18	55	37	−1 23	56	37	−0 27	55	37	00 28	56	36	01 24	55	36	222
139	−2 39	56	37	−1 43	56	36	−0 47	55	36	00 08	56	35	01 04	55	35	221

N. Lat. {LHA greater than 180°....... Zn=Z; LHA less than 180°........... Zn=360−Z}

DECLINATION (15°-29°) SAME NAME AS LATITUDE

LHA	15° Hc d Z	16° Hc d Z	17° Hc d Z	18° Hc d Z	19° Hc d Z	20° Hc d Z	21° Hc d Z	22° Hc d Z	23° Hc d Z	24° Hc d Z	25° Hc d Z	26° Hc d Z	27° Hc d Z	28° Hc d Z	29° Hc d Z	LHA
	° ′ ′ °	° ′ ′ °	° ′ ′ °	° ′ ′ °	° ′ ′ °	° ′ ′ °	° ′ ′ °	° ′ ′ °	° ′ ′ °	° ′ ′ °	° ′ ′ °	° ′ ′ °	° ′ ′ °	° ′ ′ °	° ′ ′ °	
140									−4 50 +55 36	−3 55 +56 36	−2 59 +56 36	−2 03 +56 35	−1 07 +55 35	−0 12 +56 35	00 44 +56 34	220
141									−5 11 56 36	−4 15 56 35	−3 19 56 35	−2 23 56 34	−1 27 56 34	−0 31 56 34	00 25 56 33	219
142									−5 31 57 35	−4 34 56 34	−3 38 56 34	−2 42 56 34	−1 46 56 33	−0 50 56 33	00 06 56 33	218
143										−4 54 57 33	−3 57 56 33	−3 01 56 33	−2 05 57 32	−1 08 56 32	−0 12 56 32	217
144										−5 12 56 33	−4 16 57 32	−3 19 56 32	−2 23 57 32	−1 26 56 31	−0 30 56 31	216
145										−5 31 +57 32	−4 34 +57 31	−3 37 +56 31	−2 41 +57 31	−1 44 +57 30	−0 47 +56 30	215
146											−4 52 57 31	−3 55 57 30	−2 58 57 30	−2 01 56 30	−1 05 57 29	214
147											−5 09 57 30	−4 12 57 29	−3 15 57 29	−2 18 57 29	−1 21 57 28	213
148											−5 26 57 29	−4 29 57 29	−3 32 58 28	−2 34 57 28	−1 37 57 28	212
149												−4 45 57 28	−3 48 58 27	−2 50 57 27	−1 53 57 27	211
150												−5 01 +58 27	−4 03 +57 27	−3 06 +58 26	−2 08 +57 26	210
151												−5 16 58 26	−4 18 57 26	−3 21 58 25	−2 23 57 25	209
152													−4 33 58 25	−3 35 57 25	−2 38 58 24	208
153													−4 47 58 24	−3 49 58 24	−2 51 57 23	207
154													−5 01 58 23	−4 03 58 23	−3 05 58 23	206
155													−5 14 +58 22	−4 16 +58 22	−3 18 +58 22	205
156														−4 29 59 21	−3 30 58 21	204
157														−4 41 59 20	−3 42 58 20	203
158														−4 53 59 19	−3 54 59 19	202
159														−5 04 59 18	−4 05 59 18	201
160														−5 14 +58 18	−4 16 +59 17	200
161															−4 26 59 17	199
162															−4 35 59 16	198
163															−4 44 59 15	197
164															−4 53 59 14	196
165															−5 01 +59 13	195
166															−5 09 60 12	194

LHA	15° Hc d Z	16° Hc d Z	17° Hc d Z	18° Hc d Z	19° Hc d Z	20° Hc d Z	21°	22°	23°	24°	25°	26°	27°	28°	29°	LHA
78	−5 33 50 108															282
77	−5 01 49 109	−5 50 50 110														283
76	−4 28 50 110	−5 18 50 110														284
75	−3 56 −50 111	−4 46 −50 111	−5 36 −50 112													285
74	−3 24 50 112	−4 14 50 112	−5 04 50 113	−5 54 50 113												286
73	−2 52 50 112	−3 42 50 113	−4 32 50 113	−5 22 50 114												287
72	−2 20 51 113	−3 11 50 114	−4 01 50 114	−4 51 50 115	−5 41 50 115											288
71	−1 49 50 114	−2 39 51 115	−3 30 50 115	−4 20 50 116	−5 10 51 116											289
70	−1 17 −51 115	−2 08 −50 115	−2 58 −51 116	−3 49 −50 116	−4 39 −51 117	−5 30 −50 117										290

S. Lat. {LHA greater than 180°........ Zn=180−Z; LHA less than 180°..... ..... Zn=180+Z}

DECLINATION (15°-29°) CONTRARY NAME TO LATITUDE

N. Lat. {LHA greater than 180°....... Zn=Z
{LHA less than 180°.......... Zn=360−Z

DECLINATION (15°-29°) CONTRARY NAME TO LATITUDE

LHA	15° Hc	d	Z	16° Hc	d	Z	17° Hc	d	Z	18° Hc	d	Z	19° Hc	d	Z
	° ′	′	°	° ′	′	°	° ′	′	°	° ′	′	°	° ′	′	°
69	-0 46	51	116	-1 37	51	116	-2 28	50	117	-3 18	51	117	-4 09	51	118
68	-0 15	51	116	-1 06	51	117	-1 57	51	117	-2 48	51	118	-3 39	50	119
67	00 15	51	117	-0 36	51	118	-1 27	51	118	-2 18	50	119	-3 08	51	119
66	00 46	51	118	-0 05	51	119	-0 56	51	119	-1 47	52	120	-2 39	51	120
65	01 16	-51	119	00 25	-51	119	-0 26	-52	120	-1 18	-51	120	-2 09	-51	121
64	01 46	51	120	00 55	52	120	00 03	51	121	-0 48	52	121	-1 40	51	122
63	02 16	52	121	01 24	51	121	00 33	52	122	-0 19	52	122	-1 10	52	123
62	02 45	51	121	01 54	52	122	01 02	52	122	00 10	52	123	-0 42	51	123
61	03 15	52	122	02 23	52	123	01 31	52	123	00 39	52	124	-0 13	52	124
60	03 44	-52	123	02 52	-52	124	02 00	-53	124	01 07	-52	125	00 15	-52	125
59	04 12	52	124	03 20	52	124	02 28	52	125	01 36	53	125	00 43	52	126
58	04 41	53	125	03 48	52	125	02 56	52	126	02 04	53	126	01 11	52	127
57	05 09	53	126	04 16	52	126	03 24	53	127	02 31	52	127	01 39	53	128
56	05 37	53	126	04 44	53	127	03 51	52	127	02 59	53	128	02 06	53	128
55	06 04	-53	127	05 11	-53	128	04 18	-52	128	03 26	-53	129	02 33	-53	129
54	06 32	54	128	05 38	53	129	04 45	53	129	03 52	53	130	02 59	53	130
53	06 58	53	129	06 05	53	130	05 12	53	130	04 19	54	130	03 25	53	131
52	07 25	53	130	06 32	54	130	05 38	53	131	04 45	54	131	03 51	53	132
51	07 51	53	131	06 58	54	131	06 04	54	132	05 10	53	132	04 17	54	133
50	08 17	-54	132	07 23	-53	132	06 30	-54	133	05 36	-54	133	04 42	-54	133
49	08 43	54	133	07 49	54	133	06 55	54	133	06 01	54	134	05 07	54	134
48	09 08	54	133	08 14	54	134	07 20	55	134	06 25	54	135	05 31	54	135
47	09 33	55	134	08 38	54	135	07 44	54	135	06 50	55	136	05 55	54	136
46	09 57	54	135	09 03	55	136	08 08	54	136	07 14	55	136	06 19	54	137
45	10 21	-54	136	09 27	-55	136	08 32	-55	137	07 37	-55	137	06 42	-54	138
44	10 45	55	137	09 50	55	137	08 55	55	138	08 00	55	138	07 05	55	139
43	11 08	55	138	10 13	55	138	09 18	55	139	08 23	55	139	07 28	55	139
42	11 31	55	139	10 36	55	139	09 41	55	140	08 46	56	140	07 50	55	140
41	11 54	56	140	10 58	55	140	10 03	56	140	09 07	55	141	08 12	56	141
40	12 16	-56	141	11 20	-55	141	10 25	-56	141	09 29	-56	142	08 33	-55	142
39	12 37	55	142	11 42	56	142	10 46	56	142	09 50	56	143	08 54	56	143
38	12 59	56	142	12 03	56	143	11 07	56	143	10 11	56	144	09 15	56	144
37	13 19	56	143	12 23	56	144	11 27	56	144	10 31	56	144	09 35	56	145
36	13 40	56	144	12 44	57	145	11 47	56	145	10 51	56	145	09 55	57	146
35	14 00	-57	145	13 03	-56	146	12 07	-57	146	11 10	-56	146	10 14	-57	147
34	14 19	57	146	13 22	56	147	12 26	57	147	11 29	57	147	10 32	56	148
33	14 38	57	147	13 41	57	147	12 44	56	148	11 48	57	148	10 51	57	148
32	14 57	57	148	14 00	57	148	13 03	57	149	12 06	57	149	11 09	58	149
31	15 15	58	149	14 17	57	149	13 20	57	150	12 23	57	150	11 26	57	150
30	15 32	-57	150	14 35	-58	150	13 37	-57	151	12 40	-57	151	11 43	-58	151
29	15 49	57	151	14 52	58	151	13 54	57	152	12 57	58	152	11 59	57	152
28	16 06	58	152	15 08	58	152	14 10	57	152	13 13	58	153	12 15	58	153
27	16 22	58	153	15 24	58	153	14 26	58	153	13 28	58	154	12 30	57	154
26	16 37	58	154	15 39	58	154	14 41	58	154	13 43	58	155	12 45	58	155
25	16 52	-58	155	15 54	-58	155	14 56	-58	155	13 58	-58	156	13 00	-59	156
24	17 06	58	156	16 08	58	156	15 10	58	156	14 12	59	157	13 13	58	157
23	17 20	58	157	16 22	58	157	15 24	59	157	14 25	58	157	13 27	59	158
22	17 34	59	158	16 35	58	158	15 37	59	158	14 38	58	158	13 40	59	159
21	17 46	58	159	16 48	59	159	15 49	58	159	14 51	59	159	13 52	59	160
20	17 59	-59	160	17 00	-59	160	16 01	-59	160	15 02	-58	160	14 04	-59	161
19	18 10	59	161	17 11	58	161	16 13	59	161	15 14	59	161	14 15	59	162
18	18 21	59	162	17 22	59	162	16 23	59	162	15 24	59	162	14 25	59	162
17	18 32	59	163	17 33	59	163	16 34	59	163	15 35	59	163	14 36	60	163
16	18 42	59	164	17 43	59	164	16 44	60	164	15 44	59	164	14 45	59	164
15	18 51	-59	165	17 52	-59	165	16 53	-60	165	15 53	-59	165	14 54	-59	165
14	19 00	59	166	18 01	60	166	17 01	59	166	16 02	59	166	15 03	60	166
13	19 08	59	167	18 09	60	167	17 09	59	167	16 10	60	167	15 10	59	167
12	19 16	60	168	18 16	59	168	17 17	60	168	16 17	59	168	15 18	60	168
11	19 23	60	169	18 23	59	169	17 24	60	169	16 24	60	169	15 24	59	169
10	19 29	-59	170	18 30	-60	170	17 30	-60	170	16 30	-59	170	15 31	-60	170
9	19 35	60	171	18 35	59	171	17 36	60	171	16 36	60	171	15 36	60	171
8	19 40	59	172	18 41	60	172	17 41	60	172	16 41	60	172	15 41	60	172
7	19 45	60	173	18 45	60	173	17 45	60	173	16 45	59	173	15 46	60	173
6	19 49	60	174	18 49	60	174	17 49	60	174	16 49	60	174	15 49	59	174
5	19 52	-60	175	18 52	-59	175	17 53	-60	175	16 53	-60	175	15 53	-60	175
4	19 55	60	176	18 55	60	176	17 55	60	176	16 55	60	176	15 55	60	176
3	19 57	60	177	18 57	60	177	17 57	60	177	16 57	60	177	15 57	60	177
2	19 59	60	178	18 59	60	178	17 59	60	178	16 59	60	178	15 59	60	178
1	20 00	60	179	19 00	60	179	18 00	60	179	17 00	60	179	16 00	60	179
0	20 00	-60	180	19 00	-60	180	18 00	-60	180	17 00	-60	180	16 00	-60	180

LHA	20° Hc	d	Z	21° Hc	d	Z	22° Hc	d	Z	23° Hc	d	Z	24° Hc	d	Z
	° ′	′	°	° ′	′	°	° ′	′	°	° ′	′	°	° ′	′	°
69	-5 00	50	118	-5 50	51	119	291								
68	-4 29	51	119	-5 20	51	120	292								
67	-3 59	51	120	-4 50	51	120	-5 41	51	121	293					
66	-3 30	51	121	-4 21	51	121	-5 12	51	122	294					
65	-3 00	-51	121	-3 51	-52	122	-4 43	-51	123	-5 34	-51	123	295		
64	-2 31	51	122	-3 22	52	123	-4 14	51	123	-5 05	51	124	296		
63	-2 02	52	123	-2 54	51	124	-3 45	52	124	-4 37	51	125	-5 28	52	125
62	-1 33	52	124	-2 25	52	124	-3 17	51	125	-4 08	52	125	-5 00	52	126
61	-1 05	52	125	-1 57	52	125	-2 49	52	126	-3 41	51	126	-4 32	52	127
60	-0 37	-52	126	-1 29	-52	126	-2 21	-52	127	-3 13	-52	127	-4 05	-52	128
59	-0 09	52	126	-1 01	52	127	-1 53	53	127	-2 46	52	128	-3 38	52	128
58	00 19	53	127	-0 34	52	128	-1 26	53	128	-2 19	52	129	-3 11	52	129
57	00 46	53	128	-0 07	52	128	-0 59	53	129	-1 52	52	129	-2 44	53	130
56	01 13	53	129	00 20	53	129	-0 33	52	130	-1 25	53	130	-2 18	53	131
55	01 40	-53	130	00 47	-53	130	-0 06	-53	131	-0 59	-53	131	-1 52	-53	132
54	02 06	53	130	01 13	53	131	00 20	53	131	-0 33	54	132	-1 27	53	132
53	02 32	53	131	01 39	54	132	00 45	53	132	-0 08	53	133	-1 01	54	133
52	02 58	54	132	02 04	53	133	01 11	54	133	00 17	53	134	-0 36	54	134
51	03 23	54	133	02 29	53	133	01 36	54	134	00 42	54	134	-0 12	53	135
50	03 48	-54	134	02 54	-54	134	02 00	-54	135	01 06	-54	135	00 12	-53	136
49	04 13	54	135	03 19	54	135	02 25	55	136	01 30	54	136	00 36	54	136
48	04 37	54	136	03 43	55	136	02 48	54	136	01 54	54	137	01 00	54	137
47	05 01	55	136	04 06	54	137	03 12	54	137	02 18	55	138	01 23	54	138
46	05 25	55	137	04 30	55	138	03 35	54	138	02 41	55	139	01 46	55	139
45	05 48	-55	138	04 53	-55	139	03 58	-55	139	03 03	-55	139	02 08	-54	140
44	06 10	54	139	05 16	56	139	04 20	55	140	03 25	55	140	02 30	55	141
43	06 33	55	140	05 38	56	140	04 42	55	141	03 47	55	141	02 52	55	141
42	06 55	55	141	06 00	56	141	05 04	55	142	04 09	56	142	03 13	55	142
41	07 16	55	142	06 21	56	142	05 25	55	142	04 30	56	143	03 34	55	143
40	07 38	-56	143	06 42	-56	143	05 46	-56	143	04 50	-55	144	03 55	-56	144
39	07 58	55	143	07 03	56	144	06 07	56	144	05 11	56	145	04 15	56	145
38	08 19	56	144	07 23	56	145	06 27	56	145	05 31	57	145	04 34	56	146
37	08 39	57	145	07 42	56	146	06 46	56	146	05 50	56	146	04 54	57	147
36	08 58	56	146	08 02	57	147	07 05	56	147	06 09	57	147	05 12	56	147
35	09 17	-56	147	08 21	-57	147	07 24	-57	148	06 27	-56	148	05 31	-57	148
34	09 36	57	148	08 39	57	148	07 42	57	149	06 45	56	149	05 49	57	149
33	09 54	57	149	08 57	57	149	08 00	57	149	07 03	57	150	06 06	57	150
32	10 11	57	150	09 14	57	150	08 17	57	150	07 20	57	151	06 23	57	151
31	10 29	58	151	09 31	57	151	08 34	57	151	07 37	57	151	06 40	58	152
30	10 45	-57	151	09 48	-57	152	08 51	-58	152	07 53	-57	152	06 56	-58	153
29	11 02	58	152	10 04	58	153	09 06	57	153	08 09	58	153	07 11	57	154
28	11 17	57	153	10 20	58	154	09 22	58	154	08 24	58	154	07 26	57	154
27	11 33	58	154	10 35	58	155	09 37	58	155	08 39	58	155	07 41	58	155
26	11 47	58	155	10 49	58	155	09 51	58	156	08 53	58	156	07 55	58	156
25	12 01	-58	156	11 03	-58	156	10 05	-58	157	09 07	-58	157	08 09	-58	157
24	12 15	58	157	11 17	58	157	10 19	59	158	09 20	58	158	08 22	58	158
23	12 28	58	158	11 30	58	158	10 32	59	158	09 33	58	159	08 35	59	159
22	12 41	58	159	11 43	59	159	10 44	59	159	09 45	58	160	08 47	59	160
21	12 53	58	160	11 55	59	160	10 56	59	160	09 57	58	160	08 59	59	161
20	13 05	-59	161	12 06	-59	161	11 07	-58	161	10 09	-59	161	09 10	-59	162
19	13 16	59	162	12 17	59	162	11 18	59	162	10 19	59	162	09 20	59	163
18	13 26	59	163	12 27	59	163	11 28	59	163	10 29	59	163	09 30	59	163
17	13 36	59	164	12 37	59	164	11 38	59	164	10 39	59	164	09 40	59	164
16	13 46	59	165	12 47	59	165	11 48	60	165	10 48	59	165	09 49	59	165
15	13 55	-59	166	12 56	-60	166	11 56	-59	166	10 57	-59	166	09 58	-60	166
14	14 03	59	166	13 04	60	167	12 04	59	167	11 05	59	167	10 06	60	167
13	14 11	59	167	13 12	60	168	12 12	59	168	11 13	60	168	10 13	59	168
12	14 18	59	168	13 19	60	169	12 19	59	169	11 20	60	169	10 20	60	169
11	14 25	60	169	13 25	59	169	12 26	60	170	11 26	60	170	10 26	59	170
10	14 31	-60	170	13 31	-59	170	12 32	-60	171	11 32	-60	171	10 32	-59	171
9	14 36	59	171	13 37	60	171	12 37	60	172	11 37	60	172	10 37	59	172
8	14 41	59	172	13 42	60	172	12 42	60	172	11 42	60	173	10 42	60	173
7	14 46	60	173	13 46	60	173	12 46	60	173	11 46	60	173	10 46	59	174
6	14 50	60	174	13 50	60	174	12 50	60	174	11 50	60	174	10 50	60	174
5	14 53	-60	175	13 53	-60	175	12 53	-60	175	11 53	-60	175	10 53	-60	175
4	14 55	60	176	13 55	60	176	12 55	59	176	11 56	60	176	10 56	60	176
3	14 57	60	177	13 57	60	177	12 57	59	177	11 58	60	177	10 58	60	177
2	14 59	60	178	13 59	60	178	12 59	60	178	11 59	60	178	10 59	60	178
1	15 00	60	179	14 00	60	179	13 00	60	179	12 00	60	179	11 00	60	179
0	15 00	-60	180	14 00	-60	180	13 00	-60	180	12 00	-60	180	11 00	-60	180

LHA	25° Hc	d	Z	26° Hc	d	Z	27° Hc	d	Z	28° Hc	d	Z	29° Hc	d	Z	LHA
	° ′	′	°	° ′	′	°	° ′	′	°	° ′	′	°	° ′	′	°	
63	297															
62	-5 52	51	126	298												
61	-5 24	52	127	299												
60	-4 57	-52	128	-5 49	-52	128	300									
59	-4 30	52	129	-5 22	52	129	301									
58	-4 03	53	130	-4 56	52	130	-5 48	52	131	302						
57	-3 37	53	130	-4 30	52	131	-5 22	53	131	303						
56	-3 11	53	131	-4 04	52	132	-4 56	53	132	-5 49	53	133	304			
55	-2 45	-53	132	-3 38	-53	132	-4 31	-53	133	-5 24	-53	133	305			
54	-2 20	53	133	-3 13	53	133	-4 06	53	134	-4 59	53	134	306			
53	-1 55	53	134	-2 48	53	134	-3 41	54	135	-4 35	53	135	-5 28	53	135	307
52	-1 30	53	134	-2 23	54	135	-3 17	53	135	-4 10	54	136	-5 04	53	136	308
51	-1 05	54	135	-1 59	54	136	-2 53	54	136	-3 47	53	137	-4 40	54	137	309
50	-0 41	-54	136	-1 35	-54	136	-2 29	-54	137	-3 23	-54	137	-4 17	-54	138	310
49	-0 18	54	137	-1 12	54	137	-2 06	54	138	-3 00	54	138	-3 54	54	139	311
48	00 06	55	138	-0 49	54	138	-1 43	54	139	-2 37	54	139	-3 31	55	139	312
47	00 29	55	138	-0 26	54	139	-1 20	55	139	-2 15	54	140	-3 09	55	140	313
46	00 51	54	139	-0 03	55	140	-0 58	55	140	-1 53	54	141	-2 47	55	141	314
45	01 14	-55	140	00 19	-55	141	-0 36	-55	141	-1 31	-55	141	-2 26	-55	142	315
44	01 35	55	141	00 40	55	141	-0 15	55	142	-1 10	55	142	-2 05	55	143	316
43	01 57	55	142	01 02	56	142	00 06	55	143	-0 49	55	143	-1 44	55	143	317
42	02 18	55	143	01 23	56	143	00 27	55	143	-0 28	56	144	-1 24	55	144	318
41	02 39	56	143	01 43	56	144	00 47	55	144	-0 08	56	145	-1 04	55	145	319
40	02 59	-56	144	02 03	-56	145	01 07	-55	145	00 12	-56	145	-0 44	-56	146	320
39	03 19	56	145	02 23	56	146	01 27	56	146	00 31	56	146	-0 25	56	147	321
38	03 38	56	146	02 42	56	146	01 46	56	147	00 50	56	147	-0 06	56	147	322
37	03 57	56	147	03 01	56	147	02 05	57	148	01 08	56	148	00 12	56	148	323
36	04 16	57	148	03 19	56	148	02 23	57	148	01 26	56	149	00 30	56	149	324
35	04 34	-57	149	03 37	-56	149	02 41	-57	149	01 44	-57	150	00 47	-56	150	325
34	04 52	57	149	03 55	57	150	02 58	57	150	02 01	56	150	01 05	57	151	326
33	05 09	57	150	04 12	57	151	03 15	57	151	02 18	57	151	01 21	57	152	327
32	05 26	57	151	04 29	57	151	03 32	58	152	02 34	57	152	01 37	57	152	328
31	05 42	57	152	04 45	57	152	03 48	58	153	02 50	57	153	01 53	57	153	329
30	05 58	-57	153	05 01	-58	153	04 03	-57	153	03 06	-58	154	02 08	-57	154	330
29	06 14	58	154	05 16	58	154	04 18	57	154	03 21	58	155	02 23	57	155	331
28	06 29	58	155	05 31	58	155	04 33	58	155	03 35	57	155	02 38	58	156	332
27	06 43	58	156	05 45	58	156	04 47	58	156	03 49	58	156	02 51	57	157	333
26	06 57	58	156	05 59	58	157	05 01	58	157	04 03	58	157	03 05	58	157	334
25	07 11	-58	157	06 13	-59	158	05 14	-58	158	04 16	-58	158	03 18	-58	158	335
24	07 24	59	158	06 25	58	158	05 27	58	159	04 29	59	159	03 30	58	159	336
23	07 36	59	159	06 38	59	159	05 39	58	160	04 41	59	160	03 42	58	160	337
22	07 48	58	160	06 50	59	160	05 51	58	160	04 53	59	161	03 54	59	161	338
21	08 00	59	161	07 01	59	161	06 02	58	161	05 04	59	162	04 05	59	162	339
20	08 11	-59	162	07 12	-59	162	06 13	-59	162	05 14	-58	162	04 16	-59	163	340
19	08 21	59	163	07 22	58	163	06 24	59	163	05 25	59	163	04 26	59	163	341
18	08 31	59	164	07 32	58	164	06 33	59	164	05 34	59	164	04 35	59	164	342
17	08 41	59	165	07 42	59	165	06 43	59	165	05 44	60	165	04 44	59	165	343
16	08 50	59	165	07 51	60	166	06 51	59	166	05 52	59	166	04 53	59	166	344
15	08 58	-59	166	07 59	-59	166	07 00	-60	167	06 00	-59	167	05 01	-59	167	345
14	09 06	59	167	08 07	60	167	07 07	59	168	06 08	59	168	05 09	60	168	346
13	09 14	60	168	08 14	59	168	07 15	60	168	06 15	59	169	05 16	60	169	347
12	09 20	59	169	08 21	60	169	07 21	59	169	06 22	60	169	05 22	59	170	348
11	09 27	60	170	08 27	60	170	07 27	59	170	06 28	60	170	05 28	59	170	349
10	09 33	-60	171	08 33	-60	171	07 33	-60	171	06 33	-59	171	05 34	-60	171	350
9	09 38	60	172	08 38	60	172	07 38	60	172	06 38	59	172	05 39	60	172	351
8	09 42	59	173	08 43	60	173	07 43	60	173	06 43	60	173	05 43	60	173	352
7	09 47	60	174	08 47	60	174	07 47	60	174	06 47	60	174	05 47	60	174	353
6	09 50	60	175	08 50	60	175	07 50	60	175	06 50	59	175	05 51	60	175	354
5	09 53	-60	175	08 53	-60	176	07 53	-60	176	06 53	-60	176	05 53	-59	176	355
4	09 56	60	176	08 56	60	176	07 56	60	176	06 56	60	177	05 56	60	177	356
3	09 58	60	177	08 58	60	177	07 58	60	177	06 58	60	177	05 58	60	177	357
2	09 59	60	178	08 59	60	178	07 59	60	178	06 59	60	178	05 59	60	178	358
1	10 00	60	179	09 00	60	179	08 00	60	179	07 00	60	179	06 00	60	179	359
0	10 00	-60	180	09 00	-60	180	08 00	-60	180	07 00	-60	180	06 00	-60	180	360

S. Lat. {LHA greater than 180°....... Zn=180−Z
{LHA less than 180°............ Zn=180+Z

DECLINATION (15°-29°) CONTRARY NAME TO LATITUDE

N. Lat. {LHA greater than 180°....... Zn=Z; LHA less than 180°.......... Zn=360−Z}

DECLINATION (0°-14°) SAME NAME AS LATITUDE

LHA	0° Hc	d	Z	1° Hc	d	Z	2° Hc	d	Z	3° Hc	d	Z	4° Hc	d	Z
	° ′	′	°	° ′	′	°	° ′	′	°	° ′	′	°	° ′	′	°
0	34 00	+60	180	35 00	+60	180	36 00	+60	180	37 00	+60	180	38 00	+60	180
1	34 00	60	179	35 00	60	179	36 00	60	179	37 00	60	179	38 00	60	179
2	33 59	60	178	34 59	60	178	35 59	60	178	36 59	60	178	37 59	60	178
3	33 57	60	176	34 57	60	176	35 57	60	176	36 57	60	176	37 57	60	176
4	33 54	60	175	34 54	60	175	35 54	60	175	36 54	60	175	37 54	60	175
5	33 51	+60	174	34 51	+60	174	35 51	+60	174	36 51	+60	174	37 51	+60	174
6	33 47	60	173	34 47	60	173	35 47	60	173	36 47	60	173	37 47	60	172
7	33 43	60	172	34 43	59	172	35 42	60	171	36 42	60	171	37 42	60	171
8	33 38	59	170	34 37	60	170	35 37	60	170	36 37	59	170	37 36	60	170
9	33 32	59	169	34 31	60	169	35 31	60	169	36 31	59	169	37 30	60	169
10	33 25	+60	168	34 25	+59	168	35 24	+60	168	36 24	+59	168	37 23	+60	167
11	33 18	59	167	34 17	60	167	35 17	59	167	36 16	60	166	37 16	59	166
12	33 10	59	166	34 09	59	166	35 08	60	165	36 08	59	165	37 07	60	165
13	33 01	59	164	34 00	60	164	35 00	59	164	35 59	59	164	36 58	59	164
14	32 52	59	163	33 51	59	163	34 50	59	163	35 49	59	163	36 48	59	163
15	32 42	+59	162	33 41	+59	162	34 40	+59	162	35 39	+59	162	36 38	+59	161
16	32 31	59	161	33 30	59	161	34 29	59	161	35 28	59	160	36 27	59	160
17	32 20	59	160	33 19	58	160	34 17	59	159	35 16	59	159	36 15	59	159
18	32 08	59	159	33 07	58	158	34 05	59	158	35 04	58	158	36 02	59	158
19	31 55	59	157	32 54	58	157	33 52	59	157	34 51	58	157	35 49	59	156
20	31 42	+58	156	32 40	+59	156	33 39	+58	156	34 37	+59	156	35 36	+58	155
21	31 28	59	155	32 27	58	155	33 25	58	155	34 23	58	154	35 21	58	154
22	31 14	58	154	32 12	58	154	33 10	58	153	34 08	58	153	35 06	58	153
23	30 59	58	153	31 57	58	153	32 55	58	152	33 53	58	152	34 51	57	152
24	30 43	58	152	31 41	58	151	32 39	58	151	33 37	57	151	34 34	58	151
25	30 27	+58	151	31 25	+57	150	32 22	+58	150	33 20	+58	150	34 18	+57	149
26	30 10	58	150	31 08	57	149	32 05	58	149	33 03	57	149	34 00	57	148
27	29 53	57	148	30 50	58	148	31 48	57	148	32 45	57	147	33 42	57	147
28	29 35	57	147	30 32	58	147	31 30	57	147	32 27	57	146	33 24	56	146
29	29 17	57	146	30 14	57	146	31 11	57	146	32 08	56	145	33 04	57	145
30	28 58	+57	145	29 55	+57	145	30 52	+56	144	31 48	+57	144	32 45	+56	144
31	28 39	56	144	29 35	57	144	30 32	56	143	31 28	57	143	32 25	56	143
32	28 19	56	143	29 15	56	143	30 11	57	142	31 08	56	142	32 04	56	141
33	27 58	56	142	28 54	57	142	29 51	56	141	30 47	56	141	31 43	56	140
34	27 37	56	141	28 33	56	141	29 29	56	140	30 25	56	140	31 21	56	139
35	27 16	+56	140	28 12	+56	139	29 08	+55	139	30 03	+56	139	30 59	+56	138
36	26 54	56	139	27 50	55	138	28 45	56	138	29 41	55	138	30 36	56	137
37	26 32	55	138	27 27	56	137	28 23	55	137	29 18	55	136	30 13	56	136
38	26 09	55	137	27 04	55	136	27 59	56	136	28 55	55	135	29 50	55	135
39	25 46	55	136	26 41	55	135	27 36	55	135	28 31	55	134	29 26	55	134
40	25 22	+55	135	26 17	+55	134	27 12	+55	134	28 07	+54	133	29 01	+55	133
41	24 58	55	134	25 53	54	133	26 47	55	133	27 42	55	132	28 37	54	132
42	24 33	55	133	25 28	55	132	26 23	54	132	27 17	54	131	28 11	55	131
43	24 08	55	132	25 03	54	131	25 57	55	131	26 52	54	130	27 46	54	130
44	23 43	54	131	24 37	55	130	25 32	54	130	26 26	54	129	27 20	54	129
45	23 18	+54	130	24 12	+54	129	25 06	+54	129	26 00	+53	128	26 53	+54	128
46	22 52	53	129	23 45	54	128	24 39	54	128	25 33	54	127	26 27	53	127
47	22 25	54	128	23 19	54	127	24 13	53	127	25 06	54	126	26 00	53	126
48	21 58	54	127	22 52	54	126	23 46	53	126	24 39	53	125	25 32	53	125
49	21 31	54	126	22 25	53	125	23 18	53	125	24 11	54	124	25 05	53	124
50	21 04	+53	125	21 57	+53	124	22 50	+54	124	23 44	+52	123	24 36	+53	123
51	20 36	53	124	21 29	53	123	22 22	53	123	23 15	53	122	24 08	53	122
52	20 08	53	123	21 01	53	122	21 54	53	122	22 47	52	121	23 39	53	121
53	19 40	53	122	20 33	52	122	21 25	53	121	22 18	53	121	23 11	52	120
54	19 11	53	121	20 04	53	121	20 57	52	120	21 49	52	120	22 41	53	119
55	18 43	+52	120	19 35	+52	120	20 27	+53	119	21 20	+52	119	22 12	+52	118
56	18 13	53	119	19 06	52	119	19 58	52	118	20 50	52	118	21 42	52	117
57	17 44	52	118	18 36	52	118	19 28	52	117	20 20	52	117	21 12	52	116
58	17 14	52	117	18 06	52	117	18 58	52	116	19 50	52	116	20 42	52	115
59	16 44	52	117	17 36	52	116	18 28	52	115	19 20	51	115	20 11	52	114
60	16 14	+52	116	17 06	+52	115	17 58	+51	115	18 49	+52	114	19 41	+51	113
61	15 44	51	115	16 35	52	114	17 27	52	114	18 19	51	113	19 10	51	113
62	15 13	52	114	16 05	51	113	16 56	52	113	17 48	51	112	18 39	51	112
63	14 42	52	113	15 34	51	112	16 25	51	112	17 16	52	111	18 08	51	111
64	14 11	52	112	15 03	51	112	15 54	51	111	16 45	51	110	17 36	51	110
65	13 40	+51	111	14 31	+51	111	15 22	+51	110	16 13	+51	110	17 04	+51	109
66	13 09	51	110	14 00	51	110	14 51	51	109	15 42	51	109	16 33	50	108
67	12 37	51	109	13 28	51	109	14 19	51	108	15 10	51	108	16 01	50	107
68	12 06	50	109	12 56	51	108	13 47	51	107	14 38	50	107	15 28	51	106
69	11 34	50	108	12 24	51	107	13 15	51	107	14 06	50	106	14 56	51	105

LHA	5° Hc	d	Z	6° Hc	d	Z	7° Hc	d	Z	8° Hc	d	Z	9° Hc	d	Z
	° ′	′	°	° ′	′	°	° ′	′	°	° ′	′	°	° ′	′	°
0	39 00	+60	180	40 00	+60	180	41 00	+60	180	42 00	+60	180	43 00	+60	180
1	39 00	60	179	40 00	60	179	41 00	60	179	42 00	60	179	43 00	60	179
2	38 59	60	178	39 59	60	177	40 59	59	177	41 58	60	177	42 58	60	177
3	38 57	60	176	39 57	60	176	40 57	60	176	41 57	59	176	42 56	60	176
4	38 54	60	175	39 54	60	175	40 54	60	175	41 54	60	175	42 54	60	175
5	38 51	+60	174	39 51	+59	174	40 50	+60	173	41 50	+60	173	42 50	+60	173
6	38 47	59	172	39 46	60	172	40 46	60	172	41 46	60	172	42 46	60	172
7	38 42	59	171	39 41	60	171	40 41	60	171	41 41	60	171	42 41	59	171
8	38 36	60	170	39 36	60	170	40 36	59	170	41 35	60	169	42 35	60	169
9	38 30	59	169	39 29	60	168	40 29	60	168	41 29	59	168	42 28	60	168
10	38 23	+59	167	39 22	+60	167	40 22	+59	167	41 21	+60	167	42 21	+59	167
11	38 15	59	166	39 14	60	166	40 14	59	166	41 13	60	166	42 13	59	165
12	38 07	59	165	39 06	59	165	40 05	59	164	41 04	60	164	42 04	59	164
13	37 57	60	164	38 57	59	163	39 56	59	163	40 55	59	163	41 54	59	163
14	37 47	60	162	38 47	59	162	39 46	59	162	40 45	59	162	41 44	59	161
15	37 37	+59	161	38 36	+59	161	39 35	+59	161	40 34	+59	160	41 33	+58	160
16	37 26	58	160	38 24	59	160	39 23	59	159	40 22	59	159	41 21	59	159
17	37 14	58	159	38 12	59	158	39 11	59	158	40 10	58	158	41 08	59	158
18	37 01	59	157	38 00	58	157	38 58	59	157	39 57	58	157	40 55	58	156
19	36 48	58	156	37 46	59	156	38 45	58	156	39 43	58	155	40 41	58	155
20	36 34	+58	155	37 32	+58	155	38 30	+59	154	39 29	+58	154	40 27	+58	154
21	36 19	58	154	37 17	58	153	38 15	58	153	39 13	58	153	40 11	58	152
22	36 04	58	153	37 02	58	152	38 00	58	152	38 58	58	152	39 56	57	151
23	35 48	58	151	36 46	58	151	37 44	57	151	38 41	58	150	39 39	58	150
24	35 32	58	150	36 30	57	150	37 27	58	149	38 25	57	149	39 22	57	149
25	35 15	+57	149	36 12	+58	149	37 10	+57	148	38 07	+57	148	39 04	+57	148
26	34 57	58	148	35 55	57	147	36 52	57	147	37 49	57	147	38 46	57	146
27	34 39	57	147	35 36	57	146	36 33	57	146	37 30	57	146	38 27	57	145
28	34 20	57	146	35 17	57	145	36 14	57	145	37 11	56	144	38 07	57	144
29	34 01	57	144	34 58	56	144	35 54	57	144	36 51	56	143	37 47	57	143
30	33 41	+57	143	34 38	+56	143	35 34	+57	142	36 31	+56	142	37 27	+56	142
31	33 21	56	142	34 17	57	142	35 14	56	141	36 10	56	141	37 06	56	141
32	33 00	56	141	33 56	56	141	34 52	56	140	35 48	56	140	36 44	56	139
33	32 39	56	140	33 35	56	139	34 31	55	139	35 26	56	139	36 22	55	138
34	32 17	56	139	33 13	55	138	34 08	56	138	35 04	55	137	35 59	55	137
35	31 55	+55	138	32 50	+56	137	33 46	+55	137	34 41	+55	136	35 36	+55	136
36	31 32	55	137	32 27	55	136	33 22	55	136	34 17	55	135	35 12	55	135
37	31 09	55	136	32 04	55	135	32 59	55	135	33 54	54	134	34 48	55	134
38	30 45	55	135	31 40	55	134	32 35	54	134	33 29	55	133	34 24	54	133
39	30 21	54	133	31 15	55	133	32 10	55	132	33 05	54	132	33 59	54	131
40	29 56	+55	132	30 51	+54	132	31 45	+54	131	32 39	+55	131	33 34	+54	130
41	29 31	54	131	30 25	55	131	31 20	54	130	32 14	54	130	33 08	54	129
42	29 06	54	130	30 00	54	130	30 54	54	129	31 48	54	129	32 42	53	128
43	28 40	54	129	29 34	54	129	30 28	53	128	31 21	54	128	32 15	54	127
44	28 14	54	128	29 08	53	128	30 01	54	127	30 55	53	127	31 48	53	126
45	27 47	+54	127	28 41	+53	127	29 34	+54	126	30 28	+53	126	31 21	+53	125
46	27 20	54	126	28 14	53	126	29 07	53	125	30 00	53	125	30 53	53	124
47	26 53	53	125	27 46	53	125	28 39	53	124	29 32	53	124	30 25	53	123
48	26 25	54	124	27 19	53	124	28 12	52	123	29 04	53	123	29 57	53	122
49	25 58	52	123	26 50	53	123	27 43	53	122	28 36	53	122	29 29	52	121
50	25 29	+53	122	26 22	+53	122	27 15	+52	121	28 07	+53	121	29 00	+52	120
51	25 01	52	121	25 53	53	121	26 46	52	120	27 38	52	120	28 30	53	119
52	24 32	52	120	25 24	53	120	26 17	52	119	27 09	52	119	28 01	52	118
53	24 03	52	119	24 55	52	119	25 47	52	118	26 39	52	118	27 31	52	117
54	23 34	52	119	24 26	52	118	25 18	52	117	26 10	51	117	27 01	52	116
55	23 04	+52	118	23 56	+52	117	24 48	+52	116	25 40	+51	116	26 31	+52	115
56	22 34	52	117	23 26	52	116	24 18	51	116	25 09	52	115	26 01	51	114
57	22 04	52	116	22 56	51	115	23 47	52	115	24 39	51	114	25 30	51	113
58	21 34	51	115	22 25	52	114	23 17	51	114	24 08	51	113	24 59	51	113
59	21 03	51	114	21 54	52	113	22 46	51	113	23 37	51	112	24 28	51	112
60	20 32	+51	113	21 23	+52	112	22 15	+51	112	23 06	+51	111	23 57	+51	111
61	20 01	51	112	20 52	51	111	21 43	51	111	22 34	51	110	23 25	51	110
62	19 30	51	111	20 21	51	111	21 12	51	110	22 03	51	109	22 54	50	109
63	18 59	51	110	19 50	51	110	20 40	51	109	21 31	51	109	22 22	50	108
64	18 27	51	109	19 18	51	109	20 09	50	108	20 59	51	108	21 50	50	107
65	17 55	+51	108	18 46	+51	108	19 37	+50	107	20 27	+51	107	21 18	+50	106
66	17 23	51	108	18 14	50	107	19 04	51	106	19 55	50	106	20 45	50	105
67	16 51	51	107	17 42	50	106	18 32	51	106	19 23	50	105	20 13	50	104
68	16 19	50	106	17 09	51	105	18 00	50	105	18 50	50	104	19 40	50	104
69	15 47	50	105	16 37	50	104	17 27	50	104	18 17	51	103	19 08	49	103

LHA	10° Hc	d	Z	11° Hc	d	Z	12° Hc	d	Z	13° Hc	d	Z	14° Hc	d	Z	LHA
	° ′	′	°	° ′	′	°	° ′	′	°	° ′	′	°	° ′	′	°	
0	44 00	+60	180	45 00	+60	180	46 00	+60	180	47 00	+60	180	48 00	+60	180	360
1	44 00	60	179	45 00	60	179	46 00	60	179	47 00	60	179	48 00	60	179	359
2	43 58	60	177	44 58	60	177	45 58	60	177	46 58	60	177	47 58	60	177	358
3	43 56	60	176	44 56	60	176	45 56	60	176	46 56	60	176	47 56	60	176	357
4	43 54	60	175	44 54	59	175	45 53	60	174	46 53	60	174	47 53	60	174	356
5	43 50	+60	173	44 50	+60	173	45 50	+60	173	46 50	+59	173	47 49	+60	173	355
6	43 46	59	172	44 45	60	172	45 45	60	172	46 45	60	172	47 45	60	171	354
7	43 40	60	170	44 40	60	170	45 40	60	170	46 40	59	170	47 39	60	170	353
8	43 35	59	169	44 34	60	169	45 34	59	169	46 33	60	169	47 33	60	169	352
9	43 28	59	168	44 27	60	168	45 27	59	167	46 26	60	167	47 26	59	167	351
10	43 20	+60	166	44 20	+59	166	45 19	+60	166	46 19	+59	166	47 18	+59	166	350
11	43 12	59	165	44 11	60	165	45 11	59	165	46 10	59	164	47 09	59	164	349
12	43 03	59	164	44 02	59	164	45 01	60	163	46 01	59	163	47 00	59	163	348
13	42 53	59	162	43 52	59	162	44 51	59	162	45 50	59	162	46 49	59	161	347
14	42 43	59	161	43 42	59	161	44 41	58	161	45 39	59	160	46 38	59	160	346
15	42 31	+59	160	43 30	+59	160	44 29	+59	159	45 28	+58	159	46 26	+59	159	345
16	42 20	58	159	43 18	59	158	44 17	58	158	45 15	59	158	46 14	58	157	344
17	42 07	58	157	43 05	59	157	44 04	58	157	45 02	59	156	46 01	58	156	343
18	41 53	59	156	42 52	58	156	43 50	58	155	44 48	58	155	45 46	59	155	342
19	41 39	59	155	42 38	58	154	43 36	58	154	44 34	58	154	45 32	58	153	341
20	41 25	+58	153	42 23	+58	153	43 21	+57	153	44 18	+58	152	45 16	+58	152	340
21	41 09	58	152	42 07	58	152	43 05	57	151	44 02	58	151	45 00	58	151	339
22	40 53	58	151	41 51	57	150	42 48	58	150	43 46	57	150	44 43	58	149	338
23	40 37	57	150	41 34	57	149	42 31	58	149	43 29	57	148	44 26	57	148	337
24	40 19	57	148	41 16	58	148	42 14	57	148	43 11	57	147	44 08	56	147	336
25	40 01	+57	147	40 58	+57	147	41 55	+57	146	42 52	+57	146	43 49	+56	145	335
26	39 43	57	146	40 40	56	145	41 36	57	145	42 33	56	145	43 29	57	144	334
27	39 24	56	145	40 20	57	144	41 17	56	144	42 13	57	143	43 10	56	143	333
28	39 04	56	144	40 00	57	143	40 57	56	143	41 53	56	142	42 49	56	142	332
29	38 44	56	142	39 40	56	142	40 36	56	141	41 32	56	141	42 28	56	140	331
30	38 23	+56	141	39 19	+56	141	40 15	+56	140	41 11	+55	140	42 06	+56	139	330
31	38 02	55	140	38 57	56	139	39 53	56	139	40 49	55	139	41 44	55	138	329
32	37 40	55	139	38 35	56	138	39 31	55	138	40 26	55	137	41 21	55	137	328
33	37 17	56	138	38 13	55	137	39 08	55	137	40 03	55	136	40 58	55	136	327
34	36 54	56	137	37 50	55	136	38 45	55	136	39 40	54	135	40 34	55	134	326
35	36 31	+55	135	37 26	+55	135	38 21	+55	134	39 16	+54	134	40 10	+54	133	325
36	36 07	55	134	37 02	55	134	37 57	54	133	38 51	54	133	39 45	55	132	324
37	35 43	55	133	36 38	54	133	37 32	54	132	38 26	54	132	39 20	54	131	323
38	35 18	55	132	36 13	54	132	37 07	54	131	38 01	54	130	38 55	53	130	322
39	34 53	54	131	35 47	54	130	36 41	54	130	37 35	54	129	38 29	53	129	321
40	34 28	+54	130	35 22	+53	129	36 15	+54	129	37 09	+53	128	38 02	+54	128	320
41	34 02	53	129	34 55	54	128	35 49	53	128	36 42	54	127	37 36	53	127	319
42	33 35	54	128	34 29	53	127	35 22	53	127	36 15	54	126	37 09	52	126	318
43	33 09	53	127	34 02	53	126	34 55	53	126	35 48	53	125	36 41	53	124	317
44	32 41	54	126	33 35	53	125	34 28	52	125	35 20	53	124	36 13	53	123	316
45	32 14	+53	125	33 07	+53	124	34 00	+52	124	34 52	+53	123	35 45	+52	122	315
46	31 46	53	124	32 39	53	123	33 32	52	122	34 24	52	122	35 16	53	121	314
47	31 18	53	123	32 11	52	122	33 03	52	121	33 55	53	121	34 48	52	120	313
48	30 50	52	122	31 42	52	121	32 34	53	120	33 27	51	120	34 18	52	119	312
49	30 21	52	121	31 13	52	120	32 05	52	119	32 57	52	119	33 49	52	118	311
50	29 52	+52	120	30 44	+52	119	31 36	+52	118	32 28	+51	118	33 19	+52	117	310
51	29 23	51	119	30 14	52	118	31 06	52	117	31 58	51	117	32 49	52	116	309
52	28 53	52	118	29 45	51	117	30 36	52	116	31 28	51	116	32 19	51	115	308
53	28 23	52	117	29 15	51	116	30 06	51	115	30 57	52	115	31 49	51	114	307
54	27 53	51	116	28 44	52	115	29 36	51	115	30 27	51	114	31 18	51	113	306
55	27 23	+51	115	28 14	+51	114	29 05	+51	114	29 56	+51	113	30 47	+51	112	305
56	26 52	51	114	27 43	51	113	28 34	51	113	29 25	51	112	30 16	50	111	304
57	26 21	51	113	27 12	51	112	28 03	51	112	28 54	50	111	29 44	51	110	303
58	25 50	51	112	26 41	51	111	27 32	50	111	28 22	51	110	29 13	50	110	302
59	25 19	51	111	26 10	50	110	27 00	51	110	27 51	50	109	28 41	50	109	301
60	24 48	+50	110	25 38	+51	109	26 29	+50	109	27 19	+50	108	28 09	+50	108	300
61	24 16	50	109	25 06	51	109	25 57	50	108	26 47	50	107	27 37	50	107	299
62	23 44	51	108	24 35	50	108	25 25	50	107	26 15	50	106	27 05	50	106	298
63	23 12	51	107	24 03	50	107	24 53	50	106	25 43	50	106	26 33	49	105	297
64	22 40	50	106	23 30	50	106	24 20	50	105	25 10	50	105	26 00	50	104	296
65	22 08	+50	106	22 58	+50	105	23 48	+50	104	24 38	+50	104	25 28	+49	103	295
66	21 35	50	105	22 25	50	104	23 15	50	103	24 05	50	103	24 55	49	102	294
67	21 03	50	104	21 53	50	103	22 43	49	103	23 32	50	102	24 22	49	101	293
68	20 30	50	103	21 20	50	102	22 10	50	102	23 00	49	101	23 49	49	101	292
69	19 57	50	102	20 47	50	101	21 37	50	101	22 27	49	100	23 16	49	100	291

S. Lat. {LHA greater than 180°........ Zn=180−Z; LHA less than 180°.......... Zn=180+Z}

DECLINATION (0°-14°) SAME NAME AS LATITUDE

LAT 56°

N. Lat. {LHA greater than 180°....... Zn=Z
{LHA less than 180°........... Zn=360−Z

DECLINATION (0°-14°) SAME NAME AS LATITUDE

LHA	0° Hc	d	Z	1° Hc	d	Z	2° Hc	d	Z	3° Hc	d	Z	4° Hc	d	Z	5° Hc	d	Z	6° Hc	d	Z	7° Hc	d	Z
	° ′	′	°	° ′	′	°	° ′	′	°	° ′	′	°	° ′	′	°	° ′	′	°	° ′	′	°	° ′	′	°
70	11 02	+50	107	11 52	+51	106	12 43	+50	106	13 33	+51	105	14 24	+50	105	15 14	+50	104	16 04	+51	104	16 55	+50	103
71	10 29	51	106	11 20	50	105	12 10	51	105	13 01	50	104	13 51	51	104	14 42	50	103	15 32	50	103	16 22	50	102
72	09 57	51	105	10 48	50	105	11 38	50	104	12 28	51	103	13 19	50	103	14 09	50	102	14 59	50	102	15 49	50	101
73	09 25	50	104	10 15	50	104	11 05	51	103	11 56	50	103	12 46	50	102	13 36	50	101	14 26	50	101	15 16	50	100
74	08 52	50	103	09 42	51	103	10 33	50	102	11 23	50	102	12 13	50	101	13 03	50	101	13 53	50	100	14 43	50	99
75	08 19	+51	103	09 10	+50	102	10 00	+50	101	10 50	+50	101	11 40	+50	100	12 30	+50	100	13 20	+50	99	14 10	+50	99
76	07 47	50	102	08 37	50	101	09 27	50	101	10 17	50	100	11 07	50	99	11 57	50	99	12 47	50	98	13 37	49	98
77	07 14	50	101	08 04	50	100	08 54	50	100	09 44	50	99	10 34	50	99	11 24	50	98	12 14	49	98	13 03	50	97
78	06 41	50	100	07 31	50	99	08 21	50	99	09 11	50	98	10 01	49	98	10 50	50	97	11 40	50	97	12 30	50	96
79	06 08	50	99	06 58	50	99	07 48	49	98	08 37	50	98	09 27	50	97	10 17	50	96	11 07	50	96	11 57	49	95
80	05 34	+50	98	06 24	+50	98	07 14	+50	97	08 04	+50	97	08 54	+50	96	09 44	+50	96	10 34	+49	95	11 23	+50	94
81	05 01	50	98	05 51	50	97	06 41	50	96	07 31	50	96	08 21	49	95	09 10	50	95	10 00	50	94	10 50	49	94
82	04 28	50	97	05 18	50	96	06 08	49	96	06 57	50	95	07 47	50	94	08 37	50	94	09 27	49	93	10 16	50	93
83	03 54	50	96	04 44	50	95	05 34	50	95	06 24	50	94	07 14	49	94	08 03	50	93	08 53	50	92	09 43	49	92
84	03 21	50	95	04 11	50	94	05 01	49	94	05 50	50	93	06 40	50	93	07 30	50	92	08 20	49	92	09 09	50	91
85	02 48	+49	94	03 37	+50	94	04 27	+50	93	05 17	+50	93	06 07	+49	92	06 56	+50	91	07 46	+50	91	08 36	+49	90
86	02 14	50	93	03 04	50	93	03 54	49	92	04 43	50	92	05 33	50	91	06 23	49	91	07 12	50	90	08 02	50	89
87	01 41	49	92	02 30	50	92	03 20	50	91	04 10	50	91	05 00	49	90	05 49	50	90	06 39	50	89	07 29	49	89
88	01 07	50	92	01 57	50	91	02 47	49	91	03 36	50	90	04 26	50	89	05 16	49	89	06 05	50	88	06 55	50	88
89	00 34	49	91	01 23	50	90	02 13	50	90	03 03	49	89	03 52	50	89	04 42	50	88	05 32	49	88	06 21	50	87
90	00 00	+50	90	00 50	+49	89	01 39	+50	89	02 29	+50	88	03 19	+50	88	04 09	+49	87	04 58	+50	87	05 48	+50	86
91	−0 34	50	89	00 16	50	89	01 06	50	88	01 56	49	87	02 45	50	87	03 35	50	86	04 25	50	86	05 15	49	85
92	−1 07	50	88	−0 17	49	88	00 32	50	87	01 22	50	87	02 12	50	86	03 02	49	86	03 51	50	85	04 41	50	84
93	−1 41	50	88	−0 51	50	87	−0 01	50	86	00 49	49	86	01 38	50	85	02 28	50	85	03 18	50	84	04 08	49	84
94	−2 14	50	87	−1 24	49	86	−0 35	50	86	00 15	50	85	01 05	50	84	01 55	50	84	02 45	49	83	03 34	50	83
95	−2 48	+50	86	−1 58	+50	85	−1 08	+50	85	−0 18	+50	84	00 32	+49	84	01 21	+50	83	02 11	+50	83	03 01	+50	82
96	−3 21	50	85	−2 31	50	84	−1 41	49	84	−0 52	50	83	−0 02	50	83	00 48	50	82	01 38	50	82	02 28	50	81
97	−3 54	49	84	−3 05	50	84	−2 15	50	83	−1 25	50	83	−0 35	50	82	00 15	50	81	01 05	50	81	01 55	50	80
98	−4 28	50	83	−3 38	50	83	−2 48	50	82	−1 58	50	82	−1 08	50	81	−0 18	50	81	00 32	50	80	01 22	50	79
99	−5 01	50	82	−4 11	50	82	−3 21	50	81	−2 31	50	81	−1 41	50	80	−0 51	50	80	−0 01	50	79	00 49	50	79
100	−5 34	+50	82	−4 44	+50	81	−3 54	+50	81	−3 04	+50	80	−2 14	+50	79	−1 24	+50	79	−0 34	+50	78	00 16	+50	78
101				−5 18	51	80	−4 27	50	80	−3 37	50	79	−2 47	50	79	−1 57	50	78	−1 07	50	78	−0 17	50	77
102				−5 51	51	79	−5 00	50	79	−4 10	50	78	−3 20	50	78	−2 30	50	77	−1 40	51	77	−0 49	50	76
103							−5 33	50	78	−4 43	51	78	−3 52	50	77	−3 02	50	76	−2 12	50	76	−1 22	50	75
104										−5 16	51	77	−4 25	50	76	−3 35	50	76	−2 45	51	75	−1 54	50	74
105										−5 48	+50	76	−4 58	+50	75	−4 08	+51	75	−3 17	+50	74	−2 27	+51	74
106													−5 30	50	74	−4 40	51	74	−3 49	50	73	−2 59	51	73
107													−6 03	51	74	−5 12	51	73	−4 21	50	73	−3 31	51	72
108																−5 44	51	72	−4 53	51	72	−4 02	50	71
109																			−5 25	51	71	−4 34	51	70
110																			−5 57	+51	70	−5 06	+51	69
111																						−5 37	51	69

LHA	8° Hc	d	Z	9° Hc	d	Z	10° Hc	d	Z	11° Hc	d	Z	12° Hc	d	Z	13° Hc	d	Z	14° Hc	d	Z	LHA
	° ′	′	°	° ′	′	°	° ′	′	°	° ′	′	°	° ′	′	°	° ′	′	°	° ′	′	°	
70	17 45	+50	102	18 35	+50	102	19 25	+49	101	20 14	+50	101	21 04	+50	100	21 54	+49	99	22 43	+49	99	290
71	17 12	50	101	18 02	50	101	18 52	49	100	19 41	50	100	20 31	49	99	21 20	50	99	22 10	49	98	289
72	16 39	50	101	17 29	50	100	18 19	49	99	19 08	50	99	19 58	49	98	20 47	49	98	21 36	50	97	288
73	16 06	50	100	16 56	49	99	17 45	50	99	18 35	50	98	19 25	49	97	20 14	49	97	21 03	49	96	287
74	15 33	50	99	16 23	49	98	17 12	50	98	18 02	49	97	18 51	50	97	19 41	49	96	20 30	49	95	286
75	15 00	+49	98	15 49	+50	97	16 39	+49	97	17 28	+50	96	18 18	+49	96	19 07	+49	95	19 56	+49	94	285
76	14 26	50	97	15 16	50	97	16 06	49	96	16 55	49	95	17 44	50	95	18 34	49	94	19 23	49	94	284
77	13 53	50	96	14 43	49	96	15 32	50	95	16 22	49	95	17 11	49	94	18 00	49	93	18 49	49	93	283
78	13 20	49	96	14 09	50	95	14 59	49	94	15 48	49	94	16 37	50	93	17 27	49	93	18 16	49	92	282
79	12 46	50	95	13 36	49	94	14 25	50	94	15 15	49	93	16 04	49	92	16 53	49	92	17 42	49	91	281
80	12 13	+49	94	13 02	+50	93	13 52	+49	93	14 41	+49	92	15 30	+50	92	16 20	+49	91	17 09	+49	90	280
81	11 39	50	93	12 29	49	92	13 18	50	92	14 08	49	91	14 57	49	91	15 46	49	90	16 35	49	89	279
82	11 06	49	92	11 55	50	92	12 45	49	91	13 34	49	90	14 23	50	90	15 13	49	89	16 02	49	89	278
83	10 32	50	91	11 22	49	91	12 11	50	90	13 01	49	90	13 50	49	89	14 39	49	88	15 28	49	88	277
84	09 59	49	91	10 48	50	90	11 38	49	89	12 27	49	89	13 16	49	88	14 05	50	88	14 55	49	87	276
85	09 25	+50	90	10 15	+49	89	11 04	+49	89	11 53	+50	88	12 43	+49	87	13 32	+49	87	14 21	+49	86	275
86	08 52	49	89	09 41	50	88	10 31	49	88	11 20	49	87	12 09	49	87	12 58	50	86	13 48	49	85	274
87	08 18	50	88	09 08	49	87	09 57	49	87	10 46	50	86	11 36	49	86	12 25	49	85	13 14	49	85	273
88	07 45	49	87	08 34	50	87	09 24	49	86	10 13	49	85	11 02	50	85	11 52	49	84	12 41	49	84	272
89	07 11	50	86	08 01	49	86	08 50	50	85	09 40	49	85	10 29	49	84	11 18	50	84	12 08	49	83	271
90	06 38	+49	86	07 27	+50	85	08 17	+49	84	09 06	+50	84	09 56	+49	83	10 45	+49	83	11 34	+49	82	270
91	06 04	50	85	06 54	49	84	07 43	50	84	08 33	49	83	09 22	50	82	10 12	49	82	11 01	49	81	269
92	05 31	49	84	06 20	50	83	07 10	50	83	08 00	49	82	08 49	50	82	09 39	49	81	10 28	49	80	268
93	04 57	50	83	05 47	50	83	06 37	49	82	07 26	50	81	08 16	49	81	09 05	50	80	09 55	49	80	267
94	04 24	50	82	05 14	50	82	06 04	49	81	06 53	50	81	07 43	49	80	08 32	50	79	09 22	49	79	266
95	03 51	+50	81	04 41	+49	81	05 30	+50	80	06 20	+50	80	07 10	+49	79	07 59	+50	79	08 49	+50	78	265
96	03 18	50	81	04 08	49	80	04 57	50	79	05 47	50	79	06 37	50	78	07 27	49	78	08 16	50	77	264
97	02 45	50	80	03 35	49	79	04 24	50	79	05 14	50	78	06 04	50	78	06 54	50	77	07 44	49	76	263
98	02 12	50	79	03 02	50	78	03 52	49	78	04 41	50	77	05 31	50	77	06 21	50	76	07 11	50	76	262
99	01 39	50	78	02 29	50	78	03 19	50	77	04 09	50	76	04 59	50	76	05 49	50	75	06 39	49	75	261
100	01 06	+50	77	01 56	+50	77	02 46	+50	76	03 36	+50	76	04 26	+50	75	05 16	+50	75	06 06	+50	74	260
101	00 33	51	76	01 24	50	76	02 14	50	75	03 04	50	75	03 54	50	74	04 44	50	74	05 34	50	73	259
102	00 01	50	76	00 51	50	75	01 41	51	75	02 32	50	74	03 22	50	73	04 12	50	73	05 02	50	72	258
103	−0 32	51	75	00 19	50	74	01 09	50	74	01 59	51	73	02 50	50	73	03 40	50	72	04 30	50	72	257
104	−1 04	51	74	−0 13	50	73	00 37	50	73	01 27	51	72	02 18	50	72	03 08	50	71	03 58	51	71	256
105	−1 36	+50	73	−0 46	+51	73	00 05	+50	72	00 55	+51	71	01 46	+50	71	02 36	+51	70	03 27	+50	70	255
106	−2 08	50	72	−1 18	51	72	−0 27	51	71	00 24	50	71	01 14	51	70	02 05	50	70	02 55	51	69	254
107	−2 40	51	71	−1 49	50	71	−0 59	51	70	−0 08	50	70	00 42	51	69	01 33	51	69	02 24	51	68	253
108	−3 12	51	71	−2 21	51	70	−1 30	51	70	−0 39	50	69	00 11	51	68	01 02	51	68	01 53	51	67	252
109	−3 43	51	70	−2 52	51	69	−2 01	50	69	−1 11	51	68	−0 20	51	68	00 31	51	67	01 22	51	67	251
110	−4 15	+51	69	−3 24	+51	68	−2 33	+51	68	−1 42	+51	67	−0 51	+51	67	00 00	+52	66	00 52	+51	66	250
111	−4 46	51	68	−3 55	51	68	−3 04	52	67	−2 12	51	67	−1 21	51	66	−0 30	51	65	00 21	51	65	249
112	−5 17	51	67	−4 26	52	67	−3 34	51	66	−2 43	51	66	−1 52	51	65	−1 01	52	65	−0 09	51	64	248
113	−5 48	52	66	−4 56	51	66	−4 05	51	65	−3 14	52	65	−2 22	51	64	−1 31	52	64	−0 39	51	63	247
114				−5 27	52	65	−4 35	51	64	−3 44	52	64	−2 52	51	63	−2 01	52	63	−1 09	51	62	246
115				−5 57	+51	64	−5 06	+52	64	−4 14	+52	63	−3 22	+51	63	−2 31	+52	62	−1 39	+52	62	245
116							−5 36	52	63	−4 44	52	62	−3 52	52	62	−3 00	52	61	−2 08	52	61	244
117										−5 13	52	61	−4 21	52	61	−3 29	52	60	−2 37	52	60	243
118										−5 43	52	61	−4 51	53	60	−3 58	52	60	−3 06	52	59	242
119													−5 20	53	59	−4 27	52	59	−3 35	52	58	241
120													−5 48	+52	58	−4 56	+53	58	−4 03	+52	57	240
121																−5 24	53	57	−4 31	52	57	239
122																−5 52	53	56	−4 59	52	56	238
123																			−5 27	53	55	237
124																			−5 54	53	54	236

0°	1°	2°	3°	4°	5°	6°	7°	8°	9°	10°	11°	12°	13°	14°

S. Lat. {LHA greater than 180°....... Zn=180−Z
{LHA less than 180°........... Zn=180+Z

DECLINATION (0°-14°) SAME NAME AS LATITUDE

LAT 56°

N. Lat. {LHA greater than 180°........ Zn=Z
{LHA less than 180°........... Zn=360−Z

DECLINATION (0°-14°) CONTRARY NAME TO LATITUDE

LHA	0° Hc	d	Z	1° Hc	d	Z	2° Hc	d	Z	3° Hc	d	Z	4° Hc	d	Z
	° ′	′	°	° ′	′	°	° ′	′	°	° ′	′	°	° ′	′	°
100	−5 34	−50	82	260											
99	−5 01	50	82	−5 51	50	83	261								
98	−4 28	50	83	−5 18	50	84	262								
97	−3 54	50	84	−4 44	50	85	−5 34	50	85	263					
96	−3 21	50	85	−4 11	50	86	−5 01	49	86	−5 50	50	87	264		
95	−2 48	−49	86	−3 37	−50	86	−4 27	−50	87	−5 17	−50	87	265		
94	−2 14	50	87	−3 04	50	87	−3 54	49	88	−4 43	50	88	−5 33	50	89
93	−1 41	49	88	−2 30	50	88	−3 20	50	89	−4 10	50	89	−5 00	49	90
92	−1 07	50	88	−1 57	50	89	−2 47	49	89	−3 36	50	90	−4 26	50	91
91	−0 34	49	89	−1 23	50	90	−2 13	50	90	−3 03	49	91	−3 52	50	91
90	00 00	−50	90	−0 50	−49	91	−1 39	−50	91	−2 29	−50	92	−3 19	−50	92
89	00 34	50	91	−0 16	50	91	−1 06	50	92	−1 56	49	93	−2 45	50	93
88	01 07	50	92	00 17	49	92	−0 32	50	93	−1 22	50	93	−2 12	50	94
87	01 41	50	92	00 51	50	93	00 01	50	94	−0 49	49	94	−1 38	50	95
86	02 14	50	93	01 24	49	94	00 35	50	94	−0 15	50	95	−1 05	50	96
85	02 48	−50	94	01 58	−50	95	01 08	−50	95	00 18	−50	96	−0 32	−49	96
84	03 21	50	95	02 31	50	96	01 41	49	96	00 52	50	97	00 02	50	97
83	03 54	49	96	03 05	50	96	02 15	50	97	01 25	50	97	00 35	50	98
82	04 28	50	97	03 38	50	97	02 48	50	98	01 58	50	98	01 08	50	99
81	05 01	50	98	04 11	50	98	03 21	50	99	02 31	50	99	01 41	50	100
80	05 34	−50	98	04 44	−50	99	03 54	−50	99	03 04	−50	100	02 14	−50	101
79	06 08	50	99	05 18	51	100	04 27	50	100	03 37	50	101	02 47	50	101
78	06 41	50	100	05 51	51	101	05 00	50	101	04 10	50	102	03 20	50	102
77	07 14	51	101	06 23	50	101	05 33	50	102	04 43	51	102	03 52	50	103
76	07 47	51	102	06 56	50	102	06 06	50	103	05 16	51	103	04 25	50	104
75	08 19	−50	103	07 29	−50	103	06 39	−51	104	05 48	−50	104	04 58	−50	105
74	08 52	50	103	08 02	51	104	07 11	50	105	06 21	51	105	05 30	50	106
73	09 25	51	104	08 34	50	105	07 44	51	105	06 53	50	106	06 03	51	106
72	09 57	50	105	09 07	51	106	08 16	51	106	07 25	50	107	06 35	51	107
71	10 29	50	106	09 39	51	107	08 48	51	107	07 57	50	108	07 07	51	108
70	11 02	−51	107	10 11	−51	107	09 20	−51	108	08 29	−51	108	07 38	−50	109

LHA	5° Hc	d	Z	6° Hc	d	Z	7° Hc	d	Z	8° Hc	d	Z	9° Hc	d	Z
	° ′	′	°	° ′	′	°	° ′	′	°	° ′	′	°	° ′	′	°
94	266														
93	−5 49	50	90	267											
92	−5 16	49	91	−6 05	50	92	268								
91	−4 42	50	92	−5 32	49	92	269								
90	−4 09	−49	93	−4 58	−50	93	−5 48	−50	94	270					
89	−3 35	50	94	−4 25	50	94	−5 15	49	95	−6 04	50	95	271		
88	−3 02	49	94	−3 51	50	95	−4 41	50	96	−5 31	49	96	272		
87	−2 28	50	95	−3 18	50	96	−4 08	49	96	−4 57	50	97	−5 47	50	97
86	−1 55	50	96	−2 45	49	97	−3 34	50	97	−4 24	50	98	−5 14	50	98
85	−1 21	−50	97	−2 11	−50	97	−3 01	−50	98	−3 51	−50	99	−4 41	−49	99
84	−0 48	50	98	−1 38	50	98	−2 28	50	99	−3 18	50	99	−4 08	49	100
83	−0 15	50	99	−1 05	50	99	−1 55	50	100	−2 45	50	100	−3 35	49	101
82	00 18	50	99	−0 32	50	100	−1 22	50	101	−2 12	50	101	−3 02	50	102
81	00 51	50	100	00 01	50	101	−0 49	50	101	−1 39	50	102	−2 29	50	102
80	01 24	−50	101	00 34	−50	102	−0 16	−50	102	−1 06	−50	103	−1 56	−50	103
79	01 57	50	102	01 07	50	102	00 17	50	103	−0 33	51	104	−1 24	50	104
78	02 30	50	103	01 40	51	103	00 49	50	104	−0 01	50	104	−0 51	50	105
77	03 02	50	104	02 12	50	104	01 22	50	105	00 32	51	105	−0 19	50	106
76	03 35	50	104	02 45	51	105	01 54	50	106	01 04	51	106	00 13	50	107
75	04 08	−51	105	03 17	−50	106	02 27	−51	106	01 36	−50	107	00 46	−51	107
74	04 40	51	106	03 49	50	107	02 59	51	107	02 08	50	108	01 18	51	108
73	05 12	51	107	04 21	50	107	03 31	51	108	02 40	51	109	01 49	50	109
72	05 44	51	108	04 53	51	108	04 02	50	109	03 12	51	109	02 21	51	110
71	06 16	51	109	05 25	51	109	04 34	51	110	03 43	51	110	02 52	51	111
70	06 48	−51	110	05 57	−51	110	05 06	−51	111	04 15	−51	111	03 24	−51	112

LHA	10° Hc	d	Z	11° Hc	d	Z	12° Hc	d	Z	13° Hc	d	Z	14° Hc	d	Z	LHA
	° ′	′	°	° ′	′	°	° ′	′	°	° ′	′	°	° ′	′	°	
87	273															
86	−6 04	49	99	274												
85	−5 30	−50	100	275												
84	−4 57	50	101	−5 47	50	101	276									
83	−4 24	50	101	−5 14	50	102	−6 04	50	102	277						
82	−3 52	49	102	−4 41	50	103	−5 31	50	103	278						
81	−3 19	50	103	−4 09	50	104	−4 59	50	104	−5 49	50	105	279			
80	−2 46	−50	104	−3 36	−50	104	−4 26	−50	105	−5 16	−50	105	280			
79	−2 14	50	105	−3 04	50	105	−3 54	50	106	−4 44	50	106	−5 34	50	107	281
78	−1 41	51	105	−2 32	50	106	−3 22	50	107	−4 12	50	107	−5 02	50	108	282
77	−1 09	50	106	−1 59	51	107	−2 50	50	107	−3 40	50	108	−4 30	50	108	283
76	−0 37	50	107	−1 27	51	108	−2 18	50	108	−3 08	50	109	−3 58	51	109	284
75	−0 05	−50	108	−0 55	−51	109	−1 46	−50	109	−2 36	−51	110	−3 27	−50	110	285
74	00 27	51	109	−0 24	50	109	−1 14	51	110	−2 05	50	110	−2 55	51	111	286
73	00 59	51	110	00 08	50	110	−0 42	51	111	−1 33	51	111	−2 24	51	112	287
72	01 30	51	110	00 39	50	111	−0 11	51	112	−1 02	51	112	−1 53	51	113	288
71	02 01	50	111	01 11	51	112	00 20	51	112	−0 31	51	113	−1 22	51	113	289
70	02 33	−51	112	01 42	−51	113	00 51	−51	113	00 00	−52	114	−0 52	−51	114	290

S. Lat. {LHA greater than 180°....... Zn=180−Z
{LHA less than 180°........... Zn=180+Z

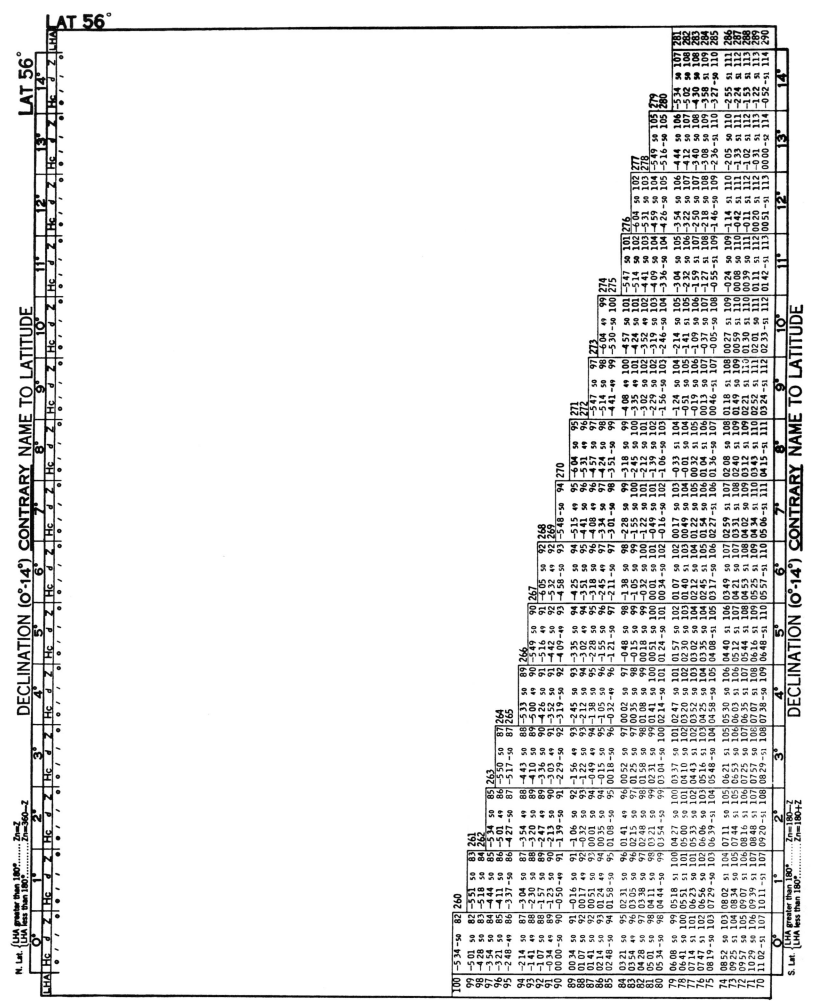

DECLINATION (0°-14°) CONTRARY NAME TO LATITUDE

N. Lat. {LHA greater than 180°....... Zn=Z; LHA less than 180°.......... Zn=360−Z}

DECLINATION (0°-14°) CONTRARY NAME TO LATITUDE

LHA	0° Hc	d	Z	1° Hc	d	Z	2° Hc	d	Z	3° Hc	d	Z	4° Hc	d	Z
	° ′	′	°	° ′	′	°	° ′	′	°	° ′	′	°	° ′	′	°
69	11 34	51	108	10 43	51	108	09 52	51	109	09 01	51	109	08 10	51	110
68	12 06	51	109	11 15	51	109	10 24	51	110	09 33	51	110	08 42	51	111
67	12 37	51	109	11 46	51	110	10 55	51	111	10 04	51	111	09 13	51	112
66	13 09	51	110	12 18	51	111	11 27	52	111	10 35	51	112	09 44	51	112
65	13 40	−51	111	12 49	−51	112	11 58	−52	112	11 06	−51	113	10 15	−51	113
64	14 11	51	112	13 20	51	113	12 29	52	113	11 37	51	114	10 46	52	114
63	14 42	51	113	13 51	52	113	12 59	51	114	12 08	52	115	11 16	52	115
62	15 13	51	114	14 22	52	114	13 30	52	115	12 38	51	115	11 47	52	116
61	15 44	52	115	14 52	52	115	14 00	52	116	13 08	51	116	12 17	52	117
60	16 14	−52	116	15 22	−52	116	14 30	−52	117	13 38	−52	117	12 46	−52	118
59	16 44	52	117	15 52	52	117	15 00	52	118	14 08	52	118	13 16	52	119
58	17 14	52	117	16 22	52	118	15 30	52	118	14 38	53	119	13 45	52	119
57	17 44	52	118	16 52	53	119	15 59	52	119	15 07	53	120	14 14	52	120
56	18 13	52	119	17 21	53	120	16 28	52	120	15 36	53	121	14 43	52	121
55	18 43	−53	120	17 50	−53	121	16 57	−52	121	16 05	−53	122	15 12	−53	122
54	19 11	52	121	18 19	53	122	17 26	53	122	16 33	53	123	15 40	53	123
53	19 40	53	122	18 47	53	123	17 54	53	123	17 01	53	124	16 08	53	124
52	20 08	53	123	19 15	53	123	18 22	53	124	17 29	53	124	16 36	54	125
51	20 36	53	124	19 43	53	124	18 50	53	125	17 57	54	125	17 03	53	126
50	21 04	−53	125	20 11	−54	125	19 17	−53	126	18 24	−54	126	17 30	−53	127
49	21 31	53	126	20 38	54	126	19 44	53	127	18 51	54	127	17 57	54	128
48	21 58	53	127	21 05	54	127	20 11	54	128	19 17	54	128	18 23	54	129
47	22 25	54	128	21 31	54	128	20 37	54	129	19 43	54	129	18 49	54	130
46	22 52	54	129	21 58	55	129	21 03	54	130	20 09	54	130	19 15	54	131
45	23 18	−55	130	22 23	−54	130	21 29	−54	131	20 35	−55	131	19 40	−54	132
44	23 43	54	131	22 49	55	131	21 54	54	132	21 00	55	132	20 05	54	133
43	24 08	54	132	23 14	55	132	22 19	54	133	21 25	55	133	20 30	55	133
42	24 33	54	133	23 39	55	133	22 44	55	134	21 49	55	134	20 54	55	134
41	24 58	55	134	24 03	55	134	23 08	55	135	22 13	55	135	21 18	55	135
40	25 22	−55	135	24 27	−55	135	23 32	−56	136	22 36	−55	136	21 41	−55	136
39	25 46	56	136	24 50	55	136	23 55	55	137	23 00	56	137	22 04	55	137
38	26 09	56	137	25 13	55	137	24 18	56	138	23 22	55	138	22 27	56	138
37	26 32	56	138	25 36	56	138	24 40	56	139	23 44	55	139	22 49	56	139
36	26 54	56	139	25 58	56	139	25 02	56	140	24 06	56	140	23 10	56	140
35	27 16	−56	140	26 20	−56	140	25 24	−56	141	24 28	−57	141	23 31	−56	141
34	27 37	56	141	26 41	56	141	25 45	57	142	24 48	56	142	23 52	56	142
33	27 58	56	142	27 02	57	142	26 05	56	143	25 09	57	143	24 12	56	143
32	28 19	57	143	27 22	57	143	26 25	56	144	25 29	57	144	24 32	57	145
31	28 39	57	144	27 42	57	144	26 45	57	145	25 48	57	145	24 51	57	146
30	28 58	−57	145	28 01	−57	146	27 04	−57	146	26 07	−57	146	25 10	−57	147
29	29 17	57	146	28 20	57	147	27 23	57	147	26 26	58	147	25 28	57	148
28	29 35	57	147	28 38	57	148	27 41	58	148	26 43	57	148	25 46	57	149
27	29 53	57	148	28 56	58	149	27 58	57	149	27 01	58	149	26 03	57	150
26	30 10	57	150	29 13	58	150	28 15	57	150	27 18	58	151	26 20	58	151
25	30 27	−58	151	29 29	−57	151	28 32	−58	151	27 34	−58	152	26 36	−58	152
24	30 43	58	152	29 45	58	152	28 47	58	152	27 49	58	153	26 51	58	153
23	30 59	58	153	30 01	58	153	29 03	58	154	28 05	59	154	27 06	58	154
22	31 14	58	154	30 16	59	154	29 17	58	155	28 19	58	155	27 21	58	155
21	31 28	58	155	30 30	58	155	29 32	59	156	28 33	58	156	27 35	59	156
20	31 42	−58	156	30 44	−59	157	29 45	−58	157	28 47	−59	157	27 48	−59	157
19	31 55	58	157	30 57	59	158	29 58	59	158	28 59	58	158	28 01	59	158
18	32 08	59	159	31 09	59	159	30 10	59	159	29 11	58	159	28 13	59	160
17	32 20	59	160	31 21	59	160	30 22	59	160	29 23	59	160	28 24	59	161
16	32 31	59	161	31 32	59	161	30 33	59	161	29 34	59	162	28 35	59	162
15	32 42	−59	162	31 43	−60	162	30 43	−59	163	29 44	−59	163	28 45	−59	163
14	32 52	60	163	31 52	59	164	30 53	59	164	29 54	59	164	28 55	60	164
13	33 01	59	164	32 02	60	165	31 02	59	165	30 03	59	165	29 04	60	165
12	33 10	60	166	32 10	59	166	31 11	60	166	30 11	59	166	29 12	60	166
11	33 18	60	167	32 18	59	167	31 19	60	167	30 19	59	167	29 20	60	167
10	33 25	−60	168	32 25	−59	168	31 26	−60	168	30 26	−59	168	29 27	−60	169
9	33 32	60	169	32 32	60	169	31 32	59	169	30 33	60	170	29 33	60	170
8	33 38	60	170	32 38	60	171	31 38	60	171	30 38	59	171	29 39	60	171
7	33 43	60	172	32 43	60	172	31 43	60	172	30 43	59	172	29 44	60	172
6	33 47	59	173	32 48	60	173	31 48	60	173	30 48	60	173	29 48	60	173
5	33 51	−60	174	32 51	−60	174	31 51	−59	174	30 52	−60	174	29 52	−60	174
4	33 54	60	175	32 54	59	175	31 55	60	175	30 55	60	175	29 55	60	175
3	33 57	60	176	32 57	60	176	31 57	60	177	30 57	60	177	29 57	60	177
2	33 59	60	178	32 59	60	178	31 59	60	178	30 59	60	178	29 59	60	178
1	34 00	60	179	33 00	60	179	32 00	60	179	31 00	60	179	30 00	60	179
0	34 00	−60	180	33 00	−60	180	32 00	−60	180	31 00	−60	180	30 00	−60	180

LHA	5° Hc	d	Z	6° Hc	d	Z	7° Hc	d	Z	8° Hc	d	Z	9° Hc	d	Z
	° ′	′	°	° ′	′	°	° ′	′	°	° ′	′	°	° ′	′	°
69	07 19	51	110	06 28	51	111	05 37	51	111	04 46	51	112	03 55	51	112
68	07 51	52	111	06 59	51	112	06 08	51	112	05 17	51	113	04 26	52	113
67	08 22	52	112	07 30	51	113	06 39	51	113	05 48	52	114	04 56	51	114
66	08 53	52	113	08 01	51	113	07 10	52	114	06 18	51	115	05 27	52	115
65	09 24	−52	114	08 32	−52	114	07 40	−51	115	06 49	−52	115	05 57	−51	116
64	09 54	52	115	09 02	51	115	08 11	52	116	07 19	52	116	06 27	51	117
63	10 24	51	116	09 33	52	116	08 41	52	117	07 49	52	117	06 57	52	118
62	10 55	52	116	10 03	52	117	09 11	52	117	08 19	52	118	07 27	52	118
61	11 25	52	117	10 33	52	118	09 41	53	118	08 48	52	119	07 56	52	119
60	11 54	−52	118	11 02	−52	119	10 10	−52	119	09 18	−53	120	08 25	−52	120
59	12 24	53	119	11 31	52	120	10 39	52	120	09 47	53	121	08 54	52	121
58	12 53	52	120	12 01	53	120	11 08	53	121	10 15	52	121	09 23	53	122
57	13 22	53	121	12 29	52	121	11 37	53	122	10 44	53	122	09 51	53	123
56	13 51	53	122	12 58	53	122	12 05	53	123	11 12	53	123	10 19	53	124
55	14 19	−53	123	13 26	−53	123	12 33	−53	124	11 40	−53	124	10 47	−53	125
54	14 47	53	124	13 54	53	124	13 01	53	125	12 08	53	125	11 15	54	125
53	15 15	53	124	14 22	54	125	13 28	53	125	12 35	53	126	11 42	54	126
52	15 42	53	125	14 49	53	126	13 56	54	126	13 02	53	127	12 09	54	127
51	16 10	54	126	15 16	53	127	14 23	54	127	13 29	54	128	12 35	54	128
50	16 37	−54	127	15 43	−54	128	14 49	−54	128	13 55	−54	129	13 01	−54	129
49	17 03	54	128	16 09	54	129	15 15	54	129	14 21	54	130	13 27	54	130
48	17 29	54	129	16 35	54	130	15 41	54	130	14 47	54	130	13 53	54	131
47	17 55	54	130	17 01	54	131	16 07	55	131	15 12	54	131	14 18	54	132
46	18 21	55	131	17 26	54	131	16 32	55	132	15 37	54	132	14 43	55	133
45	18 46	−55	132	17 51	−54	132	16 57	−55	133	16 02	−55	133	15 07	−54	134
44	19 11	55	133	18 16	55	133	17 21	55	134	16 26	55	134	15 31	55	135
43	19 35	55	134	18 40	55	134	17 45	55	135	16 50	55	135	15 55	55	136
42	19 59	55	135	19 04	55	135	18 09	55	136	17 14	56	136	16 18	55	137
41	20 23	56	136	19 27	55	136	18 32	55	137	17 37	56	137	16 41	55	137
40	20 46	−56	137	19 50	−55	137	18 55	−56	138	17 59	−55	138	17 04	−56	138
39	21 09	56	138	20 13	56	138	19 17	55	139	18 22	56	139	17 26	56	139
38	21 31	56	139	20 35	56	139	19 39	56	140	18 43	56	140	17 47	55	140
37	21 53	56	140	20 57	56	140	20 01	56	141	19 05	56	141	18 09	56	141
36	22 14	56	141	21 18	56	141	20 22	56	142	19 26	57	142	18 29	56	142
35	22 35	−56	142	21 39	−56	142	20 43	−57	143	19 46	−56	143	18 50	−57	143
34	22 56	57	143	21 59	56	143	21 03	57	144	20 06	56	144	19 10	57	144
33	23 16	57	144	22 19	57	144	21 22	56	145	20 26	57	145	19 29	57	145
32	23 35	56	145	22 39	57	145	21 42	57	146	20 45	57	146	19 48	57	146
31	23 54	57	146	22 57	57	146	22 00	57	147	21 03	57	147	20 06	57	147
30	24 13	−57	147	23 16	−57	147	22 19	−58	148	21 21	−57	148	20 24	−57	148
29	24 31	57	148	23 34	58	148	22 36	57	149	21 39	57	149	20 42	58	149
28	24 49	58	149	23 51	57	149	22 54	58	150	21 56	57	150	20 59	58	150
27	25 06	58	150	24 08	58	150	23 10	57	151	22 13	58	151	21 15	58	151
26	25 22	58	151	24 24	57	151	23 27	58	152	22 29	58	152	21 31	58	152
25	25 38	−58	152	24 40	−58	152	23 42	−58	153	22 44	−58	153	21 46	−58	153
24	25 53	58	153	24 55	58	154	23 57	58	154	22 59	58	154	22 01	58	154
23	26 08	58	154	25 10	58	155	24 12	58	155	23 14	59	155	22 15	58	155
22	26 23	59	155	25 24	58	156	24 26	59	156	23 27	58	156	22 29	58	156
21	26 36	58	157	25 38	59	157	24 39	58	157	23 41	59	157	22 42	58	157
20	26 49	−58	158	25 51	−59	158	24 52	−59	158	23 53	−58	158	22 55	−59	159
19	27 02	59	159	26 03	59	159	25 04	58	159	24 06	59	159	23 07	59	160
18	27 14	59	160	26 15	59	160	25 16	59	160	24 17	59	160	23 18	59	161
17	27 25	59	161	26 26	59	161	25 27	59	161	24 28	59	162	23 29	59	162
16	27 36	59	162	26 37	59	162	25 38	60	162	24 38	59	163	23 39	59	163
15	27 46	−59	163	26 47	−60	163	25 47	−59	163	24 48	−59	164	23 49	−59	164
14	27 55	59	164	26 56	59	164	25 57	60	165	24 57	59	165	23 58	59	165
13	28 04	59	165	27 05	60	165	26 05	59	166	25 06	59	166	24 07	60	166
12	28 12	59	166	27 13	60	167	26 13	59	167	25 14	60	167	24 14	59	167
11	28 20	60	168	27 20	59	168	26 21	60	168	25 21	59	168	24 22	60	168
10	28 27	−60	169	27 27	−59	169	26 28	−60	169	25 28	−60	169	24 28	−59	169
9	28 33	60	170	27 33	59	170	26 34	60	170	25 34	60	170	24 34	59	170
8	28 39	60	171	27 39	60	171	26 39	60	171	25 39	59	171	24 40	60	171
7	28 44	60	172	27 44	60	172	26 44	60	172	25 44	60	172	24 44	59	172
6	28 48	60	173	27 48	60	173	26 48	60	173	25 48	59	173	24 49	60	174
5	28 52	−60	174	27 52	−60	174	26 52	−60	174	25 52	−60	175	24 52	−60	175
4	28 55	60	175	27 55	60	176	26 55	60	176	25 55	60	176	24 55	60	176
3	28 57	60	177	27 57	60	177	26 57	60	177	25 57	60	177	24 57	60	177
2	28 59	60	178	27 59	60	178	26 59	60	178	25 59	60	178	24 59	60	178
1	29 00	60	179	28 00	60	179	27 00	60	179	26 00	60	179	25 00	60	179
0	29 00	−60	180	28 00	−60	180	27 00	−60	180	26 00	−60	180	25 00	−60	180

LHA	10° Hc	d	Z	11° Hc	d	Z	12° Hc	d	Z	13° Hc	d	Z	14° Hc	d	Z	LHA
	° ′	′	°	° ′	′	°	° ′	′	°	° ′	′	°	° ′	′	°	
69	03 04	52	113	02 12	51	113	01 21	51	114	00 30	51	115	−0 21	51	115	291
68	03 34	51	114	02 43	51	114	01 52	51	115	01 01	52	115	00 09	51	116	292
67	04 05	51	115	03 14	52	115	02 22	51	116	01 31	52	116	00 39	51	117	293
66	04 35	51	116	03 44	52	116	02 52	51	117	02 01	52	117	01 09	51	118	294
65	05 06	−52	116	04 14	−52	117	03 22	−51	117	02 31	−52	118	01 39	−52	118	295
64	05 36	52	117	04 44	52	118	03 52	52	118	03 00	52	119	02 08	52	119	296
63	06 05	52	118	05 13	52	119	04 21	52	119	03 29	52	120	02 37	52	120	297
62	06 35	52	119	05 43	52	119	04 51	53	120	03 58	52	120	03 06	52	121	298
61	07 04	52	120	06 12	52	120	05 20	53	121	04 27	52	121	03 35	52	122	299
60	07 33	−52	121	06 41	−53	121	05 48	−52	122	04 56	−53	122	04 03	−52	123	300
59	08 02	53	122	07 09	52	122	06 17	53	123	05 24	53	123	04 31	52	123	301
58	08 30	52	122	07 38	53	123	06 45	53	123	05 52	53	124	04 59	52	124	302
57	08 58	52	123	08 06	53	124	07 13	53	124	06 20	53	125	05 27	53	125	303
56	09 26	53	124	08 33	53	125	07 40	53	125	06 47	53	126	05 54	53	126	304
55	09 54	−53	125	09 01	−53	126	08 08	−54	126	07 14	−53	126	06 21	−53	127	305
54	10 21	53	126	09 28	53	126	08 35	54	127	07 41	53	127	06 48	54	128	306
53	10 48	53	127	09 55	54	127	09 01	53	128	08 08	54	128	07 14	53	129	307
52	11 15	54	128	10 21	53	128	09 28	54	129	08 34	54	129	07 40	53	130	308
51	11 41	53	129	10 48	54	129	09 54	54	130	09 00	54	130	08 06	54	130	309
50	12 07	−53	130	11 14	−54	130	10 20	−55	130	09 25	−54	131	08 31	−54	131	310
49	12 33	54	130	11 39	54	131	10 45	54	131	09 51	55	132	08 56	54	132	311
48	12 59	55	131	12 04	54	132	11 10	54	132	10 16	55	133	09 21	54	133	312
47	13 24	55	132	12 29	54	133	11 35	55	133	10 40	55	134	09 45	54	134	313
46	13 48	54	133	12 54	55	134	11 59	55	134	11 04	55	134	10 09	54	135	314
45	14 13	−55	134	13 18	−56	135	12 23	−55	135	11 28	−55	135	10 33	−55	136	315
44	14 36	55	135	13 41	55	135	12 46	55	136	11 51	55	136	10 56	55	137	316
43	15 00	55	136	14 05	55	136	13 10	56	137	12 14	55	137	11 19	55	138	317
42	15 23	55	137	14 28	56	137	13 32	55	138	12 37	55	138	11 42	56	139	318
41	15 46	56	138	14 50	55	138	13 55	56	139	12 59	55	139	12 04	56	139	319
40	16 08	−56	139	15 12	−55	139	14 17	−56	140	13 21	−56	140	12 25	−56	140	320
39	16 30	56	140	15 34	56	140	14 38	56	141	13 42	56	141	12 46	55	141	321
38	16 52	56	141	15 56	57	141	14 59	56	141	14 03	56	142	13 07	56	142	322
37	17 13	57	142	16 16	56	142	15 20	56	142	14 24	56	143	13 28	57	143	323
36	17 33	56	143	16 37	57	143	15 40	56	143	14 44	56	144	13 48	57	144	324
35	17 53	−56	144	16 57	−57	144	16 00	−56	144	15 04	−57	145	14 07	−57	145	325
34	18 13	57	145	17 16	56	145	16 20	57	145	15 23	57	146	14 26	57	146	326
33	18 32	57	146	17 35	57	146	16 38	56	146	15 42	57	147	14 45	57	147	327
32	18 51	57	147	17 54	57	147	16 57	57	147	16 00	57	148	15 03	57	148	328
31	19 09	57	148	18 12	57	148	17 15	57	148	16 18	58	149	15 20	57	149	329
30	19 27	−57	149	18 30	−58	149	17 32	−57	149	16 35	−57	149	15 38	−58	150	330
29	19 44	57	150	18 47	58	150	17 49	57	150	16 52	58	150	15 54	57	151	331
28	20 01	58	151	19 03	57	151	18 06	58	151	17 08	58	151	16 10	57	152	332
27	20 17	58	152	19 19	57	152	18 22	58	152	17 24	58	152	16 26	58	153	333
26	20 33	58	153	19 35	58	153	18 37	58	153	17 39	58	153	16 41	58	154	334
25	20 48	−58	154	19 50	−58	154	18 52	−58	154	17 54	−58	154	16 56	−58	155	335
24	21 03	58	155	20 05	59	155	19 06	58	155	18 08	58	155	17 10	58	156	336
23	21 17	58	156	20 19	59	156	19 20	58	156	18 22	59	156	17 23	58	157	337
22	21 31	59	157	20 32	58	157	19 34	59	157	18 35	58	157	17 37	59	158	338
21	21 44	59	158	20 45	59	158	19 46	58	158	18 48	59	158	17 49	59	159	339
20	21 56	−59	159	20 57	−58	159	19 59	−59	159	19 00	−59	159	18 01	−59	160	340
19	22 08	59	160	21 09	59	160	20 10	59	160	19 11	58	160	18 13	59	161	341
18	22 19	59	161	21 20	59	161	20 21	59	161	19 22	59	161	18 23	59	162	342
17	22 30	59	162	21 31	59	162	20 32	59	162	19 33	59	162	18 34	59	163	343
16	22 40	59	163	21 41	59	163	20 42	59	163	19 43	60	163	18 43	59	164	344
15	22 50	−60	164	21 50	−59	164	20 51	−59	164	19 52	−59	164	18 53	−60	165	345
14	22 59	60	165	21 59	59	165	21 00	59	165	20 01	60	166	19 01	59	166	346
13	23 07	59	166	22 08	60	166	21 08	59	166	20 09	60	167	19 09	59	167	347
12	23 15	60	167	22 15	59	167	21 16	60	167	20 16	59	168	19 17	60	168	348
11	23 22	60	168	22 22	59	168	21 23	60	168	20 23	59	169	19 24	60	169	349
10	23 29	−60	169	22 29	−60	169	21 29	−59	170	20 30	−60	170	19 30	−60	170	350
9	23 35	60	170	22 35	60	170	21 35	60	171	20 35	59	171	19 36	60	171	351
8	23 40	60	171	22 40	60	172	21 40	59	172	20 41	60	172	19 41	60	172	352
7	23 45	60	173	22 45	60	173	21 45	60	173	20 45	60	173	19 45	60	173	353
6	23 49	60	174	22 49	60	174	21 49	60	174	20 49	60	174	19 49	60	174	354
5	23 52	−60	175	22 52	−60	175	21 52	−60	175	20 52	−60	175	19 52	−59	175	355
4	23 55	60	176	22 55	60	176	21 55	60	176	20 55	60	176	19 55	60	176	356
3	23 57	60	177	22 57	60	177	21 57	60	177	20 57	60	177	19 57	60	177	357
2	23 59	60	178	22 59	60	178	21 59	60	178	20 59	60	178	19 59	60	178	358
1	24 00	60	179	23 00	60	179	22 00	60	179	21 00	60	179	20 00	60	179	359
0	24 00	−60	180	23 00	−60	180	22 00	−60	180	21 00	−60	180	20 00	−60	180	360

S. Lat. {LHA greater than 180°....... Zn=180−Z; LHA less than 180°.......... Zn=180+Z}

DECLINATION (0°-14°) CONTRARY NAME TO LATITUDE

N. Lat. {LHA greater than 180°....... Zn=Z; LHA less than 180°........... Zn=360−Z}

DECLINATION (15°-29°) SAME NAME AS LATITUDE

LAT 56°

LHA	15° Hc	15° d	15° Z	16° Hc	16° d	16° Z	17° Hc	17° d	17° Z	18° Hc	18° d	18° Z	19° Hc	19° d	19° Z
	° ′	′	°	° ′	′	°	° ′	′	°	° ′	′	°	° ′	′	°
0	49 00	+60	180	50 00	+60	180	51 00	+60	180	52 00	+60	180	53 00	+60	180
1	49 00	60	179	50 00	60	179	51 00	60	179	52 00	60	179	53 00	60	178
2	48 58	60	177	49 58	60	177	50 58	60	177	51 58	60	177	52 58	60	177
3	48 56	60	176	49 56	60	176	50 56	60	175	51 56	60	175	52 56	60	175
4	48 53	60	174	49 53	60	174	50 53	60	174	51 53	60	174	52 53	60	174
5	48 49	+60	173	49 49	+60	173	50 49	+60	172	51 49	+60	172	52 49	+59	172
6	48 45	59	171	49 44	60	171	50 44	60	171	51 44	60	171	52 44	59	171
7	48 39	60	170	49 39	59	170	50 38	60	169	51 38	60	169	52 38	59	169
8	48 33	59	168	49 32	60	168	50 32	59	168	51 31	60	168	52 31	59	168
9	48 25	60	167	49 25	59	167	50 24	60	166	51 24	59	166	52 23	59	166
10	48 17	+60	165	49 17	+59	165	50 16	+59	165	51 15	+60	165	52 15	+59	164
11	48 08	60	164	49 08	59	164	50 07	59	164	51 06	59	163	52 05	59	163
12	47 59	59	163	48 58	59	162	49 57	59	162	50 56	59	162	51 55	59	161
13	47 48	59	161	48 47	59	161	49 46	59	161	50 45	59	160	51 44	58	160
14	47 37	59	160	48 36	59	159	49 35	58	159	50 33	59	159	51 32	58	158
15	47 25	+59	158	48 24	+58	158	49 22	+59	158	50 21	+58	157	51 19	+58	157
16	47 12	59	157	48 11	58	157	49 09	58	156	50 07	59	156	51 06	58	156
17	46 59	58	156	47 57	58	155	48 55	58	155	49 53	58	154	50 51	58	154
18	46 45	58	154	47 43	58	154	48 41	57	153	49 38	58	153	50 36	58	153
19	46 30	57	153	47 27	58	152	48 25	58	152	49 23	57	152	50 20	58	151
20	46 14	+58	152	47 12	+57	151	48 09	+57	151	49 06	+58	150	50 04	+57	150
21	45 58	57	150	46 55	57	150	47 52	57	149	48 49	58	149	49 47	57	148
22	45 41	57	149	46 38	57	148	47 35	57	148	48 32	57	148	49 29	56	147
23	45 23	57	148	46 20	57	147	47 17	56	147	48 13	57	146	49 10	56	146
24	45 04	57	146	46 01	57	146	46 58	56	145	47 54	57	145	48 51	56	144
25	44 45	+57	145	45 42	+56	144	46 38	+57	144	47 35	+56	143	48 31	+56	143
26	44 26	56	144	45 22	56	143	46 18	56	143	47 14	56	142	48 10	56	142
27	44 06	56	142	45 02	56	142	45 58	55	141	46 53	56	141	47 49	56	140
28	43 45	56	141	44 41	55	141	45 36	56	140	46 32	55	140	47 27	56	139
29	43 24	55	140	44 19	56	139	45 15	55	139	46 10	55	138	47 05	55	138
30	43 02	+55	139	43 57	+55	138	44 52	+55	138	45 47	+55	137	46 42	+55	136
31	42 39	55	137	43 34	55	137	44 29	55	136	45 24	55	136	46 19	54	135
32	42 16	55	136	43 11	55	136	44 06	54	135	45 00	55	135	45 55	54	134
33	41 53	55	135	42 48	54	135	43 42	54	134	44 36	54	133	45 30	54	133
34	41 29	54	134	42 23	55	133	43 18	54	133	44 12	54	132	45 06	53	132
35	41 04	+55	133	41 59	+54	132	42 53	+54	132	43 47	+53	131	44 40	+54	130
36	40 40	54	132	41 34	53	131	42 27	54	130	43 21	53	130	44 14	54	129
37	40 14	54	130	41 08	54	130	42 02	53	129	42 55	53	129	43 48	53	128
38	39 48	54	129	40 42	53	129	41 35	54	128	42 29	53	128	43 22	52	127
39	39 22	54	128	40 16	53	128	41 09	53	127	42 02	52	126	42 54	53	126
40	38 56	+53	127	39 49	+53	126	40 42	+52	126	41 34	+53	125	42 27	+52	125
41	38 29	53	126	39 22	52	125	40 14	53	125	41 07	52	124	41 59	52	123
42	38 01	53	125	38 54	53	124	39 47	52	124	40 39	52	123	41 31	52	122
43	37 34	52	124	38 26	53	123	39 19	52	123	40 11	51	122	41 02	52	121
44	37 06	52	123	37 58	52	122	38 50	52	122	39 42	52	121	40 34	51	120
45	36 37	+52	122	37 29	+52	121	38 21	+52	120	39 13	+51	120	40 04	+52	119
46	36 09	51	121	37 00	52	120	37 52	52	119	38 44	51	119	39 35	51	118
47	35 40	51	120	36 31	52	119	37 23	51	118	38 14	51	118	39 05	51	117
48	35 10	52	119	36 02	51	118	36 53	51	117	37 44	51	117	38 35	51	116
49	34 41	51	118	35 32	51	117	36 23	51	116	37 14	51	116	38 05	50	115
50	34 11	+51	117	35 02	+51	116	35 53	+51	115	36 44	+50	115	37 34	+51	114
51	33 41	51	116	34 32	51	115	35 23	50	114	36 13	51	114	37 04	50	113
52	33 10	51	115	34 01	51	114	34 52	50	113	35 42	51	113	36 33	50	112
53	32 40	50	114	33 30	51	113	34 21	50	112	35 11	50	112	36 01	50	111
54	32 09	50	113	32 59	51	112	33 50	50	111	34 40	50	111	35 30	50	110
55	31 38	+50	112	32 28	+50	111	33 18	+50	110	34 08	+50	110	34 58	+50	109
56	31 06	51	111	31 57	50	110	32 47	50	109	33 37	50	109	34 27	49	108
57	30 35	50	110	31 25	50	109	32 15	50	109	33 05	50	108	33 55	49	107
58	30 03	50	109	30 53	50	108	31 43	50	108	32 33	49	107	33 22	50	106
59	29 31	50	108	30 21	50	107	31 11	50	107	32 01	49	106	32 50	49	105
60	28 59	+50	107	29 49	+50	106	30 39	+49	106	31 28	+50	105	32 18	+49	104
61	28 27	50	106	29 17	50	105	30 07	49	105	30 56	49	104	31 45	49	104
62	27 55	50	105	28 45	49	105	29 34	49	104	30 23	49	103	31 12	49	103
63	27 22	50	104	28 12	49	104	29 01	50	103	29 51	49	102	30 40	48	102
64	26 50	49	103	27 39	50	103	28 29	49	102	29 18	49	101	30 07	48	101
65	26 17	+50	103	27 07	+49	102	27 56	+49	101	28 45	+49	101	29 34	+48	100
66	25 44	50	102	26 34	49	101	27 23	49	100	28 12	49	100	29 01	48	99
67	25 11	50	101	26 01	49	100	26 50	49	99	27 39	48	99	28 27	49	98
68	24 38	50	100	25 28	49	99	26 17	49	99	27 06	48	98	27 54	49	97
69	24 05	49	99	24 54	49	98	25 43	49	98	26 32	49	97	27 21	48	96

LHA	20° Hc	20° d	20° Z	21° Hc	21° d	21° Z	22° Hc	22° d	22° Z	23° Hc	23° d	23° Z	24° Hc	24° d	24° Z
	° ′	′	°	° ′	′	°	° ′	′	°	° ′	′	°	° ′	′	°
0	54 00	+60	180	55 00	+60	180	56 00	+60	180	57 00	+60	180	58 00	+60	180
1	54 00	60	178	55 00	60	178	56 00	60	178	57 00	60	178	58 00	60	178
2	53 58	60	177	54 58	60	177	55 58	60	177	56 58	60	177	57 58	60	177
3	53 56	60	175	54 56	60	175	55 56	60	175	56 56	60	175	57 56	59	175
4	53 53	59	174	54 52	60	174	55 52	60	173	56 52	60	173	57 52	60	173
5	53 48	+60	172	54 48	+60	172	55 48	+60	172	56 48	+59	172	57 47	+60	171
6	53 43	60	170	54 43	60	170	55 43	59	170	56 42	60	170	57 42	60	170
7	53 37	60	169	54 37	59	169	55 36	60	169	56 36	59	168	57 35	60	168
8	53 30	60	167	54 30	59	167	55 29	60	167	56 29	59	167	57 28	59	166
9	53 22	60	166	54 22	59	166	55 21	59	165	56 20	60	165	57 20	59	165
10	53 14	+59	164	54 13	+59	164	55 12	+59	164	56 11	+59	163	57 10	+59	163
11	53 04	59	163	54 03	59	162	55 02	59	162	56 01	59	162	57 00	59	161
12	52 54	59	161	53 53	58	161	54 51	59	160	55 50	59	160	56 49	58	160
13	52 42	59	160	53 41	59	159	54 40	58	159	55 38	59	159	56 37	58	158
14	52 30	59	158	53 29	58	158	54 27	59	157	55 26	58	157	56 24	58	157
15	52 17	+59	157	53 16	+58	156	54 14	+58	156	55 12	+58	155	56 10	+58	155
16	52 04	58	155	53 02	58	155	54 00	58	154	54 58	57	154	55 55	58	153
17	51 49	58	154	52 47	58	153	53 45	57	153	54 42	58	152	55 40	57	152
18	51 34	57	152	52 31	58	152	53 29	57	151	54 26	57	151	55 23	58	150
19	51 18	57	151	52 15	57	150	53 12	57	150	54 09	57	149	55 06	57	149
20	51 01	+57	149	51 58	+57	149	52 55	+57	148	53 52	+57	148	54 49	+56	147
21	50 44	56	148	51 40	57	147	52 37	57	147	53 34	56	146	54 30	56	146
22	50 25	57	147	51 22	56	146	52 18	57	145	53 15	56	145	54 11	56	144
23	50 06	57	145	51 03	56	145	51 59	56	144	52 55	56	143	53 51	55	143
24	49 47	56	144	50 43	56	143	51 39	56	143	52 35	55	142	53 30	56	141
25	49 27	+56	142	50 23	+55	142	51 18	+56	141	52 14	+55	141	53 09	+55	140
26	49 06	56	141	50 02	55	140	50 57	55	140	51 52	55	139	52 47	55	139
27	48 45	55	140	49 40	55	139	50 35	55	139	51 30	54	138	52 24	55	137
28	48 23	55	138	49 18	54	138	50 12	55	137	51 07	54	137	52 01	55	136
29	48 00	55	137	48 55	54	137	49 49	55	136	50 44	54	135	51 38	54	135
30	47 37	+54	136	48 31	+55	135	49 26	+54	135	50 20	+54	134	51 14	+53	133
31	47 13	54	135	48 07	54	134	49 01	54	133	49 55	54	133	50 49	53	132
32	46 49	54	133	47 43	54	133	48 37	53	132	49 30	54	131	50 24	53	131
33	46 24	54	132	47 18	54	131	48 12	53	131	49 05	53	130	49 58	53	129
34	45 59	54	131	46 53	53	130	47 46	53	130	48 39	53	129	49 32	52	128
35	45 34	+53	130	46 27	+53	129	47 20	+53	128	48 13	+52	128	49 05	+52	127
36	45 08	53	129	46 01	52	128	46 53	53	127	47 46	52	126	48 38	52	126
37	44 41	53	127	45 34	52	127	46 26	53	126	47 19	52	125	48 11	51	125
38	44 14	53	126	45 07	52	126	45 59	52	125	46 51	52	124	47 43	51	123
39	43 47	52	125	44 39	52	124	45 31	52	124	46 23	51	123	47 14	52	122
40	43 19	+52	124	44 11	+52	123	45 03	+52	123	45 55	+51	122	46 46	+51	121
41	42 51	52	123	43 43	52	122	44 35	51	121	45 26	51	121	46 17	51	120
42	42 23	51	122	43 14	52	121	44 06	51	120	44 57	51	120	45 48	50	119
43	41 54	52	121	42 46	51	120	43 37	51	119	44 28	50	118	45 18	50	118
44	41 25	51	120	42 16	51	119	43 07	51	118	43 58	50	117	44 48	50	117
45	40 56	+51	118	41 47	+50	118	42 37	+51	117	43 28	+50	116	44 18	+50	116
46	40 26	51	117	41 17	50	117	42 07	51	116	42 58	50	115	43 48	49	114
47	39 56	51	116	40 47	50	116	41 37	50	115	42 27	50	114	43 17	49	113
48	39 26	50	115	40 16	51	115	41 07	49	114	41 56	50	113	42 46	49	112
49	38 55	51	114	39 46	50	114	40 36	50	113	41 26	49	112	42 15	49	111
50	38 25	+50	113	39 15	+50	113	40 05	+49	112	40 54	+50	111	41 44	+49	110
51	37 54	50	112	38 44	49	112	39 33	50	111	40 23	49	110	41 12	49	109
52	37 23	49	111	38 12	50	111	39 02	49	110	39 51	49	109	40 40	49	108
53	36 51	50	110	37 41	49	110	38 30	50	109	39 20	48	108	40 08	49	107
54	36 20	49	109	37 09	50	109	37 59	49	108	38 48	48	107	39 36	49	106
55	35 48	+49	108	36 37	+50	108	37 27	+48	107	38 15	+49	106	39 04	+48	106
56	35 16	49	107	36 05	49	107	36 54	49	106	37 43	49	105	38 32	48	105
57	34 44	49	107	35 33	49	106	36 22	49	105	37 11	48	104	37 59	48	104
58	34 12	49	106	35 01	49	105	35 50	48	104	36 38	48	103	37 26	48	103
59	33 39	49	105	34 28	49	104	35 17	48	103	36 05	49	103	36 54	47	102
60	33 07	+49	104	33 56	+48	103	34 44	+49	102	35 33	+48	102	36 21	+47	101
61	32 34	49	103	33 23	48	102	34 11	49	101	35 00	48	101	35 48	47	100
62	32 01	49	102	32 50	48	101	33 38	49	101	34 27	48	100	35 15	47	99
63	31 28	49	101	32 17	48	100	33 05	49	100	33 54	47	99	34 41	48	98
64	30 55	49	100	31 44	48	99	32 32	48	99	33 20	48	98	34 08	48	97
65	30 22	+49	99	31 11	+48	99	31 59	+48	98	32 47	+48	97	33 35	+47	96
66	29 49	49	98	30 38	48	98	31 26	48	97	32 14	47	96	33 01	48	96
67	29 16	48	98	30 04	48	97	30 52	48	96	31 40	48	95	32 28	47	95
68	28 43	48	97	29 31	48	96	30 19	48	95	31 07	48	95	31 55	47	94
69	28 09	49	96	28 58	48	95	29 46	47	94	30 33	48	94	31 21	47	93

LHA	25° Hc	25° d	25° Z	26° Hc	26° d	26° Z	27° Hc	27° d	27° Z	28° Hc	28° d	28° Z	29° Hc	29° d	29° Z	LHA
	° ′	′	°	° ′	′	°	° ′	′	°	° ′	′	°	° ′	′	°	
0	59 00	+60	180	60 00	+60	180	61 00	+60	180	62 00	+60	180	63 00	+60	180	360
1	59 00	60	178	60 00	60	178	61 00	59	178	61 59	60	178	62 59	60	178	359
2	58 58	60	177	59 58	60	176	60 58	60	176	61 58	60	176	62 58	60	176	358
3	58 55	60	175	59 55	60	175	60 55	60	175	61 55	60	174	62 55	60	174	357
4	58 52	60	173	59 52	59	173	60 51	60	173	61 51	60	173	62 51	60	172	356
5	58 47	+60	171	59 47	+60	171	60 47	+59	171	61 46	+60	171	62 46	+60	170	355
6	58 42	59	170	59 41	60	169	60 41	59	169	61 40	60	169	62 40	59	169	354
7	58 35	59	168	59 34	60	168	60 34	59	167	61 33	60	167	62 33	59	167	353
8	58 27	60	166	59 27	59	166	60 26	59	165	61 25	59	165	62 24	59	165	352
9	58 19	59	164	59 18	59	164	60 17	59	164	61 16	59	163	62 15	59	163	351
10	58 09	+59	163	59 08	+59	162	60 07	+59	162	61 06	+59	162	62 05	+58	161	350
11	57 59	59	161	58 58	58	161	59 56	59	160	60 55	58	160	61 53	59	159	349
12	57 47	59	159	58 46	58	159	59 44	59	158	60 43	58	158	61 41	58	158	348
13	57 35	58	158	58 33	59	157	59 32	58	157	60 30	58	156	61 28	57	156	347
14	57 22	58	156	58 20	58	156	59 18	58	155	60 16	57	155	61 13	58	154	346
15	57 08	+58	154	58 06	+57	154	59 03	+58	153	60 01	+57	153	60 58	+57	152	345
16	56 53	57	153	57 50	58	152	58 48	57	152	59 45	57	151	60 42	57	151	344
17	56 37	57	151	57 34	57	151	58 31	57	150	59 28	57	150	60 25	57	149	343
18	56 21	57	150	57 18	56	149	58 14	57	149	59 11	56	148	60 07	56	147	342
19	56 03	57	148	57 00	56	148	57 56	57	147	58 53	56	146	59 49	55	146	341
20	55 45	+56	147	56 41	+57	146	57 38	+56	145	58 34	+55	145	59 29	+56	144	340
21	55 26	56	145	56 22	56	144	57 18	56	144	58 14	55	143	59 09	55	142	339
22	55 07	55	144	56 02	56	143	56 58	55	142	57 53	55	142	58 48	55	141	338
23	54 46	56	142	55 42	55	142	56 37	55	141	57 32	55	140	58 27	54	139	337
24	54 26	55	141	55 21	55	140	56 16	54	139	57 10	54	139	58 04	54	138	336
25	54 04	+55	139	54 59	+54	139	55 53	+55	138	56 48	+54	137	57 42	+53	136	335
26	53 42	54	138	54 36	54	137	55 30	54	136	56 24	54	136	57 18	53	135	334
27	53 19	54	137	54 13	54	136	55 07	54	135	56 01	53	134	56 54	53	133	333
28	52 56	53	135	53 49	54	134	54 43	53	134	55 36	53	133	56 29	53	132	332
29	52 32	53	134	53 25	53	133	54 18	53	132	55 11	53	131	56 04	52	131	331
30	52 07	+53	132	53 00	+53	132	53 53	+53	131	54 46	+52	130	55 38	+52	129	330
31	51 42	53	131	52 35	53	130	53 28	52	130	54 20	52	129	55 12	52	128	329
32	51 17	52	130	52 09	53	129	53 02	52	128	53 54	51	127	54 45	52	127	328
33	50 51	52	129	51 43	52	128	52 35	52	127	53 27	51	126	54 18	51	125	327
34	50 24	52	127	51 16	52	127	52 08	51	126	52 59	52	125	53 51	50	124	326
35	49 57	+52	126	50 49	+52	125	51 41	+51	125	52 32	+51	124	53 23	+50	123	325
36	49 30	51	125	50 21	52	124	51 13	51	123	52 04	50	122	52 54	50	122	324
37	49 02	52	124	49 54	50	123	50 44	51	122	51 35	50	121	52 25	50	120	323
38	48 34	51	123	49 25	51	122	50 16	50	121	51 06	50	120	51 56	50	119	322
39	48 06	50	121	48 56	51	121	49 47	50	120	50 37	50	119	51 27	49	118	321
40	47 37	+50	120	48 27	+51	119	49 18	+49	119	50 07	+50	118	50 57	+49	117	320
41	47 08	50	119	47 58	50	118	48 48	50	117	49 38	49	117	50 27	49	116	319
42	46 38	50	118	47 28	50	117	48 18	49	116	49 07	50	116	49 57	48	115	318
43	46 08	50	117	46 58	50	116	47 48	49	115	48 37	49	114	49 26	48	114	317
44	45 38	50	116	46 28	49	115	47 17	49	114	48 06	49	113	48 55	48	112	316
45	45 08	+49	115	45 57	+50	114	46 47	+48	113	47 35	+49	112	48 24	+48	111	315
46	44 37	50	114	45 27	49	113	46 16	48	112	47 04	48	111	47 52	48	110	314
47	44 06	50	113	44 56	48	112	45 44	49	111	46 33	48	110	47 21	48	109	313
48	43 35	49	112	44 24	49	111	45 13	48	110	46 01	48	109	46 49	48	108	312
49	43 04	49	111	43 53	48	110	44 41	48	109	45 29	48	108	46 17	47	107	311
50	42 33	+48	110	43 21	+49	109	44 10	+47	108	44 57	+48	107	45 45	+47	106	310
51	42 01	48	109	42 49	49	108	43 38	47	107	44 25	48	106	45 13	47	105	309
52	41 29	48	108	42 17	48	107	43 05	48	106	43 53	47	105	44 40	47	104	308
53	40 57	48	107	41 45	48	106	42 33	48	105	43 21	47	104	44 08	46	103	307
54	40 25	48	106	41 13	48	105	42 01	47	104	42 48	47	103	43 35	47	102	306
55	39 52	+48	105	40 40	+48	104	41 28	+47	103	42 15	+47	102	43 02	+47	101	305
56	39 20	48	104	40 08	47	103	40 55	47	102	41 42	47	101	42 29	47	101	304
57	38 47	48	103	39 35	47	102	40 22	47	101	41 09	47	100	41 56	47	100	303
58	38 14	48	102	39 02	47	101	39 49	47	100	40 36	47	100	41 23	46	99	302
59	37 41	48	101	38 29	47	100	39 16	47	99	40 03	47	99	40 50	46	98	301
60	37 08	+48	100	37 56	+47	99	38 43	+47	99	39 30	+47	98	40 17	+46	97	300
61	36 35	48	99	37 23	47	98	38 10	47	98	38 57	46	97	39 43	46	96	299
62	36 02	48	98	36 50	47	98	37 37	46	97	38 23	47	96	39 10	46	95	298
63	35 29	47	97	36 16	47	97	37 03	47	96	37 50	46	95	38 36	46	94	297
64	34 56	47	97	35 43	47	96	36 30	47	95	37 17	46	94	38 03	46	93	296
65	34 22	+48	96	35 10	+46	95	35 56	+47	94	36 43	+46	93	37 29	+46	93	295
66	33 49	47	95	34 36	47	94	35 23	47	93	36 10	46	93	36 56	46	92	294
67	33 15	48	94	34 03	46	93	34 49	47	92	35 36	46	92	36 22	46	91	293
68	32 42	47	93	33 29	47	92	34 16	47	92	35 03	46	91	35 49	46	90	292
69	32 08	48	92	32 56	46	92	33 42	47	91	34 29	46	90	35 15	46	89	291

S. Lat. {LHA greater than 180°....... Zn=180−Z; LHA less than 180°........... Zn=180+Z}

DECLINATION (15°-29°) SAME NAME AS LATITUDE

N. Lat. {LHA greater than 180°........ Zn=Z / LHA less than 180°........... Zn=360−Z}

DECLINATION (15°-29°) SAME NAME AS LATITUDE

LHA	15° Hc	15° d	15° Z	16° Hc	16° d	16° Z	17° Hc	17° d	17° Z	18° Hc	18° d	18° Z	19° Hc	19° d	19° Z
	° ′	′	°	° ′	′	°	° ′	′	°	° ′	′	°	° ′	′	°
70	23 32	+49	98	24 21	+49	98	25 10	+49	97	25 59	+49	96	26 48	+48	96
71	22 59	49	97	23 48	49	97	24 37	49	96	25 26	48	95	26 14	48	95
72	22 26	49	96	23 15	48	96	24 03	49	95	24 52	49	95	25 41	48	94
73	21 52	49	96	22 41	49	95	23 30	49	94	24 19	48	94	25 07	48	93
74	21 19	49	95	22 08	49	94	22 57	48	93	23 45	49	93	24 34	48	92
75	20 45	+49	94	21 34	+49	93	22 23	+49	93	23 12	+48	92	24 00	+48	91
76	20 12	49	93	21 01	48	92	21 49	49	92	22 38	49	91	23 27	48	91
77	19 38	49	92	20 27	49	92	21 16	49	91	22 05	48	90	22 53	48	90
78	19 05	49	91	19 54	48	91	20 42	49	90	21 31	48	90	22 19	49	89
79	18 31	49	91	19 20	49	90	20 09	48	89	20 57	49	89	21 46	48	88
80	17 58	+49	90	18 47	+48	89	19 35	+49	88	20 24	+48	88	21 12	+49	87
81	17 24	49	89	18 13	49	88	19 02	48	88	19 50	49	87	20 39	48	86
82	16 51	48	88	17 39	49	87	18 28	49	87	19 17	48	86	20 05	49	86
83	16 17	49	87	17 06	49	87	17 55	48	86	18 43	49	85	19 32	48	85
84	15 44	49	86	16 33	48	86	17 21	49	85	18 10	49	85	18 59	48	84
85	15 10	+49	86	15 59	+49	85	16 48	+49	84	17 37	+48	84	18 25	+49	83
86	14 37	49	85	15 26	49	84	16 15	48	84	17 03	49	83	17 52	49	82
87	14 03	49	84	14 52	49	83	15 41	49	83	16 30	49	82	17 19	48	82
88	13 30	49	83	14 19	49	83	15 08	49	82	15 57	49	81	16 46	48	81
89	12 57	49	82	13 46	49	82	14 35	49	81	15 24	49	81	16 13	48	80
90	12 23	+50	82	13 13	+49	81	14 02	+49	80	14 51	+49	80	15 40	+48	79
91	11 50	50	81	12 40	49	80	13 29	49	80	14 18	49	79	15 07	49	78
92	11 17	50	80	12 07	49	79	12 56	49	79	13 45	49	78	14 34	49	78
93	10 44	50	79	11 34	49	79	12 23	49	78	13 12	49	77	14 01	49	77
94	10 11	50	78	11 01	49	78	11 50	49	77	12 39	50	77	13 29	49	76
95	09 39	+49	77	10 28	+49	77	11 17	+50	76	12 07	+49	76	12 56	+49	75
96	09 06	49	77	09 55	50	76	10 45	49	76	11 34	50	75	12 24	49	74
97	08 33	50	76	09 23	50	75	10 13	49	75	11 02	49	74	11 51	50	74
98	08 01	50	75	08 51	49	74	09 40	50	74	10 30	49	73	11 19	50	73
99	07 28	50	74	08 18	50	74	09 08	50	73	09 58	49	73	10 47	50	72
100	06 56	+50	73	07 46	+50	73	08 36	+50	72	09 26	+50	72	10 16	+49	71
101	06 24	50	73	07 14	50	72	08 04	50	72	08 54	50	71	09 44	50	70
102	05 52	50	72	06 42	50	71	07 32	50	71	08 22	50	70	09 12	50	70
103	05 20	51	71	06 11	50	70	07 01	50	70	07 51	50	69	08 41	50	69
104	04 49	50	70	05 39	50	70	06 29	51	69	07 20	50	69	08 10	50	68
105	04 17	+51	69	05 08	+50	69	05 58	+51	68	06 49	+50	68	07 39	+50	67
106	03 46	51	69	04 37	50	68	05 27	51	67	06 18	50	67	07 08	50	66
107	03 15	51	68	04 06	50	67	04 56	51	67	05 47	50	66	06 37	51	66
108	02 44	51	67	03 35	50	66	04 25	51	66	05 16	51	65	06 07	51	65
109	02 13	51	66	03 04	51	66	03 55	51	65	04 46	51	64	05 37	51	64
110	01 43	+51	65	02 34	+51	65	03 25	+51	64	04 16	+51	64	05 07	+51	63
111	01 12	51	64	02 03	52	64	02 55	51	63	03 46	51	63	04 37	51	62
112	00 42	51	64	01 33	52	63	02 25	51	63	03 16	51	62	04 07	51	62
113	00 12	52	63	01 04	51	62	01 55	51	62	02 46	52	61	03 38	51	61
114	−0 18	52	62	00 34	52	61	01 26	51	61	02 17	52	60	03 09	51	60
115	−0 47	+52	61	00 05	+51	61	00 56	+52	60	01 48	+52	60	02 40	+51	59
116	−1 16	52	60	−0 24	51	60	00 27	52	59	01 19	52	59	02 11	52	58
117	−1 45	52	59	−0 53	52	59	−0 01	52	58	00 51	52	58	01 43	52	57
118	−2 14	52	59	−1 22	52	58	−0 30	52	58	00 22	53	57	01 15	52	57
119	−2 43	53	58	−1 50	52	57	−0 58	52	57	−0 06	53	56	00 47	52	56
120	−3 11	+53	57	−2 18	+52	56	−1 26	+53	56	−0 33	+52	55	00 19	+53	55
121	−3 39	53	56	−2 46	52	56	−1 54	53	55	−1 01	53	55	−0 08	52	54
122	−4 07	53	55	−3 14	53	55	−2 21	53	54	−1 28	53	54	−0 35	53	53
123	−4 34	53	54	−3 41	53	54	−2 48	53	53	−1 55	53	53	−1 02	53	52
124	−5 01	53	53	−4 08	53	53	−3 15	53	53	−2 22	53	52	−1 29	54	52
125	−5 28	+53	53	−4 35	+54	52	−3 41	+53	52	−2 48	+53	51	−1 55	+54	51
126				−5 01	53	51	−4 08	54	51	−3 14	53	50	−2 21	54	50
127				−5 27	54	50	−4 33	53	50	−3 40	54	50	−2 46	54	49
128							−4 59	54	49	−4 05	54	49	−3 11	54	48
129							−5 24	54	48	−4 30	54	48	−3 36	54	47
130							−5 49	+54	47	−4 55	+54	47	−4 01	+55	47
131										−5 19	54	46	−4 25	55	46
132										−5 43	54	45	−4 49	55	45
133													−5 12	55	44
134													−5 35	55	43

LHA	20° Hc	20° d	20° Z	21° Hc	21° d	21° Z	22° Hc	22° d	22° Z	23° Hc	23° d	23° Z	24° Hc	24° d	24° Z
	° ′	′	°	° ′	′	°	° ′	′	°	° ′	′	°	° ′	′	°
70	27 36	+48	95	28 24	+48	94	29 12	+48	94	30 00	+48	93	30 48	+47	92
71	27 02	49	94	27 51	48	93	28 39	47	93	29 26	48	92	30 14	47	91
72	26 29	48	93	27 17	48	93	28 05	48	92	28 53	47	91	29 40	48	90
73	25 55	49	92	26 44	48	92	27 32	47	91	28 19	48	90	29 07	47	90
74	25 22	48	92	26 10	48	91	26 58	48	90	27 46	47	90	28 33	48	89
75	24 48	+49	91	25 37	+48	90	26 25	+47	89	27 12	+48	89	28 00	+47	88
76	24 15	48	90	25 03	48	89	25 51	48	89	26 39	47	88	27 26	48	87
77	23 41	48	89	24 29	48	88	25 17	48	88	26 05	48	87	26 53	47	86
78	23 08	48	88	23 56	48	88	24 44	48	87	25 32	47	86	26 19	48	86
79	22 34	48	87	23 22	48	87	24 10	48	86	24 58	48	85	25 46	47	85
80	22 01	+48	87	22 49	+48	86	23 37	+48	85	24 25	+48	85	25 13	+47	84
81	21 27	48	86	22 15	49	85	23 04	47	84	23 51	48	84	24 39	48	83
82	20 54	48	85	21 42	48	84	22 30	48	84	23 18	48	83	24 06	48	82
83	20 20	49	84	21 09	48	84	21 57	48	83	22 45	48	82	23 33	47	82
84	19 47	48	83	20 35	49	83	21 24	48	82	22 12	48	81	23 00	47	81
85	19 14	+48	83	20 02	+48	82	20 50	+49	81	21 39	+47	81	22 26	+48	80
86	18 41	48	82	19 29	48	81	20 17	48	80	21 05	48	80	21 53	48	79
87	18 07	49	81	18 56	48	80	19 44	48	80	20 32	49	79	21 21	48	78
88	17 34	49	80	18 23	48	80	19 11	49	79	20 00	48	78	20 48	48	78
89	17 01	49	79	17 50	48	79	18 38	49	78	19 27	48	77	20 15	48	77
90	16 28	+49	79	17 17	+49	78	18 06	+48	77	18 54	+48	77	19 42	+49	76
91	15 56	48	78	16 44	49	77	17 33	49	77	18 22	48	76	19 10	48	75
92	15 23	49	77	16 12	48	76	17 00	49	76	17 49	49	75	18 38	48	75
93	14 50	49	76	15 39	49	76	16 28	49	75	17 17	48	74	18 05	49	74
94	14 18	49	75	15 07	49	75	15 56	48	74	16 44	49	74	17 33	49	73
95	13 45	+49	75	14 34	+49	74	15 23	+49	73	16 12	+49	73	17 01	+49	72
96	13 13	49	74	14 02	49	73	14 51	49	73	15 40	49	72	16 29	49	71
97	12 41	49	73	13 30	49	72	14 19	50	72	15 09	49	71	15 58	49	71
98	12 09	49	72	12 58	50	72	13 48	49	71	14 37	49	70	15 26	49	70
99	11 37	50	71	12 27	49	71	13 16	49	70	14 05	50	70	14 55	49	69
100	11 05	+50	71	11 55	+49	70	12 44	+50	69	13 34	+49	69	14 23	+50	68
101	10 34	49	70	11 23	50	69	12 13	50	69	13 03	49	68	13 52	50	68
102	10 02	50	69	10 52	50	68	11 42	50	68	12 32	49	67	13 21	50	67
103	09 31	50	68	10 21	50	68	11 11	50	67	12 01	50	67	12 51	49	66
104	09 00	50	67	09 50	50	67	10 40	50	66	11 30	50	66	12 20	50	65
105	08 29	+50	67	09 19	+51	66	10 10	+50	66	11 00	+50	65	11 50	+50	64
106	07 58	51	66	08 49	50	65	09 39	50	65	10 29	51	64	11 20	50	64
107	07 28	50	65	08 18	51	65	09 09	50	64	09 59	51	63	10 50	50	63
108	06 58	50	64	07 48	51	64	08 39	50	63	09 29	51	63	10 20	50	62
109	06 28	50	63	07 18	51	63	08 09	51	62	09 00	50	62	09 50	51	61
110	05 58	+51	63	06 49	+50	62	07 39	+51	62	08 30	+51	61	09 21	+51	61
111	05 28	51	62	06 19	51	61	07 10	51	61	08 01	51	60	08 52	51	60
112	04 58	52	61	05 50	51	61	06 41	51	60	07 32	51	59	08 23	51	59
113	04 29	52	60	05 21	51	60	06 12	51	59	07 03	52	59	07 55	51	58
114	04 00	52	59	04 52	51	59	05 43	52	58	06 35	51	58	07 26	52	57
115	03 31	+52	59	04 23	+52	58	05 15	+51	58	06 06	+52	57	06 58	+52	57
116	03 03	52	58	03 55	52	57	04 47	51	57	05 38	52	56	06 30	52	56
117	02 35	52	57	03 27	52	56	04 19	52	56	05 11	52	55	06 03	52	55
118	02 07	52	56	02 59	52	56	03 51	52	55	04 43	52	55	05 35	52	54
119	01 39	52	55	02 31	53	55	03 24	52	54	04 16	52	54	05 08	53	53
120	01 12	+52	54	02 04	+53	54	02 57	+52	54	03 49	+52	53	04 41	+53	53
121	00 44	53	54	01 37	53	53	02 30	52	53	03 22	53	52	04 15	53	52
122	00 18	52	53	01 10	53	52	02 03	53	52	02 56	53	51	03 49	53	51
123	−0 09	53	52	00 44	53	52	01 37	53	51	02 30	53	51	03 23	53	50
124	−0 35	53	51	00 18	53	51	01 11	53	50	02 04	53	50	02 57	53	49
125	−1 01	+53	50	−0 08	+53	50	00 45	+54	49	01 39	+53	49	02 32	+53	48
126	−1 27	53	50	−0 34	54	49	00 20	53	49	01 13	54	48	02 07	53	48
127	−1 52	53	49	−0 59	54	48	−0 05	54	48	00 49	53	47	01 42	54	47
128	−2 17	53	48	−1 24	54	47	−0 30	54	47	00 24	54	46	01 18	54	46
129	−2 42	54	47	−1 48	54	47	−0 54	54	46	00 00	54	46	00 54	54	45
130	−3 06	+54	46	−2 12	+54	46	1 18	+54	45	−0 24	+54	45	00 30	+55	44
131	−3 30	54	45	−2 36	54	45	−1 42	55	44	−0 47	54	44	00 07	54	44
132	−3 54	54	44	−3 00	55	44	−2 05	55	44	−1 10	54	43	−0 16	55	43
133	−4 17	54	44	−3 23	55	43	−2 28	55	43	−1 33	55	42	−0 38	54	42
134	−4 40	55	43	−3 45	54	42	−2 51	55	42	−1 56	55	41	−1 01	55	41
135	−5 03	+55	42	−4 08	+55	41	−3 13	+55	41	−2 18	+55	41	−1 23	+56	40
136	−5 25	55	41	−4 30	55	41	−3 35	55	40	−2 40	56	40	−1 44	55	39
137				−4 52	56	40	−3 56	55	39	−3 01	56	39	−2 05	55	39
138				−5 13	56	39	−4 17	55	38	−3 22	56	38	−2 26	56	38
139				−5 34	56	38	−4 38	56	38	−3 42	56	37	−2 46	56	37

LHA	25° Hc	25° d	25° Z	26° Hc	26° d	26° Z	27° Hc	27° d	27° Z	28° Hc	28° d	28° Z	29° Hc	29° d	29° Z	LHA
	° ′	′	°	° ′	′	°	° ′	′	°	° ′	′	°	° ′	′	°	
70	31 35	+47	91	32 22	+47	91	33 09	+46	90	33 55	+47	89	34 42	+46	88	290
71	31 01	47	91	31 48	47	90	32 35	47	89	33 22	46	88	34 08	46	88	289
72	30 28	47	90	31 15	47	89	32 02	46	88	32 48	47	88	33 35	46	87	288
73	29 54	47	89	30 41	47	88	31 28	47	88	32 15	46	87	33 01	46	86	287
74	29 21	47	88	30 08	47	87	30 55	46	87	31 41	47	86	32 28	46	85	286
75	28 47	+47	87	29 34	+47	87	30 21	+47	86	31 08	+46	85	31 54	+46	84	285
76	28 14	47	86	29 01	47	86	29 48	47	85	30 35	46	84	31 21	46	84	284
77	27 40	47	86	28 27	47	85	29 14	47	84	30 01	47	84	30 48	46	83	283
78	27 07	47	85	27 54	47	84	28 41	47	83	29 28	46	83	30 14	47	82	282
79	26 33	48	84	27 21	47	83	28 08	47	83	28 55	46	82	29 41	47	81	281
80	26 00	+47	83	26 47	+47	83	27 34	+47	82	28 21	+47	81	29 08	+47	80	280
81	25 27	47	82	26 14	47	82	27 01	47	81	27 48	47	80	28 35	47	80	279
82	24 54	47	82	25 41	47	81	26 28	47	80	27 15	47	80	28 02	47	79	278
83	24 20	48	81	25 08	47	80	25 55	47	80	26 42	47	79	27 29	47	78	277
84	23 47	48	80	24 35	47	79	25 22	47	79	26 09	47	78	26 56	47	77	276
85	23 14	+48	79	24 02	+47	79	24 49	+48	78	25 37	+47	77	26 24	+47	77	275
86	22 41	48	79	23 29	48	78	24 17	47	77	25 04	47	77	25 51	47	76	274
87	22 09	47	78	22 56	48	77	23 44	47	76	24 31	48	76	25 19	47	75	273
88	21 36	48	77	22 24	47	76	23 11	48	76	23 59	47	75	24 46	48	74	272
89	21 03	48	76	21 51	48	76	22 39	48	75	23 27	47	74	24 14	47	74	271
90	20 31	+48	75	21 19	+48	75	22 07	+47	74	22 54	+48	73	23 42	+47	73	270
91	19 58	48	75	20 46	48	74	21 34	48	73	22 22	48	73	23 10	48	72	269
92	19 26	48	74	20 14	48	73	21 02	48	73	21 50	48	72	22 38	48	71	268
93	18 54	48	73	19 42	48	72	20 30	48	72	21 18	48	71	22 06	48	71	267
94	18 22	48	72	19 10	49	72	19 59	48	71	20 47	48	70	21 35	48	70	266
95	17 50	+48	72	18 38	+49	71	19 27	+48	70	20 15	+48	70	21 03	+49	69	265
96	17 18	49	71	18 07	48	70	18 55	49	70	19 44	48	69	20 32	48	68	264
97	16 47	48	70	17 35	49	69	18 24	49	69	19 13	48	68	20 01	48	68	263
98	16 15	49	69	17 04	49	69	17 53	49	68	18 42	48	67	19 30	49	67	262
99	15 44	49	68	16 33	49	68	17 22	49	67	18 11	48	67	18 59	49	66	261
100	15 13	+49	68	16 02	+49	67	16 51	+49	67	17 40	+49	66	18 29	+49	65	260
101	14 42	49	67	15 31	49	66	16 20	50	66	17 10	49	65	17 59	49	65	259
102	14 11	49	66	15 00	50	66	15 50	49	65	16 39	49	64	17 28	49	64	258
103	13 40	50	65	14 30	50	65	15 20	49	64	16 09	49	64	16 58	50	63	257
104	13 10	50	65	14 00	49	64	14 49	50	63	15 39	50	63	16 29	49	62	256
105	12 40	+50	64	13 30	+50	63	14 20	+49	63	15 09	+50	62	15 59	+50	62	255
106	12 10	50	63	13 00	50	63	13 50	50	62	14 40	50	61	15 30	49	61	254
107	11 40	50	62	12 30	50	62	13 20	50	61	14 10	50	61	15 00	50	60	253
108	11 10	51	62	12 01	50	61	12 51	50	60	13 41	51	60	14 32	50	59	252
109	10 41	51	61	11 32	50	60	12 22	50	60	13 12	51	59	14 03	50	59	251
110	10 12	+51	60	11 03	+50	59	11 53	+51	59	12 44	+50	58	13 34	+51	58	250
111	09 43	51	59	10 34	51	59	11 25	50	58	12 15	51	58	13 06	51	57	249
112	09 14	51	58	10 05	51	58	10 56	51	57	11 47	51	57	12 38	51	56	248
113	08 46	51	58	09 37	51	57	10 28	51	57	11 19	51	56	12 10	51	55	247
114	08 18	51	57	09 09	51	56	10 00	52	56	10 52	51	55	11 43	51	55	246
115	07 50	+51	56	08 41	+52	56	09 33	+51	55	10 24	+52	54	11 16	+51	54	245
116	07 22	52	55	08 14	51	55	09 05	52	54	09 57	52	54	10 49	51	53	244
117	06 55	51	54	07 46	52	54	08 38	52	53	09 30	52	53	10 22	52	52	243
118	06 27	52	54	07 19	52	53	08 11	52	53	09 03	52	52	09 55	52	52	242
119	06 01	52	53	06 53	52	52	07 45	52	52	08 37	52	51	09 29	52	51	241
120	05 34	+52	52	06 26	+53	52	07 19	+52	51	08 11	+52	51	09 03	+53	50	240
121	05 08	52	51	06 00	53	51	06 53	52	50	07 45	53	50	08 38	52	49	239
122	04 42	52	50	05 34	53	50	06 27	53	50	07 20	52	49	08 12	53	49	238
123	04 16	53	50	05 09	53	49	06 02	53	49	06 55	52	48	07 47	53	48	237
124	03 50	54	49	04 44	53	48	05 37	53	48	06 30	53	48	07 23	53	47	236
125	03 25	+54	48	04 19	+53	48	05 12	+53	47	06 05	+53	47	06 58	+54	46	235
126	03 00	54	47	03 54	53	47	04 47	54	46	05 41	53	46	06 34	54	45	234
127	02 36	54	46	03 30	53	46	04 23	54	46	05 17	54	45	06 11	53	45	233
128	02 12	54	46	03 06	54	45	04 00	53	45	04 53	54	44	05 47	54	44	232
129	01 48	54	45	02 42	54	44	03 36	54	44	04 30	54	43	05 24	54	43	231
130	01 25	+54	44	02 19	+54	44	03 13	+54	43	04 07	+54	43	05 01	+55	42	230
131	01 01	55	43	01 56	54	43	02 50	55	42	03 45	54	42	04 39	54	41	229
132	00 39	54	42	01 33	55	42	02 28	54	42	03 22	55	41	04 17	55	41	228
133	00 16	55	42	01 11	55	41	02 06	54	41	03 00	55	40	03 55	55	40	227
134	−0 06	55	41	00 49	55	40	01 44	55	40	02 39	55	39	03 34	55	39	226
135	−0 27	+55	40	00 28	+55	39	01 23	+55	39	02 18	+55	39	03 13	+55	38	225
136	−0 49	55	39	00 06	56	39	01 02	55	38	01 57	55	38	02 52	56	37	224
137	−1 10	56	38	−0 14	55	38	00 41	56	37	01 37	55	37	02 32	56	37	223
138	−1 30	55	37	−0 35	56	37	00 21	56	37	01 17	55	36	02 12	56	36	222
139	−1 50	55	37	−0 55	56	36	00 01	56	36	00 57	56	35	01 53	56	35	221

S. Lat. {LHA greater than 180°....... Zn=180−Z / LHA less than 180°........... Zn=180+Z}

DECLINATION (15°-29°) SAME NAME AS LATITUDE

N. Lat. {LHA greater than 180°....... Zn=Z; LHA less than 180°........... Zn=360−Z}

DECLINATION (15°-29°) SAME NAME AS LATITUDE

LHA	22° Hc	d	Z	23° Hc	d	Z	24° Hc	d	Z	25° Hc	d	Z	26° Hc	d	Z	27° Hc	d	Z	28° Hc	d	Z	29° Hc	d	Z	LHA
	° ′	′	°	° ′	′	°	° ′	′	°	° ′	′	°	° ′	′	°	° ′	′	°	° ′	′	°	° ′	′	°	
140	-4 58	+56	37	-4 02	+56	36	-3 06	+56	36	-2 10	+56	36	-1 14	+56	35	-0 18	+56	35	00 38	+56	35	01 34	+56	34	220
141	-5 18	56	36	-4 22	56	36	-3 26	56	35	-2 30	57	35	-1 33	56	34	-0 37	56	34	00 19	56	34	01 15	56	33	219
142	-5 37	56	35	-4 41	56	35	-3 45	56	34	-2 49	57	34	-1 52	56	34	-0 56	56	33	00 00	57	33	00 57	56	33	218
143				-5 00	56	34	-4 04	57	33	-3 07	56	33	-2 11	57	33	-1 14	56	32	-0 18	57	32	00 39	56	32	217
144				-5 19	57	33	-4 22	57	33	-3 25	56	32	-2 29	57	32	-1 32	57	32	-0 35	56	31	00 21	57	31	216
145							-4 40	+57	32	-3 43	+57	31	-2 46	+57	31	-1 49	+57	31	-0 52	+56	30	00 04	+57	30	215
146							-4 57	57	31	-4 00	57	31	-3 03	57	30	-2 06	57	30	-1 09	57	30	-0 12	57	29	214
147							-5 14	57	30	-4 17	57	30	-3 20	57	29	-2 23	57	29	-1 26	58	29	-0 28	57	28	213
148							-5 31	58	29	-4 33	57	29	-3 36	57	28	-2 39	58	28	-1 41	57	28	-0 44	57	28	212
149										-4 49	57	28	-3 52	58	28	-2 54	57	27	-1 57	58	27	-0 59	57	27	211
150										-5 05	+58	27	-4 07	+57	27	-3 10	+58	26	-2 12	+58	26	-1 14	+57	26	210
151										-5 20	58	26	-4 22	58	26	-3 24	57	26	-2 27	58	25	-1 29	58	25	209
152													-4 36	57	25	-3 39	58	25	-2 41	58	25	-1 43	58	24	208
153													-4 50	58	24	-3 52	58	24	-2 54	58	24	-1 56	58	23	207
154													-5 04	58	23	-4 06	58	23	-3 08	59	23	-2 09	58	23	206
155													-5 17	+58	22	-4 19	+59	22	-3 20	+58	22	-2 22	+58	22	205
156																-4 31	58	21	-3 33	59	21	-2 34	58	21	204
157																-4 43	58	20	-3 45	59	20	-2 46	59	20	203
158																-4 55	59	20	-3 56	59	19	-2 57	59	19	202
159																-5 06	59	19	-4 07	59	18	-3 08	59	18	201
160																-5 16	+59	18	-4 17	+59	18	-3 18	+59	17	200
161																			-4 27	59	17	-3 28	59	17	199
162																			-4 37	60	16	-3 37	59	16	198
163																			-4 46	60	15	-3 46	59	15	197
164																			-4 54	59	14	-3 55	60	14	196
165																			-5 02	+59	13	-4 03	+60	13	195
166																			-5 09	59	12	-4 10	60	12	194
167																						-4 17	60	11	193
168																						-4 23	59	10	192
169																						-4 29	60	10	191
170																						-4 34	+60	9	190
171																						-4 39	60	8	189
172																						-4 44	60	7	188
173																						-4 47	59	6	187
174																						-4 51	60	5	186
175																						-4 54	+60	4	185
176																						-4 56	60	4	184
177																						-4 58	60	3	183
178																						-4 59	60	2	182
179																						-5 00	60	1	181
180																						-5 00	+60	0	180

LHA	15° Hc	d	Z	16° Hc	d	Z	17° Hc	d	Z	18° Hc	d	Z	19° Hc	d	Z	20° Hc	d	Z	LHA
78	-5 52	50	108																282
77	-5 20	51	109																283
76	-4 49	50	110	-5 39	50	110													284
75	-4 17	-51	111	-5 08	-50	111	-5 58	-51	112										285
74	-3 46	51	111	-4 37	50	112	-5 27	51	113										286
73	-3 15	51	112	-4 06	50	113	-4 56	51	113	-5 47	50	114							287
72	-2 44	51	113	-3 35	50	114	-4 25	51	114	-5 16	51	115							288
71	-2 13	51	114	-3 04	51	114	-3 55	51	115	-4 46	51	116	-5 37	51	116				289
70	-1 43	-51	115	-2 34	-51	115	-3 25	-51	116	-4 16	-51	116	-5 07	-51	117	-5 58	-51	117	290

S. Lat. {LHA greater than 180°....... Zn=180−Z; LHA less than 180°........... Zn=180+Z}

DECLINATION (15°-29°) CONTRARY NAME TO LATITUDE

N. Lat. {LHA greater than 180°....... Zn=Z; LHA less than 180°.......... Zn=360−Z

DECLINATION (15°-29°) CONTRARY NAME TO LATITUDE

LHA	15° Hc	d	Z	16° Hc	d	Z	17° Hc	d	Z	18° Hc	d	Z	19° Hc	d	Z
	° ′	′	°	° ′	′	°	° ′	′	°	° ′	′	°	° ′	′	°
69	-1 12	51	116	-2 03	52	116	-2 55	51	117	-3 46	51	117	-4 37	51	118
68	-0 42	51	116	-1 33	52	117	-2 25	51	117	-3 16	51	118	-4 07	51	118
67	-0 12	52	117	-1 04	51	118	-1 55	51	118	-2 46	52	119	-3 38	51	119
66	00 18	52	118	-0 34	52	119	-1 26	51	119	-2 17	52	120	-3 09	51	120
65	00 47	-52	119	-0 05	-51	119	-0 56	-52	120	-1 48	-52	120	-2 40	-51	121
64	01 16	52	120	00 24	51	120	-0 27	52	121	-1 19	52	121	-2 11	52	122
63	01 45	52	121	00 53	52	121	00 01	52	122	-0 51	52	122	-1 43	52	123
62	02 14	52	121	01 22	52	122	00 30	52	122	-0 22	53	123	-1 15	52	123
61	02 43	53	122	01 50	52	123	00 58	52	123	00 06	53	124	-0 47	52	124
60	03 11	-53	123	02 18	-52	124	01 26	-53	124	00 33	-52	125	-0 19	-53	125
59	03 39	53	124	02 46	52	124	01 54	53	125	01 01	53	125	00 08	52	126
58	04 07	53	125	03 14	53	125	02 21	53	126	01 28	53	126	00 35	53	127
57	04 34	53	126	03 41	53	126	02 48	53	127	01 55	53	127	01 02	53	128
56	05 01	53	127	04 08	53	127	03 15	53	127	02 22	53	128	01 29	54	128
55	05 28	-53	127	04 35	-54	128	03 41	-53	128	02 48	-53	129	01 55	-54	129
54	05 54	53	128	05 01	53	129	04 08	54	129	03 14	53	130	02 21	54	130
53	06 21	54	129	05 27	54	130	04 33	53	130	03 40	54	130	02 46	54	131
52	06 47	54	130	05 53	54	130	04 59	54	131	04 05	54	131	03 11	54	132
51	07 12	54	131	06 18	54	131	05 24	54	132	04 30	54	132	03 36	54	133
50	07 37	-54	132	06 43	-54	132	05 49	-54	133	04 55	-54	133	04 01	-55	133
49	08 02	54	133	07 08	54	133	06 14	55	133	05 19	54	134	04 25	55	134
48	08 27	55	134	07 32	54	134	06 38	55	134	05 43	54	135	04 49	55	135
47	08 51	55	134	07 56	54	135	07 02	55	135	06 07	55	136	05 12	55	136
46	09 15	55	135	08 20	55	136	07 25	55	136	06 30	55	137	05 35	55	137
45	09 38	-55	136	08 43	-55	137	07 48	-55	137	06 53	-55	137	05 58	-55	138
44	10 01	55	137	09 06	55	137	08 11	55	138	07 16	56	138	06 20	55	139
43	10 24	55	138	09 29	56	138	08 33	55	139	07 38	56	139	06 42	55	140
42	10 46	55	139	09 51	56	139	08 55	55	140	08 00	56	140	07 04	56	140
41	11 08	56	140	10 12	55	140	09 17	56	141	08 21	56	141	07 25	56	141
40	11 29	-55	141	10 34	-56	141	09 38	-56	141	08 42	-56	142	07 46	-56	142
39	11 51	56	142	10 55	57	142	09 58	56	142	09 02	56	143	08 06	56	143
38	12 11	56	143	11 15	56	143	10 19	56	143	09 23	57	144	08 26	56	144
37	12 31	56	144	11 35	56	144	10 39	57	144	09 42	56	145	08 46	57	145
36	12 51	56	144	11 55	57	145	10 58	56	145	10 02	57	145	09 05	57	146
35	13 10	-56	145	12 14	-57	146	11 17	-57	146	10 20	-56	146	09 24	-57	147
34	13 29	57	146	12 32	56	147	11 36	57	147	10 39	57	147	09 42	57	148
33	13 48	57	147	12 51	57	148	11 54	57	148	10 57	57	148	10 00	57	149
32	14 06	58	148	13 08	57	149	12 11	57	149	11 14	57	149	10 17	57	149
31	14 23	57	149	13 26	58	149	12 28	57	150	11 31	57	150	10 34	58	150
30	14 40	-57	150	13 43	-58	150	12 45	-57	151	11 48	-58	151	10 50	-57	151
29	14 57	58	151	13 59	58	151	13 01	57	152	12 04	58	152	11 06	58	152
28	15 13	58	152	14 15	58	152	13 17	58	153	12 19	58	153	11 21	57	153
27	15 28	58	153	14 30	58	153	13 32	58	154	12 34	58	154	11 36	58	154
26	15 43	58	154	14 45	58	154	13 47	58	154	12 49	58	155	11 51	58	155
25	15 58	-59	155	14 59	-58	155	14 01	-58	155	13 03	-58	156	12 05	-58	156
24	16 12	59	156	15 13	58	156	14 15	58	156	13 17	59	157	12 18	58	157
23	16 25	58	157	15 27	59	157	14 28	58	157	13 30	59	158	12 31	58	158
22	16 38	59	158	15 39	58	158	14 41	59	158	13 42	58	159	12 44	59	159
21	16 50	58	159	15 52	59	159	14 53	59	159	13 54	58	159	12 56	59	160
20	17 02	-59	160	16 03	-58	160	15 05	-59	160	14 06	-59	160	13 07	-59	161
19	17 14	59	161	16 15	59	161	15 16	59	161	14 17	59	161	13 18	59	162
18	17 24	59	162	16 25	59	162	15 26	59	162	14 27	59	162	13 28	59	163
17	17 35	60	163	16 35	59	163	15 36	59	163	14 37	59	163	13 38	59	164
16	17 44	59	164	16 45	59	164	15 46	59	164	14 47	60	164	13 47	59	164
15	17 53	-59	165	16 54	-59	165	15 55	-60	165	14 55	-59	165	13 56	-59	165
14	18 02	60	166	17 02	59	166	16 03	59	166	15 04	60	166	14 04	59	166
13	18 10	60	167	17 10	59	167	16 11	60	167	15 11	59	167	14 12	60	167
12	18 17	59	168	17 18	60	168	16 18	59	168	15 19	60	168	14 19	60	168
11	18 24	60	169	17 24	59	169	16 25	60	169	15 25	59	169	14 26	60	169
10	18 30	-59	170	17 31	-60	170	16 31	-60	170	15 31	-60	170	14 31	-59	170
9	18 36	60	171	17 36	60	171	16 36	59	171	15 37	60	171	14 37	60	171
8	18 41	60	172	17 41	60	172	16 41	59	172	15 42	60	172	14 42	60	172
7	18 45	59	173	17 46	60	173	16 46	60	173	15 46	60	173	14 46	60	173
6	18 49	60	174	17 49	59	174	16 50	60	174	15 50	60	174	14 50	60	174
5	18 53	-60	175	17 53	-60	175	16 53	-60	175	15 53	-60	175	14 53	-60	175
4	18 55	60	176	17 55	60	176	16 55	60	176	15 55	60	176	14 55	59	176
3	18 57	60	177	17 57	60	177	16 57	60	177	15 57	60	177	14 57	60	177
2	18 59	60	178	17 59	60	178	16 59	60	178	15 59	60	178	14 59	60	178
1	19 00	60	179	18 00	60	179	17 00	60	179	16 00	60	179	15 00	60	179
0	19 00	-60	180	18 00	-60	180	17 00	-60	180	16 00	-60	180	15 00	-60	180

LHA	20° Hc	d	Z	21° Hc	d	Z	22° Hc	d	Z	23° Hc	d	Z	24° Hc	d	Z
	° ′	′	°	° ′	′	°	° ′	′	°	° ′	′	°	° ′	′	°
69	-5 28	51	118	291											
68	-4 58	52	119	-5 50	51	119	292								
67	-4 29	52	120	-5 21	51	120	293								
66	-4 00	52	121	-4 52	51	121	-5 43	52	122	294					
65	-3 31	-52	121	-4 23	-52	122	-5 15	-51	122	295					
64	-3 03	52	122	-3 55	52	123	-4 47	51	123	-5 38	52	124	296		
63	-2 35	52	123	-3 27	52	124	-4 19	52	124	-5 11	52	125	297		
62	-2 07	52	124	-2 59	52	124	-3 51	52	125	-4 43	52	125	-5 35	52	126
61	-1 39	52	125	-2 31	53	125	-3 24	52	126	-4 16	52	126	-5 08	53	127
60	-1 12	-52	126	-2 04	-53	126	-2 57	-52	126	-3 49	-52	127	-4 41	-53	127
59	-0 44	53	126	-1 37	53	127	-2 30	52	127	-3 22	53	128	-4 15	53	128
58	-0 18	52	127	-1 10	53	128	-2 03	53	128	-2 56	53	129	-3 49	53	129
57	00 09	53	128	-0 44	53	128	-1 37	53	129	-2 30	53	129	-3 23	53	130
56	00 35	53	129	-0 18	53	129	-1 11	53	130	-2 04	53	130	-2 57	53	131
55	01 01	-53	130	00 08	-53	130	-0 45	-54	131	-1 39	-53	131	-2 32	-53	132
54	01 27	53	130	00 34	54	131	-0 20	53	131	-1 13	54	132	-2 07	53	132
53	01 52	53	131	00 59	54	132	00 05	54	132	-0 49	53	133	-1 42	54	133
52	02 17	53	132	01 24	54	133	00 30	54	133	-0 24	54	134	-1 18	54	134
51	02 42	54	133	01 48	54	133	00 54	54	134	00 00	54	134	-0 54	54	135
50	03 06	-54	134	02 12	-54	134	01 18	-54	135	00 24	-54	135	-0 30	-55	136
49	03 30	54	135	02 36	54	135	01 42	55	136	00 47	54	136	-0 07	54	136
48	03 54	54	136	03 00	55	136	02 05	55	136	01 10	54	137	00 16	55	137
47	04 17	54	136	03 23	55	137	02 28	55	137	01 33	55	138	00 38	54	138
46	04 40	55	137	03 45	54	138	02 51	55	138	01 56	55	139	01 01	55	139
45	05 03	-55	138	04 08	-55	139	03 13	-55	139	02 18	-55	139	01 23	-56	140
44	05 25	55	139	04 30	55	139	03 35	55	140	02 40	56	140	01 44	55	141
43	05 47	55	140	04 52	56	140	03 56	55	141	03 01	56	141	02 05	55	141
42	06 08	55	141	05 13	56	141	04 17	55	142	03 22	56	142	02 26	56	142
41	06 29	55	142	05 34	56	142	04 38	56	142	03 42	56	143	02 46	56	143
40	06 50	-56	143	05 54	-56	143	04 58	-56	143	04 02	-56	144	03 06	-56	144
39	07 10	56	143	06 14	56	144	05 18	56	144	04 22	56	144	03 26	56	145
38	07 30	56	144	06 34	57	145	05 37	56	145	04 41	56	145	03 45	56	146
37	07 49	56	145	06 53	56	146	05 57	57	146	05 00	56	146	04 04	57	147
36	08 08	56	146	07 12	57	146	06 15	56	147	05 19	57	147	04 22	57	147
35	08 27	-57	147	07 30	-57	147	06 33	-56	148	05 37	-57	148	04 40	-57	148
34	08 45	57	148	07 48	57	148	06 51	57	149	05 54	57	149	04 57	57	149
33	09 03	58	149	08 05	57	149	07 08	57	149	06 11	57	150	05 14	57	150
32	09 20	58	150	08 22	57	150	07 25	57	150	06 28	57	151	05 31	58	151
31	09 36	57	151	08 39	57	151	07 42	58	151	06 44	57	152	05 47	58	152
30	09 53	-58	152	08 55	-57	152	07 58	-58	152	07 00	-58	152	06 02	-57	153
29	10 08	57	152	09 11	58	153	08 13	58	153	07 15	57	153	06 18	58	154
28	10 24	58	153	09 26	58	154	08 28	58	154	07 30	58	154	06 32	58	154
27	10 38	57	154	09 41	58	155	08 43	58	155	07 45	58	155	06 47	58	155
26	10 53	58	155	09 55	58	156	08 57	59	156	07 58	58	156	07 00	58	156
25	11 07	-59	156	10 08	-58	156	09 10	-58	157	08 12	-58	157	07 14	-59	157
24	11 20	58	157	10 22	59	157	09 23	58	158	08 25	59	158	07 26	58	158
23	11 33	59	158	10 34	58	158	09 36	59	158	08 37	58	159	07 39	59	159
22	11 45	59	159	10 46	58	159	09 48	59	159	08 49	58	160	07 51	59	160
21	11 57	59	160	10 58	59	160	09 59	58	160	09 01	59	161	08 02	59	161
20	12 08	-59	161	11 09	-58	161	10 11	-59	161	09 12	-59	161	08 13	-59	162
19	12 19	59	162	11 20	59	162	10 21	59	162	09 22	59	162	08 23	59	163
18	12 29	59	163	11 30	59	163	10 31	59	163	09 32	59	163	08 33	59	163
17	12 39	59	164	11 40	59	164	10 41	60	164	09 41	59	164	08 42	59	164
16	12 48	59	165	11 49	59	165	10 50	60	165	09 50	59	165	08 51	59	165
15	12 57	-60	166	11 57	-59	166	10 58	-59	166	09 59	-60	166	08 59	-59	166
14	13 05	60	167	12 05	59	167	11 06	59	167	10 07	60	167	09 07	59	167
13	13 12	59	168	12 13	60	168	11 13	59	168	10 14	60	168	09 14	59	168
12	13 19	59	168	12 20	60	169	11 20	59	169	10 21	60	169	09 21	59	169
11	13 26	60	169	12 26	59	170	11 27	60	170	10 27	60	170	09 27	59	170
10	13 32	-60	170	12 32	-60	170	11 32	-59	171	10 33	-60	171	09 33	-60	171
9	13 37	60	171	12 37	59	171	11 38	60	172	10 38	60	172	09 38	60	172
8	13 42	60	172	12 42	60	172	11 42	59	172	10 43	60	173	09 43	60	173
7	13 46	60	173	12 46	60	173	11 46	59	173	10 47	60	173	09 47	60	174
6	13 50	60	174	12 50	60	174	11 50	60	174	10 50	60	174	09 50	60	174
5	13 53	-60	175	12 53	-60	175	11 53	-60	175	10 53	-60	175	09 53	-60	175
4	13 56	60	176	12 56	60	176	11 56	60	176	10 56	60	176	09 56	60	176
3	13 57	59	177	12 58	60	177	11 58	60	177	10 58	60	177	09 58	60	177
2	13 59	60	178	12 59	60	178	11 59	60	178	10 59	60	178	09 59	60	178
1	14 00	60	179	13 00	60	179	12 00	60	179	11 00	60	179	10 00	60	179
0	14 00	-60	180	13 00	-60	180	12 00	-60	180	11 00	-60	180	10 00	-60	180

LHA	25° Hc	d	Z	26° Hc	d	Z	27° Hc	d	Z	28° Hc	d	Z	29° Hc	d	Z	LHA
	° ′	′	°	° ′	′	°	° ′	′	°	° ′	′	°	° ′	′	°	
62	298															
61	299															
60	-5 34	-52	128	300												
59	-5 08	52	129	301												
58	-4 42	52	130	-5 34	53	130	302									
57	-4 16	53	130	-5 09	53	131	303									
56	-3 50	54	131	-4 44	53	132	-5 37	53	132	304						
55	-3 25	-54	132	-4 19	-53	132	-5 12	-53	133	305						
54	-3 00	54	133	-3 54	53	133	-4 47	54	134	-5 41	53	134	306			
53	-2 36	54	134	-3 30	53	134	-4 23	54	134	-5 17	54	135	307			
52	-2 12	54	134	-3 06	54	135	-4 00	53	135	-4 53	54	136	308			
51	-1 48	54	135	-2 42	54	136	-3 36	54	136	-4 30	54	137	-5 24	54	137	309
50	-1 25	-54	136	-2 19	-54	136	-3 13	-54	137	-4 07	-54	137	-5 01	-55	138	310
49	-1 01	55	137	-1 56	54	137	-2 50	55	138	-3 45	54	138	-4 39	54	139	311
48	-0 39	54	138	-1 33	55	138	-2 28	54	138	-3 22	55	139	-4 17	55	139	312
47	-0 16	55	138	-1 11	55	139	-2 06	54	139	-3 00	55	140	-3 55	55	140	313
46	00 06	55	139	-0 49	55	140	-1 44	55	140	-2 39	55	141	-3 34	55	141	314
45	00 27	-55	140	-0 28	-55	141	-1 23	-55	141	-2 18	-55	141	-3 13	-55	142	315
44	00 49	55	141	-0 06	56	141	-1 02	55	142	-1 57	55	142	-2 52	56	143	316
43	01 10	56	142	00 14	55	142	-0 41	56	143	-1 37	55	143	-2 32	56	143	317
42	01 30	55	143	00 35	56	143	-0 21	56	143	-1 17	55	144	-2 12	56	144	318
41	01 50	55	143	00 55	56	144	-0 01	56	144	-0 57	56	145	-1 53	56	145	319
40	02 10	-56	144	01 14	-56	145	00 18	-56	145	-0 38	-56	145	-1 34	-56	146	320
39	02 30	57	145	01 33	56	146	00 37	56	146	-0 19	56	146	-1 15	56	147	321
38	02 49	57	146	01 52	56	146	00 56	56	147	00 00	57	147	-0 57	56	147	322
37	03 07	56	147	02 11	57	147	01 14	56	148	00 18	57	148	-0 39	56	148	323
36	03 25	56	148	02 29	57	148	01 32	57	148	00 35	56	149	-0 21	57	149	324
35	03 43	-57	149	02 46	-57	149	01 49	-57	149	00 52	-56	150	-0 04	-57	150	325
34	04 00	57	149	03 03	57	150	02 06	57	150	01 09	57	150	00 12	57	151	326
33	04 17	57	150	03 20	57	151	02 23	57	151	01 26	58	151	00 28	57	152	327
32	04 33	57	151	03 36	57	152	02 39	58	152	01 41	57	152	00 44	57	152	328
31	04 49	57	152	03 52	58	152	02 54	57	153	01 57	58	153	00 59	57	153	329
30	05 05	-58	153	04 07	-57	153	03 10	-58	154	02 12	-58	154	01 14	-57	154	330
29	05 20	58	154	04 22	58	154	03 24	57	154	02 27	58	155	01 29	58	155	331
28	05 34	58	155	04 36	57	155	03 39	58	155	02 41	58	155	01 43	58	156	332
27	05 49	59	156	04 50	58	156	03 52	58	156	02 54	58	156	01 56	58	157	333
26	06 02	58	157	05 04	58	157	04 06	58	157	03 08	59	157	02 09	58	157	334
25	06 15	-58	157	05 17	-58	158	04 19	-59	158	03 20	-58	158	02 22	-58	158	335
24	06 28	58	158	05 30	59	159	04 31	58	159	03 33	59	159	02 34	58	159	336
23	06 40	58	159	05 42	59	159	04 43	58	160	03 45	59	160	02 46	59	160	337
22	06 52	59	160	05 53	58	160	04 55	59	160	03 56	59	161	02 57	59	161	338
21	07 03	59	161	06 04	58	161	05 06	59	161	04 07	59	162	03 08	59	162	339
20	07 14	-59	162	06 15	-59	162	05 16	-59	162	04 17	-59	162	03 18	-59	163	340
19	07 24	59	163	06 25	59	163	05 26	59	163	04 27	59	163	03 28	59	163	341
18	07 34	59	164	06 35	59	164	05 36	59	164	04 37	60	164	03 37	59	164	342
17	07 43	59	165	06 44	59	165	05 45	59	165	04 46	60	165	03 46	59	165	343
16	07 52	59	165	06 53	60	166	05 53	59	166	04 54	59	166	03 55	60	166	344
15	08 00	-59	166	07 01	-60	166	06 01	-59	167	05 02	-59	167	04 03	-60	167	345
14	08 08	60	167	07 08	59	167	06 09	60	168	05 09	59	168	04 10	60	168	346
13	08 15	60	168	07 15	59	168	06 16	60	168	05 16	59	169	04 17	60	169	347
12	08 22	60	169	07 22	60	169	06 22	59	169	05 23	60	169	04 23	59	170	348
11	08 28	60	170	07 28	60	170	06 28	59	170	05 29	60	170	04 29	60	170	349
10	08 33	-59	171	07 34	-60	171	06 34	-60	171	05 34	-60	171	04 34	-60	171	350
9	08 38	59	172	07 39	60	172	06 39	60	172	05 39	60	172	04 39	60	172	351
8	08 43	60	173	07 43	60	173	06 43	60	173	05 43	59	173	04 44	60	173	352
7	08 47	60	174	07 47	60	174	06 47	60	174	05 47	60	174	04 47	59	174	353
6	08 50	59	175	07 51	60	175	06 51	60	175	05 51	60	175	04 51	60	175	354
5	08 53	-60	175	07 53	-60	176	06 53	-59	176	05 54	-60	176	04 54	-60	176	355
4	08 56	60	176	07 56	60	176	06 56	60	176	05 56	60	176	04 56	60	176	356
3	08 58	60	177	07 58	60	177	06 58	60	177	05 58	60	177	04 58	60	177	357
2	08 59	60	178	07 59	60	178	06 59	60	178	05 59	60	178	04 59	60	178	358
1	09 00	60	179	08 00	60	179	07 00	60	179	06 00	60	179	05 00	60	179	359
0	09 00	-60	180	08 00	-60	180	07 00	-60	180	06 00	-60	180	05 00	-60	180	360

S. Lat. {LHA greater than 180°....... Zn=180−Z; LHA less than 180°.......... Zn=180+Z

DECLINATION (15°-29°) CONTRARY NAME TO LATITUDE

LAT 56°

N. Lat. { LHA greater than 180° .... Zn=Z; LHA less than 180° .... Zn=360−Z }

DECLINATION (0°-14°) SAME NAME AS LATITUDE

LHA	0° Hc	d	Z	1° Hc	d	Z	2° Hc	d	Z	3° Hc	d	Z	4° Hc	d	Z	5° Hc	d	Z	6° Hc	d	Z
	° ′	′	°	° ′	′	°	° ′	′	°	° ′	′	°	° ′	′	°	° ′	′	°	° ′	′	°
0	33 00	+60	180	34 00	+60	180	35 00	+60	180	36 00	+60	180	37 00	+60	180	38 00	+60	180	39 00	+60	180
1	33 00	60	179	34 00	60	179	35 00	60	179	36 00	60	179	37 00	60	179	38 00	60	179	39 00	60	179
2	32 59	60	178	33 59	60	178	34 59	60	178	35 59	60	178	36 59	60	178	37 59	60	178	38 59	60	177
3	32 57	60	176	33 57	60	176	34 57	60	176	35 57	60	176	36 57	60	176	37 57	60	176	38 57	60	176
4	32 55	60	175	33 55	59	175	34 54	60	175	35 54	60	175	36 54	60	175	37 54	60	175	38 54	60	175
5	32 52	+59	174	33 51	+60	174	34 51	+60	174	35 51	+60	174	36 51	+60	174	37 51	+60	174	38 51	+60	174
6	32 48	60	173	33 48	60	173	34 48	59	173	35 47	60	173	36 47	60	173	37 47	60	172	38 47	60	172
7	32 43	60	172	33 43	60	172	34 43	60	172	35 43	60	171	36 43	59	171	37 42	60	171	38 42	60	171
8	32 38	60	171	33 38	60	170	34 38	60	170	35 38	59	170	36 37	60	170	37 37	60	170	38 37	60	170
9	32 33	59	169	33 32	60	169	34 32	60	169	35 32	59	169	36 31	60	169	37 31	60	169	38 31	59	169
10	32 26	+60	168	33 26	+59	168	34 25	+60	168	35 25	+60	168	36 25	+59	168	37 24	+60	167	38 24	+59	167
11	32 19	60	167	33 19	59	167	34 18	60	167	35 18	59	167	36 17	60	166	37 17	59	166	38 16	60	166
12	32 11	60	166	33 11	59	166	34 10	60	166	35 10	59	165	36 09	60	165	37 09	59	165	38 08	59	165
13	32 03	59	165	33 02	60	164	34 02	59	164	35 01	59	164	36 00	60	164	37 00	59	164	37 59	59	164
14	31 54	59	163	32 53	60	163	33 53	59	163	34 52	59	163	35 51	59	163	36 50	59	163	37 49	60	162
15	31 45	+59	162	32 44	+59	162	33 43	+59	162	34 42	+59	162	35 41	+59	162	36 40	+59	161	37 39	+59	161
16	31 34	59	161	32 33	59	161	33 32	59	161	34 31	59	161	35 30	59	160	36 29	59	160	37 28	59	160
17	31 23	59	160	32 22	59	160	33 21	59	160	34 20	59	159	35 19	59	159	36 18	59	159	37 17	58	159
18	31 12	59	159	32 11	58	159	33 09	59	158	34 08	59	158	35 07	59	158	36 06	58	158	37 04	59	157
19	31 00	58	158	31 58	59	157	32 57	59	157	33 56	58	157	34 54	59	157	35 53	58	156	36 51	59	156
20	30 47	+59	157	31 46	+58	156	32 44	+59	156	33 43	+58	156	34 41	+59	156	35 40	+58	155	36 38	+58	155
21	30 34	58	155	31 32	59	155	32 31	58	155	33 29	58	155	34 27	58	154	35 25	59	154	36 24	58	154
22	30 20	58	154	31 18	58	154	32 16	59	154	33 15	58	153	34 13	58	153	35 11	58	153	36 09	58	153
23	30 05	59	153	31 04	58	153	32 02	58	153	33 00	58	152	33 58	58	152	34 56	58	152	35 54	57	151
24	29 50	58	152	30 48	58	152	31 46	58	151	32 44	58	151	33 42	58	151	34 40	58	151	35 38	57	150
25	29 35	+58	151	30 33	+57	151	31 30	+58	150	32 28	+58	150	33 26	+57	150	34 23	+58	149	35 21	+58	149
26	29 19	57	150	30 16	58	150	31 14	57	149	32 11	58	149	33 09	58	149	34 07	57	148	35 04	57	148
27	29 02	57	149	29 59	58	148	30 57	57	148	31 54	58	148	32 52	57	147	33 49	57	147	34 46	57	147
28	28 45	57	148	29 42	57	147	30 39	58	147	31 37	57	147	32 34	57	146	33 31	57	146	34 28	57	146
29	28 27	57	147	29 24	57	146	30 21	57	146	31 18	57	146	32 15	57	145	33 12	57	145	34 09	57	144
30	28 09	+57	146	29 06	+57	145	30 03	+57	145	31 00	+56	144	31 56	+57	144	32 53	+57	144	33 50	+57	143
31	27 50	57	144	28 47	57	144	29 44	56	144	30 40	57	143	31 37	57	143	32 34	56	143	33 30	57	142
32	27 31	56	143	28 27	57	143	29 24	56	143	30 20	57	142	31 17	56	142	32 13	57	141	33 10	56	141
33	27 11	56	142	28 07	57	142	29 04	56	142	30 00	57	141	30 57	56	141	31 53	56	140	32 49	56	140
34	26 51	56	141	27 47	56	141	28 43	56	140	29 39	57	140	30 36	56	140	31 32	56	139	32 28	56	139
35	26 30	+56	140	27 26	+56	140	28 22	+56	139	29 18	+56	139	30 14	+56	139	31 10	+56	138	32 06	+56	138
36	26 09	56	139	27 05	56	139	28 01	56	138	28 57	55	138	29 52	56	138	30 48	56	137	31 44	55	137
37	25 47	56	138	26 43	56	138	27 39	55	137	28 34	56	137	29 30	56	136	30 26	55	136	31 21	55	136
38	25 25	56	137	26 21	55	137	27 16	56	136	28 12	55	136	29 07	56	135	30 03	55	135	30 58	55	134
39	25 02	56	136	25 58	55	136	26 53	56	135	27 49	55	135	28 44	55	134	29 39	55	134	30 34	55	133
40	24 40	+55	135	25 35	+55	135	26 30	+55	134	27 25	+55	134	28 20	+55	133	29 15	+55	133	30 10	+55	132
41	24 16	55	134	25 11	56	134	26 07	55	133	27 02	54	133	27 56	55	132	28 51	55	132	29 46	55	131
42	23 53	55	133	24 48	54	133	25 42	55	132	26 37	55	132	27 32	55	131	28 27	54	131	29 21	55	130
43	23 28	55	132	24 23	55	132	25 18	55	131	26 13	54	131	27 07	55	130	28 02	54	130	28 56	54	129
44	23 04	55	131	23 59	54	131	24 53	55	130	25 48	54	130	26 42	54	129	27 36	55	129	28 31	54	128
45	22 39	+55	130	23 34	+54	130	24 28	+54	129	25 22	+55	129	26 17	+54	128	27 11	+54	128	28 05	+54	127
46	22 14	54	129	23 08	54	129	24 02	55	128	24 57	54	128	25 51	54	127	26 45	54	127	27 39	53	126
47	21 48	54	128	22 42	55	128	23 37	54	127	24 31	53	127	25 24	54	126	26 18	54	126	27 12	54	125
48	21 22	54	127	22 16	54	127	23 10	54	126	24 04	54	126	24 58	54	125	25 52	53	125	26 45	53	124
49	20 56	54	126	21 50	54	126	22 44	53	125	23 37	54	125	24 31	53	124	25 24	54	124	26 18	53	123
50	20 30	+53	125	21 23	+54	125	22 17	+53	124	23 10	+54	124	24 04	+53	123	24 57	+53	123	25 50	+53	122
51	20 03	53	124	20 56	54	124	21 50	53	123	22 43	53	123	23 36	53	122	24 29	54	122	25 23	52	121
52	19 36	53	123	20 29	53	123	21 22	53	122	22 15	54	122	23 09	53	121	24 02	52	121	24 54	53	120
53	19 08	53	122	20 01	53	122	20 54	53	121	21 47	53	121	22 40	53	120	23 33	53	120	24 26	53	119
54	18 40	53	121	19 33	53	121	20 26	53	120	21 19	53	120	22 12	53	119	23 05	52	119	23 57	53	118
55	18 12	+53	120	19 05	+53	120	19 58	+53	119	20 51	+52	119	21 43	+53	118	22 36	+53	118	23 29	+52	117
56	17 44	53	120	18 37	52	119	19 29	53	119	20 22	53	118	21 15	52	118	22 07	52	117	22 59	53	116
57	17 15	53	119	18 08	53	118	19 01	52	118	19 53	52	117	20 45	53	117	21 38	52	116	22 30	52	116
58	16 47	52	118	17 39	53	117	18 32	52	117	19 24	52	116	20 16	52	116	21 08	52	115	22 00	52	115
59	16 17	53	117	17 10	52	116	18 02	52	116	18 54	53	115	19 47	52	115	20 39	52	114	21 31	51	114
60	15 48	+52	116	16 40	+53	115	17 33	+52	115	18 25	+52	114	19 17	+52	114	20 09	+52	113	21 01	+51	113
61	15 19	52	115	16 11	52	114	17 03	52	114	17 55	52	113	18 47	52	113	19 39	51	112	20 30	52	112
62	14 49	52	114	15 41	52	114	16 33	52	113	17 25	52	113	18 17	51	112	19 08	52	111	20 00	51	111
63	14 19	52	113	15 11	52	113	16 03	51	112	16 54	52	112	17 46	52	111	18 38	51	111	19 29	52	110
64	13 49	52	112	14 41	51	112	15 32	52	111	16 24	52	111	17 16	51	110	18 07	51	110	18 58	52	109
65	13 18	+52	111	14 10	+52	111	15 02	+51	110	15 53	+52	110	16 45	+51	109	17 36	+51	109	18 27	+52	108
66	12 48	52	111	13 40	51	110	14 31	51	109	15 22	52	109	16 14	51	108	17 05	51	108	17 56	51	107
67	12 17	52	110	13 09	51	109	14 00	51	109	14 51	52	108	15 43	51	108	16 34	51	107	17 25	51	106
68	11 46	52	109	12 38	51	108	13 29	51	108	14 20	51	107	15 11	52	107	16 03	51	106	16 54	51	106
69	11 15	52	108	12 07	51	107	12 58	51	107	13 49	51	106	14 40	51	106	15 31	51	105	16 22	51	105

LHA	7° Hc	d	Z	8° Hc	d	Z	9° Hc	d	Z	10° Hc	d	Z	11° Hc	d	Z	12° Hc	d	Z	13° Hc	d	Z	14° Hc	d	Z	LHA
	° ′	′	°	° ′	′	°	° ′	′	°	° ′	′	°	° ′	′	°	° ′	′	°	° ′	′	°	° ′	′	°	
0	40 00	+60	180	41 00	+60	180	42 00	+60	180	43 00	+60	180	44 00	+60	180	45 00	+60	180	46 00	+60	180	47 00	+60	180	360
1	40 00	60	179	41 00	60	179	42 00	60	179	43 00	60	179	44 00	60	179	45 00	60	179	46 00	60	179	47 00	60	179	359
2	39 59	60	177	40 59	60	177	41 59	60	177	42 59	59	177	43 58	60	177	44 58	60	177	45 58	60	177	46 58	60	177	358
3	39 57	60	176	40 57	60	176	41 57	60	176	42 57	60	176	43 57	60	176	44 57	59	176	45 56	60	176	46 56	60	176	357
4	39 54	60	175	40 54	60	175	41 54	60	175	42 54	60	175	43 54	60	175	44 54	60	175	45 54	60	174	46 54	59	174	356
5	39 51	+60	174	40 51	+60	173	41 51	+59	173	42 50	+60	173	43 50	+60	173	44 50	+60	173	45 50	+60	173	46 50	+60	173	355
6	39 47	60	172	40 47	59	172	41 46	60	172	42 46	60	172	43 46	60	172	44 46	60	172	45 46	59	172	46 45	60	172	354
7	39 42	60	171	40 42	60	171	41 42	59	171	42 41	60	171	43 41	60	171	44 41	60	170	45 41	59	170	46 40	60	170	353
8	39 37	59	170	40 36	60	170	41 36	60	169	42 36	59	169	43 35	60	169	44 35	60	169	45 35	59	169	46 34	60	169	352
9	39 30	60	168	40 30	60	168	41 30	59	168	42 29	60	168	43 29	59	168	44 28	60	168	45 28	59	167	46 27	60	167	351
10	39 23	+60	167	40 23	+59	167	41 22	+60	167	42 22	+59	167	43 21	+60	166	44 21	+59	166	45 20	+60	166	46 20	+59	166	350
11	39 16	59	166	40 15	60	166	41 15	59	166	42 14	59	165	43 13	60	165	44 13	59	165	45 12	59	165	46 11	60	165	349
12	39 07	60	165	40 07	59	164	41 06	59	164	42 05	60	164	43 05	59	164	44 04	59	164	45 03	59	163	46 02	60	163	348
13	38 58	60	163	39 58	59	163	40 57	59	163	41 56	59	163	42 55	59	163	43 54	59	162	44 53	59	162	45 52	60	162	347
14	38 49	59	162	39 48	59	162	40 47	59	162	41 46	59	161	42 45	59	161	43 44	59	161	44 43	59	161	45 42	59	160	346
15	38 38	+59	161	39 37	+59	161	40 36	+59	160	41 35	+59	160	42 34	+59	160	43 33	+59	160	44 32	+59	159	45 31	+58	159	345
16	38 27	59	160	39 26	59	159	40 25	59	159	41 24	58	159	42 22	59	159	43 21	59	158	44 20	58	158	45 18	59	158	344
17	38 15	59	158	39 14	59	158	40 13	58	158	41 11	59	158	42 10	59	157	43 09	58	157	44 07	59	157	45 06	58	156	343
18	38 03	59	157	39 02	58	157	40 00	59	157	40 59	58	156	41 57	59	156	42 56	58	156	43 54	58	155	44 52	58	155	342
19	37 50	58	156	38 48	59	156	39 47	58	155	40 45	58	155	41 43	59	155	42 42	58	154	43 40	58	154	44 38	58	154	341
20	37 36	+59	155	38 35	+58	154	39 33	+58	154	40 31	+58	154	41 29	+58	153	42 27	+58	153	43 25	+58	153	44 23	+58	152	340
21	37 22	58	153	38 20	58	153	39 18	58	153	40 16	58	152	41 14	58	152	42 12	58	152	43 10	58	151	44 08	57	151	339
22	37 07	58	152	38 05	58	152	39 03	58	152	40 01	58	151	40 59	57	151	41 56	58	151	42 54	58	150	43 52	57	150	338
23	36 51	58	151	37 49	58	151	38 47	58	150	39 45	57	150	40 42	58	150	41 40	57	149	42 37	58	149	43 35	57	148	337
24	36 35	58	150	37 33	58	150	38 31	57	149	39 28	57	149	40 25	58	148	41 23	57	148	42 20	57	148	43 17	57	147	336
25	36 19	+57	149	37 16	+57	148	38 13	+58	148	39 11	+57	148	40 08	+57	147	41 05	+57	147	42 02	+57	146	42 59	+57	146	335
26	36 01	58	148	36 59	57	147	37 56	57	147	38 53	57	146	39 50	57	146	40 47	57	146	41 44	57	145	42 41	56	145	334
27	35 43	58	146	36 41	57	146	37 38	57	146	38 35	56	145	39 31	57	145	40 28	57	144	41 25	57	144	42 22	56	143	333
28	35 25	57	145	36 22	57	145	37 19	57	144	38 16	56	144	39 12	57	144	40 09	56	143	41 05	57	143	42 02	56	142	332
29	35 06	57	144	36 03	56	144	36 59	57	143	37 56	57	143	38 53	56	142	39 49	56	142	40 45	56	141	41 41	56	141	331
30	34 47	+56	143	35 43	+57	142	36 40	+56	142	37 36	+56	142	38 32	+57	141	39 29	+56	141	40 25	+56	140	41 21	+55	140	330
31	34 27	56	142	35 23	56	141	36 19	56	141	37 15	57	140	38 12	56	140	39 08	55	140	40 03	56	139	40 59	56	139	329
32	34 06	56	141	35 02	56	140	35 58	56	140	36 54	56	139	37 50	56	139	38 46	56	138	39 42	55	138	40 37	56	137	328
33	33 45	56	139	34 41	56	139	35 37	56	139	36 33	56	138	37 29	55	138	38 24	56	137	39 20	55	137	40 15	55	136	327
34	33 24	55	138	34 19	56	138	35 15	56	137	36 11	55	137	37 06	56	137	38 02	55	136	38 57	55	136	39 52	55	135	326
35	33 02	+55	137	33 57	+56	137	34 53	+55	136	35 48	+56	136	36 44	+55	135	37 39	+55	135	38 34	+55	134	39 29	+55	134	325
36	32 39	56	136	33 35	55	136	34 30	55	135	35 25	55	135	36 20	55	134	37 15	55	134	38 10	55	133	39 05	55	133	324
37	32 16	56	135	33 12	55	135	34 07	55	134	35 02	55	134	35 57	55	133	36 52	54	133	37 46	55	132	38 41	54	132	323
38	31 53	55	134	32 48	55	134	33 43	55	133	34 38	55	133	35 33	54	132	36 27	55	132	37 22	54	131	38 16	54	131	322
39	31 29	55	133	32 24	55	132	33 19	55	132	34 14	54	131	35 08	55	131	36 03	54	130	36 57	54	130	37 51	54	129	321
40	31 05	+55	132	32 00	+54	131	32 54	+55	131	33 49	+54	130	34 43	+55	130	35 38	+54	129	36 32	+54	129	37 26	+53	128	320
41	30 41	54	131	31 35	55	130	32 30	54	130	33 24	54	129	34 18	54	129	35 12	54	128	36 06	54	128	37 00	53	127	319
42	30 16	54	130	31 10	54	129	32 04	54	129	32 58	54	128	33 52	54	128	34 46	54	127	35 40	53	127	36 33	54	126	318
43	29 50	55	129	30 45	54	128	31 39	54	128	32 33	53	127	33 26	54	127	34 20	53	126	35 13	54	126	36 07	53	125	317
44	29 25	54	128	30 19	54	127	31 13	53	127	32 06	54	126	33 00	53	126	33 53	54	125	34 47	53	125	35 40	53	124	316
45	28 59	+53	127	29 52	+54	126	30 46	+54	126	31 40	+53	125	32 33	+53	125	33 26	+54	124	34 20	+53	124	35 13	+52	123	315
46	28 32	54	126	29 26	53	125	30 19	54	125	31 13	53	124	32 06	53	124	32 59	53	123	33 52	53	122	34 45	53	122	314
47	28 06	53	125	28 59	53	124	29 52	54	124	30 46	53	123	31 39	53	123	32 32	52	122	33 24	53	121	34 17	53	121	313
48	27 38	54	124	28 32	53	123	29 25	53	123	30 18	53	122	31 11	53	122	32 04	52	121	32 56	53	120	33 49	52	120	312
49	27 11	53	123	28 04	53	122	28 57	53	122	29 50	53	121	30 43	53	121	31 36	52	120	32 28	52	119	33 20	53	119	311
50	26 43	+53	122	27 36	+53	121	28 29	+53	121	29 22	+53	120	30 15	+52	120	31 07	+52	119	31 59	+53	118	32 52	+52	118	310
51	26 15	53	121	27 08	53	120	28 01	53	120	28 54	52	119	29 46	52	119	30 38	53	118	31 31	52	117	32 23	51	117	309
52	25 47	53	120	26 40	53	119	27 33	52	119	28 25	52	118	29 17	52	118	30 09	52	117	31 01	52	116	31 53	52	116	308
53	25 19	52	119	26 11	53	118	27 04	52	118	27 56	52	117	28 48	52	117	29 40	52	116	30 32	52	115	31 24	51	115	307
54	24 50	52	118	25 42	53	117	26 35	52	117	27 27	52	116	28 19	52	116	29 11	51	115	30 02	52	114	30 54	51	114	306
55	24 21	+52	117	25 13	+52	116	26 05	+52	116	26 57	+52	115	27 49	+52	115	28 41	+52	114	29 33	+51	113	30 24	+51	113	305
56	23 52	52	116	24 44	52	115	25 36	52	115	26 28	51	114	27 19	52	114	28 11	51	113	29 02	52	113	29 54	51	112	304
57	23 22	52	115	24 14	52	114	25 06	52	114	25 58	51	113	26 49	52	113	27 41	51	112	28 32	51	112	29 23	51	111	303
58	22 52	52	114	23 44	52	114	24 36	52	113	25 28	51	112	26 19	51	112	27 10	52	111	28 02	51	111	28 53	51	110	302
59	22 22	52	113	23 14	52	113	24 06	51	112	24 57	52	111	25 49	51	111	26 40	51	110	27 31	51	110	28 22	51	109	301
60	21 52	+52	112	22 44	+51	112	23 35	+52	111	24 27	+51	111	25 18	+51	110	26 09	+51	109	27 00	+51	109	27 51	+51	108	300
61	21 22	51	111	22 13	52	111	23 05	51	110	23 56	51	110	24 47	51	109	25 38	51	108	26 29	51	108	27 20	50	107	299
62	20 51	52	110	21 43	51	110	22 34	51	109	23 25	51	109	24 16	51	108	25 07	51	108	25 58	50	107	26 48	51	106	298
63	20 21	51	109	21 12	51	109	22 03	51	108	22 54	51	108	23 45	51	107	24 36	51	107	25 27	50	106	26 17	50	105	297
64	19 50	51	109	20 41	51	108	21 32	51	107	22 23	51	107	23 14	50	106	24 04	51	106	24 55	50	105	25 45	51	105	296
65	19 19	+51	108	20 10	+51	107	21 01	+51	107	21 52	+50	106	22 42	+51	105	23 33	+50	105	24 23	+51	104	25 14	+50	104	295
66	18 47	51	107	19 38	51	106	20 29	51	106	21 20	51	105	22 11	50	104	23 01	51	104	23 52	50	103	24 42	50	103	294
67	18 16	51	106	19 07	51	105	19 58	50	105	20 48	51	104	21 39	50	104	22 29	51	103	23 20	50	102	24 10	50	102	293
68	17 45	50	105	18 35	51	104	19 26	51	104	20 17	50	103	21 07	51	103	21 58	50	102	22 48	50	102	23 38	50	101	292
69	17 13	51	104	18 04	50	104	18 54	51	103	19 45	50	102	20 35	51	102	21 26	50	101	22 16	50	101	23 06	50	100	291

S. Lat. { LHA greater than 180° .... Zn=180−Z; LHA less than 180° .... Zn=180+Z }

DECLINATION (0°-14°) SAME NAME AS LATITUDE

N. Lat. {LHA greater than 180°……. Zn=Z
{LHA less than 180°………. Zn=360−Z

DECLINATION (0°-14°) SAME NAME AS LATITUDE

LHA	0° Hc	0° d	0° Z	1° Hc	1° d	1° Z	2° Hc	2° d	2° Z	3° Hc	3° d	3° Z	4° Hc	4° d	4° Z
	° ′	′	°	° ′	′	°	° ′	′	°	° ′	′	°	° ′	′	°
70	10 44	+51	107	11 35	+52	106	12 27	+51	106	13 18	+51	105	14 09	+50	105
71	10 13	51	106	11 04	51	106	11 55	51	105	12 46	51	105	13 37	51	104
72	09 41	51	105	10 32	51	105	11 23	51	104	12 14	51	104	13 05	51	103
73	09 10	51	104	10 01	51	104	10 52	50	103	11 42	51	103	12 33	51	102
74	08 38	51	104	09 29	51	103	10 20	51	102	11 11	50	102	12 01	51	101
75	08 06	+51	103	08 57	+51	102	09 48	+51	102	10 39	+50	101	11 29	+51	101
76	07 34	51	102	08 25	51	101	09 16	50	101	10 06	51	100	10 57	51	100
77	07 02	51	101	07 53	51	100	08 44	50	100	09 34	51	99	10 25	50	99
78	06 30	51	100	07 21	50	100	08 11	51	99	09 02	50	99	09 52	51	98
79	05 58	51	99	06 49	50	99	07 39	51	98	08 30	50	98	09 20	50	97
80	05 26	+50	98	06 16	+51	98	07 07	+50	97	07 57	+51	97	08 48	+50	96
81	04 53	51	98	05 44	50	97	06 34	51	97	07 25	50	96	08 15	50	95
82	04 21	50	97	05 11	51	96	06 02	50	96	06 52	51	95	07 43	50	95
83	03 48	51	96	04 39	50	95	05 29	51	95	06 20	50	94	07 10	50	94
84	03 16	50	95	04 06	51	94	04 57	50	94	05 47	50	93	06 37	51	93
85	02 43	+51	94	03 34	+50	94	04 24	+50	93	05 14	+51	93	06 05	+50	92
86	02 11	50	93	03 01	50	93	03 51	51	92	04 42	50	92	05 32	50	91
87	01 38	50	93	02 28	51	92	03 19	50	91	04 09	50	91	04 59	51	90
88	01 05	51	92	01 56	50	91	02 46	50	91	03 36	51	90	04 27	50	89
89	00 33	50	91	01 23	50	90	02 13	51	90	03 04	50	89	03 54	50	89
90	00 00	+50	90	00 50	+51	89	01 41	+50	89	02 31	+50	88	03 21	+51	88
91	−0 33	51	89	00 18	50	89	01 08	50	88	01 58	51	88	02 49	50	87
92	−1 05	50	88	−0 15	50	88	00 35	51	87	01 26	50	87	02 16	50	86
93	−1 38	50	87	−0 48	51	87	00 03	50	86	00 53	50	86	01 43	51	85
94	−2 11	51	87	−1 20	50	86	−0 30	50	86	00 20	51	85	01 11	50	84
95	−2 43	+50	86	−1 53	+51	85	−1 02	+50	85	−0 12	+50	84	00 38	+51	84
96	−3 16	51	85	−2 25	50	84	−1 35	50	84	−0 45	51	83	00 06	50	83
97	−3 48	50	84	−2 58	51	84	−2 07	50	83	−1 17	50	82	−0 27	51	82
98	−4 21	51	83	−3 30	50	83	−2 40	51	82	−1 49	50	82	−0 59	51	81
99	−4 53	50	82	−4 03	51	82	−3 12	50	81	−2 22	51	81	−1 31	50	80
100	−5 26	+51	82	−4 35	+51	81	−3 44	+50	81	−2 54	+51	80	−2 03	+50	79
101	−5 58	51	81	−5 07	50	80	−4 17	51	80	−3 26	51	79	−2 35	50	79
102				−5 40	51	79	−4 49	51	79	−3 58	51	78	−3 07	50	78
103							−5 21	51	78	−4 30	51	77	−3 39	51	77
104							−5 53	51	77	−5 02	51	77	−4 11	51	76
105										−5 34	+51	76	−4 43	+51	75
106													−5 14	51	74
107													−5 46	52	73

LHA	5° Hc	5° d	5° Z	6° Hc	6° d	6° Z	7° Hc	7° d	7° Z	8° Hc	8° d	8° Z	9° Hc	9° d	9° Z
	° ′	′	°	° ′	′	°	° ′	′	°	° ′	′	°	° ′	′	°
70	14 59	+51	104	15 50	+51	104	16 41	+51	103	17 32	+50	103	18 22	+51	102
71	14 28	51	103	15 19	50	103	16 09	51	102	17 00	50	102	17 50	51	101
72	13 56	51	103	14 47	50	102	15 37	51	101	16 28	50	101	17 18	51	100
73	13 24	51	102	14 15	50	101	15 05	51	101	15 56	50	100	16 46	50	99
74	12 52	51	101	13 43	50	100	14 33	50	100	15 23	51	99	16 14	50	99
75	12 20	+50	100	13 10	+51	99	14 01	+50	99	14 51	+50	98	15 41	+51	98
76	11 48	50	99	12 38	50	99	13 28	51	98	14 19	50	97	15 09	50	97
77	11 15	51	98	12 06	50	98	12 56	50	97	13 46	51	97	14 37	50	96
78	10 43	50	97	11 33	51	97	12 24	50	96	13 14	50	96	14 04	50	95
79	10 10	51	97	11 01	50	96	11 51	50	95	12 41	50	95	13 31	51	94
80	09 38	+50	96	10 28	+51	95	11 19	+50	95	12 09	+50	94	12 59	+50	94
81	09 05	51	95	09 56	50	94	10 46	50	94	11 36	50	93	12 26	50	93
82	08 33	50	94	09 23	50	93	10 13	50	93	11 03	51	92	11 54	50	92
83	08 00	50	93	08 50	51	93	09 41	50	92	10 31	50	92	11 21	50	91
84	07 28	50	92	08 18	50	92	09 08	50	91	09 58	50	91	10 48	50	90
85	06 55	+50	92	07 45	+50	91	08 35	+50	90	09 25	+51	90	10 16	+50	89
86	06 22	50	91	07 12	51	90	08 03	50	90	08 53	50	89	09 43	50	88
87	05 50	50	90	06 40	50	89	07 30	50	89	08 20	50	88	09 10	50	88
88	05 17	50	89	06 07	50	88	06 57	50	88	07 47	51	87	08 38	50	87
89	04 44	50	88	05 34	51	88	06 25	50	87	07 15	50	87	08 05	50	86
90	04 12	+50	87	05 02	+50	87	05 52	+50	86	06 42	+50	86	07 32	+50	85
91	03 39	50	86	04 29	50	86	05 19	51	85	06 10	50	85	07 00	50	84
92	03 06	51	86	03 57	50	85	04 47	50	84	05 37	50	84	06 27	51	83
93	02 34	50	85	03 24	50	84	04 14	51	84	05 05	50	83	05 55	50	83
94	02 01	51	84	02 52	50	83	03 42	50	83	04 32	51	82	05 23	50	82
95	01 29	+50	83	02 19	+50	83	03 09	+51	82	04 00	+50	81	04 50	+51	81
96	00 56	51	82	01 47	50	82	02 37	51	81	03 28	50	81	04 18	50	80
97	00 24	50	81	01 14	51	81	02 05	50	80	02 55	51	80	03 46	50	79
98	−0 08	50	81	00 42	51	80	01 33	50	79	02 23	51	79	03 14	50	78
99	−0 41	50	80	00 10	51	79	01 01	50	79	01 51	51	78	02 42	50	78
100	−1 13	+51	79	−0 22	+51	78	00 29	+50	78	01 19	+51	77	02 10	+51	77
101	−1 45	51	78	−0 54	51	78	−0 03	50	77	00 47	51	76	01 38	51	76
102	−2 17	51	77	−1 26	51	77	−0 35	51	76	00 16	51	76	01 07	50	75
103	−2 48	50	76	−1 58	51	76	−1 07	51	75	−0 16	51	75	00 35	51	74
104	−3 20	51	76	−2 29	51	75	−1 38	51	74	−0 47	51	74	00 04	51	73
105	−3 52	+51	75	−3 01	+51	74	−2 10	+51	74	−1 19	+51	73	−0 28	+51	73
106	−4 23	51	74	−3 32	51	73	−2 41	51	73	−1 50	51	72	−0 59	51	72
107	−4 54	51	73	−4 03	51	72	−3 12	51	72	−2 21	51	71	−1 30	52	71
108	−5 26	52	72	−4 34	51	72	−3 43	51	71	−2 52	52	71	−2 00	51	70
109	−5 57	52	71	−5 05	51	71	−4 14	51	70	−3 23	52	70	−2 31	51	69
110				−5 36	+51	70	−4 45	+52	69	−3 53	+51	69	−3 02	+52	68
111							−5 15	52	68	−4 23	51	68	−3 32	52	67
112							−5 45	51	68	−4 54	52	67	−4 02	52	66
113										−5 24	52	66	−4 32	52	66
114										−5 54	52	65	−5 02	52	65
115													−5 31	+52	64

LHA	10° Hc	10° d	10° Z	11° Hc	11° d	11° Z	12° Hc	12° d	12° Z	13° Hc	13° d	13° Z	14° Hc	14° d	14° Z	LHA
	° ′	′	°	° ′	′	°	° ′	′	°	° ′	′	°	° ′	′	°	
70	19 13	+50	102	20 03	+50	101	20 53	+51	100	21 44	+50	100	22 34	+49	99	290
71	18 41	50	101	19 31	50	100	20 21	50	99	21 11	50	99	22 01	50	98	289
72	18 09	50	100	18 59	50	99	19 49	50	99	20 39	50	98	21 29	50	97	288
73	17 36	51	99	18 27	50	98	19 17	50	98	20 07	49	97	20 56	50	97	287
74	17 04	50	98	17 54	50	97	18 44	50	97	19 34	50	96	20 24	50	96	286
75	16 32	+50	97	17 22	+50	97	18 12	+50	96	19 02	+49	95	19 51	+50	95	285
76	15 59	50	96	16 49	50	96	17 39	50	95	18 29	50	95	19 19	50	94	284
77	15 27	50	95	16 17	50	95	17 07	50	94	17 57	49	94	18 46	50	93	283
78	14 54	50	95	15 44	50	94	16 34	50	93	17 24	50	93	18 14	49	92	282
79	14 22	50	94	15 12	49	93	16 01	50	93	16 51	50	92	17 41	50	91	281
80	13 49	+50	93	14 39	+50	92	15 29	+50	92	16 19	+49	91	17 08	+50	91	280
81	13 16	50	92	14 06	50	92	14 56	50	91	15 46	50	90	16 36	49	90	279
82	12 44	50	91	13 34	49	91	14 23	50	90	15 13	50	90	16 03	50	89	278
83	12 11	50	90	13 01	50	90	13 51	50	89	14 41	49	89	15 30	50	88	277
84	11 38	50	90	12 28	50	89	13 18	50	88	14 08	50	88	14 58	49	87	276
85	11 06	+50	89	11 56	+49	88	12 45	+50	88	13 35	+50	87	14 25	+50	86	275
86	10 33	50	88	11 23	50	87	12 13	50	87	13 03	49	86	13 52	50	86	274
87	10 00	50	87	10 50	50	86	11 40	50	86	12 30	50	85	13 20	50	85	273
88	09 28	50	86	10 18	50	86	11 08	49	85	11 57	50	85	12 47	50	84	272
89	08 55	50	85	09 45	50	85	10 35	50	84	11 25	50	84	12 15	50	83	271
90	08 22	+51	85	09 13	+50	84	10 03	+50	83	10 53	+49	83	11 42	+50	82	270
91	07 50	50	84	08 40	50	83	09 30	50	83	10 20	50	82	11 10	50	81	269
92	07 18	50	83	08 08	50	82	08 58	50	82	09 48	50	81	10 38	50	81	268
93	06 45	50	82	07 35	50	82	08 25	51	81	09 16	50	80	10 06	50	80	267
94	06 13	50	81	07 03	50	81	07 53	50	80	08 43	50	80	09 33	51	79	266
95	05 41	+50	80	06 31	+50	80	07 21	+50	79	08 11	+50	79	09 01	+51	78	265
96	05 08	51	80	05 59	50	79	06 49	50	78	07 39	51	78	08 30	50	77	264
97	04 36	51	79	05 27	50	78	06 17	50	78	07 07	51	77	07 58	50	77	263
98	04 04	51	78	04 55	50	77	05 45	51	77	06 36	50	76	07 26	50	76	262
99	03 32	51	77	04 23	50	76	05 13	51	76	06 04	50	75	06 54	51	75	261
100	03 01	+50	76	03 51	+51	76	04 42	+50	75	05 32	+51	75	06 23	+50	74	260
101	02 29	51	75	03 20	50	75	04 10	51	74	05 01	51	74	05 52	50	73	259
102	01 57	51	75	02 48	51	74	03 39	51	73	04 30	50	73	05 20	51	72	258
103	01 26	51	74	02 17	51	73	03 08	50	73	03 58	51	72	04 49	51	72	257
104	00 55	51	73	01 46	50	72	02 36	51	72	03 27	51	71	04 18	51	71	256
105	00 23	+51	72	01 14	+51	72	02 05	+51	71	02 56	+51	70	03 47	+51	70	255
106	−0 08	52	71	00 44	51	71	01 35	51	70	02 26	51	70	03 17	51	69	254
107	−0 38	51	70	00 13	51	70	01 04	51	69	01 55	51	69	02 46	52	68	253
108	−1 09	51	70	−0 18	51	69	00 33	52	68	01 25	51	68	02 16	51	67	252
109	−1 40	52	69	−0 48	51	68	00 03	52	68	00 55	51	67	01 46	51	67	251
110	−2 10	+52	68	−1 18	+51	67	−0 27	+52	67	00 25	+51	66	01 16	+52	66	250
111	−2 40	51	67	−1 49	52	66	−0 57	52	66	−0 05	51	65	00 46	52	65	249
112	−3 10	52	66	−2 18	51	66	−1 27	52	65	−0 35	52	65	00 17	52	64	248
113	−3 40	52	65	−2 48	52	65	−1 56	52	64	−1 04	52	64	−0 12	52	63	247
114	−4 10	52	64	−3 18	52	64	−2 26	53	63	−1 33	52	63	−0 41	52	62	246
115	−4 39	+52	64	−3 47	+52	63	−2 55	+53	63	−2 02	+52	62	−1 10	+52	62	245
116	−5 08	52	63	−4 16	52	62	−3 24	53	62	−2 31	52	61	−1 39	52	61	244
117	−5 37	52	62	−4 45	53	61	−3 52	52	61	−3 00	53	60	−2 07	52	60	243
118				−5 13	52	60	−4 21	53	60	−3 28	53	60	−2 35	52	59	242
119				−5 42	53	60	−4 49	53	59	−3 56	53	59	−3 03	52	58	241
120							−5 17	+53	58	−4 24	+53	58	−3 31	+53	57	240
121							−5 44	53	57	−4 51	53	57	−3 58	53	56	239
122										−5 19	54	56	−4 25	53	56	238
123										−5 46	54	55	−4 52	53	55	237
124													−5 19	54	54	236
125													−5 45	+54	53	235

LAT 57°

S. Lat. {LHA greater than 180°……. Zn=180−Z
{LHA less than 180°………. Zn=180+Z

DECLINATION (0°-14°) SAME NAME AS LATITUDE

N. Lat. {LHA greater than 180°....... Zn=Z
{LHA less than 180°........... Zn=360−Z

DECLINATION (0°-14°) CONTRARY NAME TO LATITUDE

LHA	0° Hc	0° d	0° Z	1° Hc	1° d	1° Z	2° Hc	2° d	2° Z	3° Hc	3° d	3° Z	4° Hc	4° d	4° Z	LHA
	° ′	′	°	° ′	′	°	° ′	′	°	° ′	′	°	° ′	′	°	
101	-5 58	51	81													259
100	-5 26	-50	82													260
99	-4 53	51	82	-5 44	50	83										261
98	-4 21	50	83	-5 11	51	84	-6 02	50	84							262
97	-3 48	51	84	-4 39	50	85	-5 29	51	85							263
96	-3 16	50	85	-4 06	51	86	-4 57	50	86	-5 47	50	87				264
95	-2 43	-51	86	-3 34	-50	86	-4 24	-50	87	-5 14	-51	87	-6 05	-50	88	265
94	-2 11	50	87	-3 01	50	87	-3 51	51	88	-4 42	50	88	-5 32	50	89	266
93	-1 38	50	87	-2 28	51	88	-3 19	50	89	-4 09	50	89	-4 59	51	90	267
92	-1 05	51	88	-1 56	50	89	-2 46	50	89	-3 36	51	90	-4 27	50	91	268
91	-0 33	50	89	-1 23	50	90	-2 13	51	90	-3 04	50	91	-3 54	50	91	269
90	00 00	-50	90	-0 50	-51	91	-1 41	-50	91	-2 31	-50	92	-3 21	-51	92	270
89	00 33	51	91	-0 18	50	91	-1 08	50	92	-1 58	51	92	-2 49	50	93	271
88	01 05	50	92	00 15	50	92	-0 35	51	93	-1 26	50	93	-2 16	50	94	272
87	01 38	50	93	00 48	51	93	-0 03	50	94	-0 53	50	94	-1 43	51	95	273
86	02 11	51	93	01 20	50	94	00 30	50	94	-0 20	51	95	-1 11	50	96	274
85	02 43	-50	94	01 53	-51	95	01 02	-50	95	00 12	-50	96	-0 38	-51	96	275
84	03 16	51	95	02 25	50	96	01 35	50	96	00 45	51	97	-0 06	50	97	276
83	03 48	50	96	02 58	51	96	02 07	50	97	01 17	50	98	00 27	51	98	277
82	04 21	51	97	03 30	50	97	02 40	51	98	01 49	50	98	00 59	51	99	278
81	04 53	50	98	04 03	51	98	03 12	50	99	02 22	51	99	01 31	50	100	279
80	05 26	-51	98	04 35	-51	99	03 44	-50	99	02 54	-51	100	02 03	-50	101	280
79	05 58	51	99	05 07	50	100	04 17	51	100	03 26	51	101	02 35	50	101	281
78	06 30	50	100	05 40	51	101	04 49	51	101	03 58	51	102	03 07	50	102	282
77	07 02	50	101	06 12	51	102	05 21	51	102	04 30	51	103	03 39	51	103	283
76	07 34	50	102	06 44	51	102	05 53	51	103	05 02	51	103	04 11	51	104	284
75	08 06	-51	103	07 15	-50	103	06 25	-51	104	05 34	-51	104	04 43	-51	105	285
74	08 38	51	104	07 47	51	104	06 56	51	105	06 05	51	105	05 14	51	106	286
73	09 10	51	104	08 19	51	105	07 28	51	105	06 37	51	106	05 46	52	107	287
72	09 41	51	105	08 50	51	106	07 59	51	106	07 08	51	107	06 17	51	107	288
71	10 13	51	106	09 22	51	107	08 31	52	107	07 39	51	108	06 48	51	108	289
70	10 44	-51	107	09 53	-51	108	09 02	-52	108	08 10	-51	109	07 19	-51	109	290

LHA	5° Hc	5° d	5° Z	6° Hc	6° d	6° Z	7° Hc	7° d	7° Z	8° Hc	8° d	8° Z	9° Hc	9° d	9° Z
	° ′	′	°	° ′	′	°	° ′	′	°	° ′	′	°	° ′	′	°
93	-5 50	50	90												
92	-5 17	50	91												
91	-4 44	50	92	-5 34	51	92									
90	-4 12	-50	93	-5 02	-50	93	-5 52	-50	94						
89	-3 39	50	94	-4 29	50	94	-5 19	51	95						
88	-3 06	51	94	-3 57	50	95	-4 47	50	96	-5 37	50	96			
87	-2 34	50	95	-3 24	50	96	-4 14	51	96	-5 05	50	97	-5 55	50	97
86	-2 01	51	96	-2 52	50	97	-3 42	50	97	-4 32	51	98	-5 23	50	98
85	-1 29	-50	97	-2 19	-50	97	-3 09	-51	98	-4 00	-50	99	-4 50	-51	99
84	-0 56	51	98	-1 47	50	98	-2 37	51	99	-3 28	50	99	-4 18	50	100
83	-0 24	50	99	-1 14	51	99	-2 05	50	100	-2 55	51	100	-3 46	50	101
82	00 08	50	99	-0 42	51	100	-1 33	50	101	-2 23	51	101	-3 14	50	102
81	00 41	51	100	-0 10	51	101	-1 01	50	101	-1 51	51	102	-2 42	50	102
80	01 13	-51	101	00 22	-51	102	-0 29	-50	102	-1 19	-51	103	-2 10	-51	103
79	01 45	51	102	00 54	51	102	00 03	50	103	-0 47	51	104	-1 38	51	104
78	02 17	51	103	01 26	51	103	00 35	51	104	-0 16	51	104	-1 07	50	105
77	02 48	50	104	01 58	51	104	01 07	51	105	00 16	51	105	-0 35	51	106
76	03 20	51	104	02 29	51	105	01 38	51	106	00 47	51	106	-0 04	51	107
75	03 52	-51	105	03 01	-51	106	02 10	-51	106	01 19	-51	107	00 28	-51	107
74	04 23	51	106	03 32	51	107	02 41	51	107	01 50	51	108	00 59	51	108
73	04 54	51	107	04 03	51	108	03 12	51	108	02 21	51	109	01 30	52	109
72	05 26	52	108	04 34	51	108	03 43	51	109	02 52	52	109	02 00	51	110
71	05 57	52	109	05 05	51	109	04 14	51	110	03 23	52	110	02 31	51	111
70	06 28	-52	110	05 36	-51	110	04 45	-52	111	03 53	-51	111	03 02	-52	112

LHA	10° Hc	10° d	10° Z	11° Hc	11° d	11° Z	12° Hc	12° d	12° Z	13° Hc	13° d	13° Z	14° Hc	14° d	14° Z
	° ′	′	°	° ′	′	°	° ′	′	°	° ′	′	°	° ′	′	°
85	-5 41	-50	100												
84	-5 08	51	100	-5 59	50	101									
83	-4 36	51	101	-5 27	50	102									
82	-4 04	51	102	-4 55	50	103	-5 45	51	103						
81	-3 32	51	103	-4 23	50	104	-5 13	51	104						
80	-3 01	-50	104	-3 51	-51	104	-4 42	-50	105	-5 32	-51	105			
79	-2 29	51	105	-3 20	50	105	-4 10	51	106	-5 01	51	106	-5 52	50	107
78	-1 57	51	105	-2 48	51	106	-3 39	51	107	-4 30	50	107	-5 20	51	108
77	-1 26	51	106	-2 17	51	107	-3 08	50	107	-3 58	51	108	-4 49	51	108
76	-0 55	51	107	-1 46	50	108	-2 36	51	108	-3 27	51	109	-4 18	51	109
75	-0 23	-51	108	-1 14	-51	108	-2 05	-51	109	-2 56	-51	110	-3 47	-51	110
74	00 08	52	109	-0 44	51	109	-1 35	51	110	-2 26	51	110	-3 17	51	111
73	00 38	51	110	-0 13	51	110	-1 04	51	111	-1 55	51	111	-2 46	52	112
72	01 09	51	110	00 18	51	111	-0 33	52	112	-1 25	51	112	-2 16	51	113
71	01 40	52	111	00 48	51	112	-0 03	52	112	-0 55	51	113	-1 46	51	113
70	02 10	-52	112	01 18	-51	113	00 27	-52	113	-0 25	-51	114	-1 16	-52	114

S. Lat. {LHA greater than 180°....... Zn=180−Z
{LHA less than 180°........... Zn=180+Z

DECLINATION (0°-14°) CONTRARY NAME TO LATITUDE

N. Lat. {LHA greater than 180°........ Zn=Z; LHA less than 180°........... Zn=360−Z}

DECLINATION (0°-14°) CONTRARY NAME TO LATITUDE

LHA	0° Hc	d	Z	1° Hc	d	Z	2° Hc	d	Z	3° Hc	d	Z	4° Hc	d	Z
	° ′	′	°	° ′	′	°	° ′	′	°	° ′	′	°	° ′	′	°
69	11 15	51	108	10 24	51	108	09 33	52	109	08 41	51	109	07 50	52	110
68	11 46	51	109	10 55	52	109	10 03	51	110	09 12	52	110	08 20	51	111
67	12 17	51	110	11 26	52	110	10 34	51	111	09 43	52	111	08 51	52	112
66	12 48	52	111	11 56	51	111	11 05	52	112	10 13	52	112	09 21	52	113
65	13 18	−51	111	12 27	−52	112	11 35	−52	112	10 43	−52	113	09 51	−52	113
64	13 49	52	112	12 57	52	113	12 05	52	113	11 13	52	114	10 21	52	114
63	14 19	52	113	13 27	52	114	12 35	52	114	11 43	52	115	10 51	52	115
62	14 49	52	114	13 57	52	115	13 05	53	115	12 12	52	116	11 20	52	116
61	15 19	53	115	14 26	52	115	13 34	52	116	12 42	53	117	11 49	52	117
60	15 48	−52	116	14 56	−53	116	14 03	−52	117	13 11	−53	117	12 18	−52	118
59	16 17	52	117	15 25	53	117	14 32	52	118	13 40	53	118	12 47	52	119
58	16 47	53	118	15 54	53	118	15 01	52	119	14 09	53	119	13 16	53	120
57	17 15	52	119	16 23	53	119	15 30	53	120	14 37	53	120	13 44	53	121
56	17 44	53	120	16 51	53	120	15 58	53	121	15 05	53	121	14 12	53	122
55	18 12	−53	120	17 19	−53	121	16 26	−53	121	15 33	−53	122	14 40	−53	122
54	18 40	53	121	17 47	53	122	16 54	53	122	16 01	54	123	15 07	53	123
53	19 08	53	122	18 15	54	123	17 21	53	123	16 28	54	124	15 34	53	124
52	19 36	54	123	18 42	53	124	17 49	54	124	16 55	54	125	16 01	53	125
51	20 03	54	124	19 09	54	125	18 15	53	125	17 22	54	126	16 28	54	126
50	20 30	−54	125	19 36	−54	126	18 42	−54	126	17 48	−54	127	16 54	−54	127
49	20 56	54	126	20 02	54	127	19 08	54	127	18 14	54	128	17 20	54	128
48	21 22	54	127	20 28	54	128	19 34	54	128	18 40	54	128	17 46	55	129
47	21 48	54	128	20 54	54	129	20 00	55	129	19 05	54	129	18 11	55	130
46	22 14	55	129	21 19	54	130	20 25	55	130	19 30	54	130	18 36	55	131
45	22 39	−54	130	21 45	−55	130	20 50	−55	131	19 55	−55	131	19 00	−54	132
44	23 04	55	131	22 09	55	131	21 14	54	132	20 20	55	132	19 25	55	133
43	23 28	54	132	22 34	55	132	21 39	55	133	20 44	56	133	19 48	55	134
42	23 53	56	133	22 57	55	133	22 02	55	134	21 07	55	134	20 12	55	135
41	24 16	55	134	23 21	55	134	22 26	56	135	21 30	55	135	20 35	56	136
40	24 40	−56	135	23 44	−55	135	22 49	−56	136	21 53	−55	136	20 58	−56	137
39	25 02	55	136	24 07	56	136	23 11	55	137	22 16	56	137	21 20	56	138
38	25 25	56	137	24 29	56	137	23 33	55	138	22 38	56	138	21 42	56	139
37	25 47	56	138	24 51	56	139	23 55	56	139	22 59	56	139	22 03	56	140
36	26 09	56	139	25 13	57	140	24 16	56	140	23 20	56	140	22 24	56	141
35	26 30	−56	140	25 34	−57	141	24 37	−56	141	23 41	−57	141	22 44	−56	142
34	26 51	57	141	25 54	56	142	24 58	57	142	24 01	56	142	23 05	57	143
33	27 11	57	142	26 14	56	143	25 18	57	143	24 21	57	143	23 24	57	144
32	27 31	57	143	26 34	57	144	25 37	57	144	24 40	57	144	23 43	57	145
31	27 50	57	144	26 53	57	145	25 56	57	145	24 59	57	145	24 02	57	146
30	28 09	−57	146	27 12	−58	146	26 14	−57	146	25 17	−57	147	24 20	−57	147
29	28 27	57	147	27 30	58	147	26 32	57	147	25 35	57	148	24 38	58	148
28	28 45	58	148	27 47	57	148	26 50	58	148	25 52	57	149	24 55	58	149
27	29 02	58	149	28 04	57	149	27 07	58	149	26 09	58	150	25 11	57	150
26	29 19	58	150	28 21	58	150	27 23	58	150	26 25	58	151	25 27	57	151
25	29 35	−58	151	28 37	−58	151	27 39	−58	152	26 41	−58	152	25 43	−58	152
24	29 50	58	152	28 52	58	152	27 54	58	153	26 56	58	153	25 58	58	153
23	30 05	58	153	29 07	58	153	28 09	58	154	27 11	59	154	26 12	58	154
22	30 20	58	154	29 22	59	155	28 23	58	155	27 25	59	155	26 26	58	155
21	30 34	59	155	29 35	58	156	28 37	59	156	27 38	58	156	26 40	59	156
20	30 47	−59	157	29 48	−58	157	28 50	−59	157	27 51	−58	157	26 53	−59	158
19	31 00	59	158	30 01	59	158	29 02	58	158	28 04	59	158	27 05	59	159
18	31 12	59	159	30 13	59	159	29 14	59	159	28 15	59	160	27 16	59	160
17	31 23	59	160	30 24	59	160	29 25	59	160	28 26	59	161	27 27	59	161
16	31 34	59	161	30 35	59	161	29 36	59	162	28 37	59	162	27 38	59	162
15	31 45	−60	162	30 45	−59	163	29 46	−59	163	28 47	−59	163	27 48	−60	163
14	31 54	59	163	30 55	59	164	29 56	60	164	28 56	59	164	27 57	59	164
13	32 03	59	165	31 04	60	165	30 04	59	165	29 05	59	165	28 06	60	165
12	32 11	59	166	31 12	59	166	30 13	60	166	29 13	59	166	28 14	60	166
11	32 19	59	167	31 20	60	167	30 20	59	167	29 21	60	167	28 21	60	168
10	32 26	−59	168	31 27	−60	168	30 27	−60	168	29 27	−59	169	28 28	−60	169
9	32 33	60	169	31 33	60	169	30 33	59	170	29 34	60	170	28 34	60	170
8	32 38	59	171	31 39	60	171	30 39	60	171	29 39	60	171	28 39	59	171
7	32 43	59	172	31 44	60	172	30 44	60	172	29 44	60	172	28 44	60	172
6	32 48	60	173	31 48	60	173	30 48	60	173	29 48	60	173	28 48	60	173
5	32 52	−60	174	31 52	−60	174	30 52	−60	174	29 52	−60	174	28 52	−60	174
4	32 55	60	175	31 55	60	175	30 55	60	175	29 55	60	175	28 55	60	175
3	32 57	60	176	31 57	60	177	30 57	60	177	29 57	60	177	28 57	60	177
2	32 59	60	178	31 59	60	178	30 59	60	178	29 59	60	178	28 59	60	178
1	33 00	60	179	32 00	60	179	31 00	60	179	30 00	60	179	29 00	60	179
0	33 00	−60	180	32 00	−60	180	31 00	−60	180	30 00	−60	180	29 00	−60	180

LHA	5° Hc	d	Z	6° Hc	d	Z	7° Hc	d	Z	8° Hc	d	Z	9° Hc	d	Z
	° ′	′	°	° ′	′	°	° ′	′	°	° ′	′	°	° ′	′	°
69	06 58	51	111	06 07	52	111	05 15	52	112	04 23	51	112	03 32	52	113
68	07 29	52	111	06 37	52	112	05 45	51	112	04 54	52	113	04 02	52	113
67	07 59	52	112	07 07	51	113	06 16	52	113	05 24	52	114	04 32	52	114
66	08 29	52	113	07 37	52	114	06 45	51	114	05 54	52	115	05 02	52	115
65	08 59	−52	114	08 07	−52	114	07 15	−52	115	06 23	−52	115	05 31	−52	116
64	09 29	52	115	08 37	52	115	07 45	52	116	06 53	53	116	06 00	52	117
63	09 59	53	116	09 06	52	116	08 14	52	117	07 22	53	117	06 29	52	118
62	10 28	52	117	09 36	53	117	08 43	52	118	07 51	53	118	06 58	52	119
61	10 57	52	117	10 05	53	118	09 12	53	118	08 19	52	119	07 27	53	119
60	11 26	−53	118	10 33	−52	119	09 41	−53	119	08 48	−53	120	07 55	−53	120
59	11 55	53	119	11 02	53	120	10 09	53	120	09 16	53	121	08 23	53	121
58	12 23	53	120	11 30	53	121	10 37	53	121	09 44	53	122	08 51	53	122
57	12 51	53	121	11 58	53	122	11 05	53	122	10 12	53	123	09 19	54	123
56	13 19	53	122	12 26	53	122	11 33	54	123	10 39	53	123	09 46	53	124
55	13 47	−54	123	12 53	−53	123	12 00	−54	124	11 06	−53	124	10 13	−54	125
54	14 14	54	124	13 20	53	124	12 27	54	125	11 33	53	125	10 40	54	126
53	14 41	54	125	13 47	53	125	12 54	54	126	12 00	54	126	11 06	54	127
52	15 08	54	126	14 14	54	126	13 20	54	127	12 26	54	127	11 32	54	127
51	15 34	54	127	14 40	54	127	13 46	54	127	12 52	54	128	11 58	54	128
50	16 00	−54	127	15 06	−54	128	14 12	−54	128	13 18	−54	129	12 24	−55	129
49	16 26	54	128	15 32	55	129	14 37	54	129	13 43	54	130	12 49	55	130
48	16 51	54	129	15 57	54	130	15 03	55	130	14 08	55	131	13 13	54	131
47	17 16	54	130	16 22	55	131	15 27	54	131	14 33	55	132	13 38	55	132
46	17 41	54	131	16 47	55	132	15 52	55	132	14 57	55	133	14 02	55	133
45	18 06	−55	132	17 11	−55	133	16 16	−55	133	15 21	−55	133	14 26	−55	134
44	18 30	55	133	17 35	55	134	16 40	56	134	15 44	55	134	14 49	55	135
43	18 53	55	134	17 58	55	135	17 03	55	135	16 08	56	135	15 12	55	136
42	19 17	56	135	18 21	55	136	17 26	56	136	16 30	55	136	15 35	56	137
41	19 39	55	136	18 44	56	137	17 48	55	137	16 53	56	137	15 57	56	138
40	20 02	−56	137	19 06	−56	137	18 10	−55	138	17 15	−56	138	16 19	−56	139
39	20 24	56	138	19 28	56	138	18 32	56	139	17 36	56	139	16 40	56	140
38	20 46	56	139	19 50	56	139	18 54	57	140	17 57	56	140	17 01	56	141
37	21 07	56	140	20 11	57	140	19 14	56	141	18 18	56	141	17 22	57	142
36	21 28	57	141	20 31	56	141	19 35	57	142	18 38	56	142	17 42	57	143
35	21 48	−57	142	20 51	−56	142	19 55	−57	143	18 58	−56	143	18 02	−57	143
34	22 08	57	143	21 11	57	143	20 14	56	144	19 18	57	144	18 21	57	144
33	22 27	57	144	21 30	56	144	20 34	57	145	19 37	57	145	18 40	57	145
32	22 46	57	145	21 49	57	145	20 52	57	146	19 55	57	146	18 58	57	146
31	23 05	57	146	22 08	58	146	21 10	57	147	20 13	57	147	19 16	57	147
30	23 23	−58	147	22 25	−57	148	21 28	−57	148	20 31	−58	148	19 33	−57	148
29	23 40	57	148	22 43	58	149	21 45	57	149	20 48	58	149	19 50	58	149
28	23 57	57	149	23 00	58	150	22 02	58	150	21 04	58	150	20 06	57	150
27	24 14	58	150	23 16	58	151	22 18	58	151	21 20	58	151	20 22	58	151
26	24 30	58	151	23 32	58	152	22 34	58	152	21 36	58	152	20 38	58	152
25	24 45	−58	152	23 47	−58	153	22 49	−58	153	21 51	−58	153	20 53	−59	154
24	25 00	58	153	24 02	59	154	23 03	58	154	22 05	58	154	21 07	58	155
23	25 14	58	155	24 16	59	155	23 17	58	155	22 19	58	155	21 21	59	156
22	25 28	58	156	24 30	59	156	23 31	58	156	22 33	59	156	21 34	59	157
21	25 41	58	157	24 43	59	157	23 44	59	157	22 45	58	157	21 47	59	158
20	25 54	−59	158	24 55	−59	158	23 56	−58	158	22 58	−59	158	21 59	−59	159
19	26 06	59	159	25 07	59	159	24 08	59	159	23 09	58	160	22 11	59	160
18	26 17	58	160	25 19	59	160	24 20	59	160	23 21	59	161	22 22	59	161
17	26 28	59	161	25 29	59	161	24 30	59	161	23 31	59	162	22 32	59	162
16	26 39	59	162	25 40	60	162	24 40	59	163	23 41	59	163	22 42	59	163
15	26 48	−59	163	25 49	−59	163	24 50	−59	164	23 51	−60	164	22 51	−59	164
14	26 58	60	164	25 58	59	165	24 59	59	165	24 00	60	165	23 00	59	165
13	27 06	59	165	26 07	60	166	25 07	59	166	24 08	60	166	23 08	59	166
12	27 14	59	167	26 15	60	167	25 15	60	167	24 15	59	167	23 16	60	167
11	27 21	59	168	26 22	60	168	25 22	59	168	24 23	60	168	23 23	60	168
10	27 28	−60	169	26 28	−59	169	25 29	−60	169	24 29	−60	169	23 29	−59	169
9	27 34	60	170	26 34	59	170	25 35	60	170	24 35	60	170	23 35	60	170
8	27 40	60	171	26 40	60	171	25 40	60	171	24 40	60	171	23 40	60	171
7	27 44	60	172	26 44	59	172	25 45	60	172	24 45	60	172	23 45	60	172
6	27 48	59	173	26 49	60	173	25 49	60	173	24 49	60	174	23 49	60	174
5	27 52	−60	174	26 52	−60	174	25 52	−60	175	24 52	−60	175	23 52	−60	175
4	27 55	60	176	26 55	60	176	25 55	60	176	24 55	60	176	23 55	60	176
3	27 57	60	177	26 57	60	177	25 57	60	177	24 57	60	177	23 57	60	177
2	27 59	60	178	26 59	60	178	25 59	60	178	24 59	60	178	23 59	60	178
1	28 00	60	179	27 00	60	179	26 00	60	179	25 00	60	179	24 00	60	179
0	28 00	−60	180	27 00	−60	180	26 00	−60	180	25 00	−60	180	24 00	−60	180

LHA	10° Hc	d	Z	11° Hc	d	Z	12° Hc	d	Z	13° Hc	d	Z	14° Hc	d	Z	LHA
	° ′	′	°	° ′	′	°	° ′	′	°	° ′	′	°	° ′	′	°	
69	02 40	51	113	01 49	52	114	00 57	52	114	00 05	51	115	−0 46	52	115	291
68	03 10	52	114	02 18	51	114	01 27	52	115	00 35	52	115	−0 17	52	116	292
67	03 40	52	115	02 48	52	115	01 56	52	116	01 04	52	116	00 12	52	117	293
66	04 10	52	116	03 18	52	116	02 26	53	117	01 33	52	117	00 41	52	118	294
65	04 39	−52	116	03 47	−52	117	02 55	−53	117	02 02	−52	118	01 10	−52	118	295
64	05 08	52	117	04 16	52	118	03 24	53	118	02 31	52	119	01 39	52	119	296
63	05 37	52	118	04 45	53	119	03 52	52	119	03 00	53	120	02 07	52	120	297
62	06 06	53	119	05 13	52	120	04 21	53	120	03 28	53	120	02 35	52	121	298
61	06 34	52	120	05 42	53	120	04 49	53	121	03 56	53	121	03 03	52	122	299
60	07 02	−52	121	06 10	−53	121	05 17	−53	122	04 24	−53	122	03 31	−53	123	300
59	07 30	53	122	06 37	53	122	05 44	53	123	04 51	53	123	03 58	53	124	301
58	07 58	53	123	07 05	53	123	06 12	53	123	05 19	54	124	04 25	53	124	302
57	08 25	53	123	07 32	53	124	06 39	53	124	05 46	54	125	04 52	53	125	303
56	08 53	54	124	07 59	53	125	07 06	54	125	06 12	53	126	05 19	54	126	304
55	09 19	−53	125	08 26	−54	126	07 32	−53	126	06 39	−54	127	05 45	−54	127	305
54	09 46	54	126	08 52	53	127	07 59	54	127	07 05	54	127	06 11	54	128	306
53	10 12	54	127	09 18	53	127	08 25	54	128	07 31	54	128	06 37	54	129	307
52	10 38	54	128	09 44	54	128	08 50	54	129	07 56	54	129	07 02	54	130	308
51	11 04	54	129	10 10	54	129	09 16	55	130	08 21	54	130	07 27	54	131	309
50	11 29	−54	130	10 35	−54	130	09 41	−55	131	08 46	−54	131	07 52	−55	131	310
49	11 54	54	131	11 00	55	131	10 05	54	131	09 11	55	132	08 16	54	132	311
48	12 19	55	132	11 24	54	132	10 30	55	132	09 35	55	133	08 40	55	133	312
47	12 43	55	132	11 48	54	133	10 54	55	133	09 59	55	134	09 04	55	134	313
46	13 07	55	133	12 12	55	134	11 17	55	134	10 22	55	135	09 27	55	135	314
45	13 31	−55	134	12 36	−56	135	11 40	−55	135	10 45	−55	136	09 50	−55	136	315
44	13 54	55	135	12 59	56	136	12 03	55	136	11 08	55	136	10 13	56	137	316
43	14 17	56	136	13 21	55	137	12 26	56	137	11 30	55	137	10 35	56	138	317
42	14 39	55	137	13 44	56	138	12 48	56	138	11 52	55	138	10 57	56	139	318
41	15 01	55	138	14 06	56	138	13 10	56	139	12 14	56	139	11 18	56	140	319
40	15 23	−56	139	14 27	−56	139	13 31	−56	140	12 35	−56	140	11 39	−56	140	320
39	15 44	56	140	14 48	56	140	13 52	56	141	12 56	56	141	12 00	57	141	321
38	16 05	56	141	15 09	57	141	14 12	56	142	13 16	56	142	12 20	57	142	322
37	16 25	56	142	15 29	56	142	14 33	57	143	13 36	56	143	12 40	57	143	323
36	16 45	56	143	15 49	57	143	14 52	56	144	13 56	57	144	12 59	57	144	324
35	17 05	−57	144	16 08	−57	144	15 11	−56	145	14 15	−57	145	13 18	−57	145	325
34	17 24	57	145	16 27	57	145	15 30	57	145	14 33	57	146	13 36	57	146	326
33	17 43	57	146	16 46	57	146	15 49	58	146	14 51	57	147	13 54	57	147	327
32	18 01	57	147	17 04	58	147	16 06	57	147	15 09	57	148	14 12	57	148	328
31	18 19	58	148	17 21	57	148	16 24	58	148	15 26	57	149	14 29	57	149	329
30	18 36	−58	149	17 38	−57	149	16 41	−58	149	15 43	−57	150	14 46	−58	150	330
29	18 52	57	150	17 55	58	150	16 57	58	150	15 59	57	151	15 02	58	151	331
28	19 09	58	151	18 11	58	151	17 13	58	151	16 15	58	152	15 17	57	152	332
27	19 24	57	152	18 27	58	152	17 29	58	152	16 31	58	153	15 33	58	153	333
26	19 40	58	153	18 42	58	153	17 44	59	153	16 45	58	154	15 47	58	154	334
25	19 54	−58	154	18 56	−58	154	17 58	−58	154	17 00	−58	155	16 02	−59	155	335
24	20 09	59	155	19 10	58	155	18 12	58	155	17 14	59	156	16 15	58	156	336
23	20 22	58	156	19 24	59	156	18 25	58	156	17 27	59	157	16 28	58	157	337
22	20 35	58	157	19 37	59	157	18 38	58	157	17 40	59	158	16 41	59	158	338
21	20 48	59	158	19 49	58	158	18 51	59	158	17 52	59	159	16 53	59	159	339
20	21 00	−59	159	20 01	−59	159	19 02	−58	159	18 04	−59	160	17 05	−59	160	340
19	21 12	59	160	20 13	59	160	19 14	59	160	18 15	59	161	17 16	59	161	341
18	21 23	59	161	20 24	59	161	19 25	60	161	18 25	59	162	17 26	59	162	342
17	21 33	59	162	20 34	59	162	19 35	59	162	18 36	60	163	17 36	59	163	343
16	21 43	59	163	20 44	60	163	19 44	59	163	18 45	59	164	17 46	59	164	344
15	21 52	−59	164	20 53	−60	164	19 53	−59	164	18 54	−59	165	17 55	−60	165	345
14	22 01	60	165	21 01	59	165	20 02	59	165	19 03	60	166	18 03	59	166	346
13	22 09	60	166	21 09	59	166	20 10	60	166	19 10	59	167	18 11	60	167	347
12	22 16	59	167	21 17	60	167	20 17	59	168	19 18	60	168	18 18	59	168	348
11	22 23	59	168	21 24	60	168	20 24	60	169	19 24	59	169	18 25	60	169	349
10	22 30	−60	169	21 30	−60	169	20 30	−59	170	19 31	−60	170	18 31	−60	170	350
9	22 35	59	170	21 36	60	171	20 36	60	171	19 36	60	171	18 36	59	171	351
8	22 41	60	172	21 41	60	172	20 41	60	172	19 41	60	172	18 41	59	172	352
7	22 45	60	173	21 45	60	173	20 45	59	173	19 46	60	173	18 46	60	173	353
6	22 49	60	174	21 49	60	174	20 49	60	174	19 49	59	174	18 50	60	174	354
5	22 52	−59	175	21 53	−60	175	20 53	−60	175	19 53	−60	175	18 53	−60	175	355
4	22 55	60	176	21 55	60	176	20 55	60	176	19 55	60	176	18 55	60	176	356
3	22 57	60	177	21 57	60	177	20 57	60	177	19 57	60	177	18 57	60	177	357
2	22 59	60	178	21 59	60	178	20 59	60	178	19 59	60	178	18 59	60	178	358
1	23 00	60	179	22 00	60	179	21 00	60	179	20 00	60	179	19 00	60	179	359
0	23 00	−60	180	22 00	−60	180	21 00	−60	180	20 00	−60	180	19 00	−60	180	360

S. Lat. {LHA greater than 180°........ Zn=180−Z; LHA less than 180°........... Zn=180+Z}

DECLINATION (0°-14°) CONTRARY NAME TO LATITUDE

N. Lat. {LHA greater than 180°....... Zn=Z; LHA less than 180°.......... Zn=360−Z}

DECLINATION (15°-29°) SAME NAME AS LATITUDE

LHA	15° Hc	d	Z	16° Hc	d	Z	17° Hc	d	Z	18° Hc	d	Z	19° Hc	d	Z
	° ′	′	°	° ′	′	°	° ′	′	°	° ′	′	°	° ′	′	°
0	48 00	+60	180	49 00	+60	180	50 00	+60	180	51 00	+60	180	52 00	+60	180
1	48 00	60	179	49 00	60	179	50 00	60	179	51 00	60	179	52 00	60	179
2	47 58	60	177	48 58	60	177	49 58	60	177	50 58	60	177	51 58	60	177
3	47 56	60	176	48 56	60	176	49 56	60	176	50 56	60	176	51 56	60	175
4	47 53	60	174	48 53	60	174	49 53	60	174	50 53	60	174	51 53	60	174
5	47 50	+60	173	48 50	+59	173	49 49	+60	173	50 49	+60	173	51 49	+60	172
6	47 45	60	171	48 45	60	171	49 45	60	171	50 45	59	171	51 44	60	171
7	47 40	60	170	48 40	59	170	49 39	60	170	50 39	60	170	51 39	59	169
8	47 34	59	169	48 33	60	168	49 33	60	168	50 33	59	168	51 32	60	168
9	47 27	59	167	48 26	60	167	49 26	59	167	50 25	60	167	51 25	59	166
10	47 19	+60	166	48 19	+59	166	49 18	+59	165	50 17	+60	165	51 17	+59	165
11	47 11	59	164	48 10	59	164	49 09	60	164	50 09	59	164	51 08	59	163
12	47 02	59	163	48 01	59	163	49 00	59	162	49 59	59	162	50 58	59	162
13	46 52	59	162	47 51	59	161	48 50	58	161	49 48	59	161	50 47	59	160
14	46 41	59	160	47 40	58	160	48 38	59	160	49 37	59	159	50 36	59	159
15	46 29	+57	159	47 28	+59	158	48 27	+58	158	49 25	+59	158	50 24	+58	157
16	46 17	59	157	47 16	58	157	48 14	58	157	49 12	59	156	50 11	58	156
17	46 04	58	156	47 02	59	156	48 01	58	155	48 59	58	155	49 57	58	155
18	45 50	59	155	46 49	58	154	47 47	58	154	48 45	58	154	49 43	58	153
19	45 36	58	153	46 34	58	153	47 32	58	153	48 30	58	152	49 28	57	152
20	45 21	+58	152	46 19	+58	152	47 17	+57	151	48 14	+58	151	49 12	+57	150
21	45 05	58	151	46 03	58	150	47 01	57	150	47 58	57	149	48 55	58	149
22	44 49	57	149	45 46	58	149	46 44	57	149	47 41	57	148	48 38	57	148
23	44 32	57	148	45 29	57	148	46 26	57	147	47 23	57	147	48 20	57	146
24	44 14	57	147	45 11	57	146	46 08	57	146	47 05	57	145	48 02	56	145
25	43 56	+57	146	44 53	+57	145	45 50	+56	145	46 46	+57	144	47 43	+56	144
26	43 37	57	144	44 34	56	144	45 30	57	143	46 27	56	143	47 23	56	142
27	43 18	56	143	44 14	57	143	45 11	56	142	46 07	56	142	47 03	56	141
28	42 58	56	142	43 54	56	141	44 50	56	141	45 46	56	140	46 42	55	140
29	42 37	56	141	43 33	56	140	44 29	56	140	45 25	55	139	46 20	56	138
30	42 16	+56	139	43 12	+56	139	44 08	+55	138	45 03	+55	138	45 58	+56	137
31	41 55	55	138	42 50	56	138	43 46	55	137	44 41	55	137	45 36	55	136
32	41 33	55	137	42 28	55	136	43 23	55	136	44 18	55	135	45 13	55	135
33	41 10	55	136	42 05	55	135	43 00	55	135	43 55	54	134	44 49	55	134
34	40 47	55	135	41 42	55	134	42 37	54	133	43 31	55	133	44 26	54	132
35	40 24	+54	133	41 18	+55	133	42 13	+54	132	43 07	+54	132	44 01	+54	131
36	40 00	54	132	40 54	54	132	41 48	54	131	42 42	54	131	43 36	54	130
37	39 35	54	131	40 29	54	131	41 23	54	130	42 17	54	129	43 11	53	129
38	39 10	54	130	40 04	54	129	40 58	54	129	41 52	53	128	42 45	54	128
39	38 45	54	129	39 39	53	128	40 32	54	128	41 26	53	127	42 19	53	126
40	38 19	+54	128	39 13	+53	127	40 06	+54	127	41 00	+53	126	41 53	+53	125
41	37 53	54	127	38 47	53	126	39 40	53	125	40 33	53	125	41 26	52	124
42	37 27	53	126	38 20	53	125	39 13	53	124	40 06	53	124	40 59	52	123
43	37 00	53	124	37 53	53	124	38 46	53	123	39 39	52	123	40 31	52	122
44	36 33	53	123	37 26	52	123	38 18	53	122	39 11	52	122	40 03	52	121
45	36 05	+53	122	36 58	+53	122	37 51	+52	121	38 43	+52	121	39 35	+52	120
46	35 38	52	121	36 30	52	121	37 22	53	120	38 15	51	119	39 06	52	119
47	35 10	52	120	36 02	52	120	36 54	52	119	37 46	52	118	38 38	51	118
48	34 41	52	119	35 33	52	119	36 25	52	118	37 17	52	117	38 09	51	117
49	34 13	52	118	35 05	51	118	35 56	52	117	36 48	51	116	37 39	51	116
50	33 44	+51	117	34 35	+52	117	35 27	+51	116	36 18	+52	115	37 10	+51	115
51	33 14	52	116	34 06	52	116	34 58	51	115	35 49	51	114	36 40	51	114
52	32 45	51	115	33 36	52	115	34 28	51	114	35 19	51	113	36 10	51	113
53	32 15	52	114	33 07	51	114	33 58	51	113	34 49	51	112	35 40	50	112
54	31 45	52	113	32 37	51	113	33 28	50	112	34 18	51	111	35 09	51	111
55	31 15	+51	112	32 06	+51	112	32 57	+51	111	33 48	+50	110	34 38	+51	110
56	30 45	51	111	31 36	51	111	32 27	50	110	33 17	51	109	34 08	50	109
57	30 14	51	110	31 05	51	110	31 56	50	109	32 46	51	109	33 37	50	108
58	29 44	50	109	30 34	51	109	31 25	50	108	32 15	50	108	33 05	50	107
59	29 13	50	109	30 03	51	108	30 54	50	107	31 44	50	107	32 34	50	106
60	28 42	+50	108	29 32	+50	107	30 22	+51	106	31 13	+50	106	32 03	+49	105
61	28 10	51	107	29 01	50	106	29 51	50	105	30 41	50	105	31 31	50	104
62	27 39	50	106	28 29	50	105	29 19	50	104	30 09	50	104	30 59	50	103
63	27 07	51	105	27 58	50	104	28 48	50	104	29 38	49	103	30 27	50	102
64	26 36	50	104	27 26	50	103	28 16	50	103	29 06	49	102	29 55	50	101
65	26 04	+50	103	26 54	+50	102	27 44	+50	102	28 34	+49	101	29 23	+50	100
66	25 32	50	102	26 22	50	101	27 12	50	101	28 02	49	100	28 51	49	100
67	25 00	50	101	25 50	50	101	26 40	49	100	27 29	50	99	28 19	49	99
68	24 28	50	100	25 18	49	100	26 07	50	99	26 57	49	98	27 46	50	98
69	23 56	50	99	24 46	49	99	25 35	50	98	26 25	49	98	27 14	49	97

LHA	20° Hc	d	Z	21° Hc	d	Z	22° Hc	d	Z	23° Hc	d	Z	24° Hc	d	Z
	° ′	′	°	° ′	′	°	° ′	′	°	° ′	′	°	° ′	′	°
0	53 00	+60	180	54 00	+60	180	55 00	+60	180	56 00	+60	180	57 00	+60	180
1	53 00	60	178	54 00	60	178	55 00	60	178	56 00	60	178	57 00	60	178
2	52 58	60	177	53 58	60	177	54 58	60	177	55 58	60	177	56 58	60	177
3	52 56	60	175	53 56	60	175	54 56	60	175	55 56	60	175	56 56	60	175
4	52 53	60	174	53 53	60	174	54 53	60	174	55 53	59	173	56 52	60	173
5	52 49	+60	172	53 49	+60	172	54 49	+59	172	55 48	+60	172	56 48	+60	172
6	52 44	60	171	53 44	60	171	54 44	59	170	55 43	60	170	56 43	60	170
7	52 38	60	169	53 38	60	169	54 38	59	169	55 37	60	169	56 37	59	168
8	52 32	59	168	53 31	60	168	54 31	59	167	55 30	60	167	56 30	59	167
9	52 24	60	166	53 24	59	166	54 23	59	166	55 22	60	165	56 22	59	165
10	52 16	+59	165	53 15	+59	164	54 14	+60	164	55 14	+59	164	56 13	+59	163
11	52 07	59	163	53 06	59	163	54 05	59	162	55 04	59	162	56 03	59	162
12	51 57	59	162	52 56	59	161	53 55	59	161	54 54	58	161	55 52	59	160
13	51 46	59	160	52 45	59	160	53 44	58	159	54 42	59	159	55 41	58	159
14	51 35	58	159	52 33	59	158	53 32	58	158	54 30	59	157	55 29	58	157
15	51 22	+59	157	52 21	+58	157	53 19	+58	156	54 17	+58	156	55 15	+59	156
16	51 09	58	156	52 07	59	155	53 06	58	155	54 04	58	154	55 02	57	154
17	50 55	58	154	51 53	58	154	52 51	58	153	53 49	58	153	54 47	57	152
18	50 41	57	153	51 38	58	152	52 36	58	152	53 34	57	151	54 31	58	151
19	50 25	58	151	51 23	57	151	52 20	58	150	53 18	57	150	54 15	57	149
20	50 09	+58	150	51 07	+57	149	52 04	+57	149	53 01	+57	148	53 58	+57	148
21	49 53	57	149	50 50	57	148	51 47	57	148	52 44	56	147	53 40	57	147
22	49 35	57	147	50 32	57	147	51 29	56	146	52 25	57	146	53 22	56	145
23	49 17	57	146	50 14	56	145	51 10	57	145	52 07	56	144	53 03	56	144
24	48 58	57	144	49 55	56	144	50 51	56	143	51 47	56	143	52 43	56	142
25	48 39	+56	143	49 35	+56	143	50 31	+56	142	51 27	+56	141	52 23	+55	141
26	48 19	56	142	49 15	56	141	50 11	55	141	51 06	56	140	52 02	55	139
27	47 59	55	140	48 54	56	140	49 50	55	139	50 45	55	139	51 40	55	138
28	47 37	56	139	48 33	55	139	49 28	55	138	50 23	55	137	51 18	55	137
29	47 16	55	138	48 11	55	137	49 06	55	137	50 01	54	136	50 55	55	135
30	46 54	+55	137	47 49	+54	136	48 43	+55	135	49 38	+54	135	50 32	+54	134
31	46 31	55	135	47 26	54	135	48 20	54	134	49 14	54	133	50 08	54	133
32	46 08	54	134	47 02	54	134	47 56	54	133	48 50	54	132	49 44	54	132
33	45 44	54	133	46 38	54	132	47 32	54	132	48 26	53	131	49 19	54	130
34	45 20	54	132	46 14	53	131	47 07	54	130	48 01	53	130	48 54	53	129
35	44 55	+54	130	45 49	+53	130	46 42	+54	129	47 36	+53	129	48 29	+52	128
36	44 30	53	129	45 23	54	129	46 17	53	128	47 10	53	127	48 03	52	127
37	44 04	54	128	44 58	53	127	45 51	53	127	46 44	52	126	47 36	52	125
38	43 39	53	127	44 32	52	126	45 24	53	126	46 17	52	125	47 09	52	124
39	43 12	53	126	44 05	53	125	44 58	52	125	45 50	52	124	46 42	52	123
40	42 46	+52	125	43 38	+53	124	44 31	+52	123	45 23	+52	123	46 15	+51	122
41	42 18	53	124	43 11	52	123	44 03	52	122	44 55	52	122	45 47	51	121
42	41 51	52	122	42 43	52	122	43 35	52	121	44 27	51	120	45 18	52	120
43	41 23	52	121	42 15	52	121	43 07	52	120	43 59	51	119	44 50	51	119
44	40 55	52	120	41 47	52	120	42 39	51	119	43 30	51	118	44 21	51	117
45	40 27	+51	119	41 18	+52	119	42 10	+51	118	43 01	+51	117	43 52	+50	116
46	39 58	52	118	40 50	51	117	41 41	51	117	42 32	50	116	43 22	51	115
47	39 29	51	117	40 20	51	116	41 11	51	116	42 02	51	115	42 53	50	114
48	39 00	51	116	39 51	51	115	40 42	51	115	41 33	50	114	42 23	50	113
49	38 30	51	115	39 21	51	114	40 12	51	114	41 03	50	113	41 53	50	112
50	38 01	+51	114	38 52	+50	113	39 42	+50	113	40 32	+50	112	41 22	+50	111
51	37 31	50	113	38 21	51	112	39 12	50	112	40 02	50	111	40 52	49	110
52	37 01	50	112	37 51	50	111	38 41	50	111	39 31	50	110	40 21	49	109
53	36 30	50	111	37 20	51	110	38 11	49	110	39 00	50	109	39 50	49	108
54	36 00	50	110	36 50	51	109	37 40	49	109	38 29	50	108	39 19	49	107
55	35 29	+50	109	36 19	+50	108	37 09	+49	108	37 58	+50	107	38 48	+49	106
56	34 58	50	108	35 48	49	107	36 37	50	107	37 27	49	106	38 16	49	105
57	34 27	49	107	35 16	50	106	36 06	49	106	36 55	50	105	37 45	48	104
58	33 55	50	106	34 45	50	106	35 35	49	105	36 24	49	104	37 13	49	103
59	33 24	49	105	34 13	50	105	35 03	49	104	35 52	49	103	36 41	49	103
60	32 52	+50	104	33 42	+49	104	34 31	+49	103	35 20	+49	102	36 09	+49	102
61	32 21	49	103	33 10	49	103	33 59	49	102	34 48	49	101	35 37	48	101
62	31 49	49	103	32 38	49	102	33 27	49	101	34 16	49	100	35 05	48	100
63	31 17	49	102	32 06	49	101	32 55	49	100	33 44	49	100	34 33	48	99
64	30 45	49	101	31 34	49	100	32 23	49	99	33 12	48	99	34 00	49	98
65	30 13	+49	100	31 02	+49	99	31 51	+48	98	32 39	+49	98	33 28	+48	97
66	29 40	49	99	30 29	49	98	31 18	48	98	32 07	48	97	32 55	49	96
67	29 08	49	98	29 57	49	97	30 46	48	97	31 34	49	96	32 23	48	95
68	28 36	49	97	29 25	48	97	30 13	49	96	31 02	48	95	31 50	48	94
69	28 03	49	96	28 52	49	96	29 41	48	95	30 29	49	94	31 18	48	94

LHA	25° Hc	d	Z	26° Hc	d	Z	27° Hc	d	Z	28° Hc	d	Z	29° Hc	d	Z	LHA
	° ′	′	°	° ′	′	°	° ′	′	°	° ′	′	°	° ′	′	°	
0	58 00	+60	180	59 00	+60	180	60 00	+60	180	61 00	+60	180	62 00	+60	180	360
1	58 00	60	178	59 00	60	178	60 00	60	178	61 00	60	178	62 00	60	178	359
2	57 58	60	177	58 58	60	177	59 58	60	176	60 58	60	176	61 58	60	176	358
3	57 56	60	175	58 56	59	175	59 55	60	175	60 55	60	175	61 55	60	174	357
4	57 52	60	173	58 52	60	173	59 52	60	173	60 52	60	173	61 52	59	173	356
5	57 48	+60	172	58 48	+59	171	59 47	+60	171	60 47	+60	171	61 47	+60	171	355
6	57 43	59	170	58 42	60	170	59 42	59	169	60 41	60	169	61 41	60	169	354
7	57 36	60	168	58 36	59	168	59 35	60	168	60 35	59	167	61 34	60	167	353
8	57 29	59	166	58 28	60	166	59 28	59	166	60 27	59	166	61 26	60	165	352
9	57 21	59	165	58 20	59	165	59 19	60	164	60 19	59	164	61 18	59	164	351
10	57 12	+59	163	58 11	+59	163	59 10	+59	162	60 09	+59	162	61 08	+59	162	350
11	57 02	59	162	58 01	59	161	59 00	58	161	59 58	59	160	60 57	59	160	349
12	56 51	59	160	57 50	58	160	58 48	59	159	59 47	58	159	60 45	59	158	348
13	56 39	59	158	57 38	58	158	58 36	59	157	59 35	58	157	60 33	58	156	347
14	56 27	58	157	57 25	58	156	58 23	58	156	59 21	58	155	60 19	58	155	346
15	56 14	+58	155	57 12	+57	155	58 09	+58	154	59 07	+58	154	60 05	+57	153	345
16	55 59	58	154	56 57	58	153	57 55	57	153	58 52	58	152	59 50	57	151	344
17	55 44	58	152	56 42	57	151	57 39	57	151	58 36	57	150	59 33	57	150	343
18	55 29	57	150	56 26	57	150	57 23	57	149	58 20	57	149	59 17	56	148	342
19	55 12	57	149	56 09	57	148	57 06	56	148	58 02	57	147	58 59	56	147	341
20	54 55	+57	147	55 52	+56	147	56 48	+56	146	57 44	+56	146	58 40	+56	145	340
21	54 37	56	146	55 33	56	145	56 29	56	145	57 25	56	144	58 21	56	143	339
22	54 18	56	144	55 14	56	144	56 10	56	143	57 06	55	143	58 01	56	142	338
23	53 59	56	143	54 55	55	142	55 50	56	142	56 46	55	141	57 41	55	140	337
24	53 39	55	142	54 34	56	141	55 30	55	140	56 25	55	140	57 20	54	139	336
25	53 18	+55	140	54 13	+55	140	55 08	+55	139	56 03	+55	138	56 58	+54	137	335
26	52 57	55	139	53 52	55	138	54 47	54	137	55 41	54	137	56 35	54	136	334
27	52 35	55	137	53 30	54	137	54 24	54	136	55 18	54	135	56 12	54	135	333
28	52 13	54	136	53 07	54	135	54 01	54	135	54 55	54	134	55 49	53	133	332
29	51 50	54	135	52 44	54	134	53 38	53	133	54 31	54	133	55 25	53	132	331
30	51 26	+54	133	52 20	+54	133	53 14	+53	132	54 07	+53	131	55 00	+53	130	330
31	51 02	54	132	51 56	53	131	52 49	53	131	53 42	53	130	54 35	52	129	329
32	50 38	53	131	51 31	53	130	52 24	53	129	53 17	52	129	54 09	52	128	328
33	50 13	53	130	51 06	53	129	51 59	52	128	52 51	52	127	53 43	52	126	327
34	49 47	53	128	50 40	53	128	51 33	52	127	52 25	52	126	53 17	51	125	326
35	49 21	+53	127	50 14	+52	126	51 06	+52	126	51 58	+52	125	52 50	+51	124	325
36	48 55	52	126	49 47	52	125	50 39	52	124	51 31	51	124	52 22	51	123	324
37	48 28	52	125	49 20	52	124	50 12	52	123	51 04	51	122	51 55	50	121	323
38	48 01	52	124	48 53	52	123	49 45	51	122	50 36	51	121	51 27	50	120	322
39	47 34	51	122	48 25	52	122	49 17	51	121	50 08	50	120	50 58	50	119	321
40	47 06	+51	121	47 57	+51	120	48 48	+51	120	49 39	+50	119	50 29	+50	118	320
41	46 38	51	120	47 29	51	119	48 20	50	118	49 10	50	118	50 00	50	117	319
42	46 10	50	119	47 00	51	118	47 51	50	117	48 41	50	117	49 31	50	116	318
43	45 41	50	118	46 31	51	117	47 22	50	116	48 12	49	115	49 01	50	115	317
44	45 12	50	117	46 02	50	116	46 52	50	115	47 42	50	114	48 32	49	114	316
45	44 42	+51	116	45 33	+50	115	46 23	+49	114	47 12	+50	113	48 02	+48	112	315
46	44 13	50	115	45 03	50	114	45 53	49	113	46 42	49	112	47 31	49	111	314
47	43 43	50	114	44 33	49	113	45 22	50	112	46 12	49	111	47 01	48	110	313
48	43 13	50	113	44 03	49	112	44 52	49	111	45 41	49	110	46 30	48	109	312
49	42 43	49	112	43 32	49	111	44 21	49	110	45 10	49	109	45 59	48	108	311
50	42 12	+49	110	43 01	+50	110	43 51	+48	109	44 39	+49	108	45 28	+48	107	310
51	41 41	50	109	42 31	49	109	43 20	48	108	44 08	48	107	44 56	48	106	309
52	41 10	50	108	42 00	48	108	42 48	49	107	43 37	48	106	44 25	48	105	308
53	40 39	49	107	41 28	49	107	42 17	48	106	43 05	48	105	43 53	48	104	307
54	40 08	49	107	40 57	49	106	41 46	48	105	42 34	48	104	43 22	47	103	306
55	39 37	+48	106	40 25	+49	105	41 14	+48	104	42 02	+48	103	42 50	+47	102	305
56	39 05	49	105	39 54	48	104	40 42	48	103	41 30	48	102	42 18	47	101	304
57	38 33	49	104	39 22	48	103	40 10	48	102	40 58	48	101	41 46	47	101	303
58	38 02	48	103	38 50	48	102	39 38	48	101	40 26	48	100	41 14	47	100	302
59	37 30	48	102	38 18	48	101	39 06	48	100	39 54	47	99	40 41	47	99	301
60	36 58	+48	101	37 46	+48	100	38 34	+48	99	39 22	+47	99	40 09	+47	98	300
61	36 25	49	100	37 14	48	99	38 02	47	98	38 49	48	98	39 37	47	97	299
62	35 53	48	99	36 41	48	98	37 29	48	98	38 17	47	97	39 04	47	96	298
63	35 21	48	98	36 09	48	97	36 57	47	97	37 44	48	96	38 32	46	95	297
64	34 49	48	97	35 37	47	97	36 24	48	96	37 12	47	95	37 59	47	94	296
65	34 16	+48	96	35 04	+48	96	35 52	+47	95	36 39	+47	94	37 26	+47	93	295
66	33 44	48	95	34 32	47	95	35 19	48	94	36 07	47	93	36 54	47	93	294
67	33 11	48	95	33 59	48	94	34 47	47	93	35 34	47	92	36 21	47	92	293
68	32 38	48	94	33 26	48	93	34 14	47	92	35 01	47	92	35 48	47	91	292
69	32 06	48	93	32 54	47	92	33 41	48	91	34 29	47	91	35 16	47	90	291

S. Lat. {LHA greater than 180°....... Zn=180−Z; LHA less than 180°.......... Zn=180+Z}

DECLINATION (15°-29°) SAME NAME AS LATITUDE

N. Lat. {LHA greater than 180°....... Zn=Z; LHA less than 180°........... Zn=360−Z}

DECLINATION (15°-29°) SAME NAME AS LATITUDE

LHA	15° Hc	d	Z	16° Hc	d	Z	17° Hc	d	Z	18° Hc	d	Z	19° Hc	d	Z
	° ′	′	°	° ′	′	°	° ′	′	°	° ′	′	°	° ′	′	°
70	23 23	+50	99	24 13	+50	98	25 03	+49	97	25 52	+49	97	26 41	+50	96
71	22 51	50	98	23 41	49	97	24 30	50	96	25 20	49	96	26 09	49	95
72	22 19	49	97	23 08	50	96	23 58	49	96	24 47	49	95	25 36	49	94
73	21 46	50	96	22 36	49	95	23 25	50	95	24 15	49	94	25 04	49	94
74	21 14	49	95	22 03	50	95	22 53	49	94	23 42	49	93	24 31	49	93
75	20 41	+50	94	21 31	+49	94	22 20	+49	93	23 09	+50	92	23 59	+48	92
76	20 09	49	93	20 58	49	93	21 47	50	92	22 37	49	92	23 26	49	91
77	19 36	49	93	20 25	50	92	21 15	49	91	22 04	49	91	22 53	49	90
78	19 03	50	92	19 53	49	91	20 42	49	91	21 31	49	90	22 20	49	89
79	18 31	49	91	19 20	49	90	20 09	50	90	20 59	49	89	21 48	49	88
80	17 58	+49	90	18 47	+50	89	19 37	+49	89	20 26	+49	88	21 15	+49	88
81	17 25	50	89	18 15	49	89	19 04	49	88	19 53	50	87	20 43	49	87
82	16 53	49	88	17 42	49	88	18 31	50	87	19 21	49	87	20 10	49	86
83	16 20	49	88	17 09	50	87	17 59	49	86	18 48	49	86	19 37	49	85
84	15 47	50	87	16 37	49	86	17 26	50	86	18 16	49	85	19 05	49	84
85	15 15	+49	86	16 04	+50	85	16 54	+49	85	17 43	+49	84	18 32	+49	83
86	14 42	50	85	15 32	49	84	16 21	50	84	17 11	49	83	18 00	49	83
87	14 10	49	84	14 59	50	84	15 49	49	83	16 38	49	82	17 27	50	82
88	13 37	50	83	14 27	49	83	15 16	50	82	16 06	49	82	16 55	49	81
89	13 05	49	83	13 54	50	82	14 44	49	81	15 33	50	81	16 23	49	80
90	12 32	+50	82	13 22	+50	81	14 12	+49	81	15 01	+50	80	15 51	+49	79
91	12 00	50	81	12 50	49	80	13 39	50	80	14 29	50	79	15 19	49	79
92	11 28	50	80	12 18	49	80	13 07	50	79	13 57	50	78	14 47	49	78
93	10 56	49	79	11 45	50	79	12 35	50	78	13 25	50	78	14 15	49	77
94	10 24	50	78	11 14	49	78	12 03	50	77	12 53	50	77	13 43	50	76
95	09 52	+50	78	10 42	+50	77	11 32	+50	77	12 22	+49	76	13 11	+50	75
96	09 20	50	77	10 10	50	76	11 00	50	76	11 50	50	75	12 40	50	75
97	08 48	50	76	09 38	50	75	10 28	50	75	11 18	50	74	12 08	50	74
98	08 16	51	75	09 07	50	75	09 57	50	74	10 47	50	74	11 37	50	73
99	07 45	50	74	08 35	50	74	09 25	51	73	10 16	50	73	11 06	50	72
100	07 13	+51	74	08 04	+50	73	08 54	+51	72	09 45	+50	72	10 35	+50	71
101	06 42	51	73	07 33	50	72	08 23	51	72	09 14	50	71	10 04	50	71
102	06 11	51	72	07 02	50	71	07 52	51	71	08 43	50	70	09 33	51	70
103	05 40	51	71	06 31	50	71	07 21	51	70	08 12	51	69	09 03	50	69
104	05 09	51	70	06 00	51	70	06 51	51	69	07 42	50	69	08 32	51	68
105	04 38	+51	69	05 29	+51	69	06 20	+51	68	07 11	+51	68	08 02	+51	67
106	04 08	51	69	04 59	51	68	05 50	51	67	06 41	51	67	07 32	51	67
107	03 38	51	68	04 29	51	67	05 20	51	67	06 11	51	66	07 02	51	66
108	03 07	52	67	03 59	51	66	04 50	51	66	05 41	51	65	06 32	52	65
109	02 37	52	66	03 29	51	66	04 20	52	65	05 12	51	65	06 03	51	64
110	02 08	+51	65	02 59	+52	65	03 51	+51	64	04 42	+52	64	05 34	+51	63
111	01 38	52	64	02 30	51	64	03 21	52	63	04 13	52	63	05 05	51	62
112	01 09	52	64	02 01	51	63	02 52	52	63	03 44	52	62	04 36	52	62
113	00 40	51	63	01 31	52	62	02 23	52	62	03 15	52	61	04 07	52	61
114	00 11	52	62	01 03	52	61	01 55	52	61	02 47	52	60	03 39	52	60
115	−0 18	+52	61	00 34	+52	61	01 26	+52	60	02 18	+53	60	03 11	+52	59
116	−0 47	53	60	00 06	52	60	00 58	52	59	01 50	53	59	02 43	52	58
117	−1 15	53	59	−0 22	52	59	00 30	53	58	01 23	52	58	02 15	52	57
118	−1 43	53	59	−0 50	52	58	00 02	53	58	00 55	53	57	01 48	52	57
119	−2 11	53	58	−1 18	53	57	−0 25	53	57	00 28	52	56	01 20	53	56
120	−2 38	+53	57	−1 45	+53	56	−0 52	+53	56	00 01	+52	55	00 53	+53	55
121	−3 05	53	56	−2 12	53	56	−1 19	53	55	−0 26	53	55	00 27	53	54
122	−3 32	53	55	−2 39	53	55	−1 46	53	54	−0 53	54	54	00 01	53	53
123	−3 59	53	54	−3 06	54	54	−2 12	53	53	−1 19	53	53	−0 26	54	52
124	−4 25	53	53	−3 32	54	53	−2 38	53	53	−1 45	54	52	−0 51	53	52
125	−4 51	+53	53	−3 58	+54	52	−3 04	+54	52	−2 10	+53	51	−1 17	+54	51
126	−5 17	54	52	−4 23	53	51	−3 30	54	51	−2 36	54	50	−1 42	54	50
127	−5 43	54	51	−4 49	54	50	−3 55	54	50	−3 01	54	50	−2 07	54	49
128				−5 14	54	49	−4 20	55	49	−3 25	54	49	−2 31	54	48
129				−5 39	55	49	−4 44	54	48	−3 50	54	48	−2 56	55	47
130							−5 08	+54	47	−4 14	+55	47	−3 19	+54	47
131							−5 32	54	46	−4 38	55	46	−3 43	55	46
132										−5 01	55	45	−4 06	55	45
133										−5 24	55	44	−4 29	55	44
134													−4 51	55	43
135													−5 14	+56	42
136													−5 35	55	41

LHA	20° Hc	d	Z	21° Hc	d	Z	22° Hc	d	Z	23° Hc	d	Z	24° Hc	d	Z
	° ′	′	°	° ′	′	°	° ′	′	°	° ′	′	°	° ′	′	°
70	27 31	+48	95	28 19	+49	95	29 08	+49	94	29 57	+48	93	30 45	+48	93
71	26 58	49	95	27 47	49	94	28 36	48	93	29 24	48	93	30 12	48	92
72	26 25	49	94	27 14	49	93	28 03	48	92	28 51	49	92	29 40	48	91
73	25 53	49	93	26 42	48	92	27 30	49	92	28 19	48	91	29 07	48	90
74	25 20	49	92	26 09	49	91	26 58	48	91	27 46	48	90	28 34	48	89
75	24 47	+49	91	25 36	+49	91	26 25	+48	90	27 13	+49	89	28 02	+48	89
76	24 15	49	90	25 04	48	90	25 52	49	89	26 41	48	88	27 29	48	88
77	23 42	49	89	24 31	49	89	25 20	48	88	26 08	48	88	26 56	49	87
78	23 09	49	89	23 58	49	88	24 47	48	87	25 35	49	87	26 24	48	86
79	22 37	49	88	23 26	48	87	24 14	49	87	25 03	48	86	25 51	48	85
80	22 04	+49	87	22 53	+49	86	23 42	+48	86	24 30	+49	85	25 19	+48	84
81	21 32	48	86	22 20	49	86	23 09	49	85	23 58	48	84	24 46	48	84
82	20 59	49	85	21 48	49	85	22 37	48	84	23 25	49	83	24 14	48	83
83	20 26	49	85	21 15	49	84	22 04	49	83	22 53	48	83	23 41	49	82
84	19 54	49	84	20 43	49	83	21 32	48	82	22 20	49	82	23 09	48	81
85	19 21	+49	83	20 10	+49	82	20 59	+49	82	21 48	+49	81	22 37	+48	80
86	18 49	49	82	19 38	49	81	20 27	49	81	21 16	49	80	22 05	48	80
87	18 17	49	81	19 06	49	81	19 55	49	80	20 44	48	79	21 32	49	79
88	17 44	50	80	18 34	49	80	19 23	49	79	20 12	48	79	21 00	49	78
89	17 12	50	80	18 02	49	79	18 51	49	78	19 40	49	78	20 29	48	77
90	16 40	+49	79	17 29	+50	78	18 19	+49	78	19 08	+49	77	19 57	+49	76
91	16 08	50	78	16 58	49	77	17 47	49	77	18 36	49	76	19 25	49	76
92	15 36	50	77	16 26	49	77	17 15	49	76	18 04	49	75	18 53	49	75
93	15 04	50	76	15 54	49	76	16 43	50	75	17 33	49	75	18 22	49	74
94	14 33	49	76	15 22	50	75	16 12	49	74	17 01	50	74	17 51	49	73
95	14 01	+50	75	14 51	+49	74	15 40	+50	74	16 30	+49	73	17 19	+50	72
96	13 30	49	74	14 19	50	73	15 09	50	73	15 59	49	72	16 48	50	72
97	12 58	50	73	13 48	50	73	14 38	50	72	15 28	49	71	16 17	50	71
98	12 27	50	72	13 17	50	72	14 07	50	71	14 57	50	71	15 47	49	70
99	11 56	50	72	12 46	50	71	13 36	50	71	14 26	50	70	15 16	50	69
100	11 25	+50	71	12 15	+50	70	13 05	+50	70	13 55	+50	69	14 45	+50	69
101	10 54	51	70	11 45	50	69	12 35	50	69	13 25	50	68	14 15	50	68
102	10 24	50	69	11 14	51	69	12 05	50	68	12 55	50	68	13 45	50	67
103	09 53	51	68	10 44	50	68	11 34	51	67	12 25	50	67	13 15	50	66
104	09 23	51	68	10 14	50	67	11 04	51	66	11 55	50	66	12 45	51	65
105	08 53	+51	67	09 44	+50	66	10 34	+51	66	11 25	+51	65	12 16	+50	65
106	08 23	51	66	09 14	51	65	10 05	50	65	10 55	51	64	11 46	51	64
107	07 53	51	65	08 44	51	65	09 35	51	64	10 26	51	64	11 17	51	63
108	07 24	51	64	08 15	51	64	09 06	51	63	09 57	51	63	10 48	51	62
109	06 54	52	64	07 46	51	63	08 37	51	63	09 28	51	62	10 19	51	61
110	06 25	+52	63	07 17	+51	62	08 08	+51	62	08 59	+52	61	09 51	+51	61
111	05 56	52	62	06 48	51	61	07 39	52	61	08 31	51	60	09 22	52	60
112	05 28	51	61	06 19	52	61	07 11	52	60	08 03	51	60	08 54	52	59
113	04 59	52	60	05 51	52	60	06 43	51	59	07 34	52	59	08 26	52	58
114	04 31	52	59	05 23	52	59	06 15	52	58	07 07	52	58	07 59	51	57
115	04 03	+52	59	04 55	+52	58	05 47	+52	58	06 39	+52	57	07 31	+52	57
116	03 35	52	58	04 27	53	57	05 20	52	57	06 12	52	56	07 04	52	56
117	03 07	53	57	04 00	52	56	04 52	53	56	05 45	52	56	06 37	52	55
118	02 40	52	56	03 32	53	56	04 25	53	55	05 18	52	55	06 10	53	54
119	02 13	53	55	03 06	53	55	03 59	52	54	04 51	53	54	05 44	53	53
120	01 46	+53	55	02 39	+53	54	03 32	+53	54	04 25	+53	53	05 18	+53	53
121	01 20	53	54	02 13	53	53	03 06	53	53	03 59	53	52	04 52	53	52
122	00 54	53	53	01 47	53	52	02 40	53	52	03 33	54	51	04 27	53	51
123	00 28	53	52	01 21	54	52	02 15	53	51	03 08	53	51	04 01	54	50
124	00 02	54	51	00 56	53	51	01 49	54	50	02 43	53	50	03 36	54	49
125	−0 23	+54	50	00 31	+53	50	01 24	+54	49	02 18	+54	49	03 12	+53	49
126	−0 48	54	49	00 06	54	49	01 00	54	49	01 54	53	48	02 47	54	48
127	−1 13	54	49	−0 19	54	48	00 35	54	48	01 29	54	47	02 23	54	47
128	−1 37	54	48	−0 43	54	47	00 11	54	47	01 05	55	47	02 00	54	46
129	−2 01	54	47	−1 07	55	47	−0 12	54	46	00 42	54	46	01 36	55	45
130	−2 25	+55	46	−1 30	+54	46	−0 36	+55	45	00 19	+54	45	01 13	+55	44
131	−2 48	54	45	−1 54	55	45	−0 59	55	44	−0 04	55	44	00 51	54	44
132	−3 11	55	44	−2 16	54	44	−1 22	55	44	−0 27	55	43	00 20	55	43
133	3 34	55	44	−2 39	55	43	−1 44	55	43	−0 49	55	42	00 06	55	42
134	−3 56	55	43	−3 01	55	42	−2 06	55	42	−1 11	55	41	−0 16	56	41
135	−4 18	+55	42	3 23	+55	41	−2 28	+56	41	−1 32	+55	41	−0 37	+56	40
136	−4 40	56	41	−3 44	55	41	−2 49	56	40	−1 53	55	40	−0 58	56	39
137	−5 01	56	40	−4 05	55	40	−3 10	56	39	−2 14	56	39	−1 18	55	39
138	−5 22	56	39	−4 26	56	39	−3 30	56	38	−2 34	56	38	−1 38	55	38
139				−4 46	56	38	−3 50	56	38	−2 54	56	37	−1 58	56	37

LHA	25° Hc	d	Z	26° Hc	d	Z	27° Hc	d	Z	28° Hc	d	Z	29° Hc	d	Z	LHA
	° ′	′	°	° ′	′	°	° ′	′	°	° ′	′	°	° ′	′	°	
70	31 33	+48	92	32 21	+48	91	33 09	+47	91	33 56	+47	90	34 43	+47	89	290
71	31 00	48	91	31 48	48	90	32 36	47	90	33 23	47	89	34 10	47	88	289
72	30 28	48	90	31 16	47	90	32 03	48	89	32 51	47	88	33 38	47	87	288
73	29 55	48	90	30 43	48	89	31 31	47	88	32 18	47	87	33 05	47	87	287
74	29 22	48	89	30 10	48	88	30 58	47	87	31 45	47	87	32 32	47	86	286
75	28 50	+48	88	29 38	+47	87	30 25	+48	86	31 13	+47	86	32 00	+47	85	285
76	28 17	48	87	29 05	48	86	29 53	47	86	30 40	47	85	31 27	47	84	284
77	27 45	47	86	28 32	48	86	29 20	48	85	30 08	47	84	30 55	47	83	283
78	27 12	48	85	28 00	48	85	28 48	47	84	29 35	47	83	30 22	48	83	282
79	26 39	48	85	27 27	48	84	28 15	48	83	29 03	47	83	29 50	47	82	281
80	26 07	+48	84	26 55	+48	83	27 43	+47	82	28 30	+48	82	29 18	+47	81	280
81	25 34	48	83	26 22	48	82	27 10	48	82	27 58	48	81	28 46	47	80	279
82	25 02	48	82	25 50	48	81	26 38	48	81	27 26	47	80	28 13	48	79	278
83	24 30	48	81	25 18	48	81	26 06	48	80	26 54	47	79	27 41	48	79	277
84	23 57	49	81	24 46	48	80	25 34	48	79	26 22	47	79	27 09	48	78	276
85	23 25	+49	80	24 14	+48	79	25 02	+48	78	25 50	+47	78	26 37	+48	77	275
86	22 53	48	79	23 41	49	78	24 30	48	78	25 18	48	77	26 06	47	76	274
87	22 21	49	78	23 10	48	78	23 58	48	77	24 46	48	76	25 34	48	76	273
88	21 49	49	77	22 38	48	77	23 26	48	76	24 14	48	75	25 02	48	75	272
89	21 17	49	77	22 06	48	76	22 54	49	75	23 43	48	75	24 31	48	74	271
90	20 46	+48	76	21 34	+49	75	22 23	+48	75	23 11	+49	74	24 00	+48	73	270
91	20 14	49	75	21 03	48	74	21 51	49	74	22 40	8	73	23 28	49	72	269
92	19 42	49	74	20 31	49	74	21 20	49	73	22 09	48	72	22 57	49	72	268
93	19 11	49	73	20 00	49	73	20 49	49	72	21 38	48	72	22 26	49	71	267
94	18 40	49	73	19 29	49	72	20 18	49	71	21 07	48	71	21 55	49	70	266
95	18 09	+49	72	18 58	+49	71	19 47	+49	71	20 36	+49	70	21 25	+48	69	265
96	17 38	49	71	18 27	49	70	19 16	49	70	20 05	49	69	20 54	49	69	264
97	17 07	49	70	17 56	50	70	18 46	49	69	19 35	49	69	20 24	49	68	263
98	16 36	50	70	17 26	49	69	18 15	50	68	19 05	49	68	19 54	49	67	262
99	16 06	49	69	16 55	50	68	17 45	49	68	18 34	50	67	19 24	49	66	261
100	15 35	+50	68	16 25	+50	67	17 15	+49	67	18 04	+50	66	18 54	+49	66	260
101	15 05	50	67	15 55	50	67	16 45	50	66	17 35	49	65	18 24	50	65	259
102	14 35	50	66	15 25	50	66	16 15	50	65	17 05	50	65	17 55	49	64	258
103	14 05	50	66	14 55	51	65	15 46	50	64	16 36	49	64	17 25	50	63	257
104	13 36	50	65	14 26	50	64	15 16	50	64	16 06	50	63	16 56	50	63	256
105	13 06	+51	64	13 57	+50	63	14 47	+50	63	15 37	+51	62	16 28	+50	62	255
106	12 37	50	63	13 27	51	63	14 18	50	62	15 08	51	62	15 59	50	61	254
107	12 08	51	62	12 59	50	62	13 49	51	61	14 40	50	61	15 30	51	60	253
108	11 39	51	62	12 30	51	61	13 21	51	61	14 11	51	60	15 02	51	60	252
109	11 10	51	61	12 01	51	60	12 52	51	60	13 43	51	59	14 34	51	59	251
110	10 42	+51	60	11 33	+51	60	12 24	+51	59	13 15	+51	59	14 06	+51	58	250
111	10 14	51	59	11 05	51	59	11 56	52	58	12 48	51	58	13 39	51	57	249
112	09 46	51	59	10 37	52	58	11 29	51	58	12 20	51	57	13 11	52	56	248
113	09 18	52	58	10 10	51	57	11 01	52	57	11 53	51	56	12 44	52	56	247
114	08 50	52	57	09 42	52	56	10 34	52	56	11 26	51	55	12 17	52	55	246
115	08 23	+52	56	09 15	+52	56	10 07	+52	55	10 59	+52	55	11 51	+52	54	245
116	07 56	52	55	08 48	52	55	09 40	52	54	10 32	52	54	11 24	52	53	244
117	07 29	53	55	08 22	52	54	09 14	52	54	10 06	52	53	10 58	53	53	243
118	07 03	52	54	07 55	53	53	08 48	52	53	09 40	53	52	10 33	52	52	242
119	06 37	52	53	07 29	53	53	08 22	53	52	09 15	52	52	10 07	53	51	241
120	06 11	+53	52	07 04	+52	52	07 56	+53	51	08 49	+53	51	09 42	+52	50	240
121	05 45	53	51	06 38	53	51	07 31	53	50	08 24	53	50	09 17	53	49	239
122	05 20	53	51	06 13	53	50	07 06	53	50	07 59	53	49	08 52	53	49	238
123	04 55	53	50	05 48	53	49	06 41	54	49	07 35	53	48	08 28	53	48	237
124	04 30	53	49	05 23	54	49	06 17	53	48	07 10	54	48	08 04	53	47	236
125	04 05	+54	48	04 59	+54	48	05 53	+53	47	06 46	+54	47	07 40	+53	46	235
126	03 41	54	47	04 35	54	47	05 29	54	46	06 23	53	46	07 16	54	46	234
127	03 17	54	46	04 11	54	46	05 05	54	46	05 59	54	45	06 53	54	45	233
128	02 54	54	46	03 48	54	45	04 42	54	45	05 36	54	44	06 30	55	44	232
129	02 31	54	45	03 25	54	44	04 19	55	44	05 14	54	44	06 08	54	43	231
130	02 08	+54	44	03 02	+55	44	03 57	+54	43	04 51	+55	43	05 46	+54	42	230
131	01 45	55	43	02 40	55	43	03 35	54	42	04 29	55	42	05 24	55	42	229
132	01 23	55	42	02 18	55	42	03 13	55	42	04 08	54	41	05 02	55	41	228
133	01 01	55	42	01 56	55	41	02 51	55	41	03 46	55	40	04 41	55	40	227
134	00 40	55	41	01 35	55	40	02 30	55	40	03 25	55	40	04 20	56	39	226
135	00 19	+55	40	01 14	+55	39	02 09	+56	39	03 05	+55	39	04 00	+55	38	225
136	−0 02	55	39	00 53	56	39	01 49	55	38	02 44	56	38	03 40	55	38	224
137	−0 23	56	38	00 33	56	38	01 29	56	37	02 25	55	37	03 20	56	37	223
138	−0 43	56	37	00 13	56	37	01 09	56	37	02 05	56	36	03 01	56	36	222
139	−1 02	56	36	−0 06	56	36	00 50	56	36	01 46	56	35	02 42	56	35	221

S. Lat. {LHA greater than 180°....... Zn=180−Z; LHA less than 180°........... Zn=180+Z}

DECLINATION (15°-29°) SAME NAME AS LATITUDE

LAT 57°

N. Lat. {LHA greater than 180°....... Zn=Z / LHA less than 180°........... Zn=360−Z}

DECLINATION (15°-29°) SAME NAME AS LATITUDE

LAT 57°

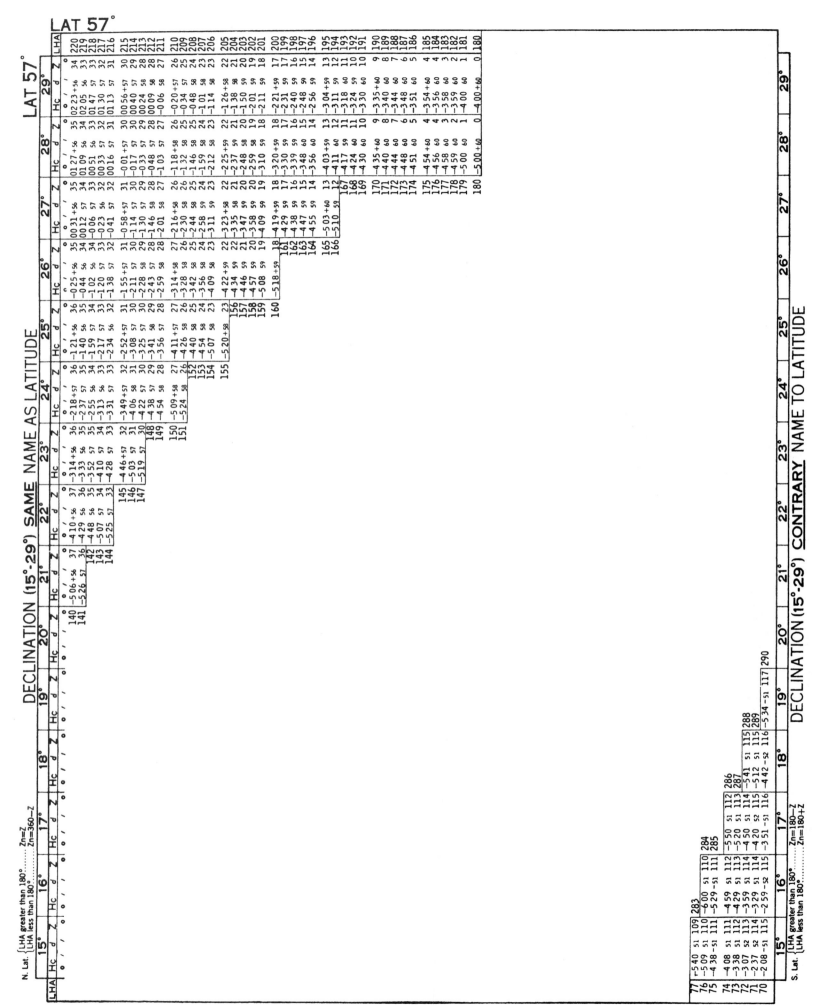

LHA	21° Hc	d	Z	22° Hc	d	Z	23° Hc	d	Z	24° Hc	d	Z	25° Hc	d	Z	26° Hc	d	Z	27° Hc	d	Z	28° Hc	d	Z	29° Hc	d	Z	LHA
	° ′	′	°	° ′	′	°	° ′	′	°	° ′	′	°	° ′	′	°	° ′	′	°	° ′	′	°	° ′	′	°	° ′	′	°	
140	−5 06	+56	37	−4 10	+56	37	−3 14	+56	36	−2 18	+57	36	−1 21	+56	36	−0 25	+56	35	00 31	+56	35	01 27	+56	35	02 23	+56	34	220
141	−5 26	57	36	−4 29	56	36	−3 33	56	35	−2 37	57	35	−1 40	56	35	−0 44	56	34	00 12	57	34	01 09	56	34	02 05	56	33	219
142				−4 48	56	35	−3 52	57	35	−2 55	56	34	−1 59	57	34	−1 02	56	34	−0 06	57	33	00 51	56	33	01 47	57	33	218
143				−5 07	57	34	−4 10	57	34	−3 13	56	33	−2 17	57	33	−1 20	57	33	−0 23	56	32	00 33	57	32	01 30	57	32	217
144				−5 25	57	33	−4 28	57	33	−3 31	57	33	−2 34	56	32	−1 38	57	32	−0 41	57	32	00 16	57	31	01 13	57	31	216
145							−4 46	+57	32	−3 49	+57	32	−2 52	+57	31	−1 55	+57	31	−0 58	+57	31	−0 01	+57	30	00 56	+57	30	215
146							−5 03	57	31	−4 06	58	31	−3 08	57	30	−2 11	57	30	−1 14	57	30	−0 17	57	30	00 40	57	29	214
147							−5 19	57	30	−4 22	57	30	−3 25	57	30	−2 28	58	29	−1 30	57	29	−0 33	57	29	00 24	58	28	213
148										−4 38	57	29	−3 41	58	29	−2 43	57	28	−1 46	58	28	−0 48	57	28	00 09	58	28	212
149										−4 54	58	28	−3 56	57	28	−2 59	58	28	−2 01	58	27	−1 03	57	27	−0 06	58	27	211
150										−5 09	+58	27	−4 11	+57	27	−3 14	+58	27	−2 16	+58	26	−1 18	+58	26	−0 20	+57	26	210
151										−5 24	58	26	−4 26	58	26	−3 28	58	26	−2 30	58	26	−1 32	58	25	−0 34	57	25	209
152													−4 40	58	25	−3 42	58	25	−2 44	58	25	−1 46	58	25	−0 48	58	24	208
153													−4 54	58	24	−3 56	58	24	−2 58	59	24	−1 59	58	24	−1 01	58	23	207
154													−5 07	58	23	−4 09	58	23	−3 11	59	23	−2 12	58	23	−1 14	58	23	206
155													−5 20	+58	23	−4 22	+59	22	−3 23	+58	22	−2 25	+59	22	−1 26	+58	22	205
156																−4 34	59	22	−3 35	58	21	−2 37	59	21	−1 38	58	21	204
157																−4 46	59	21	−3 47	59	20	−2 48	58	20	−1 50	59	20	203
158																−4 57	59	20	−3 58	59	20	−2 59	58	19	−2 01	59	19	202
159																−5 08	59	19	−4 09	59	19	−3 10	59	18	−2 11	59	18	201
160																−5 18	+59	18	−4 19	+59	18	−3 20	+59	18	−2 21	+59	17	200
161																			−4 29	59	17	−3 30	59	17	−2 31	59	17	199
162																			−4 38	59	16	−3 39	59	16	−2 40	59	16	198
163																			−4 47	59	15	−3 48	60	15	−2 48	59	15	197
164																			−4 55	59	14	−3 56	60	14	−2 56	59	14	196
165																			−5 03	+60	13	−4 03	+59	13	−3 04	+59	13	195
166																			−5 10	59	12	−4 11	60	12	−3 11	59	12	194
167																						−4 17	59	11	−3 18	60	11	193
168																						−4 24	60	11	−3 24	59	10	192
169																						−4 30	60	10	−3 30	60	10	191
170																						−4 35	+60	9	−3 35	+60	9	190
171																						−4 40	60	8	−3 40	60	8	189
172																						−4 44	60	7	−3 44	60	7	188
173																						−4 48	60	6	−3 48	60	6	187
174																						−4 51	60	5	−3 51	60	5	186
175																						−4 54	+60	4	−3 54	+60	4	185
176																						−4 56	60	4	−3 56	60	4	184
177																						−4 58	60	3	−3 58	60	3	183
178																						−4 59	60	2	−3 59	60	2	182
179																						−5 00	60	1	−4 00	60	1	181
180																						−5 00	+60	0	−4 00	+60	0	180

LHA	15° Hc	d	Z	16° Hc	d	Z	17° Hc	d	Z	18° Hc	d	Z	19° Hc	d	Z	20° Hc	d	Z	LHA
	° ′	′	°	° ′	′	°	° ′	′	°	° ′	′	°	° ′	′	°	° ′	′	°	
77	−5 40	51	109																283
76	−5 09	51	110	−6 00	51	110													284
75	−4 38	−51	111	−5 29	−51	111													285
74	−4 08	51	111	−4 59	51	112	−5 50	51	112										286
73	−3 38	51	112	−4 29	51	113	−5 20	51	113										287
72	−3 07	52	113	−3 59	51	114	−4 50	51	114	−5 41	51	115							288
71	−2 37	52	114	−3 29	51	114	−4 20	52	115	−5 12	51	115							289
70	−2 08	−51	115	−2 59	−52	115	−3 51	−51	116	−4 42	−52	116	−5 34	−51	117				290

S. Lat. {LHA greater than 180°....... Zn=180−Z / LHA less than 180°........... Zn=180+Z}

DECLINATION (15°-29°) CONTRARY NAME TO LATITUDE

N. Lat. {LHA greater than 180°....... Zn=Z; LHA less than 180°.......... Zn=360−Z}

DECLINATION (15°-29°) CONTRARY NAME TO LATITUDE

LHA	15° Hc	15° d	15° Z	16° Hc	16° d	16° Z	17° Hc	17° d	17° Z	18° Hc	18° d	18° Z	19° Hc	19° d	19° Z
	° ′	′	°	° ′	′	°	° ′	′	°	° ′	′	°	° ′	′	°
69	-1 38	52	116	-2 30	51	116	-3 21	52	117	-4 13	52	117	-5 05	51	118
68	-1 09	52	116	-2 01	51	117	-2 52	52	117	-3 44	52	118	-4 36	52	118
67	-0 40	51	117	-1 31	52	118	-2 23	52	118	-3 15	52	119	-4 07	52	119
66	-0 11	52	118	-1 03	52	119	-1 55	52	119	-2 47	52	120	-3 39	52	120
65	00 18	-52	119	-0 34	-52	119	-1 26	-52	120	-2 18	-53	120	-3 11	-52	121
64	00 47	53	120	-0 06	52	120	-0 58	52	121	-1 50	53	121	-2 43	52	122
63	01 15	53	121	00 22	52	121	-0 30	53	122	-1 23	52	122	-2 15	52	123
62	01 43	53	121	00 50	52	122	-0 02	53	122	-0 55	53	123	-1 48	52	123
61	02 11	53	122	01 18	53	123	00 25	53	123	-0 28	52	124	-1 20	53	124
60	02 38	-53	123	01 45	-53	124	00 52	-53	124	-0 01	-52	125	-0 53	-53	125
59	03 05	53	124	02 12	53	124	01 19	53	125	00 26	53	125	-0 27	53	126
58	03 32	53	125	02 39	53	125	01 46	53	126	00 53	54	126	-0 01	53	127
57	03 59	53	126	03 06	54	126	02 12	53	127	01 19	53	127	00 26	54	128
56	04 25	53	127	03 32	54	127	02 38	53	127	01 45	54	128	00 51	53	128
55	04 51	-53	127	03 58	-54	128	03 04	-54	128	02 10	-53	129	01 17	-54	129
54	05 17	54	128	04 23	53	129	03 30	54	129	02 36	54	130	01 42	54	130
53	05 43	54	129	04 49	54	130	03 55	54	130	03 01	54	130	02 07	54	131
52	06 08	54	130	05 14	54	131	04 20	55	131	03 25	54	131	02 31	54	132
51	06 33	54	131	05 39	55	131	04 44	54	132	03 50	54	132	02 56	55	133
50	06 57	-54	132	06 03	-55	132	05 08	-54	133	04 14	-55	133	03 19	-54	133
49	07 22	55	133	06 27	55	133	05 32	54	134	04 38	55	134	03 43	55	134
48	07 45	54	134	06 51	55	134	05 56	55	134	05 01	55	135	04 06	55	135
47	08 09	55	135	07 14	55	135	06 19	55	135	05 24	55	136	04 29	55	136
46	08 32	55	135	07 37	55	136	06 42	55	136	05 47	56	137	04 51	55	137
45	08 55	-55	136	08 00	-56	137	07 04	-55	137	06 09	-55	137	05 14	-56	138
44	09 17	55	137	08 22	56	138	07 26	55	138	06 31	56	138	05 35	55	139
43	09 39	55	138	08 44	56	139	07 48	56	139	06 52	55	139	05 57	56	140
42	10 01	56	139	09 05	56	139	08 09	55	140	07 14	56	140	06 18	56	141
41	10 22	56	140	09 26	56	140	08 30	56	141	07 34	56	141	06 38	56	141
40	10 43	-56	141	09 47	-56	141	08 51	-56	142	07 55	-56	142	06 59	-57	142
39	11 03	56	142	10 07	56	142	09 11	56	142	08 15	57	143	07 18	56	143
38	11 23	56	143	10 27	56	143	09 31	57	143	08 34	56	144	07 38	57	144
37	11 43	56	144	10 47	57	144	09 50	57	144	08 53	56	145	07 57	57	145
36	12 02	56	145	11 06	57	145	10 09	57	145	09 12	57	146	08 15	56	146
35	12 21	-57	145	11 24	-57	146	10 27	-57	146	09 30	-57	146	08 33	-56	147
34	12 39	57	146	11 42	57	147	10 45	57	147	09 48	57	147	08 51	57	148
33	12 57	57	147	12 00	57	148	11 03	57	148	10 06	58	148	09 08	57	149
32	13 15	58	148	12 17	57	149	11 20	57	149	10 23	58	149	09 25	57	150
31	13 32	58	149	12 34	57	150	11 37	58	150	10 39	57	150	09 42	58	150
30	13 48	-58	150	12 50	-57	151	11 53	-58	151	10 55	-57	151	09 58	-58	151
29	14 04	58	151	13 06	57	151	12 09	58	152	11 11	58	152	10 13	58	152
28	14 20	58	152	13 22	58	152	12 24	58	153	11 26	58	153	10 28	58	153
27	14 35	58	153	13 37	58	153	12 39	58	154	11 41	59	154	10 42	58	154
26	14 49	58	154	13 51	58	154	12 53	58	155	11 55	58	155	10 57	59	155
25	15 03	-58	155	14 05	-58	155	13 07	-59	156	12 08	-58	156	11 10	-58	156
24	15 17	59	156	14 18	58	156	13 20	58	156	12 22	59	157	11 23	58	157
23	15 30	59	157	14 31	58	157	13 33	59	157	12 34	58	158	11 36	59	158
22	15 42	58	158	14 44	59	158	13 45	59	158	12 46	58	159	11 48	59	159
21	15 54	58	159	14 56	59	159	13 57	59	159	12 58	59	160	11 59	58	160
20	16 06	-59	160	15 07	-59	160	14 08	-59	160	13 09	-59	161	12 10	-58	161
19	16 17	59	161	15 18	59	161	14 19	59	161	13 20	59	161	12 21	59	162
18	16 27	59	162	15 28	59	162	14 29	59	162	13 30	59	162	12 31	59	163
17	16 37	59	163	15 38	59	163	14 39	59	163	13 40	59	163	12 41	60	164
16	16 47	60	164	15 47	59	164	14 48	59	164	13 49	59	164	12 50	60	165
15	16 55	-59	165	15 56	-59	165	14 57	-60	165	13 57	-59	165	12 58	-59	166
14	17 04	60	166	16 04	59	166	15 05	60	166	14 05	59	166	13 06	59	166
13	17 11	59	167	16 12	60	167	15 12	59	167	14 13	60	167	13 13	59	167
12	17 19	60	168	16 19	60	168	15 19	59	168	14 20	60	168	13 20	59	168
11	17 25	59	169	16 26	60	169	15 26	60	169	14 26	59	169	13 27	60	169
10	17 31	-60	170	16 31	-59	170	15 32	-60	170	14 32	-60	170	13 32	-59	170
9	17 37	60	171	16 37	60	171	15 37	60	171	14 37	59	171	13 38	60	171
8	17 42	60	172	16 42	60	172	15 42	60	172	14 42	60	172	13 42	60	172
7	17 46	60	173	16 46	60	173	15 46	60	173	14 46	60	173	13 46	59	173
6	17 50	60	174	16 50	60	174	15 50	60	174	14 50	60	174	13 50	60	174
5	17 53	-60	175	16 53	-60	175	15 53	-60	175	14 53	-60	175	13 53	-60	175
4	17 55	60	176	16 55	59	176	15 56	60	176	14 56	60	176	13 56	60	176
3	17 57	60	177	16 57	60	177	15 57	59	177	14 58	60	177	13 58	60	177
2	17 59	60	178	16 59	60	178	15 59	60	178	14 59	60	178	13 59	60	178
1	18 00	60	179	17 00	60	179	16 00	60	179	15 00	60	179	14 00	60	179
0	18 00	-60	180	17 00	-60	180	16 00	-60	180	15 00	-60	180	14 00	-60	180

LHA	20° Hc	20° d	20° Z	21° Hc	21° d	21° Z	22° Hc	22° d	22° Z	23° Hc	23° d	23° Z	24° Hc	24° d	24° Z
	° ′	′	°	° ′	′	°	° ′	′	°	° ′	′	°	° ′	′	°
69	-5 56	52	118	291											
68	-5 28	51	119	292											
67	-4 59	52	120	-5 51	52	120	293								
66	-4 31	52	121	-5 23	52	121	294								
65	-4 03	-52	121	-4 55	-52	122	-5 47	-52	122	295					
64	-3 35	52	122	-4 27	53	123	-5 20	52	123	296					
63	-3 07	53	123	-4 00	52	124	-4 52	53	124	-5 45	52	124	297		
62	-2 40	52	124	-3 32	53	124	-4 25	53	125	-5 18	52	125	298		
61	-2 13	53	125	-3 06	53	125	-3 59	52	126	-4 51	53	126	-5 44	53	127
60	-1 46	-53	125	-2 39	-53	126	-3 32	-53	126	-4 25	-53	127	-5 18	-53	127
59	-1 20	53	126	-2 13	53	127	-3 06	53	127	-3 59	53	128	-4 52	53	128
58	-0 54	53	127	-1 47	53	128	-2 40	53	128	-3 33	54	129	-4 27	53	129
57	-0 28	53	128	-1 21	54	128	-2 15	53	129	-3 08	53	129	-4 01	54	130
56	-0 02	54	129	-0 56	53	129	-1 49	54	130	-2 43	53	130	-3 36	54	131
55	00 23	-54	130	-0 31	-53	130	-1 24	-54	131	-2 18	-54	131	-3 12	-53	131
54	00 48	54	131	-0 06	54	131	-1 00	54	131	-1 54	53	132	-2 47	54	132
53	01 13	54	131	00 19	54	132	-0 35	54	132	-1 29	54	133	-2 23	54	133
52	01 37	54	132	00 43	54	133	-0 11	54	133	-1 05	55	133	-2 00	54	134
51	02 01	54	133	01 07	55	133	00 12	54	134	-0 42	54	134	-1 36	55	135
50	02 25	-55	134	01 30	-54	134	00 36	-55	135	-0 19	-54	135	-1 13	-55	136
49	02 48	54	135	01 54	55	135	00 59	55	136	00 04	55	136	-0 51	54	136
48	03 11	55	136	02 16	54	136	01 22	55	136	00 27	55	137	-0 28	55	137
47	03 34	55	136	02 39	55	137	01 44	55	137	00 49	55	138	-0 06	55	138
46	03 56	55	137	03 01	55	138	02 06	55	138	01 11	55	139	00 16	56	139
45	04 18	-55	138	03 23	-55	139	02 28	-56	139	01 32	-55	139	00 37	-56	140
44	04 40	56	139	03 44	55	139	02 49	56	140	01 53	55	140	00 58	56	141
43	05 01	56	140	04 05	55	140	03 10	56	141	02 14	56	141	01 18	55	141
42	05 22	56	141	04 26	56	141	03 30	56	142	02 34	56	142	01 38	55	142
41	05 42	56	142	04 46	56	142	03 50	56	142	02 54	56	143	01 58	56	143
40	06 02	-56	143	05 06	-56	143	04 10	-56	143	03 14	-56	144	02 18	-57	144
39	06 22	56	144	05 26	57	144	04 29	56	144	03 33	56	145	02 37	57	145
38	06 41	56	144	05 45	57	145	04 48	56	145	03 52	57	145	02 55	56	146
37	07 00	57	145	06 03	56	146	05 07	57	146	04 10	57	146	03 13	56	147
36	07 19	57	146	06 22	57	147	05 25	57	147	04 28	57	147	03 31	57	147
35	07 37	-57	147	06 40	-57	147	05 43	-57	148	04 46	-57	148	03 49	-57	148
34	07 54	57	148	06 57	57	148	06 00	57	149	05 03	57	149	04 06	58	149
33	08 11	57	149	07 14	57	149	06 17	58	150	05 19	57	150	04 22	57	150
32	08 28	58	150	07 30	57	150	06 33	57	150	05 36	58	151	04 38	57	151
31	08 44	57	151	07 47	58	151	06 49	58	151	05 51	57	152	04 54	58	152
30	09 00	-58	152	08 02	-57	152	07 05	-58	152	06 07	-58	152	05 09	-58	153
29	09 15	58	153	08 17	57	153	07 20	58	153	06 22	58	153	05 24	58	154
28	09 30	58	153	08 32	58	154	07 34	58	154	06 36	58	154	05 38	58	155
27	09 44	58	154	08 46	58	155	07 48	58	155	06 50	58	155	05 52	58	155
26	09 58	58	155	09 00	58	156	08 02	58	156	07 04	59	156	06 05	58	156
25	10 12	-59	156	09 13	-58	156	08 15	-58	157	07 17	-59	157	06 18	-58	157
24	10 25	59	157	09 26	58	157	08 28	59	158	07 29	58	158	06 31	59	158
23	10 37	58	158	09 39	59	158	08 40	59	159	07 41	58	159	06 43	59	159
22	10 49	59	159	09 50	58	159	08 52	59	159	07 53	59	160	06 54	58	160
21	11 01	59	160	10 02	59	160	09 03	59	160	08 04	59	161	07 05	59	161
20	11 12	-59	161	10 13	-59	161	09 14	-59	161	08 15	-59	162	07 16	-59	162
19	11 22	59	162	10 23	59	162	09 24	59	162	08 25	59	162	07 26	59	163
18	11 32	59	163	10 33	59	163	09 34	59	163	08 35	60	163	07 35	59	164
17	11 41	59	164	10 42	59	164	09 43	59	164	08 44	59	164	07 45	60	164
16	11 50	59	165	10 51	59	165	09 52	60	165	08 52	59	165	07 53	59	165
15	11 59	-60	166	10 59	-59	166	10 00	-59	166	09 01	-60	166	08 01	-59	166
14	12 07	60	167	11 07	59	167	10 08	60	167	09 08	59	167	08 09	60	167
13	12 14	60	168	11 14	59	168	10 15	60	168	09 15	59	168	08 16	60	168
12	12 21	60	169	11 21	60	169	10 21	59	169	09 22	60	169	08 22	59	169
11	12 27	60	169	11 27	59	170	10 28	60	170	09 28	60	170	08 28	59	170
10	12 33	-60	170	11 33	-60	171	10 33	-60	171	09 33	-59	171	08 34	-60	171
9	12 38	60	171	11 38	60	171	10 38	59	172	09 39	60	172	08 39	60	172
8	12 42	59	172	11 43	60	172	10 43	60	173	09 43	60	173	08 43	60	173
7	12 47	60	173	11 47	60	173	10 47	60	173	09 47	60	174	08 47	60	174
6	12 50	60	174	11 50	60	174	10 50	60	174	09 50	59	174	08 51	60	175
5	12 53	-60	175	11 53	-60	175	10 53	-60	175	09 53	-60	175	08 53	-59	175
4	12 56	60	176	11 56	60	176	10 56	60	176	09 56	60	176	08 56	60	176
3	12 58	60	177	11 58	60	177	10 58	60	177	09 58	60	177	08 58	60	177
2	12 59	60	178	11 59	60	178	10 59	60	178	09 59	60	178	08 59	60	178
1	13 00	60	179	12 00	60	179	11 00	60	179	10 00	60	179	09 00	60	179
0	13 00	-60	180	12 00	-60	180	11 00	-60	180	10 00	-60	180	09 00	-60	180

LHA	25° Hc	25° d	25° Z	26° Hc	26° d	26° Z	27° Hc	27° d	27° Z	28° Hc	28° d	28° Z	29° Hc	29° d	29° Z	LHA
	° ′	′	°	° ′	′	°	° ′	′	°	° ′	′	°	° ′	′	°	
61	299															
60	300															
59	-5 45	53	129	301												
58	-5 20	53	129	302												
57	-4 55	53	130	-5 48	53	131	303									
56	-4 30	53	131	-5 23	54	131	304									
55	-4 05	-54	132	-4 59	-54	132	305									
54	-3 41	54	133	-4 35	54	133	-5 29	54	134	306						
53	-3 17	54	134	-4 11	54	134	-5 05	54	134	307						
52	-2 54	54	134	-3 48	54	135	-4 42	54	135	-5 36	54	136	308			
51	-2 31	54	135	-3 25	54	136	-4 19	55	136	-5 14	54	136	309			
50	-2 08	-54	136	-3 02	-55	136	-3 57	-54	137	-4 51	-55	137	310			
49	-1 45	55	137	-2 40	55	137	-3 35	54	138	-4 29	55	138	-5 24	55	138	311
48	-1 23	55	138	-2 18	55	138	-3 13	55	138	-4 08	54	139	-5 02	55	139	312
47	-1 01	55	138	-1 56	55	139	-2 51	55	139	-3 46	55	140	-4 41	55	140	313
46	-0 40	55	139	-1 35	55	140	-2 30	55	140	-3 25	55	140	-4 20	56	141	314
45	-0 19	-55	140	-1 14	-55	141	-2 09	-56	141	-3 05	-55	141	-4 00	-55	142	315
44	00 02	55	141	-0 53	56	141	-1 49	55	142	-2 44	56	142	-3 40	55	142	316
43	00 23	56	142	-0 33	56	142	-1 29	56	143	-2 25	55	143	-3 20	56	143	317
42	00 43	56	143	-0 13	56	143	-1 09	56	143	-2 05	56	144	-3 01	56	144	318
41	01 02	56	144	00 06	56	144	-0 50	56	144	-1 46	56	145	-2 42	56	145	319
40	01 21	-56	144	00 25	-56	145	-0 31	-56	145	-1 27	-56	145	-2 23	-56	146	320
39	01 40	56	145	00 44	56	146	-0 12	57	146	-1 09	56	146	-2 05	56	147	321
38	01 59	57	146	01 02	56	146	00 06	57	147	-0 51	56	147	-1 47	57	147	322
37	02 17	57	147	01 20	57	147	00 23	56	148	-0 33	57	148	-1 30	57	148	323
36	02 34	56	148	01 38	57	148	00 41	57	148	-0 16	57	149	-1 13	57	149	324
35	02 52	-57	149	01 55	-57	149	00 58	-57	149	00 01	-57	150	-0 56	-57	150	325
34	03 08	57	150	02 11	57	150	01 14	57	150	00 17	57	150	-0 40	57	151	326
33	03 25	57	150	02 28	58	151	01 30	57	151	00 33	57	151	-0 24	58	152	327
32	03 41	58	151	02 43	57	152	01 46	58	152	00 48	57	152	-0 09	58	152	328
31	03 56	57	152	02 59	58	152	02 01	58	153	01 03	57	153	00 06	58	153	329
30	04 11	-57	153	03 14	-58	153	02 16	-58	154	01 18	-58	154	00 20	-57	154	330
29	04 26	58	154	03 28	58	154	02 30	58	154	01 32	58	155	00 34	57	155	331
28	04 40	58	155	03 42	58	155	02 44	58	155	01 46	58	155	00 48	58	156	332
27	04 54	58	156	03 56	58	156	02 58	59	156	01 59	58	156	01 01	58	157	333
26	05 07	58	157	04 09	58	157	03 11	59	157	02 12	58	157	01 14	58	157	334
25	05 20	-58	157	04 22	-59	158	03 23	-58	158	02 25	-59	158	01 26	-58	158	335
24	05 32	58	158	04 34	59	158	03 35	58	159	02 37	59	159	01 38	58	159	336
23	05 44	58	159	04 46	59	159	03 47	59	160	02 48	58	160	01 50	59	160	337
22	05 56	59	160	04 57	59	160	03 58	59	160	02 59	58	161	02 01	59	161	338
21	06 06	58	161	05 08	59	161	04 09	59	161	03 10	59	162	02 11	59	162	339
20	06 17	-59	162	05 18	-59	162	04 19	-59	162	03 20	-59	162	02 21	-59	163	340
19	06 27	59	163	05 28	59	163	04 29	59	163	03 30	59	163	02 31	59	163	341
18	06 36	59	164	05 37	59	164	04 38	59	164	03 39	59	164	02 40	59	164	342
17	06 45	59	165	05 46	59	165	04 47	59	165	03 48	60	165	02 48	59	165	343
16	06 54	60	165	05 54	59	166	04 55	59	166	03 56	60	166	02 56	59	166	344
15	07 02	-60	166	06 02	-59	167	05 03	-60	167	04 03	-59	167	03 04	-59	167	345
14	07 09	59	167	06 10	60	167	05 10	59	168	04 11	60	168	03 11	59	168	346
13	07 16	59	168	06 17	60	168	05 17	60	168	04 17	59	169	03 18	60	169	347
12	07 23	60	169	06 23	60	169	05 23	59	169	04 24	60	169	03 24	59	170	348
11	07 29	60	170	06 29	60	170	05 29	59	170	04 30	60	170	03 30	60	170	349
10	07 34	-60	171	06 34	-59	171	05 35	-60	171	04 35	-60	171	03 35	-60	171	350
9	07 39	60	172	06 39	60	172	05 39	59	172	04 40	60	172	03 40	60	172	351
8	07 43	59	173	06 44	60	173	05 44	60	173	04 44	60	173	03 44	60	173	352
7	07 47	60	174	06 47	59	174	05 48	60	174	04 48	60	174	03 48	60	174	353
6	07 51	60	175	06 51	60	175	05 51	60	175	04 51	60	175	03 51	60	175	354
5	07 54	-60	175	06 54	-60	176	05 54	-60	176	04 54	-60	176	03 54	-60	176	355
4	07 56	60	176	06 56	60	176	05 56	60	176	04 56	60	176	03 56	60	176	356
3	07 58	60	177	06 58	60	177	05 58	60	177	04 58	60	177	03 58	60	177	357
2	07 59	60	178	06 59	60	178	05 59	60	178	04 59	60	178	03 59	60	178	358
1	08 00	60	179	07 00	60	179	06 00	60	179	05 00	60	179	04 00	60	179	359
0	08 00	-60	180	07 00	-60	180	06 00	-60	180	05 00	-60	180	04 00	-60	180	360

S. Lat. {LHA greater than 180°........ Zn=180−Z; LHA less than 180°........... Zn=180+Z}

DECLINATION (15°-29°) CONTRARY NAME TO LATITUDE

N. Lat. {LHA greater than 180°....... Zn=Z; LHA less than 180°........... Zn=360−Z}

DECLINATION (0°-14°) SAME NAME AS LATITUDE

LHA	0° Hc	0° d	0° Z	1° Hc	1° d	1° Z	2° Hc	2° d	2° Z	3° Hc	3° d	3° Z	4° Hc	4° d	4° Z	5° Hc	5° d	5° Z	6° Hc	6° d	6° Z	7° Hc	7° d	7° Z
	° ′	′	°	° ′	′	°	° ′	′	°	° ′	′	°	° ′	′	°	° ′	′	°	° ′	′	°	° ′	′	°
0	32 00	+60	180	33 00	+60	180	34 00	+60	180	35 00	+60	180	36 00	+60	180	37 00	+60	180	38 00	+60	180	39 00	+60	180
1	32 00	60	179	33 00	60	179	34 00	60	179	35 00	60	179	36 00	60	179	37 00	60	179	38 00	60	179	39 00	60	179
2	31 59	60	178	32 59	60	178	33 59	60	178	34 59	60	178	35 59	60	178	36 59	60	178	37 59	60	178	38 59	60	177
3	31 57	60	177	32 57	60	176	33 57	60	176	34 57	60	176	35 57	60	176	36 57	60	176	37 57	60	176	38 57	60	176
4	31 55	60	175	32 55	60	175	33 55	60	175	34 55	60	175	35 55	60	175	36 55	59	175	37 54	60	175	38 54	60	175
5	31 52	+60	174	32 52	+60	174	33 52	+60	174	34 52	+60	174	35 52	+59	174	36 51	+60	174	37 51	+60	174	38 51	+60	174
6	31 48	60	173	32 48	60	173	33 48	60	173	34 48	60	173	35 48	60	173	36 48	59	173	37 47	60	172	38 47	60	172
7	31 44	60	172	32 44	60	172	33 44	60	172	34 44	59	172	35 43	60	171	36 43	60	171	37 43	60	171	38 43	60	171
8	31 39	60	171	32 39	60	171	33 39	59	170	34 38	60	170	35 38	60	170	36 38	60	170	37 38	59	170	38 37	60	170
9	31 34	59	169	32 33	60	169	33 33	60	169	34 33	59	169	35 32	60	169	36 32	60	169	37 32	59	169	38 31	60	169
10	31 28	+59	168	32 27	+60	168	33 27	+59	168	34 26	+60	168	35 26	+60	168	36 26	+59	168	37 25	+60	167	38 25	+59	167
11	31 21	59	167	32 20	60	167	33 20	59	167	34 19	60	167	35 19	59	167	36 18	60	166	37 18	60	166	38 18	59	166
12	31 13	60	166	32 13	59	166	33 12	60	166	34 12	59	166	35 11	60	165	36 11	59	165	37 10	60	165	38 10	59	165
13	31 05	60	165	32 05	59	165	33 04	59	164	34 03	60	164	35 03	59	164	36 02	60	164	37 02	59	164	38 01	59	164
14	30 57	59	164	31 56	59	163	32 55	60	163	33 55	59	163	34 54	59	163	35 53	59	163	36 52	59	163	37 51	60	162
15	30 47	+60	163	31 47	+59	162	32 46	+59	162	33 45	+59	162	34 44	+59	162	35 43	+59	162	36 42	+59	161	37 41	+60	161
16	30 37	60	161	31 37	59	161	32 36	59	161	33 35	59	161	34 34	59	161	35 33	59	160	36 32	59	160	37 31	59	160
17	30 27	59	160	31 26	59	160	32 25	59	160	33 24	59	160	34 23	59	159	35 22	59	159	36 21	59	159	37 20	58	159
18	30 16	59	159	31 15	59	159	32 14	59	159	33 13	58	158	34 11	59	158	35 10	59	158	36 09	58	158	37 08	58	157
19	30 04	59	158	31 03	59	158	32 02	58	157	33 00	59	157	33 59	59	157	34 58	58	157	35 56	59	156	36 55	59	156
20	29 52	+59	157	30 51	+58	157	31 49	+59	156	32 48	+58	156	33 46	+59	156	34 45	+58	156	35 43	+59	155	36 42	+58	155
21	29 39	59	156	30 38	58	155	31 36	59	155	32 35	58	155	33 33	58	155	34 31	59	154	35 30	58	154	36 28	58	154
22	29 26	58	155	30 24	59	154	31 23	58	154	32 21	58	154	33 19	58	153	34 17	59	153	35 16	58	153	36 14	58	153
23	29 12	58	153	30 10	58	153	31 08	58	153	32 06	59	153	33 05	58	152	34 03	58	152	35 01	58	152	35 59	58	151
24	28 57	58	152	29 55	59	152	30 54	58	152	31 52	58	151	32 50	58	151	33 48	57	151	34 45	58	151	35 43	58	150
25	28 42	+58	151	29 40	+58	151	30 38	+58	151	31 36	+58	150	32 34	+58	150	33 32	+58	150	34 30	+57	149	35 27	+58	149
26	28 27	57	150	29 24	58	150	30 22	58	150	31 20	58	149	32 18	57	149	33 15	58	149	34 13	58	148	35 11	57	148
27	28 11	57	149	29 08	58	149	30 06	57	148	31 03	58	148	32 01	58	148	32 59	57	147	33 56	57	147	34 53	58	147
28	27 54	57	148	28 51	58	148	29 49	57	147	30 46	58	147	31 44	57	147	32 41	57	146	33 38	58	146	34 36	57	146
29	27 37	57	147	28 34	58	147	29 32	57	146	30 29	57	146	31 26	57	146	32 23	57	145	33 20	57	145	34 17	57	144
30	27 19	+57	146	28 16	+58	145	29 14	+57	145	30 11	+57	145	31 08	+57	144	32 05	+57	144	33 02	+57	144	33 59	+56	143
31	27 01	57	145	27 58	57	144	28 55	57	144	29 52	57	144	30 49	57	143	31 46	57	143	32 43	56	143	33 39	57	142
32	26 42	57	144	27 39	57	143	28 36	57	143	29 33	57	143	30 30	56	142	31 26	57	142	32 23	57	141	33 20	56	141
33	26 23	57	143	27 20	57	142	28 17	56	142	29 13	57	141	30 10	57	141	31 07	56	141	32 03	56	140	32 59	57	140
34	26 04	56	142	27 00	57	141	27 57	56	141	28 53	57	140	29 50	56	140	30 46	56	140	31 42	57	139	32 39	56	139
35	25 44	+56	141	26 40	+57	140	27 37	+56	140	28 33	+56	139	29 29	+56	139	30 25	+56	139	31 21	+56	138	32 17	+56	138
36	25 23	56	139	26 19	57	139	27 16	56	139	28 12	56	138	29 08	56	138	30 04	56	137	31 00	56	137	31 56	56	137
37	25 02	56	138	25 58	56	138	26 54	56	138	27 50	56	137	28 46	56	137	29 42	56	136	30 38	56	136	31 34	55	136
38	24 41	56	137	25 37	56	137	26 33	56	137	27 29	55	136	28 24	56	136	29 20	56	135	30 16	55	135	31 11	56	134
39	24 19	56	136	25 15	56	136	26 11	55	136	27 06	56	135	28 02	56	135	28 58	55	134	29 53	55	134	30 48	56	133
40	23 57	+56	135	24 53	+55	135	25 48	+56	135	26 44	+55	134	27 39	+56	134	28 35	+55	133	29 30	+55	133	30 25	+55	132
41	23 34	56	134	24 30	55	134	25 25	56	134	26 21	55	133	27 16	55	133	28 11	55	132	29 06	55	132	30 01	55	131
42	23 12	55	133	24 07	55	133	25 02	55	132	25 57	55	132	26 52	55	132	27 47	55	131	28 42	55	131	29 37	55	130
43	22 48	55	132	23 43	55	132	24 38	55	131	25 33	55	131	26 28	55	131	27 23	55	130	28 18	55	130	29 13	54	129
44	22 25	55	131	23 20	54	131	24 14	55	130	25 09	55	130	26 04	55	130	26 59	54	129	27 53	55	129	28 48	54	128
45	22 00	+55	130	22 55	+55	130	23 50	+55	129	24 45	+54	129	25 39	+55	129	26 34	+54	128	27 28	+55	128	28 23	+54	127
46	21 36	55	129	22 31	54	129	23 25	55	128	24 20	54	128	25 14	55	128	26 09	54	127	27 03	54	127	27 57	54	126
47	21 11	55	128	22 06	54	128	23 00	55	127	23 55	54	127	24 49	54	127	25 43	54	126	26 37	54	126	27 31	54	125
48	20 46	55	127	21 41	54	127	22 35	54	127	23 29	54	126	24 23	54	126	25 17	54	125	26 11	54	125	27 05	54	124
49	20 21	54	126	21 15	54	126	22 09	54	126	23 03	54	125	23 57	54	125	24 51	54	124	25 45	54	124	26 39	53	123
50	19 55	+54	125	20 49	+54	125	21 43	+54	125	22 37	+54	124	23 31	+54	124	24 25	+53	123	25 18	+54	123	26 12	+53	122
51	19 29	54	125	20 23	54	124	21 17	53	124	22 10	54	123	23 04	54	123	23 58	53	122	24 51	54	122	25 45	53	121
52	19 03	53	124	19 56	54	123	20 50	54	123	21 44	53	122	22 37	54	122	23 31	53	121	24 24	53	121	25 17	54	120
53	18 36	54	123	19 30	53	122	20 23	54	122	21 17	53	121	22 10	53	121	23 03	54	120	23 57	53	120	24 50	53	119
54	18 09	53	122	19 02	54	121	19 56	53	121	20 49	54	120	21 43	53	120	22 36	53	119	23 29	53	119	24 22	53	118
55	17 42	+53	121	18 35	+53	120	19 28	+54	120	20 22	+53	119	21 15	+53	119	22 08	+53	118	23 01	+53	118	23 54	+52	117
56	17 14	54	120	18 08	53	119	19 01	53	119	19 54	53	118	20 47	53	118	21 40	53	117	22 33	52	117	23 25	53	116
57	16 47	53	119	17 40	53	118	18 33	53	118	19 26	53	117	20 19	52	117	21 11	53	116	22 04	53	116	22 57	52	115
58	16 19	53	118	17 12	52	117	18 04	53	117	18 57	53	116	19 50	53	116	20 43	52	115	21 35	53	115	22 28	52	114
59	15 50	53	117	16 43	53	117	17 36	53	116	18 29	52	116	19 21	53	115	20 14	52	115	21 06	53	114	21 59	52	113
60	15 22	+53	116	16 15	+52	116	17 07	+53	115	18 00	+52	115	18 52	+53	114	19 45	+52	114	20 37	+52	113	21 29	+53	113
61	14 53	53	115	15 46	52	115	16 38	53	114	17 31	52	114	18 23	53	113	19 16	52	113	20 08	52	112	21 00	52	112
62	14 24	53	114	15 17	52	114	16 09	53	113	17 02	52	113	17 54	52	112	18 46	52	112	19 38	52	111	20 30	52	111
63	13 55	53	113	14 48	52	113	15 40	52	112	16 32	52	112	17 24	53	111	18 17	52	111	19 09	51	110	20 00	52	110
64	13 26	52	113	14 18	53	112	15 11	52	112	16 03	52	111	16 55	52	110	17 47	52	110	18 39	51	109	19 30	52	109
65	12 57	+52	112	13 49	+52	111	14 41	+52	111	15 33	+52	110	16 25	+52	110	17 17	+52	109	18 09	+51	109	19 00	+52	108
66	12 27	52	111	13 19	52	110	14 11	52	110	15 03	52	109	15 55	52	109	16 47	51	108	17 38	52	108	18 30	52	107
67	11 57	52	110	12 49	52	109	13 41	52	109	14 33	52	108	15 25	51	108	16 16	52	107	17 08	51	107	17 59	52	106
68	11 27	52	109	12 19	52	108	13 11	52	108	14 03	51	107	14 54	52	107	15 46	51	106	16 37	52	106	17 29	51	105
69	10 57	52	108	11 49	51	108	12 40	52	107	13 32	52	107	14 24	51	106	15 15	52	105	16 07	51	105	16 58	51	104

8° Hc	8° d	8° Z	9° Hc	9° d	9° Z	10° Hc	10° d	10° Z	11° Hc	11° d	11° Z	12° Hc	12° d	12° Z	13° Hc	13° d	13° Z	14° Hc	14° d	14° Z	LHA
° ′	′	°	° ′	′	°	° ′	′	°	° ′	′	°	° ′	′	°	° ′	′	°	° ′	′	°	
40 00	+60	180	41 00	+60	180	42 00	+60	180	43 00	+60	180	44 00	+60	180	45 00	+60	180	46 00	+60	180	360
40 00	60	179	41 00	60	179	42 00	60	179	43 00	60	179	44 00	60	179	45 00	60	179	46 00	60	179	359
39 59	60	177	40 59	60	177	41 59	60	177	42 59	60	177	43 59	60	177	44 59	59	177	45 58	60	177	358
39 57	60	176	40 57	60	176	41 57	60	176	42 57	60	176	43 57	60	176	44 57	60	176	45 57	60	176	357
39 54	60	175	40 54	60	175	41 54	60	175	42 54	60	175	43 54	60	175	44 54	60	175	45 54	60	174	356
39 51	+60	174	40 51	+60	174	41 51	+60	173	42 51	+60	173	43 51	+60	173	44 51	+59	173	45 50	+60	173	355
39 47	60	172	40 47	60	172	41 47	60	172	42 47	60	172	43 47	59	172	44 46	60	172	45 46	60	172	354
39 43	59	171	40 42	60	171	41 42	60	171	42 42	60	171	43 42	59	171	44 41	60	170	45 41	60	170	353
39 37	60	170	40 37	60	170	41 37	59	169	42 36	60	169	43 36	60	169	44 36	59	169	45 35	60	169	352
39 31	60	168	40 31	59	168	41 30	60	168	42 30	60	168	43 30	59	168	44 29	60	168	45 29	59	168	351
39 24	+60	167	40 24	+60	167	41 24	+59	167	42 23	+60	167	43 23	+59	167	44 22	+60	166	45 22	+59	166	350
39 17	59	166	40 16	60	166	41 16	59	166	42 15	60	165	43 15	59	165	44 14	60	165	45 14	59	165	349
39 09	59	165	40 08	60	164	41 08	59	164	42 07	59	164	43 06	60	164	44 06	59	164	45 05	59	163	348
39 00	59	163	39 59	60	163	40 59	59	163	41 58	59	163	42 57	59	163	43 56	59	162	44 55	60	162	347
38 51	59	162	39 50	59	162	40 49	59	162	41 48	59	161	42 47	59	161	43 46	59	161	44 45	59	161	346
38 41	+59	161	39 40	+59	161	40 39	+59	160	41 38	+59	160	42 37	+59	160	43 36	+58	160	44 34	+59	159	345
38 30	59	160	39 29	59	159	40 28	59	159	41 27	58	159	42 25	59	159	43 24	59	158	44 23	59	158	344
38 18	59	158	39 17	59	158	40 16	59	158	41 15	58	158	42 13	59	157	43 12	59	157	44 11	58	157	343
38 06	59	157	39 05	59	157	40 04	58	157	41 02	59	156	42 01	58	156	42 59	59	156	43 58	58	155	342
37 54	58	156	38 52	59	156	39 51	58	155	40 49	59	155	41 48	58	155	42 46	58	154	43 44	58	154	341
37 40	+59	155	38 39	+58	154	39 37	+58	154	40 35	+59	154	41 34	+58	153	42 32	+58	153	43 30	+58	153	340
37 26	59	154	38 25	58	153	39 23	58	153	40 21	58	153	41 19	58	152	42 17	58	152	43 15	58	152	339
37 12	58	152	38 10	58	152	39 08	58	152	40 06	58	151	41 04	58	151	42 02	58	151	43 00	57	150	338
36 57	58	151	37 55	58	151	38 53	57	150	39 50	58	150	40 48	58	150	41 46	57	149	42 43	58	149	337
36 41	58	150	37 39	58	150	38 37	57	149	39 34	58	149	40 32	57	148	41 29	58	148	42 27	57	148	336
36 25	+58	149	37 23	+57	148	38 20	+58	148	39 18	+57	148	40 15	+57	147	41 12	+57	147	42 09	+58	146	335
36 08	58	148	37 06	57	147	38 03	57	147	39 00	57	146	39 57	58	146	40 55	57	146	41 52	57	145	334
35 51	57	146	36 48	57	146	37 45	57	146	38 42	57	145	39 39	57	145	40 36	57	144	41 33	57	144	333
35 33	57	145	36 30	57	145	37 27	57	144	38 24	57	144	39 21	57	144	40 18	56	143	41 14	57	143	332
35 14	57	144	36 11	57	144	37 08	57	143	38 05	57	143	39 02	56	142	39 58	57	142	40 55	56	142	331
34 55	+57	143	35 52	+57	143	36 49	+56	142	37 45	+57	142	38 42	+56	141	39 38	+57	141	40 35	+56	140	330
34 36	57	142	35 33	56	141	36 29	56	141	37 25	57	141	38 22	56	140	39 18	56	140	40 14	56	139	329
34 16	56	141	35 12	57	140	36 09	56	140	37 05	56	139	38 01	56	139	38 57	56	138	39 53	56	138	328
33 56	56	140	34 52	56	139	35 48	56	139	36 44	56	138	37 40	56	138	38 36	55	137	39 31	56	137	327
33 35	56	138	34 31	56	138	35 27	56	138	36 23	55	137	37 18	56	137	38 14	55	136	39 09	56	136	326
33 13	+56	137	34 09	+56	137	35 05	+56	136	36 01	+55	136	36 56	+56	135	37 52	+55	134	38 47	+55	134	325
32 52	55	136	33 47	56	136	34 43	55	135	35 38	56	135	36 34	55	134	37 29	55	134	38 24	55	133	324
32 29	56	135	33 25	55	135	34 20	55	134	35 15	56	134	36 11	55	133	37 06	55	133	38 01	54	132	323
32 07	55	134	33 02	55	134	33 57	55	133	34 52	55	133	35 47	55	132	36 42	55	132	37 37	54	131	322
31 44	55	133	32 39	55	132	33 34	55	132	34 29	54	132	35 23	55	131	36 18	55	131	37 13	54	130	321
31 20	+55	132	32 15	+55	131	33 10	+55	131	34 05	+54	130	34 59	+55	130	35 54	+54	129	36 48	+54	129	320
30 56	55	131	31 51	55	130	32 46	54	130	33 40	55	129	34 35	54	129	35 29	54	128	36 23	54	128	319
30 32	55	130	31 27	54	129	32 21	54	129	33 15	55	128	34 10	54	128	35 04	54	127	35 58	54	127	318
30 07	55	129	31 02	54	128	31 56	54	128	32 50	54	127	33 44	54	127	34 38	54	126	35 32	54	126	317
29 42	55	128	30 37	54	127	31 31	54	127	32 25	54	126	33 19	53	126	34 12	54	125	35 06	54	125	316
29 17	+54	127	30 11	+54	126	31 05	+54	126	31 59	+54	125	32 53	+53	125	33 46	+54	124	34 40	+53	124	315
28 51	54	126	29 45	54	125	30 39	54	125	31 33	53	124	32 26	54	124	33 20	53	123	34 13	53	122	314
28 25	54	125	29 19	54	124	30 13	53	124	31 06	54	123	32 00	53	123	32 53	53	122	33 46	53	121	313
27 59	53	124	28 52	54	123	29 46	53	123	30 39	54	122	31 33	53	122	32 26	53	121	33 19	53	120	312
27 32	54	123	28 26	53	122	29 19	53	122	30 12	53	121	31 05	53	121	31 58	53	120	32 51	53	119	311
27 05	+54	122	27 59	+53	121	28 52	+53	121	29 45	+53	120	30 38	+53	119	31 31	+52	119	32 23	+53	118	310
26 38	53	121	27 31	53	120	28 24	53	120	29 17	53	119	30 10	53	118	31 03	52	118	31 55	53	117	309
26 11	53	120	27 04	52	119	27 56	53	119	28 49	53	118	29 42	53	118	30 35	52	117	31 27	52	116	308
25 43	53	119	26 36	52	118	27 28	53	118	28 21	53	117	29 14	52	117	30 06	52	116	30 58	52	115	307
25 15	52	118	26 07	53	117	27 00	53	117	27 53	52	116	28 45	52	116	29 37	52	115	30 29	52	114	306
24 46	+53	117	25 39	+53	116	26 32	+52	116	27 24	+52	115	28 16	+52	115	29 08	+52	114	30 00	+52	113	305
24 18	52	116	25 10	53	115	26 03	52	115	26 55	52	114	27 47	52	114	28 39	52	113	29 31	52	112	304
23 49	53	115	24 42	52	114	25 34	52	114	26 26	52	113	27 18	52	113	28 10	52	112	29 02	51	112	303
23 20	52	114	24 12	53	113	25 05	52	113	25 57	52	112	26 49	51	112	27 40	52	111	28 32	51	111	302
22 51	52	113	23 43	52	112	24 35	52	112	25 27	52	111	26 19	52	111	27 11	51	110	28 02	51	110	301
22 22	+52	112	23 14	+52	111	24 06	+51	111	24 57	+52	110	25 49	+52	110	26 41	+51	109	27 32	+51	109	300
21 52	52	111	22 44	52	111	23 36	51	110	24 27	52	109	25 19	51	109	26 10	52	108	27 02	51	108	299
21 22	52	110	22 14	52	110	23 06	51	109	23 57	52	109	24 49	51	108	25 40	51	107	26 31	51	107	298
20 52	52	109	21 44	52	109	22 36	51	108	23 27	52	108	24 19	51	107	25 10	51	106	26 01	51	106	297
20 22	52	108	21 14	51	108	22 05	52	107	22 57	51	107	23 48	51	106	24 39	51	106	25 30	51	105	296
19 52	+51	107	20 43	+52	107	21 35	+51	106	22 26	+51	106	23 17	+52	105	24 09	+50	105	24 59	+51	104	295
19 22	51	107	20 13	51	106	21 04	52	105	21 56	51	105	22 47	51	104	23 38	51	104	24 29	50	103	294
18 51	51	106	19 42	52	105	20 34	51	105	21 25	51	104	22 16	51	103	23 07	51	103	23 58	50	102	293
18 20	52	105	19 12	51	104	20 03	51	104	20 54	51	103	21 45	51	103	22 36	50	102	23 26	51	101	292
17 49	52	104	18 41	51	103	19 32	51	103	20 23	51	102	21 14	51	102	22 05	50	101	22 55	51	100	291

S. Lat. {LHA greater than 180°....... Zn=180−Z; LHA less than 180°........... Zn=180+Z}

DECLINATION (0°-14°) SAME NAME AS LATITUDE

N. Lat. {LHA greater than 180°....... Zn=Z; LHA less than 180°........... Zn=360−Z}

DECLINATION (0°-14°) SAME NAME AS LATITUDE

LHA	0° Hc	d	Z	1° Hc	d	Z	2° Hc	d	Z	3° Hc	d	Z	4° Hc	d	Z
	° ′	′	°	° ′	′	°	° ′	′	°	° ′	′	°	° ′	′	°
70	10 27	+51	107	11 18	+52	107	12 10	+52	106	13 02	+51	106	13 53	+52	105
71	09 56	52	106	10 48	51	106	11 39	52	105	12 31	51	105	13 22	52	104
72	09 26	51	105	10 17	52	105	11 09	51	104	12 00	51	104	12 51	52	103
73	08 55	51	105	09 46	52	104	10 38	51	104	11 29	51	103	12 20	52	102
74	08 24	51	104	09 15	52	103	10 07	51	103	10 58	51	102	11 49	52	102
75	07 53	+51	103	08 44	+52	102	09 36	+51	102	10 27	+51	101	11 18	+51	101
76	07 22	51	102	08 13	52	101	09 05	51	101	09 56	51	100	10 47	51	100
77	06 51	51	101	07 42	51	101	08 33	51	100	09 24	52	100	10 16	51	99
78	06 20	51	100	07 11	51	100	08 02	51	99	08 53	51	99	09 44	51	98
79	05 48	51	99	06 39	51	99	07 30	52	98	08 22	51	98	09 13	51	97
80	05 17	+51	99	06 08	+51	98	06 59	+51	97	07 50	+51	97	08 41	+51	96
81	04 45	51	98	05 36	51	97	06 27	51	97	07 18	51	96	08 09	51	96
82	04 14	51	97	05 05	51	96	05 56	51	96	06 47	51	95	07 38	51	95
83	03 42	51	96	04 33	51	95	05 24	51	95	06 15	51	94	07 06	51	94
84	03 11	50	95	04 01	51	95	04 52	51	94	05 43	51	94	06 34	51	93
85	02 39	+51	94	03 30	+51	94	04 21	+51	93	05 12	+50	93	06 02	+51	92
86	02 07	51	93	02 58	51	93	03 49	51	92	04 40	51	92	05 31	51	91
87	01 35	51	93	02 26	51	92	03 17	51	91	04 08	51	91	04 59	51	90
88	01 04	50	92	01 54	51	91	02 45	51	91	03 36	51	90	04 27	51	90
89	00 32	51	91	01 23	51	90	02 14	50	90	03 04	51	89	03 55	51	89
90	00 00	+51	90	00 51	+51	89	01 42	+51	89	02 33	+50	88	03 23	+51	88
91	−0 32	51	89	00 19	51	89	01 10	51	88	02 01	51	88	02 52	51	87
92	−1 04	51	88	−0 13	51	88	00 38	51	87	01 29	51	87	02 20	51	86
93	−1 35	51	87	−0 44	50	87	00 06	51	86	00 57	51	86	01 48	51	85
94	−2 07	51	87	−1 16	51	86	−0 25	51	86	00 26	51	85	01 17	51	84
95	−2 39	+51	86	−1 48	+51	85	−0 57	+51	85	−0 06	+51	84	00 45	+51	84
96	−3 11	51	85	−2 20	51	84	−1 29	51	84	−0 38	51	83	00 13	51	83
97	−3 42	51	84	−2 51	51	84	−2 00	51	83	−1 09	51	82	−0 18	51	82
98	−4 14	51	83	−3 23	51	83	−2 32	51	82	−1 41	51	82	−0 50	52	81
99	−4 45	51	82	−3 54	51	82	−3 03	51	81	−2 12	51	81	−1 21	51	80
100	−5 17	+51	81	−4 26	+51	81	−3 35	+52	80	−2 43	+51	80	−1 52	+51	79
101	−5 48	51	81	−4 57	51	80	−4 06	51	80	−3 15	52	79	−2 23	51	79
102				−5 28	51	79	−4 37	51	79	−3 46	51	78	−2 55	52	78
103				−6 00	52	78	−5 08	51	78	−4 17	51	77	−3 26	52	77
104							−5 39	51	77	−4 48	52	76	−3 56	51	76
105										−5 19	+52	76	−4 27	+51	75
106										−5 50	52	75	−4 58	52	74
107													−5 29	52	73
108													−5 59	52	72

LHA	5° Hc	d	Z	6° Hc	d	Z	7° Hc	d	Z	8° Hc	d	Z	9° Hc	d	Z
	° ′	′	°	° ′	′	°	° ′	′	°	° ′	′	°	° ′	′	°
70	14 45	+51	105	15 36	+51	104	16 27	+52	104	17 19	+51	103	18 10	+51	102
71	14 14	51	104	15 05	51	103	15 56	51	103	16 47	52	102	17 39	51	102
72	13 43	51	103	14 34	51	102	15 25	51	102	16 16	51	101	17 07	51	101
73	13 12	51	102	14 03	51	101	14 54	51	101	15 45	51	100	16 36	51	100
74	12 41	51	101	13 32	51	101	14 23	51	100	15 14	51	99	16 05	51	99
75	12 09	+51	100	13 00	+51	100	13 51	+51	99	14 42	+51	99	15 33	+51	98
76	11 38	51	99	12 29	51	99	13 20	51	98	14 11	51	98	15 02	50	97
77	11 07	51	98	11 58	50	98	12 48	51	97	13 39	51	97	14 30	51	96
78	10 35	51	98	11 26	51	97	12 17	51	97	13 08	50	96	13 58	51	95
79	10 04	50	97	10 54	51	96	11 45	51	96	12 36	51	95	13 27	50	95
80	09 32	+51	96	10 23	+51	95	11 14	+50	95	12 04	+51	94	12 55	+51	94
81	09 00	51	95	09 51	51	95	10 42	51	94	11 33	50	93	12 23	51	93
82	08 29	50	94	09 19	51	94	10 10	51	93	11 01	51	93	11 52	50	92
83	07 57	51	93	08 48	50	93	09 38	51	92	10 29	51	92	11 20	50	91
84	07 25	51	92	08 16	51	92	09 07	50	91	09 57	51	91	10 48	51	90
85	06 53	+51	92	07 44	+51	91	08 35	+51	91	09 26	+50	90	10 16	+51	89
86	06 22	50	91	07 12	51	90	08 03	51	90	08 54	50	89	09 44	51	89
87	05 50	51	90	06 41	50	89	07 31	51	89	08 22	51	88	09 13	50	88
88	05 18	51	89	06 09	50	89	06 59	51	88	07 50	51	87	08 41	51	87
89	04 46	51	88	05 37	51	88	06 28	50	87	07 18	51	87	08 09	51	86
90	04 14	+51	87	05 05	+51	87	05 56	+51	86	06 47	+50	86	07 37	+51	85
91	03 43	50	86	04 33	51	86	05 24	51	85	06 15	51	85	07 06	51	84
92	03 11	51	86	04 02	51	85	04 53	50	85	05 43	51	84	06 34	51	84
93	02 39	51	85	03 30	51	84	04 21	51	84	05 12	51	83	06 03	50	83
94	02 08	50	84	02 58	51	83	03 49	51	83	04 40	51	82	05 31	51	82
95	01 36	+51	83	02 27	+51	83	03 18	+51	82	04 09	+51	82	05 00	+51	81
96	01 04	51	82	01 55	51	82	02 46	51	81	03 37	51	81	04 28	51	80
97	00 33	51	81	01 24	51	81	02 15	51	80	03 06	51	80	03 57	51	79
98	00 02	51	81	00 53	51	80	01 44	51	80	02 35	51	79	03 26	51	78
99	−0 30	51	80	00 21	51	79	01 12	52	79	02 04	51	78	02 55	51	78
100	−1 01	+51	79	−0 10	+51	78	00 41	+51	78	01 32	+52	77	02 24	+51	77
101	−1 32	51	78	−0 41	51	78	00 10	52	77	01 02	51	76	01 53	51	76
102	−2 03	51	77	−1 12	51	77	−0 21	52	76	00 31	51	76	01 22	51	75
103	−2 34	51	76	−1 43	52	76	−0 51	51	75	00 00	51	75	00 51	52	74
104	−3 05	51	75	−2 14	52	75	−1 22	51	74	−0 31	52	74	00 21	51	73
105	−3 36	+52	75	−2 44	+51	74	−1 53	+52	74	−1 01	+51	73	−0 10	+52	73
106	−4 06	51	74	−3 15	52	73	−2 23	51	73	−1 32	52	72	−0 40	52	72
107	−4 37	52	73	−3 45	52	72	−2 53	51	72	−2 02	52	71	−1 10	52	71
108	−5 07	52	72	−4 15	51	72	−3 24	52	71	−2 32	52	71	−1 40	52	70
109	−5 37	52	71	−4 45	51	71	−3 54	52	70	−3 02	52	70	−2 10	52	69
110				−5 15	+52	70	−4 23	+52	69	−3 31	+52	69	−2 39	+52	68
111				−5 45	52	69	−4 53	52	68	−4 01	52	68	−3 09	52	67
112							−5 23	53	68	−4 30	52	67	−3 38	52	67
113							−5 52	52	67	−5 00	53	66	−4 07	52	66
114										−5 29	53	65	−4 36	52	65
115													−5 05	+53	64
116													−5 33	52	63

LHA	10° Hc	d	Z	11° Hc	d	Z	12° Hc	d	Z	13° Hc	d	Z	14° Hc	d	Z	LHA
	° ′	′	°	° ′	′	°	° ′	′	°	° ′	′	°	° ′	′	°	
70	19 01	+51	102	19 52	+51	101	20 43	+50	101	21 33	+51	100	22 24	+50	100	290
71	18 30	50	101	19 20	51	100	20 11	51	100	21 02	50	99	21 52	51	99	289
72	17 58	51	100	18 49	51	100	19 40	50	99	20 30	51	98	21 21	50	98	288
73	17 27	51	99	18 18	50	99	19 08	51	98	19 59	50	98	20 49	51	97	287
74	16 56	50	98	17 46	51	98	18 37	50	97	19 27	51	97	20 18	50	96	286
75	16 24	+51	97	17 15	+50	97	18 05	+51	96	18 56	+50	96	19 46	+51	95	285
76	15 52	51	97	16 43	51	96	17 34	50	95	18 24	51	95	19 15	50	94	284
77	15 21	50	96	16 11	51	95	17 02	50	95	17 52	51	94	18 43	50	93	283
78	14 49	51	95	15 40	50	94	16 30	51	94	17 21	50	93	18 11	50	93	282
79	14 17	51	94	15 08	51	93	15 59	50	93	16 49	50	92	17 39	51	92	281
80	13 46	+50	93	14 36	+51	93	15 27	+50	92	16 17	+51	92	17 08	+50	91	280
81	13 14	51	92	14 05	50	92	14 55	50	91	15 45	51	91	16 36	50	90	279
82	12 42	51	91	13 33	50	91	14 23	51	90	15 14	50	90	16 04	50	89	278
83	12 10	51	91	13 01	50	90	13 51	51	90	14 42	50	89	15 32	50	88	277
84	11 39	50	90	12 29	51	89	13 20	50	89	14 10	50	88	15 00	51	88	276
85	11 07	+50	89	11 57	+51	88	12 48	+50	88	13 38	+51	87	14 29	+50	87	275
86	10 35	51	88	11 26	50	88	12 16	51	87	13 07	50	86	13 57	50	86	274
87	10 03	51	87	10 54	50	87	11 44	51	86	12 35	50	86	13 25	50	85	273
88	09 32	50	86	10 22	51	86	11 13	50	85	12 03	51	85	12 54	50	84	272
89	09 00	50	86	09 50	51	85	10 41	50	84	11 31	51	84	12 22	50	83	271
90	08 28	+51	85	09 19	+50	84	10 09	+51	84	11 00	+50	83	11 50	+51	83	270
91	07 57	50	84	08 47	51	83	09 38	50	83	10 28	51	82	11 19	50	82	269
92	07 25	51	83	08 16	50	82	09 06	51	82	09 57	50	81	10 47	51	81	268
93	06 53	51	82	07 44	51	82	08 35	51	81	09 26	50	81	10 16	51	80	267
94	06 22	51	81	07 13	50	81	08 03	51	80	08 54	51	80	09 45	50	79	266
95	05 51	+50	81	06 41	+51	80	07 32	+51	79	08 23	+51	79	09 14	+50	78	265
96	05 19	51	80	06 10	51	79	07 01	51	79	07 52	51	78	08 43	50	78	264
97	04 48	51	79	05 39	51	78	06 30	51	78	07 21	51	77	08 12	50	77	263
98	04 17	51	78	05 08	51	77	05 59	51	77	06 50	51	76	07 41	51	76	262
99	03 46	51	77	04 37	51	77	05 28	51	76	06 19	51	76	07 10	51	75	261
100	03 15	+51	76	04 06	+51	76	04 57	+51	75	05 48	+51	75	06 39	+51	74	260
101	02 44	51	75	03 35	51	75	04 26	52	74	05 18	51	74	06 09	51	73	259
102	02 13	52	75	03 05	51	74	03 56	51	74	04 47	51	73	05 38	52	73	258
103	01 43	51	74	02 34	51	73	03 25	52	73	04 17	51	72	05 08	51	72	257
104	01 12	52	73	02 04	51	72	02 55	52	72	03 47	51	71	04 38	51	71	256
105	00 42	+51	72	01 33	+52	72	02 25	+52	71	03 17	+51	71	04 08	+52	70	255
106	00 12	51	71	01 03	52	71	01 55	52	70	02 47	51	70	03 38	52	69	254
107	−0 18	51	70	00 33	52	70	01 25	52	69	02 17	52	69	03 09	51	68	253
108	−0 48	52	69	00 04	51	69	00 55	52	68	01 47	52	68	02 39	52	68	252
109	−1 18	52	69	−0 26	52	68	00 26	52	68	01 18	52	67	02 10	52	67	251
110	−1 47	+52	68	−0 55	+52	67	−0 03	+52	67	00 49	+52	66	01 41	+52	66	250
111	−2 17	52	67	−1 25	53	66	−0 32	52	66	00 20	52	65	01 12	52	65	249
112	−2 46	52	66	−1 54	53	66	−1 01	52	65	−0 09	52	65	00 43	52	64	248
113	−3 15	53	65	−2 22	52	65	−1 30	52	64	−0 38	53	64	00 15	52	63	247
114	−3 44	53	64	−2 51	52	64	−1 59	53	63	−1 06	52	63	−0 14	53	62	246
115	−4 12	+52	63	−3 20	+53	63	−2 27	+53	63	−1 34	+52	62	−0 42	+53	62	245
116	−4 41	53	63	−3 48	53	62	−2 55	53	62	−2 02	52	61	−1 10	53	61	244
117	−5 09	53	62	−4 16	53	61	−3 23	53	61	−2 30	53	60	−1 37	53	60	243
118	−5 37	53	61	−4 44	53	60	−3 51	53	60	−2 58	53	59	−2 05	53	59	242
119				−5 11	53	60	−4 18	53	59	−3 25	53	59	−2 32	53	58	241
120				−5 38	+53	59	−4 45	+53	58	−3 52	+53	58	−2 59	+54	57	240
121							−5 12	53	57	−4 19	54	57	−3 25	53	56	239
122							−5 39	54	56	−4 45	53	56	−3 52	54	56	238
123										−5 11	53	55	−4 18	54	55	237
124										−5 37	54	54	−4 43	53	54	236
125													−5 09	+54	53	235
126													−5 34	54	52	234

S. Lat. {LHA greater than 180°....... Zn=180−Z; LHA less than 180°........... Zn=180+Z}

DECLINATION (0°-14°) SAME NAME AS LATITUDE

LAT 58°

N. Lat. {LHA greater than 180°....... Zn=Z; LHA less than 180°........... Zn=360−Z}

DECLINATION (0°-14°) CONTRARY NAME TO LATITUDE

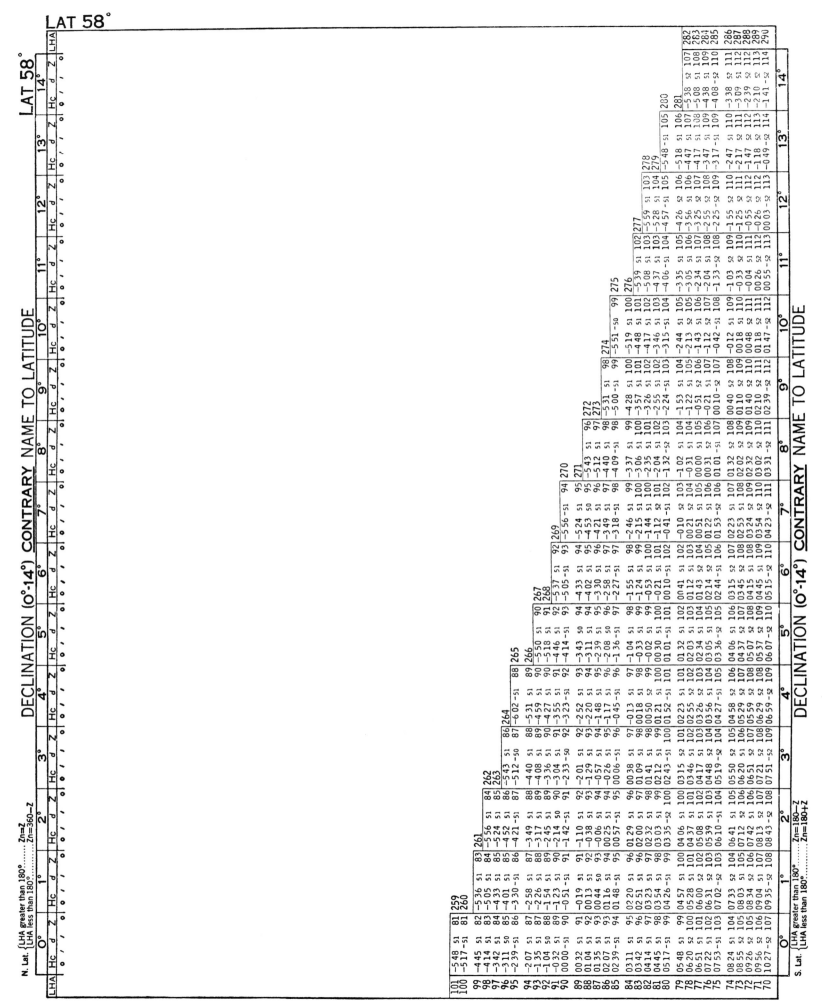

LHA	0°			1°			2°			3°			4°			5°			6°			7°			8°			9°			10°			11°			12°			13°			14°			LHA
	Hc	d	Z	Hc	d	Z	Hc	d	Z	Hc	d	Z	Hc	d	Z	Hc	d	Z	Hc	d	Z	Hc	d	Z	Hc	d	Z	Hc	d	Z	Hc	d	Z	Hc	d	Z	Hc	d	Z	Hc	d	Z	Hc	d	Z	
	° ′	′	°	° ′	′	°	° ′	′	°	° ′	′	°	° ′	′	°	° ′	′	°	° ′	′	°	° ′	′	°	° ′	′	°	° ′	′	°	° ′	′	°	° ′	′	°	° ′	′	°	° ′	′	°	° ′	′	°	
101	-5 48	51	81	259																																										
100	-5 17	-51	81	260																																										
99	-4 45	51	82	-5 36	51	83	261																																							
98	-4 14	51	83	-5 05	51	84	-5 56	51	84	262																																				
97	-3 42	51	84	-4 33	51	85	-5 24	51	85	263																																				
96	-3 11	50	85	-4 01	51	85	-4 52	51	86	-5 43	51	86	264																																	
95	-2 39	-51	86	-3 30	-51	86	-4 21	-51	87	-5 12	-50	87	-6 02	-51	88	265																														
94	-2 07	51	87	-2 58	51	87	-3 49	51	88	-4 40	51	88	-5 31	51	89	266																														
93	-1 35	51	87	-2 26	51	88	-3 17	51	89	-4 08	51	89	-4 59	51	90	-5 50	51	90	267																											
92	-1 04	50	88	-1 54	51	89	-2 45	51	89	-3 36	51	90	-4 27	51	90	-5 18	51	91	268																											
91	-0 32	51	89	-1 23	51	90	-2 14	50	90	-3 04	51	91	-3 55	51	91	-4 46	51	92	-5 37	51	92	269																								
90	00 00	-51	90	-0 51	-51	91	-1 42	-51	91	-2 33	-50	92	-3 23	-51	92	-4 14	-51	93	-5 05	-51	93	-5 56	-51	94	270																					
89	00 32	51	91	-0 19	51	91	-1 10	51	92	-2 01	51	92	-2 52	51	93	-3 43	50	94	-4 33	51	94	-5 24	51	95	271																					
88	01 04	51	92	00 13	51	92	-0 38	51	93	-1 29	51	93	-2 20	51	94	-3 11	51	94	-4 02	51	95	-4 53	50	95	-5 43	51	96	272																		
87	01 35	51	93	00 44	50	93	-0 06	51	94	-0 57	51	94	-1 48	51	95	-2 39	51	95	-3 30	51	96	-4 21	51	96	-5 12	51	97	273																		
86	02 07	51	93	01 16	51	94	00 25	51	94	-0 26	51	95	-1 17	51	96	-2 08	50	96	-2 58	51	97	-3 49	51	97	-4 40	51	98	-5 31	51	98	274															
85	02 39	-51	94	01 48	-51	95	00 57	-51	95	00 06	-51	96	-0 45	-51	96	-1 36	-51	97	-2 27	-51	97	-3 18	-51	98	-4 09	-51	98	-5 00	-51	99	-5 51	-50	99	275												
84	03 11	51	95	02 20	51	96	01 29	51	96	00 38	51	97	-0 13	51	97	-1 04	51	98	-1 55	51	98	-2 46	51	99	-3 37	51	99	-4 28	51	100	-5 19	51	100	276												
83	03 42	51	96	02 51	51	96	02 00	51	97	01 09	51	98	00 18	51	98	-0 33	51	99	-1 24	51	99	-2 15	51	100	-3 06	51	100	-3 57	51	101	-4 48	51	101	-5 39	51	102	277									
82	04 14	51	97	03 23	51	97	02 32	51	98	01 41	51	98	00 50	52	99	-0 02	51	99	-0 53	51	100	-1 44	51	100	-2 35	51	101	-3 26	51	102	-4 17	51	102	-5 08	51	103	-5 59	51	103	278						
81	04 45	51	98	03 54	51	98	03 03	51	99	02 12	51	99	01 21	51	100	00 30	51	100	-0 21	51	101	-1 12	52	101	-2 04	51	102	-2 55	51	102	-3 46	51	103	-4 37	51	103	-5 28	51	104	279						
80	05 17	-51	99	04 26	-51	99	03 35	-52	100	02 43	-51	100	01 52	-51	101	01 01	-51	101	00 10	-51	102	-0 41	-51	102	-1 32	-52	103	-2 24	-51	103	-3 15	-51	104	-4 06	-51	104	-4 57	-51	105	-5 48	-51	105	280			
79	05 48	51	99	04 57	51	100	04 06	51	100	03 15	52	101	02 23	51	101	01 32	51	102	00 41	51	102	-0 10	52	103	-1 02	51	104	-1 53	51	104	-2 44	51	105	-3 35	51	105	-4 26	52	106	-5 18	51	106	281			
78	06 20	52	100	05 28	51	101	04 37	51	101	03 46	51	102	02 55	52	102	02 03	51	103	01 12	51	103	00 21	52	104	-0 31	51	104	-1 22	51	105	-2 13	52	105	-3 05	51	106	-3 56	51	106	-4 47	51	107	-5 38	52	107	282
77	06 51	51	101	06 00	52	102	05 08	51	102	04 17	51	103	03 26	52	103	02 34	51	104	01 43	52	104	00 51	51	105	00 00	51	105	-0 51	52	106	-1 43	51	106	-2 34	51	107	-3 25	52	107	-4 17	51	108	-5 08	51	108	283
76	07 22	51	102	06 31	52	103	05 39	51	103	04 48	52	104	03 56	51	104	03 05	51	105	02 14	52	105	01 22	51	106	00 31	52	106	-0 21	51	107	-1 12	52	107	-2 04	51	108	-2 55	52	108	-3 47	51	109	-4 38	51	109	284
75	07 53	-51	103	07 02	-52	103	06 10	-51	104	05 19	-52	104	04 27	-51	105	03 36	-52	105	02 44	-51	106	01 53	-52	106	01 01	-51	107	00 10	-52	107	-0 42	-51	108	-1 33	-52	108	-2 25	-52	109	-3 17	-51	109	-4 08	-52	110	285
74	08 24	51	104	07 33	52	104	06 41	51	105	05 50	52	105	04 58	52	106	04 06	51	106	03 15	52	107	02 23	51	107	01 32	52	108	00 40	52	108	-0 12	51	109	-1 03	52	109	-1 55	52	110	-2 47	51	110	-3 38	52	111	286
73	08 55	52	105	08 03	51	105	07 12	52	106	06 20	51	106	05 29	52	107	04 37	52	107	03 45	52	108	02 53	51	108	02 02	52	109	01 10	52	109	00 18	51	110	-0 33	52	110	-1 25	52	111	-2 17	52	111	-3 09	51	112	287
72	09 26	52	105	08 34	52	106	07 42	51	106	06 51	52	107	05 59	52	108	05 07	52	108	04 15	51	108	03 24	52	109	02 32	52	109	01 40	52	110	00 48	52	111	-0 04	51	111	-0 55	52	112	-1 47	52	112	-2 39	52	112	288
71	09 56	52	106	09 04	51	107	08 13	52	107	07 21	52	108	06 29	52	108	05 37	52	109	04 45	51	109	03 54	52	110	03 02	52	110	02 10	52	111	01 18	52	111	00 26	52	112	-0 26	52	112	-1 18	52	113	-2 10	52	113	289
70	10 27	-52	107	09 35	-52	108	08 43	-52	108	07 51	-52	109	06 59	-52	109	06 07	-52	110	05 15	-52	110	04 23	-52	111	03 31	-52	111	02 39	-52	112	01 47	-52	112	00 55	-52	113	00 03	-52	113	-0 49	-52	114	-1 41	-52	114	290
	0°			1°			2°			3°			4°			5°			6°			7°			8°			9°			10°			11°			12°			13°			14°			

S. Lat. {LHA greater than 180°....... Zn=180−Z; LHA less than 180°........... Zn=180+Z}

DECLINATION (0°-14°) CONTRARY NAME TO LATITUDE

N. Lat. {LHA greater than 180°....... Zn=Z / LHA less than 180°........... Zn=360−Z}

DECLINATION (0°-14°) CONTRARY NAME TO LATITUDE

LHA	0° Hc	d	Z	1° Hc	d	Z	2° Hc	d	Z	3° Hc	d	Z	4° Hc	d	Z
	° ′	′	°	° ′	′	°	° ′	′	°	° ′	′	°	° ′	′	°
69	10 57	52	108	10 05	52	109	09 13	52	109	08 21	52	110	07 29	52	110
68	11 27	52	109	10 35	52	109	09 43	52	110	08 51	52	110	07 59	52	111
67	11 57	52	110	11 05	52	110	10 13	52	111	09 21	52	111	08 29	53	112
66	12 27	52	111	11 35	52	111	10 43	53	112	09 50	52	112	08 58	52	113
65	12 57	−53	112	12 04	−52	112	11 12	−52	113	10 20	−53	113	09 27	−52	114
64	13 26	52	113	12 34	53	113	11 41	52	114	10 49	53	114	09 56	52	115
63	13 55	52	113	13 03	53	114	12 10	52	114	11 18	53	115	10 25	52	115
62	14 24	52	114	13 32	53	115	12 39	52	115	11 47	53	116	10 54	53	116
61	14 53	52	115	14 01	53	116	13 08	53	116	12 15	53	117	11 22	53	117
60	15 22	−53	116	14 29	−53	117	13 36	−53	117	12 43	−53	118	11 50	−53	118
59	15 50	53	117	14 57	53	118	14 04	53	118	13 11	53	119	12 18	53	119
58	16 19	53	118	15 26	54	118	14 32	53	119	13 39	53	119	12 46	53	120
57	16 47	54	119	15 53	53	119	15 00	53	120	14 07	54	120	13 13	53	121
56	17 14	53	120	16 21	53	120	15 28	54	121	14 34	53	121	13 41	54	122
55	17 42	−54	121	16 48	−53	121	15 55	−54	122	15 01	−53	122	14 08	−54	123
54	18 09	54	122	17 15	53	122	16 22	54	123	15 28	54	123	14 34	54	124
53	18 36	54	123	17 42	54	123	16 48	53	124	15 55	54	124	15 01	54	124
52	19 03	54	124	18 09	54	124	17 15	54	125	16 21	54	125	15 27	54	125
51	19 29	54	125	18 35	54	125	17 41	54	125	16 47	55	126	15 52	54	126
50	19 55	−54	125	19 01	−54	126	18 07	−55	126	17 12	−54	127	16 18	−54	127
49	20 21	55	126	19 26	54	127	18 32	54	127	17 38	55	128	16 43	54	128
48	20 46	54	127	19 52	55	128	18 57	54	128	18 03	55	129	17 08	55	129
47	21 11	54	128	20 17	55	129	19 22	55	129	18 27	55	130	17 32	54	130
46	21 36	55	129	20 41	55	130	19 46	54	130	18 52	55	131	17 57	55	131
45	22 00	−54	130	21 06	−55	131	20 11	−56	131	19 15	−55	132	18 20	−55	132
44	22 25	56	131	21 29	55	132	20 34	55	132	19 39	55	133	18 44	55	133
43	22 48	55	132	21 53	55	133	20 58	56	133	20 02	55	134	19 07	56	134
42	23 12	56	133	22 16	55	134	21 21	56	134	20 25	55	135	19 30	56	135
41	23 34	55	134	22 39	56	135	21 43	55	135	20 48	56	136	19 52	56	136
40	23 57	−56	135	23 01	−55	136	22 06	−56	136	21 10	−56	137	20 14	−56	137
39	24 19	56	136	23 23	56	137	22 27	56	137	21 31	56	138	20 35	56	138
38	24 41	56	137	23 45	56	138	22 49	56	138	21 53	56	139	20 57	57	139
37	25 02	56	138	24 06	56	139	23 10	56	139	22 14	57	140	21 17	56	140
36	25 23	56	139	24 27	57	140	23 30	56	140	22 34	57	141	21 37	56	141
35	25 44	−57	141	24 47	−56	141	23 51	−57	141	22 54	−57	142	21 57	−56	142
34	26 04	57	142	25 07	57	142	24 10	56	142	23 14	57	143	22 17	56	143
33	26 23	57	143	25 26	56	143	24 30	57	143	23 33	57	144	22 36	57	144
32	26 42	57	144	25 45	57	144	24 48	57	144	23 51	57	145	22 54	57	145
31	27 01	57	145	26 04	57	145	25 07	58	145	24 09	57	146	23 12	57	146
30	27 19	−57	146	26 22	−58	146	25 24	−57	146	24 27	−57	147	23 30	−58	147
29	27 37	58	147	26 39	57	147	25 42	58	148	24 44	57	148	23 47	58	148
28	27 54	58	148	26 56	57	148	25 59	58	149	25 01	58	149	24 03	57	149
27	28 11	58	149	27 13	58	149	26 15	58	150	25 17	58	150	24 19	58	150
26	28 27	58	150	27 29	58	150	26 31	58	151	25 33	58	151	24 35	58	151
25	28 42	−58	151	27 44	−58	152	26 46	−58	152	25 48	−58	152	24 50	−58	152
24	28 57	58	152	27 59	58	153	27 01	58	153	26 03	59	153	25 04	58	153
23	29 12	59	153	28 13	58	154	27 15	58	154	26 17	59	154	25 18	58	155
22	29 26	59	155	28 27	58	155	27 29	59	155	26 30	58	155	25 32	59	156
21	29 39	58	156	28 41	59	156	27 42	59	156	26 43	58	156	25 45	59	157
20	29 52	−59	157	28 53	−59	157	27 54	−58	157	26 56	−59	158	25 57	−59	158
19	30 04	59	158	29 05	58	158	28 07	59	158	27 08	59	159	26 09	59	159
18	30 16	59	159	29 17	59	159	28 18	59	160	27 19	59	160	26 20	59	160
17	30 27	59	160	29 28	59	160	28 29	59	161	27 30	59	161	26 31	59	161
16	30 37	59	161	29 38	59	162	28 39	59	162	27 40	59	162	26 41	59	162
15	30 47	−59	163	29 48	−59	163	28 49	−59	163	27 50	−60	163	26 50	−59	163
14	30 57	60	164	29 57	59	164	28 58	59	164	27 59	60	164	26 59	59	164
13	31 05	59	165	30 06	60	165	29 06	59	165	28 07	59	165	27 08	60	165
12	31 13	59	166	30 14	60	166	29 14	59	166	28 15	60	166	27 15	59	167
11	31 21	60	167	30 21	59	167	29 22	60	167	28 22	60	168	27 22	59	168
10	31 28	−60	168	30 28	−60	168	29 28	−59	169	28 29	−60	169	27 29	−60	169
9	31 34	60	169	30 34	60	170	29 34	60	170	28 34	59	170	27 35	60	170
8	31 39	60	171	30 39	59	171	29 40	60	171	28 40	60	171	27 40	60	171
7	31 44	60	172	30 44	60	172	29 44	59	172	28 45	60	172	27 45	60	172
6	31 48	60	173	30 48	59	173	29 49	60	173	28 49	60	173	27 49	60	173
5	31 52	−60	174	30 52	−60	174	29 52	−60	174	28 52	−60	174	27 52	−60	174
4	31 55	60	175	30 55	60	175	29 55	60	175	28 55	60	175	27 55	60	176
3	31 57	60	177	30 57	60	177	29 57	60	177	28 57	60	177	27 57	60	177
2	31 59	60	178	30 59	60	178	29 59	60	178	28 59	60	178	27 59	60	178
1	32 00	60	179	31 00	60	179	30 00	60	179	29 00	60	179	28 00	60	179
0	32 00	−60	180	31 00	−60	180	30 00	−60	180	29 00	−60	180	28 00	−60	180

LHA	5° Hc	d	Z	6° Hc	d	Z	7° Hc	d	Z	8° Hc	d	Z	9° Hc	d	Z
	° ′	′	°	° ′	′	°	° ′	′	°	° ′	′	°	° ′	′	°
69	06 37	52	111	05 45	52	111	04 53	52	112	04 01	52	112	03 09	52	113
68	07 07	52	111	06 15	52	112	05 23	53	112	04 30	52	113	03 38	52	113
67	07 36	52	112	06 44	52	113	05 52	52	113	05 00	53	114	04 07	52	114
66	08 06	53	113	07 13	52	114	06 21	52	114	05 29	53	115	04 36	52	115
65	08 35	−53	114	07 42	−52	115	06 50	−53	115	05 57	−52	116	05 05	−53	116
64	09 04	53	115	08 11	52	115	07 19	53	116	06 26	53	116	05 33	52	117
63	09 33	53	116	08 40	53	116	07 47	53	117	06 54	52	117	06 02	53	118
62	10 01	53	117	09 08	53	117	08 15	53	118	07 22	52	118	06 30	53	119
61	10 29	53	118	09 36	53	118	08 43	53	119	07 50	53	119	06 57	53	120
60	10 57	−53	119	10 04	−53	119	09 11	−53	120	08 18	−53	120	07 25	−53	120
59	11 25	53	119	10 32	53	120	09 39	54	120	08 45	53	121	07 52	53	121
58	11 53	54	120	10 59	53	121	10 06	53	121	09 13	54	122	08 19	53	122
57	12 20	53	121	11 27	54	122	10 33	53	122	09 40	54	123	08 46	54	123
56	12 47	53	122	11 54	54	123	11 00	54	123	10 06	53	124	09 13	54	124
55	13 14	−54	123	12 20	−54	124	11 26	−53	124	10 33	−54	124	09 39	−54	125
54	13 40	53	124	12 47	54	124	11 53	54	125	10 59	54	125	10 05	54	126
53	14 07	54	125	13 13	54	125	12 19	55	126	11 24	54	126	10 30	54	127
52	14 33	55	126	13 38	54	126	12 44	54	127	11 50	54	127	10 56	55	128
51	14 58	54	127	14 04	54	127	13 10	55	128	12 15	54	128	11 21	55	129
50	15 24	−55	128	14 29	−54	128	13 35	−55	129	12 40	−55	129	11 45	−54	129
49	15 49	55	129	14 54	55	129	13 59	54	130	13 05	55	130	12 10	55	130
48	16 13	55	130	15 18	54	130	14 24	55	130	13 29	55	131	12 34	55	131
47	16 38	55	131	15 43	55	131	14 48	55	131	13 53	55	132	12 58	55	132
46	17 02	55	132	16 07	56	132	15 11	55	132	14 16	55	133	13 21	55	133
45	17 25	−55	132	16 30	−55	133	15 35	−56	133	14 39	−55	134	13 44	−55	134
44	17 49	56	133	16 53	55	134	15 58	56	134	15 02	55	135	14 07	56	135
43	18 11	55	134	17 16	56	135	16 20	55	135	15 25	56	136	14 29	56	136
42	18 34	56	135	17 38	55	136	16 43	56	136	15 47	56	137	14 51	56	137
41	18 56	56	136	18 00	56	137	17 04	55	137	16 09	56	137	15 13	56	138
40	19 18	−56	137	18 22	−56	138	17 26	−56	138	16 30	−56	138	15 34	−56	139
39	19 39	56	138	18 43	56	139	17 47	56	139	16 51	56	139	15 55	57	140
38	20 00	56	139	19 04	56	140	18 08	57	140	17 11	56	140	16 15	57	141
37	20 21	57	140	19 24	56	141	18 28	57	141	17 31	56	141	16 35	57	142
36	20 41	57	141	19 44	56	142	18 48	57	142	17 51	57	142	16 54	56	143
35	21 01	−57	142	20 04	−57	143	19 07	−57	143	18 10	−57	143	17 13	−57	144
34	21 20	57	143	20 23	57	144	19 26	57	144	18 29	57	144	17 32	57	145
33	21 39	57	144	20 42	58	145	19 44	57	145	18 47	57	145	17 50	57	146
32	21 57	57	145	21 00	57	146	20 03	58	146	19 05	57	146	18 08	57	147
31	22 15	58	146	21 17	57	147	20 20	57	147	19 23	58	147	18 25	57	148
30	22 32	−57	147	21 35	−58	148	20 37	−57	148	19 40	−58	148	18 42	−58	149
29	22 49	58	148	21 51	57	149	20 54	58	149	19 56	58	149	18 58	57	150
28	23 06	58	149	22 08	58	150	21 10	58	150	20 12	58	150	19 14	58	151
27	23 21	57	151	22 24	58	151	21 26	58	151	20 28	58	151	19 30	58	152
26	23 37	58	152	22 39	58	152	21 41	58	152	20 43	59	152	19 44	58	153
25	23 52	−58	153	22 54	−59	153	21 55	−58	153	20 57	−58	153	19 59	−58	154
24	24 06	58	154	23 08	59	154	22 09	58	154	21 11	58	154	20 13	59	155
23	24 20	58	155	23 22	59	155	22 23	58	155	21 25	59	155	20 26	58	156
22	24 33	58	156	23 35	59	156	22 36	58	156	21 38	59	157	20 39	59	157
21	24 46	59	157	23 47	58	157	22 49	59	157	21 50	59	158	20 51	59	158
20	24 58	−59	158	23 59	−58	158	23 01	−59	158	22 02	−59	159	21 03	−59	159
19	25 10	59	159	24 11	59	159	23 12	59	159	22 13	59	160	21 14	59	160
18	25 21	59	160	24 22	59	160	23 23	59	161	22 24	59	161	21 25	59	161
17	25 32	59	161	24 33	60	161	23 33	59	162	22 34	59	162	21 35	59	162
16	25 42	60	162	24 42	59	162	23 43	59	163	22 44	59	163	21 45	60	163
15	25 51	−59	163	24 52	−60	164	23 52	−59	164	22 53	−59	164	21 54	−60	164
14	26 00	60	164	25 00	59	165	24 01	59	165	23 02	60	165	22 02	59	165
13	26 08	59	166	25 09	60	166	24 09	59	166	23 10	60	166	22 10	59	166
12	26 16	60	167	25 16	59	167	24 17	60	167	23 17	60	167	22 17	59	167
11	26 23	60	168	25 23	60	168	24 23	59	168	23 24	60	168	22 24	59	168
10	26 29	−60	169	25 29	−59	169	24 30	−60	169	23 30	−60	169	22 30	−59	169
9	26 35	60	170	25 35	59	170	24 36	60	170	23 36	60	170	22 36	60	170
8	26 40	60	171	25 40	59	171	24 41	60	171	23 41	60	171	22 41	60	171
7	26 45	60	172	25 45	60	172	24 45	60	172	23 45	60	172	22 45	59	173
6	26 49	60	173	25 49	60	173	24 49	60	173	23 49	60	174	22 49	60	174
5	26 52	−60	174	25 52	−60	175	24 52	−59	175	23 53	−60	175	22 53	−60	175
4	26 55	60	176	25 55	60	176	24 55	60	176	23 55	60	176	22 55	60	176
3	26 57	60	177	25 57	60	177	24 57	60	177	23 57	60	177	22 57	60	177
2	26 59	60	178	25 59	60	179	24 59	60	178	23 59	60	178	22 59	60	178
1	27 00	60	179	26 00	60	179	25 00	60	179	24 00	60	179	23 00	60	179
0	27 00	−60	180	26 00	−60	180	25 00	−60	180	24 00	−60	180	23 00	−60	180

LHA	10° Hc	d	Z	11° Hc	d	Z	12° Hc	d	Z	13° Hc	d	Z	14° Hc	d	Z	LHA
	° ′	′	°	° ′	′	°	° ′	′	°	° ′	′	°	° ′	′	°	
69	02 17	52	113	01 25	53	114	00 32	52	114	−0 20	52	115	−1 12	52	115	291
68	02 46	52	114	01 54	53	114	01 01	52	115	00 09	52	115	−0 43	52	116	292
67	03 15	53	115	02 22	52	115	01 30	52	116	00 38	53	116	−0 15	52	117	293
66	03 44	53	116	02 51	52	116	01 59	53	117	01 06	52	117	00 14	53	118	294
65	04 12	−52	117	03 20	−53	117	02 27	−53	117	01 34	−52	118	00 42	−53	118	295
64	04 41	53	117	03 48	53	118	02 55	53	118	02 02	52	119	01 10	53	119	296
63	05 09	53	118	04 16	53	119	03 23	53	119	02 30	52	120	01 37	53	120	297
62	05 37	53	119	04 44	53	120	03 51	53	120	02 58	53	121	02 05	53	121	298
61	06 04	53	120	05 11	53	120	04 18	53	121	03 25	53	121	02 32	53	122	299
60	06 32	−54	121	05 38	−53	121	04 45	−53	122	03 52	−53	122	02 59	−54	123	300
59	06 59	54	122	06 05	53	122	05 12	53	123	04 19	54	123	03 25	53	124	301
58	07 26	54	123	06 32	53	123	05 39	54	124	04 45	53	124	03 52	54	124	302
57	07 52	53	124	06 59	54	124	06 05	54	124	05 11	53	125	04 18	54	125	303
56	08 19	54	124	07 25	54	125	06 31	54	125	05 37	54	126	04 43	53	126	304
55	08 45	−54	125	07 51	−54	126	06 57	−54	126	06 03	−54	127	05 09	−54	127	305
54	09 11	54	126	08 17	54	127	07 23	55	127	06 28	54	128	05 34	54	128	306
53	09 36	54	127	08 42	54	128	07 48	55	128	06 53	54	128	05 59	54	129	307
52	10 01	54	128	09 07	54	128	08 13	55	129	07 18	54	129	06 24	54	130	308
51	10 26	54	129	09 32	55	129	08 37	54	130	07 43	55	130	06 48	54	131	309
50	10 51	−55	130	09 56	−54	130	09 02	−55	131	08 07	−55	131	07 12	−55	132	310
49	11 15	55	131	10 20	55	131	09 25	54	132	08 31	55	132	07 36	55	132	311
48	11 39	55	132	10 44	55	132	09 49	55	133	08 54	55	133	07 59	55	133	312
47	12 03	55	133	11 08	56	133	10 12	55	133	09 17	55	134	08 22	55	134	313
46	12 26	55	134	11 31	56	134	10 35	55	134	09 40	55	135	08 45	56	135	314
45	12 49	−56	134	11 53	−55	135	10 58	−56	135	10 02	−55	136	09 07	−56	136	315
44	13 11	55	135	12 16	56	136	11 20	55	136	10 25	56	137	09 29	56	137	316
43	13 33	55	136	12 38	56	137	11 42	56	137	10 46	56	137	09 50	55	138	317
42	13 55	56	137	12 59	56	138	12 03	55	138	11 08	56	138	10 12	56	139	318
41	14 17	56	138	13 21	56	139	12 25	57	139	11 28	56	139	10 32	56	140	319
40	14 38	−57	139	13 41	−56	140	12 45	−56	140	11 49	−56	140	10 53	−57	141	320
39	14 58	56	140	14 02	56	140	13 06	57	141	12 09	56	141	11 13	57	142	321
38	15 18	56	141	14 22	57	141	13 25	56	142	12 29	57	142	11 32	56	142	322
37	15 38	56	142	14 42	57	142	13 45	57	143	12 48	56	143	11 52	57	143	323
36	15 58	57	143	15 01	57	143	14 04	57	144	13 07	57	144	12 10	57	144	324
35	16 16	−56	144	15 20	−57	144	14 23	−57	145	13 26	−57	145	12 29	−57	145	325
34	16 35	57	145	15 38	57	145	14 41	57	146	13 44	57	146	12 47	58	146	326
33	16 53	57	146	15 56	57	146	14 59	58	147	14 01	57	147	13 04	57	147	327
32	17 11	58	147	16 13	57	147	15 16	58	148	14 18	57	148	13 21	57	148	328
31	17 28	58	148	16 30	57	148	15 33	58	149	14 35	57	149	13 38	58	149	329
30	17 44	−57	149	16 47	−58	149	15 49	−58	149	14 51	−57	150	13 54	−58	150	330
29	18 01	58	150	17 03	58	150	16 05	58	150	15 07	58	151	14 09	58	151	331
28	18 16	58	151	17 18	58	151	16 20	57	151	15 23	58	152	14 25	58	152	332
27	18 32	58	152	17 34	59	152	16 35	58	152	15 37	58	153	14 39	58	153	333
26	18 46	58	153	17 48	58	153	16 50	58	153	15 52	58	154	14 54	59	154	334
25	19 01	−59	154	18 02	−58	154	17 04	−58	154	16 06	−59	155	15 07	−58	155	335
24	19 14	58	155	18 16	59	155	17 17	58	155	16 19	58	156	15 21	59	156	336
23	19 28	59	156	18 29	59	156	17 30	58	156	16 32	59	157	15 33	58	157	337
22	19 40	58	157	18 42	59	157	17 43	59	157	16 44	58	158	15 46	59	158	338
21	19 52	58	158	18 54	59	158	17 55	59	158	16 56	59	159	15 57	59	159	339
20	20 04	−59	159	19 05	−59	159	18 06	−59	159	17 07	−58	160	16 09	−59	160	340
19	20 15	59	160	19 16	59	160	18 17	59	160	17 18	59	161	16 19	59	161	341
18	20 26	59	161	19 27	59	161	18 28	59	161	17 29	60	162	16 29	59	162	342
17	20 36	59	162	19 37	59	162	18 38	60	162	17 38	59	163	16 39	59	163	343
16	20 45	59	163	19 46	59	163	18 47	59	164	17 48	60	164	16 48	59	164	344
15	20 54	−59	164	19 55	−59	164	18 56	−60	165	17 56	−59	165	16 57	−59	165	345
14	21 03	60	165	20 03	59	165	19 04	60	166	18 04	59	166	17 05	59	166	346
13	21 11	60	166	20 11	59	166	19 12	60	167	18 12	59	167	17 13	60	167	347
12	21 18	60	167	20 18	59	167	19 19	60	168	18 19	59	168	17 20	60	168	348
11	21 25	60	168	20 25	60	169	19 25	59	169	18 26	60	169	17 26	60	169	349
10	21 31	−60	169	20 31	−60	170	19 31	−59	170	18 32	−60	170	17 32	−60	170	350
9	21 36	60	171	20 36	59	171	19 37	60	171	18 37	60	171	17 37	60	171	351
8	21 41	60	172	20 41	60	172	19 42	60	172	18 42	60	172	17 42	60	172	352
7	21 46	60	173	20 46	60	173	19 46	60	173	18 46	60	173	17 46	60	173	353
6	21 49	59	174	20 50	60	174	19 50	60	174	18 50	60	174	17 50	60	174	354
5	21 53	−60	175	20 53	−60	175	19 53	−60	175	18 53	−60	175	17 53	−60	175	355
4	21 55	60	176	20 55	60	176	19 55	60	176	18 55	59	176	17 56	60	176	356
3	21 57	60	177	20 57	60	177	19 57	60	177	18 57	59	177	17 58	60	177	357
2	21 59	60	178	20 59	60	178	19 59	60	178	18 59	60	178	17 59	60	178	358
1	22 00	60	179	21 00	60	179	20 00	60	179	19 00	60	179	18 00	60	179	359
0	22 00	−60	180	21 00	−60	180	20 00	−60	180	19 00	−60	180	18 00	−60	180	360

S. Lat. {LHA greater than 180°....... Zn=180−Z / LHA less than 180°........... Zn=180+Z}

N. Lat. {LHA greater than 180°....... Zn=Z; LHA less than 180°........... Zn=360−Z}

DECLINATION (15°-29°) SAME NAME AS LATITUDE

LHA	15° Hc	d	Z	16° Hc	d	Z	17° Hc	d	Z	18° Hc	d	Z	19° Hc	d	Z
	° ′	′	°	° ′	′	°	° ′	′	°	° ′	′	°	° ′	′	°
0	47 00	+60	180	48 00	+60	180	49 00	+60	180	50 00	+60	180	51 00	+60	180
1	47 00	60	179	48 00	60	179	49 00	60	179	50 00	60	179	51 00	60	179
2	46 58	60	177	47 58	60	177	48 58	60	177	49 58	60	177	50 58	60	177
3	46 57	59	176	47 56	60	176	48 56	60	176	49 56	60	176	50 56	60	176
4	46 54	60	174	47 54	60	174	48 54	59	174	49 53	60	174	50 53	60	174
5	46 50	+60	173	47 50	+60	173	48 50	+60	173	49 50	+60	173	50 50	+59	173
6	46 46	60	172	47 46	60	171	48 46	59	171	49 45	60	171	50 45	60	171
7	46 41	60	170	47 41	59	170	48 40	60	170	49 40	60	170	50 40	59	170
8	46 35	60	169	47 35	59	169	48 34	60	168	49 34	60	168	50 34	59	168
9	46 28	60	167	47 28	60	167	48 28	59	167	49 27	60	167	50 27	59	167
10	46 21	+60	166	47 21	+59	166	48 20	+59	166	49 19	+60	165	50 19	+59	165
11	46 13	59	165	47 12	60	164	48 12	59	164	49 11	59	164	50 10	59	164
12	46 04	59	163	47 03	60	163	48 03	59	163	49 02	59	162	50 01	59	162
13	45 55	59	162	46 54	59	162	47 53	59	161	48 52	59	161	49 51	59	161
14	45 44	59	160	46 43	59	160	47 42	59	160	48 41	59	160	49 40	59	159
15	45 33	+59	159	46 32	+59	159	47 31	+59	159	48 30	+58	158	49 28	+59	158
16	45 22	58	158	46 20	59	157	47 19	58	157	48 17	59	157	49 16	58	157
17	45 09	59	156	46 08	58	156	47 06	59	156	48 05	58	155	49 03	58	155
18	44 56	58	155	45 54	59	155	46 53	58	154	47 51	58	154	48 49	58	154
19	44 42	59	154	45 41	58	153	46 39	58	153	47 37	58	153	48 35	58	152
20	44 28	+58	152	45 26	+58	152	46 24	+58	152	47 22	+58	151	48 20	+57	151
21	44 13	58	151	45 11	58	151	46 09	57	150	47 06	58	150	48 04	57	150
22	43 57	58	150	44 55	57	149	45 52	58	149	46 50	57	149	47 47	58	148
23	43 41	57	149	44 38	58	148	45 36	57	148	46 33	57	147	47 30	57	147
24	43 24	57	147	44 21	58	147	45 19	57	146	46 16	57	146	47 13	56	146
25	43 07	+57	146	44 04	+57	146	45 01	+57	145	45 58	+56	145	46 54	+57	144
26	42 49	56	145	43 45	57	144	44 42	57	144	45 39	56	143	46 35	57	143
27	42 30	57	144	43 27	56	143	44 23	57	143	45 20	56	142	46 16	56	142
28	42 11	56	142	43 07	57	142	44 04	56	141	45 00	56	141	45 56	56	140
29	41 51	56	141	42 47	56	141	43 43	56	140	44 39	56	140	45 35	56	139
30	41 31	+56	140	42 27	+56	139	43 23	+56	139	44 19	+55	138	45 14	+56	138
31	41 10	56	139	42 06	56	138	43 02	55	138	43 57	56	137	44 53	55	137
32	40 49	55	137	41 44	56	137	42 40	55	136	43 35	56	136	44 31	55	135
33	40 27	55	136	41 22	56	136	42 18	55	135	43 13	55	135	44 08	55	134
34	40 05	55	135	41 00	55	135	41 55	55	134	42 50	55	134	43 45	55	133
35	39 42	+55	134	40 37	+55	133	41 32	+55	133	42 27	+54	132	43 21	+55	132
36	39 19	55	133	40 14	55	132	41 09	54	132	42 03	54	131	42 57	55	131
37	38 55	55	132	39 50	55	131	40 45	54	131	41 39	54	130	42 33	54	129
38	38 31	55	131	39 26	54	130	40 20	54	129	41 14	54	129	42 08	54	128
39	38 07	54	129	39 01	55	129	39 56	53	128	40 49	54	128	41 43	54	127
40	37 42	+54	128	38 36	+54	128	39 30	+54	127	40 24	+54	127	41 18	+53	126
41	37 17	54	127	38 11	54	127	39 05	53	126	39 58	54	126	40 52	53	125
42	36 52	53	126	37 45	54	126	38 39	53	125	39 32	54	124	40 26	53	124
43	36 26	53	125	37 19	54	125	38 13	53	124	39 06	53	123	39 59	53	123
44	36 00	53	124	36 53	53	123	37 46	53	123	38 39	53	122	39 32	53	122
45	35 33	+53	123	36 26	+53	122	37 19	+53	122	38 12	+53	121	39 05	+52	121
46	35 06	53	122	35 59	53	121	36 52	53	121	37 45	52	120	38 37	53	120
47	34 39	53	121	35 32	53	120	36 25	52	120	37 17	52	119	38 09	53	118
48	34 12	52	120	35 04	53	119	35 57	52	119	36 49	52	118	37 41	52	117
49	33 44	52	119	34 36	53	118	35 29	52	118	36 21	52	117	37 13	52	116
50	33 16	+52	118	34 08	+53	117	35 01	+52	117	35 53	+51	116	36 44	+52	115
51	32 48	52	117	33 40	52	116	34 32	52	116	35 24	52	115	36 16	51	114
52	32 19	52	116	33 11	52	115	34 03	52	115	34 55	51	114	35 46	52	113
53	31 50	52	115	32 42	52	114	33 34	52	114	34 26	51	113	35 17	51	112
54	31 21	52	114	32 13	52	113	33 05	51	113	33 56	52	112	34 48	51	111
55	30 52	+52	113	31 44	+51	112	32 35	+52	112	33 27	+51	111	34 18	+51	110
56	30 23	51	112	31 14	52	111	32 06	51	111	32 57	51	110	33 48	51	109
57	29 53	52	111	30 45	51	110	31 36	51	110	32 27	51	109	33 18	51	108
58	29 23	52	110	30 15	51	109	31 06	51	109	31 57	51	108	32 48	50	108
59	28 53	52	109	29 45	51	108	30 36	51	108	31 27	50	107	32 17	51	107
60	28 23	+51	108	29 14	+51	107	30 05	+51	107	30 56	+51	106	31 47	+50	106
61	27 53	51	107	28 44	51	107	29 35	50	106	30 25	51	105	31 16	50	105
62	27 22	51	106	28 13	51	106	29 04	51	105	29 55	50	104	30 45	50	104
63	26 52	51	105	27 43	50	105	28 33	51	104	29 24	50	103	30 14	50	103
64	26 21	51	104	27 12	50	104	28 02	51	103	28 53	50	103	29 43	50	102
65	25 50	+51	103	26 41	+50	103	27 31	+51	102	28 22	+50	102	29 12	+50	101
66	25 19	51	103	26 10	50	102	27 00	51	101	27 51	50	101	28 41	50	100
67	24 48	51	102	25 39	50	101	26 29	50	100	27 19	50	100	28 09	50	99
68	24 17	50	101	25 07	51	100	25 58	50	100	26 48	50	99	27 38	50	98
69	23 46	50	100	24 36	50	99	25 26	51	99	26 17	49	98	27 06	50	97

LHA	20° Hc	d	Z	21° Hc	d	Z	22° Hc	d	Z	23° Hc	d	Z	24° Hc	d	Z
	° ′	′	°	° ′	′	°	° ′	′	°	° ′	′	°	° ′	′	°
0	52 00	+60	180	53 00	+60	180	54 00	+60	180	55 00	+60	180	56 00	+60	180
1	52 00	60	179	53 00	60	178	54 00	60	178	55 00	60	178	56 00	60	178
2	51 58	60	177	52 58	60	177	53 58	60	177	54 58	60	177	55 58	60	177
3	51 56	60	175	52 56	60	175	53 56	60	175	54 56	60	175	55 56	60	175
4	51 53	60	174	52 53	60	174	53 53	60	174	54 53	60	174	55 53	60	174
5	51 49	+60	172	52 49	+60	172	53 49	+60	172	54 49	+60	172	55 49	+60	172
6	51 45	60	171	52 45	59	171	53 44	60	171	54 44	60	170	55 44	60	170
7	51 39	60	169	52 39	60	169	53 39	59	169	54 38	60	169	55 38	60	169
8	51 33	60	168	52 33	59	168	53 32	60	168	54 32	59	167	55 31	60	167
9	51 26	59	166	52 25	60	166	53 25	59	166	54 24	60	166	55 24	59	165
10	51 18	+59	165	52 17	+60	165	53 17	+59	164	54 16	+59	164	55 15	+59	164
11	51 09	60	163	52 09	59	163	53 08	59	163	54 07	59	163	55 06	59	162
12	51 00	59	162	51 59	59	162	52 58	59	161	53 57	59	161	54 56	59	161
13	50 50	59	160	51 49	58	160	52 47	59	160	53 46	59	160	54 45	59	159
14	50 39	58	159	51 37	59	159	52 36	59	158	53 35	58	158	54 33	59	158
15	50 27	+58	158	51 25	+59	157	52 24	+58	157	53 22	+59	157	54 21	+58	156
16	50 14	59	156	51 13	58	156	52 11	58	155	53 09	58	155	54 07	59	155
17	50 01	58	155	50 59	58	154	51 57	58	154	52 55	58	154	53 53	58	153
18	49 47	58	153	50 45	58	153	51 43	58	153	52 41	58	152	53 39	57	152
19	49 33	57	152	50 30	58	152	51 28	58	151	52 26	57	151	53 23	58	150
20	49 17	+58	151	50 15	+57	150	51 12	+58	150	52 10	+57	149	53 07	+57	149
21	49 01	58	149	49 59	57	149	50 56	57	148	51 53	57	148	52 50	57	147
22	48 45	57	148	49 42	57	147	50 39	57	147	51 36	56	146	52 32	57	146
23	48 27	57	146	49 24	57	146	50 21	57	145	51 18	56	145	52 14	57	144
24	48 09	57	145	49 06	57	145	50 03	56	144	50 59	56	144	51 55	57	143
25	47 51	+56	144	48 47	+57	143	49 44	+56	143	50 40	+56	142	51 36	+56	142
26	47 32	56	142	48 28	56	142	49 24	56	141	50 20	56	141	51 16	56	140
27	47 12	56	141	48 08	56	141	49 04	56	140	50 00	55	140	50 55	56	139
28	46 52	56	140	47 48	55	139	48 43	56	139	49 39	55	138	50 34	55	138
29	46 31	56	139	47 27	55	138	48 22	55	137	49 17	55	137	50 12	55	136
30	46 10	+55	137	47 05	+55	137	48 00	+55	136	48 55	+55	136	49 50	+55	135
31	45 48	55	136	46 43	55	136	47 38	55	135	48 33	54	134	49 27	55	134
32	45 26	55	135	46 21	54	134	47 15	55	134	48 10	54	133	49 04	54	132
33	45 03	54	134	45 57	55	133	46 52	54	132	47 46	54	132	48 40	54	131
34	44 40	54	132	45 34	54	132	46 28	54	131	47 22	54	131	48 16	54	130
35	44 16	+54	131	45 10	+54	131	46 04	+54	130	46 58	+54	129	47 52	+53	129
36	43 52	54	130	44 46	54	129	45 40	53	129	46 33	54	128	47 27	53	127
37	43 27	54	129	44 21	54	128	45 15	53	128	46 08	53	127	47 01	53	126
38	43 02	54	128	43 56	53	127	44 49	53	126	45 42	53	126	46 35	53	125
39	42 37	53	127	43 30	53	126	44 23	53	125	45 16	53	125	46 09	52	124
40	42 11	+53	125	43 04	+53	125	43 57	+53	124	44 50	+52	124	45 42	+53	123
41	41 45	53	124	42 38	53	124	43 31	52	123	44 23	53	122	45 16	52	122
42	41 19	52	123	42 11	53	123	43 04	52	122	43 56	52	121	44 48	52	121
43	40 52	52	122	41 44	53	121	42 37	52	121	43 29	52	120	44 21	51	119
44	40 25	52	121	41 17	52	120	42 09	52	120	43 01	52	119	43 53	51	118
45	39 57	+52	120	40 49	+52	119	41 41	+52	119	42 33	+52	118	43 25	+51	117
46	39 30	52	119	40 22	51	118	41 13	52	118	42 05	51	117	42 56	51	116
47	39 02	51	118	39 53	52	117	40 45	52	117	41 37	51	116	42 28	51	115
48	38 33	52	117	39 25	52	116	40 17	51	115	41 08	51	115	41 59	51	114
49	38 05	51	116	38 56	52	115	39 48	51	114	40 39	51	114	41 30	50	113
50	37 36	+51	115	38 27	+52	114	39 19	+51	113	40 10	+50	113	41 00	+51	112
51	37 07	51	114	37 58	51	113	38 49	51	112	39 40	51	112	40 31	50	111
52	36 38	51	113	37 29	51	112	38 20	50	111	39 10	51	111	40 01	50	110
53	36 08	51	112	36 59	51	111	37 50	51	110	38 41	50	110	39 31	50	109
54	35 39	51	111	36 30	50	110	37 20	51	109	38 11	50	109	39 01	50	108
55	35 09	+51	110	36 00	+50	109	36 50	+50	108	37 40	+50	108	38 30	+50	107
56	34 39	50	109	35 29	51	108	36 20	50	107	37 10	50	107	38 00	50	106
57	34 09	50	108	34 59	50	107	35 49	50	107	36 39	50	106	37 29	50	105
58	33 38	51	107	34 29	50	106	35 19	50	106	36 09	50	105	36 59	49	104
59	33 08	50	106	33 58	50	105	34 48	50	105	35 38	50	104	36 28	49	103
60	32 37	+50	105	33 27	+50	104	34 17	+50	104	35 07	+50	103	35 57	+49	102
61	32 06	50	104	32 56	50	103	33 46	50	103	34 36	50	102	35 26	49	101
62	31 35	50	103	32 25	50	102	33 15	50	102	34 05	49	101	34 54	49	100
63	31 04	50	102	31 54	50	102	32 44	50	101	33 34	49	100	34 23	49	100
64	30 33	50	101	31 23	50	101	32 13	49	100	33 02	50	99	33 52	49	99
65	30 02	+50	100	30 52	+49	100	31 41	+50	99	32 31	+49	98	33 20	+49	98
66	29 31	49	99	30 20	50	99	31 10	49	98	31 59	50	98	32 49	49	97
67	28 59	50	99	29 49	50	98	30 39	49	97	31 28	49	97	32 17	49	96
68	28 28	49	98	29 17	50	97	30 07	49	96	30 56	49	96	31 45	49	95
69	27 56	50	97	28 46	49	96	29 35	50	96	30 25	49	95	31 14	48	94

LHA	25° Hc	d	Z	26° Hc	d	Z	27° Hc	d	Z	28° Hc	d	Z	29° Hc	d	Z	LHA
	° ′	′	°	° ′	′	°	° ′	′	°	° ′	′	°	° ′	′	°	
0	57 00	+60	180	58 00	+60	180	59 00	+60	180	60 00	+60	180	61 00	+60	180	360
1	57 00	60	178	58 00	60	178	59 00	60	178	60 00	60	178	61 00	60	178	359
2	56 58	60	177	57 58	60	177	58 58	60	177	59 58	60	177	60 58	60	176	358
3	56 56	60	175	57 56	60	175	58 56	60	175	59 56	60	175	60 56	59	175	357
4	56 53	60	173	57 53	59	173	58 52	60	173	59 52	60	173	60 52	60	173	356
5	56 49	+59	172	57 48	+60	172	58 48	+60	171	59 48	+60	171	60 48	+59	171	355
6	56 44	59	170	57 43	60	170	58 43	60	170	59 43	59	170	60 42	60	169	354
7	56 38	59	168	57 37	60	168	58 37	59	168	59 36	60	168	60 36	59	168	353
8	56 31	59	167	57 30	60	167	58 30	59	166	59 29	59	166	60 28	60	166	352
9	56 23	59	165	57 22	60	165	58 22	59	165	59 21	59	164	60 20	59	164	351
10	56 14	+60	164	57 14	+59	163	58 13	+59	163	59 12	+59	163	60 11	+59	162	350
11	56 05	59	162	57 04	59	162	58 03	59	161	59 02	59	161	60 01	58	161	349
12	55 55	59	160	56 54	58	160	57 52	59	160	58 51	59	159	59 50	58	159	348
13	55 44	58	159	56 42	59	158	57 41	58	158	58 39	59	158	59 38	58	157	347
14	55 32	58	157	56 30	58	157	57 28	59	156	58 27	58	156	59 25	58	155	346
15	55 19	+58	156	56 17	+58	155	57 15	+58	155	58 13	+58	154	59 11	+58	154	345
16	55 06	57	154	56 03	58	154	57 01	58	153	57 59	58	153	58 57	57	152	344
17	54 51	58	153	55 49	58	152	56 47	57	152	57 44	57	151	58 41	58	151	343
18	54 36	58	151	55 34	57	151	56 31	57	150	57 28	57	150	58 25	57	149	342
19	54 21	57	150	55 18	57	149	56 15	57	149	57 12	57	148	58 09	56	147	341
20	54 04	+57	148	55 01	+57	148	55 58	+57	147	56 55	+56	146	57 51	+56	146	340
21	53 47	57	147	54 44	56	146	55 40	57	146	56 37	56	145	57 33	56	144	339
22	53 29	57	145	54 26	56	145	55 22	56	144	56 18	56	143	57 14	56	143	338
23	53 11	56	144	54 07	56	143	55 03	56	143	55 59	55	142	56 54	56	141	337
24	52 52	56	142	53 48	55	142	54 43	56	141	55 39	55	141	56 34	55	140	336
25	52 32	+56	141	53 28	+55	140	54 23	+55	140	55 18	+55	139	56 13	+55	138	335
26	52 12	55	140	53 07	55	139	54 02	55	138	54 57	55	138	55 52	54	137	334
27	51 51	55	138	52 46	55	138	53 41	54	137	54 35	55	136	55 30	51	136	333
28	51 29	55	137	52 24	55	136	53 19	54	136	54 13	54	135	55 07	54	134	332
29	51 07	55	136	52 02	54	135	52 56	54	134	53 50	54	134	54 44	54	133	331
30	50 45	+54	134	51 39	+54	134	52 33	+54	133	53 27	+54	132	54 21	+53	131	330
31	50 22	54	133	51 16	54	132	52 10	53	132	53 03	54	131	53 57	53	130	329
32	49 58	54	132	50 52	54	131	51 46	53	130	52 39	53	130	53 32	53	129	328
33	49 34	54	130	50 28	53	130	51 21	53	129	52 14	53	128	53 07	52	128	327
34	49 10	53	129	50 03	53	129	50 56	53	128	51 49	53	127	52 42	52	126	326
35	48 45	+53	128	49 38	+53	127	50 31	+52	127	51 23	+53	126	52 16	+52	125	325
36	48 20	53	127	49 13	52	126	50 05	52	125	50 57	52	125	51 49	52	124	324
37	47 54	53	126	48 47	52	125	49 39	52	124	50 31	52	123	51 23	51	123	323
38	47 28	52	124	48 20	52	124	49 12	52	123	50 04	52	122	50 56	51	121	322
39	47 01	53	123	47 54	52	123	48 46	51	122	49 37	51	121	50 28	51	120	321
40	46 35	+52	122	47 27	+51	121	48 18	+52	121	49 10	+51	120	50 01	+51	119	320
41	46 08	51	121	46 59	52	120	47 51	51	119	48 42	51	119	49 33	50	118	319
42	45 40	52	120	46 32	51	119	47 23	51	118	48 14	51	118	49 05	50	117	318
43	45 12	52	119	46 04	51	118	46 55	51	117	47 46	50	116	48 36	50	116	317
44	44 44	52	118	45 36	50	117	46 26	51	116	47 17	50	115	48 07	50	115	316
45	44 16	+51	117	45 07	+51	116	45 58	+50	115	46 48	+50	114	47 38	+50	113	315
46	43 47	51	115	44 38	51	115	45 29	50	114	46 19	50	113	47 09	49	112	314
47	43 19	50	114	44 09	51	114	45 00	50	113	45 50	49	112	46 39	50	111	313
48	42 50	50	113	43 40	50	113	44 30	50	112	45 20	50	111	46 10	49	110	312
49	42 20	51	112	43 11	50	112	44 01	49	111	44 50	50	110	45 40	49	109	311
50	41 51	+50	111	42 41	+50	111	43 31	+49	110	44 20	+50	109	45 10	+48	108	310
51	41 21	50	110	42 11	50	110	43 01	49	109	43 50	49	108	44 39	49	107	309
52	40 51	50	109	41 41	50	109	42 31	49	108	43 20	49	107	44 09	48	106	308
53	40 21	50	108	41 11	49	108	42 00	49	107	42 49	49	106	43 38	49	105	307
54	39 51	49	107	40 40	50	107	41 30	49	106	42 19	48	105	43 07	49	104	306
55	39 20	+50	106	40 10	+49	106	40 59	+49	105	41 48	+49	104	42 37	+48	103	305
56	38 50	49	105	39 39	49	105	40 28	49	104	41 17	49	103	42 06	48	102	304
57	38 19	49	104	39 08	49	104	39 57	49	103	40 46	48	102	41 34	49	101	303
58	37 48	49	103	38 37	49	103	39 26	49	102	40 15	48	101	41 03	48	100	302
59	37 17	49	103	38 06	49	102	38 55	49	101	39 44	48	100	40 32	48	100	301
60	36 46	+49	102	37 35	+49	101	38 24	+48	100	39 12	+48	99	40 00	+48	99	300
61	36 15	49	101	37 04	48	100	37 52	49	99	38 41	48	98	39 29	48	98	299
62	35 43	49	100	36 32	49	99	37 21	48	98	38 09	48	98	38 57	48	97	298
63	35 12	49	99	36 01	49	98	36 50	48	97	37 38	48	97	38 26	48	96	297
64	34 41	48	98	35 29	49	97	36 18	48	97	37 06	48	96	37 54	48	95	296
65	34 09	+49	97	34 58	+48	96	35 46	+49	96	36 35	+47	95	37 22	+48	94	295
66	33 38	48	96	34 26	49	95	35 15	48	95	36 03	48	94	36 51	47	93	294
67	33 06	49	95	33 55	48	95	34 43	48	94	35 31	48	93	36 19	48	92	293
68	32 34	49	94	33 23	48	94	34 11	48	93	34 59	48	92	35 47	48	92	292
69	32 02	49	94	32 51	48	93	33 39	49	92	34 28	47	91	35 15	48	91	291

S. Lat. {LHA greater than 180°....... Zn=180−Z; LHA less than 180°........... Zn=180+Z}

N. Lat. {LHA greater than 180°....... Zn=Z; LHA less than 180°........... Zn=360−Z}

DECLINATION (15°-29°) SAME NAME AS LATITUDE

LHA	15° Hc	d	Z	16° Hc	d	Z	17° Hc	d	Z	18° Hc	d	Z	19° Hc	d	Z	LHA
	° ′	′	°	° ′	′	°	° ′	′	°	° ′	′	°	° ′	′	°	
70	23 14	+51	99	24 05	+50	98	24 55	+50	98	25 45	+50	97	26 35	+50	97	290
71	22 43	50	98	23 33	50	98	24 23	50	97	25 13	50	96	26 03	50	96	289
72	22 11	51	97	23 02	50	97	23 52	50	96	24 42	50	95	25 32	49	95	288
73	21 40	50	96	22 30	50	96	23 20	50	95	24 10	50	95	25 00	50	94	287
74	21 08	50	96	21 58	50	95	22 48	50	94	23 38	50	94	24 28	50	93	286
75	20 37	+50	95	21 27	+50	94	22 17	+50	93	23 07	+49	93	23 56	+50	92	285
76	20 05	50	94	20 55	50	93	21 45	50	93	22 35	50	92	23 25	49	91	284
77	19 33	50	93	20 23	50	92	21 13	50	92	22 03	50	91	22 53	49	91	283
78	19 01	50	92	19 51	50	91	20 41	50	91	21 31	50	90	22 21	50	90	282
79	18 30	50	91	19 20	50	91	20 10	50	90	21 00	49	89	21 49	50	89	281
80	17 58	+50	90	18 48	+50	90	19 38	+50	89	20 28	+50	89	21 18	+49	88	280
81	17 26	50	90	18 16	50	89	19 06	50	88	19 56	50	88	20 46	49	87	279
82	16 54	50	89	17 44	50	88	18 34	50	88	19 24	50	87	20 14	50	86	278
83	16 22	50	88	17 12	51	87	18 03	49	87	18 52	50	86	19 42	50	85	277
84	15 51	50	87	16 41	50	86	17 31	50	86	18 21	50	85	19 11	49	85	276
85	15 19	+50	86	16 09	+50	86	16 59	+50	85	17 49	+50	84	18 39	+50	84	275
86	14 47	50	85	15 37	50	85	16 27	50	84	17 17	50	84	18 07	50	83	274
87	14 15	51	84	15 06	50	84	15 56	50	83	16 46	50	83	17 36	50	82	273
88	13 44	50	84	14 34	50	83	15 24	50	83	16 14	50	82	17 04	50	81	272
89	13 12	51	83	14 03	50	82	14 53	50	82	15 43	50	81	16 33	50	81	271
90	12 41	+50	82	13 31	+50	81	14 21	+51	81	15 12	+50	80	16 02	+50	80	270
91	12 09	51	81	13 00	50	81	13 50	50	80	14 40	50	79	15 30	51	79	269
92	11 38	50	80	12 28	51	80	13 19	50	79	14 09	50	79	14 59	50	78	268
93	11 07	50	79	11 57	51	79	12 48	50	78	13 38	50	78	14 28	50	77	267
94	10 35	51	79	11 26	51	78	12 17	50	78	13 07	50	77	13 57	51	76	266
95	10 04	+51	78	10 55	+51	77	11 46	+50	77	12 36	+50	76	13 26	+51	76	265
96	09 33	51	77	10 24	51	76	11 15	50	76	12 05	51	75	12 56	50	75	264
97	09 02	51	76	09 53	51	76	10 44	51	75	11 35	50	75	12 25	51	74	263
98	08 32	50	75	09 22	51	75	10 13	51	74	11 04	51	74	11 55	50	73	262
99	08 01	51	75	08 52	51	74	09 43	50	73	10 33	51	73	11 24	51	72	261
100	07 30	+51	74	08 21	+51	73	09 12	+51	73	10 03	+51	72	10 54	+51	72	260
101	07 00	51	73	07 51	51	72	08 42	51	72	09 33	51	71	10 24	51	71	259
102	06 30	51	72	07 21	51	71	08 12	51	71	09 03	51	70	09 54	51	70	258
103	05 59	52	71	06 51	51	71	07 42	51	70	08 33	51	70	09 24	51	69	257
104	05 29	52	70	06 21	51	70	07 12	51	69	08 03	52	69	08 55	51	68	256
105	05 00	+51	69	05 51	+51	69	06 42	+52	68	07 34	+51	68	08 25	+52	67	255
106	04 30	51	69	05 21	52	68	06 13	51	68	07 04	52	67	07 56	51	67	254
107	04 00	52	68	04 52	52	67	05 44	51	67	06 35	52	66	07 27	51	66	253
108	03 31	52	67	04 23	52	66	05 15	51	66	06 06	52	66	06 58	52	65	252
109	03 02	52	66	03 54	52	66	04 46	51	65	05 37	52	65	06 29	52	64	251
110	02 33	+52	65	03 25	+52	65	04 17	+52	64	05 09	+52	64	06 01	+52	63	250
111	02 04	52	64	02 56	52	64	03 48	52	63	04 40	52	63	05 32	52	63	249
112	01 35	53	64	02 28	52	63	03 20	52	63	04 12	52	62	05 04	53	62	248
113	01 07	52	63	01 59	53	62	02 52	52	62	03 44	52	61	04 36	53	61	247
114	00 39	52	62	01 31	53	61	02 24	52	61	03 16	53	60	04 09	52	60	246
115	00 11	+53	61	01 04	+52	61	01 56	+53	60	02 49	+52	60	03 41	+53	59	245
116	-0 17	53	60	00 36	53	60	01 29	52	59	02 21	53	59	03 14	53	58	244
117	-0 44	53	59	00 09	52	59	01 01	53	58	01 54	53	58	02 47	53	58	243
118	-1 12	53	59	-0 19	53	58	00 34	54	58	01 28	53	57	02 21	53	57	242
119	-1 39	54	58	-0 45	53	57	00 08	53	57	01 01	53	56	01 54	53	56	241
120	-2 05	+53	57	-1 12	+54	56	-0 18	+53	56	00 35	+53	55	01 28	+53	55	240
121	-2 32	54	56	-1 38	53	56	-0 45	54	55	00 09	53	55	01 02	53	54	239
122	-2 58	54	55	-2 04	53	55	-1 11	54	54	-0 17	53	54	00 36	54	53	238
123	-3 24	54	54	-2 30	54	54	-1 36	53	53	-0 43	54	53	00 11	54	52	237
124	-3 50	54	53	-2 56	54	53	-2 02	54	52	-1 08	54	52	-0 14	54	52	236
125	-4 15	+54	52	-3 21	+54	52	-2 27	+54	52	-1 33	+54	51	-0 39	+54	51	235
126	-4 40	54	52	-3 46	54	51	-2 52	55	51	-1 57	54	50	-1 03	54	50	234
127	-5 05	54	51	-4 11	55	50	-3 16	54	50	-2 22	55	49	-1 27	54	49	233
128	-5 29	54	50	-4 35	55	49	-3 40	54	49	-2 46	55	49	-1 51	54	48	232
129				-4 59	55	49	-4 04	54	48	-3 10	55	48	-2 15	55	47	231
130				-5 23	+55	48	-4 28	+55	47	-3 33	+55	47	-2 38	+55	46	230
131				-5 46	55	47	-4 51	55	46	-3 56	55	46	-3 01	55	46	229
132							-5 14	55	45	-4 19	55	45	-3 24	56	45	228
133							-5 36	55	45	-4 41	55	44	-3 46	56	44	227
134										-5 03	55	43	-4 08	56	43	226
135										-5 25	+56	42	-4 29	+56	42	225
136													-4 50	56	41	224
137													-5 11	56	40	223
138													-5 31	56	39	222
139																221

LHA	20° Hc	d	Z	21° Hc	d	Z	22° Hc	d	Z	23° Hc	d	Z	24° Hc	d	Z	LHA
	° ′	′	°	° ′	′	°	° ′	′	°	° ′	′	°	° ′	′	°	
70	27 25	+49	96	28 14	+50	95	29 04	+49	95	29 53	+49	94	30 42	+49	93	290
71	26 53	50	95	27 43	49	94	28 32	49	94	29 21	49	93	30 10	49	92	289
72	26 21	50	94	27 11	49	94	28 00	49	93	28 49	49	92	29 38	49	92	288
73	25 50	49	93	26 39	49	93	27 28	50	92	28 18	49	91	29 07	48	91	287
74	25 18	49	92	26 07	50	92	26 57	49	91	27 46	49	91	28 35	49	90	286
75	24 46	+50	92	25 36	+49	91	26 25	+49	90	27 14	+49	90	28 03	+49	89	285
76	24 14	50	91	25 04	49	90	25 53	49	90	26 42	49	89	27 31	49	88	284
77	23 42	50	90	24 32	49	89	25 21	49	89	26 10	49	88	26 59	49	87	283
78	23 11	49	89	24 00	50	88	24 50	49	88	25 39	49	87	26 28	49	87	282
79	22 39	49	88	23 28	50	88	24 18	49	87	25 07	49	86	25 56	49	86	281
80	22 07	+50	87	22 57	+49	87	23 46	+49	86	24 35	+49	86	25 24	+49	85	280
81	21 35	50	87	22 25	49	86	23 14	50	85	24 04	49	85	24 53	49	84	279
82	21 04	49	86	21 53	50	85	22 43	49	85	23 32	49	84	24 21	49	83	278
83	20 32	50	85	21 22	49	84	22 11	49	84	23 00	49	83	23 49	50	82	277
84	20 00	50	84	20 50	49	83	21 39	50	83	22 29	49	82	23 18	49	82	276
85	19 29	+49	83	20 18	+50	83	21 08	+49	82	21 57	+50	81	22 47	+49	81	275
86	18 57	50	82	19 47	49	82	20 36	50	81	21 26	49	81	22 15	49	80	274
87	18 26	49	82	19 15	50	81	20 05	50	80	20 55	49	80	21 44	49	79	273
88	17 54	50	81	18 44	50	80	19 34	49	80	20 23	50	79	21 13	49	78	272
89	17 23	50	80	18 13	50	79	19 03	49	79	19 52	50	78	20 42	49	78	271
90	16 52	+50	79	17 42	+49	79	18 31	+50	78	19 21	+50	77	20 11	+49	77	270
91	16 21	50	78	17 11	49	78	18 00	50	77	18 50	50	77	19 40	49	76	269
92	15 49	50	78	16 39	50	77	17 29	50	76	18 19	50	76	19 09	50	75	268
93	15 18	51	77	16 09	50	76	16 59	50	76	17 49	49	75	18 38	50	74	267
94	14 48	50	76	15 38	50	75	16 28	50	75	17 18	50	74	18 08	50	74	266
95	14 17	+50	75	15 07	+50	74	15 57	+50	74	16 47	+50	73	17 37	+50	73	265
96	13 46	51	74	14 37	50	74	15 27	50	73	16 17	50	73	17 07	50	72	264
97	13 16	50	73	14 06	50	73	14 56	51	72	15 47	50	72	16 37	50	71	263
98	12 45	51	73	13 36	50	72	14 26	51	72	15 17	50	71	16 07	50	70	262
99	12 15	51	72	13 06	50	71	13 56	51	71	14 47	50	70	15 37	50	70	261
100	11 45	+51	71	12 36	+50	70	13 26	+51	70	14 17	+50	69	15 07	+51	69	260
101	11 15	51	70	12 06	50	70	12 56	51	69	13 47	51	69	14 38	50	68	259
102	10 45	51	69	11 36	51	69	12 27	51	68	13 18	50	68	14 08	51	67	258
103	10 15	51	69	11 06	51	68	11 57	51	67	12 48	51	67	13 39	51	66	257
104	09 46	51	68	10 37	51	67	11 28	51	67	12 19	51	66	13 10	51	66	256
105	09 17	+51	67	10 08	+51	66	10 59	+51	66	11 50	+51	65	12 41	+51	65	255
106	08 47	52	66	09 39	51	66	10 30	51	65	11 21	52	65	12 13	51	64	254
107	08 18	52	65	09 10	51	65	10 01	52	64	10 53	51	64	11 44	51	63	253
108	07 50	51	64	08 41	52	64	09 33	51	63	10 24	52	63	11 16	51	62	252
109	07 21	52	64	08 13	52	63	09 05	51	63	09 56	52	62	10 48	51	62	251
110	06 53	+52	63	07 45	+51	62	08 36	+52	62	09 28	+52	61	10 20	+52	61	250
111	06 24	53	62	07 17	51	62	08 08	52	61	09 00	52	61	09 52	52	60	249
112	05 57	52	61	06 49	52	61	07 41	52	60	08 33	52	60	09 25	52	59	248
113	05 29	52	60	06 21	52	60	07 13	53	59	08 06	52	59	08 58	52	58	247
114	05 01	53	60	05 54	52	59	06 46	52	59	07 38	53	58	08 31	52	58	246
115	04 34	+53	59	05 27	+52	58	06 19	+53	58	07 12	+52	57	08 04	+53	57	245
116	04 07	53	58	05 00	52	57	05 52	53	57	06 45	53	56	07 38	52	56	244
117	03 40	53	57	04 33	53	57	05 26	53	56	06 19	52	56	07 11	53	55	243
118	03 14	53	56	04 07	53	56	05 00	53	55	05 53	52	55	06 45	53	54	242
119	02 47	53	55	03 40	54	55	04 34	53	54	05 27	53	54	06 20	53	54	241
120	02 21	+54	55	03 15	+53	54	04 08	+53	54	05 01	+53	53	05 54	+54	53	240
121	01 55	54	54	02 49	53	53	03 42	54	53	04 36	53	52	05 29	54	52	239
122	01 30	54	53	02 24	53	52	03 17	54	52	04 11	53	52	05 04	54	51	238
123	01 05	54	52	01 59	53	52	02 52	54	51	03 46	54	51	04 40	53	50	237
124	00 40	54	51	01 34	54	51	02 28	54	50	03 22	53	50	04 15	54	49	236
125	00 15	+54	50	01 09	+54	50	02 03	+54	49	02 57	+54	49	03 51	+54	49	235
126	-0 09	54	49	00 45	54	49	01 39	55	49	02 34	54	48	03 28	54	48	234
127	-0 33	54	49	00 21	55	48	01 16	54	48	02 10	54	47	03 04	55	47	233
128	-0 57	55	48	-0 02	54	47	00 52	55	47	01 47	54	47	02 41	55	46	232
129	-1 20	54	47	-0 26	55	47	00 29	55	46	01 24	54	46	02 18	55	45	231
130	-1 43	+55	46	-0 48	+54	46	00 06	+55	45	01 01	+55	45	01 56	+55	44	230
131	-2 06	55	45	-1 11	55	45	-0 16	55	44	00 39	55	44	01 34	55	44	229
132	-2 28	55	44	-1 33	55	44	-0 38	55	44	00 17	55	43	01 12	55	43	228
133	-2 50	55	43	-1 55	55	43	-1 00	55	43	-0 05	56	42	00 51	55	42	227
134	-3 12	55	43	-2 17	56	42	-1 21	55	42	-0 26	56	41	00 30	55	41	226
135	-3 33	+55	42	-2 38	+56	41	-1 42	+55	41	-0 47	+56	41	00 09	+56	40	225
136	-3 54	55	41	-2 59	56	40	-2 03	56	40	-1 07	56	40	-0 11	55	39	224
137	-4 15	56	40	-3 19	56	40	-2 23	56	39	-1 27	56	39	-0 31	56	39	223
138	-4 35	56	39	-3 39	56	39	-2 43	56	38	-1 47	56	38	-0 51	56	38	222
139	-4 55	56	38	-3 59	56	38	-3 03	57	38	-2 06	56	37	-1 10	56	37	221

LHA	25° Hc	d	Z	26° Hc	d	Z	27° Hc	d	Z	28° Hc	d	Z	29° Hc	d	Z	LHA
	° ′	′	°	° ′	′	°	° ′	′	°	° ′	′	°	° ′	′	°	
70	31 31	+48	93	32 19	+49	92	33 08	+48	91	33 56	+48	91	34 44	+47	90	290
71	30 59	49	92	31 48	48	91	32 36	48	90	33 24	48	90	34 12	47	89	289
72	30 27	49	91	31 16	48	90	32 04	48	90	32 52	48	89	33 40	48	88	288
73	29 55	49	90	30 44	48	89	31 32	48	89	32 20	48	88	33 08	48	87	287
74	29 24	48	89	30 12	49	89	31 01	48	88	31 49	48	87	32 37	47	86	286
75	28 52	+48	88	29 40	+49	88	30 29	+48	87	31 17	+48	86	32 05	+48	86	285
76	28 20	49	88	29 09	48	87	29 57	48	86	30 45	48	86	31 33	48	85	284
77	27 48	49	87	28 37	48	86	29 25	49	85	30 14	48	85	31 02	47	84	283
78	27 17	48	86	28 05	49	85	28 54	48	85	29 42	48	84	30 30	48	83	282
79	26 45	49	85	27 34	48	84	28 22	48	84	29 10	48	83	29 58	48	82	281
80	26 13	+49	84	27 02	+48	84	27 50	+49	83	28 39	+48	82	29 27	+48	82	280
81	25 42	48	83	26 30	49	83	27 19	48	82	28 07	48	81	28 55	48	81	279
82	25 10	49	83	25 59	48	82	26 47	49	81	27 36	48	81	28 24	48	80	278
83	24 39	48	82	25 27	49	81	26 16	49	81	27 05	48	80	27 53	48	79	277
84	24 07	49	81	24 56	49	80	25 45	48	80	26 33	49	79	27 22	48	78	276
85	23 36	+49	80	24 25	+48	80	25 13	+49	79	26 02	+49	78	26 51	+48	78	275
86	23 04	49	79	23 53	49	79	24 42	49	78	25 31	49	77	26 20	48	77	274
87	22 33	49	79	23 22	49	78	24 11	49	77	25 00	49	77	25 49	48	76	273
88	22 02	49	78	22 51	49	77	23 40	49	77	24 29	49	76	25 18	48	75	272
89	21 31	49	77	22 20	49	76	23 09	49	76	23 58	49	75	24 47	49	74	271
90	21 00	+50	76	21 50	+49	76	22 39	+49	75	23 28	+49	74	24 17	+48	74	270
91	20 29	50	75	21 19	49	75	22 08	49	74	22 57	49	74	23 46	49	73	269
92	19 59	49	75	20 48	50	74	21 38	49	73	22 27	49	73	23 16	49	72	268
93	19 28	50	74	20 18	49	73	21 07	49	73	21 56	50	72	22 46	49	71	267
94	18 58	49	73	19 47	50	72	20 37	49	72	21 26	50	71	22 16	49	71	266
95	18 27	+50	72	19 17	+50	72	20 07	+49	71	20 56	+50	70	21 46	+49	70	265
96	17 57	50	71	18 47	50	71	19 37	50	70	20 27	49	70	21 16	49	69	264
97	17 27	50	71	18 17	50	70	19 07	50	69	19 57	49	69	20 46	50	68	263
98	16 57	50	70	17 47	50	69	18 37	50	69	19 27	50	68	20 17	50	67	262
99	16 27	51	69	17 18	50	68	18 08	50	68	18 58	50	67	19 48	49	67	261
100	15 58	+50	68	16 48	+50	68	17 38	+51	67	18 29	+50	67	19 19	+50	66	260
101	15 28	51	67	16 19	50	67	17 09	50	66	17 59	51	66	18 50	50	65	259
102	14 59	51	67	15 50	50	66	16 40	51	66	17 31	50	65	18 21	50	64	258
103	14 30	51	66	15 21	50	65	16 11	51	65	17 02	50	64	17 52	51	64	257
104	14 01	51	65	14 52	51	65	15 43	50	64	16 33	51	63	17 24	50	63	256
105	13 32	+51	64	14 23	+51	64	15 14	+51	63	16 05	+51	63	16 56	+50	62	255
106	13 04	51	63	13 55	51	63	14 46	51	62	15 37	51	62	16 28	51	61	254
107	12 35	52	63	13 27	51	62	14 18	51	62	15 09	51	61	16 00	51	61	253
108	12 07	52	62	12 59	51	61	13 50	51	61	14 41	51	60	15 32	52	60	252
109	11 39	52	61	12 31	51	61	13 22	52	60	14 14	51	60	15 05	51	59	251
110	11 12	+51	60	12 03	+52	60	12 55	+52	59	13 47	+51	59	14 38	+51	58	250
111	10 44	52	59	11 36	52	59	12 28	51	58	13 19	52	58	14 11	52	57	249
112	10 17	52	59	11 09	52	58	12 01	52	58	12 53	51	57	13 44	52	57	248
113	09 50	52	58	10 42	52	57	11 34	52	57	12 26	52	56	13 18	52	56	247
114	09 23	52	57	10 15	53	57	11 08	52	56	12 00	52	56	12 52	52	55	246
115	08 57	+52	56	09 49	+52	56	10 41	+53	55	11 34	+52	55	12 26	+52	54	245
116	08 30	53	56	09 23	52	55	10 15	53	55	11 08	52	54	12 00	53	54	244
117	08 04	53	55	08 57	53	54	09 50	52	54	10 42	53	53	11 35	52	53	243
118	07 38	53	54	08 31	53	53	09 24	53	53	10 17	53	52	11 10	52	52	242
119	07 13	53	53	08 06	53	53	08 59	53	52	09 52	53	52	10 45	53	51	241
120	06 48	+53	52	07 41	+53	52	08 34	+53	51	09 27	+53	51	10 20	+53	50	240
121	06 23	53	51	07 16	53	51	08 09	54	51	09 03	53	50	09 56	53	50	239
122	05 58	53	51	06 51	54	50	07 45	53	50	08 38	54	49	09 32	53	49	238
123	05 33	54	50	06 27	54	49	07 21	53	49	08 14	54	48	09 08	54	48	237
124	05 09	54	49	06 03	54	49	06 57	54	48	07 51	54	48	08 45	53	47	236
125	04 45	+54	48	05 39	+54	48	06 33	+54	47	07 27	+54	47	08 21	+54	46	235
126	04 22	54	47	05 16	54	47	06 10	54	47	07 04	54	46	07 58	55	46	234
127	03 59	54	47	04 53	54	46	05 47	55	46	06 42	54	45	07 36	54	45	233
128	03 36	54	46	04 30	55	45	05 25	54	45	06 19	55	44	07 14	54	44	232
129	03 13	55	45	04 08	54	44	05 02	55	44	05 57	55	44	06 52	54	43	231
130	02 51	+55	44	03 46	+55	44	04 41	+54	43	05 35	+56	43	06 30	+55	42	230
131	02 29	55	43	03 24	55	43	04 19	55	42	05 14	55	42	06 09	55	42	229
132	02 07	55	42	03 02	56	42	03 58	55	42	04 53	55	41	05 48	55	41	228
133	01 46	55	42	02 41	56	41	03 37	55	41	04 32	55	40	05 27	56	40	227
134	01 25	56	41	02 21	55	40	03 16	56	40	04 12	55	40	05 07	55	39	226
135	01 05	+55	40	02 00	+56	39	02 56	+55	39	03 51	+56	39	04 47	+56	38	225
136	00 44	56	39	01 40	56	39	02 36	56	38	03 32	56	38	04 28	55	38	224
137	00 25	56	38	01 21	55	38	02 16	56	37	03 12	56	37	04 08	56	37	223
138	00 05	56	37	01 01	56	37	01 57	56	37	02 53	57	36	03 50	55	36	222
139	-0 14	56	36	00 42	57	36	01 39	56	36	02 35	56	35	03 31	56	35	221

S. Lat. {LHA greater than 180°....... Zn=180−Z; LHA less than 180°........... Zn=180+Z}

DECLINATION (15°-29°) SAME NAME AS LATITUDE

LAT 58°

N. Lat. {LHA greater than 180°....... Zn=Z; LHA less than 180°........... Zn=360−Z}

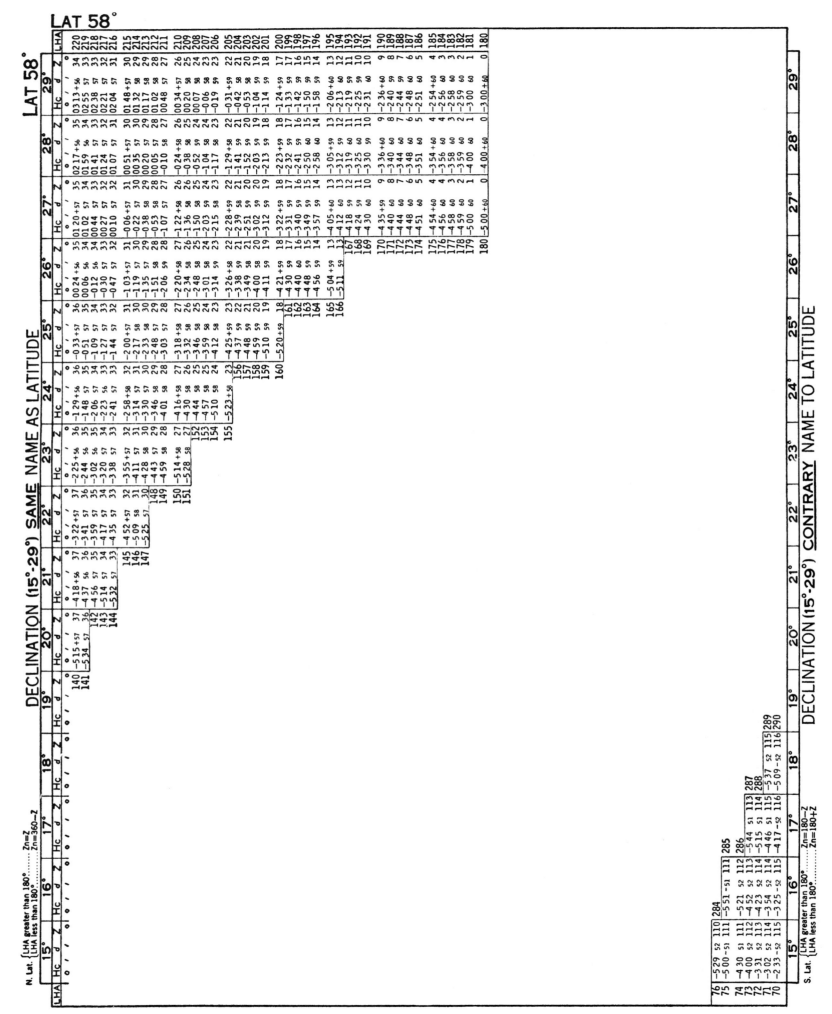

DECLINATION (15°-29°) SAME NAME AS LATITUDE

Each declination column: Hc (° ′) d (′) Z (°)

LHA	15°	16°	17°	18°	19°	20°	21°	22°	23°	24°	25°	26°	27°	28°	29°	LHA
					140	−5 15 +57 37	−4 18 +56 37	−3 22 +57 37	−2 25 +56 36	−1 29 +56 36	−0 33 +57 36	00 24 +56 35	01 20 +57 35	02 17 +56 35	03 13 +56 34	220
					141	−5 34 57 36	−4 37 56 36	−3 41 57 36	−2 44 56 35	−1 48 57 35	−0 51 57 35	00 06 56 34	01 02 57 34	01 59 56 34	02 55 57 33	219
						142	−4 56 57 35	−3 59 57 35	−3 02 56 35	−2 06 57 34	−1 09 57 34	−0 12 56 34	00 44 57 33	01 41 57 33	02 38 57 33	218
						143	−5 14 57 34	−4 17 57 34	−3 20 57 34	−2 23 56 33	−1 27 57 33	−0 30 57 33	00 27 57 32	01 24 57 32	02 21 57 32	217
						144	−5 32 57 33	−4 35 57 33	−3 38 57 33	−2 41 57 33	−1 44 57 32	−0 47 57 32	00 10 57 32	01 07 57 31	02 04 57 31	216
							145	−4 52 +57 32	−3 55 +57 32	−2 58 +58 32	−2 00 +57 31	−1 03 +57 31	−0 06 +57 31	00 51 +57 30	01 48 +57 30	215
							146	−5 09 58 31	−4 11 57 31	−3 14 57 31	−2 17 58 30	−1 19 57 30	−0 22 57 30	00 35 57 30	01 32 58 29	214
							147	−5 25 57 30	−4 28 58 30	−3 30 57 30	−2 33 58 30	−1 35 57 29	−0 38 58 29	00 20 57 29	01 17 58 29	213
								148	−4 43 57 29	−3 46 58 29	−2 48 57 29	−1 51 58 28	−0 53 58 28	00 05 57 28	01 02 58 28	212
								149	−4 59 58 28	−4 01 58 28	−3 03 57 28	−2 06 59 28	−1 07 57 27	−0 10 58 27	00 48 57 27	211
								150	−5 14 +58 27	−4 16 +58 27	−3 18 +58 27	−2 20 +58 27	−1 22 +58 26	−0 24 +58 26	00 34 +57 26	210
								151	−5 28 58 27	−4 30 58 26	−3 32 58 26	−2 34 58 26	−1 36 58 26	−0 38 58 25	00 20 58 25	209
									152	−4 44 58 25	−3 46 58 25	−2 48 58 25	−1 50 58 25	−0 52 59 24	00 07 58 24	208
									153	−4 57 58 25	−3 59 58 24	−3 01 58 24	−2 03 59 24	−1 04 58 24	−0 06 58 23	207
									154	−5 10 58 24	−4 12 58 23	−3 14 59 23	−2 15 58 23	−1 17 58 23	−0 19 59 23	206
									155	−5 23 +58 23	−4 25 +59 23	−3 26 +58 22	−2 28 +59 22	−1 29 +58 22	−0 31 +59 22	205
										156	−4 37 59 22	−3 38 59 21	−2 39 58 21	−1 41 59 21	−0 42 58 21	204
										157	−4 48 59 21	−3 49 58 21	−2 51 59 20	−1 52 59 20	−0 53 58 20	203
										158	−4 59 59 20	−4 00 58 20	−3 02 59 20	−2 03 59 19	−1 04 59 19	202
										159	−5 10 59 19	−4 11 59 19	−3 12 59 19	−2 13 59 18	−1 14 59 18	201
										160	−5 20 +59 18	−4 21 +59 18	−3 22 +59 18	−2 23 +59 18	−1 24 +59 17	200
											161	−4 30 59 17	−3 31 59 17	−2 32 59 17	−1 33 59 17	199
											162	−4 40 60 16	−3 40 59 16	−2 41 59 16	−1 42 59 16	198
											163	−4 48 59 15	−3 49 59 15	−2 50 60 15	−1 50 59 15	197
											164	−4 56 59 14	−3 57 59 14	−2 58 60 14	−1 58 59 14	196
											165	−5 04 +59 13	−4 05 +60 13	−3 05 +59 13	−2 06 +60 13	195
											166	−5 11 59 13	−4 12 60 13	−3 12 59 12	−2 13 60 12	194
												167	−4 18 59 12	−3 19 60 11	−2 19 59 11	193
												168	−4 24 59 11	−3 25 60 11	−2 25 59 10	192
												169	−4 30 60 10	−3 30 59 10	−2 31 60 10	191
												170	−4 35 +59 9	−3 36 +60 9	−2 36 +60 9	190
												171	−4 40 60 8	−3 40 60 8	−2 40 59 8	189
												172	−4 44 60 7	−3 44 60 7	−2 44 59 7	188
												173	−4 48 60 6	−3 48 60 6	−2 48 60 6	187
												174	−4 51 60 5	−3 51 60 5	−2 51 60 5	186
												175	−4 54 +60 4	−3 54 +60 4	−2 54 +60 4	185
												176	−4 56 60 4	−3 56 60 4	−2 56 60 3	184
												177	−4 58 60 3	−3 58 60 3	−2 58 60 3	183
												178	−4 59 60 2	−3 59 60 2	−2 59 60 2	182
												179	−5 00 60 1	−4 00 60 1	−3 00 60 1	181
												180	−5 00 +60 0	−4 00 +60 0	−3 00 +60 0	180

LHA	15°	16°	17°	18°	19°	20°	21°	22°	23°	24°	25°	26°	27°	28°	29°
76	−5 29 52 110	284													
75	−5 00 −51 111	−5 51 −51 111	285												
74	−4 30 51 111	−5 21 52 112	286												
73	−4 00 52 112	−4 52 52 113	−5 44 51 113	287											
72	−3 31 52 113	−4 23 52 114	−5 15 51 114	288											
71	−3 02 52 114	−3 54 52 114	−4 46 51 115	−5 37 52 115	289										
70	−2 33 −52 115	−3 25 −52 115	−4 17 −52 116	−5 09 −52 116	290										

S. Lat. {LHA greater than 180°....... Zn=180−Z; LHA less than 180°........... Zn=180+Z}

DECLINATION (15°-29°) CONTRARY NAME TO LATITUDE

N. Lat. {LHA greater than 180°....... Zn=Z; LHA less than 180°........... Zn=360−Z}

DECLINATION (15°-29°) CONTRARY NAME TO LATITUDE

LHA	15° Hc	15° d	15° Z	16° Hc	16° d	16° Z	17° Hc	17° d	17° Z	18° Hc	18° d	18° Z	19° Hc	19° d	19° Z	20° Hc	20° d	20° Z	21° Hc	21° d	21° Z	22° Hc	22° d	22° Z
	° ′	′	°	° ′	′	°	° ′	′	°	° ′	′	°	° ′	′	°	° ′	′	°	° ′	′	°	° ′	′	°
69	-2 04	52	116	-2 56	52	116	-3 48	52	117	-4 40	52	117	-5 32	52	117									
68	-1 35	53	116	-2 28	52	117	-3 20	52	117	-4 12	52	118	-5 04	53	118									
67	-1 07	52	117	-1 59	53	118	-2 52	52	118	-3 44	52	119	-4 36	53	119	-5 29	52	120						
66	-0 39	52	118	-1 31	53	119	-2 24	52	119	-3 16	53	120	-4 09	52	120	-5 01	53	120						
65	-0 11	-53	119	-1 04	-52	119	-1 56	-53	120	-2 49	-52	120	-3 41	-53	121	-4 34	-53	121	-5 27	-52	122			
64	00 17	53	120	-0 36	53	120	-1 29	52	121	-2 21	53	121	-3 14	53	122	-4 07	53	122	-5 00	52	123			
63	00 44	53	121	-0 09	52	121	-1 01	53	122	-1 54	53	122	-2 47	53	122	-3 40	53	123	-4 33	53	123	-5 26	53	124
62	01 12	53	121	00 19	53	122	-0 34	54	122	-1 28	53	123	-2 21	53	123	-3 14	53	124	-4 07	53	124	-5 00	53	125
61	01 39	54	122	00 45	53	123	-0 08	53	123	-1 01	53	124	-1 54	53	124	-2 47	53	125	-3 40	54	125	-4 34	53	126
60	02 05	-53	123	01 12	-54	124	00 18	-53	124	-0 35	-53	125	-1 28	-53	125	-2 21	-54	125	-3 15	-53	126	-4 08	-53	126
59	02 32	54	124	01 38	53	124	00 45	54	125	-0 09	53	125	-1 02	53	126	-1 55	54	126	-2 49	53	127	-3 42	54	127
58	02 58	54	125	02 04	53	125	01 11	54	126	00 17	53	126	-0 36	54	127	-1 30	54	127	-2 24	53	128	-3 17	54	128
57	03 24	54	126	02 30	54	126	01 36	53	127	00 43	54	127	-0 11	54	128	-1 05	54	128	-1 59	53	128	-2 52	54	129
56	03 50	54	127	02 56	54	127	02 02	54	128	01 08	54	128	00 14	54	128	-0 40	54	129	-1 34	54	129	-2 28	54	130
55	04 15	-54	128	03 21	-54	128	02 27	-54	128	01 33	-54	129	00 39	-54	129	-0 15	-54	130	-1 09	-54	130	-2 03	-54	131
54	04 40	54	128	03 46	54	129	02 52	55	129	01 57	54	130	01 03	54	130	00 09	54	131	-0 45	54	131	-1 39	55	131
53	05 05	54	129	04 11	55	130	03 16	54	130	02 22	55	131	01 27	54	131	00 33	54	131	-0 21	55	132	-1 16	54	132
52	05 29	54	130	04 35	55	131	03 40	54	131	02 46	55	131	01 51	54	132	00 57	55	132	00 02	54	133	-0 52	55	133
51	05 54	55	131	04 59	55	131	04 04	54	132	03 10	55	132	02 15	55	133	01 20	54	133	00 26	55	133	-0 29	55	134
50	06 17	-54	132	05 23	-55	132	04 28	-55	133	03 33	-55	133	02 38	-55	134	01 43	-55	134	00 48	-54	134	-0 06	-55	135
49	06 41	55	133	05 46	55	133	04 51	55	134	03 56	55	134	03 01	55	134	02 06	55	135	01 11	55	135	00 16	55	136
48	07 04	55	134	06 09	55	134	05 14	55	135	04 19	55	135	03 24	56	135	02 28	55	136	01 33	55	136	00 38	55	136
47	07 27	55	135	06 32	56	135	05 36	55	135	04 41	55	136	03 46	56	136	02 50	55	137	01 55	55	137	01 00	55	137
46	07 49	55	136	06 54	55	136	05 59	56	136	05 03	55	137	04 08	56	137	03 12	55	137	02 17	56	138	01 21	55	138
45	08 11	-55	136	07 16	-56	137	06 20	-55	137	05 25	-56	138	04 29	-56	138	03 33	-55	138	02 38	-56	139	01 42	-55	139
44	08 33	56	137	07 37	55	138	06 42	56	138	05 46	56	138	04 50	56	139	03 54	55	139	02 59	56	140	02 03	56	140
43	08 55	56	138	07 59	56	139	07 03	56	139	06 07	56	139	05 11	56	140	04 15	56	140	03 19	56	140	02 23	56	141
42	09 16	56	139	08 20	56	140	07 24	56	140	06 28	57	140	05 31	56	141	04 35	56	141	03 39	56	141	02 43	56	142
41	09 36	56	140	08 40	56	140	07 44	56	141	06 48	57	141	05 51	56	141	04 55	56	142	03 59	56	142	03 03	57	142
40	09 56	-56	141	09 00	-56	141	08 04	-57	142	07 07	-56	142	06 11	-56	142	05 15	-57	143	04 18	-56	143	03 22	-57	143
39	10 16	56	142	09 20	57	142	08 23	56	143	07 27	57	143	06 30	56	143	05 34	57	144	04 37	56	144	03 41	57	144
38	10 36	57	143	09 39	56	143	08 43	57	143	07 46	57	144	06 49	56	144	05 53	57	144	04 56	57	145	03 59	57	145
37	10 55	57	144	09 58	57	144	09 01	57	144	08 04	56	145	07 08	57	145	06 11	57	145	05 14	57	146	04 17	57	146
36	11 13	57	145	10 16	56	145	09 20	57	145	08 23	57	146	07 26	57	146	06 29	57	146	05 32	57	147	04 35	57	147
35	11 32	-57	146	10 35	-58	146	09 37	-57	146	08 40	-57	147	07 43	-57	147	06 46	-57	147	05 49	-57	147	04 52	-57	148
34	11 49	57	147	10 52	57	147	09 55	57	147	08 58	58	147	08 00	57	148	07 03	57	148	06 06	57	148	05 09	58	149
33	12 07	58	147	11 09	57	148	10 12	57	148	09 15	58	148	08 17	57	149	07 20	58	149	06 22	57	149	05 25	57	150
32	12 24	58	148	11 26	57	149	10 29	58	149	09 31	57	149	08 34	58	150	07 36	58	150	06 38	57	150	05 41	58	150
31	12 40	58	149	11 42	57	150	10 45	58	150	09 47	58	150	08 49	57	151	07 52	58	151	06 54	58	151	05 56	57	151
30	12 56	-58	150	11 58	-58	151	11 00	-57	151	10 03	-58	151	09 05	-58	151	08 07	-58	152	07 09	-58	152	06 11	-57	152
29	13 11	57	151	12 14	58	152	11 16	58	152	10 18	58	152	09 20	58	152	08 22	58	153	07 24	58	153	06 26	58	153
28	13 27	58	152	12 29	58	153	11 31	59	153	10 32	58	153	09 34	58	153	08 36	58	154	07 38	58	154	06 40	58	154
27	13 41	58	153	12 43	58	153	11 45	58	154	10 47	58	154	09 49	59	154	08 50	58	154	07 52	58	155	06 54	58	155
26	13 55	58	154	12 57	58	154	11 59	59	155	11 00	58	155	10 02	58	155	09 04	59	155	08 05	58	156	07 07	58	156
25	14 09	-59	155	13 10	-58	155	12 12	-58	156	11 14	-59	156	10 15	-58	156	09 17	-59	156	08 18	-58	157	07 20	-58	157
24	14 22	58	156	13 24	59	156	12 25	59	157	11 26	58	157	10 28	59	157	09 29	58	157	08 31	59	157	07 32	58	158
23	14 35	59	157	13 36	59	157	12 37	58	158	11 39	59	158	10 40	59	158	09 41	58	158	08 43	59	158	07 44	59	159
22	14 47	59	158	13 48	59	158	12 49	58	158	11 51	59	159	10 52	59	159	09 53	59	159	08 54	58	159	07 56	59	160
21	14 58	58	159	14 00	59	159	13 01	59	159	12 02	59	160	11 03	59	160	10 04	59	160	09 05	59	160	08 06	58	160
20	15 10	-59	160	14 11	-59	160	13 12	-59	160	12 13	-59	161	11 14	-59	161	10 15	-59	161	09 16	-59	161	08 17	-59	161
19	15 20	59	161	14 21	59	161	13 22	59	161	12 23	59	162	11 24	59	162	10 25	59	162	09 26	59	162	08 27	59	162
18	15 30	59	162	14 31	59	162	13 32	59	162	12 33	59	163	11 34	59	163	10 35	60	163	09 35	59	163	08 36	59	163
17	15 40	59	163	14 41	60	163	13 41	59	163	12 42	59	163	11 43	59	164	10 44	59	164	09 45	60	164	08 45	59	164
16	15 49	59	164	14 50	60	164	13 50	59	164	12 51	59	164	11 52	60	165	10 52	59	165	09 53	59	165	08 54	60	165
15	15 58	-60	165	14 58	-59	165	13 59	-60	165	12 59	-59	165	12 00	-59	166	11 01	-60	166	10 01	-59	166	09 02	-60	166
14	16 06	60	166	15 06	59	166	14 07	60	166	13 07	59	166	12 08	60	167	11 08	59	167	10 09	60	167	09 09	59	167
13	16 13	60	167	15 13	59	167	14 14	60	167	13 14	59	167	12 15	60	167	11 15	59	168	10 16	60	168	09 16	59	168
12	16 20	60	168	15 20	59	168	14 21	60	168	13 21	60	168	12 21	59	168	11 22	60	169	10 22	59	169	09 23	60	169
11	16 26	59	169	15 27	60	169	14 27	60	169	13 27	59	169	12 28	60	169	11 28	60	170	10 28	59	170	09 29	60	170
10	16 32	-60	170	15 32	-59	170	14 33	-60	170	13 33	-60	170	12 33	-60	170	11 33	-59	170	10 34	-60	171	09 34	-60	171
9	16 37	59	171	15 38	60	171	14 38	60	171	13 38	60	171	12 38	59	171	11 39	60	171	10 39	60	172	09 39	60	172
8	16 42	60	172	15 42	59	172	14 43	60	172	13 43	60	172	12 43	60	172	11 43	60	172	10 43	60	172	09 43	59	173
7	16 46	60	173	15 46	59	173	14 47	60	173	13 47	60	173	12 47	60	173	11 47	60	173	10 47	60	173	09 47	60	173
6	16 50	60	174	15 50	60	174	14 50	60	174	13 50	60	174	12 50	60	174	11 50	59	174	10 51	60	174	09 51	60	174
5	16 53	-60	175	15 53	-60	175	14 53	-60	175	13 53	-60	175	12 53	-60	175	11 53	-60	175	10 53	-59	175	09 54	-60	175
4	16 56	60	176	15 56	60	176	14 56	60	176	13 56	60	176	12 56	60	176	11 56	60	176	10 56	60	176	09 56	60	176
3	16 58	60	177	15 58	60	177	14 58	60	177	13 58	60	177	12 58	60	177	11 58	60	177	10 58	60	177	09 58	60	177
2	16 59	60	178	15 59	60	178	14 59	60	178	13 59	60	178	12 59	60	178	11 59	60	178	10 59	60	178	09 59	60	178
1	17 00	60	179	16 00	60	179	15 00	60	179	14 00	60	179	13 00	60	179	12 00	60	179	11 00	60	179	10 00	60	179
0	17 00	-60	180	16 00	-60	180	15 00	-60	180	14 00	-60	180	13 00	-60	180	12 00	-60	180	11 00	-60	180	10 00	-60	180

LHA	23° Hc	23° d	23° Z	24° Hc	24° d	24° Z	25° Hc	25° d	25° Z	26° Hc	26° d	26° Z	27° Hc	27° d	27° Z	28° Hc	28° d	28° Z	29° Hc	29° d	29° Z	LHA
	° ′	′	°	° ′	′	°	° ′	′	°	° ′	′	°	° ′	′	°	° ′	′	°	° ′	′	°	
69																						291
68																						292
67																						293
66																						294
65																						295
64																						296
63																						297
62																						298
61	-5 27	53	126																			299
60	-5 01	-53	127																			300
59	-4 36	53	128	-5 29	54	128																301
58	-4 11	53	128	-5 04	54	129																302
57	-3 46	54	129	-4 40	53	130	-5 33	54	130													303
56	-3 22	53	130	-4 15	54	131	-5 09	54	131													304
55	-2 57	-54	131	-3 51	-54	131	-4 45	-54	132	-5 39	-54	132										305
54	-2 34	54	132	-3 28	54	132	-4 22	54	133	-5 16	54	133										306
53	-2 10	54	133	-3 04	55	133	-3 59	54	133	-4 53	54	134										307
52	-1 47	54	133	-2 41	55	134	-3 36	54	134	-4 30	55	135	-5 25	54	135							308
51	-1 24	54	134	-2 18	55	135	-3 13	55	135	-4 08	54	136	-5 02	55	136							309
50	-1 01	-55	135	-1 56	-55	136	-2 51	-55	136	-3 46	-55	136	-4 41	-54	137	-5 35	-55	137				310
49	-0 39	55	136	-1 34	55	136	-2 29	55	137	-3 24	55	137	-4 19	55	138	-5 14	55	138				311
48	-0 17	55	137	-1 12	55	137	-2 07	55	138	-3 02	56	138	-3 58	55	138	-4 53	55	139				312
47	00 05	56	138	-0 51	55	138	-1 46	55	138	-2 41	56	139	-3 37	55	139	-4 32	55	140	-5 27	56	140	313
46	00 26	56	139	-0 30	55	139	-1 25	56	139	-2 21	55	140	-3 16	56	140	-4 12	55	140	-5 07	55	141	314
45	00 47	-56	139	-0 09	-56	140	-1 05	-55	140	-2 00	-56	141	-2 56	-55	141	-3 51	-56	141	-4 47	-56	142	315
44	01 07	56	140	00 11	55	141	-0 44	56	141	-1 40	56	141	-2 36	56	142	-3 32	56	142	-4 28	55	142	316
43	01 27	56	141	00 31	56	141	-0 25	56	142	-1 21	55	142	-2 16	56	143	-3 12	56	143	-4 08	56	143	317
42	01 47	56	142	00 51	56	142	-0 05	56	143	-1 01	56	143	-1 57	56	143	-2 53	57	144	-3 50	55	144	318
41	02 06	56	143	01 10	56	143	00 14	56	144	-0 42	57	144	-1 39	56	144	-2 35	56	145	-3 31	56	145	319
40	02 25	-56	144	01 29	-56	144	00 33	-57	144	-0 24	-56	145	-1 20	-57	145	-2 17	-56	145	-3 13	-56	146	320
39	02 44	56	145	01 48	57	145	00 51	57	145	-0 06	56	146	-1 02	57	146	-1 59	56	146	-2 55	57	147	321
38	03 02	56	145	02 06	57	146	01 09	57	146	00 12	56	146	-0 44	57	147	-1 41	57	147	-2 38	57	147	322
37	03 20	57	146	02 23	56	147	01 27	57	147	00 30	57	147	-0 27	57	148	-1 24	57	148	-2 21	57	148	323
36	03 38	57	147	02 41	57	147	01 44	57	148	00 47	57	148	-0 10	57	148	-1 07	57	149	-2 04	57	149	324
35	03 55	-57	148	02 58	-58	148	02 00	-57	149	01 03	-57	149	00 06	-57	149	-0 51	-57	150	-1 48	-57	150	325
34	04 11	57	149	03 14	57	149	02 17	58	150	01 19	57	150	00 22	57	150	-0 35	57	150	-1 32	58	151	326
33	04 28	58	150	03 30	57	150	02 33	58	150	01 35	57	151	00 38	58	151	-0 20	57	151	-1 17	58	151	327
32	04 43	57	151	03 46	58	151	02 48	57	151	01 51	58	152	00 53	58	152	-0 05	57	152	-1 02	58	152	328
31	04 59	58	152	04 01	58	152	03 03	57	152	02 06	59	152	01 07	57	153	00 10	58	153	-0 48	57	153	329
30	05 14	-58	153	04 16	-58	153	03 18	-58	153	02 20	-58	153	01 22	-58	154	00 24	-58	154	-0 34	-57	154	330
29	05 28	58	153	04 30	58	154	03 32	58	154	02 34	58	154	01 36	58	154	00 38	58	155	-0 20	58	155	331
28	05 42	58	154	04 44	58	155	03 46	58	155	02 48	58	155	01 50	58	155	00 52	59	156	-0 07	58	156	332
27	05 56	59	155	04 57	58	155	03 59	58	156	03 01	58	156	02 03	59	156	01 04	58	156	00 06	58	157	333
26	06 09	59	156	05 10	58	156	04 12	58	157	03 14	59	157	02 15	58	157	01 17	58	157	00 19	59	157	334
25	06 22	-59	157	05 23	-58	157	04 25	-59	157	03 26	-58	158	02 28	-59	158	01 29	-58	158	00 31	-59	158	335
24	06 34	59	158	05 35	58	158	04 37	59	158	03 38	59	159	02 39	58	159	01 41	59	159	00 42	58	159	336
23	06 45	58	159	05 47	59	159	04 48	59	159	03 49	58	159	02 51	59	160	01 52	59	160	00 53	58	160	337
22	06 57	59	160	05 58	59	160	04 59	59	160	04 00	58	160	03 02	59	160	02 03	59	161	01 04	59	161	338
21	07 08	59	161	06 09	59	161	05 10	59	161	04 11	59	161	03 12	59	161	02 13	59	162	01 14	59	162	339
20	07 18	-59	162	06 19	-59	162	05 20	-59	162	04 21	-59	162	03 22	-59	162	02 23	-59	162	01 24	-59	163	340
19	07 28	59	162	06 29	59	163	05 30	60	163	04 30	59	163	03 31	59	163	02 32	59	163	01 33	59	163	341
18	07 37	59	163	06 38	59	164	05 39	59	164	04 40	60	164	03 40	59	164	02 41	59	164	01 42	59	164	342
17	07 46	59	164	06 47	60	164	05 47	59	165	04 48	59	165	03 49	59	165	02 50	60	165	01 50	59	165	343
16	07 54	59	165	06 55	59	165	05 56	60	166	04 56	59	166	03 57	59	166	02 58	60	166	01 58	59	166	344
15	08 02	-59	166	07 03	-60	166	06 03	-59	166	05 04	-59	167	04 05	-60	167	03 05	-59	167	02 06	-60	167	345
14	08 10	60	167	07 10	59	167	06 11	60	167	05 11	59	167	04 12	60	167	03 12	59	168	02 13	60	168	346
13	08 17	60	168	07 17	60	168	06 17	59	168	05 18	60	168	04 18	59	168	03 19	60	169	02 19	59	169	347
12	08 23	60	169	07 23	59	169	06 24	60	169	05 24	60	169	04 24	59	169	03 25	60	169	02 25	59	170	348
11	08 29	60	170	07 29	59	170	06 30	60	170	05 30	60	170	04 30	60	170	03 30	59	170	02 31	60	170	349
10	08 34	-59	171	07 35	-60	171	06 35	-60	171	05 35	-60	171	04 35	-59	171	03 36	-60	171	02 36	-60	171	350
9	08 39	60	172	07 39	59	172	06 40	60	172	05 40	60	172	04 40	60	172	03 40	60	172	02 40	59	172	351
8	08 44	60	173	07 44	60	173	06 44	60	173	05 44	60	173	04 44	60	173	03 44	60	173	02 44	59	173	352
7	08 47	59	174	07 48	60	174	06 48	60	174	05 48	60	174	04 48	60	174	03 48	60	174	02 48	60	174	353
6	08 51	60	174	07 51	60	175	06 51	60	175	05 51	60	175	04 51	60	175	03 51	60	175	02 51	60	175	354
5	08 54	-60	175	07 54	-60	175	06 54	-60	175	05 54	-60	176	04 54	-60	176	03 54	-60	176	02 54	-60	176	355
4	08 56	60	176	07 56	60	176	06 56	60	176	05 56	60	176	04 56	60	176	03 56	60	176	02 56	60	177	356
3	08 58	60	177	07 58	60	177	06 58	60	177	05 58	60	177	04 58	60	177	03 58	60	177	02 58	60	177	357
2	08 59	60	178	07 59	60	178	06 59	60	178	05 59	60	178	04 59	60	178	03 59	60	178	02 59	60	178	358
1	09 00	60	179	08 00	60	179	07 00	60	179	06 00	60	179	05 00	60	179	04 00	60	179	03 00	60	179	359
0	09 00	-60	180	08 00	-60	180	07 00	-60	180	06 00	-60	180	05 00	-60	180	04 00	-60	180	03 00	-60	180	360

S. Lat. {LHA greater than 180°....... Zn=180−Z; LHA less than 180°........... Zn=180+Z}

DECLINATION (15°-29°) CONTRARY NAME TO LATITUDE

N. Lat. {LHA greater than 180°........Zn=Z; LHA less than 180°..........Zn=360−Z}

DECLINATION (0°-14°) SAME NAME AS LATITUDE

LHA	0° Hc	0° d	0° Z	1° Hc	1° d	1° Z	2° Hc	2° d	2° Z	3° Hc	3° d	3° Z	4° Hc	4° d	4° Z
	° ′	′	°	° ′	′	°	° ′	′	°	° ′	′	°	° ′	′	°
0	31 00	+60	180	32 00	+60	180	33 00	+60	180	34 00	+60	180	35 00	+60	180
1	31 00	60	179	32 00	60	179	33 00	60	179	34 00	60	179	35 00	60	179
2	30 59	60	178	31 59	60	178	32 59	60	178	33 59	60	178	34 59	60	178
3	30 57	60	177	31 57	60	177	32 57	60	176	33 57	60	176	34 57	60	176
4	30 55	60	175	31 55	60	175	32 55	60	175	33 55	60	175	34 55	60	175
5	30 52	+60	174	31 52	+60	174	32 52	+60	174	33 52	+60	174	34 52	+60	174
6	30 49	60	173	31 49	60	173	32 49	59	173	33 48	60	173	34 48	60	173
7	30 45	60	172	31 45	59	172	32 44	60	172	33 44	60	172	34 44	60	172
8	30 40	60	171	31 40	60	171	32 40	59	171	33 39	60	170	34 39	60	170
9	30 35	59	170	31 34	60	169	32 34	60	169	33 34	60	169	34 34	59	169
10	30 29	+59	168	31 28	+60	168	32 28	+60	168	33 28	+59	168	34 27	+60	168
11	30 22	60	167	31 22	59	167	32 21	60	167	33 21	60	167	34 21	59	167
12	30 15	60	166	31 15	59	166	32 14	60	166	33 14	59	166	34 13	60	166
13	30 07	60	165	31 07	59	165	32 06	60	165	33 06	59	164	34 05	59	164
14	29 59	59	164	30 58	60	164	31 58	59	163	32 57	59	163	33 56	60	163
15	29 50	+59	163	30 49	+60	163	31 49	+59	162	32 48	+59	162	33 47	+59	162
16	29 41	59	162	30 40	59	161	31 39	59	161	32 38	59	161	33 37	59	161
17	29 30	60	160	30 30	59	160	31 29	59	160	32 28	59	160	33 27	59	160
18	29 20	59	159	30 19	59	159	31 18	59	159	32 17	59	159	33 16	59	158
19	29 09	58	158	30 07	59	158	31 06	59	158	32 05	59	157	33 04	59	157
20	28 57	+59	157	29 56	+58	157	30 54	+59	157	31 53	+59	156	32 52	+58	156
21	28 44	59	156	29 43	59	156	30 42	58	155	31 40	59	155	32 39	58	155
22	28 32	58	155	29 30	59	155	30 29	58	154	31 27	58	154	32 25	59	154
23	28 18	58	154	29 16	59	153	30 15	58	153	31 13	58	153	32 11	59	153
24	28 04	58	153	29 02	59	152	30 01	58	152	30 59	58	152	31 57	58	151
25	27 50	+58	152	28 48	+58	151	29 46	+58	151	30 44	+58	151	31 42	+58	150
26	27 35	58	150	28 33	58	150	29 31	57	150	30 28	58	150	31 26	58	149
27	27 19	58	149	28 17	58	149	29 15	58	149	30 13	57	148	31 10	58	148
28	27 03	58	148	28 01	57	148	28 58	58	148	29 56	58	147	30 54	57	147
29	26 46	58	147	27 44	58	147	28 42	57	147	29 39	58	146	30 37	57	146
30	26 29	+58	146	27 27	+57	146	28 24	+58	145	29 22	+57	145	30 19	+57	145
31	26 12	57	145	27 09	57	145	28 06	58	144	29 04	57	144	30 01	57	144
32	25 54	57	144	26 51	57	144	27 48	57	143	28 45	57	143	29 42	57	143
33	25 36	57	143	26 33	56	143	27 29	57	142	28 26	57	142	29 23	57	141
34	25 17	56	142	26 13	57	141	27 10	57	141	28 07	57	141	29 04	56	140
35	24 57	+57	141	25 54	+57	140	26 51	+56	140	27 47	+57	140	28 44	+56	139
36	24 38	56	140	25 34	57	139	26 31	56	139	27 27	56	139	28 23	57	138
37	24 17	57	139	25 14	56	138	26 10	56	138	27 06	57	138	28 03	56	137
38	23 57	56	138	24 53	56	137	25 49	56	137	26 45	56	137	27 41	56	136
39	23 36	56	137	24 32	56	136	25 28	56	136	26 24	56	135	27 20	56	135
40	23 14	+56	136	24 10	+56	135	25 06	+56	135	26 02	+56	134	26 58	+55	134
41	22 52	56	135	23 48	56	134	24 44	56	134	25 40	55	133	26 35	56	133
42	22 30	56	134	23 26	56	133	24 22	55	133	25 17	55	132	26 12	56	132
43	22 08	55	133	23 03	56	132	23 59	55	132	24 54	55	131	25 49	55	131
44	21 45	55	132	22 40	55	131	23 35	56	131	24 31	55	130	25 26	55	130
45	21 22	+55	131	22 17	+55	130	23 12	+55	130	24 07	+55	129	25 02	+55	129
46	20 58	55	130	21 53	55	129	22 48	55	129	23 43	55	128	24 38	54	128
47	20 34	55	129	21 29	55	128	22 24	54	128	23 18	55	127	24 13	55	127
48	20 10	54	128	21 04	55	127	21 59	55	127	22 54	54	126	23 48	55	126
49	19 45	55	127	20 40	54	126	21 34	55	126	22 29	54	125	23 23	54	125
50	19 20	+55	126	20 15	+54	125	21 09	+54	125	22 03	+54	124	22 57	+55	124
51	18 55	54	125	19 49	54	124	20 43	55	124	21 38	54	123	22 32	54	123
52	18 29	54	124	19 23	55	123	20 18	54	123	21 12	54	122	22 06	54	122
53	18 03	55	123	18 58	54	122	19 52	53	122	20 45	54	122	21 39	54	121
54	17 37	54	122	18 31	54	122	19 25	54	121	20 19	54	121	21 13	53	120
55	17 11	+54	121	18 05	+54	121	18 59	+53	120	19 52	+54	120	20 46	+53	119
56	16 44	54	120	17 38	54	120	18 32	53	119	19 25	54	119	20 19	53	118
57	16 17	54	119	17 11	54	119	18 05	53	118	18 58	53	118	19 51	54	117
58	15 50	54	118	16 44	53	118	17 37	53	117	18 30	54	117	19 24	53	116
59	15 23	53	117	16 16	54	117	17 10	53	116	18 03	53	116	18 56	53	115
60	14 55	+54	116	15 49	+53	116	16 42	+53	115	17 35	+53	115	18 28	+53	114
61	14 28	53	115	15 21	53	115	16 14	53	114	17 07	53	114	18 00	52	114
62	14 00	53	115	14 53	52	114	15 45	53	113	16 38	53	113	17 31	53	113
63	13 31	53	114	14 24	53	113	15 17	53	113	16 10	53	112	17 02	53	112
64	13 03	53	113	13 56	52	112	14 48	53	112	15 41	53	111	16 34	52	111
65	12 34	+53	112	13 27	+53	111	14 20	+52	111	15 12	+53	110	16 05	+52	110
66	12 06	52	111	12 58	53	110	13 51	52	110	14 43	53	109	15 36	52	109
67	11 37	52	110	12 29	53	110	13 22	52	109	14 14	52	109	15 06	52	108
68	11 08	52	109	12 00	52	109	12 52	53	108	13 45	52	108	14 37	52	107
69	10 38	53	108	11 31	52	108	12 23	52	107	13 15	52	107	14 07	52	106

LHA	5° Hc	5° d	5° Z	6° Hc	6° d	6° Z	7° Hc	7° d	7° Z	8° Hc	8° d	8° Z	9° Hc	9° d	9° Z
	° ′	′	°	° ′	′	°	° ′	′	°	° ′	′	°	° ′	′	°
0	36 00	+60	180	37 00	+60	180	38 00	+60	180	39 00	+60	180	40 00	+60	180
1	36 00	60	179	37 00	60	179	38 00	60	179	39 00	60	179	40 00	60	179
2	35 59	60	178	36 59	60	178	37 59	60	178	38 59	60	178	39 59	60	177
3	35 57	60	176	36 57	60	176	37 57	60	176	38 57	60	176	39 57	60	176
4	35 55	60	175	36 55	60	175	37 55	60	175	38 55	59	175	39 54	60	175
5	35 52	+60	174	36 52	+60	174	37 52	+59	174	38 51	+60	174	39 51	+60	174
6	35 48	60	173	36 48	60	173	37 48	60	173	38 48	60	172	39 48	59	172
7	35 44	60	171	36 44	59	171	37 43	60	171	38 43	60	171	39 43	60	171
8	35 39	60	170	36 39	59	170	37 38	60	170	38 38	60	170	39 38	60	170
9	35 33	60	169	36 33	60	169	37 33	59	169	38 32	60	169	39 32	60	168
10	35 27	+60	168	36 27	+59	168	37 26	+60	168	38 26	+60	167	39 26	+59	167
11	35 20	60	167	36 20	59	166	37 19	60	166	38 19	59	166	39 18	60	166
12	35 13	59	165	36 12	60	165	37 12	59	165	38 11	59	165	39 10	60	165
13	35 04	60	164	36 04	59	164	37 03	60	164	38 03	59	164	39 02	59	163
14	34 56	59	163	35 55	59	163	36 54	60	163	37 54	59	162	38 53	59	162
15	34 46	+60	162	35 46	+59	162	36 45	+59	161	37 44	+59	161	38 43	+59	161
16	34 36	59	161	35 35	59	160	36 34	60	160	37 34	59	160	38 33	59	160
17	34 26	59	159	35 25	59	159	36 24	59	159	37 23	58	159	38 21	59	158
18	34 15	58	158	35 13	59	158	36 12	59	158	37 11	59	157	38 10	59	157
19	34 03	58	157	35 01	59	157	36 00	59	157	36 59	58	156	37 57	59	156
20	33 50	+59	156	34 49	+59	156	35 48	+58	155	36 46	+59	155	37 45	+58	155
21	33 37	59	155	34 36	58	154	35 34	59	154	36 33	58	154	37 31	58	154
22	33 24	58	153	34 22	58	153	35 20	59	153	36 19	58	153	37 17	58	152
23	33 10	58	152	34 08	58	152	35 06	58	152	36 04	58	151	37 02	58	151
24	32 55	58	151	33 53	58	151	34 51	58	151	35 49	58	150	36 47	58	150
25	32 40	+58	150	33 38	+58	150	34 36	+58	149	35 34	+57	149	36 31	+58	149
26	32 24	58	149	33 22	58	149	34 20	57	148	35 17	58	148	36 15	58	148
27	32 08	58	148	33 06	57	147	34 03	58	147	35 01	57	147	35 58	58	146
28	31 51	58	147	32 49	57	146	33 46	57	146	34 43	58	146	35 41	57	145
29	31 34	57	146	32 31	58	145	33 29	57	145	34 26	57	144	35 23	57	144
30	31 16	+57	144	32 13	+57	144	33 10	+58	144	34 08	+56	143	35 04	+57	143
31	30 58	57	143	31 55	57	143	32 52	57	143	33 49	57	142	34 46	56	142
32	30 39	57	142	31 36	57	142	32 33	57	141	33 30	56	141	34 26	57	141
33	30 20	57	141	31 17	56	141	32 13	57	140	33 10	56	140	34 06	57	140
34	30 00	57	140	30 57	56	140	31 53	57	139	32 50	56	139	33 46	56	138
35	29 40	+57	139	30 37	+56	139	31 33	+56	138	32 29	+56	138	33 25	+56	137
36	29 20	56	138	30 16	56	137	31 12	56	137	32 08	56	137	33 04	56	136
37	28 59	56	137	29 55	56	136	30 51	56	136	31 47	56	136	32 43	55	135
38	28 37	56	136	29 33	56	135	30 29	56	135	31 25	55	134	32 20	56	134
39	28 16	55	135	29 11	56	134	30 07	56	134	31 03	55	133	31 58	55	133
40	27 53	+56	134	28 49	+55	133	29 44	+56	133	30 40	+55	132	31 35	+55	132
41	27 31	55	133	28 26	56	132	29 22	55	132	30 17	55	131	31 12	55	131
42	27 08	55	131	28 03	55	131	28 58	55	131	29 53	55	130	30 48	55	130
43	26 44	56	131	27 40	55	130	28 35	55	130	29 30	54	129	30 24	55	129
44	26 21	55	129	27 16	55	129	28 11	54	129	29 05	55	128	30 00	55	128
45	25 57	+55	128	26 52	+54	128	27 46	+55	128	28 41	+54	127	29 35	+55	127
46	25 32	55	127	26 27	55	127	27 22	54	127	28 16	54	126	29 10	55	126
47	25 08	54	126	26 02	55	126	26 57	54	126	27 51	54	125	28 45	54	125
48	24 43	54	125	25 37	54	125	26 31	54	125	27 25	55	124	28 20	54	124
49	24 17	55	124	25 12	54	124	26 06	54	124	27 00	54	123	27 54	53	123
50	23 52	+54	123	24 46	+54	123	25 40	+54	123	26 34	+53	122	27 27	+54	122
51	23 26	54	123	24 20	54	122	25 14	53	122	26 07	54	121	27 01	53	121
52	23 00	53	122	23 53	54	121	24 47	54	121	25 41	53	120	26 34	54	120
53	22 33	54	121	23 27	53	120	24 20	54	120	25 14	53	119	26 07	53	119
54	22 06	54	120	23 00	53	119	23 53	54	119	24 47	53	118	25 40	53	118
55	21 39	+54	119	22 33	+53	118	23 26	+53	118	24 19	+53	117	25 12	+53	117
56	21 12	53	118	22 05	54	117	22 59	53	117	23 52	53	116	24 45	53	116
57	20 45	53	117	21 38	53	116	22 31	53	116	23 24	53	115	24 17	52	115
58	20 17	53	116	21 10	53	115	22 03	53	115	22 56	52	114	23 48	53	114
59	19 49	53	115	20 42	53	114	21 35	52	114	22 27	53	113	23 20	53	113
60	19 21	+53	114	20 14	+52	113	21 06	+53	113	21 59	+52	112	22 51	+53	112
61	18 52	53	113	19 45	53	113	20 38	52	112	21 30	53	111	22 23	52	111
62	18 24	52	112	19 16	53	112	20 09	52	111	21 01	53	111	21 54	52	110
63	17 55	53	111	18 48	52	111	19 40	52	110	20 32	53	110	21 25	52	109
64	17 26	53	110	18 19	52	110	19 11	52	109	20 03	52	109	20 55	52	108
65	16 57	+52	109	17 49	+53	109	18 42	+52	108	19 34	+52	108	20 26	+52	107
66	16 28	52	108	17 20	52	108	18 12	52	107	19 04	52	107	19 56	52	106
67	15 58	53	108	16 51	52	107	17 43	52	106	18 35	52	106	19 27	51	105
68	15 29	52	107	16 21	52	106	17 13	52	106	18 05	52	105	18 57	51	105
69	14 59	52	106	15 51	52	105	16 43	52	105	17 35	52	104	18 27	51	104

LHA	10° Hc	10° d	10° Z	11° Hc	11° d	11° Z	12° Hc	12° d	12° Z	13° Hc	13° d	13° Z	14° Hc	14° d	14° Z	LHA
	° ′	′	°	° ′	′	°	° ′	′	°	° ′	′	°	° ′	′	°	
0	41 00	+60	180	42 00	+60	180	43 00	+60	180	44 00	+60	180	45 00	+60	180	360
1	41 00	60	179	42 00	60	179	43 00	60	179	44 00	60	179	45 00	60	179	359
2	40 59	60	177	41 59	60	177	42 59	60	177	43 59	60	177	44 59	60	177	358
3	40 57	60	176	41 57	60	176	42 57	60	176	43 57	60	176	44 57	60	176	357
4	40 54	60	175	41 54	60	175	42 54	60	175	43 54	60	175	44 54	60	175	356
5	40 51	+60	174	41 51	+60	173	42 51	+60	173	43 51	+60	173	44 51	+60	173	355
6	40 47	60	172	41 47	60	172	42 47	60	172	43 47	60	172	44 47	60	172	354
7	40 43	60	171	41 43	59	171	42 42	60	171	43 42	60	171	44 42	60	170	353
8	40 38	59	170	41 37	60	170	42 37	60	169	43 37	59	169	44 36	60	169	352
9	40 32	59	168	41 31	60	168	42 31	60	168	43 31	59	168	44 30	60	168	351
10	40 25	+60	167	41 25	+59	167	42 24	+60	167	43 24	+59	167	44 23	+60	166	350
11	40 18	59	166	41 17	60	166	42 17	59	165	43 16	60	165	44 16	59	165	349
12	40 10	59	165	41 09	60	164	42 09	59	164	43 08	59	164	44 07	60	164	348
13	40 01	60	163	41 01	59	163	42 00	59	163	42 59	59	163	43 58	60	162	347
14	39 52	59	162	40 51	59	162	41 50	60	162	42 50	59	161	43 49	59	161	346
15	39 42	+59	161	40 41	+59	160	41 40	+59	160	42 39	+59	160	43 38	+59	160	345
16	39 32	58	159	40 30	59	159	41 29	59	159	42 28	59	159	43 27	59	158	344
17	39 20	59	158	40 19	59	158	41 18	59	158	42 17	58	157	43 15	59	157	343
18	39 09	58	157	40 07	59	157	41 06	59	156	42 05	58	156	43 03	59	156	342
19	38 56	59	156	39 55	58	155	40 53	59	155	41 52	58	155	42 50	58	155	341
20	38 43	+58	154	39 41	+59	154	40 40	+58	154	41 38	+58	154	42 36	+59	153	340
21	38 29	59	153	39 28	58	153	40 26	58	153	41 24	58	152	42 22	58	152	339
22	38 15	58	152	39 13	58	152	40 11	58	151	41 09	58	151	42 07	58	151	338
23	38 00	58	151	38 58	58	150	39 56	58	150	40 54	58	150	41 52	58	149	337
24	37 45	58	150	38 43	58	149	39 41	57	149	40 38	58	149	41 36	57	148	336
25	37 29	+58	148	38 27	+57	148	39 24	+58	148	40 22	+57	147	41 19	+58	147	335
26	37 13	57	147	38 10	58	147	39 08	57	146	40 05	57	146	41 02	57	146	334
27	36 56	57	146	37 53	57	146	38 50	57	145	39 47	58	145	40 45	57	145	333
28	36 38	57	145	37 35	57	144	38 32	57	144	39 29	57	144	40 26	57	143	332
29	36 20	57	144	37 17	57	143	38 14	57	143	39 11	57	143	40 08	56	142	331
30	36 01	+57	143	36 58	+57	142	37 55	+57	142	38 52	+56	141	39 48	+57	141	330
31	35 42	57	141	36 39	57	141	37 36	56	141	38 32	56	140	39 28	57	140	329
32	35 23	56	140	36 19	57	140	37 16	56	139	38 12	56	139	39 08	56	139	328
33	35 03	56	139	35 59	56	139	36 55	56	138	37 51	57	138	38 48	55	137	327
34	34 42	56	138	35 38	57	138	36 35	56	137	37 30	56	137	38 26	56	136	326
35	34 21	+56	137	35 17	+56	136	36 13	+56	136	37 09	+56	136	38 05	+55	135	325
36	34 00	56	136	34 56	56	135	35 52	55	135	36 47	56	134	37 43	55	134	324
37	33 38	56	135	34 34	55	134	35 29	56	134	36 25	55	133	37 20	55	133	323
38	33 16	56	134	34 12	55	133	35 07	55	133	36 02	55	132	36 57	55	132	322
39	32 53	56	133	33 49	55	132	34 44	55	132	35 39	55	131	36 34	55	131	321
40	32 30	+56	131	33 26	+55	131	34 21	+54	130	35 15	+55	130	36 10	+55	129	320
41	32 07	55	130	33 02	55	130	33 57	55	129	34 52	54	129	35 46	55	128	319
42	31 43	55	129	32 38	55	129	33 33	54	128	34 27	55	128	35 22	54	127	318
43	31 19	55	128	32 14	54	128	33 08	55	127	34 03	54	127	34 57	54	126	317
44	30 55	54	127	31 49	55	127	32 44	54	126	33 38	54	126	34 32	54	125	316
45	30 30	+54	126	31 24	+54	126	32 18	+55	125	33 13	+53	125	34 06	+54	124	315
46	30 05	54	125	30 59	54	125	31 53	54	124	32 47	54	124	33 41	53	123	314
47	29 39	54	124	30 33	54	124	31 27	54	123	32 21	54	123	33 15	53	122	313
48	29 14	53	123	30 07	54	123	31 01	54	122	31 55	53	122	32 48	54	121	312
49	28 47	54	122	29 41	54	122	30 35	53	121	31 28	54	120	32 22	53	120	311
50	28 21	+54	121	29 15	+53	121	30 08	+53	120	31 01	+54	119	31 55	+53	119	310
51	27 54	54	120	28 48	53	120	29 41	53	119	30 34	53	118	31 27	53	118	309
52	27 28	53	119	28 21	53	119	29 14	53	118	30 07	53	117	31 00	53	117	308
53	27 00	54	118	27 54	53	118	28 47	53	117	29 40	52	116	30 32	53	116	307
54	26 33	53	117	27 26	53	117	28 19	53	116	29 12	52	115	30 04	53	115	306
55	26 05	+53	116	26 58	+53	116	27 51	+53	115	28 44	+52	115	29 36	+53	114	305
56	25 38	52	115	26 30	53	115	27 23	53	114	28 16	52	114	29 08	52	113	304
57	25 09	53	114	26 02	53	114	26 55	52	113	27 47	52	113	28 39	53	112	303
58	24 41	53	113	25 34	52	113	26 26	53	112	27 18	53	112	28 11	52	111	302
59	24 13	52	112	25 05	52	112	25 57	53	111	26 50	52	111	27 42	52	110	301
60	23 44	+52	111	24 36	+53	111	25 29	+52	110	26 21	+52	110	27 13	+51	109	300
61	23 15	52	110	24 07	52	110	24 59	52	109	25 51	52	109	26 43	52	108	299
62	22 46	52	109	23 38	52	109	24 30	52	108	25 22	52	108	26 14	52	107	298
63	22 17	52	109	23 09	52	108	24 01	52	107	24 53	51	107	25 44	52	106	297
64	21 47	52	108	22 39	52	107	23 31	52	107	24 23	52	106	25 15	51	105	296
65	21 18	+52	107	22 10	+52	106	23 02	+51	106	23 53	+52	105	24 45	+51	105	295
66	20 48	52	106	21 40	52	105	22 32	51	105	23 23	52	104	24 15	51	104	294
67	20 18	52	105	21 10	52	104	22 02	51	104	22 53	52	103	23 45	51	103	293
68	19 48	52	104	20 40	52	103	21 32	51	103	22 23	51	102	23 14	52	102	292
69	19 18	52	103	20 10	51	103	21 01	52	102	21 53	51	101	22 44	51	101	291

S. Lat. {LHA greater than 180°........Zn=180−Z; LHA less than 180°..........Zn=180+Z}

DECLINATION (0°-14°) SAME NAME AS LATITUDE

N. Lat. {LHA greater than 180°....... Zn=Z; LHA less than 180°.......... Zn=360−Z}

DECLINATION (0°-14°) SAME NAME AS LATITUDE

LHA	0°			1°			2°			3°			4°		
	Hc	d	Z	Hc	d	Z	Hc	d	Z	Hc	d	Z	Hc	d	Z
	° ′	′	°	° ′	′	°	° ′	′	°	° ′	′	°	° ′	′	°
70	10 09	+52	107	11 01	+52	107	11 53	+52	106	12 45	+52	106	13 37	+52	105
71	09 39	52	106	10 31	52	106	11 23	53	105	12 16	52	105	13 08	51	104
72	09 10	52	106	10 02	52	105	10 54	52	105	11 46	52	104	12 38	51	104
73	08 40	52	105	09 32	52	104	10 24	52	104	11 16	51	103	12 07	52	103
74	08 10	52	104	09 02	52	103	09 54	51	103	10 45	52	102	11 37	52	102
75	07 40	+52	103	08 32	+51	102	09 23	+52	102	10 15	+52	101	11 07	+52	101
76	07 10	51	102	08 01	52	102	08 53	52	101	09 45	52	101	10 37	51	100
77	06 39	52	101	07 31	52	101	08 23	51	100	09 14	52	100	10 06	52	99
78	06 09	52	100	07 01	51	100	07 52	52	99	08 44	52	99	09 36	51	98
79	05 38	52	100	06 30	52	99	07 22	51	98	08 13	52	98	09 05	51	97
80	05 08	+52	99	06 00	+51	98	06 51	+52	98	07 43	+51	97	08 34	+52	97
81	04 37	52	98	05 29	51	97	06 20	52	97	07 12	51	96	08 03	52	96
82	04 07	51	97	04 58	52	96	05 50	51	96	06 41	52	95	07 33	51	95
83	03 36	51	96	04 27	52	95	05 19	51	95	06 10	52	95	07 02	51	94
84	03 05	52	95	03 57	51	95	04 48	52	94	05 40	51	94	06 31	51	93
85	02 34	+52	94	03 26	+51	94	04 17	+52	93	05 09	+51	93	06 00	+52	92
86	02 04	51	93	02 55	51	93	03 46	52	92	04 38	51	92	05 29	52	91
87	01 33	51	93	02 24	52	92	03 16	51	92	04 07	51	91	04 58	52	91
88	01 02	51	92	01 53	52	91	02 45	51	91	03 36	51	90	04 27	52	90
89	00 31	51	91	01 22	52	90	02 14	51	90	03 05	52	89	03 57	51	89
90	00 00	+51	90	00 51	+52	89	01 43	+51	89	02 34	+52	88	03 26	+51	88
91	−0 31	51	89	00 20	52	89	01 12	51	88	02 03	52	88	02 55	51	87
92	−1 02	52	88	−0 10	51	88	00 41	52	87	01 33	51	87	02 24	51	86
93	−1 33	52	87	−0 41	51	87	00 10	52	86	01 02	51	86	01 53	52	85
94	−2 04	52	87	−1 12	51	86	−0 21	52	86	00 31	51	85	01 22	52	85
95	−2 34	+51	86	−1 43	+52	85	−0 51	+51	85	00 00	+52	84	00 52	+51	84
96	−3 05	51	85	−2 14	52	84	−1 22	51	84	−0 31	52	83	00 21	51	83
97	−3 36	52	84	−2 44	51	83	−1 53	52	83	−1 01	51	82	−0 10	52	82
98	−4 07	52	83	−3 15	52	83	−2 23	51	82	−1 32	52	82	−0 40	51	81
99	−4 37	51	82	−3 46	52	82	−2 54	52	81	−2 02	51	81	−1 11	52	80
100	−5 08	+52	81	−4 16	+51	81	−3 25	+53	80	−2 32	+51	80	−1 41	+52	79
101	−5 38	51	80	−4 47	52	80	−3 55	52	80	−3 03	52	79	−2 11	51	79
102				−5 17	52	79	−4 25	51	79	−3 34	52	78	−2 42	52	78
103				−5 47	51	78	−4 56	52	78	−4 04	52	77	−3 12	52	77
104							−5 26	52	77	−4 34	52	76	−3 42	52	76
105							−5 56	+52	76	−5 04	+52	76	−4 12	+52	75
106										−5 34	52	75	−4 42	52	74
107													−5 11	52	73
108													−5 41	52	72

LHA	5°			6°			7°			8°			9°		
	Hc	d	Z	Hc	d	Z	Hc	d	Z	Hc	d	Z	Hc	d	Z
	° ′	′	°	° ′	′	°	° ′	′	°	° ′	′	°	° ′	′	°
70	14 29	+52	105	15 21	+52	104	16 13	+52	104	17 05	+52	103	17 57	+51	103
71	13 59	52	104	14 51	52	103	15 43	52	103	16 35	51	102	17 26	52	102
72	13 29	52	103	14 21	52	103	15 13	52	102	16 05	51	101	16 56	52	101
73	12 59	52	102	13 51	52	102	14 43	51	101	15 34	52	101	16 26	51	100
74	12 29	52	101	13 21	51	101	14 12	52	100	15 04	51	100	15 55	52	99
75	11 59	+51	100	12 50	+52	100	13 42	+51	99	14 33	+52	99	15 25	+51	98
76	11 28	52	100	12 20	51	99	13 11	52	98	14 03	51	98	14 54	51	97
77	10 58	51	99	11 49	52	98	12 41	51	98	13 32	51	97	14 23	52	97
78	10 27	52	98	11 19	51	97	12 10	51	97	13 01	52	96	13 53	51	96
79	09 56	52	97	10 48	51	96	11 39	52	96	12 31	51	95	13 22	51	95
80	09 26	+51	96	10 17	+52	96	11 09	+51	95	12 00	+51	94	12 51	+51	94
81	08 55	51	95	09 46	52	95	10 38	51	94	11 29	51	94	12 20	51	93
82	08 24	52	94	09 16	51	94	10 07	51	93	10 58	51	93	11 49	52	92
83	07 53	52	93	08 45	51	93	09 36	51	92	10 27	52	92	11 19	51	91
84	07 22	52	93	08 14	51	92	09 05	51	92	09 56	52	91	10 48	51	91
85	06 52	+51	92	07 43	+51	91	08 34	+52	91	09 26	+51	90	10 17	+51	90
86	06 21	51	91	07 12	51	90	08 03	52	90	08 55	51	89	09 46	51	89
87	05 50	51	90	06 41	51	90	07 32	52	89	08 24	51	88	09 15	51	88
88	05 19	51	89	06 10	52	89	07 02	51	88	07 53	51	88	08 44	51	87
89	04 48	51	88	05 39	52	88	06 31	51	87	07 22	51	87	08 13	51	86
90	04 17	+51	87	05 08	+52	87	06 00	+51	86	06 51	+51	86	07 42	+52	85
91	03 46	52	87	04 38	51	86	05 29	51	86	06 20	52	85	07 12	51	85
92	03 15	52	86	04 07	51	85	04 58	52	85	05 50	51	84	06 41	51	84
93	02 45	51	85	03 36	51	84	04 27	52	84	05 19	51	83	06 10	52	83
94	02 14	51	84	03 05	52	83	03 57	51	83	04 48	52	82	05 40	51	82
95	01 43	+52	83	02 35	+51	83	03 26	+52	82	04 18	+51	82	05 09	+51	81
96	01 12	52	82	02 04	51	82	02 55	52	81	03 47	51	81	04 38	52	80
97	00 42	51	81	01 33	52	81	02 25	52	80	03 17	51	80	04 08	52	79
98	00 11	52	81	01 03	52	80	01 55	51	80	02 46	52	79	03 38	51	79
99	−0 19	52	80	00 33	51	79	01 24	52	79	02 16	51	78	03 07	52	78
100	−0 49	+51	79	00 02	+52	78	00 54	+52	78	01 46	+51	77	02 37	+52	77
101	−1 20	52	78	−0 28	52	77	00 24	52	77	01 16	51	76	02 07	52	76
102	−1 50	52	77	−0 58	52	77	−0 06	52	76	00 46	51	76	01 37	52	75
103	−2 20	52	76	−1 28	52	76	−0 36	52	75	00 16	52	75	01 08	51	74
104	−2 50	52	75	−1 58	52	75	−1 06	52	74	−0 14	52	74	00 38	52	73
105	−3 20	+52	75	−2 28	+52	74	−1 36	+52	74	−0 44	+52	73	00 08	+52	73
106	−3 50	53	74	−2 57	52	73	−2 05	52	73	−1 13	52	72	−0 21	52	72
107	−4 19	52	73	−3 27	52	72	−2 35	52	72	−1 43	53	71	−0 50	52	71
108	−4 49	53	72	−3 56	52	71	−3 04	52	71	−2 12	53	70	−1 19	52	70
109	−5 18	52	71	−4 26	53	71	−3 33	52	70	−2 41	53	70	−1 48	52	69
110	−5 47	+52	70	−4 55	+53	70	−4 02	+52	69	−3 10	+53	69	−2 17	+52	68
111				−5 24	53	69	−4 31	53	68	−3 38	52	68	−2 46	53	67
112				−5 52	52	68	−5 00	53	67	−4 07	53	67	−3 14	52	67
113							−5 28	53	67	−4 35	53	66	−3 42	52	66
114							−5 56	53	66	−5 03	52	65	−4 11	53	65
115										−5 31	+53	64	−4 38	+53	64
116													−5 06	53	63
117													−5 34	54	62

LHA	10°			11°			12°			13°			14°			LHA
	Hc	d	Z	Hc	d	Z	Hc	d	Z	Hc	d	Z	Hc	d	Z	
	° ′	′	°	° ′	′	°	° ′	′	°	° ′	′	°	° ′	′	°	
70	18 48	+52	102	19 40	+51	102	20 31	+52	101	21 23	+51	101	22 14	+51	100	290
71	18 18	51	101	19 09	52	101	20 01	51	100	20 52	51	100	21 43	51	99	289
72	17 48	51	100	18 39	51	100	19 30	52	99	20 22	51	99	21 13	51	98	288
73	17 17	52	100	18 09	51	99	19 00	51	98	19 51	51	98	20 42	51	97	287
74	16 47	51	99	17 38	51	98	18 29	51	98	19 20	51	97	20 11	51	96	286
75	16 16	+51	98	17 07	+52	97	17 59	+51	97	18 50	+51	96	19 41	+51	96	285
76	15 45	52	97	16 37	51	96	17 28	51	96	18 19	51	95	19 10	51	95	284
77	15 15	51	96	16 06	51	95	16 57	51	95	17 48	51	94	18 39	51	94	283
78	14 44	51	95	15 35	51	95	16 26	51	94	17 17	51	94	18 08	51	93	282
79	14 13	51	94	15 04	51	94	15 55	51	93	16 46	51	93	17 37	51	92	281
80	13 42	+51	93	14 33	+52	93	15 25	+51	92	16 16	+50	92	17 06	+51	91	280
81	13 11	52	93	14 03	51	92	14 54	51	91	15 45	51	91	16 36	50	90	279
82	12 41	51	92	13 32	51	91	14 23	51	91	15 14	51	90	16 05	50	90	278
83	12 10	51	91	13 01	51	90	13 52	51	90	14 43	51	89	15 34	51	89	277
84	11 39	51	90	12 30	51	89	13 21	51	89	14 12	51	88	15 03	51	88	276
85	11 08	+51	89	11 59	+51	89	12 50	+51	88	13 41	+51	88	14 32	+51	87	275
86	10 37	51	88	11 28	51	88	12 19	51	87	13 10	51	87	14 01	51	86	274
87	10 06	51	87	10 57	51	87	11 48	51	86	12 39	51	86	13 30	51	85	273
88	09 35	51	87	10 26	52	86	11 18	51	85	12 09	51	85	13 00	50	84	272
89	09 04	52	86	09 56	51	85	10 47	51	85	11 38	51	84	12 29	51	84	271
90	08 34	+51	85	09 25	+51	84	10 16	+51	84	11 07	+51	83	11 58	+51	83	270
91	08 03	51	84	08 54	51	83	09 45	51	83	10 36	52	82	11 28	51	82	269
92	07 32	51	83	08 23	52	83	09 15	51	82	10 06	51	82	10 57	51	81	268
93	07 02	51	82	07 53	51	82	08 44	51	81	09 35	51	81	10 26	52	80	267
94	06 31	51	81	07 22	52	81	08 14	51	80	09 05	51	80	09 56	51	79	266
95	06 00	+52	81	06 52	+51	80	07 43	+51	80	08 34	+52	79	09 26	+51	79	265
96	05 30	51	80	06 21	52	79	07 13	51	79	08 04	52	78	08 56	51	78	264
97	05 00	51	79	05 51	52	78	06 43	51	78	07 34	51	77	08 25	52	77	263
98	04 29	52	78	05 21	51	78	06 12	52	77	07 04	51	77	07 55	52	76	262
99	03 59	52	77	04 51	51	77	05 42	52	76	06 34	51	76	07 25	52	75	261
100	03 29	+52	76	04 21	+51	76	05 12	+52	75	06 04	+52	75	06 56	+51	74	260
101	02 59	52	75	03 51	52	75	04 43	51	74	05 34	52	74	06 26	52	73	259
102	02 29	52	75	03 21	52	74	04 13	52	74	05 05	51	73	05 56	52	73	258
103	01 59	52	74	02 51	52	73	03 43	52	73	04 35	52	72	05 27	52	72	257
104	01 30	52	73	02 22	52	72	03 14	52	72	04 06	52	71	04 58	52	71	256
105	01 00	+52	72	01 52	+52	72	02 44	+52	71	03 36	+53	71	04 29	+52	70	255
106	00 31	52	71	01 23	52	71	02 15	52	70	03 07	53	70	04 00	52	69	254
107	00 02	52	70	00 54	52	70	01 46	53	69	02 39	52	69	03 31	52	68	253
108	−0 27	52	69	00 25	52	69	01 17	53	69	02 10	52	68	03 02	52	68	252
109	−0 56	52	69	−0 04	53	68	00 49	52	68	01 41	53	67	02 34	52	67	251
110	−1 25	+53	68	−0 32	+52	67	00 20	+53	67	01 13	+52	66	02 05	+53	66	250
111	−1 53	52	67	−1 01	53	66	−0 08	53	66	00 45	52	65	01 37	53	65	249
112	−2 22	53	66	−1 29	53	66	−0 36	53	65	00 17	52	65	01 09	53	64	248
113	−2 50	53	65	−1 57	53	65	−1 04	53	64	−0 11	53	64	00 42	52	63	247
114	−3 18	53	64	−2 25	53	64	−1 32	53	63	−0 39	53	63	00 14	53	62	246
115	−3 45	+53	63	−2 52	+53	63	−1 59	+53	63	−1 06	+53	62	−0 13	+53	62	245
116	−4 13	53	63	−3 20	53	62	−2 27	54	62	−1 33	53	61	−0 40	53	61	244
117	−4 40	53	62	−3 47	53	61	−2 54	54	61	−2 00	53	60	−1 07	53	60	243
118	−5 07	53	61	−4 14	53	60	−3 21	54	60	−2 27	53	59	−1 34	54	59	242
119	−5 34	53	60	−4 41	54	59	−3 47	53	59	−2 54	54	59	−2 00	54	58	241
120				−5 07	+53	59	−4 14	+54	58	−3 20	+54	58	−2 26	+54	57	240
121				−5 33	53	58	−4 40	54	57	−3 46	54	57	−2 52	54	56	239
122							−5 06	54	56	−4 12	54	56	−3 18	54	55	238
123							−5 31	54	55	−4 37	54	55	−3 43	54	55	237
124										−5 02	54	54	−4 08	54	54	236
125										−5 27	+54	53	−4 33	+55	53	235
126													−4 57	54	52	234
127													−5 22	55	51	233
128													−5 45	54	50	232

0°	1°	2°	3°	4°	5°	6°	7°	8°	9°	10°	11°	12°	13°	14°

S. Lat. {LHA greater than 180°....... Zn=180−Z; LHA less than 180°.......... Zn=180+Z}

DECLINATION (0°-14°) SAME NAME AS LATITUDE

N. Lat. {LHA greater than 180°....... Zn=Z
{LHA less than 180°........... Zn=360−Z

DECLINATION (0°-14°) CONTRARY NAME TO LATITUDE

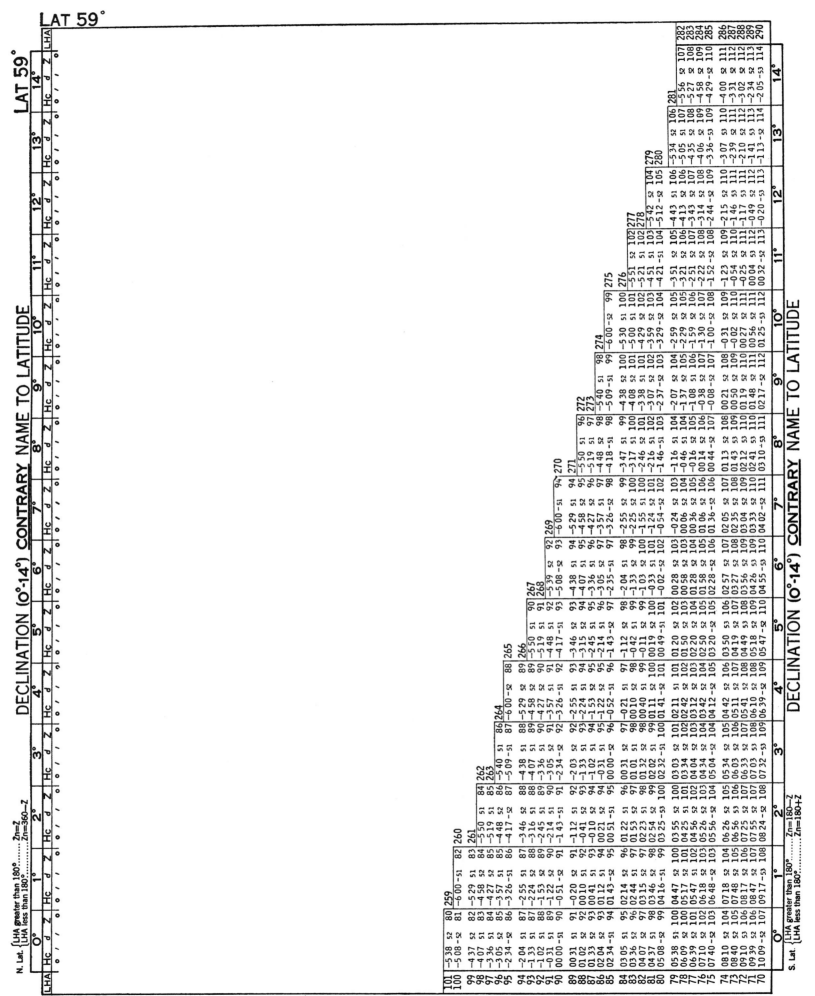

LHA	0° Hc	0° d	0° Z	1° Hc	1° d	1° Z	2° Hc	2° d	2° Z	3° Hc	3° d	3° Z	4° Hc	4° d	4° Z
	° ′	′	°	° ′	′	°	° ′	′	°	° ′	′	°	° ′	′	°
101	−5 38	52	80	259											
100	−5 08	−52	81	−6 00	−51	82	260								
99	−4 37	52	82	−5 29	51	83	261								
98	−4 07	51	83	−4 58	52	84	−5 50	51	84	262					
97	−3 36	51	84	−4 27	52	85	−5 19	51	85	263					
96	−3 05	52	85	−3 57	51	85	−4 48	52	86	−5 40	51	86	264		
95	−2 34	−52	86	−3 26	−51	86	−4 17	−52	87	−5 09	−51	87	−6 00	−52	88
94	−2 04	51	87	−2 55	51	87	−3 46	52	88	−4 38	51	88	−5 29	52	89
93	−1 33	51	87	−2 24	52	88	−3 16	51	88	−4 07	51	89	−4 58	52	89
92	−1 02	51	88	−1 53	52	89	−2 45	51	89	−3 36	51	90	−4 27	52	90
91	−0 31	51	89	−1 22	52	90	−2 14	51	90	−3 05	52	91	−3 57	51	91
90	00 00	−51	90	−0 51	−52	91	−1 43	−51	91	−2 34	−52	92	−3 26	−51	92
89	00 31	51	91	−0 20	52	91	−1 12	51	92	−2 03	52	92	−2 55	51	93
88	01 02	52	92	00 10	51	92	−0 41	52	93	−1 33	51	93	−2 24	51	94
87	01 33	52	93	00 41	51	93	−0 10	52	94	−1 02	51	94	−1 53	52	95
86	02 04	52	93	01 12	51	94	00 21	52	94	−0 31	51	95	−1 22	52	95
85	02 34	−51	94	01 43	−52	95	00 51	−51	95	00 00	−52	96	−0 52	−51	96
84	03 05	51	95	02 14	52	96	01 22	51	96	00 31	52	97	−0 21	51	97
83	03 36	52	96	02 44	51	97	01 53	52	97	01 01	51	98	00 10	52	98
82	04 07	52	97	03 15	52	97	02 23	51	98	01 32	52	98	00 40	51	99
81	04 37	51	98	03 46	52	98	02 54	52	99	02 02	51	99	01 11	52	100
80	05 08	−52	99	04 16	−51	99	03 25	−53	100	02 32	−51	100	01 41	−52	101
79	05 38	51	100	04 47	52	100	03 55	52	100	03 03	52	101	02 11	51	101
78	06 09	52	100	05 17	52	101	04 25	51	101	03 34	52	102	02 42	52	102
77	06 39	52	101	05 47	51	102	04 56	52	102	04 04	52	103	03 12	52	103
76	07 10	52	102	06 18	52	103	05 26	52	103	04 34	52	104	03 42	52	104
75	07 40	−52	103	06 48	−52	103	05 56	−52	104	05 04	−52	104	04 12	−52	105
74	08 10	52	104	07 18	52	104	06 26	52	105	05 34	52	105	04 42	52	106
73	08 40	52	105	07 48	52	105	06 56	53	106	06 03	52	106	05 11	52	107
72	09 10	53	106	08 17	52	106	07 25	52	107	06 33	52	107	05 41	52	108
71	09 39	52	106	08 47	52	107	07 55	52	107	07 03	53	108	06 10	52	108
70	10 09	−52	107	09 17	−53	108	08 24	−52	108	07 32	−53	109	06 39	−52	109

LHA	5° Hc	5° d	5° Z	6° Hc	6° d	6° Z	7° Hc	7° d	7° Z	8° Hc	8° d	8° Z	9° Hc	9° d	9° Z
	° ′	′	°	° ′	′	°	° ′	′	°	° ′	′	°	° ′	′	°
95	265														
94	266														
93	−5 50	51	90	267											
92	−5 19	51	91	268											
91	−4 48	51	92	−5 39	52	92	269								
90	−4 17	−51	93	−5 08	−52	93	−6 00	−51	94	270					
89	−3 46	52	93	−4 38	51	94	−5 29	51	94	271					
88	−3 15	52	94	−4 07	51	95	−4 58	52	95	−5 50	51	96	272		
87	−2 45	51	95	−3 36	51	96	−4 27	52	96	−5 19	51	97	273		
86	−2 14	51	96	−3 05	52	97	−3 57	51	97	−4 48	52	98	−5 40	51	98
85	−1 43	−52	97	−2 35	−51	97	−3 26	−52	98	−4 18	−51	98	−5 09	−51	99
84	−1 12	52	98	−2 04	51	98	−2 55	52	99	−3 47	51	99	−4 38	52	100
83	−0 42	51	99	−1 33	52	99	−2 25	52	100	−3 17	51	100	−4 08	52	101
82	−0 11	52	99	−1 03	52	100	−1 55	51	100	−2 46	52	101	−3 38	51	101
81	00 19	52	100	−0 33	51	101	−1 24	52	101	−2 16	51	102	−3 07	52	102
80	00 49	−51	101	−0 02	−52	102	−0 54	−52	102	−1 46	−51	103	−2 37	−52	103
79	01 20	52	102	00 28	52	103	−0 24	52	103	−1 16	51	104	−2 07	52	104
78	01 50	52	103	00 58	52	103	00 06	52	104	−0 46	51	104	−1 37	52	105
77	02 20	52	104	01 28	52	104	00 36	52	105	−0 16	52	105	−1 08	51	106
76	02 50	52	105	01 58	52	105	01 06	52	106	00 14	52	106	−0 38	52	107
75	03 20	−52	105	02 28	−52	106	01 36	−52	106	00 44	−52	107	−0 08	−52	107
74	03 50	53	106	02 57	52	107	02 05	52	107	01 13	52	108	00 21	52	108
73	04 19	52	107	03 27	52	108	02 35	52	108	01 43	53	109	00 50	52	109
72	04 49	53	108	03 56	52	109	03 04	52	109	02 12	53	110	01 19	52	110
71	05 18	52	109	04 26	53	109	03 33	52	110	02 41	53	110	01 48	52	111
70	05 47	−52	110	04 55	−53	110	04 02	−52	111	03 10	−53	111	02 17	−52	112

LHA	10° Hc	10° d	10° Z	11° Hc	11° d	11° Z	12° Hc	12° d	12° Z	13° Hc	13° d	13° Z	14° Hc	14° d	14° Z	LHA
	° ′	′	°	° ′	′	°	° ′	′	°	° ′	′	°	° ′	′	°	
86	274															
85	−6 00	−52	99	275												
84	−5 30	51	100	276												
83	−5 00	51	101	−5 51	52	102	277									
82	−4 29	52	102	−5 21	51	102	278									
81	−3 59	52	103	−4 51	51	103	−5 42	52	104	279						
80	−3 29	−52	104	−4 21	−51	104	−5 12	−52	105	280						
79	−2 59	52	105	−3 51	52	105	−4 43	51	106	−5 34	52	106	281			
78	−2 29	52	105	−3 21	52	106	−4 13	52	106	−5 05	51	107	−5 56	52	107	282
77	−1 59	52	106	−2 51	52	107	−3 43	52	107	−4 35	52	108	−5 27	52	108	283
76	−1 30	52	107	−2 22	52	108	−3 14	52	108	−4 06	52	109	−4 58	52	109	284
75	−1 00	−52	108	−1 52	−52	108	−2 44	−52	109	−3 36	−53	109	−4 29	−52	110	285
74	−0 31	52	109	−1 23	52	109	−2 15	52	110	−3 07	53	110	−4 00	52	111	286
73	−0 02	52	110	−0 54	52	110	−1 46	53	111	−2 39	52	111	−3 31	52	112	287
72	00 27	52	111	−0 25	52	111	−1 17	53	111	−2 10	52	112	−3 02	52	112	288
71	00 56	52	111	00 04	53	112	−0 49	52	112	−1 41	53	113	−2 34	52	113	289
70	01 25	−53	112	00 32	−52	113	−0 20	−53	113	−1 13	−52	114	−2 05	−53	114	290

S. Lat. {LHA greater than 180°....... Zn=180−Z
{LHA less than 180°........... Zn=180+Z

DECLINATION (0°-14°) CONTRARY NAME TO LATITUDE

N. Lat. {LHA greater than 180°....... Zn=Z; LHA less than 180°........... Zn=360−Z}

DECLINATION (0°-14°) CONTRARY NAME TO LATITUDE

LHA	0° Hc	d	Z	1° Hc	d	Z	2° Hc	d	Z	3° Hc	d	Z
	° ′	′	°	° ′	′	°	° ′	′	°	° ′	′	°
69	10 38	52	108	09 46	53	109	08 53	52	109	08 01	52	110
68	11 08	53	109	10 15	52	110	09 23	53	110	08 30	53	111
67	11 37	53	110	10 44	52	111	09 52	53	111	08 59	53	112
66	12 06	53	111	11 13	53	111	10 20	52	112	09 28	53	112
65	12 34	−52	112	11 42	−53	112	10 49	−53	113	09 56	−53	113
64	13 03	53	113	12 10	53	113	11 17	53	114	10 24	53	114
63	13 31	53	114	12 38	53	114	11 45	53	115	10 52	53	115
62	14 00	53	115	13 07	54	115	12 13	53	116	11 20	53	116
61	14 28	54	115	13 34	53	116	12 41	53	116	11 48	53	117
60	14 55	−53	116	14 02	−53	117	13 09	−54	117	12 15	−53	118
59	15 23	53	117	14 30	54	118	13 36	53	118	12 43	54	119
58	15 50	53	118	14 57	54	119	14 03	53	119	13 10	54	120
57	16 17	53	119	15 24	54	120	14 30	54	120	13 36	53	121
56	16 44	53	120	15 51	54	121	14 57	54	121	14 03	54	121
55	17 11	−54	121	16 17	−54	121	15 23	−54	122	14 29	−54	122
54	17 37	54	122	16 43	54	122	15 49	54	123	14 55	54	123
53	18 03	54	123	17 09	54	123	16 15	54	124	15 21	54	124
52	18 29	54	124	17 35	54	124	16 41	55	125	15 46	54	125
51	18 55	55	125	18 00	54	125	17 06	55	126	16 11	54	126
50	19 20	−54	126	18 26	−55	126	17 31	−55	127	16 36	−54	127
49	19 45	55	127	18 50	54	127	17 56	55	128	17 01	55	128
48	20 10	55	128	19 15	55	128	18 20	55	129	17 25	55	129
47	20 34	55	129	19 39	55	129	18 44	55	130	17 49	55	130
46	20 58	55	130	20 03	55	130	19 08	56	131	18 12	55	131
45	21 22	−56	131	20 26	−55	131	19 31	−55	131	18 36	−56	132
44	21 45	56	132	20 49	55	132	19 54	56	132	18 58	55	133
43	22 08	56	133	21 12	55	133	20 17	56	133	19 21	56	134
42	22 30	55	134	21 35	56	134	20 39	56	134	19 43	56	135
41	22 52	55	135	21 57	56	135	21 01	56	135	20 05	56	136
40	23 14	−56	136	22 18	−56	136	21 22	−56	136	20 26	−56	137
39	23 36	56	137	22 40	57	137	21 43	56	137	20 47	56	138
38	23 57	57	138	23 00	56	138	22 04	56	138	21 08	57	139
37	24 17	56	139	23 21	57	139	22 24	56	139	21 28	57	140
36	24 38	57	140	23 41	57	140	22 44	56	140	21 48	57	141
35	24 57	−56	141	24 01	−57	141	23 04	−57	142	22 07	−57	142
34	25 17	57	142	24 20	57	142	23 23	57	143	22 26	57	143
33	25 36	58	143	24 38	57	143	23 41	57	144	22 44	57	144
32	25 54	57	144	24 57	57	144	24 00	58	145	23 02	57	145
31	26 12	57	145	25 15	58	145	24 17	57	146	23 20	58	146
30	26 29	−57	146	25 32	−58	146	24 34	−57	147	23 37	−58	147
29	26 46	57	147	25 49	58	147	24 51	58	148	23 53	57	148
28	27 03	58	148	26 05	58	149	25 07	57	149	24 10	58	149
27	27 19	58	149	26 21	58	150	25 23	58	150	24 25	58	150
26	27 35	58	150	26 37	59	151	25 38	58	151	24 40	58	151
25	27 50	−59	152	26 51	−58	152	25 53	−58	152	24 55	−58	152
24	28 04	58	153	27 06	59	153	26 07	58	153	25 09	58	153
23	28 18	58	154	27 20	59	154	26 21	58	154	25 23	59	154
22	28 32	59	155	27 33	59	155	26 34	58	155	25 36	59	156
21	28 44	58	156	27 46	59	156	26 47	59	156	25 48	58	157
20	28 57	−59	157	27 58	−59	157	26 59	−59	157	26 00	−58	158
19	29 09	59	158	28 10	59	158	27 11	59	159	26 12	59	159
18	29 20	59	159	28 21	59	159	27 22	59	160	26 23	59	160
17	29 30	59	160	28 31	59	161	27 32	59	161	26 33	59	161
16	29 41	60	162	28 41	59	162	27 42	59	162	26 43	59	162
15	29 50	−59	163	28 51	−60	163	27 51	−59	163	26 52	−59	163
14	29 59	59	164	29 00	60	164	28 00	59	164	27 01	60	164
13	30 07	59	165	29 08	60	165	28 08	59	165	27 09	60	165
12	30 15	59	166	29 16	60	166	28 16	60	166	27 16	59	167
11	30 22	59	167	29 23	60	167	28 23	60	168	27 23	59	168
10	30 29	−60	168	29 29	−60	169	28 29	−59	169	27 30	−60	169
9	30 35	60	170	29 35	60	170	28 35	60	170	27 35	59	170
8	30 40	60	171	29 40	60	171	28 40	59	171	27 41	60	171
7	30 45	60	172	29 45	60	172	28 45	60	172	27 45	60	172
6	30 49	60	173	29 49	60	173	28 49	60	173	27 49	60	173
5	30 52	−60	174	29 52	−60	174	28 52	−60	174	27 52	−59	174
4	30 55	60	175	29 55	60	175	28 55	60	175	27 55	60	176
3	30 57	60	177	29 57	60	177	28 57	60	177	27 57	60	177
2	30 59	60	178	29 59	60	178	28 59	60	178	27 59	60	178
1	31 00	60	179	30 00	60	179	29 00	60	179	28 00	60	179
0	31 00	−60	180	30 00	−60	180	29 00	−60	180	28 00	−60	180

LHA	4° Hc	d	Z	5° Hc	d	Z	6° Hc	d	Z	7° Hc	d	Z
	° ′	′	°	° ′	′	°	° ′	′	°	° ′	′	°
69	07 09	53	110	06 16	52	111	05 24	53	111	04 31	53	112
68	07 37	52	111	06 45	53	112	05 52	52	112	05 00	53	113
67	08 06	52	112	07 14	53	112	06 21	53	113	05 28	53	113
66	08 35	53	113	07 42	53	113	06 49	53	114	05 56	53	114
65	09 03	−53	114	08 10	−53	114	07 17	−53	115	06 24	−53	115
64	09 31	53	115	08 38	53	115	07 45	53	116	06 52	53	116
63	09 59	53	116	09 06	53	116	08 13	53	117	07 20	53	117
62	10 27	53	116	09 34	53	117	08 41	54	117	07 47	53	118
61	10 55	54	117	10 01	53	118	09 08	53	118	08 15	54	119
60	11 22	−53	118	10 29	−54	119	09 35	−53	119	08 42	−54	120
59	11 49	53	119	10 56	54	120	10 02	54	120	09 08	53	121
58	12 16	54	120	11 22	53	121	10 29	54	121	09 35	54	121
57	12 43	54	121	11 49	54	121	10 55	54	122	10 01	54	122
56	13 09	54	122	12 15	54	122	11 21	54	123	10 27	54	123
55	13 35	−54	123	12 41	−54	123	11 47	−54	124	10 53	−54	124
54	14 01	54	124	13 07	54	124	12 13	55	125	11 18	54	125
53	14 27	55	125	13 32	54	125	12 38	55	126	11 43	54	126
52	14 52	55	126	13 57	54	126	13 03	55	126	12 08	54	127
51	15 17	55	127	14 22	54	127	13 28	55	127	12 33	55	128
50	15 42	−55	128	14 47	−55	128	13 52	−55	128	12 57	−55	129
49	16 06	55	128	15 11	55	129	14 16	55	129	13 21	55	130
48	16 30	55	129	15 35	55	130	14 40	55	130	13 45	55	131
47	16 54	55	130	15 59	56	131	15 03	55	131	14 08	55	132
46	17 17	55	131	16 22	56	132	15 26	55	132	14 31	55	133
45	17 40	−55	132	16 45	−56	133	15 49	−55	133	14 54	−56	133
44	18 03	56	133	17 07	55	134	16 12	56	134	15 16	56	134
43	18 25	56	134	17 29	55	135	16 34	56	135	15 38	56	135
42	18 47	56	135	17 51	56	136	16 55	56	136	15 59	56	136
41	19 09	56	136	18 13	56	137	17 17	57	137	16 20	56	137
40	19 30	−56	137	18 34	−56	138	17 38	−57	138	16 41	−56	138
39	19 51	57	138	18 54	56	139	17 58	56	139	17 02	57	139
38	20 11	56	139	19 15	57	140	18 18	56	140	17 22	57	140
37	20 31	56	140	19 35	57	141	18 38	57	141	17 41	57	141
36	20 51	57	141	19 54	57	142	18 57	57	142	18 00	57	142
35	21 10	−57	142	20 13	−57	143	19 16	−57	143	18 19	−57	143
34	21 29	57	143	20 32	57	144	19 35	58	144	18 37	57	144
33	21 47	57	144	20 50	57	145	19 53	58	145	18 55	57	145
32	22 05	57	145	21 08	58	146	20 10	57	146	19 13	58	146
31	22 22	57	146	21 25	58	147	20 27	57	147	19 30	58	147
30	22 39	−57	147	21 42	−58	148	20 44	−58	148	19 46	−57	148
29	22 56	58	148	21 58	58	149	21 00	58	149	20 02	58	149
28	23 12	58	149	22 14	58	150	21 16	58	150	20 18	58	150
27	23 27	58	150	22 29	58	151	21 31	58	151	20 33	58	151
26	23 42	58	152	22 44	58	152	21 46	58	152	20 48	59	152
25	23 57	−59	153	22 58	−58	153	22 00	−58	153	21 02	−59	153
24	24 11	59	154	23 12	58	154	22 14	59	154	21 15	58	154
23	24 24	58	155	23 26	59	155	22 27	58	155	21 29	59	155
22	24 37	58	156	23 39	59	156	22 40	59	156	21 41	59	156
21	24 50	59	157	23 51	59	157	22 52	59	157	21 53	59	158
20	25 02	−59	158	24 03	−59	158	23 04	−59	158	22 05	−59	159
19	25 13	59	159	24 14	59	159	23 15	59	159	22 16	59	160
18	25 24	59	160	24 25	59	160	23 26	60	160	22 26	59	161
17	25 34	59	161	24 35	59	161	23 36	60	162	22 36	59	162
16	25 44	60	162	24 44	59	162	23 45	59	163	22 46	59	163
15	25 53	−60	163	24 53	−59	164	23 54	−59	164	22 55	−60	164
14	26 01	59	164	25 02	59	165	24 03	60	165	23 03	59	165
13	26 09	59	166	25 10	60	166	24 10	59	166	23 11	60	166
12	26 17	60	167	25 17	59	167	24 18	60	167	23 18	59	167
11	26 24	60	168	25 24	60	168	24 24	59	168	23 25	60	168
10	26 30	−60	169	25 30	−59	169	24 31	−60	169	23 31	−60	169
9	26 36	60	170	25 36	60	170	24 36	60	170	23 36	59	170
8	26 41	60	171	25 41	60	171	24 41	60	171	23 41	59	171
7	26 45	60	172	25 45	59	172	24 46	60	172	23 46	60	172
6	26 49	60	173	25 49	60	173	24 49	59	173	23 50	60	174
5	26 53	−60	174	25 53	−60	175	24 53	−60	175	23 53	−60	175
4	26 55	60	176	25 55	60	176	24 55	60	176	23 55	60	176
3	26 57	60	177	25 57	60	177	24 57	60	177	23 57	60	177
2	26 59	60	178	25 59	60	178	24 59	60	178	23 59	60	178
1	27 00	60	179	26 00	60	179	25 00	60	179	24 00	60	179
0	27 00	−60	180	26 00	−60	180	25 00	−60	180	24 00	−60	180

LHA	8° Hc	d	Z	9° Hc	d	Z	10° Hc	d	Z	11° Hc	d	Z
	° ′	′	°	° ′	′	°	° ′	′	°	° ′	′	°
69	03 38	52	112	02 46	53	113	01 53	52	113	01 01	53	114
68	04 07	53	113	03 14	52	113	02 22	53	114	01 29	53	114
67	04 35	53	114	03 42	52	114	02 50	53	115	01 57	53	115
66	05 03	52	115	04 11	53	115	03 18	53	116	02 25	53	116
65	05 31	−53	116	04 38	−53	116	03 45	−53	117	02 52	−53	117
64	05 59	53	117	05 06	53	117	04 13	53	117	03 20	53	118
63	06 27	53	117	05 34	54	118	04 40	53	118	03 47	53	119
62	06 54	53	118	06 01	54	119	05 07	53	119	04 14	53	120
61	07 21	53	119	06 28	54	120	05 34	53	120	04 41	54	121
60	07 48	−54	120	06 54	−53	121	06 01	−54	121	05 07	−53	121
59	08 15	54	121	07 21	54	121	06 27	54	122	05 33	53	122
58	08 41	54	122	07 47	54	122	06 53	54	123	05 59	53	123
57	09 07	54	123	08 13	54	123	07 19	54	124	06 25	54	124
56	09 33	54	124	08 39	54	124	07 45	54	125	06 51	55	125
55	09 59	−55	125	09 04	−54	125	08 10	−54	125	07 16	−54	126
54	10 24	54	126	09 30	55	126	08 35	54	126	07 41	55	127
53	10 49	55	126	09 54	54	127	09 00	55	127	08 05	54	128
52	11 14	55	127	10 19	55	128	09 24	54	128	08 30	55	129
51	11 38	55	128	10 43	54	129	09 49	55	129	08 54	55	130
50	12 02	−55	129	11 07	−55	130	10 12	−55	130	09 17	−55	130
49	12 26	55	130	11 31	55	131	10 36	55	131	09 41	55	131
48	12 50	56	131	11 54	55	131	10 59	55	132	10 04	55	132
47	13 13	56	132	12 17	55	132	11 22	55	133	10 27	56	133
46	13 36	56	133	12 40	55	133	11 45	56	134	10 49	56	134
45	13 58	−56	134	13 02	−55	134	12 07	−56	135	11 11	−56	135
44	14 20	56	135	13 24	55	135	12 29	56	136	11 33	56	136
43	14 42	56	136	13 46	56	136	12 50	56	137	11 54	56	137
42	15 03	56	137	14 07	56	137	13 11	56	137	12 15	56	138
41	15 24	56	138	14 28	56	138	13 32	56	138	12 36	57	139
40	15 45	−56	139	14 49	−57	139	13 52	−56	139	12 56	−57	140
39	16 05	56	140	15 09	57	140	14 12	56	140	13 16	57	141
38	16 25	57	141	15 28	56	141	14 32	57	141	13 35	57	142
37	16 44	56	142	15 48	57	142	14 51	57	142	13 54	57	143
36	17 03	56	143	16 07	57	143	15 10	57	143	14 13	57	144
35	17 22	−57	144	16 25	−57	144	15 28	−57	144	14 31	−57	144
34	17 40	57	145	16 43	57	145	15 46	57	145	14 49	58	145
33	17 58	57	146	17 01	58	146	16 03	57	146	15 06	58	146
32	18 15	57	147	17 18	58	147	16 20	57	147	15 23	58	147
31	18 32	57	148	17 35	58	148	16 37	58	148	15 39	57	148
30	18 49	−58	149	17 51	−58	149	16 53	−58	149	15 55	−58	149
29	19 04	57	150	18 07	58	150	17 09	58	150	16 11	58	150
28	19 20	58	151	18 22	58	151	17 24	58	151	16 26	58	151
27	19 35	58	152	18 37	58	152	17 39	59	152	16 40	58	152
26	19 49	58	153	18 51	58	153	17 53	58	153	16 55	59	153
25	20 03	−58	154	19 05	−58	154	18 07	−59	154	17 08	−58	154
24	20 17	59	155	19 18	58	155	18 20	59	155	17 21	58	155
23	20 30	59	156	19 31	58	156	18 33	59	156	17 34	59	156
22	20 42	58	157	19 44	59	157	18 45	59	157	17 46	58	157
21	20 54	58	158	19 56	59	158	18 57	59	158	17 58	59	158
20	21 06	−59	159	20 07	−59	159	19 08	−59	159	18 09	−59	159
19	21 17	59	160	20 18	59	160	19 19	59	160	18 20	59	160
18	21 27	59	161	20 28	59	161	19 29	59	161	18 30	59	161
17	21 37	59	162	20 38	59	162	19 39	59	162	18 40	60	162
16	21 47	60	163	20 47	59	163	19 48	59	163	18 49	60	163
15	21 55	−59	164	20 56	−59	164	19 57	−60	164	18 57	−59	164
14	22 04	60	165	21 04	59	165	20 05	60	165	19 05	59	165
13	22 11	59	166	21 12	60	166	20 12	59	166	19 13	60	167
12	22 19	60	167	21 19	60	167	20 19	59	167	19 20	60	168
11	22 25	60	168	21 25	59	168	20 26	60	168	19 26	60	169
10	22 31	−60	169	21 31	−59	169	20 32	−60	170	19 32	−60	170
9	22 37	60	170	21 37	60	170	20 37	60	171	19 37	59	171
8	22 42	60	171	21 42	60	172	20 42	60	172	19 42	60	172
7	22 46	60	173	21 46	60	173	20 46	60	173	19 46	60	173
6	22 50	60	174	21 50	60	174	20 50	60	174	19 50	60	174
5	22 53	−60	175	21 53	−60	175	20 53	−60	175	19 53	−60	175
4	22 55	60	176	21 55	59	176	20 56	60	176	19 56	60	176
3	22 57	60	177	21 57	60	177	20 57	59	177	19 58	60	177
2	22 59	60	178	21 59	60	178	20 59	60	178	19 59	60	178
1	23 00	60	179	22 00	60	179	21 00	60	179	20 00	60	179
0	23 00	−60	180	22 00	−60	180	21 00	−60	180	20 00	−60	180

LHA	12° Hc	d	Z	13° Hc	d	Z	14° Hc	d	Z	LHA
	° ′	′	°	° ′	′	°	° ′	′	°	
69	00 08	53	114	−0 45	52	115	−1 37	53	115	291
68	00 36	53	115	−0 17	52	115	−1 09	53	116	292
67	01 04	53	116	00 11	53	116	−0 42	52	117	293
66	01 32	53	117	00 39	53	117	−0 14	53	118	294
65	01 59	−53	117	01 06	−53	118	00 13	−53	118	295
64	02 27	54	118	01 33	53	119	00 40	53	119	296
63	02 54	54	119	02 00	53	120	01 07	53	120	297
62	03 21	54	120	02 27	53	121	01 34	54	121	298
61	03 47	53	121	02 54	54	121	02 00	54	122	299
60	04 14	−54	122	03 20	−54	122	02 26	−54	123	300
59	04 40	54	123	03 46	54	123	02 52	54	124	301
58	05 06	54	124	04 12	54	124	03 18	54	125	302
57	05 31	54	125	04 37	54	125	03 43	54	125	303
56	05 56	54	125	05 02	54	126	04 08	54	126	304
55	06 22	−55	126	05 27	−54	127	04 33	−55	127	305
54	06 46	54	127	05 52	55	128	04 57	54	128	306
53	07 11	55	128	06 16	54	129	05 22	55	129	307
52	07 35	55	129	06 40	55	129	05 45	54	130	308
51	07 59	55	130	07 04	55	130	06 09	55	131	309
50	08 22	−55	131	07 27	−55	131	06 32	−55	132	310
49	08 46	56	132	07 50	55	132	06 55	55	133	311
48	09 09	56	133	08 13	55	133	07 18	55	133	312
47	09 31	55	134	08 36	56	134	07 40	55	134	313
46	09 53	55	134	08 58	56	135	08 02	55	135	314
45	10 15	−55	135	09 20	−56	136	08 24	−56	136	315
44	10 37	56	136	09 41	56	137	08 45	56	137	316
43	10 58	56	137	10 02	56	138	09 06	56	138	317
42	11 19	56	138	10 23	57	139	09 26	56	139	318
41	11 39	56	139	10 43	56	139	09 47	57	140	319
40	11 59	−56	140	11 03	−57	140	10 06	−56	141	320
39	12 19	57	141	11 22	56	141	10 26	57	142	321
38	12 38	56	142	11 42	57	142	10 45	57	143	322
37	12 57	57	143	12 00	57	143	11 03	57	144	323
36	13 16	57	144	12 19	58	144	11 21	57	144	324
35	13 34	−58	145	12 36	−57	145	11 39	−57	145	325
34	13 51	57	146	12 54	57	146	11 57	58	146	326
33	14 08	57	147	13 11	57	147	12 14	58	147	327
32	14 25	57	148	13 28	58	148	12 30	58	148	328
31	14 42	58	149	13 44	58	149	12 46	58	149	329
30	14 57	−57	150	14 00	−58	150	13 02	−58	150	330
29	15 13	58	151	14 15	58	151	13 17	58	151	331
28	15 28	58	152	14 30	58	152	13 32	59	152	332
27	15 42	58	153	14 44	58	153	13 46	58	153	333
26	15 56	58	154	14 58	58	154	14 00	59	154	334
25	16 10	−59	155	15 11	−58	155	14 13	−59	155	335
24	16 23	59	156	15 24	58	156	14 26	59	156	336
23	16 35	58	157	15 37	59	157	14 38	59	157	337
22	16 48	59	158	15 49	59	158	14 50	59	158	338
21	16 59	59	159	16 00	59	159	15 01	59	159	339
20	17 10	−59	160	16 11	−59	160	15 12	−59	160	340
19	17 21	59	161	16 22	59	161	15 23	60	161	341
18	17 31	59	162	16 32	60	162	15 32	59	162	342
17	17 40	59	163	16 41	59	163	15 42	59	163	343
16	17 49	59	164	16 50	59	164	15 51	60	164	344
15	17 58	−60	165	16 58	−59	165	15 59	−59	165	345
14	18 06	60	166	17 06	59	166	16 07	60	166	346
13	18 13	59	167	17 14	60	167	16 14	59	167	347
12	18 20	60	168	17 20	59	168	16 21	60	168	348
11	18 26	59	169	17 27	60	169	16 27	60	169	349
10	18 32	−59	170	17 33	−60	170	16 33	−60	170	350
9	18 38	60	171	17 38	60	171	16 38	60	171	351
8	18 42	60	172	17 42	59	172	16 43	60	172	352
7	18 46	59	173	17 47	60	173	16 47	60	173	353
6	18 50	60	174	17 50	60	174	16 50	60	174	354
5	18 53	−60	175	17 53	−60	175	16 53	−60	175	355
4	18 56	60	176	17 56	60	176	16 56	60	176	356
3	18 58	60	177	17 58	60	177	16 58	60	177	357
2	18 59	60	178	17 59	60	178	16 59	60	178	358
1	19 00	60	179	18 00	60	179	17 00	60	179	359
0	19 00	−60	180	18 00	−60	180	17 00	−60	180	360

S. Lat. {LHA greater than 180°....... Zn=180−Z; LHA less than 180°........... Zn=180+Z}

DECLINATION (0°-14°) CONTRARY NAME TO LATITUDE

LAT 59°

N. Lat. {LHA greater than 180°........ Zn=Z; LHA less than 180°........... Zn=360−Z}

DECLINATION (15°-29°) SAME NAME AS LATITUDE

	15°			16°			17°			18°			19°		
LHA	Hc	d	Z	Hc	d	Z	Hc	d	Z	Hc	d	Z	Hc	d	Z
	° ′	′	°	° ′	′	°	° ′	′	°	° ′	′	°	° ′	′	°
0	46 00	+60	180	47 00	+60	180	48 00	+60	180	49 00	+60	180	50 00	+60	180
1	46 00	60	179	47 00	60	179	48 00	60	179	49 00	60	179	50 00	60	179
2	45 59	60	177	46 59	60	177	47 59	59	177	48 58	60	177	49 58	60	177
3	45 57	60	176	46 57	60	176	47 57	60	176	48 57	59	176	49 56	60	176
4	45 54	60	174	46 54	60	174	47 54	60	174	48 54	60	174	49 54	60	174
5	45 51	+60	173	46 51	+59	173	47 50	+60	173	48 50	+60	173	49 50	+60	173
6	45 47	59	172	46 46	60	172	47 46	60	171	48 46	60	171	49 46	60	171
7	45 42	60	170	46 42	59	170	47 41	60	170	48 41	60	170	49 41	59	170
8	45 36	60	169	46 36	60	169	47 36	59	169	48 35	60	169	49 35	59	168
9	45 30	59	168	46 29	60	167	47 29	60	167	48 29	59	167	49 28	60	167
10	45 23	+59	166	46 22	+60	166	47 22	+59	166	48 21	+60	166	49 21	+59	165
11	45 15	60	165	46 15	59	165	47 14	59	164	48 13	60	164	49 13	59	164
12	45 07	59	164	46 06	59	163	47 05	59	163	48 04	60	163	49 04	59	163
13	44 58	59	162	45 57	59	162	46 56	59	162	47 55	59	161	48 54	59	161
14	44 48	59	161	45 47	59	161	46 46	59	160	47 45	59	160	48 44	59	160
15	44 37	+59	159	45 36	+59	159	46 35	+59	159	47 34	+59	159	48 33	+58	158
16	44 26	59	158	45 25	59	158	46 24	58	158	47 22	59	157	48 21	58	157
17	44 14	59	157	45 13	58	157	46 11	59	156	47 10	58	156	48 08	59	156
18	44 02	58	156	45 00	59	155	45 59	58	155	46 57	58	155	47 55	59	154
19	43 48	59	154	44 47	58	154	45 45	58	154	46 43	58	153	47 41	59	153
20	43 35	+58	153	44 33	+58	153	45 31	+58	152	46 29	+58	152	47 27	+58	151
21	43 20	58	152	44 18	58	151	45 16	58	151	46 14	58	151	47 12	58	150
22	43 05	58	150	44 03	58	150	45 01	58	150	45 59	57	149	46 56	58	149
23	42 50	57	149	43 47	58	149	44 45	57	148	45 42	58	148	46 40	57	147
24	42 33	58	148	43 31	57	147	44 28	58	147	45 26	57	147	46 23	57	146
25	42 17	+57	147	43 14	+57	146	44 11	+57	146	45 08	+57	145	46 05	+57	145
26	41 59	58	145	42 57	57	145	43 54	56	144	44 50	57	144	45 47	57	144
27	41 42	56	144	42 38	57	144	43 35	57	143	44 32	57	143	45 29	56	142
28	41 23	57	143	42 20	57	142	43 17	56	142	44 13	56	142	45 09	57	141
29	41 04	57	142	42 01	56	141	42 57	57	141	43 54	56	140	44 50	56	140
30	40 45	+56	140	41 41	+56	140	42 37	+57	140	43 34	+56	139	44 30	+55	139
31	40 25	56	139	41 21	56	139	42 17	56	138	43 13	56	138	44 09	55	137
32	40 04	56	138	41 00	56	138	41 56	56	137	42 52	56	137	43 48	55	136
33	39 43	56	137	40 39	56	136	41 35	55	136	42 30	56	135	43 26	55	135
34	39 22	56	136	40 18	55	135	41 13	56	135	42 09	55	134	43 04	55	134
35	39 00	+56	135	39 56	+55	134	40 51	+55	134	41 46	+55	133	42 41	+55	133
36	38 38	55	133	39 33	55	133	40 28	55	132	41 23	55	132	42 18	55	131
37	38 15	55	132	39 10	55	132	40 05	55	131	41 00	55	131	41 55	54	130
38	37 52	55	131	38 47	55	131	39 42	54	130	40 36	55	130	41 31	54	129
39	37 29	54	130	38 23	55	130	39 18	54	129	40 12	55	128	41 07	54	128
40	37 05	+54	129	37 59	+55	128	38 54	+54	128	39 48	+54	127	40 42	+54	127
41	36 41	54	128	37 35	54	127	38 29	54	127	39 23	54	126	40 17	54	126
42	36 16	54	127	37 10	54	126	38 04	54	126	38 58	54	125	39 52	53	125
43	35 51	54	126	36 45	54	125	37 39	54	125	38 33	53	124	39 26	54	123
44	35 26	54	125	36 20	53	124	37 13	54	124	38 07	53	123	39 00	53	122
45	35 00	+54	124	35 54	+53	123	36 47	+54	122	37 41	+53	122	38 34	+53	121
46	34 34	54	123	35 28	53	122	36 21	53	121	37 14	53	121	38 07	53	120
47	34 08	53	121	35 01	54	121	35 55	53	120	36 48	53	120	37 41	52	119
48	33 42	53	120	34 35	53	120	35 28	53	119	36 21	52	119	37 13	53	118
49	33 15	53	119	34 08	53	119	35 01	52	118	35 53	53	118	36 46	52	117
50	32 48	+53	118	33 41	+52	118	34 33	+53	117	35 26	+52	117	36 18	+53	116
51	32 20	53	117	33 13	53	117	34 06	52	116	34 58	52	116	35 50	53	115
52	31 53	52	116	32 45	53	116	33 38	52	115	34 30	52	115	35 22	52	114
53	31 25	53	115	32 18	52	115	33 10	52	114	34 02	52	114	34 54	52	113
54	30 57	52	114	31 49	53	114	32 42	52	113	33 34	51	113	34 25	52	112
55	30 29	+52	113	31 21	+52	113	32 13	+52	112	33 05	+52	112	33 57	+51	111
56	30 00	52	112	30 52	52	112	31 44	52	111	32 36	52	111	33 28	51	110
57	29 32	52	111	30 24	51	111	31 15	52	110	32 07	52	110	32 59	51	109
58	29 03	52	111	29 55	51	110	30 46	52	109	31 38	51	109	32 29	52	108
59	28 34	51	110	29 25	52	109	30 17	52	108	31 09	51	108	32 00	51	107
60	28 04	+52	109	28 56	+52	108	29 48	+51	107	30 39	+51	107	31 30	+51	106
61	27 35	52	108	28 27	51	107	29 18	51	106	30 09	52	106	31 01	50	105
62	27 06	51	107	27 57	51	106	28 48	52	106	29 40	51	105	30 31	51	104
63	26 36	51	106	27 27	52	105	28 19	51	105	29 10	51	104	30 01	50	103
64	26 06	51	105	26 57	52	104	27 49	51	104	28 40	51	103	29 31	50	102
65	25 36	+51	104	26 27	+51	103	27 18	+51	103	28 09	+51	102	29 00	+51	102
66	25 06	51	103	25 57	51	102	26 48	51	102	27 39	51	101	28 30	51	101
67	24 36	51	102	25 27	51	102	26 18	51	101	27 09	51	100	28 00	50	100
68	24 06	51	101	24 57	51	101	25 48	50	100	26 38	51	99	27 29	51	99
69	23 35	51	100	24 26	51	100	25 17	51	99	26 08	50	99	26 58	51	98

	20°			21°			22°			23°			24°		
LHA	Hc	d	Z	Hc	d	Z	Hc	d	Z	Hc	d	Z	Hc	d	Z
	° ′	′	°	° ′	′	°	° ′	′	°	° ′	′	°	° ′	′	°
0	51 00	+60	180	52 00	+60	180	53 00	+60	180	54 00	+60	180	55 00	+60	180
1	51 00	60	179	52 00	60	179	53 00	60	179	54 00	60	178	55 00	60	178
2	50 58	60	177	51 58	60	177	52 58	60	177	53 58	60	177	54 58	60	177
3	50 56	60	176	51 56	60	176	52 56	60	175	53 56	60	175	54 56	60	175
4	50 54	60	174	51 54	59	174	52 53	60	174	53 53	60	174	54 53	60	174
5	50 50	+60	173	51 50	+60	172	52 50	+60	172	53 50	+59	172	54 49	+60	172
6	50 46	59	171	51 45	60	171	52 45	60	171	53 45	60	171	54 45	59	171
7	50 40	60	170	51 40	60	169	52 40	59	169	53 39	60	169	54 39	60	169
8	50 34	60	168	51 34	60	168	52 34	59	168	53 33	60	168	54 33	59	167
9	50 28	59	167	51 27	60	166	52 27	59	166	53 26	60	166	54 26	59	166
10	50 20	+60	165	51 20	+59	165	52 19	+59	165	53 18	+60	165	54 18	+59	164
11	50 12	59	164	51 11	59	164	52 10	60	163	53 10	59	163	54 09	59	163
12	50 03	59	162	51 02	59	162	52 01	59	162	53 00	59	162	53 59	59	161
13	49 53	59	161	50 52	59	161	51 51	59	160	52 50	59	160	53 49	59	160
14	49 43	58	159	50 41	59	159	51 40	59	159	52 39	59	159	53 38	58	158
15	49 31	+59	158	50 30	+59	158	51 29	+58	157	52 27	+59	157	53 26	+58	157
16	49 19	59	157	50 18	58	156	51 16	59	156	52 15	58	156	53 13	58	155
17	49 07	58	155	50 05	58	155	51 03	59	155	52 02	58	154	53 00	58	154
18	48 54	58	154	49 52	58	153	50 50	58	153	51 48	58	153	52 46	58	152
19	48 40	58	152	49 38	57	152	50 35	58	152	51 33	58	151	52 31	58	151
20	48 25	+58	151	49 23	+57	151	50 20	+58	150	51 18	+58	150	52 16	+57	149
21	48 10	57	150	49 07	58	149	50 05	57	149	51 02	57	148	51 59	58	148
22	47 54	57	148	48 51	57	148	49 48	58	147	50 46	57	147	51 43	57	147
23	47 37	57	147	48 34	57	147	49 31	57	146	50 28	57	146	51 25	57	145
24	47 20	57	146	48 17	57	145	49 14	57	145	50 11	56	144	51 07	57	144
25	47 02	+57	144	47 59	+57	144	48 56	+56	143	49 52	+57	143	50 49	+56	142
26	46 44	57	143	47 41	56	143	48 37	56	142	49 33	57	142	50 30	56	141
27	46 25	57	142	47 22	56	141	48 18	56	141	49 14	56	140	50 10	56	140
28	46 06	56	141	47 02	56	140	47 58	56	140	48 54	56	139	49 50	55	138
29	45 46	56	139	46 42	56	139	47 38	55	138	48 33	56	138	49 29	55	137
30	45 25	+56	138	46 21	+56	137	47 17	+55	137	48 12	+55	136	49 07	+55	136
31	45 04	56	137	46 00	55	136	46 55	56	136	47 51	55	135	48 46	54	135
32	44 43	55	136	45 38	56	135	46 34	55	134	47 29	54	134	48 23	55	133
33	44 21	55	134	45 16	55	134	46 11	55	133	47 06	55	133	48 01	54	132
34	43 59	55	133	44 54	54	133	45 48	55	132	46 43	54	131	47 37	55	131
35	43 36	+55	132	44 31	+54	131	45 25	+55	131	46 20	+54	130	47 14	+54	130
36	43 13	54	131	44 07	55	130	45 02	54	130	45 56	54	129	46 50	53	128
37	42 49	55	130	43 44	54	129	44 38	54	128	45 32	53	128	46 25	54	127
38	42 25	54	128	43 19	54	128	44 13	54	127	45 07	53	127	46 00	54	126
39	42 01	54	127	42 55	53	127	43 48	54	126	44 42	53	125	45 35	53	125
40	41 36	+54	126	42 30	+53	126	43 23	+54	125	44 17	+53	124	45 10	+52	124
41	41 11	53	125	42 04	54	124	42 58	53	124	43 51	53	123	44 44	52	123
42	40 45	54	124	41 39	53	123	42 32	53	123	43 25	52	122	44 17	53	121
43	40 20	53	123	41 13	53	122	42 06	52	122	42 58	53	121	43 51	52	120
44	39 53	53	122	40 46	53	121	41 39	53	121	42 32	52	120	43 24	52	119
45	39 27	+53	121	40 20	+52	120	41 12	+53	119	42 05	+52	119	42 57	+52	118
46	39 00	53	120	39 53	52	119	40 45	53	118	41 38	52	118	42 30	51	117
47	38 33	53	119	39 26	52	118	40 18	52	117	41 10	52	117	42 02	51	116
48	38 06	52	118	38 58	52	117	39 50	52	116	40 42	52	116	41 34	51	115
49	37 38	53	116	38 31	52	116	39 23	51	115	40 14	52	115	41 06	51	114
50	37 11	+52	115	38 03	+51	115	38 54	+52	114	39 46	+51	114	40 37	+52	113
51	36 43	51	114	37 34	52	114	38 26	52	113	39 18	51	112	40 09	51	112
52	36 14	52	113	37 06	52	113	37 58	51	112	38 49	51	111	39 40	51	111
53	35 46	51	112	36 37	52	112	37 29	51	111	38 20	51	110	39 11	51	110
54	35 17	52	111	36 09	51	111	37 00	51	110	37 51	51	109	38 42	50	109
55	34 48	+52	110	35 40	+51	110	36 31	+51	109	37 22	+51	108	38 13	+50	108
56	34 19	51	109	35 10	52	109	36 02	50	108	36 52	51	108	37 43	50	107
57	33 50	51	108	34 41	51	108	35 32	51	107	36 23	50	107	37 13	51	106
58	33 21	51	108	34 12	50	107	35 02	51	106	35 53	51	106	36 44	50	105
59	32 51	51	107	33 42	51	106	34 33	50	105	35 23	51	105	36 14	50	104
60	32 21	+51	106	33 12	+51	105	34 03	+50	104	34 53	+51	104	35 44	+50	103
61	31 51	51	105	32 42	51	104	33 33	50	103	34 23	50	103	35 13	50	102
62	31 22	50	104	32 12	51	103	33 03	50	102	33 53	50	102	34 43	50	101
63	30 51	51	103	31 42	50	102	32 32	51	102	33 23	50	101	34 13	50	100
64	30 21	51	102	31 12	50	101	32 02	50	101	32 52	50	100	33 42	50	99
65	29 51	+50	101	30 41	+51	100	31 32	+50	100	32 22	+50	99	33 12	+49	98
66	29 21	50	100	30 11	50	99	31 01	50	99	31 51	50	98	32 41	50	97
67	28 50	50	99	29 40	51	99	30 31	50	98	31 21	49	97	32 10	50	97
68	28 20	50	98	29 10	50	98	30 00	50	97	30 50	50	96	31 40	49	96
69	27 49	50	97	28 39	50	97	29 29	50	96	30 19	50	95	31 09	49	95

	25°			26°			27°			28°			29°			
LHA	Hc	d	Z	Hc	d	Z	Hc	d	Z	Hc	d	Z	Hc	d	Z	LHA
	° ′	′	°	° ′	′	°	° ′	′	°	° ′	′	°	° ′	′	°	
0	56 00	+60	180	57 00	+60	180	58 00	+60	180	59 00	+60	180	60 00	+60	180	360
1	56 00	60	178	57 00	60	178	58 00	60	178	59 00	60	178	60 00	60	178	359
2	55 58	60	177	56 58	60	177	57 58	60	177	58 58	60	177	59 58	60	177	358
3	55 56	60	175	56 56	60	175	57 56	60	175	58 56	60	175	59 56	60	175	357
4	55 53	60	174	56 53	60	173	57 53	60	173	58 53	60	173	59 53	59	173	356
5	55 49	+60	172	56 49	+60	172	57 49	+60	172	58 49	+59	172	59 48	+60	171	355
6	55 44	60	170	56 44	60	170	57 44	59	170	58 43	60	170	59 43	60	170	354
7	55 39	59	169	56 38	60	169	57 38	60	168	58 38	59	168	59 37	60	168	353
8	55 32	60	167	56 32	59	167	57 31	60	167	58 31	59	166	59 30	60	166	352
9	55 25	59	166	56 24	60	165	57 24	59	165	58 23	59	165	59 22	59	164	351
10	55 17	+59	164	56 16	+59	164	57 15	+59	163	58 14	+60	163	59 14	+59	163	350
11	55 08	59	162	56 07	59	162	57 06	59	162	58 05	59	161	59 04	59	161	349
12	54 58	59	161	55 57	59	161	56 56	59	160	57 55	58	160	58 53	59	159	348
13	54 48	58	159	55 46	59	159	56 45	59	159	57 44	58	158	58 42	59	158	347
14	54 36	59	158	55 35	58	157	56 33	59	157	57 32	58	157	58 30	58	156	346
15	54 24	+59	156	55 23	+58	156	56 21	+58	155	57 19	+58	155	58 17	+58	155	345
16	54 11	59	155	55 10	58	154	56 08	58	154	57 06	57	153	58 03	58	153	344
17	53 58	58	153	54 56	58	153	55 54	57	152	56 51	58	152	57 49	57	151	343
18	53 44	57	152	54 41	58	151	55 39	57	151	56 36	58	150	57 34	57	150	342
19	53 29	57	150	54 26	58	150	55 24	57	149	56 21	57	149	57 18	57	148	341
20	53 13	+57	149	54 10	+57	148	55 07	+57	148	56 04	+57	147	57 01	+57	147	340
21	52 57	57	147	53 54	57	147	54 51	56	146	55 47	57	146	56 44	56	145	339
22	52 40	56	146	53 36	57	145	54 33	57	145	55 30	56	144	56 26	56	144	338
23	52 22	57	145	53 19	56	144	54 15	56	143	55 11	56	143	56 07	56	142	337
24	52 04	56	143	53 00	56	143	53 56	56	142	54 52	56	141	55 48	56	141	336
25	51 45	+56	142	52 41	+56	141	53 37	+56	141	54 33	+55	140	55 28	+55	139	335
26	51 26	55	140	52 21	56	140	53 17	56	139	54 13	55	139	55 08	55	138	334
27	51 06	55	139	52 01	56	139	52 57	55	138	53 52	55	137	54 47	54	137	333
28	50 45	55	138	51 40	56	137	52 36	55	137	53 31	54	136	54 25	55	135	332
29	50 24	55	136	51 19	55	136	52 14	55	135	53 09	54	135	54 03	54	134	331
30	50 02	+55	135	50 57	+55	135	51 52	+54	134	52 46	+55	133	53 41	+53	132	330
31	49 40	55	134	50 35	54	133	51 29	55	133	52 24	54	132	53 18	53	131	329
32	49 18	54	133	50 12	54	132	51 06	54	131	52 00	54	131	52 54	53	130	328
33	48 55	54	131	49 49	54	131	50 43	54	130	51 37	53	129	52 30	53	129	327
34	48 32	53	130	49 25	54	129	50 19	54	129	51 13	53	128	52 06	53	127	326
35	48 08	+53	129	49 01	+54	128	49 55	+53	128	50 48	+53	127	51 41	+52	126	325
36	47 43	54	128	48 37	53	127	49 30	53	126	50 23	53	126	51 16	52	125	324
37	47 19	53	126	48 12	53	126	49 05	53	125	49 58	52	124	50 50	52	124	323
38	46 54	53	125	47 47	52	125	48 39	53	124	49 32	52	123	50 24	52	122	322
39	46 28	53	124	47 21	53	123	48 14	52	123	49 06	52	122	49 58	52	121	321
40	46 02	+53	123	46 55	+52	122	47 47	+53	122	48 40	+51	121	49 31	+52	120	320
41	45 36	53	122	46 29	52	121	47 21	52	120	48 13	51	120	49 04	52	119	319
42	45 10	52	121	46 02	52	120	46 54	52	119	47 46	51	119	48 37	51	118	318
43	44 43	52	120	45 35	52	119	46 27	51	118	47 18	52	117	48 10	50	117	317
44	44 16	52	119	45 08	52	118	46 00	51	117	46 51	51	116	47 42	51	116	316
45	43 49	+52	117	44 41	+51	117	45 32	+51	116	46 23	+51	115	47 14	+50	114	315
46	43 21	52	116	44 13	51	116	45 04	51	115	45 55	51	114	46 46	50	113	314
47	42 53	52	115	43 45	51	115	44 36	51	114	45 27	50	113	46 17	50	112	313
48	42 25	52	114	43 17	50	113	44 07	51	113	44 58	50	112	45 48	50	111	312
49	41 57	51	113	42 48	51	112	43 39	50	112	44 29	50	111	45 19	50	110	311
50	41 29	+50	112	42 19	+51	111	43 10	+50	111	44 00	+50	110	44 50	+50	109	310
51	41 00	51	111	41 51	50	110	42 41	50	110	43 31	50	109	44 21	50	108	309
52	40 31	51	110	41 22	50	109	42 12	50	109	43 02	50	108	43 52	49	107	308
53	40 02	50	109	40 52	50	108	41 42	50	108	42 32	50	107	43 22	49	106	307
54	39 32	51	108	40 23	50	107	41 13	50	107	42 03	49	106	42 52	49	105	306
55	39 03	+50	107	39 53	+50	106	40 43	+50	106	41 33	+49	105	42 22	+49	104	305
56	38 33	51	106	39 24	49	105	40 13	50	105	41 03	49	104	41 52	49	103	304
57	38 04	50	105	38 54	49	104	39 43	50	104	40 33	49	103	41 22	49	102	303
58	37 34	50	104	38 24	49	104	39 13	50	103	40 03	49	102	40 52	49	101	302
59	37 04	50	103	37 54	49	103	38 43	50	102	39 33	49	101	40 22	48	100	301
60	36 34	+49	102	37 23	+50	102	38 13	+49	101	39 02	+49	100	39 51	+49	99	300
61	36 03	50	101	36 53	49	101	37 42	50	100	38 32	49	99	39 21	48	99	299
62	35 33	50	100	36 23	49	100	37 12	49	99	38 01	49	98	38 50	49	98	298
63	35 03	49	100	35 52	49	99	36 41	50	98	37 31	48	97	38 19	49	97	297
64	34 32	50	99	35 22	49	98	36 11	49	97	37 00	49	97	37 49	48	96	296
65	34 01	+50	98	34 51	+49	97	35 40	+49	96	36 29	+49	96	37 18	+48	95	295
66	33 31	49	97	34 20	49	96	35 09	49	95	35 58	49	95	36 47	48	94	294
67	33 00	49	96	33 49	50	95	34 39	49	95	35 28	48	94	36 16	49	93	293
68	32 29	50	95	33 19	49	94	34 08	49	94	34 57	48	93	35 45	49	92	292
69	31 58	50	94	32 48	49	93	33 37	49	93	34 26	48	92	35 14	49	91	291

S. Lat. {LHA greater than 180°........ Zn=180−Z; LHA less than 180°........... Zn=180+Z}

DECLINATION (15°-29°) SAME NAME AS LATITUDE

N. Lat. {LHA greater than 180°........ Zn=Z ; LHA less than 180°........... Zn=360−Z}

DECLINATION (15°-29°) SAME NAME AS LATITUDE

LHA	15° Hc	d	Z	16° Hc	d	Z	17° Hc	d	Z	18° Hc	d	Z	19° Hc	d	Z
	° ′	′	°	° ′	′	°	° ′	′	°	° ′	′	°	° ′	′	°
70	23 05	+51	99	23 56	+51	99	24 47	+50	98	25 37	+51	98	26 28	+50	97
71	22 34	51	99	23 25	51	98	24 16	51	97	25 07	50	97	25 57	51	96
72	22 04	51	98	22 55	50	97	23 45	51	96	24 36	50	96	25 26	51	95
73	21 33	51	97	22 24	51	96	23 15	50	96	24 05	51	95	24 56	50	94
74	21 02	51	96	21 53	51	95	22 44	50	95	23 34	51	94	24 25	50	94
75	20 32	+50	95	21 22	+51	94	22 13	+51	94	23 04	+50	93	23 54	+50	93
76	20 01	50	94	20 51	51	94	21 42	51	93	22 33	50	92	23 23	50	92
77	19 30	51	93	20 21	50	93	21 11	51	92	22 02	50	92	22 52	50	91
78	18 59	51	92	19 50	50	92	20 40	51	91	21 31	50	91	22 21	50	90
79	18 28	51	92	19 19	50	91	20 09	51	90	21 00	50	90	21 50	51	89
80	17 57	+51	91	18 48	+51	90	19 39	+50	90	20 29	+50	89	21 19	+51	88
81	17 26	51	90	18 17	51	89	19 08	50	89	19 58	51	88	20 49	50	88
82	16 55	51	89	17 46	51	88	18 37	50	88	19 27	51	87	20 18	50	87
83	16 25	50	88	17 15	51	88	18 06	50	87	18 56	51	86	19 47	50	86
84	15 54	50	87	16 44	51	87	17 35	51	86	18 26	50	86	19 16	50	85
85	15 23	+51	86	16 14	+50	86	17 04	+51	85	17 55	+50	85	18 45	+51	84
86	14 52	51	86	15 43	50	85	16 33	51	84	17 24	51	84	18 15	50	83
87	14 21	51	85	15 12	51	84	16 03	50	84	16 53	51	83	17 44	50	82
88	13 50	51	84	14 41	51	83	15 32	51	83	16 23	50	82	17 13	51	82
89	13 20	51	83	14 11	50	82	15 01	51	82	15 52	51	81	16 43	50	81
90	12 49	+51	82	13 40	+51	82	14 31	+51	81	15 22	+50	81	16 12	+51	80
91	12 19	50	81	13 09	51	81	14 00	51	80	14 51	51	80	15 42	51	79
92	11 48	51	81	12 39	51	80	13 30	51	79	14 21	51	79	15 12	50	78
93	11 18	51	80	12 09	51	79	13 00	51	79	13 51	50	78	14 41	51	78
94	10 47	51	79	11 38	51	78	12 29	51	78	13 20	51	77	14 11	51	77
95	10 17	+51	78	11 08	+51	77	11 59	+51	77	12 50	+51	76	13 41	+51	76
96	09 47	51	77	10 38	51	77	11 29	51	76	12 20	51	76	13 11	51	75
97	09 17	51	76	10 08	51	76	10 59	51	75	11 50	52	75	12 42	51	74
98	08 47	51	75	09 38	51	75	10 29	52	74	11 21	51	74	12 12	51	73
99	08 17	51	75	09 08	52	74	10 00	51	74	10 51	51	73	11 42	52	73
100	07 47	+52	74	08 39	+51	73	09 30	+52	73	10 22	+51	72	11 13	+51	72
101	07 18	51	73	08 09	52	72	09 01	51	72	09 52	52	71	10 44	51	71
102	06 48	52	72	07 40	51	72	08 31	52	71	09 23	52	71	10 15	51	70
103	06 19	52	71	07 11	51	71	08 02	52	70	08 54	52	70	09 46	51	69
104	05 50	51	70	06 41	52	70	07 33	52	69	08 25	52	69	09 17	52	68
105	05 21	+52	70	06 13	+51	69	07 04	+52	69	07 56	+52	68	08 48	+52	68
106	04 52	52	69	05 44	52	68	06 36	52	68	07 28	52	67	08 20	52	67
107	04 23	52	68	05 15	52	67	06 07	52	67	06 59	52	66	07 51	52	66
108	03 54	53	67	04 47	52	67	05 39	52	66	06 31	52	66	07 23	52	65
109	03 26	52	66	04 18	53	66	05 11	52	65	06 03	52	65	06 55	53	64
110	02 58	+52	65	03 50	+53	65	04 43	+52	64	05 35	+53	64	06 28	+52	63
111	02 30	52	64	03 22	53	64	04 15	53	64	05 08	52	63	06 00	53	63
112	02 02	53	64	02 55	52	63	03 47	53	63	04 40	53	62	05 33	52	62
113	01 34	53	63	02 27	53	62	03 20	53	62	04 13	53	61	05 06	52	61
114	01 07	53	62	02 00	53	61	02 53	53	61	03 46	53	61	04 39	53	60
115	00 40	+53	61	01 33	+53	61	02 26	+53	60	03 19	+53	60	04 12	+53	59
116	00 13	53	60	01 06	53	60	01 59	53	59	02 52	54	59	03 46	53	58
117	−0 14	54	59	00 40	53	59	01 33	53	58	02 26	53	58	03 19	54	58
118	−0 40	53	59	00 13	54	58	01 07	53	58	02 00	53	57	02 53	54	57
119	−1 06	53	58	−0 13	54	57	00 41	53	57	01 34	54	56	02 28	53	56
120	−1 32	+53	57	−0 39	+54	56	00 15	+54	56	01 09	+53	55	02 02	+54	55
121	−1 58	54	56	−1 04	53	55	−0 11	54	55	00 43	54	55	01 37	54	54
122	−2 24	54	55	−1 30	54	55	−0 36	54	54	00 18	54	54	01 12	54	53
123	−2 49	54	54	−1 55	54	54	−1 01	54	53	−0 07	55	53	00 48	54	52
124	−3 14	54	53	−2 20	55	53	−1 25	54	52	−0 31	54	52	00 23	54	52
125	−3 38	+54	52	−2 44	+54	52	−1 50	+55	52	−0 55	+54	51	−0 01	+55	51
126	−4 03	55	52	−3 08	54	51	−2 14	55	51	−1 19	54	50	−0 25	55	50
127	−4 27	55	51	−3 32	54	50	−2 38	55	50	−1 43	55	49	−0 48	55	49
128	−4 51	55	50	−3 56	55	49	−3 01	55	49	−2 06	55	49	−1 11	55	48
129	−5 14	55	49	−4 19	55	49	−3 24	55	48	−2 29	55	48	−1 34	55	47
130	−5 37	+55	48	−4 42	+55	48	−3 47	+55	47	−2 52	+55	47	−1 57	+55	46
131				−5 05	55	47	−4 10	56	46	−3 14	55	46	−2 19	55	46
132				−5 27	55	46	−4 32	56	45	−3 36	55	45	−2 41	56	45
133							−4 54	56	45	−3 58	56	44	−3 02	55	44
134							−5 15	56	44	−4 19	55	43	−3 24	56	43
135							−5 36	+56	43	−4 40	+55	42	−3 45	+56	42
136										−5 01	56	41	−4 05	56	41
137										−5 21	56	41	−4 25	56	40
138													−4 45	56	39
139													−5 05	57	38

LHA	20° Hc	d	Z	21° Hc	d	Z	22° Hc	d	Z	23° Hc	d	Z	24° Hc	d	Z
	° ′	′	°	° ′	′	°	° ′	′	°	° ′	′	°	° ′	′	°
70	27 18	+50	96	28 08	+51	96	28 59	+49	95	29 48	+50	95	30 38	+50	94
71	26 48	50	96	27 38	50	95	28 28	50	94	29 18	49	94	30 07	50	93
72	26 17	50	95	27 07	50	94	27 57	50	93	28 47	49	93	29 36	50	92
73	25 46	50	94	26 36	50	93	27 26	50	93	28 16	50	92	29 06	49	91
74	25 15	50	93	26 05	50	92	26 55	50	92	27 45	50	91	28 35	49	90
75	24 44	+50	92	25 34	+50	91	26 24	+50	91	27 14	+50	90	28 04	+49	90
76	24 13	50	91	25 03	50	91	25 53	50	90	26 43	50	89	27 33	49	89
77	23 42	51	90	24 33	49	90	25 22	50	89	26 12	50	89	27 02	49	88
78	23 11	51	90	24 02	50	89	24 52	49	88	25 41	50	88	26 31	50	87
79	22 41	50	89	23 31	50	88	24 21	50	87	25 11	49	87	26 00	50	86
80	22 10	+50	88	23 00	+50	87	23 50	+50	87	24 40	+49	86	25 29	+50	85
81	21 39	50	87	22 29	50	86	23 19	50	86	24 09	50	85	24 59	49	85
82	21 08	50	86	21 58	50	86	22 48	50	85	23 38	50	84	24 28	50	84
83	20 37	50	85	21 27	50	85	22 17	50	84	23 07	50	83	23 57	50	83
84	20 06	51	84	20 57	50	84	21 47	50	83	22 37	50	83	23 27	49	82
85	19 36	+50	84	20 26	+50	83	21 16	+50	82	22 06	+50	82	22 56	+50	81
86	19 05	50	83	19 55	50	82	20 45	51	82	21 36	50	81	22 26	49	80
87	18 34	51	82	19 25	50	81	20 15	50	81	21 05	50	80	21 55	50	80
88	18 04	50	81	18 54	51	81	19 45	50	80	20 35	50	79	21 25	50	79
89	17 33	51	80	18 24	50	80	19 14	50	79	20 04	50	79	20 54	50	78
90	17 03	+50	79	17 53	+51	79	18 44	+50	78	19 34	+50	78	20 24	+50	77
91	16 33	50	79	17 23	51	78	18 14	50	77	19 04	50	77	19 54	50	76
92	16 02	51	78	16 53	50	77	17 43	51	77	18 34	50	76	19 24	50	76
93	15 32	51	77	16 23	50	76	17 13	51	76	18 04	50	75	18 54	51	75
94	15 02	51	76	15 53	51	76	16 44	50	75	17 34	51	74	18 25	50	74
95	14 32	+51	75	15 23	+51	75	16 14	+50	74	17 04	+51	74	17 55	+51	73
96	14 02	51	74	14 53	51	74	15 44	51	73	16 35	51	73	17 26	50	72
97	13 33	51	74	14 24	51	73	15 15	50	73	16 05	51	72	16 56	51	71
98	13 03	51	73	13 54	51	72	14 45	51	72	15 36	51	71	16 27	51	71
99	12 34	51	72	13 25	51	71	14 16	51	71	15 07	51	70	15 58	51	70
100	12 04	+52	71	12 56	+51	71	13 47	+51	70	14 38	+51	70	15 29	+51	69
101	11 35	52	70	12 27	51	70	13 18	51	69	14 09	51	69	15 00	51	68
102	11 06	52	70	11 58	51	69	12 49	51	68	13 40	52	68	14 32	51	67
103	10 37	52	69	11 29	51	68	12 20	52	68	13 12	51	67	14 03	51	67
104	10 09	51	68	11 00	52	67	11 52	51	67	12 43	52	66	13 35	51	66
105	09 40	+52	67	10 32	+52	67	11 24	+51	66	12 15	+52	66	13 07	+51	65
106	09 12	52	66	10 04	51	66	10 55	52	65	11 47	52	65	12 39	52	64
107	08 43	52	65	09 35	52	65	10 27	52	64	11 19	52	64	12 11	52	63
108	08 15	53	65	09 08	52	64	10 00	52	64	10 52	52	63	11 44	52	63
109	07 48	52	64	08 40	52	63	09 32	52	63	10 24	52	62	11 16	52	62
110	07 20	+52	63	08 12	+53	62	09 05	+52	62	09 57	+52	61	10 49	+52	61
111	06 53	52	62	07 45	53	62	08 38	52	61	09 30	52	61	10 22	53	60
112	06 25	53	61	07 18	53	61	08 11	52	60	09 03	53	60	09 56	52	59
113	05 58	53	60	06 51	53	60	07 44	53	60	08 37	52	59	09 29	53	59
114	05 32	53	60	06 25	52	59	07 17	53	59	08 10	53	58	09 03	53	58
115	05 05	+53	59	05 58	+53	58	06 51	+53	58	07 44	+53	57	08 37	+53	57
116	04 39	53	58	05 32	53	58	06 25	53	57	07 18	53	57	08 11	53	56
117	04 13	53	57	05 06	53	57	05 59	53	56	06 52	54	56	07 46	53	55
118	03 47	53	56	04 40	54	56	05 34	53	55	06 27	53	55	07 20	54	54
119	03 21	54	55	04 15	53	55	05 08	54	55	06 02	53	54	06 55	54	54
120	02 56	+54	55	03 50	+53	54	04 43	+54	54	05 37	+54	53	06 31	+53	53
121	02 31	54	54	03 25	54	53	04 19	53	53	05 12	54	52	06 06	54	52
122	02 06	54	53	03 00	54	52	03 54	54	52	04 48	54	52	05 42	54	51
123	01 42	54	52	02 36	54	52	03 30	54	51	04 24	54	51	05 18	54	50
124	01 17	55	51	02 12	54	51	03 06	54	50	04 00	54	50	04 54	55	49
125	00 54	+54	50	01 48	+54	50	02 42	+55	49	03 37	+54	49	04 31	+54	49
126	00 30	54	49	01 24	55	49	02 19	54	49	03 13	55	48	04 08	55	48
127	00 07	54	49	01 01	55	48	01 56	55	48	02 51	54	47	03 45	55	47
128	−0 16	54	48	00 38	55	47	01 33	55	47	02 28	55	47	03 23	55	46
129	−0 39	55	47	00 16	55	47	01 11	55	46	02 06	55	46	03 01	55	45
130	−1 02	+56	46	−0 06	+55	46	00 49	+55	45	01 44	+55	45	02 39	+55	44
131	−1 24	56	45	−0 28	55	45	00 27	55	44	01 22	55	44	02 17	56	44
132	−1 45	55	44	−0 50	55	44	00 05	56	44	01 01	55	43	01 56	56	43
133	−2 07	56	43	−1 11	55	43	−0 16	56	43	00 40	55	42	01 35	56	42
134	−2 28	56	43	−1 32	55	42	−0 37	56	42	00 19	56	41	01 15	56	41
135	−2 49	+56	42	−1 53	+56	41	−0 57	+56	41	−0 01	+56	41	00 55	+56	40
136	−3 09	56	41	−2 13	56	40	−1 17	56	40	−0 21	56	40	00 35	56	39
137	−3 29	56	40	−2 33	56	40	−1 37	56	39	−0 41	57	39	00 16	56	39
138	−3 49	57	39	−2 52	56	39	−1 56	56	38	−1 00	57	38	−0 03	56	38
139	−4 08	56	38	−3 12	57	38	−2 15	56	37	−1 19	57	37	−0 22	56	37

LHA	25° Hc	d	Z	26° Hc	d	Z	27° Hc	d	Z	28° Hc	d	Z	29° Hc	d	Z	LHA
	° ′	′	°	° ′	′	°	° ′	′	°	° ′	′	°	° ′	′	°	
70	31 28	+49	93	32 17	+49	93	33 06	+49	92	33 55	+49	91	34 44	+48	91	290
71	30 57	49	92	31 46	49	92	32 35	49	91	33 24	49	90	34 13	48	90	289
72	30 26	49	92	31 15	49	91	32 04	49	90	32 53	49	90	33 42	48	89	288
73	29 55	49	91	30 44	49	90	31 33	49	89	32 22	49	89	33 11	48	88	287
74	29 24	49	90	30 13	49	89	31 02	49	88	31 51	49	88	32 40	48	87	286
75	28 53	+49	89	29 42	+50	88	30 32	+48	88	31 20	+49	87	32 09	+49	86	285
76	28 22	50	88	29 12	49	87	30 01	49	87	30 50	48	86	31 38	49	85	284
77	27 51	50	87	28 41	49	87	29 30	49	86	30 19	49	85	31 08	48	85	283
78	27 21	49	86	28 10	49	86	28 59	49	85	29 48	49	84	30 37	48	84	282
79	26 50	49	86	27 39	49	85	28 28	49	84	29 17	49	84	30 06	49	83	281
80	26 19	+49	85	27 08	+50	84	27 58	+49	83	28 47	+48	83	29 35	+49	82	280
81	25 48	50	84	26 38	49	83	27 27	49	83	28 16	49	82	29 05	49	81	279
82	25 18	49	83	26 07	49	82	26 56	49	82	27 45	49	81	28 34	49	81	278
83	24 47	49	82	25 36	50	82	26 26	49	81	27 15	49	80	28 04	49	80	277
84	24 16	50	81	25 06	49	81	25 55	49	80	26 44	50	80	27 34	48	79	276
85	23 46	+49	81	24 35	+50	80	25 25	+49	79	26 14	+49	79	27 03	+49	78	275
86	23 15	50	80	24 05	50	79	24 55	49	79	25 44	49	78	26 33	49	77	274
87	22 45	50	79	23 35	49	78	24 24	50	78	25 14	49	77	26 03	49	77	273
88	22 15	49	78	23 04	50	78	23 54	50	77	24 44	49	76	25 33	49	76	272
89	21 44	50	77	22 34	50	77	23 24	50	76	24 14	49	76	25 03	49	75	271
90	21 14	+50	77	22 04	+50	76	22 54	+50	75	23 44	+49	75	24 33	+50	74	270
91	20 44	50	76	21 34	50	75	22 24	50	75	23 14	50	74	24 04	49	73	269
92	20 14	51	75	21 05	50	74	21 55	49	74	22 44	50	73	23 34	50	73	268
93	19 45	50	74	20 35	50	74	21 25	50	73	22 15	50	72	23 05	49	72	267
94	19 15	50	73	20 05	51	73	20 56	50	72	21 46	49	72	22 35	50	71	266
95	18 46	+50	73	19 36	+50	72	20 26	+50	71	21 16	+50	71	22 06	+50	70	265
96	18 16	51	72	19 07	50	71	19 57	50	71	20 47	50	70	21 37	50	69	264
97	17 47	50	71	18 37	51	70	19 28	50	70	20 18	51	69	21 09	50	69	263
98	17 18	50	70	18 08	51	70	18 59	50	69	19 49	51	68	20 40	50	68	262
99	16 49	51	69	17 40	50	69	18 30	51	68	19 21	50	68	20 11	51	67	261
100	16 20	+51	68	17 11	+51	68	18 02	+50	67	18 52	+51	67	19 43	+50	66	260
101	15 51	51	68	16 42	51	67	17 33	51	67	18 24	51	66	19 15	50	65	259
102	15 23	51	67	16 14	51	66	17 05	51	66	17 56	51	65	18 47	50	65	258
103	14 54	52	66	15 46	51	66	16 37	51	65	17 28	51	64	18 19	51	64	257
104	14 26	52	65	15 18	51	65	16 09	51	64	17 00	51	64	17 51	51	63	256
105	13 58	+52	64	14 50	+51	64	15 41	+52	63	16 33	+51	63	17 24	+51	62	255
106	13 31	51	64	14 22	52	63	15 14	51	63	16 05	52	62	16 57	51	62	254
107	13 03	52	63	13 55	51	62	14 46	52	62	15 38	51	61	16 29	52	61	253
108	12 36	51	62	13 27	52	62	14 19	52	61	15 11	52	61	16 03	51	60	252
109	12 08	52	61	13 00	52	61	13 52	52	60	14 44	52	60	15 36	52	59	251
110	11 41	+53	60	12 34	+52	60	13 26	+52	59	14 18	+52	59	15 10	+51	58	250
111	11 15	52	60	12 07	52	59	12 59	52	59	13 51	52	58	14 43	52	58	249
112	10 48	53	59	11 41	52	58	12 33	52	58	13 25	52	57	14 17	53	57	248
113	10 22	52	58	11 14	53	58	12 07	52	57	12 59	53	57	13 52	52	56	247
114	09 56	52	57	10 48	53	57	11 41	53	56	12 34	52	56	13 26	53	55	246
115	09 30	+53	56	10 23	+52	56	11 15	+53	55	12 08	+53	55	13 01	+53	54	245
116	09 04	53	56	09 57	53	55	10 50	53	55	11 43	53	54	12 36	53	54	244
117	08 39	53	55	09 32	53	54	10 25	53	54	11 18	53	53	12 11	53	53	243
118	08 14	53	54	09 07	53	54	10 00	53	53	10 53	54	53	11 47	53	52	242
119	07 49	53	53	08 42	54	53	09 36	53	52	10 29	53	52	11 22	54	51	241
120	07 24	+54	52	08 18	+53	52	09 11	+54	51	10 05	+53	51	10 58	+54	51	240
121	07 00	54	52	07 54	53	51	08 47	54	51	09 41	54	50	10 35	53	50	239
122	06 36	54	51	07 30	54	50	08 24	53	50	09 17	54	49	10 11	54	49	238
123	06 12	54	50	07 06	54	49	08 00	54	49	08 54	54	49	09 48	54	48	237
124	05 49	54	49	06 43	54	49	07 37	54	48	08 31	54	48	09 25	54	47	236
125	05 25	+55	48	06 20	+54	48	07 14	+54	47	08 08	+55	47	09 03	+54	47	235
126	05 03	54	47	05 57	55	47	06 52	54	47	07 46	54	46	08 40	55	46	234
127	04 40	55	47	05 35	54	46	06 29	55	46	07 24	54	45	08 18	55	45	233
128	04 18	54	46	05 12	55	45	06 07	55	45	07 02	55	45	07 57	54	44	232
129	03 56	55	45	04 51	55	45	05 46	55	44	06 41	54	44	07 35	55	43	231
130	03 34	+55	44	04 29	+55	44	05 24	+55	43	06 19	+55	43	07 14	+55	43	230
131	03 13	55	43	04 08	55	43	05 03	55	43	05 58	56	42	06 54	55	42	229
132	02 52	55	42	03 47	55	42	04 42	56	42	05 38	55	41	06 33	56	41	228
133	02 31	56	42	03 27	55	41	04 22	56	41	05 18	55	40	06 13	56	40	227
134	02 11	55	41	03 06	56	40	04 02	56	40	04 58	56	40	05 54	55	39	226
135	01 51	+55	40	02 46	+56	40	03 42	+56	39	04 38	+56	39	05 34	+56	38	225
136	01 31	56	39	02 27	56	39	03 23	56	38	04 19	56	38	05 15	56	38	224
137	01 12	56	38	02 08	56	38	03 04	56	37	04 00	56	37	04 56	57	37	223
138	00 53	56	37	01 49	56	37	02 45	57	37	03 42	56	36	04 38	56	36	222
139	00 34	57	36	01 31	56	36	02 27	57	36	03 24	56	35	04 20	57	35	221

S. Lat. {LHA greater than 180°........ Zn=180−Z ; LHA less than 180°........... Zn=180+Z}

DECLINATION (15°-29°) SAME NAME AS LATITUDE

LAT 59°

N. Lat. {LHA greater than 180°....... Zn=Z; LHA less than 180°........... Zn=360−Z}

DECLINATION (15°-29°) SAME NAME AS LATITUDE

LAT 59°

LHA	15° Hc d Z	16° Hc d Z	17° Hc d Z	18° Hc d Z	19° Hc d Z	20° Hc d Z	21° Hc d Z	22° Hc d Z	23° Hc d Z	24° Hc d Z	25° Hc d Z	26° Hc d Z	27° Hc d Z	28° Hc d Z	29° Hc d Z	LHA
	° ′ ′ °	° ′ ′ °	° ′ ′ °	° ′ ′ °	° ′ ′ °	° ′ ′ °	° ′ ′ °	° ′ ′ °	° ′ ′ °	° ′ ′ °	° ′ ′ °	° ′ ′ °	° ′ ′ °	° ′ ′ °	° ′ ′ °	
				140	−5 24 +57 38	−4 27 +57 37	−3 30 +56 37	−2 34 +57 37	−1 37 +56 36	−0 41 +57 36	00 16 +57 36	01 13 +56 35	02 09 +57 35	03 06 +57 35	04 03 +56 34	220
					141	−4 45 56 36	−3 49 57 36	−2 52 57 36	−1 55 57 35	−0 58 56 35	−0 02 57 35	00 55 57 34	01 52 57 34	02 49 56 34	03 45 57 33	219
					142	−5 04 57 35	−4 07 57 35	−3 10 57 35	−2 13 57 35	−1 16 57 34	−0 19 57 34	00 38 57 34	01 35 57 33	02 32 56 33	03 28 57 33	218
					143	−5 21 57 35	−4 24 57 34	−3 27 57 34	−2 30 57 34	−1 33 57 33	−0 36 57 33	00 21 57 33	01 18 57 32	02 15 57 32	03 12 57 32	217
						144	−4 42 58 33	−3 44 57 33	−2 47 57 33	−1 50 57 32	−0 53 57 32	00 04 57 32	01 01 58 32	01 59 57 31	02 56 57 31	216
						145	−4 58 +57 33	−4 01 +57 32	−3 04 +58 32	−2 06 +57 32	−1 09 +57 31	−0 12 +57 31	00 45 +58 31	01 43 +57 30	02 40 +57 30	215
						146	−5 15 58 32	−4 17 57 31	−3 20 58 31	−2 22 57 31	−1 25 57 30	−0 28 58 30	00 30 57 30	01 27 58 30	02 25 57 29	214
						147	−5 31 58 31	−4 33 57 30	−3 36 58 30	−2 38 58 30	−1 40 57 30	−0 43 58 29	00 15 57 29	01 12 58 29	02 10 57 28	213
							148	−4 49 58 30	−3 51 58 29	−2 53 57 29	−1 56 58 29	−0 58 58 28	00 00 58 28	00 58 57 28	01 55 58 28	212
							149	−5 04 58 29	−4 06 58 28	−3 08 58 28	−2 10 58 28	−1 12 58 28	−0 14 57 27	00 43 58 27	01 41 58 27	211
							150	−5 18 +58 28	−4 20 +58 27	−3 22 +58 27	−2 24 +58 27	−1 26 +58 27	−0 28 +58 26	00 30 +58 26	01 28 +57 26	210
								151	−4 34 58 27	−3 36 58 26	−2 38 58 26	−1 40 58 26	−0 42 58 26	00 16 58 25	01 14 58 25	209
								152	−4 48 58 26	−3 50 58 25	−2 52 59 25	−1 53 58 25	−0 55 58 25	00 03 58 24	01 01 58 24	208
								153	−5 01 58 25	−4 03 58 25	−3 05 59 24	−2 06 58 24	−1 08 58 24	−0 10 59 24	00 49 58 23	207
								154	−5 14 59 24	−4 15 58 24	−3 17 58 23	−2 19 59 23	−1 20 58 23	−0 22 59 23	00 37 58 23	206
									155	−4 28 +59 23	−3 29 +58 23	−2 31 +59 22	−1 32 +59 22	−0 33 +58 22	00 25 +59 22	205
									156	−4 39 58 22	−3 41 59 22	−2 42 59 21	−1 43 58 21	−0 45 59 21	00 14 59 21	204
									157	−4 51 59 21	−3 52 59 21	−2 53 59 21	−1 54 58 20	−0 56 59 20	00 03 59 20	203
									158	−5 02 59 20	−4 03 59 20	−3 04 59 20	−2 05 59 20	−1 06 59 19	−0 07 59 19	202
									159	−5 12 59 19	−4 13 59 19	−3 14 59 19	−2 15 59 19	−1 16 59 18	−0 17 59 18	201
										160	−4 23 +59 18	−3 24 +59 18	−2 25 +59 18	−1 26 +59 18	−0 27 +60 17	200
										161	−4 32 59 17	−3 33 59 17	−2 34 59 17	−1 35 59 17	−0 36 60 17	199
										162	−4 41 59 16	−3 42 59 16	−2 43 60 16	−1 43 59 16	−0 44 59 16	198
										163	−4 50 60 15	−3 50 59 15	−2 51 59 15	−1 52 60 15	−0 52 59 15	197
										164	−4 58 60 15	−3 58 59 14	−2 59 60 14	−1 59 59 14	−1 00 59 14	196
										165	−5 05 +59 14	−4 06 +60 13	−3 06 +59 13	−2 07 +60 13	−1 07 +59 13	195
										166	−5 12 59 13	−4 13 60 13	−3 13 59 12	−2 14 60 12	−1 14 60 12	194
											167	−4 19 60 12	−3 19 59 12	−2 20 60 11	−1 20 59 11	193
											168	−4 25 60 11	−3 25 59 11	−2 26 60 11	−1 26 59 10	192
											169	−4 31 60 10	−3 31 60 10	−2 31 59 10	−1 32 60 10	191
											170	−4 36 +60 9	−3 36 +60 9	−2 36 +60 9	−1 36 +59 9	190
											171	−4 40 59 8	−3 41 60 8	−2 41 60 8	−1 41 60 8	189
											172	−4 44 59 7	−3 45 60 7	−2 45 60 7	−1 45 60 7	188
											173	−4 48 60 6	−3 48 60 6	−2 48 60 6	−1 48 59 6	187
											174	−4 51 60 5	−3 51 60 5	−2 51 59 5	−1 52 60 5	186
											175	−4 54 +60 5	−3 54 +60 4	−2 54 +60 4	−1 54 +60 4	185
											176	−4 56 60 4	−3 56 60 4	−2 56 60 4	−1 56 60 4	184
											177	−4 58 60 3	−3 58 60 3	−2 58 60 3	−1 58 60 3	183
											178	−4 59 60 2	−3 59 60 2	−2 59 60 2	−1 59 60 2	182
											179	−5 00 60 1	−4 00 60 1	−3 00 60 1	−2 00 60 1	181
											180	−5 00 +60 0	−4 00 +60 0	−3 00 +60 0	−2 00 +60 0	180
76	−5 50 51 110	284														
75	−5 21 −52 110	285														
74	−4 52 52 111	−5 44 52 112	286													
73	−4 23 52 112	−5 15 52 113	287													
72	−3 54 53 113	−4 47 52 113	−5 39 52 114	288												
71	−3 26 52 114	−4 18 53 114	−5 11 52 115	289												
70	−2 58 −52 115	−3 50 −53 115	−4 43 −52 116	−5 35 −53 116	290											
	15°	16°	17°	18°	19°	20°	21°	22°	23°	24°	25°	26°	27°	28°	29°	

S. Lat. {LHA greater than 180°....... Zn=180−Z; LHA less than 180°........... Zn=180+Z}

DECLINATION (15°-29°) CONTRARY NAME TO LATITUDE

N. Lat. {LHA greater than 180°……. Zn=Z; LHA less than 180°………. Zn=360−Z}

DECLINATION (15°-29°) CONTRARY NAME TO LATITUDE

LHA	15° Hc	d	Z	16° Hc	d	Z	17° Hc	d	Z	18° Hc	d	Z	19° Hc	d	Z
	° ′	′	°	° ′	′	°	° ′	′	°	° ′	′	°	° ′	′	°
69	-2 30	52	116	-3 22	53	116	-4 15	53	116	-5 08	52	117	291		
68	-2 02	53	116	-2 55	52	117	-3 47	53	117	-4 40	53	118	-5 33	52	118
67	-1 34	53	117	-2 27	53	118	-3 20	53	118	-4 13	53	119	-5 06	52	119
66	-1 07	53	118	-2 00	53	119	-2 53	53	119	-3 46	53	119	-4 39	53	120
65	-0 40	-53	119	-1 33	-53	119	-2 26	-53	120	-3 19	-53	120	-4 12	-53	121
64	-0 13	53	120	-1 06	53	120	-1 59	53	121	-2 52	54	121	-3 46	53	122
63	00 14	54	121	-0 40	53	121	-1 33	53	122	-2 26	53	122	-3 19	54	122
62	00 40	53	121	-0 13	54	122	-1 07	53	122	-2 00	53	123	-2 53	54	123
61	01 06	53	122	00 13	54	123	-0 41	53	123	-1 34	54	124	-2 28	53	124
60	01 32	-53	123	00 39	-54	124	-0 15	-54	124	-1 09	-53	125	-2 02	-54	125
59	01 58	54	124	01 04	53	125	00 11	54	125	-0 43	54	125	-1 37	54	126
58	02 24	54	125	01 30	54	125	00 36	54	126	-0 18	54	126	-1 12	54	127
57	02 49	54	126	01 55	54	126	01 01	54	127	00 07	55	127	-0 48	54	128
56	03 14	54	127	02 20	55	127	01 25	54	128	00 31	54	128	-0 23	54	128
55	03 38	-54	128	02 44	-54	128	01 50	-55	128	00 55	-54	129	00 01	-55	129
54	04 03	55	128	03 08	54	129	02 14	55	129	01 19	54	130	00 25	55	130
53	04 27	55	129	03 32	54	130	02 38	55	130	01 43	55	131	00 48	55	131
52	04 51	55	130	03 56	55	131	03 01	55	131	02 06	55	131	01 11	55	132
51	05 14	55	131	04 19	55	131	03 24	55	132	02 29	55	132	01 34	55	133
50	05 37	-55	132	04 42	-55	132	03 47	-55	133	02 52	-55	133	01 57	-55	134
49	06 00	55	133	05 05	55	133	04 10	56	134	03 14	55	134	02 19	55	134
48	06 23	56	134	05 27	55	134	04 32	56	135	03 36	55	135	02 41	56	135
47	06 45	56	135	05 49	55	135	04 54	56	135	03 58	56	136	03 02	55	136
46	07 07	56	136	06 11	56	136	05 15	56	136	04 19	55	137	03 24	56	137
45	07 28	-56	137	06 32	-56	137	05 36	-56	137	04 40	-55	138	03 45	-56	138
44	07 49	56	137	06 53	56	138	05 57	56	138	05 01	56	139	04 05	56	139
43	08 10	56	138	07 14	56	139	06 18	57	139	05 21	56	139	04 25	56	140
42	08 30	56	139	07 34	56	140	06 38	57	140	05 41	56	140	04 45	56	141
41	08 50	56	140	07 54	57	141	06 57	56	141	06 01	56	141	05 05	57	142
40	09 10	-57	141	08 13	-56	141	07 17	-57	142	06 20	-56	142	05 24	-57	142
39	09 29	57	142	08 32	56	142	07 36	57	143	06 39	57	143	05 42	57	143
38	09 48	57	143	08 51	57	143	07 54	57	144	06 57	56	144	06 01	57	144
37	10 06	57	144	09 09	57	144	08 12	57	144	07 15	57	145	06 18	57	145
36	10 24	57	145	09 27	57	145	08 30	57	145	07 33	57	146	06 36	57	146
35	10 42	-57	146	09 45	-57	146	08 48	-58	146	07 50	-57	147	06 53	-57	147
34	10 59	57	147	10 02	57	147	09 05	58	147	08 07	57	148	07 10	58	148
33	11 16	57	148	10 19	58	148	09 21	57	148	08 24	58	148	07 26	58	149
32	11 32	57	149	10 35	58	149	09 37	58	149	08 39	57	149	07 42	58	150
31	11 48	57	150	10 51	58	150	09 53	58	150	08 55	58	150	07 57	58	151
30	12 04	-58	150	11 06	-58	151	10 08	-58	151	09 10	-58	151	08 12	-58	152
29	12 19	58	151	11 21	58	152	10 23	58	152	09 25	58	152	08 27	58	152
28	12 33	58	152	11 35	58	153	10 37	58	153	09 39	58	153	08 41	58	153
27	12 48	59	153	11 49	58	154	10 51	58	154	09 53	59	154	08 54	58	154
26	13 01	58	154	12 03	59	155	11 04	58	155	10 06	58	155	09 08	59	155
25	13 14	-58	155	12 16	-59	155	11 17	-58	156	10 19	-59	156	09 20	-58	156
24	13 27	58	156	12 29	59	156	11 30	59	157	10 31	58	157	09 33	59	157
23	13 39	58	157	12 41	59	157	11 42	59	158	10 43	58	158	09 45	59	158
22	13 51	59	158	12 52	58	158	11 54	59	159	10 55	59	159	09 56	59	159
21	14 02	58	159	13 04	59	159	12 05	59	160	11 06	59	160	10 07	59	160
20	14 13	-59	160	13 14	-59	160	12 15	-59	160	11 16	-59	161	10 17	-59	161
19	14 23	59	161	13 24	59	161	12 25	59	161	11 26	59	162	10 27	59	162
18	14 33	59	162	13 34	59	162	12 35	59	162	11 36	60	163	10 36	59	163
17	14 43	60	163	13 43	59	163	12 44	59	163	11 45	60	164	10 45	59	164
16	14 51	59	164	13 52	59	164	12 53	60	164	11 53	59	165	10 54	59	165
15	15 00	-60	165	14 00	-59	165	13 01	-60	165	12 01	-59	165	11 02	-60	166
14	15 07	59	166	14 08	60	166	13 08	59	166	12 09	60	166	11 09	59	167
13	15 15	60	167	14 15	60	167	13 15	59	167	12 16	60	167	11 16	59	168
12	15 21	59	168	14 22	60	168	13 22	60	168	12 22	59	168	11 23	60	168
11	15 27	59	169	14 28	60	169	13 28	60	169	12 28	59	169	11 29	60	169
10	15 33	-60	170	14 33	-59	170	13 34	-60	170	12 34	-60	170	11 34	-60	170
9	15 38	60	171	14 38	59	171	13 39	60	171	12 39	60	171	11 39	60	171
8	15 43	60	172	14 43	60	172	13 43	60	172	12 43	60	172	11 43	59	172
7	15 47	60	173	14 47	60	173	13 47	60	173	12 47	60	173	11 47	60	173
6	15 50	60	174	14 50	60	174	13 50	59	174	12 51	60	174	11 51	60	174
5	15 53	-60	175	14 53	-60	175	13 53	-60	175	12 53	-59	175	11 54	-60	175
4	15 56	60	176	14 56	60	176	13 56	60	176	12 56	60	176	11 56	60	176
3	15 58	60	177	14 58	60	177	13 58	60	177	12 58	60	177	11 58	60	177
2	15 59	60	178	14 59	60	178	13 59	60	178	12 59	60	178	11 59	60	178
1	16 00	60	179	15 00	60	179	14 00	60	179	13 00	60	179	12 00	60	179
0	16 00	-60	180	15 00	-60	180	14 00	-60	180	13 00	-60	180	12 00	-60	180

LHA	20° Hc	d	Z	21° Hc	d	Z	22° Hc	d	Z	23° Hc	d	Z	24° Hc	d	Z
	° ′	′	°	° ′	′	°	° ′	′	°	° ′	′	°	° ′	′	°
69															
68	292														
67	293														
66	-5 32	53	120	294											
65	-5 05	-53	121	295											
64	-4 39	53	122	-5 32	53	122	296								
63	-4 13	53	123	-5 06	53	123	297								
62	-3 47	53	124	-4 40	54	124	-5 34	53	125	298					
61	-3 21	54	125	-4 15	53	125	-5 08	54	125	299					
60	-2 56	-54	125	-3 50	-53	126	-4 43	-54	126	-5 37	-54	127	300		
59	-2 31	54	126	-3 25	54	127	-4 19	53	127	-5 12	54	128	301		
58	-2 06	54	127	-3 00	54	128	-3 54	54	128	-4 48	54	128	-5 42	54	129
57	-1 42	54	128	-2 36	54	128	-3 30	54	129	-4 24	54	129	-5 18	54	130
56	-1 17	55	129	-2 12	54	129	-3 06	54	130	-4 00	54	130	-4 54	55	131
55	-0 54	-54	130	-1 48	-54	130	-2 42	-55	131	-3 37	-54	131	-4 31	-54	131
54	-0 30	54	131	-1 24	55	131	-2 19	54	131	-3 13	55	132	-4 08	55	132
53	-0 07	54	131	-1 01	55	132	-1 56	55	132	-2 51	54	133	-3 45	55	133
52	00 16	54	132	-0 38	55	133	-1 33	55	133	-2 28	55	133	-3 23	55	134
51	00 39	55	133	-0 16	55	133	-1 11	55	134	-2 06	55	134	-3 01	55	135
50	01 02	-56	134	00 06	-55	134	-0 49	-55	135	-1 44	-55	135	-2 39	-55	136
49	01 24	56	135	00 28	55	135	-0 27	55	136	-1 22	55	136	-2 17	56	136
48	01 45	55	136	00 50	55	136	-0 05	56	136	-1 01	55	137	-1 56	56	137
47	02 07	56	137	01 11	55	137	00 16	56	137	-0 40	55	138	-1 35	56	138
46	02 28	56	138	01 32	55	138	00 37	56	138	-0 19	56	139	-1 15	56	139
45	02 49	-56	138	01 53	-56	139	00 57	-56	139	00 01	-56	139	-0 55	-56	140
44	03 09	56	139	02 13	56	140	01 17	56	140	00 21	56	140	-0 35	56	141
43	03 29	56	140	02 33	56	140	01 37	56	141	00 41	57	141	-0 16	56	141
42	03 49	57	141	02 52	56	141	01 56	56	142	01 00	57	142	00 03	56	142
41	04 08	56	142	03 12	57	142	02 15	56	143	01 19	57	143	00 22	56	143
40	04 27	-57	143	03 30	-56	143	02 34	-57	143	01 37	-56	144	00 41	-57	144
39	04 45	56	144	03 49	57	144	02 52	57	144	01 55	57	145	00 58	56	145
38	05 04	57	145	04 07	57	145	03 10	57	145	02 13	57	145	01 16	57	146
37	05 21	57	145	04 24	57	146	03 27	56	146	02 30	57	146	01 33	57	147
36	05 39	57	146	04 42	58	147	03 44	57	147	02 47	57	147	01 50	57	148
35	05 56	-58	147	04 58	-57	147	04 01	-57	148	03 04	-58	148	02 06	-57	148
34	06 12	57	148	05 15	58	148	04 17	57	149	03 20	58	149	02 22	57	149
33	06 28	57	149	05 31	58	149	04 33	57	150	03 36	58	150	02 38	58	150
32	06 44	58	150	05 46	57	150	04 49	58	150	03 51	58	151	02 53	57	151
31	06 59	57	151	06 02	58	151	05 04	58	151	04 06	58	152	03 08	58	152
30	07 14	-58	152	06 16	-58	152	05 18	-58	152	04 20	-58	153	03 22	-58	153
29	07 29	58	153	06 31	58	153	05 33	59	153	04 34	58	153	03 36	58	154
28	07 43	59	154	06 44	58	154	05 46	58	154	04 48	58	154	03 50	58	155
27	07 56	58	155	06 58	58	155	06 00	59	155	05 01	58	155	04 03	58	155
26	08 09	58	155	07 11	59	156	06 12	58	156	05 14	59	156	04 15	58	156
25	08 22	-59	156	07 23	-58	157	06 25	-59	157	05 26	-58	157	04 28	-59	157
24	08 34	59	157	07 35	58	158	06 37	59	158	05 38	59	158	04 39	58	158
23	08 46	59	158	07 47	59	158	06 48	58	159	05 50	59	159	04 51	59	159
22	08 57	59	159	07 58	59	159	06 59	59	160	06 00	58	160	05 02	59	160
21	09 08	59	160	08 09	59	160	07 10	59	160	06 11	59	161	05 12	59	161
20	09 18	-59	161	08 19	-59	161	07 20	-59	161	06 21	-59	162	05 22	-59	162
19	09 28	59	162	08 29	59	162	07 30	59	162	06 31	60	162	05 31	59	163
18	09 37	59	163	08 38	59	163	07 39	59	163	06 40	60	163	05 40	59	164
17	09 46	59	164	08 47	59	164	07 48	60	164	06 48	59	164	05 49	59	164
16	09 55	60	165	08 55	59	165	07 56	60	165	06 56	59	165	05 57	59	165
15	10 02	-59	166	09 03	-60	166	08 03	-59	166	07 04	-59	166	06 05	-60	166
14	10 10	60	167	09 10	59	167	08 11	60	167	07 11	59	167	06 12	60	167
13	10 17	60	168	09 17	60	168	08 17	59	168	07 18	60	168	06 18	59	168
12	10 23	60	169	09 23	59	169	08 24	60	169	07 24	60	169	06 24	59	169
11	10 29	60	170	09 29	59	170	08 30	60	170	07 30	60	170	06 30	60	170
10	10 34	-59	170	09 35	-60	171	08 35	-60	171	07 35	-60	171	06 35	-59	171
9	10 39	60	171	09 39	59	172	08 40	60	172	07 40	60	172	06 40	60	172
8	10 44	60	172	09 44	60	172	08 44	60	173	07 44	60	173	06 44	60	173
7	10 47	59	173	09 48	60	173	08 48	60	173	07 48	60	174	06 48	60	174
6	10 51	60	174	09 51	60	174	08 51	60	174	07 51	60	174	06 51	60	175
5	10 54	-60	175	09 54	-60	175	08 54	-60	175	07 54	-60	175	06 54	-60	175
4	10 56	60	176	09 56	60	176	08 56	60	176	07 56	60	176	06 56	60	176
3	10 58	60	177	09 58	60	177	08 58	60	177	07 58	60	177	06 58	60	177
2	10 59	60	178	09 59	60	178	08 59	60	178	07 59	60	178	06 59	60	178
1	11 00	60	179	10 00	60	179	09 00	60	179	08 00	60	179	07 00	60	179
0	11 00	-60	180	10 00	-60	180	09 00	-60	180	08 00	-60	180	07 00	-60	180

LHA	25° Hc	d	Z	26° Hc	d	Z	27° Hc	d	Z	28° Hc	d	Z	29° Hc	d	Z	LHA
	° ′	′	°	° ′	′	°	° ′	′	°	° ′	′	°	° ′	′	°	
58	302															
57	303															
56	304															
55	-5 25	-55	132	305												
54	-5 03	54	133	306												
53	-4 40	55	133	-5 35	54	134	307									
52	-4 18	54	134	-5 12	55	135	308									
51	-3 56	55	135	-4 51	55	135	309									
50	-3 34	-55	136	-4 29	-55	136	-5 24	-55	137	310						
49	-3 13	55	137	-4 08	55	137	-5 03	55	137	311						
48	-2 52	55	138	-3 47	55	138	-4 42	56	138	-5 38	55	139	312			
47	-2 31	56	138	-3 27	55	139	-4 22	56	139	-5 18	55	140	313			
46	-2 11	55	139	-3 06	56	140	-4 02	56	140	-4 58	56	140	314			
45	-1 51	-55	140	-2 46	-56	140	-3 42	-56	141	-4 38	-56	141	-5 34	-56	142	315
44	-1 31	56	141	-2 27	56	141	-3 23	56	142	-4 19	56	142	-5 15	56	142	316
43	-1 12	56	142	-2 08	56	142	-3 04	56	143	-4 00	56	143	-4 56	57	143	317
42	-0 53	56	143	-1 49	56	143	-2 45	57	143	-3 42	56	144	-4 38	56	144	318
41	-0 34	57	144	-1 31	56	144	-2 27	57	144	-3 24	56	145	-4 20	57	145	319
40	-0 16	-57	144	-1 13	-56	145	-2 09	-57	145	-3 06	-57	145	-4 03	-56	146	320
39	00 02	57	145	-0 55	57	146	-1 52	57	146	-2 49	56	146	-3 45	57	147	321
38	00 19	57	146	-0 38	57	146	-1 35	57	147	-2 32	56	147	-3 28	57	147	322
37	00 36	57	147	-0 21	57	147	-1 18	57	148	-2 15	57	148	-3 12	57	148	323
36	00 53	57	148	-0 04	57	148	-1 01	58	148	-1 59	57	149	-2 56	57	149	324
35	01 09	-57	149	00 12	-57	149	-0 45	-58	149	-1 43	-57	150	-2 40	-57	150	325
34	01 25	57	150	00 28	58	150	-0 30	57	150	-1 27	58	150	-2 25	57	151	326
33	01 40	57	150	00 43	58	151	-0 15	57	151	-1 12	58	151	-2 10	57	152	327
32	01 56	58	151	00 58	58	152	00 00	58	152	-0 58	57	152	-1 55	58	152	328
31	02 10	58	152	01 12	58	152	00 14	57	153	-0 43	58	153	-1 41	58	153	329
30	02 24	-58	153	01 26	-58	153	00 28	-58	154	-0 30	-58	154	-1 28	-57	154	330
29	02 38	58	154	01 40	58	154	00 42	58	154	-0 16	58	155	-1 14	58	155	331
28	02 52	59	155	01 53	58	155	00 55	58	155	-0 03	58	156	-1 01	58	156	332
27	03 05	59	156	02 06	58	156	01 08	58	156	00 10	59	156	-0 49	58	157	333
26	03 17	58	157	02 19	59	157	01 20	58	157	00 22	59	157	-0 37	58	157	334
25	03 29	-58	157	02 31	-59	158	01 32	-59	158	00 33	-58	158	-0 25	-59	158	335
24	03 41	59	158	02 42	59	159	01 43	58	159	00 45	59	159	-0 14	59	159	336
23	03 52	59	159	02 53	59	159	01 54	58	160	00 56	59	160	-0 03	59	160	337
22	04 03	59	160	03 04	59	160	02 05	59	160	01 06	59	161	00 07	59	161	338
21	04 13	59	161	03 14	59	161	02 15	59	161	01 16	59	162	00 17	59	162	339
20	04 23	-59	162	03 24	-59	162	02 25	-59	162	01 26	-59	162	00 27	-60	163	340
19	04 32	59	163	03 33	59	163	02 34	59	163	01 35	59	163	00 36	60	163	341
18	04 41	59	164	03 42	59	164	02 43	60	164	01 43	59	164	00 44	59	164	342
17	04 50	59	165	03 51	60	165	02 51	59	165	01 52	60	165	00 52	59	165	343
16	04 58	60	165	03 58	59	166	02 59	60	166	01 59	59	166	01 00	59	166	344
15	05 05	-59	166	04 06	-60	167	03 06	-59	167	02 07	-60	167	01 07	-59	167	345
14	05 12	59	167	04 13	60	167	03 13	59	168	02 14	60	168	01 14	60	168	346
13	05 19	60	168	04 19	60	168	03 19	59	168	02 20	60	169	01 20	59	169	347
12	05 25	60	169	04 25	60	169	03 25	59	169	02 26	60	169	01 26	59	170	348
11	05 30	59	170	04 31	60	170	03 31	60	170	02 31	59	170	01 32	60	170	349
10	05 36	-60	171	04 36	-60	171	03 36	-60	171	02 36	-60	171	01 36	-59	171	350
9	05 40	60	172	04 40	59	172	03 41	60	172	02 41	60	172	01 41	60	172	351
8	05 44	60	173	04 44	59	173	03 45	60	173	02 45	60	173	01 45	60	173	352
7	05 48	60	174	04 48	60	174	03 40	60	174	02 48	60	174	01 48	59	174	353
6	05 51	60	175	04 51	60	175	03 51	60	175	02 51	59	175	01 52	60	175	354
5	05 54	-60	175	04 54	-60	175	03 54	-60	176	02 54	-60	176	01 54	-60	176	355
4	05 56	60	176	04 56	60	176	03 56	60	176	02 56	60	176	01 56	60	176	356
3	05 58	60	177	04 58	60	177	03 58	60	177	02 58	60	177	01 58	60	177	357
2	05 59	60	178	04 59	60	178	03 59	60	178	02 59	60	178	01 59	60	178	358
1	06 00	60	179	05 00	60	179	04 00	60	179	03 00	60	179	02 00	60	179	359
0	06 00	-60	180	05 00	-60	180	04 00	-60	180	03 00	-60	180	02 00	-60	180	360

S. Lat. {LHA greater than 180°……. Zn=180−Z; LHA less than 180°………. Zn=180+Z}

N. Lat. {LHA greater than 180°....... Zn=Z
{LHA less than 180°........... Zn=360−Z

DECLINATION (0°-14°) SAME NAME AS LATITUDE

LHA	0° Hc	d	Z	1° Hc	d	Z	2° Hc	d	Z	3° Hc	d	Z	4° Hc	d	Z
	° ′	′	°	° ′	′	°	° ′	′	°	° ′	′	°	° ′	′	°
0	30 00	+60	180	31 00	+60	180	32 00	+60	180	33 00	+60	180	34 00	+60	180
1	30 00	60	179	31 00	60	179	32 00	60	179	33 00	60	179	34 00	60	179
2	29 59	60	178	30 59	60	178	31 59	60	178	32 59	60	178	33 59	60	178
3	29 57	60	177	30 57	60	177	31 57	60	177	32 57	60	176	33 57	60	176
4	29 55	60	175	30 55	60	175	31 55	60	175	32 55	60	175	33 55	60	175
5	29 53	+59	174	30 52	+60	174	31 52	+60	174	32 52	+60	174	33 52	+60	174
6	29 49	60	173	30 49	60	173	31 49	60	173	32 49	60	173	33 49	60	173
7	29 45	60	172	30 45	60	172	31 45	60	172	32 45	60	172	33 45	59	172
8	29 41	60	171	30 41	59	171	31 40	60	171	32 40	60	171	33 40	60	170
9	29 36	59	170	30 35	60	170	31 35	60	169	32 35	60	169	33 35	59	169
10	29 30	+60	169	30 30	+59	168	31 29	+60	168	32 29	+60	168	33 29	+59	168
11	29 24	59	167	30 23	60	167	31 23	60	167	32 23	59	167	33 22	60	167
12	29 17	59	166	30 16	60	166	31 16	60	166	32 16	59	166	33 15	60	166
13	29 09	60	165	30 09	59	165	31 08	60	165	32 08	59	165	33 07	60	165
14	29 01	60	164	30 01	59	164	31 00	60	164	32 00	59	163	32 59	59	163
15	28 53	+59	163	29 52	+59	163	30 51	+60	163	31 51	+59	162	32 50	+59	162
16	28 44	59	162	29 43	59	162	30 42	59	161	31 41	60	161	32 41	59	161
17	28 34	59	161	29 33	59	160	30 32	59	160	31 31	59	160	32 30	60	160
18	28 24	59	159	29 23	59	159	30 22	59	159	31 21	59	159	32 20	59	159
19	28 13	59	158	29 12	59	158	30 11	59	158	31 10	59	158	32 09	58	157
20	28 02	+58	157	29 00	+59	157	29 59	+59	157	30 58	+59	157	31 57	+59	156
21	27 50	58	156	28 48	59	156	29 47	59	156	30 46	58	155	31 44	59	155
22	27 37	59	155	28 36	58	155	29 34	59	155	30 33	59	154	31 32	58	154
23	27 24	59	154	28 23	58	154	29 21	59	153	30 20	58	153	31 18	59	153
24	27 11	58	153	28 09	59	153	29 08	58	152	30 06	58	152	31 04	58	152
25	26 57	+58	152	27 55	+58	151	28 53	+59	151	29 52	+58	151	30 50	+58	151
26	26 42	59	151	27 41	58	150	28 39	58	150	29 37	58	150	30 35	58	150
27	26 27	58	150	27 25	58	149	28 23	58	149	29 21	58	149	30 19	58	148
28	26 12	58	149	27 10	58	148	28 08	57	148	29 05	58	148	30 03	58	147
29	25 56	58	147	26 54	57	147	27 51	58	147	28 49	58	147	29 47	57	146
30	25 40	+57	146	26 37	+58	146	27 35	+57	146	28 32	+58	145	29 30	+57	145
31	25 23	57	145	26 20	58	145	27 18	57	145	28 15	57	144	29 12	58	144
32	25 05	58	144	26 03	57	144	27 00	57	144	27 57	58	143	28 55	57	143
33	24 48	57	143	25 45	57	143	26 42	57	143	27 39	57	142	28 36	57	142
34	24 29	57	142	25 26	57	142	26 23	57	141	27 20	57	141	28 17	57	141
35	24 11	+57	141	25 08	+57	141	26 05	+56	140	27 01	+57	140	27 58	+57	140
36	23 52	56	140	24 48	57	140	25 45	57	139	26 42	57	139	27 39	56	139
37	23 32	57	139	24 29	56	139	25 25	57	138	26 22	56	138	27 18	57	138
38	23 12	57	138	24 09	56	138	25 05	57	137	26 02	56	137	26 58	56	136
39	22 52	56	137	23 48	57	137	24 45	56	136	25 41	56	136	26 37	56	135
40	22 31	+57	136	23 28	+56	136	24 24	+56	135	25 20	+56	135	26 16	+56	134
41	22 10	56	135	23 06	56	135	24 02	56	134	24 58	56	134	25 54	56	133
42	21 49	56	134	22 45	56	134	23 41	55	133	24 36	56	133	25 32	56	132
43	21 27	56	133	22 23	56	133	23 19	55	132	24 14	56	132	25 10	55	131
44	21 05	56	132	22 01	55	132	22 56	56	131	23 52	55	131	24 47	56	130
45	20 42	+56	131	21 38	+55	131	22 33	+56	130	23 29	+55	130	24 24	+55	129
46	20 19	56	130	21 15	55	130	22 10	55	129	23 05	56	129	24 01	55	128
47	19 56	56	129	20 52	55	129	21 47	55	128	22 42	55	128	23 37	55	127
48	19 33	55	128	20 28	55	128	21 23	55	127	22 18	55	127	23 13	55	126
49	19 09	55	127	20 04	56	127	20 59	55	126	21 54	55	126	22 49	54	125
50	18 45	+55	126	19 40	+55	126	20 35	+54	125	21 29	+55	125	22 24	+54	124
51	18 20	55	125	19 15	55	125	20 10	54	124	21 04	55	124	21 59	54	123
52	17 56	54	124	18 50	55	124	19 45	54	123	20 39	55	123	21 34	54	122
53	17 31	54	123	18 25	55	123	19 20	54	122	20 14	54	122	21 08	54	121
54	17 06	54	122	18 00	54	122	18 54	54	121	19 48	54	121	20 42	55	120
55	16 40	+54	121	17 34	+54	121	18 28	+54	120	19 22	+54	120	20 16	+54	119
56	16 14	54	120	17 08	54	120	18 02	54	119	18 56	54	119	19 50	54	119
57	15 48	54	119	16 42	54	119	17 36	54	118	18 30	54	118	19 24	53	118
58	15 22	54	118	16 16	54	118	17 10	53	118	18 03	54	117	18 57	54	117
59	14 55	54	118	15 49	54	117	16 43	53	117	17 36	54	116	18 30	54	116
60	14 29	+53	117	15 22	+54	116	16 16	+53	116	17 09	+54	115	18 03	+53	115
61	14 02	53	116	14 55	54	115	15 49	53	115	16 42	54	114	17 36	53	114
62	13 35	53	115	14 28	53	114	15 21	54	114	16 15	53	113	17 08	53	113
63	13 07	54	114	14 01	53	113	14 54	53	113	15 47	53	112	16 40	53	112
64	12 40	53	113	13 33	53	112	14 26	53	112	15 19	53	112	16 12	53	111
65	12 12	+53	112	13 05	+53	112	13 58	+53	111	14 51	+53	111	15 44	+53	110
66	11 44	53	111	12 37	53	111	13 30	53	110	14 23	53	110	15 16	53	109
67	11 16	53	110	12 09	53	110	13 02	53	109	13 55	53	109	14 48	52	108
68	10 48	53	109	11 41	52	109	12 33	53	108	13 26	53	108	14 19	53	107
69	10 19	53	108	11 12	53	108	12 05	53	107	12 58	52	107	13 50	53	106

LHA	5° Hc	d	Z	6° Hc	d	Z	7° Hc	d	Z	8° Hc	d	Z	9° Hc	d	Z
	° ′	′	°	° ′	′	°	° ′	′	°	° ′	′	°	° ′	′	°
0	35 00	+60	180	36 00	+60	180	37 00	+60	180	38 00	+60	180	39 00	+60	180
1	35 00	60	179	36 00	60	179	37 00	60	179	38 00	60	179	39 00	60	179
2	34 59	60	178	35 59	60	178	36 59	60	178	37 59	60	178	38 59	60	178
3	34 57	60	176	35 57	60	176	36 57	60	176	37 57	60	176	38 57	60	176
4	34 55	60	175	35 55	60	175	36 55	60	175	37 55	60	175	38 55	60	175
5	34 52	+60	174	35 52	+60	174	36 52	+60	174	37 52	+60	174	38 52	+60	174
6	34 49	59	173	35 48	60	173	36 48	60	173	37 48	60	173	38 48	60	172
7	34 44	60	172	35 44	60	171	36 44	60	171	37 44	60	171	38 44	60	171
8	34 40	60	170	35 40	59	170	36 39	60	170	37 39	60	170	38 39	60	170
9	34 34	60	169	35 34	60	169	36 34	60	169	37 34	59	169	38 33	60	169
10	34 28	+60	168	35 28	+60	168	36 28	+59	168	37 27	+60	168	38 27	+60	167
11	34 22	59	167	35 21	60	167	36 21	60	166	37 21	59	166	38 20	60	166
12	34 15	59	166	35 14	60	165	36 14	59	165	37 13	60	165	38 13	59	165
13	34 07	59	164	35 06	60	164	36 06	59	164	37 05	59	164	38 04	60	164
14	33 58	60	163	34 58	59	163	35 57	59	163	36 56	60	163	37 56	59	162
15	33 49	+60	162	34 49	+59	162	35 48	+59	162	36 47	+59	161	37 46	+59	161
16	33 40	59	161	34 39	59	161	35 38	59	160	36 37	59	160	37 36	59	160
17	33 30	59	160	34 29	59	159	35 28	59	159	36 27	59	159	37 26	59	159
18	33 19	59	158	34 18	59	158	35 17	59	158	36 16	58	158	37 14	59	158
19	33 07	59	157	34 06	59	157	35 05	59	157	36 04	59	157	37 03	58	156
20	32 56	+58	156	33 54	+59	156	34 53	+59	156	35 52	+58	155	36 50	+59	155
21	32 43	59	155	33 42	58	155	34 40	59	154	35 39	58	154	36 37	59	154
22	32 30	59	154	33 29	58	154	34 27	58	153	35 25	59	153	36 24	58	153
23	32 17	58	153	33 15	58	152	34 13	58	152	35 11	59	152	36 10	58	151
24	32 02	59	151	33 01	58	151	33 59	58	151	34 57	58	151	35 55	58	150
25	31 48	+58	150	32 46	+58	150	33 44	+58	150	34 42	+58	149	35 40	+58	149
26	31 33	58	149	32 31	58	149	33 29	57	149	34 26	58	148	35 24	58	148
27	31 17	58	148	32 15	58	148	33 13	57	147	34 10	58	147	35 08	58	147
28	31 01	58	147	31 59	57	147	32 56	58	146	33 54	57	146	34 51	58	146
29	30 44	58	146	31 42	57	146	32 39	58	145	33 37	57	145	34 34	58	144
30	30 27	+58	145	31 25	+57	144	32 22	+57	144	33 19	+58	144	34 17	+57	143
31	30 10	57	144	31 07	57	143	32 04	57	143	33 01	57	143	33 58	57	142
32	29 52	57	143	30 49	57	142	31 46	57	142	32 43	57	141	33 40	57	141
33	29 33	57	141	30 30	57	141	31 27	57	141	32 24	57	140	33 21	56	140
34	29 14	57	140	30 11	57	140	31 08	56	140	32 04	57	139	33 01	57	139
35	28 55	+57	139	29 52	+56	139	30 48	+57	139	31 45	+56	138	32 41	+56	138
36	28 35	57	138	29 32	56	138	30 28	56	137	31 24	57	137	32 21	56	137
37	28 15	56	137	29 11	57	137	30 08	56	136	31 04	56	136	32 00	56	136
38	27 54	56	136	28 50	57	136	29 47	56	135	30 43	56	135	31 39	56	134
39	27 33	56	135	28 29	56	135	29 25	56	134	30 21	56	134	31 17	56	133
40	27 12	+56	134	28 08	+56	134	29 04	+55	133	29 59	+56	133	30 55	+56	132
41	26 50	56	133	27 46	56	133	28 42	55	132	29 37	56	132	30 33	55	131
42	26 28	56	132	27 24	55	132	28 19	56	131	29 15	55	131	30 10	55	130
43	26 05	56	131	27 01	55	130	27 56	56	130	28 52	55	130	29 47	55	129
44	25 43	55	130	26 38	55	129	27 33	55	129	28 28	55	129	29 23	55	128
45	25 19	+55	129	26 14	+56	128	27 10	+55	128	28 05	+55	128	29 00	+54	127
46	24 56	55	128	25 51	55	127	26 46	55	127	27 41	54	127	28 35	55	126
47	24 32	55	127	25 27	55	126	26 22	54	126	27 16	55	125	28 11	55	125
48	24 08	54	126	25 02	55	125	25 57	55	125	26 52	54	124	27 46	55	124
49	23 43	55	125	24 38	54	124	25 32	55	124	26 27	54	123	27 21	54	123
50	23 18	+55	124	24 13	+54	123	25 07	+55	123	26 02	+54	122	26 56	+54	122
51	22 53	55	123	23 48	54	122	24 42	54	122	25 36	54	121	26 30	54	121
52	22 28	54	122	23 22	54	121	24 16	54	121	25 10	54	120	26 04	54	120
53	22 02	55	121	22 57	54	120	23 51	53	120	24 44	54	119	25 38	54	119
54	21 37	54	120	22 31	53	119	23 24	54	119	24 18	54	119	25 12	54	118
55	21 10	+54	119	22 04	+54	119	22 58	+54	118	23 52	+53	118	24 45	+54	117
56	20 44	54	118	21 38	53	118	22 31	54	117	23 25	53	117	24 18	54	116
57	20 17	54	117	21 11	54	117	22 05	53	116	22 58	53	116	23 51	54	115
58	19 51	53	116	20 44	54	116	21 38	53	115	22 31	53	115	23 24	53	114
59	19 24	53	115	20 17	53	115	21 10	54	114	22 04	53	114	22 57	53	113
60	18 56	+54	114	19 50	+53	114	20 43	+53	113	21 36	+53	113	22 29	+53	112
61	18 29	53	113	19 22	53	113	20 15	53	112	21 08	53	112	22 01	53	111
62	18 01	53	112	18 54	53	112	19 47	53	111	20 40	53	111	21 33	53	110
63	17 33	53	111	18 26	53	111	19 19	53	110	20 12	53	110	21 05	53	109
64	17 05	53	111	17 58	53	110	18 51	53	110	19 44	52	109	20 36	53	109
65	16 37	+53	110	17 30	+53	109	18 23	+52	109	19 15	+53	108	20 08	+52	108
66	16 09	53	109	17 02	52	108	17 54	53	108	18 47	52	107	19 39	53	107
67	15 40	53	108	16 33	53	107	17 26	52	107	18 18	52	106	19 10	53	106
68	15 12	52	107	16 04	53	106	16 57	52	106	17 49	53	105	18 42	52	105
69	14 43	52	106	15 35	53	105	16 28	52	105	17 20	52	104	18 12	53	104

10° Hc	d	Z	11° Hc	d	Z	12° Hc	d	Z	13° Hc	d	Z	14° Hc	d	Z	LHA
° ′	′	°	° ′	′	°	° ′	′	°	° ′	′	°	° ′	′	°	
40 00	+60	180	41 00	+60	180	42 00	+60	180	43 00	+60	180	44 00	+60	180	360
40 00	60	179	41 00	60	179	42 00	60	179	43 00	60	179	44 00	60	179	359
39 59	60	177	40 59	60	177	41 59	60	177	42 59	60	177	43 59	60	177	358
39 57	60	176	40 57	60	176	41 57	60	176	42 57	60	176	43 57	60	176	357
39 55	60	175	40 55	60	175	41 55	59	175	42 54	60	175	43 54	60	175	356
39 52	+60	174	40 52	+59	174	41 51	+60	173	42 51	+60	173	43 51	+60	173	355
39 48	60	172	40 48	60	172	41 48	60	172	42 48	59	172	43 47	60	172	354
39 44	59	171	40 43	60	171	41 43	60	171	42 43	60	171	43 43	60	171	353
39 39	59	170	40 38	60	170	41 38	60	170	42 38	60	169	43 38	59	169	352
39 33	60	169	40 33	59	168	41 32	60	168	42 32	60	168	43 32	59	168	351
39 27	+59	167	40 26	+60	167	41 26	+59	167	42 25	+60	167	43 25	+60	167	350
39 20	59	166	40 19	60	166	41 19	59	166	42 18	60	165	43 18	59	165	349
39 12	59	165	40 11	60	165	41 11	59	164	42 10	60	164	43 10	59	164	348
39 04	59	163	40 03	59	163	41 02	60	163	42 02	59	163	43 01	59	163	347
38 55	59	162	39 54	59	162	40 53	60	162	41 53	59	162	42 52	59	161	346
38 45	+60	161	39 45	+59	161	40 44	+59	161	41 43	+59	160	42 42	+59	160	345
38 35	59	160	39 34	59	160	40 33	59	159	41 32	59	159	42 31	59	159	344
38 25	59	158	39 24	58	158	40 22	59	158	41 21	59	158	42 20	59	157	343
38 13	59	157	39 12	59	157	40 11	59	157	41 10	58	156	42 08	59	156	342
38 01	59	156	39 00	59	156	39 59	58	155	40 57	59	155	41 56	58	155	341
37 49	+58	155	38 47	+59	155	39 46	+58	154	40 44	+59	154	41 43	+58	154	340
37 36	58	154	38 34	59	153	39 33	58	153	40 31	58	153	41 29	58	152	339
37 22	58	152	38 20	59	152	39 19	58	152	40 17	58	151	41 15	58	151	338
37 08	58	151	38 06	58	151	39 04	58	151	40 02	58	150	41 00	58	150	337
36 53	58	150	37 51	58	150	38 49	58	149	39 47	58	149	40 45	58	149	336
36 38	+58	149	37 36	+58	148	38 34	+57	148	39 31	+58	148	40 29	+58	147	335
36 22	58	148	37 20	57	147	38 17	58	147	39 15	58	147	40 13	57	146	334
36 06	57	146	37 03	58	146	38 01	57	146	38 58	58	145	39 56	57	145	333
35 49	57	145	36 46	58	145	37 44	57	145	38 41	57	144	39 38	57	144	332
35 32	57	144	36 29	57	144	37 26	57	143	38 23	57	143	39 20	57	143	331
35 14	+57	143	36 11	+57	143	37 08	+57	142	38 05	+57	142	39 02	+56	141	330
34 55	57	142	35 52	57	141	36 49	57	141	37 46	57	141	38 43	56	140	329
34 37	56	141	35 33	57	140	36 30	57	140	37 27	56	139	38 23	57	139	328
34 17	57	140	35 14	56	139	36 10	57	139	37 07	56	138	38 03	56	138	327
33 58	56	138	34 54	56	138	35 50	57	138	36 47	56	137	37 43	56	137	326
33 37	+57	137	34 34	+56	137	35 30	+56	136	36 26	+56	136	37 22	+56	136	325
33 17	56	136	34 13	56	136	35 09	56	135	36 05	56	135	37 01	56	134	324
32 56	56	135	33 52	56	135	34 48	56	134	35 44	55	134	36 39	56	133	323
32 35	55	134	33 30	56	134	34 26	56	133	35 22	55	133	36 17	56	132	322
32 13	55	133	33 08	56	133	34 04	55	132	34 59	56	132	35 55	55	131	321
31 51	+55	132	32 46	+55	131	33 41	+56	131	34 37	+55	130	35 32	+55	130	320
31 28	55	131	32 23	56	130	33 19	55	130	34 14	55	129	35 09	55	129	319
31 05	55	130	32 00	55	129	32 55	55	129	33 50	55	128	34 45	55	128	318
30 42	55	129	31 37	55	128	32 32	55	128	33 27	54	127	34 21	55	127	317
30 18	55	128	31 13	55	127	32 08	55	127	33 03	54	126	33 57	55	126	316
29 54	+55	127	30 49	+55	126	31 44	+54	126	32 38	+55	125	33 33	+54	125	315
29 30	55	126	30 25	54	125	31 19	55	125	32 14	54	124	33 08	54	124	314
29 06	54	125	30 00	54	124	30 54	55	124	31 49	54	123	32 43	54	123	313
28 41	54	124	29 35	54	123	30 29	54	123	31 23	54	122	32 17	54	122	312
28 15	55	123	29 10	54	122	30 04	54	122	30 58	53	121	31 51	54	120	311
27 50	+54	122	28 44	+54	121	29 38	+54	121	30 32	+53	120	31 25	+54	119	310
27 24	54	120	28 18	54	120	29 12	54	119	30 06	53	119	30 59	54	118	309
26 58	54	120	27 52	54	119	28 46	53	118	29 39	54	118	30 33	53	117	308
26 32	54	119	27 26	53	118	28 19	54	118	29 13	53	117	30 06	53	116	307
26 06	53	118	26 59	53	117	27 52	54	117	28 46	53	116	29 39	53	115	306
25 39	+53	117	26 32	+54	116	27 26	+53	116	28 19	+53	115	29 12	+53	114	305
25 12	53	116	26 05	53	115	26 58	53	115	27 51	53	114	28 44	53	114	304
24 45	53	115	25 38	53	114	26 31	53	114	27 24	53	113	28 17	52	113	303
24 17	53	114	25 10	53	113	26 03	53	113	26 56	53	112	27 49	52	112	302
23 50	53	113	24 43	53	112	25 36	52	112	26 28	53	111	27 21	52	111	301
23 22	+53	112	24 15	+53	111	25 08	+52	111	26 00	+53	110	26 53	+52	110	300
22 54	53	111	23 47	52	110	24 39	53	110	25 32	52	109	26 24	53	109	299
22 26	53	110	23 19	52	109	24 11	53	109	25 04	52	108	25 56	52	108	298
21 58	52	109	22 50	53	108	23 43	52	108	24 35	52	107	25 27	52	107	297
21 29	53	108	22 22	52	107	23 14	52	107	24 06	52	106	24 58	52	106	296
21 00	+53	107	21 53	+52	107	22 45	+52	106	23 37	+52	106	24 29	+52	105	295
20 32	52	106	21 24	52	106	22 16	52	105	23 08	52	105	24 00	52	104	294
20 03	52	105	20 55	52	105	21 47	52	104	22 39	52	104	23 31	52	103	293
19 34	52	104	20 26	52	104	21 18	52	103	22 10	52	103	23 02	52	102	292
19 05	52	103	19 57	52	103	20 49	52	102	21 41	52	102	22 33	51	101	291

S. Lat. {LHA greater than 180°........ Zn=180−Z
{LHA less than 180°........... Zn=180+Z

DECLINATION (0°-14°) SAME NAME AS LATITUDE

N. Lat. {LHA greater than 180°....... Zn=Z
{LHA less than 180°........... Zn=360−Z

DECLINATION (0°-14°) SAME NAME AS LATITUDE

LHA	0° Hc	0° d	0° Z	1° Hc	1° d	1° Z	2° Hc	2° d	2° Z	3° Hc	3° d	3° Z	4° Hc	4° d	4° Z
	° ′	′	°	° ′	′	°	° ′	′	°	° ′	′	°	° ′	′	°
70	09 51	+53	108	10 44	+52	107	11 36	+53	107	12 29	+52	106	13 21	+53	106
71	09 22	53	107	10 15	52	106	11 07	53	106	12 00	52	105	12 52	53	105
72	08 53	53	106	09 46	52	105	10 38	53	105	11 31	52	104	12 23	53	104
73	08 24	53	105	09 17	52	104	10 09	53	104	11 02	52	103	11 54	52	103
74	07 55	53	104	08 48	52	104	09 40	53	103	10 33	52	103	11 25	52	102
75	07 26	+53	103	08 19	+52	103	09 11	+52	102	10 03	+52	102	10 55	+53	101
76	06 57	52	102	07 49	53	102	08 42	52	101	09 34	52	101	10 26	52	100
77	06 28	52	101	07 20	52	101	08 12	52	100	09 04	52	100	09 56	53	99
78	05 58	52	100	06 50	53	100	07 43	52	99	08 35	52	99	09 27	52	98
79	05 29	52	100	06 21	52	99	07 13	52	99	08 05	52	98	08 57	52	98
80	04 59	+52	99	05 51	+52	98	06 43	+52	98	07 35	+52	97	08 27	+52	97
81	04 29	52	98	05 21	52	97	06 13	52	97	07 05	52	96	07 57	52	96
82	03 59	52	97	04 51	53	96	05 44	52	96	06 36	52	95	07 28	52	95
83	03 30	52	96	04 22	52	96	05 14	52	95	06 06	52	95	06 58	52	94
84	03 00	52	95	03 52	52	95	04 44	52	94	05 36	52	94	06 28	52	93
85	02 30	+52	94	03 22	+52	94	04 14	+52	93	05 06	+52	93	05 58	+52	92
86	02 00	52	93	02 52	52	93	03 44	52	92	04 36	52	92	05 28	52	92
87	01 30	52	93	02 22	52	92	03 14	52	92	04 06	52	91	04 58	52	91
88	01 00	52	92	01 52	52	91	02 44	52	91	03 36	52	90	04 28	52	90
89	00 30	52	91	01 22	52	90	02 14	52	90	03 06	52	89	03 58	52	89
90	00 00	+52	90	00 52	+52	90	01 44	+52	89	02 36	+52	89	03 28	+52	88
91	−0 30	52	89	00 22	52	89	01 14	52	88	02 06	52	88	02 58	52	87
92	−1 00	52	88	−0 08	52	88	00 44	52	87	01 36	52	87	02 28	52	86
93	−1 30	52	87	−0 38	52	87	00 14	52	86	01 06	52	86	01 58	52	85
94	−2 00	52	87	−1 08	52	86	−0 16	52	86	00 36	52	85	01 28	52	85
95	−2 30	+52	86	−1 38	+52	85	−0 46	+52	85	00 06	+52	84	00 58	+52	84
96	−3 00	52	85	−2 08	52	84	−1 16	52	84	−0 24	52	83	00 28	52	83
97	−3 30	52	84	−2 38	53	83	−1 45	52	83	−0 53	52	82	−0 01	52	82
98	−3 59	52	83	−3 07	52	83	−2 15	52	82	−1 23	52	82	−0 31	52	81
99	−4 29	52	82	−3 37	52	82	−2 45	52	81	−1 53	52	81	−1 01	53	80
100	−4 59	+52	81	−4 07	+53	81	−3 14	+52	80	−2 22	+52	80	−1 30	+52	79
101	−5 29	53	80	−4 36	52	80	−3 44	52	79	−2 52	52	79	−2 00	53	78
102	−5 58	52	80	−5 06	53	79	−4 13	52	79	−3 21	52	78	−2 29	52	78
103				−5 35	52	78	−4 43	53	78	−3 50	52	77	−2 58	52	77
104							−5 12	52	77	−4 20	53	76	−3 27	52	76
105							−5 41	+52	76	−4 49	+53	75	−3 56	+52	75
106										−5 18	53	75	−4 25	52	74
107										−5 47	53	74	−4 54	53	73
108													−5 23	53	72
109													−5 51	53	71

LHA	5° Hc	5° d	5° Z	6° Hc	6° d	6° Z	7° Hc	7° d	7° Z	8° Hc	8° d	8° Z	9° Hc	9° d	9° Z
	° ′	′	°	° ′	′	°	° ′	′	°	° ′	′	°	° ′	′	°
70	14 14	+52	105	15 06	+53	105	15 59	+52	104	16 51	+52	104	17 43	+52	103
71	13 45	52	104	14 37	53	104	15 30	52	103	16 22	52	103	17 14	52	102
72	13 16	52	103	14 08	52	103	15 00	53	102	15 53	52	102	16 45	52	101
73	12 46	53	102	13 39	52	102	14 31	52	101	15 23	52	101	16 15	52	100
74	12 17	52	102	13 09	53	101	14 02	52	101	14 54	52	100	15 46	52	99
75	11 48	+52	101	12 40	+52	100	13 32	+52	100	14 24	+52	99	15 16	+52	99
76	11 18	52	100	12 10	52	99	13 02	52	99	13 54	52	98	14 46	52	98
77	10 49	52	99	11 41	52	98	12 33	52	98	13 25	52	97	14 17	51	97
78	10 19	52	98	11 11	52	97	12 03	52	97	12 55	52	96	13 47	52	96
79	09 49	52	97	10 41	52	97	11 33	52	96	12 25	52	96	13 17	52	95
80	09 19	+52	96	10 11	+52	96	11 03	+52	95	11 55	+52	95	12 47	+52	94
81	08 49	52	95	09 41	52	95	10 33	52	94	11 25	52	94	12 17	52	93
82	08 20	52	94	09 12	51	94	10 03	52	93	10 55	52	93	11 47	52	92
83	07 50	52	94	08 42	51	93	09 33	52	93	10 25	52	92	11 17	52	92
84	07 20	52	93	08 12	51	92	09 03	52	92	09 55	52	91	10 47	52	91
85	06 50	+52	92	07 42	+51	91	08 33	+52	91	09 25	+52	90	10 17	+52	90
86	06 20	52	91	07 12	51	91	08 03	52	90	08 55	52	89	09 47	52	89
87	05 50	52	90	06 42	51	90	07 33	52	89	08 25	52	89	09 17	52	88
88	05 20	52	89	06 12	51	89	07 03	52	88	07 55	52	88	08 47	52	87
89	04 50	52	88	05 42	52	88	06 34	51	87	07 25	52	87	08 17	52	86
90	04 20	+52	88	05 12	+52	87	06 04	+51	87	06 55	+52	86	07 47	+52	86
91	03 50	52	87	04 42	52	86	05 34	51	86	06 25	52	85	07 17	52	85
92	03 20	52	86	04 12	52	85	05 04	52	85	05 56	51	84	06 47	52	84
93	02 50	52	85	03 42	52	84	04 34	52	84	05 26	52	83	06 18	52	83
94	02 20	52	84	03 12	52	84	04 04	52	83	04 56	52	83	05 48	52	82
95	01 50	+52	83	02 42	+52	83	03 34	+52	82	04 26	+52	82	05 18	+52	81
96	01 20	53	82	02 13	52	82	03 05	52	81	03 57	52	81	04 49	52	80
97	00 51	52	81	01 43	52	81	02 35	52	80	03 27	52	80	04 19	52	79
98	00 21	52	81	01 13	52	80	02 05	53	80	02 58	52	79	03 50	52	79
99	−0 08	52	80	00 44	52	79	01 36	52	79	02 28	52	78	03 20	52	78
100	−0 38	+52	79	00 14	+53	78	01 07	+52	78	01 59	+52	77	02 51	+52	77
101	−1 07	52	78	−0 15	52	77	00 37	53	77	01 30	52	77	02 22	52	76
102	−1 37	53	77	−0 44	52	77	00 08	52	76	01 00	53	76	01 53	52	75
103	−2 06	53	76	−1 13	52	76	−0 21	52	75	00 31	53	75	01 24	52	74
104	−2 35	53	75	−1 42	52	75	−0 50	53	74	00 03	52	74	00 55	52	73
105	−3 04	+53	74	−2 11	+52	74	−1 19	+53	74	−0 26	+52	73	00 26	+53	73
106	−3 33	53	74	−2 40	53	73	−1 47	52	73	−0 55	53	72	−0 02	52	72
107	−4 01	52	73	−3 09	53	72	−2 16	53	72	−1 23	52	71	−0 31	53	71
108	−4 30	53	72	−3 37	53	71	−2 44	52	71	−1 52	53	70	−0 59	53	70
109	−4 58	52	71	−4 06	53	71	−3 13	53	70	−2 20	53	70	−1 27	53	69
110	−5 27	+53	70	−4 34	+53	70	−3 41	+53	69	−2 48	+53	69	−1 55	+53	68
111	−5 55	53	69	−5 02	53	69	−4 09	53	68	−3 16	53	68	−2 23	53	67
112				−5 30	53	68	−4 37	54	67	−3 43	53	67	−2 50	53	66
113							−5 04	53	66	−4 11	53	66	−3 18	54	66
114							−5 32	54	66	−4 38	53	65	−3 45	53	65
115										−5 05	+53	64	−4 12	+53	64
116										−5 32	53	63	−4 39	54	63
117													−5 05	53	62
118													−5 32	54	61

LHA	10° Hc	10° d	10° Z	11° Hc	11° d	11° Z	12° Hc	12° d	12° Z	13° Hc	13° d	13° Z	14° Hc	14° d	14° Z	LHA
	° ′	′	°	° ′	′	°	° ′	′	°	° ′	′	°	° ′	′	°	
70	18 35	+53	103	19 28	+51	102	20 19	+52	101	21 11	+52	101	22 03	+52	100	290
71	18 06	52	102	18 58	52	101	19 50	52	101	20 42	52	100	21 34	51	99	289
72	17 37	52	101	18 29	52	100	19 21	51	100	20 12	52	99	21 04	52	99	288
73	17 07	52	100	17 59	52	99	18 51	52	99	19 43	51	98	20 34	52	98	287
74	16 38	51	99	17 29	52	98	18 21	52	98	19 13	51	97	20 04	52	97	286
75	16 08	+52	98	17 00	+51	98	17 51	+52	97	18 43	+52	96	19 35	+51	96	285
76	15 38	52	97	16 30	52	97	17 22	51	96	18 13	52	96	19 05	51	95	284
77	15 08	52	96	16 00	52	96	16 52	51	95	17 43	52	95	18 35	51	94	283
78	14 39	51	95	15 30	52	95	16 22	51	94	17 13	52	94	18 05	51	93	282
79	14 09	51	95	15 00	52	94	15 52	52	93	16 44	51	93	17 35	51	92	281
80	13 39	+51	94	14 30	+52	93	15 22	+52	93	16 14	+51	92	17 05	+51	92	280
81	13 09	51	93	14 00	52	92	14 52	52	92	15 44	51	91	16 35	51	91	279
82	12 39	51	92	13 30	52	91	14 22	52	91	15 14	51	90	16 05	51	90	278
83	12 09	51	91	13 00	52	91	13 52	52	90	14 44	51	89	15 35	51	89	277
84	11 39	51	90	12 30	52	90	13 22	52	89	14 14	51	89	15 05	51	88	276
85	11 09	+51	89	12 00	+52	89	12 52	+52	88	13 44	+51	88	14 35	+51	87	275
86	10 39	51	88	11 30	52	88	12 22	52	87	13 14	51	87	14 05	52	86	274
87	10 09	51	88	11 00	52	87	11 52	52	87	12 44	51	86	13 35	52	86	273
88	09 39	52	87	10 31	51	86	11 22	52	86	12 14	51	85	13 05	52	85	272
89	09 09	52	86	10 01	51	85	10 52	52	85	11 44	51	84	12 35	52	84	271
90	08 39	+52	85	09 31	+51	84	10 22	+52	84	11 14	+52	83	12 06	+51	83	270
91	08 09	52	84	09 01	52	84	09 53	51	83	10 44	52	83	11 36	51	82	269
92	07 39	52	83	08 31	52	83	09 23	52	82	10 15	51	82	11 06	52	81	268
93	07 10	51	82	08 01	52	82	08 53	52	81	09 45	52	81	10 37	51	80	267
94	06 40	52	82	07 32	52	81	08 24	51	81	09 15	52	80	10 07	52	80	266
95	06 10	+52	81	07 02	+52	80	07 54	+52	80	08 46	+52	79	09 38	+51	79	265
96	05 41	52	80	06 33	52	79	07 25	51	79	08 16	52	78	09 08	52	78	264
97	05 11	52	79	06 03	52	79	06 55	52	78	07 47	52	77	08 39	52	77	263
98	04 42	52	78	05 34	52	78	06 26	52	77	07 18	52	77	08 10	52	76	262
99	04 12	53	77	05 05	52	77	05 57	52	76	06 49	52	76	07 41	52	75	261
100	03 43	+52	76	04 35	+53	76	05 28	+52	75	06 20	+52	75	07 12	+52	74	260
101	03 14	52	76	04 06	53	75	04 59	52	75	05 51	52	74	06 43	52	74	259
102	02 45	52	75	03 37	53	74	04 30	52	74	05 22	52	73	06 14	52	73	258
103	02 16	53	74	03 09	52	73	04 01	53	73	04 54	52	72	05 46	52	72	257
104	01 47	53	73	02 40	52	72	03 32	53	72	04 25	52	71	05 17	53	71	256
105	01 19	+52	72	02 11	+53	72	03 04	+52	71	03 56	+53	71	04 49	+52	70	255
106	00 50	53	71	01 43	53	71	02 36	52	70	03 28	53	70	04 21	52	69	254
107	00 22	53	70	01 15	52	70	02 07	53	69	03 00	53	69	03 53	52	68	253
108	−0 06	53	69	00 47	52	69	01 39	53	69	02 32	53	68	03 25	53	68	252
109	−0 34	53	69	00 19	53	68	01 12	52	68	02 04	53	67	02 57	53	67	251
110	−1 02	+53	68	−0 09	+53	67	00 44	+53	67	01 37	+53	66	02 30	+53	66	250
111	−1 30	53	67	−0 37	53	66	00 16	54	66	01 10	53	65	02 03	53	65	249
112	−1 57	53	66	−1 04	53	66	−0 11	53	65	00 42	53	65	01 35	54	64	248
113	−2 24	53	65	−1 31	53	65	−0 38	53	64	00 15	54	64	01 09	53	63	247
114	−2 52	54	64	−1 58	53	64	−1 05	54	63	−0 11	53	63	00 42	53	62	246
115	−3 19	+54	63	−2 25	+53	63	−1 32	+54	62	−0 38	+53	62	00 15	+54	62	245
116	−3 45	53	62	−2 52	54	62	−1 58	54	62	−1 04	53	61	−0 11	54	61	244
117	−4 12	54	62	−3 18	54	61	−2 24	53	61	−1 31	54	60	−0 37	54	60	243
118	−4 38	54	61	−3 44	54	60	−2 50	53	60	−1 57	54	59	−1 03	54	59	242
119	−5 04	54	60	−4 10	54	59	−3 16	54	59	−2 22	54	59	−1 28	54	58	241
120	−5 30	+54	59	−4 36	+54	59	−3 42	+54	58	−2 48	+54	58	−1 54	+54	57	240
121				−5 01	54	58	−4 07	54	57	−3 13	54	57	−2 19	54	56	239
122				−5 27	55	57	−4 32	54	56	−3 38	54	56	−2 44	55	55	238
123							−4 57	54	55	−4 03	55	55	−3 08	54	55	237
124							−5 22	55	54	−4 27	54	54	−3 33	55	54	236
125							−5 46	+55	54	−4 51	+54	53	−3 57	+55	53	235
126										−5 15	55	52	−4 20	55	52	234
127										−5 39	55	51	−4 44	55	51	233
128													−5 07	55	50	232
129													−5 30	55	49	231

0° 1° 2° 3° 4° 5° 6° 7° 8° 9° 10° 11° 12° 13° 14°

S. Lat. {LHA greater than 180°....... Zn=180−Z
{LHA less than 180°........... Zn=180+Z

DECLINATION (0°-14°) SAME NAME AS LATITUDE

N. Lat. {LHA greater than 180°....... Zn=Z; LHA less than 180°........... Zn=360−Z}

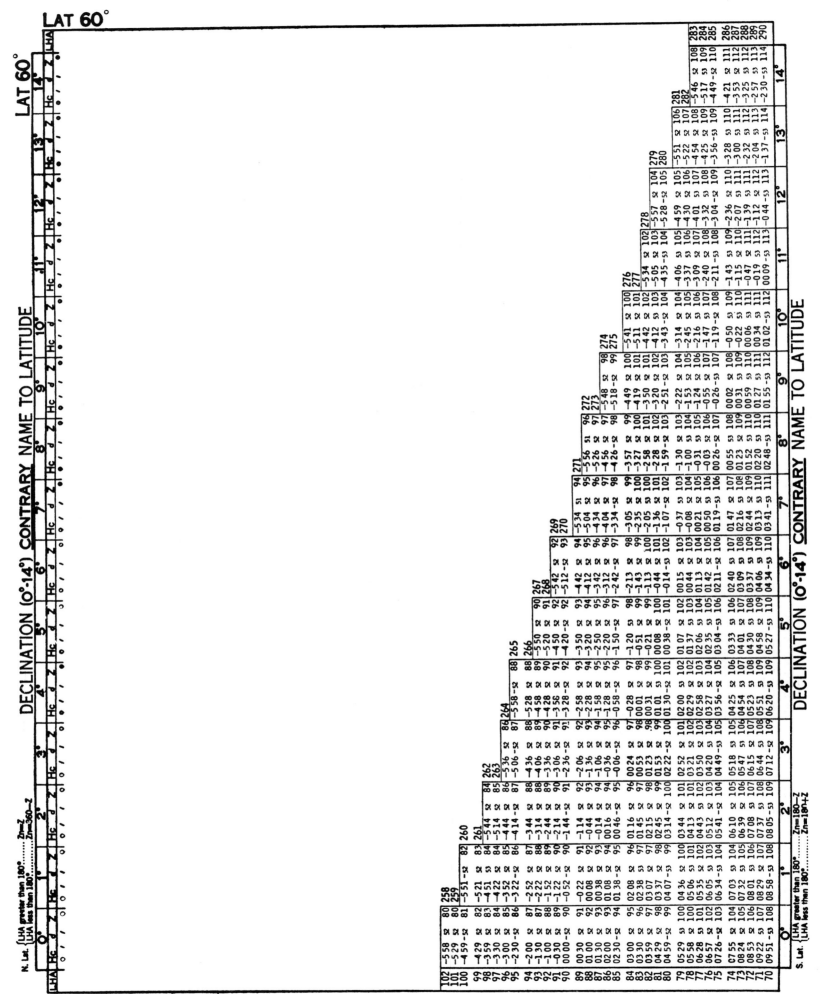

DECLINATION (0°-14°) CONTRARY NAME TO LATITUDE

LHA	0° Hc	0° d	0° Z	1° Hc	1° d	1° Z	2° Hc	2° d	2° Z	3° Hc	3° d	3° Z	4° Hc	4° d	4° Z
	° ′	′	°	° ′	′	°	° ′	′	°	° ′	′	°	° ′	′	°
102	-5 58	52	80												
101	-5 29	52	80												
100	-4 59	-52	81	-5 51	-52	82									
99	-4 29	52	82	-5 21	52	83									
98	-3 59	52	83	-4 51	53	84	-5 44	52	84						
97	-3 30	52	84	-4 22	52	84	-5 14	52	85						
96	-3 00	52	85	-3 52	52	85	-4 44	52	86	-5 36	52	86			
95	-2 30	-52	86	-3 22	-52	86	-4 14	-52	87	-5 06	-52	87	-5 58	-52	88
94	-2 00	52	87	-2 52	52	87	-3 44	52	88	-4 36	52	88	-5 28	52	88
93	-1 30	52	87	-2 22	52	88	-3 14	52	88	-4 06	52	89	-4 58	52	89
92	-1 00	52	88	-1 52	52	89	-2 44	52	89	-3 36	52	90	-4 28	52	90
91	-0 30	52	89	-1 22	52	90	-2 14	52	90	-3 06	52	91	-3 58	52	91
90	00 00	-52	90	-0 52	-52	90	-1 44	-52	91	-2 36	-52	91	-3 28	-52	92
89	00 30	52	91	-0 22	52	91	-1 14	52	92	-2 06	52	92	-2 58	52	93
88	01 00	52	92	00 08	52	92	-0 44	52	93	-1 36	52	93	-2 28	52	94
87	01 30	52	93	00 38	52	93	-0 14	52	94	-1 06	52	94	-1 58	52	95
86	02 00	52	93	01 08	52	94	00 16	52	94	-0 36	52	95	-1 28	52	95
85	02 30	-52	94	01 38	-52	95	00 46	-52	95	-0 06	-52	96	-0 58	-52	96
84	03 00	52	95	02 08	52	96	01 16	52	96	00 24	52	97	-0 28	52	97
83	03 30	52	96	02 38	53	97	01 45	52	97	00 53	52	98	00 01	52	98
82	03 59	52	97	03 07	52	97	02 15	52	98	01 23	52	.98	00 31	52	99
81	04 29	52	98	03 37	52	98	02 45	52	99	01 53	52	99	01 01	53	100
80	04 59	-52	99	04 07	-53	99	03 14	-52	100	02 22	-52	100	01 30	-52	101
79	05 29	53	100	04 36	52	100	03 44	52	101	02 52	52	101	02 00	53	102
78	05 58	52	100	05 06	53	101	04 13	52	101	03 21	52	102	02 29	52	102
77	06 28	53	101	05 35	52	102	04 43	53	102	03 50	52	103	02 58	52	103
76	06 57	52	102	06 05	53	103	05 12	52	103	04 20	53	104	03 27	52	104
75	07 26	-52	103	06 34	-53	104	05 41	-52	104	04 49	-53	105	03 56	-52	105
74	07 55	52	104	07 03	53	104	06 10	52	105	05 18	53	105	04 25	52	106
73	08 24	52	105	07 32	53	105	06 39	52	106	05 47	53	106	04 54	53	107
72	08 53	52	106	08 01	53	106	07 08	53	107	06 15	52	107	05 23	53	108
71	09 22	53	107	08 29	52	107	07 37	53	108	06 44	53	108	05 51	53	109
70	09 51	-53	108	08 58	-53	108	08 05	-53	109	07 12	-52	109	06 20	-53	109

LHA	5° Hc	5° d	5° Z	6° Hc	6° d	6° Z	7° Hc	7° d	7° Z	8° Hc	8° d	8° Z	9° Hc	9° d	9° Z
	° ′	′	°	° ′	′	°	° ′	′	°	° ′	′	°	° ′	′	°
102															
101															
100															
99															
98															
97															
96															
95															
94															
93	-5 50	52	90												
92	-5 20	52	91												
91	-4 50	52	92	-5 42	52	92									
90	-4 20	-52	92	-5 12	-52	93									
89	-3 50	52	93	-4 42	52	94	-5 34	51	94						
88	-3 20	52	94	-4 12	52	95	-5 04	52	95	-5 56	51	96			
87	-2 50	52	95	-3 42	52	96	-4 34	52	96	-5 26	52	97			
86	-2 20	52	96	-3 12	52	96	-4 04	52	97	-4 56	52	97	-5 48	52	98
85	-1 50	-52	97	-2 42	-52	97	-3 34	-52	98	-4 26	-52	98	-5 18	-52	99
84	-1 20	53	98	-2 13	52	98	-3 05	52	99	-3 57	52	99	-4 49	52	100
83	-0 51	52	99	-1 43	52	99	-2 35	52	100	-3 27	52	100	-4 19	52	101
82	-0 21	52	99	-1 13	52	100	-2 05	53	100	-2 58	52	101	-3 50	52	101
81	00 08	52	100	-0 44	52	101	-1 36	52	101	-2 28	52	102	-3 20	52	102
80	00 38	-52	101	-0 14	-53	102	-1 07	-52	102	-1 59	-52	103	-2 51	-52	103
79	01 07	52	102	00 15	52	103	-0 37	53	103	-1 30	52	103	-2 22	52	104
78	01 37	53	103	00 44	52	103	-0 08	52	104	-1 00	53	104	-1 53	52	105
77	02 06	53	104	01 13	52	104	00 21	52	105	-0 31	53	105	-1 24	52	106
76	02 35	53	105	01 42	52	105	00 50	53	106	-0 03	52	106	-0 55	52	107
75	03 04	-53	106	02 11	-52	106	01 19	-53	106	00 26	-52	107	-0 26	-53	107
74	03 33	53	106	02 40	53	107	01 47	52	107	00 55	53	108	00 02	52	108
73	04 01	52	107	03 09	53	108	02 16	53	108	01 23	52	109	00 31	53	109
72	04 30	53	108	03 37	53	109	02 44	52	109	01 52	53	110	00 59	53	110
71	04 58	52	109	04 06	53	109	03 13	53	110	02 20	53	110	01 27	53	111
70	05 27	-53	110	04 34	-53	110	03 41	-53	111	02 48	-53	111	01 55	-53	112

LHA	10° Hc	10° d	10° Z	11° Hc	11° d	11° Z	12° Hc	12° d	12° Z	13° Hc	13° d	13° Z	14° Hc	14° d	14° Z	LHA
	° ′	′	°	° ′	′	°	° ′	′	°	° ′	′	°	° ′	′	°	
102																258
101																259
100																260
99																261
98																262
97																263
96																264
95																265
94																266
93																267
92																268
91																269
90																270
89																271
88																272
87																273
86																274
85																275
84	-5 41	52	100													276
83	-5 11	52	101													277
82	-4 42	52	102	-5 34	52	102										278
81	-4 12	53	103	-5 05	52	103	-5 57	52	104							279
80	-3 43	-52	104	-4 35	-53	104	-5 28	-52	105							280
79	-3 14	52	104	-4 06	53	105	-4 59	52	105	-5 51	52	106				281
78	-2 45	52	105	-3 37	53	106	-4 30	52	106	-5 22	52	107				282
77	-2 16	53	106	-3 09	52	107	-4 01	53	107	-4 54	52	108	-5 46	52	108	283
76	-1 47	53	107	-2 40	52	108	-3 32	53	108	-4 25	52	109	-5 17	53	109	284
75	-1 19	-52	108	-2 11	-53	108	-3 04	-52	109	-3 56	-53	109	-4 49	-52	110	285
74	-0 50	53	109	-1 43	53	109	-2 36	52	110	-3 28	53	110	-4 21	52	111	286
73	-0 22	53	110	-1 15	52	110	-2 07	53	111	-3 00	53	111	-3 53	52	112	287
72	00 06	53	111	-0 47	52	111	-1 39	53	111	-2 32	53	112	-3 25	53	112	288
71	00 34	53	111	-0 19	53	112	-1 12	52	112	-2 04	53	113	-2 57	53	113	289
70	01 02	-53	112	00 09	-53	113	-0 44	-53	113	-1 37	-53	114	-2 30	-53	114	290

S. Lat. {LHA greater than 180°........ Zn=180−Z; LHA less than 180°........... Zn=180+Z}

DECLINATION (0°-14°) CONTRARY NAME TO LATITUDE

N. Lat. {LHA greater than 180°....... Zn=Z; LHA less than 180°.......... Zn=360−Z}

DECLINATION (0°-14°) CONTRARY NAME TO LATITUDE

LHA	0° Hc	0° d	0° Z	1° Hc	1° d	1° Z	2° Hc	2° d	2° Z	3° Hc	3° d	3° Z	4° Hc	4° d	4° Z	5° Hc	5° d	5° Z	6° Hc	6° d	6° Z	7° Hc	7° d	7° Z
	° ′	′	°	° ′	′	°	° ′	′	°	° ′	′	°	° ′	′	°	° ′	′	°	° ′	′	°	° ′	′	°
69	10 19	52	108	09 27	53	109	08 34	53	109	07 41	53	110	06 48	53	110	05 55	53	111	05 02	53	111	04 09	53	112
68	10 48	53	109	09 55	53	110	09 02	53	110	08 09	53	111	07 16	53	111	06 23	53	112	05 30	53	112	04 37	54	113
67	11 16	53	110	10 23	53	111	09 30	53	111	08 37	53	112	07 44	53	112	06 51	54	113	05 57	53	113	05 04	53	114
66	11 44	53	111	10 51	53	112	09 58	53	112	09 05	54	113	08 11	53	113	07 18	53	113	06 25	53	114	05 32	54	114
65	12 12	−53	112	11 19	−53	113	10 26	−54	113	09 32	−53	113	08 39	−53	114	07 46	−54	114	06 52	−53	115	05 59	−54	115
64	12 40	54	113	11 46	53	113	10 53	53	114	10 00	54	114	09 06	53	115	08 13	54	115	07 19	53	116	06 26	54	116
63	13 07	53	114	12 14	54	114	11 20	53	115	10 27	54	115	09 33	53	116	08 40	54	116	07 46	53	117	06 53	54	117
62	13 35	54	115	12 41	53	115	11 48	54	116	10 54	54	116	10 00	53	117	09 07	54	117	08 13	54	118	07 19	53	118
61	14 02	54	116	13 08	53	116	12 15	54	117	11 21	54	117	10 27	54	118	09 33	53	118	08 40	54	118	07 46	54	119
60	14 29	−54	117	13 35	−54	117	12 41	−54	118	11 47	−53	118	10 54	−54	118	10 00	−54	119	09 06	−54	119	08 12	−54	120
59	14 55	53	118	14 02	54	118	13 08	54	118	12 14	54	119	11 20	54	119	10 26	54	120	09 32	54	120	08 38	54	121
58	15 22	54	118	14 28	54	119	13 34	54	119	12 40	54	120	11 46	54	120	10 52	54	121	09 58	54	121	09 04	55	122
57	15 48	54	119	14 54	54	120	14 00	54	120	13 06	54	121	12 12	54	121	11 18	55	122	10 23	54	122	09 29	54	122
56	16 14	54	120	15 20	54	121	14 26	54	121	13 32	55	122	12 37	54	122	11 43	54	123	10 49	55	123	09 54	54	123
55	16 40	−54	121	15 46	−55	122	14 51	−54	122	13 57	−54	123	13 03	−55	123	12 08	−54	123	11 14	−55	124	10 19	−54	124
54	17 06	55	122	16 11	54	123	15 17	55	123	14 22	54	124	13 28	55	124	12 33	55	124	11 38	54	125	10 44	55	125
53	17 31	55	123	16 36	54	124	15 42	55	124	14 47	55	124	13 52	54	125	12 58	55	125	12 03	55	126	11 08	55	126
52	17 56	55	124	17 01	55	125	16 06	54	125	15 12	55	125	14 17	55	126	13 22	55	126	12 27	55	127	11 32	55	127
51	18 20	54	125	17 26	55	126	16 31	55	126	15 36	55	126	14 41	55	127	13 46	55	127	12 51	55	128	11 56	55	128
50	18 45	−55	126	17 50	−55	126	16 55	−55	127	16 00	−55	127	15 05	−55	128	14 10	−55	128	13 15	−55	129	12 20	−56	129
49	19 09	55	127	18 14	55	127	17 19	55	128	16 24	55	128	15 29	56	129	14 33	55	129	13 38	55	129	12 43	56	130
48	19 33	55	128	18 38	56	128	17 42	55	129	16 47	55	129	15 52	56	130	14 56	55	130	14 01	55	130	13 06	56	131
47	19 56	55	129	19 01	55	129	18 06	56	130	17 10	55	130	16 15	56	131	15 19	55	131	14 24	56	131	13 28	55	132
46	20 19	55	130	19 24	55	130	18 29	56	131	17 33	56	131	16 37	55	132	15 42	56	132	14 46	56	132	13 50	55	133
45	20 42	−55	131	19 47	−56	131	18 51	−56	132	17 55	−55	132	17 00	−56	133	16 04	−56	133	15 08	−56	133	14 12	−56	134
44	21 05	56	132	20 09	56	132	19 13	55	133	18 18	56	133	17 22	56	133	16 26	56	134	15 30	56	134	14 34	56	135
43	21 27	56	133	20 31	56	133	19 35	56	134	18 39	56	134	17 43	56	134	16 47	56	135	15 51	56	135	14 55	56	136
42	21 49	56	134	20 53	56	134	19 57	56	135	19 01	56	135	18 05	57	135	17 08	56	136	16 12	56	136	15 16	56	137
41	22 10	56	135	21 14	56	135	20 18	56	136	19 22	57	136	18 25	56	136	17 29	56	137	16 33	57	137	15 36	56	138
40	22 31	−56	136	21 35	−56	136	20 39	−57	137	19 42	−56	137	18 46	−57	137	17 49	−56	138	16 53	−57	138	15 56	−56	138
39	22 52	56	137	21 56	57	137	20 59	56	138	20 03	57	138	19 06	57	138	18 09	56	139	17 13	57	139	16 16	57	139
38	23 12	56	138	22 16	57	138	21 19	57	139	20 22	56	139	19 26	57	139	18 29	57	140	17 32	57	140	16 35	56	140
37	23 32	57	139	22 35	56	139	21 39	57	140	20 42	57	140	19 45	57	140	18 48	57	141	17 51	57	141	16 54	57	141
36	23 52	57	140	22 55	57	140	21 58	57	141	21 01	57	141	20 04	57	141	19 07	57	142	18 10	57	142	17 13	57	142
35	24 11	−57	141	23 14	−57	141	22 17	−57	142	21 20	−57	142	20 23	−58	142	19 25	−57	143	18 28	−57	143	17 31	−57	143
34	24 29	57	142	23 32	57	142	22 35	57	143	21 38	57	143	20 41	58	143	19 43	57	144	18 46	57	144	17 49	58	144
33	24 48	58	143	23 50	57	144	22 53	57	144	21 56	58	144	20 58	57	144	20 01	58	145	19 03	57	145	18 06	57	145
32	25 05	57	144	24 08	57	145	23 11	58	145	22 13	57	145	21 16	58	145	20 18	58	146	19 20	57	146	18 23	58	146
31	25 23	58	145	24 25	57	146	23 28	58	146	22 30	58	146	21 32	57	147	20 35	58	147	19 37	58	147	18 39	57	147
30	25 40	−58	146	24 42	−58	147	23 44	−58	147	22 46	−57	147	21 49	−58	148	20 51	−58	148	19 53	−58	148	18 55	−58	148
29	25 56	58	147	24 58	58	148	24 00	58	148	23 02	57	148	22 05	58	149	21 07	58	149	20 09	58	149	19 11	58	149
28	26 12	58	149	25 14	58	149	24 16	58	149	23 18	58	149	22 20	58	150	21 22	58	150	20 24	58	150	19 26	58	150
27	26 27	58	150	25 29	58	150	24 31	58	150	23 33	58	150	22 35	58	151	21 37	58	151	20 39	59	151	19 40	58	151
26	26 42	58	151	25 44	58	151	24 46	58	151	23 48	59	151	22 49	58	152	21 51	58	152	20 53	58	152	19 55	59	152
25	26 57	−58	152	25 59	−59	152	25 00	−58	152	24 02	−59	153	23 03	−58	153	22 05	−58	153	21 07	−59	153	20 08	−58	154
24	27 11	59	153	26 12	58	153	25 14	59	153	24 15	58	154	23 17	59	154	22 18	58	154	21 20	59	154	20 21	58	155
23	27 24	58	154	26 26	59	154	25 27	58	154	24 29	59	155	23 30	59	155	22 31	58	155	21 33	59	155	20 34	59	156
22	27 37	58	155	26 39	59	155	25 40	59	156	24 41	59	156	23 42	58	156	22 44	59	156	21 45	59	156	20 46	59	157
21	27 50	59	156	26 51	59	156	25 52	59	157	24 53	59	157	23 54	58	157	22 56	59	157	21 57	59	157	20 58	59	158
20	28 02	−59	157	27 03	−59	157	26 04	−59	158	25 05	−59	158	24 06	−59	158	23 07	−59	158	22 08	−59	159	21 09	−59	159
19	28 13	59	158	27 14	59	159	26 15	59	159	25 16	59	159	24 17	59	159	23 18	59	159	22 19	59	160	21 20	59	160
18	28 24	59	159	27 25	59	160	26 26	60	160	25 26	59	160	24 27	59	160	23 28	59	160	22 29	59	161	21 30	59	161
17	28 34	59	161	27 35	59	161	26 36	60	161	25 36	59	161	24 37	59	161	23 38	59	162	22 39	60	162	21 39	59	162
16	28 44	60	162	27 44	59	162	26 45	59	162	25 46	59	162	24 47	60	162	23 47	59	163	22 48	59	163	21 49	60	163
15	28 53	−60	163	27 53	−59	163	26 54	−59	163	25 55	−60	163	24 55	−59	164	23 56	−59	164	22 57	−60	164	21 57	−59	164
14	29 01	59	164	28 02	59	164	27 03	60	164	26 03	59	164	25 04	60	165	24 04	59	165	23 05	60	165	22 05	59	165
13	29 09	59	165	28 10	60	165	27 10	59	165	26 11	60	166	25 11	59	166	24 12	60	166	23 12	59	166	22 13	60	166
12	29 17	60	166	28 17	59	166	27 18	60	167	26 18	60	167	25 18	59	167	24 19	60	167	23 19	59	167	22 20	60	167
11	29 24	60	167	28 24	60	168	27 24	59	168	26 25	60	168	25 25	60	168	24 25	59	168	23 26	60	168	22 26	60	168
10	29 30	−60	169	28 30	−59	169	27 31	−60	169	26 31	−60	169	25 31	−60	169	24 31	−59	169	23 32	−60	169	22 32	−60	169
9	29 36	60	170	28 36	60	170	27 36	60	170	26 36	59	170	25 37	60	170	24 37	60	170	23 37	60	170	22 37	60	170
8	29 41	60	171	28 41	60	171	27 41	60	171	26 41	59	171	25 42	60	171	24 42	60	171	23 42	60	171	22 42	60	171
7	29 45	60	172	28 45	59	172	27 46	60	172	26 46	60	172	25 46	60	172	24 46	60	172	23 46	60	172	22 46	60	173
6	29 49	60	173	28 49	60	173	27 49	59	173	26 50	60	173	25 50	60	173	24 50	60	173	23 50	60	174	22 50	60	174
5	29 53	−60	174	28 53	−60	174	27 53	−60	174	26 53	−60	174	25 53	−60	175	24 53	−60	175	23 53	−60	175	22 53	−60	175
4	29 55	60	175	28 55	60	175	27 55	60	176	26 55	60	176	25 55	60	176	24 55	60	176	23 55	59	176	22 56	60	176
3	29 57	60	177	28 57	60	177	27 57	60	177	26 57	60	177	25 57	60	177	24 57	60	177	23 57	59	177	22 58	60	177
2	29 59	60	178	28 59	60	178	27 59	60	178	26 59	60	178	25 59	60	178	24 59	60	178	23 59	60	178	22 59	60	178
1	30 00	60	179	29 00	60	179	28 00	60	179	27 00	60	179	26 00	60	179	25 00	60	179	24 00	60	179	23 00	60	179
0	30 00	−60	180	29 00	−60	180	28 00	−60	180	27 00	−60	180	26 00	−60	180	25 00	−60	180	24 00	−60	180	23 00	−60	180

LHA	8° Hc	8° d	8° Z	9° Hc	9° d	9° Z	10° Hc	10° d	10° Z	11° Hc	11° d	11° Z	12° Hc	12° d	12° Z	13° Hc	13° d	13° Z	14° Hc	14° d	14° Z	LHA
	° ′	′	°	° ′	′	°	° ′	′	°	° ′	′	°	° ′	′	°	° ′	′	°	° ′	′	°	
69	03 16	53	112	02 23	53	113	01 30	53	113	00 37	53	114	−0 16	54	114	−1 10	53	115	−2 03	53	115	291
68	03 43	53	113	02 50	53	114	01 57	53	114	01 04	53	114	00 11	53	115	−0 42	53	115	−1 35	54	116	292
67	04 11	53	114	03 18	54	114	02 24	53	115	01 31	53	115	00 38	53	116	−0 15	54	116	−1 09	53	117	293
66	04 38	53	115	03 45	53	115	02 52	54	116	01 58	53	116	01 05	54	117	00 11	53	117	−0 42	53	118	294
65	05 05	−53	116	04 12	−53	116	03 19	−54	117	02 25	−53	117	01 32	−54	118	00 38	−53	118	−0 15	−54	118	295
64	05 32	53	117	04 39	54	117	03 45	53	118	02 52	54	118	01 58	54	118	01 04	53	119	00 11	54	119	296
63	05 59	54	118	05 05	53	118	04 12	54	118	03 18	54	119	02 24	53	119	01 31	54	120	00 37	54	120	297
62	06 26	54	118	05 32	54	119	04 38	54	119	03 44	54	120	02 50	53	120	01 57	54	121	01 03	54	121	298
61	06 52	54	119	05 58	54	120	05 04	54	120	04 10	54	121	03 16	54	121	02 22	54	121	01 28	54	122	299
60	07 18	−54	120	06 24	−54	121	05 30	−54	121	04 36	−54	121	03 42	−54	122	02 48	−54	122	01 54	−54	123	300
59	07 44	54	121	06 50	54	122	05 56	55	122	05 01	54	122	04 07	54	123	03 13	54	123	02 19	54	124	301
58	08 09	54	122	07 15	54	122	06 21	54	123	05 27	55	123	04 32	54	124	03 38	54	124	02 44	55	125	302
57	08 35	55	123	07 40	54	123	06 46	54	124	05 52	55	124	04 57	54	125	04 03	55	125	03 08	54	125	303
56	09 00	55	124	08 05	54	124	07 11	55	125	06 16	54	125	05 22	55	126	04 27	54	126	03 33	55	126	304
55	09 25	−55	125	08 30	−55	125	07 35	−54	126	06 41	−55	126	05 46	−55	126	04 51	−54	127	03 57	−55	127	305
54	09 49	55	126	08 54	54	126	08 00	55	126	07 05	55	127	06 10	55	127	05 15	55	128	04 20	55	128	306
53	10 13	55	127	09 18	54	127	08 24	55	127	07 29	55	128	06 34	55	128	05 39	55	129	04 44	55	129	307
52	10 37	55	127	09 42	55	128	08 47	55	128	07 52	55	129	06 57	55	129	06 02	55	130	05 07	55	130	308
51	11 01	55	128	10 06	55	129	09 11	55	129	08 16	56	130	07 20	55	130	06 25	55	130	05 30	55	131	309
50	11 24	−55	129	10 29	−55	130	09 34	−55	130	08 39	−56	131	07 43	−55	131	06 48	−56	131	05 52	−55	132	310
49	11 47	55	130	10 52	55	131	09 57	56	131	09 01	55	131	08 06	56	132	07 10	55	132	06 15	56	133	311
48	12 10	55	131	11 15	56	132	10 19	55	132	09 24	56	132	08 28	56	133	07 32	55	133	06 37	56	134	312
47	12 33	56	132	11 37	56	133	10 41	55	133	09 46	56	133	08 50	56	134	07 54	56	134	06 58	56	134	313
46	12 55	56	133	11 59	56	133	11 03	56	134	10 07	56	134	09 11	56	135	08 15	55	135	07 20	56	135	314
45	13 16	−56	134	12 20	−55	134	11 25	−56	135	10 29	−56	135	09 33	−56	136	08 37	−56	136	07 41	−57	136	315
44	13 38	56	135	12 42	56	135	11 46	56	136	10 50	57	136	09 53	56	136	08 57	56	137	08 01	56	137	316
43	13 59	56	136	13 03	57	136	12 06	56	137	11 10	56	137	10 14	56	137	09 18	57	138	08 21	56	138	317
42	14 20	57	137	13 23	56	137	12 27	56	138	11 31	57	138	10 34	56	138	09 38	57	139	08 41	56	139	318
41	14 40	57	138	13 43	56	138	12 47	57	139	11 50	56	139	10 54	57	139	09 57	56	140	09 01	57	140	319
40	15 00	−57	139	14 03	−56	139	13 07	−57	140	12 10	−57	140	11 13	−56	140	10 17	−57	141	09 20	−57	141	320
39	15 19	56	140	14 23	57	140	13 26	57	140	12 29	57	141	11 32	56	141	10 36	57	141	09 39	57	142	321
38	15 39	57	141	14 42	57	141	13 45	57	141	12 48	57	142	11 51	57	142	10 54	57	142	09 57	57	143	322
37	15 57	57	142	15 00	57	142	14 03	57	142	13 06	57	143	12 09	57	143	11 12	57	143	10 15	57	144	323
36	16 16	57	143	15 19	57	143	14 22	58	143	13 24	57	144	12 27	57	144	11 30	57	144	10 33	58	145	324
35	16 34	−57	144	15 37	−58	144	14 39	−57	144	13 42	−57	145	12 45	−58	145	11 47	−57	145	10 50	−58	146	325
34	16 51	57	145	15 54	57	145	14 57	58	145	13 59	57	146	13 02	58	146	12 04	57	146	11 07	58	146	326
33	17 09	58	146	16 11	58	146	15 13	57	146	14 16	58	147	13 18	57	147	12 21	58	147	11 23	58	147	327
32	17 25	57	147	16 28	58	147	15 30	58	147	14 32	58	148	13 34	57	148	12 37	58	148	11 39	58	148	328
31	17 42	58	148	16 44	58	148	15 46	58	148	14 48	58	149	13 50	58	149	12 52	57	149	11 55	58	149	329
30	17 57	−58	149	16 59	−57	149	16 02	−58	149	15 04	−58	150	14 06	−58	150	13 08	−58	150	12 10	−58	150	330
29	18 13	58	150	17 15	58	150	16 17	58	150	15 19	58	150	14 21	59	151	13 22	58	151	12 24	58	151	331
28	18 28	58	151	17 30	59	151	16 31	58	151	15 33	58	151	14 35	58	152	13 37	58	152	12 39	59	152	332
27	18 42	58	152	17 44	58	152	16 46	59	152	15 47	58	152	14 49	58	153	13 51	59	153	12 52	58	153	333
26	18 56	58	153	17 58	59	153	16 59	58	153	16 01	58	153	15 03	59	154	14 04	58	154	13 06	59	154	334
25	19 10	−59	154	18 11	−58	154	17 13	−59	154	16 14	−58	154	15 16	−59	155	14 17	−58	155	13 19	−59	155	335
24	19 23	59	155	18 24	58	155	17 26	59	155	16 27	59	155	15 28	58	156	14 30	59	156	13 31	59	156	336
23	19 35	58	156	18 37	59	156	17 38	59	156	16 39	59	156	15 40	58	157	14 42	59	157	13 43	59	157	337
22	19 47	58	157	18 49	59	157	17 50	59	157	16 51	59	157	15 52	59	158	14 53	59	158	13 54	59	158	338
21	19 59	59	158	19 00	59	158	18 01	59	158	17 02	59	158	16 03	59	159	15 04	59	159	14 05	59	159	339
20	20 10	−59	159	19 11	−59	159	18 12	−59	159	17 13	−59	159	16 14	−59	160	15 15	−59	160	14 16	−59	160	340
19	20 21	59	160	19 22	60	160	18 22	59	160	17 23	59	160	16 24	59	161	15 25	59	161	14 26	59	161	341
18	20 31	60	161	19 31	59	161	18 32	59	161	17 33	59	161	16 34	59	162	15 35	60	162	14 35	59	162	342
17	20 40	59	162	19 41	59	162	18 42	60	162	17 42	59	163	16 43	59	163	15 44	60	163	14 44	59	163	343
16	20 49	59	163	19 50	59	163	18 51	60	163	17 51	59	164	16 52	60	164	15 52	59	164	14 53	59	164	344
15	20 58	−60	164	19 58	−59	164	18 59	−60	164	17 59	−59	165	17 00	−59	165	16 01	−60	165	15 01	−59	165	345
14	21 06	60	165	20 06	59	165	19 07	60	165	18 07	59	166	17 08	60	166	16 08	59	166	15 09	60	166	346
13	21 13	59	166	20 14	60	166	19 14	60	166	18 14	59	167	17 15	60	167	16 15	59	167	15 16	60	167	347
12	21 20	60	167	20 20	59	167	19 21	60	168	18 21	60	168	17 21	59	168	16 22	60	168	15 22	59	168	348
11	21 26	59	168	20 27	60	168	19 27	60	169	18 27	59	169	17 28	60	169	16 28	60	169	15 28	59	169	349
10	21 32	−60	169	20 32	−59	169	19 33	−60	170	18 33	−60	170	17 33	−60	170	16 33	−59	170	15 34	−60	170	350
9	21 37	59	170	20 38	60	171	19 38	60	171	18 38	60	171	17 38	59	171	16 39	60	171	15 39	60	171	351
8	21 42	60	172	20 42	59	172	19 43	60	172	18 43	60	172	17 43	60	172	16 43	60	172	15 43	60	172	352
7	21 46	59	173	20 47	60	173	19 47	60	173	18 47	60	173	17 47	60	173	16 47	60	173	15 47	60	173	353
6	21 50	60	174	20 50	60	174	19 50	60	174	18 50	60	174	17 50	60	174	16 50	59	174	15 51	60	174	354
5	21 53	−60	175	20 53	−60	175	19 53	−60	175	18 53	−60	175	17 53	−60	175	16 53	−60	175	15 53	−59	175	355
4	21 56	60	176	20 56	60	176	19 56	60	176	18 56	60	176	17 56	60	176	16 56	60	176	15 56	60	176	356
3	21 58	60	177	20 58	60	177	19 58	60	177	18 58	60	177	17 58	60	177	16 58	60	177	15 58	60	177	357
2	21 59	60	178	20 59	60	178	19 59	60	178	18 59	60	178	17 59	60	178	16 59	60	178	15 59	60	178	358
1	22 00	60	179	21 00	60	179	20 00	60	179	19 00	60	179	18 00	60	179	17 00	60	179	16 00	60	179	359
0	22 00	−60	180	21 00	−60	180	20 00	−60	180	19 00	−60	180	18 00	−60	180	17 00	−60	180	16 00	−60	180	360

S. Lat. {LHA greater than 180°....... Zn=180−Z; LHA less than 180°.......... Zn=180+Z}

DECLINATION (0°-14°) CONTRARY NAME TO LATITUDE

LAT 60°

N. Lat. {LHA greater than 180°....... Zn=Z; LHA less than 180°........... Zn=360−Z}

DECLINATION (15°-29°) SAME NAME AS LATITUDE

LHA	15° Hc	d	Z	16° Hc	d	Z	17° Hc	d	Z	18° Hc	d	Z	19° Hc	d	Z
	° ′	′	°	° ′	′	°	° ′	′	°	° ′	′	°	° ′	′	°
0	45 00	+60	180	46 00	+60	180	47 00	+60	180	48 00	+60	180	49 00	+60	180
1	45 00	60	179	46 00	60	179	47 00	60	179	48 00	60	179	49 00	60	179
2	44 59	60	177	45 59	60	177	46 59	60	177	47 59	60	177	48 59	60	177
3	44 57	60	176	45 57	60	176	46 57	60	176	47 57	60	176	48 57	60	176
4	44 54	60	175	45 54	60	175	46 54	60	174	47 54	60	174	48 54	60	174
5	44 51	+60	173	45 51	+60	173	46 51	+60	173	47 51	+60	173	48 51	+60	173
6	44 47	60	172	45 47	60	172	46 47	60	172	47 47	60	172	48 47	59	171
7	44 43	59	171	45 42	60	170	46 42	60	170	47 42	60	170	48 42	59	170
8	44 37	60	169	45 37	60	169	46 37	59	169	47 36	60	169	48 36	60	169
9	44 31	60	168	45 31	60	168	46 31	59	167	47 30	60	167	48 30	59	167
10	44 25	+59	166	45 24	+60	166	46 24	+59	166	47 23	+60	166	48 23	+59	166
11	44 17	60	165	45 17	59	165	46 16	59	165	47 15	60	165	48 15	59	164
12	44 09	59	164	45 08	60	164	46 08	59	163	47 07	59	163	48 06	60	163
13	44 00	60	162	45 00	59	162	45 59	59	162	46 58	59	162	47 57	59	162
14	43 51	59	161	44 50	59	161	45 49	59	161	46 48	59	160	47 47	59	160
15	43 41	+59	160	44 40	+59	160	45 39	+59	159	46 38	+59	159	47 37	+59	159
16	43 30	59	159	44 29	59	158	45 28	59	158	46 27	59	158	47 26	58	157
17	43 19	59	157	44 18	58	157	45 16	59	157	46 15	59	156	47 14	58	156
18	43 07	59	156	44 06	58	156	45 04	59	155	46 03	58	155	47 01	59	155
19	42 54	59	155	43 53	58	154	44 51	59	154	45 50	58	154	46 48	58	153
20	42 41	+59	153	43 40	+58	153	44 38	+58	153	45 36	+58	152	46 34	+58	152
21	42 27	59	152	43 26	58	152	44 24	58	151	45 22	58	151	46 20	58	151
22	42 13	58	151	43 11	58	150	44 09	58	150	45 07	58	150	46 05	57	149
23	41 58	58	150	42 56	58	149	43 54	57	149	44 51	58	148	45 49	58	148
24	41 43	57	148	42 40	58	148	43 38	57	148	44 35	58	147	45 33	57	147
25	41 27	+57	147	42 24	+58	147	43 22	+57	146	44 19	+57	146	45 16	+57	145
26	41 10	57	146	42 07	58	145	43 05	57	145	44 02	57	145	44 59	57	144
27	40 53	57	145	41 50	57	144	42 47	57	144	43 44	57	143	44 41	57	143
28	40 35	57	143	41 32	57	143	42 29	57	143	43 26	57	142	44 23	56	142
29	40 17	57	142	41 14	57	142	42 11	56	141	43 07	57	141	44 04	56	140
30	39 58	+57	141	40 55	+57	141	41 52	+56	140	42 48	+56	140	43 44	+57	139
31	39 39	57	140	40 36	56	139	41 32	56	139	42 28	57	138	43 25	56	138
32	39 20	56	139	40 16	56	138	41 12	56	138	42 08	56	137	43 04	56	137
33	38 59	57	137	39 56	56	137	40 52	56	137	41 48	55	136	42 43	56	136
34	38 39	56	136	39 35	56	136	40 31	56	135	41 27	55	135	42 22	56	134
35	38 18	+56	135	39 14	+55	135	40 09	+56	134	41 05	+55	134	42 00	+56	133
36	37 57	55	134	38 52	56	134	39 48	55	133	40 43	55	133	41 38	55	132
37	37 35	55	133	38 30	56	132	39 26	55	132	40 21	55	131	41 16	55	131
38	37 13	55	132	38 08	55	131	39 03	55	131	39 58	55	130	40 53	55	130
39	36 50	55	131	37 45	55	130	38 40	55	130	39 35	55	129	40 30	54	129
40	36 27	+55	130	37 22	+55	129	38 17	+54	129	39 11	+55	128	40 06	+54	127
41	36 04	54	128	36 58	55	128	37 53	55	127	38 48	54	127	39 42	54	126
42	35 40	55	127	36 35	54	127	37 29	54	126	38 23	55	126	39 18	54	125
43	35 16	54	126	36 10	55	126	37 05	54	125	37 59	54	125	38 53	54	124
44	34 52	54	125	35 46	54	125	36 40	54	124	37 34	54	124	38 28	54	123
45	34 27	+54	124	35 21	+54	124	36 15	+54	123	37 09	+54	123	38 03	+53	122
46	34 02	54	123	34 56	54	123	35 50	53	122	36 43	54	121	37 37	53	121
47	33 37	53	122	34 30	54	121	35 24	54	121	36 18	53	120	37 11	53	120
48	33 11	54	121	34 05	53	120	34 58	54	120	35 52	53	119	36 45	53	119
49	32 45	54	120	33 39	53	119	34 32	53	119	35 25	53	118	36 18	53	118
50	32 19	+53	119	33 12	+54	118	34 06	+53	118	34 59	+53	117	35 52	+53	117
51	31 53	53	118	32 46	53	117	33 39	53	117	34 32	53	116	35 25	52	116
52	31 26	53	117	32 19	53	116	33 12	53	116	34 05	53	115	34 58	52	115
53	30 59	53	116	31 52	53	115	32 45	53	115	33 38	52	114	34 30	53	114
54	30 32	53	115	31 25	53	114	32 18	52	114	33 10	53	113	34 03	52	113
55	30 05	+52	114	30 57	+53	113	31 50	+53	113	32 43	+52	112	33 35	+52	112
56	29 37	53	113	30 30	52	112	31 22	53	112	32 15	52	112	33 07	52	111
57	29 09	53	112	30 02	52	111	30 54	53	111	31 47	52	110	32 39	52	110
58	28 41	53	111	29 34	52	110	30 26	52	110	31 18	52	109	32 10	52	109
59	28 13	53	110	29 06	52	109	29 58	52	109	30 50	52	108	31 42	52	108
60	27 45	+52	109	28 37	+52	109	29 29	+52	108	30 21	+52	107	31 13	+52	107
61	27 17	52	108	28 09	52	108	29 01	52	107	29 53	51	106	30 44	52	106
62	26 48	52	107	27 40	52	107	28 32	52	106	29 24	52	106	30 16	51	105
63	26 19	52	106	27 11	52	106	28 03	52	105	28 55	51	105	29 46	52	104
64	25 50	52	105	26 42	52	105	27 34	52	104	28 26	51	104	29 17	52	103
65	25 21	+52	104	26 13	+52	104	27 05	+52	103	27 57	+51	103	28 48	+51	102
66	24 52	52	103	25 44	52	103	26 36	51	102	27 27	52	102	28 19	51	101
67	24 23	52	103	25 15	51	102	26 06	52	101	26 58	51	101	27 49	51	100
68	23 54	51	102	24 45	52	101	25 37	51	101	26 28	52	100	27 20	51	99
69	23 24	52	101	24 16	51	100	25 07	52	100	25 59	51	99	26 50	51	98

LHA	20° Hc	d	Z	21° Hc	d	Z	22° Hc	d	Z	23° Hc	d	Z	24° Hc	d	Z
	° ′	′	°	° ′	′	°	° ′	′	°	° ′	′	°	° ′	′	°
0	50 00	+60	180	51 00	+60	180	52 00	+60	180	53 00	+60	180	54 00	+60	180
1	50 00	60	179	51 00	60	179	52 00	60	179	53 00	60	179	54 00	60	178
2	49 59	59	177	50 58	60	177	51 58	60	177	52 58	60	177	53 58	60	177
3	49 57	60	176	50 57	60	176	51 57	59	176	52 56	60	175	53 56	60	175
4	49 54	60	174	50 54	60	174	51 54	60	174	52 54	60	174	53 54	59	174
5	49 51	+59	173	50 50	+60	173	51 50	+60	173	52 50	+60	172	53 50	+60	172
6	49 46	60	171	50 46	60	171	51 46	60	171	52 46	59	171	53 45	60	171
7	49 41	60	170	50 41	60	170	51 41	60	170	52 41	59	169	53 40	60	169
8	49 36	59	168	50 35	60	168	51 35	60	168	52 35	59	168	53 34	60	168
9	49 29	60	167	50 29	59	167	51 28	60	167	52 28	59	166	53 27	60	166
10	49 22	+60	166	50 22	+59	165	51 21	+59	165	52 20	+60	165	53 20	+59	165
11	49 14	60	164	50 14	59	164	51 13	59	164	52 12	59	163	53 11	60	163
12	49 06	59	163	50 05	59	162	51 04	59	162	52 03	59	162	53 02	59	162
13	48 56	59	161	49 55	59	161	50 54	60	161	51 54	58	160	52 52	59	160
14	48 46	59	160	49 45	59	160	50 44	59	159	51 43	59	159	52 42	59	159
15	48 36	+58	158	49 34	+59	158	50 33	+59	158	51 32	+59	158	52 31	+58	157
16	48 24	59	157	49 23	59	157	50 22	58	156	51 20	59	156	52 19	58	156
17	48 12	59	156	49 11	58	155	50 09	59	155	51 08	58	155	52 06	58	154
18	48 00	58	154	48 58	58	154	49 56	58	154	50 54	59	153	51 53	58	153
19	47 46	58	153	48 44	59	153	49 43	58	152	50 41	57	152	51 38	58	151
20	47 32	+58	152	48 30	+58	151	49 28	+58	151	50 26	+58	150	51 24	+57	150
21	47 18	57	150	48 15	58	150	49 13	58	149	50 11	57	149	51 08	58	149
22	47 02	58	149	48 00	58	149	48 58	57	148	49 55	57	148	50 52	58	147
23	46 47	57	148	47 44	57	147	48 41	58	147	49 39	57	146	50 36	57	146
24	46 30	58	146	47 28	57	146	48 25	57	145	49 22	57	145	50 19	57	144
25	46 13	+57	145	47 10	+57	145	48 07	+57	144	49 04	+57	144	50 01	+57	143
26	45 56	57	144	46 53	57	143	47 50	56	143	48 46	57	142	49 43	56	142
27	45 38	57	142	46 35	56	142	47 31	57	141	48 28	56	141	49 24	56	140
28	45 19	57	141	46 16	56	141	47 12	56	140	48 08	56	140	49 04	56	139
29	45 00	56	140	45 56	57	139	46 53	56	139	47 49	56	138	48 45	55	138
30	44 41	+56	139	45 37	+56	138	46 33	+56	138	47 29	+55	137	48 24	+56	137
31	44 21	55	137	45 16	56	137	46 12	56	136	47 08	55	136	48 03	56	135
32	44 00	56	136	44 56	56	136	45 51	56	135	46 47	55	135	47 42	55	134
33	43 39	56	135	44 35	55	135	45 30	56	134	46 25	55	133	47 20	55	133
34	43 18	55	134	44 13	55	133	45 08	55	133	46 03	55	132	46 58	55	132
35	42 56	+55	133	43 51	+55	132	44 46	+55	132	45 41	+54	131	46 35	+55	130
36	42 33	55	131	43 28	55	131	44 23	55	130	45 18	54	130	46 12	54	129
37	42 11	54	130	43 05	55	130	44 00	54	129	44 54	55	129	45 49	54	128
38	41 48	54	129	42 42	55	129	43 37	54	128	44 31	54	127	45 25	54	127
39	41 24	55	128	42 19	54	127	43 13	54	127	44 07	54	126	45 01	53	126
40	41 00	+55	127	41 55	+54	126	42 49	+53	126	43 42	+54	125	44 36	+53	124
41	40 36	54	126	41 30	54	125	42 24	54	125	43 18	53	124	44 11	53	123
42	40 12	53	125	41 05	54	124	41 59	54	123	42 53	53	123	43 46	53	122
43	39 47	53	124	40 40	54	123	41 34	53	122	42 27	53	122	43 20	53	121
44	39 22	53	122	40 15	53	122	41 08	54	121	42 02	53	121	42 55	52	120
45	38 56	+53	121	39 49	+54	121	40 43	+53	120	41 36	+52	120	42 28	+53	119
46	38 30	54	120	39 24	53	120	40 17	52	119	41 09	53	118	42 02	52	118
47	38 04	53	119	38 57	53	119	39 50	53	118	40 43	52	117	41 35	53	117
48	37 38	53	118	38 31	53	118	39 24	52	117	40 16	52	116	41 08	52	116
49	37 11	53	117	38 04	53	117	38 57	52	116	39 49	52	115	40 41	52	115
50	36 45	+52	116	37 37	+53	116	38 30	+52	115	39 22	+52	114	40 14	+52	114
51	36 17	53	115	37 10	52	114	38 02	52	114	38 54	52	113	39 46	52	113
52	35 50	53	114	36 43	52	113	37 35	52	113	38 27	51	112	39 18	52	112
53	35 23	52	113	36 15	52	112	37 07	52	112	37 59	51	111	38 50	52	111
54	34 55	52	112	35 47	52	111	36 39	52	111	37 31	51	110	38 22	51	110
55	34 27	+52	111	35 19	+52	110	36 11	+51	110	37 02	+52	109	37 54	+51	109
56	33 59	52	110	34 51	52	109	35 43	51	109	36 34	51	108	37 25	51	108
57	33 31	51	109	34 22	52	108	35 14	51	108	36 05	52	107	36 57	51	107
58	33 02	52	108	33 54	51	108	34 45	52	107	35 37	51	106	36 28	51	106
59	32 34	51	107	33 25	52	107	34 17	51	106	35 08	51	105	35 59	51	105
60	32 05	+51	106	32 56	+52	106	33 48	+51	105	34 39	+51	104	35 30	+50	104
61	31 36	51	105	32 27	52	105	33 19	51	104	34 10	51	103	35 01	50	103
62	31 07	51	104	31 58	51	104	32 49	51	103	33 40	51	102	34 31	51	102
63	30 38	51	103	31 29	51	103	32 20	51	102	33 11	51	102	34 02	50	101
64	30 09	51	102	31 00	51	102	31 51	51	101	32 42	50	101	33 32	51	100
65	29 39	+51	102	30 30	+51	101	31 21	+51	100	32 12	+51	100	33 03	+50	99
66	29 10	51	101	30 01	51	100	30 52	51	99	31 43	50	99	32 33	50	98
67	28 40	51	100	29 31	51	99	30 22	51	98	31 13	50	98	32 03	51	97
68	28 11	51	99	29 02	50	98	29 52	51	98	30 43	51	97	31 34	50	96
69	27 41	51	98	28 32	51	97	29 23	50	97	30 13	51	96	31 04	50	95

LHA	25° Hc	d	Z	26° Hc	d	Z	27° Hc	d	Z	28° Hc	d	Z	29° Hc	d	Z	LHA
	° ′	′	°	° ′	′	°	° ′	′	°	° ′	′	°	° ′	′	°	
0	55 00	+60	180	56 00	+60	180	57 00	+60	180	58 00	+60	180	59 00	+60	180	360
1	55 00	60	178	56 00	60	178	57 00	60	178	58 00	60	178	59 00	60	178	359
2	54 58	60	177	55 58	60	177	56 58	60	177	57 58	60	177	58 58	60	177	358
3	54 56	60	175	55 56	60	175	56 56	60	175	57 56	60	175	58 56	60	175	357
4	54 53	60	174	55 53	60	174	56 53	60	174	57 53	60	173	58 53	60	173	356
5	54 50	+60	172	55 50	+59	172	56 49	+60	172	57 49	+60	172	58 49	+60	172	355
6	54 45	60	171	55 45	60	170	56 45	59	170	57 44	60	170	58 44	60	170	354
7	54 40	60	169	55 40	59	169	56 39	60	169	57 39	59	168	58 38	60	168	353
8	54 34	59	167	55 33	60	167	56 33	59	167	57 32	60	167	58 32	59	167	352
9	54 27	59	166	55 26	60	166	56 26	59	165	57 25	59	165	58 24	60	165	351
10	54 19	+59	164	55 18	+60	164	56 18	+59	164	57 17	+59	164	58 16	+59	163	350
11	54 11	59	163	55 10	59	163	56 09	59	162	57 08	59	162	58 07	59	162	349
12	54 01	59	161	55 00	59	161	55 59	59	161	56 58	59	160	57 57	59	160	348
13	53 51	59	160	54 50	59	159	55 49	59	159	56 48	59	159	57 47	58	158	347
14	53 41	58	158	54 39	59	158	55 38	59	158	56 37	58	157	57 35	58	157	346
15	53 29	+59	157	54 28	+58	156	55 26	+59	156	56 25	+58	156	57 23	+58	155	345
16	53 17	58	155	54 15	59	155	55 14	58	155	56 12	58	154	57 10	58	154	344
17	53 04	58	154	54 02	58	153	55 00	58	153	55 58	58	153	56 56	58	152	343
18	52 51	58	152	53 49	57	152	54 46	58	152	55 44	58	151	56 42	57	151	342
19	52 36	58	151	53 34	58	151	54 32	57	150	55 29	58	150	56 27	57	149	341
20	52 21	+58	150	53 19	+57	149	54 16	+58	149	55 14	+57	148	56 11	+57	148	340
21	52 06	57	148	53 03	57	148	54 00	57	147	54 57	57	147	55 54	57	146	339
22	51 50	57	147	52 47	57	146	53 44	57	146	54 41	56	145	55 37	57	145	338
23	51 33	57	145	52 30	57	145	53 27	56	144	54 23	57	144	55 20	56	143	337
24	51 16	56	144	52 12	57	143	53 09	56	143	54 05	56	142	55 01	56	142	336
25	50 58	+56	143	51 54	+56	142	52 50	+56	141	53 46	+56	141	54 42	+56	140	335
26	50 39	56	141	51 35	56	141	52 31	56	140	53 27	56	140	54 23	55	139	334
27	50 20	56	140	51 16	56	139	52 12	55	139	53 07	56	138	54 03	55	137	333
28	50 00	56	139	50 56	56	138	51 52	55	137	52 47	55	137	53 42	55	136	332
29	49 40	56	137	50 36	55	137	51 31	55	136	52 26	55	135	53 21	55	135	331
30	49 20	+55	136	50 15	+55	135	51 10	+55	135	52 05	+55	134	53 00	+54	133	330
31	48 59	55	135	49 54	55	134	50 49	54	133	51 43	55	133	52 38	54	132	329
32	48 37	55	133	49 32	55	133	50 27	54	132	51 21	54	132	52 15	54	131	328
33	48 15	55	132	49 10	54	132	50 04	54	131	50 58	54	130	51 52	54	130	327
34	47 53	54	131	48 47	54	130	49 41	54	130	50 35	54	129	51 29	53	128	326
35	47 30	+54	130	48 24	+54	129	49 18	+54	128	50 12	+53	128	51 05	+53	127	325
36	47 06	54	129	48 00	54	128	48 54	54	127	49 48	53	127	50 41	53	126	324
37	46 43	54	128	47 37	53	127	48 30	53	126	49 23	53	125	50 16	53	125	323
38	46 19	53	126	47 12	54	126	48 06	53	125	48 59	53	124	49 52	52	123	322
39	45 54	54	125	46 48	53	124	47 41	53	124	48 34	53	123	49 26	53	122	321
40	45 29	+54	124	46 23	+53	123	47 16	+52	122	48 08	+53	122	49 01	+52	121	320
41	45 04	53	123	45 57	53	122	46 50	53	121	47 43	52	121	48 35	52	120	319
42	44 39	53	122	45 32	52	121	46 24	53	120	47 17	52	119	48 09	52	119	318
43	44 13	53	120	45 06	52	120	45 58	52	119	46 50	52	118	47 42	52	118	317
44	43 47	53	119	44 40	52	119	45 32	52	118	46 24	52	117	47 16	51	117	316
45	43 21	+52	118	44 13	+52	118	45 05	+52	117	45 57	+52	116	46 49	+51	115	315
46	42 54	53	117	43 47	51	116	44 38	52	116	45 30	51	115	46 21	51	114	314
47	42 28	52	116	43 20	51	115	44 11	52	115	45 03	51	114	45 54	51	113	313
48	42 00	52	115	42 52	52	114	43 44	51	114	44 35	51	113	45 26	51	112	312
49	41 33	52	114	42 25	51	113	43 16	51	113	44 07	51	112	44 58	51	111	311
50	41 06	+51	113	41 57	+51	112	42 48	+52	112	43 40	+50	111	44 30	+51	110	310
51	40 38	51	112	41 29	51	111	42 20	51	111	43 11	51	110	44 02	50	109	309
52	40 10	51	111	41 01	51	110	41 52	51	110	42 43	51	109	43 34	50	108	308
53	39 42	51	110	40 33	51	109	41 24	51	108	42 15	50	108	43 05	50	107	307
54	39 13	52	109	40 05	50	108	40 55	51	107	41 46	50	107	42 36	50	106	306
55	38 45	+51	108	39 36	+51	107	40 27	+50	107	41 17	+50	106	42 07	+50	105	305
56	38 16	51	107	39 07	51	106	39 58	50	106	40 48	50	105	41 38	50	104	304
57	37 48	50	106	38 38	51	105	39 29	50	105	40 19	50	104	41 09	50	103	303
58	37 19	50	105	38 09	51	104	39 00	50	104	39 50	50	103	40 40	49	102	302
59	36 50	50	104	37 40	51	103	38 31	50	103	39 21	49	102	40 10	50	101	301
60	36 20	+51	103	37 11	+50	102	38 01	+50	102	38 51	+50	101	39 41	+49	100	300
61	35 51	51	102	36 42	50	101	37 32	50	101	38 22	49	100	39 11	50	99	299
62	35 22	50	101	36 12	50	100	37 02	50	100	37 52	50	99	38 42	49	98	298
63	34 52	51	100	35 43	50	100	36 33	49	99	37 22	50	98	38 12	49	97	297
64	34 23	50	99	35 13	50	99	36 03	50	98	36 53	49	97	37 42	49	97	296
65	33 53	+50	98	34 43	+50	98	35 33	+50	97	36 23	+49	96	37 12	+50	96	295
66	33 23	50	97	34 13	50	97	35 03	50	96	35 53	49	95	36 42	50	95	294
67	32 54	50	97	33 44	50	96	34 34	49	95	35 23	50	95	36 13	49	94	293
68	32 24	50	96	33 14	50	95	34 04	49	94	34 53	50	94	35 43	49	93	292
69	31 54	50	95	32 44	50	94	33 34	49	93	34 23	50	93	35 13	49	92	291

15° 16° 17° 18° 19° 20° 21° 22° 23° 24° 25° 26° 27° 28° 29°

S. Lat. {LHA greater than 180°....... Zn=180−Z; LHA less than 180°........... Zn=180+Z}

DECLINATION (15°-29°) SAME NAME AS LATITUDE

LAT 60°

N. Lat. {LHA greater than 180°....... Zn=Z; LHA less than 180°........... Zn=360−Z

DECLINATION (15°-29°) SAME NAME AS LATITUDE

LHA	15° Hc	15° d	15° Z	16° Hc	16° d	16° Z	17° Hc	17° d	17° Z	18° Hc	18° d	18° Z	19° Hc	19° d	19° Z
	° ′	′	°	° ′	′	°	° ′	′	°	° ′	′	°	° ′	′	°
70	22 55	+51	100	23 46	+52	99	24 38	+51	99	25 29	+51	98	26 20	+51	98
71	22 25	52	99	23 17	51	98	24 08	51	98	24 59	51	97	25 50	51	97
72	21 56	51	98	22 47	51	97	23 38	52	97	24 30	51	96	25 21	51	96
73	21 26	51	97	22 17	52	97	23 09	51	96	24 00	51	95	24 51	51	95
74	20 56	51	96	21 47	52	96	22 39	51	95	23 30	51	95	24 21	51	94
75	20 26	+52	95	21 18	+51	95	22 09	+51	94	23 00	+51	94	23 51	+51	93
76	19 56	52	95	20 48	51	94	21 39	51	93	22 30	51	93	23 21	51	92
77	19 26	52	94	20 18	51	93	21 09	51	93	22 00	51	92	22 51	51	91
78	18 56	52	93	19 48	51	92	20 39	51	92	21 30	51	91	22 21	51	91
79	18 26	52	92	19 18	51	91	20 09	51	91	21 00	51	90	21 51	51	90
80	17 56	+52	91	18 48	+51	90	19 39	+51	90	20 30	+51	89	21 21	+51	89
81	17 26	52	90	18 18	51	90	19 09	51	89	20 00	51	88	20 51	51	88
82	16 56	52	89	17 48	51	89	18 39	51	88	19 30	51	88	20 21	51	87
83	16 26	52	88	17 18	51	88	18 09	51	87	19 00	51	87	19 51	51	86
84	15 56	52	88	16 48	51	87	17 39	51	86	18 30	51	86	19 21	51	85
85	15 26	+52	87	16 18	+51	86	17 09	+51	86	18 00	+51	85	18 51	+51	85
86	14 57	51	86	15 48	51	85	16 39	51	85	17 30	51	84	18 21	51	84
87	14 27	51	85	15 18	51	84	16 09	52	84	17 01	51	83	17 52	51	83
88	13 57	51	84	14 48	52	84	15 40	51	83	16 31	51	83	17 22	51	82
89	13 27	51	83	14 18	52	83	15 10	51	82	16 01	51	82	16 52	51	81
90	12 57	+52	82	13 49	+51	82	14 40	+51	81	15 31	+52	81	16 23	+51	80
91	12 27	52	82	13 19	51	81	14 10	52	81	15 02	51	80	15 53	51	79
92	11 58	51	81	12 49	52	80	13 41	51	80	14 32	52	79	15 24	51	79
93	11 28	52	80	12 20	51	79	13 11	52	79	14 03	51	78	14 54	52	78
94	10 59	51	79	11 50	52	79	12 42	52	78	13 34	51	77	14 25	51	77
95	10 29	+52	78	11 21	+52	78	12 13	+51	77	13 04	+52	77	13 56	+51	76
96	10 00	52	77	10 52	52	77	11 44	51	76	12 35	52	76	13 27	51	75
97	09 31	52	76	10 23	51	76	11 14	52	75	12 06	52	75	12 58	51	74
98	09 02	52	76	09 54	52	75	10 46	51	75	11 37	52	74	12 29	52	74
99	08 33	52	75	09 25	52	74	10 17	52	74	11 09	51	73	12 00	52	73
100	08 04	+52	74	08 56	+52	73	09 48	+52	73	10 40	+52	72	11 32	+52	72
101	07 35	52	73	08 27	52	73	09 19	52	72	10 11	52	72	11 03	52	71
102	07 06	53	72	07 59	52	72	08 51	52	71	09 43	52	71	10 35	52	70
103	06 38	52	71	07 30	53	71	08 23	52	70	09 15	52	70	10 07	52	69
104	06 10	52	71	07 02	52	70	07 54	53	70	08 47	52	69	09 39	52	69
105	05 41	+53	70	06 34	+52	69	07 26	+53	69	08 19	+52	68	09 11	+52	68
106	05 13	53	69	06 06	52	68	06 58	53	68	07 51	52	67	08 43	53	67
107	04 45	53	68	05 38	53	68	06 31	52	67	07 23	53	67	08 16	52	66
108	04 18	53	67	05 11	52	67	06 03	53	66	06 56	53	66	07 49	52	65
109	03 50	53	66	04 43	53	66	05 36	53	65	06 29	52	65	07 21	53	64
110	03 23	+53	65	04 16	+53	65	05 09	+53	65	06 02	+52	64	06 54	+53	64
111	02 56	53	65	03 49	53	64	04 42	53	64	05 35	53	63	06 28	53	63
112	02 29	53	64	03 22	53	63	04 15	53	63	05 08	53	62	06 01	53	62
113	02 02	53	63	02 55	53	62	03 48	54	62	04 42	53	61	05 35	53	61
114	01 35	54	62	02 29	53	62	03 22	53	61	04 15	54	61	05 09	53	60
115	01 09	+53	61	02 02	+54	61	02 56	+53	60	03 49	+54	60	04 43	+53	59
116	00 43	53	60	01 36	54	60	02 30	53	59	03 23	54	59	04 17	54	58
117	00 17	54	59	01 11	53	59	02 04	54	59	02 58	54	58	03 52	53	58
118	−0 09	54	59	00 45	54	58	01 39	54	58	02 33	53	57	03 26	54	57
119	−0 34	54	58	00 20	54	57	01 14	53	57	02 07	54	56	03 01	54	56
120	−1 00	+54	57	−0 06	+55	56	00 49	+54	56	01 43	+54	55	02 37	+54	55
121	−1 25	55	56	−0 30	54	55	00 24	54	55	01 18	54	55	02 12	54	54
122	−1 49	54	55	−0 55	54	55	−0 01	55	54	00 54	54	54	01 48	54	53
123	−2 14	55	54	−1 19	54	54	−0 25	55	53	00 30	54	53	01 24	55	52
124	−2 38	55	53	−1 43	54	53	−0 49	55	52	00 06	54	52	01 00	55	52
125	−3 02	+55	52	−2 07	+55	52	−1 12	+54	52	−0 18	+55	51	00 37	+55	51
126	−3 25	54	52	−2 31	55	51	−1 36	55	51	−0 41	55	50	00 14	55	50
127	−3 49	55	51	−2 54	55	50	−1 59	55	50	−1 04	55	49	−0 09	55	49
128	−4 12	55	50	−3 17	55	49	−2 22	56	49	−1 26	55	49	−0 31	55	48
129	−4 35	56	49	−3 39	55	48	−2 44	55	48	−1 49	55	48	−0 54	56	47
130	−4 57	+55	48	−4 02	+56	48	−3 06	+55	47	−2 11	+56	47	−1 15	+55	46
131	−5 19	55	47	−4 24	56	47	−3 28	55	46	−2 33	56	46	−1 37	56	46
132	−5 41	56	46	−4 45	55	46	−3 50	56	45	−2 54	56	45	−1 58	55	45
133				−5 07	56	45	−4 11	56	45	−3 15	56	44	−2 19	56	44
134				−5 28	56	44	−4 32	56	44	−3 36	56	43	−2 40	56	43
135							−4 52	+56	43	−3 56	+56	42	−3 00	+56	42
136							−5 12	56	42	−4 16	56	41	−3 20	56	41
137							−5 32	56	41	−4 36	57	41	−3 39	56	40
138										−4 55	56	40	−3 59	57	39
139										−5 14	56	39	−4 18	57	38

LHA	20° Hc	20° d	20° Z	21° Hc	21° d	21° Z	22° Hc	22° d	22° Z	23° Hc	23° d	23° Z	24° Hc	24° d	24° Z
	° ′	′	°	° ′	′	°	° ′	′	°	° ′	′	°	° ′	′	°
70	27 11	+51	97	28 02	+51	96	28 53	+50	96	29 43	+51	95	30 34	+50	95
71	26 41	51	96	27 32	51	95	28 23	50	95	29 13	51	94	30 04	50	94
72	26 12	50	95	27 02	51	95	27 53	51	94	28 44	50	93	29 34	50	93
73	25 42	50	94	26 32	51	94	27 23	51	93	28 14	50	93	29 04	50	92
74	25 12	51	93	26 03	50	93	26 53	51	92	27 44	50	92	28 34	50	91
75	24 42	+51	93	25 33	+50	92	26 23	+51	91	27 14	+50	91	28 04	+50	90
76	24 12	51	92	25 03	50	91	25 53	51	90	26 44	50	90	27 34	50	89
77	23 42	51	91	24 33	50	90	25 23	51	90	26 14	50	89	27 04	50	88
78	23 12	51	90	24 03	50	89	24 53	51	89	25 44	50	88	26 34	50	88
79	22 42	51	89	23 33	50	88	24 23	51	88	25 14	50	87	26 04	50	87
80	22 12	+51	88	23 03	+50	88	23 53	+51	87	24 44	+50	86	25 34	+50	86
81	21 42	51	87	22 33	50	87	23 23	51	86	24 14	50	86	25 04	50	85
82	21 12	51	86	22 03	50	86	22 53	51	85	23 44	50	85	24 34	51	84
83	20 42	51	86	21 33	50	85	22 23	51	84	23 14	50	84	24 04	51	83
84	20 12	51	85	21 03	51	84	21 54	50	84	22 44	51	83	23 35	50	82
85	19 42	+51	84	20 33	+51	83	21 24	+50	83	22 14	+51	82	23 05	+50	82
86	19 12	51	83	20 03	51	83	20 54	51	82	21 45	50	81	22 35	51	81
87	18 43	51	82	19 34	50	82	20 24	51	81	21 15	51	81	22 06	50	80
88	18 13	51	81	19 04	51	81	19 55	51	80	20 46	50	80	21 36	51	79
89	17 43	51	81	18 34	51	80	19 25	51	79	20 16	51	79	21 07	50	78
90	17 14	+51	80	18 05	+51	79	18 56	+51	79	19 47	+51	78	20 38	+50	77
91	16 44	51	79	17 35	52	78	18 27	50	78	19 17	51	77	20 08	51	77
92	16 15	51	78	17 06	51	78	17 57	51	77	18 48	51	76	19 39	51	76
93	15 46	51	77	16 37	51	77	17 28	51	76	18 19	51	76	19 10	51	75
94	15 16	52	76	16 08	51	76	16 59	51	75	17 50	51	75	18 41	51	74
95	14 47	+52	76	15 39	+51	75	16 30	+51	74	17 21	+51	74	18 12	+51	73
96	14 18	52	75	15 10	51	74	16 01	52	74	16 53	51	73	17 44	51	73
97	13 49	52	74	14 41	51	73	15 32	52	73	16 24	51	72	17 15	51	72
98	13 21	51	73	14 12	52	73	15 04	51	72	15 55	52	71	16 47	51	71
99	12 52	52	72	13 44	51	72	14 35	52	71	15 27	51	71	16 18	52	70
100	12 24	+51	71	13 15	+52	71	14 07	+52	70	14 59	+51	70	15 50	+52	69
101	11 55	52	71	12 47	52	70	13 39	52	70	14 31	51	69	15 22	52	68
102	11 27	52	70	12 19	52	69	13 11	52	69	14 03	52	68	14 55	51	68
103	10 59	52	69	11 51	52	68	12 43	52	68	13 35	52	67	14 27	52	67
104	10 31	52	68	11 23	52	68	12 15	52	67	13 07	52	67	13 59	52	66
105	10 03	+53	67	10 56	+52	67	11 48	+52	66	12 40	+52	66	13 32	+52	65
106	09 36	52	66	10 28	52	66	11 20	53	65	12 13	52	65	13 05	52	64
107	09 08	53	66	10 01	52	65	10 53	53	65	11 46	52	64	12 38	52	64
108	08 41	53	65	09 34	52	64	10 26	53	64	11 19	52	63	12 11	53	63
109	08 14	53	64	09 07	52	63	09 59	53	63	10 52	53	62	11 45	52	62
110	07 47	+53	63	08 40	+53	63	09 33	+53	62	10 26	+52	62	11 18	+53	61
111	07 21	53	62	08 14	52	62	09 06	53	61	09 59	53	61	10 52	53	60
112	06 54	53	61	07 47	53	61	08 40	53	60	09 33	53	60	10 26	53	60
113	06 28	53	61	07 21	53	60	08 14	53	60	09 07	53	59	10 00	53	59
114	06 02	53	60	06 55	54	59	07 49	53	59	08 42	53	58	09 35	53	58
115	05 36	+54	59	06 30	+53	58	07 23	+53	58	08 16	+54	58	09 10	+53	57
116	05 11	53	58	06 04	54	58	06 58	53	57	07 51	54	57	08 45	53	56
117	04 45	54	57	05 39	54	57	06 33	53	56	07 26	54	56	08 20	53	55
118	04 20	54	56	05 14	54	56	06 08	54	55	07 02	53	55	07 55	54	55
119	03 55	54	55	04 49	54	55	05 43	54	55	06 37	54	54	07 31	54	54
120	03 31	+54	55	04 25	+54	54	05 19	+54	54	06 13	+54	53	07 07	+54	53
121	03 06	55	54	04 01	54	53	04 55	54	53	05 49	54	53	06 43	54	52
122	02 42	55	53	03 37	54	53	04 31	54	52	05 25	55	52	06 20	54	51
123	02 19	54	52	03 13	54	52	04 07	55	51	05 02	54	51	05 56	55	50
124	01 55	55	51	02 50	54	51	03 44	55	50	04 39	54	50	05 33	55	50
125	01 32	+55	50	02 27	+54	50	03 21	+55	50	04 16	+55	49	05 11	+54	49
126	01 09	55	50	02 04	55	49	02 59	54	49	03 53	55	48	04 48	55	48
127	00 46	55	49	01 41	55	48	02 36	55	48	03 31	55	47	04 26	55	47
128	00 24	55	48	01 19	55	47	02 14	55	47	03 09	55	47	04 04	55	46
129	00 02	55	47	00 57	55	47	01 52	56	46	02 48	55	46	03 43	55	45
130	−0 20	+55	46	00 35	+56	46	01 31	+55	45	02 26	+56	45	03 22	+55	45
131	−0 41	55	45	00 14	56	45	01 10	55	44	02 05	56	44	03 01	55	44
132	−1 03	56	44	−0 07	56	44	00 49	56	44	01 45	55	43	02 40	56	43
133	−1 23	56	43	−0 27	55	43	00 28	56	43	01 24	56	42	02 20	56	42
134	−1 44	56	43	−0 48	56	42	00 08	56	42	01 04	56	41	02 00	56	41
135	−2 04	+56	42	−1 08	+56	41	−0 12	+56	41	00 44	+57	41	01 41	+56	40
136	−2 24	57	41	−1 27	56	40	−0 31	56	40	00 25	56	40	01 21	57	39
137	−2 43	56	40	−1 47	57	40	−0 50	56	39	00 06	57	39	01 03	56	39
138	−3 02	56	39	−2 06	57	39	−1 09	56	38	−0 13	57	38	00 44	57	38
139	−3 21	57	38	−2 24	56	38	−1 28	57	37	−0 31	57	37	00 26	57	37

LHA	25° Hc	25° d	25° Z	26° Hc	26° d	26° Z	27° Hc	27° d	27° Z	28° Hc	28° d	28° Z	29° Hc	29° d	29° Z	LHA
	° ′	′	°	° ′	′	°	° ′	′	°	° ′	′	°	° ′	′	°	
70	31 24	+50	94	32 14	+50	93	33 04	+49	93	33 53	+50	92	34 43	+49	91	290
71	30 54	50	93	31 44	50	92	32 34	49	92	33 23	50	91	34 13	49	90	289
72	30 24	50	92	31 14	50	91	32 04	49	91	32 53	50	90	33 43	49	89	288
73	29 54	50	91	30 44	50	91	31 34	49	90	32 23	50	89	33 13	49	89	287
74	29 24	50	90	30 14	50	90	31 04	49	89	31 53	50	88	32 43	49	88	286
75	28 54	+50	90	29 44	+50	89	30 34	+49	88	31 23	+50	88	32 13	+49	87	285
76	28 24	50	89	29 14	50	88	30 04	49	87	30 53	50	87	31 43	49	86	284
77	27 54	50	88	28 44	50	87	29 34	49	87	30 23	50	86	31 13	49	85	283
78	27 24	50	87	28 14	50	86	29 04	50	86	29 54	49	85	30 43	49	84	282
79	26 54	50	86	27 44	50	85	28 34	50	85	29 24	49	84	30 13	49	84	281
80	26 24	+50	85	27 14	+50	85	28 04	+50	84	28 54	+49	83	29 43	+50	83	280
81	25 54	50	84	26 44	50	84	27 34	50	83	28 24	50	83	29 14	49	82	279
82	25 25	50	84	26 15	50	83	27 05	49	82	27 54	50	82	28 44	49	81	278
83	24 55	50	83	25 45	50	82	26 35	50	82	27 25	49	81	28 14	50	80	277
84	24 25	50	82	25 15	50	81	26 05	50	81	26 55	50	80	27 45	49	79	276
85	23 55	+51	81	24 46	+50	80	25 36	+50	80	26 26	+49	79	27 15	+50	79	275
86	23 26	50	80	24 16	50	80	25 06	50	79	25 56	50	78	26 46	50	78	274
87	22 56	51	79	23 47	50	79	24 37	50	78	25 27	50	78	26 17	50	77	273
88	22 27	50	79	23 17	50	78	24 07	51	77	24 58	50	77	25 48	49	76	272
89	21 57	51	78	22 48	50	77	23 38	50	77	24 28	51	76	25 19	49	75	271
90	21 28	+51	77	22 19	+50	76	23 09	+50	76	23 59	+51	75	24 50	+50	75	270
91	20 59	51	76	21 50	50	76	22 40	51	75	23 31	50	74	24 21	50	74	269
92	20 30	51	75	21 21	50	75	22 11	51	74	23 02	50	74	23 52	50	73	268
93	20 01	51	74	20 52	50	74	21 42	51	73	22 33	50	73	23 23	51	72	267
94	19 32	51	74	20 23	51	73	21 14	50	73	22 04	51	72	22 55	50	71	266
95	19 03	+51	73	19 54	+51	72	20 45	+51	72	21 36	+51	71	22 27	+50	71	265
96	18 35	51	72	19 26	51	71	20 17	51	71	21 08	50	70	21 58	51	70	264
97	18 06	52	71	18 58	51	71	19 49	50	70	20 39	51	70	21 30	51	69	263
98	17 38	51	70	18 29	51	70	19 20	51	69	20 11	51	69	21 02	51	68	262
99	17 10	51	70	18 01	51	69	18 52	52	68	19 44	51	68	20 35	51	67	261
100	16 42	+51	69	17 33	+52	68	18 25	+51	68	19 16	+51	67	20 07	+51	67	260
101	16 14	52	68	17 06	51	67	17 57	51	67	18 48	52	66	19 40	51	66	259
102	15 46	52	67	16 38	51	67	17 29	52	66	18 21	51	66	19 12	52	65	258
103	15 19	51	66	16 10	52	66	17 02	52	65	17 54	51	65	18 45	52	64	257
104	14 51	52	66	15 43	52	65	16 35	52	64	17 27	51	64	18 18	52	63	256
105	14 24	+52	65	15 16	+52	64	16 08	+52	64	17 00	+52	63	17 52	+51	63	255
106	13 57	52	64	14 49	52	63	15 41	52	63	16 33	52	62	17 25	52	62	254
107	13 30	52	63	14 22	53	63	15 15	52	62	16 07	52	62	16 59	52	61	253
108	13 04	52	62	13 56	52	62	14 48	52	61	15 40	53	61	16 33	52	60	252
109	12 37	53	61	13 30	52	61	14 22	52	60	15 14	53	60	16 07	52	59	251
110	12 11	+53	61	13 04	+52	60	13 56	+53	60	14 49	+52	59	15 41	+52	59	250
111	11 45	53	60	12 38	52	59	13 30	53	59	14 23	52	58	15 15	53	58	249
112	11 19	53	59	12 12	53	59	13 05	52	58	13 57	53	58	14 50	53	57	248
113	10 53	53	58	11 46	53	58	12 39	53	57	13 32	53	57	14 25	53	56	247
114	10 28	53	57	11 21	53	57	12 14	53	56	13 07	53	56	14 00	53	55	246
115	10 03	+53	57	10 56	+53	56	11 49	+54	56	12 43	+53	55	13 36	+53	55	245
116	09 38	53	56	10 31	54	55	11 25	53	55	12 18	53	54	13 11	54	54	244
117	09 13	54	55	10 07	53	54	11 00	54	54	11 54	53	54	12 47	54	53	243
118	08 49	54	54	09 43	53	54	10 36	54	53	11 30	53	53	12 23	54	52	242
119	08 25	54	53	09 19	53	53	10 12	54	52	11 06	54	52	12 00	53	51	241
120	08 01	+54	52	08 55	+54	52	09 49	+54	52	10 43	+53	51	11 36	+54	51	240
121	07 37	54	52	08 31	54	51	09 25	54	51	10 19	54	50	11 13	54	50	239
122	07 14	54	51	08 08	54	50	09 02	54	50	09 56	55	50	10 51	54	49	238
123	06 51	54	50	07 45	55	50	08 40	54	49	09 34	54	49	10 28	54	48	237
124	06 28	54	49	07 22	55	49	08 17	54	48	09 11	55	48	10 06	54	47	236
125	06 05	+55	48	07 00	+55	48	07 55	+54	48	08 49	+55	47	09 44	+54	47	235
126	05 43	55	48	06 38	55	47	07 33	55	47	08 28	54	46	09 22	55	46	234
127	05 21	55	47	06 16	55	46	07 11	55	46	08 06	55	45	09 01	55	45	233
128	04 59	56	46	05 55	55	45	06 50	55	45	07 45	55	45	08 40	55	44	232
129	04 38	55	45	05 33	56	45	06 29	55	44	07 24	55	44	08 19	55	43	231
130	04 17	+56	44	05 13	+55	44	06 08	+55	43	07 03	+56	43	07 59	+55	43	230
131	03 56	56	43	04 52	55	43	05 47	56	43	06 43	55	42	07 38	56	42	229
132	03 36	56	42	04 32	55	42	05 27	56	42	06 23	56	41	07 19	55	41	228
133	03 16	56	42	04 12	56	41	05 08	55	41	06 03	56	41	06 59	56	40	227
134	02 56	56	41	03 52	56	40	04 48	56	40	05 44	56	40	06 40	56	39	226
135	02 37	+56	40	03 33	+56	40	04 29	+56	39	05 25	+56	39	06 21	+56	39	225
136	02 18	56	39	03 14	56	39	04 10	56	38	05 06	57	38	06 03	56	38	224
137	01 59	56	38	02 55	57	38	03 52	56	38	04 48	57	37	05 45	56	37	223
138	01 41	56	37	02 37	57	37	03 34	56	37	04 30	57	36	05 27	56	36	222
139	01 23	56	37	02 19	57	36	03 16	57	36	04 13	56	36	05 09	57	35	221

S. Lat. {LHA greater than 180°....... Zn=180−Z; LHA less than 180°........... Zn=180+Z

DECLINATION (15°-29°) SAME NAME AS LATITUDE

LAT 60°

N. Lat. {LHA greater than 180°....... Zn=Z; LHA less than 180°........... Zn=360−Z}

DECLINATION (15°-29°) SAME NAME AS LATITUDE

LHA	18° Hc	d	Z	19° Hc	d	Z	20° Hc	d	Z	21° Hc	d	Z	22° Hc	d	Z	23° Hc	d	Z	LHA
	° ′	′	°	° ′	′	°	° ′	′	°	° ′	′	°	° ′	′	°	° ′	′	°	
140	−5 33	+57	38	−4 36	+57	38	−3 39	+57	37	−2 42	+56	37	−1 46	+57	37	−0 49	+57	36	220
141				−4 54	57	37	−3 57	57	36	−3 00	57	36	−2 03	57	36	−1 06	57	35	219
142				−5 12	57	36	−4 15	57	35	−3 18	57	35	−2 21	57	35	−1 24	58	35	218
143				−5 29	57	35	−4 32	57	35	−3 35	57	34	−2 38	58	34	−1 40	57	34	217
144							−4 49	58	34	−3 51	57	33	−2 54	57	33	−1 57	58	33	216
145							−5 05	+57	33	−4 08	+58	32	−3 10	+57	32	−2 13	+58	32	215
146							−5 21	57	32	−4 24	58	32	−3 26	58	31	−2 28	57	31	214
147										−4 39	58	31	−3 41	57	30	−2 44	58	30	213
148										−4 54	58	30	−3 56	57	30	−2 59	58	29	212
149										−5 09	58	29	−4 11	58	29	−3 13	58	28	211
150										−5 23	+58	28	−4 25	+58	28	−3 27	+58	27	210
151													−4 39	58	27	−3 41	58	27	209
152													−4 52	58	26	−3 54	58	26	208
153													−5 05	58	25	−4 07	59	25	207
154													−5 18	59	24	−4 19	58	24	206
155																−4 31	+59	23	205
156																−4 42	58	22	204
157																−4 54	59	21	203
158																−5 04	59	20	202
159																−5 14	59	19	201

LHA	24° Hc	d	Z	25° Hc	d	Z	26° Hc	d	Z	27° Hc	d	Z	28° Hc	d	Z	29° Hc	d	Z	LHA
	° ′	′	°	° ′	′	°	° ′	′	°	° ′	′	°	° ′	′	°	° ′	′	°	
140	00 08	+57	36	01 05	+57	36	02 02	+56	35	02 58	+57	35	03 55	+57	35	04 52	+57	34	220
141	−0 09	57	35	00 48	57	35	01 45	56	34	02 41	57	34	03 38	57	34	04 35	57	34	219
142	−0 26	57	34	00 31	57	34	01 28	57	34	02 25	57	33	03 22	57	33	04 19	57	33	218
143	−0 43	57	33	00 14	57	33	01 11	58	33	02 09	57	32	03 06	57	32	04 03	57	32	217
144	−0 59	57	32	−0 02	57	32	00 55	58	32	01 53	57	32	02 50	57	31	03 47	58	31	216
145	−1 15	+57	32	−0 18	+58	31	00 40	+57	31	01 37	+58	31	02 35	+57	30	03 32	+58	30	215
146	−1 31	58	31	−0 33	57	30	00 24	58	30	01 22	58	30	02 20	57	30	03 17	58	29	214
147	−1 46	58	30	−0 48	57	30	00 09	58	29	01 07	58	29	02 05	58	29	03 03	57	29	213
148	−2 01	58	29	−1 03	58	29	−0 05	58	28	00 53	58	28	01 51	58	28	02 49	57	28	212
149	−2 15	58	28	−1 17	58	28	−0 19	58	28	00 39	58	27	01 37	58	27	02 35	58	27	211
150	−2 29	+58	27	−1 31	+58	27	−0 33	+58	27	00 25	+58	26	01 23	+58	26	02 21	+59	26	210
151	−2 43	59	26	−1 44	58	26	−0 46	58	26	00 12	58	26	01 10	59	25	02 09	58	25	209
152	−2 56	59	25	−1 57	58	25	−0 59	58	25	−0 01	59	25	00 58	58	25	01 56	58	24	208
153	−3 08	58	25	−2 10	59	24	−1 11	58	24	−0 13	58	24	00 45	59	24	01 44	58	23	207
154	−3 21	59	24	−2 22	59	23	−1 23	58	23	−0 25	59	23	00 34	58	23	01 32	59	23	206
155	−3 32	+58	23	−2 34	+59	23	−1 35	+59	22	−0 36	+58	22	00 22	+59	22	01 21	+59	22	205
156	−3 44	59	22	−2 45	59	22	−1 46	58	21	−0 48	59	21	00 11	59	21	01 10	59	21	204
157	−3 55	59	21	−2 56	59	21	−1 57	59	21	−0 58	59	20	00 01	59	20	01 00	58	20	203
158	−4 05	59	20	−3 06	59	20	−2 07	59	20	−1 08	59	20	−0 09	58	19	00 49	59	19	202
159	−4 15	59	19	−3 16	59	19	−2 17	59	19	−1 18	59	19	−0 19	59	18	00 40	59	18	201
160	−4 25	+59	18	−3 26	+59	18	−2 27	+59	18	−1 28	+60	18	−0 28	+59	18	00 31	+59	17	200
161	−4 34	59	17	−3 35	59	17	−2 36	60	17	−1 36	59	17	−0 37	59	17	00 22	59	17	199
162	−4 43	59	16	−3 44	60	16	−2 44	59	16	−1 45	59	16	−0 46	60	16	00 14	59	16	198
163	−4 51	59	16	−3 52	60	15	−2 52	59	15	−1 53	59	15	−0 54	60	15	00 06	59	15	197
164	−4 59	60	15	−3 59	59	15	−3 00	59	14	−2 01	60	14	−1 01	59	14	−0 02	60	14	196
165	−5 06	+59	14	−4 07	+60	14	−3 07	+59	13	−2 08	+60	13	−1 08	+59	13	−0 09	+60	13	195
166	−5 13	59	13	−4 14	60	13	−3 14	60	13	−2 14	59	12	−1 15	60	12	−0 15	59	12	194
167				−4 20	60	12	−3 20	59	12	−2 21	60	12	−1 21	60	11	−0 21	59	11	193
168				−4 26	60	11	−3 26	60	11	−2 26	59	11	−1 27	60	11	−0 27	60	10	192
169				−4 31	59	10	−3 32	60	10	−2 32	60	10	−1 32	60	10	−0 32	60	10	191
170				−4 36	+60	9	−3 36	+59	9	−2 37	+60	9	−1 37	+60	9	−0 37	+60	9	190
171				−4 41	60	8	−3 41	60	8	−2 41	60	8	−1 41	60	8	−0 41	59	8	189
172				−4 45	60	7	−3 45	60	7	−2 45	60	7	−1 45	60	7	−0 45	60	7	188
173				−4 48	60	6	−3 48	59	6	−2 49	60	6	−1 49	60	6	−0 49	60	6	187
174				−4 51	59	5	−3 52	60	5	−2 52	60	5	−1 52	60	5	−0 52	60	5	186
175				−4 54	+60	5	−3 54	+60	5	−2 54	+60	4	−1 54	+60	4	−0 54	+60	4	185
176				−4 56	60	4	−3 56	60	4	−2 56	60	4	−1 56	60	4	−0 56	60	3	184
177				−4 58	60	3	−3 58	60	3	−2 58	60	3	−1 58	60	3	−0 58	60	3	183
178				−4 59	60	2	−3 59	60	2	−2 59	60	2	−1 59	60	2	−0 59	60	2	182
179				−5 00	60	1	−4 00	60	1	−3 00	60	1	−2 00	60	1	−1 00	60	1	181
180				−5 00	+60	0	−4 00	+60	0	−3 00	+60	0	−2 00	+60	0	−1 00	+60	0	180

LHA	15° Hc	d	Z	LHA	16° Hc	d	Z	LHA	17° Hc	d	Z	LHA
75	−5 41	−53	110	285								
74	−5 13	53	111	286								
73	−4 45	53	112		−5 38	53	112	287				
72	−4 18	53	113		−5 11	52	113	288				
71	−3 50	53	114		−4 43	53	114		−5 36	53	115	289
70	−3 23	−53	115		−4 16	−53	115		−5 09	−53	115	290

15° | 16° | 17° | 18° | 19° | 20° | 21° | 22° | 23° | 24° | 25° | 26° | 27° | 28° | 29°

S. Lat. {LHA greater than 180°....... Zn=180−Z; LHA less than 180°........... Zn=180+Z}

DECLINATION (15°-29°) CONTRARY NAME TO LATITUDE

N. Lat. {LHA greater than 180°....... Zn=Z; LHA less than 180°........... Zn=360−Z}

DECLINATION (15°-29°) CONTRARY NAME TO LATITUDE

LHA	15°			16°			17°			18°			19°		
	Hc	d	Z	Hc	d	Z	Hc	d	Z	Hc	d	Z	Hc	d	Z
	° ′	′	°	° ′	′	°	° ′	′	°	° ′	′	°	° ′	′	°
69	-2 56	53	115	-3 49	53	116	-4 42	53	116	-5 35	53	117			
68	-2 29	53	116	-3 22	53	117	-4 15	53	117	-5 08	53	118			
67	-2 02	53	117	-2 55	53	118	-3 48	54	118	-4 42	53	119	-5 35	53	119
66	-1 35	54	118	-2 29	53	118	-3 22	53	119	-4 15	54	119	-5 09	53	120
65	-1 09	-53	119	-2 02	-54	119	-2 56	-53	120	-3 49	-54	120	-4 43	-53	121
64	-0 43	53	120	-1 36	54	120	-2 30	53	121	-3 23	54	121	-4 17	54	122
63	-0 17	54	121	-1 11	53	121	-2 04	54	121	-2 58	54	122	-3 52	53	122
62	00 09	54	121	-0 45	54	122	-1 39	54	122	-2 33	53	123	-3 26	54	123
61	00 34	54	122	-0 20	54	123	-1 14	53	123	-2 07	54	124	-3 01	54	124
60	01 00	-54	123	00 06	-55	124	-0 49	-54	124	-1 43	-54	125	-2 37	-54	125
59	01 25	55	124	00 30	54	125	-0 24	54	125	-1 18	54	125	-2 12	54	126
58	01 49	54	125	00 55	54	125	00 01	55	126	-0 54	54	126	-1 48	54	127
57	02 14	55	126	01 19	54	126	00 25	55	127	-0 30	54	127	-1 24	55	128
56	02 38	55	127	01 43	54	127	00 49	55	128	-0 06	54	128	-1 00	55	128
55	03 02	-55	128	02 07	-55	128	01 12	-54	128	00 18	-55	129	-0 37	-55	129
54	03 25	54	128	02 31	55	129	01 36	55	129	00 41	55	130	-0 14	55	130
53	03 49	55	129	02 54	55	130	01 59	55	130	01 04	55	131	00 09	55	131
52	04 12	55	130	03 17	55	131	02 22	56	131	01 26	55	131	00 31	55	132
51	04 35	56	131	03 39	55	132	02 44	55	132	01 49	55	132	00 54	56	133
50	04 57	-55	132	04 02	-56	132	03 06	-55	133	02 11	-56	133	01 15	-55	134
49	05 19	55	133	04 24	56	133	03 28	55	134	02 33	56	134	01 37	56	134
48	05 41	56	134	04 45	55	134	03 50	56	135	02 54	56	135	01 58	55	135
47	06 02	55	135	05 07	56	135	04 11	56	135	03 15	56	136	02 19	56	136
46	06 24	56	136	05 28	56	136	04 32	56	136	03 36	56	137	02 40	56	137
45	06 44	-56	137	05 48	-56	137	04 52	-56	137	03 56	-56	138	03 00	-56	138
44	07 05	56	138	06 09	57	138	05 12	56	138	04 16	56	139	03 20	56	139
43	07 25	56	138	06 29	57	139	05 32	56	139	04 36	57	139	03 39	56	140
42	07 45	57	139	06 48	56	140	05 52	57	140	04 55	56	140	03 59	57	141
41	08 04	56	140	07 08	57	141	06 11	57	141	05 14	56	141	04 18	57	142
40	08 23	-57	141	07 26	-56	142	06 30	-57	142	05 33	-57	142	04 36	-57	142
39	08 42	57	142	07 45	57	142	06 48	57	143	05 51	57	143	04 54	57	143
38	09 00	57	143	08 03	57	143	07 06	57	144	06 09	57	144	05 12	57	144
37	09 18	57	144	08 21	57	144	07 24	58	145	06 26	57	145	05 29	57	145
36	09 35	57	145	08 38	57	145	07 41	57	145	06 44	58	146	05 46	57	146
35	09 52	-57	146	08 55	-57	146	07 58	-58	146	07 00	-57	147	06 03	-58	147
34	10 09	57	147	09 12	58	147	08 14	58	147	07 16	57	148	06 19	58	148
33	10 25	57	148	09 28	58	148	08 30	58	148	07 32	57	149	06 35	58	149
32	10 41	58	149	09 43	57	149	08 46	58	149	07 48	58	149	06 50	58	150
31	10 57	58	150	09 59	58	150	09 01	58	150	08 03	58	150	07 05	58	151
30	11 12	-58	151	10 14	-58	151	09 16	-58	151	08 18	-59	151	07 19	-58	152
29	11 26	58	152	10 28	58	152	09 30	58	152	08 32	58	152	07 34	59	153
28	11 40	58	152	10 42	58	153	09 44	59	153	08 45	58	153	07 47	58	153
27	11 54	58	153	10 56	59	154	09 57	58	154	08 59	59	154	08 00	58	154
26	12 07	58	154	11 09	59	155	10 10	58	155	09 12	59	155	08 13	58	155
25	12 20	-59	155	11 21	-58	156	10 23	-59	156	09 24	-58	156	08 26	-59	156
24	12 32	58	156	11 34	59	157	10 35	59	157	09 36	59	157	08 37	58	157
23	12 44	59	157	11 45	58	157	10 47	59	158	09 48	59	158	08 49	59	158
22	12 55	58	158	11 57	59	158	10 58	59	159	09 59	59	159	09 00	59	159
21	13 06	59	159	12 07	59	159	11 08	59	160	10 09	59	160	09 10	59	160
20	13 17	-59	160	12 18	-59	160	11 19	-59	161	10 20	-60	161	09 20	-59	161
19	13 27	59	161	12 28	60	161	11 28	59	162	10 29	59	162	09 30	59	162
18	13 36	59	162	12 37	59	162	11 38	60	162	10 38	59	163	09 39	59	163
17	13 45	59	163	12 46	59	163	11 47	60	163	10 47	59	164	09 48	59	164
16	13 54	60	164	12 54	59	164	11 55	60	164	10 55	59	165	09 56	59	165
15	14 02	-60	165	13 02	-59	165	12 03	-60	165	11 03	-59	166	10 04	-60	166
14	14 09	59	166	13 10	60	166	12 10	60	166	11 10	59	166	10 11	60	167
13	14 16	60	167	13 16	59	167	12 17	60	167	11 17	59	167	10 18	60	168
12	14 23	60	168	13 23	60	168	12 23	59	168	11 24	60	168	10 24	60	169
11	14 29	60	169	13 29	60	169	12 29	60	169	11 29	59	169	10 30	60	169
10	14 34	-60	170	13 34	-60	170	12 34	-59	170	11 35	-60	170	10 35	-60	170
9	14 39	60	171	13 39	60	171	12 39	60	171	11 39	59	171	10 40	60	171
8	14 43	60	172	13 43	59	172	12 44	60	172	11 44	60	172	10 44	60	172
7	14 47	60	173	13 47	60	173	12 47	59	173	11 48	60	173	10 48	60	173
6	14 51	60	174	13 51	60	174	12 51	60	174	11 51	60	174	10 51	60	174
5	14 54	-60	175	13 54	-60	175	12 54	-60	175	11 54	-60	175	10 54	-60	175
4	14 56	60	176	13 56	60	176	12 56	60	176	11 56	60	176	10 56	60	176
3	14 58	60	177	13 58	60	177	12 58	60	177	11 58	60	177	10 58	60	177
2	14 59	60	178	13 59	60	178	12 59	60	178	11 59	60	178	10 59	60	178
1	15 00	60	179	14 00	60	179	13 00	60	179	12 00	60	179	11 00	60	179
0	15 00	-60	180	14 00	-60	180	13 00	-60	180	12 00	-60	180	11 00	-60	180
	15°			16°			17°			18°			19°		

LHA	20°			21°			22°			23°			24°		
	Hc	d	Z	Hc	d	Z	Hc	d	Z	Hc	d	Z	Hc	d	Z
	° ′	′	°	° ′	′	°	° ′	′	°	° ′	′	°	° ′	′	°
69															
68															
67															
66															
65	-5 36	-54	121												
64	-5 11	53	122												
63	-4 45	54	123	-5 39	54	123									
62	-4 20	54	124	-5 14	54	124									
61	-3 55	54	125	-4 49	54	125	-5 43	54	125						
60	-3 31	-54	125	-4 25	-54	126	-5 19	-54	126						
59	-3 06	55	126	-4 01	54	127	-4 55	54	127						
58	-2 42	55	127	-3 37	54	127	-4 31	54	128	-5 25	55	128			
57	-2 19	54	128	-3 13	54	128	-4 07	55	129	-5 02	54	129			
56	-1 55	55	129	-2 50	54	129	-3 44	55	130	-4 39	54	130	-5 33	55	130
55	-1 32	-55	130	-2 27	-54	130	-3 21	-55	130	-4 16	-55	131	-5 11	-54	131
54	-1 09	55	130	-2 04	55	131	-2 59	54	131	-3 53	55	132	-4 48	55	132
53	-0 46	55	131	-1 41	55	132	-2 36	55	132	-3 31	55	133	-4 26	55	133
52	-0 24	55	132	-1 19	55	133	-2 14	55	133	-3 09	55	133	-4 04	55	134
51	-0 02	55	133	-0 57	55	133	-1 52	56	134	-2 48	55	134	-3 43	55	135
50	00 20	-55	134	-0 35	-56	134	-1 31	-55	135	-2 26	-56	135	-3 22	-55	135
49	00 41	55	135	-0 14	56	135	-1 10	55	136	-2 05	56	136	-3 01	55	136
48	01 03	56	136	00 07	56	136	-0 49	56	136	-1 45	55	137	-2 40	56	137
47	01 23	56	137	00 27	55	137	-0 28	56	137	-1 24	56	138	-2 20	56	138
46	01 44	56	137	00 48	56	138	-0 08	56	138	-1 04	56	139	-2 00	56	139
45	02 04	-56	138	01 08	-56	139	00 12	-56	139	-0 44	-57	139	-1 41	-56	140
44	02 24	57	139	01 27	56	140	00 31	56	140	-0 25	56	140	-1 21	57	141
43	02 43	56	140	01 47	57	140	00 50	56	141	-0 06	57	141	-1 03	56	141
42	03 02	56	141	02 06	57	141	01 09	56	142	00 13	57	142	-0 44	57	142
41	03 21	57	142	02 24	56	142	01 28	57	143	00 31	57	143	-0 26	57	143
40	03 39	-57	143	02 42	-56	143	01 46	-57	143	00 49	-57	144	-0 08	-57	144
39	03 57	57	144	03 00	57	144	02 03	57	144	01 06	57	145	00 09	57	145
38	04 15	57	145	03 18	57	145	02 21	57	145	01 24	58	145	00 26	57	146
37	04 32	57	145	03 35	57	146	02 38	58	146	01 40	57	146	00 43	57	147
36	04 49	58	146	03 51	57	147	02 54	57	147	01 57	58	147	00 59	57	148
35	05 05	-57	147	04 08	-58	148	03 10	-57	148	02 13	-58	148	01 15	-57	148
34	05 21	57	148	04 24	58	148	03 26	58	149	02 28	57	149	01 31	58	149
33	05 37	58	149	04 39	58	149	03 41	57	150	02 44	58	150	01 46	58	150
32	05 52	58	150	04 54	58	150	03 56	57	150	02 59	58	151	02 01	58	151
31	06 07	58	151	05 09	58	151	04 11	58	151	03 13	58	152	02 15	58	152
30	06 21	-58	152	05 23	-58	152	04 25	-58	152	03 27	-58	153	02 29	-58	153
29	06 35	58	153	05 37	58	153	04 39	58	153	03 41	58	153	02 43	59	154
28	06 49	58	154	05 51	59	154	04 52	58	154	03 54	58	154	02 56	59	155
27	07 02	58	155	06 04	59	155	05 05	58	155	04 07	59	155	03 08	58	155
26	07 15	59	156	06 16	58	156	05 18	59	156	04 19	58	156	03 21	59	156
25	07 27	-59	156	06 28	-58	157	05 30	-59	157	04 31	-59	157	03 32	-58	157
24	07 39	59	157	06 40	59	158	05 41	59	158	04 42	58	158	03 44	59	158
23	07 50	59	158	06 51	59	158	05 52	58	159	04 54	59	159	03 55	59	159
22	08 01	59	159	07 02	59	159	06 03	59	160	05 04	59	160	04 05	59	160
21	08 11	59	160	07 12	59	160	06 13	59	161	05 14	59	161	04 15	59	161
20	08 21	-59	161	07 22	-59	161	06 23	-59	161	05 24	-59	162	04 25	-59	162
19	08 31	59	162	07 32	59	162	06 33	60	162	05 33	59	163	04 34	59	163
18	08 40	59	163	07 41	60	163	06 41	59	163	05 42	59	163	04 43	59	164
17	08 49	60	164	07 49	59	164	06 50	60	164	05 50	59	164	04 51	59	164
16	08 57	60	165	07 57	59	165	06 58	60	165	05 58	59	165	04 59	60	165
15	09 04	-59	166	08 05	-60	166	07 05	-59	166	06 06	-60	166	05 06	-59	166
14	09 11	59	167	08 12	60	167	07 12	59	167	06 13	60	167	05 13	59	167
13	09 18	60	168	08 18	59	168	07 19	60	168	06 19	59	168	05 20	60	168
12	09 24	59	169	08 25	60	169	07 25	60	169	06 25	59	169	05 26	60	169
11	09 30	60	170	08 30	60	170	07 30	59	170	06 31	60	170	05 31	60	170
10	09 35	-60	171	08 35	-59	171	07 36	-60	171	06 36	-60	171	05 36	-60	171
9	09 40	60	171	08 40	60	172	07 40	60	172	06 40	59	172	05 41	60	172
8	09 44	60	172	08 44	60	172	07 44	59	173	06 45	60	173	05 45	60	173
7	09 48	60	173	08 48	60	173	07 48	60	174	06 48	60	174	05 48	60	174
6	09 51	60	174	08 51	60	174	07 51	60	174	06 51	60	174	05 51	60	175
5	09 54	-60	175	08 54	-60	175	07 54	-60	175	06 54	-60	175	05 54	-60	175
4	09 56	60	176	08 56	60	176	07 56	60	176	06 56	60	176	05 56	60	176
3	09 58	60	177	08 58	60	177	07 58	60	177	06 58	60	177	05 58	60	177
2	09 59	60	178	08 59	60	178	07 59	60	178	06 59	60	178	05 59	60	178
1	10 00	60	179	09 00	60	179	08 00	60	179	07 00	60	179	06 00	60	179
0	10 00	-60	180	09 00	-60	180	08 00	-60	180	07 00	-60	180	06 00	-60	180
	20°			21°			22°			23°			24°		

LHA	25°			26°			27°			28°			29°			LHA
	Hc	d	Z	Hc	d	Z	Hc	d	Z	Hc	d	Z	Hc	d	Z	
	° ′	′	°	° ′	′	°	° ′	′	°	° ′	′	°	° ′	′	°	
69																291
68																292
67																293
66																294
65																295
64																296
63																297
62																298
61																299
60																300
59																301
58																302
57																303
56																304
55																305
54	-5 43	55	132													306
53	-5 21	55	133													307
52	-4 59	56	134													308
51	-4 38	55	135	-5 33	56	135										309
50	-4 17	-56	136	-5 13	-55	136										310
49	-3 56	56	137	-4 52	55	137										311
48	-3 36	56	138	-4 32	55	138	-5 27	56	138							312
47	-3 16	56	138	-4 12	56	139	-5 08	55	139							313
46	-2 56	56	139	-3 52	56	140	-4 48	56	140							314
45	-2 37	-56	140	-3 33	-56	140	-4 29	-56	141	-5 25	-56	141				315
44	-2 18	56	141	-3 14	56	141	-4 10	56	142	-5 06	57	142				316
43	-1 59	56	142	-2 55	57	142	-3 52	56	142	-4 48	57	143				317
42	-1 41	56	143	-2 37	57	143	-3 34	56	143	-4 30	57	144	-5 27	56	144	318
41	-1 23	56	143	-2 19	57	144	-3 16	57	144	-4 13	56	144	-5 09	57	145	319
40	-1 05	-57	144	-2 02	-56	145	-2 58	-57	145	-3 55	-57	145	-4 52	-57	146	320
39	-0 48	57	145	-1 45	56	146	-2 41	57	146	-3 38	57	146	-4 35	57	146	321
38	-0 31	57	146	-1 28	57	146	-2 25	57	147	-3 22	57	147	-4 19	57	147	322
37	-0 14	57	147	-1 11	58	147	-2 09	57	148	-3 06	57	148	-4 03	57	148	323
36	00 02	57	148	-0 55	58	148	-1 53	57	148	-2 50	57	149	-3 47	58	149	324
35	00 18	-58	149	-0 40	-57	149	-1 37	-58	149	-2 35	-57	150	-3 32	-58	150	325
34	00 33	57	150	-0 24	58	150	-1 22	58	150	-2 20	57	150	-3 17	58	151	326
33	00 48	57	150	-0 09	58	151	-1 07	58	151	-2 05	58	151	-3 03	57	151	327
32	01 03	58	151	00 05	58	152	-0 53	58	152	-1 51	58	152	-2 49	57	152	328
31	01 17	58	152	00 19	58	152	-0 39	58	153	-1 37	58	153	-2 35	58	153	329
30	01 31	-58	153	00 33	-58	153	-0 25	-58	154	-1 23	-58	154	-2 21	-59	154	330
29	01 44	58	154	00 46	58	154	-0 12	58	154	-1 10	59	155	-2 09	58	155	331
28	01 57	58	155	00 59	58	155	00 01	59	155	-0 58	58	155	-1 56	58	156	332
27	02 10	59	156	01 11	58	156	00 13	58	156	-0 45	59	156	-1 44	58	157	333
26	02 22	59	157	01 23	58	157	00 25	59	157	-0 34	58	157	-1 32	59	157	334
25	02 34	-59	157	01 35	-59	158	00 36	-58	158	-0 22	-59	158	-1 21	-59	158	335
24	02 45	59	158	01 46	58	159	00 48	59	159	-0 11	59	159	-1 10	59	159	336
23	02 56	59	159	01 57	59	159	00 58	59	160	-0 01	59	160	-1 00	58	160	337
22	03 06	59	160	02 07	59	160	01 08	59	160	00 09	58	161	-0 49	59	161	338
21	03 16	59	161	02 17	59	161	01 18	59	161	00 19	59	162	-0 40	59	162	339
20	03 26	-59	162	02 27	-59	162	01 28	-60	162	00 28	-59	162	-0 31	-59	163	340
19	03 35	59	163	02 36	60	163	01 36	59	163	00 37	59	163	-0 22	59	163	341
18	03 44	60	164	02 44	59	164	01 45	59	164	00 46	60	164	-0 14	59	164	342
17	03 52	60	165	02 52	59	165	01 53	59	165	00 54	60	165	-0 06	59	165	343
16	03 59	59	165	03 00	59	166	02 01	60	166	01 01	59	166	00 02	60	166	344
15	04 07	-60	166	03 07	-59	167	02 08	-60	167	01 08	-59	167	00 09	-60	167	345
14	04 14	60	167	03 14	60	167	02 14	59	168	01 15	60	168	00 15	59	168	346
13	04 20	60	168	03 20	59	168	02 21	60	168	01 21	60	169	00 21	59	169	347
12	04 26	60	169	03 26	60	169	02 26	59	169	01 27	60	169	00 27	60	170	348
11	04 31	59	170	03 32	60	170	02 32	60	170	01 32	60	170	00 32	60	170	349
10	04 36	-60	171	03 36	-59	171	02 37	-60	171	01 37	-60	171	00 37	-60	171	350
9	04 41	60	172	03 41	60	172	02 41	60	172	01 41	60	172	00 41	59	172	351
8	04 45	60	173	03 45	60	173	02 45	60	173	01 45	60	173	00 45	60	173	352
7	04 48	60	174	03 48	59	174	02 49	60	174	01 49	60	174	00 49	60	174	353
6	04 51	59	175	03 52	60	175	02 52	60	175	01 52	60	175	00 52	60	175	354
5	04 54	-60	175	03 54	-60	175	02 54	-60	176	01 54	-60	176	00 54	-60	176	355
4	04 56	60	176	03 56	60	176	02 56	60	176	01 56	60	176	00 56	60	177	356
3	04 58	60	177	03 58	60	177	02 58	60	177	01 58	60	177	00 58	60	177	357
2	04 59	60	178	03 59	60	178	02 59	60	178	01 59	60	178	00 59	60	178	358
1	05 00	60	179	04 00	60	179	03 00	60	179	02 00	60	179	01 00	60	179	359
0	05 00	-60	180	04 00	-60	180	03 00	-60	180	02 00	-60	180	01 00	-60	180	360
	25°			26°			27°			28°			29°			

S. Lat. {LHA greater than 180°....... Zn=180−Z; LHA less than 180°........... Zn=180+Z}

DECLINATION (15°-29°) CONTRARY NAME TO LATITUDE

LAT 60°

N. Lat. {LHA greater than 180°....... Zn=Z; LHA less than 180°........... Zn=360−Z}

DECLINATION (0°-14°) SAME NAME AS LATITUDE

LAT 61°

LHA	0° Hc	0° d	0° Z	1° Hc	1° d	1° Z	2° Hc	2° d	2° Z	3° Hc	3° d	3° Z	4° Hc	4° d	4° Z	5° Hc	5° d	5° Z	6° Hc	6° d	6° Z	7° Hc	7° d	7° Z
	° ′	′	°	° ′	′	°	° ′	′	°	° ′	′	°	° ′	′	°	° ′	′	°	° ′	′	°	° ′	′	°
0	29 00	+60	180	30 00	+60	180	31 00	+60	180	32 00	+60	180	33 00	+60	180	34 00	+60	180	35 00	+60	180	36 00	+60	180
1	29 00	60	179	30 00	60	179	31 00	60	179	32 00	60	179	33 00	60	179	34 00	60	179	35 00	60	179	36 00	60	179
2	28 59	60	178	29 59	60	178	30 59	60	178	31 59	60	178	32 59	60	178	33 59	60	178	34 59	60	178	35 59	60	178
3	28 57	60	177	29 57	60	177	30 57	60	177	31 57	60	177	32 57	60	176	33 57	60	176	34 57	60	176	35 57	60	176
4	28 55	60	175	29 55	60	175	30 55	60	175	31 55	60	175	32 55	60	175	33 55	60	175	34 55	60	175	35 55	60	175
5	28 53	+60	174	29 53	+60	174	30 53	+60	174	31 53	+60	174	32 53	+59	174	33 52	+60	174	34 52	+60	174	35 52	+60	174
6	28 50	60	173	29 50	59	173	30 49	60	173	31 49	60	173	32 49	60	173	33 49	60	173	34 49	60	173	35 49	60	173
7	28 46	60	172	29 46	60	172	30 46	59	172	31 45	60	172	32 45	60	172	33 45	60	172	34 45	60	172	35 45	60	171
8	28 42	59	171	29 41	60	171	30 41	60	171	31 41	60	171	32 41	60	171	33 41	59	170	34 40	60	170	35 40	60	170
9	28 37	59	170	29 36	60	170	30 36	60	170	31 36	60	169	32 36	59	169	33 35	60	169	34 35	60	169	35 35	60	169
10	28 31	+60	169	29 31	+60	169	30 31	+59	168	31 30	+60	168	32 30	+60	168	33 30	+59	168	34 29	+60	168	35 29	+60	168
11	28 25	60	168	29 25	59	167	30 24	60	167	31 24	60	167	32 24	59	167	33 23	60	167	34 23	60	167	35 23	59	167
12	28 19	59	166	29 18	60	166	30 18	59	166	31 17	60	166	32 17	59	166	33 16	60	166	34 16	60	166	35 16	59	165
13	28 11	60	165	29 11	59	165	30 10	60	165	31 10	59	165	32 09	60	165	33 09	59	165	34 08	60	164	35 08	59	164
14	28 04	59	164	29 03	60	164	30 03	59	164	31 02	59	164	32 01	60	164	33 01	59	163	34 00	60	163	35 00	59	163
15	27 55	+60	163	28 55	+59	163	29 54	+60	163	30 54	+59	163	31 53	+59	162	32 52	+60	162	33 52	+59	162	34 51	+59	162
16	27 47	59	162	28 46	59	162	29 45	60	162	30 45	59	161	31 44	59	161	32 43	59	161	33 42	59	161	34 41	60	161
17	27 37	60	161	28 37	59	161	29 36	59	160	30 35	59	160	31 34	59	160	32 33	59	160	33 32	60	160	34 32	59	159
18	27 27	60	160	28 27	59	159	29 26	59	159	30 25	59	159	31 24	59	159	32 23	59	159	33 22	59	158	34 21	59	158
19	27 17	59	159	28 16	59	158	29 15	59	158	30 14	59	158	31 13	59	158	32 12	59	158	33 11	59	157	34 10	59	157
20	27 06	+59	157	28 05	+59	157	29 04	+59	157	30 03	+59	157	31 02	+59	157	32 01	+58	156	32 59	+59	156	33 58	+59	156
21	26 55	59	156	27 54	58	156	28 52	59	156	29 51	59	156	30 50	59	155	31 49	58	155	32 47	59	155	33 46	59	155
22	26 43	59	155	27 42	58	155	28 40	59	155	29 39	59	155	30 38	58	154	31 36	59	154	32 35	58	154	33 33	59	154
23	26 30	59	154	27 29	59	154	28 28	58	154	29 26	59	153	30 25	58	153	31 23	59	153	32 22	58	153	33 20	59	152
24	26 17	59	153	27 16	58	153	28 14	59	153	29 13	58	152	30 11	59	152	31 10	58	152	32 08	58	152	33 06	59	151
25	26 04	+58	152	27 02	+59	152	28 01	+58	151	28 59	+58	151	29 57	+59	151	30 56	+58	151	31 54	+58	150	32 52	+58	150
26	25 50	58	151	26 48	59	151	27 47	58	150	28 45	58	150	29 43	58	150	30 41	58	150	31 39	58	149	32 37	58	149
27	25 36	58	150	26 34	58	150	27 32	58	149	28 30	58	149	29 28	58	149	30 26	58	148	31 24	58	148	32 22	58	148
28	25 21	58	149	26 19	58	148	27 17	58	148	28 15	58	148	29 13	58	148	30 11	57	147	31 08	58	147	32 06	58	147
29	25 05	58	148	26 03	58	147	27 01	58	147	27 59	58	147	28 57	58	146	29 55	57	146	30 52	58	146	31 50	58	146
30	24 50	+57	147	25 47	+58	146	26 45	+58	146	27 43	+58	146	28 41	+57	145	29 38	+58	145	30 36	+57	145	31 33	+58	144
31	24 33	58	146	25 31	58	145	26 29	57	145	27 26	58	145	28 24	57	144	29 21	58	144	30 19	57	144	31 16	58	143
32	24 17	57	145	25 14	58	144	26 12	57	144	27 09	58	144	28 07	57	143	29 04	57	143	30 01	58	143	30 59	57	142
33	24 00	57	143	24 57	57	143	25 54	58	143	26 52	57	142	27 49	57	142	28 46	57	142	29 43	57	141	30 40	58	141
34	23 42	57	142	24 39	58	142	25 37	57	142	26 34	57	141	27 31	57	141	28 28	57	141	29 25	57	140	30 22	57	140
35	23 24	+57	141	24 21	+57	141	25 18	+57	141	26 15	+57	140	27 12	+57	140	28 09	+57	140	29 06	+57	139	30 03	+57	139
36	23 06	57	140	24 03	57	140	25 00	57	140	25 57	56	139	26 53	57	139	27 50	57	139	28 47	57	138	29 44	56	138
37	22 47	57	139	23 44	57	139	24 41	56	139	25 37	57	138	26 34	57	138	27 31	56	138	28 27	57	137	29 24	56	137
38	22 28	56	138	23 24	57	138	24 21	57	138	25 18	56	137	26 14	57	137	27 11	56	136	28 07	57	136	29 04	56	136
39	22 08	57	137	23 05	56	137	24 01	57	137	24 58	56	136	25 54	57	136	26 51	56	135	27 47	56	135	28 43	57	135
40	21 48	+57	136	22 45	+56	136	23 41	+56	136	24 37	+57	135	25 34	+56	135	26 30	+56	134	27 26	+56	134	28 22	+56	134
41	21 28	56	135	22 24	56	135	23 20	57	134	24 17	56	134	25 13	56	134	26 09	56	133	27 05	56	133	28 01	56	133
42	21 07	56	134	22 03	57	134	23 00	56	133	23 56	56	133	24 52	56	133	25 48	56	132	26 44	56	132	27 40	55	131
43	20 46	56	133	21 42	56	133	22 38	56	132	23 34	56	132	24 30	56	132	25 26	56	131	26 22	56	131	27 18	55	130
44	20 25	56	132	21 21	56	132	22 17	55	131	23 12	56	131	24 08	56	131	25 04	56	130	26 00	55	130	26 55	56	129
45	20 03	+56	131	20 59	+56	131	21 55	+55	130	22 50	+56	130	23 46	+56	130	24 42	+55	129	25 37	+56	129	26 33	+55	128
46	19 41	56	130	20 37	55	130	21 32	56	129	22 28	55	129	23 23	56	129	24 19	55	128	25 14	56	128	26 10	55	127
47	19 19	55	129	20 14	56	129	21 10	55	128	22 05	55	128	23 00	56	128	23 56	55	127	24 51	55	127	25 46	55	126
48	18 56	55	128	19 51	56	128	20 47	55	127	21 42	55	127	22 37	55	127	23 32	56	126	24 28	55	126	25 23	55	125
49	18 33	55	127	19 28	55	127	20 23	56	126	21 19	55	126	22 14	55	126	23 09	55	125	24 04	55	125	24 59	55	124
50	18 09	+56	126	19 05	+55	126	20 00	+55	125	20 55	+55	125	21 50	+55	125	22 45	+55	124	23 40	+55	124	24 35	+54	123
51	17 46	55	125	18 41	55	125	19 36	55	125	20 31	55	124	21 26	55	124	22 21	54	123	23 15	55	123	24 10	55	122
52	17 22	55	124	18 17	55	124	19 12	55	124	20 07	54	123	21 01	55	123	21 56	55	122	22 51	54	122	23 45	55	121
53	16 58	55	123	17 53	54	123	18 47	55	123	19 42	55	122	20 37	54	122	21 31	55	121	22 26	54	121	23 20	55	120
54	16 33	55	122	17 28	55	122	18 23	54	122	19 17	55	121	20 12	54	121	21 06	55	120	22 01	54	120	22 55	54	119
55	16 09	+54	122	17 03	+55	121	17 58	+54	121	18 52	+55	120	19 47	+54	120	20 41	+54	119	21 35	+55	119	22 30	+54	118
56	15 44	54	121	16 38	55	120	17 33	54	120	18 27	54	119	19 21	55	119	20 16	54	118	21 10	54	118	22 04	54	117
57	15 19	54	120	16 13	54	119	17 07	55	119	18 02	54	118	18 56	54	118	19 50	54	117	20 44	54	117	21 38	54	116
58	14 53	55	119	15 48	54	118	16 42	54	118	17 36	54	117	18 30	54	117	19 24	54	116	20 18	54	116	21 12	54	116
59	14 28	54	118	15 22	54	117	16 16	54	117	17 10	54	116	18 04	54	116	18 58	54	116	19 52	54	115	20 46	53	115
60	14 02	+54	117	14 56	+54	116	15 50	+54	116	16 44	+54	115	17 38	+54	115	18 32	+53	115	19 25	+54	114	20 19	+54	114
61	13 36	54	116	14 30	54	115	15 24	53	115	16 17	54	115	17 11	54	114	18 05	54	114	18 59	53	113	19 52	54	113
62	13 09	54	115	14 03	54	115	14 57	54	114	15 51	54	114	16 45	53	113	17 38	54	113	18 32	53	112	19 25	54	112
63	12 43	54	114	13 37	53	114	14 30	54	113	15 24	54	113	16 18	53	112	17 11	54	112	18 05	53	111	18 58	53	111
64	12 16	54	113	13 10	54	113	14 04	53	112	14 57	54	112	15 51	53	111	16 44	54	111	17 38	53	110	18 31	53	110
65	11 49	+54	112	12 43	+54	112	13 37	+53	111	14 30	+53	111	15 23	+54	110	16 17	+53	110	17 10	+53	109	18 03	+54	109
66	11 22	54	111	12 16	53	111	13 09	54	110	14 03	53	110	14 56	53	109	15 49	54	109	16 43	53	108	17 36	53	108
67	10 55	54	110	11 49	53	110	12 42	53	109	13 35	54	109	14 29	53	109	15 22	53	108	16 15	53	108	17 08	53	107
68	10 28	53	110	11 21	54	109	12 15	53	109	13 08	53	108	14 01	53	108	14 54	53	107	15 47	53	107	16 40	53	106
69	10 00	54	109	10 54	53	108	11 47	53	108	12 40	53	107	13 33	53	107	14 26	53	106	15 19	53	106	16 12	53	105

LHA	8° Hc	8° d	8° Z	9° Hc	9° d	9° Z	10° Hc	10° d	10° Z	11° Hc	11° d	11° Z	12° Hc	12° d	12° Z	13° Hc	13° d	13° Z	14° Hc	14° d	14° Z	LHA
	° ′	′	°	° ′	′	°	° ′	′	°	° ′	′	°	° ′	′	°	° ′	′	°	° ′	′	°	
0	37 00	+60	180	38 00	+60	180	39 00	+60	180	40 00	+60	180	41 00	+60	180	42 00	+60	180	43 00	+60	180	360
1	37 00	60	179	38 00	60	179	39 00	60	179	40 00	60	179	41 00	60	179	42 00	60	179	43 00	60	179	359
2	36 59	60	178	37 59	60	178	38 59	60	178	39 59	60	177	40 59	60	177	41 59	60	177	42 59	60	177	358
3	36 57	60	176	37 57	60	176	38 57	60	176	39 57	60	176	40 57	60	176	41 57	60	176	42 57	60	176	357
4	36 55	60	175	37 55	60	175	38 55	60	175	39 55	60	175	40 55	60	175	41 55	60	175	42 55	60	175	356
5	36 52	+60	174	37 52	+60	174	38 52	+60	174	39 52	+60	174	40 52	+60	174	41 52	+60	174	42 52	+60	173	355
6	36 49	60	173	37 49	59	173	38 48	60	172	39 48	60	172	40 48	60	172	41 48	60	172	42 48	60	172	354
7	36 45	60	171	37 45	59	171	38 44	60	171	39 44	60	171	40 44	60	171	41 44	60	171	42 44	59	171	353
8	36 40	60	170	37 40	60	170	38 40	59	170	39 39	60	170	40 39	60	170	41 39	60	170	42 39	59	169	352
9	36 35	59	169	37 34	60	169	38 34	60	169	39 34	60	169	40 34	59	168	41 33	60	168	42 33	60	168	351
10	36 29	+59	168	37 28	+60	168	38 28	+60	167	39 28	+59	167	40 27	+60	167	41 27	+60	167	42 27	+59	167	350
11	36 22	60	166	37 22	59	166	38 21	60	166	39 21	60	166	40 21	59	166	41 20	60	166	42 20	59	166	349
12	36 15	60	165	37 15	59	165	38 14	60	165	39 14	59	165	40 13	60	165	41 13	59	164	42 12	59	164	348
13	36 07	60	164	37 07	59	164	38 06	60	164	39 06	59	164	40 05	59	163	41 04	60	163	42 04	59	163	347
14	35 59	59	163	36 58	60	163	37 58	59	162	38 57	59	162	39 56	60	162	40 56	59	162	41 55	59	162	346
15	35 50	+59	162	36 49	+60	161	37 49	+59	161	38 48	+59	161	39 47	+59	161	40 46	+59	161	41 45	+60	160	345
16	35 41	59	160	36 40	59	160	37 39	59	160	38 38	59	160	39 37	59	160	40 36	59	159	41 35	59	159	344
17	35 31	59	159	36 30	59	159	37 29	59	159	38 28	59	159	39 27	59	158	40 26	59	158	41 25	59	158	343
18	35 20	59	158	36 19	59	158	37 18	59	158	38 17	59	157	39 16	59	157	40 15	58	157	41 13	59	157	342
19	35 09	59	157	36 08	58	157	37 06	59	156	38 05	59	156	39 04	59	156	40 03	58	156	41 01	59	155	341
20	34 57	+59	156	35 56	+59	155	36 55	+58	155	37 53	+59	155	38 52	+58	155	39 50	+59	154	40 49	+59	154	340
21	34 45	58	154	35 43	59	154	36 42	59	154	37 41	58	154	38 39	59	153	39 38	58	153	40 36	58	153	339
22	34 32	58	153	35 30	59	153	36 29	58	153	37 27	59	152	38 26	58	152	39 24	58	152	40 22	59	152	338
23	34 19	58	152	35 17	58	152	36 15	59	152	37 14	58	151	38 12	58	151	39 10	58	151	40 08	58	150	337
24	34 05	58	151	35 03	58	151	36 01	58	150	36 59	58	150	37 57	58	150	38 55	59	149	39 54	57	149	336
25	33 50	+58	150	34 48	+58	149	35 46	+59	149	36 45	+57	149	37 42	+58	149	38 40	+58	148	39 38	+58	148	335
26	33 35	58	149	34 33	58	148	35 31	58	148	36 29	58	148	37 27	58	147	38 25	58	147	39 23	57	147	334
27	33 20	58	147	34 18	58	147	35 16	57	147	36 13	58	146	37 11	58	146	38 09	57	146	39 06	58	145	333
28	33 04	58	146	34 02	57	146	34 59	58	146	35 57	58	145	36 55	57	145	37 52	58	145	38 50	57	144	332
29	32 48	57	145	33 45	58	145	34 43	57	145	35 40	58	144	36 38	57	144	37 35	57	143	38 32	57	143	331
30	32 31	+57	144	33 28	+58	144	34 26	+57	143	35 23	+57	143	36 20	+57	143	37 17	+58	142	38 15	+57	142	330
31	32 14	57	143	33 11	57	143	34 08	57	142	35 05	57	142	36 02	57	142	36 59	57	141	37 56	57	141	329
32	31 56	57	142	32 53	57	141	33 50	57	141	34 47	57	141	35 44	57	140	36 41	57	140	37 38	56	140	328
33	31 38	57	141	32 35	57	140	33 32	56	140	34 28	57	140	35 25	57	139	36 22	57	139	37 19	56	138	327
34	31 19	57	140	32 16	57	139	33 13	56	139	34 09	57	138	35 06	57	138	36 03	56	138	36 59	56	137	326
35	31 00	+57	139	31 57	+56	138	32 53	+57	138	33 50	+56	137	34 46	+57	137	35 43	+56	137	36 39	+56	136	325
36	30 40	57	137	31 37	56	137	32 33	57	137	33 30	56	136	34 26	56	136	35 22	57	135	36 19	56	135	324
37	30 20	57	136	31 17	56	136	32 13	57	136	33 10	56	135	34 06	56	135	35 02	56	134	35 58	56	134	323
38	30 00	56	135	30 56	57	135	31 53	56	134	32 49	56	134	33 45	56	134	34 41	56	133	35 37	56	133	322
39	29 40	56	134	30 36	56	134	31 32	56	133	32 28	56	133	33 24	55	133	34 19	56	132	35 15	56	132	321
40	29 18	+56	133	30 14	+56	133	31 10	+56	133	32 06	+56	132	33 02	+56	131	33 58	+55	131	34 53	+56	131	320
41	28 57	56	132	29 53	56	132	30 49	55	131	31 44	56	131	32 40	56	130	33 36	55	130	34 31	55	129	319
42	28 35	56	131	29 31	56	131	30 27	55	130	31 22	56	130	32 18	55	129	33 13	55	129	34 08	55	128	318
43	28 13	56	130	29 09	55	130	30 04	56	129	31 00	55	129	31 55	55	128	32 50	55	128	33 45	55	127	317
44	27 51	55	129	28 46	56	129	29 42	55	128	30 37	55	128	31 32	55	127	32 27	55	127	33 22	55	126	316
45	27 28	+55	128	28 23	+55	128	29 18	+56	127	30 14	+55	127	31 09	+55	126	32 04	+54	126	32 58	+55	125	315
46	27 05	55	127	28 00	55	126	28 55	55	126	29 50	55	126	30 45	55	125	31 40	54	125	32 34	55	124	314
47	26 41	55	126	27 36	55	125	28 31	55	125	29 26	55	125	30 21	55	124	31 16	54	124	32 10	55	123	313
48	26 18	55	125	27 13	54	124	28 07	55	124	29 02	55	124	29 57	54	123	30 51	55	123	31 46	54	122	312
49	25 54	54	124	26 48	55	123	27 43	55	123	28 38	54	122	29 32	55	122	30 27	54	122	31 21	54	121	311
50	25 29	+55	123	26 24	+55	122	27 19	+54	122	28 13	+54	121	29 07	+55	121	30 02	+54	120	30 56	+54	120	310
51	25 05	54	122	25 59	55	121	26 54	54	121	27 48	54	120	28 42	54	120	29 36	54	119	30 30	54	119	309
52	24 40	54	121	25 34	55	120	26 29	54	120	27 23	54	119	28 17	54	119	29 11	54	118	30 05	54	118	308
53	24 15	54	120	25 09	54	119	26 03	54	119	26 57	54	118	27 51	54	118	28 45	54	117	29 39	54	117	307
54	23 49	55	119	24 44	54	118	25 38	54	118	26 32	54	117	27 26	53	117	28 19	54	116	29 13	53	116	306
55	23 24	+54	118	24 18	+54	117	25 12	+54	117	26 06	+53	116	26 59	+54	116	27 53	+54	115	28 47	+53	115	305
56	22 58	54	117	23 52	54	116	24 46	54	116	25 40	53	116	26 33	54	115	27 27	53	115	28 20	54	114	304
57	22 32	54	116	23 26	54	116	24 20	53	115	25 13	54	115	26 07	53	114	27 00	54	114	27 54	53	113	303
58	22 06	53	115	22 59	54	115	23 53	54	114	24 47	53	114	25 40	53	113	26 33	54	113	27 27	53	112	302
59	21 39	54	114	22 33	53	114	23 26	54	113	24 20	53	113	25 13	53	113	26 06	54	112	27 00	53	111	301
60	21 13	+53	113	22 06	+54	113	23 00	+53	112	23 53	+53	112	24 46	+53	111	25 39	+53	111	26 32	+53	110	300
61	20 46	53	112	21 39	54	112	22 33	53	111	23 26	53	111	24 19	53	110	25 12	53	110	26 05	53	109	299
62	20 19	53	111	21 12	53	111	22 05	53	110	22 58	54	110	23 52	53	109	24 45	52	109	25 37	53	108	298
63	19 51	54	110	20 45	53	110	21 38	53	109	22 31	53	109	23 24	53	108	24 17	53	108	25 10	52	107	297
64	19 24	53	109	20 17	53	109	21 10	53	108	22 03	53	108	22 56	53	107	23 49	53	107	24 42	52	106	296
65	18 57	+53	108	19 50	+53	108	20 43	+53	107	21 36	+52	107	22 28	+53	106	23 21	+53	106	24 14	+52	105	295
66	18 29	53	108	19 22	53	107	20 15	53	107	21 08	52	106	22 00	53	106	22 53	53	105	23 46	52	104	294
67	18 01	53	107	18 54	53	106	19 47	53	106	20 40	52	105	21 32	53	105	22 25	52	104	23 17	53	104	293
68	17 33	53	106	18 26	53	105	19 19	53	105	20 12	52	104	21 04	53	104	21 57	52	103	22 49	52	103	292
69	17 05	53	105	17 58	53	104	18 51	52	104	19 43	53	103	20 36	52	103	21 28	53	102	22 21	52	102	291

S. Lat. {LHA greater than 180°....... Zn=180−Z; LHA less than 180°........... Zn=180+Z}

DECLINATION (0°-14°) SAME NAME AS LATITUDE

LAT 61°

N. Lat. {LHA greater than 180°........ Zn=Z
{LHA less than 180°........... Zn=360−Z

DECLINATION (0°-14°) SAME NAME AS LATITUDE

LHA	0° Hc	0° d	0° Z	1° Hc	1° d	1° Z	2° Hc	2° d	2° Z	3° Hc	3° d	3° Z	4° Hc	4° d	4° Z
	° ′	′	°	° ′	′	°	° ′	′	°	° ′	′	°	° ′	′	°
70	09 33	+53	108	10 26	+53	107	11 19	+53	107	12 12	+53	106	13 05	+53	106
71	09 05	53	107	09 58	53	106	10 51	53	106	11 44	53	105	12 37	53	105
72	08 37	53	106	09 30	53	105	10 23	53	105	11 16	53	104	12 09	53	104
73	08 09	53	105	09 02	53	105	09 55	53	104	10 48	53	104	11 41	53	103
74	07 41	53	104	08 34	53	104	09 27	53	103	10 20	52	103	11 12	53	102
75	07 13	+52	103	08 05	+53	103	08 58	+53	102	09 51	+53	102	10 44	+53	101
76	06 44	53	102	07 37	53	102	08 30	53	101	09 23	52	101	10 15	53	100
77	06 16	52	101	07 08	53	101	08 01	53	101	08 54	53	100	09 47	52	100
78	05 47	53	101	06 40	53	100	07 33	52	100	08 25	53	99	09 18	53	99
79	05 19	52	100	06 11	53	99	07 04	53	99	07 57	52	98	08 49	53	98
80	04 50	+52	99	05 42	+53	98	06 35	+53	98	07 28	+52	97	08 20	+53	97
81	04 21	53	98	05 14	52	97	06 06	53	97	06 59	52	96	07 51	53	96
82	03 52	53	97	04 45	52	97	05 37	53	96	06 30	52	96	07 22	53	95
83	03 23	53	96	04 16	52	96	05 08	53	95	06 01	52	95	06 53	53	94
84	02 54	53	95	03 47	52	95	04 39	53	94	05 32	52	94	06 24	53	93
85	02 25	+53	94	03 18	+52	94	04 10	+53	93	05 03	+52	93	05 55	+53	92
86	01 56	53	94	02 49	52	93	03 41	53	93	04 34	52	92	05 26	53	92
87	01 27	53	93	02 20	52	92	03 12	53	92	04 05	52	91	04 57	53	91
88	00 58	53	92	01 51	52	91	02 43	53	91	03 36	52	90	04 28	53	90
89	00 29	53	91	01 22	52	90	02 14	52	90	03 06	53	89	03 59	52	89
90	00 00	+52	90	00 52	+53	90	01 45	+52	89	02 37	+53	89	03 30	+52	88
91	−0 29	52	89	00 23	53	89	01 16	52	88	02 08	53	88	03 01	52	87
92	−0 58	52	88	−0 06	53	88	00 47	52	87	01 39	53	87	02 32	52	86
93	−1 27	52	87	−0 35	53	87	00 18	52	86	01 10	53	86	02 03	52	85
94	−1 56	52	86	−1 04	53	86	−0 11	52	86	00 41	53	85	01 34	52	85
95	−2 25	+52	86	−1 33	+53	85	−0 40	+52	85	00 12	+53	84	01 05	+52	84
96	−2 54	52	85	−2 02	53	84	−1 09	52	84	−0 17	53	83	00 36	53	83
97	−3 23	52	84	−2 31	53	83	−1 38	53	83	−0 45	52	82	00 07	53	82
98	−3 52	52	83	−3 00	53	83	−2 07	53	82	−1 14	52	82	−0 22	53	81
99	−4 21	53	82	−3 28	52	82	−2 36	53	81	−1 43	53	81	−0 50	52	80
100	−4 50	+53	81	−3 57	+53	81	−3 04	+52	80	−2 12	+53	80	−1 19	+53	79
101	−5 19	53	80	−4 26	53	80	−3 33	53	79	−2 40	52	79	−1 48	53	78
102	−5 47	53	79	−4 54	52	79	−4 02	53	79	−3 09	53	78	−2 16	53	78
103				−5 23	53	78	−4 30	53	78	−3 37	53	77	−2 44	53	77
104				−5 51	53	77	−4 58	53	77	−4 05	52	76	−3 13	53	76
105							−5 27	+53	76	−4 34	+53	75	−3 41	+53	75
106							−5 55	53	75	−5 02	53	74	−4 09	53	74
107										−5 30	53	74	−4 37	53	73
108													−5 04	53	72
109													−5 32	53	71

LHA	5° Hc	5° d	5° Z	6° Hc	6° d	6° Z	7° Hc	7° d	7° Z	8° Hc	8° d	8° Z	9° Hc	9° d	9° Z
	° ′	′	°	° ′	′	°	° ′	′	°	° ′	′	°	° ′	′	°
70	13 58	+53	105	14 51	+53	105	15 44	+53	104	16 37	+53	104	17 30	+52	103
71	13 30	53	104	14 23	53	104	15 16	53	103	16 09	52	103	17 01	53	102
72	13 02	53	104	13 55	52	103	14 47	53	103	15 40	53	102	16 33	52	102
73	12 34	52	103	13 26	53	102	14 19	53	102	15 12	52	101	16 04	53	101
74	12 05	53	102	12 58	52	101	13 50	53	101	14 43	53	100	15 36	52	100
75	11 37	+52	101	12 29	+53	100	13 22	+52	100	14 14	+53	99	15 07	+52	99
76	11 08	53	100	12 01	52	99	12 53	53	99	13 46	52	98	14 38	53	98
77	10 39	53	99	11 32	52	99	12 24	53	98	13 17	52	98	14 09	53	97
78	10 11	52	98	11 03	53	98	11 56	52	97	12 48	52	97	13 40	53	96
79	09 42	52	97	10 34	53	97	11 27	52	96	12 19	52	96	13 11	53	95
80	09 13	+52	96	10 05	+53	96	10 58	+52	95	11 50	+52	95	12 42	+53	94
81	08 44	52	96	09 36	53	95	10 29	52	95	11 21	52	94	12 13	53	94
82	08 15	52	95	09 07	53	94	10 00	52	94	10 52	52	93	11 44	53	93
83	07 46	52	94	08 38	53	93	09 31	52	93	10 23	52	92	11 15	53	92
84	07 17	52	93	08 09	53	92	09 02	52	92	09 54	52	91	10 46	53	91
85	06 48	+52	92	07 40	+53	92	08 33	+52	91	09 25	+52	91	10 17	+52	90
86	06 19	52	91	07 11	52	91	08 03	53	90	08 56	52	90	09 48	52	89
87	05 50	52	90	06 42	52	90	07 34	53	89	08 27	52	89	09 19	52	88
88	05 21	52	89	06 13	52	89	07 05	53	88	07 58	52	88	08 50	52	87
89	04 51	53	88	05 44	52	88	06 36	53	88	07 29	52	87	08 21	52	87
90	04 22	+53	88	05 15	+52	87	06 07	+53	87	07 00	+52	86	07 52	+52	86
91	03 53	53	87	04 46	52	86	05 38	53	86	06 31	52	85	07 23	52	85
92	03 24	53	86	04 17	52	85	05 09	53	85	06 02	52	84	06 54	52	84
93	02 55	53	85	03 48	52	84	04 40	53	84	05 33	52	84	06 25	52	83
94	02 26	53	84	03 19	52	84	04 11	53	83	05 04	52	83	05 56	53	82
95	01 57	+53	83	02 50	+52	83	03 42	+53	82	04 35	+52	82	05 27	+53	81
96	01 29	52	82	02 21	53	82	03 14	52	81	04 06	53	81	04 59	52	80
97	01 00	52	81	01 52	53	81	02 45	52	80	03 37	53	80	04 30	53	80
98	00 31	53	81	01 24	52	80	02 16	53	80	03 09	52	79	04 01	53	79
99	00 02	53	80	00 55	53	79	01 48	52	79	02 40	53	78	03 33	53	78
100	−0 26	+52	79	00 26	+53	78	01 19	+53	78	02 12	+53	77	03 05	+52	77
101	−0 55	53	78	−0 02	53	77	00 51	53	77	01 44	52	77	02 36	53	76
102	−1 23	53	77	−0 30	52	77	00 22	53	76	01 15	53	76	02 08	53	75
103	−1 51	52	76	−0 59	53	76	−0 06	53	75	00 47	53	75	01 40	53	74
104	−2 20	53	75	−1 27	53	75	−0 34	53	74	00 19	53	74	01 12	53	73
105	−2 48	+53	74	−1 55	+53	74	−1 02	+53	74	−0 09	+53	73	00 44	+53	73
106	−3 16	53	74	−2 23	53	73	−1 30	54	73	−0 36	53	72	00 17	53	72
107	−3 44	54	73	−2 50	53	72	−1 57	53	72	−1 04	53	71	−0 11	53	71
108	−4 11	53	72	−3 18	53	71	−2 25	53	71	−1 32	54	70	−0 38	53	70
109	−4 39	53	71	−3 46	54	70	−2 52	53	70	−1 59	53	70	−1 06	54	69
110	−5 06	+53	70	−4 13	+54	70	−3 19	+53	69	−2 26	+53	69	−1 33	+54	68
111	−5 34	54	69	−4 40	53	69	−3 47	54	68	−2 53	53	68	−2 00	54	67
112				−5 07	54	68	−4 13	53	67	−3 20	54	67	−2 26	53	66
113				−5 34	54	67	−4 40	53	66	−3 47	54	66	−2 53	54	66
114							−5 07	54	66	−4 13	54	65	−3 19	53	65
115							−5 33	+54	65	−4 39	+54	64	−3 45	+53	64
116										−5 05	54	63	−4 11	53	63
117										−5 31	54	62	−4 37	54	62
118													−5 03	54	61
119													−5 28	54	60

LHA	10° Hc	10° d	10° Z	11° Hc	11° d	11° Z	12° Hc	12° d	12° Z	13° Hc	13° d	13° Z	14° Hc	14° d	14° Z	LHA
	° ′	′	°	° ′	′	°	° ′	′	°	° ′	′	°	° ′	′	°	
70	18 22	+53	103	19 15	+52	102	20 07	+53	102	21 00	+52	101	21 52	+52	101	290
71	17 54	52	102	18 46	53	101	19 39	52	101	20 31	53	100	21 24	52	100	289
72	17 25	53	101	18 18	52	101	19 10	53	100	20 03	52	100	20 55	52	99	288
73	16 57	52	100	17 49	53	100	18 42	52	99	19 34	52	99	20 26	52	98	287
74	16 28	53	99	17 21	52	99	18 13	52	98	19 05	52	98	19 57	52	97	286
75	15 59	+53	98	16 52	+52	98	17 44	+52	97	18 36	+52	97	19 28	+52	96	285
76	15 31	52	97	16 23	52	97	17 15	52	96	18 07	52	96	18 59	52	95	284
77	15 02	52	97	15 54	52	96	16 46	52	96	17 38	52	95	18 30	52	95	283
78	14 33	52	96	15 25	52	95	16 17	52	95	17 09	52	94	18 01	52	94	282
79	14 04	52	95	14 56	52	94	15 48	52	94	16 40	52	93	17 32	52	93	281
80	13 35	+52	94	14 27	+52	93	15 19	+52	93	16 11	+52	92	17 03	+52	92	280
81	13 06	52	93	13 58	52	93	14 50	52	92	15 42	52	91	16 34	52	91	279
82	12 37	52	92	13 29	52	92	14 21	52	91	15 13	52	91	16 05	52	90	278
83	12 08	52	91	13 00	52	91	13 52	52	90	14 44	52	90	15 36	52	89	277
84	11 39	52	90	12 31	52	90	13 23	52	89	14 15	52	89	15 07	52	88	276
85	11 09	+53	90	12 02	+52	89	12 54	+52	89	13 46	+52	88	14 38	+52	87	275
86	10 40	53	89	11 33	52	88	12 25	52	88	13 17	52	87	14 09	52	87	274
87	10 11	52	88	11 03	53	87	11 56	52	87	12 48	52	86	13 40	52	86	273
88	09 42	52	87	10 34	53	86	11 27	52	86	12 19	52	85	13 11	52	85	272
89	09 13	52	86	10 05	53	86	10 58	52	85	11 50	52	85	12 42	52	84	271
90	08 44	+52	85	09 36	+53	85	10 29	+52	84	11 21	+52	84	12 13	+52	83	270
91	08 15	53	84	09 08	52	84	10 00	52	83	10 52	52	83	11 44	52	82	269
92	07 46	53	83	08 39	52	83	09 31	52	82	10 23	52	82	11 15	52	81	268
93	07 17	53	83	08 10	52	82	09 02	52	82	09 54	53	81	10 47	52	81	267
94	06 49	52	82	07 41	52	81	08 33	53	81	09 26	52	80	10 18	52	80	266
95	06 20	+52	81	07 12	+53	80	08 05	+52	80	08 57	+52	79	09 49	+53	79	265
96	05 51	53	80	06 44	52	79	07 36	53	79	08 29	52	78	09 21	52	78	264
97	05 23	52	79	06 15	53	79	07 08	52	78	08 00	52	78	08 52	53	77	263
98	04 54	53	78	05 47	52	78	06 39	53	77	07 32	52	77	08 24	53	76	262
99	04 26	52	77	05 18	53	77	06 11	52	76	07 03	53	76	07 56	52	75	261
100	03 57	+53	76	04 50	+53	76	05 43	+52	76	06 35	+53	75	07 28	+52	75	260
101	03 29	53	76	04 22	53	75	05 15	52	75	06 07	53	74	07 00	53	74	259
102	03 01	53	75	03 54	53	74	04 47	52	74	05 39	53	73	06 32	53	73	258
103	02 33	53	74	03 26	53	73	04 19	53	73	05 12	52	72	06 04	53	72	257
104	02 05	53	73	02 58	53	73	03 51	53	72	04 44	53	72	05 37	53	71	256
105	01 37	+53	72	02 30	+53	72	03 23	+53	71	04 16	+53	71	05 09	+53	70	255
106	01 10	53	71	02 03	53	71	02 56	53	70	03 49	53	70	04 42	53	69	254
107	00 42	53	70	01 35	54	70	02 29	53	69	03 22	53	69	04 15	53	69	253
108	00 15	53	69	01 08	53	69	02 01	54	69	02 55	53	68	03 48	53	68	252
109	−0 12	53	69	00 41	53	68	01 34	54	68	02 28	53	67	03 21	53	67	251
110	−0 39	+53	68	00 14	+54	67	01 08	+53	67	02 01	+53	66	02 54	+54	66	250
111	−1 06	53	67	−0 13	54	66	00 41	53	66	01 34	54	65	02 28	53	65	249
112	−1 33	54	66	−0 39	53	66	00 14	54	65	01 08	54	65	02 02	53	64	248
113	−1 59	53	65	−1 06	54	65	−0 12	54	64	00 42	54	64	01 36	53	63	247
114	−2 26	54	64	−1 32	54	64	−0 38	54	63	00 16	54	63	01 10	53	62	246
115	−2 52	+54	63	−1 58	+54	63	−1 04	+54	62	−0 10	+54	62	00 44	+54	62	245
116	−3 18	54	62	−2 24	54	62	−1 30	54	62	−0 36	54	61	00 18	54	61	244
117	−3 43	54	62	−2 49	54	61	−1 55	54	61	−1 01	54	60	−0 07	54	60	243
118	−4 09	55	61	−3 14	54	60	−2 20	54	60	−1 26	54	59	−0 32	54	59	242
119	−4 34	54	60	−3 40	55	59	−2 45	54	59	−1 51	54	58	−0 57	55	58	241
120	−4 59	+54	59	−4 05	+55	58	−3 10	+54	58	−2 16	+55	58	−1 21	+54	57	240
121	−5 24	55	58	−4 29	54	58	−3 35	55	57	−2 40	54	57	−1 46	55	56	239
122	−5 48	54	57	−4 54	55	57	−3 59	55	56	−3 04	54	56	−2 10	55	55	238
123				−5 18	55	56	−4 23	55	55	−3 28	55	55	−2 33	54	55	237
124				−5 42	55	55	−4 47	55	54	−3 52	55	54	−2 57	55	54	236
125							−5 10	+55	54	−4 15	+55	53	−3 20	+56	53	235
126							−5 34	56	53	−4 38	55	52	−3 43	55	52	234
127										−5 01	55	51	−4 06	55	51	233
128										−5 24	56	50	−4 28	55	50	232
129													−4 51	56	49	231
130													−5 13	+56	48	230
131													−5 34	56	47	229

S. Lat. {LHA greater than 180°........ Zn=180−Z
{LHA less than 180°........... Zn=180+Z

DECLINATION (0°-14°) SAME NAME AS LATITUDE

N. Lat. {LHA greater than 180°....... Zn=Z; LHA less than 180°........... Zn=360−Z}

DECLINATION (0°-14°) CONTRARY NAME TO LATITUDE

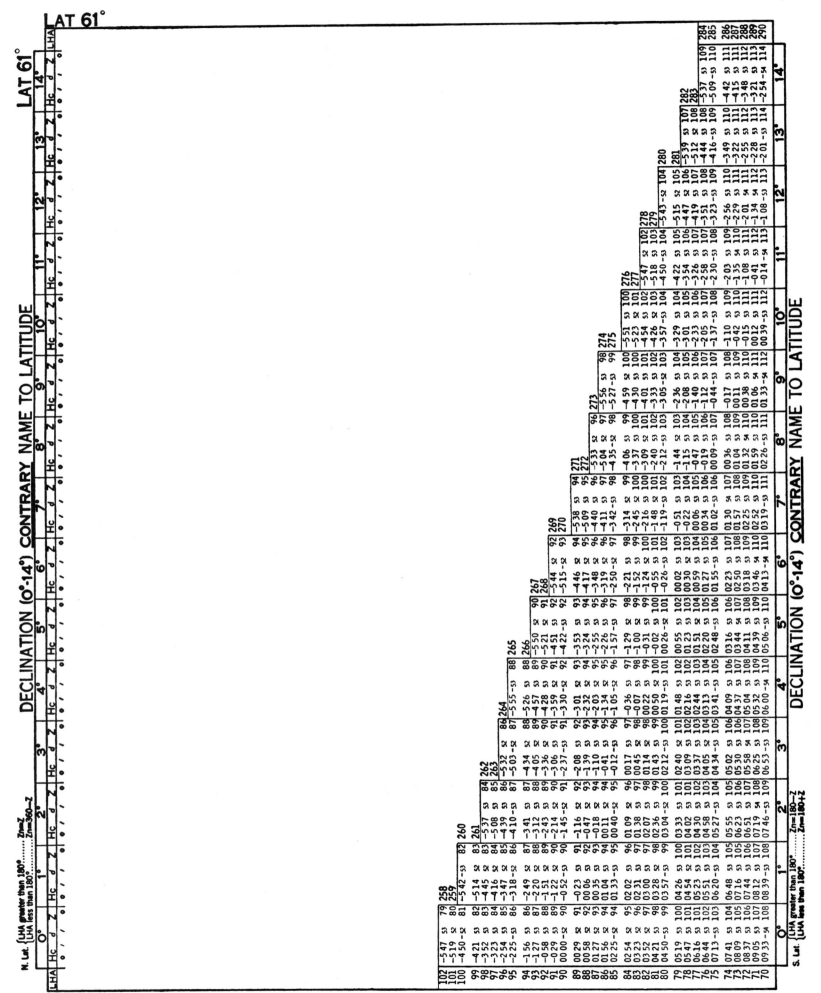

LHA	0° Hc	d	Z	1° Hc	d	Z	2° Hc	d	Z	3° Hc	d	Z	4° Hc	d	Z
°	° ′	′	°	° ′	′	°	° ′	′	°	° ′	′	°	° ′	′	°
102	-5 47	53	79												
101	-5 19	52	80												
100	-4 50	-52	81	-5 42	-53	82									
99	-4 21	53	82	-5 14	52	83									
98	-3 52	53	83	-4 45	52	83	-5 37	53	84						
97	-3 23	53	84	-4 16	52	84	-5 08	53	85						
96	-2 54	53	85	-3 47	52	85	-4 39	53	86	-5 32	52	86			
95	-2 25	-53	86	-3 18	-52	86	-4 10	-53	87	-5 03	-52	87	-5 55	-53	88
94	-1 56	53	86	-2 49	52	87	-3 41	53	87	-4 34	52	88	-5 26	53	88
93	-1 27	53	87	-2 20	52	88	-3 12	53	88	-4 05	52	89	-4 57	53	89
92	-0 58	53	88	-1 51	52	89	-2 43	53	89	-3 36	52	90	-4 28	53	90
91	-0 29	53	89	-1 22	52	90	-2 14	52	90	-3 06	53	91	-3 59	52	91
90	00 00	-52	90	-0 52	-53	90	-1 45	-52	91	-2 37	-53	91	-3 30	-52	92
89	00 29	52	91	-0 23	53	91	-1 16	52	92	-2 08	53	92	-3 01	52	93
88	00 58	52	92	00 06	53	92	-0 47	52	93	-1 39	53	93	-2 32	52	94
87	01 27	52	93	00 35	53	93	-0 18	52	94	-1 10	53	94	-2 03	52	95
86	01 56	52	94	01 04	53	94	00 11	52	94	-0 41	53	95	-1 34	52	95
85	02 25	-52	94	01 33	-53	95	00 40	-52	95	-0 12	-53	96	-1 05	-52	96
84	02 54	52	95	02 02	53	96	01 09	52	96	00 17	53	97	-0 36	53	97
83	03 23	52	96	02 31	53	97	01 38	53	97	00 45	52	98	-0 07	53	98
82	03 52	52	97	03 00	53	97	02 07	53	98	01 14	52	98	00 22	53	99
81	04 21	53	98	03 28	52	98	02 36	53	99	01 43	53	99	00 50	52	100
80	04 50	-53	99	03 57	-53	99	03 04	-52	100	02 12	-53	100	01 19	-53	101
79	05 19	53	100	04 26	53	100	03 33	53	101	02 40	52	101	01 48	53	102
78	05 47	53	101	04 54	52	101	04 02	53	101	03 09	53	102	02 16	53	102
77	06 16	53	101	05 23	53	102	04 30	53	102	03 37	53	103	02 44	53	103
76	06 44	53	102	05 51	53	103	04 58	53	103	04 05	52	104	03 13	53	104
75	07 13	-53	103	06 20	-53	104	05 27	-53	104	04 34	-53	105	03 41	-53	105
74	07 41	53	104	06 48	53	105	05 55	53	105	05 02	53	106	04 09	53	106
73	08 09	53	105	07 16	53	105	06 23	53	106	05 30	53	106	04 37	53	107
72	08 37	53	106	07 44	53	106	06 51	53	107	05 58	54	107	05 04	53	108
71	09 05	53	107	08 12	53	107	07 19	54	108	06 25	53	108	05 32	53	109
70	09 33	-54	108	08 39	-53	108	07 46	-53	109	06 53	-53	109	06 00	-54	110

LHA	5° Hc	d	Z	6° Hc	d	Z	7° Hc	d	Z	8° Hc	d	Z	9° Hc	d	Z
°	° ′	′	°	° ′	′	°	° ′	′	°	° ′	′	°	° ′	′	°
93	-5 50	52	90												
92	-5 21	52	91												
91	-4 51	53	92	-5 44	52	92									
90	-4 22	-53	92	-5 15	-52	93									
89	-3 53	53	93	-4 46	52	94	-5 38	53	94						
88	-3 24	53	94	-4 17	52	95	-5 09	53	95						
87	-2 55	53	95	-3 48	52	96	-4 40	53	96	-5 33	52	96			
86	-2 26	53	96	-3 19	52	96	-4 11	53	97	-5 04	52	97	-5 56	53	98
85	-1 57	-53	97	-2 50	-52	97	-3 42	-53	98	-4 35	-52	98	-5 27	-53	99
84	-1 29	52	98	-2 21	53	98	-3 14	52	99	-4 06	53	99	-4 59	52	100
83	-1 00	52	99	-1 52	53	99	-2 45	52	100	-3 37	53	100	-4 30	53	100
82	-0 31	53	99	-1 24	52	100	-2 16	53	100	-3 09	52	101	-4 01	53	101
81	-0 02	53	100	-0 55	53	101	-1 48	52	101	-2 40	53	102	-3 33	53	102
80	00 26	-52	101	-0 26	-53	102	-1 19	-53	102	-2 12	-53	103	-3 05	-52	103
79	00 55	53	102	00 02	53	103	-0 51	53	103	-1 44	52	103	-2 36	53	104
78	01 23	53	103	00 30	52	103	-0 22	53	104	-1 15	53	104	-2 08	53	105
77	01 51	52	104	00 59	53	104	00 06	53	105	-0 47	53	105	-1 40	53	106
76	02 20	53	105	01 27	53	105	00 34	53	106	-0 19	53	106	-1 12	53	107
75	02 48	-53	106	01 55	-53	106	01 02	-53	106	00 09	-53	107	-0 44	-53	107
74	03 16	53	106	02 23	53	107	01 30	54	107	00 36	53	108	-0 17	53	108
73	03 44	54	107	02 50	53	108	01 57	53	108	01 04	53	109	00 11	53	109
72	04 11	53	108	03 18	53	109	02 25	53	109	01 32	54	110	00 38	53	110
71	04 39	53	109	03 46	54	110	02 52	53	110	01 59	53	110	01 06	54	111
70	05 06	-53	110	04 13	-54	110	03 19	-53	111	02 26	-53	111	01 33	-54	112

LHA	10° Hc	d	Z	11° Hc	d	Z	12° Hc	d	Z	13° Hc	d	Z	14° Hc	d	Z	LHA
°	° ′	′	°	° ′	′	°	° ′	′	°	° ′	′	°	° ′	′	°	
102																258
101																259
100																260
99																261
98																262
97																263
96																264
95																265
94																266
93																267
92																268
91																269
90																270
89																271
88																272
87																273
86																274
85																275
84	-5 51	53	100													276
83	-5 23	52	101													277
82	-4 54	53	102	-5 47	52	102										278
81	-4 26	52	103	-5 18	53	103										279
80	-3 57	-53	104	-4 50	-53	104	-5 43	-52	104							280
79	-3 29	53	104	-4 22	53	105	-5 15	52	105							281
78	-3 01	53	105	-3 54	53	106	-4 47	52	106	-5 39	53	107				282
77	-2 33	53	106	-3 26	53	107	-4 19	53	107	-5 12	52	108				283
76	-2 05	53	107	-2 58	53	107	-3 51	53	108	-4 44	53	108	-5 37	53	109	284
75	-1 37	-53	108	-2 30	-53	108	-3 23	-53	109	-4 16	-53	109	-5 09	-53	110	285
74	-1 10	53	109	-2 03	53	109	-2 56	53	110	-3 49	53	110	-4 42	53	111	286
73	-0 42	53	110	-1 35	54	110	-2 29	53	111	-3 22	53	111	-4 15	53	111	287
72	-0 15	53	111	-1 08	53	111	-2 01	54	111	-2 55	53	112	-3 48	53	112	288
71	00 12	53	111	-0 41	53	112	-1 34	54	112	-2 28	53	113	-3 21	53	113	289
70	00 39	-53	112	-0 14	-54	113	-1 08	-53	113	-2 01	-53	114	-2 54	-54	114	290

S. Lat. {LHA greater than 180°....... Zn=180−Z; LHA less than 180°........... Zn=180+Z}

DECLINATION (0°-14°) CONTRARY NAME TO LATITUDE

N. Lat. {LHA greater than 180°....... Zn=Z; LHA less than 180°............ Zn=360−Z}

DECLINATION (0°-14°) CONTRARY NAME TO LATITUDE

LHA	0° Hc	d	Z	1° Hc	d	Z	2° Hc	d	Z	3° Hc	d	Z	4° Hc	d	Z
	° ′	′	°	° ′	′	°	° ′	′	°	° ′	′	°	° ′	′	°
69	10 00	53	109	09 07	53	109	08 14	54	110	07 20	53	110	06 27	53	110
68	10 28	54	110	09 34	53	110	08 41	53	110	07 48	54	111	06 54	53	111
67	10 55	53	110	10 02	54	111	09 08	53	111	08 15	54	112	07 21	53	112
66	11 22	53	111	10 29	54	112	09 35	53	112	08 42	54	113	07 48	54	113
65	11 49	−53	112	10 56	−54	113	10 02	−54	113	09 08	−53	114	08 15	−54	114
64	12 16	53	113	11 23	54	114	10 29	54	114	09 35	54	115	08 41	54	115
63	12 43	54	114	11 49	54	115	10 55	54	115	10 01	54	115	09 07	54	116
62	13 09	53	115	12 16	54	115	11 22	54	116	10 28	54	116	09 34	55	117
61	13 36	54	116	12 42	54	116	11 48	54	117	10 54	55	117	09 59	54	118
60	14 02	−54	117	13 08	−55	117	12 13	−54	118	11 19	−54	118	10 25	−54	119
59	14 28	55	118	13 33	54	118	12 39	54	119	11 45	55	119	10 50	54	120
58	14 53	54	119	13 59	54	119	13 05	55	120	12 10	54	120	11 16	55	120
57	15 19	55	120	14 24	54	120	13 30	55	121	12 35	54	121	11 41	55	121
56	15 44	55	121	14 49	54	121	13 55	55	121	13 00	55	122	12 05	54	122
55	16 09	−55	122	15 14	−55	122	14 19	−54	122	13 25	−55	123	12 30	−55	123
54	16 33	54	122	15 39	55	123	14 44	55	123	13 49	55	124	12 54	55	124
53	16 58	55	123	16 03	55	124	15 08	55	124	14 13	55	125	13 18	55	125
52	17 22	55	124	16 27	55	125	15 32	55	125	14 37	55	126	13 42	55	126
51	17 46	55	125	16 51	55	126	15 56	56	126	15 00	55	127	14 05	55	127
50	18 09	−55	126	17 14	−55	127	16 19	−55	127	15 24	−56	128	14 28	−55	128
49	18 33	56	127	17 37	55	128	16 42	55	128	15 47	56	128	14 51	56	129
48	18 56	56	128	18 00	55	129	17 05	56	129	16 09	55	129	15 14	56	130
47	19 19	56	129	18 23	56	130	17 27	56	130	16 31	55	130	15 36	56	131
46	19 41	56	130	18 45	56	131	17 49	56	131	16 53	55	131	15 58	56	132
45	20 03	−56	131	19 07	−56	132	18 11	−56	132	17 15	−56	132	16 19	−56	133
44	20 25	56	132	19 29	56	133	18 33	57	133	17 36	56	133	16 40	56	134
43	20 46	56	133	19 50	56	134	18 54	57	134	17 57	56	134	17 01	56	135
42	21 07	56	134	20 11	56	135	19 15	57	135	18 18	56	135	17 22	57	136
41	21 28	57	135	20 31	56	136	19 35	57	136	18 38	56	136	17 42	57	137
40	21 48	−56	136	20 52	−57	137	19 55	−57	137	18 58	−56	137	18 02	−57	138
39	22 08	57	137	21 11	56	138	20 15	57	138	19 18	57	138	18 21	57	139
38	22 28	57	138	21 31	57	139	20 34	57	139	19 37	57	139	18 40	57	140
37	22 47	57	139	21 50	57	140	20 53	57	140	19 56	57	140	18 59	57	141
36	23 06	57	140	22 09	58	141	21 11	57	141	20 14	57	141	19 17	57	142
35	23 24	−57	141	22 27	−57	142	21 30	−58	142	20 32	−57	142	19 35	−57	143
34	23 42	57	142	22 45	58	143	21 47	57	143	20 50	58	143	19 52	57	144
33	24 00	58	143	23 02	57	144	22 05	58	144	21 07	58	144	20 09	57	145
32	24 17	58	145	23 19	58	145	22 21	57	145	21 24	58	145	20 26	58	146
31	24 33	57	146	23 36	58	146	22 38	58	146	21 40	58	146	20 42	58	147
30	24 50	−58	147	23 52	−58	147	22 54	−58	147	21 56	−58	147	20 58	−58	148
29	25 05	58	148	24 07	58	148	23 09	58	148	22 11	58	149	21 13	58	149
28	25 21	58	149	24 23	58	149	23 25	59	149	22 26	58	150	21 28	58	150
27	25 36	59	150	24 37	58	150	23 39	58	150	22 41	58	151	21 43	59	151
26	25 50	58	151	24 52	59	151	23 53	58	151	22 55	58	152	21 57	59	152
25	26 04	−58	152	25 06	−59	152	24 07	−58	152	23 09	−59	153	22 10	−58	153
24	26 17	58	153	25 19	59	153	24 20	58	154	23 22	59	154	22 23	59	154
23	26 30	58	154	25 32	59	154	24 33	59	155	23 34	58	155	22 36	59	155
22	26 43	59	155	25 44	59	155	24 45	59	156	23 46	58	156	22 48	59	156
21	26 55	59	156	25 56	59	157	24 57	59	157	23 58	59	157	22 59	59	157
20	27 06	−59	157	26 07	−59	158	25 08	−59	158	24 09	−59	158	23 10	−59	158
19	27 17	59	159	26 18	59	159	25 19	59	159	24 20	59	159	23 21	59	159
18	27 27	59	160	26 28	59	160	25 29	59	160	24 30	59	160	23 31	59	160
17	27 37	59	161	26 38	59	161	25 39	59	161	24 40	60	161	23 40	59	161
16	27 47	60	162	26 47	59	162	25 48	59	162	24 49	60	162	23 49	59	163
15	27 55	−59	163	26 56	−59	163	25 57	−60	163	24 57	−59	163	23 58	−60	164
14	28 04	60	164	27 04	59	164	26 05	60	164	25 05	59	165	24 06	60	165
13	28 11	59	165	27 12	60	165	26 12	59	166	25 13	60	166	24 13	59	166
12	28 19	60	166	27 19	60	167	26 19	59	167	25 20	60	167	24 20	60	167
11	28 25	60	168	27 25	59	168	26 26	60	168	25 26	60	168	24 26	59	168
10	28 31	−60	169	27 31	−59	169	26 32	−60	169	25 32	−60	169	24 32	−60	169
9	28 37	60	170	27 37	60	170	26 37	60	170	25 37	60	170	24 37	59	170
8	28 42	60	171	27 42	60	171	26 42	60	171	25 42	60	171	24 42	60	171
7	28 46	60	172	27 46	60	172	26 46	60	172	25 46	60	172	24 46	59	172
6	28 50	60	173	27 50	60	173	26 50	60	173	25 50	60	173	24 50	60	173
5	28 53	−60	174	27 53	−60	174	26 53	−60	174	25 53	−60	174	24 53	−60	175
4	28 55	60	175	27 55	60	176	26 55	59	176	25 56	60	176	24 56	60	176
3	28 57	60	177	27 57	60	177	26 57	59	177	25 58	60	177	24 58	60	177
2	28 59	60	178	27 59	60	178	26 59	60	178	25 59	60	178	24 59	60	178
1	29 00	60	179	28 00	60	179	27 00	60	179	26 00	60	179	25 00	60	179
0	29 00	−60	180	28 00	−60	180	27 00	−60	180	26 00	−60	180	25 00	−60	180

LHA	5° Hc	d	Z	6° Hc	d	Z	7° Hc	d	Z	8° Hc	d	Z	9° Hc	d	Z
	° ′	′	°	° ′	′	°	° ′	′	°	° ′	′	°	° ′	′	°
69	05 34	54	111	04 40	53	111	03 47	54	112	02 53	53	112	02 00	54	113
68	06 01	54	112	05 07	54	112	04 13	53	113	03 20	54	113	02 26	53	114
67	06 28	54	113	05 34	54	113	04 40	53	114	03 47	54	114	02 53	54	114
66	06 54	53	114	06 01	54	114	05 07	54	114	04 13	54	115	03 19	53	115
65	07 21	−54	114	06 27	−54	115	05 33	−54	115	04 39	−54	116	03 45	−53	116
64	07 47	54	115	06 53	54	116	05 59	54	116	05 05	54	117	04 11	53	117
63	08 13	54	116	07 19	54	117	06 25	54	117	05 31	54	118	04 37	54	118
62	08 39	54	117	07 45	54	118	06 51	54	118	05 57	54	119	05 03	54	119
61	09 05	54	118	08 11	54	119	07 17	54	119	06 23	55	119	05 28	54	120
60	09 31	−55	119	08 36	−54	119	07 42	−54	120	06 48	−55	120	05 53	−54	121
59	09 56	54	120	09 02	55	120	08 07	54	121	07 13	55	121	06 18	54	122
58	10 21	54	121	09 27	55	121	08 32	54	122	07 38	55	122	06 43	55	123
57	10 46	55	122	09 51	54	122	08 57	55	123	08 02	55	123	07 07	54	123
56	11 11	55	123	10 16	55	123	09 21	55	124	08 26	55	124	07 31	54	124
55	11 35	−55	124	10 40	−55	124	09 45	−55	124	08 50	−55	125	07 55	−55	125
54	11 59	55	125	11 04	55	125	10 09	55	125	09 14	55	126	08 19	55	126
53	12 23	55	126	11 28	55	126	10 33	55	126	09 38	56	127	08 42	55	127
52	12 47	56	126	11 51	55	127	10 56	55	127	10 01	56	128	09 05	55	128
51	13 10	56	127	12 14	55	128	11 19	55	128	10 24	56	129	09 28	55	129
50	13 33	−56	128	12 37	−55	129	11 42	−56	129	10 46	−55	129	09 51	−56	130
49	13 55	55	129	13 00	56	130	12 04	55	130	11 09	56	130	10 13	56	131
48	14 18	56	130	13 22	56	131	12 26	55	131	11 31	56	131	10 35	56	132
47	14 40	56	131	13 44	56	132	12 48	56	132	11 52	56	132	10 56	56	133
46	15 02	56	132	14 06	56	133	13 10	56	133	12 14	56	133	11 18	57	134
45	15 23	−56	133	14 27	−56	133	13 31	−56	134	12 35	−57	134	11 38	−56	135
44	15 44	56	134	14 48	56	134	13 52	57	135	12 55	56	135	11 59	56	136
43	16 05	56	135	15 09	57	135	14 12	56	136	13 16	57	136	12 19	56	136
42	16 25	56	136	15 29	57	136	14 32	56	137	13 36	57	137	12 39	56	137
41	16 45	56	137	15 49	57	137	14 52	57	138	13 55	56	138	12 59	57	138
40	17 05	−57	138	16 08	−57	138	15 11	−56	139	14 15	−57	139	13 18	−57	139
39	17 24	57	139	16 27	56	139	15 31	57	140	14 34	57	140	13 37	57	140
38	17 43	57	140	16 46	57	140	15 49	57	141	14 52	57	141	13 55	57	141
37	18 02	57	141	17 05	58	141	16 07	57	142	15 10	57	142	14 13	57	142
36	18 20	57	142	17 23	58	142	16 25	57	143	15 28	57	143	14 31	58	143
35	18 38	−58	143	17 40	−57	143	16 43	−58	144	15 45	−57	144	14 48	−58	144
34	18 55	58	144	17 57	57	144	17 00	58	145	16 02	57	145	15 05	58	145
33	19 12	58	145	18 14	57	145	17 17	58	146	16 19	58	146	15 21	57	146
32	19 28	57	146	18 31	58	146	17 33	58	147	16 35	58	147	15 37	58	147
31	19 44	57	147	18 47	58	147	17 49	58	148	16 51	58	148	15 53	58	148
30	20 00	−58	148	19 02	−58	148	18 04	−58	149	17 06	−58	149	16 08	−58	149
29	20 15	58	149	19 17	58	149	18 19	58	150	17 21	58	150	16 23	58	150
28	20 30	58	150	19 32	58	150	18 34	59	151	17 35	58	151	16 37	58	151
27	20 44	58	151	19 46	58	151	18 48	59	152	17 49	58	152	16 51	58	152
26	20 58	58	152	20 00	59	152	19 01	58	153	18 03	59	153	17 04	58	153
25	21 12	−59	153	20 13	−59	153	19 14	−58	154	18 16	−59	154	17 17	−58	154
24	21 24	58	154	20 26	59	154	19 27	59	155	18 28	58	155	17 30	59	155
23	21 37	59	155	20 38	59	156	19 39	58	156	18 41	59	156	17 42	59	156
22	21 49	59	156	20 50	59	157	19 51	59	157	18 52	59	157	17 53	59	157
21	22 00	59	157	21 01	59	158	20 02	59	158	19 03	59	158	18 04	59	158
20	22 11	−59	158	21 12	−59	159	20 13	−59	159	19 14	−59	159	18 15	−59	159
19	22 22	59	160	21 23	60	160	20 23	59	160	19 24	59	160	18 25	59	160
18	22 32	60	161	21 32	59	161	20 33	59	161	19 34	59	161	18 35	60	161
17	22 41	59	162	21 42	60	162	20 42	59	162	19 43	59	162	18 44	60	162
16	22 50	59	163	21 51	60	163	20 51	59	163	19 52	60	163	18 52	59	163
15	22 58	−59	164	21 59	−60	164	20 59	−59	164	20 00	−59	164	19 01	−60	164
14	23 06	59	165	22 07	60	165	21 07	59	165	20 08	60	165	19 08	59	165
13	23 14	60	166	22 14	60	166	21 14	59	166	20 15	60	166	19 15	59	166
12	23 20	59	167	22 21	60	167	21 21	59	167	20 22	60	167	19 22	60	167
11	23 27	60	168	22 27	60	168	21 27	59	168	20 28	60	168	19 28	60	169
10	23 32	−59	169	22 33	−60	169	21 33	−60	169	20 33	−60	169	19 33	−59	170
9	23 38	60	170	22 38	60	170	21 38	60	170	20 38	59	171	19 39	60	171
8	23 42	59	171	22 43	60	171	21 43	60	171	20 43	60	172	19 43	60	172
7	23 47	60	172	22 47	60	172	21 47	60	173	20 47	60	173	19 47	60	173
6	23 50	60	174	22 50	60	174	21 50	60	174	20 50	60	174	19 50	59	174
5	23 53	−60	175	22 53	−60	175	21 53	−60	175	20 53	−60	175	19 53	−60	175
4	23 56	60	176	22 56	60	176	21 56	60	176	20 56	60	176	19 56	60	176
3	23 58	60	177	22 58	60	177	21 58	60	177	20 58	60	177	19 58	60	177
2	23 59	60	178	22 59	60	178	21 59	60	178	20 59	60	178	19 59	60	178
1	24 00	60	179	23 00	60	179	22 00	60	179	21 00	60	179	20 00	60	179
0	24 00	−60	180	23 00	−60	180	22 00	−60	180	21 00	−60	180	20 00	−60	180

LHA	10° Hc	d	Z	11° Hc	d	Z	12° Hc	d	Z	13° Hc	d	Z	14° Hc	d	Z	LHA
	° ′	′	°	° ′	′	°	° ′	′	°	° ′	′	°	° ′	′	°	
69	01 06	53	113	00 13	54	114	−0 41	53	114	−1 34	54	115	−2 28	53	115	291
68	01 33	54	114	00 39	53	114	−0 14	54	115	−1 08	54	115	−2 02	53	116	292
67	01 59	53	115	01 06	54	115	00 12	54	116	−0 42	54	116	−1 36	53	117	293
66	02 26	54	116	01 32	54	116	00 38	54	117	−0 16	54	117	−1 10	53	118	294
65	02 52	−54	117	01 58	−54	117	01 04	−54	118	00 10	−54	118	−0 44	−54	118	295
64	03 18	54	118	02 24	54	118	01 30	54	118	00 36	54	119	−0 18	54	119	296
63	03 43	54	118	02 49	54	119	01 55	54	119	01 01	54	120	00 07	54	120	297
62	04 09	55	119	03 14	54	120	02 20	54	120	01 26	54	121	00 32	54	121	298
61	04 34	54	120	03 40	55	121	02 45	54	121	01 51	54	122	00 57	55	122	299
60	04 59	−54	121	04 05	−55	122	03 10	−54	122	02 16	−55	122	01 21	−54	123	300
59	05 24	55	122	04 29	54	122	03 35	55	123	02 40	54	123	01 46	55	124	301
58	05 48	54	123	04 54	55	123	03 59	55	124	03 04	54	124	02 10	55	125	302
57	06 13	55	124	05 18	55	124	04 23	55	125	03 28	55	125	02 33	54	125	303
56	06 37	55	125	05 42	55	125	04 47	55	126	03 52	55	126	02 57	55	126	304
55	07 00	−55	126	06 05	−55	126	05 10	−55	126	04 15	−55	127	03 20	−55	127	305
54	07 24	55	127	06 29	55	127	05 34	56	127	04 38	55	128	03 43	55	128	306
53	07 47	55	128	06 52	55	128	05 57	56	128	05 01	55	129	04 06	55	129	307
52	08 10	55	128	07 15	56	129	06 19	55	129	05 24	56	130	04 28	55	130	308
51	08 33	56	129	07 37	55	130	06 42	56	130	05 46	55	130	04 51	56	131	309
50	08 55	−55	130	08 00	−56	131	07 04	−56	131	06 08	−55	131	05 13	−56	132	310
49	09 17	56	131	08 21	55	132	07 26	56	132	06 30	56	132	05 34	56	133	311
48	09 39	56	132	08 43	56	132	07 47	56	133	06 51	56	133	05 55	56	134	312
47	10 00	56	133	09 04	56	133	08 08	56	134	07 12	56	134	06 16	56	134	313
46	10 21	56	134	09 25	56	134	08 29	56	135	07 33	56	135	06 37	56	135	314
45	10 42	−56	135	09 46	−56	135	08 50	−57	136	07 53	−56	136	06 57	−56	136	315
44	11 03	57	136	10 06	56	136	09 10	56	137	08 14	57	137	07 17	56	137	316
43	11 23	57	137	10 26	56	137	09 30	57	137	08 33	56	138	07 37	57	138	317
42	11 43	57	138	10 46	57	138	09 49	56	138	08 53	57	139	07 56	57	139	318
41	12 02	57	139	11 05	57	139	10 08	56	139	09 12	57	140	08 15	57	140	319
40	12 21	−57	140	11 24	−57	140	10 27	−57	140	09 30	−57	141	08 33	−57	141	320
39	12 40	57	141	11 43	57	141	10 46	57	141	09 49	57	142	08 52	58	142	321
38	12 58	57	142	12 01	57	142	11 04	57	142	10 07	58	143	09 09	57	143	322
37	13 16	57	143	12 19	58	143	11 21	57	143	10 24	57	143	09 27	58	144	323
36	13 33	57	144	12 36	57	144	11 39	58	144	10 41	57	144	09 44	58	145	324
35	13 50	−57	144	12 53	−58	145	11 55	−57	145	10 58	−58	145	10 00	−57	146	325
34	14 07	57	145	13 10	58	146	12 12	58	146	11 14	57	146	10 17	58	147	326
33	14 24	58	146	13 26	58	147	12 28	58	147	11 30	58	147	10 32	57	148	327
32	14 39	57	147	13 42	58	148	12 44	58	148	11 46	58	148	10 48	58	148	328
31	14 55	58	148	13 57	58	149	12 59	58	149	12 01	58	149	11 03	58	149	329
30	15 10	−58	149	14 12	−58	150	13 14	−58	150	12 16	−58	150	11 18	−59	150	330
29	15 25	59	150	14 26	58	151	13 28	58	151	12 30	58	151	11 32	59	151	331
28	15 39	59	151	14 40	58	152	13 42	58	152	12 44	59	152	11 45	58	152	332
27	15 53	59	152	14 54	58	153	13 56	59	153	12 57	58	153	11 59	59	153	333
26	16 06	59	153	15 07	58	154	14 09	59	154	13 10	58	154	12 12	59	154	334
25	16 19	−59	154	15 20	−59	155	14 21	−58	155	13 23	−59	155	12 24	−59	155	335
24	16 31	59	155	15 32	58	156	14 34	59	156	13 35	59	156	12 36	59	156	336
23	16 43	59	156	15 44	59	157	14 45	59	157	13 46	58	157	12 48	59	157	337
22	16 54	59	157	15 55	58	158	14 57	59	158	13 58	59	158	12 59	59	158	338
21	17 05	59	158	16 06	59	159	15 07	59	159	14 08	59	159	13 09	59	159	339
20	17 16	−59	159	16 17	−59	160	15 18	−59	160	14 19	−60	160	13 19	−59	160	340
19	17 26	59	160	16 27	59	161	15 28	60	161	14 28	59	161	13 29	59	161	341
18	17 35	59	161	16 36	59	162	15 37	59	162	14 38	60	162	13 38	59	162	342
17	17 44	59	162	16 45	59	163	15 46	60	163	14 46	59	163	13 47	59	163	343
16	17 53	59	163	16 54	60	164	15 54	59	164	14 55	60	164	13 55	59	164	344
15	18 01	−59	165	17 02	−60	165	16 02	−59	165	15 03	−60	165	14 03	−59	165	345
14	18 09	60	166	17 09	59	166	16 10	60	166	15 10	60	166	14 10	59	166	346
13	18 16	60	167	17 16	60	167	16 16	59	167	15 17	60	167	14 17	59	167	347
12	18 22	59	168	17 23	60	168	16 23	60	168	15 23	59	168	14 24	60	168	348
11	18 28	60	169	17 28	59	169	16 29	60	169	15 29	60	169	14 29	59	169	349
10	18 34	−60	170	17 34	−60	170	16 34	−60	170	15 34	−59	170	14 35	−60	170	350
9	18 39	60	171	17 39	60	171	16 39	60	171	15 39	60	171	14 39	59	171	351
8	18 43	60	172	17 43	60	172	16 43	59	172	15 44	60	172	14 44	60	172	352
7	18 47	60	173	17 47	60	173	16 47	60	173	15 47	59	173	14 48	60	173	353
6	18 51	60	174	17 51	60	174	16 51	60	174	15 51	60	174	14 51	60	174	354
5	18 53	−59	175	17 54	−60	175	16 54	−60	175	15 54	−60	175	14 54	−60	175	355
4	18 56	60	176	17 56	60	176	16 56	60	176	15 56	60	176	14 56	60	176	356
3	18 58	60	177	17 58	60	177	16 58	60	177	15 58	60	177	14 58	60	177	357
2	18 59	60	178	17 59	60	178	16 59	60	178	15 59	60	178	14 59	60	178	358
1	19 00	60	179	18 00	60	179	17 00	60	179	16 00	60	179	15 00	60	179	359
0	19 00	−60	180	18 00	−60	180	17 00	−60	180	16 00	−60	180	15 00	−60	180	360

S. Lat. {LHA greater than 180°....... Zn=180−Z; LHA less than 180°............ Zn=180+Z}

DECLINATION (0°-14°) CONTRARY NAME TO LATITUDE

N. Lat. {LHA greater than 180°....... Zn=Z; LHA less than 180°............ Zn=360−Z}

DECLINATION (15°-29°) SAME NAME AS LATITUDE

LHA	15° Hc	15° d	15° Z	16° Hc	16° d	16° Z	17° Hc	17° d	17° Z	18° Hc	18° d	18° Z	19° Hc	19° d	19° Z
	° ′	′	°	° ′	′	°	° ′	′	°	° ′	′	°	° ′	′	°
0	44 00	+60	180	45 00	+60	180	46 00	+60	180	47 00	+60	180	48 00	+60	180
1	44 00	60	179	45 00	60	179	46 00	60	179	47 00	60	179	48 00	60	179
2	43 59	60	177	44 59	60	177	45 59	60	177	46 59	60	177	47 59	60	177
3	43 57	60	176	44 57	60	176	45 57	60	176	46 57	60	176	47 57	60	176
4	43 55	60	175	44 55	59	175	45 54	60	175	46 54	60	174	47 54	60	174
5	43 52	+59	173	44 51	+60	173	45 51	+60	173	46 51	+60	173	47 51	+60	173
6	43 48	60	172	44 48	60	172	45 48	59	172	46 47	60	172	47 47	60	172
7	43 43	60	171	44 43	60	171	45 43	60	170	46 43	60	170	47 43	59	170
8	43 38	60	169	44 38	60	169	45 38	60	169	46 38	59	169	47 37	60	169
9	43 33	59	168	44 32	60	168	45 32	60	168	46 32	59	168	47 31	60	167
10	43 26	+60	167	44 26	+59	167	45 25	+60	166	46 25	+59	166	47 24	+60	166
11	43 19	60	165	44 19	59	165	45 18	60	165	46 18	59	165	47 17	60	165
12	43 11	60	164	44 11	59	164	45 10	60	164	46 10	59	163	47 09	59	163
13	43 03	59	163	44 02	60	163	45 02	59	162	46 01	59	162	47 00	59	162
14	42 54	59	161	43 53	60	161	44 53	59	161	45 52	59	161	46 51	59	161
15	42 45	+59	160	43 44	+59	160	44 43	+59	160	45 42	+59	159	46 41	+59	159
16	42 34	59	159	43 33	59	159	44 32	59	158	45 31	59	158	46 30	59	158
17	42 24	58	158	43 22	59	157	44 21	59	157	45 20	59	157	46 19	58	156
18	42 12	59	156	43 11	59	156	44 10	58	156	45 08	59	155	46 07	58	155
19	42 00	59	155	42 59	58	155	43 57	59	154	44 56	58	154	45 54	59	154
20	41 48	+58	154	42 46	+58	153	43 44	+59	153	44 43	+58	153	45 41	+58	152
21	41 34	59	152	42 33	58	152	43 31	58	152	44 29	58	152	45 27	58	151
22	41 21	58	151	42 19	58	151	43 17	58	151	44 15	58	150	45 13	58	150
23	41 06	58	150	42 04	58	150	43 02	58	149	44 00	58	149	44 58	58	149
24	40 51	58	149	41 49	58	148	42 47	58	148	43 45	58	148	44 43	57	147
25	40 36	+58	148	41 34	+58	147	42 32	+57	147	43 29	+58	146	44 27	+57	146
26	40 20	58	146	41 18	57	146	42 15	58	146	43 13	57	145	44 10	57	145
27	40 04	57	145	41 01	58	145	41 59	57	144	42 56	57	144	43 53	57	143
28	39 47	57	144	40 44	57	143	41 41	57	143	42 38	57	143	43 35	57	142
29	39 29	58	143	40 27	57	142	41 24	57	142	42 21	56	141	43 17	57	141
30	39 12	+57	142	40 09	+56	141	41 05	+57	141	42 02	+57	140	42 59	+56	140
31	38 53	57	140	39 50	57	140	40 47	56	139	41 43	57	139	42 40	56	139
32	38 34	57	139	39 31	57	139	40 28	56	138	41 24	56	138	42 20	56	137
33	38 15	57	138	39 12	56	138	40 08	56	137	41 04	56	137	42 00	56	136
34	37 55	57	137	38 52	56	136	39 48	56	136	40 44	56	135	41 40	56	135
35	37 35	+56	136	38 31	+56	135	39 27	+56	135	40 23	+56	134	41 19	+56	134
36	37 15	56	135	38 11	56	134	39 07	55	134	40 02	56	133	40 58	55	133
37	36 54	56	133	37 50	55	133	38 45	56	132	39 41	55	132	40 36	56	132
38	36 32	56	132	37 28	56	132	38 24	55	131	39 19	55	131	40 14	56	130
39	36 11	55	131	37 06	56	131	38 02	55	130	38 57	55	130	39 52	55	129
40	35 49	+55	130	36 44	+55	130	37 39	+55	129	38 34	+55	129	39 29	+55	128
41	35 26	55	129	36 21	55	129	37 16	55	128	38 11	55	128	39 06	55	127
42	35 03	55	128	35 58	55	127	36 53	55	127	37 48	55	126	38 43	54	126
43	34 40	55	127	35 35	55	126	36 30	55	126	37 25	54	125	38 19	54	125
44	34 17	55	126	35 12	54	125	36 06	55	125	37 01	54	124	37 55	54	124
45	33 53	+55	125	34 48	+54	124	35 42	+54	124	36 36	+55	123	37 31	+54	123
46	33 29	54	124	34 23	55	123	35 18	54	123	36 12	54	122	37 06	54	122
47	33 05	54	123	33 59	54	122	34 53	54	122	35 47	54	121	36 41	54	120
48	32 40	54	122	33 34	54	121	34 28	54	121	35 22	54	120	36 16	53	119
49	32 15	54	121	33 09	54	120	34 03	54	119	34 57	53	119	35 50	54	118
50	31 50	+54	119	32 44	+53	119	33 37	+54	118	34 31	+54	118	35 25	+53	117
51	31 24	54	118	32 18	54	118	33 12	53	117	34 05	54	117	34 59	53	116
52	30 59	53	117	31 52	54	117	32 46	53	116	33 39	53	116	34 32	53	115
53	30 33	53	116	31 26	54	116	32 20	53	115	33 13	53	115	34 06	53	114
54	30 06	54	115	31 00	53	115	31 53	53	114	32 46	53	114	33 39	53	113
55	29 40	+53	114	30 33	+54	114	31 27	+53	113	32 20	+53	113	33 13	+52	112
56	29 14	53	113	30 07	53	113	31 00	53	112	31 53	52	112	32 45	53	111
57	28 47	53	112	29 40	53	112	30 33	53	111	31 26	52	111	32 18	53	110
58	28 20	53	112	29 13	53	111	30 06	52	110	30 58	53	110	31 51	52	109
59	27 53	52	111	28 45	53	110	29 38	53	109	30 31	52	109	31 23	53	108
60	27 25	+53	110	28 18	+53	109	29 11	+52	109	30 03	+53	108	30 56	+52	107
61	26 58	52	109	27 50	53	108	28 43	53	108	29 36	52	107	30 28	52	106
62	26 30	53	108	27 23	52	107	28 15	53	107	29 08	52	106	30 00	52	105
63	26 02	53	107	26 55	52	106	27 47	53	106	28 40	52	105	29 32	52	105
64	25 34	53	106	26 27	52	105	27 19	52	105	28 11	53	104	29 04	51	104
65	25 06	+53	105	25 59	+52	104	26 51	+52	104	27 43	+52	103	28 35	+52	103
66	24 38	52	104	25 30	53	103	26 23	52	103	27 15	52	102	28 07	52	102
67	24 10	52	103	25 02	52	102	25 54	52	102	26 46	52	101	27 38	52	101
68	23 41	53	102	24 34	52	102	25 26	52	101	26 18	52	100	27 10	51	100
69	23 13	52	101	24 05	52	101	24 57	52	100	25 49	52	100	26 41	52	99

LHA	20° Hc	20° d	20° Z	21° Hc	21° d	21° Z	22° Hc	22° d	22° Z	23° Hc	23° d	23° Z	24° Hc	24° d	24° Z
	° ′	′	°	° ′	′	°	° ′	′	°	° ′	′	°	° ′	′	°
0	49 00	+60	180	50 00	+60	180	51 00	+60	180	52 00	+60	180	53 00	+60	180
1	49 00	60	179	50 00	60	179	51 00	60	179	52 00	60	179	53 00	60	179
2	48 59	60	177	49 59	60	177	50 59	60	177	51 59	60	177	52 59	59	177
3	48 57	60	176	49 57	60	176	50 57	60	176	51 57	60	176	52 57	60	175
4	48 54	60	174	49 54	60	174	50 54	60	174	51 54	60	174	52 54	60	174
5	48 51	+60	173	49 51	+60	173	50 51	+60	173	51 51	+59	173	52 50	+60	172
6	48 47	60	171	49 47	60	171	50 47	59	171	51 46	60	171	52 46	60	171
7	48 42	60	170	49 42	60	170	50 42	60	170	51 42	59	170	52 41	60	169
8	48 37	60	169	49 37	59	168	50 36	60	168	51 36	60	168	52 36	59	168
9	48 31	59	167	49 30	60	167	50 30	60	167	51 30	59	167	52 29	60	166
10	48 24	+60	166	49 24	+59	166	50 23	+59	165	51 22	+60	165	52 22	+59	165
11	48 17	59	164	49 16	59	164	50 15	60	164	51 15	59	164	52 14	59	164
12	48 08	60	163	49 08	59	163	50 07	59	163	51 06	59	162	52 05	60	162
13	47 59	60	162	48 59	59	161	49 58	59	161	50 57	59	161	51 56	59	161
14	47 50	59	160	48 49	59	160	49 48	59	160	50 47	59	159	51 46	59	159
15	47 40	+59	159	48 39	+59	159	49 38	+58	158	50 36	+59	158	51 35	+59	158
16	47 29	59	158	48 28	58	157	49 26	59	157	50 25	59	157	51 24	58	156
17	47 17	59	156	48 16	59	156	49 15	58	156	50 13	59	155	51 12	58	155
18	47 05	59	155	48 04	58	154	49 02	59	154	50 01	58	154	50 59	58	153
19	46 53	58	153	47 51	58	153	48 49	59	153	49 48	58	152	50 46	58	152
20	46 39	+59	152	47 38	+58	152	48 36	+58	151	49 34	+58	151	50 32	+58	151
21	46 25	58	151	47 23	58	150	48 21	58	150	49 19	58	150	50 17	58	149
22	46 11	58	149	47 09	58	149	48 07	57	149	49 04	58	148	50 02	57	148
23	45 56	58	148	46 54	57	148	47 51	58	147	48 49	57	147	49 46	57	147
24	45 40	58	147	46 38	57	146	47 35	58	146	48 33	57	146	49 30	57	145
25	45 24	+57	146	46 21	+58	145	47 19	+57	145	48 16	+57	144	49 13	+57	144
26	45 07	57	144	46 04	58	144	47 02	57	143	47 59	56	143	48 55	57	142
27	44 50	57	143	45 47	57	143	46 44	57	142	47 41	56	142	48 37	57	141
28	44 32	57	142	45 29	57	141	46 26	56	141	47 22	57	140	48 19	56	140
29	44 14	57	141	45 11	56	140	46 07	57	140	47 04	56	139	48 00	56	139
30	43 55	+57	139	44 52	+56	139	45 48	+56	138	46 44	+56	138	47 40	+56	137
31	43 36	56	138	44 32	57	138	45 29	56	137	46 25	55	137	47 20	56	136
32	43 16	56	137	44 12	56	136	45 08	56	136	46 04	56	135	47 00	55	135
33	42 56	56	136	43 52	56	135	44 48	56	135	45 44	55	134	46 39	55	134
34	42 36	56	135	43 32	55	134	44 27	56	133	45 23	55	133	46 18	55	132
35	42 15	+55	133	43 10	+56	133	44 06	+55	132	45 01	+55	132	45 56	+55	131
36	41 53	56	132	42 49	55	132	43 44	55	131	44 39	55	131	45 34	55	130
37	41 32	55	131	42 27	55	130	43 22	55	130	44 17	54	129	45 11	55	129
38	41 10	55	130	42 05	54	129	42 59	55	129	43 54	55	128	44 49	54	128
39	40 47	55	129	41 42	54	128	42 36	55	128	43 31	54	127	44 25	55	126
40	40 24	+55	128	41 19	+54	127	42 13	+55	126	43 08	+54	126	44 02	+54	125
41	40 01	54	126	40 55	55	126	41 50	54	125	42 44	54	125	43 38	54	124
42	39 37	55	125	40 32	54	125	41 26	54	124	42 20	54	124	43 14	53	123
43	39 13	55	124	40 08	54	124	41 02	53	123	41 55	54	123	42 49	53	122
44	38 49	54	123	39 43	54	123	40 37	54	122	41 31	53	121	42 24	53	121
45	38 25	+53	122	39 18	+54	121	40 12	+54	121	41 06	+53	120	41 59	+53	120
46	38 00	54	121	38 54	53	120	39 47	53	120	40 40	54	119	41 34	53	119
47	37 35	53	120	38 28	54	119	39 22	53	119	40 15	53	118	41 08	53	118
48	37 09	54	119	38 03	53	118	38 56	53	118	39 49	53	117	40 42	53	116
49	36 44	53	118	37 37	53	117	38 30	53	117	39 23	53	116	40 16	52	115
50	36 18	+53	117	37 11	+53	116	38 04	+53	116	38 57	+52	115	39 49	+53	114
51	35 52	53	116	36 45	53	115	37 38	52	115	38 30	53	114	39 23	52	113
52	35 25	53	115	36 18	53	114	37 11	53	114	38 04	52	113	38 56	52	112
53	34 59	53	114	35 52	52	113	36 44	53	113	37 37	52	112	38 29	52	111
54	34 32	53	113	35 25	52	112	36 17	53	112	37 10	52	111	38 02	52	110
55	34 05	+53	112	34 58	+52	111	35 50	+52	111	36 42	+52	110	37 34	+52	109
56	33 38	53	111	34 31	52	110	35 23	52	110	36 15	52	109	37 07	52	108
57	33 11	52	110	34 03	52	109	34 55	52	109	35 47	52	108	36 39	52	107
58	32 43	53	109	33 36	52	108	34 28	52	108	35 20	51	107	36 11	52	106
59	32 16	52	108	33 08	52	107	34 00	52	107	34 52	51	106	35 43	52	105
60	31 48	+52	107	32 40	+52	106	33 32	+52	106	34 24	+51	105	35 15	+52	104
61	31 20	52	106	32 12	52	105	33 04	52	105	33 56	51	104	34 47	51	103
62	30 52	52	105	31 44	52	104	32 36	51	104	33 27	52	103	34 19	51	102
63	30 24	52	104	31 16	51	103	32 07	52	103	32 59	51	102	33 50	51	102
64	29 55	52	103	30 47	52	102	31 39	51	102	32 30	52	101	33 22	51	101
65	29 27	+52	102	30 19	+51	101	31 10	+52	101	32 02	+51	100	32 53	+51	100
66	28 59	51	101	29 50	52	101	30 42	51	100	31 33	51	99	32 24	51	99
67	28 30	52	100	29 22	51	100	30 13	51	99	31 04	51	98	31 55	51	98
68	28 01	52	99	28 53	51	99	29 44	52	98	30 36	51	98	31 27	51	97
69	27 33	51	98	28 24	51	98	29 15	52	97	30 07	51	97	30 58	51	96

LHA	25° Hc	25° d	25° Z	26° Hc	26° d	26° Z	27° Hc	27° d	27° Z	28° Hc	28° d	28° Z	29° Hc	29° d	29° Z	LHA
	° ′	′	°	° ′	′	°	° ′	′	°	° ′	′	°	° ′	′	°	
0	54 00	+60	180	55 00	+60	180	56 00	+60	180	57 00	+60	180	58 00	+60	180	360
1	54 00	60	179	55 00	60	178	56 00	60	178	57 00	60	178	58 00	60	178	359
2	53 58	60	177	54 58	60	177	55 58	60	177	56 58	60	177	57 58	60	177	358
3	53 57	59	175	54 56	60	175	55 56	60	175	56 56	60	175	57 56	60	175	357
4	53 54	60	174	54 54	60	174	55 54	59	174	56 53	60	174	57 53	60	173	356
5	53 50	+60	172	54 50	+60	172	55 50	+60	172	56 50	+60	172	57 50	+59	172	355
6	53 46	60	171	54 46	60	171	55 46	59	171	56 45	60	170	57 45	60	170	354
7	53 41	60	169	54 41	59	169	55 40	60	169	56 40	60	169	57 40	59	169	353
8	53 35	60	168	54 35	59	168	55 34	60	167	56 34	59	167	57 33	60	167	352
9	53 29	59	166	54 28	60	166	55 28	59	166	56 27	59	166	57 26	60	165	351
10	53 21	+60	165	54 21	+59	165	55 20	+59	164	56 19	+60	164	57 19	+59	164	350
11	53 13	60	163	54 13	59	163	55 12	59	163	56 11	59	162	57 10	59	162	349
12	53 05	59	162	54 04	59	161	55 03	59	161	56 02	59	161	57 01	59	161	348
13	52 55	59	160	53 54	59	160	54 53	59	160	55 52	59	159	56 51	58	159	347
14	52 45	59	159	53 44	58	158	54 42	59	158	55 41	59	158	56 40	58	157	346
15	52 34	+59	157	53 33	+58	157	54 31	+59	157	55 30	+58	156	56 28	+59	156	345
16	52 22	59	156	53 21	58	156	54 19	59	155	55 18	58	155	56 16	58	154	344
17	52 10	58	154	53 08	59	154	54 07	58	154	55 05	58	153	56 03	58	153	343
18	51 57	58	153	52 55	58	153	53 53	58	152	54 51	58	152	55 49	58	151	342
19	51 44	58	152	52 42	58	151	53 40	57	151	54 37	58	150	55 35	58	150	341
20	51 30	+57	150	52 27	+58	150	53 25	+58	149	54 23	+57	149	55 20	+57	148	340
21	51 15	57	149	52 12	58	148	53 10	57	148	54 07	57	147	55 04	58	147	339
22	50 59	58	147	51 57	57	147	52 54	57	146	53 51	57	146	54 48	57	145	338
23	50 43	58	146	51 41	57	146	52 38	57	145	53 35	56	145	54 31	57	144	337
24	50 27	57	145	51 24	57	144	52 21	56	144	53 17	57	143	54 14	56	143	336
25	50 10	+57	143	51 07	+56	143	52 03	+57	142	53 00	+56	142	53 56	+56	141	335
26	49 52	57	142	50 49	56	141	51 45	56	141	52 41	56	140	53 37	56	140	334
27	49 34	56	141	50 30	56	140	51 26	57	140	52 23	55	139	53 18	56	138	333
28	49 15	56	139	50 11	56	139	51 07	56	138	52 03	56	138	52 59	55	137	332
29	48 56	56	138	49 52	56	138	50 48	55	137	51 43	56	136	52 39	55	136	331
30	48 36	+56	137	49 32	+56	136	50 28	+55	136	51 23	+55	135	52 18	+55	134	330
31	48 16	56	136	49 12	55	135	50 07	55	134	51 02	55	134	51 57	55	133	329
32	47 55	56	134	48 51	55	134	49 46	55	133	50 41	55	132	51 36	54	132	328
33	47 34	56	133	48 30	54	132	49 24	55	132	50 19	55	131	51 14	54	131	327
34	47 13	55	132	48 08	55	131	49 03	54	131	49 57	54	130	50 51	54	129	326
35	46 51	+55	131	47 46	+54	130	48 40	+55	129	49 35	+54	129	50 29	+53	128	325
36	46 29	54	129	47 23	55	129	48 18	54	128	49 12	54	127	50 06	53	127	324
37	46 06	54	128	47 00	54	128	47 54	54	127	48 48	54	126	49 42	53	126	323
38	45 43	54	127	46 37	54	126	47 31	54	126	48 25	53	125	49 18	53	124	322
39	45 20	53	126	46 13	54	125	47 07	54	125	48 01	53	124	48 54	53	123	321
40	44 56	+54	125	45 50	+53	124	46 43	+53	123	47 36	+53	123	48 29	+53	122	320
41	44 32	53	124	45 25	54	123	46 19	53	122	47 12	53	122	48 05	52	121	319
42	44 07	54	122	45 01	53	122	45 54	53	121	46 47	53	120	47 40	52	120	318
43	43 43	53	121	44 36	53	121	45 29	53	120	46 22	52	119	47 14	52	119	317
44	43 17	54	120	44 11	52	120	45 03	53	119	45 56	52	118	46 48	53	117	316
45	42 52	+53	119	43 45	+53	118	44 38	+52	118	45 30	+52	117	46 22	+52	116	315
46	42 27	52	118	43 19	53	117	44 12	52	117	45 04	52	116	45 56	52	115	314
47	42 01	52	117	42 53	53	116	43 46	52	116	44 38	52	115	45 30	51	114	313
48	41 35	52	116	42 27	52	115	43 19	52	115	44 11	52	114	45 03	52	113	312
49	41 08	53	115	42 01	52	114	42 53	52	113	43 45	51	113	44 36	52	112	311
50	40 42	+52	114	41 34	+52	113	42 26	+52	112	43 18	+51	112	44 09	+51	111	310
51	40 15	52	113	41 07	52	112	41 59	52	111	42 51	51	111	43 42	51	110	309
52	39 48	52	112	40 40	52	111	41 32	51	111	42 23	52	110	43 15	51	109	308
53	39 21	52	111	40 13	51	110	41 04	52	109	41 56	51	109	42 47	51	108	307
54	38 54	51	110	39 45	52	109	40 37	51	108	41 28	51	108	42 19	51	107	306
55	38 26	+52	109	39 18	+51	108	40 09	+51	107	41 00	+51	107	41 51	+51	106	305
56	37 59	51	108	38 50	51	107	39 41	51	106	40 32	51	106	41 23	51	105	304
57	37 31	51	107	38 22	51	106	39 13	51	105	40 04	51	105	40 55	51	104	303
58	37 03	51	106	37 54	51	105	38 45	51	104	39 36	51	104	40 27	50	103	302
59	36 35	51	105	37 26	51	104	38 17	51	103	39 08	50	103	39 58	51	102	301
60	36 07	+51	104	36 58	+51	103	37 49	+50	102	38 39	+51	102	39 30	+50	101	300
61	35 38	51	103	36 29	51	102	37 20	51	101	38 11	50	101	39 01	50	100	299
62	35 10	51	102	36 01	51	101	36 52	50	100	37 42	51	100	38 33	50	99	298
63	34 41	51	101	35 32	51	101	36 23	51	100	37 14	50	99	38 04	50	98	297
64	34 13	51	100	35 04	50	99	35 54	51	99	36 45	50	98	37 35	50	97	296
65	33 44	+51	99	34 35	+51	98	35 26	+50	98	36 16	+50	97	37 06	+50	96	295
66	33 15	51	98	34 06	51	97	34 57	50	97	35 47	50	96	36 37	50	95	294
67	32 46	51	97	33 37	51	97	34 28	50	96	35 18	50	95	36 08	50	95	293
68	32 18	50	96	33 08	51	96	33 59	50	95	34 49	50	94	35 39	50	94	292
69	31 49	50	95	32 39	51	95	33 30	50	94	34 20	50	93	35 10	50	93	291

S. Lat. {LHA greater than 180°....... Zn=180−Z; LHA less than 180°............ Zn=180+Z}

DECLINATION (15°-29°) SAME NAME AS LATITUDE

LAT 61°

N. Lat. {LHA greater than 180°........Zn=Z; LHA less than 180°...........Zn=360−Z}

DECLINATION (15°-29°) SAME NAME AS LATITUDE

LHA	15°			16°			17°			18°			19°		
LHA	Hc	d	Z	Hc	d	Z	Hc	d	Z	Hc	d	Z	Hc	d	Z
	° ′	′	°	° ′	′	°	° ′	′	°	° ′	′	°	° ′	′	°
70	22 44	+53	100	23 37	+52	100	24 29	+51	99	25 20	+52	99	26 12	+52	98
71	22 16	52	99	23 08	52	99	24 00	52	98	24 52	51	98	25 43	52	97
72	21 47	52	98	22 39	52	98	23 31	52	97	24 23	51	97	25 14	52	96
73	21 18	52	98	22 10	52	97	23 02	52	96	23 54	51	96	24 45	52	95
74	20 49	52	97	21 41	52	96	22 33	52	96	23 25	51	95	24 16	52	94
75	20 20	+52	96	21 12	+52	95	22 04	+52	95	22 56	+51	94	23 47	+52	94
76	19 51	52	95	20 43	52	94	21 35	52	94	22 27	51	93	23 18	52	93
77	19 22	52	94	20 14	52	93	21 06	52	93	21 58	51	92	22 49	52	92
78	18 53	52	93	19 45	52	93	20 37	52	92	21 29	51	91	22 20	52	91
79	18 24	52	92	19 16	52	92	20 08	52	91	21 00	51	91	21 51	52	90
80	17 55	+52	91	18 47	+52	91	19 39	+52	90	20 31	+51	90	21 22	+52	89
81	17 26	52	90	18 18	52	90	19 10	51	89	20 01	52	89	20 53	51	88
82	16 57	52	90	17 49	52	89	18 41	51	89	19 32	52	88	20 24	51	87
83	16 28	52	89	17 20	52	88	18 12	51	88	19 03	52	87	19 55	51	87
84	15 59	52	88	16 51	52	87	17 43	51	87	18 34	52	86	19 26	51	86
85	15 30	+52	87	16 22	+52	86	17 14	+51	86	18 05	+52	85	18 57	+51	85
86	15 01	52	86	15 53	52	86	16 45	51	85	17 36	52	85	18 28	52	84
87	14 32	52	85	15 24	52	85	16 16	51	84	17 07	52	84	17 59	52	83
88	14 03	52	84	14 55	52	84	15 47	51	83	16 38	52	83	17 30	52	82
89	13 34	52	84	14 26	52	83	15 18	52	82	16 10	51	82	17 01	52	81
90	13 05	+52	83	13 57	+52	82	14 49	+52	82	15 41	+52	81	16 33	+51	81
91	12 36	52	82	13 28	52	81	14 20	52	81	15 12	52	80	16 04	52	80
92	12 07	53	81	13 00	52	80	13 52	52	80	14 44	51	79	15 35	52	79
93	11 39	52	80	12 31	52	80	13 23	52	79	14 15	52	79	15 07	52	78
94	11 10	52	79	12 02	52	79	12 54	53	78	13 47	52	78	14 39	51	77
95	10 42	+52	78	11 34	+52	78	12 26	+52	77	13 18	+52	77	14 10	+52	76
96	10 13	52	78	11 05	53	77	11 58	52	77	12 50	52	76	13 42	52	75
97	09 45	52	77	10 37	53	76	11 30	52	76	12 22	52	75	13 14	52	75
98	09 17	52	76	10 09	52	75	11 01	53	75	11 54	52	74	12 46	52	74
99	08 48	53	75	09 41	52	74	10 33	53	74	11 26	52	73	12 18	52	73
100	08 20	+53	74	09 13	+52	74	10 05	+53	73	10 58	+52	73	11 50	+53	72
101	07 53	52	73	08 45	53	73	09 38	52	72	10 30	53	72	11 23	52	71
102	07 25	52	72	08 17	53	72	09 10	53	71	10 03	52	71	10 55	53	70
103	06 57	53	72	07 50	53	71	08 43	52	71	09 35	53	70	10 28	53	70
104	06 30	52	71	07 22	53	70	08 15	53	70	09 08	53	69	10 01	52	69
105	06 02	+53	70	06 55	+53	69	07 48	+53	69	08 41	+53	68	09 34	+53	68
106	05 35	53	69	06 28	53	68	07 21	53	68	08 14	53	68	09 07	53	67
107	05 08	53	68	06 01	53	68	06 54	53	67	07 47	53	67	08 40	53	66
108	04 41	53	67	05 34	53	67	06 27	54	66	07 21	53	66	08 14	53	65
109	04 14	54	66	05 08	53	66	06 01	53	65	06 54	53	65	07 47	54	65
110	03 48	+53	65	04 41	+54	65	05 35	+53	65	06 28	+53	64	07 21	+53	64
111	03 21	54	65	04 15	53	64	05 08	54	64	06 02	53	63	06 55	54	63
112	02 55	54	64	03 49	53	63	04 42	54	63	05 36	53	62	06 29	54	62
113	02 29	54	63	03 23	54	62	04 17	53	62	05 10	54	62	06 04	53	61
114	02 03	54	62	02 57	54	62	03 51	54	61	04 45	54	61	05 39	53	60
115	01 38	+54	61	02 32	+54	61	03 26	+53	60	04 19	+54	60	05 13	+54	59
116	01 12	54	60	02 06	54	60	03 00	54	59	03 54	54	59	04 48	54	59
117	00 47	54	59	01 41	55	59	02 36	54	59	03 30	54	58	04 24	54	58
118	00 22	55	59	01 17	54	58	02 11	54	58	03 05	54	57	03 59	54	57
119	−0 02	54	58	00 52	54	57	01 46	55	57	02 41	54	56	03 35	54	56
120	−0 27	+55	57	00 28	+54	56	01 22	+55	56	02 17	+54	56	03 11	+54	55
121	−0 51	55	56	00 04	54	55	00 58	55	55	01 53	54	55	02 47	55	54
122	−1 15	55	55	−0 20	54	55	00 34	55	54	01 29	55	54	02 24	55	53
123	−1 39	55	54	−0 44	55	54	00 11	55	53	01 06	55	53	02 01	54	53
124	−2 02	55	53	−1 07	55	53	−0 12	55	52	00 43	55	52	01 38	55	52
125	−2 25	+55	52	−1 30	+55	52	−0 35	+55	52	00 20	+55	51	01 15	+55	51
126	−2 48	55	51	−1 53	55	51	−0 58	55	51	−0 03	56	50	00 53	55	50
127	−3 11	56	51	−2 15	55	50	−1 20	55	50	−0 25	56	49	00 31	55	49
128	−3 33	55	50	−2 38	56	49	−1 42	55	49	−0 47	56	49	00 09	55	48
129	−3 55	55	49	−3 00	56	48	−2 04	56	48	−1 08	55	48	−0 13	56	47
130	−4 17	+56	48	−3 21	+56	48	−2 25	+55	47	−1 30	+56	47	−0 34	+56	46
131	−4 38	56	47	−3 42	55	47	−2 47	56	46	−1 51	56	46	−0 55	56	46
132	−4 59	56	46	−4 03	56	46	−3 07	55	45	−2 12	56	45	−1 16	56	45
133	−5 20	56	45	−4 24	56	45	−3 28	56	44	−2 32	56	44	−1 36	56	44
134	−5 41	57	44	−4 44	56	44	−3 48	56	44	−2 52	56	43	−1 56	56	43
135				−5 05	+57	43	−4 08	+56	43	−3 12	+57	42	−2 15	+56	42
136				−5 24	56	42	−4 28	57	42	−3 31	56	41	−2 35	57	41
137							−4 47	57	41	−3 50	56	41	−2 54	57	40
138							−5 06	57	40	−4 09	57	40	−3 12	56	39
139							−5 24	57	39	−4 27	56	39	−3 31	57	38

LHA	20°			21°			22°			23°			24°		
LHA	Hc	d	Z	Hc	d	Z	Hc	d	Z	Hc	d	Z	Hc	d	Z
	° ′	′	°	° ′	′	°	° ′	′	°	° ′	′	°	° ′	′	°
70	27 04	+51	97	27 55	+52	97	28 47	+51	96	29 38	+51	96	30 29	+51	95
71	26 35	51	97	27 26	52	96	28 18	51	95	29 09	51	95	30 00	51	94
72	26 06	51	96	26 57	52	95	27 49	51	95	28 40	51	94	29 31	51	93
73	25 37	51	95	26 28	52	94	27 20	51	94	28 11	51	93	29 02	50	92
74	25 08	51	94	25 59	52	93	26 51	51	93	27 42	51	92	28 33	50	92
75	24 39	+51	93	25 30	+52	92	26 22	+51	92	27 13	+51	91	28 04	+50	91
76	24 10	51	92	25 01	51	92	25 52	52	91	26 44	50	90	27 34	51	90
77	23 41	51	91	24 32	51	91	25 23	51	90	26 14	51	90	27 05	51	89
78	23 12	51	90	24 03	51	90	24 54	51	89	25 45	51	89	26 36	51	88
79	22 43	51	89	23 34	51	89	24 25	51	88	25 16	51	88	26 07	51	87
80	22 14	+51	89	23 05	+51	88	23 56	+51	87	24 47	+51	87	25 38	+51	86
81	21 44	52	88	22 36	51	87	23 27	51	87	24 18	51	86	25 09	51	85
82	21 15	52	87	22 07	51	86	22 58	51	86	23 49	51	85	24 40	51	85
83	20 46	52	86	21 38	51	85	22 29	51	85	23 20	51	84	24 11	51	84
84	20 17	52	85	21 09	51	85	22 00	51	84	22 51	51	83	23 42	51	83
85	19 48	+52	84	20 40	+51	84	21 31	+51	83	22 22	+52	83	23 14	+51	82
86	19 20	51	83	20 11	51	83	21 02	52	82	21 54	51	82	22 45	51	81
87	18 51	51	83	19 42	52	82	20 34	51	82	21 25	51	81	22 16	51	80
88	18 22	51	82	19 13	52	81	20 05	51	81	20 56	51	80	21 47	52	80
89	17 53	52	81	18 45	51	80	19 36	52	80	20 28	51	79	21 19	51	79
90	17 24	+52	80	18 16	+52	80	19 08	+51	79	19 59	+51	78	20 50	+52	78
91	16 56	51	79	17 47	52	79	18 39	52	78	19 31	51	78	20 22	51	77
92	16 27	52	78	17 19	52	78	18 11	51	77	19 02	52	77	19 54	51	76
93	15 59	52	78	16 51	51	77	17 42	52	76	18 34	52	76	19 26	51	75
94	15 30	52	77	16 22	52	76	17 14	52	76	18 06	51	75	18 57	52	75
95	15 02	+52	76	15 54	+52	75	16 46	+52	75	17 38	+51	74	18 29	+52	74
96	14 34	52	75	15 26	52	74	16 18	52	74	17 10	52	73	18 02	51	73
97	14 06	52	74	14 58	52	74	15 50	52	73	16 42	52	73	17 34	52	72
98	13 38	52	73	14 30	52	73	15 22	52	72	16 14	52	72	17 06	52	71
99	13 10	53	72	14 03	52	72	14 55	52	71	15 47	52	71	16 39	52	70
100	12 43	+52	72	13 35	+52	71	14 27	+52	71	15 19	+52	70	16 11	+53	70
101	12 15	53	71	13 08	52	70	14 00	52	70	14 52	52	69	15 44	52	69
102	11 48	52	70	12 40	53	69	13 33	52	69	14 25	52	68	15 17	52	68
103	11 21	52	69	12 13	53	69	13 06	52	68	13 58	52	68	14 50	53	67
104	10 53	53	68	11 46	53	68	12 39	52	67	13 31	53	67	14 24	52	66
105	10 27	+52	67	11 19	+53	67	12 12	+53	66	13 05	+52	66	13 57	+53	65
106	10 00	53	67	10 53	52	66	11 45	53	66	12 38	53	65	13 31	52	65
107	09 33	53	66	10 26	53	65	11 19	53	65	12 12	53	64	13 05	52	64
108	09 07	53	65	10 00	53	64	10 53	53	64	11 46	53	63	12 39	52	63
109	08 41	53	64	09 34	53	64	10 27	53	63	11 20	53	63	12 13	53	62
110	08 14	+54	63	09 08	+53	63	10 01	+53	62	10 54	+53	62	11 47	+53	61
111	07 49	53	62	08 42	53	62	09 35	54	61	10 29	53	61	11 22	53	60
112	07 23	53	62	08 16	54	61	09 10	53	61	10 03	54	60	10 57	53	60
113	06 57	54	61	07 51	54	60	08 45	53	60	09 38	54	59	10 32	53	59
114	06 32	54	60	07 26	54	59	08 20	53	59	09 13	54	58	10 07	53	58
115	06 07	+54	59	07 01	+54	59	07 55	+54	58	08 49	+53	58	09 42	+54	57
116	05 42	54	58	06 36	54	58	07 30	54	57	08 24	54	57	09 18	54	56
117	05 18	54	57	06 12	54	57	07 06	54	56	08 00	54	56	08 54	54	56
118	04 53	55	56	05 48	54	56	06 42	54	56	07 36	54	55	08 30	54	55
119	04 29	55	56	05 24	54	55	06 18	54	55	07 12	54	54	08 06	55	54
120	04 05	+55	55	05 00	+54	54	05 54	+55	54	06 49	+54	53	07 43	+54	53
121	03 42	54	54	04 36	55	53	05 31	55	53	06 26	54	53	07 20	54	52
122	03 19	54	53	04 13	55	53	05 08	55	52	06 03	54	52	06 57	55	51
123	02 55	55	52	03 50	55	52	04 45	55	51	05 40	55	51	06 35	54	51
124	02 33	55	51	03 28	54	51	04 22	55	50	05 17	55	50	06 12	55	50
125	02 10	+55	50	03 05	+55	50	04 00	+55	50	04 55	+55	49	05 50	+55	49
126	01 48	55	50	02 43	55	49	03 38	55	49	04 33	56	48	05 29	55	48
127	01 26	55	49	02 21	55	48	03 16	56	48	04 12	55	47	05 07	55	47
128	01 04	56	48	02 00	55	47	02 55	55	47	03 50	56	47	04 46	55	46
129	00 43	55	47	01 38	56	47	02 34	55	46	03 29	56	46	04 25	56	45
130	00 22	+55	46	01 17	+56	46	02 13	+56	45	03 09	+55	45	04 04	+56	45
131	00 01	56	45	00 57	56	45	01 53	55	44	02 48	56	44	03 44	56	44
132	−0 20	56	44	00 36	56	44	01 32	56	44	02 28	56	43	03 24	56	43
133	−0 40	56	43	00 16	56	43	01 12	57	43	02 09	56	42	03 05	56	42
134	−1 00	57	43	−0 03	56	42	00 53	56	42	01 49	56	41	02 45	57	41
135	−1 19	+56	42	−0 23	+57	41	00 34	+56	41	01 30	+56	41	02 26	+57	40
136	−1 38	56	41	−0 42	57	40	00 15	56	40	01 11	57	40	02 08	56	39
137	−1 57	57	40	−1 00	56	40	−0 04	57	39	00 53	56	39	01 49	57	39
138	−2 16	57	39	−1 19	57	39	−0 22	57	38	00 35	56	38	01 31	57	38
139	−2 34	57	38	−1 37	57	38	−0 40	57	37	00 17	57	37	01 14	57	37

LHA	25°			26°			27°			28°			29°			LHA
LHA	Hc	d	Z	Hc	d	Z	Hc	d	Z	Hc	d	Z	Hc	d	Z	LHA
	° ′	′	°	° ′	′	°	° ′	′	°	° ′	′	°	° ′	′	°	
70	31 20	+50	94	32 10	+51	94	33 01	+50	93	33 51	+50	93	34 41	+50	92	290
71	30 51	50	94	31 41	51	93	32 32	50	92	33 22	50	92	34 12	50	91	289
72	30 22	50	93	31 12	51	92	32 03	50	91	32 53	50	91	33 43	50	90	288
73	29 52	51	92	30 43	51	91	31 34	50	91	32 24	50	90	33 14	50	89	287
74	29 23	51	91	30 14	50	90	31 04	51	90	31 55	50	89	32 45	50	88	286
75	28 54	+51	90	29 45	+50	89	30 35	+51	89	31 26	+50	88	32 16	+50	88	285
76	28 25	51	89	29 16	50	89	30 06	51	88	30 57	50	87	31 47	50	87	284
77	27 56	51	88	28 47	50	88	29 37	51	87	30 28	50	86	31 18	50	86	283
78	27 27	51	87	28 18	50	87	29 08	50	86	29 58	51	86	30 49	50	85	282
79	26 58	51	87	27 49	50	86	28 39	51	85	29 30	50	85	30 20	50	84	281
80	26 29	+51	86	27 20	+50	85	28 10	+51	85	29 01	+50	84	29 51	+50	83	280
81	26 00	51	85	26 51	50	84	27 41	51	84	28 32	50	83	29 22	50	82	279
82	25 31	51	84	26 22	50	83	27 12	51	83	28 03	50	82	28 53	50	82	278
83	25 02	51	83	25 53	51	83	26 44	50	82	27 34	50	81	28 24	50	81	277
84	24 33	51	82	25 24	51	82	26 15	50	81	27 05	51	81	27 56	50	80	276
85	24 05	+50	81	24 55	+51	81	25 46	+51	80	26 37	+50	80	27 27	+50	79	275
86	23 36	51	81	24 27	50	80	25 17	51	79	26 08	51	79	26 59	50	78	274
87	23 07	51	80	23 58	51	79	24 49	51	79	25 40	50	78	26 30	51	77	273
88	22 39	51	79	23 30	50	78	24 20	51	78	25 11	51	77	26 02	50	77	272
89	22 10	51	78	23 01	51	78	23 52	51	77	24 43	51	76	25 34	50	76	271
90	21 42	+51	77	22 33	+51	77	23 24	+51	76	24 15	+50	76	25 05	+51	75	270
91	21 13	51	76	22 04	52	76	22 56	51	75	23 47	50	75	24 37	51	74	269
92	20 45	51	76	21 36	51	75	22 27	52	75	23 19	50	74	24 09	51	73	268
93	20 17	51	75	21 08	52	74	22 00	51	74	22 51	51	73	23 42	50	73	267
94	19 49	51	74	20 40	52	73	21 32	51	73	22 23	51	72	23 14	51	72	266
95	19 21	+52	73	20 13	+51	73	21 04	+51	72	21 55	+51	72	22 46	+51	71	265
96	18 53	52	72	19 45	51	72	20 36	52	71	21 28	51	71	22 19	51	70	264
97	18 26	51	72	19 17	52	71	20 09	51	70	21 00	52	70	21 52	51	69	263
98	17 58	52	71	18 50	52	70	19 42	51	70	20 33	52	69	21 25	51	69	262
99	17 31	52	70	18 23	51	69	19 14	52	69	20 06	52	68	20 58	51	68	261
100	17 04	+51	69	17 55	+52	69	18 47	+52	68	19 39	+52	67	20 31	+51	67	260
101	16 36	52	68	17 28	52	68	18 20	52	67	19 12	52	67	20 04	52	66	259
102	16 09	53	67	17 02	52	67	17 54	52	66	18 46	52	66	19 38	51	65	258
103	15 43	52	67	16 35	52	66	17 27	52	66	18 19	52	65	19 11	52	65	257
104	15 16	52	66	16 08	53	65	17 01	52	65	17 53	52	64	18 45	52	64	256
105	14 50	+52	65	15 42	+53	64	16 35	+52	64	17 27	+52	63	18 19	+52	63	255
106	14 23	53	64	15 16	53	64	16 09	52	63	17 01	52	63	17 53	53	62	254
107	13 57	53	63	14 50	53	63	15 43	52	62	16 35	53	62	17 28	52	61	253
108	13 31	53	62	14 24	53	62	15 17	53	62	16 10	52	61	17 02	53	61	252
109	13 06	53	62	13 59	53	61	14 52	52	61	15 44	53	60	16 37	53	60	251
110	12 40	+53	61	13 33	+53	60	14 26	+53	60	15 19	+53	59	16 12	+53	59	250
111	12 15	53	60	13 08	53	60	14 01	53	59	14 54	53	59	15 47	53	58	249
112	11 50	53	59	12 43	53	59	13 36	54	58	14 30	53	58	15 23	53	57	248
113	11 25	53	58	12 18	54	58	13 12	53	57	14 05	53	57	14 58	54	56	247
114	11 00	54	58	11 54	53	57	12 47	54	57	13 41	53	56	14 34	54	56	246
115	10 36	+54	57	11 30	+53	56	12 23	+54	56	13 17	+53	55	14 10	+54	55	245
116	10 12	54	56	11 06	53	55	11 59	54	55	12 53	54	55	13 47	53	54	244
117	09 48	54	55	10 42	54	55	11 36	53	54	12 29	54	54	13 23	54	53	243
118	09 24	54	54	10 18	54	54	11 12	54	53	12 06	54	53	13 00	54	52	242
119	09 01	54	53	09 55	54	53	10 49	54	53	11 43	54	52	12 37	54	52	241
120	08 37	+55	53	09 32	+54	52	10 26	+54	52	11 20	+54	51	12 14	+55	51	240
121	08 14	55	52	09 09	54	51	10 03	55	51	10 58	54	50	11 52	54	50	239
122	07 52	54	51	08 46	55	51	09 41	54	50	10 35	55	50	11 30	54	49	238
123	07 29	55	50	08 24	55	50	09 19	54	49	10 13	55	49	11 08	55	48	237
124	07 07	55	49	08 02	55	49	08 57	55	48	09 52	54	48	10 46	55	48	236
125	06 45	+55	48	07 40	+55	48	08 35	+55	48	09 30	+55	47	10 25	+55	47	235
126	06 24	55	48	07 19	55	47	08 14	55	47	09 09	55	46	10 04	55	46	234
127	06 02	56	47	06 58	55	46	07 53	55	46	08 48	55	46	09 43	55	45	233
128	05 41	56	46	06 37	55	46	07 32	55	45	08 27	56	45	09 23	55	44	232
129	05 21	55	45	06 16	56	45	07 12	55	44	08 07	56	44	09 03	55	44	231
130	05 00	+56	44	05 56	+56	44	06 52	+55	43	07 47	+56	43	08 43	+55	43	230
131	04 40	56	43	05 36	56	43	06 32	55	43	07 27	56	42	08 23	56	42	229
132	04 20	56	42	05 16	56	42	06 12	56	42	07 08	56	41	08 04	56	41	228
133	04 01	56	42	04 57	56	41	05 53	56	41	06 49	56	41	07 45	56	40	227
134	03 42	56	41	04 38	56	40	05 34	56	40	06 30	56	40	07 26	57	39	226
135	03 23	+56	40	04 19	+56	40	05 15	+57	39	06 12	+56	39	07 08	+56	39	225
136	03 04	57	39	04 01	56	39	04 57	57	38	05 54	56	38	06 50	57	38	224
137	02 46	57	38	03 43	56	38	04 39	57	38	05 36	57	37	06 33	56	37	223
138	02 28	57	37	03 25	57	37	04 22	56	37	05 18	57	36	06 15	57	36	222
139	02 11	57	37	03 08	56	36	04 04	57	36	05 01	57	36	05 58	57	35	221

S. Lat. {LHA greater than 180°........Zn=180−Z; LHA less than 180°...........Zn=180+Z}

DECLINATION (15°-29°) SAME NAME AS LATITUDE

N. Lat. {LHA greater than 180°....... Zn=Z / LHA less than 180°.......... Zn=360−Z}

DECLINATION (15°-29°) SAME NAME AS LATITUDE

LHA	15° Hc d Z	16° Hc d Z	17° Hc d Z	18° Hc d Z	19° Hc d Z	20° Hc d Z	21° Hc d Z	22° Hc d Z	23° Hc d Z	24° Hc d Z	25° Hc d Z	26° Hc d Z	27° Hc d Z	28° Hc d Z	29° Hc d Z	LHA
	° ′ ′ °	° ′ ′ °	° ′ ′ °	° ′ ′ °	° ′ ′ °	° ′ ′ °	° ′ ′ °	° ′ ′ °	° ′ ′ °	° ′ ′ °	° ′ ′ °	° ′ ′ °	° ′ ′ °	° ′ ′ °	° ′ ′ °	
			140	−4 45 +57 38	−3 48 +57 38	−2 51 +57 37	−1 54 +57 37	−0 57 +57 37	00 00 +57 36	00 57 +57 36	01 54 +57 36	02 51 +57 35	03 48 +57 35	04 45 +57 35	05 42 +57 34	220
			141	−5 03 57 37	−4 06 57 37	−3 09 57 36	−2 12 57 36	−1 15 58 36	−0 17 57 35	00 40 57 35	01 37 57 35	02 34 57 34	03 31 57 34	04 28 57 34	05 25 57 34	219
			142	−5 20 57 36	−4 23 57 36	−3 26 57 35	−2 29 58 35	−1 31 57 35	−0 34 57 35	00 23 57 34	01 20 58 34	02 18 57 34	03 15 57 33	04 12 57 33	05 09 58 33	218
				143	−4 40 57 35	−3 43 58 35	−2 45 57 34	−1 48 58 34	−0 50 57 34	00 07 57 33	01 04 58 33	02 02 57 33	02 59 58 32	03 57 57 32	04 54 57 32	217
				144	−4 56 57 34	−3 59 58 34	−3 01 57 33	−2 04 58 33	−1 06 57 33	−0 09 58 32	00 49 57 32	01 46 58 32	02 44 57 32	03 41 58 31	04 39 57 31	216
				145	−5 12 +57 33	−4 15 +58 33	−3 17 +57 32	−2 20 +58 32	−1 22 +58 32	−0 24 +57 32	00 33 +58 31	01 31 +58 31	02 29 +57 31	03 26 +58 30	04 24 +58 30	215
				146	−5 28 58 32	−4 30 57 32	−3 33 58 32	−2 35 58 31	−1 37 58 31	−0 39 57 31	00 18 58 30	01 16 58 30	02 14 58 30	03 12 57 30	04 09 58 29	214
					147	−4 45 57 31	−3 48 58 31	−2 50 58 30	−1 52 58 30	−0 54 58 30	00 04 58 30	01 02 58 29	02 00 57 29	02 57 58 29	03 55 58 28	213
					148	−5 00 58 30	−4 02 58 30	−3 04 58 29	−2 06 58 29	−1 08 58 29	−0 10 58 29	00 48 58 28	01 46 58 28	02 44 58 28	03 42 58 28	212
					149	−5 15 59 29	−4 16 58 29	−3 18 58 29	−2 20 58 28	−1 22 58 28	−0 24 58 28	00 34 58 28	01 32 58 27	02 30 58 27	03 28 58 27	211
						150	−4 30 +58 28	−3 32 +58 28	−2 34 +58 27	−1 36 +59 27	−0 37 +58 27	00 21 +58 27	01 19 +58 26	02 17 +58 26	03 15 +59 26	210
						151	−4 44 59 27	−3 45 58 27	−2 47 58 27	−1 49 59 26	−0 50 58 26	00 08 58 26	01 06 59 26	02 05 58 25	03 03 58 25	209
						152	−4 57 59 26	−3 58 58 26	−3 00 59 26	−2 01 58 25	−1 03 58 25	−0 05 59 25	00 54 58 25	01 52 59 25	02 51 58 24	208
						153	−5 09 58 25	−4 11 59 25	−3 12 58 25	−2 14 59 25	−1 15 58 24	−0 17 59 24	00 42 58 24	01 40 59 24	02 39 58 23	207
						154	−5 21 58 24	−4 23 59 24	−3 24 58 24	−2 26 59 24	−1 27 59 23	−0 28 58 23	00 30 59 23	01 29 59 23	02 28 58 23	206
							155	−4 34 +58 23	−3 36 +59 23	−2 37 +59 23	−1 38 +58 23	−0 40 +59 22	00 19 +59 22	01 18 +59 22	02 17 +59 22	205
							156	−4 46 59 22	−3 47 59 22	−2 48 59 22	−1 49 59 22	−0 50 58 21	00 08 59 21	01 07 59 21	02 06 59 21	204
							157	−4 56 58 21	−3 58 59 21	−2 59 59 21	−2 00 59 21	−1 01 59 21	−0 02 59 20	00 57 59 20	01 56 59 20	203
							158	−5 07 59 20	−4 08 59 20	−3 09 59 20	−2 10 59 20	−1 11 59 20	−0 12 59 19	00 47 59 19	01 46 59 19	202
							159	−5 17 59 19	−4 18 59 19	−3 19 59 19	−2 20 60 19	−1 20 59 19	−0 21 59 19	00 38 59 18	01 37 59 18	201
								160	−4 27 +59 18	−3 28 +59 18	−2 29 +59 18	−1 30 +60 18	−0 30 +59 18	00 29 +59 18	01 28 +59 17	200
								161	−4 36 59 17	−3 37 59 17	−2 38 60 17	−1 38 59 17	−0 39 59 17	00 20 59 17	01 19 60 17	199
								162	−4 45 60 17	−3 45 59 16	−2 46 59 16	−1 47 60 16	−0 47 59 16	00 12 59 16	01 11 60 16	198
								163	−4 53 60 16	−3 53 59 16	−2 54 60 15	−1 54 59 15	−0 55 59 15	00 04 60 15	01 04 59 15	197
								164	−5 00 59 15	−4 01 60 15	−3 01 59 14	−2 02 60 14	−1 02 59 14	−0 03 59 14	00 56 60 14	196
								165	−5 08 +60 14	−4 08 +60 14	−3 08 +59 14	−2 09 +60 13	−1 09 +59 13	−0 10 +60 13	00 50 +59 13	195
									166	−4 15 60 13	−3 15 60 13	−2 15 59 13	−1 16 60 12	−0 16 59 12	00 43 60 12	194
									167	−4 21 60 12	−3 21 59 12	−2 22 60 12	−1 22 60 12	−0 22 59 11	00 37 60 11	193
									168	−4 27 60 11	−3 27 60 11	−2 27 59 11	−1 28 60 11	−0 28 60 10	00 32 60 10	192
									169	−4 32 60 10	−3 32 60 10	−2 32 59 10	−1 33 60 10	−0 33 60 10	00 27 60 10	191
									170	−4 37 +60 9	−3 37 +60 9	−2 37 +60 9	−1 37 +59 9	−0 38 +60 9	00 22 +60 9	190
									171	−4 41 60 8	−3 41 59 8	−2 42 60 8	−1 42 60 8	−0 42 60 8	00 18 60 8	189
									172	−4 45 60 7	−3 45 60 7	−2 45 59 7	−1 46 60 7	−0 46 60 7	00 14 60 7	188
									173	−4 49 60 6	−3 49 60 6	−2 49 60 6	−1 49 60 6	−0 49 60 6	00 11 60 6	187
									174	−4 52 60 5	−3 52 60 5	−2 52 60 5	−1 52 60 5	−0 52 60 5	00 08 60 5	186
									175	−4 54 +60 5	−3 54 +60 5	−2 54 +60 5	−1 54 +60 4	−0 54 +60 4	00 06 +59 4	185
									176	−4 56 60 4	−3 56 60 4	−2 56 60 4	−1 56 60 4	−0 56 60 4	00 04 59 4	184
									177	−4 58 60 3	−3 58 60 3	−2 58 60 3	−1 58 60 3	−0 58 60 3	00 02 60 3	183
									178	−4 59 60 2	−3 59 60 2	−2 59 60 2	−1 59 60 2	−0 59 60 2	00 01 60 2	182
									179	−5 00 60 1	−4 00 60 1	−3 00 60 1	−2 00 60 1	−1 00 60 1	00 00 60 1	181
									180	−5 00 +60 0	−4 00 +60 0	−3 00 +60 0	−2 00 +60 0	−1 00 +60 0	00 00 +60 0	180
74	−5 35 53 111	286														
73	−5 08 53 112	287														
72	−4 41 53 113	−5 34 53 113	288													
71	−4 14 54 114	−5 08 53 114	289													
70	−3 48 −53 115	−4 41 −54 115	−5 35 −53 115	290												
	15°	16°	17°	18°	19°	20°	21°	22°	23°	24°	25°	26°	27°	28°	29°	

S. Lat. {LHA greater than 180°....... Zn=180−Z / LHA less than 180°.......... Zn=180+Z}

DECLINATION (15°-29°) CONTRARY NAME TO LATITUDE

N. Lat. {LHA greater than 180°....... Zn=Z; LHA less than 180°........... Zn=360–Z}

DECLINATION (15°-29°) CONTRARY NAME TO LATITUDE

LHA	15° Hc	15° d	15° Z	16° Hc	16° d	16° Z	17° Hc	17° d	17° Z	18° Hc	18° d	18° Z	19° Hc	19° d	19° Z
	° ′	′	°	° ′	′	°	° ′	′	°	° ′	′	°	° ′	′	°
69	−3 21	54	115	−4 15	53	116	−5 08	54	116	291					
68	−2 55	54	116	−3 49	53	117	−4 42	54	117	−5 36	53	118	292		
67	−2 29	54	117	−3 23	54	118	−4 17	53	118	−5 10	54	118	293		
66	−2 03	54	118	−2 57	54	118	−3 51	54	119	−4 45	54	119	−5 39	53	120
65	−1 38	−54	119	−2 32	−54	119	−3 26	−53	120	−4 19	−54	120	−5 13	−54	121
64	−1 12	54	120	−2 06	54	120	−3 00	54	121	−3 54	54	121	−4 48	54	121
63	−0 47	54	121	−1 41	55	121	−2 36	54	121	−3 30	54	122	−4 24	54	122
62	−0 22	55	121	−1 17	54	122	−2 11	54	122	−3 05	54	123	−3 59	54	123
61	00 02	54	122	−0 52	54	123	−1 46	55	123	−2 41	54	124	−3 35	54	124
60	00 27	−55	123	−0 28	−54	124	−1 22	−55	124	−2 17	−54	124	−3 11	−54	125
59	00 51	55	124	−0 04	54	125	−0 58	55	125	−1 53	54	125	−2 47	55	126
58	01 15	55	125	00 20	54	125	−0 34	55	126	−1 29	55	126	−2 24	55	127
57	01 39	55	126	00 44	55	126	−0 11	55	127	−1 06	55	127	−2 01	54	127
56	02 02	55	127	01 07	55	127	00 12	55	128	−0 43	55	128	−1 38	55	128
55	02 25	−55	128	01 30	−55	128	00 35	−55	128	−0 20	−55	129	−1 15	−55	129
54	02 48	55	129	01 53	55	129	00 58	55	129	00 03	56	130	−0 53	55	130
53	03 11	56	129	02 15	55	130	01 20	55	130	00 25	56	131	−0 31	55	131
52	03 33	55	130	02 38	56	131	01 42	55	131	00 47	56	131	−0 09	55	132
51	03 55	55	131	03 00	56	132	02 04	56	132	01 08	55	132	00 13	56	133
50	04 17	−56	132	03 21	−56	132	02 25	−55	133	01 30	−56	133	00 34	−56	134
49	04 38	56	133	03 42	55	133	02 47	56	134	01 51	56	134	00 55	56	134
48	04 59	56	134	04 03	56	134	03 07	55	135	02 12	56	135	01 16	56	135
47	05 20	56	135	04 24	56	135	03 28	56	136	02 32	56	136	01 36	56	136
46	05 41	57	136	04 44	56	136	03 48	56	136	02 52	56	137	01 56	56	137
45	06 01	−56	137	05 05	−57	137	04 08	−56	137	03 12	−57	138	02 15	−56	138
44	06 21	57	138	05 24	56	138	04 28	57	138	03 31	56	139	02 35	57	139
43	06 40	56	139	05 44	57	139	04 47	57	139	03 50	56	139	02 54	57	140
42	06 59	56	139	06 03	57	140	05 06	57	140	04 09	57	140	03 12	56	141
41	07 18	57	140	06 21	57	141	05 24	57	141	04 27	56	141	03 31	57	142
40	07 36	−57	141	06 39	−57	142	05 42	−57	142	04 45	−57	142	03 48	−57	142
39	07 54	57	142	06 57	57	143	06 00	57	143	05 03	57	143	04 06	57	143
38	08 12	57	143	07 15	57	143	06 18	58	144	05 20	57	144	04 23	57	144
37	08 29	57	144	07 32	57	144	06 35	58	145	05 37	57	145	04 40	57	145
36	08 46	57	145	07 49	58	145	06 51	57	146	05 54	58	146	04 56	57	146
35	09 03	−58	146	08 05	−57	146	07 08	−58	146	06 10	−58	147	05 12	−57	147
34	09 19	58	147	08 21	57	147	07 24	58	147	06 26	58	148	05 28	58	148
33	09 35	58	148	08 37	58	148	07 39	58	148	06 41	58	149	05 43	58	149
32	09 50	58	149	08 52	58	149	07 54	58	149	06 56	58	150	05 58	58	150
31	10 05	58	150	09 07	58	150	08 09	58	150	07 11	58	150	06 13	58	151
30	10 19	−58	151	09 21	−58	151	08 23	−58	151	07 25	−58	151	06 27	−58	152
29	10 33	58	152	09 35	58	152	08 37	58	152	07 39	59	152	06 40	58	153
28	10 47	58	153	09 49	59	153	08 50	58	153	07 52	58	153	06 54	59	153
27	11 00	58	154	10 02	59	154	09 03	58	154	08 05	59	154	07 06	58	154
26	11 13	59	154	10 14	58	155	09 16	59	155	08 17	58	155	07 19	59	155
25	11 25	−58	155	10 27	−59	156	09 28	−59	156	08 29	−58	156	07 31	−59	156
24	11 37	58	156	10 39	59	157	09 40	59	157	08 41	59	157	07 42	59	157
23	11 49	59	157	10 50	59	158	09 51	59	158	08 52	59	158	07 53	59	158
22	12 00	59	158	11 01	59	159	10 02	59	159	09 03	59	159	08 04	59	159
21	12 10	59	159	11 11	59	159	10 12	59	160	09 13	59	160	08 14	59	160
20	12 20	−59	160	11 21	−59	160	10 22	−59	161	09 23	−59	161	08 24	−59	161
19	12 30	59	161	11 31	59	161	10 32	60	162	09 32	59	162	08 33	59	162
18	12 39	59	162	11 40	60	162	10 40	59	163	09 41	59	163	08 42	59	163
17	12 48	60	163	11 48	59	163	10 49	59	164	09 50	60	164	08 50	59	164
16	12 56	60	164	11 56	59	164	10 57	59	164	09 58	60	165	08 58	59	165
15	13 04	−60	165	12 04	−59	165	11 05	−60	165	10 05	−59	166	09 06	−60	166
14	13 11	60	166	12 11	59	166	11 12	60	166	10 12	59	167	09 13	60	167
13	13 18	60	167	12 18	60	167	11 18	59	167	10 19	60	167	09 19	60	168
12	13 24	60	168	12 24	60	168	11 24	59	168	10 25	60	168	09 25	60	169
11	13 30	60	169	12 30	60	169	11 30	60	169	10 30	59	169	09 31	60	170
10	13 35	−60	170	12 35	−60	170	11 35	−59	170	10 36	−60	170	09 36	−60	170
9	13 40	60	171	12 40	60	171	11 40	60	171	10 40	60	171	09 40	59	171
8	13 44	60	172	12 44	60	172	11 44	60	172	10 44	60	172	09 44	59	172
7	13 48	60	173	12 48	60	173	11 48	60	173	10 48	60	173	09 48	60	173
6	13 51	60	174	12 51	60	174	11 51	60	174	10 51	60	174	09 51	60	174
5	13 54	−60	175	12 54	−60	175	11 54	−60	175	10 54	−60	175	09 54	−60	175
4	13 56	60	176	12 56	60	176	11 56	60	176	10 56	60	176	09 56	60	176
3	13 58	60	177	12 58	60	177	11 58	60	177	10 58	60	177	09 58	60	177
2	13 59	60	178	12 59	60	178	11 59	60	178	10 59	60	178	09 59	60	178
1	14 00	60	179	13 00	60	179	12 00	60	179	11 00	60	179	10 00	60	179
0	14 00	−60	180	13 00	−60	180	12 00	−60	180	11 00	−60	180	10 00	−60	180

LHA	20° Hc	20° d	20° Z	21° Hc	21° d	21° Z	22° Hc	22° d	22° Z	23° Hc	23° d	23° Z	24° Hc	24° d	24° Z
	° ′	′	°	° ′	′	°	° ′	′	°	° ′	′	°	° ′	′	°
66	294														
65	295														
64	−5 42	54	122	296											
63	−5 18	54	123	297											
62	−4 53	55	124	298											
61	−4 29	55	124	−5 24	54	125	299								
60	−4 05	−55	125	−5 00	−54	126	300								
59	−3 42	54	126	−4 36	55	127	−5 31	55	127	301					
58	−3 19	54	127	−4 13	55	127	−5 08	55	128	302					
57	−2 55	55	128	−3 50	55	128	−4 45	56	129	−5 40	55	129	303		
56	−2 33	55	129	−3 28	54	129	−4 22	55	130	−5 17	55	130	304		
55	−2 10	−55	130	−3 05	−55	130	−4 00	−55	130	−4 55	−55	131	305		
54	−1 48	55	130	−2 43	55	131	−3 38	55	131	−4 33	56	132	−5 29	55	132
53	−1 26	55	131	−2 21	55	132	−3 16	56	132	−4 12	55	133	−5 07	55	133
52	−1 04	56	132	−2 00	55	133	−2 55	55	133	−3 50	56	133	−4 46	55	134
51	−0 43	55	133	−1 38	56	133	−2 34	55	134	−3 29	56	134	−4 25	56	135
50	−0 22	−55	134	−1 17	−56	134	−2 13	−56	135	−3 09	−55	135	−4 04	−56	135
49	−0 01	56	135	−0 57	56	135	−1 53	55	136	−2 48	56	136	−3 44	56	136
48	00 20	56	136	−0 36	56	136	−1 32	56	136	−2 28	56	137	−3 24	56	137
47	00 40	56	137	−0 16	56	137	−1 12	57	137	−2 09	56	138	−3 05	56	138
46	01 00	57	137	00 03	56	138	−0 53	56	138	−1 49	56	139	−2 45	57	139
45	01 19	−56	138	00 23	−57	139	−0 34	−56	139	−1 30	−56	139	−2 26	−57	140
44	01 38	56	139	00 42	57	140	−0 15	56	140	−1 11	57	140	−2 08	56	141
43	01 57	57	140	01 00	56	140	00 04	57	141	−0 53	56	141	−1 49	57	141
42	02 16	57	141	01 19	57	141	00 22	57	142	−0 35	56	142	−1 31	57	142
41	02 34	57	142	01 37	57	142	00 40	57	143	−0 17	57	143	−1 14	57	143
40	02 51	−57	143	01 54	−57	143	00 57	−57	143	00 00	−57	144	−0 57	−57	144
39	03 09	57	144	02 12	57	144	01 15	58	144	00 17	57	145	−0 40	57	145
38	03 26	57	145	02 29	58	145	01 31	57	145	00 34	57	145	−0 23	57	146
37	03 43	58	145	02 45	57	146	01 48	58	146	00 50	57	146	−0 07	57	147
36	03 59	58	146	03 01	57	147	02 04	58	147	01 06	57	147	00 09	58	148
35	04 15	−58	147	03 17	−57	148	02 20	−58	148	01 22	−58	148	00 24	−57	148
34	04 30	57	148	03 33	58	148	02 35	58	149	01 37	58	149	00 39	57	149
33	04 45	57	149	03 48	58	149	02 50	58	150	01 52	58	150	00 54	58	150
32	05 00	58	150	04 02	58	150	03 04	58	151	02 06	58	151	01 08	58	151
31	05 15	59	151	04 16	58	151	03 18	58	151	02 20	58	152	01 22	58	152
30	05 29	−59	152	04 30	−58	152	03 32	−58	152	02 34	−58	153	01 36	−59	153
29	05 42	58	153	04 44	59	153	03 45	58	153	02 47	58	153	01 49	59	154
28	05 55	58	154	04 57	59	154	03 58	58	154	03 00	59	154	02 01	58	155
27	06 08	59	155	05 09	58	155	04 11	59	155	03 12	58	155	02 14	59	155
26	06 20	59	156	05 21	58	156	04 23	59	156	03 24	58	156	02 26	59	156
25	06 32	−59	156	05 33	−59	157	04 34	−58	157	03 36	−59	157	02 37	−59	157
24	06 43	58	157	05 45	59	158	04 46	59	158	03 47	59	158	02 48	59	158
23	06 54	59	158	05 55	59	159	04 56	58	159	03 58	59	159	02 59	59	159
22	07 05	59	159	06 06	59	159	05 07	59	160	04 08	59	160	03 09	59	160
21	07 15	59	160	06 16	59	160	05 17	59	161	04 18	59	161	03 19	59	161
20	07 25	−60	161	06 25	−59	161	05 26	−59	161	04 27	−59	162	03 28	−59	162
19	07 34	59	162	06 35	60	162	05 35	59	162	04 36	59	163	03 37	59	163
18	07 43	60	163	06 43	59	163	05 44	59	163	04 45	60	163	03 45	59	164
17	07 51	60	164	06 51	59	164	05 52	59	164	04 53	60	164	03 53	59	164
16	07 59	60	165	06 59	59	165	06 00	60	165	05 00	59	165	04 01	60	165
15	08 06	−59	166	07 07	−60	166	06 07	−59	166	05 08	−60	166	04 08	−60	166
14	08 13	60	167	07 13	59	167	06 14	60	167	05 14	59	167	04 15	60	167
13	08 19	59	168	07 20	60	168	06 20	59	168	05 21	60	168	04 21	60	168
12	08 25	59	169	07 26	60	169	06 26	60	169	05 26	59	169	04 27	60	169
11	08 31	60	170	07 31	60	170	06 31	59	170	05 32	60	170	04 32	60	170
10	08 36	−60	171	07 36	−60	171	06 36	−59	171	05 37	−60	171	04 37	−60	171
9	08 41	60	171	07 41	60	172	06 41	60	172	05 41	60	172	04 41	60	172
8	08 45	60	172	07 45	60	173	06 45	60	173	05 45	60	173	04 45	60	173
7	08 48	60	173	07 48	60	173	06 48	59	174	05 49	60	174	04 49	60	174
6	08 51	60	174	07 51	59	174	06 52	60	174	05 52	60	174	04 52	60	175
5	08 54	−60	175	07 54	−60	175	06 54	−60	175	05 54	−60	175	04 54	−60	175
4	08 56	60	176	07 56	60	176	06 56	60	176	05 56	60	176	04 56	60	176
3	08 58	60	177	07 58	60	177	06 58	60	177	05 58	60	177	04 58	60	177
2	08 59	60	178	07 59	60	178	06 59	60	178	05 59	60	178	04 59	60	178
1	09 00	60	179	08 00	60	179	07 00	60	179	06 00	60	179	05 00	60	179
0	09 00	−60	180	08 00	−60	180	07 00	−60	180	06 00	−60	180	05 00	−60	180

LHA	25° Hc	25° d	25° Z	26° Hc	26° d	26° Z	27° Hc	27° d	27° Z	28° Hc	28° d	28° Z	29° Hc	29° d	29° Z	LHA
	° ′	′	°	° ′	′	°	° ′	′	°	° ′	′	°	° ′	′	°	
54	306															
53	307															
52	308															
51	−5 21	55	135	309												
50	−5 00	−56	136	310												
49	−4 40	56	137	−5 36	56	137	311									
48	−4 20	56	138	−5 16	56	138	312									
47	−4 01	56	138	−4 57	56	139	313									
46	−3 42	56	139	−4 38	56	140	−5 34	56	140	314						
45	−3 23	−56	140	−4 19	−56	140	−5 15	−57	141	315						
44	−3 04	57	141	−4 01	56	141	−4 57	57	142	316						
43	−2 46	57	142	−3 43	56	142	−4 39	57	142	317						
42	−2 28	57	143	−3 25	57	143	−4 22	56	143	−5 18	57	144	318			
41	−2 11	57	143	−3 08	56	144	−4 04	57	144	−5 01	57	144	319			
40	−1 54	−57	144	−2 51	−57	145	−3 48	−57	145	−4 45	−57	145	320			
39	−1 37	57	145	−2 34	57	146	−3 31	57	146	−4 28	57	146	−5 25	57	146	321
38	−1 20	58	146	−2 18	57	146	−3 15	57	147	−4 12	57	147	−5 09	58	147	322
37	−1 04	58	147	−2 02	57	147	−2 59	58	148	−3 57	57	148	−4 54	57	148	323
36	−0 49	57	148	−1 46	58	148	−2 44	57	148	−3 41	58	149	−4 39	57	149	324
35	−0 33	−58	149	−1 31	−58	149	−2 29	−57	149	−3 26	−58	150	−4 24	−58	150	325
34	−0 18	58	150	−1 16	58	150	−2 14	58	150	−3 12	57	150	−4 09	58	151	326
33	−0 04	58	150	−1 02	58	151	−2 00	57	151	−2 57	58	151	−3 55	58	152	327
32	00 10	58	151	−0 48	58	152	−1 46	58	152	−2 44	58	152	−3 42	58	152	328
31	00 24	58	152	−0 34	58	152	−1 32	58	153	−2 30	58	153	−3 28	58	153	329
30	00 37	−58	153	−0 21	−58	153	−1 19	−58	154	−2 17	−58	154	−3 15	−59	154	330
29	00 50	58	154	−0 08	58	154	−1 06	59	154	−2 05	58	155	−3 03	58	155	331
28	01 03	58	155	00 05	59	155	−0 54	58	155	−1 52	59	155	−2 51	58	156	332
27	01 15	58	156	00 17	59	156	−0 42	58	156	−1 40	59	156	−2 39	58	157	333
26	01 27	59	157	00 28	58	157	−0 30	59	157	−1 29	59	157	−2 28	58	157	334
25	01 38	−58	157	00 40	−59	158	−0 19	−59	158	−1 18	−59	158	−2 17	−59	158	335
24	01 49	59	158	00 50	58	159	−0 08	59	159	−1 07	59	159	−2 06	59	159	336
23	02 00	59	159	01 01	59	159	00 02	59	160	−0 57	59	160	−1 56	59	160	337
22	02 10	59	160	01 11	59	160	00 12	59	161	−0 47	59	161	−1 46	59	161	338
21	02 20	60	161	01 20	59	161	00 21	59	161	−0 38	59	162	−1 37	59	162	339
20	02 29	−59	162	01 30	−60	162	00 30	−59	162	−0 29	−59	162	−1 28	−59	163	340
19	02 38	60	163	01 38	59	163	00 39	59	163	−0 20	59	163	−1 19	60	163	341
18	02 46	59	164	01 47	60	164	00 47	59	164	−0 12	59	164	−1 11	60	164	342
17	02 54	60	165	01 54	59	165	00 55	59	165	−0 04	60	165	−1 04	59	165	343
16	03 01	59	166	02 02	60	166	01 02	59	166	00 03	59	166	−0 56	60	166	344
15	03 08	−59	166	02 09	−60	167	01 09	−59	167	00 10	−60	167	−0 50	−59	167	345
14	03 15	60	167	02 15	59	167	01 16	60	168	00 16	59	168	−0 43	60	168	346
13	03 21	59	168	02 22	60	168	01 22	60	168	00 22	59	169	−0 37	60	169	347
12	03 27	60	169	02 27	59	169	01 28	60	169	00 28	60	170	−0 32	60	170	348
11	03 32	60	170	02 32	59	170	01 33	60	170	00 33	60	170	−0 27	60	170	349
10	03 37	−60	171	02 37	−60	171	01 37	−59	171	00 38	−60	171	−0 22	−60	171	350
9	03 41	59	172	02 42	60	172	01 42	60	172	00 42	60	172	−0 18	60	172	351
8	03 45	60	173	02 45	59	173	01 46	60	173	00 46	60	173	−0 14	60	173	352
7	03 49	60	174	02 49	60	174	01 49	60	174	00 49	60	174	−0 11	60	174	353
6	03 52	60	175	02 52	60	175	01 52	60	175	00 52	60	175	−0 08	60	175	354
5	03 54	−60	175	02 54	−60	175	01 54	−60	176	00 54	−60	176	−0 06	−59	176	355
4	03 56	60	176	02 56	60	176	01 56	60	176	00 56	60	176	−0 04	59	176	356
3	03 58	60	177	02 58	60	177	01 58	60	177	00 58	60	177	−0 02	60	177	357
2	03 59	60	178	02 59	60	178	01 59	60	178	00 59	60	178	−0 01	60	178	358
1	04 00	60	179	03 00	60	179	02 00	60	179	01 00	60	179	00 00	60	179	359
0	04 00	−60	180	03 00	−60	180	02 00	−60	180	01 00	−60	180	00 00	−60	180	360

S. Lat. {LHA greater than 180°....... Zn=180–Z; LHA less than 180°........... Zn=180+Z}

DECLINATION (15°-29°) CONTRARY NAME TO LATITUDE

LAT 62°

DECLINATION (0°-14°) SAME NAME AS LATITUDE

N. Lat. {LHA greater than 180°....... Zn=Z; LHA less than 180°......... Zn=360−Z}

LHA	0° Hc	d	Z	1° Hc	d	Z	2° Hc	d	Z	3° Hc	d	Z	4° Hc	d	Z
	° ′	′	°	° ′	′	°	° ′	′	°	° ′	′	°	° ′	′	°
0	28 00	+60	180	29 00	+60	180	30 00	+60	180	31 00	+60	180	32 00	+60	180
1	28 00	60	179	29 00	60	179	30 00	60	179	31 00	60	179	32 00	60	179
2	27 59	60	178	28 59	60	178	29 59	60	178	30 59	60	178	31 59	60	178
3	27 58	60	177	28 58	59	177	29 57	60	177	30 57	60	177	31 57	60	177
4	27 56	60	176	28 56	60	175	29 56	59	175	30 55	60	175	31 55	60	175
5	27 53	+60	174	28 53	+60	174	29 53	+60	174	30 53	+60	174	31 53	+60	174
6	27 50	60	173	28 50	60	173	29 50	60	173	30 50	60	173	31 50	60	173
7	27 46	60	172	28 46	60	172	29 46	60	172	30 46	60	172	31 46	60	172
8	27 42	60	171	28 42	60	171	29 42	60	171	30 42	60	171	31 42	59	171
9	27 38	59	170	28 37	60	170	29 37	60	170	30 37	60	170	31 37	59	169
10	27 32	+60	169	28 32	+60	169	29 32	+60	169	30 32	+59	168	31 31	+60	168
11	27 27	59	168	28 26	60	168	29 26	60	167	30 26	59	167	31 25	60	167
12	27 20	60	167	28 20	59	166	29 19	60	166	30 19	60	166	31 19	59	166
13	27 13	60	165	28 13	60	165	29 13	59	165	30 12	60	165	31 12	59	165
14	27 06	59	164	28 05	60	164	29 05	59	164	30 04	60	164	31 04	59	164
15	26 58	+59	163	27 57	+60	163	28 57	+59	163	29 56	+60	163	30 56	+59	163
16	26 50	59	162	27 49	59	162	28 48	60	162	29 48	59	162	30 47	59	161
17	26 41	59	161	27 40	59	161	28 39	59	161	29 38	60	160	30 38	59	160
18	26 31	59	160	27 30	60	160	28 30	59	159	29 29	59	159	30 28	59	159
19	26 21	59	159	27 20	59	159	28 19	59	158	29 18	60	158	30 18	59	158
20	26 11	+59	158	27 10	+59	157	28 09	+59	157	29 08	+59	157	30 07	+59	157
21	26 00	59	157	26 59	59	156	27 58	58	156	28 56	59	156	29 55	59	156
22	25 48	59	155	26 47	59	155	27 46	59	155	28 45	58	155	29 43	59	155
23	25 36	59	154	26 35	59	154	27 34	58	154	28 32	59	154	29 31	59	153
24	25 24	58	153	26 22	59	153	27 21	59	153	28 20	58	153	29 18	59	152
25	25 11	+58	152	26 09	+59	152	27 08	+58	152	28 06	+59	151	29 05	+58	151
26	24 58	58	151	25 56	58	151	26 54	59	151	27 53	58	150	28 51	58	150
27	24 44	58	150	25 42	58	150	26 40	59	150	27 39	58	149	28 37	58	149
28	24 29	59	149	25 28	58	149	26 26	58	148	27 24	58	148	28 22	58	148
29	24 15	58	148	25 13	58	148	26 11	58	147	27 09	58	147	28 07	58	147
30	23 59	+58	147	24 57	+58	147	25 55	+58	146	26 53	+58	146	27 51	+58	146
31	23 44	58	146	24 42	57	146	25 39	58	145	26 37	58	145	27 35	58	145
32	23 28	57	145	24 25	58	144	25 23	58	144	26 21	57	144	27 18	58	144
33	23 11	58	144	24 09	57	143	25 06	58	143	26 04	57	143	27 01	58	142
34	22 54	58	143	23 52	57	142	24 49	58	142	25 47	57	142	26 44	57	141
35	22 37	+57	142	23 34	+58	141	24 32	+57	141	25 29	+57	141	26 26	+58	140
36	22 19	58	141	23 17	57	140	24 14	57	140	25 11	57	140	26 08	57	139
37	22 01	57	140	22 58	57	139	23 55	58	139	24 53	57	139	25 50	56	138
38	21 43	57	139	22 40	57	138	23 37	57	138	24 34	57	138	25 31	56	137
39	21 24	57	138	22 21	57	137	23 18	56	137	24 14	57	136	25 11	57	136
40	21 05	+56	137	22 01	+57	136	22 58	+57	136	23 55	+56	135	24 51	+57	135
41	20 45	57	135	21 42	56	135	22 38	57	135	23 35	56	134	24 31	57	134
42	20 25	57	134	21 22	56	134	22 18	57	134	23 15	56	133	24 11	56	133
43	20 05	56	133	21 01	57	133	21 58	56	133	22 54	56	132	23 50	56	132
44	19 44	57	132	20 41	56	132	21 37	56	132	22 33	56	131	23 29	56	131
45	19 23	+56	131	20 19	+57	131	21 16	+56	131	22 12	+56	130	23 08	+56	130
46	19 02	56	131	19 58	56	130	20 54	56	130	21 50	56	129	22 46	56	129
47	18 40	56	130	19 36	56	129	20 32	56	129	21 28	56	128	22 24	55	128
48	18 19	55	129	19 14	56	128	20 10	56	128	21 06	55	127	22 01	56	127
49	17 56	56	128	18 52	56	127	19 48	55	127	20 43	56	126	21 39	55	126
50	17 34	+55	127	18 29	+56	126	19 25	+55	126	20 20	+56	125	21 16	+55	125
51	17 11	56	126	18 07	55	125	19 02	55	125	19 57	56	124	20 53	55	124
52	16 48	55	125	17 43	56	124	18 39	55	124	19 34	55	123	20 29	55	123
53	16 25	55	124	17 20	55	123	18 15	55	123	19 10	55	122	20 05	55	122
54	16 01	55	123	16 56	55	122	17 51	55	122	18 46	55	121	19 41	55	121
55	15 37	+55	122	16 32	+55	121	17 27	+55	121	18 22	+55	121	19 17	+55	120
56	15 13	55	121	16 08	55	120	17 03	55	120	17 58	54	120	18 52	55	119
57	14 49	55	120	15 44	54	119	16 38	55	119	17 33	55	119	18 28	54	118
58	14 24	55	119	15 19	55	119	16 14	54	118	17 08	55	118	18 03	54	117
59	14 00	54	118	14 54	55	118	15 49	54	117	16 43	55	117	17 38	54	116
60	13 35	+54	117	14 29	+55	117	15 24	+54	116	16 18	+54	116	17 12	+54	115
61	13 09	55	116	14 04	54	116	14 58	54	115	15 52	55	115	16 47	54	114
62	12 44	54	115	13 38	55	115	14 33	54	114	15 27	54	114	16 21	54	113
63	12 18	55	114	13 13	54	114	14 07	54	113	15 01	54	113	15 55	54	112
64	11 53	54	113	12 47	54	113	13 41	54	112	14 35	54	112	15 29	54	112
65	11 27	+54	112	12 21	+54	112	13 15	+54	112	14 09	+54	111	15 03	+53	111
66	11 01	53	112	11 54	54	111	12 48	54	111	13 42	54	110	14 36	54	110
67	10 34	54	111	11 28	54	110	12 22	54	110	13 16	53	109	14 09	54	109
68	10 08	54	110	11 02	53	109	11 55	54	109	12 49	54	108	13 43	53	108
69	09 41	54	109	10 35	54	108	11 29	53	108	12 22	54	107	13 16	53	107

LHA	5° Hc	d	Z	6° Hc	d	Z	7° Hc	d	Z	8° Hc	d	Z	9° Hc	d	Z
	° ′	′	°	° ′	′	°	° ′	′	°	° ′	′	°	° ′	′	°
0	33 00	+60	180	34 00	+60	180	35 00	+60	180	36 00	+60	180	37 00	+60	180
1	33 00	60	179	34 00	60	179	35 00	60	179	36 00	60	179	37 00	60	179
2	32 59	60	178	33 59	60	178	34 59	60	178	35 59	60	178	36 59	60	178
3	32 57	60	176	33 57	60	176	34 57	60	176	35 57	60	176	36 57	60	176
4	32 55	60	175	33 55	60	175	34 55	60	175	35 55	60	175	36 55	60	175
5	32 53	+60	174	33 53	+60	174	34 53	+60	174	35 53	+59	174	36 52	+60	174
6	32 50	59	173	33 49	60	173	34 49	60	173	35 49	60	173	36 49	60	173
7	32 46	60	172	33 46	59	172	34 45	60	172	35 45	60	171	36 45	60	171
8	32 41	60	171	33 41	60	170	34 41	60	170	35 41	60	170	36 41	59	170
9	32 36	60	169	33 36	60	169	34 36	60	169	35 36	60	169	36 36	59	169
10	32 31	+60	168	33 31	+59	168	34 30	+60	168	35 30	+60	168	36 30	+60	168
11	32 25	60	167	33 25	59	167	34 24	60	167	35 24	60	167	36 24	59	167
12	32 18	60	166	33 18	59	166	34 17	60	166	35 17	60	165	36 17	59	165
13	32 11	60	165	33 11	59	165	34 10	60	164	35 10	59	164	36 09	60	164
14	32 03	60	164	33 03	59	163	34 02	60	163	35 02	59	163	36 01	60	163
15	31 55	+59	162	32 54	+60	162	33 54	+59	162	34 53	+60	162	35 53	+59	162
16	31 46	60	161	32 46	59	161	33 45	59	161	34 44	59	161	35 43	60	160
17	31 37	59	160	32 36	59	160	33 35	59	160	34 34	60	159	35 34	59	159
18	31 27	59	159	32 26	59	159	33 25	59	158	34 24	59	158	35 23	59	158
19	31 17	59	158	32 16	59	158	33 15	59	157	34 14	59	157	35 13	58	157
20	31 06	+59	157	32 05	+58	156	33 03	+59	156	34 02	+59	156	35 01	+59	156
21	30 54	59	155	31 53	59	155	32 52	59	155	33 51	58	155	34 49	59	155
22	30 42	59	154	31 41	59	154	32 40	58	154	33 38	59	154	34 37	59	153
23	30 30	58	153	31 28	59	153	32 27	58	153	33 25	59	152	34 24	58	152
24	30 17	58	152	31 15	59	152	32 14	58	152	33 12	59	151	34 11	58	151
25	30 03	+59	151	31 02	+58	151	32 00	+58	150	32 58	+59	150	33 57	+58	150
26	29 49	59	150	30 48	58	150	31 46	58	149	32 44	58	149	33 42	58	149
27	29 35	58	149	30 33	58	148	31 31	58	148	32 29	58	148	33 27	58	148
28	29 20	58	148	30 18	58	147	31 16	58	147	32 14	58	147	33 12	58	146
29	29 05	58	147	30 03	58	146	31 01	57	146	31 58	58	146	32 56	58	145
30	28 49	+58	145	29 47	+57	145	30 44	+58	145	31 42	+58	144	32 40	+57	144
31	28 33	57	144	29 30	58	144	30 28	58	144	31 26	57	143	32 23	58	143
32	28 16	58	143	29 14	57	143	30 11	57	143	31 08	58	142	32 06	57	142
33	27 59	57	142	28 56	58	142	29 54	57	141	30 51	57	141	31 48	57	141
34	27 41	58	141	28 39	57	141	29 36	57	140	30 33	57	140	31 30	57	140
35	27 24	+57	140	28 21	+57	140	29 18	+57	139	30 15	+57	139	31 12	+57	139
36	27 05	57	139	28 02	57	139	28 59	57	138	29 56	57	138	30 53	57	137
37	26 46	57	138	27 43	57	138	28 40	57	137	29 37	57	137	30 34	56	136
38	26 27	57	137	27 24	57	136	28 21	56	136	29 17	57	136	30 14	57	135
39	26 08	56	136	27 04	57	135	28 01	57	135	28 58	56	135	29 54	56	134
40	25 48	+57	135	26 45	+56	134	27 41	+56	134	28 37	+57	134	29 34	+56	133
41	25 28	56	134	26 24	56	133	27 20	57	133	28 17	56	133	29 13	56	132
42	25 07	56	133	26 03	57	132	27 00	56	132	27 56	56	131	28 52	56	131
43	24 46	56	132	25 42	56	131	26 38	56	131	27 34	56	130	28 30	56	130
44	24 25	56	131	25 21	56	130	26 17	56	130	27 13	56	129	28 09	55	129
45	24 04	+55	130	24 59	+56	129	25 55	+56	129	26 51	+56	128	27 47	+55	128
46	23 42	55	129	24 37	56	128	25 33	56	128	26 29	55	127	27 24	56	127
47	23 19	56	128	24 15	56	127	25 11	55	127	26 06	55	126	27 01	56	126
48	22 57	55	127	23 52	56	126	24 48	55	126	25 43	55	125	26 38	56	125
49	22 34	56	126	23 30	55	125	24 25	55	125	25 20	55	124	26 15	55	124
50	22 11	+55	125	23 06	+56	124	24 02	+55	124	24 57	+55	123	25 52	+55	123
51	21 48	55	124	22 43	55	123	23 38	55	123	24 33	55	122	25 28	55	122
52	21 24	55	123	22 19	55	122	23 14	55	122	24 09	55	121	25 04	55	121
53	21 00	55	122	21 55	55	121	22 50	55	121	23 45	54	120	24 39	55	120
54	20 36	55	121	21 31	55	120	22 26	54	120	23 20	55	119	24 15	54	119
55	20 12	+54	120	21 06	+55	119	22 01	+55	119	22 56	+54	118	23 50	+54	118
56	19 47	55	119	20 42	54	118	21 36	55	118	22 31	54	117	23 25	54	117
57	19 22	55	118	20 17	54	117	21 11	55	117	22 06	54	116	23 00	54	116
58	18 57	55	117	19 52	54	116	20 46	54	116	21 40	54	115	22 34	54	115
59	18 32	54	116	19 26	54	115	20 20	55	115	21 15	54	114	22 09	54	114
60	18 06	+55	115	19 01	+54	114	19 55	+54	114	20 49	+54	113	21 43	+54	113
61	17 41	54	114	18 35	54	113	19 29	54	113	20 23	54	113	21 17	54	112
62	17 15	54	113	18 09	54	113	19 03	54	112	19 57	54	112	20 51	53	111
63	16 49	54	112	17 43	54	112	18 37	54	111	19 31	53	111	20 24	54	110
64	16 23	54	111	17 17	53	111	18 10	54	110	19 04	54	110	19 58	53	109
65	15 56	+54	110	16 50	+54	110	17 44	+53	109	18 37	+54	109	19 31	+54	108
66	15 30	54	109	16 24	53	109	17 17	54	108	18 11	53	108	19 04	54	107
67	15 03	54	108	15 57	53	108	16 50	54	107	17 44	53	107	18 37	54	106
68	14 36	54	107	15 30	53	107	16 23	54	106	17 17	53	106	18 10	54	106
69	14 09	54	106	15 03	53	106	15 56	54	106	16 50	53	105	17 43	53	105

LHA	10° Hc	d	Z	11° Hc	d	Z	12° Hc	d	Z	13° Hc	d	Z	14° Hc	d	Z	LHA
	° ′	′	°	° ′	′	°	° ′	′	°	° ′	′	°	° ′	′	°	
0	38 00	+60	180	39 00	+60	180	40 00	+60	180	41 00	+60	180	42 00	+60	180	360
1	38 00	60	179	39 00	60	179	40 00	60	179	41 00	60	179	42 00	60	179	359
2	37 59	60	178	38 59	60	178	39 59	60	177	40 59	60	177	41 59	60	177	358
3	37 57	60	176	38 57	60	176	39 57	60	176	40 57	60	176	41 57	60	176	357
4	37 55	60	175	38 55	60	175	39 55	60	175	40 55	60	175	41 55	60	175	356
5	37 52	+60	174	38 52	+60	174	39 52	+60	174	40 52	+60	174	41 52	+60	174	355
6	37 49	60	173	38 49	60	172	39 49	60	172	40 49	60	172	41 49	59	172	354
7	37 45	60	171	38 45	60	171	39 45	60	171	40 45	59	171	41 44	60	171	353
8	37 40	60	170	38 40	60	170	39 40	60	170	40 40	60	170	41 40	59	170	352
9	37 35	60	169	38 35	60	169	39 35	59	169	40 34	60	168	41 34	60	168	351
10	37 30	+59	168	38 29	+60	167	39 29	+60	167	40 29	+59	167	41 28	+60	167	350
11	37 23	60	166	38 23	59	166	39 22	60	166	40 22	60	166	41 22	59	166	349
12	37 16	60	165	38 16	59	165	39 15	60	165	40 15	59	165	41 14	60	164	348
13	37 09	59	164	38 08	60	164	39 08	59	164	40 07	59	163	41 06	60	163	347
14	37 01	59	163	38 00	59	163	38 59	60	162	39 59	59	162	40 58	59	162	346
15	36 52	+59	161	37 51	+59	161	38 50	+60	161	39 50	+59	161	40 49	+59	161	345
16	36 43	59	160	37 42	59	160	38 41	59	160	39 40	59	160	40 39	59	159	344
17	36 33	59	159	37 32	59	159	38 31	59	159	39 30	59	158	40 29	59	158	343
18	36 22	59	158	37 21	59	158	38 20	59	157	39 19	59	157	40 18	59	157	342
19	36 11	59	157	37 10	59	156	38 09	59	156	39 08	59	156	40 07	59	156	341
20	36 00	+59	155	36 59	+59	155	37 58	+58	155	38 56	+59	155	39 55	+59	154	340
21	35 48	59	154	36 47	58	154	37 45	59	154	38 44	59	153	39 43	58	153	339
22	35 36	58	153	36 34	59	153	37 33	58	153	38 31	59	152	39 30	58	152	338
23	35 22	59	152	36 21	58	152	37 19	59	151	38 18	58	151	39 16	58	151	337
24	35 09	58	151	36 07	59	150	37 06	58	150	38 04	58	150	39 02	58	150	336
25	34 55	+58	150	35 53	+58	149	36 51	+58	149	37 49	+58	149	38 47	+58	148	335
26	34 40	58	148	35 38	58	148	36 36	58	148	37 34	58	147	38 32	58	147	334
27	34 25	58	147	35 23	58	147	36 21	58	147	37 19	58	146	38 17	57	146	333
28	34 10	58	146	35 08	57	146	36 05	58	145	37 03	58	145	38 01	57	145	332
29	33 54	58	145	34 52	57	145	35 49	58	144	36 47	57	144	37 44	58	144	331
30	33 37	+58	144	34 35	+57	143	35 32	+58	143	36 30	+57	143	37 27	+57	142	330
31	33 21	57	143	34 18	57	142	35 15	58	142	36 13	57	142	37 10	57	141	329
32	33 03	57	142	34 00	58	141	34 58	57	141	35 55	57	140	36 52	57	140	328
33	32 45	58	140	33 43	57	140	34 40	57	140	35 37	57	139	36 34	56	139	327
34	32 27	57	139	33 24	57	139	34 21	57	139	35 18	57	138	36 15	56	138	326
35	32 09	+57	138	33 06	+56	138	34 02	+57	137	34 59	+57	137	35 56	+56	137	325
36	31 50	56	137	32 46	57	137	33 43	57	136	34 40	56	136	35 36	56	136	324
37	31 30	57	136	32 27	56	136	33 23	57	135	34 20	56	135	35 16	56	134	323
38	31 11	56	135	32 07	56	135	33 03	57	134	34 00	56	134	34 56	56	133	322
39	30 50	57	134	31 47	56	133	32 43	56	133	33 39	56	133	34 35	56	132	321
40	30 30	+56	133	31 26	+56	132	32 22	+56	132	33 18	+56	132	34 14	+56	131	320
41	30 09	56	132	31 05	56	131	32 01	56	131	32 57	56	130	33 53	55	130	319
42	29 48	56	131	30 44	55	130	31 39	56	130	32 35	56	129	33 31	55	129	318
43	29 26	56	130	30 22	56	129	31 18	55	129	32 13	56	128	33 09	55	128	317
44	29 04	56	129	30 00	56	128	30 56	55	128	31 51	55	127	32 46	56	127	316
45	28 42	+56	127	29 38	+55	127	30 33	+55	127	31 28	+56	126	32 24	+55	126	315
46	28 20	55	126	29 15	55	126	30 10	55	126	31 05	56	125	32 01	55	125	314
47	27 57	55	125	28 52	55	125	29 47	55	125	30 42	55	124	31 37	55	124	313
48	27 34	55	124	28 29	55	124	29 24	55	124	30 19	55	123	31 14	54	123	312
49	27 10	55	123	28 05	55	123	29 00	55	122	29 55	55	122	30 50	54	122	311
50	26 47	+55	122	27 42	+54	122	28 36	+55	121	29 31	+55	121	30 26	+54	121	310
51	26 23	54	121	27 17	55	121	28 12	55	120	29 07	54	120	30 01	55	119	309
52	25 59	54	120	26 53	55	120	27 48	54	119	28 42	54	119	29 36	55	118	308
53	25 34	55	119	26 29	54	119	27 23	54	118	28 17	55	118	29 12	54	117	307
54	25 09	55	118	26 04	54	118	26 58	54	117	27 52	54	117	28 46	55	116	306
55	24 44	+55	117	25 39	+54	117	26 33	+54	116	27 27	+54	116	28 21	+54	115	305
56	24 19	55	116	25 14	54	116	26 08	54	115	27 02	54	115	27 56	53	114	304
57	23 54	54	115	24 48	54	115	25 42	54	114	26 36	54	114	27 30	54	114	303
58	23 28	54	114	24 22	54	114	25 16	54	114	26 10	54	113	27 04	54	113	302
59	23 03	54	114	23 57	53	113	24 50	54	113	25 44	54	112	26 38	53	112	301
60	22 37	+54	113	23 31	+53	112	24 24	+54	112	25 18	+54	111	26 12	+53	111	300
61	22 11	53	112	23 04	54	111	23 58	54	111	24 52	53	110	25 45	53	110	299
62	21 44	54	111	22 38	54	110	23 32	53	110	24 25	53	109	25 18	54	109	298
63	21 18	54	110	22 12	53	109	23 05	53	109	23 58	54	108	24 52	53	108	297
64	20 51	54	109	21 45	53	108	22 38	54	108	23 32	53	107	24 25	53	107	296
65	20 25	+53	108	21 18	+53	107	22 11	+54	107	23 05	+53	106	23 58	+53	106	295
66	19 58	53	107	20 51	53	106	21 44	53	106	22 37	54	105	23 31	53	105	294
67	19 31	53	106	20 24	53	105	21 17	53	105	22 10	53	104	23 03	53	104	293
68	19 04	53	105	19 57	53	105	20 50	53	104	21 43	53	104	22 36	53	103	292
69	18 36	53	104	19 29	53	104	20 22	53	103	21 15	53	103	22 08	53	102	291

S. Lat. {LHA greater than 180°....... Zn=180−Z; LHA less than 180°.......... Zn=180+Z}

DECLINATION (0°-14°) SAME NAME AS LATITUDE

LAT 62°

N. Lat. {LHA greater than 180°........ Zn=Z
{LHA less than 180°............ Zn=360−Z

DECLINATION (0°-14°) SAME NAME AS LATITUDE

	0°			1°			2°			3°			4°		
LHA	Hc	d	Z	Hc	d	Z	Hc	d	Z	Hc	d	Z	Hc	d	Z
	° ′	′	°	° ′	′	°	° ′	′	°	° ′	′	°	° ′	′	°
70	09 14	+54	108	10 08	+54	107	11 02	+53	107	11 55	+54	106	12 49	+53	106
71	08 48	53	107	09 41	54	107	10 35	53	106	11 28	54	106	12 22	53	105
72	08 21	53	106	09 14	54	106	10 08	53	105	11 01	53	105	11 54	54	104
73	07 53	54	105	08 47	53	105	09 40	54	104	10 34	53	104	11 27	53	103
74	07 26	54	104	08 20	53	104	09 13	53	103	10 06	54	103	11 00	53	102
75	06 59	+53	103	07 52	+53	103	08 45	+54	102	09 39	+53	102	10 32	+53	102
76	06 31	54	102	07 25	53	102	08 18	53	102	09 11	53	101	10 04	54	101
77	06 04	53	102	06 57	53	101	07 50	53	101	08 43	54	100	09 37	53	100
78	05 36	53	101	06 29	54	100	07 23	53	100	08 16	53	99	09 09	53	99
79	05 08	54	100	06 02	53	99	06 55	53	99	07 48	53	98	08 41	53	98
80	04 41	+53	99	05 34	+53	98	06 27	+53	98	07 20	+53	97	08 13	+53	97
81	04 13	53	98	05 06	53	98	05 59	53	97	06 52	53	97	07 45	53	96
82	03 45	53	97	04 38	53	97	05 31	53	96	06 24	53	96	07 17	53	95
83	03 17	53	96	04 10	53	96	05 03	53	95	05 56	53	95	06 49	53	94
84	02 49	53	95	03 42	53	95	04 35	53	94	05 28	53	94	06 21	53	93
85	02 21	+53	94	03 14	+53	94	04 07	+53	93	05 00	+53	93	05 53	+53	93
86	01 53	53	94	02 46	53	93	03 39	53	93	04 32	53	92	05 25	53	92
87	01 24	53	93	02 17	53	92	03 10	53	92	04 03	53	91	04 56	53	91
88	00 56	53	92	01 49	53	91	02 42	53	91	03 35	53	90	04 28	53	90
89	00 28	53	91	01 21	53	90	02 14	53	90	03 07	53	89	04 00	53	89
90	00 00	+53	90	00 53	+53	90	01 46	+53	89	02 39	+53	89	03 32	+53	88
91	−0 28	53	89	00 25	53	89	01 18	53	88	02 11	53	88	03 04	53	87
92	−0 56	53	88	−0 03	53	88	00 50	53	87	01 43	53	87	02 36	53	86
93	−1 24	53	87	−0 31	53	87	00 22	53	86	01 15	53	86	02 08	52	85
94	−1 53	53	86	−1 00	53	86	−0 07	53	86	00 46	53	85	01 39	53	85
95	−2 21	+53	86	−1 28	+53	85	−0 35	+53	85	00 18	+53	84	01 11	+53	84
96	−2 49	53	85	−1 56	53	84	−1 03	53	84	−0 10	53	83	00 43	54	83
97	−3 17	53	84	−2 24	53	83	−1 31	53	83	−0 38	54	82	00 16	53	82
98	−3 45	53	83	−2 52	53	82	−1 59	54	82	−1 05	53	82	−0 12	53	81
99	−4 13	53	82	−3 20	54	82	−2 26	53	81	−1 33	53	81	−0 40	53	80
100	−4 41	+54	81	−3 47	+53	81	−2 54	+53	80	−2 01	+53	80	−1 08	+53	79
101	−5 08	53	80	−4 15	53	80	−3 22	53	79	−2 29	54	79	−1 35	53	78
102	−5 36	53	79	−4 43	53	79	−3 50	54	78	−2 56	53	78	−2 03	53	78
			103	−5 10	53	78	−4 17	53	78	−3 24	54	77	−2 30	53	77
			104	−5 38	53	77	−4 45	54	77	−3 51	53	76	−2 58	54	76
						105	−5 12	+53	76	−4 19	+54	75	−3 25	+53	75
						106	−5 39	53	75	−4 46	54	74	−3 52	53	74
									107	−5 13	54	73	−4 19	53	73
									108	−5 40	54	73	−4 46	54	72
												109	−5 13	54	71
												110	−5 40	+54	70
															111
															112

	5°			6°			7°			8°			9°		
LHA	Hc	d	Z	Hc	d	Z	Hc	d	Z	Hc	d	Z	Hc	d	Z
	° ′	′	°	° ′	′	°	° ′	′	°	° ′	′	°	° ′	′	°
70	13 42	+54	106	14 36	+53	105	15 29	+53	105	16 22	+54	104	17 16	+53	104
71	13 15	53	105	14 08	54	104	15 02	53	104	15 55	53	103	16 48	53	103
72	12 48	53	104	13 41	53	103	14 34	54	103	15 28	53	102	16 21	53	102
73	12 20	54	103	13 14	53	102	14 07	53	102	15 00	53	101	15 53	53	101
74	11 53	53	102	12 46	53	101	13 39	53	101	14 32	53	101	15 25	53	100
75	11 25	+53	101	12 18	+54	101	13 12	+53	100	14 05	+53	100	14 58	+53	99
76	10 58	53	100	11 51	53	100	12 44	53	99	13 37	53	99	14 30	53	98
77	10 30	53	99	11 23	53	99	12 16	53	98	13 09	53	98	14 02	53	97
78	10 02	53	98	10 55	53	98	11 48	53	97	12 41	53	97	13 34	53	96
79	09 34	53	97	10 27	53	97	11 20	53	96	12 13	53	96	13 06	53	96
80	09 06	+53	97	09 59	+53	96	10 52	+53	96	11 45	+53	95	12 38	+53	95
81	08 38	53	96	09 31	53	95	10 24	53	95	11 17	53	94	12 10	53	94
82	08 10	53	95	09 03	53	94	09 56	53	94	10 49	53	93	11 42	52	93
83	07 42	53	94	08 35	53	93	09 28	53	93	10 21	52	92	11 13	53	92
84	07 14	53	93	08 07	53	93	09 00	52	92	09 52	53	92	10 45	53	91
85	06 46	+53	92	07 39	+52	92	08 31	+53	91	09 24	+53	91	10 17	+53	90
86	06 18	52	91	07 10	53	91	08 03	53	90	08 56	53	90	09 49	53	89
87	05 49	53	90	06 42	53	90	07 35	53	89	08 28	53	89	09 21	53	88
88	05 21	53	89	06 14	53	89	07 07	53	89	08 00	53	88	08 53	52	88
89	04 53	53	89	05 46	53	88	06 39	53	88	07 32	53	87	08 25	52	87
90	04 25	+53	88	05 18	+53	87	06 11	+53	87	07 04	+52	86	07 56	+53	86
91	03 57	53	87	04 50	53	86	05 43	52	86	06 35	53	85	07 28	53	85
92	03 29	53	86	04 22	52	85	05 14	53	85	06 07	53	85	07 00	53	84
93	03 00	53	85	03 53	53	85	04 46	53	85	05 39	53	84	06 32	53	83
94	02 32	53	84	03 25	53	84	04 18	53	84	05 11	53	83	06 04	53	82
95	02 04	+53	83	02 57	+53	83	03 50	+53	83	04 43	+53	82	05 36	+53	81
96	01 37	53	82	02 30	53	82	03 23	53	82	04 16	53	81	05 09	53	81
97	01 09	53	81	02 02	53	81	02 55	53	81	03 48	53	80	04 41	53	80
98	00 41	53	81	01 34	53	80	02 27	53	80	03 20	53	79	04 13	53	79
99	00 13	53	80	01 06	53	79	01 59	53	79	02 52	54	78	03 46	53	78
100	−0 15	+54	79	00 39	+53	78	01 32	+53	78	02 25	+53	77	03 18	+53	77
101	−0 42	53	78	00 11	53	77	01 04	54	77	01 58	53	77	02 51	53	76
102	−1 10	54	77	−0 16	53	77	00 37	53	77	01 30	53	76	02 23	54	75
	−1 37	53	76	−0 44	54	76	00 10	53	76	01 03	53	75	01 56	54	74
	−2 04	53	75	−1 11	53	75	−0 18	54	75	00 36	53	74	01 29	54	73
	−2 32	+54	74	−1 38	+53	74	−0 45	+54	74	00 09	+53	73	01 02	+54	73
	−2 59	54	74	−2 05	53	73	−1 12	54	73	−0 18	53	72	00 35	54	72
	−3 26	54	73	−2 32	54	72	−1 38	53	72	−0 45	54	71	00 09	53	71
	−3 52	53	72	−2 59	54	71	−2 05	54	71	−1 11	53	70	−0 18	54	70
	−4 19	54	71	−3 25	53	70	−2 32	54	70	−1 38	54	70	−0 44	54	69
	−4 46	+54	70	−3 52	+54	69	−2 58	+54	69	−2 04	+54	69	−1 10	+53	68
	−5 12	54	69	−4 18	54	69	−3 24	54	69	−2 30	54	68	−1 36	53	67
	−5 38	54	68	−4 44	54	68	−3 50	54	68	−2 56	54	67	−2 02	54	66
			113	−5 10	54	67	−4 16	54	67	−3 22	54	66	−2 28	54	65
			114	−5 36	54	66	−4 42	54	66	−3 48	54	65	−2 54	55	65
						115	−5 08	+55	65	−4 13	+54	64	−3 19	+54	64
						116	−5 33	55	64	−4 38	54	63	−3 44	54	63
									117	−5 04	55	62	−4 09	54	62
									118	−5 28	54	61	−4 34	55	61
												119	−4 58	54	60
												120	−5 23	+55	59
												121	−5 47	55	58
															122
															123

	10°			11°			12°			13°			14°			
LHA	Hc	d	Z	Hc	d	Z	Hc	d	Z	Hc	d	Z	Hc	d	Z	LHA
	° ′	′	°	° ′	′	°	° ′	′	°	° ′	′	°	° ′	′	°	
70	18 09	+53	103	19 02	+53	103	19 55	+53	102	20 48	+53	102	21 41	+53	101	290
71	17 41	53	102	18 34	53	102	19 27	53	101	20 20	53	101	21 13	53	100	289
72	17 14	53	101	18 07	53	101	19 00	53	100	19 53	52	100	20 45	53	99	288
73	16 46	53	100	17 39	53	100	18 32	53	99	19 25	53	99	20 18	52	98	287
74	16 18	53	100	17 11	53	99	18 04	53	99	18 57	53	98	19 50	52	98	286
75	15 51	+52	99	16 43	+53	98	17 36	+53	98	18 29	+53	97	19 22	+52	97	285
76	15 23	53	98	16 16	52	97	17 08	53	97	18 01	53	96	18 54	52	96	284
77	14 55	53	97	15 48	52	96	16 40	53	96	17 33	53	95	18 26	52	95	283
78	14 27	53	96	15 20	52	95	16 12	53	95	17 05	53	94	17 58	52	94	282
79	13 59	52	95	14 51	53	95	15 44	53	94	16 37	52	94	17 29	53	93	281
80	13 31	+52	94	14 23	+53	94	15 16	+53	93	16 09	+52	93	17 01	+53	92	280
81	13 03	52	93	13 55	53	93	14 48	53	92	15 41	52	92	16 33	53	91	279
82	12 34	53	92	13 27	53	92	14 20	52	91	15 12	53	91	16 05	52	90	278
83	12 06	53	91	12 59	53	91	13 52	52	91	14 44	53	90	15 37	52	90	277
84	11 38	53	91	12 31	52	90	13 23	53	90	14 16	53	89	15 09	52	89	276
85	11 10	+53	90	12 03	+52	89	12 55	+53	89	13 48	+52	88	14 40	+53	88	275
86	10 42	52	89	11 34	53	88	12 27	53	88	13 20	52	87	14 12	53	87	274
87	10 14	52	88	11 06	53	87	11 59	53	87	12 52	52	86	13 44	53	86	273
88	09 45	53	87	10 38	53	87	11 31	53	86	12 24	52	86	13 16	53	85	272
89	09 17	53	86	10 10	53	86	11 03	52	85	11 55	53	85	12 48	53	84	271
90	08 49	+53	85	09 42	+53	85	10 35	+52	84	11 27	+53	84	12 20	+53	83	270
91	08 21	53	84	09 14	53	84	10 07	52	83	10 59	53	83	11 52	53	83	269
92	07 53	53	84	08 46	53	83	09 39	53	83	10 32	52	82	11 24	53	82	268
93	07 25	53	83	08 18	53	82	09 11	53	82	10 04	52	81	10 56	53	81	267
94	06 57	53	82	07 50	53	81	08 43	53	81	09 36	53	80	10 29	52	80	266
95	06 29	+53	81	07 22	+53	80	08 15	+53	80	09 08	+53	80	10 01	+53	79	265
96	06 02	53	80	06 55	53	80	07 48	52	79	08 40	53	79	09 33	53	78	264
97	05 34	53	79	06 27	53	79	07 20	53	78	08 13	53	78	09 06	53	77	263
98	05 06	53	78	05 59	53	78	06 52	53	77	07 45	53	77	08 38	53	76	262
99	04 39	53	77	05 32	53	77	06 25	53	77	07 18	53	76	08 11	53	76	261
100	04 11	+54	77	05 05	+53	76	05 58	+53	76	06 51	+53	75	07 44	+53	75	260
101	03 44	53	76	04 37	53	75	05 30	54	75	06 24	53	74	07 17	53	74	259
102	03 17	53	75	04 10	53	74	05 03	54	74	05 57	53	73	06 50	53	73	258
	02 50	53	74	03 43	53	73	04 36	54	73	05 30	53	73	06 23	53	72	257
	02 23	53	73	03 16	53	73	04 09	54	72	05 03	53	72	05 56	53	71	256
	01 56	+53	72	02 49	+54	72	03 43	+53	71	04 36	+54	71	05 30	+53	70	255
	01 29	54	71	02 23	53	71	03 16	54	70	04 10	53	70	05 03	54	69	254
	01 02	54	70	01 56	54	70	02 50	53	69	03 43	54	69	04 37	53	69	253
	00 36	54	70	01 30	53	69	02 23	54	69	03 17	54	68	04 11	53	68	252
	00 10	53	69	01 03	54	68	01 57	54	68	02 51	54	67	03 45	53	67	251
	−0 17	+54	68	00 37	+54	67	01 31	+54	67	02 25	+54	66	03 19	+54	66	250
	−0 43	54	67	00 11	54	66	01 05	54	66	01 59	54	66	02 53	54	65	249
	−1 08	54	66	−0 14	54	66	00 40	54	65	01 34	54	65	02 28	54	64	248
	−1 34	54	65	−0 40	54	65	00 14	54	64	01 08	54	64	02 02	55	63	247
	−1 59	54	64	−1 05	54	64	−0 11	54	63	00 43	54	63	01 37	55	62	246
	−2 25	+55	63	−1 30	+54	63	−0 36	+54	62	00 18	+55	62	01 13	+54	62	245
	−2 50	55	62	−1 55	54	62	−1 01	54	62	−0 07	55	61	00 48	54	61	244
	−3 15	55	62	−2 20	54	61	−1 26	55	61	−0 31	54	60	00 23	55	60	243
	−3 39	54	61	−2 45	55	60	−1 50	55	60	−0 55	54	59	−0 01	55	59	242
	−4 04	55	60	−3 09	55	59	−2 14	54	59	−1 20	55	58	−0 25	55	58	241
	−4 28	+55	59	−3 33	+55	58	−2 38	+55	58	−1 43	+54	58	−0 49	+55	57	240
	−4 52	55	58	−3 57	55	57	−3 02	55	57	−2 07	55	57	−1 12	55	56	239
	−5 16	55	57	−4 21	55	57	−3 26	55	56	−2 31	55	56	−1 36	55	55	238
	−5 39	55	56	−4 44	55	56	−3 49	55	55	−2 54	55	55	−1 59	56	55	237
			124	−5 07	55	55	−4 12	55	54	−3 17	56	54	−2 21	55	54	236
			125	−5 30	+55	54	−4 35	+56	53	−3 39	+55	53	−2 44	+55	53	235
						126	−4 57	55	53	−4 02	56	52	−3 06	55	52	234
						127	−5 19	55	52	−4 24	56	51	−3 28	55	51	233
						128	−5 41	55	51	−4 46	56	50	−3 50	56	50	232
									129	−5 07	56	49	−4 11	55	49	231
									130	−5 29	+56	49	−4 33	+56	48	230
												131	−4 53	56	47	229
												132	−5 14	56	46	228
												133	−5 34	56	45	227

LAT 62°

0° 1° 2° 3° 4° 5° 6° 7° 8° 9° 10° 11° 12° 13° 14°

S. Lat. {LHA greater than 180°....... Zn=180−Z
{LHA less than 180°........... Zn=180+Z

DECLINATION (0°-14°) SAME NAME AS LATITUDE

LAT 62°

N. Lat. {LHA greater than 180°....... Zn=Z; LHA less than 180°........... Zn=360−Z}

DECLINATION (0°-14°) CONTRARY NAME TO LATITUDE

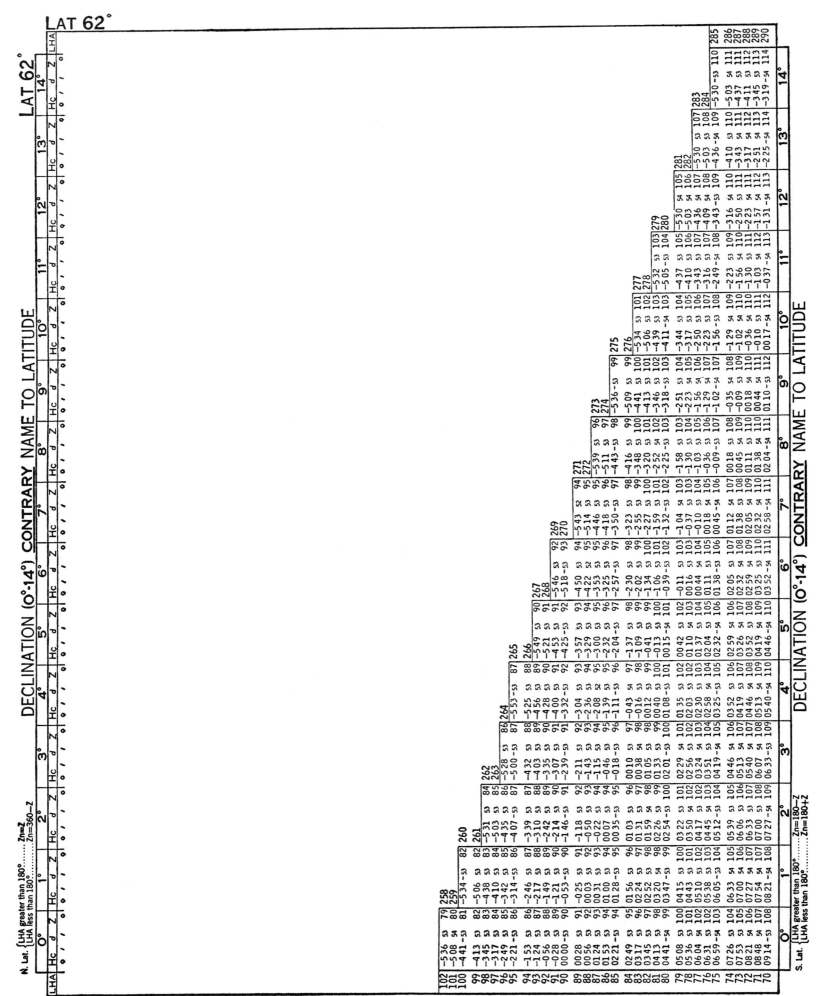

LHA	0° Hc d Z	1° Hc d Z	2° Hc d Z	3° Hc d Z	4° Hc d Z	5° Hc d Z	6° Hc d Z	7° Hc d Z	8° Hc d Z	9° Hc d Z	10° Hc d Z	11° Hc d Z	12° Hc d Z	13° Hc d Z	14° Hc d Z	LHA
	° ′ ′ °	° ′ ′ °	° ′ ′ °	° ′ ′ °	° ′ ′ °	° ′ ′ °	° ′ ′ °	° ′ ′ °	° ′ ′ °	° ′ ′ °	° ′ ′ °	° ′ ′ °	° ′ ′ °	° ′ ′ °	° ′ ′ °	
102	-5 36 53 79	258														
101	-5 08 54 80	259														
100	-4 41 -53 81	-5 34 -53 82	260													
99	-4 13 53 82	-5 06 53 82	261													
98	-3 45 53 83	-4 38 53 83	-5 31 53 84	262												
97	-3 17 53 84	-4 10 53 84	-5 03 53 85	263												
96	-2 49 53 85	-3 42 53 85	-4 35 53 86	-5 28 53 86	264											
95	-2 21 -53 86	-3 14 -53 86	-4 07 -53 87	-5 00 -53 87	-5 53 -53 87	265										
94	-1 53 53 86	-2 46 53 87	-3 39 53 87	-4 32 53 88	-5 25 53 88	266										
93	-1 24 53 87	-2 17 53 88	-3 10 53 88	-4 03 53 89	-4 56 53 89	-5 49 53 90	267									
92	-0 56 53 88	-1 49 53 89	-2 42 53 89	-3 35 53 90	-4 28 53 90	-5 21 53 91	268									
91	-0 28 53 89	-1 21 53 90	-2 14 53 90	-3 07 53 91	-4 00 53 91	-4 53 53 91	-5 46 53 92	269								
90	00 00 -53 90	-0 53 -53 90	-1 46 -53 91	-2 39 -53 91	-3 32 -53 92	-4 25 -53 92	-5 18 -53 93	270								
89	00 28 53 91	-0 25 53 91	-1 18 53 92	-2 11 53 92	-3 04 53 93	-3 57 53 93	-4 50 53 94	-5 43 52 94	271							
88	00 56 53 92	00 03 53 92	-0 50 53 93	-1 43 53 93	-2 36 53 94	-3 29 53 94	-4 22 52 95	-5 14 53 95	272							
87	01 24 53 93	00 31 53 93	-0 22 53 94	-1 15 53 94	-2 08 52 95	-3 00 53 95	-3 53 53 95	-4 46 53 95	-5 39 53 96	273						
86	01 53 53 94	01 00 53 94	00 07 53 94	-0 46 53 95	-1 39 53 95	-2 32 53 96	-3 25 53 96	-4 18 53 96	-5 11 53 97	274						
85	02 21 -53 94	01 28 -53 95	00 35 -53 95	-0 18 -53 96	-1 11 -53 96	-2 04 -53 97	-2 57 -53 97	-3 50 -53 97	-4 43 -53 98	-5 36 -53 99	275					
84	02 49 53 95	01 56 53 96	01 03 53 96	00 10 53 97	-0 43 54 97	-1 37 53 98	-2 30 53 98	-3 23 53 98	-4 16 53 99	-5 09 53 99	276					
83	03 17 53 96	02 24 53 97	01 31 53 97	00 38 54 98	-0 16 53 98	-1 09 53 99	-2 02 53 99	-2 55 53 99	-3 48 53 100	-4 41 53 100	-5 34 53 101	277				
82	03 45 53 97	02 52 53 98	01 59 54 98	01 05 53 98	00 12 53 99	-0 41 53 99	-1 34 53 100	-2 27 53 100	-3 20 53 101	-4 13 53 101	-5 06 53 102	278				
81	04 13 53 98	03 20 54 98	02 26 53 99	01 33 53 99	00 40 53 100	-0 13 53 100	-1 06 53 101	-1 59 53 101	-2 52 54 102	-3 46 53 102	-4 39 53 103	-5 32 53 103	279			
80	04 41 -54 99	03 47 -53 99	02 54 -53 100	02 01 -53 100	01 08 -53 101	00 15 -54 101	-0 39 -53 102	-1 32 -53 102	-2 25 -53 103	-3 18 -53 103	-4 11 -54 103	-5 05 -53 104	280			
79	05 08 53 100	04 15 53 100	03 22 53 101	02 29 54 101	01 35 53 102	00 42 53 102	-0 11 53 103	-1 04 54 103	-1 58 53 103	-2 51 53 104	-3 44 53 104	-4 37 53 105	-5 30 54 105	281		
78	05 36 53 101	04 43 53 101	03 50 54 102	02 56 53 102	02 03 53 102	01 10 54 103	00 16 53 103	-0 37 53 103	-1 30 53 104	-2 23 54 105	-3 17 53 105	-4 10 53 106	-5 03 54 106	282		
77	06 04 54 102	05 10 53 102	04 17 53 102	03 24 54 103	02 30 53 103	01 37 53 104	00 44 54 104	-0 10 53 104	-1 03 53 105	-1 56 54 106	-2 50 53 106	-3 43 53 107	-4 36 54 107	-5 30 53 107	283	
76	06 31 53 102	05 38 53 103	04 45 54 103	03 51 53 104	02 58 54 104	02 04 53 105	01 11 53 105	00 18 54 105	-0 36 53 106	-1 29 54 107	-2 23 53 107	-3 16 53 107	-4 09 54 108	-5 03 53 108	284	
75	06 59 -54 103	06 05 -53 104	05 12 -53 104	04 19 -54 105	03 25 -53 105	02 32 -54 106	01 38 -53 106	00 45 -54 106	-0 09 -53 107	-1 02 -54 107	-1 56 -53 108	-2 49 -54 108	-3 43 -53 109	-4 36 -54 109	-5 30 -53 110	285
74	07 26 53 104	06 33 54 105	05 39 53 105	04 46 54 106	03 52 53 106	02 59 54 106	02 05 53 107	01 12 54 107	00 18 53 108	-0 35 54 108	-1 29 54 109	-2 23 53 109	-3 16 54 110	-4 10 53 110	-5 03 54 111	286
73	07 53 53 105	07 00 54 106	06 06 53 106	05 13 54 107	04 19 53 107	03 26 54 107	02 32 54 108	01 38 53 108	00 45 54 109	-0 09 53 109	-1 02 54 110	-1 56 54 110	-2 50 53 111	-3 43 54 111	-4 37 53 111	287
72	08 21 54 106	07 27 54 107	06 33 53 107	05 40 54 107	04 46 54 108	03 52 53 108	02 59 54 109	02 05 54 109	01 11 53 110	00 18 54 110	-0 36 54 110	-1 30 53 111	-2 23 54 111	-3 17 54 112	-4 11 53 112	288
71	08 48 54 107	07 54 54 107	07 00 53 108	06 07 54 108	05 13 54 109	04 19 54 109	03 25 53 110	02 32 54 110	01 38 54 110	00 44 54 111	-0 10 53 111	-1 03 54 112	-1 57 54 112	-2 51 54 113	-3 45 53 113	289
70	09 14 -53 108	08 21 -54 108	07 27 -54 109	06 33 -53 109	05 40 -54 110	04 46 -54 110	03 52 -54 111	02 58 -54 111	02 04 -54 111	01 10 -53 112	00 17 -54 112	-0 37 -54 113	-1 31 -54 113	-2 25 -54 114	-3 19 -54 114	290
	0°	1°	2°	3°	4°	5°	6°	7°	8°	9°	10°	11°	12°	13°	14°	

S. Lat. {LHA greater than 180°....... Zn=180−Z; LHA less than 180°........... Zn=180+Z}

DECLINATION (0°-14°) CONTRARY NAME TO LATITUDE

LAT 62°

N. Lat. {LHA greater than 180°....... Zn=Z; LHA less than 180°........... Zn=360−Z}

DECLINATION (0°-14°) CONTRARY NAME TO LATITUDE

LHA	0° Hc	0° d	0° Z	1° Hc	1° d	1° Z	2° Hc	2° d	2° Z	3° Hc	3° d	3° Z	4° Hc	4° d	4° Z
	° ′	′	°	° ′	′	°	° ′	′	°	° ′	′	°	° ′	′	°
69	09 41	54	109	08 47	53	109	07 54	54	110	07 00	54	110	06 06	54	111
68	10 08	54	110	09 14	54	110	08 20	54	111	07 26	54	111	06 32	54	111
67	10 34	54	111	09 40	54	111	08 46	54	111	07 52	54	112	06 58	54	112
66	11 01	54	112	10 07	54	112	09 13	55	112	08 18	54	113	07 24	54	113
65	11 27	-54	112	10 33	-54	113	09 39	-55	113	08 44	-54	114	07 50	-54	114
64	11 53	55	113	10 58	54	114	10 04	54	114	09 10	54	115	08 16	54	115
63	12 18	54	114	11 24	54	115	10 30	54	115	09 36	55	116	08 41	54	116
62	12 44	54	115	11 50	55	116	10 55	54	116	10 01	55	116	09 06	54	117
61	13 09	54	116	12 15	54	117	11 21	55	117	10 26	55	117	09 31	54	118
60	13 35	-55	117	12 40	-54	117	11 46	-55	118	10 51	-55	118	09 56	-54	119
59	14 00	55	118	13 05	55	118	12 10	54	119	11 16	55	119	10 21	55	120
58	14 24	54	119	13 30	55	119	12 35	55	120	11 40	55	120	10 45	55	121
57	14 49	55	120	13 54	55	120	12 59	55	121	12 04	55	121	11 09	55	122
56	15 13	55	121	14 18	55	121	13 23	55	122	12 28	55	122	11 33	55	122
55	15 37	-55	122	14 42	-55	122	13 47	-55	123	12 52	-55	123	11 57	-55	123
54	16 01	55	123	15 06	55	123	14 11	55	124	13 16	56	124	12 20	55	124
53	16 25	56	124	15 29	55	124	14 34	55	124	13 39	56	125	12 43	55	125
52	16 48	55	125	15 53	56	125	14 57	55	125	14 02	56	126	13 06	55	126
51	17 11	55	126	16 16	56	126	15 20	55	126	14 25	56	127	13 29	56	127
50	17 34	-56	127	16 38	-55	127	15 43	-56	127	14 47	-56	128	13 51	-55	128
49	17 56	55	128	17 01	56	128	16 05	56	128	15 09	56	129	14 13	56	129
48	18 19	56	129	17 23	56	129	16 27	56	129	15 31	56	130	14 35	56	130
47	18 40	55	130	17 45	56	130	16 49	56	130	15 53	57	131	14 56	56	131
46	19 02	56	131	18 06	56	131	17 10	56	131	16 14	56	132	15 18	57	132
45	19 23	-56	131	18 27	-56	132	17 31	-56	132	16 35	-57	133	15 38	-56	133
44	19 44	56	132	18 48	56	133	17 52	57	133	16 55	56	134	15 59	57	134
43	20 05	57	133	19 08	56	134	18 12	56	134	17 16	57	135	16 19	57	135
42	20 25	56	134	19 29	57	135	18 32	57	135	17 35	56	136	16 39	57	136
41	20 45	57	135	19 48	56	136	18 52	57	136	17 55	57	137	16 58	57	137
40	21 05	-57	137	20 08	-57	137	19 11	-57	137	18 14	-57	138	17 17	-57	138
39	21 24	57	138	20 27	57	138	19 30	57	138	18 33	57	139	17 36	57	139
38	21 43	57	139	20 46	57	139	19 49	57	139	18 52	58	140	17 54	57	140
37	22 01	57	140	21 04	57	140	20 07	57	140	19 10	58	141	18 12	57	141
36	22 19	57	141	21 22	57	141	20 25	58	141	19 27	57	142	18 30	57	142
35	22 37	-57	142	21 40	-58	142	20 42	-57	142	19 45	-58	143	18 47	-57	143
34	22 54	57	143	21 57	58	143	20 59	57	143	20 02	58	144	19 04	58	144
33	23 11	57	144	22 14	58	144	21 16	58	144	20 18	58	145	19 20	57	145
32	23 28	58	145	22 30	58	145	21 32	58	145	20 34	58	146	19 36	57	146
31	23 44	58	146	22 46	58	146	21 48	58	146	20 50	58	147	19 52	58	147
30	23 59	-58	147	23 01	-58	147	22 03	-58	147	21 05	-58	148	20 07	-58	148
29	24 15	58	148	23 17	59	148	22 18	58	148	21 20	58	149	20 22	58	149
28	24 29	58	149	23 31	58	149	22 33	58	150	21 35	59	150	20 36	58	150
27	24 44	59	150	23 45	58	150	22 47	58	151	21 49	59	151	20 50	58	151
26	24 58	59	151	23 59	58	151	23 01	59	152	22 02	58	152	21 04	59	152
25	25 11	-59	152	24 12	-58	152	23 14	-59	153	22 15	-58	153	21 17	-59	153
24	25 24	59	153	24 25	58	154	23 27	59	154	22 28	59	154	21 29	59	154
23	25 36	58	154	24 38	59	155	23 39	59	155	22 40	59	155	21 41	59	155
22	25 48	59	155	24 49	58	156	23 51	59	156	22 52	59	156	21 53	59	156
21	26 00	59	157	25 01	59	157	24 02	59	157	23 03	59	157	22 04	59	157
20	26 11	-59	158	25 12	-59	158	24 13	-59	158	23 14	-60	158	22 14	-59	158
19	26 21	59	159	25 22	59	159	24 23	59	159	23 24	59	159	22 25	60	159
18	26 31	59	160	25 32	59	160	24 33	59	160	23 34	60	160	22 34	59	161
17	26 41	60	161	25 41	59	161	24 42	59	161	23 43	60	161	22 43	59	162
16	26 50	60	162	25 50	59	162	24 51	60	162	23 51	59	163	22 52	59	163
15	26 58	-59	163	25 59	-60	163	24 59	-59	163	24 00	-60	164	23 00	-59	164
14	27 06	60	164	26 06	59	164	25 07	60	165	24 07	59	165	23 08	60	165
13	27 13	59	165	26 14	60	166	25 14	59	166	24 15	60	166	23 15	60	166
12	27 20	59	167	26 21	60	167	25 21	60	167	24 21	59	167	23 22	60	167
11	27 27	60	168	26 27	60	168	25 27	60	168	24 27	59	168	23 28	60	168
10	27 32	-59	169	26 33	-60	169	25 33	-60	169	24 33	-60	169	23 33	-59	169
9	27 38	60	170	26 38	60	170	25 38	60	170	24 38	60	170	23 38	59	170
8	27 42	60	171	26 42	59	171	25 43	60	171	24 43	60	171	23 43	60	171
7	27 46	59	172	26 47	60	172	25 47	60	172	24 47	60	172	23 47	60	172
6	27 50	60	173	26 50	60	173	25 50	60	173	24 50	60	173	23 50	60	174
5	27 53	-60	174	26 53	-60	174	25 53	-60	174	24 53	-60	175	23 53	-60	175
4	27 56	60	176	26 56	60	176	25 56	60	176	24 56	60	176	23 56	60	176
3	27 58	60	177	26 58	60	177	25 58	60	177	24 58	60	177	23 58	60	177
2	27 59	60	178	26 59	60	178	25 59	60	178	24 59	60	178	23 59	60	178
1	28 00	60	179	27 00	60	179	26 00	60	179	25 00	60	179	24 00	60	179
0	28 00	-60	180	27 00	-60	180	26 00	-60	180	25 00	-60	180	24 00	-60	180

LHA	5° Hc	5° d	5° Z	6° Hc	6° d	6° Z	7° Hc	7° d	7° Z	8° Hc	8° d	8° Z	9° Hc	9° d	9° Z
	° ′	′	°	° ′	′	°	° ′	′	°	° ′	′	°	° ′	′	°
69	05 12	54	111	04 18	54	111	03 24	54	111	02 30	54	112	01 36	53	113
68	05 38	54	112	04 44	54	112	03 50	54	112	02 56	54	113	02 02	54	114
67	06 04	54	113	05 10	54	113	04 16	54	113	03 22	54	114	02 28	54	115
66	06 30	54	114	05 36	54	114	04 42	54	114	03 48	54	115	02 54	55	115
65	06 56	-54	115	06 02	-54	115	05 08	-55	115	04 13	-54	116	03 19	-54	116
64	07 22	55	116	06 27	54	116	05 33	55	116	04 38	54	117	03 44	54	117
63	07 47	55	116	06 52	54	117	05 58	54	117	05 04	55	118	04 09	54	118
62	08 12	55	117	07 17	54	118	06 23	55	118	05 28	54	119	04 34	55	119
61	08 37	55	118	07 42	54	119	06 48	55	119	05 53	55	120	04 58	54	120
60	09 02	-55	119	08 07	-55	120	07 12	-55	120	06 17	-54	120	05 23	-55	121
59	09 26	55	120	08 31	54	121	07 37	55	121	06 42	55	121	05 47	55	122
58	09 50	55	121	08 55	54	121	08 01	55	122	07 06	55	122	06 11	55	123
57	10 14	55	122	09 19	55	122	08 24	55	123	07 29	55	123	06 34	55	124
56	10 38	55	123	09 43	55	123	08 48	55	124	07 53	55	124	06 58	56	124
55	11 02	-55	124	10 07	-56	124	09 11	-55	125	08 16	-55	125	07 21	-56	125
54	11 25	55	125	10 30	56	125	09 34	55	126	08 39	55	126	07 44	56	126
53	11 48	55	126	10 53	56	126	09 57	55	126	09 02	56	127	08 06	55	127
52	12 11	56	127	11 15	55	127	10 20	56	127	09 24	56	128	08 28	55	128
51	12 33	55	128	11 38	56	128	10 42	56	128	09 46	56	129	08 50	55	129
50	12 56	-56	129	12 00	-56	129	11 04	-56	129	10 08	-56	130	09 12	-56	130
49	13 17	55	129	12 22	56	130	11 26	56	130	10 30	56	131	09 34	56	131
48	13 39	56	130	12 43	56	131	11 47	56	131	10 51	56	132	09 55	56	132
47	14 00	56	131	13 04	56	132	12 08	56	132	11 12	56	132	10 16	57	133
46	14 21	56	132	13 25	56	133	12 29	57	133	11 32	56	133	10 36	56	134
45	14 42	-56	133	13 46	-57	134	12 49	-56	134	11 53	-57	134	10 56	-56	135
44	15 02	56	134	14 06	57	135	13 09	56	135	12 13	57	135	11 16	56	136
43	15 22	56	135	14 26	57	136	13 29	57	136	12 32	56	136	11 36	57	137
42	15 42	57	136	14 45	56	137	13 49	57	137	12 52	57	137	11 55	57	138
41	16 01	56	137	15 05	57	138	14 08	57	138	13 11	57	138	12 14	57	139
40	16 20	-57	138	15 23	-57	139	14 26	-57	139	13 29	-57	139	12 32	-57	139
39	16 39	57	139	15 42	57	139	14 45	57	140	13 48	58	140	12 50	57	140
38	16 57	57	140	16 00	57	140	15 03	57	141	14 06	58	141	13 08	57	141
37	17 15	57	141	16 18	58	141	15 20	57	142	14 23	57	142	13 26	58	142
36	17 33	58	142	16 35	57	142	15 38	58	143	14 40	57	143	13 43	58	143
35	17 50	-58	143	16 52	-57	143	15 55	-58	144	14 57	-58	144	13 59	-57	144
34	18 06	57	144	17 09	58	144	16 11	58	145	15 13	57	145	14 16	58	145
33	18 23	58	145	17 25	58	145	16 27	58	146	15 29	58	146	14 31	57	146
32	18 39	58	146	17 41	58	146	16 43	58	147	15 45	58	147	14 47	58	147
31	18 54	58	147	17 56	58	147	16 58	58	148	16 00	58	148	15 02	58	148
30	19 09	-58	148	18 11	-58	148	17 13	-58	149	16 15	-58	149	15 17	-59	149
29	19 24	58	149	18 26	59	150	17 27	58	150	16 29	58	150	15 31	59	150
28	19 38	58	150	18 40	59	151	17 41	58	151	16 43	58	151	15 45	59	151
27	19 52	59	151	18 53	58	152	17 55	59	152	16 56	58	152	15 58	59	152
26	20 05	58	152	19 07	59	153	18 08	59	153	17 09	58	153	16 11	59	153
25	20 18	-59	153	19 19	-58	154	18 21	-59	154	17 22	-59	154	16 23	-58	154
24	20 30	58	154	19 32	59	155	18 33	59	155	17 34	59	155	16 35	59	155
23	20 42	59	155	19 43	58	156	18 45	59	156	17 46	59	156	16 47	59	156
22	20 54	59	157	19 55	59	157	18 56	59	157	17 57	59	157	16 58	59	157
21	21 05	59	158	20 06	59	158	19 07	59	158	18 08	59	158	17 09	59	158
20	21 15	-59	159	20 16	-59	159	19 17	-59	159	18 18	-59	159	17 19	-59	159
19	21 25	59	160	20 26	59	160	19 27	59	160	18 28	59	160	17 29	60	160
18	21 35	59	161	20 36	60	161	19 36	59	161	18 37	59	161	17 38	59	161
17	21 44	59	162	20 45	60	162	19 45	59	162	18 46	59	162	17 47	60	162
16	21 53	60	163	20 53	59	163	19 54	60	163	18 54	59	163	17 55	59	163
15	22 01	-60	164	21 01	-59	164	20 02	-60	164	19 02	-59	164	18 03	-60	164
14	22 08	59	165	21 09	60	165	20 09	59	165	19 10	60	165	18 10	59	165
13	22 15	59	166	21 16	60	166	20 16	59	166	19 17	60	166	18 17	60	167
12	22 22	60	167	21 22	59	167	20 23	60	167	19 23	60	167	18 23	59	168
11	22 28	60	168	21 28	59	168	20 29	60	168	19 29	60	168	18 29	60	169
10	22 34	-60	169	21 34	-60	169	20 34	-60	169	19 34	-60	170	18 34	-59	170
9	22 39	60	170	21 39	60	170	20 39	60	170	19 39	60	171	18 39	60	171
8	22 43	60	171	21 43	60	171	20 43	59	172	19 44	60	172	18 44	60	172
7	22 47	60	172	21 47	60	173	20 47	60	173	19 47	60	173	18 47	59	173
6	22 50	59	174	21 51	60	174	20 51	60	174	19 51	60	174	18 51	60	174
5	22 53	-60	175	21 53	-59	175	20 54	-60	175	19 54	-60	175	18 54	-60	175
4	22 56	60	176	21 56	60	176	20 56	60	176	19 56	60	176	18 56	60	176
3	22 58	60	177	21 58	60	177	20 58	60	177	19 58	60	177	18 58	60	177
2	22 59	60	178	21 59	60	178	20 59	60	178	19 59	60	178	18 59	60	178
1	23 00	60	179	22 00	60	179	21 00	60	179	20 00	60	179	19 00	60	179
0	23 00	-60	180	22 00	-60	180	21 00	-60	180	20 00	-60	180	19 00	-60	180

LHA	10° Hc	10° d	10° Z	11° Hc	11° d	11° Z	12° Hc	12° d	12° Z	13° Hc	13° d	13° Z	14° Hc	14° d	14° Z	LHA
	° ′	′	°	° ′	′	°	° ′	′	°	° ′	′	°	° ′	′	°	
69	00 43	54	113	-0 11	54	114	-1 05	54	114	-1 59	54	114	-2 53	54	115	291
68	01 08	54	114	00 14	54	114	-0 40	54	115	-1 34	54	115	-2 28	54	116	292
67	01 34	54	115	00 40	54	115	-0 14	54	116	-1 08	54	116	-2 02	55	117	293
66	01 59	54	116	01 05	54	116	00 11	54	117	-0 43	54	117	-1 37	55	118	294
65	02 25	-55	117	01 30	-54	117	00 36	-54	118	-0 18	-55	118	-1 13	-54	118	295
64	02 50	55	118	01 55	54	118	01 01	54	118	00 07	55	119	-0 48	54	119	296
63	03 15	55	118	02 20	54	119	01 26	55	119	00 31	54	120	-0 23	55	120	297
62	03 39	54	119	02 45	55	120	01 50	55	120	00 55	54	121	00 01	55	121	298
61	04 04	55	120	03 09	55	121	02 14	54	121	01 20	55	122	00 25	55	122	299
60	04 28	-55	121	03 33	-55	122	02 38	-55	122	01 43	-54	122	00 49	-55	123	300
59	04 52	55	122	03 57	55	123	03 02	55	123	02 07	55	123	01 12	55	124	301
58	05 16	55	123	04 21	55	123	03 26	55	124	02 31	55	124	01 36	55	125	302
57	05 39	55	124	04 44	55	124	03 49	55	125	02 54	55	125	01 59	56	125	303
56	06 02	55	125	05 07	55	125	04 12	55	126	03 17	56	126	02 21	55	126	304
55	06 25	-55	126	05 30	-55	126	04 35	-56	127	03 39	-55	127	02 44	-55	127	305
54	06 48	55	127	05 53	56	127	04 57	55	127	04 02	56	128	03 06	55	128	306
53	07 11	56	128	06 15	56	128	05 19	55	128	04 24	56	129	03 28	55	129	307
52	07 33	56	129	06 37	56	129	05 41	55	129	04 46	56	130	03 50	56	130	308
51	07 55	56	129	06 59	56	130	06 03	56	130	05 07	56	131	04 11	55	131	309
50	08 16	-56	130	07 20	-55	131	06 25	-56	131	05 29	-56	131	04 33	-56	132	310
49	08 38	56	131	07 42	56	132	06 46	56	132	05 50	57	132	04 53	56	133	311
48	08 59	56	132	08 03	57	133	07 06	56	133	06 10	56	133	05 14	56	134	312
47	09 19	56	133	08 23	56	134	07 27	56	134	06 31	57	134	05 34	56	135	313
46	09 40	57	134	08 43	56	134	07 47	56	135	06 51	57	135	05 54	56	135	314
45	10 00	-57	135	09 03	-56	135	08 07	-57	136	07 10	-56	136	06 14	-57	136	315
44	10 20	57	136	09 23	57	136	08 26	56	137	07 30	57	137	06 33	57	137	316
43	10 39	57	137	09 42	56	137	08 46	57	138	07 49	57	138	06 52	57	138	317
42	10 58	57	138	10 01	57	138	09 04	56	139	08 08	57	139	07 11	57	139	318
41	11 17	57	139	10 20	57	139	09 23	57	139	08 26	57	140	07 29	57	140	319
40	11 35	-57	140	10 38	-57	140	09 41	-57	140	08 44	-57	141	07 47	-57	141	320
39	11 53	57	141	10 56	57	141	09 59	57	141	09 02	58	142	08 04	57	142	321
38	12 11	57	142	11 14	58	142	10 16	57	142	09 19	57	143	08 22	58	143	322
37	12 28	57	143	11 31	58	143	10 33	57	143	09 36	58	144	08 38	57	144	323
36	12 45	57	144	11 48	58	144	10 50	58	144	09 52	57	145	08 55	58	145	324
35	13 02	-58	145	12 04	-58	145	11 06	-57	145	10 09	-58	145	09 11	-58	146	325
34	13 18	58	146	12 20	58	146	11 22	58	146	10 24	57	146	09 27	58	147	326
33	13 34	58	147	12 36	58	147	11 38	58	147	10 40	58	147	09 42	58	148	327
32	13 49	58	148	12 51	58	148	11 53	58	148	10 55	58	148	09 57	58	149	328
31	14 04	58	149	13 06	58	149	12 08	59	149	11 09	58	149	10 11	58	150	329
30	14 18	-58	150	13 20	-58	150	12 22	-58	150	11 24	-59	150	10 25	-58	150	330
29	14 32	58	150	13 34	58	151	12 36	59	151	11 37	58	151	10 39	58	151	331
28	14 46	58	151	13 48	59	152	12 49	58	152	11 51	59	152	10 52	58	152	332
27	14 59	58	152	14 01	59	153	13 02	58	153	12 04	59	153	11 05	58	153	333
26	15 12	58	153	14 14	59	154	13 15	59	154	12 16	58	154	11 18	59	154	334
25	15 25	-59	154	14 26	-59	155	13 27	-59	155	12 28	-58	155	11 30	-59	155	335
24	15 36	58	155	14 38	59	156	13 39	59	156	12 40	59	156	11 41	59	156	336
23	15 48	59	156	14 49	59	157	13 50	59	157	12 51	59	157	11 52	59	157	337
22	15 59	59	157	15 00	59	158	14 01	59	158	13 02	59	158	12 03	59	158	338
21	16 10	59	158	15 11	60	159	14 11	59	159	13 12	59	159	12 13	59	159	339
20	16 20	-59	160	15 21	-60	160	14 21	-59	160	13 22	-59	160	12 23	-59	160	340
19	16 29	59	161	15 30	59	161	14 31	59	161	13 32	60	161	12 32	59	161	341
18	16 39	60	162	15 39	59	162	14 40	59	162	13 41	60	162	12 41	59	162	342
17	16 47	59	163	15 48	60	163	14 48	59	163	13 49	59	163	12 50	60	163	343
16	16 56	60	164	15 56	59	164	14 57	60	164	13 57	59	164	12 58	60	164	344
15	17 03	-59	165	16 04	-60	165	15 04	-59	165	14 05	-60	165	13 05	-59	165	345
14	17 11	60	166	16 11	60	166	15 11	59	166	14 12	60	166	13 12	59	166	346
13	17 17	59	167	16 18	60	167	15 18	60	167	14 18	59	167	13 19	60	167	347
12	17 24	60	168	16 24	60	168	15 24	59	168	14 25	60	168	13 25	60	168	348
11	17 29	59	169	16 30	60	169	15 30	60	169	14 30	60	169	13 30	59	169	349
10	17 35	-60	170	16 35	-60	170	15 35	-60	170	14 35	-59	170	13 36	-60	170	350
9	17 39	59	171	16 40	60	171	15 40	60	171	14 40	60	171	13 40	60	171	351
8	17 44	60	172	16 44	60	172	15 44	60	172	14 44	60	172	13 44	60	172	352
7	17 48	60	173	16 48	60	173	15 48	60	173	14 48	60	173	13 48	60	173	353
6	17 51	60	174	16 51	60	174	15 51	60	174	14 51	60	174	13 51	60	174	354
5	17 54	-60	175	16 54	-60	175	15 54	-60	175	14 54	-60	175	13 54	-60	175	355
4	17 56	60	176	16 56	60	176	15 56	60	176	14 56	60	176	13 56	60	176	356
3	17 58	60	177	16 58	60	177	15 58	60	177	14 58	60	177	13 58	60	177	357
2	17 59	60	178	16 59	60	178	15 59	60	178	14 59	60	178	13 59	60	178	358
1	18 00	60	179	17 00	60	179	16 00	60	179	15 00	60	179	14 00	60	179	359
0	18 00	-60	180	17 00	-60	180	16 00	-60	180	15 00	-60	180	14 00	-60	180	360

S. Lat. {LHA greater than 180°....... Zn=180−Z; LHA less than 180°........... Zn=180+Z}

DECLINATION (0°-14°) CONTRARY NAME TO LATITUDE

N. Lat. {LHA greater than 180°....... Zn=Z; LHA less than 180°........... Zn=360−Z}

DECLINATION (15°-29°) **SAME** NAME AS LATITUDE

LHA	15° Hc	d	Z	16° Hc	d	Z	17° Hc	d	Z	18° Hc	d	Z	19° Hc	d	Z	LHA
	° ′	′	°	° ′	′	°	° ′	′	°	° ′	′	°	° ′	′	°	
0	43 00	+60	180	44 00	+60	180	45 00	+60	180	46 00	+60	180	47 00	+60	180	360
1	43 00	60	179	44 00	60	179	45 00	60	179	46 00	60	179	47 00	60	179	359
2	42 59	60	177	43 59	60	177	44 59	60	177	45 59	60	177	46 59	60	177	358
3	42 57	60	176	43 57	60	176	44 57	60	176	45 57	60	176	46 57	60	176	357
4	42 55	60	175	43 55	60	175	44 55	60	175	45 55	60	175	46 55	60	175	356
5	42 52	+60	173	43 52	+60	173	44 52	+60	173	45 52	+60	173	46 52	+59	173	355
6	42 48	60	172	43 48	60	172	44 48	60	172	45 48	60	172	46 48	60	172	354
7	42 44	60	171	43 44	60	171	44 44	60	171	45 44	59	170	46 43	60	170	353
8	42 39	60	170	43 39	60	169	44 39	60	169	45 39	59	169	46 38	60	169	352
9	42 34	60	168	43 34	59	168	44 33	60	168	45 33	60	168	46 33	59	168	351
10	42 28	+59	167	43 27	+60	167	44 27	+60	167	45 27	+59	166	46 26	+60	166	350
11	42 21	60	166	43 21	59	165	44 20	60	165	45 20	59	165	46 19	60	165	349
12	42 14	59	164	43 13	60	164	44 13	59	164	45 12	60	164	46 12	59	164	348
13	42 06	59	163	43 05	60	163	44 05	59	163	45 04	59	162	46 03	59	162	347
14	41 57	60	162	42 57	59	162	43 56	59	161	44 55	59	161	45 54	59	161	346
15	41 48	+59	160	42 47	+59	160	43 46	+60	160	44 46	+59	160	45 45	+59	160	345
16	41 38	59	159	42 37	60	159	43 37	59	159	44 36	59	158	45 35	58	158	344
17	41 28	59	158	42 27	59	158	43 26	59	157	44 25	59	157	45 24	59	157	343
18	41 17	59	157	42 16	59	156	43 15	59	156	44 14	58	156	45 12	59	156	342
19	41 06	58	155	42 04	59	155	43 03	59	155	44 02	58	155	45 00	59	154	341
20	40 54	+58	154	41 52	+59	154	42 51	+58	154	43 49	+59	153	44 48	+58	153	340
21	40 41	59	153	41 40	58	153	42 38	58	152	43 36	59	152	44 35	58	152	339
22	40 28	58	152	41 26	59	151	42 25	58	151	43 23	58	151	44 21	58	150	338
23	40 14	58	150	41 12	59	150	42 11	58	150	43 09	58	149	44 07	58	149	337
24	40 00	58	149	40 58	58	149	41 56	58	149	42 54	58	148	43 52	58	148	336
25	39 45	+58	148	40 43	+58	148	41 41	+58	147	42 39	+58	147	43 37	+57	147	335
26	39 30	58	147	40 28	58	146	41 26	57	146	42 23	58	146	43 21	57	145	334
27	39 14	58	146	40 12	58	145	41 10	57	145	42 07	58	144	43 05	57	144	333
28	38 58	58	144	39 56	57	144	40 53	58	144	41 51	57	143	42 48	57	143	332
29	38 42	57	143	39 39	57	143	40 36	57	142	41 33	58	142	42 31	57	142	331
30	38 24	+58	142	39 22	+57	142	40 19	+57	141	41 16	+57	141	42 13	+57	140	330
31	38 07	57	141	39 04	57	140	40 01	57	140	40 58	57	140	41 55	56	139	329
32	37 49	57	140	38 46	57	139	39 43	56	139	40 39	57	138	41 36	56	138	328
33	37 30	57	139	38 27	57	138	39 24	56	138	40 20	57	137	41 17	56	137	327
34	37 11	57	137	38 08	57	137	39 05	56	137	40 01	56	136	40 57	56	136	326
35	36 52	+57	136	37 49	+56	136	38 45	+56	135	39 41	+56	135	40 37	+56	134	325
36	36 32	57	135	37 29	56	135	38 25	56	134	39 21	56	134	40 17	56	133	324
37	36 12	57	134	37 09	56	134	38 05	56	133	39 01	55	133	39 56	56	132	323
38	35 52	56	133	36 48	56	132	37 44	56	132	38 40	55	131	39 35	56	131	322
39	35 31	56	132	36 27	56	131	37 23	55	131	38 18	56	130	39 14	55	130	321
40	35 10	+56	131	36 06	+55	130	37 01	+56	130	37 57	+55	129	38 52	+55	129	320
41	34 48	56	130	35 44	55	129	36 39	56	129	37 35	55	128	38 30	55	128	319
42	34 26	56	128	35 22	55	128	36 17	55	128	37 12	55	127	38 07	55	127	318
43	34 04	55	127	34 59	56	127	35 55	55	126	36 50	55	126	37 45	54	125	317
44	33 42	55	126	34 37	55	126	35 32	55	125	36 27	54	125	37 21	55	124	316
45	33 19	+55	125	34 14	+55	125	35 09	+54	124	36 03	+55	124	36 58	+55	123	315
46	32 56	54	124	33 50	55	124	34 45	55	123	35 40	54	123	36 34	55	122	314
47	32 32	55	123	33 27	54	123	34 21	55	122	35 16	54	122	36 10	55	121	313
48	32 08	55	122	33 03	54	122	33 57	55	121	34 52	54	121	35 46	54	120	312
49	31 44	55	121	32 39	54	121	33 33	54	120	34 27	55	120	35 22	53	119	311
50	31 20	+54	120	32 14	+55	120	33 09	+54	119	34 03	+54	118	34 57	+54	118	310
51	30 56	54	119	31 50	54	118	32 44	54	118	33 38	54	117	34 32	53	117	309
52	30 31	54	118	31 25	54	117	32 19	54	117	33 13	54	116	34 07	53	116	308
53	30 06	54	117	31 00	54	116	31 54	53	116	32 47	54	115	33 41	54	115	307
54	29 41	53	116	30 34	54	115	31 28	54	115	32 22	53	114	33 15	54	114	306
55	29 15	+54	115	30 09	+54	114	31 03	+53	114	31 56	+54	113	32 50	+53	113	305
56	28 49	54	114	29 43	54	113	30 37	53	113	31 30	53	112	32 23	54	112	304
57	28 24	53	113	29 17	54	112	30 11	53	112	31 04	53	111	31 57	53	111	303
58	27 58	53	112	28 51	53	112	29 44	54	111	30 38	53	110	31 31	53	110	302
59	27 31	54	111	28 25	53	111	29 18	53	110	30 11	53	109	31 04	53	109	301
60	27 05	+53	110	27 58	+53	110	28 51	+54	109	29 45	+53	109	30 38	+52	108	300
61	26 38	54	109	27 32	53	109	28 25	53	108	29 18	53	108	30 11	52	107	299
62	26 12	53	108	27 05	53	108	27 58	53	107	28 51	53	107	29 44	52	106	298
63	25 45	53	107	26 38	53	107	27 31	53	106	28 24	52	106	29 16	53	105	297
64	25 18	53	106	26 11	53	106	27 04	53	105	27 57	52	105	28 49	53	104	296
65	24 51	+53	105	25 44	+53	105	26 37	+52	104	27 29	+53	104	28 22	+52	103	295
66	24 24	52	104	25 16	53	104	26 09	53	103	27 02	52	103	27 54	53	102	294
67	23 56	53	103	24 49	53	103	25 42	52	102	26 34	53	102	27 27	52	101	293
68	23 29	52	103	24 21	53	102	25 14	53	101	26 07	52	101	26 59	52	100	292
69	23 01	53	102	23 54	52	101	24 46	53	101	25 39	52	100	26 31	53	99	291

LHA	20° Hc	d	Z	21° Hc	d	Z	22° Hc	d	Z	23° Hc	d	Z	24° Hc	d	Z	LHA
	° ′	′	°	° ′	′	°	° ′	′	°	° ′	′	°	° ′	′	°	
0	48 00	+60	180	49 00	+60	180	50 00	+60	180	51 00	+60	180	52 00	+60	180	360
1	48 00	60	179	49 00	60	179	50 00	60	179	51 00	60	179	52 00	60	179	359
2	47 59	60	177	48 59	60	177	49 59	60	177	50 59	60	177	51 59	60	177	358
3	47 57	60	176	48 57	60	176	49 57	60	176	50 57	60	176	51 57	60	176	357
4	47 55	59	174	48 54	60	174	49 54	60	174	50 54	60	174	51 54	60	174	356
5	47 51	+60	173	48 51	+60	173	49 51	+60	173	50 51	+60	173	51 51	+60	173	355
6	47 48	59	172	48 47	60	172	49 47	60	171	50 47	60	171	51 47	60	171	354
7	47 43	60	170	48 43	60	170	49 43	60	170	50 43	59	170	51 42	60	170	353
8	47 38	60	169	48 38	59	169	49 37	60	169	50 37	60	168	51 37	60	168	352
9	47 32	60	167	48 32	60	167	49 32	59	167	50 31	60	167	51 31	59	167	351
10	47 26	+59	166	48 25	+60	166	49 25	+59	166	50 24	+60	166	51 24	+59	165	350
11	47 19	59	165	48 18	60	165	49 18	59	164	50 17	59	164	51 16	60	164	349
12	47 11	59	163	48 10	60	163	49 10	59	163	50 09	59	163	51 08	59	162	348
13	47 02	60	162	48 02	59	162	49 01	59	162	50 00	59	161	50 59	59	161	347
14	46 53	60	161	47 53	59	160	48 52	59	160	49 51	59	160	50 50	59	160	346
15	46 44	+59	159	47 43	+59	159	48 42	+59	159	49 41	+59	158	50 40	+59	158	345
16	46 33	59	158	47 32	59	158	48 31	59	157	49 30	59	157	50 29	59	157	344
17	46 23	58	157	47 21	59	156	48 20	59	156	49 19	58	156	50 17	59	155	343
18	46 11	59	155	47 10	58	155	48 08	59	155	49 07	58	154	50 05	59	154	342
19	45 59	59	154	46 57	59	154	47 56	58	153	48 54	59	153	49 53	58	153	341
20	45 46	+59	153	46 45	+58	152	47 43	+58	152	48 41	+58	152	49 39	+58	151	340
21	45 33	58	151	46 31	58	151	47 29	58	151	48 27	58	150	49 25	58	150	339
22	45 19	58	150	46 17	58	150	47 15	58	149	48 13	58	149	49 11	58	148	338
23	45 05	58	149	46 03	57	148	47 00	58	148	47 58	58	148	48 56	57	147	337
24	44 50	58	147	45 48	57	147	46 45	58	147	47 43	57	146	48 40	58	146	336
25	44 34	+58	146	45 32	+57	146	46 29	+58	145	47 27	+57	145	48 24	+57	144	335
26	44 18	58	145	45 16	57	144	46 13	57	144	47 10	58	144	48 08	57	143	334
27	44 02	57	144	44 59	57	143	45 56	57	143	46 53	57	142	47 50	58	142	333
28	43 45	57	142	44 42	57	142	45 39	57	142	46 36	57	141	47 33	56	141	332
29	43 28	57	141	44 25	56	141	45 21	57	140	46 18	57	140	47 15	56	139	331
30	43 10	+56	140	44 06	+57	140	45 03	+57	139	46 00	+56	139	46 56	+56	138	330
31	42 51	57	139	43 48	56	138	44 44	57	138	45 41	56	137	46 37	56	137	329
32	42 32	57	138	43 29	56	137	44 25	56	137	45 21	56	136	46 17	56	136	328
33	42 13	56	136	43 09	57	136	44 06	56	135	45 02	55	135	45 57	56	134	327
34	41 54	56	135	42 50	56	135	43 46	55	134	44 41	56	134	45 37	56	133	326
35	41 33	+56	134	42 29	+56	133	43 25	+56	133	44 21	+55	132	45 16	+56	132	325
36	41 13	56	133	42 09	55	132	43 04	56	132	44 00	55	131	44 55	55	131	324
37	40 52	56	132	41 48	55	131	42 43	55	131	43 38	56	130	44 34	55	130	323
38	40 31	55	131	41 26	56	130	42 22	55	129	43 17	55	129	44 12	55	128	322
39	40 09	56	129	41 04	56	129	42 00	55	128	42 55	54	128	43 49	55	127	321
40	39 47	+55	128	40 42	+55	128	41 37	+55	127	42 32	+55	127	43 27	+54	126	320
41	39 25	55	127	40 20	55	127	41 15	54	126	42 09	55	125	43 04	54	125	319
42	39 02	55	126	39 57	55	125	40 52	54	125	41 46	55	124	42 41	54	124	318
43	38 39	55	125	39 34	55	124	40 29	54	124	41 23	54	123	42 17	54	123	317
44	38 16	55	124	39 11	54	123	40 05	54	123	40 59	54	122	41 53	54	122	316
45	37 53	+54	123	38 47	+54	122	39 41	+54	122	40 35	+54	121	41 29	+54	120	315
46	37 29	54	122	38 23	54	121	39 17	54	121	40 11	54	120	41 05	53	119	314
47	37 05	54	121	37 59	54	120	38 53	53	119	39 46	54	119	40 40	53	118	313
48	36 40	54	120	37 34	54	119	38 28	54	118	39 22	53	118	40 15	53	117	312
49	36 15	54	118	37 09	54	118	38 03	53	117	38 56	54	117	39 50	53	116	311
50	35 51	+53	117	36 44	+54	117	37 38	+53	116	38 31	+53	116	39 24	+53	115	310
51	35 25	54	116	36 19	53	116	37 12	54	115	38 06	53	115	38 59	53	114	309
52	35 00	54	115	35 54	53	115	36 47	53	114	37 40	53	114	38 33	53	113	308
53	34 35	53	114	35 28	53	114	36 21	53	113	37 14	53	113	38 07	53	112	307
54	34 09	53	113	35 02	53	113	35 55	53	112	36 48	53	112	37 41	52	111	306
55	33 43	+53	112	34 36	+53	112	35 29	+53	111	36 22	+52	111	37 14	+53	110	305
56	33 17	53	111	34 10	53	111	35 03	52	110	35 55	53	110	36 48	52	109	304
57	32 50	53	110	33 43	53	110	34 36	53	109	35 29	52	109	36 21	52	108	303
58	32 24	53	109	33 17	52	109	34 09	53	108	35 02	52	108	35 54	52	107	302
59	31 57	53	108	32 50	52	108	33 42	53	107	34 35	52	107	35 27	52	106	301
60	31 30	+53	107	32 23	+52	107	33 15	+53	106	34 08	+52	106	35 00	+52	105	300
61	31 03	53	106	31 56	52	106	32 48	53	105	33 41	52	105	34 33	52	104	299
62	30 36	53	105	31 29	52	105	32 21	52	104	33 13	52	104	34 05	52	103	298
63	30 09	52	105	31 01	53	104	31 54	52	103	32 46	52	103	33 38	52	102	297
64	29 42	52	104	30 34	52	103	31 26	52	102	32 18	52	102	33 10	52	101	296
65	29 14	+53	103	30 07	+52	102	30 59	+52	101	31 51	+52	101	32 43	+51	100	295
66	28 47	52	102	29 39	52	101	30 31	52	101	31 23	52	100	32 15	51	99	294
67	28 19	52	101	29 11	52	100	30 03	52	100	30 55	52	99	31 47	52	98	293
68	27 51	53	100	28 44	52	99	29 36	51	99	30 27	52	98	31 19	52	98	292
69	27 24	52	99	28 16	52	98	29 08	52	98	30 00	51	97	30 51	52	97	291

LHA	25° Hc	d	Z	26° Hc	d	Z	27° Hc	d	Z	28° Hc	d	Z	29° Hc	d	Z	LHA
	° ′	′	°	° ′	′	°	° ′	′	°	° ′	′	°	° ′	′	°	
0	53 00	+60	180	54 00	+60	180	55 00	+60	180	56 00	+60	180	57 00	+60	180	360
1	53 00	60	179	54 00	60	179	55 00	60	178	56 00	60	178	57 00	60	178	359
2	52 59	60	177	53 59	60	177	54 59	59	177	55 58	60	177	56 58	60	177	358
3	52 57	60	176	53 57	60	175	54 57	60	175	55 57	60	175	56 57	59	175	357
4	52 54	60	174	53 54	60	174	54 54	60	174	55 54	60	174	56 54	60	174	356
5	52 51	+60	173	53 51	+60	172	54 51	+59	172	55 50	+60	172	56 50	+60	172	355
6	52 47	60	171	53 47	59	171	54 46	60	171	55 46	60	171	56 46	60	170	354
7	52 42	60	170	53 42	59	169	54 41	60	169	55 41	60	169	56 41	59	169	353
8	52 37	59	168	53 36	60	168	54 36	59	168	55 35	60	167	56 35	60	167	352
9	52 30	60	167	53 30	59	166	54 29	60	166	55 29	59	166	56 28	60	166	351
10	52 23	+60	165	53 23	+59	165	54 22	+60	165	55 22	+59	164	56 21	+59	164	350
11	52 16	59	164	53 15	59	163	54 14	60	163	55 14	59	163	56 13	59	163	349
12	52 07	60	162	53 07	59	162	54 06	59	162	55 05	59	161	56 04	59	161	348
13	51 58	60	161	52 58	59	160	53 57	59	160	54 56	59	160	55 55	58	160	347
14	51 49	59	159	52 48	59	159	53 47	59	159	54 46	58	158	55 44	59	158	346
15	51 39	+58	158	52 37	+59	158	53 36	+59	157	54 35	+58	157	55 33	+59	156	345
16	51 28	58	156	52 26	59	156	53 25	58	156	54 23	59	155	55 22	58	155	344
17	51 16	58	155	52 14	59	155	53 13	58	154	54 11	59	154	55 10	58	153	343
18	51 04	58	154	52 02	58	153	53 00	58	153	53 58	59	152	54 57	58	152	342
19	50 51	58	152	51 49	58	152	52 47	58	151	53 45	58	151	54 43	58	151	341
20	50 37	+58	151	51 35	+58	150	52 33	+58	150	53 31	+58	150	54 29	+57	149	340
21	50 23	58	149	51 21	58	149	52 19	57	149	53 16	58	148	54 14	57	148	339
22	50 09	57	148	51 06	58	148	52 04	57	147	53 01	58	147	53 59	57	146	338
23	49 53	58	147	50 51	57	146	51 48	58	146	52 46	57	145	53 43	57	145	337
24	49 38	57	145	50 35	57	145	51 32	57	144	52 29	57	144	53 26	57	143	336
25	49 21	+57	144	50 18	+57	144	51 15	+57	143	52 12	+57	143	53 09	+57	142	335
26	49 05	56	143	50 01	57	142	50 58	57	142	51 55	56	141	52 51	57	141	334
27	48 47	57	141	49 44	57	141	50 41	56	140	51 37	56	140	52 33	56	139	333
28	48 29	57	140	49 26	56	140	50 22	57	139	51 19	56	139	52 15	55	138	332
29	48 11	56	139	49 07	57	138	50 04	56	138	51 00	55	137	51 55	56	137	331
30	47 52	+56	138	48 48	+56	137	49 44	+56	136	50 40	+56	136	51 36	+55	135	330
31	47 33	56	136	48 29	56	136	49 25	55	135	50 20	56	135	51 16	55	134	329
32	47 13	56	135	48 09	56	134	49 05	55	134	50 00	55	133	50 55	55	133	328
33	46 53	56	134	47 49	55	133	48 44	55	133	49 39	55	132	50 34	55	131	327
34	46 33	55	133	47 28	55	132	48 23	55	131	49 18	55	131	50 13	55	130	326
35	46 12	+55	131	47 07	+55	131	48 02	+55	130	48 57	+54	130	49 51	+55	129	325
36	45 50	55	130	46 45	55	130	47 40	55	129	48 35	54	128	49 29	54	128	324
37	45 29	54	129	46 23	55	128	47 18	55	128	48 13	54	127	49 07	54	127	323
38	45 07	54	128	46 01	55	127	46 56	54	127	47 50	54	126	48 44	54	125	322
39	44 44	55	127	45 39	54	126	46 33	54	125	47 27	54	125	48 21	53	124	321
40	44 21	+55	125	45 16	+54	125	46 10	+54	124	47 04	+53	124	47 57	+54	123	320
41	43 58	54	124	44 52	54	124	45 46	54	123	46 40	53	122	47 33	54	122	319
42	43 35	54	123	44 29	53	123	45 22	54	122	46 16	53	121	47 09	53	121	318
43	43 11	54	122	44 05	53	121	44 58	54	121	45 52	53	120	46 45	53	120	317
44	42 47	54	121	43 41	53	120	44 34	53	120	45 27	53	119	46 20	53	118	316
45	42 23	+53	120	43 16	+54	119	44 10	+53	119	45 03	+52	118	45 55	+53	117	315
46	41 58	53	119	42 51	54	118	43 45	53	118	44 38	52	117	45 30	53	116	314
47	41 33	54	118	42 27	52	117	43 20	52	116	44 12	53	116	45 05	52	115	313
48	41 08	53	117	42 01	53	116	42 54	53	115	43 47	52	115	44 39	52	114	312
49	40 43	53	116	41 36	53	115	42 29	52	114	43 21	52	114	44 13	52	113	311
50	40 17	+53	115	41 10	+53	114	42 03	+52	113	42 55	+52	113	43 47	+52	112	310
51	39 52	52	113	40 44	53	113	41 37	52	112	42 29	52	112	43 21	52	111	309
52	39 26	52	112	40 18	53	112	41 11	52	111	42 03	52	111	42 55	51	110	308
53	39 00	52	111	39 52	52	111	40 44	52	110	41 36	52	109	42 28	52	109	307
54	38 33	53	110	39 26	52	110	40 18	52	109	41 10	51	108	42 01	52	108	306
55	38 07	+52	109	38 59	+52	109	39 51	+52	108	40 43	+51	107	41 34	+52	107	305
56	37 40	52	108	38 32	52	108	39 24	52	107	40 16	51	106	41 07	52	106	304
57	37 13	52	107	38 05	52	107	38 57	52	106	39 49	51	105	40 40	51	105	303
58	36 46	52	106	37 38	52	106	38 30	52	105	39 22	51	104	40 13	51	104	302
59	36 19	52	105	37 11	52	105	38 03	51	104	38 54	52	104	39 46	51	103	301
60	35 52	+52	104	36 44	+51	104	37 35	+52	103	38 27	+51	103	39 18	+51	102	300
61	35 25	51	103	36 16	52	103	37 08	51	102	37 59	51	102	38 50	51	101	299
62	34 57	52	103	35 49	51	102	36 40	52	101	37 32	51	101	38 23	50	100	298
63	34 30	51	102	35 21	52	101	36 13	51	100	37 04	51	100	37 55	51	99	297
64	34 02	52	101	34 54	51	100	35 45	51	99	36 36	51	99	37 27	51	98	296
65	33 34	+52	100	34 26	+51	99	35 17	+51	98	36 08	+51	98	36 59	+51	97	295
66	33 06	52	99	33 58	51	98	34 49	51	98	35 40	51	97	36 31	51	96	294
67	32 39	51	98	33 30	51	97	34 21	51	97	35 12	51	96	36 03	51	95	293
68	32 11	51	97	33 02	51	96	33 53	51	96	34 44	51	95	35 35	51	94	292
69	31 43	51	96	32 34	51	95	33 25	51	95	34 16	51	94	35 07	50	93	291

S. Lat. {LHA greater than 180°....... Zn=180−Z; LHA less than 180°........... Zn=180+Z}

DECLINATION (15°-29°) **SAME** NAME AS LATITUDE

N. Lat. {LHA greater than 180°....... Zn=Z; LHA less than 180°........... Zn=360−Z}

DECLINATION (15°-29°) SAME NAME AS LATITUDE

LHA	15° Hc	d	Z	16° Hc	d	Z	17° Hc	d	Z	18° Hc	d	Z	19° Hc	d	Z
	° ′	′	°	° ′	′	°	° ′	′	°	° ′	′	°	° ′	′	°
70	22 34	+52	101	23 26	+53	100	24 19	+52	100	25 11	+53	99	26 04	+52	99
71	22 06	52	100	22 58	53	99	23 51	52	99	24 43	53	98	25 36	52	98
72	21 38	53	99	22 31	52	98	23 23	52	98	24 15	53	97	25 08	52	97
73	21 10	53	98	22 03	52	97	22 55	52	97	23 47	53	96	24 40	52	96
74	20 42	53	97	21 35	52	97	22 27	52	96	23 19	53	95	24 12	52	95
75	20 14	+53	96	21 07	+52	96	21 59	+52	95	22 51	+53	95	23 44	+52	94
76	19 46	53	95	20 39	52	95	21 31	52	94	22 23	52	94	23 15	52	93
77	19 18	53	94	20 11	52	94	21 03	52	93	21 55	52	93	22 47	52	92
78	18 50	52	93	19 42	53	93	20 35	52	92	21 27	52	92	22 19	52	91
79	18 22	52	93	19 14	53	92	20 07	52	92	20 59	52	91	21 51	52	90
80	17 54	+52	92	18 46	+52	91	19 38	+53	91	20 31	+52	90	21 23	+52	90
81	17 26	52	91	18 18	52	90	19 10	53	90	20 03	52	89	20 55	52	89
82	16 57	53	90	17 50	52	89	18 42	52	89	19 34	52	88	20 26	53	88
83	16 29	53	89	17 22	52	88	18 14	52	88	19 06	52	87	19 58	52	87
84	16 01	52	88	16 53	53	88	17 46	52	87	18 38	52	87	19 30	52	86
85	15 33	+52	87	16 25	+53	87	17 18	+52	86	18 10	+52	86	19 02	+52	85
86	15 05	52	86	15 57	53	86	16 50	52	85	17 42	52	85	18 34	52	84
87	14 37	52	85	15 29	53	85	16 22	52	84	17 14	52	84	18 06	52	83
88	14 09	52	85	15 01	53	84	15 54	52	84	16 46	52	83	17 38	52	83
89	13 41	52	84	14 33	53	83	15 26	52	83	16 18	52	82	17 10	52	82
90	13 13	+52	83	14 05	+53	82	14 58	+52	82	15 50	+52	81	16 42	+53	81
91	12 45	52	82	13 37	53	82	14 30	52	81	15 22	53	81	16 15	52	80
92	12 17	52	81	13 09	53	81	14 02	53	80	14 55	52	80	15 47	52	79
93	11 49	53	80	12 42	52	80	13 34	53	79	14 27	52	79	15 19	53	78
94	11 21	53	79	12 14	53	79	13 07	52	78	13 59	53	78	14 52	52	77
95	10 54	+52	79	11 46	+53	78	12 39	+53	78	13 32	+52	77	14 24	+53	77
96	10 26	53	78	11 19	53	77	12 12	52	77	13 04	53	76	13 57	53	76
97	09 59	53	77	10 52	52	76	11 44	53	76	12 37	53	75	13 30	52	75
98	09 31	53	76	10 24	53	75	11 17	53	75	12 10	53	75	13 03	52	74
99	09 04	53	75	09 57	53	75	10 50	53	74	11 43	53	74	12 36	52	73
100	08 37	+53	74	09 30	+53	74	10 23	+53	73	11 16	+53	73	12 09	+53	72
101	08 10	53	73	09 03	53	73	09 56	53	72	10 49	53	72	11 42	53	71
102	07 43	53	72	08 36	53	72	09 29	53	72	10 22	53	71	11 15	53	71
103	07 16	53	72	08 09	54	71	09 03	53	71	09 56	53	70	10 49	53	70
104	06 49	54	71	07 43	53	70	08 36	53	70	09 29	53	69	10 22	54	69
105	06 23	+53	70	07 16	+54	69	08 10	+53	69	09 03	+53	69	09 56	+54	68
106	05 57	53	69	06 50	53	69	07 43	54	68	08 37	53	68	09 30	54	67
107	05 30	54	68	06 24	53	68	07 17	54	67	08 11	53	67	09 04	54	66
108	05 04	54	67	05 58	54	67	06 52	53	66	07 45	54	66	08 39	53	65
109	04 38	54	66	05 32	54	66	06 26	53	66	07 19	54	65	08 13	54	65
110	04 13	+54	66	05 07	+53	65	06 00	+54	65	06 54	+54	64	07 48	+53	64
111	03 47	54	65	04 41	54	64	05 35	54	64	06 29	54	63	07 23	53	63
112	03 22	54	64	04 16	54	63	05 10	54	63	06 04	54	63	06 58	54	62
113	02 57	54	63	03 51	54	62	04 45	54	62	05 39	54	62	06 33	54	61
114	02 32	54	62	03 26	54	62	04 20	54	61	05 14	54	61	06 08	54	60
115	02 07	+54	61	03 01	+54	61	03 55	+55	60	04 50	+54	60	05 44	+54	60
116	01 42	55	60	02 37	54	60	03 31	54	59	04 25	55	59	05 20	54	59
117	01 18	54	59	02 12	55	59	03 07	54	59	04 01	55	58	04 56	54	58
118	00 54	54	59	01 48	55	58	02 43	55	58	03 38	54	57	04 32	55	57
119	00 30	55	58	01 25	54	57	02 19	55	57	03 14	55	56	04 09	54	56
120	00 06	+55	57	01 01	+55	56	01 56	+55	56	02 51	+54	56	03 45	+55	55
121	−0 17	55	56	00 38	55	55	01 33	54	55	02 27	55	55	03 22	55	54
122	−0 41	56	55	00 15	55	55	01 10	55	54	02 05	55	54	03 00	55	53
123	−1 03	55	54*	−0 08	55	54	00 47	55	53	01 42	55	53	02 37	55	53
124	−1 26	55	53	−0 31	55	53	00 24	56	52	01 20	55	52	02 15	55	52
125	−1 49	+56	52	−0 53	+55	52	00 02	+56	52	00 58	+55	51	01 53	+55	51
126	−2 11	56	51	−1 15	55	51	−0 20	56	51	00 36	55	50	01 31	56	50
127	−2 33	56	51	−1 37	56	50	−0 41	55	50	00 14	56	49	01 10	55	49
128	−2 54	55	50	−1 59	56	49	−1 03	56	49	−0 07	56	49	00 49	55	48
129	−3 16	56	49	−2 20	56	48	−1 24	56	48	−0 28	56	48	00 28	56	47
130	−3 37	+56	48	−2 41	+56	47	−1 45	+56	47	−0 49	+56	47	00 07	+56	46
131	−3 57	56	47	−3 01	56	47	−2 05	56	46	−1 09	56	46	−0 13	56	46
132	−4 18	56	46	−3 22	57	46	−2 25	56	45	−1 29	56	45	−0 33	56	45
133	−4 38	56	45	−3 42	57	45	−2 45	56	44	−1 49	56	44	−0 53	57	44
134	−4 58	57	44	−4 01	56	44	−3 05	57	44	−2 08	56	43	−1 12	57	43
135	−5 17	+56	43	−4 21	+57	43	−3 24	+57	43	−2 27	+56	42	−1 31	+57	42
136	−5 36	56	42	−4 40	57	42	−3 43	57	42	−2 46	56	41	−1 50	57	41
137				−4 58	56	41	−4 02	57	41	−3 05	57	41	−2 08	57	40
138				−5 17	57	40	−4 20	57	40	−3 23	57	40	−2 26	57	39
139				−5 35	57	39	−4 38	57	39	−3 41	57	39	−2 44	58	38

LHA	20° Hc	d	Z	21° Hc	d	Z	22° Hc	d	Z	23° Hc	d	Z	24° Hc	d	Z
	° ′	′	°	° ′	′	°	° ′	′	°	° ′	′	°	° ′	′	°
70	26 56	+52	98	27 48	+52	97	28 40	+52	97	29 32	+51	96	30 23	+52	96
71	26 28	52	97	27 20	52	97	28 12	52	96	29 04	51	95	29 55	52	95
72	26 00	52	96	26 52	52	96	27 44	51	95	28 35	52	94	29 27	51	94
73	25 32	52	95	26 24	52	95	27 16	51	94	28 07	52	94	28 59	51	93
74	25 04	52	94	25 56	52	94	26 48	51	93	27 39	52	93	28 31	51	92
75	24 36	+52	93	25 28	+51	93	26 19	+52	92	27 11	+52	92	28 03	+51	91
76	24 07	52	93	24 59	52	92	25 51	52	91	26 43	51	91	27 34	52	90
77	23 39	52	92	24 31	52	91	25 23	52	91	26 15	51	90	27 06	52	89
78	23 11	52	91	24 03	52	90	24 55	52	90	25 47	51	89	26 38	52	89
79	22 43	52	90	23 35	52	89	24 27	51	89	25 18	52	88	26 10	51	88
80	22 15	+52	89	23 07	+52	88	23 59	+51	88	24 50	+52	87	25 42	+51	87
81	21 47	52	88	22 39	51	88	23 30	52	87	24 22	52	87	25 14	51	86
82	21 19	51	87	22 10	52	87	23 02	52	86	23 54	52	86	24 46	51	85
83	20 50	52	86	21 42	52	86	22 34	52	85	23 26	52	85	24 18	51	84
84	20 22	52	86	21 14	52	85	22 06	52	84	22 58	52	84	23 50	51	83
85	19 54	+52	85	20 46	+52	84	21 38	+52	84	22 30	+52	83	23 22	+51	82
86	19 26	52	84	20 18	52	83	21 10	52	83	22 02	52	82	22 54	51	82
87	18 58	52	83	19 50	52	82	20 42	52	82	21 34	52	81	22 26	52	81
88	18 30	52	82	19 22	52	82	20 14	52	81	21 06	52	80	21 58	52	80
89	18 02	53	81	18 55	52	81	19 47	52	80	20 39	51	80	21 30	52	79
90	17 35	+52	80	18 27	+52	80	19 19	+52	79	20 11	+52	79	21 03	+52	78
91	17 07	52	79	17 59	52	79	18 51	52	78	19 43	52	78	20 35	52	77
92	16 39	53	79	17 32	52	78	18 24	52	78	19 16	52	77	20 08	52	77
93	16 12	52	78	17 04	52	77	17 56	52	77	18 48	53	76	19 41	52	76
94	15 44	53	77	16 37	52	76	17 29	52	76	18 21	52	75	19 13	52	75
95	15 17	+52	76	16 09	+53	76	17 02	+52	75	17 54	+52	75	18 46	+52	74
96	14 50	52	75	15 42	53	75	16 35	52	74	17 27	52	74	18 19	52	73
97	14 22	53	74	15 15	52	74	16 07	53	73	17 00	52	73	17 52	53	72
98	13 55	53	74	14 48	53	73	15 41	52	73	16 33	52	72	17 25	53	72
99	13 28	53	73	14 21	53	72	15 14	52	72	16 06	53	71	16 59	52	71
100	13 02	+52	72	13 54	+53	71	14 47	+53	71	15 40	+52	70	16 32	+53	70
101	12 35	53	71	13 28	53	70	14 21	52	70	15 13	53	70	16 06	53	69
102	12 08	53	70	13 01	53	70	13 54	53	69	14 47	53	69	15 40	52	68
103	11 42	53	69	12 35	53	69	13 28	53	68	14 21	53	68	15 14	52	67
104	11 16	53	68	12 09	53	68	13 02	53	67	13 55	53	67	14 48	53	67
105	10 50	+53	68	11 43	+53	67	12 36	+53	67	13 29	+53	66	14 22	+53	66
106	10 24	53	67	11 17	53	66	12 10	53	66	13 03	53	65	13 56	54	65
107	09 58	53	66	10 51	54	65	11 45	53	65	12 38	53	64	13 31	53	64
108	09 32	54	65	10 26	53	65	11 19	54	64	12 13	53	64	13 06	53	63
109	09 07	53	64	10 00	54	64	10 54	53	63	11 47	54	63	12 41	53	62
110	08 41	+54	63	09 35	+54	63	10 29	+53	62	11 22	+54	62	12 16	+53	62
111	08 16	54	62	09 10	54	62	10 04	54	62	10 58	53	61	11 51	54	61
112	07 52	53	62	08 45	54	61	09 39	54	61	10 33	54	60	11 27	54	60
113	07 27	54	61	08 21	54	60	09 15	54	60	10 09	54	59	11 03	53	59
114	07 02	55	60	07 57	54	59	08 51	54	59	09 45	54	59	10 39	54	58
115	06 38	+54	59	07 32	+55	59	08 27	+54	58	09 21	+54	58	10 15	+54	57
116	06 14	54	58	07 08	55	58	08 03	54	57	08 57	54	57	09 51	54	56
117	05 50	55	57	06 45	54	57	07 39	55	57	08 34	54	56	09 28	54	56
118	05 27	54	57	06 21	55	56	07 16	54	56	08 10	55	55	09 05	54	55
119	05 03	55	56	05 58	55	55	06 53	54	55	07 47	55	54	08 42	54	54
120	04 40	+55	55	05 35	+55	54	06 30	+54	54	07 24	+55	54	08 19	+55	53
121	04 17	55	54	05 12	55	54	06 07	55	53	07 02	55	53	07 57	55	52
122	03 55	55	53	04 50	55	53	05 45	55	52	06 40	55	52	07 35	55	51
123	03 32	55	52	04 27	56	52	05 23	55	51	06 18	55	51	07 13	55	51
124	03 10	55	51	04 05	56	51	05 01	55	51	05 56	55	50	06 51	55	50
125	02 48	+56	50	03 44	+55	50	04 39	+55	50	05 34	+56	49	06 30	+55	49
126	02 27	55	50	03 22	56	49	04 18	55	49	05 13	56	48	06 09	55	48
127	02 05	56	49	03 01	56	48	03 57	55	48	04 52	56	48	05 48	55	47
128	01 44	56	48	02 40	56	47	03 36	56	47	04 32	55	47	05 27	56	46
129	01 24	56	47	02 20	55	47	03 15	56	46	04 11	56	46	05 07	56	46
130	01 03	+56	46	01 59	+56	46	02 55	+56	45	03 51	+56	45	04 47	+56	45
131	00 43	56	45	01 39	56	45	02 35	56	44	03 31	57	44	04 28	56	44
132	00 23	57	44	01 20	56	44	02 16	56	44	03 12	56	43	04 08	56	43
133	00 04	56	43	01 00	57	43	01 57	56	43	02 53	56	42	03 49	57	42
134	−0 15	56	43	00 41	57	42	01 38	56	42	02 34	57	42	03 31	56	41
135	−0 34	+56	42	00 22	+57	41	01 19	+57	41	02 16	+56	41	03 12	+57	40
136	−0 53	57	41	00 04	57	40	01 01	56	40	01 57	57	40	02 54	57	39
137	−1 11	57	40	−0 14	57	40	00 43	57	39	01 40	56	39	02 36	57	39
138	−1 29	57	39	−0 32	57	39	00 25	57	38	01 22	57	38	02 19	57	38
139	−1 46	57	38	−0 49	57	38	00 08	57	37	01 05	57	37	02 02	57	37

LHA	25° Hc	d	Z	26° Hc	d	Z	27° Hc	d	Z	28° Hc	d	Z	29° Hc	d	Z	LHA
	° ′	′	°	° ′	′	°	° ′	′	°	° ′	′	°	° ′	′	°	
70	31 15	+51	95	32 06	+51	94	32 57	+51	94	33 48	+51	93	34 39	+50	93	290
71	30 47	51	94	31 38	51	94	32 29	51	93	33 20	51	92	34 11	50	92	289
72	30 18	52	93	31 10	51	93	32 01	51	92	32 52	50	91	33 42	51	91	288
73	29 50	52	92	30 42	51	92	31 33	51	91	32 24	50	91	33 14	51	90	287
74	29 22	51	92	30 13	52	91	31 05	50	90	31 55	51	90	32 46	51	89	286
75	28 54	+51	91	29 45	+51	90	30 36	+51	89	31 27	+51	89	32 18	+51	88	285
76	28 26	51	90	29 17	51	89	30 08	51	89	30 59	51	88	31 50	50	87	284
77	27 58	51	89	28 49	51	88	29 40	51	88	30 31	51	87	31 22	50	86	283
78	27 30	51	88	28 21	51	87	29 12	51	87	30 03	51	86	30 54	50	86	282
79	27 01	52	87	27 53	51	87	28 44	51	86	29 35	51	85	30 26	50	85	281
80	26 33	+52	86	27 25	+51	86	28 16	+51	85	29 07	+51	84	29 58	+50	84	280
81	26 05	51	85	26 56	52	85	27 48	51	84	28 39	51	84	29 30	50	83	279
82	25 37	51	85	26 28	52	84	27 20	51	83	28 11	51	83	29 02	50	82	278
83	25 09	51	84	26 00	52	83	26 52	51	82	27 43	51	82	28 34	51	81	277
84	24 41	52	83	25 33	51	82	26 24	51	82	27 15	51	81	28 06	51	80	276
85	24 13	+52	82	25 05	+51	81	25 56	+51	81	26 47	+51	80	27 38	+51	80	275
86	23 45	52	81	24 37	51	81	25 28	51	80	26 19	52	79	27 11	50	79	274
87	23 18	51	80	24 09	52	80	25 01	51	79	25 52	51	79	26 43	51	78	273
88	22 50	51	79	23 41	52	79	24 33	51	78	25 24	51	78	26 15	52	77	272
89	22 22	52	79	23 14	51	78	24 05	52	77	24 57	51	77	25 48	51	76	271
90	21 55	+51	78	22 46	+52	77	23 38	+51	77	24 29	+52	76	25 21	+51	75	270
91	21 27	52	77	22 19	52	76	23 11	51	76	24 02	52	75	24 54	51	75	269
92	21 00	52	76	21 52	51	75	22 43	52	75	23 35	51	74	24 26	52	74	268
93	20 33	51	75	21 24	52	75	22 16	52	74	23 08	51	74	23 59	52	73	267
94	20 05	52	74	20 57	52	74	21 49	52	73	22 41	52	73	23 33	51	72	266
95	19 38	+52	74	20 30	+52	73	21 22	+52	72	22 14	+52	72	23 06	+51	71	265
96	19 11	52	73	20 03	52	72	20 55	52	72	21 47	52	71	22 39	52	71	264
97	18 45	52	72	19 37	52	71	20 29	52	71	21 21	52	70	22 13	52	70	263
98	18 18	52	71	19 10	52	70	20 02	52	70	20 54	52	69	21 46	52	69	262
99	17 51	53	70	18 44	52	70	19 36	52	69	20 28	52	69	21 20	52	68	261
100	17 25	+52	69	18 17	+53	69	19 10	+52	68	20 02	+52	68	20 54	+52	67	260
101	16 59	52	69	17 51	53	68	18 44	52	67	19 36	52	67	20 28	52	66	259
102	16 32	53	68	17 25	53	67	18 18	52	67	19 10	53	66	20 03	52	66	258
103	16 06	53	67	16 59	53	66	17 52	52	66	18 44	53	65	19 37	52	65	257
104	15 41	53	66	16 34	52	66	17 26	53	65	18 19	53	65	19 12	52	64	256
105	15 15	+53	65	16 08	+53	65	17 01	+53	64	17 54	+52	64	18 46	+53	63	255
106	14 50	53	64	15 43	53	64	16 36	52	63	17 28	53	63	18 21	53	62	254
107	14 24	53	64	15 17	53	63	16 10	53	63	17 03	53	62	17 56	53	62	253
108	13 59	53	63	14 52	54	62	15 46	53	62	16 39	53	61	17 32	53	61	252
109	13 34	54	62	14 28	53	61	15 21	53	61	16 14	53	60	17 07	53	60	251
110	13 09	+54	61	14 03	+53	61	14 56	+54	60	15 50	+53	60	16 43	+53	59	250
111	12 45	54	60	13 39	53	60	14 32	54	59	15 26	53	59	16 19	53	58	249
112	12 21	53	59	13 14	54	59	14 08	54	58	15 02	53	58	15 55	54	58	248
113	11 56	54	59	12 50	54	58	13 44	54	58	14 38	53	57	15 31	54	57	247
114	11 33	54	58	12 27	53	57	13 20	54	57	14 14	54	56	15 08	54	56	246
115	11 09	+54	57	12 03	+54	56	12 57	+54	56	13 51	+54	56	14 45	+54	55	245
116	10 45	55	56	11 40	54	56	12 34	54	55	13 28	54	55	14 22	54	54	244
117	10 22	54	55	11 16	55	55	12 11	54	54	13 05	54	54	13 59	54	53	243
118	09 59	55	54	10 54	54	54	11 48	54	54	12 42	55	53	13 37	54	53	242
119	09 36	55	54	10 31	54	53	11 25	55	53	12 20	54	52	13 14	55	52	241
120	09 14	+55	53	10 09	+54	52	11 03	+55	52	11 58	+54	51	12 52	+55	51	240
121	08 52	54	52	09 46	55	51	10 41	55	51	11 36	55	51	12 31	54	50	239
122	08 30	54	51	09 24	55	51	10 19	55	50	11 14	55	50	12 09	55	49	238
123	08 08	55	50	09 03	55	50	09 58	55	49	10 53	55	49	11 48	55	49	237
124	07 46	56	49	08 42	55	49	09 37	55	49	10 32	55	48	11 27	55	48	236
125	07 25	+55	49	08 20	+56	48	09 16	+55	48	10 11	+55	47	11 06	+55	47	235
126	07 04	56	48	08 00	55	47	08 55	55	47	09 50	56	47	10 46	55	46	234
127	06 43	56	47	07 39	56	46	08 35	55	46	09 30	56	46	10 26	55	45	233
128	06 23	56	46	07 19	55	46	08 14	56	45	09 10	56	45	10 06	55	44	232
129	06 03	56	45	06 59	56	45	07 55	55	44	08 50	56	44	09 46	56	44	231
130	05 43	+56	44	06 39	+56	44	07 35	+56	44	08 31	+56	43	09 27	+56	43	230
131	05 24	56	43	06 20	56	43	07 16	56	43	08 12	56	42	09 08	56	42	229
132	05 04	57	43	06 01	56	42	06 57	56	42	07 53	56	42	08 49	56	41	228
133	04 46	56	42	05 42	56	41	06 38	57	41	07 35	56	41	08 31	56	40	227
134	04 27	56	41	05 23	57	41	06 20	56	40	07 16	57	40	08 13	56	40	226
135	04 09	+56	40	05 05	+57	40	06 02	+56	39	06 58	+57	39	07 55	+57	39	225
136	03 51	56	39	04 47	57	39	05 44	57	39	06 41	57	38	07 38	56	38	224
137	03 33	57	38	04 30	57	38	05 27	57	38	06 24	56	37	07 20	57	37	223
138	03 16	57	37	04 13	57	37	05 10	57	37	06 07	57	37	07 04	57	36	222
139	02 59	57	37	03 56	57	36	04 53	57	36	05 50	57	36	06 47	57	35	221

S. Lat. {LHA greater than 180°....... Zn=180−Z; LHA less than 180°........... Zn=180+Z}

DECLINATION (15°-29°) SAME NAME AS LATITUDE

LAT 62°

LAT 62°

DECLINATION (15°-29°) SAME NAME AS LATITUDE

N. Lat. {LHA greater than 180°....... Zn=Z; LHA less than 180°........... Zn=360−Z}

LHA	15° Hc	15° d	15° Z	16° Hc	16° d	16° Z	17° Hc	17° d	17° Z	18° Hc	18° d	18° Z	19° Hc	19° d	19° Z	20° Hc	20° d	20° Z	21° Hc	21° d	21° Z
	° ′	′	°	° ′	′	°	° ′	′	°	° ′	′	°	° ′	′	°	° ′	′	°	° ′	′	°
140							−4 55	+57	38	−3 58	+57	38	−3 01	+57	37	−2 04	+58	37	−1 06	+57	37
141							−5 12	57	37	−4 15	57	37	−3 18	57	37	−2 21	58	36	−1 23	57	36
142							−5 29	57	36	−4 32	58	36	−3 34	57	36	−2 37	57	35	−1 40	58	35
143										−4 48	57	35	−3 51	58	35	−2 53	57	34	−1 56	58	34
144										−5 04	57	34	−4 07	58	34	−3 09	58	34	−2 11	57	33
145										−5 20	+58	33	−4 22	+58	33	−3 24	+57	33	−2 27	+58	32
146													−4 37	58	32	−3 39	58	32	−2 41	57	32
147													−4 52	58	31	−3 54	58	31	−2 56	58	31
148													−5 06	58	30	−4 08	58	30	−3 10	58	30
149													−5 20	58	29	−4 22	58	29	−3 24	58	29
150																−4 36	+59	28	−3 37	+58	28
151																−4 49	59	27	−3 50	58	27
152																−5 01	58	26	−4 03	59	26
153																−5 14	59	25	−4 15	59	25
154																			−4 27	59	24
155																			−4 38	+59	23
156																			−4 49	59	22
157																			−5 00	59	21
158																			−5 10	59	21

LHA	22° Hc	22° d	22° Z	23° Hc	23° d	23° Z	24° Hc	24° d	24° Z	25° Hc	25° d	25° Z	26° Hc	26° d	26° Z	27° Hc	27° d	27° Z	28° Hc	28° d	28° Z	29° Hc	29° d	29° Z	LHA
	° ′	′	°	° ′	′	°	° ′	′	°	° ′	′	°	° ′	′	°	° ′	′	°	° ′	′	°	° ′	′	°	
140	−0 09	+57	37	00 48	+57	36	01 45	+57	36	02 42	+58	36	03 40	+57	35	04 37	+57	35	05 34	+57	35	06 31	+57	35	220
141	−0 26	57	36	00 31	58	35	01 29	57	35	02 26	57	35	03 23	58	35	04 21	57	34	05 18	57	34	06 15	58	34	219
142	−0 42	57	35	00 15	58	35	01 13	57	34	02 10	58	34	03 08	57	34	04 05	58	33	05 03	57	33	06 00	57	33	218
143	−0 58	58	34	00 00	57	34	00 57	58	33	01 55	57	33	02 52	58	33	03 50	57	33	04 47	58	32	05 45	57	32	217
144	−1 14	58	33	−0 16	58	33	00 42	57	32	01 39	58	32	02 37	58	32	03 35	57	32	04 32	58	31	05 30	58	31	216
145	−1 29	+58	32	−0 31	+58	32	00 27	+58	32	01 25	+57	31	02 22	+58	31	03 20	+58	31	04 18	+58	31	05 16	+58	30	215
146	−1 44	58	31	−0 46	58	31	00 12	58	31	01 10	58	30	02 08	58	30	03 06	58	30	04 04	58	30	05 02	58	29	214
147	−1 58	58	30	−1 00	58	30	−0 02	58	30	00 56	58	30	01 54	58	29	02 52	58	29	03 50	58	29	04 48	58	29	213
148	−2 12	58	29	−1 14	58	29	−0 16	58	29	00 42	58	29	01 40	59	28	02 39	58	28	03 37	58	28	04 35	58	28	212
149	−2 26	59	29	−1 27	58	28	−0 29	58	28	00 29	58	28	01 27	58	28	02 25	59	27	03 24	58	27	04 22	58	27	211
150	−2 39	+58	28	−1 41	+59	27	−0 42	+58	27	00 16	+58	27	01 14	+59	27	02 13	+58	26	03 11	+58	26	04 09	+59	26	210
151	−2 52	59	27	−1 53	58	27	−0 55	58	26	00 03	59	26	01 02	58	26	02 00	59	26	02 59	58	25	03 57	59	25	209
152	−3 04	58	26	−2 06	59	26	−1 07	58	25	−0 09	59	25	00 50	58	25	01 48	59	25	02 47	58	25	03 45	59	24	208
153	−3 16	58	25	−2 18	59	25	−1 19	59	25	−0 20	58	24	00 38	59	24	01 37	58	24	02 35	59	24	03 34	59	23	207
154	−3 28	59	24	−2 29	58	24	−1 31	59	24	−0 32	59	23	00 27	59	23	01 26	58	23	02 24	59	23	03 23	59	23	206
155	−3 39	+59	23	−2 40	+58	23	−1 42	+59	23	−0 43	+59	23	00 16	+59	22	01 15	+59	22	02 14	+58	22	03 12	+59	22	205
156	−3 50	59	22	−2 51	59	22	−1 52	59	22	−0 53	58	22	00 05	59	21	01 04	59	21	02 03	59	21	03 02	59	21	204
157	−4 01	59	21	−3 02	59	21	−2 03	59	21	−1 04	59	21	−0 05	59	21	00 54	59	20	01 53	59	20	02 52	59	20	203
158	−4 11	59	20	−3 12	60	20	−2 12	59	20	−1 13	59	20	−0 14	59	20	00 45	59	20	01 44	59	19	02 43	59	19	202
159	−4 20	59	19	−3 21	59	19	−2 22	59	19	−1 23	59	19	−0 24	60	19	00 36	59	19	01 35	59	18	02 34	59	18	201
160	−4 29	+59	19	−3 30	+59	18	−2 31	+59	18	−1 32	+60	18	−0 32	+59	18	00 27	+59	18	01 26	+59	18	02 25	+59	17	200
161	−4 38	59	18	−3 39	59	17	−2 40	60	17	−1 40	59	17	−0 41	59	17	00 18	60	17	01 18	59	17	02 17	59	17	199
162	−4 46	59	17	−3 47	59	17	−2 48	60	16	−1 48	59	16	−0 49	59	16	00 10	60	16	01 10	59	16	02 09	59	16	198
163	−4 54	59	16	−3 55	60	16	−2 55	59	16	−1 56	59	15	−0 57	60	15	00 03	59	15	01 02	60	15	02 02	59	15	197
164	−5 02	60	15	−4 02	59	15	−3 03	60	15	−2 03	59	14	−1 04	60	14	−0 04	59	14	00 55	60	14	01 55	59	14	196
165	−5 09	+60	14	−4 09	+59	14	−3 10	+60	14	−2 10	+59	14	−1 11	+60	13	−0 11	+60	13	00 49	+59	13	01 48	+60	13	195
166				−4 16	60	13	−3 16	59	13	−2 17	60	13	−1 17	59	13	−0 18	60	12	00 42	60	12	01 42	60	12	194
167				−4 22	60	12	−3 22	60	12	−2 22	59	12	−1 23	60	12	−0 23	60	11	00 37	59	11	01 36	60	11	193
168				−4 27	59	11	−3 28	60	11	−2 28	60	11	−1 28	59	11	−0 29	60	11	00 31	60	11	01 31	60	10	192
169				−4 33	60	10	−3 33	60	10	−2 33	60	10	−1 33	59	10	−0 34	60	10	00 26	60	10	01 26	60	9	191
170				−4 37	+59	9	−3 38	+60	9	−2 38	+60	9	−1 38	+60	9	−0 38	+60	9	00 22	+59	9	01 21	+60	9	190
171				−4 42	60	8	−3 42	60	8	−2 42	60	8	−1 42	60	8	−0 42	60	8	00 18	59	8	01 17	60	8	189
172				−4 45	59	7	−3 46	60	7	−2 46	60	7	−1 46	60	7	−0 46	60	7	00 14	60	7	01 14	60	7	188
173				−4 49	60	6	−3 49	60	6	−2 49	60	6	−1 49	60	6	−0 49	60	6	00 11	60	6	01 11	60	6	187
174				−4 52	60	6	−3 52	60	5	−2 52	60	5	−1 52	60	5	−0 52	60	5	00 08	60	5	01 08	60	5	186
175				−4 54	+60	5	−3 54	+60	5	−2 54	+60	5	−1 54	+59	4	−0 55	+60	4	00 05	+60	4	01 05	+60	4	185
176				−4 56	60	4	−3 56	60	4	−2 56	60	4	−1 56	60	4	−0 56	59	4	00 03	60	4	01 03	60	4	184
177				−4 58	60	3	−3 58	60	3	−2 58	60	3	−1 58	60	3	−0 58	60	3	00 02	60	3	01 02	60	3	183
178				−4 59	60	2	−3 59	60	2	−2 59	60	2	−1 59	60	2	−0 59	60	2	00 01	60	2	01 01	60	2	182
179				−5 00	60	1	−4 00	60	1	−3 00	60	1	−2 00	60	1	−1 00	60	1	00 00	60	1	01 00	60	1	181
180				−5 00	+60	0	−4 00	+60	0	−3 00	+60	0	−2 00	+60	0	−1 00	+60	0	00 00	+60	0	01 00	+60	0	180

DECLINATION (15°-29°) CONTRARY NAME TO LATITUDE

LHA	15° Hc	15° d	15° Z	16° Hc	16° d	16° Z	LHA
73	−5 30	54	112				287
72	−5 04	54	113				288
71	−4 38	54	114	−5 32	54	114	289
70	−4 13	−54	114	−5 07	−53	115	290

S. Lat. {LHA greater than 180°........ Zn=180−Z; LHA less than 180°........... Zn=180+Z}

N. Lat. {LHA greater than 180°........ Zn=Z; LHA less than 180°........... Zn=360−Z}

DECLINATION (15°-29°) CONTRARY NAME TO LATITUDE

LHA	15°			16°			17°			18°			19°		
	Hc	d	Z	Hc	d	Z	Hc	d	Z	Hc	d	Z	Hc	d	Z
	° ′	′	°	° ′	′	°	° ′	′	°	° ′	′	°	° ′	′	°
69	-3 47	54	115	-4 41	54	116	-5 35	54	116						
68	-3 22	54	116	-4 16	54	117	-5 10	54	117						
67	-2 57	54	117	-3 51	54	118	-4 45	54	118	-5 39	54	118			
66	-2 32	54	118	-3 26	54	118	-4 20	54	119	-5 14	54	119			
65	-2 07	-54	119	-3 01	-54	119	-3 55	-55	120	-4 50	-54	120	-5 44	-54	120
64	-1 42	55	120	-2 37	54	120	-3 31	54	121	-4 25	55	121	-5 20	54	121
63	-1 18	54	121	-2 12	55	121	-3 07	54	121	-4 01	55	122	-4 56	54	122
62	-0 54	54	121	-1 48	55	122	-2 43	55	122	-3 38	54	123	-4 32	55	123
61	-0 30	55	122	-1 25	54	123	-2 19	55	123	-3 14	55	124	-4 09	54	124
60	-0 06	-55	123	-1 01	-55	124	-1 56	-55	124	-2 51	-54	124	-3 45	-55	125
59	00 17	55	124	-0 38	55	125	-1 33	54	125	-2 27	55	125	-3 22	55	126
58	00 41	56	125	-0 15	55	125	-1 10	55	126	-2 05	55	126	-3 00	55	127
57	01 03	55	126	00 08	55	126	-0 47	55	127	-1 42	55	127	-2 37	55	127
56	01 26	55	127	00 31	55	127	-0 24	56	128	-1 20	55	128	-2 15	55	128
55	01 49	-56	128	00 53	-55	128	-0 02	-56	128	-0 58	-55	129	-1 53	-55	129
54	02 11	56	129	01 15	55	129	00 20	56	129	-0 36	55	130	-1 31	56	130
53	02 33	56	129	01 37	56	130	00 41	55	130	-0 14	56	131	-1 10	55	131
52	02 54	55	130	01 59	56	131	01 03	56	131	00 07	56	131	-0 49	55	132
51	03 16	56	131	02 20	56	132	01 24	56	132	00 28	56	132	-0 28	56	133
50	03 37	-56	132	02 41	-56	133	01 45	-56	133	00 49	-56	133	-0 07	-56	134
49	03 57	56	133	03 01	56	133	02 05	56	134	01 09	56	134	00 13	56	134
48	04 18	56	134	03 22	57	134	02 25	56	135	01 29	56	135	00 33	56	135
47	04 38	56	135	03 42	57	135	02 45	56	136	01 49	56	136	00 53	57	136
46	04 58	57	136	04 01	56	136	03 05	57	136	02 08	56	137	01 12	57	137
45	05 17	-56	137	04 21	-57	137	03 24	-57	137	02 27	-56	138	01 31	-57	138
44	05 36	56	138	04 40	57	138	03 43	57	138	02 46	56	139	01 50	57	139
43	05 55	57	139	04 58	56	139	04 02	57	139	03 05	57	139	02 08	57	140
42	06 14	57	139	05 17	57	140	04 20	57	140	03 23	57	140	02 26	57	141
41	06 32	57	140	05 35	57	141	04 38	57	141	03 41	57	141	02 44	58	142
40	06 50	-58	141	05 52	-57	142	04 55	-57	142	03 58	-57	142	03 01	-57	143
39	07 07	57	142	06 10	58	143	05 12	57	143	04 15	57	143	03 18	57	143
38	07 24	57	143	06 27	58	143	05 29	57	144	04 32	58	144	03 34	57	144
37	07 41	58	144	06 43	57	144	05 46	58	145	04 48	57	145	03 51	58	145
36	07 57	57	145	07 00	58	145	06 02	58	146	05 04	57	146	04 07	58	146
35	08 13	-58	146	07 15	-57	146	06 18	-58	147	05 20	-58	147	04 22	-58	147
34	08 29	58	147	07 31	58	147	06 33	58	147	05 35	58	148	04 37	58	148
33	08 44	58	148	07 46	58	148	06 48	58	148	05 50	58	149	04 52	58	149
32	08 59	58	149	08 01	58	149	07 03	59	149	06 04	58	150	05 06	58	150
31	09 13	58	150	08 15	58	150	07 17	58	150	06 19	59	151	05 20	58	151
30	09 27	-58	151	08 29	-58	151	07 31	-59	151	06 32	-58	151	05 34	-58	152
29	09 41	59	152	08 42	58	152	07 44	59	152	06 45	58	152	05 47	58	153
28	09 54	59	153	08 55	58	153	07 57	59	153	06 58	58	153	06 00	59	154
27	10 07	59	154	09 08	59	154	08 09	58	154	07 11	59	154	06 12	58	154
26	10 19	59	155	09 20	58	155	08 22	59	155	07 23	59	155	06 24	59	155
25	10 31	-59	156	09 32	-59	156	08 33	-58	156	07 35	-59	156	06 36	-59	156
24	10 42	59	156	09 43	58	157	08 45	59	157	07 46	59	157	06 47	59	157
23	10 53	59	157	09 54	59	158	08 55	58	158	07 57	59	158	06 58	59	158
22	11 04	59	158	10 05	59	159	09 06	59	159	08 07	59	159	07 08	59	159
21	11 14	59	159	10 15	59	160	09 16	59	160	08 17	59	160	07 18	59	160
20	11 24	-59	160	10 25	-60	161	09 25	-59	161	08 26	-59	161	07 27	-59	161
19	11 33	59	161	10 34	59	161	09 35	60	162	08 35	59	162	07 36	59	162
18	11 42	59	162	10 43	60	162	09 43	59	163	08 44	59	163	07 45	60	163
17	11 50	59	163	10 51	60	163	09 51	59	164	08 52	59	164	07 53	60	164
16	11 58	59	164	10 59	60	164	09 59	59	165	09 00	60	165	08 00	59	165
15	12 06	-60	165	11 06	-59	165	10 07	-60	165	09 07	-60	166	08 07	-59	166
14	12 13	60	166	11 13	60	166	10 13	59	166	09 14	60	167	08 14	59	167
13	12 19	60	167	11 19	59	167	10 20	60	167	09 20	60	168	08 20	59	168
12	12 25	60	168	11 25	59	168	10 26	60	168	09 26	60	168	08 26	59	169
11	12 31	60	169	11 31	60	169	10 31	60	169	09 31	59	169	08 32	60	170
10	12 36	-60	170	11 36	-60	170	10 36	-60	170	09 36	-59	170	08 37	-60	170
9	12 40	59	171	11 41	60	171	10 41	60	171	09 41	60	171	08 41	60	171
8	12 44	59	172	11 45	60	172	10 45	60	172	09 45	60	172	08 45	60	172
7	12 48	60	173	11 48	60	173	10 48	60	173	09 48	59	173	08 49	60	173
6	12 51	60	174	11 51	60	174	10 51	59	174	09 52	60	174	08 52	60	174
5	12 54	-60	175	11 54	-60	175	10 54	-60	175	09 54	-60	175	08 54	-60	175
4	12 56	60	176	11 56	60	176	10 56	60	176	09 56	60	176	08 56	60	176
3	12 58	60	177	11 58	60	177	10 58	60	177	09 58	60	177	08 58	60	177
2	12 59	60	178	11 59	60	178	10 59	60	178	09 59	60	178	08 59	60	178
1	13 00	60	179	12 00	60	179	11 00	60	179	10 00	60	179	09 00	60	179
0	13 00	-60	180	12 00	-60	180	11 00	-60	180	10 00	-60	180	09 00	-60	180

LHA	20°			21°			22°			23°			24°		
	Hc	d	Z	Hc	d	Z	Hc	d	Z	Hc	d	Z	Hc	d	Z
	° ′	′	°	° ′	′	°	° ′	′	°	° ′	′	°	° ′	′	°
69															
68															
67															
66															
65															
64															
63															
62	-5 27	54	123												
61	-5 03	55	124												
60	-4 40	-55	125	-5 35	-55	126									
59	-4 17	56	126	-5 12	55	127									
58	-3 55	55	127	-4 50	55	127									
57	-3 32	55	128	-4 27	56	128	-5 23	55	129						
56	-3 10	55	129	-4 05	56	129	-5 01	55	129						
55	-2 48	-56	130	-3 44	-55	130	-4 39	-55	130	-5 34	-56	131			
54	-2 27	55	130	-3 22	56	131	-4 18	55	131	-5 13	56	132			
53	-2 05	56	131	-3 01	56	132	-3 57	55	132	-4 52	56	132			
52	-1 44	56	132	-2 40	56	133	-3 36	56	133	-4 32	55	133	-5 27	56	134
51	-1 24	56	133	-2 20	55	133	-3 15	56	134	-4 11	56	134	-5 07	56	134
50	-1 03	-56	134	-1 59	-56	134	-2 55	-56	135	-3 51	-56	135	-4 47	-56	135
49	-0 43	56	135	-1 39	56	135	-2 35	56	136	-3 31	57	136	-4 28	56	136
48	-0 23	57	136	-1 20	56	136	-2 16	56	136	-3 12	56	137	-4 08	56	137
47	-0 04	56	137	-1 00	57	137	-1 57	56	137	-2 53	56	138	-3 49	57	138
46	00 15	56	137	-0 41	57	138	-1 38	56	138	-2 34	57	138	-3 31	56	139
45	00 34	-56	138	-0 22	-57	139	-1 19	-57	139	-2 16	-56	139	-3 12	-57	140
44	00 53	57	139	-0 04	57	140	-1 01	56	140	-1 57	57	140	-2 54	57	141
43	01 11	57	140	00 14	57	140	-0 43	57	141	-1 40	56	141	-2 36	57	141
42	01 29	57	141	00 32	57	141	-0 25	57	142	-1 22	57	142	-2 19	57	142
41	01 46	57	142	00 49	57	142	-0 08	57	143	-1 05	57	143	-2 02	57	143
40	02 04	-58	143	01 06	-57	143	00 09	-57	143	-0 48	-57	144	-1 45	-57	144
39	02 21	58	144	01 23	57	144	00 26	57	144	-0 31	58	145	-1 29	57	145
38	02 37	57	145	01 40	58	145	00 42	57	145	-0 15	58	145	-1 13	57	146
37	02 53	57	146	01 56	58	146	00 58	58	146	00 00	57	146	-0 57	58	147
36	03 09	58	146	02 11	57	147	01 14	58	147	00 16	58	147	-0 42	57	148
35	03 24	-57	147	02 27	-58	148	01 29	-58	148	00 31	-58	148	-0 27	-58	148
34	03 39	58	148	02 41	57	148	01 44	58	149	00 46	58	149	-0 12	58	149
33	03 54	58	149	02 56	58	149	01 58	58	150	01 00	58	150	00 02	58	150
32	04 08	58	150	03 10	58	150	02 12	58	151	01 14	58	151	00 16	58	151
31	04 22	58	151	03 24	58	151	02 26	59	151	01 27	58	152	00 29	58	152
30	04 36	-59	152	03 37	-58	152	02 39	-58	152	01 41	-59	153	00 42	-58	153
29	04 49	59	153	03 50	58	153	02 52	59	153	01 53	58	153	00 55	58	154
28	05 01	58	154	04 03	59	154	03 04	58	154	02 06	59	154	01 07	58	155
27	05 14	59	155	04 15	59	155	03 16	58	155	02 18	59	155	01 19	59	155
26	05 25	58	156	04 27	59	156	03 28	59	156	02 29	58	156	01 31	59	156
25	05 37	-59	157	04 38	-59	157	03 39	-59	157	02 40	-58	157	01 42	-59	157
24	05 48	59	157	04 49	59	158	03 50	59	158	02 51	59	158	01 52	59	158
23	05 59	59	158	05 00	59	159	04 01	59	159	03 02	59	159	02 03	59	159
22	06 09	59	159	05 10	59	159	04 11	59	160	03 12	60	160	02 12	59	160
21	06 19	60	160	05 19	59	160	04 20	59	161	03 21	59	161	02 22	59	161
20	06 28	-59	161	05 29	-60	161	04 29	-59	161	03 30	-59	162	02 31	-59	162
19	06 37	60	162	05 37	59	162	04 38	59	162	03 39	59	163	02 40	60	163
18	06 45	59	163	05 46	60	163	04 46	59	163	03 47	59	163	02 48	60	164
17	06 53	59	164	05 54	60	164	04 54	59	164	03 55	60	164	02 55	59	164
16	07 01	60	165	06 01	59	165	05 02	60	165	04 02	59	165	03 03	60	165
15	07 08	-60	166	06 08	-59	166	05 09	-60	166	04 09	-59	166	03 10	-60	166
14	07 15	60	167	06 15	60	167	05 15	59	167	04 16	60	167	03 16	59	167
13	07 21	60	168	06 21	59	168	05 22	60	168	04 22	60	168	03 22	60	168
12	07 27	60	169	06 27	60	169	05 27	60	169	04 27	59	169	03 28	60	169
11	07 32	60	170	06 32	60	170	05 32	59	170	04 33	60	170	03 33	60	170
10	07 37	-60	171	06 37	-60	171	05 37	-60	171	04 37	-59	171	03 38	-60	171
9	07 41	60	172	06 41	59	172	05 42	60	172	04 42	60	172	03 42	60	172
8	07 45	60	172	06 45	60	173	05 45	60	173	04 45	59	173	03 46	60	173
7	07 49	60	173	06 49	60	173	05 49	60	174	04 49	60	174	03 49	60	174
6	07 52	60	174	06 52	60	174	05 52	60	174	04 52	60	174	03 52	60	175
5	07 54	-60	175	06 54	-60	175	05 54	-60	175	04 54	-60	175	03 54	-60	175
4	07 56	60	176	06 56	60	176	05 56	60	176	04 56	60	176	03 56	60	176
3	07 58	60	177	06 58	60	177	05 58	60	177	04 58	60	177	03 58	60	177
2	07 59	60	178	06 59	60	178	05 59	60	178	04 59	60	178	03 59	60	178
1	08 00	60	179	07 00	60	179	06 00	60	179	05 00	60	179	04 00	60	179
0	08 00	-60	180	07 00	-60	180	06 00	-60	180	05 00	-60	180	04 00	-60	180

LHA	25°			26°			27°			28°			29°			LHA
	Hc	d	Z	Hc	d	Z	Hc	d	Z	Hc	d	Z	Hc	d	Z	
	° ′	′	°	° ′	′	°	° ′	′	°	° ′	′	°	° ′	′	°	
69																291
68																292
67																293
66																294
65																295
64																296
63																297
62																298
61																299
60																300
59																301
58																302
57																303
56																304
55																305
54																306
53																307
52																308
51																309
50																310
49	-5 24	56	137													311
48	-5 04	57	137													312
47	-4 46	56	138													313
46	-4 27	56	139	-5 23	57	139										314
45	-4 09	-56	140	-5 05	-57	140										315
44	-3 51	56	141	-4 47	57	141										316
43	-3 33	57	142	-4 30	57	142	-5 27	57	142							317
42	-3 16	57	143	-4 13	57	143	-5 10	57	143							318
41	-2 59	57	143	-3 56	57	144	-4 53	57	144							319
40	-2 42	-58	144	-3 40	-57	145	-4 37	-57	145							320
39	-2 26	57	145	-3 23	58	145	-4 21	57	146	-5 18	57	146				321
38	-2 10	58	146	-3 08	57	146	-4 05	58	147	-5 03	57	147				322
37	-1 55	57	147	-2 52	58	147	-3 50	57	147	-4 47	58	148				323
36	-1 39	58	148	-2 37	58	148	-3 35	57	148	-4 32	58	149				324
35	-1 25	-57	149	-2 22	-58	149	-3 20	-58	149	-4 18	-58	149	-5 16	-58	150	325
34	-1 10	58	150	-2 08	58	150	-3 06	58	150	-4 04	58	150	-5 02	58	151	326
33	-0 56	58	150	-1 54	58	151	-2 52	58	151	-3 50	58	151	-4 48	58	151	327
32	-0 42	58	151	-1 40	59	152	-2 39	58	152	-3 37	58	152	-4 35	58	152	328
31	-0 29	58	152	-1 27	58	152	-2 25	59	153	-3 24	58	153	-4 22	58	153	329
30	-0 16	-58	153	-1 14	-59	153	-2 13	-58	154	-3 11	-58	154	-4 09	-59	154	330
29	-0 03	59	154	-1 02	58	154	-2 00	59	154	-2 59	58	155	-3 57	59	155	331
28	00 09	59	155	-0 50	58	155	-1 48	59	155	-2 47	58	155	-3 45	59	156	332
27	00 20	58	156	-0 38	59	156	-1 37	58	156	-2 35	59	156	-3 34	59	157	333
26	00 32	59	157	-0 27	59	157	-1 26	58	157	-2 24	59	157	-3 23	59	157	334
25	00 43	-59	157	-0 16	-59	158	-1 15	-59	158	-2 14	-58	158	-3 12	-59	158	335
24	00 53	58	158	-0 05	59	159	-1 04	59	159	-2 03	59	159	-3 02	59	159	336
23	01 04	59	159	00 05	59	159	-0 54	59	160	-1 53	59	160	-2 52	59	.60	337
22	01 13	59	160	00 14	59	160	-0 45	59	160	-1 44	59	161	-2 43	59	161	338
21	01 23	59	161	00 24	60	161	-0 36	59	161	-1 35	59	162	-2 34	59	162	339
20	01 32	-60	162	00 32	-59	162	-0 27	-59	162	-1 26	-59	162	-2 25	-59	163	340
19	01 40	59	163	00 41	59	163	-0 18	60	163	-1 18	59	163	-2 17	59	163	341
18	01 48	59	164	00 49	59	164	-0 10	60	164	-1 10	59	164	-2 09	59	164	342
17	01 56	59	165	00 57	60	165	-0 03	59	165	-1 02	60	165	-2 02	59	165	343
16	02 03	59	166	01 04	60	166	00 04	59	166	-0 55	60	166	-1 55	59	166	344
15	02 10	-59	166	01 11	-60	167	00 11	-60	167	-0 49	-59	167	-1 48	-60	167	345
14	02 17	60	167	01 17	59	167	00 18	60	168	-0 42	60	168	-1 42	60	168	346
13	02 22	59	168	01 23	60	168	00 23	60	169	-0 37	59	169	-1 36	60	169	347
12	02 28	60	169	01 28	59	169	00 29	60	169	-0 31	60	169	-1 31	60	170	348
11	02 33	60	170	01 33	59	170	00 34	60	170	-0 26	60	170	-1 26	60	171	349
10	02 38	-60	171	01 38	-60	171	00 38	-60	171	-0 22	-59	171	-1 21	-60	171	350
9	02 42	60	172	01 42	60	172	00 42	60	172	-0 18	59	172	-1 17	60	172	351
8	02 46	60	173	01 46	60	173	00 46	60	173	-0 14	60	173	-1 14	60	173	352
7	02 49	60	174	01 49	60	174	00 49	60	174	-0 11	60	174	-1 11	60	174	353
6	02 52	60	175	01 52	60	175	00 52	60	175	-0 08	60	175	-1 08	60	175	354
5	02 54	-60	175	01 54	-59	176	00 55	-60	176	-0 05	-60	176	-1 05	-60	176	355
4	02 56	60	176	01 56	60	176	00 56	59	176	-0 03	60	176	-1 03	60	176	356
3	02 58	60	177	01 58	60	177	00 58	60	177	-0 02	60	177	-1 02	60	177	357
2	02 59	60	178	01 59	60	178	00 59	60	178	-0 01	60	178	-1 01	60	178	358
1	03 00	60	179	02 00	60	179	01 00	60	179	00 00	60	179	-1 00	60	179	359
0	03 00	-60	180	02 00	-60	180	01 00	-60	180	00 00	-60	180	-1 00	-60	180	360

S. Lat. {LHA greater than 180°........ Zn=180−Z; LHA less than 180°........... Zn=180+Z}

DECLINATION (15°-29°) CONTRARY NAME TO LATITUDE

LAT 62°

LAT 62°

N. Lat. {LHA greater than 180°....... Zn=Z; LHA less than 180°........... Zn=360−Z}

DECLINATION (0°-14°) SAME NAME AS LATITUDE

LHA	0° Hc	0° d	0° Z	1° Hc	1° d	1° Z	2° Hc	2° d	2° Z	3° Hc	3° d	3° Z	4° Hc	4° d	4° Z
	° ′	′	°	° ′	′	°	° ′	′	°	° ′	′	°	° ′	′	°
0	27 00	+60	180	28 00	+60	180	29 00	+60	180	30 00	+60	180	31 00	+60	180
1	27 00	60	179	28 00	60	179	29 00	60	179	30 00	60	179	31 00	60	179
2	26 59	60	178	27 59	60	178	28 59	60	178	29 59	60	178	30 59	60	178
3	26 58	60	177	27 58	60	177	28 58	60	177	29 58	60	177	30 58	60	177
4	26 56	60	176	27 56	60	176	28 56	60	175	29 56	60	175	30 56	60	175
5	26 53	+60	174	27 53	+60	174	28 53	+60	174	29 53	+60	174	30 53	+60	174
6	26 50	60	173	27 50	60	173	28 50	60	173	29 50	60	173	30 50	60	173
7	26 47	60	172	27 47	60	172	28 47	60	172	29 47	60	172	30 47	59	172
8	26 43	60	171	27 43	60	171	28 43	60	171	29 43	59	171	30 42	60	171
9	26 39	59	170	27 38	60	170	28 38	60	170	29 38	60	170	30 38	60	170
10	26 33	+60	169	27 33	+60	169	28 33	+60	169	29 33	+60	169	30 33	+59	168
11	26 28	60	168	27 28	59	168	28 27	60	168	29 27	60	167	30 27	59	167
12	26 22	60	167	27 22	59	167	28 21	60	166	29 21	59	166	30 20	60	166
13	26 15	60	166	27 15	60	165	28 15	59	165	29 14	60	165	30 14	59	165
14	26 08	60	164	27 08	59	164	28 07	60	164	29 07	59	164	30 06	60	164
15	26 01	+59	163	27 00	+60	163	28 00	+59	163	28 59	+59	163	29 58	+60	163
16	25 53	59	162	26 52	59	162	27 51	60	162	28 51	59	162	29 50	59	162
17	25 44	59	161	26 43	60	161	27 43	59	161	28 42	59	161	29 41	60	160
18	25 35	59	160	26 34	59	160	27 33	60	160	28 33	59	159	29 32	59	159
19	25 25	59	159	26 24	60	159	27 24	59	159	28 23	59	158	29 22	59	158
20	25 15	+59	158	26 14	+59	158	27 13	+59	157	28 12	+60	157	29 12	+59	157
21	25 05	59	157	26 04	59	157	27 03	59	156	28 02	59	156	29 01	59	156
22	24 54	59	156	25 53	58	155	26 51	59	155	27 50	59	155	28 49	59	155
23	24 42	59	155	25 41	59	154	26 40	59	154	27 39	58	154	28 37	59	154
24	24 30	59	153	25 29	59	153	26 28	58	153	27 26	59	153	28 25	59	153
25	24 18	+58	152	25 16	+59	152	26 15	+59	152	27 14	+58	152	28 12	+59	151
26	24 05	59	151	25 04	58	151	26 02	59	151	27 01	58	151	27 59	58	150
27	23 52	58	150	24 50	59	150	25 49	58	150	26 47	58	150	27 45	59	149
28	23 38	58	149	24 36	59	149	25 35	58	149	26 33	58	148	27 31	58	148
29	23 24	58	148	24 22	58	148	25 20	58	148	26 18	59	147	27 17	58	147
30	23 09	+58	147	24 07	+58	147	25 05	+58	147	26 03	+58	146	27 01	+58	146
31	22 54	58	146	23 52	58	146	24 50	58	145	25 48	58	145	26 46	58	145
32	22 39	58	145	23 37	57	145	24 34	58	144	25 32	58	144	26 30	58	144
33	22 23	58	144	23 21	57	144	24 18	58	143	25 16	58	143	26 14	58	143
34	22 07	57	143	23 04	58	143	24 02	58	142	25 00	57	142	25 57	58	142
35	21 50	+58	142	22 48	+57	142	23 45	+58	141	24 43	+57	141	25 40	+57	141
36	21 33	57	141	22 30	58	141	23 28	57	140	24 25	58	140	25 23	57	140
37	21 16	57	140	22 13	57	140	23 10	57	139	24 07	58	139	25 05	57	139
38	20 58	57	139	21 55	57	138	22 52	57	138	23 49	57	138	24 46	58	137
39	20 40	57	138	21 37	57	137	22 34	57	137	23 31	57	137	24 28	57	136
40	20 21	+57	137	21 18	+57	136	22 15	+57	136	23 12	+57	136	24 09	+57	135
41	20 02	57	136	20 59	57	135	21 56	57	135	22 53	57	135	23 50	56	134
42	19 43	57	135	20 40	57	134	21 37	56	134	22 33	57	134	23 30	56	133
43	19 24	56	134	20 20	57	133	21 17	56	133	22 13	57	133	23 10	56	132
44	19 04	56	133	20 00	57	132	20 57	56	132	21 53	57	132	22 50	56	131
45	18 44	+56	132	19 40	+56	131	20 36	+57	131	21 33	+56	131	22 29	+56	130
46	18 23	56	131	19 19	57	130	20 16	56	130	21 12	56	130	22 08	56	129
47	18 02	56	130	18 58	57	129	19 55	56	129	20 51	56	129	21 47	56	128
48	17 41	56	129	18 37	56	128	19 33	56	128	20 29	56	128	21 25	56	127
49	17 20	56	128	18 16	56	127	19 12	56	127	20 08	55	127	21 03	56	126
50	16 58	+56	127	17 54	+56	126	18 50	+56	126	19 46	+55	126	20 41	+56	125
51	16 36	56	126	17 32	56	125	18 28	55	125	19 23	56	125	20 19	55	124
52	16 14	56	125	17 10	55	125	18 05	56	124	19 01	55	124	19 56	56	123
53	15 51	56	124	16 47	55	124	17 42	56	123	18 38	55	123	19 33	56	122
54	15 29	55	123	16 24	56	123	17 20	55	122	18 15	55	122	19 10	55	121
55	15 06	+55	122	16 01	+59	122	16 56	+56	121	17 52	+55	121	18 47	+55	120
56	14 42	56	121	15 38	55	121	16 33	55	120	17 28	55	120	18 23	55	119
57	14 19	55	120	15 14	55	120	16 09	55	119	17 04	55	119	17 59	55	118
58	13 55	55	119	14 50	55	119	15 45	55	118	16 40	55	118	17 35	55	117
59	13 31	55	118	14 26	55	118	15 21	55	117	16 16	55	117	17 11	55	117
60	13 07	+55	117	14 02	+55	117	14 57	+55	116	15 52	+54	116	16 46	+55	116
61	12 43	55	116	13 38	54	116	14 32	55	115	15 27	55	115	16 22	54	115
62	12 18	55	115	13 13	55	115	14 08	54	115	15 02	55	114	15 57	54	114
63	11 54	54	114	12 48	55	114	13 43	54	114	14 37	55	113	15 32	54	113
64	11 29	54	114	12 23	55	113	13 18	54	113	14 12	55	112	15 07	54	112
65	11 04	+54	113	11 58	+55	112	12 53	+54	112	13 47	+54	111	14 41	+55	111
66	10 39	54	112	11 33	54	111	12 27	55	111	13 22	54	110	14 16	54	110
67	10 13	54	111	11 07	55	110	12 02	54	110	12 56	54	109	13 50	54	109
68	09 48	54	110	10 42	54	109	11 36	54	109	12 30	54	109	13 24	54	108
69	09 22	54	109	10 16	54	108	11 10	54	108	12 04	54	108	12 58	54	107

LHA	5° Hc	5° d	5° Z	6° Hc	6° d	6° Z	7° Hc	7° d	7° Z	8° Hc	8° d	8° Z	9° Hc	9° d	9° Z
	° ′	′	°	° ′	′	°	° ′	′	°	° ′	′	°	° ′	′	°
0	32 00	+60	180	33 00	+60	180	34 00	+60	180	35 00	+60	180	36 00	+60	180
1	32 00	60	179	33 00	60	179	34 00	60	179	35 00	60	179	36 00	60	179
2	31 59	60	178	32 59	60	178	33 59	60	178	34 59	60	178	35 59	60	178
3	31 58	60	177	32 58	59	176	33 57	60	176	34 57	60	176	35 57	60	176
4	31 56	60	175	32 56	60	175	33 56	59	175	34 55	60	175	35 55	60	175
5	31 53	+60	174	32 53	+60	174	33 53	+60	174	34 53	+60	174	35 53	+60	174
6	31 50	60	173	32 50	60	173	33 50	60	173	34 50	60	173	35 50	60	173
7	31 46	60	172	32 46	60	172	33 46	60	172	34 46	60	172	35 46	60	172
8	31 42	60	171	32 42	60	171	33 42	60	170	34 42	60	170	35 42	59	170
9	31 38	59	170	32 37	60	169	33 37	60	169	34 37	60	169	35 37	59	169
10	31 32	+60	168	32 32	+60	168	33 32	+59	168	34 31	+60	168	35 31	+60	168
11	31 26	60	167	32 26	60	167	33 26	60	167	34 26	59	167	35 25	60	167
12	31 20	60	166	32 20	59	166	33 19	60	166	34 19	60	166	35 19	59	165
13	31 13	60	165	32 13	59	165	33 12	60	165	34 12	59	164	35 11	60	164
14	31 06	59	164	32 05	60	164	33 05	59	163	34 04	60	163	35 04	59	163
15	30 58	+59	163	31 57	+60	162	32 57	+59	162	33 56	+60	162	34 56	+59	162
16	30 49	60	161	31 49	59	161	32 48	59	161	33 47	60	161	34 47	59	161
17	30 41	59	160	31 40	59	160	32 39	59	160	33 38	60	160	34 38	59	160
18	30 31	59	159	31 30	59	159	32 29	60	159	33 29	59	159	34 28	59	158
19	30 21	59	158	31 20	59	158	32 19	59	158	33 18	59	157	34 17	59	157
20	30 11	+59	157	31 10	+59	157	32 09	+59	156	33 08	+58	156	34 06	+59	156
21	30 00	58	156	30 58	59	155	31 57	59	155	32 56	59	155	33 55	59	155
22	29 48	59	155	30 47	59	154	31 46	59	154	32 45	58	154	33 43	59	154
23	29 36	59	153	30 35	59	153	31 34	58	153	32 32	59	153	33 31	58	152
24	29 24	58	152	30 22	59	152	31 21	59	152	32 20	58	152	33 18	59	151
25	29 11	+58	151	30 09	+59	151	31 08	+58	151	32 06	+59	150	33 05	+58	150
26	28 57	59	150	29 56	58	150	30 54	59	150	31 53	58	149	32 51	58	149
27	28 44	58	149	29 42	58	149	30 40	58	148	31 38	59	148	32 37	58	148
28	28 29	59	148	29 28	58	148	30 26	58	147	31 24	58	147	32 22	58	147
29	28 15	58	147	29 13	58	147	30 11	58	146	31 09	58	146	32 07	58	146
30	27 59	+58	146	28 57	+58	145	29 55	+58	145	30 53	+58	145	31 51	+58	145
31	27 44	58	145	28 42	58	144	29 40	57	144	30 37	58	144	31 35	58	143
32	27 28	58	144	28 26	57	143	29 23	58	143	30 21	58	143	31 19	57	142
33	27 12	57	142	28 09	58	142	29 07	57	142	30 04	58	141	31 02	57	141
34	26 55	57	141	27 52	58	141	28 50	57	141	29 47	57	140	30 44	58	140
35	26 37	+58	140	27 35	+57	140	28 32	+57	140	29 29	+58	139	30 27	+57	139
36	26 20	57	139	27 17	57	139	28 14	57	139	29 11	58	138	30 09	57	138
37	26 02	57	138	26 59	57	138	27 56	57	138	28 53	57	137	29 50	57	137
38	25 44	57	137	26 41	56	137	27 37	57	136	28 34	57	136	29 31	57	136
39	25 25	57	136	26 22	57	136	27 19	56	135	28 15	57	135	29 12	57	135
40	25 06	+56	135	26 02	+57	135	26 59	+57	134	27 56	+56	134	28 52	+57	134
41	24 46	57	134	25 43	57	134	26 40	56	133	27 36	57	133	28 33	56	133
42	24 26	57	133	25 23	57	133	26 20	56	132	27 16	56	132	28 12	57	131
43	24 06	57	132	25 03	56	132	25 59	56	131	26 55	57	131	27 52	56	130
44	23 46	56	131	24 42	56	131	25 38	57	130	26 35	56	130	27 31	56	129
45	23 25	+56	130	24 21	+57	130	25 18	+56	129	26 14	+56	129	27 10	+55	128
46	23 04	56	129	24 00	56	129	24 56	56	128	25 52	56	128	26 48	56	127
47	22 43	56	128	23 39	56	127	24 35	55	127	25 30	56	127	26 26	56	126
48	22 21	56	127	23 17	56	126	24 13	55	126	25 08	56	126	26 04	56	125
49	21 59	56	126	22 55	56	125	23 51	55	125	24 46	56	125	25 42	56	124
50	21 37	+56	125	22 33	+55	124	23 28	+56	124	24 24	+55	124	25 19	+55	123
51	21 14	56	124	22 10	55	123	23 05	56	123	24 01	55	123	24 56	55	122
52	20 52	55	123	21 47	55	122	22 42	56	122	23 38	55	122	24 33	55	121
53	20 29	55	122	21 24	55	122	22 19	55	121	23 14	55	121	24 09	55	120
54	20 05	56	121	21 01	55	121	21 56	55	120	22 51	55	120	23 46	55	119
55	19 42	+55	120	20 37	+55	120	21 32	+55	119	22 27	+55	119	23 22	+55	118
56	19 18	55	119	20 13	55	119	21 08	55	118	22 03	55	118	22 58	55	117
57	18 54	55	118	19 49	55	118	20 44	55	117	21 39	54	117	22 33	55	116
58	18 30	55	117	19 25	55	117	20 20	54	116	21 14	55	116	22 09	54	115
59	18 06	54	116	19 00	55	116	19 55	55	115	20 50	54	115	21 44	55	114
60	17 41	+55	115	18 36	+54	115	19 30	+55	114	20 25	+54	114	21 19	+55	113
61	17 16	55	114	18 11	54	114	19 05	55	113	20 00	54	113	20 54	54	112
62	16 51	55	113	17 46	54	113	18 40	55	112	19 35	54	112	20 29	54	111
63	16 26	55	112	17 21	54	112	18 15	54	111	19 09	54	111	20 03	55	111
64	16 01	54	111	16 55	55	111	17 50	54	110	18 44	54	110	19 38	54	110
65	15 36	+54	110	16 30	+54	110	17 24	+54	110	18 18	+54	109	19 12	+54	109
66	15 10	54	110	16 04	54	109	16 58	54	109	17 52	54	108	18 46	54	108
67	14 44	54	109	15 38	54	108	16 32	54	108	17 26	54	107	18 20	54	107
68	14 18	54	108	15 12	54	107	16 06	54	107	17 00	54	106	17 54	54	106
69	13 52	54	107	14 46	54	106	15 40	54	106	16 34	54	105	17 28	54	105

LHA	10° Hc	10° d	10° Z	11° Hc	11° d	11° Z	12° Hc	12° d	12° Z	13° Hc	13° d	13° Z	14° Hc	14° d	14° Z	LHA
	° ′	′	°	° ′	′	°	° ′	′	°	° ′	′	°	° ′	′	°	
0	37 00	+60	180	38 00	+60	180	39 00	+60	180	40 00	+60	180	41 00	+60	180	360
1	37 00	60	179	38 00	60	179	39 00	60	179	40 00	60	179	41 00	60	179	359
2	36 59	60	178	37 59	60	178	38 59	60	178	39 59	60	178	40 59	60	177	358
3	36 57	60	176	37 57	60	176	38 57	60	176	39 57	60	176	40 57	60	176	357
4	36 55	60	175	37 55	60	175	38 55	60	175	39 55	60	175	40 55	60	175	356
5	36 53	+60	174	37 53	+60	174	38 53	+60	174	39 53	+59	174	40 52	+60	174	355
6	36 50	59	173	37 49	60	173	38 49	60	173	39 49	60	172	40 49	60	172	354
7	36 46	60	171	37 46	59	171	38 45	60	171	39 45	60	171	40 45	60	171	353
8	36 41	60	170	37 41	60	170	38 41	60	170	39 41	60	170	40 41	59	170	352
9	36 36	60	169	37 36	60	169	38 36	60	169	39 36	59	169	40 35	60	169	351
10	36 31	+60	168	37 31	+59	168	38 30	+60	168	39 30	+60	167	40 30	+59	167	350
11	36 25	59	167	37 24	60	166	38 24	60	166	39 24	59	166	40 23	60	166	349
12	36 18	60	165	37 18	59	165	38 17	60	165	39 17	59	165	40 16	60	165	348
13	36 11	59	164	37 10	60	164	38 10	59	164	39 09	60	164	40 09	59	163	347
14	36 03	60	163	37 03	59	163	38 02	59	163	39 01	60	162	40 01	59	162	346
15	35 55	+59	162	36 54	+60	162	37 54	+59	161	38 53	+59	161	39 52	+60	161	345
16	35 46	59	161	36 45	60	160	37 45	59	160	38 44	59	160	39 43	59	160	344
17	35 37	59	159	36 36	59	159	37 35	59	159	38 34	59	158	39 33	59	158	343
18	35 27	59	158	36 26	59	158	37 25	59	158	38 24	59	157	39 23	59	157	342
19	35 16	59	157	36 15	59	157	37 14	59	156	38 13	59	156	39 12	59	156	341
20	35 05	+59	156	36 04	+59	156	37 03	+59	155	38 02	+59	155	39 01	+59	155	340
21	34 54	59	155	35 53	58	154	36 51	59	154	37 50	59	154	38 49	59	154	339
22	34 42	59	153	35 41	58	153	36 39	59	153	37 38	59	153	38 37	58	152	338
23	34 29	59	152	35 28	59	152	36 27	58	152	37 25	59	151	38 24	58	151	337
24	34 17	58	151	35 15	58	151	36 13	59	151	37 12	58	150	38 10	58	150	336
25	34 03	+58	150	35 01	+59	150	36 00	+58	149	36 58	+58	149	37 56	+58	149	335
26	33 49	58	149	34 47	59	148	35 46	58	148	36 44	58	148	37 42	58	148	334
27	33 35	58	148	34 33	58	147	35 31	58	147	36 29	58	147	37 27	58	146	333
28	33 20	58	146	34 18	58	146	35 16	58	146	36 14	58	146	37 12	57	145	332
29	33 05	58	145	34 03	57	145	35 00	58	145	35 58	58	144	36 56	57	144	331
30	32 49	+58	144	33 47	+57	144	34 44	+58	144	35 42	+58	143	36 40	+57	143	330
31	32 33	57	143	33 30	58	143	34 28	57	142	35 25	58	142	36 23	57	142	329
32	32 16	58	142	33 14	57	142	34 11	57	141	35 08	58	141	36 06	57	141	328
33	31 59	57	141	32 56	58	140	33 54	57	140	34 51	57	140	35 48	57	139	327
34	31 42	57	140	32 39	57	139	33 36	57	139	34 33	57	139	35 30	57	138	326
35	31 24	+57	139	32 21	+57	138	33 18	+57	138	34 15	+57	138	35 12	+57	137	325
36	31 06	57	138	32 03	57	137	33 00	56	137	33 56	57	136	34 53	57	136	324
37	30 47	57	136	31 44	57	136	32 41	56	136	33 37	57	135	34 34	57	135	323
38	30 28	57	135	31 25	56	135	32 21	57	135	33 18	57	134	34 15	56	134	322
39	30 09	56	134	31 05	57	134	32 02	56	133	32 58	57	133	33 55	56	133	321
40	29 49	+56	133	30 45	+57	133	31 42	+56	132	32 38	+56	132	33 34	+57	132	320
41	29 29	56	132	30 25	57	132	31 22	56	131	32 18	56	131	33 14	56	130	319
42	29 09	56	131	30 05	56	131	31 01	56	130	31 57	56	130	32 53	56	129	318
43	28 48	56	130	29 44	56	130	30 40	56	129	31 36	56	129	32 32	56	128	317
44	28 27	56	129	29 23	56	129	30 19	55	128	31 14	56	128	32 10	56	127	316
45	28 05	+56	128	29 01	+56	128	29 57	+56	127	30 53	+55	127	31 48	+56	126	315
46	27 44	56	127	28 40	55	126	29 35	56	126	30 31	55	126	31 26	56	125	314
47	27 22	55	126	28 17	56	125	29 13	55	125	30 08	56	125	31 04	55	124	313
48	27 00	55	125	27 55	56	124	28 51	55	124	29 46	55	124	30 41	55	123	312
49	26 37	56	124	27 33	55	123	28 28	55	123	29 23	55	122	30 18	55	122	311
50	26 14	+56	123	27 10	+55	122	28 05	+55	122	29 00	+55	121	29 55	+55	121	310
51	25 51	55	122	26 46	56	121	27 42	55	121	28 37	54	120	29 31	55	120	309
52	25 28	55	121	26 23	55	120	27 18	55	120	28 13	55	119	29 08	54	119	308
53	25 04	55	120	25 59	55	119	26 54	55	119	27 49	55	118	28 44	54	118	307
54	24 41	55	119	25 36	54	118	26 30	55	118	27 25	55	117	28 20	54	117	306
55	24 17	+54	118	25 11	+55	117	26 06	+55	117	27 01	+54	116	27 55	+55	116	305
56	23 53	54	117	24 47	55	116	25 42	54	116	26 36	55	115	27 31	54	115	304
57	23 28	55	116	24 23	54	115	25 17	54	115	26 11	55	114	27 06	54	114	303
58	23 03	55	115	23 58	54	114	24 52	55	114	25 47	54	113	26 41	54	113	302
59	22 39	54	114	23 33	54	113	24 27	54	113	25 21	55	112	26 16	54	112	301
60	22 14	+54	113	23 08	+54	112	24 02	+54	112	24 56	+54	112	25 50	+54	111	300
61	21 48	55	112	22 43	54	112	23 37	54	111	24 31	54	111	25 25	54	110	299
62	21 23	54	111	22 17	54	111	23 11	54	110	24 05	54	110	24 59	54	109	298
63	20 58	54	110	21 52	54	110	22 46	53	109	23 39	54	109	24 33	54	108	297
64	20 32	54	109	21 26	54	109	22 20	54	108	23 14	53	108	24 07	54	107	296
65	20 06	+54	108	21 00	+54	108	21 54	+54	107	22 48	+53	107	23 41	+54	106	295
66	19 40	54	107	20 34	54	107	21 28	53	106	22 21	54	106	23 15	53	105	294
67	19 14	54	106	20 08	54	106	21 02	53	105	21 55	54	105	22 49	53	104	293
68	18 48	54	105	19 42	53	105	20 35	54	104	21 29	53	104	22 22	54	103	292
69	18 22	53	104	19 15	54	104	20 09	53	103	21 02	54	103	21 56	53	103	291

0° 1° 2° 3° 4° 5° 6° 7° 8° 9° 10° 11° 12° 13° 14°

S. Lat. {LHA greater than 180°....... Zn=180−Z; LHA less than 180°........... Zn=180+Z}

DECLINATION (0°-14°) SAME NAME AS LATITUDE

LAT 63°

N. Lat. {LHA greater than 180°....... Zn=Z; LHA less than 180°........... Zn=360−Z}

DECLINATION (0°-14°) SAME NAME AS LATITUDE

LHA	0°			1°			2°			3°			4°		
	Hc	d	Z	Hc	d	Z	Hc	d	Z	Hc	d	Z	Hc	d	Z
	° ′	′	°	° ′	′	°	° ′	′	°	° ′	′	°	° ′	′	°
70	08 56	+54	108	09 50	+54	108	10 44	+54	107	11 38	+54	107	12 32	+54	106
71	08 30	54	107	09 24	54	107	10 18	54	106	11 12	54	106	12 06	54	105
72	08 04	54	106	08 58	54	106	09 52	54	105	10 46	54	105	11 40	53	104
73	07 38	54	105	08 32	54	105	09 26	53	104	10 19	54	104	11 13	54	104
74	07 11	54	104	08 05	54	104	08 59	54	103	09 53	54	103	10 47	53	103
75	06 45	+54	103	07 39	+54	103	08 33	+53	103	09 26	+54	102	10 20	+54	102
76	06 18	54	103	07 12	54	102	08 06	54	102	09 00	53	101	09 53	54	101
77	05 52	53	102	06 45	54	101	07 39	54	101	08 33	54	100	09 27	53	100
78	05 25	54	101	06 19	53	100	07 12	54	100	08 06	54	99	09 00	53	99
79	04 58	54	100	05 52	54	99	06 46	53	99	07 39	54	99	08 33	53	98
80	04 31	+54	99	05 25	+54	99	06 19	+53	98	07 12	+54	98	08 06	+53	97
81	04 04	54	98	04 58	54	98	05 52	53	97	06 45	54	97	07 39	53	96
82	03 37	54	97	04 31	54	97	05 25	53	96	06 18	54	96	07 12	53	95
83	03 10	54	96	04 04	53	96	04 57	54	95	05 51	53	95	06 44	54	94
84	02 43	54	95	03 37	53	95	04 30	54	94	05 24	53	94	06 17	54	94
85	02 16	+54	94	03 10	+53	94	04 03	+54	94	04 57	+53	93	05 50	+53	93
86	01 49	53	94	02 42	54	93	03 36	53	93	04 29	54	92	05 23	53	92
87	01 22	53	93	02 15	54	92	03 09	53	92	04 02	54	91	04 56	53	91
88	00 54	54	92	01 48	53	91	02 41	54	91	03 35	53	90	04 28	54	90
89	00 27	54	91	01 21	53	90	02 14	54	90	03 08	53	90	04 01	53	89
90	00 00	+53	90	00 53	+54	90	01 47	+53	89	02 40	+54	89	03 34	+53	88
91	−0 27	53	89	00 26	54	89	01 20	53	88	02 13	54	88	03 07	53	87
92	−0 54	53	88	−0 01	53	88	00 52	54	87	01 46	53	87	02 39	54	86
93	−1 22	54	87	−0 28	53	87	00 25	54	86	01 19	53	86	02 12	54	86
94	−1 49	54	86	−0 55	53	86	−0 02	54	86	00 52	53	85	01 45	54	85
95	−2 16	+53	86	−1 23	+54	85	−0 29	+53	85	00 24	+54	84	01 18	+53	84
96	−2 43	53	85	−1 50	54	84	−0 56	53	84	−0 03	54	83	00 51	53	83
97	−3 10	53	84	−2 17	54	83	−1 23	53	83	−0 30	54	82	00 24	53	82
98	−3 37	53	83	−2 44	54	82	−1 50	53	82	−0 57	54	82	−0 03	54	81
99	−4 04	53	82	−3 11	54	82	−2 17	53	81	−1 24	54	81	−0 30	54	80
100	−4 31	+53	81	−3 38	+54	81	−2 44	+54	80	−1 50	+53	80	−0 57	+54	79
101	−4 58	54	80	−4 04	53	80	−3 11	54	79	−2 17	54	79	−1 23	53	78
102	−5 25	54	79	−4 31	53	79	−3 38	54	78	−2 44	54	78	−1 50	54	77
103	−5 52	54	78	−4 58	54	78	−4 04	54	77	−3 10	53	77	−2 17	54	77
104				−5 25	54	77	−4 31	54	77	−3 37	54	76	−2 43	54	76
105				−5 51	+54	76	−4 57	+54	76	−4 03	+54	75	−3 09	+54	75
106							−5 24	54	75	−4 30	54	74	−3 36	54	74
107							−5 50	54	74	−4 56	54	73	−4 02	54	73
108										−5 22	54	72	−4 28	54	72
109										−5 48	54	72	−4 54	55	71
110													−5 19	+54	70
111													−5 45	54	69

LHA	5°			6°			7°			8°			9°		
	Hc	d	Z	Hc	d	Z	Hc	d	Z	Hc	d	Z	Hc	d	Z
	° ′	′	°	° ′	′	°	° ′	′	°	° ′	′	°	° ′	′	°
70	13 26	+54	106	14 20	+54	105	15 14	+54	105	16 08	+53	104	17 01	+54	104
71	13 00	54	105	13 54	53	104	14 47	54	104	15 41	54	104	16 35	54	103
72	12 33	54	104	13 27	54	104	14 21	54	103	15 15	53	103	16 08	54	102
73	12 07	54	103	13 01	53	103	13 54	54	102	14 48	54	102	15 42	53	101
74	11 40	54	102	12 34	54	102	13 28	53	101	14 21	54	101	15 15	53	100
75	11 14	+53	101	12 07	+54	101	13 01	+54	100	13 55	+53	100	14 48	+53	99
76	10 47	54	100	11 41	53	100	12 34	54	99	13 28	53	99	14 21	54	98
77	10 20	54	99	11 14	53	99	12 07	54	98	13 01	53	98	13 54	54	98
78	09 53	54	99	10 47	53	98	11 40	54	98	12 34	53	97	13 27	53	97
79	09 26	54	98	10 20	53	97	11 13	54	97	12 07	53	96	13 00	53	96
80	08 59	+54	97	09 53	+53	96	10 46	+54	96	11 40	+53	95	12 33	+53	95
81	08 32	54	96	09 26	53	95	10 19	53	95	11 12	54	94	12 06	53	94
82	08 05	53	95	08 58	54	94	09 52	53	94	10 45	54	94	11 39	53	93
83	07 38	53	94	08 31	54	94	09 25	53	93	10 18	53	93	11 11	54	92
84	07 11	53	93	08 04	53	93	08 57	54	92	09 51	53	92	10 44	53	91
85	06 43	+54	92	07 37	+53	92	08 30	+54	91	09 24	+53	91	10 17	+53	90
86	06 16	54	91	07 10	53	91	08 03	53	90	08 56	54	90	09 50	53	89
87	05 49	53	90	06 42	54	90	07 36	53	90	08 29	53	89	09 22	54	89
88	05 22	53	90	06 15	54	89	07 09	53	89	08 02	53	88	08 55	53	88
89	04 54	54	89	05 48	53	88	06 41	54	88	07 35	53	87	08 28	53	87
90	04 27	+54	88	05 21	+53	87	06 14	+53	87	07 07	+54	86	08 01	+53	86
91	04 00	53	87	04 53	54	86	05 47	53	86	06 40	54	86	07 34	53	85
92	03 33	53	86	04 26	54	85	05 20	53	85	06 13	54	85	07 07	53	84
93	03 06	53	85	03 59	54	85	04 53	53	84	05 46	53	84	06 39	54	83
94	02 39	53	84	03 32	53	84	04 25	54	83	05 19	53	83	06 12	54	82
95	02 11	+54	83	03 05	+53	83	03 58	+54	82	04 52	+53	82	05 45	+54	82
96	01 44	54	82	02 38	54	82	03 32	53	81	04 25	54	81	05 19	53	81
97	01 17	54	82	02 11	54	81	03 05	53	81	03 58	54	80	04 52	53	80
98	00 51	53	81	01 44	54	80	02 38	53	80	03 31	54	79	04 25	53	79
99	00 24	53	80	01 17	54	79	02 11	54	79	03 05	53	78	03 58	54	78
100	−0 03	+54	79	00 51	+53	78	01 44	+54	78	02 38	+54	77	03 32	+53	77
101	−0 30	54	78	00 24	54	77	01 18	53	77	02 11	54	77	03 05	54	76
102	−0 56	53	77	−0 03	54	77	00 51	54	76	01 45	54	76	02 39	53	75
103	−1 23	54	76	−0 29	54	76	00 25	54	75	01 19	53	75	02 12	54	74
104	−1 49	54	75	−0 55	54	75	−0 01	53	74	00 52	54	74	01 46	54	73
105	−2 15	+53	74	−1 22	+54	74	−0 28	+54	73	00 26	+54	73	01 20	+54	73
106	−2 42	54	73	−1 48	54	73	−0 54	54	73	00 00	54	72	00 54	54	72
107	−3 08	54	73	−2 14	54	72	−1 20	54	72	−0 26	54	71	00 28	55	71
108	−3 34	54	72	−2 40	55	71	−1 45	54	71	−0 51	54	70	00 03	54	70
109	−3 59	54	71	−3 05	54	70	−2 11	54	70	−1 17	54	69	−0 23	54	69
110	−4 25	+54	70	−3 31	+54	69	−2 37	+55	69	−1 42	+54	69	−0 48	+54	68
111	−4 51	55	69	−3 56	54	69	−3 02	54	68	−2 08	55	68	−1 13	54	67
112	−5 16	54	68	−4 22	55	68	−3 27	54	67	−2 33	55	67	−1 38	54	66
113	−5 41	54	67	−4 47	55	67	−3 52	54	66	−2 58	55	66	−2 03	54	65
114				−5 12	55	66	−4 17	55	65	−3 22	54	65	−2 28	55	65
115				−5 36	+54	65	−4 42	+55	64	−3 47	+55	64	−2 52	+54	64
116							−5 06	55	64	−4 11	54	63	−3 17	55	63
117							−5 31	55	63	−4 36	55	62	−3 41	55	62
118										−5 00	55	61	−4 05	55	61
119										−5 24	56	60	−4 28	55	60
120													−4 52	+55	59
121													−5 15	55	58
122													−5 38	55	57

LHA	10°			11°			12°			13°			14°			LHA
	Hc	d	Z	Hc	d	Z	Hc	d	Z	Hc	d	Z	Hc	d	Z	
	° ′	′	°	° ′	′	°	° ′	′	°	° ′	′	°	° ′	′	°	
70	17 55	+54	103	18 49	+53	103	19 42	+54	103	20 36	+53	102	21 29	+53	102	290
71	17 29	53	103	18 22	54	102	19 16	53	102	20 09	53	101	21 02	53	101	289
72	17 02	53	102	17 55	54	101	18 49	53	101	19 42	53	100	20 35	54	100	288
73	16 35	54	101	17 29	53	100	18 22	53	100	19 15	54	99	20 09	53	99	287
74	16 08	54	100	17 02	53	99	17 55	53	99	18 48	54	98	19 42	53	98	286
75	15 41	+54	99	16 35	+53	98	17 28	+53	98	18 21	+54	97	19 15	+53	97	285
76	15 15	53	98	16 08	53	98	17 01	53	97	17 54	54	97	18 48	53	96	284
77	14 48	53	97	15 41	53	97	16 34	53	96	17 27	53	96	18 20	53	95	283
78	14 20	54	96	15 14	53	96	16 07	53	95	17 00	53	95	17 53	53	94	282
79	13 53	54	95	14 47	53	95	15 40	53	94	16 33	53	94	17 26	53	93	281
80	13 26	+53	94	14 19	+54	94	15 13	+53	93	16 06	+53	93	16 59	+53	92	280
81	12 59	53	93	13 52	53	93	14 45	54	93	15 39	53	92	16 32	53	92	279
82	12 32	53	93	13 25	53	92	14 18	53	92	15 11	53	91	16 04	53	91	278
83	12 05	53	92	12 58	53	91	13 51	53	91	14 44	53	90	15 37	53	90	277
84	11 37	54	91	12 31	53	90	13 24	53	90	14 17	53	89	15 10	53	89	276
85	11 10	+53	90	12 03	+54	89	12 57	+53	89	13 50	+53	88	14 43	+53	88	275
86	10 43	53	89	11 36	53	89	12 29	53	88	13 22	54	88	14 16	53	87	274
87	10 16	53	88	11 09	53	88	12 02	53	87	12 55	53	87	13 48	53	86	273
88	09 48	54	87	10 42	53	87	11 35	53	86	12 28	53	86	13 21	53	85	272
89	09 21	54	86	10 15	53	86	11 08	53	85	12 01	53	85	12 54	53	84	271
90	08 54	+53	85	09 47	+54	85	10 41	+53	85	11 34	+53	84	12 27	+53	84	270
91	08 27	53	85	09 20	54	84	10 14	53	84	11 07	53	83	12 00	53	83	269
92	08 00	53	84	08 53	53	83	09 46	54	83	10 40	53	82	11 33	53	82	268
93	07 33	53	83	08 26	53	82	09 19	54	82	10 13	53	81	11 06	53	81	267
94	07 06	53	82	07 59	54	81	08 53	53	81	09 46	53	81	10 39	53	80	266
95	06 39	+53	81	07 32	+54	81	08 26	+53	80	09 19	+53	80	10 12	+54	79	265
96	06 12	53	80	07 05	54	80	07 59	53	79	08 52	54	79	09 46	53	78	264
97	05 45	54	79	06 39	53	79	07 32	54	78	08 26	53	78	09 19	53	77	263
98	05 18	54	78	06 12	54	78	07 06	53	77	07 59	53	77	08 52	54	77	262
99	04 52	53	77	05 45	54	77	06 39	54	77	07 33	53	76	08 26	53	76	261
100	04 25	+54	77	05 19	+54	76	06 13	+53	76	07 06	+54	75	08 00	+53	75	260
101	03 59	53	76	04 52	54	75	05 46	54	75	06 40	53	74	07 33	54	74	259
102	03 32	54	75	04 26	54	74	05 20	54	74	06 14	53	74	07 07	54	73	258
103	03 06	54	74	04 00	54	73	04 54	54	73	05 48	53	73	06 41	54	72	257
104	02 40	54	73	03 34	54	73	04 28	54	72	05 22	53	72	06 15	54	71	256
105	02 14	+54	72	03 08	+54	72	04 02	+54	71	04 56	+54	71	05 50	+54	70	255
106	01 48	54	71	02 42	54	71	03 36	54	70	04 30	54	70	05 24	54	70	254
107	01 23	54	70	02 17	54	70	03 11	54	70	04 05	54	69	04 59	54	69	253
108	00 57	54	70	01 51	54	69	02 45	54	69	03 39	54	68	04 33	54	68	252
109	00 31	55	69	01 26	54	68	02 20	54	68	03 14	54	67	04 08	54	67	251
110	00 06	+54	68	01 00	+55	67	01 55	+54	67	02 49	+54	66	03 43	+54	66	250
111	−0 19	54	67	00 35	55	66	01 30	54	66	02 24	54	66	03 18	55	65	249
112	−0 44	55	66	00 11	54	66	01 05	54	65	01 59	55	65	02 54	54	64	248
113	−1 09	55	65	−0 14	54	65	00 40	55	64	01 35	54	64	02 29	55	63	247
114	−1 33	54	64	−0 39	55	64	00 16	55	63	01 11	54	63	02 05	55	62	246
115	−1 58	+55	63	−1 03	+55	63	−0 08	+54	62	00 46	+55	62	01 41	+55	61	245
116	−2 22	55	62	−1 27	55	62	−0 32	54	62	00 22	55	61	01 17	55	61	244
117	−2 46	56	61	−1 51	55	61	−0 56	55	61	−0 01	55	60	00 54	54	60	243
118	−3 10	55	61	−2 15	55	60	−1 20	55	60	−0 25	55	59	00 30	55	59	242
119	−3 33	55	60	−2 38	55	59	−1 43	55	59	−0 48	55	58	00 07	55	58	241
120	−3 57	+55	59	−3 02	+56	58	−2 06	+55	58	−1 11	+55	58	−0 16	+55	57	240
121	−4 20	55	58	−3 25	56	57	−2 29	55	57	−1 34	55	57	−0 39	55	56	239
122	−4 43	55	57	−3 48	56	57	−2 52	55	56	−1 57	56	56	−1 01	55	55	238
123	−5 06	56	56	−4 10	55	56	−3 15	56	55	−2 19	55	55	−1 24	56	54	237
124	−5 28	55	55	−4 33	56	55	−3 37	56	54	−2 41	55	54	−1 46	56	54	236
125				−4 55	+56	54	−3 59	+56	53	−3 03	+55	53	−2 08	+56	53	235
126				−5 17	56	53	−4 21	56	53	−3 25	56	52	−2 29	56	52	234
127				−5 38	56	52	−4 42	56	52	−3 46	56	51	−2 50	56	51	233
128							−5 03	56	51	−4 07	56	50	−3 11	56	50	232
129							−5 24	56	50	−4 28	56	49	−3 32	56	49	231
130										−4 49	+56	49	−3 53	+57	48	230
131										−5 09	56	48	−4 13	57	47	229
132										−5 29	56	47	−4 33	57	46	228
133													−4 52	56	45	227
134													−5 11	56	44	226
135													−5 30	+57	44	225

0°	1°	2°	3°	4°	5°	6°	7°	8°	9°	10°	11°	12°	13°	14°

S. Lat. {LHA greater than 180°....... Zn=180−Z; LHA less than 180°........... Zn=180+Z}

DECLINATION (0°-14°) SAME NAME AS LATITUDE

LAT 63°

N. Lat. {LHA greater than 180°....... Zn=Z
LHA less than 180°.......... Zn=360−Z}

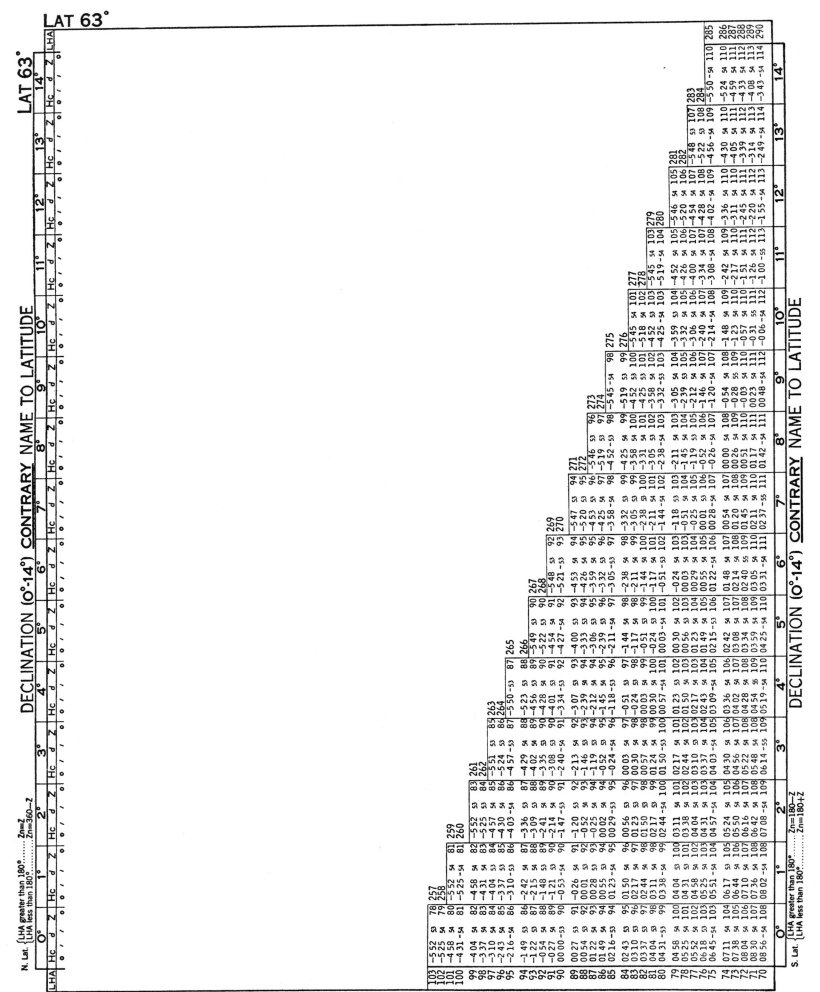

DECLINATION (0°-14°) CONTRARY NAME TO LATITUDE

LHA	0°			1°			2°			3°			4°			5°			6°			7°			8°			9°			10°			11°			12°			13°			14°			LHA
	Hc	d	Z	Hc	d	Z	Hc	d	Z	Hc	d	Z	Hc	d	Z	Hc	d	Z	Hc	d	Z	Hc	d	Z	Hc	d	Z	Hc	d	Z	Hc	d	Z	Hc	d	Z	Hc	d	Z	Hc	d	Z	Hc	d	Z	
	° ′	′	°	° ′	′	°	° ′	′	°	° ′	′	°	° ′	′	°	° ′	′	°	° ′	′	°	° ′	′	°	° ′	′	°	° ′	′	°	° ′	′	°	° ′	′	°	° ′	′	°	° ′	′	°	° ′	′	°	
103	-5 52	53	78																																											257
102	-5 25	54	79																																											258
101	-4 58	54	80	-5 52	54	81																																								259
100	-4 31	-54	81	-5 25	-54	81																																								260
99	-4 04	54	82	-4 58	54	82	-5 52	53	83																																					261
98	-3 37	54	83	-4 31	54	83	-5 25	53	84																																					262
97	-3 10	54	84	-4 04	53	84	-4 57	54	85	-5 51	53	85																																		263
96	-2 43	54	85	-3 37	53	85	-4 30	54	86	-5 24	53	86																																		264
95	-2 16	-54	86	-3 10	-53	86	-4 03	-54	86	-4 57	-53	87	-5 50	-53	87																															265
94	-1 49	53	86	-2 42	54	87	-3 36	53	87	-4 29	54	88	-5 23	53	88																															266
93	-1 22	53	87	-2 15	54	88	-3 09	53	88	-4 02	54	89	-4 56	53	89	-5 49	53	90																												267
92	-0 54	54	88	-1 48	53	89	-2 41	54	89	-3 35	53	90	-4 28	54	90	-5 22	53	90																												268
91	-0 27	54	89	-1 21	53	90	-2 14	54	90	-3 08	53	90	-4 01	53	91	-4 54	54	91	-5 48	53	92																									269
90	00 00	-53	90	-0 53	-54	90	-1 47	-53	91	-2 40	-54	91	-3 34	-53	92	-4 27	-54	92	-5 21	-53	93																									270
89	00 27	53	91	-0 26	54	91	-1 20	53	92	-2 13	54	92	-3 07	53	93	-4 00	53	93	-4 53	54	94	-5 47	53	94																						271
88	00 54	53	92	00 01	53	92	-0 52	54	93	-1 46	53	93	-2 39	54	94	-3 33	53	94	-4 26	54	95	-5 20	53	95																						272
87	01 22	54	93	00 28	53	93	-0 25	54	94	-1 19	53	94	-2 12	54	94	-3 06	53	95	-3 59	54	95	-4 53	53	96	-5 46	53	96																			273
86	01 49	54	94	00 55	53	94	00 02	54	94	-0 52	53	95	-1 45	54	95	-2 39	53	96	-3 32	53	96	-4 25	54	97	-5 19	53	97																			274
85	02 16	-53	94	01 23	-54	95	00 29	-53	95	-0 24	-54	96	-1 18	-53	96	-2 11	-54	97	-3 05	-53	97	-3 58	-54	98	-4 52	-53	98	-5 45	-54	98																275
84	02 43	53	95	01 50	54	96	00 56	53	96	00 03	54	97	-0 51	53	97	-1 44	54	98	-2 38	54	98	-3 32	53	99	-4 25	54	99	-5 19	53	99																276
83	03 10	53	96	02 17	54	97	01 23	53	97	00 30	54	98	-0 24	53	98	-1 17	54	98	-2 11	54	99	-3 05	53	99	-3 58	54	100	-4 52	53	100	-5 45	54	101													277
82	03 37	53	97	02 44	54	98	01 50	53	98	00 57	54	98	00 03	54	99	-0 51	53	99	-1 44	54	100	-2 38	53	100	-3 31	54	101	-4 25	53	101	-5 18	54	102													278
81	04 04	53	98	03 11	54	98	02 17	53	99	01 24	54	99	00 30	54	100	-0 24	53	100	-1 17	54	101	-2 11	54	101	-3 05	53	102	-3 58	54	102	-4 52	53	103	-5 45	54	103										279
80	04 31	-53	99	03 38	-54	99	02 44	-54	100	01 50	-53	100	00 57	-54	101	00 03	-54	101	-0 51	-53	102	-1 44	-54	102	-2 38	-54	103	-3 32	-53	103	-4 25	-54	103	-5 19	-54	104										280
79	04 58	54	100	04 04	53	100	03 11	54	101	02 17	54	101	01 23	53	102	00 30	54	102	-0 24	54	103	-1 18	53	103	-2 11	54	103	-3 05	54	104	-3 59	53	104	-4 52	54	105	-5 46	54	105							281
78	05 25	54	101	04 31	53	101	03 38	54	102	02 44	54	102	01 50	54	103	00 56	53	103	00 03	54	103	-0 51	54	104	-1 45	54	104	-2 39	53	105	-3 32	54	105	-4 26	54	106	-5 20	54	106							282
77	05 52	54	102	04 58	54	102	04 04	54	103	03 10	53	103	02 17	54	103	01 23	54	104	00 29	54	104	-0 25	54	105	-1 19	53	105	-2 12	54	106	-3 06	54	106	-4 00	54	107	-4 54	54	107	-5 48	53	107				283
76	06 18	53	103	05 25	54	103	04 31	54	103	03 37	54	104	02 43	54	104	01 49	54	105	00 55	54	105	00 01	53	106	-0 52	54	106	-1 46	54	107	-2 40	54	107	-3 34	54	107	-4 28	54	108	-5 22	53	108				284
75	06 45	-54	103	05 51	-54	104	04 57	-54	104	04 03	-54	105	03 09	-54	105	02 15	-53	106	01 22	-54	106	00 28	-54	107	-0 26	-54	107	-1 20	-54	107	-2 14	-54	108	-3 08	-54	108	-4 02	-54	109	-4 56	-54	109	-5 50	-54	110	285
74	07 11	54	104	06 17	53	105	05 24	54	105	04 30	54	106	03 36	54	106	02 42	54	107	01 48	54	107	00 54	54	107	00 00	54	108	-0 54	54	108	-1 48	54	109	-2 42	54	109	-3 36	54	110	-4 30	54	110	-5 24	54	110	286
73	07 38	54	105	06 44	54	106	05 50	54	106	04 56	54	107	04 02	54	107	03 08	54	107	02 14	54	108	01 20	54	108	00 26	54	109	-0 28	55	109	-1 23	54	110	-2 17	54	110	-3 11	54	110	-4 05	54	111	-4 59	54	111	287
72	08 04	54	106	07 10	54	107	06 16	54	107	05 22	54	108	04 28	54	108	03 34	54	108	02 40	55	109	01 45	54	109	00 51	54	110	-0 03	54	110	-0 57	54	110	-1 51	54	111	-2 45	54	111	-3 39	54	112	-4 33	54	112	288
71	08 30	54	107	07 36	54	108	06 42	54	108	05 48	54	108	04 54	55	109	03 59	54	109	03 05	54	110	02 11	54	110	01 17	54	111	00 23	54	111	-0 31	55	111	-1 26	54	112	-2 20	54	112	-3 14	54	113	-4 08	54	113	289
70	08 56	-54	108	08 02	-54	108	07 08	-54	109	06 14	-55	109	05 19	-54	110	04 25	-54	110	03 31	-54	111	02 37	-55	111	01 42	-54	111	00 48	-54	112	-0 06	-54	112	-1 00	-55	113	-1 55	-54	113	-2 49	-54	114	-3 43	-54	114	290
	0°			1°			2°			3°			4°			5°			6°			7°			8°			9°			10°			11°			12°			13°			14°			

S. Lat. {LHA greater than 180°....... Zn=180−Z
LHA less than 180°.......... Zn=180+Z}

DECLINATION (0°-14°) CONTRARY NAME TO LATITUDE

N. Lat. {LHA greater than 180°....... Zn=Z; LHA less than 180°....... Zn=360−Z}

DECLINATION (0°-14°) CONTRARY NAME TO LATITUDE

LHA	0° Hc	d	Z	1° Hc	d	Z	2° Hc	d	Z	3° Hc	d	Z	4° Hc	d	Z	LHA
	° ′	′	°	° ′	′	°	° ′	′	°	° ′	′	°	° ′	′	°	
69	09 22	54	109	08 28	55	109	07 33	54	110	06 39	54	110	05 45	54	111	291
68	09 48	55	110	08 53	54	110	07 59	54	111	07 05	55	111	06 10	54	112	292
67	10 13	54	111	09 19	55	111	08 24	54	112	07 30	54	112	06 36	55	112	293
66	10 39	55	112	09 44	54	112	08 50	55	113	07 55	54	113	07 01	55	113	294
65	11 04	−55	113	10 09	−54	113	09 15	−55	113	08 20	−54	114	07 26	−55	114	295
64	11 29	55	114	10 34	54	114	09 40	55	114	08 45	55	115	07 50	54	115	296
63	11 54	55	114	10 59	55	115	10 04	54	115	09 10	55	116	08 15	55	116	297
62	12 18	54	115	11 24	55	116	10 29	55	116	09 34	55	117	08 39	55	117	298
61	12 43	55	116	11 48	55	117	10 53	55	117	09 58	55	118	09 03	55	118	299
60	13 07	−55	117	12 12	−55	118	11 17	−55	118	10 22	−55	119	09 27	−55	119	300
59	13 31	55	118	12 36	55	119	11 41	55	119	10 46	55	119	09 51	55	120	301
58	13 55	55	119	13 00	55	120	12 05	55	120	11 10	55	120	10 15	56	121	302
57	14 19	55	120	13 24	55	121	12 29	56	121	11 33	55	121	10 38	55	122	303
56	14 42	55	121	13 47	55	121	12 52	56	122	11 56	55	122	11 01	55	123	304
55	15 06	−56	122	14 10	−55	122	13 15	−56	123	12 19	−55	123	11 24	−56	124	305
54	15 29	56	123	14 33	55	123	13 38	56	124	12 42	56	124	11 46	55	125	306
53	15 51	55	124	14 56	56	124	14 00	55	125	13 05	56	125	12 09	56	125	307
52	16 14	56	125	15 18	56	125	14 22	55	126	13 27	56	126	12 31	56	126	308
51	16 36	56	126	15 40	56	126	14 44	55	127	13 49	56	127	12 53	56	127	309
50	16 58	−56	127	16 02	−56	127	15 06	−56	128	14 10	−56	128	13 14	−56	128	310
49	17 20	56	128	16 24	56	128	15 28	56	129	14 32	57	129	13 35	56	129	311
48	17 41	56	129	16 45	56	129	15 49	56	130	14 53	57	130	13 56	56	130	312
47	18 02	56	130	17 06	56	130	16 10	57	130	15 13	56	131	14 17	56	131	313
46	18 23	56	131	17 27	57	131	16 30	56	131	15 34	57	132	14 37	56	132	314
45	18 44	−57	132	17 47	−56	132	16 51	−57	132	15 54	−57	133	14 57	−56	133	315
44	19 04	57	133	18 07	56	133	17 11	57	133	16 14	57	134	15 17	57	134	316
43	19 24	57	134	18 27	57	134	17 30	57	134	16 33	56	135	15 37	57	135	317
42	19 43	57	135	18 46	57	135	17 49	56	135	16 53	57	136	15 56	57	136	318
41	20 02	57	136	19 05	57	136	18 08	57	136	17 11	57	137	16 14	57	137	319
40	20 21	−57	137	19 24	−57	137	18 27	−57	137	17 30	−57	138	16 33	−57	138	320
39	20 40	58	138	19 42	57	138	18 45	57	138	17 48	57	139	16 51	57	139	321
38	20 58	57	139	20 01	58	139	19 03	57	139	18 06	57	140	17 09	58	140	322
37	21 16	58	140	20 18	57	140	19 21	58	140	18 23	57	141	17 26	58	141	323
36	21 33	58	141	20 35	57	141	19 38	58	141	18 40	57	142	17 43	58	142	324
35	21 50	−58	142	20 52	−57	142	19 55	−58	142	18 57	−58	143	17 59	−57	143	325
34	22 07	58	143	21 09	58	143	20 11	58	144	19 13	57	144	18 16	58	144	326
33	22 23	58	144	21 25	58	144	20 27	58	145	19 29	58	145	18 31	58	145	327
32	22 39	58	145	21 41	58	145	20 43	58	146	19 45	58	146	18 47	58	146	328
31	22 54	58	146	21 56	58	146	20 58	58	147	20 00	58	147	19 02	58	147	329
30	23 09	−58	147	22 11	−58	147	21 13	−58	148	20 15	−59	148	19 16	−58	148	330
29	23 24	59	148	22 25	58	148	21 27	58	149	20 29	58	149	19 31	59	149	331
28	23 38	58	149	22 40	59	149	21 41	58	150	20 43	59	150	19 44	58	150	332
27	23 52	59	150	22 53	58	151	21 55	59	151	20 56	58	151	19 58	59	151	333
26	24 05	59	151	23 06	58	152	22 08	59	152	21 09	58	152	20 11	59	152	334
25	24 18	−59	152	23 19	−59	153	22 20	−58	153	21 22	−59	153	20 23	−59	153	335
24	24 30	59	153	23 31	58	154	22 33	59	154	21 34	59	154	20 35	59	154	336
23	24 42	59	155	23 43	59	155	22 44	58	155	21 46	59	155	20 47	59	155	337
22	24 54	59	156	23 55	59	156	22 56	59	156	21 57	59	156	20 58	59	156	338
21	25 05	59	157	24 06	59	157	23 07	59	157	22 08	60	157	21 08	59	158	339
20	25 15	−59	158	24 16	−59	158	23 17	−59	158	22 18	−59	158	21 19	−59	159	340
19	25 25	59	159	24 26	59	159	23 27	59	159	22 28	60	159	21 28	59	160	341
18	25 35	59	160	24 36	60	160	23 36	59	160	22 37	59	161	21 38	60	161	342
17	25 44	59	161	24 45	60	161	23 45	59	161	22 46	60	162	21 46	59	162	343
16	25 53	60	162	24 53	59	162	23 54	60	163	22 54	59	163	21 55	60	163	344
15	26 01	−60	163	25 01	−59	163	24 02	−60	164	23 02	−59	164	22 03	−60	164	345
14	26 08	59	164	25 09	60	165	24 09	59	165	23 10	60	165	22 10	60	165	346
13	26 15	59	166	25 16	60	166	24 16	60	166	23 16	59	166	22 17	60	166	347
12	26 22	60	167	25 22	59	167	24 23	60	167	23 23	60	167	22 23	60	167	348
11	26 28	60	168	25 28	60	168	24 28	59	168	23 29	60	168	22 29	60	168	349
10	26 33	−59	169	25 34	−60	169	24 34	−60	169	23 34	−60	169	22 34	−59	169	350
9	26 39	60	170	25 39	60	170	24 39	60	170	23 39	60	170	22 39	60	170	351
8	26 43	60	171	25 43	60	171	24 43	60	171	23 43	59	171	22 44	60	171	352
7	26 47	60	172	25 47	60	172	24 47	60	172	23 47	60	172	22 47	59	172	353
6	26 50	59	173	25 51	60	173	24 51	60	173	23 51	60	173	22 51	60	174	354
5	26 53	−60	174	25 53	−59	174	24 54	−60	175	23 54	−60	175	22 54	−60	175	355
4	26 56	60	176	25 56	60	176	24 56	60	176	23 56	60	176	22 56	60	176	356
3	26 58	60	177	25 58	60	177	24 58	60	177	23 58	60	177	22 58	60	177	357
2	26 59	60	178	25 59	60	178	24 59	60	178	23 59	60	178	22 59	60	178	358
1	27 00	60	179	26 00	60	179	25 00	60	179	24 00	60	179	23 00	60	179	359
0	27 00	−60	180	26 00	−60	180	25 00	−60	180	24 00	−60	180	23 00	−60	180	360

LHA	5° Hc	d	Z	6° Hc	d	Z	7° Hc	d	Z	8° Hc	d	Z	9° Hc	d	Z	LHA
	° ′	′	°	° ′	′	°	° ′	′	°	° ′	′	°	° ′	′	°	
69	04 51	55	111	03 56	54	111	03 02	54	112	02 08	55	112	01 13	54	113	291
68	05 16	54	112	04 22	55	112	03 27	54	113	02 33	55	113	01 38	54	114	292
67	05 41	54	113	04 47	55	113	03 52	54	114	02 58	55	114	02 03	54	115	293
66	06 06	54	114	05 12	55	114	04 17	55	115	03 22	54	115	02 28	55	115	294
65	06 31	−55	115	05 36	−54	115	04 42	−55	116	03 47	−55	116	02 52	−54	116	295
64	06 56	55	116	06 01	55	116	05 06	55	116	04 11	54	117	03 17	55	117	296
63	07 20	55	117	06 25	54	117	05 31	55	117	04 36	55	118	03 41	55	118	297
62	07 44	54	117	06 50	55	118	05 55	55	118	05 00	55	119	04 05	55	119	298
61	08 08	54	118	07 14	55	119	06 19	55	119	05 24	56	120	04 28	55	120	299
60	08 32	−55	119	07 37	−55	120	06 42	−55	120	05 47	−55	121	04 52	−55	121	300
59	08 56	55	120	08 01	55	121	07 06	56	121	06 10	55	121	05 15	55	122	301
58	09 19	55	121	08 24	55	122	07 29	56	122	06 34	56	122	05 38	55	123	302
57	09 43	56	122	08 47	55	122	07 52	55	123	06 57	56	123	06 01	55	124	303
56	10 06	56	123	09 10	55	123	08 15	56	124	07 19	55	124	06 24	56	125	304
55	10 28	−55	124	09 33	−56	124	08 37	−55	125	07 42	−56	125	06 46	−56	125	305
54	10 51	56	125	09 55	56	125	08 59	56	126	08 04	56	126	07 08	56	126	306
53	11 13	56	126	10 17	55	126	09 22	56	127	08 26	56	127	07 30	56	127	307
52	11 35	56	127	10 39	56	127	09 43	56	128	08 47	56	128	07 51	56	128	308
51	11 57	56	128	11 01	56	128	10 05	56	128	09 09	56	129	08 13	56	129	309
50	12 18	−56	129	11 22	−56	129	10 26	−56	129	09 30	−56	130	08 34	−57	130	310
49	12 39	56	130	11 43	56	130	10 47	56	130	09 51	57	131	08 54	56	131	311
48	13 00	56	131	12 04	57	131	11 07	56	131	10 11	56	132	09 15	57	132	312
47	13 21	57	132	12 24	56	132	11 28	57	132	10 31	56	133	09 35	57	133	313
46	13 41	57	133	12 44	56	133	11 48	57	133	10 51	56	134	09 55	57	134	314
45	14 01	−57	133	13 04	−56	134	12 08	−57	134	11 11	−57	135	10 14	−57	135	315
44	14 20	56	134	13 24	57	135	12 27	57	135	11 30	57	135	10 33	57	136	316
43	14 40	57	135	13 43	57	136	12 46	57	136	11 49	57	136	10 52	57	137	317
42	14 59	57	136	14 02	57	137	13 05	57	137	12 08	57	137	11 11	57	138	318
41	15 17	57	137	14 20	57	138	13 23	57	138	12 26	57	138	11 29	58	139	319
40	15 36	−58	138	14 38	−57	139	13 41	−57	139	12 44	−57	139	11 47	−58	140	320
39	15 54	58	139	14 56	57	140	13 59	57	140	13 02	58	140	12 04	57	141	321
38	16 11	57	140	15 14	58	141	14 16	57	141	13 19	58	141	12 21	57	142	322
37	16 28	57	141	15 31	58	142	14 33	57	142	13 36	58	142	12 38	58	143	323
36	16 45	57	142	15 48	58	143	14 50	58	143	13 52	57	143	12 55	58	143	324
35	17 02	−58	143	16 04	−58	144	15 06	−58	144	14 08	−57	144	13 11	−58	144	325
34	17 18	58	144	16 20	58	145	15 22	58	145	14 24	58	145	13 26	58	145	326
33	17 33	58	145	16 35	58	146	15 37	58	146	14 39	58	146	13 41	58	146	327
32	17 49	58	146	16 51	58	147	15 53	59	147	14 54	58	147	13 56	58	147	328
31	18 04	59	147	17 05	58	148	16 07	58	148	15 09	58	148	14 11	58	148	329
30	18 18	−58	148	17 20	−58	149	16 22	−59	149	15 23	−58	149	14 25	−58	149	330
29	18 32	58	149	17 34	59	150	16 35	58	150	15 37	58	150	14 39	59	150	331
28	18 46	59	150	17 47	58	151	16 49	59	151	15 50	58	151	14 52	59	151	332
27	18 59	58	151	18 01	59	152	17 02	59	152	16 03	58	152	15 05	59	152	333
26	19 12	59	153	18 13	58	153	17 15	59	153	16 16	59	153	15 17	59	153	334
25	19 24	−58	154	18 26	−59	154	17 27	−59	154	16 28	−59	154	15 29	−59	154	335
24	19 36	59	155	18 37	58	155	17 39	59	155	16 40	59	155	15 41	59	155	336
23	19 48	59	156	18 49	59	156	17 50	59	156	16 51	59	156	15 52	59	156	337
22	19 59	59	157	19 00	59	157	18 01	59	157	17 02	59	157	16 03	59	157	338
21	20 09	59	158	19 10	59	158	18 11	59	158	17 12	59	158	16 13	59	158	339
20	20 20	−60	159	19 20	−59	159	18 21	−59	159	17 22	−59	159	16 23	−59	159	340
19	20 29	59	160	19 30	59	160	18 31	60	160	17 31	59	160	16 32	59	160	341
18	20 38	59	161	19 39	59	161	18 40	60	161	17 40	59	161	16 41	59	161	342
17	20 47	59	162	19 48	60	162	18 48	59	162	17 49	60	162	16 49	59	163	343
16	20 55	59	163	19 56	60	163	18 56	59	163	17 57	60	163	16 57	59	164	344
15	21 03	−59	164	20 04	−60	164	19 04	−59	164	18 05	−60	164	17 05	−60	165	345
14	21 10	59	165	20 11	60	165	19 11	59	165	18 12	60	165	17 12	60	166	346
13	21 17	59	166	20 18	60	166	19 18	60	166	18 18	59	166	17 19	60	167	347
12	21 23	59	167	20 24	60	167	19 24	60	167	18 24	59	168	17 25	60	168	348
11	21 29	59	168	20 30	60	168	19 30	60	168	18 30	60	169	17 30	59	169	349
10	21 35	−60	169	20 35	−60	169	19 35	−60	170	18 35	−60	170	17 35	−59	170	350
9	21 39	59	170	20 40	60	170	19 40	60	171	18 40	60	171	17 40	60	171	351
8	21 44	60	171	20 44	60	172	19 44	60	172	18 44	60	172	17 44	60	172	352
7	21 48	60	173	20 48	60	173	19 48	60	173	18 48	60	173	17 48	60	173	353
6	21 51	60	174	20 51	60	174	19 51	60	174	18 51	60	174	17 51	60	174	354
5	21 54	−60	175	20 54	−60	175	19 54	−60	175	18 54	−60	175	17 54	−60	175	355
4	21 56	60	176	20 56	60	176	19 56	60	176	18 56	60	176	17 56	60	176	356
3	21 58	60	177	20 58	60	177	19 58	60	177	18 58	60	177	17 58	60	177	357
2	21 59	60	178	20 59	60	178	19 59	60	178	18 59	60	178	17 59	60	178	358
1	22 00	60	179	21 00	60	179	20 00	60	179	19 00	60	179	18 00	60	179	359
0	22 00	−60	180	21 00	−60	180	20 00	−60	180	19 00	−60	180	18 00	−60	180	360

LHA	10° Hc	d	Z	11° Hc	d	Z	12° Hc	d	Z	13° Hc	d	Z	14° Hc	d	Z	LHA
	° ′	′	°	° ′	′	°	° ′	′	°	° ′	′	°	° ′	′	°	
69	00 19	54	113	−0 35	55	114	−1 30	54	114	−2 24	54	114	−3 18	55	115	291
68	00 44	55	114	−0 11	54	114	−1 05	54	115	−1 59	55	115	−2 54	54	116	292
67	01 09	55	115	00 14	54	115	−0 40	55	116	−1 35	54	116	−2 29	55	117	293
66	01 33	54	116	00 39	55	116	−0 16	55	117	−1 11	54	117	−2 05	55	118	294
65	01 58	−55	117	01 03	−55	117	00 08	−54	118	−0 46	−55	118	−1 41	−55	119	295
64	02 22	55	118	01 27	55	118	00 32	54	118	−0 22	55	119	−1 17	55	119	296
63	02 46	55	119	01 51	55	119	00 56	55	119	00 01	55	120	−0 54	54	120	297
62	03 10	55	119	02 15	55	120	01 20	55	120	00 25	55	121	−0 30	55	121	298
61	03 33	55	120	02 38	55	121	01 43	55	121	00 48	55	122	−0 07	55	122	299
60	03 57	−55	121	03 02	−56	122	02 06	−55	122	01 11	−55	122	00 16	−55	123	300
59	04 20	55	122	03 25	56	123	02 29	55	123	01 34	55	123	00 39	55	124	301
58	04 43	55	123	03 48	56	123	02 52	55	124	01 57	56	124	01 01	55	125	302
57	05 06	56	124	04 10	55	124	03 15	56	125	02 19	55	125	01 24	56	126	303
56	05 28	55	125	04 33	56	125	03 37	56	126	02 41	55	126	01 46	56	126	304
55	05 50	−55	126	04 55	−56	126	03 59	−56	127	03 03	−55	127	02 08	−56	127	305
54	06 12	55	127	05 17	56	127	04 21	56	127	03 25	56	128	02 29	56	128	306
53	06 34	56	128	05 38	56	128	04 42	56	128	03 46	56	129	02 50	56	129	307
52	06 55	56	129	05 59	56	129	05 03	56	129	04 07	56	130	03 11	56	130	308
51	07 17	56	130	06 21	57	130	05 24	56	130	04 28	56	131	03 32	56	131	309
50	07 37	−56	130	06 41	−56	131	05 45	−56	131	04 49	−56	131	03 53	−57	132	310
49	07 58	56	131	07 02	57	132	06 05	56	132	05 09	56	132	04 13	57	133	311
48	08 18	56	132	07 22	56	133	06 26	57	133	05 29	56	133	04 33	57	134	312
47	08 38	56	133	07 42	57	134	06 45	56	134	05 49	57	134	04 52	56	135	313
46	08 58	57	134	08 01	56	135	07 05	57	135	06 08	57	135	05 11	56	136	314
45	09 17	−56	135	08 21	−57	135	07 24	−57	136	06 27	−57	136	05 30	−57	136	315
44	09 36	56	136	08 40	57	136	07 43	57	137	06 46	57	137	05 49	57	137	316
43	09 55	57	137	08 58	57	137	08 01	57	138	07 04	57	138	06 07	57	138	317
42	10 14	57	138	09 17	58	138	08 19	57	139	07 22	57	139	06 25	57	139	318
41	10 32	58	139	09 34	57	139	08 37	57	140	07 40	57	140	06 43	57	140	319
40	10 49	−57	140	09 52	−57	140	08 55	−58	141	07 57	−57	141	07 00	−57	141	320
39	11 07	58	141	10 09	57	141	09 12	57	141	08 15	58	142	07 17	57	142	321
38	11 24	58	142	10 26	57	142	09 29	58	142	08 31	57	143	07 34	58	143	322
37	11 40	57	143	10 43	58	143	09 45	57	143	08 48	58	144	07 50	58	144	323
36	11 57	58	144	10 59	58	144	10 01	57	144	09 04	58	145	08 06	58	145	324
35	12 13	−58	145	11 15	−58	145	10 17	−58	145	09 19	−58	146	08 21	−58	146	325
34	12 28	58	146	11 30	58	146	10 32	58	146	09 34	58	147	08 36	58	147	326
33	12 43	58	147	11 45	58	147	10 47	58	147	09 49	58	147	08 51	58	148	327
32	12 58	58	148	12 00	58	148	11 02	58	148	10 04	58	148	09 06	59	149	328
31	13 13	59	149	12 14	58	149	11 16	58	149	10 18	58	149	09 20	59	150	329
30	13 27	−59	150	12 28	−58	150	11 30	−58	150	10 32	−59	150	09 33	−58	151	330
29	13 40	58	151	12 42	59	151	11 43	58	151	10 45	59	151	09 46	58	152	331
28	13 53	58	152	12 55	59	152	11 56	58	152	10 58	59	152	09 59	58	152	332
27	14 06	58	153	13 08	59	153	12 09	59	153	11 10	58	153	10 12	59	153	333
26	14 18	58	154	13 20	59	154	12 21	59	154	11 22	58	154	10 24	59	154	334
25	14 30	−58	155	13 32	−59	155	12 33	−59	155	11 34	−59	155	10 35	−59	155	335
24	14 42	59	156	13 43	59	156	12 44	59	156	11 45	59	156	10 46	59	156	336
23	14 53	59	157	13 54	59	157	12 55	59	157	11 56	59	157	10 57	59	157	337
22	15 04	59	158	14 05	60	158	13 05	59	158	12 06	59	158	11 07	59	158	338
21	15 14	59	159	14 15	60	159	13 15	59	159	12 16	59	159	11 17	59	159	339
20	15 24	−60	160	14 24	−59	160	13 25	−59	160	12 26	−59	160	11 27	−60	160	340
19	15 33	59	161	14 34	60	161	13 34	59	161	12 35	59	161	11 36	60	161	341
18	15 42	60	162	14 42	59	162	13 43	59	162	12 44	60	162	11 44	59	162	342
17	15 50	59	163	14 51	60	163	13 51	59	163	12 52	60	163	11 52	59	163	343
16	15 58	60	164	14 58	59	164	13 59	60	164	12 59	59	164	12 00	60	164	344
15	16 05	−59	165	15 06	−60	165	14 06	−59	165	13 07	−60	165	12 07	−59	165	345
14	16 12	59	166	15 13	60	166	14 13	59	166	13 14	60	166	12 14	60	166	346
13	16 19	60	167	15 19	59	167	14 20	60	167	13 20	60	167	12 20	59	167	347
12	16 25	60	168	15 25	59	168	14 26	60	168	13 26	60	168	12 26	60	168	348
11	16 31	60	169	15 31	60	169	14 31	60	169	13 31	59	169	12 32	60	169	349
10	16 36	−60	170	15 36	−60	170	14 36	−60	170	13 36	−60	170	12 36	−59	170	350
9	16 40	60	171	15 40	59	171	14 41	60	171	13 41	60	171	12 41	60	171	351
8	16 44	59	172	15 45	60	172	14 45	60	172	13 45	60	172	12 45	60	172	352
7	16 48	60	173	15 48	60	173	14 48	60	173	13 48	60	173	12 48	59	173	353
6	16 51	60	174	15 51	60	174	14 51	60	174	13 51	59	174	12 52	60	174	354
5	16 54	−60	175	15 54	−60	175	14 54	−60	175	13 54	−60	175	12 54	−60	175	355
4	16 56	60	176	15 56	60	176	14 56	60	176	13 56	60	176	12 56	60	176	356
3	16 58	60	177	15 58	60	177	14 58	60	177	13 58	60	177	12 58	60	177	357
2	16 59	60	178	15 59	60	178	14 59	60	178	13 59	60	178	12 59	60	178	358
1	17 00	60	179	16 00	60	179	15 00	60	179	14 00	60	179	13 00	60	179	359
0	17 00	−60	180	16 00	−60	180	15 00	−60	180	14 00	−60	180	13 00	−60	180	360

S. Lat. {LHA greater than 180°....... Zn=180−Z; LHA less than 180°....... Zn=180+Z}

DECLINATION (0°-14°) CONTRARY NAME TO LATITUDE

LAT 63°

N. Lat. {LHA greater than 180°……. Zn=Z; LHA less than 180°……….. Zn=360−Z}

DECLINATION (15°-29°) SAME NAME AS LATITUDE

LAT 63°

LHA	15°			16°			17°			18°			19°		
	Hc	d	Z	Hc	d	Z	Hc	d	Z	Hc	d	Z	Hc	d	Z
	° ′	′	°	° ′	′	°	° ′	′	°	° ′	′	°	° ′	′	°
0	42 00	+60	180	43 00	+60	180	44 00	+60	180	45 00	+60	180	46 00	+60	180
1	42 00	60	179	43 00	60	179	44 00	60	179	45 00	60	179	46 00	60	179
2	41 59	60	177	42 59	60	177	43 59	60	177	44 59	60	177	45 59	60	177
3	41 57	60	176	42 57	60	176	43 57	60	176	44 57	60	176	45 57	60	176
4	41 55	60	175	42 55	60	175	43 55	60	175	44 55	60	175	45 55	60	175
5	41 52	+60	174	42 52	+60	173	43 52	+60	173	44 52	+60	173	45 52	+60	173
6	41 49	60	172	42 49	60	172	43 49	60	172	44 49	59	172	45 48	60	172
7	41 45	60	171	42 45	60	171	43 45	59	171	44 44	60	171	45 44	60	171
8	41 40	60	170	42 40	60	170	43 40	60	169	44 40	59	169	45 39	60	169
9	41 35	60	168	42 35	60	168	43 35	59	168	44 34	60	168	45 34	60	168
10	41 29	+60	167	42 29	+60	167	43 29	+59	167	44 28	+60	167	45 28	+60	167
11	41 23	60	166	42 23	59	166	43 22	60	166	44 22	59	165	45 21	60	165
12	41 16	59	165	42 15	60	164	43 15	59	164	44 14	60	164	45 14	59	164
13	41 08	60	163	42 08	59	163	43 07	60	163	44 07	59	163	45 06	59	163
14	41 00	60	162	42 00	59	162	42 59	59	162	43 58	60	161	44 58	59	161
15	40 52	+59	161	41 51	+59	161	42 50	+59	160	43 49	+59	160	44 48	+60	160
16	40 42	59	159	41 41	60	159	42 41	59	159	43 40	59	159	44 39	59	159
17	40 32	59	158	41 31	60	158	42 31	59	158	43 30	58	158	44 28	59	157
18	40 22	59	157	41 21	59	157	42 20	59	156	43 19	59	156	44 18	58	156
19	40 11	59	156	41 10	59	155	42 09	59	155	43 08	58	155	44 06	59	155
20	40 00	+58	155	40 58	+59	154	41 57	+59	154	42 56	+58	154	43 54	+59	153
21	39 48	58	153	40 46	59	153	41 45	58	153	42 43	59	152	43 42	58	152
22	39 35	59	152	40 34	58	152	41 32	58	151	42 30	59	151	43 29	58	151
23	39 22	58	151	40 20	59	151	41 19	58	150	42 17	58	150	43 15	58	150
24	39 08	59	150	40 07	58	149	41 05	58	149	42 03	58	149	43 01	58	148
25	38 54	+59	148	39 53	+58	148	40 51	+58	148	41 49	+58	147	42 47	+57	147
26	38 40	58	147	39 38	58	147	40 36	58	147	41 34	57	146	42 31	58	146
27	38 25	58	146	39 23	58	146	40 21	57	145	41 18	58	145	42 16	58	145
28	38 09	58	145	39 07	58	144	40 05	57	144	41 02	58	144	42 00	57	143
29	37 53	58	144	38 51	58	143	39 49	57	143	40 46	57	143	41 43	58	142
30	37 37	+58	142	38 35	+57	142	39 32	+57	142	40 29	+57	141	41 26	+58	141
31	37 20	58	141	38 18	57	141	39 15	57	141	40 12	57	140	41 09	57	140
32	37 03	57	140	38 00	57	140	38 57	57	139	39 54	57	139	40 51	57	139
33	36 45	57	139	37 42	57	139	38 39	57	138	39 36	57	138	40 33	57	137
34	36 27	57	138	37 24	57	137	38 21	57	137	39 18	56	137	40 14	57	136
35	36 09	+56	137	37 05	+57	136	38 02	+57	136	38 59	+56	135	39 55	+57	135
36	35 50	56	136	36 46	57	135	37 43	56	135	38 39	57	134	39 36	56	134
37	35 31	56	134	36 27	56	134	37 23	57	134	38 20	56	133	39 16	56	133
38	35 11	56	133	36 07	57	133	37 04	56	133	38 00	56	132	38 56	56	132
39	34 51	56	132	35 47	56	132	36 43	56	131	37 39	56	131	38 35	56	130
40	34 31	+56	131	35 27	+56	131	36 23	+55	130	37 18	+56	130	38 14	+56	129
41	34 10	56	130	35 06	56	130	36 02	55	129	36 57	56	129	37 53	56	128
42	33 49	56	129	34 45	55	129	35 40	56	128	36 36	55	128	37 31	56	127
43	33 28	55	128	34 23	56	127	35 19	55	127	36 14	56	127	37 10	55	126
44	33 06	55	127	34 01	56	126	34 57	55	126	35 52	55	125	36 47	55	125
45	32 44	+55	126	33 39	+56	125	34 35	+55	125	35 30	+55	124	36 25	+55	124
46	32 22	55	125	33 17	55	124	34 12	55	124	35 07	55	123	36 02	55	123
47	31 59	55	124	32 54	55	123	33 49	55	123	34 44	55	122	35 39	55	122
48	31 36	56	123	32 31	55	122	33 26	55	122	34 21	55	121	35 16	54	121
49	31 13	55	122	32 08	55	121	33 03	55	121	33 58	54	120	34 52	55	120
50	30 50	+55	121	31 45	+54	120	32 39	+55	120	33 34	+54	119	34 28	+55	119
51	30 26	55	120	31 21	55	119	32 16	54	119	33 10	54	118	34 04	55	118
52	30 02	55	118	30 57	54	118	31 51	55	118	32 46	54	117	33 40	54	117
53	29 38	55	117	30 33	54	117	31 27	54	117	32 21	55	116	33 16	54	115
54	29 14	54	116	30 08	55	116	31 03	54	115	31 57	54	115	32 51	54	114
55	28 50	+54	115	29 44	+54	115	30 38	+54	114	31 32	+54	114	32 26	+54	113
56	28 25	54	114	29 19	54	114	30 13	54	113	31 07	54	113	32 01	54	112
57	28 00	54	113	28 54	54	113	29 48	54	112	30 42	54	112	31 36	53	111
58	27 35	54	113	28 29	54	112	29 23	54	112	30 17	53	111	31 10	54	110
59	27 10	54	112	28 04	53	111	28 57	54	111	29 51	54	110	30 45	53	109
60	26 44	+54	111	27 38	+54	110	28 32	+53	110	29 25	+54	109	30 19	+53	109
61	26 19	53	110	27 12	54	109	28 06	53	109	28 59	54	108	29 53	53	108
62	25 53	53	109	26 46	54	108	27 40	53	108	28 33	54	107	29 27	53	107
63	25 27	54	108	26 21	53	107	27 14	53	107	28 07	54	106	29 01	53	106
64	25 01	53	107	25 54	54	106	26 48	53	106	27 41	53	105	28 34	53	105
65	24 35	+53	106	25 28	+54	105	26 22	+53	105	27 15	+53	104	28 08	+53	104
66	24 08	54	105	25 02	53	104	25 55	53	104	26 48	53	103	27 41	53	103
67	23 42	53	104	24 35	54	103	25 29	53	103	26 22	53	102	27 15	53	102
68	23 16	53	103	24 09	53	102	25 02	53	102	25 55	53	101	26 48	53	101
69	22 49	53	102	23 42	53	102	24 35	53	101	25 28	53	100	26 21	53	100

LHA	20°			21°			22°			23°			24°		
	Hc	d	Z	Hc	d	Z	Hc	d	Z	Hc	d	Z	Hc	d	Z
	° ′	′	°	° ′	′	°	° ′	′	°	° ′	′	°	° ′	′	°
0	47 00	+60	180	48 00	+60	180	49 00	+60	180	50 00	+60	180	51 00	+60	180
1	47 00	60	179	48 00	60	179	49 00	60	179	50 00	60	179	51 00	60	179
2	46 59	60	177	47 59	60	177	48 59	60	177	49 59	60	177	50 59	60	177
3	46 57	60	176	47 57	60	176	48 57	60	176	49 57	60	176	50 57	60	176
4	46 55	60	175	47 55	60	174	48 55	60	174	49 55	60	174	50 55	59	174
5	46 52	+60	173	47 52	+60	173	48 52	+60	173	49 52	+59	173	50 51	+60	173
6	46 48	60	172	47 48	60	172	48 48	60	172	49 48	60	171	50 48	59	171
7	46 44	60	170	47 44	60	170	48 44	59	170	49 43	60	170	50 43	60	170
8	46 39	60	169	47 39	60	169	48 39	59	169	49 38	60	169	50 38	60	168
9	46 34	59	168	47 33	60	168	48 33	60	167	49 33	59	167	50 32	60	167
10	46 28	+59	166	47 27	+60	166	48 27	+59	166	49 26	+60	166	50 26	+59	166
11	46 21	59	165	47 20	60	165	48 20	59	165	49 19	60	164	50 19	59	164
12	46 13	60	164	47 13	59	163	48 12	60	163	49 12	59	163	50 11	59	163
13	46 05	60	162	47 05	59	162	48 04	59	162	49 03	60	162	50 03	59	161
14	45 57	59	161	46 56	59	161	47 55	59	160	48 54	60	160	49 54	59	160
15	45 48	+59	160	46 47	+59	159	47 46	+59	159	48 45	+59	159	49 44	+59	159
16	45 38	59	158	46 37	59	158	47 36	59	158	48 35	59	157	49 34	58	157
17	45 27	59	157	46 26	59	157	47 25	59	156	48 24	59	156	49 23	58	156
18	45 16	59	156	46 15	59	155	47 14	59	155	48 13	58	155	49 11	59	154
19	45 05	59	154	46 04	58	154	47 02	59	154	48 01	58	153	48 59	59	153
20	44 53	+58	153	45 51	+59	153	46 50	+58	152	47 48	+59	152	48 47	+58	152
21	44 40	59	152	45 39	58	151	46 37	58	151	47 35	58	151	48 33	59	150
22	44 27	58	151	45 25	58	150	46 23	59	150	47 22	58	149	48 20	58	149
23	44 13	58	149	45 11	58	149	46 09	58	149	47 07	58	148	48 05	58	148
24	43 59	58	148	44 57	58	148	45 55	58	147	46 53	58	147	47 51	57	146
25	43 44	+58	147	44 42	+58	146	45 40	+58	146	46 38	+57	146	47 35	+58	145
26	43 29	58	145	44 27	57	145	45 24	58	145	46 22	57	144	47 19	58	144
27	43 14	57	144	44 11	57	144	45 08	58	143	46 06	57	143	47 03	57	143
28	42 57	58	143	43 55	57	143	44 52	57	142	45 49	57	142	46 46	57	141
29	42 41	57	142	43 38	57	141	44 35	57	141	45 32	57	140	46 29	57	140
30	42 24	+57	141	43 21	+57	140	44 18	+56	140	45 14	+57	139	46 11	+57	139
31	42 06	57	139	43 03	57	139	44 00	56	138	44 56	57	138	45 53	56	138
32	41 48	57	138	42 45	56	138	43 41	57	137	44 38	56	137	45 34	57	136
33	41 30	56	137	42 26	57	137	43 23	56	136	44 19	56	136	45 15	56	135
34	41 11	56	136	42 07	57	135	43 04	56	135	44 00	56	134	44 56	56	134
35	40 52	+56	135	41 48	+56	134	42 44	+56	134	43 40	+56	133	44 36	+56	133
36	40 32	56	133	41 28	56	133	42 24	56	132	43 20	56	132	44 16	55	131
37	40 12	56	132	41 08	56	132	42 04	56	131	43 00	55	131	43 55	56	130
38	39 52	55	131	40 47	56	131	41 43	56	130	42 39	55	130	43 34	55	129
39	39 31	56	130	40 27	55	130	41 22	56	129	42 18	55	129	43 13	55	128
40	39 10	+55	129	40 05	+56	128	41 01	+55	128	41 56	+55	127	42 51	+55	127
41	38 49	55	128	39 44	55	127	40 39	56	127	41 34	55	126	42 29	55	126
42	38 27	55	127	39 22	55	126	40 17	55	126	41 12	55	125	42 07	55	125
43	38 05	55	126	39 00	55	125	39 55	55	125	40 50	54	124	41 44	55	123
44	37 42	55	124	38 37	55	124	39 32	55	123	40 27	54	123	41 21	55	122
45	37 20	+55	123	38 15	+54	123	39 09	+55	122	40 04	+54	122	40 58	+55	121
46	36 57	55	122	37 52	54	122	38 46	55	121	39 41	54	121	40 35	54	120
47	36 34	54	121	37 28	55	121	38 23	54	120	39 17	54	120	40 11	54	119
48	36 10	55	120	37 05	54	120	37 59	54	119	38 53	54	119	39 47	54	118
49	35 47	54	119	36 41	54	119	37 35	54	118	38 29	54	117	39 23	54	117
50	35 23	+54	118	36 17	+54	118	37 11	+54	117	38 05	+54	116	38 59	+53	116
51	34 59	54	117	35 53	54	116	36 47	53	116	37 40	54	115	38 34	53	115
52	34 34	54	116	35 28	54	115	36 22	54	115	37 16	53	114	38 09	53	114
53	34 10	53	115	35 03	54	114	35 57	54	114	36 51	53	113	37 44	53	113
54	33 45	54	114	34 39	53	113	35 32	54	113	36 26	53	112	37 19	53	112
55	33 20	+53	113	34 13	+54	112	35 07	+53	112	36 00	+53	111	36 53	+54	111
56	32 55	53	112	33 48	54	111	34 42	53	111	35 35	53	110	36 28	53	110
57	32 29	54	111	33 23	53	110	34 16	53	110	35 09	53	109	36 02	53	109
58	32 04	53	110	32 57	53	109	33 50	53	109	34 43	53	108	35 36	53	108
59	31 38	53	109	32 31	53	108	33 24	53	108	34 17	53	107	35 10	53	107
60	31 12	+53	108	32 05	+53	107	32 58	+53	107	33 51	+53	106	34 44	+53	106
61	30 46	53	107	31 39	53	106	32 32	53	106	33 25	53	105	34 18	52	105
62	30 20	53	106	31 13	53	106	32 06	53	105	32 59	52	104	33 51	53	104
63	29 54	53	105	30 47	53	105	31 40	52	104	32 32	53	103	33 25	52	103
64	29 27	53	104	30 20	53	104	31 13	53	103	32 06	52	102	32 58	53	102
65	29 01	+53	103	29 54	+53	103	30 47	+52	102	31 39	+53	102	32 32	+52	101
66	28 34	53	102	29 27	53	102	30 20	52	101	31 12	53	101	32 05	52	100
67	28 08	52	101	29 00	53	101	29 53	53	100	30 46	52	100	31 38	52	99
68	27 41	53	100	28 34	52	100	29 26	53	99	30 19	52	99	31 11	52	98
69	27 14	53	99	28 07	52	99	28 59	53	98	29 52	52	98	30 44	52	97

LHA	25°			26°			27°			28°			29°			LHA
	Hc	d	Z	Hc	d	Z	Hc	d	Z	Hc	d	Z	Hc	d	Z	LHA
	° ′	′	°	° ′	′	°	° ′	′	°	° ′	′	°	° ′	′	°	
0	52 00	+60	180	53 00	+60	180	54 00	+60	180	55 00	+60	180	56 00	+60	180	360
1	52 00	60	179	53 00	60	179	54 00	60	179	55 00	60	179	56 00	60	178	359
2	51 59	60	177	52 59	60	177	53 59	60	177	54 59	60	177	55 59	60	177	358
3	51 57	60	176	52 57	60	176	53 57	60	176	54 57	60	175	55 57	60	175	357
4	51 54	60	174	52 54	60	174	53 54	60	174	54 54	60	174	55 54	60	174	356
5	51 51	+60	173	52 51	+60	173	53 51	+60	172	54 51	+60	172	55 51	+60	172	355
6	51 47	60	171	52 47	60	171	53 47	60	171	54 47	60	171	55 47	59	171	354
7	51 43	60	170	52 43	59	170	53 42	60	169	54 42	60	169	55 42	60	169	353
8	51 38	59	168	52 37	60	168	53 37	60	168	54 37	59	168	55 36	60	168	352
9	51 32	60	167	52 32	59	167	53 31	60	166	54 31	59	166	55 30	60	166	351
10	51 25	+60	165	52 25	+59	165	53 24	+60	165	54 24	+59	165	55 23	+60	165	350
11	51 18	60	164	52 18	59	164	53 17	59	164	54 16	60	163	55 16	59	163	349
12	51 10	60	163	52 10	59	162	53 09	59	162	54 08	59	162	55 07	59	162	348
13	51 02	59	161	52 01	59	161	53 00	59	161	53 59	59	160	54 58	59	160	347
14	50 53	59	160	51 52	59	159	52 51	59	159	53 50	59	159	54 49	59	159	346
15	50 43	+59	158	51 42	+59	158	52 41	+59	158	53 40	+58	157	54 38	+59	157	345
16	50 32	59	157	51 31	59	157	52 30	59	156	53 29	58	156	54 27	59	156	344
17	50 21	59	156	51 20	59	155	52 19	58	155	53 17	59	154	54 16	58	154	343
18	50 10	58	154	51 08	59	154	52 07	58	153	53 05	58	153	54 03	59	153	342
19	49 58	58	153	50 56	58	152	51 54	59	152	52 53	58	152	53 51	58	151	341
20	49 45	+58	151	50 43	+58	151	51 41	+58	151	52 39	+58	150	53 37	+58	150	340
21	49 32	58	150	50 30	58	150	51 28	57	149	52 25	58	149	53 23	58	148	339
22	49 18	57	149	50 15	58	148	51 13	58	148	52 11	58	147	53 09	57	147	338
23	49 03	58	147	50 01	57	147	50 58	58	146	51 56	57	146	52 53	58	146	337
24	48 48	58	146	49 46	57	146	50 43	57	145	51 40	58	145	52 38	57	144	336
25	48 33	+57	145	49 30	+57	144	50 27	+57	144	51 24	+57	143	52 21	+57	143	335
26	48 17	57	143	49 14	57	143	50 11	57	142	51 08	57	142	52 05	56	141	334
27	48 00	57	142	48 57	57	142	49 54	57	141	50 51	57	141	51 48	56	140	333
28	47 43	57	141	48 40	57	140	49 37	56	140	50 33	57	139	51 30	56	139	332
29	47 26	56	140	48 22	57	139	49 19	56	139	50 15	57	138	51 12	56	137	331
30	47 08	+56	138	48 04	+57	138	49 01	+56	137	49 57	+56	137	50 53	+56	136	330
31	46 49	57	137	47 46	56	137	48 42	56	136	49 38	56	135	50 34	56	135	329
32	46 31	56	136	47 27	56	135	48 23	56	135	49 19	55	134	50 14	56	134	328
33	46 11	56	135	47 07	56	134	48 03	56	133	48 59	55	133	49 54	56	132	327
34	45 52	56	133	46 48	55	133	47 43	56	132	48 39	55	132	49 34	55	131	326
35	45 32	+55	132	46 27	+56	132	47 23	+55	131	48 18	+55	130	49 13	+55	130	325
36	45 11	56	131	46 07	55	130	47 02	55	130	47 57	55	129	48 52	55	129	324
37	44 51	55	130	45 46	55	129	46 41	55	129	47 36	55	128	48 31	54	127	323
38	44 29	56	129	45 25	55	128	46 20	54	127	47 14	55	127	48 09	54	126	322
39	44 08	55	127	45 03	55	127	45 58	54	126	46 52	55	126	47 47	54	125	321
40	43 46	+55	126	44 41	+55	126	45 36	+54	125	46 30	+54	125	47 24	+54	124	320
41	43 24	55	125	44 19	54	125	45 13	54	124	46 07	54	123	47 01	54	123	319
42	43 02	54	124	43 56	54	123	44 50	55	123	45 45	53	122	46 38	54	122	318
43	42 39	54	123	43 33	54	122	44 27	54	122	45 21	54	121	46 15	54	120	317
44	42 16	54	122	43 10	54	121	44 04	54	121	44 58	53	120	45 51	54	119	316
45	41 53	+54	121	42 47	+53	120	43 40	+54	119	44 34	+54	119	45 28	+53	118	315
46	41 29	54	120	42 23	54	119	43 17	53	118	44 10	53	118	45 03	53	117	314
47	41 05	54	118	41 59	53	118	42 52	54	117	43 46	53	117	44 39	53	116	313
48	40 41	54	117	41 35	53	117	42 28	53	116	43 21	53	116	44 14	53	115	312
49	40 17	53	116	41 10	54	116	42 04	53	115	42 57	53	115	43 50	52	114	311
50	39 52	+54	115	40 46	+53	115	41 39	+53	114	42 32	+53	113	43 25	+52	113	310
51	39 27	54	114	40 21	53	114	41 14	53	113	42 07	52	112	42 59	53	112	309
52	39 02	54	113	39 56	53	113	40 49	52	112	41 41	53	111	42 34	52	111	308
53	38 37	53	112	39 30	53	112	40 23	53	111	41 16	52	110	42 08	53	110	307
54	38 12	53	111	39 05	53	111	39 58	52	110	40 50	53	109	41 43	52	109	306
55	37 47	+52	110	38 39	+53	110	39 32	+53	109	40 25	+52	108	41 17	+52	108	305
56	37 21	53	109	38 14	52	109	39 06	53	108	39 59	52	107	40 51	52	107	304
57	36 55	53	108	37 48	52	108	38 40	52	107	39 32	53	106	40 25	51	106	303
58	36 29	53	107	37 22	52	107	38 14	52	106	39 06	52	105	39 58	52	105	302
59	36 03	52	106	36 55	53	106	37 48	52	105	38 40	52	104	39 32	52	104	301
60	35 37	+52	105	36 29	+52	105	37 21	+52	104	38 13	+52	103	39 05	+52	103	300
61	35 10	53	104	36 03	52	104	36 55	52	103	37 47	52	102	38 39	51	102	299
62	34 44	52	103	35 36	52	103	36 28	52	102	37 20	52	101	38 12	51	101	298
63	34 17	53	102	35 10	52	102	36 02	51	101	36 53	52	100	37 45	52	100	297
64	33 51	52	101	34 43	52	101	35 35	52	100	36 27	51	99	37 18	52	99	296
65	33 24	+52	100	34 16	+52	100	35 08	+52	99	36 00	+51	99	36 51	+52	98	295
66	32 57	52	99	33 49	52	99	34 41	52	98	35 33	51	98	36 24	52	97	294
67	32 30	52	98	33 22	52	98	34 14	52	97	35 06	51	97	35 57	51	96	293
68	32 03	52	98	32 55	52	97	33 47	52	96	34 39	51	96	35 30	51	95	292
69	31 36	52	97	32 28	52	96	33 20	52	95	34 12	51	95	35 03	51	94	291

S. Lat. {LHA greater than 180°……. Zn=180−Z; LHA less than 180°……….. Zn=180+Z}

DECLINATION (15°-29°) SAME NAME AS LATITUDE

N. Lat. {LHA greater than 180 .... Zn=Z; LHA less than 180° .... Zn=360−Z}

DECLINATION (15°-29°) SAME NAME AS LATITUDE

LHA	15° Hc	15° d	15° Z	16° Hc	16° d	16° Z	17° Hc	17° d	17° Z	18° Hc	18° d	18° Z	19° Hc	19° d	19° Z
	° ′	′	°	° ′	′	°	° ′	′	°	° ′	′	°	° ′	′	°
70	22 22	+53	101	23 15	+54	101	24 09	+53	100	25 02	+52	100	25 54	+53	99
71	21 55	54	100	22 49	53	100	23 42	53	99	24 35	52	99	25 27	53	98
72	21 29	53	99	22 22	53	99	23 15	53	98	24 08	52	98	25 00	53	97
73	21 02	53	98	21 55	53	98	22 48	53	97	23 41	52	97	24 33	53	96
74	20 35	53	97	21 28	53	97	22 21	53	96	23 14	52	96	24 06	53	95
75	20 08	+53	96	21 01	+53	96	21 54	+52	95	22 46	+53	95	23 39	+53	94
76	19 41	53	96	20 34	52	95	21 26	53	95	22 19	53	94	23 12	53	94
77	19 13	53	95	20 06	53	94	20 59	53	94	21 52	53	93	22 45	52	93
78	18 46	53	94	19 39	53	93	20 32	53	93	21 25	53	92	22 18	52	92
79	18 19	53	93	19 12	53	92	20 05	53	92	20 58	52	91	21 50	53	91
80	17 52	+53	92	18 45	+53	91	19 38	+52	91	20 30	+53	90	21 23	+53	90
81	17 25	53	91	18 18	52	91	19 10	53	90	20 03	53	90	20 56	52	89
82	16 57	53	90	17 50	53	90	18 43	53	89	19 36	53	89	20 29	52	88
83	16 30	53	89	17 23	53	89	18 16	53	88	19 09	52	88	20 01	53	87
84	16 03	53	88	16 56	53	88	17 49	53	87	18 42	52	87	19 34	53	86
85	15 36	+53	88	16 29	+53	87	17 22	+52	87	18 14	+53	86	19 07	+53	86
86	15 09	52	87	16 01	53	86	16 54	53	86	17 47	53	85	18 40	53	85
87	14 41	53	86	15 34	53	85	16 27	53	85	17 20	53	84	18 13	53	84
88	14 14	53	85	15 07	53	84	16 00	53	84	16 53	53	83	17 46	52	83
89	13 47	53	84	14 40	53	84	15 33	53	83	16 26	53	83	17 19	53	82
90	13 20	+53	83	14 13	+53	83	15 06	+53	82	15 59	+53	82	16 52	+53	81
91	12 53	53	82	13 46	53	82	14 39	53	81	15 32	53	81	16 25	53	80
92	12 26	53	81	13 19	53	81	14 12	53	80	15 05	53	80	15 58	53	79
93	11 59	53	80	12 52	53	80	13 45	53	80	14 38	53	79	15 31	53	79
94	11 32	54	80	12 26	53	79	13 19	53	79	14 12	53	78	15 05	53	78
95	11 06	+53	79	11 59	+53	78	12 52	+53	78	13 45	+53	77	14 38	+53	77
96	10 39	53	78	11 32	53	77	12 25	54	77	13 19	53	76	14 12	53	76
97	10 12	54	77	11 06	53	77	11 59	53	76	12 52	53	76	13 45	53	75
98	09 46	53	76	10 39	54	76	11 33	53	75	12 26	53	75	13 19	53	74
99	09 19	54	75	10 13	53	75	11 06	54	74	12 00	53	74	12 53	53	73
100	08 53	+54	74	09 47	+53	74	10 40	+54	73	11 34	+53	73	12 27	+53	73
101	08 27	54	74	09 21	53	73	10 14	54	73	11 08	53	72	12 01	53	72
102	08 01	54	73	08 55	53	72	09 48	54	72	10 42	53	71	11 35	54	71
103	07 35	54	72	08 29	53	71	09 22	54	71	10 16	54	70	11 10	53	70
104	07 09	54	71	08 03	54	70	08 57	53	70	09 50	54	70	10 44	54	69
105	06 44	+53	70	07 37	+54	70	08 31	+54	69	09 25	+54	69	10 19	+53	68
106	06 18	54	69	07 12	54	69	08 06	54	68	09 00	53	68	09 53	54	67
107	05 53	54	68	06 47	54	68	07 41	54	67	08 35	53	67	09 28	54	66
108	05 27	55	67	06 22	54	67	07 16	54	67	08 10	54	66	09 04	53	66
109	05 02	55	67	05 57	54	66	06 51	54	66	07 45	54	65	08 39	54	65
110	04 37	+55	66	05 32	+54	65	06 26	+54	65	07 20	+54	64	08 14	+54	64
111	04 13	54	65	05 07	54	64	06 01	55	64	06 56	54	63	07 50	54	63
112	03 48	55	64	04 43	54	63	05 37	54	63	06 31	55	63	07 26	54	62
113	03 24	54	63	04 18	55	63	05 13	54	62	06 07	55	62	07 02	54	61
114	03 00	54	62	03 54	55	62	04 49	54	61	05 43	55	61	06 38	54	60
115	02 36	+54	61	03 30	+55	61	04 25	+55	60	05 20	+54	60	06 14	+55	60
116	02 12	55	60	03 07	54	60	04 01	55	60	04 56	55	59	05 51	55	59
117	01 48	55	59	02 43	55	59	03 38	55	59	04 33	55	58	05 28	55	58
118	01 25	55	59	02 20	55	58	03 15	55	58	04 10	55	57	05 05	55	57
119	01 02	55	58	01 57	55	57	02 52	55	57	03 47	55	56	04 42	55	56
120	00 39	+55	57	01 34	+55	56	02 29	+55	56	03 24	+56	56	04 20	+55	55
121	00 16	56	56	01 12	55	56	02 07	55	55	03 02	55	55	03 57	56	54
122	−0 06	55	55	00 49	56	55	01 45	55	54	02 40	55	54	03 35	56	53
123	−0 28	55	54	00 27	56	54	01 23	55	53	02 18	56	53	03 14	55	53
124	−0 50	55	53	00 05	56	53	01 01	56	52	01 57	55	52	02 52	56	52
125	−1 12	+56	52	−0 16	+55	52	00 39	+56	52	01 35	+56	51	02 31	+56	51
126	−1 33	55	51	−0 38	56	51	00 18	56	51	01 14	56	50	02 10	56	50
127	−1 54	55	51	−0 59	56	50	−0 03	56	50	00 53	56	49	01 49	56	49
128	−2 15	56	50	−1 19	56	49	−0 23	56	49	00 33	56	49	01 29	56	48
129	−2 36	56	49	−1 40	56	48	−0 44	56	48	00 12	57	48	01 09	56	47
130	−2 56	+56	48	−2 00	+56	47	−1 04	+56	47	−0 08	+57	47	00 49	+56	46
131	−3 16	56	47	−2 20	56	47	−1 24	57	46	−0 27	56	46	00 29	56	46
132	−3 36	56	46	−2 40	57	46	−1 43	56	45	−0 47	57	45	00 10	56	45
133	−3 56	57	45	−2 59	57	45	−2 02	56	44	−1 06	57	44	−0 09	56	44
134	−4 15	57	44	−3 18	57	44	−2 21	56	44	−1 25	57	43	−0 28	57	43
135	−4 33	+56	43	−3 37	+57	43	−2 40	+57	43	−1 43	+57	42	−0 46	+57	42
136	−4 52	57	42	−3 55	57	42	−2 58	57	42	−2 01	57	41	−1 04	57	41
137	−5 10	57	41	−4 13	57	41	−3 16	57	41	−2 19	57	40	−1 22	57	40
138	−5 28	57	40	−4 31	57	40	−3 34	57	40	−2 37	58	40	−1 39	57	39
139				−4 48	57	39	−3 51	57	39	−2 54	58	39	−1 56	57	38

LHA	20° Hc	20° d	20° Z	21° Hc	21° d	21° Z	22° Hc	22° d	22° Z	23° Hc	23° d	23° Z	24° Hc	24° d	24° Z
	° ′	′	°	° ′	′	°	° ′	′	°	° ′	′	°	° ′	′	°
70	26 47	+53	98	27 40	+52	98	28 32	+53	97	29 25	+52	97	30 17	+52	96
71	26 20	53	98	27 13	52	97	28 05	53	96	28 58	52	96	29 50	52	95
72	25 53	53	97	26 46	52	96	27 38	53	96	28 31	52	95	29 23	52	94
73	25 26	53	96	26 19	52	95	27 11	52	95	28 03	53	94	28 56	52	94
74	24 59	52	95	25 51	53	94	26 44	52	94	27 36	52	93	28 28	52	93
75	24 32	+52	94	25 24	+53	93	26 17	+52	93	27 09	+52	92	28 01	+52	92
76	24 05	52	93	24 57	52	92	25 49	53	92	26 42	52	91	27 34	52	91
77	23 37	53	92	24 30	52	92	25 22	53	91	26 15	52	91	27 07	52	90
78	23 10	53	91	24 03	52	91	24 55	52	90	25 47	52	90	26 39	52	89
79	22 43	52	90	23 35	53	90	24 28	52	89	25 20	52	89	26 12	52	88
80	22 16	+52	89	23 08	+53	89	24 01	+52	88	24 53	+52	88	25 45	+52	87
81	21 48	53	89	22 41	52	88	23 33	53	87	24 26	52	87	25 18	52	86
82	21 21	53	88	22 14	52	87	23 06	52	87	23 58	53	86	24 51	52	86
83	20 54	53	87	21 47	52	86	22 39	52	86	23 31	52	85	24 23	53	85
84	20 27	52	86	21 19	53	85	22 12	52	85	23 04	52	84	23 56	52	84
85	20 00	+52	85	20 52	+53	85	21 45	+52	84	22 37	+52	83	23 29	+52	83
86	19 33	52	84	20 25	53	84	21 18	52	83	22 10	52	83	23 02	52	82
87	19 06	52	83	19 58	53	83	20 51	52	82	21 43	52	82	22 35	53	81
88	18 38	53	82	19 31	53	82	20 24	52	81	21 16	52	81	22 08	53	80
89	18 12	52	82	19 04	53	81	19 57	52	81	20 49	53	80	21 42	52	79
90	17 45	+52	81	18 37	+53	80	19 30	+52	80	20 22	+53	79	21 15	+52	79
91	17 18	53	80	18 11	52	79	19 03	53	79	19 56	52	78	20 48	53	78
92	16 51	53	79	17 44	53	78	18 37	52	78	19 29	53	77	20 22	52	77
93	16 24	53	78	17 17	53	78	18 10	53	77	19 03	52	77	19 55	53	76
94	15 58	53	77	16 51	52	77	17 43	53	76	18 36	53	76	19 29	52	75
95	15 31	+53	76	16 24	+53	76	17 17	+53	75	18 10	+53	75	19 03	+52	74
96	15 05	53	75	15 58	53	75	16 51	53	75	17 44	52	74	18 36	53	74
97	14 38	54	75	15 32	53	74	16 25	52	74	17 17	53	73	18 10	53	73
98	14 12	53	74	15 05	53	73	15 58	53	73	16 51	53	72	17 44	53	72
99	13 46	53	73	14 39	54	72	15 33	53	72	16 26	53	71	17 19	53	71
100	13 20	+53	72	14 13	+54	72	15 07	+53	71	16 00	+53	71	16 53	+53	70
101	12 54	54	71	13 48	53	71	14 41	53	70	15 34	53	70	16 27	53	69
102	12 29	53	70	13 22	53	70	14 15	54	69	15 09	53	69	16 02	53	68
103	12 03	54	69	12 57	53	69	13 50	53	69	14 43	54	68	15 37	53	68
104	11 38	53	69	12 31	54	68	13 25	53	68	14 18	54	67	15 12	53	67
105	11 12	+54	68	12 06	+54	67	13 00	+53	67	13 53	+54	66	14 47	+53	66
106	10 47	54	67	11 41	54	66	12 35	53	66	13 28	54	66	14 22	53	65
107	10 22	54	66	11 16	54	66	12 10	54	65	13 04	53	65	13 57	54	64
108	09 57	54	65	10 51	54	65	11 45	54	64	12 39	54	64	13 33	54	63
109	09 33	54	64	10 27	54	64	11 21	54	63	12 15	54	63	13 09	53	63
110	09 08	+54	63	10 02	+55	63	10 57	+54	63	11 51	+54	62	12 45	+53	62
111	08 44	54	63	09 38	54	62	10 32	55	62	11 27	54	61	12 21	54	61
112	08 20	54	62	09 14	55	61	10 09	54	61	11 03	54	60	11 57	54	60
113	07 56	55	61	08 51	54	60	09 45	54	60	10 39	55	60	11 34	54	59
114	07 32	55	60	08 27	54	60	09 21	55	59	10 16	54	59	11 10	55	58
115	07 09	+55	59	08 04	+54	59	08 58	+55	58	09 53	+54	58	10 47	+55	57
116	06 46	54	58	07 40	55	58	08 35	55	57	09 30	54	57	10 24	55	57
117	06 23	54	57	07 17	55	57	08 12	55	57	09 07	55	56	10 02	54	56
118	06 00	55	57	06 55	55	56	07 50	54	56	08 44	55	55	09 39	55	55
119	05 37	55	56	06 32	55	55	07 27	55	55	08 22	55	55	09 17	55	54
120	05 15	+55	55	06 10	+55	54	07 05	+55	54	08 00	+55	54	08 55	+55	53
121	04 53	55	54	05 48	55	54	06 43	55	53	07 38	55	53	08 33	56	52
122	04 31	55	53	05 26	55	53	06 21	56	52	07 17	55	52	08 12	55	52
123	04 09	56	52	05 05	55	52	06 00	55	51	06 55	56	51	07 51	55	51
124	03 48	55	51	04 43	56	51	05 39	55	51	06 34	56	50	07 30	55	50
125	03 27	+55	50	04 22	+56	50	05 18	+56	50	06 14	+55	49	07 09	+56	49
126	03 06	55	50	04 01	56	49	04 57	56	49	05 53	56	49	06 49	56	48
127	02 45	56	49	03 41	56	48	04 37	56	48	05 33	56	48	06 29	56	47
128	02 25	56	48	03 21	56	47	04 17	56	47	05 13	56	47	06 09	56	46
129	02 05	56	47	03 01	56	47	03 57	56	46	04 53	56	46	05 49	56	46
130	01 45	+56	46	02 41	+56	46	03 37	+57	45	04 34	+56	45	05 30	+56	45
131	01 25	57	45	02 22	56	45	03 18	57	45	04 15	56	44	05 11	56	44
132	01 06	57	44	02 03	56	44	02 59	57	44	03 56	56	43	04 52	57	43
133	00 47	57	43	01 44	57	43	02 41	56	43	03 37	57	42	04 34	56	42
134	00 29	57	43	01 26	56	42	02 22	57	42	03 19	57	42	04 16	56	41
135	00 11	+56	42	01 07	+57	41	02 04	+57	41	03 01	+57	41	03 58	+57	40
136	−0 07	57	41	00 50	57	40	01 47	56	40	02 43	57	40	03 40	57	40
137	−0 25	57	40	00 32	57	40	01 29	57	39	02 26	57	39	03 23	57	39
138	−0 42	57	39	00 15	57	39	01 12	57	38	02 09	57	38	03 06	58	38
139	−0 59	57	38	−0 02	57	38	00 55	58	37	01 53	57	37	02 50	57	37

LHA	25° Hc	25° d	25° Z	26° Hc	26° d	26° Z	27° Hc	27° d	27° Z	28° Hc	28° d	28° Z	29° Hc	29° d	29° Z	LHA
	° ′	′	°	° ′	′	°	° ′	′	°	° ′	′	°	° ′	′	°	
70	31 09	+52	96	32 01	+52	95	32 53	+51	95	33 44	+52	94	34 36	+51	93	290
71	30 42	52	95	31 34	52	94	32 26	51	94	33 17	52	93	34 09	51	92	289
72	30 15	52	94	31 07	51	93	31 58	52	93	32 50	51	92	33 41	52	91	288
73	29 48	51	93	30 39	52	92	31 31	52	92	32 23	51	91	33 14	51	91	287
74	29 20	52	92	30 12	52	91	31 04	51	91	31 55	52	90	32 47	51	90	286
75	28 53	+52	91	29 45	+52	91	30 37	+51	90	31 28	+52	89	32 20	+51	89	285
76	28 26	52	90	29 18	51	90	30 09	52	89	31 01	51	89	31 52	52	88	284
77	27 59	52	89	28 51	51	89	29 42	52	88	30 34	51	88	31 25	51	87	283
78	27 31	52	89	28 23	52	88	29 15	52	87	30 07	51	87	30 58	51	86	282
79	27 04	52	88	27 56	52	87	28 48	51	86	29 39	52	86	30 31	51	85	281
80	26 37	+52	87	27 29	+52	86	28 21	+51	86	29 12	+52	85	30 04	+51	84	280
81	26 10	52	86	27 02	51	85	27 53	52	85	28 45	52	84	29 37	51	84	279
82	25 43	52	85	26 35	51	84	27 26	52	84	28 18	52	83	29 10	51	83	278
83	25 16	52	84	26 08	51	84	26 59	52	83	27 51	52	82	28 43	51	82	277
84	24 48	52	83	25 40	52	83	26 32	52	82	27 24	52	82	28 16	51	81	276
85	24 21	+52	82	25 13	+52	82	26 05	+52	81	26 57	+52	81	27 49	+51	80	275
86	23 54	53	82	24 47	51	81	25 38	52	80	26 30	52	80	27 22	52	79	274
87	23 28	52	81	24 20	52	80	25 12	52	80	26 04	51	79	26 55	52	78	273
88	23 01	52	80	23 53	52	79	24 45	52	79	25 37	52	78	26 29	51	78	272
89	22 34	52	79	23 26	52	78	24 18	53	78	25 11	51	77	26 02	52	77	271
90	22 07	+53	78	23 00	+52	78	23 52	+52	77	24 44	+52	76	25 36	+51	76	270
91	21 41	52	77	22 33	52	77	23 25	52	76	24 17	52	76	25 09	52	75	269
92	21 14	53	76	22 07	52	76	22 59	52	75	23 51	52	75	24 43	52	74	268
93	20 48	52	76	21 40	52	75	22 32	53	74	23 25	52	74	24 17	52	73	267
94	20 21	53	75	21 14	52	74	22 06	53	74	22 59	52	73	23 51	52	73	266
95	19 55	+53	74	20 48	+52	73	21 40	+53	73	22 33	+52	72	23 25	+52	72	265
96	19 29	53	73	20 22	52	72	21 14	53	72	22 07	52	71	22 59	52	71	264
97	19 03	53	72	19 56	52	72	20 48	53	71	21 41	52	71	22 33	53	70	263
98	18 37	53	71	19 30	53	71	20 23	52	70	21 15	53	70	22 08	52	69	262
99	18 12	52	70	19 04	53	70	19 57	53	69	20 50	52	69	21 42	53	68	261
100	17 46	+53	70	18 39	+53	69	19 32	+53	69	20 25	+52	68	21 17	+53	68	260
101	17 20	53	69	18 13	53	68	19 06	53	68	19 59	53	67	20 52	53	67	259
102	16 55	53	68	17 48	53	67	18 41	53	67	19 34	53	66	20 27	53	66	258
103	16 30	53	67	17 23	53	67	18 16	53	66	19 09	53	66	20 02	53	65	257
104	16 05	53	66	16 58	53	66	17 51	54	65	18 45	53	65	19 38	53	64	256
105	15 40	+54	65	16 34	+53	65	17 27	+53	64	18 20	+53	64	19 13	+53	64	255
106	15 15	54	65	16 09	53	64	17 02	54	64	17 56	53	63	18 49	53	63	254
107	14 51	54	64	15 45	53	63	16 38	53	63	17 31	54	62	18 25	53	62	253
108	14 27	53	63	15 20	54	62	16 14	53	62	17 07	54	62	18 01	53	61	252
109	14 02	54	62	14 56	54	62	15 50	54	61	16 44	53	61	17 37	54	60	251
110	13 38	+54	61	14 32	+54	61	15 26	+54	60	16 20	+54	60	17 14	+53	59	250
111	13 15	54	60	14 09	54	60	15 03	54	60	15 57	53	59	16 50	54	59	249
112	12 51	54	60	13 45	54	59	14 39	54	59	15 33	54	58	16 27	54	58	248
113	12 28	54	59	13 22	54	58	14 16	54	58	15 10	54	57	16 04	54	57	247
114	12 05	54	58	12 59	54	57	13 53	54	57	14 47	55	57	15 42	54	56	246
115	11 42	+54	57	12 36	+54	57	13 30	+55	56	14 25	+54	56	15 19	+54	55	245
116	11 19	54	56	12 13	55	56	13 08	54	55	14 02	55	55	14 57	54	55	244
117	10 56	55	55	11 51	55	55	12 46	54	55	13 40	55	54	14 35	54	54	243
118	10 34	55	55	11 29	55	54	12 24	54	54	13 18	55	53	14 13	55	53	242
119	10 12	55	54	11 07	55	53	12 02	55	53	12 57	54	52	13 51	55	52	241
120	09 50	+55	53	10 45	+55	52	11 40	+55	52	12 35	+55	52	13 30	+55	51	240
121	09 29	55	52	10 24	55	52	11 19	55	51	12 14	55	51	13 09	55	50	239
122	09 07	56	51	10 03	55	51	10 58	55	50	11 53	55	50	12 48	55	50	238
123	08 46	56	50	09 42	55	50	10 37	55	50	11 32	55	49	12 27	56	49	237
124	08 25	56	49	09 21	55	49	10 16	56	49	11 12	55	48	12 07	56	48	236
125	08 05	+55	49	09 00	+56	48	09 56	+56	48	10 52	+55	47	11 47	+56	47	235
126	07 45	55	48	08 40	56	47	09 36	56	47	10 32	55	47	11 27	56	46	234
127	07 25	55	47	08 20	56	47	09 16	56	46	10 12	56	46	11 08	55	45	233
128	07 05	56	46	08 01	56	46	08 57	56	45	09 53	55	45	10 48	56	45	232
129	06 45	56	45	07 41	56	45	08 37	57	45	09 34	56	44	10 30	56	44	231
130	06 26	+56	44	07 22	+57	44	08 19	+56	44	09 15	+56	43	10 11	+56	43	230
131	06 07	57	44	07 04	56	43	08 00	56	43	08 56	56	42	09 52	57	42	229
132	05 49	56	43	06 45	57	42	07 42	56	42	08 38	56	42	09 34	57	41	228
133	05 30	57	42	06 27	56	41	07 23	57	41	08 20	57	41	09 17	56	40	227
134	05 12	57	41	06 09	57	41	07 06	56	40	08 02	57	40	08 59	57	40	226
135	04 55	+57	40	05 52	+56	40	06 48	+57	39	07 45	+57	39	08 42	+57	39	225
136	04 37	57	39	05 34	57	39	06 31	57	39	07 28	57	38	08 25	57	38	224
137	04 20	57	38	05 17	57	38	06 14	57	38	07 11	57	37	08 08	57	37	223
138	04 04	57	37	05 01	57	37	05 58	57	37	06 55	57	37	07 52	57	36	222
139	03 47	57	37	04 44	58	36	05 42	57	36	06 39	57	36	07 36	57	35	221

S. Lat. {LHA greater than 180° .... Zn=180−Z; LHA less than 180° .... Zn=180+Z}

DECLINATION (15°-29°) SAME NAME AS LATITUDE

LAT 63°

N. Lat. {LHA greater than 180°....... Zn=Z; LHA less than 180°........... Zn=360−Z}

DECLINATION (15°-29°) SAME NAME AS LATITUDE

Each declination column gives Hc (° ′), d (′), Z (°).

LHA	15°	16°	17°	18°	19°	20°	21°	22°	23°	24°	25°	26°	27°	28°	29°	LHA
140		−5 05 +57 38	−4 08 +57 38	−3 11 +58 38	−2 13 +57 37	−1 16 +58 37	−0 18 +57 37	00 39 +57 37	01 36 +58 36	02 34 +57 36	03 31 +57 36	04 28 +58 35	05 26 +57 35	06 23 +58 35	07 21 +57 35	220
141		−5 22 57 37	−4 25 58 37	−3 27 57 37	−2 30 58 37	−1 32 57 36	−0 35 58 36	00 23 57 36	01 20 58 35	02 18 57 35	03 15 58 35	04 13 57 35	05 10 58 34	06 08 57 34	07 05 58 34	219
142			−4 41 58 36	−3 43 57 36	−2 46 58 36	−1 48 58 35	−0 50 57 35	00 07 58 35	01 05 57 35	02 02 58 34	03 00 58 34	03 58 57 34	04 55 58 33	05 53 57 33	06 50 58 33	218
143			−4 57 58 35	−3 59 58 35	−3 01 57 35	−2 04 58 34	−1 06 58 34	−0 08 57 34	00 49 58 34	01 47 58 33	02 45 58 33	03 43 57 33	04 40 58 33	05 38 58 32	06 36 57 32	217
144			−5 12 57 34	−4 15 58 34	−3 17 58 34	−2 19 58 34	−1 21 58 33	−0 23 58 33	00 35 57 33	01 32 58 32	02 30 58 32	03 28 58 32	04 26 58 32	05 24 58 31	06 22 57 31	216
145			−5 28 +58 33	−4 30 +58 33	−3 32 +58 33	−2 34 +58 33	−1 36 +58 32	−0 38 +58 32	00 20 +58 32	01 18 +58 32	02 16 +58 31	03 14 +58 31	04 12 +58 31	05 10 +58 31	06 08 +57 30	215
146				−4 44 58 32	−3 46 58 32	−2 48 58 32	−1 50 58 31	−0 52 58 31	00 06 58 31	01 04 58 31	02 02 58 30	03 00 58 30	03 58 58 30	04 56 58 30	05 54 58 30	214
147				−4 59 58 31	−4 01 59 31	−3 02 58 31	−2 04 58 31	−1 06 58 30	−0 08 58 30	00 50 58 30	01 48 58 30	02 46 59 29	03 45 58 29	04 43 58 29	05 41 58 29	213
148				−5 13 59 30	−4 14 58 30	−3 16 58 30	−2 18 58 30	−1 20 58 29	−0 22 59 29	00 37 58 29	01 35 58 29	02 33 58 28	03 31 59 28	04 30 58 28	05 28 58 28	212
149				−5 26 58 29	−4 28 58 29	−3 30 59 29	−2 31 58 29	−1 33 58 29	−0 35 59 28	00 24 58 28	01 22 58 28	02 20 59 28	03 19 58 27	04 17 58 27	05 15 59 27	211
150					−4 41 +58 28	−3 43 +59 28	−2 44 +58 28	−1 46 +59 28	−0 47 +58 27	00 11 +59 27	01 10 +58 27	02 08 +58 27	03 06 +59 27	04 05 +58 26	05 03 +59 26	210
151					−4 54 59 27	−3 55 58 27	−2 57 59 27	−1 58 58 27	−1 00 59 27	−0 01 58 26	00 57 59 26	01 56 58 26	02 54 59 26	03 53 58 25	04 51 59 25	209
152					−5 06 58 26	−4 08 59 26	−3 09 59 26	−2 10 58 26	−1 12 59 26	−0 13 59 25	00 46 58 25	01 44 59 25	02 43 58 25	03 41 59 25	04 40 59 24	208
153					−5 18 59 25	−4 19 58 25	−3 21 59 25	−2 22 59 25	−1 23 58 25	−0 25 59 24	00 34 59 24	01 33 59 24	02 32 58 24	03 30 59 24	04 29 59 23	207
154						−4 31 59 24	−3 32 59 24	−2 33 59 24	−1 34 58 24	−0 36 59 24	00 23 59 23	01 22 59 23	02 21 59 23	03 20 58 23	04 18 59 23	206
155						−4 42 +59 23	−3 43 +59 23	−2 44 +59 23	−1 45 +59 23	−0 46 +59 23	00 13 +58 23	01 11 +59 22	02 10 +59 22	03 09 +59 22	04 08 +59 22	205
156						−4 53 59 23	−3 54 59 22	−2 55 59 22	−1 56 59 22	−0 57 59 22	00 02 59 22	01 01 59 21	02 00 59 21	02 59 59 21	03 58 59 21	204
157						−5 03 59 22	−4 04 59 21	−3 05 59 21	−2 06 59 21	−1 07 59 21	−0 08 60 21	00 52 59 20	01 51 59 20	02 50 59 20	03 49 59 20	203
158						−5 13 60 21	−4 13 59 21	−3 14 59 20	−2 15 59 20	−1 16 59 20	−0 17 59 20	00 42 59 20	01 41 59 20	02 40 60 19	03 40 59 19	202
159							−4 23 59 20	−3 24 60 19	−2 24 59 19	−1 25 59 19	−0 26 59 19	00 33 59 19	01 32 60 19	02 32 59 18	03 31 59 18	201
160							−4 32 +60 19	−3 32 +59 19	−2 33 +59 18	−1 34 +59 18	−0 35 +60 18	00 25 +59 18	01 24 +59 18	02 23 +59 18	03 22 +60 17	200
161							−4 40 59 18	−3 41 59 18	−2 42 60 17	−1 42 59 17	−0 43 59 17	00 16 60 17	01 16 59 17	02 15 59 17	03 14 60 17	199
162							−4 48 59 17	−3 49 59 17	−2 50 60 17	−1 50 59 16	−0 51 60 16	00 09 59 16	01 08 59 16	02 07 60 16	03 07 59 16	198
163							−4 56 59 16	−3 57 60 16	−2 57 59 16	−1 58 60 15	−0 58 59 15	00 01 60 15	01 01 59 15	02 00 60 15	03 00 59 15	197
164							−5 03 59 15	−4 04 60 15	−3 04 59 15	−2 05 60 15	−1 05 59 14	−0 06 60 14	00 54 59 14	01 53 60 14	02 53 59 14	196
165							−5 10 +59 14	−4 11 +60 14	−3 11 +60 14	−2 11 +59 14	−1 12 +60 14	−0 12 +59 13	00 47 +60 13	01 47 +60 13	02 47 +59 13	195
166								−4 17 60 13	−3 17 59 13	−2 18 60 13	−1 18 60 13	−0 18 59 13	00 41 60 12	01 41 60 12	02 41 59 12	194
167								−4 23 60 12	−3 23 60 12	−2 23 59 12	−1 24 60 12	−0 24 60 12	00 36 59 12	01 35 60 11	02 35 60 11	193
168								−4 28 59 11	−3 29 60 11	−2 29 60 11	−1 29 60 11	−0 29 59 11	00 30 60 11	01 30 60 11	02 30 60 10	192
169								−4 33 59 10	−3 34 60 10	−2 34 60 10	−1 34 60 10	−0 34 60 10	00 26 59 10	01 25 60 10	02 25 60 10	191
170								−4 38 +60 9	−3 38 +60 9	−2 38 +60 9	−1 38 +59 9	−0 39 +60 9	00 21 +60 9	01 21 +60 9	02 21 +60 9	190
171								−4 42 60 8	−3 42 60 8	−2 42 59 8	−1 43 60 8	−0 43 60 8	00 17 60 8	01 17 60 8	02 17 60 8	189
172								−4 46 60 7	−3 46 60 7	−2 46 60 7	−1 46 60 7	−0 46 60 7	00 14 59 7	01 13 60 7	02 13 60 7	188
173								−4 49 60 7	−3 49 60 6	−2 49 60 6	−1 49 59 6	−0 50 60 6	00 10 60 6	01 10 60 6	02 10 60 6	187
174								−4 52 60 6	−3 52 60 6	−2 52 60 5	−1 52 60 5	−0 52 60 5	00 08 60 5	01 08 59 5	02 07 60 5	186
175								−4 54 +59 5	−3 55 +60 5	−2 55 +60 5	−1 55 +60 5	−0 55 +60 4	00 05 +60 4	01 05 +60 4	02 05 +60 4	185
176								−4 56 60 4	−3 56 59 4	−2 57 60 4	−1 57 60 4	−0 57 60 4	00 03 60 4	01 03 60 4	02 03 60 4	184
177								−4 58 60 3	−3 58 60 3	−2 58 60 3	−1 58 60 3	−0 58 60 3	00 02 60 3	01 02 60 3	02 02 60 3	183
178								−4 59 60 2	−3 59 60 2	−2 59 60 2	−1 59 60 2	−0 59 60 2	00 01 60 2	01 01 60 2	02 01 60 2	182
179								−5 00 60 1	−4 00 60 1	−3 00 60 1	−2 00 60 1	−1 00 60 1	00 00 60 1	01 00 60 1	02 00 60 1	181
180								−5 00 +60 0	−4 00 +60 0	−3 00 +60 0	−2 00 +60 0	−1 00 +60 0	00 00 +60 0	01 00 +60 0	02 00 +60 0	180

LHA	15°	16°	LHA
72	−5 27 55 113		288
71	−5 02 55 113		289
70	−4 37 −55 114	−5 32 −54 115	290

15°	16°	17°	18°	19°	20°	21°	22°	23°	24°	25°	26°	27°	28°	29°

S. Lat. {LHA greater than 180°....... Zn=180−Z; LHA less than 180°........... Zn=180+Z}

DECLINATION (15°-29°) CONTRARY NAME TO LATITUDE

N. Lat. {LHA greater than 180°........ Zn=Z; LHA less than 180°............ Zn=360−Z}

DECLINATION (15°-29°) CONTRARY NAME TO LATITUDE

LHA	15° Hc	15° d	15° Z	16° Hc	16° d	16° Z	17° Hc	17° d	17° Z	18° Hc	18° d	18° Z	19° Hc	19° d	19° Z
	° ′	′	°	° ′	′	°	° ′	′	°	° ′	′	°	° ′	′	°
69	−4 13	54	115	−5 07	54	116									
68	−3 48	55	116	−4 43	54	117	−5 37	54	117						
67	−3 24	54	117	−4 18	55	117	−5 13	54	118						
66	−3 00	54	118	−3 54	55	118	−4 49	54	119	−5 43	55	119			
65	−2 36	−54	119	−3 30	−55	119	−4 25	−55	120	−5 20	−54	120			
64	−2 12	55	120	−3 07	54	120	−4 01	55	120	−4 56	55	121			
63	−1 48	55	121	−2 43	55	121	−3 38	55	121	−4 33	55	122	−5 28	55	122
62	−1 25	55	121	−2 20	55	122	−3 15	55	122	−4 10	55	123	−5 05	55	123
61	−1 02	55	122	−1 57	55	123	−2 52	55	123	−3 47	55	124	−4 42	55	124
60	−0 39	−55	123	−1 34	−55	124	−2 29	−55	124	−3 24	−56	124	−4 20	−55	125
59	−0 16	56	124	−1 12	55	124	−2 07	55	125	−3 02	55	125	−3 57	56	126
58	00 06	55	125	−0 49	56	125	−1 45	55	126	−2 40	55	126	−3 35	56	127
57	00 28	55	126	−0 27	56	126	−1 23	55	127	−2 18	56	127	−3 14	55	127
56	00 50	55	127	−0 05	56	127	−1 01	56	128	−1 57	55	128	−2 52	56	128
55	01 12	−56	128	00 16	−55	128	−0 39	−56	128	−1 35	−56	129	−2 31	−56	129
54	01 33	55	129	00 38	56	129	−0 18	56	129	−1 14	56	130	−2 10	56	130
53	01 54	55	129	00 59	56	130	00 03	56	130	−0 53	56	131	−1 49	56	131
52	02 15	56	130	01 19	56	131	00 23	56	131	−0 33	56	131	−1 29	56	132
51	02 36	56	131	01 40	56	132	00 44	56	132	−0 12	57	132	−1 09	56	133
50	02 56	−56	132	02 00	−56	133	01 04	−56	133	00 08	−57	133	−0 49	−56	134
49	03 16	56	133	02 20	56	133	01 24	57	134	00 27	56	134	−0 29	56	134
48	03 36	56	134	02 40	57	134	01 43	56	135	00 47	57	135	−0 10	56	135
47	03 56	57	135	02 59	57	135	02 02	56	136	01 06	57	136	00 09	56	136
46	04 15	57	136	03 18	57	136	02 21	56	136	01 25	57	137	00 28	57	137
45	04 33	−56	137	03 37	−57	137	02 40	−57	137	01 43	−57	138	00 46	−57	138
44	04 52	57	138	03 55	57	138	02 58	57	138	02 01	57	139	01 04	57	139
43	05 10	57	139	04 13	57	139	03 16	57	139	02 19	57	140	01 22	57	140
42	05 28	57	140	04 31	57	140	03 34	57	140	02 37	58	140	01 39	57	141
41	05 46	58	140	04 48	57	141	03 51	57	141	02 54	58	141	01 56	57	142
40	06 03	−58	141	05 05	−57	142	04 08	−57	142	03 11	−58	142	02 13	−57	143
39	06 20	58	142	05 22	57	143	04 25	58	143	03 27	57	143	02 30	58	143
38	06 36	57	143	05 39	58	144	04 41	58	144	03 43	57	144	02 46	58	144
37	06 52	57	144	05 55	58	144	04 57	58	145	03 59	58	145	03 01	57	145
36	07 08	58	145	06 10	58	145	05 12	57	146	04 15	58	146	03 17	58	146
35	07 23	−58	146	06 25	−57	146	05 28	−58	147	04 30	−58	147	03 32	−58	147
34	07 38	58	147	06 40	58	147	05 42	58	148	04 44	58	148	03 46	58	148
33	07 53	58	148	06 55	58	148	05 57	58	148	04 59	58	149	04 01	59	149
32	08 07	58	149	07 09	58	149	06 11	58	149	05 13	59	150	04 14	58	150
31	08 21	58	150	07 23	58	150	06 25	59	150	05 26	58	151	04 28	58	151
30	08 35	−59	151	07 36	−58	151	06 38	−58	151	05 40	−59	152	04 41	−58	152
29	08 48	59	152	07 49	58	152	06 51	59	152	05 52	58	152	04 54	59	153
28	09 01	59	153	08 02	59	153	07 03	58	153	06 05	59	153	05 06	58	154
27	09 13	59	154	08 14	59	154	07 15	58	154	06 17	59	154	05 18	59	155
26	09 25	59	155	08 26	59	155	07 27	59	155	06 28	58	155	05 30	59	155
25	09 36	−59	156	08 37	−58	156	07 39	−59	156	06 40	−59	156	05 41	−59	156
24	09 47	59	157	08 48	59	157	07 49	59	157	06 50	58	157	05 52	59	157
23	09 58	59	158	08 59	59	158	08 00	59	158	07 01	59	158	06 02	59	158
22	10 08	59	158	09 09	59	159	08 10	59	159	07 11	59	159	06 12	59	159
21	10 18	59	159	09 19	59	160	08 20	60	160	07 20	59	160	06 21	59	160
20	10 27	−59	160	09 28	−59	161	08 29	−59	161	07 30	−60	161	06 30	−59	161
19	10 36	59	161	09 37	59	162	08 38	60	162	07 38	59	162	06 39	59	162
18	10 45	60	162	09 45	59	163	08 46	59	163	07 47	60	163	06 47	59	163
17	10 53	60	163	09 53	59	163	08 54	60	164	07 54	59	164	06 55	59	164
16	11 00	59	164	10 01	60	164	09 01	59	165	08 02	60	165	07 02	59	165
15	11 08	−60	165	10 08	−60	165	09 08	−59	166	08 09	−60	166	07 09	−59	166
14	11 14	59	166	10 15	60	166	09 15	60	166	08 15	59	167	07 16	60	167
13	11 21	60	167	10 21	60	167	09 21	59	167	08 22	60	168	07 22	60	168
12	11 26	59	168	10 27	60	168	09 27	60	168	08 27	59	169	07 28	60	169
11	11 32	60	169	10 32	60	169	09 32	60	169	08 32	59	169	07 33	60	170
10	11 37	−60	170	10 37	−60	170	09 37	−60	170	08 37	−60	170	07 37	−59	171
9	11 41	60	171	10 41	60	171	09 41	59	171	08 42	60	171	07 42	60	171
8	11 45	60	172	10 45	60	172	09 45	60	172	08 45	59	172	07 46	60	172
7	11 49	60	173	10 49	60	173	09 49	60	173	08 49	60	173	07 49	60	173
6	11 52	60	174	10 52	60	174	09 52	60	174	08 52	60	174	07 52	60	174
5	11 54	−60	175	10 54	−60	175	09 54	−60	175	08 54	−60	175	07 54	−60	175
4	11 56	60	176	10 56	60	176	09 56	60	176	08 56	60	176	07 56	60	176
3	11 58	60	177	10 58	60	177	09 58	60	177	08 58	60	177	07 58	60	177
2	11 59	60	178	10 59	60	178	09 59	60	178	08 59	60	178	07 59	60	178
1	12 00	60	179	11 00	60	179	10 00	60	179	09 00	60	179	08 00	60	179
0	12 00	−60	180	11 00	−60	180	10 00	−60	180	09 00	−60	180	08 00	−60	180

LHA	20° Hc	20° d	20° Z	21° Hc	21° d	21° Z	22° Hc	22° d	22° Z	23° Hc	23° d	23° Z	24° Hc	24° d	24° Z
	° ′	′	°	° ′	′	°	° ′	′	°	° ′	′	°	° ′	′	°
61	−5 37	55	124												
60	−5 15	−55	125												
59	−4 53	55	126												
58	−4 31	55	127	−5 26	55	127									
57	−4 09	56	128	−5 05	55	128									
56	−3 48	55	129	−4 43	56	129	−5 39	55	129						
55	−3 27	−55	130	−4 22	−56	130	−5 18	−56	130						
54	−3 06	55	130	−4 01	56	131	−4 57	56	131						
53	−2 45	56	131	−3 41	56	132	−4 37	56	132	−5 33	56	132			
52	−2 25	56	132	−3 21	56	133	−4 17	56	133	−5 13	56	133			
51	−2 05	56	133	−3 01	56	133	−3 57	56	134	−4 53	56	134			
50	−1 45	−56	134	−2 41	−56	134	−3 37	−57	135	−4 34	−56	135	−5 30	−56	135
49	−1 25	57	135	−2 22	56	135	−3 18	57	135	−4 15	56	136	−5 11	56	136
48	−1 06	57	136	−2 03	56	136	−2 59	57	136	−3 56	56	137	−4 52	57	137
47	−0 47	57	137	−1 44	57	137	−2 41	56	137	−3 37	57	138	−4 34	56	138
46	−0 29	57	137	−1 26	56	138	−2 22	57	138	−3 19	57	138	−4 16	56	139
45	−0 11	−56	138	−1 07	−57	139	−2 04	−57	139	−3 01	−57	139	−3 58	−57	140
44	00 07	57	139	−0 50	57	140	−1 47	56	140	−2 43	57	140	−3 40	57	140
43	00 25	57	140	−0 32	57	140	−1 29	57	141	−2 26	57	141	−3 23	57	141
42	00 42	57	141	−0 15	57	141	−1 12	57	142	−2 09	57	142	−3 06	58	142
41	00 59	57	142	00 02	57	142	−0 55	58	143	−1 53	57	143	−2 50	57	143
40	01 16	−58	143	00 18	−57	143	−0 39	−57	143	−1 36	−58	144	−2 34	−57	144
39	01 32	57	144	00 35	58	144	−0 23	57	144	−1 20	58	145	−2 18	57	145
38	01 48	58	145	00 50	57	145	−0 07	58	145	−1 05	57	145	−2 02	58	146
37	02 04	58	146	01 06	58	146	00 08	57	146	−0 49	58	146	−1 47	58	147
36	02 19	58	146	01 21	58	147	00 23	58	147	−0 35	57	147	−1 32	58	148
35	02 34	−58	147	01 36	−58	148	00 38	−58	148	−0 20	−58	148	−1 18	−58	148
34	02 48	58	148	01 50	58	149	00 52	58	149	−0 06	58	149	−1 04	58	149
33	03 02	58	149	02 04	58	149	01 06	58	150	00 08	58	150	−0 50	58	150
32	03 16	58	150	02 18	58	150	01 20	58	151	00 22	59	151	−0 37	58	151
31	03 30	59	151	02 31	58	151	01 33	58	151	00 35	59	152	−0 24	58	152
30	03 43	−59	152	02 44	−58	152	01 46	−59	152	00 47	−58	153	−0 11	−59	153
29	03 55	58	153	02 57	59	153	01 58	58	153	01 00	59	153	00 01	58	154
28	04 08	59	154	03 09	59	154	02 10	58	154	01 12	59	154	00 13	59	155
27	04 19	58	155	03 21	59	155	02 22	59	155	01 23	58	155	00 25	59	156
26	04 31	59	156	03 32	59	156	02 33	59	156	01 34	58	156	00 36	59	156
25	04 42	−59	157	03 43	−59	157	02 44	−59	157	01 45	−59	157	00 46	−59	157
24	04 53	59	157	03 54	59	158	02 55	59	158	01 56	59	158	00 57	59	158
23	05 03	59	158	04 04	59	159	03 05	59	159	02 06	59	159	01 07	59	159
22	05 13	60	159	04 13	59	159	03 14	59	160	02 15	59	160	01 16	59	160
21	05 22	59	160	04 23	59	160	03 24	60	161	02 24	59	161	01 25	59	161
20	05 31	−59	161	04 32	−60	161	03 32	−59	161	02 33	−59	162	01 34	−59	162
19	05 40	60	162	04 40	59	162	03 41	59	162	02 42	60	163	01 42	59	163
18	05 48	60	163	04 48	59	163	03 49	59	163	02 50	60	163	01 50	59	164
17	05 56	60	164	04 56	59	164	03 57	60	164	02 57	59	164	01 58	60	165
16	06 03	60	165	05 03	59	165	04 04	60	165	03 04	59	165	02 05	60	165
15	06 10	−60	166	05 10	−59	166	04 11	−60	166	03 11	−60	166	02 11	−59	166
14	06 16	59	167	05 17	60	167	04 17	60	167	03 17	59	167	02 18	60	167
13	06 22	59	168	05 23	60	168	04 23	60	168	03 23	60	168	02 23	59	168
12	06 28	60	169	05 28	60	169	04 28	59	169	03 29	60	169	02 29	60	169
11	06 33	60	170	05 33	60	170	04 33	59	170	03 34	60	170	02 34	60	170
10	06 38	−60	171	05 38	−60	171	04 38	−60	171	03 38	−60	171	02 38	−60	171
9	06 42	60	172	05 42	60	172	04 42	60	172	03 42	60	172	02 42	59	172
8	06 46	60	172	05 46	60	173	04 46	60	173	03 46	60	173	02 46	60	173
7	06 49	60	173	05 49	60	173	04 49	60	173	03 49	60	174	02 49	60	174
6	06 52	60	174	05 52	60	174	04 52	60	174	03 52	60	174	02 52	60	175
5	06 54	−60	175	05 54	−60	175	04 54	−59	175	03 55	−60	175	02 55	−60	175
4	06 56	60	176	05 56	60	176	04 56	60	176	03 56	59	176	02 57	60	176
3	06 58	60	177	05 58	60	177	04 58	60	177	03 58	60	177	02 58	60	177
2	06 59	60	178	05 59	60	178	04 59	60	178	03 59	60	178	02 59	60	178
1	07 00	60	179	06 00	60	179	05 00	60	179	04 00	60	179	03 00	60	179
0	07 00	−60	180	06 00	−60	180	05 00	−60	180	04 00	−60	180	03 00	−60	180

LHA	25° Hc	25° d	25° Z	26° Hc	26° d	26° Z	27° Hc	27° d	27° Z	28° Hc	28° d	28° Z	29° Hc	29° d	29° Z	LHA
	° ′	′	°	° ′	′	°	° ′	′	°	° ′	′	°	° ′	′	°	
69																291
68																292
67																293
66																294
65																295
64																296
63																297
62																298
61																299
60																300
59																301
58																302
57																303
56																304
55																305
54																306
53																307
52																308
51																309
50																310
49																311
48																312
47	−5 30	57	138													313
46	−5 12	57	139													314
45	−4 55	−57	140													315
44	−4 37	57	141													316
43	−4 20	57	142	−5 17	57	142										317
42	−4 04	57	143	−5 01	57	143										318
41	−3 47	57	143	−4 44	58	144										319
40	−3 31	−57	144	−4 28	−58	145	−5 26	−57	145							320
39	−3 15	58	145	−4 13	57	145	−5 10	58	146							321
38	−3 00	58	146	−3 58	57	146	−4 55	58	147							322
37	−2 45	58	147	−3 43	57	147	−4 40	58	147							323
36	−2 30	58	148	−3 28	58	148	−4 26	58	148	−5 24	58	149				324
35	−2 16	−58	149	−3 14	−58	149	−4 12	−58	149	−5 10	−58	149				325
34	−2 02	58	150	−3 00	58	150	−3 58	58	150	−4 56	58	150				326
33	−1 48	58	150	−2 46	59	151	−3 45	58	151	−4 43	58	151				327
32	−1 35	58	151	−2 33	58	152	−3 31	59	152	−4 30	58	152				328
31	−1 22	58	152	−2 20	59	152	−3 19	58	153	−4 17	58	153	−5 15	59	153	329
30	−1 10	−58	153	−2 08	−58	153	−3 06	−59	153	−4 05	−58	154	−5 03	−59	154	330
29	−0 57	59	154	−1 56	58	154	−2 54	59	154	−3 53	58	155	−4 51	59	155	331
28	−0 46	58	155	−1 44	59	155	−2 43	58	155	−3 41	59	155	−4 40	59	156	332
27	−0 34	59	156	−1 33	59	156	−2 32	58	156	−3 30	59	156	−4 29	59	157	333
26	−0 23	59	157	−1 22	59	157	−2 21	59	157	−3 20	58	157	−4 18	59	157	334
25	−0 13	−58	157	−1 11	−59	158	−2 10	−59	158	−3 09	−59	158	−4 08	−59	158	335
24	−0 02	59	158	−1 01	59	159	−2 00	59	159	−2 59	59	159	−3 58	59	159	336
23	00 08	60	159	−0 52	59	160	−1 51	59	160	−2 50	59	160	−3 49	59	160	337
22	00 17	59	160	−0 42	59	160	−1 41	59	160	−2 40	60	161	−3 40	59	161	338
21	00 26	59	161	−0 33	59	161	−1 32	60	161	−2 32	59	162	−3 31	59	162	339
20	00 35	−60	162	−0 25	−59	162	−1 24	−59	162	−2 23	−59	162	−3 22	−60	163	340
19	00 43	59	163	−0 16	60	163	−1 16	59	163	−2 15	59	163	−3 14	60	163	341
18	00 51	60	164	−0 09	59	164	−1 08	59	164	−2 07	60	164	−3 07	59	164	342
17	00 58	59	165	−0 01	60	165	−1 01	59	165	−2 00	60	165	−3 00	59	165	343
16	01 05	59	166	00 06	60	166	−0 54	59	166	−1 53	60	166	−2 53	59	166	344
15	01 12	−60	166	00 12	−59	167	−0 47	−60	167	−1 47	−60	167	−2 47	−59	167	345
14	01 18	60	167	00 18	59	167	−0 41	60	168	−1 41	60	168	−2 41	59	168	346
13	01 24	60	168	00 24	60	168	−0 36	59	168	−1 35	60	169	−2 35	60	169	347
12	01 29	60	169	00 29	59	169	−0 30	60	169	−1 30	60	169	−2 30	60	170	348
11	01 34	60	170	00 34	60	170	−0 26	59	170	−1 25	60	170	−2 25	60	170	349
10	01 38	−59	171	00 39	−60	171	−0 21	−60	171	−1 21	−60	171	−2 21	−60	171	350
9	01 43	60	172	00 43	60	172	−0 17	60	172	−1 17	60	172	−2 17	60	172	351
8	01 46	60	173	00 46	60	173	−0 14	59	173	−1 13	60	173	−2 13	60	173	352
7	01 49	59	174	00 50	60	174	−0 10	60	174	−1 10	60	174	−2 10	60	174	353
6	01 52	60	175	00 52	60	175	−0 08	60	175	−1 08	59	175	−2 07	60	175	354
5	01 55	−60	175	00 55	−60	176	−0 05	−60	176	−1 05	−60	176	−2 05	−60	176	355
4	01 57	60	176	00 57	60	176	−0 03	60	176	−1 03	60	176	−2 03	60	176	356
3	01 58	60	177	00 58	60	177	−0 02	60	177	−1 02	60	177	−2 02	60	177	357
2	01 59	60	178	00 59	60	178	−0 01	60	178	−1 01	60	178	−2 01	60	178	358
1	02 00	60	179	01 00	60	179	00 00	60	179	−1 00	60	179	−2 00	60	179	359
0	02 00	−60	180	01 00	−60	180	00 00	−60	180	−1 00	−60	180	−2 00	−60	180	360

S. Lat. {LHA greater than 180°........ Zn=180−Z; LHA less than 180°............ Zn=180+Z}

DECLINATION (15°-29°) CONTRARY NAME TO LATITUDE

LAT 63°

N. Lat. {LHA greater than 180°....... Zn=Z
{LHA less than 180°........... Zn=360−Z

DECLINATION (0°-14°) SAME NAME AS LATITUDE

LAT 64°

LHA	0° Hc	0° d	0° Z	1° Hc	1° d	1° Z	2° Hc	2° d	2° Z	3° Hc	3° d	3° Z	4° Hc	4° d	4° Z
	° ′	′	°	° ′	′	°	° ′	′	°	° ′	′	°	° ′	′	°
0	26 00	+60	180	27 00	+60	180	28 00	+60	180	29 00	+60	180	30 00	+60	180
1	26 00	60	179	27 00	60	179	28 00	60	179	29 00	60	179	30 00	60	179
2	25 59	60	178	26 59	60	178	27 59	60	178	28 59	60	178	29 59	60	178
3	25 58	60	177	26 58	60	177	27 58	60	177	28 58	60	177	29 58	60	177
4	25 56	60	176	26 56	60	176	27 56	60	176	28 56	60	175	29 56	60	175
5	25 54	+60	174	26 54	+60	174	27 54	+60	174	28 54	+59	174	29 53	+60	174
6	25 51	60	173	26 51	60	173	27 51	60	173	28 51	60	173	29 51	59	173
7	25 48	59	172	26 47	60	172	27 47	60	172	28 47	60	172	29 47	60	172
8	25 44	60	171	26 44	59	171	27 43	60	171	28 43	60	171	29 43	60	171
9	25 39	60	170	26 39	60	170	27 39	60	170	28 39	60	170	29 39	60	170
10	25 35	+59	169	26 34	+60	169	27 34	+60	169	28 34	+60	169	29 34	+60	169
11	25 29	60	168	26 29	60	168	27 29	60	168	28 29	59	168	29 28	60	167
12	25 24	59	167	26 23	60	167	27 23	60	167	28 23	59	166	29 22	60	166
13	25 17	60	166	26 17	59	166	27 16	60	165	28 16	60	165	29 16	59	165
14	25 10	60	165	26 10	60	164	27 10	59	164	28 09	60	164	29 09	59	164
15	25 03	+60	163	26 03	+59	163	27 02	+60	163	28 02	+59	163	29 01	+60	163
16	24 55	60	162	25 55	59	162	26 54	60	162	27 54	59	162	28 53	60	162
17	24 47	60	161	25 47	59	161	26 46	59	161	27 45	60	161	28 45	59	161
18	24 38	60	160	25 38	59	160	26 37	59	160	27 36	60	160	28 36	59	159
19	24 29	60	159	25 29	59	159	26 28	59	159	27 27	59	159	28 26	59	158
20	24 20	+59	158	25 19	+59	158	26 18	+59	158	27 17	+59	157	28 16	+59	157
21	24 10	59	157	25 09	59	157	26 08	59	157	27 07	59	156	28 06	59	156
22	23 59	59	156	24 58	59	156	25 57	59	155	26 56	59	155	27 55	59	155
23	23 48	59	155	24 47	59	155	25 46	59	154	26 45	59	154	27 44	58	154
24	23 37	58	154	24 35	59	153	25 34	59	153	26 33	59	153	27 32	59	153
25	23 25	+58	153	24 23	+59	152	25 22	+59	152	26 21	+59	152	27 20	+58	152
26	23 12	59	152	24 11	59	151	25 10	58	151	26 08	59	151	27 07	58	151
27	23 00	58	151	23 58	59	150	24 57	58	150	25 55	59	150	26 54	58	150
28	22 46	59	149	23 45	58	149	24 43	59	149	25 42	58	149	26 40	58	148
29	22 33	58	148	23 31	58	148	24 29	59	148	25 28	58	148	26 26	58	147
30	22 19	+58	147	23 17	+58	147	24 15	+58	147	25 13	+59	147	26 12	+58	146
31	22 04	58	146	23 02	59	146	24 01	58	146	24 59	58	145	25 57	58	145
32	21 50	58	145	22 48	58	145	23 46	58	145	24 44	58	144	25 42	58	144
33	21 34	58	144	22 32	58	144	23 30	58	144	24 28	58	143	25 26	58	143
34	21 19	58	143	22 17	57	143	23 14	58	143	24 12	58	142	25 10	58	142
35	21 03	+57	142	22 00	+58	142	22 58	+58	142	23 56	+58	141	24 54	+57	141
36	20 46	58	141	21 44	58	141	22 42	57	141	23 39	58	140	24 37	57	140
37	20 30	57	140	21 27	58	140	22 25	57	139	23 22	58	139	24 20	57	139
38	20 13	57	139	21 10	57	139	22 07	58	138	23 05	57	138	24 02	57	138
39	19 55	57	138	20 52	58	138	21 50	57	137	22 47	57	137	23 44	57	137
40	19 37	+58	137	20 35	+57	137	21 32	+57	136	22 29	+57	136	23 26	+57	136
41	19 19	57	136	20 16	57	136	21 13	58	135	22 11	57	135	23 08	56	135
42	19 01	57	135	19 58	57	135	20 55	57	134	21 52	57	134	22 49	57	134
43	18 42	57	134	19 39	57	134	20 36	57	133	21 33	56	133	22 29	57	133
44	18 23	57	133	19 20	57	133	20 17	56	132	21 13	57	132	22 10	57	132
45	18 04	+56	132	19 00	+57	132	19 57	+57	131	20 54	+56	131	21 50	+57	131
46	17 44	56	131	18 40	57	131	19 37	56	130	20 33	57	130	21 30	56	130
47	17 24	56	130	18 20	57	130	19 17	56	129	20 13	57	129	21 10	56	129
48	17 03	57	129	18 00	56	129	18 56	57	128	19 53	56	128	20 49	56	128
49	16 43	56	128	17 39	56	128	18 35	57	127	19 32	56	127	20 28	56	127
50	16 22	+56	127	17 18	+56	127	18 14	+56	126	19 10	+57	126	20 07	+56	126
51	16 01	56	126	16 57	56	126	17 53	56	125	18 49	56	125	19 45	56	125
52	15 40	55	125	16 35	56	125	17 31	56	124	18 27	56	124	19 23	56	124
53	15 18	56	124	16 14	56	124	17 10	55	123	18 05	56	123	19 01	56	123
54	14 56	56	123	15 52	55	123	16 47	56	122	17 43	56	122	18 39	55	122
55	14 34	+56	122	15 30	+55	122	16 25	+56	121	17 21	+55	121	18 16	+56	121
56	14 11	56	121	15 07	56	121	16 03	55	120	16 58	56	120	17 54	55	120
57	13 49	55	120	14 44	56	120	15 40	56	120	16 35	56	119	17 31	55	119
58	13 26	55	119	14 21	56	119	15 17	55	119	16 12	55	118	17 07	56	118
59	13 03	55	118	13 58	56	118	14 54	55	118	15 49	55	117	16 44	55	117
60	12 40	+55	117	13 35	+55	117	14 30	+55	117	15 25	+55	116	16 20	+56	116
61	12 16	55	117	13 11	56	116	14 07	55	116	15 02	56	115	15 57	55	115
62	11 53	55	116	12 48	55	115	13 43	55	115	14 38	55	114	15 33	55	114
63	11 29	55	115	12 24	55	114	13 19	55	114	14 14	55	113	15 09	54	113
64	11 05	55	114	12 00	55	113	12 55	55	113	13 50	54	112	14 44	55	112
65	10 41	+55	113	11 36	+54	112	12 30	+55	112	13 25	+55	112	14 20	+55	111
66	10 16	55	112	11 11	55	111	12 06	55	111	13 01	54	111	13 55	55	110
67	09 52	55	111	10 47	54	111	11 41	55	110	12 36	54	110	13 30	55	109
68	09 27	55	110	10 22	54	110	11 16	55	109	12 11	55	109	13 06	54	108
69	09 02	55	109	09 57	55	109	10 52	54	108	11 46	55	108	12 41	54	107

LHA	5° Hc	5° d	5° Z	6° Hc	6° d	6° Z	7° Hc	7° d	7° Z	8° Hc	8° d	8° Z	9° Hc	9° d	9° Z
	° ′	′	°	° ′	′	°	° ′	′	°	° ′	′	°	° ′	′	°
0	31 00	+60	180	32 00	+60	180	33 00	+60	180	34 00	+60	180	35 00	+60	180
1	31 00	60	179	32 00	60	179	33 00	60	179	34 00	60	179	35 00	60	179
2	30 59	60	178	31 59	60	178	32 59	60	178	33 59	60	178	34 59	60	178
3	30 58	60	177	31 58	60	177	32 58	60	176	33 58	60	176	34 58	60	176
4	30 56	60	175	31 56	60	175	32 56	60	175	33 56	60	175	34 56	60	175
5	30 53	+60	174	31 53	+60	174	32 53	+60	174	33 53	+60	174	34 53	+60	174
6	30 50	60	173	31 50	60	173	32 50	60	173	33 50	60	173	34 50	60	173
7	30 47	60	172	31 47	60	172	32 47	60	172	33 47	60	172	34 47	59	172
8	30 43	60	171	31 43	60	171	32 43	60	171	33 43	59	171	34 42	60	170
9	30 39	59	170	31 38	60	170	32 38	60	169	33 38	60	169	34 38	60	169
10	30 34	+59	168	31 33	+60	168	32 33	+60	168	33 33	+60	168	34 33	+59	168
11	30 28	60	167	31 28	59	167	32 27	60	167	33 27	60	167	34 27	59	167
12	30 22	60	166	31 22	59	166	32 21	60	166	33 21	60	166	34 21	59	166
13	30 15	60	165	31 15	60	165	32 15	59	165	33 14	60	165	34 14	59	164
14	30 08	60	164	31 08	59	164	32 07	60	164	33 07	59	163	34 06	60	163
15	30 01	+59	163	31 00	+60	163	32 00	+59	162	32 59	+60	162	33 59	+59	162
16	29 53	59	162	30 52	59	161	31 51	60	161	32 51	59	161	33 50	60	161
17	29 44	59	160	30 43	60	160	31 43	59	160	32 42	59	160	33 41	60	160
18	29 35	59	159	30 34	59	159	31 33	60	159	32 33	59	159	33 32	59	159
19	29 25	60	158	30 25	59	158	31 24	59	158	32 23	59	158	33 22	59	157
20	29 15	+59	157	30 14	+60	157	31 14	+59	157	32 13	+59	156	33 12	+59	156
21	29 05	59	156	30 04	59	156	31 03	59	156	32 02	59	155	33 01	59	155
22	28 54	59	155	29 53	59	155	30 52	59	154	31 51	58	154	32 49	59	154
23	28 42	59	154	29 41	59	153	30 40	59	153	31 39	59	153	32 38	58	153
24	28 31	58	153	29 29	59	152	30 28	59	152	31 27	58	152	32 25	59	152
25	28 18	+59	151	29 17	+58	151	30 15	+59	151	31 14	+59	151	32 13	+58	150
26	28 05	59	150	29 04	58	150	30 02	59	150	31 01	58	150	31 59	59	149
27	27 52	59	149	28 51	58	149	29 49	58	149	30 47	59	148	31 46	58	148
28	27 38	59	148	28 37	58	148	29 35	58	148	30 33	59	147	31 32	58	147
29	27 24	59	147	28 23	58	147	29 21	58	147	30 19	58	146	31 17	58	146
30	27 10	+58	146	28 08	+58	146	29 06	+58	145	30 04	+58	145	31 02	+58	145
31	26 55	58	145	27 53	58	145	28 51	58	144	29 49	58	144	30 47	58	144
32	26 40	58	144	27 38	57	144	28 35	58	143	29 33	58	143	30 31	58	143
33	26 24	58	143	27 22	57	142	28 19	58	142	29 17	58	142	30 15	57	142
34	26 08	57	142	27 05	58	141	28 03	58	141	29 01	57	141	29 58	58	140
35	25 51	+58	141	26 49	+57	140	27 46	+58	140	28 44	+57	140	29 41	+58	139
36	25 34	58	140	26 32	57	139	27 29	58	139	28 27	57	139	29 24	57	138
37	25 17	57	139	26 14	58	138	27 12	57	138	28 09	57	138	29 06	58	137
38	24 59	58	137	25 57	57	137	26 54	57	137	27 51	57	136	28 48	57	136
39	24 41	58	136	25 39	57	136	26 36	57	136	27 33	57	135	28 30	57	135
40	24 23	+57	135	25 20	+57	135	26 17	+57	135	27 14	+57	134	28 11	+57	134
41	24 04	57	134	25 01	57	134	25 58	57	134	26 55	57	133	27 52	57	133
42	23 46	56	133	24 42	57	133	25 39	57	133	26 36	57	132	27 32	57	132
43	23 26	57	132	24 23	57	132	25 20	56	132	26 16	57	131	27 13	56	131
44	23 07	56	131	24 03	57	131	25 00	56	131	25 56	57	130	26 53	56	130
45	22 47	+56	130	23 43	+57	130	24 40	+56	129	25 36	+56	129	26 32	+56	129
46	22 26	57	129	23 23	56	129	24 19	56	128	25 15	57	128	26 12	56	128
47	22 06	56	128	23 02	56	128	23 58	56	127	24 54	57	127	25 51	56	127
48	21 45	56	127	22 41	56	127	23 37	56	126	24 33	56	126	25 29	56	126
49	21 24	56	126	22 20	56	126	23 16	56	125	24 12	56	125	25 08	56	125
50	21 03	+55	125	21 58	+56	125	22 54	+56	124	23 50	+56	124	24 46	+56	124
51	20 41	56	124	21 37	56	124	22 33	55	123	23 28	56	123	24 24	56	123
52	20 19	56	123	21 15	55	123	22 10	56	122	23 06	56	122	24 02	55	122
53	19 57	56	122	20 53	55	122	21 48	56	121	22 44	55	121	23 39	56	121
54	19 34	56	121	20 30	56	121	21 26	55	120	22 21	55	120	23 16	56	120
55	19 12	+55	120	20 07	+56	120	21 03	+55	119	21 58	+55	119	22 53	+56	119
56	18 49	55	119	19 44	56	119	20 40	55	118	21 35	55	118	22 30	55	118
57	18 26	55	118	19 21	55	118	20 16	56	118	21 12	55	117	22 07	55	117
58	18 03	55	117	18 58	55	117	19 53	55	117	20 48	55	116	21 43	55	116
59	17 39	55	116	18 34	55	116	19 29	55	116	20 24	55	115	21 19	55	115
60	17 16	+55	115	18 11	+55	115	19 06	+54	115	20 00	+55	114	20 55	+55	114
61	16 52	55	114	17 47	55	114	18 42	54	114	19 36	55	113	20 31	55	113
62	16 28	55	114	17 23	54	113	18 17	55	113	19 12	55	112	20 07	54	112
63	16 03	55	113	16 58	55	112	17 53	55	112	18 48	54	111	19 42	55	111
64	15 39	55	112	16 34	54	111	17 28	55	111	18 23	55	110	19 18	54	110
65	15 15	+54	111	16 09	+55	110	17 04	+54	110	17 58	+55	109	18 53	+54	109
66	14 50	54	110	15 44	55	109	16 39	54	109	17 33	55	108	18 28	54	108
67	14 25	55	109	15 20	54	108	16 14	54	108	17 08	55	108	18 03	54	107
68	14 00	55	108	14 55	54	107	15 49	54	107	16 43	55	107	17 38	54	106
69	13 35	54	107	14 29	55	107	15 24	54	106	16 18	54	106	17 12	54	105

LHA	10° Hc	10° d	10° Z	11° Hc	11° d	11° Z	12° Hc	12° d	12° Z	13° Hc	13° d	13° Z	14° Hc	14° d	14° Z	LHA
	° ′	′	°	° ′	′	°	° ′	′	°	° ′	′	°	° ′	′	°	
0	36 00	+60	180	37 00	+60	180	38 00	+60	180	39 00	+60	180	40 00	+60	180	360
1	36 00	60	179	37 00	60	179	38 00	60	179	39 00	60	179	40 00	60	179	359
2	35 59	60	178	36 59	60	178	37 59	60	178	38 59	60	178	39 59	60	178	358
3	35 58	60	176	36 58	59	176	37 57	60	176	38 57	60	176	39 57	60	176	357
4	35 56	60	175	36 56	59	175	37 55	60	175	38 55	60	175	39 55	60	175	356
5	35 53	+60	174	36 53	+60	174	37 53	+60	174	38 53	+60	174	39 53	+60	174	355
6	35 50	60	173	36 50	60	173	37 50	60	173	38 50	60	173	39 50	59	172	354
7	35 46	60	172	36 46	60	171	37 46	60	171	38 46	60	171	39 46	60	171	353
8	35 42	60	170	36 42	60	170	37 42	60	170	38 42	60	170	39 42	59	170	352
9	35 38	59	169	36 37	60	169	37 37	60	169	38 37	60	169	39 37	59	169	351
10	35 32	+60	168	36 32	+60	168	37 32	+59	168	38 31	+60	168	39 31	+60	167	350
11	35 26	60	167	36 26	60	167	37 26	59	166	38 25	60	166	39 25	60	166	349
12	35 20	60	166	36 20	59	165	37 19	60	165	38 19	60	165	39 19	59	165	348
13	35 13	60	164	36 13	59	164	37 12	60	164	38 12	59	164	39 11	60	164	347
14	35 06	59	163	36 05	60	163	37 05	59	163	38 04	60	163	39 04	59	162	346
15	34 58	+59	162	35 57	+60	162	36 57	+59	162	37 56	+60	161	38 56	+59	161	345
16	34 50	59	161	35 49	59	161	36 48	59	160	37 47	60	160	38 47	59	160	344
17	34 41	59	160	35 40	59	159	36 39	59	159	37 38	59	159	38 37	60	159	343
18	34 31	59	158	35 30	59	158	36 29	60	158	37 29	59	158	38 28	59	158	342
19	34 21	59	157	35 20	59	157	36 19	59	157	37 18	59	157	38 17	59	156	341
20	34 11	+59	156	35 10	+59	156	36 09	+59	156	37 08	+58	155	38 06	+59	155	340
21	34 00	59	155	34 59	58	155	35 57	59	154	36 56	59	154	37 55	59	154	339
22	33 48	59	154	34 47	59	153	35 46	59	153	36 45	58	153	37 43	59	153	338
23	33 36	59	153	34 35	59	152	35 34	58	152	36 32	59	152	37 31	59	151	337
24	33 24	59	151	34 23	58	151	35 21	59	151	36 20	58	151	37 18	59	150	336
25	33 11	+59	150	34 10	+58	150	35 08	+58	150	36 06	+59	149	37 05	+58	149	335
26	32 58	58	149	33 56	59	149	34 55	58	149	35 53	58	148	36 51	58	148	334
27	32 44	58	148	33 42	59	148	34 41	58	147	35 39	58	147	36 37	58	147	333
28	32 30	58	147	33 28	58	147	34 26	58	146	35 24	58	146	36 22	58	146	332
29	32 15	58	146	33 13	58	145	34 11	58	145	35 09	58	145	36 07	58	144	331
30	32 00	+58	145	32 58	+58	144	33 56	+58	144	34 54	+58	144	35 52	+57	143	330
31	31 45	58	143	32 43	57	143	33 40	58	143	34 38	58	142	35 36	57	142	329
32	31 29	57	142	32 26	58	142	33 24	58	142	34 22	57	141	35 19	58	141	328
33	31 12	58	141	32 10	58	141	33 08	57	141	34 05	58	140	35 03	57	140	327
34	30 56	57	140	31 53	58	140	32 51	57	139	33 48	57	139	34 45	58	139	326
35	30 39	+57	139	31 36	+57	139	32 33	+58	138	33 31	+57	138	34 28	+57	138	325
36	30 21	58	138	31 19	57	138	32 16	57	137	33 13	57	137	34 10	57	136	324
37	30 03	58	137	31 01	57	136	31 58	57	136	32 55	57	136	33 52	56	135	323
38	29 45	57	136	30 42	57	135	31 39	57	135	32 36	57	135	33 33	57	134	322
39	29 27	57	135	30 24	56	134	31 20	57	134	32 17	57	134	33 14	56	133	321
40	29 08	+57	134	30 05	+56	133	31 01	+57	133	31 58	+56	132	32 54	+57	132	320
41	28 49	56	133	29 45	57	132	30 42	56	132	31 38	57	131	32 35	56	131	319
42	28 29	57	131	29 26	56	131	30 22	56	131	31 18	57	130	32 15	56	130	318
43	28 09	57	130	29 06	56	130	30 02	56	130	30 58	56	129	31 54	56	129	317
44	27 49	56	129	28 45	56	129	29 41	57	129	30 38	56	128	31 34	56	128	316
45	27 28	+57	128	28 25	+56	128	29 21	+56	128	30 17	+56	127	31 13	+56	127	315
46	27 08	56	127	28 04	56	127	29 00	56	126	29 56	56	126	30 52	55	126	314
47	26 47	56	126	27 43	55	126	28 38	56	125	29 34	56	125	30 30	56	125	313
48	26 25	56	125	27 21	56	125	28 17	56	124	29 13	55	124	30 08	56	124	312
49	26 04	55	124	26 59	56	124	27 55	56	123	28 51	55	123	29 46	56	123	311
50	25 42	+55	123	26 37	+56	123	27 33	+55	122	28 28	+56	122	29 24	+55	121	310
51	25 20	55	122	26 15	56	122	27 11	55	121	28 06	55	121	29 01	55	120	309
52	24 57	56	121	25 53	55	121	26 48	55	120	27 43	55	120	28 38	56	119	308
53	24 35	55	120	25 30	55	120	26 25	55	119	27 20	55	119	28 15	55	118	307
54	24 12	55	119	25 07	55	119	26 02	55	118	26 57	55	118	27 52	55	117	306
55	23 49	+55	118	24 44	+55	118	25 39	+55	117	26 34	+55	117	27 29	+55	116	305
56	23 25	55	117	24 20	55	117	25 15	55	116	26 10	55	116	27 05	55	115	304
57	23 02	55	116	23 57	55	116	24 52	54	115	25 46	55	115	26 41	55	114	303
58	22 38	55	115	23 33	55	115	24 28	55	114	25 23	54	114	26 17	55	113	302
59	22 14	55	114	23 09	55	114	24 04	54	113	24 58	55	113	25 53	54	112	301
60	21 50	+55	113	22 45	+54	113	23 39	+55	112	24 34	+55	112	25 29	+54	111	300
61	21 26	55	112	22 21	54	112	23 15	55	111	24 10	54	111	25 04	54	111	299
62	21 01	55	111	21 56	55	111	22 51	54	110	23 45	54	110	24 39	54	110	298
63	20 37	54	110	21 31	55	110	22 26	54	110	23 20	54	109	24 14	55	109	297
64	20 12	55	109	21 07	54	109	22 01	54	109	22 55	54	108	23 49	54	108	296
65	19 47	+55	109	20 42	+54	108	21 36	+54	108	22 30	+54	107	23 24	+54	107	295
66	19 22	55	108	20 17	54	107	21 11	54	107	22 05	54	106	22 59	54	106	294
67	18 57	54	107	19 51	54	106	20 45	55	106	21 40	54	105	22 34	54	105	293
68	18 32	54	106	19 26	54	105	20 20	54	105	21 14	54	104	22 08	54	104	292
69	18 06	55	105	19 01	54	104	19 55	54	104	20 49	54	103	21 43	53	103	291

S. Lat. {LHA greater than 180°........ Zn=180−Z
{LHA less than 180°.......... Zn=180+Z

DECLINATION (0°-14°) SAME NAME AS LATITUDE

LAT 64°

N. Lat. {LHA greater than 180°……. Zn=Z
LHA less than 180°………. Zn=360−Z}

DECLINATION (0°-14°) SAME NAME AS LATITUDE

LHA	0° Hc	0° d	0° Z	1° Hc	1° d	1° Z	2° Hc	2° d	2° Z	3° Hc	3° d	3° Z	4° Hc	4° d	4° Z
	° ′	′	°	° ′	′	°	° ′	′	°	° ′	′	°	° ′	′	°
70	08 37	+55	108	09 32	+54	108	10 26	+55	107	11 21	+54	107	12 15	+55	106
71	08 12	55	107	09 07	54	107	10 01	55	106	10 56	54	106	11 50	54	106
72	07 47	55	106	08 42	54	106	09 36	54	105	10 30	55	105	11 25	54	105
73	07 22	54	105	08 16	55	105	09 11	54	105	10 05	54	104	10 59	54	104
74	06 56	55	105	07 51	54	104	08 45	54	104	09 39	55	103	10 34	54	103
75	06 31	+54	104	07 25	+54	103	08 19	+55	103	09 14	+54	102	10 08	+54	102
76	06 05	55	103	07 00	54	102	07 54	54	102	08 48	54	101	09 42	54	101
77	05 40	54	102	06 34	54	101	07 28	54	101	08 22	54	100	09 16	54	100
78	05 14	54	101	06 08	54	100	07 02	54	100	07 56	54	100	08 50	54	99
79	04 48	54	100	05 42	54	100	06 36	54	99	07 30	54	99	08 24	54	98
80	04 22	+54	99	05 16	+54	99	06 10	+54	98	07 04	+54	98	07 58	+54	97
81	03 56	54	98	04 50	54	98	05 44	54	97	06 38	54	97	07 32	54	96
82	03 30	54	97	04 24	54	97	05 18	54	96	06 12	54	96	07 06	54	95
83	03 04	54	96	03 58	54	96	04 52	54	95	05 46	54	95	06 40	54	95
84	02 38	54	95	03 32	54	95	04 26	54	95	05 20	53	94	06 13	54	94
85	02 11	+54	94	03 05	+54	94	03 59	+54	94	04 53	+54	93	05 47	+54	93
86	01 45	54	94	02 39	54	93	03 33	54	93	04 27	54	92	05 21	54	92
87	01 19	54	93	02 13	54	92	03 07	54	92	04 01	54	91	04 55	54	91
88	00 53	54	92	01 47	53	91	02 40	54	91	03 34	54	90	04 28	54	90
89	00 26	54	91	01 20	54	90	02 14	54	90	03 08	54	90	04 02	54	89
90	00 00	+54	90	00 54	+54	90	01 48	+54	89	02 42	+54	89	03 36	+54	88
91	−0 26	54	89	00 28	54	89	01 22	53	88	02 15	54	88	03 09	54	87
92	−0 53	54	88	00 01	54	88	00 55	54	87	01 49	54	87	02 43	54	86
93	−1 19	54	87	−0 25	54	87	00 29	54	86	01 23	54	86	02 17	54	86
94	−1 45	54	86	−0 51	54	86	00 03	54	86	00 57	54	85	01 51	54	85
95	−2 11	+54	86	−1 17	+54	85	−0 23	+54	85	00 31	+54	84	01 25	+53	84
96	−2 38	54	85	−1 44	54	84	−0 50	54	84	00 04	54	83	00 58	54	83
97	−3 04	54	84	−2 10	54	83	−1 16	54	83	−0 22	54	82	00 32	54	82
98	−3 30	54	83	−2 36	54	82	−1 42	54	82	−0 48	54	81	00 06	54	81
99	−3 56	54	82	−3 02	54	81	−2 08	54	81	−1 14	54	81	−0 20	54	80
100	−4 22	+54	81	−3 28	+54	81	−2 34	+54	80	−1 40	+54	80	−0 46	+55	79
101	−4 48	54	80	−3 54	54	80	−3 00	55	79	−2 05	54	79	−1 11	54	78
102	−5 14	54	79	−4 20	55	79	−3 25	54	78	−2 31	54	78	−1 37	54	77
103	−5 40	55	78	−4 45	54	78	−3 51	54	77	−2 57	54	77	−2 03	55	77
104				−5 11	54	77	−4 17	55	77	−3 22	54	76	−2 28	54	76
105				−5 37	+55	76	−4 42	+54	76	−3 48	+54	75	−2 54	+55	75
106							−5 08	55	75	−4 13	54	74	−3 19	54	74
107							−5 33	54	74	−4 39	55	73	−3 44	54	73
108										−5 04	55	72	−4 09	54	72
109										−5 29	55	71	−4 34	54	71
110													−4 59	+55	70
111													−5 24	55	69
112													−5 48	55	68

LHA	5° Hc	5° d	5° Z	6° Hc	6° d	6° Z	7° Hc	7° d	7° Z	8° Hc	8° d	8° Z	9° Hc	9° d	9° Z
	° ′	′	°	° ′	′	°	° ′	′	°	° ′	′	°	° ′	′	°
70	13 10	+54	106	14 04	+54	106	14 58	+55	105	15 53	+54	105	16 47	+54	104
71	12 44	55	105	13 39	54	105	14 33	54	104	15 27	54	104	16 21	54	103
72	12 19	54	104	13 13	54	104	14 07	55	103	15 02	54	103	15 56	54	102
73	11 53	55	103	12 48	54	103	13 42	54	102	14 36	54	102	15 30	54	101
74	11 28	54	102	12 22	54	102	13 16	54	101	14 10	54	101	15 04	54	101
75	11 02	+54	101	11 56	+54	101	12 50	+54	101	13 44	+54	100	14 38	+54	100
76	10 36	54	101	11 30	54	100	12 24	54	100	13 18	54	99	14 12	54	99
77	10 10	54	100	11 04	54	99	11 58	54	99	12 52	54	98	13 46	54	98
78	09 44	54	99	10 38	54	98	11 32	54	98	12 26	54	97	13 20	54	97
79	09 18	54	98	10 12	54	97	11 06	54	97	12 00	54	96	12 54	54	96
80	08 52	+54	97	09 46	+54	96	10 40	+54	96	11 34	+54	96	12 28	+54	95
81	08 26	54	96	09 20	54	96	10 14	54	95	11 08	54	95	12 02	53	94
82	08 00	54	95	08 54	54	95	09 48	53	94	10 41	54	94	11 35	54	93
83	07 34	54	94	08 28	53	94	09 21	54	93	10 15	54	93	11 09	54	92
84	07 07	54	93	08 01	54	93	08 55	54	92	09 49	54	92	10 43	53	91
85	06 41	+54	92	07 35	+54	92	08 29	+54	91	09 23	+53	91	10 16	+54	91
86	06 15	54	91	07 09	54	91	08 03	53	91	08 56	54	90	09 50	54	90
87	05 49	53	91	06 42	54	90	07 36	54	90	08 30	54	89	09 24	54	89
88	05 22	54	90	06 16	54	89	07 10	54	89	08 04	54	88	08 58	53	88
89	04 56	54	89	05 50	54	88	06 44	53	88	07 37	54	87	08 31	54	87
90	04 30	+54	88	05 24	+53	87	06 17	+54	87	07 11	+54	87	08 05	+54	86
91	04 03	54	87	04 57	54	86	05 51	54	86	06 45	54	86	07 39	54	85
92	03 37	54	86	04 31	54	86	05 25	54	85	06 19	54	85	07 13	53	84
93	03 11	54	85	04 05	54	85	04 59	54	84	05 53	53	84	06 46	54	83
94	02 45	54	84	03 39	54	84	04 33	53	83	05 26	54	83	06 20	54	83
95	02 18	+54	83	03 12	+54	83	04 06	+54	82	05 00	+54	82	05 54	+54	82
96	01 52	54	82	02 46	54	82	03 40	54	82	04 34	54	81	05 28	54	81
97	01 26	54	82	02 20	54	81	03 14	54	81	04 08	54	80	05 02	54	80
98	01 00	54	81	01 54	54	80	02 48	54	80	03 42	55	79	04 37	54	79
99	00 34	55	80	01 29	54	79	02 23	54	79	03 17	54	78	04 11	54	78
100	00 09	+54	79	01 03	+54	78	01 57	+54	78	02 51	+54	78	03 45	+54	77
101	−0 17	54	78	00 37	54	77	01 31	54	77	02 25	54	77	03 19	55	76
102	−0 43	54	77	00 11	55	77	01 06	54	76	02 00	54	76	02 54	54	75
103	−1 08	54	76	−0 14	54	76	00 40	54	75	01 34	55	75	02 29	54	74
104	−1 34	54	75	−0 40	55	75	00 15	54	74	01 09	54	74	02 03	55	74
105	−1 59	+54	74	−1 05	+54	74	−0 11	+55	73	00 44	+54	73	01 38	+54	73
106	−2 25	55	73	−1 30	54	73	−0 36	55	73	00 19	54	72	01 13	54	72
107	−2 50	55	73	−1 55	54	72	−1 01	55	72	−0 06	54	71	00 48	55	71
108	−3 15	55	72	−2 20	54	71	−1 26	55	71	−0 31	54	70	00 23	55	70
109	−3 40	55	71	−2 45	55	70	−1 50	54	70	−0 56	55	69	−0 01	54	69
110	−4 04	+54	70	−3 10	+55	69	−2 15	+55	69	−1 20	+54	69	−0 26	+55	68
111	−4 29	55	69	−3 34	54	68	−2 40	55	68	−1 45	55	68	−0 50	55	67
112	−4 53	54	68	−3 59	55	68	−3 04	55	67	−2 09	55	67	−1 14	55	66
113	−5 18	55	67	−4 23	55	67	−3 28	55	66	−2 33	55	66	−1 38	55	65
114	−5 42	55	66	−4 47	55	66	−3 52	55	65	−2 57	55	65	−2 02	55	65
115				−5 11	+55	65	−4 16	+55	64	−3 21	+55	64	−2 26	+55	64
116				−5 35	56	64	−4 39	55	64	−3 44	55	63	−2 49	55	63
117							−5 03	55	63	−4 08	56	62	−3 12	55	62
118							−5 26	55	62	−4 31	55	61	−3 36	56	61
119										−4 54	56	60	−3 58	55	60
120										−5 17	+56	59	−4 21	+55	59
121										−5 39	55	58	−4 44	56	58
122													−5 06	56	57
123													−5 28	56	56

LHA	10° Hc	10° d	10° Z	11° Hc	11° d	11° Z	12° Hc	12° d	12° Z	13° Hc	13° d	13° Z	14° Hc	14° d	14° Z	LHA
	° ′	′	°	° ′	′	°	° ′	′	°	° ′	′	°	° ′	′	°	
70	17 41	+54	104	18 35	+54	103	19 29	+54	103	20 23	+54	102	21 17	+54	102	290
71	17 15	54	103	18 09	54	102	19 03	54	102	19 57	54	101	20 51	54	101	289
72	16 50	54	102	17 44	54	101	18 38	53	101	19 31	54	101	20 25	54	100	288
73	16 24	54	101	17 18	54	101	18 12	54	100	19 06	53	100	19 59	54	99	287
74	15 58	54	100	16 52	54	100	17 46	54	99	18 40	53	99	19 33	54	98	286
75	15 32	+54	99	16 26	+54	99	17 20	+53	98	18 13	+54	98	19 07	+54	97	285
76	15 06	54	98	16 00	54	98	16 54	53	97	17 47	54	97	18 41	54	96	284
77	14 40	54	97	15 34	54	97	16 28	53	96	17 21	54	96	18 15	53	95	283
78	14 14	54	96	15 08	53	96	16 01	54	96	16 55	54	95	17 49	53	95	282
79	13 48	54	96	14 42	53	95	15 35	54	95	16 29	53	94	17 22	54	94	281
80	13 22	+53	95	14 15	+54	94	15 09	+54	94	16 03	+53	93	16 56	+54	93	280
81	12 55	54	94	13 49	54	93	14 43	53	93	15 36	54	92	16 30	53	92	279
82	12 29	54	93	13 23	53	92	14 16	54	92	15 10	54	91	16 04	53	91	278
83	12 03	53	92	12 56	54	91	13 50	54	91	14 44	53	91	15 37	54	90	277
84	11 36	54	91	12 30	54	91	13 24	53	90	14 17	54	90	15 11	54	89	276
85	11 10	+54	90	12 04	+54	90	12 58	+53	89	13 51	+54	89	14 45	+53	88	275
86	10 44	54	89	11 38	53	89	12 31	54	88	13 25	53	88	14 18	54	87	274
87	10 18	53	88	11 11	54	88	12 05	54	87	12 59	53	87	13 52	54	86	273
88	09 51	54	87	10 45	54	87	11 39	53	87	12 32	54	86	13 26	53	86	272
89	09 25	54	87	10 19	53	86	11 12	54	86	12 06	54	85	13 00	53	85	271
90	08 59	+54	86	09 53	+53	85	10 46	+54	85	11 40	+54	84	12 34	+53	84	270
91	08 33	53	85	09 26	54	84	10 20	54	84	11 14	53	83	12 07	54	83	269
92	08 06	54	84	09 00	54	83	09 54	54	83	10 48	53	82	11 41	54	82	268
93	07 40	54	83	08 34	54	83	09 28	54	82	10 22	53	82	11 15	54	81	267
94	07 14	54	82	08 08	54	82	09 02	54	81	09 56	53	81	10 49	54	80	266
95	06 48	+54	81	07 42	+54	81	08 36	+54	80	09 30	+54	80	10 24	+53	79	265
96	06 22	54	80	07 16	54	80	08 10	54	79	09 04	54	79	09 58	53	79	264
97	05 56	54	79	06 50	54	79	07 44	54	79	08 38	54	78	09 32	54	78	263
98	05 31	54	78	06 25	53	78	07 18	54	78	08 12	54	77	09 06	54	77	262
99	05 05	54	78	05 59	54	77	06 53	54	77	07 47	54	76	08 41	54	76	261
100	04 39	+54	77	05 33	+54	76	06 27	+54	76	07 21	+54	75	08 15	+54	75	260
101	04 14	54	76	05 08	54	75	06 02	54	75	06 56	54	75	07 50	54	74	259
102	03 48	54	75	04 42	55	74	05 37	54	74	06 31	54	74	07 25	54	73	258
103	03 23	54	74	04 17	54	74	05 11	54	73	06 05	55	73	07 00	54	72	257
104	02 58	54	73	03 52	54	73	04 46	54	72	05 40	55	72	06 35	54	71	256
105	02 32	+55	72	03 27	+54	72	04 21	+55	71	05 16	+54	71	06 10	+54	71	255
106	02 07	55	71	03 02	54	71	03 56	55	70	04 51	54	70	05 45	54	70	254
107	01 43	54	70	02 37	55	70	03 32	54	70	04 26	54	69	05 20	55	69	253
108	01 18	54	70	02 12	55	69	03 07	55	69	04 02	54	68	04 56	55	68	252
109	00 53	55	69	01 48	55	68	02 43	54	68	03 37	55	67	04 32	54	67	251
110	00 29	+55	68	01 24	+54	67	02 18	+55	67	03 13	+55	67	04 08	+54	66	250
111	00 05	54	67	00 59	55	66	01 54	55	66	02 49	55	66	03 44	54	65	249
112	−0 19	54	66	00 35	55	66	01 30	55	65	02 25	55	65	03 20	55	64	248
113	−0 43	55	65	00 12	54	65	01 06	55	64	02 01	55	64	02 56	55	63	247
114	−1 07	55	64	−0 12	55	64	00 43	55	63	01 38	55	63	02 33	55	63	246
115	−1 31	+55	63	−0 36	+55	63	00 19	+55	62	01 14	+56	62	02 10	+55	62	245
116	−1 54	55	62	−0 59	55	62	−0 04	55	62	00 51	56	61	01 47	55	61	244
117	−2 17	55	61	−1 22	55	61	−0 27	55	61	00 28	56	60	01 24	55	60	243
118	−2 40	55	61	−1 45	55	60	−0 50	56	60	00 06	55	59	01 01	55	59	242
119	−3 03	55	60	−2 08	56	59	−1 12	55	59	−0 17	56	58	00 39	55	58	241
120	−3 26	+56	59	−2 30	+55	58	−1 35	+56	58	−0 39	+55	58	00 16	+56	57	240
121	−3 48	56	58	−2 52	55	57	−1 57	56	57	−1 01	55	57	−0 06	56	56	239
122	−4 10	56	57	−3 14	55	56	−2 19	56	56	−1 23	56	56	−0 27	55	55	238
123	−4 32	56	56	−3 36	56	56	−2 40	55	55	−1 45	56	55	−0 49	56	54	237
124	−4 54	56	55	−3 58	56	55	−3 02	56	54	−2 06	56	54	−1 10	56	54	236
125	−5 15	+56	54	−4 19	+56	54	−3 23	+56	53	−2 27	+56	53	−1 31	+56	53	235
126	−5 36	56	53	−4 40	56	53	−3 44	56	52	−2 48	56	52	−1 52	56	52	234
127				−5 01	56	52	−4 05	56	52	−3 09	56	51	−2 13	57	51	233
128				−5 22	57	51	−4 25	56	51	−3 29	56	50	−2 33	57	50	232
129							−4 46	57	50	−3 49	56	49	−2 53	57	49	231
130							−5 06	+57	49	−4 09	+56	48	−3 13	+57	48	230
131							−5 25	56	48	−4 29	57	48	−3 32	57	47	229
132										−4 48	57	47	−3 51	57	46	228
133										−5 07	57	46	−4 10	57	45	227
134										−5 26	57	45	−4 29	57	44	226
135													−4 47	+57	44	225
136													−5 05	57	43	224
137													−5 22	57	42	223

S. Lat. {LHA greater than 180°……. Zn=180−Z
LHA less than 180°………. Zn=180+Z}

DECLINATION (0°-14°) SAME NAME AS LATITUDE

LAT 64°

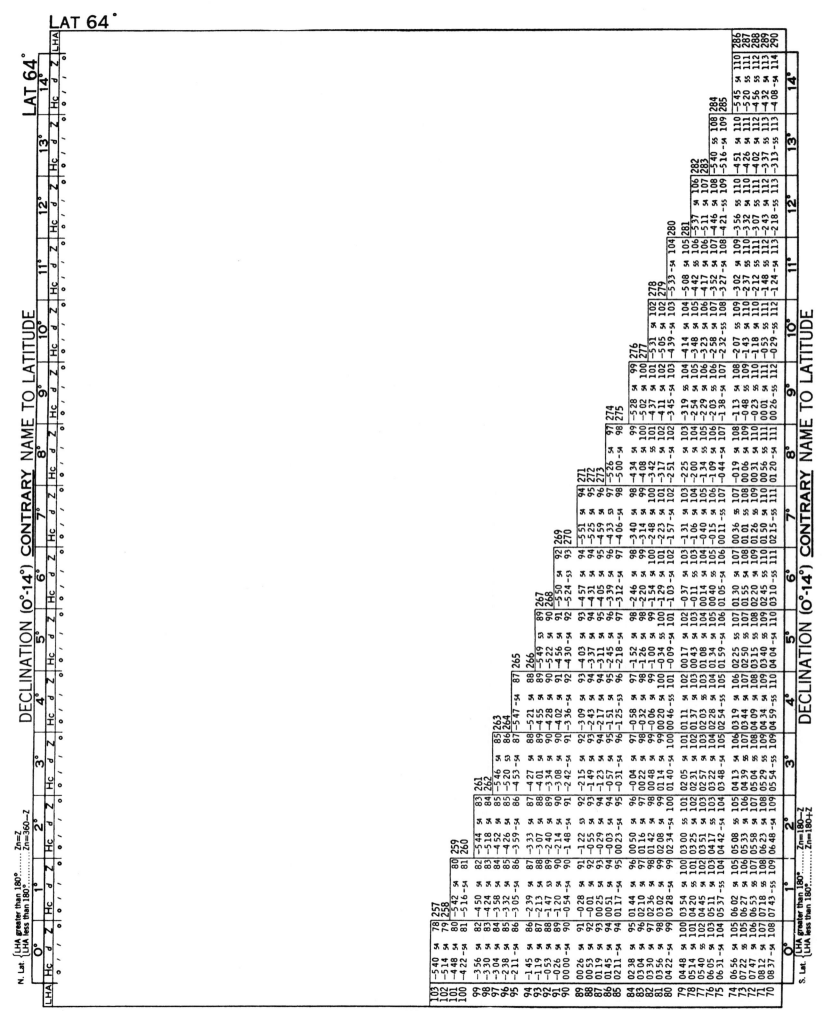

LAT 64°

DECLINATION (0°-14°) CONTRARY NAME TO LATITUDE

N. Lat. {LHA greater than 180°........Zn=Z; LHA less than 180°..........Zn=360−Z}

LHA	0° Hc	d	Z	1° Hc	d	Z	2° Hc	d	Z	3° Hc	d	Z	4° Hc	d	Z	5° Hc	d	Z	6° Hc	d	Z	7° Hc	d	Z
	° ′	′	°	° ′	′	°	° ′	′	°	° ′	′	°	° ′	′	°	° ′	′	°	° ′	′	°	° ′	′	°
103	-5 40	54	78																					
102	-5 14	54	79																					
101	-4 48	54	80	-5 42	54	80																		
100	-4 22	-54	81	-5 16	-54	81																		
99	-3 56	54	82	-4 50	54	82	-5 44	54	83															
98	-3 30	54	83	-4 24	54	83	-5 18	54	84															
97	-3 04	54	84	-3 58	54	84	-4 52	54	85	-5 46	54	85												
96	-2 38	54	85	-3 32	54	85	-4 26	54	85	-5 20	53	86												
95	-2 11	-54	86	-3 05	-54	86	-3 59	-54	86	-4 53	-54	87	-5 47	-54	87									
94	-1 45	54	86	-2 39	54	87	-3 33	54	87	-4 27	54	88	-5 21	54	88									
93	-1 19	54	87	-2 13	54	88	-3 07	54	88	-4 01	54	89	-4 55	54	89	-5 49	53	89						
92	-0 53	54	88	-1 47	53	89	-2 40	54	89	-3 34	54	90	-4 28	54	90	-5 22	54	90						
91	-0 26	54	89	-1 20	54	90	-2 14	54	90	-3 08	54	90	-4 02	54	91	-4 56	54	91	-5 50	54	92			
90	00 00	-54	90	-0 54	-54	90	-1 48	-54	91	-2 42	-54	91	-3 36	-54	92	-4 30	-54	92	-5 24	-53	93			
89	00 26	54	91	-0 28	54	91	-1 22	53	92	-2 15	54	92	-3 09	54	93	-4 03	54	93	-4 57	54	94	-5 51	54	94
88	00 53	54	92	-0 01	54	92	-0 55	54	93	-1 49	54	93	-2 43	54	94	-3 37	54	94	-4 31	54	94	-5 25	54	95
87	01 19	54	93	00 25	54	93	-0 29	54	94	-1 23	54	94	-2 17	54	94	-3 11	54	95	-4 05	54	95	-4 59	54	96
86	01 45	54	94	00 51	54	94	-0 03	54	94	-0 57	54	95	-1 51	54	95	-2 45	54	96	-3 39	54	96	-4 33	53	97
85	02 11	-54	94	01 17	-54	95	00 23	-54	95	-0 31	-54	96	-1 25	-53	96	-2 18	-54	97	-3 12	-54	97	-4 06	-54	98
84	02 38	54	95	01 44	54	96	00 50	54	96	-0 04	54	97	-0 58	54	97	-1 52	54	98	-2 46	54	98	-3 40	54	98
83	03 04	54	96	02 10	54	97	01 16	54	97	00 22	54	98	-0 32	54	98	-1 26	54	98	-2 20	54	99	-3 14	54	99
82	03 30	54	97	02 36	54	98	01 42	54	98	00 48	54	99	-0 06	54	99	-1 00	54	99	-1 54	54	100	-2 48	54	100
81	03 56	54	98	03 02	54	99	02 08	54	99	01 14	54	99	00 20	54	100	-0 34	55	100	-1 29	54	101	-2 23	54	101
80	04 22	-54	99	03 28	-54	99	02 34	-54	100	01 40	-54	100	00 46	-55	101	-0 09	-54	101	-1 03	-54	102	-1 57	-54	102
79	04 48	54	100	03 54	54	100	03 00	55	101	02 05	54	101	01 11	54	102	00 17	54	102	-0 37	54	103	-1 31	54	103
78	05 14	54	101	04 20	55	101	03 25	54	102	02 31	54	102	01 37	54	103	00 43	54	103	-0 11	55	103	-1 06	54	104
77	05 40	55	102	04 45	54	102	03 51	54	103	02 57	54	103	02 03	55	103	01 08	54	104	00 14	54	104	-0 40	54	105
76	06 05	54	103	05 11	54	103	04 17	55	103	03 22	54	104	02 28	54	104	01 34	54	105	00 40	55	105	-0 15	54	106
75	06 31	-54	104	05 37	-55	104	04 42	-54	104	03 48	-54	105	02 54	-55	105	01 59	-54	106	01 05	-54	106	00 11	-55	107
74	06 56	54	105	06 02	54	105	05 08	55	105	04 13	54	106	03 19	54	106	02 25	55	107	01 30	54	107	00 36	55	107
73	07 22	55	105	06 27	54	106	05 33	54	106	04 39	55	107	03 44	54	107	02 50	55	107	01 55	54	108	01 01	55	108
72	07 47	54	106	06 53	55	107	05 58	54	107	05 04	55	108	04 09	54	108	03 15	55	108	02 20	54	109	01 26	55	109
71	08 12	54	107	07 18	55	108	06 23	54	108	05 29	55	109	04 34	54	109	03 40	55	109	02 45	55	110	01 50	54	110
70	08 37	-54	108	07 43	-55	109	06 48	-54	109	05 54	-55	109	04 59	-55	110	04 04	-54	110	03 10	-55	111	02 15	-55	111

LHA	8° Hc	d	Z	9° Hc	d	Z	10° Hc	d	Z	11° Hc	d	Z	12° Hc	d	Z	13° Hc	d	Z	14° Hc	d	Z	LHA
	° ′	′	°	° ′	′	°	° ′	′	°	° ′	′	°	° ′	′	°	° ′	′	°	° ′	′	°	
103																						257
102																						258
101																						259
100																						260
99																						261
98																						262
97																						263
96																						264
95																						265
94																						266
93																						267
92																						268
91																						269
90																						270
89																						271
88																						272
87																						273
86	-5 26	54	97																			274
85	-5 00	-54	98																			275
84	-4 34	54	99	-5 28	54	99																276
83	-4 08	54	100	-5 02	54	100																277
82	-3 42	55	101	-4 37	54	101	-5 31	54	102													278
81	-3 17	54	102	-4 11	54	102	-5 05	54	102													279
80	-2 51	-54	102	-3 45	-54	103	-4 39	-54	103	-5 33	-54	104										280
79	-2 25	54	103	-3 19	55	104	-4 14	54	104	-5 08	54	105										281
78	-2 00	54	104	-2 54	54	105	-3 48	54	105	-4 42	55	106	-5 37	54	106							282
77	-1 34	55	105	-2 29	54	106	-3 23	54	106	-4 17	54	106	-5 11	54	107							283
76	-1 09	54	106	-2 03	55	106	-2 58	54	107	-3 52	54	107	-4 46	54	108	-5 40	55	108				284
75	-0 44	-54	107	-1 38	-54	107	-2 32	-55	108	-3 27	-54	108	-4 21	-55	109	-5 16	-54	109				285
74	-0 19	54	108	-1 13	54	108	-2 07	55	109	-3 02	54	109	-3 56	55	110	-4 51	54	110	-5 45	54	110	286
73	00 06	54	109	-0 48	55	109	-1 43	54	110	-2 37	55	110	-3 32	54	110	-4 26	54	111	-5 20	55	111	287
72	00 31	54	110	-0 23	55	110	-1 18	54	110	-2 12	55	111	-3 07	55	111	-4 02	54	112	-4 56	55	112	288
71	00 56	55	111	00 01	54	111	-0 53	55	111	-1 48	55	112	-2 43	54	112	-3 37	55	113	-4 32	54	113	289
70	01 20	-54	111	00 26	-55	112	-0 29	-55	112	-1 24	-54	113	-2 18	-55	113	-3 13	-55	113	-4 08	-54	114	290

S. Lat. {LHA greater than 180°........Zn=180−Z; LHA less than 180°..........Zn=180+Z}

DECLINATION (0°-14°) CONTRARY NAME TO LATITUDE

LAT 64°

N. Lat. {LHA greater than 180°.......Zn=Z; LHA less than 180°..........Zn=360−Z}

DECLINATION (0°-14°) CONTRARY NAME TO LATITUDE

LHA	0° Hc	0° d	0° Z	1° Hc	1° d	1° Z	2° Hc	2° d	2° Z	3° Hc	3° d	3° Z	4° Hc	4° d	4° Z
	° ′	′	°	° ′	′	°	° ′	′	°	° ′	′	°	° ′	′	°
69	09 02	54	109	08 08	55	110	07 13	55	110	06 18	54	110	05 24	55	111
68	09 27	55	110	08 32	54	110	07 38	55	111	06 43	55	111	05 48	55	112
67	09 52	55	111	08 57	55	111	08 02	55	112	07 07	54	112	06 13	55	113
66	10 16	55	112	09 21	54	112	08 27	55	113	07 32	55	113	06 37	55	113
65	10 41	-55	113	09 46	-55	113	08 51	-55	114	07 56	-55	114	07 01	-55	114
64	11 05	55	114	10 10	55	114	09 15	55	115	08 20	55	115	07 25	55	115
63	11 29	55	115	10 34	55	115	09 39	55	115	08 44	56	116	07 48	55	116
62	11 53	55	116	10 58	56	116	10 02	55	116	09 07	55	117	08 12	55	117
61	12 16	55	117	11 21	55	117	10 26	55	117	09 31	56	118	08 35	55	118
60	12 40	-56	117	11 44	-55	118	10 49	-55	118	09 54	-56	119	08 58	-55	119
59	13 03	55	118	12 08	56	119	11 12	55	119	10 17	56	120	09 21	55	120
58	13 26	55	119	12 31	56	120	11 35	55	120	10 40	56	121	09 44	56	121
57	13 49	56	120	12 53	55	121	11 58	56	121	11 02	56	121	10 06	55	122
56	14 11	55	121	13 16	56	122	12 20	56	122	11 24	55	122	10 29	56	123
55	14 34	-56	122	13 38	-56	123	12 42	-55	123	11 47	-56	123	10 51	-56	124
54	14 56	56	123	14 00	56	124	13 04	56	124	12 08	56	124	11 12	56	125
53	15 18	56	124	14 22	56	125	13 26	56	125	12 30	56	125	11 34	56	126
52	15 40	57	125	14 43	56	125	13 47	56	126	12 51	56	126	11 55	56	127
51	16 01	56	126	15 05	56	126	14 09	57	127	13 12	56	127	12 16	56	128
50	16 22	-56	127	15 26	-56	127	14 30	-57	128	13 33	-56	128	12 37	-56	129
49	16 43	56	128	15 47	57	128	14 50	56	129	13 54	57	129	12 57	56	129
48	17 03	56	129	16 07	56	129	15 11	57	130	14 14	56	130	13 18	57	130
47	17 24	57	130	16 27	56	130	15 31	57	131	14 34	57	131	13 37	56	131
46	17 44	57	131	16 47	57	131	15 50	56	132	14 54	57	132	13 57	57	132
45	18 04	-57	132	17 07	-57	132	16 10	-57	133	15 13	-57	133	14 16	-56	133
44	18 23	57	133	17 26	57	133	16 29	57	134	15 32	57	134	14 35	57	134
43	18 42	57	134	17 45	57	134	16 48	57	135	15 51	57	135	14 54	57	135
42	19 01	57	135	18 04	57	135	17 07	57	136	16 10	58	136	15 12	57	136
41	19 19	57	136	18 22	57	136	17 25	57	137	16 28	58	137	15 30	57	137
40	19 37	-57	137	18 40	-57	137	17 43	-58	138	16 45	-57	138	15 48	-57	138
39	19 55	57	138	18 58	58	138	18 00	57	139	17 03	58	139	16 05	57	139
38	20 13	58	139	19 15	57	139	18 18	58	140	17 20	58	140	16 22	57	140
37	20 30	58	140	19 32	58	140	18 34	57	141	17 37	58	141	16 39	58	141
36	20 46	57	141	19 49	58	141	18 51	58	142	17 53	58	142	16 55	57	142
35	21 03	-58	142	20 05	-58	142	19 07	-58	143	18 09	-58	143	17 11	-58	143
34	21 19	58	143	20 21	58	143	19 23	58	144	18 25	58	144	17 27	58	144
33	21 34	58	144	20 36	58	144	19 38	58	145	18 40	58	145	17 42	58	145
32	21 50	59	145	20 51	58	146	19 53	58	146	18 55	58	146	17 57	58	146
31	22 04	58	146	21 06	58	147	20 08	58	147	19 10	59	147	18 11	58	147
30	22 19	-59	147	21 20	-58	148	20 22	-58	148	19 24	-59	148	18 25	-58	148
29	22 33	59	148	21 34	58	149	20 36	59	149	19 37	58	149	18 39	58	149
28	22 46	58	149	21 48	59	150	20 49	58	150	19 51	59	150	18 52	58	150
27	23 00	59	151	22 01	59	151	21 02	58	151	20 04	59	151	19 05	59	151
26	23 12	58	152	22 14	59	152	21 15	59	152	20 16	59	152	19 17	58	152
25	23 25	-59	153	22 26	-59	153	21 27	-59	153	20 28	-59	153	19 29	-58	153
24	23 37	59	154	22 38	59	154	21 39	59	154	20 40	59	154	19 41	59	155
23	23 48	59	155	22 49	59	155	21 50	59	155	20 51	59	155	19 52	59	156
22	23 59	59	156	23 00	59	156	22 01	59	156	21 02	59	156	20 03	59	157
21	24 10	60	157	23 10	59	157	22 11	59	157	21 12	59	157	20 13	59	158
20	24 20	-60	158	23 20	-59	158	22 21	-59	158	21 22	-59	159	20 23	-59	159
19	24 29	59	159	23 30	59	159	22 31	60	159	21 31	59	160	20 32	59	160
18	24 38	59	160	23 39	59	160	22 40	60	160	21 40	59	161	20 41	59	161
17	24 47	59	161	23 48	60	161	22 48	59	162	21 49	60	162	20 49	59	162
16	24 55	59	162	23 56	60	163	22 56	59	163	21 57	60	163	20 57	59	163
15	25 03	-59	163	24 04	-60	164	23 04	-59	164	22 05	-60	164	21 05	-60	164
14	25 10	59	165	24 11	60	165	23 11	59	165	22 12	60	165	21 12	60	165
13	25 17	59	166	24 18	60	166	23 18	60	166	22 18	59	166	21 19	60	166
12	25 24	60	167	24 24	60	167	23 24	60	167	22 24	59	167	21 25	60	167
11	25 29	59	168	24 30	60	168	23 30	60	168	22 30	60	168	21 30	59	168
10	25 35	-60	169	24 35	-60	169	23 35	-60	169	22 35	-60	169	21 35	-59	169
9	25 39	59	170	24 40	60	170	23 40	60	170	22 40	60	170	21 40	60	170
8	25 44	60	171	24 44	60	171	23 44	60	171	22 44	60	171	21 44	60	171
7	25 48	60	172	24 48	60	172	23 48	60	172	22 48	60	172	21 48	60	173
6	25 51	60	173	24 51	60	173	23 51	60	173	22 51	60	174	21 51	60	174
5	25 54	-60	174	24 54	-60	175	23 54	-60	175	22 54	-60	175	21 54	-60	175
4	25 56	60	176	24 56	60	176	23 56	60	176	22 56	60	176	21 56	60	176
3	25 58	60	177	24 58	60	177	23 58	60	177	22 58	60	177	21 58	60	177
2	25 59	60	178	24 59	60	178	23 59	60	178	22 59	60	178	21 59	60	178
1	26 00	60	179	25 00	60	179	24 00	60	179	23 00	60	179	22 00	60	179
0	26 00	-60	180	25 00	-60	180	24 00	-60	180	23 00	-60	180	22 00	-60	180

LHA	5° Hc	5° d	5° Z	6° Hc	6° d	6° Z	7° Hc	7° d	7° Z	8° Hc	8° d	8° Z	9° Hc	9° d	9° Z
	° ′	′	°	° ′	′	°	° ′	′	°	° ′	′	°	° ′	′	°
69	04 29	55	111	03 34	54	112	02 40	55	112	01 45	55	112	00 50	55	113
68	04 53	54	112	03 59	55	112	03 04	55	113	02 09	55	113	01 14	55	114
67	05 18	55	113	04 23	55	113	03 28	55	114	02 33	55	114	01 38	55	115
66	05 42	55	114	04 47	55	114	03 52	55	115	02 57	55	115	02 02	55	115
65	06 06	-55	115	05 11	-55	115	04 16	-55	116	03 21	-55	116	02 26	-55	116
64	06 30	55	116	05 35	56	116	04 39	55	116	03 44	55	117	02 49	55	117
63	06 53	55	117	05 58	55	117	05 03	55	117	04 08	56	118	03 12	55	118
62	07 17	56	118	06 21	55	118	05 26	55	118	04 31	55	119	03 36	56	119
61	07 40	55	119	06 45	56	119	05 49	55	119	04 54	56	120	03 58	55	120
60	08 03	-55	119	07 08	-56	120	06 12	-55	120	05 17	-56	121	04 21	-55	121
59	08 26	56	120	07 30	55	121	06 35	56	121	05 39	55	122	04 44	56	122
58	08 48	55	121	07 53	56	122	06 57	55	122	06 02	56	122	05 06	56	123
57	09 11	56	122	08 15	56	123	07 19	55	123	06 24	56	123	05 28	56	124
56	09 33	56	123	08 37	56	124	07 41	56	124	06 45	55	124	05 50	56	125
55	09 55	-56	124	08 59	-56	124	08 03	-56	125	07 07	-56	125	06 11	-56	126
54	10 16	56	125	09 20	56	125	08 24	56	126	07 28	56	126	06 32	56	127
53	10 38	56	126	09 42	56	126	08 46	56	127	07 50	57	127	06 53	56	127
52	10 59	56	127	10 03	56	127	09 07	57	128	08 10	56	128	07 14	56	128
51	11 20	56	128	10 24	57	128	09 27	56	129	08 31	56	129	07 35	57	129
50	11 41	-57	129	10 44	-56	129	09 48	-57	130	08 51	-56	130	07 55	-56	130
49	12 01	57	130	11 04	56	130	10 08	57	131	09 11	56	131	08 15	57	131
48	12 21	57	131	11 24	56	131	10 28	57	131	09 31	56	132	08 35	57	132
47	12 41	57	132	11 44	57	132	10 47	56	132	09 51	57	133	08 54	57	133
46	13 00	56	133	12 04	57	133	11 07	57	133	10 10	57	134	09 13	57	134
45	13 20	-57	134	12 23	-57	134	11 26	-57	134	10 29	-57	135	09 32	-57	135
44	13 38	57	135	12 41	57	135	11 44	57	135	10 47	57	136	09 50	57	136
43	13 57	57	136	13 00	57	136	12 03	57	136	11 06	58	137	10 08	57	137
42	14 15	57	137	13 18	57	137	12 21	57	137	11 24	58	138	10 26	57	138
41	14 33	57	138	13 36	57	138	12 39	58	138	11 41	57	138	10 44	58	139
40	14 51	-58	139	13 53	-57	139	12 56	-58	139	11 58	-57	139	11 01	-58	140
39	15 08	58	140	14 10	57	140	13 13	58	140	12 15	57	140	11 18	58	141
38	15 25	58	141	14 27	57	141	13 30	58	141	12 32	58	141	11 34	57	142
37	15 41	57	142	14 44	58	142	13 46	58	142	12 48	58	142	11 50	57	143
36	15 58	58	143	15 00	58	143	14 02	58	143	13 04	58	143	12 06	58	144
35	16 13	-57	144	15 16	-58	144	14 18	-58	144	13 20	-58	144	12 22	-58	145
34	16 29	58	145	15 31	58	145	14 33	58	145	13 35	58	145	12 37	58	146
33	16 44	58	146	15 46	58	146	14 48	58	146	13 50	59	146	12 51	58	147
32	16 59	58	147	16 01	59	147	15 02	58	147	14 04	58	147	13 06	58	148
31	17 13	58	148	16 15	59	148	15 16	58	148	14 18	58	148	13 20	59	149
30	17 27	-58	149	16 29	-59	149	15 30	-58	149	14 32	-59	149	13 33	-58	150
29	17 41	59	150	16 42	58	150	15 44	59	150	14 45	59	150	13 46	58	151
28	17 54	59	151	16 55	59	151	15 56	58	151	14 58	59	151	13 59	58	152
27	18 06	58	152	17 08	59	152	16 09	59	152	15 10	58	152	14 12	59	153
26	18 19	59	153	17 20	59	153	16 21	59	153	15 22	58	153	14 24	59	153
25	18 31	-59	154	17 32	-59	154	16 33	-59	154	15 34	-59	154	14 35	-59	154
24	18 42	59	155	17 43	59	155	16 44	59	155	15 45	59	155	14 46	59	156
23	18 53	59	156	17 54	59	156	16 55	59	156	15 56	59	156	14 57	59	157
22	19 04	59	157	18 05	60	157	17 05	59	157	16 06	59	157	15 07	59	158
21	19 14	59	158	18 15	59	158	17 16	60	158	16 16	59	158	15 17	59	159
20	19 24	-60	159	18 24	-59	159	17 25	-59	159	16 26	-59	159	15 27	-60	160
19	19 33	59	160	18 34	60	160	17 34	59	160	16 35	59	160	15 36	60	161
18	19 42	60	161	18 42	59	161	17 43	59	161	16 44	60	161	15 44	59	162
17	19 50	59	162	18 51	60	162	17 51	59	162	16 52	60	162	15 52	59	163
16	19 58	60	163	18 58	59	163	17 59	60	163	16 59	59	163	16 00	60	164
15	20 05	-59	164	19 06	-60	164	18 06	-59	164	17 07	-60	164	16 07	-59	165
14	20 12	59	165	19 13	60	165	18 13	59	165	17 14	60	166	16 14	60	166
13	20 19	60	166	19 19	59	166	18 20	60	166	17 20	60	167	16 20	59	167
12	20 25	60	167	19 25	59	167	18 26	60	167	17 26	60	168	16 26	60	168
11	20 31	60	168	19 31	60	168	18 31	60	169	17 31	60	169	16 31	59	169
10	20 36	-60	169	19 36	-60	169	18 36	-60	170	17 36	-60	170	16 36	-59	170
9	20 40	60	170	19 40	59	171	18 41	60	171	17 41	60	171	16 41	60	171
8	20 44	59	172	19 45	60	172	18 45	60	172	17 45	60	172	16 45	60	172
7	20 48	60	173	19 48	60	173	18 48	60	173	17 48	60	173	16 48	59	173
6	20 51	60	174	19 51	60	174	18 51	60	174	17 51	59	174	16 52	60	174
5	20 54	-60	175	19 54	-60	175	18 54	-60	175	17 54	-60	175	16 54	-60	175
4	20 56	60	176	19 56	60	176	18 56	60	176	17 56	60	176	16 56	60	176
3	20 58	60	177	19 58	60	177	18 58	60	177	17 58	60	177	16 58	60	177
2	20 59	60	178	19 59	60	178	18 59	60	178	17 59	60	178	16 59	60	178
1	21 00	60	179	20 00	60	179	19 00	60	179	18 00	60	179	17 00	60	179
0	21 00	-60	180	20 00	-60	180	19 00	-60	180	18 00	-60	180	17 00	-60	180

LHA	10° Hc	10° d	10° Z	11° Hc	11° d	11° Z	12° Hc	12° d	12° Z	13° Hc	13° d	13° Z	14° Hc	14° d	14° Z	LHA
	° ′	′	°	° ′	′	°	° ′	′	°	° ′	′	°	° ′	′	°	
69	-0 05	54	113	-0 59	55	114	-1 54	55	114	-2 49	55	114	-3 44	54	115	291
68	00 19	54	114	-0 35	55	114	-1 30	55	115	-2 25	55	115	-3 20	55	116	292
67	00 43	55	115	-0 12	54	115	-1 06	55	116	-2 01	55	116	-2 56	55	117	293
66	01 07	55	116	00 12	55	116	-0 43	55	117	-1 38	55	117	-2 33	55	117	294
65	01 31	-55	117	00 36	-55	117	-0 19	-55	118	-1 14	-56	118	-2 10	-55	118	295
64	01 54	55	118	00 59	55	118	00 04	55	118	-0 51	56	119	-1 47	55	119	296
63	02 17	55	119	01 22	55	119	00 27	55	119	-0 28	56	120	-1 24	55	120	297
62	02 40	55	119	01 45	55	120	00 50	56	120	-0 06	55	121	-1 01	55	121	298
61	03 03	55	120	02 08	56	121	01 12	55	121	00 17	56	122	-0 39	55	122	299
60	03 26	-56	121	02 30	-55	122	01 35	-56	122	00 39	-55	122	-0 16	-56	123	300
59	03 48	56	122	02 52	55	123	01 57	56	123	01 01	55	123	00 06	56	124	301
58	04 10	56	123	03 14	55	124	02 19	56	124	01 23	56	124	00 27	55	125	302
57	04 32	56	124	03 36	56	124	02 40	55	125	01 45	56	125	00 49	56	126	303
56	04 54	56	125	03 58	56	125	03 02	56	126	02 06	56	126	01 10	56	126	304
55	05 15	-56	126	04 19	-56	126	03 23	-56	127	02 27	-56	127	01 31	-56	127	305
54	05 36	56	127	04 40	56	127	03 44	56	128	02 48	56	128	01 52	56	128	306
53	05 57	56	128	05 01	56	128	04 05	56	128	03 09	56	129	02 13	57	129	307
52	06 18	56	129	05 22	57	129	04 25	56	129	03 29	56	130	02 33	57	130	308
51	06 38	56	130	05 42	56	130	04 46	57	130	03 49	56	131	02 53	57	131	309
50	06 59	-57	131	06 02	-56	131	05 06	-57	131	04 09	-56	132	03 13	-57	132	310
49	07 18	56	132	06 22	57	132	05 25	56	132	04 29	57	132	03 32	57	133	311
48	07 38	57	132	06 41	56	133	05 45	57	133	04 48	57	133	03 51	57	134	312
47	07 57	57	133	07 00	56	134	06 04	57	134	05 07	57	134	04 10	57	135	313
46	08 16	57	134	07 19	57	135	06 22	56	135	05 26	57	135	04 29	57	136	314
45	08 35	-57	135	07 38	-57	136	06 41	-57	136	05 44	-57	136	04 47	-57	136	315
44	08 53	57	136	07 56	57	137	06 59	57	137	06 02	57	137	05 05	57	137	316
43	09 11	57	137	08 14	57	137	07 17	57	138	06 20	58	138	05 22	57	138	317
42	09 29	57	138	08 32	58	138	07 34	57	139	06 37	57	139	05 40	58	139	318
41	09 46	57	139	08 49	57	139	07 52	58	140	06 54	57	140	05 57	58	140	319
40	10 03	-57	140	09 06	-58	140	08 08	-57	141	07 11	-58	141	06 13	-57	141	320
39	10 20	57	141	09 23	58	141	08 25	58	142	07 27	57	142	06 30	58	142	321
38	10 37	58	142	09 39	58	142	08 41	58	143	07 43	57	143	06 46	58	143	322
37	10 53	58	143	09 55	58	143	08 57	58	143	07 59	58	144	07 01	57	144	323
36	11 08	58	144	10 10	57	144	09 13	58	144	08 15	58	145	07 17	58	145	324
35	11 24	-59	145	10 26	-58	145	09 28	-58	145	08 30	-58	146	07 32	-58	146	325
34	11 39	58	146	10 41	59	146	09 42	58	146	08 44	58	147	07 46	58	147	326
33	11 53	58	147	10 55	58	147	09 57	58	147	08 59	59	148	08 00	58	148	327
32	12 08	59	148	11 09	58	148	10 11	58	148	09 13	59	149	08 14	58	149	328
31	12 21	58	149	11 23	58	149	10 25	59	149	09 26	58	149	08 28	59	150	329
30	12 35	-59	150	11 36	-58	150	10 38	-59	150	09 39	-58	150	08 41	-59	151	330
29	12 48	59	151	11 49	58	151	10 51	59	151	09 52	58	151	08 54	59	152	331
28	13 01	59	152	12 02	59	152	11 03	58	152	10 05	59	152	09 06	59	153	332
27	13 13	59	153	12 14	59	153	11 15	58	153	10 17	59	153	09 18	59	154	333
26	13 25	59	154	12 26	59	154	11 27	59	154	10 28	59	154	09 29	58	155	334
25	13 36	-59	155	12 37	-59	155	11 38	-59	155	10 39	-58	155	09 41	-59	155	335
24	13 47	59	156	12 48	59	156	11 49	59	156	10 50	59	156	09 51	59	156	336
23	13 58	59	157	12 59	59	157	12 00	59	157	11 01	59	157	10 02	59	157	337
22	14 08	59	158	13 09	59	158	12 10	59	158	11 11	59	158	10 12	60	158	338
21	14 18	59	159	13 19	60	159	12 19	59	159	11 20	59	159	10 21	59	159	339
20	14 27	-59	160	13 28	-59	160	12 29	-60	160	11 29	-59	160	10 30	-59	160	340
19	14 36	59	161	13 37	59	161	12 38	60	161	11 38	59	161	10 39	60	161	341
18	14 45	60	162	13 45	59	162	12 46	60	162	11 46	59	162	10 47	59	162	342
17	14 53	60	163	13 53	59	163	12 54	60	163	11 54	59	163	10 55	60	163	343
16	15 00	59	164	14 01	60	164	13 01	59	164	12 02	60	164	11 02	59	164	344
15	15 08	-60	165	14 08	-60	165	13 08	-59	165	12 09	-60	165	11 09	-59	165	345
14	15 14	59	166	14 15	60	166	13 15	60	166	12 15	59	166	11 16	60	166	346
13	15 21	60	167	14 21	60	167	13 21	60	167	12 21	59	167	11 22	60	167	347
12	15 26	59	168	14 27	60	168	13 27	60	168	12 27	60	168	11 27	59	168	348
11	15 32	60	169	14 32	60	169	13 32	60	169	12 32	59	169	11 33	60	169	349
10	15 37	-60	170	14 37	-60	170	13 37	-60	170	12 37	-60	170	11 37	-59	170	350
9	15 41	60	171	14 41	60	171	13 41	59	171	12 42	60	171	11 42	60	171	351
8	15 45	60	172	14 45	60	172	13 45	60	172	12 45	59	172	11 46	60	172	352
7	15 49	60	173	14 49	60	173	13 49	60	173	12 49	60	173	11 49	60	173	353
6	15 52	60	174	14 52	60	174	13 52	60	174	12 52	60	174	11 52	60	174	354
5	15 54	-60	175	14 54	-60	175	13 54	-60	175	12 54	-60	175	11 54	-60	175	355
4	15 56	60	176	14 56	60	176	13 56	60	176	12 56	60	176	11 56	60	176	356
3	15 58	60	177	14 58	60	177	13 58	60	177	12 58	60	177	11 58	60	177	357
2	15 59	60	178	14 59	60	178	13 59	60	178	12 59	60	178	11 59	60	178	358
1	16 00	60	179	15 00	60	179	14 00	60	179	13 00	60	179	12 00	60	179	359
0	16 00	-60	180	15 00	-60	180	14 00	-60	180	13 00	-60	180	12 00	-60	180	360

S. Lat. {LHA greater than 180°.......Zn=180−Z; LHA less than 180°..........Zn=180+Z}

DECLINATION (0°-14°) CONTRARY NAME TO LATITUDE

LAT 64°

N. Lat. {LHA greater than 180°....... Zn=Z; LHA less than 180°........... Zn=360−Z}

DECLINATION (15°-29°) SAME NAME AS LATITUDE

LAT 64°

LHA	15° Hc	15° d	15° Z	16° Hc	16° d	16° Z	17° Hc	17° d	17° Z	18° Hc	18° d	18° Z	19° Hc	19° d	19° Z	LHA
	° ′	′	°	° ′	′	°	° ′	′	°	° ′	′	°	° ′	′	°	
0	41 00	+60	180	42 00	+60	180	43 00	+60	180	44 00	+60	180	45 00	+60	180	360
1	41 00	60	179	42 00	60	179	43 00	60	179	44 00	60	179	45 00	60	179	359
2	40 59	60	177	41 59	60	177	42 59	60	177	43 59	60	177	44 59	60	177	358
3	40 57	60	176	41 57	60	176	42 57	60	176	43 57	60	176	44 57	60	176	357
4	40 55	60	175	41 55	60	175	42 55	60	175	43 55	60	175	44 55	60	175	356
5	40 53	+60	174	41 53	+60	174	42 53	+59	174	43 52	+60	173	44 52	+60	173	355
6	40 49	60	172	41 49	60	172	42 49	60	172	43 49	60	172	44 49	60	172	354
7	40 46	60	171	41 46	59	171	42 45	60	171	43 45	60	171	44 45	60	171	353
8	40 41	60	170	41 41	60	170	42 41	60	170	43 41	59	170	44 40	60	169	352
9	40 36	60	169	41 36	60	168	42 36	60	168	43 36	59	168	44 35	60	168	351
10	40 31	+60	167	41 31	+59	167	42 30	+60	167	43 30	+60	167	44 30	+59	167	350
11	40 25	59	166	41 24	60	166	42 24	60	166	43 24	59	166	44 23	60	165	349
12	40 18	60	165	41 18	59	165	42 17	60	164	43 17	59	164	44 16	60	164	348
13	40 11	59	164	41 10	60	163	42 10	59	163	43 09	60	163	44 09	59	163	347
14	40 03	60	162	41 03	59	162	42 02	59	162	43 01	60	162	44 01	59	162	346
15	39 55	+59	161	40 54	+60	161	41 54	+59	161	42 53	+59	160	43 52	+59	160	345
16	39 46	59	160	40 45	59	160	41 44	60	159	42 44	59	159	43 43	59	159	344
17	39 37	59	159	40 36	59	158	41 35	59	158	42 34	59	158	43 33	59	158	343
18	39 27	59	157	40 26	59	157	41 25	59	157	42 24	59	157	43 23	59	156	342
19	39 16	59	156	40 15	59	156	41 14	59	156	42 13	59	155	43 12	59	155	341
20	39 05	+59	155	40 04	+59	155	41 03	+59	154	42 02	+59	154	43 01	+58	154	340
21	38 54	59	154	39 53	58	153	40 51	59	153	41 50	59	153	42 49	58	153	339
22	38 42	59	152	39 41	58	152	40 39	59	152	41 38	58	152	42 36	59	151	338
23	38 30	58	151	39 28	59	151	40 27	58	151	41 25	58	150	42 23	59	150	337
24	38 17	58	150	39 15	58	150	40 13	59	149	41 12	58	149	42 10	58	149	336
25	38 03	+59	149	39 02	+58	149	40 00	+58	148	40 58	+58	148	41 56	+58	148	335
26	37 49	59	148	38 48	58	147	39 46	58	147	40 44	58	147	41 42	58	146	334
27	37 35	58	146	38 33	58	146	39 31	58	146	40 29	58	145	41 27	58	145	333
28	37 20	58	145	38 18	58	145	39 16	58	145	40 14	58	144	41 12	57	144	332
29	37 05	58	144	38 03	58	144	39 01	57	143	39 58	58	143	40 56	57	143	331
30	36 49	+58	143	37 47	+58	143	38 45	+57	142	39 42	+58	142	40 40	+57	141	330
31	36 33	58	142	37 31	57	141	38 28	58	141	39 26	57	141	40 23	57	140	329
32	36 17	57	141	37 14	58	140	38 12	57	140	39 09	57	140	40 06	57	139	328
33	36 00	57	139	36 57	57	139	37 54	58	139	38 52	57	138	39 49	57	138	327
34	35 43	57	138	36 40	57	138	37 37	57	138	38 34	57	137	39 31	57	137	326
35	35 25	+57	137	36 22	+57	137	37 19	+57	136	38 16	+57	136	39 13	+56	136	325
36	35 07	57	136	36 04	57	136	37 01	56	135	37 57	57	135	38 54	57	134	324
37	34 48	57	135	35 45	57	135	36 42	56	134	37 38	57	134	38 35	56	133	323
38	34 30	56	134	35 26	57	133	36 23	56	133	37 19	57	133	38 16	56	132	322
39	34 10	57	133	35 07	56	132	36 03	57	132	37 00	56	132	37 56	56	131	321
40	33 51	+56	132	34 47	+57	131	35 44	+56	131	36 40	+56	130	37 36	+56	130	320
41	33 31	56	131	34 27	57	130	35 24	56	130	36 20	56	129	37 16	56	129	319
42	33 11	56	129	34 07	56	129	35 03	56	129	35 59	56	128	36 55	56	128	318
43	32 50	57	128	33 47	55	128	34 42	56	128	35 38	56	127	36 34	56	127	317
44	32 30	56	127	33 26	55	127	34 21	56	126	35 17	56	126	36 13	55	126	316
45	32 09	+55	126	33 04	+56	126	34 00	+56	125	34 56	+55	125	35 51	+56	124	315
46	31 47	56	125	32 43	56	125	33 39	55	124	34 34	55	124	35 29	56	123	314
47	31 26	55	124	32 21	56	124	33 17	55	123	34 12	55	123	35 07	55	122	313
48	31 04	55	123	31 59	56	123	32 55	55	122	33 50	55	122	34 45	55	121	312
49	30 42	55	122	31 37	55	122	32 32	55	121	33 27	55	121	34 22	55	120	311
50	30 19	+55	121	31 14	+56	121	32 10	+55	120	33 05	+54	120	33 59	+55	119	310
51	29 56	56	120	30 52	55	120	31 47	55	119	32 42	54	119	33 36	55	118	309
52	29 34	55	119	30 29	55	119	31 24	54	118	32 18	55	118	33 13	55	117	308
53	29 10	55	118	30 05	55	118	31 00	55	117	31 55	55	117	32 50	54	116	307
54	28 47	55	117	29 42	55	117	30 37	54	116	31 31	55	116	32 26	54	115	306
55	28 24	+54	116	29 18	+55	115	30 13	+54	115	31 07	+55	115	32 02	+54	114	305
56	28 00	54	115	28 54	55	114	29 49	54	114	30 43	55	114	31 38	54	113	304
57	27 36	54	114	28 30	55	114	29 25	54	113	30 19	54	113	31 13	55	112	303
58	27 12	54	113	28 06	55	113	29 01	54	112	29 55	54	112	30 49	54	111	302
59	26 47	55	112	27 42	54	112	28 36	54	111	29 30	54	111	30 24	54	110	301
60	26 23	+54	111	27 17	+54	111	28 11	+55	110	29 06	+54	110	30 00	+53	109	300
61	25 58	55	110	26 53	54	110	27 47	54	109	28 41	54	109	29 35	53	108	299
62	25 33	55	109	26 28	54	109	27 22	54	108	28 16	53	108	29 09	54	107	298
63	25 09	54	108	26 03	54	108	26 57	54	107	27 51	53	107	28 44	54	106	297
64	24 43	55	107	25 38	53	107	26 31	54	106	27 25	54	106	28 19	54	105	296
65	24 18	+54	106	25 12	+54	106	26 06	+54	105	27 00	+54	105	27 54	+53	104	295
66	23 53	54	105	24 47	54	105	25 41	53	104	26 34	54	104	27 28	53	103	294
67	23 28	55	104	24 21	54	104	25 15	54	103	26 09	53	103	27 02	54	102	293
68	23 02	54	103	23 56	53	103	24 49	54	102	25 43	54	102	26 37	53	101	292
69	22 36	54	102	23 30	54	102	24 24	53	101	25 17	54	101	26 11	53	100	291

LHA	20° Hc	20° d	20° Z	21° Hc	21° d	21° Z	22° Hc	22° d	22° Z	23° Hc	23° d	23° Z	24° Hc	24° d	24° Z	LHA
	° ′	′	°	° ′	′	°	° ′	′	°	° ′	′	°	° ′	′	°	
0	46 00	+60	180	47 00	+60	180	48 00	+60	180	49 00	+60	180	50 00	+60	180	360
1	46 00	60	179	47 00	60	179	48 00	60	179	49 00	60	179	50 00	60	179	359
2	45 59	60	177	46 59	60	177	47 59	60	177	48 59	60	177	49 59	60	177	358
3	45 57	60	176	46 57	60	176	47 57	60	176	48 57	60	176	49 57	60	176	357
4	45 55	60	175	46 55	60	175	47 55	60	175	48 55	60	174	49 55	60	174	356
5	45 52	+60	173	46 52	+60	173	47 52	+60	173	48 52	+60	173	49 52	+60	173	355
6	45 49	60	172	46 49	60	172	47 49	59	172	48 48	60	172	49 48	60	172	354
7	45 45	60	171	46 45	60	170	47 45	59	170	48 44	60	170	49 44	60	170	353
8	45 40	60	169	46 40	60	169	47 40	60	169	48 40	59	169	49 39	60	169	352
9	45 35	60	168	46 35	59	168	47 34	60	168	48 34	60	167	49 34	59	167	351
10	45 29	+60	167	46 29	+59	166	47 28	+60	166	48 28	+60	166	49 28	+59	166	350
11	45 23	59	165	46 22	60	165	47 22	59	165	48 21	60	165	49 21	59	165	349
12	45 16	59	164	46 15	60	164	47 15	59	164	48 14	60	163	49 14	59	163	348
13	45 08	60	163	46 08	59	162	47 07	59	162	48 06	60	162	49 06	59	162	347
14	45 00	59	161	45 59	60	161	46 59	59	161	47 58	59	161	48 57	59	160	346
15	44 51	+60	160	45 51	+59	160	46 50	+59	160	47 49	+59	159	48 48	+59	159	345
16	44 42	59	159	45 41	59	158	46 40	59	158	47 39	59	158	48 38	59	158	344
17	44 32	59	157	45 31	59	157	46 30	59	157	47 29	59	157	48 28	59	156	343
18	44 22	59	156	45 21	58	156	46 19	59	156	47 18	59	155	48 17	59	155	342
19	44 11	59	155	45 10	58	155	46 08	59	154	47 07	59	154	48 06	58	154	341
20	43 59	+59	154	44 58	+59	153	45 57	+58	153	46 55	+59	153	47 54	+58	152	340
21	43 47	59	152	44 46	58	152	45 44	59	152	46 43	58	151	47 41	58	151	339
22	43 35	58	151	44 33	59	151	45 32	58	150	46 30	58	150	47 28	58	150	338
23	43 22	58	150	44 20	58	149	45 18	58	149	46 16	58	149	47 14	58	148	337
24	43 08	58	148	44 06	58	148	45 04	58	148	46 02	58	147	47 00	58	147	336
25	42 54	+58	147	43 52	+58	147	44 50	+58	147	45 48	+58	146	46 46	+58	146	335
26	42 40	58	146	43 38	57	146	44 35	58	145	45 33	58	145	46 31	57	144	334
27	42 25	57	145	43 22	58	144	44 20	58	144	45 18	57	144	46 15	58	143	333
28	42 09	58	144	43 07	57	143	44 04	58	143	45 02	57	142	45 59	57	142	332
29	41 53	58	142	42 51	57	142	43 48	58	142	44 46	57	141	45 43	57	141	331
30	41 37	+57	141	42 34	+58	141	43 32	+57	140	44 29	+57	140	45 26	+57	139	330
31	41 20	58	140	42 18	57	140	43 15	57	139	44 12	57	139	45 09	56	138	329
32	41 03	57	139	42 00	57	138	42 57	57	138	43 54	57	137	44 51	56	137	328
33	40 46	57	138	41 43	56	137	42 39	57	137	43 36	57	136	44 33	56	136	327
34	40 28	56	136	41 24	57	136	42 21	57	135	43 18	56	135	44 14	56	135	326
35	40 09	+57	135	41 06	+56	135	42 02	+57	134	42 59	+56	134	43 55	+56	133	325
36	39 51	56	134	40 47	56	134	41 43	57	133	42 40	56	133	43 36	56	132	324
37	39 31	57	133	40 28	56	132	41 24	56	132	42 20	56	132	43 16	56	131	323
38	39 12	56	132	40 08	56	131	41 04	56	131	42 00	56	130	42 56	56	130	322
39	38 52	56	131	39 48	56	130	40 44	56	130	41 40	56	129	42 36	55	129	321
40	38 32	+56	130	39 28	+56	129	40 24	+55	129	41 19	+56	128	42 15	+55	128	320
41	38 12	55	128	39 07	56	128	40 03	56	127	40 59	55	127	41 54	55	126	319
42	37 51	55	127	38 46	56	127	39 42	55	126	40 37	56	126	41 33	55	125	318
43	37 30	55	126	38 25	56	126	39 21	55	125	40 16	55	125	41 11	55	124	317
44	37 08	56	125	38 04	55	125	38 59	55	124	39 54	55	124	40 49	55	123	316
45	36 47	+55	124	37 42	+55	124	38 37	+55	123	39 32	+55	122	40 27	+55	122	315
46	36 25	55	123	37 20	55	122	38 15	55	122	39 10	54	121	40 04	55	121	314
47	36 02	55	122	36 57	55	121	37 52	55	121	38 47	55	120	39 42	54	120	313
48	35 40	55	121	36 35	55	120	37 30	54	120	38 24	55	119	39 19	54	119	312
49	35 17	55	120	36 12	55	119	37 07	54	119	38 01	55	118	38 56	54	118	311
50	34 54	+55	119	35 49	+54	118	36 43	+55	118	37 38	+54	117	38 32	+54	117	310
51	34 31	55	118	35 26	54	117	36 20	54	117	37 14	55	116	38 09	54	116	309
52	34 08	54	117	35 02	54	116	35 56	55	116	36 51	54	115	37 45	54	114	308
53	33 44	54	116	34 38	55	115	35 33	54	115	36 27	54	114	37 21	53	113	307
54	33 20	54	115	34 14	55	114	35 09	54	114	36 03	53	113	36 56	54	112	306
55	32 56	+54	114	33 50	+54	113	34 44	+54	112	35 38	+54	112	36 32	+54	111	305
56	32 32	54	113	33 26	54	112	34 20	54	111	35 14	53	111	36 07	54	110	304
57	32 08	54	112	33 02	53	111	33 55	54	110	34 49	54	110	35 43	53	109	303
58	31 43	54	111	32 37	54	110	33 31	53	109	34 24	54	109	35 18	53	108	302
59	31 18	54	110	32 12	54	109	33 06	53	108	33 59	54	108	34 53	53	107	301
60	30 53	+54	109	31 47	+54	108	32 41	+53	108	33 34	+54	107	34 28	+53	106	300
61	30 28	54	108	31 22	54	107	32 16	53	107	33 09	53	106	34 02	53	105	299
62	30 03	54	107	30 57	53	106	31 50	54	106	32 44	53	105	33 37	53	104	298
63	29 38	53	106	30 31	54	105	31 25	53	105	32 18	53	104	33 11	53	103	297
64	29 13	53	105	30 06	53	104	30 59	54	104	31 53	53	103	32 46	53	103	296
65	28 47	+53	104	29 40	+54	103	30 34	+53	103	31 27	+53	102	32 20	+53	102	295
66	28 21	54	103	29 15	53	102	30 08	53	102	31 01	53	101	31 54	53	101	294
67	27 56	53	102	28 49	53	101	29 42	53	101	30 35	53	100	31 28	53	100	293
68	27 30	53	101	28 23	53	100	29 16	53	100	30 09	53	99	31 02	53	99	292
69	27 04	53	100	27 57	53	99	28 50	53	99	29 43	53	98	30 36	53	98	291

LHA	25° Hc	25° d	25° Z	26° Hc	26° d	26° Z	27° Hc	27° d	27° Z	28° Hc	28° d	28° Z	29° Hc	29° d	29° Z	LHA
	° ′	′	°	° ′	′	°	° ′	′	°	° ′	′	°	° ′	′	°	
0	51 00	+60	180	52 00	+60	180	53 00	+60	180	54 00	+60	180	55 00	+60	180	360
1	51 00	60	179	52 00	60	179	53 00	60	179	54 00	60	179	55 00	60	179	359
2	50 59	60	177	51 59	60	177	52 59	60	177	53 59	60	177	54 59	60	177	358
3	50 57	60	176	51 57	60	176	52 57	60	176	53 57	60	176	54 57	60	175	357
4	50 55	60	174	51 55	60	174	52 55	60	174	53 55	59	174	54 54	60	174	356
5	50 52	+60	173	51 52	+60	173	52 52	+59	173	53 51	+60	173	54 51	+60	172	355
6	50 48	60	171	51 48	60	171	52 48	60	171	53 48	59	171	54 47	60	171	354
7	50 44	60	170	51 44	59	170	52 43	60	170	53 43	60	170	54 43	60	169	353
8	50 39	60	169	51 39	59	168	52 38	60	168	53 38	60	168	54 38	59	168	352
9	50 33	60	167	51 33	60	167	52 33	59	167	53 32	60	167	54 32	59	166	351
10	50 27	+60	166	51 27	+59	166	52 26	+60	165	53 26	+59	165	54 25	+60	165	350
11	50 20	60	164	51 20	59	164	52 19	60	164	53 19	59	164	54 18	60	163	349
12	50 13	59	163	51 12	60	163	52 12	59	162	53 11	59	162	54 10	60	162	348
13	50 05	59	162	51 04	59	161	52 03	60	161	53 03	59	161	54 02	59	160	347
14	49 56	59	160	50 55	60	160	51 55	59	160	52 54	59	159	53 53	59	159	346
15	49 47	+59	159	50 46	+59	158	51 45	+59	158	52 44	+59	158	53 43	+59	158	345
16	49 37	59	157	50 36	59	157	51 35	59	157	52 34	59	156	53 33	58	156	344
17	49 27	59	156	50 26	58	156	51 24	59	155	52 23	59	155	53 22	58	155	343
18	49 16	58	155	50 14	59	154	51 13	59	154	52 12	58	154	53 10	58	153	342
19	49 04	59	153	50 03	58	153	51 01	59	153	52 00	58	152	52 58	58	152	341
20	48 52	+58	152	49 50	+59	152	50 49	+58	151	51 47	+58	151	52 45	+58	150	340
21	48 39	59	151	49 38	58	150	50 36	58	150	51 34	58	149	52 32	58	149	339
22	48 26	58	149	49 24	58	149	50 22	58	148	51 20	58	148	52 18	58	148	338
23	48 12	58	148	49 10	58	148	50 08	58	147	51 06	58	147	52 04	57	146	337
24	47 58	58	147	48 56	58	146	49 54	57	146	50 51	58	145	51 49	57	145	336
25	47 44	+57	145	48 41	+58	145	49 39	+57	144	50 36	+57	144	51 33	+58	144	335
26	47 28	58	144	48 26	57	144	49 23	57	143	50 20	58	143	51 18	57	142	334
27	47 13	57	143	48 10	57	142	49 07	57	142	50 04	57	141	51 01	57	141	333
28	46 56	58	142	47 54	57	141	48 51	57	141	49 48	56	140	50 44	57	140	332
29	46 40	57	140	47 37	57	140	48 34	56	139	49 30	57	139	50 27	57	138	331
30	46 23	+57	139	47 20	+56	139	48 16	+57	138	49 13	+56	138	50 09	+57	137	330
31	46 05	57	138	47 02	57	137	47 59	56	137	48 55	56	136	49 51	56	136	329
32	45 47	57	137	46 44	56	136	47 40	57	136	48 37	56	135	49 33	56	134	328
33	45 29	56	135	46 25	57	135	47 22	56	134	48 18	56	134	49 14	55	133	327
34	45 10	57	134	46 07	56	134	47 03	56	133	47 59	55	133	48 54	56	132	326
35	44 51	+56	133	45 47	+56	132	46 43	+56	132	47 39	+56	131	48 35	+55	131	325
36	44 32	56	132	45 28	55	131	46 23	56	131	47 19	55	130	48 14	56	130	324
37	44 12	56	131	45 08	55	130	46 03	56	129	46 59	55	129	47 54	55	128	323
38	43 52	55	129	44 47	56	129	45 43	55	128	46 38	55	128	47 33	55	127	322
39	43 31	56	128	44 27	55	128	45 22	55	127	46 17	55	127	47 12	55	126	321
40	43 10	+56	127	44 06	+55	126	45 01	+55	126	45 56	+54	125	46 50	+55	125	320
41	42 49	55	126	43 44	55	125	44 39	55	125	45 34	55	124	46 29	54	124	319
42	42 28	55	125	43 23	55	124	44 18	54	124	45 12	55	123	46 07	54	122	318
43	42 06	55	124	43 01	54	123	43 55	55	123	44 50	54	122	45 44	54	121	317
44	41 44	55	123	42 39	54	122	43 33	55	121	44 28	54	121	45 22	54	120	316
45	41 22	+54	121	42 16	+55	121	43 11	+54	120	44 05	+54	120	44 59	+54	119	315
46	40 59	54	120	41 53	55	120	42 48	54	119	43 42	54	119	44 36	53	118	314
47	40 36	54	119	41 30	55	119	42 25	54	118	43 19	53	117	44 12	54	117	313
48	40 13	54	118	41 07	54	118	42 01	54	117	42 55	54	116	43 49	53	116	312
49	39 50	54	117	40 44	54	117	41 38	53	116	42 31	54	115	43 25	53	115	311
50	39 26	+54	116	40 20	+54	115	41 14	+54	115	42 08	+53	114	43 01	+53	114	310
51	39 03	53	115	39 56	54	114	40 50	53	114	41 43	54	113	42 37	53	113	309
52	38 39	53	114	39 32	54	113	40 26	53	113	41 19	53	112	42 12	53	112	308
53	38 14	54	113	39 08	53	112	40 01	54	112	40 55	53	111	41 48	53	111	307
54	37 50	54	112	38 44	53	111	39 37	53	111	40 30	53	110	41 23	53	109	306
55	37 26	+53	111	38 19	+53	110	39 12	+53	110	40 05	+53	109	40 58	+53	108	305
56	37 01	53	110	37 54	53	109	38 47	53	109	39 40	53	108	40 33	53	107	304
57	36 36	53	109	37 29	53	108	38 22	53	108	39 15	53	107	40 08	53	106	303
58	36 11	53	108	37 04	53	107	37 57	53	107	38 50	53	106	39 43	52	105	302
59	35 46	53	107	36 39	53	106	37 32	53	106	38 25	52	105	39 17	53	104	301
60	35 21	+53	106	36 14	+53	105	37 07	+52	105	37 59	+53	104	38 52	+52	103	300
61	34 55	53	105	35 48	53	104	36 41	53	104	37 34	52	103	38 26	52	102	299
62	34 30	53	104	35 23	53	103	36 16	52	103	37 08	52	102	38 00	53	102	298
63	34 04	53	103	34 57	53	102	35 50	52	102	36 42	53	101	37 35	52	101	297
64	33 39	52	102	34 31	53	101	35 24	52	101	36 16	53	100	37 09	52	100	296
65	33 13	+53	101	34 06	+52	100	34 58	+53	100	35 51	+52	99	36 43	+52	99	295
66	32 47	53	100	33 40	52	99	34 32	53	99	35 25	52	98	36 17	52	98	294
67	32 21	53	99	33 14	52	99	34 06	52	98	34 58	53	97	35 51	52	97	293
68	31 55	53	98	32 48	52	98	33 40	52	97	34 32	52	96	35 24	52	96	292
69	31 29	53	97	32 22	52	97	33 14	52	96	34 06	52	95	34 58	52	95	291

S. Lat. {LHA greater than 180°....... Zn=180−Z; LHA less than 180°........... Zn=180+Z}

DECLINATION (15°-29°) SAME NAME AS LATITUDE

N. Lat. {LHA greater than 180°....... Zn=Z; LHA less than 180°........... Zn=360−Z}

DECLINATION (15°-29°) SAME NAME AS LATITUDE

LHA	15° Hc	15° d	15° Z	16° Hc	16° d	16° Z	17° Hc	17° d	17° Z	18° Hc	18° d	18° Z	19° Hc	19° d	19° Z
	° ′	′	°	° ′	′	°	° ′	′	°	° ′	′	°	° ′	′	°
70	22 11	+53	101	23 04	+54	101	23 58	+53	101	24 51	+54	100	25 45	+53	100
71	21 45	53	101	22 38	54	100	23 32	53	100	24 25	54	99	25 19	53	99
72	21 19	53	100	22 12	54	99	23 06	53	99	23 59	54	98	24 53	53	98
73	20 53	53	99	21 46	54	98	22 40	53	98	23 33	54	97	24 27	53	97
74	20 27	53	98	21 20	54	97	22 14	53	97	23 07	54	96	24 01	53	96
75	20 01	+53	97	20 54	+54	96	21 48	+53	96	22 41	+53	95	23 34	+54	95
76	19 35	53	96	20 28	54	95	21 22	53	95	22 15	53	94	23 08	53	94
77	19 08	54	95	20 02	53	95	20 55	54	94	21 49	53	94	22 42	53	93
78	18 42	54	94	19 36	53	94	20 29	53	93	21 22	54	93	22 16	53	92
79	18 16	53	93	19 09	54	93	20 03	53	92	20 56	53	92	21 49	53	91
80	17 50	+53	92	18 43	+54	92	19 37	+53	91	20 30	+53	91	21 23	+53	90
81	17 23	54	91	18 17	53	91	19 10	53	90	20 03	54	90	20 57	53	89
82	16 57	54	90	17 51	53	90	18 44	53	90	19 37	53	89	20 30	54	89
83	16 31	53	90	17 24	54	89	18 18	53	89	19 11	53	88	20 04	53	88
84	16 05	53	89	16 58	53	88	17 51	54	88	18 45	53	87	19 38	53	87
85	15 38	+54	88	16 32	+53	87	17 25	+53	87	18 18	+54	86	19 12	+53	86
86	15 12	53	87	16 05	54	86	16 59	53	86	17 52	53	85	18 45	54	85
87	14 46	53	86	15 39	54	86	16 33	53	85	17 26	53	85	18 19	53	84
88	14 19	54	85	15 13	53	85	16 06	54	84	17 00	53	84	17 53	53	83
89	13 53	54	84	14 47	53	84	15 40	54	83	16 34	53	83	17 27	53	82
90	13 27	+54	83	14 21	+53	83	15 14	+54	82	16 08	+53	82	17 01	+53	81
91	13 01	54	82	13 55	53	82	14 48	54	82	15 42	53	81	16 35	53	81
92	12 35	54	82	13 29	53	81	14 22	54	81	15 16	53	80	16 09	53	80
93	12 09	54	81	13 03	53	80	13 56	54	80	14 50	53	79	15 43	54	79
94	11 43	54	80	12 37	53	79	13 30	54	79	14 24	53	78	15 17	54	78
95	11 17	+54	79	12 11	+54	78	13 05	+53	78	13 58	+54	78	14 52	+53	77
96	10 51	54	78	11 45	54	78	12 39	54	77	13 33	53	77	14 26	54	76
97	10 26	54	77	11 20	54	77	12 13	54	76	13 07	54	76	14 01	53	75
98	10 00	54	76	10 54	54	76	11 48	54	75	12 42	53	75	13 35	54	74
99	09 35	54	75	10 29	53	75	11 22	54	75	12 16	54	74	13 10	54	74
100	09 09	+54	75	10 03	+54	74	10 57	+54	74	11 51	+54	73	12 45	+54	73
101	08 44	54	74	09 38	54	73	10 32	54	73	11 26	54	72	12 20	54	72
102	08 19	54	73	09 13	54	72	10 07	54	72	11 01	54	71	11 55	54	71
103	07 54	54	72	08 48	54	71	09 42	54	71	10 36	54	71	11 30	54	70
104	07 29	54	71	08 23	54	71	09 17	54	70	10 11	54	70	11 05	54	69
105	07 04	+54	70	07 58	+55	70	08 53	+54	69	09 47	+54	69	10 41	+54	68
106	06 39	55	69	07 34	54	69	08 28	54	68	09 22	55	68	10 17	54	68
107	06 15	54	68	07 09	55	68	08 04	54	68	08 58	54	67	09 52	55	67
108	05 51	54	67	06 45	54	67	07 39	55	67	08 34	54	66	09 28	55	66
109	05 26	55	67	06 21	54	66	07 15	55	66	08 10	54	65	09 04	55	65
110	05 02	+55	66	05 57	+55	65	06 52	+54	65	07 46	+55	64	08 41	+54	64
111	04 38	55	65	05 33	55	64	06 28	54	64	07 22	55	64	08 17	55	63
112	04 15	54	64	05 09	55	64	06 04	55	63	06 59	55	63	07 54	54	62
113	03 51	55	63	04 46	55	63	05 41	55	62	06 36	55	62	07 31	54	61
114	03 28	55	62	04 23	55	62	05 18	55	61	06 13	55	61	07 08	54	61
115	03 05	+55	61	04 00	+55	61	04 55	+55	60	05 50	+55	60	06 45	+55	60
116	02 42	55	60	03 37	55	60	04 32	55	60	05 27	55	59	06 22	56	59
117	02 19	55	59	03 14	55	59	04 09	56	59	05 05	55	58	06 00	55	58
118	01 56	56	59	02 52	55	58	03 47	55	58	04 42	56	57	05 38	55	57
119	01 34	55	58	02 29	56	57	03 25	55	57	04 20	56	57	05 16	55	56
120	01 12	+55	57	02 07	+56	56	03 03	+55	56	03 58	+56	56	04 54	+55	55
121	00 50	56	56	01 46	55	56	02 41	56	55	03 37	55	55	04 32	56	54
122	00 28	56	55	01 24	56	55	02 20	55	54	03 15	56	54	04 11	56	54
123	00 07	56	54	01 03	55	54	01 58	56	53	02 54	56	53	03 50	56	53
124	−0 14	56	53	00 42	56	53	01 38	55	52	02 33	56	52	03 29	56	52
125	−0 35	+56	52	00 21	+56	52	01 17	+56	52	02 13	+56	51	03 09	+56	51
126	−0 56	56	51	00 00	56	51	00 56	56	51	01 52	56	50	02 48	57	50
127	−1 16	56	50	−0 20	56	50	00 36	56	50	01 32	56	49	02 28	57	49
128	−1 36	56	50	−0 40	56	49	00 16	56	49	01 12	57	49	02 09	56	48
129	−1 56	56	49	−1 00	56	48	−0 04	57	48	00 53	56	48	01 49	57	47
130	−2 16	+57	48	−1 19	+56	47	−0 23	+57	47	00 34	+56	47	01 30	+57	46
131	−2 35	56	47	−1 39	57	47	−0 42	57	46	00 15	56	46	01 11	57	46
132	−2 54	56	46	−1 58	57	46	−1 01	57	45	−0 04	57	45	00 53	56	45
133	−3 13	57	45	−2 16	57	45	−1 19	56	44	−0 23	57	44	00 34	57	44
134	−3 32	57	44	−2 35	57	44	−1 38	57	43	−0 41	57	43	00 16	57	43
135	−3 50	+57	43	−2 53	+57	43	−1 56	+57	43	−0 59	+57	42	−0 02	+57	42
136	−4 08	58	42	−3 10	57	42	−2 13	57	42	−1 16	57	41	−0 19	57	41
137	−4 25	57	41	−3 28	57	41	−2 31	58	41	−1 33	57	40	−0 36	57	40
138	−4 42	57	40	−3 45	57	40	−2 48	58	40	−1 50	57	40	−0 53	57	39
139	−4 59	57	39	−4 02	58	39	−3 04	57	39	−2 07	58	39	−1 09	57	38

LHA	20° Hc	20° d	20° Z	21° Hc	21° d	21° Z	22° Hc	22° d	22° Z	23° Hc	23° d	23° Z	24° Hc	24° d	24° Z
	° ′	′	°	° ′	′	°	° ′	′	°	° ′	′	°	° ′	′	°
70	26 38	+53	99	27 31	+53	98	28 24	+53	98	29 17	+53	97	30 10	+53	97
71	26 12	53	98	27 05	53	98	27 58	53	97	28 51	53	96	29 44	53	96
72	25 46	53	97	26 39	53	97	27 32	53	96	28 25	53	96	29 18	52	95
73	25 20	53	96	26 13	53	96	27 06	53	95	27 59	53	95	28 52	52	94
74	24 54	53	95	25 47	53	95	26 40	53	94	27 33	52	94	28 25	53	93
75	24 28	+53	94	25 21	+53	94	26 14	+52	93	27 06	+53	93	27 59	+53	92
76	24 01	53	93	24 54	53	93	25 47	53	92	26 40	53	92	27 33	52	91
77	23 35	53	93	24 28	53	92	25 21	53	92	26 14	52	91	27 06	53	90
78	23 09	53	92	24 02	53	91	24 55	52	91	25 47	53	90	26 40	53	90
79	22 42	53	91	23 35	53	90	24 28	53	90	25 21	53	89	26 14	52	89
80	22 16	+53	90	23 09	+53	89	24 02	+53	89	24 55	+53	88	25 48	+52	88
81	21 50	53	89	22 43	53	88	23 36	53	88	24 29	52	87	25 21	53	87
82	21 24	53	88	22 17	53	88	23 10	52	87	24 02	53	87	24 55	53	86
83	20 57	53	87	21 50	53	87	22 43	53	86	23 36	53	86	24 29	53	85
84	20 31	53	86	21 24	53	86	22 17	53	85	23 10	53	85	24 03	52	84
85	20 05	+53	85	20 58	+53	85	21 51	+53	84	22 44	+53	84	23 37	+52	83
86	19 39	53	85	20 32	53	84	21 25	53	84	22 18	52	83	23 10	53	82
87	19 12	54	84	20 06	53	83	20 59	53	83	21 52	52	82	22 44	53	82
88	18 46	53	83	19 39	54	82	20 33	52	82	21 25	53	81	22 18	53	81
89	18 20	53	82	19 13	54	81	20 07	53	81	21 00	52	80	21 52	53	80
90	17 54	+53	81	18 47	+54	80	19 41	+53	80	20 34	+53	80	21 27	+53	79
91	17 28	54	80	18 22	53	80	19 15	53	79	20 08	53	79	21 01	53	78
92	17 02	54	79	17 56	53	79	18 49	53	78	19 42	53	78	20 35	53	77
93	16 37	53	78	17 30	53	78	18 23	53	77	19 16	54	77	20 10	53	76
94	16 11	53	77	17 04	54	77	17 58	53	77	18 51	53	76	19 44	53	76
95	15 45	+54	77	16 39	+53	76	17 32	+53	76	18 25	+54	75	19 19	+53	75
96	15 20	53	76	16 13	54	75	17 07	53	75	18 00	53	74	18 53	54	74
97	14 54	54	75	15 48	53	74	16 41	54	74	17 35	53	73	18 28	53	73
98	14 29	54	74	15 23	53	73	16 16	54	73	17 10	53	73	18 03	53	72
99	14 04	53	73	14 57	54	73	15 51	54	72	16 45	53	72	17 38	53	71
100	13 39	+53	72	14 32	+54	72	15 26	+54	71	16 20	+53	71	17 13	+54	70
101	13 14	53	71	14 07	54	71	15 01	54	70	15 55	54	70	16 49	53	70
102	12 49	54	71	13 43	53	70	14 36	54	70	15 30	54	69	16 24	54	69
103	12 24	54	70	13 18	54	69	14 12	54	69	15 06	54	68	16 00	53	68
104	11 59	54	69	12 53	54	68	13 47	54	68	14 41	54	67	15 35	54	67
105	11 35	+54	68	12 29	+54	68	13 23	+54	67	14 17	+54	67	15 11	+54	66
106	11 11	54	67	12 05	54	67	12 59	54	66	13 53	54	66	14 47	54	65
107	10 47	54	66	11 41	54	66	12 35	54	65	13 29	54	65	14 23	54	64
108	10 23	54	65	11 17	54	65	12 11	54	64	13 05	55	64	14 00	54	63
109	09 59	54	64	10 53	55	64	11 48	54	64	12 42	54	63	13 36	54	63
110	09 35	+55	64	10 30	+54	63	11 24	+55	63	12 19	+54	62	13 13	+54	62
111	09 12	54	63	10 06	55	62	11 01	54	62	11 55	55	61	12 50	54	61
112	08 48	55	62	09 43	55	61	10 38	54	61	11 32	55	61	12 27	54	60
113	08 25	55	61	09 20	55	61	10 15	55	60	11 10	54	60	12 04	55	59
114	08 02	55	60	08 57	55	60	09 52	55	59	10 47	55	59	11 42	54	59
115	07 40	+55	59	08 35	+55	59	09 30	+55	59	10 25	+54	58	11 19	+55	58
116	07 17	55	58	08 12	55	58	09 07	55	58	10 02	55	57	10 57	55	57
117	06 55	55	58	07 50	55	57	08 45	55	57	09 40	55	56	10 35	55	56
118	06 33	56	57	07 28	55	56	08 23	56	56	09 19	55	55	10 14	55	55
119	06 11	55	56	07 06	56	55	08 02	55	55	08 57	55	55	09 52	56	54
120	05 49	+56	55	06 45	+55	55	07 40	+56	54	08 36	+55	54	09 31	+55	53
121	05 28	56	54	06 24	55	54	07 19	56	53	08 15	55	53	09 10	56	53
122	05 07	55	53	06 02	56	53	06 58	56	52	07 54	55	52	08 49	56	52
123	04 46	56	52	05 42	55	52	06 37	56	52	07 33	56	51	08 29	56	51
124	04 25	56	51	05 21	56	51	06 17	56	50	07 13	56	50	08 09	55	50
125	04 05	+56	51	05 01	+56	50	05 57	+56	50	06 53	+56	49	07 49	+56	49
126	03 45	56	50	04 41	56	49	05 37	56	49	06 33	56	49	07 29	56	48
127	03 25	56	49	04 21	56	48	05 17	56	48	06 13	56	48	07 09	57	47
128	03 05	56	48	04 01	57	48	04 58	56	47	05 54	56	47	06 50	56	47
129	02 46	56	47	03 42	56	47	04 38	57	46	05 35	56	46	06 31	57	46
130	02 27	+56	46	03 23	+57	46	04 20	+56	45	05 16	+57	45	06 13	+56	45
131	02 08	56	45	03 04	57	45	04 01	57	45	04 58	56	44	05 54	57	44
132	01 49	57	44	02 46	57	44	03 43	56	44	04 39	57	43	05 36	57	43
133	01 31	57	43	02 28	57	43	03 25	56	43	04 21	57	42	05 18	57	42
134	01 13	57	43	02 10	57	42	03 07	57	42	04 04	57	42	05 01	57	41
135	00 55	+57	42	01 52	+58	41	02 50	+57	41	03 47	+57	41	04 44	+57	40
136	00 38	57	41	01 35	57	40	02 32	58	40	03 30	57	40	04 27	57	40
137	00 21	57	40	01 18	58	40	02 16	57	39	03 13	57	39	04 10	57	39
138	00 04	58	39	01 02	57	39	01 59	57	38	02 56	58	38	03 54	57	38
139	−0 12	57	38	00 45	58	38	01 43	57	37	02 40	58	37	03 38	57	37

LHA	25° Hc	25° d	25° Z	26° Hc	26° d	26° Z	27° Hc	27° d	27° Z	28° Hc	28° d	28° Z	29° Hc	29° d	29° Z	LHA
	° ′	′	°	° ′	′	°	° ′	′	°	° ′	′	°	° ′	′	°	
70	31 03	+52	96	31 55	+53	96	32 48	+52	95	33 40	+52	95	34 32	+52	94	290
71	30 37	52	95	31 29	53	95	32 22	52	94	33 14	52	94	34 06	52	93	289
72	30 10	53	94	31 03	52	94	31 55	52	93	32 47	52	93	33 39	52	92	288
73	29 44	53	94	30 37	52	93	31 29	52	92	32 21	52	92	33 13	52	91	287
74	29 18	52	93	30 10	53	92	31 03	52	92	31 55	52	91	32 47	52	90	286
75	28 52	+52	92	29 44	+52	91	30 36	+53	91	31 29	+52	90	32 21	+51	89	285
76	28 25	53	91	29 18	52	90	30 10	53	90	31 02	52	89	31 54	52	89	284
77	27 59	53	90	28 52	52	89	29 44	52	89	30 36	52	88	31 28	52	88	283
78	27 33	52	89	28 25	53	88	29 18	52	88	30 10	52	87	31 02	52	87	282
79	27 06	53	88	27 59	52	88	28 51	52	87	29 43	52	86	30 35	52	86	281
80	26 40	+53	87	27 33	+52	87	28 25	+52	86	29 17	+52	86	30 09	+52	85	280
81	26 14	52	86	27 06	53	86	27 59	52	85	28 51	52	85	29 43	52	84	279
82	25 48	52	86	26 40	53	85	27 33	52	84	28 25	52	84	29 17	52	83	278
83	25 22	52	85	26 14	52	84	27 06	53	84	27 59	52	83	28 51	52	82	277
84	24 55	53	84	25 48	52	83	26 40	53	83	27 33	52	82	28 25	52	82	276
85	24 29	+53	83	25 22	+52	82	26 14	+53	82	27 07	+52	81	27 59	+52	81	275
86	24 03	53	82	24 56	52	81	25 48	53	81	26 41	52	80	27 33	52	80	274
87	23 37	53	81	24 30	52	81	25 22	53	80	26 15	52	79	27 07	52	79	273
88	23 11	53	80	24 04	52	80	24 56	53	79	25 49	52	79	26 41	53	78	272
89	22 45	53	79	23 38	53	79	24 31	52	78	25 23	53	78	26 16	52	77	271
90	22 20	+52	78	23 12	+53	78	24 05	+53	77	24 58	+52	77	25 50	+52	76	270
91	21 54	53	78	22 47	52	77	23 39	53	77	24 32	52	76	25 24	53	76	269
92	21 28	53	77	22 21	52	76	23 14	53	76	24 07	52	75	24 59	53	75	268
93	21 03	53	76	21 56	52	75	22 48	53	75	23 41	53	74	24 34	52	74	267
94	20 37	53	75	21 30	53	75	22 23	53	74	23 16	53	74	24 09	52	73	266
95	20 12	+53	74	21 05	+53	74	21 58	+53	73	22 51	+52	73	23 43	+53	72	265
96	19 47	53	73	20 40	53	73	21 33	53	72	22 26	53	72	23 19	52	71	264
97	19 21	54	72	20 15	53	72	21 08	53	71	22 01	53	71	22 54	52	70	263
98	18 56	54	72	19 50	53	71	20 43	53	71	21 36	53	70	22 29	53	70	262
99	18 31	54	71	19 25	53	70	20 18	53	70	21 11	53	69	22 04	53	69	261
100	18 07	+53	70	19 00	+53	69	19 53	+54	69	20 47	+53	68	21 40	+53	68	260
101	17 42	54	69	18 36	53	69	19 29	53	68	20 22	54	68	21 16	53	67	259
102	17 18	53	68	18 11	54	68	19 05	53	67	19 58	53	67	20 51	54	66	258
103	16 53	54	67	17 47	53	67	18 40	54	66	19 34	53	66	20 27	54	65	257
104	16 29	54	67	17 23	53	66	18 16	54	66	19 10	54	65	20 04	53	65	256
105	16 05	+54	66	16 59	+54	65	17 53	+53	65	18 46	+54	64	19 40	+53	64	255
106	15 41	54	65	16 35	54	64	17 29	54	64	18 23	53	63	19 16	54	63	254
107	15 17	54	64	16 11	54	64	17 05	54	63	17 59	54	63	18 53	54	62	253
108	14 54	54	63	15 48	54	63	16 42	54	62	17 36	54	62	18 30	54	61	252
109	14 30	55	62	15 25	54	62	16 19	54	61	17 13	54	61	18 07	54	61	251
110	14 07	+55	61	15 02	+54	61	15 56	+54	61	16 50	+54	60	17 44	+54	60	250
111	13 44	55	61	14 39	54	60	15 33	54	60	16 27	55	59	17 22	54	59	249
112	13 21	55	60	14 16	54	59	15 10	55	59	16 05	54	58	16 59	54	58	248
113	12 59	54	59	13 53	55	59	14 48	54	58	15 42	55	58	16 37	54	57	247
114	12 36	55	58	13 31	55	58	14 26	54	57	15 20	55	57	16 15	54	56	246
115	12 14	+55	57	13 09	+55	57	14 04	+54	56	14 58	+55	56	15 53	+55	56	245
116	11 52	55	56	12 47	55	56	13 42	55	56	14 37	55	55	15 32	54	55	244
117	11 30	55	56	12 25	55	55	13 20	55	55	14 15	55	54	15 10	55	54	243
118	11 09	55	55	12 04	55	54	12 59	55	54	13 54	55	53	14 49	55	53	242
119	10 48	55	54	11 43	55	53	12 38	55	53	13 33	55	53	14 28	55	52	241
120	10 26	+56	53	11 22	+55	53	12 17	+55	52	13 12	+56	52	14 08	+55	51	240
121	10 06	55	52	11 01	55	52	11 56	56	51	12 52	55	51	13 47	55	51	239
122	09 45	55	51	10 40	56	51	11 36	55	51	12 31	56	50	13 27	55	50	238
123	09 25	55	50	10 20	56	50	11 16	55	50	12 11	56	49	13 07	56	49	237
124	09 04	56	50	10 00	56	49	10 56	56	49	11 52	55	48	12 47	56	48	236
125	08 45	+55	49	09 40	+56	48	10 36	+56	48	11 32	+56	48	12 28	+56	47	235
126	08 25	56	48	09 21	56	48	10 17	56	47	11 13	56	47	12 09	56	46	234
127	08 06	56	47	09 02	56	47	09 58	56	46	10 54	56	46	11 50	56	46	233
128	07 46	57	46	08 43	56	46	09 39	56	45	10 35	56	45	11 31	56	45	232
129	07 28	56	45	08 24	56	45	09 20	57	45	10 17	56	44	11 13	56	44	231
130	07 09	+57	44	08 06	+56	44	09 02	+56	44	09 58	+57	43	10 55	+56	43	230
131	06 51	56	44	07 47	57	43	08 44	56	43	09 40	57	43	10 37	56	42	229
132	06 33	56	43	07 29	57	42	08 26	57	42	09 23	56	42	10 19	57	41	228
133	06 15	57	42	07 12	57	42	08 09	56	41	09 05	57	41	10 02	57	41	227
134	05 58	57	41	06 55	57	41	07 52	56	40	08 48	57	40	09 45	57	40	226
135	05 41	+57	40	06 38	+57	40	07 35	+57	40	08 32	+57	39	09 29	+57	39	225
136	05 24	57	39	06 21	57	39	07 18	57	39	08 15	57	38	09 12	57	38	224
137	05 07	58	38	06 05	57	38	07 02	57	38	07 59	57	38	08 56	57	37	223
138	04 51	58	37	05 49	57	37	06 46	57	37	07 43	58	37	08 41	57	36	222
139	04 35	58	37	05 33	57	36	06 30	58	36	07 28	57	36	08 25	57	36	221

S. Lat. {LHA greater than 180°....... Zn=180−Z; LHA less than 180°........... Zn=180+Z}

DECLINATION (15°-29°) SAME NAME AS LATITUDE

N. Lat. {LHA greater than 180°....... Zn=Z; LHA less than 180°........... Zn=360−Z}

DECLINATION (15°-29°) SAME NAME AS LATITUDE

LHA	15°			16°			17°			18°			19°			20°			21°		
	Hc	d	Z	Hc	d	Z	Hc	d	Z	Hc	d	Z	Hc	d	Z	Hc	d	Z	Hc	d	Z
	° ′	′	°	° ′	′	°	° ′	′	°	° ′	′	°	° ′	′	°	° ′	′	°	° ′	′	°
140	−5 16	+58	39	−4 18	+57	38	−3 21	+58	38	−2 23	+57	38	−1 26	+58	37	−0 28	+58	37	00 30	+57	37
141	−5 32	58	38	−4 34	57	37	−3 37	58	37	−2 39	58	37	−1 41	57	37	−0 44	58	36	00 14	58	36
142				−4 50	58	36	−3 52	57	36	−2 55	58	36	−1 57	58	36	−0 59	58	35	−0 01	57	35
143				−5 06	58	35	−4 08	58	35	−3 10	58	35	−2 12	58	35	−1 14	58	34	−0 16	58	34
144				−5 21	58	35	−4 23	58	34	−3 25	58	34	−2 27	58	34	−1 29	58	34	−0 31	58	33
145							−4 37	+58	33	−3 39	+58	33	−2 41	+58	33	−1 43	+58	33	−0 45	+58	32
146							−4 52	58	32	−3 54	59	32	−2 55	58	32	−1 57	58	32	−0 59	58	31
147							−5 06	59	31	−4 07	58	31	−3 09	58	31	−2 11	58	31	−1 13	59	31
148							−5 19	58	31	−4 21	58	30	−3 23	59	30	−2 24	58	30	−1 26	59	30
149										−4 34	58	29	−3 36	59	29	−2 37	58	29	−1 39	59	29
150										−4 47	+59	28	−3 48	+58	28	−2 50	+59	28	−1 51	+58	28
151										−4 59	59	28	−4 00	58	27	−3 02	59	27	−2 03	58	27
152										−5 11	59	27	−4 12	58	26	−3 14	59	26	−2 15	59	26
153										−5 23	59	26	−4 24	59	25	−3 25	59	25	−2 26	58	25
154													−4 35	59	25	−3 36	59	24	−2 37	59	24
155													−4 46	+59	24	−3 47	+59	23	−2 48	+59	23
156													−4 56	59	23	−3 57	59	23	−2 58	59	22
157													−5 06	59	22	−4 07	59	22	−3 08	59	21
158													−5 16	60	21	−4 16	59	21	−3 17	59	21
159																−4 26	60	20	−3 26	59	20
160																−4 34	+59	19	−3 35	+59	19
161																−4 43	60	18	−3 43	59	18
162																−4 50	59	17	−3 51	60	17
163																−4 58	60	16	−3 58	59	16
164																−5 05	60	15	−4 05	59	15
165																−5 12	+60	14	−4 12	+60	14
166																			−4 18	60	13
167																			−4 24	60	12
168																			−4 29	60	11
169																			−4 34	60	10
170																			−4 39	+60	9
171																			−4 43	60	8
172																			−4 46	60	7
173																			−4 49	59	7
174																			−4 52	60	6
175																			−4 55	+60	5
176																			−4 57	60	4
177																			−4 58	60	3
178																			−4 59	60	2
179																			−5 00	60	1
180																			−5 00	+60	0
71	−5 26	55	113																		
70	−5 02	−55	114																		

LHA	22°			23°			24°			25°			26°			27°			28°			29°			LHA
	Hc	d	Z	Hc	d	Z	Hc	d	Z	Hc	d	Z	Hc	d	Z	Hc	d	Z	Hc	d	Z	Hc	d	Z	
	° ′	′	°	° ′	′	°	° ′	′	°	° ′	′	°	° ′	′	°	° ′	′	°	° ′	′	°	° ′	′	°	
140	01 27	+58	37	02 25	+57	36	03 22	+58	36	04 20	+57	36	05 17	+58	36	06 15	+57	35	07 12	+58	35	08 10	+58	35	220
141	01 12	57	36	02 09	58	35	03 07	58	35	04 05	57	35	05 02	58	35	06 00	58	34	06 58	57	34	07 55	58	34	219
142	00 56	58	35	01 54	58	35	02 52	58	34	03 50	57	34	04 47	58	34	05 45	58	34	06 43	58	33	07 41	57	33	218
143	00 42	57	34	01 39	58	34	02 37	58	33	03 35	58	33	04 33	58	33	05 31	58	33	06 29	58	32	07 27	57	32	217
144	00 27	58	33	01 25	58	33	02 23	58	33	03 21	58	32	04 19	58	32	05 17	58	32	06 15	58	32	07 13	58	31	216
145	00 13	+58	32	01 11	+58	32	02 09	+58	32	03 07	+58	31	04 05	+58	31	05 03	+58	31	06 01	+58	31	06 59	+58	30	215
146	−0 01	58	31	00 57	58	31	01 55	59	31	02 54	58	31	03 52	58	30	04 50	58	30	05 48	58	30	06 46	58	30	214
147	−0 14	58	30	00 44	58	30	01 42	58	30	02 40	59	30	03 39	58	29	04 37	58	29	05 35	58	29	06 33	59	29	213
148	−0 27	58	29	00 31	58	29	01 29	59	29	02 28	58	29	03 26	58	29	04 24	59	28	05 23	58	28	06 21	58	28	212
149	−0 40	58	29	00 18	59	28	01 17	58	28	02 15	59	28	03 14	58	28	04 12	59	27	05 11	58	27	06 09	58	27	211
150	−0 53	+59	28	00 06	+58	27	01 04	+59	27	02 03	+59	27	03 02	+58	27	04 00	+59	27	04 59	+58	26	05 57	+59	26	210
151	−1 05	59	27	−0 06	59	26	00 53	58	26	01 51	59	26	02 50	59	26	03 49	58	26	04 47	59	25	05 46	58	25	209
152	−1 16	58	26	−0 18	59	26	00 41	59	25	01 40	59	25	02 39	58	25	03 37	59	25	04 36	59	25	05 35	58	24	208
153	−1 28	59	25	−0 29	59	25	00 30	59	24	01 29	59	24	02 28	58	24	03 26	59	24	04 25	59	24	05 24	59	24	207
154	−1 38	58	24	−0 40	59	24	00 19	59	24	01 18	59	23	02 17	59	23	03 16	59	23	04 15	59	23	05 14	59	23	206
155	−1 49	+59	23	−0 50	+59	23	00 09	+59	23	01 08	+59	23	02 07	+59	22	03 06	+59	22	04 05	+59	22	05 04	+59	22	205
156	−1 59	59	22	−1 00	59	22	−0 01	59	22	00 58	59	22	01 57	59	21	02 56	59	21	03 55	59	21	04 54	59	21	204
157	−2 09	59	21	−1 10	59	21	−0 11	60	21	00 49	59	21	01 48	59	21	02 47	59	20	03 46	59	20	04 45	59	20	203
158	−2 18	59	20	−1 19	59	20	−0 20	59	20	00 39	60	20	01 39	59	20	02 38	59	20	03 37	59	19	04 36	59	19	202
159	−2 27	59	19	−1 28	59	19	−0 29	60	19	00 31	59	19	01 30	59	19	02 29	59	19	03 28	60	18	04 28	59	18	201
160	−2 36	+60	19	−1 36	+59	18	−0 37	+59	18	00 22	+60	18	01 22	+59	18	02 21	+59	18	03 20	+60	18	04 20	+59	17	200
161	−2 44	60	18	−1 44	59	17	−0 45	59	17	00 14	60	17	01 14	59	17	02 13	60	17	03 13	59	17	04 12	59	17	199
162	−2 51	59	17	−1 52	59	17	−0 53	60	16	00 07	59	16	01 06	60	16	02 06	59	16	03 05	60	16	04 05	59	16	198
163	−2 59	60	16	−1 59	59	16	−1 00	60	15	00 00	59	15	00 59	60	15	01 59	59	15	02 58	60	15	03 58	59	15	197
164	−3 06	60	15	−2 06	59	15	−1 07	60	15	−0 07	59	14	00 52	60	14	01 52	60	14	02 52	59	14	03 51	60	14	196
165	−3 12	+59	14	−2 13	+60	14	−1 13	+60	14	−0 13	+59	14	00 46	+60	13	01 46	+59	13	02 45	+60	13	03 45	+60	13	195
166	−3 18	59	13	−2 19	60	13	−1 19	60	13	−0 19	59	13	00 40	60	13	01 40	60	12	02 40	59	12	03 39	60	12	194
167	−3 24	60	12	−2 24	59	12	−1 25	60	12	−0 25	60	12	00 35	59	12	01 34	60	12	02 34	60	11	03 34	60	11	193
168	−3 29	59	11	−2 30	60	11	−1 30	60	11	−0 30	60	11	00 30	59	11	01 29	60	11	02 29	60	11	03 29	60	11	192
169	−3 34	60	10	−2 34	59	10	−1 35	60	10	−0 35	60	10	00 25	60	10	01 25	59	10	02 24	60	10	03 24	60	10	191
170	−3 39	+60	9	−2 39	+60	9	−1 39	+60	9	−0 39	+60	9	00 21	+59	9	01 20	+60	9	02 20	+60	9	03 20	+60	9	190
171	−3 43	60	8	−2 43	60	8	−1 43	60	8	−0 43	60	8	00 17	60	8	01 17	59	8	02 16	60	8	03 16	60	8	189
172	−3 46	60	7	−2 46	59	7	−1 47	60	7	−0 47	60	7	00 13	60	7	01 13	60	7	02 13	60	7	03 13	60	7	188
173	−3 50	60	6	−2 50	60	6	−1 50	60	6	−0 50	60	6	00 10	60	6	01 10	60	6	02 10	60	6	03 10	60	6	187
174	−3 52	60	6	−2 52	60	6	−1 52	59	5	−0 53	60	5	00 07	60	5	01 07	60	5	02 07	60	5	03 07	60	5	186
175	−3 55	+60	5	−2 55	+60	5	−1 55	+60	5	−0 55	+60	5	00 05	+60	4	01 05	+60	4	02 05	+60	4	03 05	+60	4	185
176	−3 57	60	4	−2 57	60	4	−1 57	60	4	−0 57	60	4	00 03	60	4	01 03	60	4	02 03	60	4	03 03	60	4	184
177	−3 58	60	3	−2 58	60	3	−1 58	60	3	−0 58	60	3	00 02	60	3	01 02	60	3	02 02	60	3	03 02	60	3	183
178	−3 59	60	2	−2 59	60	2	−1 59	60	2	−0 59	60	2	00 01	60	2	01 01	60	2	02 01	60	2	03 01	60	2	182
179	−4 00	60	1	−3 00	60	1	−2 00	60	1	−1 00	60	1	00 00	60	1	01 00	60	1	02 00	60	1	03 00	60	1	181
180	−4 00	+60	0	−3 00	+60	0	−2 00	+60	0	−1 00	+60	0	00 00	+60	0	01 00	+60	0	02 00	+60	0	03 00	+60	0	180
71																									289
70																									290

15°	16°	17°	18°	19°	20°	21°	22°	23°	24°	25°	26°	27°	28°	29°

S. Lat. {LHA greater than 180°....... Zn=180−Z; LHA less than 180°........... Zn=180+Z}

DECLINATION (15°-29°) CONTRARY NAME TO LATITUDE

N. Lat. {LHA greater than 180°....... Zn=Z; LHA less than 180°........... Zn=360−Z}

DECLINATION (15°-29°) CONTRARY NAME TO LATITUDE

LHA	15° Hc	d	Z	16° Hc	d	Z	17° Hc	d	Z	18° Hc	d	Z	19° Hc	d	Z
	° ′	′	°	° ′	′	°	° ′	′	°	° ′	′	°	° ′	′	°
69	−4 38	55	115	−5 33	55	116									
68	−4 15	54	116	−5 09	55	116									
67	−3 51	55	117	−4 46	55	117	−5 41	55	118						
66	−3 28	55	118	−4 23	55	118	−5 18	55	119						
65	−3 05	−55	119	−4 00	−55	119	−4 55	−55	120						
64	−2 42	55	120	−3 37	55	120	−4 32	55	120	−5 27	55	121			
63	−2 19	55	121	−3 14	55	121	−4 09	56	121	−5 05	55	122			
62	−1 56	56	121	−2 52	55	122	−3 47	55	122	−4 42	56	123	−5 38	55	123
61	−1 34	55	122	−2 29	56	123	−3 25	55	123	−4 20	56	123	−5 16	55	124
60	−1 12	−55	123	−2 07	−56	124	−3 03	−55	124	−3 58	−56	124	−4 54	−55	125
59	−0 50	56	124	−1 46	55	124	−2 41	56	125	−3 37	55	125	−4 32	56	126
58	−0 28	56	125	−1 24	56	125	−2 20	55	126	−3 15	56	126	−4 11	56	126
57	−0 07	56	126	−1 03	55	126	−1 58	56	127	−2 54	56	127	−3 50	56	127
56	00 14	56	127	−0 42	56	127	−1 38	55	128	−2 33	56	128	−3 29	56	128
55	00 35	−56	128	−0 21	−56	128	−1 17	−56	128	−2 13	−56	129	−3 09	−56	129
54	00 56	56	129	00 00	56	129	−0 56	56	129	−1 52	56	130	−2 48	57	130
53	01 16	56	129	00 20	56	130	−0 36	56	130	−1 32	56	131	−2 28	57	131
52	01 36	56	130	00 40	56	131	−0 16	56	131	−1 12	57	131	−2 09	56	132
51	01 56	56	131	01 00	56	132	00 04	57	132	−0 53	56	132	−1 49	57	133
50	02 16	−57	132	01 19	−56	133	00 23	−57	133	−0 34	−56	133	−1 30	−57	134
49	02 35	56	133	01 39	57	133	00 42	57	134	−0 15	56	134	−1 11	57	134
48	02 54	56	134	01 58	57	134	01 01	57	135	00 04	57	135	−0 53	56	135
47	03 13	57	135	02 16	57	135	01 19	56	136	00 23	57	136	−0 34	57	136
46	03 32	57	136	02 35	57	136	01 38	57	136	00 41	57	137	−0 16	57	137
45	03 50	−57	137	02 53	−57	137	01 56	−57	137	00 59	−57	138	00 02	−57	138
44	04 08	58	138	03 10	57	138	02 13	57	138	01 16	57	139	00 19	57	139
43	04 25	57	139	03 28	57	139	02 31	58	139	01 33	57	140	00 36	57	140
42	04 42	57	140	03 45	57	140	02 48	58	140	01 50	57	140	00 53	57	141
41	04 59	57	141	04 02	58	141	03 04	57	141	02 07	58	141	01 09	57	142
40	05 16	−58	141	04 18	−57	142	03 21	−58	142	02 23	−57	142	01 26	−58	143
39	05 32	58	142	04 34	57	143	03 37	58	143	02 39	58	143	01 41	57	143
38	05 48	58	143	04 50	58	144	03 52	57	144	02 55	58	144	01 57	58	144
37	06 04	58	144	05 06	58	145	04 08	58	145	03 10	58	145	02 12	58	145
36	06 19	58	145	05 21	58	145	04 23	58	146	03 25	58	146	02 27	58	146
35	06 34	−58	146	05 36	−59	146	04 37	−58	147	03 39	−58	147	02 41	−58	147
34	06 48	58	147	05 50	58	147	04 52	58	148	03 54	59	148	02 55	58	148
33	07 02	58	148	06 04	58	148	05 06	59	149	04 07	58	149	03 09	58	149
32	07 16	58	149	06 18	59	149	05 19	58	149	04 21	58	150	03 23	59	150
31	07 29	58	150	06 31	58	150	05 33	59	150	04 34	58	151	03 36	59	151
30	07 42	−58	151	06 44	−59	151	05 45	−58	151	04 47	−59	152	03 48	−58	152
29	07 55	59	152	06 56	58	152	05 58	59	152	04 59	59	152	04 00	58	153
28	08 07	58	153	07 09	59	153	06 10	59	153	05 11	59	153	04 12	58	154
27	08 19	59	154	07 20	58	154	06 22	59	154	05 23	59	154	04 24	59	155
26	08 31	59	155	07 32	59	155	06 33	59	155	05 34	59	155	04 35	59	155
25	08 42	−59	156	07 43	−59	156	06 44	−59	156	05 45	−59	156	04 46	−59	156
24	08 52	59	157	07 53	59	157	06 54	59	157	05 55	59	157	04 56	59	157
23	09 03	60	158	08 03	59	158	07 04	59	158	06 05	59	158	05 06	59	158
22	09 12	59	159	08 13	59	159	07 14	59	159	06 15	59	159	05 16	60	159
21	09 22	59	160	08 23	60	160	07 23	59	160	06 24	59	160	05 25	59	160
20	09 31	−59	160	08 32	−60	161	07 32	−59	161	06 33	−59	161	05 34	−60	161
19	09 39	59	161	08 40	59	162	07 41	60	162	06 41	59	162	05 42	59	162
18	09 48	60	162	08 48	59	163	07 49	60	163	06 49	59	163	05 50	60	163
17	09 55	59	163	08 56	60	164	07 56	59	164	06 57	60	164	05 57	59	164
16	10 03	60	164	09 03	59	164	08 04	60	165	07 04	60	165	06 04	59	165
15	10 10	−60	165	09 10	−60	165	08 10	−59	166	07 11	−60	166	06 11	−59	166
14	10 16	60	166	09 16	59	166	08 17	60	167	07 17	60	167	06 17	59	167
13	10 22	60	167	09 22	59	167	08 23	60	167	07 23	60	168	06 23	59	168
12	10 28	60	168	09 28	60	168	08 28	60	168	07 28	59	169	06 29	60	169
11	10 33	60	169	09 33	60	169	08 33	60	169	07 33	59	170	06 34	60	170
10	10 38	−60	170	09 38	−60	170	08 38	−60	170	07 38	−60	170	06 38	−60	171
9	10 42	60	171	09 42	60	171	08 42	60	171	07 42	60	171	06 42	59	171
8	10 46	60	172	09 46	60	172	08 46	60	172	07 46	60	172	06 46	60	172
7	10 49	60	173	09 49	60	173	08 49	60	173	07 49	60	173	06 49	60	173
6	10 52	60	174	09 52	60	174	08 52	60	174	07 52	60	174	06 52	60	174
5	10 54	−60	175	09 54	−60	175	08 54	−59	175	07 55	−60	175	06 55	−60	175
4	10 56	60	176	09 56	60	176	08 56	59	176	07 57	60	176	06 57	60	176
3	10 58	60	177	09 58	60	177	08 58	60	177	07 58	60	177	06 58	60	177
2	10 59	60	178	09 59	60	178	08 59	60	178	07 59	60	178	06 59	60	178
1	11 00	60	179	10 00	60	179	09 00	60	179	08 00	60	179	07 00	60	179
0	11 00	−60	180	10 00	−60	180	09 00	−60	180	08 00	−60	180	07 00	−60	180

LHA	20° Hc	d	Z	21° Hc	d	Z	22° Hc	d	Z	23° Hc	d	Z	24° Hc	d	Z
	° ′	′	°	° ′	′	°	° ′	′	°	° ′	′	°	° ′	′	°
59	−5 28	56	126												
58	−5 07	55	127												
57	−4 46	56	128												
56	−4 25	56	129	−5 21	56	129									
55	−4 05	−56	129	−5 01	−56	130									
54	−3 45	56	130	−4 41	56	131	−5 37	56	131						
53	−3 25	56	131	−4 21	56	132	−5 17	56	132						
52	−3 05	56	132	−4 01	57	132	−4 58	56	133						
51	−2 46	56	133	−3 42	56	133	−4 38	57	134	−5 35	56	134			
50	−2 27	−56	134	−3 23	−57	134	−4 20	−56	135	−5 16	−57	135			
49	−2 08	56	135	−3 04	57	135	−4 01	57	135	−4 58	56	136			
48	−1 49	57	136	−2 46	57	136	−3 43	56	136	−4 39	57	137			
47	−1 31	57	137	−2 28	57	137	−3 25	56	137	−4 21	57	138	−5 18	57	138
46	−1 13	57	137	−2 10	57	138	−3 07	57	138	−4 04	57	138	−5 01	57	139
45	−0 55	−57	138	−1 52	−58	139	−2 50	−57	139	−3 47	−57	139	−4 44	−57	140
44	−0 38	57	139	−1 35	57	140	−2 32	58	140	−3 30	57	140	−4 27	57	140
43	−0 21	57	140	−1 18	58	140	−2 16	57	141	−3 13	57	141	−4 10	57	141
42	−0 04	58	141	−1 02	57	141	−1 59	57	142	−2 56	58	142	−3 54	57	142
41	00 12	57	142	−0 45	58	142	−1 43	57	143	−2 40	58	143	−3 38	57	143
40	00 28	−58	143	−0 30	−57	143	−1 27	−58	143	−2 25	−57	144	−3 22	−58	144
39	00 44	58	144	−0 14	58	144	−1 12	57	144	−2 09	58	145	−3 07	58	145
38	00 59	58	145	00 01	57	145	−0 56	58	145	−1 54	58	145	−2 52	58	146
37	01 14	58	146	00 16	58	146	−0 42	57	146	−1 39	58	146	−2 37	58	147
36	01 29	58	146	00 31	58	147	−0 27	58	147	−1 25	58	147	−2 23	58	147
35	01 43	−58	147	00 45	−58	148	−0 13	−58	148	−1 11	−58	148	−2 09	−58	148
34	01 57	58	148	00 59	58	149	00 01	58	149	−0 57	58	149	−1 55	59	149
33	02 11	58	149	01 13	59	149	00 14	58	150	−0 44	58	150	−1 42	58	150
32	02 24	58	150	01 26	59	150	00 27	58	151	−0 31	58	151	−1 29	59	151
31	02 37	58	151	01 39	59	151	00 40	58	151	−0 18	59	152	−1 17	58	152
30	02 50	−59	152	01 51	−58	152	00 53	−59	152	−0 06	−58	153	−1 04	−59	153
29	03 02	59	153	02 03	58	153	01 05	59	153	00 06	59	154	−0 53	58	154
28	03 14	59	154	02 15	59	154	01 16	58	154	00 18	59	154	−0 41	59	155
27	03 25	59	155	02 26	58	155	01 28	59	155	00 29	59	155	−0 30	59	156
26	03 36	59	156	02 37	59	156	01 38	58	156	00 40	59	156	−0 19	59	156
25	03 47	−59	157	02 48	−59	157	01 49	−59	157	00 50	−59	157	−0 09	−59	157
24	03 57	59	157	02 58	59	158	01 59	59	158	01 00	59	158	00 01	59	158
23	04 07	59	158	03 08	59	159	02 09	59	159	01 10	59	159	00 11	60	159
22	04 16	59	159	03 17	59	159	02 18	59	160	01 19	59	160	00 20	59	160
21	04 26	60	160	03 26	59	160	02 27	59	161	01 28	59	161	00 29	60	161
20	04 34	−59	161	03 35	−59	161	02 36	−60	161	01 36	−59	162	00 37	−59	162
19	04 43	60	162	03 43	59	162	02 44	60	162	01 44	59	163	00 45	59	163
18	04 50	59	163	03 51	60	163	02 51	59	163	01 52	59	163	00 53	60	164
17	04 58	60	164	03 58	59	164	02 59	60	164	01 59	59	164	01 00	60	165
16	05 05	60	165	04 05	59	165	03 06	60	165	02 06	59	165	01 07	60	165
15	05 12	−60	166	04 12	−60	166	03 12	−59	166	02 13	−60	166	01 13	−60	166
14	05 18	60	167	04 18	60	167	03 18	59	167	02 19	60	167	01 19	60	167
13	05 24	60	168	04 24	60	168	03 24	60	168	02 24	59	168	01 25	60	168
12	05 29	60	169	04 29	60	169	03 29	59	169	02 30	60	169	01 30	60	169
11	05 34	60	170	04 34	60	170	03 34	60	170	02 34	59	170	01 35	60	170
10	05 38	−59	171	04 39	−60	171	03 39	−60	171	02 39	−60	171	01 39	−60	171
9	05 43	60	172	04 43	60	172	03 43	60	172	02 43	60	172	01 43	60	172
8	05 46	60	172	04 46	60	173	03 46	60	173	02 46	59	173	01 47	60	173
7	05 49	60	173	04 49	59	173	03 50	60	174	02 50	60	174	01 50	60	174
6	05 52	60	174	04 52	60	174	03 52	60	174	02 52	60	174	01 52	59	175
5	05 55	−60	175	04 55	−60	175	03 55	−60	175	02 55	−60	175	01 55	−60	175
4	05 57	60	176	04 57	60	176	03 57	60	176	02 57	60	176	01 57	60	176
3	05 58	60	177	04 58	60	177	03 58	60	177	02 58	60	177	01 58	60	177
2	05 59	60	178	04 59	60	178	03 59	60	178	02 59	60	178	01 59	60	178
1	06 00	60	179	05 00	60	179	04 00	60	179	03 00	60	179	02 00	60	179
0	06 00	−60	180	05 00	−60	180	04 00	−60	180	03 00	−60	180	02 00	−60	180

LHA	25° Hc	d	Z	26° Hc	d	Z	27° Hc	d	Z	28° Hc	d	Z	29° Hc	d	Z	LHA
	° ′	′	°	° ′	′	°	° ′	′	°	° ′	′	°	° ′	′	°	
69																291
68																292
67																293
66																294
65																295
64																296
63																297
62																298
61																299
60																300
59																301
58																302
57																303
56																304
55																305
54																306
53																307
52																308
51																309
50																310
49																311
48																312
47																313
46																314
45																315
44	−5 24	57	141													316
43	−5 07	58	142													317
42	−4 51	58	143													318
41	−4 35	58	143													319
40	−4 20	−57	144	−5 17	−58	144										320
39	−4 05	57	145	−5 02	58	145										321
38	−3 50	57	146	−4 47	58	146										322
37	−3 35	58	147	−4 33	58	147										323
36	−3 21	58	148	−4 19	58	148	−5 17	58	148							324
35	−3 07	−58	149	−4 05	−58	149	−5 03	−58	149							325
34	−2 54	58	149	−3 52	58	150	−4 50	58	150							326
33	−2 40	59	150	−3 39	58	151	−4 37	58	151							327
32	−2 28	58	151	−3 26	58	151	−4 24	59	152	−5 23	58	152				328
31	−2 15	59	152	−3 14	58	152	−4 12	59	153	−5 11	58	153				329
30	−2 03	−59	153	−3 02	−58	153	−4 00	−59	153	−4 59	−58	154				330
29	−1 51	59	154	−2 50	59	154	−3 49	58	154	−4 47	59	155				331
28	−1 40	59	155	−2 39	58	155	−3 37	59	155	−4 36	59	155				332
27	−1 29	59	156	−2 28	58	156	−3 26	59	156	−4 25	59	156				333
26	−1 18	59	157	−2 17	59	157	−3 16	59	157	−4 15	59	157	−5 14	59	157	334
25	−1 08	−59	157	−2 07	−59	158	−3 06	−59	158	−4 05	−59	158	−5 04	−59	158	335
24	−0 58	59	158	−1 57	59	159	−2 56	59	159	−3 55	59	159	−4 54	59	159	336
23	−0 49	59	159	−1 48	59	159	−2 47	59	160	−3 46	59	160	−4 45	59	160	337
22	−0 39	60	160	−1 39	59	160	−2 38	59	160	−3 37	59	161	−4 36	59	161	338
21	−0 31	59	161	−1 30	59	161	−2 29	59	161	−3 28	60	162	−4 28	59	162	339
20	−0 22	−60	162	−1 22	−59	162	−2 21	−59	162	−3 20	−60	162	−4 20	−59	163	340
19	−0 14	60	163	−1 14	59	163	−2 13	60	163	−3 13	59	163	−4 12	59	163	341
18	−0 07	59	164	−1 06	60	164	−2 06	59	164	−3 05	60	164	−4 05	59	164	342
17	00 00	59	165	−0 59	60	165	−1 59	59	165	−2 58	60	165	−3 58	59	165	343
16	00 07	59	166	−0 52	60	166	−1 52	60	166	−2 52	59	166	−3 51	60	166	344
15	00 13	−59	166	−0 46	−60	167	−1 46	−59	167	−2 45	−60	167	−3 45	−60	167	345
14	00 19	59	167	−0 40	60	167	−1 40	60	168	−2 40	59	168	−3 39	60	168	346
13	00 25	60	168	−0 35	59	168	−1 34	60	168	−2 34	60	169	−3 34	60	169	347
12	00 30	60	169	−0 30	59	169	−1 29	60	169	−2 29	60	169	−3 29	60	169	348
11	00 35	60	170	−0 25	60	170	−1 25	59	170	−2 24	60	170	−3 24	60	170	349
10	00 39	−60	171	−0 21	−59	171	−1 20	−60	171	−2 20	−60	171	−3 20	−60	171	350
9	00 43	60	172	−0 17	60	172	−1 17	59	172	−2 16	60	172	−3 16	60	172	351
8	00 47	60	173	−0 13	60	173	−1 13	60	173	−2 13	60	173	−3 13	60	173	352
7	00 50	60	174	−0 10	60	174	−1 10	60	174	−2 10	60	174	−3 10	60	174	353
6	00 53	60	175	−0 07	60	175	−1 07	60	175	−2 07	60	175	−3 07	60	175	354
5	00 55	−60	175	−0 05	−60	176	−1 05	−60	176	−2 05	−60	176	−3 05	−60	176	355
4	00 57	60	176	−0 03	60	176	−1 03	60	176	−2 03	60	176	−3 03	60	176	356
3	00 58	60	177	−0 02	60	177	−1 02	60	177	−2 02	60	177	−3 02	60	177	357
2	00 59	60	178	−0 01	60	178	−1 01	60	178	−2 01	60	178	−3 01	60	178	358
1	01 00	60	179	00 00	60	179	−1 00	60	179	−2 00	60	179	−3 00	60	179	359
0	01 00	−60	180	00 00	−60	180	−1 00	−60	180	−2 00	−60	180	−3 00	−60	180	360

S. Lat. {LHA greater than 180°....... Zn=180−Z; LHA less than 180°........... Zn=180+Z}

DECLINATION (15°-29°) CONTRARY NAME TO LATITUDE

LHA	0° Hc	d	Z	1° Hc	d	Z	2° Hc	d	Z	3° Hc	d	Z	4° Hc	d	Z
	° ′	′	°	° ′	′	°	° ′	′	°	° ′	′	°	° ′	′	°
0	25 00	+60	180	26 00	+60	180	27 00	+60	180	28 00	+60	180	29 00	+60	180
1	25 00	60	179	26 00	60	179	27 00	60	179	28 00	60	179	29 00	60	179
2	24 59	60	178	25 59	60	178	26 59	60	178	27 59	60	178	28 59	60	178
3	24 58	60	177	25 58	60	177	26 58	60	177	27 58	60	177	28 58	60	177
4	24 56	60	176	25 56	60	176	26 56	60	176	27 56	60	176	28 56	60	175
5	24 54	+60	175	25 54	+60	174	26 54	+60	174	27 54	+60	174	28 54	+60	174
6	24 51	60	173	25 51	60	173	26 51	60	173	27 51	60	173	28 51	60	173
7	24 48	60	172	25 48	60	172	26 48	60	172	27 48	60	172	28 48	60	172
8	24 44	60	171	25 44	60	171	26 44	60	171	27 44	60	171	28 44	60	171
9	24 40	60	170	25 40	60	170	26 40	60	170	27 40	60	170	28 40	60	170
10	24 36	+60	169	25 36	+59	169	26 35	+60	169	27 35	+60	169	28 35	+60	169
11	24 31	59	168	25 30	60	168	26 30	60	168	27 30	60	168	28 30	59	168
12	24 25	60	167	25 25	60	167	26 25	59	167	27 24	60	167	28 24	60	166
13	24 19	60	166	25 19	59	166	26 18	60	166	27 18	60	165	28 18	59	165
14	24 13	59	165	25 12	60	165	26 12	59	164	27 11	60	164	28 11	60	164
15	24 06	+59	164	25 05	+60	163	26 05	+59	163	27 04	+60	163	28 04	+59	163
16	23 58	60	162	24 58	59	162	25 57	60	162	26 57	59	162	27 56	60	162
17	23 50	60	161	24 50	59	161	25 49	60	161	26 49	59	161	27 48	59	161
18	23 42	59	160	24 41	60	160	25 41	59	160	26 40	59	160	27 39	60	160
19	23 33	60	159	24 33	59	159	25 32	59	159	26 31	59	159	27 30	60	159
20	23 24	+59	158	24 23	+59	158	25 22	+60	158	26 22	+59	158	27 21	+59	157
21	23 14	59	157	24 13	60	157	25 13	59	157	26 12	59	157	27 11	59	156
22	23 04	59	156	24 03	59	156	25 02	59	156	26 01	60	155	27 01	59	155
23	22 54	59	155	23 53	59	155	24 52	59	155	25 51	59	154	26 50	59	154
24	22 43	59	154	23 42	59	154	24 41	58	153	25 39	59	153	26 38	59	153
25	22 31	+59	153	23 30	+59	153	24 29	+59	152	25 28	+59	152	26 27	+58	152
26	22 20	58	152	23 18	59	152	24 17	59	151	25 16	58	151	26 14	59	151
27	22 07	59	151	23 06	59	150	24 05	58	150	25 03	59	150	26 02	59	150
28	21 55	58	150	22 53	59	149	23 52	58	149	24 50	59	149	25 49	58	149
29	21 42	58	149	22 40	59	148	23 39	58	148	24 37	59	148	25 36	58	148
30	21 28	+59	148	22 27	+58	147	23 25	+58	147	24 23	+59	147	25 22	+58	147
31	21 14	59	147	22 13	58	146	23 11	58	146	24 09	59	146	25 08	58	145
32	21 00	58	145	21 58	59	145	22 57	58	145	23 55	58	145	24 53	58	144
33	20 46	58	144	21 44	58	144	22 42	58	144	23 40	58	144	24 38	58	143
34	20 31	58	143	21 29	58	143	22 27	58	143	23 25	58	143	24 23	58	142
35	20 15	+58	142	21 13	+58	142	22 11	+59	142	23 09	+58	142	24 07	+58	141
36	20 00	57	141	20 57	58	141	21 55	58	141	22 53	58	140	23 51	58	140
37	19 44	57	140	20 41	58	140	21 39	58	140	22 37	57	139	23 34	58	139
38	19 27	58	139	20 25	57	139	21 22	58	139	22 20	58	138	23 18	57	138
39	19 10	58	138	20 08	58	138	21 06	57	138	22 03	58	137	23 01	57	137
40	18 53	+58	137	19 51	+57	137	20 48	+58	137	21 46	+57	136	22 43	+57	136
41	18 36	57	136	19 33	58	136	20 31	57	136	21 28	57	135	22 25	57	135
42	18 18	58	135	19 16	57	135	20 13	57	135	21 10	57	134	22 07	57	134
43	18 00	57	134	18 57	58	134	19 55	57	134	20 52	57	133	21 49	57	133
44	17 42	57	133	18 39	57	133	19 36	57	133	20 33	57	132	21 30	57	132
45	17 23	+57	132	18 20	+57	132	19 17	+57	132	20 14	+57	131	21 11	+57	131
46	17 04	57	131	18 01	57	131	18 58	57	131	19 55	57	130	20 52	56	130
47	16 45	57	130	17 42	57	130	18 39	56	130	19 35	57	129	20 32	57	129
48	16 26	56	129	17 22	57	129	18 19	57	129	19 16	56	128	20 12	57	128
49	16 06	56	128	17 02	57	128	17 59	56	128	18 55	57	127	19 52	56	127
50	15 46	+56	127	16 42	+57	127	17 39	+56	127	18 35	+57	126	19 32	+56	126
51	15 25	57	126	16 22	56	126	17 18	57	126	18 15	56	125	19 11	56	125
52	15 05	56	125	16 01	56	125	16 57	57	125	17 54	56	124	18 50	56	124
53	14 44	56	124	15 40	56	124	16 36	57	124	17 33	56	123	18 29	56	123
54	14 23	56	123	15 19	56	123	16 15	56	123	17 11	56	122	18 07	56	122
55	14 02	+56	122	14 58	+56	122	15 54	+56	122	16 50	+56	121	17 46	+56	121
56	13 40	56	121	14 36	56	121	15 32	56	121	16 28	56	120	17 24	56	120
57	13 18	56	121	14 14	56	120	15 10	56	120	16 06	56	119	17 02	55	119
58	12 57	55	120	13 52	56	119	14 48	56	119	15 44	55	118	16 39	56	118
59	12 34	56	119	13 30	56	118	14 26	55	118	15 21	56	117	16 17	55	117
60	12 12	+56	118	13 08	+55	117	14 03	+56	117	14 59	+55	117	15 54	+56	116
61	11 49	56	117	12 45	55	116	13 40	56	116	14 36	55	116	15 31	56	115
62	11 27	55	116	12 22	56	115	13 18	55	115	14 13	55	115	15 08	56	114
63	11 04	55	115	11 59	55	114	12 54	56	114	13 50	55	114	14 45	55	113
64	10 41	55	114	11 36	55	114	12 31	56	113	13 27	55	113	14 22	55	112
65	10 17	+56	113	11 13	+55	113	12 08	+55	112	13 03	+55	112	13 58	+55	111
66	09 54	55	112	10 49	55	112	11 44	55	111	12 39	55	111	13 34	56	110
67	09 30	55	111	10 25	56	111	11 21	55	110	12 16	55	110	13 11	55	109
68	09 07	55	110	10 02	55	110	10 57	55	109	11 52	55	109	12 47	55	109
69	08 43	55	109	09 38	55	109	10 33	55	108	11 28	55	108	12 23	54	108

LHA	5° Hc	d	Z	6° Hc	d	Z	7° Hc	d	Z	8° Hc	d	Z	9° Hc	d	Z
	° ′	′	°	° ′	′	°	° ′	′	°	° ′	′	°	° ′	′	°
0	30 00	+60	180	31 00	+60	180	32 00	+60	180	33 00	+60	180	34 00	+60	180
1	30 00	60	179	31 00	60	179	32 00	60	179	33 00	60	179	34 00	60	179
2	29 59	60	178	30 59	60	178	31 59	60	178	32 59	60	178	33 59	60	178
3	29 58	60	177	30 58	60	177	31 58	60	177	32 58	60	177	33 58	60	176
4	29 56	60	175	30 56	60	175	31 56	60	175	32 56	60	175	33 56	60	175
5	29 54	+60	174	30 54	+60	174	31 54	+60	174	32 54	+59	174	33 53	+60	174
6	29 51	60	173	30 51	60	173	31 51	60	173	32 51	60	173	33 51	59	173
7	29 48	59	172	30 47	60	172	31 47	60	172	32 47	60	172	33 47	60	172
8	29 44	60	171	30 44	60	171	31 44	59	171	32 43	60	171	33 43	60	171
9	29 40	59	170	30 39	60	170	31 39	60	170	32 39	60	169	33 39	60	169
10	29 35	+59	169	30 34	+60	168	31 34	+60	168	32 34	+60	168	33 34	+60	168
11	29 29	60	167	30 29	60	167	31 29	60	167	32 29	59	167	33 28	60	167
12	29 24	59	166	30 23	60	166	31 23	60	166	32 23	59	166	33 22	60	166
13	29 17	60	165	30 17	60	165	31 17	59	165	32 16	60	165	33 16	59	165
14	29 11	59	164	30 10	60	164	31 10	59	164	32 09	60	164	33 09	59	163
15	29 03	+60	163	30 03	+59	163	31 02	+60	163	32 02	+59	162	33 01	+60	162
16	28 56	59	162	29 55	60	162	30 55	59	161	31 54	59	161	32 53	60	161
17	28 47	60	161	29 47	59	160	30 46	60	160	31 46	59	160	32 45	59	160
18	28 39	59	160	29 38	59	159	30 37	60	159	31 37	59	159	32 36	59	159
19	28 30	59	158	29 29	59	158	30 28	59	158	31 27	60	158	32 27	59	158
20	28 20	+59	157	29 19	+59	157	30 18	+60	157	31 18	+59	157	32 17	+59	156
21	28 10	59	156	29 09	59	156	30 08	59	156	31 07	59	156	32 06	59	155
22	28 00	59	155	28 59	59	155	29 58	59	155	30 57	59	154	31 56	58	154
23	27 49	59	154	28 48	58	154	29 46	59	154	30 45	59	153	31 44	59	153
24	27 37	59	153	28 36	59	153	29 35	59	152	30 34	58	152	31 32	59	152
25	27 25	+59	152	28 24	+59	152	29 23	+59	151	30 22	+58	151	31 20	+59	151
26	27 13	59	151	28 12	59	150	29 11	58	150	30 09	59	150	31 08	58	150
27	27 01	58	150	27 59	59	149	28 58	58	149	29 56	59	149	30 55	58	149
28	26 47	59	148	27 46	58	148	28 44	59	148	29 43	58	148	30 41	59	147
29	26 34	58	147	27 32	59	147	28 31	58	147	29 29	58	147	30 27	59	146
30	26 20	+58	146	27 18	+59	146	28 17	+58	146	29 15	+58	145	30 13	+58	145
31	26 06	58	145	27 04	58	145	28 02	58	145	29 00	58	144	29 58	58	144
32	25 51	58	144	26 49	58	144	27 47	58	144	28 45	58	143	29 43	58	143
33	25 36	58	143	26 34	58	143	27 32	58	142	28 30	58	142	29 28	58	142
34	25 21	57	142	26 18	58	142	27 16	58	141	28 14	58	141	29 12	58	141
35	25 05	+58	141	26 03	+57	141	27 00	+58	140	27 58	+58	140	28 56	+57	140
36	24 49	57	140	25 46	58	140	26 44	58	139	27 42	57	139	28 39	58	139
37	24 32	58	139	25 30	57	139	26 27	58	138	27 25	57	138	28 22	58	138
38	24 15	58	138	25 13	57	137	26 10	58	137	27 08	57	137	28 05	57	136
39	23 58	57	137	24 55	58	136	25 53	57	136	26 50	57	136	27 47	57	135
40	23 40	+58	136	24 38	+57	135	25 35	+57	135	26 32	+57	135	27 29	+57	134
41	23 22	58	135	24 20	57	134	25 17	57	134	26 14	57	134	27 11	57	133
42	23 04	57	134	24 01	57	133	24 58	57	133	25 55	57	133	26 52	57	132
43	22 46	57	133	23 43	57	132	24 40	57	132	25 37	56	132	26 33	57	131
44	22 27	57	132	23 24	57	131	24 21	56	131	25 17	57	131	26 14	57	130
45	22 08	+57	131	23 05	+56	130	24 01	+57	130	24 58	+57	129	25 55	+56	129
46	21 48	57	130	22 45	57	129	23 42	56	129	24 38	57	128	25 35	56	128
47	21 29	56	129	22 25	57	128	23 22	56	128	24 18	57	127	25 15	56	127
48	21 09	56	128	22 05	57	127	23 02	56	127	23 58	56	126	24 54	56	126
49	20 48	57	127	21 45	56	126	22 41	56	126	23 37	57	125	24 34	56	125
50	20 28	+56	126	21 24	+56	125	22 20	+57	125	23 17	+56	124	24 13	+56	124
51	20 07	56	125	21 03	56	124	21 59	56	124	22 55	57	123	23 52	55	123
52	19 46	56	124	20 42	56	123	21 38	56	123	22 34	56	122	23 30	56	122
53	19 25	56	123	20 21	56	122	21 17	56	122	22 13	55	121	23 08	56	121
54	19 03	56	122	19 59	56	121	20 55	56	121	21 51	56	120	22 47	55	120
55	18 42	+55	121	19 37	+56	120	20 33	+56	120	21 29	+56	119	22 25	+55	119
56	18 20	55	120	19 15	56	119	20 11	56	119	21 07	55	118	22 02	56	118
57	17 57	56	119	18 53	56	118	19 49	55	118	20 44	56	117	21 40	55	117
58	17 35	56	118	18 31	55	117	19 26	56	117	20 22	55	116	21 17	55	116
59	17 12	56	117	18 08	55	116	19 03	56	116	19 59	55	115	20 54	55	115
60	16 50	+55	116	17 45	+55	115	18 40	+56	115	19 36	+55	114	20 31	+55	114
61	16 27	55	115	17 22	55	114	18 17	56	114	19 13	55	113	20 08	55	113
62	16 04	55	114	16 59	55	113	17 54	55	113	18 49	55	113	19 44	55	112
63	15 40	56	113	16 36	55	112	17 31	55	112	18 26	55	112	19 21	55	111
64	15 17	55	112	16 12	55	111	17 07	55	111	18 02	55	111	18 57	55	110
65	14 53	+55	111	15 48	+55	111	16 43	+55	110	17 38	+55	110	18 33	+55	109
66	14 30	55	110	15 25	54	110	16 19	55	109	17 14	55	109	18 09	55	108
67	14 06	55	109	15 01	54	109	15 55	55	108	16 50	55	108	17 45	55	107
68	13 42	54	108	14 36	55	108	15 31	55	107	16 26	55	107	17 21	55	106
69	13 17	55	107	14 12	55	107	15 07	55	106	16 02	54	106	16 56	55	105

LHA	10° Hc	d	Z	11° Hc	d	Z	12° Hc	d	Z	13° Hc	d	Z	14° Hc	d	Z	LHA
	° ′	′	°	° ′	′	°	° ′	′	°	° ′	′	°	° ′	′	°	
0	35 00	+60	180	36 00	+60	180	37 00	+60	180	38 00	+60	180	39 00	+60	180	360
1	35 00	60	179	36 00	60	179	37 00	60	179	38 00	60	179	39 00	60	179	359
2	34 59	60	178	35 59	60	178	36 59	60	178	37 59	60	178	38 59	60	178	358
3	34 58	60	176	35 58	60	176	36 58	60	176	37 58	60	176	38 58	60	176	357
4	34 56	60	175	35 56	60	175	36 56	60	175	37 56	60	175	38 56	60	175	356
5	34 53	+60	174	35 53	+60	174	36 53	+60	174	37 53	+60	174	38 53	+60	174	355
6	34 50	60	173	35 50	60	173	36 50	60	173	37 50	60	173	38 50	60	173	354
7	34 47	60	172	35 47	60	172	36 47	60	171	37 47	60	171	38 47	59	171	353
8	34 43	60	170	35 43	60	170	36 43	60	170	37 43	59	170	38 42	60	170	352
9	34 39	59	169	35 38	60	169	36 38	60	169	37 38	60	169	38 38	60	169	351
10	34 34	+59	168	35 33	+60	168	36 33	+60	168	37 33	+60	168	38 33	+59	168	350
11	34 28	60	167	35 28	59	167	36 27	60	167	37 27	60	167	38 27	60	166	349
12	34 22	60	166	35 22	59	166	36 21	60	165	37 21	60	165	38 21	59	165	348
13	34 15	60	165	35 15	60	164	36 15	59	164	37 14	60	164	38 14	59	164	347
14	34 08	60	163	35 08	59	163	36 07	60	163	37 07	60	163	38 07	59	163	346
15	34 01	+59	162	35 00	+60	162	36 00	+59	162	36 59	+60	162	37 59	+59	161	345
16	33 53	59	161	34 52	60	161	35 52	59	161	36 51	59	160	37 50	60	160	344
17	33 44	60	160	34 44	59	160	35 43	59	159	36 42	60	159	37 42	59	159	343
18	33 35	60	159	34 35	59	158	35 34	59	158	36 33	59	158	37 32	59	158	342
19	33 26	59	157	34 25	59	157	35 24	59	157	36 23	59	157	37 22	59	157	341
20	33 16	+59	156	34 15	+59	156	35 14	+59	156	36 13	+59	156	37 12	+59	155	340
21	33 05	59	155	34 04	59	155	35 03	59	155	36 02	59	154	37 01	59	154	339
22	32 54	59	154	33 53	59	154	34 52	59	154	35 51	59	153	36 50	59	153	338
23	32 43	59	153	33 42	59	153	34 41	58	152	35 39	59	152	36 38	59	152	337
24	32 31	59	152	33 30	59	151	34 29	58	151	35 27	59	151	36 26	59	151	336
25	32 19	+59	151	33 18	+58	150	34 16	+59	150	35 15	+58	150	36 13	+59	149	335
26	32 06	59	149	33 05	58	149	34 03	59	149	35 02	58	149	36 00	59	148	334
27	31 53	59	148	32 52	58	148	33 50	58	148	34 48	59	147	35 47	58	147	333
28	31 40	58	147	32 38	58	147	33 36	58	147	34 34	59	146	35 33	58	146	332
29	31 26	58	146	32 24	58	146	33 22	58	145	34 20	58	145	35 18	58	145	331
30	31 11	+58	145	32 09	+58	145	33 07	+58	144	34 05	+58	144	35 03	+58	144	330
31	30 56	58	144	31 54	58	143	32 52	58	143	33 50	58	143	34 48	58	143	329
32	30 41	58	143	31 39	58	142	32 37	58	142	33 35	58	142	34 33	57	141	328
33	30 26	57	142	31 23	58	141	32 21	58	141	33 19	58	141	34 17	57	140	327
34	30 10	57	140	31 07	58	140	32 05	58	140	33 03	57	140	34 00	58	139	326
35	29 53	+58	139	30 51	+57	139	31 48	+58	139	32 46	+57	138	33 43	+58	138	325
36	29 37	57	138	30 34	58	138	31 32	57	138	32 29	57	137	33 26	57	137	324
37	29 20	57	137	30 17	57	137	31 14	58	137	32 12	57	136	33 09	57	136	323
38	29 02	57	136	29 59	58	136	30 57	57	135	31 54	57	135	32 51	57	135	322
39	28 44	58	135	29 42	57	135	30 39	57	134	31 36	57	134	32 33	57	134	321
40	28 26	+57	134	29 23	+57	134	30 20	+57	133	31 17	+57	133	32 14	+57	133	320
41	28 08	57	133	29 05	57	133	30 02	57	132	30 59	56	132	31 55	57	131	319
42	27 49	57	132	28 46	57	131	29 43	56	131	30 39	57	131	31 36	57	130	318
43	27 30	57	131	28 27	56	130	29 23	57	130	30 20	57	130	31 17	56	129	317
44	27 11	56	130	28 07	57	129	29 04	56	129	30 00	57	129	30 57	56	128	316
45	26 51	+57	129	27 48	+56	128	28 44	+56	128	29 40	+57	128	30 37	+56	127	315
46	26 31	57	128	27 28	56	127	28 24	56	127	29 20	56	127	30 16	57	126	314
47	26 11	56	127	27 07	57	126	28 04	56	126	29 00	56	125	29 56	56	125	313
48	25 50	57	126	26 47	56	125	27 43	56	125	28 39	56	124	29 35	56	124	312
49	25 30	56	125	26 26	56	124	27 22	56	124	28 18	56	123	29 14	56	123	311
50	25 09	+56	124	26 05	+56	123	27 01	+56	123	27 57	+55	122	28 52	+56	122	310
51	24 47	56	123	25 43	56	122	26 39	56	122	27 35	56	121	28 31	55	121	309
52	24 26	56	122	25 22	56	121	26 18	55	121	27 13	56	120	28 09	55	120	308
53	24 04	56	121	25 00	56	120	25 56	55	120	26 51	56	119	27 47	55	119	307
54	23 42	56	120	24 38	55	119	25 33	56	119	26 29	55	118	27 24	56	118	306
55	23 20	+56	119	24 16	+55	118	25 11	+56	118	26 07	+55	117	27 02	+55	117	305
56	22 58	55	118	23 53	56	117	24 49	55	117	25 44	55	116	26 39	55	116	304
57	22 35	56	117	23 31	55	116	24 26	55	116	25 21	55	115	26 16	55	115	303
58	22 12	56	116	23 08	55	115	24 03	55	115	24 58	55	114	25 53	55	114	302
59	21 49	56	115	22 45	55	114	23 40	55	114	24 35	55	113	25 30	55	113	301
60	21 26	+55	114	22 21	+55	113	23 16	+55	113	24 11	+55	112	25 06	+55	112	300
61	21 03	55	113	21 58	55	112	22 53	55	112	23 48	55	111	24 43	55	111	299
62	20 39	55	112	21 34	55	111	22 29	55	111	23 24	55	110	24 19	55	110	298
63	20 16	55	111	21 11	55	110	22 06	54	110	23 00	55	109	23 55	55	109	297
64	19 52	55	110	20 47	55	109	21 42	54	109	22 36	55	108	23 31	55	108	296
65	19 28	+55	109	20 23	+55	108	21 18	+54	108	22 12	+55	108	23 07	+54	107	295
66	19 04	55	108	19 59	54	107	20 53	55	107	21 48	55	107	22 43	54	106	294
67	18 40	55	107	19 35	54	107	20 29	55	106	21 24	54	106	22 18	55	105	293
68	18 16	54	106	19 10	55	106	20 05	54	105	20 59	55	105	21 54	54	104	292
69	17 51	55	105	18 46	54	105	19 40	55	104	20 35	54	104	21 29	54	103	291

N. Lat. {LHA greater than 180°....... Zn=Z; LHA less than 180°........... Zn=360−Z}

DECLINATION (0°-14°) SAME NAME AS LATITUDE

LHA	0° Hc	0° d	0° Z	1° Hc	1° d	1° Z	2° Hc	2° d	2° Z	3° Hc	3° d	3° Z	4° Hc	4° d	4° Z	LHA
	° ′	′	°	° ′	′	°	° ′	′	°	° ′	′	°	° ′	′	°	
70	08 19	+55	108	09 14	+55	108	10 09	+54	107	11 03	+55	107	11 58	+55	107	290
71	07 55	54	107	08 49	55	107	09 44	55	107	10 39	55	106	11 34	55	106	289
72	07 30	55	106	08 25	55	106	09 20	55	106	10 15	54	105	11 09	55	105	288
73	07 06	55	106	08 01	54	105	08 55	55	105	09 50	55	104	10 45	55	104	287
74	06 41	55	105	07 36	55	104	08 31	55	104	09 26	54	103	10 20	55	103	286
75	06 17	+55	104	07 12	+54	103	08 06	+55	103	09 01	+54	102	09 55	+55	102	285
76	05 52	55	103	06 47	54	102	07 41	55	102	08 36	55	102	09 31	54	101	284
77	05 27	55	102	06 22	55	101	07 17	54	101	08 11	55	101	09 06	54	100	283
78	05 03	54	101	05 57	55	101	06 52	54	100	07 46	55	100	08 41	54	99	282
79	04 38	54	100	05 32	55	100	06 27	54	99	07 21	55	99	08 16	54	98	281
80	04 13	+54	99	05 07	+55	99	06 02	+54	98	06 56	+55	98	07 51	+54	97	280
81	03 47	55	98	04 42	54	98	05 36	55	97	06 31	54	97	07 25	55	97	279
82	03 22	55	97	04 17	54	97	05 11	55	96	06 06	54	96	07 00	55	96	278
83	02 57	55	96	03 52	54	96	04 46	54	96	05 40	55	95	06 35	54	95	277
84	02 32	54	95	03 26	55	95	04 21	54	95	05 15	56	94	06 10	54	94	276
85	02 07	+54	95	03 01	+54	94	03 55	+55	94	04 50	+54	93	05 44	+55	93	275
86	01 41	55	94	02 36	54	93	03 30	55	93	04 25	54	92	05 19	54	92	274
87	01 16	54	93	02 10	56	92	03 05	54	92	03 59	55	91	04 54	54	91	273
88	00 51	54	92	01 45	54	91	02 39	55	91	03 34	54	91	04 28	55	90	272
89	00 25	55	91	01 20	54	90	02 14	54	90	03 08	55	90	04 03	54	89	271
90	00 00	+54	90	00 54	+55	90	01 49	+54	89	02 43	+54	89	03 37	+55	88	270
91	−0 25	54	89	00 29	54	89	01 23	55	88	02 18	54	88	03 12	54	87	269
92	−0 51	55	88	00 04	54	88	00 58	54	87	01 52	55	87	02 47	54	87	268
93	−1 16	54	87	−0 22	55	87	00 33	54	86	01 27	55	86	02 22	54	86	267
94	−1 41	54	86	−0 47	54	86	00 07	55	86	01 02	54	85	01 56	55	85	266
95	−2 07	+55	85	−1 12	+54	85	−0 18	+55	85	00 37	+54	84	01 31	+54	84	265
96	−2 32	55	85	−1 37	54	84	−0 43	54	84	00 11	55	83	01 06	54	83	264
97	−2 57	54	84	−2 03	55	83	−1 08	54	83	−0 14	56	82	00 41	54	82	263
98	−3 22	54	83	−2 28	55	82	−1 33	54	82	−0 39	55	81	00 16	54	81	262
99	−3 47	54	82	−2 53	55	81	−1 58	54	81	−1 04	55	81	−0 09	54	80	261
100	−4 13	+55	81	−3 18	+55	80	−2 23	+54	80	−1 29	+55	80	−0 34	+54	79	260
101	−4 38	55	80	−3 43	55	80	−2 48	54	79	−1 54	55	79	−0 59	54	78	259
102	−5 03	55	79	−4 08	55	79	−3 13	54	78	−2 19	55	78	−1 24	55	77	258
103	−5 27	54	78	−4 33	55	78	−3 38	55	77	−2 43	54	77	−1 49	55	77	257
104				−4 57	54	77	−4 03	55	76	−3 08	55	76	−2 13	54	76	256
105				−5 22	+55	76	−4 27	+54	76	−3 33	+55	75	−2 38	+55	75	255
106				−5 47	55	75	−4 52	55	75	−3 57	56	74	−3 02	55	74	254
107							−5 16	55	74	−4 21	54	73	−3 27	55	73	253
108							−5 41	55	73	−4 46	56	72	−3 51	55	72	252
109										−5 10	55	71	−4 15	55	71	251
110										−5 34	+55	70	−4 39	+55	70	250
111													−5 02	56	69	249
112													−5 26	56	68	248

LHA	5° Hc	5° d	5° Z	6° Hc	6° d	6° Z	7° Hc	7° d	7° Z	8° Hc	8° d	8° Z	9° Hc	9° d	9° Z	LHA
	° ′	′	°	° ′	′	°	° ′	′	°	° ′	′	°	° ′	′	°	
70	12 53	+55	106	13 48	+55	106	14 43	+54	105	15 37	+55	105	16 32	+55	105	290
71	12 29	54	105	13 23	55	105	14 18	55	104	15 13	54	104	16 07	55	104	289
72	12 04	55	104	12 59	55	104	13 54	54	104	14 48	55	103	15 43	54	103	288
73	11 40	54	103	12 34	55	103	13 29	54	103	14 23	55	102	15 18	54	102	287
74	11 15	54	103	12 09	55	102	13 04	55	102	13 59	54	101	14 53	54	101	286
75	10 50	+55	102	11 45	+54	101	12 39	+55	101	13 34	+54	100	14 28	+54	100	285
76	10 25	55	101	11 20	54	100	12 14	55	100	13 09	54	99	14 03	54	99	284
77	10 00	55	100	10 55	54	99	11 49	55	99	12 44	54	98	13 38	54	98	283
78	09 35	55	99	10 30	54	98	11 24	54	98	12 18	55	98	13 13	54	97	282
79	09 10	55	98	10 05	54	98	10 59	54	97	11 53	55	97	12 48	54	96	281
80	08 45	+54	97	09 39	+55	97	10 34	+54	96	11 28	+54	96	12 22	+55	95	280
81	08 20	54	96	09 14	55	96	10 09	54	95	11 03	54	95	11 57	54	94	279
82	07 55	54	95	08 49	54	95	09 43	55	94	10 38	54	94	11 32	54	93	278
83	07 29	55	94	08 24	54	94	09 18	54	93	10 12	54	93	11 06	55	93	277
84	07 04	54	93	07 58	55	93	08 53	54	93	09 47	54	92	10 41	54	92	276
85	06 39	+54	92	07 33	+54	92	08 27	+55	92	09 22	+54	91	10 16	+54	91	275
86	06 13	55	92	07 08	54	91	08 02	54	91	08 56	54	90	09 50	55	90	274
87	05 48	54	91	06 42	55	90	07 37	54	90	08 31	54	89	09 25	54	89	273
88	05 23	54	90	06 17	54	89	07 11	54	89	08 05	55	88	09 00	54	88	272
89	04 57	55	89	05 52	54	88	06 46	54	88	07 40	54	88	08 34	55	87	271
90	04 32	+54	88	05 26	+55	88	06 21	+54	87	07 15	+54	87	08 09	+54	86	270
91	04 06	55	87	05 01	54	87	05 55	55	86	06 50	54	86	07 44	54	85	269
92	03 41	55	86	04 36	54	86	05 30	54	85	06 24	55	85	07 19	54	84	268
93	03 16	54	85	04 10	55	85	05 05	54	84	05 59	54	84	06 53	55	84	267
94	02 51	54	84	03 45	54	84	04 39	55	83	05 34	54	83	06 28	54	83	266
95	02 25	+55	83	03 20	+54	83	04 14	+55	83	05 09	+54	82	06 03	+54	82	265
96	02 00	55	82	02 55	54	82	03 49	55	82	04 44	54	81	05 38	54	81	264
97	01 35	55	82	02 30	54	81	03 24	55	81	04 19	54	80	05 13	54	80	263
98	01 10	55	81	02 05	54	80	02 59	55	80	03 54	54	79	04 48	55	79	262
99	00 45	55	80	01 40	54	79	02 34	55	79	03 29	54	78	04 23	55	78	261
100	00 20	+55	79	01 15	+54	78	02 09	+55	78	03 04	+54	78	03 58	+55	77	260
101	−0 05	55	78	00 50	55	78	01 45	54	77	02 39	55	77	03 34	54	76	259
102	−0 29	54	77	00 25	55	77	01 20	55	76	02 15	54	76	03 09	55	75	258
103	−0 54	55	76	00 01	54	76	00 55	55	75	01 50	55	75	02 45	54	74	257
104	−1 19	55	75	−0 24	55	75	00 31	55	74	01 26	54	74	02 20	55	74	256
105	−1 43	+55	74	−0 48	+54	74	00 06	+55	73	01 01	+55	73	01 56	+55	73	255
106	−2 07	54	73	−1 13	55	73	−0 18	55	73	00 37	55	72	01 32	55	72	254
107	−2 32	55	72	−1 37	55	72	−0 42	55	72	00 13	55	71	01 08	55	71	253
108	−2 56	55	72	−2 01	55	71	−1 06	55	71	−0 11	55	70	00 44	55	70	252
109	−3 20	55	71	−2 25	55	70	−1 30	55	70	−0 35	55	69	00 20	55	69	251
110	−3 44	+55	70	−2 49	+55	69	−1 54	+56	69	−0 58	+55	69	−0 03	+55	68	250
111	−4 07	55	69	−3 12	55	68	−2 17	56	68	−1 22	55	68	−0 27	55	67	249
112	−4 31	55	68	−3 36	55	68	−2 41	56	67	−1 45	55	67	−0 50	56	66	248
113	−4 54	55	67	−3 59	55	67	−3 04	55	66	−2 09	56	66	−1 13	55	65	247
114	−5 18	56	66	−4 22	55	66	−3 27	55	65	−2 32	56	65	−1 36	55	64	246
115	−5 41	+56	65	−4 45	+55	65	−3 50	+56	64	−2 54	+55	64	−1 59	+55	64	245
116				−5 08	55	64	−4 13	56	63	−3 17	55	63	−2 22	56	63	244
117				−5 31	56	63	−4 35	55	63	−3 40	56	62	−2 44	55	62	243
118							−4 58	56	62	−4 02	56	61	−3 06	55	61	242
119							−5 20	56	61	−4 24	56	60	−3 28	55	60	241
120							−5 42	+56	60	−4 46	+56	59	−3 50	+56	59	240
121										−5 08	56	58	−4 12	56	58	239
122										−5 29	56	57	−4 33	56	57	238
123													−4 55	57	56	237
124													−5 16	57	55	236
125													−5 36	+56	54	235

LHA	10° Hc	10° d	10° Z	11° Hc	11° d	11° Z	12° Hc	12° d	12° Z	13° Hc	13° d	13° Z	14° Hc	14° d	14° Z	LHA
	° ′	′	°	° ′	′	°	° ′	′	°	° ′	′	°	° ′	′	°	
70	17 27	+54	104	18 21	+55	104	19 16	+54	103	20 10	+54	103	21 04	+54	102	290
71	17 02	54	103	17 56	55	103	18 51	54	102	19 45	54	102	20 39	55	101	289
72	16 37	55	102	17 32	54	102	18 26	54	101	19 20	55	101	20 15	54	100	288
73	16 12	55	101	17 07	54	101	18 01	54	100	18 55	55	100	19 50	54	100	287
74	15 47	55	100	16 42	54	100	17 36	54	99	18 30	55	99	19 25	54	99	286
75	15 22	+55	99	16 17	+54	99	17 11	+54	99	18 05	+54	98	18 59	+54	98	285
76	14 57	55	99	15 52	54	98	16 46	54	98	17 40	54	97	18 34	54	97	284
77	14 32	55	98	15 27	54	97	16 21	54	97	17 15	54	96	18 09	54	96	283
78	14 07	54	97	15 01	55	96	15 56	54	96	16 50	54	95	17 44	54	95	282
79	13 42	54	96	14 36	54	95	15 30	54	95	16 24	54	94	17 18	55	94	281
80	13 17	+54	95	14 11	+54	94	15 05	+54	94	15 59	+54	94	16 53	+54	93	280
81	12 51	55	94	13 46	54	94	14 40	54	93	15 34	54	93	16 28	54	92	279
82	12 26	54	93	13 20	54	93	14 14	54	92	15 08	55	92	16 03	53	91	278
83	12 01	54	92	12 55	54	92	13 49	54	91	14 43	54	91	15 37	54	90	277
84	11 35	55	91	12 30	54	91	13 24	54	90	14 18	54	90	15 12	54	89	276
85	11 10	+54	90	12 04	+54	90	12 58	+54	89	13 52	+54	89	14 46	+54	89	275
86	10 45	54	89	11 39	54	89	12 33	54	89	13 27	54	88	14 21	54	88	274
87	10 19	54	88	11 13	55	88	12 08	54	88	13 02	54	87	13 56	54	87	273
88	09 54	54	88	10 48	54	87	11 42	54	87	12 36	54	86	13 30	54	86	272
89	09 29	54	87	10 23	54	86	11 17	54	86	12 11	54	85	13 05	54	85	271
90	09 03	+55	86	09 58	+54	85	10 52	+54	85	11 46	+54	84	12 40	+54	84	270
91	08 38	54	85	09 32	54	84	10 26	55	84	11 21	54	84	12 15	54	83	269
92	08 13	54	84	09 07	54	84	10 01	54	83	10 55	55	83	11 50	54	82	268
93	07 48	54	83	08 42	54	83	09 36	54	82	10 30	55	82	11 25	54	81	267
94	07 22	55	82	08 17	54	82	09 11	54	81	10 05	54	81	10 59	55	80	266
95	06 57	+55	81	07 52	+54	81	08 46	+54	80	09 40	+55	80	10 35	+54	80	265
96	06 32	55	80	07 27	54	80	08 21	54	80	09 15	55	79	10 10	54	79	264
97	06 07	55	79	07 02	54	79	07 56	55	79	08 51	54	78	09 45	54	78	263
98	05 43	54	79	06 37	54	78	07 31	55	78	08 26	54	77	09 20	54	77	262
99	05 18	54	78	06 12	55	77	07 07	54	77	08 01	54	76	08 55	55	76	261
100	04 53	+54	77	05 47	+55	76	06 42	+54	76	07 36	+55	76	08 31	+54	75	260
101	04 28	55	76	05 23	54	75	06 17	55	75	07 12	54	75	08 06	55	74	259
102	04 04	54	75	04 58	55	75	05 53	55	74	06 48	54	74	07 42	55	73	258
103	03 39	55	74	04 34	55	74	05 29	54	73	06 23	55	73	07 18	54	72	257
104	03 15	55	73	04 10	54	73	05 04	55	72	05 59	55	72	06 54	54	72	256
105	02 51	+55	72	03 46	+54	72	04 40	+55	71	05 35	+55	71	06 30	+54	71	255
106	02 27	55	71	03 22	54	71	04 16	55	71	05 11	55	70	06 06	55	70	254
107	02 03	55	70	02 58	54	70	03 52	55	70	04 47	55	69	05 42	55	69	253
108	01 39	55	70	02 34	55	69	03 29	55	69	04 24	55	68	05 19	55	68	252
109	01 15	55	69	02 10	55	68	03 05	55	68	04 00	55	67	04 55	55	67	251
110	00 52	+55	68	01 47	+55	67	02 42	+55	67	03 37	+55	67	04 32	+55	66	250
111	00 28	55	67	01 23	56	66	02 19	55	66	03 14	55	66	04 09	55	65	249
112	00 05	55	66	01 00	55	66	01 55	56	65	02 51	55	65	03 46	55	64	248
113	−0 18	55	65	00 37	56	65	01 33	55	64	02 28	55	64	03 23	55	63	247
114	−0 41	55	64	00 14	56	64	01 10	55	63	02 05	55	63	03 00	56	63	246
115	−1 04	+56	63	−0 08	+55	63	00 47	+56	62	01 43	+55	62	02 38	+55	62	245
116	−1 26	55	62	−0 31	56	62	00 25	55	62	01 20	56	61	02 16	55	61	244
117	−1 49	56	61	−0 53	56	61	00 03	55	61	00 58	56	60	01 54	55	60	243
118	−2 11	56	60	−1 15	56	60	−0 19	55	60	00 36	56	59	01 32	56	59	242
119	−2 33	56	60	−1 37	56	59	−0 41	56	59	00 15	55	58	01 10	56	58	241
120	−2 54	+55	59	−1 59	+56	58	−1 03	+56	58	−0 07	+56	58	00 49	+56	57	240
121	−3 16	56	58	−2 20	56	57	−1 24	56	57	−0 28	56	57	00 28	56	56	239
122	−3 37	56	57	−2 41	56	56	−1 45	56	56	−0 49	56	56	00 07	56	55	238
123	−3 58	56	56	−3 02	56	56	−2 06	56	55	−1 10	56	55	−0 14	56	54	237
124	−4 19	56	55	−3 23	56	55	−2 27	56	54	−1 31	56	54	−0 35	57	54	236
125	−4 40	+56	54	−3 44	+57	54	−2 47	+56	53	−1 51	+56	53	−0 55	+56	53	235
126	−5 00	56	53	−4 04	56	53	−3 08	57	52	−2 11	56	52	−1 15	57	52	234
127	−5 21	57	52	−4 24	56	52	−3 28	57	51	−2 31	56	51	−1 35	57	51	233
128				−4 44	57	51	−3 47	56	51	−2 51	57	50	−1 54	56	50	232
129				−5 03	56	50	−4 07	57	50	−3 10	57	49	−2 13	56	49	231
130				−5 23	+57	49	−4 26	+57	49	−3 29	+57	48	−2 32	+56	48	230
131							−4 45	57	48	−3 48	57	47	−2 51	57	47	229
132							−5 04	57	47	−4 07	57	47	−3 10	57	46	228
133							−5 22	57	46	−4 25	57	46	−3 28	57	45	227
134										−4 43	57	45	−3 46	57	44	226
135										−5 01	+58	44	−4 03	+57	43	225
136										−5 18	57	43	−4 21	58	43	224
137													−4 38	58	42	223
138													−4 54	57	41	222
139													−5 11	58	40	221

S. Lat. {LHA greater than 180°....... Zn=180−Z; LHA less than 180°........... Zn=180+Z}

DECLINATION (0°-14°) SAME NAME AS LATITUDE

N. Lat. {LHA greater than 180°....... Zn=Z
{LHA less than 180°.......... Zn=360−Z

DECLINATION (0°-14°) SAME NAME AS LATITUDE

LHA	0°			1°			2°			3°			4°		
	Hc	d	Z	Hc	d	Z	Hc	d	Z	Hc	d	Z	Hc	d	Z
	° ′	′	°	° ′	′	°	° ′	′	°	° ′	′	°	° ′	′	°
103	−5 27	55	78	257											
102	−5 03	54	79	258											
101	−4 38	54	80	−5 32	55	80	259								
100	−4 13	−54	81	−5 07	−55	81	260								
99	−3 47	55	82	−4 42	54	82	−5 36	55	83	261					
98	−3 22	55	83	−4 17	54	83	−5 11	55	84	262					
97	−2 57	55	84	−3 52	54	84	−4 46	54	84	−5 40	55	85	263		
96	−2 32	54	85	−3 26	55	85	−4 21	54	85	−5 15	55	86	264		
95	−2 07	−54	85	−3 01	−54	86	−3 55	−55	86	−4 50	−54	87	−5 44	−55	87
94	−1 41	55	86	−2 36	54	87	−3 30	55	87	−4 25	54	88	−5 19	54	88
93	−1 16	54	87	−2 10	55	88	−3 05	54	88	−3 59	55	89	−4 54	54	89
92	−0 51	54	88	−1 45	54	89	−2 39	55	89	−3 34	54	89	−4 28	55	90
91	−0 25	55	89	−1 20	54	90	−2 14	54	90	−3 08	55	90	−4 03	54	91
90	00 00	−54	90	−0 54	−55	90	−1 49	−54	91	−2 43	−54	91	−3 37	−55	92
89	00 25	54	91	−0 29	54	91	−1 23	55	92	−2 18	54	92	−3 12	54	93
88	00 51	55	92	−0 04	54	92	−0 58	54	93	−1 52	55	93	−2 47	54	93
87	01 16	54	93	00 22	55	93	−0 33	54	94	−1 27	55	94	−2 22	54	94
86	01 41	54	94	00 47	54	94	−0 07	55	94	−1 02	54	95	−1 56	55	95
85	02 07	−55	95	01 12	−54	95	00 18	−55	95	−0 37	−54	96	−1 31	−54	96
84	02 32	55	95	01 37	54	96	00 43	54	96	−0 11	55	97	−1 06	54	97
83	02 57	54	96	02 03	55	97	01 08	54	97	00 14	55	98	−0 41	54	98
82	03 22	54	97	02 28	55	98	01 33	54	98	00 39	55	99	−0 16	54	99
81	03 47	54	98	02 53	55	99	01 58	54	99	01 04	55	99	00 09	54	100
80	04 13	−55	99	03 18	−55	100	02 23	−54	100	01 29	−55	100	00 34	−54	101
79	04 38	55	100	03 43	55	100	02 48	54	101	01 54	55	101	00 59	54	102
78	05 03	55	101	04 08	55	101	03 13	54	102	02 19	55	102	01 24	55	103
77	05 27	54	102	04 33	55	102	03 38	55	103	02 43	54	103	01 49	55	103
76	05 52	55	103	04 57	54	103	04 03	55	104	03 08	55	104	02 13	54	104
75	06 17	−55	104	05 22	−55	104	04 27	−54	104	03 33	−55	105	02 38	−55	105
74	06 41	54	105	05 47	55	105	04 52	55	105	03 57	55	106	03 02	55	106
73	07 06	55	106	06 11	55	106	05 16	55	106	04 21	54	107	03 27	55	107
72	07 30	55	106	06 35	54	107	05 41	55	107	04 46	55	108	03 51	55	108
71	07 55	55	107	07 00	55	108	06 05	55	108	05 10	55	109	04 15	55	109
70	08 19	−55	108	07 24	−55	109	06 29	−55	109	05 34	−55	110	04 39	−55	110

LHA	5°			6°			7°			8°			9°		
	Hc	d	Z	Hc	d	Z	Hc	d	Z	Hc	d	Z	Hc	d	Z
	° ′	′	°	° ′	′	°	° ′	′	°	° ′	′	°	° ′	′	°
95	265														
94	266														
93	−5 48	54	89	267											
92	−5 23	54	90	268											
91	−4 57	55	91	269											
90	−4 32	−54	92	−5 26	−55	92	270								
89	−4 06	55	93	−5 01	54	93	271								
88	−3 41	55	94	−4 36	54	94	−5 30	54	95	272					
87	−3 16	54	95	−4 10	55	95	−5 05	54	96	273					
86	−2 51	54	96	−3 45	54	96	−4 39	55	97	−5 34	54	97	274		
85	−2 25	−55	97	−3 20	−54	97	−4 14	−55	97	−5 09	−54	98	275		
84	−2 00	55	98	−2 55	54	98	−3 49	55	98	−4 44	54	99	−5 38	54	99
83	−1 35	55	98	−2 30	54	99	−3 24	55	99	−4 19	54	100	−5 13	54	100
82	−1 10	55	99	−2 05	54	100	−2 59	55	100	−3 54	54	101	−4 48	55	101
81	−0 45	55	100	−1 40	54	101	−2 34	55	101	−3 29	54	102	−4 23	55	102
80	−0 20	−55	101	−1 15	−54	102	−2 09	−55	102	−3 04	−54	102	−3 58	−55	103
79	00 05	55	102	−0 50	55	102	−1 45	54	103	−2 39	55	103	−3 34	54	104
78	00 29	54	103	−0 25	55	103	−1 20	55	104	−2 15	54	104	−3 09	55	105
77	00 54	55	104	−0 01	54	104	−0 55	55	105	−1 50	55	105	−2 45	54	106
76	01 19	55	105	00 24	55	105	−0 31	55	106	−1 26	54	106	−2 20	55	106
75	01 43	−55	106	00 48	−54	106	−0 06	−55	107	−1 01	−55	107	−1 56	−55	107
74	02 07	54	107	01 13	55	107	00 18	55	107	−0 37	55	108	−1 32	55	108
73	02 32	55	108	01 37	55	108	00 42	55	108	−0 13	55	109	−1 08	55	109
72	02 56	55	108	02 01	55	109	01 06	55	109	00 11	55	110	−0 44	55	110
71	03 20	55	109	02 25	55	110	01 30	55	110	00 35	55	111	−0 20	56	111
70	03 44	−55	110	02 49	−55	111	01 54	−56	111	00 58	−55	111	00 03	−55	112

LHA	10°			11°			12°			13°			14°			LHA
	Hc	d	Z	Hc	d	Z	Hc	d	Z	Hc	d	Z	Hc	d	Z	
	° ′	′	°	° ′	′	°	° ′	′	°	° ′	′	°	° ′	′	°	
												140	−5 27	+58	39	220
84	276															
83	277															
82	−5 43	54	101	278												
81	−5 18	54	102	279												
80	−4 53	−54	103	−5 47	−55	104	280									
79	−4 28	55	104	−5 23	54	105	281									
78	−4 04	54	105	−4 58	55	105	282									
77	−3 39	55	106	−4 34	55	106	−5 29	54	107	283						
76	−3 15	55	107	−4 10	54	107	−5 04	55	108	284						
75	−2 51	−55	108	−3 46	−54	108	−4 40	−55	109	−5 35	−55	109	285			
74	−2 27	55	109	−3 22	54	109	−4 16	55	109	−5 11	55	110	286			
73	−2 03	55	110	−2 58	54	110	−3 52	55	110	−4 47	55	111	−5 42	55	111	287
72	−1 39	55	110	−2 34	55	111	−3 29	55	111	−4 24	55	112	−5 19	55	112	288
71	−1 15	55	111	−2 10	55	112	−3 05	55	112	−4 00	55	113	−4 55	55	113	289
70	−0 52	−55	112	−1 47	−55	113	−2 42	−55	113	−3 37	−55	113	−4 32	−55	114	290

S. Lat. {LHA greater than 180°....... Zn=180−Z
{LHA less than 180°.......... Zn=180+Z

DECLINATION (0°-14°) CONTRARY NAME TO LATITUDE

N. Lat. {LHA greater than 180°....... Zn=Z / LHA less than 180°........... Zn=360−Z

DECLINATION (0°-14°) CONTRARY NAME TO LATITUDE

LHA	0° Hc	0° d	0° Z	1° Hc	1° d	1° Z	2° Hc	2° d	2° Z	3° Hc	3° d	3° Z	4° Hc	4° d	4° Z
	° ′	′	°	° ′	′	°	° ′	′	°	° ′	′	°	° ′	′	°
69	08 43	55	109	07 48	55	110	06 53	55	110	05 58	56	110	05 02	55	111
68	09 07	55	110	08 12	56	111	07 16	55	111	06 21	55	111	05 26	55	112
67	09 30	55	111	08 35	55	111	07 40	55	112	06 45	55	112	05 50	56	113
66	09 54	55	112	08 59	56	112	08 03	55	113	07 08	55	113	06 13	55	114
65	10 17	−55	113	09 22	−55	113	08 27	−56	114	07 31	−55	114	06 36	−55	115
64	10 41	56	114	09 45	55	114	08 50	55	115	07 55	56	115	06 59	55	115
63	11 04	56	115	10 08	55	115	09 13	56	116	08 17	55	116	07 22	56	116
62	11 27	56	116	10 31	55	116	09 36	56	117	08 40	55	117	07 45	56	117
61	11 49	55	117	10 54	56	117	09 58	55	117	09 03	56	118	08 07	56	118
60	12 12	−56	118	11 16	−55	118	10 21	−56	118	09 25	−56	119	08 29	−56	119
59	12 34	55	119	11 39	56	119	10 43	56	119	09 47	56	120	08 51	56	120
58	12 57	56	120	12 01	56	120	11 05	56	120	10 09	56	121	09 13	56	121
57	13 18	55	121	12 23	56	121	11 27	56	121	10 31	56	122	09 35	56	122
56	13 40	56	121	12 44	56	122	11 48	56	122	10 52	56	123	09 56	56	123
55	14 02	−56	122	13 06	−56	123	12 10	−57	123	11 13	−56	124	10 17	−56	124
54	14 23	56	123	13 27	56	124	12 31	57	124	11 34	56	124	10 38	56	125
53	14 44	56	124	13 48	56	125	12 52	57	125	11 55	56	125	10 59	56	126
52	15 05	56	125	14 09	57	126	13 12	56	126	12 16	57	126	11 19	56	127
51	15 25	56	126	14 29	56	127	13 33	57	127	12 36	56	127	11 40	57	128
50	15 46	−57	127	14 49	−56	128	13 53	−57	128	12 56	−56	128	12 00	−57	129
49	16 06	57	128	15 09	56	129	14 13	57	129	13 16	57	129	12 19	56	130
48	16 26	57	129	15 29	57	130	14 32	57	130	13 35	56	130	12 39	57	131
47	16 45	57	130	15 48	56	131	14 52	57	131	13 55	57	131	12 58	57	132
46	17 04	57	131	16 07	56	132	15 11	57	132	14 14	57	132	13 17	57	133
45	17 23	−57	132	16 26	−57	133	15 29	−57	133	14 32	−57	133	13 35	−57	134
44	17 42	57	133	16 45	57	134	15 48	57	134	14 51	58	134	13 53	57	135
43	18 00	57	134	17 03	57	135	16 06	57	135	15 09	58	135	14 11	57	135
42	18 18	57	135	17 21	57	136	16 24	58	136	15 26	57	136	14 29	57	136
41	18 36	57	136	17 39	58	137	16 41	57	137	15 44	58	137	14 46	57	137
40	18 53	−57	137	17 56	−58	138	16 58	−57	138	16 01	−58	138	15 03	−57	138
39	19 10	57	138	18 13	58	139	17 15	57	139	16 18	58	139	15 20	58	139
38	19 27	57	139	18 30	58	140	17 32	58	140	16 34	58	140	15 36	57	140
37	19 44	58	140	18 46	58	141	17 48	58	141	16 50	58	141	15 52	58	141
36	20 00	58	141	19 02	58	142	18 04	58	142	17 06	58	142	16 08	58	142
35	20 15	−58	142	19 17	−58	143	18 19	−58	143	17 21	−58	143	16 23	−58	143
34	20 31	58	143	19 33	59	144	18 34	58	144	17 36	58	144	16 38	58	144
33	20 46	59	144	19 47	58	145	18 49	58	145	17 51	58	145	16 53	58	145
32	21 00	58	145	20 02	58	146	19 04	59	146	18 05	58	146	17 07	58	146
31	21 14	58	147	20 16	58	147	19 18	59	147	18 19	58	147	17 21	59	147
30	21 28	−58	148	20 30	−59	148	19 31	−58	148	18 33	−59	148	17 34	−58	149
29	21 42	59	149	20 43	58	149	19 45	59	149	18 46	59	149	17 47	58	150
28	21 55	59	150	20 56	59	150	19 57	58	150	18 59	59	150	18 00	59	151
27	22 07	58	151	21 09	59	151	20 10	59	151	19 11	59	151	18 12	58	152
26	22 20	59	152	21 21	59	152	20 22	59	152	19 23	59	152	18 24	59	153
25	22 31	−59	153	21 32	−58	153	20 34	−59	153	19 35	−59	153	18 36	−59	154
24	22 43	59	154	21 44	59	154	20 45	59	154	19 46	59	154	18 47	59	155
23	22 54	59	155	21 55	59	155	20 56	59	155	19 57	60	156	18 57	59	156
22	23 04	59	156	22 05	59	156	21 06	59	156	20 07	59	157	19 08	59	157
21	23 14	59	157	22 15	59	157	21 16	59	157	20 17	59	158	19 18	60	158
20	23 24	−59	158	22 25	−60	158	21 25	−59	159	20 26	−59	159	19 27	−59	159
19	23 33	59	159	22 34	59	159	21 35	60	160	20 35	59	160	19 36	60	160
18	23 42	59	160	22 43	60	160	21 43	59	161	20 44	60	161	19 44	59	161
17	23 50	59	161	22 51	60	162	21 51	59	162	20 52	60	162	19 52	59	162
16	23 58	59	162	22 59	60	163	21 59	59	163	21 00	60	163	20 00	59	163
15	24 06	−60	164	23 06	−60	164	22 06	−59	164	21 07	−60	164	20 07	−59	164
14	24 13	60	165	23 13	60	165	22 13	59	165	21 14	60	165	20 14	60	165
13	24 19	60	166	23 19	59	166	22 20	60	166	21 20	60	166	20 20	59	166
12	24 25	60	167	23 25	59	167	22 26	60	167	21 26	60	167	20 26	60	167
11	24 31	60	168	23 31	60	168	22 31	60	168	21 31	59	168	20 32	60	168
10	24 36	−60	169	23 36	−60	169	22 36	−60	169	21 36	−60	169	20 36	−59	169
9	24 40	60	170	23 40	59	170	22 41	60	170	21 41	60	170	20 41	60	170
8	24 44	59	171	23 45	60	171	22 45	60	171	21 45	60	171	20 45	60	172
7	24 48	60	172	23 48	60	172	22 48	60	172	21 48	60	173	20 48	59	173
6	24 51	60	173	23 51	60	173	22 51	60	174	21 51	59	174	20 52	60	174
5	24 54	−60	175	23 54	−60	175	22 54	−60	175	21 54	−60	175	20 54	−60	175
4	24 56	60	176	23 56	60	176	22 56	60	176	21 56	60	176	20 56	60	176
3	24 58	60	177	23 58	60	177	22 58	60	177	21 58	60	177	20 58	60	177
2	24 59	60	178	23 59	60	178	22 59	60	178	21 59	60	178	20 59	60	178
1	25 00	60	179	24 00	60	179	23 00	60	179	22 00	60	179	21 00	60	179
0	25 00	−60	180	24 00	−60	180	23 00	−60	180	22 00	−60	180	21 00	−60	180

LHA	5° Hc	5° d	5° Z	6° Hc	6° d	6° Z	7° Hc	7° d	7° Z	8° Hc	8° d	8° Z	9° Hc	9° d	9° Z
	° ′	′	°	° ′	′	°	° ′	′	°	° ′	′	°	° ′	′	°
69	04 07	55	111	03 12	55	112	02 17	55	112	01 22	55	112	00 27	55	113
68	04 31	55	112	03 36	55	112	02 41	56	113	01 45	55	113	00 50	55	114
67	04 54	55	113	03 59	55	113	03 04	55	114	02 09	56	114	01 13	55	115
66	05 18	56	114	04 22	55	114	03 27	55	115	02 32	56	115	01 36	55	116
65	05 41	−56	115	04 45	−55	115	03 50	−56	116	02 54	−55	116	01 59	−55	116
64	06 04	56	116	05 08	55	116	04 13	56	117	03 17	55	117	02 22	56	117
63	06 26	55	117	05 31	56	117	04 35	55	117	03 40	56	118	02 44	55	118
62	06 49	56	118	05 53	55	118	04 58	56	118	04 02	56	119	03 06	55	119
61	07 11	55	119	06 16	56	119	05 20	56	119	04 24	56	120	03 28	55	120
60	07 33	−55	120	06 38	−56	120	05 42	−56	120	04 46	−56	121	03 50	−56	121
59	07 55	55	120	07 00	56	121	06 04	56	121	05 08	56	122	04 12	56	122
58	08 17	56	121	07 21	56	122	06 25	56	122	05 29	56	123	04 33	56	123
57	08 39	56	122	07 43	56	123	06 47	56	123	05 51	56	123	04 55	57	124
56	09 00	56	123	08 04	56	124	07 08	56	124	06 12	56	124	05 16	57	125
55	09 21	−56	124	08 25	−56	125	07 29	−57	125	06 32	−56	125	05 36	−56	126
54	09 42	56	125	08 46	57	126	07 49	56	126	06 53	56	126	05 57	57	127
53	10 03	57	126	09 06	56	126	08 10	57	127	07 13	56	127	06 17	56	128
52	10 23	56	127	09 27	57	127	08 30	56	128	07 34	57	128	06 37	57	128
51	10 43	56	128	09 47	57	128	08 50	57	129	07 53	56	129	06 57	57	129
50	11 03	−57	129	10 06	−56	129	09 10	−57	130	08 13	−57	130	07 16	−57	130
49	11 23	57	130	10 26	57	130	09 29	57	131	08 32	57	131	07 35	56	131
48	11 42	57	131	10 45	57	131	09 48	57	132	08 51	57	132	07 54	57	132
47	12 01	57	132	11 04	57	132	10 07	57	133	09 10	57	133	08 13	57	133
46	12 20	57	133	11 23	57	133	10 26	58	134	09 28	57	134	08 31	57	134
45	12 38	−57	134	11 41	−57	134	10 44	−57	134	09 47	−58	135	08 49	−57	135
44	12 56	57	135	11 59	57	135	11 02	58	135	10 04	57	136	09 07	57	136
43	13 14	57	136	12 17	58	136	11 19	57	136	10 22	57	137	09 25	58	137
42	13 32	58	137	12 34	57	137	11 37	58	137	10 39	57	138	09 42	58	138
41	13 49	58	138	12 51	57	138	11 54	58	138	10 56	57	139	09 59	58	139
40	14 06	−58	139	13 08	−58	139	12 10	−57	139	11 13	−58	140	10 15	−57	140
39	14 22	57	140	13 25	58	140	12 27	58	140	11 29	58	141	10 31	57	141
38	14 39	58	141	13 41	58	141	12 43	58	141	11 45	58	142	10 47	58	142
37	14 54	57	142	13 57	58	142	12 59	58	142	12 01	58	143	11 03	58	143
36	15 10	58	143	14 12	58	143	13 14	58	143	12 16	58	143	11 18	58	144
35	15 25	−58	144	14 27	−58	144	13 29	−58	144	12 31	−58	144	11 33	−58	145
34	15 40	58	145	14 42	58	145	13 44	59	145	12 45	58	145	11 47	58	146
33	15 55	59	146	14 56	58	146	13 58	58	146	13 00	59	146	12 01	58	147
32	16 09	59	147	15 10	58	147	14 12	58	147	13 14	59	147	12 15	58	148
31	16 22	58	148	15 24	58	148	14 26	59	148	13 27	58	148	12 29	59	149
30	16 36	−59	149	15 37	−58	149	14 39	−59	149	13 40	−58	149	12 42	−59	150
29	16 49	59	150	15 50	58	150	14 52	59	150	13 53	59	150	12 54	58	151
28	17 01	58	151	16 03	59	151	15 04	59	151	14 05	59	151	13 06	58	152
27	17 14	59	152	16 15	59	152	15 16	59	152	14 17	59	152	13 18	58	153
26	17 25	58	153	16 27	59	153	15 28	59	153	14 29	59	153	13 30	59	154
25	17 37	−59	154	16 38	−59	154	15 39	−59	154	14 40	−59	154	13 41	−59	155
24	17 48	59	155	16 49	59	155	15 50	59	155	14 51	59	155	13 52	59	156
23	17 58	59	156	16 59	59	156	16 00	59	156	15 01	59	156	14 02	59	157
22	18 09	60	157	17 09	59	157	16 10	59	157	15 11	59	157	14 12	59	158
21	18 18	59	158	17 19	59	158	16 20	59	158	15 21	60	158	14 21	59	159
20	18 28	−60	159	17 28	−59	159	16 29	−59	159	15 30	−60	159	14 30	−59	160
19	18 36	59	160	17 37	59	160	16 38	60	160	15 38	59	160	14 39	59	161
18	18 45	59	161	17 46	60	161	16 46	59	161	15 47	60	162	14 47	59	162
17	18 53	60	162	17 53	59	162	16 54	60	162	15 54	59	163	14 55	60	163
16	19 01	60	163	18 01	60	163	17 01	59	163	16 02	60	164	15 02	59	164
15	19 08	−60	164	18 08	−59	164	17 09	−60	164	16 09	−60	165	15 09	−59	165
14	19 14	59	165	18 15	60	165	17 15	60	165	16 15	59	166	15 16	60	166
13	19 21	60	166	18 21	60	166	17 21	59	167	16 22	60	167	15 22	60	167
12	19 26	59	167	18 27	60	167	17 27	60	168	16 27	60	168	15 27	59	168
11	19 32	60	168	18 32	60	169	17 32	60	169	16 32	59	169	15 33	60	169
10	19 37	−60	169	18 37	−60	170	17 37	−60	170	16 37	−60	170	15 37	−59	170
9	19 41	60	171	18 41	60	171	17 41	59	171	16 42	60	171	15 42	60	171
8	19 45	60	172	18 45	60	172	17 45	60	172	16 45	59	172	15 46	60	172
7	19 49	60	173	18 49	60	173	17 49	60	173	16 49	60	173	15 49	60	173
6	19 52	60	174	18 52	60	174	17 52	60	174	16 52	60	174	15 52	60	174
5	19 54	−60	175	18 54	−60	175	17 54	−60	175	16 54	−60	175	15 54	−60	175
4	19 56	60	176	18 56	60	176	17 56	60	176	16 56	60	176	15 56	60	176
3	19 58	60	177	18 58	60	177	17 58	60	177	16 58	60	177	15 58	60	177
2	19 59	60	178	18 59	60	178	17 59	60	178	16 59	60	178	15 59	60	178
1	20 00	60	179	19 00	60	179	18 00	60	179	17 00	60	179	16 00	60	179
0	20 00	−60	180	19 00	−60	180	18 00	−60	180	17 00	−60	180	16 00	−60	180

10° Hc	10° d	10° Z	11° Hc	11° d	11° Z	12° Hc	12° d	12° Z	13° Hc	13° d	13° Z	14° Hc	14° d	14° Z	LHA
° ′	′	°	° ′	′	°	° ′	′	°	° ′	′	°	° ′	′	°	
−0 28	55	113	−1 23	56	114	−2 19	55	114	−3 14	55	114	−4 09	55	115	291
−0 05	55	114	−1 00	55	114	−1 55	56	115	−2 51	55	115	−3 46	55	116	292
00 18	55	115	−0 37	56	115	−1 33	55	116	−2 28	55	116	−3 23	55	117	293
00 41	55	116	−0 14	56	116	−1 10	55	117	−2 05	55	117	−3 00	56	117	294
01 04	−56	117	00 08	−55	117	−0 47	−56	118	−1 43	−55	118	−2 38	−55	118	295
01 26	55	118	00 31	56	118	−0 25	55	118	−1 20	56	119	−2 16	55	119	296
01 49	56	119	00 53	56	119	−0 03	55	119	−0 58	56	120	−1 54	55	120	297
02 11	56	120	01 15	56	120	00 19	55	120	−0 36	56	121	−1 32	56	121	298
02 33	56	120	01 37	56	121	00 41	56	121	−0 15	55	122	−1 10	56	122	299
02 54	−55	121	01 59	−56	122	01 03	−56	122	00 07	−56	122	−0 49	−56	123	300
03 16	56	122	02 20	56	123	01 24	56	123	00 28	56	123	−0 28	56	124	301
03 37	56	123	02 41	56	124	01 45	56	124	00 49	56	124	−0 07	56	125	302
03 58	56	124	03 02	56	124	02 06	56	125	01 10	56	125	00 14	56	126	303
04 19	56	125	03 23	56	125	02 27	56	126	01 31	56	126	00 35	57	126	304
04 40	−56	126	03 44	−57	126	02 47	−56	127	01 51	−56	127	00 55	−56	127	305
05 00	56	127	04 04	56	127	03 08	57	128	02 11	56	128	01 15	57	128	306
05 21	57	128	04 24	56	128	03 28	57	129	02 31	56	129	01 35	57	129	307
05 40	56	129	04 44	57	129	03 47	56	129	02 51	57	130	01 54	56	130	308
06 00	57	130	05 03	56	130	04 07	57	130	03 10	57	131	02 13	56	131	309
06 19	−56	131	05 23	−57	131	04 26	−57	131	03 29	−57	132	02 32	−56	132	310
06 39	57	132	05 42	57	132	04 45	57	132	03 48	57	133	02 51	57	133	311
06 57	56	133	06 01	57	133	05 04	57	133	04 07	57	133	03 10	57	134	312
07 16	57	133	06 19	57	134	05 22	57	134	04 25	57	134	03 28	57	135	313
07 34	57	134	06 37	57	135	05 40	57	135	04 43	57	135	03 46	57	136	314
07 52	−57	135	06 55	−57	136	05 58	−57	136	05 01	−58	136	04 03	−57	137	315
08 10	57	136	07 13	58	137	06 15	57	137	05 18	57	137	04 21	58	137	316
08 27	57	137	07 30	58	138	06 32	57	138	05 35	57	138	04 38	58	138	317
08 44	57	138	07 47	58	139	06 49	57	139	05 52	58	139	04 54	57	139	318
09 01	58	139	08 03	57	139	07 06	58	140	06 08	57	140	05 11	58	140	319
09 18	−58	140	08 20	−58	140	07 22	−58	141	06 24	−57	141	05 27	−58	141	320
09 34	58	141	08 36	58	141	07 38	58	142	06 40	58	142	05 42	57	142	321
09 49	58	142	08 51	57	142	07 54	58	143	06 56	58	143	05 58	58	143	322
10 05	58	143	09 07	58	143	08 09	58	144	07 11	58	144	06 13	58	144	323
10 20	58	144	09 22	58	144	08 24	58	145	07 26	58	145	06 28	59	145	324
10 35	−59	145	09 36	−58	145	08 38	−58	145	07 40	−58	146	06 42	−58	146	325
10 49	58	146	09 51	58	146	08 53	59	146	07 54	58	147	06 56	58	147	326
11 03	58	147	10 05	59	147	09 06	58	147	08 08	58	148	07 10	59	148	327
11 17	59	148	10 18	58	148	09 20	59	148	08 21	58	149	07 23	58	149	328
11 30	58	149	10 32	59	149	09 33	58	149	08 35	59	150	07 36	59	150	329
11 43	−59	150	10 44	−58	150	09 46	−59	150	08 47	−58	151	07 49	−59	151	330
11 56	59	151	10 57	59	151	09 58	58	151	09 00	59	151	08 01	59	152	331
12 08	59	152	11 09	59	152	10 10	59	152	09 11	58	152	08 13	59	153	332
12 20	59	153	11 21	59	153	10 22	59	153	09 23	59	153	08 24	59	154	333
12 31	59	154	11 32	59	154	10 33	59	154	09 34	59	154	08 35	59	154	334
12 42	−59	155	11 43	−59	155	10 44	−59	155	09 45	−59	155	08 46	−59	156	335
12 53	59	156	11 54	60	156	10 54	59	156	09 55	59	156	08 56	59	157	336
13 03	59	157	12 04	59	157	11 05	60	157	10 05	59	157	09 06	59	157	337
13 13	60	158	12 13	59	158	11 14	59	158	10 15	59	158	09 16	59	158	338
13 22	59	159	12 23	60	159	11 23	59	159	10 24	59	159	09 25	59	159	339
13 31	−59	160	12 32	−60	160	11 32	−59	160	10 33	−59	160	09 34	−60	160	340
13 40	60	161	12 40	59	161	11 41	60	161	10 41	59	161	09 42	59	161	341
13 48	60	162	12 48	59	162	11 49	60	162	10 49	59	162	09 50	60	162	342
13 55	59	163	12 56	60	163	11 56	59	163	10 57	60	163	09 57	59	163	343
14 03	60	164	13 03	59	164	12 04	60	164	11 04	59	164	10 05	60	164	344
14 10	−60	165	13 10	−60	165	12 10	−59	165	11 11	−60	165	10 11	−59	165	345
14 16	60	166	13 16	59	166	12 17	60	166	11 17	60	166	10 17	59	166	346
14 22	60	167	13 22	59	167	12 23	60	167	11 23	60	167	10 23	59	167	347
14 28	60	168	13 28	60	168	12 28	60	168	11 28	59	168	10 29	60	168	348
14 33	60	169	13 33	60	169	12 33	60	169	11 33	59	169	10 34	60	169	349
14 38	−60	170	13 38	−60	170	12 38	−60	170	11 38	−60	170	10 38	−60	170	350
14 42	60	171	13 42	60	171	12 42	60	171	11 42	60	171	10 42	59	171	351
14 46	60	172	13 46	60	172	12 46	60	172	11 46	60	172	10 46	60	172	352
14 49	60	173	13 49	60	173	12 49	60	173	11 49	60	173	10 49	60	173	353
14 52	60	174	13 52	60	174	12 52	60	174	11 52	60	174	10 52	60	174	354
14 54	−60	175	13 54	−59	175	12 55	−60	175	11 55	−60	175	10 55	−60	175	355
14 56	60	176	13 56	60	176	12 56	59	176	11 57	60	176	10 57	60	176	356
14 58	60	177	13 58	60	177	12 58	60	177	11 58	60	177	10 58	60	177	357
14 59	60	178	13 59	60	178	12 59	60	178	11 59	60	178	10 59	60	178	358
15 00	60	179	14 00	60	179	13 00	60	179	12 00	60	179	11 00	60	179	359
15 00	−60	180	14 00	−60	180	13 00	−60	180	12 00	−60	180	11 00	−60	180	360

S. Lat. {LHA greater than 180°....... Zn=180−Z / LHA less than 180°........... Zn=180+Z

DECLINATION (0°-14°) CONTRARY NAME TO LATITUDE

N. Lat. {LHA greater than 180°....... Zn=Z; LHA less than 180°.......... Zn=360−Z}

DECLINATION (15°-29°) SAME NAME AS LATITUDE

LHA	15°			16°			17°			18°			19°		
	Hc	d	Z	Hc	d	Z	Hc	d	Z	Hc	d	Z	Hc	d	Z
	° ′	′	°	° ′	′	°	° ′	′	°	° ′	′	°	° ′	′	°
0	40 00	+60	180	41 00	+60	180	42 00	+60	180	43 00	+60	180	44 00	+60	180
1	40 00	60	179	41 00	60	179	42 00	60	179	43 00	60	179	44 00	60	179
2	39 59	60	178	40 59	60	178	41 59	60	177	42 59	60	177	43 59	60	177
3	39 58	60	176	40 58	59	176	41 57	60	176	42 57	60	176	43 57	60	176
4	39 56	60	175	40 56	59	175	41 55	60	175	42 55	60	175	43 55	60	175
5	39 53	+60	174	40 53	+60	174	41 53	+60	174	42 53	+60	174	43 53	+60	173
6	39 50	60	172	40 50	60	172	41 50	60	172	42 50	60	172	43 50	59	172
7	39 46	60	171	40 46	60	171	41 46	60	171	42 46	60	171	43 46	60	171
8	39 42	60	170	40 42	60	170	41 42	60	170	42 42	60	170	43 42	59	170
9	39 38	59	169	40 37	60	169	41 37	60	169	42 37	60	168	43 37	59	168
10	39 32	+60	167	40 32	+60	167	41 32	+59	167	42 31	+60	167	43 31	+60	167
11	39 27	59	166	40 26	60	166	41 26	59	166	42 25	60	166	43 25	60	166
12	39 20	60	165	40 20	59	165	41 19	60	165	42 19	60	165	43 19	59	164
13	39 13	60	164	40 13	59	164	41 12	60	163	42 12	59	163	43 11	60	163
14	39 06	59	163	40 05	60	162	41 05	59	162	42 04	60	162	43 04	59	162
15	38 58	+59	161	39 57	+60	161	40 57	+59	161	41 56	+60	161	42 56	+59	161
16	38 50	59	160	39 49	59	160	40 48	60	160	41 48	59	159	42 47	59	159
17	38 41	59	159	39 40	59	159	40 39	59	158	41 38	60	158	42 38	59	158
18	38 31	59	158	39 30	60	157	40 30	59	157	41 29	59	157	42 28	59	157
19	38 21	59	156	39 20	60	156	40 20	59	156	41 19	58	156	42 17	59	155
20	38 11	+59	155	39 10	+59	155	40 09	+59	155	41 08	+59	154	42 07	+58	154
21	38 00	59	154	38 59	59	154	39 58	59	153	40 57	58	153	41 55	59	153
22	37 49	58	153	38 47	59	153	39 46	59	152	40 45	59	152	41 44	58	152
23	37 37	59	152	38 36	58	151	39 34	59	151	40 33	58	151	41 31	59	150
24	37 25	58	150	38 23	59	150	39 22	58	150	40 20	59	150	41 19	58	149
25	37 12	+58	149	38 10	+59	149	39 09	+58	149	40 07	+58	148	41 05	+59	148
26	36 59	58	148	37 57	58	148	38 55	58	147	39 53	59	147	40 52	58	147
27	36 45	58	147	37 43	58	147	38 41	58	146	39 39	59	146	40 38	58	146
28	36 31	58	146	37 29	58	145	38 27	58	145	39 25	58	145	40 23	58	144
29	36 16	58	145	37 14	58	144	38 12	58	144	39 10	58	144	40 08	58	143
30	36 01	+58	143	36 59	+58	143	37 57	+58	143	38 55	+58	142	39 53	+57	142
31	35 46	58	142	36 44	58	142	37 42	57	142	38 39	58	141	39 37	57	141
32	35 30	58	141	36 28	58	141	37 26	57	140	38 23	58	140	39 21	57	140
33	35 14	58	140	36 12	57	140	37 09	58	139	38 07	57	139	39 04	57	139
34	34 58	57	139	35 55	57	138	36 52	58	138	37 50	57	138	38 47	57	137
35	34 41	+57	138	35 38	+57	137	36 35	+57	137	37 32	+58	137	38 30	+57	136
36	34 23	58	137	35 21	57	136	36 18	57	136	37 15	57	135	38 12	57	135
37	34 06	57	135	35 03	57	135	36 00	57	135	36 57	57	134	37 54	56	134
38	33 48	57	134	34 45	57	134	35 42	56	134	36 38	57	133	37 35	57	133
39	33 30	56	133	34 26	57	133	35 23	57	132	36 20	56	132	37 16	57	132
40	33 11	+57	132	34 08	+56	132	35 04	+57	131	36 01	+56	131	36 57	+57	131
41	32 52	57	131	33 49	56	131	34 45	56	130	35 41	57	130	36 38	56	129
42	32 33	56	130	33 29	57	130	34 26	56	129	35 22	56	129	36 18	56	128
43	32 13	56	129	33 09	57	129	34 06	56	128	35 02	56	128	35 58	56	127
44	31 53	56	128	32 49	57	127	33 46	56	127	34 42	56	127	35 38	56	126
45	31 33	+56	127	32 29	+56	126	33 25	+56	126	34 21	+56	126	35 17	+56	125
46	31 13	56	126	32 09	56	125	33 05	55	125	34 00	56	124	34 56	56	124
47	30 52	56	125	31 48	56	124	32 44	55	124	33 39	56	123	34 35	56	123
48	30 31	56	124	31 27	55	123	32 22	56	123	33 18	56	122	34 14	55	122
49	30 10	55	123	31 05	56	122	32 01	55	122	32 56	56	121	33 52	55	121
50	29 48	+56	122	30 44	+55	121	31 39	+56	121	32 35	+55	120	33 30	+55	120
51	29 26	56	121	30 22	55	120	31 17	56	120	32 13	55	119	33 08	55	119
52	29 04	56	119	30 00	55	119	30 55	55	119	31 50	55	118	32 45	56	118
53	28 42	55	118	29 37	56	118	30 33	55	118	31 28	55	117	32 23	55	117
54	28 20	55	117	29 15	55	117	30 10	55	117	31 05	55	116	32 00	55	116
55	27 57	+55	116	28 52	+55	116	29 47	+55	116	30 42	+55	115	31 37	+55	115
56	27 34	55	115	28 29	55	115	29 24	55	115	30 19	55	114	31 14	55	114
57	27 11	55	114	28 06	55	114	29 01	55	114	29 56	55	113	30 51	54	113
58	26 48	55	113	27 43	55	113	28 38	55	113	29 33	54	112	30 27	55	112
59	26 25	55	112	27 20	54	112	28 14	55	112	29 09	55	111	30 04	54	111
60	26 01	+55	111	26 56	+55	111	27 51	+54	111	28 45	+55	110	29 40	+54	110
61	25 38	54	111	26 32	55	110	27 27	54	110	28 21	55	109	29 16	54	109
62	25 14	54	110	26 08	55	109	27 03	54	109	27 57	55	108	28 52	54	108
63	24 50	54	109	25 44	55	108	26 39	54	108	27 33	54	107	28 27	55	107
64	24 26	54	108	25 20	55	107	26 15	54	107	27 09	54	106	28 03	54	106
65	24 01	+55	107	24 56	+54	106	25 50	+54	106	26 44	+55	105	27 39	+54	105
66	23 37	54	106	24 31	55	105	25 26	54	105	26 20	54	104	27 14	54	104
67	23 13	54	105	24 07	54	104	25 01	54	104	25 55	54	103	26 49	54	103
68	22 48	54	104	23 42	54	103	24 36	55	103	25 31	54	102	26 25	53	102
69	22 23	54	103	23 17	55	102	24 12	54	102	25 06	54	101	26 00	54	101

LHA	20°			21°			22°			23°			24°		
	Hc	d	Z	Hc	d	Z	Hc	d	Z	Hc	d	Z	Hc	d	Z
	° ′	′	°	° ′	′	°	° ′	′	°	° ′	′	°	° ′	′	°
0	45 00	+60	180	46 00	+60	180	47 00	+60	180	48 00	+60	180	49 00	+60	180
1	45 00	60	179	46 00	60	179	47 00	60	179	48 00	60	179	49 00	60	179
2	44 59	60	177	45 59	60	177	46 59	60	177	47 59	60	177	48 59	60	177
3	44 57	60	176	45 57	60	176	46 57	60	176	47 57	60	176	48 57	60	176
4	44 55	60	175	45 55	60	175	46 55	60	175	47 55	60	175	48 55	60	174
5	44 53	+60	173	45 53	+60	173	46 53	+59	173	47 52	+60	173	48 52	+60	173
6	44 49	60	172	45 49	60	172	46 49	60	172	47 49	60	172	48 49	60	172
7	44 46	60	171	45 46	59	171	46 45	60	171	47 45	60	170	48 45	60	170
8	44 41	60	169	45 41	60	169	46 41	60	169	47 41	59	169	48 40	60	169
9	44 36	60	168	45 36	60	168	46 36	60	168	47 36	59	168	48 35	60	168
10	44 31	+60	167	45 31	+59	167	46 30	+60	167	47 30	+59	166	48 29	+60	166
11	44 25	59	166	45 24	60	165	46 24	60	165	47 24	59	165	48 23	60	165
12	44 18	60	164	45 18	59	164	46 17	60	164	47 17	59	164	48 16	60	163
13	44 11	59	163	45 10	60	163	46 10	59	163	47 09	60	162	48 09	59	162
14	44 03	60	162	45 03	59	161	46 02	59	161	47 01	60	161	48 01	59	161
15	43 55	+59	160	44 54	+59	160	45 53	+60	160	46 53	+59	160	47 52	+59	159
16	43 46	59	159	44 45	59	159	45 44	60	159	46 44	59	158	47 43	59	158
17	43 37	59	158	44 36	59	158	45 35	59	157	46 34	59	157	47 33	59	157
18	43 27	59	156	44 26	59	156	45 25	59	156	46 24	59	156	47 23	58	155
19	43 16	59	155	44 15	59	155	45 14	59	155	46 13	59	154	47 12	59	154
20	43 05	+59	154	44 04	+59	154	45 03	+59	153	46 02	+58	153	47 00	+59	153
21	42 54	59	153	43 53	58	152	44 51	59	152	45 50	59	152	46 49	58	151
22	42 42	59	151	43 41	58	151	44 39	59	151	45 38	58	151	46 36	59	150
23	42 30	58	150	43 28	59	150	44 27	58	150	45 25	58	149	46 23	59	149
24	42 17	58	149	43 15	59	149	44 14	58	148	45 12	58	148	46 10	58	148
25	42 04	+58	148	43 02	+58	147	44 00	+58	147	44 58	+58	147	45 56	+58	146
26	41 50	58	146	42 48	58	146	43 46	58	146	44 44	58	145	45 42	58	145
27	41 36	58	145	42 34	57	145	43 31	58	145	44 29	58	144	45 27	58	144
28	41 21	58	144	42 19	57	144	43 16	58	143	44 14	58	143	45 12	57	143
29	41 06	57	143	42 03	58	142	43 01	58	142	43 59	57	142	44 56	58	141
30	40 50	+58	142	41 48	+57	141	42 45	+58	141	43 43	+57	141	44 40	+57	140
31	40 34	58	140	41 32	57	140	42 29	57	140	43 26	58	139	44 24	57	139
32	40 18	57	139	41 15	57	139	42 12	58	138	43 10	57	138	44 07	57	138
33	40 01	57	138	40 58	57	138	41 55	57	137	42 52	57	137	43 49	57	136
34	39 44	57	137	40 41	57	137	41 38	57	136	42 35	57	136	43 32	56	135
35	39 27	+56	136	40 23	+57	135	41 20	+57	135	42 17	+57	135	43 14	+56	134
36	39 09	56	135	40 05	57	134	41 02	57	134	41 59	56	133	42 55	57	133
37	38 50	57	133	39 47	57	133	40 44	56	133	41 40	56	132	42 36	57	132
38	38 32	56	132	39 28	57	132	40 25	56	131	41 21	56	131	42 17	56	131
39	38 13	56	131	39 09	57	131	40 06	56	130	41 02	56	130	41 58	56	129
40	37 54	+56	130	38 50	+56	130	39 46	+56	129	40 42	+56	129	41 38	+56	128
41	37 34	56	129	38 30	56	129	39 26	56	128	40 22	56	128	41 18	56	127
42	37 14	56	128	38 10	56	127	39 06	56	127	40 02	56	126	40 58	55	126
43	36 54	56	127	37 50	56	126	38 46	55	126	39 41	56	125	40 37	55	125
44	36 34	55	126	37 29	56	125	38 25	56	125	39 21	55	124	40 16	55	124
45	36 13	+56	125	37 09	+55	124	38 04	+56	124	39 00	+55	123	39 55	+55	123
46	35 52	55	124	36 47	56	123	37 43	55	123	38 38	55	122	39 33	55	122
47	35 31	55	122	36 26	55	122	37 21	56	122	38 17	55	121	39 12	55	121
48	35 09	55	121	36 04	56	121	37 00	55	120	37 55	55	120	38 50	54	119
49	34 47	55	120	35 42	56	120	36 38	55	119	37 33	54	119	38 27	55	118
50	34 25	+55	119	35 20	+55	119	36 15	+55	118	37 10	+55	118	38 05	+55	117
51	34 03	55	118	34 58	55	118	35 53	55	117	36 48	54	117	37 42	55	116
52	33 41	54	117	34 35	55	117	35 30	55	116	36 25	54	116	37 19	55	115
53	33 18	55	116	34 13	54	116	35 07	55	115	36 02	54	115	36 56	55	114
54	32 55	55	115	33 50	54	115	34 44	55	114	35 39	54	114	36 33	54	113
55	32 32	+55	114	33 27	+54	114	34 21	+55	113	35 16	+54	113	36 10	+54	112
56	32 09	54	113	33 03	55	113	33 58	54	112	34 52	54	112	35 46	54	111
57	31 45	55	112	32 40	54	112	33 34	54	111	34 28	54	111	35 22	54	110
58	31 22	54	111	32 16	54	111	33 10	55	110	34 05	54	110	34 59	53	109
59	30 58	54	110	31 52	54	110	32 46	55	109	33 41	54	109	34 35	53	108
60	30 34	+54	109	31 28	+54	109	32 22	+54	108	33 16	+54	108	34 10	+54	107
61	30 10	54	108	31 04	54	108	31 58	54	107	32 52	54	107	33 46	54	106
62	29 46	54	107	30 40	54	107	31 34	54	106	32 28	54	106	33 22	53	105
63	29 22	54	106	30 16	54	106	31 10	53	105	32 03	54	105	32 57	54	104
64	28 57	54	105	29 51	54	105	30 45	54	104	31 39	53	104	32 32	54	103
65	28 33	+54	104	29 27	+53	104	30 20	+54	103	31 14	+54	103	32 08	+53	102
66	28 08	54	103	29 02	54	103	29 56	53	102	30 49	54	102	31 43	53	101
67	27 43	54	102	28 37	54	102	29 31	53	101	30 24	54	101	31 18	53	100
68	27 18	54	101	28 12	54	101	29 06	53	100	29 59	54	100	30 53	53	99
69	26 54	53	100	27 47	54	100	28 41	53	99	29 34	54	99	30 28	53	98

25°			26°			27°			28°			29°			LHA
Hc	d	Z	Hc	d	Z	Hc	d	Z	Hc	d	Z	Hc	d	Z	
° ′	′	°	° ′	′	°	° ′	′	°	° ′	′	°	° ′	′	°	
50 00	+60	180	51 00	+60	180	52 00	+60	180	53 00	+60	180	54 00	+60	180	360
50 00	60	179	51 00	60	179	52 00	60	179	53 00	60	179	54 00	60	179	359
49 59	60	177	50 59	60	177	51 59	60	177	52 59	60	177	53 59	60	177	358
49 57	60	176	50 57	60	176	51 57	60	176	52 57	60	176	53 57	60	176	357
49 55	60	174	50 55	60	174	51 55	60	174	52 55	60	174	53 55	60	174	356
49 52	+60	173	50 52	+60	173	51 52	+60	173	52 52	+60	173	53 52	+60	173	355
49 49	60	172	50 49	60	171	51 49	59	171	52 48	60	171	53 48	60	171	354
49 45	60	170	50 45	59	170	51 44	60	170	52 44	60	170	53 44	60	170	353
49 40	60	169	50 40	60	169	51 40	59	169	52 39	60	168	53 39	60	168	352
49 35	60	167	50 35	59	167	51 34	60	167	52 34	60	167	53 34	59	167	351
49 29	+60	166	50 29	+59	166	51 28	+60	166	52 28	+59	165	53 27	+60	165	350
49 23	59	165	50 22	60	164	51 22	59	164	52 21	60	164	53 21	59	164	349
49 16	59	163	50 15	59	163	51 14	60	163	52 14	59	163	53 13	60	162	348
49 08	59	162	50 07	60	162	51 07	59	161	52 06	59	161	53 05	59	161	347
49 00	59	161	49 59	59	160	50 58	59	160	51 57	60	160	52 57	59	159	346
48 51	+59	159	49 50	+59	159	50 49	+59	159	51 48	+59	158	52 47	+59	158	345
48 42	59	158	49 41	59	158	50 40	59	157	51 39	59	157	52 38	59	157	344
48 32	59	156	49 31	59	156	50 30	59	156	51 29	58	156	52 27	59	155	343
48 21	59	155	49 20	59	155	50 19	59	155	51 18	58	154	52 16	59	154	342
48 11	58	154	49 09	59	153	50 08	58	153	51 06	59	153	52 05	58	152	341
47 59	+59	152	48 58	+58	152	49 56	+59	152	50 55	+58	151	51 53	+58	151	340
47 47	58	151	48 45	59	151	49 44	58	150	50 42	58	150	51 40	58	150	339
47 35	58	150	48 33	58	149	49 31	58	149	50 29	58	149	51 27	58	148	338
47 22	58	149	48 20	58	148	49 18	58	148	50 16	58	147	51 14	57	147	337
47 08	58	147	48 06	58	147	49 04	58	146	50 02	58	146	51 00	57	146	336
46 54	+58	146	47 52	+58	146	48 50	+57	145	49 47	+58	145	50 45	+58	144	335
46 40	57	145	47 37	58	144	48 35	58	144	49 33	57	143	50 30	57	143	334
46 25	57	143	47 22	58	143	48 20	57	143	49 17	57	142	50 14	58	142	333
46 09	58	142	47 07	57	142	48 04	57	141	49 01	57	141	49 58	57	140	332
45 54	57	141	46 51	57	140	47 48	57	140	48 45	57	140	49 42	57	139	331
45 37	+57	140	46 34	+57	139	47 31	+57	139	48 28	+57	138	49 25	+57	138	330
45 21	57	138	46 18	57	138	47 15	56	138	48 11	57	137	49 08	56	137	329
45 04	56	137	46 00	57	137	46 57	57	136	47 54	56	136	48 50	57	135	328
44 46	57	136	45 43	56	136	46 39	57	135	47 36	56	135	48 32	56	134	327
44 28	57	135	45 25	56	134	46 21	57	134	47 18	56	133	48 14	56	133	326
44 10	+57	134	45 07	+56	133	46 03	+56	133	46 59	+56	132	47 55	+56	132	325
43 52	56	132	44 48	56	132	45 44	56	131	46 40	56	131	47 36	56	130	324
43 33	56	131	44 29	56	131	45 25	56	130	46 21	55	130	47 16	56	129	323
43 13	56	130	44 09	56	130	45 05	56	129	46 01	56	129	46 57	55	128	322
42 54	56	129	43 50	55	128	44 45	56	128	45 41	55	127	46 36	56	127	321
42 34	+56	128	43 30	+55	127	44 25	+56	127	45 21	+55	126	46 16	+55	126	320
42 14	55	127	43 09	56	126	44 05	55	126	45 00	55	125	45 55	55	124	319
41 53	56	126	42 49	55	125	43 44	55	124	44 39	55	124	45 34	55	123	318
41 32	56	124	42 28	55	124	43 23	55	123	44 18	55	123	45 13	54	122	317
41 11	56	123	42 07	55	123	43 02	54	122	43 56	55	122	44 51	55	121	316
40 50	+55	122	41 45	+55	122	42 40	+55	121	43 35	+54	121	44 29	+55	120	315
40 28	55	121	41 23	55	121	42 18	55	120	43 13	54	119	44 07	54	119	314
40 07	54	120	41 01	55	119	41 56	55	119	42 51	54	118	43 45	54	118	313
39 44	55	119	40 39	55	118	41 34	54	118	42 28	54	117	43 22	54	117	312
39 22	55	118	40 17	54	117	41 11	54	117	42 05	55	116	43 00	53	116	311
39 00	+54	117	39 54	+54	116	40 48	+55	116	41 43	+54	115	42 37	+53	115	310
38 37	54	116	39 31	54	115	40 25	54	115	41 19	54	114	42 13	54	113	309
38 14	54	115	39 08	54	114	40 02	54	114	40 56	54	113	41 50	54	112	308
37 51	54	114	38 45	54	113	39 39	54	113	40 33	53	112	41 26	54	111	307
37 27	55	113	38 22	53	112	39 15	54	111	40 09	54	111	41 03	53	110	306
37 04	+54	112	37 58	+54	111	38 52	+53	110	39 45	+54	110	40 39	+53	109	305
36 40	54	111	37 34	54	110	38 28	53	109	39 21	54	109	40 15	53	108	304
36 16	54	110	37 10	54	109	38 04	53	108	38 57	54	108	39 51	53	107	303
35 52	54	109	36 46	54	108	37 40	53	107	38 33	53	107	39 26	53	106	302
35 28	54	108	36 22	53	107	37 15	54	106	38 09	53	106	39 02	53	105	301
35 04	+54	107	35 58	+53	106	36 51	+53	105	37 44	+53	105	38 37	+53	104	300
34 40	53	106	35 33	54	105	36 27	53	104	37 20	53	104	38 13	53	103	299
34 15	54	105	35 09	53	104	36 02	53	103	36 55	53	103	37 48	53	102	298
33 51	53	104	34 44	53	103	35 37	53	102	36 30	53	102	37 23	53	101	297
33 26	53	103	34 19	53	102	35 12	53	101	36 05	53	101	36 58	53	100	296
33 01	+53	102	33 54	+54	101	34 48	+53	101	35 41	+52	100	36 33	+53	99	295
32 36	53	101	33 29	54	100	34 23	53	100	35 16	52	99	36 08	53	98	294
32 11	53	100	33 04	54	99	33 58	52	99	34 50	53	98	35 43	53	97	293
31 46	53	99	32 39	53	98	33 32	53	98	34 25	53	97	35 18	53	97	292
31 21	53	98	32 14	53	97	33 07	53	97	34 00	53	96	34 53	52	96	291

S. Lat. {LHA greater than 180°....... Zn=180−Z; LHA less than 180°.......... Zn=180+Z}

DECLINATION (15°-29°) SAME NAME AS LATITUDE

N. Lat. {LHA greater than 180°....... Zn=Z; LHA less than 180°.......... Zn=360−Z}

DECLINATION (15°-29°) SAME NAME AS LATITUDE

LHA	15° Hc	d	Z	16° Hc	d	Z	17° Hc	d	Z	18° Hc	d	Z	19° Hc	d	Z
	° ′	′	°	° ′	′	°	° ′	′	°	° ′	′	°	° ′	′	°
70	21 58	+55	102	22 53	+54	101	23 47	+54	101	24 41	+54	100	25 35	+54	100
71	21 34	54	101	22 28	54	100	23 22	54	100	24 16	54	100	25 10	53	99
72	21 09	54	100	22 03	54	100	22 57	54	99	23 51	54	99	24 45	53	98
73	20 44	54	99	21 38	54	99	22 32	54	98	23 26	53	98	24 19	54	97
74	20 19	54	98	21 13	54	98	22 07	54	97	23 01	53	97	23 54	54	96
75	19 53	+54	97	20 47	+54	97	21 41	+54	96	22 35	+54	96	23 29	+54	95
76	19 28	54	96	20 22	54	96	21 16	54	95	22 10	54	95	23 04	53	94
77	19 03	54	95	19 57	54	95	20 51	54	94	21 45	54	94	22 39	53	93
78	18 38	54	94	19 32	54	94	20 26	53	94	21 19	54	93	22 13	54	93
79	18 13	53	94	19 06	54	93	20 00	54	93	20 54	54	92	21 48	53	92
80	17 47	+54	93	18 41	+54	92	19 35	+54	92	20 29	+53	91	21 22	+54	91
81	17 22	54	92	18 16	54	91	19 10	53	91	20 03	54	90	20 57	54	90
82	16 56	54	91	17 50	54	90	18 44	54	90	19 38	54	89	20 32	53	89
83	16 31	54	90	17 25	54	89	18 19	54	89	19 13	53	88	20 06	54	88
84	16 06	54	89	17 00	54	89	17 54	53	88	18 47	54	88	19 41	54	87
85	15 40	+54	88	16 34	+54	88	17 28	+54	87	18 22	+54	87	19 16	+53	86
86	15 15	54	87	16 09	54	87	17 03	54	86	17 57	53	86	18 50	54	85
87	14 50	54	86	15 44	54	86	16 38	53	85	17 31	54	85	18 25	54	84
88	14 24	54	85	15 18	54	85	16 12	54	84	17 06	54	84	18 00	54	84
89	13 59	54	84	14 53	54	84	15 47	54	84	16 41	54	83	17 35	54	83
90	13 34	+54	84	14 28	+54	83	15 22	+54	83	16 16	+54	82	17 10	+54	82
91	13 09	54	83	14 03	54	82	14 57	54	82	15 51	54	81	16 45	53	81
92	12 44	54	82	13 38	54	81	14 32	54	81	15 26	54	80	16 20	54	80
93	12 19	54	81	13 13	54	80	14 07	54	80	15 01	54	80	15 55	54	79
94	11 54	54	80	12 48	54	80	13 42	54	79	14 36	54	79	15 30	54	78
95	11 29	+54	79	12 23	+54	79	13 17	+54	78	14 11	+54	78	15 05	+54	77
96	11 04	54	78	11 58	54	78	12 52	54	77	13 46	54	77	14 40	54	76
97	10 39	54	77	11 33	55	77	12 28	54	76	13 22	54	76	14 16	54	76
98	10 14	55	76	11 09	54	76	12 03	54	76	12 57	54	75	13 51	54	75
99	09 50	54	76	10 44	54	75	11 38	55	75	12 33	54	74	13 27	54	74
100	09 25	+55	75	10 20	+54	74	11 14	+54	74	12 08	+55	73	13 03	+54	73
101	09 01	54	74	09 55	55	73	10 50	54	73	11 44	54	73	12 38	55	72
102	08 37	54	73	09 31	55	72	10 26	54	72	11 20	54	72	12 14	55	71
103	08 12	55	72	09 07	55	72	10 02	54	71	10 56	54	71	11 50	55	70
104	07 48	55	71	08 43	55	71	09 38	54	70	10 32	55	70	11 27	54	69
105	07 24	+55	70	08 19	+55	70	09 14	+54	69	10 08	+55	69	11 03	+55	69
106	07 01	54	69	07 55	55	69	08 50	55	69	09 45	54	68	10 39	55	68
107	06 37	55	68	07 32	55	68	08 27	54	68	09 21	55	67	10 16	55	67
108	06 14	55	67	07 08	55	67	08 03	55	67	08 58	55	66	09 53	55	66
109	05 50	55	67	06 45	55	66	07 40	55	66	08 35	55	65	09 30	55	65
110	05 27	+55	66	06 22	+55	65	07 17	+55	65	08 12	+55	65	09 07	+55	64
111	05 04	55	65	05 59	55	65	06 54	55	64	07 49	55	64	08 44	55	63
112	04 41	55	64	05 36	55	64	06 31	55	63	07 26	56	63	08 22	55	62
113	04 18	56	63	05 14	55	63	06 09	55	62	07 04	55	62	07 59	55	62
114	03 56	55	62	04 51	55	62	05 46	56	61	06 42	55	61	07 37	55	61
115	03 33	+56	61	04 29	+55	61	05 24	+56	61	06 20	+55	60	07 15	+55	60
116	03 11	56	60	04 07	55	60	05 02	56	60	05 58	55	59	06 53	56	59
117	02 49	56	60	03 45	55	59	04 40	56	59	05 36	56	58	06 32	55	58
118	02 28	55	59	03 23	56	58	04 19	56	58	05 15	55	58	06 10	56	57
119	02 06	56	58	03 02	56	57	03 58	55	57	04 53	56	57	05 49	56	56
120	01 45	+56	57	02 41	+55	56	03 36	+56	56	04 32	+56	56	05 28	+56	55
121	01 24	56	56	02 20	55	56	03 15	56	55	04 11	56	55	05 07	56	55
122	01 03	56	55	01 59	56	55	02 55	56	54	03 51	56	54	04 47	56	54
123	00 42	56	54	01 38	56	54	02 34	56	53	03 30	56	53	04 26	57	53
124	00 22	56	53	01 18	56	53	02 14	56	53	03 10	56	52	04 06	57	52
125	00 01	+57	52	00 58	+56	52	01 54	+56	52	02 50	+57	51	03 47	+56	51
126	−0 18	56	51	00 38	56	51	01 34	57	51	02 31	56	50	03 27	56	50
127	−0 38	56	50	00 18	57	50	01 15	56	50	02 11	57	49	03 08	56	49
128	−0 58	57	50	−0 01	57	49	00 56	56	49	01 52	57	48	02 49	56	48
129	−1 17	57	49	−0 20	57	48	00 37	56	48	01 33	57	48	02 30	57	47
130	−1 36	+57	48	−0 39	+57	47	00 18	+57	47	01 15	+56	47	02 11	+57	46
131	−1 54	57	47	−0 57	56	47	−0 01	57	46	00 56	57	46	01 53	57	46
132	−2 13	57	46	−1 16	57	46	−0 19	57	45	00 38	57	45	01 35	57	45
133	−2 31	57	45	−1 34	57	45	−0 37	57	44	00 20	58	44	01 18	57	44
134	−2 49	58	44	−1 51	57	44	−0 54	57	43	00 03	57	43	01 00	57	43
135	−3 06	+57	43	−2 09	+57	43	−1 12	+58	43	−0 14	+57	42	00 43	+57	42
136	−3 23	57	42	−2 26	57	42	−1 29	58	42	−0 31	57	41	00 26	58	41
137	−3 40	57	41	−2 43	53	41	−1 45	57	41	−0 48	58	40	00 10	57	40
138	−3 57	58	40	−2 59	57	40	−2 02	58	40	−1 04	58	40	−0 06	57	39
139	−4 13	58	39	−3 15	57	39	−2 18	58	39	−1 20	58	39	−0 22	57	38

LHA	20° Hc	d	Z	21° Hc	d	Z	22° Hc	d	Z	23° Hc	d	Z	24° Hc	d	Z
	° ′	′	°	° ′	′	°	° ′	′	°	° ′	′	°	° ′	′	°
70	26 29	+53	99	27 22	+54	99	28 16	+53	98	29 09	+54	98	30 03	+53	97
71	26 03	54	99	26 57	54	98	27 51	53	98	28 44	54	97	29 38	53	97
72	25 38	54	98	26 32	54	97	27 26	53	97	28 19	53	96	29 12	54	96
73	25 13	54	97	26 07	53	96	27 00	54	96	27 54	53	95	28 47	53	95
74	24 48	54	96	25 42	53	95	26 35	54	95	27 29	53	94	28 22	53	94
75	24 23	+53	95	25 16	+54	94	26 10	+53	94	27 03	+53	93	27 56	+54	93
76	23 57	54	94	24 51	54	93	25 45	53	93	26 38	53	92	27 31	53	92
77	23 32	54	93	24 26	53	92	25 19	54	92	26 13	53	91	27 06	53	91
78	23 07	53	92	24 00	54	92	24 54	53	91	25 47	53	91	26 40	54	90
79	22 41	54	91	23 35	53	91	24 28	54	90	25 22	53	90	26 15	53	89
80	22 16	+54	90	23 10	+53	90	24 03	+53	89	24 56	+54	89	25 50	+53	88
81	21 51	53	89	22 44	54	89	23 38	53	88	24 31	53	88	25 24	54	87
82	21 25	54	88	22 19	53	88	23 12	54	87	24 06	53	87	24 59	53	86
83	21 00	54	88	21 54	53	87	22 47	53	87	23 40	54	86	24 34	53	86
84	20 35	53	87	21 28	54	86	22 22	53	86	23 15	54	85	24 09	53	85
85	20 09	+54	86	21 03	+54	85	21 57	+53	85	22 50	+53	84	23 43	+54	84
86	19 44	54	85	20 38	53	84	21 31	54	84	22 25	53	83	23 18	53	83
87	19 19	54	84	20 13	53	83	21 06	54	83	22 00	53	83	22 53	53	82
88	18 54	53	83	19 47	54	83	20 41	53	82	21 34	54	82	22 28	53	81
89	18 29	53	82	19 22	54	82	20 16	53	81	21 09	54	81	22 03	53	80
90	18 04	+53	81	18 57	+54	81	19 51	+53	80	20 44	+54	80	21 38	+53	79
91	17 38	54	80	18 32	54	80	19 26	54	79	20 20	53	79	21 13	53	79
92	17 14	53	80	18 07	54	79	19 01	54	79	19 55	53	78	20 48	54	78
93	16 49	53	79	17 42	54	78	18 36	54	78	19 30	54	77	20 24	53	77
94	16 24	54	78	17 18	53	77	18 11	54	77	19 05	54	76	19 59	53	76
95	15 59	+54	77	16 53	+54	76	17 47	+54	76	18 41	+53	76	19 34	+54	75
96	15 34	54	76	16 28	54	76	17 22	54	75	18 16	54	75	19 10	54	74
97	15 10	54	75	16 04	54	75	16 58	54	74	17 52	54	74	18 46	53	73
98	14 45	54	74	15 39	54	74	16 33	54	73	17 27	54	73	18 21	54	72
99	14 21	54	73	15 15	54	73	16 09	54	73	17 03	54	72	17 57	54	72
100	13 57	+54	73	14 51	+54	72	15 45	+54	72	16 39	+54	71	17 33	+54	71
101	13 33	54	72	14 27	54	71	15 21	54	71	16 15	54	70	17 09	54	70
102	13 09	54	71	14 03	54	70	14 57	54	70	15 51	55	69	16 46	54	69
103	12 45	54	70	13 39	55	69	14 34	54	69	15 28	54	69	16 22	54	68
104	12 21	55	69	13 16	54	69	14 10	54	68	15 04	55	68	15 59	54	67
105	11 58	+54	68	12 52	+54	68	13 46	+55	67	14 41	+54	67	15 35	+55	66
106	11 34	55	67	12 29	54	67	13 23	55	66	14 18	54	66	15 12	55	66
107	11 11	54	66	12 05	55	66	13 00	55	66	13 55	54	65	14 49	55	65
108	10 48	54	66	11 42	55	65	12 37	55	65	13 32	54	64	14 26	55	64
109	10 25	54	65	11 19	55	64	12 14	55	64	13 09	55	63	14 04	54	63
110	10 02	+55	64	10 57	+55	63	11 52	+54	63	12 46	+55	63	13 41	+55	62
111	09 39	55	63	10 34	55	63	11 29	55	62	12 24	55	62	13 19	55	61
112	09 17	55	62	10 12	55	62	11 07	55	61	12 02	55	61	12 57	55	60
113	08 54	56	61	09 50	55	61	10 45	55	60	11 40	55	60	12 35	55	60
114	08 32	55	60	09 27	56	60	10 23	55	59	11 18	55	59	12 13	55	59
115	08 10	+56	59	09 06	+55	59	10 01	+55	59	10 56	+55	58	11 51	+56	58
116	07 49	55	59	08 44	55	58	09 39	56	58	10 35	55	57	11 30	55	57
117	07 27	56	58	08 23	55	57	09 18	56	57	10 14	55	57	11 09	55	56
118	07 06	56	57	08 01	56	56	08 57	56	56	09 53	55	56	10 48	56	55
119	06 45	55	56	07 40	56	56	08 36	56	55	09 32	55	55	10 27	56	54
120	06 24	+56	55	07 20	+55	55	08 15	+56	54	09 11	+56	54	10 07	+56	54
121	06 03	56	54	06 59	56	54	07 55	56	53	08 51	56	53	09 47	55	53
122	05 43	56	53	06 39	56	53	07 35	56	53	08 31	56	52	09 27	55	52
123	05 23	56	52	06 19	56	52	07 15	56	52	08 11	56	51	09 07	56	51
124	05 03	56	52	05 59	56	51	06 55	56	51	07 51	56	50	08 47	56	50
125	04 43	+56	51	05 39	+56	50	06 35	+57	50	07 32	+56	50	08 28	+56	49
126	04 23	57	50	05 20	56	49	06 16	56	49	07 12	57	49	08 09	56	48
127	04 04	57	49	05 01	56	49	05 57	57	48	06 54	56	48	07 50	56	48
128	03 45	57	48	04 42	56	48	05 38	57	47	06 35	56	47	07 31	57	47
129	03 27	56	47	04 23	57	47	05 20	57	46	06 17	56	46	07 13	57	46
130	03 08	+57	46	04 05	+57	46	05 02	+56	46	05 58	+57	45	06 55	+57	45
131	02 50	57	45	03 47	57	45	04 44	57	45	05 41	56	44	06 37	57	44
132	02 32	57	44	03 29	57	44	04 26	57	44	05 23	57	43	06 20	57	43
133	02 15	57	43	03 12	57	43	04 09	57	43	05 06	57	43	06 03	57	42
134	01 57	57	43	02 54	58	42	03 52	57	42	04 49	57	42	05 46	57	41
135	01 40	+58	42	02 38	+57	41	03 35	+57	41	04 32	+57	41	05 29	+58	41
136	01 24	57	41	02 21	57	40	03 18	58	40	04 16	57	40	05 13	57	40
137	01 07	58	40	02 05	57	40	03 02	57	39	03 59	58	39	04 57	57	39
138	00 51	58	39	01 49	57	39	02 46	58	38	03 44	57	38	04 41	58	38
139	00 35	58	38	01 33	58	38	02 31	57	38	03 28	58	37	04 26	58	37

LHA	25° Hc	d	Z	26° Hc	d	Z	27° Hc	d	Z	28° Hc	d	Z	29° Hc	d	Z	LHA
	° ′	′	°	° ′	′	°	° ′	′	°	° ′	′	°	° ′	′	°	
70	30 56	+53	97	31 49	+53	96	32 42	+53	96	33 35	+53	95	34 28	+52	95	290
71	30 31	53	96	31 24	53	95	32 17	53	95	33 10	52	94	34 02	53	94	289
72	30 06	53	95	30 59	53	94	31 52	52	94	32 44	53	93	33 37	52	93	288
73	29 40	53	94	30 33	53	94	31 26	53	93	32 19	53	92	33 12	52	92	287
74	29 15	53	93	30 08	53	93	31 01	53	92	31 54	52	92	32 46	53	91	286
75	28 50	+53	92	29 43	+53	92	30 36	+52	91	31 28	+53	91	32 21	+52	90	285
76	28 24	53	91	29 17	53	91	30 10	53	90	31 03	53	90	31 56	52	89	284
77	27 59	53	90	28 52	53	90	29 45	53	89	30 38	52	89	31 30	53	88	283
78	27 34	53	90	28 27	52	89	29 19	53	88	30 12	53	88	31 05	52	87	282
79	27 08	53	89	28 01	53	88	28 54	53	88	29 47	53	87	30 40	52	86	281
80	26 43	+53	88	27 36	+53	87	28 29	+53	87	29 22	+52	86	30 14	+53	86	280
81	26 18	53	87	27 11	53	86	28 04	52	86	28 56	53	85	29 49	53	85	279
82	25 52	53	86	26 45	53	85	27 38	53	85	28 31	53	84	29 24	52	84	278
83	25 27	53	85	26 20	53	85	27 13	53	84	28 06	53	83	28 59	52	83	277
84	25 02	53	84	25 55	53	84	26 48	53	83	27 41	52	83	28 33	53	82	276
85	24 37	+53	83	25 30	+53	83	26 23	+53	82	27 16	+52	82	28 08	+53	81	275
86	24 11	54	82	25 05	53	82	25 58	53	81	26 51	52	81	27 43	53	80	274
87	23 46	53	82	24 39	54	81	25 33	53	81	26 26	52	80	27 18	53	79	273
88	23 21	53	81	24 14	54	80	25 08	53	80	26 01	52	79	26 53	53	79	272
89	22 56	53	80	23 49	54	79	24 43	53	79	25 36	53	78	26 29	53	78	271
90	22 31	+54	79	23 25	+53	78	24 18	+53	78	25 11	+53	77	26 04	+53	77	270
91	22 06	54	78	23 00	53	78	23 53	53	77	24 46	53	77	25 39	53	76	269
92	21 42	53	77	22 35	53	77	23 28	54	76	24 22	53	76	25 15	53	75	268
93	21 17	53	76	22 10	54	76	23 04	53	75	23 57	53	75	24 50	53	74	267
94	20 52	54	75	21 46	53	75	22 39	54	74	23 33	53	74	24 26	53	73	266
95	20 28	+54	75	21 22	+53	74	22 15	+53	74	23 08	+54	73	24 02	+53	73	265
96	20 04	53	74	20 57	54	73	21 51	53	73	22 44	54	72	23 38	53	72	264
97	19 39	54	73	20 33	54	72	21 27	53	72	22 20	54	71	23 14	53	71	263
98	19 15	54	72	20 09	54	72	21 03	53	71	21 56	54	71	22 50	53	70	262
99	18 51	54	71	19 45	54	71	20 39	53	70	21 32	54	70	22 26	53	69	261
100	18 27	+54	70	19 21	+54	70	20 15	+54	69	21 09	+53	69	22 02	+54	68	260
101	18 03	54	69	18 57	54	69	19 51	54	68	20 45	54	68	21 39	53	68	259
102	17 40	54	69	18 34	54	68	19 28	54	68	20 22	53	67	21 15	54	67	258
103	17 16	54	68	18 10	54	67	19 04	54	67	19 58	54	66	20 52	54	66	257
104	16 53	54	67	17 47	54	66	18 41	54	66	19 35	54	65	20 29	54	65	256
105	16 30	+54	66	17 24	+54	66	18 18	+54	65	19 12	+54	65	20 06	+54	64	255
106	16 07	54	65	17 01	54	65	17 55	54	64	18 49	55	64	19 44	54	63	254
107	15 44	54	64	16 38	54	64	17 32	55	63	18 27	54	63	19 21	54	62	253
108	15 21	54	63	16 15	55	63	17 10	54	63	18 04	55	62	18 59	54	62	252
109	14 58	55	63	15 53	54	62	16 47	55	62	17 42	54	61	18 36	55	61	251
110	14 36	+55	62	15 31	+54	61	16 25	+55	61	17 20	+54	60	18 14	+55	60	250
111	14 14	54	61	15 08	55	60	16 03	55	60	16 58	54	60	17 52	55	59	249
112	13 52	54	60	14 46	55	60	15 41	55	59	16 36	55	59	17 31	54	58	248
113	13 30	55	59	14 25	55	59	15 20	55	58	16 15	54	58	17 09	55	57	247
114	13 08	55	58	14 03	55	58	14 58	55	57	15 53	55	57	16 48	55	57	246
115	12 47	+55	57	13 42	+55	57	14 37	+55	57	15 32	+55	56	16 27	+55	56	245
116	12 25	56	57	13 21	55	56	14 16	55	56	15 11	55	55	16 06	55	55	244
117	12 04	56	56	13 00	55	55	13 55	55	55	14 50	56	55	15 46	55	54	243
118	11 44	55	55	12 39	55	54	13 34	56	54	14 30	55	54	15 25	55	53	242
119	11 23	55	54	12 18	56	54	13 14	55	53	14 09	56	53	15 05	55	52	241
120	11 03	+55	53	11 58	+56	53	12 54	+55	52	13 49	+56	52	14 45	+55	52	240
121	10 42	56	52	11 38	56	52	12 34	56	52	13 30	55	51	14 25	56	51	239
122	10 22	56	51	11 18	56	51	12 14	56	51	13 10	56	50	14 06	55	50	238
123	10 03	56	51	10 59	56	50	11 55	56	50	12 51	55	49	13 46	56	49	237
124	09 43	56	50	10 39	56	49	11 35	56	49	12 31	56	49	13 27	56	48	236
125	09 24	+56	49	10 20	+56	49	11 16	+57	48	12 13	+56	48	13 09	+56	47	235
126	09 05	56	48	10 01	57	48	10 58	56	47	11 54	56	47	12 50	56	47	234
127	08 46	57	47	09 43	56	47	10 39	56	46	11 35	57	46	12 32	56	46	233
128	08 28	56	46	09 24	57	46	10 21	56	46	11 17	57	45	12 14	56	45	232
129	08 10	56	45	09 06	57	45	10 03	57	45	11 00	56	44	11 56	57	44	231
130	07 52	+57	45	08 49	+56	44	09 45	+57	44	10 42	+57	44	11 39	+56	43	230
131	07 34	57	44	08 31	57	43	09 28	57	43	10 25	56	43	11 21	57	42	229
132	07 17	57	43	08 14	57	43	09 11	57	42	10 08	56	42	11 04	57	42	228
133	07 00	57	42	07 57	57	42	08 54	57	41	09 51	57	41	10 48	57	41	227
134	06 43	57	41	07 40	57	41	08 37	57	40	09 34	57	40	10 31	57	40	226
135	06 27	+57	40	07 24	+57	40	08 21	+57	40	09 18	+57	39	10 15	+57	39	225
136	06 10	58	39	07 08	57	39	08 05	57	39	09 02	58	38	10 00	57	38	224
137	05 54	58	38	06 52	57	38	07 49	58	38	08 47	57	38	09 44	57	37	223
138	05 39	57	38	06 36	58	37	07 34	57	37	08 31	58	37	09 29	57	36	222
139	05 24	57	37	06 21	58	36	07 19	57	36	08 16	58	36	09 14	58	36	221

S. Lat. {LHA greater than 180°....... Zn=180−Z; LHA less than 180°.......... Zn=180+Z}

LAT 65°

N. Lat. {LHA greater than 180°.... Zn=Z; LHA less than 180°.......... Zn=360−Z}

DECLINATION (15°-29°) SAME NAME AS LATITUDE

LHA	15° Hc	d	Z	16° Hc	d	Z	17° Hc	d	Z	18° Hc	d	Z	19° Hc	d	Z
	° ′	′	°	° ′	′	°	° ′	′	°	° ′	′	°	° ′	′	°
140	−4 29	+58	39	−3 31	+58	38	−2 33	+57	38	−1 36	+58	38	−0 38	+58	37
141	−4 45	58	38	−3 47	58	37	−2 49	58	37	−1 51	58	37	−0 53	58	37
142	−5 00	58	37	−4 02	58	36	−3 04	58	36	−2 06	58	36	−1 08	58	36
143	−5 15	58	36	−4 17	58	35	−3 19	58	35	−2 21	58	35	−1 23	58	35
144				−4 31	58	35	−3 33	58	34	−2 35	58	34	−1 37	58	34
145				−4 46	+59	34	−3 47	+58	33	−2 49	+58	33	−1 51	+58	33
146				−4 59	58	33	−4 01	58	32	−3 03	58	32	−2 05	59	32
147				−5 13	58	32	−4 15	59	31	−3 16	58	31	−2 18	59	31
148				−5 26	58	31	−4 28	59	31	−3 29	58	30	−2 31	59	30
149							−4 40	58	30	−3 42	59	29	−2 43	58	29
150							−4 53	+59	29	−3 54	+59	28	−2 55	+58	28
151							−5 05	59	28	−4 06	59	28	−3 07	59	27
152							−5 16	59	27	−4 17	58	27	−3 19	59	26
153										−4 29	59	26	−3 30	59	25
154										−4 39	59	25	−3 40	58	25
155										−4 50	+59	24	−3 51	+59	24
156										−5 00	59	23	−4 01	59	23
157										−5 10	60	22	−4 10	59	22
158													−4 20	60	21
159													−4 28	59	20
160													−4 37	+60	19
161													−4 45	60	18
162													−4 52	59	17
163													−5 00	60	16
164													−5 07	60	15
165															
166															
167															
168															
169															
170															
171															
172															
173															
174															
175															
176															
177															
178															
179															
180															

LHA	20° Hc	d	Z	21° Hc	d	Z	22° Hc	d	Z	23° Hc	d	Z	24° Hc	d	Z
	° ′	′	°	° ′	′	°	° ′	′	°	° ′	′	°	° ′	′	°
140	00 20	+58	37	01 18	+57	37	02 15	+58	37	03 13	+58	36	04 11	+58	36
141	00 05	57	36	01 02	58	36	02 00	58	36	02 58	58	35	03 56	58	35
142	−0 10	58	35	00 48	58	35	01 46	58	35	02 44	58	35	03 42	57	34
143	−0 25	58	34	00 33	58	34	01 31	58	34	02 29	58	34	03 27	58	33
144	−0 39	58	34	00 19	58	33	01 17	58	33	02 15	59	33	03 14	58	33
145	−0 53	+58	33	00 05	+59	32	01 04	+58	32	02 02	+58	32	03 00	+58	32
146	−1 06	58	32	−0 08	58	31	00 50	59	31	01 49	58	31	02 47	58	31
147	−1 19	58	31	−0 21	58	31	00 37	58	30	01 35	59	30	02 34	59	30
148	−1 32	58	30	−0 34	59	30	00 25	58	29	01 23	59	29	02 22	58	29
149	−1 45	59	29	−0 46	58	29	00 12	59	29	01 11	59	28	02 10	58	28
150	−1 57	+59	28	−0 58	+59	28	00 01	+58	28	00 59	+59	27	01 58	+58	27
151	−2 08	58	27	−1 10	59	27	−0 11	59	27	00 48	58	27	01 46	59	26
152	−2 20	59	26	−1 21	59	26	−0 22	59	26	00 37	58	26	01 35	59	25
153	−2 31	59	25	−1 32	59	25	−0 33	59	25	00 26	59	25	01 25	59	25
154	−2 42	59	24	−1 43	59	24	−0 44	59	24	00 15	59	24	01 14	59	24
155	−2 52	+59	23	−1 53	+59	23	−0 54	+59	23	00 05	+59	23	01 04	+59	23
156	−3 02	59	23	−2 03	60	22	−1 03	59	22	−0 04	59	22	00 55	59	22
157	−3 11	59	22	−2 12	59	21	−1 13	59	21	−0 14	60	21	00 46	59	21
158	−3 20	59	21	−2 21	59	20	−1 22	59	20	−0 23	60	20	00 37	59	20
159	−3 29	59	20	−2 30	60	20	−1 30	59	19	−0 31	59	19	00 28	59	19
160	−3 37	+59	19	−2 38	+59	19	−1 39	+60	19	−0 39	+59	18	00 20	+59	18
161	−3 45	59	18	−2 46	59	18	−1 47	60	18	−0 47	59	17	00 12	60	17
162	−3 53	60	17	−2 53	59	17	−1 54	59	17	−0 55	60	17	00 05	59	16
163	−4 00	59	16	−3 01	60	16	−2 01	59	16	−1 02	60	16	−0 02	60	15
164	−4 07	60	15	−3 07	59	15	−2 08	60	15	−1 08	59	15	−0 09	60	15
165	−4 13	+59	14	−3 14	+60	14	−2 14	+60	14	−1 14	+59	14	−0 15	+60	14
166	−4 19	59	13	−3 20	60	13	−2 20	60	13	−1 20	59	13	−0 21	60	13
167	−4 25	60	12	−3 25	60	12	−2 25	59	12	−1 26	60	12	−0 26	60	12
168	−4 30	60	11	−3 30	59	11	−2 31	60	11	−1 31	60	11	−0 31	60	11
169	−4 35	60	10	−3 35	60	10	−2 35	60	10	−1 35	59	10	−0 36	60	10
170	−4 39	+60	9	−3 39	+59	9	−2 40	+60	9	−1 40	+60	9	−0 40	+60	9
171	−4 43	60	8	−3 43	60	8	−2 43	59	8	−1 44	60	8	−0 44	60	8
172	−4 47	60	8	−3 47	60	7	−2 47	60	7	−1 47	60	7	−0 47	60	7
173	−4 50	60	7	−3 50	60	7	−2 50	60	6	−1 50	60	6	−0 50	60	6
174	−4 52	59	6	−3 53	60	6	−2 53	60	6	−1 53	60	6	−0 53	60	5
175	−4 55	+60	5	−3 55	+60	5	−2 55	+60	5	−1 55	+60	5	−0 55	+60	5
176	−4 57	60	4	−3 57	60	4	−2 57	60	4	−1 57	60	4	−0 57	60	4
177	−4 58	60	3	−3 58	60	3	−2 58	60	3	−1 58	60	3	−0 58	60	3
178	−4 59	60	2	−3 59	60	2	−2 59	60	2	−1 59	60	2	−0 59	60	2
179	−5 00	60	1	−4 00	60	1	−3 00	60	1	−2 00	60	1	−1 00	60	1
180	−5 00	+60	0	−4 00	+60	0	−3 00	+60	0	−2 00	+60	0	−1 00	+60	0

LHA	25° Hc	d	Z	26° Hc	d	Z	27° Hc	d	Z	28° Hc	d	Z	29° Hc	d	Z	LHA
	° ′	′	°	° ′	′	°	° ′	′	°	° ′	′	°	° ′	′	°	
140	05 09	+57	36	06 06	+58	36	07 04	+58	35	08 02	+57	35	08 59	+58	35	220
141	04 54	58	35	05 52	57	35	06 49	58	34	07 47	58	34	08 45	58	34	219
142	04 39	58	34	05 37	58	34	06 35	58	34	07 33	58	33	08 31	58	33	218
143	04 25	58	33	05 23	58	33	06 21	58	33	07 19	58	32	08 17	58	32	217
144	04 12	58	32	05 10	58	32	06 08	58	32	07 06	58	32	08 04	58	31	216
145	03 58	+59	31	04 57	+58	31	05 55	+58	31	06 53	+58	31	07 51	+58	30	215
146	03 45	59	31	04 44	58	30	05 42	58	30	06 40	58	30	07 38	59	30	214
147	03 33	58	30	04 31	58	29	05 29	59	29	06 28	58	29	07 26	58	29	213
148	03 20	59	29	04 19	58	29	05 17	59	28	06 16	58	28	07 14	59	28	212
149	03 08	59	28	04 07	58	28	05 05	59	27	06 04	58	27	07 02	59	27	211
150	02 56	+59	27	03 55	+59	27	04 54	+58	27	05 52	+59	26	06 51	+59	26	210
151	02 45	59	26	03 44	59	26	04 43	58	26	05 41	59	26	06 40	59	25	209
152	02 34	59	25	03 33	59	25	04 32	59	25	05 31	58	25	06 29	59	24	208
153	02 24	58	24	03 22	59	24	04 21	59	24	05 20	59	24	06 19	59	24	207
154	02 13	59	23	03 12	59	23	04 11	59	23	05 10	59	23	06 09	59	23	206
155	02 03	+59	23	03 02	+59	22	04 01	+60	22	05 01	+59	22	06 00	+59	22	205
156	01 54	59	22	02 53	59	21	03 52	59	21	04 51	59	21	05 50	59	21	204
157	01 45	59	21	02 44	59	21	03 43	59	20	04 42	59	20	05 41	60	20	203
158	01 36	59	20	02 35	59	20	03 34	60	20	04 34	59	19	05 33	59	19	202
159	01 27	60	19	02 27	59	19	03 26	59	19	04 25	60	19	05 25	59	18	201
160	01 19	+60	18	02 19	+59	18	03 18	+60	18	04 18	+59	18	05 17	+59	18	200
161	01 12	59	17	02 11	60	17	03 11	59	17	04 10	60	17	05 10	59	17	199
162	01 04	60	16	02 04	59	16	03 03	60	16	04 03	59	16	05 02	60	16	198
163	00 58	59	15	01 57	60	15	02 57	59	15	03 56	60	15	04 56	59	15	197
164	00 51	60	14	01 51	59	14	02 50	60	14	03 50	59	14	04 49	60	14	196
165	00 45	+60	14	01 45	+59	13	02 44	+60	13	03 44	+59	13	04 43	+60	13	195
166	00 39	60	13	01 39	59	13	02 38	60	12	03 38	60	12	04 38	60	12	194
167	00 34	59	12	01 33	60	12	02 33	60	12	03 33	60	11	04 33	59	11	193
168	00 29	60	11	01 29	59	11	02 28	60	11	03 28	60	11	04 28	60	10	192
169	00 24	60	10	01 24	60	10	02 24	60	10	03 24	59	10	04 23	60	10	191
170	00 20	+60	9	01 20	+60	9	02 20	+60	9	03 20	+59	9	04 19	+60	9	190
171	00 16	60	8	01 16	60	8	02 16	60	8	03 16	60	8	04 16	60	8	189
172	00 13	60	7	01 13	60	7	02 13	60	7	03 13	59	7	04 12	60	7	188
173	00 10	60	6	01 10	60	6	02 10	60	6	03 10	59	6	04 09	60	6	187
174	00 07	60	5	01 07	60	5	02 07	60	5	03 07	60	5	04 07	60	5	186
175	00 05	+60	5	01 05	+60	4	02 05	+60	4	03 05	+60	4	04 05	+60	4	185
176	00 03	60	4	01 03	60	4	02 03	60	4	03 03	60	4	04 03	60	4	184
177	00 02	60	3	01 02	60	3	02 02	60	3	03 02	60	3	04 02	60	3	183
178	00 01	60	2	01 01	60	2	02 01	60	2	03 01	60	2	04 01	60	2	182
179	00 00	60	1	01 00	60	1	02 00	60	1	03 00	60	1	04 00	60	1	181
180	00 00	+60	0	01 00	+60	0	02 00	+60	0	03 00	+60	0	04 00	+60	0	180

70	−5 27 −55 114	290

15°	16°	17°	18°	19°	20°	21°	22°	23°	24°	25°	26°	27°	28°	29°

S. Lat. {LHA greater than 180°....... Zn=180−Z; LHA less than 180°........... Zn=180+Z}

DECLINATION (15°-29°) CONTRARY NAME TO LATITUDE

N. Lat. {LHA greater than 180°....... Zn=Z; LHA less than 180°........... Zn=360−Z}

DECLINATION (15°-29°) CONTRARY NAME TO LATITUDE

	15°			16°			17°			18°			19°			20°			21°			22°		
LHA	Hc	d	Z	Hc	d	Z	Hc	d	Z	Hc	d	Z	Hc	d	Z	Hc	d	Z	Hc	d	Z	Hc	d	Z
	° ′	′	°	° ′	′	°	° ′	′	°	° ′	′	°	° ′	′	°	° ′	′	°	° ′	′	°	° ′	′	°
69	−5 04	55	115	291																				
68	−4 41	55	116	−5 36	55	116	292																	
67	−4 18	56	117	−5 14	55	117	293																	
66	−3 56	55	118	−4 51	55	118	294																	
65	−3 33	−56	119	−4 29	−55	119	−5 24	−56	119	295														
64	−3 11	56	120	−4 07	55	120	−5 02	56	120	296														
63	−2 49	56	120	−3 45	55	121	−4 40	56	121	−5 36	56	122	297											
62	−2 28	55	121	−3 23	56	122	−4 19	56	122	−5 15	55	122	298											
61	−2 06	56	122	−3 02	56	123	−3 58	55	123	−4 53	56	123	299											
60	−1 45	−56	123	−2 41	−55	124	−3 36	−56	124	−4 32	−56	124	−5 28	−56	125	300								
59	−1 24	56	124	−2 20	55	124	−3 15	56	125	−4 11	56	125	−5 07	56	125	301								
58	−1 03	56	125	−1 59	56	125	−2 55	56	126	−3 51	56	126	−4 47	56	126	302								
57	−0 42	56	126	−1 38	56	126	−2 34	56	127	−3 30	56	127	−4 26	57	127	−5 23	56	128	303					
56	−0 22	56	127	−1 18	56	127	−2 14	56	127	−3 10	56	128	−4 06	57	128	−5 03	56	128	304					
55	−0 01	−57	128	−0 58	−56	128	−1 54	−56	128	−2 50	−57	129	−3 47	−56	129	−4 43	−56	129	305					
54	00 18	56	129	−0 38	56	129	−1 34	57	129	−2 31	56	130	−3 27	56	130	−4 23	57	130	−5 20	56	131	306		
53	00 38	56	130	−0 18	57	130	−1 15	56	130	−2 11	57	131	−3 08	56	131	−4 04	57	131	−5 01	56	131	307		
52	00 58	57	130	00 01	57	131	−0 56	56	131	−1 52	57	131	−2 49	56	132	−3 45	57	132	−4 42	56	132	308		
51	01 17	57	131	00 20	57	132	−0 37	56	132	−1 33	57	132	−2 30	57	133	−3 27	56	133	−4 23	57	133	−5 20	57	134
50	01 36	−57	132	00 39	−57	133	−0 18	−57	133	−1 15	−56	133	−2 11	−57	134	−3 08	−57	134	−4 05	−57	134	−5 02	−56	134
49	01 54	57	133	00 57	56	133	00 01	57	134	−0 56	57	134	−1 53	57	134	−2 50	57	135	−3 47	57	135	−4 44	57	135
48	02 13	57	134	01 16	57	134	00 19	57	135	−0 38	57	135	−1 35	57	135	−2 32	57	136	−3 29	57	136	−4 26	57	136
47	02 31	57	135	01 34	57	135	00 37	57	136	−0 20	58	136	−1 18	57	136	−2 15	57	137	−3 12	57	137	−4 09	57	137
46	02 49	58	136	01 51	57	136	00 54	57	137	−0 03	57	137	−1 00	57	137	−1 57	57	137	−2 54	58	138	−3 52	57	138
45	03 06	−57	137	02 09	−57	137	01 12	−58	137	00 14	−57	138	−0 43	−57	138	−1 40	−58	138	−2 38	−57	139	−3 35	−57	139
44	03 23	57	138	02 26	57	138	01 29	58	138	00 31	57	139	−0 26	58	139	−1 24	57	139	−2 21	57	140	−3 18	58	140
43	03 40	57	139	02 43	58	139	01 45	57	139	00 48	58	140	−0 10	57	140	−1 07	58	140	−2 05	57	140	−3 02	57	141
42	03 57	58	140	02 59	57	140	02 02	58	140	01 04	58	140	00 06	57	141	−0 51	58	141	−1 49	57	141	−2 46	58	142
41	04 13	58	141	03 15	57	141	02 18	58	141	01 20	58	141	00 22	57	142	−0 35	58	142	−1 33	58	142	−2 31	57	142
40	04 29	−58	141	03 31	−58	142	02 33	−57	142	01 36	−58	142	00 38	−58	143	−0 20	−58	143	−1 18	−57	143	−2 15	−58	143
39	04 45	58	142	03 47	58	143	02 49	58	143	01 51	58	143	00 53	58	143	−0 05	57	144	−1 02	58	144	−2 00	58	144
38	05 00	58	143	04 02	58	144	03 04	58	144	02 06	58	144	01 08	58	144	00 10	58	145	−0 48	58	145	−1 46	58	145
37	05 15	58	144	04 17	58	145	03 19	58	145	02 21	58	145	01 23	58	145	00 25	58	146	−0 33	58	146	−1 31	58	146
36	05 29	58	145	04 31	58	145	03 33	58	146	02 35	58	146	01 37	58	146	00 39	58	146	−0 19	58	147	−1 17	58	147
35	05 44	−58	146	04 46	−59	146	03 47	−58	147	02 49	−58	147	01 51	−58	147	00 53	−58	147	−0 05	−59	148	−1 04	−58	148
34	05 58	59	147	04 59	58	147	04 01	58	148	03 03	58	148	02 05	59	148	01 06	58	148	00 08	58	149	−0 50	59	149
33	06 11	58	148	05 13	58	148	04 15	59	149	03 16	58	149	02 18	59	149	01 19	58	149	00 21	58	149	−0 37	58	150
32	06 25	59	149	05 26	58	149	04 28	59	149	03 29	58	150	02 31	59	150	01 32	58	150	00 34	59	150	−0 25	58	151
31	06 37	58	150	05 39	59	150	04 40	58	150	03 42	59	151	02 43	58	151	01 45	59	151	00 46	58	151	−0 12	59	151
30	06 50	−59	151	05 51	−58	151	04 53	−59	151	03 54	−59	152	02 55	−58	152	01 57	−59	152	00 58	−59	152	−0 01	−58	152
29	07 02	59	152	06 03	58	152	05 05	59	152	04 06	59	152	03 07	59	153	02 08	58	153	01 10	59	153	00 11	59	153
28	07 14	59	153	06 15	59	153	05 16	59	153	04 17	58	153	03 19	59	154	02 20	59	154	01 21	59	154	00 22	59	154
27	07 25	59	154	06 26	58	154	05 28	59	154	04 29	59	154	03 30	59	155	02 31	59	155	01 32	59	155	00 33	59	155
26	07 36	59	155	06 37	59	155	05 38	59	155	04 39	59	155	03 40	58	155	02 42	59	156	01 43	59	156	00 44	59	156
25	07 47	−59	156	06 48	−59	156	05 49	−59	156	04 50	−59	156	03 51	−59	156	02 52	−59	157	01 53	−59	157	00 54	−59	157
24	07 57	59	157	06 58	59	157	05 59	59	157	05 00	59	157	04 01	59	157	03 02	59	157	02 03	60	158	01 03	59	158
23	08 07	59	158	07 08	59	158	06 09	59	158	05 10	60	158	04 10	59	158	03 11	59	158	02 12	59	159	01 13	59	159
22	08 17	60	159	07 17	59	159	06 18	59	159	05 19	59	159	04 20	60	159	03 20	59	159	02 21	59	160	01 22	59	160
21	08 26	60	160	07 26	59	160	06 27	59	160	05 28	60	160	04 28	59	160	03 29	59	160	02 30	60	160	01 30	59	161
20	08 34	−59	161	07 35	−59	161	06 36	−60	161	05 36	−59	161	04 37	−60	161	03 37	−59	161	02 38	−59	161	01 39	−60	161
19	08 43	60	161	07 43	59	162	06 44	60	162	05 44	59	162	04 45	60	162	03 45	59	162	02 46	59	162	01 47	60	162
18	08 50	59	162	07 51	60	163	06 51	59	163	05 52	60	163	04 52	59	163	03 53	60	163	02 53	59	163	01 54	59	163
17	08 58	60	163	07 58	59	164	06 59	60	164	05 59	59	164	05 00	60	164	04 00	59	164	03 01	60	164	02 01	59	164
16	09 05	60	164	08 05	59	165	07 06	60	165	06 06	59	165	05 07	60	165	04 07	60	165	03 07	59	165	02 08	60	165
15	09 12	−60	165	08 12	−60	165	07 12	−59	166	06 13	−60	166	05 13	−60	166	04 13	−59	166	03 14	−60	166	02 14	−60	166
14	09 18	60	166	08 18	60	166	07 18	60	167	06 18	59	167	05 19	60	167	04 19	59	167	03 20	60	167	02 20	60	167
13	09 24	60	167	08 24	60	167	07 24	60	168	06 24	59	168	05 25	60	168	04 25	60	168	03 25	60	168	02 25	59	168
12	09 29	60	168	08 29	60	168	07 29	59	168	06 30	60	169	05 30	60	169	04 30	60	169	03 30	59	169	02 31	60	169
11	09 34	60	169	08 34	60	169	07 34	60	169	06 34	59	170	05 35	60	170	04 35	60	170	03 35	60	170	02 35	60	170
10	09 38	−59	170	08 39	−60	170	07 39	−60	170	06 39	−60	170	05 39	−60	171	04 39	−60	171	03 39	−59	171	02 40	−60	171
9	09 43	60	171	08 43	60	171	07 43	60	171	06 43	60	171	05 43	60	172	04 43	60	172	03 43	60	172	02 43	59	172
8	09 46	60	172	08 46	60	172	07 46	59	172	06 47	60	172	05 47	60	172	04 47	60	172	03 47	60	173	02 47	60	173
7	09 49	59	173	08 50	60	173	07 50	60	173	06 50	60	173	05 50	60	173	04 50	60	173	03 50	60	173	02 50	60	174
6	09 52	60	174	08 52	60	174	07 52	60	174	06 52	60	174	05 52	60	174	04 52	59	174	03 53	60	174	02 53	60	174
5	09 55	−60	175	08 55	−60	175	07 55	−60	175	06 55	−60	175	05 55	−60	175	04 55	−60	175	03 55	−60	175	02 55	−60	175
4	09 57	60	176	08 57	60	176	07 57	60	176	06 57	60	176	05 57	60	176	04 57	60	176	03 57	60	176	02 57	60	176
3	09 58	60	177	08 58	60	177	07 58	60	177	06 58	60	177	05 58	60	177	04 58	60	177	03 58	60	177	02 58	60	177
2	09 59	60	178	08 59	60	178	07 59	60	178	06 59	60	178	05 59	60	178	04 59	60	178	03 59	60	178	02 59	60	178
1	10 00	60	179	09 00	60	179	08 00	60	179	07 00	60	179	06 00	60	179	05 00	60	179	04 00	60	179	03 00	60	179
0	10 00	−60	180	09 00	−60	180	08 00	−60	180	07 00	−60	180	06 00	−60	180	05 00	−60	180	04 00	−60	180	03 00	−60	180
	15°			16°			17°			18°			19°			20°			21°			22°		

	23°			24°			25°			26°			27°			28°			29°			
LHA	Hc	d	Z	Hc	d	Z	Hc	d	Z	Hc	d	Z	Hc	d	Z	Hc	d	Z	Hc	d	Z	LHA
	° ′	′	°	° ′	′	°	° ′	′	°	° ′	′	°	° ′	′	°	° ′	′	°	° ′	′	°	
51	309																					
50	310																					
49	311																					
48	−5 23	57	137	312																		
47	−5 06	57	137	313																		
46	−4 49	57	138	314																		
45	−4 32	−57	139	−5 29	−58	139	315															
44	−4 16	57	140	−5 13	57	140	316															
43	−3 59	58	141	−4 57	57	141	317															
42	−3 44	57	142	−4 41	58	142	318															
41	−3 28	58	143	−4 26	58	143	−5 24	57	143	319												
40	−3 13	−58	144	−4 11	−58	144	−5 09	−57	144	320												
39	−2 58	58	145	−3 56	58	145	−4 54	58	145	321												
38	−2 44	58	145	−3 42	57	146	−4 39	58	146	322												
37	−2 29	58	146	−3 27	58	147	−4 25	58	147	−5 23	58	147	323									
36	−2 15	59	147	−3 14	58	147	−4 12	58	148	−5 10	58	148	324									
35	−2 02	−58	148	−3 00	−58	148	−3 58	−59	149	−4 57	−58	149	325									
34	−1 49	58	149	−2 47	58	149	−3 45	59	149	−4 44	58	150	326									
33	−1 35	59	150	−2 34	59	150	−3 33	58	150	−4 31	58	151	327									
32	−1 23	59	151	−2 22	58	151	−3 20	59	151	−4 19	58	151	−5 17	59	152	328						
31	−1 11	59	152	−2 10	58	152	−3 08	59	152	−4 07	58	152	−5 05	59	153	329						
30	−0 59	−59	153	−1 58	−58	153	−2 56	−59	153	−3 55	−59	153	−4 54	−58	153	330						
29	−0 48	58	153	−1 46	59	154	−2 45	59	154	−3 44	59	154	−4 43	58	154	331						
28	−0 37	58	154	−1 35	59	155	−2 34	59	155	−3 33	59	155	−4 32	59	155	332						
27	−0 26	59	155	−1 25	59	155	−2 24	58	156	−3 22	59	156	−4 21	59	156	333						
26	−0 15	59	156	−1 14	59	156	−2 13	59	157	−3 12	59	157	−4 11	59	157	−5 10	59	157	334			
25	−0 05	−59	157	−1 04	−59	157	−2 03	−59	157	−3 02	−59	158	−4 01	−60	158	−5 01	−59	158	335			
24	00 04	59	158	−0 55	59	158	−1 54	59	158	−2 53	59	159	−3 52	59	159	−4 51	59	159	336			
23	00 14	60	159	−0 46	59	159	−1 45	59	159	−2 44	59	159	−3 43	59	160	−4 42	59	160	337			
22	00 23	60	160	−0 37	59	160	−1 36	59	160	−2 35	59	160	−3 34	60	160	−4 34	59	161	338			
21	00 31	59	161	−0 28	59	161	−1 27	60	161	−2 27	59	161	−3 26	59	161	−4 25	60	161	339			
20	00 39	−59	162	−0 20	−59	162	−1 19	−60	162	−2 19	−59	162	−3 18	−60	162	−4 18	−59	162	340			
19	00 47	59	163	−0 12	60	163	−1 12	59	163	−2 11	60	163	−3 11	59	163	−4 10	60	163	−5 10	59	163	341
18	00 55	60	163	−0 05	59	164	−1 04	60	164	−2 04	59	164	−3 03	60	164	−4 03	59	164	−5 02	60	164	342
17	01 02	60	164	00 02	60	165	−0 58	59	165	−1 57	60	165	−2 57	59	165	−3 56	60	165	−4 56	59	165	343
16	01 08	59	165	00 09	60	165	−0 51	60	166	−1 51	59	166	−2 50	60	166	−3 50	59	166	−4 49	60	166	344
15	01 14	−59	166	00 15	−60	166	−0 45	−60	166	−1 45	−59	167	−2 44	−60	167	−3 44	−59	167	−4 43	−60	167	345
14	01 20	59	167	00 21	60	167	−0 39	60	167	−1 39	59	167	−2 38	60	168	−3 38	60	168	−4 38	60	168	346
13	01 26	60	168	00 26	60	168	−0 34	59	168	−1 33	60	168	−2 33	60	168	−3 33	60	169	−4 33	59	169	347
12	01 31	60	169	00 31	60	169	−0 29	60	169	−1 29	59	169	−2 28	60	169	−3 28	60	169	−4 28	60	170	348
11	01 35	59	170	00 36	60	170	−0 24	60	170	−1 24	60	170	−2 24	60	170	−3 24	59	170	−4 23	60	170	349
10	01 40	−60	171	00 40	−60	171	−0 20	−60	171	−1 20	−60	171	−2 20	−60	171	−3 20	−59	171	−4 19	−60	171	350
9	01 44	60	172	00 44	60	172	−0 16	60	172	−1 16	60	172	−2 16	60	172	−3 16	60	172	−4 16	60	172	351
8	01 47	60	173	00 47	60	173	−0 13	60	173	−1 13	60	173	−2 13	60	173	−3 13	59	173	−4 12	60	173	352
7	01 50	60	174	00 50	60	174	−0 10	60	174	−1 10	60	174	−2 10	60	174	−3 10	59	174	−4 09	60	174	353
6	01 53	60	174	00 53	60	175	−0 07	60	175	−1 07	60	175	−2 07	60	175	−3 07	60	175	−4 07	60	175	354
5	01 55	−60	175	00 55	−60	175	−0 05	−60	175	−1 05	−60	176	−2 05	−60	176	−3 05	−60	176	−4 05	−60	176	355
4	01 57	60	176	00 57	60	176	−0 03	60	176	−1 03	60	176	−2 03	60	176	−3 03	60	176	−4 03	60	176	356
3	01 58	60	177	00 58	60	177	−0 02	60	177	−1 02	60	177	−2 02	60	177	−3 02	60	177	−4 02	60	177	357
2	01 59	60	178	00 59	60	178	−0 01	60	178	−1 01	60	178	−2 01	60	178	−3 01	60	178	−4 01	60	178	358
1	02 00	60	179	01 00	60	179	00 00	60	179	−1 00	60	179	−2 00	60	179	−3 00	60	179	−4 00	60	179	359
0	02 00	−60	180	01 00	−60	180	00 00	−60	180	−1 00	−60	180	−2 00	−60	180	−3 00	−60	180	−4 00	−60	180	360
	23°			24°			25°			26°			27°			28°			29°			

S. Lat. {LHA greater than 180°....... Zn=180−Z; LHA less than 180°........... Zn=180+Z}

DECLINATION (15°-29°) CONTRARY NAME TO LATITUDE

N. Lat. {LHA greater than 180°........ Zn=Z; LHA less than 180°........... Zn=360−Z}

DECLINATION (0°-14°) SAME NAME AS LATITUDE

LHA	0° Hc	0° d	0° Z	1° Hc	1° d	1° Z	2° Hc	2° d	2° Z	3° Hc	3° d	3° Z	4° Hc	4° d	4° Z	5° Hc	5° d	5° Z	6° Hc	6° d	6° Z	7° Hc	7° d	7° Z
	° ′	′	°	° ′	′	°	° ′	′	°	° ′	′	°	° ′	′	°	° ′	′	°	° ′	′	°	° ′	′	°
0	24 00	+60	180	25 00	+60	180	26 00	+60	180	27 00	+60	180	28 00	+60	180	29 00	+60	180	30 00	+60	180	31 00	+60	180
1	24 00	60	179	25 00	60	179	26 00	60	179	27 00	60	179	28 00	60	179	29 00	60	179	30 00	60	179	31 00	60	179
2	23 59	60	178	24 59	60	178	25 59	60	178	26 59	60	178	27 59	60	178	28 59	60	178	29 59	60	178	30 59	60	178
3	23 58	60	177	24 58	60	177	25 58	60	177	26 58	60	177	27 58	60	177	28 58	60	177	29 58	60	177	30 58	60	177
4	23 56	60	176	24 56	60	176	25 56	60	176	26 56	60	176	27 56	60	176	28 56	60	175	29 56	60	175	30 56	60	175
5	23 54	+60	175	24 54	+60	175	25 54	+60	174	26 54	+60	174	27 54	+60	174	28 54	+60	174	29 54	+60	174	30 54	+60	174
6	23 52	60	173	24 52	60	173	25 52	59	173	26 51	60	173	27 51	60	173	28 51	60	173	29 51	60	173	30 51	60	173
7	23 49	60	172	24 49	59	172	25 48	60	172	26 48	60	172	27 48	60	172	28 48	60	172	29 48	60	172	30 48	60	172
8	23 45	60	171	24 45	60	171	25 45	60	171	26 45	60	171	27 45	60	171	28 45	59	171	29 44	60	171	30 44	60	171
9	23 41	60	170	24 41	60	170	25 41	60	170	26 41	60	170	27 41	59	170	28 40	60	170	29 40	60	170	30 40	60	170
10	23 37	+60	169	24 37	+59	169	25 36	+60	169	26 36	+60	169	27 36	+60	169	28 36	+60	169	29 36	+60	169	30 36	+59	169
11	23 32	60	168	24 32	60	168	25 32	59	168	26 31	60	168	27 31	60	168	28 31	60	168	29 31	59	167	30 30	60	167
12	23 27	59	167	24 26	60	167	25 26	60	167	26 26	60	167	27 26	59	167	28 25	60	166	29 25	60	166	30 25	59	166
13	23 21	60	166	24 21	59	166	25 20	60	166	26 20	60	166	27 20	59	165	28 19	60	165	29 19	60	165	30 19	59	165
14	23 15	59	165	24 14	60	165	25 14	60	165	26 14	59	164	27 13	60	164	28 13	60	164	29 13	59	164	30 12	60	164
15	23 08	+60	164	24 08	+59	164	25 07	+60	163	26 07	+59	163	27 06	+60	163	28 06	+60	163	29 06	+59	163	30 05	+60	163
16	23 01	60	163	24 01	59	162	25 00	60	162	26 00	59	162	26 59	60	162	27 59	59	162	28 58	60	162	29 58	59	162
17	22 53	60	162	23 53	59	161	24 52	60	161	25 52	59	161	26 51	60	161	27 51	59	161	28 50	60	161	29 50	59	161
18	22 45	60	160	23 45	59	160	24 44	60	160	25 44	59	160	26 43	60	160	27 43	59	160	28 42	59	160	29 41	60	159
19	22 37	59	159	23 36	60	159	24 36	59	159	25 35	60	159	26 35	59	159	27 34	59	159	28 33	59	158	29 32	60	158
20	22 28	+60	158	23 28	+59	158	24 27	+59	158	25 26	+59	158	26 25	+60	158	27 25	+59	157	28 24	+59	157	29 23	+59	157
21	22 19	59	157	23 18	60	157	24 18	59	157	25 17	59	157	26 16	59	157	27 15	59	156	28 14	59	156	29 13	60	156
22	22 09	60	156	23 09	59	156	24 08	59	156	25 07	59	156	26 06	59	155	27 05	59	155	28 04	59	155	29 03	59	155
23	21 59	59	155	22 58	59	155	23 57	60	155	24 57	59	155	25 56	59	154	26 55	59	154	27 54	59	154	28 53	59	154
24	21 49	59	154	22 48	59	154	23 47	59	154	24 46	59	153	25 45	59	153	26 44	59	153	27 43	59	153	28 42	59	153
25	21 38	+59	153	22 37	+59	153	23 36	+59	153	24 35	+59	152	25 34	+59	152	26 33	+58	152	27 31	+59	152	28 30	+59	152
26	21 27	58	152	22 25	59	152	23 24	59	152	24 23	59	151	25 22	59	151	26 21	59	151	27 20	58	151	28 18	59	150
27	21 15	59	151	22 14	59	151	23 13	58	150	24 11	59	150	25 10	59	150	26 09	58	150	27 07	59	150	28 06	59	149
28	21 03	59	150	22 02	58	150	23 00	59	149	23 59	59	149	24 58	58	149	25 56	59	149	26 55	58	148	27 53	59	148
29	20 50	59	149	21 49	59	149	22 48	58	148	23 46	59	148	24 45	58	148	25 43	59	148	26 42	58	147	27 40	59	147
30	20 38	+58	148	21 36	+59	148	22 35	+58	147	23 33	+59	147	24 32	+58	147	25 30	+59	147	26 29	+58	146	27 27	+58	146
31	20 24	59	147	21 23	58	146	22 21	59	146	23 20	58	146	24 18	58	146	25 16	59	145	26 15	58	145	27 13	58	145
32	20 11	58	146	21 09	58	145	22 07	59	145	23 06	58	145	24 04	58	145	25 02	59	144	26 01	58	144	26 59	58	144
33	19 57	58	145	20 55	58	144	21 53	59	144	22 52	58	144	23 50	58	144	24 48	58	143	25 46	58	143	26 44	58	143
34	19 42	59	144	20 41	58	143	21 39	58	143	22 37	58	143	23 35	58	143	24 33	58	142	25 31	58	142	26 29	58	142
35	19 28	+58	143	20 26	+58	142	21 24	+58	142	22 22	+58	142	23 20	+58	142	24 18	+58	141	25 16	+58	141	26 14	+58	141
36	19 13	58	142	20 11	58	141	21 09	58	141	22 07	58	141	23 05	58	140	24 03	58	140	25 01	57	140	25 58	58	140
37	18 57	58	141	19 55	58	140	20 53	58	140	21 51	58	140	22 49	58	139	23 47	58	139	24 45	57	139	25 42	58	139
38	18 42	58	140	19 40	57	139	20 37	58	139	21 35	58	139	22 33	58	138	23 31	57	138	24 28	58	138	25 26	58	137
39	18 26	57	138	19 23	58	138	20 21	58	138	21 19	58	138	22 17	57	137	23 14	58	137	24 12	57	137	25 09	58	136
40	18 09	+58	137	19 07	+58	137	20 05	+57	137	21 02	+58	137	22 00	+57	136	22 57	+58	136	23 55	+57	136	24 52	+58	135
41	17 53	57	136	18 50	58	136	19 48	57	136	20 45	58	136	21 43	57	135	22 40	58	135	23 38	57	135	24 35	57	134
42	17 36	57	135	18 33	58	135	19 31	57	135	20 28	57	135	21 25	58	134	22 23	57	134	23 20	57	134	24 17	58	133
43	17 18	58	134	18 16	57	134	19 13	57	134	20 10	58	134	21 08	57	133	22 05	57	133	23 02	57	133	23 59	58	132
44	17 01	57	133	17 58	57	133	18 55	58	133	19 53	57	133	20 50	57	132	21 47	57	132	22 44	57	132	23 41	57	131
45	16 43	+57	132	17 40	+57	132	18 37	+57	132	19 34	+58	132	20 32	+57	131	21 29	+57	131	22 26	+57	131	23 23	+57	130
46	16 25	57	131	17 22	57	131	18 19	57	131	19 16	57	131	20 13	57	130	21 10	57	130	22 07	57	129	23 04	57	129
47	16 06	57	130	17 03	57	130	18 00	57	130	18 57	57	129	19 54	57	129	20 51	57	129	21 48	57	128	22 45	57	128
48	15 48	57	129	16 45	56	129	17 41	57	129	18 38	57	128	19 35	57	128	20 32	57	128	21 29	57	127	22 26	56	127
49	15 29	57	129	16 26	56	128	17 22	57	128	18 19	57	127	19 16	57	127	20 13	56	127	21 09	57	126	22 06	57	126
50	15 09	+57	128	16 06	+57	127	17 03	+57	127	18 00	+56	127	18 56	+57	126	19 53	+57	126	20 50	+56	125	21 46	+57	125
51	14 50	57	127	15 47	56	126	16 43	57	126	17 40	56	126	18 36	57	125	19 33	56	125	20 29	57	124	21 26	56	124
52	14 30	57	126	15 27	56	125	16 23	57	125	17 20	56	125	18 16	57	124	19 13	56	124	20 09	57	123	21 06	56	123
53	14 10	57	125	15 07	56	124	16 03	57	124	17 00	56	124	17 56	56	123	18 52	57	123	19 49	56	122	20 45	56	122
54	13 50	56	124	14 46	57	123	15 43	56	123	16 39	56	123	17 35	57	122	18 32	56	122	19 28	56	121	20 24	56	121
55	13 30	+56	123	14 26	+56	122	15 22	+56	122	16 18	+57	122	17 15	+56	121	18 11	+56	121	19 07	+56	120	20 03	+56	120
56	13 09	56	122	14 05	56	121	15 01	57	121	15 58	56	121	16 54	56	120	17 50	56	120	18 46	56	120	19 42	56	119
57	12 48	55	121	13 44	56	120	14 40	56	120	15 36	57	120	16 33	56	119	17 29	56	119	18 25	56	119	19 21	55	118
58	12 27	56	120	13 23	56	119	14 19	56	119	15 15	56	119	16 11	56	118	17 07	56	118	18 03	56	118	18 59	56	117
59	12 06	56	119	13 02	56	118	13 58	56	118	14 54	56	118	15 50	55	117	16 45	56	117	17 41	56	117	18 37	56	116
60	11 44	+56	118	12 40	+56	117	13 36	+56	117	14 32	+56	117	15 28	+56	116	16 24	+55	116	17 19	+56	116	18 15	+56	115
61	11 22	56	117	12 18	56	117	13 14	56	116	14 10	56	116	15 06	56	115	16 02	55	115	16 57	56	115	17 53	56	114
62	11 01	55	116	11 56	56	116	12 52	56	115	13 48	56	115	14 44	55	114	15 39	56	114	16 35	56	114	17 31	55	113
63	10 39	55	115	11 34	56	115	12 30	56	114	13 26	55	114	14 21	56	113	15 17	56	113	16 13	55	113	17 08	56	112
64	10 16	56	114	11 12	56	114	12 08	55	113	13 03	56	113	13 59	55	113	14 54	56	112	15 50	55	112	16 45	56	111
65	09 54	+56	113	10 50	+55	113	11 45	+56	112	12 41	+55	112	13 36	+56	112	14 32	+55	111	15 27	+56	111	16 23	+55	110
66	09 31	56	112	10 27	56	112	11 23	55	111	12 18	55	111	13 13	56	111	14 09	55	110	15 04	56	110	16 00	55	109
67	09 09	55	111	10 04	56	111	11 00	55	110	11 55	56	110	12 51	55	110	13 46	55	109	14 41	56	109	15 37	55	108
68	08 46	55	110	09 41	56	110	10 37	55	110	11 32	56	109	12 28	55	109	13 23	55	108	14 18	55	108	15 13	56	108
69	08 23	55	109	09 18	56	109	10 14	55	109	11 09	55	108	12 04	56	108	13 00	55	107	13 55	55	107	14 50	55	107

8° Hc	8° d	8° Z	9° Hc	9° d	9° Z	10° Hc	10° d	10° Z	11° Hc	11° d	11° Z	12° Hc	12° d	12° Z	13° Hc	13° d	13° Z	14° Hc	14° d	14° Z	LHA
° ′	′	°	° ′	′	°	° ′	′	°	° ′	′	°	° ′	′	°	° ′	′	°	° ′	′	°	
32 00	+60	180	33 00	+60	180	34 00	+60	180	35 00	+60	180	36 00	+60	180	37 00	+60	180	38 00	+60	180	360
32 00	60	179	33 00	60	179	34 00	60	179	35 00	60	179	36 00	60	179	37 00	60	179	38 00	60	179	359
31 59	60	178	32 59	60	178	33 59	60	178	34 59	60	178	35 59	60	178	36 59	60	178	37 59	60	178	358
31 58	60	177	32 58	60	177	33 58	60	176	34 58	60	176	35 58	60	176	36 58	60	176	37 58	60	176	357
31 56	60	175	32 56	60	175	33 56	60	175	34 56	60	175	35 56	60	175	36 56	60	175	37 56	60	175	356
31 54	+60	174	32 54	+60	174	33 54	+60	174	34 54	+60	174	35 54	+60	174	36 54	+60	174	37 54	+59	174	355
31 51	60	173	32 51	60	173	33 51	60	173	34 51	60	173	35 51	60	173	36 51	60	173	37 51	60	173	354
31 48	60	172	32 48	60	172	33 48	60	172	34 48	59	172	35 47	60	172	36 47	60	172	37 47	60	171	353
31 44	60	171	32 44	60	171	33 44	60	171	34 44	60	170	35 44	59	170	36 43	60	170	37 43	60	170	352
31 40	60	170	32 40	60	169	33 40	59	169	34 39	60	169	35 39	60	169	36 39	60	169	37 39	60	169	351
31 35	+60	168	32 35	+60	168	33 35	+60	168	34 35	+59	168	35 34	+60	168	36 34	+60	168	37 34	+60	168	350
31 30	60	167	32 30	60	167	33 30	59	167	34 29	60	167	35 29	60	167	36 29	60	167	37 29	59	167	349
31 24	60	166	32 24	60	166	33 24	60	166	34 24	59	166	35 23	60	166	36 23	60	165	37 23	59	165	348
31 18	60	165	32 18	60	165	33 18	59	165	34 17	60	165	35 17	60	164	36 17	59	164	37 16	60	164	347
31 12	59	164	32 11	60	164	33 11	60	164	34 11	59	163	35 10	60	163	36 10	59	163	37 09	60	163	346
31 05	+59	163	32 04	+60	162	33 04	+59	162	34 03	+60	162	35 03	+59	162	36 02	+60	162	37 02	+59	162	345
30 57	60	161	31 57	59	161	32 56	60	161	33 56	59	161	34 55	59	161	35 54	60	161	36 54	59	161	344
30 49	60	160	31 49	59	160	32 48	59	160	33 47	60	160	34 47	59	160	35 46	59	159	36 45	60	159	343
30 41	59	159	31 40	59	159	32 39	60	159	33 39	59	159	34 38	59	158	35 37	60	158	36 37	59	158	342
30 32	59	158	31 31	59	158	32 30	60	158	33 30	59	158	34 29	59	157	35 28	59	157	36 27	59	157	341
30 22	+60	157	31 22	+59	157	32 21	+59	157	33 20	+59	156	34 19	+59	156	35 18	+59	156	36 17	+59	156	340
30 13	59	156	31 12	59	156	32 11	59	155	33 10	59	155	34 09	59	155	35 08	59	155	36 07	59	155	339
30 02	59	155	31 01	59	154	32 00	59	154	32 59	59	154	33 58	59	154	34 57	59	154	35 56	59	153	338
29 52	59	154	30 51	59	153	31 50	59	153	32 49	58	153	33 47	59	153	34 46	59	152	35 45	59	152	337
29 41	59	152	30 40	58	152	31 38	59	152	32 37	59	152	33 36	59	152	34 35	59	151	35 34	58	151	336
29 29	+59	151	30 28	+59	151	31 27	+58	151	32 25	+59	151	33 24	+59	150	34 23	+59	150	35 22	+58	150	335
29 17	59	150	30 16	59	150	31 15	58	150	32 13	59	149	33 12	58	149	34 10	59	149	35 09	59	149	334
29 05	58	149	30 03	59	149	31 02	59	149	32 01	58	148	32 59	59	148	33 58	58	148	34 56	59	148	333
28 52	59	148	29 51	58	148	30 49	59	147	31 48	58	147	32 46	58	147	33 44	59	147	34 43	58	146	332
28 39	58	147	29 37	59	147	30 36	58	146	31 34	59	146	32 33	58	146	33 31	58	146	34 29	58	145	331
28 25	+59	146	29 24	+58	146	30 22	+58	145	31 20	+59	145	32 19	+58	145	33 17	+58	144	34 15	+58	144	330
28 11	59	145	29 10	58	144	30 08	58	144	31 06	58	144	32 04	58	144	33 02	58	143	34 00	58	143	329
27 57	58	144	28 55	58	143	29 53	59	143	30 52	58	143	31 50	58	142	32 48	58	142	33 46	57	142	328
27 42	59	143	28 41	58	142	29 39	58	142	30 37	57	142	31 34	58	141	32 32	58	141	33 30	58	141	327
27 27	58	141	28 25	58	141	29 23	58	141	30 21	58	141	31 19	58	140	32 17	58	140	33 15	57	140	326
27 12	+58	140	28 10	+58	140	29 08	+57	140	30 05	+58	139	31 03	+58	139	32 01	+58	139	32 59	+57	138	325
26 56	58	139	27 54	58	139	28 52	57	139	29 49	58	138	30 47	58	138	31 45	57	138	32 42	58	137	324
26 40	58	138	27 38	57	138	28 35	58	138	29 33	58	137	30 31	57	137	31 28	58	137	32 26	57	136	323
26 24	57	137	27 21	58	137	28 19	57	137	29 16	58	136	30 14	57	136	31 11	57	136	32 08	58	135	322
26 07	57	136	27 04	58	136	28 02	57	135	28 59	58	135	29 57	57	135	30 54	57	134	31 51	57	134	321
25 50	+57	135	26 47	+58	135	27 45	+57	134	28 42	+57	134	29 39	+57	134	30 36	+57	133	31 33	+57	133	320
25 32	58	134	26 30	57	134	27 27	57	133	28 24	57	133	29 21	57	133	30 18	57	132	31 15	57	132	319
25 15	57	133	26 12	57	133	27 09	57	132	28 06	57	132	29 03	57	132	30 00	57	131	30 57	57	131	318
24 57	57	132	25 54	57	132	26 51	57	131	27 48	57	131	28 45	57	131	29 42	56	130	30 38	57	130	317
24 38	57	131	25 35	57	131	26 32	57	130	27 29	57	130	28 26	57	129	29 23	57	129	30 20	56	129	316
24 20	+57	130	25 17	+56	129	26 13	+57	129	27 10	+57	129	28 07	+57	128	29 04	+56	128	30 00	+57	128	315
24 01	57	129	24 58	56	128	25 54	57	128	26 51	57	128	27 48	56	127	28 44	57	127	29 41	56	127	314
23 42	56	128	24 38	57	127	25 35	57	127	26 32	56	127	27 28	57	126	28 25	56	126	29 21	56	126	313
23 22	57	127	24 19	56	126	25 15	57	126	26 12	56	126	27 08	57	125	28 05	56	125	29 01	56	125	312
23 03	56	126	23 59	57	125	24 56	56	125	25 52	56	125	26 48	57	124	27 45	56	124	28 41	56	123	311
22 43	+56	125	23 39	+56	124	24 35	+57	124	25 32	+56	124	26 28	+56	123	27 24	+56	123	28 20	+56	122	310
22 22	57	124	23 19	56	123	24 15	56	123	25 11	56	123	26 07	57	122	27 04	56	122	28 00	56	121	309
22 02	56	123	22 58	56	122	23 54	57	122	24 51	56	122	25 47	56	121	26 43	56	121	27 39	56	120	308
21 41	56	122	22 37	57	121	23 34	56	121	24 30	56	121	25 26	56	120	26 22	56	120	27 18	55	119	307
21 20	57	121	22 17	56	120	23 13	56	120	24 09	55	120	25 04	56	119	26 00	56	119	26 56	56	118	306
20 59	+56	120	21 55	+56	119	22 51	+56	119	23 47	+56	119	24 43	+56	118	25 39	+56	118	26 35	+55	117	305
20 38	56	119	21 34	56	118	22 30	56	118	23 26	55	118	24 21	56	117	25 17	56	117	26 13	55	116	304
20 16	56	118	21 12	56	117	22 08	56	117	23 04	56	117	24 00	55	116	24 55	56	116	25 51	55	115	303
19 55	56	117	20 51	55	116	21 46	56	116	22 42	56	116	23 38	55	115	24 33	56	115	25 29	55	114	302
19 33	56	116	20 29	55	115	21 24	56	115	22 20	55	115	23 15	56	114	24 11	55	114	25 06	56	113	301
19 11	+55	115	20 06	+56	114	21 02	+56	114	21 58	+55	114	22 53	+55	113	23 48	+56	113	24 44	+55	112	300
18 49	55	114	19 44	56	113	20 40	55	113	21 35	56	113	22 31	55	112	23 26	55	112	24 21	55	111	299
18 26	56	113	19 22	55	112	20 17	56	112	21 13	55	112	22 08	55	111	23 03	55	111	23 58	55	110	298
18 04	55	112	18 59	55	112	19 54	56	111	20 50	55	111	21 45	55	110	22 40	55	110	23 35	55	109	297
17 41	55	111	18 36	56	111	19 32	55	110	20 27	55	110	21 22	55	109	22 17	55	109	23 12	55	108	296
17 18	+55	110	18 13	+56	110	19 09	+55	109	20 04	+55	109	20 59	+55	108	21 54	+55	108	22 49	+55	107	295
16 55	55	109	17 50	55	109	18 45	56	108	19 41	55	108	20 36	55	107	21 31	55	107	22 26	55	107	294
16 32	55	108	17 27	55	108	18 22	55	107	19 17	55	107	20 12	55	106	21 07	55	106	22 02	55	106	293
16 09	55	107	17 04	55	107	17 59	55	106	18 54	55	106	19 49	55	105	20 44	55	105	21 39	55	105	292
15 45	55	106	16 40	55	106	17 35	55	105	18 30	55	105	19 25	55	105	20 20	55	104	21 15	55	104	291

S. Lat. {LHA greater than 180°........ Zn=180−Z; LHA less than 180°........... Zn=180+Z}

DECLINATION (0°-14°) SAME NAME AS LATITUDE

LAT 66°

N. Lat. {LHA greater than 180°....... Zn=Z
{LHA less than 180°........... Zn=360−Z

DECLINATION (0°-14°) SAME NAME AS LATITUDE

LHA	0° Hc	d	Z	1° Hc	d	Z	2° Hc	d	Z	3° Hc	d	Z	4° Hc	d	Z
	° ′	′	°	° ′	′	°	° ′	′	°	° ′	′	°	° ′	′	°
70	08 00	+55	108	08 55	+55	108	09 50	+56	108	10 46	+55	107	11 41	+55	107
71	07 37	55	108	08 32	55	107	09 27	55	107	10 22	56	106	11 18	55	106
72	07 13	56	107	08 09	55	106	09 04	55	106	09 59	55	105	10 54	55	105
73	06 50	55	106	07 45	55	105	08 40	55	105	09 35	55	104	10 30	56	104
74	06 26	55	105	07 21	56	104	08 17	55	104	09 12	55	104	10 07	55	103
75	06 03	+55	104	06 58	+55	103	07 53	+55	103	08 48	+55	103	09 43	+55	102
76	05 39	55	103	06 34	55	102	07 29	55	102	08 24	55	102	09 19	55	101
77	05 15	55	102	06 10	55	102	07 05	55	101	08 00	55	101	08 55	55	100
78	04 51	55	101	05 46	55	101	06 41	55	100	07 36	55	100	08 31	55	99
79	04 27	55	100	05 22	55	100	06 17	55	99	07 12	55	99	08 07	55	99
80	04 03	+55	99	04 58	+55	99	05 53	+55	98	06 48	+55	98	07 43	+55	98
81	03 39	55	98	04 34	55	98	05 29	55	97	06 24	55	97	07 19	54	97
82	03 15	55	97	04 10	55	97	05 05	54	97	05 59	55	96	06 54	55	96
83	02 50	55	96	03 45	55	96	04 40	55	96	05 35	55	95	06 30	55	95
84	02 26	55	95	03 21	55	95	04 16	55	95	05 11	55	94	06 06	54	94
85	02 02	+55	95	02 57	+55	94	03 52	+54	94	04 46	+55	93	05 41	+55	93
86	01 38	54	94	02 32	55	93	03 27	55	93	04 22	55	92	05 17	55	92
87	01 13	55	93	02 08	55	92	03 03	55	92	03 58	54	92	04 52	55	91
88	00 49	55	92	01 44	54	91	02 38	55	91	03 33	55	91	04 28	55	90
89	00 24	55	91	01 19	55	91	02 14	55	90	03 09	55	90	04 04	54	89
90	00 00	+55	90	00 55	+55	90	01 50	+54	89	02 44	+55	89	03 39	+55	88
91	−0 24	54	89	00 30	55	89	01 25	55	88	02 20	55	88	03 15	55	87
92	−0 49	55	88	00 06	55	88	01 01	55	87	01 56	54	87	02 50	55	87
93	−1 13	55	87	−0 18	54	87	00 36	55	86	01 31	55	86	02 26	55	86
94	−1 38	55	86	−0 43	55	86	00 12	55	86	01 07	55	85	02 02	55	85
95	−2 02	+55	85	−1 07	+55	85	−0 12	+55	85	00 43	+55	84	01 38	+54	84
96	−2 26	55	85	−1 31	55	84	−0 36	54	84	00 18	55	83	01 13	55	83
97	−2 50	54	84	−1 56	55	83	−1 01	55	83	−0 06	55	82	00 49	55	82
98	−3 15	55	83	−2 20	55	82	−1 25	55	82	−0 30	55	81	00 25	55	81
99	−3 39	55	82	−2 44	55	81	−1 49	55	81	−0 54	55	81	00 01	55	80
100	−4 03	+55	81	−3 08	+55	80	−2 13	+55	80	−1 18	+55	80	−0 23	+55	79
101	−4 27	55	80	−3 32	55	80	−2 37	55	79	−1 42	55	79	−0 47	55	78
102	−4 51	55	79	−3 56	55	79	−3 01	55	78	−2 06	55	78	−1 11	55	77
103	−5 15	55	78	−4 20	55	78	−3 25	55	77	−2 30	55	77	−1 35	55	76
104	−5 39	55	77	−4 44	55	77	−3 49	55	76	−2 54	56	76	−1 58	55	76
105				−5 07	+55	76	−4 12	+55	75	−3 17	+55	75	−2 22	+55	75
106				−5 31	55	75	−4 36	55	75	−3 41	56	74	−2 45	55	74
107							−4 59	55	74	−4 04	55	73	−3 09	55	73
108							−5 23	56	73	−4 27	55	72	−3 32	55	72
109							−5 46	55	72	−4 51	56	71	−3 55	55	71
110										−5 14	+56	70	−4 18	+55	70
111										−5 37	56	69	−4 41	55	69
112													−5 04	56	68
113													−5 26	55	67

LHA	5° Hc	d	Z	6° Hc	d	Z	7° Hc	d	Z	8° Hc	d	Z	9° Hc	d	Z
	° ′	′	°	° ′	′	°	° ′	′	°	° ′	′	°	° ′	′	°
70	12 36	+55	106	13 31	+56	106	14 27	+55	106	15 22	+55	105	16 17	+55	105
71	12 13	55	106	13 08	55	105	14 03	55	105	14 58	55	104	15 53	55	104
72	11 49	55	105	12 44	55	104	13 39	55	104	14 34	55	103	15 29	55	103
73	11 26	55	104	12 21	55	103	13 16	55	103	14 11	55	102	15 06	54	102
74	11 02	55	103	11 57	55	102	12 52	55	102	13 47	55	101	14 42	54	101
75	10 38	+55	102	11 33	+55	101	12 28	+55	101	13 23	+55	101	14 18	+54	100
76	10 14	55	101	11 09	55	100	12 04	55	100	12 59	55	100	13 54	54	99
77	09 50	55	100	10 45	55	100	11 40	55	99	12 35	54	99	13 29	55	98
78	09 26	55	99	10 21	55	99	11 16	54	98	12 10	55	98	13 05	55	97
79	09 02	55	98	09 57	54	98	10 51	55	97	11 46	55	97	12 41	55	96
80	08 38	+54	97	09 32	+55	97	10 27	+55	96	11 22	+55	96	12 17	+54	96
81	08 13	55	96	09 08	56	96	10 03	55	95	10 58	54	95	11 52	55	95
82	07 49	55	95	08 44	55	95	09 39	54	95	10 33	55	94	11 28	55	94
83	07 25	55	94	08 20	54	94	09 14	55	94	10 09	55	93	11 04	54	93
84	07 00	55	93	07 55	55	93	08 50	55	93	09 45	54	92	10 39	55	92
85	06 36	+55	93	07 31	+55	92	08 26	+54	92	09 20	+55	91	10 15	+55	91
86	06 12	54	92	07 06	55	91	08 01	55	91	08 56	55	90	09 51	54	90
87	05 47	55	91	06 42	55	90	07 37	54	90	08 31	55	90	09 26	55	89
88	05 23	55	90	06 18	54	89	07 12	55	89	08 07	55	89	09 02	54	88
89	04 58	55	89	05 53	55	89	06 48	55	88	07 43	54	88	08 37	55	87
90	04 34	+55	88	05 29	+55	88	06 24	+54	87	07 18	+55	87	08 13	+55	86
91	04 10	54	87	05 04	55	87	05 59	55	86	06 54	55	86	07 49	54	85
92	03 45	55	86	04 40	55	86	05 35	55	85	06 30	54	85	07 24	55	85
93	03 21	55	85	04 16	55	85	05 11	54	84	06 05	55	84	07 00	55	84
94	02 57	54	84	03 51	55	84	04 46	55	84	05 41	55	83	06 36	55	83
95	02 32	+55	83	03 27	+55	83	04 22	+55	83	05 17	+55	82	06 12	+54	82
96	02 08	55	82	03 03	55	82	03 58	55	82	04 53	55	81	05 48	54	81
97	01 44	55	82	02 39	55	81	03 34	55	81	04 29	55	80	05 24	54	80
98	01 20	55	81	02 15	55	80	03 10	55	80	04 05	54	79	04 59	55	79
99	00 56	55	80	01 51	55	79	02 46	55	79	03 41	55	78	04 36	54	78
100	00 32	+55	79	01 27	+55	78	02 22	+55	78	03 17	+55	78	04 12	+55	77
101	00 08	55	78	01 03	55	78	01 58	55	77	02 53	55	77	03 48	55	76
102	−0 16	55	77	00 39	55	77	01 34	55	76	02 29	55	76	03 24	55	75
103	−0 40	55	76	00 15	56	76	01 11	55	75	02 06	55	75	03 01	55	75
104	−1 03	55	75	−0 08	55	75	00 47	55	74	01 42	55	74	02 37	55	74
105	−1 27	+55	74	−0 32	+56	74	00 24	+55	73	01 19	+55	73	02 14	+55	73
106	−1 50	55	73	−0 55	55	73	00 00	55	73	00 55	56	72	01 51	55	72
107	−2 14	56	72	−1 18	55	72	−0 23	55	72	00 32	56	71	01 28	55	71
108	−2 37	56	72	−1 41	55	71	−0 46	55	71	00 09	56	70	01 05	55	70
109	−3 00	56	71	−2 04	55	70	−1 09	55	70	−0 14	56	69	00 42	55	69
110	−3 23	+56	70	−2 27	+55	69	−1 32	+55	69	−0 37	+56	69	00 19	+55	68
111	−3 46	56	69	−2 50	55	68	−1 55	56	68	−0 59	55	68	−0 04	56	67
112	−4 08	55	68	−3 13	56	67	−2 17	55	67	−1 22	56	67	−0 26	56	66
113	−4 31	56	67	−3 35	55	67	−2 40	56	66	−1 44	56	66	−0 48	55	65
114	−4 53	55	66	−3 58	56	66	−3 02	56	65	−2 06	56	65	−1 10	55	64
115	−5 15	+55	65	−4 20	+56	65	−3 24	+56	64	−2 28	+56	64	−1 32	+55	64
116	−5 37	55	64	−4 42	56	64	−3 46	56	63	−2 50	56	63	−1 54	56	63
117				−5 03	55	63	−4 08	56	62	−3 12	56	62	−2 16	56	62
118				−5 25	56	62	−4 29	56	62	−3 33	56	61	−2 37	56	61
119							−4 50	56	61	−3 54	56	60	−2 58	56	60
120							−5 12	+57	60	−4 15	+56	59	−3 19	+56	59
121							−5 33	57	59	−4 36	56	58	−3 40	56	58
122										−4 57	56	58	−4 01	57	57
123										−5 18	57	56	−4 21	56	56
124										−5 38	57	56	−4 41	56	55
125													−5 01	+56	54
126													−5 21	57	53

LHA	10° Hc	d	Z	11° Hc	d	Z	12° Hc	d	Z	13° Hc	d	Z	14° Hc	d	Z	LHA
	° ′	′	°	° ′	′	°	° ′	′	°	° ′	′	°	° ′	′	°	
70	17 12	+55	104	18 07	+55	104	19 02	+55	104	19 57	+54	103	20 51	+55	103	290
71	16 48	55	103	17 43	55	103	18 38	55	103	19 33	54	102	20 27	55	102	289
72	16 24	55	103	17 19	55	102	18 14	55	102	19 09	54	101	20 03	55	101	288
73	16 00	55	102	16 55	55	101	17 50	55	101	18 45	54	100	19 39	55	100	287
74	15 36	55	101	16 31	55	100	17 26	55	100	18 21	54	99	19 15	55	99	286
75	15 12	+55	100	16 07	+55	99	17 02	+55	99	17 57	+54	98	18 51	+55	98	285
76	14 48	55	99	15 43	55	98	16 38	54	98	17 32	55	98	18 27	55	97	284
77	14 24	55	98	15 19	55	97	16 14	54	97	17 08	55	97	18 03	54	96	283
78	14 00	55	97	14 55	54	97	15 49	55	96	16 44	55	96	17 39	54	95	282
79	13 36	54	96	14 30	55	96	15 25	55	95	16 20	54	95	17 14	55	94	281
80	13 11	+55	95	14 06	+55	95	15 01	+54	94	15 55	+55	94	16 50	+54	93	280
81	12 47	55	94	13 42	54	94	14 36	55	93	15 31	54	93	16 25	55	92	279
82	12 23	54	93	13 17	55	93	14 12	55	92	15 07	54	92	16 01	55	92	278
83	11 58	55	92	12 53	55	92	13 48	54	91	14 42	55	91	15 37	54	91	277
84	11 34	54	91	12 28	55	91	13 23	55	91	14 18	54	90	15 12	55	90	276
85	11 10	+54	91	12 04	+55	90	12 59	+54	90	13 53	+55	89	14 48	+54	89	275
86	10 45	55	90	11 40	54	89	12 34	55	89	13 29	55	88	14 24	54	88	274
87	10 21	54	89	11 15	55	88	12 10	55	88	13 05	54	87	13 59	55	87	273
88	09 56	55	88	10 51	55	87	11 46	54	87	12 40	55	86	13 35	54	86	272
89	09 32	55	87	10 27	54	86	11 21	55	86	12 16	54	86	13 10	55	85	271
90	09 08	+54	86	10 02	+55	86	10 57	+55	85	11 52	+54	85	12 46	+55	84	270
91	08 43	55	85	09 38	55	85	10 33	54	84	11 27	55	84	12 22	54	83	269
92	08 19	55	84	09 14	54	84	10 08	55	83	11 03	55	83	11 58	54	82	268
93	07 55	55	83	08 50	54	83	09 44	55	82	10 39	55	82	11 34	54	82	267
94	07 31	54	82	08 25	55	82	09 20	55	81	10 15	54	81	11 09	55	81	266
95	07 06	+55	81	08 01	+55	81	08 56	+55	81	09 51	+54	80	10 45	+55	80	265
96	06 42	55	81	07 37	55	80	08 32	55	80	09 27	54	79	10 21	55	79	264
97	06 18	55	80	07 13	55	79	08 08	55	79	09 03	54	78	09 57	55	78	263
98	05 54	55	79	06 49	55	78	07 44	55	78	08 39	55	77	09 34	54	77	262
99	05 30	55	78	06 25	55	77	07 20	55	77	08 15	55	77	09 10	55	76	261
100	05 07	+55	77	06 02	+55	76	06 57	+54	76	07 51	+55	76	08 46	+55	75	260
101	04 43	55	76	05 38	55	76	06 33	55	75	07 28	55	75	08 23	55	74	259
102	04 19	55	75	05 14	55	75	06 09	55	74	07 04	55	74	07 59	55	73	258
103	03 56	55	74	04 51	55	74	05 46	55	73	06 41	55	73	07 36	55	73	257
104	03 32	55	73	04 27	56	73	05 23	55	72	06 18	55	72	07 13	55	72	256
105	03 09	+55	72	04 04	+55	72	04 59	+56	72	05 55	+55	71	06 50	+55	71	255
106	02 46	55	71	03 41	55	71	04 36	55	71	05 31	56	70	06 27	55	70	254
107	02 23	55	70	03 18	55	70	04 13	56	70	05 09	55	69	06 04	55	69	253
108	02 00	55	70	02 55	55	69	03 50	56	69	04 46	55	68	05 41	55	68	252
109	01 37	55	69	02 32	56	68	03 28	55	68	04 23	56	68	05 19	55	67	251
110	01 14	+56	68	02 10	+55	67	03 05	+56	67	04 01	+55	67	04 56	+56	66	250
111	00 52	55	67	01 47	56	66	02 43	55	66	03 38	56	66	04 34	55	65	249
112	00 30	55	66	01 25	56	66	02 21	55	65	03 16	56	65	04 12	55	64	248
113	00 07	56	65	01 03	56	65	01 59	55	64	02 54	56	64	03 50	55	64	247
114	−0 15	56	64	00 41	56	64	01 37	55	63	02 32	56	63	03 28	56	63	246
115	−0 37	+56	63	00 19	+56	63	01 15	+56	62	02 11	+55	62	03 06	+56	62	245
116	−0 58	56	62	−0 02	55	62	00 53	56	62	01 49	56	61	02 45	56	61	244
117	−1 20	56	61	−0 24	56	61	00 32	56	61	01 28	56	60	02 24	56	60	243
118	−1 41	56	60	−0 45	56	60	00 11	56	60	01 07	56	59	02 03	56	59	242
119	−2 02	56	60	−1 06	56	59	−0 10	56	59	00 46	56	58	01 42	56	58	241
120	−2 23	+56	59	−1 27	+56	58	−0 31	+56	58	00 25	+56	58	01 21	+57	57	240
121	−2 44	56	58	−1 48	57	57	−0 51	56	57	00 05	56	57	01 01	56	56	239
122	−3 04	56	57	−2 08	56	56	−1 12	56	56	−0 16	57	56	00 41	56	55	238
123	−3 25	57	56	−2 28	56	55	−1 32	56	55	−0 36	57	55	00 21	56	54	237
124	−3 45	57	55	−2 48	56	55	−1 52	57	54	−0 55	56	54	00 01	57	54	236
125	−4 05	+57	54	−3 08	+56	54	−2 12	+57	53	−1 15	+57	53	−0 18	+56	53	235
126	−4 24	56	53	−3 28	57	53	−2 31	57	52	−1 34	56	52	−0 38	57	52	234
127	−4 44	57	52	−3 47	57	52	−2 50	57	51	−1 53	56	51	−0 57	57	51	233
128	−5 03	57	51	−4 06	57	51	−3 09	57	51	−2 12	56	50	−1 16	57	50	232
129	−5 22	57	50	−4 25	57	50	−3 28	57	50	−2 31	57	49	−1 34	57	49	231
130				−4 43	+57	49	−3 46	+57	49	−2 49	+57	48	−1 52	+57	48	230
131				−5 02	57	48	−4 05	58	48	−3 07	57	47	−2 10	57	47	229
132				−5 20	58	47	−4 22	57	47	−3 25	57	46	−2 28	57	46	228
133							−4 40	57	46	−3 43	57	46	−2 46	58	45	227
134							−4 58	58	45	−4 00	57	45	−3 03	58	44	226
135							−5 15	+58	44	−4 17	+57	44	−3 20	+58	43	225
136							−5 31	57	43	−4 34	58	43	−3 36	57	42	224
137										−4 50	57	42	−3 53	58	42	223
138										−5 06	57	41	−4 09	58	41	222
139										−5 22	58	40	−4 24	57	40	221

S. Lat. {LHA greater than 180°....... Zn=180−Z
{LHA less than 180°........... Zn=180+Z

DECLINATION (0°-14°) SAME NAME AS LATITUDE

N. Lat. {LHA greater than 180°....... Zn=Z; LHA less than 180°........... Zn=360−Z}

DECLINATION (0°-14°) SAME NAME AS LATITUDE

LHA	0° Hc d Z	1° Hc d Z	2° Hc d Z	3° Hc d Z	4° Hc d Z	5° Hc d Z	6° Hc d Z	7° Hc d Z	8° Hc d Z	9° Hc d Z	10° Hc d Z	11° Hc d Z	12° Hc d Z	13° Hc d Z	14° Hc d Z	LHA
140															−4 40 +58 39	220
141															−4 55 58 38	219
142															−5 10 58 37	218
143															−5 24 58 36	217
104	−5 39 55 77															256
103	−5 15 55 78															257
102	−4 51 55 79	−5 46 55 79														258
101	−4 27 55 80	−5 22 55 80														259
100	−4 03 −55 81	−4 58 −55 81														260
99	−3 39 55 82	−4 34 55 82	−5 29 55 83													261
98	−3 15 55 83	−4 10 55 83	−5 05 54 83													262
97	−2 50 55 84	−3 45 55 84	−4 40 55 84	−5 35 55 85												263
96	−2 26 55 85	−3 21 55 85	−4 16 55 85	−5 11 55 86												264
95	−2 02 −55 85	−2 57 −55 86	−3 52 −54 86	−4 46 −55 87	−5 41 −55 87											265
94	−1 38 54 86	−2 32 55 87	−3 27 55 87	−4 22 55 88	−5 17 55 88											266
93	−1 13 55 87	−2 08 55 88	−3 03 55 88	−3 58 54 88	−4 52 55 89	−5 47 55 89										267
92	−0 49 55 88	−1 44 54 89	−2 38 55 89	−3 33 55 89	−4 28 55 90	−5 23 55 90										268
91	−0 24 55 89	−1 19 55 89	−2 14 55 90	−3 09 55 90	−4 04 54 91	−4 58 55 91										269
90	00 00 −55 90	−0 55 −55 90	−1 50 −54 91	−2 44 −55 91	−3 39 −55 92	−4 34 −55 92	−5 29 −55 92									270
89	00 24 54 91	−0 30 55 91	−1 25 55 92	−2 20 55 92	−3 15 55 93	−4 10 54 93	−5 04 55 93									271
88	00 49 55 92	−0 06 55 92	−1 01 55 93	−1 56 54 93	−2 50 55 93	−3 45 55 94	−4 40 55 94	−5 35 55 95								272
87	01 13 55 93	00 18 54 93	−0 36 55 94	−1 31 55 94	−2 26 55 94	−3 21 55 95	−4 16 55 95	−5 11 54 96								273
86	01 38 55 94	00 43 55 94	−0 12 55 94	−1 07 55 95	−2 02 55 95	−2 57 54 96	−3 51 55 96	−4 46 55 96	−5 41 55 97							274
85	02 02 −55 95	01 07 −55 95	00 12 −55 95	−0 43 −55 96	−1 38 −54 96	−2 32 −55 97	−3 27 −55 97	−4 22 −55 97	−5 17 −55 98							275
84	02 26 55 95	01 31 55 96	00 36 54 96	−0 18 55 97	−1 13 55 97	−2 08 55 98	−3 03 55 98	−3 58 55 98	−4 53 55 99	−5 48 54 99						276
83	02 50 54 96	01 56 55 97	01 01 55 97	00 06 55 98	−0 49 55 98	−1 44 55 98	−2 39 55 99	−3 34 55 99	−4 29 55 100	−5 24 54 100						277
82	03 15 55 97	02 20 55 98	01 25 55 98	00 30 55 99	−0 25 55 99	−1 20 55 99	−2 15 55 100	−3 10 55 100	−4 05 54 101	−4 59 55 101						278
81	03 39 55 98	02 44 56 99	01 49 55 99	00 54 55 99	−0 01 55 100	−0 56 55 100	−1 51 55 101	−2 46 55 101	−3 41 55 102	−4 36 54 102	−5 30 55 102					279
80	04 03 −55 99	03 08 −55 100	02 13 −55 100	01 18 −55 100	00 23 −55 101	−0 32 −55 101	−1 27 −55 102	−2 22 −55 102	−3 17 −55 102	−4 12 −55 103	−5 07 −55 103					280
79	04 27 55 100	03 32 55 100	02 37 55 101	01 42 55 101	00 47 55 102	−0 08 55 102	−1 03 55 102	−1 58 55 103	−2 53 55 103	−3 48 55 104	−4 43 55 104	−5 38 55 104				281
78	04 51 55 101	03 56 55 101	03 01 55 102	02 06 55 102	01 11 55 103	00 16 55 103	−0 39 55 103	−1 34 55 104	−2 29 55 104	−3 24 55 105	−4 19 55 105	−5 14 55 105				282
77	05 15 55 102	04 20 55 102	03 25 55 103	02 30 55 103	01 35 55 104	00 40 55 104	−0 15 56 104	−1 11 55 105	−2 06 55 105	−3 01 55 105	−3 56 55 106	−4 51 55 106	−5 46 55 107			283
76	05 39 55 103	04 44 55 103	03 49 55 104	02 54 56 104	01 58 55 104	01 03 55 105	00 08 55 105	−0 47 55 106	−1 42 55 106	−2 37 55 106	−3 32 55 107	−4 27 56 107	−5 23 55 108			284
75	06 03 −56 104	05 07 −55 104	04 12 −55 105	03 17 −55 105	02 22 −55 105	01 27 −55 106	00 32 −56 106	−0 24 −55 107	−1 19 −55 107	−2 14 −55 107	−3 09 −55 108	−4 04 −55 108	−4 59 −56 108			285
74	06 26 55 105	05 31 55 105	04 36 55 105	03 41 56 106	02 45 55 106	01 50 55 107	00 55 55 107	00 00 55 107	−0 55 56 108	−1 51 55 108	−2 46 55 109	−3 41 55 109	−4 36 55 109	−5 31 56 110		286
73	06 50 55 106	05 55 56 106	04 59 55 106	04 04 55 107	03 09 55 107	02 14 56 108	01 18 55 108	00 23 55 108	−0 32 56 109	−1 28 55 109	−2 23 55 110	−3 18 55 110	−4 13 56 110	−5 09 55 111		287
72	07 13 55 107	06 18 55 107	05 23 56 107	04 27 55 108	03 32 55 108	02 37 56 108	01 41 55 109	00 46 55 109	−0 09 56 110	−1 05 55 110	−2 00 55 110	−2 55 55 111	−3 50 56 111	−4 46 55 112	−5 41 55 112	288
71	07 37 56 108	06 41 55 108	05 46 55 108	04 51 56 109	03 55 55 109	03 00 56 109	02 04 55 110	01 09 55 110	00 14 56 111	−0 42 55 111	−1 37 55 111	−2 32 56 112	−3 28 55 112	−4 23 56 112	−5 19 55 113	289
70	08 00 −56 108	07 04 −55 109	06 09 −55 109	05 14 −56 110	04 18 −55 110	03 23 −56 110	02 27 −55 111	01 32 −55 111	00 37 −56 111	−0 19 −55 112	−1 14 −56 112	−2 10 −55 113	−3 05 −56 113	−4 01 −55 113	−4 56 −56 114	290

S. Lat. {LHA greater than 180°....... Zn=180−Z; LHA less than 180°........... Zn=180+Z}

DECLINATION (0°-14°) CONTRARY NAME TO LATITUDE

N. Lat. {LHA greater than 180°....... Zn=Z; LHA less than 180°........... Zn=360−Z}

DECLINATION (0°-14°) CONTRARY NAME TO LATITUDE

LHA	0° Hc	d	Z	1° Hc	d	Z	2° Hc	d	Z	3° Hc	d	Z	4° Hc	d	Z	5° Hc	d	Z	6° Hc	d	Z	7° Hc	d	Z
	° ′	′	°	° ′	′	°	° ′	′	°	° ′	′	°	° ′	′	°	° ′	′	°	° ′	′	°	° ′	′	°
69	08 23	55	109	07 28	56	110	06 32	55	110	05 37	56	111	04 41	55	111	03 46	56	111	02 50	55	112	01 55	56	112
68	08 46	56	110	07 50	55	111	06 55	56	111	05 59	56	111	05 04	56	112	04 08	55	112	03 13	56	113	02 17	55	113
67	09 09	56	111	08 13	55	112	07 18	56	112	06 22	56	112	05 26	55	113	04 31	56	113	03 35	55	113	02 40	56	114
66	09 31	55	112	08 36	56	113	07 40	55	113	06 45	56	113	05 49	56	114	04 53	55	114	03 58	56	114	03 02	56	115
65	09 54	−56	113	08 58	−55	114	08 03	−56	114	07 07	−56	114	06 11	−56	115	05 15	−55	115	04 20	−56	115	03 24	−56	116
64	10 16	55	114	09 21	56	114	08 25	56	115	07 29	56	115	06 33	56	116	05 37	55	116	04 42	56	116	03 46	56	117
63	10 39	56	115	09 43	56	115	08 47	56	116	07 51	56	116	06 55	56	116	05 59	56	117	05 03	55	117	04 08	56	118
62	11 01	56	116	10 05	56	116	09 09	56	117	08 13	56	117	07 17	56	117	06 21	56	118	05 25	56	118	04 29	56	118
61	11 22	56	117	10 26	55	117	09 31	56	118	08 35	56	118	07 39	56	118	06 43	56	119	05 47	57	119	04 50	56	119
60	11 44	−56	118	10 48	−56	118	09 52	−56	119	08 56	−56	119	08 00	−56	119	07 04	−56	120	06 08	−56	120	05 12	−57	120
59	12 06	56	119	11 10	57	119	10 13	56	120	09 17	56	120	08 21	56	120	07 25	56	121	06 29	56	121	05 33	57	121
58	12 27	56	120	11 31	56	120	10 35	57	120	09 38	56	121	08 42	56	121	07 46	56	122	06 50	57	122	05 53	56	122
57	12 48	56	121	11 52	57	121	10 55	56	121	09 59	56	122	09 03	56	122	08 07	57	122	07 10	56	123	06 14	56	123
56	13 09	56	122	12 13	57	122	11 16	56	122	10 20	57	123	09 23	56	123	08 27	56	123	07 31	57	124	06 34	56	124
55	13 30	−57	123	12 33	−56	123	11 37	−57	123	10 40	−56	124	09 44	−57	124	08 47	−56	124	07 51	−57	125	06 54	−56	125
54	13 50	57	124	12 53	56	124	11 57	57	124	11 00	56	125	10 04	57	125	09 07	56	125	08 11	57	126	07 14	56	126
53	14 10	56	125	13 14	57	125	12 17	57	125	11 20	56	126	10 24	57	126	09 27	56	126	08 31	57	127	07 34	57	127
52	14 30	56	126	13 34	57	126	12 37	57	126	11 40	57	127	10 43	56	127	09 47	57	127	08 50	57	128	07 53	57	128
51	14 50	57	127	13 53	57	127	12 56	56	127	12 00	57	128	11 03	57	128	10 06	57	128	09 09	57	129	08 12	56	129
50	15 09	−56	128	14 13	−57	128	13 16	−57	128	12 19	−57	129	11 22	−57	129	10 25	−57	129	09 28	−57	129	08 31	−57	130
49	15 29	57	129	14 32	57	129	13 35	57	129	12 38	57	129	11 41	57	130	10 44	57	130	09 47	57	130	08 50	57	131
48	15 48	57	129	14 51	57	130	13 54	57	130	12 57	57	130	12 00	58	131	11 02	57	131	10 05	57	131	09 08	57	132
47	16 06	57	130	15 09	57	131	14 12	57	131	13 15	57	131	12 18	57	132	11 21	57	132	10 24	58	132	09 26	57	133
46	16 25	57	131	15 28	58	132	14 30	57	132	13 33	57	132	12 36	57	133	11 39	58	133	10 41	57	133	09 44	57	134
45	16 43	−57	132	15 46	−58	133	14 48	−57	133	13 51	−57	133	12 54	−58	134	11 56	−57	134	10 59	−57	134	10 02	−58	135
44	17 01	58	133	16 03	57	134	15 06	57	134	14 09	58	134	13 11	57	135	12 14	58	135	11 16	57	135	10 19	58	136
43	17 18	57	134	16 21	57	135	15 24	58	135	14 26	57	135	13 29	58	136	12 31	58	136	11 33	57	136	10 36	58	137
42	17 36	58	135	16 38	57	136	15 41	58	136	14 43	58	136	13 45	57	137	12 48	58	137	11 50	57	137	10 53	58	137
41	17 53	58	136	16 55	58	137	15 57	57	137	15 00	58	137	14 02	58	138	13 04	57	138	12 07	58	138	11 09	58	138
40	18 09	−57	137	17 12	−58	138	16 14	−58	138	15 16	−58	138	14 18	−57	139	13 21	−58	139	12 23	−58	139	11 25	−58	139
39	18 26	58	138	17 28	58	139	16 30	58	139	15 32	58	139	14 34	57	140	13 37	58	140	12 39	58	140	11 41	58	140
38	18 42	58	140	17 44	58	140	16 46	58	140	15 48	58	140	14 50	58	141	13 52	58	141	12 54	58	141	11 56	58	141
37	18 57	58	141	17 59	58	141	17 01	58	141	16 03	58	141	15 05	58	142	14 07	58	142	13 09	58	142	12 11	58	142
36	19 13	58	142	18 15	58	142	17 17	58	142	16 19	59	142	15 20	58	143	14 22	58	143	13 24	58	143	12 26	58	143
35	19 28	−58	143	18 30	−59	143	17 31	−58	143	16 33	−58	143	15 35	−58	144	14 37	−58	144	13 39	−59	144	12 40	−58	144
34	19 42	58	144	18 44	58	144	17 46	58	144	16 48	59	144	15 49	58	145	14 51	58	145	13 53	59	145	12 54	58	145
33	19 57	59	145	18 58	58	145	18 00	58	145	17 02	59	145	16 03	58	146	15 05	58	146	14 07	59	146	13 08	58	146
32	20 11	59	146	19 12	58	146	18 14	59	146	17 15	58	146	16 17	59	147	15 18	58	147	14 20	58	147	13 22	59	147
31	20 24	58	147	19 26	59	147	18 27	58	147	17 29	59	147	16 30	58	148	15 32	59	148	14 33	58	148	13 35	59	148
30	20 38	−59	148	19 39	−59	148	18 40	−58	148	17 42	−59	148	16 43	−59	149	15 44	−58	149	14 46	−59	149	13 47	−59	149
29	20 50	58	149	19 52	59	149	18 53	59	149	17 54	58	149	16 56	59	150	15 57	59	150	14 58	59	150	13 59	58	150
28	21 03	59	150	20 04	59	150	19 05	58	150	18 07	59	150	17 08	59	151	16 09	59	151	15 10	59	151	14 11	58	151
27	21 15	59	151	20 16	59	151	19 17	59	151	18 18	58	152	17 20	59	152	16 21	59	152	15 22	59	152	14 23	59	152
26	21 27	59	152	20 28	59	152	19 29	59	152	18 30	59	153	17 31	59	153	16 32	59	153	15 33	59	153	14 34	59	153
25	21 38	−59	153	20 39	−59	153	19 40	−59	153	18 41	−59	154	17 42	−59	154	16 43	−59	154	15 44	−59	154	14 45	−59	154
24	21 49	59	154	20 50	59	154	19 51	59	154	18 52	59	155	17 53	60	155	16 53	59	155	15 54	59	155	14 55	59	155
23	21 59	59	155	21 00	59	155	20 01	59	155	19 02	59	156	18 03	59	156	17 04	60	156	16 04	59	156	15 05	59	156
22	22 09	59	156	21 10	59	156	20 11	59	157	19 12	59	157	18 13	60	157	17 13	59	157	16 14	59	157	15 15	59	157
21	22 19	59	157	21 20	59	157	20 21	60	158	19 21	59	158	18 22	59	158	17 23	60	158	16 23	59	158	15 24	59	158
20	22 28	−59	158	21 29	−59	158	20 30	−60	159	19 30	−59	159	18 31	−59	159	17 32	−60	159	16 32	−59	159	15 33	−60	159
19	22 37	59	159	21 38	60	160	20 38	59	160	19 39	59	160	18 40	60	160	17 40	59	160	16 41	60	160	15 41	59	160
18	22 45	59	160	21 46	59	161	20 47	60	161	19 47	59	161	18 48	60	161	17 48	59	161	16 49	60	161	15 49	59	161
17	22 53	59	162	21 54	60	162	20 54	59	162	19 55	60	162	18 55	59	162	17 56	60	162	16 56	59	162	15 57	60	162
16	23 01	60	163	22 01	59	163	21 02	60	163	20 02	59	163	19 03	60	163	18 03	59	163	17 04	60	163	16 04	60	164
15	23 08	−60	164	22 08	−59	164	21 09	−60	164	20 09	−59	164	19 10	−60	164	18 10	−60	164	17 10	−59	164	16 11	−60	165
14	23 15	60	165	22 15	60	165	21 15	59	165	20 16	60	165	19 16	60	165	18 16	59	165	17 17	60	165	16 17	60	166
13	23 21	60	166	22 21	59	166	21 22	60	166	20 22	60	166	19 22	60	166	18 22	59	166	17 23	60	166	16 23	60	167
12	23 27	60	167	22 27	60	167	21 27	60	167	20 27	59	167	19 28	60	167	18 28	60	167	17 28	60	168	16 28	59	168
11	23 32	60	168	22 32	60	168	21 32	59	168	20 33	60	168	19 33	60	168	18 33	60	168	17 33	60	169	16 33	59	169
10	23 37	−60	169	22 37	−60	169	21 37	−60	169	20 37	−59	169	19 38	−60	169	18 38	−60	170	17 38	−60	170	16 38	−60	170
9	23 41	60	170	22 41	59	170	21 42	60	170	20 42	60	170	19 42	60	171	18 42	60	171	17 42	60	171	16 42	60	171
8	23 45	60	171	22 45	60	171	21 45	59	171	20 46	60	172	19 46	60	172	18 46	60	172	17 46	60	172	16 46	60	172
7	23 49	60	172	22 49	60	172	21 49	60	173	20 49	60	173	19 49	60	173	18 49	60	173	17 49	60	173	16 49	60	173
6	23 52	60	173	22 52	60	174	21 52	60	174	20 52	60	174	19 52	60	174	18 52	60	174	17 52	60	174	16 52	60	174
5	23 54	−60	175	22 54	−60	175	21 54	−60	175	20 54	−60	175	19 54	−60	175	18 54	−60	175	17 54	−59	175	16 55	−60	175
4	23 56	60	176	22 56	60	176	21 56	60	176	20 56	60	176	19 56	60	176	18 56	60	176	17 56	59	176	16 57	60	176
3	23 58	60	177	22 58	60	177	21 58	60	177	20 58	60	177	19 58	60	177	18 58	60	177	17 58	60	177	16 58	60	177
2	23 59	60	178	22 59	60	178	21 59	60	178	20 59	60	178	19 59	60	178	18 59	60	178	17 59	60	178	16 59	60	178
1	24 00	60	179	23 00	60	179	22 00	60	179	21 00	60	179	20 00	60	179	19 00	60	179	18 00	60	179	17 00	60	179
0	24 00	−60	180	23 00	−60	180	22 00	−60	180	21 00	−60	180	20 00	−60	180	19 00	−60	180	18 00	−60	180	17 00	−60	180

LHA	8° Hc	d	Z	9° Hc	d	Z	10° Hc	d	Z	11° Hc	d	Z	12° Hc	d	Z	13° Hc	d	Z	14° Hc	d	Z	LHA
	° ′	′	°	° ′	′	°	° ′	′	°	° ′	′	°	° ′	′	°	° ′	′	°	° ′	′	°	
69	00 59	55	112	00 04	56	113	−0 52	55	113	−1 47	56	114	−2 43	55	114	−3 38	56	114	−4 34	55	115	291
68	01 22	56	113	00 26	56	114	−0 30	55	114	−1 25	56	114	−2 21	55	115	−3 16	56	115	−4 12	55	116	292
67	01 44	56	114	00 48	55	115	−0 07	56	115	−1 03	56	115	−1 59	55	116	−2 54	56	116	−3 50	55	116	293
66	02 06	56	115	01 10	55	116	00 15	56	116	−0 41	56	116	−1 37	55	117	−2 32	56	117	−3 28	56	117	294
65	02 28	−56	116	01 32	−55	116	00 37	−56	117	−0 19	−56	117	−1 15	−56	118	−2 11	−55	118	−3 06	−56	118	295
64	02 50	56	117	01 54	56	117	00 58	56	118	00 02	55	118	−0 53	56	118	−1 49	56	119	−2 45	56	119	296
63	03 12	56	118	02 16	56	118	01 20	56	119	00 24	56	119	−0 32	56	119	−1 28	56	120	−2 24	56	120	297
62	03 33	56	119	02 37	56	119	01 41	56	120	00 45	56	120	−0 11	56	120	−1 07	56	121	−2 03	56	121	298
61	03 54	56	120	02 58	56	120	02 02	56	120	01 06	56	121	00 10	56	121	−0 46	56	122	−1 42	56	122	299
60	04 15	−56	121	03 19	−56	121	02 23	−56	121	01 27	−56	122	00 31	−56	122	−0 25	−56	122	−1 21	−57	123	300
59	04 36	56	122	03 40	56	122	02 44	56	122	01 48	57	123	00 51	56	123	−0 05	56	123	−1 01	56	124	301
58	04 57	56	122	04 01	57	123	03 04	56	123	02 08	56	124	01 12	56	124	00 16	57	124	−0 41	56	125	302
57	05 18	57	124	04 21	56	124	03 25	57	124	02 28	56	125	01 32	56	125	00 36	57	125	−0 21	56	126	303
56	05 38	57	124	04 41	56	125	03 45	57	125	02 48	56	125	01 52	57	126	00 55	56	126	−0 01	57	126	304
55	05 58	−57	125	05 01	−56	126	04 05	−57	126	03 08	−56	126	02 12	−57	127	01 15	−57	127	00 18	−56	127	305
54	06 18	57	126	05 21	57	127	04 24	56	127	03 28	57	127	02 31	57	128	01 34	56	128	00 38	57	128	306
53	06 37	57	127	05 40	56	128	04 44	57	128	03 47	57	128	02 50	57	129	01 53	56	129	00 57	57	129	307
52	06 56	56	128	06 00	57	129	05 03	57	129	04 06	57	129	03 09	57	129	02 12	56	130	01 16	57	130	308
51	07 16	57	129	06 19	57	129	05 22	57	130	04 25	57	130	03 28	57	130	02 31	57	131	01 34	57	131	309
50	07 34	−57	130	06 37	−57	130	05 40	−57	131	04 43	−57	131	03 46	−57	131	02 49	−57	132	01 52	−57	132	310
49	07 53	57	131	06 56	57	131	05 59	57	132	05 02	57	132	04 05	58	132	03 07	57	133	02 10	57	133	311
48	08 11	57	132	07 14	57	132	06 17	57	133	05 20	58	133	04 22	57	133	03 25	57	134	02 28	57	134	312
47	08 29	57	133	07 32	57	133	06 35	58	134	05 37	57	134	04 40	57	134	03 43	57	134	02 46	58	135	313
46	08 47	57	134	07 50	58	134	06 52	57	135	05 55	57	135	04 58	57	135	04 00	57	135	03 03	58	136	314
45	09 04	−57	135	08 07	−57	135	07 10	−58	135	06 12	−57	136	05 15	−58	136	04 17	−57	136	03 20	−58	137	315
44	09 21	57	136	08 24	58	136	07 26	57	136	06 29	58	137	05 31	57	137	04 34	58	137	03 36	57	138	316
43	09 38	57	137	08 41	58	137	07 43	57	137	06 46	58	138	05 48	58	138	04 50	57	138	03 53	58	138	317
42	09 55	58	138	08 57	57	138	08 00	58	138	07 02	58	139	06 04	58	139	05 06	57	139	04 09	58	139	318
41	10 11	58	139	09 13	57	139	08 16	58	139	07 18	58	140	06 20	58	140	05 22	58	140	04 24	57	140	319
40	10 27	−58	140	09 29	−58	140	08 31	−57	140	07 34	−58	141	06 36	−58	141	05 38	−58	141	04 40	−58	141	320
39	10 43	58	141	09 45	58	141	08 47	58	141	07 49	58	141	06 51	58	142	05 53	58	142	04 55	58	142	321
38	10 58	58	142	10 00	58	142	09 02	58	142	08 04	58	142	07 06	58	143	06 08	58	143	05 10	58	143	322
37	11 13	58	143	10 15	58	143	09 17	58	143	08 19	58	143	07 21	59	144	06 22	58	144	05 24	58	144	323
36	11 28	58	144	10 30	59	144	09 31	58	144	08 33	58	144	07 35	58	145	06 37	59	145	05 38	58	145	324
35	11 42	−58	145	10 44	−58	145	09 46	−59	145	08 47	−58	145	07 49	−58	146	06 51	−59	146	05 52	−58	146	325
34	11 56	58	146	10 58	59	146	09 59	58	146	09 01	58	146	08 03	59	147	07 04	58	147	06 06	59	147	326
33	12 10	59	147	11 11	58	147	10 13	59	147	09 14	58	147	08 16	59	147	07 17	58	148	06 19	59	148	327
32	12 23	59	148	11 24	58	148	10 26	59	148	09 27	58	148	08 29	59	148	07 30	58	149	06 32	59	149	328
31	12 36	59	149	11 37	58	149	10 39	59	149	09 40	59	149	08 41	58	149	07 43	59	150	06 44	58	150	329
30	12 48	−58	150	11 50	−59	150	10 51	−59	150	09 52	−58	150	08 54	−59	150	07 55	−59	151	06 56	−58	151	330
29	13 01	59	151	12 02	59	151	11 03	59	151	10 04	58	151	09 06	59	151	08 07	59	152	07 08	59	152	331
28	13 13	59	152	12 14	59	152	11 15	59	152	10 16	59	152	09 17	59	152	08 18	59	153	07 19	58	153	332
27	13 24	59	153	12 25	59	153	11 26	59	153	10 27	59	153	09 28	59	153	08 29	59	153	07 30	59	154	333
26	13 35	59	154	12 36	59	154	11 37	59	154	10 38	59	154	09 39	59	154	08 40	59	154	07 41	59	155	334
25	13 46	−59	155	12 47	−59	155	11 48	−59	155	10 49	−59	155	09 50	−60	155	08 50	−59	155	07 51	−59	156	335
24	13 56	59	156	12 57	59	156	11 58	59	156	10 59	59	156	10 00	60	156	09 00	59	156	08 01	59	157	336
23	14 06	59	157	13 07	59	157	12 08	60	157	11 08	59	157	10 09	59	157	09 10	59	157	08 11	59	158	337
22	14 16	60	158	13 16	59	158	12 17	59	158	11 18	59	158	10 19	60	158	09 19	59	158	08 20	59	158	338
21	14 25	60	159	13 25	59	159	12 26	59	159	11 27	60	159	10 27	59	159	09 28	59	159	08 29	60	159	339
20	14 33	−59	160	13 34	−59	160	12 35	−60	160	11 35	−59	160	10 36	−59	160	09 37	−60	160	08 37	−59	160	340
19	14 42	60	161	13 42	59	161	12 43	60	161	11 43	59	161	10 44	59	161	09 45	60	161	08 45	59	161	341
18	14 50	60	162	13 50	59	162	12 51	60	162	11 51	59	162	10 52	60	162	09 52	59	162	08 53	60	162	342
17	14 57	59	163	13 58	60	163	12 58	59	163	11 59	60	163	10 59	59	163	10 00	60	163	09 00	60	163	343
16	15 04	59	164	14 05	60	164	13 05	59	164	12 06	60	164	11 06	60	164	10 06	59	164	09 07	60	164	344
15	15 11	−60	165	14 11	−59	165	13 12	−60	165	12 12	−60	165	11 12	−59	165	10 13	−60	165	09 13	−59	165	345
14	15 17	59	166	14 18	60	166	13 18	60	166	12 18	59	166	11 19	60	166	10 19	60	166	09 19	60	166	346
13	15 23	60	167	14 23	59	167	13 24	60	167	12 24	60	167	11 24	59	167	10 25	60	167	09 25	60	167	347
12	15 29	60	168	14 29	60	168	13 29	60	168	12 29	59	168	11 30	60	168	10 30	60	168	09 30	60	168	348
11	15 34	60	169	14 34	60	169	13 34	60	169	12 34	60	169	11 34	59	169	10 35	60	169	09 35	60	169	349
10	15 38	−60	170	14 38	−59	170	13 39	−60	170	12 39	−60	170	11 39	−60	170	10 39	−60	170	09 39	−60	170	350
9	15 42	60	171	14 42	59	171	13 43	60	171	12 43	60	171	11 43	60	171	10 43	60	171	09 43	60	171	351
8	15 46	60	172	14 46	60	172	13 46	60	172	12 46	60	172	11 46	59	172	10 47	60	172	09 47	60	172	352
7	15 49	60	173	14 49	60	173	13 49	59	173	12 50	60	173	11 50	60	173	10 50	60	173	09 50	60	173	353
6	15 52	60	174	14 52	60	174	13 52	60	174	12 52	60	174	11 52	60	174	10 52	59	174	09 53	60	174	354
5	15 55	−60	175	14 55	−60	175	13 55	−60	175	12 55	−60	175	11 55	−60	175	10 55	−60	175	09 55	−60	175	355
4	15 57	60	176	14 57	60	176	13 57	60	176	12 57	60	176	11 57	60	176	10 57	60	176	09 57	60	176	356
3	15 58	60	177	14 58	60	177	13 58	60	177	12 58	60	177	11 58	60	177	10 58	60	177	09 58	60	177	357
2	15 59	60	178	14 59	60	178	13 59	60	178	12 59	60	178	11 59	60	178	10 59	60	178	09 59	60	178	358
1	16 00	60	179	15 00	60	179	14 00	60	179	13 00	60	179	12 00	60	179	11 00	60	179	10 00	60	179	359
0	16 00	−60	180	15 00	−60	180	14 00	−60	180	13 00	−60	180	12 00	−60	180	11 00	−60	180	10 00	−60	180	360

S. Lat. {LHA greater than 180°....... Zn=180−Z; LHA less than 180°........... Zn=180+Z}

DECLINATION (0°-14°) CONTRARY NAME TO LATITUDE

N. Lat. {LHA greater than 180°....... Zn=Z; LHA less than 180°........... Zn=360−Z}

DECLINATION (15°-29°) SAME NAME AS LATITUDE

LHA	15° Hc	d	Z	16° Hc	d	Z	17° Hc	d	Z	18° Hc	d	Z	19° Hc	d	Z	LHA
	° ′	′	°	° ′	′	°	° ′	′	°	° ′	′	°	° ′	′	°	
0	39 00	+60	180	40 00	+60	180	41 00	+60	180	42 00	+60	180	43 00	+60	180	360
1	39 00	60	179	40 00	60	179	41 00	60	179	42 00	60	179	43 00	60	179	359
2	38 59	60	178	39 59	60	178	40 59	60	178	41 59	60	177	42 59	60	177	358
3	38 58	60	176	39 58	60	176	40 58	60	176	41 58	60	176	42 58	60	176	357
4	38 56	60	175	39 56	60	175	40 56	60	175	41 56	60	175	42 56	60	175	356
5	38 53	+60	174	39 53	+60	174	40 53	+60	174	41 53	+60	174	42 53	+60	174	355
6	38 51	59	173	39 50	60	173	40 50	60	172	41 50	60	172	42 50	60	172	354
7	38 47	60	171	39 47	60	171	40 47	60	171	41 47	60	171	42 47	59	171	353
8	38 43	60	170	39 43	60	170	40 43	60	170	41 43	59	170	42 42	60	170	352
9	38 39	60	169	39 39	59	169	40 38	60	169	41 38	60	169	42 38	60	168	351
10	38 34	+59	168	39 33	+60	168	40 33	+60	167	41 33	+60	167	42 33	+59	167	350
11	38 28	60	166	39 28	60	166	40 28	59	166	41 27	60	166	42 27	60	166	349
12	38 22	60	165	39 22	60	165	40 22	59	165	41 21	60	165	42 21	59	165	348
13	38 16	59	164	39 15	60	164	40 15	59	164	41 14	60	164	42 14	60	163	347
14	38 09	59	163	39 08	60	163	40 08	59	162	41 07	60	162	42 07	59	162	346
15	38 01	+60	162	39 01	+59	161	40 00	+60	161	41 00	+59	161	41 59	+59	161	345
16	37 53	60	160	38 53	59	160	39 52	59	160	40 51	60	160	41 51	59	160	344
17	37 45	59	159	38 44	59	159	39 43	60	159	40 43	59	159	41 42	59	158	343
18	37 36	59	158	38 35	59	158	39 34	59	158	40 33	60	157	41 33	59	157	342
19	37 26	60	157	38 26	59	157	39 25	59	156	40 24	59	156	41 23	59	156	341
20	37 16	+60	156	38 16	+59	155	39 15	+59	155	40 14	+59	155	41 13	+59	155	340
21	37 06	59	154	38 05	59	154	39 04	59	154	40 03	59	154	41 02	59	153	339
22	36 55	59	153	37 54	59	153	38 53	59	153	39 52	59	152	40 51	58	152	338
23	36 44	59	152	37 43	59	152	38 42	58	151	39 40	59	151	40 39	59	151	337
24	36 32	59	151	37 31	59	151	38 30	58	150	39 28	59	150	40 27	58	150	336
25	36 20	+59	150	37 19	+58	149	38 17	+59	149	39 16	+58	149	40 14	+59	148	335
26	36 08	58	148	37 06	59	148	38 05	58	148	39 03	58	148	40 01	59	147	334
27	35 55	58	147	36 53	58	147	37 51	59	147	38 50	58	146	39 48	58	146	333
28	35 41	58	146	36 39	59	146	37 38	58	146	38 36	58	145	39 34	58	145	332
29	35 27	59	145	36 26	58	145	37 24	58	144	38 22	58	144	39 20	58	144	331
30	35 13	+58	144	36 11	+58	144	37 09	+58	143	38 07	+58	143	39 05	+58	143	330
31	34 58	58	143	35 56	58	142	36 54	58	142	37 52	58	142	38 50	58	141	329
32	34 43	58	142	35 41	58	141	36 39	58	141	37 37	58	141	38 35	57	140	328
33	34 28	58	140	35 26	58	140	36 24	57	140	37 21	58	139	38 19	57	139	327
34	34 12	58	139	35 10	58	139	36 08	57	139	37 05	58	138	38 03	57	138	326
35	33 56	+58	138	34 54	+57	138	35 51	+58	137	36 49	+57	137	37 46	+57	137	325
36	33 40	57	137	34 37	58	137	35 35	57	136	36 32	57	136	37 29	57	136	324
37	33 23	57	136	34 20	58	136	35 18	57	135	36 15	57	135	37 12	57	134	323
38	33 06	57	135	34 03	57	134	35 00	57	134	35 57	57	134	36 54	57	133	322
39	32 48	57	134	33 45	57	133	34 42	57	133	35 39	57	133	36 36	57	132	321
40	32 30	+57	133	33 27	+57	132	34 24	+57	132	35 21	+57	131	36 18	+57	131	320
41	32 12	57	132	33 09	57	131	34 06	57	131	35 03	57	130	36 00	56	130	319
42	31 54	57	130	32 51	56	130	33 47	57	130	34 44	57	129	35 41	56	129	318
43	31 35	57	129	32 32	57	129	33 29	56	129	34 25	57	128	35 22	56	128	317
44	31 16	57	128	32 13	56	128	33 09	57	128	34 06	56	127	35 02	56	127	316
45	30 57	+56	127	31 53	+57	127	32 50	+56	126	33 46	+56	126	34 42	+57	126	315
46	30 37	57	126	31 34	56	126	32 30	56	125	33 26	56	125	34 22	56	125	314
47	30 17	57	125	31 14	56	125	32 10	56	124	33 06	56	124	34 02	56	123	313
48	29 57	57	124	30 54	56	124	31 50	56	123	32 46	56	123	33 42	56	122	312
49	29 37	56	123	30 33	56	123	31 29	56	122	32 25	56	122	33 21	56	121	311
50	29 16	+56	122	30 12	+56	122	31 08	+56	121	32 04	+56	121	33 00	+56	120	310
51	28 56	56	121	29 52	55	121	30 47	56	120	31 43	56	120	32 39	55	119	309
52	28 35	55	120	29 30	56	120	30 26	56	119	31 22	55	119	32 17	56	118	308
53	28 13	56	119	29 09	56	119	30 05	55	118	31 00	56	118	31 56	55	117	307
54	27 52	56	118	28 48	55	118	29 43	56	117	30 39	55	117	31 34	55	116	306
55	27 30	+56	117	28 26	+55	116	29 21	+56	116	30 17	+55	116	31 12	+55	115	305
56	27 08	56	116	28 04	55	115	28 59	56	115	29 55	55	115	30 50	55	114	304
57	26 46	56	115	27 42	55	114	28 37	55	114	29 32	55	114	30 27	55	113	303
58	26 24	55	114	27 19	56	113	28 15	55	113	29 10	55	113	30 05	55	112	302
59	26 02	55	113	26 57	55	112	27 52	55	112	28 47	55	112	29 42	55	111	301
60	25 39	+55	112	26 34	+55	111	27 29	+55	111	28 24	+55	111	29 19	+55	110	300
61	25 16	55	111	26 11	56	111	27 07	54	110	28 01	55	110	28 56	55	109	299
62	24 53	56	110	25 49	55	110	26 44	54	109	27 38	55	109	28 33	55	108	298
63	24 30	55	109	25 25	55	109	26 20	55	108	27 15	55	108	28 10	55	107	297
64	24 07	55	108	25 02	55	108	25 57	55	107	26 52	55	107	27 47	54	106	296
65	23 44	+55	107	24 39	+55	107	25 34	+54	106	26 28	+55	106	27 23	+55	105	295
66	23 21	54	106	24 15	55	106	25 10	55	105	26 05	54	105	26 59	55	104	294
67	22 57	55	105	23 52	55	105	24 47	54	104	25 41	55	104	26 36	54	103	293
68	22 34	54	104	23 28	55	104	24 23	54	103	25 17	55	103	26 12	54	102	292
69	22 10	54	103	23 04	55	103	23 59	55	102	24 54	54	102	25 48	54	101	291

LHA	20° Hc	d	Z	21° Hc	d	Z	22° Hc	d	Z	23° Hc	d	Z	24° Hc	d	Z	LHA
	° ′	′	°	° ′	′	°	° ′	′	°	° ′	′	°	° ′	′	°	
0	44 00	+60	180	45 00	+60	180	46 00	+60	180	47 00	+60	180	48 00	+60	180	360
1	44 00	60	179	45 00	60	179	46 00	60	179	47 00	60	179	48 00	60	179	359
2	43 59	60	177	44 59	60	177	45 59	60	177	46 59	60	177	47 59	60	177	358
3	43 58	60	176	44 58	59	176	45 57	60	176	46 57	60	176	47 57	60	176	357
4	43 56	60	175	44 56	60	175	45 56	59	175	46 55	60	175	47 55	60	175	356
5	43 53	+60	174	44 53	+60	173	45 53	+60	173	46 53	+60	173	47 53	+60	173	355
6	43 50	60	172	44 50	60	172	45 50	60	172	46 50	60	172	47 50	59	172	354
7	43 46	60	171	44 46	60	171	45 46	60	171	46 46	60	171	47 46	60	171	353
8	43 42	60	170	44 42	60	170	45 42	60	169	46 42	60	169	47 42	59	169	352
9	43 38	59	168	44 37	60	168	45 37	60	168	46 37	60	168	47 37	59	168	351
10	43 32	+60	167	44 32	+60	167	45 32	+60	167	46 32	+59	167	47 31	+60	166	350
11	43 27	59	166	44 26	60	166	45 26	60	165	46 26	59	165	47 25	60	165	349
12	43 20	60	164	44 20	60	164	45 20	59	164	46 19	60	164	47 19	59	164	348
13	43 14	59	163	44 13	60	163	45 13	59	163	46 12	60	163	47 12	59	162	347
14	43 06	60	162	44 06	59	162	45 05	59	162	46 04	60	161	47 04	59	161	346
15	42 58	+60	161	43 58	+59	160	44 57	+59	160	45 56	+60	160	46 56	+59	160	345
16	42 50	59	159	43 49	60	159	44 49	59	159	45 48	59	159	46 47	59	158	344
17	42 41	59	158	43 40	59	158	44 39	60	158	45 39	59	157	46 38	59	157	343
18	42 32	59	157	43 31	59	157	44 30	59	156	45 29	59	156	46 28	59	156	342
19	42 22	59	156	43 21	59	155	44 20	59	155	45 19	59	155	46 18	59	155	341
20	42 12	+58	154	43 10	+59	154	44 09	+59	154	45 08	+59	154	46 07	+59	153	340
21	42 01	59	153	43 00	58	153	43 58	59	153	44 57	59	152	45 56	58	152	339
22	41 49	59	152	42 48	59	152	43 47	58	151	44 45	59	151	45 44	59	151	338
23	41 38	58	151	42 36	59	150	43 35	58	150	44 33	59	150	45 32	58	149	337
24	41 25	59	149	42 24	58	149	43 22	59	149	44 21	58	148	45 19	58	148	336
25	41 13	+58	148	42 11	+59	148	43 10	+58	148	44 08	+58	147	45 06	+58	147	335
26	41 00	58	147	41 58	58	147	42 56	58	146	43 54	58	146	44 52	58	146	334
27	40 46	58	146	41 44	58	145	42 42	58	145	43 40	58	145	44 38	58	144	333
28	40 32	58	145	41 30	58	144	42 28	58	144	43 26	58	144	44 24	58	143	332
29	40 18	58	143	41 16	58	143	42 14	57	143	43 11	58	142	44 09	58	142	331
30	40 03	+58	142	41 01	+58	142	41 59	+57	141	42 56	+58	141	43 54	+57	141	330
31	39 48	58	141	40 46	57	141	41 43	58	140	42 41	57	140	43 38	58	139	329
32	39 32	58	140	40 30	57	139	41 27	58	139	42 25	57	139	43 22	58	138	328
33	39 16	58	139	40 14	57	138	41 11	57	138	42 08	58	138	43 06	57	137	327
34	39 00	57	138	39 57	58	137	40 55	57	137	41 52	57	136	42 49	57	136	326
35	38 43	+58	136	39 41	+57	136	40 38	+57	136	41 35	+57	135	42 32	+57	135	325
36	38 26	57	135	39 23	57	135	40 20	57	134	41 17	57	134	42 14	57	134	324
37	38 09	57	134	39 06	57	134	40 03	57	133	41 00	56	133	41 56	57	132	323
38	37 51	57	133	38 48	57	133	39 45	57	132	40 42	56	132	41 38	57	131	322
39	37 33	57	132	38 30	57	131	39 27	56	131	40 23	57	131	41 20	56	130	321
40	37 15	+56	131	38 11	+57	130	39 08	+56	130	40 04	+57	129	41 01	+56	129	320
41	36 56	57	130	37 53	56	129	38 49	56	129	39 45	57	128	40 42	56	128	319
42	36 37	57	128	37 34	56	128	38 30	56	128	39 26	56	127	40 22	56	127	318
43	36 18	57	127	37 14	56	127	38 10	56	127	39 06	56	126	40 02	56	126	317
44	35 58	57	126	36 55	56	126	37 51	56	125	38 47	55	125	39 42	56	124	316
45	35 39	+56	125	36 35	+56	125	37 31	+55	124	38 26	+56	124	39 22	+56	123	315
46	35 18	56	124	36 14	56	124	37 10	56	123	38 06	56	123	39 02	55	122	314
47	34 58	56	123	35 54	56	123	36 50	55	122	37 45	56	122	38 41	55	121	313
48	34 38	55	122	35 33	56	122	36 29	55	121	37 24	56	121	38 20	55	120	312
49	34 17	55	121	35 12	56	120	36 08	55	120	37 03	56	120	37 59	55	119	311
50	33 56	+55	120	34 51	+56	119	35 47	+55	119	36 42	+55	118	37 37	+55	118	310
51	33 34	56	119	34 30	55	118	35 25	55	118	36 20	56	117	37 16	55	117	309
52	33 13	55	118	34 08	55	117	35 03	56	117	35 59	55	116	36 54	55	116	308
53	32 51	55	117	33 46	56	116	34 42	55	116	35 37	55	115	36 32	54	115	307
54	32 29	55	116	33 24	56	115	34 20	55	115	35 15	54	114	36 09	55	114	306
55	32 07	+55	115	33 02	+55	114	33 57	+55	114	34 52	+55	113	35 47	+55	113	305
56	31 45	55	114	32 40	55	113	33 35	55	113	34 30	54	112	35 24	55	112	304
57	31 22	55	113	32 17	55	112	33 12	55	112	34 07	55	111	35 02	54	111	303
58	31 00	55	112	31 55	55	111	32 50	54	111	33 44	55	110	34 39	54	110	302
59	30 37	55	111	31 32	55	110	32 27	54	110	33 21	55	109	34 16	54	109	301
60	30 14	+55	110	31 09	+55	109	32 04	+54	109	32 58	+54	108	33 52	+55	108	300
61	29 51	55	109	30 46	54	108	31 40	55	108	32 35	54	107	33 29	54	107	299
62	29 28	55	108	30 23	54	107	31 17	54	107	32 11	55	106	33 06	54	106	298
63	29 05	54	107	29 59	55	106	30 54	54	106	31 48	54	105	32 42	54	105	297
64	28 41	55	106	29 36	54	105	30 30	54	105	31 24	54	104	32 18	55	104	296
65	28 18	+54	105	29 12	+54	104	30 06	+55	104	31 01	+54	103	31 55	+54	103	295
66	27 54	54	104	28 48	55	103	29 43	54	103	30 37	54	102	31 31	54	102	294
67	27 30	55	103	28 25	54	102	29 19	54	102	30 13	54	101	31 07	54	101	293
68	27 06	55	102	28 01	54	101	28 55	54	101	29 49	54	100	30 43	54	100	292
69	26 42	55	101	27 37	54	100	28 31	54	100	29 25	54	99	30 19	54	99	291

LHA	25° Hc	d	Z	26° Hc	d	Z	27° Hc	d	Z	28° Hc	d	Z	29° Hc	d	Z	LHA
	° ′	′	°	° ′	′	°	° ′	′	°	° ′	′	°	° ′	′	°	
0	49 00	+60	180	50 00	+60	180	51 00	+60	180	52 00	+60	180	53 00	+60	180	360
1	49 00	60	179	50 00	60	179	51 00	60	179	52 00	60	179	53 00	60	179	359
2	48 59	60	177	49 59	60	177	50 59	60	177	51 59	60	177	52 59	60	177	358
3	48 57	60	176	49 57	60	176	50 57	60	176	51 57	60	176	52 57	60	176	357
4	48 55	60	175	49 55	60	174	50 55	60	174	51 55	60	174	52 55	60	174	356
5	48 53	+60	173	49 53	+60	173	50 53	+59	173	51 52	+60	173	52 52	+60	173	355
6	48 49	60	172	49 49	60	172	50 49	60	172	51 49	60	171	52 49	60	171	354
7	48 46	60	170	49 46	59	170	50 45	60	170	51 45	60	170	52 45	60	170	353
8	48 41	60	169	49 41	60	169	50 41	60	169	51 41	59	169	52 40	60	168	352
9	48 36	60	168	49 36	60	168	50 36	59	167	51 35	60	167	52 35	60	167	351
10	48 31	+59	166	49 30	+60	166	50 30	+60	166	51 30	+59	166	52 29	+60	166	350
11	48 25	59	165	49 24	60	165	50 24	59	165	51 23	60	164	52 23	59	164	349
12	48 18	60	164	49 18	59	163	50 17	60	163	51 17	59	163	52 16	59	163	348
13	48 11	59	162	49 10	60	162	50 10	59	162	51 09	59	162	52 08	60	161	347
14	48 03	60	161	49 03	59	161	50 02	59	160	51 01	59	160	52 00	60	160	346
15	47 55	+59	160	48 54	+59	159	49 53	+60	159	50 53	+59	159	51 52	+59	159	345
16	47 46	59	158	48 45	59	158	49 44	59	158	50 43	59	157	51 42	59	157	344
17	47 37	59	157	48 36	59	157	49 35	59	156	50 34	59	156	51 33	59	156	343
18	47 27	59	156	48 26	59	155	49 25	59	155	50 24	58	155	51 22	59	154	342
19	47 17	58	154	48 15	59	154	49 14	59	154	50 13	59	153	51 12	58	153	341
20	47 06	+58	153	48 04	+59	153	49 03	+59	152	50 02	+58	152	51 00	+59	152	340
21	46 54	59	152	47 53	58	151	48 51	59	151	49 50	58	151	50 48	59	150	339
22	46 43	58	150	47 41	58	150	48 39	59	150	49 38	58	149	50 36	58	149	338
23	46 30	59	149	47 29	58	149	48 27	58	148	49 25	58	148	50 23	58	148	337
24	46 17	59	148	47 16	58	147	48 14	58	147	49 12	58	147	50 10	58	146	336
25	46 04	+58	147	47 02	+58	146	48 00	+58	146	48 58	+58	145	49 56	+58	145	335
26	45 50	58	145	46 48	58	145	47 46	58	145	48 44	58	144	49 42	57	144	334
27	45 36	58	144	46 34	58	144	47 32	58	143	48 30	57	143	49 27	58	142	333
28	45 22	57	143	46 19	58	142	47 17	58	142	48 15	57	142	49 12	57	141	332
29	45 07	57	142	46 04	58	141	47 02	57	141	47 59	58	140	48 57	57	140	331
30	44 51	+58	140	45 49	+57	140	46 46	+57	139	47 43	+58	139	48 41	+57	139	330
31	44 36	57	139	45 33	57	139	46 30	57	138	47 27	57	138	48 24	57	137	329
32	44 19	58	138	45 17	57	137	46 14	57	137	47 11	56	137	48 07	57	136	328
33	44 03	57	137	45 00	57	136	45 57	57	136	46 54	56	135	47 50	57	135	327
34	43 46	57	135	44 43	57	135	45 40	56	135	46 36	57	134	47 33	56	134	326
35	43 29	+56	134	44 25	+57	134	45 22	+57	133	46 19	+56	133	47 15	+56	132	325
36	43 11	57	133	44 08	56	133	45 04	56	132	46 00	57	132	46 57	56	131	324
37	42 53	56	132	43 49	57	131	44 46	56	131	45 42	56	131	46 38	56	130	323
38	42 35	56	131	43 31	56	130	44 27	56	130	45 23	56	129	46 19	56	129	322
39	42 16	56	130	43 12	56	129	44 08	56	129	45 04	56	128	46 00	56	128	321
40	41 57	+56	128	42 53	+56	128	43 49	+56	128	44 45	+56	127	45 41	+55	126	320
41	41 38	56	127	42 34	56	127	43 30	55	126	44 25	56	126	45 21	55	125	319
42	41 18	56	126	42 14	56	126	43 10	55	125	44 05	56	125	45 01	55	124	318
43	40 58	56	125	41 54	56	125	42 50	55	124	43 45	56	124	44 40	56	123	317
44	40 38	56	124	41 34	55	123	42 29	56	123	43 25	55	122	44 20	55	122	316
45	40 18	+55	123	41 13	+56	122	42 09	+55	122	43 04	+55	121	43 59	+55	121	315
46	39 57	56	122	40 53	55	121	41 48	55	121	42 43	55	120	43 38	55	120	314
47	39 36	56	121	40 32	55	120	41 27	55	120	42 22	55	119	43 17	54	119	313
48	39 15	55	120	40 10	55	119	41 05	55	119	42 00	55	118	42 55	55	117	312
49	38 54	55	119	39 49	55	118	40 44	55	118	41 39	54	117	42 33	55	116	311
50	38 32	+55	117	39 27	+55	117	40 22	+55	116	41 17	+54	116	42 11	+55	115	310
51	38 11	54	116	39 05	55	116	40 00	55	115	40 55	54	115	41 49	54	114	309
52	37 49	54	115	38 43	55	115	39 38	54	114	40 32	55	114	41 27	54	113	308
53	37 26	55	114	38 21	55	114	39 16	54	113	40 10	54	113	41 04	54	112	307
54	37 04	55	113	37 59	54	113	38 53	54	112	39 47	55	112	40 42	54	111	306
55	36 42	+54	112	37 36	+54	112	38 30	+55	111	39 25	+54	111	40 19	+54	110	305
56	36 19	54	111	37 13	55	111	38 08	54	110	39 02	54	110	39 56	54	109	304
57	35 56	54	110	36 50	55	110	37 45	54	109	38 39	54	109	39 33	53	108	303
58	35 33	54	109	36 27	55	109	37 22	53	108	38 15	54	108	39 09	54	107	302
59	35 10	54	108	36 04	54	108	36 58	54	107	37 52	54	107	38 46	53	106	301
60	34 47	+54	107	35 41	+54	107	36 35	+54	106	37 29	+53	106	38 22	+54	105	300
61	34 23	54	106	35 17	54	106	36 11	54	105	37 05	54	105	37 59	53	104	299
62	34 00	54	105	34 54	54	105	35 48	53	104	36 41	54	104	37 35	53	103	298
63	33 36	54	104	34 30	54	104	35 24	54	103	36 18	53	103	37 11	54	102	297
64	33 13	53	103	34 06	54	103	35 00	54	102	35 54	53	102	36 47	54	101	296
65	32 49	+54	102	33 43	+53	102	34 36	+54	101	35 30	+53	101	36 23	+54	100	295
66	32 25	54	101	33 19	53	101	34 12	54	100	35 06	53	100	35 59	53	99	294
67	32 01	54	100	32 55	53	100	33 48	54	99	34 42	53	99	35 35	53	98	293
68	31 37	54	99	32 31	53	99	33 24	54	98	34 18	53	98	35 11	53	97	292
69	31 13	53	98	32 06	54	98	33 00	53	97	33 53	54	97	34 47	53	96	291

S. Lat. {LHA greater than 180°....... Zn=180−Z; LHA less than 180°........... Zn=180+Z}

DECLINATION (15°-29°) SAME NAME AS LATITUDE

N. Lat. {LHA greater than 180°....... Zn=Z; LHA less than 180° .... Zn=360−Z}

DECLINATION (15°-29°) SAME NAME AS LATITUDE

	15°			16°			17°			18°			19°		
LHA	Hc	d	Z	Hc	d	Z	Hc	d	Z	Hc	d	Z	Hc	d	Z
	° ′	′	°	° ′	′	°	° ′	′	°	° ′	′	°	° ′	′	°
70	21 46	+55	102	22 41	+54	102	23 35	+55	101	24 30	+54	101	25 24	+54	100
71	21 22	55	101	22 17	54	101	23 11	55	100	24 06	54	100	25 00	54	99
72	20 58	55	100	21 53	54	100	22 47	56	99	23 42	54	99	24 36	54	99
73	20 34	55	99	21 29	54	99	22 23	55	99	23 18	54	98	24 12	54	98
74	20 10	54	99	21 04	55	98	21 59	54	98	22 53	55	97	23 48	54	97
75	19 46	+54	98	20 40	+55	97	21 35	+54	97	22 29	+54	96	23 23	+55	96
76	19 22	54	97	20 16	54	96	21 10	55	96	22 05	54	95	22 59	54	95
77	18 57	55	96	19 52	54	95	20 46	54	95	21 40	55	94	22 35	54	94
78	18 33	54	95	19 27	55	94	20 22	54	94	21 16	54	93	22 10	54	93
79	18 09	54	94	19 03	54	93	19 57	55	93	20 52	54	93	21 46	54	92
80	17 44	+55	93	18 39	+54	92	19 33	+54	92	20 27	+55	92	21 22	+54	91
81	17 20	54	92	18 14	55	92	19 09	54	91	20 03	54	91	20 57	54	90
82	16 56	54	91	17 50	54	91	18 44	55	90	19 39	54	90	20 33	54	89
83	16 31	55	90	17 26	54	90	18 20	54	89	19 14	54	89	20 08	54	88
84	16 07	54	89	17 01	54	89	17 55	55	88	18 50	54	88	19 44	54	87
85	15 42	+55	88	16 37	+54	88	17 31	+54	87	18 25	+55	87	19 20	+54	87
86	15 18	54	87	16 12	55	87	17 07	54	87	18 01	54	86	18 55	54	86
87	14 54	54	87	15 48	54	86	16 42	55	86	17 37	54	85	18 31	54	85
88	14 29	55	86	15 24	54	85	16 18	54	85	17 12	55	84	18 07	54	84
89	14 05	54	85	14 59	55	84	15 54	54	84	16 48	54	83	17 42	55	83
90	13 41	+54	84	14 35	+55	83	15 30	+54	83	16 24	+54	83	17 18	+54	82
91	13 16	55	83	14 11	54	82	15 05	55	82	16 00	54	82	16 54	54	81
92	12 52	55	82	13 47	54	82	14 41	55	81	15 36	54	81	16 30	54	80
93	12 28	55	81	13 23	54	81	14 17	55	80	15 12	54	80	16 06	54	79
94	12 04	55	80	12 59	54	80	13 53	55	79	14 48	54	79	15 42	54	79
95	11 40	+55	79	12 35	+54	79	13 29	+55	78	14 24	+54	78	15 18	+55	78
96	11 16	55	78	12 11	54	78	13 05	55	78	14 00	54	77	14 54	55	77
97	10 52	55	78	11 47	55	77	12 42	54	77	13 36	55	76	14 31	54	76
98	10 28	55	77	11 23	55	76	12 18	54	76	13 12	55	75	14 07	55	75
99	10 05	54	76	10 59	55	75	11 54	55	75	12 49	55	74	13 44	54	74
100	09 41	+55	75	10 36	+55	74	11 31	+54	74	12 25	+55	74	13 20	+55	73
101	09 18	54	74	10 12	55	74	11 07	56	73	12 02	55	73	12 57	55	72
102	08 54	55	73	09 49	55	73	10 44	55	72	11 39	55	72	12 34	54	71
103	08 31	55	72	09 26	55	72	10 21	55	71	11 16	55	71	12 11	54	71
104	08 08	55	71	09 03	55	71	09 58	55	70	10 53	55	70	11 48	55	70
105	07 45	+55	70	08 40	+55	70	09 35	+55	70	10 30	+55	69	11 25	+55	69
106	07 22	55	69	08 17	55	69	09 12	55	69	10 07	55	68	11 02	55	68
107	06 59	55	69	07 54	55	68	08 49	56	68	09 45	55	67	10 40	55	67
108	06 36	56	68	07 32	55	67	08 27	55	67	09 22	56	67	10 17	55	66
109	06 14	55	67	07 09	56	66	08 05	55	66	09 00	55	66	09 55	55	65
110	05 52	+55	66	06 47	+55	66	07 42	+56	65	08 38	+55	65	09 33	+55	64
111	05 29	56	65	06 25	55	65	07 20	56	64	08 16	55	64	09 11	56	63
112	05 07	56	64	06 03	55	64	06 58	56	63	07 54	55	63	08 49	56	63
113	04 45	56	63	05 41	56	63	06 37	55	62	07 32	56	62	08 28	55	62
114	04 24	55	62	05 19	56	62	06 15	56	62	07 11	55	61	08 06	56	61
115	04 02	+56	61	04 58	+56	61	05 54	+55	61	06 49	+56	60	07 45	+56	60
116	03 41	56	60	04 37	56	60	05 33	55	60	06 28	56	59	07 24	56	59
117	03 20	56	60	04 16	56	59	05 12	56	59	06 08	55	59	07 03	56	58
118	02 59	56	59	03 55	56	58	04 51	56	58	05 47	56	58	06 43	56	57
119	02 38	56	58	03 34	56	57	04 30	56	57	05 26	56	57	06 22	56	56
120	02 18	+56	57	03 14	+56	56	04 10	+56	56	05 06	+56	56	06 02	+56	55
121	01 57	56	56	02 53	57	56	03 50	56	55	04 46	56	55	05 42	56	55
122	01 37	56	55	02 33	57	55	03 30	56	54	04 26	56	54	05 22	57	54
123	01 17	57	54	02 14	56	54	03 10	56	53	04 06	57	53	05 03	56	53
124	00 58	56	53	01 54	57	53	02 51	56	53	03 47	56	52	04 43	57	52
125	00 38	+57	52	01 35	+56	52	02 31	+57	52	03 28	+56	51	04 24	+57	51
126	00 19	57	51	01 16	56	51	02 12	57	51	03 09	57	50	04 06	56	50
127	00 00	57	50	00 57	57	50	01 54	56	50	02 50	57	50	03 47	57	49
128	−0 19	57	50	00 38	57	49	01 35	57	49	02 32	57	49	03 29	56	48
129	−0 37	57	49	00 20	57	48	01 17	57	48	02 14	57	48	03 11	56	47
130	−0 55	+57	48	00 02	+57	47	00 59	+57	47	01 56	+57	47	02 53	+57	46
131	−1 13	57	47	−0 16	57	47	00 41	57	46	01 38	57	46	02 35	57	46
132	−1 31	57	46	−0 34	57	46	00 23	58	45	01 21	57	45	02 18	57	45
133	−1 48	57	45	−0 51	57	45	00 06	58	44	01 04	57	44	02 01	57	44
134	−2 05	57	44	−1 08	57	44	−0 11	58	43	00 47	57	43	01 44	57	43
135	−2 22	+57	43	−1 25	+58	43	−0 27	+57	43	00 30	+58	42	01 28	+57	42
136	−2 39	58	42	−1 41	57	42	−0 44	58	42	00 14	57	41	01 11	58	41
137	−2 55	58	41	−1 57	57	41	−1 00	58	41	−0 02	58	40	00 56	57	40
138	−3 11	58	40	−2 13	57	40	−1 16	58	40	−0 18	58	40	00 40	58	39
139	−3 27	58	39	−2 29	58	39	−1 31	58	39	−0 33	58	39	00 25	57	38

	20°			21°			22°			23°			24°		
LHA	Hc	d	Z	Hc	d	Z	Hc	d	Z	Hc	d	Z	Hc	d	Z
	° ′	′	°	° ′	′	°	° ′	′	°	° ′	′	°	° ′	′	°
70	26 18	+55	100	27 13	+54	99	28 07	+54	99	29 01	+54	99	29 55	+54	98
71	25 54	55	99	26 49	54	99	27 43	54	98	28 37	54	98	29 31	53	97
72	25 30	54	98	26 24	54	98	27 18	54	97	28 12	54	97	29 06	54	96
73	25 06	54	97	26 00	54	97	26 54	54	96	27 48	54	96	28 42	54	95
74	24 42	54	96	25 36	54	96	26 30	54	95	27 24	54	95	28 18	53	94
75	24 18	+54	95	25 12	+54	95	26 06	+54	94	27 00	+53	94	27 53	+54	93
76	23 53	54	94	24 47	54	94	25 41	54	93	26 35	54	93	27 29	54	92
77	23 29	54	93	24 23	54	93	25 17	54	92	26 11	54	92	27 05	53	91
78	23 04	55	93	23 59	54	92	24 53	53	92	25 46	54	91	26 40	54	91
79	22 40	54	92	23 34	54	91	24 28	54	91	25 22	54	90	26 16	53	90
80	22 16	+54	91	23 10	+54	90	24 04	+54	90	24 58	+53	89	25 51	+54	89
81	21 51	54	90	22 45	54	89	23 39	54	89	24 33	54	88	25 27	54	88
82	21 27	54	89	22 21	54	88	23 15	54	88	24 09	54	87	25 03	53	87
83	21 02	55	88	21 57	54	87	22 51	53	87	23 44	54	87	24 38	54	86
84	20 38	54	87	21 32	54	87	22 26	54	86	23 20	54	86	24 14	54	85
85	20 14	+54	86	21 08	+54	86	22 02	+54	85	22 56	+54	85	23 50	+53	84
86	19 49	55	85	20 44	54	85	21 38	53	84	22 31	54	84	23 25	54	83
87	19 25	54	84	20 19	54	84	21 13	54	83	22 07	54	83	23 01	54	82
88	19 01	54	83	19 55	54	83	20 49	54	83	21 43	54	82	22 37	54	82
89	18 37	54	83	19 31	54	82	20 25	54	82	21 19	54	81	22 13	54	81
90	18 12	+55	82	19 07	+54	81	20 01	+54	81	20 55	+54	80	21 49	+54	80
91	17 48	55	81	18 43	54	80	19 37	54	80	20 31	54	79	21 25	54	79
92	17 24	55	80	18 19	54	79	19 13	54	79	20 07	54	78	21 01	54	78
93	17 00	55	79	17 55	54	79	18 49	54	78	19 43	54	78	20 37	54	77
94	16 36	55	78	17 31	54	78	18 25	54	77	19 19	54	77	20 13	54	76
95	16 13	+54	77	17 07	+54	77	18 01	+55	76	18 56	+54	76	19 50	+54	75
96	15 49	54	76	16 43	55	76	17 38	54	75	18 32	54	75	19 26	54	75
97	15 25	55	75	16 20	54	75	17 14	54	75	18 08	55	74	19 03	54	74
98	15 02	54	75	15 56	55	74	16 51	54	74	17 45	54	73	18 39	55	73
99	14 38	55	74	15 33	54	73	16 27	55	73	17 22	54	72	18 16	54	72
100	14 15	+54	73	15 09	+55	72	16 04	+54	72	16 58	+55	71	17 53	+54	71
101	13 52	54	72	14 46	55	71	15 41	54	71	16 35	55	71	17 30	54	70
102	13 28	55	71	14 23	55	71	15 18	54	70	16 12	55	70	17 07	55	69
103	13 05	55	70	14 00	55	70	14 55	55	69	15 50	54	69	16 44	55	68
104	12 43	54	69	13 37	55	69	14 32	55	68	15 27	55	68	16 22	54	68
105	12 20	+55	68	13 15	+55	68	14 10	+54	68	15 04	+55	67	15 59	+55	67
106	11 57	55	67	12 52	55	67	13 47	55	67	14 42	55	66	15 37	55	66
107	11 35	55	67	12 30	55	66	13 25	55	66	14 20	55	65	15 15	55	65
108	11 12	56	66	12 08	55	65	13 03	56	65	13 58	55	64	14 53	55	64
109	10 50	55	65	11 45	56	64	12 41	55	64	13 36	55	64	14 31	55	63
110	10 28	+56	64	11 24	+55	64	12 19	+55	63	13 14	+55	63	14 09	+55	62
111	10 06	56	63	11 02	55	63	11 57	55	62	12 52	56	62	13 48	55	61
112	09 45	55	62	10 40	56	62	11 36	55	61	12 31	55	61	13 26	56	61
113	09 23	56	61	10 19	55	61	11 14	56	61	12 10	55	60	13 05	55	60
114	09 02	56	60	09 58	55	60	10 53	56	60	11 49	55	59	12 44	56	59
115	08 41	+56	60	09 37	+55	59	10 32	+56	59	11 28	+55	58	12 23	+56	58
116	08 20	56	59	09 16	55	58	10 11	56	58	11 07	56	58	12 03	55	57
117	07 59	56	58	08 55	56	57	09 51	56	57	10 47	55	57	11 42	56	56
118	07 39	56	57	08 35	55	57	09 30	56	56	10 26	56	56	11 22	56	55
119	07 18	56	56	08 14	56	56	09 10	56	55	10 06	56	55	11 02	56	55
120	06 58	+56	55	07 54	+56	55	08 50	+56	54	09 46	+56	54	10 42	+56	54
121	06 38	57	54	07 35	56	54	08 31	56	54	09 27	56	53	10 23	56	53
122	06 19	56	53	07 15	56	53	08 11	56	53	09 07	57	52	10 04	56	52
123	05 59	57	52	06 56	56	52	07 52	56	52	08 48	57	51	09 45	56	51
124	05 40	56	52	06 36	57	51	07 33	56	51	08 29	57	51	09 26	56	50
125	05 21	+57	51	06 18	+56	50	07 14	+57	50	08 11	+56	50	09 07	+57	49
126	05 02	57	50	05 59	56	49	06 55	57	49	07 52	57	49	08 49	56	48
127	04 44	56	49	05 40	57	49	06 37	57	48	07 34	57	48	08 31	56	48
128	04 25	57	48	05 22	57	48	06 19	57	47	07 16	57	47	08 13	56	47
129	04 07	57	47	05 04	57	47	06 01	57	46	06 58	57	46	07 55	57	46
130	03 50	+57	46	04 47	+57	46	05 44	+57	46	06 41	+57	45	07 38	+57	45
131	03 32	57	45	04 29	57	45	05 26	58	45	06 24	57	44	07 21	57	44
132	03 15	57	44	04 12	57	44	05 09	58	44	06 07	57	44	07 04	57	43
133	02 58	57	43	03 55	58	43	04 53	57	43	05 50	57	43	06 47	57	42
134	02 41	58	43	03 39	57	42	04 36	58	42	05 34	57	42	06 31	57	41
135	02 25	+58	42	03 23	+57	41	04 20	+57	41	05 17	+58	41	06 15	+57	41
136	02 09	58	41	03 07	57	41	04 04	58	40	05 02	57	40	05 59	58	40
137	01 53	58	40	02 51	57	40	03 48	58	39	04 46	58	39	05 44	57	39
138	01 38	57	39	02 35	58	39	03 33	58	38	04 31	58	38	05 29	57	38
139	01 22	58	38	02 20	58	38	03 18	58	38	04 16	58	37	05 14	58	37

	25°			26°			27°			28°			29°			
LHA	Hc	d	Z	Hc	d	Z	Hc	d	Z	Hc	d	Z	Hc	d	Z	LHA
	° ′	′	°	° ′	′	°	° ′	′	°	° ′	′	°	° ′	′	°	
70	30 49	+53	97	31 42	+54	97	32 36	+53	96	33 29	+53	96	34 22	+53	95	290
71	30 24	54	97	31 18	53	96	32 11	54	95	33 05	53	95	33 58	53	94	289
72	30 00	54	96	30 54	53	95	31 47	53	95	32 40	54	94	33 34	53	93	288
73	29 36	53	95	30 29	54	94	31 23	53	94	32 16	53	93	33 09	53	93	287
74	29 11	54	94	30 05	53	93	30 58	54	93	31 52	53	92	32 45	53	92	286
75	28 47	+54	93	29 41	+53	92	30 34	+53	92	31 27	+54	91	32 21	+53	91	285
76	28 23	53	92	29 16	54	91	30 10	53	91	31 03	53	90	31 56	53	90	284
77	27 58	54	91	28 52	53	90	29 45	54	90	30 39	53	89	31 32	53	89	283
78	27 34	53	90	28 27	54	90	29 21	53	89	30 14	53	89	31 07	53	88	282
79	27 09	54	89	28 03	53	89	28 56	54	88	29 50	53	88	30 43	53	87	281
80	26 45	+54	88	27 39	+53	88	28 32	+53	87	29 25	+54	87	30 19	+53	86	280
81	26 21	53	87	27 14	54	87	28 08	53	86	29 01	53	86	29 54	53	85	279
82	25 56	54	86	26 50	53	86	27 43	54	85	28 37	53	85	29 30	53	84	278
83	25 32	54	86	26 26	53	85	27 19	53	85	28 12	54	84	29 06	53	83	277
84	25 08	53	85	26 01	54	84	26 55	53	84	27 48	53	83	28 41	54	83	276
85	24 43	+54	84	25 37	+54	83	26 31	+53	83	27 24	+53	82	28 17	+54	82	275
86	24 19	54	83	25 13	53	82	26 06	54	82	27 00	53	81	27 53	53	81	274
87	23 55	54	82	24 49	53	81	25 42	54	81	26 36	53	80	27 29	53	80	273
88	23 31	54	81	24 25	53	81	25 18	54	80	26 12	53	80	27 05	53	79	272
89	23 07	53	80	24 00	54	80	24 54	54	79	25 48	53	79	26 41	54	78	271
90	22 43	+54	79	23 37	+53	79	24 30	+54	78	25 24	+53	78	26 17	+54	77	270
91	22 19	54	78	23 13	53	78	24 06	54	77	25 00	54	77	25 54	53	76	269
92	21 55	54	78	22 49	54	77	23 43	53	77	24 36	54	76	25 30	53	76	268
93	21 31	54	77	22 25	54	76	23 19	54	76	24 13	53	75	25 06	54	75	267
94	21 07	54	76	22 01	54	75	22 55	54	75	23 49	54	74	24 43	53	74	266
95	20 44	+54	75	21 38	+54	74	22 32	+54	74	23 26	+53	74	24 19	+54	73	265
96	20 20	54	74	21 14	54	74	22 08	54	73	23 02	54	73	23 56	54	72	264
97	19 57	54	73	20 51	54	73	21 45	54	72	22 39	54	72	23 33	54	71	263
98	19 34	54	72	20 28	54	72	21 22	54	71	22 16	54	71	23 10	54	70	262
99	19 10	55	71	20 05	54	71	20 59	54	71	21 53	54	70	22 47	54	70	261
100	18 47	+55	71	19 42	+54	70	20 36	+54	70	21 30	+54	69	22 24	+54	69	260
101	18 24	55	70	19 19	54	69	20 13	54	69	21 07	55	68	22 02	54	68	259
102	18 02	54	69	18 56	54	68	19 50	55	68	20 45	54	67	21 39	54	67	258
103	17 39	54	68	18 33	55	68	19 28	54	67	20 22	55	67	21 17	54	66	257
104	17 16	55	67	18 11	55	67	19 06	54	66	20 00	54	66	20 54	55	65	256
105	16 54	+55	66	17 49	+54	66	18 43	+55	65	19 38	+54	65	20 32	+55	64	255
106	16 32	54	65	17 26	55	65	18 21	55	65	19 16	54	64	20 10	55	64	254
107	16 10	54	65	17 04	55	64	17 59	55	64	18 54	55	63	19 49	54	63	253
108	15 48	55	64	16 43	54	63	17 37	55	63	18 32	55	62	19 27	55	62	252
109	15 26	55	63	16 21	55	62	17 16	55	62	18 11	55	62	19 06	54	61	251
110	15 04	+55	62	15 59	+55	62	16 54	+55	61	17 49	+55	61	18 44	+55	60	250
111	14 43	55	61	15 38	55	61	16 33	55	60	17 28	55	60	18 23	55	59	249
112	14 22	55	60	15 17	55	60	16 12	55	59	17 07	55	59	18 02	55	59	248
113	14 00	56	59	14 56	55	59	15 51	55	59	16 46	56	58	17 42	55	58	247
114	13 40	55	58	14 35	55	58	15 30	56	58	16 26	55	57	17 21	55	57	246
115	13 19	+55	58	14 14	+56	57	15 10	+55	57	16 05	+56	56	17 01	+55	56	245
116	12 58	56	57	13 54	56	56	14 50	55	56	15 45	56	56	16 41	55	55	244
117	12 38	56	56	13 34	55	56	14 29	56	55	15 25	56	55	16 21	55	54	243
118	12 18	56	55	13 14	56	55	14 10	55	54	15 05	56	54	16 01	56	54	242
119	11 58	56	54	12 54	56	54	13 50	56	53	14 46	55	53	15 41	56	53	241
120	11 38	+56	53	12 34	+56	53	13 30	+56	53	14 26	+56	52	15 22	+56	52	240
121	11 19	56	52	12 15	56	52	13 11	56	52	14 07	56	51	15 03	56	51	239
122	11 00	56	52	11 56	56	51	12 52	56	51	13 48	56	50	14 44	56	50	238
123	10 41	56	51	11 37	56	50	12 33	56	50	13 29	57	50	14 26	56	49	237
124	10 22	56	50	11 18	57	50	12 15	56	49	13 11	56	49	14 07	57	48	236
125	10 04	+56	49	11 00	+56	49	11 56	+57	48	12 53	+56	48	13 49	+57	48	235
126	09 45	57	48	10 42	56	48	11 38	57	47	12 35	56	47	13 31	57	47	234
127	09 27	57	47	10 24	56	47	11 20	57	47	12 17	57	46	13 14	56	46	233
128	09 09	57	46	10 06	57	46	11 03	57	46	12 00	56	45	12 56	57	45	232
129	08 52	57	46	09 49	57	45	10 46	56	45	11 42	57	45	12 39	57	44	231
130	08 35	+57	45	09 32	+56	44	10 28	+57	44	11 25	+57	44	12 22	+57	43	230
131	08 18	57	44	09 15	57	43	10 12	57	43	11 09	57	43	12 06	57	43	229
132	08 01	57	43	08 58	57	43	09 55	57	42	10 52	57	42	11 49	57	42	228
133	07 44	58	42	08 42	57	42	09 39	57	41	10 36	57	41	11 33	57	41	227
134	07 28	58	41	08 26	57	41	09 23	57	41	10 20	57	40	11 17	58	40	226
135	07 12	+58	40	08 10	+57	40	09 07	+58	40	10 05	+57	39	11 02	+57	39	225
136	06 57	57	39	07 54	58	39	08 52	57	39	09 49	58	39	10 47	57	38	224
137	06 41	58	39	07 39	58	38	08 37	57	38	09 34	58	38	10 32	57	37	223
138	06 26	58	38	07 24	58	37	08 22	57	37	09 19	58	37	10 17	58	37	222
139	06 12	57	37	07 09	58	37	08 07	58	36	09 05	58	36	10 03	57	36	221

S. Lat. {LHA greater than 180°....... Zn=180−Z; LHA less than 180° .... Zn=180+Z}

DECLINATION (15°-29°) SAME NAME AS LATITUDE

LAT 66°

N. Lat. {LHA greater than 180°....... Zn=Z
{LHA less than 180°........... Zn=360−Z

DECLINATION (15°-29°) SAME NAME AS LATITUDE

	15°			16°			17°			18°			19°		
LHA	Hc	d	Z	Hc	d	Z	Hc	d	Z	Hc	d	Z	Hc	d	Z
	° ′	′	°	° ′	′	°	° ′	′	°	° ′	′	°	° ′	′	°
140	−3 42	+58	38	−2 44	+58	38	−1 46	+58	38	−0 48	+58	38	00 10	+58	37
141	−3 57	58	38	−2 59	58	37	−2 01	58	37	−1 03	58	37	−0 05	58	37
142	−4 12	58	37	−3 14	58	36	−2 16	59	36	−1 17	58	36	−0 19	58	36
143	−4 26	58	36	−3 28	58	35	−2 30	58	35	−1 32	59	35	−0 33	58	35
144	−4 40	58	35	−3 42	58	34	−2 44	59	34	−1 45	58	34	−0 47	58	34
145	−4 54	+58	34	−3 56	+59	34	−2 57	+58	33	−1 59	+58	33	−1 01	+59	33
146	−5 07	58	33	−4 09	59	33	−3 10	58	32	−2 12	58	32	−1 14	59	32
147	−5 20	58	32	−4 22	59	32	−3 23	58	31	−2 25	59	31	−1 26	58	31
148				−4 34	58	31	−3 36	59	31	−2 37	58	30	−1 39	59	30
149				−4 47	59	30	−3 48	59	30	−2 49	58	29	−1 51	59	29
150				−4 59	+59	29	−4 00	+59	29	−3 01	+58	28	−2 03	+59	28
151				−5 10	58	28	−4 12	59	28	−3 13	59	28	−2 14	59	27
152				−5 22	59	27	−4 23	59	27	−3 24	59	27	−2 25	59	26
153							−4 34	59	26	−3 35	59	26	−2 36	59	25
154							−4 44	59	25	−3 45	59	25	−2 46	59	25
155							−4 54	+59	24	−3 55	+59	24	−2 56	+59	24
156							−5 04	59	23	−4 05	60	23	−3 05	59	23
157							−5 13	59	22	−4 14	59	22	−3 15	60	22
158										−4 23	60	21	−3 23	59	21
159										−4 31	59	20	−3 32	59	20
160										−4 39	+59	19	−3 40	+59	19
161										−4 47	59	18	−3 48	60	18
162										−4 55	60	17	−3 55	59	17
163										−5 02	60	16	−4 02	60	16
164										−5 08	59	15	−4 09	60	15
165													−4 15	+60	14
166													−4 21	60	13
167													−4 26	60	12
168													−4 31	60	11
169													−4 36	60	10
170													−4 40	+60	9
171													−4 44	60	9
172													−4 47	60	8
173													−4 50	60	7
174													−4 53	60	6
175													−4 55	+60	5
176													−4 57	60	4
177													−4 58	60	3
178													−4 59	60	2
179													−5 00	60	1
180													−5 00	+60	0

	20°			21°			22°			23°			24°		
LHA	Hc	d	Z	Hc	d	Z	Hc	d	Z	Hc	d	Z	Hc	d	Z
	° ′	′	°	° ′	′	°	° ′	′	°	° ′	′	°	° ′	′	°
140	01 08	+58	37	02 06	+57	37	03 03	+58	37	04 01	+58	36	04 59	+58	36
141	00 53	58	36	01 51	58	36	02 49	58	36	03 47	58	35	04 45	58	35
142	00 39	58	35	01 37	58	35	02 35	58	35	03 33	58	35	04 31	58	34
143	00 25	58	34	01 23	58	34	02 21	58	34	03 19	58	34	04 17	59	33
144	00 11	58	34	01 09	59	33	02 08	58	33	03 06	58	33	04 04	58	33
145	−0 02	+58	33	00 56	+59	32	01 55	+58	32	02 53	+58	32	03 51	+59	32
146	−0 15	58	32	00 43	59	31	01 42	58	31	02 40	59	31	03 39	58	31
147	−0 28	59	31	00 31	58	31	01 29	59	30	02 28	58	30	03 26	59	30
148	−0 40	58	30	00 18	59	30	01 17	59	29	02 16	58	29	03 14	59	29
149	−0 52	59	29	00 07	58	29	01 05	59	29	02 04	59	28	03 03	58	28
150	−1 04	+59	28	−0 05	+59	28	00 54	+58	28	01 52	+59	27	02 51	+59	27
151	−1 15	59	27	−0 16	59	27	00 43	58	27	01 41	59	27	02 40	59	26
152	−1 26	59	26	−0 27	59	26	00 32	59	26	01 31	59	26	02 30	58	25
153	−1 37	59	25	−0 38	59	25	00 21	59	25	01 20	59	25	02 19	59	25
154	−1 47	59	24	−0 48	59	24	00 11	59	24	01 10	59	24	02 09	59	24
155	−1 57	+59	23	−0 58	+59	23	00 01	+60	23	01 01	+59	23	02 00	+59	23
156	−2 06	59	22	−1 07	59	22	−0 08	59	22	00 51	59	22	01 50	60	22
157	−2 15	59	22	−1 16	59	21	−0 17	59	21	00 42	60	21	01 42	59	21
158	−2 24	59	21	−1 25	59	20	−0 26	60	20	00 34	59	20	01 33	59	20
159	−2 33	60	20	−1 33	59	20	−0 34	59	19	00 25	60	19	01 25	59	19
160	−2 41	+60	19	−1 41	+59	19	−0 42	+60	18	00 18	+59	18	01 17	+59	18
161	−2 48	59	18	−1 49	60	18	−0 49	59	18	00 10	60	17	01 10	59	17
162	−2 56	60	17	−1 56	59	17	−0 57	60	17	00 03	60	17	01 03	59	16
163	−3 02	59	16	−2 03	60	16	−1 03	59	16	−0 04	60	16	00 56	59	15
164	−3 09	60	15	−2 09	59	15	−1 10	60	15	−0 10	59	15	00 49	60	15
165	−3 15	+60	14	−2 15	+59	14	−1 16	+60	14	−0 16	+60	14	00 44	+59	14
166	−3 21	60	13	−2 21	60	13	−1 21	59	13	−0 22	60	13	00 38	60	13
167	−3 26	59	12	−2 27	60	12	−1 27	60	12	−0 27	60	12	00 33	59	12
168	−3 31	60	11	−2 31	59	11	−1 32	60	11	−0 32	60	11	00 28	60	11
169	−3 36	60	10	−2 36	60	10	−1 36	60	10	−0 36	59	10	00 23	60	10
170	−3 40	+60	9	−2 40	+60	9	−1 40	+60	9	−0 40	+59	9	00 19	+60	9
171	−3 44	60	8	−2 44	60	8	−1 44	60	8	−0 44	60	8	00 16	60	8
172	−3 47	60	8	−2 47	60	7	−1 47	60	7	−0 47	59	7	00 12	60	7
173	−3 50	60	7	−2 50	60	7	−1 50	60	6	−0 50	60	6	00 10	59	6
174	−3 53	60	6	−2 53	60	6	−1 53	60	6	−0 53	60	6	00 07	60	5
175	−3 55	+60	5	−2 55	+60	5	−1 55	+60	5	−0 55	+60	5	00 05	+60	5
176	−3 57	60	4	−2 57	60	4	−1 57	60	4	−0 57	60	4	00 03	60	4
177	−3 58	60	3	−2 58	60	3	−1 58	60	3	−0 58	60	3	00 02	60	3
178	−3 59	60	2	−2 59	60	2	−1 59	60	2	−0 59	60	2	00 01	60	2
179	−4 00	60	1	−3 00	60	1	−2 00	60	1	−1 00	60	1	00 00	60	1
180	−4 00	+60	0	−3 00	+60	0	−2 00	+60	0	−1 00	+60	0	00 00	+60	0

	25°			26°			27°			28°			29°			
LHA	Hc	d	Z	Hc	d	Z	Hc	d	Z	Hc	d	Z	Hc	d	Z	LHA
	° ′	′	°	° ′	′	°	° ′	′	°	° ′	′	°	° ′	′	°	
140	05 57	+58	36	06 55	+58	36	07 53	+58	35	08 51	+58	35	09 49	+57	35	220
141	05 43	58	35	06 41	58	35	07 39	58	35	08 37	58	34	09 35	58	34	219
142	05 29	58	34	06 27	58	34	07 25	58	34	08 23	58	33	09 21	58	33	218
143	05 16	58	33	06 14	58	33	07 12	58	33	08 10	58	33	09 08	58	32	217
144	05 02	59	32	06 01	58	32	06 59	58	32	07 57	58	32	08 55	59	31	216
145	04 50	+58	31	05 48	+58	31	06 46	+59	31	07 45	+58	31	08 43	+58	31	215
146	04 37	58	31	05 35	59	30	06 34	58	30	07 32	59	30	08 31	58	30	214
147	04 25	58	30	05 23	59	30	06 22	58	29	07 20	59	29	08 19	58	29	213
148	04 13	58	29	05 11	59	29	06 10	59	28	07 09	58	28	08 07	59	28	212
149	04 01	59	28	05 00	59	28	05 59	58	28	06 57	59	27	07 56	59	27	211
150	03 50	+59	27	04 49	+58	27	05 47	+59	27	06 46	+59	26	07 45	+59	26	210
151	03 39	59	26	04 38	59	26	05 37	59	26	06 36	58	26	07 34	59	25	209
152	03 28	59	25	04 27	59	25	05 26	59	25	06 25	59	25	07 24	59	25	208
153	03 18	59	24	04 17	59	24	05 16	59	24	06 15	59	24	07 14	59	24	207
154	03 08	59	23	04 07	59	23	05 06	59	23	06 05	60	23	07 05	59	23	206
155	02 59	+59	23	03 58	+59	22	04 57	+59	22	05 56	+59	22	06 55	+59	22	205
156	02 50	59	22	03 49	59	21	04 48	59	21	05 47	59	21	06 46	60	21	204
157	02 41	59	21	03 40	59	21	04 39	60	20	05 39	59	20	06 38	59	20	203
158	02 32	60	20	03 32	59	20	04 31	59	20	05 30	60	19	06 30	59	19	202
159	02 24	60	19	03 24	59	19	04 23	59	19	05 22	60	19	06 22	59	18	201
160	02 16	+60	18	03 16	+59	18	04 15	+60	18	05 15	+59	18	06 14	+60	18	200
161	02 09	60	17	03 09	59	17	04 08	60	17	05 08	59	17	06 07	59	17	199
162	02 02	60	16	03 02	59	16	04 01	60	16	05 01	59	16	06 00	60	16	198
163	01 55	60	15	02 55	60	15	03 55	59	15	04 54	60	15	05 54	59	15	197
164	01 49	60	14	02 49	59	14	03 48	60	14	04 48	60	14	05 48	59	14	196
165	01 43	+60	14	02 43	+60	13	03 43	+59	13	04 42	+60	13	05 42	+60	13	195
166	01 38	59	13	02 37	60	13	03 37	60	12	04 37	60	12	05 37	59	12	194
167	01 32	60	12	02 32	60	12	03 32	60	12	04 32	60	11	05 32	59	11	193
168	01 28	59	11	02 27	60	11	03 27	60	11	04 27	60	11	05 27	60	11	192
169	01 23	60	10	02 23	60	10	03 23	60	10	04 23	60	10	05 23	59	10	191
170	01 19	+60	9	02 19	+60	9	03 19	+60	9	04 19	+60	9	05 19	+60	9	190
171	01 16	59	8	02 15	60	8	03 15	60	8	04 15	60	8	05 15	60	8	189
172	01 12	60	7	02 12	60	7	03 12	60	7	04 12	60	7	05 12	60	7	188
173	01 09	60	6	02 09	60	6	03 09	60	6	04 09	60	6	05 09	60	6	187
174	01 07	60	5	02 07	60	5	03 07	60	5	04 07	60	5	05 07	60	5	186
175	01 05	+60	5	02 05	+60	5	03 05	+60	4	04 05	+60	4	05 05	+60	4	185
176	01 03	60	4	02 03	60	4	03 03	60	4	04 03	60	4	05 03	60	4	184
177	01 02	60	3	02 02	60	3	03 02	60	3	04 02	60	3	05 02	60	3	183
178	01 01	60	2	02 01	60	2	03 01	60	2	04 01	60	2	05 01	60	2	182
179	01 00	60	1	02 00	60	1	03 00	60	1	04 00	60	1	05 00	60	1	181
180	01 00	+60	0	02 00	+60	0	03 00	+60	0	04 00	+60	0	05 00	+60	0	180

15°	16°	17°	18°	19°	20°	21°	22°	23°	24°	25°	26°	27°	28°	29°

S. Lat. {LHA greater than 180°....... Zn=180−Z
{LHA less than 180°........... Zn=180+Z

DECLINATION (15°-29°) SAME NAME AS LATITUDE

N. Lat. {LHA greater than 180°........ Zn=Z / LHA less than 180°........... Zn=360−Z}

DECLINATION (15°-29°) CONTRARY NAME TO LATITUDE

LHA	15° Hc	d	Z	16° Hc	d	Z	17° Hc	d	Z	18° Hc	d	Z	19° Hc	d	Z
	° ′	′	°	° ′	′	°	° ′	′	°	° ′	′	°	° ′	′	°
69	-5 29	56	115												
68	-5 07	56	116												
67	-4 45	56	117	-5 41	56	117									
66	-4 24	55	118	-5 19	56	118									
65	-4 02	-56	119	-4 58	-56	119									
64	-3 41	56	120	-4 37	56	120	-5 33	55	120						
63	-3 20	56	120	-4 16	56	121	-5 12	56	121						
62	-2 59	56	121	-3 55	56	122	-4 51	56	122						
61	-2 38	56	122	-3 34	56	123	-4 30	56	123	-5 26	56	123			
60	-2 18	-56	123	-3 14	-56	124	-4 10	-56	124	-5 06	-56	124			
59	-1 57	56	124	-2 53	57	124	-3 50	56	125	-4 46	56	125			
58	-1 37	56	125	-2 33	57	125	-3 30	56	126	-4 26	56	126	-5 22	57	126
57	-1 17	57	126	-2 14	56	126	-3 10	56	127	-4 06	57	127	-5 03	56	127
56	-0 58	56	127	-1 54	57	127	-2 51	56	127	-3 47	56	128	-4 43	57	128
55	-0 38	-57	128	-1 35	-56	128	-2 31	-57	128	-3 28	-56	129	-4 24	-57	129
54	-0 19	57	129	-1 16	56	129	-2 12	57	129	-3 09	57	130	-4 06	56	130
53	00 00	57	130	-0 57	57	130	-1 54	56	130	-2 50	57	130	-3 47	57	131
52	00 19	57	130	-0 38	57	131	-1 35	57	131	-2 32	57	131	-3 29	56	132
51	00 37	57	131	-0 20	57	132	-1 17	57	132	-2 14	57	132	-3 11	56	133
50	00 55	-57	132	-0 02	-57	133	-0 59	-57	133	-1 56	-57	133	-2 53	-57	134
49	01 13	57	133	00 16	57	133	-0 41	57	134	-1 38	57	134	-2 35	57	134
48	01 31	57	134	00 34	57	134	-0 23	58	135	-1 21	57	135	-2 18	57	135
47	01 48	57	135	00 51	57	135	-0 06	58	136	-1 04	57	136	-2 01	57	136
46	02 05	57	136	01 08	57	136	00 11	58	137	-0 47	57	137	-1 44	57	137
45	02 22	-57	137	01 25	-58	137	00 27	-57	137	-0 30	-58	138	-1 28	-57	138
44	02 39	58	138	01 41	57	138	00 44	58	138	-0 14	57	139	-1 11	58	139
43	02 55	58	139	01 57	57	139	01 00	58	139	00 02	58	140	-0 56	57	140
42	03 11	58	140	02 13	57	140	01 16	58	140	00 18	58	140	-0 40	58	141
41	03 27	58	141	02 29	58	141	01 31	58	141	00 33	58	141	-0 25	57	142
40	03 42	-58	142	02 44	-58	142	01 46	-58	142	00 48	-58	142	-0 10	-58	143
39	03 57	58	142	02 59	58	143	02 01	58	143	01 03	58	143	00 05	58	143
38	04 12	58	143	03 14	58	144	02 16	59	144	01 17	58	144	00 19	58	144
37	04 26	58	144	03 28	58	145	02 30	58	145	01 32	59	145	00 33	58	145
36	04 40	58	145	03 42	58	146	02 44	59	146	01 45	58	146	00 47	58	146
35	04 54	-58	146	03 56	-59	146	02 57	-58	147	01 59	-58	147	01 01	-59	147
34	05 07	58	147	04 09	59	147	03 10	58	148	02 12	58	148	01 14	59	148
33	05 20	58	148	04 22	59	148	03 23	58	149	02 25	59	149	01 26	58	149
32	05 33	59	149	04 34	58	149	03 36	59	149	02 37	58	150	01 39	59	150
31	05 46	59	150	04 47	59	150	03 48	59	150	02 49	58	151	01 51	59	151
30	05 58	-59	151	04 59	-59	151	04 00	-59	151	03 01	-58	152	02 03	-59	152
29	06 09	59	152	05 10	58	152	04 12	59	152	03 13	59	152	02 14	59	153
28	06 21	59	153	05 22	59	153	04 23	59	153	03 24	59	153	02 25	59	154
27	06 31	58	154	05 33	59	154	04 34	59	154	03 35	59	154	02 36	59	155
26	06 42	59	155	05 43	59	155	04 44	59	155	03 45	59	155	02 46	59	155
25	06 52	-59	156	05 53	-59	156	04 54	-59	156	03 55	-59	156	02 56	-59	156
24	07 02	59	157	06 03	59	157	05 04	59	157	04 05	60	157	03 05	59	157
23	07 12	60	158	06 12	59	158	05 13	59	158	04 14	59	158	03 15	60	158
22	07 21	60	159	06 21	59	159	05 22	59	159	04 23	60	159	03 23	59	159
21	07 29	59	160	06 30	59	160	05 31	60	160	04 31	59	160	03 32	59	160
20	07 38	-60	161	06 38	-59	161	05 39	-60	161	04 39	-59	161	03 40	-59	161
19	07 46	60	162	06 46	59	162	05 47	60	162	04 47	59	162	03 48	60	162
18	07 53	59	163	06 54	60	163	05 54	59	163	04 55	60	163	03 55	59	163
17	08 00	59	163	07 01	60	164	06 01	59	164	05 02	60	164	04 02	60	164
16	08 07	59	164	07 08	60	165	06 08	60	165	05 08	59	165	04 09	60	165
15	08 14	-60	165	07 14	-60	166	06 14	-59	166	05 15	-60	166	04 15	-60	166
14	08 19	59	166	07 20	60	166	06 20	60	167	05 20	59	167	04 21	60	167
13	08 25	60	167	07 25	59	167	06 26	60	168	05 26	60	168	04 26	60	168
12	08 30	60	168	07 30	59	168	06 31	60	169	05 31	60	169	04 31	60	169
11	08 35	60	169	07 35	60	169	06 35	60	169	05 35	59	170	04 36	60	170
10	08 39	-60	170	07 39	-59	170	06 40	-60	170	05 40	-60	170	04 40	-60	171
9	08 43	60	171	07 43	60	171	06 43	59	171	05 44	60	171	04 44	60	171
8	08 47	60	172	07 47	60	172	06 47	60	172	05 47	60	172	04 47	60	172
7	08 50	60	173	07 50	60	173	06 50	60	173	05 50	60	173	04 50	60	173
6	08 53	60	174	07 53	60	174	06 53	60	174	05 53	60	174	04 53	60	174
5	08 55	-60	175	07 55	-60	175	06 55	-60	175	05 55	-60	175	04 55	-60	175
4	08 57	60	176	07 57	60	176	06 57	60	176	05 57	60	176	04 57	60	176
3	08 58	60	177	07 58	60	177	06 58	60	177	05 58	60	177	04 58	60	177
2	08 59	60	178	07 59	60	178	06 59	60	178	05 59	60	178	04 59	60	178
1	09 00	60	179	08 00	60	179	07 00	60	179	06 00	60	179	05 00	60	179
0	09 00	-60	180	08 00	-60	180	07 00	-60	180	06 00	-60	180	05 00	-60	180

LHA	20° Hc	d	Z	21° Hc	d	Z	22° Hc	d	Z	23° Hc	d	Z	24° Hc	d	Z
	° ′	′	°	° ′	′	°	° ′	′	°	° ′	′	°	° ′	′	°
55	-5 21	-57	129												
54	-5 02	57	130												
53	-4 44	56	131												
52	-4 25	57	132	-5 22	57	132									
51	-4 07	57	133	-5 04	57	133									
50	-3 50	-57	134	-4 47	-57	134									
49	-3 32	57	135	-4 29	57	135	-5 26	58	135						
48	-3 15	57	136	-4 12	57	136	-5 09	58	136						
47	-2 58	57	137	-3 55	58	137	-4 53	57	137						
46	-2 41	58	137	-3 39	57	138	-4 36	58	138						
45	-2 25	-58	138	-3 23	-57	139	-4 20	-57	139	-5 17	-58	139			
44	-2 09	58	139	-3 07	57	139	-4 04	58	140	-5 02	57	140			
43	-1 53	58	140	-2 51	57	140	-3 48	58	141	-4 46	58	141			
42	-1 38	57	141	-2 35	58	141	-3 33	58	142	-4 31	58	142	-5 29	57	142
41	-1 22	58	142	-2 20	58	142	-3 18	58	142	-4 16	58	143	-5 14	58	143
40	-1 08	-58	143	-2 06	-57	143	-3 03	-58	143	-4 01	-58	144	-4 59	-58	144
39	-0 53	58	144	-1 51	58	144	-2 49	58	144	-3 47	58	145	-4 45	58	145
38	-0 39	58	145	-1 37	58	145	-2 35	58	145	-3 33	58	145	-4 31	58	146
37	-0 25	58	146	-1 23	58	146	-2 21	58	146	-3 19	58	146	-4 17	59	147
36	-0 11	58	146	-1 09	59	147	-2 08	58	147	-3 06	58	147	-4 04	58	147
35	00 02	-58	147	-0 56	-59	148	-1 55	-58	148	-2 53	-58	148	-3 51	-59	148
34	00 15	58	148	-0 43	59	149	-1 42	58	149	-2 40	59	149	-3 39	58	149
33	00 28	59	149	-0 31	58	149	-1 29	59	150	-2 28	58	150	-3 26	59	150
32	00 40	58	150	-0 18	59	150	-1 17	59	151	-2 16	58	151	-3 14	59	151
31	00 52	59	151	-0 07	58	151	-1 05	59	151	-2 04	59	152	-3 03	58	152
30	01 04	-59	152	00 05	-59	152	-0 54	-58	152	-1 52	-59	153	-2 51	-59	153
29	01 15	59	153	00 16	59	153	-0 43	58	153	-1 41	59	153	-2 40	59	154
28	01 26	59	154	00 27	59	154	-0 32	59	154	-1 31	59	154	-2 30	58	155
27	01 37	59	155	00 38	59	155	-0 21	59	155	-1 20	59	155	-2 19	59	155
26	01 47	59	156	00 48	59	156	-0 11	59	156	-1 10	59	156	-2 09	59	156
25	01 57	-59	157	00 58	-59	157	-0 01	-60	157	-1 01	-59	157	-2 00	-59	157
24	02 06	59	158	01 07	59	158	00 08	59	158	-0 51	59	158	-1 50	60	158
23	02 15	59	158	01 16	59	159	00 17	59	159	-0 42	60	159	-1 42	59	159
22	02 24	59	159	01 25	59	160	00 26	60	160	-0 34	59	160	-1 33	59	160
21	02 33	60	160	01 33	59	160	00 34	59	161	-0 25	60	161	-1 25	59	161
20	02 41	-60	161	01 41	-59	161	00 42	-60	162	-0 18	-59	162	-1 17	-59	162
19	02 48	59	162	01 49	60	162	00 49	59	162	-0 10	60	163	-1 10	59	163
18	02 56	60	163	01 56	59	163	00 57	60	163	-0 03	60	163	-1 03	59	164
17	03 02	59	164	02 03	60	164	01 03	59	164	00 04	60	164	-0 56	59	165
16	03 09	60	165	02 09	59	165	01 10	60	165	00 10	59	165	-0 49	60	165
15	03 15	-60	166	02 15	-59	166	01 16	-60	166	00 16	-60	166	-0 44	-59	166
14	03 21	60	167	02 21	60	167	01 21	59	167	00 22	60	167	-0 38	60	167
13	03 26	59	168	02 27	60	168	01 27	60	168	00 27	60	168	-0 33	59	168
12	03 31	60	169	02 31	59	169	01 32	60	169	00 32	60	169	-0 28	60	169
11	03 36	60	170	02 36	60	170	01 36	60	170	00 36	59	170	-0 23	60	170
10	03 40	-60	171	02 40	-60	171	01 40	-60	171	00 40	-59	171	-0 19	-60	171
9	03 44	60	172	02 44	60	172	01 44	60	172	00 44	60	172	-0 16	60	172
8	03 47	60	172	02 47	60	173	01 47	60	173	00 47	59	173	-0 12	60	173
7	03 50	60	173	02 50	60	173	01 50	60	174	00 50	60	174	-0 10	59	174
6	03 53	60	174	02 53	60	174	01 53	60	174	00 53	60	174	-0 07	60	175
5	03 55	-60	175	02 55	-60	175	01 55	-60	175	00 55	-60	175	-0 05	-60	175
4	03 57	60	176	02 57	60	176	01 57	60	176	00 57	60	176	-0 03	60	176
3	03 58	60	177	02 58	60	177	01 58	60	177	00 58	60	177	-0 02	60	177
2	03 59	60	178	02 59	60	178	01 59	60	178	00 59	60	178	-0 01	60	178
1	04 00	60	179	03 00	60	179	02 00	60	179	01 00	60	179	00 00	60	179
0	04 00	-60	180	03 00	-60	180	02 00	-60	180	01 00	-60	180	00 00	-60	180

LHA	25° Hc	d	Z	26° Hc	d	Z	27° Hc	d	Z	28° Hc	d	Z	29° Hc	d	Z	LHA
	° ′	′	°	° ′	′	°	° ′	′	°	° ′	′	°	° ′	′	°	
69																291
68																292
67																293
66																294
65																295
64																296
63																297
62																298
61																299
60																300
59																301
58																302
57																303
56																304
55																305
54																306
53																307
52																308
51																309
50																310
49																311
48																312
47																313
46																314
45																315
44																316
43																317
42																318
41																319
40																320
39																321
38																322
37	-5 16	58	147													323
36	-5 02	59	148													324
35	-4 50	-58	149													325
34	-4 37	58	149													326
33	-4 25	58	150													327
32	-4 13	58	151	-5 11	59	151										328
31	-4 01	59	152	-5 00	59	152										329
30	-3 50	-59	153	-4 49	-58	153										330
29	-3 39	59	154	-4 38	59	154										331
28	-3 28	59	155	-4 27	59	155										332
27	-3 18	59	156	-4 17	59	156	-5 16	59	156							333
26	-3 08	59	157	-4 07	59	157	-5 06	59	157							334
25	-2 59	-59	157	-3 58	-59	158	-4 57	-59	158							335
24	-2 50	59	158	-3 49	59	159	-4 48	59	159							336
23	-2 41	59	159	-3 40	59	159	-4 39	60	160							337
22	-2 32	60	160	-3 32	59	160	-4 31	59	160							338
21	-2 24	60	161	-3 24	59	161	-4 23	59	161							339
20	-2 16	-60	162	-3 16	-59	162	-4 15	-60	162							340
19	-2 09	60	163	-3 09	59	163	-4 08	60	163	-5 08	59	163				341
18	-2 02	60	164	-3 02	59	164	-4 01	60	164	-5 01	59	164				342
17	-1 55	60	165	-2 55	60	165	-3 55	59	165	-4 54	60	165				343
16	-1 49	60	166	-2 49	59	166	-3 48	60	166	-4 48	60	166				344
15	-1 43	-60	166	-2 43	-60	167	-3 43	-59	167	-4 42	-60	167				345
14	-1 38	59	167	-2 37	60	167	-3 37	60	168	-4 37	60	168				346
13	-1 32	60	168	-2 32	60	168	-3 32	60	168	-4 32	60	169				347
12	-1 28	59	169	-2 27	60	169	-3 27	60	169	-4 27	60	169				348
11	-1 23	60	170	-2 23	60	170	-3 23	60	170	-4 23	60	170				349
10	-1 19	-60	171	-2 19	-60	171	-3 19	-60	171	-4 19	-60	171				350
9	-1 16	59	172	-2 15	60	172	-3 15	60	172	-4 15	60	172				351
8	-1 12	60	173	-2 12	60	173	-3 12	60	173	-4 12	60	173				352
7	-1 09	60	174	-2 09	60	174	-3 09	60	174	-4 09	60	174				353
6	-1 07	60	175	-2 07	60	175	-3 07	60	175	-4 07	60	175				354
5	-1 05	-60	175	-2 05	-60	175	-3 05	-60	176	-4 05	-60	176				355
4	-1 03	60	176	-2 03	60	176	-3 03	60	176	-4 03	60	176				356
3	-1 02	60	177	-2 02	60	177	-3 02	60	177	-4 02	60	177				357
2	-1 01	60	178	-2 01	60	178	-3 01	60	178	-4 01	60	178				358
1	-1 00	60	179	-2 00	60	179	-3 00	60	179	-4 00	60	179	-5 00	60	179	359
0	-1 00	-60	180	-2 00	-60	180	-3 00	-60	180	-4 00	-60	180	-5 00	-60	180	360

S. Lat. {LHA greater than 180°........ Zn=180−Z / LHA less than 180°........... Zn=180+Z}

DECLINATION (15°-29°) CONTRARY NAME TO LATITUDE

LAT 66°

N. Lat. {LHA greater than 180°....... Zn=Z; LHA less than 180°........... Zn=360−Z}

DECLINATION (0°-14°) SAME NAME AS LATITUDE

LHA	0° Hc	0° d	0° Z	1° Hc	1° d	1° Z	2° Hc	2° d	2° Z	3° Hc	3° d	3° Z	4° Hc	4° d	4° Z
	° ′	′	°	° ′	′	°	° ′	′	°	° ′	′	°	° ′	′	°
0	23 00	+60	180	24 00	+60	180	25 00	+60	180	26 00	+60	180	27 00	+60	180
1	23 00	60	179	24 00	60	179	25 00	60	179	26 00	60	179	27 00	60	179
2	22 59	60	178	23 59	60	178	24 59	60	178	25 59	60	178	26 59	60	178
3	22 58	60	177	23 58	60	177	24 58	60	177	25 58	60	177	26 58	60	177
4	22 56	60	176	23 56	60	176	24 56	60	176	25 56	60	176	26 56	60	176
5	22 54	+60	175	23 54	+60	175	24 54	+60	175	25 54	+60	174	26 54	+60	174
6	22 52	60	174	23 52	60	173	24 52	60	173	25 52	60	173	26 52	60	173
7	22 49	60	172	23 49	60	172	24 49	60	172	25 49	60	172	26 49	60	172
8	22 46	60	171	23 46	60	171	24 46	60	171	25 46	59	171	26 45	60	171
9	22 42	60	170	23 42	60	170	24 42	60	170	25 42	60	170	26 42	59	170
10	22 38	+60	169	23 38	+60	169	24 38	+59	169	25 37	+60	169	26 37	+60	169
11	22 33	60	168	23 33	60	168	24 33	60	168	25 33	59	168	26 32	60	168
12	22 28	60	167	23 28	60	167	24 28	60	167	25 28	59	167	26 27	60	167
13	22 23	59	166	23 22	60	166	24 22	60	166	25 22	60	166	26 22	59	166
14	22 17	60	165	23 17	59	165	24 16	60	165	25 16	60	165	26 16	59	164
15	22 10	+60	164	23 10	+60	164	24 10	+59	164	25 09	+60	163	26 09	+60	163
16	22 04	59	163	23 03	60	163	24 03	59	162	25 02	60	162	26 02	60	162
17	21 57	59	162	22 56	60	162	23 56	59	161	24 55	60	161	25 55	59	161
18	21 49	59	161	22 48	60	160	23 48	59	160	24 47	60	160	25 47	59	160
19	21 41	59	160	22 40	60	159	23 40	59	159	24 39	60	159	25 39	59	159
20	21 33	+59	158	22 32	+59	158	23 31	+60	158	24 31	+59	158	25 30	+59	158
21	21 24	59	157	22 23	59	157	23 22	60	157	24 22	59	157	25 21	59	157
22	21 14	60	156	22 14	59	156	23 13	59	156	24 12	59	156	25 11	60	156
23	21 05	59	155	22 04	59	155	23 03	59	155	24 02	60	155	25 02	59	155
24	20 55	59	154	21 54	59	154	22 53	59	154	23 52	59	154	24 51	59	153
25	20 44	+59	153	21 43	+60	153	22 43	+59	153	23 42	+59	153	24 41	+59	152
26	20 34	59	152	21 33	59	152	22 32	59	152	23 31	58	152	24 29	59	151
27	20 22	59	151	21 21	59	151	22 20	59	151	23 19	59	150	24 18	59	150
28	20 11	59	150	21 10	59	150	22 09	58	150	23 07	59	149	24 06	59	149
29	19 59	59	149	20 58	59	149	21 57	58	149	22 55	59	148	23 54	59	148
30	19 47	+58	148	20 45	+59	148	21 44	+59	148	22 43	+58	147	23 41	+59	147
31	19 34	59	147	20 33	58	147	21 31	59	146	22 30	58	146	23 28	59	146
32	19 21	59	146	20 20	58	146	21 18	59	145	22 17	58	145	23 15	59	145
33	19 08	58	145	20 06	59	145	21 05	58	144	22 03	58	144	23 01	59	144
34	18 54	58	144	19 52	59	144	20 51	58	143	21 49	58	143	22 47	59	143
35	18 40	+58	143	19 38	+59	143	20 37	+58	142	21 35	+58	142	22 33	+58	142
36	18 26	58	142	19 24	58	142	20 22	58	141	21 20	58	141	22 18	59	141
37	18 11	58	141	19 09	58	140	20 07	58	140	21 05	58	140	22 03	58	140
38	17 56	58	140	18 54	58	139	19 52	58	139	20 50	58	139	21 48	58	139
39	17 41	58	139	18 39	58	138	19 37	57	138	20 34	58	138	21 32	58	138
40	17 25	+58	138	18 23	+58	137	19 21	+58	137	20 19	+57	137	21 16	+58	137
41	17 09	58	137	18 07	58	136	19 05	57	136	20 02	58	136	21 00	58	136
42	16 53	58	136	17 51	57	135	18 48	58	135	19 46	58	135	20 44	57	135
43	16 36	58	135	17 34	58	134	18 32	57	134	19 29	58	134	20 27	57	133
44	16 19	58	134	17 17	58	133	18 15	57	133	19 12	57	133	20 09	58	132
45	16 02	+58	133	17 00	+57	132	17 57	+58	132	18 55	+57	132	19 52	+57	131
46	15 45	57	132	16 42	58	131	17 40	57	131	18 37	57	131	19 34	58	130
47	15 27	58	131	16 25	57	130	17 22	57	130	18 19	57	130	19 16	57	129
48	15 09	58	130	16 07	57	129	17 04	57	129	18 01	57	129	18 58	57	128
49	14 51	57	129	15 48	57	128	16 45	58	128	17 43	57	128	18 40	57	127
50	14 33	+57	128	15 30	+57	127	16 27	+57	127	17 24	+57	127	18 21	+57	126
51	14 14	57	127	15 11	57	126	16 08	57	126	17 05	57	126	18 02	57	125
52	13 55	57	126	14 52	57	125	15 49	57	125	16 46	57	125	17 43	56	124
53	13 36	57	125	14 33	57	124	15 30	56	124	16 26	57	124	17 23	57	123
54	13 17	56	124	14 13	57	123	15 10	57	123	16 07	56	123	17 03	57	122
55	12 57	+57	123	13 54	+56	123	14 50	+57	122	15 47	+57	122	16 44	+56	121
56	12 37	57	122	13 34	56	122	14 30	57	121	15 27	56	121	16 23	57	121
57	12 17	57	121	13 14	56	121	14 10	57	120	15 07	56	120	16 03	57	120
58	11 57	56	120	12 53	57	120	13 50	56	119	14 46	57	119	15 43	56	119
59	11 37	56	119	12 33	56	119	13 29	57	118	14 26	56	118	15 22	56	118
60	11 16	+56	118	12 12	+57	118	13 09	+56	117	14 05	+56	117	15 01	+56	117
61	10 55	56	117	11 51	57	117	12 48	56	116	13 44	56	116	14 40	56	116
62	10 34	56	116	11 30	57	116	12 27	56	115	13 23	56	115	14 19	56	115
63	10 13	56	115	11 09	56	115	12 05	56	114	13 01	56	114	13 57	56	114
64	09 52	56	114	10 48	56	114	11 44	56	114	12 40	56	113	13 36	56	113
65	09 30	+56	113	10 26	+56	113	11 22	+56	113	12 18	+56	112	13 14	+56	112
66	09 09	56	112	10 05	56	112	11 01	55	112	11 56	56	111	12 52	56	111
67	08 47	56	111	09 43	56	111	10 39	56	111	11 35	55	110	12 30	56	110
68	08 25	56	110	09 21	56	110	10 17	55	110	11 12	56	109	12 08	56	109
69	08 03	56	110	08 59	56	109	09 55	55	109	10 50	56	108	11 46	56	108

LHA	5° Hc	5° d	5° Z	6° Hc	6° d	6° Z	7° Hc	7° d	7° Z	8° Hc	8° d	8° Z	9° Hc	9° d	9° Z
	° ′	′	°	° ′	′	°	° ′	′	°	° ′	′	°	° ′	′	°
0	28 00	+60	180	29 00	+60	180	30 00	+60	180	31 00	+60	180	32 00	+60	180
1	28 00	60	179	29 00	60	179	30 00	60	179	31 00	60	179	32 00	60	179
2	27 59	60	178	28 59	60	178	29 59	60	178	30 59	60	178	31 59	60	178
3	27 58	60	177	28 58	60	177	29 58	60	177	30 58	60	177	31 58	60	177
4	27 56	60	176	28 56	60	176	29 56	60	175	30 56	60	175	31 56	60	175
5	27 54	+60	174	28 54	+60	174	29 54	+60	174	30 54	+60	174	31 54	+60	174
6	27 52	60	173	28 52	60	173	29 52	60	173	30 52	59	173	31 51	60	173
7	27 49	60	172	28 49	60	172	29 49	59	172	30 48	60	172	31 48	60	172
8	27 45	60	171	28 45	60	171	29 45	60	171	30 45	60	171	31 45	60	171
9	27 41	60	170	28 41	60	170	29 41	60	170	30 41	60	170	31 41	60	170
10	27 37	+60	169	28 37	+60	169	29 37	+60	169	30 37	+59	169	31 36	+60	168
11	27 32	60	168	28 32	60	168	29 32	60	167	30 32	59	167	31 31	60	167
12	27 27	60	167	28 27	60	166	29 27	59	166	30 26	60	166	31 26	60	166
13	27 21	60	165	28 21	60	165	29 21	59	165	30 20	60	165	31 20	60	165
14	27 15	60	164	28 15	59	164	29 14	60	164	30 14	60	164	31 14	59	164
15	27 09	+59	163	28 08	+60	163	29 08	+59	163	30 07	+60	163	31 07	+60	163
16	27 02	59	162	28 01	60	162	29 01	59	162	30 00	60	162	31 00	59	162
17	26 54	60	161	27 54	59	161	28 53	60	161	29 53	59	161	30 52	60	160
18	26 46	60	160	27 46	59	160	28 45	60	160	29 45	59	159	30 44	59	159
19	26 38	59	159	27 37	60	159	28 37	59	158	29 36	59	158	30 35	60	158
20	26 29	+60	158	27 29	+59	158	28 28	+59	157	29 27	+59	157	30 26	+60	157
21	26 20	59	157	27 19	60	156	28 19	59	156	29 18	59	156	30 17	59	156
22	26 11	59	155	27 10	59	155	28 09	59	155	29 08	59	155	30 07	59	155
23	26 01	59	154	27 00	59	154	27 59	59	154	28 58	59	154	29 57	59	154
24	25 50	59	153	26 49	59	153	27 48	59	153	28 47	59	153	29 46	59	152
25	25 40	+59	152	26 39	+58	152	27 37	+59	152	28 36	+59	152	29 35	+59	151
26	25 28	59	151	26 27	59	151	27 26	59	151	28 25	59	150	29 24	59	150
27	25 17	59	150	26 16	58	150	27 14	59	150	28 13	59	149	29 12	59	149
28	25 05	59	149	26 04	58	149	27 02	59	149	28 01	59	148	29 00	58	148
29	24 53	58	148	25 51	59	148	26 50	59	147	27 49	58	147	28 47	59	147
30	24 40	+59	147	25 39	+58	147	26 37	+59	146	27 36	+58	146	28 34	+59	146
31	24 27	58	146	25 25	59	145	26 24	58	145	27 22	59	145	28 21	58	145
32	24 14	58	145	25 12	58	144	26 10	59	144	27 09	58	144	28 07	58	144
33	24 00	58	144	24 58	58	143	25 56	59	143	26 55	58	143	27 53	58	143
34	23 46	58	143	24 44	58	142	25 42	58	142	26 40	59	142	27 39	58	141
35	23 31	+58	142	24 29	+59	141	25 28	+58	141	26 26	+58	141	27 24	+58	140
36	23 17	58	140	24 15	58	140	25 13	58	140	26 11	58	140	27 09	58	139
37	23 01	58	139	23 59	58	139	24 57	58	139	25 55	58	139	26 53	58	138
38	22 46	58	138	23 44	58	138	24 42	58	138	25 40	57	137	26 37	58	137
39	22 30	58	137	23 28	58	137	24 26	58	137	25 24	57	136	26 21	58	136
40	22 14	+58	136	23 12	+58	136	24 10	+57	136	25 07	+58	135	26 05	+57	135
41	21 58	57	135	22 55	58	135	23 53	58	135	24 51	57	134	25 48	58	134
42	21 41	58	134	22 39	57	134	23 36	58	134	24 34	57	133	25 31	58	133
43	21 24	58	133	22 22	57	133	23 19	57	133	24 16	58	132	25 14	57	132
44	21 07	57	132	22 04	58	132	23 02	57	132	23 59	57	131	24 56	57	131
45	20 49	+58	131	21 47	+57	131	22 44	+57	131	23 41	+57	130	24 38	+57	130
46	20 32	57	130	21 29	57	130	22 26	57	129	23 23	57	129	24 20	57	129
47	20 13	58	129	21 11	57	129	22 08	57	128	23 05	57	128	24 02	57	128
48	19 55	57	128	20 52	57	128	21 49	57	127	22 46	57	127	23 43	57	127
49	19 37	57	127	20 34	56	127	21 30	57	126	22 27	57	126	23 24	57	126
50	19 18	+57	126	20 15	+56	126	21 11	+57	125	22 08	+57	125	23 05	+57	125
51	18 59	56	125	19 55	57	125	20 52	57	124	21 49	57	124	22 46	56	124
52	18 39	57	124	19 36	57	124	20 33	56	123	21 29	57	123	22 26	57	123
53	18 20	56	123	19 16	57	123	20 13	57	122	21 10	56	122	22 06	57	122
54	18 00	57	122	18 57	56	122	19 53	57	121	20 50	56	121	21 46	56	121
55	17 40	+57	121	18 37	+56	121	19 33	+56	120	20 29	+57	120	21 26	+56	120
56	17 20	56	120	18 16	57	120	19 13	56	119	20 09	56	119	21 05	57	119
57	17 00	56	119	17 56	56	119	18 52	56	118	19 48	57	118	20 45	56	118
58	16 39	56	118	17 35	56	118	18 31	57	117	19 28	56	117	20 24	56	117
59	16 18	56	117	17 14	57	117	18 11	56	116	19 07	56	116	20 03	56	116
60	15 57	+56	116	16 53	+56	116	17 49	+57	116	18 46	+56	115	19 42	+56	115
61	15 36	56	115	16 32	56	115	17 28	56	115	18 24	56	114	19 20	56	114
62	15 15	56	114	16 11	56	114	17 07	56	114	18 03	56	113	18 59	55	113
63	14 53	56	113	15 49	56	113	16 45	56	113	17 41	56	112	18 37	56	112
64	14 32	56	112	15 28	56	112	16 24	55	112	17 19	56	111	18 15	56	111
65	14 10	+56	111	15 06	+56	111	16 02	+55	111	16 57	+56	110	17 53	+56	110
66	13 48	56	110	14 44	56	110	15 40	55	110	16 35	56	109	17 31	56	109
67	13 26	56	110	14 22	55	109	15 17	56	109	16 13	56	108	17 09	55	108
68	13 04	56	109	14 00	55	108	14 55	56	108	15 51	55	107	16 46	56	107
69	12 42	55	108	13 37	56	107	14 33	55	107	15 28	56	106	16 24	55	106

10° Hc	10° d	10° Z	11° Hc	11° d	11° Z	12° Hc	12° d	12° Z	13° Hc	13° d	13° Z	14° Hc	14° d	14° Z	LHA
° ′	′	°	° ′	′	°	° ′	′	°	° ′	′	°	° ′	′	°	
33 00	+60	180	34 00	+60	180	35 00	+60	180	36 00	+60	180	37 00	+60	180	360
33 00	60	179	34 00	60	179	35 00	60	179	36 00	60	179	37 00	60	179	359
32 59	60	178	33 59	60	178	34 59	60	178	35 59	60	178	36 59	60	178	358
32 58	60	177	33 58	60	176	34 58	60	176	35 58	60	176	36 58	60	176	357
32 56	60	175	33 56	60	175	34 56	60	175	35 56	60	175	36 56	60	175	356
32 54	+60	174	33 54	+60	174	34 54	+60	174	35 54	+60	174	36 54	+60	174	355
32 51	60	173	33 51	60	173	34 51	60	173	35 51	60	173	36 51	60	173	354
32 48	60	172	33 48	60	172	34 48	60	172	35 48	60	172	36 48	60	172	353
32 45	60	171	33 45	59	171	34 44	60	171	35 44	60	170	36 44	60	170	352
32 41	60	170	33 41	59	169	34 40	60	169	35 40	60	169	36 40	60	169	351
32 36	+60	168	33 36	+60	168	34 36	+60	168	35 36	+59	168	36 35	+60	168	350
32 31	60	167	33 31	60	167	34 31	59	167	35 30	60	167	36 30	60	167	349
32 26	59	166	33 25	60	166	34 25	60	166	35 25	60	166	36 25	59	166	348
32 20	59	165	33 19	60	165	34 19	60	165	35 19	59	164	36 18	60	164	347
32 13	60	164	33 13	60	164	34 13	59	163	35 12	60	163	36 12	59	163	346
32 07	+59	163	33 06	+60	162	34 06	+59	162	35 05	+60	162	36 05	+59	162	345
31 59	60	161	32 59	59	161	33 58	60	161	34 58	59	161	35 57	60	161	344
31 52	59	160	32 51	59	160	33 50	60	160	34 50	59	160	35 49	60	160	343
31 43	60	159	32 43	59	159	33 42	60	159	34 42	59	159	35 41	59	158	342
31 35	59	158	32 34	59	158	33 33	60	158	34 33	59	157	35 32	59	157	341
31 26	+59	157	32 25	+59	157	33 24	+59	156	34 23	+60	156	35 23	+59	156	340
31 16	59	156	32 15	60	155	33 15	59	155	34 14	59	155	35 13	59	155	339
31 06	60	155	32 06	59	154	33 05	59	154	34 04	59	154	35 03	59	154	338
30 56	59	153	31 55	59	153	32 54	59	153	33 53	59	153	34 52	59	153	337
30 45	59	152	31 44	59	152	32 43	59	152	33 42	59	152	34 41	59	151	336
30 34	+59	151	31 33	+59	151	32 32	+59	151	33 31	+59	150	34 30	+58	150	335
30 23	58	150	31 21	59	150	32 20	59	150	33 19	59	149	34 18	58	149	334
30 11	58	149	31 09	59	149	32 08	59	148	33 07	58	148	34 05	59	148	333
29 58	59	148	30 57	59	148	31 56	58	147	32 54	59	147	33 53	58	147	332
29 46	58	147	30 44	59	146	31 43	58	146	32 41	59	146	33 40	58	146	331
29 33	+58	146	30 31	+59	145	31 30	+58	145	32 28	+58	145	33 26	+59	145	330
29 19	59	144	30 18	58	144	31 16	58	144	32 14	58	144	33 12	59	143	329
29 05	59	143	30 04	58	143	31 02	58	143	32 00	58	143	32 58	58	142	328
28 51	58	142	29 49	59	142	30 48	58	142	31 46	58	141	32 44	58	141	327
28 37	58	141	29 35	58	141	30 33	58	141	31 31	58	140	32 29	58	140	326
28 22	+58	140	29 20	+58	140	30 18	+58	140	31 16	+58	139	32 14	+57	139	325
28 07	57	139	29 04	58	139	30 02	58	138	31 00	58	138	31 58	58	138	324
27 51	58	138	28 49	58	138	29 47	57	137	30 44	58	137	31 42	58	137	323
27 35	58	137	28 33	58	137	29 31	57	136	30 28	58	136	31 26	57	136	322
27 19	58	136	28 17	57	136	29 14	58	135	30 12	57	135	31 09	58	135	321
27 02	+58	135	28 00	+57	134	28 57	+58	134	29 55	+57	134	30 52	+58	133	320
26 46	57	134	27 43	58	133	28 41	57	133	29 38	57	133	30 35	57	132	319
26 29	57	133	27 26	57	132	28 23	57	132	29 20	58	132	30 18	57	131	318
26 11	57	132	27 08	58	131	28 06	57	131	29 03	57	131	30 00	57	130	317
25 53	58	131	26 51	57	130	27 48	57	130	28 45	57	130	29 42	57	129	316
25 35	+58	130	26 33	+57	129	27 30	+57	129	28 27	+57	128	29 24	+56	128	315
25 17	57	128	26 14	57	128	27 11	57	128	28 08	57	127	29 05	57	127	314
24 59	57	127	25 56	57	127	26 53	56	127	27 49	57	126	28 46	57	126	313
24 40	57	126	25 37	57	126	26 34	56	126	27 30	57	125	28 27	57	125	312
24 21	57	125	25 18	56	125	26 14	57	125	27 11	57	124	28 08	56	124	311
24 02	+56	124	24 58	+57	124	25 55	+57	124	26 52	+56	123	27 48	+56	123	310
23 42	57	123	24 39	56	123	25 35	57	123	26 32	56	122	27 28	57	122	309
23 23	56	122	24 19	56	122	25 15	57	122	26 12	56	121	27 08	56	121	308
23 03	56	121	23 59	56	121	24 55	57	121	25 52	56	120	26 48	56	120	307
22 42	57	120	23 39	56	120	24 35	56	120	25 31	57	119	26 28	56	119	306
22 22	+56	119	23 18	+57	119	24 15	+56	119	25 11	+56	118	26 07	+56	118	305
22 02	56	118	22 58	56	118	23 54	56	118	24 50	56	117	25 46	56	117	304
21 41	56	117	22 37	56	117	23 33	56	117	24 29	56	116	25 25	56	116	303
21 20	56	116	22 16	56	116	23 12	56	116	24 08	56	115	25 04	56	115	302
20 59	56	115	21 55	56	115	22 51	56	115	23 47	55	114	24 42	56	114	301
20 38	+55	114	21 33	+56	114	22 29	+56	114	23 25	+56	113	24 21	+56	113	300
20 16	56	113	21 12	56	113	22 08	55	113	23 03	56	112	23 59	56	112	299
19 54	56	112	20 50	56	112	21 46	56	112	22 42	55	111	23 37	56	111	298
19 33	55	111	20 28	56	111	21 24	56	111	22 20	55	110	23 15	56	110	297
19 11	55	110	20 06	56	110	21 02	56	110	21 58	55	109	22 53	56	109	296
18 49	+55	110	19 44	+56	109	20 40	+55	109	21 35	+56	108	22 31	+55	108	295
18 27	55	109	19 22	56	108	20 18	55	108	21 13	56	107	22 09	55	107	294
18 04	56	108	19 00	55	107	19 55	56	107	20 51	55	106	21 46	55	106	293
17 42	55	107	18 37	56	106	19 33	55	106	20 28	55	105	21 23	56	105	292
17 19	56	106	18 15	55	105	19 10	55	105	20 05	56	104	21 01	55	104	291

S. Lat. {LHA greater than 180°....... Zn=180−Z; LHA less than 180°........... Zn=180+Z}

N. Lat. {LHA greater than 180°....... Zn=Z / LHA less than 180°........... Zn=360−Z}

DECLINATION (0°-14°) SAME NAME AS LATITUDE

LHA	0° Hc	d	Z	1° Hc	d	Z	2° Hc	d	Z	3° Hc	d	Z	4° Hc	d	Z	LHA
	° ′	′	°	° ′	′	°	° ′	′	°	° ′	′	°	° ′	′	°	
70	07 41	+56	109	08 37	+55	108	09 32	+56	108	10 28	+56	107	11 24	+55	107	290
71	07 19	55	108	08 14	56	107	09 10	56	107	10 06	55	107	11 01	56	106	289
72	06 56	56	107	07 52	55	106	08 47	56	106	09 43	56	106	10 39	55	105	288
73	06 34	55	106	07 29	56	105	08 25	55	105	09 20	56	105	10 16	55	104	287
74	06 11	56	105	07 07	55	104	08 02	56	104	08 58	55	104	09 53	56	103	286
75	05 48	+56	104	06 44	+55	104	07 39	+56	103	08 35	+55	103	09 30	+56	102	285
76	05 25	56	103	06 21	55	103	07 16	56	102	08 12	55	102	09 07	56	101	284
77	05 03	55	102	05 58	55	102	06 53	56	101	07 49	55	101	08 44	56	101	283
78	04 40	55	101	05 35	55	101	06 30	56	100	07 26	55	100	08 21	55	100	282
79	04 17	55	100	05 12	55	100	06 07	56	99	07 03	55	99	07 58	55	99	281
80	03 53	+56	99	04 49	+55	99	05 44	+55	98	06 39	+56	98	07 35	+55	98	280
81	03 30	56	98	04 26	55	98	05 21	55	98	06 16	56	97	07 12	55	97	279
82	03 07	55	97	04 02	56	97	04 58	55	97	05 53	56	96	06 48	56	96	278
83	02 44	55	96	03 39	55	96	04 34	56	96	05 30	55	95	06 25	55	95	277
84	02 20	56	96	03 16	55	95	04 11	55	95	05 06	56	94	06 02	55	94	276
85	01 57	+55	95	02 52	+56	94	03 48	+55	94	04 43	+55	93	05 38	+55	93	275
86	01 34	55	94	02 29	55	93	03 24	56	93	04 19	56	93	05 15	55	92	274
87	01 10	56	93	02 06	55	92	03 01	55	92	03 56	55	92	04 51	55	91	273
88	00 47	55	92	01 42	55	91	02 37	56	91	03 33	55	91	04 28	55	90	272
89	00 23	56	91	01 19	55	91	02 14	55	90	03 09	55	90	04 04	56	89	271
90	00 00	+55	90	00 55	+55	90	01 50	+56	89	02 46	+55	89	03 41	+55	88	270
91	−0 23	55	89	00 32	55	89	01 27	55	88	02 22	55	88	03 17	56	88	269
92	−0 47	55	88	00 08	56	88	01 04	56	87	01 59	55	87	02 54	55	87	268
93	−1 10	55	87	−0 15	55	87	00 40	55	86	01 35	55	86	02 31	55	86	267
94	−1 34	56	86	−0 38	55	86	00 17	55	86	01 12	55	85	02 07	56	85	266
95	−1 57	+55	85	−1 02	+55	85	−0 07	+56	85	00 49	+55	84	01 44	+55	84	265
96	−2 20	55	84	−1 25	55	84	−0 30	56	84	00 25	56	83	01 21	55	83	264
97	−2 44	56	84	−1 48	55	83	−0 53	55	83	00 02	55	82	00 57	56	82	263
98	−3 07	55	83	−2 12	56	82	−1 16	55	82	−0 21	55	81	00 34	56	81	262
99	−3 30	55	82	−2 35	55	81	−1 40	56	81	−0 44	55	81	00 11	55	80	261
100	−3 53	+55	81	−2 58	+55	80	−2 03	+56	80	−1 07	+55	80	−0 12	+55	79	260
101	−4 17	56	80	−3 21	55	79	−2 26	56	79	−1 30	55	79	−0 35	55	78	259
102	−4 40	56	79	−3 44	55	79	−2 49	56	78	−1 53	55	78	−0 58	56	77	258
103	−5 03	56	78	−4 07	55	78	−3 12	56	77	−2 16	55	77	−1 21	56	76	257
104	−5 25	55	77	−4 30	56	77	−3 34	56	76	−2 39	56	76	−1 43	55	76	256
105				−4 53	+56	76	−3 57	+55	75	−3 02	+56	75	−2 06	+55	75	255
106				−5 15	55	75	−4 20	56	74	−3 24	56	74	−2 29	56	74	254
107				−5 38	56	74	−4 42	56	74	−3 47	56	73	−2 51	56	73	253
108							−5 05	56	73	−4 09	56	72	−3 13	56	72	252
109							−5 27	56	72	−4 31	55	71	−3 36	56	71	251
110										−4 54	+56	70	−3 58	+56	70	250
111										−5 16	56	69	−4 20	56	69	249
112										−5 37	55	68	−4 42	56	68	248
113													−5 03	56	67	247
114													−5 25	56	66	246

LHA	5° Hc	d	Z	6° Hc	d	Z	7° Hc	d	Z	8° Hc	d	Z	9° Hc	d	Z	LHA
	° ′	′	°	° ′	′	°	° ′	′	°	° ′	′	°	° ′	′	°	
70	12 19	+56	107	13 15	+55	106	14 10	+56	106	15 06	+55	106	16 01	+56	105	290
71	11 57	55	106	12 52	56	105	13 48	55	105	14 43	56	105	15 39	55	104	289
72	11 34	56	105	12 30	55	104	13 25	56	104	14 20	56	104	15 16	55	103	288
73	11 11	56	104	12 07	55	103	13 02	56	103	13 58	55	103	14 53	55	102	287
74	10 49	55	103	11 44	55	103	12 39	56	102	13 35	55	102	14 30	55	101	286
75	10 26	+55	102	11 21	+55	102	12 16	+56	101	13 12	+55	101	14 07	+55	100	285
76	10 03	55	101	10 58	55	101	11 53	56	100	12 49	55	100	13 44	55	99	284
77	09 40	55	100	10 35	55	100	11 30	56	99	12 26	55	99	13 21	55	99	283
78	09 16	56	99	10 12	55	99	11 07	55	98	12 02	56	98	12 58	55	98	282
79	08 53	56	98	09 49	55	98	10 44	55	97	11 39	55	97	12 34	55	97	281
80	08 30	+55	97	09 25	+56	97	10 21	+55	97	11 16	+55	96	12 11	+55	96	280
81	08 07	55	96	09 02	56	96	09 57	56	96	10 52	56	95	11 48	55	95	279
82	07 43	56	95	08 39	55	95	09 34	55	95	10 29	55	94	11 24	55	94	278
83	07 20	55	95	08 15	56	94	09 11	55	94	10 06	55	93	11 01	55	93	277
84	06 57	55	94	07 52	55	93	08 47	55	93	09 42	55	92	10 37	55	92	276
85	06 33	+56	93	07 29	+55	92	08 24	+55	92	09 19	+55	92	10 14	+55	91	275
86	06 10	55	92	07 05	55	91	08 00	55	91	08 55	56	91	09 51	55	90	274
87	05 46	56	91	06 42	55	90	07 37	55	90	08 32	55	90	09 27	55	89	273
88	05 23	55	90	06 18	55	90	07 13	56	89	08 09	55	89	09 04	55	88	272
89	05 00	55	89	05 55	55	89	06 50	55	88	07 45	55	88	08 40	56	87	271
90	04 36	+55	88	05 31	+56	88	06 27	+55	87	07 22	+55	87	08 17	+55	87	270
91	04 13	55	87	05 08	55	87	06 03	55	86	06 58	55	86	07 53	56	86	269
92	03 49	55	86	04 44	56	86	05 40	55	85	06 35	55	85	07 30	55	85	268
93	03 26	55	85	04 21	55	85	05 16	56	85	06 12	56	84	07 07	55	84	267
94	03 03	55	84	03 58	55	84	04 53	55	84	05 48	55	83	06 43	56	83	266
95	02 39	+55	83	03 34	+56	83	04 30	+55	83	05 25	+55	82	06 20	+55	82	265
96	02 16	55	83	03 11	56	82	04 07	55	82	05 02	55	81	05 57	55	81	264
97	01 53	55	82	02 48	56	81	03 43	56	81	04 39	55	80	05 34	55	80	263
98	01 30	55	81	02 25	55	80	03 20	56	80	04 16	55	80	05 11	55	79	262
99	01 06	56	80	02 02	55	79	02 57	56	79	03 53	55	79	04 48	55	78	261
100	00 43	+56	79	01 39	+55	78	02 34	+56	78	03 30	+55	77	04 25	+55	77	260
101	00 20	56	78	01 16	55	78	02 11	56	77	03 07	55	77	04 02	55	76	259
102	−0 02	55	77	00 53	55	76	01 48	56	76	02 44	55	76	03 39	56	75	258
103	−0 25	56	76	00 30	56	76	01 26	55	75	02 21	56	75	03 17	55	75	257
104	−0 48	56	75	00 08	55	75	01 03	56	74	01 59	55	74	02 54	56	74	256
105	−1 11	+56	74	−0 15	+56	74	00 41	+55	73	01 36	+56	73	02 32	+55	73	255
106	−1 33	56	73	−0 37	56	73	00 18	56	73	01 14	55	72	02 09	56	72	254
107	−1 55	56	72	−1 00	56	72	−0 04	56	72	00 52	55	71	01 47	56	71	253
108	−2 18	56	71	−1 22	56	71	−0 26	55	71	00 29	56	70	01 25	56	70	252
109	−2 40	56	71	−1 44	56	70	−0 48	55	70	00 07	56	69	01 03	56	69	251
110	−3 02	+56	70	−2 06	+56	69	−1 10	+55	69	−0 15	+56	69	00 41	+56	68	250
111	−3 24	56	69	−2 28	56	68	−1 32	56	68	−0 36	56	68	00 20	56	67	249
112	−3 46	56	68	−2 50	56	67	−1 54	56	67	−0 58	56	67	−0 02	56	66	248
113	−4 07	56	67	−3 11	56	66	−2 15	56	66	−1 19	56	66	−0 23	56	65	247
114	−4 29	56	66	−3 33	56	66	−2 37	56	65	−1 41	56	65	−0 45	56	64	246
115	−4 50	+56	65	−3 54	+56	65	−2 58	+56	64	−2 02	+56	64	−1 06	+56	64	245
116	−5 11	56	64	−4 15	56	64	−3 19	56	63	−2 23	56	63	−1 27	57	63	244
117	−5 32	56	63	−4 36	56	63	−3 40	56	62	−2 44	57	62	−1 47	56	62	243
118				−4 57	57	62	−4 00	56	61	−3 04	56	61	−2 08	56	61	242
119				−5 17	56	61	−4 21	56	61	−3 25	57	60	−2 28	56	60	241
120				−5 38	+57	60	−4 41	+56	60	−3 45	+57	59	−2 48	+56	59	240
121							−5 01	56	59	−4 05	57	58	−3 08	56	58	239
122							−5 21	56	58	−4 25	57	57	−3 28	56	57	238
123										−4 44	56	56	−3 48	57	56	237
124										−5 04	57	55	−4 07	57	55	236
125										−5 23	+57	55	−4 26	+57	54	235
126													−4 45	57	53	234
127													−5 04	57	52	233
128													−5 22	57	51	232

LHA	10° Hc	d	Z	11° Hc	d	Z	12° Hc	d	Z	13° Hc	d	Z	14° Hc	d	Z	LHA
	° ′	′	°	° ′	′	°	° ′	′	°	° ′	′	°	° ′	′	°	
70	16 57	+55	105	17 52	+55	104	18 47	+56	104	19 43	+55	103	20 38	+55	103	290
71	16 34	55	104	17 29	56	103	18 25	55	103	19 20	55	103	20 15	55	102	289
72	16 11	55	103	17 06	56	102	18 02	55	102	18 57	55	102	19 52	55	101	288
73	15 48	56	102	16 44	55	101	17 39	55	101	18 34	55	101	19 29	55	100	287
74	15 25	56	101	16 21	55	101	17 16	55	100	18 11	55	100	19 06	55	99	286
75	15 02	+55	100	15 57	+56	100	16 53	+55	99	17 48	+55	99	18 43	+55	98	285
76	14 39	55	99	15 34	55	99	16 29	56	98	17 25	55	98	18 20	55	97	284
77	14 16	55	98	15 11	55	98	16 06	55	97	17 01	55	97	17 56	55	96	283
78	13 53	55	97	14 48	55	97	15 43	55	96	16 38	55	96	17 33	55	96	282
79	13 29	56	96	14 25	55	96	15 20	55	95	16 15	55	95	17 10	55	95	281
80	13 06	+55	95	14 01	+55	95	14 56	+55	95	15 51	+55	94	16 46	+55	94	280
81	12 43	55	94	13 38	55	94	14 33	55	94	15 28	55	93	16 23	55	93	279
82	12 19	55	93	13 14	55	93	14 09	55	93	15 04	55	92	15 59	55	92	278
83	11 56	55	93	12 51	55	92	13 46	55	92	14 41	55	91	15 36	55	91	277
84	11 32	56	92	12 28	55	91	13 23	55	91	14 18	55	90	15 13	54	90	276
85	11 09	+55	91	12 04	+55	90	12 59	+55	90	13 54	+55	89	14 49	+55	89	275
86	10 46	55	90	11 41	55	89	12 36	55	89	13 31	55	89	14 26	55	88	274
87	10 22	55	89	11 17	55	88	12 12	55	88	13 07	55	88	14 02	55	87	273
88	09 59	55	88	10 54	55	88	11 49	55	87	12 44	55	87	13 39	55	86	272
89	09 35	55	87	10 30	55	87	11 25	55	86	12 20	55	86	13 15	55	85	271
90	09 12	+55	86	10 07	+55	86	11 02	+55	85	11 57	+55	85	12 52	+55	84	270
91	08 49	55	85	09 44	55	85	10 39	55	84	11 34	55	84	12 29	55	84	269
92	08 25	55	84	09 20	55	84	10 15	55	83	11 10	55	83	12 05	55	83	268
93	08 02	55	83	08 57	55	83	09 52	55	83	10 47	55	82	11 42	55	82	267
94	07 39	55	83	08 34	55	82	09 29	55	82	10 24	55	81	11 19	55	81	266
95	07 15	+56	82	08 11	+55	81	09 06	+55	81	10 01	+55	80	10 56	+55	80	265
96	06 52	56	81	07 47	56	80	08 43	55	80	09 38	55	79	10 33	55	79	264
97	06 29	55	80	07 24	56	79	08 20	55	79	09 15	55	78	10 10	55	78	263
98	06 06	55	79	07 01	56	78	07 57	55	78	08 52	55	78	09 47	55	77	262
99	05 43	55	78	06 38	56	77	07 34	55	77	08 29	55	77	09 24	55	76	261
100	05 20	+56	77	06 16	+55	77	07 11	+55	76	08 06	+56	76	09 02	+56	75	260
101	04 57	56	76	05 53	55	76	06 48	56	75	07 44	55	75	08 39	55	75	259
102	04 35	55	75	05 30	56	75	06 26	55	74	07 21	55	74	08 16	56	74	258
103	04 12	56	74	05 08	55	74	06 03	55	73	06 59	55	73	07 54	56	73	257
104	03 50	55	73	04 45	56	73	05 41	55	73	06 36	56	72	07 32	55	72	256
105	03 27	+56	72	04 23	+55	72	05 18	+56	72	06 14	+55	71	07 09	+56	71	255
106	03 05	56	71	04 01	55	71	04 56	56	71	05 52	55	70	06 47	56	70	254
107	02 43	55	71	03 38	56	70	04 34	56	70	05 30	55	69	06 25	56	69	253
108	02 21	55	70	03 16	56	69	04 12	56	69	05 08	56	69	06 04	55	68	252
109	01 59	55	69	02 55	56	68	03 50	56	68	04 46	56	68	05 42	56	67	251
110	01 37	+56	68	02 33	+56	67	03 29	+55	67	04 24	+56	67	05 20	+56	66	250
111	01 15	56	67	02 11	56	67	03 07	56	66	04 03	56	66	04 59	56	65	249
112	00 54	56	66	01 50	56	66	02 46	56	65	03 42	56	65	04 38	56	65	248
113	00 33	56	65	01 29	56	65	02 25	56	64	03 21	56	64	04 17	56	64	247
114	00 11	57	64	01 08	56	64	02 04	56	63	03 00	56	63	03 56	56	63	246
115	−0 10	+57	63	00 47	+56	63	01 43	+56	62	02 39	+56	62	03 35	+56	62	245
116	−0 30	56	62	00 26	56	62	01 22	56	62	02 18	56	61	03 14	56	61	244
117	−0 51	56	61	00 05	56	61	01 01	57	61	01 58	56	60	02 54	56	60	243
118	−1 12	57	60	−0 15	56	60	00 41	56	60	01 37	56	59	02 34	56	59	242
119	−1 32	57	59	−0 35	56	59	00 21	56	59	01 17	57	58	02 14	56	58	241
120	−1 52	+57	59	−0 55	+56	58	00 01	+56	58	00 57	+57	58	01 54	+56	57	240
121	−2 12	57	58	−1 15	56	57	−0 19	57	57	00 38	56	57	01 34	57	56	239
122	−2 32	57	57	−1 35	57	56	−0 38	56	56	00 18	57	56	01 15	57	55	238
123	−2 51	57	56	−1 54	56	55	−0 58	57	55	−0 01	57	55	00 56	56	54	237
124	−3 10	56	55	−2 14	57	55	−1 17	57	54	−0 20	57	54	00 37	57	54	236
125	−3 29	+56	54	−2 33	+57	54	−1 36	+57	53	−0 39	+57	53	00 18	+57	53	235
126	−3 48	57	53	−2 51	57	53	−1 54	57	52	−0 57	56	52	−0 01	57	52	234
127	−4 07	57	52	−3 10	57	52	−2 13	57	51	−1 16	57	51	−0 19	57	51	233
128	−4 25	57	51	−3 28	57	51	−2 31	57	50	−1 34	57	50	−0 37	57	50	232
129	−4 43	57	50	−3 46	57	50	−2 49	57	50	−1 52	57	49	−0 55	58	49	231
130	−5 01	+57	49	−4 04	+57	49	−3 07	+58	49	−2 09	+57	48	−1 12	+57	48	230
131	−5 19	58	48	−4 21	57	48	−3 24	57	48	−2 27	57	47	−1 30	58	47	229
132				−4 39	58	47	−3 41	57	47	−2 44	57	46	−1 47	58	46	228
133				−4 56	58	46	−3 58	57	46	−3 01	58	46	−2 03	57	45	227
134				−5 13	58	45	−4 15	58	45	−3 17	57	45	−2 20	58	44	226
135				−5 29	+58	44	−4 31	+57	44	−3 34	+58	44	−2 36	+58	43	225
136							−4 48	58	43	−3 50	58	43	−2 52	58	42	224
137							−5 03	57	42	−4 06	58	42	−3 08	58	42	223
138							−5 19	58	41	−4 21	58	41	−3 23	58	41	222
139										−4 36	58	40	−3 38	58	40	221

	0°	1°	2°	3°	4°	5°	6°	7°	8°	9°	10°	11°	12°	13°	14°

S. Lat. {LHA greater than 180°........ Zn=180−Z / LHA less than 180°........... Zn=180+Z}

DECLINATION (0°-14°) SAME NAME AS LATITUDE

LAT 67°

N. Lat. {LHA greater than 180°....... Zn=Z; LHA less than 180°........... Zn=360−Z}

DECLINATION (0°-14°) SAME NAME AS LATITUDE

LAT 67°

LHA	0° Hc d Z	1° Hc d Z	2° Hc d Z	3° Hc d Z	4° Hc d Z	5° Hc d Z	6° Hc d Z	7° Hc d Z	8° Hc d Z	9° Hc d Z	10° Hc d Z	11° Hc d Z	12° Hc d Z	13° Hc d Z	14° Hc d Z	LHA
	° ′ ′ °	° ′ ′ °	° ′ ′ °	° ′ ′ °	° ′ ′ °	° ′ ′ °	° ′ ′ °	° ′ ′ °	° ′ ′ °	° ′ ′ °	° ′ ′ °	° ′ ′ °	° ′ ′ °	° ′ ′ °	° ′ ′ °	
													140	-4 51 +58 39	-3 53 +58 39	220
													141	-5 06 58 38	-4 08 59 38	219
													142	-5 20 58 37	-4 22 58 37	218
														143	-4 36 59 36	217
														144	-4 49 58 35	216
														145	-5 03 +59 34	215
														146	-5 15 58 33	214
104	-5 25 56 77	256														
103	-5 03 55 78	257														
102	-4 40 55 79	-5 35 55 79	258													
101	-4 17 55 80	-5 12 55 80	259													
100	-3 53 -56 81	-4 49 -55 81	-5 44 -55 82	260												
99	-3 30 56 82	-4 26 55 82	-5 21 55 82	261												
98	-3 07 55 83	-4 02 56 83	-4 58 55 83	262												
97	-2 44 55 84	-3 39 55 84	-4 34 56 84	-5 30 55 85	263											
96	-2 20 56 84	-3 16 55 85	-4 11 55 85	-5 06 56 86	264											
95	-1 57 -55 85	-2 52 -56 86	-3 48 -55 86	-4 43 -55 87	-5 38 -55 87	265										
94	-1 34 55 86	-2 29 55 87	-3 24 55 87	-4 19 56 87	-5 15 55 88	266										
93	-1 10 56 87	-2 06 55 88	-3 01 55 88	-3 56 55 88	-4 51 55 89	267										
92	-0 47 55 88	-1 42 55 89	-2 37 56 89	-3 33 55 89	-4 28 55 90	-5 23 55 90	268									
91	-0 23 56 89	-1 19 55 89	-2 14 55 90	-3 09 55 90	-4 04 56 91	-5 00 55 91	269									
90	00 00 -55 90	-0 55 -55 90	-1 50 -56 91	-2 46 -55 91	-3 41 -55 92	-4 36 -55 92	-5 31 -56 92	270								
89	00 23 55 91	-0 32 55 91	-1 27 55 92	-2 22 55 92	-3 17 56 92	-4 13 55 93	-5 08 55 93	271								
88	00 47 55 92	-0 08 56 92	-1 04 55 93	-1 59 55 93	-2 54 55 93	-3 49 55 94	-4 44 56 94	-5 40 55 95	272							
87	01 10 55 93	00 15 55 93	-0 40 55 94	-1 35 56 94	-2 31 55 94	-3 26 55 95	-4 21 55 95	-5 16 56 95	273							
86	01 34 56 94	00 38 55 94	-0 17 55 94	-1 12 55 95	-2 07 56 95	-3 03 55 96	-3 58 55 96	-4 53 55 96	274							
85	01 57 -55 95	01 02 -55 95	00 07 -56 95	-0 49 -55 96	-1 44 -55 96	-2 39 -55 97	-3 34 -56 97	-4 30 -55 97	-5 25 -55 98	275						
84	02 20 55 96	01 25 55 96	00 30 55 96	-0 25 56 97	-1 21 55 97	-2 16 55 97	-3 11 56 98	-4 07 55 98	-5 02 55 99	276						
83	02 44 56 96	01 48 55 97	00 53 55 97	-0 02 55 98	-0 57 56 98	-1 53 55 98	-2 48 55 99	-3 43 56 99	-4 39 55 100	-5 34 55 100	277					
82	03 07 55 97	02 12 56 98	01 16 55 98	00 21 55 99	-0 34 56 99	-1 30 55 99	-2 25 55 100	-3 20 56 100	-4 16 55 100	-5 11 55 101	278					
81	03 30 55 98	02 35 55 99	01 40 56 99	00 44 55 99	-0 11 55 100	-1 06 56 100	-2 02 55 101	-2 57 56 101	-3 53 55 101	-4 48 55 102	-5 43 55 102	279				
80	03 53 -55 99	02 58 -55 100	02 03 -56 100	01 07 -55 100	00 12 -55 101	-0 43 -56 101	-1 39 -55 102	-2 34 -56 102	-3 30 -55 102	-4 25 -55 103	-5 20 -56 103	280				
79	04 17 56 100	03 21 55 101	02 26 56 101	01 30 55 101	00 35 55 102	-0 20 56 102	-1 16 55 102	-2 11 56 103	-3 07 55 103	-4 02 55 104	-4 57 56 104	281				
78	04 40 56 101	03 44 55 101	02 49 56 102	01 53 55 102	00 58 56 103	00 02 55 103	-0 53 55 103	-1 48 56 104	-2 44 55 104	-3 39 56 105	-4 35 55 105	-5 30 56 105	282			
77	05 03 56 102	04 07 55 102	03 12 56 103	02 16 55 103	01 21 56 104	00 25 55 104	-0 30 56 104	-1 26 55 105	-2 21 56 105	-3 17 55 105	-4 12 56 106	-5 08 55 106	283			
76	05 25 55 103	04 30 56 103	03 34 55 104	02 39 56 104	01 43 55 104	00 48 56 105	-0 08 55 105	-1 03 56 106	-1 59 55 106	-2 54 56 106	-3 50 55 107	-4 45 56 107	-5 41 55 107	284		
75	05 48 -55 104	04 53 -56 104	03 57 -55 105	03 02 -56 105	02 06 -55 105	01 11 -56 106	00 15 -56 106	-0 41 -55 107	-1 36 -56 107	-2 32 -55 107	-3 27 -56 108	-4 23 -55 108	-5 18 -56 108	285		
74	06 11 56 105	05 15 55 105	04 20 56 106	03 24 55 106	02 29 56 106	01 33 56 107	00 37 55 107	-0 18 56 107	-1 14 55 108	-2 09 56 108	-3 05 56 109	-4 01 55 109	-4 56 56 109	286		
73	06 34 56 106	05 38 56 106	04 42 55 106	03 47 56 107	02 51 56 107	01 55 55 108	01 00 56 108	00 04 56 108	-0 52 55 109	-1 47 56 109	-2 43 55 109	-3 38 56 110	-4 34 56 110	-5 30 55 111	287	
72	06 56 55 107	06 01 56 107	05 05 56 107	04 09 56 108	03 13 55 108	02 18 56 109	01 22 56 109	00 26 55 109	-0 29 56 110	-1 25 56 110	-2 21 55 110	-3 16 56 111	-4 12 56 111	-5 08 56 111	288	
71	07 19 56 108	06 23 56 108	05 27 56 108	04 31 55 109	03 36 56 109	02 40 56 109	01 44 56 110	00 48 55 110	-0 07 56 111	-1 03 56 111	-1 59 56 111	-2 55 55 112	-3 50 56 112	-4 46 56 112	-5 42 56 113	289
70	07 41 -56 109	06 45 -56 109	05 49 -55 109	04 54 -56 110	03 58 -56 110	03 02 -56 110	02 06 -56 111	01 10 -55 111	00 15 -56 111	-0 41 -56 112	-1 37 -56 112	-2 33 -56 113	-3 29 -55 113	-4 24 -56 113	-5 20 -56 114	290
	0°	1°	2°	3°	4°	5°	6°	7°	8°	9°	10°	11°	12°	13°	14°	

S. Lat. {LHA greater than 180°........ Zn=180−Z; LHA less than 180°........... Zn=180+Z}

DECLINATION (0°-14°) CONTRARY NAME TO LATITUDE

N. Lat. {LHA greater than 180°....... Zn=Z
{LHA less than 180°........... Zn=360−Z

DECLINATION (0°-14°) CONTRARY NAME TO LATITUDE

LHA	0° Hc	d	Z	1° Hc	d	Z	2° Hc	d	Z	3° Hc	d	Z	4° Hc	d	Z
	° ′	′	°	° ′	′	°	° ′	′	°	° ′	′	°	° ′	′	°
69	08 03	56	110	07 07	56	110	06 11	55	110	05 16	56	111	04 20	56	111
68	08 25	56	110	07 29	56	111	06 33	56	111	05 37	55	112	04 42	56	112
67	08 47	56	111	07 51	56	112	06 55	56	112	05 59	56	112	05 03	56	113
66	09 09	56	112	08 13	56	113	07 17	56	113	06 21	56	113	05 25	56	114
65	09 30	−56	113	08 34	−56	114	07 38	−56	114	06 42	−56	114	05 46	−56	115
64	09 52	56	114	08 56	56	115	08 00	56	115	07 04	57	115	06 07	56	116
63	10 13	56	115	09 17	56	116	08 21	56	116	07 25	57	116	06 28	56	117
62	10 34	56	116	09 38	56	116	08 42	56	117	07 46	57	117	06 49	56	118
61	10 55	56	117	09 59	56	117	09 03	57	118	08 06	56	118	07 10	56	118
60	11 16	−56	118	10 20	−57	118	09 23	−56	119	08 27	−56	119	07 31	−57	119
59	11 37	57	119	10 40	56	119	09 44	57	120	08 47	56	120	07 51	57	120
58	11 57	56	120	11 01	57	120	10 04	56	121	09 08	57	121	08 11	56	121
57	12 17	56	121	11 21	57	121	10 24	56	122	09 28	57	122	08 31	57	122
56	12 37	56	122	11 41	57	122	10 44	57	123	09 47	56	123	08 51	57	123
55	12 57	−57	123	12 00	−56	123	11 04	−57	124	10 07	−57	124	09 10	−57	124
54	13 17	57	124	12 20	57	124	11 23	57	124	10 26	56	125	09 30	57	125
53	13 36	57	125	12 39	57	125	11 42	57	125	10 45	56	126	09 49	57	126
52	13 55	57	126	12 58	57	126	12 01	57	126	11 04	57	127	10 07	57	127
51	14 14	57	127	13 17	57	127	12 20	57	127	11 23	57	128	10 26	57	128
50	14 33	−57	128	13 36	−57	128	12 39	−57	128	11 42	−58	129	10 44	−57	129
49	14 51	57	129	13 54	57	129	12 57	57	129	12 00	58	130	11 02	57	130
48	15 09	57	130	14 12	57	130	13 15	57	130	12 18	58	131	11 20	57	131
47	15 27	57	131	14 30	57	131	13 33	58	131	12 35	57	132	11 38	57	132
46	15 45	57	132	14 48	58	132	13 50	57	132	12 53	58	133	11 55	57	133
45	16 02	−57	133	15 05	−58	133	14 07	−57	133	13 10	−58	134	12 12	−57	134
44	16 19	57	134	15 22	58	134	14 24	57	134	13 27	58	135	12 29	58	135
43	16 36	57	135	15 39	58	135	14 41	58	135	13 43	57	136	12 46	58	136
42	16 53	58	136	15 55	58	136	14 57	57	136	14 00	58	137	13 02	58	137
41	17 09	58	137	16 11	58	137	15 13	57	137	14 16	58	138	13 18	58	138
40	17 25	−58	138	16 27	−58	138	15 29	−58	138	14 31	−58	139	13 33	−58	139
39	17 41	58	139	16 43	58	139	15 45	58	139	14 47	58	140	13 49	58	140
38	17 56	58	140	16 58	58	140	16 00	58	140	15 02	58	141	14 04	58	141
37	18 11	58	141	17 13	58	141	16 15	58	141	15 17	59	142	14 18	58	142
36	18 26	59	142	17 27	58	142	16 29	58	142	15 31	58	143	14 33	59	143
35	18 40	−58	143	17 42	−59	143	16 43	−58	143	15 45	−58	144	14 47	−59	144
34	18 54	58	144	17 56	59	144	16 57	58	144	15 59	59	145	15 00	58	145
33	19 08	59	145	18 09	58	145	17 11	59	145	16 12	58	146	15 14	59	146
32	19 21	58	146	18 23	59	146	17 24	59	146	16 25	58	147	15 27	59	147
31	19 34	59	147	18 35	58	147	17 37	59	147	16 38	58	148	15 40	59	148
30	19 47	−59	148	18 48	−59	148	17 49	−58	148	16 51	−59	149	15 52	−59	149
29	19 59	59	149	19 00	59	149	18 01	58	149	17 03	59	150	16 04	59	150
28	20 11	59	150	19 12	59	150	18 13	59	150	17 14	59	151	16 15	58	151
27	20 22	58	151	19 24	59	151	18 25	59	151	17 26	59	152	16 27	59	152
26	20 34	59	152	19 35	59	152	18 36	59	153	17 37	59	153	16 38	59	153
25	20 44	−59	153	19 45	−59	153	18 46	−59	154	17 47	−59	154	16 48	−59	154
24	20 55	59	154	19 56	59	154	18 57	60	155	17 57	59	155	16 58	59	155
23	21 05	59	155	20 06	60	155	19 06	59	156	18 07	59	156	17 08	59	156
22	21 14	59	156	20 15	59	157	19 16	59	157	18 17	60	157	17 17	59	157
21	21 24	60	157	20 24	59	158	19 25	59	158	18 26	60	158	17 26	59	158
20	21 33	−60	158	20 33	−59	159	19 34	−60	159	18 34	−59	159	17 35	−59	159
19	21 41	60	160	20 41	59	160	19 42	59	160	18 43	60	160	17 43	59	160
18	21 49	60	161	20 49	59	161	19 50	60	161	18 50	59	161	17 51	60	161
17	21 57	60	162	20 57	60	162	19 57	59	162	18 58	60	162	17 58	59	162
16	22 04	60	163	21 04	59	163	20 05	60	163	19 05	60	163	18 05	59	163
15	22 10	−59	164	21 11	−60	164	20 11	−59	164	19 12	−60	164	18 12	−60	164
14	22 17	60	165	21 17	60	165	20 17	59	165	19 18	60	165	18 18	60	165
13	22 23	60	166	21 23	60	166	20 23	59	166	19 24	60	166	18 24	60	166
12	22 28	60	167	21 28	59	167	20 29	60	167	19 29	60	167	18 29	60	167
11	22 33	60	168	21 33	59	168	20 34	60	168	19 34	60	168	18 34	60	168
10	22 38	−60	169	21 38	−60	169	20 38	−60	169	19 38	−59	169	18 39	−60	170
9	22 42	60	170	21 42	60	170	20 42	60	170	19 42	59	170	18 43	60	171
8	22 46	60	171	21 46	60	171	20 46	60	171	19 46	60	172	18 46	60	172
7	22 49	60	172	21 49	60	173	20 49	60	173	19 49	60	173	18 49	59	173
6	22 52	60	174	21 52	60	174	20 52	60	174	19 52	60	174	18 52	60	174
5	22 54	−59	175	21 55	−60	175	20 55	−60	175	19 55	−60	175	18 55	−60	175
4	22 56	59	176	21 57	60	176	20 57	60	176	19 57	60	176	18 57	60	176
3	22 58	60	177	21 58	60	177	20 58	60	177	19 58	60	177	18 58	60	177
2	22 59	60	178	21 59	60	178	20 59	60	178	19 59	60	178	18 59	60	178
1	23 00	60	179	22 00	60	179	21 00	60	179	20 00	60	179	19 00	60	179
0	23 00	−60	180	22 00	−60	180	21 00	−60	180	20 00	−60	180	19 00	−60	180

LHA	5° Hc	d	Z	6° Hc	d	Z	7° Hc	d	Z	8° Hc	d	Z	9° Hc	d	Z
	° ′	′	°	° ′	′	°	° ′	′	°	° ′	′	°	° ′	′	°
69	03 24	56	111	02 28	56	112	01 32	56	112	00 36	56	112	−0 20	55	113
68	03 46	56	112	02 50	56	113	01 54	56	113	00 58	56	113	00 02	56	114
67	04 07	56	113	03 11	56	114	02 15	56	114	01 19	56	114	00 23	56	115
66	04 29	56	114	03 33	56	114	02 37	56	115	01 41	56	115	00 45	56	116
65	04 50	−56	115	03 54	−56	115	02 58	−56	116	02 02	−56	116	01 06	−56	116
64	05 11	56	116	04 15	56	116	03 19	56	117	02 23	56	117	01 27	57	117
63	05 32	56	117	04 36	56	117	03 40	56	118	02 44	57	118	01 47	56	118
62	05 53	56	118	04 57	57	118	04 00	56	119	03 04	56	119	02 08	56	119
61	06 14	57	119	05 17	56	119	04 21	56	119	03 25	57	120	02 28	56	120
60	06 34	−56	120	05 38	−57	120	04 41	−56	120	03 45	−57	121	02 48	−56	121
59	06 54	56	121	05 58	57	121	05 01	56	121	04 05	57	122	03 08	56	122
58	07 15	57	122	06 18	57	122	05 21	56	122	04 25	57	123	03 28	56	123
57	07 34	56	123	06 38	57	123	05 41	57	123	04 44	56	124	03 48	57	124
56	07 54	57	124	06 57	56	124	06 01	57	124	05 04	57	125	04 07	57	125
55	08 13	−56	125	07 17	−57	125	06 20	−57	125	05 23	−57	125	04 26	−57	126
54	08 33	57	125	07 36	57	126	06 39	57	126	05 42	57	126	04 45	57	127
53	08 52	57	126	07 55	57	127	06 58	57	127	06 01	57	127	05 04	57	128
52	09 10	57	127	08 13	57	128	07 16	57	128	06 19	57	128	05 22	57	129
51	09 29	57	128	08 32	57	129	07 35	57	129	06 38	58	129	05 40	57	130
50	09 47	−57	129	08 50	−57	130	07 53	−57	130	06 56	−58	130	05 58	−57	131
49	10 05	57	130	09 08	57	131	08 11	58	131	07 13	57	131	06 16	57	131
48	10 23	57	131	09 26	58	132	08 28	57	132	07 31	57	132	06 34	58	132
47	10 41	58	132	09 43	57	132	08 46	58	133	07 48	57	133	06 51	58	133
46	10 58	58	133	10 00	57	133	09 03	58	134	08 05	57	134	07 08	58	134
45	11 15	−58	134	10 17	−57	134	09 20	−58	135	08 22	−58	135	07 24	−57	135
44	11 31	57	135	10 34	58	135	09 36	58	136	08 38	57	136	07 41	58	136
43	11 48	58	136	10 50	58	136	09 52	57	137	08 55	58	137	07 57	58	137
42	12 04	58	137	11 06	58	137	10 08	58	138	09 10	57	138	08 13	58	138
41	12 20	58	138	11 22	58	138	10 24	58	139	09 26	58	139	08 28	58	139
40	12 35	−58	139	11 37	−58	139	10 39	−58	140	09 41	−58	140	08 43	−58	140
39	12 51	58	140	11 53	59	140	10 54	58	141	09 56	58	141	08 58	58	141
38	13 06	59	141	12 07	58	141	11 09	58	142	10 11	58	142	09 13	58	142
37	13 20	58	142	12 22	58	142	11 24	59	143	10 25	58	143	09 27	58	143
36	13 34	58	143	12 36	58	143	11 38	59	143	10 39	58	144	09 41	58	144
35	13 48	−58	144	12 50	−58	144	11 52	−59	144	10 53	−58	145	09 55	−59	145
34	14 02	58	145	13 04	59	145	12 05	58	145	11 07	59	146	10 08	58	146
33	14 15	58	146	13 17	59	146	12 18	58	146	11 20	59	147	10 21	59	147
32	14 28	58	147	13 30	59	147	12 31	59	147	11 32	58	148	10 34	59	148
31	14 41	59	148	13 42	59	148	12 43	58	148	11 45	59	149	10 46	59	149
30	14 53	−59	149	13 54	−58	149	12 56	−59	149	11 57	−59	150	10 58	−59	150
29	15 05	59	150	14 06	59	150	13 07	59	150	12 08	58	151	11 10	59	151
28	15 17	59	151	14 18	59	151	13 19	59	151	12 20	59	152	11 21	59	152
27	15 28	59	152	14 29	59	152	13 30	59	152	12 31	59	153	11 32	59	153
26	15 39	59	153	14 40	60	153	13 40	59	153	12 41	59	154	11 42	59	154
25	15 49	−59	154	14 50	−59	154	13 51	−59	154	12 52	−59	155	11 53	−60	155
24	15 59	59	155	15 00	59	155	14 01	59	155	13 02	60	156	12 02	59	156
23	16 09	59	156	15 10	60	156	14 10	59	156	13 11	59	157	12 12	60	157
22	16 18	59	157	15 19	60	157	14 19	59	157	13 20	59	158	12 21	59	158
21	16 27	59	158	15 28	60	158	14 28	59	158	13 29	59	159	12 30	60	159
20	16 36	−60	159	15 36	−59	159	14 37	−60	160	13 37	−59	160	12 38	−60	160
19	16 44	60	160	15 44	59	160	14 45	60	161	13 45	59	161	12 46	60	161
18	16 51	59	161	15 52	60	161	14 52	59	162	13 53	60	162	12 53	59	162
17	16 59	60	162	15 59	59	162	15 00	60	163	14 00	60	163	13 00	59	163
16	17 06	60	163	16 06	60	163	15 06	59	164	14 07	60	164	13 07	59	164
15	17 12	−59	164	16 13	−60	165	15 13	−60	165	14 13	−59	165	13 14	−60	165
14	17 18	59	165	16 19	60	166	15 19	60	166	14 19	60	166	13 19	59	166
13	17 24	60	166	16 24	59	167	15 25	60	167	14 25	60	167	13 25	60	167
12	17 29	59	168	16 30	60	168	15 30	60	168	14 30	60	168	13 30	60	168
11	17 34	60	169	16 34	59	169	15 35	60	169	14 35	60	169	13 35	60	169
10	17 39	−60	170	16 39	−60	170	15 39	−60	170	14 39	−60	170	13 39	−60	170
9	17 43	60	171	16 43	60	171	15 43	60	171	14 43	60	171	13 43	60	171
8	17 46	60	172	16 46	59	172	15 47	60	172	14 47	60	172	13 47	60	172
7	17 50	60	173	16 50	60	173	15 50	60	173	14 50	60	173	13 50	60	173
6	17 52	60	174	16 52	60	174	15 52	59	174	14 53	60	174	13 53	60	174
5	17 55	−60	175	16 55	−60	175	15 55	−60	175	14 55	−60	175	13 55	−60	175
4	17 57	60	176	16 57	60	176	15 57	60	176	14 57	60	176	13 57	60	176
3	17 58	60	177	16 58	60	177	15 58	60	177	14 58	60	177	13 58	60	177
2	17 59	60	178	16 59	60	178	15 59	60	178	14 59	60	178	13 59	60	178
1	18 00	60	179	17 00	60	179	16 00	60	179	15 00	60	179	14 00	60	179
0	18 00	−60	180	17 00	−60	180	16 00	−60	180	15 00	−60	180	14 00	−60	180

LHA	10° Hc	d	Z	11° Hc	d	Z	12° Hc	d	Z	13° Hc	d	Z	14° Hc	d	Z	LHA
	° ′	′	°	° ′	′	°	° ′	′	°	° ′	′	°	° ′	′	°	
69	−1 15	56	113	−2 11	56	113	−3 07	56	114	−4 03	56	114	−4 59	56	115	291
68	−0 54	56	114	−1 50	56	114	−2 46	56	115	−3 42	56	115	−4 38	56	115	292
67	−0 33	56	115	−1 29	56	115	−2 25	56	116	−3 21	56	116	−4 17	56	116	293
66	−0 11	57	116	−1 08	56	116	−2 04	56	117	−3 00	56	117	−3 56	56	117	294
65	00 10	−57	117	−0 47	−56	117	−1 43	−56	118	−2 39	−56	118	−3 35	−56	118	295
64	00 30	56	118	−0 26	56	118	−1 22	56	118	−2 18	56	119	−3 14	56	119	296
63	00 51	56	119	−0 05	56	119	−1 01	57	119	−1 58	56	120	−2 54	56	120	297
62	01 12	57	120	00 15	56	120	−0 41	56	120	−1 37	57	121	−2 34	56	121	298
61	01 32	57	121	00 35	56	121	−0 21	56	121	−1 17	57	122	−2 14	56	122	299
60	01 52	−57	121	00 55	−56	122	−0 01	−56	122	−0 57	−57	122	−1 54	−56	123	300
59	02 12	57	122	01 15	56	123	00 19	57	123	−0 38	56	123	−1 34	57	124	301
58	02 32	57	123	01 35	57	124	00 38	56	124	−0 18	57	124	−1 15	57	125	302
57	02 51	57	124	01 54	56	125	00 58	57	125	00 01	57	125	−0 56	56	126	303
56	03 10	56	125	02 14	57	125	01 17	57	126	00 20	57	126	−0 37	57	126	304
55	03 29	−56	126	02 33	−57	126	01 36	−57	127	00 39	−57	127	−0 18	−57	127	305
54	03 48	57	127	02 51	57	127	01 54	57	128	00 57	56	128	00 01	57	128	306
53	04 07	57	128	03 10	57	128	02 13	57	129	01 16	57	129	00 19	57	129	307
52	04 25	57	129	03 28	57	129	02 31	57	130	01 34	57	130	00 37	57	130	308
51	04 43	57	130	03 46	57	130	02 49	57	130	01 52	57	131	00 55	58	131	309
50	05 01	−57	131	04 04	−57	131	03 07	−58	131	02 09	−57	132	01 12	−57	132	310
49	05 19	58	132	04 21	57	132	03 24	57	132	02 27	57	133	01 30	58	133	311
48	05 36	57	133	04 39	58	133	03 41	57	133	02 44	57	134	01 47	58	134	312
47	05 53	57	134	04 56	58	134	03 58	57	134	03 01	58	134	02 03	57	135	313
46	06 10	57	135	05 13	58	135	04 15	58	135	03 17	57	135	02 20	58	136	314
45	06 27	−58	136	05 29	−58	136	04 31	−57	136	03 34	−58	136	02 36	−58	137	315
44	06 43	58	137	05 45	57	137	04 48	58	137	03 50	58	137	02 52	58	138	316
43	06 59	58	137	06 01	58	138	05 03	57	138	04 06	58	138	03 08	58	138	317
42	07 15	58	138	06 17	58	139	05 19	58	139	04 21	58	139	03 23	58	139	318
41	07 30	58	139	06 32	58	140	05 34	58	140	04 36	58	140	03 38	58	140	319
40	07 45	−58	140	06 47	−58	141	05 49	−58	141	04 51	−58	141	03 53	−58	141	320
39	08 00	58	141	07 02	58	142	06 04	58	142	05 06	58	142	04 08	59	142	321
38	08 15	59	142	07 16	58	143	06 18	58	143	05 20	58	143	04 22	58	143	322
37	08 29	58	143	07 31	59	143	06 32	58	144	05 34	58	144	04 36	59	144	323
36	08 43	59	144	07 44	58	144	06 46	58	145	05 48	59	145	04 49	58	145	324
35	08 56	−58	145	07 58	−59	145	06 59	−58	146	06 01	−58	146	05 03	−59	146	325
34	09 10	59	146	08 11	58	146	07 13	59	147	06 14	59	147	05 15	58	147	326
33	09 22	58	147	08 24	59	147	07 25	58	148	06 27	59	148	05 28	59	148	327
32	09 35	59	148	08 36	58	148	07 38	59	149	06 39	59	149	05 40	58	149	328
31	09 47	58	149	08 49	59	149	07 50	59	149	06 51	59	150	05 52	59	150	329
30	09 59	−59	150	09 00	−58	150	08 02	−59	150	07 03	−59	151	06 04	−59	151	330
29	10 11	59	151	09 12	59	151	08 13	59	151	07 14	59	152	06 15	59	152	331
28	10 22	59	152	09 23	59	152	08 24	59	152	07 25	59	153	06 26	59	153	332
27	10 33	59	153	09 34	59	153	08 35	59	153	07 36	59	154	06 37	59	154	333
26	10 43	59	154	09 44	59	154	08 45	59	154	07 46	59	155	06 47	59	155	334
25	10 53	−59	155	09 54	−59	155	08 55	−59	155	07 56	−59	155	06 57	−59	156	335
24	11 03	59	156	10 04	59	156	09 05	60	156	08 05	59	156	07 06	59	157	336
23	11 12	59	157	10 13	59	157	09 14	59	157	08 15	60	157	07 15	59	158	337
22	11 22	60	158	10 22	59	158	09 23	59	158	08 24	60	158	07 24	59	159	338
21	11 30	59	159	10 31	60	159	09 31	59	159	08 32	59	159	07 33	60	160	339
20	11 38	−59	160	10 39	−59	160	09 40	−60	160	08 40	−59	160	07 41	−60	160	340
19	11 46	59	161	10 47	60	161	09 47	59	161	08 48	60	161	07 48	59	161	341
18	11 54	60	162	10 54	59	162	09 55	60	162	08 55	59	162	07 56	60	162	342
17	12 01	60	163	11 01	59	163	10 02	60	163	09 02	60	163	08 02	59	163	343
16	12 08	60	164	11 08	60	164	10 08	59	164	09 09	60	164	08 09	60	164	344
15	12 14	−60	165	11 14	−60	165	10 14	−59	165	09 15	−60	165	08 15	−60	165	345
14	12 20	60	166	11 20	60	166	10 20	59	166	09 21	60	166	08 21	60	166	346
13	12 25	59	167	11 26	60	167	10 26	60	167	09 26	60	167	08 26	60	167	347
12	12 30	59	168	11 31	60	168	10 31	60	168	09 31	60	168	08 31	60	168	348
11	12 35	60	169	11 35	60	169	10 35	59	169	09 36	60	169	08 36	60	169	349
10	12 39	−59	170	11 40	−60	170	10 40	−60	170	09 40	−60	170	08 40	−60	170	350
9	12 43	60	171	11 43	59	171	10 44	60	171	09 44	60	171	08 44	60	171	351
8	12 47	60	172	11 47	60	172	10 47	60	172	09 47	60	172	08 47	60	172	352
7	12 50	60	173	11 50	60	173	10 50	60	173	09 50	60	173	08 50	60	173	353
6	12 53	60	174	11 53	60	174	10 53	60	174	09 53	60	174	08 53	60	174	354
5	12 55	−60	175	11 55	−60	175	10 55	−60	175	09 55	−60	175	08 55	−60	175	355
4	12 57	60	176	11 57	60	176	10 57	60	176	09 57	60	176	08 57	60	176	356
3	12 58	60	177	11 58	60	177	10 58	60	177	09 58	60	177	08 58	60	177	357
2	12 59	60	178	11 59	60	178	10 59	60	178	09 59	60	178	08 59	60	178	358
1	13 00	60	179	12 00	60	179	11 00	60	179	10 00	60	179	09 00	60	179	359
0	13 00	−60	180	12 00	−60	180	11 00	−60	180	10 00	−60	180	09 00	−60	180	360

0° 1° 2° 3° 4° 5° 6° 7° 8° 9° 10° 11° 12° 13° 14°

S. Lat. {LHA greater than 180°....... Zn=180−Z
{LHA less than 180°........... Zn=180+Z

DECLINATION (0°-14°) CONTRARY NAME TO LATITUDE

N. Lat. {LHA greater than 180°....... Zn=Z; LHA less than 180°.......... Zn=360−Z}

DECLINATION (15°-29°) SAME NAME AS LATITUDE

LHA	15° Hc	d	Z	16° Hc	d	Z	17° Hc	d	Z	18° Hc	d	Z	19° Hc	d	Z	LHA
	° ′	′	°	° ′	′	°	° ′	′	°	° ′	′	°	° ′	′	°	
0	38 00	+60	180	39 00	+60	180	40 00	+60	180	41 00	+60	180	42 00	+60	180	360
1	38 00	60	179	39 00	60	179	40 00	60	179	41 00	60	179	42 00	60	179	359
2	37 59	60	178	38 59	60	178	39 59	60	178	40 59	60	178	41 59	60	178	358
3	37 58	60	176	38 58	60	176	39 58	60	176	40 58	60	176	41 58	60	176	357
4	37 56	60	175	38 56	60	175	39 56	60	175	40 56	60	175	41 56	60	175	356
5	37 54	+60	174	38 54	+60	174	39 54	+60	174	40 54	+60	174	41 54	+59	174	355
6	37 51	60	173	38 51	60	173	39 51	60	173	40 51	60	172	41 51	60	172	354
7	37 48	60	171	38 48	60	171	39 48	59	171	40 47	60	171	41 47	60	171	353
8	37 44	60	170	38 44	60	170	39 44	60	170	40 44	59	170	41 43	60	170	352
9	37 40	60	169	38 40	59	169	39 39	60	169	40 39	60	169	41 39	60	169	351
10	37 35	+60	168	38 35	+60	168	39 35	+59	168	40 34	+60	167	41 34	+60	167	350
11	37 30	60	167	38 30	59	166	39 29	60	166	40 29	60	166	41 29	59	166	349
12	37 24	60	165	38 24	60	165	39 24	59	165	40 23	60	165	41 23	60	165	348
13	37 18	60	164	38 18	59	164	39 17	60	164	40 17	59	164	41 16	60	164	347
14	37 11	60	163	38 11	60	163	39 11	59	163	40 10	60	163	41 10	59	162	346
15	37 04	+60	162	38 04	+59	162	39 03	+60	161	40 03	+59	161	41 02	+60	161	345
16	36 57	59	161	37 56	60	160	38 56	59	160	39 55	59	160	40 54	60	160	344
17	36 49	59	159	37 48	59	159	38 47	60	159	39 47	59	159	40 46	59	159	343
18	36 40	59	158	37 39	60	158	38 39	59	158	39 38	59	158	40 37	60	157	342
19	36 31	59	157	37 30	60	157	38 30	59	157	39 29	59	156	40 28	59	156	341
20	36 22	+59	156	37 21	+59	156	38 20	+59	155	39 19	+59	155	40 18	+59	155	340
21	36 12	59	155	37 11	59	154	38 10	59	154	39 09	59	154	40 08	59	154	339
22	36 02	59	153	37 01	59	153	38 00	59	153	38 59	59	153	39 58	58	153	338
23	35 51	59	152	36 50	59	152	37 49	59	152	38 48	58	152	39 46	59	151	337
24	35 40	59	151	36 39	59	151	37 38	58	151	38 36	59	150	39 35	59	150	336
25	35 28	+59	150	36 27	+59	150	37 26	+58	149	38 24	+59	149	39 23	+59	149	335
26	35 16	59	149	36 15	59	149	37 14	58	148	38 12	59	148	39 11	58	148	334
27	35 04	59	148	36 03	58	147	37 01	59	147	38 00	58	147	38 58	58	147	333
28	34 51	59	147	35 50	58	146	36 48	59	146	37 47	58	146	38 45	58	145	332
29	34 38	58	145	35 36	59	145	36 35	58	145	37 33	58	144	38 31	59	144	331
30	34 25	+58	144	35 23	+58	144	36 21	+58	144	37 19	+58	143	38 17	+59	143	330
31	34 11	58	143	35 09	58	143	36 07	58	142	37 05	58	142	38 03	58	142	329
32	33 56	58	142	34 54	59	142	35 53	57	141	36 50	58	141	37 48	58	141	328
33	33 42	58	141	34 40	58	141	35 38	58	140	36 36	57	140	37 33	58	140	327
34	33 27	58	140	34 25	57	139	35 22	58	139	36 20	58	139	37 18	58	138	326
35	33 11	+58	139	34 09	+58	138	35 07	+58	138	36 05	+57	138	37 02	+58	137	325
36	32 56	57	137	33 53	58	137	34 51	58	137	35 49	57	136	36 46	58	136	324
37	32 40	57	136	33 37	58	136	34 35	57	136	35 32	58	135	36 30	57	135	323
38	32 23	58	135	33 21	57	135	34 18	58	135	35 16	57	134	36 13	57	134	322
39	32 07	57	134	33 04	57	134	34 01	58	133	34 59	57	133	35 56	57	133	321
40	31 50	+57	133	32 47	+57	133	33 44	+57	132	34 41	+57	132	35 38	+58	132	320
41	31 32	58	132	32 30	57	132	33 27	57	131	34 24	57	131	35 21	57	131	319
42	31 15	57	131	32 12	57	131	33 09	57	130	34 06	57	130	35 03	57	129	318
43	30 57	57	130	31 54	57	129	32 51	57	129	33 48	57	129	34 45	56	128	317
44	30 39	57	129	31 36	57	128	32 33	56	128	33 29	57	128	34 26	57	127	316
45	30 20	+57	128	31 17	+57	127	32 14	+57	127	33 11	+56	127	34 07	+57	126	315
46	30 02	56	127	30 58	57	126	31 55	57	126	32 52	56	126	33 48	57	125	314
47	29 43	56	126	30 39	57	125	31 36	56	125	32 32	57	124	33 29	56	124	313
48	29 24	56	125	30 20	57	124	31 17	56	124	32 13	56	123	33 09	57	123	312
49	29 04	57	124	30 01	56	123	30 57	56	123	31 53	57	122	32 50	56	122	311
50	28 44	+57	122	29 41	+56	122	30 37	+56	122	31 33	+56	121	32 29	+57	121	310
51	28 25	56	121	29 21	56	121	30 17	56	121	31 13	56	120	32 09	56	120	309
52	28 04	57	120	29 01	56	120	29 57	56	120	30 53	56	119	31 49	56	119	308
53	27 44	56	119	28 40	56	119	29 36	56	119	30 32	56	118	31 28	56	118	307
54	27 24	56	118	28 20	56	118	29 16	55	118	30 11	56	117	31 07	56	117	306
55	27 03	+56	117	27 59	+56	117	28 55	+56	117	29 51	+55	116	30 46	+56	116	305
56	26 42	56	116	27 38	56	116	28 34	55	116	29 29	56	115	30 25	56	115	304
57	26 21	56	115	27 17	55	115	28 12	56	115	29 08	56	114	30 04	56	114	303
58	26 00	55	114	26 55	56	114	27 51	56	114	28 47	55	113	29 42	55	113	302
59	25 38	56	113	26 34	55	113	27 29	56	113	28 25	55	112	29 20	56	112	301
60	25 17	+55	112	26 12	+56	112	27 08	+55	112	28 03	+55	111	28 58	+56	111	300
61	24 55	55	111	25 50	56	111	26 46	55	111	27 41	55	110	28 36	56	110	299
62	24 33	55	110	25 28	56	110	26 24	55	110	27 19	55	109	28 14	55	109	298
63	24 11	55	109	25 06	56	109	26 02	55	109	26 57	55	108	27 52	55	108	297
64	23 49	55	108	24 44	55	108	25 39	55	108	26 34	56	107	27 30	55	107	296
65	23 26	+55	107	24 22	+55	107	25 17	+55	107	26 12	+55	106	27 07	+55	106	295
66	23 04	55	106	23 59	55	106	24 54	55	106	25 49	55	105	26 44	55	105	294
67	22 41	56	106	23 37	55	105	24 32	55	105	25 27	55	104	26 22	55	104	293
68	22 19	55	105	23 14	55	104	24 09	55	104	25 04	55	103	25 59	55	103	292
69	21 56	55	104	22 51	55	103	23 46	55	103	24 41	55	102	25 36	55	102	291

LHA	20° Hc	d	Z	21° Hc	d	Z	22° Hc	d	Z	23° Hc	d	Z	24° Hc	d	Z	LHA
	° ′	′	°	° ′	′	°	° ′	′	°	° ′	′	°	° ′	′	°	
0	43 00	+60	180	44 00	+60	180	45 00	+60	180	46 00	+60	180	47 00	+60	180	360
1	43 00	60	179	44 00	60	179	45 00	60	179	46 00	60	179	47 00	60	179	359
2	42 59	60	177	43 59	60	177	44 59	60	177	45 59	60	177	46 59	60	177	358
3	42 58	60	176	43 58	60	176	44 58	60	176	45 58	60	176	46 58	60	176	357
4	42 56	60	175	43 56	60	175	44 56	60	175	45 56	60	175	46 56	60	175	356
5	42 53	+60	174	43 53	+60	174	44 53	+60	174	45 53	+60	173	46 53	+60	173	355
6	42 51	60	172	43 51	59	172	44 50	60	172	45 50	60	172	46 50	60	172	354
7	42 47	60	171	43 47	60	171	44 47	60	171	45 47	60	171	46 47	60	171	353
8	42 43	60	170	43 43	60	170	44 43	60	170	45 43	60	169	46 43	59	169	352
9	42 39	60	169	43 39	59	168	44 38	60	168	45 38	60	168	46 38	60	168	351
10	42 34	+60	167	43 34	+59	167	44 33	+60	167	45 33	+60	167	46 33	+60	167	350
11	42 28	60	166	43 28	60	166	44 28	60	166	45 28	59	166	46 27	60	165	349
12	42 23	59	165	43 22	60	165	44 22	59	164	45 21	60	164	46 21	60	164	348
13	42 16	60	163	43 16	59	163	44 15	60	163	45 15	59	163	46 14	60	163	347
14	42 09	60	162	43 09	59	162	44 08	60	162	45 08	59	162	46 07	59	161	346
15	42 02	+59	161	43 01	+60	161	44 01	+59	161	45 00	+59	160	45 59	+60	160	345
16	41 54	59	160	42 53	59	159	43 52	60	159	44 52	59	159	45 51	59	159	344
17	41 45	60	158	42 45	59	158	43 44	59	158	44 43	59	158	45 42	60	158	343
18	41 37	59	157	42 36	59	157	43 35	59	157	44 34	59	157	45 33	59	156	342
19	41 27	59	156	42 26	59	156	43 25	59	155	44 24	59	155	45 23	59	155	341
20	41 17	+59	155	42 16	+59	154	43 15	+59	154	44 14	+59	154	45 13	+59	154	340
21	41 07	59	153	42 06	59	153	43 05	59	153	44 04	59	153	45 03	58	152	339
22	40 56	59	152	41 55	59	152	42 54	59	152	43 53	59	151	44 52	58	151	338
23	40 45	59	151	41 44	59	151	42 43	58	151	43 41	59	150	44 40	59	150	337
24	40 34	58	150	41 32	59	150	42 31	59	149	43 30	58	149	44 28	59	149	336
25	40 22	+58	149	41 20	+59	148	42 19	+58	148	43 17	+59	148	44 16	+58	147	335
26	40 09	59	147	41 08	58	147	42 06	58	147	43 04	59	147	44 03	58	146	334
27	39 56	59	146	40 55	58	146	41 53	58	146	42 51	59	145	43 50	58	145	333
28	39 43	58	145	40 41	59	145	41 40	58	144	42 38	58	144	43 36	58	144	332
29	39 30	58	144	40 28	58	144	41 26	58	143	42 24	58	143	43 22	58	143	331
30	39 16	+58	143	40 14	+58	142	41 12	+57	142	42 09	+58	142	43 07	+58	141	330
31	39 01	58	142	39 59	58	141	40 57	58	141	41 55	57	140	42 52	58	140	329
32	38 46	58	140	39 44	58	140	40 42	58	140	41 40	57	139	42 37	58	139	328
33	38 31	58	139	39 29	57	139	40 26	58	138	41 24	58	138	42 22	57	138	327
34	38 16	57	138	39 13	58	138	40 11	57	137	41 08	58	137	42 06	57	137	326
35	38 00	+57	137	38 57	+58	137	39 55	+57	136	40 52	+57	136	41 49	+57	135	325
36	37 44	57	136	38 41	57	135	39 38	57	135	40 35	58	135	41 33	57	134	324
37	37 27	57	135	38 24	57	134	39 21	58	134	40 19	57	133	41 16	57	133	323
38	37 10	57	133	38 07	57	133	39 04	57	133	40 01	57	132	40 58	57	132	322
39	36 53	57	132	37 50	57	132	38 47	57	132	39 44	57	131	40 41	56	131	321
40	36 36	+56	131	37 32	+57	131	38 29	+57	130	39 26	+57	130	40 23	+56	130	320
41	36 18	57	130	37 15	56	130	38 11	57	129	39 08	57	129	40 05	56	128	319
42	36 00	56	129	36 56	57	129	37 53	57	128	38 50	56	128	39 46	56	127	318
43	35 41	57	128	36 38	56	128	37 34	57	127	38 31	56	127	39 27	57	126	317
44	35 23	56	127	36 19	57	126	37 16	56	126	38 12	56	126	39 08	56	125	316
45	35 04	+56	126	36 00	+57	125	36 57	+56	125	37 53	+56	124	38 49	+56	124	315
46	34 45	56	125	35 41	56	124	36 37	56	124	37 33	56	123	38 29	56	123	314
47	34 25	56	124	35 21	57	123	36 18	56	123	37 14	56	122	38 10	55	122	313
48	34 06	56	123	35 02	56	122	35 58	56	122	36 54	56	121	37 50	55	121	312
49	33 46	56	122	34 42	56	121	35 38	56	121	36 34	55	120	37 29	56	120	311
50	33 26	+55	120	34 21	+56	120	35 17	+56	120	36 13	+56	119	37 09	+55	119	310
51	33 05	56	119	34 01	56	119	34 57	56	119	35 53	55	118	36 48	56	118	309
52	32 45	56	118	33 40	56	118	34 36	56	117	35 32	55	117	36 27	56	117	308
53	32 24	56	117	33 20	55	117	34 15	56	116	35 11	55	116	36 06	55	115	307
54	32 03	56	116	32 59	55	116	33 54	56	115	34 50	55	115	35 45	55	114	306
55	31 42	+55	115	32 37	+56	115	33 33	+55	114	34 28	+55	114	35 23	+56	113	305
56	31 21	55	114	32 16	55	114	33 11	56	113	34 07	55	113	35 02	55	112	304
57	30 59	56	113	31 55	55	113	32 50	55	112	33 45	55	112	34 40	55	111	303
58	30 37	56	112	31 33	55	112	32 28	55	111	33 23	55	111	34 18	55	110	302
59	30 16	55	111	31 11	55	111	32 06	55	110	33 01	55	110	33 56	55	109	301
60	29 54	+55	110	30 49	+55	110	31 44	+55	109	32 39	+55	109	33 34	+55	108	300
61	29 32	55	109	30 27	55	109	31 22	55	108	32 17	55	108	33 12	54	107	299
62	29 09	56	108	30 05	55	108	31 00	54	107	31 54	55	107	32 49	55	106	298
63	28 47	55	107	29 42	55	107	30 37	54	106	31 32	55	106	32 27	54	105	297
64	28 25	55	106	29 20	55	106	30 15	54	105	31 09	55	105	32 04	54	104	296
65	28 02	+55	105	28 57	+55	105	29 52	+55	104	30 47	+54	104	31 41	+55	103	295
66	27 39	55	104	28 34	55	104	29 29	55	103	30 24	54	103	31 18	55	102	294
67	27 17	55	103	28 12	54	103	29 06	55	102	30 01	54	102	30 55	55	101	293
68	26 54	55	102	27 49	54	102	28 43	55	101	29 38	54	101	30 32	55	100	292
69	26 31	55	101	27 26	54	101	28 20	55	100	29 15	54	100	30 09	55	100	291

LHA	25° Hc	d	Z	26° Hc	d	Z	27° Hc	d	Z	28° Hc	d	Z	29° Hc	d	Z	LHA
	° ′	′	°	° ′	′	°	° ′	′	°	° ′	′	°	° ′	′	°	
0	48 00	+60	180	49 00	+60	180	50 00	+60	180	51 00	+60	180	52 00	+60	180	360
1	48 00	60	179	49 00	60	179	50 00	60	179	51 00	60	179	52 00	60	179	359
2	47 59	60	177	48 59	60	177	49 59	60	177	50 59	60	177	51 59	60	177	358
3	47 58	60	176	48 58	59	176	49 57	60	176	50 57	60	176	51 57	60	176	357
4	47 56	60	175	48 56	60	175	49 56	59	175	50 55	60	174	51 55	60	174	356
5	47 53	+60	173	48 53	+60	173	49 53	+60	173	50 53	+60	173	51 53	+60	173	355
6	47 50	60	172	48 50	60	172	49 50	60	172	50 50	60	172	51 50	59	172	354
7	47 47	59	171	48 46	60	170	49 46	60	170	50 46	60	170	51 46	60	170	353
8	47 42	60	169	48 42	60	169	49 42	60	169	50 42	60	169	51 42	59	169	352
9	47 38	59	168	48 37	60	168	49 37	60	168	50 37	60	167	51 37	59	167	351
10	47 33	+59	167	48 32	+60	166	49 32	+60	166	50 32	+59	166	51 31	+60	166	350
11	47 27	59	165	48 26	60	165	49 26	60	165	50 26	59	165	51 25	60	165	349
12	47 21	59	164	48 20	60	164	49 20	59	164	50 19	60	163	51 19	59	163	348
13	47 14	59	163	48 13	60	162	49 13	59	162	50 12	60	162	51 12	59	162	347
14	47 06	60	161	48 06	59	161	49 05	60	161	50 05	59	161	51 04	59	160	346
15	46 59	+59	160	47 58	+59	160	48 57	+60	159	49 57	+59	159	50 56	+59	159	345
16	46 50	60	159	47 50	59	158	48 49	59	158	49 48	59	158	50 47	59	158	344
17	46 42	59	157	47 41	59	157	48 40	59	157	49 39	59	157	50 38	59	156	343
18	46 32	59	156	47 31	59	156	48 30	59	155	49 29	59	155	50 28	59	155	342
19	46 22	59	155	47 21	59	154	48 20	59	154	49 19	59	154	50 18	59	154	341
20	46 12	+59	153	47 11	+59	153	48 10	+59	153	49 09	+58	153	50 07	+59	152	340
21	46 01	59	152	47 00	59	152	47 59	59	152	48 58	58	151	49 56	59	151	339
22	45 50	59	151	46 49	58	151	47 47	59	150	48 46	58	150	49 44	59	150	338
23	45 39	58	150	46 37	59	150	47 36	58	149	48 34	58	149	49 32	59	148	337
24	45 27	58	148	46 25	58	148	47 23	59	148	48 22	58	147	49 20	58	147	336
25	45 14	+58	147	46 12	+59	147	47 11	+58	146	48 09	+58	146	49 07	+58	146	335
26	45 01	58	146	45 59	58	146	46 57	58	145	47 55	58	145	48 53	58	144	334
27	44 48	58	145	45 46	58	144	46 44	58	144	47 42	57	144	48 39	58	143	333
28	44 34	58	143	45 32	58	143	46 30	57	143	47 27	58	142	48 25	58	142	332
29	44 20	57	142	45 17	58	142	46 15	58	141	47 13	57	141	48 10	58	141	331
30	44 05	+58	141	45 03	+57	141	46 00	+58	140	46 58	+57	140	47 55	+58	139	330
31	43 50	58	140	44 48	57	139	45 45	58	139	46 43	57	139	47 40	57	138	329
32	43 35	57	139	44 32	58	138	45 30	57	138	46 27	57	137	47 24	57	137	328
33	43 19	57	137	44 16	58	137	45 14	57	136	46 11	57	136	47 08	57	136	327
34	43 03	57	136	44 00	57	136	44 57	57	135	45 54	57	135	46 51	57	134	326
35	42 46	+58	135	43 44	+57	135	44 41	+56	134	45 37	+57	134	46 34	+57	133	325
36	42 30	57	134	43 27	57	133	44 24	56	133	45 20	57	132	46 17	56	132	324
37	42 13	56	133	43 09	57	132	44 06	57	132	45 03	56	131	45 59	57	131	323
38	41 55	57	131	42 52	57	131	43 49	56	131	44 45	56	130	45 41	57	130	322
39	41 37	57	130	42 34	57	130	43 31	56	129	44 27	56	129	45 23	56	128	321
40	41 19	+57	129	42 16	+56	129	43 12	+57	128	44 09	+56	128	45 05	+56	127	320
41	41 01	56	128	41 57	57	128	42 54	56	127	43 50	56	127	44 46	56	126	319
42	40 42	57	127	41 39	56	126	42 35	56	126	43 31	56	125	44 27	56	125	318
43	40 24	56	126	41 20	56	125	42 16	56	125	43 12	55	124	44 07	56	124	317
44	40 04	56	125	41 00	56	124	41 56	56	124	42 52	56	123	43 48	55	123	316
45	39 45	+56	124	40 41	+56	123	41 37	+55	123	42 32	+56	122	43 28	+55	122	315
46	39 25	56	122	40 21	56	122	41 17	55	122	42 12	56	121	43 08	55	120	314
47	39 05	56	121	40 01	56	121	40 57	55	120	41 52	56	120	42 48	55	119	313
48	38 45	56	120	39 41	55	120	40 36	56	119	41 32	55	119	42 27	55	118	312
49	38 25	55	119	39 20	56	119	40 16	55	118	41 11	55	118	42 06	55	117	311
50	38 04	+56	118	39 00	+55	118	39 55	+55	117	40 50	+55	117	41 45	+55	116	310
51	37 44	55	117	38 39	55	117	39 34	55	116	40 29	55	116	41 24	55	115	309
52	37 23	55	116	38 18	55	116	39 13	55	115	40 08	55	115	41 03	55	114	308
53	37 01	56	115	37 57	55	115	38 52	55	114	39 47	54	113	40 41	55	113	307
54	36 40	55	114	37 35	55	113	38 30	55	113	39 25	55	112	40 20	54	112	306
55	36 19	+55	113	37 14	+54	112	38 08	+55	112	39 03	+55	111	39 58	+54	111	305
56	35 57	55	112	36 52	55	111	37 47	54	111	38 41	55	110	39 36	54	110	304
57	35 35	55	111	36 30	55	110	37 25	54	110	38 19	55	109	39 14	54	109	303
58	35 13	55	110	36 08	55	109	37 03	54	109	37 57	54	108	38 51	55	108	302
59	34 51	55	109	35 46	54	108	36 40	55	108	37 35	54	107	38 29	54	107	301
60	34 29	+54	108	35 23	+55	107	36 18	+54	107	37 12	+55	106	38 07	+54	106	300
61	34 06	55	107	35 01	54	106	35 55	55	106	36 50	54	105	37 44	54	105	299
62	33 44	54	106	34 38	55	105	35 33	54	105	36 27	54	104	37 21	54	104	298
63	33 21	55	105	34 16	54	104	35 10	54	104	36 04	54	103	36 58	54	103	297
64	32 58	55	104	33 53	54	103	34 47	54	103	35 41	54	102	36 35	54	102	296
65	32 36	+54	103	33 30	+54	102	34 24	+54	102	35 18	+54	101	36 12	+54	101	295
66	32 13	54	102	33 07	54	101	34 01	54	101	34 55	54	100	35 49	54	100	294
67	31 50	54	101	32 44	54	100	33 38	54	100	34 32	54	99	35 26	54	99	293
68	31 27	54	100	32 21	54	99	33 15	54	99	34 09	54	98	35 03	54	98	292
69	31 04	54	99	31 58	54	99	32 52	54	98	33 46	54	98	34 40	53	97	291

S. Lat. {LHA greater than 180°....... Zn=180−Z; LHA less than 180°.......... Zn=180+Z}

DECLINATION (15°-29°) SAME NAME AS LATITUDE

N. Lat. {LHA greater than 180°....... Zn=Z; LHA less than 180°.......... Zn=360−Z}

DECLINATION (15°-29°) SAME NAME AS LATITUDE

LHA	15° Hc	d	Z	16° Hc	d	Z	17° Hc	d	Z	18° Hc	d	Z	19° Hc	d	Z	20° Hc	d	Z	21° Hc	d	Z
	° ′	′	°	° ′	′	°	° ′	′	°	° ′	′	°	° ′	′	°	° ′	′	°	° ′	′	°
70	21 33	+55	103	22 28	+55	102	23 23	+55	102	24 18	+55	101	25 13	+55	101	26 08	+55	100	27 03	+54	100
71	21 10	55	102	22 05	55	101	23 00	55	101	23 55	55	100	24 50	55	100	25 45	54	100	26 39	55	99
72	20 47	55	101	21 42	55	100	22 37	55	100	23 32	55	99	24 27	55	99	25 22	54	99	26 16	55	98
73	20 24	55	100	21 19	55	99	22 14	55	99	23 09	55	99	24 04	54	98	24 58	55	98	25 53	55	97
74	20 01	55	99	20 56	55	98	21 51	55	98	22 46	54	98	23 40	55	97	24 35	55	97	25 30	54	96
75	19 38	+55	98	20 33	+55	97	21 28	+54	97	22 22	+55	97	23 17	+55	96	24 12	+54	96	25 06	+55	95
76	19 15	54	97	20 09	55	97	21 04	55	96	21 59	55	96	22 54	54	95	23 48	55	95	24 43	55	94
77	18 51	55	96	19 46	55	96	20 41	55	95	21 36	54	95	22 30	55	94	23 25	55	94	24 20	54	93
78	18 28	55	95	19 23	55	95	20 18	54	94	21 12	55	94	22 07	55	93	23 02	54	93	23 56	55	92
79	18 05	54	94	18 59	55	94	19 54	55	93	20 49	55	93	21 44	54	92	22 38	55	92	23 33	54	92
80	17 41	+55	93	18 36	+55	93	19 31	+55	92	20 26	+54	92	21 20	+55	92	22 15	+54	91	23 09	+55	91
81	17 18	55	92	18 13	54	92	19 07	55	91	20 02	55	91	20 57	54	91	21 51	55	90	22 46	54	90
82	16 54	55	91	17 49	55	91	18 44	55	91	19 39	54	90	20 33	55	90	21 28	54	89	22 22	55	89
83	16 31	55	90	17 26	54	90	18 20	55	90	19 15	55	89	20 10	55	89	21 05	54	88	21 59	55	88
84	16 07	55	90	17 02	55	89	17 57	55	89	18 52	54	88	19 46	55	88	20 41	55	87	21 36	54	87
85	15 44	+55	89	16 39	+55	88	17 34	+54	88	18 28	+55	87	19 23	+55	87	20 18	+54	86	21 12	+55	86
86	15 21	54	88	16 15	55	87	17 10	55	87	18 05	55	86	19 00	54	86	19 54	55	86	20 49	55	85
87	14 57	55	87	15 52	55	86	16 47	55	86	17 42	54	86	18 36	55	85	19 31	55	85	20 26	54	84
88	14 34	55	86	15 29	54	85	16 23	55	85	17 18	55	85	18 13	55	84	19 08	54	84	20 02	55	83
89	14 10	55	85	15 05	55	85	16 00	55	84	16 55	55	84	17 50	54	83	18 44	55	83	19 39	55	82
90	13 47	+55	84	14 42	+55	84	15 37	+55	83	16 32	+54	83	17 26	+55	82	18 21	+55	82	19 16	+54	82
91	13 24	55	83	14 19	55	83	15 14	54	82	16 08	55	82	17 03	55	81	17 58	55	81	18 53	54	81
92	13 00	55	82	13 55	55	82	14 50	55	81	15 45	55	81	16 40	55	81	17 35	54	80	18 29	55	80
93	12 37	55	81	13 32	55	81	14 27	55	80	15 22	55	80	16 17	55	80	17 12	54	79	18 06	55	79
94	12 14	55	80	13 09	55	80	14 04	55	80	14 59	55	79	15 54	55	79	16 49	54	78	17 43	55	78
95	11 51	+55	80	12 46	+55	79	13 41	+55	79	14 36	+55	78	15 31	+55	78	16 26	+55	77	17 21	+54	77
96	11 28	55	79	12 23	55	78	13 18	55	78	14 13	55	77	15 08	55	77	16 03	55	77	16 58	55	76
97	11 05	55	78	12 00	55	77	12 55	55	77	13 50	55	77	14 45	55	76	15 40	55	76	16 35	55	75
98	10 42	55	77	11 37	55	76	12 32	56	76	13 28	55	76	14 23	55	75	15 18	54	75	16 12	55	74
99	10 19	56	76	11 15	55	76	12 10	55	75	13 05	55	75	14 00	55	74	14 55	55	74	15 50	55	73
100	09 57	+55	75	10 52	+55	75	11 47	+55	74	12 42	+55	74	13 37	+56	73	14 33	+55	73	15 28	+55	73
101	09 34	55	74	10 29	56	74	11 25	55	73	12 20	55	73	13 15	55	73	14 10	55	72	15 05	55	72
102	09 12	55	73	10 07	55	73	11 02	56	72	11 58	55	72	12 53	55	72	13 48	55	71	14 43	55	71
103	08 49	56	72	09 45	55	72	10 40	55	72	11 35	56	71	12 31	55	71	13 26	55	70	14 21	55	70
104	08 27	55	71	09 22	56	71	10 18	55	71	11 13	55	70	12 08	56	70	13 04	55	69	13 59	55	69
105	08 05	+55	71	09 00	+56	70	09 56	+55	70	10 51	+56	69	11 47	+55	69	12 42	+55	69	13 37	+55	68
106	07 43	55	70	08 38	56	69	09 34	55	69	10 29	56	68	11 25	55	68	12 20	56	68	13 16	55	67
107	07 21	56	69	08 17	55	68	09 12	56	68	10 08	55	68	11 03	56	67	11 59	55	67	12 54	55	66
108	06 59	56	68	07 55	55	67	08 50	56	67	09 46	56	67	10 42	55	66	11 37	56	66	12 33	55	65
109	06 38	55	67	07 33	56	67	08 29	56	66	09 25	55	66	10 20	56	65	11 16	55	65	12 11	56	65
110	06 16	+56	66	07 12	+56	66	08 08	+55	65	09 03	+56	65	09 59	+56	64	10 55	+55	64	11 50	+56	64
111	05 55	56	65	06 51	55	65	07 46	56	64	08 42	56	64	09 38	56	64	10 34	55	63	11 29	56	63
112	05 34	56	64	06 29	56	64	07 25	56	63	08 21	56	63	09 17	56	63	10 13	56	62	11 09	55	62
113	05 13	55	63	06 08	56	63	07 04	56	63	08 00	56	62	08 56	56	62	09 52	56	61	10 48	56	61
114	04 52	56	62	05 48	56	62	06 44	56	62	07 40	56	61	08 36	56	61	09 32	56	61	10 28	55	60
115	04 31	+56	61	05 27	+56	61	06 23	+56	61	07 19	+56	60	08 15	+56	60	09 11	+56	60	10 07	+56	59
116	04 10	57	61	05 07	56	60	06 03	56	60	06 59	56	60	07 55	56	59	08 51	56	59	09 47	56	58
117	03 50	56	60	04 46	57	59	05 43	56	59	06 39	56	59	07 35	56	58	08 31	56	58	09 27	56	58
118	03 30	56	59	04 26	57	58	05 23	56	58	06 19	56	58	07 15	56	57	08 11	57	57	09 08	56	57
119	03 10	56	58	04 06	57	57	05 03	56	57	05 59	57	57	06 56	56	56	07 52	56	56	08 48	56	56
120	02 50	+57	57	03 47	+56	57	04 43	+57	56	05 40	+56	56	06 36	+57	56	07 33	+56	55	08 29	+56	55
121	02 31	56	56	03 27	57	56	04 24	56	55	05 20	57	55	06 17	56	55	07 13	57	54	08 10	56	54
122	02 12	56	55	03 08	57	55	04 05	56	54	05 01	57	54	05 58	56	54	06 54	57	53	07 51	57	53
123	01 52	57	54	02 49	57	54	03 46	56	53	04 42	57	53	05 39	57	53	06 36	57	53	07 32	57	52
124	01 34	56	53	02 30	57	53	03 27	57	53	04 24	57	52	05 21	56	52	06 17	57	52	07 14	57	51
125	01 15	+57	52	02 12	+57	52	03 09	+56	52	04 05	+57	51	05 02	+57	51	05 59	+57	51	06 56	+57	50
126	00 56	57	51	01 53	57	51	02 50	57	51	03 47	57	50	04 44	57	50	05 41	57	50	06 38	57	50
127	00 38	57	50	01 35	57	50	02 32	57	50	03 29	57	50	04 26	57	49	05 23	57	49	06 20	57	49
128	00 20	57	50	01 17	57	49	02 14	57	49	03 11	58	49	04 09	57	48	05 06	57	48	06 03	57	48
129	00 03	57	49	01 00	57	48	01 57	57	48	02 54	57	48	03 51	57	47	04 48	57	47	05 45	58	47
130	−0 15	+57	48	00 42	+58	47	01 40	+57	47	02 37	+57	47	03 34	+57	47	04 31	+58	46	05 29	+57	46
131	−0 32	57	47	00 25	57	47	01 22	58	46	02 20	57	46	03 17	57	46	04 14	58	45	05 12	57	45
132	−0 49	57	46	00 08	58	46	01 06	57	45	02 03	57	45	03 00	58	45	03 58	57	44	04 55	58	44
133	−1 06	58	45	−0 08	57	45	00 49	58	44	01 47	57	44	02 44	58	44	03 42	57	44	04 39	58	43
134	−1 22	57	44	−0 25	58	44	00 33	57	43	01 30	58	43	02 28	58	43	03 26	57	43	04 23	58	42
135	−1 38	+57	43	−0 41	+58	43	00 17	+58	42	01 15	+57	42	02 12	+58	42	03 10	+58	42	04 08	+57	41
136	−1 54	57	42	−0 57	58	42	00 01	58	42	00 59	58	41	01 57	57	41	02 54	58	41	03 52	58	41
137	−2 10	58	41	−1 12	58	41	−0 14	58	41	00 44	57	40	01 41	58	40	02 39	58	40	03 37	58	40
138	−2 25	58	40	−1 27	58	40	−0 29	58	40	00 29	57	40	01 26	58	39	02 24	58	39	03 22	58	39
139	−2 40	58	39	−1 42	58	39	−0 44	58	39	00 14	58	39	01 12	58	38	02 10	58	38	03 08	58	38

LHA	22° Hc	d	Z	23° Hc	d	Z	24° Hc	d	Z	25° Hc	d	Z	26° Hc	d	Z	27° Hc	d	Z	28° Hc	d	Z	29° Hc	d	Z	LHA
	° ′	′	°	° ′	′	°	° ′	′	°	° ′	′	°	° ′	′	°	° ′	′	°	° ′	′	°	° ′	′	°	
70	27 57	+55	100	28 52	+54	99	29 46	+54	99	30 40	+55	98	31 35	+54	98	32 29	+54	97	33 23	+53	97	34 16	+54	96	290
71	27 34	55	99	28 29	54	98	29 23	54	98	30 17	54	97	31 11	54	97	32 05	54	96	32 59	54	96	33 53	54	95	289
72	27 11	54	98	28 05	54	97	29 00	54	97	29 54	54	96	30 48	54	96	31 42	54	95	32 36	54	95	33 30	53	94	288
73	26 48	54	97	27 42	54	96	28 36	55	96	29 31	54	95	30 25	54	95	31 19	54	94	32 13	53	94	33 06	54	93	287
74	26 24	55	96	27 19	54	95	28 13	54	95	29 07	54	94	30 01	54	94	30 55	54	93	31 49	54	93	32 43	54	92	286
75	26 01	+54	95	26 55	+55	94	27 50	+54	94	28 44	+54	93	29 38	+54	93	30 32	+54	92	31 26	+54	92	32 20	+53	91	285
76	25 38	54	94	26 32	54	93	27 26	54	93	28 20	55	92	29 15	53	92	30 08	54	91	31 02	54	91	31 56	54	90	284
77	25 14	54	93	26 08	55	92	27 03	54	92	27 57	54	92	28 51	54	91	29 45	54	91	30 39	54	90	31 33	53	89	283
78	24 51	54	92	25 45	54	92	26 39	55	91	27 34	54	91	28 28	54	90	29 22	53	90	30 15	54	89	31 09	54	89	282
79	24 27	55	91	25 22	54	91	26 16	54	90	27 10	54	90	28 04	54	89	28 58	54	89	29 52	54	88	30 46	53	88	281
80	24 04	+54	90	24 58	+54	90	25 52	+55	89	26 47	+54	89	27 41	+54	88	28 35	+54	88	29 29	+53	87	30 22	+54	87	280
81	23 40	55	89	24 35	54	89	25 29	54	88	26 23	54	88	27 17	54	87	28 11	54	87	29 05	54	86	29 59	54	86	279
82	23 17	54	88	24 11	55	88	25 06	54	87	26 00	54	87	26 54	54	86	27 48	54	86	28 42	54	85	29 36	53	85	278
83	22 54	54	87	23 48	54	87	24 42	54	86	25 36	55	86	26 31	54	86	27 25	53	85	28 18	54	85	29 12	54	84	277
84	22 30	54	87	23 24	55	86	24 19	54	86	25 13	54	85	26 07	54	85	27 01	54	84	27 55	54	84	28 49	54	83	276
85	22 07	+54	86	23 01	+54	85	23 55	+55	85	24 50	+54	84	25 44	+54	84	26 38	+54	83	27 32	+54	83	28 26	+53	82	275
86	21 43	55	85	22 38	54	84	23 32	55	84	24 26	55	83	25 21	54	83	26 15	54	82	27 09	54	82	28 03	53	81	274
87	21 20	54	84	22 14	55	83	23 09	54	83	24 03	54	82	24 57	54	82	25 51	54	81	26 45	54	81	27 39	54	80	273
88	20 57	54	83	21 51	55	82	22 46	54	82	23 40	54	82	24 34	54	81	25 28	54	81	26 22	54	80	27 16	54	80	272
89	20 34	54	82	21 28	54	82	22 22	55	81	23 17	54	81	24 11	54	80	25 05	54	80	25 59	54	79	26 53	54	79	271
90	20 10	+55	81	21 05	+54	81	21 59	+55	80	22 54	+54	80	23 48	+54	79	24 42	+54	79	25 36	+54	78	26 30	+54	78	270
91	19 47	55	80	20 42	54	80	21 36	55	79	22 31	54	79	23 25	54	78	24 19	54	78	25 13	54	77	26 07	54	77	269
92	19 24	55	79	20 19	54	79	21 13	55	78	22 08	54	78	23 02	54	77	23 56	55	77	24 51	54	77	25 45	54	76	268
93	19 01	55	78	19 56	54	78	20 50	55	78	21 45	54	77	22 39	55	77	23 34	54	76	24 28	54	76	25 22	54	75	267
94	18 38	55	78	19 33	54	77	20 27	55	77	21 22	54	76	22 16	55	76	23 11	54	75	24 05	54	75	24 59	54	74	266
95	18 15	+55	77	19 10	+55	76	20 05	+54	76	20 59	+55	75	21 54	+54	75	22 48	+55	74	23 43	+54	74	24 37	+54	73	265
96	17 53	54	76	18 47	55	75	19 42	55	75	20 37	54	74	21 31	55	74	22 26	54	74	23 20	54	73	24 14	55	73	264
97	17 30	55	75	18 25	54	74	19 19	55	74	20 14	55	74	21 09	54	73	22 03	55	73	22 58	54	72	23 52	54	72	263
98	17 07	55	74	18 02	55	74	18 57	55	73	19 52	54	73	20 46	55	72	21 41	55	72	22 35	55	71	23 30	54	71	262
99	16 45	55	73	17 40	55	73	18 35	54	72	19 29	55	72	20 24	55	71	21 19	54	71	22 13	55	70	23 08	54	70	261
100	16 23	+54	72	17 17	+55	72	18 12	+55	71	19 07	+55	71	20 02	+55	70	20 57	+54	70	21 51	+55	70	22 46	+54	69	260
101	16 00	55	71	16 55	55	71	17 50	55	70	18 45	55	70	19 40	55	70	20 35	54	69	21 29	55	69	22 24	55	68	259
102	15 38	55	70	16 33	55	70	17 28	55	70	18 23	55	69	19 18	55	69	20 13	55	68	21 08	54	68	22 02	55	67	258
103	15 16	55	70	16 11	55	69	17 06	55	69	18 01	55	68	18 56	55	68	19 51	55	67	20 46	55	67	21 41	54	67	257
104	14 54	55	69	15 49	56	68	16 45	55	68	17 40	55	67	18 35	55	67	19 30	54	67	20 24	55	66	21 19	55	66	256
105	14 32	+56	68	15 28	+55	67	16 23	+55	67	17 18	+55	67	18 13	+55	66	19 08	+55	66	20 03	+55	65	20 58	+55	65	255
106	14 11	55	67	15 06	55	66	16 01	56	66	16 57	55	66	17 52	55	65	18 47	55	65	19 42	55	64	20 37	55	64	254
107	13 49	56	66	14 45	55	66	15 40	55	65	16 35	56	65	17 31	55	64	18 26	55	64	19 21	55	64	20 16	55	63	253
108	13 28	55	65	14 23	56	65	15 19	55	64	16 14	56	64	17 10	55	64	18 05	55	63	19 00	55	63	19 55	55	62	252
109	13 07	55	64	14 02	56	64	14 58	55	63	15 53	56	63	16 49	55	63	17 44	55	62	18 39	55	62	19 34	56	61	251
110	12 46	+55	63	13 41	+56	63	14 37	+55	63	15 32	+56	62	16 28	+55	62	17 23	+56	61	18 19	+55	61	19 14	+55	61	250
111	12 25	56	62	13 21	55	62	14 16	56	62	15 12	55	61	16 07	56	61	17 03	55	61	17 58	56	60	18 54	55	60	249
112	12 04	56	62	13 00	56	61	13 56	55	61	14 51	56	60	15 47	55	60	16 42	56	60	17 38	55	59	18 33	56	59	248
113	11 44	56	61	12 40	55	60	13 35	56	60	14 31	56	60	15 27	55	59	16 22	56	59	17 18	56	58	18 14	55	58	247
114	11 23	56	60	12 19	56	59	13 15	56	59	14 11	56	59	15 07	55	58	16 02	56	58	16 58	56	58	17 54	55	57	246
115	11 03	+56	59	11 59	+56	58	12 55	+56	58	13 51	+56	58	14 47	+56	57	15 43	+55	57	16 38	+56	57	17 34	+56	56	245
116	10 43	56	58	11 39	56	58	12 35	56	57	13 31	56	57	14 27	56	56	15 23	56	56	16 19	56	56	17 15	56	55	244
117	10 23	57	57	11 20	56	57	12 16	56	56	13 12	56	56	14 08	56	56	15 04	56	55	16 00	56	55	16 56	56	55	243
118	10 04	56	56	11 00	56	56	11 56	56	56	12 52	56	55	13 48	57	55	14 45	56	54	15 41	56	54	16 37	56	54	242
119	09 44	57	55	10 41	56	55	11 37	56	55	12 33	56	54	13 29	57	54	14 26	56	54	15 22	56	53	16 18	56	53	241
120	09 25	+57	55	10 22	+56	54	11 18	+56	54	12 14	+57	53	13 11	+56	53	14 07	+56	53	15 03	+56	52	15 59	+56	52	240
121	09 06	57	54	10 03	56	53	10 59	57	53	11 56	56	53	12 52	56	52	13 48	57	52	14 45	56	52	15 41	56	51	239
122	08 48	56	53	09 44	57	52	10 41	56	52	11 37	57	52	12 34	56	51	13 30	56	51	14 26	57	51	15 23	56	50	238
123	08 29	57	52	09 26	56	52	10 22	57	51	11 19	56	51	12 15	57	51	13 12	56	50	14 08	57	50	15 05	56	49	237
124	08 11	56	51	09 07	57	51	10 04	57	50	11 01	56	50	11 57	57	50	12 54	57	49	13 51	56	49	14 47	57	49	236
125	07 53	+56	50	08 49	+57	50	09 46	+57	49	10 43	+57	49	11 40	+56	49	12 36	+57	48	13 33	+57	48	14 30	+56	48	235
126	07 35	57	49	08 32	56	49	09 28	57	49	10 25	57	48	11 22	57	48	12 19	57	48	13 16	56	47	14 12	57	47	234
127	07 17	57	48	08 14	57	48	09 11	57	48	10 08	57	47	11 05	57	47	12 02	57	47	12 59	56	46	13 55	57	46	233
128	07 00	57	47	07 57	57	47	08 54	57	47	09 51	57	47	10 48	57	46	11 45	57	46	12 42	57	46	13 39	57	45	232
129	06 43	57	47	07 40	57	46	08 37	57	46	09 34	57	46	10 31	57	45	11 28	57	45	12 25	57	45	13 22	57	44	231
130	06 26	+57	46	07 23	+57	45	08 20	+57	45	09 17	+57	45	10 14	+58	44	11 12	+57	44	12 09	+57	44	13 06	+57	44	230
131	06 09	57	45	07 06	58	44	08 04	57	44	09 01	57	44	09 58	57	44	10 55	58	43	11 53	57	43	12 50	57	43	229
132	05 53	57	44	06 50	57	44	07 47	58	43	08 45	57	43	09 42	58	43	10 40	57	42	11 37	57	42	12 34	57	42	228
133	05 37	57	43	06 34	58	43	07 32	57	42	08 29	57	42	09 26	58	42	10 24	57	42	11 21	58	41	12 19	57	41	227
134	05 21	57	42	06 18	58	42	07 16	57	42	08 13	58	41	09 11	57	41	10 08	58	41	11 06	57	40	12 03	58	40	226
135	05 05	+58	41	06 03	+58	41	07 01	+57	41	07 58	+58	40	08 56	+57	40	09 53	+58	40	10 51	+57	40	11 48	+58	39	225
136	04 50	58	40	05 48	57	40	06 45	58	40	07 43	58	39	08 41	57	39	09 38	58	39	10 36	58	39	11 34	58	38	224
137	04 35	58	39	05 33	58	39	06 31	57	39	07 28	58	39	08 26	58	38	09 24	58	38	10 22	58	38	11 19	58	38	223
138	04 20	58	38	05 18	58	38	06 16	58	38	07 14	58	38	08 12	58	37	09 10	57	37	10 07	58	37	11 05	58	37	222
139	04 06	58	38	05 04	58	37	06 02	58	37	07 00	58	37	07 58	58	37	08 56	58	36	09 54	57	36	10 51	58	36	221

S. Lat. {LHA greater than 180°....... Zn=180−Z; LHA less than 180°.......... Zn=180+Z}

DECLINATION (15°-29°) SAME NAME AS LATITUDE

LAT 67°

N. Lat. {LHA greater than 180°....... Zn=Z; LHA less than 180°........... Zn=360−Z}

DECLINATION (15°-29°) SAME NAME AS LATITUDE

LHA	15° Hc	d	Z	16° Hc	d	Z	17° Hc	d	Z	18° Hc	d	Z	19° Hc	d	Z
	° ′	′	°	° ′	′	°	° ′	′	°	° ′	′	°	° ′	′	°
140	−2 55	+58	38	−1 57	+58	38	−0 59	+58	38	−0 01	+58	38	00 57	+59	37
141	−3 09	58	37	−2 11	58	37	−1 13	58	37	−0 15	58	37	00 43	58	37
142	−3 24	59	37	−2 25	58	36	−1 27	58	36	−0 29	58	36	00 29	59	36
143	−3 37	58	36	−2 39	58	35	−1 41	59	35	−0 42	58	35	00 16	58	35
144	−3 51	59	35	−2 52	58	34	−1 54	58	34	−0 56	59	34	00 03	58	34
145	−4 04	+58	34	−3 06	+59	34	−2 07	+58	33	−1 09	+59	33	−0 10	+58	33
146	−4 17	59	33	−3 18	58	33	−2 20	59	32	−1 21	58	32	−0 23	59	32
147	−4 29	58	32	−3 31	59	32	−2 32	58	31	−1 34	59	31	−0 35	59	31
148	−4 42	59	31	−3 43	59	31	−2 44	58	30	−1 46	59	30	−0 47	59	30
149	−4 53	58	30	−3 55	59	30	−2 56	59	30	−1 57	59	29	−0 58	58	29
150	−5 05	+59	29	−4 06	+59	29	−3 07	+59	29	−2 08	+58	28	−1 10	+59	28
151	−5 16	59	28	−4 17	59	28	−3 18	59	28	−2 19	58	27	−1 21	59	27
152				−4 28	59	27	−3 29	59	27	−2 30	59	27	−1 31	59	26
153				−4 39	60	26	−3 39	59	26	−2 40	59	26	−1 41	59	25
154				−4 49	59	25	−3 50	60	25	−2 50	59	25	−1 51	59	24
155				−4 58	+59	24	−3 59	+59	24	−3 00	+59	24	−2 01	+59	24
156				−5 08	59	23	−4 09	60	23	−3 09	59	23	−2 10	59	23
157				−5 17	59	22	−4 18	60	22	−3 18	59	22	−2 19	59	22
158							−4 26	59	21	−3 27	60	21	−2 27	59	21
159							−4 34	59	20	−3 35	59	20	−2 36	60	20
160							−4 42	+59	19	−3 43	+60	19	−2 43	+59	19
161							−4 50	60	18	−3 50	59	18	−2 51	60	18
162							−4 57	60	17	−3 57	59	17	−2 58	60	17
163							−5 04	60	16	−4 04	60	16	−3 04	59	16
164							−5 10	60	15	−4 10	59	15	−3 11	60	15
165										−4 16	+59	14	−3 17	+60	14
166										−4 22	60	13	−3 22	60	13
167										−4 27	60	12	−3 27	59	12
168										−4 32	60	11	−3 32	60	11
169										−4 36	59	10	−3 37	60	10
170										−4 41	+60	10	−3 41	+60	9
171										−4 44	60	9	−3 44	60	9
172										−4 48	60	8	−3 48	60	8
173										−4 50	59	7	−3 51	60	7
174										−4 53	60	6	−3 53	60	6
175										−4 55	+60	5	−3 55	+60	5
176										−4 57	60	4	−3 57	60	4
177										−4 58	60	3	−3 58	60	3
178										−4 59	60	2	−3 59	60	2
179										−5 00	60	1	−4 00	60	1
180										−5 00	+60	0	−4 00	+60	0

LHA	20° Hc	d	Z	21° Hc	d	Z	22° Hc	d	Z	23° Hc	d	Z	24° Hc	d	Z
	° ′	′	°	° ′	′	°	° ′	′	°	° ′	′	°	° ′	′	°
140	01 55	+58	37	02 53	+59	37	03 52	+58	37	04 50	+58	36	05 48	+58	36
141	01 41	59	36	02 40	58	36	03 38	58	36	04 36	58	36	05 34	58	35
142	01 28	58	35	02 26	58	35	03 24	58	35	04 22	59	35	05 21	58	34
143	01 14	59	34	02 13	58	34	03 11	58	34	04 09	59	34	05 08	58	34
144	01 01	59	34	02 00	58	33	02 58	58	33	03 56	59	33	04 55	58	33
145	00 48	+59	33	01 47	+58	32	02 45	+59	32	03 44	+58	32	04 42	+59	32
146	00 36	58	32	01 34	59	31	02 33	59	31	03 32	58	31	04 30	59	31
147	00 24	58	31	01 22	59	31	02 21	59	30	03 20	58	30	04 18	59	30
148	00 12	59	30	01 11	58	30	02 09	59	29	03 08	59	29	04 07	58	29
149	00 00	59	29	00 59	59	29	01 58	59	29	02 57	58	28	03 55	59	28
150	−0 11	+59	28	00 48	+59	28	01 47	+59	28	02 46	+59	27	03 45	+58	27
151	−0 22	59	27	00 37	59	27	01 36	59	27	02 35	59	27	03 34	59	26
152	−0 32	59	26	00 27	59	26	01 26	59	26	02 25	59	26	03 24	59	25
153	−0 42	59	25	00 17	59	25	01 16	59	25	02 15	59	25	03 14	59	25
154	−0 52	59	24	00 07	59	24	01 06	59	24	02 05	59	24	03 04	59	24
155	−1 02	+60	23	−0 02	+59	23	00 57	+59	23	01 56	+59	23	02 55	+59	23
156	−1 11	59	22	−0 12	60	22	00 48	59	22	01 47	59	22	02 46	59	22
157	−1 20	60	22	−0 20	59	21	00 39	59	21	01 38	60	21	02 38	59	21
158	−1 28	59	21	−0 29	60	20	00 31	59	20	01 30	59	20	02 29	60	20
159	−1 36	59	20	−0 37	60	20	00 23	59	19	01 22	60	19	02 22	59	19
160	−1 44	+60	19	−0 44	+59	19	00 15	+60	18	01 15	+59	18	02 14	+59	18
161	−1 51	59	18	−0 52	60	18	00 08	59	18	01 07	60	17	02 07	59	17
162	−1 58	59	17	−0 59	60	17	00 01	60	17	01 01	59	17	02 00	60	16
163	−2 05	60	16	−1 05	59	16	−0 06	60	16	00 54	60	16	01 54	59	16
164	−2 11	60	15	−1 11	59	15	−0 12	60	15	00 48	60	15	01 48	59	15
165	−2 17	+60	14	−1 17	+59	14	−0 18	+60	14	00 42	+60	14	01 42	+60	14
166	−2 22	59	13	−1 23	60	13	−0 23	60	13	00 37	59	13	01 36	60	13
167	−2 28	60	12	−1 28	60	12	−0 28	60	12	00 32	59	12	01 31	60	12
168	−2 32	59	11	−1 33	60	11	−0 33	60	11	00 27	60	11	01 27	60	11
169	−2 37	60	10	−1 37	60	10	−0 37	60	10	00 23	60	10	01 23	59	10
170	−2 41	+60	9	−1 41	+60	9	−0 41	+60	9	00 19	+60	9	01 19	+60	9
171	−2 44	59	8	−1 45	60	8	−0 45	60	8	00 15	60	8	01 15	60	8
172	−2 48	60	8	−1 48	60	7	−0 48	60	7	00 12	60	7	01 12	60	7
173	−2 51	60	7	−1 51	60	7	−0 51	60	6	00 09	60	6	01 09	60	6
174	−2 53	60	6	−1 53	60	6	−0 53	60	6	00 07	60	6	01 07	60	6
175	−2 55	+60	5	−1 55	+60	5	−0 55	+60	5	00 05	+60	5	01 05	+60	5
176	−2 57	60	4	−1 57	60	4	−0 57	60	4	00 03	60	4	01 03	60	4
177	−2 58	60	3	−1 58	60	3	−0 58	60	3	00 02	60	3	01 02	60	3
178	−2 59	60	2	−1 59	60	2	−0 59	60	2	00 01	60	2	01 01	60	2
179	−3 00	60	1	−2 00	60	1	−1 00	60	1	00 00	60	1	01 00	60	1
180	−3 00	+60	0	−2 00	+60	0	−1 00	+60	0	00 00	+60	0	01 00	+60	0

LHA	25° Hc	d	Z	26° Hc	d	Z	27° Hc	d	Z	28° Hc	d	Z	29° Hc	d	Z	LHA
	° ′	′	°	° ′	′	°	° ′	′	°	° ′	′	°	° ′	′	°	
140	06 46	+58	36	07 44	+58	36	08 42	+58	35	09 40	+58	35	10 38	+58	35	220
141	06 32	58	35	07 30	58	35	08 28	59	35	09 27	58	34	10 25	58	34	219
142	06 19	58	34	07 17	58	34	08 15	58	34	09 13	59	33	10 12	58	33	218
143	06 06	58	33	07 04	58	33	08 02	59	33	09 01	58	33	09 59	58	32	217
144	05 53	59	32	06 52	58	32	07 50	58	32	08 48	59	32	09 47	58	31	216
145	05 41	+58	32	06 39	+59	31	07 38	+58	31	08 36	+59	31	09 35	+58	31	215
146	05 29	58	31	06 27	59	30	07 26	58	30	08 24	59	30	09 23	58	30	214
147	05 17	58	30	06 15	59	30	07 14	59	29	08 13	58	29	09 11	59	29	213
148	05 05	59	29	06 04	59	29	07 03	58	28	08 01	59	28	09 00	59	28	212
149	04 54	59	28	05 53	59	28	06 52	59	28	07 51	58	27	08 49	59	27	211
150	04 43	+59	27	05 42	+59	27	06 41	+59	27	07 40	+59	27	08 39	+59	26	210
151	04 33	59	26	05 32	59	26	06 31	59	26	07 30	59	26	08 29	58	25	209
152	04 23	59	25	05 22	59	25	06 21	59	25	07 20	59	25	08 19	59	25	208
153	04 13	59	24	05 12	59	24	06 11	59	24	07 10	59	24	08 09	59	24	207
154	04 03	60	23	05 03	59	23	06 02	59	23	07 01	59	23	08 00	59	23	206
155	03 54	+59	23	04 53	+60	22	05 53	+59	22	06 52	+59	22	07 51	+59	22	205
156	03 45	60	22	04 45	59	22	05 44	59	21	06 43	59	21	07 42	60	21	204
157	03 37	59	21	04 36	60	21	05 36	59	21	06 35	59	20	07 34	59	20	203
158	03 29	59	20	04 28	59	20	05 27	60	20	06 27	59	19	07 26	60	19	202
159	03 21	59	19	04 20	60	19	05 20	59	19	06 19	60	19	07 19	59	18	201
160	03 13	+60	18	04 13	+59	18	05 12	+60	18	06 12	+59	18	07 11	+60	18	200
161	03 06	60	17	04 06	59	17	05 05	60	17	06 05	59	17	07 04	60	17	199
162	03 00	59	16	03 59	60	16	04 59	59	16	05 58	60	16	06 58	59	16	198
163	02 53	60	15	03 53	59	15	04 52	60	15	05 52	60	15	06 52	59	15	197
164	02 47	60	14	03 47	59	14	04 46	60	14	05 46	60	14	06 46	59	14	196
165	02 42	+59	14	03 41	+60	13	04 41	+60	13	05 41	+59	13	06 40	+60	13	195
166	02 36	60	13	03 36	60	13	04 36	59	12	05 35	60	12	06 35	60	12	194
167	02 31	60	12	03 31	60	12	04 31	60	12	05 31	59	12	06 30	60	11	193
168	02 27	59	11	03 26	60	11	04 26	60	11	05 26	60	11	06 26	60	11	192
169	02 22	60	10	03 22	60	10	04 22	60	10	05 22	60	10	06 22	60	10	191
170	02 19	+59	9	03 18	+60	9	04 18	+60	9	05 18	+60	9	06 18	+60	9	190
171	02 15	60	8	03 15	60	8	04 15	60	8	05 15	60	8	06 15	59	8	189
172	02 12	60	7	03 12	60	7	04 12	60	7	05 12	60	7	06 12	59	7	188
173	02 09	60	6	03 09	60	6	04 09	60	6	05 09	60	6	06 09	60	6	187
174	02 07	60	5	03 07	60	5	04 07	60	5	05 07	60	5	06 07	59	5	186
175	02 05	+60	5	03 05	+60	5	04 05	+60	4	05 05	+60	4	06 05	+60	4	185
176	02 03	60	4	03 03	60	4	04 03	60	4	05 03	60	4	06 03	60	4	184
177	02 02	60	3	03 02	60	3	04 02	60	3	05 02	60	3	06 02	60	3	183
178	02 01	60	2	03 01	60	2	04 01	60	2	05 01	60	2	06 01	60	2	182
179	02 00	60	1	03 00	60	1	04 00	60	1	05 00	60	1	06 00	60	1	181
180	02 00	+60	0	03 00	+60	0	04 00	+60	0	05 00	+60	0	06 00	+60	0	180

LAT 67°

| 15° | 16° | 17° | 18° | 19° | 20° | 21° | 22° | 23° | 24° | 25° | 26° | 27° | 28° | 29° |

S. Lat. {LHA greater than 180°....... Zn=180−Z; LHA less than 180°........... Zn=180+Z}

DECLINATION (15°-29°) SAME NAME AS LATITUDE

N. Lat. {LHA greater than 180°....... Zn=Z; LHA less than 180°........... Zn=360−Z}

DECLINATION (15°-29°) CONTRARY NAME TO LATITUDE

LHA	15°			16°			17°			18°			19°			20°			21°			22°			23°			24°			25°			26°			27°			28°			29°			LHA
	Hc	d	Z	Hc	d	Z	Hc	d	Z	Hc	d	Z	Hc	d	Z	Hc	d	Z	Hc	d	Z	Hc	d	Z	Hc	d	Z	Hc	d	Z	Hc	d	Z	Hc	d	Z	Hc	d	Z	Hc	d	Z	Hc	d	Z	
	° ′	′	°	° ′	′	°	° ′	′	°	° ′	′	°	° ′	′	°	° ′	′	°	° ′	′	°	° ′	′	°	° ′	′	°	° ′	′	°	° ′	′	°	° ′	′	°	° ′	′	°	° ′	′	°	° ′	′	°	
68	−5 34	55	116																																											292
67	−5 13	55	117																																											293
66	−4 52	56	118																																											294
65	−4 31	−56	119	−5 27	−56	119																																								295
64	−4 10	57	119	−5 07	56	120																																								296
63	−3 50	56	120	−4 46	57	121																																								297
62	−3 30	56	121	−4 26	57	122	−5 23	56	122																																					298
61	−3 10	56	122	−4 06	57	123	−5 03	56	123																																					299
60	−2 50	−57	123	−3 47	−56	123	−4 43	−57	124																																					300
59	−2 31	56	124	−3 27	57	124	−4 24	56	125	−5 20	57	125																																		301
58	−2 12	56	125	−3 08	57	125	−4 05	56	126	−5 01	57	126																																		302
57	−1 52	57	126	−2 49	57	126	−3 46	56	127	−4 42	57	127																																		303
56	−1 34	56	127	−2 30	57	127	−3 27	57	127	−4 24	57	128	−5 21	56	128																															304
55	−1 15	−57	128	−2 12	−57	128	−3 09	−56	128	−4 05	−57	129	−5 02	−57	129																															305
54	−0 56	57	129	−1 53	57	129	−2 50	57	129	−3 47	57	130	−4 44	57	130																															306
53	−0 38	57	130	−1 35	57	130	−2 32	57	130	−3 29	57	130	−4 26	57	131	−5 23	57	131																												307
52	−0 20	57	130	−1 17	57	131	−2 14	57	131	−3 11	58	131	−4 09	57	132	−5 06	57	132																												308
51	−0 03	57	131	−1 00	57	132	−1 57	57	132	−2 54	57	132	−3 51	57	133	−4 48	57	133																												309
50	00 15	−57	132	−0 42	−58	133	−1 40	−57	133	−2 37	−57	133	−3 34	−57	133	−4 31	−58	134	−5 29	−57	134																									310
49	00 32	57	133	−0 25	57	133	−1 22	58	134	−2 20	57	134	−3 17	57	134	−4 14	58	135	−5 12	57	135																									311
48	00 49	57	134	−0 08	58	134	−1 06	57	135	−2 03	57	135	−3 00	58	135	−3 58	57	136	−4 55	58	136																									312
47	01 06	58	135	00 08	57	135	−0 49	58	136	−1 47	57	136	−2 44	58	136	−3 42	57	136	−4 39	58	137																									313
46	01 22	57	136	00 25	58	136	−0 33	57	137	−1 30	58	137	−2 28	58	137	−3 26	57	137	−4 23	58	138	−5 21	57	138																						314
45	01 38	−57	137	00 41	−58	137	−0 17	−58	137	−1 15	−57	138	−2 12	−58	138	−3 10	−58	138	−4 08	−57	139	−5 05	−58	139																						315
44	01 54	57	138	00 57	58	138	−0 01	58	138	−0 59	58	139	−1 57	57	139	−2 54	58	139	−3 52	58	139	−4 50	58	140																						316
43	02 10	58	139	01 12	58	139	00 14	58	139	−0 44	57	140	−1 41	58	140	−2 39	58	140	−3 37	58	140	−4 35	58	141																						317
42	02 25	58	140	01 27	58	140	00 29	58	140	−0 29	57	140	−1 26	58	141	−2 24	58	141	−3 22	58	141	−4 20	58	142	−5 18	58	142																			318
41	02 40	58	141	01 42	58	141	00 44	58	141	−0 14	58	141	−1 12	58	142	−2 10	58	142	−3 08	58	142	−4 06	58	142	−5 04	58	143																			319
40	02 55	−58	142	01 57	−58	142	00 59	−58	142	00 01	−58	142	−0 57	−58	143	−1 55	−58	143	−2 53	−59	143	−3 52	−58	143	−4 50	−58	144																			320
39	03 09	58	143	02 11	58	143	01 13	58	143	00 15	58	143	−0 43	58	143	−1 41	59	144	−2 40	58	144	−3 38	58	144	−4 36	58	144																			321
38	03 24	59	143	02 25	58	144	01 27	58	144	00 29	58	144	−0 29	59	144	−1 28	58	145	−2 26	58	145	−3 24	58	145	−4 22	59	145	−5 21	58	146																322
37	03 37	58	144	02 39	58	145	01 41	59	145	00 42	58	145	−0 16	58	145	−1 14	59	146	−2 13	58	146	−3 11	58	146	−4 09	59	146	−5 08	58	146																323
36	03 51	59	145	02 52	58	146	01 54	58	146	00 56	59	146	−0 03	58	146	−1 01	59	146	−2 00	58	147	−2 58	58	147	−3 56	59	147	−4 55	58	147																324
35	04 04	−58	146	03 06	−59	146	02 07	−58	147	01 09	−59	147	00 10	−58	147	−0 48	−59	147	−1 47	−58	148	−2 45	−59	148	−3 44	−58	148	−4 42	−59	148																325
34	04 17	59	147	03 18	58	147	02 20	59	148	01 21	58	148	00 23	59	148	−0 36	58	148	−1 34	59	149	−2 33	59	149	−3 32	58	149	−4 30	59	149																326
33	04 29	58	148	03 31	59	148	02 32	58	149	01 34	59	149	00 35	59	149	−0 24	58	149	−1 22	59	149	−2 21	59	150	−3 20	58	150	−4 18	59	150	−5 17	58	150													327
32	04 42	59	149	03 43	59	149	02 44	58	150	01 46	59	150	00 47	59	150	−0 12	59	150	−1 11	58	150	−2 09	59	151	−3 08	59	151	−4 07	58	151	−5 05	59	151													328
31	04 53	58	150	03 55	59	150	02 56	59	150	01 57	59	151	00 58	58	151	00 00	59	151	−0 59	59	151	−1 58	59	151	−2 57	58	152	−3 55	59	152	−4 54	59	152													329
30	05 05	−59	151	04 06	−59	151	03 07	−59	151	02 08	−58	152	01 10	−59	152	00 11	−59	152	−0 48	−59	152	−1 47	−59	152	−2 46	−59	153	−3 45	−58	153	−4 43	−59	153													330
29	05 16	59	152	04 17	59	152	03 18	59	152	02 19	58	153	01 21	59	153	00 22	59	153	−0 37	59	153	−1 36	59	153	−2 35	59	153	−3 34	59	154	−4 33	59	154													331
28	05 27	59	153	04 28	59	153	03 29	59	153	02 30	59	153	01 31	59	154	00 32	59	154	−0 27	59	154	−1 26	59	154	−2 25	59	154	−3 24	59	155	−4 23	59	155													332
27	05 38	59	154	04 39	60	154	03 39	59	154	02 40	59	154	01 41	59	155	00 42	59	155	−0 17	59	155	−1 16	59	155	−2 15	59	155	−3 14	59	155	−4 13	59	156	−5 12	59	156										333
26	05 48	59	155	04 49	59	155	03 50	60	155	02 50	59	155	01 51	59	156	00 52	59	156	−0 07	59	156	−1 06	59	156	−2 05	59	156	−3 04	59	156	−4 03	60	157	−5 03	59	157										334
25	05 58	−60	156	04 58	−59	156	03 59	−59	156	03 00	−59	156	02 01	−59	156	01 02	−60	157	00 02	−59	157	−0 57	−59	157	−1 56	−59	157	−2 55	−59	157	−3 54	−59	157	−4 53	−60	158										335
24	06 07	59	157	05 08	59	157	04 09	60	157	03 09	59	157	02 10	59	157	01 11	59	158	00 12	60	158	−0 48	59	158	−1 47	59	158	−2 46	59	158	−3 45	60	158	−4 45	59	158										336
23	06 16	59	158	05 17	59	158	04 18	60	158	03 18	59	158	02 19	59	158	01 20	60	158	00 20	59	159	−0 39	59	159	−1 38	60	159	−2 38	59	159	−3 37	59	159	−4 36	60	159										337
22	06 25	60	159	05 25	59	159	04 26	59	159	03 27	60	159	02 27	59	159	01 28	59	159	00 29	60	160	−0 31	59	160	−1 30	59	160	−2 29	60	160	−3 29	59	160	−4 28	59	160										338
21	06 33	59	160	05 34	60	160	04 34	59	160	03 35	59	160	02 36	60	160	01 36	59	160	00 37	60	160	−0 23	59	161	−1 22	60	161	−2 22	59	161	−3 21	59	161	−4 20	60	161										339
20	06 41	−59	161	05 42	−60	161	04 42	−59	161	03 43	−60	161	02 43	−59	161	01 44	−60	161	00 44	−59	161	−0 15	−60	162	−1 15	−59	162	−2 14	−59	162	−3 13	−60	162	−4 13	−59	162	−5 12	−60	162							340
19	06 49	60	162	05 49	59	162	04 50	60	162	03 50	59	162	02 51	60	162	01 51	59	162	00 52	60	162	−0 08	59	162	−1 07	60	163	−2 07	59	163	−3 06	60	163	−4 06	59	163	−5 05	60	163							341
18	06 56	60	163	05 56	59	163	04 57	60	163	03 57	59	163	02 58	60	163	01 58	59	163	00 59	60	163	−0 01	60	163	−1 01	59	163	−2 00	60	164	−3 00	59	164	−3 59	60	164	−4 59	59	164							342
17	07 03	60	164	06 03	59	164	05 04	60	164	04 04	60	164	03 04	59	164	02 05	60	164	01 05	59	164	00 06	60	164	−0 54	60	164	−1 54	59	164	−2 53	60	165	−3 53	59	165	−4 52	60	165							343
16	07 09	59	164	06 10	60	165	05 10	60	165	04 10	59	165	03 11	60	165	02 11	60	165	01 11	59	165	00 12	60	165	−0 48	60	165	−1 48	59	165	−2 47	60	166	−3 47	59	166	−4 46	60	166							344
15	07 15	−59	165	06 16	−60	166	05 16	−60	166	04 16	−59	166	03 17	−60	166	02 17	−60	166	01 17	−59	166	00 18	−60	166	−0 42	−60	166	−1 42	−60	166	−2 42	−59	166	−3 41	−60	167	−4 41	−60	167							345
14	07 21	60	166	06 21	59	167	05 22	60	167	04 22	60	167	03 22	60	167	02 22	59	167	01 23	60	167	00 23	60	167	−0 37	59	167	−1 36	60	167	−2 36	60	167	−3 36	60	167	−4 36	59	168							346
13	07 26	59	167	06 27	60	167	05 27	60	168	04 27	60	168	03 27	59	168	02 28	60	168	01 28	60	168	00 28	60	168	−0 32	59	168	−1 31	60	168	−2 31	60	168	−3 31	60	168	−4 31	60	168							347
12	07 31	59	168	06 32	60	168	05 32	60	169	04 32	60	169	03 32	60	169	02 32	59	169	01 33	60	169	00 33	60	169	−0 27	60	169	−1 27	60	169	−2 27	59	169	−3 26	60	169	−4 26	60	169							348
11	07 36	60	169	06 36	60	169	05 36	60	169	04 36	59	170	03 37	60	170	02 37	60	170	01 37	60	170	00 37	60	170	−0 23	60	170	−1 23	59	170	−2 22	60	170	−3 22	60	170	−4 22	60	170							349
10	07 40	−60	170	06 40	−60	170	05 40	−59	170	04 41	−60	170	03 41	−60	171	02 41	−60	171	01 41	−60	171	00 41	−60	171	−0 19	−60	171	−1 19	−60	171	−2 19	−59	171	−3 18	−60	171	−4 18	−60	171							350
9	07 44	60	171	06 44	60	171	05 44	60	171	04 44	60	171	03 44	60	171	02 44	59	172	01 45	60	172	00 45	60	172	−0 15	60	172	−1 15	60	172	−2 15	60	172	−3 15	60	172	−4 15	60	172							351
8	07 47	60	172	06 47	60	172	05 47	59	172	04 48	60	172	03 48	60	172	02 48	60	172	01 48	60	173	00 48	60	173	−0 12	60	173	−1 12	60	173	−2 12	60	173	−3 12	60	173	−4 12	60	173							352
7	07 50	60	173	06 50	60	173	05 50	60	173	04 50	59	173	03 51	60	173	02 51	60	173	01 51	60	173	00 51	60	174	−0 09	60	174	−1 09	60	174	−2 09	60	174	−3 09	60	174	−4 09	60	174							353
6	07 53	60	174	06 53	60	174	05 53	60	174	04 53	60	174	03 53	60	174	02 53	60	174	01 53	60	174	00 53	60	174	−0 07	60	174	−1 07	60	175	−2 07	60	175	−3 07	60	175	−4 07	60	175							354
5	07 55	−60	175	06 55	−60	175	05 55	−60	175	04 55	−60	175	03 55	−60	175	02 55	−60	175	01 55	−60	175	00 55	−60	175	−0 05	−60	175	−1 05	−60	175	−2 05	−60	175	−3 05	−60	175	−4 05	−60	176							355
4	07 57	60	176	06 57	60	176	05 57	60	176	04 57	60	176	03 57	60	176	02 57	60	176	01 57	60	176	00 57	60	176	−0 03	60	176	−1 03	60	176	−2 03	60	176	−3 03	60	176	−4 03	60	176							356
3	07 58	60	177	06 58	60	177	05 58	60	177	04 58	60	177	03 58	60	177	02 58	60	177	01 58	60	177	00 58	60	177	−0 02	60	177	−1 02	60	177	−2 02	60	177	−3 02	60	177	−4 02	60	177							357
2	07 59	60	178	06 59	60	178	05 59	60	178	04 59	60	178	03 59	60	178	02 59	60	178	01 59	60	178	00 59	60	178	−0 01	60	178	−1 01	60	178	−2 01	60	178	−3 01	60	178	−4 01	60	178							358
1	08 00	60	179	07 00	60	179	06 00	60	179	05 00	60	179	04 00	60	179	03 00	60	179	02 00	60	179	01 00	60	179	00 00	60	179	−1 00	60	179	−2 00	60	179	−3 00	60	179	−4 00	60	179	−5 00	60	179				359
0	08 00	−60	180	07 00	−60	180	06 00	−60	180	05 00	−60	180	04 00	−60	180	03 00	−60	180	02 00	−60	180	01 00	−60	180	00 00	−60	180	−1 00	−60	180	−2 00	−60	180	−3 00	−60	180	−4 00	−60	180	−5 00	−60	180				360
	15°			16°			17°			18°			19°			20°			21°			22°			23°			24°			25°			26°			27°			28°			29°			

S. Lat. {LHA greater than 180°....... Zn=180−Z; LHA less than 180°........... Zn=180+Z}

DECLINATION (15°-29°) CONTRARY NAME TO LATITUDE

N. Lat. { LHA greater than 180°........ Zn=Z
LHA less than 180°............ Zn=360−Z

DECLINATION (0°-14°) SAME NAME AS LATITUDE

	0°			1°			2°			3°			4°		
LHA	Hc	d	Z	Hc	d	Z	Hc	d	Z	Hc	d	Z	Hc	d	Z
	° ′	′	°	° ′	′	°	° ′	′	°	° ′	′	°	° ′	′	°
0	22 00	+60	180	23 00	+60	180	24 00	+60	180	25 00	+60	180	26 00	+60	180
1	22 00	60	179	23 00	60	179	24 00	60	179	25 00	60	179	26 00	60	179
2	21 59	60	178	22 59	60	178	23 59	60	178	24 59	60	178	25 59	60	178
3	21 58	60	177	22 58	60	177	23 58	60	177	24 58	60	177	25 58	60	177
4	21 57	60	176	22 57	60	176	23 57	60	176	24 57	60	176	25 57	60	176
5	21 55	+60	175	22 55	+60	175	23 55	+60	175	24 55	+60	175	25 55	+60	175
6	21 52	60	174	22 52	60	174	23 52	60	173	24 52	60	173	25 52	60	173
7	21 50	60	173	22 50	60	172	23 50	59	172	24 49	60	172	25 49	60	172
8	21 47	59	171	22 46	60	171	23 46	60	171	24 46	60	171	25 46	60	171
9	21 43	60	170	22 43	60	170	23 43	60	170	24 43	59	170	25 42	60	170
10	21 39	+60	169	22 39	+60	169	23 39	+60	169	24 39	+59	169	25 38	+60	169
11	21 35	59	168	22 34	60	168	23 34	60	168	24 34	60	168	25 34	60	168
12	21 30	60	167	22 30	59	167	23 29	60	167	24 29	60	167	25 29	60	167
13	21 25	59	166	22 24	60	166	23 24	60	166	24 24	60	166	25 24	59	166
14	21 19	60	165	22 19	59	165	23 18	60	165	24 18	60	165	25 18	59	165
15	21 13	+60	164	22 13	+59	164	23 12	+60	164	24 12	+60	164	25 12	+59	163
16	21 06	60	163	22 06	60	163	23 06	59	163	24 05	60	163	25 05	59	162
17	21 00	59	162	21 59	60	162	22 59	59	162	23 58	60	161	24 58	59	161
18	20 52	60	161	21 52	59	161	22 51	60	160	23 51	59	160	24 50	60	160
19	20 45	59	160	21 44	60	160	22 44	59	159	23 43	60	159	24 43	59	159
20	20 37	+59	159	21 36	+60	158	22 36	+59	158	23 35	+59	158	24 34	+60	158
21	20 28	60	158	21 28	59	157	22 27	59	157	23 26	60	157	24 26	59	157
22	20 19	60	157	21 19	59	156	22 18	59	156	23 17	60	156	24 17	59	156
23	20 10	60	155	21 10	59	155	22 09	59	155	23 08	59	155	24 07	60	155
24	20 01	59	154	21 00	59	154	21 59	59	154	22 58	60	154	23 58	59	154
25	19 51	+59	153	20 50	+59	153	21 49	+59	153	22 48	+59	153	23 47	+59	153
26	19 41	59	152	20 40	59	152	21 39	59	152	22 38	59	152	23 37	59	152
27	19 30	59	151	20 29	59	151	21 28	59	151	22 27	59	151	23 26	59	150
28	19 19	59	150	20 18	59	150	21 17	59	150	22 16	59	150	23 15	59	149
29	19 08	58	149	20 06	59	149	21 05	59	149	22 04	59	149	23 03	59	148
30	18 56	+59	148	19 55	+58	148	20 53	+59	148	21 52	+59	148	22 51	+59	147
31	18 44	59	147	19 43	58	147	20 41	59	147	21 40	59	146	22 39	58	146
32	18 31	59	146	19 30	59	146	20 29	58	146	21 27	59	145	22 26	59	145
33	18 19	58	145	19 17	59	145	20 16	58	145	21 14	59	144	22 13	58	144
34	18 06	58	144	19 04	59	144	20 03	58	144	21 01	59	143	22 00	58	143
35	17 52	+59	143	18 51	+58	143	19 49	+59	143	20 48	+58	142	21 46	+58	142
36	17 39	58	142	18 37	58	142	19 35	59	141	20 34	58	141	21 32	58	141
37	17 25	58	141	18 23	58	141	19 21	58	140	20 19	59	140	21 18	58	140
38	17 10	58	140	18 08	59	140	19 07	58	139	20 05	58	139	21 03	58	139
39	16 56	58	139	17 54	58	139	18 52	58	138	19 50	58	138	20 48	58	138
40	16 41	+58	138	17 39	+58	138	18 37	+58	137	19 35	+58	137	20 33	+58	137
41	16 25	58	137	17 23	58	137	18 21	58	136	19 19	58	136	20 17	58	136
42	16 10	58	136	17 08	58	136	18 06	58	135	19 04	57	135	20 01	58	135
43	15 54	58	135	16 52	58	135	17 50	58	134	18 48	57	134	19 45	58	134
44	15 38	58	134	16 36	58	134	17 34	57	133	18 31	58	133	19 29	58	133
45	15 22	+57	133	16 19	+58	133	17 17	+58	132	18 15	+57	132	19 12	+58	132
46	15 05	58	132	16 03	57	132	17 00	58	131	17 58	57	131	18 55	58	131
47	14 48	58	131	15 46	57	131	16 43	58	130	17 41	57	130	18 38	58	130
48	14 31	58	130	15 29	57	130	16 26	57	129	17 23	58	129	18 21	57	129
49	14 14	57	129	15 11	57	129	16 08	58	128	17 06	57	128	18 03	57	128
50	13 56	+57	128	14 53	+58	128	15 51	+57	127	16 48	+57	127	17 45	+57	127
51	13 38	57	127	14 35	58	127	15 33	57	126	16 30	57	126	17 27	57	126
52	13 20	57	126	14 17	57	126	15 14	58	125	16 12	57	125	17 09	57	125
53	13 02	57	125	13 59	57	125	14 56	57	124	15 53	57	124	16 50	57	124
54	12 43	57	124	13 40	57	124	14 37	57	123	15 34	57	123	16 31	57	123
55	12 25	+56	123	13 21	+57	123	14 18	+57	122	15 15	+57	122	16 12	+57	122
56	12 06	56	122	13 02	57	122	13 59	57	121	14 56	57	121	15 53	57	121
57	11 46	57	121	12 43	57	121	13 40	57	120	14 37	56	120	15 33	57	120
58	11 27	57	120	12 24	57	120	13 21	56	119	14 17	57	119	15 14	57	119
59	11 08	56	119	12 04	57	119	13 01	56	119	13 57	57	118	14 54	57	118
60	10 48	+56	118	11 44	+57	118	12 41	+57	118	13 38	+56	117	14 34	+57	117
61	10 28	56	117	11 24	57	117	12 21	56	117	13 17	57	116	14 14	56	116
62	10 08	56	116	11 04	57	116	12 01	56	116	12 57	57	115	13 54	56	115
63	09 48	56	115	10 44	56	115	11 40	57	115	12 37	56	114	13 33	57	114
64	09 27	57	114	10 24	56	114	11 20	56	114	12 16	57	113	13 13	56	113
65	09 07	+56	113	10 03	+56	113	10 59	+57	113	11 56	+56	112	12 52	+56	112
66	08 46	56	112	09 42	56	112	10 38	57	112	11 35	56	111	12 31	56	111
67	08 25	56	112	09 21	56	111	10 17	57	111	11 14	56	110	12 10	56	110
68	08 04	56	111	09 00	56	110	09 56	57	110	10 53	56	110	11 49	56	109
69	07 43	56	110	08 39	56	109	09 35	56	109	10 31	56	109	11 27	56	108

	5°			6°			7°			8°			9°		
LHA	Hc	d	Z	Hc	d	Z	Hc	d	Z	Hc	d	Z	Hc	d	Z
	° ′	′	°	° ′	′	°	° ′	′	°	° ′	′	°	° ′	′	°
0	27 00	+60	180	28 00	+60	180	29 00	+60	180	30 00	+60	180	31 00	+60	180
1	27 00	60	179	28 00	60	179	29 00	60	179	30 00	60	179	31 00	60	179
2	26 59	60	178	27 59	60	178	28 59	60	178	29 59	60	178	30 59	60	178
3	26 58	60	177	27 58	60	177	28 58	60	177	29 58	60	177	30 58	60	177
4	26 57	60	176	27 57	59	176	28 56	60	176	29 56	60	175	30 56	60	175
5	26 55	+60	174	27 55	+59	174	28 54	+60	174	29 54	+60	174	30 54	+60	174
6	26 52	60	173	27 52	60	173	28 52	60	173	29 52	60	173	30 52	60	173
7	26 49	60	172	27 49	60	172	28 49	60	172	29 49	60	172	30 49	60	172
8	26 46	60	171	27 46	60	171	28 46	60	171	29 46	60	171	30 46	60	171
9	26 42	60	170	27 42	60	170	28 42	60	170	29 42	60	170	30 42	50	170
10	26 38	+60	169	27 38	+60	169	28 38	+60	169	29 38	+60	169	30 38	+59	169
11	26 34	59	168	27 33	60	168	28 33	60	168	29 33	60	168	30 33	60	167
12	26 29	59	167	27 28	60	167	28 28	60	166	29 28	60	166	30 28	59	166
13	26 23	60	166	27 23	60	165	28 23	59	165	29 22	60	165	30 22	60	165
14	26 17	60	164	27 17	60	164	28 17	59	164	29 16	60	164	30 16	60	164
15	26 11	+60	163	27 11	+59	163	28 10	+60	163	29 10	+60	163	30 10	+59	163
16	26 04	60	162	27 04	60	162	28 04	59	162	29 03	60	162	30 03	59	162
17	25 57	60	161	26 57	60	161	27 57	59	161	28 56	60	161	29 56	59	161
18	25 50	59	160	26 49	60	160	27 49	59	160	28 48	60	160	29 48	59	159
19	25 42	59	159	26 41	60	159	27 41	59	159	28 40	60	158	29 40	59	158
20	25 34	+59	158	26 33	+60	158	27 33	+59	158	28 32	+59	157	29 31	+60	157
21	25 25	59	157	26 24	60	157	27 24	59	156	28 23	59	156	29 22	60	156
22	25 16	59	156	26 15	60	156	27 15	59	155	28 14	59	155	29 13	59	155
23	25 07	59	155	26 06	59	154	27 05	59	154	28 04	59	154	29 03	59	154
24	24 57	59	154	25 56	59	153	26 55	59	153	27 54	59	153	28 53	59	153
25	24 46	+60	152	25 46	+59	152	26 45	+59	152	27 44	+59	152	28 43	+59	152
26	24 36	59	151	25 35	59	151	26 34	59	151	27 33	59	151	28 32	59	151
27	24 25	59	150	25 24	59	150	26 23	59	150	27 22	58	150	28 20	59	149
28	24 14	58	149	25 12	59	149	26 11	59	149	27 10	59	149	28 09	59	148
29	24 02	59	148	25 01	58	148	25 59	59	148	26 58	59	147	27 57	59	147
30	23 50	+58	147	24 48	+59	147	25 47	+59	147	26 46	+58	146	27 44	+59	146
31	23 37	59	146	24 36	59	146	25 35	58	146	26 33	59	145	27 32	58	145
32	23 25	58	145	24 23	59	145	25 22	58	144	26 20	59	144	27 19	58	144
33	23 11	59	144	24 10	58	144	25 08	59	143	26 07	58	143	27 05	59	143
34	22 58	58	143	23 56	59	143	24 55	58	142	25 53	59	142	26 52	58	142
35	22 44	+59	142	23 43	+58	142	24 41	+58	141	25 39	+58	141	26 37	+59	141
36	22 30	58	141	23 28	59	140	24 27	58	140	25 25	58	140	26 23	58	140
37	22 16	58	140	23 14	58	139	24 12	58	139	25 10	58	139	26 08	58	139
38	22 01	58	139	22 59	58	138	23 57	58	138	24 55	58	138	25 53	58	138
39	21 46	58	138	22 44	58	137	23 42	58	137	24 40	58	137	25 38	58	136
40	21 31	+58	137	22 29	+58	136	23 27	+57	136	24 24	+58	136	25 22	+58	135
41	21 15	58	136	22 13	58	135	23 11	58	135	24 09	57	135	25 06	58	134
42	20 59	58	134	21 57	58	134	22 55	57	134	23 52	58	134	24 50	58	133
43	20 43	58	133	21 41	57	133	22 38	58	133	23 36	58	133	24 34	57	132
44	20 27	57	132	21 24	58	132	22 22	57	132	23 19	58	132	24 17	57	131
45	20 10	+57	131	21 07	+58	131	22 05	+57	131	23 02	+58	131	24 00	+57	130
46	19 53	57	130	20 50	58	130	21 48	57	130	22 45	57	129	23 42	58	129
47	19 36	57	129	20 33	57	129	21 30	58	129	22 28	57	128	23 25	57	128
48	19 18	57	128	20 15	58	128	21 13	57	128	22 10	57	127	23 07	57	127
49	19 00	58	127	19 58	57	127	20 55	57	127	21 52	57	126	22 49	57	126
50	18 42	+57	126	19 39	+58	126	20 37	+57	126	21 34	+57	125	22 31	+57	125
51	18 24	57	125	19 21	57	125	20 18	57	125	21 15	57	124	22 12	57	124
52	18 06	57	124	19 03	57	124	20 00	57	124	20 57	56	123	21 53	57	123
53	17 47	57	123	18 44	57	123	19 41	57	123	20 38	57	122	21 35	56	122
54	17 28	57	122	18 25	57	122	19 22	57	122	20 19	56	121	21 15	57	121
55	17 09	+57	121	18 06	+57	121	19 03	+56	121	19 59	+57	120	20 56	+57	120
56	16 50	56	120	17 46	57	120	18 43	57	120	19 40	56	119	20 36	57	119
57	16 30	57	119	17 27	57	119	18 24	56	119	19 20	57	118	20 17	56	118
58	16 11	56	118	17 07	57	118	18 04	56	118	19 00	57	117	19 57	56	117
59	15 51	56	117	16 47	57	117	17 44	56	117	18 40	57	116	19 37	56	116
60	15 31	+56	116	16 27	+57	116	17 24	+56	116	18 20	+56	115	19 16	+57	115
61	15 10	57	116	16 07	56	115	17 03	57	115	18 00	56	114	18 56	56	114
62	14 50	56	115	15 46	57	114	16 43	56	114	17 39	56	113	18 35	56	113
63	14 30	56	114	15 26	56	113	16 22	56	113	17 18	57	113	18 15	56	112
64	14 09	56	113	15 05	56	112	16 01	56	112	16 57	57	112	17 54	56	111
65	13 48	+56	112	14 44	+56	111	15 40	+57	111	16 37	+56	111	17 33	+56	110
66	13 27	56	111	14 23	56	110	15 19	56	110	16 15	56	110	17 11	56	109
67	13 06	56	110	14 02	56	109	14 58	56	109	15 54	56	109	16 50	56	108
68	12 45	56	109	13 41	56	108	14 37	56	108	15 33	56	108	16 29	56	107
69	12 23	56	108	13 19	56	107	14 15	56	107	15 11	56	107	16 07	56	106

	10°			11°			12°			13°			14°			
LHA	Hc	d	Z	Hc	d	Z	Hc	d	Z	Hc	d	Z	Hc	d	Z	LHA
	° ′	′	°	° ′	′	°	° ′	′	°	° ′	′	°	° ′	′	°	
0	32 00	+60	180	33 00	+60	180	34 00	+60	180	35 00	+60	180	36 00	+60	180	360
1	32 00	60	179	33 00	60	179	34 00	60	179	35 00	60	179	36 00	60	179	359
2	31 59	60	178	32 59	60	178	33 59	60	178	34 59	60	178	35 59	60	178	358
3	31 58	60	177	32 58	60	177	33 58	60	177	34 58	60	176	35 58	60	176	357
4	31 56	60	175	32 56	60	175	33 56	60	175	34 56	60	175	35 56	60	175	356
5	31 54	+60	174	32 54	+60	174	33 54	+60	174	34 54	+60	174	35 54	+60	174	355
6	31 52	60	173	32 52	60	173	33 52	60	173	34 52	60	173	35 52	60	173	354
7	31 49	60	172	32 49	60	172	33 49	60	172	34 49	60	172	35 49	59	172	353
8	31 46	59	171	32 45	60	171	33 45	60	171	34 45	60	171	35 45	60	170	352
9	31 42	60	170	32 42	59	170	33 41	60	169	34 41	60	169	35 41	60	169	351
10	31 37	+60	168	32 37	+60	168	33 37	+60	168	34 37	+60	168	35 37	+59	168	350
11	31 33	59	167	32 32	60	167	33 32	60	167	34 32	60	167	35 32	60	167	349
12	31 27	60	166	32 27	60	166	33 27	60	166	34 27	59	166	35 26	60	166	348
13	31 22	60	165	32 22	59	165	33 21	60	165	34 21	60	165	35 21	59	165	347
14	31 16	59	164	32 15	60	164	33 15	60	164	34 15	59	163	35 14	60	163	346
15	31 09	+60	163	32 09	+60	163	33 09	+59	162	34 08	+60	162	35 08	+59	162	345
16	31 02	60	162	32 02	60	161	33 02	59	161	34 01	60	161	35 01	59	161	344
17	30 55	60	160	31 55	59	160	32 54	60	160	33 54	59	160	34 53	59	160	343
18	30 47	60	159	31 47	59	159	32 46	60	159	33 46	59	159	34 45	59	159	342
19	30 39	60	158	31 39	59	158	32 38	59	158	33 37	60	158	34 37	59	157	341
20	30 31	+59	157	31 30	+59	157	32 29	+60	157	33 29	+59	157	34 28	+59	156	340
21	30 22	59	156	31 21	59	156	32 20	59	156	33 19	60	155	34 19	59	155	339
22	30 12	59	155	31 11	60	155	32 11	59	154	33 10	59	154	34 09	59	154	338
23	30 02	60	154	31 02	59	153	32 01	59	153	33 00	59	153	33 59	59	153	337
24	29 52	59	153	30 51	59	152	31 50	59	152	32 49	59	152	33 48	59	152	336
25	29 42	+59	151	30 41	+59	151	31 40	+59	151	32 39	+58	151	33 37	+59	151	335
26	29 31	59	150	30 30	58	150	31 28	59	150	32 27	59	150	33 26	59	149	334
27	29 19	59	149	30 18	59	149	31 17	59	149	32 16	59	149	33 15	58	148	333
28	29 08	58	148	30 06	59	148	31 05	59	148	32 04	59	147	33 03	58	147	332
29	28 56	58	147	29 54	59	147	30 53	59	147	31 52	58	146	32 50	59	146	331
30	28 43	+59	146	29 42	+58	146	30 40	+59	145	31 39	+58	145	32 37	+59	145	330
31	28 30	59	145	29 29	58	145	30 27	59	144	31 26	58	144	32 24	59	144	329
32	28 17	59	144	29 16	58	143	30 14	58	143	31 12	59	143	32 11	58	143	328
33	28 04	58	143	29 02	58	142	30 00	59	142	30 59	58	142	31 57	58	142	327
34	27 50	58	142	28 48	58	141	29 46	59	141	30 45	58	141	31 43	58	140	326
35	27 36	+58	140	28 34	+58	140	29 32	+58	140	30 30	+58	140	31 28	+58	139	325
36	27 21	58	139	28 19	58	139	29 17	58	139	30 15	58	139	31 13	58	138	324
37	27 06	58	138	28 04	58	138	29 02	58	138	30 00	58	137	30 58	58	137	323
38	26 51	58	137	27 49	58	137	28 47	58	137	29 45	58	136	30 43	58	136	322
39	26 36	58	136	27 34	58	136	28 32	57	136	29 29	58	135	30 27	58	135	321
40	26 20	+58	135	27 18	+58	135	28 16	+57	135	29 13	+58	134	30 11	+58	134	320
41	26 04	58	134	27 02	57	134	27 59	58	133	28 57	58	133	29 55	57	133	319
42	25 48	57	133	26 45	58	133	27 43	57	132	28 40	58	132	29 38	57	132	318
43	25 31	58	132	26 29	57	132	27 26	58	131	28 24	57	131	29 21	57	131	317
44	25 14	58	131	26 12	57	131	27 09	58	130	28 07	57	130	29 04	57	130	316
45	24 57	+58	130	25 55	+57	130	26 52	+57	129	27 49	+57	129	28 46	+58	129	315
46	24 40	57	129	25 37	57	129	26 34	58	128	27 32	57	128	28 29	57	127	314
47	24 22	57	128	25 19	58	127	26 17	57	127	27 14	57	127	28 11	57	126	313
48	24 04	57	127	25 01	57	126	25 58	57	126	26 55	57	126	27 52	57	125	312
49	23 46	57	126	24 43	57	125	25 40	57	125	26 37	57	125	27 34	57	124	311
50	23 28	+57	125	24 25	+57	124	25 22	+57	124	26 19	+56	124	27 15	+57	123	310
51	23 09	57	124	24 06	57	123	25 03	57	123	26 00	56	123	26 56	57	122	309
52	22 50	57	123	23 47	57	122	24 44	57	122	25 41	56	122	26 37	57	121	308
53	22 31	57	122	23 28	57	121	24 25	56	121	25 21	57	121	26 18	57	120	307
54	22 12	57	121	23 09	56	120	24 05	57	120	25 02	56	120	25 58	57	119	306
55	21 53	+56	120	22 49	+57	119	23 46	+56	119	24 42	+57	119	25 39	+56	118	305
56	21 33	57	119	22 30	56	118	23 26	56	118	24 22	57	118	25 19	56	117	304
57	21 13	57	118	22 10	56	117	23 06	56	117	24 02	57	117	24 59	56	116	303
58	20 53	57	117	21 50	56	116	22 46	56	116	23 42	56	116	24 38	57	115	302
59	20 33	56	116	21 29	57	115	22 26	56	115	23 22	56	115	24 18	56	114	301
60	20 13	+56	115	21 09	+56	114	22 05	+56	114	23 01	+56	114	23 57	+57	113	300
61	19 52	56	114	20 48	57	113	21 45	56	113	22 41	56	113	23 37	56	112	299
62	19 31	57	113	20 28	56	112	21 24	56	112	22 20	56	112	23 16	56	111	298
63	19 11	56	112	20 07	56	111	21 03	56	111	21 59	56	111	22 55	56	110	297
64	18 50	56	111	19 46	56	110	20 42	56	110	21 38	56	110	22 34	55	109	296
65	18 29	+56	110	19 25	+56	109	20 21	+55	109	21 16	+56	109	22 12	+56	108	295
66	18 07	56	109	19 03	56	108	19 59	56	108	20 55	56	108	21 51	56	107	294
67	17 46	56	108	18 42	56	108	19 38	56	107	20 34	55	107	21 29	56	106	293
68	17 25	55	107	18 20	56	107	19 16	56	106	20 12	56	106	21 08	55	105	292
69	17 03	56	106	17 59	56	106	18 55	55	105	19 50	56	105	20 46	56	104	291

S. Lat. { LHA greater than 180°........ Zn=180−Z
LHA less than 180°............ Zn=180+Z

DECLINATION (0°-14°) SAME NAME AS LATITUDE

LAT 68°

N. Lat. {LHA greater than 180°....... Zn=Z; LHA less than 180°........... Zn=360−Z

DECLINATION (0°-14°) SAME NAME AS LATITUDE

LHA	0° Hc	0° d	0° Z	1° Hc	1° d	1° Z	2° Hc	2° d	2° Z	3° Hc	3° d	3° Z	4° Hc	4° d	4° Z	LHA
	° ′	′	°	° ′	′	°	° ′	′	°	° ′	′	°	° ′	′	°	
70	07 22	+56	109	08 18	+56	108	09 14	+56	108	10 10	+56	108	11 06	+56	107	290
71	07 00	56	108	07 56	56	107	08 52	56	107	09 48	56	107	10 44	56	106	289
72	06 39	56	107	07 35	56	106	08 31	56	106	09 27	56	106	10 23	56	105	288
73	06 17	56	106	07 13	56	106	08 09	56	105	09 05	56	105	10 01	56	104	287
74	05 56	56	105	06 52	55	105	07 47	56	104	08 43	56	104	09 39	56	103	286
75	05 34	+56	104	06 30	+56	104	07 26	+55	103	08 21	+56	103	09 17	+56	103	285
76	05 12	56	103	06 08	56	103	07 04	56	102	08 00	55	102	08 55	56	102	284
77	04 50	56	102	05 46	56	102	06 42	56	101	07 38	55	101	08 33	56	101	283
78	04 28	56	101	05 24	56	101	06 20	55	100	07 15	56	100	08 11	56	100	282
79	04 06	56	100	05 02	56	100	05 58	55	100	06 53	56	99	07 49	56	99	281
80	03 44	+56	99	04 40	+55	99	05 35	+56	99	06 31	+56	98	07 27	+55	98	280
81	03 22	55	98	04 17	56	98	05 13	56	98	06 09	55	97	07 04	56	97	279
82	02 59	56	97	03 55	56	97	04 51	55	97	05 46	56	96	06 42	56	96	278
83	02 37	56	96	03 33	55	96	04 28	56	96	05 24	56	95	06 20	55	95	277
84	02 15	55	96	03 10	56	95	04 06	56	95	05 02	55	94	05 57	56	94	276
85	01 52	+56	95	02 48	+56	94	03 44	+55	94	04 39	+56	94	05 35	+56	93	275
86	01 30	55	94	02 25	56	93	03 21	56	93	04 17	55	93	05 12	56	92	274
87	01 07	56	93	02 03	56	92	02 59	55	92	03 54	56	92	04 50	56	91	273
88	00 45	56	92	01 41	55	91	02 36	56	91	03 32	55	91	04 27	56	90	272
89	00 22	56	91	01 18	56	91	02 14	55	90	03 09	56	90	04 05	56	89	271
90	00 00	+56	90	00 56	+55	90	01 51	+56	89	02 47	+55	89	03 42	+56	89	270
91	−0 22	55	89	00 33	56	89	01 29	55	88	02 24	56	88	03 20	56	88	269
92	−0 45	55	88	00 11	55	88	01 06	56	87	02 02	56	87	02 58	55	87	268
93	−1 07	55	87	−0 12	56	87	00 44	56	86	01 40	55	86	02 35	56	86	267
94	−1 30	56	86	−0 34	55	86	00 21	56	86	01 17	56	85	02 13	55	85	266
95	−1 52	+55	85	−0 57	+56	85	−0 01	+56	85	00 55	+55	84	01 50	+56	84	265
96	−2 15	56	84	−1 19	56	84	−0 23	55	84	00 32	56	83	01 28	56	83	264
97	−2 37	56	84	−1 41	55	83	−0 46	56	83	00 10	56	82	01 06	55	82	263
98	−2 59	55	83	−2 04	56	82	−1 08	56	82	−0 12	56	81	00 44	55	81	262
99	−3 22	56	82	−2 26	56	81	−1 30	56	81	−0 34	55	81	00 21	56	80	261
100	−3 44	+56	81	−2 48	+56	80	−1 52	+55	80	−0 57	+56	80	−0 01	+56	79	260
101	−4 06	56	80	−3 10	56	79	−2 14	55	79	−1 19	56	79	−0 23	56	78	259
102	−4 28	56	79	−3 32	56	78	−2 36	55	78	−1 41	56	78	−0 45	56	77	258
103	−4 50	56	78	−3 54	56	78	−2 58	55	77	−2 03	56	77	−1 07	56	76	257
104	−5 12	56	77	−4 16	56	77	−3 20	56	76	−2 24	56	76	−1 28	55	76	256
105	−5 34	+56	76	−4 38	+56	76	−3 42	+56	75	−2 46	+56	75	−1 50	+56	75	255
106				−5 00	56	75	−4 04	56	74	−3 08	56	74	−2 12	56	74	254
107				−5 21	56	74	−4 25	56	73	−3 29	56	73	−2 33	56	73	253
108							−4 47	56	73	−3 51	56	72	−2 55	56	72	252
109							−5 08	56	72	−4 12	56	71	−3 16	56	71	251
110							−5 30	+57	71	−4 33	+56	70	−3 37	+56	70	250
111										−4 54	56	69	−3 58	56	69	249
112										−5 15	56	68	−4 19	56	68	248
113										−5 36	56	67	−4 40	56	67	247
114													−5 01	57	66	246
115													−5 21	+56	65	245

LHA	5° Hc	5° d	5° Z	6° Hc	6° d	6° Z	7° Hc	7° d	7° Z	8° Hc	8° d	8° Z	9° Hc	9° d	9° Z	LHA
	° ′	′	°	° ′	′	°	° ′	′	°	° ′	′	°	° ′	′	°	
70	12 02	+56	107	12 58	+56	107	13 54	+56	106	14 50	+56	106	15 46	+55	105	290
71	11 40	56	106	12 36	56	106	13 32	56	105	14 28	56	105	15 24	56	104	289
72	11 19	56	105	12 15	55	105	13 10	56	104	14 06	56	104	15 02	56	103	288
73	10 57	56	104	11 53	56	104	12 49	55	103	13 44	56	103	14 40	56	103	287
74	10 35	56	103	11 31	56	103	12 27	55	102	13 22	56	102	14 18	56	102	286
75	10 13	+56	102	11 09	+56	102	12 05	+55	101	13 00	+56	101	13 56	+56	101	285
76	09 51	56	101	10 47	56	101	11 43	55	100	12 38	56	100	13 34	56	100	284
77	09 29	56	100	10 25	55	100	11 20	56	100	12 16	56	99	13 12	55	99	283
78	09 07	56	99	10 03	55	99	10 58	56	99	11 54	56	98	12 50	55	98	282
79	08 45	55	98	09 40	56	98	10 36	56	98	11 32	55	97	12 27	56	97	281
80	08 22	+56	97	09 18	+56	97	10 14	+55	97	11 09	+56	96	12 05	+55	96	280
81	08 00	56	97	08 56	55	96	09 51	56	96	10 47	56	95	11 43	55	95	279
82	07 38	55	96	08 33	56	95	09 29	56	95	10 25	55	94	11 20	56	94	278
83	07 15	56	95	08 11	56	94	09 07	55	94	10 02	56	94	10 58	55	93	277
84	06 53	56	94	07 49	55	93	08 44	56	93	09 40	55	93	10 35	56	92	276
85	06 31	+55	93	07 26	+56	92	08 22	+55	92	09 17	+56	92	10 13	+55	91	275
86	06 08	56	92	07 04	55	92	07 59	56	91	08 55	55	91	09 50	56	90	274
87	05 46	55	91	06 41	56	91	07 37	55	90	08 32	56	90	09 28	55	89	273
88	05 23	56	90	06 19	55	90	07 14	56	89	08 10	55	89	09 05	56	89	272
89	05 01	55	89	05 56	56	89	06 52	55	88	07 47	56	88	08 43	55	88	271
90	04 38	+56	88	05 34	+55	88	06 29	+56	87	07 25	+55	87	08 20	+56	87	270
91	04 16	55	87	05 11	56	87	06 07	55	86	07 02	56	86	07 58	56	86	269
92	03 53	56	86	04 49	55	86	05 44	56	86	06 40	56	85	07 36	55	85	268
93	03 31	55	85	04 26	56	85	05 22	56	85	06 18	55	84	07 13	56	84	267
94	03 08	56	84	04 04	56	84	05 00	55	84	05 55	56	83	06 51	56	83	266
95	02 46	+56	83	03 42	+55	83	04 37	+56	83	05 33	+56	82	06 29	+55	82	265
96	02 24	55	83	03 19	56	82	04 15	56	82	05 11	55	81	06 06	56	81	264
97	02 01	56	82	02 57	56	81	03 53	56	81	04 49	55	81	05 44	56	80	263
98	01 39	56	81	02 35	56	80	03 31	55	80	04 26	56	80	05 22	56	79	262
99	01 17	56	80	02 13	56	79	03 09	55	79	04 04	56	79	05 00	56	78	261
100	00 55	+56	79	01 51	+56	79	02 47	+55	78	03 42	+56	78	04 38	+56	77	260
101	00 33	56	78	01 29	56	78	02 25	55	77	03 20	56	77	04 16	56	76	259
102	00 11	56	77	01 07	56	77	02 03	56	76	02 59	55	76	03 54	56	76	258
103	−0 11	56	76	00 45	56	76	01 41	56	75	02 37	56	75	03 33	55	75	257
104	−0 33	56	75	00 23	56	75	01 19	56	74	02 15	56	74	03 11	56	74	256
105	−0 54	+56	74	00 02	+56	74	00 58	+56	74	01 54	+55	73	02 49	+56	73	255
106	−1 16	56	73	−0 20	56	73	00 36	56	73	01 32	56	72	02 28	56	72	254
107	−1 37	56	72	−0 41	56	72	00 15	56	72	01 11	56	71	02 07	56	71	253
108	−1 59	56	71	−1 03	56	71	−0 07	57	71	00 50	56	70	01 46	56	70	252
109	−2 20	56	71	−1 24	56	70	−0 28	56	70	00 28	57	69	01 25	56	69	251
110	−2 41	+56	70	−1 45	+56	69	−0 49	+56	69	00 07	+57	69	01 04	+56	68	250
111	−3 02	56	69	−2 06	56	68	−1 10	57	68	−0 13	56	68	00 43	56	67	249
112	−3 23	56	68	−2 27	57	67	−1 30	56	67	−0 34	56	67	00 22	56	66	248
113	−3 44	57	67	−2 47	56	66	−1 51	56	66	−0 55	57	66	00 02	56	65	247
114	−4 04	56	66	−3 08	57	65	−2 11	56	65	−1 15	56	65	−0 19	57	64	246
115	−4 25	+57	65	−3 28	+56	65	−2 32	+57	64	−1 35	+56	64	−0 39	+57	64	245
116	−4 45	57	64	−3 48	56	64	−2 52	57	63	−1 55	56	63	−0 59	57	63	244
117	−5 05	57	63	−4 08	56	63	−3 12	57	62	−2 15	56	62	−1 19	57	62	243
118	−5 25	57	62	−4 28	56	62	−3 32	57	61	−2 35	56	61	−1 39	57	61	242
119				−4 48	57	61	−3 51	56	60	−2 55	57	60	−1 58	57	60	241
120				−5 08	+57	60	−4 11	+57	60	−3 14	+57	59	−2 17	+56	59	240
121				−5 27	57	59	−4 30	57	59	−3 33	56	58	−2 37	57	58	239
122							−4 49	57	58	−3 52	57	57	−2 55	56	57	238
123							−5 08	57	57	−4 11	57	56	−3 14	57	56	237
124							−5 27	57	56	−4 30	57	55	−3 33	57	55	236
125										−4 48	+57	54	−3 51	+57	54	235
126										−5 06	57	53	−4 09	57	53	234
127										−5 24	57	53	−4 27	57	52	233
128													−4 45	58	51	232
129													−5 02	57	50	231
130													−5 19	+57	49	230

LHA	10° Hc	10° d	10° Z	11° Hc	11° d	11° Z	12° Hc	12° d	12° Z	13° Hc	13° d	13° Z	14° Hc	14° d	14° Z	LHA
	° ′	′	°	° ′	′	°	° ′	′	°	° ′	′	°	° ′	′	°	
70	16 41	+56	105	17 37	+56	105	18 33	+56	104	19 29	+55	104	20 24	+56	103	290
71	16 20	55	104	17 15	56	104	18 11	56	103	19 07	55	103	20 02	56	102	289
72	15 58	55	103	16 53	56	103	17 49	56	102	18 45	55	102	19 40	56	102	288
73	15 36	56	102	16 32	55	102	17 27	56	101	18 23	55	101	19 18	56	101	287
74	15 14	55	101	16 09	56	101	17 05	56	100	18 01	55	100	18 56	56	100	286
75	14 52	+55	100	15 47	+56	100	16 43	+55	99	17 38	+56	99	18 34	+55	99	285
76	14 30	55	99	15 25	56	99	16 21	55	99	17 16	56	98	18 12	55	98	284
77	14 07	56	98	15 03	55	98	15 58	56	98	16 54	55	97	17 49	56	97	283
78	13 45	56	97	14 41	55	97	15 36	56	97	16 32	55	96	17 27	55	96	282
79	13 23	55	96	14 18	56	96	15 14	55	96	16 09	56	95	17 05	55	95	281
80	13 00	+56	96	13 56	+55	95	14 51	+56	95	15 47	+55	94	16 42	+56	94	280
81	12 38	56	95	13 34	55	94	14 29	55	94	15 24	56	93	16 20	55	93	279
82	12 16	55	94	13 11	56	93	14 07	55	93	15 02	55	93	15 57	56	92	278
83	11 53	56	93	12 49	55	92	13 44	56	92	14 40	55	92	15 35	55	91	277
84	11 31	55	92	12 26	56	91	13 22	55	91	14 17	55	91	15 12	56	90	276
85	11 08	+56	91	12 04	+55	91	12 59	+56	90	13 55	+55	90	14 50	+55	89	275
86	10 46	55	90	11 41	56	90	12 37	55	89	13 32	55	89	14 27	56	88	274
87	10 23	56	89	11 19	55	89	12 14	56	88	13 10	55	88	14 05	55	87	273
88	10 01	55	88	10 56	56	88	11 52	55	87	12 47	56	87	13 43	55	87	272
89	09 38	56	87	10 34	55	87	11 29	56	86	12 25	55	86	13 20	56	86	271
90	09 16	+55	86	10 11	+56	86	11 07	+55	85	12 02	+56	85	12 58	+55	85	270
91	08 54	55	85	09 49	56	85	10 45	55	85	11 40	55	84	12 35	56	84	269
92	08 31	56	84	09 27	55	84	10 22	56	84	11 18	55	83	12 13	55	83	268
93	08 09	55	84	09 04	56	83	10 00	55	83	10 55	56	82	11 51	55	82	267
94	07 47	55	83	08 42	56	82	09 38	55	82	10 33	56	81	11 29	55	81	266
95	07 24	+56	82	08 20	+55	81	09 15	+56	81	10 11	+55	81	11 06	+56	80	265
96	07 02	56	81	07 58	55	80	08 53	56	80	09 49	55	80	10 44	56	79	264
97	06 40	56	80	07 36	55	79	08 31	56	79	09 27	55	79	10 22	56	78	263
98	06 18	55	79	07 13	56	79	08 09	56	78	09 05	55	78	10 00	56	77	262
99	05 56	55	78	06 51	56	78	07 47	56	77	08 43	55	77	09 38	56	76	261
100	05 34	+56	77	06 30	+55	77	07 25	+56	76	08 21	+56	76	09 17	+55	76	260
101	05 12	56	76	06 08	55	76	07 03	56	75	07 59	56	75	08 55	56	75	259
102	04 50	56	75	05 46	56	75	06 42	56	74	07 38	55	74	08 33	56	74	258
103	04 28	56	74	05 24	56	74	06 20	56	74	07 16	56	73	08 12	56	73	257
104	04 07	56	73	05 03	56	73	05 59	56	73	06 55	55	72	07 50	56	72	256
105	03 45	+56	72	04 41	+56	72	05 37	+56	72	06 33	+56	71	07 29	+56	71	255
106	03 24	56	72	04 20	56	71	05 16	56	71	06 12	56	70	07 08	56	70	254
107	03 03	56	71	03 59	56	70	04 55	56	70	05 51	56	70	06 47	56	69	253
108	02 42	56	70	03 38	56	69	04 34	56	69	05 30	56	69	06 26	56	68	252
109	02 21	56	69	03 17	56	68	04 13	56	68	05 09	56	68	06 05	56	67	251
110	02 00	+56	68	02 56	+56	67	03 52	+56	67	04 48	+56	67	05 44	+56	66	250
111	01 39	56	67	02 35	56	67	03 31	57	66	04 28	56	66	05 24	56	66	249
112	01 18	57	66	02 15	56	66	03 11	56	65	04 07	56	65	05 03	57	65	248
113	00 58	56	65	01 54	57	65	02 51	56	64	03 47	56	64	04 43	57	64	247
114	00 38	56	64	01 34	56	64	02 30	57	63	03 27	56	63	04 23	57	63	246
115	00 18	+56	63	01 14	+56	63	02 10	+57	63	03 07	+56	62	04 03	+57	62	245
116	−0 02	56	62	00 54	57	62	01 51	56	62	02 47	56	61	03 43	57	61	244
117	−0 22	56	61	00 34	57	61	01 31	56	61	02 27	57	60	03 24	56	60	243
118	−0 42	57	60	00 15	56	60	01 11	57	60	02 08	57	59	03 05	56	59	242
119	−1 01	56	59	−0 05	57	59	00 52	57	59	01 49	56	59	02 45	57	58	241
120	−1 21	+57	59	−0 24	+57	58	00 33	+57	58	01 30	+56	58	02 26	+57	57	240
121	−1 40	57	58	−0 43	57	57	00 14	57	57	01 11	57	57	02 08	56	56	239
122	−1 59	57	57	−1 02	57	56	−0 05	57	56	00 52	57	56	01 49	57	55	238
123	−2 17	57	56	−1 20	57	55	−0 23	57	55	00 34	57	55	01 31	57	54	237
124	−2 36	57	55	−1 39	57	55	−0 42	57	54	00 15	57	54	01 12	57	54	236
125	−2 54	+57	54	−1 57	+57	54	−1 00	+57	53	−0 03	+57	53	00 54	+58	53	235
126	−3 12	57	53	−2 15	57	53	−1 18	57	52	−0 21	58	52	00 37	57	52	234
127	−3 30	57	52	−2 33	58	52	−1 35	57	51	−0 38	57	51	00 19	57	51	233
128	−3 47	57	51	−2 50	57	51	−1 53	57	50	−0 56	58	50	00 02	57	50	232
129	−4 05	58	50	−3 07	57	50	−2 10	57	50	−1 13	58	49	−0 15	57	49	231
130	−4 22	+57	49	−3 25	+58	49	−2 27	+57	49	−1 30	+58	48	−0 32	+57	48	230
131	−4 39	58	48	−3 41	57	48	−2 44	58	48	−1 46	57	47	−0 49	58	47	229
132	−4 55	57	47	−3 58	58	47	−3 00	57	47	−2 03	58	46	−1 05	58	46	228
133	−5 12	58	46	−4 14	58	46	−3 16	57	46	−2 19	58	45	−1 21	58	45	227
134	−5 28	58	45	−4 30	58	45	−3 32	57	45	−2 35	58	45	−1 37	58	44	226
135				−4 46	+58	44	−3 48	+58	44	−2 50	+58	44	−1 52	+57	43	225
136				−5 02	58	43	−4 04	58	43	−3 06	58	43	−2 08	58	42	224
137				−5 17	58	42	−4 19	58	42	−3 21	58	42	−2 23	58	41	223
138							−4 34	58	41	−3 36	58	41	−2 38	59	41	222
139							−4 48	58	40	−3 50	58	40	−2 52	58	40	221

LAT 68°

S. Lat. {LHA greater than 180°....... Zn=180−Z; LHA less than 180°........... Zn=180+Z

DECLINATION (0°-14°) SAME NAME AS LATITUDE

LAT 68°

N. Lat. {LHA greater than 180°……. Zn=Z
{LHA less than 180°………….Zn=360−Z

DECLINATION (0°-14°) SAME NAME AS LATITUDE

LHA	0°			1°			2°			3°			4°			5°			6°			7°			8°			9°			10°			11°			12°			13°			14°			LHA
	Hc	d	Z	Hc	d	Z	Hc	d	Z	Hc	d	Z	Hc	d	Z	Hc	d	Z	Hc	d	Z	Hc	d	Z	Hc	d	Z	Hc	d	Z	Hc	d	Z	Hc	d	Z	Hc	d	Z	Hc	d	Z	Hc	d	Z	
	° ′	′	°	° ′	′	°	° ′	′	°	° ′	′	°	° ′	′	°	° ′	′	°	° ′	′	°	° ′	′	°	° ′	′	°	° ′	′	°	° ′	′	°	° ′	′	°	° ′	′	°	° ′	′	°	° ′	′	°	
																																		140	-5 03	+59	39	-4 04	+58	39	-3 06	+58	39	220
																																		141	-5 17	59	38	-4 18	58	38	-3 20	58	38	219
																																					142	-4 32	58	37	-3 34	59	37	218
																																					143	-4 45	58	36	-3 47	58	36	217
																																					144	-4 59	59	35	-4 00	59	35	216
																																					145	-5 11	+58	34	-4 13	+59	34	215
																																					146	-5 24	59	33	-4 25	59	33	214
																																								147	-4 37	59	32	213
																																								148	-4 49	59	31	212
																																								149	-5 00	59	30	211
																																								150	-5 12	+59	29	210
105	-5 34	-56	76	255																																										
104	-5 12	55	77	256																																										
103	-4 50	56	78	257																																										
102	-4 28	56	79	-5 24	55	79	258																																						
101	-4 06	56	80	-5 02	56	80	259																																						
100	-3 44	-56	81	-4 40	-55	81	-5 35	-56	81	260																																			
99	-3 22	55	82	-4 17	56	82	-5 13	55	82	261																																			
98	-2 59	56	83	-3 55	56	83	-4 51	56	83	262																																			
97	-2 37	56	84	-3 33	55	84	-4 28	56	84	-5 24	55	85	263																																
96	-2 15	55	84	-3 10	56	85	-4 06	56	85	-5 02	56	86	264																																
95	-1 52	-56	85	-2 48	-56	86	-3 44	-55	86	-4 39	-56	86	-5 35	-56	87	265																													
94	-1 30	55	86	-2 25	56	87	-3 21	56	87	-4 17	55	87	-5 12	56	88	266																													
93	-1 07	56	87	-2 03	56	88	-2 59	55	88	-3 54	56	88	-4 50	56	89	267																													
92	-0 45	56	88	-1 41	55	89	-2 36	56	89	-3 32	55	89	-4 27	56	90	-5 23	56	90	268																										
91	-0 22	56	89	-1 18	56	89	-2 14	55	90	-3 09	56	90	-4 05	56	91	-5 01	55	91	269																										
90	00 00	-56	90	-0 56	-55	90	-1 51	-56	91	-2 47	-55	91	-3 42	-56	91	-4 38	-56	92	-5 34	-55	92	270																							
89	00 22	55	91	-0 33	56	91	-1 29	55	92	-2 24	56	92	-3 20	56	92	-4 16	55	93	-5 11	56	93	271																							
88	00 45	56	92	-0 11	55	92	-1 06	56	93	-2 02	56	93	-2 58	55	93	-3 53	56	94	-4 49	55	94	272																							
87	01 07	55	93	00 12	56	93	-0 44	56	94	-1 40	55	94	-2 35	56	94	-3 31	55	95	-4 26	56	95	-5 22	56	95	273																				
86	01 30	56	94	00 34	55	94	-0 21	56	94	-1 17	56	95	-2 13	55	95	-3 08	56	96	-4 04	56	96	-5 00	55	96	274																				
85	01 52	-55	95	00 57	-56	95	00 01	-56	95	-0 55	-55	96	-1 50	-56	96	-2 46	-56	97	-3 42	-55	97	-4 37	-56	97	-5 33	-56	98	275																	
84	02 15	56	96	01 19	56	96	00 23	55	96	-0 32	56	97	-1 28	56	97	-2 24	55	97	-3 19	56	98	-4 15	56	98	-5 11	55	99	276																	
83	02 37	56	96	01 41	55	97	00 46	56	97	-0 10	56	98	-1 06	55	98	-2 01	56	98	-2 57	56	99	-3 53	56	99	-4 49	55	99	277																	
82	02 59	55	97	02 04	56	98	01 08	56	98	00 12	56	99	-0 44	55	99	-1 39	56	99	-2 35	56	100	-3 31	55	100	-4 26	56	100	-5 22	56	101	278													
81	03 22	56	98	02 26	56	99	01 30	56	99	00 34	55	99	-0 21	56	100	-1 17	56	100	-2 13	56	101	-3 09	55	101	-4 04	56	101	-5 00	56	102	279													
80	03 44	-56	99	02 48	-56	100	01 52	-55	100	00 57	-56	100	00 01	-56	101	-0 55	-56	101	-1 51	-56	101	-2 47	-55	102	-3 42	-56	102	-4 38	-56	103	-5 34	-56	103	280									
79	04 06	56	100	03 10	56	101	02 14	55	101	01 19	56	101	00 23	56	102	-0 33	56	102	-1 29	56	102	-2 25	55	103	-3 20	56	103	-4 16	56	104	-5 12	56	104	281									
78	04 28	56	101	03 32	56	102	02 36	55	102	01 41	56	102	00 45	56	103	-0 11	56	103	-1 07	56	103	-2 03	56	104	-2 59	55	104	-3 54	56	104	-4 50	56	105	282									
77	04 50	56	102	03 54	56	102	02 58	55	103	02 03	56	103	01 07	56	104	00 11	56	104	-0 45	56	104	-1 41	56	105	-2 37	56	105	-3 33	55	105	-4 28	56	106	-5 24	56	106	283						
76	05 12	56	103	04 16	56	103	03 20	56	104	02 24	56	104	01 28	55	104	00 33	56	105	-0 23	56	105	-1 19	56	106	-2 15	56	106	-3 11	56	106	-4 07	56	107	-5 03	56	107	284						
75	05 34	-56	104	04 38	-56	104	03 42	-56	105	02 46	-56	105	01 50	-56	105	00 54	-56	106	-0 02	-56	106	-0 58	-56	106	-1 54	-55	107	-2 49	-56	107	-3 45	-56	108	-4 41	-56	108	-5 37	-56	108	285			
74	05 56	56	105	05 00	56	105	04 04	56	106	03 08	56	106	02 12	56	106	01 16	56	107	00 20	56	107	-0 36	56	107	-1 32	56	108	-2 28	56	108	-3 24	56	108	-4 20	56	109	-5 16	56	109	286			
73	06 17	56	106	05 21	56	106	04 25	56	107	03 29	56	107	02 33	56	107	01 37	56	108	00 41	56	108	-0 15	56	108	-1 11	56	109	-2 07	56	109	-3 03	56	109	-3 59	56	110	-4 55	56	110	287			
72	06 39	56	107	05 43	56	107	04 47	56	107	03 51	56	108	02 55	56	108	01 59	56	109	01 03	56	109	00 07	57	109	-0 50	56	110	-1 46	56	110	-2 42	56	110	-3 38	56	111	-4 34	56	111	-5 30	56	111	288
71	07 00	56	108	06 04	56	108	05 08	56	108	04 12	56	109	03 16	56	109	02 20	56	109	01 24	56	110	00 28	56	110	-0 28	57	111	-1 25	56	111	-2 21	56	111	-3 17	56	112	-4 13	56	112	-5 09	56	112	289
70	07 22	-56	109	06 26	-56	109	05 30	-57	109	04 33	-56	110	03 37	-56	110	02 41	-56	110	01 45	-56	111	00 49	-56	111	-0 07	-57	111	-1 04	-56	112	-2 00	-56	112	-2 56	-56	113	-3 52	-56	113	-4 48	-56	113	290
	0°			1°			2°			3°			4°			5°			6°			7°			8°			9°			10°			11°			12°			13°			14°			

S. Lat. {LHA greater than 180°……. Zn=180−Z
{LHA less than 180°………….Zn=180+Z

DECLINATION (0°-14°) CONTRARY NAME TO LATITUDE

N. Lat. {LHA greater than 180°……Zn=Z; LHA less than 180°……Zn=360−Z}

DECLINATION (0°-14°) CONTRARY NAME TO LATITUDE

Each declination cell gives Hc (° ′), d (′), Z (°).

LHA	0° Hc d Z	1° Hc d Z	2° Hc d Z	3° Hc d Z	4° Hc d Z	5° Hc d Z	6° Hc d Z	7° Hc d Z	8° Hc d Z	9° Hc d Z	10° Hc d Z	11° Hc d Z	12° Hc d Z	13° Hc d Z	14° Hc d Z	LHA
69	07 43 56 110	06 47 56 110	05 51 57 110	04 54 56 111	03 58 56 111	03 02 56 111	02 06 56 112	01 10 57 112	00 13 56 112	−0 43 56 113	−1 39 56 113	−2 35 56 113	−3 31 57 114	−4 28 56 114	−5 24 56 114	291
68	08 04 56 111	07 08 56 111	06 12 57 111	05 15 56 112	04 19 56 112	03 23 56 112	02 27 57 113	01 30 56 113	00 34 56 113	−0 22 56 114	−1 18 57 114	−2 15 56 114	−3 11 56 115	−4 07 56 115	−5 03 57 115	292
67	08 25 56 112	07 29 56 112	06 33 57 112	05 36 56 113	04 40 56 113	03 44 57 113	02 47 56 114	01 51 56 114	00 55 57 114	−0 02 56 115	−0 58 56 115	−1 54 57 115	−2 51 56 116	−3 47 56 116	−4 43 57 116	293
66	08 46 56 112	07 50 57 113	06 53 56 113	05 57 56 114	05 01 57 114	04 04 56 114	03 08 57 115	02 11 56 115	01 15 56 115	00 19 57 116	−0 38 56 116	−1 34 56 116	−2 30 57 117	−3 27 56 117	−4 23 57 117	294
65	09 07 −57 113	08 10 −56 114	07 14 −57 114	06 17 −56 114	05 21 −56 115	04 25 −57 115	03 28 −56 115	02 32 −57 116	01 35 −56 116	00 39 −57 116	−0 18 −56 117	−1 14 −56 117	−2 10 −57 117	−3 07 −56 118	−4 03 −57 118	295
64	09 27 56 114	08 31 57 115	07 34 56 115	06 38 57 115	05 41 56 116	04 45 57 116	03 48 56 116	02 52 57 117	01 55 56 117	00 59 57 117	00 02 56 118	−0 54 57 118	−1 51 56 118	−2 47 56 119	−3 43 57 119	296
63	09 48 57 115	08 51 56 116	07 55 57 116	06 58 56 116	06 02 57 117	05 05 57 117	04 08 56 117	03 12 57 118	02 15 56 118	01 19 57 118	00 22 56 119	−0 34 57 119	−1 31 56 119	−2 27 57 120	−3 24 56 120	297
62	10 08 57 116	09 11 56 117	08 15 57 117	07 18 56 117	06 22 57 118	05 25 57 118	04 28 56 118	03 32 57 119	02 35 56 119	01 39 57 119	00 42 57 120	−0 15 56 120	−1 11 57 120	−2 08 57 121	−3 05 56 121	298
61	10 28 57 117	09 31 56 118	08 35 57 118	07 38 57 118	06 41 56 119	05 45 57 119	04 48 57 119	03 51 56 120	02 55 57 120	01 58 57 120	01 01 56 121	00 05 57 121	−0 52 57 121	−1 49 56 121	−2 45 57 122	299
60	10 48 −57 118	09 51 −57 119	08 54 −56 119	07 58 −57 119	07 01 −57 120	06 04 −56 120	05 08 −57 120	04 11 −57 120	03 14 −57 121	02 17 −56 121	01 21 −57 121	00 24 −57 122	−0 33 −57 122	−1 30 −56 122	−2 26 −57 123	300
59	11 08 57 119	10 11 57 120	09 14 57 120	08 17 56 120	07 21 57 120	06 24 57 121	05 27 57 121	04 30 57 121	03 33 56 122	02 37 57 122	01 40 57 122	00 43 57 123	−0 14 57 123	−1 11 57 123	−2 08 56 124	301
58	11 27 57 120	10 30 57 120	09 33 56 121	08 37 57 121	07 40 57 121	06 43 57 122	05 46 57 122	04 49 57 122	03 52 57 123	02 55 56 123	01 59 57 123	01 02 57 124	00 05 57 124	−0 52 57 124	−1 49 57 125	302
57	11 46 56 121	10 50 57 121	09 53 57 122	08 56 57 122	07 59 57 122	07 02 57 123	06 05 57 123	05 08 57 123	04 11 57 124	03 14 57 124	02 17 57 124	01 20 57 125	00 23 57 125	−0 34 57 125	−1 31 57 126	303
56	12 06 57 122	11 09 57 122	10 12 57 123	09 15 57 123	08 18 57 123	07 21 57 124	06 24 57 124	05 27 57 124	04 30 57 125	03 33 57 125	02 36 57 125	01 39 57 125	00 42 57 126	−0 15 57 126	−1 12 57 126	304
55	12 25 −57 123	11 28 −57 123	10 31 −57 124	09 34 −57 124	08 37 −58 124	07 39 −57 125	06 42 −57 125	05 45 −57 125	04 48 −57 126	03 51 −57 126	02 54 −57 126	01 57 −57 126	01 00 −57 127	00 03 −57 127	−0 54 −58 127	305
54	12 43 57 124	11 46 57 124	10 49 57 125	09 52 57 125	08 55 57 125	07 58 57 126	07 01 57 126	06 04 58 126	05 06 57 127	04 09 57 127	03 12 57 127	02 15 57 127	01 18 57 128	00 21 58 128	−0 37 57 128	306
53	13 02 57 125	12 05 57 125	11 08 58 126	10 10 57 126	09 13 57 126	08 16 57 127	07 19 57 127	06 22 58 127	05 24 57 127	04 27 57 128	03 30 57 128	02 33 58 128	01 35 57 129	00 38 57 129	−0 19 57 129	307
52	13 20 57 126	12 23 57 126	11 26 58 127	10 28 57 127	09 31 57 127	08 34 57 128	07 37 58 128	06 39 57 128	05 42 57 128	04 45 58 129	03 47 57 129	02 50 57 129	01 53 57 130	00 56 58 130	−0 02 57 130	308
51	13 38 57 127	12 41 57 127	11 44 58 128	10 46 57 128	09 49 57 128	08 52 58 128	07 54 57 129	06 57 57 129	06 00 58 129	05 02 57 130	04 05 58 130	03 07 57 130	02 10 57 130	01 13 58 131	00 15 57 131	309
50	13 56 −57 128	12 59 −58 128	12 01 −57 129	11 04 −57 129	10 07 −58 129	09 09 −57 129	08 12 −58 130	07 14 −57 130	06 17 −58 130	05 19 −57 131	04 22 −57 131	03 25 −58 131	02 27 −57 131	01 30 −58 132	00 32 −57 132	310
49	14 14 58 129	13 16 57 129	12 19 58 130	11 21 57 130	10 24 58 130	09 26 57 130	08 29 58 131	07 31 57 131	06 34 58 131	05 36 57 132	04 39 58 132	03 41 57 132	02 44 58 132	01 46 57 133	00 49 58 133	311
48	14 31 57 130	13 34 58 130	12 36 57 130	11 39 58 131	10 41 58 131	09 43 57 131	08 46 58 132	07 48 57 132	06 51 58 132	05 53 58 133	04 55 57 133	03 58 58 133	03 00 57 133	02 03 58 134	01 05 58 134	312
47	14 48 57 131	13 51 58 131	12 53 58 131	11 55 57 132	10 58 58 132	10 00 57 132	09 03 58 133	08 05 58 133	07 07 57 133	06 10 58 133	05 12 58 134	04 14 58 134	03 16 57 134	02 19 58 135	01 21 58 135	313
46	15 05 58 132	14 07 57 132	13 10 58 132	12 12 58 133	11 14 57 133	10 17 58 133	09 19 58 134	08 21 57 134	07 24 58 134	06 26 58 134	05 28 58 135	04 30 58 135	03 32 57 135	02 35 58 135	01 37 58 136	314
45	15 22 −58 133	14 24 −58 133	13 26 −58 133	12 28 −57 134	11 31 −58 134	10 33 −58 134	09 35 −58 135	08 37 −57 135	07 40 −58 135	06 42 −58 135	05 44 −58 136	04 46 −58 136	03 48 −58 136	02 50 −58 136	01 52 −57 137	315
44	15 38 58 134	14 40 58 134	13 42 57 134	12 45 58 135	11 47 58 135	10 49 58 135	09 51 58 136	08 53 58 136	07 55 58 136	06 57 57 136	06 00 58 137	05 02 58 137	04 04 58 137	03 06 58 137	02 08 58 138	316
43	15 54 58 135	14 56 58 135	13 58 58 135	13 00 58 136	12 03 58 136	11 05 58 136	10 07 58 137	09 09 58 137	08 11 58 137	07 13 58 137	06 15 58 138	05 17 58 138	04 19 58 138	03 21 58 138	02 23 58 139	317
42	16 10 58 136	15 12 58 136	14 14 58 136	13 16 58 137	12 18 58 137	11 20 58 137	10 22 58 137	09 24 58 138	08 26 58 138	07 28 58 138	06 30 58 139	05 32 58 139	04 34 58 139	03 36 58 139	02 38 58 139	318
41	16 25 58 137	15 27 58 137	14 29 58 137	13 31 58 138	12 33 58 138	11 35 58 138	10 37 58 138	09 39 58 139	08 41 58 139	07 43 58 139	06 45 58 139	05 47 59 140	04 48 58 140	03 50 58 140	02 52 58 140	319
40	16 41 −58 138	15 43 −59 138	14 44 −58 138	13 46 −58 139	12 48 −58 139	11 50 −58 139	10 52 −58 139	09 54 −58 140	08 56 −59 140	07 57 −58 140	06 59 −58 140	06 01 −58 141	05 03 −59 141	04 04 −58 141	03 06 −58 141	320
39	16 56 59 139	15 57 58 139	14 59 58 139	14 01 58 140	13 03 58 140	12 05 59 140	11 06 58 140	10 08 58 141	09 10 58 141	08 12 59 141	07 13 58 141	06 15 58 142	05 17 59 142	04 18 58 142	03 20 58 142	321
38	17 10 58 140	16 12 58 140	15 14 59 140	14 15 58 141	13 17 58 141	12 19 58 141	11 21 59 141	10 22 58 142	09 24 58 142	08 26 59 142	07 27 58 142	06 29 59 143	05 30 58 143	04 32 58 143	03 34 59 143	322
37	17 25 59 141	16 26 58 141	15 28 58 141	14 30 59 142	13 31 58 142	12 33 59 142	11 34 58 142	10 36 58 143	09 38 59 143	08 39 58 143	07 41 59 143	06 42 58 144	05 44 59 144	04 45 58 144	03 47 58 144	323
36	17 39 59 142	16 40 58 142	15 42 59 142	14 43 58 143	13 45 59 143	12 46 58 143	11 48 58 143	10 50 59 144	09 51 58 144	08 53 59 144	07 54 58 144	06 56 59 145	05 57 58 145	04 59 59 145	04 00 59 145	324
35	17 52 −58 143	16 54 −59 143	15 55 −58 143	14 57 −59 144	13 58 −58 144	13 00 −59 144	12 01 −58 144	11 03 −59 145	10 04 −58 145	09 06 −59 145	08 07 −59 145	07 08 −58 145	06 10 −59 146	05 11 −58 146	04 13 −59 146	325
34	18 06 59 144	17 07 58 144	16 09 59 144	15 10 59 145	14 11 58 145	13 13 59 145	12 14 58 145	11 16 59 146	10 17 59 146	09 18 58 146	08 20 59 146	07 21 59 146	06 22 58 147	05 24 59 147	04 25 59 147	326
33	18 19 59 145	17 20 59 145	16 21 58 145	15 23 59 146	14 24 58 146	13 26 59 146	12 27 59 146	11 28 59 147	10 29 58 147	09 31 59 147	08 32 59 147	07 33 58 147	06 35 59 148	05 36 59 148	04 37 59 148	327
32	18 31 58 146	17 33 59 146	16 34 59 147	15 35 58 147	14 37 59 147	13 38 59 147	12 39 59 147	11 40 58 148	10 42 59 148	09 43 59 148	08 44 59 148	07 45 58 148	06 47 59 149	05 48 59 149	04 49 59 149	328
31	18 44 59 147	17 45 59 147	16 46 58 148	15 48 59 148	14 49 59 148	13 50 59 148	12 51 59 148	11 52 59 149	10 53 58 149	09 55 59 149	08 56 59 149	07 57 59 149	06 58 59 150	05 59 59 150	05 00 59 150	329
30	18 56 −59 148	17 57 −59 148	16 58 −59 149	15 59 −58 149	15 01 −59 149	14 02 −59 149	13 03 −59 149	12 04 −59 150	11 05 −59 150	10 06 −59 150	09 07 −59 150	08 08 −59 150	07 09 −59 151	06 10 −58 151	05 12 −59 151	330
29	19 08 59 149	18 09 59 149	17 10 59 150	16 11 59 150	15 12 59 150	14 13 59 150	13 14 59 150	12 15 59 151	11 16 59 151	10 17 59 151	09 18 59 151	08 19 59 151	07 20 59 151	06 21 59 152	05 22 59 152	331
28	19 19 59 150	18 20 59 150	17 21 59 151	16 22 59 151	15 23 59 151	14 24 59 151	13 25 59 151	12 26 59 152	11 27 59 152	10 28 59 152	09 29 59 152	08 30 59 152	07 31 59 152	06 32 59 153	05 33 59 153	332
27	19 30 59 151	18 31 59 151	17 32 59 152	16 33 59 152	15 34 59 152	14 35 59 152	13 36 59 152	12 37 60 153	11 37 59 153	10 38 59 153	09 39 59 153	08 40 59 153	07 41 59 153	06 42 59 154	05 43 59 154	333
26	19 41 60 152	18 41 59 152	17 42 59 153	16 43 59 153	15 44 59 153	14 45 59 153	13 46 59 153	12 47 59 154	11 48 60 154	10 48 59 154	09 49 59 154	08 50 59 154	07 51 59 154	06 52 59 155	05 53 60 155	334
25	19 51 −59 153	18 52 −59 154	17 53 −60 154	16 53 −59 154	15 54 −59 154	14 55 −59 154	13 56 −59 154	12 57 −60 155	11 57 −59 155	10 58 −59 155	09 59 −59 155	09 00 −59 155	08 01 −60 155	07 01 −59 156	06 02 −59 156	335
24	20 01 59 154	19 02 60 155	18 02 59 155	17 03 59 155	16 04 59 155	15 05 60 155	14 05 59 155	13 06 59 156	12 07 59 156	11 08 60 156	10 08 59 156	09 09 59 156	08 10 60 156	07 10 59 157	06 11 59 157	336
23	20 10 59 155	19 11 59 156	18 12 60 156	17 12 59 156	16 13 59 156	15 14 59 156	14 15 60 156	13 15 59 157	12 16 59 157	11 17 60 157	10 17 59 157	09 18 59 157	08 19 60 157	07 19 59 157	06 20 59 158	337
22	20 19 59 157	19 20 59 157	18 21 60 157	17 21 59 157	16 22 59 157	15 23 60 157	14 23 59 157	13 24 59 158	12 25 60 158	11 25 59 158	10 26 59 158	09 27 60 158	08 27 59 158	07 28 60 158	06 28 59 159	338
21	20 28 59 158	19 29 59 158	18 30 60 158	17 30 59 158	16 31 60 158	15 31 59 158	14 32 60 158	13 32 59 159	12 33 59 159	11 34 60 159	10 34 59 159	09 35 60 159	08 35 59 159	07 36 60 159	06 36 59 160	339
20	20 37 −60 159	19 37 −59 159	18 38 −60 159	17 38 −59 159	16 39 −60 159	15 39 −59 159	14 40 −60 159	13 40 −59 160	12 41 −59 160	11 42 −60 160	10 42 −59 160	09 43 −60 160	08 43 −59 160	07 44 −60 160	06 44 −59 161	340
19	20 45 60 160	19 45 59 160	18 46 60 160	17 46 59 160	16 47 60 160	15 47 59 160	14 48 60 160	13 48 59 161	12 49 60 161	11 49 59 161	10 50 60 161	09 50 60 161	08 50 59 161	07 51 60 161	06 51 59 161	341
18	20 52 59 161	19 53 60 161	18 53 59 161	17 54 60 161	16 54 59 161	15 55 60 161	14 55 60 162	13 55 59 162	12 56 60 162	11 56 59 162	10 57 60 162	09 57 59 162	08 58 60 162	07 58 60 162	06 58 59 162	342
17	21 00 60 162	20 00 60 162	19 00 59 162	18 01 60 162	17 01 59 162	16 02 60 162	15 02 60 163	14 02 59 163	13 03 60 163	12 03 60 163	11 03 59 163	10 04 60 163	09 04 59 163	08 05 60 163	07 05 60 163	343
16	21 06 59 163	20 07 60 163	19 07 60 163	18 07 59 163	17 08 60 163	16 08 59 163	15 09 60 164	14 09 60 164	13 09 59 164	12 10 60 164	11 10 60 164	10 10 59 164	09 11 60 164	08 11 60 164	07 11 59 164	344
15	21 13 −60 164	20 13 −60 164	19 13 −59 164	18 14 −60 164	17 14 −60 164	16 14 −59 164	15 15 −60 165	14 15 −60 165	13 15 −59 165	12 16 −60 165	11 16 −60 165	10 16 −59 165	09 17 −60 165	08 17 −60 165	07 17 −60 165	345
14	21 19 60 165	20 19 60 165	19 19 59 165	18 20 60 165	17 20 60 165	16 20 59 166	15 21 60 166	14 21 60 166	13 21 60 166	12 21 59 166	11 22 60 166	10 22 60 166	09 22 60 166	08 22 59 166	07 23 60 166	346
13	21 25 60 166	20 25 60 166	19 25 60 166	18 25 60 166	17 25 59 166	16 26 60 167	15 26 60 167	14 26 60 167	13 26 59 167	12 27 60 167	11 27 60 167	10 27 60 167	09 27 59 167	08 28 60 167	07 28 60 167	347
12	21 30 60 167	20 30 60 167	19 30 60 167	18 30 59 167	17 31 60 167	16 31 60 168	15 31 60 168	14 31 60 168	13 31 59 168	12 32 60 168	11 32 60 168	10 32 60 168	09 32 60 168	08 32 60 168	07 32 59 168	348
11	21 35 60 168	20 35 60 168	19 35 60 168	18 35 60 168	17 35 60 169	16 35 59 169	15 36 60 169	14 36 60 169	13 36 60 169	12 36 60 169	11 36 60 169	10 36 59 169	09 37 60 169	08 37 60 169	07 37 60 169	349
10	21 39 −60 169	20 39 −60 169	19 39 −60 169	18 39 −59 170	17 40 −60 170	16 40 −60 170	15 40 −60 170	14 40 −60 170	13 40 −60 170	12 40 −60 170	11 40 −60 170	10 40 −59 170	09 41 −60 170	08 41 −60 170	07 41 −60 170	350
9	21 43 60 170	20 43 60 170	19 43 60 170	18 43 60 171	17 43 59 171	16 44 60 171	15 44 60 171	14 44 60 171	13 44 60 171	12 44 60 171	11 44 60 171	10 44 60 171	09 44 60 171	08 44 59 171	07 45 60 171	351
8	21 47 60 171	20 47 60 171	19 47 60 172	18 47 60 172	17 47 60 172	16 47 60 172	15 47 60 172	14 47 60 172	13 47 60 172	12 47 60 172	11 47 59 172	10 48 60 172	09 48 60 172	08 48 60 172	07 48 60 172	352
7	21 50 60 173	20 50 60 173	19 50 60 173	18 50 60 173	17 50 60 173	16 50 60 173	15 50 60 173	14 50 60 173	13 50 60 173	12 50 60 173	11 50 60 173	10 50 59 173	09 51 60 173	08 51 60 173	07 51 60 173	353
6	21 52 60 174	20 52 59 174	19 53 60 174	18 53 60 174	17 53 60 174	16 53 60 174	15 53 60 174	14 53 60 174	13 53 60 174	12 53 60 174	11 53 60 174	10 53 60 174	09 53 60 174	08 53 60 174	07 53 60 174	354
5	21 55 −60 175	20 55 −60 175	19 55 −60 175	18 55 −60 175	17 55 −60 175	16 55 −60 175	15 55 −60 175	14 55 −60 175	13 55 −60 175	12 55 −60 175	11 55 −60 175	10 55 −60 175	09 55 −60 175	08 55 −60 175	07 55 −60 175	355
4	21 57 60 176	20 57 60 176	19 57 60 176	18 57 60 176	17 57 60 176	16 57 60 176	15 57 60 176	14 57 60 176	13 57 60 176	12 57 60 176	11 57 60 176	10 57 60 176	09 57 60 176	08 57 60 176	07 57 60 176	356
3	21 58 60 177	20 58 60 177	19 58 60 177	18 58 60 177	17 58 60 177	16 58 60 177	15 58 60 177	14 58 60 177	13 58 60 177	12 58 60 177	11 58 60 177	10 58 60 177	09 58 60 177	08 58 60 177	07 58 60 177	357
2	21 59 60 178	20 59 60 178	19 59 60 178	18 59 60 178	17 59 60 178	16 59 60 178	15 59 60 178	14 59 60 178	13 59 60 178	12 59 60 178	11 59 60 178	10 59 60 178	09 59 60 178	08 59 60 178	07 59 60 178	358
1	22 00 60 179	21 00 60 179	20 00 60 179	19 00 60 179	18 00 60 179	17 00 60 179	16 00 60 179	15 00 60 179	14 00 60 179	13 00 60 179	12 00 60 179	11 00 60 179	10 00 60 179	09 00 60 179	08 00 60 179	359
0	22 00 −60 180	21 00 −60 180	20 00 −60 180	19 00 −60 180	18 00 −60 180	17 00 −60 180	16 00 −60 180	15 00 −60 180	14 00 −60 180	13 00 −60 180	12 00 −60 180	11 00 −60 180	10 00 −60 180	09 00 −60 180	08 00 −60 180	360

S. Lat. {LHA greater than 180°……Zn=180−Z; LHA less than 180°……Zn=180+Z}

DECLINATION (0°-14°) CONTRARY NAME TO LATITUDE

N. Lat. {LHA greater than 180°....... Zn=Z; LHA less than 180°........... Zn=360−Z}

DECLINATION (15°-29°) SAME NAME AS LATITUDE

LHA	15° Hc	d	Z	16° Hc	d	Z	17° Hc	d	Z	18° Hc	d	Z	19° Hc	d	Z
	° ′	′	°	° ′	′	°	° ′	′	°	° ′	′	°	° ′	′	°
0	37 00	+60	180	38 00	+60	180	39 00	+60	180	40 00	+60	180	41 00	+60	180
1	37 00	60	179	38 00	60	179	39 00	60	179	40 00	60	179	41 00	60	179
2	36 59	60	178	37 59	60	178	38 59	60	178	39 59	60	178	40 59	60	178
3	36 58	60	176	37 58	60	176	38 58	60	176	39 58	60	176	40 58	60	176
4	36 56	60	175	37 56	60	175	38 56	60	175	39 56	60	175	40 56	60	175
5	36 54	+60	174	37 54	+60	174	38 54	+60	174	39 54	+60	174	40 54	+60	174
6	36 52	59	173	37 51	60	173	38 51	60	173	39 51	60	173	40 51	60	173
7	36 48	60	172	37 48	60	172	38 48	60	171	39 48	60	171	40 48	60	171
8	36 45	60	170	37 45	60	170	38 45	60	170	39 45	59	170	40 44	60	170
9	36 41	60	169	37 41	60	169	38 41	59	169	39 40	60	169	40 40	60	169
10	36 36	+60	168	37 36	+60	168	38 36	+60	168	39 36	+60	168	40 36	+59	168
11	36 32	59	167	37 31	60	167	38 31	60	167	39 31	60	166	40 31	59	166
12	36 26	60	166	37 26	60	165	38 26	59	165	39 25	60	165	40 25	60	165
13	36 20	60	164	37 20	60	164	38 20	59	164	39 19	60	164	40 19	60	164
14	36 14	60	163	37 14	59	163	38 13	60	163	39 13	59	163	40 12	60	163
15	36 07	+60	162	37 07	+59	162	38 06	+60	162	39 06	+59	162	40 05	+60	161
16	36 00	60	161	37 00	59	161	37 59	60	161	38 59	59	160	39 58	59	160
17	35 52	60	160	36 52	59	159	37 51	60	159	38 51	59	159	39 50	60	159
18	35 44	60	158	36 44	59	158	37 43	60	158	38 43	59	158	39 42	59	158
19	35 36	59	157	36 35	60	157	37 35	59	157	38 34	59	157	39 33	59	157
20	35 27	+59	156	36 26	+60	156	37 26	+59	156	38 25	+59	156	39 24	+59	155
21	35 18	59	155	36 17	59	155	37 16	59	155	38 15	59	154	39 14	59	154
22	35 08	59	154	36 07	59	154	37 06	59	153	38 05	59	153	39 04	59	153
23	34 58	59	153	35 57	59	152	36 56	59	152	37 55	59	152	38 54	59	152
24	34 47	59	151	35 46	59	151	36 45	59	151	37 44	59	151	38 43	59	151
25	34 36	+59	150	35 35	+59	150	36 34	+59	150	37 33	+59	150	38 32	+58	149
26	34 25	59	149	35 24	59	149	36 23	58	149	37 21	59	148	38 20	59	148
27	34 13	59	148	35 12	59	148	36 11	58	148	37 09	59	147	38 08	58	147
28	34 01	59	147	35 00	58	147	35 58	59	146	36 57	58	146	37 55	59	146
29	33 49	58	146	34 47	59	145	35 46	58	145	36 44	59	145	37 43	58	145
30	33 36	+58	145	34 34	+59	144	35 33	+58	144	36 31	+58	144	37 29	+59	143
31	33 23	58	143	34 21	58	143	35 19	59	143	36 18	58	143	37 16	58	142
32	33 09	58	142	34 07	59	142	35 06	58	142	36 04	58	141	37 02	58	141
33	32 55	58	141	33 53	58	141	34 51	59	141	35 50	58	140	36 48	58	140
34	32 41	58	140	33 39	58	140	34 37	58	140	35 35	58	139	36 33	58	139
35	32 26	+58	139	33 24	+58	139	34 22	+58	138	35 20	+58	138	36 18	+58	138
36	32 11	58	138	33 09	58	138	34 07	58	137	35 05	58	137	36 03	57	137
37	31 56	58	137	32 54	58	136	33 52	57	136	34 49	58	136	35 47	58	136
38	31 41	57	136	32 38	58	135	33 36	58	135	34 34	57	135	35 31	58	134
39	31 25	57	135	32 22	58	134	33 20	57	134	34 17	58	134	35 15	57	133
40	31 09	+57	134	32 06	+58	133	33 04	+57	133	34 01	+57	133	34 58	+58	132
41	30 52	58	132	31 50	57	132	32 47	57	132	33 44	58	131	34 42	57	131
42	30 35	58	131	31 33	57	131	32 30	57	131	33 27	58	130	34 25	57	130
43	30 18	58	130	31 16	57	130	32 13	57	130	33 10	57	129	34 07	57	129
44	30 01	57	129	30 58	57	129	31 55	58	129	32 53	57	128	33 50	56	128
45	29 44	+57	128	30 41	+57	128	31 38	+57	127	32 35	+57	127	33 32	+56	127
46	29 26	57	127	30 23	57	127	31 20	57	126	32 17	56	126	33 13	57	126
47	29 08	57	126	30 05	57	126	31 02	56	125	31 58	57	125	32 55	57	125
48	28 49	57	125	29 46	57	125	30 43	57	124	31 40	56	124	32 36	57	124
49	28 31	57	124	29 28	56	124	30 24	57	123	31 21	57	123	32 18	56	122
50	28 12	+57	123	29 09	+56	123	30 05	+57	122	31 02	+56	122	31 58	+57	121
51	27 53	57	122	28 50	56	122	29 46	57	121	30 43	56	121	31 39	57	120
52	27 34	56	121	28 30	57	121	29 27	56	120	30 23	57	120	31 20	56	119
53	27 15	56	120	28 11	56	119	29 07	57	119	30 04	56	119	31 00	56	118
54	26 55	56	119	27 51	57	118	28 48	56	118	29 44	56	118	30 40	56	117
55	26 35	+56	118	27 31	+57	117	28 28	+56	117	29 24	+56	117	30 20	+56	116
56	26 15	56	117	27 11	57	116	28 08	56	116	29 04	56	116	30 00	56	115
57	25 55	56	116	26 51	56	115	27 47	56	115	28 43	56	115	29 39	56	114
58	25 35	56	115	26 31	56	114	27 27	56	114	28 23	56	114	29 19	56	113
59	25 14	56	114	26 10	56	113	27 06	56	113	28 02	56	113	28 58	56	112
60	24 54	+56	113	25 50	+55	112	26 45	+56	112	27 41	+56	112	28 37	+56	111
61	24 33	56	112	25 29	56	111	26 25	55	111	27 20	56	111	28 16	56	110
62	24 12	56	111	25 08	55	110	26 03	56	110	26 59	56	110	27 55	55	109
63	23 51	56	110	24 47	55	109	25 42	56	109	26 38	56	109	27 34	55	108
64	23 29	56	109	24 25	56	108	25 21	56	108	26 17	55	108	27 12	56	107
65	23 08	+56	108	24 04	+56	107	25 00	+55	107	25 55	+56	107	26 51	+55	106
66	22 47	55	107	23 42	56	106	24 38	56	106	25 34	55	106	26 29	55	105
67	22 25	56	106	23 21	55	106	24 16	56	105	25 12	55	105	26 07	56	104
68	22 03	56	105	22 59	56	105	23 55	55	104	24 50	55	104	25 45	56	103
69	21 42	55	104	22 37	56	104	23 33	55	103	24 28	56	103	25 24	55	102

LHA	20° Hc	d	Z	21° Hc	d	Z	22° Hc	d	Z	23° Hc	d	Z	24° Hc	d	Z
	° ′	′	°	° ′	′	°	° ′	′	°	° ′	′	°	° ′	′	°
0	42 00	+60	180	43 00	+60	180	44 00	+60	180	45 00	+60	180	46 00	+60	180
1	42 00	60	179	43 00	60	179	44 00	60	179	45 00	60	179	46 00	60	179
2	41 59	60	178	42 59	60	177	43 59	60	177	44 59	60	177	45 59	60	177
3	41 58	60	176	42 58	60	176	43 58	60	176	44 58	60	176	45 58	60	176
4	41 56	60	175	42 56	60	175	43 56	60	175	44 56	60	175	45 56	60	175
5	41 54	+60	174	42 54	+60	174	43 54	+60	174	44 54	+60	174	45 54	+60	173
6	41 51	60	172	42 51	60	172	43 51	60	172	44 51	60	172	45 51	60	172
7	41 48	60	171	42 48	60	171	43 48	60	171	44 48	59	171	45 47	60	171
8	41 44	60	170	42 44	60	170	43 44	60	170	44 44	60	170	45 44	59	170
9	41 40	60	169	42 40	60	169	43 40	59	168	44 39	60	168	45 39	60	168
10	41 35	+60	167	42 35	+60	167	43 35	+60	167	44 35	+59	167	45 34	+60	167
11	41 30	60	166	42 30	60	166	43 30	59	166	44 29	60	166	45 29	60	166
12	41 25	59	165	42 24	60	165	43 24	60	165	44 24	59	165	45 23	60	164
13	41 19	59	164	42 18	60	164	43 18	59	163	44 17	60	163	45 17	59	163
14	41 12	60	162	42 12	59	162	43 11	60	162	44 11	59	162	45 10	60	162
15	41 05	+59	161	42 04	+60	161	43 04	+59	161	44 03	+60	161	45 03	+59	160
16	40 57	60	160	41 57	59	160	42 56	60	160	43 56	59	159	44 55	59	159
17	40 50	59	159	41 49	59	159	42 48	60	158	43 48	59	158	44 47	59	158
18	40 41	59	158	41 40	60	157	42 40	59	157	43 39	59	157	44 38	59	157
19	40 32	60	156	41 32	59	156	42 31	59	156	43 30	59	156	44 29	59	155
20	40 23	+59	155	41 22	+59	155	42 21	+59	155	43 20	+59	154	44 19	+59	154
21	40 13	59	154	41 12	59	154	42 11	59	153	43 10	59	153	44 09	59	153
22	40 03	59	153	41 02	59	152	42 01	59	152	43 00	59	152	43 59	59	152
23	39 53	59	151	40 52	58	151	41 50	59	151	42 49	59	151	43 48	59	150
24	39 42	59	150	40 41	58	150	41 39	59	150	42 38	59	149	43 37	58	149
25	39 30	+59	149	40 29	+59	149	41 28	+58	149	42 26	+59	148	43 25	+58	148
26	39 19	58	148	40 17	59	148	41 16	58	147	42 14	59	147	43 13	58	147
27	39 06	59	147	40 05	58	146	41 03	59	146	42 02	58	146	43 00	59	146
28	38 54	58	146	39 52	59	145	40 51	58	145	41 49	58	145	42 47	59	144
29	38 41	58	144	39 39	59	144	40 38	58	144	41 36	58	143	42 34	58	143
30	38 28	+58	143	39 26	+58	143	40 24	+58	143	41 22	+58	142	42 20	+58	142
31	38 14	58	142	39 12	58	142	40 10	58	141	41 08	58	141	42 06	58	141
32	38 00	58	141	38 58	58	141	39 56	58	140	40 54	58	140	41 52	58	140
33	37 46	58	140	38 44	57	139	39 41	58	139	40 39	58	139	41 37	58	138
34	37 31	58	139	38 29	57	138	39 26	58	138	40 24	58	138	41 22	57	137
35	37 16	+58	137	38 14	+57	137	39 11	+58	137	40 09	+57	136	41 06	+58	136
36	37 00	58	136	37 58	58	136	38 56	57	136	39 53	58	135	40 51	57	135
37	36 45	57	135	37 42	58	135	38 40	57	134	39 37	57	134	40 34	58	134
38	36 29	57	134	37 26	58	134	38 24	57	133	39 21	57	133	40 18	57	133
39	36 12	58	133	37 10	57	133	38 07	57	132	39 04	57	132	40 01	57	131
40	35 56	+57	132	36 53	+57	131	37 50	+57	131	38 47	+57	131	39 44	+57	130
41	35 39	57	131	36 36	57	130	37 33	57	130	38 30	57	130	39 27	57	129
42	35 22	57	130	36 19	57	129	37 16	57	129	38 13	56	128	39 09	57	128
43	35 04	57	129	36 01	57	128	36 58	57	128	37 55	57	127	38 52	56	127
44	34 46	57	127	35 43	57	127	36 40	57	127	37 37	56	126	38 33	57	126
45	34 28	+57	126	35 25	+57	126	36 22	+57	126	37 19	+56	125	38 15	+57	125
46	34 10	57	125	35 07	57	125	36 04	56	124	37 00	56	124	37 56	57	124
47	33 52	56	124	34 48	57	124	35 45	56	123	36 41	57	123	37 38	56	123
48	33 33	57	123	34 30	56	123	35 26	56	122	36 22	57	122	37 19	56	121
49	33 14	57	122	34 11	56	122	35 07	56	121	36 03	56	121	36 59	56	120
50	32 55	+56	121	33 51	+57	121	34 48	+56	120	35 44	+56	120	36 40	+56	119
51	32 36	56	120	33 32	56	120	34 28	56	119	35 24	56	119	36 20	56	118
52	32 16	56	119	33 12	56	119	34 08	56	118	35 04	56	118	36 00	56	117
53	31 56	56	118	32 52	56	117	33 48	56	117	34 44	56	117	35 40	56	116
54	31 36	56	117	32 32	56	116	33 28	56	116	34 24	56	116	35 20	55	115
55	31 16	+56	116	32 12	+56	115	33 08	+56	115	34 04	+55	115	34 59	+56	114
56	30 56	56	115	31 52	55	114	32 47	56	114	33 43	56	113	34 39	55	113
57	30 35	56	114	31 31	56	113	32 27	55	113	33 22	56	112	34 18	55	112
58	30 15	55	113	31 10	56	112	32 06	56	112	33 02	55	111	33 57	55	111
59	29 54	55	112	30 49	56	111	31 45	56	111	32 41	55	110	33 36	55	110
60	29 33	+55	111	30 28	+56	110	31 24	+55	110	32 19	+56	109	33 15	+55	109
61	29 12	55	110	30 07	56	109	31 03	55	109	31 58	55	108	32 53	56	108
62	28 50	56	109	29 46	55	108	30 41	56	108	31 37	55	107	32 32	55	107
63	28 29	56	108	29 25	55	107	30 20	55	107	31 15	55	106	32 10	56	106
64	28 08	55	107	29 03	55	106	29 58	56	106	30 54	55	105	31 49	55	105
65	27 46	+55	106	28 41	+56	105	29 37	+55	105	30 32	+55	104	31 27	+55	104
66	27 24	56	105	28 20	55	104	29 15	55	104	30 10	55	103	31 05	55	103
67	27 03	55	104	27 58	55	103	28 53	55	103	29 48	55	103	30 43	55	102
68	26 41	55	103	27 36	55	102	28 31	55	102	29 26	55	102	30 21	55	101
69	26 19	55	102	27 14	55	101	28 09	55	101	29 04	55	101	29 59	55	100

LHA	25° Hc	d	Z	26° Hc	d	Z	27° Hc	d	Z	28° Hc	d	Z	29° Hc	d	Z	LHA
	° ′	′	°	° ′	′	°	° ′	′	°	° ′	′	°	° ′	′	°	
0	47 00	+60	180	48 00	+60	180	49 00	+60	180	50 00	+60	180	51 00	+60	180	360
1	47 00	60	179	48 00	60	179	49 00	60	179	50 00	60	179	51 00	60	179	359
2	46 59	60	177	47 59	60	177	48 59	60	177	49 59	60	177	50 59	60	177	358
3	46 58	60	176	47 58	60	176	48 58	60	176	49 58	60	176	50 58	60	176	357
4	46 56	60	175	47 56	60	175	48 56	60	175	49 56	60	175	50 56	60	174	356
5	46 54	+59	173	47 53	+60	173	48 53	+60	173	49 53	+60	173	50 53	+60	173	355
6	46 51	60	172	47 51	59	172	48 50	60	172	49 50	60	172	50 50	60	172	354
7	46 47	60	171	47 47	60	171	48 47	60	171	49 47	60	170	50 47	60	170	353
8	46 43	60	169	47 43	60	169	48 43	60	169	49 43	60	169	50 43	59	169	352
9	46 39	60	168	47 39	60	168	48 39	59	168	49 38	60	168	50 38	60	168	351
10	46 34	+60	167	47 34	+60	167	48 34	+59	167	49 33	+60	166	50 33	+60	166	350
11	46 29	59	166	47 28	60	165	48 28	60	165	49 28	59	165	50 27	60	165	349
12	46 23	59	164	47 22	60	164	48 22	60	164	49 22	59	164	50 21	60	163	348
13	46 16	60	163	47 16	60	163	48 16	59	163	49 15	60	162	50 15	59	162	347
14	46 10	59	162	47 09	60	161	48 09	59	161	49 08	59	161	50 07	60	161	346
15	46 02	+60	160	47 02	+59	160	48 01	+59	160	49 00	+60	160	50 00	+59	159	345
16	45 54	60	159	46 54	59	159	47 53	59	159	48 52	60	158	49 52	59	158	344
17	45 46	59	158	46 45	60	157	47 45	59	157	48 44	59	157	49 43	59	157	343
18	45 37	60	156	46 37	59	156	47 36	59	156	48 35	59	156	49 34	59	155	342
19	45 28	59	155	46 27	59	155	47 26	59	155	48 25	59	154	49 24	59	154	341
20	45 18	+59	154	46 17	+59	154	47 16	+59	153	48 15	+59	153	49 14	+59	153	340
21	45 08	59	153	46 07	59	152	47 06	59	152	48 05	59	152	49 04	58	151	339
22	44 58	59	151	45 57	58	151	46 55	59	151	47 54	59	150	48 53	58	150	338
23	44 47	58	150	45 45	59	150	46 44	59	150	47 43	58	149	48 41	59	149	337
24	44 35	59	149	45 34	58	149	46 32	59	148	47 31	58	148	48 29	59	148	336
25	44 23	+59	148	45 22	+58	147	46 20	+59	147	47 19	+58	147	48 17	+58	146	335
26	44 11	59	146	45 10	58	146	46 08	58	146	47 06	58	145	48 04	59	145	334
27	43 59	58	145	44 57	58	145	45 55	58	144	46 53	58	144	47 51	58	144	333
28	43 46	58	144	44 44	58	144	45 42	58	143	46 40	58	143	47 38	58	143	332
29	43 32	58	143	44 30	58	142	45 28	58	142	46 26	58	142	47 24	58	141	331
30	43 18	+58	142	44 16	+58	141	45 14	+58	141	46 12	+58	140	47 10	+57	140	330
31	43 04	58	140	44 02	58	140	45 00	57	140	45 57	58	139	46 55	57	139	329
32	42 50	57	139	43 47	58	139	44 45	58	138	45 43	57	138	46 40	57	138	328
33	42 35	57	138	43 32	58	138	44 30	57	137	45 27	58	137	46 25	57	136	327
34	42 19	58	137	43 17	57	136	44 14	58	136	45 12	57	136	46 09	57	135	326
35	42 04	+57	136	43 01	+58	135	43 59	+57	135	44 56	+57	134	45 53	+57	134	325
36	41 48	57	134	42 45	57	134	43 42	58	134	44 40	57	133	45 37	56	133	324
37	41 32	57	133	42 29	57	133	43 26	57	132	44 23	57	132	45 20	57	132	323
38	41 15	57	132	42 12	57	132	43 09	57	131	44 06	57	131	45 03	57	130	322
39	40 58	57	131	41 55	57	131	42 52	57	130	43 49	57	130	44 46	56	129	321
40	40 41	+57	130	41 38	+57	129	42 35	+57	129	43 32	+56	129	44 28	+56	128	320
41	40 24	57	129	41 21	56	128	42 17	57	128	43 14	56	127	44 10	57	127	319
42	40 06	57	128	41 03	56	127	41 59	57	127	42 56	56	126	43 52	56	126	318
43	39 48	57	126	40 45	56	126	41 41	57	126	42 38	56	125	43 34	56	125	317
44	39 30	56	125	40 26	57	125	41 23	56	124	42 19	56	124	43 15	56	124	316
45	39 12	+56	124	40 08	+56	124	41 04	+56	123	42 00	+56	123	42 56	+56	122	315
46	38 53	56	123	39 49	56	123	40 45	56	122	41 41	56	122	42 37	56	121	314
47	38 34	56	122	39 30	56	122	40 26	56	121	41 22	56	121	42 18	55	120	313
48	38 15	56	121	39 11	56	121	40 07	56	120	41 03	55	120	41 58	56	119	312
49	37 55	56	120	38 51	56	119	39 47	56	119	40 43	55	119	41 38	56	118	311
50	37 36	+56	119	38 32	+55	118	39 27	+56	118	40 23	+56	117	41 19	+55	117	310
51	37 16	56	118	38 12	55	117	39 07	56	117	40 03	55	116	40 58	56	116	309
52	36 56	56	117	37 52	55	116	38 47	56	116	39 43	55	115	40 38	55	115	308
53	36 36	55	116	37 31	56	115	38 27	55	115	39 22	56	114	40 18	55	114	307
54	36 15	56	115	37 11	55	114	38 06	56	114	39 02	55	113	39 57	55	113	306
55	35 55	+55	114	36 50	+56	113	37 46	+55	113	38 41	+55	112	39 36	+55	112	305
56	35 34	56	113	36 30	55	112	37 25	55	112	38 20	55	111	39 15	55	111	304
57	35 13	56	112	36 09	55	111	37 04	55	111	37 59	55	110	38 54	55	110	303
58	34 52	56	111	35 48	55	110	36 43	55	110	37 38	55	109	38 33	55	109	302
59	34 31	55	110	35 26	56	109	36 22	55	109	37 17	54	108	38 11	55	108	301
60	34 10	+55	108	35 05	+55	108	36 00	+55	108	36 55	+55	107	37 50	+55	107	300
61	33 49	55	107	34 44	55	107	35 39	55	107	36 34	54	106	37 28	55	106	299
62	33 27	55	106	34 22	55	106	35 17	55	106	36 12	55	105	37 07	54	105	298
63	33 06	55	105	34 01	54	105	34 55	55	105	35 50	55	104	36 45	54	104	297
64	32 44	55	105	33 39	55	104	34 34	54	104	35 28	55	103	36 23	54	103	296
65	32 22	+55	104	33 17	+55	103	34 12	+54	103	35 06	+55	102	36 01	+54	102	295
66	32 00	55	103	32 55	55	102	33 50	54	102	34 44	55	101	35 39	54	101	294
67	31 38	55	102	32 33	55	101	33 28	54	101	34 22	55	100	35 17	54	100	293
68	31 16	55	101	32 11	54	100	33 05	55	100	34 00	54	99	34 54	55	99	292
69	30 54	55	100	31 49	54	99	32 43	55	99	33 38	54	98	34 32	54	98	291

S. Lat. {LHA greater than 180°....... Zn=180−Z; LHA less than 180°........... Zn=180+Z}

DECLINATION (15°-29°) SAME NAME AS LATITUDE

N. Lat. {LHA greater than 180°……Zn=Z; LHA less than 180°……Zn=360−Z}

DECLINATION (15°-29°) SAME NAME AS LATITUDE

LHA	15° Hc	d	Z	16° Hc	d	Z	17° Hc	d	Z	18° Hc	d	Z	19° Hc	d	Z
	° ′	′	°	° ′	′	°	° ′	′	°	° ′	′	°	° ′	′	°
70	21 20	+55	103	22 15	+56	103	23 11	+55	102	24 06	+56	102	25 02	+55	101
71	20 58	55	102	21 53	56	102	22 49	55	101	23 44	55	101	24 39	56	100
72	20 36	55	101	21 31	56	101	22 27	55	100	23 22	55	100	24 17	55	99
73	20 14	55	100	21 09	56	100	22 05	55	99	23 00	55	99	23 55	55	99
74	19 52	55	99	20 47	55	99	21 42	56	98	22 38	55	98	23 33	55	98
75	19 29	+56	98	20 25	+55	98	21 20	+55	97	22 15	+56	97	23 11	+55	97
76	19 07	55	97	20 02	56	97	20 58	55	97	21 53	55	96	22 48	55	96
77	18 45	55	96	19 40	55	96	20 35	56	96	21 31	55	95	22 26	55	95
78	18 22	56	95	19 18	55	95	20 13	55	95	21 08	55	94	22 03	55	94
79	18 00	55	95	18 55	56	94	19 51	55	94	20 46	55	93	21 41	55	93
80	17 38	+55	94	18 33	+55	93	19 28	+55	93	20 23	+55	92	21 18	+56	92
81	17 15	55	93	18 10	56	92	19 06	55	92	20 01	55	91	20 56	55	91
82	16 53	55	92	17 48	55	91	18 43	55	91	19 38	56	90	20 34	55	90
83	16 30	56	91	17 26	56	90	18 21	55	90	19 16	55	90	20 11	55	89
84	16 08	55	90	17 03	55	89	17 58	55	89	18 53	56	89	19 49	55	88
85	15 45	+56	89	16 41	+55	89	17 36	+55	88	18 31	+55	88	19 26	+55	87
86	15 23	55	88	16 18	55	88	17 13	56	87	18 09	55	87	19 04	55	86
87	15 00	56	87	15 56	55	87	16 51	55	86	17 46	55	86	18 41	55	85
88	14 38	55	86	15 33	56	86	16 29	55	85	17 24	55	85	18 19	55	85
89	14 16	55	85	15 11	55	85	16 06	55	84	17 01	56	84	17 57	55	84
90	13 53	+55	84	14 48	+56	84	15 44	+55	84	16 39	+55	83	17 34	+55	83
91	13 31	55	83	14 26	55	83	15 21	56	83	16 17	55	82	17 12	55	82
92	13 08	56	82	14 04	55	82	14 59	55	82	15 54	56	81	16 50	55	81
93	12 46	56	82	13 42	55	81	14 37	55	81	15 32	56	80	16 28	55	80
94	12 24	55	81	13 19	56	80	14 15	55	80	15 10	55	79	16 05	56	79
95	12 02	+55	80	12 57	+56	79	13 53	+55	79	14 48	+55	79	15 43	+56	78
96	11 40	55	79	12 35	56	78	13 31	55	78	14 26	55	78	15 21	56	77
97	11 18	55	78	12 13	56	78	13 09	56	77	14 04	56	77	15 00	55	76
98	10 56	55	77	11 51	56	77	12 47	55	76	13 42	56	76	14 38	55	75
99	10 34	56	76	11 30	56	76	12 25	56	75	13 21	55	75	14 16	56	75
100	10 12	+56	75	11 08	+55	75	12 03	+56	74	12 59	+56	74	13 55	+55	74
101	09 51	55	74	10 46	56	74	11 42	55	74	12 37	56	73	13 33	56	73
102	09 29	56	73	10 25	55	73	11 20	56	73	12 16	56	72	13 12	55	72
103	09 08	55	72	10 03	56	72	10 59	56	72	11 55	55	71	12 50	56	71
104	08 46	56	72	09 42	56	71	10 38	55	71	11 33	56	70	12 29	56	70
105	08 25	+56	71	09 21	+56	70	10 17	+55	70	11 12	+56	70	12 08	+56	69
106	08 04	56	70	09 00	55	69	09 55	56	69	10 51	56	69	11 47	56	68
107	07 43	56	69	08 39	56	68	09 35	55	68	10 30	56	68	11 26	56	67
108	07 22	56	68	08 18	56	68	09 14	56	67	10 10	56	67	11 06	56	66
109	07 01	56	67	07 57	56	67	08 53	56	66	09 49	56	66	10 45	56	66
110	06 40	+57	66	07 37	+56	66	08 33	+56	65	09 29	+56	65	10 25	+56	65
111	06 20	56	65	07 16	56	65	08 12	56	64	09 08	57	64	10 05	56	64
112	06 00	56	64	06 56	56	64	07 52	56	64	08 48	56	63	09 44	57	63
113	05 40	56	63	06 36	56	63	07 32	56	63	08 28	57	62	09 25	56	62
114	05 20	56	62	06 16	56	62	07 12	56	62	08 08	57	61	09 05	56	61
115	05 00	+56	61	05 56	+56	61	06 52	+57	61	07 49	+56	61	08 45	+57	60
116	04 40	56	61	05 36	57	60	06 33	56	60	07 29	57	60	08 26	56	59
117	04 20	57	60	05 17	57	59	06 14	56	59	07 10	57	59	08 07	56	58
118	04 01	57	59	04 58	56	58	05 54	57	58	06 51	57	58	07 48	56	57
119	03 42	57	58	04 39	56	58	05 35	57	57	06 32	57	57	07 29	56	57
120	03 23	+57	57	04 20	+57	57	05 17	+56	56	06 13	+57	56	07 10	+57	56
121	03 04	57	56	04 01	57	56	04 58	57	55	05 55	57	55	06 52	56	55
122	02 46	57	55	03 43	57	55	04 40	57	54	05 37	56	54	06 33	57	54
123	02 28	56	54	03 24	57	54	04 21	57	54	05 18	57	53	06 15	57	53
124	02 09	57	53	03 06	57	53	04 03	58	53	05 01	57	52	05 58	57	52
125	01 52	+57	52	02 49	+57	52	03 46	+57	52	04 43	+57	51	05 40	+57	51
126	01 34	57	51	02 31	57	51	03 28	57	51	04 25	58	51	05 23	57	50
127	01 16	58	51	02 14	57	50	03 11	57	50	04 08	57	50	05 05	58	49
128	00 59	57	50	01 56	58	49	02 54	57	49	03 51	57	49	04 48	58	48
129	00 42	58	49	01 40	57	48	02 37	57	48	03 34	58	48	04 32	57	47
130	00 25	+58	48	01 23	+57	47	02 20	+58	47	03 18	+57	47	04 15	+58	47
131	00 09	57	47	01 06	58	47	02 04	58	46	03 02	57	46	03 59	58	46
132	−0 07	57	46	00 50	58	46	01 48	57	45	02 45	58	45	03 43	58	45
133	−0 23	57	45	00 34	58	45	01 32	58	44	02 30	57	44	03 27	58	44
134	−0 39	58	44	00 19	57	44	01 16	58	43	02 14	58	43	03 12	58	43
135	−0 55	+58	43	00 03	+58	43	01 01	+58	43	01 59	+58	42	02 57	+58	42
136	−1 10	58	42	−0 12	58	42	00 46	58	42	01 44	58	41	02 42	58	41
137	−1 25	58	41	−0 27	58	41	00 31	58	41	01 29	58	40	02 27	58	40
138	−1 39	58	40	−0 41	58	40	00 17	58	40	01 15	58	40	02 13	58	39
139	−1 54	58	39	−0 56	58	39	00 02	59	39	01 01	58	39	01 59	58	38

LHA	20° Hc	d	Z	21° Hc	d	Z	22° Hc	d	Z	23° Hc	d	Z	24° Hc	d	Z
	° ′	′	°	° ′	′	°	° ′	′	°	° ′	′	°	° ′	′	°
70	25 57	+55	101	26 52	+55	101	27 47	+55	100	28 42	+55	100	29 37	+55	99
71	25 35	55	100	26 30	55	100	27 25	55	99	28 20	55	99	29 15	54	98
72	25 12	55	99	26 08	55	99	27 03	55	98	27 58	54	98	28 52	55	97
73	24 50	55	98	25 45	55	98	26 40	55	97	27 35	55	97	28 30	55	96
74	24 28	55	97	25 23	55	97	26 18	55	96	27 13	55	96	28 08	54	95
75	24 06	+55	96	25 01	+55	96	25 56	+55	95	26 51	+54	95	27 45	+55	94
76	23 43	55	95	24 38	55	95	25 33	55	94	26 28	55	94	27 23	55	93
77	23 21	55	94	24 16	55	94	25 11	55	93	26 06	54	93	27 00	55	93
78	22 58	55	93	23 53	55	93	24 48	55	92	25 43	55	92	26 38	55	92
79	22 36	55	92	23 31	55	92	24 26	55	92	25 21	55	91	26 16	54	91
80	22 14	+55	91	23 09	+54	91	24 03	+55	91	24 58	+55	90	25 53	+55	90
81	21 51	55	91	22 46	55	90	23 41	55	90	24 36	55	89	25 31	54	89
82	21 29	55	90	22 24	55	89	23 19	54	89	24 13	55	88	25 08	55	88
83	21 06	55	89	22 01	55	88	22 56	55	88	23 51	55	87	24 46	54	87
84	20 44	55	88	21 39	55	87	22 34	54	87	23 28	55	86	24 23	55	86
85	20 21	+55	87	21 16	+55	86	22 11	+55	86	23 06	+55	85	24 01	+55	85
86	19 59	55	86	20 54	55	86	21 49	55	85	22 44	54	85	23 38	55	84
87	19 36	55	85	20 31	55	85	21 26	55	84	22 21	55	84	23 16	55	83
88	19 14	55	84	20 09	55	84	21 04	55	83	21 59	55	83	22 54	55	82
89	18 52	55	83	19 47	55	83	20 42	55	82	21 37	55	82	22 32	54	81
90	18 29	+55	82	19 24	+55	82	20 19	+55	81	21 14	+55	81	22 09	+55	81
91	18 07	55	81	19 02	55	81	19 57	55	81	20 52	55	80	21 47	55	80
92	17 45	55	80	18 40	55	80	19 35	55	80	20 30	55	79	21 25	55	79
93	17 23	55	80	18 18	55	79	19 13	55	79	20 08	55	78	21 03	55	78
94	17 01	55	79	17 56	55	78	18 51	55	78	19 46	55	78	20 41	55	77
95	16 39	+55	78	17 34	+55	77	18 29	+55	77	19 24	+55	77	20 19	+55	76
96	16 17	55	77	17 12	55	76	18 07	55	76	19 02	56	76	19 58	55	75
97	15 55	55	76	16 50	56	76	17 46	55	75	18 41	55	75	19 36	55	74
98	15 33	56	75	16 29	55	75	17 24	55	74	18 19	55	74	19 14	55	73
99	15 12	55	74	16 07	55	74	17 02	56	73	17 58	55	73	18 53	55	73
100	14 50	+55	73	15 45	+56	73	16 41	+55	72	17 36	+55	72	18 31	+56	72
101	14 29	55	72	15 24	55	72	16 19	56	72	17 15	55	71	18 10	55	71
102	14 07	56	71	15 03	55	71	15 58	56	71	16 54	55	70	17 49	55	70
103	13 46	55	71	14 41	56	70	15 37	56	70	16 33	55	69	17 28	55	69
104	13 25	55	70	14 20	56	69	15 16	56	69	16 12	55	68	17 07	56	68
105	13 04	+55	69	13 59	+56	68	14 55	+56	68	15 51	+55	68	16 46	+56	67
106	12 43	56	68	13 39	55	67	14 34	56	67	15 30	56	67	16 26	55	66
107	12 22	56	67	13 18	56	67	14 14	55	66	15 09	56	66	16 05	56	65
108	12 02	56	66	12 57	56	66	13 53	56	65	14 49	56	65	15 45	56	65
109	11 41	56	65	12 37	56	65	13 33	56	64	14 29	56	64	15 25	55	64
110	11 21	+56	64	12 17	+56	64	13 13	+56	64	14 09	+56	63	15 05	+55	63
111	11 01	56	63	11 57	56	63	12 53	56	63	13 49	56	62	14 45	56	62
112	10 41	56	63	11 37	56	62	12 33	56	62	13 29	56	61	14 25	56	61
113	10 21	56	62	11 17	56	61	12 13	56	61	13 09	56	61	14 05	56	60
114	10 01	56	61	10 57	57	60	11 54	56	60	12 50	56	60	13 46	56	59
115	09 42	+56	60	10 38	+56	59	11 34	+56	59	12 30	+57	59	13 27	+56	58
116	09 22	57	59	10 19	56	59	11 15	56	58	12 11	57	58	13 08	56	58
117	09 03	57	58	10 00	56	58	10 56	56	57	11 52	57	57	12 49	56	57
118	08 44	57	57	09 41	56	57	10 37	57	56	11 34	56	56	12 30	57	56
119	08 25	57	56	09 22	57	56	10 19	56	56	11 15	57	55	12 12	56	55
120	08 07	+56	55	09 03	+57	55	10 00	+57	54	10 57	+56	54	11 53	+57	54
121	07 48	57	54	08 45	57	54	09 42	57	54	10 39	56	53	11 35	57	53
122	07 30	57	54	08 27	57	53	09 24	57	53	10 21	56	53	11 17	57	52
123	07 12	57	53	08 09	57	52	09 06	57	52	10 03	57	52	11 00	57	51
124	06 55	56	52	07 51	57	51	08 48	57	51	09 45	57	51	10 42	57	50
125	06 37	+57	51	07 34	+57	51	08 31	+57	50	09 28	+57	50	10 25	+57	50
126	06 20	57	50	07 17	57	50	08 14	57	49	09 11	57	49	10 08	57	49
127	06 03	57	49	07 00	57	49	07 57	57	48	08 54	57	48	09 51	58	48
128	05 46	57	48	06 43	57	48	07 40	58	48	08 38	57	47	09 35	57	47
129	05 29	58	47	06 27	57	47	07 24	57	47	08 21	58	46	09 19	57	46
130	05 13	+57	46	06 10	+58	46	07 08	+57	46	08 05	+58	45	09 03	+57	45
131	04 57	57	45	05 54	58	45	06 52	58	45	07 49	58	45	08 47	57	44
132	04 41	57	44	05 38	58	44	06 36	58	44	07 34	57	44	08 31	58	43
133	04 25	58	44	05 23	58	43	06 21	57	43	07 18	58	43	08 16	58	43
134	04 10	58	43	05 08	57	42	06 05	58	42	07 03	58	42	08 01	58	42
135	03 55	+57	42	04 52	+58	42	05 50	+58	41	06 48	+58	41	07 46	+58	41
136	03 40	58	41	04 38	58	41	05 36	58	40	06 34	58	40	07 32	57	40
137	03 25	58	40	04 23	58	40	05 21	58	39	06 19	58	39	07 17	58	39
138	03 11	58	39	04 09	58	39	05 07	58	39	06 05	58	38	07 03	58	38
139	02 57	58	38	03 55	58	38	04 53	58	38	05 51	59	37	06 50	58	37

LHA	25° Hc	d	Z	26° Hc	d	Z	27° Hc	d	Z	28° Hc	d	Z	29° Hc	d	Z	LHA
	° ′	′	°	° ′	′	°	° ′	′	°	° ′	′	°	° ′	′	°	
70	30 32	+54	99	31 26	+55	98	32 21	+55	98	33 16	+54	97	34 10	+54	97	290
71	30 09	55	98	31 04	55	97	31 59	54	97	32 53	55	96	33 48	54	96	289
72	29 47	55	97	30 42	54	96	31 36	55	96	32 31	54	95	33 25	54	95	288
73	29 25	54	96	30 19	55	95	31 14	54	95	32 08	55	94	33 03	54	94	287
74	29 02	55	95	29 57	55	94	30 52	54	94	31 46	54	93	32 40	54	93	286
75	28 40	+55	94	29 35	+54	93	30 29	+55	93	31 24	+54	92	32 18	+54	92	285
76	28 18	54	93	29 12	55	93	30 07	54	92	31 01	54	92	31 55	54	91	284
77	27 55	55	92	28 50	54	92	29 44	55	91	30 39	54	91	31 33	54	90	283
78	27 33	54	91	28 27	55	91	29 22	54	90	30 16	54	90	31 10	55	89	282
79	27 10	55	90	28 05	54	90	28 59	55	89	29 54	54	89	30 48	54	88	281
80	26 48	+54	89	27 42	+55	89	28 37	+54	88	29 31	+55	88	30 26	+54	87	280
81	26 25	55	88	27 20	54	88	28 14	55	87	29 09	54	87	30 03	54	86	279
82	26 03	54	87	26 57	55	87	27 52	54	86	28 46	55	86	29 41	54	86	278
83	25 40	55	86	26 35	55	86	27 30	54	86	28 24	54	85	29 18	54	85	277
84	25 18	55	86	26 13	54	85	27 07	55	85	28 02	54	84	28 56	54	84	276
85	24 56	+54	85	25 50	+55	84	26 45	+54	84	27 39	+55	83	28 34	+54	83	275
86	24 33	55	84	25 28	54	83	26 22	55	83	27 17	54	82	28 11	55	82	274
87	24 11	55	83	25 06	54	82	26 00	55	82	26 55	54	81	27 49	54	81	273
88	23 49	54	82	24 43	55	81	25 38	54	81	26 32	55	81	27 27	54	80	272
89	23 26	55	81	24 21	55	81	25 16	54	80	26 10	55	80	27 05	54	79	271
90	23 04	+55	80	23 59	+55	80	24 54	+54	79	25 48	+55	79	26 43	+54	78	270
91	22 42	55	79	23 37	55	79	24 32	54	78	25 26	55	78	26 21	54	77	269
92	22 20	55	78	23 15	55	78	24 10	54	77	25 04	55	77	25 59	54	77	268
93	21 58	55	77	22 53	55	77	23 48	54	77	24 42	55	76	25 37	55	76	267
94	21 36	55	77	22 31	55	76	23 26	55	76	24 21	54	75	25 15	55	75	266
95	21 14	+55	76	22 09	+55	75	23 04	+55	75	23 59	+55	74	24 54	+54	74	265
96	20 53	55	75	21 48	55	74	22 43	54	74	23 37	55	73	24 32	55	73	264
97	20 31	55	74	21 26	55	73	22 21	55	73	23 16	55	73	24 11	55	72	263
98	20 09	56	73	21 05	55	73	22 00	55	72	22 55	54	72	23 49	55	71	262
99	19 48	55	72	20 43	55	72	21 38	55	71	22 33	55	71	23 28	55	70	261
100	19 27	+55	71	20 22	+55	71	21 17	+55	70	22 12	+55	70	23 07	+55	70	260
101	19 05	56	70	20 01	55	70	20 56	55	70	21 51	55	69	22 46	55	69	259
102	18 44	56	69	19 40	55	69	20 35	55	69	21 30	55	68	22 25	55	68	258
103	18 23	56	69	19 19	55	68	20 14	55	68	21 09	55	67	22 04	56	67	257
104	18 03	55	68	18 58	55	67	19 53	56	67	20 49	55	66	21 44	55	66	256
105	17 42	+55	67	18 37	+56	66	19 33	+55	66	20 28	+55	66	21 23	+56	65	255
106	17 21	56	66	18 17	55	66	19 12	56	65	20 08	55	65	21 03	55	64	254
107	17 01	55	65	17 56	56	65	18 52	55	64	19 47	56	64	20 43	55	63	253
108	16 41	55	64	17 36	56	64	18 32	55	63	19 27	56	63	20 23	55	63	252
109	16 20	56	63	17 16	56	63	18 12	55	63	19 07	56	62	20 03	56	62	251
110	16 00	+56	62	16 56	+56	62	17 52	+56	62	18 48	+55	61	19 43	+56	61	250
111	15 41	55	62	16 36	56	61	17 32	56	61	18 28	56	60	19 24	55	60	249
112	15 21	56	61	16 17	56	60	17 13	56	60	18 09	55	60	19 04	56	59	248
113	15 01	56	60	15 57	56	59	16 53	56	59	17 49	56	59	18 45	56	58	247
114	14 42	56	59	15 38	56	59	16 34	56	58	17 30	56	58	18 26	56	57	246
115	14 23	+56	58	15 19	+56	58	16 15	+56	57	17 11	+56	57	18 07	+56	57	245
116	14 04	56	57	15 00	56	57	15 56	57	56	16 53	56	56	17 49	56	56	244
117	13 45	56	56	14 41	57	56	15 38	56	56	16 34	56	55	17 30	56	55	243
118	13 27	56	55	14 23	56	55	15 19	57	55	16 16	56	54	17 12	56	54	242
119	13 08	57	55	14 05	56	54	15 01	57	54	15 58	56	53	16 54	56	53	241
120	12 50	+57	54	13 47	+56	53	14 43	+57	53	15 40	+56	53	16 36	+56	52	240
121	12 32	57	53	13 29	56	52	14 25	57	52	15 22	56	52	16 18	57	51	239
122	12 14	57	52	13 11	57	52	14 08	56	51	15 04	57	51	16 01	57	51	238
123	11 57	56	51	12 53	57	51	13 50	57	50	14 47	57	50	15 44	56	50	237
124	11 39	57	50	12 36	57	50	13 33	57	49	14 30	57	49	15 27	56	49	236
125	11 22	+57	49	12 19	+57	49	13 16	+57	49	14 13	+57	48	15 10	+57	48	235
126	11 05	57	48	12 02	57	48	12 59	57	48	13 56	57	47	14 53	57	47	234
127	10 49	57	48	11 46	57	47	12 43	57	47	13 40	57	47	14 37	57	46	233
128	10 32	57	47	11 29	58	46	12 27	57	46	13 24	57	46	14 21	57	45	232
129	10 16	57	46	11 13	57	45	12 10	58	45	13 08	57	45	14 05	57	45	231
130	10 00	+57	45	10 57	+58	45	11 55	+57	44	12 52	+57	44	13 49	+58	44	230
131	09 44	58	44	10 42	57	44	11 39	58	43	12 37	57	43	13 34	57	43	229
132	09 29	57	43	10 26	58	43	11 24	57	43	12 21	58	42	13 19	57	42	228
133	09 14	57	42	10 11	58	42	11 09	57	42	12 06	58	41	13 04	58	41	227
134	08 59	57	41	09 56	58	41	10 54	58	41	11 52	57	41	12 49	58	40	226
135	08 44	+58	40	09 42	+57	40	10 39	+58	40	11 37	+58	39	12 35	+58	39	225
136	08 29	58	40	09 27	58	39	10 25	58	39	11 23	58	39	12 21	58	39	224
137	08 15	58	39	09 13	58	38	10 11	58	38	11 09	58	38	12 07	58	38	223
138	08 01	58	38	08 59	58	38	09 57	58	37	10 55	58	37	11 53	58	37	222
139	07 48	58	37	08 46	58	37	09 44	58	36	10 42	58	36	11 40	58	36	221

S. Lat. {LHA greater than 180°……Zn=180−Z; LHA less than 180°……Zn=180+Z}

DECLINATION (15°-29°) SAME NAME AS LATITUDE

N. Lat. {LHA greater than 180°....... Zn=Z; LHA less than 180°........... Zn=360−Z}

DECLINATION (15°-29°) SAME NAME AS LATITUDE

LAT 68°

LHA	15° Hc	15° d	15° Z	16° Hc	16° d	16° Z	17° Hc	17° d	17° Z	18° Hc	18° d	18° Z	19° Hc	19° d	19° Z	20° Hc	20° d	20° Z	21° Hc	21° d	21° Z	22° Hc	22° d	22° Z
	° ′	′	°	° ′	′	°	° ′	′	°	° ′	′	°	° ′	′	°	° ′	′	°	° ′	′	°	° ′	′	°
140	−2 08	+58	38	−1 10	+59	38	−0 11	+58	38	00 47	+58	38	01 45	+58	37	02 43	+58	37	03 41	+59	37	04 40	+58	37
141	−2 22	59	37	−1 23	58	37	−0 25	58	37	00 33	58	37	01 31	59	37	02 30	58	36	03 28	58	36	04 26	59	36
142	−2 35	58	37	−1 37	58	36	−0 39	59	36	00 20	58	36	01 18	59	36	02 17	58	35	03 15	58	35	04 13	59	35
143	−2 49	59	36	−1 50	58	35	−0 52	59	35	00 07	58	35	01 05	59	35	02 04	58	34	03 02	59	34	04 01	58	34
144	−3 01	58	35	−2 03	59	34	−1 04	58	34	−0 06	59	34	00 53	58	34	01 51	59	34	02 50	58	33	03 48	59	33
145	−3 14	+58	34	−2 16	+59	33	−1 17	+59	33	−0 18	+58	33	00 40	+59	33	01 39	+58	33	02 37	+59	32	03 36	+59	32
146	−3 26	58	33	−2 28	59	33	−1 29	59	32	−0 30	58	32	00 28	59	32	01 27	59	32	02 26	58	32	03 24	59	31
147	−3 38	58	32	−2 40	59	32	−1 41	59	31	−0 42	59	31	00 17	58	31	01 15	59	31	02 14	59	31	03 13	58	30
148	−3 50	59	31	−2 51	58	31	−1 53	59	30	−0 54	59	30	00 05	59	30	01 04	59	30	02 03	59	30	03 02	58	29
149	−4 01	58	30	−3 03	59	30	−2 04	59	30	−1 05	59	29	−0 06	59	29	00 53	59	29	01 52	59	29	02 51	58	29
150	−4 13	+59	29	−3 14	+59	29	−2 15	+59	29	−1 16	+59	28	−0 17	+59	28	00 42	+59	28	01 41	+59	28	02 40	+59	28
151	−4 23	59	28	−3 24	59	28	−2 25	59	28	−1 26	59	27	−0 27	59	27	00 32	59	27	01 31	59	27	02 30	59	27
152	−4 34	59	27	−3 35	59	27	−2 36	60	27	−1 36	59	27	−0 37	59	26	00 22	59	26	01 21	59	26	02 20	59	26
153	−4 44	59	26	−3 45	60	26	−2 45	59	26	−1 46	59	26	−0 47	59	25	00 12	59	25	01 11	59	25	02 10	59	25
154	−4 53	59	25	−3 54	59	25	−2 55	59	25	−1 56	59	25	−0 57	59	24	00 02	60	24	01 02	59	24	02 01	59	24
155	−5 03	+59	24	−4 04	+60	24	−3 04	+59	24	−2 05	+59	24	−1 06	+59	24	−0 07	+60	23	00 53	+59	23	01 52	+59	23
156	−5 12	59	23	−4 13	60	23	−3 13	59	23	−2 14	59	23	−1 15	60	23	−0 15	59	22	00 44	59	22	01 43	60	22
157				−4 21	59	22	−3 22	60	22	−2 22	59	22	−1 23	59	22	−0 24	60	22	00 36	59	21	01 35	59	21
158				−4 29	59	21	−3 30	59	21	−2 31	60	21	−1 31	59	21	−0 32	60	21	00 28	59	20	01 27	59	20
159				−4 37	59	20	−3 38	59	20	−2 39	60	20	−1 39	59	20	−0 40	60	20	00 20	59	20	01 19	60	19
160				−4 45	+59	19	−3 46	+60	19	−2 46	+59	19	−1 47	+60	19	−0 47	+60	19	00 13	+59	19	01 12	+60	18
161				−4 52	59	18	−3 53	60	18	−2 53	59	18	−1 54	60	18	−0 54	60	18	00 06	59	18	01 05	60	18
162				−4 59	59	17	−4 00	60	17	−3 00	60	17	−2 00	59	17	−1 01	60	17	−0 01	59	17	00 58	60	17
163				−5 06	60	16	−4 06	60	16	−3 06	59	16	−2 07	60	16	−1 07	60	16	−0 07	59	16	00 52	60	16
164				−5 12	60	15	−4 12	60	15	−3 12	59	15	−2 13	60	15	−1 13	60	15	−0 13	59	15	00 46	60	15
165							−4 18	+60	14	−3 18	+60	14	−2 18	+59	14	−1 19	+60	14	−0 19	+60	14	00 41	+59	14
166							−4 23	59	13	−3 24	60	13	−2 24	60	13	−1 24	60	13	−0 24	59	13	00 35	60	13
167							−4 28	59	12	−3 29	60	12	−2 29	60	12	−1 29	60	12	−0 29	60	12	00 31	59	12
168							−4 33	60	11	−3 33	60	11	−2 33	59	11	−1 34	60	11	−0 34	60	11	00 26	60	11
169							−4 37	60	11	−3 37	59	10	−2 38	60	10	−1 38	60	10	−0 38	60	10	00 22	60	10
170							−4 41	+60	10	−3 41	+60	10	−2 41	+59	9	−1 42	+60	9	−0 42	+60	9	00 18	+60	9
171							−4 45	60	9	−3 45	60	9	−2 45	60	9	−1 45	60	8	−0 45	60	8	00 15	60	8
172							−4 48	60	8	−3 48	60	8	−2 48	60	8	−1 48	60	8	−0 48	60	7	00 12	60	7
173							−4 51	60	7	−3 51	60	7	−2 51	60	7	−1 51	60	7	−0 51	60	7	00 09	60	6
174							−4 53	60	6	−3 53	60	6	−2 53	60	6	−1 53	60	6	−0 53	60	6	00 07	59	6
175							−4 55	+60	5	−3 55	+60	5	−2 55	+60	5	−1 55	+60	5	−0 55	+60	5	00 05	+60	5
176							−4 57	60	4	−3 57	60	4	−2 57	60	4	−1 57	60	4	−0 57	60	4	00 03	60	4
177							−4 58	60	3	−3 58	60	3	−2 58	60	3	−1 58	60	3	−0 58	60	3	00 02	60	3
178							−4 59	60	2	−3 59	60	2	−2 59	60	2	−1 59	60	2	−0 59	60	2	00 01	60	2
179							−5 00	60	1	−4 00	60	1	−3 00	60	1	−2 00	60	1	−1 00	60	1	00 00	60	1
180							−5 00	+60	0	−4 00	+60	0	−3 00	+60	0	−2 00	+60	0	−1 00	+60	0	00 00	+60	0

LHA	23° Hc	23° d	23° Z	24° Hc	24° d	24° Z	25° Hc	25° d	25° Z	26° Hc	26° d	26° Z	27° Hc	27° d	27° Z	28° Hc	28° d	28° Z	29° Hc	29° d	29° Z	LHA
	° ′	′	°	° ′	′	°	° ′	′	°	° ′	′	°	° ′	′	°	° ′	′	°	° ′	′	°	
140	05 38	+58	37	06 36	+58	36	07 34	+59	36	08 33	+58	36	09 31	+58	36	10 29	+58	35	11 27	+58	35	220
141	05 25	58	36	06 23	58	35	07 21	59	35	08 20	58	35	09 18	58	35	10 16	58	34	11 14	59	34	219
142	05 12	58	35	06 10	58	35	07 08	59	34	08 07	58	34	09 05	59	34	10 04	58	34	11 02	58	33	218
143	04 59	59	34	05 58	58	34	06 56	58	33	07 54	59	33	08 53	58	33	09 51	59	33	10 50	58	32	217
144	04 47	58	33	05 45	59	33	06 44	58	32	07 42	59	32	08 41	58	32	09 39	59	32	10 38	58	32	216
145	04 35	+58	32	05 33	+59	32	06 32	+58	32	07 30	+59	31	08 29	+59	31	09 28	+58	31	10 26	+59	31	215
146	04 23	59	31	05 22	58	31	06 20	59	31	07 19	59	30	08 18	58	30	09 16	59	30	10 15	58	30	214
147	04 11	59	30	05 10	59	30	06 09	59	30	07 08	58	30	08 06	59	29	09 05	59	29	10 04	59	29	213
148	04 00	59	29	04 59	59	29	05 58	59	29	06 57	59	29	07 56	58	29	08 54	59	28	09 53	59	28	212
149	03 49	59	28	04 48	59	28	05 47	59	28	06 46	59	28	07 45	59	28	08 44	59	27	09 43	59	27	211
150	03 39	+59	27	04 38	+59	27	05 37	+59	27	06 36	+59	27	07 35	+59	27	08 34	+59	27	09 33	+58	26	210
151	03 29	59	27	04 28	59	26	05 27	59	26	06 26	59	26	07 25	59	26	08 24	59	26	09 23	59	26	209
152	03 19	59	26	04 18	59	25	05 17	59	25	06 16	59	25	07 15	59	25	08 14	59	25	09 13	59	25	208
153	03 09	59	25	04 08	60	25	05 08	59	24	06 07	59	24	07 06	59	24	08 05	59	24	09 04	59	24	207
154	03 00	59	24	03 59	59	24	04 58	60	24	05 58	59	23	06 57	59	23	07 56	59	23	08 55	59	23	206
155	02 51	+59	23	03 50	+60	23	04 50	+59	23	05 49	+59	22	06 48	+59	22	07 47	+60	22	08 47	+59	22	205
156	02 43	59	22	03 42	59	22	04 41	59	22	05 40	60	22	06 40	59	21	07 39	59	21	08 38	60	21	204
157	02 34	60	21	03 34	59	21	04 33	59	21	05 32	60	21	06 32	59	21	07 31	59	20	08 30	60	20	203
158	02 26	60	20	03 26	59	20	04 25	60	20	05 25	59	20	06 24	59	20	07 23	60	20	08 23	59	19	202
159	02 19	59	19	03 18	60	19	04 18	59	19	05 17	60	19	06 17	59	19	07 16	60	19	08 16	59	19	201
160	02 12	+59	18	03 11	+60	18	04 11	+59	18	05 10	+60	18	06 10	+59	18	07 09	+60	18	08 09	+59	18	200
161	02 05	59	17	03 04	60	17	04 04	59	17	05 03	60	17	06 03	59	17	07 02	60	17	08 02	59	17	199
162	01 58	60	17	02 58	59	16	03 57	60	16	04 57	59	16	05 56	60	16	06 56	60	16	07 56	59	16	198
163	01 52	59	16	02 51	60	16	03 51	60	15	04 51	59	15	05 50	60	15	06 50	60	15	07 50	59	15	197
164	01 46	60	15	02 46	59	15	03 45	60	15	04 45	60	14	05 45	59	14	06 44	60	14	07 44	60	14	196
165	01 40	+60	14	02 40	+60	14	03 40	+60	14	04 40	+59	14	05 39	+60	13	06 39	+60	13	07 39	+59	13	195
166	01 35	60	13	02 35	60	13	03 35	59	13	04 34	60	13	05 34	60	13	06 34	60	12	07 34	60	12	194
167	01 30	60	12	02 30	60	12	03 30	60	12	04 30	60	12	05 30	59	12	06 29	60	12	07 29	60	11	193
168	01 26	60	11	02 26	60	11	03 26	59	11	04 25	60	11	05 25	60	11	06 25	60	11	07 25	60	11	192
169	01 22	60	10	02 22	59	10	03 21	60	10	04 21	60	10	05 21	60	10	06 21	60	10	07 21	60	10	191
170	01 18	+60	9	02 18	+60	9	03 18	+60	9	04 18	+60	9	05 18	+59	9	06 17	+60	9	07 17	+60	9	190
171	01 15	59	8	02 14	60	8	03 14	60	8	04 14	60	8	05 14	60	8	06 14	60	8	07 14	60	8	189
172	01 12	59	7	02 11	60	7	03 11	60	7	04 11	60	7	05 11	60	7	06 11	60	7	07 11	60	7	188
173	01 09	60	6	02 09	60	6	03 09	60	6	04 09	60	6	05 09	60	6	06 09	60	6	07 09	59	6	187
174	01 06	60	6	02 06	60	5	03 06	60	5	04 06	60	5	05 06	60	5	06 06	60	5	07 06	60	5	186
175	01 05	+59	5	02 04	+60	5	03 04	+60	5	04 04	+60	5	05 04	+60	5	06 04	+60	4	07 04	+60	4	185
176	01 03	60	4	02 03	60	4	03 03	60	4	04 03	60	4	05 03	60	4	06 03	60	4	07 03	60	4	184
177	01 02	60	3	02 02	60	3	03 02	60	3	04 02	60	3	05 02	60	3	06 02	60	3	07 02	60	3	183
178	01 01	60	2	02 01	60	2	03 01	60	2	04 01	60	2	05 01	60	2	06 01	60	2	07 01	60	2	182
179	01 00	60	1	02 00	60	1	03 00	60	1	04 00	60	1	05 00	60	1	06 00	60	1	07 00	60	1	181
180	01 00	+60	0	02 00	+60	0	03 00	+60	0	04 00	+60	0	05 00	+60	0	06 00	+60	0	07 00	+60	0	180

S. Lat. {LHA greater than 180°....... Zn=180−Z; LHA less than 180°........... Zn=180+Z}

DECLINATION (15°-29°) SAME NAME AS LATITUDE

N. Lat. {LHA greater than 180°....... Zn=Z; LHA less than 180°........... Zn=360−Z}

DECLINATION (15°-29°) CONTRARY NAME TO LATITUDE

LHA	15° Hc d Z	16° Hc d Z	17° Hc d Z	18° Hc d Z	19° Hc d Z	20° Hc d Z	21° Hc d Z	22° Hc d Z	23° Hc d Z	24° Hc d Z	25° Hc d Z	26° Hc d Z	27° Hc d Z	28° Hc d Z	29° Hc d Z
°	° ′ ′ °	° ′ ′ °	° ′ ′ °	° ′ ′ °	° ′ ′ °	° ′ ′ °	° ′ ′ °	° ′ ′ °	° ′ ′ °	° ′ ′ °	° ′ ′ °	° ′ ′ °	° ′ ′ °	° ′ ′ °	° ′ ′ °
66	−5 20 56 118	294													
65	−5 00 −56 119	295													
64	−4 40 56 119	−5 36 57 120	296												
63	−4 20 57 120	−5 17 57 121	297												
62	−4 01 57 121	−4 58 56 122	298												
61	−3 42 57 122	−4 39 56 122	−5 35 57 123	299											
60	−3 23 −57 123	−4 20 −57 123	−5 17 −56 124	300											
59	−3 04 57 124	−4 01 57 124	−4 58 57 125	301											
58	−2 46 57 125	−3 43 57 125	−4 40 57 126	302											
57	−2 28 56 126	−3 24 57 126	−4 21 57 126	−5 18 57 127	303										
56	−2 09 57 127	−3 06 57 127	−4 03 58 127	−5 01 57 128	304										
55	−1 52 −57 128	−2 49 −57 128	−3 46 −57 128	−4 43 −57 129	305										
54	−1 34 57 129	−2 31 57 129	−3 28 57 129	−4 25 58 129	−5 23 57 130	306									
53	−1 16 58 129	−2 14 57 130	−3 11 57 130	−4 08 57 130	−5 05 58 131	307									
52	−0 59 57 130	−1 56 58 131	−2 54 57 131	−3 51 57 131	−4 48 58 132	308									
51	−0 42 58 131	−1 40 57 132	−2 37 57 132	−3 34 58 132	−4 32 57 133	−5 29 58 133	309								
50	−0 25 −58 132	−1 23 −57 133	−2 20 −58 133	−3 18 −57 133	−4 15 −58 133	−5 13 −57 134	310								
49	−0 09 57 133	−1 06 58 133	−2 04 58 134	−3 02 57 134	−3 59 58 134	−4 57 57 135	311								
48	00 07 57 134	−0 50 58 134	−1 48 57 135	−2 45 58 135	−3 43 58 135	−4 41 57 136	312								
47	00 23 57 135	−0 34 58 135	−1 32 58 136	−2 30 57 136	−3 27 58 136	−4 25 58 136	−5 23 58 137	313							
46	00 39 58 136	−0 19 57 136	−1 16 58 137	−2 14 58 137	−3 12 58 137	−4 10 58 137	−5 08 57 138	314							
45	00 55 −58 137	−0 03 −58 137	−1 01 −58 137	−1 59 −58 138	−2 57 −58 138	−3 55 −57 138	−4 52 −58 138	315							
44	01 10 58 138	00 12 58 138	−0 46 58 138	−1 44 58 139	−2 42 58 139	−3 40 58 139	−4 38 58 139	316							
43	01 25 58 139	00 27 58 139	−0 31 58 139	−1 29 58 140	−2 27 58 140	−3 25 58 140	−4 23 58 140	−5 21 58 141	317						
42	01 39 58 140	00 41 58 140	−0 17 58 140	−1 15 58 140	−2 13 58 141	−3 11 58 141	−4 09 58 141	−5 07 58 141	318						
41	01 54 58 141	00 56 58 141	−0 02 59 141	−1 01 58 141	−1 59 58 142	−2 57 58 142	−3 55 58 142	−4 53 58 142	319						
40	02 08 −58 142	01 10 −59 142	00 11 −58 142	−0 47 −58 142	−1 45 −58 143	−2 43 −58 143	−3 41 −59 143	−4 40 −58 143	320						
39	02 22 59 143	01 23 58 143	00 25 58 143	−0 33 58 143	−1 31 59 143	−2 30 58 144	−3 28 58 144	−4 26 59 144	−5 25 58 144	321					
38	02 35 58 143	01 37 58 144	00 39 59 144	−0 20 58 144	−1 18 59 144	−2 17 58 145	−3 15 58 145	−4 13 59 145	−5 12 58 145	322					
37	02 49 59 144	01 50 58 145	00 52 59 145	−0 07 58 145	−1 05 59 145	−2 04 58 146	−3 02 59 146	−4 01 58 146	−4 59 59 146	323					
36	03 01 58 145	02 03 59 146	01 04 58 146	00 06 59 146	−0 53 58 146	−1 51 59 146	−2 50 58 147	−3 48 59 147	−4 47 58 147	324					
35	03 14 −58 146	02 16 −59 147	01 17 −59 147	00 18 −58 147	−0 40 −59 147	−1 39 −58 147	−2 37 −59 148	−3 36 −59 148	−4 35 −58 148	325					
34	03 26 58 147	02 28 59 147	01 29 59 148	00 30 58 148	−0 28 59 148	−1 27 59 148	−2 26 58 148	−3 24 59 149	−4 23 59 149	−5 22 58 149	326				
33	03 38 58 148	02 40 59 148	01 41 59 149	00 42 59 149	−0 17 58 149	−1 15 59 149	−2 14 59 149	−3 13 58 150	−4 11 59 150	−5 10 59 150	327				
32	03 50 59 149	02 51 58 149	01 53 59 150	00 54 59 150	−0 05 59 150	−1 04 59 150	−2 03 59 150	−3 02 58 151	−4 00 59 151	−4 59 59 151	328				
31	04 01 58 150	03 03 59 150	02 04 59 150	01 05 59 151	00 06 59 151	−0 53 59 151	−1 52 59 151	−2 51 58 151	−3 49 59 152	−4 48 59 152	329				
30	04 13 −59 151	03 14 −59 151	02 15 −59 151	01 16 −59 152	00 17 −59 152	−0 42 −59 152	−1 41 −59 152	−2 40 −59 152	−3 39 −59 153	−4 38 −59 153	330				
29	04 23 59 152	03 24 59 152	02 25 59 152	01 26 59 153	00 27 59 153	−0 32 59 153	−1 31 59 153	−2 30 59 153	−3 29 59 153	−4 28 59 154	331				
28	04 34 59 153	03 35 59 153	02 36 60 153	01 36 59 153	00 37 59 154	−0 22 59 154	−1 21 59 154	−2 20 59 154	−3 19 59 154	−4 18 59 155	−5 17 59 155	332			
27	04 44 59 154	03 45 60 154	02 45 59 154	01 46 59 154	00 47 59 155	−0 12 59 155	−1 11 59 155	−2 10 59 155	−3 09 59 155	−4 08 60 155	−5 08 59 156	333			
26	04 53 59 155	03 54 59 155	02 55 59 155	01 56 59 155	00 57 59 156	−0 02 60 156	−1 02 59 156	−2 01 59 156	−3 00 59 156	−3 59 59 156	−4 58 60 156	334			
25	05 03 −59 156	04 04 −60 156	03 04 −59 156	02 05 −59 156	01 06 −59 156	00 07 −60 157	−0 53 −59 157	−1 52 −59 157	−2 51 −59 157	−3 50 −60 157	−4 50 −59 157	335			
24	05 12 59 157	04 13 60 157	03 13 59 157	02 14 59 157	01 15 60 157	00 15 59 158	−0 44 59 158	−1 43 60 158	−2 43 59 158	−3 42 59 158	−4 41 59 158	336			
23	05 21 60 158	04 21 59 158	03 22 60 158	02 22 59 158	01 23 59 158	00 24 60 158	−0 36 59 159	−1 35 59 159	−2 34 60 159	−3 34 59 159	−4 33 59 159	337			
22	05 29 60 159	04 29 59 159	03 30 59 159	02 31 60 159	01 31 59 159	00 32 60 159	−0 28 59 160	−1 27 59 160	−2 26 60 160	−3 26 59 160	−4 25 60 160	338			
21	05 37 60 160	04 37 59 160	03 38 59 160	02 39 60 160	01 39 59 160	00 40 60 160	−0 20 59 160	−1 19 60 161	−2 19 59 161	−3 18 60 161	−4 18 59 161	339			
20	05 45 −60 161	04 45 −59 161	03 46 −60 161	02 46 −59 161	01 47 −60 161	00 47 −60 161	−0 13 −59 161	−1 12 −60 162	−2 12 −59 162	−3 11 −60 162	−4 11 −59 162	−5 10 −60 162	340		
19	05 52 60 162	04 52 59 162	03 53 60 162	02 53 59 162	01 54 60 162	00 54 60 162	−0 06 59 162	−1 05 60 162	−2 05 59 163	−3 04 60 163	−4 04 59 163	−5 03 60 163	341		
18	05 59 60 163	04 59 59 163	04 00 60 163	03 00 60 163	02 00 59 163	01 01 60 163	00 01 59 163	−0 58 60 163	−1 58 59 164	−2 58 59 164	−3 57 60 164	−4 57 59 164	342		
17	06 05 59 164	05 06 60 164	04 06 60 164	03 06 59 164	02 07 60 164	01 07 60 164	00 07 59 164	−0 52 60 164	−1 52 59 164	−2 51 60 164	−3 51 60 165	−4 51 59 165	343		
16	06 12 60 165	05 12 60 165	04 12 60 165	03 12 59 165	02 13 60 165	01 13 60 165	00 13 59 165	−0 46 60 165	−1 46 59 165	−2 46 59 165	−3 45 60 165	−4 45 60 166	344		
15	06 17 −59 165	05 18 −60 166	04 18 −60 166	03 18 −60 166	02 18 −59 166	01 19 −60 166	00 19 −60 166	−0 41 −59 166	−1 40 −60 166	−2 40 −60 166	−3 40 −60 166	−4 40 −59 166	345		
14	06 23 60 166	05 23 60 167	04 23 59 167	03 24 60 167	02 24 60 167	01 24 60 167	00 24 59 167	−0 35 60 167	−1 35 60 167	−2 35 60 167	−3 35 59 167	−4 34 60 167	346		
13	06 28 60 167	05 28 60 168	04 28 59 168	03 29 60 168	02 29 60 168	01 29 60 168	00 29 60 168	−0 31 59 168	−1 30 60 168	−2 30 60 168	−3 30 60 168	−4 30 60 168	347		
12	06 33 60 168	05 33 60 168	04 33 60 169	03 33 60 169	02 33 59 169	01 34 60 169	00 34 60 169	−0 26 60 169	−1 26 60 169	−2 26 60 169	−3 26 59 169	−4 25 60 169	348		
11	06 37 60 169	05 37 60 169	04 37 60 169	03 37 59 170	02 38 60 170	01 38 60 170	00 38 60 170	−0 22 60 170	−1 22 60 170	−2 22 59 170	−3 21 60 170	−4 21 60 170	349		
10	06 41 −60 170	05 41 −60 170	04 41 −60 170	03 41 −60 170	02 41 −59 171	01 42 −60 171	00 42 −60 171	−0 18 −60 171	−1 18 −60 171	−2 18 −60 171	−3 18 −60 171	−4 18 −60 171	350		
9	06 45 60 171	05 45 60 171	04 45 60 171	03 45 60 171	02 45 60 171	01 45 60 172	00 45 60 172	−0 15 60 172	−1 15 59 172	−2 14 60 172	−3 14 60 172	−4 14 60 172	351		
8	06 48 60 172	05 48 60 172	04 48 60 172	03 48 60 172	02 48 60 172	01 48 60 172	00 48 60 173	−0 12 60 173	−1 12 59 173	−2 11 60 173	−3 11 60 173	−4 11 60 173	352		
7	06 51 60 173	05 51 60 173	04 51 60 173	03 51 60 173	02 51 60 173	01 51 60 173	00 51 60 173	−0 09 60 174	−1 09 60 174	−2 09 60 174	−3 09 60 174	−4 09 60 174	353		
6	06 53 60 174	05 53 60 174	04 53 60 174	03 53 60 174	02 53 60 174	01 53 60 174	00 53 60 174	−0 07 59 174	−1 06 60 174	−2 06 60 175	−3 06 60 175	−4 06 60 175	354		
5	06 55 −60 175	05 55 −60 175	04 55 −60 175	03 55 −60 175	02 55 −60 175	01 55 −60 175	00 55 −60 175	−0 05 −60 175	−1 05 −59 175	−2 04 −60 175	−3 04 −60 175	−4 04 −60 175	355		
4	06 57 60 176	05 57 60 176	04 57 60 176	03 57 60 176	02 57 60 176	01 57 60 176	00 57 60 176	−0 03 60 176	−1 03 60 176	−2 03 60 176	−3 03 60 176	−4 03 60 176	356		
3	06 58 60 177	05 58 60 177	04 58 60 177	03 58 60 177	02 58 60 177	01 58 60 177	00 58 60 177	−0 02 60 177	−1 02 60 177	−2 02 60 177	−3 02 60 177	−4 02 60 177	357		
2	06 59 60 178	05 59 60 178	04 59 60 178	03 59 60 178	02 59 60 178	01 59 60 178	00 59 60 178	−0 01 60 178	−1 01 60 178	−2 01 60 178	−3 01 60 178	−4 01 60 178	358		
1	07 00 60 179	06 00 60 179	05 00 60 179	04 00 60 179	03 00 60 179	02 00 60 179	01 00 60 179	00 00 60 179	−1 00 60 179	−2 00 60 179	−3 00 60 179	−4 00 60 179	−5 00 60 179	359	
0	07 00 −60 180	06 00 −60 180	05 00 −60 180	04 00 −60 180	03 00 −60 180	02 00 −60 180	01 00 −60 180	00 00 −60 180	−1 00 −60 180	−2 00 −60 180	−3 00 −60 180	−4 00 −60 180	−5 00 −60 180	360	
	15°	16°	17°	18°	19°	20°	21°	22°	23°	24°	25°	26°	27°	28°	29°

S. Lat. {LHA greater than 180°....... Zn=180−Z; LHA less than 180°........... Zn=180+Z}

DECLINATION (15°-29°) CONTRARY NAME TO LATITUDE

N. Lat. {LHA greater than 180°....... Zn=Z; LHA less than 180°........... Zn=360−Z}

DECLINATION (0°-14°) SAME NAME AS LATITUDE

LHA	0° Hc	d	Z	1° Hc	d	Z	2° Hc	d	Z	3° Hc	d	Z	4° Hc	d	Z
	° ′	′	°	° ′	′	°	° ′	′	°	° ′	′	°	° ′	′	°
0	21 00	+60	180	22 00	+60	180	23 00	+60	180	24 00	+60	180	25 00	+60	180
1	21 00	60	179	22 00	60	179	23 00	60	179	24 00	60	179	25 00	60	179
2	20 59	60	178	21 59	60	178	22 59	60	178	23 59	60	178	24 59	60	178
3	20 58	60	177	21 58	60	177	22 58	60	177	23 58	60	177	24 58	60	177
4	20 57	60	176	21 57	60	176	22 57	60	176	23 57	60	176	24 57	60	176
5	20 55	+60	175	21 55	+60	175	22 55	+60	175	23 55	+60	175	24 55	+60	175
6	20 53	60	174	21 53	60	174	22 53	60	174	23 53	60	173	24 53	60	173
7	20 50	60	173	21 50	60	173	22 50	60	172	23 50	60	172	24 50	60	172
8	20 47	60	171	21 47	60	171	22 47	60	171	23 47	60	171	24 47	60	171
9	20 44	60	170	21 44	60	170	22 44	59	170	23 43	60	170	24 43	60	170
10	20 40	+60	169	21 40	+60	169	22 40	+60	169	23 40	+59	169	24 39	+60	169
11	20 36	60	168	21 36	60	168	22 36	59	168	23 35	60	168	24 35	60	168
12	20 31	60	167	21 31	60	167	22 31	60	167	23 31	59	167	24 30	60	167
13	20 26	60	166	21 26	60	166	22 26	60	166	23 26	59	166	24 25	60	166
14	20 21	60	165	21 21	59	165	22 20	60	165	23 20	60	165	24 20	60	165
15	20 15	+60	164	21 15	+60	164	22 15	+59	164	23 14	+60	164	24 14	+60	164
16	20 09	60	163	21 09	59	163	22 08	60	163	23 08	60	163	24 08	59	163
17	20 03	59	162	21 02	60	162	22 02	59	162	23 01	60	162	24 01	60	161
18	19 56	59	161	20 55	60	161	21 55	59	161	22 54	60	160	23 54	60	160
19	19 48	60	160	20 48	59	160	21 47	60	160	22 47	60	159	23 47	59	159
20	19 41	+59	159	20 40	+60	159	21 40	+59	158	22 39	+60	158	23 39	+59	158
21	19 33	59	158	20 32	60	158	21 32	59	157	22 31	60	157	23 31	59	157
22	19 24	60	157	20 24	59	156	21 23	60	156	22 23	59	156	23 22	59	156
23	19 16	59	156	20 15	59	155	21 14	60	155	22 14	59	155	23 13	59	155
24	19 07	59	155	20 06	59	154	21 05	59	154	22 04	60	154	23 04	59	154
25	18 57	+59	154	19 56	+60	153	20 56	+59	153	21 55	+59	153	22 54	+59	153
26	18 47	60	152	19 47	59	152	20 46	59	152	21 45	59	152	22 44	59	152
27	18 37	59	151	19 36	60	151	20 36	59	151	21 35	59	151	22 34	59	151
28	18 27	59	150	19 26	59	150	20 25	59	150	21 24	59	150	22 23	59	150
29	18 16	59	149	19 15	59	149	20 14	59	149	21 13	59	149	22 12	59	149
30	18 05	+59	148	19 04	+59	148	20 03	+59	148	21 02	+58	148	22 00	+59	148
31	17 53	59	147	18 52	59	147	19 51	59	147	20 50	59	147	21 49	59	146
32	17 42	58	146	18 40	59	146	19 39	59	146	20 38	59	146	21 37	58	145
33	17 29	59	145	18 28	59	145	19 27	59	145	20 26	58	145	21 24	59	144
34	17 17	59	144	18 16	58	144	19 14	59	144	20 13	59	144	21 12	58	143
35	17 04	+59	143	18 03	+58	143	19 01	+59	143	20 00	+59	142	20 59	+58	142
36	16 51	59	142	17 50	58	142	18 48	59	142	19 47	58	141	20 45	59	141
37	16 38	58	141	17 36	59	141	18 35	58	141	19 33	59	140	20 32	58	140
38	16 24	59	140	17 23	58	140	18 21	58	140	19 19	59	139	20 18	58	139
39	16 10	59	139	17 09	58	139	18 07	58	139	19 05	58	138	20 03	59	138
40	15 56	+58	138	16 54	+59	138	17 53	+58	138	18 51	+58	137	19 49	+58	137
41	15 42	58	137	16 40	58	137	17 38	58	137	18 36	58	136	19 34	58	136
42	15 27	58	136	16 25	58	136	17 23	58	136	18 21	58	135	19 19	58	135
43	15 12	58	135	16 10	58	135	17 08	58	135	18 06	58	134	19 04	58	134
44	14 56	58	134	15 54	58	134	16 52	58	134	17 50	58	133	18 48	58	133
45	14 41	+58	133	15 39	+58	133	16 37	+57	133	17 34	+58	132	18 32	+58	132
46	14 25	58	132	15 23	58	132	16 21	57	132	17 18	58	131	18 16	58	131
47	14 09	58	131	15 07	57	131	16 04	58	131	17 02	58	130	18 00	57	130
48	13 53	57	130	14 50	58	130	15 48	58	130	16 46	57	129	17 43	58	129
49	13 36	58	129	14 34	57	129	15 31	58	129	16 29	57	128	17 26	58	128
50	13 19	+58	128	14 17	+57	128	15 14	+58	128	16 12	+57	127	17 09	+58	127
51	13 02	58	127	14 00	57	127	14 57	57	127	15 54	58	126	16 52	57	126
52	12 45	57	126	13 42	58	126	14 40	57	126	15 37	57	125	16 34	58	125
53	12 27	58	125	13 25	57	125	14 22	57	125	15 19	58	124	16 17	57	124
54	12 10	57	124	13 07	57	124	14 04	57	124	15 01	58	123	15 59	57	123
55	11 52	+57	123	12 49	+57	123	13 46	+57	123	14 43	+58	122	15 41	+57	122
56	11 34	57	122	12 31	57	122	13 28	57	122	14 25	57	121	15 22	57	121
57	11 15	57	121	12 12	58	121	13 10	57	121	14 07	57	120	15 04	57	120
58	10 57	57	120	11 54	57	120	12 51	57	120	13 48	57	119	14 45	57	119
59	10 38	57	119	11 35	57	119	12 32	57	119	13 29	57	118	14 26	57	118
60	10 19	+57	118	11 16	+57	118	12 13	+57	118	13 10	+57	117	14 07	+57	117
61	10 00	57	117	10 57	57	117	11 54	57	117	12 51	57	116	13 48	56	116
62	09 41	57	116	10 38	57	116	11 35	57	116	12 32	56	115	13 28	57	115
63	09 22	57	115	10 19	56	115	11 15	57	115	12 12	57	114	13 09	56	114
64	09 02	57	115	09 59	57	114	10 56	56	114	11 52	57	114	12 49	57	113
65	08 43	+56	114	09 39	+57	113	10 36	+57	113	11 33	+56	113	12 29	+57	112
66	08 23	57	113	09 20	56	112	10 16	57	112	11 13	56	112	12 09	57	111
67	08 03	57	112	09 00	56	111	09 56	57	111	10 53	56	111	11 49	57	110
68	07 43	56	111	08 39	57	110	09 36	56	110	10 32	57	110	11 29	56	109
69	07 23	56	110	08 19	57	109	09 16	56	109	10 12	57	109	11 09	56	108

LHA	5° Hc	d	Z	6° Hc	d	Z	7° Hc	d	Z	8° Hc	d	Z	9° Hc	d	Z
	° ′	′	°	° ′	′	°	° ′	′	°	° ′	′	°	° ′	′	°
0	26 00	+60	180	27 00	+60	180	28 00	+60	180	29 00	+60	180	30 00	+60	180
1	26 00	60	179	27 00	60	179	28 00	60	179	29 00	60	179	30 00	60	179
2	25 59	60	178	26 59	60	178	27 59	60	178	28 59	60	178	29 59	60	178
3	25 58	60	177	26 58	60	177	27 58	60	177	28 58	60	177	29 58	60	177
4	25 57	60	176	26 57	60	176	27 57	60	176	28 57	60	176	29 57	60	175
5	25 55	+60	175	26 55	+60	174	27 55	+60	174	28 55	+60	174	29 55	+60	174
6	25 53	60	173	26 53	59	173	27 52	60	173	28 52	60	173	29 52	60	173
7	25 50	60	172	26 50	60	172	27 50	60	172	28 50	60	172	29 50	60	172
8	25 47	60	171	26 47	60	171	27 47	59	171	28 46	60	171	29 46	60	171
9	25 43	60	170	26 43	60	170	27 43	60	170	28 43	60	170	29 43	60	170
10	25 39	+60	169	26 39	+60	169	27 39	+60	169	28 39	+60	169	29 39	+60	169
11	25 35	60	168	26 35	60	168	27 35	59	168	28 34	60	168	29 34	60	168
12	25 30	60	167	26 30	60	167	27 30	60	167	28 30	59	167	29 29	60	166
13	25 25	60	166	26 25	60	166	27 25	59	165	28 24	60	165	29 24	60	165
14	25 20	59	165	26 19	60	164	27 19	60	164	28 19	59	164	29 18	60	164
15	25 14	+59	163	26 13	+60	163	27 13	+60	163	28 13	+59	163	29 12	+60	163
16	25 07	60	162	26 07	60	162	27 07	59	162	28 06	60	162	29 06	59	162
17	25 01	59	161	26 00	60	161	27 00	59	161	27 59	60	161	28 59	60	161
18	24 54	59	160	25 53	60	160	26 53	59	160	27 52	60	160	28 52	59	160
19	24 46	60	159	25 46	59	159	26 45	60	159	27 45	59	159	28 44	59	159
20	24 38	+60	158	25 38	+59	158	26 37	+59	158	27 36	+60	158	28 36	+59	157
21	24 30	59	157	25 29	60	157	26 29	59	157	27 28	59	156	28 27	60	156
22	24 21	60	156	25 21	59	156	26 20	59	156	27 19	60	155	28 19	59	155
23	24 12	60	155	25 12	59	155	26 11	59	154	27 10	59	154	28 09	60	154
24	24 03	59	154	25 02	59	154	26 01	60	153	27 01	59	153	28 00	59	153
25	23 53	+59	153	24 52	+60	152	25 52	+59	152	26 51	+59	152	27 50	+59	152
26	23 43	59	152	24 42	59	151	25 41	59	151	26 40	59	151	27 39	60	151
27	23 33	59	150	24 32	59	150	25 31	59	150	26 30	59	150	27 29	59	150
28	23 22	59	149	24 21	59	149	25 20	59	149	26 19	59	149	27 18	59	149
29	23 11	59	148	24 10	59	148	25 09	58	148	26 07	59	148	27 06	59	148
30	22 59	+59	147	23 58	+59	147	24 57	+59	147	25 56	+59	147	26 55	+58	146
31	22 48	58	146	23 46	59	146	24 45	59	146	25 44	59	146	26 43	58	145
32	22 35	59	145	23 34	59	145	24 33	58	145	25 31	59	144	26 30	59	144
33	22 23	59	144	23 22	58	144	24 20	59	144	25 19	58	143	26 17	59	143
34	22 10	59	143	23 09	58	143	24 07	59	143	25 06	58	142	26 04	59	142
35	21 57	+59	142	22 56	+58	142	23 54	+59	142	24 53	+58	141	25 51	+58	141
36	21 44	58	141	22 42	59	141	23 41	58	140	24 39	58	140	25 37	59	140
37	21 30	58	140	22 28	59	140	23 27	58	139	24 25	58	139	25 23	59	139
38	21 16	58	139	22 14	59	139	23 13	58	138	24 11	58	138	25 09	58	138
39	21 02	58	138	22 00	58	138	22 58	58	137	23 56	58	137	24 54	58	137
40	20 47	+58	137	21 45	+58	137	22 43	+58	136	23 41	+58	136	24 39	+59	136
41	20 32	58	136	21 30	58	136	22 28	58	135	23 26	58	135	24 24	58	135
42	20 17	58	135	21 15	58	134	22 13	58	134	23 11	58	134	24 09	58	134
43	20 02	58	134	21 00	57	133	21 57	58	133	22 55	58	133	23 53	58	133
44	19 46	58	133	20 44	58	132	21 42	57	132	22 39	58	132	23 37	58	132
45	19 30	+58	132	20 28	+58	131	21 26	+57	131	22 23	+58	131	23 21	+58	131
46	19 14	58	131	20 12	57	130	21 09	58	130	22 07	58	130	23 05	57	129
47	18 57	58	130	19 55	58	129	20 53	57	129	21 50	58	129	22 48	57	128
48	18 41	57	129	19 38	58	128	20 36	57	128	21 33	58	128	22 31	57	127
49	18 24	57	128	19 21	58	127	20 19	57	127	21 16	58	127	22 14	57	126
50	18 07	+57	127	19 04	+57	126	20 01	+58	126	20 59	+57	126	21 56	+57	125
51	17 49	58	126	18 47	57	125	19 44	57	125	20 41	58	125	21 39	57	124
52	17 32	57	125	18 29	57	124	19 26	57	124	20 23	58	124	21 21	57	123
53	17 14	57	124	18 11	57	123	19 08	57	123	20 05	58	123	21 03	57	122
54	16 56	57	123	17 53	57	122	18 50	57	122	19 47	57	122	20 44	57	121
55	16 38	+57	122	17 35	+57	121	18 32	+57	121	19 29	+57	121	20 26	+57	120
56	16 19	57	121	17 16	57	120	18 13	57	120	19 10	57	120	20 07	57	119
57	16 01	57	120	16 58	57	119	17 55	56	119	18 51	57	119	19 48	57	118
58	15 42	57	119	16 39	57	118	17 36	57	118	18 33	56	118	19 29	57	117
59	15 23	57	118	16 20	57	117	17 17	56	117	18 13	57	117	19 10	57	116
60	15 04	+57	117	16 01	+56	116	16 57	+57	116	17 54	+57	116	18 51	+56	115
61	14 44	57	116	15 41	57	115	16 38	57	115	17 35	56	115	18 31	57	114
62	14 25	57	115	15 22	56	114	16 18	57	114	17 15	57	114	18 12	56	113
63	14 05	57	114	15 02	57	113	15 59	56	113	16 55	57	113	17 52	56	112
64	13 46	56	113	14 42	57	113	15 39	56	112	16 35	57	112	17 32	56	111
65	13 26	+56	112	14 22	+57	112	15 19	+56	111	16 15	+57	111	17 12	+56	110
66	13 06	56	111	14 02	57	111	14 59	56	110	15 55	57	110	16 52	56	110
67	12 46	56	110	13 42	56	110	14 38	57	109	15 35	56	109	16 31	57	109
68	12 25	57	109	13 22	56	109	14 18	56	108	15 14	57	108	16 11	56	108
69	12 05	56	108	13 01	57	108	13 58	56	107	14 54	56	107	15 50	56	107

LHA	10° Hc	d	Z	11° Hc	d	Z	12° Hc	d	Z	13° Hc	d	Z	14° Hc	d	Z	LHA
	° ′	′	°	° ′	′	°	° ′	′	°	° ′	′	°	° ′	′	°	
0	31 00	+60	180	32 00	+60	180	33 00	+60	180	34 00	+60	180	35 00	+60	180	360
1	31 00	60	179	32 00	60	179	33 00	60	179	34 00	60	179	35 00	60	179	359
2	30 59	60	178	31 59	60	178	32 59	60	178	33 59	60	178	34 59	60	178	358
3	30 58	60	177	31 58	60	177	32 58	60	177	33 58	60	177	34 58	60	176	357
4	30 57	60	175	31 57	60	175	32 57	60	175	33 57	59	175	34 56	60	175	356
5	30 55	+60	174	31 55	+60	174	32 55	+60	174	33 55	+60	174	34 55	+59	174	355
6	30 52	60	173	31 52	60	173	32 52	60	173	33 52	60	173	34 52	60	173	354
7	30 50	59	172	31 49	60	172	32 49	60	172	33 49	60	172	34 49	60	172	353
8	30 46	60	171	31 46	60	171	32 46	60	171	33 46	60	171	34 46	60	171	352
9	30 43	60	170	31 43	59	170	32 42	60	170	33 42	60	169	34 42	60	169	351
10	30 39	+59	169	31 38	+60	169	32 38	+60	168	33 38	+60	168	34 38	+60	168	350
11	30 34	60	167	31 34	60	167	32 34	60	167	33 34	59	167	34 33	60	167	349
12	30 29	60	166	31 29	60	166	32 29	60	166	33 29	59	166	34 28	60	166	348
13	30 24	60	165	31 24	59	165	32 23	60	165	33 23	60	165	34 23	59	165	347
14	30 18	60	164	31 18	60	164	32 18	59	164	33 17	60	164	34 17	60	164	346
15	30 12	+60	163	31 12	+59	163	32 11	+60	163	33 11	+60	163	34 11	+59	162	345
16	30 05	60	162	31 05	60	162	32 05	59	161	33 04	60	161	34 04	59	161	344
17	29 59	59	161	30 58	60	160	31 58	59	160	32 57	60	160	33 57	59	160	343
18	29 51	60	160	30 51	59	159	31 50	60	159	32 50	59	159	33 49	60	159	342
19	29 43	60	158	30 43	59	158	31 42	60	158	32 42	59	158	33 41	60	158	341
20	29 35	+60	157	30 35	+59	157	31 34	+59	157	32 33	+60	157	33 33	+59	157	340
21	29 27	59	156	30 26	59	156	31 25	60	156	32 25	59	156	33 24	59	155	339
22	29 18	59	155	30 17	59	155	31 16	60	155	32 16	59	154	33 15	59	154	338
23	29 09	59	154	30 08	59	154	31 07	59	154	32 06	59	153	33 05	60	153	337
24	28 59	59	153	29 58	59	153	30 57	59	152	31 56	59	152	32 55	60	152	336
25	28 49	+59	152	29 48	+59	151	30 47	+59	151	31 46	+59	151	32 45	+59	151	335
26	28 39	59	151	29 38	59	150	30 37	59	150	31 36	58	150	32 34	59	150	334
27	28 28	59	149	29 27	59	149	30 26	59	149	31 25	58	149	32 23	59	149	333
28	28 17	59	148	29 16	58	148	30 14	59	148	31 13	59	148	32 12	59	147	332
29	28 05	59	147	29 04	59	147	30 03	59	147	31 02	58	147	32 00	59	146	331
30	27 53	+59	146	28 52	+59	146	29 51	+59	146	30 50	+58	145	31 48	+59	145	330
31	27 41	59	145	28 40	59	145	29 39	58	145	30 37	59	144	31 36	58	144	329
32	27 29	58	144	28 27	59	144	29 26	58	144	30 24	59	143	31 23	58	143	328
33	27 16	58	143	28 14	59	143	29 13	58	142	30 11	59	142	31 10	58	142	327
34	27 03	58	142	28 01	59	142	29 00	58	141	29 58	58	141	30 56	59	141	326
35	26 49	+59	141	27 48	+58	141	28 46	+58	140	29 44	+59	140	30 43	+58	140	325
36	26 36	58	140	27 34	58	139	28 32	58	139	29 30	59	139	30 29	58	139	324
37	26 22	58	139	27 20	58	138	28 18	58	138	29 16	58	138	30 14	58	138	323
38	26 07	58	138	27 05	58	137	28 03	58	137	29 01	59	137	30 00	58	136	322
39	25 52	59	137	26 51	58	136	27 49	58	136	28 47	58	136	29 45	57	135	321
40	25 38	+58	135	26 36	+57	135	27 33	+58	135	28 31	+58	135	29 29	+58	134	320
41	25 22	58	134	26 20	58	134	27 18	58	134	28 16	58	134	29 14	57	133	319
42	25 07	58	133	26 05	57	133	27 02	58	133	28 00	58	132	28 58	58	132	318
43	24 51	58	132	25 49	57	132	26 46	58	132	27 44	58	131	28 42	57	131	317
44	24 35	58	131	25 33	57	131	26 30	58	131	27 28	57	130	28 25	58	130	316
45	24 19	+57	130	25 16	+58	130	26 14	+57	130	27 11	+58	129	28 09	+57	129	315
46	24 02	58	129	25 00	57	129	25 57	58	129	26 55	57	128	27 52	57	128	314
47	23 45	58	128	24 43	57	128	25 40	58	128	26 38	57	127	27 35	57	127	313
48	23 28	58	127	24 26	57	127	25 23	57	126	26 20	58	126	27 18	57	126	312
49	23 11	57	126	24 08	58	126	25 06	57	125	26 03	57	125	27 00	57	125	311
50	22 53	+58	125	23 51	+57	125	24 48	+57	124	25 45	+57	124	26 42	+57	124	310
51	22 36	57	124	23 33	57	124	24 30	57	123	25 27	57	123	26 24	57	123	309
52	22 18	57	123	23 15	57	123	24 12	57	122	25 09	57	122	26 06	57	122	308
53	22 00	57	122	22 57	57	122	23 54	57	121	24 51	57	121	25 48	56	121	307
54	21 41	57	121	22 38	57	121	23 35	57	120	24 32	57	120	25 29	57	120	306
55	21 23	+57	120	22 20	+57	120	23 17	+56	119	24 13	+57	119	25 10	+57	119	305
56	21 04	57	119	22 01	57	119	22 58	57	118	23 55	56	118	24 51	57	118	304
57	20 45	57	118	21 42	57	118	22 39	56	117	23 35	57	117	24 32	57	117	303
58	20 26	57	117	21 23	57	117	22 20	56	116	23 16	57	116	24 13	56	116	302
59	20 07	57	116	21 04	56	116	22 00	57	115	22 57	56	115	23 53	57	115	301
60	19 47	+57	115	20 44	+57	115	21 41	+56	114	22 37	+57	114	23 34	+56	114	300
61	19 28	56	114	20 24	57	114	21 21	56	113	22 17	57	113	23 14	56	113	299
62	19 08	57	113	20 05	56	113	21 01	57	112	21 58	56	112	22 54	56	112	298
63	18 48	57	112	19 45	56	112	20 41	57	111	21 38	56	111	22 34	56	111	297
64	18 28	57	111	19 25	56	111	20 21	56	110	21 17	57	110	22 14	56	110	296
65	18 08	+57	110	19 05	+56	110	20 01	+56	109	20 57	+56	109	21 53	+57	109	295
66	17 48	56	109	18 44	57	109	19 41	56	108	20 37	56	108	21 33	56	108	294
67	17 28	56	108	18 24	56	108	19 20	56	107	20 16	56	107	21 12	56	107	293
68	17 07	56	107	18 03	56	107	18 59	57	106	19 56	56	106	20 52	56	106	292
69	16 46	57	106	17 43	56	106	18 39	56	106	19 35	56	105	20 31	56	105	291

S. Lat. {LHA greater than 180°....... Zn=180−Z; LHA less than 180°........... Zn=180+Z}

DECLINATION (0°-14°) SAME NAME AS LATITUDE

LAT 69°

N. Lat. {LHA greater than 180°........ Zn=Z; LHA less than 180°........... Zn=360−Z}

DECLINATION (0°-14°) SAME NAME AS LATITUDE

LHA	0°			1°			2°			3°			4°		
	Hc	d	Z	Hc	d	Z	Hc	d	Z	Hc	d	Z	Hc	d	Z
	° ′	′	°	° ′	′	°	° ′	′	°	° ′	′	°	° ′	′	°
70	07 02	+57	109	07 59	+56	108	08 55	+57	108	09 52	+56	108	10 48	+56	107
71	06 42	56	108	07 38	57	108	08 35	56	107	09 31	57	107	10 28	56	106
72	06 22	56	107	07 18	56	107	08 14	57	106	09 11	56	106	10 07	56	106
73	06 01	56	106	06 57	57	106	07 54	56	105	08 50	56	105	09 46	56	105
74	05 40	56	105	06 36	57	105	07 33	56	104	08 29	56	104	09 25	56	104
75	05 19	+57	104	06 16	+56	104	07 12	+56	103	08 08	+56	103	09 04	+56	103
76	04 58	57	103	05 55	56	103	06 51	56	102	07 47	56	102	08 43	56	102
77	04 37	57	102	05 34	56	102	06 30	56	102	07 26	56	101	08 22	56	101
78	04 16	57	101	05 13	56	101	06 09	56	101	07 05	56	100	08 01	56	100
79	03 55	56	100	04 51	57	100	05 48	56	100	06 44	56	99	07 40	56	99
80	03 34	+56	99	04 30	+56	99	05 26	+56	99	06 22	+57	98	07 19	+56	98
81	03 13	56	98	04 09	56	98	05 05	56	98	06 01	56	97	06 57	56	97
82	02 52	56	97	03 48	56	97	04 44	56	97	05 40	56	96	06 36	56	96
83	02 30	56	97	03 26	56	96	04 22	56	96	05 18	56	96	06 14	56	95
84	02 09	56	96	03 05	56	95	04 01	56	95	04 57	56	95	05 53	56	94
85	01 47	+56	95	02 43	+56	94	03 39	+56	94	04 35	+57	94	05 32	+56	93
86	01 26	56	94	02 22	56	93	03 18	56	93	04 14	56	93	05 10	56	92
87	01 04	57	93	02 01	56	92	02 57	56	92	03 53	56	92	04 49	56	91
88	00 43	56	92	01 39	56	92	02 35	56	91	03 31	56	91	04 27	56	90
89	00 22	56	91	01 18	56	91	02 14	56	90	03 10	56	90	04 06	56	89
90	00 00	+56	90	00 56	+56	90	01 52	+56	89	02 48	+56	89	03 44	+56	89
91	-0 22	57	89	00 35	56	89	01 31	56	88	02 27	56	88	03 23	56	88
92	-0 43	56	88	00 13	56	88	01 09	56	87	02 05	56	87	03 01	56	87
93	-1 04	56	87	-0 08	56	87	00 48	56	86	01 44	56	86	02 40	56	86
94	-1 26	56	86	-0 30	56	86	00 26	56	86	01 22	56	85	02 18	56	85
95	-1 47	+56	85	-0 51	+56	85	00 05	+56	85	01 01	+56	84	01 57	+56	84
96	-2 09	56	84	-1 13	56	84	-0 17	56	84	00 39	56	83	01 35	56	83
97	-2 30	56	83	-1 34	56	83	-0 38	56	83	00 18	56	82	01 14	56	82
98	-2 52	57	83	-1 55	56	82	-0 59	56	82	-0 03	56	81	00 53	56	81
99	-3 13	56	82	-2 17	56	81	-1 21	57	81	-0 24	56	81	00 32	56	80
100	-3 34	+56	81	-2 38	+56	80	-1 42	+56	80	-0 46	+56	80	00 10	+57	79
101	-3 55	56	80	-2 59	56	79	-2 03	56	79	-1 07	56	79	-0 11	57	78
102	-4 16	56	79	-3 20	56	78	-2 24	56	78	-1 28	56	78	-0 32	57	77
103	-4 37	56	78	-3 41	56	77	-2 45	56	77	-1 49	56	77	-0 53	57	76
104	-4 58	56	77	-4 02	56	77	-3 06	56	76	-2 10	57	76	-1 13	56	75
105	-5 19	+56	76	-4 23	+56	76	-3 27	+56	75	-2 31	+57	75	-1 34	+56	75
106	-5 40	56	75	-4 44	56	75	-3 48	57	74	-2 51	56	74	-1 55	56	74
107				-5 05	57	74	-4 08	56	73	-3 12	57	73	-2 15	56	73
108				-5 25	56	73	-4 29	57	72	-3 32	56	72	-2 36	56	72
109							-4 49	56	71	-3 53	57	71	-2 56	56	71
110							-5 10	+57	71	-4 13	+56	70	-3 17	+57	70
111							-5 30	57	70	-4 33	56	69	-3 37	57	69
112										-4 53	56	68	-3 57	57	68
113										-5 13	56	67	-4 17	57	67
114										-5 33	57	66	-4 36	56	66
115													-4 56	+57	65
116													-5 15	56	64
117													-5 35	57	63

LHA	5°			6°			7°			8°			9°		
	Hc	d	Z	Hc	d	Z	Hc	d	Z	Hc	d	Z	Hc	d	Z
	° ′	′	°	° ′	′	°	° ′	′	°	° ′	′	°	° ′	′	°
70	11 44	+57	107	12 41	+56	107	13 37	+56	106	14 33	+57	106	15 30	+56	106
71	11 24	56	106	12 20	56	106	13 16	57	105	14 13	56	105	15 09	56	105
72	11 03	56	105	11 59	57	105	12 56	56	104	13 52	56	104	14 48	56	104
73	10 42	57	104	11 39	56	104	12 35	56	104	13 31	56	103	14 27	56	103
74	10 21	57	103	11 18	56	103	12 14	56	103	13 10	56	102	14 06	56	102
75	10 00	+57	102	10 57	+56	102	11 53	+56	102	12 49	+56	101	13 45	+56	101
76	09 39	57	101	10 36	56	101	11 32	56	101	12 28	56	100	13 24	56	100
77	09 18	56	100	10 14	56	100	11 10	57	100	12 07	56	99	13 03	56	99
78	08 57	56	99	09 53	56	99	10 49	56	99	11 45	56	98	12 41	56	98
79	08 36	56	99	09 32	56	98	10 28	56	98	11 24	56	97	12 20	56	97
80	08 15	+56	98	09 11	+56	97	10 07	+56	97	11 03	+56	97	11 59	+56	96
81	07 53	56	97	08 49	56	96	09 45	56	96	10 41	56	96	11 37	56	95
82	07 32	56	96	08 28	56	95	09 24	56	95	10 20	56	95	11 16	56	94
83	07 10	56	95	08 06	56	94	09 02	56	94	09 58	56	94	10 54	56	93
84	06 49	56	94	07 45	56	93	08 41	56	93	09 37	56	93	10 33	56	92
85	06 28	+56	93	07 24	+56	93	08 20	+55	92	09 15	+56	92	10 11	+56	91
86	06 06	56	92	07 02	56	92	07 58	56	91	08 54	56	91	09 50	56	91
87	05 45	56	91	06 41	56	91	07 37	55	90	08 32	56	90	09 28	56	90
88	05 23	56	90	06 19	56	90	07 15	56	89	08 11	56	89	09 07	56	89
89	05 02	56	89	05 58	56	89	06 54	55	88	07 49	56	88	08 45	56	88
90	04 40	+56	88	05 36	+56	88	06 32	+56	88	07 28	+56	87	08 24	+56	87
91	04 19	56	87	05 15	56	87	06 11	56	87	07 07	55	86	08 02	56	86
92	03 57	56	86	04 53	56	86	05 49	56	86	06 45	56	85	07 41	56	85
93	03 36	56	85	04 32	56	85	05 28	56	85	06 24	56	84	07 20	56	84
94	03 14	56	84	04 10	56	84	05 06	56	84	06 02	56	83	06 58	56	83
95	02 53	+56	84	03 49	+56	83	04 45	+56	83	05 41	+56	82	06 37	+56	82
96	02 31	57	83	03 28	56	82	04 24	56	82	05 20	56	82	06 16	56	81
97	02 10	56	82	03 06	56	81	04 02	56	81	04 58	56	81	05 54	56	80
98	01 49	56	81	02 45	56	80	03 41	56	80	04 37	56	80	05 33	56	79
99	01 28	56	80	02 24	56	79	03 20	56	79	04 16	56	79	05 12	56	78
100	01 07	+56	79	02 03	+56	79	02 59	+56	78	03 55	+56	78	04 51	+56	77
101	00 46	56	78	01 42	56	78	02 38	56	77	03 34	56	77	04 30	56	77
102	00 25	56	77	01 21	56	77	02 17	56	76	03 13	56	76	04 09	57	76
103	00 04	56	76	01 00	56	76	01 56	56	75	02 52	57	75	03 49	56	75
104	-0 17	56	75	00 39	56	75	01 35	57	74	02 32	56	74	03 28	56	74
105	-0 38	+56	74	00 18	+57	74	01 15	+56	74	02 11	+56	73	03 07	+56	73
106	-0 59	57	73	-0 02	56	73	00 54	56	73	01 50	57	72	02 47	56	72
107	-1 19	56	72	-0 23	57	72	00 34	56	72	01 30	56	71	02 26	57	71
108	-1 40	57	71	-0 43	56	71	00 13	57	71	01 10	56	70	02 06	56	70
109	-2 00	57	70	-1 03	56	70	-0 07	56	70	00 49	57	69	01 46	56	69
110	-2 20	+56	70	-1 24	+57	69	-0 27	+56	69	00 29	+57	69	01 26	+56	68
111	-2 40	56	69	-1 44	57	68	-0 47	56	68	00 09	57	68	01 06	57	67
112	-3 00	56	68	-2 04	57	67	-1 07	57	67	-0 10	56	67	00 46	57	66
113	-3 20	57	67	-2 23	56	66	-1 27	57	66	-0 30	57	66	00 27	56	65
114	-3 40	57	66	-2 43	57	65	-1 46	56	65	-0 50	57	65	00 07	57	64
115	-3 59	+57	65	-3 02	+56	64	-2 06	+57	64	-1 09	+57	64	-0 12	+57	64
116	-4 19	57	64	-3 22	57	64	-2 25	57	63	-1 28	57	63	-0 31	56	63
117	-4 38	57	63	-3 41	57	63	-2 44	57	62	-1 47	57	62	-0 50	56	62
118	-4 57	57	62	-4 00	57	62	-3 03	57	61	-2 06	57	61	-1 09	57	61
119	-5 16	57	61	-4 19	57	61	-3 22	57	60	-2 25	57	60	-1 28	57	60
120	-5 35	+58	60	-4 37	+57	60	-3 40	+57	59	-2 43	+57	59	-1 46	+57	59
121				-4 56	57	59	-3 59	57	59	-3 02	57	58	-2 05	57	58
122				-5 14	57	58	-4 17	57	58	-3 20	57	57	-2 23	57	57
123				-5 32	57	57	-4 35	57	57	-3 38	57	56	-2 41	58	56
124							-4 53	57	56	-3 56	58	55	-2 58	57	55
125							-5 11	+58	55	-4 13	+57	54	-3 16	+57	54
126							-5 28	57	54	-4 31	58	53	-3 33	57	53
127										-4 48	58	53	-3 50	57	52
128										-5 05	58	52	-4 07	57	51
129										-5 22	58	51	-4 24	58	50
130													-4 40	+57	49
131													-4 57	58	48
132													-5 13	58	47
133													-5 28	58	46

LHA	10°			11°			12°			13°			14°			LHA
	Hc	d	Z	Hc	d	Z	Hc	d	Z	Hc	d	Z	Hc	d	Z	
	° ′	′	°	° ′	′	°	° ′	′	°	° ′	′	°	° ′	′	°	
70	16 26	+56	105	17 22	+56	105	18 18	+56	105	19 14	+56	104	20 10	+56	104	290
71	16 05	56	104	17 01	56	104	17 57	56	104	18 53	56	103	19 49	56	103	289
72	15 44	56	103	16 40	56	103	17 36	56	103	18 32	56	102	19 28	56	102	288
73	15 23	56	102	16 19	56	102	17 15	56	102	18 11	56	101	19 07	56	101	287
74	15 02	56	101	15 58	56	101	16 54	56	101	17 50	56	100	18 46	56	100	286
75	14 41	+56	101	15 37	+56	100	16 33	+56	100	17 29	+56	99	18 25	+56	99	285
76	14 20	56	100	15 16	56	99	16 12	56	99	17 08	56	98	18 04	55	98	284
77	13 59	56	99	14 55	55	98	15 50	56	98	16 46	56	97	17 42	56	97	283
78	13 37	56	98	14 33	56	97	15 29	56	97	16 25	56	97	17 21	56	96	282
79	13 16	56	97	14 12	56	96	15 08	56	96	16 04	55	96	16 59	56	95	281
80	12 55	+55	96	13 50	+56	95	14 46	+56	95	15 42	+56	95	16 38	+56	94	280
81	12 33	56	95	13 29	56	94	14 25	56	94	15 21	56	94	16 17	55	93	279
82	12 12	56	94	13 08	55	94	14 03	56	93	14 59	56	93	15 55	56	92	278
83	11 50	56	93	12 46	56	93	13 42	56	92	14 38	56	92	15 34	55	91	277
84	11 29	56	92	12 25	56	92	13 21	55	91	14 16	56	91	15 12	56	91	276
85	11 07	+56	91	12 03	+56	91	12 59	+56	90	13 55	+56	90	14 51	+55	90	275
86	10 46	56	90	11 42	55	90	12 37	56	89	13 33	56	89	14 29	56	89	274
87	10 24	56	89	11 20	56	89	12 16	56	88	13 12	56	88	14 08	55	88	273
88	10 03	56	88	10 59	56	88	11 55	55	88	12 50	56	87	13 46	56	87	272
89	09 41	56	87	10 37	56	87	11 33	56	87	12 29	56	86	13 25	55	86	271
90	09 20	+56	86	10 16	+56	86	11 12	+55	86	12 07	+56	85	13 03	+56	85	270
91	08 58	56	86	09 54	56	85	10 50	56	85	11 46	56	84	12 42	56	84	269
92	08 37	56	85	09 33	56	84	10 29	56	84	11 25	55	83	12 20	56	83	268
93	08 16	56	84	09 12	55	83	10 07	56	83	11 03	56	83	11 59	56	82	267
94	07 54	56	83	08 50	56	82	09 46	56	82	10 42	56	82	11 38	56	81	266
95	07 33	+56	82	08 29	+56	81	09 25	+56	81	10 21	+56	81	11 17	+56	80	265
96	07 12	56	81	08 08	56	81	09 04	56	80	10 00	55	80	10 55	56	79	264
97	06 50	56	80	07 46	56	80	08 42	56	79	09 38	56	79	10 34	56	78	263
98	06 29	56	79	07 25	56	79	08 21	56	78	09 17	56	78	10 13	56	78	262
99	06 08	56	78	07 04	56	78	08 00	56	77	08 56	56	77	09 52	56	77	261
100	05 47	+56	77	06 43	+56	77	07 39	+56	76	08 35	+57	76	09 32	+56	76	260
101	05 26	56	76	06 22	57	76	07 19	56	76	08 15	56	75	09 11	56	75	259
102	05 06	56	75	06 02	56	75	06 58	56	75	07 54	56	74	08 50	56	74	258
103	04 45	56	74	05 41	56	74	06 37	56	74	07 33	56	73	08 29	57	73	257
104	04 24	56	73	05 20	57	73	06 17	56	73	07 13	56	72	08 09	56	72	256
105	04 03	+57	72	05 00	+56	72	05 56	+56	72	06 52	+57	71	07 49	+56	71	255
106	03 43	56	72	04 39	57	71	05 36	56	71	06 32	56	71	07 28	57	70	254
107	03 23	56	71	04 19	56	70	05 15	57	70	06 12	56	70	07 08	56	69	253
108	03 02	57	70	03 59	56	69	04 55	57	69	05 52	56	69	06 48	56	68	252
109	02 42	57	69	03 39	56	68	04 35	57	68	05 32	56	68	06 28	57	67	251
110	02 22	+57	68	03 19	+56	68	04 15	+57	67	05 12	+56	67	06 08	+57	67	250
111	02 03	56	67	02 59	57	67	03 56	56	66	04 52	57	66	05 49	56	66	249
112	01 43	56	66	02 39	57	66	03 36	57	65	04 33	56	65	05 29	57	65	248
113	01 23	57	65	02 20	57	65	03 17	56	64	04 13	57	64	05 10	56	64	247
114	01 04	57	64	02 01	56	64	02 57	57	63	03 54	57	63	04 51	56	63	246
115	00 45	+56	63	01 41	+57	63	02 38	+57	63	03 35	+57	62	04 32	+56	62	245
116	00 25	57	62	01 22	57	62	02 19	57	62	03 16	57	61	04 13	56	61	244
117	00 06	57	61	01 03	57	61	02 00	57	61	02 57	57	60	03 54	57	60	243
118	-0 12	57	60	00 45	57	60	01 42	56	60	02 38	57	59	03 35	57	59	242
119	-0 31	57	59	00 26	57	59	01 23	57	59	02 20	57	59	03 17	57	58	241
120	-0 49	+57	59	00 08	+57	58	01 05	+57	58	02 02	+57	58	02 59	+57	57	240
121	-1 08	58	58	-0 10	57	57	00 47	57	57	01 44	57	57	02 41	57	56	239
122	-1 26	58	57	-0 28	57	56	00 29	57	56	01 26	57	56	02 23	57	55	238
123	-1 43	57	56	-0 46	57	55	00 11	57	55	01 08	57	55	02 05	58	55	237
124	-2 01	57	55	-1 04	57	54	-0 07	58	54	00 51	57	54	01 48	57	54	236
125	-2 19	+58	54	-1 21	+57	54	-0 24	+57	53	00 33	+58	53	01 31	+57	53	235
126	-2 36	58	53	-1 38	57	53	-0 41	57	52	00 16	58	52	01 14	57	52	234
127	-2 53	58	52	-1 55	57	52	-0 58	58	51	00 00	57	51	00 57	58	51	233
128	-3 10	58	51	-2 12	57	51	-1 15	58	50	-0 17	57	50	00 40	58	50	232
129	-3 26	57	50	-2 29	58	50	-1 31	58	49	-0 33	57	49	00 24	58	49	231
130	-3 43	+58	49	-2 45	+58	49	-1 47	+57	49	-0 50	+58	48	00 08	+58	48	230
131	-3 59	58	48	-3 01	58	48	-2 03	57	48	-1 06	58	47	-0 08	58	47	229
132	-4 15	58	47	-3 17	58	47	-2 19	58	47	-1 21	58	46	-0 23	58	46	228
133	-4 30	57	46	-3 33	58	46	-2 35	58	46	-1 37	58	45	-0 39	58	45	227
134	-4 46	58	45	-3 48	58	45	-2 50	58	45	-1 52	58	45	-0 54	58	44	226
135	-5 01	+58	44	-4 03	+58	44	-3 05	+58	44	-2 07	+58	44	-1 09	+58	43	225
136	-5 16	58	43	-4 18	58	43	-3 20	58	43	-2 22	59	43	-1 23	58	42	224
137				-4 32	58	42	-3 34	58	42	-2 36	58	42	-1 38	58	41	223
138				-4 47	59	41	-3 48	58	41	-2 50	58	41	-1 52	58	41	222
139				-5 01	59	40	-4 02	58	40	-3 04	58	40	-2 06	59	40	221

0°	1°	2°	3°	4°	5°	6°	7°	8°	9°	10°	11°	12°	13°	14°

S. Lat. {LHA greater than 180°........ Zn=180−Z; LHA less than 180°........... Zn=180+Z}

DECLINATION (0°-14°) SAME NAME AS LATITUDE

N. Lat. {LHA greater than 180°....... Zn=Z / LHA less than 180°........... Zn=360−Z}

DECLINATION (0°-14°) SAME NAME AS LATITUDE

LHA	11° Hc	d	Z	12° Hc	d	Z	13° Hc	d	Z	14° Hc	d	Z	LHA
	° ′	′	°	° ′	′	°	° ′	′	°	° ′	′	°	
140	-5 15	+59	39	-4 16	+58	39	-3 18	+59	39	-2 19	+58	39	220
141				-4 30	59	38	-3 31	58	38	-2 33	59	38	219
142				-4 43	59	37	-3 44	58	37	-2 46	59	37	218
143				-4 55	58	36	-3 57	59	36	-2 58	58	36	217
144				-5 08	59	35	-4 09	58	35	-3 11	59	35	216
145				-5 20	+58	34	-4 22	+59	34	-3 23	+59	34	215
146							-4 34	59	33	-3 35	59	33	214
147							-4 45	59	32	-3 46	59	32	213
148							-4 56	58	31	-3 58	59	31	212
149							-5 07	59	30	-4 08	59	30	211
150							-5 18	+59	29	-4 19	+59	29	210
151										-4 29	59	28	209
152										-4 39	59	27	208
153										-4 49	59	26	207
154										-4 58	59	25	206
155										-5 07	+59	24	205
156										-5 16	59	23	204

LHA	0° Hc	d	Z	1° Hc	d	Z	2° Hc	d	Z	3° Hc	d	Z	4° Hc	d	Z	5° Hc	d	Z	6° Hc	d	Z	7° Hc	d	Z
106	-5 40	56	75	254																				
105	-5 19	-57	76	255																				
104	-4 58	57	77	256																				
103	-4 37	57	78	-5 34	56	78	257																	
102	-4 16	57	79	-5 13	56	79	258																	
101	-3 55	56	80	-4 51	57	80	259																	
100	-3 34	-56	81	-4 30	-56	81	-5 26	-56	81	260														
99	-3 13	56	82	-4 09	56	82	-5 05	56	82	261														
98	-2 52	56	83	-3 48	56	83	-4 44	56	83	-5 40	56	84	262											
97	-2 30	56	83	-3 26	56	84	-4 22	56	84	-5 18	56	84	263											
96	-2 09	56	84	-3 05	56	85	-4 01	56	85	-4 57	56	85	264											
95	-1 47	-56	85	-2 43	-56	86	-3 39	-56	86	-4 35	-57	86	-5 32	-56	87	265								
94	-1 26	56	86	-2 22	56	87	-3 18	56	87	-4 14	56	87	-5 10	56	88	266								
93	-1 04	57	87	-2 01	56	88	-2 57	56	88	-3 53	56	88	-4 49	56	89	267								
92	-0 43	56	88	-1 39	56	88	-2 35	56	89	-3 31	56	89	-4 27	56	90	-5 23	56	90	268					
91	-0 22	56	89	-1 18	56	89	-2 14	56	90	-3 10	56	90	-4 06	56	91	-5 02	56	91	269					
90	00 00	-56	90	-0 56	-56	90	-1 52	-56	91	-2 48	-56	91	-3 44	-56	91	-4 40	-56	92	-5 36	-56	92	270		
89	00 22	57	91	-0 35	56	91	-1 31	56	92	-2 27	56	92	-3 23	56	92	-4 19	56	93	-5 15	56	93	271		
88	00 43	56	92	-0 13	56	92	-1 09	56	93	-2 05	56	93	-3 01	56	93	-3 57	56	94	-4 53	56	94	272		
87	01 04	56	93	00 08	56	93	-0 48	56	94	-1 44	56	94	-2 40	56	94	-3 36	56	95	-4 32	56	95	-5 28	56	95
86	01 26	56	94	00 30	56	94	-0 26	56	94	-1 22	56	95	-2 18	56	95	-3 14	56	96	-4 10	56	96	-5 06	56	96
85	01 47	-56	95	00 51	-56	95	-0 05	-56	95	-1 01	-56	96	-1 57	-56	96	-2 53	-56	96	-3 49	-56	97	-4 45	-56	97
84	02 09	56	96	01 13	56	96	00 17	56	96	-0 39	56	97	-1 35	56	97	-2 31	57	97	-3 28	56	98	-4 24	56	98
83	02 30	56	97	01 34	56	97	00 38	56	97	-0 18	56	98	-1 14	56	98	-2 10	56	98	-3 06	56	99	-4 02	56	99
82	02 52	57	97	01 55	56	98	00 59	56	98	00 03	56	99	-0 53	56	99	-1 49	56	99	-2 45	56	100	-3 41	56	100
81	03 13	56	98	02 17	56	99	01 21	57	99	00 24	56	99	-0 32	56	100	-1 28	56	100	-2 24	56	101	-3 20	56	101
80	03 34	-56	99	02 38	-56	100	01 42	-56	100	00 46	-56	100	-0 10	-57	101	-1 07	-56	101	-2 03	-56	101	-2 59	-56	102
79	03 55	56	100	02 59	56	101	02 03	56	101	01 07	56	101	00 11	57	102	-0 46	56	102	-1 42	56	102	-2 38	56	103
78	04 16	56	101	03 20	56	102	02 24	56	102	01 28	56	102	00 32	57	103	-0 25	56	103	-1 21	56	103	-2 17	56	104
77	04 37	56	102	03 41	56	103	02 45	56	103	01 49	56	103	00 53	57	104	-0 04	56	104	-1 00	56	104	-1 56	56	105
76	04 58	56	103	04 02	56	103	03 06	56	104	02 10	57	104	01 13	56	105	00 17	56	105	-0 39	56	105	-1 35	57	106
75	05 19	-56	104	04 23	-56	104	03 27	-56	105	02 31	-57	105	01 34	-56	105	00 38	-56	106	-0 18	-57	106	-1 15	-56	106
74	05 40	56	105	04 44	56	105	03 48	57	106	02 51	56	106	01 55	56	106	00 59	57	107	00 02	56	107	-0 54	56	107
73	06 01	56	106	05 05	57	106	04 08	56	107	03 12	57	107	02 15	56	107	01 19	56	108	00 23	57	108	-0 34	56	108
72	06 22	57	107	05 25	56	107	04 29	57	108	03 32	56	108	02 36	56	108	01 40	57	109	00 43	56	109	-0 13	57	109
71	06 42	56	108	05 46	57	108	04 49	56	109	03 53	57	109	02 56	56	109	02 00	57	110	01 03	56	110	00 07	56	110
70	07 02	-56	109	06 06	-56	109	05 10	-57	109	04 13	-56	110	03 17	-57	110	02 20	-56	110	01 24	-57	111	00 27	-56	111

LHA	8° Hc	d	Z	9° Hc	d	Z	10° Hc	d	Z	11° Hc	d	Z	12° Hc	d	Z	13° Hc	d	Z	14° Hc	d	Z
87	273																				
86	274																				
85	-5 41	-56	98	275																	
84	-5 20	56	98	276																	
83	-4 58	56	99	277																	
82	-4 37	56	100	-5 33	56	101	278														
81	-4 16	56	101	-5 12	56	102	279														
80	-3 55	-56	102	-4 51	-56	103	280														
79	-3 34	56	103	-4 30	56	103	-5 26	56	104	281											
78	-3 13	56	104	-4 09	57	104	-5 06	56	105	282											
77	-2 52	57	105	-3 49	56	105	-4 45	56	106	283											
76	-2 32	56	106	-3 28	56	106	-4 24	56	107	-5 20	57	107	284								
75	-2 11	-56	107	-3 07	-56	107	-4 03	-57	108	-5 00	-56	108	285								
74	-1 50	57	108	-2 47	56	108	-3 43	56	108	-4 39	57	109	-5 36	56	109	286					
73	-1 30	56	109	-2 26	57	109	-3 23	56	109	-4 19	56	110	-5 15	57	110	287					
72	-1 10	56	110	-2 06	56	110	-3 02	57	110	-3 59	56	111	-4 55	57	111	288					
71	-0 49	57	111	-1 46	56	111	-2 42	57	111	-3 39	56	112	-4 35	57	112	-5 32	56	112	289		
70	-0 29	-57	111	-1 26	-56	112	-2 22	-57	112	-3 19	-56	112	-4 15	-57	113	-5 12	-56	113	290		

S. Lat. {LHA greater than 180°....... Zn=180−Z / LHA less than 180°........... Zn=180+Z}

DECLINATION (0°-14°) CONTRARY NAME TO LATITUDE

N. Lat. {LHA greater than 180°........ Zn=Z; LHA less than 180°........... Zn=360−Z}

DECLINATION (0°-14°) CONTRARY NAME TO LATITUDE

LHA	0° Hc	0° d	0° Z	1° Hc	1° d	1° Z	2° Hc	2° d	2° Z	3° Hc	3° d	3° Z	4° Hc	4° d	4° Z
	° ′	′	°	° ′	′	°	° ′	′	°	° ′	′	°	° ′	′	°
69	07 23	57	110	06 26	56	110	05 30	57	110	04 33	56	111	03 37	57	111
68	07 43	57	111	06 46	56	111	05 50	57	111	04 53	56	112	03 57	57	112
67	08 03	57	112	07 06	56	112	06 10	57	112	05 13	56	113	04 17	57	113
66	08 23	57	113	07 26	56	113	06 30	57	113	05 33	57	114	04 36	56	114
65	08 43	−57	114	07 46	−57	114	06 49	−56	114	05 53	−57	115	04 56	−57	115
64	09 02	56	115	08 06	57	115	07 09	57	115	06 12	57	116	05 15	56	116
63	09 22	57	115	08 25	57	116	07 28	57	116	06 31	56	116	05 35	57	117
62	09 41	57	116	08 44	56	117	07 48	57	117	06 51	57	117	05 54	57	118
61	10 00	57	117	09 03	56	118	08 07	57	118	07 10	57	118	06 13	57	119
60	10 19	−57	118	09 22	−57	119	08 25	−57	119	07 28	−56	119	06 32	−57	120
59	10 38	57	119	09 41	57	120	08 44	57	120	07 47	57	120	06 50	57	121
58	10 57	57	120	10 00	57	121	09 03	57	121	08 06	57	121	07 09	58	122
57	11 15	57	121	10 18	57	122	09 21	57	122	08 24	57	122	07 27	57	123
56	11 34	58	122	10 36	57	123	09 39	57	123	08 42	57	123	07 45	57	123
55	11 52	−57	123	10 55	−58	124	09 57	−57	124	09 00	−57	124	08 03	−58	124
54	12 10	58	124	11 12	57	125	10 15	57	125	09 18	58	125	08 20	57	125
53	12 27	57	125	11 30	57	125	10 33	58	126	09 35	57	126	08 38	58	126
52	12 45	58	126	11 47	57	126	10 50	58	127	09 52	57	127	08 55	58	127
51	13 02	57	127	12 05	58	127	11 07	57	128	10 10	58	128	09 12	58	128
50	13 19	−57	128	12 22	−58	128	11 24	−58	129	10 26	−57	129	09 29	−58	129
49	13 36	58	129	12 38	57	129	11 41	58	130	10 43	58	130	09 45	57	130
48	13 53	58	130	12 55	58	130	11 57	58	131	10 59	57	131	10 02	58	131
47	14 09	58	131	13 11	58	131	12 13	58	132	11 15	57	132	10 18	58	132
46	14 25	58	132	13 27	58	132	12 29	58	133	11 31	58	133	10 33	57	133
45	14 41	−58	133	13 43	−58	133	12 45	−58	134	11 47	−58	134	10 49	−58	134
44	14 56	58	134	13 58	58	134	13 00	58	135	12 02	58	135	11 04	58	135
43	15 12	58	135	14 14	58	135	13 16	58	136	12 18	59	136	11 19	58	136
42	15 27	58	136	14 29	58	136	13 31	59	137	12 32	58	137	11 34	58	137
41	15 42	59	137	14 43	58	137	13 45	58	138	12 47	58	138	11 49	59	138
40	15 56	−58	138	14 58	−58	138	14 00	−59	139	13 01	−58	139	12 03	−58	139
39	16 10	58	139	15 12	58	139	14 14	59	140	13 15	58	140	12 17	58	140
38	16 24	58	140	15 26	59	140	14 27	58	141	13 29	58	141	12 31	59	141
37	16 38	59	141	15 39	58	141	14 41	59	142	13 42	58	142	12 44	59	142
36	16 51	58	142	15 53	59	142	14 54	58	143	13 56	59	143	12 57	59	143
35	17 04	−58	143	16 06	−59	143	15 07	−59	144	14 08	−58	144	13 10	−59	144
34	17 17	59	144	16 18	58	144	15 20	59	145	14 21	59	145	13 22	58	145
33	17 29	58	145	16 31	59	145	15 32	59	146	14 33	59	146	13 34	58	146
32	17 42	59	146	16 43	59	146	15 44	59	147	14 45	59	147	13 46	59	147
31	17 53	58	147	16 55	59	147	15 56	59	148	14 57	59	148	13 58	59	148
30	18 05	−59	148	17 06	−59	149	16 07	−59	149	15 08	−59	149	14 09	−59	149
29	18 16	59	149	17 17	59	150	16 18	59	150	15 19	59	150	14 20	59	150
28	18 27	59	150	17 28	59	151	16 29	59	151	15 30	59	151	14 31	60	151
27	18 37	59	151	17 38	59	152	16 39	59	152	15 40	59	152	14 41	59	152
26	18 47	59	152	17 48	59	153	16 49	59	153	15 50	59	153	14 51	60	153
25	18 57	−59	154	17 58	−59	154	16 59	−59	154	16 00	−60	154	15 00	−59	154
24	19 07	60	155	18 07	59	155	17 08	59	155	16 09	60	155	15 09	59	155
23	19 16	60	156	18 16	59	156	17 17	59	156	16 18	60	156	15 18	59	156
22	19 24	59	157	18 25	59	157	17 26	60	157	16 26	59	157	15 27	60	157
21	19 33	60	158	18 33	59	158	17 34	60	158	16 34	59	158	15 35	59	158
20	19 41	−60	159	18 41	−59	159	17 42	−60	159	16 42	−59	159	15 43	−60	159
19	19 48	59	160	18 49	60	160	17 49	59	160	16 50	60	160	15 50	59	160
18	19 56	60	161	18 56	59	161	17 57	60	161	16 57	60	161	15 57	59	161
17	20 03	60	162	19 03	60	162	18 03	59	162	17 04	60	162	16 04	60	162
16	20 09	60	163	19 09	59	163	18 10	60	163	17 10	60	163	16 10	59	163
15	20 15	−60	164	19 15	−59	164	18 16	−60	164	17 16	−60	164	16 16	−59	164
14	20 21	60	165	19 21	60	165	18 21	59	165	17 22	60	165	16 22	60	165
13	20 26	59	166	19 27	60	166	18 27	60	166	17 27	60	166	16 27	60	167
12	20 31	60	167	19 31	59	167	18 32	60	167	17 32	60	167	16 32	60	168
11	20 36	60	168	19 36	60	168	18 36	60	168	17 36	60	169	16 36	59	169
10	20 40	−60	169	19 40	−60	169	18 40	−60	169	17 40	−59	170	16 41	−60	170
9	20 44	60	170	19 44	60	170	18 44	60	171	17 44	60	171	16 44	60	171
8	20 47	60	171	19 47	60	172	18 47	60	172	17 47	59	172	16 48	60	172
7	20 50	60	173	19 50	60	173	18 50	60	173	17 50	60	173	16 50	59	173
6	20 53	60	174	19 53	60	174	18 53	60	174	17 53	60	174	16 53	60	174
5	20 55	−60	175	19 55	−60	175	18 55	−60	175	17 55	−60	175	16 55	−60	175
4	20 57	60	176	19 57	60	176	18 57	60	176	17 57	60	176	16 57	60	176
3	20 58	60	177	19 58	60	177	18 58	60	177	17 58	60	177	16 58	60	177
2	20 59	60	178	19 59	60	178	18 59	60	178	17 59	60	178	16 59	60	178
1	21 00	60	179	20 00	60	179	19 00	60	179	18 00	60	179	17 00	60	179
0	21 00	−60	180	20 00	−60	180	19 00	−60	180	18 00	−60	180	17 00	−60	180

LHA	5° Hc	5° d	5° Z	6° Hc	6° d	6° Z	7° Hc	7° d	7° Z	8° Hc	8° d	8° Z	9° Hc	9° d	9° Z
	° ′	′	°	° ′	′	°	° ′	′	°	° ′	′	°	° ′	′	°
69	02 40	56	111	01 44	57	112	00 47	56	112	−0 09	57	112	−1 06	57	113
68	03 00	56	112	02 04	57	113	01 07	57	113	00 10	56	113	−0 46	57	114
67	03 20	57	113	02 23	56	114	01 27	57	114	00 30	57	114	−0 27	56	115
66	03 40	57	114	02 43	57	115	01 46	56	115	00 50	57	115	−0 07	57	116
65	03 59	−57	115	03 02	−56	116	02 06	−57	116	01 09	−57	116	00 12	−57	116
64	04 19	57	116	03 22	57	116	02 25	57	117	01 28	57	117	00 31	56	117
63	04 38	57	117	03 41	57	117	02 44	57	118	01 47	57	118	00 50	56	118
62	04 57	57	118	04 00	57	118	03 03	57	119	02 06	57	119	01 09	57	119
61	05 16	57	119	04 19	57	119	03 22	57	120	02 25	57	120	01 28	57	120
60	05 35	−58	120	04 37	−57	120	03 40	−57	121	02 43	−57	121	01 46	−57	121
59	05 53	57	121	04 56	57	121	03 59	57	121	03 02	57	122	02 05	57	122
58	06 11	57	122	05 14	57	122	04 17	57	122	03 20	57	123	02 23	57	123
57	06 30	58	123	05 32	57	123	04 35	57	123	03 38	57	124	02 41	58	124
56	06 48	58	124	05 50	57	124	04 53	57	124	03 56	58	125	02 58	57	125
55	07 05	−57	125	06 08	−57	125	05 11	−58	125	04 13	−57	126	03 16	−57	126
54	07 23	57	126	06 26	58	126	05 28	57	126	04 31	58	127	03 33	57	127
53	07 40	57	127	06 43	58	127	05 45	57	127	04 48	58	127	03 50	57	128
52	07 57	57	128	07 00	58	128	06 02	57	128	05 05	58	128	04 07	57	129
51	08 14	57	129	07 17	58	129	06 19	57	129	05 22	58	129	04 24	58	130
50	08 31	−58	130	07 33	−57	130	06 36	−58	130	05 38	−58	130	04 40	−57	131
49	08 48	58	131	07 50	58	131	06 52	58	131	05 54	57	131	04 57	58	132
48	09 04	58	131	08 06	58	132	07 08	58	132	06 10	57	132	05 13	58	133
47	09 20	58	132	08 22	58	133	07 24	58	133	06 26	58	133	05 28	58	134
46	09 36	58	133	08 38	58	134	07 40	58	134	06 42	58	134	05 44	58	134
45	09 51	−58	134	08 53	−58	135	07 55	−58	135	06 57	−58	135	05 59	−58	135
44	10 06	58	135	09 08	58	136	08 10	58	136	07 12	58	136	06 14	58	136
43	10 21	58	136	09 23	58	137	08 25	58	137	07 27	58	137	06 29	58	137
42	10 36	58	137	09 38	58	138	08 40	59	138	07 41	58	138	06 43	58	138
41	10 50	58	138	09 52	58	139	08 54	58	139	07 56	59	139	06 57	58	139
40	11 05	−59	139	10 06	−58	140	09 08	−58	140	08 10	−59	140	07 11	−58	140
39	11 19	59	140	10 20	58	141	09 22	59	141	08 23	58	141	07 25	59	141
38	11 32	58	141	10 34	59	142	09 35	58	142	08 37	59	142	07 38	58	142
37	11 45	58	142	10 47	59	143	09 48	58	143	08 50	59	143	07 51	58	143
36	11 58	58	143	11 00	59	144	10 01	58	144	09 03	59	144	08 04	59	144
35	12 11	−58	144	11 13	−59	144	10 14	−59	145	09 15	−59	145	08 16	−58	145
34	12 24	59	145	11 25	59	145	10 26	59	146	09 27	58	146	08 29	59	146
33	12 36	59	146	11 37	59	146	10 38	59	147	09 39	59	147	08 40	58	147
32	12 47	58	147	11 49	59	147	10 50	59	148	09 51	59	148	08 52	59	148
31	12 59	59	148	12 00	59	148	11 01	59	149	10 02	59	149	09 03	59	149
30	13 10	−59	149	12 11	−59	149	11 12	−59	150	10 13	−59	150	09 14	−59	150
29	13 21	59	150	12 22	59	150	11 23	59	151	10 24	59	151	09 25	59	151
28	13 31	59	151	12 32	59	151	11 33	59	152	10 34	59	152	09 35	59	152
27	13 42	60	152	12 42	59	152	11 43	59	153	10 44	59	153	09 45	59	153
26	13 51	59	153	12 52	59	153	11 53	59	154	10 54	59	154	09 55	60	154
25	14 01	−59	154	13 02	−60	154	12 02	−59	155	11 03	−59	155	10 04	−59	155
24	14 10	59	155	13 11	59	156	12 12	60	156	11 12	59	156	10 13	60	156
23	14 19	59	156	13 20	60	157	12 20	59	157	11 21	60	157	10 21	59	157
22	14 27	59	157	13 28	59	158	12 29	60	158	11 29	59	158	10 30	60	158
21	14 36	60	158	13 36	59	159	12 37	60	159	11 37	59	159	10 38	60	159
20	14 43	−59	159	13 44	−60	160	12 44	−59	160	11 45	−60	160	10 45	−59	160
19	14 51	60	160	13 51	59	161	12 52	60	161	11 52	60	161	10 52	59	161
18	14 58	60	161	13 58	59	162	12 59	60	162	11 59	60	162	10 59	59	162
17	15 04	59	162	14 05	60	163	13 05	60	163	12 05	59	163	11 06	60	163
16	15 11	60	164	14 11	60	164	13 11	59	164	12 12	60	164	11 12	60	164
15	15 17	−60	165	14 17	−60	165	13 17	−60	165	12 17	−59	165	11 18	−60	165
14	15 22	60	166	14 22	59	166	13 23	60	166	12 23	60	166	11 23	60	166
13	15 27	59	167	14 28	60	167	13 28	60	167	12 28	60	167	11 28	60	167
12	15 32	60	168	14 32	59	168	13 33	60	168	12 33	60	168	11 33	60	168
11	15 37	60	169	14 37	60	169	13 37	60	169	12 37	60	169	11 37	60	169
10	15 41	−60	170	14 41	−60	170	13 41	−60	170	12 41	−60	170	11 41	−60	170
9	15 44	60	171	14 44	59	171	13 45	60	171	12 45	60	171	11 45	60	171
8	15 48	60	172	14 48	60	172	13 48	60	172	12 48	60	172	11 48	60	172
7	15 51	60	173	14 51	60	173	13 51	60	173	12 51	60	173	11 51	60	173
6	15 53	60	174	14 53	60	174	13 53	60	174	12 53	60	174	11 53	60	174
5	15 55	−60	175	14 55	−60	175	13 55	−60	175	12 55	−60	175	11 55	−60	175
4	15 57	60	176	14 57	60	176	13 57	60	176	12 57	60	176	11 57	60	176
3	15 58	60	177	14 58	60	177	13 58	60	177	12 58	60	177	11 58	60	177
2	15 59	60	178	14 59	60	178	13 59	60	178	12 59	60	178	11 59	60	178
1	16 00	60	179	15 00	60	179	14 00	60	179	13 00	60	179	12 00	60	179
0	16 00	−60	180	15 00	−60	180	14 00	−60	180	13 00	−60	180	12 00	−60	180

LHA	10° Hc	10° d	10° Z	11° Hc	11° d	11° Z	12° Hc	12° d	12° Z	13° Hc	13° d	13° Z	14° Hc	14° d	14° Z	LHA
	° ′	′	°	° ′	′	°	° ′	′	°	° ′	′	°	° ′	′	°	
69	−2 03	56	113	−2 59	57	113	−3 56	56	114	−4 52	57	114	291			
68	−1 43	56	114	−2 39	57	114	−3 36	57	115	−4 33	56	115	−5 29	57	115	292
67	−1 23	57	115	−2 20	57	115	−3 17	56	116	−4 13	57	116	−5 10	56	116	293
66	−1 04	57	116	−2 01	56	116	−2 57	57	117	−3 54	57	117	−4 51	56	117	294
65	−0 45	−56	117	−1 41	−57	117	−2 38	−57	117	−3 35	−57	118	−4 32	−56	118	295
64	−0 25	57	118	−1 22	57	118	−2 19	57	118	−3 16	57	119	−4 13	56	119	296
63	−0 06	57	119	−1 03	57	119	−2 00	57	119	−2 57	57	120	−3 54	57	120	297
62	00 12	57	120	−0 45	57	120	−1 42	56	120	−2 38	57	121	−3 35	57	121	298
61	00 31	57	121	−0 26	57	121	−1 23	57	121	−2 20	57	121	−3 17	57	122	299
60	00 49	−57	121	−0 08	−57	122	−1 05	−57	122	−2 02	−57	122	−2 59	−57	123	300
59	01 08	58	122	00 10	57	123	−0 47	57	123	−1 44	57	123	−2 41	57	124	301
58	01 26	58	123	00 28	57	124	−0 29	57	124	−1 26	57	124	−2 23	57	125	302
57	01 43	57	124	00 46	57	125	−0 11	57	125	−1 08	57	125	−2 05	58	125	303
56	02 01	57	125	01 04	57	126	00 07	58	126	−0 51	57	126	−1 48	57	126	304
55	02 19	−58	126	01 21	−57	126	00 24	−57	127	−0 33	−58	127	−1 31	−57	127	305
54	02 36	58	127	01 38	57	127	00 41	57	128	−0 16	58	128	−1 14	57	128	306
53	02 53	58	128	01 55	57	128	00 58	58	129	00 00	57	129	−0 57	58	129	307
52	03 10	58	129	02 12	57	129	01 15	58	130	00 17	57	130	−0 40	58	130	308
51	03 26	57	130	02 29	58	130	01 31	58	131	00 33	57	131	−0 24	58	131	309
50	03 43	−58	131	02 45	−58	131	01 47	−57	131	00 50	−58	132	−0 08	−58	132	310
49	03 59	58	132	03 01	58	132	02 03	57	132	01 06	58	133	00 08	58	133	311
48	04 15	58	133	03 17	58	133	02 19	58	133	01 21	58	134	00 23	58	134	312
47	04 30	57	134	03 33	58	134	02 35	58	134	01 37	58	135	00 39	58	135	313
46	04 46	58	135	03 48	58	135	02 50	58	135	01 52	58	135	00 54	58	136	314
45	05 01	−58	136	04 03	−58	136	03 05	−58	136	02 07	−58	136	01 09	−58	137	315
44	05 16	58	137	04 18	58	137	03 20	58	137	02 22	59	137	01 23	58	138	316
43	05 31	59	138	04 32	58	138	03 34	58	138	02 36	58	138	01 38	58	139	317
42	05 45	58	139	04 47	59	139	03 48	58	139	02 50	58	139	01 52	58	139	318
41	05 59	58	140	05 01	59	140	04 02	58	140	03 04	58	140	02 06	59	140	319
40	06 13	−58	140	05 15	−59	141	04 16	−58	141	03 18	−59	141	02 19	−58	141	320
39	06 26	58	141	05 28	58	142	04 30	59	142	03 31	58	142	02 33	59	142	321
38	06 40	59	142	05 41	58	143	04 43	59	143	03 44	58	143	02 46	59	143	322
37	06 53	59	143	05 54	59	144	04 55	58	144	03 57	59	144	02 58	58	144	323
36	07 05	58	144	06 07	59	145	05 08	59	145	04 09	58	145	03 11	59	145	324
35	07 18	−59	145	06 19	−59	146	05 20	−58	146	04 22	−59	146	03 23	−59	146	325
34	07 30	59	146	06 31	59	147	05 32	58	147	04 34	59	147	03 35	59	147	326
33	07 42	59	147	06 43	59	147	05 44	59	148	04 45	59	148	03 46	59	148	327
32	07 53	59	148	06 54	59	148	05 55	59	149	04 56	58	149	03 58	59	149	328
31	08 04	59	149	07 05	59	149	06 06	59	150	05 07	59	150	04 08	59	150	329
30	08 15	−59	150	07 16	−59	150	06 17	−59	151	05 18	−59	151	04 19	−59	151	330
29	08 26	59	151	07 27	59	151	06 28	60	152	05 28	59	152	04 29	59	152	331
28	08 36	59	152	07 37	59	152	06 38	59	153	05 39	60	153	04 39	59	153	332
27	08 46	59	153	07 47	60	153	06 47	59	153	05 48	59	154	04 49	59	154	333
26	08 55	59	154	07 56	59	154	06 57	59	154	05 58	60	155	04 58	59	155	334
25	09 05	−60	155	08 05	−59	155	07 06	−59	155	06 07	−60	156	05 07	−59	156	335
24	09 13	59	156	08 14	59	156	07 15	60	156	06 15	59	157	05 16	59	157	336
23	09 22	59	157	08 23	60	157	07 23	59	157	06 24	60	158	05 24	59	158	337
22	09 30	59	158	08 31	60	158	07 31	59	158	06 32	60	158	05 32	59	159	338
21	09 38	59	159	08 39	60	159	07 39	59	159	06 40	60	159	05 40	59	160	339
20	09 46	−60	160	08 46	−59	160	07 47	−60	160	06 47	−59	160	05 48	−60	161	340
19	09 53	60	161	08 53	59	161	07 54	60	161	06 54	59	161	05 55	60	162	341
18	10 00	60	162	09 00	60	162	08 00	59	162	07 01	60	162	06 01	59	163	342
17	10 06	60	163	09 06	59	163	08 07	60	163	07 07	60	163	06 07	59	163	343
16	10 12	59	164	09 13	60	164	08 13	60	164	07 13	60	164	06 13	59	164	344
15	10 18	−60	165	09 18	−59	165	08 19	−60	165	07 19	−60	165	06 19	−60	165	345
14	10 23	59	166	09 24	60	166	08 24	60	166	07 24	60	166	06 24	59	166	346
13	10 28	59	167	09 29	60	167	08 29	60	167	07 29	60	167	06 29	60	167	347
12	10 33	60	168	09 33	60	168	08 33	59	168	07 34	60	168	06 34	60	168	348
11	10 37	59	169	09 38	60	169	08 38	60	169	07 38	60	169	06 38	60	169	349
10	10 41	−60	170	09 41	−59	170	08 42	−60	170	07 42	−60	170	06 42	−60	170	350
9	10 45	60	171	09 45	60	171	08 45	60	171	07 45	60	171	06 45	60	171	351
8	10 48	60	172	09 48	60	172	08 48	60	172	07 48	60	172	06 48	60	172	352
7	10 51	60	173	09 51	60	173	08 51	60	173	07 51	60	173	06 51	60	173	353
6	10 53	60	174	09 53	60	174	08 53	60	174	07 53	60	174	06 53	60	174	354
5	10 55	−60	175	09 55	−60	175	08 55	−60	175	07 55	−60	175	06 55	−60	175	355
4	10 57	60	176	09 57	60	176	08 57	60	176	07 57	60	176	06 57	60	176	356
3	10 58	60	177	09 58	60	177	08 58	60	177	07 58	60	177	06 58	60	177	357
2	10 59	60	178	09 59	60	178	08 59	60	178	07 59	60	178	06 59	60	178	358
1	11 00	60	179	10 00	60	179	09 00	60	179	08 00	60	179	07 00	60	179	359
0	11 00	−60	180	10 00	−60	180	09 00	−60	180	08 00	−60	180	07 00	−60	180	360

S. Lat. {LHA greater than 180°....... Zn=180−Z; LHA less than 180°........... Zn=180+Z}

DECLINATION (0°-14°) CONTRARY NAME TO LATITUDE

N. Lat. {LHA greater than 180°....... Zn=Z; LHA less than 180°.......... Zn=360−Z}

DECLINATION (15°-29°) **SAME** NAME AS LATITUDE

LHA	15° Hc	15° d	15° Z	16° Hc	16° d	16° Z	17° Hc	17° d	17° Z	18° Hc	18° d	18° Z	19° Hc	19° d	19° Z
	° ′	′	°	° ′	′	°	° ′	′	°	° ′	′	°	° ′	′	°
0	36 00	+60	180	37 00	+60	180	38 00	+60	180	39 00	+60	180	40 00	+60	180
1	36 00	60	179	37 00	60	179	38 00	60	179	39 00	60	179	40 00	60	179
2	35 59	60	178	36 59	60	178	37 59	60	178	38 59	60	178	39 59	60	178
3	35 58	60	176	36 58	60	176	37 58	60	176	38 58	60	176	39 58	60	176
4	35 56	60	175	36 56	60	175	37 56	60	175	38 56	60	175	39 56	60	175
5	35 54	+60	174	36 54	+60	174	37 54	+60	174	38 54	+60	174	39 54	+60	174
6	35 52	60	173	36 52	60	173	37 52	60	173	38 52	60	173	39 52	60	173
7	35 49	60	172	36 49	60	172	37 49	60	172	38 49	60	171	39 49	60	171
8	35 46	60	171	36 46	60	170	37 46	59	170	38 45	60	170	39 45	60	170
9	35 42	60	169	36 42	60	169	37 42	60	169	38 42	59	169	39 41	60	169
10	35 38	+60	168	36 38	+59	168	37 37	+60	168	38 37	+60	168	39 37	+60	168
11	35 33	60	167	36 33	60	167	37 33	59	167	38 32	60	167	39 32	60	167
12	35 28	60	166	36 28	59	166	37 27	60	166	38 27	60	165	39 27	60	165
13	35 22	60	165	36 22	60	164	37 22	60	164	38 22	59	164	39 21	60	164
14	35 17	59	163	36 16	60	163	37 16	59	163	38 15	60	163	39 15	60	163
15	35 10	+60	162	36 10	+59	162	37 09	+60	162	38 09	+60	162	39 09	+59	162
16	35 03	60	161	36 03	60	161	37 03	59	161	38 02	60	161	39 02	59	160
17	34 56	60	160	35 56	59	160	36 55	60	160	37 55	59	159	38 54	60	159
18	34 49	59	159	35 48	59	159	36 47	60	158	37 47	59	158	38 46	60	158
19	34 41	59	158	35 40	59	157	36 39	60	157	37 39	59	157	38 38	59	157
20	34 32	+59	156	35 31	+60	156	36 31	+59	156	37 30	+59	156	38 29	+60	156
21	34 23	60	155	35 23	59	155	36 22	59	155	37 21	59	155	38 20	59	154
22	34 14	59	154	35 13	59	154	36 12	60	154	37 12	59	153	38 11	59	153
23	34 05	59	153	35 04	59	153	36 03	59	153	37 02	59	152	38 01	59	152
24	33 55	59	152	34 54	59	152	35 53	59	151	36 52	59	151	37 51	59	151
25	33 44	+59	151	34 43	+59	150	35 42	+59	150	36 41	+59	150	37 40	+59	150
26	33 33	59	150	34 32	59	149	35 31	59	149	36 30	59	149	37 29	59	149
27	33 22	59	148	34 21	59	148	35 20	59	148	36 19	58	148	37 17	59	147
28	33 11	59	147	34 10	58	147	35 08	59	147	36 07	59	146	37 06	58	146
29	32 59	59	146	33 58	58	146	34 56	59	146	35 55	59	145	36 54	58	145
30	32 47	+58	145	33 45	+59	145	34 44	+59	144	35 43	+58	144	36 41	+59	144
31	32 34	59	144	33 33	58	144	34 31	59	143	35 30	58	143	36 28	59	143
32	32 21	59	143	33 20	58	142	34 18	59	142	35 17	58	142	36 15	58	142
33	32 08	59	142	33 07	58	141	34 05	58	141	35 03	58	141	36 01	59	141
34	31 55	58	141	32 53	58	140	33 51	58	140	34 49	59	140	35 48	58	139
35	31 41	+58	139	32 39	+58	139	33 37	+58	139	34 35	+58	139	35 33	+58	138
36	31 27	58	138	32 25	58	138	33 23	58	138	34 21	58	137	35 19	58	137
37	31 12	58	137	32 10	58	137	33 08	58	137	34 06	58	136	35 04	58	136
38	30 58	57	136	31 55	58	136	32 53	58	136	33 51	58	135	34 49	58	135
39	30 42	58	135	31 40	58	135	32 38	58	134	33 36	58	134	34 34	57	134
40	30 27	+58	134	31 25	+58	134	32 23	+57	133	33 20	+58	133	34 18	+58	133
41	30 11	58	133	31 09	58	133	32 07	57	132	33 04	58	132	34 02	58	132
42	29 56	57	132	30 53	58	132	31 51	57	131	32 48	58	131	33 46	57	130
43	29 39	58	131	30 37	57	130	31 34	58	130	32 32	57	130	33 29	58	129
44	29 23	57	130	30 20	58	129	31 18	57	129	32 15	58	129	33 13	57	128
45	29 06	+58	129	30 04	+57	128	31 01	+57	128	31 58	+58	128	32 56	+57	127
46	28 49	58	128	29 47	57	127	30 44	57	127	31 41	57	127	32 38	57	126
47	28 32	57	127	29 29	58	126	30 27	57	126	31 24	57	125	32 21	57	125
48	28 15	57	125	29 12	57	125	30 09	57	125	31 06	57	124	32 03	57	124
49	27 57	57	124	28 54	57	124	29 51	57	124	30 48	57	123	31 45	57	123
50	27 39	+57	123	28 36	+57	123	29 33	+57	123	30 30	+57	122	31 27	+57	122
51	27 21	57	122	28 18	57	122	29 15	57	122	30 12	57	121	31 09	56	121
52	27 03	57	121	28 00	57	121	28 57	56	121	29 53	57	120	30 50	57	120
53	26 44	57	120	27 41	57	120	28 38	57	120	29 35	56	119	30 31	57	119
54	26 26	57	119	27 23	56	119	28 19	57	119	29 16	56	118	30 12	57	118
55	26 07	+57	118	27 04	+56	118	28 00	+57	118	28 57	+56	117	29 53	+57	117
56	25 48	57	117	26 45	56	117	27 41	57	117	28 38	56	116	29 34	56	116
57	25 29	56	116	26 25	57	116	27 22	56	115	28 18	57	115	29 15	56	115
58	25 09	57	115	26 06	56	115	27 02	57	114	27 59	56	114	28 55	56	114
59	24 50	56	114	25 46	57	114	26 43	56	113	27 39	56	113	28 35	56	113
60	24 30	+56	113	25 26	+57	113	26 23	+56	112	27 19	+56	112	28 15	+56	112
61	24 10	57	112	25 07	56	112	26 03	56	111	26 59	56	111	27 55	56	111
62	23 50	57	111	24 47	56	111	25 43	56	110	26 39	56	110	27 35	56	110
63	23 30	56	110	24 26	57	110	25 23	56	109	26 19	56	109	27 15	56	109
64	23 10	56	109	24 06	56	109	25 02	56	108	25 58	56	108	26 54	56	108
65	22 50	+56	108	23 46	+56	108	24 42	+56	108	25 38	+56	107	26 34	+56	107
66	22 29	56	107	23 25	56	107	24 21	56	107	25 17	56	106	26 13	56	106
67	22 08	57	106	23 05	56	106	24 01	56	106	24 56	56	105	25 52	56	105
68	21 48	56	105	22 44	56	105	23 40	56	105	24 36	55	104	25 31	56	104
69	21 27	56	104	22 23	56	104	23 19	56	104	24 15	56	103	25 11	55	103

LHA	20° Hc	20° d	20° Z	21° Hc	21° d	21° Z	22° Hc	22° d	22° Z	23° Hc	23° d	23° Z	24° Hc	24° d	24° Z
	° ′	′	°	° ′	′	°	° ′	′	°	° ′	′	°	° ′	′	°
0	41 00	+60	180	42 00	+60	180	43 00	+60	180	44 00	+60	180	45 00	+60	180
1	41 00	60	179	42 00	60	179	43 00	60	179	44 00	60	179	45 00	60	179
2	40 59	60	178	41 59	60	178	42 59	60	178	43 59	60	177	44 59	60	177
3	40 58	60	176	41 58	60	176	42 58	60	176	43 58	60	176	44 58	60	176
4	40 56	60	175	41 56	60	175	42 56	60	175	43 56	60	175	44 56	60	175
5	40 54	+60	174	41 54	+60	174	42 54	+60	174	43 54	+60	174	44 54	+60	174
6	40 52	60	173	41 52	60	173	42 52	59	172	43 51	60	172	44 51	60	172
7	40 49	60	171	41 49	59	171	42 48	60	171	43 48	60	171	44 48	60	171
8	40 45	60	170	41 45	60	170	42 45	60	170	43 45	60	170	44 45	59	170
9	40 41	60	169	41 41	60	169	42 41	60	169	43 41	60	169	44 41	59	168
10	40 37	+60	168	41 37	+59	168	42 36	+60	167	43 36	+60	167	44 36	+60	167
11	40 32	60	166	41 32	59	166	42 31	60	166	43 31	60	166	44 31	60	166
12	40 27	59	165	41 26	60	165	42 26	60	165	43 26	59	165	44 25	60	165
13	40 21	60	164	41 21	59	164	42 20	60	164	43 20	59	164	44 19	60	163
14	40 15	59	163	41 14	60	163	42 14	60	162	43 14	59	162	44 13	60	162
15	40 08	+60	162	41 08	+59	161	42 07	+60	161	43 07	+59	161	44 06	+60	161
16	40 01	60	160	41 01	59	160	42 00	59	160	42 59	60	160	43 59	59	160
17	39 54	59	159	40 53	59	159	41 52	60	159	42 52	59	159	43 51	60	158
18	39 46	59	158	40 45	59	158	41 44	60	157	42 44	59	157	43 43	59	157
19	39 37	60	157	40 37	59	156	41 36	59	156	42 35	59	156	43 34	60	156
20	39 29	+59	155	40 28	+59	155	41 27	+59	155	42 26	+59	155	43 25	+59	155
21	39 19	60	154	40 19	59	154	41 18	59	154	42 17	59	154	43 16	59	153
22	39 10	59	153	40 09	59	153	41 08	59	153	42 07	59	152	43 06	59	152
23	39 00	59	152	39 59	59	152	40 58	59	151	41 57	59	151	42 56	59	151
24	38 50	58	151	39 48	59	150	40 47	59	150	41 46	59	150	42 45	59	150
25	38 39	+59	149	39 38	+58	149	40 36	+59	149	41 35	+59	149	42 34	+59	148
26	38 28	58	148	39 26	59	148	40 25	59	148	41 24	59	148	42 23	58	147
27	38 16	59	147	39 15	59	147	40 14	58	147	41 12	59	146	42 11	58	146
28	38 04	59	146	39 03	58	146	40 01	59	145	41 00	58	145	41 58	59	145
29	37 52	59	145	38 51	58	145	39 49	58	144	40 47	59	144	41 46	58	144
30	37 40	+58	144	38 38	+58	143	39 36	+59	143	40 35	+58	143	41 33	+58	142
31	37 27	58	142	38 25	58	142	39 23	58	142	40 21	59	142	41 20	58	141
32	37 13	59	141	38 12	58	141	39 10	58	141	40 08	58	140	41 06	58	140
33	37 00	58	140	37 58	58	140	38 56	58	140	39 54	58	139	40 52	58	139
34	36 46	58	139	37 44	58	139	38 42	58	138	39 40	58	138	40 38	58	138
35	36 31	+58	138	37 29	+58	138	38 27	+58	137	39 25	+58	137	40 23	+58	137
36	36 17	58	137	37 15	58	136	38 13	57	136	39 10	58	136	40 08	58	135
37	36 02	58	136	37 00	58	135	37 58	57	135	38 55	58	135	39 53	57	134
38	35 47	58	135	36 45	57	134	37 42	58	134	38 40	57	134	39 37	58	133
39	35 31	58	133	36 29	58	133	37 27	57	133	38 24	57	132	39 21	58	132
40	35 16	+57	132	36 13	+58	132	37 11	+57	132	38 08	+57	131	39 05	+58	131
41	35 00	57	131	35 57	57	131	36 54	58	131	37 52	57	130	38 49	57	130
42	34 43	58	130	35 41	57	130	36 38	57	129	37 35	57	129	38 32	57	129
43	34 27	57	129	35 24	57	129	36 21	57	128	37 18	57	128	38 15	57	128
44	34 10	57	128	35 07	57	128	36 04	57	127	37 01	57	127	37 58	57	126
45	33 53	+57	127	34 50	+57	127	35 47	+57	126	36 44	+57	126	37 41	+57	125
46	33 35	57	126	34 32	57	125	35 29	57	125	36 26	57	125	37 23	57	124
47	33 18	57	125	34 15	57	124	35 12	56	124	36 08	57	124	37 05	57	123
48	33 00	57	124	33 57	57	123	34 54	56	123	35 50	57	123	36 47	57	122
49	32 42	57	123	33 39	57	122	34 36	56	122	35 32	57	121	36 29	56	121
50	32 24	+57	122	33 21	+56	121	34 17	+57	121	35 14	+56	120	36 10	+57	120
51	32 05	57	121	33 02	57	120	33 59	56	120	34 55	56	119	35 51	57	119
52	31 47	56	119	32 43	57	119	33 40	56	119	34 36	56	118	35 32	57	118
53	31 28	56	118	32 24	57	118	33 21	56	118	34 17	56	117	35 13	57	117
54	31 09	56	117	32 05	57	117	33 02	56	117	33 58	56	116	34 54	56	116
55	30 50	+56	116	31 46	+56	116	32 42	+57	116	33 39	+56	115	34 35	+56	115
56	30 30	57	115	31 27	56	115	32 23	56	115	33 19	56	114	34 15	56	114
57	30 11	56	114	31 07	56	114	32 03	56	113	32 59	56	113	33 55	56	113
58	29 51	56	113	30 47	56	113	31 43	56	112	32 39	56	112	33 35	56	112
59	29 31	56	112	30 27	56	112	31 23	56	111	32 19	56	111	33 15	56	111
60	29 11	+56	111	30 07	+56	111	31 03	+56	110	31 59	+56	110	32 55	+56	110
61	28 51	56	110	29 47	56	110	30 43	56	109	31 39	56	109	32 35	55	109
62	28 31	56	109	29 27	56	109	30 23	56	108	31 19	55	108	32 14	56	108
63	28 11	56	108	29 07	55	108	30 02	56	107	30 58	56	107	31 54	55	107
64	27 50	56	107	28 46	56	107	29 42	55	106	30 37	56	106	31 33	56	106
65	27 30	+55	106	28 25	+56	106	29 21	+56	105	30 17	+55	105	31 12	+56	105
66	27 09	56	105	28 05	55	105	29 00	56	104	29 56	55	104	30 51	56	104
67	26 48	56	104	27 44	55	104	28 39	56	103	29 35	55	103	30 30	56	103
68	26 27	56	103	27 23	55	103	28 18	56	103	29 14	56	102	30 09	56	102
69	26 06	56	102	27 02	55	102	27 57	56	102	28 53	55	101	29 48	56	101

LHA	25° Hc	25° d	25° Z	26° Hc	26° d	26° Z	27° Hc	27° d	27° Z	28° Hc	28° d	28° Z	29° Hc	29° d	29° Z	LHA
	° ′	′	°	° ′	′	°	° ′	′	°	° ′	′	°	° ′	′	°	
0	46 00	+60	180	47 00	+60	180	48 00	+60	180	49 00	+60	180	50 00	+60	180	360
1	46 00	60	179	47 00	60	179	48 00	60	179	49 00	60	179	50 00	60	179	359
2	45 59	60	177	46 59	60	177	47 59	60	177	48 59	60	177	49 59	60	177	358
3	45 58	60	176	46 58	60	176	47 58	60	176	48 58	60	176	49 58	60	176	357
4	45 56	60	175	46 56	60	175	47 56	60	175	48 56	60	175	49 56	60	175	356
5	45 54	+60	174	46 54	+60	173	47 54	+60	173	48 54	+60	173	49 54	+60	173	355
6	45 51	60	172	46 51	60	172	47 51	60	172	48 51	60	172	49 51	60	172	354
7	45 48	60	171	46 48	60	171	47 48	60	171	48 48	60	171	49 48	59	171	353
8	45 44	60	170	46 44	60	170	47 44	60	169	48 44	60	169	49 44	60	169	352
9	45 40	60	168	46 40	60	168	47 40	60	168	48 40	59	168	49 39	60	168	351
10	45 36	+59	167	46 35	+60	167	47 35	+60	167	48 35	+60	167	49 35	+59	167	350
11	45 31	59	166	46 30	60	166	47 30	60	165	48 30	59	165	49 29	60	165	349
12	45 25	60	164	46 25	59	164	47 24	60	164	48 24	60	164	49 24	59	164	348
13	45 19	60	163	46 19	59	163	47 18	60	163	48 18	59	163	49 17	60	162	347
14	45 13	59	162	46 12	60	162	47 12	59	162	48 11	60	161	49 11	59	161	346
15	45 06	+59	161	46 05	+60	160	47 05	+59	160	48 04	+59	160	49 03	+60	160	345
16	44 58	60	159	45 58	59	159	46 57	59	159	47 56	60	159	48 56	59	159	344
17	44 51	59	158	45 50	59	158	46 49	59	158	47 48	60	157	48 48	59	157	343
18	44 42	60	157	45 42	59	157	46 41	59	156	47 40	59	156	48 39	59	156	342
19	44 34	59	156	45 33	59	155	46 32	59	155	47 31	59	155	48 30	59	155	341
20	44 24	+60	154	45 24	+59	154	46 23	+59	154	47 22	+59	154	48 21	+59	153	340
21	44 15	59	153	45 14	59	153	46 13	59	153	47 12	59	152	48 11	59	152	339
22	44 05	59	152	45 04	59	152	46 03	59	151	47 02	58	151	48 00	59	151	338
23	43 55	58	151	44 53	59	150	45 52	59	150	46 51	59	150	47 50	58	149	337
24	43 44	59	149	44 43	58	149	45 41	59	149	46 40	59	148	47 39	58	148	336
25	43 33	+58	148	44 31	+59	148	45 30	+58	148	46 28	+59	147	47 27	+58	147	335
26	43 21	59	147	44 20	58	147	45 18	59	146	46 17	58	146	47 15	58	146	334
27	43 09	59	146	44 08	58	145	45 06	58	145	46 04	59	145	47 03	58	144	333
28	42 57	58	145	43 55	59	144	44 54	58	144	45 52	58	144	46 50	58	143	332
29	42 44	58	143	43 42	59	143	44 41	58	143	45 39	58	142	46 37	58	142	331
30	42 31	+58	142	43 29	+58	142	44 27	+58	141	45 25	+58	141	46 23	+58	141	330
31	42 18	58	141	43 16	58	141	44 14	58	140	45 12	58	140	46 10	57	139	329
32	42 04	58	140	43 02	58	139	44 00	58	139	44 58	57	139	45 55	58	138	328
33	41 50	58	139	42 48	58	138	43 46	57	138	44 43	58	137	45 41	58	137	327
34	41 36	57	137	42 33	58	137	43 31	58	137	44 29	57	136	45 26	58	136	326
35	41 21	+57	136	42 18	+58	136	43 16	+58	135	44 14	+57	135	45 11	+57	135	325
36	41 06	57	135	42 03	58	135	43 01	57	134	43 58	58	134	44 56	57	133	324
37	40 50	58	134	41 48	57	134	42 45	58	133	43 43	57	133	44 40	57	132	323
38	40 35	57	133	41 32	57	132	42 29	58	132	43 27	57	132	44 24	57	131	322
39	40 19	57	132	41 16	57	131	42 13	57	131	43 10	57	130	44 07	57	130	321
40	40 03	+57	131	41 00	+57	130	41 57	+57	130	42 54	+57	129	43 51	+57	129	320
41	39 46	57	129	40 43	57	129	41 40	57	129	42 37	57	128	43 34	57	128	319
42	39 29	57	128	40 26	57	128	41 23	57	127	42 20	57	127	43 17	56	127	318
43	39 12	57	127	40 09	57	127	41 06	57	126	42 03	56	126	42 59	57	125	317
44	38 55	57	126	39 52	57	126	40 49	56	125	41 45	57	125	42 42	56	124	316
45	38 38	+56	125	39 34	+57	125	40 31	+56	124	41 27	+57	124	42 24	+56	123	315
46	38 20	56	124	39 16	57	123	40 13	56	123	41 09	57	123	42 06	56	122	314
47	38 02	56	123	38 58	57	122	39 55	56	122	40 51	56	121	41 47	56	121	313
48	37 44	56	122	38 40	56	121	39 36	57	121	40 33	56	120	41 29	56	120	312
49	37 25	57	121	38 22	56	120	39 18	56	120	40 14	56	119	41 10	56	119	311
50	37 07	+56	120	38 03	+56	119	38 59	+56	119	39 55	+56	118	40 51	+56	118	310
51	36 48	56	118	37 44	56	118	38 40	56	118	39 36	56	117	40 32	56	117	309
52	36 29	56	117	37 25	56	117	38 21	56	117	39 17	56	116	40 13	55	116	308
53	36 10	56	116	37 06	56	116	38 02	55	115	38 57	56	115	39 53	56	115	307
54	35 50	56	115	36 46	56	115	37 42	56	114	38 38	55	114	39 33	56	113	306
55	35 31	+56	114	36 27	+55	114	37 22	+56	113	38 18	+56	113	39 14	+55	112	305
56	35 11	56	113	36 07	56	113	37 03	55	112	37 58	56	112	38 54	55	111	304
57	34 51	56	112	35 47	56	112	36 43	55	111	37 38	56	111	38 34	55	110	303
58	34 31	56	111	35 27	55	111	36 22	56	110	37 18	55	110	38 13	56	109	302
59	34 11	56	110	35 07	55	110	36 02	56	109	36 58	55	109	37 53	55	108	301
60	33 51	+55	109	34 46	+56	109	35 42	+55	108	36 37	+55	108	37 32	+56	107	300
61	33 30	56	108	34 26	55	108	35 21	56	107	36 17	55	107	37 12	55	106	299
62	33 10	55	107	34 05	56	107	35 01	55	106	35 56	56	106	36 51	55	105	298
63	32 49	56	106	33 45	55	106	34 40	55	105	35 35	55	105	36 30	55	104	297
64	32 29	55	105	33 24	55	105	34 19	55	104	35 14	56	104	36 10	54	103	296
65	32 08	+55	104	33 03	+55	104	33 58	+55	103	34 53	+56	103	35 49	+54	102	295
66	31 47	55	103	32 42	55	103	33 37	55	102	34 32	55	102	35 27	55	101	294
67	31 26	55	102	32 21	55	102	33 16	55	101	34 11	55	101	35 06	55	100	293
68	31 05	55	101	32 00	55	101	32 55	55	100	33 50	55	100	34 45	55	99	292
69	30 44	55	100	31 39	55	100	32 34	55	99	33 29	55	99	34 24	55	98	291

S. Lat. {LHA greater than 180°....... Zn=180−Z; LHA less than 180°.......... Zn=180+Z}

DECLINATION (15°-29°) **SAME** NAME AS LATITUDE

N. Lat. {LHA greater than 180°....... Zn=Z; LHA less than 180°.......... Zn=360−Z}

DECLINATION (15°-29°) SAME NAME AS LATITUDE

LHA	15° Hc	d	Z	16° Hc	d	Z	17° Hc	d	Z	18° Hc	d	Z	19° Hc	d	Z
	° ′	′	°	° ′	′	°	° ′	′	°	° ′	′	°	° ′	′	°
70	21 06	+55	103	22 02	+56	103	22 58	+56	103	23 54	+56	102	24 50	+55	102
71	20 45	56	102	21 41	56	102	22 37	56	102	23 33	55	101	24 28	56	101
72	20 24	56	101	21 20	56	101	22 16	56	101	23 12	56	100	24 07	56	100
73	20 03	55	101	20 59	56	100	21 55	55	100	22 50	56	99	23 46	56	99
74	19 42	56	100	20 38	55	99	21 33	56	99	22 29	56	98	23 25	55	98
75	19 21	+55	99	20 16	+56	98	21 12	+56	98	22 08	+55	97	23 03	+56	97
76	18 59	56	98	19 55	56	97	20 51	55	97	21 46	56	96	22 42	56	96
77	18 38	56	97	19 34	55	96	20 29	56	96	21 25	56	96	22 21	55	95
78	18 17	55	96	19 12	56	95	20 08	56	95	21 04	55	95	21 59	56	94
79	17 55	56	95	18 51	56	94	19 47	55	94	20 42	56	94	21 38	55	93
80	17 34	+55	94	18 29	+56	93	19 25	+56	93	20 21	+55	93	21 16	+56	92
81	17 12	56	93	18 08	56	93	19 04	55	92	19 59	56	92	20 55	55	91
82	16 51	56	92	17 47	55	92	18 42	56	91	19 38	55	91	20 33	56	90
83	16 29	56	91	17 25	56	91	18 21	55	90	19 16	56	90	20 12	55	89
84	16 08	56	90	17 04	55	90	17 59	56	89	18 55	55	89	19 50	56	88
85	15 46	+56	89	16 42	+56	89	17 38	+55	88	18 33	+56	88	19 29	+55	88
86	15 25	56	88	16 21	55	88	17 16	56	87	18 12	55	87	19 07	56	87
87	15 03	56	87	15 59	56	87	16 55	55	87	17 50	56	86	18 46	55	86
88	14 42	56	86	15 38	56	86	16 33	56	86	17 29	55	85	18 24	56	85
89	14 20	56	85	15 16	56	85	16 12	55	85	17 07	56	84	18 03	56	84
90	13 59	+56	85	14 55	+55	84	15 50	+56	84	16 46	+56	83	17 42	+55	83
91	13 38	55	84	14 33	56	83	15 29	56	83	16 25	55	82	17 20	56	82
92	13 16	56	83	14 12	56	82	15 08	56	82	16 03	56	82	16 59	56	81
93	12 55	56	82	13 51	56	81	14 47	55	81	15 42	56	81	16 38	56	80
94	12 34	56	81	13 30	55	80	14 25	56	80	15 21	56	80	16 17	55	79
95	12 13	+55	80	13 08	+56	80	14 04	+56	79	15 00	+56	79	15 56	+55	78
96	11 51	56	79	12 47	56	79	13 43	56	78	14 39	56	78	15 35	55	78
97	11 30	56	78	12 26	56	78	13 22	56	77	14 18	56	77	15 14	55	77
98	11 09	56	77	12 05	56	77	13 01	56	76	13 57	56	76	14 53	56	76
99	10 48	56	76	11 44	56	76	12 40	56	76	13 36	56	75	14 32	56	75
100	10 28	+56	75	11 24	+55	75	12 19	+56	75	13 15	+56	74	14 11	+56	74
101	10 07	56	74	11 03	56	74	11 59	56	74	12 55	56	73	13 51	56	73
102	09 46	56	74	10 42	56	73	11 38	56	73	12 34	56	72	13 30	56	72
103	09 26	56	73	10 22	56	72	11 18	56	72	12 14	56	72	13 10	56	71
104	09 05	56	72	10 01	56	71	10 57	56	71	11 53	57	71	12 50	56	70
105	08 45	+56	71	09 41	+56	70	10 37	+56	70	11 33	+56	70	12 29	+56	69
106	08 25	56	70	09 21	56	70	10 17	56	69	11 13	56	69	12 09	56	68
107	08 04	57	69	09 01	56	69	09 57	56	68	10 53	56	68	11 49	57	68
108	07 44	57	68	08 41	56	68	09 37	56	67	10 33	57	67	11 30	56	67
109	07 25	56	67	08 21	56	67	09 17	57	66	10 14	56	66	11 10	56	66
110	07 05	+56	66	08 01	+57	66	08 58	+56	66	09 54	+56	65	10 50	+57	65
111	06 45	57	65	07 42	56	65	08 38	57	65	09 35	56	64	10 31	56	64
112	06 26	56	64	07 22	57	64	08 19	56	64	09 15	57	63	10 12	56	63
113	06 06	57	63	07 03	57	63	08 00	56	63	08 56	57	62	09 53	56	62
114	05 47	57	63	06 44	57	62	07 41	56	62	08 37	57	62	09 34	56	61
115	05 28	+57	62	06 25	+57	61	07 22	+56	61	08 18	+57	61	09 15	+57	60
116	05 09	57	61	06 06	57	60	07 03	57	60	08 00	56	60	08 56	57	59
117	04 51	57	60	05 48	56	59	06 44	57	59	07 41	57	59	08 38	57	58
118	04 32	57	59	05 29	57	59	06 26	57	58	07 23	57	58	08 20	57	58
119	04 14	57	58	05 11	57	58	06 08	57	57	07 05	57	57	08 02	57	57
120	03 56	+57	57	04 53	+57	57	05 50	+57	56	06 47	+57	56	07 44	+57	56
121	03 38	57	56	04 35	57	56	05 32	57	55	06 29	57	55	07 26	57	55
122	03 20	57	55	04 17	58	55	05 15	57	55	06 12	57	54	07 09	57	54
123	03 03	57	54	04 00	57	54	04 57	57	54	05 54	57	53	06 51	58	53
124	02 45	58	53	03 43	57	53	04 40	57	53	05 37	57	52	06 34	58	52
125	02 28	+57	52	03 25	+58	52	04 23	+57	52	05 20	+58	52	06 18	+57	51
126	02 11	58	51	03 09	57	51	04 06	58	51	05 04	57	51	06 01	57	50
127	01 55	57	51	02 52	57	50	03 49	58	50	04 47	57	50	05 44	58	49
128	01 38	58	50	02 36	57	49	03 33	58	49	04 31	57	49	05 28	58	49
129	01 22	57	49	02 19	58	48	03 17	58	48	04 15	57	48	05 12	58	48
130	01 06	+57	48	02 03	+58	47	03 01	+58	47	03 59	+57	47	04 56	+58	47
131	00 50	58	47	01 48	57	47	02 45	58	46	03 43	58	46	04 41	58	46
132	00 35	57	46	01 32	58	46	02 30	58	45	03 28	58	45	04 26	58	45
133	00 19	58	45	01 17	58	45	02 15	58	44	03 13	58	44	04 11	58	44
134	00 04	58	44	01 02	58	44	02 00	58	44	02 58	58	43	03 56	58	43
135	−0 11	+58	43	00 47	+58	43	01 45	+58	43	02 43	+58	42	03 41	+58	42
136	−0 25	58	42	00 33	58	42	01 31	58	42	02 29	58	41	03 27	58	41
137	−0 40	59	41	00 19	58	41	01 17	58	41	02 15	58	40	03 13	58	40
138	−0 54	59	40	00 05	58	40	01 03	58	40	02 01	58	40	02 59	59	39
139	−1 07	58	39	−0 09	58	39	00 49	59	39	01 48	58	39	02 46	58	38

LHA	20° Hc	d	Z	21° Hc	d	Z	22° Hc	d	Z	23° Hc	d	Z	24° Hc	d	Z
	° ′	′	°	° ′	′	°	° ′	′	°	° ′	′	°	° ′	′	°
70	25 45	+56	101	26 41	+55	101	27 36	+56	101	28 32	+55	100	29 27	+55	100
71	25 24	56	100	26 20	55	100	27 15	56	100	28 11	55	99	29 06	55	99
72	25 03	55	99	25 58	56	99	26 54	55	99	27 49	56	98	28 45	55	98
73	24 42	55	99	25 37	56	98	26 33	55	98	27 28	55	97	28 23	56	97
74	24 20	56	98	25 16	55	97	26 11	56	97	27 07	55	96	28 02	55	96
75	23 59	+56	97	24 55	+55	96	25 50	+55	96	26 45	+56	95	27 41	+55	95
76	23 38	55	96	24 33	56	95	25 29	55	95	26 24	56	94	27 19	55	94
77	23 16	56	95	24 12	55	94	25 07	55	94	26 02	56	93	26 58	55	93
78	22 55	55	94	23 50	56	93	24 46	55	93	25 41	55	93	26 36	55	92
79	22 33	56	93	23 29	55	92	24 24	55	92	25 19	56	92	26 15	55	91
80	22 12	+55	92	23 07	+56	91	24 03	+55	91	24 58	+55	91	25 53	+55	90
81	21 50	56	91	22 46	55	91	23 41	55	90	24 36	56	90	25 32	55	89
82	21 29	55	90	22 24	56	90	23 20	55	89	24 15	55	89	25 10	55	88
83	21 07	56	89	22 03	55	89	22 58	55	88	23 53	56	88	24 49	55	87
84	20 46	55	88	21 41	56	88	22 37	55	87	23 32	55	87	24 27	55	86
85	20 24	+56	87	21 20	+55	87	22 15	+56	86	23 11	+55	86	24 06	+55	86
86	20 03	55	86	20 58	56	86	21 54	55	85	22 49	55	85	23 44	56	85
87	19 41	56	85	20 37	55	85	21 32	56	85	22 28	55	84	23 23	55	84
88	19 20	56	84	20 16	55	84	21 11	55	84	22 06	56	83	23 02	55	83
89	18 59	55	84	19 54	56	83	20 50	55	83	21 45	55	82	22 40	56	82
90	18 37	+56	83	19 33	+55	82	20 28	+56	82	21 24	+55	81	22 19	+55	81
91	18 16	56	82	19 12	55	81	20 07	55	81	21 02	56	80	21 58	55	80
92	17 55	56	81	18 50	56	80	19 46	55	80	20 41	56	80	21 37	55	79
93	17 34	55	80	18 29	56	79	19 25	55	79	20 20	56	79	21 16	55	78
94	17 12	56	79	18 08	56	79	19 04	55	78	19 59	56	78	20 55	55	77
95	16 51	+56	78	17 47	+56	78	18 43	+55	77	19 38	+56	77	20 34	+55	76
96	16 30	56	77	17 26	56	77	18 22	55	76	19 17	56	76	20 13	55	76
97	16 09	56	76	17 05	56	76	18 01	55	75	18 56	56	75	19 52	56	75
98	15 49	55	75	16 44	56	75	17 40	56	75	18 36	55	74	19 31	56	74
99	15 28	56	74	16 24	55	74	17 19	56	74	18 15	56	73	19 11	55	73
100	15 07	+56	74	16 03	+56	73	16 59	+56	73	17 55	+55	72	18 50	+56	72
101	14 47	56	73	15 43	55	72	16 38	56	72	17 34	56	71	18 30	56	71
102	14 26	56	72	15 22	56	71	16 18	56	71	17 14	56	71	18 10	55	70
103	14 06	56	71	15 02	56	70	15 58	56	70	16 54	55	70	17 49	56	69
104	13 46	56	70	14 42	56	70	15 38	56	69	16 34	55	69	17 29	56	68
105	13 25	+57	69	14 22	+56	69	15 18	+56	68	16 14	+55	68	17 09	+56	67
106	13 05	57	68	14 02	56	68	14 58	56	67	15 54	56	67	16 50	56	67
107	12 46	56	67	13 42	56	67	14 38	56	66	15 34	56	66	16 30	56	66
108	12 26	56	66	13 22	56	66	14 18	56	66	15 14	56	65	16 10	57	65
109	12 06	56	65	13 02	57	65	13 59	56	65	14 55	56	64	15 51	56	64
110	11 47	+56	64	12 43	+56	64	13 39	+57	64	14 36	+56	63	15 32	+56	63
111	11 27	57	64	12 24	56	63	13 20	56	63	14 16	57	63	15 13	56	62
112	11 08	57	63	12 05	56	62	13 01	57	62	13 58	56	62	14 54	56	61
113	10 49	57	62	11 46	56	61	12 42	57	61	13 39	56	61	14 35	56	60
114	10 30	57	61	11 27	57	61	12 24	56	60	13 20	56	60	14 16	57	59
115	10 12	+56	60	11 08	+57	60	12 05	+57	59	13 02	+56	59	13 58	+57	59
116	09 53	57	59	10 50	57	59	11 47	56	58	12 43	57	58	13 40	56	58
117	09 35	57	58	10 32	56	58	11 28	57	58	12 25	57	57	13 22	56	57
118	09 17	56	57	10 13	57	57	11 10	57	57	12 07	57	56	13 04	57	56
119	08 59	57	56	09 56	56	56	10 52	57	56	11 49	57	55	12 46	57	55
120	08 41	+57	55	09 38	+57	55	10 35	+57	55	11 32	+57	54	12 29	+56	54
121	08 23	57	55	09 20	57	54	10 17	57	54	11 14	57	54	12 11	57	53
122	08 06	57	54	09 03	57	53	10 00	57	53	10 57	57	53	11 54	57	52
123	07 49	57	53	08 46	57	52	09 43	57	52	10 40	57	52	11 37	57	52
124	07 32	57	52	08 29	57	52	09 26	57	51	10 23	58	51	11 21	57	51
125	07 15	+57	51	08 12	+57	51	09 09	+58	50	10 07	+57	50	11 04	+57	50
126	06 58	58	50	07 56	57	50	08 53	57	49	09 50	58	49	10 48	57	49
127	06 42	57	49	07 39	58	49	08 37	57	49	09 34	58	48	10 32	57	48
128	06 26	57	48	07 23	58	48	08 21	57	48	09 18	58	47	10 16	57	47
129	06 10	57	47	07 07	58	47	08 05	58	47	09 03	57	46	10 00	58	46
130	05 54	+58	46	06 52	+58	46	07 50	+57	46	08 47	+58	46	09 45	+57	45
131	05 39	58	46	06 37	57	45	07 34	58	45	08 32	58	45	09 30	57	44
132	05 24	57	45	06 21	58	44	07 19	58	44	08 17	58	44	09 15	58	44
133	05 09	57	44	06 06	58	43	07 04	58	43	08 02	58	43	09 00	58	43
134	04 54	58	43	05 52	58	43	06 50	58	42	07 48	58	42	08 46	58	42
135	04 39	+58	42	05 37	+58	42	06 35	+58	41	07 33	+58	41	08 31	+58	41
136	04 25	58	41	05 23	58	41	06 21	59	40	07 20	58	40	08 18	58	40
137	04 11	58	40	05 09	59	40	06 08	58	40	07 06	58	39	08 04	58	39
138	03 58	58	39	04 56	58	39	05 54	58	39	06 52	59	38	07 51	58	38
139	03 44	58	38	04 42	59	38	05 41	58	38	06 39	58	37	07 37	59	37

25° Hc	d	Z	26° Hc	d	Z	27° Hc	d	Z	28° Hc	d	Z	29° Hc	d	Z	LHA
° ′	′	°	° ′	′	°	° ′	′	°	° ′	′	°	° ′	′	°	
30 22	+56	99	31 18	+55	99	32 13	+55	98	33 08	+55	98	34 03	+54	97	290
30 01	55	98	30 56	55	98	31 51	55	97	32 46	55	97	33 41	55	96	289
29 40	55	97	30 35	55	97	31 30	55	96	32 25	55	96	33 20	55	95	288
29 19	55	96	30 14	55	96	31 09	55	95	32 04	54	95	32 58	55	94	287
28 57	55	95	29 52	55	95	30 47	55	94	31 42	55	94	32 37	55	94	286
28 36	+55	94	29 31	+55	94	30 26	+55	94	31 21	+55	93	32 16	+54	93	285
28 14	55	94	29 09	55	93	30 04	55	93	30 59	55	92	31 54	55	92	284
27 53	55	93	28 48	55	92	29 43	55	92	30 38	55	91	31 33	54	91	283
27 31	55	92	28 26	55	91	29 21	55	91	30 16	55	90	31 11	55	90	282
27 10	55	91	28 05	55	90	29 00	55	90	29 55	55	89	30 50	54	89	281
26 48	+55	90	27 43	+55	89	28 38	+55	89	29 33	+55	88	30 28	+55	88	280
26 27	55	89	27 22	55	88	28 17	55	88	29 12	55	87	30 07	54	87	279
26 05	55	88	27 00	55	87	27 55	55	87	28 50	55	87	29 45	55	86	278
25 44	55	87	26 39	55	87	27 34	55	86	28 29	55	86	29 24	54	85	277
25 22	55	86	26 17	55	86	27 12	55	85	28 07	55	85	29 02	55	84	276
25 01	+55	85	25 56	+55	85	26 51	+55	84	27 46	+55	84	28 41	+55	83	275
24 40	55	84	25 35	55	84	26 30	55	83	27 25	55	83	28 20	54	82	274
24 18	55	83	25 13	55	83	26 08	55	82	27 03	55	82	27 58	55	82	273
23 57	55	82	24 52	55	82	25 47	55	82	26 42	55	81	27 37	55	81	272
23 36	55	81	24 31	55	81	25 26	55	81	26 21	55	80	27 16	55	80	271
23 14	+56	81	24 10	+55	80	25 05	+55	80	26 00	+55	79	26 55	+55	79	270
22 53	55	80	23 48	56	79	24 44	55	79	25 39	55	78	26 34	55	78	269
22 32	55	79	23 27	55	78	24 22	56	78	25 18	55	77	26 13	55	77	268
22 11	55	78	23 06	56	77	24 02	55	77	24 57	55	77	25 52	55	76	267
21 50	55	77	22 45	56	77	23 41	55	76	24 36	55	76	25 31	55	75	266
21 29	+55	76	22 24	+56	76	23 20	+55	75	24 15	+55	75	25 10	+55	74	265
21 08	56	75	22 04	55	75	22 59	55	74	23 54	56	74	24 50	55	73	264
20 48	55	74	21 43	56	74	22 38	56	73	23 34	55	73	24 29	55	73	263
20 27	55	73	21 22	56	73	22 18	55	73	23 13	56	72	24 09	55	72	262
20 06	56	72	21 02	55	72	21 57	56	72	22 53	55	71	23 48	55	71	261
19 46	+55	72	20 41	+56	71	21 37	+56	71	22 33	+55	70	23 28	+55	70	260
19 26	55	71	20 21	56	70	21 17	55	70	22 12	56	69	23 08	55	69	259
19 05	56	70	20 01	56	69	20 57	55	69	21 52	56	69	22 48	55	68	258
18 45	56	69	19 41	56	69	20 37	55	68	21 32	56	68	22 28	55	67	257
18 25	56	68	19 21	56	68	20 17	55	67	21 12	56	67	22 08	56	66	256
18 05	+56	67	19 01	+56	67	19 57	+56	66	20 53	+55	66	21 48	+56	66	255
17 46	56	66	18 42	55	66	19 37	56	65	20 33	56	65	21 29	56	65	254
17 26	56	65	18 22	56	65	19 18	56	65	20 14	56	64	21 10	55	64	253
17 07	56	64	18 03	56	64	18 59	56	64	19 55	55	63	20 50	56	63	252
16 47	56	64	17 43	56	63	18 39	56	63	19 35	56	62	20 31	56	62	251
16 28	+56	63	17 24	+56	62	18 20	+56	62	19 16	+56	62	20 12	+56	61	250
16 09	56	62	17 05	56	61	18 01	57	61	18 58	56	61	19 54	56	60	249
15 50	56	61	16 46	57	61	17 43	56	60	18 39	56	60	19 35	56	59	248
15 31	57	60	16 28	56	60	17 24	56	59	18 20	57	59	19 17	56	59	247
15 13	56	59	16 09	57	59	17 06	56	58	18 02	56	58	18 58	57	58	246
14 55	+56	58	15 51	+57	58	16 48	+56	58	17 44	+56	57	18 40	+57	57	245
14 36	57	57	15 33	56	57	16 29	57	57	17 26	56	56	18 22	56	56	244
14 18	57	56	15 15	57	56	16 12	56	56	17 08	57	55	18 05	56	55	243
14 01	56	56	14 57	57	55	15 54	57	55	16 51	56	55	17 47	57	54	242
13 43	57	55	14 40	56	54	15 36	57	54	16 33	57	54	17 30	57	53	241
13 25	+57	54	14 22	+57	54	15 19	+57	53	16 16	+57	53	17 13	+56	53	240
13 08	57	53	14 05	57	53	15 02	57	52	15 59	57	52	16 56	57	52	239
12 51	57	52	13 48	57	52	14 45	57	51	15 42	57	51	16 39	57	51	238
12 34	57	51	13 31	57	51	14 28	57	51	15 25	57	50	16 22	57	50	237
12 18	57	50	13 15	57	50	14 12	57	50	15 09	57	49	16 06	57	49	236
12 01	+57	49	12 58	+58	49	13 56	+57	49	14 53	+57	48	15 50	+57	48	235
11 45	57	49	12 42	58	48	13 40	57	48	14 37	57	48	15 34	57	47	234
11 29	57	48	12 26	58	47	13 24	57	47	14 21	57	47	15 18	58	46	233
11 13	58	47	12 11	57	46	13 08	58	46	14 06	57	46	15 03	57	46	232
10 58	57	46	11 55	58	46	12 53	57	45	13 50	58	45	14 48	57	45	231
10 42	+58	45	11 40	+58	45	12 38	+57	44	13 35	+58	44	14 33	+57	44	230
10 27	58	44	11 25	58	44	12 23	57	44	13 20	58	43	14 18	58	43	229
10 13	57	43	11 10	58	43	12 08	58	43	13 06	57	42	14 03	58	42	228
09 58	58	42	10 56	58	42	11 54	57	42	12 51	58	42	13 49	58	41	227
09 44	57	41	10 41	58	41	11 39	58	41	12 37	58	41	13 35	58	40	226
09 29	+58	41	10 27	+58	40	11 25	+58	40	12 23	+58	40	13 21	+58	40	225
09 16	58	40	10 14	58	39	11 12	58	39	12 10	58	39	13 08	58	39	224
09 02	58	39	10 00	58	39	10 58	58	38	11 56	58	38	12 54	59	38	223
08 49	58	38	09 47	58	38	10 45	58	37	11 43	58	37	12 41	59	37	222
08 36	58	37	09 34	58	37	10 32	58	37	11 30	59	36	12 29	58	36	221

S. Lat. {LHA greater than 180°....... Zn=180−Z; LHA less than 180°.......... Zn=180+Z}

DECLINATION (15°-29°) SAME NAME AS LATITUDE

N. Lat. {LHA greater than 180°....... Zn=Z
LHA less than 180°........... Zn=360−Z}

DECLINATION (15°-29°) **SAME** NAME AS LATITUDE

LHA	15° Hc	d	Z	16° Hc	d	Z	17° Hc	d	Z	18° Hc	d	Z	19° Hc	d	Z
	° ′	′	°	° ′	′	°	° ′	′	°	° ′	′	°	° ′	′	°
140	-1 21	+58	38	-0 23	+59	38	00 36	+58	38	01 34	+59	38	02 33	+58	37
141	-1 34	58	37	-0 36	59	37	00 23	58	37	01 21	59	37	02 20	58	37
142	-1 47	58	37	-0 49	59	36	00 10	58	36	01 08	59	36	02 07	59	36
143	-2 00	59	36	-1 01	58	35	-0 03	59	35	00 56	59	35	01 55	58	35
144	-2 12	59	35	-1 13	58	34	-0 15	59	34	00 44	59	34	01 43	58	34
145	-2 24	+59	34	-1 25	+58	33	-0 27	+59	33	00 32	+59	33	01 31	+58	33
146	-2 36	59	33	-1 37	59	33	-0 38	58	32	00 20	59	32	01 19	59	32
147	-2 47	58	32	-1 49	59	32	-0 50	59	31	00 09	59	31	01 08	59	31
148	-2 59	59	31	-2 00	59	31	-1 01	59	30	-0 02	59	30	00 57	59	30
149	-3 09	58	30	-2 11	59	30	-1 12	59	30	-0 13	59	29	00 46	59	29
150	-3 20	+59	29	-2 21	+59	29	-1 22	+59	29	-0 23	+59	28	00 36	+59	28
151	-3 30	59	28	-2 31	59	28	-1 32	59	28	-0 33	59	27	00 26	59	27
152	-3 40	59	27	-2 41	59	27	-1 42	59	27	-0 43	59	27	00 16	60	26
153	-3 50	59	26	-2 51	60	26	-1 51	59	26	-0 52	59	26	00 07	59	25
154	-3 59	59	25	-3 00	59	25	-2 01	60	25	-1 01	59	25	-0 02	59	24
155	-4 08	+59	24	-3 09	+60	24	-2 09	+59	24	-1 10	+59	24	-0 11	+59	24
156	-4 17	60	23	-3 17	59	23	-2 18	59	23	-1 19	60	23	-0 19	59	23
157	-4 25	59	22	-3 26	60	22	-2 26	59	22	-1 27	60	22	-0 27	59	22
158	-4 33	59	21	-3 34	60	21	-2 34	59	21	-1 35	60	21	-0 35	59	21
159	-4 41	60	20	-3 41	59	20	-2 42	60	20	-1 42	59	20	-0 43	60	20
160	-4 48	+60	19	-3 48	+59	19	-2 49	+60	19	-1 49	+59	19	-0 50	+60	19
161	-4 55	60	18	-3 55	59	18	-2 56	60	18	-1 56	59	18	-0 57	60	18
162	-5 02	60	17	-4 02	60	17	-3 02	59	17	-2 03	60	17	-1 03	60	17
163	-5 08	60	16	-4 08	60	16	-3 08	59	16	-2 09	60	16	-1 09	60	16
164				-4 14	60	15	-3 14	59	15	-2 15	60	15	-1 15	60	15
165				-4 20	+60	14	-3 20	+60	14	-2 20	+60	14	-1 20	+59	14
166				-4 25	60	13	-3 25	60	13	-2 25	60	13	-1 25	59	13
167				-4 30	60	13	-3 30	60	12	-2 30	60	12	-1 30	60	12
168				-4 34	60	12	-3 34	60	11	-2 34	59	11	-1 35	60	11
169				-4 38	60	11	-3 38	60	11	-2 38	59	10	-1 39	60	10
170				-4 42	+60	10	-3 42	+60	10	-2 42	+60	10	-1 42	+60	9
171				-4 45	60	9	-3 45	59	9	-2 46	60	9	-1 46	60	9
172				-4 48	59	8	-3 49	60	8	-2 49	60	8	-1 49	60	8
173				-4 51	60	7	-3 51	60	7	-2 51	60	7	-1 51	60	7
174				-4 53	59	6	-3 54	60	6	-2 54	60	6	-1 54	60	6
175				-4 55	+59	5	-3 56	+60	5	-2 56	+60	5	-1 56	+60	5
176				-4 57	60	4	-3 57	60	4	-2 57	60	4	-1 57	60	4
177				-4 58	60	3	-3 58	60	3	-2 58	60	3	-1 58	60	3
178				-4 59	60	2	-3 59	60	2	-2 59	60	2	-1 59	60	2
179				-5 00	60	1	-4 00	60	1	-3 00	60	1	-2 00	60	1
180				-5 00	+60	0	-4 00	+60	0	-3 00	+60	0	-2 00	+60	0

LHA	20° Hc	d	Z	21° Hc	d	Z	22° Hc	d	Z	23° Hc	d	Z	24° Hc	d	Z
	° ′	′	°	° ′	′	°	° ′	′	°	° ′	′	°	° ′	′	°
140	03 31	+58	37	04 29	+59	37	05 28	+58	37	06 26	+59	37	07 25	+58	36
141	03 18	59	36	04 17	58	36	05 15	58	36	06 13	59	36	07 12	58	35
142	03 06	58	35	04 04	59	35	05 03	58	35	06 01	59	35	07 00	58	35
143	02 53	59	34	03 52	58	34	04 50	59	34	05 49	59	34	06 48	58	34
144	02 41	59	34	03 40	58	33	04 38	59	33	05 37	59	33	06 36	58	33
145	02 29	+59	33	03 28	+59	32	04 27	+59	32	05 26	+58	32	06 24	+59	32
146	02 18	59	32	03 17	59	32	04 16	58	31	05 14	59	31	06 13	59	31
147	02 07	59	31	03 06	58	31	04 04	59	30	05 03	59	30	06 02	59	30
148	01 56	59	30	02 55	59	30	03 54	59	30	04 53	59	29	05 52	58	29
149	01 45	59	29	02 44	59	29	03 43	59	29	04 42	59	28	05 41	59	28
150	01 35	+59	28	02 34	+59	28	03 33	+59	28	04 32	+59	28	05 31	+59	27
151	01 25	59	27	02 24	59	27	03 23	59	27	04 22	60	27	05 22	59	26
152	01 16	59	26	02 15	59	26	03 14	59	26	04 13	59	26	05 12	59	26
153	01 06	59	25	02 05	60	25	03 05	59	25	04 04	59	25	05 03	59	25
154	00 57	59	24	01 56	60	24	02 56	59	24	03 55	59	24	04 54	59	24
155	00 48	+60	23	01 48	+59	23	02 47	+59	23	03 46	+60	23	04 46	+59	23
156	00 40	59	22	01 39	60	22	02 39	59	22	03 38	60	22	04 38	59	22
157	00 32	59	22	01 31	60	21	02 31	59	21	03 30	60	21	04 30	59	21
158	00 24	60	21	01 24	59	20	02 23	60	20	03 23	59	20	04 22	60	20
159	00 17	59	20	01 16	60	20	02 16	59	19	03 15	60	19	04 15	59	19
160	00 10	+59	19	01 09	+60	19	02 09	+59	19	03 08	+60	18	04 08	+60	18
161	00 03	60	18	01 03	59	18	02 02	60	18	03 02	59	17	04 01	60	17
162	-0 03	59	17	00 56	60	17	01 56	60	17	02 56	59	17	03 55	60	16
163	-0 09	59	16	00 50	60	16	01 50	60	16	02 50	59	16	03 49	60	16
164	-0 15	60	15	00 45	59	15	01 44	60	15	02 44	60	15	03 44	59	15
165	-0 21	+60	14	00 39	+60	14	01 39	+60	14	02 39	+59	14	03 38	+60	14
166	-0 26	60	13	00 34	60	13	01 34	60	13	02 34	59	13	03 33	60	13
167	-0 30	59	12	00 29	60	12	01 29	60	12	02 29	60	12	03 29	60	12
168	-0 35	60	11	00 25	60	11	01 25	60	11	02 25	60	11	03 25	59	11
169	-0 39	60	10	00 21	60	10	01 21	60	10	02 21	60	10	03 21	60	10
170	-0 42	+59	9	00 17	+60	9	01 17	+60	9	02 17	+60	9	03 17	+60	9
171	-0 46	60	8	00 14	60	8	01 14	60	8	02 14	60	8	03 14	60	8
172	-0 49	60	8	00 11	60	7	01 11	60	7	02 11	60	7	03 11	60	7
173	-0 51	60	7	00 09	60	7	01 09	59	6	02 08	60	6	03 08	60	6
174	-0 54	60	6	00 06	60	6	01 06	60	6	02 06	60	6	03 06	60	5
175	-0 56	+60	5	00 04	+60	5	01 04	+60	5	02 04	+60	5	03 04	+60	5
176	-0 57	60	4	00 03	60	4	01 03	60	4	02 03	60	4	03 03	60	4
177	-0 58	60	3	00 02	60	3	01 02	60	3	02 02	60	3	03 02	60	3
178	-0 59	60	2	00 01	60	2	01 01	60	2	02 01	60	2	03 01	60	2
179	-1 00	60	1	00 00	60	1	01 00	60	1	02 00	60	1	03 00	60	1
180	-1 00	+60	0	00 00	+60	0	01 00	+60	0	02 00	+60	0	03 00	+60	0

LHA	25° Hc	d	Z	26° Hc	d	Z	27° Hc	d	Z	28° Hc	d	Z	29° Hc	d	Z	LHA
	° ′	′	°	° ′	′	°	° ′	′	°	° ′	′	°	° ′	′	°	
140	08 23	+58	36	09 21	+59	36	10 20	+58	36	11 18	+58	35	12 16	+58	35	220
141	08 10	59	35	09 09	58	35	10 07	59	35	11 06	58	35	12 04	58	34	219
142	07 58	59	34	08 57	58	34	09 55	59	34	10 54	58	34	11 52	58	33	218
143	07 46	59	33	08 45	58	33	09 43	59	33	10 42	58	33	11 40	59	33	217
144	07 34	59	33	08 33	59	32	09 32	58	32	10 30	59	32	11 29	58	32	216
145	07 23	+59	32	08 22	+58	31	09 20	+59	31	10 19	+59	31	11 18	+58	31	215
146	07 12	59	31	08 11	58	31	09 09	59	30	10 08	59	30	11 07	59	30	214
147	07 01	59	30	08 00	59	30	08 59	58	29	09 57	59	29	10 56	59	29	213
148	06 50	59	29	07 49	59	29	08 48	59	29	09 47	59	28	10 46	59	28	212
149	06 40	59	28	07 39	59	28	08 38	59	28	09 37	59	28	10 36	59	27	211
150	06 30	+59	27	07 29	+59	27	08 28	+59	27	09 27	+59	27	10 26	+59	26	210
151	06 21	59	26	07 20	59	26	08 19	59	26	09 18	59	26	10 17	59	26	209
152	06 11	59	25	07 10	60	25	08 10	59	25	09 09	59	25	10 08	59	25	208
153	06 02	59	24	07 01	60	24	08 01	59	24	09 00	59	24	09 59	59	24	207
154	05 53	60	24	06 53	59	23	07 52	59	23	08 51	59	23	09 50	60	23	206
155	05 45	+59	23	06 44	+60	23	07 44	+59	22	08 43	+59	22	09 42	+60	22	205
156	05 37	59	22	06 36	60	22	07 36	59	21	08 35	59	21	09 34	60	21	204
157	05 29	60	21	06 29	59	21	07 28	59	21	08 27	60	20	09 27	59	20	203
158	05 22	59	20	06 21	60	20	07 21	59	20	08 20	59	20	09 19	60	19	202
159	05 14	60	19	06 14	59	19	07 13	60	19	08 13	59	19	09 12	60	19	201
160	05 08	+59	18	06 07	+60	18	07 07	+59	18	08 06	+60	18	09 06	+59	18	200
161	05 01	60	17	06 01	59	17	07 00	60	17	08 00	59	17	08 59	60	17	199
162	04 55	59	16	05 54	60	16	06 54	60	16	07 54	59	16	08 53	60	16	198
163	04 49	60	15	05 49	59	15	06 48	60	15	07 48	60	15	08 48	59	15	197
164	04 43	60	15	05 43	60	14	06 43	60	14	07 43	59	14	08 42	60	14	196
165	04 38	+60	14	05 38	+60	14	06 38	+59	13	07 37	+60	13	08 37	+60	13	195
166	04 33	60	13	05 33	60	13	06 33	60	13	07 33	59	12	08 32	60	12	194
167	04 29	60	12	05 29	59	12	06 28	60	12	07 28	60	12	08 28	60	12	193
168	04 24	60	11	05 24	60	11	06 24	60	11	07 24	60	11	08 24	60	11	192
169	04 21	59	10	05 20	60	10	06 20	60	10	07 20	60	10	08 20	60	10	191
170	04 17	+60	9	05 17	+60	9	06 17	+60	9	07 17	+60	9	08 17	+59	9	190
171	04 14	60	8	05 14	60	8	06 14	60	8	07 14	59	8	08 13	60	8	189
172	04 11	60	7	05 11	60	7	06 11	60	7	07 11	60	7	08 11	60	7	188
173	04 08	60	6	05 08	60	6	06 08	60	6	07 08	60	6	08 08	60	6	187
174	04 06	60	5	05 06	60	5	06 06	60	5	07 06	60	5	08 06	60	5	186
175	04 04	+60	5	05 04	+60	5	06 04	+60	5	07 04	+60	4	08 04	+60	4	185
176	04 03	60	4	05 03	60	4	06 03	60	4	07 03	60	4	08 03	60	4	184
177	04 02	60	3	05 02	60	3	06 02	60	3	07 02	60	3	08 02	60	3	183
178	04 01	60	2	05 01	60	2	06 01	60	2	07 01	60	2	08 01	60	2	182
179	04 00	60	1	05 00	60	1	06 00	60	1	07 00	60	1	08 00	60	1	181
180	04 00	+60	0	05 00	+60	0	06 00	+60	0	07 00	+60	0	08 00	+60	0	180

15° 16° 17° 18° 19° 20° 21° 22° 23° 24° 25° 26° 27° 28° 29°

S. Lat. {LHA greater than 180°....... Zn=180−Z
LHA less than 180°........... Zn=180+Z}

DECLINATION (15°-29°) SAME NAME AS LATITUDE

LAT 69°

N. Lat. {LHA greater than 180°........ Zn=Z; LHA less than 180°............ Zn=360−Z}

LAT 69°

DECLINATION (15°-29°) CONTRARY NAME TO LATITUDE

LHA	15° Hc d Z	16° Hc d Z	17° Hc d Z	18° Hc d Z	19° Hc d Z	20° Hc d Z	21° Hc d Z	22° Hc d Z	23° Hc d Z	24° Hc d Z	25° Hc d Z	26° Hc d Z	27° Hc d Z	28° Hc d Z	29° Hc d Z	LHA
	° ′ ′ °	° ′ ′ °	° ′ ′ °	° ′ ′ °	° ′ ′ °	° ′ ′ °	° ′ ′ °	° ′ ′ °	° ′ ′ °	° ′ ′ °	° ′ ′ °	° ′ ′ °	° ′ ′ °	° ′ ′ °	° ′ ′ °	
65	-5 28 -57 118															295
64	-5 09 57 119															296
63	-4 51 57 120															297
62	-4 32 57 121	-5 29 57 121														298
61	-4 14 57 122	-5 11 57 122														299
60	-3 56 -57 123	-4 53 -57 123														300
59	-3 38 57 124	-4 35 57 124	-5 32 57 125													301
58	-3 20 57 125	-4 17 58 125	-5 15 57 125													302
57	-3 03 57 126	-4 00 57 126	-4 57 57 126													303
56	-2 45 58 127	-3 43 57 127	-4 40 57 127													304
55	-2 28 -57 128	-3 25 -58 128	-4 23 -57 128	-5 20 -58 128												305
54	-2 11 58 129	-3 09 57 129	-4 06 58 129	-5 04 57 129												306
53	-1 55 57 129	-2 52 57 130	-3 49 58 130	-4 47 57 130												307
52	-1 38 58 130	-2 36 57 131	-3 33 58 131	-4 31 57 131	-5 28 58 131											308
51	-1 22 57 131	-2 19 58 132	-3 17 58 132	-4 15 57 132	-5 12 58 132											309
50	-1 06 -57 132	-2 03 -58 133	-3 01 -58 133	-3 59 -57 133	-4 56 -58 133											310
49	-0 50 58 133	-1 48 57 133	-2 45 58 134	-3 43 58 134	-4 41 58 134											311
48	-0 35 57 134	-1 32 58 134	-2 30 58 135	-3 28 58 135	-4 26 58 135	-5 24 57 135										312
47	-0 19 58 135	-1 17 58 135	-2 15 58 136	-3 13 58 136	-4 11 58 136	-5 09 57 136										313
46	-0 04 58 136	-1 02 58 136	-2 00 58 136	-2 58 58 137	-3 56 58 137	-4 54 58 137										314
45	00 11 -58 137	-0 47 -58 137	-1 45 -58 137	-2 43 -58 138	-3 41 -58 138	-4 39 -58 138										315
44	00 25 58 138	-0 33 58 138	-1 31 58 138	-2 29 58 139	-3 27 58 139	-4 25 58 139	-5 23 58 139									316
43	00 40 59 139	-0 19 58 139	-1 17 58 139	-2 15 58 140	-3 13 58 140	-4 11 58 140	-5 09 59 140									317
42	00 54 59 140	-0 05 58 140	-1 03 58 140	-2 01 58 140	-2 59 59 141	-3 58 58 141	-4 56 58 141									318
41	01 07 58 141	00 09 58 141	-0 49 59 141	-1 48 58 141	-2 46 58 142	-3 44 58 142	-4 42 59 142									319
40	01 21 -58 142	00 23 -59 142	-0 36 -58 142	-1 34 -59 142	-2 33 -58 143	-3 31 -58 143	-4 29 -59 143									320
39	01 34 58 143	00 36 59 143	-0 23 58 143	-1 21 59 143	-2 20 58 143	-3 18 59 144	-4 17 58 144	-5 15 58 144								321
38	01 47 58 143	00 49 59 144	-0 10 58 144	-1 08 59 144	-2 07 59 144	-3 06 58 145	-4 04 59 145	-5 03 58 145								322
37	02 00 59 144	01 01 58 145	00 03 59 145	-0 56 59 145	-1 55 58 145	-2 53 59 146	-3 52 58 146	-4 50 59 146								323
36	02 12 59 145	01 13 58 146	00 15 59 146	-0 44 59 146	-1 43 58 146	-2 41 59 146	-3 40 58 147	-4 38 59 147								324
35	02 24 -59 146	01 25 -58 147	00 27 -59 147	-0 32 -59 147	-1 31 -58 147	-2 29 -59 147	-3 28 -59 148	-4 27 -59 148								325
34	02 36 59 147	01 37 59 147	00 38 58 148	-0 20 59 148	-1 19 59 148	-2 18 59 148	-3 17 59 148	-4 16 58 149	-5 14 59 149							326
33	02 47 58 148	01 49 59 148	00 50 59 149	-0 09 59 149	-1 08 59 149	-2 07 59 149	-3 06 58 149	-4 04 59 150	-5 03 59 150							327
32	02 59 59 149	02 00 59 149	01 01 59 150	00 02 59 150	-0 57 59 150	-1 56 59 150	-2 55 59 150	-3 54 59 150	-4 53 59 151							328
31	03 09 58 150	02 11 59 150	01 12 59 150	00 13 59 151	-0 46 59 151	-1 45 59 151	-2 44 59 151	-3 43 59 151	-4 42 59 152							329
30	03 20 -59 151	02 21 -59 151	01 22 -59 151	00 23 -59 152	-0 36 -59 152	-1 35 -59 152	-2 34 -59 152	-3 33 -59 152	-4 32 -59 152							330
29	03 30 59 152	02 31 59 152	01 32 59 152	00 33 59 153	-0 26 59 153	-1 25 59 153	-2 24 59 153	-3 23 59 153	-4 22 60 153							331
28	03 40 59 153	02 41 59 153	01 42 59 153	00 43 59 153	-0 16 60 154	-1 16 59 154	-2 15 59 154	-3 14 59 154	-4 13 59 154	-5 12 59 154						332
27	03 50 59 154	02 51 60 154	01 51 59 154	00 52 59 154	-0 07 59 155	-1 06 59 155	-2 05 60 155	-3 05 59 155	-4 04 59 155	-5 03 59 155						333
26	03 59 59 155	03 00 59 155	02 01 60 155	01 01 59 155	00 02 59 156	-0 57 59 156	-1 56 60 156	-2 56 59 156	-3 55 59 156	-4 54 59 156						334
25	04 08 -59 156	03 09 -60 156	02 09 -59 156	01 10 -59 156	00 11 -59 156	-0 48 -60 157	-1 48 -59 157	-2 47 -59 157	-3 46 -60 157	-4 46 -59 157						335
24	04 17 60 157	03 17 59 157	02 18 59 157	01 19 60 157	00 19 59 157	-0 40 59 158	-1 39 60 158	-2 39 59 158	-3 38 60 158	-4 38 59 158						336
23	04 25 59 158	03 26 60 158	02 26 59 158	01 27 60 158	00 27 59 158	-0 32 59 158	-1 31 60 159	-2 31 59 159	-3 30 60 159	-4 30 59 159						337
22	04 33 59 159	03 34 60 159	02 34 59 159	01 35 60 159	00 35 59 159	-0 24 60 159	-1 24 59 160	-2 23 60 160	-3 23 59 160	-4 22 60 160						338
21	04 41 60 160	03 41 59 160	02 42 60 160	01 42 59 160	00 43 60 160	-0 17 59 160	-1 16 60 160	-2 16 59 161	-3 15 60 161	-4 15 59 161						339
20	04 48 -60 161	03 48 -59 161	02 49 -60 161	01 49 -59 161	00 50 -60 161	-0 10 -59 161	-1 09 -60 161	-2 09 -59 161	-3 08 -60 162	-4 08 -60 162	-5 08 -59 162					340
19	04 55 60 162	03 55 59 162	02 56 60 162	01 56 59 162	00 57 60 162	-0 03 60 162	-1 03 59 162	-2 02 60 162	-3 02 59 163	-4 01 60 163	-5 01 60 163					341
18	05 02 60 163	04 02 60 163	03 02 59 163	02 03 60 163	01 03 60 163	00 03 59 163	-0 56 60 163	-1 56 60 163	-2 56 59 163	-3 55 60 164	-4 55 59 164					342
17	05 08 60 164	04 08 60 164	03 08 59 164	02 09 60 164	01 09 60 164	00 09 59 164	-0 50 60 164	-1 50 60 164	-2 50 59 164	-3 49 60 164	-4 49 60 165					343
16	05 14 60 165	04 14 60 165	03 14 59 165	02 15 60 165	01 15 60 165	00 15 60 165	-0 45 59 165	-1 44 60 165	-2 44 60 165	-3 44 59 165	-4 43 60 165					344
15	05 19 -59 166	04 20 -60 166	03 20 -60 166	02 20 -60 166	01 20 -59 166	00 21 -60 166	-0 39 -60 166	-1 39 -60 166	-2 39 -59 166	-3 38 -60 166	-4 38 -60 166					345
14	05 25 60 166	04 25 60 167	03 25 60 167	02 25 60 167	01 25 59 167	00 26 60 167	-0 34 60 167	-1 34 60 167	-2 34 59 167	-3 33 60 167	-4 33 60 167					346
13	05 29 59 167	04 30 60 167	03 30 60 168	02 30 60 168	01 30 60 168	00 30 59 168	-0 29 60 168	-1 29 60 168	-2 29 60 168	-3 29 60 168	-4 29 60 168					347
12	05 34 60 168	04 34 60 168	03 34 60 169	02 34 59 169	01 35 60 169	00 35 60 169	-0 25 60 169	-1 25 60 169	-2 25 60 169	-3 25 59 169	-4 24 60 169					348
11	05 38 60 169	04 38 60 169	03 38 60 169	02 38 59 170	01 39 60 170	00 39 60 170	-0 21 60 170	-1 21 60 170	-2 21 60 170	-3 21 60 170	-4 21 59 170					349
10	05 42 -60 170	04 42 -60 170	03 42 -60 170	02 42 -60 170	01 42 -60 171	00 42 -59 171	-0 17 -60 171	-1 17 -60 171	-2 17 -60 171	-3 17 -60 171	-4 17 -60 171					350
9	05 45 60 171	04 45 60 171	03 45 59 171	02 46 60 171	01 46 60 171	00 46 60 172	-0 14 60 172	-1 14 60 172	-2 14 60 172	-3 14 60 172	-4 14 60 172					351
8	05 48 60 172	04 48 59 172	03 49 60 172	02 49 60 172	01 49 60 172	00 49 60 172	-0 11 60 173	-1 11 60 173	-2 11 60 173	-3 11 60 173	-4 11 60 173					352
7	05 51 60 173	04 51 60 173	03 51 60 173	02 51 60 173	01 51 60 173	00 51 60 173	-0 09 60 173	-1 09 59 174	-2 08 60 174	-3 08 60 174	-4 08 60 174					353
6	05 53 60 174	04 53 59 174	03 54 60 174	02 54 60 174	01 54 60 174	00 54 60 174	-0 06 60 174	-1 06 60 174	-2 06 60 174	-3 06 60 175	-4 06 60 175					354
5	05 55 -60 175	04 55 -59 175	03 56 -60 175	02 56 -60 175	01 56 -60 175	00 56 -60 175	-0 04 -60 175	-1 04 -60 175	-2 04 -60 175	-3 04 -60 175	-4 04 -60 175					355
4	05 57 60 176	04 57 60 176	03 57 60 176	02 57 60 176	01 57 60 176	00 57 60 176	-0 03 60 176	-1 03 60 176	-2 03 60 176	-3 03 60 176	-4 03 60 176					356
3	05 58 60 177	04 58 60 177	03 58 60 177	02 58 60 177	01 58 60 177	00 58 60 177	-0 02 60 177	-1 02 60 177	-2 02 60 177	-3 02 60 177	-4 02 60 177					357
2	05 59 60 178	04 59 60 178	03 59 60 178	02 59 60 178	01 59 60 178	00 59 60 178	-0 01 60 178	-1 01 60 178	-2 01 60 178	-3 01 60 178	-4 01 60 178					358
1	06 00 60 179	05 00 60 179	04 00 60 179	03 00 60 179	02 00 60 179	01 00 60 179	00 00 60 179	-1 00 60 179	-2 00 60 179	-3 00 60 179	-4 00 60 179	-5 00 60 179				359
0	06 00 -60 180	05 00 -60 180	04 00 -60 180	03 00 -60 180	02 00 -60 180	01 00 -60 180	00 00 -60 180	-1 00 -60 180	-2 00 -60 180	-3 00 -60 180	-4 00 -60 180	-5 00 -60 180				360
	15°	16°	17°	18°	19°	20°	21°	22°	23°	24°	25°	26°	27°	28°	29°	

S. Lat. {LHA greater than 180°........ Zn=180−Z; LHA less than 180°............ Zn=180+Z}

DECLINATION (15°-29°) CONTRARY NAME TO LATITUDE

LAT 69°

LAT 70°

DECLINATION (0°-14°) SAME NAME AS LATITUDE

N. Lat. {LHA greater than 180°........ Zn=Z; LHA less than 180°............ Zn=360−Z}

LHA	0° Hc	d	Z	1° Hc	d	Z	2° Hc	d	Z	3° Hc	d	Z	4° Hc	d	Z	LHA
	° ′	′	°	° ′	′	°	° ′	′	°	° ′	′	°	° ′	′	°	
0	20 00	+60	180	21 00	+60	180	22 00	+60	180	23 00	+60	180	24 00	+60	180	360
2	19 59	60	178	20 59	60	178	21 59	60	178	22 59	60	178	23 59	60	178	358
4	19 57	60	176	20 57	60	176	21 57	60	176	22 57	60	176	23 57	60	176	356
6	19 53	60	174	20 53	60	174	21 53	60	174	22 53	60	174	23 53	60	174	354
8	19 48	60	172	20 48	60	171	21 48	60	171	22 48	60	171	23 48	59	171	352
10	19 41	+60	169	20 41	+60	169	21 41	+60	169	22 41	+60	169	23 41	+59	169	350
12	19 33	60	167	20 33	59	167	21 32	60	167	22 32	60	167	23 32	60	167	348
14	19 23	60	165	20 23	59	165	21 22	60	165	22 22	60	165	23 22	60	165	346
16	19 12	59	163	20 11	60	163	21 11	60	163	22 11	59	163	23 10	60	163	344
18	18 59	60	161	19 59	59	161	20 58	60	161	21 58	59	161	22 57	60	160	342
20	18 45	+59	159	19 44	+60	159	20 44	+59	159	21 43	+60	158	22 43	+60	158	340
22	18 29	60	157	19 29	59	157	20 28	60	156	21 28	59	156	22 27	60	156	338
24	18 12	60	155	19 12	59	155	20 11	59	154	21 10	60	154	22 10	59	154	336
26	17 54	59	153	18 53	60	152	19 53	59	152	20 52	59	152	21 51	59	152	334
28	17 35	59	151	18 34	59	150	19 33	59	150	20 32	59	150	21 31	59	150	332
30	17 14	+59	148	18 13	+59	148	19 12	+59	148	20 11	+59	148	21 10	+59	148	330
32	16 52	59	146	17 51	59	146	18 50	58	146	19 48	59	146	20 47	59	146	328
34	16 28	59	144	17 27	59	144	18 26	59	144	19 25	58	144	20 23	59	144	326
36	16 04	59	142	17 03	58	142	18 01	59	142	19 00	58	142	19 58	59	141	324
38	15 38	59	140	16 37	58	140	17 35	59	140	18 34	58	140	19 32	59	139	322
40	15 11	+59	138	16 10	+58	138	17 08	+59	138	18 07	+58	138	19 05	+58	137	320
42	14 44	58	136	15 42	58	136	16 40	58	136	17 38	59	136	18 37	58	135	318
44	14 15	58	134	15 13	58	134	16 11	58	134	17 09	58	133	18 07	58	133	316
46	13 45	58	132	14 43	58	132	15 41	58	132	16 39	58	131	17 37	58	131	314
48	13 14	58	130	14 12	58	130	15 10	58	130	16 08	57	129	17 05	58	129	312
50	12 42	+58	128	13 40	+58	128	14 38	+57	128	15 35	+58	127	16 33	+58	127	310
52	12 09	58	126	13 07	58	126	14 05	57	126	15 02	58	125	16 00	58	125	308
54	11 36	57	124	12 33	58	124	13 31	57	124	14 28	58	123	15 26	57	123	306
56	11 02	57	122	11 59	57	122	12 56	58	122	13 54	57	122	14 51	58	121	304
58	10 27	57	120	11 24	57	120	12 21	57	120	13 18	58	120	14 16	57	119	302
60	09 51	+57	119	10 48	+57	118	11 45	+57	118	12 42	+58	118	13 40	+57	117	300
62	09 14	58	117	10 12	57	116	11 09	57	116	12 06	57	116	13 03	57	115	298
64	08 37	57	115	09 34	57	114	10 31	57	114	11 28	57	114	12 25	57	113	296
66	08 00	57	113	08 57	57	112	09 54	57	112	10 51	56	112	11 47	57	111	294
68	07 22	57	111	08 19	56	111	09 15	57	110	10 12	57	110	11 09	57	110	292
70	06 43	+57	109	07 40	+57	109	08 37	+56	108	09 33	+57	108	10 30	+57	108	290
72	06 04	57	107	07 01	56	107	07 57	57	106	08 54	57	106	09 51	56	106	288
74	05 25	56	105	06 21	57	105	07 18	56	104	08 14	57	104	09 11	57	104	286
76	04 45	56	103	05 41	57	103	06 38	56	103	07 34	57	102	08 31	57	102	284
78	04 05	56	101	05 01	57	101	05 58	56	101	06 54	57	100	07 51	56	100	282
80	03 24	+57	99	04 21	+56	99	05 17	+57	99	06 14	+56	98	07 10	+57	98	280
82	02 44	56	98	03 40	57	97	04 37	56	97	05 33	56	97	06 29	57	96	278
84	02 03	56	96	02 59	57	95	03 56	56	95	04 52	57	95	05 49	56	94	276
86	01 22	56	94	02 18	57	93	03 15	56	93	04 11	57	93	05 08	56	92	274
88	00 41	56	92	01 37	57	91	02 34	56	91	03 30	57	91	04 27	56	90	272
90	00 00	+56	90	00 56	+57	90	01 53	+56	89	02 49	+57	89	03 46	+56	89	270
92	−0 41	56	88	00 15	57	88	01 12	56	87	02 08	56	87	03 04	57	87	268
94	−1 22	56	86	−0 26	57	86	00 31	56	86	01 27	57	85	02 24	56	85	266
96	−2 03	57	84	−1 06	56	84	−0 10	56	84	00 46	57	83	01 43	56	83	264
98	−2 44	57	82	−1 47	56	82	−0 51	57	82	00 06	56	81	01 02	57	81	262
100	−3 24	+56	81	−2 28	+57	80	−1 31	+56	80	−0 35	+57	80	00 22	+56	79	260
102	−4 05	57	79	−3 08	56	78	−2 12	57	78	−1 15	56	78	−0 19	57	77	258
104	−4 45	57	77	−3 48	56	76	−2 52	57	76	−1 55	57	76	−0 58	56	75	256
106	−5 25	57	75	−4 28	57	75	−3 31	56	74	−2 35	57	74	−1 38	57	74	254
108	−6 04	57	73	−5 07	56	73	−4 11	57	72	−3 14	57	72	−2 17	57	72	252
110	−6 43	+57	71	−5 46	+56	71	−4 50	+57	70	−3 53	+57	70	−2 56	+57	70	250
112	−7 22	57	69	−6 25	57	69	−5 28	57	69	−4 31	57	68	−3 34	57	68	248
114	−8 00	57	67	−7 03	57	67	−6 06	57	67	−5 09	57	66	−4 12	57	66	246
116				−7 40	57	65	−6 43	57	65	−5 46	57	64	−4 49	57	64	244
118							−7 20	57	63	−6 23	57	62	−5 26	57	62	242
120							−7 56	+57	61	−6 59	+57	61	−6 02	+57	60	240
122										−7 35	58	59	−6 37	57	58	238
124										−8 09	57	57	−7 12	58	56	236
126													−7 46	58	54	234

LHA	5° Hc	d	Z	6° Hc	d	Z	7° Hc	d	Z	8° Hc	d	Z	9° Hc	d	Z	LHA
	° ′	′	°	° ′	′	°	° ′	′	°	° ′	′	°	° ′	′	°	
0	25 00	+60	180	26 00	+60	180	27 00	+60	180	28 00	+60	180	29 00	+60	180	360
2	24 59	60	178	25 59	60	178	26 59	60	178	27 59	60	178	28 59	60	178	358
4	24 57	60	176	25 57	60	176	26 57	60	176	27 57	60	176	28 57	60	176	356
6	24 53	60	173	25 53	60	173	26 53	60	173	27 53	60	173	28 53	60	173	354
8	24 47	60	171	25 47	60	171	26 47	60	171	27 47	60	171	28 47	60	171	352
10	24 40	+60	169	25 40	+60	169	26 40	+60	169	27 40	+60	169	28 40	+60	169	350
12	24 32	60	167	25 32	59	167	26 31	60	167	27 31	60	167	28 31	60	167	348
14	24 22	60	165	25 22	59	165	26 21	60	165	27 21	60	164	28 21	59	164	346
16	24 10	60	163	25 10	59	162	26 09	60	162	27 09	60	162	28 09	59	162	344
18	23 57	60	160	24 57	59	160	25 56	60	160	26 56	59	160	27 55	60	160	342
20	23 43	+59	158	24 42	+60	158	25 42	+59	158	26 41	+59	158	27 40	+60	158	340
22	23 27	59	156	24 26	59	156	25 25	60	156	26 25	59	156	27 24	59	155	338
24	23 09	59	154	24 08	60	154	25 08	59	154	26 07	59	153	27 06	60	153	336
26	22 50	60	152	23 50	59	152	24 49	59	151	25 48	59	151	26 47	59	151	334
28	22 30	59	150	23 29	59	149	24 28	59	149	25 27	59	149	26 26	59	149	332
30	22 09	+59	148	23 08	+59	147	24 07	+59	147	25 06	+59	147	26 05	+58	147	330
32	21 46	59	145	22 45	59	145	23 44	59	145	24 43	58	145	25 41	59	145	328
34	21 22	59	143	22 21	59	143	23 20	58	143	24 18	59	143	25 17	59	142	326
36	20 57	59	141	21 56	58	141	22 54	59	141	23 53	58	141	24 51	59	140	324
38	20 31	58	139	21 29	59	139	22 28	58	139	23 26	58	138	24 24	59	138	322
40	20 03	+59	137	21 02	+58	137	22 00	+58	137	22 58	+58	136	23 56	+59	136	320
42	19 35	58	135	20 33	58	135	21 31	58	134	22 29	58	134	23 27	58	134	318
44	19 05	58	133	20 03	58	133	21 01	58	132	21 59	58	132	22 57	58	132	316
46	18 35	58	131	19 33	58	131	20 31	57	130	21 28	58	130	22 26	58	130	314
48	18 03	58	129	19 01	58	129	19 59	58	128	20 57	57	128	21 54	58	128	312
50	17 31	+57	127	18 28	+58	127	19 26	+58	126	20 24	+57	126	21 21	+58	126	310
52	16 58	57	125	17 55	58	125	18 53	57	124	19 50	58	124	20 48	57	124	308
54	16 23	58	123	17 21	57	123	18 18	58	122	19 16	57	122	20 13	57	122	306
56	15 49	57	121	16 46	57	121	17 43	57	120	18 40	58	120	19 38	57	120	304
58	15 13	57	119	16 10	57	119	17 07	58	118	18 05	57	118	19 02	57	118	302
60	14 37	+57	117	15 34	+57	117	16 31	+57	116	17 28	+57	116	18 25	+57	116	300
62	14 00	57	115	14 57	57	115	15 54	57	114	16 51	57	114	17 48	57	114	298
64	13 22	57	113	14 19	57	113	15 16	57	112	16 13	57	112	17 10	57	112	296
66	12 44	57	111	13 41	57	111	14 38	57	110	15 35	56	110	16 31	57	110	294
68	12 06	57	109	13 03	56	109	13 59	57	109	14 56	57	108	15 53	56	108	292
70	11 27	+56	107	12 23	+57	107	13 20	+57	107	14 17	+56	106	15 13	+57	106	290
72	10 47	57	105	11 44	57	105	12 41	56	105	13 37	57	104	14 34	56	104	288
74	10 08	56	103	11 04	57	103	12 01	56	103	12 57	57	102	13 54	56	102	286
76	09 28	56	102	10 24	57	101	11 21	56	101	12 17	56	101	13 13	57	100	284
78	08 47	57	100	09 44	56	99	10 40	56	99	11 36	57	99	12 33	56	98	282
80	08 07	+56	98	09 03	+56	97	09 59	+57	97	10 56	+56	97	11 52	+56	96	280
82	07 26	56	96	08 22	57	96	09 19	56	95	10 15	56	95	11 11	57	94	278
84	06 45	56	94	07 41	57	94	08 38	56	93	09 34	56	93	10 30	57	93	276
86	06 04	56	92	07 00	57	92	07 57	56	91	08 53	56	91	09 49	57	91	274
88	05 23	56	90	06 19	57	90	07 16	56	90	08 12	56	89	09 08	57	89	272
90	04 42	+56	88	05 38	+57	88	06 35	+56	88	07 31	+56	87	08 27	+57	87	270
92	04 01	56	86	04 57	57	86	05 54	56	86	06 50	56	85	07 46	57	85	268
94	03 20	56	84	04 16	57	84	05 13	56	84	06 09	56	84	07 05	57	83	266
96	02 39	57	83	03 36	56	82	04 32	56	82	05 28	57	82	06 25	56	81	264
98	01 59	56	81	02 55	56	80	03 51	57	80	04 48	56	80	05 44	57	79	262
100	01 18	+57	79	02 15	+56	79	03 11	+57	78	04 08	+56	78	05 04	+57	78	260
102	00 38	57	77	01 35	56	77	02 31	57	76	03 28	56	76	04 24	57	76	258
104	−0 02	57	75	00 55	56	75	01 51	57	74	02 48	57	74	03 45	56	74	256
106	−0 41	56	73	00 15	57	73	01 12	57	73	02 09	56	72	03 05	57	72	254
108	−1 20	56	71	−0 24	57	71	00 33	57	71	01 30	56	70	02 26	57	70	252
110	−1 59	+57	69	−1 02	+57	69	−0 05	+56	69	00 51	+57	69	01 48	+57	68	250
112	−2 37	57	68	−1 40	57	67	−0 43	56	67	00 13	57	67	01 10	57	66	248
114	−3 15	57	66	−2 18	57	65	−1 21	57	65	−0 24	57	65	00 33	57	64	246
116	−3 52	57	64	−2 55	57	64	−1 58	57	63	−1 01	57	63	−0 04	57	63	244
118	−4 29	58	62	−3 31	57	62	−2 34	57	61	−1 37	57	61	−0 40	57	61	242
120	−5 05	+58	60	−4 07	+57	60	−3 10	+57	59	−2 13	+58	59	−1 15	+57	59	240
122	−5 40	58	58	−4 42	57	58	−3 45	58	58	−2 47	57	57	−1 50	57	57	238
124	−6 14	57	56	−5 17	58	56	−4 19	57	56	−3 22	58	55	−2 24	57	55	236
126	−6 48	58	54	−5 50	57	54	−4 53	58	54	−3 55	58	53	−2 57	57	53	234
128	−7 21	58	52	−6 23	58	52	−5 25	57	52	−4 28	58	52	−3 30	58	51	232
130	−7 53	+58	50	−6 55	+58	50	−5 57	+58	50	−4 59	+58	50	−4 01	+58	49	230
132				−7 26	58	48	−6 28	58	48	−5 30	58	48	−4 32	58	47	228
134				−7 56	58	46	−6 58	58	46	−6 00	58	46	−5 02	58	45	226
136							−7 27	58	44	−6 29	58	44	−5 31	59	44	224
138							−7 55	58	42	−6 57	59	42	−5 58	58	42	222

LHA	10° Hc	d	Z	11° Hc	d	Z	12° Hc	d	Z	13° Hc	d	Z	14° Hc	d	Z	LHA
	° ′	′	°	° ′	′	°	° ′	′	°	° ′	′	°	° ′	′	°	
0	30 00	+60	180	31 00	+60	180	32 00	+60	180	33 00	+60	180	34 00	+60	180	360
2	29 59	60	178	30 59	60	178	31 59	60	178	32 59	60	178	33 59	60	178	358
4	29 57	60	176	30 57	60	175	31 57	60	175	32 57	60	175	33 57	60	175	356
6	29 53	60	173	30 53	60	173	31 53	60	173	32 53	60	173	33 53	59	173	354
8	29 47	60	171	30 47	60	171	31 47	60	171	32 47	60	171	33 47	60	171	352
10	29 40	+60	169	30 40	+59	169	31 39	+60	169	32 39	+60	168	33 39	+60	168	350
12	29 31	60	166	30 31	59	166	31 30	60	166	32 30	60	166	33 30	60	166	348
14	29 20	60	164	30 20	60	164	31 20	60	164	32 20	59	164	33 19	60	164	346
16	29 08	60	162	30 08	60	162	31 08	59	162	32 07	60	162	33 07	60	161	344
18	28 55	60	160	29 55	59	160	30 54	60	159	31 54	59	159	32 53	60	159	342
20	28 40	+59	157	29 39	+60	157	30 39	+59	157	31 38	+60	157	32 38	+59	157	340
22	28 23	60	155	29 23	59	155	30 22	59	155	31 21	60	155	32 21	59	155	338
24	28 06	59	153	29 05	59	153	30 04	59	153	31 03	59	152	32 02	60	152	336
26	27 46	59	151	28 45	59	151	29 44	60	150	30 44	59	150	31 43	59	150	334
28	27 25	59	149	28 24	59	148	29 23	59	148	30 22	59	148	31 21	59	148	332
30	27 03	+59	146	28 02	+59	146	29 01	+59	146	30 00	+59	146	30 59	+59	146	330
32	26 40	59	144	27 39	59	144	28 38	58	144	29 36	59	144	30 35	59	143	328
34	26 16	58	142	27 14	59	142	28 13	58	142	29 11	59	141	30 10	58	141	326
36	25 50	58	140	26 48	59	140	27 47	58	140	28 45	58	139	29 43	59	139	324
38	25 23	58	138	26 21	58	138	27 19	59	137	28 18	58	137	29 16	58	137	322
40	24 55	+58	136	25 53	+58	136	26 51	+58	135	27 49	+58	135	28 47	+58	135	320
42	24 25	59	134	25 24	58	133	26 22	58	133	27 20	58	133	28 18	57	133	318
44	23 55	58	132	24 53	58	131	25 51	58	131	26 49	58	131	27 47	58	130	316
46	23 24	58	130	24 22	58	129	25 20	57	129	26 17	58	129	27 15	58	128	314
48	22 52	58	127	23 50	57	127	24 47	58	127	25 45	57	127	26 42	58	126	312
50	22 19	+57	125	23 16	+58	125	24 14	+57	125	25 11	+58	124	26 09	+57	124	310
52	21 45	57	123	22 42	56	123	23 40	57	123	24 37	57	122	25 34	58	122	308
54	21 10	58	121	22 08	57	121	23 05	57	121	24 02	57	120	24 59	57	120	306
56	20 35	57	119	21 32	57	119	22 29	57	119	23 26	57	118	24 23	57	118	304
58	19 59	57	117	20 56	57	117	21 53	57	117	22 50	57	116	23 47	57	116	302
60	19 22	+57	115	20 19	+57	115	21 16	+57	115	22 13	+57	114	23 10	+56	114	300
62	18 45	56	113	19 41	57	113	20 38	57	113	21 35	57	112	22 32	56	112	298
64	18 07	56	111	19 03	57	111	20 00	57	111	20 57	56	110	21 53	57	110	296
66	17 28	57	109	18 25	56	109	19 21	57	109	20 18	57	108	21 15	56	108	294
68	16 49	57	108	17 46	56	107	18 42	57	107	19 39	56	106	20 35	57	106	292
70	16 10	+56	106	17 06	+57	105	18 03	+56	105	18 59	+57	105	19 56	+56	104	290
72	15 30	57	104	16 27	56	103	17 23	56	103	18 19	57	103	19 16	56	102	288
74	14 50	56	102	15 46	57	101	16 43	56	101	17 39	56	101	18 35	57	100	286
76	14 10	56	100	15 06	56	99	16 02	57	99	16 59	56	99	17 55	56	98	284
78	13 29	57	98	14 26	56	98	15 22	56	97	16 18	56	97	17 14	56	96	282
80	12 48	+57	96	13 45	+56	96	14 41	+56	95	15 37	+56	95	16 33	+57	95	280
82	12 08	56	94	13 04	56	94	14 00	56	93	14 56	56	93	15 52	57	93	278
84	11 27	56	92	12 23	56	92	13 19	56	92	14 15	56	91	15 11	57	91	276
86	10 46	56	90	11 42	56	90	12 38	56	90	13 34	56	89	14 30	57	89	274
88	10 05	56	88	11 01	56	88	11 57	56	88	12 53	56	87	13 49	57	87	272
90	09 24	+56	87	10 20	+56	86	11 16	+56	86	12 12	+56	86	13 08	+57	85	270
92	08 43	56	85	09 39	56	84	10 35	56	84	11 31	57	84	12 28	56	83	268
94	08 02	56	83	08 58	56	83	09 54	57	82	10 51	56	82	11 47	56	81	266
96	07 21	57	81	08 18	56	81	09 14	56	80	10 10	56	80	11 06	57	80	264
98	06 41	56	79	07 37	57	79	08 34	56	78	09 30	56	78	10 26	57	78	262
100	06 01	+56	77	06 57	+56	77	07 53	+57	77	08 50	+56	76	09 46	+57	76	260
102	05 21	56	75	06 17	57	75	07 14	56	75	08 10	57	74	09 07	56	74	258
104	04 41	57	74	05 38	56	73	06 34	57	73	07 31	56	73	08 27	57	72	256
106	04 02	57	72	04 59	56	71	05 55	57	71	06 52	57	71	07 49	56	70	254
108	03 23	57	70	04 20	57	69	05 17	56	69	06 13	57	69	07 10	57	68	252
110	02 45	+57	68	03 42	+57	68	04 39	+56	67	05 35	+57	67	06 32	+57	67	250
112	02 07	57	66	03 04	57	66	04 01	57	65	04 58	57	65	05 55	57	65	248
114	01 30	57	64	02 27	57	64	03 24	57	64	04 21	57	63	05 18	57	63	246
116	00 53	57	62	01 50	58	62	02 48	57	62	03 45	57	61	04 42	57	61	244
118	00 17	57	60	01 14	58	60	02 12	57	60	03 09	57	60	04 06	57	59	242
120	−0 18	+57	59	00 39	+58	58	01 37	+57	58	02 34	+57	58	03 31	+57	57	240
122	−0 53	58	57	00 05	57	56	01 02	58	56	02 00	57	56	02 57	57	56	238
124	−1 27	58	55	−0 29	58	54	00 29	57	54	01 26	58	54	02 24	57	54	236
126	−2 00	58	53	−1 02	58	53	−0 04	57	52	00 53	58	52	01 51	58	52	234
128	−2 32	58	51	−1 34	58	51	−0 36	57	50	00 21	58	50	01 19	58	50	232
130	−3 03	+57	49	−2 06	+58	49	−1 08	+58	49	−0 10	+58	48	00 48	+58	48	230
132	−3 34	58	47	−2 36	58	47	−1 38	58	47	−0 40	58	46	00 18	58	46	228
134	−4 04	58	45	−3 06	59	45	−2 07	58	45	−1 09	58	45	−0 11	58	44	226
136	−4 32	58	43	−3 34	58	43	−2 36	59	43	−1 37	58	43	−0 39	58	42	224
138	−5 00	58	41	−4 02	59	41	−3 03	58	41	−2 05	59	41	−1 06	58	40	222

S Lat {LHA greater than 180°........ Zn=180−Z; LHA less than 180°........ Zn=180+Z}

DECLINATION (0°-14°) SAME NAME AS LATITUDE

LAT 70°

N. Lat. {LHA greater than 180°……. Zn=Z; LHA less than 180°………. Zn=360−Z}

DECLINATION (0°-14°) SAME NAME AS LATITUDE

LHA	0° Hc d Z	1° Hc d Z	2° Hc d Z	3° Hc d Z	4° Hc d Z	5° Hc d Z	6° Hc d Z	7° Hc d Z	8° Hc d Z	9° Hc d Z	10° Hc d Z	11° Hc d Z	12° Hc d Z	13° Hc d Z	14° Hc d Z	LHA
	° ′ ′ °	° ′ ′ °	° ′ ′ °	° ′ ′ °	° ′ ′ °	° ′ ′ °	° ′ ′ °	° ′ ′ °	° ′ ′ °	° ′ ′ °	° ′ ′ °	° ′ ′ °	° ′ ′ °	° ′ ′ °	° ′ ′ °	
								140	−7 24 +59 40	−6 25 +58 40	−5 27 +59 39	−4 28 +58 39	−3 30 +59 39	−2 31 +59 39	−1 32 +58 39	220
								142	−7 49 58 38	−6 51 59 38	−5 52 58 38	−4 54 59 37	−3 55 59 37	−2 56 58 37	−1 58 59 37	218
									144	−7 15 58 36	−6 17 59 36	−5 18 59 35	−4 19 59 35	−3 20 58 35	−2 22 59 35	216
									146	−7 39 59 34	−6 40 59 34	−5 41 59 33	−4 42 59 33	−3 43 59 33	−2 44 58 33	214
										148	−7 02 59 32	−6 03 59 31	−5 04 59 31	−4 05 59 31	−3 06 59 31	212
										150	−7 23 +59 30	−6 24 +59 30	−5 25 +59 29	−4 26 +59 29	−3 27 +59 29	210
											152	−6 44 60 28	−5 44 59 27	−4 45 59 27	−3 46 59 27	208
											154	−7 02 59 26	−6 03 60 25	−5 03 59 25	−4 04 59 25	206
											156	−7 19 59 24	−6 20 60 24	−5 20 59 23	−4 21 59 23	204
												158	−6 36 60 22	−5 36 59 21	−4 37 60 21	202
												160	−6 50 +59 20	−5 51 +60 20	−4 51 +60 19	200
												162	−7 03 59 18	−6 04 60 18	−5 04 60 17	198
												164	−7 15 60 16	−6 15 59 16	−5 16 60 16	196
													166	−6 26 60 14	−5 26 60 14	194
													168	−6 35 60 12	−5 35 60 12	192
													170	−6 43 +60 10	−5 43 +60 10	190
													172	−6 49 60 8	−5 49 60 8	188
													174	−6 54 60 6	−5 54 60 6	186
													176	−6 57 60 4	−5 57 60 4	184
													178	−6 59 60 2	−5 59 60 2	182
													180	−7 00 +60 0	−6 00 +60 0	180
114	−8 00 57 67	246														
112	−7 22 57 69	248														
110	−6 43 −57 71	−7 40 −57 71	250													
108	−6 04 57 73	−7 01 56 73	−7 57 57 74	252												
106	−5 25 56 75	−6 21 57 75	−7 18 56 76	−8 14 57 76	254											
104	−4 45 56 77	−5 41 57 77	−6 38 56 77	−7 34 57 78	256											
102	−4 05 56 79	−5 01 57 79	−5 58 56 79	−6 54 57 80	−7 51 56 80	258										
100	−3 24 −57 81	−4 21 −56 81	−5 17 −57 81	−6 14 −56 82	−7 10 −57 82	−8 07 −56 82	260									
98	−2 44 56 82	−3 40 57 83	−4 37 56 83	−5 33 56 83	−6 29 57 84	−7 26 56 84	262									
96	−2 03 56 84	−2 59 57 85	−3 56 56 85	−4 52 57 85	−5 49 56 86	−6 45 56 86	−7 41 57 86	264								
94	−1 22 56 86	−2 18 57 87	−3 15 56 87	−4 11 57 87	−5 08 56 88	−6 04 56 88	−7 00 57 88	−7 57 56 89	266							
92	−0 41 56 88	−1 37 57 89	−2 34 56 89	−3 30 57 89	−4 27 56 90	−5 23 56 90	−6 19 57 90	−7 16 56 90	−8 12 56 91	268						
90	00 00 −56 90	−0 56 −57 90	−1 53 −56 91	−2 49 −57 91	−3 46 −56 91	−4 42 −56 92	−5 38 −57 92	−6 35 −56 92	−7 31 −56 93	270						
88	00 41 56 92	−0 15 57 92	−1 12 56 93	−2 08 56 93	−3 04 57 93	−4 01 56 94	−4 57 57 94	−5 54 56 94	−6 50 56 95	−7 46 57 95	272					
86	01 22 56 94	00 26 57 94	−0 31 56 94	−1 27 57 95	−2 24 56 95	−3 20 56 96	−4 16 57 96	−5 13 56 96	−6 09 56 96	−7 05 57 97	−8 02 56 97	274				
84	02 03 57 96	01 06 56 96	00 10 56 96	−0 46 57 97	−1 43 56 97	−2 39 57 97	−3 36 56 98	−4 32 56 98	−5 28 57 98	−6 25 56 99	−7 21 57 99	−8 18 56 99	276			
82	02 44 57 98	01 47 56 98	00 51 57 98	−0 06 56 99	−1 02 57 99	−1 59 56 99	−2 55 56 100	−3 51 57 100	−4 48 56 100	−5 44 57 101	−6 41 56 101	−7 37 57 101	278			
80	03 24 −56 99	02 28 −57 100	01 31 −56 100	00 35 −57 100	−0 22 −56 101	−1 18 −57 101	−2 15 −56 101	−3 11 −57 102	−4 08 −56 102	−5 04 −57 102	−6 01 −56 103	−6 57 −56 103	−7 53 −57 103	280		
78	04 05 57 101	03 08 56 102	02 12 57 102	01 15 56 102	00 19 57 103	−0 38 57 103	−1 35 56 103	−2 31 57 104	−3 28 56 104	−4 24 57 104	−5 21 56 105	−6 17 57 105	−7 14 56 105	−8 10 57 106	282	
76	04 45 57 103	03 48 56 104	02 52 57 104	01 55 57 104	00 58 56 105	00 02 57 105	−0 55 56 105	−1 51 57 106	−2 48 57 106	−3 45 56 106	−4 41 57 106	−5 38 56 107	−6 34 57 107	−7 31 56 107	284	
74	05 25 57 105	04 28 57 105	03 31 56 106	02 35 57 106	01 38 57 106	00 41 56 107	−0 15 57 107	−1 12 57 107	−2 09 56 108	−3 05 57 108	−4 02 57 108	−4 59 56 109	−5 55 57 109	−6 52 57 109	−7 49 56 110	286
72	06 04 57 107	05 07 56 107	04 11 57 108	03 14 57 108	02 17 57 108	01 20 56 109	00 24 57 109	−0 33 57 109	−1 30 56 110	−2 26 57 110	−3 23 57 110	−4 20 57 111	−5 17 56 111	−6 13 57 111	−7 10 57 112	288
70	06 43 −57 109	05 46 −56 109	04 50 −57 110	03 53 −57 110	02 56 −57 110	01 59 −57 111	01 02 −57 111	00 05 −56 111	−0 51 −57 111	−1 48 −57 112	−2 45 −57 112	−3 42 −57 112	−4 39 −56 113	−5 35 −57 113	−6 32 −57 113	290
68	07 22 57 111	06 25 57 111	05 28 57 111	04 31 57 112	03 34 57 112	02 37 57 112	01 40 57 113	00 43 56 113	−0 13 57 113	−1 10 57 114	−2 07 57 114	−3 04 57 114	−4 01 57 115	−4 58 57 115	−5 55 57 115	292
66	08 00 57 113	07 03 57 113	06 06 57 113	05 09 57 114	04 12 57 114	03 15 57 114	02 18 57 115	01 21 57 115	00 24 57 115	−0 33 57 116	−1 30 57 116	−2 27 57 116	−3 24 57 116	−4 21 57 117	−5 18 57 117	294
64	08 37 57 115	07 40 57 115	06 43 57 115	05 46 57 116	04 49 57 116	03 52 57 116	02 55 57 116	01 58 57 117	01 01 57 117	00 04 57 117	−0 53 57 118	−1 50 58 118	−2 48 57 118	−3 45 57 119	−4 42 57 119	296
62	09 14 57 117	08 17 57 117	07 20 57 117	06 23 57 118	05 26 57 118	04 29 58 118	03 31 57 118	02 34 57 119	01 37 57 119	00 40 57 119	−0 17 57 120	−1 14 58 120	−2 12 57 120	−3 09 57 120	−4 06 57 121	298
60	09 51 −57 119	08 54 −58 119	07 56 −57 119	06 59 −57 119	06 02 −57 120	05 05 −58 120	04 07 −57 120	03 10 −57 121	02 13 −58 121	01 15 −57 121	00 18 −57 121	−0 39 −58 122	−1 37 −57 122	−2 34 −57 122	−3 31 −57 123	300
58	10 27 58 120	09 29 57 121	08 32 57 121	07 35 58 121	06 37 57 122	05 40 58 122	04 42 57 122	03 45 58 122	02 47 57 123	01 50 57 123	00 53 58 123	−0 05 57 124	−1 02 58 124	−2 00 57 124	−2 57 57 124	302
56	11 02 58 122	10 04 57 123	09 07 58 123	08 09 57 123	07 12 58 124	06 14 57 124	05 17 58 124	04 19 57 124	03 22 58 125	02 24 57 125	01 27 58 125	00 29 58 126	−0 29 57 126	−1 26 58 126	−2 24 57 126	304
54	11 36 58 124	10 38 57 125	09 41 58 125	08 43 57 125	07 46 58 126	06 48 58 126	05 50 57 126	04 53 58 126	03 55 58 127	02 57 57 127	02 00 58 127	01 02 58 127	00 04 57 128	−0 53 58 128	−1 51 58 128	306
52	12 09 57 126	11 12 58 127	10 14 58 127	09 16 57 127	08 19 58 127	07 21 58 128	06 23 58 128	05 25 57 128	04 28 58 128	03 30 58 129	02 32 58 129	01 34 58 129	00 36 57 130	−0 21 58 130	−1 19 58 130	308
50	12 42 −58 128	11 44 −58 129	10 46 −57 129	09 49 −58 129	08 51 −58 129	07 53 −58 130	06 55 −58 130	05 57 −58 130	04 59 −58 130	04 01 −58 131	03 03 −57 131	02 06 −58 131	01 08 −58 131	00 10 −58 132	−0 48 −58 132	310
48	13 14 58 130	12 16 58 131	11 18 58 131	10 20 58 131	09 22 58 131	08 24 58 132	07 26 58 132	06 28 58 132	05 30 58 132	04 32 58 133	03 34 58 133	02 36 58 133	01 38 58 133	00 40 58 134	−0 18 58 134	312
46	13 45 58 132	12 47 58 133	11 49 58 133	10 51 59 133	09 52 58 133	08 54 58 134	07 56 58 134	06 58 58 134	06 00 58 134	05 02 58 135	04 04 58 135	03 06 59 135	02 07 58 135	01 09 58 135	00 11 58 136	314
44	14 15 59 134	13 16 58 135	12 18 58 135	11 20 58 135	10 22 58 135	09 24 59 136	08 25 58 136	07 27 58 136	06 29 58 136	05 31 59 136	04 32 58 137	03 34 58 137	02 36 59 137	01 37 58 137	00 39 58 138	316
42	14 44 59 136	13 45 58 137	12 47 58 137	11 49 59 137	10 50 58 137	09 52 58 137	08 54 59 138	07 55 58 138	06 57 59 138	05 58 58 138	05 00 58 139	04 02 59 139	03 03 58 139	02 05 59 139	01 06 58 140	318
40	15 11 −58 138	14 13 −58 139	13 15 −59 139	12 16 −58 139	11 18 −59 139	10 19 −58 139	09 21 −59 140	08 22 −58 140	07 24 −59 140	06 25 −58 140	05 27 −59 141	04 28 −58 141	03 30 −59 141	02 31 −59 141	01 32 −58 141	320
38	15 38 58 140	14 40 59 141	13 41 59 141	12 42 58 141	11 44 59 141	10 45 58 141	09 47 59 142	08 48 59 142	07 49 58 142	06 51 59 142	05 52 58 142	04 54 59 143	03 55 59 143	02 56 58 143	01 58 59 143	322
36	16 04 59 142	15 05 59 143	14 06 58 143	13 08 59 143	12 09 59 143	11 10 58 143	10 12 59 144	09 13 59 144	08 14 59 144	07 15 58 144	06 17 59 144	05 18 59 145	04 19 59 145	03 20 58 145	02 22 59 145	324
34	16 28 58 144	15 30 59 145	14 31 59 145	13 32 59 145	12 33 59 145	11 34 59 145	10 35 58 146	09 37 59 146	08 38 59 146	07 39 59 146	06 40 59 146	05 41 59 147	04 42 59 147	03 43 59 147	02 44 58 147	326
32	16 52 59 146	15 53 59 147	14 54 59 147	13 55 59 147	12 56 59 147	11 57 59 147	10 58 59 148	09 59 59 148	09 00 59 148	08 01 59 148	07 02 59 148	06 03 59 149	05 04 59 149	04 05 59 149	03 06 59 149	328
30	17 14 −59 148	16 15 −59 149	15 16 −59 149	14 17 −59 149	13 18 −59 149	12 19 −60 149	11 19 −59 150	10 20 −59 150	09 21 −59 150	08 22 −59 150	07 23 −59 150	06 24 −59 150	05 25 −59 151	04 26 −59 151	03 27 −59 151	330
28	17 35 59 151	16 36 60 151	15 36 59 151	14 37 59 151	13 38 59 151	12 39 59 151	11 40 60 152	10 40 59 152	09 41 59 152	08 42 59 152	07 43 59 152	06 44 60 152	05 44 59 153	04 45 59 153	03 46 59 153	332
26	17 54 59 153	16 55 59 153	15 56 60 153	14 56 59 153	13 57 59 153	12 58 59 153	11 59 60 154	10 59 59 154	10 00 59 154	09 01 60 154	08 01 59 154	07 02 59 154	06 03 60 155	05 03 59 155	04 04 59 155	334
24	18 12 59 155	17 13 59 155	16 14 60 155	15 14 59 155	14 15 59 155	13 16 60 155	12 16 59 156	11 17 60 156	10 17 59 156	09 18 59 156	08 19 60 156	07 19 59 156	06 20 60 156	05 20 59 157	04 21 59 157	336
22	18 29 59 157	17 30 60 157	16 30 59 157	15 31 59 157	14 32 60 157	13 32 59 157	12 33 60 158	11 33 59 158	10 34 60 158	09 34 59 158	08 35 60 158	07 35 59 158	06 36 60 158	05 36 59 159	04 37 60 159	338
20	18 45 −60 159	17 45 −59 159	16 46 −60 159	15 46 −59 159	14 47 −60 159	13 47 −59 160	12 48 −60 160	11 48 −60 160	10 48 −59 160	09 49 −60 160	08 49 −59 160	07 50 −60 160	06 50 −59 160	05 51 −60 160	04 51 −60 161	340
18	18 59 60 161	17 59 59 161	17 00 60 161	16 00 60 161	15 00 59 161	14 01 60 162	13 01 59 162	12 02 60 162	11 02 60 162	10 02 59 162	09 03 60 162	08 03 60 162	07 03 59 162	06 04 60 162	05 04 60 163	342
16	19 12 60 163	18 12 60 163	17 12 59 163	16 13 60 163	15 13 60 163	14 13 60 164	13 13 59 164	12 14 60 164	11 14 60 164	10 14 59 164	09 15 60 164	08 15 60 164	07 15 60 164	06 15 59 164	05 16 60 164	344
14	19 23 60 165	18 23 60 165	17 23 59 165	16 24 60 165	15 24 60 166	14 24 60 166	13 24 59 166	12 25 60 166	11 25 60 166	10 25 60 166	09 25 60 166	08 25 59 166	07 26 60 166	06 26 60 166	05 26 60 166	346
12	19 33 60 167	18 33 60 167	17 33 60 167	16 33 60 168	15 33 59 168	14 34 60 168	13 34 60 168	12 34 60 168	11 34 60 168	10 34 60 168	09 34 59 168	08 35 60 168	07 35 60 168	06 35 60 168	05 35 60 168	348
10	19 41 −60 169	18 41 −60 169	17 41 −60 170	16 41 −59 170	15 42 −60 170	14 42 −60 170	13 42 −60 170	12 42 −60 170	11 42 −60 170	10 42 −60 170	09 42 −60 170	08 42 −60 170	07 42 −59 170	06 43 −60 170	05 43 −60 170	350
8	19 48 60 172	18 48 60 172	17 48 60 172	16 48 60 172	15 48 60 172	14 48 60 172	13 48 60 172	12 48 60 172	11 48 59 172	10 49 60 172	09 49 60 172	08 49 60 172	07 49 60 172	06 49 60 172	05 49 60 172	352
6	19 53 60 174	18 53 60 174	17 53 60 174	16 53 60 174	15 53 60 174	14 53 60 174	13 53 60 174	12 53 59 174	11 54 60 174	10 54 60 174	09 54 60 174	08 54 60 174	07 54 60 174	06 54 60 174	05 54 60 174	354
4	19 57 60 176	18 57 60 176	17 57 60 176	16 57 60 176	15 57 60 176	14 57 60 176	13 57 60 176	12 57 60 176	11 57 60 176	10 57 60 176	09 57 60 176	08 57 60 176	07 57 60 176	06 57 60 176	05 57 60 176	356
2	19 59 60 178	18 59 60 178	17 59 60 178	16 59 60 178	15 59 60 178	14 59 60 178	13 59 60 178	12 59 60 178	11 59 60 178	10 59 60 178	09 59 60 178	08 59 60 178	07 59 60 178	06 59 60 178	05 59 60 178	358
0	20 00 −60 180	19 00 −60 180	18 00 −60 180	17 00 −60 180	16 00 −60 180	15 00 −60 180	14 00 −60 180	13 00 −60 180	12 00 −60 180	11 00 −60 180	10 00 −60 180	09 00 −60 180	08 00 −60 180	07 00 −60 180	06 00 −60 180	360
	0°	1°	2°	3°	4°	5°	6°	7°	8°	9°	10°	11°	12°	13°	14°	

S. Lat. {LHA greater than 180°……. Zn=180−Z; LHA less than 180°………. Zn=180+Z}

DECLINATION (0°-14°) CONTRARY NAME TO LATITUDE

N. Lat. {LHA greater than 180°....... Zn=Z; LHA less than 180°........... Zn=360−Z}

DECLINATION (15°-29°) SAME NAME AS LATITUDE

LHA	15° Hc	d	Z	16° Hc	d	Z	17° Hc	d	Z	18° Hc	d	Z	19° Hc	d	Z
	° ′	′	°	° ′	′	°	° ′	′	°	° ′	′	°	° ′	′	°
0	35 00	+60	180	36 00	+60	180	37 00	+60	180	38 00	+60	180	39 00	+60	180
2	34 59	60	178	35 59	60	178	36 59	60	178	37 59	60	178	38 59	60	178
4	34 57	60	175	35 57	60	175	36 57	60	175	37 57	60	175	38 57	60	175
6	34 52	60	173	35 52	60	173	36 52	60	173	37 52	60	173	38 52	60	173
8	34 47	59	171	35 46	60	171	36 46	60	170	37 46	60	170	38 46	60	170
10	34 39	+60	168	35 39	+60	168	36 39	+60	168	37 39	+59	168	38 38	+60	168
12	34 30	60	166	35 30	59	166	36 29	60	166	37 29	60	166	38 29	60	166
14	34 19	60	164	35 19	59	163	36 18	60	163	37 18	60	163	38 18	59	163
16	34 07	59	161	35 06	60	161	36 06	59	161	37 05	60	161	38 05	60	161
18	33 53	59	159	34 52	60	159	35 52	59	159	36 51	60	159	37 51	59	158
20	33 37	+60	157	34 37	+59	157	35 36	+59	156	36 35	+60	156	37 35	+59	156
22	33 20	59	154	34 19	60	154	35 19	59	154	36 18	59	154	37 17	59	154
24	33 02	59	152	34 01	59	152	35 00	59	152	35 59	59	151	36 58	59	151
26	32 42	59	150	33 41	59	150	34 40	59	149	35 39	59	149	36 38	59	149
28	32 20	59	148	33 19	59	147	34 18	59	147	35 17	59	147	36 16	59	147
30	31 58	+58	145	32 56	+59	145	33 55	+59	145	34 54	+58	145	35 52	+59	144
32	31 34	58	143	32 32	59	143	33 31	58	143	34 29	59	142	35 28	58	142
34	31 08	59	141	32 07	58	141	33 05	59	140	34 04	58	140	35 02	58	140
36	30 42	58	139	31 40	58	138	32 38	59	138	33 37	58	138	34 35	58	138
38	30 14	58	137	31 12	58	136	32 10	59	136	33 09	58	136	34 07	58	135
40	29 45	+58	134	30 43	+58	134	31 41	+58	134	32 39	+58	133	33 37	+58	133
42	29 15	58	132	30 13	58	132	31 11	58	132	32 09	58	131	33 07	57	131
44	28 45	57	130	29 42	58	130	30 40	58	129	31 38	57	129	32 35	58	129
46	28 13	57	128	29 10	58	128	30 08	57	127	31 05	58	127	32 03	57	127
48	27 40	57	126	28 37	58	126	29 35	57	125	30 32	57	125	31 29	58	125
50	27 06	+57	124	28 03	+58	123	29 01	+57	123	29 58	+57	123	30 55	+57	122
52	26 32	57	122	27 29	57	121	28 26	57	121	29 23	57	121	30 20	57	120
54	25 56	57	120	26 53	57	119	27 50	57	119	28 47	57	119	29 44	57	118
56	25 20	57	118	26 17	57	117	27 14	57	117	28 11	57	117	29 08	56	116
58	24 44	56	116	25 40	57	115	26 37	57	115	27 34	57	115	28 31	56	114
60	24 06	+57	114	25 03	+57	113	26 00	+56	113	26 56	+57	113	27 53	+56	112
62	23 28	57	112	24 25	57	111	25 22	56	111	26 18	57	111	27 15	56	110
64	22 50	57	110	23 47	56	109	24 43	56	109	25 39	57	109	26 36	56	108
66	22 11	57	108	23 08	56	107	24 04	56	107	25 00	57	107	25 57	56	106
68	21 32	56	106	22 28	56	105	23 24	57	105	24 21	56	105	25 17	56	104
70	20 52	+56	104	21 48	+57	103	22 45	+56	103	23 41	+56	103	24 37	+56	102
72	20 12	56	102	21 08	57	101	22 05	56	101	23 01	56	101	23 57	56	100
74	19 32	56	100	20 28	56	100	21 24	55	99	22 20	56	99	23 16	56	98
76	18 51	56	98	19 47	56	98	20 43	57	97	21 40	56	97	22 36	56	96
78	18 10	57	96	19 07	56	96	20 03	56	95	20 59	56	95	21 55	56	95
80	17 30	+56	94	18 26	+56	94	19 22	+56	93	20 18	+56	93	21 14	+56	93
82	16 49	56	92	17 45	56	92	18 41	56	92	19 37	56	91	20 33	56	91
84	16 08	56	90	17 04	56	90	18 00	56	90	18 56	56	89	19 52	56	89
86	15 27	56	89	16 23	56	88	17 19	56	88	18 15	56	87	19 11	56	87
88	14 46	56	87	15 42	56	86	16 38	56	86	17 34	56	86	18 30	56	85
90	14 05	+56	85	15 01	+56	84	15 57	+56	84	16 53	+56	84	17 49	+56	83
92	13 24	56	83	14 20	56	83	15 16	56	82	16 12	56	82	17 08	56	81
94	12 43	56	81	13 39	57	81	14 36	56	80	15 32	56	80	16 28	56	80
96	12 03	56	79	12 59	56	79	13 55	56	79	14 51	57	78	15 48	56	78
98	11 23	56	77	12 19	56	77	13 15	56	77	14 11	57	76	15 08	56	76
100	10 43	+56	76	11 39	+56	75	12 35	+57	75	13 32	+56	74	14 28	+56	74
102	10 03	57	74	11 00	56	73	11 56	56	73	12 52	57	73	13 49	56	72
104	09 24	56	72	10 20	57	72	11 17	56	71	12 13	57	71	13 10	56	70
106	08 45	57	70	09 42	56	70	10 38	57	69	11 35	56	69	12 31	57	69
108	08 07	56	68	09 03	57	68	10 00	57	67	10 57	56	67	11 53	57	67
110	07 29	+57	66	08 26	+56	66	09 22	+57	66	10 19	+57	65	11 16	+57	65
112	06 52	57	64	07 49	56	64	08 45	57	64	09 42	57	64	10 39	57	63
114	06 15	57	63	07 12	57	62	08 09	57	62	09 06	57	62	10 03	57	61
116	05 39	57	61	06 36	57	60	07 33	57	60	08 30	57	60	09 27	57	60
118	05 03	58	59	06 01	57	59	06 58	57	58	07 55	57	58	08 52	57	58
120	04 28	+58	57	05 26	+57	57	06 23	+57	56	07 20	+58	56	08 18	+57	56
122	03 54	58	55	04 52	57	55	05 49	58	55	06 47	57	54	07 44	57	54
124	03 21	58	53	04 19	57	53	05 16	58	53	06 14	57	53	07 11	58	52
126	02 49	57	52	03 46	58	51	04 44	58	51	05 42	57	51	06 39	58	50
128	02 17	58	50	03 15	57	49	04 12	58	49	05 10	58	49	06 08	58	49
130	01 46	+58	48	02 44	+58	48	03 42	+58	47	04 40	+58	47	05 38	+58	47
132	01 16	58	46	02 14	58	46	03 12	58	45	04 10	58	45	05 08	58	45
134	00 47	58	44	01 45	59	44	02 44	58	44	03 42	58	43	04 40	58	43
136	00 19	58	42	01 17	59	42	02 16	58	42	03 14	58	41	04 12	59	41
138	−0 08	59	40	00 51	58	40	01 49	58	40	02 47	59	40	03 46	58	39

LHA	20° Hc	d	Z	21° Hc	d	Z	22° Hc	d	Z	23° Hc	d	Z	24° Hc	d	Z
	° ′	′	°	° ′	′	°	° ′	′	°	° ′	′	°	° ′	′	°
0	40 00	+60	180	41 00	+60	180	42 00	+60	180	43 00	+60	180	44 00	+60	180
2	39 59	60	178	40 59	60	178	41 59	60	178	42 59	60	178	43 59	60	178
4	39 57	60	175	40 57	59	175	41 56	60	175	42 56	60	175	43 56	60	175
6	39 52	60	173	40 52	60	173	41 52	60	173	42 52	60	173	43 52	60	172
8	39 46	60	170	40 46	60	170	41 46	60	170	42 46	60	170	43 46	59	170
10	39 38	+60	168	40 38	+60	168	41 38	+60	168	42 38	+59	168	43 37	+60	167
12	39 29	59	165	40 28	60	165	41 28	60	165	42 28	60	165	43 28	59	165
14	39 17	60	163	40 17	60	163	41 17	59	163	42 16	60	163	43 16	60	162
16	39 05	59	161	40 04	60	160	41 04	59	160	42 03	60	160	43 03	59	160
18	38 50	59	158	39 49	60	158	40 49	59	158	41 48	60	158	42 48	59	157
20	38 34	+59	156	39 33	+60	156	40 33	+59	155	41 32	+59	155	42 31	+59	155
22	38 16	60	153	39 16	59	153	40 15	59	153	41 14	59	153	42 13	59	153
24	37 57	59	151	38 56	59	151	39 55	59	151	40 54	59	150	41 53	59	150
26	37 37	58	149	38 35	59	148	39 34	59	148	40 33	59	148	41 32	59	148
28	37 15	58	146	38 13	59	146	39 12	59	146	40 11	58	146	41 09	59	145
30	36 51	+59	144	37 50	+58	144	38 48	+59	144	39 47	+58	143	40 45	+59	143
32	36 26	59	142	37 25	58	142	38 23	59	141	39 22	58	141	40 20	58	141
34	36 00	59	140	36 59	58	139	37 57	58	139	38 55	58	139	39 53	58	138
36	35 33	58	137	36 31	58	137	37 29	58	137	38 27	58	136	39 25	58	136
38	35 05	58	135	36 03	57	135	37 00	58	134	37 58	58	134	38 56	58	134
40	34 35	+58	133	35 33	+58	133	36 31	+57	132	37 28	+58	132	38 26	+57	131
42	34 04	58	131	35 02	58	130	36 00	57	130	36 57	58	130	37 55	57	129
44	33 33	57	128	34 30	58	128	35 28	57	128	36 25	57	127	37 22	57	127
46	33 00	57	126	33 57	58	126	34 55	57	126	35 52	57	125	36 49	57	125
48	32 27	57	124	33 24	57	124	34 21	57	123	35 18	57	123	36 15	57	123
50	31 52	+57	122	32 49	+57	122	33 46	+57	121	34 43	+57	121	35 40	+57	121
52	31 17	57	120	32 14	57	120	33 11	57	119	34 08	56	119	35 04	57	118
54	30 41	57	118	31 38	57	118	32 35	56	117	33 31	57	117	34 28	56	116
56	30 04	57	116	31 01	57	115	31 58	56	115	32 54	57	115	33 51	56	114
58	29 27	57	114	30 24	56	113	31 20	57	113	32 17	56	113	33 13	56	112
60	28 49	+57	112	29 46	+56	111	30 42	+56	111	31 38	+57	111	32 35	+56	110
62	28 11	56	110	29 07	57	109	30 04	56	109	31 00	56	109	31 56	56	108
64	27 32	56	108	28 28	57	107	29 25	56	107	30 21	56	107	31 17	56	106
66	26 53	56	106	27 49	56	105	28 45	56	105	29 41	56	105	30 37	56	104
68	26 13	56	104	27 09	56	103	28 05	56	103	29 01	56	103	29 57	56	102
70	25 33	+56	102	26 29	+56	101	27 25	+56	101	28 21	+56	101	29 17	+56	100
72	24 53	56	100	25 49	56	100	26 45	56	99	27 41	55	99	28 36	56	98
74	24 12	56	98	25 08	56	98	26 04	56	97	27 00	56	97	27 56	55	96
76	23 32	55	96	24 27	56	96	25 23	56	95	26 19	56	95	27 15	55	94
78	22 51	56	94	23 47	55	94	24 42	56	93	25 38	56	93	26 34	55	93
80	22 10	+56	92	23 06	+55	92	24 01	+56	92	24 57	+56	91	25 53	+55	91
82	21 29	56	90	22 25	55	90	23 20	56	90	24 16	56	89	25 12	55	89
84	20 48	55	89	21 43	56	88	22 39	56	88	23 35	56	87	24 31	55	87
86	20 07	55	87	21 02	56	86	21 58	56	86	22 54	56	85	23 50	55	85
88	19 26	56	85	20 22	55	84	21 17	56	84	22 13	56	84	23 09	56	83
90	18 45	+56	83	19 41	+56	83	20 37	+56	82	21 33	+55	82	22 28	+56	81
92	18 04	56	81	19 00	56	81	19 56	56	80	20 52	56	80	21 48	56	80
94	17 24	56	79	18 20	56	79	19 16	56	79	20 12	56	78	21 08	55	78
96	16 44	56	77	17 40	56	77	18 36	56	77	19 32	56	76	20 28	56	76
98	16 04	56	76	17 00	56	75	17 56	56	75	18 52	56	74	19 48	56	74
100	15 24	+56	74	16 20	+57	73	17 17	+56	73	18 13	+56	73	19 09	+56	72
102	14 45	56	72	15 41	56	72	16 37	57	71	17 34	56	71	18 30	56	70
104	14 06	57	70	15 03	56	70	15 59	56	69	16 55	56	69	17 51	57	69
106	13 28	56	68	14 24	57	68	15 21	56	68	16 17	56	67	17 13	57	67
108	12 50	56	66	13 46	57	66	14 43	56	66	15 39	57	65	16 36	56	65
110	12 13	+56	65	13 09	+57	64	14 06	+56	64	15 02	+57	64	15 59	+57	63
112	11 36	57	63	12 33	56	63	13 29	57	62	14 26	57	62	15 23	56	62
114	11 00	56	61	11 56	57	61	12 53	57	60	13 50	57	60	14 47	57	60
116	10 24	57	59	11 21	57	59	12 18	57	59	13 15	57	58	14 12	57	58
118	09 49	57	57	10 46	57	57	11 43	57	57	12 40	57	56	13 37	57	56
120	09 15	+57	56	10 12	+57	55	11 09	+58	55	12 07	+57	55	13 04	+57	54
122	08 41	58	54	09 39	57	53	10 36	57	53	11 33	58	53	12 31	57	53
124	08 09	57	52	09 06	58	52	10 04	57	51	11 01	58	51	11 59	57	51
126	07 37	57	50	08 34	58	50	09 32	58	50	10 30	57	49	11 27	58	49
128	07 06	58	48	08 04	57	48	09 01	58	48	09 59	58	47	10 57	57	47
130	06 36	+57	46	07 33	+58	46	08 31	+58	46	09 29	+58	46	10 27	+58	45
132	06 06	58	45	07 04	58	44	08 02	58	44	09 00	58	44	09 58	58	44
134	05 38	58	43	06 36	58	43	07 34	58	42	08 32	58	42	09 30	59	42
136	05 11	58	41	06 09	58	41	07 07	58	41	08 05	59	40	09 04	58	40
138	04 44	59	39	05 43	58	39	06 41	58	39	07 39	59	38	08 38	58	38

LHA	25° Hc	d	Z	26° Hc	d	Z	27° Hc	d	Z	28° Hc	d	Z	29° Hc	d	Z	LHA
	° ′	′	°	° ′	′	°	° ′	′	°	° ′	′	°	° ′	′	°	
0	45 00	+60	180	46 00	+60	180	47 00	+60	180	48 00	+60	180	49 00	+60	180	360
2	44 59	60	177	45 59	60	177	46 59	60	177	47 59	60	177	48 59	60	177	358
4	44 56	60	175	45 56	60	175	46 56	60	175	47 56	60	175	48 56	60	175	356
6	44 52	60	172	45 52	60	172	46 52	60	172	47 52	59	172	48 51	60	172	354
8	44 45	60	170	45 45	60	170	46 45	60	170	47 45	60	170	48 45	60	169	352
10	44 37	+60	167	45 37	+60	167	46 37	+60	167	47 37	+59	167	48 36	+60	167	350
12	44 27	60	165	45 27	60	165	46 27	59	164	47 26	60	164	48 26	60	164	348
14	44 16	59	162	45 15	60	162	46 15	59	162	47 14	60	162	48 14	59	162	346
16	44 02	60	160	45 02	59	160	46 01	60	159	47 01	59	159	48 00	59	159	344
18	43 47	59	157	44 46	60	157	45 46	59	157	46 45	59	157	47 44	60	156	342
20	43 30	+60	155	44 30	+59	155	45 29	+59	154	46 28	+59	154	47 27	+59	154	340
22	43 12	59	152	44 11	59	152	45 10	59	152	46 09	59	152	47 08	59	151	338
24	42 52	59	150	43 51	59	150	44 50	59	149	45 49	58	149	46 47	59	149	336
26	42 31	58	147	43 29	59	147	44 28	59	147	45 27	58	147	46 25	59	146	334
28	42 08	58	145	43 06	59	145	44 05	58	144	45 03	59	144	46 02	58	144	332
30	41 44	+58	143	42 42	+58	142	43 40	+59	142	44 39	+58	142	45 37	+58	141	330
32	41 18	58	140	42 16	58	140	43 14	58	140	44 12	59	139	45 11	57	139	328
34	40 51	58	138	41 49	58	138	42 47	58	137	43 45	58	137	44 43	58	137	326
36	40 23	58	136	41 21	58	135	42 19	57	135	43 16	58	135	44 14	58	134	324
38	39 54	57	133	40 51	58	133	41 49	58	133	42 47	57	132	43 44	57	132	322
40	39 23	+58	131	40 21	+57	131	41 18	+58	130	42 16	+57	130	43 13	+57	130	320
42	38 52	57	129	39 49	57	129	40 46	58	128	41 44	57	128	42 41	57	127	318
44	38 19	58	127	39 17	57	126	40 14	57	126	41 11	57	125	42 08	56	125	316
46	37 46	57	124	38 43	57	124	39 40	57	124	40 37	56	123	41 33	57	123	314
48	37 12	57	122	38 09	56	122	39 05	57	122	40 02	57	121	40 59	56	121	312
50	36 37	+56	120	37 33	+57	120	38 30	+56	119	39 26	+57	119	40 23	+56	118	310
52	36 01	56	118	36 57	57	118	37 54	56	117	38 50	56	117	39 46	57	116	308
54	35 24	57	116	36 21	56	116	37 17	56	115	38 13	56	115	39 09	56	114	306
56	34 47	56	114	35 43	56	113	36 39	57	113	37 36	56	113	38 32	55	112	304
58	34 09	56	112	35 05	56	111	36 01	56	111	36 57	56	110	37 53	56	110	302
60	33 31	+56	110	34 27	+56	109	35 23	+56	109	36 19	+55	108	37 14	+56	108	300
62	32 52	56	108	33 48	56	107	34 44	55	107	35 39	56	106	36 35	56	106	298
64	32 13	55	106	33 08	56	105	34 04	56	105	35 00	55	104	35 55	56	104	296
66	31 33	56	104	32 29	55	103	33 24	56	103	34 20	55	102	35 15	56	102	294
68	30 53	56	102	31 49	55	101	32 44	56	101	33 40	55	100	34 35	55	100	292
70	30 13	+55	100	31 08	+56	99	32 04	+55	99	32 59	+56	98	33 55	+55	98	290
72	29 32	56	98	30 28	55	97	31 23	56	97	32 19	55	97	33 14	55	96	288
74	28 51	56	96	29 47	55	96	30 42	56	95	31 38	55	95	32 33	55	94	286
76	28 10	56	94	29 06	55	94	30 01	56	93	30 57	55	93	31 52	55	92	284
78	27 29	56	92	28 25	55	92	29 20	56	91	30 16	55	91	31 11	55	90	282
80	26 48	+56	90	27 44	+55	90	28 39	+56	89	29 35	+55	89	30 30	+55	89	280
82	26 07	56	88	27 03	55	88	27 58	56	88	28 54	55	87	29 49	55	87	278
84	25 26	56	87	26 22	55	86	27 17	56	86	28 13	55	85	29 08	55	85	276
86	24 45	56	85	25 41	55	84	26 36	56	84	27 32	55	83	28 27	55	83	274
88	24 05	55	83	25 00	56	82	25 56	55	82	26 51	56	82	27 47	55	81	272
90	23 24	+56	81	24 20	+55	81	25 15	+56	80	26 11	+55	80	27 06	+56	79	270
92	22 44	55	79	23 39	56	79	24 35	55	78	25 30	56	78	26 26	55	78	268
94	22 03	56	77	22 59	56	77	23 55	55	77	24 50	56	76	25 46	56	76	266
96	21 24	55	76	22 19	56	75	23 15	56	75	24 11	55	74	25 06	56	74	264
98	20 44	56	74	21 40	56	73	22 36	55	73	23 31	56	73	24 27	56	72	262
100	20 05	+56	72	21 01	+56	72	21 57	+56	71	22 53	+55	71	23 48	+56	70	260
102	19 26	56	70	20 22	56	70	21 18	56	69	22 14	56	69	23 10	56	69	258
104	18 48	56	68	19 44	56	68	20 40	56	68	21 36	56	67	22 32	56	67	256
106	18 10	56	67	19 06	56	66	20 02	56	66	20 58	57	65	21 55	56	65	254
108	17 32	57	65	18 29	56	64	19 25	56	64	20 21	57	64	21 18	56	63	252
110	16 56	+56	63	17 52	+56	63	18 48	+57	62	19 45	+56	62	20 41	+57	62	250
112	16 19	57	61	17 16	56	61	18 12	57	60	19 09	57	60	20 06	56	60	248
114	15 44	56	59	16 40	57	59	17 37	57	59	18 34	56	58	19 30	57	58	246
116	15 09	57	58	16 06	56	57	17 02	57	57	17 59	57	57	18 56	57	56	244
118	14 34	57	56	15 31	57	55	16 28	57	55	17 25	57	55	18 22	57	55	242
120	14 01	+57	54	14 58	+57	54	15 55	+57	53	16 52	+57	53	17 49	+57	53	240
122	13 28	57	52	14 25	58	52	15 23	57	52	16 20	57	51	17 17	57	51	238
124	12 56	57	50	13 53	58	50	14 51	57	50	15 48	57	50	16 45	58	49	236
126	12 25	57	49	13 22	58	48	14 20	57	48	15 17	58	48	16 15	57	48	234
128	11 54	58	47	12 52	58	47	13 50	57	46	14 47	58	46	15 45	58	46	232
130	11 25	+58	45	12 23	+57	45	13 20	+58	45	14 18	+58	44	15 16	+58	44	230
132	10 56	58	43	11 54	58	43	12 52	58	43	13 50	58	43	14 48	58	42	228
134	10 29	58	42	11 27	58	41	12 25	58	41	13 23	58	41	14 21	58	41	226
136	10 02	58	40	11 00	58	40	11 58	58	39	12 56	59	39	13 55	58	39	224
138	09 36	58	38	10 34	59	38	11 33	58	38	12 31	58	37	13 29	59	37	222

S. Lat. {LHA greater than 180°....... Zn=180−Z; LHA less than 180°........... Zn=180+Z}

DECLINATION (15°-29°) SAME NAME AS LATITUDE

LAT 70°

N. Lat. {LHA greater than 180°....... Zn=Z; LHA less than 180°........... Zn=360−Z}

DECLINATION (15°-29°) SAME NAME AS LATITUDE

LHA	15° Hc d Z	16° Hc d Z	17° Hc d Z	18° Hc d Z	19° Hc d Z	20° Hc d Z	21° Hc d Z	22° Hc d Z	23° Hc d Z	24° Hc d Z	25° Hc d Z	26° Hc d Z	27° Hc d Z	28° Hc d Z	29° Hc d Z	LHA
	° ′ ′ °	° ′ ′ °	° ′ ′ °	° ′ ′ °	° ′ ′ °	° ′ ′ °	° ′ ′ °	° ′ ′ °	° ′ ′ °	° ′ ′ °	° ′ ′ °	° ′ ′ °	° ′ ′ °	° ′ ′ °	° ′ ′ °	
140	−0 34 +59 38	00 25 +58 38	01 23 +59 38	02 22 +58 38	03 20 +59 38	04 19 +58 37	05 17 +59 37	06 16 +58 37	07 14 +59 37	08 13 +58 36	09 11 +59 36	10 10 +58 36	11 08 +59 36	12 07 +58 36	13 05 +59 35	220
142	−0 59 59 37	00 00 58 36	00 58 59 36	01 57 59 36	02 56 58 36	03 54 59 35	04 53 59 35	05 52 58 35	06 50 59 35	07 49 59 35	08 48 58 34	09 46 59 34	10 45 58 34	11 43 59 34	12 42 59 34	218
144	−1 23 59 35	−0 24 59 34	00 35 59 34	01 34 58 34	02 32 59 34	03 31 59 34	04 30 59 33	05 29 58 33	06 27 59 33	07 26 59 33	08 25 59 33	09 24 58 32	10 22 59 32	11 21 59 32	12 20 59 32	216
146	−1 46 59 33	−0 47 59 33	00 12 59 32	01 11 59 32	02 10 59 32	03 09 59 32	04 08 59 32	05 07 59 31	06 06 59 31	07 05 58 31	08 03 59 31	09 02 59 31	10 01 59 30	11 00 59 30	11 59 59 30	214
148	−2 07 59 31	−1 08 59 31	−0 09 59 30	00 50 59 30	01 49 59 30	02 48 59 30	03 47 59 30	04 46 59 30	05 45 59 29	06 44 59 29	07 43 59 29	08 42 59 29	09 41 59 29	10 40 59 28	11 39 59 28	212
150	−2 28 +60 29	−1 28 +59 29	−0 29 +59 29	00 30 +59 28	01 29 +59 28	02 28 +59 28	03 27 +59 28	04 26 +59 28	05 25 +60 28	06 25 +59 27	07 24 +59 27	08 23 +59 27	09 22 +59 27	10 21 +59 27	11 20 +59 27	210
152	−2 47 59 27	−1 48 60 27	−0 48 59 27	00 11 59 27	01 10 59 26	02 09 60 26	03 09 59 26	04 08 59 26	05 07 59 26	06 06 59 26	07 05 60 25	08 05 59 25	09 04 59 25	10 03 59 25	11 02 59 25	208
154	−3 05 59 25	−2 06 60 25	−1 06 59 25	−0 07 60 25	00 53 59 24	01 52 59 24	02 51 59 24	03 50 60 24	04 50 59 24	05 49 59 24	06 48 60 24	07 48 59 23	08 47 59 23	09 46 60 23	10 46 59 23	206
156	−3 22 60 23	−2 22 59 23	−1 23 60 23	−0 23 59 23	00 36 60 23	01 36 59 22	02 35 59 22	03 34 60 22	04 34 59 22	05 33 60 22	06 33 59 22	07 32 59 22	08 31 60 22	09 31 59 21	10 30 60 21	204
158	−3 37 59 21	−2 38 60 21	−1 38 59 21	−0 39 60 21	00 21 59 21	01 20 60 21	02 20 60 20	03 20 59 20	04 19 60 20	05 19 59 20	06 18 60 20	07 18 59 20	08 17 60 20	09 17 59 20	10 16 59 19	202
160	−3 51 +59 19	−2 52 +60 19	−1 52 +59 19	−0 53 +60 19	00 07 +60 19	01 07 +59 19	02 06 +60 19	03 06 +59 19	04 05 +60 18	05 05 +60 18	06 05 +59 18	07 04 +60 18	08 04 +59 18	09 03 +60 18	10 03 +60 18	200
162	−4 04 59 17	−3 05 60 17	−2 05 60 17	−1 05 59 17	−0 06 60 17	00 54 60 17	01 54 59 17	02 53 60 17	03 53 60 17	04 53 59 17	05 52 60 16	06 52 60 16	07 52 59 16	08 51 60 16	09 51 60 16	198
164	−4 16 60 15	−3 16 60 15	−2 16 59 15	−1 17 60 15	−0 17 60 15	00 43 59 15	01 42 60 15	02 42 60 15	03 42 60 15	04 42 60 15	05 42 59 15	06 41 60 14	07 41 60 14	08 41 59 14	09 40 60 14	196
166	−4 26 60 14	−3 26 59 14	−2 27 60 13	−1 27 60 13	−0 27 60 13	00 33 60 13	01 33 59 13	02 32 60 13	03 32 60 13	04 32 60 13	05 32 60 13	06 32 59 13	07 31 60 13	08 31 60 13	09 31 60 12	194
168	−4 35 60 12	−3 35 60 12	−2 35 59 12	−1 36 60 11	−0 36 60 11	00 24 60 11	01 24 60 11	02 24 60 11	03 24 60 11	04 24 59 11	05 23 60 11	06 23 60 11	07 23 60 11	08 23 60 11	09 23 60 11	192
170	−4 43 +60 10	−3 43 +60 10	−2 43 +60 10	−1 43 +60 10	−0 43 +60 9	00 17 +60 9	01 17 +60 9	02 17 +59 9	03 16 +60 9	04 16 +60 9	05 16 +60 9	06 16 +60 9	07 16 +60 9	08 16 +60 9	09 16 +60 9	190
172	−4 49 60 8	−3 49 60 8	−2 49 60 8	−1 49 60 8	−0 49 60 8	00 11 60 8	01 11 60 8	02 11 60 7	03 11 59 7	04 10 60 7	05 10 60 7	06 10 60 7	07 10 60 7	08 10 60 7	09 10 60 7	188
174	−4 54 60 6	−3 54 60 6	−2 54 60 6	−1 54 60 6	−0 54 60 6	00 06 60 6	01 06 60 6	02 06 60 6	03 06 60 6	04 06 60 6	05 06 60 6	06 06 60 5	07 06 60 5	08 06 60 5	09 06 60 5	186
176	−4 57 60 4	−3 57 60 4	−2 57 60 4	−1 57 60 4	−0 57 60 4	00 03 60 4	01 03 60 4	02 03 60 4	03 03 60 4	04 03 60 4	05 03 60 4	06 03 60 4	07 03 60 4	08 03 60 4	09 03 60 4	184
178	−4 59 60 2	−3 59 60 2	−2 59 60 2	−1 59 60 2	−0 59 60 2	00 01 60 2	01 01 60 2	02 01 60 2	03 01 60 2	04 01 60 2	05 01 60 2	06 01 60 2	07 01 60 2	08 01 60 2	09 01 60 2	182
180	−5 00 +60 0	−4 00 +60 0	−3 00 +60 0	−2 00 +60 0	−1 00 +60 0	00 00 +60 0	01 00 +60 0	02 00 +60 0	03 00 +60 0	04 00 +60 0	05 00 +60 0	06 00 +60 0	07 00 +60 0	08 00 +60 0	09 00 +60 0	180

LHA	15° Hc d Z	16° Hc d Z	17° Hc d Z	18° Hc d Z	19° Hc d Z	20° Hc d Z	21° Hc d Z	22° Hc d Z	23° Hc d Z	24° Hc d Z	25° Hc d Z	26° Hc d Z	27° Hc d Z	28° Hc d Z	29° Hc d Z
72	−8 07 56 112	288													
70	−7 29 −57 114	290													
68	−6 52 57 116	−7 49 56 116	292												
66	−6 15 57 117	−7 12 57 118	−8 09 57 118	294											
64	−5 39 57 119	−6 36 57 120	−7 33 57 120	296											
62	−5 03 58 121	−6 01 57 121	−6 58 57 122	−7 55 57 122	298										
60	−4 28 −58 123	−5 26 −57 123	−6 23 −57 124	−7 20 −58 124	300										
58	−3 54 58 125	−4 52 57 125	−5 49 58 125	−6 47 57 126	−7 44 57 126	302									
56	−3 21 58 127	−4 19 57 127	−5 16 58 127	−6 14 57 127	−7 11 58 128	304									
54	−2 49 57 128	−3 46 58 129	−4 44 58 129	−5 42 57 129	−6 39 58 130	−7 37 57 130	306								
52	−2 17 58 130	−3 15 57 131	−4 12 58 131	−5 10 58 131	−6 08 58 131	−7 06 58 132	308								
50	−1 46 −58 132	−2 44 −58 132	−3 42 −58 133	−4 40 −58 133	−5 38 −58 133	−6 36 −57 134	−7 33 −58 134	310							
48	−1 16 58 134	−2 14 58 134	−3 12 58 135	−4 10 58 135	−5 08 58 135	−6 06 58 135	−7 04 58 136	312							
46	−0 47 58 136	−1 45 59 136	−2 44 58 136	−3 42 58 137	−4 40 58 137	−5 38 58 137	−6 36 58 137	−7 34 58 138	314						
44	−0 19 58 138	−1 17 59 138	−2 16 58 138	−3 14 58 139	−4 12 59 139	−5 11 58 139	−6 09 58 139	−7 07 58 139	316						
42	00 08 59 140	−0 51 58 140	−1 49 58 140	−2 47 59 140	−3 46 58 141	−4 44 59 141	−5 43 58 141	−6 41 58 141	−7 39 59 142	318					
40	00 34 −59 142	−0 25 −58 142	−1 23 −59 142	−2 22 −58 142	−3 20 −59 142	−4 19 −58 143	−5 17 −59 143	−6 16 −58 143	−7 14 −59 143	320					
38	00 59 59 143	00 00 58 144	−0 58 59 144	−1 57 59 144	−2 56 58 144	−3 54 59 145	−4 53 59 145	−5 52 58 145	−6 50 59 145	322					
36	01 23 59 145	00 24 59 146	−0 35 59 146	−1 34 58 146	−2 32 59 146	−3 31 59 146	−4 30 59 147	−5 29 58 147	−6 27 59 147	−7 26 59 147	324				
34	01 46 59 147	00 47 59 147	−0 12 59 148	−1 11 59 148	−2 10 59 148	−3 09 59 148	−4 08 59 148	−5 07 59 149	−6 06 59 149	−7 05 58 149	326				
32	02 07 59 149	01 08 59 149	00 09 59 150	−0 50 59 150	−1 49 59 150	−2 48 59 150	−3 47 59 150	−4 46 59 150	−5 45 59 151	−6 44 59 151	328				
30	02 28 −60 151	01 28 −59 151	00 29 −59 151	−0 30 −59 152	−1 29 −59 152	−2 28 −59 152	−3 27 −59 152	−4 26 −59 152	−5 25 −60 152	−6 25 −59 153	−7 24 −59 153	330			
28	02 47 59 153	01 48 60 153	00 48 59 153	−0 11 59 153	−1 10 59 154	−2 09 60 154	−3 09 59 154	−4 08 59 154	−5 07 59 154	−6 06 59 154	−7 05 60 155	332			
26	03 05 59 155	02 06 60 155	01 06 59 155	00 07 60 155	−0 53 59 156	−1 52 59 156	−2 51 59 156	−3 50 60 156	−4 50 59 156	−5 49 59 156	−6 48 60 156	334			
24	03 22 60 157	02 22 59 157	01 23 60 157	00 23 59 157	−0 36 60 157	−1 36 59 158	−2 35 59 158	−3 34 60 158	−4 34 59 158	−5 33 60 158	−6 33 59 158	336			
22	03 37 59 159	02 38 60 159	01 38 59 159	00 39 60 159	−0 21 59 159	−1 20 60 159	−2 20 60 160	−3 20 59 160	−4 19 60 160	−5 19 59 160	−6 18 60 160	−7 18 59 160	338		
20	03 51 −59 161	02 52 −60 161	01 52 −59 161	00 53 −60 161	−0 07 −60 161	−1 07 −59 161	−2 06 −60 161	−3 06 −59 161	−4 05 −60 162	−5 05 −60 162	−6 05 −59 162	−7 04 −60 162	340		
18	04 04 59 163	03 05 60 163	02 05 60 163	01 05 59 163	00 06 60 163	−0 54 60 163	−1 54 59 163	−2 53 60 163	−3 53 60 163	−4 53 59 163	−5 52 60 164	−6 52 60 164	342		
16	04 16 60 165	03 16 60 165	02 16 59 165	01 17 60 165	00 17 60 165	−0 43 59 165	−1 42 60 165	−2 42 60 165	−3 42 60 165	−4 42 60 165	−5 42 59 165	−6 41 60 166	344		
14	04 26 60 166	03 26 59 166	02 27 60 167	01 27 60 167	00 27 60 167	−0 33 60 167	−1 33 59 167	−2 32 60 167	−3 32 60 167	−4 32 60 167	−5 32 60 167	−6 32 59 167	346		
12	04 35 60 168	03 35 60 168	02 35 59 168	01 36 60 169	00 36 60 169	−0 24 60 169	−1 24 60 169	−2 24 60 169	−3 24 60 169	−4 24 59 169	−5 23 60 169	−6 23 60 169	348		
10	04 43 −60 170	03 43 −60 170	02 43 −60 170	01 43 −60 170	00 43 −60 171	−0 17 −60 171	−1 17 −60 171	−2 17 −59 171	−3 16 −60 171	−4 16 −60 171	−5 16 −60 171	−6 16 −60 171	350		
8	04 49 60 172	03 49 60 172	02 49 60 172	01 49 60 172	00 49 60 172	−0 11 60 172	−1 11 60 172	−2 11 60 173	−3 11 59 173	−4 10 60 173	−5 10 60 173	−6 10 60 173	352		
6	04 54 60 174	03 54 60 174	02 54 60 174	01 54 60 174	00 54 60 174	−0 06 60 174	−1 06 60 174	−2 06 60 174	−3 06 60 174	−4 06 60 174	−5 06 60 174	−6 06 60 175	354		
4	04 57 60 176	03 57 60 176	02 57 60 176	01 57 60 176	00 57 60 176	−0 03 60 176	−1 03 60 176	−2 03 60 176	−3 03 60 176	−4 03 60 176	−5 03 60 176	−6 03 60 176	356		
2	04 59 60 178	03 59 60 178	02 59 60 178	01 59 60 178	00 59 60 178	−0 01 60 178	−1 01 60 178	−2 01 60 178	−3 01 60 178	−4 01 60 178	−5 01 60 178	−6 01 60 178	−7 01 60 178	358	
0	05 00 −60 180	04 00 −60 180	03 00 −60 180	02 00 −60 180	01 00 −60 180	00 00 −60 180	−1 00 −60 180	−2 00 −60 180	−3 00 −60 180	−4 00 −60 180	−5 00 −60 180	−6 00 −60 180	−7 00 −60 180	360	
	15°	16°	17°	18°	19°	20°	21°	22°	23°	24°	25°	26°	27°	28°	29°

S. Lat. {LHA greater than 180°....... Zn=180−Z; LHA less than 180°........... Zn=180+Z}

DECLINATION (15°-29°) CONTRARY NAME TO LATITUDE

N. Lat. {LHA greater than 180°....... Zn=Z; LHA less than 180°........... Zn=360−Z}

DECLINATION (0°-14°) SAME NAME AS LATITUDE

LAT 71°

LHA	0° Hc	0° d	0° Z	1° Hc	1° d	1° Z	2° Hc	2° d	2° Z	3° Hc	3° d	3° Z	4° Hc	4° d	4° Z
	° ′	′	°	° ′	′	°	° ′	′	°	° ′	′	°	° ′	′	°
0	19 00	+60	180	20 00	+60	180	21 00	+60	180	22 00	+60	180	23 00	+60	180
2	18 59	60	178	19 59	60	178	20 59	60	178	21 59	60	178	22 59	60	178
4	18 57	60	176	19 57	60	176	20 57	60	176	21 57	60	176	22 57	60	176
6	18 54	60	174	19 54	59	174	20 53	60	174	21 53	60	174	22 53	60	174
8	18 49	59	172	19 48	60	172	20 48	60	171	21 48	60	171	22 48	60	171
10	18 42	+60	169	19 42	+60	169	20 42	+60	169	21 42	+60	169	22 42	+60	169
12	18 34	60	167	19 34	60	167	20 34	60	167	21 34	60	167	22 34	59	167
14	18 25	60	165	19 25	60	165	20 25	59	165	21 24	60	165	22 24	60	165
16	18 14	60	163	19 14	60	163	20 14	59	163	21 13	60	163	22 13	60	163
18	18 02	60	161	19 02	60	161	20 02	59	161	21 01	60	161	22 01	60	161
20	17 49	+59	159	18 48	+60	159	19 48	+60	159	20 48	+59	159	21 47	+60	158
22	17 34	60	157	18 34	59	157	19 33	60	157	20 33	59	157	21 32	60	156
24	17 18	60	155	18 18	59	155	19 17	59	155	20 16	60	154	21 16	59	154
26	17 01	59	153	18 00	60	153	19 00	59	152	19 59	59	152	20 58	59	152
28	16 42	60	151	17 42	59	151	18 41	59	150	19 40	59	150	20 39	59	150
30	16 23	+59	149	17 22	+59	148	18 21	+59	148	19 20	+59	148	20 19	+59	148
32	16 02	59	147	17 01	59	146	18 00	59	146	18 59	59	146	19 58	59	146
34	15 40	58	145	16 38	59	144	17 37	59	144	18 36	59	144	19 35	59	144
36	15 16	59	143	16 15	59	142	17 14	59	142	18 13	58	142	19 11	59	142
38	14 52	59	140	15 51	58	140	16 49	59	140	17 48	59	140	18 47	58	140
40	14 27	+58	138	15 25	+59	138	16 24	+58	138	17 22	+59	138	18 21	+58	138
42	14 00	59	136	14 59	58	136	15 57	58	136	16 55	59	136	17 54	58	136
44	13 33	58	134	14 31	58	134	15 29	59	134	16 28	58	134	17 26	58	133
46	13 04	59	132	14 03	58	132	15 01	58	132	15 59	58	132	16 57	58	131
48	12 35	58	130	13 33	58	130	14 31	58	130	15 29	58	130	16 27	58	129
50	12 05	+58	128	13 03	+58	128	14 01	+58	128	14 59	+58	128	15 57	+58	127
52	11 34	58	127	12 32	58	126	13 30	57	126	14 27	58	126	15 25	58	125
54	11 02	58	125	12 00	58	124	12 58	57	124	13 55	58	124	14 53	58	123
56	10 29	58	123	11 27	58	122	12 25	57	122	13 22	58	122	14 20	58	121
58	09 56	58	121	10 54	57	120	11 51	58	120	12 49	57	120	13 46	58	119
60	09 22	+58	119	10 20	+57	118	11 17	+58	118	12 15	+57	118	13 12	+57	118
62	08 48	57	117	09 45	57	116	10 42	58	116	11 40	57	116	12 37	57	116
64	08 12	58	115	09 10	57	115	10 07	57	114	11 04	58	114	12 02	57	114
66	07 37	57	113	08 34	57	113	09 31	57	112	10 28	57	112	11 25	58	112
68	07 00	58	111	07 58	57	111	08 55	57	110	09 52	57	110	10 49	57	110
70	06 24	+57	109	07 21	+57	109	08 18	+57	108	09 15	+57	108	10 12	+57	108
72	05 46	58	107	06 44	57	107	07 41	57	106	08 38	56	106	09 34	57	106
74	05 09	57	105	06 06	57	105	07 03	57	105	08 00	57	104	08 57	57	104
76	04 31	57	103	05 28	57	103	06 25	57	103	07 22	57	102	08 19	56	102
78	03 53	57	101	04 50	57	101	05 47	56	101	06 43	57	100	07 40	57	100
80	03 14	+57	100	04 11	+57	99	05 08	+57	99	06 05	+57	99	07 02	+57	98
82	02 36	57	98	03 33	56	97	04 29	57	97	05 26	57	97	06 23	57	96
84	01 57	57	96	02 54	57	95	03 51	56	95	04 47	57	95	05 44	57	94
86	01 18	57	94	02 15	57	94	03 12	56	93	04 08	57	93	05 05	57	93
88	00 39	57	92	01 36	56	92	02 32	57	91	03 29	57	91	04 26	57	91
90	00 00	+57	90	00 57	+57	90	01 54	+56	89	02 50	+57	89	03 47	+57	89
92	−0 39	57	88	00 18	56	88	01 14	57	87	02 11	57	87	03 08	57	87
94	−1 18	57	86	−0 21	56	86	00 35	57	86	01 32	57	85	02 29	57	85
96	−1 57	57	84	−1 00	57	84	−0 03	56	84	00 53	57	83	01 50	57	83
98	−2 36	57	82	−1 39	57	82	−0 42	57	82	00 15	56	81	01 11	57	81
100	−3 14	+56	80	−2 18	+57	80	−1 21	+57	80	−0 24	+57	80	00 33	+57	79
102	−3 53	57	79	−2 56	57	78	−1 59	57	78	−1 02	57	78	−0 05	56	77
104	−4 31	57	77	−3 34	57	76	−2 37	57	76	−1 40	57	76	−0 43	57	75
106	−5 09	57	75	−4 12	57	74	−3 15	57	74	−2 18	57	74	−1 21	57	74
108	−5 46	57	73	−4 49	57	73	−3 52	57	72	−2 55	57	72	−1 58	57	72
110	−6 24	+57	71	−5 27	+58	71	−4 29	+57	70	−3 32	+57	70	−2 35	+57	70
112	−7 00	57	69	−6 03	57	69	−5 06	57	68	−4 09	57	68	−3 12	58	68
114	−7 37	58	67	−6 39	57	67	−5 42	57	67	−4 45	57	66	−3 48	58	66
116				−7 15	57	65	−6 18	58	65	−5 20	57	64	−4 23	57	64
118				−7 50	57	63	−6 53	58	63	−5 55	57	62	−4 58	58	62
120							−7 27	+57	61	−6 30	+58	60	−5 32	+58	60
122							−8 01	58	59	−7 03	57	59	−6 06	58	58
124										−7 36	57	57	−6 39	58	56
126													−7 11	58	54
128													−7 42	58	52

LHA	5° Hc	5° d	5° Z	6° Hc	6° d	6° Z	7° Hc	7° d	7° Z	8° Hc	8° d	8° Z	9° Hc	9° d	9° Z
	° ′	′	°	° ′	′	°	° ′	′	°	° ′	′	°	° ′	′	°
0	24 00	+60	180	25 00	+60	180	26 00	+60	180	27 00	+60	180	28 00	+60	180
2	23 59	60	178	24 59	60	178	25 59	60	178	26 59	60	178	27 59	60	178
4	23 57	60	176	24 57	60	176	25 57	60	176	26 57	60	176	27 57	60	176
6	23 53	60	174	24 53	60	173	25 53	60	173	26 53	60	173	27 53	60	173
8	23 48	60	171	24 48	60	171	25 48	60	171	26 48	60	171	27 48	60	171
10	23 42	+59	169	24 41	+60	169	25 41	+60	169	26 41	+60	169	27 41	+60	169
12	23 33	60	167	24 33	60	167	25 33	60	167	26 33	60	167	27 33	60	167
14	23 24	60	165	24 24	59	165	25 23	60	165	26 23	60	165	27 23	60	164
16	23 13	60	163	24 13	59	163	25 12	60	162	26 12	60	162	27 12	59	162
18	23 01	59	161	24 00	60	160	25 00	59	160	25 59	60	160	26 59	60	160
20	22 47	+59	158	23 46	+60	158	24 46	+59	158	25 45	+60	158	26 45	+60	158
22	22 32	59	156	23 31	60	156	24 31	59	156	25 30	60	156	26 30	59	156
24	22 15	60	154	23 15	59	154	24 14	59	154	25 13	60	154	26 13	59	153
26	21 57	60	152	22 57	59	152	23 56	59	152	24 55	60	151	25 55	59	151
28	21 38	60	150	22 38	59	150	23 37	59	149	24 36	59	149	25 35	59	149
30	21 18	+59	148	22 17	+59	148	23 16	+59	147	24 15	+59	147	25 14	+59	147
32	20 57	59	146	21 56	59	145	22 55	59	145	23 54	58	145	24 52	59	145
34	20 34	59	144	21 33	59	143	22 32	59	143	23 31	58	143	24 29	59	143
36	20 10	59	141	21 09	59	141	22 08	58	141	23 06	59	141	24 05	59	141
38	19 45	59	139	20 44	59	139	21 43	58	139	22 41	59	139	23 40	58	138
40	19 19	+59	137	20 18	+58	137	21 16	+59	137	22 15	+58	137	23 13	+59	136
42	18 52	59	135	19 51	58	135	20 49	58	135	21 47	59	135	22 46	58	134
44	18 24	59	133	19 23	58	133	20 21	58	133	21 19	58	132	22 17	58	132
46	17 55	58	131	18 53	59	131	19 52	58	131	20 50	58	130	21 48	58	130
48	17 25	58	129	18 23	58	129	19 21	58	129	20 19	58	128	21 17	58	128
50	16 55	+58	127	17 53	+58	127	18 51	+57	127	19 48	+58	126	20 46	+58	126
52	16 23	58	125	17 21	58	125	18 19	57	125	19 16	58	124	20 14	58	124
54	15 51	57	123	16 48	58	123	17 46	58	123	18 44	57	122	19 41	58	122
56	15 18	57	121	16 15	58	121	17 13	57	121	18 10	58	120	19 08	57	120
58	14 44	57	119	15 41	58	119	16 39	57	119	17 36	58	118	18 34	57	118
60	14 09	+58	117	15 07	+57	117	16 04	+58	117	17 02	+57	116	17 59	+57	116
62	13 34	58	115	14 32	57	115	15 29	57	115	16 26	57	114	17 23	58	114
64	12 59	57	113	13 56	57	113	14 53	57	113	15 50	57	112	16 47	58	112
66	12 23	57	111	13 20	57	111	14 17	57	111	15 14	57	110	16 11	57	110
68	11 46	57	109	12 43	57	109	13 40	57	109	14 37	57	108	15 34	57	108
70	11 09	+57	107	12 06	+57	107	13 03	+57	107	14 00	+57	107	14 57	+57	106
72	10 31	57	106	11 28	57	105	12 25	57	105	13 22	57	105	14 19	57	104
74	09 54	56	104	10 50	57	103	11 47	57	103	12 44	57	103	13 41	57	102
76	09 15	57	102	10 12	57	101	11 09	57	101	12 06	57	101	13 03	56	100
78	08 37	57	100	09 34	57	99	10 31	56	99	11 27	57	99	12 24	57	98
80	07 59	+56	98	08 55	+57	98	09 52	+57	97	10 49	+56	97	11 45	+57	97
82	07 20	56	96	08 16	57	96	09 13	57	95	10 10	57	95	11 07	56	95
84	06 41	57	94	07 38	56	94	08 34	57	93	09 31	57	93	10 28	56	93
86	06 02	56	92	06 58	57	92	07 55	57	92	08 52	57	91	09 49	56	91
88	05 23	56	90	06 19	57	90	07 16	57	90	08 13	56	89	09 09	57	89
90	04 44	+56	88	05 40	+57	88	06 37	+57	88	07 34	+56	87	08 30	+57	87
92	04 05	56	86	05 01	57	86	05 58	57	86	06 55	56	86	07 51	57	85
94	03 26	56	85	04 22	57	84	05 19	57	84	06 16	57	84	07 13	56	83
96	02 47	57	83	03 44	56	82	04 40	57	82	05 37	57	82	06 34	57	81
98	02 08	57	81	03 05	57	80	04 02	57	80	04 59	56	80	05 55	57	80
100	01 30	+56	79	02 26	+57	79	03 23	+57	78	04 20	+57	78	05 17	+57	78
102	00 51	57	77	01 48	57	77	02 45	57	76	03 42	57	76	04 39	57	76
104	00 14	56	75	01 10	57	75	02 07	57	74	03 04	57	74	04 01	57	74
106	−0 24	57	73	00 33	57	73	01 30	57	73	02 27	57	72	03 24	57	72
108	−1 01	57	71	−0 04	57	71	00 53	57	71	01 50	57	70	02 47	57	70
110	−1 38	+57	70	−0 41	+57	69	00 16	+57	69	01 13	+57	69	02 10	+58	68
112	−2 14	57	68	−1 17	57	67	−0 20	57	67	00 37	57	67	01 34	58	66
114	−2 50	57	66	−1 53	57	65	−0 56	58	65	00 02	57	65	00 59	57	64
116	−3 26	58	64	−2 28	57	64	−1 31	58	63	−0 33	57	63	00 24	57	63
118	−4 00	57	62	−3 03	58	62	−2 05	57	61	−1 08	58	61	−0 10	57	61
120	−4 34	+57	60	−3 37	+58	60	−2 39	+57	59	−1 42	+58	59	−0 44	+57	59
122	−5 08	58	58	−4 10	57	58	−3 13	58	58	−2 15	58	57	−1 17	57	57
124	−5 41	58	56	−4 43	58	56	−3 45	58	56	−2 47	57	55	−1 50	58	55
126	−6 13	58	54	−5 15	58	54	−4 17	58	54	−3 19	58	53	−2 21	58	53
128	−6 44	58	52	−5 46	58	52	−4 48	58	52	−3 50	58	52	−2 52	58	51
130	−7 15	+58	50	−6 17	+59	50	−5 18	+58	50	−4 20	+58	50	−3 22	+58	49
132	−7 44	58	48	−6 46	58	48	−5 48	58	48	−4 50	59	48	−3 51	58	47
134				−7 15	59	46	−6 16	58	46	−5 18	58	46	−4 20	59	45
136				−7 42	58	44	−6 44	58	44	−5 46	59	44	−4 47	58	44
138							−7 11	59	42	−6 12	58	42	−5 14	59	42

LHA	10° Hc	10° d	10° Z	11° Hc	11° d	11° Z	12° Hc	12° d	12° Z	13° Hc	13° d	13° Z	14° Hc	14° d	14° Z	LHA
	° ′	′	°	° ′	′	°	° ′	′	°	° ′	′	°	° ′	′	°	
0	29 00	+60	180	30 00	+60	180	31 00	+60	180	32 00	+60	180	33 00	+60	180	360
2	28 59	60	178	29 59	60	178	30 59	60	178	31 59	60	178	32 59	60	178	358
4	28 57	60	176	29 57	60	176	30 57	60	175	31 57	60	175	32 57	60	175	356
6	28 53	60	173	29 53	60	173	30 53	60	173	31 53	60	173	32 53	60	173	354
8	28 48	60	171	29 48	60	171	30 48	60	171	31 48	59	171	32 47	60	171	352
10	28 41	+60	169	29 41	+60	169	30 41	+60	169	31 41	+59	169	32 40	+60	169	350
12	28 33	59	167	29 32	60	166	30 32	60	166	31 32	60	166	32 32	60	166	348
14	28 23	59	164	29 22	60	164	30 22	60	164	31 22	60	164	32 22	59	164	346
16	28 11	60	162	29 11	60	162	30 11	59	162	31 10	60	162	32 10	60	162	344
18	27 59	59	160	28 58	60	160	29 58	59	160	30 57	60	159	31 57	60	159	342
20	27 45	+59	158	28 44	+60	158	29 44	+59	157	30 43	+60	157	31 43	+59	157	340
22	27 29	59	155	28 28	60	155	29 28	59	155	30 27	60	155	31 27	59	155	338
24	27 12	59	153	28 11	60	153	29 11	59	153	30 10	59	153	31 09	60	153	336
26	26 54	59	151	27 53	59	151	28 52	59	151	29 51	60	151	30 51	59	150	334
28	26 34	59	149	27 33	59	149	28 32	59	149	29 31	60	148	30 31	59	148	332
30	26 13	+59	147	27 12	+59	147	28 11	+59	146	29 10	+59	146	30 09	+59	146	330
32	25 51	59	145	26 50	59	144	27 49	59	144	28 48	59	144	29 47	59	144	328
34	25 28	59	142	26 27	59	142	27 26	58	142	28 24	59	142	29 23	59	142	326
36	25 04	58	140	26 02	59	140	27 01	59	140	28 00	58	140	28 58	59	139	324
38	24 38	59	138	25 37	58	138	26 35	59	138	27 34	58	137	28 32	58	137	322
40	24 12	+58	136	25 10	+58	136	26 08	+59	136	27 07	+59	135	28 05	+58	135	320
42	23 44	58	134	24 42	58	134	25 40	59	133	26 39	58	133	27 37	58	133	318
44	23 15	58	132	24 13	59	132	25 12	58	131	26 10	58	131	27 08	58	131	316
46	22 46	58	130	23 44	58	130	24 42	58	129	25 40	58	129	26 38	58	129	314
48	22 15	58	128	23 13	58	128	24 11	58	127	25 09	58	127	26 07	57	127	312
50	21 44	+58	126	22 42	+58	125	23 40	+57	125	24 37	+58	125	25 35	+58	125	310
52	21 12	58	124	22 10	57	123	23 07	58	123	24 05	57	123	25 02	58	122	308
54	20 39	58	122	21 37	57	121	22 34	58	121	23 32	57	121	24 29	57	120	306
56	20 05	58	120	21 03	57	119	22 00	58	119	22 58	57	119	23 55	57	118	304
58	19 31	57	118	20 28	58	117	21 26	57	117	22 23	57	117	23 20	57	116	302
60	18 56	+57	116	19 53	+58	115	20 51	+57	115	21 48	+57	115	22 45	+57	114	300
62	18 21	57	114	19 18	57	113	20 15	57	113	21 12	57	113	22 09	57	112	298
64	17 45	57	112	18 42	57	111	19 39	57	111	20 36	57	111	21 33	57	110	296
66	17 08	57	110	18 05	57	109	19 02	57	109	19 59	57	109	20 56	57	108	294
68	16 31	57	108	17 28	57	107	18 25	57	107	19 22	57	107	20 19	56	106	292
70	15 54	+57	106	16 51	+56	106	17 47	+57	105	18 44	+57	105	19 41	+57	105	290
72	15 16	57	104	16 13	56	104	17 09	57	103	18 06	57	103	19 03	57	103	288
74	14 38	57	102	15 35	56	102	16 31	57	101	17 28	57	101	18 25	56	101	286
76	13 59	57	100	14 56	57	100	15 53	57	99	16 50	56	99	17 46	57	99	284
78	13 21	57	98	14 18	56	98	15 14	57	97	16 11	56	97	17 07	57	97	282
80	12 42	+57	96	13 39	+56	96	14 35	+57	96	15 32	+57	95	16 29	+56	95	280
82	12 03	57	94	13 00	56	94	13 56	57	94	14 53	57	93	15 50	56	93	278
84	11 24	57	92	12 21	56	92	13 17	57	92	14 14	57	91	15 11	56	91	276
86	10 45	57	91	11 42	56	90	12 38	57	90	13 35	56	90	14 31	57	89	274
88	10 06	57	89	11 03	56	88	11 59	57	88	12 56	56	88	13 52	57	87	272
90	09 27	+57	87	10 24	+56	86	11 20	+57	86	12 17	+56	86	13 13	+57	85	270
92	08 48	57	85	09 45	56	85	10 41	57	84	11 38	57	84	12 35	56	84	268
94	08 09	57	83	09 06	57	83	10 03	56	82	10 59	57	82	11 56	56	82	266
96	07 31	56	81	08 27	57	81	09 24	57	80	10 21	56	80	11 17	57	80	264
98	06 52	57	79	07 49	57	79	08 46	56	79	09 42	57	78	10 39	57	78	262
100	06 14	+57	77	07 11	+56	77	08 07	+57	77	09 04	+57	76	10 01	+57	76	260
102	05 36	57	75	06 33	57	75	07 30	56	75	08 26	57	75	09 23	57	74	258
104	04 58	57	74	05 55	57	73	06 52	57	73	07 49	57	73	08 46	57	72	256
106	04 21	57	72	05 18	57	71	06 15	57	71	07 12	57	71	08 09	57	70	254
108	03 44	57	70	04 41	57	70	05 38	57	69	06 35	57	69	07 32	57	69	252
110	03 08	+57	68	04 05	+57	68	05 02	+57	67	05 59	+57	67	06 56	+57	67	250
112	02 32	57	66	03 29	57	66	04 26	57	65	05 23	57	65	06 20	58	65	248
114	01 56	57	64	02 53	58	64	03 51	57	64	04 48	57	63	05 45	58	63	246
116	01 21	58	62	02 19	57	62	03 16	57	62	04 13	58	61	05 11	57	61	244
118	00 47	57	60	01 44	58	60	02 42	57	60	03 39	58	60	04 37	57	59	242
120	00 13	+58	59	01 11	+57	58	02 08	+58	58	03 06	+58	58	04 04	+57	57	240
122	−0 20	58	57	00 38	58	56	01 36	57	56	02 33	58	56	03 31	58	56	238
124	−0 52	58	55	00 06	57	54	01 03	58	54	02 01	58	54	02 59	58	54	236
126	−1 23	57	53	−0 26	58	53	00 32	58	52	01 30	58	52	02 28	58	52	234
128	−1 54	58	51	−0 56	58	51	00 02	58	50	01 00	58	50	01 58	58	50	232
130	−2 24	+58	49	−1 26	+58	49	−0 28	+58	49	00 30	+58	48	01 28	+58	48	230
132	−2 53	58	47	−1 55	58	47	−0 57	58	47	00 01	59	46	01 00	58	46	228
134	−3 21	58	45	−2 23	58	45	−1 25	59	45	−0 26	58	45	00 32	58	44	226
136	−3 49	59	43	−2 50	58	43	−1 52	59	43	−0 53	58	43	00 05	59	42	224
138	−4 15	59	41	−3 16	58	41	−2 18	59	41	−1 19	58	41	−0 21	59	40	222

S. Lat. {LHA greater than 180°....... Zn=180−Z; LHA less than 180°........... Zn=180+Z}

DECLINATION (0°-14°) SAME NAME AS LATITUDE

N. Lat. {LHA greater than 180°....... Zn=Z; LHA less than 180°........... Zn=360−Z}

DECLINATION (0°-14°) SAME NAME AS LATITUDE

LHA	0° Hc	d	Z	1° Hc	d	Z	2° Hc	d	Z	3° Hc	d	Z	4° Hc	d	Z	5° Hc	d	Z	6° Hc	d	Z	7° Hc	d	Z	8° Hc	d	Z	9° Hc	d	Z	10° Hc	d	Z	11° Hc	d	Z	12° Hc	d	Z	13° Hc	d	Z	14° Hc	d	Z	LHA
	° ′	′	°	° ′	′	°	° ′	′	°	° ′	′	°	° ′	′	°	° ′	′	°	° ′	′	°	° ′	′	°	° ′	′	°	° ′	′	°	° ′	′	°	° ′	′	°	° ′	′	°	° ′	′	°	° ′	′	°	
																					140	-7 36	+58	40	-6 38	+59	40	-5 39	+59	40	-4 40	+58	39	-3 42	+59	39	-2 43	+59	39	-1 44	+58	39	-0 46	+59	39	220
																								142	-7 02	59	38	-6 03	58	38	-5 05	59	37	-4 06	59	37	-3 07	59	37	-2 08	59	37	-1 09	58	37	218
																								144	-7 26	59	36	-6 27	59	36	-5 28	59	36	-4 29	59	35	-3 30	59	35	-2 31	59	35	-1 32	59	35	216
																											146	-6 49	59	34	-5 50	59	34	-4 51	59	33	-3 52	59	33	-2 53	59	33	-1 54	59	33	214
																											148	-7 10	59	32	-6 11	59	32	-5 12	59	31	-4 13	59	31	-3 14	59	31	-2 15	59	31	212
																											150	-7 30	+59	30	-6 31	+59	30	-5 32	+59	29	-4 33	+60	29	-3 33	+59	29	-2 34	+59	29	210
																														152	-6 50	60	28	-5 50	59	28	-4 51	59	27	-3 52	59	27	-2 53	60	27	208
																														154	-7 07	59	26	-6 08	59	26	-5 09	60	25	-4 09	59	25	-3 10	60	25	206
																														156	-7 24	60	24	-6 24	59	24	-5 25	60	24	-4 25	59	23	-3 26	60	23	204
																																	158	-6 39	59	22	-5 40	60	22	-4 40	59	22	-3 41	60	21	202
																																	160	-6 53	+59	20	-5 54	+60	20	-4 54	+60	20	-3 54	+59	19	200
																																	162	-7 06	60	18	-6 06	60	18	-5 06	59	18	-4 07	60	18	198
																																	164	-7 17	60	16	-6 17	59	16	-5 18	60	16	-4 18	60	16	196
																																				166	-6 27	60	14	-5 27	59	14	-4 28	60	14	194
																																				168	-6 36	60	12	-5 36	60	12	-4 36	60	12	192
																																				170	-6 43	+60	10	-5 43	+60	10	-4 43	+59	10	190
																																				172	-6 49	60	8	-5 49	60	8	-4 49	59	8	188
																																				174	-6 54	60	6	-5 54	60	6	-4 54	60	6	186
																																				176	-6 57	60	4	-5 57	60	4	-4 57	60	4	184
																																				178	-6 59	60	2	-5 59	60	2	-4 59	60	2	182
																																				180	-7 00	+60	0	-6 00	+60	0	-5 00	+60	0	180
114	-7 37	57	67	246																																										
112	-7 00	58	69	-7 58	57	69	248																																							
110	-6 24	-57	71	-7 21	-57	71	250																																							
108	-5 46	58	73	-6 44	57	73	-7 41	57	74	252																																				
106	-5 09	57	75	-6 06	57	75	-7 03	57	75	-8 00	57	76	254																																	
104	-4 31	57	77	-5 28	57	77	-6 25	57	77	-7 22	57	78	256																																	
102	-3 53	57	79	-4 50	57	79	-5 47	56	79	-6 43	57	80	-7 40	57	80	258																														
100	-3 14	-57	80	-4 11	-57	81	-5 08	-57	81	-6 05	-57	81	-7 02	-57	82	-7 59	-56	82	260																											
98	-2 36	57	82	-3 33	56	83	-4 29	57	83	-5 26	57	83	-6 23	57	84	-7 20	56	84	-8 16	57	84	262																								
96	-1 57	57	84	-2 54	57	85	-3 51	56	85	-4 47	57	85	-5 44	57	86	-6 41	57	86	-7 38	56	86	264																								
94	-1 18	57	86	-2 15	57	86	-3 12	56	87	-4 08	57	87	-5 05	57	87	-6 02	56	88	-6 58	57	88	-7 55	57	88	266																					
92	-0 39	57	88	-1 36	56	88	-2 32	57	89	-3 29	57	89	-4 26	57	89	-5 23	56	90	-6 19	57	90	-7 16	57	90	-8 13	56	91	268																		
90	00 00	-57	90	-0 57	-57	90	-1 54	-56	91	-2 50	-57	91	-3 47	-57	91	-4 44	-56	92	-5 40	-57	92	-6 37	-57	92	-7 34	-56	93	270																		
88	00 39	57	92	-0 18	56	92	-1 14	57	93	-2 11	57	93	-3 08	57	93	-4 05	56	94	-5 01	57	94	-5 58	57	94	-6 55	56	94	-7 51	57	95	272															
86	01 18	57	94	00 21	56	94	-0 35	57	94	-1 32	57	95	-2 29	57	95	-3 26	56	95	-4 22	57	96	-5 19	57	96	-6 16	57	96	-7 13	56	97	-8 09	57	97	274												
84	01 57	57	96	01 00	57	96	00 03	56	96	-0 53	57	97	-1 50	57	97	-2 47	57	97	-3 44	56	98	-4 40	57	98	-5 37	57	98	-6 34	57	99	-7 31	56	99	276												
82	02 36	57	98	01 39	57	98	00 42	57	98	-0 15	56	99	-1 11	57	99	-2 08	57	99	-3 05	57	100	-4 02	57	100	-4 59	56	100	-5 55	57	100	-6 52	57	101	-7 49	57	101	278									
80	03 14	-56	100	02 18	-57	100	01 21	-57	100	00 24	-57	100	-0 33	-57	101	-1 30	-56	101	-2 26	-57	101	-3 23	-57	102	-4 20	-57	102	-5 17	-57	102	-6 14	-57	103	-7 11	-56	103	-8 07	-57	103	280						
78	03 53	57	101	02 56	57	102	01 59	57	102	01 02	57	102	00 05	56	103	-0 51	57	103	-1 48	57	103	-2 45	57	104	-3 42	57	104	-4 39	57	104	-5 36	57	105	-6 33	57	105	-7 30	56	105	282						
76	04 31	57	103	03 34	57	104	02 37	57	104	01 40	57	104	00 43	57	105	-0 14	56	105	-1 10	57	105	-2 07	57	106	-3 04	57	106	-4 01	57	106	-4 58	57	106	-5 55	57	107	-6 52	57	107	-7 49	57	107	284			
74	05 09	57	105	04 12	57	106	03 15	57	106	02 18	57	106	01 21	57	106	00 24	57	107	-0 33	57	107	-1 30	57	107	-2 27	57	108	-3 24	57	108	-4 21	57	108	-5 18	57	109	-6 15	57	109	-7 12	57	109	-8 09	57	110	286
72	05 46	57	107	04 49	57	107	03 52	57	108	02 55	57	108	01 58	57	108	01 01	57	109	00 04	57	109	-0 53	57	109	-1 50	57	110	-2 47	57	110	-3 44	57	110	-4 41	57	110	-5 38	57	111	-6 35	57	111	-7 32	57	111	288
70	06 24	-57	109	05 27	-58	109	04 29	-57	110	03 32	-57	110	02 35	-57	110	01 38	-57	110	00 41	-57	111	-0 16	-57	111	-1 13	-57	111	-2 10	-58	112	-3 08	-57	112	-4 05	-57	112	-5 02	-57	113	-5 59	-57	113	-6 56	-57	113	290
68	07 00	57	111	06 03	57	111	05 06	57	112	04 09	57	112	03 12	58	112	02 14	57	112	01 17	57	113	00 20	57	113	-0 37	57	113	-1 34	58	114	-2 32	57	114	-3 29	57	114	-4 26	57	115	-5 23	57	115	-6 20	58	115	292
66	07 37	58	113	06 39	57	113	05 42	57	113	04 45	57	114	03 48	58	114	02 50	57	114	01 53	57	115	00 56	58	115	-0 02	57	115	-0 59	57	116	-1 56	57	116	-2 53	58	116	-3 51	57	116	-4 48	57	117	-5 45	58	117	294
64	08 12	57	115	07 15	57	115	06 18	58	115	05 20	57	116	04 23	57	116	03 26	58	116	02 28	57	116	01 31	58	117	00 33	57	117	-0 24	57	117	-1 21	58	118	-2 19	57	118	-3 16	57	118	-4 13	58	119	-5 11	57	119	296
62	08 48	58	117	07 50	57	117	06 53	58	117	05 55	57	118	04 58	58	118	04 00	57	118	03 03	58	118	02 05	57	119	01 08	58	119	00 10	57	119	-0 47	57	120	-1 44	58	120	-2 42	57	120	-3 39	58	120	-4 37	57	121	298
60	09 22	-57	119	08 25	-58	119	07 27	-57	119	06 30	-58	120	05 32	-58	120	04 34	-57	120	03 37	-58	120	02 39	-57	121	01 42	-58	121	00 44	-57	121	-0 13	-58	121	-1 11	-57	122	-2 08	-58	122	-3 06	-58	122	-4 04	-57	123	300
58	09 56	57	121	08 59	58	121	08 01	58	121	07 03	57	121	06 06	58	122	05 08	58	122	04 10	57	122	03 13	58	122	02 15	58	123	01 17	57	123	00 20	58	123	-0 38	58	124	-1 36	57	124	-2 33	58	124	-3 31	58	124	302
56	10 29	57	123	09 32	58	123	08 34	58	123	07 36	57	123	06 39	58	124	05 41	58	124	04 43	58	124	03 45	58	124	02 47	57	125	01 50	58	125	00 52	58	125	-0 06	57	126	-1 03	58	126	-2 01	58	126	-2 59	58	126	304
54	11 02	58	125	10 04	58	125	09 06	57	125	08 09	58	125	07 11	58	126	06 13	58	126	05 15	58	126	04 17	58	126	03 19	58	127	02 21	58	127	01 23	57	127	00 26	58	127	-0 32	58	128	-1 30	58	128	-2 28	58	128	306
52	11 34	58	127	10 36	58	127	09 38	58	127	08 40	58	127	07 42	58	128	06 44	58	128	05 46	58	128	04 48	58	128	03 50	58	128	02 52	58	129	01 54	58	129	00 56	58	129	-0 02	58	130	-1 00	58	130	-1 58	58	130	308
50	12 05	-58	128	11 07	-58	129	10 09	-58	129	09 11	-58	129	08 13	-58	130	07 15	-58	130	06 17	-59	130	05 18	-58	130	04 20	-58	130	03 22	-58	131	02 24	-58	131	01 26	-58	131	00 28	-58	131	-0 30	-58	132	-1 28	-58	132	310
48	12 35	58	130	11 37	58	131	10 39	58	131	09 41	59	131	08 42	58	131	07 44	58	132	06 46	58	132	05 48	58	132	04 50	59	132	03 51	58	133	02 53	58	133	01 55	58	133	00 57	58	133	-0 01	59	134	-1 00	58	134	312
46	13 04	58	132	12 06	58	133	11 08	58	133	10 10	59	133	09 11	58	133	08 13	58	134	07 15	59	134	06 16	58	134	05 18	58	134	04 20	59	135	03 21	58	135	02 23	58	135	01 25	59	135	00 26	58	135	-0 32	58	136	314
44	13 33	59	134	12 34	58	135	11 36	58	135	10 38	59	135	09 39	58	135	08 41	59	136	07 42	58	136	06 44	58	136	05 46	59	136	04 47	58	136	03 49	59	137	02 50	58	137	01 52	59	137	00 53	58	137	-0 05	59	138	316
42	14 00	58	136	13 02	59	137	12 03	58	137	11 05	59	137	10 06	58	137	09 08	59	138	08 09	58	138	07 11	59	138	06 12	58	138	05 14	59	138	04 15	59	139	03 16	58	139	02 18	59	139	01 19	58	139	00 21	59	140	318
40	14 27	-59	138	13 28	-59	139	12 29	-58	139	11 31	-59	139	10 32	-58	139	09 34	-59	140	08 35	-59	140	07 36	-58	140	06 38	-59	140	05 39	-59	140	04 40	-58	141	03 42	-59	141	02 43	-59	141	01 44	-58	141	00 46	-59	141	320
38	14 52	59	140	13 53	58	141	12 55	59	141	11 56	59	141	10 57	59	141	09 58	58	142	09 00	59	142	08 01	59	142	07 02	59	142	06 03	58	142	05 05	59	143	04 06	59	143	03 07	59	143	02 08	59	143	01 09	58	143	322
36	15 16	58	143	14 18	59	143	13 19	59	143	12 20	59	143	11 21	59	143	10 22	59	144	09 23	59	144	08 24	58	144	07 26	59	144	06 27	59	144	05 28	59	144	04 29	59	145	03 30	59	145	02 31	59	145	01 32	59	145	324
34	15 40	59	145	14 41	59	145	13 42	59	145	12 43	59	145	11 44	59	145	10 45	59	146	09 46	59	146	08 47	59	146	07 48	59	146	06 49	59	146	05 50	59	146	04 51	59	147	03 52	59	147	02 53	59	147	01 54	59	147	326
32	16 02	59	147	15 03	59	147	14 04	59	147	13 05	59	147	12 06	59	147	11 06	59	148	10 07	59	148	09 08	59	148	08 09	59	148	07 10	59	148	06 11	59	148	05 12	59	149	04 13	59	149	03 14	59	149	02 15	59	149	328
30	16 23	-59	149	15 24	-60	149	14 24	-59	149	13 25	-59	149	12 26	-59	149	11 27	-59	150	10 28	-59	150	09 29	-60	150	08 29	-59	150	07 30	-59	150	06 31	-59	150	05 32	-59	151	04 33	-60	151	03 33	-59	151	02 34	-59	151	330
28	16 42	59	151	15 43	59	151	14 44	59	151	13 45	60	151	12 45	59	151	11 46	59	152	10 47	59	152	09 48	60	152	08 48	59	152	07 49	59	152	06 50	60	152	05 50	59	152	04 51	59	153	03 52	59	153	02 53	60	153	332
26	17 01	59	153	16 02	60	153	15 02	59	153	14 03	59	153	13 04	60	153	12 04	59	154	11 05	60	154	10 05	59	154	09 06	59	154	08 07	60	154	07 07	59	154	06 08	59	154	05 09	60	155	04 09	59	155	03 10	60	155	334
24	17 18	59	155	16 19	60	155	15 19	59	155	14 20	60	155	13 20	59	155	12 21	59	156	11 22	60	156	10 22	59	156	09 23	60	156	08 23	59	156	07 24	60	156	06 24	59	156	05 25	60	156	04 25	59	157	03 26	60	157	336
22	17 34	59	157	16 35	60	157	15 35	59	157	14 36	60	157	13 36	59	157	12 37	60	158	11 37	59	158	10 38	60	158	09 38	60	158	08 38	59	158	07 39	60	158	06 39	59	158	05 40	60	158	04 40	59	158	03 41	60	159	338
20	17 49	-60	159	16 49	-59	159	15 50	-60	159	14 50	-59	159	13 51	-60	159	12 51	-60	160	11 51	-59	160	10 52	-60	160	09 52	-60	160	08 52	-59	160	07 53	-60	160	06 53	-59	160	05 54	-60	160	04 54	-60	160	03 54	-59	161	340
18	18 02	59	161	17 03	60	161	16 03	60	161	15 03	59	161	14 04	60	162	13 04	60	162	12 04	59	162	11 05	60	162	10 05	60	162	09 05	60	162	08 05	59	162	07 06	60	162	06 06	60	162	05 06	59	162	04 07	60	162	342
16	18 14	59	163	17 15	60	163	16 15	60	163	15 15	60	163	14 15	59	164	13 16	60	164	12 16	60	164	11 16	60	164	10 16	59	164	09 17	60	164	08 17	60	164	07 17	60	164	06 17	59	164	05 18	60	164	04 18	60	164	344
14	18 25	60	165	17 25	60	165	16 25	59	165	15 26	60	166	14 26	60	166	13 26	60	166	12 26	60	166	11 26	59	166	10 27	60	166	09 27	60	166	08 27	60	166	07 27	60	166	06 27	60	166	05 27	59	166	04 28	60	166	346
12	18 34	60	167	17 34	59	167	16 35	60	168	15 35	60	168	14 35	60	168	13 35	60	168	12 35	60	168	11 35	60	168	10 35	59	168	09 36	60	168	08 36	60	168	07 36	60	168	06 36	60	168	05 36	60	168	04 36	60	168	348
10	18 42	-60	169	17 42	-60	170	16 42	-60	170	15 42	-59	170	14 43	-60	170	13 43	-60	170	12 43	-60	170	11 43	-60	170	10 43	-60	170	09 43	-60	170	08 43	-60	170	07 43	-60	170	06 43	-60	170	05 43	-60	170	04 43	-59	170	350
8	18 49	60	172	17 49	60	172	16 49	60	172	15 49	60	172	14 49	60	172	13 49	60	172	12 49	60	172	11 49	60	172	10 49	60	172	09 49	60	172	08 49	60	172	07 49	60	172	06 49	60	172	05 49	60	172	04 49	59	172	352
6	18 54	60	174	17 54	60	174	16 54	60	174	15 54	60	174	14 54	60	174	13 54	60	174	12 54	60	174	11 54	60	174	10 54	60	174	09 54	60	174	08 54	60	174	07 54	60	174	06 54	60	174	05 54	60	174	04 54	60	174	354
4	18 57	60	176	17 57	60	176	16 57	60	176	15 57	60	176	14 57	60	176	13 57	60	176	12 57	60	176	11 57	60	176	10 57	60	176	09 57	60	176	08 57	60	176	07 57	60	176	06 57	60	176	05 57	60	176	04 57	60	176	356
2	18 59	60	178	17 59	60	178	16 59	60	178	15 59	60	178	14 59	60	178	13 59	60	178	12 59	60	178	11 59	60	178	10 59	60	178	09 59	60	178	08 59	60	178	07 59	60	178	06 59	60	178	05 59	60	178	04 59	60	178	358
0	19 00	-60	180	18 00	-60	180	17 00	-60	180	16 00	-60	180	15 00	-60	180	14 00	-60	180	13 00	-60	180	12 00	-60	180	11 00	-60	180	10 00	-60	180	09 00	-60	180	08 00	-60	180	07 00	-60	180	06 00	-60	180	05 00	-60	180	360
	0°			1°			2°			3°			4°			5°			6°			7°			8°			9°			10°			11°			12°			13°			14°			

S. Lat. {LHA greater than 180°....... Zn=180−Z; LHA less than 180°........... Zn=180+Z}

DECLINATION (0°-14°) CONTRARY NAME TO LATITUDE

N. Lat. {LHA greater than 180°....... Zn=Z
{LHA less than 180°.......... Zn=360−Z

DECLINATION (15°-29°) SAME NAME AS LATITUDE

LHA	15° Hc	15° d	15° Z	16° Hc	16° d	16° Z	17° Hc	17° d	17° Z	18° Hc	18° d	18° Z	19° Hc	19° d	19° Z
	° ′	′	°	° ′	′	°	° ′	′	°	° ′	′	°	° ′	′	°
0	34 00	+60	180	35 00	+60	180	36 00	+60	180	37 00	+60	180	38 00	+60	180
2	33 59	60	178	34 59	60	178	35 59	60	178	36 59	60	178	37 59	60	178
4	33 57	60	175	34 57	60	175	35 57	60	175	36 57	60	175	37 57	60	175
6	33 53	60	173	34 53	60	173	35 53	60	173	36 53	60	173	37 53	60	173
8	33 47	60	171	34 47	60	171	35 47	60	171	36 47	60	171	37 47	60	170
10	33 40	+60	168	34 40	+60	168	35 40	+60	168	36 40	+60	168	37 40	+60	168
12	33 32	59	166	34 31	60	166	35 31	60	166	36 31	60	166	37 31	60	166
14	33 21	60	164	34 21	60	164	35 21	60	164	36 21	59	163	37 20	60	163
16	33 10	59	162	34 09	60	161	35 09	60	161	36 09	59	161	37 08	60	161
18	32 57	59	159	33 56	60	159	34 56	59	159	35 55	60	159	36 55	59	159
20	32 42	+59	157	33 41	+60	157	34 41	+59	157	35 40	+60	156	36 40	+59	156
22	32 26	59	155	33 25	60	154	34 25	59	154	35 24	59	154	36 23	60	154
24	32 09	59	152	33 08	59	152	34 07	59	152	35 06	59	152	36 05	60	152
26	31 50	59	150	32 49	59	150	33 48	59	150	34 47	59	150	35 46	59	149
28	31 30	59	148	32 29	59	148	33 28	59	147	34 27	59	147	35 26	58	147
30	31 08	+59	146	32 07	+59	145	33 06	+59	145	34 05	+59	145	35 04	+58	145
32	30 46	58	143	31 44	59	143	32 43	59	143	33 42	58	143	34 40	59	143
34	30 22	58	141	31 20	59	141	32 19	58	141	33 17	59	141	34 16	59	140
36	29 57	58	139	30 55	59	139	31 54	58	139	32 52	58	138	33 50	59	138
38	29 30	59	137	30 29	58	137	31 27	58	136	32 25	59	136	33 24	58	136
40	29 03	+58	135	30 01	+59	135	31 00	+58	134	31 58	+58	134	32 56	+58	134
42	28 35	58	133	29 33	58	132	30 31	58	132	31 29	58	132	32 27	58	131
44	28 06	58	131	29 04	58	130	30 02	58	130	31 00	57	130	31 57	58	129
46	27 36	57	128	28 33	58	128	29 31	58	128	30 29	58	128	31 27	57	127
48	27 04	58	126	28 02	58	126	29 00	58	126	29 58	57	125	30 55	58	125
50	26 33	+57	124	27 30	+58	124	28 28	+57	124	29 25	+58	123	30 23	+57	123
52	26 00	57	122	26 57	58	122	27 55	57	122	28 52	58	121	29 50	57	121
54	25 26	58	120	26 24	57	120	27 21	57	119	28 18	58	119	29 16	57	119
56	24 52	58	118	25 50	57	118	26 47	57	117	27 44	57	117	28 41	57	117
58	24 17	58	116	25 15	57	116	26 12	57	115	27 09	57	115	28 06	57	115
60	23 42	+57	114	24 39	+57	114	25 36	+57	113	26 33	+57	113	27 30	+57	113
62	23 06	57	112	24 03	57	112	25 00	57	111	25 57	57	111	26 54	56	111
64	22 30	57	110	23 27	56	110	24 23	57	109	25 20	57	109	26 17	57	109
66	21 53	57	108	22 50	56	108	23 46	57	107	24 43	57	107	25 40	56	107
68	21 15	57	106	22 12	57	106	23 09	56	105	24 05	57	105	25 02	57	105
70	20 38	+56	104	21 34	+57	104	22 31	+57	103	23 28	+56	103	24 24	+57	103
72	20 00	56	102	20 56	57	102	21 53	56	102	22 49	57	101	23 46	56	101
74	19 21	57	100	20 18	56	100	21 14	57	100	22 11	56	99	23 07	57	99
76	18 43	56	98	19 39	57	98	20 36	56	98	21 32	57	97	22 29	56	97
78	18 04	56	96	19 00	57	96	19 57	56	96	20 53	57	95	21 50	56	95
80	17 25	+57	95	18 22	+56	94	19 18	+56	94	20 14	+57	93	21 11	+56	93
82	16 46	57	93	17 43	56	92	18 39	56	92	19 35	57	92	20 32	56	91
84	16 07	57	91	17 04	56	90	18 00	56	90	18 56	57	90	19 53	56	89
86	15 28	56	89	16 24	57	88	17 21	56	88	18 17	57	88	19 14	56	87
88	14 49	56	87	15 45	57	87	16 42	56	86	17 38	57	86	18 35	56	86
90	14 10	+56	85	15 06	+57	85	16 03	+56	84	16 59	+57	84	17 56	+56	84
92	13 31	57	83	14 28	56	83	15 24	57	82	16 21	56	82	17 17	56	82
94	12 52	57	81	13 49	56	81	14 45	57	81	15 42	56	80	16 38	57	80
96	12 14	56	79	13 10	57	79	14 07	57	79	15 04	56	78	16 00	57	78
98	11 36	56	78	12 32	57	77	13 29	56	77	14 25	57	77	15 22	57	76
100	10 58	+56	76	11 54	+57	75	12 51	+57	75	13 48	+56	75	14 44	+57	74
102	10 20	57	74	11 17	56	74	12 13	57	73	13 10	57	73	14 07	56	73
104	09 43	56	72	10 39	57	72	11 36	57	71	12 33	57	71	13 30	56	71
106	09 06	57	70	10 03	56	70	10 59	57	70	11 56	57	69	12 53	57	69
108	08 29	57	68	09 26	57	68	10 23	57	68	11 20	57	67	12 17	57	67
110	07 53	+57	66	08 50	+57	66	09 47	+57	66	10 44	+57	66	11 41	+57	65
112	07 18	57	65	08 15	57	64	09 12	57	64	10 09	57	64	11 06	57	63
114	06 43	57	63	07 40	57	62	08 37	57	62	09 34	57	62	10 31	58	62
116	06 08	57	61	07 05	58	61	08 03	57	60	09 00	57	60	09 57	58	60
118	05 34	58	59	06 32	57	59	07 29	58	58	08 27	57	58	09 24	57	58
120	05 01	+58	57	05 59	+57	57	06 56	+58	57	07 54	+57	56	08 51	+58	56
122	04 29	57	55	05 26	58	55	06 24	58	55	07 22	57	54	08 19	58	54
124	03 57	58	53	04 55	57	53	05 52	58	53	06 50	58	53	07 48	58	52
126	03 26	58	52	04 24	58	51	05 22	58	51	06 20	57	51	07 17	58	51
128	02 56	58	50	03 54	58	49	04 52	58	49	05 50	58	49	06 48	58	49
130	02 26	+58	48	03 24	+59	48	04 23	+58	47	05 21	+58	47	06 19	+58	47
132	01 58	58	46	02 56	58	46	03 54	59	45	04 53	58	45	05 51	58	45
134	01 30	59	44	02 29	58	44	03 27	58	44	04 25	59	43	05 24	58	43
136	01 04	58	42	02 02	58	42	03 00	59	42	03 59	58	42	04 57	59	41
138	00 38	58	40	01 36	59	40	02 35	59	40	03 34	58	40	04 32	59	39

LHA	20° Hc	20° d	20° Z	21° Hc	21° d	21° Z	22° Hc	22° d	22° Z	23° Hc	23° d	23° Z	24° Hc	24° d	24° Z
	° ′	′	°	° ′	′	°	° ′	′	°	° ′	′	°	° ′	′	°
0	39 00	+60	180	40 00	+60	180	41 00	+60	180	42 00	+60	180	43 00	+60	180
2	38 59	60	178	39 59	60	178	40 59	60	178	41 59	60	178	42 59	60	178
4	38 57	60	175	39 57	60	175	40 57	60	175	41 57	60	175	42 57	60	175
6	38 53	60	173	39 53	60	173	40 53	59	173	41 52	60	173	42 52	60	173
8	38 47	60	170	39 47	60	170	40 47	60	170	41 47	59	170	42 46	60	170
10	38 40	+59	168	39 39	+60	168	40 39	+60	168	41 39	+60	168	42 39	+60	168
12	38 31	59	166	39 30	60	165	40 30	60	165	41 30	60	165	42 30	59	165
14	38 20	60	163	39 20	59	163	40 19	60	163	41 19	60	163	42 19	59	163
16	38 08	60	161	39 08	59	161	40 07	60	161	41 07	59	160	42 06	60	160
18	37 54	60	158	38 54	59	158	39 53	60	158	40 53	59	158	41 52	60	158
20	37 39	+60	156	38 39	+59	156	39 38	+59	156	40 37	+60	156	41 37	+59	155
22	37 23	59	154	38 22	59	154	39 21	59	153	40 20	60	153	41 20	59	153
24	37 05	59	151	38 04	59	151	39 03	59	151	40 02	59	151	41 01	59	151
26	36 45	59	149	37 44	59	149	38 43	59	149	39 42	59	148	40 41	59	148
28	36 24	59	147	37 23	59	147	38 22	59	146	39 21	59	146	40 20	59	146
30	36 02	+59	145	37 01	+59	144	38 00	+59	144	38 59	+58	144	39 57	+59	143
32	35 39	59	142	36 38	58	142	37 36	59	142	38 35	58	141	39 33	59	141
34	35 15	58	140	36 13	58	140	37 11	59	139	38 10	58	139	39 08	58	139
36	34 49	58	138	35 47	58	137	36 45	59	137	37 44	58	137	38 42	58	137
38	34 22	58	136	35 20	58	135	36 18	58	135	37 16	58	135	38 14	58	134
40	33 54	+58	133	34 52	+58	133	35 50	+58	133	36 48	+58	132	37 46	+58	132
42	33 25	58	131	34 23	58	131	35 21	58	131	36 19	57	130	37 16	58	130
44	32 55	58	129	33 53	58	129	34 51	57	128	35 48	58	128	36 46	57	128
46	32 24	58	127	33 22	58	127	34 20	57	126	35 17	58	126	36 15	57	125
48	31 53	57	125	32 50	58	124	33 48	57	124	34 45	57	124	35 42	57	123
50	31 20	+57	123	32 17	+58	122	33 15	+57	122	34 12	+57	122	35 09	+57	121
52	30 47	57	121	31 44	57	120	32 41	57	120	33 38	57	119	34 35	57	119
54	30 13	57	118	31 10	57	118	32 07	57	118	33 04	57	117	34 01	57	117
56	29 38	57	116	30 35	57	116	31 32	57	116	32 29	57	115	33 26	56	115
58	29 03	57	114	30 00	57	114	30 57	56	114	31 53	57	113	32 50	57	113
60	28 27	+57	112	29 24	+56	112	30 20	+57	112	31 17	+57	111	32 14	+56	111
62	27 50	57	110	28 47	57	110	29 44	56	110	30 40	57	109	31 37	56	109
64	27 14	56	108	28 10	57	108	29 07	56	108	30 03	57	107	31 00	56	107
66	26 36	57	106	27 33	56	106	28 29	57	106	29 26	56	105	30 22	56	105
68	25 59	56	104	26 55	57	104	27 52	56	104	28 48	56	103	29 44	56	103
70	25 21	+56	102	26 17	+56	102	27 13	+57	102	28 10	+56	101	29 06	+56	101
72	24 42	57	100	25 39	56	100	26 35	56	100	27 31	56	99	28 27	57	99
74	24 04	56	98	25 00	56	98	25 56	57	98	26 53	56	97	27 49	56	97
76	23 25	56	97	24 21	57	96	25 18	56	96	26 14	56	95	27 10	56	95
78	22 46	56	95	23 42	57	94	24 39	56	94	25 35	56	93	26 31	56	93
80	22 07	+56	93	23 03	+57	92	24 00	+56	92	24 56	+56	92	25 52	+56	91
82	21 28	56	91	22 24	57	90	23 21	56	90	24 17	56	90	25 13	56	89
84	20 49	56	89	21 45	56	89	22 41	57	88	23 38	56	88	24 34	56	87
86	20 10	56	87	21 06	56	87	22 02	57	86	22 59	56	86	23 55	56	86
88	19 31	56	85	20 27	57	85	21 24	56	84	22 20	56	84	23 16	56	84
90	18 52	+56	83	19 48	+57	83	20 45	+56	83	21 41	+56	82	22 37	+56	82
92	18 13	57	81	19 10	56	81	20 06	56	81	21 02	57	80	21 59	56	80
94	17 35	56	80	18 31	57	79	19 28	56	79	20 24	56	78	21 20	56	78
96	16 57	56	78	17 53	56	77	18 49	57	77	19 46	56	77	20 42	56	76
98	16 19	56	76	17 15	57	76	18 12	56	75	19 08	56	75	20 04	57	74
100	15 41	+56	74	16 37	+57	74	17 34	+56	73	18 30	+57	73	19 27	+56	73
102	15 03	57	72	16 00	57	72	16 57	56	72	17 53	57	71	18 50	56	71
104	14 26	57	70	15 23	57	70	16 20	56	70	17 16	57	69	18 13	57	69
106	13 50	57	69	14 47	56	68	15 43	57	68	16 40	57	68	17 37	57	67
108	13 14	57	67	14 11	57	66	15 08	56	66	16 04	57	66	17 01	57	65
110	12 38	+57	65	13 35	+57	65	14 32	+57	64	15 29	+57	64	16 26	+57	64
112	12 03	57	63	13 00	57	63	13 57	57	62	14 54	57	62	15 51	57	62
114	11 29	57	61	12 26	57	61	13 23	57	61	14 20	57	60	15 17	57	60
116	10 55	57	59	11 52	57	59	12 49	57	59	13 46	58	58	14 44	57	58
118	10 21	58	58	11 19	57	57	12 16	57	57	13 13	58	57	14 11	57	56
120	09 49	+57	56	10 46	+58	55	11 44	+57	55	12 41	+58	55	13 39	+57	55
122	09 17	57	54	10 14	58	54	11 12	58	53	12 10	57	53	13 07	58	53
124	08 46	57	52	09 43	58	52	10 41	58	52	11 39	57	51	12 36	58	51
126	08 15	58	50	09 13	58	50	10 11	58	50	11 09	58	49	12 07	57	49
128	07 46	58	48	08 44	58	48	09 42	58	48	10 40	57	48	11 37	58	47
130	07 17	+58	46	08 15	+58	46	09 13	+58	46	10 11	+58	46	11 09	+58	46
132	06 49	58	45	07 47	58	44	08 45	59	44	09 44	58	44	10 42	58	44
134	06 22	58	43	07 20	59	43	08 19	58	42	09 17	58	42	10 15	58	42
136	05 56	58	41	06 54	59	41	07 53	58	41	08 51	59	40	09 50	58	40
138	05 31	58	39	06 29	59	39	07 28	58	39	08 26	59	39	09 25	58	38

LHA	25° Hc	25° d	25° Z	26° Hc	26° d	26° Z	27° Hc	27° d	27° Z	28° Hc	28° d	28° Z	29° Hc	29° d	29° Z	LHA
	° ′	′	°	° ′	′	°	° ′	′	°	° ′	′	°	° ′	′	°	
0	44 00	+60	180	45 00	+60	180	46 00	+60	180	47 00	+60	180	48 00	+60	180	360
2	43 59	60	178	44 59	60	178	45 59	60	177	46 59	60	177	47 59	60	177	358
4	43 57	60	175	44 57	60	175	45 57	60	175	46 57	59	175	47 56	60	175	356
6	43 52	60	172	44 52	60	172	45 52	60	172	46 52	60	172	47 52	60	172	354
8	43 46	60	170	44 46	60	170	45 46	60	170	46 46	60	170	47 46	60	170	352
10	43 39	+60	167	44 39	+59	167	45 38	+60	167	46 38	+60	167	47 38	+60	167	350
12	43 29	60	165	44 29	60	165	45 29	60	165	46 29	59	165	47 28	60	164	348
14	43 18	60	163	44 18	60	162	45 18	59	162	46 17	60	162	47 17	59	162	346
16	43 06	59	160	44 05	60	160	45 05	59	160	46 04	60	160	47 04	59	159	344
18	42 52	59	158	43 51	60	157	44 51	59	157	45 50	59	157	46 49	60	157	342
20	42 36	+59	155	43 35	+60	155	44 35	+59	155	45 34	+59	154	46 33	+59	154	340
22	42 19	59	153	43 18	59	152	44 17	59	152	45 16	59	152	46 15	59	152	338
24	42 00	59	150	42 59	59	150	43 58	59	150	44 57	59	150	45 56	59	149	336
26	41 40	59	148	42 39	59	148	43 38	59	147	44 37	58	147	45 35	59	147	334
28	41 19	58	146	42 17	59	145	43 16	59	145	44 15	58	145	45 13	59	144	332
30	40 56	+58	143	41 54	+59	143	42 53	+58	143	43 51	+59	142	44 50	+58	142	330
32	40 32	58	141	41 30	59	141	42 29	58	140	43 27	58	140	44 25	58	140	328
34	40 06	59	139	41 05	58	138	42 03	58	138	43 01	58	138	43 59	58	137	326
36	39 40	58	136	40 38	58	136	41 36	58	136	42 34	58	135	43 32	58	135	324
38	39 12	58	134	40 10	58	134	41 08	58	133	42 06	58	133	43 04	57	133	322
40	38 44	+58	132	39 42	+57	131	40 39	+58	131	41 37	+57	131	42 34	+58	130	320
42	38 14	58	130	39 12	57	129	40 09	58	129	41 07	57	128	42 04	57	128	318
44	37 43	58	127	38 41	57	127	39 38	58	127	40 36	57	126	41 33	57	126	316
46	37 12	57	125	38 09	57	125	39 06	58	124	40 04	57	124	41 01	57	124	314
48	36 39	58	123	37 37	57	123	38 34	57	122	39 31	57	122	40 28	57	121	312
50	36 06	+57	121	37 03	+57	120	38 00	+57	120	38 57	+57	120	39 54	+57	119	310
52	35 32	57	119	36 29	57	118	37 26	57	118	38 23	56	117	39 19	57	117	308
54	34 58	57	117	35 55	56	116	36 51	57	116	37 48	56	115	38 44	57	115	306
56	34 22	57	114	35 19	57	114	36 16	56	114	37 12	57	113	38 09	56	113	304
58	33 47	56	112	34 43	57	112	35 40	56	112	36 36	56	111	37 32	57	111	302
60	33 10	+57	110	34 07	+56	110	35 03	+56	110	35 59	+57	109	36 56	+56	109	300
62	32 33	57	108	33 30	56	108	34 26	56	108	35 22	56	107	36 18	56	107	298
64	31 56	56	106	32 52	57	106	33 49	56	106	34 45	56	105	35 41	56	105	296
66	31 18	57	104	32 15	56	104	33 11	56	104	34 07	56	103	35 03	56	103	294
68	30 40	57	102	31 37	56	102	32 33	56	102	33 29	55	101	34 24	56	101	292
70	30 02	+56	100	30 58	+56	100	31 54	+56	100	32 50	+56	99	33 46	+56	99	290
72	29 24	56	98	30 20	56	98	31 16	55	98	32 11	56	97	33 07	56	97	288
74	28 45	56	97	29 41	56	96	30 37	56	96	31 33	55	95	32 28	56	95	286
76	28 06	56	95	29 02	56	94	29 58	56	94	30 54	55	93	31 49	56	93	284
78	27 27	56	93	28 23	56	92	29 19	56	92	30 15	55	91	31 10	56	91	282
80	26 48	+56	91	27 44	+56	90	28 40	+56	90	29 36	+55	90	30 31	+56	89	280
82	26 09	56	89	27 05	56	88	28 01	55	88	28 56	56	88	29 52	56	87	278
84	25 30	56	87	26 26	56	87	27 22	55	86	28 17	56	86	29 13	56	85	276
86	24 51	56	85	25 47	56	85	26 43	56	84	27 39	55	84	28 34	56	84	274
88	24 12	56	83	25 08	56	83	26 04	56	82	27 00	56	82	27 56	55	82	272
90	23 33	+56	81	24 29	+56	81	25 25	+56	81	26 21	+56	80	27 17	+56	80	270
92	22 55	56	80	23 51	56	79	24 47	56	79	25 43	56	78	26 39	56	78	268
94	22 16	57	78	23 13	56	77	24 09	56	77	25 05	56	77	26 01	56	76	266
96	21 38	57	76	22 35	56	76	23 31	56	75	24 27	56	75	25 23	56	74	264
98	21 01	56	74	21 57	56	74	22 53	56	73	23 49	56	73	24 45	57	73	262
100	20 23	+57	72	21 20	+56	72	22 16	+56	72	23 12	+56	71	24 08	+57	71	260
102	19 46	57	70	20 43	56	70	21 39	56	70	22 35	57	69	23 32	56	69	258
104	19 10	56	69	20 06	57	68	21 03	56	68	21 59	56	68	22 55	57	67	256
106	18 34	56	67	19 30	57	66	20 27	56	66	21 23	57	66	22 20	56	65	254
108	17 58	57	65	18 55	56	65	19 51	57	64	20 48	56	64	21 44	57	64	252
110	17 23	+57	63	18 20	+56	63	19 16	+57	63	20 13	+57	62	21 10	+56	62	250
112	16 48	57	61	17 45	57	61	18 42	57	61	19 39	57	60	20 36	56	60	248
114	16 14	57	60	17 11	57	59	18 08	57	59	19 05	57	59	20 02	57	58	246
116	15 41	57	58	16 38	57	58	17 35	57	57	18 32	57	57	19 29	57	57	244
118	15 08	57	56	16 05	58	56	17 03	57	55	18 00	57	55	18 57	57	55	242
120	14 36	+57	54	15 33	+58	54	16 31	+57	54	17 28	+57	53	18 25	+58	53	240
122	14 05	57	52	15 02	58	52	16 00	57	52	16 57	58	52	17 55	57	51	238
124	13 34	58	51	14 32	57	50	15 29	58	50	16 27	58	50	17 25	57	50	236
126	13 04	58	49	14 02	58	49	15 00	58	48	15 58	57	48	16 55	58	48	234
128	12 35	58	47	13 33	58	47	14 31	58	47	15 29	58	46	16 27	58	46	232
130	12 07	+58	45	13 05	+58	45	14 03	+58	45	15 01	+58	45	15 59	+58	44	230
132	11 40	58	43	12 38	58	43	13 36	58	43	14 34	58	43	15 32	58	42	228
134	11 13	59	42	12 12	58	41	13 10	58	41	14 08	58	41	15 06	59	41	226
136	10 48	58	40	11 46	59	40	12 45	58	39	13 43	58	39	14 41	59	39	224
138	10 23	59	38	11 22	58	38	12 20	59	38	13 19	58	37	14 17	59	37	222

15° 16° 17° 18° 19° 20° 21° 22° 23° 24° 25° 26° 27° 28° 29°

S. Lat. {LHA greater than 180°....... Zn=180−Z
{LHA less than 180°.......... Zn=180+Z

DECLINATION (15°-29°) SAME NAME AS LATITUDE

LAT 71°

N. Lat. {LHA greater than 180°....... Zn=Z; LHA less than 180°........... Zn=360−Z}

DECLINATION (15°-29°) SAME NAME AS LATITUDE

Each declination cell gives Hc (° ′), d (′), Z (°).

LHA	15°	16°	17°	18°	19°	20°	21°	22°	23°	24°	25°	26°	27°	28°	29°	LHA
	Hc d Z	Hc d Z	Hc d Z	Hc d Z	Hc d Z	Hc d Z	Hc d Z	Hc d Z	Hc d Z	Hc d Z	Hc d Z	Hc d Z	Hc d Z	Hc d Z	Hc d Z	
140	00 13 +59 38	01 12 +58 38	02 10 +59 38	03 09 +59 38	04 08 +59 38	05 07 +58 37	06 05 +59 37	07 04 +58 37	08 02 +59 37	09 01 +59 37	10 00 +58 36	10 58 +59 36	11 57 +59 36	12 56 +58 36	13 54 +59 35	220
142	−0 11 59 36	00 48 59 36	01 47 59 36	02 46 58 36	03 44 59 36	04 43 59 36	05 42 59 35	06 41 59 35	07 40 58 35	08 38 59 35	09 37 59 35	10 36 59 34	11 35 58 34	12 33 59 34	13 32 59 34	218
144	−0 33 59 35	00 26 58 34	01 24 59 34	02 23 59 34	03 22 59 34	04 21 59 34	05 20 59 33	06 19 59 33	07 18 59 33	08 17 59 33	09 16 58 33	10 14 59 33	11 13 59 32	12 12 59 32	13 11 59 32	216
146	−0 55 59 33	00 04 59 33	01 03 59 32	02 02 59 32	03 01 59 32	04 00 59 32	04 59 59 32	05 58 59 31	06 57 59 31	07 56 59 31	08 55 59 31	09 54 59 31	10 53 59 31	11 52 59 30	12 51 59 30	214
148	−1 16 60 31	−0 16 59 31	00 43 59 30	01 42 59 30	02 41 59 30	03 40 59 30	04 39 59 30	05 38 59 30	06 37 59 29	07 36 59 29	08 35 60 29	09 35 59 29	10 34 59 29	11 33 59 29	12 32 59 28	212
150	−1 35 +59 29	−0 36 +59 29	00 23 +60 29	01 23 +59 28	02 22 +59 28	03 21 +59 28	04 20 +59 28	05 19 +60 28	06 19 +59 28	07 18 +59 27	08 17 +59 27	09 16 +59 27	10 15 +60 27	11 15 +59 27	12 14 +59 27	210
152	−1 53 59 27	−0 54 59 27	00 05 60 27	01 05 59 27	02 04 59 26	03 03 59 26	04 02 60 26	05 02 59 26	06 01 59 26	07 00 60 26	08 00 59 25	08 59 59 25	09 58 60 25	10 58 59 25	11 57 59 25	208
154	−2 10 59 25	−1 11 59 25	−0 12 60 25	00 48 59 25	01 47 59 24	02 46 60 24	03 46 59 24	04 45 60 24	05 45 59 24	06 44 59 24	07 43 60 24	08 43 59 24	09 42 60 23	10 42 59 23	11 41 59 23	206
156	−2 26 59 23	−1 27 60 23	−0 27 59 23	00 32 60 23	01 32 59 23	02 31 59 22	03 30 60 22	04 30 59 22	05 29 60 22	06 29 59 22	07 28 60 22	08 28 59 22	09 27 60 22	10 27 59 21	11 26 60 21	204
158	−2 41 59 21	−1 42 60 21	−0 42 60 21	00 18 59 21	01 17 60 21	02 17 59 21	03 16 60 21	04 16 59 20	05 15 60 20	06 15 59 20	07 14 60 20	08 14 59 20	09 13 60 20	10 13 60 20	11 13 59 20	202
160	−2 55 +60 19	−1 55 +60 19	−0 55 +59 19	00 04 +60 19	01 04 +60 19	02 04 +59 19	03 03 +60 19	04 03 +59 19	05 02 +60 18	06 02 +60 18	07 02 +59 18	08 01 +60 18	09 01 +59 18	10 00 +60 18	11 00 +60 18	200
162	−3 07 60 17	−2 07 59 17	−1 08 60 17	−0 08 60 17	00 52 60 17	01 52 59 17	02 51 60 17	03 51 60 17	04 51 59 17	05 50 60 17	06 50 60 16	07 50 59 16	08 49 60 16	09 49 60 16	10 49 59 16	198
164	−3 18 60 16	−2 18 60 15	−1 18 59 15	−0 19 60 15	00 41 60 15	01 41 59 15	02 40 60 15	03 40 60 15	04 40 60 15	05 40 60 15	06 40 59 15	07 39 60 15	08 39 60 14	09 39 60 14	10 39 59 14	196
166	−3 28 60 14	−2 28 60 13	−1 28 60 13	−0 28 59 13	00 31 60 13	01 31 60 13	02 31 60 13	03 31 60 13	04 31 60 13	05 31 59 13	06 30 60 13	07 30 60 13	08 30 60 13	09 30 60 13	10 30 59 12	194
168	−3 36 60 12	−2 36 59 12	−1 37 60 12	−0 37 60 11	00 23 60 11	01 23 60 11	02 23 60 11	03 23 60 11	04 23 59 11	05 22 60 11	06 22 60 11	07 22 60 11	08 22 60 11	09 22 60 11	10 22 60 11	192
170	−3 44 +60 10	−2 44 +60 10	−1 44 +60 10	−0 44 +60 10	00 16 +60 9	01 16 +60 9	02 16 +60 9	03 16 +60 9	04 16 +60 9	05 16 +60 9	06 16 +59 9	07 15 +60 9	08 15 +60 9	09 15 +60 9	10 15 +60 9	190
172	−3 50 60 8	−2 50 60 8	−1 50 60 8	−0 50 60 8	00 10 60 8	01 10 60 8	02 10 60 8	03 10 60 7	04 10 60 7	05 10 60 7	06 10 60 7	07 10 60 7	08 10 60 7	09 10 60 7	10 10 60 7	188
174	−3 54 60 6	−2 54 60 6	−1 54 60 6	−0 54 60 6	00 06 60 6	01 06 60 6	02 06 60 6	03 06 60 6	04 06 60 6	05 06 60 6	06 06 60 6	07 06 60 5	08 06 60 5	09 06 59 5	10 05 60 5	186
176	−3 57 60 4	−2 57 60 4	−1 57 60 4	−0 57 60 4	00 03 60 4	01 03 60 4	02 03 60 4	03 03 60 4	04 03 60 4	05 03 60 4	06 03 60 4	07 03 60 4	08 03 59 4	09 02 60 4	10 02 60 4	184
178	−3 59 60 2	−2 59 60 2	−1 59 60 2	−0 59 60 2	00 01 60 2	01 01 60 2	02 01 60 2	03 01 60 2	04 01 60 2	05 01 60 2	06 01 60 2	07 01 60 2	08 01 60 2	09 01 60 2	10 01 60 2	182
180	−4 00 +60 0	−3 00 +60 0	−2 00 +60 0	−1 00 +60 0	00 00 +60 0	01 00 +60 0	02 00 +60 0	03 00 +60 0	04 00 +60 0	05 00 +60 0	06 00 +60 0	07 00 +60 0	08 00 +60 0	09 00 +60 0	10 00 +60 0	180

LHA	15°	16°	17°	18°	19°	20°	21°	22°	23°	24°	25°	26°	27°	28°	29°
70	−7 53 −57 114	290													
68	−7 18 57 115	292													
66	−6 43 57 117	−7 40 57 118	294												
64	−6 08 57 119	−7 05 58 119	−8 03 57 120	296											
62	−5 34 58 121	−6 32 57 121	−7 29 58 122	298											
60	−5 01 −58 123	−5 59 −57 123	−6 56 −58 123	−7 54 −57 124	300										
58	−4 29 57 125	−5 26 58 125	−6 24 58 125	−7 22 57 126	302										
56	−3 57 58 127	−4 55 57 127	−5 52 58 127	−6 50 58 127	−7 48 58 128	304									
54	−3 26 58 128	−4 24 58 129	−5 22 58 129	−6 20 57 129	−7 17 58 129	306									
52	−2 56 58 130	−3 54 58 131	−4 52 58 131	−5 50 58 131	−6 48 58 131	−7 46 58 132	308								
50	−2 26 −58 132	−3 24 −59 132	−4 23 −58 133	−5 21 −58 133	−6 19 −58 133	−7 17 −58 134	310								
48	−1 58 58 134	−2 56 58 134	−3 54 59 135	−4 53 58 135	−5 51 58 135	−6 49 58 135	−7 47 58 136	312							
46	−1 30 59 136	−2 29 58 136	−3 27 58 136	−4 25 59 137	−5 24 58 137	−6 22 58 137	−7 20 59 137	314							
44	−1 04 58 138	−2 02 58 138	−3 00 59 138	−3 59 58 138	−4 57 59 139	−5 56 58 139	−6 54 59 139	316							
42	−0 38 58 140	−1 36 59 140	−2 35 59 140	−3 34 58 140	−4 32 59 141	−5 31 58 141	−6 29 59 141	−7 28 58 141	318						
40	−0 13 −59 142	−1 12 −58 142	−2 10 −59 142	−3 09 −59 142	−4 08 −59 142	−5 07 −58 143	−6 05 −59 143	−7 04 −58 143	320						
38	00 11 59 144	−0 48 59 144	−1 47 59 144	−2 46 58 144	−3 44 59 144	−4 43 59 144	−5 42 59 145	−6 41 59 145	−7 40 58 145	322					
36	00 33 59 145	−0 26 58 146	−1 24 59 146	−2 23 59 146	−3 22 59 146	−4 21 59 146	−5 20 59 147	−6 19 59 147	−7 18 59 147	324					
34	00 55 59 147	−0 04 59 147	−1 03 59 148	−2 02 59 148	−3 01 59 148	−4 00 59 148	−4 59 59 148	−5 58 59 149	−6 57 59 149	326					
32	01 16 60 149	00 16 59 149	−0 43 59 150	−1 42 59 150	−2 41 59 150	−3 40 59 150	−4 39 59 150	−5 38 59 150	−6 37 59 151	328					
30	01 35 −59 151	00 36 −59 151	−0 23 −60 151	−1 23 −59 152	−2 22 −59 152	−3 21 −59 152	−4 20 −59 152	−5 19 −60 152	−6 19 −59 152	−7 18 −59 153	330				
28	01 53 59 153	00 54 59 153	−0 05 60 153	−1 05 59 153	−2 04 59 154	−3 03 59 154	−4 02 60 154	−5 02 59 154	−6 01 59 154	−7 00 60 154	332				
26	02 10 59 155	01 11 59 155	00 12 60 155	−0 48 59 155	−1 47 59 156	−2 46 60 156	−3 46 59 156	−4 45 60 156	−5 45 59 156	−6 44 59 156	334				
24	02 26 59 157	01 27 60 157	00 27 59 157	−0 32 60 157	−1 32 59 157	−2 31 59 158	−3 30 60 158	−4 30 59 158	−5 29 60 158	−6 29 59 158	336				
22	02 41 59 159	01 42 60 159	00 42 60 159	−0 18 59 159	−1 17 60 159	−2 17 59 159	−3 16 60 159	−4 16 59 160	−5 15 60 160	−6 15 59 160	−7 14 60 160	338			
20	02 55 −60 161	01 55 −60 161	00 55 −59 161	−0 04 −60 161	−1 04 −60 161	−2 04 −59 161	−3 03 −60 161	−4 03 −59 161	−5 02 −60 162	−6 02 −60 162	−7 02 −59 162	340			
18	03 07 60 163	02 07 59 163	01 08 60 163	00 08 60 163	−0 52 60 163	−1 52 59 163	−2 51 60 163	−3 51 60 163	−4 51 59 163	−5 50 60 163	−6 50 60 164	342			
16	03 18 60 164	02 18 60 165	01 18 59 165	00 19 60 165	−0 41 60 165	−1 41 59 165	−2 40 60 165	−3 40 60 165	−4 40 60 165	−5 40 60 165	−6 40 59 165	344			
14	03 28 60 166	02 28 60 167	01 28 60 167	00 28 59 167	−0 31 60 167	−1 31 60 167	−2 31 60 167	−3 31 60 167	−4 31 60 167	−5 31 59 167	−6 30 60 167	346			
12	03 36 60 168	02 36 59 168	01 37 60 168	00 37 60 169	−0 23 60 169	−1 23 60 169	−2 23 60 169	−3 23 60 169	−4 23 59 169	−5 22 60 169	−6 22 60 169	348			
10	03 44 −60 170	02 44 −60 170	01 44 −60 170	00 44 −60 170	−0 16 −60 171	−1 16 −60 171	−2 16 −60 171	−3 16 −60 171	−4 16 −60 171	−5 16 −60 171	−6 16 −59 171	350			
8	03 50 60 172	02 50 60 172	01 50 60 172	00 50 60 172	−0 10 60 172	−1 10 60 172	−2 10 60 172	−3 10 60 173	−4 10 60 173	−5 10 60 173	−6 10 60 173	352			
6	03 54 60 174	02 54 60 174	01 54 60 174	00 54 60 174	−0 06 60 174	−1 06 60 174	−2 06 60 174	−3 06 60 174	−4 06 60 174	−5 06 60 174	−6 06 60 174	354			
4	03 57 60 176	02 57 60 176	01 57 60 176	00 57 60 176	−0 03 60 176	−1 03 60 176	−2 03 60 176	−3 03 60 176	−4 03 60 176	−5 03 60 176	−6 03 60 176	356			
2	03 59 60 178	02 59 60 178	01 59 60 178	00 59 60 178	−0 01 60 178	−1 01 60 178	−2 01 60 178	−3 01 60 178	−4 01 60 178	−5 01 60 178	−6 01 60 178	−7 01 60 178	358		
0	04 00 −60 180	03 00 −60 180	02 00 −60 180	01 00 −60 180	00 00 −60 180	−1 00 −60 180	−2 00 −60 180	−3 00 −60 180	−4 00 −60 180	−5 00 −60 180	−6 00 −60 180	−7 00 −60 180	360		

S. Lat. {LHA greater than 180°....... Zn=180−Z; LHA less than 180°........... Zn=180+Z}

DECLINATION (15°-29°) CONTRARY NAME TO LATITUDE

LAT 71°

N. Lat. {LHA greater than 180°....... Zn=Z; LHA less than 180°.......... Zn=360−Z}

DECLINATION (0°-14°) SAME NAME AS LATITUDE

LHA	0° Hc	0° d	0° Z	1° Hc	1° d	1° Z	2° Hc	2° d	2° Z	3° Hc	3° d	3° Z	4° Hc	4° d	4° Z
	° ′	′	°	° ′	′	°	° ′	′	°	° ′	′	°	° ′	′	°
0	18 00	+60	180	19 00	+60	180	20 00	+60	180	21 00	+60	180	22 00	+60	180
2	17 59	60	178	18 59	60	178	19 59	60	178	20 59	60	178	21 59	60	178
4	17 57	60	176	18 57	60	176	19 57	60	176	20 57	60	176	21 57	60	176
6	17 54	60	174	18 54	60	174	19 54	60	174	20 54	60	174	21 54	60	174
8	17 49	60	172	18 49	60	172	19 49	60	172	20 49	60	171	21 49	60	171
10	17 43	+60	170	18 43	+60	169	19 43	+60	169	20 43	+60	169	21 43	+60	169
12	17 36	60	167	18 36	59	167	19 35	60	167	20 35	60	167	21 35	60	167
14	17 27	60	165	18 27	60	165	19 27	59	165	20 26	60	165	21 26	60	165
16	17 17	60	163	18 17	59	163	19 16	60	163	20 16	60	163	21 16	60	163
18	17 06	59	161	18 05	60	161	19 05	60	161	20 05	59	161	21 04	60	161
20	16 53	+60	159	17 53	+59	159	18 52	+60	159	19 52	+59	159	20 51	+60	159
22	16 39	60	157	17 39	59	157	18 38	60	157	19 38	59	157	20 37	60	157
24	16 24	59	155	17 23	60	155	18 23	59	155	19 22	60	155	20 22	59	154
26	16 08	59	153	17 07	59	153	18 06	60	153	19 06	59	152	20 05	59	152
28	15 50	59	151	16 49	60	151	17 49	59	151	18 48	59	150	19 47	60	150
30	15 31	+60	149	16 31	+59	149	17 30	+59	148	18 29	+59	148	19 28	+59	148
32	15 12	59	147	16 11	59	147	17 10	59	146	18 09	59	146	19 08	59	146
34	14 51	59	145	15 50	59	145	16 49	59	144	17 48	59	144	18 47	59	144
36	14 29	59	143	15 28	59	142	16 27	58	142	17 25	59	142	18 24	59	142
38	14 06	59	141	15 05	58	140	16 03	59	140	17 02	59	140	18 01	59	140
40	13 42	+58	139	14 40	+59	138	15 39	+59	138	16 38	+58	138	17 36	+59	138
42	13 17	58	137	14 15	59	136	15 14	58	136	16 12	59	136	17 11	59	136
44	12 51	58	135	13 49	59	134	14 48	58	134	15 46	59	134	16 45	58	134
46	12 24	58	133	13 22	59	132	14 21	58	132	15 19	58	132	16 17	59	132
48	11 56	58	131	12 54	59	130	13 53	58	130	14 51	58	130	15 49	58	130
50	11 27	+59	129	12 26	+58	128	13 24	+58	128	14 22	+58	128	15 20	+58	128
52	10 58	58	127	11 56	58	126	12 54	58	126	13 52	58	126	14 50	59	126
54	10 28	58	125	11 26	58	124	12 24	58	124	13 22	58	124	14 20	58	124
56	09 57	58	123	10 55	58	122	11 53	58	122	12 51	58	122	13 49	58	122
58	09 26	57	121	10 23	58	121	11 21	58	120	12 19	58	120	13 17	58	120
60	08 53	+58	119	09 51	+58	119	10 49	+58	118	11 47	+57	118	12 44	+58	118
62	08 21	57	117	09 18	58	117	10 16	58	116	11 14	57	116	12 11	58	116
64	07 47	58	115	08 45	57	115	09 42	58	114	10 40	57	114	11 37	58	114
66	07 13	58	113	08 11	57	113	09 08	58	112	10 06	57	112	11 03	58	112
68	06 39	57	111	07 36	58	111	08 34	57	110	09 31	58	110	10 29	57	110
70	06 04	+57	109	07 01	+58	109	07 59	+57	109	08 56	+58	108	09 54	+57	108
72	05 29	57	107	06 26	57	107	07 23	58	107	08 21	57	106	09 18	57	106
74	04 53	57	105	05 50	58	105	06 48	57	105	07 45	57	104	08 42	57	104
76	04 17	58	103	05 15	57	103	06 12	57	103	07 09	57	102	08 06	57	102
78	03 41	57	101	04 38	57	101	05 35	58	101	06 33	57	101	07 30	57	100
80	03 05	+57	100	04 02	+57	99	04 59	+57	99	05 56	+57	99	06 53	+57	98
82	02 28	57	98	03 25	57	97	04 22	57	97	05 19	57	97	06 16	57	96
84	01 51	57	96	02 48	57	95	03 45	57	95	04 42	57	95	05 39	58	95
86	01 14	57	94	02 11	57	94	03 08	57	93	04 05	57	93	05 02	57	93
88	00 37	57	92	01 34	57	92	02 31	57	91	03 28	57	91	04 25	57	91
90	00 00	+57	90	00 57	+57	90	01 54	+57	89	02 51	+57	89	03 48	+57	89
92	−0 37	57	88	00 20	57	88	01 17	57	87	02 14	57	87	03 11	57	87
94	−1 14	57	86	−0 17	57	86	00 40	57	86	01 37	57	85	02 34	57	85
96	−1 51	57	84	−0 54	57	84	00 03	57	84	01 00	57	83	01 57	57	83
98	−2 28	57	82	−1 31	57	82	−0 34	57	82	00 23	58	81	01 21	57	81
100	−3 05	+58	80	−2 07	+57	80	−1 10	+57	80	−0 13	+57	80	00 44	+57	79
102	−3 41	57	79	−2 44	57	78	−1 47	58	78	−0 49	57	78	00 08	57	77
104	−4 17	57	77	−3 20	57	76	−2 23	57	76	−1 26	58	76	−0 28	57	75
106	−4 53	57	75	−3 56	57	74	−2 59	58	74	−2 01	57	74	−1 04	57	74
108	−5 29	57	73	−4 32	58	72	−3 34	57	72	−2 37	58	72	−1 39	57	72
110	−6 04	+57	71	−5 07	+58	71	−4 09	+57	70	−3 12	+58	70	−2 14	+57	70
112	−6 39	58	69	−5 41	57	69	−4 44	58	68	−3 46	57	68	−2 49	57	68
114	−7 13	57	67	−6 16	58	67	−5 18	57	66	−4 21	58	66	−3 23	57	66
116	−7 47	57	65	−6 50	58	65	−5 52	58	65	−4 54	57	64	−3 57	58	64
118				−7 23	58	63	−6 25	58	63	−5 27	57	62	−4 30	58	62
120				−7 56	+58	61	−6 58	+58	61	−6 00	+58	60	−5 02	+58	60
122							−7 30	58	59	−6 32	58	58	−5 34	58	58
124							−8 01	58	57	−7 03	58	56	−6 05	58	56
126										−7 34	58	55	−6 36	58	54
128													−7 06	59	52
130													−7 34	+58	50

LHA	5° Hc	5° d	5° Z	6° Hc	6° d	6° Z	7° Hc	7° d	7° Z	8° Hc	8° d	8° Z	9° Hc	9° d	9° Z
	° ′	′	°	° ′	′	°	° ′	′	°	° ′	′	°	° ′	′	°
0	23 00	+60	180	24 00	+60	180	25 00	+60	180	26 00	+60	180	27 00	+60	180
2	22 59	60	178	23 59	60	178	24 59	60	178	25 59	60	178	26 59	60	178
4	22 57	60	176	23 57	60	176	24 57	60	176	25 57	60	176	26 57	60	176
6	22 54	60	174	23 54	60	174	24 54	60	173	25 54	60	173	26 54	60	173
8	22 49	60	171	23 49	60	171	24 49	60	171	25 49	60	171	26 49	60	171
10	22 43	+59	169	23 42	+60	169	24 42	+60	169	25 42	+60	169	26 42	+60	169
12	22 35	60	167	23 35	60	167	24 35	60	167	25 35	59	167	26 34	60	167
14	22 26	60	165	23 26	60	165	24 26	59	165	25 25	60	165	26 25	60	165
16	22 16	59	163	23 15	60	163	24 15	60	163	25 15	60	162	26 15	59	162
18	22 04	60	161	23 04	59	161	24 03	60	160	25 03	60	160	26 03	59	160
20	21 51	+60	159	22 51	+59	158	23 50	+60	158	24 50	+59	158	25 49	+60	158
22	21 37	59	156	22 36	60	156	23 36	59	156	24 35	60	156	25 35	59	156
24	21 21	60	154	22 21	59	154	23 20	60	154	24 20	59	154	25 19	59	154
26	21 04	60	152	22 04	59	152	23 03	60	152	24 03	59	152	25 02	59	152
28	20 47	59	150	21 46	59	150	22 45	59	150	23 44	60	150	24 44	59	149
30	20 27	+60	148	21 27	+59	148	22 26	+59	148	23 25	+59	147	24 24	+59	147
32	20 07	59	146	21 06	59	146	22 05	59	145	23 04	59	145	24 03	59	145
34	19 46	59	144	20 45	59	144	21 44	59	143	22 43	59	143	23 42	58	143
36	19 23	59	142	20 22	59	141	21 21	59	141	22 20	59	141	23 19	58	141
38	19 00	58	140	19 58	59	139	20 57	59	139	21 56	59	139	22 55	58	139
40	18 35	+59	138	19 34	+58	137	20 32	+59	137	21 31	+59	137	22 30	+58	137
42	18 10	58	136	19 08	59	135	20 07	58	135	21 05	59	135	22 04	58	135
44	17 43	59	133	18 42	58	133	19 40	58	133	20 38	59	133	21 37	58	132
46	17 16	58	131	18 14	58	131	19 12	59	131	20 11	58	131	21 09	58	130
48	16 47	59	129	17 46	58	129	18 44	58	129	19 42	58	129	20 40	58	128
50	16 18	+59	127	17 17	+58	127	18 15	+58	127	19 13	+58	127	20 11	+58	126
52	15 49	58	125	16 47	58	125	17 45	58	125	18 43	58	125	19 41	58	124
54	15 18	58	123	16 16	58	123	17 14	58	123	18 12	58	123	19 10	57	122
56	14 47	57	121	15 44	58	121	16 42	58	121	17 40	58	121	18 38	58	120
58	14 15	57	119	15 12	58	119	16 10	58	119	17 08	57	119	18 05	58	118
60	13 42	+58	117	14 40	+57	117	15 37	+58	117	16 35	+57	117	17 32	+58	116
62	13 09	57	115	14 06	58	115	15 04	57	115	16 01	58	115	16 59	57	114
64	12 35	57	114	13 32	58	113	14 30	57	113	15 27	58	113	16 25	57	112
66	12 01	57	112	12 58	58	111	13 56	57	111	14 53	57	111	15 50	58	110
68	11 26	57	110	12 23	58	109	13 21	57	109	14 18	57	109	15 15	58	108
70	10 51	+57	108	11 48	+57	107	12 45	+58	107	13 43	+57	107	14 40	+57	106
72	10 15	58	106	11 13	57	105	12 10	57	105	13 07	57	105	14 04	57	104
74	09 39	58	104	10 37	57	103	11 34	57	103	12 31	57	103	13 28	57	103
76	09 03	57	102	10 00	58	102	10 58	57	101	11 55	57	101	12 52	57	101
78	08 27	57	100	09 24	57	100	10 21	57	99	11 18	57	99	12 15	57	99
80	07 50	+57	98	08 47	+57	98	09 44	+57	97	10 41	+58	97	11 39	+57	97
82	07 13	57	96	08 10	58	96	09 08	57	95	10 05	57	95	11 02	57	95
84	06 37	57	94	07 34	57	94	08 31	57	94	09 28	57	93	10 25	57	93
86	05 59	58	92	06 57	57	92	07 54	57	92	08 51	57	91	09 48	57	91
88	05 22	57	90	06 19	57	90	07 16	57	90	08 13	57	89	09 10	57	89
90	04 45	+57	88	05 42	+57	88	06 39	+57	88	07 36	+57	88	08 33	+57	87
92	04 08	57	87	05 05	57	86	06 02	57	86	06 59	57	86	07 56	57	85
94	03 31	57	85	04 28	57	84	05 25	57	84	06 22	58	84	07 20	57	83
96	02 54	58	83	03 52	57	82	04 49	57	82	05 46	57	82	06 43	57	82
98	02 18	57	81	03 15	57	80	04 12	57	80	05 09	57	80	06 06	57	80
100	01 41	+57	79	02 38	+58	79	03 36	+57	78	04 33	+57	78	05 30	+57	78
102	01 05	57	77	02 02	57	77	02 59	58	76	03 57	57	76	04 54	57	76
104	00 29	57	75	01 26	57	75	02 23	58	75	03 21	57	74	04 18	57	74
106	−0 07	58	73	00 51	57	73	01 48	57	73	02 45	57	72	03 42	58	72
108	−0 42	57	71	00 15	58	71	01 13	57	71	02 10	57	70	03 07	58	70
110	−1 17	+57	69	−0 20	+58	69	00 38	+58	69	01 36	+57	69	02 33	+57	68
112	−1 52	58	68	−0 54	57	67	00 03	58	67	01 01	57	67	01 58	58	66
114	−2 26	58	66	−1 28	58	65	−0 30	57	65	00 27	58	65	01 25	57	65
116	−2 59	58	64	−2 01	57	63	−1 04	58	63	−0 06	58	63	00 52	57	63
118	−3 32	58	62	−2 34	57	62	−1 37	58	61	−0 39	58	61	00 19	58	61
120	−4 04	+57	60	−3 07	+58	60	−2 09	+58	59	−1 11	+58	59	−0 13	+58	59
122	−4 36	58	58	−3 38	58	58	−2 40	58	57	−1 42	57	57	−0 45	58	57
124	−5 07	58	56	−4 09	58	56	−3 11	58	56	−2 13	58	55	−1 15	58	55
126	−5 38	58	54	−4 40	58	54	−3 42	59	54	−2 43	58	53	−1 45	58	53
128	−6 07	58	52	−5 09	58	52	−4 11	58	52	−3 13	59	51	−2 14	58	51
130	−6 36	+58	50	−5 38	+58	50	−4 40	+59	50	−3 41	+58	50	−2 43	+58	49
132	−7 04	58	48	−6 06	58	48	−5 08	59	48	−4 09	58	48	−3 11	59	47
134	−7 32	59	46	−6 33	58	46	−5 35	59	46	−4 36	58	46	−3 38	59	45
136				−6 59	58	44	−6 01	59	44	−5 02	58	44	−4 04	59	43
138				−7 25	59	42	−6 26	59	42	−5 27	59	42	−4 28	58	42

10° Hc	10° d	10° Z	11° Hc	11° d	11° Z	12° Hc	12° d	12° Z	13° Hc	13° d	13° Z	14° Hc	14° d	14° Z	LHA
° ′	′	°	° ′	′	°	° ′	′	°	° ′	′	°	° ′	′	°	
28 00	+60	180	29 00	+60	180	30 00	+60	180	31 00	+60	180	32 00	+60	180	360
27 59	60	178	28 59	60	178	29 59	60	178	30 59	60	178	31 59	60	178	358
27 57	60	176	28 57	60	176	29 57	60	176	30 57	60	176	31 57	60	175	356
27 54	60	173	28 54	59	173	29 53	60	173	30 53	60	173	31 53	60	173	354
27 49	59	171	28 48	60	171	29 48	60	171	30 48	60	171	31 48	60	171	352
27 42	+60	169	28 42	+60	169	29 42	+60	169	30 42	+60	169	31 42	+59	169	350
27 34	60	167	28 34	60	167	29 34	60	167	30 34	60	166	31 34	59	166	348
27 25	60	164	28 25	60	164	29 25	59	164	30 24	60	164	31 24	60	164	346
27 14	60	162	28 14	60	162	29 14	59	162	30 13	60	162	31 13	60	162	344
27 02	60	160	28 02	60	160	29 02	59	160	30 01	60	160	31 01	59	160	342
26 49	+60	158	27 49	+59	158	28 48	+60	158	29 48	+59	157	30 47	+60	157	340
26 34	60	156	27 34	59	156	28 33	60	155	29 33	59	155	30 32	60	155	338
26 18	60	154	27 18	59	153	28 17	60	153	29 17	59	153	30 16	59	153	336
26 01	60	151	27 01	59	151	28 00	59	151	28 59	59	151	29 58	60	151	334
25 43	59	149	26 42	59	149	27 41	59	149	28 40	60	149	29 40	59	148	332
25 23	+59	147	26 22	+59	147	27 21	+59	147	28 20	+59	146	29 19	+60	146	330
25 02	59	145	26 01	59	145	27 00	59	144	27 59	59	144	28 58	59	144	328
24 40	59	143	25 39	59	143	26 38	59	142	27 37	59	142	28 36	59	142	326
24 17	59	141	25 16	59	140	26 15	59	140	27 14	58	140	28 12	59	140	324
23 53	59	139	24 52	59	138	25 51	58	138	26 49	59	138	27 48	59	138	322
23 28	+59	136	24 27	+58	136	25 25	+59	136	26 24	+58	136	27 22	+59	135	320
23 02	59	134	24 01	58	134	24 59	58	134	25 57	59	134	26 56	58	133	318
22 35	59	132	23 34	58	132	24 32	58	132	25 30	58	131	26 28	59	131	316
22 07	58	130	23 05	59	130	24 04	58	130	25 02	58	129	26 00	58	129	314
21 38	59	128	22 37	58	128	23 35	58	128	24 33	58	127	25 31	58	127	312
21 09	+58	126	22 07	+58	126	23 05	+58	126	24 03	+58	125	25 01	+58	125	310
20 39	57	124	21 36	58	124	22 34	58	123	23 32	58	123	24 30	58	123	308
20 07	58	122	21 05	58	122	22 03	58	121	23 01	57	121	23 58	58	121	306
19 36	57	120	20 33	58	120	21 31	58	119	22 29	57	119	23 26	58	119	304
19 03	58	118	20 01	57	118	20 58	58	117	21 56	57	117	22 53	58	117	302
18 30	+58	116	19 28	+57	116	20 25	+58	115	21 23	+57	115	22 20	+57	115	300
17 56	58	114	18 54	57	114	19 51	58	113	20 49	57	113	21 46	57	113	298
17 22	58	112	18 20	57	112	19 17	57	111	20 14	58	111	21 12	57	111	296
16 48	57	110	17 45	57	110	18 42	58	109	19 40	57	109	20 37	57	109	294
16 13	57	108	17 10	57	108	18 07	57	107	19 04	57	107	20 01	58	107	292
15 37	+57	106	16 34	+58	106	17 32	+57	105	18 29	+57	105	19 26	+57	105	290
15 01	58	104	15 59	57	104	16 56	57	104	17 53	57	103	18 50	57	103	288
14 25	57	102	15 22	57	102	16 19	57	102	17 16	57	101	18 13	57	101	286
13 49	57	100	14 46	57	100	15 43	57	100	16 40	57	99	17 37	57	99	284
13 12	57	98	14 09	57	98	15 06	57	98	16 03	57	97	17 00	57	97	282
12 36	+57	96	13 33	+56	96	14 29	+57	96	15 26	+57	95	16 23	+57	95	280
11 59	57	95	12 56	57	94	13 53	56	94	14 49	57	94	15 46	57	93	278
11 22	57	93	12 19	57	92	13 16	56	92	14 12	57	92	15 09	57	91	276
10 45	56	91	11 41	57	90	12 38	57	90	13 35	57	90	14 32	57	89	274
10 07	57	89	11 04	57	89	12 01	57	88	12 58	57	88	13 55	57	88	272
09 30	+57	87	10 27	+57	87	11 24	+57	86	12 21	+57	86	13 18	+57	86	270
08 53	57	85	09 50	57	85	10 47	57	84	11 44	57	84	12 41	57	84	268
08 17	57	83	09 14	57	83	10 11	57	83	11 08	56	82	12 04	57	82	266
07 40	57	81	08 37	57	81	09 34	57	81	10 31	57	80	11 28	57	80	264
07 03	57	79	08 00	57	79	08 57	57	79	09 54	57	78	10 51	57	78	262
06 27	+57	77	07 24	+57	77	08 21	+57	77	09 18	+57	77	10 15	+57	76	260
05 51	57	76	06 48	57	75	07 45	57	75	08 42	57	75	09 39	58	74	258
05 15	57	74	06 12	58	73	07 10	57	73	08 07	57	73	09 04	57	72	256
04 40	57	72	05 37	57	72	06 34	58	71	07 32	57	71	08 29	57	71	254
04 05	57	70	05 02	57	70	05 59	58	69	06 57	57	69	07 54	57	69	252
03 30	+58	68	04 28	+57	68	05 25	+57	67	06 22	+58	67	07 20	+57	67	250
02 56	57	66	03 53	58	66	04 51	57	66	05 48	58	65	06 46	57	65	248
02 22	58	64	03 20	57	64	04 17	58	64	05 15	57	63	06 12	58	63	246
01 49	58	62	02 47	57	62	03 44	58	62	04 42	58	62	05 40	57	61	244
01 17	57	60	02 14	58	60	03 12	58	60	04 10	58	60	05 08	57	59	242
00 45	+57	59	01 42	+58	58	02 40	+58	58	03 38	+58	58	04 36	+58	58	240
00 13	58	57	01 11	58	56	02 09	58	56	03 07	58	56	04 05	58	56	238
−0 17	58	55	00 41	58	54	01 39	58	54	02 37	58	54	03 35	58	54	236
−0 47	58	53	00 11	58	53	01 09	58	52	02 07	58	52	03 05	58	52	234
−1 16	58	51	−0 18	58	51	00 40	58	50	01 38	58	50	02 36	59	50	232
−1 45	+59	49	−0 46	+58	49	00 12	+58	49	01 10	+58	48	02 08	+59	48	230
−2 12	58	47	−1 14	58	47	−0 16	59	47	00 43	58	46	01 41	59	46	228
−2 39	58	45	−1 41	59	45	−0 42	58	45	00 16	59	45	01 15	58	44	226
−3 05	59	43	−2 06	58	43	−1 08	59	43	−0 09	58	43	00 49	59	42	224
−3 30	59	41	−2 31	59	41	−1 32	58	41	−0 34	59	41	00 25	59	40	222

S. Lat. {LHA greater than 180°....... Zn=180−Z; LHA less than 180°.......... Zn=180+Z}

DECLINATION (0°-14°) SAME NAME AS LATITUDE

N. Lat. {LHA greater than 180°........Zn=Z / LHA less than 180°...........Zn=360−Z}

DECLINATION (0°-14°) SAME NAME AS LATITUDE

LHA	0° Hc	0° d	0° Z	1° Hc	1° d	1° Z	2° Hc	2° d	2° Z	3° Hc	3° d	3° Z	4° Hc	4° d	4° Z	5° Hc	5° d	5° Z	6° Hc	6° d	6° Z	7° Hc	7° d	7° Z	8° Hc	8° d	8° Z	9° Hc	9° d	9° Z	10° Hc	10° d	10° Z	11° Hc	11° d	11° Z	12° Hc	12° d	12° Z	13° Hc	13° d	13° Z	14° Hc	14° d	14° Z	LHA
	° ′	′	°	° ′	′	°	° ′	′	°	° ′	′	°	° ′	′	°	° ′	′	°	° ′	′	°	° ′	′	°	° ′	′	°	° ′	′	°	° ′	′	°	° ′	′	°	° ′	′	°	° ′	′	°	° ′	′	°	
																		140	-7 49	+59	40	-6 50	+58	40	-5 52	+59	40	-4 53	+59	40	-3 54	+59	39	-2 55	+59	39	-1 56	+59	39	-0 57	+58	39	00 01	+59	39	220
																					142	-7 14	59	38	-6 15	59	38	-5 16	59	38	-4 17	59	37	-3 18	59	37	-2 19	59	37	-1 20	59	37	-0 21	59	37	218
																					144	-7 36	59	36	-6 37	59	36	-5 38	59	36	-4 39	59	36	-3 40	59	35	-2 41	59	35	-1 42	59	35	-0 43	59	35	216
																								146	-6 58	59	34	-5 59	59	34	-5 00	59	34	-4 01	59	33	-3 02	59	33	-2 03	59	33	-1 04	60	33	214
																								148	-7 18	59	32	-6 19	59	32	-5 20	59	32	-4 21	59	31	-3 22	60	31	-2 22	59	31	-1 23	59	31	212
																								150	-7 37	+59	30	-6 38	+59	30	-5 39	+59	30	-4 40	+60	30	-3 40	+59	29	-2 41	+59	29	-1 42	+60	29	210
																											152	-6 56	59	28	-5 57	60	28	-4 57	59	28	-3 58	60	28	-2 58	59	27	-1 59	59	27	208
																											154	-7 13	60	26	-6 13	59	26	-5 14	60	26	-4 14	59	26	-3 15	59	25	-2 16	60	25	206
																											156	-7 28	59	24	-6 29	60	24	-5 29	59	24	-4 30	60	24	-3 30	59	23	-2 31	60	23	204
																														158	-6 43	59	22	-5 44	60	22	-4 44	60	22	-3 44	59	21	-2 45	60	21	202
																														160	-6 56	+59	20	-5 57	+60	20	-4 57	+60	20	-3 57	+59	20	-2 58	+60	19	200
																														162	-7 08	59	18	-6 09	60	18	-5 09	60	18	-4 09	59	18	-3 10	60	18	198
																														164	-7 19	60	16	-6 19	59	16	-5 20	60	16	-4 20	60	16	-3 20	60	16	196
																																	166	-6 29	60	14	-5 29	60	14	-4 29	60	14	-3 29	59	14	194
																																	168	-6 37	60	12	-5 37	60	12	-4 37	60	12	-3 37	59	12	192
																																	170	-6 44	+60	10	-5 44	+60	10	-4 44	+60	10	-3 44	+60	10	190
																																	172	-6 50	60	8	-5 50	60	8	-4 50	60	8	-3 50	60	8	188
																																	174	-6 54	60	6	-5 54	60	6	-4 54	60	6	-3 54	60	6	186
																																	176	-6 57	59	4	-5 58	60	4	-4 58	60	4	-3 58	60	4	184
																																	178	-6 59	60	2	-5 59	60	2	-4 59	60	2	-3 59	60	2	182
																																	180	-7 00	+60	0	-6 00	+60	0	-5 00	+60	0	-4 00	+60	0	180
116	-7 47	58	65	244																																										
114	-7 13	58	67	246																																										
112	-6 39	57	69	-7 36	58	69	248																																							
110	-6 04	-57	71	-7 01	-58	71	-7 59	-57	71	250																																				
108	-5 29	57	73	-6 26	57	73	-7 23	58	73	252																																				
106	-4 53	57	75	-5 50	58	75	-6 48	57	75	-7 45	57	76	254																																	
104	-4 17	58	77	-5 15	57	77	-6 12	57	77	-7 09	57	78	-8 06	57	78	256																														
102	-3 41	57	79	-4 38	57	79	-5 35	58	79	-6 33	57	79	-7 30	57	80	258																														
100	-3 05	-57	80	-4 02	-57	81	-4 59	-57	81	-5 56	-57	81	-6 53	-57	82	-7 50	-57	82	260																											
98	-2 28	57	82	-3 25	57	83	-4 22	57	83	-5 19	57	83	-6 16	57	84	-7 13	57	84	-8 10	58	84	262																								
96	-1 51	57	84	-2 48	57	85	-3 45	57	85	-4 42	57	85	-5 39	58	85	-6 37	57	86	-7 34	57	86	264																								
94	-1 14	57	86	-2 11	57	86	-3 08	57	87	-4 05	57	87	-5 02	57	87	-5 59	58	88	-6 57	57	88	-7 54	57	88	266																					
92	-0 37	57	88	-1 34	57	88	-2 31	57	89	-3 28	57	89	-4 25	57	89	-5 22	57	90	-6 19	57	90	-7 16	57	90	-8 13	57	91	268																		
90	00 00	-57	90	-0 57	-57	90	-1 54	-57	91	-2 51	-57	91	-3 48	-57	91	-4 45	-57	92	-5 42	-57	92	-6 39	-57	92	-7 36	-57	92	270																		
88	00 37	57	92	-0 20	57	92	-1 17	57	93	-2 14	57	93	-3 11	57	93	-4 08	57	93	-5 05	57	94	-6 02	57	94	-6 59	57	94	-7 56	57	95	272															
86	01 14	57	94	00 17	57	94	-0 40	57	94	-1 37	57	95	-2 34	57	95	-3 31	57	95	-4 28	57	96	-5 25	57	96	-6 22	58	96	-7 20	57	97	274															
84	01 51	57	96	00 54	57	96	-0 03	57	96	-1 00	57	97	-1 57	57	97	-2 54	58	97	-3 52	57	98	-4 49	57	98	-5 46	57	98	-6 43	57	98	-7 40	57	99	276												
82	02 28	57	98	01 31	57	98	00 34	57	98	-0 23	58	99	-1 21	57	99	-2 18	57	99	-3 15	57	100	-4 12	57	100	-5 09	57	100	-6 06	57	100	-7 03	57	101	-8 00	57	101	278									
80	03 05	-58	100	02 07	-57	100	01 10	-57	100	00 13	-57	100	-0 44	-57	101	-1 41	-57	101	-2 38	-58	101	-3 36	-57	102	-4 33	-57	102	-5 30	-57	102	-6 27	-57	103	-7 24	-57	103	280									
78	03 41	57	101	02 44	57	102	01 47	58	102	00 49	57	102	-0 08	57	103	-1 05	57	103	-2 02	57	103	-2 59	58	104	-3 57	57	104	-4 54	57	104	-5 51	57	104	-6 48	57	105	-7 45	57	105	282						
76	04 17	57	103	03 20	57	104	02 23	57	104	01 26	58	104	00 28	57	105	-0 29	57	105	-1 26	57	105	-2 23	58	105	-3 21	57	106	-4 18	57	106	-5 15	57	106	-6 12	58	107	-7 10	57	107	-8 07	57	107	284			
74	04 53	57	105	03 56	57	106	02 59	58	106	02 01	57	106	01 04	57	106	00 07	58	107	-0 51	57	107	-1 48	57	107	-2 45	57	108	-3 42	58	108	-4 40	57	108	-5 37	57	108	-6 34	58	109	-7 32	57	109	286			
72	05 29	57	107	04 32	58	108	03 34	57	108	02 37	58	108	01 39	57	108	00 42	57	109	-0 15	58	109	-1 13	57	109	-2 10	57	110	-3 07	58	110	-4 05	57	110	-5 02	57	110	-5 59	58	111	-6 57	57	111	-7 54	57	111	288
70	06 04	-57	109	05 07	-58	109	04 09	-57	110	03 12	-58	110	02 14	-57	110	01 17	-57	111	00 20	-58	111	-0 38	-58	111	-1 36	-57	111	-2 33	-57	112	-3 30	-58	112	-4 28	-57	112	-5 25	-57	113	-6 22	-58	113	-7 20	-57	113	290
68	06 39	58	111	05 41	57	111	04 44	58	112	03 46	57	112	02 49	57	112	01 52	58	112	00 54	57	113	-0 03	58	113	-1 01	57	113	-1 58	58	114	-2 56	57	114	-3 53	58	114	-4 51	57	114	-5 48	58	115	-6 46	57	115	292
66	07 13	57	113	06 16	58	113	05 18	57	114	04 21	58	114	03 23	57	114	02 26	58	114	01 28	58	115	00 30	57	115	-0 27	58	115	-1 25	57	115	-2 22	58	116	-3 20	57	116	-4 17	58	116	-5 15	57	117	-6 12	58	117	294
64	07 47	57	115	06 50	58	115	05 52	58	115	04 54	57	116	03 57	58	116	02 59	58	116	02 01	57	117	01 04	58	117	00 06	58	117	-0 52	57	117	-1 49	58	118	-2 47	57	118	-3 44	58	118	-4 42	58	118	-5 40	57	119	296
62	08 21	58	117	07 23	58	117	06 25	58	117	05 27	57	118	04 30	58	118	03 32	58	118	02 34	57	118	01 37	58	119	00 39	58	119	-0 19	58	119	-1 17	57	120	-2 14	58	120	-3 12	58	120	-4 10	58	120	-5 08	57	121	298
60	08 53	-57	119	07 56	-58	119	06 58	-58	119	06 00	-58	120	05 02	-58	120	04 04	-57	120	03 07	-58	120	02 09	-58	121	01 11	-58	121	00 13	-58	121	-0 45	-57	121	-1 42	-58	122	-2 40	-58	122	-3 38	-58	122	-4 36	-58	122	300
58	09 26	58	121	08 28	58	121	07 30	58	121	06 32	58	122	05 34	58	122	04 36	58	122	03 38	58	122	02 40	58	123	01 42	57	123	00 45	58	123	-0 13	58	123	-1 11	58	124	-2 09	58	124	-3 07	58	124	-4 05	58	124	302
56	09 57	58	123	08 59	58	123	08 01	58	123	07 03	58	124	06 05	58	124	05 07	58	124	04 09	58	124	03 11	58	124	02 13	58	125	01 15	58	125	00 17	58	125	-0 41	58	126	-1 39	58	126	-2 37	58	126	-3 35	58	126	304
54	10 28	58	125	09 30	58	125	08 32	58	125	07 34	58	125	06 36	58	126	05 38	58	126	04 40	58	126	03 42	59	126	02 43	58	127	01 45	58	127	00 47	58	127	-0 11	58	127	-1 09	58	128	-2 07	58	128	-3 05	58	128	306
52	10 58	58	127	10 00	58	127	09 02	58	127	08 04	58	127	07 06	59	128	06 07	58	128	05 09	58	128	04 11	58	128	03 13	59	129	02 14	58	129	01 16	58	129	00 18	58	129	-0 40	58	130	-1 38	58	130	-2 36	59	130	308
50	11 27	-58	129	10 29	-58	129	09 31	-58	129	08 33	-59	129	07 34	-58	130	06 36	-58	130	05 38	-58	130	04 40	-59	130	03 41	-58	130	02 43	-58	131	01 45	-59	131	00 46	-58	131	-0 12	-58	131	-1 10	-58	132	-2 08	-59	132	310
48	11 56	58	131	10 58	59	131	09 59	58	131	09 01	58	131	08 03	59	132	07 04	58	132	06 06	58	132	05 08	59	132	04 09	58	132	03 11	59	133	02 12	58	133	01 14	58	133	00 16	59	133	-0 43	58	134	-1 41	59	134	312
46	12 24	59	133	11 25	58	133	10 27	59	133	09 28	58	133	08 30	58	134	07 32	59	134	06 33	58	134	05 35	59	134	04 36	58	134	03 38	59	135	02 39	58	135	01 41	59	135	00 42	58	135	-0 16	59	135	-1 15	58	136	314
44	12 51	59	135	11 52	58	135	10 54	59	135	09 55	59	135	08 56	58	136	07 58	59	136	06 59	58	136	06 01	59	136	05 02	58	136	04 04	59	137	03 05	59	137	02 06	58	137	01 08	59	137	00 09	58	137	-0 49	59	138	316
42	13 17	59	137	12 18	59	137	11 19	58	137	10 21	59	137	09 22	59	137	08 23	58	138	07 25	59	138	06 26	59	138	05 27	59	138	04 28	58	138	03 30	59	139	02 31	59	139	01 32	58	139	00 34	59	139	-0 25	59	140	318
40	13 42	-59	139	12 43	-59	139	11 44	-59	139	10 45	-58	139	09 47	-59	139	08 48	-59	140	07 49	-59	140	06 50	-58	140	05 52	-59	140	04 53	-59	140	03 54	-59	141	02 55	-59	141	01 56	-59	141	00 57	-58	141	-0 01	-59	141	320
38	14 06	59	141	13 07	59	141	12 08	59	141	11 09	59	141	10 10	59	141	09 11	58	142	08 13	59	142	07 14	59	142	06 15	59	142	05 16	59	142	04 17	59	143	03 18	59	143	02 19	59	143	01 20	59	143	00 21	59	143	322
36	14 29	59	143	13 30	59	143	12 31	59	143	11 32	59	143	10 33	59	143	09 34	59	144	08 35	59	144	07 36	59	144	06 37	59	144	05 38	59	144	04 39	59	144	03 40	59	145	02 41	59	145	01 42	59	145	00 43	59	145	324
34	14 51	59	145	13 52	59	145	12 53	59	145	11 54	60	145	10 54	59	145	09 55	59	146	08 56	59	146	07 57	59	146	06 58	59	146	05 59	59	146	05 00	59	146	04 01	59	147	03 02	59	147	02 03	59	147	01 04	60	147	326
32	15 12	60	147	14 12	59	147	13 13	59	147	12 14	59	147	11 15	59	147	10 16	59	148	09 17	59	148	08 18	60	148	07 18	59	148	06 19	59	148	05 20	59	148	04 21	59	149	03 22	60	149	02 22	59	149	01 23	59	149	328
30	15 31	-59	149	14 32	-59	149	13 33	-59	149	12 34	-60	149	11 34	-59	149	10 35	-59	150	09 36	-59	150	08 37	-60	150	07 37	-59	150	06 38	-59	150	05 39	-59	150	04 40	-60	150	03 40	-59	151	02 41	-59	151	01 42	-60	151	330
28	15 50	59	151	14 51	60	151	13 51	59	151	12 52	59	151	11 53	60	151	10 53	59	152	09 54	59	152	08 55	60	152	07 55	59	152	06 56	59	152	05 57	60	152	04 57	59	152	03 58	60	152	02 58	59	153	01 59	59	153	332
26	16 08	60	153	15 08	59	153	14 09	60	153	13 09	59	153	12 10	59	153	11 11	60	154	10 11	59	154	09 12	60	154	08 12	59	154	07 13	60	154	06 13	59	154	05 14	60	154	04 14	59	154	03 15	59	155	02 16	60	155	334
24	16 24	60	155	15 24	59	155	14 25	60	155	13 25	59	155	12 26	60	156	11 26	59	156	10 27	60	156	09 27	59	156	08 28	60	156	07 28	59	156	06 29	60	156	05 29	59	156	04 30	60	156	03 30	59	157	02 31	60	157	336
22	16 39	60	157	15 39	59	157	14 40	60	157	13 40	59	157	12 41	60	158	11 41	59	158	10 42	60	158	09 42	60	158	08 42	59	158	07 43	60	158	06 43	59	158	05 44	60	158	04 44	60	158	03 44	59	159	02 45	60	159	338
20	16 53	-60	159	15 53	-59	159	14 54	-60	159	13 54	-60	159	12 54	-59	160	11 55	-60	160	10 55	-60	160	09 55	-59	160	08 56	-60	160	07 56	-60	160	06 56	-59	160	05 57	-60	160	04 57	-60	160	03 57	-59	160	02 58	-60	161	340
18	17 06	60	161	16 06	60	161	15 06	60	161	14 06	59	161	13 07	60	162	12 07	60	162	11 07	59	162	10 08	60	162	09 08	60	162	08 08	60	162	07 08	59	162	06 09	60	162	05 09	60	162	04 09	59	162	03 10	60	162	342
16	17 17	60	163	16 17	60	163	15 17	59	163	14 18	60	164	13 18	60	164	12 18	60	164	11 18	60	164	10 18	59	164	09 19	60	164	08 19	60	164	07 19	60	164	06 19	59	164	05 20	60	164	04 20	60	164	03 20	60	164	344
14	17 27	60	165	16 27	60	165	15 27	60	166	14 27	59	166	13 28	60	166	12 28	60	166	11 28	60	166	10 28	60	166	09 28	59	166	08 29	60	166	07 29	60	166	06 29	60	166	05 29	60	166	04 29	60	166	03 29	59	166	346
12	17 36	60	167	16 36	60	168	15 36	60	168	14 36	60	168	13 36	60	168	12 36	60	168	11 36	59	168	10 37	60	168	09 37	60	168	08 37	60	168	07 37	60	168	06 37	60	168	05 37	60	168	04 37	60	168	03 37	59	168	348
10	17 43	-60	170	16 43	-60	170	15 43	-60	170	14 43	-60	170	13 43	-59	170	12 44	-60	170	11 44	-60	170	10 44	-60	170	09 44	-60	170	08 44	-60	170	07 44	-60	170	06 44	-60	170	05 44	-60	170	04 44	-60	170	03 44	-60	170	350
8	17 49	60	172	16 49	60	172	15 49	60	172	14 49	60	172	13 49	60	172	12 49	59	172	11 50	60	172	10 50	60	172	09 50	60	172	08 50	60	172	07 50	60	172	06 50	60	172	05 50	60	172	04 50	60	172	03 50	60	172	352
6	17 54	60	174	16 54	60	174	15 54	60	174	14 54	60	174	13 54	60	174	12 54	60	174	11 54	60	174	10 54	60	174	09 54	60	174	08 54	60	174	07 54	60	174	06 54	60	174	05 54	60	174	04 54	60	174	03 54	60	174	354
4	17 57	60	176	16 57	60	176	15 57	60	176	14 57	60	176	13 57	60	176	12 57	60	176	11 57	60	176	10 57	60	176	09 57	60	176	08 57	60	176	07 57	60	176	06 57	59	176	05 58	60	176	04 58	60	176	03 58	60	176	356
2	17 59	60	178	16 59	60	178	15 59	60	178	14 59	60	178	13 59	60	178	12 59	60	178	11 59	60	178	10 59	60	178	09 59	60	178	08 59	60	178	07 59	60	178	06 59	60	178	05 59	60	178	04 59	60	178	03 59	60	178	358
0	18 00	-60	180	17 00	-60	180	16 00	-60	180	15 00	-60	180	14 00	-60	180	13 00	-60	180	12 00	-60	180	11 00	-60	180	10 00	-60	180	09 00	-60	180	08 00	-60	180	07 00	-60	180	06 00	-60	180	05 00	-60	180	04 00	-60	180	360
	0°			1°			2°			3°			4°			5°			6°			7°			8°			9°			10°			11°			12°			13°			14°			

S. Lat. {LHA greater than 180°........Zn=180−Z / LHA less than 180°...........Zn=180+Z}

DECLINATION (0°-14°) CONTRARY NAME TO LATITUDE

LAT 72°

N. Lat. {LHA greater than 180°........ Zn=Z
{LHA less than 180°............ Zn=360−Z

DECLINATION (15°-29°) SAME NAME AS LATITUDE

LHA	15° Hc	d	Z	16° Hc	d	Z	17° Hc	d	Z	18° Hc	d	Z	19° Hc	d	Z
	° ′	′	°	° ′	′	°	° ′	′	°	° ′	′	°	° ′	′	°
0	33 00	+60	180	34 00	+60	180	35 00	+60	180	36 00	+60	180	37 00	+60	180
2	32 59	60	178	33 59	60	178	34 59	60	178	35 59	60	178	36 59	60	178
4	32 57	60	175	33 57	60	175	34 57	60	175	35 57	60	175	36 57	60	175
6	32 53	60	173	33 53	60	173	34 53	60	173	35 53	60	173	36 53	60	173
8	32 48	60	171	33 48	60	171	34 48	60	171	35 48	60	171	36 48	60	171
10	32 41	+60	169	33 41	+60	168	34 41	+60	168	35 41	+60	168	36 41	+60	168
12	32 33	60	166	33 33	60	166	34 33	60	166	35 33	60	166	36 33	59	166
14	32 24	60	164	33 24	59	164	34 23	60	164	35 23	60	164	36 23	60	164
16	32 13	60	162	33 13	59	162	34 12	60	161	35 12	60	161	36 12	59	161
18	32 00	60	159	33 00	60	159	34 00	59	159	34 59	60	159	35 59	59	159
20	31 47	+59	157	32 46	+60	157	33 46	+59	157	34 45	+60	157	35 45	+59	157
22	31 32	59	155	32 31	60	155	33 31	59	155	34 30	59	154	35 29	60	154
24	31 15	60	153	32 15	59	153	33 14	59	152	34 13	60	152	35 13	59	152
26	30 58	59	150	31 57	59	150	32 56	59	150	33 55	59	150	34 54	60	150
28	30 39	59	148	31 38	59	148	32 37	59	148	33 36	59	148	34 35	59	147
30	30 19	+59	146	31 18	+59	146	32 17	+59	146	33 16	+58	145	34 14	+59	145
32	29 57	59	144	30 56	59	144	31 55	59	143	32 54	59	143	33 53	59	143
34	29 35	59	142	30 34	58	141	31 32	59	141	32 31	59	141	33 30	58	141
36	29 11	59	139	30 10	58	139	31 08	59	139	32 07	59	139	33 06	58	138
38	28 47	58	137	29 45	59	137	30 44	58	137	31 42	59	137	32 41	58	136
40	28 21	+58	135	29 19	+59	135	30 18	+58	135	31 16	+58	134	32 14	+59	134
42	27 54	59	133	28 53	58	133	29 51	58	133	30 49	58	132	31 47	58	132
44	27 27	58	131	28 25	58	131	29 23	58	130	30 21	58	130	31 19	58	130
46	26 58	58	129	27 56	58	129	28 54	58	128	29 52	58	128	30 50	58	128
48	26 29	58	127	27 27	58	126	28 25	58	126	29 23	57	126	30 20	58	126
50	25 59	+58	125	26 57	+57	124	27 54	+58	124	28 52	+58	124	29 50	+58	123
52	25 28	58	123	26 26	57	122	27 23	58	122	28 21	58	122	29 19	57	121
54	24 56	58	121	25 54	57	120	26 51	58	120	27 49	58	120	28 47	57	119
56	24 24	57	118	25 21	58	118	26 19	57	118	27 16	58	118	28 14	57	117
58	23 51	57	116	24 48	58	116	25 46	57	116	26 43	58	115	27 41	57	115
60	23 17	+58	114	24 15	+57	114	25 12	+57	114	26 09	+58	113	27 07	+57	113
62	22 43	58	112	23 41	57	112	24 38	57	112	25 35	57	111	26 32	57	111
64	22 09	57	110	23 06	57	110	24 03	58	110	25 01	57	109	25 58	57	109
66	21 34	57	108	22 31	57	108	23 28	57	108	24 25	57	107	25 22	57	107
68	20 59	57	106	21 56	57	106	22 53	57	106	23 50	57	105	24 47	57	105
70	20 23	+57	105	21 20	+57	104	22 17	+57	104	23 14	+57	104	24 11	+57	103
72	19 47	57	103	20 44	57	102	21 41	57	102	22 38	56	102	23 34	57	101
74	19 10	57	101	20 07	57	100	21 04	57	100	22 01	57	100	22 58	57	99
76	18 34	57	99	19 31	57	98	20 28	56	98	21 24	57	98	22 21	57	97
78	17 57	57	97	18 54	57	96	19 51	57	96	20 48	56	96	21 44	57	95
80	17 20	+57	95	18 17	+57	94	19 14	+57	94	20 11	+56	94	21 07	+57	93
82	16 43	57	93	17 40	57	93	18 37	57	92	19 34	56	92	20 30	57	92
84	16 06	57	91	17 03	57	91	18 00	57	90	18 57	56	90	19 53	57	90
86	15 29	57	89	16 26	57	89	17 23	57	88	18 20	56	88	19 16	57	88
88	14 52	57	87	15 49	57	87	16 46	56	87	17 42	57	86	18 39	57	86
90	14 15	+57	85	15 12	+57	85	16 09	+57	85	17 06	+56	84	18 02	+57	84
92	13 38	57	83	14 35	57	83	15 32	57	83	16 29	56	82	17 25	57	82
94	13 01	57	82	13 58	57	81	14 55	57	81	15 52	57	81	16 49	57	80
96	12 25	57	80	13 22	57	79	14 19	57	79	15 16	56	79	16 12	57	78
98	11 48	57	78	12 45	57	77	13 42	57	77	14 39	57	77	15 36	57	76
100	11 12	+57	76	12 09	+57	76	13 06	+57	75	14 03	+57	75	15 00	+57	75
102	10 37	57	74	11 34	57	74	12 31	57	73	13 28	57	73	14 25	57	73
104	10 01	57	72	10 58	57	72	11 55	57	72	12 52	58	71	13 50	57	71
106	09 26	57	70	10 23	57	70	11 20	58	70	12 18	57	69	13 15	57	69
108	08 51	58	68	09 49	57	68	10 46	57	68	11 43	57	68	12 40	57	67
110	08 17	+57	67	09 14	+58	66	10 12	+57	66	11 09	+57	66	12 06	+58	65
112	07 43	58	65	08 41	57	64	09 38	58	64	10 36	57	64	11 33	57	64
114	07 10	58	63	08 08	57	63	09 05	58	62	10 03	57	62	11 00	57	62
116	06 37	58	61	07 35	58	61	08 33	57	60	09 30	58	60	10 28	57	60
118	06 05	58	59	07 03	58	59	08 01	57	59	08 58	58	58	09 56	58	58
120	05 34	+58	57	06 32	+57	57	07 29	+58	57	08 27	+58	56	09 25	+58	56
122	05 03	58	55	06 01	58	55	06 59	58	55	07 57	57	55	08 54	58	54
124	04 33	58	53	05 31	58	53	06 29	58	53	07 27	58	53	08 25	58	52
126	04 03	58	52	05 01	58	51	05 59	59	51	06 58	58	51	07 56	58	51
128	03 35	58	50	04 33	58	50	05 31	58	49	06 29	58	49	07 27	59	49
130	03 07	+58	48	04 05	+58	48	05 03	+59	47	06 02	+58	47	07 00	+58	47
132	02 40	58	46	03 38	58	46	04 36	59	46	05 35	58	45	06 33	59	45
134	02 13	59	44	03 12	58	44	04 10	59	44	05 09	58	43	06 07	59	43
136	01 48	59	42	02 47	58	42	03 45	59	42	04 44	59	42	05 43	58	41
138	01 24	58	40	02 22	59	40	03 21	59	40	04 20	58	40	05 18	59	40

LHA	20° Hc	d	Z	21° Hc	d	Z	22° Hc	d	Z	23° Hc	d	Z	24° Hc	d	Z
	° ′	′	°	° ′	′	°	° ′	′	°	° ′	′	°	° ′	′	°
0	38 00	+60	180	39 00	+60	180	40 00	+60	180	41 00	+60	180	42 00	+60	180
2	37 59	60	178	38 59	60	178	39 59	60	178	40 59	60	178	41 59	60	178
4	37 57	60	175	38 57	60	175	39 57	60	175	40 57	60	175	41 57	60	175
6	37 53	60	173	38 53	60	173	39 53	60	173	40 53	60	173	41 53	60	173
8	37 48	60	171	38 48	60	170	39 48	59	170	40 47	60	170	41 47	60	170
10	37 41	+60	168	38 41	+60	168	39 41	+59	168	40 40	+60	168	41 40	+60	168
12	37 32	60	166	38 32	60	166	39 32	60	166	40 32	60	165	41 32	59	165
14	37 23	59	163	38 22	60	163	39 22	60	163	40 22	59	163	41 21	60	163
16	37 11	60	161	38 11	60	161	39 11	59	161	40 10	60	161	41 10	59	161
18	36 58	60	159	37 58	60	159	38 58	59	158	39 57	60	158	40 57	59	158
20	36 44	+60	156	37 44	+59	156	38 43	+60	156	39 43	+59	156	40 42	+59	156
22	36 29	59	154	37 28	59	154	38 27	60	154	39 27	59	154	40 26	59	153
24	36 12	59	152	37 11	59	152	38 10	60	151	39 10	59	151	40 09	59	151
26	35 54	59	149	36 53	59	149	37 52	59	149	38 51	59	149	39 50	59	149
28	35 34	59	147	36 33	59	147	37 32	59	147	38 31	59	147	39 30	59	146
30	35 13	+59	145	36 12	+59	145	37 11	+59	144	38 10	+59	144	39 09	+59	144
32	34 52	58	143	35 50	59	142	36 49	59	142	37 48	58	142	38 46	59	142
34	34 28	59	140	35 27	59	140	36 26	58	140	37 24	59	140	38 23	58	139
36	34 04	59	138	35 03	58	138	36 01	59	138	37 00	58	137	37 58	58	137
38	33 39	58	136	34 37	59	136	35 36	58	135	36 34	58	135	37 32	59	135
40	33 13	+58	134	34 11	+58	134	35 09	+58	133	36 07	+59	133	37 06	+58	133
42	32 45	59	132	33 44	58	131	34 42	58	131	35 40	58	131	36 38	58	130
44	32 17	58	130	33 15	58	129	34 13	58	129	35 11	58	129	36 09	58	128
46	31 48	58	127	32 46	58	127	33 44	58	127	34 42	57	126	35 39	58	126
48	31 18	58	125	32 16	58	125	33 14	57	125	34 11	58	124	35 09	58	124
50	30 48	+57	123	31 45	+58	123	32 43	+57	122	33 40	+58	122	34 38	+57	122
52	30 16	58	121	31 14	57	121	32 11	58	120	33 09	57	120	34 06	57	120
54	29 44	57	119	30 41	58	119	31 39	57	118	32 36	57	118	33 33	58	118
56	29 11	58	117	30 09	57	117	31 06	57	116	32 03	57	116	33 00	57	115
58	28 38	57	115	29 35	57	114	30 32	57	114	31 29	57	114	32 26	57	113
60	28 04	+57	113	29 01	+57	112	29 58	+57	112	30 55	+57	112	31 52	+57	111
62	27 29	58	111	28 27	57	110	29 24	57	110	30 21	56	110	31 17	57	109
64	26 55	57	109	27 52	57	108	28 49	56	108	29 45	57	108	30 42	57	107
66	26 19	57	107	27 16	57	106	28 13	57	106	29 10	57	106	30 07	56	105
68	25 44	56	105	26 40	57	104	27 37	57	104	28 34	57	104	29 31	56	103
70	25 08	+56	103	26 04	+57	102	27 01	+57	102	27 58	+56	102	28 54	+57	101
72	24 31	57	101	25 28	57	100	26 25	56	100	27 21	57	100	28 18	56	99
74	23 55	56	99	24 51	57	99	25 48	57	98	26 45	56	98	27 41	57	97
76	23 18	57	97	24 15	56	97	25 11	57	96	26 08	56	96	27 04	57	95
78	22 41	57	95	23 38	56	95	24 34	57	94	25 31	56	94	26 27	57	94
80	22 04	+57	93	23 01	+56	93	23 57	+57	92	24 54	+56	92	25 50	+57	92
82	21 27	57	91	22 24	56	91	23 20	57	90	24 17	56	90	25 13	57	90
84	20 50	57	89	21 47	56	89	22 43	57	89	23 40	56	88	24 36	57	88
86	20 13	57	87	21 10	56	87	22 06	57	87	23 03	56	86	23 59	57	86
88	19 36	57	86	20 33	56	85	21 29	57	85	22 26	56	84	23 22	57	84
90	18 59	+57	84	19 56	+56	83	20 52	+57	83	21 49	+56	83	22 45	+57	82
92	18 22	57	82	19 19	57	81	20 16	56	81	21 12	57	81	22 09	56	80
94	17 46	56	80	18 42	57	80	19 39	57	79	20 36	56	79	21 32	57	78
96	17 09	57	78	18 06	57	78	19 03	57	77	20 00	56	77	20 56	57	77
98	16 33	57	76	17 30	57	76	18 27	57	75	19 24	56	75	20 20	57	75
100	15 57	+57	74	16 54	+57	74	17 51	+57	74	18 48	+57	73	19 45	+56	73
102	15 22	57	72	16 19	57	72	17 16	57	72	18 13	56	71	19 09	57	71
104	14 47	57	71	15 44	57	70	16 41	57	70	17 38	57	70	18 35	56	69
106	14 12	57	69	15 09	57	68	16 06	57	68	17 03	57	68	18 00	57	67
108	13 37	58	67	14 35	57	67	15 32	57	66	16 29	57	66	17 26	57	66
110	13 04	+57	65	14 01	+57	65	14 58	+57	64	15 55	+58	64	16 53	+57	64
112	12 30	58	63	13 28	57	63	14 25	57	63	15 22	58	62	16 20	57	62
114	11 57	58	61	12 55	57	61	13 52	58	61	14 50	57	60	15 47	57	60
116	11 25	58	60	12 23	57	59	13 20	58	59	14 18	57	59	15 15	58	58
118	10 54	57	58	11 51	58	57	12 49	57	57	13 46	58	57	14 44	58	57
120	10 23	+57	56	11 20	+58	56	12 18	+58	55	13 16	+57	55	14 13	+58	55
122	09 52	58	54	10 50	58	54	11 48	58	53	12 46	57	53	13 43	58	53
124	09 23	58	52	10 21	57	52	11 18	58	52	12 16	58	51	13 14	58	51
126	08 54	58	50	09 52	58	50	10 50	58	50	11 48	58	50	12 46	58	49
128	08 26	58	49	09 24	58	48	10 22	58	48	11 20	58	48	12 18	58	48
130	07 58	+58	47	08 56	+59	46	09 55	+58	46	10 53	+58	46	11 51	+58	46
132	07 32	58	45	08 30	58	45	09 28	59	44	10 27	58	44	11 25	58	44
134	07 06	58	43	08 04	59	43	09 03	58	43	10 01	59	42	11 00	58	42
136	06 41	59	41	07 40	58	41	08 38	59	41	09 37	58	40	10 35	59	40
138	06 17	59	39	07 16	59	39	08 15	58	39	09 13	59	39	10 12	59	38

LHA	25° Hc	d	Z	26° Hc	d	Z	27° Hc	d	Z	28° Hc	d	Z	29° Hc	d	Z	LHA
	° ′	′	°	° ′	′	°	° ′	′	°	° ′	′	°	° ′	′	°	
0	43 00	+60	180	44 00	+60	180	45 00	+60	180	46 00	+60	180	47 00	+60	180	360
2	42 59	60	178	43 59	60	178	44 59	60	178	45 59	60	178	46 59	60	177	358
4	42 57	60	175	43 57	60	175	44 57	60	175	45 57	60	175	46 57	60	175	356
6	42 53	60	173	43 53	60	173	44 53	60	172	45 53	60	172	46 53	60	172	354
8	42 47	60	170	43 47	60	170	44 47	60	170	45 47	60	170	46 47	60	170	352
10	42 40	+60	168	43 40	+60	168	44 40	+60	167	45 40	+59	167	46 39	+60	167	350
12	42 31	60	165	43 31	60	165	44 31	60	165	45 31	59	165	46 30	60	165	348
14	42 21	60	163	43 21	60	163	44 21	59	163	45 20	60	162	46 20	59	162	346
16	42 09	60	160	43 09	60	160	44 09	59	160	45 08	60	160	46 08	59	160	344
18	41 56	60	158	42 56	59	158	43 55	60	158	44 55	59	157	45 54	59	157	342
20	41 41	+60	156	42 41	+59	155	43 40	+60	155	44 40	+59	155	45 39	+59	155	340
22	41 25	60	153	42 25	59	153	43 24	59	153	44 23	59	152	45 22	59	152	338
24	41 08	59	151	42 07	59	151	43 06	59	150	44 05	59	150	45 04	59	150	336
26	40 49	59	148	41 48	59	148	42 47	59	148	43 46	59	148	44 45	59	147	334
28	40 29	59	146	41 28	59	146	42 27	59	146	43 26	58	145	44 24	59	145	332
30	40 08	+58	144	41 06	+59	143	42 05	+59	143	43 04	+58	143	44 02	+59	143	330
32	39 45	59	141	40 44	58	141	41 42	59	141	42 41	58	141	43 39	59	140	328
34	39 21	59	139	40 20	58	139	41 18	59	139	42 17	58	138	43 15	58	138	326
36	38 56	59	137	39 55	58	137	40 53	58	136	41 51	58	136	42 49	59	136	324
38	38 31	58	135	39 29	58	134	40 27	58	134	41 25	58	134	42 23	58	133	322
40	38 04	+58	132	39 02	+58	132	40 00	+58	132	40 58	+57	131	41 55	+58	131	320
42	37 36	58	130	38 34	57	130	39 31	58	129	40 29	58	129	41 27	58	129	318
44	37 07	58	128	38 05	57	128	39 02	58	127	40 00	57	127	40 57	58	126	316
46	36 37	58	126	37 35	57	125	38 32	58	125	39 30	57	125	40 27	58	124	314
48	36 07	57	124	37 04	58	123	38 02	57	123	38 59	57	122	39 56	57	122	312
50	35 35	+58	121	36 33	+57	121	37 30	+57	121	38 27	+57	120	39 24	+57	120	310
52	35 03	58	119	36 01	57	119	36 58	57	119	37 55	57	118	38 52	57	118	308
54	34 31	57	117	35 28	57	117	36 25	57	116	37 22	57	116	38 19	57	116	306
56	33 57	57	115	34 54	57	115	35 51	57	114	36 48	57	114	37 45	57	114	304
58	33 23	57	113	34 20	57	113	35 17	57	112	36 14	57	112	37 11	56	111	302
60	32 49	+57	111	33 46	+57	111	34 43	+56	110	35 39	+57	110	36 36	+57	109	300
62	32 14	57	109	33 11	57	109	34 08	56	108	35 04	57	108	36 01	56	107	298
64	31 39	57	107	32 36	56	107	33 32	57	106	34 29	56	106	35 25	57	105	296
66	31 03	57	105	32 00	56	105	32 56	57	104	33 53	56	104	34 49	57	103	294
68	30 27	57	103	31 24	56	103	32 20	57	102	33 17	56	102	34 13	56	101	292
70	29 51	+57	101	30 48	+56	101	31 44	+56	100	32 40	+57	100	33 37	+56	99	290
72	29 14	57	99	30 11	56	99	31 07	57	98	32 04	56	98	33 00	56	97	288
74	28 38	56	97	29 34	57	97	30 31	56	96	31 27	56	96	32 23	56	95	286
76	28 01	56	95	28 57	57	95	29 54	56	94	30 50	56	94	31 46	56	94	284
78	27 24	56	93	28 20	57	93	29 17	56	92	30 13	56	92	31 09	56	92	282
80	26 47	+56	91	27 43	+57	91	28 40	+56	90	29 36	+56	90	30 32	+56	90	280
82	26 10	56	89	27 06	56	89	28 02	57	89	28 59	56	88	29 55	56	88	278
84	25 33	56	87	26 29	56	87	27 25	57	87	28 22	56	86	29 18	56	86	276
86	24 56	56	86	25 52	56	85	26 48	57	85	27 45	56	84	28 41	56	84	274
88	24 19	56	84	25 15	57	83	26 12	56	83	27 08	56	83	28 04	56	82	272
90	23 42	+56	82	24 38	+57	81	25 35	+56	81	26 31	+56	81	27 27	+57	80	270
92	23 05	57	80	24 02	56	80	24 58	57	79	25 55	56	79	26 51	56	78	268
94	22 29	57	78	23 26	56	78	24 22	56	77	25 18	57	77	26 15	56	77	266
96	21 53	56	76	22 49	57	76	23 46	56	76	24 42	57	75	25 39	56	75	264
98	21 17	57	74	22 14	56	74	23 10	57	74	24 07	56	73	25 03	57	73	262
100	20 41	+57	73	21 38	+57	72	22 35	+56	72	23 31	+57	72	24 28	+57	71	260
102	20 06	57	71	21 03	57	70	22 00	56	70	22 56	57	70	23 53	57	69	258
104	19 31	57	69	20 28	57	69	21 25	57	68	22 22	57	68	23 19	56	68	256
106	18 57	57	67	19 54	57	67	20 51	57	66	21 48	57	66	22 45	56	66	254
108	18 23	57	65	19 20	57	65	20 17	57	65	21 14	57	64	22 11	57	64	252
110	17 50	+57	64	18 47	+57	63	19 44	+57	63	20 41	+57	63	21 38	+57	62	250
112	17 17	57	62	18 14	57	61	19 11	57	61	20 08	57	61	21 05	58	60	248
114	16 44	58	60	17 42	57	60	18 39	57	59	19 36	58	59	20 34	57	59	246
116	16 13	57	58	17 10	57	58	18 07	58	57	19 05	57	57	20 02	57	57	244
118	15 42	57	56	16 39	58	56	17 37	57	56	18 34	57	55	19 31	58	55	242
120	15 11	+58	54	16 09	+57	54	17 06	+58	54	18 04	+57	54	19 01	+58	53	240
122	14 41	58	53	15 39	58	52	16 37	57	52	17 34	58	52	18 32	58	52	238
124	14 12	58	51	15 10	58	51	16 08	58	50	17 06	57	50	18 03	58	50	236
126	13 44	58	49	14 42	58	49	15 40	58	49	16 38	58	48	17 36	57	48	234
128	13 16	58	47	14 14	58	47	15 12	58	47	16 10	58	46	17 08	58	46	232
130	12 49	+59	45	13 48	+58	45	14 46	+58	45	15 44	+58	45	16 42	+58	44	230
132	12 23	59	44	13 22	58	43	14 20	58	43	15 18	58	43	16 16	59	43	228
134	11 58	59	42	12 57	58	42	13 55	58	41	14 53	59	41	15 52	58	41	226
136	11 34	58	40	12 32	59	40	13 31	59	40	14 30	58	39	15 28	58	39	224
138	11 11	58	38	12 09	59	38	13 08	58	38	14 06	59	38	15 05	59	37	222

S. Lat. {LHA greater than 180°........ Zn=180−Z
{LHA less than 180°............ Zn=180+Z

DECLINATION (15°-29°) SAME NAME AS LATITUDE

N. Lat. {LHA greater than 180°....... Zn=Z; LHA less than 180°........... Zn=360−Z}

DECLINATION (15°-29°) SAME NAME AS LATITUDE

LHA	15° Hc	d	Z	16° Hc	d	Z	17° Hc	d	Z	18° Hc	d	Z	19° Hc	d	Z	20° Hc	d	Z	21° Hc	d	Z	22° Hc	d	Z
	° ′	′	°	° ′	′	°	° ′	′	°	° ′	′	°	° ′	′	°	° ′	′	°	° ′	′	°	° ′	′	°
140	01 00	+59	38	01 59	+59	38	02 58	+59	38	03 57	+58	38	04 55	+59	38	05 54	+59	37	06 53	+59	37	07 52	+59	37
142	00 38	58	36	01 36	59	36	02 35	59	36	03 34	59	36	04 33	59	36	05 32	59	36	06 31	59	35	07 30	59	35
144	00 16	59	35	01 15	59	34	02 14	59	34	03 13	59	34	04 12	59	34	05 11	59	34	06 10	59	34	07 09	59	33
146	−0 04	59	33	00 55	59	33	01 54	59	32	02 53	59	32	03 52	59	32	04 51	59	32	05 50	59	32	06 49	59	32
148	−0 24	59	31	00 35	59	31	01 34	60	30	02 34	59	30	03 33	59	30	04 32	59	30	05 31	59	30	06 30	60	30
150	−0 42	+59	29	00 17	+59	29	01 16	+59	29	02 15	+60	28	03 15	+59	28	04 14	+59	28	05 13	+60	28	06 13	+59	28
152	−1 00	60	27	00 00	59	27	00 59	59	27	01 58	60	26	02 58	59	26	03 57	59	26	04 56	60	26	05 56	59	26
154	−1 16	59	25	−0 17	60	25	00 43	59	25	01 42	60	25	02 42	59	24	03 41	60	24	04 41	59	24	05 40	60	24
156	−1 31	59	23	−0 32	60	23	00 28	59	23	01 27	60	23	02 27	59	23	03 26	60	23	04 26	59	22	05 25	60	22
158	−1 45	59	21	−0 46	60	21	00 14	60	21	01 14	59	21	02 13	60	21	03 13	59	21	04 12	60	21	05 12	60	20
160	−1 58	+60	19	−0 58	+59	19	00 01	+60	19	01 01	+60	19	02 01	+59	19	03 00	+60	19	04 00	+60	19	05 00	+59	19
162	−2 10	60	17	−1 10	60	17	−0 10	59	17	00 49	60	17	01 49	60	17	02 49	60	17	03 49	59	17	04 48	60	17
164	−2 20	60	16	−1 20	59	15	−0 21	60	15	00 39	60	15	01 39	60	15	02 39	59	15	03 38	60	15	04 38	60	15
166	−2 30	60	14	−1 30	60	14	−0 30	60	13	00 30	60	13	01 30	60	13	02 30	60	13	03 30	59	13	04 29	60	13
168	−2 38	60	12	−1 38	60	12	−0 38	60	11	00 22	60	11	01 22	60	11	02 22	60	11	03 22	60	11	04 22	60	11
170	−2 44	+60	10	−1 44	+59	10	−0 45	+60	10	00 15	+60	10	01 15	+60	10	02 15	+60	9	03 15	+60	9	04 15	+60	9
172	−2 50	60	8	−1 50	60	8	−0 50	60	8	00 10	60	8	01 10	60	8	02 10	60	8	03 10	60	8	04 10	60	7
174	−2 54	60	6	−1 54	60	6	−0 54	60	6	00 06	60	6	01 06	60	6	02 06	59	6	03 05	60	6	04 05	60	6
176	−2 58	60	4	−1 58	60	4	−0 58	60	4	00 02	60	4	01 02	60	4	02 02	60	4	03 02	60	4	04 02	60	4
178	−2 59	60	2	−1 59	60	2	−0 59	60	2	00 01	60	2	01 01	60	2	02 01	60	2	03 01	60	2	04 01	60	2
180	−3 00	+60	0	−2 00	+60	0	−1 00	+60	0	00 00	+60	0	01 00	+60	0	02 00	+60	0	03 00	+60	0	04 00	+60	0

LHA	23° Hc	d	Z	24° Hc	d	Z	25° Hc	d	Z	26° Hc	d	Z	27° Hc	d	Z	28° Hc	d	Z	29° Hc	d	Z	LHA
	° ′	′	°	° ′	′	°	° ′	′	°	° ′	′	°	° ′	′	°	° ′	′	°	° ′	′	°	
140	08 51	+58	37	09 49	+59	37	10 48	+59	36	11 47	+59	36	12 46	+58	36	13 44	+59	36	14 43	+59	36	220
142	08 29	59	35	09 28	59	35	10 27	58	35	11 25	59	34	12 24	59	34	13 23	59	34	14 22	59	34	218
144	08 08	59	33	09 07	59	33	10 06	59	33	11 05	59	33	12 04	59	32	13 03	59	32	14 02	59	32	216
146	07 48	59	31	08 47	59	31	09 46	60	31	10 46	59	31	11 45	59	31	12 44	59	30	13 43	59	30	214
148	07 30	59	30	08 29	59	29	09 28	59	29	10 27	59	29	11 26	59	29	12 25	60	29	13 25	59	29	212
150	07 12	+59	28	08 11	+59	28	09 10	+60	27	10 10	+59	27	11 09	+59	27	12 08	+59	27	13 07	+60	27	210
152	06 55	59	26	07 54	60	26	08 54	59	26	09 53	60	25	10 53	59	25	11 52	59	25	12 51	60	25	208
154	06 40	59	24	07 39	59	24	08 38	60	24	09 38	59	24	10 37	60	23	11 37	59	23	12 36	60	23	206
156	06 25	60	22	07 25	59	22	08 24	60	22	09 24	59	22	10 23	60	22	11 23	59	22	12 22	60	21	204
158	06 12	59	20	07 11	60	20	08 11	59	20	09 10	60	20	10 10	60	20	11 10	59	20	12 09	60	20	202
160	05 59	+60	19	06 59	+60	18	07 59	+59	18	08 58	+60	18	09 58	+60	18	10 58	+59	18	11 57	+60	18	200
162	05 48	60	17	06 48	60	17	07 48	59	16	08 47	60	16	09 47	60	16	10 47	59	16	11 46	60	16	198
164	05 38	60	15	06 38	60	15	07 38	59	15	08 37	60	15	09 37	60	14	10 37	60	14	11 37	60	14	196
166	05 29	60	13	06 29	60	13	07 29	60	13	08 29	60	13	09 29	59	13	10 28	60	13	11 28	60	13	194
168	05 22	59	11	06 21	60	11	07 21	60	11	08 21	60	11	09 21	60	11	10 21	60	11	11 21	60	11	192
170	05 15	+60	9	06 15	+60	9	07 15	+60	9	08 15	+60	9	09 15	+60	9	10 15	+59	9	11 14	+60	9	190
172	05 10	60	7	06 10	59	7	07 09	60	7	08 09	60	7	09 09	60	7	10 09	60	7	11 09	60	7	188
174	05 05	60	6	06 05	60	6	07 05	60	6	08 05	60	5	09 05	60	5	10 05	60	5	11 05	60	5	186
176	05 02	60	4	06 02	60	4	07 02	60	4	08 02	60	4	09 02	60	4	10 02	60	4	11 02	60	4	184
178	05 01	60	2	06 01	60	2	07 01	60	2	08 01	60	2	09 01	60	2	10 01	60	2	11 01	60	2	182
180	05 00	+60	0	06 00	+60	0	07 00	+60	0	08 00	+60	0	09 00	+60	0	10 00	+60	0	11 00	+60	0	180

DECLINATION (15°-29°) CONTRARY NAME TO LATITUDE

LHA	15° Hc	d	Z	16° Hc	d	Z	17° Hc	d	Z	18° Hc	d	Z	19° Hc	d	Z	20° Hc	d	Z
68	−7 43	58	115															
66	−7 10	58	117															
64	−6 37	58	119	−7 35	58	119												
62	−6 05	58	121	−7 03	58	121	−8 01	57	121									
60	−5 34	−58	123	−6 32	−57	123	−7 29	−58	123									
58	−5 03	58	125	−6 01	58	125	−6 59	58	125	−7 57	57	125						
56	−4 33	58	127	−5 31	58	127	−6 29	58	127	−7 27	58	127						
54	−4 03	58	128	−5 01	58	129	−5 59	59	129	−6 58	58	129						
52	−3 35	58	130	−4 33	58	130	−5 31	58	131	−6 29	58	131	−7 27	59	131			
50	−3 07	−58	132	−4 05	−58	132	−5 03	−59	133	−6 02	−58	133	−7 00	−58	133			
48	−2 40	58	134	−3 38	58	134	−4 36	59	134	−5 35	58	135	−6 33	59	135	−7 32	58	135
46	−2 13	59	136	−3 12	58	136	−4 10	59	136	−5 09	58	137	−6 07	59	137	−7 06	58	137
44	−1 48	59	138	−2 47	58	138	−3 45	59	138	−4 44	59	138	−5 43	58	139	−6 41	59	139
42	−1 24	58	140	−2 22	59	140	−3 21	59	140	−4 20	58	140	−5 18	59	140	−6 17	59	141
40	−1 00	−59	142	−1 59	−59	142	−2 58	−59	142	−3 57	−58	142	−4 55	−59	142	−5 54	−59	143
38	−0 38	58	144	−1 36	59	144	−2 35	59	144	−3 34	59	144	−4 33	59	144	−5 32	59	144
36	−0 16	59	145	−1 15	59	146	−2 14	59	146	−3 13	59	146	−4 12	59	146	−5 11	59	146
34	00 04	59	147	−0 55	59	147	−1 54	59	148	−2 53	59	148	−3 52	59	148	−4 51	59	148
32	00 24	59	149	−0 35	59	149	−1 34	60	150	−2 34	59	150	−3 33	59	150	−4 32	59	150
30	00 42	−59	151	−0 17	−59	151	−1 16	−59	151	−2 15	−60	152	−3 15	−59	152	−4 14	−59	152
28	01 00	60	153	00 00	59	153	−0 59	59	153	−1 58	60	154	−2 58	59	154	−3 57	59	154
26	01 16	59	155	00 17	60	155	−0 43	59	155	−1 42	60	155	−2 42	59	156	−3 41	60	156
24	01 31	59	157	00 32	60	157	−0 28	59	157	−1 27	60	157	−2 27	59	157	−3 26	60	157
22	01 45	59	159	00 46	60	159	−0 14	60	159	−1 14	59	159	−2 13	60	159	−3 13	59	159
20	01 58	−60	161	00 58	−59	161	−0 01	−60	161	−1 01	−60	161	−2 01	−59	161	−3 00	−60	161
18	02 10	60	163	01 10	60	163	00 10	59	163	−0 49	60	163	−1 49	60	163	−2 49	60	163
16	02 20	60	164	01 20	59	165	00 21	60	165	−0 39	60	165	−1 39	60	165	−2 39	59	165
14	02 30	60	166	01 30	60	166	00 30	60	167	−0 30	60	167	−1 30	60	167	−2 30	60	167
12	02 38	60	168	01 38	60	168	00 38	60	169	−0 22	60	169	−1 22	60	169	−2 22	60	169
10	02 44	−60	170	01 44	−59	170	00 45	−60	170	−0 15	−60	170	−1 15	−60	170	−2 15	−60	171
8	02 50	60	172	01 50	60	172	00 50	60	172	−0 10	60	172	−1 10	60	172	−2 10	60	172
6	02 54	60	174	01 54	60	174	00 54	60	174	−0 06	60	174	−1 06	60	174	−2 06	59	174
4	02 58	60	176	01 58	60	176	00 58	60	176	−0 02	60	176	−1 02	60	176	−2 02	60	176
2	02 59	60	178	01 59	60	178	00 59	60	178	−0 01	60	178	−1 01	60	178	−2 01	60	178
0	03 00	−60	180	02 00	−60	180	01 00	−60	180	00 00	−60	180	−1 00	−60	180	−2 00	−60	180

LHA	21° Hc	d	Z	22° Hc	d	Z	23° Hc	d	Z	24° Hc	d	Z	25° Hc	d	Z	26°	27°	28°	29°	LHA
68																				292
66																				294
64																				296
62																				298
60																				300
58																				302
56																				304
54																				306
52																				308
50																				310
48																				312
46																				314
44	−7 40	58	139																	316
42	−7 16	59	141																	318
40	−6 53	−59	143																	320
38	−6 31	59	145	−7 30	59	145														322
36	−6 10	59	146	−7 09	59	147														324
34	−5 50	59	148	−6 49	59	148														326
32	−5 31	59	150	−6 30	60	150	−7 30	59	150											328
30	−5 13	−60	152	−6 13	−59	152	−7 12	−59	152											330
28	−4 56	60	154	−5 56	59	154	−6 55	59	154											332
26	−4 41	59	156	−5 40	60	156	−6 40	59	156											334
24	−4 26	59	158	−5 25	60	158	−6 25	60	158	−7 25	59	158								336
22	−4 12	60	159	−5 12	60	160	−6 12	59	160	−7 11	60	160								338
20	−4 00	−60	161	−5 00	−59	161	−5 59	−60	161	−6 59	−60	162								340
18	−3 49	59	163	−4 48	60	163	−5 48	60	163	−6 48	60	163								342
16	−3 38	60	165	−4 38	60	165	−5 38	60	165	−6 38	60	165								344
14	−3 30	59	167	−4 29	60	167	−5 29	60	167	−6 29	60	167								346
12	−3 22	60	169	−4 22	60	169	−5 22	59	169	−6 21	60	169								348
10	−3 15	−60	171	−4 15	−60	171	−5 15	−60	171	−6 15	−60	171								350
8	−3 10	60	172	−4 10	60	173	−5 10	60	173	−6 10	59	173								352
6	−3 05	60	174	−4 05	60	174	−5 05	60	174	−6 05	60	174								354
4	−3 02	60	176	−4 02	60	176	−5 02	60	176	−6 02	60	176								356
2	−3 01	60	178	−4 01	60	178	−5 01	60	178	−6 01	60	178	−7 01	60	178					358
0	−3 00	−60	180	−4 00	−60	180	−5 00	−60	180	−6 00	−60	180	−7 00	−60	180					360

S. Lat. {LHA greater than 180°....... Zn=180−Z; LHA less than 180°........... Zn=180+Z}

N. Lat. {LHA greater than 180°....... Zn=Z
{LHA less than 180°........... Zn=360−Z

DECLINATION (0°-14°) SAME NAME AS LATITUDE

LHA	0° Hc	d	Z	1° Hc	d	Z	2° Hc	d	Z	3° Hc	d	Z	4° Hc	d	Z
	° ′	′	°	° ′	′	°	° ′	′	°	° ′	′	°	° ′	′	°
0	17 00	+60	180	18 00	+60	180	19 00	+60	180	20 00	+60	180	21 00	+60	180
2	16 59	60	178	17 59	60	178	18 59	60	178	19 59	60	178	20 59	60	178
4	16 57	60	176	17 57	60	176	18 57	60	176	19 57	60	176	20 57	60	176
6	16 54	60	174	17 54	60	174	18 54	60	174	19 54	60	174	20 54	60	174
8	16 50	60	172	17 50	60	172	18 50	60	172	19 50	60	172	20 50	60	172
10	16 44	+60	170	17 44	+60	170	18 44	+60	169	19 44	+60	169	20 44	+60	169
12	16 37	60	168	17 37	60	167	18 37	60	167	19 37	60	167	20 37	59	167
14	16 29	60	165	17 29	60	165	18 29	59	165	19 28	60	165	20 28	60	165
16	16 19	60	163	17 19	60	163	18 19	60	163	19 19	60	163	20 19	59	163
18	16 09	59	161	17 08	60	161	18 08	60	161	19 08	60	161	20 08	59	161
20	15 57	+60	159	16 57	+59	159	17 56	+60	159	18 56	+60	159	19 56	+59	159
22	15 44	59	157	16 43	60	157	17 43	60	157	18 43	59	157	19 42	60	157
24	15 30	59	155	16 29	60	155	17 29	59	155	18 28	60	155	19 28	59	155
26	15 14	60	153	16 14	59	153	17 13	60	153	18 13	59	153	19 12	59	152
28	14 58	59	151	15 57	59	151	16 56	60	151	17 56	59	151	18 55	60	150
30	14 40	+59	149	15 39	+60	149	16 39	+59	149	17 38	+59	148	18 37	+60	148
32	14 21	60	147	15 21	59	147	16 20	59	147	17 19	59	146	18 18	59	146
34	14 02	59	145	15 01	59	145	16 00	59	145	16 59	59	144	17 58	59	144
36	13 41	59	143	14 40	59	143	15 39	59	142	16 38	59	142	17 37	59	142
38	13 19	59	141	14 18	59	141	15 17	59	140	16 16	59	140	17 15	59	140
40	12 57	+58	139	13 55	+59	139	14 54	+59	138	15 53	+59	138	16 52	+59	138
42	12 33	59	137	13 32	59	137	14 31	58	136	15 29	59	136	16 28	59	136
44	12 08	59	135	13 07	59	135	14 06	59	134	15 05	58	134	16 03	59	134
46	11 43	59	133	12 42	58	133	13 40	59	132	14 39	58	132	15 37	59	132
48	11 17	58	131	12 15	59	131	13 14	58	130	14 12	59	130	15 11	58	130
50	10 50	+58	129	11 48	+59	129	12 47	+58	128	13 45	+59	128	14 44	+58	128
52	10 22	59	127	11 21	58	127	12 19	58	126	13 17	58	126	14 15	59	126
54	09 54	58	125	10 52	58	125	11 50	58	124	12 48	59	124	13 47	58	124
56	09 25	58	123	10 23	58	123	11 21	58	122	12 19	58	122	13 17	58	122
58	08 55	58	121	09 53	58	120	10 51	58	120	11 49	58	120	12 47	58	120
60	08 24	+58	119	09 22	+58	119	10 20	+58	118	11 18	+58	118	12 16	+58	118
62	07 53	58	117	08 51	58	117	09 49	58	116	10 47	58	116	11 45	58	116
64	07 22	58	115	08 20	58	115	09 18	57	115	10 15	58	114	11 13	58	114
66	06 50	58	113	07 48	57	113	08 45	58	113	09 43	58	112	10 41	58	112
68	06 17	58	111	07 15	58	111	08 13	57	111	09 10	58	110	10 08	58	110
70	05 44	+58	109	06 42	+58	109	07 40	+57	109	08 37	+58	108	09 35	+58	108
72	05 11	58	107	06 09	57	107	07 06	58	107	08 04	57	106	09 01	58	106
74	04 37	58	105	05 35	58	105	06 33	57	105	07 30	58	105	08 28	57	104
76	04 03	58	103	05 01	57	103	05 58	58	103	06 56	57	103	07 53	58	102
78	03 29	58	102	04 27	57	101	05 24	58	101	06 22	57	101	07 19	57	100
80	02 55	+57	100	03 52	+58	99	04 50	+57	99	05 47	+57	99	06 44	+58	98
82	02 20	57	98	03 17	58	97	04 15	57	97	05 12	58	97	06 10	57	97
84	01 45	57	96	02 42	58	95	03 40	57	95	04 37	58	95	05 35	57	95
86	01 10	58	94	02 08	57	94	03 05	57	93	04 02	58	93	05 00	57	93
88	00 35	57	92	01 32	58	92	02 30	57	91	03 27	58	91	04 25	57	91
90	00 00	+57	90	00 57	+58	90	01 55	+57	89	02 52	+58	89	03 50	+57	89
92	−0 35	57	88	00 22	58	88	01 20	57	88	02 17	57	87	03 14	58	87
94	−1 10	57	86	−0 13	58	86	00 45	57	86	01 42	57	85	02 39	58	85
96	−1 45	57	84	−0 48	58	84	00 10	57	84	01 07	57	83	02 04	58	83
98	−2 20	58	82	−1 22	57	82	−0 25	57	82	00 32	58	81	01 30	57	81
100	−2 55	+58	80	−1 57	+57	80	−1 00	+58	80	−0 02	+57	80	00 55	+58	79
102	−3 29	57	78	−2 32	58	78	−1 34	57	78	−0 37	58	78	00 21	57	77
104	−4 03	57	77	−3 06	58	76	−2 08	57	76	−1 11	58	76	−0 13	57	75
106	−4 37	57	75	−3 40	58	74	−2 42	57	74	−1 45	58	74	−0 47	58	74
108	−5 11	58	73	−4 13	57	72	−3 16	58	72	−2 18	58	72	−1 20	57	72
110	−5 44	+57	71	−4 47	+58	70	−3 49	+58	70	−2 51	+57	70	−1 54	+58	70
112	−6 17	57	69	−5 20	58	69	−4 22	58	68	−3 24	58	68	−2 26	57	68
114	−6 50	58	67	−5 52	58	67	−4 54	58	66	−3 56	57	66	−2 59	58	66
116	−7 22	58	65	−6 24	58	65	−5 26	58	64	−4 28	58	64	−3 30	58	64
118	−7 53	58	63	−6 55	57	63	−5 58	58	62	−5 00	58	62	−4 02	58	62
120				−7 26	+58	61	−6 28	+58	61	−5 30	+58	60	−4 32	+58	60
122				−7 57	58	59	−6 59	58	59	−6 01	59	58	−5 02	58	58
124							−7 28	58	57	−6 30	58	56	−5 32	58	56
126							−7 57	58	55	−6 59	58	54	−6 01	59	54
128										−7 27	58	52	−6 29	59	52
130										−7 55	+59	51	−6 56	+58	50
132													−7 23	59	48
134													−7 49	59	46

LHA	5° Hc	d	Z	6° Hc	d	Z	7° Hc	d	Z	8° Hc	d	Z	9° Hc	d	Z
	° ′	′	°	° ′	′	°	° ′	′	°	° ′	′	°	° ′	′	°
0	22 00	+60	180	23 00	+60	180	24 00	+60	180	25 00	+60	180	26 00	+60	180
2	21 59	60	178	22 59	60	178	23 59	60	178	24 59	60	178	25 59	60	178
4	21 57	60	176	22 57	60	176	23 57	60	176	24 57	60	176	25 57	60	176
6	21 54	60	174	22 54	60	174	23 54	60	174	24 54	60	173	25 54	60	173
8	21 50	59	171	22 49	60	171	23 49	60	171	24 49	60	171	25 49	60	171
10	21 44	+60	169	22 44	+59	169	23 43	+60	169	24 43	+60	169	25 43	+60	169
12	21 36	60	167	22 36	60	167	23 36	60	167	24 36	60	167	25 36	60	167
14	21 28	60	165	22 28	60	165	23 28	59	165	24 27	60	165	25 27	60	165
16	21 18	60	163	22 18	60	163	23 18	60	163	24 18	59	163	25 17	60	163
18	21 07	60	161	22 07	60	161	23 07	59	161	24 06	60	160	25 06	60	160
20	20 55	+60	159	21 55	+59	159	22 54	+60	158	23 54	+60	158	24 54	+59	158
22	20 42	59	157	21 41	60	156	22 41	60	156	23 41	59	156	24 40	60	156
24	20 27	60	154	21 27	59	154	22 26	60	154	23 26	59	154	24 25	60	154
26	20 11	60	152	21 11	59	152	22 10	60	152	23 10	59	152	24 09	60	152
28	19 55	59	150	20 54	59	150	21 53	60	150	22 53	59	150	23 52	59	150
30	19 37	+59	148	20 36	+59	148	21 35	+59	148	22 34	+60	148	23 34	+59	147
32	19 17	60	146	20 17	59	146	21 16	59	146	22 15	59	146	23 14	59	145
34	18 57	59	144	19 56	59	144	20 55	60	144	21 55	59	143	22 54	59	143
36	18 36	59	142	19 35	59	142	20 34	59	142	21 33	59	141	22 32	59	141
38	18 14	59	140	19 13	59	140	20 12	59	139	21 11	59	139	22 10	59	139
40	17 51	+59	138	18 50	+58	138	19 48	+59	137	20 47	+59	137	21 46	+59	137
42	17 27	58	136	18 25	59	136	19 24	59	135	20 23	59	135	21 22	58	135
44	17 02	58	134	18 00	59	133	18 59	59	133	19 58	58	133	20 56	59	133
46	16 36	59	132	17 35	58	131	18 33	59	131	19 32	58	131	20 30	58	131
48	16 09	59	130	17 08	58	129	18 06	59	129	19 05	58	129	20 03	58	129
50	15 42	+58	128	16 40	+59	127	17 39	+58	127	18 37	+58	127	19 35	+58	127
52	15 14	58	126	16 12	58	125	17 10	58	125	18 08	59	125	19 07	58	125
54	14 45	58	124	15 43	58	123	16 41	58	123	17 39	58	123	18 37	59	123
56	14 15	58	122	15 13	58	121	16 11	58	121	17 09	59	121	18 08	58	121
58	13 45	58	120	14 43	58	119	15 41	58	119	16 39	58	119	17 37	58	119
60	13 14	+58	118	14 12	+58	117	15 10	+58	117	16 08	+58	117	17 06	+58	117
62	12 43	58	116	13 41	58	115	14 39	57	115	15 36	58	115	16 34	58	115
64	12 11	58	114	13 09	58	113	14 07	57	113	15 04	58	113	16 02	58	113
66	11 39	57	112	12 36	58	111	13 34	58	111	14 32	57	111	15 29	58	111
68	11 06	57	110	12 03	58	110	13 01	58	109	13 59	57	109	14 56	58	109
70	10 33	+57	108	11 30	+58	108	12 28	+57	107	13 25	+58	107	14 23	+57	107
72	09 59	58	106	10 57	57	106	11 54	58	105	12 52	57	105	13 49	58	105
74	09 25	58	104	10 23	57	104	11 20	58	103	12 18	57	103	13 15	57	103
76	08 51	57	102	09 48	58	102	10 46	57	101	11 43	58	101	12 41	57	101
78	08 16	58	100	09 14	57	100	10 11	58	100	11 09	57	99	12 06	57	99
80	07 42	+57	98	08 39	+58	98	09 37	+57	98	10 34	+57	97	11 31	+58	97
82	07 07	57	96	08 04	58	96	09 02	57	96	09 59	57	95	10 56	58	95
84	06 32	57	94	07 29	58	94	08 27	57	94	09 24	57	93	10 21	58	93
86	05 57	57	92	06 54	58	92	07 52	57	92	08 49	57	92	09 46	58	91
88	05 22	57	90	06 19	58	90	07 17	57	90	08 14	57	90	09 11	58	89
90	04 47	+57	88	05 44	+58	88	06 42	+57	88	07 39	+57	87	08 36	+58	87
92	04 12	57	87	05 09	58	86	06 07	57	86	07 04	57	86	08 01	58	85
94	03 37	57	85	04 34	58	84	05 32	57	84	06 29	57	84	07 26	58	84
96	03 02	57	83	03 59	58	82	04 57	57	82	05 54	58	82	06 52	57	81
98	02 27	58	81	03 25	57	81	04 22	58	80	05 20	57	80	06 17	57	80
100	01 53	+57	79	02 50	+58	79	03 48	+57	78	04 45	+58	78	05 43	+57	78
102	01 18	58	77	02 16	57	77	03 13	58	76	04 11	57	76	05 08	58	76
104	00 44	58	75	01 42	57	75	02 39	58	75	03 37	57	74	04 34	58	74
106	00 11	57	73	01 08	58	73	02 06	57	73	03 03	58	72	04 01	57	72
108	−0 23	58	71	00 35	57	71	01 32	58	71	02 30	58	70	03 28	57	70
110	−0 56	+58	69	00 02	+57	69	00 59	+58	69	01 57	+58	69	02 55	+57	68
112	−1 29	58	67	−0 31	58	67	00 27	58	67	01 25	57	67	02 22	58	66
114	−2 01	58	66	−1 03	58	65	−0 05	58	65	00 53	57	65	01 50	58	64
116	−2 32	57	64	−1 35	58	63	−0 37	58	63	00 21	58	63	01 19	58	63
118	−3 04	58	62	−2 06	58	62	−1 08	58	61	−0 10	58	61	00 48	58	61
120	−3 34	+58	60	−2 36	+58	60	−1 38	+58	59	−0 40	+58	59	00 18	+58	59
122	−4 04	58	58	−3 06	58	58	−2 08	58	57	−1 10	58	57	−0 12	58	57
124	−4 34	58	56	−3 36	59	56	−2 37	58	56	−1 39	58	55	−0 41	58	55
126	−5 02	58	54	−4 04	58	54	−3 06	58	54	−2 08	59	53	−1 09	58	53
128	−5 30	58	52	−4 32	58	52	−3 34	59	52	−2 35	58	51	−1 37	58	51
130	−5 58	+59	50	−4 59	+58	50	−4 01	+59	50	−3 02	+58	49	−2 04	+59	49
132	−6 24	58	48	−5 26	59	48	−4 27	58	48	−3 29	59	47	−2 30	58	47
134	−6 50	59	46	−5 51	58	46	−4 53	59	46	−3 54	59	46	−2 55	58	45
136	−7 15	59	44	−6 16	59	44	−5 17	58	44	−4 19	59	44	−3 20	59	43
138	−7 39	59	42	−6 40	59	42	−5 41	59	42	−4 42	58	42	−3 44	59	42

10° Hc	d	Z	11° Hc	d	Z	12° Hc	d	Z	13° Hc	d	Z	14° Hc	d	Z	LHA
° ′	′	°	° ′	′	°	° ′	′	°	° ′	′	°	° ′	′	°	
27 00	+60	180	28 00	+60	180	29 00	+60	180	30 00	+60	180	31 00	+60	180	360
26 59	60	178	27 59	60	178	28 59	60	178	29 59	60	178	30 59	60	178	358
26 57	60	176	27 57	60	176	28 57	60	176	29 57	60	176	30 57	60	176	356
26 54	60	173	27 54	60	173	28 54	60	173	29 54	60	173	30 54	60	173	354
26 49	60	171	27 49	60	171	28 49	60	171	29 49	60	171	30 49	60	171	352
26 43	+60	169	27 43	+60	169	28 43	+60	169	29 43	+60	169	30 43	+60	169	350
26 36	60	167	27 36	60	167	28 36	59	167	29 35	60	167	30 35	60	166	348
26 27	60	165	27 27	60	165	28 27	60	164	29 27	59	164	30 26	60	164	346
26 17	60	162	27 17	60	162	28 17	59	162	29 16	60	162	30 16	60	162	344
26 06	60	160	27 06	59	160	28 05	60	160	29 05	60	160	30 05	59	160	342
25 53	+60	158	26 53	+60	158	27 53	+59	158	28 52	+60	158	29 52	+59	158	340
25 40	59	156	26 39	60	156	27 39	59	156	28 38	60	155	29 38	59	155	338
25 25	59	154	26 24	60	154	27 24	59	153	28 23	60	153	29 23	59	153	336
25 09	59	152	26 08	59	151	27 07	60	151	28 07	59	151	29 06	59	151	334
24 51	60	149	25 51	59	149	26 50	59	149	27 49	59	149	28 48	60	149	332
24 33	+59	147	25 32	+59	147	26 31	+59	147	27 30	+60	147	28 30	+59	147	330
24 13	59	145	25 12	59	145	26 11	60	145	27 11	59	145	28 10	59	144	328
23 53	59	143	24 52	59	143	25 51	59	143	26 50	59	142	27 49	59	142	326
23 31	59	141	24 30	59	141	25 29	59	140	26 28	59	140	27 27	58	140	324
23 08	59	139	24 07	59	139	25 06	59	138	26 05	59	138	27 04	58	138	322
22 45	+58	137	23 43	+59	136	24 42	+59	136	25 41	+59	136	26 40	+58	136	320
22 20	59	135	23 19	58	134	24 17	59	134	25 16	59	134	26 15	58	134	318
21 55	58	133	22 53	59	132	23 52	58	132	24 50	59	132	25 49	58	132	316
21 28	59	130	22 27	58	130	23 25	59	130	24 24	58	130	25 22	58	129	314
21 01	59	128	22 00	58	128	22 58	58	128	23 56	59	128	24 55	58	127	312
20 33	+59	126	21 32	+58	126	22 30	+58	126	23 28	+58	126	24 26	+58	125	310
20 05	58	124	21 03	58	124	22 01	58	124	22 59	58	124	23 57	58	123	308
19 36	58	122	20 34	58	122	21 32	58	122	22 30	58	121	23 28	58	121	306
19 06	57	120	20 03	58	120	21 01	58	120	21 59	58	119	22 57	58	119	304
18 35	58	118	19 33	58	118	20 31	58	118	21 29	57	117	22 26	58	117	302
18 04	+58	116	19 02	+57	116	19 59	+58	116	20 57	+58	115	21 55	+58	115	300
17 32	58	114	18 30	57	114	19 27	58	114	20 25	58	113	21 23	57	113	298
17 00	57	112	17 57	58	112	18 55	58	112	19 53	57	111	20 50	58	111	296
16 27	58	110	17 25	57	110	18 22	58	110	19 20	57	109	20 17	58	109	294
15 54	57	108	16 51	58	108	17 49	58	108	18 47	57	107	19 44	57	107	292
15 20	+58	106	16 18	+57	106	17 15	+58	106	18 13	+57	105	19 10	+58	105	290
14 47	57	104	15 44	57	104	16 41	58	104	17 39	57	104	18 36	58	103	288
14 12	58	102	15 10	57	102	16 07	58	102	17 05	57	102	18 02	57	101	286
13 38	57	101	14 35	58	100	15 33	57	100	16 30	57	100	17 27	58	99	284
13 03	58	99	14 01	57	98	14 58	57	98	15 55	58	98	16 53	57	97	282
12 29	+57	97	13 26	+57	96	14 23	+58	96	15 21	+57	96	16 18	+57	95	280
11 54	57	95	12 51	57	94	13 48	58	94	14 46	57	94	15 43	57	94	278
11 19	57	93	12 16	57	93	13 13	58	92	14 11	57	92	15 08	57	92	276
10 44	57	91	11 41	57	91	12 38	58	90	13 36	57	90	14 33	57	90	274
10 09	57	89	11 06	57	89	12 03	57	88	13 00	58	88	13 58	57	88	272
09 34	+57	87	10 31	+57	87	11 28	+57	86	12 25	+58	86	13 23	+57	86	270
08 59	57	85	09 56	57	85	10 53	57	85	11 50	58	84	12 48	57	84	268
08 24	57	83	09 21	57	83	10 18	58	83	11 16	57	82	12 13	57	82	266
07 49	57	81	08 46	58	81	09 44	57	81	10 41	57	80	11 38	58	80	264
07 14	58	79	08 12	57	79	09 09	57	79	10 06	58	79	11 04	57	78	262
06 40	+57	78	07 37	+58	77	08 35	+57	77	09 32	+58	77	10 30	+57	76	260
06 06	57	76	07 03	58	75	08 01	57	75	08 58	58	75	09 56	57	75	258
05 32	57	74	06 29	58	74	07 27	57	73	08 24	58	73	09 22	57	73	256
04 58	57	72	05 56	58	72	06 54	57	71	07 51	58	71	08 49	57	71	254
04 25	58	70	05 23	58	70	06 21	57	69	07 18	58	69	08 16	57	69	252
03 52	+58	68	04 50	+58	68	05 48	+58	68	06 46	+57	67	07 43	+58	67	250
03 20	58	66	04 18	58	66	05 16	57	66	06 13	58	65	07 11	58	65	248
02 48	58	64	03 46	58	64	04 44	58	64	05 42	58	64	06 40	57	63	246
02 17	58	62	03 15	58	62	04 13	58	62	05 11	58	62	06 09	57	61	244
01 46	58	60	02 44	58	60	03 42	58	60	04 40	58	60	05 38	58	59	242
01 16	+58	59	02 14	+58	58	03 12	+58	58	04 10	+58	58	05 08	+58	58	240
00 46	58	57	01 44	59	56	02 43	58	56	03 41	58	56	04 39	58	56	238
00 17	59	55	01 16	58	54	02 14	58	54	03 12	58	54	04 10	58	54	236
−0 11	58	53	00 47	59	53	01 46	58	52	02 44	58	52	03 42	58	52	234
−0 39	59	51	00 20	58	51	01 18	59	50	02 17	58	50	03 15	58	50	232
−1 05	+58	49	−0 07	+59	49	00 52	+58	49	01 50	+58	48	02 48	+59	48	230
−1 32	59	47	−0 33	59	47	00 26	58	47	01 24	59	46	02 23	58	46	228
−1 57	59	45	−0 58	59	45	00 01	58	45	00 59	59	45	01 58	59	44	226
−2 21	59	43	−1 22	58	43	−0 24	59	43	00 35	59	43	01 34	59	42	224
−2 45	59	41	−1 46	59	41	−0 47	59	41	00 12	59	41	01 11	58	40	222

S. Lat. {LHA greater than 180°....... Zn=180−Z
{LHA less than 180°........... Zn=180+Z

DECLINATION (0°-14°) SAME NAME AS LATITUDE

N. Lat. {LHA greater than 180°……. Zn=Z; LHA less than 180°……….. Zn=360−Z}

DECLINATION (0°-14°) SAME NAME AS LATITUDE

LHA	0° Hc	0° d	0° Z	1° Hc	1° d	1° Z	2° Hc	2° d	2° Z	3° Hc	3° d	3° Z	4° Hc	4° d	4° Z	5° Hc	5° d	5° Z	6° Hc	6° d	6° Z	7° Hc	7° d	7° Z	8° Hc	8° d	8° Z	9° Hc	9° d	9° Z	10° Hc	10° d	10° Z	11° Hc	11° d	11° Z	12° Hc	12° d	12° Z	13° Hc	13° d	13° Z	14° Hc	14° d	14° Z	LHA
	° ′	′	°	° ′	′	°	° ′	′	°	° ′	′	°	° ′	′	°	° ′	′	°	° ′	′	°	° ′	′	°	° ′	′	°	° ′	′	°	° ′	′	°	° ′	′	°	° ′	′	°	° ′	′	°	° ′	′	°	
140																			-7 03	+59	40	-6 04	+59	40	-5 05	+59	40	-4 06	+58	40	-3 08	+59	39	-2 09	+59	39	-1 10	+59	39	-0 11	+59	39	00 48	+59	39	220
142																			-7 25	59	38	-6 26	59	38	-5 27	59	38	-4 28	59	38	-3 29	59	37	-2 30	59	37	-1 31	59	37	-0 32	59	37	00 27	59	37	218
144																						-6 47	59	36	-5 48	59	36	-4 49	59	36	-3 50	59	36	-2 51	59	35	-1 52	59	35	-0 53	59	35	00 06	59	35	216
146																						-7 08	60	34	-6 08	59	34	-5 09	59	34	-4 10	59	34	-3 11	59	33	-2 12	60	33	-1 12	59	33	-0 13	59	33	214
148																						-7 27	60	32	-6 27	59	32	-5 28	59	32	-4 29	59	32	-3 30	60	31	-2 30	59	31	-1 31	59	31	-0 32	60	31	212
150																									-6 45	+59	30	-5 46	+59	30	-4 47	+60	30	-3 47	+59	30	-2 48	+59	29	-1 49	+60	29	-0 49	+59	29	210
152																									-7 02	59	28	-6 03	59	28	-5 04	60	28	-4 04	59	28	-3 05	60	27	-2 05	59	27	-1 06	60	27	208
154																									-7 18	59	26	-6 19	60	26	-5 19	59	26	-4 20	60	26	-3 20	59	26	-2 21	60	25	-1 21	59	25	206
156																												-6 34	60	24	-5 34	60	24	-4 34	59	24	-3 35	60	24	-2 35	59	23	-1 36	60	23	204
158																												-6 47	59	22	-5 48	60	22	-4 48	60	22	-3 48	59	22	-2 49	60	21	-1 49	60	21	202
160																												-7 00	+60	20	-6 00	+60	20	-5 00	+60	20	-4 00	+59	20	-3 01	+60	20	-2 01	+60	19	200
162																												-7 11	60	18	-6 11	59	18	-5 12	60	18	-4 12	60	18	-3 12	60	18	-2 12	60	18	198
164																															-6 21	59	16	-5 22	60	16	-4 22	60	16	-3 22	60	16	-2 22	60	16	196
166																															-6 30	59	14	-5 31	60	14	-4 31	60	14	-3 31	60	14	-2 31	60	14	194
168																															-6 38	60	12	-5 38	60	12	-4 38	59	12	-3 39	60	12	-2 39	60	12	192
170																															-6 45	+60	10	-5 45	+60	10	-4 45	+60	10	-3 45	+60	10	-2 45	+60	10	190
172																															-6 50	60	8	-5 50	60	8	-4 50	60	8	-3 50	60	8	-2 50	59	8	188
174																															-6 55	60	6	-5 55	60	6	-4 55	60	6	-3 55	60	6	-2 55	60	6	186
176																															-6 58	60	4	-5 58	60	4	-4 58	60	4	-3 58	60	4	-2 58	60	4	184
178																															-6 59	60	2	-5 59	60	2	-4 59	60	2	-3 59	60	2	-2 59	60	2	182
180																															-7 00	+60	0	-6 00	+60	0	-5 00	+60	0	-4 00	+60	0	-3 00	+60	0	180
118	-7 53	58	63																																											242
116	-7 22	58	65																																											244
114	-6 50	58	67	-7 48	57	67																																								246
112	-6 17	58	69	-7 15	58	69																																								248
110	-5 44	-58	71	-6 42	-58	71	-7 40	-57	71																																					250
108	-5 11	58	73	-6 09	57	73	-7 06	58	73	-8 04	57	74																																		252
106	-4 37	58	75	-5 35	58	75	-6 33	57	75	-7 30	58	75																																		254
104	-4 03	58	77	-5 01	57	77	-5 58	58	77	-6 56	57	77	-7 53	58	78																															256
102	-3 29	58	78	-4 27	57	79	-5 24	58	79	-6 22	57	79	-7 19	57	80																															258
100	-2 55	-57	80	-3 52	-58	81	-4 50	-57	81	-5 47	-57	81	-6 44	-58	82	-7 42	-57	82																												260
98	-2 20	57	82	-3 17	58	83	-4 15	57	83	-5 12	58	83	-6 10	57	83	-7 07	57	84	-8 04	58	84																									262
96	-1 45	57	84	-2 42	58	85	-3 40	57	85	-4 37	58	85	-5 35	57	85	-6 32	57	86	-7 29	58	86																									264
94	-1 10	58	86	-2 08	57	86	-3 05	57	87	-4 02	58	87	-5 00	57	87	-5 57	57	88	-6 54	58	88	-7 52	57	88																						266
92	-0 35	57	88	-1 32	58	88	-2 30	57	89	-3 27	58	89	-4 25	57	89	-5 22	57	90	-6 19	58	90	-7 17	57	90																						268
90	00 00	-57	90	-0 57	-58	90	-1 55	-57	91	-2 52	-58	91	-3 50	-57	91	-4 47	-57	92	-5 44	-58	92	-6 42	-57	92	-7 39	-57	92																			270
88	00 35	57	92	-0 22	58	92	-1 20	57	92	-2 17	57	93	-3 14	58	93	-4 12	57	93	-5 09	58	94	-6 07	57	94	-7 04	57	94	-8 01	58	95																272
86	01 10	57	94	00 13	58	94	-0 45	57	94	-1 42	57	95	-2 39	58	95	-3 37	57	95	-4 34	58	96	-5 32	57	96	-6 29	57	96	-7 26	58	96																274
84	01 45	57	96	00 48	58	96	-0 10	57	96	-1 07	57	97	-2 04	58	97	-3 02	57	97	-3 59	58	98	-4 57	57	98	-5 54	58	98	-6 52	57	98	-7 49	57	99													276
82	02 20	58	98	01 22	57	98	00 25	57	98	-0 32	58	99	-1 30	57	99	-2 27	58	99	-3 25	57	99	-4 22	58	100	-5 20	57	100	-6 17	57	100	-7 14	58	101													278
80	02 55	-58	100	01 57	-57	100	01 00	-58	100	00 02	-57	100	-0 55	-58	101	-1 53	-57	101	-2 50	-58	101	-3 48	-57	102	-4 45	-58	102	-5 43	-57	102	-6 40	-57	102	-7 37	-58	103										280
78	03 29	57	102	02 32	58	102	01 34	57	102	00 37	58	102	-0 21	57	103	-1 18	58	103	-2 16	57	103	-3 13	58	104	-4 11	57	104	-5 08	58	104	-6 06	57	104	-7 03	58	105	-8 01	57	105							282
76	04 03	57	103	03 06	58	104	02 08	57	104	01 11	58	104	00 13	57	105	-0 44	58	105	-1 42	57	105	-2 39	58	105	-3 37	57	106	-4 34	58	106	-5 32	57	106	-6 29	58	106	-7 27	57	107							284
74	04 37	57	105	03 40	58	106	02 42	57	106	01 45	58	106	00 47	58	106	-0 11	57	107	-1 08	58	107	-2 06	57	107	-3 03	58	108	-4 01	57	108	-4 58	58	108	-5 56	58	108	-6 54	57	109	-7 51	58	109				286
72	05 11	58	107	04 13	57	108	03 16	58	108	02 18	58	108	01 20	57	108	00 23	58	109	-0 35	57	109	-1 32	58	109	-2 30	58	110	-3 28	57	110	-4 25	58	110	-5 23	58	110	-6 21	57	111	-7 18	58	111				288
70	05 44	-57	109	04 47	-58	110	03 49	-58	110	02 51	-57	110	01 54	-58	110	00 56	-58	111	-0 02	-57	111	-0 59	-58	111	-1 57	-58	111	-2 55	-57	112	-3 52	-58	112	-4 50	-58	112	-5 48	-58	112	-6 46	-57	113	-7 43	-58	113	290
68	06 17	57	111	05 20	58	111	04 22	58	112	03 24	58	112	02 26	57	112	01 29	58	113	00 31	58	113	-0 27	58	113	-1 25	57	113	-2 22	58	114	-3 20	58	114	-4 18	58	114	-5 16	57	114	-6 13	58	115	-7 11	58	115	292
66	06 50	58	113	05 52	58	113	04 54	58	114	03 56	57	114	02 59	58	114	02 01	58	114	01 03	58	115	00 05	58	115	-0 53	57	115	-1 50	58	116	-2 48	58	116	-3 46	58	116	-4 44	58	116	-5 42	58	116	-6 40	57	117	294
64	07 22	58	115	06 24	58	115	05 26	58	116	04 28	58	116	03 30	58	116	02 32	57	116	01 35	58	117	00 37	58	117	-0 21	58	117	-1 19	58	117	-2 17	58	118	-3 15	58	118	-4 13	58	118	-5 11	58	118	-6 09	57	119	296
62	07 53	58	117	06 55	57	117	05 58	58	118	05 00	58	118	04 02	58	118	03 04	58	118	02 06	58	118	01 08	58	119	00 10	58	119	-0 48	58	119	-1 46	58	120	-2 44	58	120	-3 42	58	120	-4 40	58	120	-5 38	58	121	298
60	08 24	-58	119	07 26	-58	119	06 28	-58	119	05 30	-58	120	04 32	-58	120	03 34	-58	120	02 36	-58	120	01 38	-58	121	00 40	-58	121	-0 18	-58	121	-1 16	-58	121	-2 14	-58	122	-3 12	-58	122	-4 10	-58	122	-5 08	-58	122	300
58	08 55	58	121	07 57	58	121	06 59	58	121	06 01	59	122	05 02	58	122	04 04	58	122	03 06	58	122	02 08	58	123	01 10	58	123	00 12	58	123	-0 46	58	123	-1 44	59	124	-2 43	58	124	-3 41	58	124	-4 39	58	124	302
56	09 25	59	123	08 26	58	123	07 28	58	123	06 30	58	124	05 32	58	124	04 34	58	124	03 36	59	124	02 37	58	124	01 39	58	125	00 41	58	125	-0 17	59	125	-1 16	58	126	-2 14	58	126	-3 12	58	126	-4 10	58	126	304
54	09 54	58	125	08 56	59	125	07 57	58	125	06 59	58	126	06 01	59	126	05 02	58	126	04 04	58	126	03 06	58	126	02 08	59	127	01 09	58	127	00 11	58	127	-0 47	59	127	-1 46	58	128	-2 44	58	128	-3 42	58	128	306
52	10 22	58	127	09 24	58	127	08 26	59	127	07 27	58	128	06 29	59	128	05 30	58	128	04 32	58	128	03 34	59	128	02 35	58	129	01 37	58	129	00 39	59	129	-0 20	58	129	-1 18	59	130	-2 17	58	130	-3 15	58	130	308
50	10 50	-58	129	09 52	-59	129	08 53	-58	129	07 55	-59	129	06 56	-58	130	05 58	-59	130	04 59	-58	130	04 01	-59	130	03 02	-58	131	02 04	-59	131	01 05	-58	131	00 07	-59	131	-0 52	-58	131	-1 50	-58	132	-2 48	-59	132	310
48	11 17	59	131	10 18	58	131	09 20	59	131	08 21	58	131	07 23	59	132	06 24	58	132	05 26	59	132	04 27	58	132	03 29	59	133	02 30	58	133	01 32	59	133	00 33	59	133	-0 26	58	133	-1 24	59	134	-2 23	58	134	312
46	11 43	58	133	10 45	59	133	09 46	59	133	08 47	58	133	07 49	59	134	06 50	59	134	05 51	58	134	04 53	59	134	03 54	59	134	02 55	58	135	01 57	59	135	00 58	59	135	-0 01	58	135	-0 59	59	135	-1 58	59	136	314
44	12 08	58	135	11 10	59	135	10 11	59	135	09 12	58	135	08 14	59	136	07 15	59	136	06 16	59	136	05 17	58	136	04 19	59	136	03 20	59	137	02 21	59	137	01 22	58	137	00 24	59	137	-0 35	59	137	-1 34	59	138	316
42	12 33	59	137	11 34	59	137	10 35	58	137	09 37	59	137	08 38	59	138	07 39	59	138	06 40	59	138	05 41	59	138	04 42	58	138	03 44	59	138	02 45	59	139	01 46	59	139	00 47	59	139	-0 12	59	139	-1 11	58	140	318
40	12 57	-59	139	11 58	-59	139	10 59	-59	139	10 00	-59	139	09 01	-59	140	08 02	-59	140	07 03	-59	140	06 04	-59	140	05 05	-59	140	04 06	-58	140	03 08	-59	141	02 09	-59	141	01 10	-59	141	00 11	-59	141	-0 48	-59	141	320
38	13 19	59	141	12 20	59	141	11 21	59	141	10 22	59	141	09 23	59	142	08 24	59	142	07 25	59	142	06 26	59	142	05 27	59	142	04 28	59	142	03 29	59	143	02 30	59	143	01 31	59	143	00 32	59	143	-0 27	59	143	322
36	13 41	59	143	12 42	59	143	11 43	59	143	10 44	59	143	09 45	59	144	08 46	59	144	07 47	60	144	06 47	59	144	05 48	59	144	04 49	59	144	03 50	59	144	02 51	59	145	01 52	59	145	00 53	59	145	-0 06	59	145	324
34	14 02	59	145	13 03	60	145	12 03	59	145	11 04	59	145	10 05	59	146	09 06	59	146	08 07	59	146	07 08	60	146	06 08	59	146	05 09	59	146	04 10	59	146	03 11	59	147	02 12	60	147	01 12	59	147	00 13	59	147	326
32	14 21	59	147	13 22	59	147	12 23	59	147	11 24	60	147	10 24	59	148	09 25	59	148	08 26	59	148	07 27	60	148	06 27	59	148	05 28	59	148	04 29	59	148	03 30	60	149	02 30	59	149	01 31	59	149	00 32	60	149	328
30	14 40	-59	149	13 41	-60	149	12 41	-59	149	11 42	-59	149	10 43	-60	150	09 43	-59	150	08 44	-59	150	07 45	-60	150	06 45	-59	150	05 46	-59	150	04 47	-60	150	03 47	-59	150	02 48	-59	151	01 49	-60	151	00 49	-59	151	330
28	14 58	60	151	13 58	59	151	12 59	60	151	11 59	59	151	11 00	59	152	10 01	60	152	09 01	59	152	08 02	60	152	07 02	59	152	06 03	59	152	05 04	60	152	04 04	59	152	03 05	60	153	02 05	59	153	01 06	60	153	332
26	15 14	59	153	14 15	60	153	13 15	59	153	12 16	60	153	11 16	59	154	10 17	60	154	09 17	59	154	08 18	60	154	07 18	59	154	06 19	60	154	05 19	59	154	04 20	60	154	03 20	59	154	02 21	60	155	01 21	59	155	334
24	15 30	60	155	14 30	60	155	13 30	59	155	12 31	60	155	11 31	59	156	10 32	60	156	09 32	59	156	08 33	60	156	07 33	59	156	06 34	60	156	05 34	60	156	04 34	59	156	03 35	60	156	02 35	59	157	01 36	60	157	336
22	15 44	60	157	14 44	59	157	13 45	60	157	12 45	60	157	11 45	59	158	10 46	60	158	09 46	60	158	08 46	59	158	07 47	60	158	06 47	59	158	05 48	60	158	04 48	60	158	03 48	59	158	02 49	60	159	01 49	60	159	338
20	15 57	-60	159	14 57	-60	159	13 57	-59	159	12 58	-60	160	11 58	-60	160	10 58	-59	160	09 59	-60	160	08 59	-60	160	07 59	-59	160	07 00	-60	160	06 00	-60	160	05 00	-60	160	04 00	-59	160	03 01	-60	160	02 01	-60	161	340
18	16 09	60	161	15 09	60	161	14 09	59	161	13 10	60	162	12 10	60	162	11 10	60	162	10 10	59	162	09 11	60	162	08 11	60	162	07 11	60	162	06 11	59	162	05 12	60	162	04 12	60	162	03 12	60	162	02 12	60	162	342
16	16 19	59	163	15 20	60	163	14 20	60	164	13 20	60	164	12 20	60	164	11 20	59	164	10 21	60	164	09 21	60	164	08 21	60	164	07 21	60	164	06 21	59	164	05 22	60	164	04 22	60	164	03 22	60	164	02 22	60	164	344
14	16 29	60	165	15 29	60	166	14 29	60	166	13 29	59	166	12 30	60	166	11 30	60	166	10 30	60	166	09 30	60	166	08 30	60	166	07 30	60	166	06 30	59	166	05 31	60	166	04 31	60	166	03 31	60	166	02 31	60	166	346
12	16 37	60	168	15 37	60	168	14 37	60	168	13 37	59	168	12 38	60	168	11 38	60	168	10 38	60	168	09 38	60	168	08 38	60	168	07 38	60	168	06 38	60	168	05 38	60	168	04 38	59	168	03 39	60	168	02 39	60	168	348
10	16 44	-60	170	15 44	-60	170	14 44	-60	170	13 44	-60	170	12 44	-59	170	11 45	-60	170	10 45	-60	170	09 45	-60	170	08 45	-60	170	07 45	-60	170	06 45	-60	170	05 45	-60	170	04 45	-60	170	03 45	-60	170	02 45	-60	170	350
8	16 50	60	172	15 50	60	172	14 50	60	172	13 50	60	172	12 50	60	172	11 50	60	172	10 50	60	172	09 50	60	172	08 50	60	172	07 50	60	172	06 50	60	172	05 50	60	172	04 50	60	172	03 50	60	172	02 50	59	172	352
6	16 54	60	174	15 54	60	174	14 54	60	174	13 54	60	174	12 54	60	174	11 54	60	174	10 54	59	174	09 55	60	174	08 55	60	174	07 55	60	174	06 55	60	174	05 55	60	174	04 55	60	174	03 55	60	174	02 55	60	174	354
4	16 57	59	176	15 58	60	176	14 58	60	176	13 58	60	176	12 58	60	176	11 58	60	176	10 58	60	176	09 58	60	176	08 58	60	176	07 58	60	176	06 58	60	176	05 58	60	176	04 58	60	176	03 58	60	176	02 58	60	176	356
2	16 59	60	178	15 59	60	178	14 59	60	178	13 59	60	178	12 59	60	178	11 59	60	178	10 59	60	178	09 59	60	178	08 59	60	178	07 59	60	178	06 59	60	178	05 59	60	178	04 59	60	178	03 59	60	178	02 59	60	178	358
0	17 00	-60	180	16 00	-60	180	15 00	-60	180	14 00	-60	180	13 00	-60	180	12 00	-60	180	11 00	-60	180	10 00	-60	180	09 00	-60	180	08 00	-60	180	07 00	-60	180	06 00	-60	180	05 00	-60	180	04 00	-60	180	03 00	-60	180	360
	0°			1°			2°			3°			4°			5°			6°			7°			8°			9°			10°			11°			12°			13°			14°			

S. Lat. {LHA greater than 180°…….. Zn=180−Z; LHA less than 180°……….. Zn=180+Z}

DECLINATION (0°-14°) CONTRARY NAME TO LATITUDE

LAT 73°

N. Lat. {LHA greater than 180°....... Zn=Z; LHA less than 180°.......... Zn=360−Z}

DECLINATION (15°-29°) <u>SAME</u> NAME AS LATITUDE

LHA	15° Hc	d	Z	16° Hc	d	Z	17° Hc	d	Z	18° Hc	d	Z	19° Hc	d	Z	LHA
	° ′	′	°	° ′	′	°	° ′	′	°	° ′	′	°	° ′	′	°	
0	32 00	+60	180	33 00	+60	180	34 00	+60	180	35 00	+60	180	36 00	+60	180	360
2	31 59	60	178	32 59	60	178	33 59	60	178	34 59	60	178	35 59	60	178	358
4	31 57	60	175	32 57	60	175	33 57	60	175	34 57	60	175	35 57	60	175	356
6	31 54	60	173	32 54	60	173	33 54	60	173	34 54	60	173	35 54	60	173	354
8	31 49	60	171	32 49	60	171	33 49	60	171	34 49	60	171	35 49	60	171	352
10	31 43	+60	169	32 43	+59	169	33 42	+60	169	34 42	+60	168	35 42	+60	168	350
12	31 35	60	166	32 35	60	166	33 35	60	166	34 35	59	166	35 34	60	166	348
14	31 26	60	164	32 26	60	164	33 26	60	164	34 26	59	164	35 25	60	164	346
16	31 16	60	162	32 16	59	162	33 15	60	162	34 15	60	162	35 15	59	161	344
18	31 04	60	160	32 04	60	160	33 04	59	159	34 03	60	159	35 03	60	159	342
20	30 51	+60	157	31 51	+60	157	32 51	+59	157	33 50	+60	157	34 50	+59	157	340
22	30 37	60	155	31 37	59	155	32 36	60	155	33 36	59	155	34 35	60	155	338
24	30 22	59	153	31 21	60	153	32 21	59	153	33 20	60	152	34 20	59	152	336
26	30 05	60	151	31 05	59	151	32 04	59	150	33 03	60	150	34 03	59	150	334
28	29 48	59	149	30 47	59	148	31 46	59	148	32 45	59	148	33 44	60	148	332
30	29 29	+59	146	30 28	+59	146	31 27	+59	146	32 26	+59	146	33 25	+59	146	330
32	29 09	59	144	30 08	59	144	31 07	59	144	32 06	59	144	33 05	59	143	328
34	28 48	59	142	29 47	58	142	30 45	59	142	31 44	59	141	32 43	59	141	326
36	28 25	59	140	29 24	59	140	30 23	59	139	31 22	59	139	32 21	58	139	324
38	28 02	59	138	29 01	59	137	30 00	58	137	30 58	59	137	31 57	59	137	322
40	27 38	+59	136	28 37	+58	135	29 35	+59	135	30 34	+59	135	31 33	+58	135	320
42	27 13	59	133	28 12	58	133	29 10	59	133	30 09	58	133	31 07	58	132	318
44	26 47	59	131	27 46	58	131	28 44	58	131	29 42	59	131	30 41	58	130	316
46	26 20	59	129	27 19	58	129	28 17	58	129	29 15	58	128	30 13	59	128	314
48	25 53	58	127	26 51	58	127	27 49	58	127	28 47	58	126	29 45	59	126	312
50	25 24	+59	125	26 23	+58	125	27 21	+58	124	28 19	+58	124	29 17	+58	124	310
52	24 55	58	123	25 53	58	123	26 51	58	122	27 49	58	122	28 47	58	122	308
54	24 26	57	121	25 23	58	121	26 21	58	120	27 19	58	120	28 17	58	120	306
56	23 55	58	119	24 53	58	119	25 51	58	118	26 49	57	118	27 46	58	118	304
58	23 24	58	117	24 22	58	117	25 20	57	116	26 17	58	116	27 15	58	116	302
60	22 53	+57	115	23 50	+58	115	24 48	+57	114	25 45	+58	114	26 43	+58	114	300
62	22 20	58	113	23 18	58	113	24 16	57	112	25 13	58	112	26 11	57	112	298
64	21 48	57	111	22 45	58	111	23 43	57	110	24 40	58	110	25 38	57	110	296
66	21 15	57	109	22 12	58	109	23 10	57	108	24 07	57	108	25 04	58	108	294
68	20 41	58	107	21 39	57	107	22 36	58	106	23 34	57	106	24 31	57	106	292
70	20 08	+57	105	21 05	+57	105	22 02	+58	104	23 00	+57	104	23 57	+57	104	290
72	19 34	57	103	20 31	57	103	21 28	57	102	22 25	58	102	23 23	57	102	288
74	18 59	58	101	19 57	57	101	20 54	57	100	21 51	57	100	22 48	57	100	286
76	18 25	57	99	19 22	57	99	20 19	57	98	21 16	57	98	22 13	58	98	284
78	17 50	57	97	18 47	57	97	19 44	58	96	20 42	57	96	21 39	57	96	282
80	17 15	+57	95	18 12	+57	95	19 09	+58	95	20 07	+57	94	21 04	+57	94	280
82	16 40	57	93	17 37	57	93	18 34	58	93	19 32	57	92	20 29	57	92	278
84	16 05	57	91	17 02	57	91	17 59	57	91	18 56	58	90	19 54	57	90	276
86	15 30	57	89	16 27	57	89	17 24	57	89	18 21	57	88	19 18	58	88	274
88	14 55	57	87	15 52	57	87	16 49	57	87	17 46	57	87	18 43	57	86	272
90	14 20	+57	86	15 17	+57	85	16 14	+57	85	17 11	+57	85	18 08	+58	84	270
92	13 45	57	84	14 42	57	83	15 39	57	83	16 36	58	83	17 34	57	82	268
94	13 10	57	82	14 07	58	81	15 05	57	81	16 02	57	81	16 59	57	81	266
96	12 36	57	80	13 33	58	80	14 30	57	79	15 27	57	79	16 24	58	79	264
98	12 01	57	78	12 58	58	78	13 56	57	77	14 53	57	77	15 50	57	77	262
100	11 27	+57	76	12 24	+58	76	13 22	+57	76	14 19	+57	75	15 16	+57	75	260
102	10 53	57	74	11 50	58	74	12 48	57	74	13 45	57	73	14 42	58	73	258
104	10 19	58	72	11 17	57	72	12 14	58	72	13 12	57	71	14 09	57	71	256
106	09 46	58	70	10 44	57	70	11 41	58	70	12 39	57	70	13 36	57	69	254
108	09 13	58	69	10 11	57	68	11 08	58	68	12 06	57	68	13 03	58	67	252
110	08 41	+57	67	09 38	+58	66	10 36	+58	66	11 34	+57	66	12 31	+58	66	250
112	08 09	58	65	09 07	57	65	10 04	58	64	11 02	58	64	12 00	57	64	248
114	07 37	58	63	08 35	58	63	09 33	58	62	10 31	57	62	11 28	58	62	246
116	07 06	58	61	08 04	58	61	09 02	58	61	10 00	58	60	10 58	58	60	244
118	06 36	58	59	07 34	58	59	08 32	58	59	09 30	58	58	10 28	58	58	242
120	06 06	+58	57	07 04	+58	57	08 02	+58	57	09 00	+58	57	09 58	+58	56	240
122	05 37	58	55	06 35	58	55	07 33	58	55	08 31	58	55	09 29	58	54	238
124	05 08	59	54	06 07	58	53	07 05	58	53	08 03	58	53	09 01	58	53	236
126	04 40	59	52	05 39	58	51	06 37	58	51	07 35	59	51	08 34	58	51	234
128	04 13	59	50	05 12	58	50	06 10	59	49	07 09	58	49	08 07	58	49	232
130	03 47	+59	48	04 46	+58	48	05 44	+58	47	06 42	+59	47	07 41	+58	47	230
132	03 21	59	46	04 20	59	46	05 19	58	46	06 17	59	45	07 16	58	45	228
134	02 57	58	44	03 55	59	44	04 54	59	44	05 53	58	44	06 51	59	43	226
136	02 33	58	42	03 31	59	42	04 30	59	42	05 29	59	42	06 28	58	41	224
138	02 09	59	40	03 08	59	40	04 07	59	40	05 06	59	40	06 05	59	40	222

LHA	20° Hc	d	Z	21° Hc	d	Z	22° Hc	d	Z	23° Hc	d	Z	24° Hc	d	Z	LHA
	° ′	′	°	° ′	′	°	° ′	′	°	° ′	′	°	° ′	′	°	
0	37 00	+60	180	38 00	+60	180	39 00	+60	180	40 00	+60	180	41 00	+60	180	360
2	36 59	60	178	37 59	60	178	38 59	60	178	39 59	60	178	40 59	60	178	358
4	36 57	60	175	37 57	60	175	38 57	60	175	39 57	60	175	40 57	60	175	356
6	36 54	60	173	37 54	59	173	38 53	60	173	39 53	60	173	40 53	60	173	354
8	36 49	59	171	37 48	60	171	38 48	60	171	39 48	60	170	40 48	60	170	352
10	36 42	+60	168	37 42	+60	168	38 42	+60	168	39 42	+60	168	40 42	+59	168	350
12	36 34	60	166	37 34	60	166	38 34	60	166	39 34	60	166	40 34	59	166	348
14	36 25	60	164	37 25	60	164	38 25	59	163	39 24	60	163	40 24	60	163	346
16	36 14	60	161	37 14	60	161	38 14	60	161	39 14	59	161	40 13	60	161	344
18	36 03	59	159	37 02	60	159	38 02	59	159	39 01	60	159	40 01	60	158	342
20	35 49	+60	157	36 49	+59	157	37 48	+60	156	38 48	+59	156	39 47	+60	156	340
22	35 35	59	154	36 34	60	154	37 34	59	154	38 33	59	154	39 32	60	154	338
24	35 19	59	152	36 18	60	152	37 18	59	152	38 17	59	152	39 16	59	151	336
26	35 02	59	150	36 01	59	150	37 00	60	149	38 00	59	149	38 59	59	149	334
28	34 44	59	148	35 43	59	147	36 42	59	147	37 41	59	147	38 40	59	147	332
30	34 24	+59	145	35 23	+59	145	36 22	+59	145	37 21	+59	145	38 20	+59	144	330
32	34 04	59	143	35 03	58	143	36 02	58	143	37 00	59	142	37 59	59	142	328
34	33 42	59	141	34 41	59	141	35 40	58	140	36 38	59	140	37 37	59	140	326
36	33 19	59	139	34 18	59	138	35 17	58	138	36 15	59	138	37 14	59	138	324
38	32 56	58	136	33 54	59	136	34 53	58	136	35 51	59	136	36 50	58	135	322
40	32 31	+58	134	33 29	+59	134	34 28	+58	134	35 26	+59	133	36 25	+58	133	320
42	32 05	59	132	33 04	58	132	34 02	58	132	35 00	59	131	35 59	58	131	318
44	31 39	58	130	32 37	58	130	33 35	59	129	34 34	58	129	35 32	58	129	316
46	31 12	58	128	32 10	58	128	33 08	58	127	34 06	58	127	35 04	58	127	314
48	30 44	58	126	31 42	58	125	32 40	57	125	33 37	58	125	34 35	58	124	312
50	30 15	+58	124	31 13	+57	123	32 10	+58	123	33 08	+58	123	34 06	+58	122	310
52	29 45	58	122	30 43	58	121	31 41	57	121	32 38	58	121	33 36	58	120	308
54	29 15	58	119	30 13	57	119	31 10	58	119	32 08	57	118	33 05	58	118	306
56	28 44	58	117	29 42	57	117	30 39	58	117	31 37	57	116	32 34	58	116	304
58	28 12	58	115	29 10	58	115	30 08	57	115	31 05	57	114	32 02	58	114	302
60	27 41	+57	113	28 38	+57	113	29 35	+58	113	30 33	+57	112	31 30	+57	112	300
62	27 08	57	111	28 05	58	111	29 03	57	111	30 00	57	110	30 57	58	110	298
64	26 35	57	109	27 32	58	109	28 30	57	109	29 27	57	108	30 24	57	108	296
66	26 02	57	107	26 59	57	107	27 56	57	107	28 53	58	106	29 51	57	106	294
68	25 28	57	105	26 25	57	105	27 22	58	105	28 20	57	104	29 17	57	104	292
70	24 54	+57	103	25 51	+57	103	26 48	+57	103	27 45	+57	102	28 42	+57	102	290
72	24 20	57	101	25 17	57	101	26 14	57	101	27 11	57	100	28 08	57	100	288
74	23 45	57	99	24 42	57	99	25 39	57	99	26 36	57	98	27 33	57	98	286
76	23 11	57	97	24 08	57	97	25 05	57	97	26 02	56	96	26 58	57	96	284
78	22 36	57	95	23 33	57	95	24 30	57	95	25 27	57	94	26 24	56	94	282
80	22 01	+57	94	22 58	+57	93	23 55	+57	93	24 52	+56	92	25 48	+57	92	280
82	21 26	57	92	22 23	57	91	23 20	57	91	24 17	56	91	25 13	57	90	278
84	20 51	57	90	21 48	57	89	22 45	56	89	23 41	57	89	24 38	57	88	276
86	20 16	57	88	21 13	56	87	22 09	57	87	23 06	57	87	24 03	57	86	274
88	19 40	58	86	20 37	57	86	21 34	57	85	22 31	57	85	23 28	57	85	272
90	19 06	+57	84	20 03	+57	84	21 00	+57	83	21 57	+56	83	22 53	+57	83	270
92	18 31	57	82	19 28	57	82	20 25	57	81	21 22	57	81	22 19	57	81	268
94	17 56	58	80	18 53	57	80	19 50	58	80	20 47	57	79	21 44	57	79	266
96	17 22	57	78	18 19	57	78	19 16	57	78	20 13	57	77	21 10	57	77	264
98	16 47	58	76	17 45	57	76	18 42	57	76	19 39	57	75	20 36	57	75	262
100	16 13	+58	75	17 11	+57	74	18 08	+57	74	19 05	+57	74	20 02	+57	73	260
102	15 40	57	73	16 37	57	72	17 34	57	72	18 31	58	72	19 29	57	71	258
104	15 06	58	71	16 04	57	71	17 01	57	70	17 58	58	70	18 56	57	70	256
106	14 33	58	69	15 31	57	69	16 28	58	68	17 26	57	68	18 23	57	68	254
108	14 01	57	67	14 58	58	67	15 56	57	67	16 53	58	66	17 51	57	66	252
110	13 29	+57	65	14 26	+58	65	15 24	+57	65	16 21	+58	64	17 19	+57	64	250
112	12 57	58	63	13 55	57	63	14 52	58	63	15 50	58	63	16 48	57	62	248
114	12 26	58	62	13 24	58	61	14 22	57	61	15 19	58	61	16 17	57	60	246
116	11 56	57	60	12 53	58	59	13 51	58	59	14 49	58	59	15 47	57	59	244
118	11 26	57	58	12 23	58	58	13 21	58	57	14 19	58	57	15 17	58	57	242
120	10 56	+58	56	11 54	+58	56	12 52	+58	56	13 50	+58	55	14 48	+58	55	240
122	10 27	58	54	11 25	59	54	12 24	58	54	13 22	58	53	14 20	58	53	238
124	09 59	58	52	10 57	59	52	11 56	58	52	12 54	58	52	13 52	58	51	236
126	09 32	58	50	10 30	58	50	11 28	59	50	12 27	58	50	13 25	58	49	234
128	09 05	59	49	10 04	58	48	11 02	58	48	12 00	59	48	12 59	58	48	232
130	08 39	+59	47	09 38	+58	47	10 36	+59	46	11 35	+58	46	12 33	+58	46	230
132	08 14	59	45	09 13	58	45	10 11	59	44	11 10	58	44	12 08	59	44	228
134	07 50	58	43	08 48	59	43	09 47	59	43	10 46	58	42	11 44	59	42	226
136	07 26	59	41	08 25	59	41	09 24	58	41	10 22	59	41	11 21	59	40	224
138	07 04	58	39	08 02	59	39	09 01	59	39	10 00	59	39	10 59	59	39	222

LHA	25° Hc	d	Z	26° Hc	d	Z	27° Hc	d	Z	28° Hc	d	Z	29° Hc	d	Z	LHA
	° ′	′	°	° ′	′	°	° ′	′	°	° ′	′	°	° ′	′	°	
0	42 00	+60	180	43 00	+60	180	44 00	+60	180	45 00	+60	180	46 00	+60	180	360
2	41 59	60	178	42 59	60	178	43 59	60	178	44 59	60	178	45 59	60	178	358
4	41 57	60	175	42 57	60	175	43 57	60	175	44 57	60	175	45 57	60	175	356
6	41 53	60	173	42 53	60	173	43 53	60	173	44 53	60	173	45 53	60	173	354
8	41 48	60	170	42 48	60	170	43 48	60	170	44 48	60	170	45 48	60	170	352
10	41 41	+60	168	42 41	+60	168	43 41	+60	168	44 41	+60	168	45 41	+60	167	350
12	41 33	60	165	42 33	60	165	43 33	60	165	44 33	60	165	45 33	59	165	348
14	41 24	60	163	42 24	59	163	43 23	60	163	44 23	60	163	45 23	59	163	346
16	41 13	60	161	42 13	59	161	43 12	60	160	44 12	59	160	45 11	60	160	344
18	41 01	59	158	42 00	60	158	43 00	59	158	43 59	60	158	44 59	59	158	342
20	40 47	+59	156	41 46	+60	156	42 46	+59	156	43 45	+60	155	44 45	+59	155	340
22	40 32	59	154	41 31	60	153	42 31	59	153	43 30	59	153	44 29	59	153	338
24	40 15	60	151	41 15	59	151	42 14	59	151	43 13	59	151	44 12	60	150	336
26	39 58	59	149	40 57	59	149	41 56	59	148	42 55	59	148	43 54	59	148	334
28	39 39	59	147	40 38	59	146	41 37	59	146	42 36	59	146	43 35	59	146	332
30	39 19	+59	144	40 18	+59	144	41 17	+59	144	42 16	+59	143	43 15	+58	143	330
32	38 58	59	142	39 57	59	142	40 56	58	141	41 54	59	141	42 53	59	141	328
34	38 36	58	140	39 34	59	139	40 33	59	139	41 32	58	139	42 30	59	138	326
36	38 13	58	137	39 11	59	137	40 10	58	137	41 08	58	136	42 06	59	136	324
38	37 48	59	135	38 47	58	135	39 45	58	135	40 43	59	134	41 42	58	134	322
40	37 23	+58	133	38 21	+59	133	39 20	+58	132	40 18	+58	132	41 16	+58	132	320
42	36 57	58	131	37 55	58	130	38 53	58	130	39 51	58	130	40 49	58	129	318
44	36 30	58	129	37 28	58	128	38 26	58	128	39 24	58	128	40 22	57	127	316
46	36 02	58	126	37 00	58	126	37 58	57	126	38 55	58	125	39 53	58	125	314
48	35 33	58	124	36 31	58	124	37 29	57	123	38 26	58	123	39 24	58	123	312
50	35 04	+58	122	36 02	+57	122	36 59	+58	121	37 57	+57	121	38 54	+58	121	310
52	34 34	57	120	35 31	58	120	36 29	57	119	37 26	58	119	38 24	57	118	308
54	34 03	57	118	35 00	58	117	35 58	57	117	36 55	58	117	37 53	57	116	306
56	33 32	57	116	34 29	57	115	35 26	58	115	36 24	57	115	37 21	57	114	304
58	33 00	57	114	33 57	57	113	34 54	57	113	35 51	58	113	36 49	57	112	302
60	32 27	+58	112	33 25	+57	111	34 22	+57	111	35 19	+57	110	36 16	+57	110	300
62	31 55	57	110	32 52	57	109	33 49	57	109	34 46	57	108	35 43	56	108	298
64	31 21	57	108	32 18	57	107	33 15	57	107	34 12	57	106	35 09	57	106	296
66	30 48	57	106	31 45	57	105	32 42	56	105	33 38	57	104	34 35	57	104	294
68	30 14	57	104	31 11	56	103	32 07	57	103	33 04	57	102	34 01	57	102	292
70	29 39	+57	102	30 36	+57	101	31 33	+57	101	32 30	+57	100	33 27	+56	100	290
72	29 05	57	100	30 02	57	99	30 59	56	99	31 55	57	98	32 52	56	98	288
74	28 30	57	98	29 27	57	97	30 24	56	97	31 20	57	96	32 17	57	96	286
76	27 55	57	96	28 52	57	95	29 49	57	95	30 46	56	95	31 42	57	94	284
78	27 20	57	94	28 17	57	93	29 14	56	93	30 10	57	93	31 07	57	92	282
80	26 45	+57	92	27 42	+57	91	28 39	+56	91	29 35	+57	91	30 32	+57	90	280
82	26 10	57	90	27 07	57	90	28 04	56	89	29 00	57	89	29 57	56	88	278
84	25 35	57	88	26 32	57	88	27 29	56	87	28 25	57	87	29 22	56	86	276
86	25 00	57	86	25 57	57	86	26 54	56	85	27 50	57	85	28 47	56	85	274
88	24 25	57	84	25 22	57	84	26 19	56	83	27 15	57	83	28 12	57	83	272
90	23 50	+57	82	24 47	+57	82	25 44	+57	82	26 41	+56	81	27 37	+57	81	270
92	23 16	57	80	24 13	56	80	25 09	57	80	26 06	57	79	27 03	56	79	268
94	22 41	57	79	23 38	57	78	24 35	57	78	25 32	56	77	26 28	57	77	266
96	22 07	57	77	23 04	57	76	24 01	57	76	24 58	56	76	25 54	57	75	264
98	21 33	57	75	22 30	57	74	23 27	57	74	24 24	57	74	25 21	56	73	262
100	20 59	+57	73	21 56	+57	73	22 53	+57	72	23 50	+57	72	24 47	+57	72	260
102	20 26	57	71	21 23	57	71	22 20	57	70	23 17	57	70	24 14	57	70	258
104	19 53	57	69	20 50	57	69	21 47	57	69	22 44	57	68	23 41	57	68	256
106	19 20	57	67	20 17	58	67	21 15	57	67	22 12	57	66	23 09	57	66	254
108	18 48	57	66	19 45	58	65	20 43	57	65	21 40	57	65	22 37	57	64	252
110	18 16	+58	64	19 14	+57	63	20 11	+58	63	21 09	+57	63	22 06	+57	63	250
112	17 45	58	62	18 43	57	62	19 40	58	61	20 38	57	61	21 35	57	61	248
114	17 14	58	60	18 12	58	60	19 10	57	60	20 07	58	59	21 05	57	59	246
116	16 44	58	58	17 42	58	58	18 40	57	58	19 37	58	57	20 35	57	57	244
118	16 15	58	57	17 13	57	56	18 10	58	56	19 08	58	56	20 06	57	55	242
120	15 46	+58	55	16 44	+58	54	17 42	+57	54	18 39	+58	54	19 37	+58	54	240
122	15 18	58	53	16 16	57	53	17 13	58	52	18 11	58	52	19 09	58	52	238
124	14 50	58	51	15 48	58	51	16 46	58	51	17 44	58	50	18 42	58	50	236
126	14 23	58	49	15 21	58	49	16 19	59	49	17 17	59	48	18 16	58	48	234
128	13 57	58	47	14 55	58	47	15 53	59	47	16 52	58	47	17 50	58	46	232
130	13 31	+59	46	14 30	+58	45	15 28	+58	45	16 26	+59	45	17 25	+58	45	230
132	13 07	58	44	14 05	59	44	15 04	58	43	16 02	59	43	17 01	58	43	228
134	12 43	58	42	13 41	59	42	14 40	59	42	15 39	59	41	16 37	59	41	226
136	12 20	59	40	13 19	58	40	14 17	59	40	15 16	59	40	16 15	58	39	224
138	11 58	58	38	12 56	59	38	13 55	59	38	14 54	59	38	15 53	58	38	222

S. Lat. {LHA greater than 180°....... Zn=180−Z; LHA less than 180°.......... Zn=180+Z}

DECLINATION (15°-29°) <u>SAME</u> NAME AS LATITUDE

N. Lat. {LHA greater than 180°....... Zn=Z; LHA less than 180°........... Zn=360−Z}

DECLINATION (15°-29°) SAME NAME AS LATITUDE

LHA	15° Hc d Z	16° Hc d Z	17° Hc d Z	18° Hc d Z	19° Hc d Z	20° Hc d Z	21° Hc d Z	22° Hc d Z	23° Hc d Z	24° Hc d Z	25° Hc d Z	26° Hc d Z	27° Hc d Z	28° Hc d Z	29° Hc d Z	LHA
	° ′ ′ °	° ′ ′ °	° ′ ′ °	° ′ ′ °	° ′ ′ °	° ′ ′ °	° ′ ′ °	° ′ ′ °	° ′ ′ °	° ′ ′ °	° ′ ′ °	° ′ ′ °	° ′ ′ °	° ′ ′ °	° ′ ′ °	
140	01 47 +59 38	02 46 +59 38	03 45 +59 38	04 44 +59 38	05 43 +59 38	06 42 +59 38	07 41 +59 37	08 40 +59 37	09 39 +58 37	10 37 +59 37	11 36 +59 37	12 35 +59 36	13 34 +59 36	14 33 +59 36	15 32 +59 36	220
142	01 26 59 36	02 25 59 36	03 24 59 36	04 23 59 36	05 22 59 36	06 21 59 36	07 20 59 35	08 19 59 35	09 18 59 35	10 17 59 35	11 16 59 35	12 15 59 35	13 14 59 34	14 13 59 34	15 12 59 34	218
144	01 05 60 35	02 05 59 34	03 04 59 34	04 03 59 34	05 02 59 34	06 01 59 34	07 00 59 34	07 59 59 33	08 58 59 33	09 57 59 33	10 56 60 33	11 56 59 33	12 55 59 33	13 54 59 32	14 53 59 32	216
146	00 46 59 33	01 45 59 32	02 44 60 32	03 44 59 32	04 43 59 32	05 42 59 32	06 41 59 32	07 40 60 32	08 40 59 31	09 39 59 31	10 38 59 31	11 37 59 31	12 36 59 31	13 35 59 31	14 34 60 30	214
148	00 28 59 31	01 27 59 31	02 26 59 30	03 25 60 30	04 25 59 30	05 24 59 30	06 23 59 30	07 22 60 30	08 22 59 30	09 21 59 29	10 20 60 29	11 20 59 29	12 19 59 29	13 18 59 29	14 17 59 29	212
150	00 10 +60 29	01 10 +59 29	02 09 +59 29	03 08 +60 28	04 08 +59 28	05 07 +59 28	06 06 +60 28	07 06 +59 28	08 05 +59 28	09 04 +60 28	10 04 +59 27	11 03 +59 27	12 02 +60 27	13 02 +59 27	14 01 +59 27	210
152	-0 06 59 27	00 53 59 27	01 52 60 27	02 52 59 27	03 51 60 26	04 51 59 26	05 50 60 26	06 50 59 26	07 49 60 26	08 49 59 26	09 48 59 26	10 47 60 25	11 47 59 25	12 46 60 25	13 46 59 25	208
154	-0 22 60 25	00 38 59 25	01 37 60 25	02 37 59 25	03 36 60 25	04 36 59 24	05 35 60 24	06 35 59 24	07 34 60 24	08 34 59 24	09 33 60 24	10 33 59 24	11 32 60 24	12 32 59 23	13 31 60 23	206
156	-0 36 60 23	00 24 59 23	01 23 60 23	02 23 59 23	03 22 60 23	04 22 59 23	05 21 60 22	06 21 60 22	07 21 59 22	08 20 60 22	09 20 59 22	10 19 60 22	11 19 59 22	12 18 60 22	13 18 59 21	204
158	-0 49 59 21	00 10 60 21	01 10 60 21	02 10 59 21	03 09 60 21	04 09 60 21	05 09 59 21	06 08 60 20	07 08 59 20	08 07 60 20	09 07 60 20	10 07 59 20	11 06 60 20	12 06 60 20	13 06 59 20	202
160	-1 01 +59 19	-0 02 +60 19	00 58 +60 19	01 58 +59 19	02 57 +60 19	03 57 +60 19	04 57 +60 19	05 57 +59 19	06 56 +60 19	07 56 +60 18	08 56 +59 18	09 55 +60 18	10 55 +60 18	11 55 +59 18	12 54 +60 18	200
162	-1 12 59 17	-0 13 60 17	00 47 60 17	01 47 60 17	02 47 59 17	03 46 60 17	04 46 60 17	05 46 60 17	06 46 59 17	07 45 60 17	08 45 60 17	09 45 60 16	10 45 59 16	11 44 60 16	12 44 60 16	198
164	-1 22 59 15	-0 23 60 15	00 37 60 15	01 37 60 15	02 37 60 15	03 37 59 15	04 36 60 15	05 36 60 15	06 36 60 15	07 36 60 15	08 36 60 15	09 36 59 15	10 35 60 15	11 35 60 14	12 35 60 14	196
166	-1 31 60 14	-0 31 60 13	00 29 59 13	01 28 60 13	02 28 60 13	03 28 60 13	04 28 60 13	05 28 60 13	06 28 60 13	07 28 59 13	08 27 60 13	09 27 60 13	10 27 60 13	11 27 60 13	12 27 60 13	194
168	-1 39 60 12	-0 39 60 12	00 21 60 11	01 21 60 11	02 21 60 11	03 21 60 11	04 21 59 11	05 20 60 11	06 20 60 11	07 20 60 11	08 20 60 11	09 20 60 11	10 20 60 11	11 20 60 11	12 20 60 11	192
170	-1 45 +60 10	-0 45 +60 10	00 15 +59 10	01 14 +60 10	02 14 +60 10	03 14 +60 9	04 14 +60 9	05 14 +60 9	06 14 +60 9	07 14 +60 9	08 14 +60 9	09 14 +60 9	10 14 +60 9	11 14 +60 9	12 14 +60 9	190
172	-1 51 60 8	-0 51 60 8	00 09 60 8	01 09 60 8	02 09 60 8	03 09 60 8	04 09 60 8	05 09 60 7	06 09 60 7	07 09 60 7	08 09 60 7	09 09 60 7	10 09 60 7	11 09 60 7	12 09 60 7	188
174	-1 55 60 6	-0 55 60 6	00 05 60 6	01 05 60 6	02 05 60 6	03 05 60 6	04 05 60 6	05 05 60 6	06 05 60 6	07 05 60 6	08 05 60 6	09 05 60 6	10 05 60 5	11 05 60 5	12 05 60 5	186
176	-1 58 60 4	-0 58 60 4	00 02 60 4	01 02 60 4	02 02 60 4	03 02 60 4	04 02 60 4	05 02 60 4	06 02 60 4	07 02 60 4	08 02 60 4	09 02 60 4	10 02 60 4	11 02 60 4	12 02 60 4	184
178	-1 59 60 2	-0 59 60 2	00 01 60 2	01 01 60 2	02 01 60 2	03 01 60 2	04 01 60 2	05 01 60 2	06 01 60 2	07 01 60 2	08 01 60 2	09 01 60 2	10 01 60 2	11 01 60 2	12 01 60 2	182
180	-2 00 +60 0	-1 00 +60 0	00 00 +60 0	01 00 +60 0	02 00 +60 0	03 00 +60 0	04 00 +60 0	05 00 +60 0	06 00 +60 0	07 00 +60 0	08 00 +60 0	09 00 +60 0	10 00 +60 0	11 00 +60 0	12 00 +60 0	180

LHA	15° Hc d Z	16° Hc d Z	17° Hc d Z	18° Hc d Z	19° Hc d Z	20° Hc d Z	21° Hc d Z	22° Hc d Z	23° Hc d Z	24° Hc d Z	LHA
66	-7 37 58 117										294
64	-7 06 58 119										296
62	-6 36 58 121	-7 34 58 121									298
60	-6 06 -58 123	-7 04 -58 123									300
58	-5 37 58 125	-6 35 58 125	-7 33 58 125								302
56	-5 08 59 126	-6 07 58 127	-7 05 58 127								304
54	-4 40 59 128	-5 39 58 129	-6 37 58 129	-7 35 59 129							306
52	-4 13 59 130	-5 12 58 130	-6 10 59 131	-7 09 58 131							308
50	-3 47 -59 132	-4 46 -58 132	-5 44 -58 133	-6 42 -59 133	-7 41 -58 133						310
48	-3 21 59 134	-4 20 59 134	-5 19 58 134	-6 17 59 135	-7 16 58 135						312
46	-2 57 58 136	-3 55 59 136	-4 54 59 136	-5 53 58 136	-6 51 59 137						314
44	-2 33 58 138	-3 31 59 138	-4 30 59 138	-5 29 59 138	-6 28 58 139	-7 26 59 139					316
42	-2 09 59 140	-3 08 59 140	-4 07 59 140	-5 06 59 140	-6 05 59 140	-7 04 58 141					318
40	-1 47 -59 142	-2 46 -59 142	-3 45 -59 142	-4 44 -59 142	-5 43 -59 142	-6 42 -59 142					320
38	-1 26 59 144	-2 25 59 144	-3 24 59 144	-4 23 59 144	-5 22 59 144	-6 21 59 144	-7 20 59 145				322
36	-1 05 60 145	-2 05 59 146	-3 04 59 146	-4 03 59 146	-5 02 59 146	-6 01 59 146	-7 00 59 146				324
34	-0 46 59 147	-1 45 59 148	-2 44 60 148	-3 44 59 148	-4 43 59 148	-5 42 59 148	-6 41 59 148				326
32	-0 28 59 149	-1 27 59 149	-2 26 59 150	-3 25 60 150	-4 25 59 150	-5 24 59 150	-6 23 59 150	-7 22 60 150			328
30	-0 10 -60 151	-1 10 -59 151	-2 09 -59 151	-3 08 -60 152	-4 08 -59 152	-5 07 -59 152	-6 06 -60 152	-7 06 -59 152			330
28	00 06 59 153	-0 53 59 153	-1 52 60 153	-2 52 59 153	-3 51 60 154	-4 51 59 154	-5 50 60 154	-6 50 59 154			332
26	00 22 60 155	-0 38 59 155	-1 37 60 155	-2 37 59 155	-3 36 60 155	-4 36 59 156	-5 35 60 156	-6 35 59 156			334
24	00 36 60 157	-0 24 59 157	-1 23 60 157	-2 23 59 157	-3 22 60 157	-4 22 59 157	-5 21 60 158	-6 21 60 158	-7 21 59 158		336
22	00 49 59 159	-0 10 60 159	-1 10 60 159	-2 10 59 159	-3 09 60 159	-4 09 60 159	-5 09 59 159	-6 08 60 160	-7 08 59 160		338
20	01 01 -59 161	00 02 -60 161	-0 58 -60 161	-1 58 -59 161	-2 57 -60 161	-3 57 -60 161	-4 57 -60 161	-5 57 -59 161	-6 56 -60 161		340
18	01 12 59 163	00 13 60 163	-0 47 60 163	-1 47 60 163	-2 47 59 163	-3 46 60 163	-4 46 60 163	-5 46 60 163	-6 46 59 163		342
16	01 22 59 165	00 23 60 165	-0 37 60 165	-1 37 60 165	-2 37 60 165	-3 37 59 165	-4 36 60 165	-5 36 60 165	-6 36 60 165		344
14	01 31 60 166	00 31 60 167	-0 29 59 167	-1 28 60 167	-2 28 60 167	-3 28 60 167	-4 28 60 167	-5 28 60 167	-6 28 60 167		346
12	01 39 60 168	00 39 60 168	-0 21 60 169	-1 21 60 169	-2 21 60 169	-3 21 60 169	-4 21 59 169	-5 20 60 169	-6 20 60 169		348
10	01 45 -60 170	00 45 -60 170	-0 15 -59 170	-1 14 -60 170	-2 14 -60 170	-3 14 -60 171	-4 14 -60 171	-5 14 -60 171	-6 14 -60 171		350
8	01 51 60 172	00 51 60 172	-0 09 60 172	-1 09 60 172	-2 09 60 172	-3 09 60 172	-4 09 60 172	-5 09 60 173	-6 09 60 173		352
6	01 55 60 174	00 55 60 174	-0 05 60 174	-1 05 60 174	-2 05 60 174	-3 05 60 174	-4 05 60 174	-5 05 60 174	-6 05 60 174		354
4	01 58 60 176	00 58 60 176	-0 02 60 176	-1 02 60 176	-2 02 60 176	-3 02 60 176	-4 02 60 176	-5 02 60 176	-6 02 60 176		356
2	01 59 60 178	00 59 60 178	-0 01 60 178	-1 01 60 178	-2 01 60 178	-3 01 60 178	-4 01 60 178	-5 01 60 178	-6 01 60 178	-7 01 60 178	358
0	02 00 -60 180	01 00 -60 180	00 00 -60 180	-1 00 -60 180	-2 00 -60 180	-3 00 -60 180	-4 00 -60 180	-5 00 -60 180	-6 00 -60 180	-7 00 -60 180	360

15°	16°	17°	18°	19°	20°	21°	22°	23°	24°	25°	26°	27°	28°	29°

S. Lat. {LHA greater than 180°....... Zn=180−Z; LHA less than 180°........... Zn=180+Z}

DECLINATION (15°-29°) CONTRARY NAME TO LATITUDE

N. Lat. {LHA greater than 180°....... Zn=Z; LHA less than 180°........... Zn=360−Z}

DECLINATION (0°-14°) <u>SAME</u> NAME AS LATITUDE

LAT 74°

LHA	0° Hc	0° d	0° Z	1° Hc	1° d	1° Z	2° Hc	2° d	2° Z	3° Hc	3° d	3° Z	4° Hc	4° d	4° Z
	° ′	′	°	° ′	′	°	° ′	′	°	° ′	′	°	° ′	′	°
0	16 00	+60	180	17 00	+60	180	18 00	+60	180	19 00	+60	180	20 00	+60	180
2	15 59	60	178	16 59	60	178	17 59	60	178	18 59	60	178	19 59	60	178
4	15 58	60	176	16 58	60	176	17 58	60	176	18 58	60	176	19 58	60	176
6	15 55	60	174	16 55	60	174	17 55	60	174	18 55	60	174	19 55	60	174
8	15 50	60	172	16 50	60	172	17 50	60	172	18 50	60	172	19 50	60	172
10	15 45	+60	170	16 45	+60	170	17 45	+60	170	18 45	+60	169	19 45	+60	169
12	15 39	59	168	16 38	60	168	17 38	60	167	18 38	60	167	19 38	60	167
14	15 31	60	166	16 31	60	165	17 31	59	165	18 30	60	165	19 30	60	165
16	15 22	60	163	16 22	60	163	17 22	59	163	18 21	60	163	19 21	60	163
18	15 12	60	161	16 12	59	161	17 11	60	161	18 11	60	161	19 11	60	161
20	15 01	+59	159	16 00	+60	159	17 00	+60	159	18 00	+60	159	19 00	+59	159
22	14 48	60	157	15 48	60	157	16 48	59	157	17 47	60	157	18 47	60	157
24	14 35	60	155	15 35	59	155	16 34	60	155	17 34	59	155	18 33	60	155
26	14 21	59	153	15 20	60	153	16 20	59	153	17 19	60	153	18 19	59	153
28	14 05	60	151	15 05	59	151	16 04	60	151	17 04	59	151	18 03	59	151
30	13 49	+59	149	14 48	+59	149	15 47	+60	149	16 47	+59	149	17 46	+60	148
32	13 31	59	147	14 30	60	147	15 30	59	147	16 29	59	147	17 28	60	146
34	13 13	59	145	14 12	59	145	15 11	59	145	16 10	60	144	17 10	59	144
36	12 53	59	143	13 52	59	143	14 51	60	143	15 51	59	142	16 50	59	142
38	12 33	59	141	13 32	59	141	14 31	59	141	15 30	59	140	16 29	59	140
40	12 11	+59	139	13 10	+59	139	14 09	+59	139	15 08	+59	138	16 07	+59	138
42	11 49	59	137	12 48	59	137	13 47	59	137	14 46	59	136	15 45	59	136
44	11 26	59	135	12 25	59	135	13 24	59	135	14 23	59	134	15 22	58	134
46	11 02	59	133	12 01	59	133	13 00	59	133	13 59	58	132	14 57	59	132
48	10 38	58	131	11 36	59	131	12 35	59	131	13 34	58	130	14 32	59	130
50	10 12	+59	129	11 11	+59	129	12 10	+58	129	13 08	+59	128	14 07	+58	128
52	09 46	59	127	10 45	58	127	11 43	59	127	12 42	58	126	13 40	59	126
54	09 19	59	125	10 18	58	125	11 16	59	125	12 15	58	124	13 13	59	124
56	08 52	58	123	09 50	59	123	10 49	58	123	11 47	58	122	12 45	59	122
58	08 24	58	121	09 22	59	121	10 21	58	121	11 19	58	120	12 17	58	120
60	07 55	+59	119	08 54	+58	119	09 52	+58	119	10 50	+58	118	11 48	+58	118
62	07 26	58	117	08 24	58	117	09 22	59	117	10 21	58	116	11 19	58	116
64	06 56	59	115	07 55	58	115	08 53	58	115	09 51	58	114	10 49	58	114
66	06 26	58	113	07 24	58	113	08 22	58	113	09 20	58	112	10 18	58	112
68	05 56	58	111	06 54	58	111	07 52	58	111	08 50	58	110	09 48	57	110
70	05 25	+58	109	06 23	+57	109	07 20	+58	109	08 18	+58	109	09 16	+58	108
72	04 53	58	107	05 51	58	107	06 49	58	107	07 47	58	107	08 45	58	106
74	04 21	58	105	05 19	58	105	06 17	58	105	07 15	58	105	08 13	58	104
76	03 49	58	104	04 47	58	103	05 45	58	103	06 43	58	103	07 41	57	102
78	03 17	58	102	04 15	58	101	05 13	57	101	06 10	58	101	07 08	58	101
80	02 45	+57	100	03 42	+58	99	04 40	+58	99	05 38	+58	99	06 36	+57	99
82	02 12	58	98	03 10	57	97	04 07	58	97	05 05	58	97	06 03	57	97
84	01 39	58	96	02 37	57	96	03 34	58	95	04 32	58	95	05 30	58	95
86	01 06	58	94	02 04	58	94	03 02	57	93	03 59	58	93	04 57	58	93
88	00 33	58	92	01 31	57	92	02 28	58	91	03 26	58	91	04 24	57	91
90	00 00	+58	90	00 58	+57	90	01 55	+58	89	02 53	+58	89	03 51	+57	89
92	−0 33	58	88	00 25	57	88	01 22	58	88	02 20	58	87	03 18	57	87
94	−1 06	58	86	−0 08	57	86	00 49	58	86	01 47	58	85	02 45	57	85
96	−1 39	58	84	−0 41	57	84	00 16	58	84	01 14	58	83	02 12	57	83
98	−2 12	58	82	−1 14	58	82	−0 16	57	82	00 41	58	81	01 39	58	81
100	−2 45	+58	80	−1 47	+58	80	−0 49	+58	80	00 09	+57	80	01 06	+58	79
102	−3 17	58	78	−2 19	57	78	−1 22	58	78	−0 24	58	78	00 34	58	77
104	−3 49	57	76	−2 52	58	76	−1 54	58	76	−0 56	58	76	00 02	58	75
106	−4 21	57	75	−3 24	58	74	−2 26	58	74	−1 28	58	74	−0 30	58	74
108	−4 53	58	73	−3 55	58	72	−2 57	57	72	−2 00	58	72	−1 02	58	72
110	−5 25	+58	71	−4 27	+58	70	−3 29	+58	70	−2 31	+58	70	−1 33	+58	70
112	−5 56	58	69	−4 58	58	68	−4 00	58	68	−3 02	58	68	−2 04	58	68
114	−6 26	58	67	−5 28	58	67	−4 30	58	66	−3 32	58	66	−2 34	58	66
116	−6 56	58	65	−5 58	58	65	−5 00	58	64	−4 02	58	64	−3 04	58	64
118	−7 26	58	63	−6 28	58	63	−5 30	58	62	−4 32	59	62	−3 33	58	62
120	−7 55	+58	61	−6 57	+58	61	−5 59	+58	60	−5 01	+59	60	−4 02	+58	60
122				−7 26	59	59	−6 27	58	58	−5 29	58	58	−4 31	59	58
124				−7 54	59	57	−6 55	58	57	−5 57	59	56	−4 58	58	56
126							−7 23	59	55	−6 24	58	54	−5 26	59	54
128							−7 49	58	53	−6 51	59	52	−5 52	58	52
130										−7 17	+59	50	−6 18	+59	50
132										−7 42	59	48	−6 43	59	48
134													−7 07	59	46
136													−7 31	59	44
138															

LHA	5° Hc	5° d	5° Z	6° Hc	6° d	6° Z	7° Hc	7° d	7° Z	8° Hc	8° d	8° Z	9° Hc	9° d	9° Z
	° ′	′	°	° ′	′	°	° ′	′	°	° ′	′	°	° ′	′	°
0	21 00	+60	180	22 00	+60	180	23 00	+60	180	24 00	+60	180	25 00	+60	180
2	20 59	60	178	21 59	60	178	22 59	60	178	23 59	60	178	24 59	60	178
4	20 58	60	176	21 58	60	176	22 58	60	176	23 58	60	176	24 58	60	176
6	20 55	59	174	21 54	60	174	22 54	60	174	23 54	60	174	24 54	60	174
8	20 50	60	172	21 50	60	171	22 50	60	171	23 50	60	171	24 50	60	171
10	20 45	+60	169	21 45	+60	169	22 45	+59	169	23 44	+60	169	24 44	+60	169
12	20 38	60	167	21 38	60	167	22 38	60	167	23 38	60	167	24 38	59	167
14	20 30	60	165	21 30	60	165	22 30	60	165	23 30	59	165	24 29	60	165
16	20 21	60	163	21 21	60	163	22 21	59	163	23 20	60	163	24 20	60	163
18	20 11	59	161	21 10	60	161	22 10	60	161	23 10	60	161	24 10	59	161
20	19 59	+60	159	20 59	+60	159	21 59	+59	159	22 58	+60	158	23 58	+60	158
22	19 47	59	157	20 46	60	157	21 46	60	156	22 46	59	156	23 45	60	156
24	19 33	60	155	20 33	59	154	21 32	60	154	22 32	59	154	23 31	60	154
26	19 18	60	152	20 18	59	152	21 17	60	152	22 17	59	152	23 16	60	152
28	19 02	60	150	20 02	59	150	21 01	60	150	22 01	59	150	23 00	60	150
30	18 46	+59	148	19 45	+59	148	20 44	+60	148	21 44	+59	148	22 43	+59	148
32	18 28	59	146	19 27	59	146	20 26	59	146	21 25	60	146	22 25	59	146
34	18 09	59	144	19 08	59	144	20 07	59	144	21 06	59	144	22 05	60	143
36	17 49	59	142	18 48	59	142	19 47	59	142	20 46	59	142	21 45	59	141
38	17 28	59	140	18 27	59	140	19 26	59	140	20 25	59	139	21 24	59	139
40	17 06	+59	138	18 05	+59	138	19 04	+59	138	20 03	+59	137	21 02	+59	137
42	16 44	59	136	17 43	58	136	18 41	59	136	19 40	59	135	20 39	59	135
44	16 20	59	134	17 19	59	134	18 18	59	133	19 17	58	133	20 15	59	133
46	15 56	59	132	16 55	58	132	17 53	59	131	18 52	59	131	19 51	58	131
48	15 31	59	130	16 30	58	130	17 28	59	129	18 27	58	129	19 25	59	129
50	15 05	+59	128	16 04	+58	128	17 02	+59	127	18 01	+58	127	18 59	+59	127
52	14 39	58	126	15 37	59	126	16 36	58	125	17 34	59	125	18 33	58	125
54	14 12	58	124	15 10	58	124	16 08	59	123	17 07	58	123	18 05	58	123
56	13 44	58	122	14 42	58	122	15 40	59	121	16 39	58	121	17 37	58	121
58	13 15	59	120	14 14	58	120	15 12	58	119	16 10	58	119	17 08	58	119
60	12 46	+59	118	13 45	+58	118	14 43	+58	117	15 41	+58	117	16 39	+58	117
62	12 17	58	116	13 15	58	116	14 13	58	115	15 11	58	115	16 09	58	115
64	11 47	58	114	12 45	58	114	13 43	58	113	14 41	58	113	15 39	58	113
66	11 16	58	112	12 14	58	112	13 12	58	111	14 10	58	111	15 08	58	111
68	10 45	58	110	11 43	58	110	12 41	58	109	13 39	58	109	14 37	58	109
70	10 14	+58	108	11 12	+58	108	12 10	+58	107	13 08	+58	107	14 06	+57	107
72	09 43	57	106	10 40	58	106	11 38	58	106	12 36	58	105	13 34	58	105
74	09 11	57	104	10 08	58	104	11 06	58	104	12 04	58	103	13 02	57	103
76	08 38	58	102	09 36	58	102	10 34	58	102	11 32	57	101	12 29	58	101
78	08 06	58	100	09 04	57	100	10 01	58	100	10 59	58	99	11 57	57	99
80	07 33	+58	98	08 31	+58	98	09 29	+57	98	10 26	+58	97	11 24	+58	97
82	07 00	58	96	07 58	58	96	08 56	57	96	09 53	58	96	10 51	58	95
84	06 28	57	94	07 25	58	94	08 23	58	94	09 21	57	94	10 18	58	93
86	05 55	57	93	06 52	58	92	07 50	57	92	08 47	58	92	09 45	58	91
88	05 21	58	91	06 19	58	90	07 17	57	90	08 14	58	90	09 12	58	89
90	04 48	+58	89	05 46	+58	88	06 44	+57	88	07 41	+58	88	08 39	+58	88
92	04 15	58	87	05 13	58	86	06 11	57	86	07 08	58	86	08 06	58	86
94	03 42	58	85	04 40	58	84	05 38	57	84	06 35	58	84	07 33	58	84
96	03 09	58	83	04 07	58	83	05 05	58	82	06 03	57	82	07 00	58	82
98	02 37	57	81	03 34	58	81	04 32	58	80	05 30	58	80	06 28	57	80
100	02 04	+58	79	03 02	+58	79	04 00	+57	78	04 57	+58	78	05 55	+58	78
102	01 32	58	77	02 30	57	77	03 27	58	77	04 25	58	76	05 23	58	76
104	01 00	58	75	01 58	57	75	02 55	58	75	03 53	58	74	04 51	58	74
106	00 28	58	73	01 26	58	73	02 24	57	73	03 21	58	72	04 19	58	72
108	−0 04	58	71	00 54	58	71	01 52	58	71	02 50	58	71	03 48	58	70
110	−0 35	+58	69	00 23	+58	69	01 21	+58	69	02 19	+58	69	03 17	+58	68
112	−1 06	58	67	−0 08	58	67	00 50	58	67	01 48	58	67	02 46	58	66
114	−1 36	58	66	−0 38	58	65	00 20	58	65	01 18	58	65	02 16	58	65
116	−2 06	58	64	−1 08	58	63	−0 10	59	63	00 49	58	63	01 47	58	63
118	−2 35	58	62	−1 37	58	62	−0 39	58	61	00 19	59	61	01 18	58	61
120	−3 04	+58	60	−2 06	+58	60	−1 08	+59	59	−0 09	+58	59	00 49	+58	59
122	−3 32	58	58	−2 34	58	58	−1 36	59	57	−0 37	58	57	00 21	58	57
124	−4 00	58	56	−3 02	59	56	−2 03	58	55	−1 05	59	55	−0 06	58	55
126	−4 27	58	54	−3 29	59	54	−2 30	58	54	−1 32	59	53	−0 33	58	53
128	−4 54	59	52	−3 55	59	52	−2 56	58	52	−1 58	58	51	−1 00	59	51
130	−5 19	+58	50	−4 21	+59	50	−3 22	+59	50	−2 23	+58	49	−1 25	+59	49
132	−5 44	58	48	−4 46	59	48	−3 47	59	48	−2 48	59	47	−1 49	58	47
134	−6 08	58	46	−5 10	59	46	−4 11	59	46	−3 12	59	45	−2 13	59	45
136	−6 32	59	44	−5 33	59	44	−4 34	59	44	−3 35	59	44	−2 36	58	43
138	−6 55	59	42	−5 56	59	42	−4 57	59	42	−3 58	59	42	−2 59	59	41

LHA	10° Hc	10° d	10° Z	11° Hc	11° d	11° Z	12° Hc	12° d	12° Z	13° Hc	13° d	13° Z	14° Hc	14° d	14° Z	LHA
	° ′	′	°	° ′	′	°	° ′	′	°	° ′	′	°	° ′	′	°	
0	26 00	+60	180	27 00	+60	180	28 00	+60	180	29 00	+60	180	30 00	+60	180	360
2	25 59	60	178	26 59	60	178	27 59	60	178	28 59	60	178	29 59	60	178	358
4	25 58	60	176	26 58	59	176	27 57	60	176	28 57	60	176	29 57	60	176	356
6	25 54	60	173	26 54	60	173	27 54	60	173	28 54	60	173	29 54	60	173	354
8	25 50	60	171	26 50	60	171	27 50	60	171	28 50	60	171	29 50	60	171	352
10	25 44	+60	169	26 44	+60	169	27 44	+60	169	28 44	+60	169	29 44	+60	169	350
12	25 37	60	167	26 37	60	167	27 37	60	167	28 37	60	167	29 37	60	167	348
14	25 29	60	165	26 29	60	165	27 29	60	165	28 29	60	164	29 29	59	164	346
16	25 20	60	163	26 20	60	162	27 20	59	162	28 19	60	162	29 19	60	162	344
18	25 09	60	160	26 09	60	160	27 09	60	160	28 09	59	160	29 08	60	160	342
20	24 58	+59	158	25 57	+60	158	26 57	+60	158	27 57	+59	158	28 56	+60	158	340
22	24 45	59	156	25 44	60	156	26 44	60	156	27 44	59	156	28 43	60	156	338
24	24 31	59	154	25 30	60	154	26 30	59	154	27 29	60	154	28 29	59	153	336
26	24 16	59	152	25 15	60	152	26 15	59	151	27 14	60	151	28 14	59	151	334
28	24 00	59	150	24 59	59	149	25 58	60	149	26 58	59	149	27 57	59	149	332
30	23 42	+60	148	24 42	+59	147	25 41	+59	147	26 40	+59	147	27 39	+60	147	330
32	23 24	59	145	24 23	59	145	25 22	60	145	26 22	59	145	27 21	59	145	328
34	23 05	59	143	24 04	59	143	25 03	59	143	26 02	59	143	27 01	59	143	326
36	22 44	59	141	23 43	59	141	24 42	60	141	25 42	59	141	26 41	59	140	324
38	22 23	59	139	23 22	59	139	24 21	59	139	25 20	59	138	26 19	59	138	322
40	22 01	+59	137	23 00	+59	137	23 59	+59	137	24 58	+58	136	25 56	+59	136	320
42	21 38	59	135	22 37	59	135	23 36	58	134	24 34	59	134	25 33	59	134	318
44	21 14	59	133	22 13	59	133	23 12	58	132	24 10	59	132	25 09	58	132	316
46	20 49	59	131	21 48	59	131	22 47	58	130	23 45	59	130	24 44	58	130	314
48	20 24	59	129	21 23	58	128	22 21	59	128	23 20	58	128	24 18	58	128	312
50	19 58	+58	127	20 56	+59	126	21 55	+58	126	22 53	+59	126	23 52	+58	126	310
52	19 31	58	125	20 29	59	124	21 28	58	124	22 26	58	124	23 24	59	124	308
54	19 03	59	123	20 02	58	122	21 00	58	122	21 58	58	122	22 56	59	122	306
56	18 35	58	121	19 33	59	120	20 32	58	120	21 30	58	120	22 28	58	120	304
58	18 06	59	119	19 05	58	118	20 03	58	118	21 01	58	118	21 59	58	118	302
60	17 37	+58	117	18 35	+58	116	19 33	+58	116	20 31	+58	116	21 29	+58	115	300
62	17 07	58	115	18 05	58	114	19 03	58	114	20 01	58	114	20 59	58	113	298
64	16 37	58	113	17 35	58	112	18 33	58	112	19 31	58	112	20 29	57	111	296
66	16 06	58	111	17 04	58	110	18 02	58	110	19 00	58	110	19 58	57	109	294
68	15 35	58	109	16 33	58	108	17 31	57	108	18 28	58	108	19 26	58	107	292
70	15 03	+58	107	16 01	+58	106	16 59	+58	106	17 57	+57	106	18 54	+58	106	290
72	14 32	57	105	15 29	58	104	16 27	58	104	17 25	57	104	18 22	58	104	288
74	13 59	58	103	14 57	58	102	15 55	57	102	16 52	58	102	17 50	58	102	286
76	13 27	58	101	14 25	57	101	15 22	58	100	16 20	58	100	17 18	57	100	284
78	12 54	58	99	13 52	58	99	14 50	57	98	15 47	58	98	16 45	57	98	282
80	12 22	+57	97	13 19	+58	97	14 17	+57	96	15 14	+58	96	16 12	+58	96	280
82	11 49	57	95	12 46	58	95	13 44	58	94	14 42	57	94	15 39	58	94	278
84	11 16	57	93	12 13	58	93	13 11	58	92	14 09	57	92	15 06	58	92	276
86	10 43	57	91	11 40	58	91	12 38	57	91	13 35	58	90	14 33	58	90	274
88	10 10	57	89	11 07	58	89	12 05	57	89	13 02	58	88	14 00	57	88	272
90	09 37	+57	87	10 34	+58	87	11 32	+57	87	12 29	+58	86	13 27	+57	86	270
92	09 04	57	85	10 01	58	85	10 59	57	85	11 56	58	84	12 54	57	84	268
94	08 31	57	83	09 28	58	83	10 26	58	83	11 24	57	83	12 21	58	82	266
96	07 58	58	82	08 56	57	81	09 53	58	81	10 51	57	81	11 48	58	80	264
98	07 25	58	80	08 23	58	79	09 21	57	79	10 18	58	79	11 16	58	78	262
100	06 53	+58	78	07 51	+57	77	08 48	+58	77	09 46	+58	77	10 44	+57	77	260
102	06 21	57	76	07 18	58	76	08 16	58	75	09 14	58	75	10 12	57	75	258
104	05 49	58	74	06 47	57	74	07 44	58	73	08 42	58	73	09 40	58	73	256
106	05 17	58	72	06 15	58	72	07 13	58	71	08 11	57	71	09 08	58	71	254
108	04 46	58	70	05 44	58	70	06 42	57	70	07 39	58	69	08 37	58	69	252
110	04 15	+58	68	05 13	+58	68	06 11	+58	68	07 09	+58	67	08 07	+58	67	250
112	03 44	58	66	04 42	58	66	05 40	58	66	06 38	58	65	07 36	58	65	248
114	03 14	58	64	04 12	59	64	05 11	58	64	06 09	58	64	07 07	58	63	246
116	02 45	58	62	03 43	58	62	04 41	58	62	05 39	58	62	06 37	58	61	244
118	02 16	58	60	03 14	58	60	04 12	58	60	05 10	59	60	06 09	58	60	242
120	01 47	+59	59	02 46	+58	58	03 44	+58	58	04 42	+58	58	05 40	+59	58	240
122	01 19	59	57	02 18	58	56	03 16	58	56	04 14	59	56	05 13	58	56	238
124	00 52	58	55	01 50	59	54	02 49	58	54	03 47	59	54	04 46	58	54	236
126	00 25	59	53	01 24	58	53	02 22	59	52	03 21	58	52	04 19	59	52	234
128	−0 01	59	51	00 58	58	51	01 56	59	50	02 55	59	50	03 54	58	50	232
130	−0 26	+59	49	00 33	+58	49	01 31	+59	48	02 30	+59	48	03 29	+58	48	230
132	−0 51	59	47	00 08	59	47	01 07	59	47	02 06	58	46	03 04	59	46	228
134	−1 14	58	45	−0 16	59	45	00 43	59	45	01 42	59	44	02 41	59	44	226
136	−1 38	59	43	−0 39	59	43	00 20	59	43	01 19	59	43	02 18	59	42	224
138	−2 00	59	41	−1 01	59	41	−0 02	59	41	00 57	59	41	01 56	59	40	222

S. Lat. {LHA greater than 180°....... Zn=180−Z; LHA less than 180°........... Zn=180+Z}

DECLINATION (0°-14°) <u>SAME</u> NAME AS LATITUDE

N. Lat. {LHA greater than 180°……. Zn=Z; LHA less than 180°………. Zn=360−Z}

DECLINATION (0°-14°) SAME NAME AS LATITUDE

LHA	0° Hc	0° d	0° Z	1° Hc	1° d	1° Z	2° Hc	2° d	2° Z	3° Hc	3° d	3° Z	4° Hc	4° d	4° Z	LHA
	° ′	′	°	° ′	′	°	° ′	′	°	° ′	′	°	° ′	′	°	
															140	220
															142	218
																216
																214
																212
																210
																208
																206
																204
																202
																200
																198
																196
																194
																192
																190
																188
																186
																184
																182
																180
120	-7 55	-59	61	240												
118	-7 26	58	63	242												
116	-6 56	59	65	-7 55	58	65	244									
114	-6 26	58	67	-7 24	58	67	246									
112	-5 56	58	69	-6 54	58	69	-7 52	58	69	248						
110	-5 25	-58	71	-6 23	-57	71	-7 20	-58	71	250						
108	-4 53	58	73	-5 51	58	73	-6 49	58	73	-7 47	58	73	252			
106	-4 21	58	75	-5 19	58	75	-6 17	58	75	-7 15	58	75	254			
104	-3 49	58	76	-4 47	58	77	-5 45	58	77	-6 43	58	77	-7 41	57	78	
102	-3 17	58	78	-4 15	58	79	-5 13	57	79	-6 10	58	79	-7 08	58	79	
100	-2 45	-57	80	-3 42	-58	81	-4 40	-58	81	-5 38	-58	81	-6 36	-57	81	
98	-2 12	58	82	-3 10	57	83	-4 07	58	83	-5 05	58	83	-6 03	57	83	
96	-1 39	58	84	-2 37	57	84	-3 34	58	85	-4 32	58	85	-5 30	58	85	
94	-1 06	58	86	-2 04	58	86	-3 02	57	87	-3 59	58	87	-4 57	58	87	
92	-0 33	58	88	-1 31	57	88	-2 28	58	89	-3 26	58	89	-4 24	57	89	
90	00 00	-58	90	-0 58	-57	90	-1 55	-58	91	-2 53	-58	91	-3 51	-57	91	
88	00 33	58	92	-0 25	57	92	-1 22	58	92	-2 20	58	93	-3 18	57	93	
86	01 06	58	94	00 08	57	94	-0 49	58	94	-1 47	58	95	-2 45	57	95	
84	01 39	58	96	00 41	57	96	-0 16	58	96	-1 14	58	97	-2 12	57	97	
82	02 12	58	98	01 14	58	98	00 16	57	98	-0 41	58	99	-1 39	58	99	
80	02 45	-58	100	01 47	-58	100	00 49	-58	100	-0 09	-57	100	-1 06	-58	101	
78	03 17	58	102	02 19	57	102	01 22	58	102	00 24	58	102	-0 34	58	103	
76	03 49	57	104	02 52	58	104	01 54	58	104	00 56	58	104	-0 02	58	105	
74	04 21	57	105	03 24	58	106	02 26	58	106	01 28	58	106	00 30	58	106	
72	04 53	58	107	03 55	58	108	02 57	57	108	02 00	58	108	01 02	58	108	
70	05 25	-58	109	04 27	-58	110	03 29	-58	110	02 31	-58	110	01 33	-58	110	
68	05 56	58	111	04 58	58	112	04 00	58	112	03 02	58	112	02 04	58	112	292
66	06 26	58	113	05 28	58	113	04 30	58	114	03 32	58	114	02 34	58	114	294
64	06 56	58	115	05 58	58	115	05 00	58	116	04 02	58	116	03 04	58	116	296
62	07 26	58	117	06 28	58	117	05 30	58	118	04 32	59	118	03 33	58	118	298
60	07 55	-58	119	06 57	-58	119	05 59	-58	120	05 01	-59	120	04 02	-58	120	300
58	08 24	58	121	07 26	59	121	06 27	58	122	05 29	58	122	04 31	59	122	302
56	08 52	58	123	07 54	59	123	06 55	58	123	05 57	59	124	04 58	58	124	304
54	09 19	58	125	08 21	58	125	07 23	59	125	06 24	58	126	05 26	59	126	306
52	09 46	58	127	08 48	59	127	07 49	58	127	06 51	59	128	05 52	58	128	308
50	10 12	-58	129	09 14	-59	129	08 15	-58	129	07 17	-59	130	06 18	-59	130	310
48	10 38	59	131	09 39	59	131	08 40	58	131	07 42	59	132	06 43	59	132	312
46	11 02	58	133	10 04	59	133	09 05	59	133	08 06	59	134	07 07	59	134	314
44	11 26	59	135	10 27	58	135	09 29	59	135	08 30	59	136	07 31	59	136	316
42	11 49	59	137	10 50	59	137	09 51	59	137	08 52	59	137	07 53	58	138	318
40	12 11	-59	139	11 12	-59	139	10 13	-59	139	09 14	-59	139	08 15	-59	140	320
38	12 33	59	141	11 34	59	141	10 35	60	141	09 35	59	141	08 36	59	142	322
36	12 53	59	143	11 54	59	143	10 55	59	143	09 56	60	143	08 56	59	144	324
34	13 13	60	145	12 13	59	145	11 14	59	145	10 15	59	145	09 16	60	146	326
32	13 31	59	147	12 32	60	147	11 32	59	147	10 33	59	147	09 34	60	148	328
30	13 49	-60	149	12 49	-59	149	11 50	-60	149	10 50	-59	149	09 51	-59	150	330
28	14 05	59	151	13 06	60	151	12 06	59	151	11 07	60	152	10 07	59	152	332
26	14 21	60	153	13 21	59	153	12 22	60	153	11 22	59	154	10 23	60	154	334
24	14 35	59	155	13 36	60	155	12 36	60	155	11 36	59	156	10 37	60	156	336
22	14 48	59	157	13 49	60	157	12 49	60	157	11 49	59	158	10 50	60	158	338
20	15 01	-60	159	14 01	-60	159	13 01	-59	160	12 02	-60	160	11 02	-60	160	340
18	15 12	60	161	14 12	60	161	13 12	59	162	12 13	60	162	11 13	60	162	342
16	15 22	60	163	14 22	60	164	13 22	60	164	12 22	59	164	11 23	60	164	344
14	15 31	60	166	14 31	60	166	13 31	60	166	12 31	60	166	11 31	59	166	346
12	15 39	60	168	14 39	60	168	13 39	60	168	12 39	60	168	11 39	60	168	348
10	15 45	-60	170	14 45	-60	170	13 45	-60	170	12 45	-60	170	11 45	-60	170	350
8	15 50	59	172	14 51	60	172	13 51	60	172	12 51	60	172	11 51	60	172	352
6	15 55	60	174	14 55	60	174	13 55	60	174	12 55	60	174	11 55	60	174	354
4	15 58	60	176	14 58	60	176	13 58	60	176	12 58	60	176	11 58	60	176	356
2	15 59	60	178	14 59	60	178	13 59	60	178	12 59	60	178	11 59	60	178	358
0	16 00	-60	180	15 00	-60	180	14 00	-60	180	13 00	-60	180	12 00	-60	180	360

LHA	5° Hc	5° d	5° Z	6° Hc	6° d	6° Z	7° Hc	7° d	7° Z	8° Hc	8° d	8° Z	9° Hc	9° d	9° Z	LHA
	° ′	′	°	° ′	′	°	° ′	′	°	° ′	′	°	° ′	′	°	
	-7 16	+59	40	-6 17	+59	40	-5 18	+59	40	-4 19	+59	40	-3 20	+59	40	220
	-7 37	59	38	-6 38	59	38	-5 39	59	38	-4 40	59	38	-3 41	59	38	218
			144	-6 58	59	36	-5 59	59	36	-5 00	60	36	-4 00	59	36	216
			146	-7 17	59	34	-6 18	59	34	-5 19	60	34	-4 19	59	34	214
			148	-7 35	59	32	-6 36	60	32	-5 36	59	32	-4 37	59	32	212
						150	-6 53	+60	30	-5 53	+59	30	-4 54	+60	30	210
						152	-7 09	60	28	-6 09	59	28	-5 10	60	28	208
						154	-7 24	60	26	-6 24	59	26	-5 25	60	26	206
									156	-6 38	59	24	-5 39	60	24	204
									158	-6 51	60	22	-5 51	59	22	202
									160	-7 03	+60	20	-6 03	+59	20	200
									162	-7 14	60	18	-6 14	60	18	198
												164	-6 24	60	16	196
												166	-6 32	60	14	194
												168	-6 39	59	12	192
												170	-6 46	+60	10	190
												172	-6 51	60	8	188
												174	-6 55	60	6	186
												176	-6 58	60	4	184
												178	-6 59	60	2	182
												180	-7 00	+60	0	180
120																
118																
116																
114																
112																
110																
108																
106																
104	256															
102	258															
100	-7 33	-58	82	260												
98	-7 00	58	84	-7 58	58	84	262									
96	-6 28	57	86	-7 25	58	86	264									
94	-5 55	57	87	-6 52	58	88	-7 50	57	88	266						
92	-5 21	58	89	-6 19	58	90	-7 17	57	90	268						
90	-4 48	-58	91	-5 46	-58	92	-6 44	-57	92	-7 41	-58	92	270			
88	-4 15	58	93	-5 13	58	94	-6 11	57	94	-7 08	58	94	272			
86	-3 42	58	95	-4 40	58	96	-5 38	57	96	-6 35	58	96	-7 33	58	96	
84	-3 09	58	97	-4 07	58	97	-5 05	58	98	-6 03	57	98	-7 00	58	98	
82	-2 37	57	99	-3 34	58	99	-4 32	58	100	-5 30	58	100	-6 28	57	100	
80	-2 04	-58	101	-3 02	-58	101	-4 00	-57	102	-4 57	-58	102	-5 55	-58	102	
78	-1 32	58	103	-2 30	57	103	-3 27	58	103	-4 25	58	104	-5 23	58	104	
76	-1 00	58	105	-1 58	57	105	-2 55	58	105	-3 53	58	106	-4 51	58	106	
74	-0 28	58	107	-1 26	58	107	-2 24	57	107	-3 21	58	108	-4 19	58	108	
72	00 04	58	109	-0 54	58	109	-1 52	58	109	-2 50	58	109	-3 48	58	110	
70	00 35	-58	111	-0 23	-58	111	-1 21	-58	111	-2 19	-58	111	-3 17	-58	112	
68	01 06	58	113	00 08	58	113	-0 50	58	113	-1 48	58	113	-2 46	58	114	292
66	01 36	58	114	00 38	58	115	-0 20	58	115	-1 18	58	115	-2 16	58	115	294
64	02 06	58	116	01 08	58	117	00 10	59	117	-0 49	58	117	-1 47	58	117	296
62	02 35	58	118	01 37	58	118	00 39	58	119	-0 19	59	119	-1 18	58	119	298
60	03 04	-58	120	02 06	-58	120	01 08	-59	121	00 09	-58	121	-0 49	-58	121	300
58	03 32	58	122	02 34	58	122	01 36	59	123	00 37	58	123	-0 21	58	123	302
56	04 00	58	124	03 02	59	124	02 03	58	125	01 05	59	125	00 06	58	125	304
54	04 27	58	126	03 29	59	126	02 30	58	126	01 32	59	127	00 33	58	127	306
52	04 54	59	128	03 55	59	128	02 56	58	128	01 58	58	129	01 00	59	129	308
50	05 19	-58	130	04 21	-59	130	03 22	-59	130	02 23	-58	131	01 25	-59	131	310
48	05 44	58	132	04 46	59	132	03 47	59	132	02 48	59	133	01 49	58	133	312
46	06 08	58	134	05 10	59	134	04 11	59	134	03 12	59	135	02 13	59	135	314
44	06 32	59	136	05 33	59	136	04 34	59	136	03 35	59	136	02 36	58	137	316
42	06 55	59	138	05 56	59	138	04 57	59	138	03 58	59	138	02 59	59	139	318
40	07 16	-59	140	06 17	-59	140	05 18	-59	140	04 19	-59	140	03 20	-59	140	320
38	07 37	59	142	06 38	59	142	05 39	59	142	04 40	59	142	03 41	59	142	322
36	07 57	59	144	06 58	59	144	05 59	59	144	05 00	60	144	04 00	59	144	324
34	08 16	59	146	07 17	59	146	06 18	59	146	05 19	60	146	04 19	59	146	326
32	08 34	59	148	07 35	59	148	06 36	60	148	05 36	59	148	04 37	59	148	328
30	08 52	-60	150	07 52	-59	150	06 53	-60	150	05 53	-59	150	04 54	-60	150	330
28	09 08	60	152	08 08	59	152	07 09	60	152	06 09	59	152	05 10	60	152	332
26	09 23	60	154	08 23	59	154	07 24	60	154	06 24	59	154	05 25	60	154	334
24	09 37	60	156	08 37	59	156	07 38	60	156	06 38	59	156	05 39	60	156	336
22	09 50	60	158	08 50	59	158	07 51	60	158	06 51	60	158	05 51	59	158	338
20	10 02	-60	160	09 02	-59	160	08 03	-60	160	07 03	-60	160	06 03	-59	160	340
18	10 13	60	162	09 13	60	162	08 13	59	162	07 14	60	162	06 14	60	162	342
16	10 23	60	164	09 23	60	164	08 23	60	164	07 23	59	164	06 24	60	164	344
14	10 32	60	166	09 32	60	166	08 32	60	166	07 32	60	166	06 32	60	166	346
12	10 39	60	168	09 39	60	168	08 39	60	168	07 39	60	168	06 39	59	168	348
10	10 45	-59	170	09 46	-60	170	08 46	-60	170	07 46	-60	170	06 46	-60	170	350
8	10 51	60	172	09 51	60	172	08 51	60	172	07 51	60	172	06 51	60	172	352
6	10 55	60	174	09 55	60	174	08 55	60	174	07 55	60	174	06 55	60	174	354
4	10 58	60	176	09 58	60	176	08 58	60	176	07 58	60	176	06 58	60	176	356
2	10 59	60	178	09 59	60	178	08 59	60	178	07 59	60	178	06 59	60	178	358
0	11 00	-60	180	10 00	-60	180	09 00	-60	180	08 00	-60	180	07 00	-60	180	360

LHA	10° Hc	10° d	10° Z	11° Hc	11° d	11° Z	12° Hc	12° d	12° Z	13° Hc	13° d	13° Z	14° Hc	14° d	14° Z	LHA
	° ′	′	°	° ′	′	°	° ′	′	°	° ′	′	°	° ′	′	°	
	-2 21	+59	39	-1 22	+59	39	-0 23	+59	39	00 36	+59	39	01 35	+59	39	220
	-2 42	60	37	-1 42	59	37	-0 43	59	37	00 16	59	37	01 15	59	37	218
	-3 01	59	35	-2 02	59	35	-1 03	59	35	-0 04	60	35	00 56	59	35	216
	-3 20	59	34	-2 21	60	33	-1 21	59	33	-0 22	59	33	00 37	59	33	214
	-3 38	60	32	-2 38	59	31	-1 39	59	31	-0 40	60	31	00 20	59	31	212
	-3 54	+59	30	-2 55	+59	29	-1 56	+60	29	-0 56	+59	29	00 03	+60	29	210
	-4 10	59	28	-3 11	60	28	-2 11	59	27	-1 12	60	27	-0 12	59	27	208
	-4 25	59	26	-3 26	60	26	-2 26	60	26	-1 26	59	25	-0 27	60	25	206
	-4 39	60	24	-3 39	59	24	-2 40	60	24	-1 40	60	23	-0 40	59	23	204
	-4 52	60	22	-3 52	60	22	-2 52	59	22	-1 53	60	21	-0 53	60	21	202
	-5 04	+60	20	-4 04	+60	20	-3 04	+60	20	-2 04	+60	20	-1 04	+59	19	200
	-5 14	60	18	-4 14	60	18	-3 14	59	18	-2 15	60	18	-1 15	60	18	198
	-5 24	60	16	-4 24	60	16	-3 24	60	16	-2 24	60	16	-1 24	59	16	196
	-5 32	60	14	-4 32	60	14	-3 32	59	14	-2 33	60	14	-1 33	60	14	194
	-5 40	60	12	-4 40	60	12	-3 40	60	12	-2 40	60	12	-1 40	60	12	192
	-5 46	+60	10	-4 46	+60	10	-3 46	+60	10	-2 46	+60	10	-1 46	+60	10	190
	-5 51	60	8	-4 51	60	8	-3 51	60	8	-2 51	60	8	-1 51	60	8	188
	-5 55	60	6	-4 55	60	6	-3 55	60	6	-2 55	60	6	-1 55	60	6	186
	-5 58	60	4	-4 58	60	4	-3 58	60	4	-2 58	60	4	-1 58	60	4	184
	-5 59	60	2	-4 59	60	2	-3 59	60	2	-2 59	60	2	-1 59	60	2	182
	-6 00	+60	0	-5 00	+60	0	-4 00	+60	0	-3 00	+60	0	-2 00	+60	0	180
120																
118																
116																
114																
112																
110																
108																
106																
104																
102																
100																
98																
96																
94																
92																
90																
88																
86	274															
84	-7 58	58	98	276												
82	-7 25	58	100	278												
80	-6 53	-58	102	-7 51	-57	103	280									
78	-6 21	57	104	-7 18	58	104	282									
76	-5 49	58	106	-6 47	57	106	-7 44	58	107	284						
74	-5 17	58	108	-6 15	58	108	-7 13	58	109	286						
72	-4 46	58	110	-5 44	58	110	-6 42	57	110	-7 39	58	111	288			
70	-4 15	-58	112	-5 13	-58	112	-6 11	-58	112	-7 09	-58	113	290			
68	-3 44	58	114	-4 42	58	114	-5 40	58	114	-6 38	58	115	-7 36	58	115	292
66	-3 14	58	116	-4 12	59	116	-5 11	58	116	-6 09	58	116	-7 07	58	117	294
64	-2 45	58	118	-3 43	58	118	-4 41	58	118	-5 39	58	118	-6 37	58	119	296
62	-2 16	58	120	-3 14	58	120	-4 12	58	120	-5 10	59	120	-6 09	58	120	298
60	-1 47	-59	121	-2 46	-58	122	-3 44	-58	122	-4 42	-58	122	-5 40	-59	122	300
58	-1 19	59	123	-2 18	58	124	-3 16	58	124	-4 14	59	124	-5 13	58	124	302
56	-0 52	58	125	-1 50	59	126	-2 49	58	126	-3 47	59	126	-4 46	58	126	304
54	-0 25	59	127	-1 24	58	127	-2 22	59	128	-3 21	58	128	-4 19	59	128	306
52	00 01	59	129	-0 58	58	129	-1 56	59	130	-2 55	59	130	-3 54	58	130	308
50	00 26	-59	131	-0 33	-58	131	-1 31	-59	132	-2 30	-59	132	-3 29	-58	132	310
48	00 51	59	133	-0 08	59	133	-1 07	59	133	-2 06	58	134	-3 04	59	134	312
46	01 14	58	135	00 16	59	135	-0 43	59	135	-1 42	59	136	-2 41	59	136	314
44	01 38	59	137	00 39	59	137	-0 20	59	137	-1 19	59	137	-2 18	59	138	316
42	02 00	59	139	01 01	59	139	00 02	59	139	-0 57	59	139	-1 56	59	140	318
40	02 21	-59	141	01 22	-59	141	00 23	-59	141	-0 36	-59	141	-1 35	-59	141	320
38	02 42	60	143	01 42	59	143	00 43	59	143	-0 16	59	143	-1 15	59	143	322
36	03 01	59	145	02 02	59	145	01 03	59	145	00 04	60	145	-0 56	59	145	324
34	03 20	59	146	02 21	60	147	01 21	59	147	00 22	59	147	-0 37	59	147	326
32	03 38	60	148	02 38	59	149	01 39	59	149	00 40	60	149	-0 20	59	149	328
30	03 54	-59	150	02 55	-59	151	01 56	-60	151	00 56	-59	151	-0 03	-60	151	330
28	04 10	59	152	03 11	60	152	02 11	59	153	01 12	60	153	00 12	59	153	332
26	04 25	59	154	03 26	60	154	02 26	60	154	01 26	59	155	00 27	60	155	334
24	04 39	60	156	03 39	59	156	02 40	60	156	01 40	60	157	00 40	59	157	336
22	04 52	60	158	03 52	60	158	02 52	59	158	01 53	60	159	00 53	60	159	338
20	05 04	-60	160	04 04	-60	160	03 04	-60	160	02 04	-60	160	01 04	-59	161	340
18	05 14	60	162	04 14	60	162	03 14	59	162	02 15	60	162	01 15	60	162	342
16	05 24	60	164	04 24	60	164	03 24	60	164	02 24	60	164	01 24	59	164	344
14	05 32	60	166	04 32	60	166	03 32	59	166	02 33	60	166	01 33	60	166	346
12	05 40	60	168	04 40	60	168	03 40	60	168	02 40	60	168	01 40	60	168	348
10	05 46	-60	170	04 46	-60	170	03 46	-60	170	02 46	-60	170	01 46	-60	170	350
8	05 51	60	172	04 51	60	172	03 51	60	172	02 51	60	172	01 51	60	172	352
6	05 55	60	174	04 55	60	174	03 55	60	174	02 55	60	174	01 55	60	174	354
4	05 58	60	176	04 58	60	176	03 58	60	176	02 58	60	176	01 58	60	176	356
2	05 59	60	178	04 59	60	178	03 59	60	178	02 59	60	178	01 59	60	178	358
0	06 00	-60	180	05 00	-60	180	04 00	-60	180	03 00	-60	180	02 00	-60	180	360

S. Lat. {LHA greater than 180°……. Zn=180−Z; LHA less than 180°………. Zn=180+Z}

DECLINATION (0°-14°) CONTRARY NAME TO LATITUDE

LAT 74°

N. Lat. {LHA greater than 180°....... Zn=Z; LHA less than 180°........... Zn=360−Z}

DECLINATION (15°-29°) SAME NAME AS LATITUDE

LAT 74°

LHA	15° Hc	d	Z	16° Hc	d	Z	17° Hc	d	Z	18° Hc	d	Z	19° Hc	d	Z
	° ′	′	°	° ′	′	°	° ′	′	°	° ′	′	°	° ′	′	°
0	31 00	+60	180	32 00	+60	180	33 00	+60	180	34 00	+60	180	35 00	+60	180
2	30 59	60	178	31 59	60	178	32 59	60	178	33 59	60	178	34 59	60	178
4	30 57	60	176	31 57	60	176	32 57	60	175	33 57	60	175	34 57	60	175
6	30 54	60	173	31 54	60	173	32 54	60	173	33 54	60	173	34 54	60	173
8	30 50	60	171	31 50	60	171	32 50	59	171	33 49	60	171	34 49	60	171
10	30 44	+60	169	31 44	+60	169	32 44	+60	169	33 44	+59	169	34 43	+60	169
12	30 37	60	167	31 37	59	166	32 36	60	166	33 36	60	166	34 36	60	166
14	30 28	60	164	31 28	60	164	32 28	60	164	33 28	60	164	34 28	59	164
16	30 19	60	162	31 19	59	162	32 18	60	162	33 18	60	162	34 18	60	162
18	30 08	60	160	31 08	59	160	32 07	60	160	33 07	60	160	34 07	59	159
20	29 56	+60	158	30 56	+59	158	31 55	+60	157	32 55	+60	157	33 55	+59	157
22	29 43	59	155	30 42	60	155	31 42	59	155	32 41	60	155	33 41	60	155
24	29 28	60	153	30 28	59	153	31 27	60	153	32 27	59	153	33 26	60	153
26	29 13	59	151	30 12	60	151	31 12	59	151	32 11	60	151	33 11	59	150
28	28 56	60	149	29 56	59	149	30 55	59	148	31 54	60	148	32 54	59	148
30	28 39	+59	147	29 38	+59	146	30 37	+59	146	31 36	+60	146	32 36	+59	146
32	28 20	59	144	29 19	59	144	30 18	59	144	31 17	60	144	32 17	59	144
34	28 00	59	142	28 59	59	142	29 58	59	142	30 57	59	142	31 56	59	142
36	27 40	58	140	28 38	59	140	29 37	59	140	30 36	59	140	31 35	59	139
38	27 18	59	138	28 17	59	138	29 16	58	138	30 14	59	137	31 13	59	137
40	26 55	+59	136	27 54	+59	136	28 53	+59	135	29 52	+58	135	30 50	+59	135
42	26 32	58	134	27 30	59	134	28 29	59	133	29 28	58	133	30 26	59	133
44	26 07	59	132	27 06	59	131	28 05	58	131	29 03	59	131	30 02	58	131
46	25 42	59	130	26 41	58	129	27 39	59	129	28 38	58	129	29 36	59	129
48	25 16	59	128	26 15	58	127	27 13	59	127	28 12	58	127	29 10	58	126
50	24 50	+58	125	25 48	+59	125	26 47	+58	125	27 45	+58	125	28 43	+58	124
52	24 23	58	123	25 21	58	123	26 19	58	123	27 17	58	123	28 15	59	122
54	23 55	58	121	24 53	58	121	25 51	58	121	26 49	58	120	27 47	58	120
56	23 26	58	119	24 24	58	119	25 22	58	119	26 20	58	118	27 18	58	118
58	22 57	58	117	23 55	58	117	24 53	58	117	25 51	58	116	26 49	58	116
60	22 27	+58	115	23 25	+58	115	24 23	+58	115	25 21	+58	114	26 19	+58	114
62	21 57	58	113	22 55	58	113	23 53	58	113	24 51	57	112	25 48	58	112
64	21 26	58	111	22 24	58	111	23 22	58	111	24 20	57	110	25 17	58	110
66	20 55	58	109	21 53	58	109	22 51	58	109	23 49	57	108	24 46	58	108
68	20 24	58	107	21 22	57	107	22 19	58	107	23 17	58	106	24 15	57	106
70	19 52	+58	105	20 50	+57	105	21 47	+58	105	22 45	+58	104	23 43	+57	104
72	19 20	58	103	20 18	57	103	21 15	58	103	22 13	57	102	23 10	58	102
74	18 48	57	101	19 45	58	101	20 43	57	101	21 40	58	100	22 38	57	100
76	18 15	58	99	19 13	57	99	20 10	58	99	21 08	57	98	22 05	58	98
78	17 42	58	97	18 40	58	97	19 38	57	97	20 35	57	96	21 32	58	96
80	17 10	+57	95	18 07	+58	95	19 05	+57	95	20 02	+57	95	20 59	+58	94
82	16 37	57	94	17 34	58	93	18 32	57	93	19 29	57	93	20 26	58	92
84	16 04	57	92	17 01	58	91	17 59	57	91	18 56	57	91	19 53	58	90
86	15 31	57	90	16 28	57	89	17 25	58	89	18 23	57	89	19 20	58	88
88	14 57	58	88	15 55	57	87	16 52	58	87	17 50	57	87	18 47	58	87
90	14 24	+58	86	15 22	+57	86	16 19	+58	85	17 17	+57	85	18 14	+58	85
92	13 51	58	84	14 49	57	84	15 46	58	83	16 44	57	83	17 41	58	83
94	13 19	57	82	14 16	58	82	15 14	57	81	16 11	58	81	17 09	57	81
96	12 46	58	80	13 44	57	80	14 41	58	80	15 39	57	79	16 36	58	79
98	12 14	57	78	13 11	58	78	14 09	57	78	15 06	58	77	16 04	57	77
100	11 41	+58	76	12 39	+58	76	13 37	+57	76	14 34	+59	75	15 32	+57	75
102	11 09	58	74	12 07	58	74	13 05	57	74	14 02	58	74	15 00	57	73
104	10 38	57	73	11 35	58	72	12 33	58	72	13 31	57	72	14 28	58	71
106	10 06	58	71	11 04	58	70	12 02	57	70	12 59	58	70	13 57	58	70
108	09 35	58	69	10 33	58	68	11 31	58	68	12 29	57	68	13 26	58	68
110	09 05	+57	67	10 02	+58	67	11 00	+58	66	11 58	+58	66	12 56	+58	66
112	08 34	58	65	09 32	58	65	10 30	58	64	11 28	58	64	12 26	58	64
114	08 05	58	63	09 03	58	63	10 01	58	63	10 59	58	62	11 57	58	62
116	07 35	59	61	08 34	58	61	09 32	58	61	10 30	58	60	11 28	58	60
118	07 07	58	59	08 05	58	59	09 03	58	59	10 01	58	59	10 59	58	58
120	06 39	+58	57	07 37	+58	57	08 35	+58	57	09 33	+58	57	10 31	+59	56
122	06 11	58	56	07 09	59	55	08 08	58	55	09 06	58	55	10 04	59	55
124	05 44	58	54	06 42	59	53	07 41	58	53	08 39	59	53	09 38	58	53
126	05 18	58	52	06 16	59	52	07 15	58	51	08 13	59	51	09 12	58	51
128	04 52	59	50	05 51	58	50	06 49	59	49	07 48	58	49	08 46	59	49
130	04 27	+59	48	05 26	+59	48	06 25	+58	48	07 23	+59	47	08 22	+58	47
132	04 03	59	46	05 02	59	46	06 01	58	46	06 59	59	45	07 58	59	45
134	03 40	58	44	04 38	59	44	05 37	59	44	06 36	59	44	07 35	59	43
136	03 17	59	42	04 16	59	42	05 15	59	42	06 14	59	42	07 13	58	42
138	02 55	59	40	03 54	59	40	04 53	59	40	05 52	59	40	06 51	59	40

LHA	20° Hc	d	Z	21° Hc	d	Z	22° Hc	d	Z	23° Hc	d	Z	24° Hc	d	Z
	° ′	′	°	° ′	′	°	° ′	′	°	° ′	′	°	° ′	′	°
0	36 00	+60	180	37 00	+60	180	38 00	+60	180	39 00	+60	180	40 00	+60	180
2	35 59	60	178	36 59	60	178	37 59	60	178	38 59	60	178	39 59	60	178
4	35 57	60	175	36 57	60	175	37 57	60	175	38 57	60	175	39 57	60	175
6	35 54	60	173	36 54	60	173	37 54	60	173	38 54	60	173	39 54	60	173
8	35 49	60	171	36 49	60	171	37 49	60	171	38 49	60	171	39 49	60	171
10	35 43	+60	168	36 43	+60	168	37 43	+60	168	38 43	+60	168	39 43	+60	168
12	35 36	60	166	36 36	60	166	37 36	60	166	38 36	59	166	39 35	60	166
14	35 27	60	164	36 27	60	164	37 27	60	164	38 27	60	164	39 27	59	163
16	35 18	59	162	36 17	60	161	37 17	60	161	38 17	60	161	39 17	59	161
18	35 06	60	159	36 06	60	159	37 06	59	159	38 05	60	159	39 05	60	159
20	34 54	+60	157	35 54	+59	157	36 53	+60	157	37 53	+59	157	38 52	+60	156
22	34 41	59	155	35 40	60	155	36 40	59	154	37 39	60	154	38 39	59	154
24	34 26	59	152	35 25	60	152	36 25	59	152	37 24	59	152	38 23	60	152
26	34 10	59	150	35 09	60	150	36 09	59	150	37 08	59	150	38 07	59	149
28	33 53	59	148	34 52	59	148	35 51	60	148	36 51	59	147	37 50	59	147
30	33 35	+59	146	34 34	+59	146	35 33	+59	145	36 32	+59	145	37 31	+59	145
32	33 16	59	144	34 15	59	143	35 14	59	143	36 13	59	143	37 12	59	143
34	32 55	59	141	33 54	59	141	34 53	59	141	35 52	59	141	36 51	59	140
36	32 34	59	139	33 33	59	139	34 32	59	139	35 31	59	138	36 30	58	138
38	32 12	59	137	33 11	59	137	34 10	58	136	35 08	59	136	36 07	59	136
40	31 49	+59	135	32 48	+58	134	33 46	+59	134	34 45	+58	134	35 43	+59	134
42	31 25	59	133	32 24	58	132	33 22	59	132	34 21	58	132	35 19	59	132
44	31 00	59	130	31 59	58	130	32 57	59	130	33 56	58	130	34 54	58	129
46	30 35	58	128	31 33	58	128	32 31	59	128	33 30	58	127	34 28	58	127
48	30 08	59	126	31 07	58	126	32 05	58	126	33 03	58	125	34 01	58	125
50	29 41	+58	124	30 39	+59	124	31 38	+58	124	32 36	+58	123	33 34	+58	123
52	29 14	58	122	30 12	58	122	31 10	58	121	32 08	58	121	33 06	58	121
54	28 45	58	120	29 43	58	120	30 41	58	119	31 39	58	119	32 37	58	118
56	28 16	58	118	29 14	58	118	30 12	58	117	31 10	58	117	32 08	57	117
58	27 47	58	116	28 45	57	116	29 42	58	115	30 40	58	115	31 38	57	115
60	27 17	+57	114	28 14	+58	113	29 12	+58	113	30 10	+57	113	31 07	+58	113
62	26 46	58	112	27 44	57	111	28 41	58	111	29 39	58	111	30 37	57	110
64	26 15	58	110	27 13	57	109	28 10	58	109	29 08	57	109	30 05	58	108
66	25 44	57	108	26 41	58	107	27 39	57	107	28 36	58	107	29 34	57	106
68	25 12	58	106	26 10	57	105	27 07	58	105	28 05	57	105	29 02	57	104
70	24 40	+58	104	25 38	+57	103	26 35	+57	103	27 32	+58	103	28 30	+57	102
72	24 08	57	102	25 05	58	101	26 03	57	101	27 00	57	101	27 57	58	100
74	23 35	58	100	24 33	57	99	25 30	57	99	26 27	58	99	27 25	57	98
76	23 03	57	98	24 00	57	97	24 57	58	97	25 55	57	97	26 52	57	97
78	22 30	57	96	23 27	58	96	24 25	57	95	25 22	57	95	26 19	57	95
80	21 57	+57	94	22 54	+58	94	23 52	+57	93	24 49	+57	93	25 46	+57	93
82	21 24	57	92	22 21	57	92	23 18	58	91	24 16	57	91	25 13	57	91
84	20 51	57	90	21 48	57	90	22 45	58	89	23 43	57	89	24 40	57	89
86	20 18	57	88	21 15	57	88	22 12	58	88	23 10	57	87	24 07	57	87
88	19 45	57	86	20 42	57	86	21 39	58	86	22 37	57	85	23 34	57	85
90	19 12	+57	84	20 09	+57	84	21 06	+58	84	22 04	+57	83	23 01	+57	83
92	18 39	57	82	19 36	58	82	20 34	57	82	21 31	57	81	22 28	57	81
94	18 06	58	81	19 04	57	80	20 01	57	80	20 58	58	80	21 56	57	79
96	17 34	57	79	18 31	57	78	19 28	58	78	20 26	57	78	21 23	58	77
98	17 01	58	77	17 59	57	76	18 56	58	76	19 54	57	76	20 51	57	76
100	16 29	+58	75	17 27	+57	75	18 24	+58	74	19 22	+57	74	20 19	+58	74
102	15 57	58	73	16 55	58	73	17 53	57	72	18 50	58	72	19 48	57	72
104	15 26	58	71	16 24	57	71	17 21	58	71	18 19	57	70	19 16	58	70
106	14 55	58	69	15 53	57	69	16 50	58	69	17 48	58	68	18 46	57	68
108	14 24	58	67	15 22	58	67	16 20	57	67	17 17	58	67	18 15	58	66
110	13 54	+58	66	14 52	+57	65	15 49	+58	65	16 47	+58	65	17 45	+58	64
112	13 24	58	64	14 22	58	63	15 20	58	63	16 18	57	63	17 15	58	63
114	12 55	58	62	13 53	58	62	14 51	57	61	15 48	58	61	16 46	58	61
116	12 26	58	60	13 24	58	60	14 22	58	59	15 20	58	59	16 18	58	59
118	11 57	59	58	12 56	58	58	13 54	58	58	14 52	58	57	15 50	58	57
120	11 30	+58	56	12 28	+58	56	13 26	+58	56	14 24	+58	55	15 22	+58	55
122	11 03	58	54	12 01	58	54	12 59	58	54	13 57	59	54	14 56	58	53
124	10 36	58	52	11 34	59	52	12 33	58	52	13 31	58	52	14 29	59	52
126	10 10	59	51	11 09	58	50	12 07	58	50	13 05	59	50	14 04	58	50
128	09 45	58	49	10 43	59	48	11 42	58	48	12 40	59	48	13 39	58	48
130	09 20	+59	47	10 19	+59	47	11 18	+58	46	12 16	+59	46	13 15	+58	46
132	08 57	58	45	09 55	59	45	10 54	59	45	11 53	58	44	12 51	59	44
134	08 34	58	43	09 32	59	43	10 31	59	43	11 30	59	43	12 29	58	42
136	08 11	59	41	09 10	59	41	10 09	59	41	11 08	59	41	12 07	59	41
138	07 50	59	39	08 49	59	39	09 48	59	39	10 47	59	39	11 46	59	39

LHA	25° Hc	d	Z	26° Hc	d	Z	27° Hc	d	Z	28° Hc	d	Z	29° Hc	d	Z	LHA
	° ′	′	°	° ′	′	°	° ′	′	°	° ′	′	°	° ′	′	°	
0	41 00	+60	180	42 00	+60	180	43 00	+60	180	44 00	+60	180	45 00	+60	180	360
2	40 59	60	178	41 59	60	178	42 59	60	178	43 59	60	178	44 59	60	178	358
4	40 57	60	175	41 57	60	175	42 57	60	175	43 57	60	175	44 57	60	175	356
6	40 54	60	173	41 54	60	173	42 54	60	173	43 54	60	173	44 54	60	173	354
8	40 49	60	170	41 49	60	170	42 49	60	170	43 49	60	170	44 49	60	170	352
10	40 43	+60	168	41 43	+60	168	42 43	+59	168	43 42	+60	168	44 42	+60	168	350
12	40 35	60	166	41 35	60	166	42 35	60	165	43 35	60	165	44 35	59	165	348
14	40 26	60	163	41 26	60	163	42 26	60	163	43 26	59	163	44 25	60	163	346
16	40 16	60	161	41 16	60	161	42 16	59	161	43 15	60	161	44 15	60	160	344
18	40 05	59	159	41 04	60	158	42 04	60	158	43 04	59	158	44 03	60	158	342
20	39 52	+60	156	40 52	+59	156	41 51	+60	156	42 51	+59	156	43 50	+60	156	340
22	39 38	59	154	40 37	60	154	41 37	59	154	42 36	60	153	43 36	59	153	338
24	39 23	59	152	40 22	60	151	41 22	59	151	42 21	59	151	43 20	59	151	336
26	39 06	60	149	40 06	59	149	41 05	59	149	42 04	59	149	43 03	60	148	334
28	38 49	59	147	39 48	59	147	40 47	59	147	41 46	59	146	42 45	60	146	332
30	38 30	+59	145	39 29	+59	144	40 28	+59	144	41 27	+59	144	42 26	+59	144	330
32	38 11	59	142	39 10	59	142	40 09	58	142	41 07	59	142	42 06	59	141	328
34	37 50	59	140	38 49	59	140	39 48	58	140	40 46	59	139	41 45	59	139	326
36	37 28	59	138	38 27	59	138	39 26	58	137	40 24	59	137	41 23	58	137	324
38	37 06	58	136	38 04	59	135	39 03	58	135	40 01	59	135	41 00	58	135	322
40	36 42	+59	133	37 41	+58	133	38 39	+58	133	39 37	+59	133	40 36	+58	132	320
42	36 18	58	131	37 16	58	131	38 14	59	131	39 13	58	130	40 11	58	130	318
44	35 52	59	129	36 51	58	129	37 49	58	128	38 47	58	128	39 45	58	128	316
46	35 26	58	127	36 24	58	127	37 22	59	126	38 21	58	126	39 19	58	126	314
48	34 59	58	125	35 57	58	124	36 55	58	124	37 53	58	124	38 51	58	123	312
50	34 32	+58	123	35 30	+58	122	36 28	+58	122	37 26	+57	122	38 23	+58	121	310
52	34 04	57	121	35 01	58	120	35 59	58	120	36 57	58	120	37 55	57	119	308
54	33 35	58	118	34 33	57	118	35 30	58	118	36 28	58	117	37 26	57	117	306
56	33 05	58	116	34 03	58	116	35 01	57	116	35 58	58	115	36 56	57	115	304
58	32 35	58	114	33 33	58	114	34 31	57	114	35 28	58	113	36 26	57	113	302
60	32 05	+58	112	33 03	+57	112	34 00	+58	111	34 58	+57	111	35 55	+57	111	300
62	31 34	58	110	32 32	57	110	33 29	57	109	34 26	58	109	35 24	57	109	298
64	31 03	57	108	32 00	58	108	32 58	57	107	33 55	57	107	34 52	57	107	296
66	30 31	58	106	31 29	57	106	32 26	57	105	33 23	57	105	34 20	57	105	294
68	29 59	58	104	30 57	57	104	31 54	57	103	32 51	57	103	33 48	57	103	292
70	29 27	+57	102	30 24	+58	102	31 22	+57	101	32 19	+57	101	33 16	+57	101	290
72	28 55	57	100	29 52	57	100	30 49	57	99	31 46	57	99	32 43	57	99	288
74	28 22	57	98	29 19	57	98	30 16	57	97	31 13	57	97	32 10	57	97	286
76	27 49	57	96	28 46	57	96	29 43	58	95	30 41	57	95	31 38	56	95	284
78	27 16	57	94	28 13	57	94	29 10	58	94	30 08	57	93	31 05	56	93	282
80	26 43	+57	92	27 40	+57	92	28 37	+57	92	29 34	+57	91	30 31	+57	91	280
82	26 10	57	90	27 07	57	90	28 04	57	90	29 01	57	89	29 58	57	89	278
84	25 37	57	88	26 34	57	88	27 31	57	88	28 28	57	87	29 25	57	87	276
86	25 04	57	87	26 01	57	86	26 58	57	86	27 55	57	85	28 52	57	85	274
88	24 31	57	85	25 28	57	84	26 25	57	84	27 22	57	84	28 19	57	83	272
90	23 58	+57	83	24 55	+58	82	25 53	+57	82	26 50	+57	82	27 47	+57	81	270
92	23 25	58	81	24 23	57	81	25 20	57	80	26 17	57	80	27 14	57	79	268
94	22 53	57	79	23 50	57	79	24 47	58	78	25 45	57	78	26 42	57	78	266
96	22 21	57	77	23 18	57	77	24 15	57	76	25 12	57	76	26 09	58	76	264
98	21 48	58	76	22 46	57	75	23 43	57	75	24 40	58	74	25 38	57	74	262
100	21 17	+57	73	22 14	+57	73	23 11	+58	73	24 09	+57	72	25 06	+57	72	260
102	20 45	58	71	21 43	57	71	22 40	57	71	23 37	58	71	24 35	57	70	258
104	20 14	57	70	21 11	58	69	22 09	57	69	23 06	58	69	24 04	57	68	256
106	19 43	58	68	20 41	57	67	21 38	58	67	22 36	57	67	23 33	58	67	254
108	19 13	57	66	20 10	58	66	21 08	58	65	22 06	57	65	23 03	58	65	252
110	18 43	+57	64	19 40	+58	64	20 38	+58	64	21 36	+57	63	22 33	+58	63	250
112	18 13	58	62	19 11	58	62	20 09	57	62	21 06	58	61	22 04	58	61	248
114	17 44	58	60	18 42	58	60	19 40	58	60	20 38	57	60	21 35	58	59	246
116	17 16	58	59	18 14	58	58	19 12	57	58	20 09	58	58	21 07	58	57	244
118	16 48	58	57	17 46	58	56	18 44	58	56	19 42	58	56	20 40	58	56	242
120	16 20	+59	55	17 19	+58	55	18 17	+58	54	19 15	+58	54	20 13	+58	54	240
122	15 54	58	53	16 52	58	53	17 50	58	53	18 48	58	52	19 46	58	52	238
124	15 28	58	51	16 26	58	51	17 24	58	51	18 22	59	51	19 21	58	50	236
126	15 02	59	49	16 01	58	49	16 59	58	49	17 57	59	49	18 56	58	48	234
128	14 37	59	48	15 36	58	47	16 34	59	47	17 33	58	47	18 31	59	47	232
130	14 13	+59	46	15 12	+58	46	16 10	+59	45	17 09	+58	45	18 07	+59	45	230
132	13 50	59	44	14 49	58	44	15 47	59	44	16 46	59	43	17 45	58	43	228
134	13 27	59	42	14 26	59	42	15 25	59	42	16 24	58	42	17 22	59	41	226
136	13 06	59	40	14 05	58	40	15 03	59	40	16 02	59	40	17 01	59	39	224
138	12 45	59	38	13 44	58	38	14 43	58	38	15 41	59	38	16 40	59	38	222

S. Lat. {LHA greater than 180°....... Zn=180−Z; LHA less than 180°........... Zn=180+Z}

DECLINATION (15°-29°) SAME NAME AS LATITUDE

LAT 74°

N. Lat. {LHA greater than 180°....... Zn=Z; LHA less than 180°........... Zn=360−Z}

DECLINATION (15°-29°) SAME NAME AS LATITUDE

LHA	15° Hc	15° d	15° Z	16° Hc	16° d	16° Z	17° Hc	17° d	17° Z	18° Hc	18° d	18° Z	19° Hc	19° d	19° Z
	° ′	′	°	° ′	′	°	° ′	′	°	° ′	′	°	° ′	′	°
140	02 34	+59	38	03 33	+59	38	04 32	+59	38	05 31	+59	38	06 30	+59	38
142	02 14	59	36	03 13	59	36	04 12	59	36	05 11	60	36	06 11	59	36
144	01 55	59	35	02 54	59	34	03 53	59	34	04 52	60	34	05 52	59	34
146	01 36	60	33	02 36	59	32	03 35	59	32	04 34	60	32	05 34	59	32
148	01 19	59	31	02 18	60	31	03 18	59	30	04 17	60	30	05 17	59	30
150	01 03	+59	29	02 02	+60	29	03 02	+59	29	04 01	+59	29	05 00	+60	28
152	00 47	60	27	01 47	59	27	02 46	60	27	03 46	59	27	04 45	60	27
154	00 33	59	25	01 32	60	25	02 32	59	25	03 31	60	25	04 31	59	25
156	00 19	60	23	01 19	59	23	02 18	60	23	03 18	60	23	04 18	59	23
158	00 07	59	21	01 06	60	21	02 06	60	21	03 06	59	21	04 05	60	21
160	−0 05	+60	19	00 55	+60	19	01 55	+59	19	02 54	+60	19	03 54	+60	19
162	−0 15	60	17	00 45	59	17	01 44	60	17	02 44	60	17	03 44	60	17
164	−0 25	60	15	00 35	60	15	01 35	60	15	02 35	60	15	03 35	60	15
166	−0 33	60	14	00 27	60	13	01 27	60	13	02 27	60	13	03 27	59	13
168	−0 40	60	12	00 20	60	12	01 20	60	11	02 20	60	11	03 20	60	11
170	−0 46	+60	10	00 14	+60	10	01 14	+60	10	02 14	+60	10	03 14	+60	10
172	−0 51	60	8	00 09	60	8	01 09	60	8	02 09	60	8	03 09	60	8
174	−0 55	60	6	00 05	60	6	01 05	60	6	02 05	60	6	03 05	60	6
176	−0 58	60	4	00 02	60	4	01 02	60	4	02 02	60	4	03 02	60	4
178	−0 59	60	2	00 01	60	2	01 01	60	2	02 01	60	2	03 01	60	2
180	−1 00	+60	0	00 00	+60	0	01 00	+60	0	02 00	+60	0	03 00	+60	0

LHA	20° Hc	20° d	20° Z	21° Hc	21° d	21° Z	22° Hc	22° d	22° Z	23° Hc	23° d	23° Z	24° Hc	24° d	24° Z
	° ′	′	°	° ′	′	°	° ′	′	°	° ′	′	°	° ′	′	°
140	07 29	+59	38	08 28	+60	37	09 28	+59	37	10 27	+59	37	11 26	+59	37
142	07 10	59	36	08 09	59	36	09 08	59	35	10 07	59	35	11 06	59	35
144	06 51	59	34	07 50	59	34	08 49	59	34	09 48	60	33	10 48	59	33
146	06 33	59	32	07 32	59	32	08 31	60	32	09 31	59	32	10 30	59	31
148	06 16	59	30	07 15	60	30	08 15	59	30	09 14	59	30	10 13	60	30
150	06 00	+59	28	06 59	+60	28	07 59	+59	28	08 58	+59	28	09 57	+60	28
152	05 45	59	26	06 44	60	26	07 44	59	26	08 43	60	26	09 43	59	26
154	05 30	60	24	06 30	60	24	07 30	59	24	08 29	60	24	09 29	59	24
156	05 17	60	23	06 17	60	23	07 17	59	22	08 16	60	22	09 16	59	22
158	05 05	60	21	06 05	59	21	07 04	60	21	08 04	60	20	09 04	59	20
160	04 54	+60	19	05 54	+59	19	06 53	+60	19	07 53	+60	19	08 53	+60	18
162	04 44	60	17	05 44	59	17	06 43	60	17	07 43	60	17	08 43	60	17
164	04 35	59	15	05 34	60	15	06 34	60	15	07 34	60	15	08 34	60	15
166	04 26	60	13	05 26	60	13	06 26	60	13	07 26	60	13	08 26	60	13
168	04 20	59	11	05 19	60	11	06 19	60	11	07 19	60	11	08 19	60	11
170	04 14	+60	9	05 14	+59	9	06 13	+60	9	07 13	+60	9	08 13	+60	9
172	04 09	60	8	05 09	60	8	06 09	60	8	07 09	60	7	08 09	60	7
174	04 05	60	6	05 05	60	6	06 05	60	6	07 05	60	6	08 05	60	6
176	04 02	60	4	05 02	60	4	06 02	60	4	07 02	60	4	08 02	60	4
178	04 01	60	2	05 01	60	2	06 01	60	2	07 01	60	2	08 01	60	2
180	04 00	+60	0	05 00	+60	0	06 00	+60	0	07 00	+60	0	08 00	+60	0

LHA	25° Hc	25° d	25° Z	26° Hc	26° d	26° Z	27° Hc	27° d	27° Z	28° Hc	28° d	28° Z	29° Hc	29° d	29° Z	LHA
	° ′	′	°	° ′	′	°	° ′	′	°	° ′	′	°	° ′	′	°	
140	12 25	+59	37	13 24	+59	36	14 23	+59	36	15 22	+59	36	16 21	+58	36	220
142	12 05	59	35	13 04	59	35	14 03	59	34	15 02	60	34	16 02	59	34	218
144	11 47	59	33	12 46	59	33	13 45	59	33	14 44	59	33	15 43	60	32	216
146	11 29	60	31	12 29	59	31	13 28	59	31	14 27	59	31	15 26	59	31	214
148	11 13	59	29	12 12	59	29	13 11	60	29	14 11	59	29	15 10	59	29	212
150	10 57	+59	28	11 56	+60	27	12 56	+59	27	13 55	+59	27	14 54	+60	27	210
152	10 42	60	26	11 42	59	26	12 41	59	25	13 40	60	25	14 40	59	25	208
154	10 28	60	24	11 28	59	24	12 27	60	24	13 27	59	24	14 26	60	23	206
156	10 15	60	22	11 15	60	22	12 15	59	22	13 14	60	22	14 14	59	22	204
158	10 03	60	20	11 03	60	20	12 03	59	20	13 02	60	20	14 02	60	20	202
160	09 53	+59	18	10 52	+60	18	11 52	+60	18	12 52	+59	18	13 51	+60	18	200
162	09 43	59	17	10 42	60	16	11 42	60	16	12 42	60	16	13 42	60	16	198
164	09 34	60	15	10 34	59	15	11 33	60	15	12 33	60	14	13 33	60	14	196
166	09 26	60	13	10 26	60	13	11 26	59	13	12 25	60	13	13 25	60	13	194
168	09 19	60	11	10 19	60	11	11 19	60	11	12 19	60	11	13 19	60	11	192
170	09 13	+60	9	10 13	+60	9	11 13	+60	9	12 13	+60	9	13 13	+60	9	190
172	09 09	59	7	10 08	60	7	11 08	60	7	12 08	60	7	13 08	60	7	188
174	09 05	60	6	10 05	60	6	11 05	60	5	12 05	60	5	13 05	60	5	186
176	09 02	60	4	10 02	60	4	11 02	60	4	12 02	60	4	13 02	60	4	184
178	09 01	60	2	10 01	60	2	11 01	60	2	12 01	60	2	13 01	60	2	182
180	09 00	+60	0	10 00	+60	0	11 00	+60	0	12 00	+60	0	13 00	+60	0	180

LHA	15° Hc	15° d	15° Z	16° Hc	16° d	16° Z	17° Hc	17° d	17° Z	18° Hc	18° d	18° Z	19° Hc	19° d	19° Z	20° Hc	20° d	20° Z	21° Hc	21° d	21° Z	22° Hc	22° d	22° Z	23° Hc	23° d	23° Z	LHA
64	−7 35	59	119																									296
62	−7 07	58	121																									298
60	−6 39	−58	123	−7 37	−58	123																						300
58	−6 11	58	124	−7 09	59	125																						302
56	−5 44	58	126	−6 42	59	127	−7 41	58	127																			304
54	−5 18	58	128	−6 16	59	128	−7 15	58	129																			306
52	−4 52	59	130	−5 51	58	130	−6 49	59	131	−7 48	58	131																308
50	−4 27	−59	132	−5 26	−59	132	−6 25	−58	132	−7 23	−59	133																310
48	−4 03	59	134	−5 02	59	134	−6 01	58	134	−6 59	59	135																312
46	−3 40	58	136	−4 38	59	136	−5 37	59	136	−6 36	59	136	−7 35	59	137													314
44	−3 17	59	138	−4 16	59	138	−5 15	59	138	−6 14	59	138	−7 13	58	138													316
42	−2 55	59	140	−3 54	59	140	−4 53	59	140	−5 52	59	140	−6 51	59	140													318
40	−2 34	−59	142	−3 33	−59	142	−4 32	−59	142	−5 31	−59	142	−6 30	−59	142	−7 29	−59	142										320
38	−2 14	59	144	−3 13	59	144	−4 12	59	144	−5 11	60	144	−6 11	59	144	−7 10	59	144										322
36	−1 55	59	145	−2 54	59	146	−3 53	59	146	−4 52	60	146	−5 52	59	146	−6 51	59	146										324
34	−1 36	60	147	−2 36	59	148	−3 35	59	148	−4 34	60	148	−5 34	59	148	−6 33	59	148	−7 32	59	148							326
32	−1 19	59	149	−2 18	60	149	−3 18	59	150	−4 17	60	150	−5 17	59	150	−6 16	59	150	−7 15	59	150							328
30	−1 03	−59	151	−2 02	−60	151	−3 02	−59	151	−4 01	−59	151	−5 00	−60	152	−6 00	−59	152	−6 59	−60	152							330
28	−0 47	60	153	−1 47	59	153	−2 46	60	153	−3 46	59	153	−4 45	60	153	−5 45	59	154	−6 44	60	154							332
26	−0 33	59	155	−1 32	60	155	−2 32	59	155	−3 31	60	155	−4 31	59	155	−5 30	60	156	−6 30	60	156							334
24	−0 19	60	157	−1 19	59	157	−2 18	60	157	−3 18	60	157	−4 18	59	157	−5 17	60	157	−6 17	60	157	−7 17	59	158				336
22	−0 07	59	159	−1 06	60	159	−2 06	60	159	−3 06	59	159	−4 05	60	159	−5 05	60	159	−6 05	59	159	−7 04	60	159				338
20	00 05	−60	161	−0 55	−60	161	−1 55	−59	161	−2 54	−60	161	−3 54	−60	161	−4 54	−60	161	−5 54	−59	161	−6 53	−60	161				340
18	00 15	60	163	−0 45	59	163	−1 44	60	163	−2 44	60	163	−3 44	60	163	−4 44	60	163	−5 44	59	163	−6 43	60	163				342
16	00 25	60	165	−0 35	60	165	−1 35	60	165	−2 35	60	165	−3 35	60	165	−4 35	59	165	−5 34	60	165	−6 34	60	165				344
14	00 33	60	166	−0 27	60	167	−1 27	60	167	−2 27	60	167	−3 27	59	167	−4 26	60	167	−5 26	60	167	−6 26	60	167				346
12	00 40	60	168	−0 20	60	168	−1 20	60	169	−2 20	60	169	−3 20	60	169	−4 20	59	169	−5 19	60	169	−6 19	60	169				348
10	00 46	−60	170	−0 14	−60	170	−1 14	−60	170	−2 14	−60	170	−3 14	−60	170	−4 14	−60	171	−5 14	−59	171	−6 13	−60	171				350
8	00 51	60	172	−0 09	60	172	−1 09	60	172	−2 09	60	172	−3 09	60	172	−4 09	60	172	−5 09	60	172	−6 09	60	172				352
6	00 55	60	174	−0 05	60	174	−1 05	60	174	−2 05	60	174	−3 05	60	174	−4 05	60	174	−5 05	60	174	−6 05	60	174				354
4	00 58	60	176	−0 02	60	176	−1 02	60	176	−2 02	60	176	−3 02	60	176	−4 02	60	176	−5 02	60	176	−6 02	60	176				356
2	00 59	60	178	−0 01	60	178	−1 01	60	178	−2 01	60	178	−3 01	60	178	−4 01	60	178	−5 01	60	178	−6 01	60	178	−7 01	60	178	358
0	01 00	−60	180	00 00	−60	180	−1 00	−60	180	−2 00	−60	180	−3 00	−60	180	−4 00	−60	180	−5 00	−60	180	−6 00	−60	180	−7 00	−60	180	360

15°	16°	17°	18°	19°	20°	21°	22°	23°	24°	25°	26°	27°	28°	29°

S. Lat. {LHA greater than 180°........ Zn=180−Z; LHA less than 180°.......... Zn=180+Z}

DECLINATION (15°-29°) CONTRARY NAME TO LATITUDE

N. Lat. {LHA greater than 180°....... Zn=Z
{LHA less than 180°........... Zn=360−Z

DECLINATION (0°-14°) SAME NAME AS LATITUDE

LHA	0° Hc	d	Z	1° Hc	d	Z	2° Hc	d	Z	3° Hc	d	Z	4° Hc	d	Z
	° ′	′	°	° ′	′	°	° ′	′	°	° ′	′	°	° ′	′	°
0	15 00	+60	180	16 00	+60	180	17 00	+60	180	18 00	+60	180	19 00	+60	180
2	14 59	60	178	15 59	60	178	16 59	60	178	17 59	60	178	18 59	60	178
4	14 58	60	176	15 58	60	176	16 58	60	176	17 58	60	176	18 58	60	176
6	14 55	60	174	15 55	60	174	16 55	60	174	17 55	60	174	18 55	60	174
8	14 51	60	172	15 51	60	172	16 51	60	172	17 51	60	172	18 51	60	172
10	14 46	+60	170	15 46	+60	170	16 46	+60	170	17 46	+60	170	18 46	+60	170
12	14 40	60	168	15 40	60	168	16 40	60	168	17 40	60	167	18 40	59	167
14	14 33	60	166	15 33	59	166	16 32	60	165	17 32	60	165	18 32	60	165
16	14 24	60	164	15 24	60	163	16 24	60	163	17 24	60	163	18 24	60	163
18	14 15	60	161	15 15	60	161	16 15	59	161	17 14	60	161	18 14	60	161
20	14 05	+59	159	15 04	+60	159	16 04	+60	159	17 04	+60	159	18 04	+59	159
22	13 53	60	157	14 53	60	157	15 53	59	157	16 52	60	157	17 52	60	157
24	13 41	59	155	14 40	60	155	15 40	60	155	16 40	59	155	17 39	60	155
26	13 27	60	153	14 27	59	153	15 26	60	153	16 26	59	153	17 25	60	153
28	13 13	59	151	14 12	60	151	15 12	59	151	16 11	60	151	17 11	59	151
30	12 57	+60	149	13 57	+59	149	14 56	+60	149	15 56	+59	149	16 55	+59	149
32	12 41	59	147	13 40	60	147	14 40	59	147	15 39	59	147	16 38	60	147
34	12 23	60	145	13 23	59	145	14 22	59	145	15 21	60	145	16 21	59	145
36	12 05	60	143	13 05	59	143	14 04	59	143	15 03	59	143	16 02	60	142
38	11 46	59	141	12 45	60	141	13 45	59	141	14 44	59	141	15 43	59	140
40	11 26	+59	139	12 25	+59	139	13 24	+60	139	14 24	+59	139	15 23	+59	138
42	11 05	59	137	12 04	60	137	13 04	59	137	14 03	59	137	15 02	59	136
44	10 44	59	135	11 43	59	135	12 42	59	135	13 41	59	134	14 40	59	134
46	10 22	58	133	11 20	59	133	12 19	59	133	13 18	59	132	14 17	59	132
48	09 58	59	131	10 57	59	131	11 56	59	131	12 55	59	130	13 54	59	130
50	09 35	+58	129	10 33	+59	129	11 32	+59	129	12 31	+59	128	13 30	+58	128
52	09 10	59	127	10 09	59	127	11 08	58	127	12 06	59	126	13 05	59	126
54	08 45	59	125	09 44	58	125	10 42	59	125	11 41	59	124	12 40	58	124
56	08 19	59	123	09 18	58	123	10 16	59	123	11 15	59	122	12 14	58	122
58	07 53	59	121	08 52	58	121	09 50	59	121	10 49	58	120	11 47	58	120
60	07 26	+59	119	08 25	+58	119	09 23	+58	119	10 21	+59	119	11 20	+58	118
62	06 59	58	117	07 57	59	117	08 56	58	117	09 54	58	117	10 52	59	116
64	06 31	58	115	07 29	59	115	08 28	58	115	09 26	58	115	10 24	58	114
66	06 03	58	113	07 01	58	113	07 59	58	113	08 57	59	113	09 56	58	112
68	05 34	58	111	06 32	58	111	07 30	59	111	08 29	58	111	09 27	58	110
70	05 05	+58	109	06 03	+58	109	07 01	+58	109	07 59	+58	109	08 57	+59	108
72	04 35	58	107	05 33	59	107	06 32	58	107	07 30	58	107	08 28	58	106
74	04 06	58	106	05 04	58	105	06 02	58	105	07 00	58	105	07 58	58	105
76	03 35	59	104	04 34	58	103	05 32	58	103	06 30	58	103	07 28	58	103
78	03 05	58	102	04 03	58	101	05 01	58	101	05 59	58	101	06 57	58	101
80	02 35	+58	100	03 33	+58	99	04 31	+58	99	05 29	+58	99	06 27	+58	99
82	02 04	58	98	03 02	58	98	04 00	58	97	04 58	58	97	05 56	58	97
84	01 33	58	96	02 31	58	96	03 29	58	95	04 27	58	95	05 25	58	95
86	01 02	58	94	02 00	58	94	02 58	58	93	03 56	58	93	04 54	58	93
88	00 31	58	92	01 29	58	92	02 27	58	91	03 25	58	91	04 23	58	91
90	00 00	+58	90	00 58	+58	90	01 56	+58	90	02 54	+58	89	03 52	+58	89
92	−0 31	58	88	00 27	58	88	01 25	58	88	02 23	58	87	03 21	58	87
94	−1 02	58	86	−0 04	58	86	00 54	58	86	01 52	58	85	02 50	58	85
96	−1 33	58	84	−0 35	58	84	00 23	58	84	01 21	58	83	02 19	58	83
98	−2 04	58	82	−1 06	58	82	−0 08	58	82	00 50	58	82	01 48	58	81
100	−2 35	+58	80	−1 37	+58	80	−0 39	+58	80	00 19	+59	80	01 18	+58	79
102	−3 05	58	78	−2 07	58	78	−1 09	58	78	−0 11	58	78	00 47	58	77
104	−3 35	58	76	−2 37	58	76	−1 39	58	76	−0 41	58	76	00 17	58	75
106	−4 06	59	74	−3 07	58	74	−2 09	58	74	−1 11	58	74	−0 13	58	74
108	−4 35	58	73	−3 37	58	72	−2 39	58	72	−1 41	58	72	−0 43	59	72
110	−5 05	+59	71	−4 06	+58	70	−3 08	+58	70	−2 10	+58	70	−1 12	+58	70
112	−5 34	58	69	−4 36	59	68	−3 37	58	68	−2 39	58	68	−1 41	58	68
114	−6 03	59	67	−5 04	58	66	−4 06	58	66	−3 08	59	66	−2 09	58	66
116	−6 31	58	65	−5 33	59	64	−4 34	58	64	−3 36	58	64	−2 38	59	64
118	−6 59	59	63	−6 00	58	63	−5 02	58	62	−4 04	59	62	−3 05	58	62
120	−7 26	+58	61	−6 28	+59	61	−5 29	+58	60	−4 31	+59	60	−3 32	+58	60
122	−7 53	58	59	−6 55	59	59	−5 56	59	58	−4 57	58	58	−3 59	59	58
124				−7 21	59	57	−6 22	58	56	−5 24	59	56	−4 25	59	56
126				−7 46	58	55	−6 48	59	54	−5 49	59	54	−4 50	58	54
128							−7 13	59	52	−6 14	59	52	−5 15	59	52
130							−7 37	+59	51	−6 38	+59	50	−5 39	+58	50
132										−7 02	59	48	−6 03	59	48
134										−7 25	59	46	−6 26	59	46
136													−6 48	59	44
138													−7 09	59	42

LHA	5° Hc	d	Z	6° Hc	d	Z	7° Hc	d	Z	8° Hc	d	Z	9° Hc	d	Z
	° ′	′	°	° ′	′	°	° ′	′	°	° ′	′	°	° ′	′	°
0	20 00	+60	180	21 00	+60	180	22 00	+60	180	23 00	+60	180	24 00	+60	180
2	19 59	60	178	20 59	60	178	21 59	60	178	22 59	60	178	23 59	60	178
4	19 58	60	176	20 58	60	176	21 58	60	176	22 58	60	176	23 58	60	176
6	19 55	60	174	20 55	60	174	21 55	60	174	22 55	60	174	23 55	60	174
8	19 51	60	172	20 51	60	172	21 51	60	171	22 51	60	171	23 51	60	171
10	19 46	+60	169	20 46	+60	169	21 46	+60	169	22 46	+59	169	23 45	+60	169
12	19 39	60	167	20 39	60	167	21 39	60	167	22 39	60	167	23 39	60	167
14	19 32	60	165	20 32	60	165	21 32	60	165	22 32	60	165	23 32	59	165
16	19 24	59	163	20 23	60	163	21 23	60	163	22 23	60	163	23 23	60	163
18	19 14	60	161	20 14	60	161	21 14	59	161	22 13	60	161	23 13	60	161
20	19 03	+60	159	20 03	+60	159	21 03	+60	159	22 03	+59	159	23 02	+60	159
22	18 52	59	157	19 51	60	157	20 51	60	157	21 51	59	156	22 50	60	156
24	18 39	59	155	19 38	60	155	20 38	60	154	21 38	59	154	22 37	60	154
26	18 25	60	153	19 25	59	153	20 24	60	152	21 24	59	152	22 23	60	152
28	18 10	60	151	19 10	59	150	20 09	60	150	21 09	59	150	22 08	60	150
30	17 54	+60	148	18 54	+59	148	19 53	+60	148	20 53	+59	148	21 52	+60	148
32	17 38	59	146	18 37	59	146	19 36	60	146	20 36	59	146	21 35	60	146
34	17 20	59	144	18 19	60	144	19 19	59	144	20 18	59	144	21 17	60	144
36	17 02	59	142	18 01	59	142	19 00	59	142	19 59	59	142	20 58	60	142
38	16 42	59	140	17 41	59	140	18 40	60	140	19 40	59	140	20 39	59	140
40	16 22	+59	138	17 21	+59	138	18 20	+59	138	19 19	+59	138	20 18	+59	137
42	16 01	59	136	17 00	59	136	17 59	59	136	18 58	59	136	19 57	59	135
44	15 39	59	134	16 38	59	134	17 37	58	134	18 35	59	134	19 34	59	133
46	15 16	59	132	16 15	59	132	17 14	59	132	18 13	58	131	19 11	59	131
48	14 53	58	130	15 51	59	130	16 50	59	130	17 49	59	129	18 48	58	129
50	14 28	+59	128	15 27	+59	128	16 26	+59	128	17 25	+58	127	18 23	+59	127
52	14 04	58	126	15 02	59	126	16 01	59	126	17 00	58	125	17 58	59	125
54	13 38	59	124	14 37	58	124	15 35	59	124	16 34	58	123	17 32	59	123
56	13 12	59	122	14 11	58	122	15 09	59	122	16 08	58	121	17 06	59	121
58	12 45	59	120	13 44	58	120	14 42	59	120	15 41	58	119	16 39	59	119
60	12 18	+59	118	13 17	+58	118	14 15	+58	118	15 13	+59	117	16 12	+58	117
62	11 51	58	116	12 49	58	116	13 47	59	116	14 46	58	115	15 44	58	115
64	11 22	59	114	12 21	58	114	13 19	58	114	14 17	59	113	15 16	58	113
66	10 54	58	112	11 52	58	112	12 50	59	112	13 49	58	111	14 47	58	111
68	10 25	58	110	11 23	58	110	12 21	58	110	13 19	59	109	14 18	58	109
70	09 56	+58	108	10 54	+58	108	11 52	+58	108	12 50	+58	107	13 48	+58	107
72	09 26	58	106	10 24	58	106	11 22	58	106	12 20	58	105	13 18	58	105
74	08 56	58	104	09 54	58	104	10 52	58	104	11 50	58	103	12 48	58	103
76	08 26	58	102	09 24	58	102	10 22	58	102	11 20	58	102	12 18	58	101
78	07 55	58	100	08 53	58	100	09 51	58	100	10 49	58	100	11 47	58	99
80	07 25	+58	98	08 23	+58	98	09 21	+58	98	10 19	+57	98	11 16	+58	97
82	06 54	58	96	07 52	58	96	08 50	58	96	09 48	58	96	10 46	58	95
84	06 23	58	95	07 21	58	94	08 19	58	94	09 17	58	94	10 15	58	94
86	05 52	58	93	06 50	58	92	07 48	58	92	08 46	58	92	09 44	58	92
88	05 21	58	91	06 19	58	90	07 17	58	90	08 15	58	90	09 13	57	90
90	04 50	+58	89	05 48	+58	88	06 46	+58	88	07 44	+58	88	08 42	+57	88
92	04 19	58	87	05 17	58	87	06 15	58	86	07 13	57	86	08 10	58	86
94	03 48	58	85	04 46	58	85	05 44	58	84	06 42	58	84	07 40	57	84
96	03 17	58	83	04 15	58	83	05 13	58	82	06 11	58	82	07 09	58	82
98	02 46	58	81	03 44	58	81	04 42	58	81	05 40	58	80	06 38	58	80
100	02 16	+58	79	03 14	+58	79	04 12	+58	79	05 10	+58	78	06 08	+58	78
102	01 45	58	77	02 43	58	77	03 41	58	77	04 39	58	76	05 37	58	76
104	01 15	58	75	02 13	58	75	03 11	58	75	04 09	58	74	05 07	58	74
106	00 45	58	73	01 43	58	73	02 41	58	73	03 39	59	73	04 38	58	72
108	00 16	58	71	01 14	58	71	02 12	58	71	03 10	58	71	04 08	58	70
110	−0 14	+58	69	00 44	+59	69	01 43	+58	69	02 41	÷58	69	03 39	+58	68
112	−0 43	59	67	00 16	58	67	01 14	58	67	02 12	58	67	03 10	59	67
114	−1 11	58	65	−0 13	58	65	00 45	59	65	01 44	58	65	02 42	58	65
116	−1 39	58	64	−0 41	59	63	00 18	58	63	01 16	58	63	02 14	59	63
118	−2 07	59	62	−1 08	58	61	−0 10	58	61	00 48	59	61	01 47	58	61
120	−2 34	+59	60	−1 35	+58	59	−0 37	+59	59	00 22	+58	59	01 20	+58	59
122	−3 00	58	58	−2 02	59	58	−1 03	58	57	−0 05	59	57	00 54	58	57
124	−3 26	58	56	−2 28	59	56	−1 29	58	55	−0 31	59	55	00 28	59	55
126	−3 52	59	54	−2 53	59	54	−1 54	58	53	−0 56	59	53	00 03	59	53
128	−4 16	58	52	−3 18	59	52	−2 19	59	51	−1 20	58	51	−0 22	59	51
130	−4 41	+59	50	−3 42	+59	50	−2 43	+59	50	−1 44	+59	49	−0 45	+58	49
132	−5 04	59	48	−4 05	59	48	−3 06	59	48	−2 07	58	47	−1 09	59	47
134	−5 27	59	46	−4 28	59	46	−3 29	59	46	−2 30	59	45	−1 31	59	45
136	−5 49	59	44	−4 50	59	44	−3 51	59	44	−2 52	59	44	−1 53	59	43
138	−6 10	59	42	−5 11	59	42	−4 12	59	42	−3 13	59	42	−2 14	59	41

LHA	10° Hc	d	Z	11° Hc	d	Z	12° Hc	d	Z	13° Hc	d	Z	14° Hc	d	Z	LHA
	° ′	′	°	° ′	′	°	° ′	′	°	° ′	′	°	° ′	′	°	
0	25 00	+60	180	26 00	+60	180	27 00	+60	180	28 00	+60	180	29 00	+60	180	360
2	24 59	60	178	25 59	60	178	26 59	60	178	27 59	60	178	28 59	60	178	358
4	24 58	60	176	25 58	60	176	26 58	60	176	27 58	60	176	28 58	60	176	356
6	24 55	60	174	25 55	60	173	26 55	60	173	27 55	60	173	28 55	60	173	354
8	24 51	60	171	25 51	60	171	26 51	60	171	27 51	59	171	28 50	60	171	352
10	24 45	+60	169	25 45	+60	169	26 45	+60	169	27 45	+60	169	28 45	+60	169	350
12	24 39	60	167	25 39	60	167	26 39	60	167	27 39	60	167	28 39	59	167	348
14	24 31	60	165	25 31	60	165	26 31	60	165	27 31	60	165	28 31	60	165	346
16	24 23	60	163	25 23	59	163	26 22	60	163	27 22	60	162	28 22	60	162	344
18	24 13	60	161	25 13	59	160	26 12	60	160	27 12	60	160	28 12	60	160	342
20	24 02	+60	158	25 02	+59	158	26 01	+60	158	27 01	+60	158	28 01	+59	158	340
22	23 50	60	156	24 50	59	156	25 49	60	156	26 49	60	156	27 49	59	156	338
24	23 37	60	154	24 37	59	154	25 36	60	154	26 36	59	154	27 35	60	154	336
26	23 23	59	152	24 22	60	152	25 22	59	152	26 21	60	152	27 21	59	151	334
28	23 08	59	150	24 07	60	150	25 07	59	150	26 06	60	149	27 06	59	149	332
30	22 52	+59	148	23 51	+59	148	24 50	+60	147	25 50	+59	147	26 49	+60	147	330
32	22 35	59	146	23 34	59	145	24 33	59	145	25 32	60	145	26 32	59	145	328
34	22 17	59	144	23 16	59	143	24 15	59	143	25 14	59	143	26 13	60	143	326
36	21 58	59	141	22 57	59	141	23 56	59	141	24 55	59	141	25 54	59	141	324
38	21 38	59	139	22 37	59	139	23 36	59	139	24 35	59	139	25 34	59	139	322
40	21 17	+59	137	22 16	+59	137	23 15	+59	137	24 14	+59	137	25 13	+59	136	320
42	20 56	59	135	21 55	58	135	22 53	59	135	23 52	59	135	24 51	59	134	318
44	20 33	59	133	21 32	59	133	22 31	59	133	23 30	59	132	24 29	58	132	316
46	20 10	59	131	21 09	59	131	22 08	59	131	23 07	58	130	24 05	59	130	314
48	19 46	59	129	20 45	59	129	21 44	59	129	22 43	58	128	23 41	59	128	312
50	19 22	+59	127	20 21	+58	127	21 19	+59	127	22 18	+59	126	23 16	+59	126	310
52	18 57	59	125	19 55	59	125	20 54	58	124	21 52	59	124	22 51	58	124	308
54	18 31	58	123	19 29	59	123	20 28	58	122	21 26	59	122	22 25	58	122	306
56	18 05	58	121	19 03	58	121	20 01	59	120	21 00	58	120	21 58	59	120	304
58	17 38	58	119	18 36	58	119	19 34	59	118	20 33	58	118	21 31	58	118	302
60	17 10	+58	117	18 08	+59	117	19 07	+58	116	20 05	+58	116	21 03	+59	116	300
62	16 42	58	115	17 40	59	115	18 39	58	114	19 37	58	114	20 35	58	114	298
64	16 14	58	113	17 12	58	113	18 10	58	112	19 08	58	112	20 06	59	112	296
66	15 45	58	111	16 43	58	111	17 41	58	110	18 39	58	110	19 37	58	110	294
68	15 16	58	109	16 14	58	109	17 12	58	108	18 10	58	108	19 08	58	108	292
70	14 46	+58	107	15 44	+58	107	16 42	+58	106	17 40	+58	106	18 38	+58	106	290
72	14 16	58	105	15 14	58	105	16 12	58	104	17 10	58	104	18 08	58	104	288
74	13 46	58	103	14 44	58	103	15 42	58	102	16 40	58	102	17 38	58	102	286
76	13 16	58	101	14 14	58	101	15 12	58	100	16 10	57	100	17 07	58	100	284
78	12 45	58	99	13 43	58	99	14 41	58	99	15 39	58	98	16 37	58	98	282
80	12 14	+58	97	13 12	+58	97	14 10	+58	97	15 08	+58	96	16 06	+58	96	280
82	11 44	57	95	12 41	58	95	13 39	58	95	14 37	58	94	15 35	58	94	278
84	11 13	57	93	12 10	58	93	13 08	58	93	14 06	58	92	15 04	58	92	276
86	10 42	57	91	11 39	58	91	12 37	58	91	13 35	58	90	14 33	58	90	274
88	10 10	58	89	11 08	58	89	12 06	58	89	13 04	58	89	14 02	58	88	272
90	09 39	+58	87	10 37	+58	87	11 35	+58	87	12 33	+58	87	13 31	+58	86	270
92	09 08	58	86	10 06	58	85	11 04	58	85	12 02	58	85	13 00	58	84	268
94	08 37	58	84	09 35	58	83	10 33	58	83	11 31	58	83	12 29	58	83	266
96	08 07	58	82	09 05	58	81	10 03	57	81	11 00	58	81	11 58	58	81	264
98	07 36	58	80	08 34	58	79	09 32	58	79	10 30	58	79	11 28	58	79	262
100	07 06	+58	78	08 04	+58	78	09 02	+58	77	10 00	+57	77	10 57	+58	77	260
102	06 35	58	76	07 33	58	76	08 31	58	75	09 29	58	75	10 27	58	75	258
104	06 05	58	74	07 03	58	74	08 01	59	73	09 00	58	73	09 58	58	73	256
106	05 36	58	72	06 34	58	72	07 32	58	72	08 30	58	71	09 28	58	71	254
108	05 06	58	70	06 04	59	70	07 03	58	70	08 01	58	69	08 59	58	69	252
110	04 37	+58	68	05 35	+59	68	06 34	+58	68	07 32	+58	68	08 30	+58	67	250
112	04 09	58	66	05 07	58	66	06 05	58	66	07 03	59	66	08 02	58	65	248
114	03 40	59	64	04 39	58	64	05 37	58	64	06 35	59	64	07 34	58	63	246
116	03 13	58	62	04 11	58	62	05 09	59	62	06 08	58	62	07 06	58	62	244
118	02 45	59	61	03 44	58	60	04 42	59	60	05 41	58	60	06 39	58	60	242
120	02 18	+59	59	03 17	+59	58	04 16	+58	58	05 14	+58	58	06 12	+59	58	240
122	01 52	59	57	02 51	58	57	03 49	59	56	04 48	58	56	05 46	59	56	238
124	01 27	58	55	02 25	59	55	03 24	58	54	04 22	59	54	05 21	59	54	236
126	01 02	58	53	02 00	59	53	02 59	59	52	03 58	58	52	04 56	59	52	234
128	00 37	59	51	01 36	59	51	02 35	58	51	03 33	59	50	04 32	59	50	232
130	00 13	+59	49	01 12	+59	49	02 11	+59	49	03 10	+59	48	04 09	+58	48	230
132	−0 10	59	47	00 49	59	47	01 48	59	47	02 47	59	47	03 46	59	46	228
134	−0 32	59	45	00 27	59	45	01 26	59	45	02 25	59	45	03 24	59	44	226
136	−0 54	59	43	00 05	59	43	01 04	59	43	02 03	59	43	03 02	59	43	224
138	−1 15	60	41	−0 15	59	41	00 44	59	41	01 43	59	41	02 42	59	41	222

S. Lat. {LHA greater than 180°....... Zn=180−Z
{LHA less than 180°........... Zn=180+Z

DECLINATION (0°-14°) SAME NAME AS LATITUDE

N. Lat. {LHA greater than 180°....... Zn=Z
{LHA less than 180°........... Zn=360−Z

DECLINATION (0°-14°) **SAME** NAME AS LATITUDE

	0°			1°			2°			3°			4°			5°			6°			7°			8°			9°			10°			11°			12°			13°			14°			
LHA	Hc	d	Z	Hc	d	Z	Hc	d	Z	Hc	d	Z	Hc	d	Z	Hc	d	Z	Hc	d	Z	Hc	d	Z	Hc	d	Z	Hc	d	Z	Hc	d	Z	Hc	d	Z	Hc	d	Z	Hc	d	Z	Hc	d	Z	LHA
	° ′	′	°	° ′	′	°	° ′	′	°	° ′	′	°	° ′	′	°	° ′	′	°	° ′	′	°	° ′	′	°	° ′	′	°	° ′	′	°	° ′	′	°	° ′	′	°	° ′	′	°	° ′	′	°	° ′	′	°	
140													−7 30	+60	40	−6 30	+59	40	−5 31	+59	40	−4 32	+59	40	−3 33	+59	40	−2 34	+59	39	−1 35	+60	39	−0 35	+59	39	00 24	+59	39	01 23	+59	39	02 22	+59	39	220
142																−6 50	59	38	−5 51	59	38	−4 52	60	38	−3 52	59	38	−2 53	59	37	−1 54	59	37	−0 55	60	37	00 05	59	37	01 04	59	37	02 03	59	37	218
144																−7 09	59	36	−6 10	60	36	−5 10	59	36	−4 11	59	36	−3 12	60	36	−2 12	59	35	−1 13	59	35	−0 14	60	35	00 46	59	35	01 45	59	35	216
146																−7 27	60	34	−6 27	59	34	−5 28	59	34	−4 29	60	34	−3 29	59	34	−2 30	60	33	−1 30	59	33	−0 31	59	33	00 28	60	33	01 28	59	33	214
148																			−6 44	59	32	−5 45	60	32	−4 45	59	32	−3 46	60	32	−2 46	59	31	−1 47	59	31	−0 48	60	31	00 12	59	31	01 11	60	31	212
150																			−7 00	+59	30	−6 01	+60	30	−5 01	+59	30	−4 02	+60	30	−3 02	+59	29	−2 03	+60	29	−1 03	+59	29	−0 04	+60	29	00 56	+59	29	210
152																			−7 15	59	28	−6 16	60	28	−5 16	59	28	−4 17	60	28	−3 17	59	28	−2 18	60	27	−1 18	60	27	−0 18	59	27	00 41	60	27	208
154																						−6 30	60	26	−5 30	59	26	−4 31	60	26	−3 31	59	26	−2 32	60	25	−1 32	60	25	−0 32	59	25	00 27	60	25	206
156																						−6 43	60	24	−5 43	59	24	−4 44	60	24	−3 44	60	24	−2 44	59	24	−1 45	60	23	−0 45	60	23	00 15	59	23	204
158																						−6 55	60	22	−5 55	59	22	−4 56	60	22	−3 56	60	22	−2 56	59	22	−1 57	60	21	−0 57	60	21	00 03	60	21	202
160																						−7 06	+59	20	−6 07	+60	20	−5 07	+60	20	−4 07	+60	20	−3 07	+59	20	−2 08	+60	20	−1 08	+60	19	−0 08	+60	19	200
162																						−7 16	59	18	−6 17	60	18	−5 17	60	18	−4 17	60	18	−3 17	60	18	−2 17	59	18	−1 18	60	17	−0 18	60	17	198
164																									−6 26	60	16	−5 26	60	16	−4 26	60	16	−3 26	60	16	−2 26	60	16	−1 26	59	16	−0 27	60	16	196
166																									−6 34	60	14	−5 34	60	14	−4 34	60	14	−3 34	60	14	−2 34	60	14	−1 34	60	14	−0 34	60	14	194
168																									−6 41	60	12	−5 41	60	12	−4 41	60	12	−3 41	60	12	−2 41	60	12	−1 41	60	12	−0 41	60	12	192
170																									−6 47	+60	10	−5 47	+60	10	−4 47	+60	10	−3 47	+60	10	−2 47	+60	10	−1 47	+60	10	−0 47	+60	10	190
172																									−6 51	60	8	−5 51	59	8	−4 52	60	8	−3 52	60	8	−2 52	60	8	−1 52	60	8	−0 52	60	8	188
174																									−6 55	60	6	−5 55	60	6	−4 55	60	6	−3 55	60	6	−2 55	60	6	−1 55	60	6	−0 55	60	6	186
176																									−6 58	60	4	−5 58	60	4	−4 58	60	4	−3 58	60	4	−2 58	60	4	−1 58	60	4	−0 58	60	4	184
178																									−7 00	60	2	−6 00	60	2	−5 00	60	2	−4 00	60	2	−3 00	60	2	−2 00	60	2	−1 00	60	2	182
180																									−7 00	+60	0	−6 00	+60	0	−5 00	+60	0	−4 00	+60	0	−3 00	+60	0	−2 00	+60	0	−1 00	+60	0	180

0°	1°	2°	3°	4°	5°	6°	7°	8°	9°	10°	11°	12°	13°	14°

S. Lat. {LHA greater than 180°....... Zn=180−Z
{LHA less than 180°........... Zn=180+Z

DECLINATION (0°-14°) **SAME** NAME AS LATITUDE

N. Lat. {LHA greater than 180°....... Zn=Z / LHA less than 180°........... Zn=360−Z}

DECLINATION (0°-14°) CONTRARY NAME TO LATITUDE

LAT 75°

LHA	0°			1°			2°			3°			4°		
	Hc	d	Z	Hc	d	Z	Hc	d	Z	Hc	d	Z	Hc	d	Z
	° ′	′	°	° ′	′	°	° ′	′	°	° ′	′	°	° ′	′	°
122	-7 53	59	59	238											
120	-7 26	-59	61	240											
118	-6 59	58	63	242											
116	-6 31	58	65	-7 29	59	65	244								
114	-6 03	58	67	-7 01	58	67	246								
112	-5 34	58	69	-6 32	58	69	-7 30	59	69	248					
110	-5 05	-58	71	-6 03	-58	71	-7 01	-58	71	250					
108	-4 35	58	73	-5 33	59	73	-6 32	58	73	-7 30	58	73	252		
106	-4 06	58	74	-5 04	58	75	-6 02	58	75	-7 00	58	75	-7 58	58	75
104	-3 35	59	76	-4 34	58	77	-5 32	58	77	-6 30	58	77	-7 28	58	77
102	-3 05	58	78	-4 03	58	79	-5 01	58	79	-5 59	58	79	-6 57	58	79
100	-2 35	-58	80	-3 33	-58	81	-4 31	-58	81	-5 29	-58	81	-6 27	-58	81
98	-2 04	58	82	-3 02	58	82	-4 00	58	83	-4 58	58	83	-5 56	58	83
96	-1 33	58	84	-2 31	58	84	-3 29	58	85	-4 27	58	85	-5 25	58	85
94	-1 02	58	86	-2 00	58	86	-2 58	58	87	-3 56	58	87	-4 54	58	87
92	-0 31	58	88	-1 29	58	88	-2 27	58	89	-3 25	58	89	-4 23	58	89
90	00 00	-58	90	-0 58	-58	90	-1 56	-58	90	-2 54	-58	91	-3 52	-58	91
88	00 31	58	92	-0 27	58	92	-1 25	58	92	-2 23	58	93	-3 21	58	93
86	01 02	58	94	00 04	58	94	-0 54	58	94	-1 52	58	95	-2 50	58	95
84	01 33	58	96	00 35	58	96	-0 23	58	96	-1 21	58	97	-2 19	58	97
82	02 04	58	98	01 06	58	98	00 08	58	98	-0 50	58	98	-1 48	58	99
80	02 35	-58	100	01 37	-58	100	00 39	-58	100	-0 19	-59	100	-1 18	-58	101
78	03 05	58	102	02 07	58	102	01 09	58	102	00 11	58	102	-0 47	58	103
76	03 35	58	104	02 37	58	104	01 39	58	104	00 41	58	104	-0 17	58	105
74	04 06	59	106	03 07	58	106	02 09	58	106	01 11	58	106	00 13	58	106
72	04 35	58	107	03 37	58	108	02 39	58	108	01 41	58	108	00 43	59	108
70	05 05	-59	109	04 06	-58	110	03 08	-58	110	02 10	-58	110	01 12	-58	110
68	05 34	58	111	04 36	59	112	03 37	58	112	02 39	58	112	01 41	58	112
66	06 03	59	113	05 04	58	114	04 06	58	114	03 08	59	114	02 09	58	114
64	06 31	58	115	05 33	59	116	04 34	58	116	03 36	58	116	02 38	59	116
62	06 59	59	117	06 00	58	117	05 02	58	118	04 04	59	118	03 05	58	118
60	07 26	-58	119	06 28	-59	119	05 29	-58	120	04 31	-59	120	03 32	-58	120
58	07 53	58	121	06 55	59	121	05 56	59	122	04 57	58	122	03 59	59	122
56	08 19	58	123	07 21	59	123	06 22	58	124	05 24	59	124	04 25	59	124
54	08 45	59	125	07 46	58	125	06 48	59	126	05 49	59	126	04 50	58	126
52	09 10	59	127	08 11	58	127	07 13	59	128	06 14	59	128	05 15	59	128
50	09 35	-59	129	08 36	-59	129	07 37	-59	129	06 38	-59	130	05 39	-58	130
48	09 58	58	131	09 00	59	131	08 01	59	131	07 02	59	132	06 03	59	132
46	10 22	59	133	09 23	59	133	08 24	59	133	07 25	59	134	06 26	59	134
44	10 44	59	135	09 45	59	135	08 46	59	135	07 47	59	136	06 48	59	136
42	11 05	59	137	10 06	59	137	09 07	59	137	08 08	59	138	07 09	59	138
40	11 26	-59	139	10 27	-59	139	09 28	-59	139	08 29	-59	140	07 30	-60	140
38	11 46	59	141	10 47	59	141	09 48	59	141	08 49	60	142	07 49	59	142
36	12 05	59	143	11 06	59	143	10 07	60	143	09 07	59	144	08 08	59	144
34	12 23	59	145	11 24	59	145	10 25	60	145	09 25	59	146	08 26	59	146
32	12 41	60	147	11 41	59	147	10 42	59	147	09 43	60	148	08 43	59	148
30	12 57	-59	149	11 58	-60	149	10 58	-59	149	09 59	-60	150	08 59	-59	150
28	13 13	60	151	12 13	59	151	11 14	60	151	10 14	59	152	09 15	60	152
26	13 27	59	153	12 28	60	153	11 28	60	153	10 28	59	154	09 29	60	154
24	13 41	60	155	12 41	60	155	11 41	59	156	10 42	60	156	09 42	60	156
22	13 53	60	157	12 53	59	157	11 54	60	158	10 54	60	158	09 54	59	158
20	14 05	-60	159	13 05	-60	159	12 05	-60	160	11 05	-59	160	10 06	-60	160
18	14 15	60	161	13 15	60	162	12 15	59	162	11 16	60	162	10 16	60	162
16	14 24	59	164	13 25	60	164	12 25	60	164	11 25	60	164	10 25	60	164
14	14 33	60	166	13 33	60	166	12 33	60	166	11 33	60	166	10 33	60	166
12	14 40	60	168	13 40	60	168	12 40	60	168	11 40	60	168	10 40	60	168
10	14 46	-60	170	13 46	-60	170	12 46	-60	170	11 46	-60	170	10 46	-60	170
8	14 51	60	172	13 51	60	172	12 51	60	172	11 51	60	172	10 51	60	172
6	14 55	60	174	13 55	60	174	12 55	60	174	11 55	60	174	10 55	60	174
4	14 58	60	176	13 58	60	176	12 58	60	176	11 58	60	176	10 58	60	176
2	14 59	60	178	13 59	60	178	12 59	60	178	11 59	60	178	10 59	59	178
0	15 00	-60	180	14 00	-60	180	13 00	-60	180	12 00	-60	180	11 00	-60	180

LHA	5°			6°			7°			8°			9°		
	Hc	d	Z	Hc	d	Z	Hc	d	Z	Hc	d	Z	Hc	d	Z
	° ′	′	°	° ′	′	°	° ′	′	°	° ′	′	°	° ′	′	°
122															
120															
118															
116															
114															
112															
110															
108															
106	254														
104	256														
102	-7 55	58	80	258											
100	-7 25	-58	82	260											
98	-6 54	58	84	-7 52	58	84	262								
96	-6 23	58	85	-7 21	58	86	264								
94	-5 52	58	87	-6 50	58	88	-7 48	58	88	266					
92	-5 21	58	89	-6 19	58	90	-7 17	58	90	268					
90	-4 50	-58	91	-5 48	-58	92	-6 46	-58	92	-7 44	-58	92	270		
88	-4 19	58	93	-5 17	58	93	-6 15	58	94	-7 13	57	94	272		
86	-3 48	58	95	-4 46	58	95	-5 44	58	96	-6 42	58	96	-7 40	57	96
84	-3 17	58	97	-4 15	58	97	-5 13	58	98	-6 11	58	98	-7 09	58	98
82	-2 46	58	99	-3 44	58	99	-4 42	58	99	-5 40	58	100	-6 38	58	100
80	-2 16	-58	101	-3 14	-58	101	-4 12	-58	101	-5 10	-58	102	-6 08	-58	102
78	-1 45	58	103	-2 43	58	103	-3 41	58	103	-4 39	58	104	-5 37	58	104
76	-1 15	58	105	-2 13	58	105	-3 11	58	105	-4 09	58	106	-5 07	58	106
74	-0 45	58	107	-1 43	58	107	-2 41	58	107	-3 39	59	107	-4 38	58	108
72	-0 16	58	109	-1 14	58	109	-2 12	58	109	-3 10	58	109	-4 08	58	110
70	00 14	-58	111	-0 44	-59	111	-1 43	-58	111	-2 41	-58	111	-3 39	-58	112
68	00 43	59	113	-0 16	58	113	-1 14	58	113	-2 12	58	113	-3 10	59	113
66	01 11	58	115	00 13	58	115	-0 45	59	115	-1 44	58	115	-2 42	58	115
64	01 39	58	116	00 41	59	117	-0 18	58	117	-1 16	58	117	-2 14	59	117
62	02 07	59	118	01 08	58	119	00 10	58	119	-0 48	59	119	-1 47	58	119
60	02 34	-59	120	01 35	-58	121	00 37	-59	121	-0 22	-58	121	-1 20	-58	121
58	03 00	58	122	02 02	59	122	01 03	58	123	00 05	59	123	-0 54	58	123
56	03 26	58	124	02 28	59	124	01 29	58	125	00 31	59	125	-0 28	59	125
54	03 52	59	126	02 53	59	126	01 54	58	127	00 56	59	127	-0 03	59	127
52	04 16	58	128	03 18	59	128	02 19	59	129	01 20	58	129	00 22	59	129
50	04 41	-59	130	03 42	-59	130	02 43	-59	130	01 44	-59	131	00 45	-58	131
48	05 04	59	132	04 05	59	132	03 06	59	132	02 07	58	133	01 09	59	133
46	05 27	59	134	04 28	59	134	03 29	59	134	02 30	59	135	01 31	59	135
44	05 49	59	136	04 50	59	136	03 51	59	136	02 52	59	136	01 53	59	137
42	06 10	59	138	05 11	59	138	04 12	59	138	03 13	59	138	02 14	59	139
40	06 30	-59	140	05 31	-59	140	04 32	-59	140	03 33	-59	140	02 34	-59	141
38	06 50	59	142	05 51	59	142	04 52	60	142	03 52	59	142	02 53	59	143
36	07 09	59	144	06 10	60	144	05 10	59	144	04 11	59	144	03 12	60	144
34	07 27	60	146	06 27	59	146	05 28	59	146	04 29	60	146	03 29	59	146
32	07 44	60	148	06 44	59	148	05 45	60	148	04 45	59	148	03 46	60	148
30	08 00	-60	150	07 00	-59	150	06 01	-60	150	05 01	-59	150	04 02	-60	150
28	08 15	60	152	07 15	59	152	06 16	60	152	05 16	59	152	04 17	60	152
26	08 29	59	154	07 30	60	154	06 30	60	154	05 30	59	154	04 31	60	154
24	08 42	59	156	07 43	60	156	06 43	60	156	05 43	59	156	04 44	60	156
22	08 55	60	158	07 55	60	158	06 55	60	158	05 55	59	158	04 56	60	158
20	09 06	-60	160	08 06	-60	160	07 06	-59	160	06 07	-60	160	05 07	-60	160
18	09 16	60	162	08 16	60	162	07 16	59	162	06 17	60	162	05 17	60	162
16	09 25	60	164	08 25	59	164	07 26	60	164	06 26	60	164	05 26	60	164
14	09 33	60	166	08 33	59	166	07 34	60	166	06 34	60	166	05 34	60	166
12	09 40	60	168	08 40	59	168	07 41	60	168	06 41	60	168	05 41	60	168
10	09 46	-60	170	08 46	-59	170	07 47	-60	170	06 47	-60	170	05 47	-60	170
8	09 51	60	172	08 51	60	172	07 51	60	172	06 51	60	172	05 51	59	172
6	09 55	60	174	08 55	60	174	07 55	60	174	06 55	60	174	05 55	60	174
4	09 58	60	176	08 58	60	176	07 58	60	176	06 58	60	176	05 58	60	176
2	10 00	60	178	09 00	60	178	08 00	60	178	07 00	60	178	06 00	60	178
0	10 00	-60	180	09 00	-60	180	08 00	-60	180	07 00	-60	180	06 00	-60	180

LHA	10°			11°			12°			13°			14°			LHA
	Hc	d	Z	Hc	d	Z	Hc	d	Z	Hc	d	Z	Hc	d	Z	
	° ′	′	°	° ′	′	°	° ′	′	°	° ′	′	°	° ′	′	°	
122																
120																
118																
116																
114																
112																
110																
108																
106																
104																
102																
100																
98																
96																
94																
92																
90																
88																
86	274															
84	276															
82	-7 36	58	100	278												
80	-7 06	-58	102	280												
78	-6 35	58	104	-7 33	58	104	282									
76	-6 05	58	106	-7 03	58	106	284									
74	-5 36	58	108	-6 34	58	108	-7 32	58	108	286						
72	-5 06	58	110	-6 04	59	110	-7 03	58	110	288						
70	-4 37	-58	112	-5 35	-59	112	-6 34	-58	112	-7 32	-58	112	290			
68	-4 09	58	114	-5 07	58	114	-6 05	58	114	-7 03	59	114	292			
66	-3 40	59	116	-4 39	58	116	-5 37	58	116	-6 35	59	116	-7 34	58	117	294
64	-3 13	58	118	-4 11	58	118	-5 09	59	118	-6 08	58	118	-7 06	58	118	296
62	-2 45	59	119	-3 44	58	120	-4 42	59	120	-5 41	58	120	-6 39	58	120	298
60	-2 18	-59	121	-3 17	-59	122	-4 16	-58	122	-5 14	-58	122	-6 12	-59	122	300
58	-1 52	59	123	-2 51	58	123	-3 49	59	124	-4 48	58	124	-5 46	59	124	302
56	-1 27	58	125	-2 25	59	125	-3 24	58	126	-4 22	59	126	-5 21	59	126	304
54	-1 02	58	127	-2 00	59	127	-2 59	59	128	-3 58	58	128	-4 56	59	128	306
52	-0 37	59	129	-1 36	59	129	-2 35	58	129	-3 33	59	130	-4 32	59	130	308
50	-0 13	-59	131	-1 12	-59	131	-2 11	-59	131	-3 10	-59	132	-4 09	-58	132	310
48	00 10	59	133	-0 49	59	133	-1 48	59	133	-2 47	59	133	-3 46	59	134	312
46	00 32	59	135	-0 27	59	135	-1 26	59	135	-2 25	59	135	-3 24	59	136	314
44	00 54	59	137	-0 05	59	137	-1 04	59	137	-2 03	59	137	-3 02	59	137	316
42	01 15	60	139	00 15	59	139	-0 44	59	139	-1 43	59	139	-2 42	59	139	318
40	01 35	-60	141	00 35	-59	141	-0 24	-59	141	-1 23	-59	141	-2 22	-59	141	320
38	01 54	59	143	00 55	60	143	-0 05	59	143	-1 04	59	143	-2 03	59	143	322
36	02 12	59	145	01 13	59	145	00 14	60	145	-0 46	59	145	-1 45	59	145	324
34	02 30	60	147	01 30	59	147	00 31	59	147	-0 28	60	147	-1 28	59	147	326
32	02 46	59	149	01 47	59	149	00 48	60	149	-0 12	59	149	-1 11	60	149	328
30	03 02	-59	151	02 03	-60	151	01 03	-59	151	00 04	-60	151	-0 56	-59	151	330
28	03 17	59	152	02 18	60	153	01 18	60	153	00 18	59	153	-0 41	60	153	332
26	03 31	59	154	02 32	60	155	01 32	60	155	00 32	59	155	-0 27	60	155	334
24	03 44	60	156	02 44	59	156	01 45	60	157	00 45	60	157	-0 15	59	157	336
22	03 56	60	158	02 56	59	158	01 57	60	159	00 57	60	159	-0 03	60	159	338
20	04 07	-60	160	03 07	-59	160	02 08	-60	160	01 08	-60	161	00 08	-60	161	340
18	04 17	60	162	03 17	60	162	02 17	59	162	01 18	60	163	00 18	60	163	342
16	04 26	60	164	03 26	60	164	02 26	60	164	01 26	59	164	00 27	60	164	344
14	04 34	60	166	03 34	60	166	02 34	60	166	01 34	60	166	00 34	60	166	346
12	04 41	60	168	03 41	60	168	02 41	60	168	01 41	60	168	00 41	60	168	348
10	04 47	-60	170	03 47	-60	170	02 47	-60	170	01 47	-60	170	00 47	-60	170	350
8	04 52	60	172	03 52	60	172	02 52	60	172	01 52	60	172	00 52	60	172	352
6	04 55	60	174	03 55	60	174	02 55	60	174	01 55	60	174	00 55	60	174	354
4	04 58	60	176	03 58	60	176	02 58	60	176	01 58	60	176	00 58	60	176	356
2	05 00	60	178	04 00	60	178	03 00	60	178	02 00	60	178	01 00	60	178	358
0	05 00	-60	180	04 00	-60	180	03 00	-60	180	02 00	-60	180	01 00	-60	180	360

S. Lat. {LHA greater than 180°....... Zn=180−Z / LHA less than 180°........... Zn=180+Z}

DECLINATION (0°-14°) CONTRARY NAME TO LATITUDE

N. Lat. {LHA greater than 180°....... Zn=Z
{LHA less than 180°........... Zn=360−Z

DECLINATION (15°-29°) SAME NAME AS LATITUDE

LHA	15° Hc	d	Z	16° Hc	d	Z	17° Hc	d	Z	18° Hc	d	Z	19° Hc	d	Z
	° ′	′	°	° ′	′	°	° ′	′	°	° ′	′	°	° ′	′	°
0	30 00	+60	180	31 00	+60	180	32 00	+60	180	33 00	+60	180	34 00	+60	180
2	29 59	60	178	30 59	60	178	31 59	60	178	32 59	60	178	33 59	60	178
4	29 58	60	176	30 58	60	176	31 58	60	176	32 58	60	176	33 58	60	175
6	29 55	60	173	30 55	60	173	31 55	60	173	32 55	59	173	33 54	60	173
8	29 50	60	171	30 50	60	171	31 50	60	171	32 50	60	171	33 50	60	171
10	29 45	+60	169	30 45	+60	169	31 45	+60	169	32 45	+60	169	33 45	+60	169
12	29 38	60	167	30 38	60	167	31 38	60	167	32 38	60	166	33 38	60	166
14	29 31	59	164	30 30	60	164	31 30	60	164	32 30	60	164	33 30	60	164
16	29 22	60	162	30 22	59	162	31 21	60	162	32 21	60	162	33 21	60	162
18	29 12	59	160	30 11	60	160	31 11	60	160	32 11	60	160	33 11	59	160
20	29 00	+60	158	30 00	+60	158	31 00	+60	158	32 00	+59	157	32 59	+60	157
22	28 48	60	156	29 48	59	156	30 47	60	155	31 47	60	155	32 47	59	155
24	28 35	59	153	29 34	60	153	30 34	60	153	31 34	59	153	32 33	60	153
26	28 20	60	151	29 20	59	151	30 19	60	151	31 19	59	151	32 18	60	151
28	28 05	59	149	29 04	60	149	30 04	59	149	31 03	60	149	32 03	59	148
30	27 49	+59	147	28 48	+59	147	29 47	+60	147	30 47	+59	146	31 46	+59	146
32	27 31	59	145	28 30	60	145	29 30	59	144	30 29	59	144	31 28	59	144
34	27 13	59	143	28 12	59	142	29 11	59	142	30 10	59	142	31 09	59	142
36	26 53	59	141	27 52	60	140	28 52	59	140	29 51	59	140	30 50	59	140
38	26 33	59	138	27 32	59	138	28 31	59	138	29 30	59	138	30 29	59	138
40	26 12	+59	136	27 11	+59	136	28 10	+59	136	29 09	+59	136	30 08	+59	135
42	25 50	59	134	26 49	59	134	27 48	59	134	28 47	59	133	29 46	58	133
44	25 27	59	132	26 26	59	132	27 25	59	132	28 24	58	131	29 22	59	131
46	25 04	59	130	26 03	58	130	27 01	59	129	28 00	59	129	28 59	58	129
48	24 40	58	128	25 38	59	128	26 37	59	127	27 36	58	127	28 34	59	127
50	24 15	+59	126	25 14	+58	126	26 12	+59	125	27 11	+58	125	28 09	+58	125
52	23 49	59	124	24 48	58	123	25 46	59	123	26 45	58	123	27 43	59	123
54	23 23	59	122	24 22	58	121	25 20	58	121	26 18	59	121	27 17	58	121
56	22 57	58	120	23 55	58	119	24 53	58	119	25 51	59	119	26 50	58	119
58	22 29	59	118	23 28	58	117	24 26	58	117	25 24	58	117	26 22	58	117
60	22 02	+58	116	23 00	+58	115	23 58	+58	115	24 56	+58	115	25 54	+58	115
62	21 33	58	114	22 31	59	113	23 30	58	113	24 28	58	113	25 26	58	112
64	21 05	58	112	22 03	58	111	23 01	58	111	23 59	58	111	24 57	58	110
66	20 35	59	110	21 34	58	109	22 32	58	109	23 30	57	109	24 27	58	108
68	20 06	58	108	21 04	58	107	22 02	58	107	23 00	58	107	23 58	58	106
70	19 36	+58	106	20 34	+58	105	21 32	+58	105	22 30	+58	105	23 28	+58	104
72	19 06	58	104	20 04	58	103	21 02	58	103	22 00	58	103	22 58	57	102
74	18 36	58	102	19 34	58	101	20 32	57	101	21 29	58	101	22 27	58	100
76	18 05	58	100	19 03	58	99	20 01	58	99	20 59	58	99	21 57	57	99
78	17 35	57	98	18 32	58	97	19 30	58	97	20 28	58	97	21 26	58	97
80	17 04	+58	96	18 02	+57	95	18 59	+58	95	19 57	+58	95	20 55	+58	95
82	16 33	58	94	17 31	57	94	18 28	58	93	19 26	58	93	20 24	58	93
84	16 02	58	92	17 00	57	92	17 57	58	91	18 55	58	91	19 53	58	91
86	15 31	58	90	16 29	57	90	17 26	58	89	18 24	58	89	19 22	58	89
88	15 00	58	88	15 58	57	88	16 55	58	87	17 53	58	87	18 51	57	87
90	14 29	+58	86	15 27	+57	86	16 24	+58	86	17 22	+58	85	18 20	+58	85
92	13 58	58	84	14 56	57	84	15 53	58	84	16 51	58	83	17 49	58	83
94	13 27	58	82	14 25	58	82	15 23	57	82	16 20	58	81	17 18	58	81
96	12 56	58	80	13 54	58	80	14 52	58	80	15 50	58	80	16 48	57	79
98	12 26	58	78	13 24	57	78	14 21	58	78	15 19	58	78	16 17	58	77
100	11 55	+58	77	12 53	+58	76	13 51	+58	76	14 49	+58	76	15 47	+58	75
102	11 25	58	75	12 23	58	74	13 21	58	74	14 19	58	74	15 17	58	74
104	10 56	58	73	11 54	58	72	12 52	57	72	13 49	58	72	14 47	58	72
106	10 26	58	71	11 24	58	71	12 22	58	70	13 20	58	70	14 18	58	70
108	09 57	58	69	10 55	58	69	11 53	58	68	12 51	58	68	13 49	58	68
110	09 28	+58	67	10 26	+58	67	11 24	+59	67	12 23	+58	66	13 21	+58	66
112	09 00	58	65	09 58	58	65	10 56	58	65	11 54	58	64	12 52	59	64
114	08 32	58	63	09 30	58	63	10 28	59	63	11 27	58	62	12 25	58	62
116	08 04	59	61	09 03	58	61	10 01	58	61	10 59	59	61	11 58	58	60
118	07 37	59	59	08 36	58	59	09 34	58	59	10 32	59	59	11 31	58	58
120	07 11	+58	58	08 09	+59	57	09 08	+58	57	10 06	+59	57	11 05	+58	57
122	06 45	59	56	07 44	58	55	08 42	59	55	09 41	58	55	10 39	58	55
124	06 20	58	54	07 18	59	54	08 17	58	53	09 15	59	53	10 14	59	53
126	05 55	59	52	06 54	58	52	07 52	59	51	08 51	59	51	09 50	58	51
128	05 31	59	50	06 30	58	50	07 28	59	50	08 27	59	49	09 26	58	49
130	05 07	+59	48	06 06	+59	48	07 05	+59	48	08 04	+59	47	09 03	+58	47
132	04 45	59	46	05 44	58	46	06 42	59	46	07 41	59	46	08 40	59	45
134	04 23	59	44	05 22	59	44	06 21	59	44	07 20	58	44	08 18	59	43
136	04 01	59	42	05 00	59	42	05 59	59	42	06 58	60	42	07 58	59	42
138	03 41	59	40	04 40	59	40	05 39	59	40	06 38	59	40	07 37	59	40

LHA	20° Hc	d	Z	21° Hc	d	Z	22° Hc	d	Z	23° Hc	d	Z	24° Hc	d	Z
	° ′	′	°	° ′	′	°	° ′	′	°	° ′	′	°	° ′	′	°
0	35 00	+60	180	36 00	+60	180	37 00	+60	180	38 00	+60	180	39 00	+60	180
2	34 59	60	178	35 59	60	178	36 59	60	178	37 59	60	178	38 59	60	178
4	34 58	60	175	35 58	60	175	36 58	60	175	37 58	60	175	38 58	59	175
6	34 54	60	173	35 54	60	173	36 54	60	173	37 54	60	173	38 54	60	173
8	34 50	60	171	35 50	60	171	36 50	60	171	37 50	60	171	38 50	60	171
10	34 45	+59	169	35 44	+60	169	36 44	+60	168	37 44	+60	168	38 44	+60	168
12	34 38	60	166	35 38	60	166	36 38	59	166	37 37	60	166	38 37	60	166
14	34 30	60	164	35 30	59	164	36 29	60	164	37 29	60	164	38 29	60	164
16	34 21	59	162	35 20	60	162	36 20	60	162	37 20	60	161	38 20	59	161
18	34 10	60	160	35 10	60	159	36 10	59	159	37 09	60	159	38 09	60	159
20	33 59	+60	157	34 59	+59	157	35 58	+60	157	36 58	+59	157	37 57	+60	157
22	33 46	60	155	34 46	59	155	35 45	60	155	36 45	60	155	37 45	59	154
24	33 33	59	153	34 32	60	153	35 32	59	152	36 31	60	152	37 31	59	152
26	33 18	59	151	34 17	60	150	35 17	59	150	36 16	59	150	37 15	60	150
28	33 02	59	148	34 01	60	148	35 01	59	148	36 00	59	148	36 59	60	148
30	32 45	+59	146	33 44	+60	146	34 44	+59	146	35 43	+59	146	36 42	+59	145
32	32 27	59	144	33 26	60	144	34 26	59	143	35 25	59	143	36 24	59	143
34	32 08	60	142	33 08	59	141	34 07	59	141	35 06	59	141	36 05	59	141
36	31 49	59	140	32 48	59	139	33 47	59	139	34 46	59	139	35 45	59	139
38	31 28	59	137	32 27	59	137	33 26	59	137	34 25	59	137	35 24	59	136
40	31 07	+58	135	32 05	+59	135	33 04	+59	135	34 03	+59	134	35 02	+59	134
42	30 44	59	133	31 43	59	133	32 42	58	133	33 40	59	132	34 39	59	132
44	30 21	59	131	31 20	59	131	32 19	58	130	33 17	59	130	34 16	58	130
46	29 57	59	129	30 56	58	129	31 54	59	128	32 53	58	128	33 51	59	128
48	29 33	58	127	30 31	59	126	31 30	58	126	32 28	59	126	33 27	58	126
50	29 07	+59	125	30 06	+58	124	31 04	+59	124	32 03	+58	124	33 01	+58	123
52	28 42	58	122	29 40	58	122	30 38	58	122	31 36	59	122	32 35	58	121
54	28 15	58	120	29 13	59	120	30 12	58	120	31 10	58	120	32 08	58	119
56	27 48	58	118	28 46	58	118	29 44	58	118	30 42	59	117	31 41	58	117
58	27 20	58	116	28 18	59	116	29 17	58	116	30 15	58	115	31 13	58	115
60	26 52	+58	114	27 50	+58	114	28 48	+58	114	29 46	+58	113	30 44	+58	113
62	26 24	58	112	27 22	58	112	28 20	58	112	29 18	57	111	30 15	58	111
64	25 55	58	110	26 53	58	110	27 51	57	110	28 48	58	109	29 46	58	109
66	25 25	58	108	26 23	58	108	27 21	58	108	28 19	58	107	29 17	57	107
68	24 56	58	106	25 54	57	106	26 51	58	106	27 49	58	105	28 47	58	105
70	24 26	+58	104	25 24	+57	104	26 21	+58	104	27 19	+58	103	28 17	+57	103
72	23 55	58	102	24 53	58	102	25 51	58	102	26 49	57	101	27 46	58	101
74	23 25	58	100	24 23	57	100	25 20	58	100	26 18	58	99	27 16	57	99
76	22 54	58	98	23 52	58	98	24 50	57	98	25 47	58	97	26 45	58	97
78	22 24	57	96	23 21	58	96	24 19	58	96	25 17	57	95	26 14	58	95
80	21 53	+57	94	22 50	+58	94	23 48	+58	94	24 46	+57	93	25 43	+58	93
82	21 22	57	92	22 19	58	92	23 17	58	92	24 15	57	91	25 12	58	91
84	20 51	57	90	21 48	58	90	22 46	57	90	23 43	58	90	24 41	58	89
86	20 20	57	89	21 17	58	88	22 15	57	88	23 12	58	88	24 10	57	87
88	19 48	58	87	20 46	58	86	21 44	57	86	22 41	58	86	23 39	58	85
90	19 18	+57	85	20 15	+58	84	21 13	+57	84	22 10	+58	84	23 08	+58	83
92	18 47	57	83	19 44	58	82	20 42	58	82	21 40	57	82	22 37	58	82
94	18 16	58	81	19 14	57	81	20 11	58	80	21 09	58	80	22 07	57	80
96	17 45	58	79	18 43	58	79	19 41	58	78	20 39	57	78	21 36	58	78
98	17 15	58	77	18 13	58	77	19 11	57	76	20 08	58	76	21 06	58	76
100	16 45	+58	75	17 43	+57	75	18 40	+58	75	19 38	+58	74	20 36	+58	74
102	16 15	58	73	17 13	58	73	18 11	57	73	19 08	58	72	20 06	58	72
104	15 45	58	71	16 43	58	71	17 41	58	71	18 39	58	71	19 37	58	70
106	15 16	58	69	16 14	58	69	17 12	58	69	18 10	58	69	19 08	58	68
108	14 47	58	68	15 45	58	67	16 43	58	67	17 41	58	67	18 39	58	67
110	14 19	+58	66	15 17	+58	65	16 15	+58	65	17 13	+58	65	18 11	+58	65
112	13 51	58	64	14 49	58	64	15 47	58	63	16 45	58	63	17 43	58	63
114	13 23	58	62	14 21	58	62	15 19	59	61	16 18	58	61	17 16	58	61
116	12 56	58	60	13 54	58	60	14 52	59	60	15 51	58	59	16 49	58	59
118	12 29	58	58	13 27	59	58	14 26	58	58	15 24	58	58	16 22	59	57
120	12 03	+58	56	13 01	+59	56	14 00	+58	56	14 58	+59	56	15 57	+58	55
122	11 37	59	54	12 36	58	54	13 34	59	54	14 33	58	54	15 31	59	54
124	11 13	58	53	12 11	59	52	13 10	58	52	14 08	59	52	15 07	58	52
126	10 48	59	51	11 47	58	51	12 45	59	50	13 44	59	50	14 43	58	50
128	10 24	59	49	11 23	59	49	12 22	58	48	13 20	59	48	14 19	59	48
130	10 01	+59	47	11 00	+59	47	11 59	+59	47	12 58	+58	46	13 56	+59	46
132	09 39	59	45	10 38	59	45	11 37	59	45	12 36	58	45	13 34	59	44
134	09 17	59	43	10 16	59	43	11 15	59	43	12 14	59	43	13 13	59	43
136	08 57	58	41	09 55	59	41	10 54	59	41	11 53	59	41	12 52	59	41
138	08 36	59	40	09 35	59	39	10 34	60	39	11 34	59	39	12 33	59	39

LHA	25° Hc	d	Z	26° Hc	d	Z	27° Hc	d	Z	28° Hc	d	Z	29° Hc	d	Z	LHA
	° ′	′	°	° ′	′	°	° ′	′	°	° ′	′	°	° ′	′	°	
0	40 00	+60	180	41 00	+60	180	42 00	+60	180	43 00	+60	180	44 00	+60	180	360
2	39 59	60	178	40 59	60	178	41 59	60	178	42 59	60	178	43 59	60	178	358
4	39 57	60	175	40 57	60	175	41 57	60	175	42 57	60	175	43 57	60	175	356
6	39 54	60	173	40 54	60	173	41 54	60	173	42 54	60	173	43 54	60	173	354
8	39 50	60	171	40 50	60	171	41 50	60	170	42 50	60	170	43 50	59	170	352
10	39 44	+60	168	40 44	+60	168	41 44	+60	168	42 44	+60	168	43 44	+60	168	350
12	39 37	60	166	40 37	60	166	41 37	60	166	42 37	59	166	43 36	60	166	348
14	39 29	60	164	40 29	59	163	41 28	60	163	42 28	60	163	43 28	60	163	346
16	39 19	60	161	40 19	60	161	41 19	60	161	42 19	59	161	43 18	60	161	344
18	39 09	60	159	40 09	59	159	41 08	60	159	42 08	59	158	43 07	60	158	342
20	38 57	+60	157	39 57	+59	156	40 56	+60	156	41 56	+59	156	42 55	+60	156	340
22	38 44	60	154	39 44	59	154	40 43	60	154	41 43	59	154	42 42	60	154	338
24	38 30	59	152	39 29	60	152	40 29	59	152	41 28	60	151	42 28	59	151	336
26	38 15	59	150	39 14	60	149	40 14	59	149	41 13	59	149	42 12	59	149	334
28	37 59	59	147	38 58	59	147	39 57	59	147	40 56	60	147	41 56	59	147	332
30	37 41	+60	145	38 41	+59	145	39 40	+59	145	40 39	+59	144	41 38	+59	144	330
32	37 23	59	143	38 22	59	143	39 21	59	142	40 20	59	142	41 19	59	142	328
34	37 04	59	141	38 03	59	140	39 02	59	140	40 01	59	140	41 00	58	140	326
36	36 44	59	138	37 43	58	138	38 41	59	138	39 40	59	138	40 39	59	137	324
38	36 23	58	136	37 21	59	136	38 20	59	136	39 19	59	135	40 18	58	135	322
40	36 01	+58	134	36 59	+59	134	37 58	+59	133	38 57	+58	133	39 55	+59	133	320
42	35 38	58	132	36 36	59	132	37 35	59	131	38 34	58	131	39 32	58	131	318
44	35 14	59	130	36 13	58	129	37 11	59	129	38 10	58	129	39 08	58	128	316
46	34 50	58	127	35 48	59	127	36 47	58	127	37 45	58	127	38 43	59	126	314
48	34 25	58	125	35 23	59	125	36 22	58	125	37 20	58	124	38 18	58	124	312
50	33 59	+58	123	34 57	+59	123	35 56	+58	123	36 54	+58	122	37 52	+58	122	310
52	33 33	58	121	34 31	58	121	35 29	58	120	36 27	58	120	37 25	58	120	308
54	33 06	58	119	34 04	58	119	35 02	58	118	36 00	58	118	36 58	58	118	306
56	32 39	58	117	33 37	58	117	34 35	57	116	35 32	58	116	36 30	58	116	304
58	32 11	58	115	33 09	57	115	34 06	58	114	35 04	58	114	36 02	58	114	302
60	31 42	+58	113	32 40	+58	112	33 38	+58	112	34 36	+57	112	35 33	+58	111	300
62	31 13	58	111	32 11	58	110	33 09	58	110	34 07	57	110	35 04	58	109	298
64	30 44	58	109	31 42	57	108	32 39	58	108	33 37	58	108	34 35	57	107	296
66	30 14	58	107	31 12	58	106	32 10	57	106	33 07	58	106	34 05	57	105	294
68	29 45	57	105	30 42	58	104	31 40	57	104	32 37	58	104	33 35	57	103	292
70	29 14	+58	103	30 12	+58	102	31 10	+57	102	32 07	+57	102	33 04	+58	101	290
72	28 44	57	101	29 41	58	100	30 39	57	100	31 36	58	100	32 34	57	99	288
74	28 13	58	99	29 11	57	98	30 08	58	98	31 06	57	98	32 03	57	97	286
76	27 43	57	97	28 40	58	96	29 38	57	96	30 35	57	96	31 32	58	95	284
78	27 12	57	95	28 09	58	94	29 07	57	94	30 04	57	94	31 01	58	93	282
80	26 41	+57	93	27 38	+58	92	28 36	+57	92	29 33	+57	92	30 30	+58	91	280
82	26 10	57	91	27 07	58	91	28 05	57	90	29 02	57	90	29 59	58	90	278
84	25 39	57	89	26 36	57	89	27 33	58	88	28 31	57	88	29 28	57	88	276
86	25 07	58	87	26 05	57	87	27 02	58	86	28 00	57	86	28 57	57	86	274
88	24 37	57	85	25 34	57	85	26 31	58	84	27 29	57	84	28 26	58	84	272
90	24 06	+57	83	25 03	+58	83	26 01	+57	83	26 58	+57	82	27 55	+58	82	270
92	23 35	57	81	24 32	58	81	25 30	57	81	26 27	58	80	27 25	57	80	268
94	23 04	58	79	24 02	57	79	24 59	58	79	25 57	57	78	26 54	58	78	266
96	22 34	57	77	23 31	58	77	24 29	58	77	25 27	57	77	26 24	57	76	264
98	22 04	57	76	23 01	58	75	23 59	57	75	24 56	58	75	25 54	57	74	262
100	21 34	+57	74	22 31	+58	73	23 29	+58	73	24 27	+57	73	25 24	+58	73	260
102	21 04	58	72	22 02	57	72	22 59	58	71	23 57	58	71	24 55	57	71	258
104	20 35	57	70	21 32	58	70	22 30	58	69	23 28	58	69	24 26	57	69	256
106	20 06	58	68	21 04	57	68	22 01	58	68	22 59	58	67	23 57	58	67	254
108	19 37	58	66	20 35	58	66	21 33	58	66	22 31	58	65	23 29	57	65	252
110	19 09	+58	64	20 07	+58	64	21 05	+58	64	22 03	+58	64	23 01	+57	63	250
112	18 41	58	63	19 39	58	62	20 37	58	62	21 35	58	62	22 33	58	61	248
114	18 14	58	61	19 12	58	60	20 10	58	60	21 08	58	60	22 06	58	60	246
116	17 47	58	59	18 45	58	59	19 43	58	58	20 41	58	58	21 39	59	58	244
118	17 21	58	57	18 19	58	57	19 17	58	57	20 15	58	56	21 13	59	56	242
120	16 55	+58	55	17 53	+59	55	18 52	+58	55	19 50	+58	54	20 48	+58	54	240
122	16 30	58	53	17 28	58	53	18 26	59	53	19 25	58	53	20 23	58	52	238
124	16 05	59	51	17 04	58	51	18 02	58	51	19 00	59	51	19 59	58	51	236
126	15 41	59	50	16 40	58	49	17 38	59	49	18 37	58	49	19 35	59	49	234
128	15 18	58	48	16 16	59	48	17 15	59	47	18 14	58	47	19 12	59	47	232
130	14 55	+59	46	15 54	+59	46	16 53	+58	46	17 51	+59	45	18 50	+59	45	230
132	14 33	59	44	15 32	59	44	16 31	59	44	17 30	58	44	18 28	59	43	228
134	14 12	59	42	15 11	59	42	16 10	59	42	17 09	58	42	18 07	59	42	226
136	13 51	59	40	14 50	59	40	15 49	59	40	16 48	59	40	17 47	59	40	224
138	13 32	59	39	14 31	59	38	15 30	59	38	16 29	59	38	17 28	59	38	222

S. Lat. {LHA greater than 180°....... Zn=180−Z
{LHA less than 180°........... Zn=180+Z

DECLINATION (15°-29°) SAME NAME AS LATITUDE

LAT 75°

N. Lat. {LHA greater than 180°....... Zn=Z; LHA less than 180°.......... Zn=360−Z}

DECLINATION (15°-29°) SAME NAME AS LATITUDE

LAT 75°

LHA	15° Hc	15° d	15° Z	16° Hc	16° d	16° Z	17° Hc	17° d	17° Z	18° Hc	18° d	18° Z	19° Hc	19° d	19° Z	20° Hc	20° d	20° Z	21° Hc	21° d	21° Z	22° Hc	22° d	22° Z
	° ′	′	°	° ′	′	°	° ′	′	°	° ′	′	°	° ′	′	°	° ′	′	°	° ′	′	°	° ′	′	°
140	03 21	+59	39	04 20	+60	38	05 20	+59	38	06 19	+59	38	07 18	+59	38	08 17	+59	38	09 16	+59	37	10 15	+59	37
142	03 02	60	37	04 02	59	36	05 01	59	36	06 00	59	36	06 59	59	36	07 58	60	36	08 58	59	36	09 57	59	35
144	02 44	60	35	03 44	59	35	04 43	59	34	05 42	59	34	06 41	60	34	07 41	59	34	08 40	59	34	09 39	60	34
146	02 27	59	33	03 26	60	33	04 26	59	32	05 25	59	32	06 24	60	32	07 24	59	32	08 23	60	32	09 23	59	32
148	02 11	59	31	03 10	60	31	04 10	59	31	05 09	59	30	06 08	60	30	07 08	59	30	08 07	60	30	09 07	59	30
150	01 55	+60	29	02 55	+59	29	03 54	+60	29	04 54	+59	29	05 53	+60	28	06 53	+59	28	07 52	+60	28	08 52	+59	28
152	01 41	59	27	02 40	60	27	03 40	59	27	04 39	60	27	05 39	59	27	06 38	60	26	07 38	60	26	08 38	59	26
154	01 27	60	25	02 27	59	25	03 26	60	25	04 26	59	25	05 25	60	25	06 25	60	25	07 25	59	24	08 24	60	24
156	01 14	60	23	02 14	60	23	03 14	59	23	04 13	60	23	05 13	60	23	06 13	59	23	07 12	60	23	08 12	60	22
158	01 03	59	21	02 02	60	21	03 02	60	21	04 02	59	21	05 01	60	21	06 01	60	21	07 01	60	21	08 01	59	21
160	00 52	+60	19	01 52	+59	19	02 51	+60	19	03 51	+60	19	04 51	+60	19	05 51	+59	19	06 50	+60	19	07 50	+60	19
162	00 42	60	17	01 42	60	17	02 42	60	17	03 42	59	17	04 41	60	17	05 41	60	17	06 41	60	17	07 41	60	17
164	00 33	60	15	01 33	60	15	02 33	60	15	03 33	60	15	04 33	60	15	05 33	59	15	06 32	60	15	07 32	60	15
166	00 26	59	14	01 25	60	14	02 25	60	13	03 25	60	13	04 25	60	13	05 25	60	13	06 25	60	13	07 25	60	13
168	00 19	60	12	01 19	60	12	02 19	59	12	03 18	60	11	04 18	60	11	05 18	60	11	06 18	60	11	07 18	60	11
170	00 13	+60	10	01 13	+60	10	02 13	+60	10	03 13	+60	10	04 13	+60	10	05 13	+60	9	06 13	+60	9	07 13	+60	9
172	00 08	60	8	01 08	60	8	02 08	60	8	03 08	60	8	04 08	60	8	05 08	60	8	06 08	60	8	07 08	60	8
174	00 05	60	6	01 05	60	6	02 05	60	6	03 05	60	6	04 05	60	6	05 05	60	6	06 05	60	6	07 05	60	6
176	00 02	60	4	01 02	60	4	02 02	60	4	03 02	60	4	04 02	60	4	05 02	60	4	06 02	60	4	07 02	60	4
178	00 00	60	2	01 00	60	2	02 00	60	2	03 00	60	2	04 00	60	2	05 00	60	2	06 00	60	2	07 00	60	2
180	00 00	+60	0	01 00	+60	0	02 00	+60	0	03 00	+60	0	04 00	+60	0	05 00	+60	0	06 00	+60	0	07 00	+60	0

LHA	23° Hc	23° d	23° Z	24° Hc	24° d	24° Z	25° Hc	25° d	25° Z	26° Hc	26° d	26° Z	27° Hc	27° d	27° Z	28° Hc	28° d	28° Z	29° Hc	29° d	29° Z	LHA
	° ′	′	°	° ′	′	°	° ′	′	°	° ′	′	°	° ′	′	°	° ′	′	°	° ′	′	°	
140	11 14	+60	37	12 14	+59	37	13 13	+59	37	14 12	+59	37	15 11	+59	36	16 10	+59	36	17 09	+59	36	220
142	10 56	59	35	11 55	59	35	12 54	60	35	13 54	59	35	14 53	59	35	15 52	59	34	16 51	59	34	218
144	10 39	59	33	11 38	59	33	12 37	59	33	13 36	60	33	14 36	59	33	15 35	59	33	16 34	59	32	216
146	10 22	59	32	11 21	60	31	12 21	59	31	13 20	59	31	14 19	60	31	15 19	59	31	16 18	59	31	214
148	10 06	59	30	11 05	60	30	12 05	59	29	13 04	60	29	14 04	59	29	15 03	59	29	16 02	60	29	212
150	09 51	+60	28	10 51	+59	28	11 50	+60	28	12 50	+59	27	13 49	+59	27	14 48	+60	27	15 48	+59	27	210
152	09 37	60	26	10 37	59	26	11 36	60	26	12 36	59	26	13 35	60	26	14 35	59	25	15 34	60	25	208
154	09 24	60	24	10 24	59	24	11 23	60	24	12 23	59	24	13 22	60	24	14 22	59	24	15 21	60	23	206
156	09 12	59	22	10 11	60	22	11 11	60	22	12 11	59	22	13 10	60	22	14 10	60	22	15 10	59	22	204
158	09 00	60	20	10 00	60	20	11 00	59	20	11 59	60	20	12 59	60	20	13 59	60	20	14 59	59	20	202
160	08 50	+60	19	09 50	+59	19	10 49	+60	18	11 49	+60	18	12 49	+60	18	13 49	+60	18	14 49	+59	18	200
162	08 41	59	17	09 40	60	17	10 40	60	17	11 40	60	17	12 40	60	16	13 40	59	16	14 39	60	16	198
164	08 32	60	15	09 32	60	15	10 32	60	15	11 32	59	15	12 31	60	15	13 31	60	15	14 31	60	14	196
166	08 25	60	13	09 25	59	13	10 24	60	13	11 24	60	13	12 24	60	13	13 24	60	13	14 24	60	13	194
168	08 18	60	11	09 18	60	11	10 18	60	11	11 18	60	11	12 18	60	11	13 18	60	11	14 18	59	11	192
170	08 13	+60	9	09 13	+59	9	10 12	+60	9	11 12	+60	9	12 12	+60	9	13 12	+60	9	14 12	+60	9	190
172	08 08	60	7	09 08	60	7	10 08	60	7	11 08	60	7	12 08	60	7	13 08	60	7	14 08	60	7	188
174	08 05	60	6	09 05	60	6	10 05	60	6	11 05	59	6	12 04	60	6	13 04	60	5	14 04	60	5	186
176	08 02	60	4	09 02	60	4	10 02	60	4	11 02	60	4	12 02	60	4	13 02	60	4	14 02	60	4	184
178	08 00	60	2	09 00	60	2	10 00	60	2	11 00	60	2	12 00	60	2	13 00	60	2	14 00	60	2	182
180	08 00	+60	0	09 00	+60	0	10 00	+60	0	11 00	+60	0	12 00	+60	0	13 00	+60	0	14 00	+60	0	180

15°	16°	17°	18°	19°	20°	21°	22°	23°	24°	25°	26°	27°	28°	29°

S. Lat. {LHA greater than 180°....... Zn=180−Z; LHA less than 180°.......... Zn=180+Z}

DECLINATION (15°-29°) SAME NAME AS LATITUDE

LAT 75°

N. Lat. {LHA greater than 180°....... Zn=Z; LHA less than 180°........... Zn=360−Z}

DECLINATION (15°-29°) CONTRARY NAME TO LATITUDE

LHA	15°			16°			17°			18°			19°			20°			21°			22°			23°			24°			25°			26°			27°			28°			29°			LHA
	Hc	d	Z	Hc	d	Z	Hc	d	Z	Hc	d	Z	Hc	d	Z	Hc	d	Z	Hc	d	Z	Hc	d	Z	Hc	d	Z	Hc	d	Z	Hc	d	Z	Hc	d	Z	Hc	d	Z	Hc	d	Z	Hc	d	Z	
°	° ′	′	°	° ′	′	°	° ′	′	°	° ′	′	°	° ′	′	°	° ′	′	°	° ′	′	°	° ′	′	°	° ′	′	°	° ′	′	°	° ′	′	°	° ′	′	°	° ′	′	°	° ′	′	°	° ′	′	°	°
62	−7 37	59	121																																											298
60	−7 11	−58	122																																											300
58	−6 45	59	124	−7 44	58	125																																								302
56	−6 20	58	126	−7 18	59	126																																								304
54	−5 55	59	128	−6 54	58	128																																								306
52	−5 31	59	130	−6 30	58	130	−7 28	59	130																																					308
50	−5 07	−59	132	−6 06	−59	132	−7 05	−59	132																																					310
48	−4 45	59	134	−5 44	58	134	−6 42	59	134	−7 41	59	134																																		312
46	−4 23	59	136	−5 22	59	136	−6 21	59	136	−7 20	58	136																																		314
44	−4 01	59	138	−5 00	59	138	−5 59	59	138	−6 58	60	138																																		316
42	−3 41	59	140	−4 40	59	140	−5 39	59	140	−6 38	59	140	−7 37	59	140																															318
40	−3 21	−59	141	−4 20	−60	142	−5 20	−59	142	−6 19	−59	142	−7 18	−59	142																															320
38	−3 02	60	143	−4 02	59	144	−5 01	59	144	−6 00	59	144	−6 59	59	144																															322
36	−2 44	60	145	−3 44	59	145	−4 43	59	146	−5 42	59	146	−6 41	60	146																															324
34	−2 27	59	147	−3 26	60	147	−4 26	59	148	−5 25	59	148	−6 24	60	148	−7 24	59	148																												326
32	−2 11	59	149	−3 10	60	149	−4 10	59	149	−5 09	59	150	−6 08	60	150	−7 08	59	150																												328
30	−1 55	−60	151	−2 55	−59	151	−3 54	−60	151	−4 54	−59	151	−5 53	−60	152	−6 53	−59	152																												330
28	−1 41	59	153	−2 40	60	153	−3 40	59	153	−4 39	60	153	−5 39	59	153	−6 38	60	154																												332
26	−1 27	60	155	−2 27	59	155	−3 26	60	155	−4 26	59	155	−5 25	60	155	−6 25	60	155																												334
24	−1 14	60	157	−2 14	60	157	−3 14	59	157	−4 13	60	157	−5 13	60	157	−6 13	59	157	−7 12	60	157																									336
22	−1 03	59	159	−2 02	60	159	−3 02	60	159	−4 02	59	159	−5 01	60	159	−6 01	60	159	−7 01	60	159																									338
20	−0 52	−60	161	−1 52	−59	161	−2 51	−60	161	−3 51	−60	161	−4 51	−60	161	−5 51	−59	161	−6 50	−60	161																									340
18	−0 42	60	163	−1 42	60	163	−2 42	60	163	−3 42	59	163	−4 41	60	163	−5 41	60	163	−6 41	60	163																									342
16	−0 33	60	165	−1 33	60	165	−2 33	60	165	−3 33	60	165	−4 33	60	165	−5 33	59	165	−6 32	60	165																									344
14	−0 26	59	166	−1 25	60	166	−2 25	60	167	−3 25	60	167	−4 25	60	167	−5 25	60	167	−6 25	60	167																									346
12	−0 19	60	168	−1 19	60	168	−2 19	59	168	−3 18	60	169	−4 18	60	169	−5 18	60	169	−6 18	60	169																									348
10	−0 13	−60	170	−1 13	−60	170	−2 13	−60	170	−3 13	−60	170	−4 13	−60	170	−5 13	−60	171	−6 13	−60	171																									350
8	−0 08	60	172	−1 08	60	172	−2 08	60	172	−3 08	60	172	−4 08	60	172	−5 08	60	172	−6 08	60	172																									352
6	−0 05	60	174	−1 05	60	174	−2 05	60	174	−3 05	60	174	−4 05	60	174	−5 05	60	174	−6 05	60	174																									354
4	−0 02	60	176	−1 02	60	176	−2 02	60	176	−3 02	60	176	−4 02	60	176	−5 02	60	176	−6 02	60	176																									356
2	00 00	60	178	−1 00	60	178	−2 00	60	178	−3 00	60	178	−4 00	60	178	−5 00	60	178	−6 00	60	178	−7 00	60	178																						358
0	00 00	−60	180	−1 00	−60	180	−2 00	−60	180	−3 00	−60	180	−4 00	−60	180	−5 00	−60	180	−6 00	−60	180	−7 00	−60	180																						360
	15°			16°			17°			18°			19°			20°			21°			22°			23°			24°			25°			26°			27°			28°			29°			

S. Lat. {LHA greater than 180°....... Zn=180−Z; LHA less than 180°........... Zn=180+Z}

DECLINATION (15°-29°) CONTRARY NAME TO LATITUDE

LAT 75°

N. Lat. {LHA greater than 180°....... Zn=Z
{LHA less than 180°.......... Zn=360−Z

DECLINATION (0°-14°) SAME NAME AS LATITUDE

LHA	0° Hc	0° d	0° Z	1° Hc	1° d	1° Z	2° Hc	2° d	2° Z	3° Hc	3° d	3° Z	4° Hc	4° d	4° Z	LHA
	° ′	′	°	° ′	′	°	° ′	′	°	° ′	′	°	° ′	′	°	
0	14 00	+60	180	15 00	+60	180	16 00	+60	180	17 00	+60	180	18 00	+60	180	360
2	14 00	60	178	15 00	60	178	16 00	60	178	17 00	60	178	18 00	60	178	358
4	13 58	60	176	14 58	60	176	15 58	60	176	16 58	60	176	17 58	60	176	356
6	13 55	60	174	14 55	60	174	15 55	60	174	16 55	60	174	17 55	60	174	354
8	13 52	60	172	14 52	60	172	15 52	60	172	16 52	60	172	17 52	60	172	352
10	13 47	+60	170	14 47	+60	170	15 47	+60	170	16 47	+60	170	17 47	+60	170	350
12	13 41	60	168	14 41	60	168	15 41	60	168	16 41	60	168	17 41	60	167	348
14	13 35	60	166	14 35	59	166	15 34	60	166	16 34	60	165	17 34	60	165	346
16	13 27	60	164	14 27	60	164	15 27	59	163	16 26	60	163	17 26	60	163	344
18	13 18	60	162	14 18	60	161	15 18	60	161	16 18	59	161	17 17	60	161	342
20	13 08	+60	159	14 08	+60	159	15 08	+60	159	16 08	+60	159	17 08	+59	159	340
22	12 58	60	157	13 58	59	157	14 57	60	157	15 57	60	157	16 57	59	157	338
24	12 46	60	155	13 46	60	155	14 46	59	155	15 45	60	155	16 45	60	155	336
26	12 34	59	153	13 33	60	153	14 33	59	153	15 32	60	153	16 32	60	153	334
28	12 20	60	151	13 20	59	151	14 19	60	151	15 19	59	151	16 18	60	151	332
30	12 06	+59	149	13 05	+60	149	14 05	+59	149	15 04	+60	149	16 04	+59	149	330
32	11 50	60	147	12 50	59	147	13 49	60	147	14 49	59	147	15 48	60	147	328
34	11 34	60	145	12 34	59	145	13 33	59	145	14 32	60	145	15 32	59	145	326
36	11 17	60	143	12 17	59	143	13 16	59	143	14 15	60	143	15 15	59	143	324
38	10 59	60	141	11 59	59	141	12 58	59	141	13 57	60	141	14 57	59	141	322
40	10 41	+59	139	11 40	+59	139	12 39	+60	139	13 39	+59	139	14 38	+59	139	320
42	10 21	60	137	11 21	59	137	12 20	59	137	13 19	59	137	14 18	59	137	318
44	10 01	59	135	11 00	60	135	12 00	59	135	12 59	59	135	13 58	59	134	316
46	09 41	59	133	10 40	59	133	11 39	59	133	12 38	59	133	13 37	59	132	314
48	09 19	59	131	10 18	59	131	11 17	59	131	12 16	59	131	13 15	59	130	312
50	08 57	+59	129	09 56	+59	129	10 55	+59	129	11 54	+58	129	12 52	+59	128	310
52	08 34	59	127	09 33	59	127	10 32	59	127	11 31	58	127	12 29	59	126	308
54	08 11	58	125	09 09	59	125	10 08	59	125	11 07	59	125	12 06	59	124	306
56	07 47	58	123	08 45	59	123	09 44	59	123	10 43	59	123	11 42	58	122	304
58	07 22	59	121	08 21	58	121	09 19	59	121	10 18	59	121	11 17	58	120	302
60	06 57	+59	119	07 56	+58	119	08 54	+59	119	09 53	+58	119	10 51	+59	118	300
62	06 31	59	117	07 30	59	117	08 29	58	117	09 27	59	117	10 26	58	116	298
64	06 05	59	115	07 04	58	115	08 02	59	115	09 01	58	115	09 59	59	114	296
66	05 39	58	113	06 37	59	113	07 36	58	113	08 34	59	113	09 33	58	113	294
68	05 12	58	111	06 10	59	111	07 09	58	111	08 07	59	111	09 06	58	111	292
70	04 45	+58	110	05 43	+59	109	06 42	+58	109	07 40	+58	109	08 38	+59	109	290
72	04 17	59	108	05 16	58	107	06 14	58	107	07 12	59	107	08 11	58	107	288
74	03 49	59	106	04 48	58	105	05 46	58	105	06 44	59	105	07 43	58	105	286
76	03 21	59	104	04 20	58	103	05 18	58	103	06 16	59	103	07 15	58	103	284
78	02 53	58	102	03 51	59	101	04 50	58	101	05 48	58	101	06 46	58	101	282
80	02 24	+59	100	03 23	+58	100	04 21	+58	99	05 19	+59	99	06 18	+58	99	280
82	01 56	58	98	02 54	58	98	03 52	58	97	04 50	59	97	05 49	58	97	278
84	01 27	58	96	02 25	58	96	03 23	59	95	04 22	58	95	05 20	58	95	276
86	00 58	58	94	01 56	58	94	02 54	59	93	03 53	58	93	04 51	58	93	274
88	00 29	58	92	01 27	59	92	02 26	58	92	03 24	58	91	04 22	58	91	272
90	00 00	+58	90	00 58	+58	90	01 56	+59	90	02 55	+58	89	03 53	+58	89	270
92	−0 29	58	88	00 29	58	88	01 27	59	88	02 26	58	87	03 24	58	87	268
94	−0 58	58	86	00 00	58	86	00 58	59	86	01 57	58	85	02 55	58	85	266
96	−1 27	58	84	−0 29	59	84	00 30	58	84	01 28	58	84	02 26	58	83	264
98	−1 56	58	82	−0 58	59	82	00 01	58	82	00 59	58	82	01 57	58	81	262
100	−2 24	+58	80	−1 26	+58	80	−0 28	+58	80	00 30	+59	80	01 29	+58	79	260
102	−2 53	58	78	−1 55	59	78	−0 56	58	78	00 02	58	78	01 00	58	77	258
104	−3 21	58	76	−2 23	58	76	−1 25	59	76	−0 26	58	76	00 32	58	75	256
106	−3 49	58	74	−2 51	58	74	−1 53	59	74	−0 54	58	74	00 04	58	74	254
108	−4 17	58	72	−3 19	59	72	−2 20	58	72	−1 22	58	72	−0 24	59	72	252
110	−4 45	+59	70	−3 46	+58	70	−2 48	+58	70	−1 50	+59	70	−0 51	+58	70	250
112	−5 12	58	69	−4 14	59	68	−3 15	58	68	−2 17	59	68	−1 18	58	68	248
114	−5 39	59	67	−4 40	58	66	−3 42	59	66	−2 43	58	66	−1 45	59	66	246
116	−6 05	58	65	−5 07	59	64	−4 08	58	64	−3 10	59	64	−2 11	59	64	244
118	−6 31	58	63	−5 33	59	62	−4 34	58	62	−3 36	59	62	−2 37	59	62	242
120	−6 57	+59	61	−5 58	+58	60	−5 00	+59	60	−4 01	+59	60	−3 02	+58	60	240
122	−7 22	59	59	−6 23	58	59	−5 25	59	58	−4 26	59	58	−3 27	59	58	238
124	−7 47	59	57	−6 48	59	57	−5 49	59	56	−4 50	59	56	−3 51	58	56	236
126				−7 12	59	55	−6 13	59	54	−5 14	59	54	−4 15	59	54	234
128				−7 35	59	53	−6 36	59	52	−5 37	59	52	−4 38	58	52	232
130							−6 59	+59	50	−6 00	+59	50	−5 01	+59	50	230
132							−7 21	59	48	−6 22	59	48	−5 23	59	48	228
134							−7 42	59	46	−6 43	59	46	−5 44	59	46	226
136										−7 04	59	44	−6 05	59	44	224
138										−7 24	59	42	−6 25	59	42	222

LHA	5° Hc	5° d	5° Z	6° Hc	6° d	6° Z	7° Hc	7° d	7° Z	8° Hc	8° d	8° Z	9° Hc	9° d	9° Z	LHA
	° ′	′	°	° ′	′	°	° ′	′	°	° ′	′	°	° ′	′	°	
0	19 00	+60	180	20 00	+60	180	21 00	+60	180	22 00	+60	180	23 00	+60	180	360
2	19 00	60	178	20 00	60	178	21 00	60	178	22 00	60	178	23 00	60	178	358
4	18 58	60	176	19 58	60	176	20 58	60	176	21 58	60	176	22 58	60	176	356
6	18 55	60	174	19 55	60	174	20 55	60	174	21 55	60	174	22 55	60	174	354
8	18 52	59	172	19 51	60	172	20 51	60	172	21 51	60	172	22 51	60	171	352
10	18 47	+60	170	19 47	+60	169	20 47	+60	169	21 47	+60	169	22 47	+59	169	350
12	18 41	60	167	19 41	60	167	20 41	60	167	21 41	60	167	22 41	59	167	348
14	18 34	60	165	19 34	60	165	20 34	60	165	21 34	60	165	22 34	59	165	346
16	18 26	60	163	19 26	60	163	20 26	60	163	21 26	60	163	22 26	59	163	344
18	18 17	60	161	19 17	60	161	20 17	60	161	21 17	59	161	22 16	60	161	342
20	18 07	+60	159	19 07	+60	159	20 07	+60	159	21 07	+59	159	22 06	+60	159	340
22	17 56	60	157	18 56	60	157	19 56	60	157	20 56	59	157	21 55	60	157	338
24	17 45	59	155	18 44	60	155	19 44	60	155	20 44	59	155	21 43	60	154	336
26	17 32	59	153	18 31	60	153	19 31	60	153	20 31	59	152	21 30	60	152	334
28	17 18	60	151	18 18	59	151	19 17	60	150	20 17	59	150	21 16	60	150	332
30	17 03	+60	149	18 03	+59	149	19 02	+60	148	20 02	+59	148	21 01	+60	148	330
32	16 48	59	147	17 47	60	146	18 47	59	146	19 46	60	146	20 46	59	146	328
34	16 31	60	145	17 31	59	144	18 30	59	144	19 29	60	144	20 29	59	144	326
36	16 14	59	142	17 13	60	142	18 13	59	142	19 12	59	142	20 11	60	142	324
38	15 56	59	140	16 55	59	140	17 54	60	140	18 54	59	140	19 53	59	140	322
40	15 37	+59	138	16 36	+59	138	17 35	+60	138	18 35	+59	138	19 34	+59	138	320
42	15 17	59	136	16 16	60	136	17 16	59	136	18 15	59	136	19 14	59	136	318
44	14 57	59	134	15 56	59	134	16 55	59	134	17 54	59	134	18 53	59	134	316
46	14 36	59	132	15 35	59	132	16 34	59	132	17 33	59	132	18 32	59	132	314
48	14 14	59	130	15 13	59	130	16 12	59	130	17 11	59	130	18 10	59	129	312
50	13 51	+59	128	14 50	+59	128	15 49	+59	128	16 48	+59	128	17 47	+59	127	310
52	13 28	59	126	14 27	59	126	15 26	59	126	16 25	59	126	17 24	58	125	308
54	13 05	58	124	14 03	59	124	15 02	59	124	16 01	59	124	17 00	58	123	306
56	12 40	59	122	13 39	59	122	14 38	58	122	15 36	59	122	16 35	59	121	304
58	12 15	59	120	13 14	59	120	14 13	58	120	15 11	59	120	16 10	59	119	302
60	11 50	+59	118	12 49	+58	118	13 47	+59	118	14 46	+58	118	15 44	+59	117	300
62	11 24	59	116	12 23	58	116	13 21	59	116	14 20	58	116	15 18	59	115	298
64	10 58	58	114	11 56	59	114	12 55	58	114	13 53	59	114	14 52	58	113	296
66	10 31	59	112	11 30	58	112	12 28	59	112	13 27	58	112	14 25	58	111	294
68	10 04	59	110	11 03	58	110	12 01	58	110	12 59	59	110	13 58	58	109	292
70	09 37	+58	108	10 35	+59	108	11 34	+58	108	12 32	+58	108	13 30	+59	107	290
72	09 09	58	106	10 07	59	106	11 06	58	106	12 04	58	106	13 02	59	105	288
74	08 41	58	104	09 39	59	104	10 38	58	104	11 36	58	104	12 34	59	103	286
76	08 13	58	102	09 11	58	102	10 09	59	102	11 08	58	102	12 06	58	101	284
78	07 44	59	101	08 43	58	100	09 41	58	100	10 39	58	100	11 37	59	100	282
80	07 16	+58	99	08 14	+58	98	09 12	+58	98	10 10	+59	98	11 09	+58	98	280
82	06 47	58	97	07 45	58	96	08 43	59	96	09 42	58	96	10 40	58	96	278
84	06 18	58	95	07 16	59	94	08 15	58	94	09 13	58	94	10 11	58	94	276
86	05 49	58	93	06 47	59	92	07 46	58	92	08 44	58	92	09 42	58	92	274
88	05 20	58	91	06 18	59	91	07 17	58	90	08 15	58	90	09 13	58	90	272
90	04 51	+58	89	05 49	+59	89	06 48	+58	88	07 46	+58	88	08 44	+58	88	270
92	04 22	58	87	05 20	59	87	06 19	58	86	07 17	58	86	08 15	58	86	268
94	03 53	58	85	04 51	59	85	05 50	58	84	06 48	58	84	07 46	58	84	266
96	03 24	58	83	04 22	59	83	05 21	58	83	06 19	58	82	07 17	58	82	264
98	02 55	59	81	03 54	58	81	04 52	58	81	05 50	58	80	06 48	59	80	262
100	02 27	+58	79	03 25	+58	79	04 23	+59	79	05 22	+58	78	06 20	+58	78	260
102	01 58	59	77	02 57	58	77	03 55	58	77	04 53	59	77	05 52	58	76	258
104	01 30	59	75	02 29	58	75	03 27	58	75	04 25	59	75	05 24	58	74	256
106	01 02	59	73	02 01	58	73	02 59	58	73	03 57	59	73	04 56	58	72	254
108	00 35	58	71	01 33	59	71	02 32	58	71	03 30	58	71	04 28	59	70	252
110	00 07	+59	69	01 06	+58	69	02 04	+59	69	03 03	+58	69	04 01	+59	69	250
112	−0 20	59	67	00 39	58	67	01 37	59	67	02 36	58	67	03 34	59	67	248
114	−0 46	58	66	00 12	59	65	01 11	58	65	02 09	59	65	03 08	58	65	246
116	−1 12	58	64	−0 14	59	63	00 45	58	63	01 43	59	63	02 42	58	63	244
118	−1 38	58	62	−0 40	59	61	00 19	59	61	01 18	58	61	02 16	59	61	242
120	−2 04	+59	60	−1 05	+59	59	−0 06	+58	59	00 52	+59	59	01 51	+59	59	240
122	−2 28	58	58	−1 30	59	57	−0 31	59	57	00 28	58	57	01 26	59	57	238
124	−2 53	59	56	−1 54	59	56	−0 55	59	55	00 04	58	55	01 02	59	55	236
126	−3 16	58	54	−2 18	59	54	−1 19	59	53	−0 20	59	53	00 39	59	53	234
128	−3 40	59	52	−2 41	59	52	−1 42	59	51	−0 43	59	51	00 16	59	51	232
130	−4 02	+59	50	−3 03	+59	50	−2 04	+59	49	−1 05	+59	49	−0 06	+59	49	230
132	−4 24	59	48	−3 25	59	48	−2 26	59	48	−1 27	59	47	−0 28	59	47	228
134	−4 45	59	46	−3 46	59	46	−2 47	59	46	−1 48	59	45	−0 49	59	45	226
136	−5 06	60	44	−4 06	59	44	−3 07	59	44	−2 08	59	43	−1 09	59	43	224
138	−5 26	60	42	−4 26	59	42	−3 27	59	42	−2 28	59	41	−1 29	60	41	222

LHA	10° Hc	10° d	10° Z	11° Hc	11° d	11° Z	12° Hc	12° d	12° Z	13° Hc	13° d	13° Z	14° Hc	14° d	14° Z	LHA
	° ′	′	°	° ′	′	°	° ′	′	°	° ′	′	°	° ′	′	°	
0	24 00	+60	180	25 00	+60	180	26 00	+60	180	27 00	+60	180	28 00	+60	180	360
2	24 00	60	178	25 00	59	178	25 59	60	178	26 59	60	178	27 59	60	178	358
4	23 58	60	176	24 58	60	176	25 58	60	176	26 58	60	176	27 58	60	176	356
6	23 55	60	174	24 55	60	174	25 55	60	174	26 55	60	173	27 55	60	173	354
8	23 51	60	171	24 51	60	171	25 51	60	171	26 51	60	171	27 51	60	171	352
10	23 46	+60	169	24 46	+60	169	25 46	+60	169	26 46	+60	169	27 46	+60	169	350
12	23 40	60	167	24 40	60	167	25 40	60	167	26 40	60	167	27 40	60	167	348
14	23 33	60	165	24 33	60	165	25 33	60	165	26 33	60	165	27 33	60	165	346
16	23 25	60	163	24 25	60	163	25 25	60	163	26 25	60	163	27 25	60	163	344
18	23 16	60	161	24 16	60	161	25 16	60	161	26 16	59	160	27 15	60	160	342
20	23 06	+60	159	24 06	+60	158	25 06	+59	158	26 05	+60	158	27 05	+60	158	340
22	22 55	60	156	23 55	59	156	24 54	60	156	25 54	60	156	26 54	60	156	338
24	22 43	60	154	23 43	59	154	24 42	60	154	25 42	60	154	26 42	59	154	336
26	22 30	59	152	23 29	60	152	24 29	60	152	25 29	59	152	26 28	60	152	334
28	22 16	59	150	23 15	60	150	24 15	59	150	25 14	60	150	26 14	59	150	332
30	22 01	+59	148	23 00	+60	148	24 00	+59	148	24 59	+60	148	25 59	+59	147	330
32	21 45	59	146	22 44	60	146	23 44	59	146	24 43	60	145	25 43	59	145	328
34	21 28	60	144	22 28	59	144	23 27	59	143	24 26	60	143	25 26	59	143	326
36	21 11	59	142	22 10	59	142	23 09	59	141	24 08	60	141	25 08	59	141	324
38	20 52	59	140	21 51	60	139	22 51	59	139	23 50	59	139	24 49	59	139	322
40	20 33	+59	138	21 32	+59	137	22 31	+59	137	23 30	+60	137	24 30	+59	137	320
42	20 13	59	135	21 12	59	135	22 11	59	135	23 10	59	135	24 09	59	135	318
44	19 52	59	133	20 51	59	133	21 50	59	133	22 49	59	133	23 48	59	133	316
46	19 31	59	131	20 30	59	131	21 29	59	131	22 28	58	131	23 26	59	131	314
48	19 09	58	129	20 07	59	129	21 06	59	129	22 05	59	129	23 04	59	128	312
50	18 46	+59	127	19 45	+58	127	20 43	+59	127	21 42	+59	127	22 41	+59	126	310
52	18 22	59	125	19 21	59	125	20 20	59	125	21 19	58	125	22 17	59	124	308
54	17 58	59	123	18 57	59	123	19 56	58	123	20 54	59	123	21 53	59	122	306
56	17 34	58	121	18 32	59	121	19 31	59	121	20 30	58	120	21 28	59	120	304
58	17 09	58	119	18 07	59	119	19 06	58	119	20 04	59	118	21 03	58	118	302
60	16 43	+58	117	17 41	+59	117	18 40	+59	117	19 39	+58	116	20 37	+58	116	300
62	16 17	58	115	17 15	59	115	18 14	58	115	19 12	59	114	20 11	58	114	298
64	15 50	59	113	16 49	58	113	17 47	59	113	18 46	58	112	19 44	58	112	296
66	15 23	59	111	16 22	58	111	17 20	59	111	18 19	58	110	19 17	58	110	294
68	14 56	59	109	15 55	58	109	16 53	58	109	17 51	59	108	18 50	58	108	292
70	14 29	+58	107	15 27	+58	107	16 25	+59	107	17 24	+58	106	18 22	+58	106	290
72	14 01	58	105	14 59	58	105	15 57	59	105	16 56	58	104	17 54	58	104	288
74	13 33	58	103	14 31	58	103	15 29	58	103	16 27	58	102	17 25	59	102	286
76	13 04	58	101	14 02	59	101	15 01	58	101	15 59	58	100	16 57	58	100	284
78	12 36	58	99	13 34	58	99	14 32	58	99	15 30	58	99	16 28	58	98	282
80	12 07	+58	97	13 05	+58	97	14 03	+58	97	15 01	+59	97	16 00	+58	96	280
82	11 38	58	95	12 36	58	95	13 34	59	95	14 33	58	95	15 31	58	94	278
84	11 09	58	93	12 07	58	93	13 05	59	93	14 04	58	93	15 02	58	92	276
86	10 40	58	91	11 38	58	91	12 36	59	91	13 35	58	91	14 33	58	90	274
88	10 11	58	90	11 09	58	89	12 07	59	89	13 06	58	89	14 04	58	89	272
90	09 42	+58	88	10 40	+58	87	11 38	+58	87	12 36	+59	87	13 35	+58	87	270
92	09 13	58	86	10 11	58	85	11 09	59	85	12 08	58	85	13 06	58	85	268
94	08 44	58	84	09 42	59	83	10 41	58	83	11 39	58	83	12 37	58	83	266
96	08 15	59	82	09 14	58	82	10 12	58	81	11 10	58	81	12 08	58	81	264
98	07 47	58	80	08 45	58	80	09 43	58	79	10 41	59	79	11 40	58	79	262
100	07 18	+58	78	08 16	+59	78	09 15	+58	77	10 13	+58	77	11 11	+58	77	260
102	06 50	58	76	07 48	58	76	08 46	59	76	09 45	58	75	10 43	58	75	258
104	06 22	58	74	07 20	59	74	08 19	58	74	09 17	58	73	10 15	58	73	256
106	05 54	58	72	06 52	59	72	07 51	58	72	08 49	58	71	09 47	59	71	254
108	05 27	58	70	06 25	58	70	07 23	59	70	08 22	58	70	09 20	58	69	252
110	05 00	+58	68	05 58	+58	68	06 56	+59	68	07 55	+58	68	08 53	+59	67	250
112	04 33	58	66	05 31	59	66	06 30	58	66	07 28	59	66	08 27	58	65	248
114	04 06	59	64	05 05	58	64	06 03	59	64	07 02	58	64	08 00	59	64	246
116	03 40	59	63	04 39	58	62	05 37	59	62	06 36	59	62	07 35	58	62	244
118	03 15	58	61	04 13	59	60	05 12	59	60	06 11	58	60	07 09	59	60	242
120	02 50	+58	59	03 48	+59	58	04 47	+59	58	05 46	+58	58	06 44	+59	58	240
122	02 25	59	57	03 24	59	57	04 23	58	56	05 21	59	56	06 20	59	56	238
124	02 01	59	55	03 00	59	55	03 59	59	54	04 58	58	54	05 56	59	54	236
126	01 38	59	53	02 37	59	53	03 36	58	52	04 34	59	52	05 33	59	52	234
128	01 15	59	51	02 14	59	51	03 13	59	51	04 12	59	50	05 11	59	50	232
130	00 53	+59	49	01 52	+59	49	02 51	+59	49	03 50	+59	48	04 49	+59	48	230
132	00 31	59	47	01 30	59	47	02 29	59	47	03 28	59	47	04 27	59	46	228
134	00 10	59	45	01 09	59	45	02 08	60	45	03 08	59	45	04 07	59	44	226
136	−0 10	59	43	00 49	59	43	01 48	60	43	02 48	59	43	03 47	59	43	224
138	−0 29	59	41	00 30	59	41	01 29	59	41	02 28	59	41	03 27	60	41	222

S. Lat. {LHA greater than 180°....... Zn=180−Z
{LHA less than 180°.......... Zn=180+Z

DECLINATION (0°-14°) SAME NAME AS LATITUDE

LAT 76°

N. Lat. {LHA greater than 180°....... Zn=Z; LHA less than 180°........... Zn=360−Z}

DECLINATION (0°-14°) SAME NAME AS LATITUDE

LHA	0° Hc d Z	1° Hc d Z	2° Hc d Z	3° Hc d Z	4° Hc d Z	5° Hc d Z	6° Hc d Z	7° Hc d Z	8° Hc d Z
220				140	−6 44 +59 40	−5 45 +60 40	−4 45 +59 40	−3 46 +59 40	−2 47 +59 40
218				142	−7 02 59 38	−6 03 59 38	−5 04 60 38	−4 04 59 38	−3 05 59 38
216				144	−7 20 60 36	−6 20 59 36	−5 21 59 36	−4 22 60 36	−3 22 59 36
214					146	−6 37 59 34	−5 38 60 34	−4 38 59 34	−3 39 60 34
212					148	−6 53 60 32	−5 53 59 32	−4 54 60 32	−3 54 59 32
210					150	−7 08 +60 30	−6 08 +59 30	−5 09 +60 30	−4 09 +59 30
208					152	−7 22 60 28	−6 22 59 28	−5 23 60 28	−4 23 59 28
206						154	−6 36 60 26	−5 36 60 26	−4 36 59 26
204						156	−6 48 60 24	−5 48 60 24	−4 48 59 24
202						158	−6 59 59 22	−6 00 60 22	−5 00 60 22
200						160	−7 10 +60 20	−6 10 +60 20	−5 10 +60 20
198						162	−7 19 60 18	−6 19 59 18	−5 20 60 18
196							164	−6 28 60 16	−5 28 60 16
194							166	−6 35 60 14	−5 35 59 14
192							168	−6 42 60 12	−5 42 60 12
190							170	−6 47 +60 10	−5 47 +59 10
188							172	−6 52 60 8	−5 52 60 8
186							174	−6 55 59 6	−5 56 60 6
184							176	−6 58 60 4	−5 58 60 4
182							178	−7 00 60 2	−6 00 60 2
180							180	−7 00 +60 0	−6 00 +60 0

LHA	9° Hc d Z	10° Hc d Z	11° Hc d Z	12° Hc d Z	13° Hc d Z	14° Hc d Z
220	−1 48 +60 39	−0 48 +59 39	00 11 +59 39	01 10 +60 39	02 10 +59 39	03 09 +59 39
218	−2 06 60 37	−1 06 59 37	−0 07 59 37	00 52 60 37	01 52 59 37	02 51 59 37
216	−2 23 60 35	−1 23 59 35	−0 24 59 35	00 35 60 35	01 35 59 35	02 34 60 35
214	−2 39 59 34	−1 40 60 33	−0 40 59 33	00 19 60 33	01 19 59 33	02 18 60 33
212	−2 55 60 32	−1 55 59 31	−0 56 60 31	00 04 59 31	01 03 60 31	02 03 59 31
210	−3 10 +60 30	−2 10 +59 29	−1 11 +60 29	−0 11 +60 29	00 49 +59 29	01 48 +60 29
208	−3 24 60 28	−2 24 60 28	−1 24 59 27	−0 25 60 27	00 35 59 27	01 34 60 27
206	−3 37 60 26	−2 37 60 26	−1 37 59 25	−0 38 60 25	00 22 60 25	01 22 59 25
204	−3 49 60 24	−2 49 60 24	−1 49 59 23	−0 50 60 23	00 10 60 23	01 10 60 23
202	−4 00 60 22	−3 00 60 22	−2 00 59 22	−1 01 60 21	−0 01 60 21	00 59 59 21
200	−4 10 +60 20	−3 10 +59 20	−2 11 +60 20	−1 11 +60 20	−0 11 +60 19	00 49 +59 19
198	−4 20 60 18	−3 20 60 18	−2 20 60 18	−1 20 60 18	−0 20 59 18	00 39 60 17
196	−4 28 60 16	−3 28 60 16	−2 28 60 16	−1 28 59 16	−0 29 60 16	00 31 60 15
194	−4 36 60 14	−3 36 60 14	−2 36 60 14	−1 36 60 14	−0 36 60 14	00 24 60 13
192	−4 42 60 12	−3 42 60 12	−2 42 60 12	−1 42 60 12	−0 42 60 12	00 18 60 12
190	−4 48 +60 10	−3 48 +60 10	−2 48 +60 10	−1 48 +60 10	−0 48 +60 10	00 12 +60 10
188	−4 52 60 8	−3 52 60 8	−2 52 60 8	−1 52 60 8	−0 52 60 8	00 08 60 8
186	−4 56 60 6	−3 56 60 6	−2 56 60 6	−1 56 60 6	−0 56 60 6	00 04 60 6
184	−4 58 60 4	−3 58 60 4	−2 58 60 4	−1 58 60 4	−0 58 60 4	00 02 60 4
182	−5 00 60 2	−4 00 60 2	−3 00 60 2	−2 00 60 2	−1 00 60 2	00 00 60 2
180	−5 00 +60 0	−4 00 +60 0	−3 00 +60 0	−2 00 +60 0	−1 00 +60 0	00 00 +60 0

0° 1° 2° 3° 4° 5° 6° 7° 8° 9° 10° 11° 12° 13° 14°

S. Lat. {LHA greater than 180°....... Zn=180−Z; LHA less than 180°........... Zn=180+Z}

DECLINATION (0°-14°) SAME NAME AS LATITUDE

N. Lat. {LHA greater than 180°....... Zn=Z; LHA less than 180°.......... Zn=360−Z}

DECLINATION (0°-14°) CONTRARY NAME TO LATITUDE

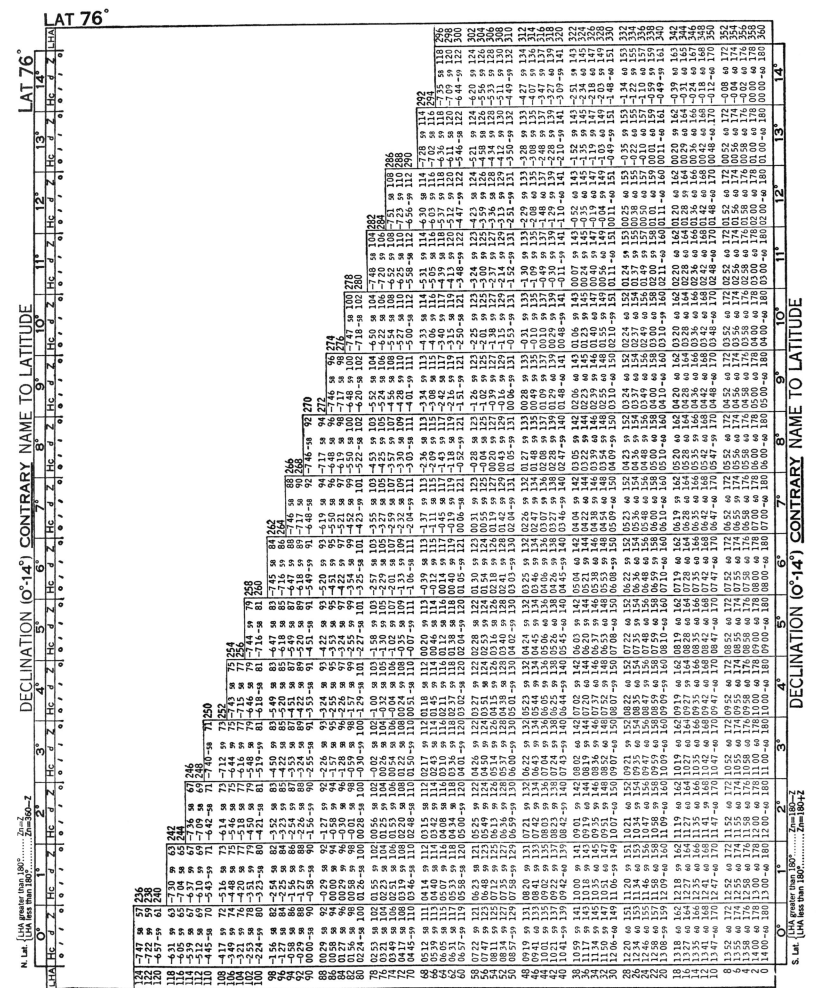

LHA	0° Hc	0° d	0° Z	1° Hc	1° d	1° Z	2° Hc	2° d	2° Z	3° Hc	3° d	3° Z	4° Hc	4° d	4° Z
	° ′	′	°	° ′	′	°	° ′	′	°	° ′	′	°	° ′	′	°
124	−7 47	58	57												
122	−7 22	59	59												
120	−6 57	−59	61												
118	−6 31	59	63	−7 30	59	63									
116	−6 05	59	65	−7 04	58	65									
114	−5 39	58	67	−6 37	59	67	−7 36	58	67						
112	−5 12	58	69	−6 10	59	69	−7 09	58	69						
110	−4 45	−58	70	−5 43	−59	71	−6 42	−58	71	−7 40	−58	71			
108	−4 17	59	72	−5 16	58	73	−6 14	58	73	−7 12	59	73			
106	−3 49	59	74	−4 48	58	75	−5 46	58	75	−6 44	59	75	−7 43	58	75
104	−3 21	59	76	−4 20	58	77	−5 18	58	77	−6 16	59	77	−7 15	58	77
102	−2 53	58	78	−3 51	59	79	−4 50	58	79	−5 48	58	79	−6 46	58	79
100	−2 24	−59	80	−3 23	−58	80	−4 21	−58	81	−5 19	−59	81	−6 18	−58	81
98	−1 56	58	82	−2 54	58	82	−3 52	58	83	−4 50	59	83	−5 49	58	83
96	−1 27	58	84	−2 25	58	84	−3 23	59	85	−4 22	58	85	−5 20	58	85
94	−0 58	58	86	−1 56	58	86	−2 54	59	87	−3 53	58	87	−4 51	58	87
92	−0 29	58	88	−1 27	59	88	−2 26	58	88	−3 24	58	89	−4 22	58	89
90	00 00	−58	90	−0 58	−58	90	−1 56	−59	90	−2 55	−58	91	−3 53	−58	91
88	00 29	58	92	−0 29	58	92	−1 27	59	92	−2 26	58	93	−3 24	58	93
86	00 58	58	94	00 00	58	94	−0 58	59	94	−1 57	58	95	−2 55	58	95
84	01 27	58	96	00 29	59	96	−0 30	58	96	−1 28	58	96	−2 26	58	97
82	01 56	58	98	00 58	59	98	−0 01	58	98	−0 59	58	98	−1 57	58	99
80	02 24	−58	100	01 26	−58	100	00 28	−58	100	−0 30	−59	100	−1 29	−58	101
78	02 53	58	102	01 55	59	102	00 56	58	102	−0 02	58	102	−1 00	58	103
76	03 21	58	104	02 23	58	104	01 25	59	104	00 26	58	104	−0 32	58	105
74	03 49	58	106	02 51	58	106	01 53	59	106	00 54	58	106	−0 04	58	106
72	04 17	58	108	03 19	59	108	02 20	58	108	01 22	58	108	00 24	59	108
70	04 45	−59	110	03 46	−58	110	02 48	−58	110	01 50	−59	110	00 51	−58	110
68	05 12	58	111	04 14	59	112	03 15	58	112	02 17	59	112	01 18	58	112
66	05 39	59	113	04 40	58	114	03 42	59	114	02 43	58	114	01 45	59	114
64	06 05	58	115	05 07	59	116	04 08	58	116	03 10	59	116	02 11	59	116
62	06 31	58	117	05 33	59	118	04 34	58	118	03 36	59	118	02 37	59	118
60	06 57	−59	119	05 58	−58	120	05 00	−59	120	04 01	−59	120	03 02	−58	120
58	07 22	59	121	06 23	58	121	05 25	59	122	04 26	59	122	03 27	59	122
56	07 47	59	123	06 48	59	123	05 49	59	124	04 50	59	124	03 51	58	124
54	08 11	59	125	07 12	59	125	06 13	59	126	05 14	59	126	04 15	59	126
52	08 34	59	127	07 35	59	127	06 36	59	128	05 37	59	128	04 38	58	128
50	08 57	−59	129	07 58	−59	129	06 59	−59	130	06 00	−59	130	05 01	−59	130
48	09 19	59	131	08 20	59	131	07 21	59	132	06 22	59	132	05 23	59	132
46	09 41	60	133	08 41	59	133	07 42	59	134	06 43	59	134	05 44	59	134
44	10 01	59	135	09 02	59	135	08 03	59	136	07 04	59	136	06 05	59	136
42	10 21	59	137	09 22	59	137	08 23	59	138	07 24	59	138	06 25	59	138
40	10 41	−59	139	09 42	−60	139	08 42	−59	140	07 43	−59	140	06 44	−59	140
38	10 59	59	141	10 00	59	141	09 01	59	142	08 02	60	142	07 02	59	142
36	11 17	59	143	10 18	59	143	09 19	60	144	08 19	59	144	07 20	60	144
34	11 34	59	145	10 35	60	145	09 35	59	146	08 36	59	146	07 37	60	146
32	11 50	59	147	10 51	60	147	09 51	59	148	08 52	60	148	07 52	59	148
30	12 06	−60	149	11 06	−59	149	10 07	−60	150	09 07	−60	150	08 07	−59	150
28	12 20	60	151	11 20	59	151	10 21	60	152	09 21	59	152	08 22	60	152
26	12 34	60	153	11 34	60	153	10 34	59	154	09 35	60	154	08 35	60	154
24	12 46	60	155	11 46	59	156	10 47	60	156	09 47	60	156	08 47	59	156
22	12 58	60	157	11 58	60	158	10 58	59	158	09 59	60	158	08 59	60	158
20	13 08	−59	159	12 09	−60	160	11 09	−60	160	10 09	−60	160	09 09	−59	160
18	13 18	60	162	12 18	59	162	11 19	60	162	10 19	60	162	09 19	60	162
16	13 27	60	164	12 27	60	164	11 27	60	164	10 27	60	164	09 27	59	164
14	13 35	60	166	12 35	60	166	11 35	60	166	10 35	60	166	09 35	60	166
12	13 41	60	168	12 41	60	168	11 41	59	168	10 42	60	168	09 42	60	168
10	13 47	−60	170	12 47	−60	170	11 47	−60	170	10 47	−60	170	09 47	−60	170
8	13 52	60	172	12 52	60	172	11 52	60	172	10 52	60	172	09 52	60	172
6	13 55	60	174	12 55	60	174	11 55	60	174	10 55	60	174	09 55	60	174
4	13 58	60	176	12 58	60	176	11 58	60	176	10 58	60	176	09 58	60	176
2	14 00	60	178	13 00	60	178	12 00	60	178	11 00	60	178	10 00	60	178
0	14 00	−60	180	13 00	−60	180	12 00	−60	180	11 00	−60	180	10 00	−60	180

LHA	5° Hc	5° d	5° Z	6° Hc	6° d	6° Z	7° Hc	7° d	7° Z	8° Hc	8° d	8° Z	9° Hc	9° d	9° Z
	° ′	′	°	° ′	′	°	° ′	′	°	° ′	′	°	° ′	′	°
102	−7 44	59	79												
100	−7 16	−58	81												
98	−6 47	58	83	−7 45	58	84									
96	−6 18	58	85	−7 16	59	86									
94	−5 49	58	87	−6 47	59	88	−7 46	58	88						
92	−5 20	58	89	−6 18	59	89	−7 17	58	90						
90	−4 51	−58	91	−5 49	−59	91	−6 48	−58	92	−7 46	−58	92			
88	−4 22	58	93	−5 20	59	93	−6 19	58	94	−7 17	58	94			
86	−3 53	58	95	−4 51	59	95	−5 50	58	96	−6 48	58	96	−7 46	58	96
84	−3 24	58	97	−4 22	59	97	−5 21	58	97	−6 19	58	98	−7 17	58	98
82	−2 55	59	99	−3 54	58	99	−4 52	58	99	−5 50	58	100	−6 48	59	100
80	−2 27	−58	101	−3 25	−58	101	−4 23	−59	101	−5 22	−58	102	−6 20	−58	102
78	−1 58	59	103	−2 57	58	103	−3 55	58	103	−4 53	59	103	−5 52	58	104
76	−1 30	59	105	−2 29	58	105	−3 27	58	105	−4 25	59	105	−5 24	58	106
74	−1 02	59	107	−2 01	58	107	−2 59	58	107	−3 57	59	107	−4 56	58	108
72	−0 35	58	109	−1 33	59	109	−2 32	58	109	−3 30	58	109	−4 28	59	110
70	−0 07	−59	111	−1 06	−58	111	−2 04	−59	111	−3 03	−58	111	−4 01	−59	111
68	00 20	59	113	−0 39	58	113	−1 37	59	113	−2 36	58	113	−3 34	59	113
66	00 46	58	114	−0 12	59	115	−1 11	58	115	−2 09	59	115	−3 08	58	115
64	01 12	58	116	00 14	59	117	−0 45	58	117	−1 43	59	117	−2 42	58	117
62	01 38	58	118	00 40	59	119	−0 19	59	119	−1 18	58	119	−2 16	59	119
60	02 04	−59	120	01 05	−59	121	00 06	−58	121	−0 52	−59	121	−1 51	−59	121
58	02 28	58	122	01 30	59	123	00 31	59	123	−0 28	58	123	−1 26	59	123
56	02 53	59	124	01 54	59	124	00 55	59	125	−0 04	58	125	−1 02	59	125
54	03 16	58	126	02 18	59	126	01 19	59	127	00 20	59	127	−0 39	59	127
52	03 40	59	128	02 41	59	128	01 42	59	129	00 43	59	129	−0 16	59	129
50	04 02	−59	130	03 03	−59	130	02 04	−59	131	01 05	−59	131	00 06	−59	131
48	04 24	59	132	03 25	59	132	02 26	59	132	01 27	59	133	00 28	59	133
46	04 45	59	134	03 46	59	134	02 47	59	134	01 48	59	135	00 49	59	135
44	05 06	60	136	04 06	59	136	03 07	59	136	02 08	59	137	01 09	59	137
42	05 26	60	138	04 26	59	138	03 27	59	138	02 28	59	139	01 29	60	139
40	05 45	−60	140	04 45	−59	140	03 46	−59	140	02 47	−59	140	01 48	−60	141
38	06 03	59	142	05 04	60	142	04 04	59	142	03 05	59	142	02 06	60	143
36	06 20	59	144	05 21	59	144	04 22	60	144	03 22	59	144	02 23	60	145
34	06 37	59	146	05 38	60	146	04 38	59	146	03 39	60	146	02 39	59	146
32	06 53	60	148	05 53	59	148	04 54	60	148	03 54	59	148	02 55	60	148
30	07 08	−60	150	06 08	−59	150	05 09	−60	150	04 09	−59	150	03 10	−60	150
28	07 22	60	152	06 22	59	152	05 23	60	152	04 23	59	152	03 24	60	152
26	07 35	59	154	06 36	60	154	05 36	60	154	04 36	59	154	03 37	60	154
24	07 48	60	156	06 48	60	156	05 48	60	156	04 48	59	156	03 49	60	156
22	07 59	60	158	06 59	59	158	06 00	60	158	05 00	60	158	04 00	60	158
20	08 10	−60	160	07 10	−60	160	06 10	−60	160	05 10	−60	160	04 10	−60	160
18	08 19	60	162	07 19	60	162	06 19	59	162	05 20	60	162	04 20	60	162
16	08 28	60	164	07 28	60	164	06 28	60	164	05 28	60	164	04 28	60	164
14	08 35	60	166	07 35	60	166	06 35	60	166	05 35	59	166	04 36	60	166
12	08 42	60	168	07 42	60	168	06 42	60	168	05 42	60	168	04 42	60	168
10	08 47	−60	170	07 47	−60	170	06 47	−60	170	05 47	−59	170	04 48	−60	170
8	08 52	60	172	07 52	60	172	06 52	60	172	05 52	60	172	04 52	60	172
6	08 55	60	174	07 55	60	174	06 55	59	174	05 56	60	174	04 56	60	174
4	08 58	60	176	07 58	60	176	06 58	60	176	05 58	60	176	04 58	60	176
2	09 00	60	178	08 00	60	178	07 00	60	178	06 00	60	178	05 00	60	178
0	09 00	−60	180	08 00	−60	180	07 00	−60	180	06 00	−60	180	05 00	−60	180

LHA	10° Hc	10° d	10° Z	11° Hc	11° d	11° Z	12° Hc	12° d	12° Z	13° Hc	13° d	13° Z	14° Hc	14° d	14° Z	LHA
	° ′	′	°	° ′	′	°	° ′	′	°	° ′	′	°	° ′	′	°	
124																236
122																238
120																240
118																242
116																244
114																246
112																248
110																250
108																252
106																254
104																256
102																258
100																260
98																262
96																264
94																266
92																268
90																270
88																272
86																274
84																276
82	−7 47	58	100													278
80	−7 18	−58	102													280
78	−6 50	58	104	−7 48	58	104										282
76	−6 22	58	106	−7 20	59	106										284
74	−5 54	58	108	−6 52	59	108	−7 51	58	108							286
72	−5 27	58	110	−6 25	58	110	−7 23	59	110							288
70	−5 00	−58	112	−5 58	−58	112	−6 56	−59	112							290
68	−4 33	58	114	−5 31	59	114	−6 30	58	114	−7 28	59	114				292
66	−4 06	59	116	−5 05	58	116	−6 03	59	116	−7 02	58	116				294
64	−3 40	59	117	−4 39	58	118	−5 37	59	118	−6 36	59	118	−7 35	58	118	296
62	−3 15	58	119	−4 13	59	120	−5 12	59	120	−6 11	58	120	−7 09	59	120	298
60	−2 50	−58	121	−3 48	−59	122	−4 47	−59	122	−5 46	−58	122	−6 44	−59	122	300
58	−2 25	59	123	−3 24	59	123	−4 23	58	124	−5 21	59	124	−6 20	59	124	302
56	−2 01	59	125	−3 00	59	125	−3 59	59	126	−4 58	58	126	−5 56	59	126	304
54	−1 38	59	127	−2 37	59	127	−3 36	58	128	−4 34	59	128	−5 33	59	128	306
52	−1 15	59	129	−2 14	59	129	−3 13	59	129	−4 12	59	130	−5 11	59	130	308
50	−0 53	−59	131	−1 52	−59	131	−2 51	−59	131	−3 50	−59	132	−4 49	−59	132	310
48	−0 31	59	133	−1 30	59	133	−2 29	59	133	−3 28	59	133	−4 27	59	134	312
46	−0 10	59	135	−1 09	59	135	−2 08	60	135	−3 08	59	135	−4 07	59	136	314
44	00 10	59	137	−0 49	59	137	−1 48	60	137	−2 48	59	137	−3 47	59	137	316
42	00 29	59	139	−0 30	59	139	−1 29	59	139	−2 28	59	139	−3 27	60	139	318
40	00 48	−59	141	−0 11	−59	141	−1 10	−60	141	−2 10	−59	141	−3 09	−59	141	320
38	01 06	59	143	00 07	59	143	−0 52	60	143	−1 52	59	143	−2 51	59	143	322
36	01 23	59	145	00 24	59	145	−0 35	60	145	−1 35	59	145	−2 34	60	145	324
34	01 40	60	147	00 40	59	147	−0 19	60	147	−1 19	59	147	−2 18	60	147	326
32	01 55	59	149	00 56	60	149	−0 04	59	149	−1 03	60	149	−2 03	59	149	328
30	02 10	−59	151	01 11	−60	151	00 11	−60	151	−0 49	−59	151	−1 48	−60	151	330
28	02 24	60	152	01 24	59	153	00 25	60	153	−0 35	59	153	−1 34	60	153	332
26	02 37	60	154	01 37	59	155	00 38	60	155	−0 22	60	155	−1 22	59	155	334
24	02 49	60	156	01 49	59	157	00 50	60	157	−0 10	60	157	−1 10	60	157	336
22	03 00	60	158	02 00	59	158	01 01	60	159	00 01	60	159	−0 59	59	159	338
20	03 10	−59	160	02 11	−60	160	01 11	−60	160	00 11	−60	161	−0 49	−59	161	340
18	03 20	60	162	02 20	60	162	01 20	60	162	00 20	59	162	−0 39	60	163	342
16	03 28	60	164	02 28	60	164	01 28	59	164	00 29	60	164	−0 31	60	165	344
14	03 36	60	166	02 36	60	166	01 36	60	166	00 36	60	166	−0 24	60	167	346
12	03 42	60	168	02 42	60	168	01 42	60	168	00 42	60	168	−0 18	60	168	348
10	03 48	−60	170	02 48	−60	170	01 48	−60	170	00 48	−60	170	−0 12	−60	170	350
8	03 52	60	172	02 52	60	172	01 52	60	172	00 52	60	172	−0 08	60	172	352
6	03 56	60	174	02 56	60	174	01 56	60	174	00 56	60	174	−0 04	60	174	354
4	03 58	60	176	02 58	60	176	01 58	60	176	00 58	60	176	−0 02	60	176	356
2	04 00	60	178	03 00	60	178	02 00	60	178	01 00	60	178	00 00	60	178	358
0	04 00	−60	180	03 00	−60	180	02 00	−60	180	01 00	−60	180	00 00	−60	180	360

S. Lat. {LHA greater than 180°....... Zn=180−Z; LHA less than 180°.......... Zn=180+Z}

DECLINATION (0°-14°) CONTRARY NAME TO LATITUDE

LAT 76°

N. Lat. {LHA greater than 180°....... Zn=Z; LHA less than 180°........... Zn=360−Z}

DECLINATION (15°-29°) SAME NAME AS LATITUDE

	15°			16°			17°			18°			19°		
LHA	Hc	d	Z	Hc	d	Z	Hc	d	Z	Hc	d	Z	Hc	d	Z
	° ′	′	°	° ′	′	°	° ′	′	°	° ′	′	°	° ′	′	°
0	29 00	+60	180	30 00	+60	180	31 00	+60	180	32 00	+60	180	33 00	+60	180
2	28 59	60	178	29 59	60	178	30 59	60	178	31 59	60	178	32 59	60	178
4	28 58	60	176	29 58	60	176	30 58	60	176	31 58	60	176	32 58	60	176
6	28 55	60	173	29 55	60	173	30 55	60	173	31 55	60	173	32 55	60	173
8	28 51	60	171	29 51	60	171	30 51	60	171	31 51	60	171	32 51	60	171
10	28 46	+60	169	29 46	+60	169	30 46	+60	169	31 46	+60	169	32 46	+60	169
12	28 40	60	167	29 40	60	167	30 40	60	167	31 40	60	167	32 40	59	167
14	28 33	60	165	29 33	60	165	30 33	59	164	31 32	60	164	32 32	60	164
16	28 25	59	162	29 24	60	162	30 24	60	162	31 24	60	162	32 24	60	162
18	28 15	60	160	29 15	60	160	30 15	60	160	31 15	59	160	32 14	60	160
20	28 05	+60	158	29 05	+59	158	30 04	+60	158	31 04	+60	158	32 04	+60	158
22	27 54	59	156	28 53	60	156	29 53	60	156	30 53	59	156	31 52	60	155
24	27 41	60	154	28 41	59	154	29 40	60	153	30 40	60	153	31 40	59	153
26	27 28	59	152	28 27	60	151	29 27	59	151	30 26	60	151	31 26	60	151
28	27 13	60	149	28 13	59	149	29 12	60	149	30 12	59	149	31 11	60	149
30	26 58	+60	147	27 58	+59	147	28 57	+59	147	29 56	+60	147	30 56	+59	147
32	26 42	59	145	27 41	60	145	28 41	59	145	29 40	59	145	30 39	60	144
34	26 25	59	143	27 24	60	143	28 24	59	143	29 23	59	142	30 22	59	142
36	26 07	59	141	27 06	59	141	28 05	60	140	29 05	59	140	30 04	59	140
38	25 48	59	139	26 47	60	139	27 47	59	138	28 46	59	138	29 45	59	138
40	25 29	+59	137	26 28	+59	136	27 27	+59	136	28 26	+59	136	29 25	+59	136
42	25 08	59	134	26 07	59	134	27 06	59	134	28 05	59	134	29 04	59	134
44	24 47	59	132	25 46	59	132	26 45	59	132	27 44	59	132	28 43	59	132
46	24 25	59	130	25 24	59	130	26 23	59	130	27 22	59	130	28 21	59	129
48	24 03	59	128	25 02	59	128	26 01	58	128	26 59	59	128	27 58	59	127
50	23 40	+59	126	24 39	+58	126	25 37	+59	126	26 36	+59	125	27 35	+58	125
52	23 16	59	124	24 15	58	124	25 13	59	124	26 12	59	123	27 11	58	123
54	22 52	58	122	23 50	59	122	24 49	58	122	25 47	59	121	26 46	59	121
56	22 27	58	120	23 25	59	120	24 24	58	120	25 22	59	119	26 21	58	119
58	22 01	59	118	23 00	58	118	23 58	59	117	24 57	58	117	25 55	59	117
60	21 35	+59	116	22 34	+58	116	23 32	+59	115	24 31	+58	115	25 29	+58	115
62	21 09	59	114	22 08	58	114	23 06	58	113	24 04	59	113	25 03	58	113
64	20 42	59	112	21 41	58	112	22 39	58	111	23 37	59	111	24 36	58	111
66	20 15	59	110	21 14	58	110	22 12	58	109	23 10	58	109	24 08	59	109
68	19 48	58	108	20 46	58	108	21 44	59	107	22 43	58	107	23 41	58	107
70	19 20	+58	106	20 18	+58	106	21 16	+59	105	22 15	+58	105	23 13	+58	105
72	18 52	58	104	19 50	58	104	20 48	58	103	21 46	59	103	22 45	58	103
74	18 24	58	102	19 22	58	102	20 20	58	101	21 18	58	101	22 16	58	101
76	17 55	58	100	18 53	58	100	19 51	58	99	20 49	59	99	21 48	58	99
78	17 26	59	98	18 25	58	98	19 23	58	97	20 21	58	97	21 19	58	97
80	16 58	+58	96	17 56	+58	96	18 54	+58	96	19 52	+58	95	20 50	+58	95
82	16 29	58	94	17 27	58	94	18 25	58	94	19 23	58	93	20 21	58	93
84	16 00	58	92	16 58	58	92	17 56	58	92	18 54	58	91	19 52	58	91
86	15 31	58	90	16 29	58	90	17 27	58	90	18 25	58	89	19 23	58	89
88	15 02	58	88	16 00	59	88	16 58	58	88	17 56	58	87	18 54	58	87
90	14 33	+58	86	15 31	+58	86	16 29	+58	86	17 27	+58	86	18 25	+58	85
92	14 04	58	84	15 02	58	84	16 00	58	84	16 58	58	84	17 56	58	83
94	13 35	58	82	14 33	58	82	15 31	58	82	16 29	58	82	17 27	58	81
96	13 06	58	81	14 04	58	80	15 02	59	80	16 01	58	80	16 59	58	80
98	12 38	58	79	13 36	58	78	14 34	58	78	15 32	58	78	16 30	58	78
100	12 09	+59	77	13 08	+58	76	14 06	+58	76	15 04	+58	76	16 02	+58	76
102	11 41	58	75	12 39	59	75	13 38	58	74	14 36	58	74	15 34	58	74
104	11 13	59	73	12 12	58	73	13 10	58	72	14 08	58	72	15 06	58	72
106	10 46	58	71	11 44	58	71	12 42	59	70	13 41	58	70	14 39	58	70
108	10 18	59	69	11 17	58	69	12 15	58	69	13 13	59	68	14 12	58	68
110	09 52	+58	67	10 50	+58	67	11 48	+59	67	12 47	+58	66	13 45	+58	66
112	09 25	58	65	10 23	59	65	11 22	58	65	12 20	59	65	13 19	58	64
114	08 59	58	63	09 57	59	63	10 56	58	63	11 54	59	63	12 53	58	62
116	08 33	59	61	09 32	58	61	10 30	59	61	11 29	58	61	12 27	59	61
118	08 08	58	60	09 06	59	59	10 05	59	59	11 04	58	59	12 02	59	59
120	07 43	+59	58	08 42	+58	57	09 40	+59	57	10 39	+59	57	11 38	+58	57
122	07 19	59	56	08 18	58	56	09 16	59	55	10 15	59	55	11 14	58	55
124	06 55	59	54	07 54	59	54	08 53	58	53	09 51	59	53	10 50	59	53
126	06 32	59	52	07 31	59	52	08 30	58	52	09 28	59	51	10 27	59	51
128	06 10	58	50	07 08	59	50	08 07	59	50	09 06	59	49	10 05	59	49
130	05 48	+59	48	06 47	+58	48	07 45	+59	48	08 44	+59	48	09 43	+59	47
132	05 26	59	46	06 25	59	46	07 24	59	46	08 23	59	46	09 22	59	45
134	05 06	59	44	06 05	59	44	07 04	59	44	08 03	59	44	09 02	59	44
136	04 46	59	42	05 45	59	42	06 44	59	42	07 43	59	42	08 42	60	42
138	04 27	59	40	05 26	59	40	06 25	59	40	07 24	59	40	08 23	60	40
	15°			16°			17°			18°			19°		

	20°			21°			22°			23°			24°		
LHA	Hc	d	Z	Hc	d	Z	Hc	d	Z	Hc	d	Z	Hc	d	Z
	° ′	′	°	° ′	′	°	° ′	′	°	° ′	′	°	° ′	′	°
0	34 00	+60	180	35 00	+60	180	36 00	+60	180	37 00	+60	180	38 00	+60	180
2	33 59	60	178	34 59	60	178	35 59	60	178	36 59	60	178	37 59	60	178
4	33 58	60	176	34 58	60	175	35 58	60	175	36 58	60	175	37 58	60	175
6	33 55	60	173	34 55	60	173	35 55	60	173	36 55	60	173	37 55	60	173
8	33 51	60	171	34 51	60	171	35 51	60	171	36 51	60	171	37 51	60	171
10	33 46	+60	169	34 46	+60	169	35 46	+60	169	36 46	+59	169	37 45	+60	168
12	33 39	60	166	34 39	60	166	35 39	60	166	36 39	60	166	37 39	60	166
14	33 32	60	164	34 32	60	164	35 32	60	164	36 32	60	164	37 32	59	164
16	33 24	59	162	34 23	60	162	35 23	60	162	36 23	60	162	37 23	60	162
18	33 14	60	160	34 14	60	160	35 14	59	160	36 13	60	159	37 13	60	159
20	33 04	+59	158	34 03	+60	157	35 03	+60	157	36 03	+59	157	37 02	+60	157
22	32 52	60	155	33 52	59	155	34 51	60	155	35 51	59	155	36 50	60	155
24	32 39	60	153	33 39	59	153	34 38	60	153	35 38	59	153	36 37	60	152
26	32 26	59	151	33 25	60	151	34 25	59	151	35 24	60	150	36 24	59	150
28	32 11	59	149	33 10	60	148	34 10	59	148	35 09	60	148	36 09	59	148
30	31 55	+60	146	32 55	+59	146	33 54	+59	146	34 53	+60	146	35 53	+59	146
32	31 39	59	144	32 38	59	144	33 37	60	144	34 37	59	144	35 36	59	144
34	31 21	60	142	32 21	59	142	33 20	59	142	34 19	59	141	35 18	59	141
36	31 03	59	140	32 02	59	140	33 01	59	140	34 00	60	139	35 00	59	139
38	30 44	59	138	31 43	59	138	32 42	59	137	33 41	59	137	34 40	59	137
40	30 24	+59	136	31 23	+59	135	32 22	+59	135	33 21	+59	135	34 20	+59	135
42	30 03	59	133	31 02	59	133	32 01	59	133	33 00	59	133	33 59	59	133
44	29 42	59	131	30 41	58	131	31 39	59	131	32 38	59	131	33 37	59	130
46	29 20	58	129	30 18	59	129	31 17	59	129	32 16	59	129	33 15	58	128
48	28 57	58	127	29 55	59	127	30 54	59	127	31 53	58	126	32 51	59	126
50	28 33	+59	125	29 32	+59	125	30 31	+58	125	31 29	+59	124	32 28	+58	124
52	28 09	59	123	29 08	58	123	30 06	59	122	31 05	58	122	32 03	59	122
54	27 45	58	121	28 43	59	121	29 42	58	120	30 40	58	120	31 38	59	120
56	27 19	59	119	28 18	58	119	29 16	59	118	30 15	58	118	31 13	58	118
58	26 54	58	117	27 52	58	116	28 50	59	116	29 49	58	116	30 47	58	116
60	26 27	+59	115	27 26	+58	114	28 24	+58	114	29 22	+59	114	30 21	+58	114
62	26 01	58	113	26 59	58	112	27 57	59	112	28 56	58	112	29 54	58	112
64	25 34	58	111	26 32	58	110	27 30	58	110	28 28	59	110	29 27	58	110
66	25 07	58	109	26 05	58	108	27 03	58	108	28 01	58	108	28 59	58	107
68	24 39	58	107	25 37	58	106	26 35	58	106	27 33	58	106	28 31	58	105
70	24 11	+58	105	25 09	+58	104	26 07	+58	104	27 05	+58	104	28 03	+58	103
72	23 43	58	103	24 41	58	102	25 39	58	102	26 37	58	102	27 35	58	101
74	23 14	58	101	24 12	58	100	25 10	58	100	26 08	58	100	27 06	58	99
76	22 46	58	99	23 44	58	98	24 42	58	98	25 40	57	98	26 37	58	98
78	22 17	58	97	23 15	58	96	24 13	58	96	25 11	58	96	26 09	57	96
80	21 48	+58	95	22 46	+58	94	23 44	+58	94	24 42	+58	94	25 40	+58	94
82	21 19	58	93	22 17	58	92	23 15	58	92	24 13	58	92	25 11	58	92
84	20 50	58	91	21 48	58	91	22 46	58	90	23 44	58	90	24 42	57	90
86	20 21	58	89	21 19	58	89	22 17	58	88	23 15	58	88	24 13	57	88
88	19 52	58	87	20 50	58	87	21 48	58	86	22 46	58	86	23 44	57	86
90	19 23	+58	85	20 21	+58	85	21 19	+58	84	22 17	+58	84	23 15	+58	84
92	18 54	58	83	19 52	58	83	20 50	58	83	21 48	58	82	22 46	58	82
94	18 25	58	81	19 23	58	81	20 21	58	81	21 19	58	80	22 17	58	80
96	17 57	58	79	18 55	58	79	19 53	58	79	20 51	58	78	21 49	58	78
98	17 28	58	77	18 26	58	77	19 24	58	77	20 22	58	77	21 20	58	76
100	17 00	+58	75	17 58	+58	75	18 56	+58	75	19 54	+58	75	20 52	+58	74
102	16 32	58	74	17 30	58	73	18 28	58	73	19 26	59	73	20 25	58	72
104	16 04	59	72	17 03	58	71	18 01	58	71	18 59	58	71	19 57	58	71
106	15 37	58	70	16 35	58	70	17 33	59	69	18 32	58	69	19 30	58	69
108	15 10	58	68	16 08	58	68	17 06	59	67	18 05	58	67	19 03	58	67
110	14 43	+59	66	15 42	+58	66	16 40	+58	65	17 38	+58	65	18 36	+59	65
112	14 17	58	64	15 15	59	64	16 14	58	64	17 12	58	63	18 10	59	63
114	13 51	59	62	14 50	58	62	15 48	58	62	16 46	59	61	17 45	58	61
116	13 26	58	60	14 24	59	60	15 23	58	60	16 21	58	60	17 19	59	59
118	13 01	58	58	13 59	59	58	14 58	58	58	15 56	59	58	16 55	58	58
120	12 36	+59	57	13 35	+58	56	14 33	+59	56	15 32	+59	56	16 31	+58	56
122	12 12	59	55	13 11	59	54	14 10	58	54	15 08	59	54	16 07	58	54
124	11 49	59	53	12 48	58	53	13 46	59	52	14 45	59	52	15 44	58	52
126	11 26	59	51	12 25	59	51	13 24	58	51	14 22	59	50	15 21	59	50
128	11 04	59	49	12 03	59	49	13 02	58	49	14 00	59	48	14 59	59	48
130	10 42	+59	47	11 41	+59	47	12 40	+59	47	13 39	+59	47	14 38	+59	46
132	10 21	59	45	11 20	59	45	12 19	59	45	13 18	59	45	14 17	59	45
134	10 01	59	43	11 00	59	43	11 59	59	43	12 58	59	43	13 57	59	43
136	09 42	59	42	10 41	59	41	11 40	59	41	12 39	59	41	13 38	59	41
138	09 23	59	40	10 22	59	39	11 21	59	39	12 20	59	39	13 19	59	39
	20°			21°			22°			23°			24°		

	25°			26°			27°			28°			29°			
LHA	Hc	d	Z	Hc	d	Z	Hc	d	Z	Hc	d	Z	Hc	d	Z	LHA
	° ′	′	°	° ′	′	°	° ′	′	°	° ′	′	°	° ′	′	°	
0	39 00	+60	180	40 00	+60	180	41 00	+60	180	42 00	+60	180	43 00	+60	180	360
2	38 59	60	178	39 59	60	178	40 59	60	178	41 59	60	178	42 59	60	178	358
4	38 58	60	175	39 58	60	175	40 58	60	175	41 58	60	175	42 58	60	175	356
6	38 55	60	173	39 55	60	173	40 55	60	173	41 55	60	173	42 55	60	173	354
8	38 51	60	171	39 51	60	171	40 51	59	171	41 50	60	171	42 50	60	170	352
10	38 45	+60	168	39 45	+60	168	40 45	+60	168	41 45	+60	168	42 45	+60	168	350
12	38 39	60	166	39 39	60	166	40 39	60	166	41 39	59	166	42 38	60	166	348
14	38 31	60	164	39 31	60	164	40 31	60	164	41 31	60	163	42 31	59	163	346
16	38 23	59	161	39 22	60	161	40 22	60	161	41 22	60	161	42 22	59	161	344
18	38 13	60	159	39 13	59	159	40 12	60	159	41 12	60	159	42 12	59	159	342
20	38 02	+60	157	39 02	+59	157	40 01	+60	157	41 01	+60	156	42 01	+59	156	340
22	37 50	60	155	38 50	59	154	39 49	60	154	40 49	59	154	41 48	60	154	338
24	37 37	60	152	38 37	59	152	39 36	60	152	40 36	59	152	41 35	60	152	336
26	37 23	59	150	38 22	60	150	39 22	59	150	40 21	60	150	41 21	59	149	334
28	37 08	59	148	38 07	60	148	39 07	59	147	40 06	59	147	41 05	60	147	332
30	36 52	+59	146	37 51	+60	145	38 51	+59	145	39 50	+59	145	40 49	+59	145	330
32	36 35	59	143	37 34	60	143	38 34	59	143	39 33	59	143	40 32	59	142	328
34	36 17	59	141	37 16	60	141	38 16	59	141	39 15	59	140	40 14	59	140	326
36	35 59	59	139	36 58	59	139	37 57	59	138	38 56	59	138	39 55	59	138	324
38	35 39	59	137	36 38	59	136	37 37	59	136	38 36	59	136	39 35	59	136	322
40	35 19	+59	134	36 18	+58	134	37 16	+59	134	38 15	+59	134	39 14	+59	134	320
42	34 58	58	132	35 56	59	132	36 55	59	132	37 54	59	132	38 53	58	131	318
44	34 36	59	130	35 35	58	130	36 33	59	130	37 32	58	129	38 30	59	129	316
46	34 13	59	128	35 12	58	128	36 10	59	127	37 09	59	127	38 08	58	127	314
48	33 50	59	126	34 49	58	126	35 47	59	125	36 46	58	125	37 44	58	125	312
50	33 26	+59	124	34 25	+58	123	35 23	+59	123	36 22	+58	123	37 20	+58	123	310
52	33 02	58	122	34 00	59	121	34 59	58	121	35 57	58	121	36 55	58	121	308
54	32 37	58	120	33 35	58	119	34 33	59	119	35 32	58	119	36 30	58	118	306
56	32 11	58	117	33 09	59	117	34 08	58	117	35 06	58	117	36 04	58	116	304
58	31 45	58	115	32 43	59	115	33 42	58	115	34 40	58	114	35 38	58	114	302
60	31 19	+58	113	32 17	+58	113	33 15	+58	113	34 13	+58	112	35 11	+58	112	300
62	30 52	58	111	31 50	58	111	32 48	58	111	33 46	58	110	34 44	58	110	298
64	30 25	58	109	31 23	58	109	32 21	58	109	33 19	58	108	34 17	57	108	296
66	29 57	58	107	30 55	58	107	31 53	58	107	32 51	58	106	33 49	58	106	294
68	29 29	58	105	30 27	58	105	31 25	58	105	32 23	58	104	33 21	57	104	292
70	29 01	+58	103	29 59	+58	103	30 57	+58	103	31 55	+57	102	32 52	+58	102	290
72	28 33	58	101	29 31	57	101	30 28	58	101	31 26	58	100	32 24	58	100	288
74	28 04	58	99	29 02	58	99	30 00	58	99	30 58	57	98	31 55	58	98	286
76	27 35	58	97	28 33	58	97	29 31	58	97	30 29	57	96	31 26	58	96	284
78	27 06	58	95	28 04	58	95	29 02	58	95	30 00	57	94	30 57	58	94	282
80	26 38	+57	93	27 35	+58	93	28 33	+58	93	29 31	+58	92	30 29	+57	92	280
82	26 09	57	91	27 06	58	91	28 04	58	91	29 02	57	90	29 59	58	90	278
84	25 39	58	89	26 37	58	89	27 35	58	89	28 33	57	88	29 30	58	88	276
86	25 10	58	87	26 08	58	87	27 06	58	87	28 04	57	87	29 01	58	86	274
88	24 41	58	86	25 39	58	85	26 37	58	85	27 35	58	85	28 33	57	84	272
90	24 13	+57	84	25 10	+58	83	26 08	+58	83	27 06	+58	83	28 04	+57	82	270
92	23 44	58	82	24 42	57	81	25 39	58	81	26 37	58	81	27 35	58	81	268
94	23 15	58	80	24 13	58	80	25 11	58	79	26 09	57	79	27 06	58	79	266
96	22 47	58	78	23 45	57	78	24 42	58	77	25 40	58	77	26 38	58	77	264
98	22 18	58	76	23 16	58	76	24 14	58	75	25 12	58	75	26 10	58	75	262
100	21 50	+58	74	22 48	+58	74	23 46	+58	74	24 44	+58	73	25 42	+58	73	260
102	21 23	58	72	22 21	58	72	23 19	58	72	24 17	57	71	25 14	58	71	258
104	20 55	58	70	21 53	58	70	22 51	58	70	23 49	58	70	24 47	58	69	256
106	20 28	58	68	21 26	58	68	22 24	58	68	23 22	58	68	24 20	58	67	254
108	20 01	58	67	20 59	58	66	21 57	59	66	22 56	58	66	23 54	58	66	252
110	19 35	+58	65	20 33	+58	64	21 31	+58	64	22 29	+58	64	23 27	+59	64	250
112	19 09	58	63	20 07	58	63	21 05	58	62	22 03	59	62	23 02	58	62	248
114	18 43	58	61	19 41	59	61	20 40	58	61	21 38	58	60	22 36	58	60	246
116	18 18	58	59	19 16	59	59	20 15	58	59	21 13	58	58	22 11	59	58	244
118	17 53	59	57	18 52	58	57	19 50	59	57	20 49	58	57	21 47	58	56	242
120	17 29	+59	55	18 28	+58	55	19 26	+59	55	20 25	+58	55	21 23	+59	54	240
122	17 05	59	54	18 04	59	53	19 03	58	53	20 01	59	53	21 00	58	53	238
124	16 42	59	52	17 41	59	52	18 40	58	51	19 38	59	51	20 37	59	51	236
126	16 20	59	50	17 19	58	50	18 17	59	49	19 16	59	49	20 15	58	49	234
128	15 58	59	48	16 57	59	48	17 56	58	48	18 54	59	47	19 53	59	47	232
130	15 37	+59	46	16 36	+59	46	17 35	+58	46	18 33	+59	46	19 32	+59	45	230
132	15 16	59	44	16 15	59	44	17 14	59	44	18 13	59	44	19 12	59	44	228
134	14 56	59	42	15 55	59	42	16 54	59	42	17 53	59	42	18 52	59	42	226
136	14 37	59	41	15 36	59	40	16 35	59	40	17 34	59	40	18 33	59	40	224
138	14 18	60	39	15 18	59	39	16 17	59	38	17 16	59	38	18 15	59	38	222
	25°			26°			27°			28°			29°			

S. Lat. {LHA greater than 180°....... Zn=180−Z; LHA less than 180°........... Zn=180+Z}

N. Lat. {LHA greater than 180°....... Zn=Z; LHA less than 180°........... Zn=360−Z}

DECLINATION (15°-29°) **SAME** NAME AS LATITUDE

LAT 76°

LHA	15° Hc	15° d	15° Z	16° Hc	16° d	16° Z	17° Hc	17° d	17° Z	18° Hc	18° d	18° Z	19° Hc	19° d	19° Z	20° Hc	20° d	20° Z	21° Hc	21° d	21° Z
	° ′	′	°	° ′	′	°	° ′	′	°	° ′	′	°	° ′	′	°	° ′	′	°	° ′	′	°
140	04 08	+59	39	05 07	+60	38	06 07	+59	38	07 06	+59	38	08 05	+60	38	09 05	+59	38	10 04	+59	38
142	03 50	60	37	04 50	59	36	05 49	59	36	06 48	60	36	07 48	59	36	08 47	59	36	09 46	60	36
144	03 34	59	35	04 33	59	35	05 32	60	34	06 32	59	34	07 31	60	34	08 31	59	34	09 30	59	34
146	03 18	59	33	04 17	59	33	05 16	60	33	06 16	59	32	07 15	60	32	08 15	59	32	09 14	60	32
148	03 02	60	31	04 02	59	31	05 01	60	31	06 01	59	30	07 00	60	30	08 00	59	30	08 59	60	30
150	02 48	+59	29	03 47	+60	29	04 47	+59	29	05 46	+60	29	06 46	+60	28	07 46	+59	28	08 45	+60	28
152	02 34	60	27	03 34	59	27	04 33	60	27	05 33	60	27	06 33	59	27	07 32	60	26	08 32	59	26
154	02 21	60	25	03 21	60	25	04 21	59	25	05 20	60	25	06 20	60	25	07 20	59	25	08 19	60	24
156	02 10	59	23	03 09	60	23	04 09	60	23	05 09	59	23	06 08	60	23	07 08	60	23	08 08	59	23
158	01 58	60	21	02 58	60	21	03 58	60	21	04 58	60	21	05 58	59	21	06 57	60	21	07 57	60	21
160	01 48	+60	19	02 48	+60	19	03 48	+60	19	04 48	+60	19	05 48	+59	19	06 47	+60	19	07 47	+60	19
162	01 39	60	17	02 39	60	17	03 39	60	17	04 39	60	17	05 39	60	17	06 39	59	17	07 38	60	17
164	01 31	60	15	02 31	60	15	03 31	60	15	04 31	60	15	05 31	60	15	06 31	59	15	07 30	60	15
166	01 24	60	14	02 24	60	14	03 24	60	14	04 24	60	13	05 24	59	13	06 23	60	13	07 23	60	13
168	01 18	60	12	02 18	59	12	03 17	60	12	04 17	60	11	05 17	60	11	06 17	60	11	07 17	60	11
170	01 12	+60	10	02 12	+60	10	03 12	+60	10	04 12	+60	10	05 12	+60	10	06 12	+60	9	07 12	+60	9
172	01 08	60	8	02 08	60	8	03 08	60	8	04 08	60	8	05 08	60	8	06 08	60	8	07 08	60	8
174	01 04	60	6	02 04	60	6	03 04	60	6	04 04	60	6	05 04	60	6	06 04	60	6	07 04	60	6
176	01 02	60	4	02 02	60	4	03 02	60	4	04 02	60	4	05 02	60	4	06 02	60	4	07 02	60	4
178	01 00	60	2	02 00	60	2	03 00	60	2	04 00	60	2	05 00	60	2	06 00	60	2	07 00	60	2
180	01 00	+60	0	02 00	+60	0	03 00	+60	0	04 00	+60	0	05 00	+60	0	06 00	+60	0	07 00	+60	0

22° Hc	22° d	22° Z	23° Hc	23° d	23° Z	24° Hc	24° d	24° Z	25° Hc	25° d	25° Z	26° Hc	26° d	26° Z	27° Hc	27° d	27° Z	28° Hc	28° d	28° Z	29° Hc	29° d	29° Z	LHA
° ′	′	°	° ′	′	°	° ′	′	°	° ′	′	°	° ′	′	°	° ′	′	°	° ′	′	°	° ′	′	°	
11 03	+59	37	12 02	+59	37	13 01	+60	37	14 01	+59	37	15 00	+59	37	15 59	+59	37	16 58	+60	36	17 58	+59	36	220
10 46	59	36	11 45	59	35	12 44	60	35	13 44	59	35	14 43	59	35	15 42	59	35	16 41	60	35	17 41	59	34	218
10 29	60	34	11 29	59	34	12 28	59	33	13 27	60	33	14 27	59	33	15 26	59	33	16 25	60	33	17 25	59	33	216
10 14	59	32	11 13	59	32	12 12	60	32	13 12	59	31	14 11	60	31	15 11	59	31	16 10	59	31	17 09	60	31	214
09 59	59	30	10 58	60	30	11 58	59	30	12 57	60	30	13 57	59	29	14 56	60	29	15 56	59	29	16 55	59	29	212
09 45	+59	28	10 44	+60	28	11 44	+59	28	12 43	+60	28	13 43	+59	28	14 42	+60	27	15 42	+59	27	16 41	+60	27	210
09 31	60	26	10 31	60	26	11 31	59	26	12 30	60	26	13 30	59	26	14 29	60	26	15 29	60	26	16 29	59	25	208
09 19	60	24	10 19	59	24	11 18	60	24	12 18	60	24	13 18	59	24	14 17	60	24	15 17	59	24	16 16	60	24	206
09 07	60	23	10 07	60	22	11 07	60	22	12 07	59	22	13 06	60	22	14 06	60	22	15 06	59	22	16 05	60	22	204
08 57	60	21	09 57	59	21	10 56	60	20	11 56	60	20	12 56	60	20	13 56	59	20	14 55	60	20	15 55	60	20	202
08 47	+60	19	09 47	+60	19	10 47	+59	19	11 46	+60	19	12 46	+60	18	13 46	+60	18	14 46	+60	18	15 46	+59	18	200
08 38	60	17	09 38	60	17	10 38	60	17	11 38	59	17	12 37	60	17	13 37	60	17	14 37	60	16	15 37	60	16	198
08 30	60	15	09 30	60	15	10 30	60	15	11 30	60	15	12 30	60	15	13 30	59	15	14 29	60	15	15 29	60	15	196
08 23	60	13	09 23	60	13	10 23	60	13	11 23	60	13	12 23	60	13	13 23	60	13	14 23	59	13	15 22	60	13	194
08 17	60	11	09 17	60	11	10 17	60	11	11 17	60	11	12 17	60	11	13 17	60	11	14 17	60	11	15 17	59	11	192
08 12	+60	9	09 12	+60	9	10 12	+60	9	11 12	+60	9	12 12	+60	9	13 12	+60	9	14 12	+59	9	15 11	+60	9	190
08 08	60	8	09 08	60	8	10 08	60	7	11 08	59	7	12 07	60	7	13 07	60	7	14 07	60	7	15 07	60	7	188
08 04	60	6	09 04	60	6	10 04	60	6	11 04	60	6	12 04	60	6	13 04	60	6	14 04	60	6	15 04	60	5	186
08 02	60	4	09 02	60	4	10 02	60	4	11 02	60	4	12 02	60	4	13 02	60	4	14 02	60	4	15 02	60	4	184
08 00	60	2	09 00	60	2	10 00	60	2	11 00	60	2	12 00	60	2	13 00	60	2	14 00	60	2	15 00	60	2	182
08 00	+60	0	09 00	+60	0	10 00	+60	0	11 00	+60	0	12 00	+60	0	13 00	+60	0	14 00	+60	0	15 00	+60	0	180

15° 16° 17° 18° 19° 20° 21° 22° 23° 24° 25° 26° 27° 28° 29°

S. Lat. {LHA greater than 180°....... Zn=180−Z; LHA less than 180°........... Zn=180+Z}

DECLINATION (15°-29°) **SAME** NAME AS LATITUDE

N. Lat. {LHA greater than 180°....... Zn=Z; LHA less than 180°........... Zn=360−Z}

DECLINATION (15°-29°) CONTRARY NAME TO LATITUDE

LHA	15°			16°			17°			18°			19°			20°			21°			22°	23°	24°	25°	26°	27°	28°	29°	LHA
	Hc	d	Z	Hc	d	Z	Hc	d	Z	Hc	d	Z	Hc	d	Z	Hc	d	Z	Hc	d	Z	Hc d Z	Hc d Z	Hc d Z	Hc d Z	Hc d Z	Hc d Z	Hc d Z	Hc d Z	
	° ′	′	°	° ′	′	°	° ′	′	°	° ′	′	°	° ′	′	°	° ′	′	°	° ′	′	°	° ′ ′ °	° ′ ′ °	° ′ ′ °	° ′ ′ °	° ′ ′ °	° ′ ′ °	° ′ ′ °	° ′ ′ °	
60	−7 43	−59	122																											300
58	−7 19	59	124																											302
56	−6 55	59	126																											304
54	−6 32	59	128	−7 31	59	128																								306
52	−6 10	58	130	−7 08	59	130																								308
50	−5 48	−59	132	−6 47	−58	132																								310
48	−5 26	59	134	−6 25	59	134	−7 24	59	134																					312
46	−5 06	59	136	−6 05	59	136	−7 04	59	136																					314
44	−4 46	59	138	−5 45	59	138	−6 44	59	138																					316
42	−4 27	59	140	−5 26	59	140	−6 25	59	140	−7 24	59	140																		318
40	−4 08	−59	141	−5 07	−60	142	−6 07	−59	142	−7 06	−59	142																		320
38	−3 50	60	143	−4 50	59	144	−5 49	59	144	−6 48	60	144																		322
36	−3 34	59	145	−4 33	59	145	−5 32	60	146	−6 32	59	146																		324
34	−3 18	59	147	−4 17	59	147	−5 16	60	147	−6 16	59	148	−7 15	60	148															326
32	−3 02	60	149	−4 02	59	149	−5 01	60	149	−6 01	59	150	−7 00	60	150															328
30	−2 48	−59	151	−3 47	−60	151	−4 47	−59	151	−5 46	−60	151	−6 46	−60	152															330
28	−2 34	60	153	−3 34	59	153	−4 33	60	153	−5 33	60	153	−6 33	59	153															332
26	−2 21	60	155	−3 21	60	155	−4 21	59	155	−5 20	60	155	−6 20	60	155	−7 20	59	155												334
24	−2 10	59	157	−3 09	60	157	−4 09	60	157	−5 09	59	157	−6 08	60	157	−7 08	60	157												336
22	−1 58	60	159	−2 58	60	159	−3 58	60	159	−4 58	60	159	−5 58	59	159	−6 57	60	159												338
20	−1 48	−60	161	−2 48	−60	161	−3 48	−60	161	−4 48	−60	161	−5 48	−59	161	−6 47	−60	161												340
18	−1 39	60	163	−2 39	60	163	−3 39	60	163	−4 39	60	163	−5 39	60	163	−6 39	59	163												342
16	−1 31	60	165	−2 31	60	165	−3 31	60	165	−4 31	60	165	−5 31	60	165	−6 31	59	165												344
14	−1 24	60	166	−2 24	60	166	−3 24	60	166	−4 24	60	167	−5 24	59	167	−6 23	60	167												346
12	−1 18	60	168	−2 18	59	168	−3 17	60	168	−4 17	60	169	−5 17	60	169	−6 17	60	169												348
10	−1 12	−60	170	−2 12	−60	170	−3 12	−60	170	−4 12	−60	170	−5 12	−60	170	−6 12	−60	171												350
8	−1 08	60	172	−2 08	60	172	−3 08	60	172	−4 08	60	172	−5 08	60	172	−6 08	60	172												352
6	−1 04	60	174	−2 04	60	174	−3 04	60	174	−4 04	60	174	−5 04	60	174	−6 04	60	174												354
4	−1 02	60	176	−2 02	60	176	−3 02	60	176	−4 02	60	176	−5 02	60	176	−6 02	60	176												356
2	−1 00	60	178	−2 00	60	178	−3 00	60	178	−4 00	60	178	−5 00	60	178	−6 00	60	178	−7 00	60	178									358
0	−1 00	−60	180	−2 00	−60	180	−3 00	−60	180	−4 00	−60	180	−5 00	−60	180	−6 00	−60	180	−7 00	−60	180									360
	15°			16°			17°			18°			19°			20°			21°			22°	23°	24°	25°	26°	27°	28°	29°	

S. Lat. {LHA greater than 180°....... Zn=180−Z; LHA less than 180°........... Zn=180+Z}

DECLINATION (15°-29°) CONTRARY NAME TO LATITUDE

N. Lat. {LHA greater than 180°....... Zn=Z; LHA less than 180°........... Zn=360−Z}

DECLINATION (0°-14°) SAME NAME AS LATITUDE

LAT 77°

LHA	0° Hc	0° d	0° Z	1° Hc	1° d	1° Z	2° Hc	2° d	2° Z	3° Hc	3° d	3° Z	4° Hc	4° d	4° Z
	° ′	′	°	° ′	′	°	° ′	′	°	° ′	′	°	° ′	′	°
0	13 00	+60	180	14 00	+60	180	15 00	+60	180	16 00	+60	180	17 00	+60	180
2	13 00	60	178	14 00	60	178	15 00	60	178	16 00	60	178	17 00	60	178
4	12 58	60	176	13 58	60	176	14 58	60	176	15 58	60	176	16 58	60	176
6	12 56	60	174	13 56	60	174	14 56	60	174	15 56	60	174	16 56	60	174
8	12 52	60	172	13 52	60	172	14 52	60	172	15 52	60	172	16 52	60	172
10	12 48	+60	170	13 48	+60	170	14 48	+60	170	15 48	+60	170	16 48	+60	170
12	12 43	60	168	13 43	60	168	14 43	60	168	15 43	59	168	16 42	60	168
14	12 36	60	166	13 36	60	166	14 36	60	166	15 36	60	166	16 36	60	165
16	12 29	60	164	13 29	60	164	14 29	60	164	15 29	60	163	16 29	60	163
18	12 21	60	162	13 21	60	162	14 21	60	161	15 21	60	161	16 21	59	161
20	12 12	+60	160	13 12	+60	159	14 12	+60	159	15 12	+60	159	16 12	+59	159
22	12 02	60	158	13 02	60	157	14 02	60	157	15 02	59	157	16 01	60	157
24	11 52	59	155	12 51	60	155	13 51	60	155	14 51	60	155	15 51	59	155
26	11 40	60	153	12 40	59	153	13 39	60	153	14 39	60	153	15 39	59	153
28	11 27	60	151	12 27	60	151	13 27	59	151	14 26	60	151	15 26	60	151
30	11 14	+60	149	12 14	+59	149	13 13	+60	149	14 13	+59	149	15 12	+60	149
32	11 00	59	147	11 59	60	147	12 59	60	147	13 59	59	147	14 58	60	147
34	10 45	59	145	11 44	60	145	12 44	59	145	13 43	60	145	14 43	59	145
36	10 29	60	143	11 29	59	143	12 28	60	143	13 28	59	143	14 27	59	143
38	10 13	59	141	11 12	59	141	12 11	60	141	13 11	59	141	14 10	60	141
40	09 55	+60	139	10 55	+59	139	11 54	+59	139	12 53	+60	139	13 53	+59	139
42	09 37	60	137	10 37	59	137	11 36	59	137	12 35	60	137	13 35	59	137
44	09 19	59	135	10 18	59	135	11 17	59	135	12 16	60	135	13 16	59	135
46	08 59	60	133	09 59	59	133	10 58	59	133	11 57	59	133	12 56	59	133
48	08 39	60	131	09 39	59	131	10 38	59	131	11 37	59	131	12 36	59	131
50	08 19	+59	129	09 18	+59	129	10 17	+59	129	11 16	+59	129	12 15	+59	129
52	07 58	59	127	08 57	59	127	09 56	59	127	10 55	59	127	11 54	59	127
54	07 36	59	125	08 35	59	125	09 34	59	125	10 33	59	125	11 32	59	125
56	07 14	59	123	08 13	58	123	09 11	59	123	10 10	59	123	11 09	59	123
58	06 51	59	121	07 50	59	121	08 49	58	121	09 47	59	121	10 46	59	121
60	06 28	+58	119	07 26	+59	119	08 25	+59	119	09 24	+59	119	10 23	+59	119
62	06 04	59	117	07 03	58	117	08 01	59	117	09 00	59	117	09 59	59	117
64	05 40	58	115	06 38	59	115	07 37	59	115	08 36	59	115	09 35	58	115
66	05 15	59	114	06 14	58	113	07 12	59	113	08 11	59	113	09 10	59	113
68	04 50	59	112	05 49	58	111	06 47	59	111	07 46	59	111	08 45	58	111
70	04 25	+58	110	05 23	+59	109	06 22	+59	109	07 21	+58	109	08 19	+59	109
72	03 59	59	108	04 58	58	107	05 56	59	107	06 55	59	107	07 54	58	107
74	03 33	59	106	04 32	58	105	05 30	59	105	06 29	59	105	07 28	58	105
76	03 07	59	104	04 06	58	103	05 04	59	103	06 03	58	103	07 01	59	103
78	02 41	58	102	03 39	59	102	04 38	58	101	05 36	59	101	06 35	58	101
80	02 14	+59	100	03 13	+58	100	04 11	+59	99	05 10	+58	99	06 08	+59	99
82	01 48	58	98	02 46	59	98	03 45	58	97	04 43	59	97	05 42	58	97
84	01 21	58	96	02 19	59	96	03 18	58	95	04 16	59	95	05 15	58	95
86	00 54	58	94	01 52	59	94	02 51	58	93	03 49	59	93	04 48	58	93
88	00 27	58	92	01 25	59	92	02 24	58	92	03 22	59	91	04 21	58	91
90	00 00	+58	90	00 58	+59	90	01 57	+58	90	02 55	+59	89	03 54	+58	89
92	−0 27	58	88	00 31	59	88	01 30	58	88	02 28	59	87	03 27	58	87
94	−0 54	59	86	00 05	58	86	01 03	59	86	02 02	58	85	03 00	58	85
96	−1 21	59	84	−0 22	58	84	00 36	59	84	01 35	58	84	02 33	59	83
98	−1 48	59	82	−0 49	58	82	00 09	59	82	01 08	58	82	02 06	59	81
100	−2 14	+58	80	−1 16	+59	80	−0 17	+58	80	00 41	+59	80	01 40	+58	79
102	−2 41	59	78	−1 42	58	78	−0 44	59	78	00 15	58	78	01 13	59	77
104	−3 07	58	76	−2 09	59	76	−1 10	58	76	−0 12	59	76	00 47	59	76
106	−3 33	58	74	−2 35	59	74	−1 36	58	74	−0 38	59	74	00 21	59	74
108	−3 59	58	72	−3 01	59	72	−2 02	59	72	−1 03	58	72	−0 05	59	72
110	−4 25	+59	70	−3 26	+58	70	−2 28	+59	70	−1 29	+59	70	−0 30	+58	70
112	−4 50	59	68	−3 51	58	68	−2 53	59	68	−1 54	59	68	−0 55	58	68
114	−5 15	59	66	−4 16	58	66	−3 18	59	66	−2 19	59	66	−1 20	59	66
116	−5 40	59	65	−4 41	59	64	−3 42	59	64	−2 43	59	64	−1 44	58	64
118	−6 04	59	63	−5 05	59	62	−4 06	59	62	−3 07	59	62	−2 08	58	62
120	−6 28	+59	61	−5 29	+59	60	−4 30	+59	60	−3 31	+59	60	−2 32	+59	60
122	−6 51	59	59	−5 52	59	58	−4 53	59	58	−3 54	59	58	−2 55	59	58
124	−7 14	59	57	−6 15	59	56	−5 16	59	56	−4 17	59	56	−3 18	59	56
126	−7 36	59	55	−6 37	59	54	−5 38	59	54	−4 39	59	54	−3 40	59	54
128				−6 59	59	52	−6 00	59	52	−5 01	59	52	−4 02	60	52
130				−7 20	+59	51	−6 21	+59	50	−5 22	+60	50	−4 22	+59	50
132				−7 40	59	49	−6 41	59	48	−5 42	59	48	−4 43	59	48
134							−7 01	59	46	−6 02	59	46	−5 03	60	46
136							−7 20	59	44	−6 21	59	44	−5 22	60	44
138										−6 40	60	42	−5 40	59	42

LHA	5° Hc	5° d	5° Z	6° Hc	6° d	6° Z	7° Hc	7° d	7° Z	8° Hc	8° d	8° Z	9° Hc	9° d	9° Z
	° ′	′	°	° ′	′	°	° ′	′	°	° ′	′	°	° ′	′	°
0	18 00	+60	180	19 00	+60	180	20 00	+60	180	21 00	+60	180	22 00	+60	180
2	18 00	60	178	19 00	60	178	20 00	60	178	21 00	60	178	22 00	60	178
4	17 58	60	176	18 58	60	176	19 58	60	176	20 58	60	176	21 58	60	176
6	17 56	60	174	18 56	60	174	19 56	60	174	20 56	60	174	21 56	60	174
8	17 52	60	172	18 52	60	172	19 52	60	172	20 52	60	172	21 52	60	172
10	17 48	+60	170	18 48	+60	170	19 48	+60	169	20 48	+60	169	21 48	+59	169
12	17 42	60	167	18 42	60	167	19 42	60	167	20 42	60	167	21 42	60	167
14	17 36	60	165	18 36	60	165	19 36	60	165	20 36	60	165	21 36	60	165
16	17 29	60	163	18 29	59	163	19 28	60	163	20 28	60	163	21 28	60	163
18	17 20	60	161	18 20	60	161	19 20	60	161	20 20	60	161	21 20	60	161
20	17 11	+60	159	18 11	+60	159	19 11	+60	159	20 11	+60	159	21 11	+59	159
22	17 01	60	157	18 01	60	157	19 01	60	157	20 01	59	157	21 00	60	157
24	16 50	60	155	17 50	60	155	18 50	59	155	19 49	60	155	20 49	60	155
26	16 38	60	153	17 38	60	153	18 38	59	153	19 37	60	153	20 37	60	152
28	16 26	59	151	17 25	60	151	18 25	60	151	19 25	59	151	20 24	60	150
30	16 12	+60	149	17 12	+59	149	18 11	+60	149	19 11	+59	148	20 10	+60	148
32	15 58	59	147	16 57	60	147	17 57	59	146	18 56	60	146	19 56	59	146
34	15 42	60	145	16 42	59	145	17 41	60	144	18 41	59	144	19 40	60	144
36	15 26	60	143	16 26	59	142	17 25	60	142	18 25	59	142	19 24	59	142
38	15 10	59	141	16 09	59	140	17 08	60	140	18 08	59	140	19 07	59	140
40	14 52	+59	139	15 51	+60	138	16 51	+59	138	17 50	+59	138	18 49	+60	138
42	14 34	59	137	15 33	59	136	16 32	60	136	17 32	59	136	18 31	59	136
44	14 15	59	134	15 14	59	134	16 13	60	134	17 13	59	134	18 12	59	134
46	13 55	59	132	14 54	60	132	15 54	59	132	16 53	59	132	17 52	59	132
48	13 35	59	130	14 34	59	130	15 33	59	130	16 32	59	130	17 31	60	130
50	13 14	+59	128	14 13	+59	128	15 12	+59	128	16 11	+59	128	17 10	+59	128
52	12 53	59	126	13 52	59	126	14 51	59	126	15 50	59	126	16 49	59	126
54	12 31	59	124	13 30	59	124	14 29	59	124	15 28	58	124	16 26	59	124
56	12 08	59	122	13 07	59	122	14 06	59	122	15 05	59	122	16 04	59	122
58	11 45	59	120	12 44	59	120	13 43	59	120	14 42	58	120	15 40	59	120
60	11 22	+58	118	12 20	+59	118	13 19	+59	118	14 18	+59	118	15 17	+59	118
62	10 58	58	116	11 56	59	116	12 55	59	116	13 54	59	116	14 53	58	116
64	10 33	59	114	11 32	59	114	12 31	58	114	13 29	59	114	14 28	59	114
66	10 09	58	112	11 07	59	112	12 06	58	112	13 04	59	112	14 03	59	112
68	09 43	59	110	10 42	59	110	11 41	58	110	12 39	59	110	13 38	58	110
70	09 18	+59	109	10 17	+58	108	11 15	+59	108	12 14	+58	108	13 12	+59	108
72	08 52	59	107	09 51	58	106	10 49	59	106	11 48	58	106	12 46	59	106
74	08 26	59	105	09 25	58	104	10 23	59	104	11 22	58	104	12 20	59	104
76	08 00	58	103	08 58	59	102	09 57	58	102	10 55	59	102	11 54	58	102
78	07 33	59	101	08 32	58	100	09 30	59	100	10 29	58	100	11 27	59	100
80	07 07	+58	99	08 05	+59	98	09 04	+58	98	10 02	+59	98	11 01	+58	98
82	06 40	59	97	07 39	58	97	08 37	58	96	09 35	59	96	10 34	58	96
84	06 13	59	95	07 12	58	95	08 10	59	94	09 09	58	94	10 07	58	94
86	05 46	59	93	06 45	58	93	07 43	59	92	08 42	58	92	09 40	58	92
88	05 19	59	91	06 18	58	91	07 16	59	90	08 15	58	90	09 13	59	90
90	04 52	+59	89	05 51	+58	89	06 49	+59	88	07 48	+58	88	08 46	+59	88
92	04 25	59	87	05 24	58	87	06 22	59	87	07 21	58	86	08 19	59	86
94	03 58	59	85	04 57	58	85	05 55	59	85	06 54	58	84	07 52	59	84
96	03 32	58	83	04 30	59	83	05 29	58	83	06 27	58	82	07 25	59	82
98	03 05	58	81	04 03	59	81	05 02	58	81	06 00	59	80	06 59	58	80
100	02 38	+59	79	03 37	+58	79	04 35	+59	79	05 34	+58	79	06 32	+59	78
102	02 12	58	77	03 10	59	77	04 09	58	77	05 07	59	77	06 06	58	76
104	01 46	58	75	02 44	59	75	03 43	58	75	04 41	59	75	05 40	58	74
106	01 20	58	73	02 18	59	73	03 17	58	73	04 15	59	73	05 14	59	72
108	00 54	58	71	01 52	59	71	02 51	59	71	03 50	58	71	04 48	59	71
110	00 28	+59	69	01 27	+59	69	02 26	+58	69	03 24	+59	69	04 23	+59	69
112	00 03	59	67	01 02	59	67	02 01	58	67	02 59	59	67	03 58	59	67
114	−0 21	58	66	00 37	59	65	01 36	59	65	02 35	59	65	03 34	58	65
116	−0 46	59	64	00 13	59	63	01 12	59	63	02 11	58	63	03 09	59	63
118	−1 10	59	62	−0 11	59	61	00 48	59	61	01 47	59	61	02 46	58	61
120	−1 33	+59	60	−0 34	+58	59	00 24	+59	59	01 23	+59	59	02 22	+59	59
122	−1 56	59	58	−0 57	58	58	00 01	59	57	01 00	59	57	01 59	59	57
124	−2 19	59	56	−1 20	59	56	−0 21	59	55	00 38	59	55	01 37	59	55
126	−2 41	59	54	−1 42	59	54	−0 43	59	54	00 16	59	53	01 15	59	53
128	−3 02	59	52	−2 03	59	52	−1 04	59	51	−0 05	59	51	00 54	59	51
130	−3 23	+59	50	−2 24	+59	50	−1 25	+59	49	−0 26	+59	49	00 33	+59	49
132	−3 44	59	48	−2 45	60	48	−1 45	59	48	−0 46	59	47	00 13	59	47
134	−4 03	59	46	−3 04	59	46	−2 05	59	46	−1 06	59	45	−0 07	60	45
136	−4 22	59	44	−3 23	59	44	−2 24	59	44	−1 25	60	43	−0 25	59	43
138	−4 41	59	42	−3 42	60	42	−2 42	59	42	−1 43	59	41	−0 44	60	41

LHA	10° Hc	10° d	10° Z	11° Hc	11° d	11° Z	12° Hc	12° d	12° Z	13° Hc	13° d	13° Z	14° Hc	14° d	14° Z	LHA
	° ′	′	°	° ′	′	°	° ′	′	°	° ′	′	°	° ′	′	°	
0	23 00	+60	180	24 00	+60	180	25 00	+60	180	26 00	+60	180	27 00	+60	180	360
2	23 00	60	178	24 00	60	178	25 00	60	178	26 00	60	178	27 00	60	178	358
4	22 58	60	176	23 58	60	176	24 58	60	176	25 58	60	176	26 58	60	176	356
6	22 56	59	174	23 55	60	174	24 55	60	174	25 55	60	174	26 55	60	174	354
8	22 52	60	171	23 52	60	171	24 52	60	171	25 52	60	171	26 52	60	171	352
10	22 47	+60	169	23 47	+60	169	24 47	+60	169	25 47	+60	169	26 47	+60	169	350
12	22 42	60	167	23 42	60	167	24 42	60	167	25 42	60	167	26 42	60	167	348
14	22 36	59	165	23 35	60	165	24 35	60	165	25 35	60	165	26 35	60	165	346
16	22 28	60	163	23 28	60	163	24 28	60	163	25 28	60	163	26 28	59	163	344
18	22 20	59	161	23 19	60	161	24 19	60	161	25 19	60	161	26 19	60	161	342
20	22 10	+60	159	23 10	+60	159	24 10	+60	159	25 10	+59	158	26 09	+60	158	340
22	22 00	60	157	23 00	60	157	24 00	59	156	24 59	60	156	25 59	60	156	338
24	21 49	60	154	22 49	59	154	23 48	60	154	24 48	60	154	25 48	59	154	336
26	21 37	59	152	22 36	60	152	23 36	60	152	24 36	59	152	25 35	60	152	334
28	21 24	59	150	22 23	60	150	23 23	60	150	24 23	59	150	25 22	60	150	332
30	21 10	+59	148	22 09	+60	148	23 09	+60	148	24 09	+59	148	25 08	+60	148	330
32	20 55	60	146	21 55	59	146	22 54	60	146	23 54	59	146	24 53	60	146	328
34	20 40	59	144	21 39	60	144	22 39	59	144	23 38	60	144	24 38	59	143	326
36	20 23	60	142	21 23	59	142	22 22	60	142	23 22	59	141	24 21	59	141	324
38	20 06	60	140	21 06	59	140	22 05	59	140	23 04	60	139	24 04	59	139	322
40	19 49	+59	138	20 48	+59	138	21 47	+59	137	22 46	+60	137	23 46	+59	137	320
42	19 30	59	136	20 29	60	136	21 29	59	135	22 28	59	135	23 27	59	135	318
44	19 11	59	134	20 10	59	133	21 09	59	133	22 08	60	133	23 08	59	133	316
46	18 51	59	132	19 50	59	131	20 49	59	131	21 48	59	131	22 47	59	131	314
48	18 31	59	130	19 30	59	129	20 29	59	129	21 28	59	129	22 27	59	129	312
50	18 09	+59	127	19 08	+59	127	20 07	+59	127	21 06	+59	127	22 05	+59	127	310
52	17 48	59	125	18 47	59	125	19 46	58	125	20 44	59	125	21 43	59	125	308
54	17 25	59	123	18 24	59	123	19 23	59	123	20 22	59	123	21 21	59	123	306
56	17 03	58	121	18 01	59	121	19 00	59	121	19 59	59	121	20 58	59	121	304
58	16 39	59	119	17 38	59	119	18 37	59	119	19 36	58	119	20 34	59	119	302
60	16 16	+58	117	17 14	+59	117	18 13	+59	117	19 12	+58	117	20 10	+59	117	300
62	15 51	59	115	16 50	59	115	17 49	58	115	18 47	59	115	19 46	59	114	298
64	15 27	58	113	16 25	59	113	17 24	59	113	18 23	58	113	19 21	59	112	296
66	15 02	58	111	16 00	59	111	16 59	59	111	17 58	58	111	18 56	59	110	294
68	14 36	59	109	15 35	59	109	16 34	58	109	17 32	59	109	18 31	58	108	292
70	14 11	+58	107	15 09	+59	107	16 08	+58	107	17 06	+59	107	18 05	+58	106	290
72	13 45	58	105	14 43	59	105	15 42	58	105	16 40	59	105	17 39	58	104	288
74	13 19	58	103	14 17	59	103	15 16	58	103	16 14	59	103	17 13	58	103	286
76	12 52	59	101	13 51	58	101	14 49	59	101	15 48	58	101	16 46	59	101	284
78	12 26	58	100	13 24	59	99	14 23	58	99	15 21	59	99	16 20	58	99	282
80	11 59	+59	98	12 58	+58	97	13 56	+58	97	14 54	+59	97	15 53	+58	97	280
82	11 32	59	96	12 31	58	95	13 29	59	95	14 28	58	95	15 26	58	95	278
84	11 05	59	94	12 04	58	93	13 02	59	93	14 01	58	93	14 59	58	93	276
86	10 38	59	92	11 37	58	91	12 35	59	91	13 34	58	91	14 32	58	91	274
88	10 12	58	90	11 10	58	89	12 08	59	89	13 07	58	89	14 05	58	89	272
90	09 45	+58	88	10 43	+58	88	11 41	+59	87	12 40	+58	87	13 38	+58	87	270
92	09 18	58	86	10 16	58	86	11 14	59	85	12 13	58	85	13 11	59	85	268
94	08 51	58	84	09 49	59	84	10 48	58	83	11 46	58	83	12 44	59	83	266
96	08 24	58	82	09 22	59	82	10 21	58	81	11 19	59	81	12 18	58	81	264
98	07 57	59	80	08 56	58	80	09 54	59	80	10 53	58	79	11 51	58	79	262
100	07 31	+58	78	08 29	+59	78	09 28	+58	78	10 26	+59	77	11 25	+58	77	260
102	07 04	59	76	08 03	58	76	09 01	59	76	10 00	58	75	10 58	59	75	258
104	06 38	59	74	07 37	58	74	08 35	59	74	09 34	58	74	10 32	59	73	256
106	06 13	58	72	07 11	59	72	08 10	58	72	09 08	59	72	10 07	58	71	254
108	05 47	59	70	06 46	58	70	07 44	59	70	08 43	58	70	09 41	59	69	252
110	05 22	+58	68	06 20	+59	68	07 19	+59	68	08 18	+58	68	09 16	+59	68	250
112	04 57	58	66	05 55	59	66	06 54	59	66	07 53	58	66	08 51	59	66	248
114	04 32	59	65	05 31	59	64	06 30	58	64	07 28	59	64	08 27	59	64	246
116	04 08	59	63	05 07	59	62	06 06	58	62	07 04	59	62	08 03	59	62	244
118	03 44	59	61	04 43	59	60	05 42	58	60	06 41	58	60	07 39	59	60	242
120	03 21	+59	59	04 20	+59	59	05 19	+59	58	06 18	+58	58	07 16	+59	58	240
122	02 58	59	57	03 57	59	57	04 56	59	56	05 55	59	56	06 54	59	56	238
124	02 36	59	55	03 35	59	55	04 34	59	54	05 33	59	54	06 32	59	54	236
126	02 14	59	53	03 13	59	53	04 12	59	53	05 11	59	52	06 10	59	52	234
128	01 53	59	51	02 52	59	51	03 51	59	51	04 50	59	50	05 49	59	50	232
130	01 32	+59	49	02 31	+59	49	03 30	+59	49	04 29	+60	49	05 29	+59	48	230
132	01 12	59	47	02 11	59	47	03 10	60	47	04 10	59	47	05 09	59	46	228
134	00 53	59	45	01 52	59	45	02 51	59	45	03 50	60	45	04 50	59	45	226
136	00 34	59	43	01 33	59	43	02 32	60	43	03 32	59	43	04 31	59	43	224
138	00 16	59	41	01 15	59	41	02 14	60	41	03 14	59	41	04 13	59	41	222

S. Lat. {LHA greater than 180°....... Zn=180−Z; LHA less than 180°........... Zn=180+Z}

DECLINATION (0°-14°) SAME NAME AS LATITUDE

N. Lat. {LHA greater than 180°....... Zn=Z; LHA less than 180°.......... Zn=360−Z}

DECLINATION (0°-14°) SAME NAME AS LATITUDE

LHA	0° Hc	0° d	0° Z	1° Hc	1° d	1° Z	2° Hc	2° d	2° Z	3° Hc	3° d	3° Z	4° Hc	4° d	4° Z	5° Hc	5° d	5° Z	6° Hc	6° d	6° Z	7° Hc	7° d	7° Z
	° ′	′	°	° ′	′	°	° ′	′	°	° ′	′	°	° ′	′	°	° ′	′	°	° ′	′	°	° ′	′	°
140										−6 57	+59	40	−5 58	+59	40	−4 59	+60	40	−3 59	+59	40	−3 00	+60	40
142										−7 14	59	38	−6 15	59	38	−5 16	60	38	−4 16	59	38	−3 17	60	38
144										−7 31	60	36	−6 31	59	36	−5 32	60	36	−4 32	59	36	−3 33	60	36
146													−6 47	60	34	−5 47	59	34	−4 48	60	34	−3 48	59	34
148													−7 02	60	32	−6 02	59	32	−5 03	60	32	−4 03	60	32
150													−7 16	+60	30	−6 16	+60	30	−5 16	+59	30	−4 17	+60	30
152																−6 29	60	28	−5 29	59	28	−4 30	60	28
154																−6 41	59	26	−5 42	60	26	−4 42	60	26
156																−6 53	60	24	−5 53	60	24	−4 53	59	24
158																−7 03	59	22	−6 04	60	22	−5 04	60	22
160																−7 13	+60	20	−6 13	+59	20	−5 14	+60	20
162																			−6 22	60	18	−5 22	60	18
164																			−6 30	60	16	−5 30	60	16
166																			−6 37	60	14	−5 37	60	14
168																			−6 43	60	12	−5 43	60	12
170																			−6 48	+60	10	−5 48	+60	10
172																			−6 53	60	8	−5 53	60	8
174																			−6 56	60	6	−5 56	60	6
176																			−6 58	60	4	−5 58	60	4
178																			−7 00	60	2	−6 00	60	2
180																			−7 00	+60	0	−6 00	+60	0

LHA	8° Hc	8° d	8° Z	9° Hc	9° d	9° Z	10° Hc	10° d	10° Z	11° Hc	11° d	11° Z	12° Hc	12° d	12° Z	13° Hc	13° d	13° Z	14° Hc	14° d	14° Z	LHA
	° ′	′	°	° ′	′	°	° ′	′	°	° ′	′	°	° ′	′	°	° ′	′	°	° ′	′	°	
140	−2 00	+59	40	−1 01	+59	39	−0 02	+60	39	00 58	+59	39	01 57	+59	39	02 56	+60	39	03 56	+59	39	220
142	−2 17	59	38	−1 18	60	37	−0 18	59	37	00 41	59	37	01 40	60	37	02 40	59	37	03 39	60	37	218
144	−2 33	59	36	−1 34	60	35	−0 34	59	35	00 25	59	35	01 24	60	35	02 24	59	35	03 23	60	35	216
146	−2 49	60	34	−1 49	59	34	−0 50	60	33	00 10	59	33	01 09	60	33	02 09	59	33	03 08	60	33	214
148	−3 03	59	32	−2 04	60	32	−1 04	59	31	−0 05	60	31	00 55	59	31	01 54	60	31	02 54	60	31	212
150	−3 17	+59	30	−2 18	+60	30	−1 18	+60	29	−0 18	+59	29	00 41	+60	29	01 41	+60	29	02 41	+59	29	210
152	−3 30	60	28	−2 30	59	28	−1 31	60	27	−0 31	60	27	00 29	59	27	01 28	60	27	02 28	60	27	208
154	−3 42	59	26	−2 43	60	26	−1 43	60	26	−0 43	60	25	00 17	59	25	01 16	60	25	02 16	60	25	206
156	−3 54	60	24	−2 54	60	24	−1 54	60	24	−0 54	59	24	00 05	60	23	01 05	60	23	02 05	60	23	204
158	−4 04	60	22	−3 04	60	22	−2 04	59	22	−1 05	60	22	−0 05	60	22	00 55	60	21	01 55	59	21	202
160	−4 14	+60	20	−3 14	+60	20	−2 14	+60	20	−1 14	+60	20	−0 14	+59	20	00 45	+60	19	01 45	+60	19	200
162	−4 22	60	18	−3 22	59	18	−2 23	60	18	−1 23	60	18	−0 23	60	18	00 37	60	18	01 37	60	18	198
164	−4 30	60	16	−3 30	60	16	−2 30	59	16	−1 31	60	16	−0 31	60	16	00 29	60	16	01 29	60	16	196
166	−4 37	60	14	−3 37	60	14	−2 37	60	14	−1 37	59	14	−0 38	60	14	00 22	60	14	01 22	60	14	194
168	−4 43	60	12	−3 43	60	12	−2 43	60	12	−1 43	60	12	−0 43	59	12	00 16	60	12	01 16	60	12	192
170	−4 48	+60	10	−3 48	+60	10	−2 48	+60	10	−1 48	+59	10	−0 49	+60	10	00 11	+60	10	01 11	+60	10	190
172	−4 53	60	8	−3 53	60	8	−2 53	60	8	−1 53	60	8	−0 53	60	8	00 07	60	8	01 07	60	8	188
174	−4 56	60	6	−3 56	60	6	−2 56	60	6	−1 56	60	6	−0 56	60	6	00 04	60	6	01 04	60	6	186
176	−4 58	60	4	−3 58	60	4	−2 58	60	4	−1 58	60	4	−0 58	60	4	00 02	60	4	01 02	60	4	184
178	−5 00	60	2	−4 00	60	2	−3 00	60	2	−2 00	60	2	−1 00	60	2	00 00	60	2	01 00	60	2	182
180	−5 00	+60	0	−4 00	+60	0	−3 00	+60	0	−2 00	+60	0	−1 00	+60	0	00 00	+60	0	01 00	+60	0	180

LAT 77°

0°	1°	2°	3°	4°	5°	6°	7°	8°	9°	10°	11°	12°	13°	14°

S. Lat. {LHA greater than 180°....... Zn=180−Z; LHA less than 180°.......... Zn=180+Z}

N. Lat. {LHA greater than 180°........ Zn=Z
{LHA less than 180°........... Zn=360−Z

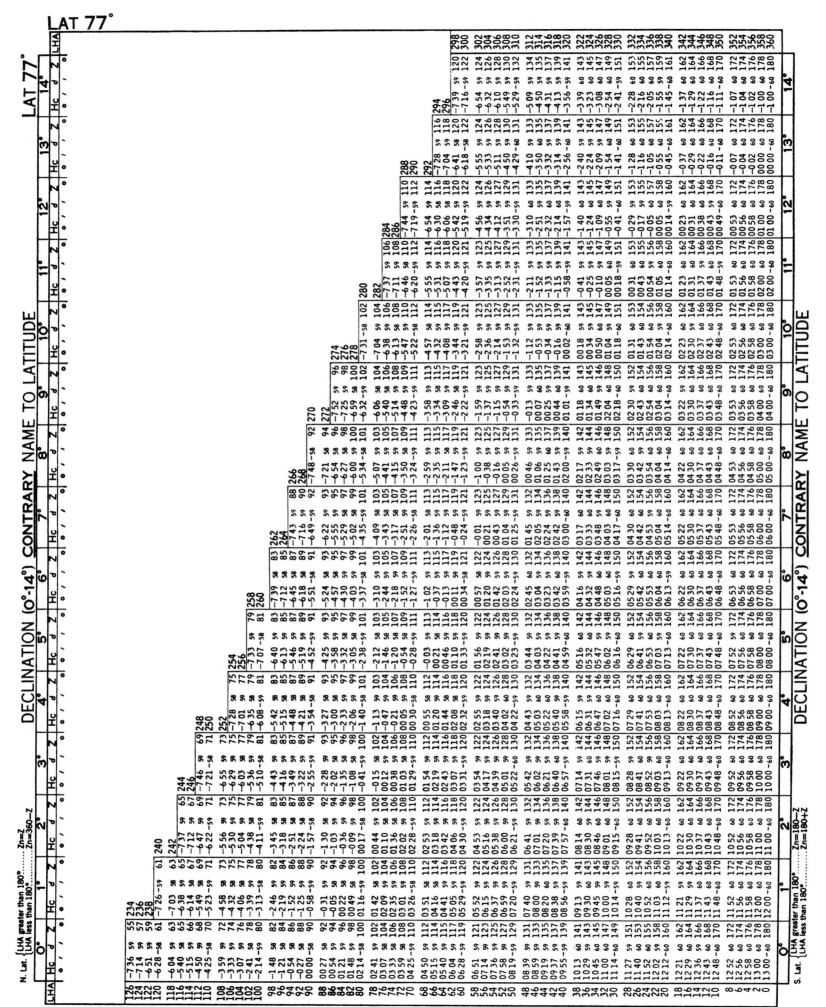

DECLINATION (0°-14°) CONTRARY NAME TO LATITUDE

LHA	0° Hc	d	Z	1° Hc	d	Z	2° Hc	d	Z	3° Hc	d	Z	4° Hc	d	Z
	° ′	′	°	° ′	′	°	° ′	′	°	° ′	′	°	° ′	′	°
126	-7 36	59	55	234											
124	-7 14	59	57	236											
122	-6 51	59	59	238											
120	-6 28	-58	61	-7 26	-59	61	240								
118	-6 04	59	63	-7 03	58	63	242								
116	-5 40	58	65	-6 38	59	65	-7 37	59	65	244					
114	-5 15	59	66	-6 14	58	67	-7 12	59	67	246					
112	-4 50	59	68	-5 49	58	69	-6 47	59	69	-7 46	59	69	248		
110	-4 25	-58	70	-5 23	-59	71	-6 22	-59	71	-7 21	-58	71	250		
108	-3 59	59	72	-4 58	58	73	-5 56	59	73	-6 55	59	73	252		
106	-3 33	59	74	-4 32	58	75	-5 30	59	75	-6 29	59	75	-7 28	58	75
104	-3 07	59	76	-4 06	58	77	-5 04	59	77	-6 03	58	77	-7 01	59	77
102	-2 41	58	78	-3 39	59	78	-4 38	58	79	-5 36	59	79	-6 35	58	79
100	-2 14	-59	80	-3 13	-58	80	-4 11	-59	81	-5 10	-58	81	-6 08	-59	81
98	-1 48	58	82	-2 46	59	82	-3 45	58	83	-4 43	59	83	-5 42	58	83
96	-1 21	58	84	-2 19	59	84	-3 18	58	85	-4 16	59	85	-5 15	58	85
94	-0 54	58	86	-1 52	59	86	-2 51	58	87	-3 49	59	87	-4 48	58	87
92	-0 27	58	88	-1 25	59	88	-2 24	58	88	-3 22	59	89	-4 21	58	89
90	00 00	-58	90	-0 58	-59	90	-1 57	-58	90	-2 55	-59	91	-3 54	-58	91
88	00 27	58	92	-0 31	59	92	-1 30	58	92	-2 28	59	93	-3 27	58	93
86	00 54	59	94	-0 05	58	94	-1 03	59	94	-2 02	58	95	-3 00	58	95
84	01 21	59	96	00 22	58	96	-0 36	59	96	-1 35	58	96	-2 33	59	97
82	01 48	59	98	00 49	58	98	-0 09	59	98	-1 08	58	98	-2 06	59	99
80	02 14	-58	100	01 16	-59	100	00 17	-58	100	-0 41	-59	100	-1 40	-58	101
78	02 41	59	102	01 42	58	102	00 44	59	102	-0 15	58	102	-1 13	59	103
76	03 07	58	104	02 09	59	104	01 10	58	104	00 12	59	104	-0 47	59	104
74	03 33	58	106	02 35	59	106	01 36	58	106	00 38	59	106	-0 21	59	106
72	03 59	58	108	03 01	59	108	02 02	59	108	01 03	58	108	00 05	59	108
70	04 25	-59	110	03 26	-58	110	02 28	-59	110	01 29	-59	110	00 30	-58	110
68	04 50	59	112	03 51	58	112	02 53	59	112	01 54	59	112	00 55	58	112
66	05 15	59	114	04 16	58	114	03 18	59	114	02 19	59	114	01 20	59	114
64	05 40	59	115	04 41	59	116	03 42	59	116	02 43	59	116	01 44	58	116
62	06 04	59	117	05 05	59	118	04 06	59	118	03 07	59	118	02 08	58	118
60	06 28	-59	119	05 29	-59	120	04 30	-59	120	03 31	-59	120	02 32	-59	120
58	06 51	59	121	05 52	59	122	04 53	59	122	03 54	59	122	02 55	59	122
56	07 14	59	123	06 15	59	124	05 16	59	124	04 17	59	124	03 18	59	124
54	07 36	59	125	06 37	59	126	05 38	59	126	04 39	59	126	03 40	59	126
52	07 58	59	127	06 59	59	128	06 00	59	128	05 01	59	128	04 02	60	128
50	08 19	-59	129	07 20	-59	129	06 21	-59	130	05 22	-60	130	04 22	-59	130
48	08 39	59	131	07 40	59	131	06 41	59	132	05 42	59	132	04 43	59	132
46	08 59	59	133	08 00	59	133	07 01	59	134	06 02	59	134	05 03	60	134
44	09 19	59	135	08 20	60	135	07 20	59	136	06 21	59	136	05 22	60	136
42	09 37	59	137	08 38	59	137	07 39	59	138	06 40	60	138	05 40	59	138
40	09 55	-59	139	08 56	-59	139	07 57	-60	140	06 57	-59	140	05 58	-59	140
38	10 13	60	141	09 13	59	141	08 14	60	142	07 14	59	142	06 15	59	142
36	10 29	59	143	09 30	60	143	08 30	59	144	07 31	60	144	06 31	59	144
34	10 45	60	145	09 45	59	145	08 46	60	146	07 46	59	146	06 47	60	146
32	11 00	60	147	10 00	59	148	09 01	60	148	08 01	59	148	07 02	60	148
30	11 14	-60	149	10 14	-59	150	09 15	-60	150	08 15	-59	150	07 16	-60	150
28	11 27	59	151	10 28	60	152	09 28	60	152	08 28	59	152	07 29	60	152
26	11 40	60	153	10 40	59	154	09 41	60	154	08 41	60	154	07 41	60	154
24	11 52	60	155	10 52	60	156	09 52	60	156	08 52	59	156	07 53	60	156
22	12 02	59	158	11 03	60	158	10 03	60	158	09 03	60	158	08 03	60	158
20	12 12	-60	160	11 12	-59	160	10 13	-60	160	09 13	-60	160	08 13	-60	160
18	12 21	60	162	11 21	59	162	10 22	60	162	09 22	60	162	08 22	60	162
16	12 29	60	164	11 29	59	164	10 30	60	164	09 30	60	164	08 30	60	164
14	12 36	59	166	11 37	60	166	10 37	60	166	09 37	60	166	08 37	60	166
12	12 43	60	168	11 43	60	168	10 43	60	168	09 43	60	168	08 43	60	168
10	12 48	-60	170	11 48	-60	170	10 48	-60	170	09 48	-60	170	08 48	-60	170
8	12 52	60	172	11 52	60	172	10 52	60	172	09 52	60	172	08 52	60	172
6	12 56	60	174	11 56	60	174	10 56	60	174	09 56	60	174	08 56	60	174
4	12 58	60	176	11 58	60	176	10 58	60	176	09 58	60	176	08 58	60	176
2	13 00	60	178	12 00	60	178	11 00	60	178	10 00	60	178	09 00	60	178
0	13 00	-60	180	12 00	-60	180	11 00	-60	180	10 00	-60	180	09 00	-60	180

LHA	5° Hc	d	Z	6° Hc	d	Z	7° Hc	d	Z	8° Hc	d	Z	9° Hc	d	Z
	° ′	′	°	° ′	′	°	° ′	′	°	° ′	′	°	° ′	′	°
106	254														
104	256														
102	-7 33	59	79	258											
100	-7 07	-58	81	260											
98	-6 40	59	83	-7 39	58	83	262								
96	-6 13	59	85	-7 12	58	85	264								
94	-5 46	59	87	-6 45	58	87	-7 43	59	88	266					
92	-5 19	59	89	-6 18	58	89	-7 16	59	90	268					
90	-4 52	-59	91	-5 51	-58	91	-6 49	-59	92	-7 48	-58	92	270		
88	-4 25	59	93	-5 24	58	93	-6 22	59	93	-7 21	58	94	272		
86	-3 58	59	95	-4 57	58	95	-5 55	59	95	-6 54	58	96	-7 52	59	96
84	-3 32	58	97	-4 30	59	97	-5 29	58	97	-6 27	58	98	-7 25	59	98
82	-3 05	58	99	-4 03	59	99	-5 02	58	99	-6 00	59	100	-6 59	58	100
80	-2 38	-59	101	-3 37	-58	101	-4 35	-59	101	-5 34	-58	101	-6 32	-59	102
78	-2 12	58	103	-3 10	59	103	-4 09	58	103	-5 07	59	103	-6 06	58	104
76	-1 46	58	105	-2 44	59	105	-3 43	58	105	-4 41	59	105	-5 40	58	106
74	-1 20	58	107	-2 18	59	107	-3 17	58	107	-4 15	59	107	-5 14	59	108
72	-0 54	58	109	-1 52	59	109	-2 51	59	109	-3 50	58	109	-4 48	59	109
70	-0 28	-59	111	-1 27	-59	111	-2 26	-58	111	-3 24	-59	111	-4 23	-59	111
68	-0 03	59	113	-1 02	59	113	-2 01	58	113	-2 59	59	113	-3 58	59	113
66	00 21	58	114	-0 37	59	115	-1 36	59	115	-2 35	59	115	-3 34	58	115
64	00 46	59	116	-0 13	59	117	-1 12	59	117	-2 11	58	117	-3 09	59	117
62	01 10	59	118	00 11	59	119	-0 48	59	119	-1 47	59	119	-2 46	58	119
60	01 33	-59	120	00 34	-58	121	-0 24	-59	121	-1 23	-59	121	-2 22	-59	121
58	01 56	59	122	00 57	58	122	-0 01	59	123	-1 00	59	123	-1 59	59	123
56	02 19	59	124	01 20	59	124	00 21	59	125	-0 38	59	125	-1 37	59	125
54	02 41	59	126	01 42	59	126	00 43	59	127	-0 16	59	127	-1 15	59	127
52	03 02	59	128	02 03	59	128	01 04	59	129	00 05	59	129	-0 54	59	129
50	03 23	-59	130	02 24	-59	130	01 25	-59	131	00 26	-59	131	-0 33	-59	131
48	03 44	59	132	02 45	60	132	01 45	59	132	00 46	59	133	-0 13	59	133
46	04 03	59	134	03 04	59	134	02 05	59	134	01 06	59	135	00 07	60	135
44	04 22	59	136	03 23	59	136	02 24	59	136	01 25	60	137	00 25	59	137
42	04 41	59	138	03 42	60	138	02 42	59	138	01 43	59	139	00 44	60	139
40	04 59	-60	140	03 59	-59	140	03 00	-60	140	02 00	-59	140	01 01	-59	141
38	05 16	60	142	04 16	59	142	03 17	60	142	02 17	59	142	01 18	60	143
36	05 32	60	144	04 32	59	144	03 33	60	144	02 33	59	144	01 34	60	145
34	05 47	59	146	04 48	60	146	03 48	59	146	02 49	60	146	01 49	59	146
32	06 02	59	148	05 03	60	148	04 03	60	148	03 03	59	148	02 04	60	148
30	06 16	-60	150	05 16	-59	150	04 17	-60	150	03 17	-59	150	02 18	-60	150
28	06 29	60	152	05 29	59	152	04 30	60	152	03 30	60	152	02 30	59	152
26	06 41	59	154	05 42	59	154	04 42	60	154	03 42	59	154	02 43	60	154
24	06 53	59	156	05 53	60	156	04 53	59	156	03 54	60	156	02 54	60	156
22	07 03	59	158	06 04	60	158	05 04	60	158	04 04	60	158	03 04	60	158
20	07 13	-60	160	06 13	-59	160	05 14	-60	160	04 14	-60	160	03 14	-60	160
18	07 22	60	162	06 22	60	162	05 22	60	162	04 22	60	162	03 22	59	162
16	07 30	60	164	06 30	60	164	05 30	60	164	04 30	60	164	03 30	60	164
14	07 37	60	166	06 37	60	166	05 37	60	166	04 37	60	166	03 37	60	166
12	07 43	60	168	06 43	60	168	05 43	60	168	04 43	60	168	03 43	60	168
10	07 48	-60	170	06 48	-60	170	05 48	-60	170	04 48	-60	170	03 48	-60	170
8	07 52	59	172	06 53	60	172	05 53	60	172	04 53	60	172	03 53	60	172
6	07 56	60	174	06 56	60	174	05 56	60	174	04 56	60	174	03 56	60	174
4	07 58	60	176	06 58	60	176	05 58	60	176	04 58	60	176	03 58	60	176
2	08 00	60	178	07 00	60	178	06 00	60	178	05 00	60	178	04 00	60	178
0	08 00	-60	180	07 00	-60	180	06 00	-60	180	05 00	-60	180	04 00	-60	180

LHA	10° Hc	d	Z	11° Hc	d	Z	12° Hc	d	Z	13° Hc	d	Z	14° Hc	d	Z	LHA
	° ′	′	°	° ′	′	°	° ′	′	°	° ′	′	°	° ′	′	°	
86	274															
84	276															
82	278															
80	-7 31	-58	102	280												
78	-7 04	59	104	282												
76	-6 38	59	106	-7 37	59	106	284									
74	-6 13	58	108	-7 11	59	108	286									
72	-5 47	59	110	-6 46	58	110	-7 44	59	110	288						
70	-5 22	-58	112	-6 20	-59	112	-7 19	-59	112	290						
68	-4 57	58	114	-5 55	59	114	-6 54	59	114	292						
66	-4 32	59	115	-5 31	59	116	-6 30	58	116	-7 28	59	116	294			
64	-4 08	59	117	-5 07	59	118	-6 06	58	118	-7 04	59	118	296			
62	-3 44	59	119	-4 43	59	120	-5 42	59	120	-6 41	58	120	-7 39	59	120	298
60	-3 21	-59	121	-4 20	-59	121	-5 19	-59	122	-6 18	-58	122	-7 16	-59	122	300
58	-2 58	59	123	-3 57	59	123	-4 56	59	124	-5 55	59	124	-6 54	59	124	302
56	-2 36	59	125	-3 35	59	125	-4 34	59	126	-5 33	59	126	-6 32	59	126	304
54	-2 14	59	127	-3 13	59	127	-4 12	59	127	-5 11	59	128	-6 10	59	128	306
52	-1 53	59	129	-2 52	59	129	-3 51	59	129	-4 50	59	130	-5 49	59	130	308
50	-1 32	-59	131	-2 31	-59	131	-3 30	-59	131	-4 29	-60	131	-5 29	-59	132	310
48	-1 12	59	133	-2 11	59	133	-3 10	60	133	-4 10	59	133	-5 09	59	134	312
46	-0 53	59	135	-1 52	59	135	-2 51	60	135	-3 50	60	135	-4 50	59	135	314
44	-0 34	59	137	-1 33	59	137	-2 32	60	137	-3 32	59	137	-4 31	59	137	316
42	-0 16	59	139	-1 15	59	139	-2 14	60	139	-3 14	59	139	-4 13	59	139	318
40	00 02	-60	141	-0 58	-59	141	-1 57	-59	141	-2 56	-60	141	-3 56	-59	141	320
38	00 18	59	143	-0 41	59	143	-1 40	60	143	-2 40	59	143	-3 39	60	143	322
36	00 34	59	145	-0 25	59	145	-1 24	60	145	-2 24	59	145	-3 23	60	145	324
34	00 50	60	147	-0 10	59	147	-1 09	60	147	-2 09	59	147	-3 08	60	147	326
32	01 04	59	149	00 05	60	149	-0 55	59	149	-1 54	60	149	-2 54	60	149	328
30	01 18	-60	151	00 18	-59	151	-0 41	-60	151	-1 41	-60	151	-2 41	-59	151	330
28	01 31	60	153	00 31	60	153	-0 29	59	153	-1 28	60	153	-2 28	60	153	332
26	01 43	60	154	00 43	60	155	-0 17	59	155	-1 16	60	155	-2 16	60	155	334
24	01 54	60	156	00 54	59	156	-0 05	60	157	-1 05	60	157	-2 05	60	157	336
22	02 04	59	158	01 05	60	158	00 05	60	158	-0 55	60	159	-1 55	59	159	338
20	02 14	-60	160	01 14	-60	160	00 14	-59	160	-0 45	-60	161	-1 45	-60	161	340
18	02 23	60	162	01 23	60	162	00 23	60	162	-0 37	60	162	-1 37	60	162	342
16	02 30	59	164	01 31	60	164	00 31	60	164	-0 29	60	164	-1 29	60	164	344
14	02 37	60	166	01 37	59	166	00 38	60	166	-0 22	60	166	-1 22	60	166	346
12	02 43	60	168	01 43	60	168	00 43	59	168	-0 16	60	168	-1 16	60	168	348
10	02 48	-60	170	01 48	-59	170	00 49	-60	170	-0 11	-60	170	-1 11	-60	170	350
8	02 53	60	172	01 53	60	172	00 53	60	172	-0 07	60	172	-1 07	60	172	352
6	02 56	60	174	01 56	60	174	00 56	60	174	-0 04	60	174	-1 04	60	174	354
4	02 58	60	176	01 58	60	176	00 58	60	176	-0 02	60	176	-1 02	60	176	356
2	03 00	60	178	02 00	60	178	01 00	60	178	00 00	60	178	-1 00	60	178	358
0	03 00	-60	180	02 00	-60	180	01 00	-60	180	00 00	-60	180	-1 00	-60	180	360

S. Lat. {LHA greater than 180°........ Zn=180−Z
{LHA less than 180°........... Zn=180+Z

DECLINATION (0°-14°) CONTRARY NAME TO LATITUDE

N. Lat. {LHA greater than 180°....... Zn=Z
{LHA less than 180°........... Zn=360−Z

DECLINATION (15°-29°) **SAME** NAME AS LATITUDE

LHA	15° Hc	d	Z	16° Hc	d	Z	17° Hc	d	Z	18° Hc	d	Z	19° Hc	d	Z	LHA
	° ′	′	°	° ′	′	°	° ′	′	°	° ′	′	°	° ′	′	°	
0	28 00	+60	180	29 00	+60	180	30 00	+60	180	31 00	+60	180	32 00	+60	180	360
2	28 00	60	178	29 00	60	178	30 00	60	178	31 00	60	178	32 00	60	178	358
4	27 58	60	176	28 58	60	176	29 58	60	176	30 58	60	176	31 58	60	176	356
6	27 55	60	173	28 55	60	173	29 55	60	173	30 55	60	173	31 55	60	173	354
8	27 52	60	171	28 52	60	171	29 52	60	171	30 52	60	171	31 52	60	171	352
10	27 47	+60	169	28 47	+60	169	29 47	+60	169	30 47	+60	169	31 47	+60	169	350
12	27 42	60	167	28 42	59	167	29 41	60	167	30 41	60	167	31 41	60	167	348
14	27 35	60	165	28 35	60	165	29 35	60	165	30 35	59	165	31 34	60	164	346
16	27 27	60	163	28 27	60	163	29 27	60	162	30 27	60	162	31 27	60	162	344
18	27 19	60	160	28 19	59	160	29 18	60	160	30 18	60	160	31 18	60	160	342
20	27 09	+60	158	28 09	+60	158	29 09	+60	158	30 09	+59	158	31 08	+60	158	340
22	26 59	59	156	27 58	60	156	28 58	60	156	29 58	60	156	30 58	59	156	338
24	26 47	60	154	27 47	60	154	28 47	59	154	29 46	60	154	30 46	60	153	336
26	26 35	60	152	27 35	59	152	28 34	60	152	29 34	59	151	30 33	60	151	334
28	26 22	59	150	27 21	60	150	28 21	59	149	29 20	60	149	30 20	60	149	332
30	26 08	+59	148	27 07	+60	147	28 07	+59	147	29 06	+60	147	30 06	+59	147	330
32	25 53	59	145	26 52	60	145	27 52	59	145	28 51	60	145	29 51	59	145	328
34	25 37	59	143	26 36	60	143	27 36	59	143	28 35	60	143	29 35	59	143	326
36	25 20	60	141	26 20	59	141	27 19	59	141	28 18	60	141	29 18	59	140	324
38	25 03	59	139	26 02	60	139	27 02	59	139	28 01	59	139	29 00	59	138	322
40	24 45	+59	137	25 44	+59	137	26 43	+60	137	27 43	+59	136	28 42	+59	136	320
42	24 26	59	135	25 25	59	135	26 24	60	134	27 24	59	134	28 23	59	134	318
44	24 07	59	133	25 06	59	133	26 05	59	132	27 04	59	132	28 03	59	132	316
46	23 46	60	131	24 46	59	130	25 45	59	130	26 44	59	130	27 43	59	130	314
48	23 26	59	129	24 25	59	128	25 24	59	128	26 23	59	128	27 22	58	128	312
50	23 04	+59	127	24 03	+59	126	25 02	+59	126	26 01	+59	126	27 00	+59	126	310
52	22 42	59	124	23 41	59	124	24 40	59	124	25 39	59	124	26 38	58	124	308
54	22 20	59	122	23 19	58	122	24 17	59	122	25 16	59	122	26 15	59	122	306
56	21 57	58	120	22 55	59	120	23 54	59	120	24 53	59	120	25 52	58	119	304
58	21 33	59	118	22 32	59	118	23 31	58	118	24 29	59	118	25 28	58	117	302
60	21 09	+59	116	22 08	+58	116	23 06	+59	116	24 05	+59	116	25 04	+58	115	300
62	20 45	58	114	21 43	59	114	22 42	59	114	23 41	58	114	24 39	59	113	298
64	20 20	58	112	21 18	59	112	22 17	59	112	23 16	58	112	24 14	59	111	296
66	19 55	58	110	20 53	59	110	21 52	58	110	22 50	59	110	23 49	58	109	294
68	19 29	59	108	20 28	58	108	21 26	59	108	22 25	58	108	23 23	59	107	292
70	19 03	+59	106	20 02	+58	106	21 00	+59	106	21 59	+58	106	22 57	+59	105	290
72	18 37	59	104	19 36	58	104	20 34	59	104	21 33	58	104	22 31	58	103	288
74	18 11	59	102	19 10	58	102	20 08	58	102	21 06	59	102	22 05	58	101	286
76	17 45	58	100	18 43	58	100	19 41	59	100	20 40	58	100	21 38	58	99	284
78	17 18	58	98	18 16	59	98	19 15	58	98	20 13	58	98	21 11	59	97	282
80	16 51	+59	96	17 50	+58	96	18 48	+58	96	19 46	+59	96	20 45	+58	95	280
82	16 24	59	94	17 23	58	94	18 21	58	94	19 19	59	94	20 18	58	93	278
84	15 57	59	92	16 56	58	92	17 54	58	92	18 52	59	92	19 51	58	91	276
86	15 30	59	90	16 29	58	90	17 27	58	90	18 25	59	90	19 24	58	90	274
88	15 03	59	89	16 02	58	88	17 00	58	88	17 58	59	88	18 57	58	88	272
90	14 36	+59	87	15 35	+58	86	16 33	+58	86	17 31	+59	86	18 30	+58	86	270
92	14 10	58	85	15 08	58	84	16 06	59	84	17 05	58	84	18 03	58	84	268
94	13 43	58	83	14 41	58	82	15 39	58	82	16 38	58	82	17 36	58	82	266
96	13 16	58	81	14 14	59	81	15 13	58	80	16 11	58	80	17 09	59	80	264
98	12 49	59	79	13 48	58	79	14 46	59	78	15 45	58	78	16 43	58	78	262
100	12 23	+58	77	13 21	+59	77	14 20	+58	76	15 18	+59	76	16 17	+58	76	260
102	11 57	58	75	12 55	59	75	13 54	58	75	14 52	59	74	15 51	58	74	258
104	11 31	58	73	12 29	59	73	13 28	58	73	14 26	59	72	15 25	58	72	256
106	11 05	59	71	12 04	58	71	13 02	59	71	14 01	58	70	14 59	59	70	254
108	10 40	58	69	11 38	59	69	12 37	58	69	13 35	59	69	14 34	59	68	252
110	10 15	+58	67	11 13	+59	67	12 12	+59	67	13 11	+58	67	14 09	+59	66	250
112	09 50	59	65	10 49	58	65	11 47	59	65	12 46	58	65	13 45	58	65	248
114	09 26	58	63	10 24	59	63	11 23	59	63	12 22	58	63	13 20	59	63	246
116	09 02	59	62	10 01	58	61	10 59	59	61	11 58	59	61	12 57	58	61	244
118	08 38	59	60	09 37	59	59	10 36	59	59	11 35	58	59	12 33	59	59	242
120	08 15	+59	58	09 14	+59	58	10 13	+59	57	11 12	+58	57	12 10	+59	57	240
122	07 53	59	56	08 52	58	56	09 50	59	55	10 49	58	55	11 48	58	55	238
124	07 31	59	54	08 30	58	54	09 28	59	54	10 27	59	53	11 26	59	53	236
126	07 09	59	52	08 08	59	52	09 07	59	52	10 06	59	51	11 05	59	51	234
128	06 48	59	50	07 47	59	50	08 46	59	50	09 45	59	50	10 44	59	49	232
130	06 28	+59	48	07 27	+59	48	08 26	+59	48	09 25	+59	48	10 24	+59	48	230
132	06 08	59	46	07 07	59	46	08 06	59	46	09 05	59	46	10 04	60	46	228
134	05 49	59	44	06 48	59	44	07 47	59	44	08 46	59	44	09 45	60	44	226
136	05 30	59	42	06 29	60	42	07 29	59	42	08 28	59	42	09 27	60	42	224
138	05 12	60	41	06 12	59	40	07 11	59	40	08 10	60	40	09 10	59	40	222

LHA	20° Hc	d	Z	21° Hc	d	Z	22° Hc	d	Z	23° Hc	d	Z	24° Hc	d	Z	LHA
	° ′	′	°	° ′	′	°	° ′	′	°	° ′	′	°	° ′	′	°	
0	33 00	+60	180	34 00	+60	180	35 00	+60	180	36 00	+60	180	37 00	+60	180	360
2	33 00	60	178	34 00	60	178	35 00	60	178	36 00	60	178	37 00	60	178	358
4	32 58	60	176	33 58	60	176	34 58	60	176	35 58	60	175	36 58	60	175	356
6	32 55	60	173	33 55	60	173	34 55	60	173	35 55	60	173	36 55	60	173	354
8	32 52	60	171	33 52	60	171	34 52	59	171	35 51	60	171	36 51	60	171	352
10	32 47	+60	169	33 47	+60	169	34 47	+60	169	35 47	+60	169	36 47	+60	169	350
12	32 41	60	167	33 41	60	167	34 41	60	166	35 41	60	166	36 41	60	166	348
14	32 34	60	164	33 34	60	164	34 34	60	164	35 34	60	164	36 34	60	164	346
16	32 27	59	162	33 26	60	162	34 26	60	162	35 26	60	162	36 26	60	162	344
18	32 18	60	160	33 18	59	160	34 17	60	160	35 17	60	160	36 17	60	160	342
20	32 08	+60	158	33 08	+60	158	34 08	+59	158	35 07	+60	157	36 07	+60	157	340
22	31 57	60	156	32 57	60	155	33 57	59	155	34 56	60	155	35 56	60	155	338
24	31 46	59	153	32 45	60	153	33 45	60	153	34 45	59	153	35 44	60	153	336
26	31 33	60	151	32 33	59	151	33 32	60	151	34 32	59	151	35 31	60	151	334
28	31 20	59	149	32 19	60	149	33 19	59	149	34 18	60	149	35 18	59	148	332
30	31 05	+60	147	32 05	+59	147	33 04	+60	146	34 04	+59	146	35 03	+59	146	330
32	30 50	59	145	31 49	60	144	32 49	59	144	33 48	60	144	34 48	59	144	328
34	30 34	59	142	31 33	60	142	32 33	59	142	33 32	59	142	34 31	59	142	326
36	30 17	59	140	31 16	60	140	32 16	59	140	33 15	59	140	34 14	59	140	324
38	29 59	60	138	30 59	59	138	31 58	59	138	32 57	59	138	33 56	59	137	322
40	29 41	+59	136	30 40	+59	136	31 39	+59	136	32 38	+59	135	33 37	+60	135	320
42	29 22	59	134	30 21	59	134	31 20	59	133	32 19	59	133	33 18	59	133	318
44	29 02	59	132	30 01	59	132	31 00	59	131	31 59	59	131	32 58	59	131	316
46	28 42	59	130	29 41	58	129	30 39	59	129	31 38	59	129	32 37	59	129	314
48	28 20	59	128	29 19	59	127	30 18	59	127	31 17	59	127	32 16	59	127	312
50	27 59	+59	125	28 58	+58	125	29 56	+59	125	30 55	+59	125	31 54	+59	125	310
52	27 36	59	123	28 35	59	123	29 34	59	123	30 33	58	123	31 31	59	122	308
54	27 14	58	121	28 12	59	121	29 11	59	121	30 10	58	121	31 08	59	120	306
56	26 50	59	119	27 49	59	119	28 48	58	119	29 46	59	119	30 45	58	118	304
58	26 26	59	117	27 25	59	117	28 24	58	117	29 22	59	116	30 21	58	116	302
60	26 02	+59	115	27 01	+58	115	27 59	+59	115	28 58	+58	114	29 56	+59	114	300
62	25 38	58	113	26 36	59	113	27 35	58	113	28 33	58	112	29 31	59	112	298
64	25 13	58	111	26 11	58	111	27 09	59	111	28 08	58	110	29 06	59	110	296
66	24 47	59	109	25 46	58	109	26 44	58	109	27 42	59	108	28 41	58	108	294
68	24 22	58	107	25 20	58	107	26 18	59	107	27 17	58	106	28 15	58	106	292
70	23 56	+58	105	24 54	+58	105	25 52	+59	105	26 51	+58	104	27 49	+58	104	290
72	23 29	59	103	24 28	58	103	25 26	58	103	26 24	59	102	27 23	58	102	288
74	23 03	58	101	24 01	59	101	25 00	58	101	25 58	58	100	26 56	58	100	286
76	22 36	59	99	23 35	58	99	24 33	58	99	25 31	58	98	26 29	59	98	284
78	22 10	58	97	23 08	58	97	24 06	58	97	25 04	59	96	26 03	58	96	282
80	21 43	+58	95	22 41	+58	95	23 39	+59	95	24 38	+58	94	25 36	+58	94	280
82	21 16	58	93	22 14	58	93	23 12	59	93	24 11	58	92	25 09	58	92	278
84	20 49	58	91	21 47	58	91	22 45	59	91	23 44	58	90	24 42	58	90	276
86	20 22	58	89	21 20	58	89	22 18	59	89	23 17	58	88	24 15	58	88	274
88	19 55	58	87	20 53	58	87	21 51	59	87	22 50	58	87	23 48	58	86	272
90	19 28	+58	85	20 26	+59	85	21 25	+58	85	22 23	+58	85	23 21	+58	84	270
92	19 01	58	83	19 59	59	83	20 58	58	83	21 56	58	83	22 54	58	82	268
94	18 34	59	82	19 33	58	81	20 31	58	81	21 29	58	81	22 27	59	80	266
96	18 08	58	80	19 06	58	79	20 04	59	79	21 03	58	79	22 01	58	79	264
98	17 41	59	78	18 40	58	77	19 38	58	77	20 36	59	77	21 35	58	77	262
100	17 15	+58	76	18 13	+59	76	19 12	+58	75	20 10	+58	75	21 08	+59	75	260
102	16 49	58	74	17 47	59	74	18 46	58	73	19 44	58	73	20 42	59	73	258
104	16 23	59	72	17 22	58	72	18 20	58	71	19 18	59	71	20 17	58	71	256
106	15 58	58	70	16 56	59	70	17 55	58	70	18 53	58	69	19 51	59	69	254
108	15 33	58	68	16 31	59	68	17 30	58	68	18 28	58	67	19 26	59	67	252
110	15 08	+58	66	16 06	+59	66	17 05	+58	66	18 03	+59	66	19 02	+58	65	250
112	14 43	59	64	15 42	58	64	16 40	59	64	17 39	58	64	18 37	59	63	248
114	14 19	59	62	15 18	58	62	16 16	59	62	17 15	58	62	18 13	59	62	246
116	13 55	59	61	14 54	59	60	15 53	58	60	16 51	59	60	17 50	59	60	244
118	13 32	59	59	14 31	59	58	15 30	58	58	16 28	59	58	17 27	59	58	242
120	13 09	+59	57	14 08	+59	57	15 07	+59	56	16 06	+58	56	17 04	+59	56	240
122	12 47	59	55	13 46	59	55	14 45	58	54	15 43	59	54	16 42	59	54	238
124	12 25	59	53	13 24	59	53	14 23	59	53	15 22	58	52	16 21	59	52	236
126	12 04	59	51	13 03	59	51	14 02	59	51	15 01	59	50	16 00	59	50	234
128	11 43	59	49	12 42	59	49	13 41	59	49	14 40	59	48	15 39	59	48	232
130	11 23	+59	47	12 22	+59	47	13 21	+59	47	14 20	+59	47	15 19	+59	47	230
132	11 04	59	45	12 03	59	45	13 02	59	45	14 01	59	45	15 00	59	45	228
134	10 45	59	44	11 44	59	43	12 43	59	43	13 42	59	43	14 41	59	43	226
136	10 26	60	42	11 26	59	41	12 25	59	41	13 24	59	41	14 23	60	41	224
138	10 09	59	40	11 08	59	40	12 07	60	39	13 07	59	39	14 06	59	39	222

LHA	25° Hc	d	Z	26° Hc	d	Z	27° Hc	d	Z	28° Hc	d	Z	29° Hc	d	Z	LHA
	° ′	′	°	° ′	′	°	° ′	′	°	° ′	′	°	° ′	′	°	
0	38 00	+60	180	39 00	+60	180	40 00	+60	180	41 00	+60	180	42 00	+60	180	360
2	38 00	60	178	39 00	60	178	40 00	59	178	40 59	60	178	41 59	60	178	358
4	37 58	60	175	38 58	60	175	39 58	60	175	40 58	60	175	41 58	60	175	356
6	37 55	60	173	38 55	60	173	39 55	60	173	40 55	60	173	41 55	60	173	354
8	37 51	60	171	38 51	60	171	39 51	60	171	40 51	60	171	41 51	60	171	352
10	37 47	+59	169	38 46	+60	169	39 46	+60	168	40 46	+60	168	41 46	+60	168	350
12	37 41	60	166	38 41	59	166	39 40	60	166	40 40	60	166	41 40	60	166	348
14	37 34	60	164	38 34	59	164	39 33	60	164	40 33	60	164	41 33	60	164	346
16	37 26	60	162	38 26	59	162	39 25	60	162	40 25	60	161	41 25	60	161	344
18	37 17	59	159	38 16	60	159	39 16	60	159	40 16	60	159	41 16	59	159	342
20	37 07	+59	157	38 06	+60	157	39 06	+60	157	40 06	+60	157	41 06	+59	157	340
22	36 56	59	155	37 55	60	155	38 55	60	155	39 55	59	155	40 54	60	154	338
24	36 44	59	153	37 43	60	153	38 43	60	152	39 43	59	152	40 42	60	152	336
26	36 31	59	150	37 30	60	150	38 30	60	150	39 30	59	150	40 29	60	150	334
28	36 17	60	148	37 17	59	148	38 16	60	148	39 16	59	148	40 15	59	148	332
30	36 02	+60	146	37 02	+59	146	38 01	+60	146	39 01	+59	145	40 00	+59	145	330
32	35 47	59	144	36 46	60	144	37 46	59	143	38 45	59	143	39 44	59	143	328
34	35 30	60	142	36 30	59	141	37 29	59	141	38 28	59	141	39 27	60	141	326
36	35 13	59	139	36 12	60	139	37 12	59	139	38 11	59	139	39 10	59	139	324
38	34 55	59	137	35 54	60	137	36 54	59	137	37 53	59	137	38 52	59	136	322
40	34 37	+59	135	35 36	+59	135	36 35	+59	135	37 34	+59	134	38 33	+59	134	320
42	34 17	59	133	35 16	59	133	36 15	59	132	37 14	59	132	38 13	59	132	318
44	33 57	59	131	34 56	59	130	35 55	59	130	36 54	58	130	37 52	59	130	316
46	33 36	59	129	34 35	59	128	35 34	59	128	36 33	58	128	37 31	59	128	314
48	33 15	58	126	34 13	59	126	35 12	59	126	36 11	59	126	37 10	58	125	312
50	32 53	+58	124	33 51	+59	124	34 50	+59	124	35 49	+58	124	36 47	+59	123	310
52	32 30	59	122	33 29	58	122	34 27	59	122	35 26	58	121	36 24	59	121	308
54	32 07	59	120	33 06	58	120	34 04	59	120	35 03	58	119	36 01	59	119	306
56	31 43	59	118	32 42	58	118	33 40	59	117	34 39	58	117	35 37	59	117	304
58	31 19	59	116	32 18	58	116	33 16	59	115	34 15	58	115	35 13	58	115	302
60	30 55	+58	114	31 53	+59	114	32 52	+58	113	33 50	+58	113	34 48	+58	113	300
62	30 30	58	112	31 28	59	112	32 27	58	111	33 25	58	111	34 23	58	111	298
64	30 05	58	110	31 03	58	110	32 01	59	109	33 00	58	109	33 58	58	109	296
66	29 39	58	108	30 37	59	107	31 36	58	107	32 34	58	107	33 32	58	107	294
68	29 13	58	106	30 11	59	105	31 10	58	105	32 08	58	105	33 06	58	105	292
70	28 47	+58	104	29 45	+59	103	30 44	+58	103	31 42	+58	103	32 40	+58	103	290
72	28 21	58	102	29 19	58	101	30 17	58	101	31 15	58	101	32 13	58	101	288
74	27 54	58	100	28 52	59	99	29 51	58	99	30 49	58	99	31 47	58	99	286
76	27 28	58	98	28 26	58	97	29 24	58	97	30 22	58	97	31 20	58	97	284
78	27 01	58	96	27 59	58	95	28 57	58	95	29 55	58	95	30 53	58	95	282
80	26 34	+58	94	27 32	+58	94	28 30	+58	93	29 28	+58	93	30 26	+58	93	280
82	26 07	58	92	27 05	58	92	28 03	58	91	29 01	58	91	29 59	58	91	278
84	25 40	58	90	26 38	58	90	27 36	58	89	28 34	58	89	29 32	58	89	276
86	25 13	58	88	26 11	58	88	27 09	58	87	28 07	58	87	29 05	58	87	274
88	24 46	58	86	25 44	58	86	26 42	58	85	27 40	58	85	28 38	58	85	272
90	24 19	+58	84	25 17	+58	84	26 15	+58	84	27 13	+58	83	28 11	+58	83	270
92	23 52	58	82	24 50	59	82	25 49	58	82	26 47	58	81	27 45	58	81	268
94	23 26	58	80	24 24	58	80	25 22	58	80	26 20	58	79	27 18	58	79	266
96	22 59	58	78	23 57	58	78	24 55	59	78	25 54	58	77	26 52	58	77	264
98	22 33	58	76	23 31	58	76	24 29	58	76	25 27	58	76	26 25	59	75	262
100	22 07	+58	74	23 05	+58	74	24 03	+58	74	25 01	+58	74	25 59	+59	73	260
102	21 41	58	73	22 39	58	72	23 37	59	72	24 36	58	72	25 34	58	72	258
104	21 15	58	71	22 13	59	70	23 12	58	70	24 10	58	70	25 08	58	70	256
106	20 50	58	69	21 48	59	69	22 47	58	68	23 45	58	68	24 43	58	68	254
108	20 25	58	67	21 23	59	67	22 22	58	66	23 20	58	66	24 18	59	66	252
110	20 00	+59	65	20 59	+58	65	21 57	+58	65	22 55	+59	64	23 54	+58	64	250
112	19 36	58	63	20 34	59	63	21 33	58	63	22 31	59	62	23 30	58	62	248
114	19 12	59	61	20 11	58	61	21 09	59	61	22 08	58	61	23 06	59	60	246
116	18 49	58	59	19 47	59	59	20 46	58	59	21 44	59	59	22 43	58	59	244
118	18 26	58	58	19 24	59	57	20 23	59	57	21 22	58	57	22 20	59	57	242
120	18 03	+59	56	19 02	+58	55	20 00	+59	55	20 59	+59	55	21 58	+58	55	240
122	17 41	59	54	18 40	59	54	19 39	58	53	20 37	59	53	21 36	59	53	238
124	17 20	58	52	18 18	59	52	19 17	59	52	20 16	59	51	21 15	59	51	236
126	16 59	58	50	17 57	59	50	18 56	59	50	19 55	59	49	20 54	59	49	234
128	16 38	59	48	17 37	59	48	18 36	59	48	19 35	59	48	20 34	59	47	232
130	16 18	+59	46	17 17	+59	46	18 16	+59	46	19 15	+59	46	20 14	+59	46	230
132	15 59	59	45	16 58	59	44	17 57	59	44	18 56	59	44	19 55	59	44	228
134	15 40	60	43	16 40	59	42	17 39	59	42	18 38	59	42	19 37	59	42	226
136	15 23	59	41	16 22	59	41	17 21	59	40	18 20	59	40	19 19	59	40	224
138	15 05	60	39	16 05	59	39	17 04	59	39	18 03	59	38	19 02	59	38	222

S. Lat. {LHA greater than 180°....... Zn=180−Z
{LHA less than 180°........... Zn=180+Z

DECLINATION (15°-29°) **SAME** NAME AS LATITUDE

LAT 77°

N. Lat. {LHA greater than 180°....... Zn=Z; LHA less than 180°........... Zn=360−Z}

DECLINATION (15°-29°) SAME NAME AS LATITUDE

LHA	15° Hc	15° d	15° Z	16° Hc	16° d	16° Z	17° Hc	17° d	17° Z	18° Hc	18° d	18° Z	19° Hc	19° d	19° Z	20° Hc	20° d	20° Z	21° Hc	21° d	21° Z	22° Hc	22° d	22° Z
	° ′	′	°	° ′	′	°	° ′	′	°	° ′	′	°	° ′	′	°	° ′	′	°	° ′	′	°	° ′	′	°
140	04 55	+60	39	05 55	+59	38	06 54	+59	38	07 53	+60	38	08 53	+59	38	09 52	+59	38	10 51	+60	38	11 51	+59	38
142	04 39	59	37	05 38	60	37	06 38	59	36	07 37	59	36	08 36	60	36	09 36	59	36	10 35	60	36	11 35	59	36
144	04 23	59	35	05 22	60	35	06 22	59	34	07 21	60	34	08 21	59	34	09 20	60	34	10 20	59	34	11 19	60	34
146	04 08	59	33	05 07	60	33	06 07	60	33	07 07	59	32	08 06	60	32	09 06	59	32	10 05	60	32	11 05	59	32
148	03 54	59	31	04 53	60	31	05 53	59	31	06 52	60	31	07 52	60	30	08 52	59	30	09 51	60	30	10 51	59	30
150	03 40	+60	29	04 40	+59	29	05 39	+60	29	06 39	+60	29	07 39	+59	29	08 38	+60	28	09 38	+60	28	10 38	+59	28
152	03 28	59	27	04 27	60	27	05 27	60	27	06 27	59	27	07 26	60	27	08 26	60	27	09 26	59	26	10 25	60	26
154	03 16	59	25	04 15	60	25	05 15	60	25	06 15	60	25	07 15	59	25	08 14	60	25	09 14	60	25	10 14	59	25
156	03 05	59	23	04 04	60	23	05 04	60	23	06 04	60	23	07 04	59	23	08 03	60	23	09 03	60	23	10 03	60	23
158	02 54	60	21	03 54	60	21	04 54	60	21	05 54	60	21	06 54	59	21	07 53	60	21	08 53	60	21	09 53	60	21
160	02 45	+60	19	03 45	+60	19	04 45	+60	19	05 45	+59	19	06 44	+60	19	07 44	+60	19	08 44	+60	19	09 44	+60	19
162	02 37	59	17	03 36	60	17	04 36	60	17	05 36	60	17	06 36	60	17	07 36	60	17	08 36	60	17	09 36	59	17
164	02 29	60	16	03 29	60	15	04 29	60	15	05 29	60	15	06 29	59	15	07 28	60	15	08 28	60	15	09 28	60	15
166	02 22	60	14	03 22	60	14	04 22	60	13	05 22	60	13	06 22	60	13	07 22	60	13	08 22	60	13	09 22	60	13
168	02 16	60	12	03 16	60	12	04 16	60	12	05 16	60	12	06 16	60	11	07 16	60	11	08 16	60	11	09 16	60	11
170	02 11	+60	10	03 11	+60	10	04 11	+60	10	05 11	+60	10	06 11	+60	10	07 11	+60	10	08 11	+60	9	09 11	+60	9
172	02 07	60	8	03 07	60	8	04 07	60	8	05 07	60	8	06 07	60	8	07 07	60	8	08 07	60	8	09 07	60	8
174	02 04	60	6	03 04	60	6	04 04	60	6	05 04	60	6	06 04	60	6	07 04	60	6	08 04	60	6	09 04	60	6
176	02 02	60	4	03 02	60	4	04 02	60	4	05 02	60	4	06 02	60	4	07 02	60	4	08 02	60	4	09 02	60	4
178	02 00	60	2	03 00	60	2	04 00	60	2	05 00	60	2	06 00	60	2	07 00	60	2	08 00	60	2	09 00	60	2
180	02 00	+60	0	03 00	+60	0	04 00	+60	0	05 00	+60	0	06 00	+60	0	07 00	+60	0	08 00	+60	0	09 00	+60	0

LHA	23° Hc	23° d	23° Z	24° Hc	24° d	24° Z	25° Hc	25° d	25° Z	26° Hc	26° d	26° Z	27° Hc	27° d	27° Z	28° Hc	28° d	28° Z	29° Hc	29° d	29° Z	LHA
	° ′	′	°	° ′	′	°	° ′	′	°	° ′	′	°	° ′	′	°	° ′	′	°	° ′	′	°	
140	12 50	+59	37	13 49	+60	37	14 49	+59	37	15 48	+59	37	16 47	+60	37	17 47	+59	37	18 46	+59	36	220
142	12 34	59	36	13 33	60	35	14 33	59	35	15 32	59	35	16 31	60	35	17 31	59	35	18 30	60	35	218
144	12 19	59	34	13 18	60	34	14 18	59	33	15 17	59	33	16 16	60	33	17 16	59	33	18 15	60	33	216
146	12 04	60	32	13 04	59	32	14 03	60	32	15 03	59	31	16 02	60	31	17 02	59	31	18 01	59	31	214
148	11 50	60	30	12 50	59	30	13 49	60	30	14 49	59	30	15 48	60	29	16 48	59	29	17 47	60	29	212
150	11 37	+60	28	12 37	+59	28	13 36	+60	28	14 36	+60	28	15 36	+59	28	16 35	+60	27	17 35	+59	27	210
152	11 25	60	26	12 25	59	26	13 24	60	26	14 24	59	26	15 23	60	26	16 23	60	26	17 23	59	26	208
154	11 13	60	24	12 13	60	24	13 13	59	24	14 12	60	24	15 12	60	24	16 12	59	24	17 11	60	24	206
156	11 03	59	22	12 02	60	22	13 02	60	22	14 02	60	22	15 02	59	22	16 01	60	22	17 01	60	22	204
158	10 53	60	21	11 53	59	21	12 52	60	20	13 52	60	20	14 52	60	20	15 52	59	20	16 51	60	20	202
160	10 44	+60	19	11 44	+59	19	12 43	+60	19	13 43	+60	18	14 43	+60	18	15 43	+60	18	16 43	+59	18	200
162	10 35	60	17	11 35	60	17	12 35	60	17	13 35	60	17	14 35	60	17	15 35	60	17	16 35	59	16	198
164	10 28	60	15	11 28	60	15	12 28	60	15	13 28	60	15	14 28	59	15	15 27	60	15	16 27	60	15	196
166	10 22	59	13	11 21	60	13	12 21	60	13	13 21	60	13	14 21	60	13	15 21	60	13	16 21	60	13	194
168	10 16	60	11	11 16	60	11	12 16	60	11	13 16	60	11	14 16	60	11	15 16	59	11	16 15	60	11	192
170	10 11	+60	9	11 11	+60	9	12 11	+60	9	13 11	+60	9	14 11	+60	9	15 11	+60	9	16 11	+60	9	190
172	10 07	60	8	11 07	60	7	12 07	60	7	13 07	60	7	14 07	60	7	15 07	60	7	16 07	60	7	188
174	10 04	60	6	11 04	60	6	12 04	60	6	13 04	60	6	14 04	60	6	15 04	60	6	16 04	60	6	186
176	10 02	60	4	11 02	60	4	12 02	60	4	13 02	60	4	14 02	60	4	15 02	60	4	16 02	60	4	184
178	10 00	60	2	11 00	60	2	12 00	60	2	13 00	60	2	14 00	60	2	15 00	60	2	16 00	60	2	182
180	10 00	+60	0	11 00	+60	0	12 00	+60	0	13 00	+60	0	14 00	+60	0	15 00	+60	0	16 00	+60	0	180

15°	16°	17°	18°	19°	20°	21°	22°	23°	24°	25°	26°	27°	28°	29°

S. Lat. {LHA greater than 180°....... Zn=180−Z; LHA less than 180°........... Zn=180+Z}

DECLINATION (15°-29°) SAME NAME AS LATITUDE

N. Lat. {LHA greater than 180°....... Zn=Z; LHA less than 180°........... Zn=360−Z}

DECLINATION (15°-29°) CONTRARY NAME TO LATITUDE

LHA	15°			16°			17°			18°			19°			20°			21°			22°			23°			24°			25°			26°			27°			28°			29°			LHA
	Hc	d	Z	Hc	d	Z	Hc	d	Z	Hc	d	Z	Hc	d	Z	Hc	d	Z	Hc	d	Z	Hc	d	Z	Hc	d	Z	Hc	d	Z	Hc	d	Z	Hc	d	Z	Hc	d	Z	Hc	d	Z	Hc	d	Z	
	° ′	′	°	° ′	′	°	° ′	′	°	° ′	′	°	° ′	′	°	° ′	′	°	° ′	′	°	° ′	′	°	° ′	′	°	° ′	′	°	° ′	′	°	° ′	′	°	° ′	′	°	° ′	′	°	° ′	′	°	
56	−7 31	59	126																																										304
54	−7 09	59	128																																										306
52	−6 48	59	130																																										308
50	−6 28	−59	132	−7 27	−59	132																																							310
48	−6 08	59	134	−7 07	59	134																																							312
46	−5 49	59	136	−6 48	59	136																																							314
44	−5 30	59	138	−6 29	60	138	−7 29	59	138																																				316
42	−5 12	60	139	−6 12	59	140	−7 11	59	140																																				318
40	−4 55	−60	141	−5 55	−59	142	−6 54	−59	142																																				320
38	−4 39	59	143	−5 38	60	143	−6 38	59	144																																				322
36	−4 23	59	145	−5 22	60	145	−6 22	59	146	−7 21	60	146																																	324
34	−4 08	59	147	−5 07	60	147	−6 07	60	147	−7 07	59	148																																	326
32	−3 54	59	149	−4 53	60	149	−5 53	59	149	−6 52	60	149																																	328
30	−3 40	−60	151	−4 40	−59	151	−5 39	−60	151	−6 39	−60	151																																	330
28	−3 28	59	153	−4 27	60	153	−5 27	60	153	−6 27	59	153																																	332
26	−3 16	59	155	−4 15	60	155	−5 15	60	155	−6 15	60	155	−7 15	59	155																														334
24	−3 05	59	157	−4 04	60	157	−5 04	60	157	−6 04	60	157	−7 04	59	157																														336
22	−2 54	60	159	−3 54	60	159	−4 54	60	159	−5 54	60	159	−6 54	59	159																														338
20	−2 45	−60	161	−3 45	−60	161	−4 45	−60	161	−5 45	−59	161	−6 44	−60	161																														340
18	−2 37	59	163	−3 36	60	163	−4 36	60	163	−5 36	60	163	−6 36	60	163																														342
16	−2 29	60	164	−3 29	60	165	−4 29	60	165	−5 29	60	165	−6 29	59	165																														344
14	−2 22	60	166	−3 22	60	166	−4 22	60	167	−5 22	60	167	−6 22	60	167																														346
12	−2 16	60	168	−3 16	60	168	−4 16	60	168	−5 16	60	168	−6 16	60	169																														348
10	−2 11	−60	170	−3 11	−60	170	−4 11	−60	170	−5 11	−60	170	−6 11	−60	170																														350
8	−2 07	60	172	−3 07	60	172	−4 07	60	172	−5 07	60	172	−6 07	60	172																														352
6	−2 04	60	174	−3 04	60	174	−4 04	60	174	−5 04	60	174	−6 04	60	174																														354
4	−2 02	60	176	−3 02	60	176	−4 02	60	176	−5 02	60	176	−6 02	60	176																														356
2	−2 00	60	178	−3 00	60	178	−4 00	60	178	−5 00	60	178	−6 00	60	178	−7 00	60	178																											358
0	−2 00	−60	180	−3 00	−60	180	−4 00	−60	180	−5 00	−60	180	−6 00	−60	180	−7 00	−60	180																											360
	15°			16°			17°			18°			19°			20°			21°			22°			23°			24°			25°			26°			27°			28°			29°			

S. Lat. {LHA greater than 180°....... Zn=180−Z; LHA less than 180°........... Zn=180+Z}

DECLINATION (15°-29°) CONTRARY NAME TO LATITUDE

N. Lat. {LHA greater than 180°....... Zn=Z; LHA less than 180°........... Zn=360−Z}

DECLINATION (0°-14°) SAME NAME AS LATITUDE

LHA	0° Hc	d	Z	1° Hc	d	Z	2° Hc	d	Z	3° Hc	d	Z	4° Hc	d	Z
0	12 00	+60	180	13 00	+60	180	14 00	+60	180	15 00	+60	180	16 00	+60	180
2	12 00	60	178	13 00	60	178	14 00	60	178	15 00	60	178	16 00	60	178
4	11 58	60	176	12 58	60	176	13 58	60	176	14 58	60	176	15 58	60	176
6	11 56	60	174	12 56	60	174	13 56	60	174	14 56	60	174	15 56	60	174
8	11 53	60	172	12 53	60	172	13 53	60	172	14 53	60	172	15 53	60	172
10	11 49	+60	170	12 49	+60	170	13 49	+60	170	14 49	+60	170	15 49	+60	170
12	11 44	60	168	12 44	60	168	13 44	60	168	14 44	60	168	15 44	60	168
14	11 38	60	166	12 38	60	166	13 38	60	166	14 38	60	166	15 38	60	166
16	11 32	60	164	12 32	60	164	13 32	59	164	14 31	60	164	15 31	60	163
18	11 24	60	162	12 24	60	162	13 24	60	162	14 24	60	161	15 24	60	161
20	11 16	+60	160	12 16	+60	160	13 16	+60	159	14 16	+59	159	15 15	+60	159
22	11 07	60	158	12 07	60	158	13 07	59	157	14 06	60	157	15 06	60	157
24	10 57	60	156	11 57	60	155	12 57	59	155	13 56	60	155	14 56	60	155
26	10 46	60	154	11 46	60	153	12 46	59	153	13 45	60	153	14 45	60	153
28	10 35	59	152	11 34	60	151	12 34	60	151	13 34	60	151	14 34	59	151
30	10 22	+60	149	11 22	+60	149	12 22	+59	149	13 21	+60	149	14 21	+60	149
32	10 09	60	147	11 09	60	147	12 09	59	147	13 08	60	147	14 08	59	147
34	09 56	59	145	10 55	60	145	11 55	59	145	12 54	60	145	13 54	59	145
36	09 41	60	143	10 41	59	143	11 40	60	143	12 40	59	143	13 39	60	143
38	09 26	59	141	10 25	60	141	11 25	59	141	12 24	60	141	13 24	59	141
40	09 10	+59	139	10 09	+60	139	11 09	+59	139	12 08	+60	139	13 08	+59	139
42	08 53	60	137	09 53	59	137	10 52	60	137	11 52	59	137	12 51	59	137
44	08 36	59	135	09 35	60	135	10 35	59	135	11 34	60	135	12 34	59	135
46	08 18	60	133	09 18	59	133	10 17	59	133	11 16	60	133	12 16	59	133
48	08 00	59	131	08 59	59	131	09 58	60	131	10 58	59	131	11 57	59	131
50	07 41	+59	129	08 40	+59	129	09 39	+60	129	10 39	+59	129	11 38	+59	129
52	07 21	59	127	08 20	60	127	09 20	59	127	10 19	59	127	11 18	59	127
54	07 01	59	125	08 00	59	125	08 59	60	125	09 59	59	125	10 58	59	125
56	06 41	59	123	07 40	59	123	08 39	59	123	09 38	59	123	10 37	59	123
58	06 20	59	121	07 19	59	121	08 18	59	121	09 17	59	121	10 16	59	121
60	05 58	+59	120	06 57	+59	119	07 56	+59	119	08 55	+59	119	09 54	+59	119
62	05 36	59	118	06 35	59	117	07 34	59	117	08 33	59	117	09 32	59	117
64	05 14	59	116	06 13	59	115	07 12	59	115	08 11	59	115	09 10	58	115
66	04 51	59	114	05 50	59	113	06 49	59	113	07 48	59	113	08 47	59	113
68	04 28	59	112	05 27	59	111	06 26	59	111	07 25	59	111	08 24	58	111
70	04 05	+59	110	05 04	+58	109	06 02	+59	109	07 01	+59	109	08 00	+59	109
72	03 41	59	108	04 40	59	107	05 39	58	107	06 37	59	107	07 36	59	107
74	03 17	59	106	04 16	59	106	05 15	59	105	06 14	58	105	07 12	59	105
76	02 53	59	104	03 52	58	104	04 50	59	103	05 49	59	103	06 48	59	103
78	02 29	58	102	03 27	59	102	04 26	59	101	05 25	59	101	06 24	58	101
80	02 04	+59	100	03 03	+59	100	04 02	+58	99	05 00	+59	99	05 59	+59	99
82	01 40	58	98	02 38	59	98	03 37	59	97	04 36	58	97	05 34	59	97
84	01 15	58	96	02 13	59	96	03 12	59	95	04 11	59	95	05 10	58	95
86	00 50	59	94	01 49	58	94	02 47	59	94	03 46	59	93	04 45	58	93
88	00 25	59	92	01 24	58	92	02 22	59	92	03 21	59	91	04 20	58	91
90	00 00	+59	90	00 59	+58	90	01 57	+59	90	02 56	+59	89	03 55	+58	89
92	−0 25	59	88	00 34	58	88	01 32	59	88	02 31	59	87	03 30	58	87
94	−0 50	59	86	00 09	59	86	01 08	58	86	02 06	59	86	03 05	59	85
96	−1 15	59	84	−0 16	59	84	00 43	58	84	01 41	59	84	02 40	59	83
98	−1 40	59	82	−0 41	59	82	00 18	59	82	01 17	58	82	02 15	59	81
100	−2 04	+59	80	−1 05	+58	80	−0 07	+59	80	00 52	+59	80	01 51	+59	79
102	−2 29	59	78	−1 30	59	78	−0 31	59	78	00 28	58	78	01 26	59	77
104	−2 53	59	76	−1 54	59	76	−0 55	58	76	00 03	59	76	01 02	59	76
106	−3 17	59	74	−2 18	58	74	−1 20	59	74	−0 21	59	74	00 38	59	74
108	−3 41	59	72	−2 42	59	72	−1 43	58	72	−0 45	59	72	00 14	59	72
110	−4 05	+59	70	−3 06	+59	70	−2 07	+59	70	−1 08	+59	70	−0 09	+59	70
112	−4 28	59	68	−3 29	59	68	−2 30	59	68	−1 31	58	68	−0 33	59	68
114	−4 51	59	66	−3 52	59	66	−2 53	59	66	−1 54	59	66	−0 55	58	66
116	−5 14	59	64	−4 15	59	64	−3 16	59	64	−2 17	59	64	−1 18	59	64
118	−5 36	59	62	−4 37	59	62	−3 38	59	62	−2 39	59	62	−1 40	59	62
120	−5 58	+59	60	−4 59	+59	60	−4 00	+59	60	−3 01	+59	60	−2 02	+59	60
122	−6 20	59	59	−5 21	60	58	−4 21	59	58	−3 22	59	58	−2 23	59	58
124	−6 41	59	57	−5 42	60	56	−4 42	59	56	−3 43	59	56	−2 44	59	56
126	−7 01	59	55	−6 02	59	54	−5 03	59	54	−4 04	59	54	−3 05	59	54
128	−7 21	59	53	−6 22	59	52	−5 23	59	52	−4 24	60	52	−3 24	59	52
130				−6 42	+60	50	−5 42	+59	50	−4 43	+59	50	−3 44	+59	50
132				−7 01	60	48	−6 01	59	48	−5 02	59	48	−4 03	59	48
134				−7 19	59	46	−6 20	60	46	−5 20	59	46	−4 21	59	46
136							−6 37	59	44	−5 38	59	44	−4 39	60	44
138							−6 55	60	42	−5 55	59	42	−4 56	60	42

LHA	5° Hc	d	Z	6° Hc	d	Z	7° Hc	d	Z	8° Hc	d	Z	9° Hc	d	Z
0	17 00	+60	180	18 00	+60	180	19 00	+60	180	20 00	+60	180	21 00	+60	180
2	17 00	60	178	18 00	60	178	19 00	60	178	20 00	60	178	21 00	60	178
4	16 58	60	176	17 58	60	176	18 58	60	176	19 58	60	176	20 58	60	176
6	16 56	60	174	17 56	60	174	18 56	60	174	19 56	60	174	20 56	60	174
8	16 53	60	172	17 53	60	172	18 53	60	172	19 53	60	172	20 53	60	172
10	16 49	+60	170	17 49	+60	170	18 49	+60	170	19 49	+60	170	20 49	+60	169
12	16 44	60	168	17 44	60	168	18 44	60	167	19 44	60	167	20 44	59	167
14	16 38	60	165	17 38	60	165	18 38	60	165	19 38	60	165	20 38	60	165
16	16 31	60	163	17 31	60	163	18 31	60	163	19 31	60	163	20 31	60	163
18	16 24	60	161	17 24	59	161	18 23	60	161	19 23	60	161	20 23	60	161
20	16 15	+60	159	17 15	+60	159	18 15	+60	159	19 15	+60	159	20 15	+59	159
22	16 06	60	157	17 06	60	157	18 06	59	157	19 05	60	157	20 05	60	157
24	15 56	60	155	16 56	59	155	17 55	60	155	18 55	60	155	19 55	60	155
26	15 45	60	153	16 45	59	153	17 44	60	153	18 44	60	153	19 44	60	153
28	15 33	60	151	16 33	60	151	17 33	59	151	18 32	60	151	19 32	60	151
30	15 21	+59	149	16 20	+60	149	17 20	+60	149	18 20	+59	149	19 19	+60	148
32	15 07	60	147	16 07	60	147	17 07	59	147	18 06	60	147	19 06	59	146
34	14 53	60	145	15 53	60	145	16 53	59	145	17 52	60	144	18 52	59	144
36	14 39	59	143	15 38	60	143	16 38	59	143	17 37	60	142	18 37	59	142
38	14 23	60	141	15 23	59	141	16 22	60	140	17 22	59	140	18 21	60	140
40	14 07	+60	139	15 07	+59	139	16 06	+59	138	17 05	+60	138	18 05	+59	138
42	13 50	60	137	14 50	59	137	15 49	59	136	16 48	60	136	17 48	59	136
44	13 33	59	135	14 32	60	135	15 32	59	134	16 31	59	134	17 30	59	134
46	13 15	59	133	14 14	59	132	15 13	60	132	16 13	59	132	17 12	59	132
48	12 56	59	131	13 55	60	130	14 55	59	130	15 54	59	130	16 53	59	130
50	12 37	+59	129	13 36	+59	128	14 35	+59	128	15 34	+60	128	16 34	+59	128
52	12 17	59	127	13 16	59	126	14 15	60	126	15 15	59	126	16 14	59	126
54	11 57	59	125	12 56	59	124	13 55	59	124	14 54	59	124	15 53	59	124
56	11 36	59	123	12 35	59	122	13 34	59	122	14 33	59	122	15 32	59	122
58	11 15	59	121	12 14	59	120	13 13	59	120	14 12	59	120	15 11	59	120
60	10 53	+59	119	11 52	+59	118	12 51	+59	118	13 50	+59	118	14 49	+59	118
62	10 31	59	117	11 30	59	116	12 29	59	116	13 28	59	116	14 27	59	116
64	10 08	59	115	11 07	59	114	12 06	59	114	13 05	59	114	14 04	59	114
66	09 46	58	113	10 44	59	112	11 43	59	112	12 42	59	112	13 41	59	112
68	09 22	59	111	10 21	59	110	11 20	59	110	12 19	59	110	13 18	58	110
70	08 59	+59	109	09 58	+58	108	10 56	+59	108	11 55	+59	108	12 54	+59	108
72	08 35	59	107	09 34	59	106	10 33	58	106	11 31	59	106	12 30	59	106
74	08 11	59	105	09 10	59	105	10 09	58	104	11 07	59	104	12 06	59	104
76	07 47	59	103	08 46	58	103	09 44	59	102	10 43	59	102	11 42	58	102
78	07 22	59	101	08 21	59	101	09 20	59	100	10 19	58	100	11 17	59	100
80	06 58	+58	99	07 56	+59	99	08 55	+59	98	09 54	+59	98	10 53	+58	98
82	06 33	59	97	07 32	58	97	08 30	59	96	09 29	59	96	10 28	58	96
84	06 08	59	95	07 07	59	95	08 06	58	94	09 04	59	94	10 03	59	94
86	05 43	59	93	06 42	59	93	07 41	58	93	08 39	59	92	09 38	59	92
88	05 18	59	91	06 17	59	91	07 16	58	91	08 14	59	90	09 13	59	90
90	04 53	+59	89	05 52	+59	89	06 51	+58	89	07 49	+59	88	08 48	+59	88
92	04 28	59	87	05 27	59	87	06 26	59	87	07 25	58	86	08 23	59	86
94	04 04	58	85	05 02	59	85	06 01	59	85	07 00	58	84	07 58	59	84
96	03 39	59	83	04 38	58	83	05 36	59	83	06 35	59	83	07 34	58	82
98	03 14	59	81	04 13	59	81	05 12	58	81	06 10	59	81	07 09	59	80
100	02 50	+58	79	03 48	+59	79	04 47	+59	79	05 46	+58	79	06 44	+59	78
102	02 25	59	77	03 24	59	77	04 23	58	77	05 21	59	77	06 20	59	76
104	02 01	59	75	03 00	58	75	03 58	59	75	04 57	59	75	05 56	59	75
106	01 37	59	73	02 36	58	73	03 34	59	73	04 33	59	73	05 32	59	73
108	01 13	59	71	02 12	59	71	03 11	59	71	04 10	58	71	05 08	59	71
110	00 50	+58	69	01 48	+59	69	02 47	+59	69	03 46	+59	69	04 45	+59	69
112	00 26	59	67	01 25	59	67	02 24	59	67	03 23	59	67	04 22	59	67
114	00 03	59	66	01 02	59	65	02 01	59	65	03 00	59	65	03 59	59	65
116	−0 19	59	64	00 40	59	63	01 39	59	63	02 38	59	63	03 37	59	63
118	−0 41	59	62	00 18	59	61	01 17	59	61	02 16	59	61	03 15	59	61
120	−1 03	+59	60	−0 04	+59	59	00 55	+59	59	01 54	+59	59	02 53	+59	59
122	−1 24	59	58	−0 25	59	58	00 34	59	57	01 33	59	57	02 32	59	57
124	−1 45	59	56	−0 46	59	56	00 13	59	55	01 12	59	55	02 11	59	55
126	−2 06	60	54	−1 06	59	54	−0 07	59	53	00 52	59	53	01 51	59	53
128	−2 25	59	52	−1 26	59	52	−0 27	59	51	00 32	59	51	01 31	60	51
130	−2 45	+60	50	−1 45	+59	50	−0 46	+59	50	00 13	+59	49	01 12	+60	49
132	−3 04	60	48	−2 04	59	48	−1 05	59	48	−0 06	60	47	00 54	59	47
134	−3 22	60	46	−2 22	59	46	−1 23	59	46	−0 24	60	45	00 36	59	45
136	−3 39	59	44	−2 40	60	44	−1 40	59	44	−0 41	59	44	00 18	60	43
138	−3 56	59	42	−2 57	60	42	−1 57	59	42	−0 58	59	42	00 01	60	41

LHA	10° Hc	d	Z	11° Hc	d	Z	12° Hc	d	Z	13° Hc	d	Z	14° Hc	d	Z	LHA
0	22 00	+60	180	23 00	+60	180	24 00	+60	180	25 00	+60	180	26 00	+60	180	360
2	22 00	60	178	23 00	60	178	24 00	60	178	25 00	60	178	26 00	60	178	358
4	21 58	60	176	22 58	60	176	23 58	60	176	24 58	60	176	25 58	60	176	356
6	21 56	60	174	22 56	60	174	23 56	60	174	24 56	60	174	25 56	60	174	354
8	21 53	60	172	22 53	60	172	23 53	60	171	24 53	60	171	25 53	60	171	352
10	21 49	+59	169	22 48	+60	169	23 48	+60	169	24 48	+60	169	25 48	+60	169	350
12	21 43	60	167	22 43	60	167	23 43	60	167	24 43	60	167	25 43	60	167	348
14	21 38	59	165	22 37	60	165	23 37	60	165	24 37	60	165	25 37	60	165	346
16	21 31	60	163	22 31	59	163	23 30	60	163	24 30	60	163	25 30	60	163	344
18	21 23	60	161	22 23	60	161	23 23	60	161	24 23	59	161	25 22	60	161	342
20	21 14	+60	159	22 14	+60	159	23 14	+60	159	24 14	+60	159	25 14	+59	159	340
22	21 05	60	157	22 05	60	157	23 05	59	157	24 04	60	156	25 04	60	156	338
24	20 55	59	155	21 54	60	155	22 54	60	154	23 54	60	154	24 54	59	154	336
26	20 44	59	153	21 43	60	152	22 43	60	152	23 43	59	152	24 42	60	152	334
28	20 32	59	150	21 31	60	150	22 31	60	150	23 31	59	150	24 30	60	150	332
30	20 19	+60	148	21 19	+59	148	22 18	+60	148	23 18	+59	148	24 17	+60	148	330
32	20 05	60	146	21 05	60	146	22 05	59	146	23 04	60	146	24 04	59	146	328
34	19 51	60	144	20 51	59	144	21 50	60	144	22 50	59	144	23 49	60	144	326
36	19 36	60	142	20 36	59	142	21 35	60	142	22 35	59	142	23 34	60	142	324
38	19 21	59	140	20 20	59	140	21 19	60	140	22 19	59	140	23 18	60	139	322
40	19 04	+60	138	20 04	+59	138	21 03	+59	138	22 02	+60	138	23 02	+59	137	320
42	18 47	59	136	19 46	60	136	20 46	59	136	21 45	59	135	22 44	60	135	318
44	18 29	60	134	19 29	59	134	20 28	59	134	21 27	60	133	22 27	59	133	316
46	18 11	59	132	19 10	60	132	20 10	59	131	21 09	59	131	22 08	59	131	314
48	17 52	59	130	18 51	60	130	19 51	59	129	20 50	59	129	21 49	59	129	312
50	17 33	+59	128	18 32	+59	128	19 31	+59	127	20 30	+59	127	21 29	+59	127	310
52	17 13	59	126	18 12	59	126	19 11	59	125	20 10	59	125	21 09	59	125	308
54	16 52	59	124	17 51	59	124	18 50	59	123	19 49	59	123	20 48	59	123	306
56	16 31	59	122	17 30	59	121	18 29	59	121	19 28	59	121	20 27	59	121	304
58	16 10	59	120	17 09	59	119	18 08	59	119	19 07	59	119	20 06	59	119	302
60	15 48	+59	118	16 47	+59	117	17 46	+59	117	18 45	+59	117	19 44	+58	117	300
62	15 26	58	116	16 24	59	115	17 23	59	115	18 22	59	115	19 21	59	115	298
64	15 03	59	114	16 02	59	113	17 01	58	113	17 59	59	113	18 58	59	113	296
66	14 40	59	112	15 39	58	111	16 37	59	111	17 36	59	111	18 35	59	111	294
68	14 16	59	110	15 15	59	109	16 14	59	109	17 13	59	109	18 12	58	109	292
70	13 53	+59	108	14 52	+58	107	15 50	+59	107	16 49	+59	107	17 48	+59	107	290
72	13 29	59	106	14 28	58	105	15 26	59	105	16 25	59	105	17 24	59	105	288
74	13 05	58	104	14 03	59	103	15 02	59	103	16 01	59	103	17 00	58	103	286
76	12 40	59	102	13 39	59	101	14 38	58	101	15 36	59	101	16 35	59	101	284
78	12 16	59	100	13 15	58	100	14 13	59	99	15 12	59	99	16 11	58	99	282
80	11 51	+59	98	12 50	+59	98	13 49	+58	97	14 47	+59	97	15 46	+58	97	280
82	11 26	59	96	12 25	59	96	13 24	58	95	14 22	59	95	15 21	59	95	278
84	11 02	58	94	12 00	59	94	12 59	59	93	13 58	58	93	14 56	59	93	276
86	10 37	58	92	11 35	59	92	12 34	59	91	13 33	58	91	14 31	59	91	274
88	10 12	58	90	11 10	59	90	12 09	59	89	13 08	58	89	14 06	59	89	272
90	09 47	+58	88	10 45	+59	88	11 44	+59	88	12 43	+58	87	13 41	+59	87	270
92	09 22	59	86	10 21	58	86	11 19	59	86	12 18	58	85	13 16	59	85	268
94	08 57	59	84	09 56	58	84	10 54	59	84	11 53	59	83	12 52	58	83	266
96	08 32	59	82	09 31	59	82	10 30	58	82	11 28	59	81	12 27	59	81	264
98	08 08	58	80	09 06	59	80	10 05	59	80	11 04	58	80	12 02	59	79	262
100	07 43	+59	78	08 42	+59	78	09 41	+58	78	10 39	+59	78	11 38	+59	77	260
102	07 19	59	76	08 18	58	76	09 16	59	76	10 15	59	76	11 14	58	75	258
104	06 55	58	74	07 53	59	74	08 52	59	74	09 51	59	74	10 50	58	73	256
106	06 31	59	72	07 30	58	72	08 28	59	72	09 27	59	72	10 26	59	72	254
108	06 07	59	70	07 06	59	70	08 05	59	70	09 04	58	70	10 02	59	70	252
110	05 44	+59	68	06 43	+58	68	07 41	+59	68	08 40	+59	68	09 39	+59	68	250
112	05 21	59	67	06 20	58	66	07 18	59	66	08 17	59	66	09 16	59	66	248
114	04 58	59	65	05 57	59	64	06 56	59	64	07 55	59	64	08 54	58	64	246
116	04 36	59	63	05 35	59	62	06 34	58	62	07 32	59	62	08 31	59	62	244
118	04 14	59	61	05 13	59	61	06 12	59	60	07 11	59	60	08 10	59	60	242
120	03 52	+59	59	04 51	+59	59	05 50	+59	58	06 49	+59	58	07 48	+59	58	240
122	03 31	59	57	04 30	59	57	05 29	59	56	06 28	59	56	07 27	59	56	238
124	03 10	60	55	04 10	59	55	05 09	59	55	06 08	59	54	07 07	59	54	236
126	02 50	59	53	03 49	59	53	04 48	60	53	05 48	59	52	06 47	59	52	234
128	02 31	59	51	03 30	59	51	04 29	59	51	05 28	59	51	06 27	60	50	232
130	02 12	+59	49	03 11	+59	49	04 10	+59	49	05 09	+59	49	06 08	+60	48	230
132	01 53	59	47	02 52	60	47	03 52	59	47	04 51	59	47	05 50	59	47	228
134	01 35	59	45	02 34	60	45	03 34	59	45	04 33	59	45	05 32	60	45	226
136	01 18	59	43	02 17	59	43	03 16	60	43	04 16	59	43	05 15	59	43	224
138	01 01	59	41	02 00	60	41	03 00	59	41	03 59	59	41	04 58	60	41	222

S. Lat. {LHA greater than 180°....... Zn=180−Z; LHA less than 180°........... Zn=180+Z}

DECLINATION (0°-14°) SAME NAME AS LATITUDE

N. Lat. {LHA greater than 180°....... Zn=Z
{LHA less than 180°.......... Zn=360−Z

DECLINATION (0°-14°) SAME NAME AS LATITUDE

LHA	0° Hc	0° d	0° Z	1° Hc	1° d	1° Z	2° Hc	2° d	2° Z	3° Hc	3° d	3° Z	4° Hc	4° d	4° Z	LHA
	° ′	′	°	° ′	′	°	° ′	′	°	° ′	′	°	° ′	′	°	
140							−7 11	+59	40	−6 12	+60	40	−5 12	+59	40	220
142							−7 27	60	38	−6 27	59	38	−5 28	60	38	218
144										−6 42	59	36	−5 43	60	36	216
146										−6 57	60	34	−5 57	59	34	214
148										−7 10	59	32	−6 11	60	32	212
150										−7 23	+59	30	−6 24	+60	30	210
152													−6 36	60	28	208
154													−6 47	59	26	206
156													−6 58	60	24	204
158													−7 08	60	22	202
160													−7 17	+60	20	200
162																198
164																196
166																194
168																192
170																190
172																188
174																186
176																184
178																182
180																180

LHA	5° Hc	5° d	5° Z	6° Hc	6° d	6° Z	7° Hc	7° d	7° Z	8° Hc	8° d	8° Z	9° Hc	9° d	9° Z
	° ′	′	°	° ′	′	°	° ′	′	°	° ′	′	°	° ′	′	°
220	−4 13	+60	40	−3 13	+59	40	−2 14	+60	40	−1 14	+59	40	−0 15	+60	39
218	−4 28	59	38	−3 29	60	38	−2 29	59	38	−1 30	60	38	−0 30	59	37
216	−4 43	59	36	−3 44	60	36	−2 44	59	36	−1 45	60	36	−0 45	59	35
214	−4 58	60	34	−3 58	60	34	−2 58	59	34	−1 59	60	34	−0 59	59	34
212	−5 11	59	32	−4 12	60	32	−3 12	60	32	−2 12	59	32	−1 13	60	32
210	−5 24	+60	30	−4 24	+59	30	−3 25	+60	30	−2 25	+60	30	−1 25	+59	30
208	−5 36	60	28	−4 36	59	28	−3 37	60	28	−2 37	60	28	−1 37	59	28
206	−5 48	60	26	−4 48	60	26	−3 48	60	26	−2 48	59	26	−1 49	60	26
204	−5 58	60	24	−4 58	60	24	−3 58	59	24	−2 59	60	24	−1 59	60	24
202	−6 08	60	22	−5 08	60	22	−4 08	60	22	−3 08	60	22	−2 08	59	22
200	−6 17	+60	20	−5 17	+60	20	−4 17	+60	20	−3 17	+60	20	−2 17	+59	20
198	−6 25	60	18	−5 25	60	18	−4 25	60	18	−3 25	60	18	−2 25	59	18
196	−6 32	60	16	−5 32	60	16	−4 32	59	16	−3 33	60	16	−2 33	60	16
194	−6 39	60	14	−5 39	60	14	−4 39	60	14	−3 39	60	14	−2 39	60	14
192	−6 44	60	12	−5 44	60	12	−4 44	59	12	−3 45	61	12	−2 44	59	12
190	−6 49	+60	10	−5 49	+60	10	−4 49	+60	10	−3 49	+60	10	−2 49	+60	10
188	−6 53	60	8	−5 53	60	8	−4 53	60	8	−3 53	60	8	−2 53	60	8
186	−6 56	60	6	−5 56	60	6	−4 56	60	6	−3 56	60	6	−2 56	60	6
184	−6 58	60	4	−5 58	60	4	−4 58	60	4	−3 58	60	4	−2 58	60	4
182	−7 00	60	2	−6 00	60	2	−5 00	60	2	−4 00	60	2	−3 00	60	2
180	−7 00	+60	0	−6 00	+60	0	−5 00	+60	0	−4 00	+60	0	−3 00	+60	0

10° Hc	10° d	10° Z	11° Hc	11° d	11° Z	12° Hc	12° d	12° Z	13° Hc	13° d	13° Z	14° Hc	14° d	14° Z	LHA
° ′	′	°	° ′	′	°	° ′	′	°	° ′	′	°	° ′	′	°	
00 45	+59	39	01 44	+60	39	02 44	+59	39	03 43	+60	39	04 43	+59	39	220
00 29	60	37	01 29	59	37	02 28	60	37	03 28	59	37	04 27	60	37	218
00 14	60	35	01 14	60	35	02 14	59	35	03 13	60	35	04 13	59	35	216
00 00	60	33	01 00	60	33	02 00	59	33	02 59	60	33	03 59	59	33	214
−0 13	60	31	00 47	59	31	01 46	60	31	02 46	60	31	03 46	59	31	212
−0 26	+60	30	00 34	+60	29	01 34	+59	29	02 33	+60	29	03 33	+60	29	210
−0 38	60	28	00 22	60	27	01 22	60	27	02 22	59	27	03 21	60	27	208
−0 49	60	26	00 11	60	25	01 11	59	25	02 10	60	25	03 10	60	25	206
−0 59	60	24	00 01	59	24	01 00	60	23	02 00	60	23	03 00	60	23	204
−1 09	60	22	−0 09	60	22	00 51	60	22	01 51	60	21	02 51	59	21	202
−1 18	+60	20	−0 18	+60	20	00 42	+60	20	01 42	+60	20	02 42	+60	19	200
−1 26	60	18	−0 26	60	18	00 34	60	18	01 34	60	18	02 34	60	18	198
−1 33	60	16	−0 33	60	16	00 27	60	16	01 27	60	16	02 27	60	16	196
−1 39	60	14	−0 39	60	14	00 21	60	14	01 21	60	14	02 21	59	14	194
−1 45	60	12	−0 45	60	12	00 15	60	12	01 15	60	12	02 15	60	12	192
−1 49	+60	10	−0 49	+60	10	00 11	+60	10	01 11	+60	10	02 11	+59	10	190
−1 53	60	8	−0 53	60	8	00 07	60	8	01 07	60	8	02 07	60	8	188
−1 56	60	6	−0 56	60	6	00 04	60	6	01 04	60	6	02 04	60	6	186
−1 58	60	4	−0 58	60	4	00 02	60	4	01 02	60	4	02 02	60	4	184
−2 00	60	2	−1 00	60	2	00 00	60	2	01 00	60	2	02 00	60	2	182
−2 00	+60	0	−1 00	+60	0	00 00	+60	0	01 00	+60	0	02 00	+60	0	180

LAT 78°

0° 1° 2° 3° 4° 5° 6° 7° 8° 9° 10° 11° 12° 13° 14°

S. Lat. {LHA greater than 180°....... Zn=180−Z
{LHA less than 180°.......... Zn=180+Z

DECLINATION (0°-14°) SAME NAME AS LATITUDE

LAT 78°

N. Lat. {LHA greater than 180°....... Zn=Z
{LHA less than 180°.......... Zn=360−Z

DECLINATION (0°-14°) CONTRARY NAME TO LATITUDE

LHA	0°			1°			2°			3°			4°			5°			6°			7°			8°			9°			10°			11°			12°			13°			14°			LHA
	Hc	d	Z	Hc	d	Z	Hc	d	Z	Hc	d	Z	Hc	d	Z	Hc	d	Z	Hc	d	Z	Hc	d	Z	Hc	d	Z	Hc	d	Z	Hc	d	Z	Hc	d	Z	Hc	d	Z	Hc	d	Z	Hc	d	Z	
	° ′	′	°	° ′	′	°	° ′	′	°	° ′	′	°	° ′	′	°	° ′	′	°	° ′	′	°	° ′	′	°	° ′	′	°	° ′	′	°	° ′	′	°	° ′	′	°	° ′	′	°	° ′	′	°	° ′	′	°	
128	-7 21	59	53	232																																									
126	-7 01	59	55	234																																									
124	-6 41	59	57	-7 40	59	57	236																																						
122	-6 20	59	59	-7 19	59	59	238																																						
120	-5 58	-59	60	-6 57	-59	61	240																																						
118	-5 36	59	62	-6 35	59	63	-7 34	59	63	242																																			
116	-5 14	59	64	-6 13	59	65	-7 12	59	65	244																																			
114	-4 51	59	66	-5 50	59	67	-6 49	59	67	246																																			
112	-4 28	59	68	-5 27	59	69	-6 26	59	69	-7 25	59	69	248																																
110	-4 05	-59	70	-5 04	-58	71	-6 02	-59	71	-7 01	-59	71	250																																
108	-3 41	59	72	-4 40	59	73	-5 39	58	73	-6 37	59	73	-7 36	59	73	252																													
106	-3 17	59	74	-4 16	59	74	-5 15	59	75	-6 14	58	75	-7 12	59	75	254																													
104	-2 53	59	76	-3 52	58	76	-4 50	59	77	-5 49	59	77	-6 48	59	77	-7 47	59	77	256																										
102	-2 29	58	78	-3 27	59	78	-4 26	59	79	-5 25	59	79	-6 24	58	79	-7 22	59	79	258																										
100	-2 04	-59	80	-3 03	-59	80	-4 02	-58	81	-5 00	-59	81	-5 59	-59	81	-6 58	-58	81	260																										
98	-1 40	58	82	-2 38	59	82	-3 37	59	83	-4 36	58	83	-5 34	59	83	-6 33	59	83	-7 32	58	83	262																							
96	-1 15	58	84	-2 13	59	84	-3 12	59	85	-4 11	59	85	-5 10	58	85	-6 08	59	85	-7 07	59	85	264																							
94	-0 50	59	86	-1 49	58	86	-2 47	59	86	-3 46	59	87	-4 45	58	87	-5 43	59	87	-6 42	59	87	-7 41	58	87	266																				
92	-0 25	59	88	-1 24	58	88	-2 22	59	88	-3 21	59	89	-4 20	58	89	-5 18	59	89	-6 17	59	89	-7 16	58	89	268																				
90	00 00	-59	90	-0 59	-58	90	-1 57	-59	90	-2 56	-59	91	-3 55	-58	91	-4 53	-59	91	-5 52	-59	91	-6 51	-58	91	270																				
88	00 25	59	92	-0 34	58	92	-1 32	59	92	-2 31	59	93	-3 30	58	93	-4 28	59	93	-5 27	59	93	-6 26	59	93	-7 25	58	94	272																	
86	00 50	59	94	-0 09	59	94	-1 08	58	94	-2 06	59	94	-3 05	59	95	-4 04	58	95	-5 02	59	95	-6 01	59	95	-7 00	58	96	274																	
84	01 15	59	96	00 16	59	96	-0 43	58	96	-1 41	59	96	-2 40	59	97	-3 39	59	97	-4 38	58	97	-5 36	59	97	-6 35	59	97	-7 34	58	98	276														
82	01 40	59	98	00 41	59	98	-0 18	59	98	-1 17	58	98	-2 15	59	99	-3 14	59	99	-4 13	59	99	-5 12	58	99	-6 10	59	99	-7 09	59	100	278														
80	02 04	-59	100	01 05	-58	100	00 07	-59	100	-0 52	-59	100	-1 51	-59	101	-2 50	-58	101	-3 48	-59	101	-4 47	-59	101	-5 46	-58	101	-6 44	-59	102	-7 43	-59	102	280											
78	02 29	59	102	01 30	59	102	00 31	59	102	-0 28	58	102	-1 26	59	103	-2 25	59	103	-3 24	59	103	-4 23	58	103	-5 21	59	103	-6 20	59	104	-7 19	59	104	282											
76	02 53	59	104	01 54	59	104	00 55	58	104	-0 03	59	104	-1 02	59	104	-2 01	59	105	-3 00	58	105	-3 58	59	105	-4 57	59	105	-5 56	59	105	-6 55	58	106	284											
74	03 17	59	106	02 18	58	106	01 20	59	106	00 21	59	106	-0 38	59	106	-1 37	59	107	-2 36	58	107	-3 34	59	107	-4 33	59	107	-5 32	59	107	-6 31	59	108	-7 30	58	108	286								
72	03 41	59	108	02 42	59	108	01 43	58	108	00 45	59	108	-0 14	59	108	-1 13	59	109	-2 12	59	109	-3 11	59	109	-4 10	58	109	-5 08	59	109	-6 07	59	110	-7 06	59	110	288								
70	04 05	-59	110	03 06	-59	110	02 07	-59	110	01 08	-59	110	00 09	-59	110	-0 50	-58	111	-1 48	-59	111	-2 47	-59	111	-3 46	-59	111	-4 45	-59	112	-5 44	-59	112	-6 43	-58	112	-7 41	-59	112	290					
68	04 28	59	112	03 29	59	112	02 30	59	112	01 31	58	112	00 33	59	112	-0 26	59	113	-1 25	59	113	-2 24	59	113	-3 23	59	113	-4 22	59	113	-5 21	59	113	-6 20	58	114	-7 18	59	114	292					
66	04 51	59	114	03 52	59	114	02 53	59	114	01 54	59	114	00 55	58	114	-0 03	59	114	-1 02	59	115	-2 01	59	115	-3 00	59	115	-3 59	59	115	-4 58	59	115	-5 57	59	116	-6 56	59	116	294					
64	05 14	59	116	04 15	59	116	03 16	59	116	02 17	59	116	01 18	59	116	00 19	59	116	-0 40	59	117	-1 39	59	117	-2 38	59	117	-3 37	59	117	-4 36	59	117	-5 35	59	118	-6 34	58	118	-7 32	59	118	296			
62	05 36	59	118	04 37	59	118	03 38	59	118	02 39	59	118	01 40	59	118	00 41	59	118	-0 18	59	119	-1 17	59	119	-2 16	59	119	-3 15	59	119	-4 14	59	119	-5 13	59	119	-6 12	59	120	-7 11	59	120	298			
60	05 58	-59	120	04 59	-59	120	04 00	-59	120	03 01	-59	120	02 02	-59	120	01 03	-59	120	00 04	-59	121	-0 55	-59	121	-1 54	-59	121	-2 53	-59	121	-3 52	-59	121	-4 51	-59	121	-5 50	-59	122	-6 49	-59	122	300			
58	06 20	59	121	05 21	60	122	04 21	59	122	03 22	59	122	02 23	59	122	01 24	59	122	00 25	59	122	-0 34	59	123	-1 33	59	123	-2 32	59	123	-3 31	59	123	-4 30	59	123	-5 29	59	124	-6 28	59	124	-7 27	59	124	302
56	06 41	59	123	05 42	60	124	04 42	59	124	03 43	59	124	02 44	59	124	01 45	59	124	00 46	59	124	-0 13	59	125	-1 12	59	125	-2 11	59	125	-3 10	60	125	-4 10	59	125	-5 09	59	125	-6 08	59	126	-7 07	59	126	304
54	07 01	59	125	06 02	59	126	05 03	59	126	04 04	59	126	03 05	59	126	02 06	60	126	01 06	59	126	00 07	59	127	-0 52	59	127	-1 51	59	127	-2 50	59	127	-3 49	59	127	-4 48	60	127	-5 48	59	128	-6 47	59	128	306
52	07 21	59	127	06 22	59	128	05 23	59	128	04 24	60	128	03 24	59	128	02 25	59	128	01 26	59	128	00 27	59	129	-0 32	59	129	-1 31	60	129	-2 31	59	129	-3 30	59	129	-4 29	59	129	-5 28	59	129	-6 27	60	130	308
50	07 41	-59	129	06 42	-60	130	05 42	-59	130	04 43	-59	130	03 44	-59	130	02 45	-60	130	01 45	-59	130	00 46	-59	130	-0 13	-59	131	-1 12	-60	131	-2 12	-59	131	-3 11	-59	131	-4 10	-59	131	-5 09	-59	131	-6 08	-60	132	310
48	08 00	59	131	07 01	60	132	06 01	59	132	05 02	59	132	04 03	59	132	03 04	60	132	02 04	59	132	01 05	59	132	00 06	60	133	-0 54	59	133	-1 53	59	133	-2 52	60	133	-3 52	59	133	-4 51	59	133	-5 50	59	133	312
46	08 18	59	133	07 19	59	134	06 20	60	134	05 20	59	134	04 21	59	134	03 22	60	134	02 22	59	134	01 23	59	134	00 24	60	135	-0 36	59	135	-1 35	59	135	-2 34	60	135	-3 34	59	135	-4 33	59	135	-5 32	60	135	314
44	08 36	59	135	07 37	60	136	06 37	59	136	05 38	59	136	04 39	60	136	03 39	59	136	02 40	60	136	01 40	59	136	00 41	59	136	-0 18	60	137	-1 18	59	137	-2 17	59	137	-3 16	60	137	-4 16	59	137	-5 15	59	137	316
42	08 53	59	137	07 54	59	138	06 55	60	138	05 55	59	138	04 56	60	138	03 56	59	138	02 57	60	138	01 57	59	138	00 58	59	138	-0 01	60	139	-1 01	59	139	-2 00	60	139	-3 00	59	139	-3 59	59	139	-4 58	60	139	318
40	09 10	-60	139	08 10	-59	140	07 11	-59	140	06 12	-60	140	05 12	-59	140	04 13	-60	140	03 13	-59	140	02 14	-60	140	01 14	-59	140	00 15	-60	141	-0 45	-59	141	-1 44	-60	141	-2 44	-59	141	-3 43	-60	141	-4 43	-59	141	320
38	09 26	60	141	08 26	59	142	07 27	60	142	06 27	59	142	05 28	60	142	04 28	59	142	03 29	60	142	02 29	59	142	01 30	60	142	00 30	59	143	-0 29	60	143	-1 29	59	143	-2 28	60	143	-3 28	59	143	-4 27	60	143	322
36	09 41	59	143	08 42	60	144	07 42	60	144	06 42	59	144	05 43	60	144	04 43	59	144	03 44	60	144	02 44	59	144	01 45	60	144	00 45	59	145	-0 14	60	145	-1 14	60	145	-2 14	59	145	-3 13	60	145	-4 13	59	145	324
34	09 56	60	145	08 56	60	146	07 56	59	146	06 57	60	146	05 57	59	146	04 58	60	146	03 58	60	146	02 58	59	146	01 59	60	146	00 59	59	146	00 00	60	147	-1 00	60	147	-2 00	59	147	-2 59	60	147	-3 59	59	147	326
32	10 09	59	147	09 10	60	148	08 10	60	148	07 10	59	148	06 11	60	148	05 11	59	148	04 12	60	148	03 12	60	148	02 12	59	148	01 13	60	148	00 13	60	149	-0 47	59	149	-1 46	60	149	-2 46	60	149	-3 46	59	149	328
30	10 22	-59	149	09 23	-60	150	08 23	-60	150	07 23	-59	150	06 24	-60	150	05 24	-60	150	04 24	-59	150	03 25	-60	150	02 25	-60	150	01 25	-59	150	00 26	-60	150	-0 34	-60	151	-1 34	-59	151	-2 33	-60	151	-3 33	-60	151	330
28	10 35	60	152	09 35	60	152	08 35	59	152	07 36	60	152	06 36	60	152	05 36	60	152	04 36	59	152	03 37	60	152	02 37	60	152	01 37	59	152	00 38	60	152	-0 22	60	153	-1 22	60	153	-2 22	59	153	-3 21	60	153	332
26	10 46	59	154	09 47	60	154	08 47	60	154	07 47	60	154	06 47	59	154	05 48	60	154	04 48	60	154	03 48	60	154	02 48	59	154	01 49	60	154	00 49	60	154	-0 11	60	155	-1 11	59	155	-2 10	60	155	-3 10	60	155	334
24	10 57	60	156	09 57	60	156	08 57	59	156	07 58	60	156	06 58	60	156	05 58	60	156	04 58	60	156	03 58	59	156	02 59	60	156	01 59	60	156	00 59	60	156	-0 01	59	156	-1 00	60	157	-2 00	60	157	-3 00	60	157	336
22	11 07	60	158	10 07	60	158	09 07	60	158	08 07	59	158	07 08	60	158	06 08	60	158	05 08	60	158	04 08	60	158	03 08	60	158	02 08	59	158	01 09	60	158	00 09	60	158	-0 51	60	158	-1 51	60	159	-2 51	59	159	338
20	11 16	-60	160	10 16	-60	160	09 16	-59	160	08 17	-60	160	07 17	-60	160	06 17	-60	160	05 17	-60	160	04 17	-60	160	03 17	-60	160	02 17	-59	160	01 18	-60	160	00 18	-60	160	-0 42	-60	160	-1 42	-60	160	-2 42	-60	161	340
18	11 24	60	162	10 24	59	162	09 25	60	162	08 25	60	162	07 25	60	162	06 25	60	162	05 25	60	162	04 25	60	162	03 25	60	162	02 25	59	162	01 26	60	162	00 26	60	162	-0 34	60	162	-1 34	60	162	-2 34	60	162	342
16	11 32	60	164	10 32	60	164	09 32	60	164	08 32	60	164	07 32	60	164	06 32	60	164	05 32	60	164	04 32	59	164	03 33	60	164	02 33	60	164	01 33	60	164	00 33	60	164	-0 27	60	164	-1 27	60	164	-2 27	60	164	344
14	11 38	60	166	10 38	59	166	09 39	60	166	08 39	60	166	07 39	60	166	06 39	60	166	05 39	60	166	04 39	60	166	03 39	60	166	02 39	60	166	01 39	60	166	00 39	60	166	-0 21	60	166	-1 21	60	166	-2 21	59	166	346
12	11 44	60	168	10 44	60	168	09 44	60	168	08 44	60	168	07 44	60	168	06 44	60	168	05 44	60	168	04 44	59	168	03 45	61	168	02 44	59	168	01 45	60	168	00 45	60	168	-0 15	60	168	-1 15	60	168	-2 15	60	168	348
10	11 49	-60	170	10 49	-60	170	09 49	-60	170	08 49	-60	170	07 49	-60	170	06 49	-60	170	05 49	-60	170	04 49	-60	170	03 49	-60	170	02 49	-60	170	01 49	-60	170	00 49	-60	170	-0 11	-60	170	-1 11	-60	170	-2 11	-59	170	350
8	11 53	60	172	10 53	60	172	09 53	60	172	08 53	60	172	07 53	60	172	06 53	60	172	05 53	60	172	04 53	60	172	03 53	60	172	02 53	60	172	01 53	60	172	00 53	60	172	-0 07	60	172	-1 07	60	172	-2 07	60	172	352
6	11 56	60	174	10 56	60	174	09 56	60	174	08 56	60	174	07 56	60	174	06 56	60	174	05 56	60	174	04 56	60	174	03 56	60	174	02 56	60	174	01 56	60	174	00 56	60	174	-0 04	60	174	-1 04	60	174	-2 04	60	174	354
4	11 58	60	176	10 58	60	176	09 58	60	176	08 58	60	176	07 58	60	176	06 58	60	176	05 58	60	176	04 58	60	176	03 58	60	176	02 58	60	176	01 58	60	176	00 58	60	176	-0 02	60	176	-1 02	60	176	-2 02	60	176	356
2	12 00	60	178	11 00	60	178	10 00	60	178	09 00	60	178	08 00	60	178	07 00	60	178	06 00	60	178	05 00	60	178	04 00	60	178	03 00	60	178	02 00	60	178	01 00	60	178	00 00	60	178	-1 00	60	178	-2 00	60	178	358
0	12 00	-60	180	11 00	-60	180	10 00	-60	180	09 00	-60	180	08 00	-60	180	07 00	-60	180	06 00	-60	180	05 00	-60	180	04 00	-60	180	03 00	-60	180	02 00	-60	180	01 00	-60	180	00 00	-60	180	-1 00	-60	180	-2 00	-60	180	360
	0°			1°			2°			3°			4°			5°			6°			7°			8°			9°			10°			11°			12°			13°			14°			

S. Lat. {LHA greater than 180°....... Zn=180−Z
{LHA less than 180°.......... Zn=180+Z

DECLINATION (0°-14°) CONTRARY NAME TO LATITUDE

LHA	15° Hc	d	Z	16° Hc	d	Z	17° Hc	d	Z	18° Hc	d	Z	19° Hc	d	Z	LHA
	° ′	′	°	° ′	′	°	° ′	′	°	° ′	′	°	° ′	′	°	
0	27 00	+60	180	28 00	+60	180	29 00	+60	180	30 00	+60	180	31 00	+60	180	360
2	27 00	60	178	28 00	60	178	29 00	60	178	30 00	60	178	31 00	60	178	358
4	26 58	60	176	27 58	60	176	28 58	60	176	29 58	60	176	30 58	60	176	356
6	26 56	60	174	27 56	60	174	28 56	60	173	29 56	60	173	30 56	60	173	354
8	26 53	59	171	27 52	60	171	28 52	60	171	29 52	60	171	30 52	60	171	352
10	26 48	+60	169	27 48	+60	169	28 48	+60	169	29 48	+60	169	30 48	+60	169	350
12	26 43	60	167	27 43	60	167	28 43	60	167	29 43	60	167	30 43	60	167	348
14	26 37	60	165	27 37	60	165	28 37	60	165	29 37	60	165	30 37	60	165	346
16	26 30	60	163	27 30	60	163	28 30	60	163	29 30	60	163	30 30	59	162	344
18	26 22	60	161	27 22	60	161	28 22	60	160	29 22	60	160	30 22	59	160	342
20	26 13	+60	158	27 13	+60	158	28 13	+60	158	29 13	+60	158	30 13	+59	158	340
22	26 04	60	156	27 04	59	156	28 03	60	156	29 03	60	156	30 03	60	156	338
24	25 53	60	154	26 53	60	154	27 53	60	154	28 53	59	154	29 52	60	154	336
26	25 42	60	152	26 42	59	152	27 41	60	152	28 41	60	152	29 41	59	152	334
28	25 30	60	150	26 30	59	150	27 29	60	150	28 29	59	150	29 28	60	149	332
30	25 17	+60	148	26 17	+59	148	27 16	+60	148	28 16	+59	147	29 15	+60	147	330
32	25 03	60	146	26 03	59	146	27 02	60	145	28 02	59	145	29 01	60	145	328
34	24 49	59	144	25 48	60	143	26 48	59	143	27 47	60	143	28 47	59	143	326
36	24 34	59	141	25 33	60	141	26 33	59	141	27 32	59	141	28 31	60	141	324
38	24 18	59	139	25 17	59	139	26 16	60	139	27 16	59	139	28 15	60	139	322
40	24 01	+59	137	25 00	+60	137	26 00	+59	137	26 59	+59	137	27 58	+60	137	320
42	23 44	59	135	24 43	59	135	25 42	60	135	26 42	59	135	27 41	59	134	318
44	23 26	59	133	24 25	59	133	25 24	60	133	26 24	59	133	27 23	59	132	316
46	23 07	59	131	24 06	60	131	25 06	59	131	26 05	59	130	27 04	59	130	314
48	22 48	59	129	23 47	59	129	24 46	60	129	25 46	59	128	26 45	59	128	312
50	22 28	+60	127	23 28	+59	127	24 27	+59	126	25 26	+59	126	26 25	+59	126	310
52	22 08	59	125	23 07	59	125	24 06	59	124	25 05	59	124	26 04	59	124	308
54	21 47	59	123	22 46	59	123	23 45	59	122	24 44	59	122	25 43	59	122	306
56	21 26	59	121	22 25	59	121	23 24	59	120	24 23	59	120	25 22	59	120	304
58	21 05	58	119	22 03	59	118	23 02	59	118	24 01	59	118	25 00	59	118	302
60	20 42	+59	117	21 41	+59	116	22 40	+59	116	23 39	+59	116	24 38	+59	116	300
62	20 20	59	115	21 19	59	114	22 18	58	114	23 16	59	114	24 15	59	114	298
64	19 57	59	113	20 56	59	112	21 55	58	112	22 53	59	112	23 52	59	112	296
66	19 34	59	111	20 33	58	110	21 31	59	110	22 30	59	110	23 29	58	110	294
68	19 10	59	109	20 09	59	108	21 08	58	108	22 06	59	108	23 05	59	108	292
70	18 47	+58	107	19 45	+59	106	20 44	+59	106	21 43	+58	106	22 41	+59	106	290
72	18 23	58	105	19 21	59	104	20 20	58	104	21 18	59	104	22 17	59	104	288
74	17 58	59	103	18 57	59	102	19 56	58	102	20 54	59	102	21 53	58	102	286
76	17 34	58	101	18 32	59	100	19 31	59	100	20 30	58	100	21 28	59	100	284
78	17 09	59	99	18 08	58	98	19 06	59	98	20 05	59	98	21 04	58	98	282
80	16 44	+59	97	17 43	+59	96	18 42	+58	96	19 40	+59	96	20 39	+58	96	280
82	16 20	58	95	17 18	59	94	18 17	58	94	19 15	59	94	20 14	58	94	278
84	15 55	58	93	16 53	59	93	17 52	58	92	18 50	59	92	19 49	59	92	276
86	15 30	58	91	16 28	59	91	17 27	59	90	18 26	58	90	19 24	59	90	274
88	15 05	58	89	16 03	59	89	17 02	59	88	18 01	58	88	18 59	59	88	272
90	14 40	+59	87	15 39	+58	87	16 37	+59	86	17 36	+58	86	18 34	+59	86	270
92	14 15	59	85	15 14	58	85	16 12	59	84	17 11	58	84	18 09	59	84	268
94	13 50	58	83	14 49	58	83	15 47	59	83	16 46	59	82	17 45	58	82	266
96	13 26	58	81	14 24	59	81	15 23	58	81	16 21	59	80	17 20	59	80	264
98	13 01	59	79	14 00	58	79	14 58	59	79	15 57	58	78	16 55	59	78	262
100	12 37	+58	77	13 35	+59	77	14 34	+59	77	15 33	+58	76	16 31	+59	76	260
102	12 12	59	75	13 11	59	75	14 10	58	75	15 08	59	75	16 07	59	74	258
104	11 48	59	73	12 47	59	73	13 46	58	73	14 44	59	73	15 43	59	72	256
106	11 25	58	71	12 23	59	71	13 22	59	71	14 21	58	71	15 19	59	71	254
108	11 01	59	69	12 00	59	69	12 59	59	69	13 57	59	69	14 56	59	69	252
110	10 38	+59	67	11 37	+58	67	12 35	+59	67	13 34	+59	67	14 33	+59	67	250
112	10 15	59	66	11 14	59	65	12 13	58	65	13 11	59	65	14 10	59	65	248
114	09 52	59	64	10 51	59	63	11 50	59	63	12 49	59	63	13 48	59	63	246
116	09 30	59	62	10 29	59	62	11 28	59	61	12 27	59	61	13 26	59	61	244
118	09 09	59	60	10 08	58	60	11 06	59	59	12 05	59	59	13 04	59	59	242
120	08 47	+59	58	09 46	+59	58	10 45	+59	58	11 44	+59	57	12 43	+59	57	240
122	08 26	59	56	09 25	59	56	10 24	59	56	11 23	59	55	12 22	59	55	238
124	08 06	59	54	09 05	59	54	10 04	59	54	11 03	59	54	12 02	59	53	236
126	07 46	59	52	08 45	59	52	09 44	59	52	10 43	59	52	11 42	60	51	234
128	07 27	59	50	08 26	59	50	09 25	59	50	10 24	59	50	11 23	59	50	232
130	07 08	+59	48	08 07	+59	48	09 06	+59	48	10 05	+60	48	11 05	+59	48	230
132	06 49	60	46	07 49	59	46	08 48	59	46	09 47	59	46	10 46	60	46	228
134	06 32	59	44	07 31	59	44	08 30	60	44	09 30	59	44	10 29	59	44	226
136	06 14	60	43	07 14	59	42	08 13	60	42	09 13	59	42	10 12	59	42	224
138	05 58	59	41	06 57	60	40	07 57	59	40	08 56	60	40	09 56	59	40	222

LHA	20° Hc	d	Z	21° Hc	d	Z	22° Hc	d	Z	23° Hc	d	Z	24° Hc	d	Z	LHA
	° ′	′	°	° ′	′	°	° ′	′	°	° ′	′	°	° ′	′	°	
0	32 00	+60	180	33 00	+60	180	34 00	+60	180	35 00	+60	180	36 00	+60	180	360
2	32 00	60	178	33 00	60	178	34 00	60	178	35 00	60	178	36 00	60	178	358
4	31 58	60	176	32 58	60	176	33 58	60	176	34 58	60	176	35 58	60	176	356
6	31 56	60	173	32 56	60	173	33 56	60	173	34 56	60	173	35 56	60	173	354
8	31 52	60	171	32 52	60	171	33 52	60	171	34 52	60	171	35 52	60	171	352
10	31 48	+60	169	32 48	+60	169	33 48	+60	169	34 48	+60	169	35 48	+60	169	350
12	31 43	60	167	32 43	60	167	33 43	60	167	34 43	59	167	35 42	60	167	348
14	31 37	59	165	32 36	60	164	33 36	60	164	34 36	60	164	35 36	60	164	346
16	31 29	60	162	32 29	60	162	33 29	60	162	34 29	60	162	35 29	60	162	344
18	31 21	60	160	32 21	60	160	33 21	60	160	34 21	60	160	35 21	60	160	342
20	31 12	+60	158	32 12	+60	158	33 12	+60	158	34 12	+60	158	35 12	+59	158	340
22	31 03	59	156	32 02	60	156	33 02	60	156	34 02	60	155	35 02	59	155	338
24	30 52	60	154	31 52	59	153	32 51	60	153	33 51	60	153	34 51	59	153	336
26	30 40	60	151	31 40	60	151	32 40	59	151	33 39	60	151	34 39	60	151	334
28	30 28	60	149	31 28	59	149	32 27	60	149	33 27	59	149	34 26	60	149	332
30	30 15	+59	147	31 14	+60	147	32 14	+60	147	33 14	+59	147	34 13	+60	147	330
32	30 01	59	145	31 00	60	145	32 00	59	145	32 59	60	144	33 59	59	144	328
34	29 46	60	143	30 46	59	143	31 45	60	142	32 45	59	142	33 44	59	142	326
36	29 31	59	141	30 30	60	140	31 30	59	140	32 29	59	140	33 28	60	140	324
38	29 15	59	139	30 14	59	138	31 13	60	138	32 13	59	138	33 12	59	138	322
40	28 58	+59	136	29 57	+59	136	30 56	+60	136	31 56	+59	136	32 55	+59	136	320
42	28 40	59	134	29 39	60	134	30 39	59	134	31 38	59	134	32 37	59	134	318
44	28 22	59	132	29 21	59	132	30 20	59	132	31 19	60	132	32 19	59	131	316
46	28 03	59	130	29 02	59	130	30 01	59	130	31 00	60	129	32 00	59	129	314
48	27 44	59	128	28 43	59	128	29 42	59	128	30 41	59	127	31 40	59	127	312
50	27 24	+59	126	28 23	+59	126	29 22	+59	125	30 21	+59	125	31 20	+59	125	310
52	27 03	59	124	28 02	59	124	29 01	59	123	30 00	59	123	30 59	59	123	308
54	26 42	59	122	27 41	59	122	28 40	59	121	29 39	59	121	30 38	59	121	306
56	26 21	59	120	27 20	59	119	28 19	58	119	29 17	59	119	30 16	59	119	304
58	25 59	59	118	26 58	59	117	27 57	58	117	28 55	59	117	29 54	59	117	302
60	25 37	+58	116	26 35	+59	115	27 34	+59	115	28 33	+59	115	29 32	+58	115	300
62	25 14	59	114	26 13	58	113	27 11	59	113	28 10	59	113	29 09	58	113	298
64	24 51	59	111	25 50	58	111	26 48	59	111	27 47	59	111	28 46	58	111	296
66	24 27	59	109	25 26	59	109	26 25	58	109	27 23	59	109	28 22	59	109	294
68	24 04	58	107	25 02	59	107	26 01	59	107	27 00	58	107	27 58	59	107	292
70	23 40	+58	105	24 38	+59	105	25 37	+59	105	26 36	+58	105	27 34	+59	104	290
72	23 16	58	103	24 14	59	103	25 13	58	103	26 11	59	103	27 10	58	102	288
74	22 51	59	101	23 50	58	101	24 48	59	101	25 47	58	101	26 45	59	100	286
76	22 27	58	99	23 25	59	99	24 24	58	99	25 22	59	99	26 21	58	98	284
78	22 02	59	97	23 01	58	97	23 59	59	97	24 58	59	97	25 56	59	97	282
80	21 37	+59	96	22 36	+58	95	23 34	+59	95	24 33	+58	95	25 31	+59	95	280
82	21 12	59	94	22 11	58	93	23 09	59	93	24 08	58	93	25 06	59	93	278
84	20 48	58	92	21 46	59	91	22 45	58	91	23 43	58	91	24 41	59	91	276
86	20 23	58	90	21 21	59	89	22 20	58	89	23 18	58	89	24 16	59	89	274
88	19 58	58	88	20 56	59	87	21 55	58	87	22 53	59	87	23 52	58	87	272
90	19 33	+58	86	20 31	+59	85	21 30	+58	85	22 28	+59	85	23 27	+58	85	270
92	19 08	58	84	20 06	59	84	21 05	58	83	22 03	59	83	23 02	58	83	268
94	18 43	59	82	19 42	58	82	20 40	59	81	21 39	58	81	22 37	59	81	266
96	18 19	58	80	19 17	59	80	20 16	58	79	21 14	59	79	22 13	58	79	264
98	17 54	59	78	18 53	58	78	19 51	59	78	20 50	58	77	21 48	59	77	262
100	17 30	+58	76	18 28	+59	76	19 27	+58	76	20 25	+59	75	21 24	+59	75	260
102	17 06	58	74	18 04	59	74	19 03	58	74	20 01	59	73	21 00	59	73	258
104	16 42	58	72	17 40	59	72	18 39	59	72	19 38	58	72	20 36	59	71	256
106	16 18	59	70	17 17	58	70	18 15	59	70	19 14	59	70	20 13	58	69	254
108	15 55	59	68	16 54	58	68	17 52	59	68	18 51	59	68	19 50	58	68	252
110	15 32	+59	66	16 31	+58	66	17 29	+59	66	18 28	+59	66	19 27	+58	66	250
112	15 09	59	65	16 08	59	64	17 07	58	64	18 05	59	64	19 04	59	64	248
114	14 47	59	63	15 46	58	62	16 44	59	62	17 43	59	62	18 42	59	62	246
116	14 25	59	61	15 24	59	61	16 23	58	60	17 21	59	60	18 20	59	60	244
118	14 03	59	59	15 02	59	59	16 01	59	58	17 00	59	58	17 59	59	58	242
120	13 42	+59	57	14 41	+59	57	15 40	+59	57	16 39	+59	56	17 38	+59	56	240
122	13 21	59	55	14 20	59	55	15 19	59	55	16 18	59	54	17 17	59	54	238
124	13 01	59	53	14 00	59	53	14 59	59	53	15 58	59	53	16 57	59	52	236
126	12 42	59	51	13 41	59	51	14 40	59	51	15 39	59	51	16 38	59	51	234
128	12 22	60	49	13 22	59	49	14 21	59	49	15 20	59	49	16 19	59	49	232
130	12 04	+59	47	13 03	+59	47	14 02	+59	47	15 01	+59	47	16 00	+60	47	230
132	11 46	59	46	12 45	59	45	13 44	59	45	14 43	60	45	15 43	60	45	228
134	11 28	59	44	12 27	60	44	13 27	59	43	14 26	59	43	15 25	60	43	226
136	11 11	60	42	12 11	59	42	13 10	59	41	14 09	60	41	15 09	59	41	224
138	10 55	59	40	11 54	60	40	12 54	59	40	13 53	60	39	14 53	59	39	222

LHA	25° Hc	d	Z	26° Hc	d	Z	27° Hc	d	Z	28° Hc	d	Z	29° Hc	d	Z	LHA
	° ′	′	°	° ′	′	°	° ′	′	°	° ′	′	°	° ′	′	°	
0	37 00	+60	180	38 00	+60	180	39 00	+60	180	40 00	+60	180	41 00	+60	180	360
2	37 00	60	178	38 00	60	178	39 00	60	178	40 00	60	178	41 00	60	178	358
4	36 58	60	176	37 58	60	175	38 58	60	175	39 58	60	175	40 58	60	175	356
6	36 56	60	173	37 56	60	173	38 56	60	173	39 56	60	173	40 56	59	173	354
8	36 52	60	171	37 52	60	171	38 52	60	171	39 52	60	171	40 52	60	171	352
10	36 48	+60	169	37 48	+60	169	38 48	+60	169	39 48	+59	169	40 47	+60	168	350
12	36 42	60	166	37 42	60	166	38 42	60	166	39 42	60	166	40 42	60	166	348
14	36 36	60	164	37 36	60	164	38 36	60	164	39 36	60	164	40 36	59	164	346
16	36 29	60	162	37 29	59	162	38 28	60	162	39 28	60	162	40 28	60	162	344
18	36 21	59	160	37 20	60	160	38 20	60	160	39 20	60	159	40 20	59	159	342
20	36 11	+60	157	37 11	+60	157	38 11	+60	157	39 11	+59	157	40 10	+60	157	340
22	36 01	60	155	37 01	60	155	38 01	59	155	39 00	60	155	40 00	60	155	338
24	35 50	60	153	36 50	60	153	37 50	59	153	38 49	60	153	39 49	60	152	336
26	35 39	59	151	36 38	60	151	37 38	59	150	38 37	60	150	39 37	60	150	334
28	35 26	60	149	36 26	59	148	37 25	60	148	38 25	59	148	39 24	60	148	332
30	35 13	+59	146	36 12	+60	146	37 12	+59	146	38 11	+60	146	39 11	+59	146	330
32	34 58	60	144	35 58	59	144	36 57	60	144	37 57	59	144	38 56	59	143	328
34	34 43	60	142	35 43	59	142	36 42	60	142	37 42	59	141	38 41	59	141	326
36	34 28	59	140	35 27	59	140	36 26	60	139	37 26	59	139	38 25	59	139	324
38	34 11	59	138	35 10	60	137	36 10	59	137	37 09	59	137	38 08	59	137	322
40	33 54	+59	135	34 53	+59	135	35 52	+60	135	36 52	+59	135	37 51	+59	135	320
42	33 36	59	133	34 35	59	133	35 34	60	133	36 34	59	133	37 33	59	132	318
44	33 18	59	131	34 17	59	131	35 16	59	131	36 15	59	131	37 14	59	130	316
46	32 59	59	129	33 58	59	129	34 57	59	129	35 56	59	128	36 55	58	128	314
48	32 39	59	127	33 38	59	127	34 37	59	126	35 36	59	126	36 35	58	126	312
50	32 19	+59	125	33 18	+58	125	34 16	+59	124	35 15	+59	124	36 14	+59	124	310
52	31 58	59	123	32 57	59	122	33 56	58	122	34 54	59	122	35 53	59	122	308
54	31 37	58	121	32 35	59	120	33 34	59	120	34 33	59	120	35 32	58	120	306
56	31 15	59	119	32 14	58	118	33 12	59	118	34 11	59	118	35 10	58	118	304
58	30 53	59	116	31 52	58	116	32 50	59	116	33 49	58	116	34 47	59	115	302
60	30 30	+59	114	31 29	+59	114	32 28	+58	114	33 26	+59	114	34 25	+58	113	300
62	30 07	59	112	31 06	59	112	32 05	58	112	33 03	59	112	34 02	58	111	298
64	29 44	59	110	30 43	58	110	31 41	59	110	32 40	58	110	33 38	59	109	296
66	29 21	58	108	30 19	59	108	31 18	58	108	32 16	59	108	33 15	58	107	294
68	28 57	58	106	29 55	59	106	30 54	58	106	31 52	59	105	32 51	58	105	292
70	28 33	+58	104	29 31	+59	104	30 30	+58	104	31 28	+58	103	32 26	+59	103	290
72	28 08	59	102	29 07	58	102	30 05	59	102	31 04	58	101	32 02	58	101	288
74	27 44	58	100	28 42	59	100	29 41	58	100	30 39	58	99	31 37	59	99	286
76	27 19	59	98	28 18	58	98	29 16	58	98	30 14	59	97	31 13	58	97	284
78	26 55	58	96	27 53	58	96	28 51	59	96	29 50	58	95	30 48	58	95	282
80	26 30	+58	94	27 28	+58	94	28 26	+59	94	29 25	+58	93	30 23	+58	93	280
82	26 05	58	92	27 03	59	92	28 02	58	92	29 00	58	92	29 58	58	91	278
84	25 40	58	90	26 38	59	90	27 37	58	90	28 35	58	90	29 33	58	89	276
86	25 15	58	88	26 13	59	88	27 12	58	88	28 10	58	88	29 08	59	87	274
88	24 50	58	86	25 48	59	86	26 47	58	86	27 45	58	86	28 43	59	85	272
90	24 25	+59	85	25 24	+58	84	26 22	+58	84	27 20	+59	84	28 19	+58	83	270
92	24 00	59	83	24 59	58	82	25 57	58	82	26 55	59	82	27 54	58	82	268
94	23 36	58	81	24 34	58	80	25 32	59	80	26 31	58	80	27 29	58	80	266
96	23 11	59	79	24 10	58	78	25 08	58	78	26 06	59	78	27 05	58	78	264
98	22 47	58	77	23 45	59	77	24 44	58	77	25 42	58	76	26 40	59	76	262
100	22 23	+58	75	23 21	+59	75	24 20	+58	74	25 18	+58	74	26 16	+59	74	260
102	21 59	58	73	22 57	59	73	23 56	58	73	24 54	59	72	25 53	58	72	258
104	21 35	58	71	22 33	59	71	23 32	58	71	24 30	59	70	25 29	58	70	256
106	21 11	59	69	22 10	59	69	23 09	58	69	24 07	59	68	25 06	58	68	254
108	20 48	59	67	21 47	58	67	22 45	59	67	23 44	59	67	24 43	58	66	252
110	20 25	+59	65	21 24	+59	65	22 23	+58	65	23 21	+59	65	24 20	+59	64	250
112	20 03	59	63	21 02	58	63	22 00	59	63	22 59	59	63	23 58	58	63	248
114	19 41	59	62	20 40	58	61	21 38	59	61	22 37	59	61	23 36	58	61	246
116	19 19	59	60	20 18	59	60	21 17	58	59	22 15	59	59	23 14	59	59	244
118	18 58	59	58	19 57	58	58	20 55	59	57	21 54	59	57	22 53	59	57	242
120	18 37	+59	56	19 36	+59	56	20 35	+58	56	21 33	+59	55	22 32	+59	55	240
122	18 16	59	54	19 15	59	54	20 14	59	54	21 13	59	53	22 12	59	53	238
124	17 56	59	52	18 55	59	52	19 54	59	52	20 53	59	52	21 52	59	51	236
126	17 37	59	50	18 36	59	50	19 35	59	50	20 34	59	50	21 33	59	50	234
128	17 18	59	48	18 17	59	48	19 16	59	48	20 15	59	48	21 14	59	48	232
130	17 00	+59	47	17 59	+59	46	18 58	+59	46	19 57	+59	46	20 56	+59	46	230
132	16 42	59	45	17 41	59	45	18 40	59	44	19 39	60	44	20 39	59	44	228
134	16 25	59	43	17 24	59	43	18 23	59	43	19 22	60	42	20 22	59	42	226
136	16 08	59	41	17 07	60	41	18 07	59	41	19 06	59	41	20 05	59	40	224
138	15 52	59	39	16 51	60	39	17 51	59	39	18 50	59	39	19 49	60	39	222

LHA	15° Hc	15° d	15° Z	16° Hc	16° d	16° Z	17° Hc	17° d	17° Z	18° Hc	18° d	18° Z	19° Hc	19° d	19° Z	20° Hc	20° d	20° Z	21° Hc	21° d	21° Z
	° ′	′	°	° ′	′	°	° ′	′	°	° ′	′	°	° ′	′	°	° ′	′	°	° ′	′	°
140	05 42	+60	39	06 42	+59	39	07 41	+59	38	08 40	+60	38	09 40	+59	38	10 39	+60	38	11 39	+59	38
142	05 27	59	37	06 26	60	37	07 26	59	36	08 25	60	36	09 25	59	36	10 24	60	36	11 24	59	36
144	05 12	60	35	06 12	59	35	07 11	60	35	08 11	59	34	09 10	60	34	10 10	59	34	11 09	60	34
146	04 58	60	33	05 58	60	33	06 58	59	33	07 57	60	33	08 57	59	32	09 56	60	32	10 56	59	32
148	04 45	60	31	05 45	59	31	06 44	60	31	07 44	60	31	08 44	59	31	09 43	60	30	10 43	60	30
150	04 33	+59	29	05 32	+60	29	06 32	+60	29	07 32	+59	29	08 31	+60	29	09 31	+60	29	10 31	+59	28
152	04 21	60	27	05 21	59	27	06 20	60	27	07 20	60	27	08 20	60	27	09 20	59	27	10 19	60	27
154	04 10	60	25	05 10	60	25	06 10	59	25	07 09	60	25	08 09	60	25	09 09	60	25	10 09	59	25
156	04 00	60	23	05 00	59	23	05 59	60	23	06 59	60	23	07 59	60	23	08 59	60	23	09 59	59	23
158	03 50	60	21	04 50	60	21	05 50	60	21	06 50	60	21	07 50	59	21	08 49	60	21	09 49	60	21
160	03 42	+60	19	04 42	+59	19	05 41	+60	19	06 41	+60	19	07 41	+60	19	08 41	+60	19	09 41	+60	19
162	03 34	60	17	04 34	60	17	05 34	60	17	06 34	59	17	07 33	60	17	08 33	60	17	09 33	60	17
164	03 27	60	16	04 27	60	15	05 27	60	15	06 27	59	15	07 26	60	15	08 26	60	15	09 26	60	15
166	03 20	60	14	04 20	60	14	05 20	60	13	06 20	60	13	07 20	60	13	08 20	60	13	09 20	60	13
168	03 15	60	12	04 15	60	12	05 15	60	12	06 15	60	12	07 15	60	11	08 15	60	11	09 15	60	11
170	03 10	+60	10	04 10	+60	10	05 10	+60	10	06 10	+60	10	07 10	+60	10	08 10	+60	10	09 10	+60	10
172	03 07	60	8	04 07	60	8	05 07	60	8	06 07	60	8	07 07	60	8	08 07	60	8	09 07	60	8
174	03 04	60	6	04 04	60	6	05 04	60	6	06 04	60	6	07 04	60	6	08 04	60	6	09 04	60	6
176	03 02	60	4	04 02	60	4	05 02	60	4	06 02	60	4	07 02	60	4	08 02	60	4	09 02	60	4
178	03 00	60	2	04 00	60	2	05 00	60	2	06 00	60	2	07 00	60	2	08 00	60	2	09 00	60	2
180	03 00	+60	0	04 00	+60	0	05 00	+60	0	06 00	+60	0	07 00	+60	0	08 00	+60	0	09 00	+60	0

22° Hc	22° d	22° Z	23° Hc	23° d	23° Z	24° Hc	24° d	24° Z	25° Hc	25° d	25° Z	26° Hc	26° d	26° Z	27° Hc	27° d	27° Z	28° Hc	28° d	28° Z	29° Hc	29° d	29° Z	LHA
° ′	′	°	° ′	′	°	° ′	′	°	° ′	′	°	° ′	′	°	° ′	′	°	° ′	′	°	° ′	′	°	
12 38	+60	38	13 38	+59	38	14 37	+59	37	15 36	+60	37	16 36	+59	37	17 35	+60	37	18 35	+59	37	19 34	+59	37	220
12 23	60	36	13 23	59	36	14 22	60	36	15 22	59	35	16 21	60	35	17 21	59	35	18 20	60	35	19 20	59	35	218
12 09	60	34	13 09	59	34	14 08	60	34	15 08	59	34	16 07	60	33	17 07	59	33	18 06	60	33	19 06	59	33	216
11 55	60	32	12 55	60	32	13 55	59	32	14 54	60	32	15 54	59	32	16 53	60	31	17 53	59	31	18 52	60	31	214
11 43	59	30	12 42	60	30	13 42	59	30	14 41	60	30	15 41	60	30	16 41	59	30	17 40	60	29	18 40	59	29	212
11 30	+60	28	12 30	+60	28	13 30	+59	28	14 29	+60	28	15 29	+60	28	16 29	+59	28	17 28	+60	28	18 28	+60	28	210
11 19	60	26	12 19	59	26	13 18	60	26	14 18	60	26	15 18	59	26	16 17	60	26	17 17	60	26	18 17	60	26	208
11 08	60	25	12 08	60	24	13 08	59	24	14 07	60	24	15 07	60	24	16 07	60	24	17 07	59	24	18 06	60	24	206
10 58	60	23	11 58	60	23	12 58	60	22	13 58	59	22	14 57	60	22	15 57	60	22	16 57	60	22	17 57	59	22	204
10 49	60	21	11 49	60	21	12 49	60	21	13 49	59	21	14 48	60	20	15 48	60	20	16 48	60	20	17 48	60	20	202
10 41	+60	19	11 41	+59	19	12 40	+60	19	13 40	+60	19	14 40	+60	19	15 40	+60	19	16 40	+60	18	17 40	+59	18	200
10 33	60	17	11 33	60	17	12 33	60	17	13 33	59	17	14 32	60	17	15 32	60	17	16 32	60	17	17 32	60	17	198
10 26	60	15	11 26	60	15	12 26	60	15	13 26	60	15	14 26	60	15	15 26	60	15	16 26	59	15	17 25	60	15	196
10 20	60	13	11 20	60	13	12 20	60	13	13 20	60	13	14 20	60	13	15 20	60	13	16 20	59	13	17 19	60	13	194
10 15	60	11	11 15	60	11	12 15	60	11	13 15	60	11	14 15	59	11	15 14	60	11	16 14	60	11	17 14	60	11	192
10 10	+60	9	11 10	+60	9	12 10	+60	9	13 10	+60	9	14 10	+60	9	15 10	+60	9	16 10	+60	9	17 10	+60	9	190
10 07	60	8	11 07	60	8	12 07	60	8	13 07	59	7	14 06	60	7	15 06	60	7	16 06	60	7	17 06	60	7	188
10 04	60	6	11 04	60	6	12 04	60	6	13 04	60	6	14 04	60	6	15 04	60	6	16 04	60	6	17 04	60	6	186
10 02	60	4	11 02	60	4	12 02	60	4	13 02	60	4	14 02	60	4	15 02	60	4	16 02	60	4	17 02	60	4	184
10 00	60	2	11 00	60	2	12 00	60	2	13 00	60	2	14 00	60	2	15 00	60	2	16 00	60	2	17 00	60	2	182
10 00	+60	0	11 00	+60	0	12 00	+60	0	13 00	+60	0	14 00	+60	0	15 00	+60	0	16 00	+60	0	17 00	+60	0	180

N. Lat. {LHA greater than 180°....... Zn=Z; LHA less than 180°........... Zn=360−Z}

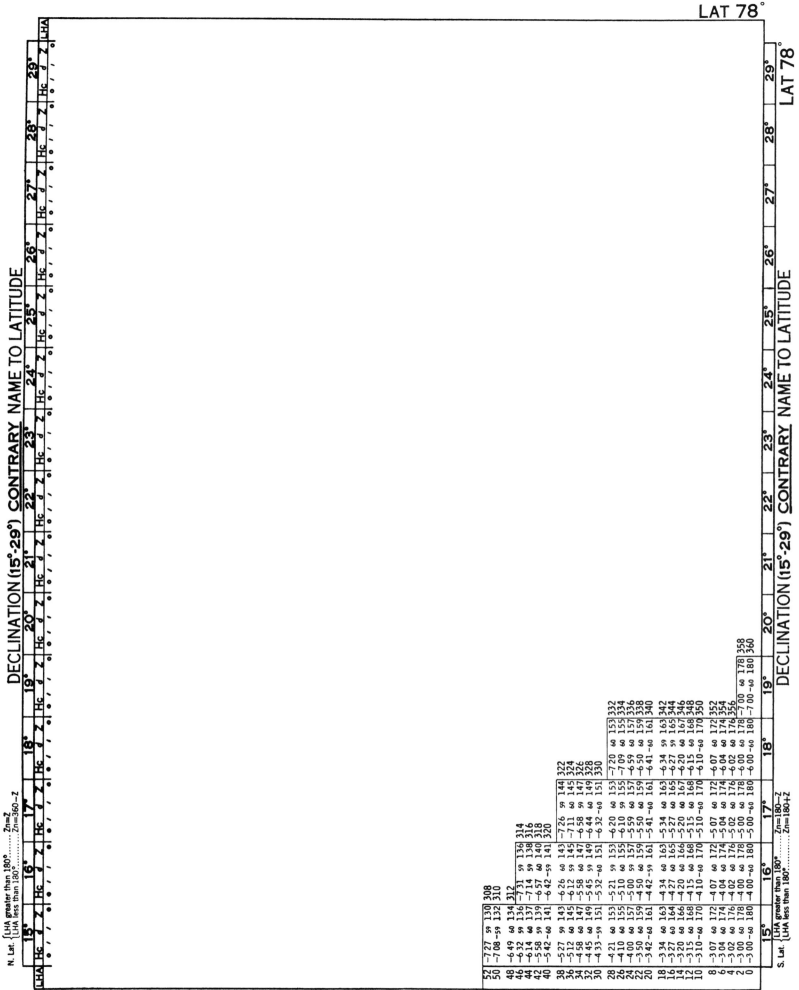

DECLINATION (15°-29°) CONTRARY NAME TO LATITUDE

LHA	15° Hc d Z	16° Hc d Z	17° Hc d Z	18° Hc d Z	19° Hc d Z	20° Hc d Z	21° Hc d Z	22° Hc d Z	23° Hc d Z	24° Hc d Z	25° Hc d Z	26° Hc d Z	27° Hc d Z	28° Hc d Z	29° Hc d Z	LHA
°	° ′ ′ °	° ′ ′ °	° ′ ′ °	° ′ ′ °	° ′ ′ °	° ′ ′ °	° ′ ′ °	° ′ ′ °	° ′ ′ °	° ′ ′ °	° ′ ′ °	° ′ ′ °	° ′ ′ °	° ′ ′ °	° ′ ′ °	°
52	−7 27 59 130															308
50	−7 08 −59 132															310
48	−6 49 60 134															312
46	−6 32 59 136	−7 31 59 136														314
44	−6 14 60 137	−7 14 59 138														316
42	−5 58 59 139	−6 57 60 140														318
40	−5 42 −60 141	−6 42 −59 141														320
38	−5 27 59 143	−6 26 60 143	−7 26 59 144													322
36	−5 12 60 145	−6 12 59 145	−7 11 60 145													324
34	−4 58 60 147	−5 58 60 147	−6 58 59 147													326
32	−4 45 60 149	−5 45 59 149	−6 44 60 149													328
30	−4 33 −59 151	−5 32 −60 151	−6 32 −60 151													330
28	−4 21 60 153	−5 21 59 153	−6 20 60 153	−7 20 60 153												332
26	−4 10 60 155	−5 10 60 155	−6 10 59 155	−7 09 60 155												334
24	−4 00 60 157	−5 00 59 157	−5 59 60 157	−6 59 60 157												336
22	−3 50 60 159	−4 50 60 159	−5 50 60 159	−6 50 60 159												338
20	−3 42 −60 161	−4 42 −59 161	−5 41 −60 161	−6 41 −60 161												340
18	−3 34 60 163	−4 34 60 163	−5 34 60 163	−6 34 59 163												342
16	−3 27 60 164	−4 27 60 165	−5 27 60 165	−6 27 59 165												344
14	−3 20 60 166	−4 20 60 166	−5 20 60 167	−6 20 60 167												346
12	−3 15 60 168	−4 15 60 168	−5 15 60 168	−6 15 60 168												348
10	−3 10 −60 170	−4 10 −60 170	−5 10 −60 170	−6 10 −60 170												350
8	−3 07 60 172	−4 07 60 172	−5 07 60 172	−6 07 60 172												352
6	−3 04 60 174	−4 04 60 174	−5 04 60 174	−6 04 60 174												354
4	−3 02 60 176	−4 02 60 176	−5 02 60 176	−6 02 60 176												356
2	−3 00 60 178	−4 00 60 178	−5 00 60 178	−6 00 60 178	−7 00 60 178											358
0	−3 00 −60 180	−4 00 −60 180	−5 00 −60 180	−6 00 −60 180	−7 00 −60 180											360
	15°	16°	17°	18°	19°	20°	21°	22°	23°	24°	25°	26°	27°	28°	29°	

S. Lat. {LHA greater than 180°....... Zn=180−Z; LHA less than 180°........... Zn=180+Z}

DECLINATION (15°-29°) CONTRARY NAME TO LATITUDE

LAT 78°

N. Lat. {LHA greater than 180°....... Zn=Z
{LHA less than 180°.......... Zn=360−Z

DECLINATION (0°-14°) SAME NAME AS LATITUDE

LHA	0° Hc	d	Z	1° Hc	d	Z	2° Hc	d	Z	3° Hc	d	Z	4° Hc	d	Z
	° ′	′	°	° ′	′	°	° ′	′	°	° ′	′	°	° ′	′	°
0	11 00	+60	180	12 00	+60	180	13 00	+60	180	14 00	+60	180	15 00	+60	180
2	11 00	60	178	12 00	60	178	13 00	60	178	14 00	60	178	15 00	60	178
4	10 58	60	176	11 58	60	176	12 58	60	176	13 58	60	176	14 58	60	176
6	10 56	60	174	11 56	60	174	12 56	60	174	13 56	60	174	14 56	60	174
8	10 54	60	172	11 54	60	172	12 54	59	172	13 53	60	172	14 53	60	172
10	10 50	+60	170	11 50	+60	170	12 50	+60	170	13 50	+60	170	14 50	+60	170
12	10 45	60	168	11 45	60	168	12 45	60	168	13 45	60	168	14 45	60	168
14	10 40	60	166	11 40	60	166	12 40	60	166	13 40	60	166	14 40	60	166
16	10 34	60	164	11 34	60	164	12 34	60	164	13 34	60	164	14 34	60	164
18	10 27	60	162	11 27	60	162	12 27	60	162	13 27	60	162	14 27	60	161
20	10 20	+60	160	11 20	+60	160	12 20	+59	160	13 19	+60	160	14 19	+60	159
22	10 11	60	158	11 11	60	158	12 11	60	158	13 11	60	157	14 11	60	157
24	10 02	60	156	11 02	60	156	12 02	60	155	13 02	60	155	14 02	59	155
26	09 53	59	154	10 52	60	154	11 52	60	153	12 52	60	153	13 52	59	153
28	09 42	60	152	10 42	59	152	11 41	60	151	12 41	60	151	13 41	60	151
30	09 31	+59	150	10 30	+60	149	11 30	+60	149	12 30	+60	149	13 30	+59	149
32	09 19	59	148	10 18	60	147	11 18	60	147	12 18	60	147	13 18	59	147
34	09 06	60	146	10 06	59	145	11 05	60	145	12 05	60	145	13 05	59	145
36	08 53	59	144	09 52	60	143	10 52	60	143	11 52	59	143	12 51	60	143
38	08 39	59	142	09 38	60	141	10 38	60	141	11 38	59	141	12 37	60	141
40	08 24	+60	140	09 24	+59	139	10 23	+60	139	11 23	+59	139	12 22	+60	139
42	08 09	60	138	09 09	59	137	10 08	60	137	11 08	59	137	12 07	60	137
44	07 53	60	136	08 53	59	135	09 52	60	135	10 52	59	135	11 51	60	135
46	07 37	59	134	08 36	60	133	09 36	59	133	10 35	60	133	11 35	59	133
48	07 20	60	132	08 20	59	131	09 19	59	131	10 18	60	131	11 18	59	131
50	07 03	+59	130	08 02	+59	129	09 01	+60	129	10 01	+59	129	11 00	+59	129
52	06 45	59	128	07 44	59	127	08 43	60	127	09 43	59	127	10 42	59	127
54	06 26	60	126	07 26	59	125	08 25	59	125	09 24	59	125	10 23	60	125
56	06 08	59	124	07 07	59	123	08 06	59	123	09 05	59	123	10 04	60	123
58	05 48	59	122	06 47	60	121	07 47	59	121	08 46	59	121	09 45	59	121
60	05 29	+59	120	06 28	+59	119	07 27	+59	119	08 26	+59	119	09 25	+59	119
62	05 08	60	118	06 08	59	117	07 07	59	117	08 06	59	117	09 05	59	117
64	04 48	59	116	05 47	59	115	06 46	59	115	07 45	59	115	08 44	59	115
66	04 27	59	114	05 26	59	113	06 25	59	113	07 24	59	113	08 23	59	113
68	04 06	59	112	05 05	59	112	06 04	59	111	07 03	59	111	08 02	59	111
70	03 45	+59	110	04 44	+59	110	05 43	+59	109	06 42	+59	109	07 41	+59	109
72	03 23	59	108	04 22	59	108	05 21	59	107	06 20	59	107	07 19	59	107
74	03 01	59	106	04 00	59	106	04 59	59	105	05 58	59	105	06 57	59	105
76	02 39	59	104	03 38	59	104	04 37	59	103	05 36	59	103	06 35	59	103
78	02 16	59	102	03 15	59	102	04 14	59	101	05 13	59	101	06 12	59	101
80	01 54	+59	100	02 53	+59	100	03 52	+59	99	04 51	+59	99	05 50	+59	99
82	01 31	59	98	02 30	59	98	03 29	59	98	04 28	59	97	05 27	59	97
84	01 09	59	96	02 08	58	96	03 06	59	96	04 05	59	95	05 04	59	95
86	00 46	59	94	01 45	59	94	02 44	58	94	03 42	59	93	04 41	59	93
88	00 23	59	92	01 22	59	92	02 21	59	92	03 20	58	91	04 18	59	91
90	00 00	+59	90	00 59	+59	90	01 58	+59	90	02 57	+59	89	03 56	+58	89
92	−0 23	59	88	00 36	59	88	01 35	59	88	02 34	59	88	03 33	59	87
94	−0 46	59	86	00 13	59	86	01 12	59	86	02 11	59	86	03 10	59	85
96	−1 09	59	84	−0 10	59	84	00 49	59	84	01 48	59	84	02 47	59	83
98	−1 31	59	82	−0 32	59	82	00 27	59	82	01 26	58	82	02 24	59	81
100	−1 54	+59	80	−0 55	+59	80	00 04	+59	80	01 03	+59	80	02 02	+59	79
102	−2 16	58	78	−1 18	59	78	−0 19	59	78	00 40	59	78	01 39	59	78
104	−2 39	59	76	−1 40	59	76	−0 41	59	76	00 18	59	76	01 17	59	76
106	−3 01	59	74	−2 02	59	74	−1 03	59	74	−0 04	59	74	00 55	59	74
108	−3 23	59	72	−2 24	59	72	−1 25	59	72	−0 26	59	72	00 33	59	72
110	−3 45	+59	70	−2 46	+60	70	−1 46	+59	70	−0 47	+59	70	00 12	+59	70
112	−4 06	59	68	−3 07	59	68	−2 08	59	68	−1 09	59	68	−0 10	59	68
114	−4 27	59	66	−3 28	59	66	−2 29	59	66	−1 30	59	66	−0 31	59	66
116	−4 48	59	64	−3 49	59	64	−2 50	59	64	−1 51	60	64	−0 51	59	64
118	−5 08	59	62	−4 09	59	62	−3 10	59	62	−2 11	59	62	−1 12	59	62
120	−5 29	+60	60	−4 29	+59	60	−3 30	+59	60	−2 31	+59	60	−1 32	+59	60
122	−5 48	59	58	−4 49	59	58	−3 50	59	58	−2 51	60	58	−1 51	59	58
124	−6 08	60	56	−5 08	59	56	−4 09	59	56	−3 10	60	56	−2 10	59	56
126	−6 26	59	54	−5 27	59	54	−4 28	60	54	−3 28	59	54	−2 29	59	54
128	−6 45	59	52	−5 46	60	52	−4 46	59	52	−3 47	59	52	−2 48	60	52
130	−7 03	+60	50	−6 03	+59	50	−5 04	+59	50	−4 05	+60	50	−3 05	+59	50
132	−7 20	59	48	−6 21	60	48	−5 21	59	48	−4 22	59	48	−3 23	60	48
134				−6 38	60	46	−5 38	59	46	−4 39	60	46	−3 39	59	46
136				−6 54	60	44	−5 54	59	44	−4 55	59	44	−3 56	60	44
138				−7 10	60	42	−6 10	59	42	−5 11	60	42	−4 11	59	42

LHA	5° Hc	d	Z	6° Hc	d	Z	7° Hc	d	Z	8° Hc	d	Z	9° Hc	d	Z
	° ′	′	°	° ′	′	°	° ′	′	°	° ′	′	°	° ′	′	°
0	16 00	+60	180	17 00	+60	180	18 00	+60	180	19 00	+60	180	20 00	+60	180
2	16 00	60	178	17 00	60	178	18 00	60	178	19 00	60	178	20 00	60	178
4	15 58	60	176	16 58	60	176	17 58	60	176	18 58	60	176	19 58	60	176
6	15 56	60	174	16 56	60	174	17 56	60	174	18 56	60	174	19 56	60	174
8	15 53	60	172	16 53	60	172	17 53	60	172	18 53	60	172	19 53	60	172
10	15 50	+60	170	16 50	+60	170	17 50	+60	170	18 50	+60	170	19 50	+60	170
12	15 45	60	168	16 45	60	168	17 45	60	168	18 45	60	167	19 45	60	167
14	15 40	60	166	16 40	60	166	17 40	60	165	18 40	60	165	19 40	60	165
16	15 34	60	163	16 34	60	163	17 34	59	163	18 33	60	163	19 33	60	163
18	15 27	60	161	16 27	60	161	17 27	59	161	18 26	60	161	19 26	60	161
20	15 19	+60	159	16 19	+60	159	17 19	+60	159	18 19	+60	159	19 19	+59	159
22	15 11	59	157	16 10	60	157	17 10	60	157	18 10	60	157	19 10	60	157
24	15 01	60	155	16 01	60	155	17 01	60	155	18 01	60	155	19 01	59	155
26	14 51	60	153	15 51	60	153	16 51	60	153	17 51	60	153	18 51	59	153
28	14 41	59	151	15 40	60	151	16 40	60	151	17 40	60	151	18 40	59	151
30	14 29	+60	149	15 29	+60	149	16 29	+59	149	17 28	+60	149	18 28	+60	149
32	14 17	60	147	15 17	60	147	16 17	59	147	17 16	60	147	18 16	60	147
34	14 04	60	145	15 04	60	145	16 04	59	145	17 03	60	145	18 03	60	145
36	13 51	59	143	14 50	60	143	15 50	60	143	16 50	59	143	17 49	60	142
38	13 37	59	141	14 36	60	141	15 36	59	141	16 35	60	141	17 35	60	140
40	13 22	+60	139	14 22	+59	139	15 21	+60	139	16 21	+59	138	17 20	+60	138
42	13 07	59	137	14 06	60	137	15 06	59	137	16 05	60	136	17 05	59	136
44	12 51	59	135	13 50	60	135	14 50	59	135	15 49	59	134	16 48	60	134
46	12 34	60	133	13 34	59	133	14 33	59	133	15 32	60	132	16 32	59	132
48	12 17	59	131	13 16	60	131	14 16	59	130	15 15	59	130	16 14	60	130
50	11 59	+60	129	12 59	+59	129	13 58	+59	128	14 57	+60	128	15 57	+59	128
52	11 41	60	127	12 41	59	127	13 40	59	126	14 39	59	126	15 38	60	126
54	11 23	59	125	12 22	59	125	13 21	59	124	14 20	60	124	15 20	59	124
56	11 04	59	123	12 03	59	123	13 02	59	122	14 01	60	122	15 01	59	122
58	10 44	59	121	11 43	60	121	12 43	59	120	13 42	59	120	14 41	59	120
60	10 24	+59	119	11 23	+60	119	12 23	+59	118	13 22	+59	118	14 21	+59	118
62	10 04	59	117	11 03	59	117	12 02	59	116	13 01	59	116	14 00	60	116
64	09 43	59	115	10 42	60	115	11 42	59	114	12 41	59	114	13 40	59	114
66	09 22	60	113	10 22	59	113	11 21	59	112	12 20	59	112	13 19	59	112
68	09 01	59	111	10 00	59	111	10 59	59	110	11 58	59	110	12 57	59	110
70	08 40	+59	109	09 39	+59	109	10 38	+59	108	11 37	+59	108	12 36	+59	108
72	08 18	59	107	09 17	59	107	10 16	59	106	11 15	59	106	12 14	59	106
74	07 56	59	105	08 55	59	105	09 54	59	104	10 53	59	104	11 52	59	104
76	07 34	59	103	08 33	58	103	09 31	59	102	10 30	59	102	11 29	59	102
78	07 11	59	101	08 10	59	101	09 09	59	101	10 08	59	100	11 07	59	100
80	06 49	+59	99	07 48	+58	99	08 46	+59	99	09 45	+59	98	10 44	+59	98
82	06 26	59	97	07 25	59	97	08 24	59	97	09 23	58	96	10 21	59	96
84	06 03	59	95	07 02	59	95	08 01	59	95	09 00	59	94	09 59	59	94
86	05 40	59	93	06 39	59	93	07 38	59	93	08 37	59	92	09 36	59	92
88	05 17	59	91	06 16	59	91	07 15	59	91	08 14	59	90	09 13	59	90
90	04 54	+59	89	05 53	+59	89	06 52	+59	89	07 51	+59	89	08 50	+59	88
92	04 32	59	87	05 31	58	87	06 29	59	87	07 28	59	87	08 27	59	86
94	04 09	59	85	05 08	59	85	06 07	58	85	07 05	59	85	08 04	59	84
96	03 46	59	83	04 45	59	83	05 44	59	83	06 43	59	83	07 42	59	82
98	03 23	59	81	04 22	59	81	05 21	59	81	06 20	59	81	07 19	59	80
100	03 01	+59	79	04 00	+59	79	04 59	+59	79	05 58	+58	79	06 56	+59	79
102	02 38	59	77	03 37	59	77	04 36	59	77	05 35	59	77	06 34	59	77
104	02 16	59	75	03 15	59	75	04 14	59	75	05 13	59	75	06 12	59	75
106	01 54	59	73	02 53	59	73	03 52	59	73	04 51	59	73	05 50	59	73
108	01 32	59	71	02 31	59	71	03 30	59	71	04 29	59	71	05 28	59	71
110	01 11	+59	69	02 10	+59	69	03 09	+59	69	04 08	+59	69	05 07	+59	69
112	00 49	59	67	01 48	59	67	02 47	59	67	03 46	60	67	04 46	59	67
114	00 28	59	66	01 27	59	65	02 26	60	65	03 26	59	65	04 25	59	65
116	00 08	59	64	01 07	59	63	02 06	59	63	03 05	59	63	04 04	59	63
118	−0 13	59	62	00 46	60	61	01 46	59	61	02 45	59	61	03 44	59	61
120	−0 33	+60	60	00 27	+59	59	01 26	+59	59	02 25	+59	59	03 24	+59	59
122	−0 52	59	58	00 07	59	58	01 06	59	57	02 05	60	57	03 05	59	57
124	−1 11	59	56	−0 12	59	56	00 47	59	55	01 46	60	55	02 46	59	55
126	−1 30	59	54	−0 31	60	54	00 29	59	53	01 28	59	53	02 27	59	53
128	−1 48	59	52	−0 49	59	52	00 10	60	51	01 10	59	51	02 09	59	51
130	−2 06	+59	50	−1 07	+60	50	−0 07	+59	49	00 52	+60	49	01 52	+59	49
132	−2 23	59	48	−1 24	60	48	−0 24	59	48	00 35	59	47	01 34	60	47
134	−2 40	60	46	−1 40	59	46	−0 41	59	46	00 18	60	45	01 18	59	45
136	−2 56	59	44	−1 57	60	44	−0 57	59	44	00 02	60	43	01 02	59	43
138	−3 12	60	42	−2 12	59	42	−1 13	60	42	−0 13	59	42	00 46	60	41

LHA	10° Hc	d	Z	11° Hc	d	Z	12° Hc	d	Z	13° Hc	d	Z	14° Hc	d	Z	LHA
	° ′	′	°	° ′	′	°	° ′	′	°	° ′	′	°	° ′	′	°	
0	21 00	+60	180	22 00	+60	180	23 00	+60	180	24 00	+60	180	25 00	+60	180	360
2	21 00	60	178	22 00	60	178	23 00	60	178	24 00	60	178	25 00	60	178	358
4	20 58	60	176	21 58	60	176	22 58	60	176	23 58	60	176	24 58	60	176	356
6	20 56	60	174	21 56	60	174	22 56	60	174	23 56	60	174	24 56	60	174	354
8	20 53	60	172	21 53	60	172	22 53	60	172	23 53	60	172	24 53	60	171	352
10	20 50	+60	170	21 50	+59	169	22 49	+60	169	23 49	+60	169	24 49	+60	169	350
12	20 45	60	167	21 45	60	167	22 45	60	167	23 45	60	167	24 45	60	167	348
14	20 40	59	165	21 39	60	165	22 39	60	165	23 39	60	165	24 39	60	165	346
16	20 33	60	163	21 33	60	163	22 33	60	163	23 33	60	163	24 33	60	163	344
18	20 26	60	161	21 26	60	161	22 26	60	161	23 26	60	161	24 26	60	161	342
20	20 18	+60	159	21 18	+60	159	22 18	+60	159	23 18	+60	159	24 18	+60	159	340
22	20 10	60	157	21 10	59	157	22 09	60	157	23 09	60	157	24 09	60	157	338
24	20 00	60	155	21 00	60	155	22 00	60	155	23 00	60	155	24 00	59	154	336
26	19 50	60	153	20 50	60	153	21 50	60	153	22 50	59	152	23 49	60	152	334
28	19 39	60	151	20 39	60	151	21 39	60	150	22 39	59	150	23 38	60	150	332
30	19 28	+59	149	20 27	+60	148	21 27	+60	148	22 27	+60	148	23 27	+59	148	330
32	19 16	59	146	20 15	60	146	21 15	59	146	22 14	60	146	23 14	60	146	328
34	19 03	59	144	20 02	60	144	21 02	59	144	22 01	60	144	23 01	60	144	326
36	18 49	59	142	19 48	60	142	20 48	60	142	21 48	59	142	22 47	60	142	324
38	18 35	59	140	19 34	60	140	20 34	59	140	21 33	60	140	22 33	59	140	322
40	18 20	+59	138	19 19	+60	138	20 19	+59	138	21 18	+59	138	22 17	+60	138	320
42	18 04	59	136	19 03	60	136	20 03	59	136	21 02	60	136	22 02	59	136	318
44	17 48	59	134	18 47	60	134	19 47	59	134	20 46	59	134	21 45	60	134	316
46	17 31	59	132	18 30	60	132	19 30	59	132	20 29	60	132	21 29	59	131	314
48	17 14	59	130	18 13	59	130	19 12	60	130	20 12	59	130	21 11	59	129	312
50	16 56	+59	128	17 55	+60	128	18 55	+59	128	19 54	+59	128	20 53	+59	127	310
52	16 38	59	126	17 37	59	126	18 36	59	126	19 35	60	125	20 35	59	125	308
54	16 19	59	124	17 18	59	124	18 17	60	124	19 17	59	123	20 16	59	123	306
56	16 00	59	122	16 59	59	122	17 58	59	122	18 57	59	121	19 56	59	121	304
58	15 40	59	120	16 39	59	120	17 38	59	120	18 37	60	119	19 37	59	119	302
60	15 20	+59	118	16 19	+59	118	17 18	+59	118	18 17	+59	117	19 16	+59	117	300
62	15 00	59	116	15 59	59	116	16 58	59	116	17 57	59	115	18 56	59	115	298
64	14 39	59	114	15 38	59	114	16 37	59	113	17 36	59	113	18 35	59	113	296
66	14 18	59	112	15 17	59	112	16 16	59	111	17 15	59	111	18 14	59	111	294
68	13 56	59	110	14 55	59	110	15 54	59	109	16 53	59	109	17 52	59	109	292
70	13 35	+59	108	14 34	+59	108	15 33	+58	107	16 31	+59	107	17 30	+59	107	290
72	13 13	59	106	14 12	59	106	15 11	58	105	16 09	59	105	17 08	59	105	288
74	12 51	58	104	13 49	59	104	14 48	59	104	15 47	59	103	16 46	59	103	286
76	12 28	59	102	13 27	59	102	14 26	59	102	15 25	59	101	16 24	59	101	284
78	12 06	59	100	13 05	59	100	14 04	58	100	15 02	59	99	16 01	59	99	282
80	11 43	+59	98	12 42	+59	98	13 41	+59	98	14 40	+59	97	15 39	+58	97	280
82	11 20	59	96	12 19	59	96	13 18	59	96	14 17	59	95	15 16	59	95	278
84	10 58	58	94	11 56	59	94	12 55	59	94	13 54	59	93	14 53	59	93	276
86	10 35	59	92	11 34	58	92	12 32	59	92	13 31	59	91	14 30	59	91	274
88	10 12	59	90	11 11	59	90	12 10	58	90	13 08	59	89	14 07	59	89	272
90	09 49	+59	88	10 48	+59	88	11 47	+58	88	12 45	+59	88	13 44	+59	87	270
92	09 26	59	86	10 25	59	86	11 24	59	86	12 23	58	86	13 21	59	85	268
94	09 03	59	84	10 02	59	84	11 01	59	84	12 00	59	84	12 59	59	83	266
96	08 41	58	82	09 39	59	82	10 38	59	82	11 37	59	82	12 36	59	81	264
98	08 18	59	80	09 17	59	80	10 16	59	80	11 15	58	80	12 13	59	80	262
100	07 55	+59	78	08 54	+59	78	09 53	+59	78	10 52	+59	78	11 51	+59	78	260
102	07 33	59	76	08 32	59	76	09 31	59	76	10 30	59	76	11 29	59	76	258
104	07 11	59	74	08 10	59	74	09 09	59	74	10 08	59	74	11 07	59	74	256
106	06 49	59	72	07 48	59	72	08 47	59	72	09 46	59	72	10 45	59	72	254
108	06 27	59	71	07 26	59	70	08 25	59	70	09 24	59	70	10 23	59	70	252
110	06 06	+59	69	07 05	+59	68	08 04	+59	68	09 03	+59	68	10 02	+59	68	250
112	05 45	59	67	06 44	59	66	07 43	59	66	08 42	59	66	09 41	59	66	248
114	05 24	59	65	06 23	59	65	07 22	59	64	08 21	59	64	09 20	59	64	246
116	05 03	59	63	06 02	59	63	07 01	60	62	08 01	59	62	09 00	59	62	244
118	04 43	59	61	05 42	59	61	06 41	59	60	07 40	60	60	08 40	59	60	242
120	04 23	+59	59	05 22	+60	59	06 22	+59	59	07 21	+59	58	08 20	+59	58	240
122	04 04	59	57	05 03	59	57	06 02	60	57	07 02	59	56	08 01	59	56	238
124	03 45	59	55	04 44	59	55	05 43	60	55	06 43	59	54	07 42	59	54	236
126	03 26	60	53	04 26	59	53	05 25	59	53	06 24	60	53	07 24	59	52	234
128	03 08	60	51	04 08	59	51	05 07	59	51	06 06	60	51	07 06	59	50	232
130	02 51	+59	49	03 50	+60	49	04 50	+59	49	05 49	+59	49	06 48	+60	49	230
132	02 34	59	47	03 33	60	47	04 33	59	47	05 32	59	47	06 31	60	47	228
134	02 17	60	45	03 17	59	45	04 16	60	45	05 16	59	45	06 15	59	45	226
136	02 01	60	43	03 01	59	43	04 00	60	43	05 00	59	43	05 59	60	43	224
138	01 46	60	41	02 46	59	41	03 45	59	41	04 44	60	41	05 44	60	41	222

S. Lat. {LHA greater than 180°....... Zn=180−Z
{LHA less than 180°.......... Zn=180+Z

DECLINATION (0°-14°) SAME NAME AS LATITUDE

LAT 79°

N. Lat. {LHA greater ' / LHA less than 180°..........Zn=360−Z

DECL… N (0°-14°) SAME NAME AS LATITUDE

LHA	0° Hc	d	Z	1° Hc	d	Z	2° Hc	d	Z	3° Hc	d	Z	4° Hc	d	Z	5° Hc	d	Z	6° Hc	d	Z	7° Hc	d	Z
	° ′	′	°	° ′	′	°	° ′	′	°	° ′	′	°	° ′	′	°	° ′	′	°	° ′	′	°	° ′	′	°
140				−7 25	+60	40	−6 25	+59	40	−5 26	+60	40	−4 26	+59	40	−3 27	+60	40	−2 27	+59	40	−1 28	+60	40
142							−6 40	60	38	−5 40	59	38	−4 41	60	38	−3 41	60	38	−2 41	59	38	−1 42	60	38
144							−6 54	60	36	−5 54	60	36	−4 54	59	36	−3 55	60	36	−2 55	59	36	−1 56	60	36
146							−7 07	60	34	−6 07	59	34	−5 08	60	34	−4 08	60	34	−3 08	60	34	−2 08	59	34
148							−7 19	59	32	−6 20	60	32	−5 20	60	32	−4 20	59	32	−3 21	60	32	−2 21	60	32
150										−6 32	+60	30	−5 32	+60	30	−4 32	+60	30	−3 32	+59	30	−2 33	+60	30
152										−6 43	60	28	−5 43	60	28	−4 43	60	28	−3 43	59	28	−2 44	60	28
154										−6 53	60	26	−5 53	59	26	−4 54	60	26	−3 54	60	26	−2 54	60	26
156										−7 03	60	24	−6 03	60	24	−5 03	60	24	−4 03	59	24	−3 04	60	24
158										−7 12	60	22	−6 12	60	22	−5 12	60	22	−4 12	60	22	−3 12	59	22
160													−6 20	+60	20	−5 20	+60	20	−4 20	+59	20	−3 21	+60	20
162													−6 28	60	18	−5 28	60	18	−4 28	60	18	−3 28	60	18
164													−6 35	60	16	−5 35	60	16	−4 35	60	16	−3 35	60	16
166													−6 40	59	14	−5 41	60	14	−4 41	60	14	−3 41	60	14
168													−6 46	60	12	−5 46	60	12	−4 46	60	12	−3 46	60	12
170													−6 50	+60	10	−5 50	+60	10	−4 50	+60	10	−3 50	+60	10
172													−6 54	60	8	−5 54	60	8	−4 54	60	8	−3 54	60	8
174													−6 56	60	6	−5 56	60	6	−4 56	60	6	−3 56	60	6
176													−6 58	60	4	−5 58	60	4	−4 58	60	4	−3 58	60	4
178													−7 00	60	2	−6 00	60	2	−5 00	60	2	−4 00	60	2
180													−7 00	+60	0	−6 00	+60	0	−5 00	+60	0	−4 00	+60	0

LHA	8° Hc	d	Z	9° Hc	d	Z	10° Hc	d	Z	11° Hc	d	Z	12° Hc	d	Z	13° Hc	d	Z	14° Hc	d	Z	LHA
	° ′	′	°	° ′	′	°	° ′	′	°	° ′	′	°	° ′	′	°	° ′	′	°	° ′	′	°	
140	−0 28	+60	40	00 32	+59	39	01 31	+60	39	02 31	+59	39	03 30	+60	39	04 30	+59	39	05 29	+60	39	220
142	−0 42	59	38	00 17	60	37	01 17	59	37	02 16	60	37	03 16	60	37	04 16	59	37	05 15	60	37	218
144	−0 56	60	36	00 04	59	35	01 03	60	35	02 03	60	35	03 03	59	35	04 02	60	35	05 02	60	35	216
146	−1 09	60	34	−0 09	59	34	00 50	60	33	01 50	60	33	02 50	59	33	03 49	60	33	04 49	60	33	214
148	−1 21	59	32	−0 22	60	32	00 38	60	31	01 38	60	31	02 38	59	31	03 37	60	31	04 37	60	31	212
150	−1 33	+60	30	−0 33	+60	30	00 27	+59	30	01 26	+60	29	02 26	+60	29	03 26	+60	29	04 26	+59	29	210
152	−1 44	60	28	−0 44	60	28	00 16	59	28	01 15	60	27	02 15	60	27	03 15	60	27	04 15	59	27	208
154	−1 54	60	26	−0 54	59	26	00 05	60	26	01 05	60	25	02 05	60	25	03 05	59	25	04 04	60	25	206
156	−2 04	60	24	−1 04	60	24	−0 04	60	24	00 56	60	24	01 56	59	23	02 55	60	23	03 55	60	23	204
158	−2 13	60	22	−1 13	60	22	−0 13	60	22	00 47	60	22	01 47	60	22	02 47	59	21	03 46	60	21	202
160	−2 21	+60	20	−1 21	+60	20	−0 21	+60	20	00 39	+59	20	01 38	+60	20	02 38	+60	20	03 38	+60	19	200
162	−2 28	60	18	−1 28	60	18	−0 28	60	18	00 32	59	18	01 31	60	18	02 31	60	18	03 31	60	18	198
164	−2 35	60	16	−1 35	60	16	−0 35	60	16	00 25	60	16	01 25	60	16	02 25	60	16	03 25	60	16	196
166	−2 41	60	14	−1 41	60	14	−0 41	60	14	00 19	60	14	01 19	60	14	02 19	60	14	03 19	60	14	194
168	−2 46	60	12	−1 46	60	12	−0 46	60	12	00 14	60	12	01 14	60	12	02 14	60	12	03 14	60	12	192
170	−2 50	+60	10	−1 50	+60	10	−0 50	+60	10	00 10	+60	10	01 10	+60	10	02 10	+60	10	03 10	+60	10	190
172	−2 54	60	8	−1 54	60	8	−0 54	60	8	00 06	60	8	01 06	60	8	02 06	60	8	03 06	60	8	188
174	−2 56	60	6	−1 56	60	6	−0 56	60	6	00 04	60	6	01 04	60	6	02 04	60	6	03 04	60	6	186
176	−2 58	60	4	−1 58	60	4	−0 58	60	4	00 02	60	4	01 02	60	4	02 02	60	4	03 02	60	4	184
178	−3 00	60	2	−2 00	60	2	−1 00	60	2	00 00	60	2	01 00	60	2	02 00	60	2	03 00	60	2	182
180	−3 00	+60	0	−2 00	+60	0	−1 00	+60	0	00 00	+60	0	01 00	+60	0	02 00	+60	0	03 00	+60	0	180

0°	1°	2°	3°	4°	5°	6°	7°	8°	9°	10°	11°	12°	13°	14°

S. Lat. {LHA greater than 180°.......Zn=180−Z / LHA less than 180°...........Zn=180+Z

DECLINATION (0°-14°) SAME NAME AS LATITUDE

LAT 79°

LAT 79°

N. Lat. {LHA greater than 180°....... Zn=Z; LHA less than 180°........... Zn=360−Z}

DECLINATION (0°-14°) CONTRARY NAME TO LATITUDE

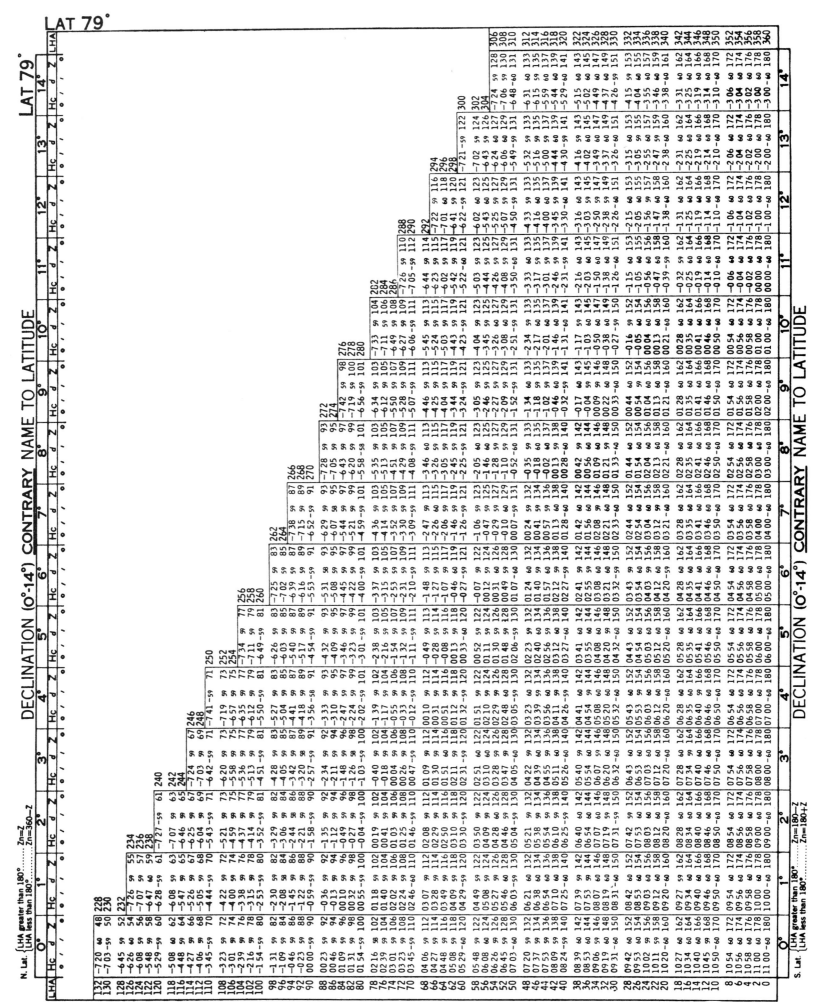

LHA	0° Hc d Z	1° Hc d Z	2° Hc d Z	3° Hc d Z	4° Hc d Z	5° Hc d Z	6° Hc d Z	7° Hc d Z	8° Hc d Z	9° Hc d Z	10° Hc d Z	11° Hc d Z	12° Hc d Z	13° Hc d Z	14° Hc d Z	LHA
	° ′ ′ °	° ′ ′ °	° ′ ′ °	° ′ ′ °	° ′ ′ °	° ′ ′ °	° ′ ′ °	° ′ ′ °	° ′ ′ °	° ′ ′ °	° ′ ′ °	° ′ ′ °	° ′ ′ °	° ′ ′ °	° ′ ′ °	
132	−7 20 60 48	228														
130	−7 03 −59 50	230														
128	−6 45 59 52	232														
126	−6 26 60 54	−7 26 59 55	234													
124	−6 08 59 56	−7 07 59 57	236													
122	−5 48 59 58	−6 47 60 59	238													
120	−5 29 −59 60	−6 28 −59 61	−7 27 −59 61	240												
118	−5 08 60 62	−6 08 59 63	−7 07 59 63	242												
116	−4 48 59 64	−5 47 59 65	−6 46 59 65	244												
114	−4 27 59 66	−5 26 59 67	−6 25 59 67	−7 24 59 67	246											
112	−4 06 59 68	−5 05 59 68	−6 04 59 69	−7 03 59 69	248											
110	−3 45 −59 70	−4 44 −59 70	−5 43 −59 71	−6 42 −59 71	−7 41 −59 71	250										
108	−3 23 59 72	−4 22 59 72	−5 21 59 73	−6 20 59 73	−7 19 59 73	252										
106	−3 01 59 74	−4 00 59 74	−4 59 59 75	−5 58 59 75	−6 57 59 75	254										
104	−2 39 59 76	−3 38 59 76	−4 37 59 77	−5 36 59 77	−6 35 59 77	−7 34 59 77	256									
102	−2 16 59 78	−3 15 59 78	−4 14 59 79	−5 13 59 79	−6 12 59 79	−7 11 59 79	258									
100	−1 54 −59 80	−2 53 −59 80	−3 52 −59 81	−4 51 −59 81	−5 50 −59 81	−6 49 −59 81	260									
98	−1 31 59 82	−2 30 59 82	−3 29 59 82	−4 28 59 83	−5 27 59 83	−6 26 59 83	−7 25 59 83	262								
96	−1 09 59 84	−2 08 58 84	−3 06 59 84	−4 05 59 85	−5 04 59 85	−6 03 59 85	−7 02 59 85	264								
94	−0 46 59 86	−1 45 59 86	−2 44 58 86	−3 42 59 87	−4 41 59 87	−5 40 59 87	−6 39 59 87	−7 38 59 87	266							
92	−0 23 59 88	−1 22 59 88	−2 21 59 88	−3 20 58 89	−4 18 59 89	−5 17 59 89	−6 16 59 89	−7 15 59 89	268							
90	00 00 −59 90	−0 59 −59 90	−1 58 −59 90	−2 57 −59 91	−3 56 −58 91	−4 54 −59 91	−5 53 −59 91	−6 52 −59 91	270							
88	00 23 59 92	−0 36 59 92	−1 35 59 92	−2 34 59 92	−3 33 59 93	−4 32 59 93	−5 31 58 93	−6 29 59 93	−7 28 59 93	272						
86	00 46 59 94	−0 13 59 94	−1 12 59 94	−2 11 59 94	−3 10 59 95	−4 09 59 95	−5 08 59 95	−6 07 58 95	−7 05 59 95	274						
84	01 09 59 96	00 10 59 96	−0 49 59 96	−1 48 59 96	−2 47 59 97	−3 46 59 97	−4 45 59 97	−5 44 59 97	−6 43 59 97	−7 42 59 98	276					
82	01 31 59 98	00 32 59 98	−0 27 59 98	−1 26 58 98	−2 24 59 99	−3 23 59 99	−4 22 59 99	−5 21 59 99	−6 20 59 99	−7 19 59 100	278					
80	01 54 −59 100	00 55 −59 100	−0 04 −59 100	−1 03 −59 100	−2 02 −59 101	−3 01 −59 101	−4 00 −59 101	−4 59 −59 101	−5 58 −58 101	−6 56 −59 101	280					
78	02 16 58 102	01 18 59 102	00 19 59 102	−0 40 59 102	−1 39 59 102	−2 38 59 103	−3 37 59 103	−4 36 59 103	−5 35 59 103	−6 34 59 103	−7 33 59 104	282				
76	02 39 59 104	01 40 59 104	00 41 59 104	−0 18 59 104	−1 17 59 104	−2 16 59 105	−3 15 59 105	−4 14 59 105	−5 13 59 105	−6 12 59 105	−7 11 59 106	284				
74	03 01 59 106	02 02 59 106	01 03 59 106	00 04 59 106	−0 55 59 106	−1 54 59 107	−2 53 59 107	−3 52 59 107	−4 51 59 107	−5 50 59 107	−6 49 59 108	286				
72	03 23 59 108	02 24 59 108	01 25 59 108	00 26 59 108	−0 33 59 108	−1 32 59 109	−2 31 59 109	−3 30 59 109	−4 29 59 109	−5 28 59 109	−6 27 59 109	−7 26 59 110	288			
70	03 45 −59 110	02 46 −60 110	01 46 −59 110	00 47 −59 110	−0 12 −59 110	−1 11 −59 111	−2 10 −59 111	−3 09 −59 111	−4 08 −59 111	−5 07 −59 111	−6 06 −59 111	−7 05 −59 112	290			
68	04 06 59 112	03 07 59 112	02 08 59 112	01 09 59 112	00 10 59 112	−0 49 59 113	−1 48 59 113	−2 47 59 113	−3 46 60 113	−4 46 59 113	−5 45 59 113	−6 44 59 114	292			
66	04 27 59 114	03 28 59 114	02 29 59 114	01 30 59 114	00 31 59 114	−0 28 59 114	−1 27 59 115	−2 26 60 115	−3 26 59 115	−4 25 59 115	−5 24 59 115	−6 23 59 115	−7 22 59 116	294		
64	04 48 59 116	03 49 59 116	02 50 59 116	01 51 60 116	00 51 59 116	−0 08 59 116	−1 07 59 117	−2 06 59 117	−3 05 59 117	−4 04 59 117	−5 03 59 117	−6 02 59 117	−7 01 60 118	296		
62	05 08 59 118	04 09 59 118	03 10 59 118	02 11 59 118	01 12 59 118	00 13 59 118	−0 46 60 119	−1 46 59 119	−2 45 59 119	−3 44 59 119	−4 43 59 119	−5 42 59 119	−6 41 59 120	298		
60	05 29 −60 120	04 29 −59 120	03 30 −59 120	02 31 −59 120	01 32 −59 120	00 33 −60 120	−0 27 −59 121	−1 26 −59 121	−2 25 −59 121	−3 24 −59 121	−4 23 −59 121	−5 22 −60 121	−6 22 −59 121	−7 21 −59 122	300	
58	05 48 59 122	04 49 59 122	03 50 59 122	02 51 60 122	01 51 59 122	00 52 59 122	−0 07 59 122	−1 06 59 123	−2 05 60 123	−3 05 59 123	−4 04 59 123	−5 03 59 123	−6 02 60 123	−7 02 59 124	302	
56	06 08 60 124	05 08 59 124	04 09 59 124	03 10 60 124	02 10 59 124	01 11 59 124	00 12 59 124	−0 47 59 125	−1 46 60 125	−2 46 59 125	−3 45 59 125	−4 44 59 125	−5 43 60 125	−6 43 59 126	304	
54	06 26 59 126	05 27 59 126	04 28 60 126	03 28 59 126	02 29 59 126	01 30 59 126	00 31 60 126	−0 29 59 127	−1 28 59 127	−2 27 59 127	−3 26 60 127	−4 26 59 127	−5 25 59 127	−6 24 60 127	−7 24 59 128	306
52	06 45 59 128	05 46 60 128	04 46 59 128	03 47 59 128	02 48 60 128	01 48 59 128	00 49 59 128	−0 10 60 129	−1 10 59 129	−2 09 59 129	−3 08 60 129	−4 08 59 129	−5 07 59 129	−6 06 60 129	−7 06 59 130	308
50	07 03 −60 130	06 03 −59 130	05 04 −59 130	04 05 −60 130	03 05 −59 130	02 06 −59 130	01 07 −60 130	00 07 −59 131	−0 52 −60 131	−1 52 −59 131	−2 51 −59 131	−3 50 −60 131	−4 50 −59 131	−5 49 −59 131	−6 48 −60 131	310
48	07 20 59 132	06 21 60 132	05 21 59 132	04 22 59 132	03 23 60 132	02 23 59 132	01 24 60 132	00 24 59 132	−0 35 59 133	−1 34 60 133	−2 34 59 133	−3 33 60 133	−4 33 59 133	−5 32 59 133	−6 31 60 133	312
46	07 37 59 134	06 38 60 134	05 38 59 134	04 39 60 134	03 39 59 134	02 40 60 134	01 40 59 134	00 41 59 134	−0 18 60 135	−1 18 59 135	−2 17 60 135	−3 17 59 135	−4 16 60 135	−5 16 59 135	−6 15 59 135	314
44	07 53 59 136	06 54 60 136	05 54 59 136	04 55 59 136	03 56 60 136	02 56 59 136	01 57 60 136	00 57 59 136	−0 02 60 137	−1 02 59 137	−2 01 60 137	−3 01 59 137	−4 00 60 137	−5 00 59 137	−5 59 60 137	316
42	08 09 59 138	07 10 60 138	06 10 59 138	05 11 60 138	04 11 59 138	03 12 60 138	02 12 59 138	01 13 60 138	00 13 59 138	−0 46 60 139	−1 46 60 139	−2 46 59 139	−3 45 59 139	−4 44 60 139	−5 44 60 139	318
40	08 24 −59 140	07 25 −60 140	06 25 −59 140	05 26 −60 140	04 26 −59 140	03 27 −60 140	02 27 −59 140	01 28 −60 140	00 28 −60 140	−0 32 −59 141	−1 31 −60 141	−2 31 −59 141	−3 30 −60 141	−4 30 −59 141	−5 29 −60 141	320
38	08 39 60 142	07 39 59 142	06 40 60 142	05 40 59 142	04 41 60 142	03 41 60 142	02 41 59 142	01 42 60 142	00 42 59 142	−0 17 60 143	−1 17 59 143	−2 16 60 143	−3 16 60 143	−4 16 59 143	−5 15 60 143	322
36	08 53 60 144	07 53 59 144	06 54 60 144	05 54 60 144	04 54 59 144	03 55 60 144	02 55 59 144	01 56 60 144	00 56 60 144	−0 04 59 145	−1 03 60 145	−2 03 60 145	−3 03 59 145	−4 02 60 145	−5 02 60 145	324
34	09 06 59 146	08 07 60 146	07 07 60 146	06 07 59 146	05 08 60 146	04 08 60 146	03 08 60 146	02 08 59 146	01 09 60 146	00 09 59 146	−0 50 60 147	−1 50 60 147	−2 50 59 147	−3 49 60 147	−4 49 60 147	326
32	09 19 60 148	08 19 60 148	07 19 59 148	06 20 60 148	05 20 60 148	04 20 59 148	03 21 60 148	02 21 60 148	01 21 59 148	00 22 60 148	−0 38 60 149	−1 38 60 149	−2 38 59 149	−3 37 60 149	−4 37 60 149	328
30	09 31 −60 150	08 31 −60 150	07 31 −59 150	06 32 −60 150	05 32 −60 150	04 32 −60 150	03 32 −59 150	02 33 −60 150	01 33 −60 150	00 33 −60 150	−0 27 −59 150	−1 26 −60 151	−2 26 −60 151	−3 26 −60 151	−4 26 −59 151	330
28	09 42 60 152	08 42 60 152	07 42 59 152	06 43 60 152	05 43 60 152	04 43 60 152	03 43 59 152	02 44 60 152	01 44 60 152	00 44 60 152	−0 16 59 152	−1 15 60 153	−2 15 60 153	−3 15 60 153	−4 15 59 153	332
26	09 53 60 154	08 53 60 154	07 53 60 154	06 53 60 154	05 53 59 154	04 54 60 154	03 54 60 154	02 54 60 154	01 54 60 154	00 54 59 154	−0 05 60 154	−1 05 60 155	−2 05 60 155	−3 05 59 155	−4 04 60 155	334
24	10 02 59 156	09 03 60 156	08 03 60 156	07 03 60 156	06 03 60 156	05 03 60 156	04 03 59 156	03 04 60 156	02 04 60 156	01 04 60 156	00 04 60 156	−0 56 60 156	−1 56 59 157	−2 55 60 157	−3 55 60 157	336
22	10 11 59 158	09 12 60 158	08 12 60 158	07 12 60 158	06 12 60 158	05 12 60 158	04 12 60 158	03 12 59 158	02 13 60 158	01 13 60 158	00 13 60 158	−0 47 60 158	−1 47 60 158	−2 47 59 159	−3 46 60 159	338
20	10 20 −60 160	09 20 −60 160	08 20 −60 160	07 20 −60 160	06 20 −60 160	05 20 −60 160	04 20 −59 160	03 21 −60 160	02 21 −60 160	01 21 −60 160	00 21 −60 160	−0 39 −59 160	−1 38 −60 160	−2 38 −60 160	−3 38 −60 161	340
18	10 27 60 162	09 27 59 162	08 28 60 162	07 28 60 162	06 28 60 162	05 28 60 162	04 28 60 162	03 28 60 162	02 28 60 162	01 28 60 162	00 28 60 162	−0 32 59 162	−1 31 60 162	−2 31 60 162	−3 31 60 162	342
16	10 34 60 164	09 34 60 164	08 34 60 164	07 34 59 164	06 35 60 164	05 35 60 164	04 35 60 164	03 35 60 164	02 35 60 164	01 35 60 164	00 35 60 164	−0 25 60 164	−1 25 60 164	−2 25 60 164	−3 25 60 164	344
14	10 40 60 166	09 40 60 166	08 40 60 166	07 40 60 166	06 40 59 166	05 41 60 166	04 41 60 166	03 41 60 166	02 41 60 166	01 41 60 166	00 41 60 166	−0 19 60 166	−1 19 60 166	−2 19 60 166	−3 19 60 166	346
12	10 45 59 168	09 46 60 168	08 46 60 168	07 46 60 168	06 46 60 168	05 46 60 168	04 46 60 168	03 46 60 168	02 46 60 168	01 46 60 168	00 46 60 168	−0 14 60 168	−1 14 60 168	−2 14 60 168	−3 14 60 168	348
10	10 50 −60 170	09 50 −60 170	08 50 −60 170	07 50 −60 170	06 50 −60 170	05 50 −60 170	04 50 −60 170	03 50 −60 170	02 50 −60 170	01 50 −60 170	00 50 −60 170	−0 10 −60 170	−1 10 −60 170	−2 10 −60 170	−3 10 −60 170	350
8	10 54 60 172	09 54 60 172	08 54 60 172	07 54 60 172	06 54 60 172	05 54 60 172	04 54 60 172	03 54 60 172	02 54 60 172	01 54 60 172	00 54 60 172	−0 06 60 172	−1 06 60 172	−2 06 60 172	−3 06 60 172	352
6	10 56 60 174	09 56 60 174	08 56 60 174	07 56 60 174	06 56 60 174	05 56 60 174	04 56 60 174	03 56 60 174	02 56 60 174	01 56 60 174	00 56 60 174	−0 04 60 174	−1 04 60 174	−2 04 60 174	−3 04 60 174	354
4	10 58 60 176	09 58 60 176	08 58 60 176	07 58 60 176	06 58 60 176	05 58 60 176	04 58 60 176	03 58 60 176	02 58 60 176	01 58 60 176	00 58 60 176	−0 02 60 176	−1 02 60 176	−2 02 60 176	−3 02 60 176	356
2	11 00 60 178	10 00 60 178	09 00 60 178	08 00 60 178	07 00 60 178	06 00 60 178	05 00 60 178	04 00 60 178	03 00 60 178	02 00 60 178	01 00 60 178	00 00 60 178	−1 00 60 178	−2 00 60 178	−3 00 60 178	358
0	11 00 −60 180	10 00 −60 180	09 00 −60 180	08 00 −60 180	07 00 −60 180	06 00 −60 180	05 00 −60 180	04 00 −60 180	03 00 −60 180	02 00 −60 180	01 00 −60 180	00 00 −60 180	−1 00 −60 180	−2 00 −60 180	−3 00 −60 180	360
	0°	1°	2°	3°	4°	5°	6°	7°	8°	9°	10°	11°	12°	13°	14°	

S. Lat. {LHA greater than 180°....... Zn=180−Z; LHA less than 180°........... Zn=180+Z}

DECLINATION (0°-14°) CONTRARY NAME TO LATITUDE

LAT 79°

N. Lat. {LHA greater than 180°……. Zn=Z; LHA less than 180°……….Zn=360−Z}

DECLINATION (15°-29°) SAME NAME AS LATITUDE

LHA	15° Hc	15° d	15° Z	16° Hc	16° d	16° Z	17° Hc	17° d	17° Z	18° Hc	18° d	18° Z	19° Hc	19° d	19° Z
	° ′	′	°	° ′	′	°	° ′	′	°	° ′	′	°	° ′	′	°
0	26 00	+60	180	27 00	+60	180	28 00	+60	180	29 00	+60	180	30 00	+60	180
2	26 00	60	178	27 00	60	178	28 00	60	178	29 00	60	178	30 00	60	178
4	25 58	60	176	26 58	60	176	27 58	60	176	28 58	60	176	29 58	60	176
6	25 56	60	174	26 56	60	174	27 56	60	174	28 56	60	174	29 56	60	174
8	25 53	60	171	26 53	60	171	27 53	60	171	28 53	60	171	29 53	60	171
10	25 49	+60	169	26 49	+60	169	27 49	+60	169	28 49	+60	169	29 49	+60	169
12	25 45	60	167	26 45	60	167	27 45	59	167	28 44	60	167	29 44	60	167
14	25 39	60	165	26 39	60	165	27 39	60	165	28 39	60	165	29 39	60	165
16	25 33	60	163	26 33	60	163	27 33	59	163	28 32	60	163	29 32	60	163
18	25 26	60	161	26 26	59	161	27 25	60	161	28 25	60	161	29 25	60	160
20	25 18	+60	159	26 18	+59	159	27 17	+60	158	28 17	+60	158	29 17	+60	158
22	25 09	60	156	26 09	60	156	27 09	59	156	28 08	60	156	29 08	60	156
24	24 59	60	154	25 59	60	154	26 59	60	154	27 59	59	154	28 58	60	154
26	24 49	60	152	25 49	60	152	26 49	59	152	27 48	60	152	28 48	60	152
28	24 38	60	150	25 38	59	150	26 37	60	150	27 37	60	150	28 37	59	150
30	24 26	+60	148	25 26	+60	148	26 26	+59	148	27 25	+60	148	28 25	+59	148
32	24 14	59	146	25 13	60	146	26 13	60	146	27 13	59	146	28 12	60	145
34	24 01	59	144	25 00	60	144	26 00	59	144	26 59	60	143	27 59	59	143
36	23 47	59	142	24 46	60	142	25 46	59	141	26 45	60	141	27 45	59	141
38	23 32	60	140	24 32	59	139	25 31	60	139	26 31	59	139	27 30	60	139
40	23 17	+59	138	24 16	+60	137	25 16	+59	137	26 15	+60	137	27 15	+59	137
42	23 01	60	135	24 01	59	135	25 00	59	135	25 59	60	135	26 59	59	135
44	22 45	59	133	23 44	60	133	24 44	59	133	25 43	59	133	26 42	60	133
46	22 28	59	131	23 27	60	131	24 27	59	131	25 26	59	131	26 25	59	131
48	22 10	60	129	23 10	59	129	24 09	59	129	25 08	59	129	26 07	60	129
50	21 52	+60	127	22 52	+59	127	23 51	+59	127	24 50	+59	127	25 49	+59	126
52	21 34	59	125	22 33	59	125	23 32	59	125	24 31	60	125	25 31	59	124
54	21 15	59	123	22 14	59	123	23 13	59	123	24 12	59	123	25 11	60	122
56	20 55	60	121	21 55	59	121	22 54	59	121	23 53	59	120	24 52	59	120
58	20 36	59	119	21 35	59	119	22 34	59	119	23 33	59	118	24 32	59	118
60	20 15	+59	117	21 14	+60	117	22 14	+59	117	23 13	+59	116	24 12	+59	116
62	19 55	59	115	20 54	59	115	21 53	59	115	22 52	59	114	23 51	59	114
64	19 34	59	113	20 33	59	113	21 32	59	113	22 31	59	112	23 30	59	112
66	19 13	59	111	20 12	59	111	21 11	58	111	22 09	59	110	23 08	59	110
68	18 51	59	109	19 50	59	109	20 49	59	109	21 48	59	108	22 47	59	108
70	18 29	+59	107	19 28	+59	107	20 27	+59	106	21 26	+59	106	22 25	+59	106
72	18 07	59	105	19 06	59	105	20 05	59	104	21 04	59	104	22 03	59	104
74	17 45	59	103	18 44	59	103	19 43	59	103	20 42	58	102	21 40	59	102
76	17 23	59	101	18 22	58	101	19 20	59	101	20 19	59	100	21 18	59	100
78	17 00	59	99	17 59	59	99	18 58	59	99	19 57	58	98	20 55	59	98
80	16 37	+59	97	17 36	+59	97	18 35	+59	97	19 34	+59	96	20 33	+58	96
82	16 15	58	95	17 13	59	95	18 12	59	95	19 11	59	94	20 10	59	94
84	15 52	59	93	16 51	58	93	17 49	59	93	18 48	59	92	19 47	59	92
86	15 29	59	91	16 28	59	91	17 27	58	91	18 25	59	90	19 24	59	90
88	15 06	59	89	16 05	59	89	17 04	58	89	18 02	59	88	19 01	59	88
90	14 43	+59	87	15 42	+59	87	16 41	+59	87	17 40	+58	87	18 38	+59	86
92	14 20	59	85	15 19	59	85	16 18	59	85	17 17	59	85	18 16	58	84
94	13 58	58	83	14 56	59	83	15 55	59	83	16 54	59	83	17 53	59	82
96	13 35	59	81	14 34	59	81	15 33	58	81	16 31	59	81	17 30	59	80
98	13 12	59	79	14 11	59	79	15 10	59	79	16 09	59	79	17 08	58	79
100	12 50	+59	77	13 49	+59	77	14 48	+58	77	15 46	+59	77	16 45	+59	77
102	12 28	58	75	13 26	59	75	14 25	59	75	15 24	59	75	16 23	59	75
104	12 06	58	73	13 04	59	73	14 03	59	73	15 02	59	73	16 01	59	73
106	11 44	59	72	12 43	59	71	13 42	58	71	14 40	59	71	15 39	59	71
108	11 22	59	70	12 21	59	69	13 20	59	69	14 19	59	69	15 18	59	69
110	11 01	+59	68	12 00	+59	67	12 59	+59	67	13 58	+59	67	14 57	+59	67
112	10 40	59	66	11 39	59	66	12 38	59	65	13 37	59	65	14 36	59	65
114	10 19	59	64	11 18	59	64	12 17	59	63	13 16	59	63	14 15	59	63
116	09 59	59	62	10 58	59	62	11 57	59	62	12 56	59	61	13 55	59	61
118	09 39	59	60	10 38	59	60	11 37	59	60	12 36	59	59	13 35	59	59
120	09 19	+59	58	10 18	+59	58	11 17	+60	58	12 17	+59	57	13 16	+59	57
122	09 00	59	56	09 59	59	56	10 58	59	56	11 57	60	56	12 57	59	55
124	08 41	59	54	09 40	60	54	10 40	59	54	11 39	59	54	12 38	59	53
126	08 23	59	52	09 22	59	52	10 21	60	52	11 21	59	52	12 20	59	52
128	08 05	59	50	09 04	60	50	10 04	59	50	11 03	59	50	12 02	59	50
130	07 48	+59	48	08 47	+59	48	09 46	+60	48	10 46	+59	48	11 45	+59	48
132	07 31	59	46	08 30	60	46	09 30	59	46	10 29	59	46	11 28	60	46
134	07 14	60	45	08 14	59	44	09 13	60	44	10 13	59	44	11 12	60	44
136	06 59	59	43	07 58	60	42	08 58	59	42	09 57	60	42	10 57	59	42
138	06 44	59	41	07 43	60	41	08 43	59	40	09 42	60	40	10 42	59	40

LHA	20° Hc	20° d	20° Z	21° Hc	21° d	21° Z	22° Hc	22° d	22° Z	23° Hc	23° d	23° Z	24° Hc	24° d	24° Z
	° ′	′	°	° ′	′	°	° ′	′	°	° ′	′	°	° ′	′	°
0	31 00	+60	180	32 00	+60	180	33 00	+60	180	34 00	+60	180	35 00	+60	180
2	31 00	60	178	32 00	60	178	33 00	60	178	34 00	60	178	35 00	60	178
4	30 58	60	176	31 58	60	176	32 58	60	176	33 58	60	176	34 58	60	176
6	30 56	60	173	31 56	60	173	32 56	60	173	33 56	60	173	34 56	60	173
8	30 53	60	171	31 53	60	171	32 53	60	171	33 53	60	171	34 53	60	171
10	30 49	+60	169	31 49	+60	169	32 49	+60	169	33 49	+60	169	34 49	+60	169
12	30 44	60	167	31 44	60	167	32 44	60	167	33 44	60	167	34 44	60	167
14	30 39	60	165	31 39	60	165	32 39	59	165	33 38	60	165	34 38	60	164
16	30 32	60	163	31 32	60	162	32 32	60	162	33 32	60	162	34 32	60	162
18	30 25	60	160	31 25	60	160	32 25	60	160	33 25	59	160	34 24	60	160
20	30 17	+60	158	31 17	+59	158	32 16	+60	158	33 16	+60	158	34 16	+60	158
22	30 08	60	156	31 08	60	156	32 08	59	156	33 07	60	156	34 07	60	156
24	29 58	60	154	30 58	60	154	31 58	59	154	32 57	60	154	33 57	60	153
26	29 48	59	152	30 47	60	152	31 47	60	151	32 47	60	151	33 47	59	151
28	29 36	60	150	30 36	60	149	31 36	59	149	32 35	60	149	33 35	60	149
30	29 24	+60	147	30 24	+60	147	31 24	+59	147	32 23	+60	147	33 23	+60	147
32	29 12	59	145	30 11	60	145	31 11	60	145	32 11	59	145	33 10	60	145
34	28 58	60	143	29 58	59	143	30 57	60	143	31 57	60	143	32 57	59	143
36	28 44	60	141	29 44	59	141	30 43	60	141	31 43	59	141	32 42	60	140
38	28 30	59	139	29 29	59	139	30 28	60	139	31 28	59	138	32 27	60	138
40	28 14	+60	137	29 14	+59	137	30 13	+59	136	31 12	+60	136	32 12	+59	136
42	27 58	60	135	28 58	59	134	29 57	59	134	30 56	60	134	31 56	59	134
44	27 42	59	133	28 41	59	132	29 40	59	132	30 39	60	132	31 39	59	132
46	27 24	60	130	28 24	59	130	29 23	59	130	30 22	59	130	31 21	60	130
48	27 07	59	128	28 06	59	128	29 05	59	128	30 04	60	128	31 04	59	128
50	26 48	+60	126	27 48	+59	126	28 47	+59	126	29 46	+59	126	30 45	+59	126
52	26 30	59	124	27 29	59	124	28 28	59	124	29 27	59	124	30 26	59	123
54	26 11	59	122	27 10	59	122	28 09	59	122	29 08	59	122	30 07	59	121
56	25 51	59	120	26 50	59	120	27 49	59	120	28 48	59	119	29 47	59	119
58	25 31	59	118	26 30	59	118	27 29	59	118	28 28	59	117	29 27	59	117
60	25 11	+59	116	26 10	+59	116	27 09	+58	116	28 07	+59	115	29 06	+59	115
62	24 50	59	114	25 49	59	114	26 48	59	114	27 47	58	113	28 45	59	113
64	24 29	59	112	25 28	59	112	26 27	58	112	27 25	59	111	28 24	59	111
66	24 07	59	110	25 06	59	110	26 05	59	109	27 04	59	109	28 03	59	109
68	23 46	58	108	24 44	59	108	25 43	59	107	26 42	59	107	27 41	59	107
70	23 24	+59	106	24 23	+58	106	25 21	+59	105	26 20	+59	105	27 19	+59	105
72	23 02	58	104	24 00	59	104	24 59	59	103	25 58	59	103	26 57	58	103
74	22 39	59	102	23 38	59	102	24 37	59	101	25 36	58	101	26 34	59	101
76	22 17	59	100	23 16	58	100	24 14	59	99	25 13	59	99	26 12	58	99
78	21 54	59	98	22 53	59	98	23 52	58	97	24 50	59	97	25 49	59	97
80	21 31	+59	96	22 30	+59	96	23 29	+59	95	24 28	+58	95	25 26	+59	95
82	21 09	58	94	22 07	59	94	23 06	59	93	24 05	58	93	25 03	59	93
84	20 46	58	92	21 44	59	92	22 43	59	92	23 42	59	91	24 41	58	91
86	20 23	59	90	21 22	58	90	22 20	59	90	23 19	59	89	24 18	58	89
88	20 00	59	88	20 59	58	88	21 57	59	88	22 56	59	87	23 55	58	87
90	19 37	+59	86	20 36	+59	86	21 35	+58	86	22 33	+59	85	23 32	+59	85
92	19 14	59	84	20 13	59	84	21 12	58	84	22 10	59	83	23 09	59	83
94	18 52	58	82	19 50	59	82	20 49	59	82	21 48	59	82	22 47	58	81
96	18 29	59	80	19 28	58	80	20 26	59	80	21 25	59	80	22 24	59	79
98	18 06	59	78	19 05	59	78	20 04	59	78	21 03	59	78	22 02	58	77
100	17 44	+59	76	18 43	+59	76	19 42	+58	76	20 40	+59	76	21 39	+59	76
102	17 22	59	74	18 21	59	74	19 20	58	74	20 18	59	74	21 17	59	74
104	17 00	59	72	17 59	59	72	18 58	59	72	19 57	58	72	20 55	59	72
106	16 38	59	71	17 37	59	70	18 36	59	70	19 35	59	70	20 34	59	70
108	16 17	59	69	17 16	59	68	18 15	59	68	19 14	59	68	20 12	59	68
110	15 56	+59	67	16 55	+59	67	17 54	+58	66	18 52	+59	66	19 51	+59	66
112	15 35	59	65	16 34	59	65	17 33	59	64	18 32	59	64	19 31	59	64
114	15 14	59	63	16 13	59	63	17 12	59	63	18 11	59	62	19 10	59	62
116	14 54	59	61	15 53	59	61	16 52	59	61	17 51	59	60	18 50	59	60
118	14 34	59	59	15 33	59	59	16 32	59	59	17 31	60	59	18 30	59	58
120	14 15	+59	57	15 14	+59	57	16 13	+59	57	17 12	+59	57	18 11	+59	56
122	13 56	59	55	14 55	59	55	15 54	59	55	16 53	59	55	17 52	59	55
124	13 37	59	53	14 36	60	53	15 36	59	53	16 35	59	53	17 34	59	53
126	13 19	59	51	14 18	60	51	15 18	59	51	16 17	59	51	17 16	59	51
128	13 01	60	50	14 01	59	49	15 00	59	49	15 59	60	49	16 59	59	49
130	12 44	+60	48	13 44	+59	47	14 43	+59	47	15 42	+60	47	16 42	+59	47
132	12 28	59	46	13 27	59	46	14 26	60	45	15 26	59	45	16 25	59	45
134	12 12	59	44	13 11	59	44	14 10	60	44	15 10	59	43	16 09	60	43
136	11 56	59	42	12 55	60	42	13 55	59	42	14 54	60	41	15 54	59	41
138	11 41	59	40	12 40	60	40	13 40	59	40	14 39	60	40	15 39	59	39

LHA	25° Hc	25° d	25° Z	26° Hc	26° d	26° Z	27° Hc	27° d	27° Z	28° Hc	28° d	28° Z	29° Hc	29° d	29° Z	LHA
	° ′	′	°	° ′	′	°	° ′	′	°	° ′	′	°	° ′	′	°	
0	36 00	+60	180	37 00	+60	180	38 00	+60	180	39 00	+60	180	40 00	+60	180	360
2	36 00	60	178	37 00	60	178	38 00	60	178	39 00	60	178	40 00	60	178	358
4	35 58	60	176	36 58	60	176	37 58	60	176	38 58	60	176	39 58	60	175	356
6	35 56	60	173	36 56	60	173	37 56	60	173	38 56	60	173	39 56	60	173	354
8	35 53	60	171	36 53	60	171	37 53	60	171	38 53	60	171	39 53	60	171	352
10	35 49	+60	169	36 49	+60	169	37 49	+60	169	38 49	+60	169	39 49	+60	169	350
12	35 44	60	167	36 44	60	167	37 44	60	167	38 44	60	166	39 44	60	166	348
14	35 38	60	164	36 38	60	164	37 38	60	164	38 38	60	164	39 38	60	164	346
16	35 32	60	162	36 32	59	162	37 31	60	162	38 31	60	162	39 31	60	162	344
18	35 24	60	160	36 24	60	160	37 24	60	160	38 24	60	160	39 24	59	160	342
20	35 16	+60	158	36 16	+60	158	37 16	+59	158	38 15	+60	157	39 15	+60	157	340
22	35 07	60	156	36 07	59	155	37 06	60	155	38 06	60	155	39 06	60	155	338
24	34 57	60	153	35 57	59	153	36 56	60	153	37 56	60	153	38 56	59	153	336
26	34 46	60	151	35 46	60	151	36 46	59	151	37 45	60	151	38 45	60	151	334
28	34 35	59	149	35 34	60	149	36 34	60	149	37 34	59	149	38 33	60	148	332
30	34 23	+59	147	35 22	+60	147	36 22	+59	146	37 21	+60	146	38 21	+59	146	330
32	34 10	59	145	35 09	60	144	36 09	59	144	37 08	60	144	38 08	59	144	328
34	33 56	60	142	34 56	59	142	35 55	59	142	36 54	60	142	37 54	59	142	326
36	33 42	59	140	34 41	60	140	35 41	59	140	36 40	59	140	37 39	60	140	324
38	33 27	59	138	34 26	59	138	35 25	60	138	36 25	59	138	37 24	60	137	322
40	33 11	+59	136	34 10	+60	136	35 10	+59	136	36 09	+59	135	37 08	+60	135	320
42	32 55	59	134	33 54	59	134	34 53	60	133	35 53	59	133	36 52	59	133	318
44	32 38	59	132	33 37	59	131	34 36	60	131	35 36	59	131	36 35	59	131	316
46	32 21	59	130	33 20	59	129	34 19	59	129	35 18	59	129	36 17	59	129	314
48	32 03	59	127	33 02	59	127	34 01	59	127	35 00	59	127	35 59	59	127	312
50	31 44	+59	125	32 43	+59	125	33 42	+59	125	34 41	+59	125	35 40	+60	124	310
52	31 25	59	123	32 24	59	123	33 23	59	123	34 22	59	123	35 21	59	122	308
54	31 06	59	121	32 05	59	121	33 04	59	121	34 03	59	120	35 02	59	120	306
56	30 46	59	119	31 45	59	119	32 44	59	119	33 43	59	118	34 42	59	118	304
58	30 26	59	117	31 25	59	117	32 24	59	117	33 23	58	116	34 21	59	116	302
60	30 05	+59	115	31 04	+59	115	32 03	+59	114	33 02	+59	114	34 01	+58	114	300
62	29 44	59	113	30 43	59	113	31 42	59	112	32 41	59	112	33 40	58	112	298
64	29 23	59	111	30 22	59	111	31 21	58	110	32 19	59	110	33 18	59	110	296
66	29 02	58	109	30 00	59	109	30 59	59	108	31 58	59	108	32 57	58	108	294
68	28 40	58	107	29 38	59	107	30 37	59	106	31 36	59	106	32 35	58	106	292
70	28 18	+58	105	29 16	+59	105	30 15	+59	104	31 14	+58	104	32 12	+59	104	290
72	27 55	59	103	28 54	59	103	29 53	59	102	30 52	58	102	31 50	59	102	288
74	27 33	59	101	28 32	58	101	29 30	59	100	30 29	59	100	31 28	58	100	286
76	27 10	59	99	28 09	59	99	29 08	58	98	30 06	59	98	31 05	59	98	284
78	26 48	58	97	27 46	59	97	28 45	59	96	29 44	58	96	30 42	59	96	282
80	26 25	+59	95	27 24	+58	95	28 22	+59	94	29 21	+58	94	30 19	+59	94	280
82	26 02	59	93	27 01	58	93	27 59	59	92	28 58	59	92	29 57	58	92	278
84	25 39	59	91	26 38	59	91	27 37	58	90	28 35	59	90	29 34	58	90	276
86	25 16	59	89	26 15	59	89	27 14	58	88	28 12	59	88	29 11	58	88	274
88	24 53	59	87	25 52	59	87	26 51	58	86	27 49	59	86	28 48	58	86	272
90	24 31	+58	85	25 29	+59	85	26 28	+59	84	27 27	+58	84	28 25	+59	84	270
92	24 08	59	83	25 07	58	83	26 05	59	83	27 04	58	82	28 02	59	82	268
94	23 45	59	81	24 44	59	81	25 43	58	81	26 41	59	80	27 40	58	80	266
96	23 23	58	79	24 21	59	79	25 20	59	79	26 19	58	78	27 17	59	78	264
98	23 00	59	78	23 59	59	77	24 58	58	77	25 56	59	77	26 55	59	76	262
100	22 38	+59	75	23 37	+58	75	24 35	+59	75	25 34	+59	75	26 33	+58	74	260
102	22 16	59	73	23 15	58	73	24 13	59	73	25 12	59	73	26 11	59	72	258
104	21 54	59	71	22 53	59	71	23 52	58	71	24 50	59	71	25 49	59	71	256
106	21 33	58	70	22 31	59	69	23 30	59	69	24 29	59	69	25 28	58	69	254
108	21 11	59	68	22 10	59	67	23 09	59	67	24 08	59	67	25 07	58	67	252
110	20 50	+59	66	21 49	+59	66	22 48	+59	65	23 47	+59	65	24 46	+58	65	250
112	20 30	58	64	21 28	59	64	22 27	59	63	23 26	59	63	24 25	59	63	248
114	20 09	59	62	21 08	59	62	22 07	59	62	23 06	59	61	24 05	59	61	246
116	19 49	59	60	20 48	59	60	21 47	59	60	22 46	59	59	23 45	59	59	244
118	19 30	59	58	20 29	59	58	21 28	59	58	22 27	59	58	23 26	59	57	242
120	19 10	+59	56	20 09	+59	56	21 08	+59	56	22 07	+60	56	23 07	+59	55	240
122	18 51	60	54	19 51	59	54	20 50	59	54	21 49	59	54	22 48	59	54	238
124	18 33	59	52	19 32	59	52	20 31	60	52	21 31	59	52	22 30	59	52	236
126	18 15	59	51	19 14	60	50	20 14	59	50	21 13	59	50	22 12	59	50	234
128	17 58	59	49	18 57	59	49	19 56	59	48	20 55	60	48	21 55	59	48	232
130	17 41	+59	47	18 40	+59	47	19 39	+60	47	20 39	+59	46	21 38	+59	46	230
132	17 24	60	45	18 24	59	45	19 23	59	45	20 22	60	44	21 22	59	44	228
134	17 09	59	43	18 08	59	43	19 07	60	43	20 07	59	43	21 06	59	42	226
136	16 53	60	41	17 53	59	41	18 52	59	41	19 51	60	41	20 51	59	41	224
138	16 38	60	39	17 38	59	39	18 37	60	39	19 37	59	39	20 36	60	39	222

15° 16° 17° 18° 19° 20° 21° 22° 23° 24° 25° 26° 27° 28° 29°

S. Lat. {LHA greater than 180°…….Zn=180−Z; LHA less than 180°……….Zn=180+Z}

DECLINATION (15°-29°) SAME NAME AS LATITUDE

N. Lat. {LHA greater than 180°....... Zn=Z / LHA less than 180°........... Zn=360−Z}

DECLINATION (15°-29°) SAME NAME AS LATITUDE

LAT 79°

LHA	15° Hc	15° d	15° Z	16° Hc	16° d	16° Z	17° Hc	17° d	17° Z	18° Hc	18° d	18° Z	19° Hc	19° d	19° Z
	° ′	′	°	° ′	′	°	° ′	′	°	° ′	′	°	° ′	′	°
140	06 29	+59	39	07 28	+60	39	08 28	+60	38	09 28	+59	38	10 27	+60	38
142	06 15	59	37	07 14	60	37	08 14	60	37	09 14	59	36	10 13	60	36
144	06 02	59	35	07 01	60	35	08 01	59	35	09 00	60	35	10 00	60	34
146	05 49	59	33	06 48	60	33	07 48	60	33	08 48	59	33	09 47	60	32
148	05 37	59	31	06 36	60	31	07 36	60	31	08 36	59	31	09 35	60	31
150	05 25	+60	29	06 25	+60	29	07 25	+59	29	08 24	+60	29	09 24	+60	29
152	05 14	60	27	06 14	60	27	07 14	60	27	08 14	59	27	09 13	60	27
154	05 04	60	25	06 04	60	25	07 04	60	25	08 04	60	25	09 04	59	25
156	04 55	60	23	05 55	60	23	06 55	59	23	07 54	60	23	08 54	60	23
158	04 46	60	21	05 46	60	21	06 46	60	21	07 46	60	21	08 46	60	21
160	04 38	+60	19	05 38	+60	19	06 38	+60	19	07 38	+60	19	08 38	+60	19
162	04 31	60	17	05 31	60	17	06 31	60	17	07 31	60	17	08 31	60	17
164	04 25	60	16	05 25	59	15	06 24	60	15	07 24	60	15	08 24	60	15
166	04 19	60	14	05 19	60	14	06 19	60	14	07 19	60	13	08 19	60	13
168	04 14	60	12	05 14	60	12	06 14	60	12	07 14	60	12	08 14	60	12
170	04 10	+60	10	05 10	+60	10	06 10	+60	10	07 10	+60	10	08 10	+60	10
172	04 06	60	8	05 06	60	8	06 06	60	8	07 06	60	8	08 06	60	8
174	04 04	60	6	05 04	60	6	06 04	59	6	07 03	60	6	08 03	60	6
176	04 02	60	4	05 02	60	4	06 02	60	4	07 02	60	4	08 02	60	4
178	04 00	60	2	05 00	60	2	06 00	60	2	07 00	60	2	08 00	60	2
180	04 00	+60	0	05 00	+60	0	06 00	+60	0	07 00	+60	0	08 00	+60	0

LHA	20° Hc	20° d	20° Z	21° Hc	21° d	21° Z	22° Hc	22° d	22° Z	23° Hc	23° d	23° Z	24° Hc	24° d	24° Z
	° ′	′	°	° ′	′	°	° ′	′	°	° ′	′	°	° ′	′	°
140	11 27	+59	38	12 26	+60	38	13 26	+59	38	14 25	+60	38	15 25	+59	38
142	11 13	59	36	12 12	60	36	13 12	59	36	14 11	60	36	15 11	60	36
144	11 00	59	34	11 59	60	34	12 59	59	34	13 58	60	34	14 58	60	34
146	10 47	60	32	11 47	59	32	12 46	60	32	13 46	60	32	14 46	59	32
148	10 35	60	30	11 35	59	30	12 34	60	30	13 34	60	30	14 34	59	30
150	10 24	+60	29	11 24	+59	28	12 23	+60	28	13 23	+60	28	14 23	+59	28
152	10 13	60	27	11 13	60	27	12 13	59	26	13 12	60	26	14 12	60	26
154	10 03	60	25	11 03	60	25	12 03	60	25	13 03	59	25	14 02	60	24
156	09 54	60	23	10 54	60	23	11 54	60	23	12 54	59	23	13 53	60	23
158	09 46	59	21	10 45	60	21	11 45	60	21	12 45	60	21	13 45	60	21
160	09 38	+60	19	10 38	+59	19	11 37	+60	19	12 37	+60	19	13 37	+60	19
162	09 31	60	17	10 31	59	17	11 30	60	17	12 30	60	17	13 30	60	17
164	09 24	60	15	10 24	60	15	11 24	60	15	12 24	60	15	13 24	60	15
166	09 19	60	13	10 19	59	13	11 18	60	13	12 18	60	13	13 18	60	13
168	09 14	60	11	10 14	60	11	11 14	60	11	12 14	59	11	13 13	60	11
170	09 10	+59	10	10 09	+60	10	11 09	+60	9	12 09	+60	9	13 09	+60	9
172	09 06	60	8	10 06	60	8	11 06	60	8	12 06	60	8	13 06	60	8
174	09 03	60	6	10 03	60	6	11 03	60	6	12 03	60	6	13 03	60	6
176	09 02	60	4	10 02	60	4	11 02	60	4	12 02	60	4	13 02	60	4
178	09 00	60	2	10 00	60	2	11 00	60	2	12 00	60	2	13 00	60	2
180	09 00	+60	0	10 00	+60	0	11 00	+60	0	12 00	+60	0	13 00	+60	0

LHA	25° Hc	25° d	25° Z	26° Hc	26° d	26° Z	27° Hc	27° d	27° Z	28° Hc	28° d	28° Z	29° Hc	29° d	29° Z	LHA
	° ′	′	°	° ′	′	°	° ′	′	°	° ′	′	°	° ′	′	°	
140	16 24	+60	37	17 24	+59	37	18 23	+60	37	19 23	+59	37	20 22	+60	37	220
142	16 11	59	36	17 10	60	35	18 10	59	35	19 09	60	35	20 09	59	35	218
144	15 58	59	34	16 57	60	34	17 57	59	33	18 56	60	33	19 56	59	33	216
146	15 45	60	32	16 45	59	32	17 44	60	32	18 44	60	31	19 44	59	31	214
148	15 33	60	30	16 33	60	30	17 33	59	30	18 32	60	30	19 32	60	30	212
150	15 22	+60	28	16 22	+60	28	17 22	+59	28	18 21	+60	28	19 21	+60	28	210
152	15 12	60	26	16 12	59	26	17 11	60	26	18 11	60	26	19 11	60	26	208
154	15 02	60	24	16 02	60	24	17 02	60	24	18 02	59	24	19 01	60	24	206
156	14 53	60	22	15 53	60	22	16 53	60	22	17 53	59	22	18 52	60	22	204
158	14 45	60	21	15 45	59	21	16 44	60	20	17 44	60	20	18 44	60	20	202
160	14 37	+60	19	15 37	+60	19	16 37	+60	19	17 37	+59	19	18 36	+60	18	200
162	14 30	60	17	15 30	60	17	16 30	60	17	17 30	60	17	18 30	59	17	198
164	14 24	60	15	15 24	60	15	16 24	60	15	17 24	59	15	18 23	60	15	196
166	14 18	60	13	15 18	60	13	16 18	60	13	17 18	60	13	18 18	60	13	194
168	14 13	60	11	15 13	60	11	16 13	60	11	17 13	60	11	18 13	60	11	192
170	14 09	+60	9	15 09	+60	9	16 09	+60	9	17 09	+60	9	18 09	+60	9	190
172	14 06	60	8	15 06	60	7	16 06	60	7	17 06	60	7	18 06	60	7	188
174	14 03	60	6	15 03	60	6	16 03	60	6	17 03	60	6	18 03	60	6	186
176	14 02	60	4	15 02	60	4	16 02	60	4	17 02	60	4	18 02	60	4	184
178	14 00	60	2	15 00	60	2	16 00	60	2	17 00	60	2	18 00	60	2	182
180	14 00	+60	0	15 00	+60	0	16 00	+60	0	17 00	+60	0	18 00	+60	0	180

15°	16°	17°	18°	19°	20°	21°	22°	23°	24°	25°	26°	27°	28°	29°

S. Lat. {LHA greater than 180°........ Zn=180−Z / LHA less than 180°........... Zn=180+Z}

DECLINATION (15°-29°) SAME NAME AS LATITUDE

N. Lat. {LHA greater than 180°........Zn=Z; LHA less than 180°..........Zn=360−Z}

DECLINATION (15°-29°) CONTRARY NAME TO LATITUDE

	15°			16°			17°			18°			19°			20°			21°			22°			23°			24°			25°			26°			27°			28°			29°			
LHA	Hc	d	Z	Hc	d	Z	Hc	d	Z	Hc	d	Z	Hc	d	Z	Hc	d	Z	Hc	d	Z	Hc	d	Z	Hc	d	Z	Hc	d	Z	Hc	d	Z	Hc	d	Z	Hc	d	Z	Hc	d	Z	Hc	d	Z	LHA
	° ′	′	°	° ′	′	°	° ′	′	°	° ′	′	°	° ′	′	°	° ′	′	°	° ′	′	°	° ′	′	°	° ′	′	°	° ′	′	°	° ′	′	°	° ′	′	°	° ′	′	°	° ′	′	°	° ′	′	°	
48	−7 31	59	134																																											312
46	−7 14	60	135																																											314
44	−6 59	60	137																																											316
42	−6 44	59	139																																											318
40	−6 29	−59	141																																											320
38	−6 15	59	143	−7 14	60	143																																						322
36	−6 02	59	145	−7 01	60	145																																						324
34	−5 49	59	147	−6 48	60	147																																						326
32	−5 37	59	149	−6 36	60	149																																						328
30	−5 25	−60	151	−6 25	−60	151																																						330
28	−5 14	60	153	−6 14	60	153	−7 14	60	153																																			332
26	−5 04	60	155	−6 04	60	155	−7 04	60	155																																			334
24	−4 55	60	157	−5 55	60	157	−6 55	59	157																																			336
22	−4 46	60	159	−5 46	60	159	−6 46	60	159																																			338
20	−4 38	−60	161	−5 38	−60	161	−6 38	−60	161																																			340
18	−4 31	60	163	−5 31	60	163	−6 31	60	163																																			342
16	−4 25	60	164	−5 25	59	165	−6 24	60	165																																			344
14	−4 19	60	166	−5 19	60	166	−6 19	60	166																																			346
12	−4 14	60	168	−5 14	60	168	−6 14	60	168																																			348
10	−4 10	−60	170	−5 10	−60	170	−6 10	−60	170																																			350
8	−4 06	60	172	−5 06	60	172	−6 06	60	172																																			352
6	−4 04	60	174	−5 04	60	174	−6 04	59	174																																			354
4	−4 02	60	176	−5 02	60	176	−6 02	60	176																																			356
2	−4 00	60	178	−5 00	60	178	−6 00	60	178	−7 00	60	178																																358
0	−4 00	−60	180	−5 00	−60	180	−6 00	−60	180	−7 00	−60	180																																360
	15°			16°			17°			18°			19°			20°			21°			22°			23°			24°			25°			26°			27°			28°			29°			

LAT 79°

S. Lat. {LHA greater than 180°.......Zn=180−Z; LHA less than 180°...........Zn=180+Z}

DECLINATION (15°-29°) CONTRARY NAME TO LATITUDE

N. Lat. {LHA greater than 180°....... Zn=Z
{LHA less than 180°........... Zn=360−Z

DECLINATION (0°-14°) SAME NAME AS LATITUDE

LHA	0° Hc	0° d	0° Z	1° Hc	1° d	1° Z	2° Hc	2° d	2° Z	3° Hc	3° d	3° Z	4° Hc	4° d	4° Z
	° ′	′	°	° ′	′	°	° ′	′	°	° ′	′	°	° ′	′	°
0	10 00	+60	180	11 00	+60	180	12 00	+60	180	13 00	+60	180	14 00	+60	180
2	10 00	60	178	11 00	60	178	12 00	60	178	13 00	60	178	14 00	60	178
4	09 59	60	176	10 59	60	176	11 59	60	176	12 59	60	176	13 59	60	176
6	09 57	60	174	10 57	60	174	11 57	60	174	12 57	60	174	13 57	60	174
8	09 54	60	172	10 54	60	172	11 54	60	172	12 54	60	172	13 54	60	172
10	09 51	+60	170	10 51	+60	170	11 51	+60	170	12 51	+60	170	13 51	+60	170
12	09 47	60	168	10 47	60	168	11 47	60	168	12 47	60	168	13 47	60	168
14	09 42	60	166	10 42	60	166	11 42	60	166	12 42	60	166	13 42	60	166
16	09 37	60	164	10 37	59	164	11 36	60	164	12 36	60	164	13 36	60	164
18	09 30	60	162	10 30	60	162	11 30	60	162	12 30	60	162	13 30	60	162
20	09 24	+59	160	10 23	+60	160	11 23	+60	160	12 23	+60	160	13 23	+60	160
22	09 16	60	158	10 16	60	158	11 16	60	158	12 16	59	158	13 15	60	157
24	09 08	60	156	10 08	59	156	11 07	60	156	12 07	60	156	13 07	60	155
26	08 59	60	154	09 59	59	154	10 58	60	154	11 58	60	153	12 58	60	153
28	08 49	60	152	09 49	60	152	10 49	60	152	11 49	59	151	12 48	60	151
30	08 39	+60	150	09 39	+60	150	10 39	+59	149	11 38	+60	149	12 38	+60	149
32	08 28	60	148	09 28	60	148	10 28	59	147	11 27	60	147	12 27	60	147
34	08 17	59	146	09 16	60	146	10 16	60	145	11 16	60	145	12 16	59	145
36	08 05	59	144	09 04	60	144	10 04	60	143	11 04	59	143	12 03	60	143
38	07 52	60	142	08 52	59	142	09 51	60	141	10 51	60	141	11 51	59	141
40	07 39	+59	140	08 38	+60	140	09 38	+60	139	10 38	+59	139	11 37	+60	139
42	07 25	60	138	08 25	59	137	09 24	60	137	10 24	59	137	11 23	60	137
44	07 11	59	136	08 10	60	135	09 10	59	135	10 09	60	135	11 09	59	135
46	06 56	59	134	07 55	60	133	08 55	59	133	09 54	60	133	10 54	59	133
48	06 40	60	132	07 40	59	131	08 39	60	131	09 39	59	131	10 38	60	131
50	06 25	+59	130	07 24	+59	129	08 23	+60	129	09 23	+59	129	10 22	+60	129
52	06 08	60	128	07 08	59	127	08 07	60	127	09 07	59	127	10 06	59	127
54	05 52	59	126	06 51	59	125	07 50	60	125	08 50	59	125	09 49	60	125
56	05 34	60	124	06 34	59	123	07 33	59	123	08 32	60	123	09 32	59	123
58	05 17	59	122	06 16	60	122	07 16	59	121	08 15	59	121	09 14	60	121
60	04 59	+59	120	05 58	+60	120	06 58	+59	119	07 57	+59	119	08 56	+59	119
62	04 41	59	118	05 40	59	118	06 39	59	117	07 38	60	117	08 38	59	117
64	04 22	59	116	05 21	60	116	06 21	59	115	07 20	59	115	08 19	59	115
66	04 03	59	114	05 02	60	114	06 02	59	113	07 01	59	113	08 00	59	113
68	03 44	59	112	04 43	59	112	05 42	59	111	06 41	60	111	07 41	59	111
70	03 24	+59	110	04 23	+60	110	05 23	+59	109	06 22	+59	109	07 21	+59	109
72	03 05	59	108	04 04	59	108	05 03	59	107	06 02	59	107	07 01	59	107
74	02 45	59	106	03 44	59	106	04 43	59	106	05 42	59	105	06 41	59	105
76	02 24	60	104	03 24	59	104	04 23	59	104	05 22	59	103	06 21	59	103
78	02 04	59	102	03 03	59	102	04 02	60	102	05 02	59	101	06 01	59	101
80	01 44	+59	100	02 43	+59	100	03 42	+59	100	04 41	+59	99	05 40	+59	99
82	01 23	59	98	02 22	59	98	03 21	59	98	04 20	60	97	05 20	59	97
84	01 02	59	96	02 01	60	96	03 01	59	96	04 00	60	95	05 00	58	95
86	00 42	59	94	01 41	59	94	02 40	59	94	03 39	60	93	04 39	58	93
88	00 21	59	92	01 20	59	92	02 19	59	92	03 18	60	91	04 18	58	91
90	00 00	+59	90	00 59	+59	90	01 58	+59	90	02 57	+60	90	03 57	+58	89
92	−0 21	59	88	00 38	59	88	01 37	59	88	02 36	60	88	03 36	59	87
94	−0 42	59	86	00 17	60	86	01 17	59	86	02 16	59	86	03 15	59	85
96	−1 02	59	84	−0 03	59	84	00 56	59	84	01 55	59	84	02 54	59	83
98	−1 23	59	82	−0 24	59	82	00 35	59	82	01 34	59	82	02 33	60	81
100	−1 44	+59	80	−0 45	+60	80	00 15	+59	80	01 14	+59	80	02 13	+59	79
102	−2 04	59	78	−1 05	59	78	−0 06	59	78	00 53	59	78	01 52	60	77
104	−2 24	59	76	−1 25	59	76	−0 26	59	76	00 33	59	76	01 32	59	75
106	−2 45	60	74	−1 45	59	74	−0 46	59	74	00 13	59	74	01 12	59	73
108	−3 05	60	72	−2 05	59	72	−1 06	59	72	−0 07	60	72	00 53	58	71
110	−3 24	+59	70	−2 25	+59	70	−1 26	+59	70	−0 27	+60	70	00 33	+59	69
112	−3 44	59	68	−2 45	60	68	−1 45	59	68	−0 46	60	68	00 14	58	67
114	−4 03	59	66	−3 04	59	66	−2 05	60	66	−1 05	59	66	−0 06	59	66
116	−4 22	59	64	−3 23	60	64	−2 23	59	64	−1 24	59	64	−0 25	59	64
118	−4 41	60	62	−3 41	59	62	−2 42	59	62	−1 43	60	62	−0 43	59	62
120	−4 59	+59	60	−4 00	+60	60	−3 00	+59	60	−2 01	+59	60	−1 02	+60	60
122	−5 17	60	58	−4 17	59	58	−3 18	59	58	−2 19	60	58	−1 19	59	58
124	−5 34	59	56	−4 35	59	56	−3 36	60	56	−2 36	59	56	−1 37	60	56
126	−5 52	60	54	−4 52	59	54	−3 53	60	54	−2 53	59	54	−1 54	60	54
128	−6 08	59	52	−5 09	60	52	−4 09	59	52	−3 10	60	52	−2 10	59	52
130	−6 25	+60	50	−5 25	+59	50	−4 26	+60	50	−3 26	+59	50	−2 27	+60	50
132	−6 40	59	48	−5 41	60	48	−4 41	59	48	−3 42	60	48	−2 42	59	48
134	−6 56	60	46	−5 56	59	46	−4 57	60	46	−3 57	59	46	−2 58	60	46
136	−7 11	60	44	−6 11	60	44	−5 11	59	44	−4 12	60	44	−3 12	59	44
138	−7 25	60	42	−6 25	59	42	−5 26	60	42	−4 26	59	42	−3 27	60	42

LHA	5° Hc	5° d	5° Z	6° Hc	6° d	6° Z	7° Hc	7° d	7° Z	8° Hc	8° d	8° Z	9° Hc	9° d	9° Z
	° ′	′	°	° ′	′	°	° ′	′	°	° ′	′	°	° ′	′	°
0	15 00	+60	180	16 00	+60	180	17 00	+60	180	18 00	+60	180	19 00	+60	180
2	15 00	60	178	16 00	60	178	17 00	60	178	18 00	60	178	19 00	60	178
4	14 59	60	176	15 59	60	176	16 59	60	176	17 59	60	176	18 59	60	176
6	14 57	60	174	15 57	60	174	16 57	60	174	17 57	60	174	18 57	60	174
8	14 54	60	172	15 54	60	172	16 54	60	172	17 54	60	172	18 54	60	172
10	14 51	+60	170	15 51	+60	170	16 51	+60	170	17 51	+60	170	18 51	+60	170
12	14 47	60	168	15 47	60	168	16 47	59	168	17 46	60	168	18 46	60	168
14	14 42	60	166	15 42	60	166	16 42	60	166	17 42	60	165	18 42	59	165
16	14 36	60	164	15 36	60	164	16 36	60	163	17 36	60	163	18 36	60	163
18	14 30	60	162	15 30	60	161	16 30	60	161	17 30	60	161	18 30	59	161
20	14 23	+60	159	15 23	+60	159	16 23	+60	159	17 23	+60	159	18 23	+59	159
22	14 15	60	157	15 15	60	157	16 15	60	157	17 15	60	157	18 15	60	157
24	14 07	60	155	15 07	60	155	16 07	59	155	17 06	60	155	18 06	60	155
26	13 58	60	153	14 58	60	153	15 58	59	153	16 57	60	153	17 57	60	153
28	13 48	60	151	14 48	60	151	15 48	60	151	16 48	59	151	17 47	60	151
30	13 38	+60	149	14 38	+59	149	15 37	+60	149	16 37	+60	149	17 37	+60	149
32	13 27	60	147	14 27	59	147	15 26	60	147	16 26	60	147	17 26	59	147
34	13 15	60	145	14 15	60	145	15 15	59	145	16 14	60	145	17 14	60	145
36	13 03	60	143	14 03	59	143	15 02	60	143	16 02	60	143	17 02	59	143
38	12 50	60	141	13 50	59	141	14 49	60	141	15 49	60	141	16 49	59	141
40	12 37	+59	139	13 36	+60	139	14 36	+60	139	15 36	+59	139	16 35	+60	139
42	12 23	59	137	13 22	60	137	14 22	60	137	15 22	59	137	16 21	60	137
44	12 08	60	135	13 08	59	135	14 07	60	135	15 07	59	135	16 06	60	134
46	11 53	60	133	12 53	59	133	13 52	60	133	14 52	59	133	15 51	60	132
48	11 38	59	131	12 37	60	131	13 37	59	131	14 36	60	131	15 36	59	130
50	11 22	+59	129	12 21	+60	129	13 21	+59	129	14 20	+60	129	15 20	+59	128
52	11 05	60	127	12 05	59	127	13 04	60	127	14 04	59	126	15 03	59	126
54	10 49	59	125	11 48	59	125	12 47	60	125	13 47	59	124	14 46	59	124
56	10 31	60	123	11 31	59	123	12 30	59	123	13 29	60	122	14 29	59	122
58	10 14	59	121	11 13	59	121	12 12	59	121	13 11	60	120	14 11	59	120
60	09 55	+60	119	10 55	+59	119	11 54	+59	119	12 53	+60	118	13 53	+59	118
62	09 37	59	117	10 36	60	117	11 36	59	117	12 35	59	116	13 34	59	116
64	09 18	60	115	10 18	59	115	11 17	59	115	12 16	59	114	13 15	59	114
66	08 59	59	113	09 58	60	113	10 58	59	113	11 57	59	112	12 56	59	112
68	08 40	59	111	09 39	59	111	10 38	59	111	11 37	60	110	12 37	59	110
70	08 20	+59	109	09 19	+60	109	10 19	+59	109	11 18	+59	108	12 17	+59	108
72	08 00	60	107	09 00	59	107	09 59	59	107	10 58	59	106	11 57	59	106
74	07 40	60	105	08 40	59	105	09 39	59	105	10 38	59	104	11 37	59	104
76	07 20	59	103	08 19	59	103	09 18	60	103	10 18	59	102	11 17	59	102
78	07 00	59	101	07 59	59	101	08 58	59	101	09 57	59	100	10 56	59	100
80	06 39	+59	99	07 38	+59	99	08 37	+60	99	09 37	+59	99	10 36	+59	98
82	06 19	59	97	07 18	59	97	08 17	59	97	09 16	59	97	10 15	59	96
84	05 58	59	95	06 57	59	95	07 56	59	95	08 55	59	95	09 54	59	94
86	05 37	59	93	06 36	59	93	07 35	59	93	08 34	59	93	09 33	60	92
88	05 16	59	91	06 15	59	91	07 14	60	91	08 14	59	91	09 13	59	90
90	04 55	+60	89	05 55	+59	89	06 54	+59	89	07 53	+59	89	08 52	+59	88
92	04 35	59	87	05 34	59	87	06 33	59	87	07 32	59	87	08 31	59	87
94	04 14	59	85	05 13	59	85	06 12	59	85	07 11	59	85	08 10	59	85
96	03 53	59	83	04 52	59	83	05 51	59	83	06 50	59	83	07 49	60	83
98	03 33	59	81	04 32	59	81	05 31	59	81	06 30	59	81	07 29	59	81
100	03 12	+59	79	04 11	+59	79	05 10	+59	79	06 09	+59	79	07 08	+59	79
102	02 52	59	77	03 51	59	77	04 50	59	77	05 49	59	77	06 48	59	77
104	02 31	59	75	03 30	60	75	04 30	59	75	05 29	59	75	06 28	59	75
106	02 11	59	73	03 10	59	73	04 09	60	73	05 09	59	73	06 08	59	73
108	01 51	59	71	02 50	60	71	03 50	59	71	04 49	59	71	05 48	59	71
110	01 32	+59	69	02 31	+59	69	03 30	+59	69	04 29	+60	69	05 29	+59	69
112	01 12	60	67	02 12	59	67	03 11	59	67	04 10	59	67	05 09	59	67
114	00 53	59	66	01 52	60	65	02 52	59	65	03 51	59	65	04 50	59	65
116	00 34	60	64	01 34	59	63	02 33	59	63	03 32	59	63	04 31	60	63
118	00 16	59	62	01 15	59	61	02 14	60	61	03 14	59	61	04 13	59	61
120	−0 02	+59	60	00 57	+59	60	01 56	+60	59	02 56	+59	59	03 55	+59	59
122	−0 20	59	58	00 39	60	58	01 39	59	57	02 38	59	57	03 37	60	57
124	−0 37	59	56	00 22	59	56	01 21	60	55	02 21	59	55	03 20	59	55
126	−0 54	59	54	00 05	59	54	01 04	60	53	02 04	59	53	03 03	60	53
128	−1 11	59	52	−0 12	60	52	00 48	59	51	01 47	60	51	02 47	59	51
130	−1 27	+59	50	−0 28	+60	50	00 32	+59	49	01 31	+60	49	02 31	+59	49
132	−1 43	60	48	−0 43	59	48	00 16	60	47	01 16	59	47	02 15	60	47
134	−1 58	59	46	−0 59	60	46	00 01	60	46	01 01	59	45	02 00	60	45
136	−2 13	60	44	−1 13	59	44	−0 14	60	44	00 46	59	43	01 45	60	43
138	−2 27	60	42	−1 27	59	42	−0 28	60	42	00 32	59	41	01 31	60	41

LHA	10° Hc	10° d	10° Z	11° Hc	11° d	11° Z	12° Hc	12° d	12° Z	13° Hc	13° d	13° Z	14° Hc	14° d	14° Z	LHA
	° ′	′	°	° ′	′	°	° ′	′	°	° ′	′	°	° ′	′	°	
0	20 00	+60	180	21 00	+60	180	22 00	+60	180	23 00	+60	180	24 00	+60	180	360
2	20 00	60	178	21 00	60	178	22 00	60	178	23 00	60	178	24 00	60	178	358
4	19 59	60	176	20 59	60	176	21 59	60	176	22 59	60	176	23 59	60	176	356
6	19 57	60	174	20 57	60	174	21 57	60	174	22 57	60	174	23 57	60	174	354
8	19 54	60	172	20 54	60	172	21 54	60	172	22 54	60	172	23 54	60	172	352
10	19 51	+60	170	20 51	+59	170	21 50	+60	170	22 50	+60	169	23 50	+60	169	350
12	19 46	60	167	20 46	60	167	21 46	60	167	22 46	60	167	23 46	60	167	348
14	19 41	60	165	20 41	60	165	21 41	60	165	22 41	60	165	23 41	60	165	346
16	19 36	60	163	20 36	60	163	21 36	60	163	22 36	60	163	23 36	59	163	344
18	19 29	60	161	20 29	60	161	21 29	60	161	22 29	60	161	23 29	60	161	342
20	19 22	+60	159	20 22	+60	159	21 22	+60	159	22 22	+60	159	23 22	+60	159	340
22	19 15	59	157	20 14	60	157	21 14	60	157	22 14	60	157	23 14	60	157	338
24	19 06	60	155	20 06	60	155	21 06	60	155	22 06	59	155	23 05	60	155	336
26	18 57	60	153	19 57	60	153	20 57	59	153	21 56	60	153	22 56	60	153	334
28	18 47	60	151	19 47	60	151	20 47	59	151	21 46	60	151	22 46	60	150	332
30	18 37	+59	149	19 36	+60	149	20 36	+60	149	21 36	+60	148	22 36	+59	148	330
32	18 25	60	147	19 25	60	147	20 25	60	146	21 25	59	146	22 24	60	146	328
34	18 14	59	145	19 13	60	145	20 13	60	144	21 13	59	144	22 12	60	144	326
36	18 01	60	143	19 01	60	142	20 01	59	142	21 00	60	142	22 00	60	142	324
38	17 48	60	140	18 48	60	140	19 48	59	140	20 47	60	140	21 47	59	140	322
40	17 35	+59	138	18 34	+60	138	19 34	+59	138	20 33	+60	138	21 33	+60	138	320
42	17 21	59	136	18 20	60	136	19 20	59	136	20 19	60	136	21 19	59	136	318
44	17 06	60	134	18 06	59	134	19 05	60	134	20 05	59	134	21 04	60	134	316
46	16 51	59	132	17 50	60	132	18 50	59	132	19 49	60	132	20 49	59	132	314
48	16 35	60	130	17 35	59	130	18 34	59	130	19 33	60	130	20 33	59	130	312
50	16 19	+59	128	17 18	+60	128	18 18	+59	128	19 17	+60	128	20 17	+59	128	310
52	16 02	60	126	17 02	59	126	18 01	60	126	19 01	59	126	20 00	59	126	308
54	15 45	60	124	16 45	59	124	17 44	59	124	18 43	60	124	19 43	59	124	306
56	15 28	59	122	16 27	60	122	17 27	59	122	18 26	59	122	19 25	59	122	304
58	15 10	59	120	16 09	60	120	17 09	59	120	18 08	59	120	19 07	59	119	302
60	14 52	+59	118	15 51	+59	118	16 50	+60	118	17 50	+59	118	18 49	+59	117	300
62	14 33	60	116	15 33	59	116	16 32	59	116	17 31	59	116	18 30	59	115	298
64	14 14	60	114	15 14	59	114	16 13	59	114	17 12	59	114	18 11	59	113	296
66	13 55	59	112	14 54	60	112	15 54	59	112	16 53	59	112	17 52	59	111	294
68	13 36	59	110	14 35	59	110	15 34	59	110	16 33	59	110	17 32	60	109	292
70	13 16	+59	108	14 15	+59	108	15 14	+60	108	16 14	+59	108	17 13	+59	107	290
72	12 56	59	106	13 55	59	106	14 54	60	106	15 54	59	106	16 53	59	105	288
74	12 36	59	104	13 35	59	104	14 34	59	104	15 33	59	104	16 32	60	103	286
76	12 16	59	102	13 15	59	102	14 14	59	102	15 13	59	102	16 12	59	101	284
78	11 55	59	100	12 54	59	100	13 53	60	100	14 53	59	100	15 52	59	99	282
80	11 35	+59	98	12 34	+59	98	13 33	+59	98	14 32	+59	98	15 31	+59	97	280
82	11 14	59	96	12 13	59	96	13 12	59	96	14 11	59	96	15 10	59	95	278
84	10 53	59	94	11 52	59	94	12 51	59	94	13 50	60	94	14 50	59	93	276
86	10 33	59	92	11 32	59	92	12 31	59	92	13 30	59	92	14 29	59	92	274
88	10 12	59	90	11 11	59	90	12 10	59	90	13 09	59	90	14 08	59	90	272
90	09 51	+59	88	10 50	+59	88	11 49	+59	88	12 48	+59	88	13 47	+59	88	270
92	09 30	59	86	10 29	59	86	11 28	59	86	12 27	59	86	13 26	59	86	268
94	09 09	59	84	10 08	59	84	11 07	59	84	12 06	59	84	13 05	60	84	266
96	08 49	59	82	09 48	59	82	10 47	59	82	11 46	59	82	12 45	59	82	264
98	08 28	59	80	09 27	59	80	10 26	59	80	11 25	59	80	12 24	59	80	262
100	08 07	+60	78	09 07	+59	78	10 06	+59	78	11 05	+59	78	12 04	+59	78	260
102	07 47	59	77	08 46	59	76	09 45	59	76	10 44	60	76	11 44	59	76	258
104	07 27	59	75	08 26	59	74	09 25	59	74	10 24	59	74	11 23	60	74	256
106	07 07	59	73	08 06	59	72	09 05	59	72	10 04	60	72	11 04	59	72	254
108	06 47	59	71	07 46	60	70	08 46	59	70	09 45	59	70	10 44	59	70	252
110	06 28	+59	69	07 27	+59	69	08 26	+59	68	09 25	+59	68	10 24	+60	68	250
112	06 08	60	67	07 08	59	67	08 07	59	66	09 06	59	66	10 05	59	66	248
114	05 49	60	65	06 49	59	65	07 48	59	64	08 47	59	64	09 46	60	64	246
116	05 31	59	63	06 30	59	63	07 29	59	63	08 28	60	62	09 28	59	62	244
118	05 12	60	61	06 12	59	61	07 11	59	61	08 10	59	60	09 09	60	60	242
120	04 54	+60	59	05 54	+59	59	06 53	+59	59	07 52	+60	58	08 52	+59	58	240
122	04 37	59	57	05 36	59	57	06 35	60	57	07 35	59	57	08 34	59	56	238
124	04 19	60	55	05 19	59	55	06 18	60	55	07 18	59	55	08 17	59	54	236
126	04 03	59	53	05 02	59	53	06 01	60	53	07 01	59	53	08 00	60	52	234
128	03 46	60	51	04 46	59	51	05 45	59	51	06 44	60	51	07 44	59	51	232
130	03 30	+60	49	04 30	+59	49	05 29	+60	49	06 29	+59	49	07 28	+59	49	230
132	03 15	59	47	04 14	60	47	05 14	59	47	06 13	60	47	07 13	59	47	228
134	03 00	59	45	03 59	60	45	04 59	59	45	05 58	60	45	06 58	59	45	226
136	02 45	60	43	03 45	59	43	04 44	60	43	05 44	59	43	06 43	60	43	224
138	02 31	60	41	03 31	59	41	04 30	60	41	05 30	59	41	06 29	60	41	222

S. Lat. {LHA greater than 180°....... Zn=180−Z
{LHA less than 180°........... Zn=180+Z

DECLINATION (0°-14°) SAME NAME AS LATITUDE

LAT 80°

N. Lat. {LHA greater than 180°....... Zn=Z / LHA less than 180°........... Zn=360−Z

DECLINATION (0°-14°) SAME NAME AS LATITUDE

LHA	0° Hc	d	Z	1° Hc	d	Z	2° Hc	d	Z	3° Hc	d	Z	4° Hc	d	Z	5° Hc	d	Z	6° Hc	d	Z	7° Hc	d	Z
	° ′	′	°	° ′	′	°	° ′	′	°	° ′	′	°	° ′	′	°	° ′	′	°	° ′	′	°	° ′	′	°
140				-6 39	+60	40	-5 39	+59	40	-4 40	+60	40	-3 40	+59	40	-2 41	+60	40	-1 41	+60	40	-0 41	+59	40
142				-6 52	59	38	-5 53	60	38	-4 53	60	38	-3 53	59	38	-2 54	60	38	-1 54	60	38	-0 54	59	38
144				-7 05	60	36	-6 05	59	36	-5 06	60	36	-4 06	60	36	-3 06	60	36	-2 06	59	36	-1 07	60	36
146				-7 17	60	34	-6 17	59	34	-5 18	60	34	-4 18	60	34	-3 18	60	34	-2 18	59	34	-1 19	60	34
148							-6 29	60	32	-5 29	60	32	-4 29	60	32	-3 29	59	32	-2 30	60	32	-1 30	60	32
150							-6 39	+59	30	-5 40	+60	30	-4 40	+60	30	-3 40	+60	30	-2 40	+59	30	-1 41	+60	30
152							-6 50	60	28	-5 50	60	28	-4 50	60	28	-3 50	60	28	-2 50	59	28	-1 51	60	28
154							-6 59	60	26	-5 59	60	26	-4 59	59	26	-4 00	60	26	-3 00	60	26	-2 00	60	26
156							-7 08	60	24	-6 08	60	24	-5 08	60	24	-4 08	59	24	-3 09	60	24	-2 09	60	24
158							-7 16	60	22	-6 16	60	22	-5 16	59	22	-4 17	60	22	-3 17	60	22	-2 17	60	22
160										-6 24	+60	20	-5 24	+60	20	-4 24	+60	20	-3 24	+60	20	-2 24	+60	20
162										-6 31	60	18	-5 31	60	18	-4 31	60	18	-3 31	60	18	-2 31	60	18
164										-6 37	60	16	-5 37	60	16	-4 37	60	16	-3 37	60	16	-2 37	60	16
166										-6 42	60	14	-5 42	60	14	-4 42	60	14	-3 42	60	14	-2 42	60	14
168										-6 47	60	12	-5 47	60	12	-4 47	60	12	-3 47	60	12	-2 47	60	12
170										-6 51	+60	10	-5 51	+60	10	-4 51	+60	10	-3 51	+60	10	-2 51	+60	10
172										-6 54	60	8	-5 54	60	8	-4 54	60	8	-3 54	60	8	-2 54	60	8
174										-6 57	60	6	-5 57	60	6	-4 57	60	6	-3 57	60	6	-2 57	60	6
176										-6 59	60	4	-5 59	60	4	-4 59	60	4	-3 59	60	4	-2 59	60	4
178										-7 00	60	2	-6 00	60	2	-5 00	60	2	-4 00	60	2	-3 00	60	2
180										-7 00	+60	0	-6 00	+60	0	-5 00	+60	0	-4 00	+60	0	-3 00	+60	0

LHA	8° Hc	d	Z	9° Hc	d	Z	10° Hc	d	Z	11° Hc	d	Z	12° Hc	d	Z	13° Hc	d	Z	14° Hc	d	Z	LHA
	° ′	′	°	° ′	′	°	° ′	′	°	° ′	′	°	° ′	′	°	° ′	′	°	° ′	′	°	
140	00 18	+60	40	01 18	+60	39	02 18	+59	39	03 17	+60	39	04 17	+59	39	05 16	+60	39	06 16	+60	39	220
142	00 05	60	38	01 05	60	37	02 05	59	37	03 04	60	37	04 04	60	37	05 04	59	37	06 03	60	37	218
144	-0 07	60	36	00 53	59	35	01 52	60	35	02 52	60	35	03 52	59	35	04 51	60	35	05 51	60	35	216
146	-0 19	60	34	00 41	60	34	01 41	59	33	02 40	60	33	03 40	60	33	04 40	59	33	05 39	60	33	214
148	-0 30	60	32	00 30	59	32	01 29	60	31	02 29	60	31	03 29	60	31	04 29	59	31	05 28	60	31	212
150	-0 41	+60	30	00 19	+60	30	01 19	+60	30	02 19	+59	29	03 18	+60	29	04 18	+60	29	05 18	+60	29	210
152	-0 51	60	28	00 09	60	28	01 09	60	28	02 09	59	27	03 08	60	27	04 08	60	27	05 08	60	27	208
154	-1 00	60	26	00 00	60	26	01 00	59	26	01 59	60	25	02 59	60	25	03 59	60	25	04 59	60	25	206
156	-1 09	60	24	-0 09	60	24	00 51	60	24	01 51	59	24	02 50	60	23	03 50	60	23	04 50	60	23	204
158	-1 17	60	22	-0 17	60	22	00 43	60	22	01 43	60	22	02 43	59	21	03 42	60	21	04 42	60	21	202
160	-1 24	+60	20	-0 24	+59	20	00 35	+60	20	01 35	+60	20	02 35	+60	20	03 35	+60	19	04 35	+60	20	200
162	-1 31	60	18	-0 31	60	18	00 29	60	18	01 29	60	18	02 29	59	18	03 28	60	18	04 28	60	18	198
164	-1 37	60	16	-0 37	60	16	00 23	60	16	01 23	60	16	02 23	60	16	03 23	60	16	04 23	59	16	196
166	-1 42	59	14	-0 43	60	14	00 17	60	14	01 17	60	14	02 17	60	14	03 17	60	14	04 17	60	14	194
168	-1 47	60	12	-0 47	60	12	00 13	60	12	01 13	60	12	02 13	60	12	03 13	60	12	04 13	60	12	192
170	-1 51	+60	10	-0 51	+60	10	00 09	+60	10	01 09	+60	10	02 09	+60	10	03 09	+60	10	04 09	+60	10	190
172	-1 54	60	8	-0 54	60	8	00 06	60	8	01 06	60	8	02 06	60	8	03 06	60	8	04 06	60	8	188
174	-1 57	60	6	-0 57	60	6	00 03	60	6	01 03	60	6	02 03	60	6	03 03	60	6	04 03	60	6	186
176	-1 59	60	4	-0 59	60	4	00 01	60	4	01 01	60	4	02 01	60	4	03 01	60	4	04 01	60	4	184
178	-2 00	60	2	-1 00	60	2	00 00	60	2	01 00	60	2	02 00	60	2	03 00	60	2	04 00	60	2	182
180	-2 00	+60	0	-1 00	+60	0	00 00	+60	0	01 00	+60	0	02 00	+60	0	03 00	+60	0	04 00	+60	0	180

0°	1°	2°	3°	4°	5°	6°	7°	8°	9°	10°	11°	12°	13°	14°

S. Lat. {LHA greater than 180°....... Zn=180−Z / LHA less than 180°........... Zn=180+Z

DECLINATION (0°-14°) SAME NAME AS LATITUDE

LAT 80°

N. Lat. {LHA greater than 180°....... Zn=Z; LHA less than 180°........... Zn=360−Z}

DECLINATION (0°-14°) CONTRARY NAME TO LATITUDE

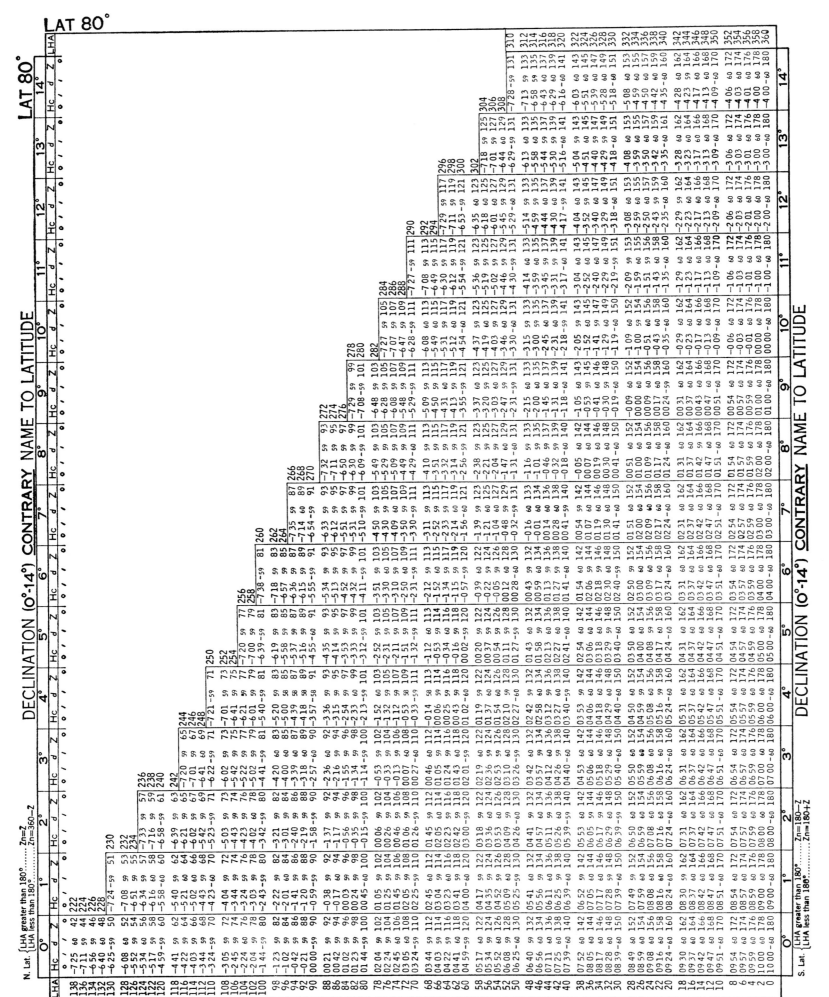

LHA	0°			1°			2°			3°			4°			5°			6°			7°			8°			9°			10°			11°			12°			13°			14°			LHA
	Hc	d	Z	Hc	d	Z	Hc	d	Z	Hc	d	Z	Hc	d	Z	Hc	d	Z	Hc	d	Z	Hc	d	Z	Hc	d	Z	Hc	d	Z	Hc	d	Z	Hc	d	Z	Hc	d	Z	Hc	d	Z	Hc	d	Z	
	° ′	′	°	° ′	′	°	° ′	′	°	° ′	′	°	° ′	′	°	° ′	′	°	° ′	′	°	° ′	′	°	° ′	′	°	° ′	′	°	° ′	′	°	° ′	′	°	° ′	′	°	° ′	′	°	° ′	′	°	
138	−7 25	60	42																																											222
136	−7 11	59	44																																											224
134	−6 56	59	46																																											226
132	−6 40	60	48																																											228
130	−6 25	−59	50	−7 24	−59	51																																								230
128	−6 08	60	52	−7 08	59	53																																								232
126	−5 52	59	54	−6 51	59	55																																								234
124	−5 34	60	56	−6 34	59	57	−7 33	59	57																																					236
122	−5 17	59	58	−6 16	60	58	−7 16	59	59																																					238
120	−4 59	−59	60	−5 58	−60	60	−6 58	−59	61																																					240
118	−4 41	59	62	−5 40	59	62	−6 39	59	63																																					242
116	−4 22	59	64	−5 21	60	64	−6 21	59	65	−7 20	59	65																																		244
114	−4 03	59	66	−5 02	60	66	−6 02	59	67	−7 01	59	67																																		246
112	−3 44	59	68	−4 43	59	68	−5 42	59	69	−6 41	60	69																																		248
110	−3 24	−59	70	−4 23	−60	70	−5 23	−59	71	−6 22	−59	71	−7 21	−59	71																															250
108	−3 05	59	72	−4 04	59	72	−5 03	59	73	−6 02	59	73	−7 01	59	73																															252
106	−2 45	59	74	−3 44	59	74	−4 43	59	74	−5 42	59	75	−6 41	59	75																															254
104	−2 24	60	76	−3 24	59	76	−4 23	59	76	−5 22	59	77	−6 21	59	77	−7 20	59	77																												256
102	−2 04	59	78	−3 03	59	78	−4 02	60	78	−5 02	59	79	−6 01	59	79	−7 00	59	79																												258
100	−1 44	−59	80	−2 43	−59	80	−3 42	−59	80	−4 41	−59	81	−5 40	−59	81	−6 39	−59	81	−7 38	−59	81																									260
98	−1 23	59	82	−2 22	59	82	−3 21	59	82	−4 20	60	83	−5 20	59	83	−6 19	59	83	−7 18	59	83																									262
96	−1 02	59	84	−2 01	60	84	−3 01	59	84	−4 00	60	85	−5 00	58	85	−5 58	59	85	−6 57	59	85																									264
94	−0 42	59	86	−1 41	59	86	−2 40	59	86	−3 39	60	87	−4 39	58	87	−5 37	59	87	−6 36	59	87	−7 35	59	87																						266
92	−0 21	59	88	−1 20	59	88	−2 19	59	88	−3 18	60	89	−4 18	58	89	−5 16	59	89	−6 15	59	89	−7 14	60	89																						268
90	00 00	−59	90	−0 59	−59	90	−1 58	−59	90	−2 57	−60	90	−3 57	−58	91	−4 55	−60	91	−5 55	−59	91	−6 54	−59	91																						270
88	00 21	59	92	−0 38	59	92	−1 37	59	92	−2 36	60	92	−3 36	59	93	−4 35	59	93	−5 34	59	93	−6 33	59	93	−7 32	59	93																			272
86	00 42	59	94	−0 17	60	94	−1 17	59	94	−2 16	59	94	−3 15	59	95	−4 14	59	95	−5 13	59	95	−6 12	59	95	−7 11	59	95																			274
84	01 02	59	96	00 03	59	96	−0 56	59	96	−1 55	59	96	−2 54	59	97	−3 53	59	97	−4 52	59	97	−5 51	59	97	−6 50	59	97																			276
82	01 23	59	98	00 24	59	98	−0 35	59	98	−1 34	59	98	−2 33	60	99	−3 33	59	99	−4 32	59	99	−5 31	59	99	−6 30	59	99	−7 29	59	99																278
80	01 44	−59	100	00 45	−60	100	−0 15	−59	100	−1 14	−59	100	−2 13	−59	101	−3 12	−59	101	−4 11	−59	101	−5 10	−59	101	−6 09	−59	101	−7 08	−59	101																280
78	02 04	59	102	01 05	59	102	00 06	59	102	−0 53	59	102	−1 52	60	103	−2 52	59	103	−3 51	59	103	−4 50	59	103	−5 49	59	103	−6 48	59	103																282
76	02 24	59	104	01 25	59	104	00 26	59	104	−0 33	59	104	−1 32	59	105	−2 31	59	105	−3 30	60	105	−4 30	59	105	−5 29	59	105	−6 28	59	105	−7 27	59	105													284
74	02 45	60	106	01 45	59	106	00 46	59	106	−0 13	59	106	−1 12	59	107	−2 11	59	107	−3 10	59	107	−4 09	60	107	−5 09	59	107	−6 08	59	107	−7 07	59	107													286
72	03 05	60	108	02 05	59	108	01 06	59	108	00 07	60	108	−0 53	58	109	−1 51	59	109	−2 50	60	109	−3 50	59	109	−4 49	59	109	−5 48	59	109	−6 47	59	109													288
70	03 24	−59	110	02 25	−59	110	01 26	−59	110	00 27	−60	110	−0 33	−59	111	−1 32	−59	111	−2 31	−59	111	−3 30	−59	111	−4 29	−60	111	−5 29	−59	111	−6 28	−59	111	−7 27	−59	111										290
68	03 44	59	112	02 45	60	112	01 45	59	112	00 46	60	112	−0 14	58	113	−1 12	60	113	−2 12	59	113	−3 11	59	113	−4 10	59	113	−5 09	59	113	−6 08	60	113	−7 08	59	113										292
66	04 03	59	114	03 04	59	114	02 05	60	114	01 05	59	114	00 06	59	114	−0 53	59	114	−1 52	60	115	−2 52	59	115	−3 51	59	115	−4 50	59	115	−5 49	60	115	−6 49	59	115										294
64	04 22	59	116	03 23	60	116	02 23	59	116	01 24	59	116	00 25	59	116	−0 34	60	116	−1 34	59	117	−2 33	59	117	−3 32	59	117	−4 31	60	117	−5 31	59	117	−6 30	59	117	−7 29	59	117							296
62	04 41	60	118	03 41	59	118	02 42	59	118	01 43	60	118	00 43	59	118	−0 16	59	118	−1 15	59	119	−2 14	60	119	−3 14	59	119	−4 13	59	119	−5 12	60	119	−6 12	59	119	−7 11	59	119							298
60	04 59	−59	120	04 00	−60	120	03 00	−59	120	02 01	−59	120	01 02	−60	120	00 02	−59	120	−0 57	−59	120	−1 56	−60	121	−2 56	−59	121	−3 55	−59	121	−4 54	−60	121	−5 54	−59	121	−6 53	−59	121							300
58	05 17	60	122	04 17	59	122	03 18	59	122	02 19	60	122	01 19	59	122	00 20	59	122	−0 39	60	122	−1 39	59	123	−2 38	59	123	−3 37	60	123	−4 37	59	123	−5 36	59	123	−6 35	60	123							302
56	05 34	59	124	04 35	59	124	03 36	60	124	02 36	59	124	01 37	60	124	00 37	59	124	−0 22	59	124	−1 21	60	125	−2 21	59	125	−3 20	59	125	−4 19	60	125	−5 19	59	125	−6 18	60	125	−7 18	59	125				304
54	05 52	60	126	04 52	59	126	03 53	60	126	02 53	59	126	01 54	60	126	00 54	59	126	−0 05	59	126	−1 04	60	127	−2 04	59	127	−3 03	60	127	−4 03	59	127	−5 02	59	127	−6 01	60	127	−7 01	59	127				306
52	06 08	59	128	05 09	60	128	04 09	59	128	03 10	60	128	02 10	59	128	01 11	59	128	00 12	60	128	−0 48	59	129	−1 47	60	129	−2 47	59	129	−3 46	60	129	−4 46	59	129	−5 45	59	129	−6 44	60	129				308
50	06 25	−60	130	05 25	−59	130	04 26	−60	130	03 26	−59	130	02 27	−60	130	01 27	−59	130	00 28	−60	130	−0 32	−59	131	−1 31	−60	131	−2 31	−59	131	−3 30	−60	131	−4 30	−59	131	−5 29	−60	131	−6 29	−59	131	−7 28	−59	131	310
48	06 40	59	132	05 41	60	132	04 41	59	132	03 42	60	132	02 42	59	132	01 43	60	132	00 43	59	132	−0 16	60	133	−1 16	59	133	−2 15	60	133	−3 15	59	133	−4 14	60	133	−5 14	59	133	−6 13	60	133	−7 13	59	133	312
46	06 56	60	134	05 56	59	134	04 57	60	134	03 57	59	134	02 58	60	134	01 58	59	134	00 59	60	134	−0 01	60	134	−1 01	59	135	−2 00	60	135	−3 00	59	135	−3 59	60	135	−4 59	59	135	−5 58	60	135	−6 58	59	135	314
44	07 11	60	136	06 11	60	136	05 11	59	136	04 12	60	136	03 12	59	136	02 13	60	136	01 13	59	136	00 14	60	136	−0 46	59	137	−1 45	60	137	−2 45	60	137	−3 45	59	137	−4 44	60	137	−5 44	59	137	−6 43	60	137	316
42	07 25	60	138	06 25	59	138	05 26	60	138	04 26	59	138	03 27	60	138	02 27	60	138	01 27	59	138	00 28	60	138	−0 32	59	139	−1 31	60	139	−2 31	60	139	−3 31	59	139	−4 30	60	139	−5 30	59	139	−6 29	60	139	318
40	07 39	−60	140	06 39	−60	140	05 39	−59	140	04 40	−60	140	03 40	−59	140	02 41	−60	140	01 41	−60	140	00 41	−59	140	−0 18	−60	140	−1 18	−60	141	−2 18	−59	141	−3 17	−60	141	−4 17	−59	141	−5 16	−60	141	−6 16	−60	141	320
38	07 52	60	142	06 52	59	142	05 53	60	142	04 53	60	142	03 53	59	142	02 54	60	142	01 54	60	142	00 54	59	142	−0 05	60	142	−1 05	60	143	−2 05	59	143	−3 04	60	143	−4 04	60	143	−5 04	59	143	−6 03	60	143	322
36	08 05	60	144	07 05	60	144	06 05	59	144	05 06	60	144	04 06	60	144	03 06	60	144	02 06	59	144	01 07	60	144	00 07	60	144	−0 53	59	145	−1 52	60	145	−2 52	60	145	−3 52	59	145	−4 51	60	145	−5 51	60	145	324
34	08 17	60	146	07 17	60	146	06 17	59	146	05 18	60	146	04 18	60	146	03 18	60	146	02 18	59	146	01 19	60	146	00 19	60	146	−0 41	60	146	−1 41	59	147	−2 40	60	147	−3 40	60	147	−4 40	59	147	−5 39	60	147	326
32	08 28	60	148	07 28	59	148	06 29	60	148	05 29	60	148	04 29	60	148	03 29	59	148	02 30	60	148	01 30	60	148	00 30	60	148	−0 30	59	148	−1 29	60	149	−2 29	60	149	−3 29	60	149	−4 29	59	149	−5 28	60	149	328
30	08 39	−60	150	07 39	−60	150	06 39	−59	150	05 40	−60	150	04 40	−60	150	03 40	−60	150	02 40	−59	150	01 41	−60	150	00 41	−60	150	−0 19	−60	150	−1 19	−60	150	−2 19	−59	151	−3 18	−60	151	−4 18	−60	151	−5 18	−60	151	330
28	08 49	60	152	07 49	59	152	06 50	60	152	05 50	60	152	04 50	60	152	03 50	60	152	02 50	59	152	01 51	60	152	00 51	60	152	−0 09	60	152	−1 09	60	152	−2 09	59	153	−3 08	60	153	−4 08	60	153	−5 08	60	153	332
26	08 59	60	154	07 59	60	154	06 59	60	154	05 59	60	154	04 59	59	154	04 00	60	154	03 00	60	154	02 00	60	154	01 00	60	154	00 00	60	154	−1 00	59	154	−1 59	60	155	−2 59	60	155	−3 59	60	155	−4 59	60	155	334
24	09 08	60	156	08 08	60	156	07 08	60	156	06 08	60	156	05 08	60	156	04 08	59	156	03 09	60	156	02 09	60	156	01 09	60	156	00 09	60	156	−0 51	60	156	−1 51	59	156	−2 50	60	157	−3 50	60	157	−4 50	60	157	336
22	09 16	60	158	08 16	60	158	07 16	60	158	06 16	60	158	05 16	59	158	04 17	60	158	03 17	60	158	02 17	60	158	01 17	60	158	00 17	60	158	−0 43	60	158	−1 43	60	158	−2 43	59	159	−3 42	60	159	−4 42	60	159	338
20	09 24	−60	160	08 24	−60	160	07 24	−60	160	06 24	−60	160	05 24	−60	160	04 24	−60	160	03 24	−60	160	02 24	−60	160	01 24	−60	160	00 24	−59	160	−0 35	−60	160	−1 35	−60	160	−2 35	−60	160	−3 35	−60	161	−4 35	−60	160	340
18	09 30	60	162	08 30	59	162	07 31	60	162	06 31	60	162	05 31	60	162	04 31	60	162	03 31	60	162	02 31	60	162	01 31	60	162	00 31	60	162	−0 29	60	162	−1 29	60	162	−2 29	59	162	−3 28	60	162	−4 28	60	162	342
16	09 37	60	164	08 37	60	164	07 37	60	164	06 37	60	164	05 37	60	164	04 37	60	164	03 37	60	164	02 37	60	164	01 37	60	164	00 37	60	164	−0 23	60	164	−1 23	60	164	−2 23	60	164	−3 23	60	164	−4 23	59	164	344
14	09 42	60	166	08 42	60	166	07 42	60	166	06 42	60	166	05 42	60	166	04 42	60	166	03 42	60	166	02 42	60	166	01 42	59	166	00 43	60	166	−0 17	60	166	−1 17	60	166	−2 17	60	166	−3 17	60	166	−4 17	60	166	346
12	09 47	60	168	08 47	60	168	07 47	60	168	06 47	60	168	05 47	60	168	04 47	60	168	03 47	60	168	02 47	60	168	01 47	60	168	00 47	60	168	−0 13	60	168	−1 13	60	168	−2 13	60	168	−3 13	60	168	−4 13	60	168	348
10	09 51	−60	170	08 51	−60	170	07 51	−60	170	06 51	−60	170	05 51	−60	170	04 51	−60	170	03 51	−60	170	02 51	−60	170	01 51	−60	170	00 51	−60	170	−0 09	−60	170	−1 09	−60	170	−2 09	−60	170	−3 09	−60	170	−4 09	−60	170	350
8	09 54	60	172	08 54	60	172	07 54	60	172	06 54	60	172	05 54	60	172	04 54	60	172	03 54	60	172	02 54	60	172	01 54	60	172	00 54	60	172	−0 06	60	172	−1 06	60	172	−2 06	60	172	−3 06	60	172	−4 06	60	172	352
6	09 57	60	174	08 57	60	174	07 57	60	174	06 57	60	174	05 57	60	174	04 57	60	174	03 57	60	174	02 57	60	174	01 57	60	174	00 57	60	174	−0 03	60	174	−1 03	60	174	−2 03	60	174	−3 03	60	174	−4 03	60	174	354
4	09 59	60	176	08 59	60	176	07 59	60	176	06 59	60	176	05 59	60	176	04 59	60	176	03 59	60	176	02 59	60	176	01 59	60	176	00 59	60	176	−0 01	60	176	−1 01	60	176	−2 01	60	176	−3 01	60	176	−4 01	60	176	356
2	10 00	60	178	09 00	60	178	08 00	60	178	07 00	60	178	06 00	60	178	05 00	60	178	04 00	60	178	03 00	60	178	02 00	60	178	01 00	60	178	00 00	60	178	−1 00	60	178	−2 00	60	178	−3 00	60	178	−4 00	60	178	358
0	10 00	−60	180	09 00	−60	180	08 00	−60	180	07 00	−60	180	06 00	−60	180	05 00	−60	180	04 00	−60	180	03 00	−60	180	02 00	−60	180	01 00	−60	180	00 00	−60	180	−1 00	−60	180	−2 00	−60	180	−3 00	−60	180	−4 00	−60	180	360
	0°			1°			2°			3°			4°			5°			6°			7°			8°			9°			10°			11°			12°			13°			14°			

S. Lat. {LHA greater than 180°....... Zn=180−Z; LHA less than 180°........... Zn=180+Z}

DECLINATION (0°-14°) CONTRARY NAME TO LATITUDE

LAT 80°

N. Lat. {LHA greater than 180°....... Zn=Z; LHA less than 180°........... Zn=360−Z}

DECLINATION (15°-29°) SAME NAME AS LATITUDE

LHA	15° Hc	d	Z	16° Hc	d	Z	17° Hc	d	Z	18° Hc	d	Z	19° Hc	d	Z
	° ′	′	°	° ′	′	°	° ′	′	°	° ′	′	°	° ′	′	°
0	25 00	+60	180	26 00	+60	180	27 00	+60	180	28 00	+60	180	29 00	+60	180
2	25 00	60	178	26 00	60	178	27 00	60	178	28 00	60	178	29 00	60	178
4	24 59	59	176	25 58	60	176	26 58	60	176	27 58	60	176	28 58	60	176
6	24 57	60	174	25 57	60	174	26 57	60	174	27 57	60	174	28 57	60	174
8	24 54	60	172	25 54	60	171	26 54	60	171	27 54	60	171	28 54	60	171
10	24 50	+60	169	25 50	+60	169	26 50	+60	169	27 50	+60	169	28 50	+60	169
12	24 46	60	167	25 46	60	167	26 46	60	167	27 46	60	167	28 46	60	167
14	24 41	60	165	25 41	60	165	26 41	60	165	27 41	60	165	28 41	60	165
16	24 35	60	163	25 35	60	163	26 35	60	163	27 35	60	163	28 35	60	163
18	24 29	60	161	25 29	60	161	26 29	60	161	27 29	60	161	28 29	59	161
20	24 22	+60	159	25 22	+60	159	26 22	+59	159	27 21	+60	159	28 21	+60	158
22	24 14	60	157	25 14	60	157	26 14	59	157	27 13	60	156	28 13	60	156
24	24 05	60	155	25 05	60	154	26 05	60	154	27 05	60	154	28 05	59	154
26	23 56	60	152	24 56	60	152	25 56	59	152	26 55	60	152	27 55	60	152
28	23 46	60	150	24 46	59	150	25 45	60	150	26 45	60	150	27 45	60	150
30	23 35	+60	148	24 35	+60	148	25 35	+59	148	26 34	+60	148	27 34	+60	148
32	23 24	60	146	24 24	59	146	25 23	60	145	26 23	60	146	27 23	59	146
34	23 12	60	144	24 12	59	144	25 11	60	144	26 11	60	144	27 11	59	144
36	23 00	59	142	23 59	60	142	24 59	59	142	25 58	60	142	26 58	60	141
38	22 46	60	140	23 46	60	140	24 46	59	140	25 45	60	140	26 45	59	139
40	22 33	+59	138	23 32	+60	138	24 32	+59	138	25 31	+60	137	26 31	+59	137
42	22 18	60	136	23 18	59	136	24 17	60	135	25 17	59	135	26 16	60	135
44	22 04	59	134	23 03	59	134	24 02	60	133	25 02	59	133	26 01	60	133
46	21 48	60	132	22 48	59	131	23 47	60	131	24 47	59	131	25 46	59	131
48	21 32	60	130	22 32	59	129	23 31	60	129	24 31	59	129	25 30	59	129
50	21 16	+59	127	22 15	+60	127	23 15	+59	127	24 14	+59	127	25 13	+60	127
52	20 59	60	125	21 59	59	125	22 58	59	125	23 57	60	125	24 57	59	125
54	20 42	59	123	21 41	60	123	22 41	59	123	23 40	59	123	24 39	60	123
56	20 24	60	121	21 24	59	121	22 23	59	121	23 22	60	121	24 22	59	121
58	20 06	60	119	21 06	59	119	22 05	59	119	23 04	59	119	24 03	60	119
60	19 48	+59	117	20 47	+60	117	21 47	+59	117	22 46	+59	117	23 45	+59	117
62	19 29	60	115	20 29	59	115	21 28	59	115	22 27	59	115	23 26	59	115
64	19 10	60	113	20 10	59	113	21 09	59	113	22 08	59	113	23 07	59	113
66	18 51	59	111	19 50	59	111	20 49	60	111	21 49	59	111	22 48	59	111
68	18 32	59	109	19 31	59	109	20 30	59	109	21 29	59	109	22 28	59	108
70	18 12	+59	107	19 11	+59	107	20 10	+59	107	21 09	+59	107	22 08	+59	106
72	17 52	59	105	18 51	59	105	19 50	59	105	20 49	59	105	21 48	59	104
74	17 32	59	103	18 31	59	103	19 30	59	103	20 29	59	103	21 28	59	102
76	17 11	59	101	18 10	59	101	19 09	59	101	20 08	59	101	21 07	59	100
78	16 51	59	99	17 50	59	99	18 49	59	99	19 48	59	99	20 47	59	98
80	16 30	+59	97	17 29	+59	97	18 28	+59	97	19 27	+59	97	20 26	+59	96
82	16 09	59	95	17 08	59	95	18 07	59	95	19 06	59	95	20 05	59	95
84	15 49	59	93	16 48	59	93	17 47	59	93	18 46	59	93	19 45	59	93
86	15 28	59	91	16 27	59	91	17 26	59	91	18 25	59	91	19 24	59	91
88	15 07	59	89	16 06	59	89	17 05	59	89	18 04	59	89	19 03	59	89
90	14 46	+59	87	15 45	+59	87	16 44	+59	87	17 43	+59	87	18 42	+59	87
92	14 25	59	85	15 24	59	85	16 23	59	85	17 22	59	85	18 21	59	85
94	14 05	59	83	15 04	59	83	16 03	59	83	17 02	59	83	18 01	59	83
96	13 44	59	82	14 43	59	81	15 42	59	81	16 41	59	81	17 40	59	81
98	13 23	59	80	14 22	59	79	15 21	59	79	16 20	59	79	17 19	59	79
100	13 03	+59	78	14 02	+59	77	15 01	+59	77	16 00	+59	77	16 59	+59	77
102	12 43	59	76	13 42	59	75	14 41	59	75	15 40	59	75	16 39	59	75
104	12 23	59	74	13 22	59	74	14 21	59	73	15 20	59	73	16 19	59	73
106	12 03	59	72	13 02	59	72	14 01	59	71	15 00	59	71	15 59	59	71
108	11 43	59	70	12 42	59	70	13 41	59	69	14 40	59	69	15 39	60	69
110	11 24	+59	68	12 23	+59	68	13 22	+59	68	14 21	+59	67	15 20	+59	67
112	11 04	60	66	12 04	59	66	13 03	59	66	14 02	59	65	15 01	59	65
114	10 46	59	64	11 45	59	64	12 44	59	64	13 43	59	63	14 42	60	63
116	10 27	59	62	11 26	59	62	12 25	60	62	13 25	59	62	14 24	59	61
118	10 09	59	60	11 08	59	60	12 07	60	60	13 07	59	60	14 06	59	59
120	09 51	+59	58	10 50	+59	58	11 49	+60	58	12 49	+59	58	13 48	+59	58
122	09 33	60	56	10 33	59	56	11 32	59	56	12 31	60	56	13 31	59	56
124	09 16	60	54	10 16	59	54	11 15	59	54	12 14	60	54	13 14	59	54
126	09 00	59	52	09 59	59	52	10 58	60	52	11 58	59	52	12 57	59	52
128	08 43	60	50	09 43	59	50	10 42	60	50	11 42	59	50	12 41	59	50
130	08 27	+60	48	09 27	+59	48	10 26	+60	48	11 26	+59	48	12 25	+60	48
132	08 12	60	47	09 12	59	46	10 11	60	46	11 11	59	46	12 10	60	46
134	07 57	60	45	08 57	59	44	09 56	60	44	10 56	59	44	11 55	60	44
136	07 43	59	43	08 42	60	43	09 42	60	42	10 42	59	42	11 41	60	42
138	07 29	60	41	08 29	59	41	09 28	60	40	10 28	59	40	11 27	60	40

LHA	20° Hc	d	Z	21° Hc	d	Z	22° Hc	d	Z	23° Hc	d	Z	24° Hc	d	Z
	° ′	′	°	° ′	′	°	° ′	′	°	° ′	′	°	° ′	′	°
0	30 00	+60	180	31 00	+60	180	32 00	+60	180	33 00	+60	180	34 00	+60	180
2	30 00	60	178	31 00	60	178	32 00	60	178	33 00	60	178	34 00	60	178
4	29 58	60	176	30 58	60	176	31 58	60	176	32 58	60	176	33 58	60	176
6	29 57	59	174	30 56	60	174	31 56	60	173	32 56	60	173	33 56	60	173
8	29 54	60	171	30 54	60	171	31 54	60	171	32 54	60	171	33 54	60	171
10	29 50	+60	169	30 50	+60	169	31 50	+60	169	32 50	+60	169	33 50	+60	169
12	29 46	60	167	30 46	60	167	31 46	60	167	32 46	60	167	33 46	60	167
14	29 41	60	165	30 41	60	165	31 41	60	165	32 41	60	165	33 41	59	165
16	29 35	60	163	30 35	60	163	31 35	60	163	32 35	60	163	33 35	60	162
18	29 28	60	161	30 28	60	160	31 28	60	160	32 28	60	160	33 28	60	160
20	29 21	+60	158	30 21	+60	158	31 21	+60	158	32 21	+60	158	33 21	+59	158
22	29 13	60	156	30 13	60	156	31 13	60	156	32 13	59	156	33 12	60	156
24	29 04	60	154	30 04	60	154	31 04	60	154	32 04	59	154	33 03	60	154
26	28 55	60	152	29 55	59	152	30 54	60	152	31 54	60	152	32 54	60	152
28	28 45	59	150	29 44	60	150	30 44	60	150	31 44	60	150	32 44	59	149
30	28 34	+60	148	29 34	+59	148	30 33	+60	147	31 33	+60	147	32 33	+59	147
32	28 22	60	146	29 22	60	145	30 22	59	145	31 21	60	145	32 21	60	145
34	28 10	60	143	29 10	60	143	30 10	59	143	31 09	60	143	32 09	59	143
36	27 58	59	141	28 57	60	141	29 57	59	141	30 56	60	141	31 56	59	141
38	27 44	60	139	28 44	59	139	29 43	60	139	30 43	59	139	31 42	60	139
40	27 30	+60	137	28 30	+59	137	29 29	+60	137	30 29	+59	137	31 28	+60	137
42	27 16	59	135	28 15	60	135	29 15	59	135	30 14	60	135	31 14	59	134
44	27 01	59	133	28 00	60	133	29 00	59	133	29 59	60	132	30 59	59	132
46	26 45	60	131	27 45	59	131	28 44	60	131	29 44	59	130	30 43	59	130
48	26 29	60	129	27 29	59	129	28 28	59	128	29 27	60	128	30 27	59	128
50	26 13	+59	127	27 12	+59	127	28 11	+60	126	29 11	+59	126	30 10	+59	126
52	25 56	59	125	26 55	59	124	27 54	60	124	28 54	59	124	29 53	59	124
54	25 39	59	123	26 38	59	122	27 37	59	122	28 36	59	122	29 35	60	122
56	25 21	59	121	26 20	59	120	27 19	59	120	28 18	60	120	29 18	59	120
58	25 03	59	118	26 02	59	118	27 01	59	118	28 00	59	118	28 59	59	118
60	24 44	+59	116	25 43	+59	116	26 42	+60	116	27 42	+59	116	28 41	+59	116
62	24 25	59	114	25 24	60	114	26 24	59	114	27 23	59	114	28 22	59	114
64	24 06	59	112	25 05	59	112	26 04	59	112	27 03	59	112	28 02	60	112
66	23 47	59	110	24 46	59	110	25 45	59	110	26 44	59	110	27 43	59	110
68	23 27	59	108	24 26	59	108	25 25	59	108	26 24	59	108	27 23	59	108
70	23 07	+59	106	24 06	+59	106	25 05	+59	106	26 04	+59	106	27 03	+59	105
72	22 47	59	104	23 46	59	104	24 45	59	104	25 44	59	104	26 43	59	103
74	22 27	59	102	23 26	59	102	24 25	59	102	25 24	59	102	26 23	59	101
76	22 06	59	100	23 05	59	100	24 04	59	100	25 03	59	100	26 02	59	99
78	21 46	59	98	22 45	59	98	23 44	59	98	24 43	59	98	25 42	59	97
80	21 25	+59	96	22 24	+59	96	23 23	+59	96	24 22	+59	96	25 21	+59	95
82	21 04	59	94	22 03	59	94	23 02	59	94	24 01	59	94	25 00	59	94
84	20 44	59	92	21 43	58	92	22 41	59	92	23 40	59	92	24 39	59	92
86	20 23	59	90	21 22	59	90	22 21	59	90	23 20	58	90	24 18	59	90
88	20 02	59	88	21 01	59	88	22 00	59	88	22 59	59	88	23 58	59	88
90	19 41	+59	86	20 40	+59	86	21 39	+59	86	22 38	+59	86	23 37	+59	86
92	19 20	59	84	20 19	59	84	21 18	59	84	22 17	59	84	23 16	59	84
94	19 00	59	83	19 59	59	82	20 58	58	82	21 56	59	82	22 55	59	82
96	18 39	59	81	19 38	59	80	20 37	59	80	21 36	59	80	22 35	59	80
98	18 18	59	79	19 17	59	78	20 16	59	78	21 15	59	78	22 14	59	78
100	17 58	+59	77	18 57	+59	76	19 56	+59	76	20 55	+59	76	21 54	+59	76
102	17 38	59	75	18 37	59	75	19 36	59	74	20 35	59	74	21 34	59	74
104	17 18	59	73	18 17	59	73	19 16	59	72	20 15	59	72	21 14	59	72
106	16 58	59	71	17 57	59	71	18 56	59	70	19 55	59	70	20 54	59	70
108	16 39	59	69	17 38	59	69	18 37	59	69	19 36	59	68	20 35	59	68
110	16 19	+59	67	17 18	+60	67	18 18	+59	67	19 17	+59	66	20 16	+59	66
112	16 00	59	65	16 59	60	65	17 59	59	65	18 58	59	65	19 57	59	64
114	15 42	59	63	16 41	59	63	17 40	59	63	18 39	59	63	19 38	59	62
116	15 23	59	61	16 22	60	61	17 22	59	61	18 21	59	61	19 20	59	61
118	15 05	59	59	16 04	59	59	17 03	60	59	18 03	59	59	19 02	59	59
120	14 47	+60	57	15 47	+59	57	16 46	+59	57	17 45	+59	57	18 44	+60	57
122	14 30	59	55	15 29	60	55	16 29	59	55	17 28	59	55	18 27	59	55
124	14 13	59	54	15 12	60	53	16 12	59	53	17 11	59	53	18 10	60	53
126	13 56	60	52	14 56	59	51	15 55	60	51	16 55	59	51	17 54	59	51
128	13 40	60	50	14 40	59	50	15 39	60	49	16 39	59	49	17 38	59	49
130	13 25	+59	48	14 24	+60	48	15 24	+59	47	16 23	+59	47	17 22	+60	47
132	13 10	59	46	14 09	59	46	15 08	60	46	16 08	59	45	17 07	60	45
134	12 55	59	44	13 54	60	44	14 54	59	44	15 53	60	44	16 53	59	43
136	12 41	59	42	13 40	60	42	14 40	59	42	15 39	60	42	16 39	59	42
138	12 27	60	40	13 27	59	40	14 26	60	40	15 26	59	40	16 25	60	40

25° Hc	d	Z	26° Hc	d	Z	27° Hc	d	Z	28° Hc	d	Z	29° Hc	d	Z	LHA
° ′	′	°	° ′	′	°	° ′	′	°	° ′	′	°	° ′	′	°	
35 00	+60	180	36 00	+60	180	37 00	+60	180	38 00	+60	180	39 00	+60	180	360
35 00	60	178	36 00	60	178	37 00	60	178	38 00	60	178	39 00	60	178	358
34 58	60	176	35 58	60	176	36 58	60	176	37 58	60	176	38 58	60	176	356
34 56	60	173	35 56	60	173	36 56	60	173	37 56	60	173	38 56	60	173	354
34 54	60	171	35 54	60	171	36 54	60	171	37 54	60	171	38 54	59	171	352
34 50	+60	169	35 50	+60	169	36 50	+60	169	37 50	+60	169	38 50	+60	169	350
34 46	60	167	35 46	60	167	36 46	59	167	37 45	60	167	38 45	60	167	348
34 40	60	165	35 40	60	165	36 40	60	164	37 40	60	164	38 40	60	164	346
34 35	59	162	35 34	60	162	36 34	60	162	37 34	60	162	38 34	60	162	344
34 28	60	160	35 28	60	160	36 28	59	160	37 27	60	160	38 27	60	160	342
34 20	+60	158	35 20	+60	158	36 20	+60	158	37 20	+60	158	38 20	+60	158	340
34 12	60	156	35 12	60	156	36 12	60	156	37 12	59	156	38 11	60	155	338
34 03	60	154	35 03	60	154	36 03	60	153	37 03	59	153	38 02	60	153	336
33 54	59	151	34 53	60	151	35 53	60	151	36 53	60	151	37 53	59	151	334
33 43	60	149	34 43	60	149	35 43	59	149	36 42	60	149	37 42	60	149	332
33 32	+60	147	34 32	+60	147	35 32	+59	147	36 31	+60	147	37 31	+60	147	330
33 21	59	145	34 20	60	145	35 20	60	145	36 20	59	145	37 19	60	144	328
33 08	60	143	34 08	60	143	35 08	59	143	36 07	60	142	37 07	59	142	326
32 55	60	141	33 55	60	141	34 55	59	140	35 54	60	140	36 54	59	140	324
32 42	59	139	33 41	60	138	34 41	59	138	35 40	60	138	36 40	59	138	322
32 28	+59	136	33 27	+60	136	34 27	+59	136	35 26	+60	136	36 26	+59	136	320
32 13	60	134	33 13	59	134	34 12	59	134	35 11	60	134	36 11	59	134	318
31 58	59	132	32 57	60	132	33 57	59	132	34 56	59	132	35 55	60	131	316
31 42	60	130	32 42	59	130	33 41	59	130	34 40	60	129	35 40	59	129	314
31 26	59	128	32 25	60	128	33 25	59	128	34 24	59	127	35 23	59	127	312
31 09	+60	126	32 09	+59	126	33 08	+59	125	34 07	+59	125	35 06	+60	125	310
30 52	59	124	31 51	60	124	32 51	59	123	33 50	59	123	34 49	59	123	308
30 35	59	122	31 34	59	121	32 33	59	121	33 32	59	121	34 31	59	121	306
30 17	59	120	31 16	59	119	32 15	59	119	33 14	59	119	34 13	59	119	304
29 58	60	118	30 58	59	117	31 57	59	117	32 56	59	117	33 55	59	117	302
29 40	+59	115	30 39	+59	115	31 38	+59	115	32 37	+59	115	33 36	+59	115	300
29 21	59	113	30 20	59	113	31 19	59	113	32 18	59	113	33 17	59	113	298
29 02	59	111	30 01	59	111	31 00	59	111	31 59	59	111	32 58	58	111	296
28 42	59	109	29 41	59	109	30 40	59	109	31 39	59	109	32 38	59	108	294
28 22	59	107	29 21	59	107	30 20	59	107	31 19	59	107	32 18	59	106	292
28 02	+59	105	29 01	+59	105	30 00	+59	105	30 59	+59	105	31 58	+59	104	290
27 42	59	103	28 41	59	103	29 40	59	103	30 39	59	103	31 38	58	102	288
27 22	59	101	28 21	58	101	29 19	59	101	30 18	59	101	31 17	59	100	286
27 01	59	99	28 00	59	99	28 59	59	99	29 58	59	99	30 57	58	98	284
26 41	58	97	27 39	59	97	28 38	59	97	29 37	59	97	30 36	59	96	282
26 20	+59	95	27 19	+59	95	28 18	+58	95	29 16	+59	95	30 15	+59	94	280
25 59	59	93	26 58	59	93	27 57	59	93	28 56	58	93	29 54	59	92	278
25 38	59	91	26 37	59	91	27 36	59	91	28 35	59	91	29 34	58	90	276
25 17	59	89	26 16	59	89	27 15	59	89	28 14	59	89	29 13	59	88	274
24 57	58	87	25 55	59	87	26 54	59	87	27 53	59	87	28 52	59	87	272
24 36	+59	85	25 35	+58	85	26 33	+59	85	27 32	+59	85	28 31	+59	85	270
24 15	59	83	25 14	59	83	26 13	59	83	27 12	58	83	28 10	59	83	268
23 54	59	82	24 53	59	81	25 52	59	81	26 51	59	81	27 50	59	81	266
23 34	59	80	24 33	59	79	25 32	58	79	26 30	59	79	27 29	59	79	264
23 13	59	78	24 12	59	77	25 11	59	77	26 10	59	77	27 09	59	77	262
22 53	+59	76	23 52	+59	75	24 51	+59	75	25 50	+59	75	26 49	+59	75	260
22 33	59	74	23 32	59	74	24 31	59	73	25 30	59	73	26 29	59	73	258
22 13	59	72	23 12	59	72	24 11	59	71	25 10	59	71	26 09	59	71	256
21 53	59	70	22 52	59	70	23 51	59	70	24 50	59	69	25 49	59	69	254
21 34	59	68	22 33	59	68	23 32	59	68	24 31	59	67	25 30	59	67	252
21 15	+59	66	22 14	+59	66	23 13	+59	66	24 12	+59	66	25 11	+59	65	250
20 56	59	64	21 55	59	64	22 54	59	64	23 53	59	64	24 52	59	63	248
20 37	59	62	21 36	60	62	22 36	59	62	23 35	59	62	24 34	59	62	246
20 19	59	60	21 18	59	60	22 17	59	60	23 16	60	60	24 16	59	60	244
20 01	59	58	21 00	59	58	21 59	60	58	22 59	59	58	23 58	59	58	242
19 44	+59	57	20 43	+59	56	21 42	+59	56	22 41	+59	56	23 40	+60	56	240
19 26	60	55	20 26	59	54	21 25	59	54	22 24	59	54	23 23	60	54	238
19 10	59	53	20 09	59	53	21 08	59	52	22 07	60	52	23 07	59	52	236
18 53	60	51	19 53	59	51	20 52	59	51	21 51	60	50	22 51	59	50	234
18 37	60	49	19 37	59	49	20 36	59	49	21 35	60	48	22 35	59	48	232
18 22	+59	47	19 21	+60	47	20 21	+59	47	21 20	+59	47	22 19	+60	46	230
18 07	59	45	19 06	60	45	20 06	59	45	21 05	60	45	22 05	59	45	228
17 52	60	43	18 52	59	43	19 51	60	43	20 51	59	43	21 50	60	43	226
17 38	60	41	18 38	59	41	19 37	60	41	20 37	59	41	21 36	60	41	224
17 25	59	40	18 24	60	39	19 24	59	39	20 23	60	39	21 23	59	39	222

S. Lat. {LHA greater than 180°....... Zn=180−Z; LHA less than 180°........... Zn=180+Z}

DECLINATION (15°-29°) SAME NAME AS LATITUDE

N. Lat. {LHA greater than 180°....... Zn=Z; LHA less than 180°........... Zn=360−Z}

DECLINATION (15°-29°) SAME NAME AS LATITUDE

LAT 80°

LHA	15° Hc	15° d	15° Z	16° Hc	16° d	16° Z	17° Hc	17° d	17° Z	18° Hc	18° d	18° Z	19° Hc	19° d	19° Z	20° Hc	20° d	20° Z	21° Hc	21° d	21° Z
	° ′	′	°	° ′	′	°	° ′	′	°	° ′	′	°	° ′	′	°	° ′	′	°	° ′	′	°
140	07 16	+59	39	08 15	+60	39	09 15	+60	39	10 15	+59	38	11 14	+60	38	12 14	+59	38	13 13	+60	38
142	07 03	60	37	08 03	59	37	09 02	60	37	10 02	60	37	11 02	59	36	12 01	60	36	13 01	59	36
144	06 51	59	35	07 50	60	35	08 50	60	35	09 50	59	35	10 49	60	35	11 49	60	34	12 49	60	34
146	06 39	60	33	07 39	60	33	08 39	59	33	09 38	60	33	10 38	60	33	11 38	59	32	12 37	60	32
148	06 28	60	31	07 28	60	31	08 28	59	31	09 27	60	31	10 27	60	31	11 27	60	31	12 27	59	30
150	06 18	+59	29	07 17	+60	29	08 17	+60	29	09 17	+60	29	10 17	+60	29	11 17	+59	29	12 16	+60	29
152	06 08	60	27	07 08	59	27	08 07	60	27	09 07	60	27	10 07	60	27	11 07	60	27	12 07	59	27
154	05 59	59	25	06 58	60	25	07 58	60	25	08 58	60	25	09 58	60	25	10 58	60	25	11 58	59	25
156	05 50	60	23	06 50	60	23	07 50	60	23	08 50	60	23	09 50	59	23	10 49	60	23	11 49	60	23
158	05 42	60	21	06 42	60	21	07 42	60	21	08 42	60	21	09 42	60	21	10 42	59	21	11 41	60	21
160	05 35	+60	19	06 35	+60	19	07 35	+60	19	08 35	+60	19	09 35	+59	19	10 34	+60	19	11 34	+60	19
162	05 28	60	17	06 28	60	17	07 28	60	17	08 28	60	17	09 28	60	17	10 28	60	17	11 28	60	17
164	05 22	60	16	06 22	60	16	07 22	60	15	08 22	60	15	09 22	60	15	10 22	60	15	11 22	60	15
166	05 17	60	14	06 17	60	14	07 17	60	14	08 17	60	13	09 17	60	13	10 17	60	13	11 17	60	13
168	05 13	60	12	06 13	60	12	07 13	60	12	08 13	60	12	09 13	60	12	10 13	59	12	11 12	60	11
170	05 09	+60	10	06 09	+60	10	07 09	+60	10	08 09	+60	10	09 09	+60	10	10 09	+60	10	11 09	+60	10
172	05 06	60	8	06 06	60	8	07 06	60	8	08 06	60	8	09 06	60	8	10 06	60	8	11 06	60	8
174	05 03	60	6	06 03	60	6	07 03	60	6	08 03	60	6	09 03	60	6	10 03	60	6	11 03	60	6
176	05 01	60	4	06 01	60	4	07 01	60	4	08 01	60	4	09 01	60	4	10 01	60	4	11 01	60	4
178	05 00	60	2	06 00	60	2	07 00	60	2	08 00	60	2	09 00	60	2	10 00	60	2	11 00	60	2
180	05 00	+60	0	06 00	+60	0	07 00	+60	0	08 00	+60	0	09 00	+60	0	10 00	+60	0	11 00	+60	0

22° Hc	22° d	22° Z	23° Hc	23° d	23° Z	24° Hc	24° d	24° Z	25° Hc	25° d	25° Z	26° Hc	26° d	26° Z	27° Hc	27° d	27° Z	28° Hc	28° d	28° Z	29° Hc	29° d	29° Z	LHA
° ′	′	°	° ′	′	°	° ′	′	°	° ′	′	°	° ′	′	°	° ′	′	°	° ′	′	°	° ′	′	°	
14 13	+60	38	15 13	+59	38	16 12	+60	38	17 12	+59	38	18 11	+60	38	19 11	+60	37	20 11	+59	37	21 10	+60	37	220
14 00	60	36	15 00	60	36	16 00	59	36	16 59	60	36	17 59	60	36	18 59	59	36	19 58	60	35	20 58	59	35	218
13 49	59	34	14 48	60	34	15 48	59	34	16 47	60	34	17 47	60	34	18 47	59	34	19 46	60	34	20 46	60	33	216
13 37	60	32	14 37	59	32	15 36	60	32	16 36	60	32	17 36	60	32	18 36	59	32	19 35	60	32	20 35	60	32	214
13 26	60	30	14 26	60	30	15 26	59	30	16 25	60	30	17 25	60	30	18 25	60	30	19 25	59	30	20 24	60	30	212
13 16	+60	28	14 16	+60	28	15 16	+59	28	16 15	+60	28	17 15	+60	28	18 15	+60	28	19 15	+59	28	20 14	+60	28	210
13 06	60	27	14 06	60	27	15 06	60	26	16 06	60	26	17 06	59	26	18 05	60	26	19 05	60	26	20 05	60	26	208
12 57	60	25	13 57	60	25	14 57	60	25	15 57	60	24	16 57	59	24	17 56	60	24	18 56	60	24	19 56	60	24	206
12 49	60	23	13 49	60	23	14 49	60	23	15 49	59	23	16 48	60	23	17 48	60	22	18 48	60	22	19 48	60	22	204
12 41	60	21	13 41	60	21	14 41	60	21	15 41	60	21	16 41	60	21	17 41	59	21	18 40	60	20	19 40	60	20	202
12 34	+60	19	13 34	+60	19	14 34	+60	19	15 34	+60	19	16 34	+60	19	17 34	+60	19	18 34	+59	19	19 33	+60	19	200
12 28	60	17	13 28	60	17	14 28	59	17	15 27	60	17	16 27	60	17	17 27	60	17	18 27	60	17	19 27	60	17	198
12 22	60	15	13 22	60	15	14 22	60	15	15 22	60	15	16 22	60	15	17 22	60	15	18 22	59	15	19 21	60	15	196
12 17	60	13	13 17	60	13	14 17	60	13	15 17	60	13	16 17	60	13	17 17	60	13	18 17	59	13	19 16	60	13	194
12 12	60	11	13 12	60	11	14 12	60	11	15 12	60	11	16 12	60	11	17 12	60	11	18 12	60	11	19 12	60	11	192
12 09	+60	10	13 09	+60	9	14 09	+60	9	15 09	+60	9	16 09	+60	9	17 09	+59	9	18 08	+60	9	19 08	+60	9	190
12 06	60	8	13 06	60	8	14 06	60	8	15 06	59	8	16 05	60	8	17 05	60	8	18 05	60	7	19 05	60	7	188
12 03	60	6	13 03	60	6	14 03	60	6	15 03	60	6	16 03	60	6	17 03	60	6	18 03	60	6	19 03	60	6	186
12 01	60	4	13 01	60	4	14 01	60	4	15 01	60	4	16 01	60	4	17 01	60	4	18 01	60	4	19 01	60	4	184
12 00	60	2	13 00	60	2	14 00	60	2	15 00	60	2	16 00	60	2	17 00	60	2	18 00	60	2	19 00	60	2	182
12 00	+60	0	13 00	+60	0	14 00	+60	0	15 00	+60	0	16 00	+60	0	17 00	+60	0	18 00	+60	0	19 00	+60	0	180

LAT 80°

15°	16°	17°	18°	19°	20°	21°	22°	23°	24°	25°	26°	27°	28°	29°

S. Lat. {LHA greater than 180°....... Zn=180−Z; LHA less than 180°........... Zn=180+Z}

DECLINATION (15°-29°) SAME NAME AS LATITUDE

N. Lat. {LHA greater than 180°....... Zn=Z; LHA less than 180°........... Zn=360−Z}

DECLINATION (15°-29°) CONTRARY NAME TO LATITUDE

LHA	15° Hc	15° d	15° Z	16° Hc	16° d	16° Z	17° Hc	17° d	17° Z	LHA
	° ′	′	°	° ′	′	°	° ′	′	°	
40	−7 16	−59	141							320
38	−7 03	60	143							322
36	−6 51	59	145							324
34	−6 39	60	147							326
32	−6 28	60	149							328
30	−6 18	−59	151	−7 17	−60	151				330
28	−6 08	60	153	−7 08	59	153				332
26	−5 59	59	155	−6 58	60	155				334
24	−5 50	60	157	−6 50	60	157				336
22	−5 42	60	159	−6 42	60	159				338
20	−5 35	−60	161	−6 35	−60	161				340
18	−5 28	60	163	−6 28	60	163				342
16	−5 22	60	164	−6 22	60	164				344
14	−5 17	60	166	−6 17	60	166				346
12	−5 13	60	168	−6 13	60	168				348
10	−5 09	−60	170	−6 09	−60	170				350
8	−5 06	60	172	−6 06	60	172				352
6	−5 03	60	174	−6 03	60	174				354
4	−5 01	60	176	−6 01	60	176				356
2	−5 00	60	178	−6 00	60	178	−7 00	60	178	358
0	−5 00	−60	180	−6 00	−60	180	−7 00	−60	180	360

S. Lat. {LHA greater than 180°....... Zn=180−Z; LHA less than 180°........... Zn=180+Z}

DECLINATION (15°-29°) CONTRARY NAME TO LATITUDE

LAT 80°

LAT 81°

N. Lat. {LHA greater than 180°....... Zn=Z; LHA less than 180°........... Zn=360−Z}

DECLINATION (0°-14°) SAME NAME AS LATITUDE

LHA	0° Hc	d	Z	1° Hc	d	Z	2° Hc	d	Z	3° Hc	d	Z	4° Hc	d	Z
	° ′	′	°	° ′	′	°	° ′	′	°	° ′	′	°	° ′	′	°
0	09 00	+60	180	10 00	+60	180	11 00	+60	180	12 00	+60	180	13 00	+60	180
2	09 00	60	178	10 00	60	178	11 00	60	178	12 00	60	178	13 00	60	178
4	08 59	60	176	09 59	60	176	10 59	60	176	11 59	60	176	12 59	60	176
6	08 57	60	174	09 57	60	174	10 57	60	174	11 57	60	174	12 57	60	174
8	08 55	60	172	09 55	60	172	10 55	60	172	11 55	60	172	12 55	60	172
10	08 52	+60	170	09 52	+60	170	10 52	+60	170	11 52	+60	170	12 52	+60	170
12	08 48	60	168	09 48	60	168	10 48	60	168	11 48	60	168	12 48	60	168
14	08 44	60	166	09 44	60	166	10 44	60	166	11 44	60	166	12 44	60	166
16	08 39	60	164	09 39	60	164	10 39	60	164	11 39	60	164	12 39	60	164
18	08 33	60	162	09 33	60	162	10 33	60	162	11 33	60	162	12 33	60	162
20	08 27	+60	160	09 27	+60	160	10 27	+60	160	11 27	+60	160	12 27	+60	160
22	08 20	60	158	09 20	60	158	10 20	60	158	11 20	60	158	12 20	60	158
24	08 13	60	156	09 13	60	156	10 13	60	156	11 13	60	156	12 13	59	156
26	08 05	60	154	09 05	60	154	10 05	60	154	11 05	59	154	12 04	60	153
28	07 56	60	152	08 56	60	152	09 56	60	152	10 56	60	152	11 56	60	151
30	07 47	+60	150	08 47	+60	150	09 47	+60	150	10 47	+59	150	11 46	+60	149
32	07 37	60	148	08 37	60	148	09 37	60	148	10 37	60	147	11 37	59	147
34	07 27	60	146	08 27	60	146	09 27	59	146	10 26	60	145	11 26	60	145
36	07 16	60	144	08 16	60	144	09 16	60	144	10 16	59	143	11 15	60	143
38	07 05	60	142	08 05	59	142	09 04	60	142	10 04	60	141	11 04	59	141
40	06 53	+60	140	07 53	+59	140	08 52	+60	139	09 52	+60	139	10 52	+59	139
42	06 41	59	138	07 40	60	138	08 40	60	137	09 40	59	137	10 39	60	137
44	06 28	59	136	07 27	60	136	08 27	60	135	09 27	59	135	10 26	60	135
46	06 14	60	134	07 14	60	134	08 14	59	133	09 13	60	133	10 13	59	133
48	06 01	59	132	07 00	60	132	08 00	59	131	08 59	60	131	09 59	59	131
50	05 46	+60	130	06 46	+59	130	07 45	+60	129	08 45	+60	129	09 45	+59	129
52	05 32	59	128	06 31	60	128	07 31	59	127	08 30	60	127	09 30	59	127
54	05 17	59	126	06 16	60	126	07 16	59	125	08 15	60	125	09 15	59	125
56	05 01	60	124	06 01	59	124	07 00	60	123	08 00	59	123	08 59	60	123
58	04 45	60	122	05 45	59	122	06 44	60	121	07 44	59	121	08 43	60	121
60	04 29	+60	120	05 29	+59	120	06 28	+60	119	07 28	+59	119	08 27	+59	119
62	04 13	59	118	05 12	60	118	06 12	59	117	07 11	59	117	08 10	60	117
64	03 56	59	116	04 55	60	116	05 55	59	115	06 54	60	115	07 54	59	115
66	03 39	59	114	04 38	60	114	05 38	59	113	06 37	59	113	07 36	60	113
68	03 22	59	112	04 21	59	112	05 20	60	112	06 20	59	111	07 19	59	111
70	03 04	+59	110	04 03	+60	110	05 03	+59	110	06 02	+59	109	07 01	+60	109
72	02 46	60	108	03 46	59	108	04 45	59	108	05 44	60	107	06 44	59	107
74	02 28	60	106	03 28	59	106	04 27	59	106	05 26	60	105	06 26	59	105
76	02 10	59	104	03 09	60	104	04 09	59	104	05 08	59	103	06 07	60	103
78	01 52	59	102	02 51	59	102	03 50	60	102	04 50	59	101	05 49	59	101
80	01 33	+60	100	02 33	+59	100	03 32	+59	100	04 31	+60	99	05 31	+59	99
82	01 15	59	98	02 14	59	98	03 13	60	98	04 13	59	97	05 12	59	97
84	00 56	59	96	01 55	60	96	02 55	59	96	03 54	59	95	04 53	60	95
86	00 38	59	94	01 37	59	94	02 36	59	94	03 35	60	93	04 35	59	93
88	00 19	59	92	01 18	59	92	02 17	60	92	03 17	59	91	04 16	59	91
90	00 00	+59	90	00 59	+60	90	01 59	+59	90	02 58	+59	90	03 57	+59	89
92	−0 19	60	88	00 41	59	88	01 40	59	88	02 39	59	88	03 38	60	87
94	−0 38	60	86	00 22	59	86	01 21	60	86	02 21	59	86	03 20	59	85
96	−0 56	59	84	00 03	59	84	01 02	60	84	02 02	59	84	03 01	59	83
98	−1 15	59	82	−0 16	60	82	00 44	59	82	01 43	59	82	02 42	60	81
100	−1 33	+59	80	−0 34	+59	80	00 25	+59	80	01 24	+60	80	02 24	+59	80
102	−1 52	59	78	−0 53	60	78	00 07	59	78	01 06	59	78	02 05	60	78
104	−2 10	59	76	−1 11	59	76	−0 12	60	76	00 48	59	76	01 47	59	76
106	−2 28	59	74	−1 29	59	74	−0 30	60	74	00 30	59	74	01 29	59	74
108	−2 46	59	72	−1 47	59	72	−0 48	60	72	00 12	59	72	01 11	59	72
110	−3 04	+60	70	−2 04	+59	70	−1 05	+59	70	−0 06	+59	70	00 53	+60	70
112	−3 22	60	68	−2 22	59	68	−1 23	60	68	−0 23	59	68	00 36	59	68
114	−3 39	60	66	−2 39	59	66	−1 40	59	66	−0 41	60	66	00 19	59	66
116	−3 56	59	64	−2 57	60	64	−1 57	59	64	−0 58	60	64	00 02	59	64
118	−4 13	60	62	−3 13	59	62	−2 14	60	62	−1 14	59	62	−0 15	59	62
120	−4 29	+59	60	−3 30	+60	60	−2 30	+59	60	−1 31	+60	60	−0 31	+59	60
122	−4 45	59	58	−3 46	60	58	−2 46	59	58	−1 47	60	58	−0 47	59	58
124	−5 01	59	56	−4 02	60	56	−3 02	59	56	−2 03	60	56	−1 03	59	56
126	−5 17	60	54	−4 17	59	54	−3 18	60	54	−2 18	60	54	−1 18	59	54
128	−5 32	60	52	−4 32	59	52	−3 33	60	52	−2 33	60	52	−1 33	59	52
130	−5 46	+59	50	−4 47	+60	50	−3 47	+59	50	−2 48	+60	50	−1 48	+60	50
132	−6 01	60	48	−5 01	60	48	−4 01	59	48	−3 02	60	48	−2 02	59	48
134	−6 14	59	46	−5 15	60	46	−4 15	60	46	−3 15	59	46	−2 16	60	46
136	−6 28	60	44	−5 28	60	44	−4 28	59	44	−3 29	60	44	−2 29	60	44
138	−6 41	60	42	−5 41	60	42	−4 41	59	42	−3 42	60	42	−2 42	60	42

LHA	5° Hc	d	Z	6° Hc	d	Z	7° Hc	d	Z	8° Hc	d	Z	9° Hc	d	Z
	° ′	′	°	° ′	′	°	° ′	′	°	° ′	′	°	° ′	′	°
0	14 00	+60	180	15 00	+60	180	16 00	+60	180	17 00	+60	180	18 00	+60	180
2	14 00	60	178	15 00	60	178	16 00	60	178	17 00	60	178	18 00	60	178
4	13 59	60	176	14 59	60	176	15 59	60	176	16 59	60	176	17 59	60	176
6	13 57	60	174	14 57	60	174	15 57	60	174	16 57	60	174	17 57	60	174
8	13 55	60	172	14 55	60	172	15 55	60	172	16 55	60	172	17 55	60	172
10	13 52	+60	170	14 52	+60	170	15 52	+60	170	16 52	+60	170	17 52	+60	170
12	13 48	60	168	14 48	60	168	15 48	60	168	16 48	60	168	17 48	60	168
14	13 44	60	166	14 44	60	166	15 44	60	166	16 44	59	166	17 43	60	166
16	13 39	60	164	14 39	60	164	15 39	59	164	16 38	60	163	17 38	60	163
18	13 33	60	162	14 33	60	162	15 33	60	161	16 33	60	161	17 33	60	161
20	13 27	+60	160	14 27	+60	159	15 27	+60	159	16 27	+59	159	17 26	+60	159
22	13 20	60	157	14 20	60	157	15 20	60	157	16 20	59	157	17 19	60	157
24	13 12	60	155	14 12	60	155	15 12	60	155	16 12	60	155	17 12	60	155
26	13 04	60	153	14 04	60	153	15 04	60	153	16 04	60	153	17 04	60	153
28	12 56	59	151	13 55	60	151	14 55	60	151	15 55	60	151	16 55	60	151
30	12 46	+60	149	13 46	+60	149	14 46	+60	149	15 46	+59	149	16 45	+60	149
32	12 36	60	147	13 36	60	147	14 36	60	147	15 36	60	147	16 36	59	147
34	12 26	60	145	13 26	59	145	14 25	60	145	15 25	60	145	16 25	60	145
36	12 15	60	143	13 15	59	143	14 14	60	143	15 14	60	143	16 14	60	143
38	12 03	60	141	13 03	60	141	14 03	60	141	15 03	59	141	16 02	60	141
40	11 51	+60	139	12 51	+60	139	13 51	+59	139	14 50	+60	139	15 50	+60	139
42	11 39	60	137	12 39	59	137	13 38	60	137	14 38	60	137	15 38	59	137
44	11 26	60	135	12 26	59	135	13 25	60	135	14 25	59	135	15 24	60	135
46	11 12	60	133	12 12	60	133	13 12	59	133	14 11	60	133	15 11	59	133
48	10 58	60	131	11 58	60	131	12 58	59	131	13 57	60	131	14 57	59	131
50	10 44	+60	129	11 44	+59	129	12 43	+60	129	13 43	+59	129	14 42	+60	129
52	10 29	60	127	11 29	59	127	12 28	60	127	13 28	59	127	14 27	60	127
54	10 14	60	125	11 14	59	125	12 13	60	125	13 13	59	125	14 12	60	125
56	09 59	59	123	10 58	60	123	11 58	59	123	12 57	59	123	13 56	60	123
58	09 43	59	121	10 42	60	121	11 42	59	121	12 41	59	121	13 40	60	121
60	09 26	+60	119	10 26	+59	119	11 25	+60	119	12 25	+59	119	13 24	+60	118
62	09 10	59	117	10 09	60	117	11 09	59	117	12 08	59	117	13 07	60	116
64	08 53	59	115	09 52	60	115	10 52	59	115	11 51	59	115	12 50	60	114
66	08 36	59	113	09 35	60	113	10 35	59	113	11 34	59	113	12 33	60	112
68	08 18	60	111	09 18	59	111	10 17	59	111	11 16	60	111	12 16	59	110
70	08 01	+59	109	09 00	+59	109	09 59	+60	109	10 59	+59	109	11 58	+59	108
72	07 43	59	107	08 42	60	107	09 42	59	107	10 41	59	107	11 40	59	106
74	07 25	59	105	08 24	59	105	09 23	60	105	10 23	59	105	11 22	59	104
76	07 07	59	103	08 06	59	103	09 05	60	103	10 05	59	103	11 04	59	102
78	06 48	60	101	07 48	59	101	08 47	59	101	09 46	59	101	10 45	60	101
80	06 30	+59	99	07 29	+59	99	08 28	+60	99	09 28	+59	99	10 27	+59	99
82	06 11	60	97	07 11	59	97	08 10	59	97	09 09	59	97	10 08	60	97
84	05 53	59	95	06 52	59	95	07 51	59	95	08 50	60	95	09 50	59	95
86	05 34	59	93	06 33	59	93	07 32	60	93	08 32	59	93	09 31	59	93
88	05 15	59	91	06 14	60	91	07 14	59	91	08 13	59	91	09 12	59	91
90	04 56	+60	89	05 56	+59	89	06 55	+59	89	07 54	+59	89	08 53	+60	89
92	04 38	59	87	05 37	59	87	06 36	59	87	07 35	60	87	08 35	59	87
94	04 19	59	85	05 18	59	85	06 17	60	85	07 17	59	85	08 16	59	85
96	04 00	59	83	04 59	60	83	05 59	59	83	06 58	59	83	07 57	59	83
98	03 42	59	81	04 41	59	81	05 40	59	81	06 39	60	81	07 39	59	81
100	03 23	+59	79	04 22	+60	79	05 22	+59	79	06 21	+59	79	07 20	+59	79
102	03 05	59	77	04 04	59	77	05 03	60	77	06 03	59	77	07 02	59	77
104	02 46	60	75	03 46	59	75	04 45	59	75	05 44	60	75	06 44	59	75
106	02 28	60	73	03 28	59	73	04 27	59	73	05 26	60	73	06 26	59	73
108	02 10	60	71	03 10	59	71	04 09	59	71	05 08	60	71	06 08	59	71
110	01 53	+59	69	02 52	+59	69	03 51	+60	69	04 51	+59	69	05 50	+59	69
112	01 35	60	67	02 35	59	67	03 34	59	67	04 33	60	67	05 33	59	67
114	01 18	59	66	02 17	60	65	03 17	59	65	04 16	60	65	05 16	59	65
116	01 01	59	64	02 00	60	63	03 00	59	63	03 59	60	63	04 59	59	63
118	00 44	60	62	01 44	59	61	02 43	60	61	03 43	59	61	04 42	60	61
120	00 28	+60	60	01 28	+59	60	02 27	+59	59	03 26	+60	59	04 26	+59	59
122	00 12	60	58	01 12	59	58	02 11	59	57	03 10	60	57	04 10	59	57
124	−0 04	60	56	00 56	59	56	01 55	60	55	02 55	59	55	03 54	60	55
126	−0 19	60	54	00 41	59	54	01 40	60	53	02 40	59	53	03 39	60	53
128	−0 34	60	52	00 26	59	52	01 25	60	51	02 25	59	51	03 24	60	51
130	−0 48	+59	50	00 11	+60	50	01 11	+59	50	02 10	+60	49	03 10	+59	49
132	−1 03	60	48	−0 03	60	48	00 57	59	48	01 56	60	47	02 56	59	47
134	−1 16	59	46	−0 17	60	46	00 43	60	46	01 43	59	45	02 42	60	45
136	−1 29	59	44	−0 30	60	44	00 30	59	44	01 29	60	43	02 29	60	43
138	−1 42	59	42	−0 43	60	42	00 17	60	42	01 17	59	41	02 16	60	41

LHA	10° Hc	d	Z	11° Hc	d	Z	12° Hc	d	Z	13° Hc	d	Z	14° Hc	d	Z	LHA
	° ′	′	°	° ′	′	°	° ′	′	°	° ′	′	°	° ′	′	°	
0	19 00	+60	180	20 00	+60	180	21 00	+60	180	22 00	+60	180	23 00	+60	180	360
2	19 00	60	178	20 00	60	178	21 00	60	178	22 00	60	178	23 00	60	178	358
4	18 59	60	176	19 59	60	176	20 59	60	176	21 59	60	176	22 59	60	176	356
6	18 57	60	174	19 57	60	174	20 57	60	174	21 57	60	174	22 57	60	174	354
8	18 55	60	172	19 55	60	172	20 55	60	172	21 55	60	172	22 55	60	172	352
10	18 52	+60	170	19 52	+59	170	20 51	+60	170	21 51	+60	170	22 51	+60	170	350
12	18 48	60	168	19 48	60	168	20 48	60	167	21 48	60	167	22 48	60	167	348
14	18 43	60	165	19 43	60	165	20 43	60	165	21 43	60	165	22 43	60	165	346
16	18 38	60	163	19 38	60	163	20 38	60	163	21 38	60	163	22 38	60	163	344
18	18 33	60	161	19 33	60	161	20 33	59	161	21 32	60	161	22 32	60	161	342
20	18 26	+60	159	19 26	+60	159	20 26	+60	159	21 26	+60	159	22 26	+60	159	340
22	18 19	60	157	19 19	60	157	20 19	60	157	21 19	60	157	22 19	60	157	338
24	18 12	60	155	19 12	59	155	20 11	60	155	21 11	60	155	22 11	60	155	336
26	18 04	59	153	19 03	60	153	20 03	60	153	21 03	60	153	22 03	60	153	334
28	17 55	60	151	18 55	59	151	19 54	60	151	20 54	60	151	21 54	60	151	332
30	17 45	+60	149	18 45	+60	149	19 45	+60	149	20 45	+59	149	21 44	+60	149	330
32	17 35	60	147	18 35	60	147	19 35	60	147	20 35	59	147	21 34	60	146	328
34	17 25	59	145	18 24	60	145	19 24	60	145	20 24	60	145	21 24	59	144	326
36	17 14	59	143	18 13	60	143	19 13	60	143	20 13	59	142	21 12	60	142	324
38	17 02	60	141	18 02	59	141	19 01	60	140	20 01	60	140	21 01	59	140	322
40	16 50	+59	139	17 49	+60	139	18 49	+60	138	19 49	+59	138	20 48	+60	138	320
42	16 37	60	137	17 37	59	136	18 36	60	136	19 36	60	136	20 36	59	136	318
44	16 24	60	135	17 24	59	134	18 23	60	134	19 23	59	134	20 22	60	134	316
46	16 10	60	133	17 10	60	132	18 10	59	132	19 09	60	132	20 09	59	132	314
48	15 56	60	130	16 56	59	130	17 55	60	130	18 55	60	130	19 55	59	130	312
50	15 42	+59	128	16 41	+60	128	17 41	+59	128	18 40	+60	128	19 40	+59	128	310
52	15 27	59	126	16 26	60	126	17 26	59	126	18 25	60	126	19 25	59	126	308
54	15 12	59	124	16 11	60	124	17 11	59	124	18 10	59	124	19 09	60	124	306
56	14 56	59	122	15 55	60	122	16 55	59	122	17 54	60	122	18 54	59	122	304
58	14 40	59	120	15 39	60	120	16 39	59	120	17 38	60	120	18 38	59	120	302
60	14 24	+59	118	15 23	+59	118	16 22	+60	118	17 22	+59	118	18 21	+59	118	300
62	14 07	59	116	15 06	60	116	16 06	59	116	17 05	59	116	18 04	60	116	298
64	13 50	59	114	14 49	60	114	15 49	59	114	16 48	59	114	17 47	60	114	296
66	13 33	59	112	14 32	59	112	15 31	60	112	16 31	59	112	17 30	59	112	294
68	13 15	59	110	14 14	60	110	15 14	59	110	16 13	59	110	17 12	60	110	292
70	12 57	+60	108	13 57	+59	108	14 56	+59	108	15 55	+60	108	16 55	+59	108	290
72	12 39	60	106	13 39	59	106	14 38	59	106	15 37	60	106	16 37	59	106	288
74	12 21	60	104	13 21	59	104	14 20	59	104	15 19	59	104	16 18	60	104	286
76	12 03	59	102	13 02	60	102	14 02	59	102	15 01	59	102	16 00	59	102	284
78	11 45	59	100	12 44	59	100	13 43	59	100	14 42	60	100	15 42	59	100	282
80	11 26	+59	98	12 25	+60	98	13 25	+59	98	14 24	+59	98	15 23	+59	98	280
82	11 08	59	96	12 07	59	96	13 06	59	96	14 05	59	96	15 04	60	96	278
84	10 49	59	94	11 48	59	94	12 47	60	94	13 47	59	94	14 46	59	94	276
86	10 30	59	92	11 29	60	92	12 29	59	92	13 28	59	92	14 27	59	92	274
88	10 11	60	90	11 11	59	90	12 10	59	90	13 09	59	90	14 08	59	90	272
90	09 53	+59	88	10 52	+59	88	11 51	+59	88	12 50	+60	88	13 50	+59	88	270
92	09 34	59	86	10 33	59	86	11 32	60	86	12 32	59	86	13 31	59	86	268
94	09 15	59	85	10 14	60	84	11 14	59	84	12 13	59	84	13 12	59	84	266
96	08 56	60	83	09 56	59	82	10 55	59	82	11 54	59	82	12 53	60	82	264
98	08 38	59	81	09 37	59	80	10 36	60	80	11 36	59	80	12 35	59	80	262
100	08 19	+60	79	09 19	+59	78	10 18	+59	78	11 17	+59	78	12 16	+60	78	260
102	08 01	59	77	09 00	60	76	10 00	59	76	10 59	59	76	11 58	59	76	258
104	07 43	59	75	08 42	60	75	09 42	59	74	10 41	59	74	11 40	59	74	256
106	07 25	59	73	08 24	60	73	09 24	59	72	10 23	59	72	11 22	59	72	254
108	07 07	59	71	08 06	60	71	09 06	59	70	10 05	59	70	11 04	60	70	252
110	06 49	+60	69	07 49	+59	69	08 48	+59	69	09 47	+60	68	10 47	+59	68	250
112	06 32	59	67	07 31	60	67	08 31	59	67	09 30	60	66	10 30	59	66	248
114	06 15	59	65	07 14	60	65	08 14	59	65	09 13	59	64	10 12	60	64	246
116	05 58	60	63	06 58	59	63	07 57	59	63	08 56	60	62	09 56	59	62	244
118	05 42	59	61	06 41	59	61	07 40	60	61	08 40	59	61	09 39	60	60	242
120	05 25	+60	59	06 25	+59	59	07 24	+60	59	08 24	+59	59	09 23	+60	58	240
122	05 09	60	57	06 09	59	57	07 08	60	57	08 08	59	57	09 07	60	56	238
124	04 54	59	55	05 53	60	55	06 53	59	55	07 52	60	55	08 52	59	55	236
126	04 39	59	53	05 38	60	53	06 38	59	53	07 37	60	53	08 37	59	53	234
128	04 24	59	51	05 23	60	51	06 23	59	51	07 22	60	51	08 22	60	51	232
130	04 09	+60	49	05 09	+60	49	06 09	+59	49	07 08	+60	49	08 08	+59	49	230
132	03 55	60	47	04 55	60	47	05 55	59	47	06 54	60	47	07 54	59	47	228
134	03 42	59	45	04 41	60	45	05 41	60	45	06 41	59	45	07 40	60	45	226
136	03 29	59	43	04 28	60	43	05 28	60	43	06 28	59	43	07 27	60	43	224
138	03 16	60	41	04 16	60	41	05 16	59	41	06 15	60	41	07 15	60	41	222

S. Lat. {LHA greater than 180°....... Zn=180−Z; LHA less than 180°........... Zn=180+Z}

DECLINATION (0°-14°) SAME NAME AS LATITUDE

LAT 81°

N. Lat. {LHA greater than 180°....... Zn=Z; LHA less than 180°.......... Zn=360−Z}

DECLINATION (0°-14°) SAME NAME AS LATITUDE

LHA	0° Hc	0° d	0° Z	1° Hc	1° d	1° Z	2° Hc	2° d	2° Z	3° Hc	3° d	3° Z	4° Hc	4° d	4° Z	5° Hc	5° d	5° Z	6° Hc	6° d	6° Z	7° Hc	7° d	7° Z	8° Hc	8° d	8° Z	9° Hc	9° d	9° Z	10° Hc	10° d	10° Z	11° Hc	11° d	11° Z	12° Hc	12° d	12° Z	13° Hc	13° d	13° Z	14° Hc	14° d	14° Z	LHA
	° ′	′	°	° ′	′	°	° ′	′	°	° ′	′	°	° ′	′	°	° ′	′	°	° ′	′	°	° ′	′	°	° ′	′	°	° ′	′	°	° ′	′	°	° ′	′	°	° ′	′	°	° ′	′	°	° ′	′	°	
140	−6 53	+60	40	−5 53	+59	40	−4 54	+60	40	−3 54	+60	40	−2 54	+60	40	−1 54	+59	40	−0 55	+60	40	00 05	+60	40	01 05	+59	40	02 04	+60	39	03 04	+60	39	04 04	+59	39	05 03	+60	39	06 03	+60	39	07 03	+60	39	220
142	−7 05	60	38	−6 05	60	38	−5 05	59	38	−4 06	60	38	−3 06	60	38	−2 06	59	38	−1 07	60	38	−0 07	60	38	00 53	60	38	01 53	59	37	02 52	60	37	03 52	60	37	04 52	60	37	05 52	59	37	06 51	60	37	218
144	−7 16	59	36	−6 17	60	36	−5 17	60	36	−4 17	60	36	−3 17	60	36	−2 17	59	36	−1 18	60	36	−0 18	60	36	00 42	59	36	01 41	60	36	02 41	60	35	03 41	60	35	04 41	59	35	05 40	60	35	06 40	60	35	216
146				−6 27	59	34	−5 28	60	34	−4 28	60	34	−3 28	60	34	−2 28	60	34	−1 28	59	34	−0 29	60	34	00 31	60	34	01 31	60	34	02 31	59	33	03 30	60	33	04 30	60	33	05 30	60	33	06 30	59	33	214
148				−6 38	60	32	−5 38	60	32	−4 38	60	32	−3 38	60	32	−2 38	59	32	−1 39	60	32	−0 39	60	32	00 21	60	32	01 21	60	32	02 21	59	31	03 20	60	31	04 20	60	31	05 20	60	31	06 20	60	31	212
150				−6 47	+59	30	−5 48	+60	30	−4 48	+60	30	−3 48	+60	30	−2 48	+60	30	−1 48	+60	30	−0 48	+59	30	00 11	+60	30	01 11	+60	30	02 11	+60	30	03 11	+60	29	04 11	+59	29	05 10	+60	29	06 10	+60	29	210
152				−6 57	60	28	−5 57	60	28	−4 57	60	28	−3 57	60	28	−2 57	60	28	−1 57	60	28	−0 57	59	28	00 02	60	28	01 02	60	28	02 02	60	28	03 02	60	27	04 02	60	27	05 02	59	27	06 01	60	27	208
154				−7 05	60	26	−6 05	60	26	−5 05	59	26	−4 06	60	26	−3 06	60	26	−2 06	60	26	−1 06	60	26	−0 06	60	26	00 54	60	26	01 54	59	26	02 53	60	26	03 53	60	26	04 53	60	25	05 53	60	25	206
156				−7 13	60	24	−6 13	60	24	−5 13	60	24	−4 13	59	24	−3 14	60	24	−2 14	60	24	−1 14	60	24	−0 14	60	24	00 46	60	24	01 46	60	24	02 46	60	24	03 46	59	24	04 45	60	23	05 45	60	23	204
158							−6 21	60	22	−5 21	60	22	−4 21	60	22	−3 21	60	22	−2 21	60	22	−1 21	60	22	−0 21	60	22	00 39	60	22	01 39	59	22	02 38	60	22	03 38	60	22	04 38	60	21	05 38	60	21	202
160							−6 27	+60	20	−5 27	+59	20	−4 28	+60	20	−3 28	+60	20	−2 28	+60	20	−1 28	+60	20	−0 28	+60	20	00 32	+60	20	01 32	+60	20	02 32	+60	20	03 32	+60	20	04 32	+60	20	05 32	+60	20	200
162							−6 34	60	18	−5 34	60	18	−4 34	60	18	−3 34	60	18	−2 34	60	18	−1 34	60	18	−0 34	60	18	00 26	60	18	01 26	60	18	02 26	60	18	03 26	60	18	04 26	60	18	05 26	60	18	198
164							−6 39	60	16	−5 39	60	16	−4 39	60	16	−3 39	60	16	−2 39	60	16	−1 39	60	16	−0 39	60	16	00 21	60	16	01 21	59	16	02 20	60	16	03 20	60	16	04 20	60	16	05 20	60	16	196
166							−6 44	60	14	−5 44	60	14	−4 44	60	14	−3 44	60	14	−2 44	60	14	−1 44	60	14	−0 44	60	14	00 16	60	14	01 16	60	14	02 16	60	14	03 16	60	14	04 16	60	14	05 16	60	14	194
168							−6 48	60	12	−5 48	60	12	−4 48	60	12	−3 48	60	12	−2 48	60	12	−1 48	60	12	−0 48	60	12	00 12	60	12	01 12	60	12	02 12	60	12	03 12	59	12	04 11	60	12	05 11	60	12	192
170							−6 52	+60	10	−5 52	+60	10	−4 52	+60	10	−3 52	+60	10	−2 52	+60	10	−1 52	+60	10	−0 52	+60	10	00 08	+60	10	01 08	+60	10	02 08	+60	10	03 08	+60	10	04 08	+60	10	05 08	+60	10	190
172							−6 55	60	8	−5 55	60	8	−4 55	60	8	−3 55	60	8	−2 55	60	8	−1 55	60	8	−0 55	60	8	00 05	60	8	01 05	60	8	02 05	60	8	03 05	60	8	04 05	60	8	05 05	60	8	188
174							−6 57	60	6	−5 57	60	6	−4 57	60	6	−3 57	60	6	−2 57	60	6	−1 57	60	6	−0 57	60	6	00 03	60	6	01 03	60	6	02 03	60	6	03 03	60	6	04 03	60	6	05 03	60	6	186
176							−6 59	60	4	−5 59	60	4	−4 59	60	4	−3 59	60	4	−2 59	60	4	−1 59	60	4	−0 59	60	4	00 01	60	4	01 01	60	4	02 01	60	4	03 01	60	4	04 01	60	4	05 01	60	4	184
178							−7 00	60	2	−6 00	60	2	−5 00	60	2	−4 00	60	2	−3 00	60	2	−2 00	60	2	−1 00	60	2	00 00	60	2	01 00	60	2	02 00	60	2	03 00	60	2	04 00	60	2	05 00	60	2	182
180							−7 00	+60	0	−6 00	+60	0	−5 00	+60	0	−4 00	+60	0	−3 00	+60	0	−2 00	+60	0	−1 00	+60	0	00 00	+60	0	01 00	+60	0	02 00	+60	0	03 00	+60	0	04 00	+60	0	05 00	+60	0	180

LHA	0° Hc	0° d	0° Z	LHA
144	−7 16	60	36	216
142	−7 05	60	38	218
140	−6 53	−60	40	220

0° | 1° | 2° | 3° | 4° | 5° | 6° | 7° | 8° | 9° | 10° | 11° | 12° | 13° | 14°

S. Lat. {LHA greater than 180°....... Zn=180−Z; LHA less than 180°.......... Zn=180+Z}

DECLINATION (0°-14°) CONTRARY NAME TO LATITUDE

LAT 81°

N. Lat. {LHA greater than 180°....... Zn=Z
{LHA less than 180°........... Zn=360−Z

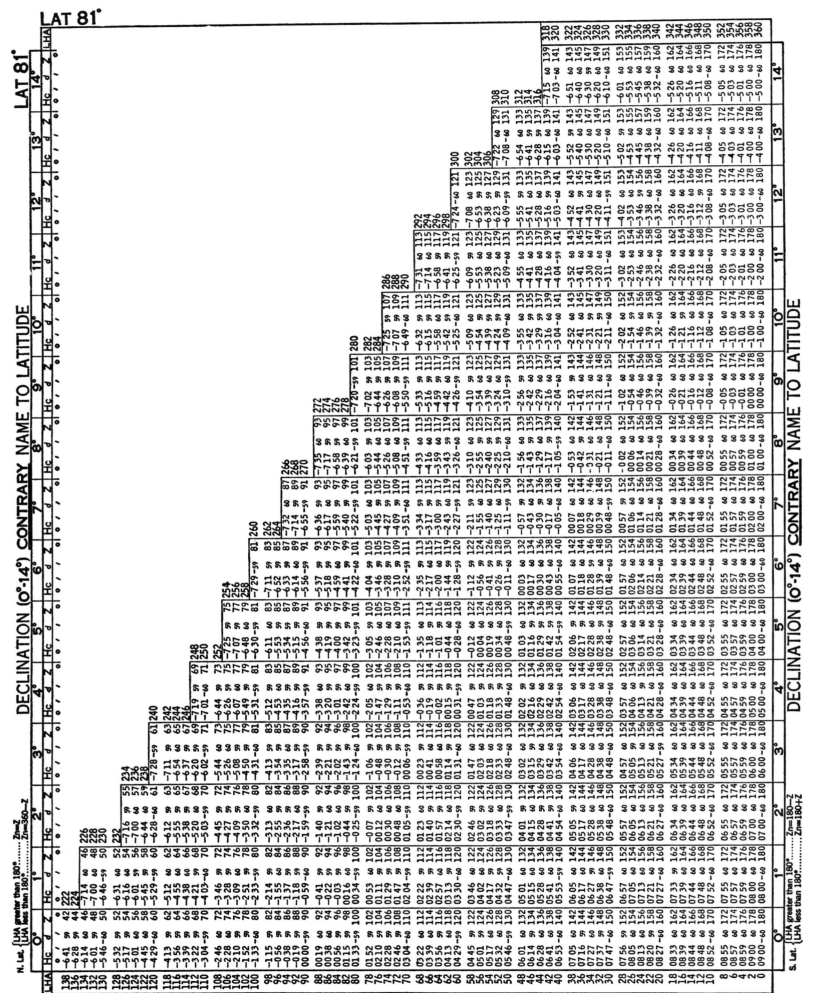

DECLINATION (0°-14°) CONTRARY NAME TO LATITUDE

LHA	0° Hc	0° d	0° Z	1° Hc	1° d	1° Z	2° Hc	2° d	2° Z	3° Hc	3° d	3° Z	4° Hc	4° d	4° Z
	° ′	′	°	° ′	′	°	° ′	′	°	° ′	′	°	° ′	′	°
138	-6 41	59	42	222											
136	-6 28	59	44	224											
134	-6 14	60	46	-7 14	60	46	226								
132	-6 01	59	48	-7 00	60	48	228								
130	-5 46	-60	50	-6 46	-59	50	230								
128	-5 32	59	52	-6 31	60	52	232								
126	-5 17	59	54	-6 16	60	54	-7 16	59	55	234					
124	-5 01	60	56	-6 01	59	56	-7 00	60	57	236					
122	-4 45	60	58	-5 45	59	58	-6 44	60	59	238					
120	-4 29	-60	60	-5 29	-59	60	-6 28	-60	61	-7 28	-59	61	240		
118	-4 13	59	62	-5 12	60	62	-6 12	59	63	-7 11	59	63	242		
116	-3 56	59	64	-4 55	60	64	-5 55	59	65	-6 54	60	65	244		
114	-3 39	59	66	-4 38	60	66	-5 38	59	67	-6 37	59	67	246		
112	-3 22	59	68	-4 21	59	68	-5 20	60	68	-6 20	59	69	-7 19	59	69
110	-3 04	-59	70	-4 03	-60	70	-5 03	-59	70	-6 02	-59	71	-7 01	-60	71
108	-2 46	60	72	-3 46	59	72	-4 45	59	72	-5 44	60	73	-6 44	59	73
106	-2 28	60	74	-3 28	59	74	-4 27	59	74	-5 26	60	75	-6 26	59	75
104	-2 10	59	76	-3 09	60	76	-4 09	59	76	-5 08	59	77	-6 07	60	77
102	-1 52	59	78	-2 51	59	78	-3 50	60	78	-4 50	59	79	-5 49	59	79
100	-1 33	-60	80	-2 33	-59	80	-3 32	-59	80	-4 31	-60	81	-5 31	-59	81
98	-1 15	59	82	-2 14	59	82	-3 13	60	82	-4 13	59	83	-5 12	59	83
96	-0 56	59	84	-1 55	60	84	-2 55	59	84	-3 54	59	85	-4 53	60	85
94	-0 38	59	86	-1 37	59	86	-2 36	59	86	-3 35	60	87	-4 35	59	87
92	-0 19	59	88	-1 18	59	88	-2 17	60	88	-3 17	59	89	-4 16	59	89
90	00 00	-59	90	-0 59	-60	90	-1 59	-59	90	-2 58	-59	90	-3 57	-59	91
88	00 19	60	92	-0 41	59	92	-1 40	59	92	-2 39	59	92	-3 38	60	93
86	00 38	60	94	-0 22	59	94	-1 21	60	94	-2 21	59	94	-3 20	59	95
84	00 56	59	96	-0 03	59	96	-1 02	60	96	-2 02	59	96	-3 01	59	97
82	01 15	59	98	00 16	60	98	-0 44	59	98	-1 43	59	98	-2 42	60	99
80	01 33	-59	100	00 34	-59	100	-0 25	-59	100	-1 24	-60	100	-2 24	-59	100
78	01 52	59	102	00 53	60	102	-0 07	59	102	-1 06	59	102	-2 05	60	102
76	02 10	59	104	01 11	59	104	00 12	60	104	-0 48	59	104	-1 47	59	104
74	02 28	59	106	01 29	59	106	00 30	60	106	-0 30	59	106	-1 29	59	106
72	02 46	59	108	01 47	59	108	00 48	60	108	-0 12	59	108	-1 11	59	108
70	03 04	-60	110	02 04	-59	110	01 05	-59	110	00 06	-59	110	-0 53	-60	110
68	03 22	60	112	02 22	59	112	01 23	60	112	00 23	59	112	-0 36	59	112
66	03 39	60	114	02 39	59	114	01 40	59	114	00 41	60	114	-0 19	59	114
64	03 56	59	116	02 57	60	116	01 57	59	116	00 58	60	116	-0 02	59	116
62	04 13	60	118	03 13	59	118	02 14	60	118	01 14	59	118	00 15	59	118
60	04 29	-59	120	03 30	-60	120	02 30	-59	120	01 31	-60	120	00 31	-59	120
58	04 45	59	122	03 46	60	122	02 46	59	122	01 47	60	122	00 47	59	122
56	05 01	59	124	04 02	60	124	03 02	59	124	02 03	60	124	01 03	59	124
54	05 17	60	126	04 17	59	126	03 18	60	126	02 18	60	126	01 18	59	126
52	05 32	60	128	04 32	59	128	03 33	60	128	02 33	60	128	01 33	59	128
50	05 46	-59	130	04 47	-60	130	03 47	-59	130	02 48	-60	130	01 48	-60	130
48	06 01	60	132	05 01	60	132	04 01	59	132	03 02	60	132	02 02	59	132
46	06 14	59	134	05 15	60	134	04 15	60	134	03 15	59	134	02 16	60	134
44	06 28	60	136	05 28	60	136	04 28	59	136	03 29	60	136	02 29	60	136
42	06 41	60	138	05 41	60	138	04 41	59	138	03 42	60	138	02 42	60	138
40	06 53	-60	140	05 53	-59	140	04 54	-60	140	03 54	-60	140	02 54	-60	140
38	07 05	60	142	06 05	60	142	05 05	59	142	04 06	60	142	03 06	60	142
36	07 16	59	144	06 17	60	144	05 17	60	144	04 17	60	144	03 17	60	144
34	07 27	60	146	06 27	59	146	05 28	60	146	04 28	60	146	03 28	60	146
32	07 37	59	148	06 38	60	148	05 38	60	148	04 38	60	148	03 38	60	148
30	07 47	-60	150	06 47	-59	150	05 48	-60	150	04 48	-60	150	03 48	-60	150
28	07 56	59	152	06 57	60	152	05 57	60	152	04 57	60	152	03 57	60	152
26	08 05	60	154	07 05	60	154	06 05	60	154	05 05	59	154	04 06	60	154
24	08 13	60	156	07 13	60	156	06 13	60	156	05 13	60	156	04 13	59	156
22	08 20	59	158	07 21	60	158	06 21	60	158	05 21	60	158	04 21	60	158
20	08 27	-60	160	07 27	-60	160	06 27	-60	160	05 27	-59	160	04 28	-60	160
18	08 33	60	162	07 33	59	162	06 34	60	162	05 34	60	162	04 34	60	162
16	08 39	60	164	07 39	60	164	06 39	60	164	05 39	60	164	04 39	60	164
14	08 44	60	166	07 44	60	166	06 44	60	166	05 44	60	166	04 44	60	166
12	08 48	60	168	07 48	60	168	06 48	60	168	05 48	60	168	04 48	60	168
10	08 52	-60	170	07 52	-60	170	06 52	-60	170	05 52	-60	170	04 52	-60	170
8	08 55	60	172	07 55	60	172	06 55	60	172	05 55	60	172	04 55	60	172
6	08 57	60	174	07 57	60	174	06 57	60	174	05 57	60	174	04 57	60	174
4	08 59	60	176	07 59	60	176	06 59	60	176	05 59	60	176	04 59	60	176
2	09 00	60	178	08 00	60	178	07 00	60	178	06 00	60	178	05 00	60	178
0	09 00	-60	180	08 00	-60	180	07 00	-60	180	06 00	-60	180	05 00	-60	180

LHA	5° Hc	5° d	5° Z	6° Hc	6° d	6° Z	7° Hc	7° d	7° Z	8° Hc	8° d	8° Z	9° Hc	9° d	9° Z
	° ′	′	°	° ′	′	°	° ′	′	°	° ′	′	°	° ′	′	°
112	248														
110	250														
108	252														
106	-7 25	59	75	254											
104	-7 07	59	77	256											
102	-6 48	60	79	258											
100	-6 30	-59	81	-7 29	-59	81	260								
98	-6 11	60	83	-7 11	59	83	262								
96	-5 53	59	85	-6 52	59	85	264								
94	-5 34	59	87	-6 33	59	87	-7 32	60	87	266					
92	-5 15	59	89	-6 14	60	89	-7 14	59	89	268					
90	-4 56	-60	91	-5 56	-59	91	-6 55	-59	91	270					
88	-4 38	59	93	-5 37	59	93	-6 36	59	93	-7 35	60	93	272		
86	-4 19	59	95	-5 18	59	95	-6 17	60	95	-7 17	59	95	274		
84	-4 00	59	97	-4 59	60	97	-5 59	59	97	-6 58	59	97	276		
82	-3 42	59	99	-4 41	59	99	-5 40	59	99	-6 39	60	99	278		
80	-3 23	-59	101	-4 22	-60	101	-5 22	-59	101	-6 21	-59	101	-7 20	-59	101
78	-3 05	59	103	-4 04	59	103	-5 03	60	103	-6 03	59	103	-7 02	59	103
76	-2 46	60	105	-3 46	59	105	-4 45	59	105	-5 44	60	105	-6 44	59	105
74	-2 28	60	107	-3 28	59	107	-4 27	59	107	-5 26	60	107	-6 26	59	107
72	-2 10	60	109	-3 10	59	109	-4 09	59	109	-5 08	60	109	-6 08	59	109
70	-1 53	-59	111	-2 52	-59	111	-3 51	-60	111	-4 51	-59	111	-5 50	-59	111
68	-1 35	60	113	-2 35	59	113	-3 34	59	113	-4 33	60	113	-5 33	59	113
66	-1 18	59	114	-2 17	60	115	-3 17	59	115	-4 16	60	115	-5 16	59	115
64	-1 01	59	116	-2 00	60	117	-3 00	59	117	-3 59	60	117	-4 59	59	117
62	-0 44	60	118	-1 44	59	119	-2 43	60	119	-3 43	59	119	-4 42	60	119
60	-0 28	-60	120	-1 28	-59	120	-2 27	-59	121	-3 26	-60	121	-4 26	-59	121
58	-0 12	60	122	-1 12	59	122	-2 11	59	123	-3 10	60	123	-4 10	59	123
56	00 04	60	124	-0 56	59	124	-1 55	60	125	-2 55	59	125	-3 54	60	125
54	00 19	60	126	-0 41	59	126	-1 40	60	127	-2 40	59	127	-3 39	60	127
52	00 34	60	128	-0 26	59	128	-1 25	60	129	-2 25	59	129	-3 24	60	129
50	00 48	-59	130	-0 11	-60	130	-1 11	-59	130	-2 10	-60	131	-3 10	-59	131
48	01 03	60	132	00 03	60	132	-0 57	59	132	-1 56	60	133	-2 56	59	133
46	01 16	59	134	00 17	60	134	-0 43	60	134	-1 43	59	135	-2 42	60	135
44	01 29	59	136	00 30	60	136	-0 30	59	136	-1 29	60	137	-2 29	60	137
42	01 42	59	138	00 43	60	138	-0 17	60	138	-1 17	59	139	-2 16	60	139
40	01 54	-59	140	00 55	-60	140	-0 05	-60	140	-1 05	-59	140	-2 04	-60	141
38	02 06	59	142	01 07	60	142	00 07	60	142	-0 53	60	142	-1 53	59	143
36	02 17	59	144	01 18	60	144	00 18	60	144	-0 42	59	144	-1 41	60	144
34	02 28	60	146	01 28	59	146	00 29	60	146	-0 31	60	146	-1 31	60	146
32	02 38	59	148	01 39	60	148	00 39	60	148	-0 21	60	148	-1 21	60	148
30	02 48	-60	150	01 48	-60	150	00 48	-59	150	-0 11	-60	150	-1 11	-60	150
28	02 57	60	152	01 57	60	152	00 57	59	152	-0 02	60	152	-1 02	60	152
26	03 06	60	154	02 06	60	154	01 06	60	154	00 06	60	154	-0 54	60	154
24	03 14	60	156	02 14	60	156	01 14	60	156	00 14	60	156	-0 46	60	156
22	03 21	60	158	02 21	60	158	01 21	60	158	00 21	60	158	-0 39	60	158
20	03 28	-60	160	02 28	-60	160	01 28	-60	160	00 28	-60	160	-0 32	-60	160
18	03 34	60	162	02 34	60	162	01 34	60	162	00 34	60	162	-0 26	60	162
16	03 39	60	164	02 39	60	164	01 39	60	164	00 39	60	164	-0 21	60	164
14	03 44	60	166	02 44	60	166	01 44	60	166	00 44	60	166	-0 16	60	166
12	03 48	60	168	02 48	60	168	01 48	60	168	00 48	60	168	-0 12	60	168
10	03 52	-60	170	02 52	-60	170	01 52	-60	170	00 52	-60	170	-0 08	-60	170
8	03 55	60	172	02 55	60	172	01 55	60	172	00 55	60	172	-0 05	60	172
6	03 57	60	174	02 57	60	174	01 57	60	174	00 57	60	174	-0 03	60	174
4	03 59	60	176	02 59	60	176	01 59	60	176	00 59	60	176	-0 01	60	176
2	04 00	60	178	03 00	60	178	02 00	60	178	01 00	60	178	00 00	60	178
0	04 00	-60	180	03 00	-60	180	02 00	-60	180	01 00	-60	180	00 00	-60	180

LHA	10° Hc	10° d	10° Z	11° Hc	11° d	11° Z	12° Hc	12° d	12° Z	13° Hc	13° d	13° Z	14° Hc	14° d	14° Z	LHA
	° ′	′	°	° ′	′	°	° ′	′	°	° ′	′	°	° ′	′	°	
80	280															
78	282															
76	284															
74	-7 25	59	107	286												
72	-7 07	59	109	288												
70	-6 49	-60	111	290												
68	-6 32	59	113	-7 31	60	113	292									
66	-6 15	59	115	-7 14	60	115	294									
64	-5 58	60	117	-6 58	59	117	296									
62	-5 42	59	119	-6 41	59	119	298									
60	-5 25	-60	121	-6 25	-59	121	-7 24	-60	121	300						
58	-5 09	60	123	-6 09	59	123	-7 08	60	123	302						
56	-4 54	59	125	-5 53	60	125	-6 53	59	125	304						
54	-4 39	59	127	-5 38	60	127	-6 38	59	127	306						
52	-4 24	59	129	-5 23	60	129	-6 23	59	129	-7 22	60	129	308			
50	-4 09	-60	131	-5 09	-60	131	-6 09	-59	131	-7 08	-60	131	310			
48	-3 55	60	133	-4 55	60	133	-5 55	59	133	-6 54	60	133	312			
46	-3 42	59	135	-4 41	60	135	-5 41	60	135	-6 41	59	135	314			
44	-3 29	59	137	-4 28	60	137	-5 28	60	137	-6 28	59	137	316			
42	-3 16	60	139	-4 16	60	139	-5 16	59	139	-6 15	60	139	-7 15	60	139	318
40	-3 04	-60	141	-4 04	-59	141	-5 03	-60	141	-6 03	-60	141	-7 03	-60	141	320
38	-2 52	60	143	-3 52	60	143	-4 52	60	143	-5 52	59	143	-6 51	60	143	322
36	-2 41	60	145	-3 41	60	145	-4 41	59	145	-5 40	60	145	-6 40	60	145	324
34	-2 31	59	147	-3 30	60	147	-4 30	60	147	-5 30	60	147	-6 30	59	147	326
32	-2 21	59	149	-3 20	60	149	-4 20	60	149	-5 20	60	149	-6 20	60	149	328
30	-2 11	-60	150	-3 11	-60	151	-4 11	-59	151	-5 10	-60	151	-6 10	-60	151	330
28	-2 02	60	152	-3 02	60	153	-4 02	60	153	-5 02	59	153	-6 01	60	153	332
26	-1 54	59	154	-2 53	60	154	-3 53	60	154	-4 53	60	155	-5 53	60	155	334
24	-1 46	60	156	-2 46	60	156	-3 46	59	156	-4 45	60	157	-5 45	60	157	336
22	-1 39	59	158	-2 38	60	158	-3 38	60	158	-4 38	60	159	-5 38	60	159	338
20	-1 32	-60	160	-2 32	-60	160	-3 32	-60	160	-4 32	-60	160	-5 32	-60	160	340
18	-1 26	60	162	-2 26	60	162	-3 26	60	162	-4 26	60	162	-5 26	60	162	342
16	-1 21	59	164	-2 20	60	164	-3 20	60	164	-4 20	60	164	-5 20	60	164	344
14	-1 16	60	166	-2 16	60	166	-3 16	60	166	-4 16	60	166	-5 16	60	166	346
12	-1 12	60	168	-2 12	60	168	-3 12	59	168	-4 11	60	168	-5 11	60	168	348
10	-1 08	-60	170	-2 08	-60	170	-3 08	-60	170	-4 08	-60	170	-5 08	-60	170	350
8	-1 05	60	172	-2 05	60	172	-3 05	60	172	-4 05	60	172	-5 05	60	172	352
6	-1 03	60	174	-2 03	60	174	-3 03	60	174	-4 03	60	174	-5 03	60	174	354
4	-1 01	60	176	-2 01	60	176	-3 01	60	176	-4 01	60	176	-5 01	60	176	356
2	-1 00	60	178	-2 00	60	178	-3 00	60	178	-4 00	60	178	-5 00	60	178	358
0	-1 00	-60	180	-2 00	-60	180	-3 00	-60	180	-4 00	-60	180	-5 00	-60	180	360

S. Lat. {LHA greater than 180°....... Zn=180−Z
{LHA less than 180°........... Zn=180+Z

DECLINATION (0°-14°) CONTRARY NAME TO LATITUDE

N. Lat. {LHA greater than 180°....... Zn=Z; LHA less than 180°........... Zn=360−Z}

DECLINATION (15°-29°) SAME NAME AS LATITUDE

LHA	15°			16°			17°			18°			19°		
	Hc	d	Z	Hc	d	Z	Hc	d	Z	Hc	d	Z	Hc	d	Z
	° '	'	°	° '	'	°	° '	'	°	° '	'	°	° '	'	°
0	24 00	+60	180	25 00	+60	180	26 00	+60	180	27 00	+60	180	28 00	+60	180
2	24 00	60	178	25 00	60	178	26 00	60	178	27 00	60	178	28 00	60	178
4	23 59	60	176	24 59	60	176	25 59	60	176	26 59	60	176	27 59	60	176
6	23 57	60	174	24 57	60	174	25 57	60	174	26 57	60	174	27 57	60	174
8	23 55	60	172	24 55	59	172	25 54	60	172	26 54	60	172	27 54	60	171
10	23 51	+60	169	24 51	+60	169	25 51	+60	169	26 51	+60	169	27 51	+60	169
12	23 48	60	167	24 48	60	167	25 48	60	167	26 48	59	167	27 47	60	167
14	23 43	60	165	24 43	60	165	25 43	60	165	26 43	60	165	27 43	60	165
16	23 38	60	163	24 38	60	163	25 38	60	163	26 38	60	163	27 38	60	163
18	23 32	60	161	24 32	60	161	25 32	60	161	26 32	60	161	27 32	60	161
20	23 26	+60	159	24 26	+60	159	25 26	+60	159	26 26	+59	159	27 25	+60	159
22	23 19	60	157	24 19	60	157	25 19	59	157	26 18	60	157	27 18	60	157
24	23 11	60	155	24 11	60	155	25 11	60	155	26 11	59	155	27 10	60	154
26	23 03	60	153	24 03	59	153	25 02	60	152	26 02	60	152	27 02	60	152
28	22 54	60	151	23 54	59	150	24 53	60	150	25 53	60	150	26 53	60	150
30	22 44	+60	148	23 44	+60	148	24 44	+60	148	25 44	+59	148	26 43	+60	148
32	22 34	60	146	23 34	60	146	24 34	59	146	25 33	60	146	26 33	60	146
34	22 23	60	144	23 23	60	144	24 23	60	144	25 23	59	144	26 22	60	144
36	22 12	60	142	23 12	60	142	24 12	59	142	25 11	60	142	26 11	60	142
38	22 00	60	140	23 00	60	140	24 00	59	140	24 59	60	140	25 59	60	140
40	21 48	+60	138	22 48	+59	138	23 47	+60	138	24 47	+60	138	25 47	+59	138
42	21 35	60	136	22 35	60	136	23 35	59	136	24 34	60	136	25 34	59	136
44	21 22	60	134	22 22	59	134	23 21	60	134	24 21	59	134	25 20	60	133
46	21 08	60	132	22 08	59	132	23 07	60	132	24 07	59	131	25 06	60	131
48	20 54	60	130	21 54	59	130	22 53	60	130	23 53	59	129	24 52	60	129
50	20 39	+60	128	21 39	+59	128	22 38	+60	128	23 38	+59	127	24 37	+60	127
52	20 24	60	126	21 24	59	126	22 23	60	125	23 23	59	125	24 22	60	125
54	20 09	59	124	21 08	60	124	22 08	59	123	23 07	60	123	24 07	59	123
56	19 53	60	122	20 53	59	122	21 52	59	121	22 51	60	121	23 51	59	121
58	19 37	59	120	20 36	60	119	21 36	59	119	22 35	60	119	23 35	59	119
60	19 20	+60	118	20 20	+59	117	21 19	+60	117	22 19	+59	117	23 18	+59	117
62	19 04	59	116	20 03	59	115	21 02	60	115	22 02	59	115	23 01	59	115
64	18 47	59	114	19 46	59	113	20 45	60	113	21 45	59	113	22 44	59	113
66	18 29	60	112	19 29	59	111	20 28	59	111	21 27	59	111	22 26	60	111
68	18 12	59	110	19 11	59	109	20 10	60	109	21 10	59	109	22 09	59	109
70	17 54	+59	108	18 53	+59	107	19 52	+60	107	20 52	+59	107	21 51	+59	107
72	17 36	59	106	18 35	59	105	19 34	60	105	20 34	59	105	21 33	59	105
74	17 18	59	104	18 17	59	103	19 16	59	103	20 15	60	103	21 15	59	103
76	16 59	60	102	17 59	59	101	18 58	59	101	19 57	59	101	20 56	59	101
78	16 41	59	100	17 40	59	99	18 39	60	99	19 39	59	99	20 38	59	99
80	16 22	+60	98	17 22	+59	97	18 21	+59	97	19 20	+59	97	20 19	+59	97
82	16 04	59	96	17 03	59	95	18 02	59	95	19 01	60	95	20 01	59	95
84	15 45	59	94	16 44	59	93	17 43	60	93	18 43	59	93	19 42	59	93
86	15 26	59	92	16 25	60	91	17 25	59	91	18 24	59	91	19 23	59	91
88	15 07	60	90	16 07	59	89	17 06	59	89	18 05	59	89	19 04	59	89
90	14 49	+59	88	15 48	+59	87	16 47	+59	87	17 46	+59	87	18 45	+60	87
92	14 30	59	86	15 29	59	86	16 28	60	85	17 28	59	85	18 27	59	85
94	14 11	60	84	15 11	59	84	16 10	59	83	17 09	59	83	18 08	59	83
96	13 53	59	82	14 52	59	82	15 51	59	81	16 50	60	81	17 50	59	81
98	13 34	59	80	14 33	60	80	15 33	59	79	16 32	59	79	17 31	59	79
100	13 16	+59	78	14 15	+59	78	15 14	+59	77	16 13	+60	77	17 13	+59	77
102	12 57	60	76	13 57	59	76	14 56	59	76	15 55	59	75	16 54	60	75
104	12 39	60	74	13 39	59	74	14 38	59	74	15 37	59	73	16 36	60	73
106	12 21	60	72	13 21	59	72	14 20	59	72	15 19	59	71	16 18	60	71
108	12 04	59	70	13 03	59	70	14 02	60	70	15 02	59	70	16 01	59	69
110	11 46	+59	68	12 45	+60	68	13 45	+59	68	14 44	+59	68	15 43	+60	67
112	11 29	59	66	12 28	60	66	13 28	59	66	14 27	59	66	15 26	59	65
114	11 12	59	64	12 11	60	64	13 11	59	64	14 10	59	64	15 09	60	64
116	10 55	59	62	11 54	60	62	12 54	59	62	13 53	60	62	14 53	59	62
118	10 39	59	60	11 38	59	60	12 37	60	60	13 37	59	60	14 36	60	60
120	10 23	+59	58	11 22	+59	58	12 21	+60	58	13 21	+59	58	14 20	+60	58
122	10 07	59	56	11 06	60	56	12 06	59	56	13 05	60	56	14 05	59	56
124	09 51	60	54	10 51	59	54	11 50	60	54	12 50	59	54	13 49	60	54
126	09 36	60	52	10 36	59	52	11 35	60	52	12 35	59	52	13 34	60	52
128	09 22	59	51	10 21	60	50	11 21	59	50	12 20	60	50	13 20	59	50
130	09 07	+60	49	10 07	+59	48	11 06	+60	48	12 06	+59	48	13 05	+60	48
132	08 53	60	47	09 53	60	47	10 53	59	46	11 52	60	46	12 52	59	46
134	08 40	60	45	09 40	59	45	10 39	60	44	11 39	59	44	12 38	60	44
136	08 27	60	43	09 27	59	43	10 26	60	43	11 26	60	42	12 26	59	42
138	08 15	59	41	09 14	60	41	10 14	60	41	11 14	59	41	12 13	60	40

LHA	20°			21°			22°			23°			24°		
	Hc	d	Z	Hc	d	Z	Hc	d	Z	Hc	d	Z	Hc	d	Z
	° '	'	°	° '	'	°	° '	'	°	° '	'	°	° '	'	°
0	29 00	+60	180	30 00	+60	180	31 00	+60	180	32 00	+60	180	33 00	+60	180
2	29 00	60	178	30 00	60	178	31 00	60	178	32 00	60	178	33 00	60	178
4	28 59	60	176	29 59	60	176	30 59	60	176	31 59	60	176	32 59	60	176
6	28 57	60	174	29 57	60	174	30 57	60	174	31 57	60	174	32 57	60	174
8	28 54	60	171	29 54	60	171	30 54	60	171	31 54	60	171	32 54	60	171
10	28 51	+60	169	29 51	+60	169	30 51	+60	169	31 51	+60	169	32 51	+60	169
12	28 47	60	167	29 47	60	167	30 47	60	167	31 47	60	167	32 47	60	167
14	28 43	60	165	29 43	60	165	30 43	60	165	31 43	60	165	32 43	60	165
16	28 38	60	163	29 38	60	163	30 38	59	163	31 37	60	163	32 37	60	163
18	28 32	60	161	29 32	60	161	30 32	60	161	31 32	59	161	32 31	60	160
20	28 25	+60	159	29 25	+60	159	30 25	+60	158	31 25	+60	158	32 25	+60	158
22	28 18	60	156	29 18	60	156	30 18	60	156	31 18	60	156	32 18	59	156
24	28 10	60	154	29 10	60	154	30 10	60	154	31 10	60	154	32 10	59	154
26	28 02	60	152	29 02	59	152	30 01	60	152	31 01	60	152	32 01	60	152
28	27 53	60	150	28 53	59	150	29 52	60	150	30 52	60	150	31 52	60	150
30	27 43	+60	148	28 43	+60	148	29 43	+59	148	30 42	+60	148	31 42	+60	148
32	27 33	60	146	28 33	59	146	29 32	60	146	30 32	60	146	31 32	59	145
34	27 22	60	144	28 22	59	144	29 21	60	144	30 21	60	143	31 21	59	143
36	27 11	59	142	28 10	60	142	29 10	60	141	30 10	59	141	31 09	60	141
38	26 59	59	140	27 58	60	139	28 58	60	139	29 58	59	139	30 57	60	139
40	26 46	+60	137	27 46	+60	137	28 46	+59	137	29 45	+60	137	30 45	+59	137
42	26 33	60	135	27 33	59	135	28 32	60	135	29 32	60	135	30 32	59	135
44	26 20	59	133	27 19	60	133	28 19	60	133	29 19	59	133	30 18	60	133
46	26 06	60	131	27 06	59	131	28 05	60	131	29 05	59	131	30 04	60	131
48	25 52	59	129	26 51	60	129	27 51	59	129	28 50	60	129	29 50	59	129
50	25 37	+59	127	26 36	+60	127	27 36	+59	127	28 35	+60	127	29 35	+59	126
52	25 22	59	125	26 21	60	125	27 21	59	125	28 20	59	125	29 19	60	124
54	25 06	60	123	26 06	59	123	27 05	59	123	28 04	60	122	29 04	59	122
56	24 50	60	121	25 50	59	121	26 49	59	121	27 48	60	120	28 48	59	120
58	24 34	59	119	25 33	60	119	26 33	59	119	27 32	59	118	28 31	60	118
60	24 17	+60	117	25 17	+59	117	26 16	+59	116	27 15	+60	116	28 15	+59	116
62	24 00	60	115	25 00	59	115	25 59	59	114	26 58	60	114	27 58	59	114
64	23 43	59	113	24 42	60	113	25 42	59	112	26 41	59	112	27 40	59	112
66	23 26	59	111	24 25	59	111	25 24	59	110	26 23	60	110	27 23	59	110
68	23 08	59	109	24 07	60	109	25 07	59	108	26 06	59	108	27 05	59	108
70	22 50	+59	107	23 49	+60	107	24 49	+59	106	25 48	+59	106	26 47	+59	106
72	22 32	59	105	23 31	60	105	24 31	59	104	25 30	59	104	26 29	59	104
74	22 14	59	103	23 13	59	102	24 12	59	102	25 11	60	102	26 11	59	102
76	21 55	60	101	22 55	59	100	23 54	59	100	24 53	59	100	25 52	59	100
78	21 37	59	99	22 36	59	98	23 35	59	98	24 34	60	98	25 34	59	98
80	21 18	+60	97	22 18	+59	97	23 17	+59	96	24 16	+59	96	25 15	+59	96
82	21 00	59	95	21 59	59	95	22 58	59	94	23 57	59	94	24 56	59	94
84	20 41	59	93	21 40	59	93	22 39	59	92	23 38	60	92	24 38	59	92
86	20 22	59	91	21 21	59	91	22 20	60	90	23 20	59	90	24 19	59	90
88	20 03	60	89	21 03	59	89	22 02	59	88	23 01	59	88	24 00	59	88
90	19 45	+59	87	20 44	+59	87	21 43	+59	86	22 42	+59	86	23 41	+59	86
92	19 26	59	85	20 25	59	85	21 24	59	84	22 23	60	84	23 23	59	84
94	19 07	59	83	20 06	60	83	21 06	59	83	22 05	59	82	23 04	59	82
96	18 49	59	81	19 48	59	81	20 47	59	81	21 46	59	80	22 45	59	80
98	18 30	59	79	19 29	60	79	20 29	59	79	21 28	59	78	22 27	59	78
100	18 12	+59	77	19 11	+59	77	20 10	+59	77	21 09	+60	76	22 09	+59	76
102	17 54	59	75	18 53	59	75	19 52	59	75	20 51	59	75	21 50	60	74
104	17 36	59	73	18 35	59	73	19 34	59	73	20 33	59	73	21 32	60	72
106	17 18	59	71	18 17	59	71	19 16	59	71	20 15	60	71	21 15	59	70
108	17 00	59	69	17 59	60	69	18 59	59	69	19 58	59	69	20 57	59	69
110	16 43	+59	67	17 42	+59	67	18 41	+59	67	19 40	+60	67	20 40	+59	67
112	16 25	60	65	17 25	59	65	18 24	59	65	19 23	60	65	20 23	59	65
114	16 09	59	63	17 08	59	63	18 07	60	63	19 07	59	63	20 06	59	63
116	15 52	59	61	16 51	60	61	17 51	59	61	18 50	59	61	19 49	60	61
118	15 36	59	60	16 35	59	59	17 34	60	59	18 34	59	59	19 33	59	59
120	15 20	+59	58	16 19	+59	57	17 18	+60	57	18 18	+59	57	19 17	+60	57
122	15 04	59	56	16 03	60	56	17 03	59	55	18 02	60	55	19 02	59	55
124	14 49	59	54	15 48	60	54	16 48	59	53	17 47	59	53	18 46	60	53
126	14 34	59	52	15 33	60	52	16 33	59	52	17 32	60	51	18 32	59	51
128	14 19	60	50	15 19	59	50	16 18	60	50	17 18	59	49	18 17	60	49
130	14 05	+60	48	15 05	+59	48	16 04	+60	48	17 04	+59	48	18 03	+60	47
132	13 51	60	46	14 51	59	46	15 50	60	46	16 50	60	46	17 50	59	46
134	13 38	60	44	14 38	59	44	15 37	60	44	16 37	59	44	17 36	60	44
136	13 25	60	42	14 25	59	42	15 24	60	42	16 24	60	42	17 24	59	42
138	13 13	59	40	14 12	60	40	15 12	60	40	16 12	59	40	17 11	60	40

LHA	25°			26°			27°			28°			29°			LHA
	Hc	d	Z	Hc	d	Z	Hc	d	Z	Hc	d	Z	Hc	d	Z	
	° '	'	°	° '	'	°	° '	'	°	° '	'	°	° '	'	°	
0	34 00	+60	180	35 00	+60	180	36 00	+60	180	37 00	+60	180	38 00	+60	180	360
2	34 00	60	178	35 00	60	178	36 00	60	178	37 00	60	178	38 00	60	178	358
4	33 59	60	176	34 59	60	176	35 59	60	176	36 59	60	176	37 59	60	176	356
6	33 57	60	173	34 57	60	173	35 57	60	173	36 57	60	173	37 57	60	173	354
8	33 54	60	171	34 54	60	171	35 54	60	171	36 54	60	171	37 54	60	171	352
10	33 51	+60	169	34 51	+60	169	35 51	+60	169	36 51	+60	169	37 51	+60	169	350
12	33 47	60	167	34 47	60	167	35 47	60	167	36 47	60	167	37 47	60	167	348
14	33 43	60	165	34 43	59	165	35 42	60	165	36 42	60	165	37 42	60	165	346
16	33 37	60	163	34 37	60	163	35 37	60	162	36 37	60	162	37 37	60	162	344
18	33 31	60	160	34 31	60	160	35 31	60	160	36 31	60	160	37 31	60	160	342
20	33 25	+60	158	34 25	+59	158	35 24	+60	158	36 24	+60	158	37 24	+60	158	340
22	33 17	60	156	34 17	60	156	35 17	60	156	36 17	60	156	37 17	60	156	338
24	33 09	60	154	34 09	60	154	35 09	60	154	36 09	60	154	37 09	60	154	336
26	33 01	60	152	34 01	59	152	35 00	60	152	36 00	60	151	37 00	60	151	334
28	32 52	59	150	33 51	60	150	34 51	60	149	35 51	60	149	36 51	59	149	332
30	32 42	+60	147	33 42	+59	147	34 41	+60	147	35 41	+60	147	36 41	+59	147	330
32	32 31	60	145	33 31	60	145	34 31	60	145	35 31	59	145	36 30	60	145	328
34	32 20	60	143	33 20	60	143	34 20	59	143	35 19	60	143	36 19	60	143	326
36	32 09	60	141	33 09	59	141	34 08	60	141	35 08	59	141	36 07	60	141	324
38	31 57	59	139	32 56	60	139	33 56	60	139	34 56	59	139	35 55	60	138	322
40	31 44	+60	137	32 44	+59	137	33 43	+60	137	34 43	+60	136	35 43	+59	136	320
42	31 31	60	135	32 31	59	135	33 30	60	134	34 30	59	134	35 29	60	134	318
44	31 18	59	133	32 17	60	132	33 17	59	132	34 16	60	132	35 16	59	132	316
46	31 04	59	130	32 03	59	130	33 02	60	130	34 02	59	130	35 01	60	130	314
48	30 49	59	128	31 48	60	128	32 48	59	128	33 47	60	128	34 47	59	128	312
50	30 34	+59	126	31 33	+60	126	32 33	+59	126	33 32	+60	126	34 32	+59	126	310
52	30 19	59	124	31 18	59	124	32 17	60	124	33 17	59	124	34 16	59	124	308
54	30 03	59	122	31 02	60	122	32 02	59	122	33 01	59	122	34 00	60	121	306
56	29 47	59	120	30 46	60	120	31 46	59	120	32 45	59	120	33 44	59	119	304
58	29 31	59	118	30 30	59	118	31 29	59	118	32 28	60	117	33 28	59	117	302
60	29 14	+59	116	30 13	+59	116	31 12	+60	116	32 12	+59	115	33 11	+59	115	300
62	28 57	59	114	29 56	59	114	30 55	59	114	31 54	60	113	32 54	59	113	298
64	28 39	60	112	29 39	59	112	30 38	59	112	31 37	59	111	32 36	59	111	296
66	28 22	59	110	29 21	59	110	30 20	59	109	31 19	60	109	32 19	59	109	294
68	28 04	59	108	29 03	59	108	30 02	60	107	31 02	59	107	32 01	59	107	292
70	27 46	+59	106	28 45	+59	106	29 44	+60	105	30 44	+59	105	31 43	+59	105	290
72	27 28	59	104	28 27	59	104	29 26	59	103	30 25	59	103	31 24	60	103	288
74	27 10	59	102	28 09	59	102	29 08	59	101	30 07	59	101	31 06	59	101	286
76	26 51	59	100	27 50	59	100	28 49	60	99	29 49	59	99	30 48	59	99	284
78	26 33	59	98	27 32	59	98	28 31	59	97	29 30	59	97	30 29	59	97	282
80	26 14	+59	96	27 13	+59	96	28 12	+59	95	29 11	+59	95	30 10	+59	95	280
82	25 55	59	94	26 54	60	94	27 54	59	93	28 53	59	93	29 52	59	93	278
84	25 37	59	92	26 36	59	92	27 35	59	91	28 34	59	91	29 33	59	91	276
86	25 18	59	90	26 17	59	90	27 16	59	89	28 15	59	89	29 14	59	89	274
88	24 59	59	88	25 58	59	88	26 57	59	87	27 56	59	87	28 55	59	87	272
90	24 40	+59	86	25 39	+60	86	26 39	+59	85	27 38	+59	85	28 37	+59	85	270
92	24 22	59	84	25 21	59	84	26 20	59	84	27 19	59	83	28 18	59	83	268
94	24 03	59	82	25 02	59	82	26 01	59	82	27 00	59	81	27 59	59	81	266
96	23 44	60	80	24 44	59	80	25 43	59	80	26 42	59	79	27 41	59	79	264
98	23 26	59	78	24 25	59	78	25 24	59	78	26 23	59	77	27 22	60	77	262
100	23 08	+59	76	24 07	+59	76	25 06	+59	76	26 05	+59	76	27 04	+59	75	260
102	22 50	59	74	23 49	59	74	24 48	59	74	25 47	59	74	26 46	59	73	258
104	22 32	59	72	23 31	59	72	24 30	59	72	25 29	59	72	26 28	59	71	256
106	22 14	59	70	23 13	59	70	24 12	59	70	25 11	60	70	26 11	59	70	254
108	21 56	60	68	22 56	59	68	23 55	59	68	24 54	59	68	25 53	59	68	252
110	21 39	+59	66	22 38	+59	66	23 37	+60	66	24 37	+59	66	25 36	+59	66	250
112	21 22	59	65	22 21	59	64	23 20	60	64	24 20	59	64	25 19	59	64	248
114	21 05	59	63	22 04	60	62	23 04	59	62	24 03	59	62	25 02	59	62	246
116	20 49	59	61	21 48	59	61	22 47	60	60	23 47	59	60	24 46	59	60	244
118	20 32	60	59	21 32	59	59	22 31	59	58	23 30	60	58	24 30	59	58	242
120	20 17	+59	57	21 16	+59	57	22 15	+60	57	23 15	+59	56	24 14	+59	56	240
122	20 01	59	55	21 00	60	55	22 00	59	55	22 59	60	54	23 59	59	54	238
124	19 46	59	53	20 45	60	53	21 45	59	53	22 44	59	53	23 43	60	52	236
126	19 31	60	51	20 31	59	51	21 30	59	51	22 29	60	51	23 29	59	51	234
128	19 17	59	49	20 16	60	49	21 16	59	49	22 15	60	49	23 15	59	49	232
130	19 03	+59	47	20 02	+60	47	21 02	+59	47	22 01	+60	47	23 01	+59	47	230
132	18 49	60	45	19 49	59	45	20 48	60	45	21 48	59	45	22 47	60	45	228
134	18 36	60	44	19 36	59	43	20 35	60	43	21 35	59	43	22 34	60	43	226
136	18 23	60	42	19 23	59	41	20 22	60	41	21 22	60	41	22 22	59	41	224
138	18 11	60	40	19 11	59	40	20 10	60	39	21 10	60	39	22 10	59	39	222

S. Lat. {LHA greater than 180°....... Zn=180−Z; LHA less than 180°........... Zn=180+Z}

DECLINATION (15°-29°) SAME NAME AS LATITUDE

LHA	15° Hc	15° d	15° Z	16° Hc	16° d	16° Z	17° Hc	17° d	17° Z	18° Hc	18° d	18° Z	19° Hc	19° d	19° Z
	° ′	′	°	° ′	′	°	° ′	′	°	° ′	′	°	° ′	′	°
140	08 03	+59	39	09 02	+60	39	10 02	+60	39	11 02	+59	39	12 01	+60	38
142	07 51	60	37	08 51	59	37	09 50	60	37	10 50	60	37	11 50	60	37
144	07 40	60	35	08 40	59	35	09 39	60	35	10 39	60	35	11 39	60	35
146	07 29	60	33	08 29	60	33	09 29	60	33	10 29	60	33	11 29	59	33
148	07 20	59	31	08 19	60	31	09 19	60	31	10 19	60	31	11 19	59	31
150	07 10	+60	29	08 10	+60	29	09 10	+60	29	10 10	+59	29	11 09	+60	29
152	07 01	60	27	08 01	60	27	09 01	60	27	10 01	60	27	11 01	59	27
154	06 53	60	25	07 53	60	25	08 53	60	25	09 53	59	25	10 52	60	25
156	06 45	60	23	07 45	60	23	08 45	60	23	09 45	60	23	10 45	60	23
158	06 38	60	21	07 38	60	21	08 38	60	21	09 38	60	21	10 38	60	21
160	06 32	+59	19	07 31	+60	19	08 31	+60	19	09 31	+60	19	10 31	+60	19
162	06 26	60	18	07 26	59	17	08 25	60	17	09 25	60	17	10 25	60	17
164	06 20	60	16	07 20	60	16	08 20	60	16	09 20	60	15	10 20	60	15
166	06 16	60	14	07 16	59	14	08 15	60	14	09 15	60	14	10 15	60	13
168	06 11	60	12	07 11	60	12	08 11	60	12	09 11	60	12	10 11	60	12
170	06 08	+60	10	07 08	+60	10	08 08	+60	10	09 08	+60	10	10 08	+60	10
172	06 05	60	8	07 05	60	8	08 05	60	8	09 05	60	8	10 05	60	8
174	06 03	60	6	07 03	60	6	08 03	60	6	09 03	60	6	10 03	60	6
176	06 01	60	4	07 01	60	4	08 01	60	4	09 01	60	4	10 01	60	4
178	06 00	60	2	07 00	60	2	08 00	60	2	09 00	60	2	10 00	60	2
180	06 00	+60	0	07 00	+60	0	08 00	+60	0	09 00	+60	0	10 00	+60	0

LHA	20° Hc	20° d	20° Z	21° Hc	21° d	21° Z	22° Hc	22° d	22° Z	23° Hc	23° d	23° Z	24° Hc	24° d	24° Z
	° ′	′	°	° ′	′	°	° ′	′	°	° ′	′	°	° ′	′	°
140	13 01	+60	38	14 01	+59	38	15 00	+60	38	16 00	+60	38	17 00	+59	38
142	12 50	59	36	13 49	60	36	14 49	60	36	15 49	59	36	16 48	60	36
144	12 39	59	35	13 38	60	34	14 38	60	34	15 38	60	34	16 38	59	34
146	12 28	60	33	13 28	60	33	14 28	60	32	15 28	59	32	16 27	60	32
148	12 18	60	31	13 18	60	31	14 18	60	31	15 18	60	30	16 18	59	30
150	12 09	+60	29	13 09	+60	29	14 09	+60	29	15 09	+59	29	16 08	+60	28
152	12 00	60	27	13 00	60	27	14 00	60	27	15 00	60	27	16 00	60	27
154	11 52	60	25	12 52	60	25	13 52	60	25	14 52	60	25	15 52	59	25
156	11 45	59	23	12 44	60	23	13 44	60	23	14 44	60	23	15 44	60	23
158	11 38	59	21	12 37	60	21	13 37	60	21	14 37	60	21	15 37	60	21
160	11 31	+60	19	12 31	+60	19	13 31	+60	19	14 31	+60	19	15 31	+60	19
162	11 25	60	17	12 25	60	17	13 25	60	17	14 25	60	17	15 25	60	17
164	11 20	60	15	12 20	60	15	13 20	60	15	14 20	60	15	15 20	60	15
166	11 15	60	13	12 15	60	13	13 15	60	13	14 15	60	13	15 15	60	13
168	11 11	60	12	12 11	60	12	13 11	60	11	14 11	60	11	15 11	60	11
170	11 08	+60	10	12 08	+60	10	13 08	+60	10	14 08	+60	10	15 08	+60	10
172	11 05	60	8	12 05	60	8	13 05	60	8	14 05	60	8	15 05	60	8
174	11 03	60	6	12 03	60	6	13 03	60	6	14 03	60	6	15 03	60	6
176	11 01	60	4	12 01	60	4	13 01	60	4	14 01	60	4	15 01	60	4
178	11 00	60	2	12 00	60	2	13 00	60	2	14 00	60	2	15 00	60	2
180	11 00	+60	0	12 00	+60	0	13 00	+60	0	14 00	+60	0	15 00	+60	0

25° Hc	25° d	25° Z	26° Hc	26° d	26° Z	27° Hc	27° d	27° Z	28° Hc	28° d	28° Z	29° Hc	29° d	29° Z	LHA
° ′	′	°	° ′	′	°	° ′	′	°	° ′	′	°	° ′	′	°	
17 59	+60	38	18 59	+60	38	19 59	+59	38	20 58	+60	37	21 58	+60	37	220
17 48	60	36	18 48	59	36	19 47	60	36	20 47	60	36	21 47	59	35	218
17 37	60	34	18 37	60	34	19 37	59	34	20 36	60	34	21 36	60	34	216
17 27	60	32	18 27	60	32	19 27	59	32	20 26	60	32	21 26	60	32	214
17 17	60	30	18 17	60	30	19 17	60	30	20 17	59	30	21 16	60	30	212
17 08	+60	28	18 08	+60	28	19 08	+60	28	20 08	+59	28	21 07	+60	28	210
17 00	59	26	17 59	60	26	18 59	60	26	19 59	60	26	20 59	60	26	208
16 51	60	25	17 51	60	25	18 51	60	24	19 51	60	24	20 51	60	24	206
16 44	60	23	17 44	60	23	18 44	60	23	19 44	59	22	20 43	60	22	204
16 37	60	21	17 37	60	21	18 37	60	21	19 37	60	21	20 37	59	21	202
16 31	+60	19	17 31	+59	19	18 30	+60	19	19 30	+60	19	20 30	+60	19	200
16 25	60	17	17 25	60	17	18 25	60	17	19 25	60	17	20 25	60	17	198
16 20	60	15	17 20	60	15	18 20	60	15	19 20	59	15	20 19	60	15	196
16 15	60	13	17 15	60	13	18 15	60	13	19 15	60	13	20 15	60	13	194
16 11	60	11	17 11	60	11	18 11	60	11	19 11	60	11	20 11	60	11	192
16 08	+60	9	17 08	+60	9	18 08	+60	9	19 08	+60	9	20 08	+60	9	190
16 05	60	8	17 05	60	8	18 05	60	8	19 05	60	8	20 05	60	7	188
16 03	60	6	17 03	60	6	18 03	60	6	19 03	60	6	20 03	60	6	186
16 01	60	4	17 01	60	4	18 01	60	4	19 01	60	4	20 01	60	4	184
16 00	60	2	17 00	60	2	18 00	60	2	19 00	60	2	20 00	60	2	182
16 00	+60	0	17 00	+60	0	18 00	+60	0	19 00	+60	0	20 00	+60	0	180

N. Lat. {LHA greater than 180°....... Zn=Z; LHA less than 180°........... Zn=360−Z}

DECLINATION (15°-29°) CONTRARY NAME TO LATITUDE

LHA	15° Hc	15° d	15° Z	16° Hc	16° d	16° Z	17°–29°	LHA
	° ′	′	°	° ′	′	°		
30	−7 10	−60	151					330
28	−7 01	60	153					332
26	−6 53	60	155					334
24	−6 45	60	157					336
22	−6 38	60	159					338
20	−6 32	−60	161					340
18	−6 26	60	162					342
16	−6 20	60	164					344
14	−6 16	60	166					346
12	−6 11	60	168					348
10	−6 08	−60	170					350
8	−6 05	60	172					352
6	−6 03	60	174					354
4	−6 01	60	176					356
2	−6 00	60	178	−7 00	60	178		358
0	−6 00	−60	180	−7 00	−60	180		360

Column headings 15° 16° 17° 18° 19° 20° 21° 22° 23° 24° 25° 26° 27° 28° 29°, each with Hc, d, Z.

S. Lat. {LHA greater than 180°....... Zn=180−Z; LHA less than 180°........... Zn=180+Z}

DECLINATION (15°-29°) CONTRARY NAME TO LATITUDE

LAT 81°

N. Lat. {LHA greater than 180°....... Zn=Z; LHA less than 180°........... Zn=360−Z}

DECLINATION (0°-14°) SAME NAME AS LATITUDE

LHA	0° Hc	0° d	0° Z	1° Hc	1° d	1° Z	2° Hc	2° d	2° Z	3° Hc	3° d	3° Z	4° Hc	4° d	4° Z
	° ′	′	°	° ′	′	°	° ′	′	°	° ′	′	°	° ′	′	°
0	08 00	+60	180	09 00	+60	180	10 00	+60	180	11 00	+60	180	12 00	+60	180
2	08 00	60	178	09 00	60	178	10 00	60	178	11 00	60	178	12 00	60	178
4	07 59	60	176	08 59	60	176	09 59	60	176	10 59	60	176	11 59	60	176
6	07 57	60	174	08 57	60	174	09 57	60	174	10 57	60	174	11 57	60	174
8	07 55	60	172	08 55	60	172	09 55	60	172	10 55	60	172	11 55	60	172
10	07 53	+60	170	08 53	+60	170	09 53	+60	170	10 53	+60	170	11 53	+60	170
12	07 49	60	168	08 49	60	168	09 49	60	168	10 49	60	168	11 49	60	168
14	07 46	60	166	08 46	60	166	09 46	60	166	10 46	60	166	11 46	60	166
16	07 41	60	164	08 41	60	164	09 41	60	164	10 41	60	164	11 41	60	164
18	07 36	60	162	08 36	60	162	09 36	60	162	10 36	60	162	11 36	60	162
20	07 31	+60	160	08 31	+60	160	09 31	+60	160	10 31	+60	160	11 31	+60	160
22	07 25	60	158	08 25	60	158	09 25	60	158	10 25	60	158	11 25	59	158
24	07 18	60	156	08 18	60	156	09 18	60	156	10 18	60	156	11 18	60	156
26	07 11	60	154	08 11	60	154	09 11	60	154	10 11	60	154	11 11	60	154
28	07 04	59	152	08 03	60	152	09 03	60	152	10 03	60	152	11 03	60	152
30	06 55	+60	150	07 55	+60	150	08 55	+60	150	09 55	+60	150	10 55	+60	150
32	06 47	60	148	07 47	59	148	08 46	60	148	09 46	60	148	10 46	60	147
34	06 38	59	146	07 37	60	146	08 37	60	146	09 37	60	146	10 37	60	145
36	06 28	60	144	07 28	60	144	08 28	59	144	09 27	60	144	10 27	60	143
38	06 18	60	142	07 18	59	142	08 17	60	142	09 17	60	142	10 17	60	141
40	06 07	+60	140	07 07	+60	140	08 07	+60	140	09 07	+59	140	10 06	+60	139
42	05 56	60	138	06 56	60	138	07 56	59	138	08 55	60	137	09 55	60	137
44	05 45	60	136	06 45	59	136	07 44	60	136	08 44	60	135	09 44	59	135
46	05 33	60	134	06 33	59	134	07 32	60	134	08 32	60	133	09 32	59	133
48	05 21	59	132	06 20	60	132	07 20	60	132	08 20	59	131	09 19	60	131
50	05 08	+60	130	06 08	+59	130	07 07	+60	130	08 07	+60	129	09 07	+59	129
52	04 55	60	128	05 55	59	128	06 54	60	128	07 54	59	127	08 53	60	127
54	04 42	59	126	05 41	60	126	06 41	59	126	07 40	60	125	08 40	60	125
56	04 28	59	124	05 27	60	124	06 27	60	124	07 27	59	123	08 26	60	123
58	04 14	59	122	05 13	60	122	06 13	60	122	07 13	59	121	08 12	60	121
60	03 59	+60	120	04 59	+60	120	05 59	+59	120	06 58	+60	119	07 58	+59	119
62	03 45	59	118	04 44	60	118	05 44	59	118	06 43	60	117	07 43	60	117
64	03 30	59	116	04 29	60	116	05 29	59	116	06 28	60	115	07 28	60	115
66	03 15	59	114	04 14	60	114	05 14	59	114	06 13	60	113	07 13	59	113
68	02 59	60	112	03 59	59	112	04 58	60	112	05 58	59	111	06 57	60	111
70	02 44	+59	110	03 43	+60	110	04 43	+59	110	05 42	+60	109	06 42	+59	109
72	02 28	59	108	03 27	60	108	04 27	59	108	05 26	60	107	06 26	59	107
74	02 12	59	106	03 11	60	106	04 11	59	106	05 10	60	105	06 10	59	105
76	01 56	59	104	02 55	60	104	03 55	59	104	04 54	60	104	05 54	59	103
78	01 39	60	102	02 39	59	102	03 38	60	102	04 38	59	102	05 37	60	101
80	01 23	+60	100	02 23	+59	100	03 22	+59	100	04 21	+60	100	05 21	+59	99
82	01 07	59	98	02 06	59	98	03 05	60	98	04 05	59	98	05 04	60	97
84	00 50	59	96	01 49	60	96	02 49	59	96	03 48	60	96	04 48	59	95
86	00 33	60	94	01 33	59	94	02 32	60	94	03 32	59	94	04 31	60	93
88	00 17	59	92	01 16	60	92	02 16	59	92	03 15	59	92	04 14	60	91
90	00 00	+59	90	00 59	+60	90	01 59	+59	90	02 58	+60	90	03 58	+59	90
92	−0 17	60	88	00 43	59	88	01 42	60	88	02 42	59	88	03 41	59	88
94	−0 33	59	86	00 26	59	86	01 25	60	86	02 25	59	86	03 24	60	86
96	−0 50	59	84	00 09	60	84	01 09	59	84	02 08	60	84	03 08	59	84
98	−1 07	60	82	−0 07	59	82	00 52	60	82	01 52	59	82	02 51	60	82
100	−1 23	+59	80	−0 24	+60	80	00 36	+59	80	01 35	+60	80	02 35	+59	80
102	−1 39	59	78	−0 40	59	78	00 19	60	78	01 19	59	78	02 18	60	78
104	−1 56	60	76	−0 56	59	76	00 03	60	76	01 03	59	76	02 02	59	76
106	−2 12	60	74	−1 12	59	74	−0 13	59	74	00 46	60	74	01 46	59	74
108	−2 28	60	72	−1 28	59	72	−0 29	60	72	00 31	59	72	01 30	59	72
110	−2 44	+60	70	−1 44	+59	70	−0 45	+60	70	00 15	+59	70	01 14	+60	70
112	−2 59	59	68	−2 00	60	68	−1 00	59	68	−0 01	60	68	00 59	59	68
114	−3 15	60	66	−2 15	59	66	−1 16	60	66	−0 16	59	66	00 43	60	66
116	−3 30	60	64	−2 30	59	64	−1 31	60	64	−0 31	59	64	00 28	60	64
118	−3 45	60	62	−2 45	59	62	−1 46	60	62	−0 46	59	62	00 13	60	62
120	−3 59	+59	60	−3 00	+60	60	−2 00	+59	60	−1 01	+60	60	−0 01	+59	60
122	−4 14	60	58	−3 14	59	58	−2 15	60	58	−1 15	60	58	−0 15	59	58
124	−4 28	60	56	−3 28	59	56	−2 29	60	56	−1 29	60	56	−0 29	59	56
126	−4 42	60	54	−3 42	60	54	−2 42	59	54	−1 43	60	54	−0 43	60	54
128	−4 55	60	52	−3 55	59	52	−2 56	60	52	−1 56	60	52	−0 56	59	52
130	−5 08	+60	50	−4 08	+59	50	−3 09	+60	50	−2 09	+60	50	−1 09	+59	50
132	−5 21	60	48	−4 21	60	48	−3 21	59	48	−2 22	60	48	−1 22	60	48
134	−5 33	60	46	−4 33	60	46	−3 33	59	46	−2 34	60	46	−1 34	60	46
136	−5 45	60	44	−4 45	60	44	−3 45	59	44	−2 46	60	44	−1 46	60	44
138	−5 56	60	42	−4 56	59	42	−3 57	60	42	−2 57	60	42	−1 57	60	42

LHA	5° Hc	5° d	5° Z	6° Hc	6° d	6° Z	7° Hc	7° d	7° Z	8° Hc	8° d	8° Z	9° Hc	9° d	9° Z
	° ′	′	°	° ′	′	°	° ′	′	°	° ′	′	°	° ′	′	°
0	13 00	+60	180	14 00	+60	180	15 00	+60	180	16 00	+60	180	17 00	+60	180
2	13 00	60	178	14 00	60	178	15 00	60	178	16 00	60	178	17 00	60	178
4	12 59	60	176	13 59	60	176	14 59	60	176	15 59	60	176	16 59	60	176
6	12 57	60	174	13 57	60	174	14 57	60	174	15 57	60	174	16 57	60	174
8	12 55	60	172	13 55	60	172	14 55	60	172	15 55	60	172	16 55	60	172
10	12 53	+60	170	13 53	+60	170	14 53	+60	170	15 53	+60	170	16 53	+60	170
12	12 49	60	168	13 49	60	168	14 49	60	168	15 49	60	168	16 49	60	168
14	12 46	59	166	13 45	60	166	14 45	60	166	15 45	60	166	16 45	60	166
16	12 41	60	164	13 41	60	164	14 41	60	164	15 41	60	164	16 41	60	164
18	12 36	60	162	13 36	60	162	14 36	60	162	15 36	60	162	16 36	60	161
20	12 31	+60	160	13 31	+59	160	14 30	+60	160	15 30	+60	159	16 30	+60	159
22	12 24	60	158	13 24	60	158	14 24	60	157	15 24	60	157	16 24	60	157
24	12 18	60	156	13 18	60	155	14 18	60	155	15 18	59	155	16 17	60	155
26	12 11	60	154	13 11	59	153	14 10	60	153	15 10	60	153	16 10	60	153
28	12 03	60	151	13 03	60	151	14 03	59	151	15 02	60	151	16 02	60	151
30	11 55	+60	149	12 55	+59	149	13 54	+60	149	14 54	+60	149	15 54	+60	149
32	11 46	60	147	12 46	60	147	13 46	59	147	14 45	60	147	15 45	60	147
34	11 37	59	145	12 36	60	145	13 36	60	145	14 36	60	145	15 36	60	145
36	11 27	60	143	12 27	59	143	13 26	60	143	14 26	60	143	15 26	60	143
38	11 17	59	141	12 16	60	141	13 16	60	141	14 16	60	141	15 16	60	141
40	11 06	+60	139	12 06	+60	139	13 06	+59	139	14 05	+60	139	15 05	+60	139
42	10 55	60	137	11 55	59	137	12 54	60	137	13 54	60	137	14 54	60	137
44	10 43	60	135	11 43	60	135	12 43	59	135	13 42	60	135	14 42	60	135
46	10 31	60	133	11 31	60	133	12 31	59	133	13 30	60	133	14 30	60	133
48	10 19	60	131	11 19	59	131	12 18	60	131	13 18	60	131	14 18	59	131
50	10 06	+60	129	11 06	+60	129	12 06	+59	129	13 05	+60	129	14 05	+59	129
52	09 53	60	127	10 53	59	127	11 52	60	127	12 52	60	127	13 52	59	127
54	09 40	59	125	10 39	60	125	11 39	59	125	12 38	60	125	13 38	60	125
56	09 26	59	123	10 25	60	123	11 25	60	123	12 25	59	123	13 24	60	123
58	09 12	59	121	10 11	60	121	11 11	59	121	12 10	60	121	13 10	59	121
60	08 57	+60	119	09 57	+59	119	10 56	+60	119	11 56	+59	119	12 55	+60	119
62	08 43	59	117	09 42	60	117	10 42	59	117	11 41	60	117	12 41	59	117
64	08 28	59	115	09 27	60	115	10 27	59	115	11 26	60	115	12 26	59	115
66	08 12	60	113	09 12	59	113	10 11	60	113	11 11	59	113	12 10	60	113
68	07 57	59	111	08 56	60	111	09 56	59	111	10 55	60	111	11 55	59	111
70	07 41	+60	109	08 41	+59	109	09 40	+60	109	10 40	+59	109	11 39	+59	109
72	07 25	60	107	08 25	59	107	09 24	60	107	10 24	59	107	11 23	60	107
74	07 09	60	105	08 09	59	105	09 08	60	105	10 08	59	105	11 07	59	105
76	06 53	59	103	07 52	60	103	08 52	59	103	09 51	60	103	10 51	59	103
78	06 37	59	101	07 36	60	101	08 36	59	101	09 35	59	101	10 34	60	101
80	06 20	+60	99	07 20	+59	99	08 19	+60	99	09 19	+59	99	10 18	+59	99
82	06 04	59	97	07 03	60	97	08 03	59	97	09 02	59	97	10 01	60	97
84	05 47	60	95	06 47	59	95	07 46	59	95	08 45	60	95	09 45	59	95
86	05 31	59	93	06 30	59	93	07 29	60	93	08 29	59	93	09 28	60	93
88	05 14	59	91	06 13	60	91	07 13	59	91	08 12	59	91	09 11	60	91
90	04 57	+60	89	05 57	+59	89	06 56	+59	89	07 55	+60	89	08 55	+59	89
92	04 40	60	87	05 40	59	87	06 39	60	87	07 39	59	87	08 38	59	87
94	04 24	59	85	05 23	60	85	06 23	59	85	07 22	59	85	08 21	60	85
96	04 07	60	83	05 07	59	83	06 06	59	83	07 05	60	83	08 05	59	83
98	03 51	59	81	04 50	59	81	05 49	60	81	06 49	59	81	07 48	60	81
100	03 34	+60	79	04 34	+59	79	05 33	+59	79	06 32	+60	79	07 32	+59	79
102	03 18	59	77	04 17	60	77	05 17	59	77	06 16	60	77	07 16	59	77
104	03 01	60	75	04 01	59	75	05 00	60	75	06 00	59	75	06 59	60	75
106	02 45	60	73	03 45	59	73	04 44	60	73	05 44	59	73	06 43	60	73
108	02 29	60	71	03 29	59	71	04 28	60	71	05 28	59	71	06 27	60	71
110	02 14	+59	70	03 13	+60	69	04 13	+59	69	05 12	+60	69	06 12	+59	69
112	01 58	60	68	02 58	59	67	03 57	60	67	04 57	59	67	05 56	60	67
114	01 43	59	66	02 42	60	65	03 42	59	65	04 41	60	65	05 41	59	65
116	01 28	59	64	02 27	60	63	03 27	59	63	04 26	60	63	05 26	59	63
118	01 13	59	62	02 12	60	61	03 12	60	61	04 12	59	61	05 11	60	61
120	00 58	+60	60	01 58	+60	60	02 58	+59	59	03 57	+60	59	04 57	+59	59
122	00 44	60	58	01 44	59	58	02 43	60	57	03 43	59	57	04 42	60	57
124	00 30	60	56	01 30	59	56	02 29	60	55	03 29	60	55	04 29	59	55
126	00 17	59	54	01 16	60	54	02 16	59	53	03 15	60	53	04 15	60	53
128	00 03	60	52	01 03	60	52	02 03	59	51	03 02	60	51	04 02	60	51
130	−0 10	+60	50	00 50	+60	50	01 50	+59	50	02 49	+60	49	03 49	+60	49
132	−0 22	59	48	00 37	60	48	01 37	60	48	02 37	59	47	03 36	60	47
134	−0 34	59	46	00 25	60	46	01 25	60	46	02 25	59	45	03 24	60	45
136	−0 46	60	44	00 14	59	44	01 13	60	44	02 13	60	43	03 13	59	43
138	−0 57	59	42	00 02	60	42	01 02	60	42	02 02	59	42	03 01	60	41

LHA	10° Hc	10° d	10° Z	11° Hc	11° d	11° Z	12° Hc	12° d	12° Z	13° Hc	13° d	13° Z	14° Hc	14° d	14° Z	LHA
	° ′	′	°	° ′	′	°	° ′	′	°	° ′	′	°	° ′	′	°	
0	18 00	+60	180	19 00	+60	180	20 00	+60	180	21 00	+60	180	22 00	+60	180	360
2	18 00	60	178	19 00	60	178	20 00	60	178	21 00	60	178	22 00	60	178	358
4	17 59	60	176	18 59	60	176	19 59	60	176	20 59	60	176	21 59	60	176	356
6	17 57	60	174	18 57	60	174	19 57	60	174	20 57	60	174	21 57	60	174	354
8	17 55	60	172	18 55	60	172	19 55	60	172	20 55	60	172	21 55	60	172	352
10	17 53	+60	170	18 53	+59	170	19 52	+60	170	20 52	+60	170	21 52	+60	170	350
12	17 49	60	168	18 49	60	168	19 49	60	168	20 49	60	168	21 49	60	167	348
14	17 45	60	166	18 45	60	166	19 45	60	165	20 45	60	165	21 45	60	165	346
16	17 41	60	163	18 41	60	163	19 41	60	163	20 41	60	163	21 41	60	163	344
18	17 36	60	161	18 36	60	161	19 36	60	161	20 36	60	161	21 36	60	161	342
20	17 30	+60	159	18 30	+60	159	19 30	+60	159	20 30	+60	159	21 30	+60	159	340
22	17 24	60	157	18 24	60	157	19 24	60	157	20 24	60	157	21 24	60	157	338
24	17 17	60	155	18 17	60	155	19 17	60	155	20 17	60	155	21 17	60	155	336
26	17 10	60	153	18 10	60	153	19 10	60	153	20 10	60	153	21 10	59	153	334
28	17 02	60	151	18 02	60	151	19 02	60	151	20 02	60	151	21 02	59	151	332
30	16 54	+60	149	17 54	+60	149	18 54	+59	149	19 53	+60	149	20 53	+60	149	330
32	16 45	60	147	17 45	60	147	18 45	59	147	19 44	60	147	20 44	60	147	328
34	16 36	59	145	17 35	60	145	18 35	60	145	19 35	60	145	20 35	60	145	326
36	16 26	60	143	17 26	59	143	18 25	60	143	19 25	60	143	20 25	60	143	324
38	16 16	59	141	17 15	60	141	18 15	60	141	19 15	60	141	20 15	59	141	322
40	16 05	+59	139	17 04	+60	139	18 04	+60	139	19 04	+60	139	20 04	+59	138	320
42	15 54	59	137	16 53	60	137	17 53	60	137	18 53	59	136	19 52	60	136	318
44	15 42	60	135	16 42	59	135	17 41	60	135	18 41	60	134	19 41	59	134	316
46	15 30	59	133	16 29	60	133	17 29	60	133	18 29	59	132	19 28	60	132	314
48	15 17	60	131	16 17	60	131	17 17	59	130	18 16	60	130	19 16	60	130	312
50	15 04	+60	129	16 04	+60	129	17 04	+59	128	18 03	+60	128	19 03	+60	128	310
52	14 51	60	127	15 51	59	127	16 50	60	126	17 50	60	126	18 50	59	126	308
54	14 38	59	125	15 37	60	125	16 37	59	124	17 36	60	124	18 36	60	124	306
56	14 24	59	123	15 23	60	122	16 23	59	122	17 22	60	122	18 22	60	122	304
58	14 09	60	121	15 09	60	120	16 09	59	120	17 08	60	120	18 08	59	120	302
60	13 55	+60	119	14 55	+59	118	15 54	+60	118	16 54	+59	118	17 53	+60	118	300
62	13 40	60	117	14 40	59	116	15 39	60	116	16 39	59	116	17 38	60	116	298
64	13 25	60	115	14 25	59	114	15 24	60	114	16 24	59	114	17 23	60	114	296
66	13 10	59	113	14 09	60	112	15 09	59	112	16 08	60	112	17 08	59	112	294
68	12 54	60	111	13 54	59	110	14 53	60	110	15 53	59	110	16 52	60	110	292
70	12 38	+60	109	13 38	+59	108	14 37	+60	108	15 37	+59	108	16 36	+60	108	290
72	12 23	59	107	13 22	59	106	14 21	60	106	15 21	59	106	16 20	60	106	288
74	12 06	60	105	13 06	59	104	14 05	60	104	15 05	59	104	16 04	60	104	286
76	11 50	60	103	12 50	59	102	13 49	59	102	14 48	60	102	15 48	59	102	284
78	11 34	59	101	12 33	60	100	13 33	59	100	14 32	59	100	15 31	60	100	282
80	11 17	+60	99	12 17	+59	98	13 16	+60	98	14 16	+59	98	15 15	+59	98	280
82	11 01	59	97	12 00	60	96	13 00	59	96	13 59	59	96	14 58	60	96	278
84	10 44	60	95	11 44	59	94	12 43	59	94	13 42	60	94	14 42	59	94	276
86	10 28	59	93	11 27	59	92	12 26	60	92	13 26	59	92	14 25	59	92	274
88	10 11	59	91	11 10	60	90	12 10	59	90	13 09	59	90	14 08	60	90	272
90	09 54	+60	89	10 54	+59	89	11 53	+59	88	12 52	+60	88	13 52	+59	88	270
92	09 37	60	87	10 37	59	87	11 36	60	86	12 36	59	86	13 35	59	86	268
94	09 21	59	85	10 20	60	85	11 20	59	84	12 19	59	84	13 18	60	84	266
96	09 04	60	83	10 04	59	83	11 03	59	82	12 02	60	82	13 02	59	82	264
98	08 48	59	81	09 47	60	81	10 47	59	80	11 46	59	80	12 45	60	80	262
100	08 31	+60	79	09 31	+59	79	10 30	+60	78	11 30	+59	78	12 29	+59	78	260
102	08 15	59	77	09 14	60	77	10 14	59	77	11 13	60	76	12 13	59	76	258
104	07 59	59	75	08 58	60	75	09 58	59	75	10 57	59	74	11 56	60	74	256
106	07 43	59	73	08 42	60	73	09 42	59	73	10 41	59	72	11 40	60	72	254
108	07 27	59	71	08 26	60	71	09 26	59	71	10 25	60	70	11 25	59	70	252
110	07 11	+60	69	08 11	+59	69	09 10	+60	69	10 10	+59	69	11 09	+60	68	250
112	06 56	59	67	07 55	60	67	08 55	59	67	09 54	60	67	10 54	59	66	248
114	06 40	60	65	07 40	59	65	08 39	60	65	09 39	59	65	10 38	60	64	246
116	06 25	60	63	07 25	59	63	08 24	60	63	09 24	60	63	10 24	59	63	244
118	06 11	59	61	07 10	60	61	08 10	59	61	09 09	60	61	10 09	59	61	242
120	05 56	+60	59	06 56	+59	59	07 55	+60	59	08 55	+59	59	09 54	+60	59	240
122	05 42	60	57	06 42	59	57	07 41	60	57	08 41	59	57	09 40	60	57	238
124	05 28	60	55	06 28	59	55	07 27	60	55	08 27	60	55	09 27	59	55	236
126	05 15	59	53	06 14	60	53	07 14	60	53	08 14	59	53	09 13	60	53	234
128	05 02	59	51	06 01	60	51	07 01	59	51	08 00	60	51	09 00	60	51	232
130	04 49	+59	49	05 48	+60	49	06 48	+60	49	07 48	+59	49	08 47	+60	49	230
132	04 36	60	47	05 36	60	47	06 36	59	47	07 35	60	47	08 35	60	47	228
134	04 24	60	45	05 24	60	45	06 24	59	45	07 23	60	45	08 23	60	45	226
136	04 12	60	43	05 12	60	43	06 12	60	43	07 12	59	43	08 11	60	43	224
138	04 01	60	41	05 01	60	41	06 01	59	41	07 00	60	41	08 00	60	41	222

S. Lat. {LHA greater than 180°....... Zn=180−Z; LHA less than 180°........... Zn=180+Z}

DECLINATION (0°-14°) SAME NAME AS LATITUDE

LAT 82°

N. Lat. {LHA greater than 180°....... Zn=Z
{LHA less than 180°.......... Zn=360−Z

DECLINATION (0°-14°) SAME NAME AS LATITUDE

LHA	0° Hc	d	Z	1° Hc	d	Z	2° Hc	d	Z	3° Hc	d	Z	4° Hc	d	Z
	° ′	′	°	° ′	′	°	° ′	′	°	° ′	′	°	° ′	′	°
140	−6 07	+60	40	−5 07	+59	40	−4 08	+60	40	−3 08	+60	40	−2 08	+60	40
142	−6 18	60	38	−5 18	60	38	−4 18	60	38	−3 18	59	38	−2 19	60	38
144	−6 28	60	36	−5 28	60	36	−4 28	60	36	−3 28	59	36	−2 29	60	36
146	−6 38	60	34	−5 38	60	34	−4 38	60	34	−3 38	60	34	−2 38	60	34
148	−6 47	60	32	−5 47	60	32	−4 47	60	32	−3 47	60	32	−2 47	60	32
150	−6 55	+59	30	−5 56	+60	30	−4 56	+60	30	−3 56	+60	30	−2 56	+60	30
152	−7 04	60	28	−6 04	60	28	−5 04	60	28	−4 04	60	28	−3 04	60	28
154	−7 11	60	26	−6 11	60	26	−5 11	60	26	−4 11	59	26	−3 12	60	26
156				−6 18	59	24	−5 19	60	24	−4 19	60	24	−3 19	60	24
158				−6 25	60	22	−5 25	60	22	−4 25	60	22	−3 25	60	22
160				−6 31	+60	20	−5 31	+60	20	−4 31	+60	20	−3 31	+60	20
162				−6 36	59	18	−5 37	60	18	−4 37	60	18	−3 37	60	18
164				−6 41	60	16	−5 41	60	16	−4 41	60	16	−3 41	60	16
166				−6 46	60	14	−5 46	60	14	−4 46	60	14	−3 46	60	14
168				−6 50	60	12	−5 50	60	12	−4 50	60	12	−3 50	60	12
170				−6 53	+60	10	−5 53	+60	10	−4 53	+60	10	−3 53	+60	10
172				−6 55	60	8	−5 55	60	8	−4 55	60	8	−3 55	60	8
174				−6 57	60	6	−5 57	60	6	−4 57	60	6	−3 57	60	6
176				−6 59	60	4	−5 59	60	4	−4 59	60	4	−3 59	60	4
178				−7 00	60	2	−6 00	60	2	−5 00	60	2	−4 00	60	2
180				−7 00	+60	0	−6 00	+60	0	−5 00	+60	0	−4 00	+60	0

LHA	5° Hc	d	Z	6° Hc	d	Z	7° Hc	d	Z	8° Hc	d	Z	9° Hc	d	Z
	° ′	′	°	° ′	′	°	° ′	′	°	° ′	′	°	° ′	′	°
140	−1 08	+59	40	−0 09	+60	40	00 51	+60	40	01 51	+60	40	02 51	+59	39
142	−1 19	60	38	−0 19	60	38	00 41	59	38	01 40	60	38	02 40	60	37
144	−1 29	60	36	−0 29	60	36	00 31	59	36	01 30	60	36	02 30	60	36
146	−1.38	59	34	−0 39	60	34	00 21	60	34	01 21	60	34	02 21	60	34
148	−1 47	59	32	−0 48	60	32	00 12	60	32	01 12	60	32	02 12	60	32
150	−1 56	+60	30	−0 56	+60	30	00 04	+59	30	01 03	+60	30	02 03	+60	30
152	−2 04	60	28	−1 04	60	28	−0 04	59	28	00 55	60	28	01 55	60	28
154	−2 12	60	26	−1 12	60	26	−0 12	60	26	00 48	60	26	01 48	60	26
156	−2 19	60	24	−1 19	60	24	−0 19	60	24	00 41	60	24	01 41	60	24
158	−2 25	60	22	−1 25	60	22	−0 25	60	22	00 35	59	22	01 34	60	22
160	−2 31	+60	20	−1 31	+60	20	−0 31	+60	20	00 29	+59	20	01 28	+60	20
162	−2 37	60	18	−1 37	60	18	−0 37	60	18	00 23	60	18	01 23	60	18
164	−2 41	59	16	−1 42	60	16	−0 42	60	16	00 18	60	16	01 18	60	16
166	−2 46	60	14	−1 46	60	14	−0 46	60	14	00 14	60	14	01 14	60	14
168	−2 50	60	12	−1 50	60	12	−0 50	60	12	00 10	60	12	01 10	60	12
170	−2 53	+60	10	−1 53	+60	10	−0 53	+60	10	00 07	+60	10	01 07	+60	10
172	−2 55	60	8	−1 55	60	8	−0 55	60	8	00 05	60	8	01 05	60	8
174	−2 57	60	6	−1 57	60	6	−0 57	60	6	00 03	60	6	01 03	60	6
176	−2 59	60	4	−1 59	60	4	−0 59	60	4	00 01	60	4	01 01	60	4
178	−3 00	60	2	−2 00	60	2	−1 00	60	2	00 00	60	2	01 00	60	2
180	−3 00	+60	0	−2 00	+60	0	−1 00	+60	0	00 00	+60	0	01 00	+60	0

LHA	10° Hc	d	Z	11° Hc	d	Z	12° Hc	d	Z	13° Hc	d	Z	14° Hc	d	Z	LHA
	° ′	′	°	° ′	′	°	° ′	′	°	° ′	′	°	° ′	′	°	
140	03 50	+60	39	04 50	+60	39	05 50	+60	39	06 50	+59	39	07 49	+60	39	220
142	03 40	60	37	04 40	60	37	05 40	59	37	06 39	60	37	07 39	60	37	218
144	03 30	60	35	04 30	60	35	05 30	60	35	06 30	59	35	07 29	60	35	216
146	03 21	59	33	04 20	60	33	05 20	60	33	06 20	60	33	07 20	60	33	214
148	03 12	60	31	04 12	59	31	05 11	60	31	06 11	60	31	07 11	60	31	212
150	03 03	+60	30	04 03	+60	30	05 03	+60	29	06 03	+60	29	07 03	+60	29	210
152	02 55	60	28	03 55	60	28	04 55	60	27	05 55	60	27	06 55	60	27	208
154	02 48	60	26	03 48	60	26	04 48	59	25	05 47	60	25	06 47	60	25	206
156	02 41	60	24	03 41	60	24	04 41	60	24	05 41	59	24	06 40	60	23	204
158	02 34	60	22	03 34	60	22	04 34	60	22	05 34	60	22	06 34	60	22	202
160	02 28	+60	20	03 28	+60	20	04 28	+60	20	05 28	+60	20	06 28	+60	20	200
162	02 23	60	18	03 23	60	18	04 23	60	18	05 23	60	18	06 23	60	18	198
164	02 18	60	16	03 18	60	16	04 18	60	16	05 18	60	16	06 18	60	16	196
166	02 14	60	14	03 14	60	14	04 14	60	14	05 14	60	14	06 14	60	14	194
168	02 10	60	12	03 10	60	12	04 10	60	12	05 10	60	12	06 10	60	12	192
170	02 07	+60	10	03 07	+60	10	04 07	+60	10	05 07	+60	10	06 07	+60	10	190
172	02 05	60	8	03 05	60	8	04 05	60	8	05 05	60	8	06 05	60	8	188
174	02 03	60	6	03 03	60	6	04 03	60	6	05 03	60	6	06 03	60	6	186
176	02 01	60	4	03 01	60	4	04 01	60	4	05 01	60	4	06 01	60	4	184
178	02 00	60	2	03 00	60	2	04 00	60	2	05 00	60	2	06 00	60	2	182
180	02 00	+60	0	03 00	+60	0	04 00	+60	0	05 00	+60	0	06 00	+60	0	180

0°	1°	2°	3°	4°	5°	6°	7°	8°	9°	10°	11°	12°	13°	14°

S. Lat. {LHA greater than 180°....... Zn=180−Z
{LHA less than 180°.......... Zn=180+Z

DECLINATION (0°-14°) SAME NAME AS LATITUDE

N. Lat. {LHA greater than 180°....... Zn=Z; LHA less than 180°........... Zn=360−Z}

DECLINATION (0°-14°) CONTRARY NAME TO LATITUDE

LHA	0° Hc	0° d	0° Z	1° Hc	1° d	1° Z	LHA
	° ′	′	°	° ′	′	°	
154	−7 11	60	26				206
152	−7 04	59	28				208
150	−6 55	−60	30				210
148	−6 47	60	32				212
146	−6 38	59	34				214
144	−6 28	60	36				216
142	−6 18	60	38	−7 18	59	38	218
140	−6 07	−60	40	−7 07	−60	40	220

S. Lat. {LHA greater than 180°....... Zn=180−Z; LHA less than 180°........... Zn=180+Z}

DECLINATION (0°-14°) CONTRARY NAME TO LATITUDE

LAT 82°

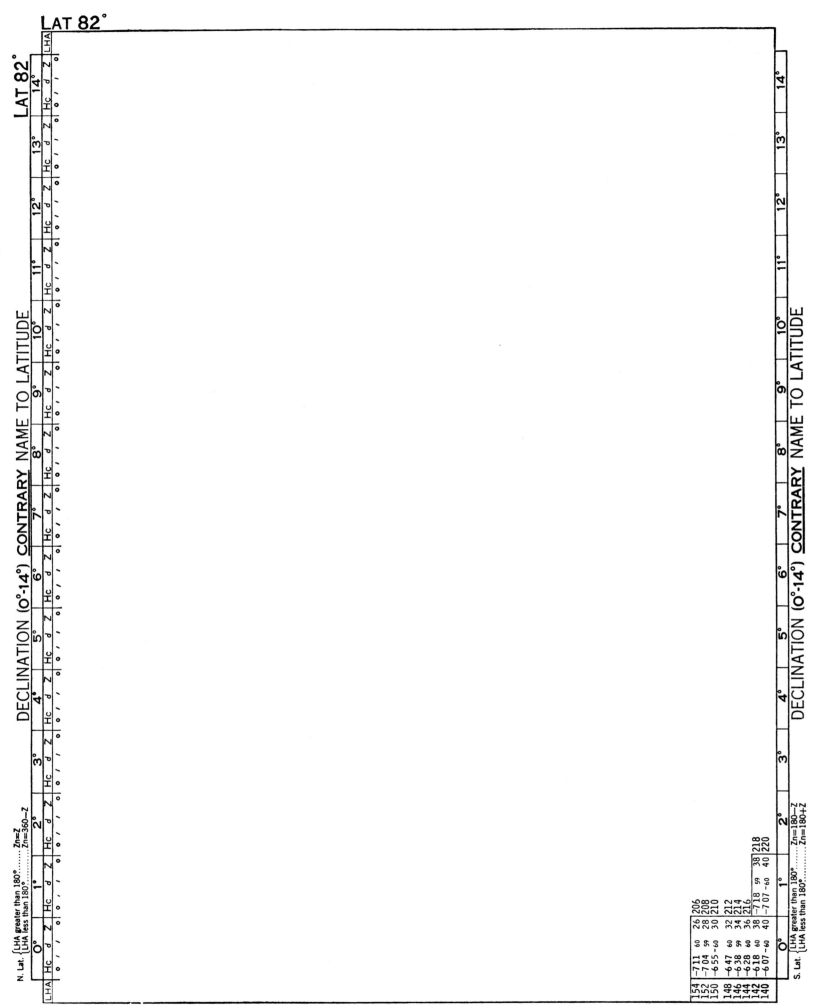

N. Lat. {LHA greater than 180°....... Zn=Z
{LHA less than 180°............ Zn=360−Z

DECLINATION (0°-14°) CONTRARY NAME TO LATITUDE

LHA	0° Hc	d	Z	1° Hc	d	Z	2° Hc	d	Z	3° Hc	d	Z	4° Hc	d	Z
	° ′	′	°	° ′	′	°	° ′	′	°	° ′	′	°	° ′	′	°
138	-5 56	60	42	-6 56	60	42									
136	-5 45	60	44	-6 45	59	44									
134	-5 33	60	46	-6 33	59	46									
132	-5 21	59	48	-6 20	60	48	-7 20	60	48						
130	-5 08	-60	50	-6 08	-59	50	-7 07	-60	50						
128	-4 55	60	52	-5 55	59	52	-6 54	60	52						
126	-4 42	59	54	-5 41	60	54	-6 41	59	54						
124	-4 28	59	56	-5 27	60	56	-6 27	60	56	-7 27	59	57			
122	-4 14	59	58	-5 13	60	58	-6 13	60	58	-7 13	59	59			
120	-3 59	-60	60	-4 59	-60	60	-5 59	-59	60	-6 58	-60	61			
118	-3 45	59	62	-4 44	60	62	-5 44	59	62	-6 43	60	63			
116	-3 30	59	64	-4 29	60	64	-5 29	59	64	-6 28	60	65	-7 28	60	65
114	-3 15	59	66	-4 14	60	66	-5 14	59	66	-6 13	60	67	-7 13	59	67
112	-2 59	60	68	-3 59	59	68	-4 58	60	68	-5 58	59	69	-6 57	60	69
110	-2 44	-59	70	-3 43	-60	70	-4 43	-59	70	-5 42	-60	71	-6 42	-59	71
108	-2 28	59	72	-3 27	60	72	-4 27	59	72	-5 26	60	73	-6 26	59	73
106	-2 12	59	74	-3 11	60	74	-4 11	59	74	-5 10	60	75	-6 10	59	75
104	-1 56	59	76	-2 55	60	76	-3 55	59	76	-4 54	60	76	-5 54	59	77
102	-1 39	60	78	-2 39	59	78	-3 38	60	78	-4 38	59	78	-5 37	60	79
100	-1 23	-60	80	-2 23	-59	80	-3 22	-59	80	-4 21	-60	80	-5 21	-59	81
98	-1 07	59	82	-2 06	59	82	-3 05	60	82	-4 05	59	82	-5 04	60	83
96	-0 50	59	84	-1 49	60	84	-2 49	59	84	-3 48	60	84	-4 48	59	85
94	-0 33	60	86	-1 33	59	86	-2 32	60	86	-3 32	59	86	-4 31	60	87
92	-0 17	59	88	-1 16	60	88	-2 16	59	88	-3 15	59	88	-4 14	60	89
90	00 00	-59	90	-0 59	-60	90	-1 59	-59	90	-2 58	-60	90	-3 58	-59	90
88	00 17	60	92	-0 43	59	92	-1 42	60	92	-2 42	59	92	-3 41	59	92
86	00 33	59	94	-0 26	59	94	-1 25	60	94	-2 25	59	94	-3 24	60	94
84	00 50	59	96	-0 09	60	96	-1 09	59	96	-2 08	60	96	-3 08	59	96
82	01 07	60	98	00 07	59	98	-0 52	60	98	-1 52	59	98	-2 51	60	98
80	01 23	-59	100	00 24	-60	100	-0 36	-59	100	-1 35	-60	100	-2 35	-59	100
78	01 39	59	102	00 40	59	102	-0 19	60	102	-1 19	59	102	-2 18	60	102
76	01 56	60	104	00 56	59	104	-0 03	60	104	-1 03	59	104	-2 02	59	104
74	02 12	60	106	01 12	59	106	00 13	59	106	-0 46	60	106	-1 46	59	106
72	02 28	60	108	01 28	59	108	00 29	60	108	-0 31	59	108	-1 30	59	108
70	02 44	-60	110	01 44	-59	110	00 45	-60	110	-0 15	-59	110	-1 14	-60	110
68	02 59	59	112	02 00	60	112	01 00	59	112	00 01	60	112	-0 59	59	112
66	03 15	60	114	02 15	59	114	01 16	60	114	00 16	59	114	-0 43	60	114
64	03 30	60	116	02 30	59	116	01 31	60	116	00 31	59	116	-0 28	60	116
62	03 45	60	118	02 45	59	118	01 46	60	118	00 46	59	118	-0 13	60	118
60	03 59	-59	120	03 00	-60	120	02 00	-59	120	01 01	-60	120	00 01	-59	120
58	04 14	60	122	03 14	59	122	02 15	60	122	01 15	60	122	00 15	59	122
56	04 28	60	124	03 28	59	124	02 29	60	124	01 29	60	124	00 29	59	124
54	04 42	60	126	03 42	60	126	02 42	59	126	01 43	60	126	00 43	60	126
52	04 55	60	128	03 55	59	128	02 56	60	128	01 56	60	128	00 56	59	128
50	05 08	-60	130	04 08	-59	130	03 09	-60	130	02 09	-60	130	01 09	-59	130
48	05 21	60	132	04 21	60	132	03 21	59	132	02 22	60	132	01 22	60	132
46	05 33	60	134	04 33	60	134	03 33	59	134	02 34	60	134	01 34	60	134
44	05 45	60	136	04 45	60	136	03 45	59	136	02 46	60	136	01 46	60	136
42	05 56	60	138	04 56	59	138	03 57	60	138	02 57	60	138	01 57	60	138
40	06 07	-60	140	05 07	-59	140	04 08	-60	140	03 08	-60	140	02 08	-60	140
38	06 18	60	142	05 18	60	142	04 18	60	142	03 18	59	142	02 19	60	142
36	06 28	60	144	05 28	60	144	04 28	60	144	03 28	59	144	02 29	60	144
34	06 38	60	146	05 38	60	146	04 38	60	146	03 38	60	146	02 38	60	146
32	06 47	60	148	05 47	60	148	04 47	60	148	03 47	60	148	02 47	60	148
30	06 55	-59	150	05 56	-60	150	04 56	-60	150	03 56	-60	150	02 56	-60	150
28	07 04	60	152	06 04	60	152	05 04	60	152	04 04	60	152	03 04	60	152
26	07 11	60	154	06 11	60	154	05 11	60	154	04 11	59	154	03 12	60	154
24	07 18	60	156	06 18	59	156	05 19	60	156	04 19	60	156	03 19	60	156
22	07 25	60	158	06 25	60	158	05 25	60	158	04 25	60	158	03 25	60	158
20	07 31	-60	160	06 31	-60	160	05 31	-60	160	04 31	-60	160	03 31	-60	160
18	07 36	60	162	06 36	59	162	05 37	60	162	04 37	60	162	03 37	60	162
16	07 41	60	164	06 41	60	164	05 41	60	164	04 41	60	164	03 41	60	164
14	07 46	60	166	06 46	60	166	05 46	60	166	04 46	60	166	03 46	60	166
12	07 49	59	168	06 50	60	168	05 50	60	168	04 50	60	168	03 50	60	168
10	07 53	-60	170	06 53	-60	170	05 53	-60	170	04 53	-60	170	03 53	-60	170
8	07 55	60	172	06 55	60	172	05 55	60	172	04 55	60	172	03 55	60	172
6	07 57	60	174	06 57	60	174	05 57	60	174	04 57	60	174	03 57	60	174
4	07 59	60	176	06 59	60	176	05 59	60	176	04 59	60	176	03 59	60	176
2	08 00	60	178	07 00	60	178	06 00	60	178	05 00	60	178	04 00	60	178
0	08 00	-60	180	07 00	-60	180	06 00	-60	180	05 00	-60	180	04 00	-60	180

LHA	5° Hc	d	Z	6° Hc	d	Z	7° Hc	d	Z	8° Hc	d	Z	9° Hc	d	Z
	° ′	′	°	° ′	′	°	° ′	′	°	° ′	′	°	° ′	′	°
108	-7 25	60	73												
106	-7 09	60	75												
104	-6 53	59	77												
102	-6 37	59	79												
100	-6 20	-60	81	-7 20	-59	81									
98	-6 04	59	83	-7 03	60	83									
96	-5 47	60	85	-6 47	59	85									
94	-5 31	59	87	-6 30	59	87	-7 29	60	87						
92	-5 14	59	89	-6 13	60	89	-7 13	59	89						
90	-4 57	-60	91	-5 57	-59	91	-6 56	-59	91						
88	-4 40	60	93	-5 40	59	93	-6 39	60	93						
86	-4 24	59	95	-5 23	60	95	-6 23	59	95	-7 22	59	95			
84	-4 07	60	97	-5 07	59	97	-6 06	59	97	-7 05	60	97			
82	-3 51	59	99	-4 50	59	99	-5 49	60	99	-6 49	59	99			
80	-3 34	-60	101	-4 34	-59	101	-5 33	-59	101	-6 32	-60	101	-7 32	-59	101
78	-3 18	59	103	-4 17	60	103	-5 17	59	103	-6 16	60	103	-7 16	59	103
76	-3 01	60	105	-4 01	59	105	-5 00	60	105	-6 00	59	105	-6 59	60	105
74	-2 45	60	107	-3 45	59	107	-4 44	60	107	-5 44	59	107	-6 43	60	107
72	-2 29	60	109	-3 29	59	109	-4 28	60	109	-5 28	60	109	-6 27	60	109
70	-2 14	-59	110	-3 13	-60	111	-4 13	-59	111	-5 12	-60	111	-6 12	-59	111
68	-1 58	60	112	-2 58	59	113	-3 57	60	113	-4 57	59	113	-5 56	60	113
66	-1 43	59	114	-2 42	60	115	-3 42	59	115	-4 41	60	115	-5 41	59	115
64	-1 28	59	116	-2 27	60	117	-3 27	59	117	-4 26	60	117	-5 26	59	117
62	-1 13	59	118	-2 12	60	119	-3 12	60	119	-4 12	59	119	-5 11	60	119
60	-0 58	-60	120	-1 58	-60	120	-2 58	-59	121	-3 57	-60	121	-4 57	-59	121
58	-0 44	60	122	-1 44	59	122	-2 43	60	123	-3 43	59	123	-4 42	60	123
56	-0 30	60	124	-1 30	59	124	-2 29	60	125	-3 29	60	125	-4 29	59	125
54	-0 17	59	126	-1 16	60	126	-2 16	59	127	-3 15	60	127	-4 15	60	127
52	-0 03	60	128	-1 03	60	128	-2 03	59	129	-3 02	60	129	-4 02	60	129
50	00 10	-60	130	-0 50	-60	130	-1 50	-59	130	-2 49	-60	131	-3 49	-60	131
48	00 22	59	132	-0 37	60	132	-1 37	60	132	-2 37	59	133	-3 36	60	133
46	00 34	59	134	-0 25	60	134	-1 25	60	134	-2 25	59	135	-3 24	60	135
44	00 46	60	136	-0 14	59	136	-1 13	60	136	-2 13	60	137	-3 13	59	137
42	00 57	59	138	-0 02	60	138	-1 02	60	138	-2 02	59	138	-3 01	60	139
40	01 08	-59	140	00 09	-60	140	-0 51	-60	140	-1 51	-60	140	-2 51	-59	141
38	01 19	60	142	00 19	60	142	-0 41	59	142	-1 40	60	142	-2 40	60	143
36	01 29	60	144	00 29	60	144	-0 31	59	144	-1 30	60	144	-2 30	60	144
34	01 38	59	146	00 39	60	146	-0 21	60	146	-1 21	60	146	-2 21	60	146
32	01 47	59	148	00 48	60	148	-0 12	60	148	-1 12	60	148	-2 12	60	148
30	01 56	-60	150	00 56	-60	150	-0 04	-59	150	-1 03	-60	150	-2 03	-60	150
28	02 04	60	152	01 04	60	152	00 04	59	152	-0 55	60	152	-1 55	60	152
26	02 12	60	154	01 12	60	154	00 12	60	154	-0 48	60	154	-1 48	60	154
24	02 19	60	156	01 19	60	156	00 19	60	156	-0 41	60	156	-1 41	60	156
22	02 25	60	158	01 25	60	158	00 25	60	158	-0 35	59	158	-1 34	60	158
20	02 31	-60	160	01 31	-60	160	00 31	-60	160	-0 29	-59	160	-1 28	-60	160
18	02 37	60	162	01 37	60	162	00 37	60	162	-0 23	60	162	-1 23	60	162
16	02 41	59	164	01 42	60	164	00 42	60	164	-0 18	60	164	-1 18	60	164
14	02 46	60	166	01 46	60	166	00 46	60	166	-0 14	60	166	-1 14	60	166
12	02 50	60	168	01 50	60	168	00 50	60	168	-0 10	60	168	-1 10	60	168
10	02 53	-60	170	01 53	-60	170	00 53	-60	170	-0 07	-60	170	-1 07	-60	170
8	02 55	60	172	01 55	60	172	00 55	60	172	-0 05	60	172	-1 05	60	172
6	02 57	60	174	01 57	60	174	00 57	60	174	-0 03	60	174	-1 03	60	174
4	02 59	60	176	01 59	60	176	00 59	60	176	-0 01	60	176	-1 01	60	176
2	03 00	60	178	02 00	60	178	01 00	60	178	00 00	60	178	-1 00	60	178
0	03 00	-60	180	02 00	-60	180	01 00	-60	180	00 00	-60	180	-1 00	-60	180

LHA	10° Hc	d	Z	11° Hc	d	Z	12° Hc	d	Z	13° Hc	d	Z	14° Hc	d	Z	LHA
	° ′	′	°	° ′	′	°	° ′	′	°	° ′	′	°	° ′	′	°	
138																222
136																224
134																226
132																228
130																230
128																232
126																234
124																236
122																238
120																240
118																242
116																244
114																246
112																248
110																250
108																252
106																254
104																256
102																258
100																260
98																262
96																264
94																266
92																268
90																270
88																272
86																274
84																276
82																278
80																280
78																282
76																284
74																286
72	-7 27	59	109													288
70	-7 11	-60	111													290
68	-6 56	59	113													292
66	-6 40	60	115													294
64	-6 25	60	117	-7 25	59	117										296
62	-6 11	59	119	-7 10	60	119										298
60	-5 56	-60	121	-6 56	-59	121										300
58	-5 42	60	123	-6 42	59	123										302
56	-5 28	60	125	-6 28	59	125										304
54	-5 15	59	127	-6 14	60	127	-7 14	60	127							306
52	-5 02	59	129	-6 01	60	129	-7 01	59	129							308
50	-4 49	-59	131	-5 48	-60	131	-6 48	-60	131							310
48	-4 36	60	133	-5 36	60	133	-6 36	59	133							312
46	-4 24	60	135	-5 24	60	135	-6 24	59	135							314
44	-4 12	60	137	-5 12	60	137	-6 12	60	137	-7 12	59	137				316
42	-4 01	60	139	-5 01	60	139	-6 01	59	139	-7 00	60	139				318
40	-3 50	-60	141	-4 50	-60	141	-5 50	-60	141	-6 50	-59	141				320
38	-3 40	60	143	-4 40	60	143	-5 40	59	143	-6 39	60	143				322
36	-3 30	60	145	-4 30	60	145	-5 30	60	145	-6 30	59	145				324
34	-3 21	59	147	-4 20	60	147	-5 20	60	147	-6 20	60	147				326
32	-3 12	60	149	-4 12	59	149	-5 11	60	149	-6 11	60	149	-7 11	60	149	328
30	-3 03	-60	150	-4 03	-60	150	-5 03	-60	151	-6 03	-60	151	-7 03	-60	151	330
28	-2 55	60	152	-3 55	60	152	-4 55	60	153	-5 55	60	153	-6 55	60	153	332
26	-2 48	60	154	-3 48	60	154	-4 48	59	155	-5 47	60	155	-6 47	60	155	334
24	-2 41	60	156	-3 41	60	156	-4 41	60	156	-5 41	59	156	-6 40	60	157	336
22	-2 34	60	158	-3 34	60	158	-4 34	60	158	-5 34	60	158	-6 34	60	158	338
20	-2 28	-60	160	-3 28	-60	160	-4 28	-60	160	-5 28	-60	160	-6 28	-60	160	340
18	-2 23	60	162	-3 23	60	162	-4 23	60	162	-5 23	60	162	-6 23	60	162	342
16	-2 18	60	164	-3 18	60	164	-4 18	60	164	-5 18	60	164	-6 18	60	164	344
14	-2 14	60	166	-3 14	60	166	-4 14	60	166	-5 14	60	166	-6 14	60	166	346
12	-2 10	60	168	-3 10	60	168	-4 10	60	168	-5 10	60	168	-6 10	60	168	348
10	-2 07	-60	170	-3 07	-60	170	-4 07	-60	170	-5 07	-60	170	-6 07	-60	170	350
8	-2 05	60	172	-3 05	60	172	-4 05	60	172	-5 05	60	172	-6 05	60	172	352
6	-2 03	60	174	-3 03	60	174	-4 03	60	174	-5 03	60	174	-6 03	60	174	354
4	-2 01	60	176	-3 01	60	176	-4 01	60	176	-5 01	60	176	-6 01	60	176	356
2	-2 00	60	178	-3 00	60	178	-4 00	60	178	-5 00	60	178	-6 00	60	178	358
0	-2 00	-60	180	-3 00	-60	180	-4 00	-60	180	-5 00	-60	180	-6 00	-60	180	360

S. Lat. {LHA greater than 180°....... Zn=180−Z
{LHA less than 180°............ Zn=180+Z

N. Lat. {LHA greater than 180°....... Zn=Z; LHA less than 180°........... Zn=360−Z}

DECLINATION (15°-29°) SAME NAME AS LATITUDE

LHA	15° Hc	15° d	15° Z	16° Hc	16° d	16° Z	17° Hc	17° d	17° Z	18° Hc	18° d	18° Z	19° Hc	19° d	19° Z
	° ′	′	°	° ′	′	°	° ′	′	°	° ′	′	°	° ′	′	°
0	23 00	+60	180	24 00	+60	180	25 00	+60	180	26 00	+60	180	27 00	+60	180
2	23 00	60	178	24 00	60	178	25 00	60	178	26 00	60	178	27 00	60	178
4	22 59	60	176	23 59	60	176	24 59	60	176	25 59	60	176	26 59	60	176
6	22 57	60	174	23 57	60	174	24 57	60	174	25 57	60	174	26 57	60	174
8	22 55	60	172	23 55	60	172	24 55	60	172	25 55	60	172	26 55	60	172
10	22 52	+60	170	23 52	+60	170	24 52	+60	170	25 52	+60	169	26 52	+60	169
12	22 49	60	167	23 49	60	167	24 49	60	167	25 49	60	167	26 49	60	167
14	22 45	60	165	23 45	60	165	24 45	60	165	25 45	60	165	26 45	60	165
16	22 41	60	163	23 41	60	163	24 41	59	163	25 40	60	163	26 40	60	163
18	22 36	59	161	23 35	60	161	24 35	60	161	25 35	60	161	26 35	60	161
20	22 30	+60	159	23 30	+60	159	24 30	+60	159	25 30	+60	159	26 30	+59	159
22	22 24	59	157	23 23	60	157	24 23	60	157	25 23	60	157	26 23	60	157
24	22 17	60	155	23 17	60	155	24 17	59	155	25 16	60	155	26 16	60	155
26	22 09	60	153	23 09	60	153	24 09	60	153	25 09	60	153	26 09	60	153
28	22 01	60	151	23 01	60	151	24 01	60	151	25 01	60	151	26 01	60	150
30	21 53	+60	149	22 53	+60	149	23 53	+60	149	24 53	+59	148	25 52	+60	148
32	21 44	60	147	22 44	60	147	23 44	60	146	24 44	59	146	25 43	60	146
34	21 35	59	145	22 34	60	144	23 34	60	144	24 34	60	144	25 34	60	144
36	21 25	59	142	22 24	60	142	23 24	60	142	24 24	60	142	25 24	60	142
38	21 14	60	140	22 14	60	140	23 14	60	140	24 14	59	140	25 13	60	140
40	21 03	+60	138	22 03	+60	138	23 03	+60	138	24 03	+59	138	25 02	+60	138
42	20 52	60	136	21 52	59	136	22 51	60	136	23 51	60	136	24 51	60	136
44	20 40	60	134	21 40	60	134	22 40	59	134	23 39	60	134	24 39	60	134
46	20 28	60	132	21 28	59	132	22 27	60	132	23 27	60	132	24 27	59	132
48	20 16	59	130	21 15	60	130	22 15	59	130	23 14	60	130	24 14	60	130
50	20 03	+59	128	21 02	+60	128	22 02	+59	128	23 01	+60	128	24 01	+60	128
52	19 49	60	126	20 49	59	126	21 48	60	126	22 48	60	126	23 48	59	126
54	19 36	59	124	20 35	60	124	21 35	59	124	22 34	60	124	23 34	59	123
56	19 22	59	122	20 21	60	122	21 21	59	122	22 20	60	122	23 20	59	121
58	19 07	60	120	20 07	59	120	21 06	60	120	22 06	59	120	23 05	60	119
60	18 53	+59	118	19 52	+60	118	20 52	+59	118	21 51	+60	118	22 51	+59	117
62	18 38	59	116	19 37	60	116	20 37	59	116	21 36	60	115	22 36	59	115
64	18 23	59	114	19 22	59	114	20 21	60	114	21 21	59	113	22 20	60	113
66	18 07	60	112	19 07	59	112	20 06	59	112	21 05	60	111	22 05	59	111
68	17 52	59	110	18 51	59	110	19 50	60	110	20 50	59	109	21 49	60	109
70	17 36	+59	108	18 35	+60	108	19 35	+59	108	20 34	+59	107	21 33	+60	107
72	17 20	59	106	18 19	60	106	19 19	59	106	20 18	59	105	21 17	60	105
74	17 04	59	104	18 03	59	104	19 02	60	104	20 02	59	103	21 01	60	103
76	16 47	60	102	17 47	59	102	18 46	59	102	19 45	60	101	20 45	59	101
78	16 31	59	100	17 30	60	100	18 30	59	100	19 29	59	99	20 28	60	99
80	16 14	+60	98	17 14	+59	98	18 13	+60	98	19 13	+59	97	20 12	+59	97
82	15 58	59	96	16 57	60	96	17 57	59	96	18 56	59	95	19 55	60	95
84	15 41	60	94	16 41	59	94	17 40	59	94	18 39	60	93	19 39	59	93
86	15 24	60	92	16 24	59	92	17 23	60	92	18 23	59	91	19 22	59	91
88	15 08	59	90	16 07	60	90	17 07	59	90	18 06	59	89	19 05	60	89
90	14 51	+59	88	15 50	+60	88	16 50	+59	88	17 49	+60	87	18 49	+59	87
92	14 34	60	86	15 34	59	86	16 33	60	86	17 33	59	85	18 32	59	85
94	14 18	59	84	15 17	60	84	16 17	59	84	17 16	59	84	18 15	60	83
96	14 01	60	82	15 01	59	82	16 00	59	82	16 59	60	82	17 59	59	81
98	13 45	59	80	14 44	59	80	15 43	60	80	16 43	59	80	17 42	60	79
100	13 28	+60	78	14 28	+59	78	15 27	+60	78	16 27	+59	78	17 26	+59	77
102	13 12	59	76	14 11	60	76	15 11	59	76	16 10	60	76	17 10	59	76
104	12 56	59	74	13 55	60	74	14 55	59	74	15 54	60	74	16 54	59	74
106	12 40	59	72	13 39	60	72	14 39	59	72	15 38	60	72	16 38	59	72
108	12 24	60	70	13 24	59	70	14 23	59	70	15 22	60	70	16 22	59	70
110	12 09	+59	68	13 08	+59	68	14 07	+60	68	15 07	+59	68	16 06	+60	68
112	11 53	60	66	12 53	59	66	13 52	60	66	14 52	59	66	15 51	59	66
114	11 38	59	64	12 37	60	64	13 37	59	64	14 36	60	64	15 36	59	64
116	11 23	60	62	12 23	59	62	13 22	60	62	14 22	59	62	15 21	60	62
118	11 08	60	60	12 08	59	60	13 07	60	60	14 07	59	60	15 06	60	60
120	10 54	+60	58	11 54	+59	58	12 53	+60	58	13 53	+59	58	14 52	+60	58
122	10 40	60	57	11 40	59	56	12 39	60	56	13 39	59	56	14 38	60	56
124	10 26	60	55	11 26	59	54	12 25	60	54	13 25	59	54	14 24	60	54
126	10 13	59	53	11 12	60	52	12 12	60	52	13 12	59	52	14 11	60	52
128	10 00	59	51	10 59	60	51	11 59	60	50	12 59	59	50	13 58	60	50
130	09 47	+60	49	10 47	+59	49	11 46	+60	48	12 46	+60	48	13 46	+59	48
132	09 35	59	47	10 34	60	47	11 34	60	47	12 34	59	46	13 33	60	46
134	09 23	59	45	10 22	60	45	11 22	60	45	12 22	59	45	13 21	60	44
136	09 11	60	43	10 11	59	43	11 10	60	43	12 10	60	43	13 10	60	42
138	09 00	60	41	10 00	59	41	10 59	60	41	11 59	60	41	12 59	60	41

LHA	20° Hc	20° d	20° Z	21° Hc	21° d	21° Z	22° Hc	22° d	22° Z	23° Hc	23° d	23° Z	24° Hc	24° d	24° Z
	° ′	′	°	° ′	′	°	° ′	′	°	° ′	′	°	° ′	′	°
0	28 00	+60	180	29 00	+60	180	30 00	+60	180	31 00	+60	180	32 00	+60	180
2	28 00	60	178	29 00	60	178	30 00	60	178	31 00	60	178	32 00	60	178
4	27 59	60	176	28 59	60	176	29 59	60	176	30 59	60	176	31 59	60	176
6	27 57	60	174	28 57	60	174	29 57	60	174	30 57	60	174	31 57	60	174
8	27 55	60	172	28 55	60	172	29 55	60	171	30 55	60	171	31 55	60	171
10	27 52	+60	169	28 52	+60	169	29 52	+60	169	30 52	+60	169	31 52	+60	169
12	27 49	60	167	28 49	60	167	29 49	60	167	30 49	60	167	31 49	60	167
14	27 45	60	165	28 45	60	165	29 45	60	165	30 45	60	165	31 45	60	165
16	27 40	60	163	28 40	60	163	29 40	60	163	30 40	60	163	31 40	60	163
18	27 35	60	161	28 35	60	161	29 35	60	161	30 35	60	161	31 35	60	161
20	27 29	+60	159	28 29	+60	159	29 29	+60	159	30 29	+60	159	31 29	+60	159
22	27 23	60	157	28 23	60	157	29 23	60	157	30 23	60	156	31 23	60	156
24	27 16	60	155	28 16	60	155	29 16	60	154	30 16	60	154	31 16	60	154
26	27 09	60	152	28 09	59	152	29 08	60	152	30 08	60	152	31 08	60	152
28	27 01	60	150	28 01	59	150	29 00	60	150	30 00	60	150	31 00	60	150
30	26 52	+60	148	27 52	+60	148	28 52	+60	148	29 52	+59	148	30 51	+60	148
32	26 43	60	146	27 43	60	146	28 43	59	146	29 42	60	146	30 42	60	146
34	26 34	59	144	27 33	60	144	28 33	60	144	29 33	60	144	30 33	59	144
36	26 24	59	142	27 23	60	142	28 23	60	142	29 23	59	142	30 22	60	142
38	26 13	60	140	27 13	59	140	28 12	60	140	29 12	60	140	30 12	60	139
40	26 02	+60	138	27 02	+59	138	28 01	+60	138	29 01	+60	137	30 01	+59	137
42	25 51	59	136	26 50	60	136	27 50	60	135	28 50	59	135	29 49	60	135
44	25 39	59	134	26 38	60	134	27 38	60	133	28 38	59	133	29 37	60	133
46	25 26	60	132	26 26	60	131	27 26	59	131	28 25	60	131	29 25	59	131
48	25 14	59	130	26 13	60	129	27 13	59	129	28 12	60	129	29 12	60	129
50	25 01	+59	127	26 00	+60	127	27 00	+59	127	27 59	+60	127	28 59	+59	127
52	24 47	60	125	25 47	59	125	26 46	60	125	27 46	59	125	28 45	60	125
54	24 33	60	123	25 33	59	123	26 32	60	123	27 32	59	123	28 31	60	123
56	24 19	60	121	25 19	59	121	26 18	60	121	27 18	59	121	28 17	60	121
58	24 05	59	119	25 04	60	119	26 04	59	119	27 03	60	119	28 03	59	119
60	23 50	+60	117	24 50	+59	117	25 49	+59	117	26 48	+60	117	27 48	+59	117
62	23 35	60	115	24 35	59	115	25 34	59	115	26 33	60	115	27 33	59	115
64	23 20	59	113	24 19	60	113	25 19	59	113	26 18	60	113	27 18	59	113
66	23 04	60	111	24 04	59	111	25 03	60	111	26 03	59	111	27 02	59	111
68	22 49	59	109	23 48	59	109	24 47	60	109	25 47	59	109	26 46	60	108
70	22 33	+59	107	23 32	+60	107	24 32	+59	107	25 31	+59	107	26 30	+60	106
72	22 17	59	105	23 16	59	105	24 15	60	105	25 15	59	105	26 14	60	104
74	22 01	59	103	23 00	59	103	23 59	60	103	24 59	59	103	25 58	59	102
76	21 44	60	101	22 44	59	101	23 43	59	101	24 42	60	101	25 42	59	100
78	21 28	59	99	22 27	59	99	23 26	60	99	24 26	59	99	25 25	59	98
80	21 11	+60	97	22 11	+59	97	23 10	+59	97	24 09	+60	97	25 09	+59	96
82	20 55	59	95	21 54	59	95	22 53	60	95	23 53	59	95	24 52	59	94
84	20 38	59	93	21 37	60	93	22 37	59	93	23 36	59	93	24 35	60	92
86	20 21	60	91	21 21	59	91	22 20	59	91	23 19	60	91	24 19	59	90
88	20 05	59	89	21 04	59	89	22 03	60	89	23 03	59	89	24 02	59	88
90	19 48	+59	87	20 47	+60	87	21 47	+59	87	22 46	+59	87	23 45	+59	87
92	19 31	60	85	20 31	59	85	21 30	59	85	22 29	60	85	23 29	59	85
94	19 15	59	83	20 14	59	83	21 13	60	83	22 13	59	83	23 12	59	83
96	18 58	59	81	19 57	60	81	20 57	59	81	21 56	59	81	22 55	60	81
98	18 42	59	79	19 41	59	79	20 40	60	79	21 40	59	79	22 39	59	79
100	18 25	+60	77	19 25	+59	77	20 24	+59	77	21 23	+60	77	22 23	+59	77
102	18 09	59	75	19 08	60	75	20 08	59	75	21 07	59	75	22 06	60	75
104	17 53	59	73	18 52	60	73	19 52	59	73	20 51	59	73	21 50	60	73
106	17 37	59	71	18 36	60	71	19 36	59	71	20 35	60	71	21 35	59	71
108	17 21	60	69	18 21	59	69	19 20	60	69	20 20	59	69	21 19	59	69
110	17 06	+59	68	18 05	+60	67	19 05	+59	67	20 04	+59	67	21 03	+60	67
112	16 50	60	66	17 50	59	65	18 49	60	65	19 49	59	65	20 48	60	65
114	16 35	60	64	17 35	59	64	18 34	60	63	19 34	59	63	20 33	60	63
116	16 21	59	62	17 20	60	62	18 20	59	61	19 19	59	61	20 18	60	61
118	16 06	59	60	17 05	60	60	18 05	59	59	19 04	60	59	20 04	59	59
120	15 52	+59	58	16 51	+60	58	17 51	+59	57	18 50	+60	57	19 50	+59	57
122	15 38	59	56	16 37	60	56	17 37	59	56	18 36	60	56	19 36	59	55
124	15 24	60	54	16 24	59	54	17 23	60	54	18 23	59	54	19 22	60	53
126	15 11	59	52	16 10	60	52	17 10	59	52	18 09	60	52	19 09	60	52
128	14 58	59	50	15 57	60	50	16 57	60	50	17 57	59	50	18 56	60	50
130	14 45	+60	48	15 45	+59	48	16 44	+60	48	17 44	+60	48	18 44	+59	48
132	14 33	60	46	15 33	59	46	16 32	60	46	17 32	59	46	18 31	60	46
134	14 21	60	44	15 21	59	44	16 20	60	44	17 20	60	44	18 20	59	44
136	14 10	59	42	15 09	60	42	16 09	60	42	17 09	59	42	18 08	60	42
138	13 59	59	40	14 58	60	40	15 58	60	40	16 58	59	40	17 57	60	40

25° Hc	25° d	25° Z	26° Hc	26° d	26° Z	27° Hc	27° d	27° Z	28° Hc	28° d	28° Z	29° Hc	29° d	29° Z	LHA
° ′	′	°	° ′	′	°	° ′	′	°	° ′	′	°	° ′	′	°	
33 00	+60	180	34 00	+60	180	35 00	+60	180	36 00	+60	180	37 00	+60	180	360
33 00	60	178	34 00	60	178	35 00	60	178	36 00	60	178	37 00	60	178	358
32 59	60	176	33 59	60	176	34 59	60	176	35 59	60	176	36 59	60	176	356
32 57	60	174	33 57	60	174	34 57	60	174	35 57	60	174	36 57	60	173	354
32 55	60	171	33 55	60	171	34 55	60	171	35 55	60	171	36 55	60	171	352
32 52	+60	169	33 52	+60	169	34 52	+60	169	35 52	+60	169	36 52	+60	169	350
32 49	60	167	33 49	60	167	34 49	60	167	35 49	60	167	36 49	60	167	348
32 45	60	165	33 45	60	165	34 45	60	165	35 45	60	165	36 45	59	165	346
32 40	60	163	33 40	60	163	34 40	60	163	35 40	60	163	36 40	60	163	344
32 35	60	161	33 35	60	161	34 35	60	161	35 35	59	160	36 34	60	160	342
32 29	+60	158	33 29	+60	158	34 29	+60	158	35 29	+60	158	36 29	+59	158	340
32 23	59	156	33 22	60	156	34 22	60	156	35 22	60	156	36 22	60	156	338
32 16	59	154	33 15	60	154	34 15	60	154	35 15	60	154	36 15	60	154	336
32 08	60	152	33 08	60	152	34 08	59	152	35 07	60	152	36 07	60	152	334
32 00	60	150	33 00	60	150	34 00	59	150	34 59	60	150	35 59	60	150	332
31 51	+60	148	32 51	+60	148	33 51	+60	148	34 51	+59	148	35 50	+60	147	330
31 42	60	146	32 42	60	146	33 42	59	145	34 41	60	145	35 41	60	145	328
31 32	60	144	32 32	60	143	33 32	60	143	34 32	59	143	35 31	60	143	326
31 22	60	141	32 22	60	141	33 22	59	141	34 21	60	141	35 21	60	141	324
31 12	59	139	32 11	60	139	33 11	60	139	34 11	59	139	35 10	60	139	322
31 00	+60	137	32 00	+60	137	33 00	+59	137	33 59	+60	137	34 59	+60	137	320
30 49	59	135	31 48	60	135	32 48	60	135	33 48	59	135	34 47	60	135	318
30 37	59	133	31 36	60	133	32 36	60	133	33 36	59	133	34 35	60	132	316
30 24	60	131	31 24	60	131	32 24	59	131	33 23	60	131	34 23	59	130	314
30 12	59	129	31 11	60	129	32 11	59	129	33 10	60	128	34 10	59	128	312
29 58	+60	127	30 58	+59	127	31 57	+60	126	32 57	+59	126	33 56	+60	126	310
29 45	59	125	30 44	60	125	31 44	59	124	32 43	60	124	33 43	59	124	308
29 31	59	123	30 30	60	122	31 30	59	122	32 29	60	122	33 29	59	122	306
29 17	59	121	30 16	60	120	31 16	59	120	32 15	59	120	33 14	60	120	304
29 02	60	119	30 02	59	118	31 01	59	118	32 00	60	118	33 00	59	118	302
28 47	+60	116	29 47	+59	116	30 46	+60	116	31 46	+59	116	32 45	+59	116	300
28 32	60	114	29 32	59	114	30 31	59	114	31 30	60	114	32 30	59	114	298
28 17	59	112	29 16	60	112	30 16	59	112	31 15	59	112	32 14	60	112	296
28 01	60	110	29 01	59	110	30 00	59	110	30 59	60	110	31 59	59	110	294
27 46	59	108	28 45	59	108	29 44	60	108	30 44	59	108	31 43	59	108	292
27 30	+59	106	28 29	+59	106	29 28	+60	106	30 28	+59	106	31 27	+59	106	290
27 14	59	104	28 13	59	104	29 12	59	104	30 11	60	104	31 11	59	104	288
26 57	60	102	27 57	59	102	28 56	59	102	29 55	59	102	30 54	60	102	286
26 41	59	100	27 40	59	100	28 39	60	100	29 39	59	100	30 38	59	100	284
26 24	60	98	27 24	59	98	28 23	59	98	29 22	60	98	30 22	59	98	282
26 08	+59	96	27 07	+59	96	28 06	+60	96	29 06	+59	96	30 05	+59	96	280
25 51	60	94	26 51	59	94	27 50	59	94	28 49	59	94	29 48	60	94	278
25 35	59	92	26 34	59	92	27 33	59	92	28 32	60	92	29 32	59	92	276
25 18	59	90	26 17	59	90	27 16	60	90	28 16	59	90	29 15	59	90	274
25 01	59	88	26 00	60	88	27 00	59	88	27 59	59	88	28 58	59	88	272
24 44	+60	86	25 44	+59	86	26 43	+59	86	27 42	+60	86	28 42	+59	86	270
24 28	59	84	25 27	59	84	26 26	60	84	27 26	59	84	28 25	59	84	268
24 11	60	82	25 11	59	82	26 10	59	82	27 09	59	82	28 08	60	82	266
23 55	59	80	24 54	59	80	25 53	60	80	26 53	59	80	27 52	59	80	264
23 38	60	78	24 38	59	78	25 37	59	78	26 36	59	78	27 35	60	78	262
23 22	+59	77	24 21	+60	76	25 21	+59	76	26 20	+59	76	27 19	+60	76	260
23 06	59	75	24 05	59	74	25 04	60	74	26 04	59	74	27 03	59	74	258
22 50	59	73	23 49	60	72	24 49	59	72	25 48	59	72	26 47	59	72	256
22 34	59	71	23 33	60	71	24 33	59	70	25 32	59	70	26 31	60	70	254
22 18	60	69	23 18	59	69	24 17	59	68	25 16	60	68	26 16	59	68	252
22 03	+59	67	23 02	+60	67	24 02	+59	66	25 01	+59	66	26 00	+60	66	250
21 48	59	65	22 47	59	65	23 46	60	65	24 46	59	64	25 45	60	64	248
21 33	59	63	22 32	59	63	23 31	60	63	24 31	59	62	25 30	60	62	246
21 18	59	61	22 17	60	61	23 17	59	61	24 16	60	61	25 16	60	60	244
21 03	60	59	22 03	59	59	23 02	60	59	24 02	59	59	25 01	60	59	242
20 49	+60	57	21 49	+59	57	22 48	+60	57	23 48	+59	57	24 47	+60	57	240
20 35	60	55	21 35	59	55	22 34	60	55	23 34	59	55	24 33	60	55	238
20 22	59	53	21 21	60	53	22 21	59	53	23 20	60	53	24 20	59	53	236
20 09	59	51	21 08	60	51	22 08	59	51	23 07	60	51	24 07	59	51	234
19 56	59	49	20 55	60	49	21 55	60	49	22 55	59	49	23 54	60	49	232
19 43	+60	48	20 43	+59	47	21 42	+60	47	22 42	+60	47	23 42	+59	47	230
19 31	60	46	20 31	59	46	21 30	60	45	22 30	60	45	23 30	59	45	228
19 19	60	44	20 19	60	44	21 19	59	44	22 18	60	43	23 18	60	43	226
19 08	60	42	20 08	59	42	21 07	60	42	22 07	60	42	23 07	59	41	224
18 57	60	40	19 57	60	40	20 57	59	40	21 56	60	40	22 56	60	40	222

S. Lat. {LHA greater than 180°....... Zn=180−Z; LHA less than 180°........... Zn=180+Z}

DECLINATION (15°-29°) SAME NAME AS LATITUDE

N. Lat. {LHA greater than 180°....... Zn=Z
{LHA less than 180°.......... Zn=360−Z

DECLINATION (15°-29°) SAME NAME AS LATITUDE

LHA	15° Hc	15° d	15° Z	16° Hc	16° d	16° Z	17° Hc	17° d	17° Z	18° Hc	18° d	18° Z	19° Hc	19° d	19° Z
	° ′	′	°	° ′	′	°	° ′	′	°	° ′	′	°	° ′	′	°
140	08 49	+60	39	09 49	+60	39	10 49	+59	39	11 48	+60	39	12 48	+60	39
142	08 39	60	37	09 39	59	37	10 38	60	37	11 38	60	37	12 38	60	37
144	08 29	60	35	09 29	60	35	10 29	60	35	11 29	59	35	12 28	60	35
146	08 20	60	33	09 20	59	33	10 19	60	33	11 19	60	33	12 19	60	33
148	08 11	60	31	09 11	60	31	10 11	59	31	11 10	60	31	12 10	60	31
150	08 03	+59	29	09 02	+60	29	10 02	+60	29	11 02	+60	29	12 02	+60	29
152	07 55	59	27	08 54	60	27	09 54	60	27	10 54	60	27	11 54	60	27
154	07 47	60	25	08 47	60	25	09 47	60	25	10 47	60	25	11 47	60	25
156	07 40	60	23	08 40	60	23	09 40	60	23	10 40	60	23	11 40	60	23
158	07 34	60	21	08 34	60	21	09 34	60	21	10 34	60	21	11 34	60	21
160	07 28	+60	20	08 28	+60	19	09 28	+60	19	10 28	+60	19	11 28	+60	19
162	07 23	60	18	08 23	60	18	09 23	60	17	10 23	60	17	11 23	60	17
164	07 18	60	16	08 18	60	16	09 18	60	16	10 18	60	16	11 18	60	15
166	07 14	60	14	08 14	60	14	09 14	60	14	10 14	60	14	11 14	60	14
168	07 10	60	12	08 10	60	12	09 10	60	12	10 10	60	12	11 10	60	12
170	07 07	+60	10	08 07	+60	10	09 07	+60	10	10 07	+60	10	11 07	+60	10
172	07 05	60	8	08 05	60	8	09 05	60	8	10 05	60	8	11 05	60	8
174	07 03	60	6	08 03	60	6	09 03	60	6	10 03	60	6	11 03	60	6
176	07 01	60	4	08 01	60	4	09 01	60	4	10 01	60	4	11 01	60	4
178	07 00	60	2	08 00	60	2	09 00	60	2	10 00	60	2	11 00	60	2
180	07 00	+60	0	08 00	+60	0	09 00	+60	0	10 00	+60	0	11 00	+60	0

LHA	20° Hc	20° d	20° Z	21° Hc	21° d	21° Z	22° Hc	22° d	22° Z	23° Hc	23° d	23° Z	24° Hc	24° d	24° Z
	° ′	′	°	° ′	′	°	° ′	′	°	° ′	′	°	° ′	′	°
140	13 48	+60	39	14 48	+59	38	15 47	+60	38	16 47	+60	38	17 47	+60	38
142	13 38	60	37	14 38	59	36	15 37	60	36	16 37	60	36	17 37	60	36
144	13 28	60	35	14 28	60	35	15 28	59	34	16 27	60	34	17 27	60	34
146	13 19	60	33	14 19	59	33	15 18	60	33	16 18	60	32	17 18	60	32
148	13 10	60	31	14 10	60	31	15 10	60	31	16 10	59	31	17 09	60	30
150	13 02	+60	29	14 02	+59	29	15 01	+60	29	16 01	+60	29	17 01	+60	29
152	12 54	60	27	13 54	60	27	14 54	60	27	15 54	59	27	16 53	60	27
154	12 47	60	25	13 47	59	25	14 46	60	25	15 46	60	25	16 46	60	25
156	12 40	60	23	13 40	60	23	14 40	60	23	15 40	59	23	16 39	60	23
158	12 34	59	21	13 33	60	21	14 33	60	21	15 33	60	21	16 33	60	21
160	12 28	+60	19	13 28	+60	19	14 28	+60	19	15 28	+60	19	16 28	+59	19
162	12 23	60	17	13 23	59	17	14 22	60	17	15 22	60	17	16 22	60	17
164	12 18	60	15	13 18	60	15	14 18	60	15	15 18	60	15	16 18	60	15
166	12 14	60	14	13 14	60	13	14 14	60	13	15 14	60	13	16 14	60	13
168	12 10	60	12	13 10	60	12	14 10	60	12	15 10	60	11	16 10	60	11
170	12 07	+60	10	13 07	+60	10	14 07	+60	10	15 07	+60	10	16 07	+60	10
172	12 05	60	8	13 05	59	8	14 04	60	8	15 04	60	8	16 04	60	8
174	12 03	60	6	13 03	60	6	14 03	60	6	15 03	60	6	16 03	60	6
176	12 01	60	4	13 01	60	4	14 01	60	4	15 01	60	4	16 01	60	4
178	12 00	60	2	13 00	60	2	14 00	60	2	15 00	60	2	16 00	60	2
180	12 00	+60	0	13 00	+60	0	14 00	+60	0	15 00	+60	0	16 00	+60	0

LHA	25° Hc	25° d	25° Z	26° Hc	26° d	26° Z	27° Hc	27° d	27° Z	28° Hc	28° d	28° Z	29° Hc	29° d	29° Z	LHA
	° ′	′	°	° ′	′	°	° ′	′	°	° ′	′	°	° ′	′	°	
140	18 47	+59	38	19 46	+60	38	20 46	+60	38	21 46	+60	38	22 46	+59	38	220
142	18 37	59	36	19 36	60	36	20 36	60	36	21 36	60	36	22 36	59	36	218
144	18 27	60	34	19 27	60	34	20 27	59	34	21 26	60	34	22 26	60	34	216
146	18 18	60	32	19 18	59	32	20 17	60	32	21 17	60	32	22 17	60	32	214
148	18 09	60	30	19 09	60	30	20 09	60	30	21 09	59	30	22 08	60	30	212
150	18 01	+60	29	19 01	+60	28	20 01	+59	28	21 00	+60	28	22 00	+60	28	210
152	17 53	60	27	18 53	60	27	19 53	60	26	20 53	60	26	21 53	60	26	208
154	17 46	60	25	18 46	60	25	19 46	60	25	20 46	60	25	21 46	59	24	206
156	17 39	60	23	18 39	60	23	19 39	60	23	20 39	60	23	21 39	60	23	204
158	17 33	60	21	18 33	60	21	19 33	60	21	20 33	60	21	21 33	60	21	202
160	17 27	+60	19	18 27	+60	19	19 27	+60	19	20 27	+60	19	21 27	+60	19	200
162	17 22	60	17	18 22	60	17	19 22	60	17	20 22	60	17	21 22	60	17	198
164	17 18	60	15	18 18	60	15	19 18	59	15	20 17	60	15	21 17	60	15	196
166	17 14	59	13	18 13	60	13	19 13	60	13	20 13	60	13	21 13	60	13	194
168	17 10	60	11	18 10	60	11	19 10	60	11	20 10	60	11	21 10	60	11	192
170	17 07	+60	10	18 07	+60	10	19 07	+60	9	20 07	+60	9	21 07	+60	9	190
172	17 04	60	8	18 04	60	8	19 04	60	8	20 04	60	8	21 04	60	8	188
174	17 03	60	6	18 03	60	6	19 03	60	6	20 03	60	6	21 03	59	6	186
176	17 01	60	4	18 01	60	4	19 01	60	4	20 01	60	4	21 01	60	4	184
178	17 00	60	2	18 00	60	2	19 00	60	2	20 00	60	2	21 00	60	2	182
180	17 00	+60	0	18 00	+60	0	19 00	+60	0	20 00	+60	0	21 00	+60	0	180

15°	16°	17°	18°	19°	20°	21°	22°	23°	24°	25°	26°	27°	28°	29°

S. Lat. {LHA greater than 180°....... Zn=180−Z
{LHA less than 180°.......... Zn=180+Z

DECLINATION (15°-29°) SAME NAME AS LATITUDE

LAT 82°

N. Lat. {LHA greater than 180°....... Zn=Z; LHA less than 180°.......... Zn=360−Z}

DECLINATION (0°-14°) SAME NAME AS LATITUDE

LHA	0° Hc	d	Z	1° Hc	d	Z	2° Hc	d	Z	3° Hc	d	Z	4° Hc	d	Z	LHA
	° ′	′	°	° ′	′	°	° ′	′	°	° ′	′	°	° ′	′	°	
0	07 00	+60	180	08 00	+60	180	09 00	+60	180	10 00	+60	180	11 00	+60	180	360
2	07 00	60	178	08 00	60	178	09 00	60	178	10 00	60	178	11 00	60	178	358
4	06 59	60	176	07 59	60	176	08 59	60	176	09 59	60	176	10 59	60	176	356
6	06 58	60	174	07 58	60	174	08 58	60	174	09 58	60	174	10 58	60	174	354
8	06 56	60	172	07 56	60	172	08 56	60	172	09 56	60	172	10 56	60	172	352
10	06 54	+60	170	07 54	+60	170	08 54	+60	170	09 54	+60	170	10 54	+60	170	350
12	06 51	60	168	07 51	60	168	08 51	60	168	09 51	60	168	10 51	60	168	348
14	06 48	59	166	07 47	60	166	08 47	60	166	09 47	60	166	10 47	60	166	346
16	06 44	60	164	07 44	60	164	08 44	60	164	09 44	60	164	10 44	60	164	344
18	06 39	60	162	07 39	60	162	08 39	60	162	09 39	60	162	10 39	60	162	342
20	06 35	+60	160	07 35	+59	160	08 34	+60	160	09 34	+60	160	10 34	+60	160	340
22	06 29	60	158	07 29	60	158	08 29	60	158	09 29	60	158	10 29	60	158	338
24	06 24	60	156	07 24	59	156	08 23	60	156	09 23	60	156	10 23	60	156	336
26	06 17	60	154	07 17	60	154	08 17	60	154	09 17	60	154	10 17	60	154	334
28	06 11	60	152	07 11	59	152	08 10	60	152	09 10	60	152	10 10	60	152	332
30	06 04	+59	150	07 03	+60	150	08 03	+60	150	09 03	+60	150	10 03	+60	150	330
32	05 56	60	148	06 56	60	148	07 56	60	148	08 56	59	148	09 55	60	148	328
34	05 48	60	146	06 48	60	146	07 48	60	146	08 48	59	146	09 47	60	146	326
36	05 40	59	144	06 39	60	144	07 39	60	144	08 39	60	144	09 39	60	144	324
38	05 31	60	142	06 31	59	142	07 30	60	142	08 30	60	142	09 30	60	142	322
40	05 21	+60	140	06 21	+60	140	07 21	+60	140	08 21	+60	140	09 21	+60	140	320
42	05 12	60	138	06 12	59	138	07 11	60	138	08 11	60	138	09 11	60	138	318
44	05 02	60	136	06 02	59	136	07 01	60	136	08 01	60	136	09 01	60	135	316
46	04 51	60	134	05 51	60	134	06 51	60	134	07 51	59	134	08 50	60	133	314
48	04 41	59	132	05 40	60	132	06 40	60	132	07 40	60	132	08 40	59	131	312
50	04 30	+59	130	05 29	+60	130	06 29	+60	130	07 29	+60	130	08 29	+59	129	310
52	04 18	60	128	05 18	60	128	06 18	59	128	07 17	60	128	08 17	60	127	308
54	04 06	60	126	05 06	60	126	06 06	60	126	07 06	59	126	08 05	60	125	306
56	03 54	60	124	04 54	60	124	05 54	60	124	06 54	59	124	07 53	60	123	304
58	03 42	60	122	04 42	60	122	05 42	59	122	06 41	60	122	07 41	60	121	302
60	03 30	+59	120	04 29	+60	120	05 29	+60	120	06 29	+59	120	07 28	+60	119	300
62	03 17	59	118	04 16	60	118	05 16	60	118	06 16	59	118	07 15	60	117	298
64	03 04	59	116	04 03	60	116	05 03	60	116	06 03	59	116	07 02	60	115	296
66	02 50	60	114	03 50	60	114	04 50	59	114	05 49	60	114	06 49	60	113	294
68	02 37	60	112	03 37	59	112	04 36	60	112	05 36	60	112	06 36	59	111	292
70	02 23	+60	110	03 23	+60	110	04 23	+59	110	05 22	+60	110	06 22	+59	109	290
72	02 09	60	108	03 09	60	108	04 09	59	108	05 08	60	108	06 08	60	107	288
74	01 56	59	106	02 55	60	106	03 55	59	106	04 54	60	106	05 54	59	105	286
76	01 41	60	104	02 41	60	104	03 41	59	104	04 40	60	104	05 40	59	103	284
78	01 27	60	102	02 27	59	102	03 26	60	102	04 26	59	102	05 25	60	101	282
80	01 13	+59	100	02 12	+60	100	03 12	+60	100	04 12	+59	100	05 11	+60	99	280
82	00 58	60	98	01 58	59	98	02 57	60	98	03 57	60	98	04 57	59	97	278
84	00 44	59	96	01 43	60	96	02 43	59	96	03 42	60	96	04 42	60	95	276
86	00 29	60	94	01 29	59	94	02 28	60	94	03 28	59	94	04 27	60	93	274
88	00 15	59	92	01 14	60	92	02 14	59	92	03 13	60	92	04 13	59	91	272
90	00 00	+60	90	01 00	+59	90	01 59	+60	90	02 59	+59	90	03 58	+60	90	270
92	-0 15	60	88	00 45	59	88	01 44	60	88	02 44	60	88	03 44	59	88	268
94	-0 29	59	86	00 30	60	86	01 30	59	86	02 29	60	86	03 29	60	86	266
96	-0 44	60	84	00 16	59	84	01 15	60	84	02 15	59	84	03 14	60	84	264
98	-0 58	59	82	00 01	60	82	01 01	59	82	02 00	60	82	03 00	60	82	262
100	-1 13	+60	80	-0 13	+59	80	00 46	+60	80	01 46	+60	80	02 46	+59	80	260
102	-1 27	59	78	-0 28	60	78	00 32	60	78	01 32	59	78	02 31	60	78	258
104	-1 41	59	76	-0 42	60	76	00 18	59	76	01 17	60	76	02 17	60	76	256
106	-1 56	60	74	-0 56	60	74	00 04	59	74	01 03	60	74	02 03	59	74	254
108	-2 09	59	72	-1 10	60	72	-0 10	59	72	00 49	60	72	01 49	59	72	252
110	-2 23	+59	70	-1 24	+60	70	-0 24	+59	70	00 35	+60	70	01 35	+60	70	250
112	-2 37	60	68	-1 37	59	68	-0 38	60	68	00 22	59	68	01 21	60	68	248
114	-2 50	59	66	-1 51	60	66	-0 51	59	66	00 08	60	66	01 08	60	66	246
116	-3 04	60	64	-2 04	60	64	-1 04	59	64	-0 05	60	64	00 55	59	64	244
118	-3 17	60	62	-2 17	60	62	-1 17	59	62	-0 18	60	62	00 42	59	62	242
120	-3 30	+60	60	-2 30	+60	60	-1 30	+59	60	-0 31	+60	60	00 29	+60	60	240
122	-3 42	60	58	-2 42	59	58	-1 43	60	58	-0 43	60	58	00 17	59	58	238
124	-3 54	59	56	-2 55	60	56	-1 55	60	56	-0 55	59	56	00 04	60	56	236
126	-4 06	59	54	-3 07	60	54	-2 07	60	54	-1 07	59	54	-0 08	60	54	234
128	-4 18	60	52	-3 18	59	52	-2 19	60	52	-1 19	60	52	-0 19	59	52	232
130	-4 30	+60	50	-3 30	+60	50	-2 30	+60	50	-1 30	+59	50	-0 31	+60	50	230
132	-4 41	60	48	-3 41	60	48	-2 41	60	48	-1 41	59	48	-0 42	60	48	228
134	-4 51	59	46	-3 52	60	46	-2 52	60	46	-1 52	60	46	-0 52	59	46	226
136	-5 02	60	44	-4 02	60	44	-3 02	60	44	-2 02	59	44	-1 03	60	44	224
138	-5 12	60	42	-4 12	60	42	-3 12	60	42	-2 12	59	42	-1 13	60	42	222

LHA	5° Hc	d	Z	6° Hc	d	Z	7° Hc	d	Z	8° Hc	d	Z	9° Hc	d	Z	LHA
	° ′	′	°	° ′	′	°	° ′	′	°	° ′	′	°	° ′	′	°	
0	12 00	+60	180	13 00	+60	180	14 00	+60	180	15 00	+60	180	16 00	+60	180	360
2	12 00	60	178	13 00	60	178	14 00	60	178	15 00	60	178	16 00	60	178	358
4	11 59	60	176	12 59	60	176	13 59	60	176	14 59	60	176	15 59	60	176	356
6	11 58	60	174	12 58	60	174	13 58	60	174	14 58	60	174	15 58	60	174	354
8	11 56	60	172	12 56	60	172	13 56	60	172	14 56	60	172	15 56	60	172	352
10	11 54	+60	170	12 54	+60	170	13 54	+60	170	14 54	+60	170	15 54	+59	170	350
12	11 51	60	168	12 51	60	168	13 51	60	168	14 51	60	168	15 51	60	168	348
14	11 47	60	166	12 47	60	166	13 47	60	166	14 47	60	166	15 47	60	166	346
16	11 44	59	164	12 43	60	164	13 43	60	164	14 43	60	164	15 43	60	164	344
18	11 39	60	162	12 39	60	162	13 39	60	162	14 39	60	162	15 39	60	162	342
20	11 34	+60	160	12 34	+60	160	13 34	+60	160	14 34	+60	160	15 34	+60	160	340
22	11 29	60	158	12 29	60	158	13 29	60	158	14 29	60	158	15 29	60	157	338
24	11 23	60	156	12 23	60	156	13 23	60	156	14 23	60	155	15 23	60	155	336
26	11 17	60	154	12 17	60	154	13 17	60	153	14 17	60	153	15 17	59	153	334
28	11 10	60	152	12 10	60	152	13 10	60	151	14 10	60	151	15 10	60	151	332
30	11 03	+60	150	12 03	+60	149	13 03	+60	149	14 03	+60	149	15 03	+59	149	330
32	10 55	60	148	11 55	60	147	12 55	60	147	13 55	60	147	14 55	60	147	328
34	10 47	60	146	11 47	60	145	12 47	60	145	13 47	60	145	14 47	60	145	326
36	10 39	60	143	11 39	59	143	12 38	60	143	13 38	60	143	14 38	60	143	324
38	10 30	60	141	11 30	59	141	12 29	60	141	13 29	60	141	14 29	60	141	322
40	10 21	+59	139	11 20	+60	139	12 20	+60	139	13 20	+60	139	14 20	+60	139	320
42	10 11	60	137	11 11	59	137	12 10	60	137	13 10	60	137	14 10	60	137	318
44	10 01	59	135	11 00	60	135	12 00	60	135	13 00	60	135	14 00	60	135	316
46	09 50	60	133	10 50	60	133	11 50	60	133	12 50	59	133	13 49	60	133	314
48	09 39	60	131	10 39	60	131	11 39	60	131	12 39	59	131	13 38	60	131	312
50	09 28	+60	129	10 28	+60	129	11 28	+59	129	12 27	+60	129	13 27	+60	129	310
52	09 17	60	127	10 17	59	127	11 16	60	127	12 16	60	127	13 16	59	127	308
54	09 05	60	125	10 05	59	125	11 04	60	125	12 04	60	125	13 04	60	125	306
56	08 53	60	123	09 53	59	123	10 52	60	123	11 52	60	123	12 52	59	123	304
58	08 41	59	121	09 40	60	121	10 40	60	121	11 40	59	121	12 39	60	121	302
60	08 28	+60	119	09 28	+59	119	10 27	+60	119	11 27	+60	119	12 27	+59	119	300
62	08 15	60	117	09 15	59	117	10 14	60	117	11 14	60	117	12 14	59	117	298
64	08 02	60	115	09 02	59	115	10 01	60	115	11 01	59	115	12 00	60	115	296
66	07 49	59	113	08 48	60	113	09 48	59	113	10 47	60	113	11 47	60	113	294
68	07 35	60	111	08 35	59	111	09 34	60	111	10 34	60	111	11 34	59	111	292
70	07 21	+60	109	08 21	+60	109	09 21	+59	109	10 20	+60	109	11 20	+59	109	290
72	07 08	59	107	08 07	60	107	09 07	59	107	10 06	60	107	11 06	59	107	288
74	06 53	60	105	07 53	60	105	08 53	59	105	09 52	60	105	10 52	59	105	286
76	06 39	60	103	07 39	59	103	08 38	60	103	09 38	60	103	10 38	59	103	284
78	06 25	60	101	07 25	59	101	08 24	60	101	09 24	59	101	10 23	60	101	282
80	06 11	+59	99	07 10	+60	99	08 10	+59	99	09 09	+60	99	10 09	+59	99	280
82	05 56	60	97	06 56	59	97	07 55	60	97	08 55	59	97	09 54	60	97	278
84	05 42	59	95	06 41	60	95	07 41	59	95	08 40	60	95	09 40	59	95	276
86	05 27	60	93	06 27	59	93	07 26	60	93	08 26	59	93	09 25	60	93	274
88	05 12	60	91	06 12	60	91	07 12	59	91	08 11	60	91	09 11	59	91	272
90	04 58	+59	89	05 57	+60	89	06 57	+59	89	07 56	+60	89	08 56	+60	89	270
92	04 43	60	87	05 43	59	87	06 42	60	87	07 42	59	87	08 41	60	87	268
94	04 29	59	85	05 28	60	85	06 28	59	85	07 27	60	85	08 27	59	85	266
96	04 14	60	83	05 14	59	83	06 13	60	83	07 13	59	83	08 12	60	83	264
98	04 00	59	81	04 59	60	81	05 59	59	81	06 58	60	81	07 58	59	81	262
100	03 45	+60	80	04 45	+59	79	05 44	+60	79	06 44	+59	79	07 43	+60	79	260
102	03 31	59	78	04 30	60	77	05 30	59	77	06 29	60	77	07 29	60	77	258
104	03 17	59	76	04 16	60	75	05 16	59	75	06 15	60	75	07 15	59	75	256
106	03 02	60	74	04 02	60	73	05 02	59	73	06 01	60	73	07 01	59	73	254
108	02 48	60	72	03 48	60	71	04 48	59	71	05 47	60	71	06 47	59	71	252
110	02 35	+59	70	03 34	+60	69	04 34	+60	69	05 34	+59	69	06 33	+60	69	250
112	02 21	60	68	03 21	59	67	04 20	60	67	05 20	60	67	06 20	59	67	248
114	02 08	59	66	03 07	60	65	04 07	60	65	05 07	59	65	06 06	60	65	246
116	01 54	60	64	02 54	60	63	03 54	59	63	04 53	60	63	05 53	60	63	244
118	01 41	60	62	02 41	60	61	03 41	59	61	04 40	60	61	05 40	60	61	242
120	01 29	+59	60	02 28	+60	60	03 28	+60	59	04 28	+59	59	05 27	+60	59	240
122	01 16	60	58	02 16	60	58	03 16	59	57	04 15	60	57	05 15	60	57	238
124	01 04	60	56	02 04	59	56	03 03	60	55	04 03	60	55	05 03	60	55	236
126	00 52	60	54	01 52	59	54	02 51	60	53	03 51	60	53	04 51	60	53	234
128	00 40	60	52	01 40	60	52	02 40	60	52	03 40	59	51	04 39	60	51	232
130	00 29	+60	50	01 29	+60	50	02 29	+59	50	03 28	+60	49	04 28	+60	49	230
132	00 18	60	48	01 18	60	48	02 18	59	48	03 17	60	47	04 17	60	47	228
134	00 07	60	46	01 07	60	46	02 07	60	46	03 07	60	46	04 07	59	45	226
136	-0 03	60	44	00 57	60	44	01 57	60	44	02 57	59	44	03 56	60	44	224
138	-0 13	60	42	00 47	60	42	01 47	60	42	02 47	59	42	03 46	60	42	222

LHA	10° Hc	d	Z	11° Hc	d	Z	12° Hc	d	Z	13° Hc	d	Z	14° Hc	d	Z	LHA
	° ′	′	°	° ′	′	°	° ′	′	°	° ′	′	°	° ′	′	°	
0	17 00	+60	180	18 00	+60	180	19 00	+60	180	20 00	+60	180	21 00	+60	180	360
2	17 00	60	178	18 00	60	178	19 00	60	178	20 00	60	178	21 00	60	178	358
4	16 59	60	176	17 59	60	176	18 59	60	176	19 59	60	176	20 59	60	176	356
6	16 58	60	174	17 58	60	174	18 58	60	174	19 58	60	174	20 58	60	174	354
8	16 56	60	172	17 56	60	172	18 56	60	172	19 56	60	172	20 56	60	172	352
10	16 53	+60	170	17 53	+60	170	18 53	+60	170	19 53	+60	170	20 53	+60	170	350
12	16 51	60	168	17 51	60	168	18 51	60	168	19 51	60	168	20 51	60	168	348
14	16 47	60	166	17 47	60	166	18 47	60	166	19 47	60	166	20 47	60	166	346
16	16 43	60	164	17 43	60	164	18 43	60	164	19 43	60	163	20 43	60	163	344
18	16 39	60	162	17 39	60	161	18 39	60	161	19 39	60	161	20 39	60	161	342
20	16 34	+60	159	17 34	+60	159	18 34	+60	159	19 34	+60	159	20 34	+60	159	340
22	16 29	60	157	17 29	60	157	18 29	59	157	19 28	60	157	20 28	60	157	338
24	16 23	60	155	17 23	60	155	18 23	60	155	19 23	59	155	20 22	60	155	336
26	16 16	60	153	17 16	60	153	18 16	60	153	19 16	60	153	20 16	60	153	334
28	16 10	60	151	17 10	59	151	18 09	60	151	19 09	60	151	20 09	60	151	332
30	16 02	+60	149	17 02	+60	149	18 02	+60	149	19 02	+60	149	20 02	+60	149	330
32	15 55	60	147	16 55	59	147	17 54	60	147	18 54	60	147	19 54	60	147	328
34	15 47	59	145	16 46	60	145	17 46	60	145	18 46	60	145	19 46	60	145	326
36	15 38	60	143	16 38	60	143	17 38	59	143	18 37	60	143	19 37	60	143	324
38	15 29	60	141	16 29	60	141	17 29	59	141	18 28	60	141	19 28	60	141	322
40	15 20	+59	139	16 19	+60	139	17 19	+60	139	18 19	+60	139	19 19	+60	139	320
42	15 10	60	137	16 10	59	137	17 09	60	137	18 09	60	137	19 09	60	137	318
44	15 00	59	135	15 59	60	135	16 59	60	135	17 59	60	135	18 59	59	135	316
46	14 49	60	133	15 49	60	133	16 49	59	133	17 48	60	133	18 48	60	133	314
48	14 38	60	131	15 38	60	131	16 38	59	131	17 37	60	131	18 37	60	131	312
50	14 27	+60	129	15 27	+59	129	16 26	+60	129	17 26	+60	129	18 26	+59	128	310
52	14 15	60	127	15 15	60	127	16 15	59	127	17 14	60	127	18 14	60	126	308
54	14 04	59	125	15 03	60	125	16 03	60	125	17 03	59	125	18 02	60	124	306
56	13 51	60	123	14 51	60	123	15 51	59	123	16 50	60	122	17 50	60	122	304
58	13 39	60	121	14 39	59	121	15 38	60	121	16 38	60	120	17 38	59	120	302
60	13 26	+60	119	14 26	+60	119	15 26	+59	119	16 25	+60	118	17 25	+59	118	300
62	13 13	60	117	14 13	60	117	15 13	59	117	16 12	60	116	17 12	59	116	298
64	13 00	60	115	14 00	59	115	14 59	60	115	15 59	60	114	16 59	59	114	296
66	12 47	59	113	13 46	60	113	14 46	60	113	15 46	59	112	16 45	60	112	294
68	12 33	60	111	13 33	59	111	14 32	60	111	15 32	59	110	16 31	60	110	292
70	12 19	+60	109	13 19	+60	109	14 19	+59	109	15 18	+60	108	16 18	+59	108	290
72	12 05	60	107	13 05	60	107	14 05	59	107	15 04	60	106	16 04	59	106	288
74	11 51	60	105	12 51	59	105	13 50	60	104	14 50	60	104	15 50	59	104	286
76	11 37	60	103	12 37	59	103	13 36	60	102	14 36	59	102	15 35	60	102	284
78	11 23	59	101	12 22	60	101	13 22	59	101	14 21	60	100	15 21	60	100	282
80	11 08	+60	99	12 08	+59	99	13 07	+60	99	14 07	+60	98	15 07	+59	98	280
82	10 54	59	97	11 53	60	97	12 53	60	97	13 53	59	96	14 52	60	96	278
84	10 39	60	95	11 39	59	95	12 38	60	95	13 38	60	94	14 38	59	94	276
86	10 25	59	93	11 24	60	93	12 24	59	93	13 23	60	92	14 23	59	92	274
88	10 10	60	91	11 10	59	91	12 09	60	91	13 09	59	90	14 08	60	90	272
90	09 56	+59	89	10 55	+60	89	11 55	+59	89	12 54	+60	88	13 54	+59	88	270
92	09 41	59	87	10 40	60	87	11 40	60	87	12 40	59	86	13 39	60	86	268
94	09 26	60	85	10 26	59	85	11 25	60	85	12 25	59	84	13 24	60	84	266
96	09 12	59	83	10 11	60	83	11 11	59	83	12 10	60	82	13 10	59	82	264
98	08 57	60	81	09 57	59	81	10 56	60	81	11 56	60	81	12 56	59	80	262
100	08 43	+59	79	09 42	+60	79	10 42	+60	79	11 42	+59	79	12 41	+60	78	260
102	08 29	59	77	09 28	60	77	10 28	59	77	11 27	60	77	12 27	59	76	258
104	08 14	60	75	09 14	60	75	10 14	59	75	11 13	60	75	12 13	59	74	256
106	08 00	60	73	09 00	60	73	10 00	59	73	10 59	60	73	11 59	59	73	254
108	07 46	60	71	08 46	60	71	09 46	59	71	10 45	60	71	11 45	59	71	252
110	07 33	+59	69	08 32	+60	69	09 32	+60	69	10 32	+59	69	11 31	+60	69	250
112	07 19	60	67	08 19	59	67	09 18	60	67	10 18	60	67	11 18	59	67	248
114	07 06	59	65	08 05	60	65	09 05	60	65	10 05	59	65	11 04	60	65	246
116	06 53	59	63	07 52	60	63	08 52	60	63	09 52	59	63	10 51	60	63	244
118	06 40	59	61	07 39	60	61	08 39	60	61	09 39	59	61	10 38	60	61	242
120	06 27	+60	59	07 27	+59	59	08 26	+60	59	09 26	+60	59	10 26	+59	59	240
122	06 15	59	57	07 14	60	57	08 14	60	57	09 14	59	57	10 13	60	57	238
124	06 03	59	55	07 02	60	55	08 02	60	55	09 02	59	55	10 01	60	55	236
126	05 51	59	53	06 50	60	53	07 50	60	53	08 50	59	53	09 49	60	53	234
128	05 39	60	51	06 39	60	51	07 39	59	51	08 38	60	51	09 38	60	51	232
130	05 28	+60	49	06 28	+59	49	07 27	+60	49	08 27	+60	49	09 27	+60	49	230
132	05 17	60	47	06 17	59	47	07 16	60	47	08 16	60	47	09 16	60	47	228
134	05 06	60	45	06 06	60	45	07 06	60	45	08 06	59	45	09 05	60	45	226
136	04 56	60	43	05 56	60	43	06 56	59	43	07 55	60	43	08 55	60	43	224
138	04 46	60	42	05 46	60	41	06 46	60	41	07 46	59	41	08 45	60	41	222

S. Lat. {LHA greater than 180°....... Zn=180−Z; LHA less than 180°.......... Zn=180+Z}

DECLINATION (0°-14°) SAME NAME AS LATITUDE

N. Lat. {LHA greater than 180°....... Zn=Z; LHA less than 180°.......... Zn=360−Z}

DECLINATION (0°-14°) SAME NAME AS LATITUDE

LHA	0° Hc	d	Z	1° Hc	d	Z	2° Hc	d	Z	3° Hc	d	Z	4° Hc	d	Z	5° Hc	d	Z	6° Hc	d	Z
	° ′	′	°	° ′	′	°	° ′	′	°	° ′	′	°	° ′	′	°	° ′	′	°	° ′	′	°
140	−5 21	+59	40	−4 22	+60	40	−3 22	+60	40	−2 22	+60	40	−1 22	+60	40	−0 22	+59	40	00 37	+60	40
142	−5 31	60	38	−4 31	60	38	−3 31	60	38	−2 31	60	38	−1 31	59	38	−0 32	60	38	00 28	60	38
144	−5 40	60	36	−4 40	60	36	−3 40	60	36	−2 40	60	36	−1 40	60	36	−0 40	60	36	00 20	59	36
146	−5 48	60	34	−4 48	60	34	−3 48	60	34	−2 48	60	34	−1 48	59	34	−0 49	60	34	00 11	60	34
148	−5 56	60	32	−4 56	60	32	−3 56	60	32	−2 56	60	32	−1 56	59	32	−0 57	60	32	00 03	60	32
150	−6 04	+60	30	−5 04	+60	30	−4 04	+60	30	−3 04	+60	30	−2 04	+60	30	−1 04	+60	30	−0 04	+60	30
152	−6 11	60	28	−5 11	60	28	−4 11	60	28	−3 11	60	28	−2 11	60	28	−1 11	60	28	−0 11	60	28
154	−6 17	60	26	−5 17	60	26	−4 17	59	26	−3 18	60	26	−2 18	60	26	−1 18	60	26	−0 18	60	26
156	−6 24	60	24	−5 24	60	24	−4 24	60	24	−3 24	60	24	−2 24	60	24	−1 24	60	24	−0 24	60	24
158	−6 29	60	22	−5 29	60	22	−4 29	60	22	−3 29	59	22	−2 30	60	22	−1 30	60	22	−0 30	60	22
160	−6 35	+60	20	−5 35	+60	20	−4 35	+60	20	−3 35	+60	20	−2 35	+60	20	−1 35	+60	20	−0 35	+60	20
162	−6 39	60	18	−5 39	60	18	−4 39	60	18	−3 39	59	18	−2 40	60	18	−1 40	60	18	−0 40	60	18
164	−6 44	60	16	−5 44	60	16	−4 44	60	16	−3 44	60	16	−2 44	60	16	−1 44	60	16	−0 44	60	16
166	−6 48	60	14	−5 48	60	14	−4 48	60	14	−3 48	60	14	−2 48	60	14	−1 48	60	14	−0 48	60	14
168	−6 51	60	12	−5 51	60	12	−4 51	60	12	−3 51	60	12	−2 51	60	12	−1 51	60	12	−0 51	60	12
170	−6 54	+60	10	−5 54	+60	10	−4 54	+60	10	−3 54	+60	10	−2 54	+60	10	−1 54	+60	10	−0 54	+60	10
172	−6 56	60	8	−5 56	60	8	−4 56	60	8	−3 56	60	8	−2 56	60	8	−1 56	60	8	−0 56	60	8
174	−6 58	60	6	−5 58	60	6	−4 58	60	6	−3 58	60	6	−2 58	60	6	−1 58	60	6	−0 58	60	6
176	−6 59	60	4	−5 59	60	4	−4 59	60	4	−3 59	60	4	−2 59	60	4	−1 59	60	4	−0 59	60	4
178	−7 00	60	2	−6 00	60	2	−5 00	60	2	−4 00	60	2	−3 00	60	2	−2 00	60	2	−1 00	60	2
180	−7 00	+60	0	−6 00	+60	0	−5 00	+60	0	−4 00	+60	0	−3 00	+60	0	−2 00	+60	0	−1 00	+60	0

LHA	7° Hc	d	Z	8° Hc	d	Z	9° Hc	d	Z	10° Hc	d	Z	11° Hc	d	Z	12° Hc	d	Z	13° Hc	d	Z	14° Hc	d	Z	LHA
	° ′	′	°	° ′	′	°	° ′	′	°	° ′	′	°	° ′	′	°	° ′	′	°	° ′	′	°	° ′	′	°	
140	01 37	+60	40	02 37	+60	40	03 37	+60	40	04 37	+60	40	05 37	+59	39	06 36	+60	39	07 36	+60	39	08 36	+60	39	220
142	01 28	60	38	02 28	60	38	03 28	60	38	04 28	60	38	05 28	59	37	06 27	60	37	07 27	60	37	08 27	60	37	218
144	01 19	60	36	02 19	60	36	03 19	60	36	04 19	60	36	05 19	60	35	06 19	60	35	07 19	59	35	08 18	60	35	216
146	01 11	60	34	02 11	60	34	03 11	60	34	04 11	60	34	05 11	59	33	06 10	60	33	07 10	60	33	08 10	60	33	214
148	01 03	60	32	02 03	60	32	03 03	60	32	04 03	60	32	05 03	60	32	06 03	59	31	07 02	60	31	08 02	60	31	212
150	00 56	+60	30	01 56	+59	30	02 55	+60	30	03 55	+60	30	04 55	+60	30	05 55	+60	30	06 55	+60	29	07 55	+60	29	210
152	00 49	60	28	01 49	59	28	02 48	60	28	03 48	60	28	04 48	60	28	05 48	60	28	06 48	60	27	07 48	60	27	208
154	00 42	60	26	01 42	60	26	02 42	60	26	03 42	60	26	04 42	60	26	05 42	60	26	06 42	60	26	07 42	59	25	206
156	00 36	60	24	01 36	60	24	02 36	60	24	03 36	60	24	04 36	60	24	05 36	60	24	06 36	59	24	07 35	60	24	204
158	00 30	60	22	01 30	60	22	02 30	60	22	03 30	60	22	04 30	60	22	05 30	60	22	06 30	60	22	07 30	60	22	202
160	00 25	+60	20	01 25	+60	20	02 25	+60	20	03 25	+60	20	04 25	+60	20	05 25	+60	20	06 25	+60	20	07 25	+60	20	200
162	00 20	60	18	01 20	60	18	02 20	60	18	03 20	60	18	04 20	60	18	05 20	60	18	06 20	60	18	07 20	60	18	198
164	00 16	60	16	01 16	60	16	02 16	60	16	03 16	60	16	04 16	60	16	05 16	60	16	06 16	60	16	07 16	60	16	196
166	00 12	60	14	01 12	60	14	02 12	60	14	03 12	60	14	04 12	60	14	05 12	60	14	06 12	60	14	07 12	60	14	194
168	00 09	60	12	01 09	60	12	02 09	60	12	03 09	60	12	04 09	60	12	05 09	60	12	06 09	60	12	07 09	60	12	192
170	00 06	+60	10	01 06	+60	10	02 06	+60	10	03 06	+60	10	04 06	+60	10	05 06	+60	10	06 06	+60	10	07 06	+60	10	190
172	00 04	60	8	01 04	60	8	02 04	60	8	03 04	60	8	04 04	60	8	05 04	60	8	06 04	60	8	07 04	60	8	188
174	00 02	60	6	01 02	60	6	02 02	60	6	03 02	60	6	04 02	60	6	05 02	60	6	06 02	60	6	07 02	60	6	186
176	00 01	60	4	01 01	60	4	02 01	60	4	03 01	60	4	04 01	60	4	05 01	60	4	06 01	60	4	07 01	60	4	184
178	00 00	60	2	01 00	60	2	02 00	60	2	03 00	60	2	04 00	60	2	05 00	60	2	06 00	60	2	07 00	60	2	182
180	00 00	+60	0	01 00	+60	0	02 00	+60	0	03 00	+60	0	04 00	+60	0	05 00	+60	0	06 00	+60	0	07 00	+60	0	180

0°	1°	2°	3°	4°	5°	6°	7°	8°	9°	10°	11°	12°	13°	14°

S. Lat. {LHA greater than 180°....... Zn=180−Z; LHA less than 180°.......... Zn=180+Z}

DECLINATION (0°-14°) SAME NAME AS LATITUDE

LAT 83°

N. Lat. {LHA greater than 180°....... Zn=Z; LHA less than 180°........... Zn=360−Z}

DECLINATION (0°-14°) CONTRARY NAME TO LATITUDE

LAT 83°

LHA	0° Hc	0° d	0° Z	1° Hc	1° d	1° Z	LHA
	° ′	′	°	° ′	′	°	
180	−7 00	−60	0				180
178	−7 00	60	2				182
176	−6 59	60	4				184
174	−6 58	60	6				186
172	−6 56	60	8				188
170	−6 54	−60	10				190
168	−6 51	50	12				192
166	−6 48	59	14				194
164	−6 44	60	16				196
162	−6 39	60	18				198
160	−6 35	−60	20				200
158	−6 29	60	22				202
156	−6 24	60	24				204
154	−6 17	60	26				206
152	−6 11	60	28	−7 11	59	28	208
150	−6 04	−59	30	−7 03	−60	30	210
148	−5 56	60	32	−6 56	60	32	212
146	−5 48	60	34	−6 48	60	34	214
144	−5 40	59	36	−6 39	60	36	216
142	−5 31	60	38	−6 31	59	38	218
140	−5 21	−60	40	−6 21	−60	40	220

S. Lat. {LHA greater than 180°....... Zn=180−Z; LHA less than 180°........... Zn=180+Z}

DECLINATION (0°-14°) CONTRARY NAME TO LATITUDE

N. Lat. {LHA greater than 180°....... Zn=Z; LHA less than 180°........... Zn=360−Z}

DECLINATION (0°-14°) CONTRARY NAME TO LATITUDE

LHA	0°			1°			2°			3°			4°		
LHA	Hc	d	Z	Hc	d	Z	Hc	d	Z	Hc	d	Z	Hc	d	Z
	° ′	′	°	° ′	′	°	° ′	′	°	° ′	′	°	° ′	′	°
138	-5 12	60	42	-6 12	59	42	-7 11	60	42						
136	-5 02	60	44	-6 02	59	44	-7 01	60	44						
134	-4 51	60	46	-5 51	60	46	-6 51	60	46						
132	-4 41	59	48	-5 40	60	48	-6 40	60	48						
130	-4 30	-59	50	-5 29	-60	50	-6 29	-60	50						
128	-4 18	60	52	-5 18	60	52	-6 18	59	52	-7 17	60	52			
126	-4 06	60	54	-5 06	60	54	-6 06	60	54	-7 06	59	54			
124	-3 54	60	56	-4 54	60	56	-5 54	60	56	-6 54	59	56			
122	-3 42	60	58	-4 42	60	58	-5 42	59	58	-6 41	60	58			
120	-3 30	-59	60	-4 29	-60	60	-5 29	-60	60	-6 29	-59	60			
118	-3 17	59	62	-4 16	60	62	-5 16	60	62	-6 16	59	62	-7 15	60	63
116	-3 04	59	64	-4 03	60	64	-5 03	60	64	-6 03	59	64	-7 02	60	65
114	-2 50	60	66	-3 50	60	66	-4 50	59	66	-5 49	60	66	-6 49	60	67
112	-2 37	60	68	-3 37	59	68	-4 36	60	68	-5 36	60	68	-6 36	59	69
110	-2 23	-60	70	-3 23	-60	70	-4 23	-59	70	-5 22	-60	70	-6 22	-59	71
108	-2 09	60	72	-3 09	60	72	-4 09	59	72	-5 08	60	72	-6 08	60	73
106	-1 56	59	74	-2 55	60	74	-3 55	59	74	-4 54	60	74	-5 54	59	75
104	-1 41	60	76	-2 41	60	76	-3 41	59	76	-4 40	60	76	-5 40	59	77
102	-1 27	60	78	-2 27	59	78	-3 26	60	78	-4 26	59	78	-5 25	60	79
100	-1 13	-59	80	-2 12	-60	80	-3 12	-60	80	-4 12	-59	80	-5 11	-60	81
98	-0 58	60	82	-1 58	59	82	-2 57	60	82	-3 57	60	82	-4 57	59	83
96	-0 44	59	84	-1 43	60	84	-2 43	59	84	-3 42	60	84	-4 42	60	85
94	-0 29	60	86	-1 29	59	86	-2 28	60	86	-3 28	59	86	-4 27	60	87
92	-0 15	59	88	-1 14	60	88	-2 14	59	88	-3 13	60	88	-4 13	59	89
90	00 00	-60	90	-1 00	-59	90	-1 59	-60	90	-2 59	-59	90	-3 58	-60	90
88	00 15	60	92	-0 45	59	92	-1 44	60	92	-2 44	60	92	-3 44	59	92
86	00 29	59	94	-0 30	60	94	-1 30	59	94	-2 29	60	94	-3 29	60	94
84	00 44	60	96	-0 16	59	96	-1 15	60	96	-2 15	59	96	-3 14	60	96
82	00 58	59	98	-0 01	60	98	-1 01	59	98	-2 00	60	98	-3 00	60	98
80	01 13	-60	100	00 13	-59	100	-0 46	-60	100	-1 46	-60	100	-2 46	-59	100
78	01 27	59	102	00 28	60	102	-0 32	60	102	-1 32	59	102	-2 31	60	102
76	01 41	59	104	00 42	60	104	-0 18	59	104	-1 17	60	104	-2 17	60	104
74	01 56	60	106	00 56	60	106	-0 04	59	106	-1 03	60	106	-2 03	59	106
72	02 09	59	108	01 10	60	108	00 10	59	108	-0 49	60	108	-1 49	59	108
70	02 23	-59	110	01 24	-60	110	00 24	-59	110	-0 35	-60	110	-1 35	-60	110
68	02 37	60	112	01 37	59	112	00 38	60	112	-0 22	59	112	-1 21	60	112
66	02 50	59	114	01 51	60	114	00 51	59	114	-0 08	60	114	-1 08	60	114
64	03 04	60	116	02 04	60	116	01 04	59	116	00 05	60	116	-0 55	59	116
62	03 17	60	118	02 17	60	118	01 17	59	118	00 18	60	118	-0 42	59	118
60	03 30	-60	120	02 30	-60	120	01 30	-59	120	00 31	-60	120	-0 29	-60	120
58	03 42	60	122	02 42	59	122	01 43	60	122	00 43	60	122	-0 17	59	122
56	03 54	59	124	02 55	60	124	01 55	60	124	00 55	59	124	-0 04	60	124
54	04 06	59	126	03 07	60	126	02 07	60	126	01 07	59	126	00 08	60	126
52	04 18	60	128	03 18	59	128	02 19	60	128	01 19	60	128	00 19	59	128
50	04 30	-60	130	03 30	-60	130	02 30	-60	130	01 30	-59	130	00 31	-60	130
48	04 41	60	132	03 41	60	132	02 41	60	132	01 41	59	132	00 42	60	132
46	04 51	59	134	03 52	60	134	02 52	60	134	01 52	60	134	00 52	59	134
44	05 02	60	136	04 02	60	136	03 02	60	136	02 02	59	136	01 03	60	136
42	05 12	60	138	04 12	60	138	03 12	60	138	02 12	59	138	01 13	60	138
40	05 21	-59	140	04 22	-60	140	03 22	-60	140	02 22	-60	140	01 22	-60	140
38	05 31	60	142	04 31	60	142	03 31	60	142	02 31	60	142	01 31	59	142
36	05 40	60	144	04 40	60	144	03 40	60	144	02 40	60	144	01 40	60	144
34	05 48	60	146	04 48	60	146	03 48	60	146	02 48	60	146	01 48	59	146
32	05 56	60	148	04 56	60	148	03 56	60	148	02 56	60	148	01 56	59	148
30	06 04	-60	150	05 04	-60	150	04 04	-60	150	03 04	-60	150	02 04	-60	150
28	06 11	60	152	05 11	60	152	04 11	60	152	03 11	60	152	02 11	60	152
26	06 17	60	154	05 17	60	154	04 17	59	154	03 18	60	154	02 18	60	154
24	06 24	60	156	05 24	60	156	04 24	60	156	03 24	60	156	02 24	60	156
22	06 29	60	158	05 29	60	158	04 29	60	158	03 29	59	158	02 30	60	158
20	06 35	-60	160	05 35	-60	160	04 35	-60	160	03 35	-60	160	02 35	-60	160
18	06 39	60	162	05 39	60	162	04 39	60	162	03 39	59	162	02 40	60	162
16	06 44	60	164	05 44	60	164	04 44	60	164	03 44	60	164	02 44	60	164
14	06 48	60	166	05 48	60	166	04 48	60	166	03 48	60	166	02 48	60	166
12	06 51	60	168	05 51	60	168	04 51	60	168	03 51	60	168	02 51	60	168
10	06 54	-60	170	05 54	-60	170	04 54	-60	170	03 54	-60	170	02 54	-60	170
8	06 56	60	172	05 56	60	172	04 56	60	172	03 56	60	172	02 56	60	172
6	06 58	60	174	05 58	60	174	04 58	60	174	03 58	60	174	02 58	60	174
4	06 59	60	176	05 59	60	176	04 59	60	176	03 59	60	176	02 59	60	176
2	07 00	60	178	06 00	60	178	05 00	60	178	04 00	60	178	03 00	60	178
0	07 00	-60	180	06 00	-60	180	05 00	-60	180	04 00	-60	180	03 00	-60	180

LHA	5°			6°			7°			8°			9°		
LHA	Hc	d	Z	Hc	d	Z	Hc	d	Z	Hc	d	Z	Hc	d	Z
	° ′	′	°	° ′	′	°	° ′	′	°	° ′	′	°	° ′	′	°
138															
136															
134															
132															
130															
128															
126															
124															
122															
120															
118															
116															
114															
112															
110	-7 21	-60	71												
108	-7 08	59	73												
106	-6 53	60	75												
104	-6 39	60	77												
102	-6 25	60	79	-7 25	59	79									
100	-6 11	-59	81	-7 10	-60	81									
98	-5 56	60	83	-6 56	59	83									
96	-5 42	59	85	-6 41	60	85									
94	-5 27	60	87	-6 27	59	87	-7 26	60	87						
92	-5 12	60	89	-6 12	60	89	-7 12	59	89						
90	-4 58	-59	91	-5 57	-60	91	-6 57	-59	91						
88	-4 43	60	93	-5 43	59	93	-6 42	60	93						
86	-4 29	59	95	-5 28	60	95	-6 28	59	95	-7 27	59	95			
84	-4 14	60	97	-5 14	59	97	-6 13	60	97	-7 13	59	97			
82	-4 00	59	99	-4 59	60	99	-5 59	59	99	-6 58	60	99			
80	-3 45	-60	100	-4 45	-59	101	-5 44	-60	101	-6 44	-59	101			
78	-3 31	59	102	-4 30	60	103	-5 30	59	103	-6 29	60	103			
76	-3 17	59	104	-4 16	60	105	-5 16	59	105	-6 15	60	105	-7 15	59	105
74	-3 02	60	106	-4 02	60	107	-5 02	59	107	-6 01	60	107	-7 01	59	107
72	-2 48	60	108	-3 48	60	109	-4 48	59	109	-5 47	60	109	-6 47	59	109
70	-2 35	-59	110	-3 34	-60	111	-4 34	-60	111	-5 34	-59	111	-6 33	-60	111
68	-2 21	60	112	-3 21	59	113	-4 20	60	113	-5 20	60	113	-6 20	59	113
66	-2 08	59	114	-3 07	60	115	-4 07	60	115	-5 07	59	115	-6 06	60	115
64	-1 54	60	116	-2 54	60	117	-3 54	59	117	-4 53	60	117	-5 53	60	117
62	-1 41	60	118	-2 41	60	119	-3 41	59	119	-4 40	60	119	-5 40	60	119
60	-1 29	-59	120	-2 28	-60	120	-3 28	-60	121	-4 28	-59	121	-5 27	-60	121
58	-1 16	60	122	-2 16	60	122	-3 16	59	123	-4 15	60	123	-5 15	60	123
56	-1 04	60	124	-2 04	59	124	-3 03	60	125	-4 03	60	125	-5 03	60	125
54	-0 52	60	126	-1 52	59	126	-2 51	60	127	-3 51	60	127	-4 51	60	127
52	-0 40	60	128	-1 40	60	128	-2 40	60	128	-3 40	59	129	-4 39	60	129
50	-0 29	-60	130	-1 29	-60	130	-2 29	-59	130	-3 28	-60	131	-4 28	-60	131
48	-0 18	60	132	-1 18	60	132	-2 18	59	132	-3 17	60	133	-4 17	60	133
46	-0 07	60	134	-1 07	60	134	-2 07	60	134	-3 07	60	134	-4 07	59	135
44	00 03	60	136	-0 57	60	136	-1 57	60	136	-2 57	59	136	-3 56	60	136
42	00 13	60	138	-0 47	60	138	-1 47	60	138	-2 47	59	138	-3 46	60	138
40	00 22	-59	140	-0 37	-60	140	-1 37	-60	140	-2 37	-60	140	-3 37	-60	140
38	00 32	60	142	-0 28	60	142	-1 28	60	142	-2 28	60	142	-3 28	60	142
36	00 40	60	144	-0 20	59	144	-1 19	60	144	-2 19	60	144	-3 19	60	144
34	00 49	60	146	-0 11	60	146	-1 11	60	146	-2 11	60	146	-3 11	60	146
32	00 57	60	148	-0 03	60	148	-1 03	60	148	-2 03	60	148	-3 03	60	148
30	01 04	-60	150	00 04	-60	150	-0 56	-60	150	-1 56	-59	150	-2 55	-60	150
28	01 11	60	152	00 11	60	152	-0 49	60	152	-1 49	59	152	-2 48	60	152
26	01 18	60	154	00 18	60	154	-0 42	60	154	-1 42	60	154	-2 42	60	154
24	01 24	60	156	00 24	60	156	-0 36	60	156	-1 36	60	156	-2 36	60	156
22	01 30	60	158	00 30	60	158	-0 30	60	158	-1 30	60	158	-2 30	60	158
20	01 35	-60	160	00 35	-60	160	-0 25	-60	160	-1 25	-60	160	-2 25	-60	160
18	01 40	60	162	00 40	60	162	-0 20	60	162	-1 20	60	162	-2 20	60	162
16	01 44	60	164	00 44	60	164	-0 16	60	164	-1 16	60	164	-2 16	60	164
14	01 48	60	166	00 48	60	166	-0 12	60	166	-1 12	60	166	-2 12	60	166
12	01 51	60	168	00 51	60	168	-0 09	60	168	-1 09	60	168	-2 09	60	168
10	01 54	-60	170	00 54	-60	170	-0 06	-60	170	-1 06	-60	170	-2 06	-60	170
8	01 56	60	172	00 56	60	172	-0 04	60	172	-1 04	60	172	-2 04	60	172
6	01 58	60	174	00 58	60	174	-0 02	60	174	-1 02	60	174	-2 02	60	174
4	01 59	60	176	00 59	60	176	-0 01	60	176	-1 01	60	176	-2 01	60	176
2	02 00	60	178	01 00	60	178	00 00	60	178	-1 00	60	178	-2 00	60	178
0	02 00	-60	180	01 00	-60	180	00 00	-60	180	-1 00	-60	180	-2 00	-60	180

LHA	10°			11°			12°			13°			14°			LHA
LHA	Hc	d	Z	Hc	d	Z	Hc	d	Z	Hc	d	Z	Hc	d	Z	LHA
	° ′	′	°	° ′	′	°	° ′	′	°	° ′	′	°	° ′	′	°	
138																222
136																224
134																226
132																228
130																230
128																232
126																234
124																236
122																238
120																240
118																242
116																244
114																246
112																248
110																250
108																252
106																254
104																256
102																258
100																260
98																262
96																264
94																266
92																268
90																270
88																272
86																274
84																276
82																278
80																280
78																282
76																284
74																286
72																288
70																290
68	-7 19	60	113													292
66	-7 06	59	115													294
64	-6 53	59	117													296
62	-6 40	59	119													298
60	-6 27	-60	121													300
58	-6 15	59	123	-7 14	60	123										302
56	-6 03	59	125	-7 02	60	125										304
54	-5 51	59	127	-6 50	60	127										306
52	-5 39	60	129	-6 39	60	129										308
50	-5 28	-60	131	-6 28	-59	131										310
48	-5 17	60	133	-6 17	59	133	-7 16	60	133							312
46	-5 06	60	135	-6 06	60	135	-7 06	60	135							314
44	-4 56	60	137	-5 56	60	137	-6 56	59	137							316
42	-4 46	60	138	-5 46	60	139	-6 46	60	139							318
40	-4 37	-60	140	-5 37	-59	141	-6 36	-60	141							320
38	-4 28	60	142	-5 28	59	143	-6 27	60	143							322
36	-4 19	60	144	-5 19	60	145	-6 19	60	145							324
34	-4 11	60	146	-5 11	59	147	-6 10	60	147	-7 10	60	147				326
32	-4 03	60	148	-5 03	60	148	-6 03	59	149	-7 02	60	149				328
30	-3 55	-60	150	-4 55	-60	150	-5 55	-60	150	-6 55	-60	151				330
28	-3 48	60	152	-4 48	60	152	-5 48	60	152	-6 48	60	153				332
26	-3 42	60	154	-4 42	60	154	-5 42	60	154	-6 42	60	154				334
24	-3 36	60	156	-4 36	60	156	-5 36	60	156	-6 36	59	156				336
22	-3 30	60	158	-4 30	60	158	-5 30	60	158	-6 30	60	158				338
20	-3 25	-60	160	-4 25	-60	160	-5 25	-60	160	-6 25	-60	160				340
18	-3 20	60	162	-4 20	60	162	-5 20	60	162	-6 20	60	162				342
16	-3 16	60	164	-4 16	60	164	-5 16	60	164	-6 16	60	164				344
14	-3 12	60	166	-4 12	60	166	-5 12	60	166	-6 12	60	166				346
12	-3 09	60	168	-4 09	60	168	-5 09	60	168	-6 09	60	168				348
10	-3 06	-60	170	-4 06	-60	170	-5 06	-60	170	-6 06	-60	170				350
8	-3 04	60	172	-4 04	60	172	-5 04	60	172	-6 04	60	172				352
6	-3 02	60	174	-4 02	60	174	-5 02	60	174	-6 02	60	174				354
4	-3 01	60	176	-4 01	60	176	-5 01	60	176	-6 01	60	176				356
2	-3 00	60	178	-4 00	60	178	-5 00	60	178	-6 00	60	178	-7 00	60	178	358
0	-3 00	-60	180	-4 00	-60	180	-5 00	-60	180	-6 00	-60	180	-7 00	-60	180	360

S. Lat. {LHA greater than 180°....... Zn=180−Z; LHA less than 180°........... Zn=180+Z}

DECLINATION (0°-14°) CONTRARY NAME TO LATITUDE

N. Lat. {LHA greater than 180°....... Zn=Z; LHA less than 180°........... Zn=360−Z}

DECLINATION (15°-29°) SAME NAME AS LATITUDE

LAT 83°

LHA	15° Hc	15° d	15° Z	16° Hc	16° d	16° Z	17° Hc	17° d	17° Z	18° Hc	18° d	18° Z	19° Hc	19° d	19° Z
	° ′	′	°	° ′	′	°	° ′	′	°	° ′	′	°	° ′	′	°
0	22 00	+60	180	23 00	+60	180	24 00	+60	180	25 00	+60	180	26 00	+60	180
2	22 00	60	178	23 00	60	178	24 00	60	178	25 00	60	178	26 00	60	178
4	21 59	60	176	22 59	60	176	23 59	60	176	24 59	60	176	25 59	60	176
6	21 58	60	174	22 58	60	174	23 58	60	174	24 58	60	174	25 58	60	174
8	21 56	60	172	22 56	60	172	23 56	60	172	24 56	60	172	25 56	60	172
10	21 53	+60	170	22 53	+60	170	23 53	+60	170	24 53	+60	170	25 53	+60	170
12	21 51	59	168	22 50	60	168	23 50	60	167	24 50	60	167	25 50	60	167
14	21 47	60	165	22 47	60	165	23 47	60	165	24 47	60	165	25 47	60	165
16	21 43	60	163	22 43	60	163	23 43	60	163	24 43	60	163	25 43	60	163
18	21 39	60	161	22 39	60	161	23 39	60	161	24 39	60	161	25 39	59	161
20	21 34	+60	159	22 34	+60	159	23 34	+60	159	24 34	+60	159	25 34	+59	159
22	21 28	60	157	22 28	60	157	23 28	60	157	24 28	60	157	25 28	60	157
24	21 22	60	155	22 22	60	155	23 22	60	155	24 22	60	155	25 22	60	155
26	21 16	60	153	22 16	60	153	23 16	60	153	24 16	60	153	25 16	59	153
28	21 09	60	151	22 09	60	151	23 09	60	151	24 09	60	151	25 09	60	151
30	21 02	+60	149	22 02	+60	149	23 02	+59	149	24 01	+60	149	25 01	+60	149
32	20 54	60	147	21 54	60	147	22 54	60	147	23 54	59	147	24 53	60	147
34	20 46	60	145	21 46	59	145	22 45	60	145	23 45	60	145	24 45	60	144
36	20 37	60	143	21 37	60	143	22 37	60	143	23 37	59	142	24 36	60	142
38	20 28	60	141	21 28	60	141	22 28	59	140	23 27	60	140	24 27	60	140
40	20 19	+59	139	21 18	+60	139	22 18	+60	138	23 18	+60	138	24 18	+59	138
42	20 09	59	137	21 08	60	136	22 08	60	136	23 08	60	136	24 08	59	136
44	19 58	60	134	20 58	60	134	21 58	60	134	22 58	59	134	23 57	60	134
46	19 48	60	132	20 48	59	132	21 47	60	132	22 47	60	132	23 47	59	132
48	19 37	60	130	20 37	59	130	21 36	60	130	22 36	60	130	23 36	59	130
50	19 25	+60	128	20 25	+60	128	21 25	+60	128	22 25	+59	128	23 24	+60	128
52	19 14	60	126	20 14	59	126	21 13	60	126	22 13	60	126	23 13	59	126
54	19 02	60	124	20 02	59	124	21 01	60	124	22 01	60	124	23 01	59	124
56	18 50	59	122	19 49	60	122	20 49	60	122	21 49	59	122	22 48	60	122
58	18 37	60	120	19 37	59	120	20 36	60	120	21 36	60	120	22 36	59	120
60	18 24	+60	118	19 24	+60	118	20 24	+59	118	21 23	+60	118	22 23	+59	118
62	18 11	60	116	19 11	60	116	20 11	59	116	21 10	60	116	22 10	59	116
64	17 58	60	114	18 58	59	114	19 57	60	114	20 57	60	114	21 57	59	114
66	17 45	59	112	18 44	60	112	19 44	59	112	20 43	60	112	21 43	60	112
68	17 31	60	110	18 31	59	110	19 30	60	110	20 30	59	110	21 29	60	110
70	17 17	+60	108	18 17	+59	108	19 16	+60	108	20 16	+59	108	21 15	+60	108
72	17 03	60	106	18 03	59	106	19 02	60	106	20 02	59	106	21 01	60	106
74	16 49	60	104	17 49	59	104	18 48	60	104	19 48	59	104	20 47	60	104
76	16 35	59	102	17 34	60	102	18 34	60	102	19 34	59	102	20 33	60	102
78	16 21	59	100	17 20	60	100	18 20	59	100	19 19	60	100	20 19	59	100
80	16 06	+60	98	17 06	+59	98	18 05	+60	98	19 05	+59	98	20 04	+60	98
82	15 52	59	96	16 51	60	96	17 51	59	96	18 50	60	96	19 50	59	96
84	15 37	60	94	16 37	59	94	17 36	60	94	18 36	59	94	19 35	60	94
86	15 22	60	92	16 22	59	92	17 21	60	92	18 21	59	92	19 20	60	92
88	15 08	59	90	16 07	60	90	17 07	59	90	18 06	60	90	19 06	59	90
90	14 53	+60	88	15 53	+59	88	16 52	+60	88	17 52	+59	88	18 51	+60	88
92	14 39	59	86	15 38	60	86	16 38	59	86	17 37	60	86	18 37	59	86
94	14 24	60	84	15 24	59	84	16 23	60	84	17 23	59	84	18 22	60	84
96	14 09	60	82	15 09	60	82	16 09	59	82	17 08	60	82	18 08	59	82
98	13 55	60	80	14 55	59	80	15 54	60	80	16 54	59	80	17 53	60	80
100	13 41	+59	78	14 40	+60	78	15 40	+59	78	16 39	+60	78	17 39	+59	78
102	13 26	60	76	14 26	59	76	15 25	60	76	16 25	60	76	17 25	59	76
104	13 12	60	74	14 12	59	74	15 11	60	74	16 11	59	74	17 10	60	74
106	12 58	60	72	13 58	59	72	14 57	60	72	15 57	59	72	16 56	60	72
108	12 44	60	70	13 44	60	70	14 44	59	70	15 43	60	70	16 43	59	70
110	12 31	+59	68	13 30	+60	68	14 30	+59	68	15 29	+60	68	16 29	+60	68
112	12 17	60	66	13 17	59	66	14 16	60	66	15 16	60	66	16 16	59	66
114	12 04	60	65	13 04	59	64	14 03	60	64	15 03	59	64	16 02	60	64
116	11 51	59	63	12 50	60	62	13 50	60	62	14 50	59	62	15 49	60	62
118	11 38	60	61	12 38	59	60	13 37	60	60	14 37	59	60	15 36	60	60
120	11 25	+60	59	12 25	+60	59	13 25	+59	58	14 24	+60	58	15 24	+60	58
122	11 13	60	57	12 13	59	57	13 12	60	56	14 12	60	56	15 12	59	56
124	11 01	60	55	12 01	59	55	13 00	60	55	14 00	60	54	15 00	59	54
126	10 49	60	53	11 49	60	53	12 49	59	53	13 48	60	52	14 48	60	52
128	10 38	59	51	11 37	60	51	12 37	60	51	13 37	60	51	14 37	59	50
130	10 27	+59	49	11 26	+60	49	12 26	+60	49	13 26	+59	49	14 25	+60	48
132	10 16	59	47	11 15	60	47	12 15	60	47	13 15	60	47	14 15	59	47
134	10 05	60	45	11 05	60	45	12 05	59	45	13 04	60	45	14 04	60	45
136	09 55	60	43	10 55	60	43	11 55	59	43	12 54	60	43	13 54	60	43
138	09 45	60	41	10 45	60	41	11 45	60	41	12 45	59	41	13 44	60	41

LHA	20° Hc	20° d	20° Z	21° Hc	21° d	21° Z	22° Hc	22° d	22° Z	23° Hc	23° d	23° Z	24° Hc	24° d	24° Z
	° ′	′	°	° ′	′	°	° ′	′	°	° ′	′	°	° ′	′	°
0	27 00	+60	180	28 00	+60	180	29 00	+60	180	30 00	+60	180	31 00	+60	180
2	27 00	60	178	28 00	60	178	29 00	60	178	30 00	60	178	31 00	60	178
4	26 59	60	176	27 59	60	176	28 59	60	176	29 59	60	176	30 59	60	176
6	26 58	60	174	27 58	60	174	28 58	60	174	29 58	60	174	30 58	60	174
8	26 56	60	172	27 56	60	172	28 56	60	172	29 56	60	172	30 56	60	172
10	26 53	+60	170	27 53	+60	169	28 53	+60	169	29 53	+60	169	30 53	+60	169
12	26 50	60	167	27 50	60	167	28 50	60	167	29 50	60	167	30 50	60	167
14	26 47	60	165	27 47	60	165	28 47	60	165	29 47	60	165	30 47	60	165
16	26 43	60	163	27 43	60	163	28 43	60	163	29 43	60	163	30 43	60	163
18	26 38	60	161	27 38	60	161	28 38	60	161	29 38	60	161	30 38	60	161
20	26 33	+60	159	27 33	+60	159	28 33	+60	159	29 33	+60	159	30 33	+60	159
22	26 28	60	157	27 28	60	157	28 28	60	157	29 28	60	157	30 28	60	157
24	26 22	60	155	27 22	60	155	28 22	60	155	29 22	60	155	30 22	59	155
26	26 15	60	153	27 15	60	153	28 15	60	153	29 15	60	153	30 15	60	152
28	26 09	59	151	27 08	60	151	28 08	60	150	29 08	60	150	30 08	60	150
30	26 01	+60	149	27 01	+60	148	28 01	+60	148	29 01	+60	148	30 01	+59	148
32	25 53	60	146	26 53	60	146	27 53	60	146	28 53	60	146	29 53	59	146
34	25 45	60	144	26 45	60	144	27 45	59	144	28 44	60	144	29 44	60	144
36	25 36	60	142	26 36	60	142	27 36	60	142	28 36	59	142	29 35	60	142
38	25 27	60	140	26 27	60	140	27 27	59	140	28 26	60	140	29 26	60	140
40	25 17	+60	138	26 17	+60	138	27 17	+60	138	28 17	+60	138	29 17	+59	138
42	25 07	60	136	26 07	60	136	27 07	60	136	28 07	59	136	29 06	60	136
44	24 57	60	134	25 57	60	134	26 57	59	134	27 56	60	134	28 56	60	134
46	24 46	60	132	25 46	60	132	26 46	60	132	27 46	59	132	28 45	60	131
48	24 35	60	130	25 35	60	130	26 35	59	130	27 34	60	130	28 34	60	129
50	24 24	+60	128	25 24	+59	128	26 23	+60	128	27 23	+60	127	28 23	+59	127
52	24 12	60	126	25 12	60	126	26 12	59	126	27 11	60	125	28 11	60	125
54	24 00	60	124	25 00	60	124	26 00	59	123	26 59	60	123	27 59	59	123
56	23 48	60	122	24 48	59	122	25 47	60	121	26 47	59	121	27 46	60	121
58	23 35	60	120	24 35	60	120	25 35	59	119	26 34	60	119	27 34	59	119
60	23 22	+60	118	24 22	+60	117	25 22	+59	117	26 21	+60	117	27 21	+59	117
62	23 09	60	116	24 09	60	115	25 09	59	115	26 08	60	115	27 08	59	115
64	22 56	60	114	23 56	59	113	24 55	60	113	25 55	59	113	26 54	60	113
66	22 43	59	112	23 42	60	111	24 42	59	111	25 41	60	111	26 41	59	111
68	22 29	59	110	23 28	60	109	24 28	60	109	25 28	59	109	26 27	60	109
70	22 15	+60	107	23 15	+59	107	24 14	+60	107	25 14	+59	107	26 13	+60	107
72	22 01	60	105	23 01	59	105	24 00	60	105	25 00	59	105	25 59	60	105
74	21 47	59	103	22 46	60	103	23 46	59	103	24 45	60	103	25 45	59	103
76	21 33	59	101	22 32	60	101	23 32	59	101	24 31	60	101	25 31	59	101
78	21 18	60	99	22 18	59	99	23 17	60	99	24 17	59	99	25 16	60	99
80	21 04	+59	97	22 03	+60	97	23 03	+59	97	24 02	+60	97	25 02	+59	97
82	20 49	60	95	21 49	59	95	22 48	60	95	23 48	59	95	24 47	60	95
84	20 35	59	93	21 34	60	93	22 34	59	93	23 33	60	93	24 33	59	93
86	20 20	59	91	21 19	60	91	22 19	59	91	23 18	60	91	24 18	59	91
88	20 05	60	89	21 05	59	89	22 04	60	89	23 04	59	89	24 03	60	89
90	19 51	+59	88	20 50	+60	87	21 50	+59	87	22 49	+60	87	23 49	+59	87
92	19 36	60	86	20 36	59	85	21 35	60	85	22 35	59	85	23 34	60	85
94	19 22	59	84	20 21	60	83	21 21	59	83	22 20	60	83	23 20	59	83
96	19 07	60	82	20 07	59	81	21 06	60	81	22 06	59	81	23 05	60	81
98	18 53	59	80	19 52	60	79	20 52	59	79	21 51	60	79	22 51	59	79
100	18 38	+60	78	19 38	+59	78	20 37	+60	77	21 37	+59	77	22 36	+60	77
102	18 24	60	76	19 24	59	76	20 23	60	75	21 23	59	75	22 22	60	75
104	18 10	60	74	19 10	59	74	20 09	60	73	21 09	59	73	22 08	60	73
106	17 56	60	72	18 56	59	72	19 55	60	71	20 55	59	71	21 54	60	71
108	17 42	60	70	18 42	59	70	19 41	60	70	20 41	59	69	21 40	60	69
110	17 29	+59	68	18 28	+60	68	19 28	+59	68	20 27	+60	67	21 27	+59	67
112	17 15	60	66	18 15	59	66	19 14	60	66	20 14	59	65	21 13	60	65
114	17 02	60	64	18 02	59	64	19 01	60	64	20 01	59	64	21 00	60	63
116	16 49	60	62	17 49	59	62	18 48	60	62	19 48	59	62	20 47	60	61
118	16 36	60	60	17 36	59	60	18 35	60	60	19 35	60	60	20 35	59	60
120	16 24	+59	58	17 23	+60	58	18 23	+59	58	19 22	+60	58	20 22	+60	58
122	16 11	60	56	17 11	60	56	18 11	59	56	19 10	60	56	20 10	60	56
124	15 59	60	54	16 59	60	54	17 59	59	54	18 58	60	54	19 58	60	54
126	15 48	59	52	16 47	60	52	17 47	60	52	18 47	59	52	19 46	60	52
128	15 36	60	50	16 36	60	50	17 36	59	50	18 35	60	50	19 35	60	50
130	15 25	+60	48	16 25	+60	48	17 25	+59	48	18 24	+60	48	19 24	+60	48
132	15 14	60	46	16 14	60	46	17 14	60	46	18 14	59	46	19 13	60	46
134	15 04	60	44	16 04	59	44	17 03	60	44	18 03	60	44	19 03	60	44
136	14 54	60	43	15 54	59	42	16 53	60	42	17 53	60	42	18 53	60	42
138	14 44	60	41	15 44	60	41	16 44	60	40	17 44	59	40	18 43	60	40

LHA	25° Hc	25° d	25° Z	26° Hc	26° d	26° Z	27° Hc	27° d	27° Z	28° Hc	28° d	28° Z	29° Hc	29° d	29° Z	LHA
	° ′	′	°	° ′	′	°	° ′	′	°	° ′	′	°	° ′	′	°	
0	32 00	+60	180	33 00	+60	180	34 00	+60	180	35 00	+60	180	36 00	+60	180	360
2	32 00	60	178	33 00	60	178	34 00	60	178	35 00	60	178	36 00	60	178	358
4	31 59	60	176	32 59	60	176	33 59	60	176	34 59	60	176	35 59	60	176	356
6	31 58	60	174	32 58	60	174	33 58	60	174	34 58	60	174	35 58	60	174	354
8	31 56	60	172	32 56	60	171	33 56	60	171	34 56	60	171	35 56	60	171	352
10	31 53	+60	169	32 53	+60	169	33 53	+60	169	34 53	+60	169	35 53	+60	169	350
12	31 50	60	167	32 50	60	167	33 50	60	167	34 50	60	167	35 50	60	167	348
14	31 47	60	165	32 47	60	165	33 47	60	165	34 47	60	165	35 47	60	165	346
16	31 43	60	163	32 43	60	163	33 43	60	163	34 43	60	163	35 43	59	163	344
18	31 38	60	161	32 38	60	161	33 38	60	161	34 38	60	161	35 38	60	161	342
20	31 33	+60	159	32 33	+60	159	33 33	+60	159	34 33	+60	159	35 33	+60	158	340
22	31 28	59	157	32 27	60	157	33 27	60	156	34 27	60	156	35 27	60	156	338
24	31 21	60	154	32 21	60	154	33 21	60	154	34 21	60	154	35 21	60	154	336
26	31 15	60	152	32 15	60	152	33 15	60	152	34 15	59	152	35 14	60	152	334
28	31 08	60	150	32 08	60	150	33 08	59	150	34 07	60	150	35 07	60	150	332
30	31 00	+60	148	32 00	+60	148	33 00	+60	148	34 00	+60	148	35 00	+60	148	330
32	30 52	60	146	31 52	60	146	32 52	60	146	33 52	60	146	34 52	60	146	328
34	30 44	60	144	31 44	60	144	32 44	59	144	33 43	60	144	34 43	60	144	326
36	30 35	60	142	31 35	60	142	32 35	60	142	33 35	59	142	34 34	60	141	324
38	30 26	60	140	31 26	59	140	32 25	60	140	33 25	60	139	34 25	60	139	322
40	30 16	+60	138	31 16	+60	138	32 16	+59	137	33 15	+60	137	34 15	+60	137	320
42	30 06	60	136	31 06	60	135	32 06	59	135	33 05	60	135	34 05	60	135	318
44	29 56	59	133	30 55	60	133	31 55	60	133	32 55	60	133	33 55	59	133	316
46	29 45	60	131	30 45	59	131	31 44	60	131	32 44	60	131	33 44	59	131	314
48	29 34	59	129	30 33	60	129	31 33	60	129	32 33	59	129	33 32	60	129	312
50	29 22	+60	127	30 22	+60	127	31 22	+59	127	32 21	+60	127	33 21	+59	127	310
52	29 11	59	125	30 10	60	125	31 10	59	125	32 09	60	125	33 09	60	125	308
54	28 58	60	123	29 58	60	123	30 58	59	123	31 57	60	123	32 57	59	123	306
56	28 46	60	121	29 46	59	121	30 45	60	121	31 45	59	121	32 44	60	121	304
58	28 33	60	119	29 33	99	119	30 32	60	119	31 32	60	119	32 32	59	118	302
60	28 20	+60	117	29 20	+60	117	30 20	+59	117	31 19	+60	117	32 19	+59	116	300
62	28 07	60	115	29 07	59	115	30 06	60	115	31 06	59	114	32 05	60	114	298
64	27 54	59	113	28 53	60	113	29 53	59	113	30 52	60	112	31 52	59	112	296
66	27 40	60	111	28 40	59	111	29 39	60	111	30 39	59	110	31 38	60	110	294
68	27 27	59	109	28 26	60	109	29 26	59	109	30 25	60	108	31 25	59	108	292
70	27 13	+59	107	28 12	+60	107	29 12	+59	106	30 11	+60	106	31 11	+59	106	290
72	26 59	59	105	27 58	60	105	28 58	59	104	29 57	59	104	30 56	60	104	288
74	26 44	60	103	27 44	59	103	28 43	60	102	29 43	59	102	30 42	60	102	286
76	26 30	59	101	27 29	60	101	28 29	59	100	29 28	60	100	30 28	59	100	284
78	26 16	59	99	27 15	60	99	28 15	59	98	29 14	59	98	30 13	60	98	282
80	26 01	+60	97	27 01	+59	97	28 00	+59	96	28 59	+60	96	29 59	+59	96	280
82	25 47	59	95	26 46	59	95	27 45	60	94	28 45	59	94	29 44	60	94	278
84	25 32	59	93	26 31	60	93	27 31	59	92	28 30	60	92	29 30	59	92	276
86	25 17	60	91	26 17	59	91	27 16	60	90	28 16	59	90	29 15	59	90	274
88	25 03	59	89	26 02	60	89	27 02	59	88	28 01	59	88	29 00	60	88	272
90	24 48	+60	87	25 48	+59	87	26 47	+59	86	27 46	+60	86	28 46	+59	86	270
92	24 34	59	85	25 33	59	85	26 32	60	85	27 32	59	84	28 31	60	84	268
94	24 19	59	83	25 18	60	83	26 18	59	83	27 17	60	82	28 17	59	82	266
96	24 05	59	81	25 04	59	81	26 03	60	81	27 03	59	80	28 02	60	80	264
98	23 50	60	79	24 50	59	79	25 49	60	79	26 49	59	78	27 48	59	78	262
100	23 36	+59	77	24 35	+60	77	25 35	+59	77	26 34	+60	77	27 34	+59	76	260
102	23 22	59	75	24 21	60	75	25 21	59	75	26 20	60	75	27 20	59	74	258
104	23 08	59	73	24 07	60	73	25 07	59	73	26 06	60	73	27 06	59	72	256
106	22 54	59	71	23 53	60	71	24 53	59	71	25 52	60	71	26 52	59	71	254
108	22 40	59	69	23 39	60	69	24 39	59	69	25 38	60	69	26 38	59	69	252
110	22 26	+60	67	23 26	+59	67	24 25	+60	67	25 25	+59	67	26 24	+60	67	250
112	22 13	60	65	23 13	59	65	24 12	60	65	25 12	59	65	26 11	60	65	248
114	22 00	59	63	22 59	60	63	23 59	59	63	24 58	60	63	25 58	60	63	246
116	21 47	59	61	22 46	60	61	23 46	60	61	24 46	59	61	25 45	60	61	244
118	21 34	60	59	22 34	59	59	23 33	60	59	24 33	60	59	25 33	59	59	242
120	21 22	+59	57	22 21	+60	57	23 21	+60	57	24 21	+59	57	25 20	+60	57	240
122	21 10	59	56	22 09	60	55	23 09	59	55	24 08	60	55	25 08	60	55	238
124	20 58	59	54	21 57	60	54	22 57	60	53	23 57	59	53	24 56	60	53	236
126	20 46	60	52	21 46	59	52	22 45	60	51	23 45	60	51	24 45	59	51	234
128	20 35	59	50	21 34	60	50	22 34	60	50	23 34	59	49	24 33	60	49	232
130	20 24	+59	48	21 23	+60	48	22 23	+60	48	23 23	+59	48	24 22	+60	47	230
132	20 13	60	46	21 13	59	46	22 12	60	46	23 12	60	46	24 12	60	45	228
134	20 03	59	44	21 02	60	44	22 02	60	44	23 02	60	44	24 02	59	44	226
136	19 53	59	42	20 52	60	42	21 52	60	42	22 52	60	42	23 52	59	42	224
138	19 43	60	40	20 43	60	40	21 43	59	40	22 42	60	40	23 42	60	40	222

15° 16° 17° 18° 19° 20° 21° 22° 23° 24° 25° 26° 27° 28° 29°

S. Lat. {LHA greater than 180°....... Zn=180−Z; LHA less than 180°........... Zn=180+Z}

DECLINATION (15°-29°) SAME NAME AS LATITUDE

LAT 83°

N. Lat. {LHA greater than 180°....... Zn=Z
{LHA less than 180°........... Zn=360−Z

DECLINATION (15°-29°) SAME NAME AS LATITUDE

	15°			16°			17°			18°			19°		
LHA	Hc	d	Z	Hc	d	Z	Hc	d	Z	Hc	d	Z	Hc	d	Z
	° ′	′	°	° ′	′	°	° ′	′	°	° ′	′	°	° ′	′	°
140	09 36	+60	39	10 36	+59	39	11 35	+60	39	12 35	+60	39	13 35	+60	39
142	09 27	60	37	10 27	59	37	11 26	60	37	12 26	60	37	13 26	60	37
144	09 18	60	35	10 18	60	35	11 18	60	35	12 18	60	35	13 18	59	35
146	09 10	60	33	10 10	60	33	11 10	60	33	12 10	59	33	13 09	60	33
148	09 02	60	31	10 02	60	31	11 02	60	31	12 02	60	31	13 02	60	31
150	08 55	+60	29	09 55	+60	29	10 55	+60	29	11 55	+59	29	12 54	+60	29
152	08 48	60	27	09 48	60	27	10 48	60	27	11 48	60	27	12 48	59	27
154	08 41	60	25	09 41	60	25	10 41	60	25	11 41	60	25	12 41	60	25
156	08 35	60	23	09 35	60	23	10 35	60	23	11 35	60	23	12 35	60	23
158	08 30	60	22	09 30	60	21	10 30	60	21	11 30	60	21	12 30	60	21
160	08 25	+60	20	09 25	+60	20	10 25	+60	19	11 25	+59	19	12 24	+60	19
162	08 20	60	18	09 20	60	18	10 20	60	18	11 20	60	17	12 20	60	17
164	08 16	60	16	09 16	60	16	10 16	60	16	11 16	60	16	12 16	60	16
166	08 12	60	14	09 12	60	14	10 12	60	14	11 12	60	14	12 12	60	14
168	08 09	60	12	09 09	60	12	10 09	60	12	11 09	60	12	12 09	60	12
170	08 06	+60	10	09 06	+60	10	10 06	+60	10	11 06	+60	10	12 06	+60	10
172	08 04	60	8	09 04	60	8	10 04	60	8	11 04	60	8	12 04	60	8
174	08 02	60	6	09 02	60	6	10 02	60	6	11 02	60	6	12 02	60	6
176	08 01	60	4	09 01	60	4	10 01	60	4	11 01	60	4	12 01	60	4
178	08 00	60	2	09 00	60	2	10 00	60	2	11 00	60	2	12 00	60	2
180	08 00	+60	0	09 00	+60	0	10 00	+60	0	11 00	+60	0	12 00	+60	0

	20°			21°			22°			23°			24°		
LHA	Hc	d	Z	Hc	d	Z	Hc	d	Z	Hc	d	Z	Hc	d	Z
	° ′	′	°	° ′	′	°	° ′	′	°	° ′	′	°	° ′	′	°
140	14 35	+60	39	15 35	+59	39	16 34	+60	38	17 34	+60	38	18 34	+60	38
142	14 26	60	37	15 26	60	37	16 26	59	37	17 25	60	36	18 25	60	36
144	14 17	60	35	15 17	60	35	16 17	60	35	17 17	60	35	18 17	60	34
146	14 09	60	33	15 09	60	33	16 09	60	33	17 09	60	33	18 09	60	33
148	14 02	59	31	15 01	60	31	16 01	60	31	17 01	60	31	18 01	60	31
150	13 54	+60	29	14 54	+60	29	15 54	+60	29	16 54	+60	29	17 54	+60	29
152	13 47	60	27	14 47	60	27	15 47	60	27	16 47	60	27	17 47	60	27
154	13 41	60	25	14 41	60	25	15 41	60	25	16 41	60	25	17 41	60	25
156	13 35	60	23	14 35	60	23	15 35	60	23	16 35	60	23	17 35	60	23
158	13 30	59	21	14 29	60	21	15 29	60	21	16 29	60	21	17 29	60	21
160	13 24	+60	19	14 24	+60	19	15 24	+60	19	16 24	+60	19	17 24	+60	19
162	13 20	60	17	14 20	60	17	15 20	60	17	16 20	60	17	17 20	60	17
164	13 16	60	15	14 16	60	15	15 16	60	15	16 16	60	15	17 16	60	15
166	13 12	60	14	14 12	60	14	15 12	60	13	16 12	60	13	17 12	60	13
168	13 09	60	12	14 09	60	12	15 09	60	12	16 09	60	12	17 09	60	12
170	13 06	+60	10	14 06	+60	10	15 06	+60	10	16 06	+60	10	17 06	+60	10
172	13 04	60	8	14 04	60	8	15 04	60	8	16 04	60	8	17 04	60	8
174	13 02	60	6	14 02	60	6	15 02	60	6	16 02	60	6	17 02	60	6
176	13 01	60	4	14 01	60	4	15 01	60	4	16 01	60	4	17 01	60	4
178	13 00	60	2	14 00	60	2	15 00	60	2	16 00	60	2	17 00	60	2
180	13 00	+60	0	14 00	+60	0	15 00	+60	0	16 00	+60	0	17 00	+60	0

25°			26°			27°			28°			29°			
Hc	d	Z	Hc	d	Z	Hc	d	Z	Hc	d	Z	Hc	d	Z	LHA
° ′	′	°	° ′	′	°	° ′	′	°	° ′	′	°	° ′	′	°	
19 34	+60	38	20 34	+59	38	21 33	+60	38	22 33	+60	38	23 33	+60	38	220
19 25	60	36	20 25	60	36	21 25	59	36	22 24	60	36	23 24	60	36	218
19 17	59	34	20 16	60	34	21 16	60	34	22 16	60	34	23 16	60	34	216
19 09	59	32	20 08	60	32	21 08	60	32	22 08	60	32	23 08	60	32	214
19 01	60	31	20 01	60	31	21 01	59	30	22 00	60	30	23 00	60	30	212
18 54	+60	29	19 54	+59	29	20 53	+60	29	21 53	+60	28	22 53	+60	28	210
18 47	60	27	19 47	60	27	20 47	60	27	21 47	59	27	22 46	60	26	208
18 41	59	25	19 40	60	25	20 40	60	25	21 40	60	25	22 40	60	25	206
18 35	60	23	19 35	59	23	20 34	60	23	21 34	60	23	22 34	60	23	204
18 29	60	21	19 29	60	21	20 29	60	21	21 29	60	21	22 29	60	21	202
18 24	+60	19	19 24	+60	19	20 24	+60	19	21 24	+68	19	22 24	+60	19	200
18 20	60	17	19 20	60	17	20 20	59	17	21 19	60	17	22 19	60	17	198
18 16	59	15	19 15	60	15	20 15	60	15	21 15	60	15	22 15	60	15	196
18 12	60	13	19 12	60	13	20 12	60	13	21 12	60	13	22 12	60	13	194
18 09	60	11	19 09	60	11	20 09	60	11	21 09	60	11	22 09	60	11	192
18 06	+60	10	19 06	+60	10	20 06	+60	10	21 06	+60	10	22 06	+60	9	190
18 04	60	8	19 04	60	8	20 04	60	8	21 04	60	8	22 04	60	8	188
18 02	60	6	19 02	60	6	20 02	60	6	21 02	60	6	22 02	60	6	186
18 01	60	4	19 01	60	4	20 01	60	4	21 01	60	4	22 01	60	4	184
18 00	60	2	19 00	60	2	20 00	60	2	21 00	60	2	22 00	60	2	182
18 00	+60	0	19 00	+60	0	20 00	+60	0	21 00	+60	0	22 00	+60	0	180

N. Lat. {LHA greater than 180°....... Zn=Z
LHA less than 180°.......... Zn=360−Z}

DECLINATION (0°-14°) SAME NAME AS LATITUDE

LHA	0° Hc	d	Z	1° Hc	d	Z	2° Hc	d	Z	3° Hc	d	Z	4° Hc	d	Z
	° ′	′	°	° ′	′	°	° ′	′	°	° ′	′	°	° ′	′	°
0	06 00	+60	180	07 00	+60	180	08 00	+60	180	09 00	+60	180	10 00	+60	180
2	06 00	60	178	07 00	60	178	08 00	60	178	09 00	60	178	10 00	60	178
4	05 59	60	176	06 59	60	176	07 59	60	176	08 59	60	176	09 59	60	176
6	05 58	60	174	06 58	60	174	07 58	60	174	08 58	60	174	09 58	60	174
8	05 57	60	172	06 57	60	172	07 57	60	172	08 57	60	172	09 57	60	172
10	05 55	+60	170	06 55	+60	170	07 55	+60	170	08 55	+60	170	09 55	+60	170
12	05 52	60	168	06 52	60	168	07 52	60	168	08 52	60	168	09 52	60	168
14	05 49	60	166	06 49	60	166	07 49	60	166	08 49	60	166	09 49	60	166
16	05 46	60	164	06 46	60	164	07 46	60	164	08 46	60	164	09 46	60	164
18	05 42	60	162	06 42	60	162	07 42	60	162	08 42	60	162	09 42	60	162
20	05 38	+60	160	06 38	+60	160	07 38	+60	160	08 38	+60	160	09 38	+60	160
22	05 34	60	158	06 34	60	158	07 34	60	158	08 34	60	158	09 34	60	158
24	05 29	60	156	06 29	60	156	07 29	60	156	08 29	60	156	09 29	60	156
26	05 24	59	154	06 23	60	154	07 23	60	154	08 23	60	154	09 23	60	154
28	05 18	60	152	06 18	60	152	07 18	60	152	08 18	59	152	09 17	60	152
30	05 12	+60	150	06 12	+60	150	07 12	+59	150	08 11	+60	150	09 11	+60	150
32	05 05	60	148	06 05	60	148	07 05	60	148	08 05	60	148	09 05	60	148
34	04 58	60	146	05 58	60	146	06 58	60	146	07 58	60	146	08 58	60	146
36	04 51	60	144	05 51	60	144	06 51	60	144	07 51	60	144	08 51	60	144
38	04 43	60	142	05 43	60	142	06 43	60	142	07 43	60	142	08 43	60	142
40	04 36	+59	140	05 35	+60	140	06 35	+60	140	07 35	+60	140	08 35	+60	140
42	04 27	60	138	05 27	60	138	06 27	60	138	07 27	60	138	08 27	60	138
44	04 19	60	136	05 19	59	136	06 18	60	136	07 18	60	136	08 18	60	136
46	04 10	60	134	05 10	60	134	06 10	59	134	07 09	60	134	08 09	60	134
48	04 01	60	132	05 01	59	132	06 00	60	132	07 00	60	132	08 00	60	132
50	03 51	+60	130	04 51	+60	130	05 51	+60	130	06 51	+59	130	07 50	+60	130
52	03 41	60	128	04 41	60	128	05 41	60	128	06 41	60	128	07 41	59	128
54	03 31	60	126	04 31	60	126	05 31	60	126	06 31	60	126	07 31	59	126
56	03 21	60	124	04 21	60	124	05 21	59	124	06 20	60	124	07 20	60	124
58	03 11	59	122	04 10	60	122	05 10	60	122	06 10	60	122	07 10	59	122
60	03 00	+60	120	04 00	+59	120	04 59	+60	120	05 59	+60	120	06 59	+60	120
62	02 49	59	118	03 48	60	118	04 48	60	118	05 48	60	118	06 48	60	118
64	02 38	59	116	03 37	60	116	04 37	60	116	05 37	60	116	06 37	59	116
66	02 26	60	114	03 26	60	114	04 26	59	114	05 25	60	114	06 25	60	114
68	02 15	59	112	03 14	60	112	04 14	60	112	05 14	60	112	06 14	59	112
70	02 03	+60	110	03 03	+59	110	04 02	+60	110	05 02	+60	110	06 02	+60	110
72	01 51	60	108	02 51	59	108	03 50	60	108	04 50	60	108	05 50	60	108
74	01 39	60	106	02 39	59	106	03 38	60	106	04 38	60	106	05 38	60	106
76	01 27	60	104	02 27	59	104	03 26	60	104	04 26	60	104	05 26	59	104
78	01 15	59	102	02 14	60	102	03 14	60	102	04 14	60	102	05 14	59	102
80	01 02	+60	100	02 02	+60	100	03 02	+59	100	04 01	+60	100	05 01	+60	100
82	00 50	60	98	01 50	59	98	02 49	60	98	03 49	60	98	04 49	59	98
84	00 38	59	96	01 37	60	96	02 37	60	96	03 37	59	96	04 36	60	96
86	00 25	60	94	01 25	59	94	02 24	60	94	03 24	60	94	04 24	59	94
88	00 13	59	92	01 12	60	92	02 12	60	92	03 12	59	92	04 11	60	92
90	00 00	+60	90	01 00	+59	90	01 59	+60	90	02 59	+60	90	03 59	+59	90
92	−0 13	60	88	00 47	60	88	01 47	59	88	02 46	60	88	03 46	60	88
94	−0 25	60	86	00 35	59	86	01 34	60	86	02 34	60	86	03 34	59	86
96	−0 38	60	84	00 22	60	84	01 22	59	84	02 21	60	84	03 21	60	84
98	−0 50	60	82	00 10	59	82	01 09	60	82	02 09	60	82	03 09	59	82
100	−1 02	+59	80	−0 03	+60	80	00 57	+60	80	01 57	+59	80	02 56	+60	80
102	−1 15	60	78	−0 15	60	78	00 45	59	78	01 44	60	78	02 44	60	78
104	−1 27	60	76	−0 27	59	76	00 32	60	76	01 32	60	76	02 32	60	76
106	−1 39	60	74	−0 39	59	74	00 20	60	74	01 20	60	74	02 20	59	74
108	−1 51	60	72	−0 51	59	72	00 08	60	72	01 08	60	72	02 08	59	72
110	−2 03	+60	70	−1 03	+59	70	−0 04	+60	70	00 56	+60	70	01 56	+60	70
112	−2 15	60	68	−1 15	60	68	−0 15	60	68	00 45	59	68	01 44	60	68
114	−2 26	60	66	−1 26	59	66	−0 27	60	66	00 33	60	66	01 33	59	66
116	−2 38	60	64	−1 38	60	64	−0 38	60	64	00 22	59	64	01 21	60	64
118	−2 49	60	62	−1 49	60	62	−0 49	59	62	00 10	60	62	01 10	60	62
120	−3 00	+60	60	−2 00	+60	60	−1 00	+60	60	00 00	+59	60	00 59	+60	60
122	−3 11	60	58	−2 11	60	58	−1 11	60	58	−0 11	60	58	00 49	59	58
124	−3 21	60	56	−2 21	59	56	−1 22	60	56	−0 22	60	56	00 38	60	56
126	−3 31	59	54	−2 32	60	54	−1 32	60	54	−0 32	60	54	00 28	60	54
128	−3 41	59	52	−2 42	60	52	−1 42	60	52	−0 42	60	52	00 18	60	52
130	−3 51	+60	50	−2 51	+59	50	−1 52	+60	50	−0 52	+60	50	00 08	+60	50
132	−4 01	60	48	−3 01	60	48	−2 01	60	48	−1 01	60	48	−0 01	59	48
134	−4 10	60	46	−3 10	60	46	−2 10	60	46	−1 10	60	46	−0 10	59	46
136	−4 19	60	44	−3 19	60	44	−2 19	60	44	−1 19	60	44	−0 19	59	44
138	−4 27	60	42	−3 27	59	42	−2 28	60	42	−1 28	60	42	−0 28	60	42

LHA	5° Hc	d	Z	6° Hc	d	Z	7° Hc	d	Z	8° Hc	d	Z	9° Hc	d	Z
	° ′	′	°	° ′	′	°	° ′	′	°	° ′	′	°	° ′	′	°
0	11 00	+60	180	12 00	+60	180	13 00	+60	180	14 00	+60	180	15 00	+60	180
2	11 00	60	178	12 00	60	178	13 00	60	178	14 00	60	178	15 00	60	178
4	10 59	60	176	11 59	60	176	12 59	60	176	13 59	60	176	14 59	60	176
6	10 58	60	174	11 58	60	174	12 58	60	174	13 58	60	174	14 58	60	174
8	10 57	59	172	11 56	60	172	12 56	60	172	13 56	60	172	14 56	60	172
10	10 55	+60	170	11 55	+59	170	12 54	+60	170	13 54	+60	170	14 54	+60	170
12	10 52	60	168	11 52	60	168	12 52	60	168	13 52	60	168	14 52	60	168
14	10 49	60	166	11 49	60	166	12 49	60	166	13 49	60	166	14 49	60	166
16	10 46	60	164	11 46	60	164	12 46	60	164	13 46	60	164	14 46	60	164
18	10 42	60	162	11 42	60	162	12 42	60	162	13 42	60	162	14 42	60	162
20	10 38	+60	160	11 38	+60	160	12 38	+60	160	13 38	+60	160	14 38	+60	160
22	10 34	59	158	11 33	60	158	12 33	60	158	13 33	60	158	14 33	60	158
24	10 29	59	156	11 28	60	156	12 28	60	156	13 28	60	156	14 28	60	156
26	10 23	60	154	11 23	60	154	12 23	60	154	13 23	60	154	14 23	60	154
28	10 17	60	152	11 17	60	152	12 17	60	152	13 17	60	152	14 17	60	151
30	10 11	+60	150	11 11	+60	150	12 11	+60	150	13 11	+60	149	14 11	+60	149
32	10 05	60	148	11 05	60	148	12 05	59	148	13 04	60	147	14 04	60	147
34	09 58	60	146	10 58	60	146	11 58	59	145	12 57	60	145	13 57	60	145
36	09 51	59	144	10 50	60	144	11 50	60	143	12 50	60	143	13 50	60	143
38	09 43	60	142	10 43	60	142	11 43	60	141	12 43	59	141	13 42	60	141
40	09 35	+60	140	10 35	+60	139	11 35	+60	139	12 35	+59	139	13 34	+60	139
42	09 27	59	138	10 26	60	137	11 26	60	137	12 26	60	137	13 26	60	137
44	09 18	60	136	10 18	60	135	11 18	59	135	12 17	60	135	13 17	60	135
46	09 09	60	134	10 09	60	133	11 09	60	133	12 09	59	133	13 08	60	133
48	09 00	60	132	10 00	59	131	10 59	60	131	11 59	60	131	12 59	60	131
50	08 50	+60	129	09 50	+60	129	10 50	+60	129	11 50	+59	129	12 49	+60	129
52	08 40	60	127	09 40	60	127	10 40	60	127	11 40	60	127	12 40	59	127
54	08 30	60	125	09 30	60	125	10 30	60	125	11 30	59	125	12 29	60	125
56	08 20	60	123	09 20	60	123	10 20	59	123	11 19	60	123	12 19	60	123
58	08 09	60	121	09 09	60	121	10 09	60	121	11 09	59	121	12 08	60	121
60	07 59	+59	119	08 58	+60	119	09 58	+60	119	10 58	+60	119	11 58	+59	119
62	07 48	59	117	08 47	60	117	09 47	60	117	10 47	59	117	11 46	60	117
64	07 36	60	115	08 36	60	115	09 36	59	115	10 35	60	115	11 35	60	115
66	07 25	60	113	08 25	59	113	09 24	60	113	10 24	60	113	11 24	59	113
68	07 13	60	111	08 13	60	111	09 13	59	111	10 12	60	111	11 12	60	111
70	07 02	+59	109	08 01	+60	109	09 01	+60	109	10 01	+59	109	11 00	+60	109
72	06 50	59	107	07 49	60	107	08 49	60	107	09 49	59	107	10 48	60	107
74	06 38	59	105	07 37	60	105	08 37	60	105	09 37	59	105	10 36	60	105
76	06 25	60	103	07 25	60	103	08 25	59	103	09 24	60	103	10 24	60	103
78	06 13	60	101	07 13	60	101	08 13	59	101	09 12	60	101	10 12	60	101
80	06 01	+60	99	07 01	+59	99	08 00	+60	99	09 00	+60	99	10 00	+59	99
82	05 48	60	97	06 48	60	97	07 48	59	97	08 47	60	97	09 47	60	97
84	05 36	60	95	06 36	59	95	07 35	60	95	08 35	60	95	09 35	59	95
86	05 23	60	94	06 23	60	93	07 23	59	93	08 22	60	93	09 22	60	93
88	05 11	60	92	06 11	59	91	07 10	60	91	08 10	60	91	09 10	59	91
90	04 58	+60	90	05 58	+60	89	06 58	+59	89	07 57	+60	89	08 57	+60	89
92	04 46	60	88	05 46	59	87	06 45	60	87	07 45	60	87	08 45	59	87
94	04 33	60	86	05 33	60	85	06 33	59	85	07 32	60	85	08 32	60	85
96	04 21	60	84	05 21	59	83	06 20	60	83	07 20	60	83	08 20	59	83
98	04 08	60	82	05 08	60	81	06 08	59	81	07 07	60	81	08 07	60	81
100	03 56	+60	80	04 56	+59	80	05 55	+60	79	06 55	+60	79	07 55	+59	79
102	03 44	59	78	04 43	60	78	05 43	60	77	06 43	59	77	07 42	60	77
104	03 32	59	76	04 31	60	76	05 31	60	75	06 31	59	75	07 30	60	75
106	03 19	60	74	04 19	60	74	05 19	60	73	06 19	59	73	07 18	60	73
108	03 07	60	72	04 07	60	72	05 07	60	71	06 07	59	71	07 06	60	71
110	02 56	+59	70	03 55	+60	70	04 55	+60	69	05 55	+59	69	06 54	+60	69
112	02 44	60	68	03 44	59	68	04 43	60	67	05 43	60	67	06 43	60	67
114	02 32	60	66	03 32	60	66	04 32	60	65	05 32	59	65	06 31	60	65
116	02 21	60	64	03 21	60	64	04 21	59	63	05 20	60	63	06 20	60	63
118	02 10	60	62	03 10	59	62	04 09	60	61	05 09	60	61	06 09	60	61
120	01 59	+60	60	02 59	+60	60	03 59	+59	60	04 58	+60	59	05 58	+60	59
122	01 48	60	58	02 48	60	58	03 48	60	58	04 48	59	57	05 47	60	57
124	01 38	60	56	02 38	59	56	03 37	60	56	04 37	60	55	05 37	60	55
126	01 28	59	54	02 27	60	54	03 27	60	54	04 27	60	53	05 27	60	53
128	01 18	59	52	02 17	60	52	03 17	60	52	04 17	60	51	05 17	60	51
130	01 08	+60	50	02 08	+59	50	03 07	+60	50	04 07	+60	49	05 07	+60	49
132	00 58	60	48	01 58	60	48	02 58	60	48	03 58	60	47	04 58	60	47
134	00 49	60	46	01 49	60	46	02 49	60	46	03 49	60	45	04 49	60	45
136	00 40	60	44	01 40	60	44	02 40	60	44	03 40	60	43	04 40	60	43
138	00 32	60	42	01 32	60	42	02 32	60	42	03 32	59	41	04 31	60	42

LHA	10° Hc	d	Z	11° Hc	d	Z	12° Hc	d	Z	13° Hc	d	Z	14° Hc	d	Z	LHA
	° ′	′	°	° ′	′	°	° ′	′	°	° ′	′	°	° ′	′	°	
0	16 00	+60	180	17 00	+60	180	18 00	+60	180	19 00	+60	180	20 00	+60	180	360
2	16 00	60	178	17 00	60	178	18 00	60	178	19 00	60	178	20 00	60	178	358
4	15 59	60	176	16 59	60	176	17 59	60	176	18 59	60	176	19 59	60	176	356
6	15 58	60	174	16 58	60	174	17 58	60	174	18 58	60	174	19 58	60	174	354
8	15 56	60	172	16 56	60	172	17 56	60	172	18 56	60	172	19 56	60	172	352
10	15 54	+60	170	16 54	+60	170	17 54	+60	170	18 54	+60	170	19 54	+60	170	350
12	15 52	60	168	16 52	60	168	17 52	60	168	18 52	60	168	19 52	60	168	348
14	15 49	60	166	16 49	60	166	17 49	60	166	18 49	60	166	19 49	60	166	346
16	15 46	60	164	16 46	60	164	17 46	60	164	18 46	60	164	19 46	60	164	344
18	15 42	60	162	16 42	60	162	17 42	60	162	18 42	60	162	19 42	60	161	342
20	15 38	+60	160	16 38	+60	160	17 38	+60	159	18 38	+60	159	19 38	+60	159	340
22	15 33	60	158	16 33	60	157	17 33	60	157	18 33	60	157	19 33	60	157	338
24	15 28	60	155	16 28	60	155	17 28	60	155	18 28	60	155	19 28	60	155	336
26	15 23	60	153	16 23	60	153	17 23	60	153	18 23	60	153	19 23	60	153	334
28	15 17	60	151	16 17	60	151	17 17	60	151	18 17	60	151	19 17	60	151	332
30	15 11	+60	149	16 11	+60	149	17 11	+60	149	18 11	+59	149	19 10	+60	149	330
32	15 04	60	147	16 04	60	147	17 04	60	147	18 04	60	147	19 04	60	147	328
34	14 57	60	145	15 57	60	145	16 57	60	145	17 57	60	145	18 57	60	145	326
36	14 50	60	143	15 50	60	143	16 50	60	143	17 50	59	143	18 49	60	143	324
38	14 42	60	141	15 42	60	141	16 42	60	141	17 42	60	141	18 42	60	141	322
40	14 34	+60	139	15 34	+60	139	16 34	+60	139	17 34	+60	139	18 34	+59	139	320
42	14 26	60	137	15 26	60	137	16 26	59	137	17 25	60	137	18 25	60	137	318
44	14 17	60	135	15 17	60	135	16 17	60	135	17 17	59	135	18 16	60	135	316
46	14 08	60	133	15 08	60	133	16 08	60	133	17 08	59	133	18 07	60	133	314
48	13 59	60	131	14 59	59	131	15 58	60	131	16 58	60	131	17 58	60	131	312
50	13 49	+60	129	14 49	+60	129	15 49	+60	129	16 49	+59	129	17 48	+60	129	310
52	13 39	60	127	14 39	60	127	15 39	60	127	16 39	59	127	17 38	60	127	308
54	13 29	60	125	14 29	60	125	15 29	60	125	16 29	59	125	17 28	60	125	306
56	13 19	60	123	14 19	59	123	15 18	60	123	16 18	60	123	17 18	60	123	304
58	13 08	60	121	14 08	60	121	15 08	59	121	16 07	60	121	17 07	60	121	302
60	12 57	+60	119	13 57	+60	119	14 57	+59	119	15 56	+60	119	16 56	+60	119	300
62	12 46	60	117	13 46	60	117	14 46	59	117	15 45	60	117	16 45	60	117	298
64	12 35	60	115	13 35	59	115	14 34	60	115	15 34	60	115	16 34	59	115	296
66	12 23	60	113	13 23	60	113	14 23	60	113	15 23	59	113	16 22	60	113	294
68	12 12	60	111	13 12	59	111	14 11	60	111	15 11	60	111	16 11	59	111	292
70	12 00	+60	109	13 00	+59	109	13 59	+60	109	14 59	+60	109	15 59	+59	109	290
72	11 48	60	107	12 48	59	107	13 47	60	107	14 47	60	107	15 47	60	107	288
74	11 36	60	105	12 36	59	105	13 35	60	105	14 35	60	105	15 35	59	105	286
76	11 24	60	103	12 24	59	103	13 23	60	103	14 23	60	103	15 23	59	103	284
78	11 12	59	101	12 11	60	101	13 11	60	101	14 11	59	101	15 10	60	101	282
80	10 59	+60	99	11 59	+60	99	12 59	+59	99	13 58	+60	99	14 58	+60	99	280
82	10 47	59	97	11 46	60	97	12 46	60	97	13 46	59	97	14 45	60	97	278
84	10 34	60	95	11 34	60	95	12 34	59	95	13 33	60	95	14 33	60	95	276
86	10 22	59	93	11 21	60	93	12 21	60	93	13 21	59	93	14 20	60	93	274
88	10 09	60	91	11 09	60	91	12 09	59	91	13 08	60	91	14 08	60	91	272
90	09 57	+59	89	10 56	+60	89	11 56	+60	89	12 56	+59	89	13 55	+60	89	270
92	09 44	60	87	10 44	60	87	11 44	59	87	12 43	60	87	13 43	59	87	268
94	09 32	59	85	10 31	60	85	11 31	60	85	12 31	59	85	13 30	60	85	266
96	09 19	60	83	10 19	60	83	11 19	59	83	12 18	60	83	13 18	60	83	264
98	09 07	59	81	10 06	60	81	11 06	60	81	12 06	59	81	13 05	60	81	262
100	08 54	+60	79	09 54	+60	79	10 54	+59	79	11 53	+60	79	12 53	+60	79	260
102	08 42	60	77	09 42	60	77	10 42	59	77	11 41	60	77	12 41	60	77	258
104	08 30	60	75	09 30	59	75	10 29	60	75	11 29	60	75	12 29	59	75	256
106	08 18	60	73	09 18	59	73	10 17	60	73	11 17	60	73	12 17	59	73	254
108	08 06	60	71	09 06	59	71	10 05	60	71	11 05	60	71	12 05	59	71	252
110	07 54	+60	69	08 54	+60	69	09 54	+59	69	10 53	+60	69	11 53	+60	69	250
112	07 43	59	67	08 42	60	67	09 42	60	67	10 42	59	67	11 41	60	67	248
114	07 31	60	65	08 31	60	65	09 31	59	65	10 30	60	65	11 30	60	65	246
116	07 20	60	63	08 20	59	63	09 19	60	63	10 19	60	63	11 19	59	63	244
118	07 09	59	61	08 08	60	61	09 08	60	61	10 08	60	61	11 08	59	61	242
120	06 58	+60	59	07 58	+59	59	08 57	+60	59	09 57	+60	59	10 57	+60	59	240
122	06 47	60	57	07 47	60	57	08 47	59	57	09 46	60	57	10 46	60	57	238
124	06 37	59	55	07 36	60	55	08 36	60	55	09 36	60	55	10 36	60	55	236
126	06 27	59	53	07 26	60	53	08 26	60	53	09 26	60	53	10 26	59	53	234
128	06 17	59	51	07 16	60	51	08 16	60	51	09 16	60	51	10 16	60	51	232
130	06 07	+60	49	07 07	+60	49	08 07	+59	49	09 06	+60	49	10 06	+60	49	230
132	05 58	59	47	06 57	60	47	07 57	60	47	08 57	60	47	09 57	60	47	228
134	05 49	59	45	06 48	60	45	07 48	60	45	08 48	60	45	09 48	60	45	226
136	05 40	60	43	06 40	59	43	07 39	60	43	08 39	60	43	09 39	60	43	224
138	05 31	60	42	06 31	60	41	07 31	60	41	08 31	60	41	09 31	60	41	222

S. Lat. {LHA greater than 180°....... Zn=180−Z
LHA less than 180°.......... Zn=180+Z}

DECLINATION (0°-14°) SAME NAME AS LATITUDE

LAT 84°

N. Lat. {LHA greater than 180°....... Zn=Z; LHA less than 180°........... Zn=360−Z}

DECLINATION (0°-14°) SAME NAME AS LATITUDE

LHA	0° Hc	0° d	0° Z	1° Hc	1° d	1° Z	2° Hc	2° d	2° Z	3° Hc	3° d	3° Z	4° Hc	4° d	4° Z	5° Hc	5° d	5° Z	6° Hc	6° d	6° Z
	° ′	′	°	° ′	′	°	° ′	′	°	° ′	′	°	° ′	′	°	° ′	′	°	° ′	′	°
140	−4 36	+60	40	−3 36	+60	40	−2 36	+60	40	−1 36	+60	40	−0 36	+60	40	00 24	+60	40	01 24	+60	40
142	−4 43	59	38	−3 44	60	38	−2 44	60	38	−1 44	60	38	−0 44	60	38	00 16	60	38	01 16	60	38
144	−4 51	60	36	−3 51	60	36	−2 51	60	36	−1 51	60	36	−0 51	59	36	00 08	60	36	01 08	60	36
146	−4 58	60	34	−3 58	60	34	−2 58	59	34	−1 59	60	34	−0 59	60	34	00 01	60	34	01 01	60	34
148	−5 05	60	32	−4 05	60	32	−3 05	60	32	−2 05	60	32	−1 05	59	32	−0 06	60	32	00 54	60	32
150	−5 12	+60	30	−4 12	+60	30	−3 12	+60	30	−2 12	+60	30	−1 12	+60	30	−0 12	+60	30	00 48	+60	30
152	−5 18	60	28	−4 18	60	28	−3 18	60	28	−2 18	60	28	−1 18	60	28	−0 18	60	28	00 42	60	28
154	−5 24	60	26	−4 24	60	26	−3 24	60	26	−2 24	60	26	−1 24	60	26	−0 24	60	26	00 36	60	26
156	−5 29	60	24	−4 29	60	24	−3 29	60	24	−2 29	60	24	−1 29	60	24	−0 29	60	24	00 31	60	24
158	−5 34	60	22	−4 34	60	22	−3 34	60	22	−2 34	60	22	−1 34	60	22	−0 34	60	22	00 26	60	22
160	−5 38	+60	20	−4 38	+60	20	−3 38	+60	20	−2 38	+60	20	−1 38	+60	20	−0 38	+60	20	00 22	+60	20
162	−5 42	60	18	−4 42	60	18	−3 42	60	18	−2 42	60	18	−1 42	60	18	−0 42	59	18	00 17	60	18
164	−5 46	60	16	−4 46	60	16	−3 46	60	16	−2 46	60	16	−1 46	60	16	−0 46	60	16	00 14	60	16
166	−5 49	60	14	−4 49	60	14	−3 49	60	14	−2 49	60	14	−1 49	60	14	−0 49	60	14	00 11	60	14
168	−5 52	60	12	−4 52	60	12	−3 52	60	12	−2 52	60	12	−1 52	60	12	−0 52	60	12	00 08	60	12
170	−5 55	+60	10	−4 55	+60	10	−3 55	+60	10	−2 55	+60	10	−1 55	+60	10	−0 55	+60	10	00 05	+60	10
172	−5 57	60	8	−4 57	60	8	−3 57	60	8	−2 57	60	8	−1 57	60	8	−0 57	60	8	00 03	60	8
174	−5 58	60	6	−4 58	60	6	−3 58	60	6	−2 58	60	6	−1 58	60	6	−0 58	60	6	00 02	60	6
176	−5 59	60	4	−4 59	60	4	−3 59	60	4	−2 59	60	4	−1 59	60	4	−0 59	60	4	00 01	60	4
178	−6 00	60	2	−5 00	60	2	−4 00	60	2	−3 00	60	2	−2 00	60	2	−1 00	60	2	00 00	60	2
180	−6 00	+60	0	−5 00	+60	0	−4 00	+60	0	−3 00	+60	0	−2 00	+60	0	−1 00	+60	0	00 00	+60	0

7° Hc	7° d	7° Z	8° Hc	8° d	8° Z	9° Hc	9° d	9° Z	10° Hc	10° d	10° Z	11° Hc	11° d	11° Z	12° Hc	12° d	12° Z	13° Hc	13° d	13° Z	14° Hc	14° d	14° Z	LHA
° ′	′	°	° ′	′	°	° ′	′	°	° ′	′	°	° ′	′	°	° ′	′	°	° ′	′	°	° ′	′	°	
02 24	+59	40	03 23	+60	40	04 23	+60	40	05 23	+60	40	06 23	+60	39	07 23	+60	39	08 23	+60	39	09 23	+59	39	220
02 16	60	38	03 16	59	38	04 15	60	38	05 15	60	38	06 15	60	37	07 15	60	37	08 15	60	37	09 15	60	37	218
02 08	60	36	03 08	60	36	04 08	60	36	05 08	60	36	06 08	60	36	07 08	60	35	08 08	59	35	09 07	60	35	216
02 01	60	34	03 01	60	34	04 01	60	34	05 01	60	34	06 01	60	34	07 01	59	33	08 00	60	33	09 00	60	33	214
01 54	60	32	02 54	60	32	03 54	60	32	04 54	60	32	05 54	60	32	06 54	60	32	07 54	60	31	08 54	60	31	212
01 48	+60	30	02 48	+60	30	03 48	+60	30	04 48	+60	30	05 48	+59	30	06 47	+60	30	07 47	+60	30	08 47	+60	29	210
01 42	60	28	02 42	60	28	03 42	60	28	04 42	60	28	05 42	59	28	06 41	60	28	07 41	60	28	08 41	60	27	208
01 36	60	26	02 36	60	26	03 36	60	26	04 36	60	26	05 36	60	26	06 36	60	26	07 36	60	26	08 36	60	26	206
01 31	60	24	02 31	60	24	03 31	60	24	04 31	60	24	05 31	60	24	06 31	60	24	07 31	60	24	08 31	59	24	204
01 26	60	22	02 26	60	22	03 26	60	22	04 26	60	22	05 26	60	22	06 26	60	22	07 26	60	22	08 26	60	22	202
01 22	+59	20	02 21	+60	20	03 21	+60	20	04 21	+60	20	05 21	+60	20	06 21	+60	20	07 21	+60	20	08 21	+60	20	200
01 17	60	18	02 17	60	18	03 17	60	18	04 17	60	18	05 17	60	18	06 17	60	18	07 17	60	18	08 17	60	18	198
01 14	60	16	02 14	60	16	03 14	60	16	04 14	60	16	05 14	60	16	06 14	60	16	07 14	60	16	08 14	60	16	196
01 11	60	14	02 11	60	14	03 11	60	14	04 11	60	14	05 11	60	14	06 11	60	14	07 11	60	14	08 11	59	14	194
01 08	60	12	02 08	60	12	03 08	60	12	04 08	60	12	05 08	60	12	06 08	60	12	07 08	60	12	08 08	60	12	192
01 05	+60	10	02 05	+60	10	03 05	+60	10	04 05	+60	10	05 05	+60	10	06 05	+60	10	07 05	+60	10	08 05	+60	10	190
01 03	60	8	02 03	60	8	03 03	60	8	04 03	60	8	05 03	60	8	06 03	60	8	07 03	60	8	08 03	60	8	188
01 02	60	6	02 02	60	6	03 02	60	6	04 02	60	6	05 02	60	6	06 02	60	6	07 02	60	6	08 02	60	6	186
01 01	60	4	02 01	60	4	03 01	60	4	04 01	60	4	05 01	60	4	06 01	60	4	07 01	60	4	08 01	60	4	184
01 00	60	2	02 00	60	2	03 00	60	2	04 00	60	2	05 00	60	2	06 00	60	2	07 00	60	2	08 00	60	2	182
01 00	+60	0	02 00	+60	0	03 00	+60	0	04 00	+60	0	05 00	+60	0	06 00	+60	0	07 00	+60	0	08 00	+60	0	180

0°	1°	2°	3°	4°	5°	6°	7°	8°	9°	10°	11°	12°	13°	14°

S. Lat. {LHA greater than 180°....... Zn=180−Z; LHA less than 180°........... Zn=180+Z}

DECLINATION (0°-14°) SAME NAME AS LATITUDE

N. Lat. {LHA greater than 180°....... Zn=Z; LHA less than 180°........... Zn=360−Z}

DECLINATION (0°-14°) CONTRARY NAME TO LATITUDE

LHA	0° Hc	0° d	0° Z	1° Hc	1° d	1° Z	2° Hc	2° d	2° Z	LHA
	° ′	′	°	° ′	′	°	° ′	′	°	
180	−6 00	−60	0	−7 00	−60	0				180
178	−6 00	60	2	−7 00	60	2				182
176	−5 59	60	4	−6 59	60	4				184
174	−5 58	60	6	−6 58	60	6				186
172	−5 57	60	8	−6 57	60	8				188
170	−5 55	−60	10	−6 55	−60	10				190
168	−5 52	60	12	−6 52	60	12				192
166	−5 49	60	14	−6 49	60	14				194
164	−5 46	60	16	−6 46	60	16				196
162	−5 42	60	18	−6 42	60	18				198
160	−5 38	−60	20	−6 38	−60	20				200
158	−5 34	60	22	−6 34	60	22				202
156	−5 29	60	24	−6 29	60	24				204
154	−5 24	59	26	−6 23	60	26				206
152	−5 18	60	28	−6 18	60	28				208
150	−5 12	−60	30	−6 12	−60	30	−7 12	−59	30	210
148	−5 05	60	32	−6 05	60	32	−7 05	60	32	212
146	−4 58	60	34	−5 58	60	34	−6 58	60	34	214
144	−4 51	60	36	−5 51	60	36	−6 51	60	36	216
142	−4 43	60	38	−5 43	60	38	−6 43	60	38	218
140	−4 36	−59	40	−5 35	−60	40	−6 35	−60	40	220

3° Hc	d	Z	4° Hc	d	Z	5° Hc	d	Z	6° Hc	d	Z	7° Hc	d	Z	8° Hc	d	Z	9° Hc	d	Z	10° Hc	d	Z	11° Hc	d	Z	12° Hc	d	Z	13° Hc	d	Z	14° Hc	d	Z
° ′	′	°	° ′	′	°	° ′	′	°	° ′	′	°	° ′	′	°	° ′	′	°	° ′	′	°	° ′	′	°	° ′	′	°	° ′	′	°	° ′	′	°	° ′	′	°

S. Lat. {LHA greater than 180°....... Zn=180−Z; LHA less than 180°........... Zn=180+Z}

DECLINATION (0°-14°) CONTRARY NAME TO LATITUDE

N. Lat. {LHA greater than 180°....... Zn=Z; LHA less than 180°........... Zn=360−Z}

DECLINATION (0°-14°) CONTRARY NAME TO LATITUDE

Each declination column gives Hc (° ′), d (′), Z (°).

LHA	0° Hc d Z	1° Hc d Z	2° Hc d Z	3° Hc d Z	4° Hc d Z	5° Hc d Z	6° Hc d Z	7° Hc d Z	8° Hc d Z	9° Hc d Z	10° Hc d Z	11° Hc d Z	12° Hc d Z	13° Hc d Z	14° Hc d Z	LHA
°	° ′ ′ °	° ′ ′ °	° ′ ′ °	° ′ ′ °	° ′ ′ °	° ′ ′ °	° ′ ′ °	° ′ ′ °	° ′ ′ °	° ′ ′ °	° ′ ′ °	° ′ ′ °	° ′ ′ °	° ′ ′ °	° ′ ′ °	
138	−4 27 60 42	−5 27 60 42	−6 27 60 42	222												
136	−4 19 60 44	−5 19 59 44	−6 18 60 44	224												
134	−4 10 60 46	−5 10 60 46	−6 10 59 46	−7 09 60 46	226											
132	−4 01 60 48	−5 01 59 48	−6 00 60 48	−7 00 60 48	228											
130	−3 51 −60 50	−4 51 −60 50	−5 51 −60 50	−6 51 −59 50	230											
128	−3 41 60 52	−4 41 60 52	−5 41 60 52	−6 41 60 52	232											
126	−3 31 60 54	−4 31 60 54	−5 31 60 54	−6 31 60 54	234											
124	−3 21 60 56	−4 21 60 56	−5 21 59 56	−6 20 60 56	−7 20 60 56	236										
122	−3 11 59 58	−4 10 60 58	−5 10 60 58	−6 10 60 58	−7 10 59 58	238										
120	−3 00 −60 60	−4 00 −59 60	−4 59 −60 60	−5 59 −60 60	−6 59 −60 60	240										
118	−2 49 59 62	−3 48 60 62	−4 48 60 62	−5 48 60 62	−6 48 60 62	242										
116	−2 38 59 64	−3 37 60 64	−4 37 60 64	−5 37 60 64	−6 37 59 64	244										
114	−2 26 60 66	−3 26 60 66	−4 26 59 66	−5 25 60 66	−6 25 60 66	246										
112	−2 15 59 68	−3 14 60 68	−4 14 60 68	−5 14 60 68	−6 14 59 68	−7 13 60 69	248									
110	−2 03 −60 70	−3 03 −59 70	−4 02 −60 70	−5 02 −60 70	−6 02 −60 70	−7 02 −59 71	250									
108	−1 51 60 72	−2 51 59 72	−3 50 60 72	−4 50 60 72	−5 50 60 72	−6 50 59 73	252									
106	−1 39 60 74	−2 39 59 74	−3 38 60 74	−4 38 60 74	−5 38 60 74	−6 38 59 75	254									
104	−1 27 60 76	−2 27 59 76	−3 26 60 76	−4 26 60 76	−5 26 59 76	−6 25 60 77	256									
102	−1 15 59 78	−2 14 60 78	−3 14 60 78	−4 14 60 78	−5 14 59 78	−6 13 60 79	−7 13 60 79	258								
100	−1 02 −60 80	−2 02 −60 80	−3 02 −59 80	−4 01 −60 80	−5 01 −60 80	−6 01 −60 81	−7 01 −59 81	260								
98	−0 50 60 82	−1 50 59 82	−2 49 60 82	−3 49 60 82	−4 49 59 82	−5 48 60 83	−6 48 60 83	262								
96	−0 38 59 84	−1 37 60 84	−2 37 60 84	−3 37 59 84	−4 36 60 84	−5 36 60 85	−6 36 59 85	264								
94	−0 25 60 86	−1 25 59 86	−2 24 60 86	−3 24 60 86	−4 24 59 86	−5 23 60 86	−6 23 60 87	−7 23 59 87	266							
92	−0 13 59 88	−1 12 60 88	−2 12 60 88	−3 12 59 88	−4 11 60 88	−5 11 60 88	−6 11 59 89	−7 10 60 89	268							
90	00 00 −60 90	−1 00 −59 90	−1 59 −60 90	−2 59 −60 90	−3 59 −59 90	−4 58 −60 90	−5 58 −60 91	−6 58 −59 91	270							
88	00 13 60 92	−0 47 60 92	−1 47 59 92	−2 46 60 92	−3 46 60 92	−4 46 60 92	−5 46 59 93	−6 45 60 93	272							
86	00 25 60 94	−0 35 59 94	−1 34 60 94	−2 34 60 94	−3 34 59 94	−4 33 60 94	−5 33 60 95	−6 33 59 95	274							
84	00 38 60 96	−0 22 60 96	−1 22 59 96	−2 21 60 96	−3 21 60 96	−4 21 60 96	−5 21 59 97	−6 20 60 97	−7 20 60 97	276						
82	00 50 60 98	−0 10 59 98	−1 09 60 98	−2 09 60 98	−3 09 59 98	−4 08 60 98	−5 08 60 99	−6 08 59 99	−7 07 60 99	278						
80	01 02 −59 100	00 03 −60 100	−0 57 −60 100	−1 57 −59 100	−2 56 −60 100	−3 56 −60 100	−4 56 −59 100	−5 55 −60 101	−6 55 −60 101	280						
78	01 15 60 102	00 15 60 102	−0 45 59 102	−1 44 60 102	−2 44 60 102	−3 44 59 102	−4 43 60 102	−5 43 60 103	−6 43 59 103	282						
76	01 27 60 104	00 27 59 104	−0 32 60 104	−1 32 60 104	−2 32 60 104	−3 32 59 104	−4 31 60 104	−5 31 60 105	−6 31 59 105	284						
74	01 39 60 106	00 39 59 106	−0 20 60 106	−1 20 60 106	−2 20 59 106	−3 19 60 106	−4 19 60 106	−5 19 60 107	−6 19 59 107	−7 18 60 107	286					
72	01 51 60 108	00 51 59 108	−0 08 60 108	−1 08 60 108	−2 08 59 108	−3 07 60 108	−4 07 60 108	−5 07 60 109	−6 07 59 109	−7 06 60 109	288					
70	02 03 −60 110	01 03 −59 110	00 04 −60 110	−0 56 −60 110	−1 56 −60 110	−2 56 −59 110	−3 55 −60 110	−4 55 −60 111	−5 55 −59 111	−6 54 −60 111	290					
68	02 15 60 112	01 15 60 112	00 15 60 112	−0 45 59 112	−1 44 60 112	−2 44 60 112	−3 44 59 112	−4 43 60 113	−5 43 60 113	−6 43 60 113	292					
66	02 26 60 114	01 26 59 114	00 27 60 114	−0 33 60 114	−1 33 59 114	−2 32 60 114	−3 32 60 114	−4 32 60 115	−5 32 59 115	−6 31 60 115	294					
64	02 38 60 116	01 38 60 116	00 38 60 116	−0 22 59 116	−1 21 60 116	−2 21 60 116	−3 21 60 116	−4 21 59 117	−5 20 60 117	−6 20 60 117	−7 20 60 117	296				
62	02 49 60 118	01 49 60 118	00 49 59 118	−0 10 60 118	−1 10 60 118	−2 10 60 118	−3 10 59 118	−4 09 60 119	−5 09 60 119	−6 09 60 119	−7 09 59 119	298				
60	03 00 −60 120	02 00 −60 120	01 00 −60 120	00 00 −59 120	−0 59 −60 120	−1 59 −60 120	−2 59 −60 120	−3 59 −59 120	−4 58 −60 121	−5 58 −60 121	−6 58 −60 121	300				
58	03 11 60 122	02 11 60 122	01 11 60 122	00 11 60 122	−0 49 59 122	−1 48 60 122	−2 48 60 122	−3 48 60 122	−4 48 59 123	−5 47 60 123	−6 47 60 123	302				
56	03 21 60 124	02 21 59 124	01 22 60 124	00 22 60 124	−0 38 60 124	−1 38 60 124	−2 38 59 124	−3 37 60 124	−4 37 60 125	−5 37 60 125	−6 37 59 125	304				
54	03 31 59 126	02 32 60 126	01 32 60 126	00 32 60 126	−0 28 60 126	−1 28 59 126	−2 27 60 126	−3 27 60 126	−4 27 60 127	−5 27 60 127	−6 27 59 127	306				
52	03 41 59 128	02 42 60 128	01 42 60 128	00 42 60 128	−0 18 60 128	−1 18 59 128	−2 17 60 128	−3 17 60 128	−4 17 60 129	−5 17 60 129	−6 17 59 129	−7 16 60 129	308			
50	03 51 −60 130	02 51 −59 130	01 52 −60 130	00 52 −60 130	−0 08 −60 130	−1 08 −60 130	−2 08 −59 130	−3 07 −60 130	−4 07 −60 131	−5 07 −60 131	−6 07 −60 131	−7 07 −60 131	310			
48	04 01 60 132	03 01 60 132	02 01 60 132	01 01 60 132	00 01 59 132	−0 58 60 132	−1 58 60 132	−2 58 60 132	−3 58 60 133	−4 58 60 133	−5 58 59 133	−6 57 60 133	312			
46	04 10 60 134	03 10 60 134	02 10 60 134	01 10 60 134	00 10 59 134	−0 49 60 134	−1 49 60 134	−2 49 60 134	−3 49 60 135	−4 49 60 135	−5 49 59 135	−6 48 60 135	314			
44	04 19 60 136	03 19 60 136	02 19 60 136	01 19 60 136	00 19 59 136	−0 40 60 136	−1 40 60 136	−2 40 60 136	−3 40 60 137	−4 40 60 137	−5 40 60 137	−6 40 59 137	316			
42	04 27 60 138	03 27 59 138	02 28 60 138	01 28 60 138	00 28 60 138	−0 32 60 138	−1 32 60 138	−2 32 60 138	−3 32 59 139	−4 31 60 138	−5 31 60 138	−6 31 60 139	318			
40	04 36 −60 140	03 36 −60 140	02 36 −60 140	01 36 −60 140	00 36 −60 140	−0 24 −60 140	−1 24 −60 140	−2 24 −59 140	−3 23 −60 140	−4 23 −60 140	−5 23 −60 140	−6 23 −60 141	320			
38	04 43 59 142	03 44 60 142	02 44 60 142	01 44 60 142	00 44 60 142	−0 16 60 142	−1 16 60 142	−2 16 60 142	−3 16 59 142	−4 15 60 142	−5 15 60 142	−6 15 60 143	322			
36	04 51 60 144	03 51 60 144	02 51 60 144	01 51 60 144	00 51 59 144	−0 08 60 144	−1 08 60 144	−2 08 60 144	−3 08 60 144	−4 08 60 144	−5 08 60 144	−6 08 60 144	−7 08 60 145	324		
34	04 58 60 146	03 58 60 146	02 58 59 146	01 59 60 146	00 59 60 146	−0 01 60 146	−1 01 60 146	−2 01 60 146	−3 01 60 146	−4 01 60 146	−5 01 60 146	−6 01 60 146	−7 01 59 147	326		
32	05 05 60 148	04 05 60 148	03 05 60 148	02 05 60 148	01 05 59 148	00 06 60 148	−0 54 60 148	−1 54 60 148	−2 54 60 148	−3 54 60 148	−4 54 60 148	−5 54 60 148	−6 54 60 148	328		
30	05 12 −60 150	04 12 −60 150	03 12 −60 150	02 12 −60 150	01 12 −60 150	00 12 −60 150	−0 48 −60 150	−1 48 −60 150	−2 48 −60 150	−3 48 −60 150	−4 48 −60 150	−5 48 −59 150	−6 47 −60 150	330		
28	05 18 60 152	04 18 60 152	03 18 60 152	02 18 60 152	01 18 60 152	00 18 60 152	−0 42 60 152	−1 42 60 152	−2 42 60 152	−3 42 60 152	−4 42 60 152	−5 42 59 152	−6 41 60 152	332		
26	05 24 60 154	04 24 60 154	03 24 60 154	02 24 60 154	01 24 60 154	00 24 60 154	−0 36 60 154	−1 36 60 154	−2 36 60 154	−3 36 60 154	−4 36 60 154	−5 36 60 154	−6 36 60 154	334		
24	05 29 60 156	04 29 60 156	03 29 60 156	02 29 60 156	01 29 60 156	00 29 60 156	−0 31 60 156	−1 31 60 156	−2 31 60 156	−3 31 60 156	−4 31 60 156	−5 31 60 156	−6 31 60 156	336		
22	05 34 60 158	04 34 60 158	03 34 60 158	02 34 60 158	01 34 60 158	00 34 60 158	−0 26 60 158	−1 26 60 158	−2 26 60 158	−3 26 60 158	−4 26 60 158	−5 26 60 158	−6 26 60 158	338		
20	05 38 −60 160	04 38 −60 160	03 38 −60 160	02 38 −60 160	01 38 −60 160	00 38 −60 160	−0 22 −60 160	−1 22 −59 160	−2 21 −60 160	−3 21 −60 160	−4 21 −60 160	−5 21 −60 160	−6 21 −60 160	340		
18	05 42 60 162	04 42 60 162	03 42 60 162	02 42 60 162	01 42 60 162	00 42 59 162	−0 17 60 162	−1 17 60 162	−2 17 60 162	−3 17 60 162	−4 17 60 162	−5 17 60 162	−6 17 60 162	342		
16	05 46 60 164	04 46 60 164	03 46 60 164	02 46 60 164	01 46 60 164	00 46 60 164	−0 14 60 164	−1 14 60 164	−2 14 60 164	−3 14 60 164	−4 14 60 164	−5 14 60 164	−6 14 60 164	344		
14	05 49 60 166	04 49 60 166	03 49 60 166	02 49 60 166	01 49 60 166	00 49 60 166	−0 11 60 166	−1 11 60 166	−2 11 60 166	−3 11 60 166	−4 11 60 166	−5 11 60 166	−6 11 60 166	346		
12	05 52 60 168	04 52 60 168	03 52 60 168	02 52 60 168	01 52 60 168	00 52 60 168	−0 08 60 168	−1 08 60 168	−2 08 60 168	−3 08 60 168	−4 08 60 168	−5 08 60 168	−6 08 60 168	348		
10	05 55 −60 170	04 55 −60 170	03 55 −60 170	02 55 −60 170	01 55 −60 170	00 55 −60 170	−0 05 −60 170	−1 05 −60 170	−2 05 −60 170	−3 05 −60 170	−4 05 −60 170	−5 05 −60 170	−6 05 −60 170	350		
8	05 57 60 172	04 57 60 172	03 57 60 172	02 57 60 172	01 57 60 172	00 57 60 172	−0 03 60 172	−1 03 60 172	−2 03 60 172	−3 03 60 172	−4 03 60 172	−5 03 60 172	−6 03 60 172	352		
6	05 58 60 174	04 58 60 174	03 58 60 174	02 58 60 174	01 58 60 174	00 58 60 174	−0 02 60 174	−1 02 60 174	−2 02 60 174	−3 02 60 174	−4 02 60 174	−5 02 60 174	−6 02 60 174	354		
4	05 59 60 176	04 59 60 176	03 59 60 176	02 59 60 176	01 59 60 176	00 59 60 176	−0 01 60 176	−1 01 60 176	−2 01 60 176	−3 01 60 176	−4 01 60 176	−5 01 60 176	−6 01 60 176	356		
2	06 00 60 178	05 00 60 178	04 00 60 178	03 00 60 178	02 00 60 178	01 00 60 178	00 00 60 178	−1 00 60 178	−2 00 60 178	−3 00 60 178	−4 00 60 178	−5 00 60 178	−6 00 60 178	−7 00 60 178	358	
0	06 00 −60 180	05 00 −60 180	04 00 −60 180	03 00 −60 180	02 00 −60 180	01 00 −60 180	00 00 −60 180	−1 00 −60 180	−2 00 −60 180	−3 00 −60 180	−4 00 −60 180	−5 00 −60 180	−6 00 −60 180	−7 00 −60 180	360	
	0°	1°	2°	3°	4°	5°	6°	7°	8°	9°	10°	11°	12°	13°	14°	

S. Lat. {LHA greater than 180°....... Zn=180−Z; LHA less than 180°........... Zn=180+Z}

N. Lat. {LHA greater than 180°....... Zn=Z; LHA less than 180°........... Zn=360−Z}

DECLINATION (15°-29°) SAME NAME AS LATITUDE

LHA	15°			16°			17°			18°			19°		
	Hc	d	Z	Hc	d	Z	Hc	d	Z	Hc	d	Z	Hc	d	Z
	° ′	′	°	° ′	′	°	° ′	′	°	° ′	′	°	° ′	′	°
0	21 00	+60	180	22 00	+60	180	23 00	+60	180	24 00	+60	180	25 00	+60	180
2	21 00	60	178	22 00	60	178	23 00	60	178	24 00	60	178	25 00	60	178
4	20 59	60	176	21 59	60	176	22 59	60	176	23 59	60	176	24 59	60	176
6	20 58	60	174	21 58	60	174	22 58	60	174	23 58	60	174	24 58	60	174
8	20 56	60	172	21 56	60	172	22 56	60	172	23 56	60	172	24 56	60	172
10	20 54	+60	170	21 54	+60	170	22 54	+60	170	23 54	+60	170	24 54	+60	170
12	20 52	60	168	21 52	60	168	22 52	60	168	23 52	60	168	24 52	60	168
14	20 49	60	166	21 49	60	166	22 49	60	166	23 49	60	165	24 49	60	165
16	20 46	60	164	21 46	60	163	22 46	60	163	23 46	60	163	24 46	60	163
18	20 42	60	161	21 42	60	161	22 42	60	161	23 42	60	161	24 42	60	161
20	20 38	+60	159	21 38	+60	159	22 38	+60	159	23 38	+59	159	24 37	+60	159
22	20 33	60	157	21 33	60	157	22 33	60	157	23 33	60	157	24 33	60	157
24	20 28	60	155	21 28	60	155	22 28	60	155	23 28	60	155	24 28	60	155
26	20 23	59	153	21 22	60	153	22 22	60	153	23 22	60	153	24 22	60	153
28	20 17	60	151	21 17	59	151	22 16	60	151	23 16	60	151	24 16	60	151
30	20 10	+60	149	21 10	+60	149	22 10	+60	149	23 10	+60	149	24 10	+60	149
32	20 04	60	147	21 04	60	147	22 04	59	147	23 03	60	147	24 03	60	147
34	19 57	60	145	20 57	59	145	21 56	60	145	22 56	60	145	23 56	60	145
36	19 49	60	143	20 49	60	143	21 49	60	143	22 49	60	143	23 49	60	143
38	19 42	59	141	20 41	60	141	21 41	60	141	22 41	60	141	23 41	60	141
40	19 33	+60	139	20 33	+60	139	21 33	+60	139	22 33	+60	139	23 33	+60	139
42	19 25	60	137	20 25	60	137	21 25	60	137	22 25	59	137	23 24	60	136
44	19 16	60	135	20 16	60	135	21 16	60	135	22 16	60	134	23 16	59	134
46	19 07	60	133	20 07	60	133	21 07	60	133	22 07	59	132	23 06	60	132
48	18 58	60	131	19 58	59	131	20 57	60	130	21 57	60	130	22 57	60	130
50	18 48	+60	129	19 48	+60	129	20 48	+60	128	21 48	+59	128	22 47	+60	128
52	18 38	60	127	19 38	60	127	20 38	60	126	21 38	59	126	22 37	60	126
54	18 28	60	125	19 28	60	125	20 28	59	124	21 27	60	124	22 27	60	124
56	18 18	59	123	19 17	60	122	20 17	60	122	21 17	60	122	22 17	59	122
58	18 07	60	121	19 07	59	120	20 06	60	120	21 06	60	120	22 06	60	120
60	17 56	+60	119	18 56	+59	118	19 55	+60	118	20 55	+60	118	21 55	+60	118
62	17 45	60	116	18 45	59	116	19 44	60	116	20 44	60	116	21 44	59	116
64	17 33	60	114	18 33	60	114	19 33	60	114	20 33	59	114	21 32	60	114
66	17 22	60	112	18 22	59	112	19 21	60	112	20 21	60	112	21 21	59	112
68	17 10	60	110	18 10	60	110	19 10	59	110	20 09	60	110	21 09	60	110
70	16 58	+60	108	17 58	+60	108	18 58	+60	108	19 58	+59	108	20 57	+60	108
72	16 47	59	106	17 46	60	106	18 46	60	106	19 46	59	106	20 45	60	106
74	16 34	60	104	17 34	60	104	18 34	59	104	19 33	60	104	20 33	60	104
76	16 22	60	102	17 22	60	102	18 22	59	102	19 21	60	102	20 21	59	102
78	16 10	60	100	17 10	59	100	18 09	60	100	19 09	60	100	20 09	59	100
80	15 58	+59	98	16 57	+60	98	17 57	+59	98	18 56	+60	98	19 56	+60	98
82	15 45	60	96	16 45	59	96	17 44	60	96	18 44	60	96	19 44	59	96
84	15 33	59	94	16 32	60	94	17 32	60	94	18 32	59	94	19 31	60	94
86	15 20	60	92	16 20	59	92	17 19	60	92	18 19	60	92	19 19	59	92
88	15 08	59	90	16 07	60	90	17 07	59	90	18 06	60	90	19 06	60	90
90	14 55	+60	88	15 55	+59	88	16 54	+60	88	17 54	+60	88	18 54	+59	88
92	14 42	60	86	15 42	60	86	16 42	59	86	17 41	60	86	18 41	60	86
94	14 30	60	84	15 30	59	84	16 29	60	84	17 29	60	84	18 29	59	84
96	14 18	59	82	15 17	60	82	16 17	59	82	17 16	60	82	18 16	60	82
98	14 05	60	81	15 05	59	80	16 04	60	80	17 04	60	80	18 04	59	80
100	13 53	+59	79	14 52	+60	78	15 52	+60	78	16 52	+59	78	17 51	+60	78
102	13 41	59	77	14 40	60	76	15 40	60	76	16 40	59	76	17 39	60	76
104	13 28	60	75	14 28	60	74	15 28	59	74	16 27	60	74	17 27	60	74
106	13 16	60	73	14 16	60	72	15 16	59	72	16 15	60	72	17 15	60	72
108	13 04	60	71	14 04	60	71	15 04	60	70	16 04	59	70	17 03	60	70
110	12 53	+59	69	13 52	+60	69	14 52	+60	68	15 52	+59	68	16 51	+60	68
112	12 41	60	67	13 41	60	67	14 41	59	66	15 40	60	66	16 40	60	66
114	12 30	59	65	13 29	60	65	14 29	60	65	15 29	60	64	16 29	59	64
116	12 18	60	63	13 18	60	63	14 18	60	63	15 18	59	62	16 17	60	62
118	12 07	60	61	13 07	60	61	14 07	60	61	15 07	59	60	16 06	60	60
120	11 57	+59	59	12 56	+60	59	13 56	+60	59	14 56	+60	59	15 56	+59	58
122	11 46	60	57	12 46	59	57	13 45	60	57	14 45	60	57	15 45	60	56
124	11 36	59	55	12 35	60	55	13 35	60	55	14 35	60	55	15 35	59	55
126	11 25	60	53	12 25	60	53	13 25	60	53	14 25	60	53	15 25	59	53
128	11 16	59	51	12 15	60	51	13 15	60	51	14 15	60	51	15 15	59	51
130	11 06	+60	49	12 06	+60	49	13 06	+59	49	14 05	+60	49	15 05	+59	49
132	10 57	59	47	11 56	60	47	12 56	60	47	13 56	60	47	14 56	60	47
134	10 48	59	45	11 47	60	45	12 47	60	45	13 47	60	45	14 47	60	45
136	10 39	60	43	11 39	60	43	12 39	59	43	13 38	60	43	14 38	60	43
138	10 31	59	41	11 30	60	41	12 30	60	41	13 30	60	41	14 30	60	41

LHA	20°			21°			22°			23°			24°		
	Hc	d	Z	Hc	d	Z	Hc	d	Z	Hc	d	Z	Hc	d	Z
	° ′	′	°	° ′	′	°	° ′	′	°	° ′	′	°	° ′	′	°
0	26 00	+60	180	27 00	+60	180	28 00	+60	180	29 00	+60	180	30 00	+60	180
2	26 00	60	178	27 00	60	178	28 00	60	178	29 00	60	178	30 00	60	178
4	25 59	60	176	26 59	60	176	27 59	60	176	28 59	60	176	29 59	60	176
6	25 58	60	174	26 58	60	174	27 58	60	174	28 58	60	174	29 58	60	174
8	25 56	60	172	26 56	60	172	27 56	60	172	28 56	60	172	29 56	60	172
10	25 54	+60	170	26 54	+60	170	27 54	+60	170	28 54	+60	170	29 54	+60	170
12	25 52	60	168	26 52	60	167	27 52	60	167	28 52	60	167	29 52	60	167
14	25 49	60	165	26 49	60	165	27 49	60	165	28 49	60	165	29 49	60	165
16	25 46	59	163	26 45	60	163	27 45	60	163	28 45	60	163	29 45	60	163
18	25 42	60	161	26 42	60	161	27 42	60	161	28 42	60	161	29 42	59	161
20	25 37	+60	159	26 37	+60	159	27 37	+60	159	28 37	+60	159	29 37	+60	159
22	25 33	60	157	26 33	60	157	27 33	60	157	28 33	60	157	29 33	59	157
24	25 28	60	155	26 28	60	155	27 28	59	155	28 27	60	155	29 27	60	155
26	25 22	60	153	26 22	60	153	27 22	60	153	28 22	60	153	29 22	60	153
28	25 16	60	151	26 16	60	151	27 16	60	151	28 16	60	151	29 16	60	151
30	25 10	+60	149	26 10	+60	149	27 10	+60	149	28 10	+59	149	29 09	+60	149
32	25 03	60	147	26 03	60	147	27 03	60	147	28 03	60	146	29 03	60	146
34	24 56	60	145	25 56	60	145	26 56	60	144	27 56	60	144	28 56	59	144
36	24 49	60	143	25 49	59	142	26 48	60	142	27 48	60	142	28 48	60	142
38	24 41	60	141	25 41	60	140	26 41	59	140	27 40	60	140	28 40	60	140
40	24 33	+60	138	25 33	+59	138	26 32	+60	138	27 32	+60	138	28 32	+60	138
42	24 24	60	136	25 24	60	136	26 24	60	136	27 24	59	136	28 23	60	136
44	24 15	60	134	25 15	60	134	26 15	60	134	27 15	60	134	28 15	59	134
46	24 06	60	132	25 06	60	132	26 06	60	132	27 06	59	132	28 05	60	132
48	23 57	60	130	24 57	59	130	25 56	60	130	26 56	60	130	27 56	60	130
50	23 47	+60	128	24 47	+60	128	25 47	+59	128	26 46	+60	128	27 46	+60	128
52	23 37	60	126	24 37	60	126	25 37	59	126	26 36	60	126	27 36	60	126
54	23 27	60	124	24 27	59	124	25 26	60	124	26 26	60	124	27 26	59	124
56	23 16	60	122	24 16	60	122	25 16	59	122	26 15	60	122	27 15	60	122
58	23 06	59	120	24 05	60	120	25 05	60	120	26 05	59	120	27 04	60	120
60	22 55	+59	118	23 54	+60	118	24 54	+60	118	25 54	+59	118	26 53	+60	118
62	22 43	60	116	23 43	60	116	24 43	59	116	25 42	60	116	26 42	60	116
64	22 32	60	114	23 32	59	114	24 31	60	114	25 31	60	114	26 31	59	113
66	22 20	60	112	23 20	60	112	24 20	59	112	25 19	60	112	26 19	60	111
68	22 09	59	110	23 08	60	110	24 08	60	110	25 08	59	110	26 07	60	109
70	21 57	+60	108	22 57	+59	108	23 56	+60	108	24 56	+59	108	25 55	+60	107
72	21 45	59	106	22 44	60	106	23 44	60	106	24 44	59	106	25 43	60	105
74	21 33	59	104	22 32	60	104	23 32	60	104	24 32	59	103	25 31	60	103
76	21 20	60	102	22 20	60	102	23 20	59	102	24 19	60	101	25 19	60	101
78	21 08	60	100	22 08	59	100	23 07	60	100	24 07	60	99	25 07	59	99
80	20 56	+59	98	21 55	+60	98	22 55	+60	98	23 55	+59	97	24 54	+60	97
82	20 43	60	96	21 43	60	96	22 43	59	96	23 42	60	95	24 42	59	95
84	20 31	59	94	21 30	60	94	22 30	60	94	23 30	59	93	24 29	60	93
86	20 18	60	92	21 18	60	92	22 18	59	92	23 17	60	91	24 17	59	91
88	20 06	59	90	21 05	60	90	22 05	60	90	23 05	59	89	24 04	60	89
90	19 53	+60	88	20 53	+59	88	21 52	+60	88	22 52	+60	88	23 52	+59	87
92	19 41	59	86	20 40	60	86	21 40	60	86	22 40	59	86	23 39	60	85
94	19 28	60	84	20 28	59	84	21 27	60	84	22 27	60	84	23 27	59	83
96	19 16	59	82	20 15	60	82	21 15	60	82	22 15	59	82	23 14	60	81
98	19 03	60	80	20 03	60	80	21 03	59	80	22 02	60	80	23 02	59	79
100	18 51	+60	78	19 51	+59	78	20 50	+60	78	21 50	+60	78	22 50	+59	77
102	18 39	59	76	19 38	60	76	20 38	60	76	21 38	59	76	22 37	60	76
104	18 27	59	74	19 26	60	74	20 26	60	74	21 26	59	74	22 25	60	74
106	18 15	59	72	19 14	60	72	20 14	60	72	21 14	59	72	22 13	60	72
108	18 03	60	70	19 03	59	70	20 02	60	70	21 02	60	70	22 02	59	70
110	17 51	+60	68	18 51	+59	68	19 50	+60	68	20 50	+60	68	21 50	+59	68
112	17 40	59	66	18 39	60	66	19 39	60	66	20 39	59	66	21 38	60	66
114	17 28	60	64	18 28	60	64	19 28	59	64	20 27	60	64	21 27	60	64
116	17 17	60	62	18 17	59	62	19 16	60	62	20 16	60	62	21 16	60	62
118	17 06	60	60	18 06	59	60	19 05	60	60	20 05	60	60	21 05	60	60
120	16 55	+60	58	17 55	+60	58	18 55	+59	58	19 54	+60	58	20 54	+60	58
122	16 45	59	56	17 44	60	56	18 44	60	56	19 44	60	56	20 44	59	56
124	16 34	60	54	17 34	60	54	18 34	60	54	19 34	59	54	20 33	60	54
126	16 24	60	52	17 24	60	52	18 24	60	52	19 24	59	52	20 23	60	52
128	16 14	60	51	17 14	60	50	18 14	60	50	19 14	60	50	20 14	59	50
130	16 05	+60	49	17 05	+60	48	18 05	+59	48	19 04	+60	48	20 04	+60	48
132	15 56	60	47	16 56	59	47	17 55	60	46	18 55	60	46	19 55	60	46
134	15 47	60	45	16 47	59	45	17 46	60	45	18 46	60	44	19 46	60	44
136	15 38	60	43	16 38	60	43	17 38	60	43	18 38	59	42	19 37	60	42
138	15 30	60	41	16 30	59	41	17 29	60	41	18 29	60	41	19 29	60	40

LHA	25°			26°			27°			28°			29°			LHA
	Hc	d	Z	Hc	d	Z	Hc	d	Z	Hc	d	Z	Hc	d	Z	
	° ′	′	°	° ′	′	°	° ′	′	°	° ′	′	°	° ′	′	°	
0	31 00	+60	180	32 00	+60	180	33 00	+60	180	34 00	+60	180	35 00	+60	180	360
2	31 00	60	178	32 00	60	178	33 00	60	178	34 00	60	178	35 00	60	178	358
4	30 59	60	176	31 59	60	176	32 59	60	176	33 59	60	176	34 59	60	176	356
6	30 58	60	174	31 58	60	174	32 58	60	174	33 58	60	174	34 58	60	174	354
8	30 56	60	172	31 56	60	172	32 56	60	172	33 56	60	172	34 56	60	172	352
10	30 54	+60	169	31 54	+60	169	32 54	+60	169	33 54	+60	169	34 54	+60	169	350
12	30 52	60	167	31 52	60	167	32 52	60	167	33 52	60	167	34 52	60	167	348
14	30 49	60	165	31 49	60	165	32 49	60	165	33 49	60	165	34 49	60	165	346
16	30 45	60	163	31 45	60	163	32 45	60	163	33 45	60	163	34 45	60	163	344
18	30 41	60	161	31 41	60	161	32 41	60	161	33 41	60	161	34 41	60	161	342
20	30 37	+60	159	31 37	+60	159	32 37	+60	159	33 37	+60	159	34 37	+60	159	340
22	30 32	60	157	31 32	60	157	32 32	60	157	33 32	60	157	34 32	60	157	338
24	30 27	60	155	31 27	60	155	32 27	60	155	33 27	60	155	34 27	60	154	336
26	30 22	60	153	31 22	60	153	32 22	59	153	33 21	60	152	34 21	60	152	334
28	30 16	60	151	31 16	60	150	32 16	59	150	33 15	60	150	34 15	60	150	332
30	30 09	+60	148	31 09	+60	148	32 09	+60	148	33 09	+60	148	34 09	+60	148	330
32	30 03	59	146	31 02	60	146	32 02	60	146	33 02	60	146	34 02	60	146	328
34	29 55	60	144	30 55	60	144	31 55	60	144	32 55	60	144	33 55	60	144	326
36	29 48	60	142	30 48	60	142	31 48	59	142	32 47	60	142	33 47	60	142	324
38	29 40	60	140	30 40	60	140	31 40	60	140	32 40	59	140	33 39	60	140	322
40	29 32	+60	138	30 32	+59	138	31 31	+60	138	32 31	+60	138	33 31	+60	138	320
42	29 23	60	136	30 23	60	136	31 23	60	136	32 23	59	136	33 22	60	136	318
44	29 14	60	134	30 14	60	134	31 14	60	134	32 14	60	134	33 14	59	133	316
46	29 05	60	132	30 05	60	132	31 05	59	132	32 04	60	131	33 04	60	131	314
48	28 56	59	130	29 55	60	130	30 55	60	130	31 55	60	129	32 55	59	129	312
50	28 46	+60	128	29 46	+59	128	30 45	+60	127	31 45	+60	127	32 45	+60	127	310
52	28 36	60	126	29 36	59	126	30 35	60	125	31 35	60	125	32 35	59	125	308
54	28 25	60	124	29 25	60	123	30 25	60	123	31 25	59	123	32 24	60	123	306
56	28 15	60	122	29 15	59	121	30 14	60	121	31 14	60	121	32 14	59	121	304
58	28 04	60	119	29 04	59	119	30 03	60	119	31 03	60	119	32 03	59	119	302
60	27 53	+60	117	28 53	+59	117	29 52	+60	117	30 52	+60	117	31 52	+59	117	300
62	27 42	59	115	28 41	60	115	29 41	60	115	30 41	59	115	31 40	60	115	298
64	27 30	60	113	28 30	60	113	29 30	59	113	30 29	60	113	31 29	60	113	296
66	27 19	59	111	28 18	60	111	29 18	60	111	30 18	59	111	31 17	60	111	294
68	27 07	60	109	28 07	59	109	29 06	60	109	30 06	60	109	31 06	59	109	292
70	26 55	+60	107	27 55	+59	107	28 54	+60	107	29 54	+60	107	30 54	+59	107	290
72	26 43	60	105	27 43	59	105	28 42	60	105	29 42	59	105	30 41	60	105	288
74	26 31	60	103	27 31	59	103	28 30	60	103	29 30	59	103	30 29	60	103	286
76	26 19	59	101	27 18	60	101	28 18	59	101	29 17	60	101	30 17	60	101	284
78	26 06	60	99	27 06	59	99	28 05	60	99	29 05	60	99	30 05	59	99	282
80	25 54	+59	97	26 53	+60	97	27 53	+60	97	28 53	+59	97	29 52	+60	97	280
82	25 41	60	95	26 41	60	95	27 41	59	95	28 40	60	95	29 40	59	95	278
84	25 29	59	93	26 28	60	93	27 28	60	93	28 28	59	93	29 27	60	93	276
86	25 16	60	91	26 16	60	91	27 16	59	91	28 15	60	91	29 15	59	91	274
88	25 04	59	89	26 03	60	89	27 03	60	89	28 03	59	89	29 02	60	89	272
90	24 51	+60	87	25 51	+59	87	26 50	+60	87	27 50	+60	87	28 50	+59	87	270
92	24 39	59	85	25 38	60	85	26 38	60	85	27 38	59	85	28 37	60	85	268
94	24 26	60	83	25 26	59	83	26 25	60	83	27 25	60	83	28 25	59	83	266
96	24 14	59	81	25 13	60	81	26 13	60	81	27 13	59	81	28 12	60	81	264
98	24 01	60	79	25 01	60	79	26 01	59	79	27 00	60	79	28 00	59	79	262
100	23 49	+60	77	24 49	+59	77	25 48	+60	77	26 48	+60	77	27 48	+59	77	260
102	23 37	60	75	24 37	59	75	25 36	60	75	26 36	59	75	27 35	60	75	258
104	23 25	60	73	24 25	59	73	25 24	60	73	26 24	59	73	27 23	60	73	256
106	23 13	60	71	24 13	59	71	25 12	60	71	26 12	59	71	27 11	60	71	254
108	23 01	60	70	24 01	59	69	25 00	60	69	26 00	60	69	27 00	59	69	252
110	22 49	+60	68	23 49	+60	67	24 49	+59	67	25 48	+60	67	26 48	+60	67	250
112	22 38	60	66	23 38	59	65	24 37	60	65	25 37	60	65	26 37	59	65	248
114	22 27	59	64	23 26	60	64	24 26	60	63	25 26	59	63	26 25	60	63	246
116	22 16	59	62	23 15	60	62	24 15	60	61	25 15	59	61	26 14	60	61	244
118	22 05	59	60	23 04	60	60	24 04	60	60	25 04	59	59	26 03	60	59	242
120	21 54	+60	58	22 54	+59	58	23 53	+60	58	24 53	+60	57	25 53	+59	57	240
122	21 43	60	56	22 43	60	56	23 43	60	56	24 43	59	56	25 42	60	55	238
124	21 33	60	54	22 33	60	54	23 33	59	54	24 32	60	54	25 32	60	54	236
126	21 23	60	52	22 23	60	52	23 23	59	52	24 22	60	52	25 22	60	52	234
128	21 13	60	50	22 13	60	50	23 13	60	50	24 13	59	50	25 12	60	50	232
130	21 04	+60	48	22 04	+59	48	23 03	+60	48	24 03	+60	48	25 03	+60	48	230
132	20 55	59	46	21 54	60	46	22 54	60	46	23 54	60	46	24 54	60	46	228
134	20 46	60	44	21 46	59	44	22 45	60	44	23 45	60	44	24 45	60	44	226
136	20 37	60	42	21 37	60	42	22 37	60	42	23 37	59	42	24 36	60	42	224
138	20 29	60	40	21 29	60	40	22 29	59	40	23 28	60	40	24 28	60	40	222

S. Lat. {LHA greater than 180°....... Zn=180−Z; LHA less than 180°........... Zn=180+Z}

DECLINATION (15°-29°) SAME NAME AS LATITUDE

N. Lat. {LHA greater than 180°....... Zn=Z
LHA less than 180°.......... Zn=360−Z}

DECLINATION (15°-29°) SAME NAME AS LATITUDE

LHA	15° Hc	d	Z	16° Hc	d	Z	17° Hc	d	Z	18° Hc	d	Z	19° Hc	d	Z	20° Hc	d	Z	21° Hc	d	Z
	° ′	′	°	° ′	′	°	° ′	′	°	° ′	′	°	° ′	′	°	° ′	′	°	° ′	′	°
140	10 22	+60	39	11 22	+60	39	12 22	+60	39	13 22	+60	39	14 22	+60	39	15 22	+60	39	16 22	+59	39
142	10 15	60	37	11 15	59	37	12 14	60	37	13 14	60	37	14 14	60	37	15 14	60	37	16 14	60	37
144	10 07	60	35	11 07	60	35	12 07	60	35	13 07	60	35	14 07	60	35	15 07	60	35	16 07	59	35
146	10 00	60	33	11 00	60	33	12 00	60	33	13 00	60	33	14 00	60	33	15 00	60	33	16 00	59	33
148	09 54	59	31	10 53	60	31	11 53	60	31	12 53	60	31	13 53	60	31	14 53	60	31	15 53	60	31
150	09 47	+60	29	10 47	+60	29	11 47	+60	29	12 47	+60	29	13 47	+60	29	14 47	+60	29	15 47	+60	29
152	09 41	60	27	10 41	60	27	11 41	60	27	12 41	60	27	13 41	60	27	14 41	60	27	15 41	60	27
154	09 36	60	25	10 36	60	25	11 36	59	25	12 35	60	25	13 35	60	25	14 35	60	25	15 35	60	25
156	09 30	60	24	10 30	60	23	11 30	60	23	12 30	60	23	13 30	60	23	14 30	60	23	15 30	60	23
158	09 26	60	22	10 26	60	22	11 26	60	21	12 26	59	21	13 25	60	21	14 25	60	21	15 25	60	21
160	09 21	+60	20	10 21	+60	20	11 21	+60	20	12 21	+60	20	13 21	+60	19	14 21	+60	19	15 21	+60	19
162	09 17	60	18	10 17	60	18	11 17	60	18	12 17	60	18	13 17	60	18	14 17	60	17	15 17	60	17
164	09 14	60	16	10 14	60	16	11 14	60	16	12 14	60	16	13 14	60	16	14 14	60	16	15 14	59	16
166	09 10	60	14	10 10	60	14	11 10	60	14	12 10	60	14	13 10	60	14	14 10	60	14	15 10	60	14
168	09 08	60	12	10 08	60	12	11 08	60	12	12 08	60	12	13 08	60	12	14 08	60	12	15 08	60	12
170	09 05	+60	10	10 05	+60	10	11 05	+60	10	12 05	+60	10	13 05	+60	10	14 05	+60	10	15 05	+60	10
172	09 03	60	8	10 03	60	8	11 03	60	8	12 03	60	8	13 03	60	8	14 03	60	8	15 03	60	8
174	09 02	60	6	10 02	60	6	11 02	60	6	12 02	60	6	13 02	60	6	14 02	60	6	15 02	60	6
176	09 01	60	4	10 01	60	4	11 01	60	4	12 01	60	4	13 01	60	4	14 01	60	4	15 01	60	4
178	09 00	60	2	10 00	60	2	11 00	60	2	12 00	60	2	13 00	60	2	14 00	60	2	15 00	60	2
180	09 00	+60	0	10 00	+60	0	11 00	+60	0	12 00	+60	0	13 00	+60	0	14 00	+60	0	15 00	+60	0

LHA	22° Hc	d	Z	23° Hc	d	Z	24° Hc	d	Z	25° Hc	d	Z	26° Hc	d	Z	27° Hc	d	Z	28° Hc	d	Z	29° Hc	d	Z	LHA
	° ′	′	°	° ′	′	°	° ′	′	°	° ′	′	°	° ′	′	°	° ′	′	°	° ′	′	°	° ′	′	°	
140	17 21	+60	39	18 21	+60	39	19 21	+60	39	20 21	+60	38	21 21	+60	38	22 21	+59	38	23 20	+60	38	24 20	+60	38	220
142	17 14	60	37	18 14	59	37	19 13	60	37	20 13	60	37	21 13	60	36	22 13	60	36	23 13	60	36	24 13	60	36	218
144	17 06	60	35	18 06	60	35	19 06	60	35	20 06	60	35	21 06	60	35	22 06	60	34	23 06	60	34	24 06	59	34	216
146	16 59	60	33	17 59	60	33	18 59	60	33	19 59	60	33	20 59	60	33	21 59	60	33	22 59	60	32	23 59	60	32	214
148	16 53	60	31	17 53	60	31	18 53	60	31	19 53	59	31	20 52	60	31	21 52	60	31	22 52	60	31	23 52	60	31	212
150	16 47	+59	29	17 46	+60	29	18 46	+60	29	19 46	+60	29	20 46	+60	29	21 46	+60	29	22 46	+60	29	23 46	+60	29	210
152	16 41	60	27	17 41	60	27	18 41	59	27	19 40	60	27	20 40	60	27	21 40	60	27	22 40	60	27	23 40	60	27	208
154	16 35	60	25	17 35	60	25	18 35	60	25	19 35	60	25	20 35	60	25	21 35	60	25	22 35	60	25	23 35	60	25	206
156	16 30	60	23	17 30	60	23	18 30	60	23	19 30	60	23	20 30	60	23	21 30	60	23	22 30	60	23	23 30	60	23	204
158	16 25	60	21	17 25	60	21	18 25	60	21	19 25	60	21	20 25	60	21	21 25	60	21	22 25	60	21	23 25	60	21	202
160	16 21	+60	19	17 21	+60	19	18 21	+60	19	19 21	+60	19	20 21	+60	19	21 21	+60	19	22 21	+60	19	23 21	+60	19	200
162	16 17	60	17	17 17	60	17	18 17	60	17	19 17	60	17	20 17	60	17	21 17	60	17	22 17	60	17	23 17	60	17	198
164	16 13	60	15	17 13	60	15	18 13	60	15	19 13	60	15	20 13	60	15	21 13	60	15	22 13	60	15	23 13	60	15	196
166	16 10	60	14	17 10	60	14	18 10	60	14	19 10	60	13	20 10	60	13	21 10	60	13	22 10	60	13	23 10	60	13	194
168	16 08	60	12	17 08	60	12	18 08	60	12	19 08	60	12	20 08	60	12	21 08	60	12	22 08	60	11	23 08	59	11	192
170	16 05	+60	10	17 05	+60	10	18 05	+60	10	19 05	+60	10	20 05	+60	10	21 05	+60	10	22 05	+60	10	23 05	+60	10	190
172	16 03	60	8	17 03	60	8	18 03	60	8	19 03	60	8	20 03	60	8	21 03	60	8	22 03	60	8	23 03	60	8	188
174	16 02	60	6	17 02	60	6	18 02	60	6	19 02	60	6	20 02	60	6	21 02	60	6	22 02	60	6	23 02	60	6	186
176	16 01	60	4	17 01	60	4	18 01	60	4	19 01	60	4	20 01	60	4	21 01	60	4	22 01	60	4	23 01	60	4	184
178	16 00	60	2	17 00	60	2	18 00	60	2	19 00	60	2	20 00	60	2	21 00	60	2	22 00	60	2	23 00	60	2	182
180	16 00	+60	0	17 00	+60	0	18 00	+60	0	19 00	+60	0	20 00	+60	0	21 00	+60	0	22 00	+60	0	23 00	+60	0	180

LAT 84°

15° 16° 17° 18° 19° 20° 21° 22° 23° 24° 25° 26° 27° 28° 29°

S. Lat. {LHA greater than 180°....... Zn=180−Z
LHA less than 180°.......... Zn=180+Z}

DECLINATION (15°-29°) SAME NAME AS LATITUDE

LAT 84°

N. Lat. {LHA greater than 180°....... Zn=Z; LHA less than 180°........... Zn=360−Z}

DECLINATION (0°-14°) SAME NAME AS LATITUDE

LHA	0° Hc	d	Z	1° Hc	d	Z	2° Hc	d	Z	3° Hc	d	Z	4° Hc	d	Z
	° ′	′	°	° ′	′	°	° ′	′	°	° ′	′	°	° ′	′	°
0	05 00	+60	180	06 00	+60	180	07 00	+60	180	08 00	+60	180	09 00	+60	180
2	05 00	60	178	06 00	60	178	07 00	60	178	08 00	60	178	09 00	60	178
4	04 59	60	176	05 59	60	176	06 59	60	176	07 59	60	176	08 59	60	176
6	04 58	60	174	05 58	60	174	06 58	60	174	07 58	60	174	08 58	60	174
8	04 57	60	172	05 57	60	172	06 57	60	172	07 57	60	172	08 57	60	172
10	04 55	+60	170	05 55	+60	170	06 55	+60	170	07 55	+60	170	08 55	+60	170
12	04 53	60	168	05 53	60	168	06 53	60	168	07 53	60	168	08 53	60	168
14	04 51	60	166	05 51	60	166	06 51	60	166	07 51	60	166	08 51	60	166
16	04 48	60	164	05 48	60	164	06 48	60	164	07 48	60	164	08 48	60	164
18	04 45	60	162	05 45	60	162	06 45	60	162	07 45	60	162	08 45	60	162
20	04 42	+60	160	05 42	+60	160	06 42	+60	160	07 42	+60	160	08 42	+60	160
22	04 38	60	158	05 38	60	158	06 38	60	158	07 38	60	158	08 38	60	158
24	04 34	60	156	05 34	60	156	06 34	60	156	07 34	60	156	08 34	60	156
26	04 30	60	154	05 30	60	154	06 30	59	154	07 29	60	154	08 29	60	154
28	04 25	60	152	05 25	60	152	06 25	60	152	07 25	60	152	08 25	60	152
30	04 20	+60	150	05 20	+60	150	06 20	+60	150	07 20	+60	150	08 20	+59	150
32	04 14	60	148	05 14	60	148	06 14	60	148	07 14	60	148	08 14	60	148
34	04 09	60	146	05 09	60	146	06 09	59	146	07 08	60	146	08 08	60	146
36	04 03	60	144	05 03	59	144	06 02	60	144	07 02	60	144	08 02	60	144
38	03 56	60	142	04 56	60	142	05 56	60	142	06 56	60	142	07 56	60	142
40	03 50	+60	140	04 50	+60	140	05 50	+59	140	06 49	+60	140	07 49	+60	140
42	03 43	60	138	04 43	60	138	05 43	60	138	06 43	59	138	07 42	60	138
44	03 36	60	136	04 36	59	136	05 35	60	136	06 35	60	136	07 35	60	136
46	03 28	60	134	04 28	60	134	05 28	60	134	06 28	60	134	07 28	60	134
48	03 21	59	132	04 20	60	132	05 20	60	132	06 20	60	132	07 20	60	132
50	03 13	+60	130	04 13	+59	130	05 12	+60	130	06 12	+60	130	07 12	+60	130
52	03 05	59	128	04 04	60	128	05 04	60	128	06 04	60	128	07 04	60	128
54	02 56	60	126	03 56	60	126	04 56	60	126	05 56	60	126	06 56	59	126
56	02 48	59	124	03 47	60	124	04 47	60	124	05 47	60	124	06 47	60	124
58	02 39	60	122	03 39	60	122	04 39	59	122	05 38	60	122	06 38	60	122
60	02 30	+60	120	03 30	+60	120	04 30	+59	120	05 29	+60	120	06 29	+60	120
62	02 21	60	118	03 21	59	118	04 20	60	118	05 20	60	118	06 20	60	118
64	02 11	60	116	03 11	60	116	04 11	60	116	05 11	60	116	06 11	59	116
66	02 02	60	114	03 02	60	114	04 02	59	114	05 01	60	114	06 01	60	114
68	01 52	60	112	02 52	60	112	03 52	60	112	04 52	60	112	05 52	59	112
70	01 42	+60	110	02 42	+60	110	03 42	+60	110	04 42	+60	110	05 42	+60	110
72	01 33	59	108	02 32	60	108	03 32	60	108	04 32	60	108	05 32	60	108
74	01 23	59	106	02 22	60	106	03 22	60	106	04 22	60	106	05 22	60	106
76	01 12	60	104	02 12	60	104	03 12	60	104	04 12	60	104	05 12	59	104
78	01 02	60	102	02 02	60	102	03 02	60	102	04 02	59	102	05 01	60	102
80	00 52	+60	100	01 52	+60	100	02 52	+59	100	03 51	+60	100	04 51	+60	100
82	00 42	59	98	01 41	60	98	02 41	60	98	03 41	60	98	04 41	60	98
84	00 31	60	96	01 31	60	96	02 31	60	96	03 31	59	96	04 30	60	96
86	00 21	60	94	01 21	59	94	02 20	60	94	03 20	60	94	04 20	60	94
88	00 10	60	92	01 10	60	92	02 10	60	92	03 10	60	92	04 10	59	92
90	00 00	+60	90	01 00	+60	90	02 00	+59	90	02 59	+60	90	03 59	+60	90
92	−0 10	59	88	00 49	60	88	01 49	60	88	02 49	60	88	03 49	59	88
94	−0 21	60	86	00 39	60	86	01 39	59	86	02 38	60	86	03 38	60	86
96	−0 31	59	84	00 28	60	84	01 28	60	84	02 28	60	84	03 28	60	84
98	−0 42	60	82	00 18	60	82	01 18	60	82	02 18	59	82	03 17	60	82
100	−0 52	+60	80	00 08	+60	80	01 08	+59	80	02 07	+60	80	03 07	+60	80
102	−1 02	59	78	−0 03	60	78	00 57	60	78	01 57	60	78	02 57	60	78
104	−1 12	59	76	−0 13	60	76	00 47	60	76	01 47	60	76	02 47	59	76
106	−1 23	60	74	−0 23	60	74	00 37	60	74	01 37	60	74	02 37	59	74
108	−1 33	60	72	−0 33	60	72	00 27	60	72	01 27	60	72	02 27	59	72
110	−1 42	+59	70	−0 43	+60	70	00 17	+60	70	01 17	+60	70	02 17	+60	70
112	−1 52	60	68	−0 52	59	68	00 07	60	68	01 07	60	68	02 07	60	68
114	−2 02	60	66	−1 02	60	66	−0 02	60	66	00 58	59	66	01 57	60	66
116	−2 11	59	64	−1 12	60	64	−0 12	60	64	00 48	60	64	01 48	60	64
118	−2 21	60	62	−1 21	60	62	−0 21	60	62	00 39	60	62	01 39	59	62
120	−2 30	+60	60	−1 30	+60	60	−0 30	+60	60	00 30	+59	60	01 29	+60	60
122	−2 39	60	58	−1 39	60	58	−0 39	60	58	00 21	59	58	01 20	60	58
124	−2 48	60	56	−1 48	60	56	−0 48	60	56	00 12	60	56	01 12	60	56
126	−2 56	60	54	−1 56	60	54	−0 56	59	54	00 03	60	54	01 03	60	54
128	−3 05	60	52	−2 05	60	52	−1 05	60	52	−0 05	60	52	00 55	60	52
130	−3 13	+60	50	−2 13	+60	50	−1 13	+60	50	−0 13	+60	50	00 47	+60	50
132	−3 21	60	48	−2 21	60	48	−1 21	60	48	−0 21	60	48	00 39	60	48
134	−3 28	60	46	−2 28	59	46	−1 29	60	46	−0 29	60	46	00 31	60	46
136	−3 36	60	44	−2 36	60	44	−1 36	60	44	−0 36	60	44	00 24	60	44
138	−3 43	60	42	−2 43	60	42	−1 43	60	42	−0 43	60	42	00 17	60	42

LHA	5° Hc	d	Z	6° Hc	d	Z	7° Hc	d	Z	8° Hc	d	Z	9° Hc	d	Z
	° ′	′	°	° ′	′	°	° ′	′	°	° ′	′	°	° ′	′	°
0	10 00	+60	180	11 00	+60	180	12 00	+60	180	13 00	+60	180	14 00	+60	180
2	10 00	60	178	11 00	60	178	12 00	60	178	13 00	60	178	14 00	60	178
4	09 59	60	176	10 59	60	176	11 59	60	176	12 59	60	176	13 59	60	176
6	09 58	60	174	10 58	60	174	11 58	60	174	12 58	60	174	13 58	60	174
8	09 57	60	172	10 57	60	172	11 57	60	172	12 57	60	172	13 57	60	172
10	09 55	+60	170	10 55	+60	170	11 55	+60	170	12 55	+60	170	13 55	+60	170
12	09 53	60	168	10 53	60	168	11 53	60	168	12 53	60	168	13 53	60	168
14	09 51	60	166	10 51	60	166	11 51	60	166	12 51	60	166	13 51	60	166
16	09 48	60	164	10 48	60	164	11 48	60	164	12 48	60	164	13 48	60	164
18	09 45	60	162	10 45	60	162	11 45	60	162	12 45	60	162	13 45	60	162
20	09 42	+60	160	10 42	+60	160	11 42	+60	160	12 42	+60	160	13 42	+60	160
22	09 38	60	158	10 38	60	158	11 38	60	158	12 38	60	158	13 38	60	158
24	09 34	60	156	10 34	60	156	11 34	60	156	12 34	60	156	13 34	60	156
26	09 29	60	154	10 29	60	154	11 29	60	154	12 29	60	154	13 29	60	154
28	09 25	60	152	10 25	60	152	11 25	59	152	12 24	60	152	13 24	60	152
30	09 19	+60	150	10 19	+60	150	11 19	+60	150	12 19	+60	150	13 19	+60	150
32	09 14	60	148	10 14	60	148	11 14	60	148	12 14	60	148	13 14	60	148
34	09 08	60	146	10 08	60	146	11 08	60	146	12 08	60	146	13 08	60	145
36	09 02	60	144	10 02	60	144	11 02	60	144	12 02	60	144	13 02	60	143
38	08 56	60	142	09 56	60	142	10 56	60	142	11 56	60	142	12 56	59	141
40	08 49	+60	140	09 49	+60	140	10 49	+60	140	11 49	+60	139	12 49	+60	139
42	08 42	60	138	09 42	60	138	10 42	60	138	11 42	60	137	12 42	60	137
44	08 35	60	136	09 35	60	136	10 35	60	136	11 35	60	135	12 35	60	135
46	08 28	60	134	09 28	59	134	10 27	60	133	11 27	60	133	12 27	60	133
48	08 20	60	132	09 20	60	132	10 20	60	131	11 20	59	131	12 19	60	131
50	08 12	+60	130	09 12	+60	130	10 12	+60	129	11 12	+60	129	12 12	+59	129
52	08 04	60	128	09 04	60	128	10 04	59	127	11 03	60	127	12 03	60	127
54	07 55	60	126	08 55	60	126	09 55	60	125	10 55	60	125	11 55	60	125
56	07 47	60	124	08 47	60	124	09 47	59	123	10 46	60	123	11 46	60	123
58	07 38	60	122	08 38	60	122	09 38	60	121	10 38	59	121	11 37	60	121
60	07 29	+60	120	08 29	+60	119	09 29	+60	119	10 29	+59	119	11 28	+60	119
62	07 20	60	118	08 20	59	117	09 19	60	117	10 19	60	117	11 19	60	117
64	07 10	60	116	08 10	60	115	09 10	60	115	10 10	60	115	11 10	60	115
66	07 01	60	114	08 01	60	113	09 01	59	113	10 00	60	113	11 00	60	113
68	06 51	60	112	07 51	60	111	08 51	60	111	09 51	60	111	10 51	59	111
70	06 42	+59	110	07 41	+60	109	08 41	+60	109	09 41	+60	109	10 41	+59	109
72	06 32	59	108	07 31	60	107	08 31	60	107	09 31	60	107	10 31	60	107
74	06 22	59	106	07 21	60	105	08 21	60	105	09 21	60	105	10 21	60	105
76	06 11	60	104	07 11	60	103	08 11	60	103	09 11	60	103	10 11	59	103
78	06 01	60	102	07 01	60	101	08 01	60	101	09 01	59	101	10 00	60	101
80	05 51	+60	100	06 51	+60	99	07 51	+59	99	08 50	+60	99	09 50	+60	99
82	05 41	59	98	06 40	60	98	07 40	60	97	08 40	60	97	09 40	59	97
84	05 30	60	96	06 30	60	96	07 30	60	95	08 30	59	95	09 29	60	95
86	05 20	60	94	06 20	59	94	07 19	60	93	08 19	60	93	09 19	60	93
88	05 09	60	92	06 09	60	92	07 09	60	91	08 09	59	91	09 08	60	91
90	04 59	+60	90	05 59	+59	90	06 58	+60	89	07 58	+60	89	08 58	+60	89
92	04 48	60	88	05 48	60	88	06 48	60	87	07 48	60	87	08 48	59	87
94	04 38	60	86	05 38	60	86	06 38	59	85	07 37	60	85	08 37	60	85
96	04 28	59	84	05 27	60	84	06 27	60	83	07 27	60	83	08 27	59	83
98	04 17	60	82	05 17	60	82	06 17	60	81	07 17	59	81	08 16	60	81
100	04 07	+60	80	05 07	+59	80	06 06	+60	79	07 06	+60	79	08 06	+60	79
102	03 57	59	78	04 56	60	78	05 56	60	77	06 56	60	77	07 56	60	77
104	03 46	60	76	04 46	60	76	05 46	60	76	06 46	60	75	07 46	59	75
106	03 36	60	74	04 36	60	74	05 36	60	74	06 36	60	73	07 36	59	73
108	03 26	60	72	04 26	60	72	05 26	60	72	06 26	60	71	07 26	59	71
110	03 17	+59	70	04 16	+60	70	05 16	+60	70	06 16	+60	69	07 16	+60	69
112	03 07	60	68	04 07	59	68	05 06	60	68	06 06	60	67	07 06	60	67
114	02 57	60	66	03 57	60	66	04 57	60	65	05 57	59	65	06 56	60	65
116	02 48	60	64	03 48	59	64	04 47	60	63	05 47	60	64	06 47	60	63
118	02 38	60	62	03 38	60	62	04 38	60	61	05 38	60	62	06 38	60	61
120	02 29	+60	60	03 29	+60	60	04 29	+60	60	05 29	+60	60	06 29	+59	59
122	02 20	60	58	03 20	60	58	04 20	60	58	05 20	60	58	06 20	60	57
124	02 12	59	56	03 11	60	56	04 11	60	56	05 11	60	56	06 11	60	55
126	02 03	60	54	03 03	60	54	04 03	60	54	05 03	60	54	06 03	59	54
128	01 55	60	52	02 55	59	52	03 54	60	52	04 54	60	52	05 54	60	52
130	01 47	+59	50	02 46	+60	50	03 46	+60	50	04 46	+60	50	05 46	+60	50
132	01 39	60	48	02 39	60	48	03 39	59	48	04 38	60	48	05 38	60	48
134	01 31	60	46	02 31	60	46	03 31	60	46	04 31	60	46	05 31	60	46
136	01 24	60	44	02 24	60	44	03 24	59	44	04 23	60	44	05 23	60	44
138	01 17	60	42	02 17	59	42	03 16	60	42	04 16	60	42	05 16	60	42

LHA	10° Hc	d	Z	11° Hc	d	Z	12° Hc	d	Z	13° Hc	d	Z	14° Hc	d	Z	LHA
	° ′	′	°	° ′	′	°	° ′	′	°	° ′	′	°	° ′	′	°	
0	15 00	+60	180	16 00	+60	180	17 00	+60	180	18 00	+60	180	19 00	+60	180	360
2	15 00	60	178	16 00	60	178	17 00	60	178	18 00	60	178	19 00	60	178	358
4	14 59	60	176	15 59	60	176	16 59	60	176	17 59	60	176	18 59	60	176	356
6	14 58	60	174	15 58	60	174	16 58	60	174	17 58	60	174	18 58	60	174	354
8	14 57	60	172	15 57	60	172	16 57	60	172	17 57	60	172	18 57	60	172	352
10	14 55	+60	170	15 55	+60	170	16 55	+60	170	17 55	+60	170	18 55	+60	170	350
12	14 53	60	168	15 53	60	168	16 53	60	168	17 53	60	168	18 53	60	168	348
14	14 51	60	166	15 51	60	166	16 51	60	166	17 51	60	166	18 51	60	166	346
16	14 48	60	164	15 48	60	164	16 48	60	164	17 48	60	164	18 48	60	164	344
18	14 45	60	162	15 45	60	162	16 45	60	162	17 45	60	162	18 45	60	162	342
20	14 42	+60	160	15 42	+60	160	16 42	+60	160	17 42	+60	160	18 42	+59	160	340
22	14 38	60	158	15 38	60	158	16 38	60	158	17 38	60	158	18 38	60	157	338
24	14 34	60	156	15 34	60	156	16 34	60	156	17 34	60	155	18 34	59	155	336
26	14 29	60	154	15 29	60	154	16 29	60	153	17 29	60	153	18 29	60	153	334
28	14 24	60	152	15 24	60	151	16 24	60	151	17 24	60	151	18 24	60	151	332
30	14 19	+60	150	15 19	+60	149	16 19	+60	149	17 19	+60	149	18 19	+60	149	330
32	14 14	60	147	15 14	60	147	16 14	60	147	17 14	59	147	18 13	60	147	328
34	14 08	60	145	15 08	60	145	16 08	60	145	17 08	60	145	18 08	60	145	326
36	14 02	60	143	15 02	60	143	16 02	60	143	17 02	59	143	18 01	60	143	324
38	13 55	60	141	14 55	60	141	15 55	60	141	16 55	60	141	17 55	60	141	322
40	13 49	+60	139	14 49	+60	139	15 49	+59	139	16 48	+60	139	17 48	+60	139	320
42	13 42	60	137	14 42	60	137	15 42	59	137	16 41	60	137	17 41	60	137	318
44	13 35	59	135	14 34	60	135	15 34	60	135	16 34	60	135	17 34	60	135	316
46	13 27	60	133	14 27	60	133	15 27	60	133	16 27	60	133	17 27	59	133	314
48	13 19	60	131	14 19	60	131	15 19	60	131	16 19	60	131	17 19	60	131	312
50	13 11	+60	129	14 11	+60	129	15 11	+60	129	16 11	+60	129	17 11	+60	129	310
52	13 03	60	127	14 03	60	127	15 03	60	127	16 03	60	127	17 03	59	127	308
54	12 55	60	125	13 55	59	125	14 54	60	125	15 54	60	125	16 54	60	125	306
56	12 46	60	123	13 46	60	123	14 46	60	123	15 46	59	123	16 45	60	123	304
58	12 37	60	121	13 37	60	121	14 37	60	121	15 37	60	121	16 37	59	121	302
60	12 28	+60	119	13 28	+60	119	14 28	+60	119	15 28	+59	119	16 27	+60	119	300
62	12 19	60	117	13 19	60	117	14 19	59	117	15 18	60	117	16 18	60	117	298
64	12 10	59	115	13 09	60	115	14 09	60	115	15 09	60	115	16 09	60	115	296
66	12 00	60	113	13 00	60	113	14 00	59	113	14 59	60	113	15 59	60	113	294
68	11 50	60	111	12 50	60	111	13 50	60	111	14 50	59	111	15 49	60	111	292
70	11 40	+60	109	12 40	+60	109	13 40	+60	109	14 40	+60	109	15 40	+59	109	290
72	11 31	59	107	12 30	60	107	13 30	60	107	14 30	60	107	15 30	59	107	288
74	11 21	59	105	12 20	60	105	13 20	60	105	14 20	60	105	15 20	59	105	286
76	11 10	60	103	12 10	60	103	13 10	60	103	14 10	59	103	15 09	60	103	284
78	11 00	60	101	12 00	60	101	13 00	59	101	13 59	60	101	14 59	60	101	282
80	10 50	+60	99	11 50	+59	99	12 49	+60	99	13 49	+60	99	14 49	+60	99	280
82	10 39	60	97	11 39	60	97	12 39	60	97	13 39	60	97	14 39	59	97	278
84	10 29	60	95	11 29	60	95	12 29	59	95	13 28	60	95	14 28	60	95	276
86	10 19	59	93	11 18	60	93	12 18	60	93	13 18	60	93	14 18	59	93	274
88	10 08	60	91	11 08	60	91	12 08	59	91	13 07	60	91	14 07	60	91	272
90	09 58	+60	89	10 58	+59	89	11 57	+60	89	12 57	+60	89	13 57	+60	89	270
92	09 47	60	87	10 47	60	87	11 47	60	87	12 47	59	87	13 46	60	87	268
94	09 37	60	85	10 37	59	85	11 36	60	85	12 36	60	85	13 36	60	85	266
96	09 26	60	83	10 26	60	83	11 26	60	83	12 26	60	83	13 26	59	83	264
98	09 16	60	81	10 16	60	81	11 16	59	81	12 15	60	81	13 15	60	81	262
100	09 06	+60	79	10 06	+59	79	11 05	+60	79	12 05	+60	79	13 05	+60	79	260
102	08 56	59	77	09 55	60	77	10 55	60	77	11 55	60	77	12 55	59	77	258
104	08 45	60	75	09 45	60	75	10 45	60	75	11 45	60	75	12 45	59	75	256
106	08 35	60	73	09 35	60	73	10 35	60	73	11 35	59	73	12 34	60	73	254
108	08 25	60	71	09 25	60	71	10 25	60	71	11 25	60	71	12 25	59	71	252
110	08 16	+59	69	09 15	+60	69	10 15	+60	69	11 15	+60	69	12 15	+59	69	250
112	08 06	60	67	09 06	59	67	10 05	60	67	11 05	60	67	12 05	60	67	248
114	07 56	60	65	08 56	60	65	09 56	60	65	10 56	59	65	11 55	60	65	246
116	07 47	60	63	08 47	59	63	09 46	60	63	10 46	60	63	11 46	60	63	244
118	07 38	59	61	08 37	60	61	09 37	60	61	10 37	60	61	11 37	60	61	242
120	07 28	+60	59	08 28	+60	59	09 28	+60	59	10 28	+60	59	11 28	+60	59	240
122	07 20	59	57	08 19	60	57	09 19	60	57	10 19	60	57	11 19	60	57	238
124	07 11	60	55	08 11	60	55	09 11	59	55	10 10	60	55	11 10	60	55	236
126	07 02	60	53	08 02	60	53	09 02	60	53	10 02	60	53	11 02	60	53	234
128	06 54	60	51	07 54	60	51	08 54	60	51	09 54	59	51	10 53	60	51	232
130	06 46	+60	49	07 46	+60	49	08 46	+60	49	09 46	+59	49	10 45	+60	49	230
132	06 38	60	48	07 38	60	47	08 38	60	47	09 38	60	47	10 38	60	47	228
134	06 31	59	46	07 30	60	45	08 30	60	45	09 30	60	45	10 30	60	45	226
136	06 23	60	44	07 23	60	43	08 23	60	43	09 23	60	43	10 23	60	43	224
138	06 16	60	42	07 16	60	42	08 16	60	41	09 16	60	41	10 16	60	41	222

S. Lat. {LHA greater than 180°........ Zn=180−Z; LHA less than 180°........... Zn=180+Z}

DECLINATION (0°-14°) SAME NAME AS LATITUDE

LAT 85°

LAT 85°

N. Lat. {LHA greater than 180°....... Zn=Z; LHA less than 180°.......... Zn=360−Z}

DECLINATION (0°-14°) SAME NAME AS LATITUDE

LHA	0° Hc	d	Z	1° Hc	d	Z	2° Hc	d	Z	3° Hc	d	Z	4° Hc	d	Z	LHA
	° ′	′	°	° ′	′	°	° ′	′	°	° ′	′	°	° ′	′	°	
140	−3 50	+60	40	−2 50	+60	40	−1 50	+60	40	−0 50	+60	40	00 10	+60	40	220
142	−3 56	60	38	−2 56	60	38	−1 56	59	38	−0 57	60	38	00 03	60	38	218
144	−4 03	60	36	−3 03	60	36	−2 03	60	36	−1 03	60	36	−0 03	60	36	216
146	−4 09	60	34	−3 09	60	34	−2 09	60	34	−1 09	60	34	−0 09	60	34	214
148	−4 14	60	32	−3 14	60	32	−2 14	59	32	−1 15	60	32	−0 15	60	32	212
150	−4 20	+60	30	−3 20	+60	30	−2 20	+60	30	−1 20	+60	30	−0 20	+60	30	210
152	−4 25	60	28	−3 25	60	28	−2 25	60	28	−1 25	60	28	−0 25	60	28	208
154	−4 30	60	26	−3 30	60	26	−2 30	60	26	−1 30	60	26	−0 30	60	26	206
156	−4 34	60	24	−3 34	60	24	−2 34	60	24	−1 34	60	24	−0 34	60	24	204
158	−4 38	60	22	−3 38	60	22	−2 38	60	22	−1 38	60	22	−0 38	60	22	202
160	−4 42	+60	20	−3 42	+60	20	−2 42	+60	20	−1 42	+60	20	−0 42	+60	20	200
162	−4 45	60	18	−3 45	60	18	−2 45	60	18	−1 45	60	18	−0 45	60	18	198
164	−4 48	60	16	−3 48	60	16	−2 48	60	16	−1 48	60	16	−0 48	60	16	196
166	−4 51	60	14	−3 51	60	14	−2 51	60	14	−1 51	60	14	−0 51	60	14	194
168	−4 53	60	12	−3 53	60	12	−2 53	60	12	−1 53	60	12	−0 53	60	12	192
170	−4 55	+60	10	−3 55	+60	10	−2 55	+60	10	−1 55	+60	10	−0 55	+60	10	190
172	−4 57	60	8	−3 57	60	8	−2 57	60	8	−1 57	60	8	−0 57	60	8	188
174	−4 58	60	6	−3 58	60	6	−2 58	60	6	−1 58	60	6	−0 58	60	6	186
176	−4 59	60	4	−3 59	60	4	−2 59	60	4	−1 59	60	4	−0 59	60	4	184
178	−5 00	60	2	−4 00	60	2	−3 00	60	2	−2 00	60	2	−1 00	60	2	182
180	−5 00	+60	0	−4 00	+60	0	−3 00	+60	0	−2 00	+60	0	−1 00	+60	0	180

LHA	5° Hc	d	Z	6° Hc	d	Z	7° Hc	d	Z	8° Hc	d	Z	9° Hc	d	Z	LHA
	° ′	′	°	° ′	′	°	° ′	′	°	° ′	′	°	° ′	′	°	
140	01 10	+60	40	02 10	+60	40	03 10	+60	40	04 10	+60	40	05 10	+59	40	220
142	01 03	60	38	02 03	60	38	03 03	60	38	04 03	60	38	05 03	60	38	218
144	00 57	60	36	01 57	60	36	02 57	60	36	03 57	60	36	04 57	60	36	216
146	00 51	60	34	01 51	60	34	02 51	60	34	03 51	60	34	04 51	60	34	214
148	00 45	60	32	01 45	60	32	02 45	60	32	03 45	60	32	04 45	60	32	212
150	00 40	+60	30	01 40	+60	30	02 40	+60	30	03 40	+60	30	04 40	+60	30	210
152	00 35	60	28	01 35	60	28	02 35	60	28	03 35	60	28	04 35	60	28	208
154	00 30	60	26	01 30	60	26	02 30	60	26	03 30	60	26	04 30	60	26	206
156	00 26	60	24	01 26	60	24	02 26	60	24	03 26	60	24	04 26	60	24	204
158	00 22	60	22	01 22	60	22	02 22	60	22	03 22	60	22	04 22	60	22	202
160	00 18	+60	20	01 18	+60	20	02 18	+60	20	03 18	+60	20	04 18	+60	20	200
162	00 15	60	18	01 15	60	18	02 15	60	18	03 15	60	18	04 15	60	18	198
164	00 12	60	16	01 12	60	16	02 12	59	16	03 11	60	16	04 11	60	16	196
166	00 09	60	14	01 09	60	14	02 09	60	14	03 09	60	14	04 09	60	14	194
168	00 07	60	12	01 07	60	12	02 07	60	12	03 07	60	12	04 07	60	12	192
170	00 05	+60	10	01 05	+60	10	02 05	+60	10	03 05	+60	10	04 05	+60	10	190
172	00 03	60	8	01 03	60	8	02 03	60	8	03 03	60	8	04 03	60	8	188
174	00 02	60	6	01 02	60	6	02 02	60	6	03 02	60	6	04 02	60	6	186
176	00 01	60	4	01 01	60	4	02 01	60	4	03 01	60	4	04 01	60	4	184
178	00 00	60	2	01 00	60	2	02 00	60	2	03 00	60	2	04 00	60	2	182
180	00 00	+60	0	01 00	+60	0	02 00	+60	0	03 00	+60	0	04 00	+60	0	180

LHA	10° Hc	d	Z	11° Hc	d	Z	12° Hc	d	Z	13° Hc	d	Z	14° Hc	d	Z	LHA
	° ′	′	°	° ′	′	°	° ′	′	°	° ′	′	°	° ′	′	°	
140	06 09	+60	40	07 09	+60	40	08 09	+60	39	09 09	+60	39	10 09	+60	39	220
142	06 03	60	38	07 03	60	38	08 03	60	38	09 03	60	37	10 03	59	37	218
144	05 57	60	36	06 57	60	36	07 57	59	36	08 56	60	35	09 56	60	35	216
146	05 51	60	34	06 51	60	34	07 51	60	34	08 51	59	34	09 50	60	33	214
148	05 45	60	32	06 45	60	32	07 45	60	32	08 45	60	32	09 45	60	31	212
150	05 40	+60	30	06 40	+60	30	07 40	+60	30	08 40	+60	30	09 40	+59	30	210
152	05 35	60	28	06 35	60	28	07 35	60	28	08 35	60	28	09 35	59	28	208
154	05 30	60	26	06 30	60	26	07 30	60	26	08 30	60	26	09 30	60	26	206
156	05 26	60	24	06 26	60	24	07 26	60	24	08 26	60	24	09 26	59	24	204
158	05 22	60	22	06 22	60	22	07 22	60	22	08 22	59	22	09 21	60	22	202
160	05 18	+60	20	06 18	+60	20	07 18	+60	20	08 18	+60	20	09 18	+60	20	200
162	05 15	60	18	06 15	60	18	07 15	59	18	08 14	60	18	09 14	60	18	198
164	05 11	60	16	06 11	60	16	07 11	60	16	08 11	60	16	09 11	60	16	196
166	05 09	60	14	06 09	60	14	07 09	60	14	08 09	60	14	09 09	60	14	194
168	05 07	60	12	06 07	60	12	07 07	59	12	08 06	60	12	09 06	60	12	192
170	05 05	+60	10	06 05	+60	10	07 05	+60	10	08 05	+60	10	09 05	+60	10	190
172	05 03	60	8	06 03	60	8	07 03	60	8	08 03	60	8	09 03	60	8	188
174	05 02	60	6	06 02	60	6	07 02	60	6	08 02	60	6	09 02	60	6	186
176	05 01	60	4	06 01	60	4	07 01	60	4	08 01	60	4	09 01	60	4	184
178	05 00	60	2	06 00	60	2	07 00	60	2	08 00	60	2	09 00	60	2	182
180	05 00	+60	0	06 00	+60	0	07 00	+60	0	08 00	+60	0	09 00	+60	0	180

0°	1°	2°	3°	4°	5°	6°	7°	8°	9°	10°	11°	12°	13°	14°

S. Lat. {LHA greater than 180°....... Zn=180−Z; LHA less than 180°.......... Zn=180+Z}

DECLINATION (0°-14°) SAME NAME AS LATITUDE

LAT 85°

LAT 85°

N. Lat. {LHA greater than 180°....... Zn=Z; LHA less than 180°.......... Zn=360−Z}

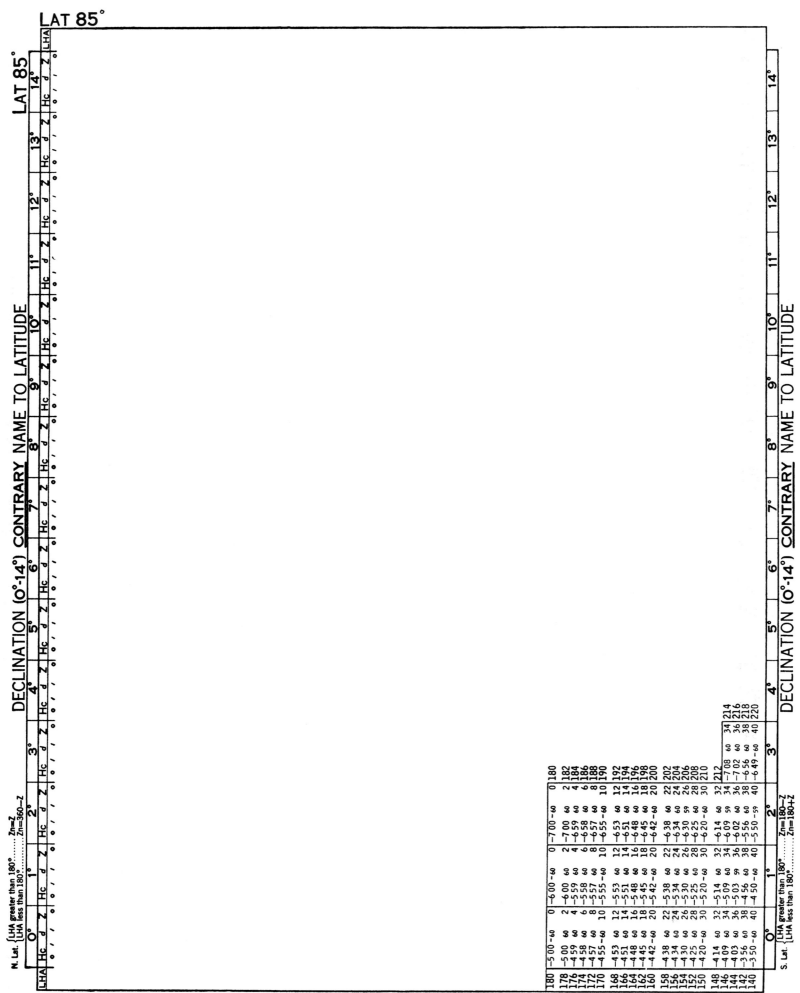

DECLINATION (0°-14°) CONTRARY NAME TO LATITUDE

LHA	0° Hc	0° d	0° Z	1° Hc	1° d	1° Z	2° Hc	2° d	2° Z	3° Hc	3° d	3° Z	LHA
	° ′	′	°	° ′	′	°	° ′	′	°	° ′	′	°	
180	−5 00	−60	0	−6 00	−60	0	−7 00	−60	0				180
178	−5 00	60	2	−6 00	60	2	−7 00	60	2				182
176	−4 59	60	4	−5 59	60	4	−6 59	60	4				184
174	−4 58	60	6	−5 58	60	6	−6 58	60	6				186
172	−4 57	60	8	−5 57	60	8	−6 57	60	8				188
170	−4 55	−60	10	−5 55	−60	10	−6 55	−60	10				190
168	−4 53	60	12	−5 53	60	12	−6 53	60	12				192
166	−4 51	60	14	−5 51	60	14	−6 51	60	14				194
164	−4 48	60	16	−5 48	60	16	−6 48	60	16				196
162	−4 45	60	18	−5 45	60	18	−6 45	60	18				198
160	−4 42	−60	20	−5 42	−60	20	−6 42	−60	20				200
158	−4 38	60	22	−5 38	60	22	−6 38	60	22				202
156	−4 34	60	24	−5 34	60	24	−6 34	60	24				204
154	−4 30	60	26	−5 30	60	26	−6 30	59	26				206
152	−4 25	60	28	−5 25	60	28	−6 25	60	28				208
150	−4 20	−60	30	−5 20	−60	30	−6 20	−60	30				210
148	−4 14	60	32	−5 14	60	32	−6 14	60	32				212
146	−4 09	60	34	−5 09	60	34	−6 09	59	34	−7 08	60	34	214
144	−4 03	60	36	−5 03	59	36	−6 02	60	36	−7 02	60	36	216
142	−3 56	60	38	−4 56	60	38	−5 56	60	38	−6 56	60	38	218
140	−3 50	−60	40	−4 50	−60	40	−5 50	−59	40	−6 49	−60	40	220

S. Lat. {LHA greater than 180°....... Zn=180−Z; LHA less than 180°.......... Zn=180+Z}

DECLINATION (0°-14°) CONTRARY NAME TO LATITUDE

N. Lat. {LHA greater than 180°....... Zn=Z; LHA less than 180°.......... Zn=360−Z}

DECLINATION (0°-14°) CONTRARY NAME TO LATITUDE

LHA	0° Hc	d	Z	1° Hc	d	Z	2° Hc	d	Z	3° Hc	d	Z	4° Hc	d	Z
	° ′	′	°	° ′	′	°	° ′	′	°	° ′	′	°	° ′	′	°
138	-3 43	60	42	-4 43	60	42	-5 43	60	42	-6 43	59	42			
136	-3 36	60	44	-4 36	59	44	-5 35	60	44	-6 35	60	44			
134	-3 28	60	46	-4 28	60	46	-5 28	60	46	-6 28	60	46			
132	-3 21	59	48	-4 20	60	48	-5 20	60	48	-6 20	60	48			
130	-3 13	-60	50	-4 13	-59	50	-5 12	-60	50	-6 12	-60	50	-7 12	-60	50
128	-3 05	59	52	-4 04	60	52	-5 04	60	52	-6 04	60	52	-7 04	60	52
126	-2 56	60	54	-3 56	60	54	-4 56	60	54	-5 56	60	54	-6 56	60	54
124	-2 48	59	56	-3 47	60	56	-4 47	60	56	-5 47	60	56	-6 47	60	56
122	-2 39	60	58	-3 39	60	58	-4 39	59	58	-5 38	60	58	-6 38	60	58
120	-2 30	-60	60	-3 30	-60	60	-4 30	-59	60	-5 29	-60	60	-6 29	-60	60
118	-2 21	60	62	-3 21	59	62	-4 20	60	62	-5 20	60	62	-6 20	59	62
116	-2 11	60	64	-3 11	60	64	-4 11	60	64	-5 11	60	64	-6 11	59	64
114	-2 02	60	66	-3 02	60	66	-4 02	59	66	-5 01	60	66	-6 01	60	66
112	-1 52	60	68	-2 52	60	68	-3 52	60	68	-4 52	60	68	-5 52	59	68
110	-1 42	-60	70	-2 42	-60	70	-3 42	-60	70	-4 42	-60	70	-5 42	-60	70
108	-1 33	59	72	-2 32	60	72	-3 32	60	72	-4 32	60	72	-5 32	60	72
106	-1 23	59	74	-2 22	60	74	-3 22	60	74	-4 22	60	74	-5 22	60	74
104	-1 12	60	76	-2 12	60	76	-3 12	60	76	-4 12	60	76	-5 12	59	76
102	-1 02	60	78	-2 02	60	78	-3 02	60	78	-4 02	59	78	-5 01	60	78
100	-0 52	-60	80	-1 52	-60	80	-2 52	-59	80	-3 51	-60	80	-4 51	-60	80
98	-0 42	59	82	-1 41	60	82	-2 41	60	82	-3 41	60	82	-4 41	60	82
96	-0 31	60	84	-1 31	60	84	-2 31	60	84	-3 31	59	84	-4 30	60	84
94	-0 21	60	86	-1 21	59	86	-2 20	60	86	-3 20	60	86	-4 20	60	86
92	-0 10	60	88	-1 10	60	88	-2 10	60	88	-3 10	60	88	-4 10	59	88
90	00 00	-60	90	-1 00	-60	90	-2 00	-59	90	-2 59	-60	90	-3 59	-60	90
88	00 10	59	92	-0 49	60	92	-1 49	60	92	-2 49	60	92	-3 49	59	92
86	00 21	60	94	-0 39	60	94	-1 39	59	94	-2 38	60	94	-3 38	60	94
84	00 31	59	96	-0 28	60	96	-1 28	60	96	-2 28	60	96	-3 28	60	96
82	00 42	60	98	-0 18	60	98	-1 18	60	98	-2 18	59	98	-3 17	60	98
80	00 52	-60	100	-0 08	-60	100	-1 08	-59	100	-2 07	-60	100	-3 07	-60	100
78	01 02	59	102	00 03	60	102	-0 57	60	102	-1 57	60	102	-2 57	60	102
76	01 12	59	104	00 13	60	104	-0 47	60	104	-1 47	60	104	-2 47	59	104
74	01 23	60	106	00 23	60	106	-0 37	60	106	-1 37	60	106	-2 37	59	106
72	01 33	60	108	00 33	60	108	-0 27	60	108	-1 27	60	108	-2 27	59	108
70	01 42	-59	110	00 43	-60	110	-0 17	-60	110	-1 17	-60	110	-2 17	-60	110
68	01 52	60	112	00 52	59	112	-0 07	60	112	-1 07	60	112	-2 07	60	112
66	02 02	60	114	01 02	60	114	00 02	60	114	-0 58	59	114	-1 57	60	114
64	02 11	59	116	01 12	60	116	00 12	60	116	-0 48	60	116	-1 48	60	116
62	02 21	60	118	01 21	60	118	00 21	60	118	-0 39	60	118	-1 39	59	118
60	02 30	-60	120	01 30	-60	120	00 30	-60	120	-0 30	-59	120	-1 29	-60	120
58	02 39	60	122	01 39	60	122	00 39	60	122	-0 21	59	122	-1 20	60	122
56	02 48	60	124	01 48	60	124	00 48	60	124	-0 12	60	124	-1 12	60	124
54	02 56	60	126	01 56	60	126	00 56	59	126	-0 03	60	126	-1 03	60	126
52	03 05	60	128	02 05	60	128	01 05	60	128	00 05	60	128	-0 55	60	128
50	03 13	-60	130	02 13	-60	130	01 13	-60	130	00 13	-60	130	-0 47	-60	130
48	03 21	60	132	02 21	60	132	01 21	60	132	00 21	60	132	-0 39	60	132
46	03 28	60	134	02 28	59	134	01 29	60	134	00 29	60	134	-0 31	60	134
44	03 36	60	136	02 36	60	136	01 36	60	136	00 36	60	136	-0 24	60	136
42	03 43	60	138	02 43	60	138	01 43	60	138	00 43	60	138	-0 17	60	138
40	03 50	-60	140	02 50	-60	140	01 50	-60	140	00 50	-60	140	-0 10	-60	140
38	03 56	60	142	02 56	60	142	01 56	59	142	00 57	60	142	-0 03	60	142
36	04 03	60	144	03 03	60	144	02 03	60	144	01 03	60	144	00 03	60	144
34	04 09	60	146	03 09	60	146	02 09	60	146	01 09	60	146	00 09	60	146
32	04 14	60	148	03 14	60	148	02 14	59	148	01 15	60	148	00 15	60	148
30	04 20	-60	150	03 20	-60	150	02 20	-60	150	01 20	-60	150	00 20	-60	150
28	04 25	60	152	03 25	60	152	02 25	60	152	01 25	60	152	00 25	60	152
26	04 30	60	154	03 30	60	154	02 30	60	154	01 30	60	154	00 30	60	154
24	04 34	60	156	03 34	60	156	02 34	60	156	01 34	60	156	00 34	60	156
22	04 38	60	158	03 38	60	158	02 38	60	158	01 38	60	158	00 38	60	158
20	04 42	-60	160	03 42	-60	160	02 42	-60	160	01 42	-60	160	00 42	-60	160
18	04 45	60	162	03 45	60	162	02 45	60	162	01 45	60	162	00 45	60	162
16	04 48	60	164	03 48	60	164	02 48	60	164	01 48	60	164	00 48	60	164
14	04 51	60	166	03 51	60	166	02 51	60	166	01 51	60	166	00 51	60	166
12	04 53	60	168	03 53	60	168	02 53	60	168	01 53	60	168	00 53	60	168
10	04 55	-60	170	03 55	-60	170	02 55	-60	170	01 55	-60	170	00 55	-60	170
8	04 57	60	172	03 57	60	172	02 57	60	172	01 57	60	172	00 57	60	172
6	04 58	60	174	03 58	60	174	02 58	60	174	01 58	60	174	00 58	60	174
4	04 59	60	176	03 59	60	176	02 59	60	176	01 59	60	176	00 59	60	176
2	05 00	60	178	04 00	60	178	03 00	60	178	02 00	60	178	01 00	60	178
0	05 00	-60	180	04 00	-60	180	03 00	-60	180	02 00	-60	180	01 00	-60	180

LHA	5° Hc	d	Z	6° Hc	d	Z	7° Hc	d	Z	8° Hc	d	Z	9° Hc	d	Z
	° ′	′	°	° ′	′	°	° ′	′	°	° ′	′	°	° ′	′	°
138															
136															
134															
132															
130															
128															
126															
124															
122															
120															
118															
116	-7 10	60	64												
114	-7 01	60	66												
112	-6 51	59	68												
110	-6 42	-60	70												
108	-6 32	60	72												
106	-6 22	60	74												
104	-6 11	60	76	-7 11	60	77									
102	-6 01	60	78	-7 01	60	79									
100	-5 51	-60	80	-6 51	-60	81									
98	-5 41	59	82	-6 40	59	82									
96	-5 30	60	84	-6 30	60	84									
94	-5 20	60	86	-6 20	59	86	-7 19	59	87						
92	-5 09	60	88	-6 09	60	88	-7 09	60	89						
90	-4 59	-60	90	-5 59	-59	90	-6 58	-60	91						
88	-4 48	60	92	-5 48	60	92	-6 48	60	93						
86	-4 38	60	94	-5 38	60	94	-6 38	60	95						
84	-4 28	59	96	-5 27	60	96	-6 27	59	97						
82	-4 17	60	98	-5 17	60	98	-6 17	60	99	-7 17	59	99			
80	-4 07	-60	100	-5 07	-59	100	-6 06	-60	101	-7 06	-60	101			
78	-3 57	59	102	-4 56	60	102	-5 56	60	103	-6 56	60	103			
76	-3 46	60	104	-4 46	60	104	-5 46	60	104	-6 46	60	105			
74	-3 36	60	106	-4 36	60	106	-5 36	60	106	-6 36	60	107			
72	-3 26	60	108	-4 26	60	108	-5 26	60	108	-6 26	60	109			
70	-3 17	-59	110	-4 16	-60	110	-5 16	-60	110	-6 16	-60	111	-7 16	-60	111
68	-3 07	60	112	-4 07	59	112	-5 06	60	112	-6 06	60	113	-7 06	60	113
66	-2 57	60	114	-3 57	60	114	-4 57	60	115	-5 57	59	115	-6 56	60	115
64	-2 48	60	116	-3 48	59	116	-4 47	60	117	-5 47	60	116	-6 47	60	117
62	-2 38	60	118	-3 38	60	118	-4 38	60	119	-5 38	60	118	-6 38	60	119
60	-2 29	-60	120	-3 29	-60	120	-4 29	-60	120	-5 29	-60	120	-6 29	-59	121
58	-2 20	60	122	-3 20	60	122	-4 20	60	122	-5 20	60	122	-6 20	60	123
56	-2 12	59	124	-3 11	60	124	-4 11	60	124	-5 11	60	124	-6 11	60	125
54	-2 03	60	126	-3 03	60	126	-4 03	60	126	-5 03	60	126	-6 03	59	126
52	-1 55	60	128	-2 55	59	128	-3 54	60	128	-4 54	60	128	-5 54	60	128
50	-1 47	-59	130	-2 46	-60	130	-3 46	-60	130	-4 46	-60	130	-5 46	-60	130
48	-1 39	60	132	-2 39	60	132	-3 39	59	132	-4 38	60	132	-5 38	60	132
46	-1 31	60	134	-2 31	60	134	-3 31	60	134	-4 31	60	134	-5 31	60	134
44	-1 24	60	136	-2 24	60	136	-3 24	59	136	-4 23	60	136	-5 23	60	136
42	-1 17	60	138	-2 17	59	138	-3 16	60	138	-4 16	60	138	-5 16	60	138
40	-1 10	-60	140	-2 10	-60	140	-3 10	-60	140	-4 10	-60	140	-5 10	-59	140
38	-1 03	60	142	-2 03	60	142	-3 03	60	142	-4 03	60	142	-5 03	60	142
36	-0 57	60	144	-1 57	60	144	-2 57	60	144	-3 57	60	144	-4 57	60	144
34	-0 51	60	146	-1 51	60	146	-2 51	60	146	-3 51	60	146	-4 51	60	146
32	-0 45	60	148	-1 45	60	148	-2 45	60	148	-3 45	60	148	-4 45	60	148
30	-0 40	-60	150	-1 40	-60	150	-2 40	-60	150	-3 40	-60	150	-4 40	-60	150
28	-0 35	60	152	-1 35	60	152	-2 35	60	152	-3 35	60	152	-4 35	60	152
26	-0 30	60	154	-1 30	60	154	-2 30	60	154	-3 30	60	154	-4 30	60	154
24	-0 26	60	156	-1 26	60	156	-2 26	60	156	-3 26	60	156	-4 26	60	156
22	-0 22	60	158	-1 22	60	158	-2 22	60	158	-3 22	60	158	-4 22	60	158
20	-0 18	-60	160	-1 18	-60	160	-2 18	-60	160	-3 18	-60	160	-4 18	-60	160
18	-0 15	60	162	-1 15	60	162	-2 15	60	162	-3 15	60	162	-4 15	60	162
16	-0 12	60	164	-1 12	60	164	-2 12	59	164	-3 11	60	164	-4 11	60	164
14	-0 09	60	166	-1 09	60	166	-2 09	60	166	-3 09	60	166	-4 09	60	166
12	-0 07	60	168	-1 07	60	168	-2 07	60	168	-3 07	60	168	-4 07	60	168
10	-0 05	-60	170	-1 05	-60	170	-2 05	-60	170	-3 05	-60	170	-4 05	-60	170
8	-0 03	60	172	-1 03	60	172	-2 03	60	172	-3 03	60	172	-4 03	60	172
6	-0 02	60	174	-1 02	60	174	-2 02	60	174	-3 02	60	174	-4 02	60	174
4	-0 01	60	176	-1 01	60	176	-2 01	60	176	-3 01	60	176	-4 01	60	176
2	00 00	60	178	-1 00	60	178	-2 00	60	178	-3 00	60	178	-4 00	60	178
0	00 00	-60	180	-1 00	-60	180	-2 00	-60	180	-3 00	-60	180	-4 00	-60	180

LHA	10° Hc	d	Z	11° Hc	d	Z	12° Hc	d	Z	13° Hc	d	Z	14° Hc	d	Z	LHA
	° ′	′	°	° ′	′	°	° ′	′	°	° ′	′	°	° ′	′	°	
138																222
136																224
134																226
132																228
130																230
128																232
126																234
124																236
122																238
120																240
118																242
116																244
114																246
112																248
110																250
108																252
106																254
104																256
102																258
100																260
98																262
96																264
94																266
92																268
90																270
88																272
86																274
84																276
82																278
80																280
78																282
76																284
74																286
72																288
70																290
68																292
66																294
64																296
62																298
60																300
58																302
56	-7 11	60	125													304
54	-7 02	60	127													306
52	-6 54	60	129													308
50	-6 46	-60	131													310
48	-6 38	60	132													312
46	-6 31	59	134													314
44	-6 23	60	136													316
42	-6 16	60	138													318
40	-6 09	-60	140	-7 09	-60	140										320
38	-6 03	60	142	-7 03	60	142										322
36	-5 57	60	144	-6 57	60	144										324
34	-5 51	60	146	-6 51	60	146										326
32	-5 45	60	148	-6 45	60	148										328
30	-5 40	-60	150	-6 40	-60	150										330
28	-5 35	60	152	-6 35	60	152										332
26	-5 30	60	154	-6 30	60	154										334
24	-5 26	60	156	-6 26	60	156										336
22	-5 22	60	158	-6 22	60	158										338
20	-5 18	-60	160	-6 18	-60	160										340
18	-5 15	60	162	-6 15	60	162										342
16	-5 11	60	164	-6 11	60	164										344
14	-5 09	60	166	-6 09	60	166										346
12	-5 07	60	168	-6 07	60	168										348
10	-5 05	-60	170	-6 05	-60	170										350
8	-5 03	60	172	-6 03	60	172										352
6	-5 02	60	174	-6 02	60	174										354
4	-5 01	60	176	-6 01	60	176										356
2	-5 00	60	178	-6 00	60	178	-7 00	60	178							358
0	-5 00	-60	180	-6 00	-60	180	-7 00	-60	180							360

S. Lat. {LHA greater than 180°....... Zn=180−Z; LHA less than 180°.......... Zn=180+Z}

N. Lat. {LHA greater than 180°....... Zn=Z / LHA less than 180°.......... Zn=360−Z

DECLINATION (15°-29°) SAME NAME AS LATITUDE

LAT 85°

LHA	15° Hc	d	Z	16° Hc	d	Z	17° Hc	d	Z	18° Hc	d	Z	19° Hc	d	Z
	° ′	′	°	° ′	′	°	° ′	′	°	° ′	′	°	° ′	′	°
0	20 00	+60	180	21 00	+60	180	22 00	+60	180	23 00	+60	180	24 00	+60	180
2	20 00	60	178	21 00	60	178	22 00	60	178	23 00	60	178	24 00	60	178
4	19 59	60	176	20 59	60	176	21 59	60	176	22 59	60	176	23 59	60	176
6	19 58	60	174	20 58	60	174	21 58	60	174	22 58	60	174	23 58	60	174
8	19 57	60	172	20 57	60	172	21 57	60	172	22 57	60	172	23 57	60	172
10	19 55	+60	170	20 55	+60	170	21 55	+60	170	22 55	+60	170	23 55	+60	170
12	19 53	60	168	20 53	60	168	21 53	60	168	22 53	60	168	23 53	60	168
14	19 51	60	166	20 51	60	166	21 51	60	166	22 51	60	166	23 51	60	166
16	19 48	60	164	20 48	60	164	21 48	60	164	22 48	60	164	23 48	60	164
18	19 45	60	162	20 45	60	162	21 45	60	161	22 45	60	161	23 45	60	161
20	19 41	+60	160	20 41	+60	159	21 41	+60	159	22 41	+60	159	23 41	+60	159
22	19 38	60	157	20 38	60	157	21 38	60	157	22 38	60	157	23 38	59	157
24	19 33	60	155	20 33	60	155	21 33	60	155	22 33	60	155	23 33	60	155
26	19 29	60	153	20 29	60	153	21 29	60	153	22 29	60	153	23 29	60	153
28	19 24	60	151	20 24	60	151	21 24	60	151	22 24	60	151	23 24	60	151
30	19 19	+60	149	20 19	+60	149	21 19	+60	149	22 19	+60	149	23 19	+60	149
32	19 13	60	147	20 13	60	147	21 13	60	147	22 13	60	147	23 13	60	147
34	19 08	59	145	20 07	60	145	21 07	60	145	22 07	60	145	23 07	60	145
36	19 01	60	143	20 01	60	143	21 01	60	143	22 01	60	143	23 01	60	143
38	18 55	60	141	19 55	60	141	20 55	60	141	21 55	60	141	22 55	59	141
40	18 48	+60	139	19 48	+60	139	20 48	+60	139	21 48	+60	139	22 48	+60	139
42	18 41	60	137	19 41	60	137	20 41	60	137	21 41	60	137	22 41	60	137
44	18 34	60	135	19 34	60	135	20 34	60	135	21 34	59	135	22 33	60	135
46	18 26	60	133	19 26	60	133	20 26	60	133	21 26	60	133	22 26	60	133
48	18 19	60	131	19 19	59	131	20 18	60	131	21 18	60	131	22 18	60	131
50	18 11	+59	129	19 10	+60	129	20 10	+60	129	21 10	+60	129	22 10	+60	129
52	18 02	60	127	19 02	60	127	20 02	60	127	21 02	60	127	22 02	60	127
54	17 54	60	125	18 54	60	125	19 54	59	125	20 53	60	125	21 53	60	125
56	17 45	60	123	18 45	60	123	19 45	60	123	20 45	60	123	21 45	59	122
58	17 36	60	121	18 36	60	121	19 36	60	121	20 36	60	121	21 36	59	120
60	17 27	+60	119	18 27	+60	119	19 27	+60	119	20 27	+59	119	21 26	+60	118
62	17 18	60	117	18 18	60	117	19 18	59	117	20 17	60	117	21 17	60	116
64	17 09	59	115	18 08	60	115	19 08	60	115	20 08	60	114	21 08	60	114
66	16 59	60	113	17 59	60	113	18 59	59	113	19 58	60	112	20 58	60	112
68	16 49	60	111	17 49	60	111	18 49	60	111	19 49	59	110	20 48	60	110
70	16 39	+60	109	17 39	+60	109	18 39	+60	109	19 39	+60	108	20 39	+59	108
72	16 29	60	107	17 29	60	107	18 29	60	107	19 29	60	106	20 29	59	106
74	16 19	60	105	17 19	60	105	18 19	60	105	19 19	59	104	20 18	60	104
76	16 09	60	103	17 09	60	103	18 09	60	103	19 09	59	102	20 08	60	102
78	15 59	60	101	16 59	59	101	17 58	60	101	18 58	60	100	19 58	60	100
80	15 49	+59	99	16 48	+60	99	17 48	+60	99	18 48	+60	98	19 48	+59	98
82	15 38	60	97	16 38	60	97	17 38	60	97	18 38	59	96	19 37	60	96
84	15 28	60	95	16 28	59	95	17 27	60	95	18 27	60	94	19 27	60	94
86	15 17	60	93	16 17	60	93	17 17	60	93	18 17	59	92	19 16	60	92
88	15 07	60	91	16 07	60	91	17 07	59	91	18 06	60	90	19 06	60	90
90	14 57	+59	89	15 56	+60	89	16 56	+60	89	17 56	+60	88	18 56	+59	88
92	14 46	60	87	15 46	60	87	16 46	59	87	17 45	60	86	18 45	60	86
94	14 36	59	85	15 35	60	85	16 35	60	85	17 35	60	84	18 35	59	84
96	14 25	60	83	15 25	60	83	16 25	60	83	17 25	59	82	18 24	60	82
98	14 15	60	81	15 15	59	81	16 14	60	81	17 14	60	80	18 14	60	80
100	14 05	+59	79	15 04	+60	79	16 04	+60	79	17 04	+60	78	18 04	+59	78
102	13 54	60	77	14 54	60	77	15 54	60	77	16 54	59	77	17 53	60	76
104	13 44	60	75	14 44	60	75	15 44	60	75	16 44	59	75	17 43	60	74
106	13 34	60	73	14 34	60	73	15 34	60	73	16 34	59	73	17 33	60	72
108	13 24	60	71	14 24	60	71	15 24	60	71	16 24	59	71	17 23	60	70
110	13 14	+60	69	14 14	+60	69	15 14	+60	69	16 14	+60	69	17 14	+59	69
112	13 05	60	67	14 05	59	67	15 04	60	67	16 04	60	67	17 04	60	67
114	12 55	60	65	13 55	60	65	14 55	60	65	15 55	59	65	16 54	60	65
116	12 46	60	63	13 46	59	63	14 45	60	63	15 45	60	63	16 45	60	63
118	12 37	59	61	13 36	60	61	14 36	60	61	15 36	60	61	16 36	60	61
120	12 28	+59	59	13 27	+60	59	14 27	+60	59	15 27	+60	59	16 27	+60	59
122	12 19	60	57	13 19	59	57	14 18	60	57	15 18	60	57	16 18	60	57
124	12 10	60	55	13 10	60	55	14 10	60	55	15 10	59	55	16 09	60	55
126	12 02	59	53	13 01	60	53	14 01	60	53	15 01	60	53	16 01	60	53
128	11 53	60	51	12 53	60	51	13 53	60	51	14 53	60	51	15 53	60	51
130	11 45	+60	49	12 45	+60	49	13 45	+60	49	14 45	+60	49	15 45	+60	49
132	11 38	59	47	12 37	60	47	13 37	60	47	14 37	60	47	15 37	60	47
134	11 30	60	45	12 30	60	45	13 30	60	45	14 30	60	45	15 30	59	45
136	11 23	60	43	12 23	59	43	13 22	60	43	14 22	60	43	15 22	60	43
138	11 16	60	41	12 16	59	41	13 15	60	41	14 15	60	41	15 15	60	41

LHA	20° Hc	d	Z	21° Hc	d	Z	22° Hc	d	Z	23° Hc	d	Z	24° Hc	d	Z
	° ′	′	°	° ′	′	°	° ′	′	°	° ′	′	°	° ′	′	°
0	25 00	+60	180	26 00	+60	180	27 00	+60	180	28 00	+60	180	29 00	+60	180
2	25 00	60	178	26 00	60	178	27 00	60	178	28 00	60	178	29 00	60	178
4	24 59	60	176	25 59	60	176	26 59	60	176	27 59	60	176	28 59	60	176
6	24 58	60	174	25 58	60	174	26 58	60	174	27 58	60	174	28 58	60	174
8	24 57	60	172	25 57	60	172	26 57	60	172	27 57	60	172	28 57	60	172
10	24 55	+60	170	25 55	+60	170	26 55	+60	170	27 55	+60	170	28 55	+60	170
12	24 53	60	168	25 53	60	168	26 53	60	168	27 53	60	168	28 53	60	168
14	24 51	60	166	25 51	60	166	26 51	60	165	27 51	60	165	28 51	60	165
16	24 48	60	163	25 48	60	163	26 48	60	163	27 48	60	163	28 48	60	163
18	24 45	60	161	25 45	60	161	26 45	60	161	27 45	60	161	28 45	60	161
20	24 41	+60	159	25 41	+60	159	26 41	+60	159	27 41	+60	159	28 41	+60	159
22	24 37	60	157	25 37	60	157	26 37	60	157	27 37	60	157	28 37	60	157
24	24 33	60	155	25 33	60	155	26 33	60	155	27 33	60	155	28 33	60	155
26	24 29	60	153	25 29	60	153	26 29	60	153	27 29	59	153	28 28	60	153
28	24 24	60	151	25 24	60	151	26 24	60	151	27 24	60	151	28 24	59	151
30	24 19	+59	149	25 18	+60	149	26 18	+60	149	27 18	+60	149	28 18	+60	149
32	24 13	60	147	25 13	60	147	26 13	60	147	27 13	60	147	28 13	60	147
34	24 07	60	145	25 07	60	145	26 07	60	145	27 07	60	145	28 07	60	145
36	24 01	60	143	25 01	60	143	26 01	60	143	27 01	60	143	28 01	59	143
38	23 54	60	141	24 54	60	141	25 54	60	141	26 54	60	141	27 54	60	141
40	23 48	+60	139	24 48	+59	139	25 47	+60	139	26 47	+60	139	27 47	+60	138
42	23 41	60	137	24 41	59	137	25 40	60	137	26 40	60	136	27 40	60	136
44	23 33	60	135	24 33	60	135	25 33	60	134	26 33	60	134	27 33	60	134
46	23 26	60	133	24 26	59	133	25 25	60	132	26 25	60	132	27 25	60	132
48	23 18	60	131	24 18	60	130	25 18	59	130	26 17	60	130	27 17	60	130
50	23 10	+60	129	24 10	+60	128	25 10	+59	128	26 09	+60	128	27 09	+60	128
52	23 02	59	126	24 01	60	126	25 01	60	126	26 01	60	126	27 01	60	126
54	22 53	60	124	23 53	60	124	24 53	60	124	25 53	59	124	26 52	60	124
56	22 44	60	122	23 44	60	122	24 44	60	122	25 44	60	122	26 44	59	122
58	22 35	60	120	23 35	60	120	24 35	60	120	25 35	60	120	26 35	59	120
60	22 26	+60	118	23 26	+60	118	24 26	+60	118	25 26	+59	118	26 25	+60	118
62	22 17	60	116	23 17	60	116	24 17	59	116	25 16	60	116	26 16	60	116
64	22 08	59	114	23 07	60	114	24 07	60	114	25 07	60	114	26 07	59	114
66	21 58	60	112	22 58	59	112	23 57	60	112	24 57	60	112	25 57	60	112
68	21 48	60	110	22 48	60	110	23 48	59	110	24 47	60	110	25 47	60	110
70	21 38	+60	108	22 38	+60	108	23 38	+60	108	24 38	+59	108	25 37	+60	108
72	21 28	60	106	22 28	60	106	23 28	60	106	24 28	59	106	25 27	60	106
74	21 18	60	104	22 18	60	104	23 18	59	104	24 17	60	104	25 17	60	104
76	21 08	60	102	22 08	60	102	23 08	59	102	24 07	60	102	25 07	60	102
78	20 58	60	100	21 58	59	100	22 57	60	100	23 57	60	100	24 57	59	100
80	20 47	+60	98	21 47	+60	98	22 47	+60	98	23 47	+59	98	24 46	+60	98
82	20 37	60	96	21 37	60	96	22 37	59	96	23 36	60	96	24 36	60	96
84	20 27	59	94	21 26	60	94	22 26	60	94	23 26	60	94	24 26	59	94
86	20 16	60	92	21 16	60	92	22 16	59	92	23 15	60	92	24 15	60	92
88	20 06	59	90	21 05	60	90	22 05	60	90	23 05	60	90	24 05	59	90
90	19 55	+60	88	20 55	+60	88	21 55	+59	88	22 54	+60	88	23 54	+60	88
92	19 45	60	86	20 45	59	86	21 44	60	86	22 44	60	86	23 44	60	86
94	19 34	60	84	20 34	60	84	21 34	60	84	22 34	59	84	23 33	60	84
96	19 24	60	82	20 24	60	82	21 24	59	82	22 23	60	82	23 23	60	82
98	19 14	59	80	20 13	60	80	21 13	60	80	22 13	60	80	23 13	59	80
100	19 03	+60	78	20 03	+60	78	21 03	+60	78	22 03	+59	78	23 02	+60	78
102	18 53	60	76	19 53	60	76	20 53	59	76	21 52	60	76	22 52	60	76
104	18 43	60	74	19 43	60	74	20 43	59	74	21 42	60	74	22 42	60	74
106	18 33	60	72	19 33	60	72	20 33	59	72	21 32	60	72	22 32	60	72
108	18 23	60	70	19 23	60	70	20 23	59	70	21 22	60	70	22 22	60	70
110	18 13	+60	68	19 13	+60	68	20 13	+60	68	21 13	+59	68	22 12	+60	68
112	18 04	60	66	19 04	59	66	20 03	60	66	21 03	60	66	22 03	60	66
114	17 54	60	64	18 54	60	64	19 54	60	64	20 54	59	64	21 53	60	64
116	17 45	60	63	18 45	59	62	19 44	60	62	20 44	60	62	21 44	60	62
118	17 36	59	61	18 35	60	60	19 35	60	60	20 35	60	60	21 35	60	60
120	17 27	+59	59	18 26	+60	59	19 26	+60	58	20 26	+60	58	21 26	+60	58
122	17 18	60	57	18 18	59	57	19 17	60	56	20 17	60	56	21 17	60	56
124	17 09	60	55	18 09	60	55	19 09	60	55	20 09	60	54	21 09	59	54
126	17 01	60	53	18 01	59	53	19 00	60	53	20 00	60	52	21 00	60	52
128	16 53	59	51	17 52	60	51	18 52	60	51	19 52	60	51	20 52	60	50
130	16 45	+59	49	17 44	+60	49	18 44	+60	49	19 44	+60	49	20 44	+60	48
132	16 37	60	47	17 37	60	47	18 37	59	47	19 36	60	47	20 36	60	47
134	16 29	60	45	17 29	60	45	18 29	60	45	19 29	60	45	20 29	60	45
136	16 22	60	43	17 22	60	43	18 22	60	43	19 22	60	43	20 22	60	43
138	16 15	60	41	17 15	60	41	18 15	60	41	19 15	60	41	20 15	60	41

LHA	25° Hc	d	Z	26° Hc	d	Z	27° Hc	d	Z	28° Hc	d	Z	29° Hc	d	Z	LHA
	° ′	′	°	° ′	′	°	° ′	′	°	° ′	′	°	° ′	′	°	
0	30 00	+60	180	31 00	+60	180	32 00	+60	180	33 00	+60	180	34 00	+60	180	360
2	30 00	60	178	31 00	60	178	32 00	60	178	33 00	60	178	34 00	60	178	358
4	29 59	60	176	30 59	60	176	31 59	60	176	32 59	60	176	33 59	60	176	356
6	29 58	60	174	30 58	60	174	31 58	60	174	32 58	60	174	33 58	60	174	354
8	29 57	60	172	30 57	60	172	31 57	60	172	32 57	60	172	33 57	60	172	352
10	29 55	+60	170	30 55	+60	170	31 55	+60	170	32 55	+60	170	33 55	+60	170	350
12	29 53	60	167	30 53	60	167	31 53	60	167	32 53	60	167	33 53	60	167	348
14	29 51	60	165	30 51	60	165	31 51	60	165	32 51	60	165	33 51	60	165	346
16	29 48	60	163	30 48	60	163	31 48	60	163	32 48	60	163	33 48	60	163	344
18	29 45	60	161	30 45	60	161	31 45	60	161	32 45	60	161	33 45	60	161	342
20	29 41	+60	159	30 41	+60	159	31 41	+60	159	32 41	+60	159	33 41	+60	159	340
22	29 37	60	157	30 37	60	157	31 37	60	157	32 37	60	157	33 37	60	157	338
24	29 33	60	155	30 33	60	155	31 33	60	155	32 33	60	155	33 33	60	155	336
26	29 28	60	153	30 28	60	153	31 28	60	153	32 28	60	153	33 28	60	153	334
28	29 23	60	151	30 23	60	151	31 23	60	151	32 23	60	151	33 23	60	151	332
30	29 18	+60	149	30 18	+60	149	31 18	+60	149	32 18	+60	149	33 18	+60	149	330
32	29 13	60	147	30 13	59	147	31 12	60	147	32 12	60	146	33 12	60	146	328
34	29 07	60	145	30 07	59	145	31 06	60	144	32 06	60	144	33 06	60	144	326
36	29 00	60	143	30 00	60	142	31 00	60	142	32 00	60	142	33 00	60	142	324
38	28 54	60	140	29 54	60	140	30 54	60	140	31 54	59	140	32 53	60	140	322
40	28 47	+60	138	29 47	+60	138	30 47	+60	138	31 47	+60	138	32 47	+59	138	320
42	28 40	60	136	29 40	60	136	30 40	60	136	31 40	59	136	32 39	60	136	318
44	28 33	60	134	29 33	59	134	30 32	60	134	31 32	60	134	32 32	60	134	316
46	28 25	60	132	29 25	60	132	30 25	60	132	31 25	59	132	32 24	60	132	314
48	28 17	60	130	29 17	60	130	30 17	60	130	31 17	60	130	32 17	59	130	312
50	28 09	+60	128	29 09	+60	128	30 09	+60	128	31 09	+59	128	32 08	+60	128	310
52	28 01	60	126	29 01	59	126	30 00	60	126	31 00	60	126	32 00	60	126	308
54	27 52	60	124	28 52	60	124	29 52	60	124	30 52	59	124	31 51	60	124	306
56	27 43	60	122	28 43	60	122	29 43	60	122	30 43	60	122	31 43	59	122	304
58	27 34	60	120	28 34	60	120	29 34	60	120	30 34	60	120	31 34	59	120	302
60	27 25	+60	118	28 25	+60	118	29 25	+60	118	30 25	+59	118	31 24	+60	117	300
62	27 16	60	116	28 16	59	116	29 15	60	116	30 15	60	116	31 15	60	115	298
64	27 06	60	114	28 06	60	114	29 06	60	114	30 06	59	114	31 05	60	113	296
66	26 57	60	112	27 57	59	112	28 56	60	112	29 56	60	111	30 56	60	111	294
68	26 47	60	110	27 47	59	110	28 46	60	110	29 46	60	109	30 46	60	109	292
70	26 37	+60	108	27 37	+60	108	28 37	+59	108	29 36	+60	107	30 36	+60	107	290
72	26 27	60	106	27 27	60	106	28 27	59	106	29 26	60	105	30 26	60	105	288
74	26 17	60	104	27 17	59	104	28 16	60	104	29 16	60	103	30 16	60	103	286
76	26 07	59	102	27 06	60	102	28 06	60	102	29 06	60	101	30 06	59	101	284
78	25 56	60	100	26 56	60	100	27 56	60	99	28 56	59	99	29 55	60	99	282
80	25 46	+60	98	26 46	+60	98	27 46	+59	97	28 45	+60	97	29 45	+60	97	280
82	25 36	59	96	26 35	60	96	27 35	60	95	28 35	60	95	29 35	59	95	278
84	25 25	60	94	26 25	60	94	27 25	59	93	28 24	60	93	29 24	60	93	276
86	25 15	60	92	26 15	59	92	27 14	60	91	28 14	60	91	29 14	59	91	274
88	25 04	60	90	26 04	60	90	27 04	60	89	28 04	59	89	29 03	60	89	272
90	24 54	+60	88	25 54	+59	88	26 53	+60	88	27 53	+60	87	28 53	+60	87	270
92	24 44	59	86	25 43	60	86	26 43	60	86	27 43	59	85	28 42	60	85	268
94	24 33	60	84	25 33	60	84	26 33	59	84	27 32	60	83	28 32	60	83	266
96	24 23	59	82	25 22	60	82	26 22	60	82	27 22	60	81	28 22	59	81	264
98	24 12	60	80	25 12	60	80	26 12	60	80	27 12	59	79	28 11	60	79	262
100	24 02	+60	78	25 02	+60	78	26 02	+59	78	27 01	+60	77	28 01	+60	77	260
102	23 52	60	76	24 52	59	76	25 51	60	76	26 51	60	76	27 51	60	75	258
104	23 42	60	74	24 42	59	74	25 41	60	74	26 41	60	74	27 41	60	73	256
106	23 32	60	72	24 32	59	72	25 31	60	72	26 31	60	72	27 31	60	71	254
108	23 22	60	70	24 22	60	70	25 22	59	70	26 21	60	70	27 21	60	70	252
110	23 12	+60	68	24 12	+60	68	25 12	+60	68	26 12	+59	68	27 11	+60	68	250
112	23 03	59	66	24 02	60	66	25 02	60	66	26 02	60	66	27 02	59	66	248
114	22 53	60	64	23 53	60	64	24 53	59	64	25 52	60	64	26 52	60	64	246
116	22 44	60	62	23 44	59	62	24 43	60	62	25 43	60	62	26 43	60	62	244
118	22 35	59	60	23 34	60	60	24 34	60	60	25 34	60	60	26 34	60	60	242
120	22 26	+60	58	23 26	+59	58	24 25	+60	58	25 25	+60	58	26 25	+60	58	240
122	22 17	60	56	23 17	60	56	24 17	59	56	25 16	60	56	26 16	60	56	238
124	22 08	60	54	23 08	60	54	24 08	60	54	25 08	60	54	26 08	59	54	236
126	22 00	60	52	23 00	60	52	24 00	59	52	24 59	60	52	25 59	60	52	234
128	21 52	60	50	22 52	59	50	23 51	60	50	24 51	60	50	25 51	60	50	232
130	21 44	+60	48	22 44	+60	48	23 44	+59	48	24 43	+60	48	25 43	+60	48	230
132	21 36	60	46	22 36	60	46	23 36	60	46	24 36	60	46	25 36	59	46	228
134	21 29	60	45	22 29	59	44	23 28	60	44	24 28	60	44	25 28	60	44	226
136	21 22	59	43	22 21	60	43	23 21	60	43	24 21	60	42	25 21	60	42	224
138	21 15	59	41	22 14	60	41	23 14	60	41	24 14	60	40	25 14	60	40	222

S. Lat. {LHA greater than 180°....... Zn=180−Z / LHA less than 180°.......... Zn=180+Z

DECLINATION (15°-29°) SAME NAME AS LATITUDE

N. Lat. {LHA greater than 180°....... Zn=Z; LHA less than 180°.......... Zn=360−Z}

DECLINATION (15°-29°) SAME NAME AS LATITUDE

LHA	15° Hc	15° d	15° Z	16° Hc	16° d	16° Z	17° Hc	17° d	17° Z	18° Hc	18° d	18° Z	19° Hc	19° d	19° Z	20° Hc	20° d	20° Z	21° Hc	21° d	21° Z
	° ′	′	°	° ′	′	°	° ′	′	°	° ′	′	°	° ′	′	°	° ′	′	°	° ′	′	°
140	11 09	+60	39	12 09	+60	39	13 09	+60	39	14 09	+60	39	15 09	+59	39	16 08	+60	39	17 08	+60	39
142	11 02	60	37	12 02	60	37	13 02	60	37	14 02	60	37	15 02	60	37	16 02	60	37	17 02	60	37
144	10 56	60	35	11 56	60	35	12 56	60	35	13 56	60	35	14 56	60	35	15 56	60	35	16 56	60	35
146	10 50	60	33	11 50	60	33	12 50	60	33	13 50	60	33	14 50	60	33	15 50	60	33	16 50	60	33
148	10 45	60	31	11 45	60	31	12 45	60	31	13 45	59	31	14 44	60	31	15 44	60	31	16 44	60	31
150	10 39	+60	29	11 39	+60	29	12 39	+60	29	13 39	+60	29	14 39	+60	29	15 39	+60	29	16 39	+60	29
152	10 34	60	28	11 34	60	27	12 34	60	27	13 34	60	27	14 34	60	27	15 34	60	27	16 34	60	27
154	10 30	60	26	11 30	60	26	12 30	60	25	13 30	60	25	14 30	60	25	15 30	60	25	16 30	59	25
156	10 25	60	24	11 25	60	24	12 25	60	24	13 25	60	23	14 25	60	23	15 25	60	23	16 25	60	23
158	10 21	60	22	11 21	60	22	12 21	60	22	13 21	60	22	14 21	60	21	15 21	60	21	16 21	60	21
160	10 18	+60	20	11 18	+60	20	12 18	+60	20	13 18	+60	20	14 18	+60	20	15 18	+60	20	16 18	+60	19
162	10 14	60	18	11 14	60	18	12 14	60	18	13 14	60	18	14 14	60	18	15 14	60	18	16 14	60	18
164	10 11	60	16	11 11	60	16	12 11	60	16	13 11	60	16	14 11	60	16	15 11	60	16	16 11	60	16
166	10 09	60	14	11 09	60	14	12 09	60	14	13 09	60	14	14 09	60	14	15 09	60	14	16 09	60	14
168	10 06	60	12	11 06	60	12	12 06	60	12	13 06	60	12	14 06	60	12	15 06	60	12	16 06	60	12
170	10 05	+60	10	11 05	+60	10	12 05	+59	10	13 04	+60	10	14 04	+60	10	15 04	+60	10	16 04	+60	10
172	10 03	60	8	11 03	60	8	12 03	60	8	13 03	60	8	14 03	60	8	15 03	60	8	16 03	60	8
174	10 02	60	6	11 02	60	6	12 02	60	6	13 02	60	6	14 02	60	6	15 02	60	6	16 02	60	6
176	10 01	60	4	11 01	60	4	12 01	60	4	13 01	60	4	14 01	60	4	15 01	60	4	16 01	60	4
178	10 00	60	2	11 00	60	2	12 00	60	2	13 00	60	2	14 00	60	2	15 00	60	2	16 00	60	2
180	10 00	+60	0	11 00	+60	0	12 00	+60	0	13 00	+60	0	14 00	+60	0	15 00	+60	0	16 00	+60	0

22° Hc	22° d	22° Z	23° Hc	23° d	23° Z	24° Hc	24° d	24° Z	25° Hc	25° d	25° Z	26° Hc	26° d	26° Z	27° Hc	27° d	27° Z	28° Hc	28° d	28° Z	29° Hc	29° d	29° Z	LHA
° ′	′	°	° ′	′	°	° ′	′	°	° ′	′	°	° ′	′	°	° ′	′	°	° ′	′	°	° ′	′	°	
18 08	+60	39	19 08	+60	39	20 08	+60	39	21 08	+60	39	22 08	+60	39	23 08	+60	39	24 08	+59	39	25 07	+60	38	220
18 02	60	37	19 02	60	37	20 02	60	37	21 02	59	37	22 01	60	37	23 01	60	37	24 01	60	37	25 01	60	37	218
17 56	60	35	18 56	59	35	19 55	60	35	20 55	60	35	21 55	60	35	22 55	60	35	23 55	60	35	24 55	60	35	216
17 50	60	33	18 50	60	33	19 50	60	33	20 50	60	33	21 50	59	33	22 49	60	33	23 49	60	33	24 49	60	33	214
17 44	60	31	18 44	60	31	19 44	60	31	20 44	60	31	21 44	60	31	22 44	60	31	23 44	60	31	24 44	60	31	212
17 39	+60	29	18 39	+60	29	19 39	+60	29	20 39	+60	29	21 39	+60	29	22 39	+60	29	23 39	+60	29	24 39	+60	29	210
17 34	60	27	18 34	60	27	19 34	60	27	20 34	60	27	21 34	60	27	22 34	60	27	23 34	60	27	24 34	60	27	208
17 29	60	25	18 29	60	25	19 29	60	25	20 29	60	25	21 29	60	25	22 29	60	25	23 29	60	25	24 29	60	25	206
17 25	60	23	18 25	60	23	19 25	60	23	20 25	60	23	21 25	60	23	22 25	60	23	23 25	60	23	24 25	60	23	204
17 21	60	21	18 21	60	21	19 21	60	21	20 21	60	21	21 21	60	21	22 21	60	21	23 21	60	21	24 21	60	21	202
17 18	+60	19	18 18	+60	19	19 18	+59	19	20 17	+60	19	21 17	+60	19	22 17	+60	19	23 17	+60	19	24 17	+60	19	200
17 14	60	18	18 14	60	17	19 14	60	17	20 14	60	17	21 14	60	17	22 14	60	17	23 14	60	17	24 14	60	17	198
17 11	60	16	18 11	60	16	19 11	60	16	20 11	60	15	21 11	60	15	22 11	60	15	23 11	60	15	24 11	60	15	196
17 09	60	14	18 09	60	14	19 09	60	14	20 09	60	14	21 09	60	14	22 09	60	14	23 09	60	13	24 09	60	13	194
17 06	60	12	18 06	60	12	19 06	60	12	20 06	60	12	21 06	60	12	22 06	60	12	23 06	60	12	24 06	60	12	192
17 04	+60	10	18 04	+60	10	19 04	+60	10	20 04	+60	10	21 04	+60	10	22 04	+60	10	23 04	+60	10	24 04	+60	10	190
17 03	60	8	18 03	60	8	19 03	60	8	20 03	60	8	21 03	60	8	22 03	60	8	23 03	60	8	24 03	60	8	188
17 02	60	6	18 02	60	6	19 02	60	6	20 02	60	6	21 02	60	6	22 02	60	6	23 02	60	6	24 02	60	6	186
17 01	60	4	18 01	60	4	19 01	60	4	20 01	60	4	21 01	60	4	22 01	60	4	23 01	60	4	24 01	60	4	184
17 00	60	2	18 00	60	2	19 00	60	2	20 00	60	2	21 00	60	2	22 00	60	2	23 00	60	2	24 00	60	2	182
17 00	+60	0	18 00	+60	0	19 00	+60	0	20 00	+60	0	21 00	+60	0	22 00	+60	0	23 00	+60	0	24 00	+60	0	180

N. Lat. {LHA greater than 180°....... Zn=Z; LHA less than 180°........... Zn=360−Z}

DECLINATION (0°-14°) SAME NAME AS LATITUDE

LHA	0° Hc	d	Z	1° Hc	d	Z	2° Hc	d	Z	3° Hc	d	Z	4° Hc	d	Z
	° ′	′	°	° ′	′	°	° ′	′	°	° ′	′	°	° ′	′	°
0	04 00	+60	180	05 00	+60	180	06 00	+60	180	07 00	+60	180	08 00	+60	180
2	04 00	60	178	05 00	60	178	06 00	60	178	07 00	60	178	08 00	60	178
4	03 59	60	176	04 59	60	176	05 59	60	176	06 59	60	176	07 59	60	176
6	03 59	60	174	04 59	60	174	05 59	60	174	06 59	60	174	07 59	60	174
8	03 58	60	172	04 58	60	172	05 58	60	172	06 58	60	172	07 58	60	172
10	03 56	+60	170	04 56	+60	170	05 56	+60	170	06 56	+60	170	07 56	+60	170
12	03 55	60	168	04 55	60	168	05 55	60	168	06 55	60	168	07 55	60	168
14	03 53	60	166	04 53	60	166	05 53	60	166	06 53	60	166	07 53	60	166
16	03 51	60	164	04 51	60	164	05 51	60	164	06 51	60	164	07 51	60	164
18	03 48	60	162	04 48	60	162	05 48	60	162	06 48	60	162	07 48	60	162
20	03 46	+60	160	04 46	+60	160	05 46	+60	160	06 46	+59	160	07 45	+60	160
22	03 43	60	158	04 43	60	158	05 43	59	158	06 42	60	158	07 42	60	158
24	03 39	60	156	04 39	60	156	05 39	60	156	06 39	60	156	07 39	60	156
26	03 36	60	154	04 36	60	154	05 36	60	154	06 36	60	154	07 36	60	154
28	03 32	60	152	04 32	60	152	05 32	60	152	06 32	60	152	07 32	60	152
30	03 28	+60	150	04 28	+60	150	05 28	+60	150	06 28	+60	150	07 28	+60	150
32	03 23	60	148	04 23	60	148	05 23	60	148	06 23	60	148	07 23	60	148
34	03 19	60	146	04 19	60	146	05 19	60	146	06 19	60	146	07 19	60	146
36	03 14	60	144	04 14	60	144	05 14	60	144	06 14	60	144	07 14	60	144
38	03 09	60	142	04 09	60	142	05 09	60	142	06 09	60	142	07 09	60	142
40	03 04	+60	140	04 04	+60	140	05 04	+60	140	06 04	+60	140	07 04	+60	140
42	02 58	60	138	03 58	60	138	04 58	60	138	05 58	60	138	06 58	60	138
44	02 53	60	136	03 53	59	136	04 52	60	136	05 52	60	136	06 52	60	136
46	02 47	60	134	03 47	59	134	04 46	60	134	05 46	60	134	06 46	60	134
48	02 41	59	132	03 40	60	132	04 40	60	132	05 40	60	132	06 40	60	132
50	02 34	+60	130	03 34	+60	130	04 34	+60	130	05 34	+60	130	06 34	+60	130
52	02 28	60	128	03 28	59	128	04 27	60	128	05 27	60	128	06 27	60	128
54	02 21	60	126	03 21	60	126	04 21	60	126	05 21	60	126	06 21	60	126
56	02 14	60	124	03 14	60	124	04 14	60	124	05 14	60	124	06 14	60	124
58	02 07	60	122	03 07	60	122	04 07	60	122	05 07	60	122	06 07	60	122
60	02 00	+60	120	03 00	+60	120	04 00	+60	120	05 00	+60	120	06 00	+59	120
62	01 53	59	118	02 52	60	118	03 52	60	118	04 52	60	118	05 52	60	118
64	01 45	60	116	02 45	60	116	03 45	60	116	04 45	60	116	05 45	60	116
66	01 38	59	114	02 37	60	114	03 37	60	114	04 37	60	114	05 37	60	114
68	01 30	60	112	02 30	60	112	03 30	59	112	04 29	60	112	05 29	60	112
70	01 22	+60	110	02 22	+60	110	03 22	+60	110	04 22	+60	110	05 22	+59	110
72	01 14	60	108	02 14	60	108	03 14	60	108	04 14	60	108	05 14	59	108
74	01 06	60	106	02 06	60	106	03 06	60	106	04 06	60	106	05 06	59	106
76	00 58	60	104	01 58	60	104	02 58	60	104	03 58	59	104	04 57	60	104
78	00 50	60	102	01 50	60	102	02 50	59	102	03 49	60	102	04 49	60	102
80	00 42	+60	100	01 42	+59	100	02 41	+60	100	03 41	+60	100	04 41	+60	100
82	00 33	60	98	01 33	60	98	02 33	60	98	03 33	60	98	04 33	60	98
84	00 25	60	96	01 25	60	96	02 25	60	96	03 25	59	96	04 24	60	96
86	00 17	60	94	01 17	59	94	02 16	60	94	03 16	60	94	04 16	60	94
88	00 08	60	92	01 08	60	92	02 08	60	92	03 08	60	92	04 08	60	92
90	00 00	+60	90	01 00	+60	90	02 00	+60	90	03 00	+59	90	03 59	+60	90
92	−0 08	59	88	00 51	60	88	01 51	60	88	02 51	60	88	03 51	60	88
94	−0 17	60	86	00 43	60	86	01 43	60	86	02 43	60	86	03 43	60	86
96	−0 25	60	84	00 35	60	84	01 35	60	84	02 35	59	84	03 34	60	84
98	−0 33	59	82	00 26	60	82	01 26	60	82	02 26	60	82	03 26	60	82
100	−0 42	+60	80	00 18	+60	80	01 18	+60	80	02 18	+60	80	03 18	+60	80
102	−0 50	60	78	00 10	60	78	01 10	60	78	02 10	60	78	03 10	59	78
104	−0 58	60	76	00 02	60	76	01 02	60	76	02 02	59	76	03 01	60	76
106	−1 06	60	74	−0 06	60	74	00 54	59	74	01 53	60	74	02 53	60	74
108	−1 14	60	72	−0 14	60	72	00 46	59	72	01 45	60	72	02 45	60	72
110	−1 22	+60	70	−0 22	+60	70	00 38	+60	70	01 38	+59	70	02 37	+60	70
112	−1 30	60	68	−0 30	60	68	00 30	60	68	01 30	60	68	02 30	60	68
114	−1 38	60	66	−0 38	60	66	00 22	60	66	01 22	60	66	02 22	60	66
116	−1 45	60	64	−0 45	60	64	00 15	60	64	01 15	59	64	02 14	60	64
118	−1 53	60	62	−0 53	60	62	00 07	60	62	01 07	60	62	02 07	60	62
120	−2 00	+60	60	−1 00	+60	60	00 00	+60	60	01 00	+60	60	02 00	+60	60
122	−2 07	60	58	−1 07	60	58	−0 07	60	58	00 53	59	58	01 52	60	58
124	−2 14	60	56	−1 14	60	56	−0 14	60	56	00 46	59	56	01 45	60	56
126	−2 21	60	54	−1 21	60	54	−0 21	60	54	00 39	60	54	01 39	60	54
128	−2 28	60	52	−1 28	60	52	−0 28	60	52	00 32	60	52	01 32	60	52
130	−2 34	+60	50	−1 34	+60	50	−0 34	+60	50	00 26	+59	50	01 25	+60	50
132	−2 41	60	48	−1 41	60	48	−0 41	60	48	00 19	60	48	01 19	60	48
134	−2 47	60	46	−1 47	60	46	−0 47	60	46	00 13	60	46	01 13	60	46
136	−2 53	60	44	−1 53	60	44	−0 53	60	44	00 07	60	44	01 07	60	44
138	−2 58	60	42	−1 58	60	42	−0 58	60	42	00 02	59	42	01 01	60	42

LHA	5° Hc	d	Z	6° Hc	d	Z	7° Hc	d	Z	8° Hc	d	Z	9° Hc	d	Z
	° ′	′	°	° ′	′	°	° ′	′	°	° ′	′	°	° ′	′	°
0	09 00	+60	180	10 00	+60	180	11 00	+60	180	12 00	+60	180	13 00	+60	180
2	09 00	60	178	10 00	60	178	11 00	60	178	12 00	60	178	13 00	60	178
4	08 59	60	176	09 59	60	176	10 59	60	176	11 59	60	176	12 59	60	176
6	08 59	60	174	09 59	60	174	10 59	60	174	11 59	60	174	12 59	60	174
8	08 58	60	172	09 58	60	172	10 58	60	172	11 58	60	172	12 58	60	172
10	08 56	+60	170	09 56	+60	170	10 56	+60	170	11 56	+60	170	12 56	+60	170
12	08 55	60	168	09 55	60	168	10 55	60	168	11 55	60	168	12 55	60	168
14	08 53	60	166	09 53	60	166	10 53	60	166	11 53	60	166	12 53	60	166
16	08 51	60	164	09 51	60	164	10 51	60	164	11 51	60	164	12 51	60	164
18	08 48	60	162	09 48	60	162	10 48	60	162	11 48	60	162	12 48	60	162
20	08 45	+60	160	09 45	+60	160	10 45	+60	160	11 45	+60	160	12 45	+60	160
22	08 42	60	158	09 42	60	158	10 42	60	158	11 42	60	158	12 42	60	158
24	08 39	60	156	09 39	60	156	10 39	60	156	11 39	60	156	12 39	60	156
26	08 36	60	154	09 36	60	154	10 36	59	154	11 35	60	154	12 35	60	154
28	08 32	60	152	09 32	60	152	10 32	60	152	11 32	60	152	12 32	60	152
30	08 28	+60	150	09 28	+60	150	10 28	+60	150	11 28	+60	150	12 28	+59	150
32	08 23	60	148	09 23	60	148	10 23	60	148	11 23	60	148	12 23	60	148
34	08 19	60	146	09 19	60	146	10 19	60	146	11 19	60	146	12 19	60	146
36	08 14	60	144	09 14	60	144	10 14	60	144	11 14	60	144	12 14	60	144
38	08 09	60	142	09 09	60	142	10 09	60	142	11 09	60	142	12 09	60	142
40	08 04	+59	140	09 03	+60	140	10 03	+60	140	11 03	+60	140	12 03	+60	140
42	07 58	60	138	08 58	60	138	09 58	60	138	10 58	60	138	11 58	60	138
44	07 52	60	136	08 52	60	136	09 52	60	136	10 52	60	136	11 52	60	136
46	07 46	60	134	08 46	60	134	09 46	60	134	10 46	60	134	11 46	60	134
48	07 40	60	132	08 40	60	132	09 40	60	132	10 40	60	132	11 40	60	132
50	07 34	+60	130	08 34	+60	130	09 34	+60	130	10 34	+59	130	11 33	+60	129
52	07 27	60	128	08 27	60	128	09 27	60	128	10 27	60	128	11 27	60	127
54	07 21	59	126	08 20	60	126	09 20	60	126	10 20	60	126	11 20	60	125
56	07 14	60	124	08 14	59	124	09 13	60	124	10 13	60	124	11 13	60	123
58	07 07	60	122	08 07	59	122	09 06	60	122	10 06	60	122	11 06	60	121
60	06 59	+60	120	07 59	+60	120	08 59	+60	120	09 59	+60	119	10 59	+60	119
62	06 52	60	118	07 52	60	118	08 52	60	118	09 52	60	117	10 52	59	117
64	06 45	59	116	07 44	60	116	08 44	60	116	09 44	60	115	10 44	60	115
66	06 37	60	114	07 37	60	114	08 37	60	114	09 37	59	113	10 36	60	113
68	06 29	60	112	07 29	60	112	08 29	60	112	09 29	60	111	10 29	60	111
70	06 21	+60	110	07 21	+60	110	08 21	+60	110	09 21	+60	109	10 21	+60	109
72	06 13	60	108	07 13	60	108	08 13	60	108	09 13	60	107	10 13	60	107
74	06 05	60	106	07 05	60	106	08 05	60	106	09 05	60	105	10 05	60	105
76	05 57	60	104	06 57	60	104	07 57	60	104	08 57	60	103	09 57	60	103
78	05 49	60	102	06 49	60	102	07 49	60	102	08 49	60	101	09 49	59	101
80	05 41	+60	100	06 41	+60	100	07 41	+60	100	08 41	+59	99	09 40	+60	99
82	05 33	60	98	06 33	59	98	07 32	60	98	08 32	60	97	09 32	60	97
84	05 24	60	96	06 24	60	96	07 24	60	96	08 24	60	95	09 24	60	95
86	05 16	60	94	06 16	60	94	07 16	60	94	08 16	59	93	09 15	60	93
88	05 08	60	92	06 08	59	92	07 07	60	92	08 07	60	91	09 07	60	91
90	04 59	+60	90	05 59	+60	90	06 59	+60	90	07 59	+60	89	08 59	+60	89
92	04 51	60	88	05 51	60	88	06 51	60	88	07 51	59	87	08 50	60	87
94	04 43	59	86	05 42	60	86	06 42	60	86	07 42	60	85	08 42	60	85
96	04 34	60	84	05 34	60	84	06 34	60	84	07 34	60	84	08 34	60	83
98	04 26	60	82	05 26	60	82	06 26	60	82	07 26	59	82	08 25	60	81
100	04 18	+60	80	05 18	+59	80	06 17	+60	80	07 17	+60	80	08 17	+60	79
102	04 09	60	78	05 09	60	78	06 09	60	78	07 09	60	78	08 09	60	77
104	04 01	60	76	05 01	60	76	06 01	60	76	07 01	60	76	08 01	60	75
106	03 53	60	74	04 53	60	74	05 53	60	74	06 53	60	74	07 53	60	73
108	03 45	60	72	04 45	60	72	05 45	60	72	06 45	60	72	07 45	60	71
110	03 37	+60	70	04 37	+60	70	05 37	+60	70	06 37	+60	70	07 37	+60	70
112	03 30	59	68	04 29	60	68	05 29	60	68	06 29	60	68	07 29	60	68
114	03 22	60	66	04 22	60	66	05 22	60	66	06 22	59	66	07 21	60	66
116	03 14	60	64	04 14	60	64	05 14	60	64	06 14	60	64	07 14	60	64
118	03 07	60	62	04 07	60	62	05 07	60	62	06 07	59	62	07 06	60	62
120	03 00	+59	60	03 59	+60	60	04 59	+60	60	05 59	+60	60	06 59	+60	60
122	02 52	60	58	03 52	60	58	04 52	60	58	05 52	60	58	06 52	60	58
124	02 45	60	56	03 45	60	56	04 45	60	56	05 45	60	56	06 45	60	56
126	02 39	59	54	03 38	60	54	04 38	60	54	05 38	60	54	06 38	60	54
128	02 32	60	52	03 32	60	52	04 32	60	52	05 32	60	52	06 32	59	52
130	02 25	+60	50	03 25	+60	50	04 25	+60	50	05 25	+60	50	06 25	+60	50
132	02 19	60	48	03 19	60	48	04 19	60	48	05 19	60	48	06 19	60	48
134	02 13	60	46	03 13	60	46	04 13	60	46	05 13	60	46	06 13	60	46
136	02 07	60	44	03 07	60	44	04 07	60	44	05 07	60	44	06 07	60	44
138	02 01	60	42	03 01	60	42	04 01	60	42	05 01	60	42	06 01	60	42

LHA	10° Hc	d	Z	11° Hc	d	Z	12° Hc	d	Z	13° Hc	d	Z	14° Hc	d	Z	LHA
	° ′	′	°	° ′	′	°	° ′	′	°	° ′	′	°	° ′	′	°	
0	14 00	+60	180	15 00	+60	180	16 00	+60	180	17 00	+60	180	18 00	+60	180	360
2	14 00	60	178	15 00	60	178	16 00	60	178	17 00	60	178	18 00	60	178	358
4	13 59	60	176	14 59	60	176	15 59	60	176	16 59	60	176	17 59	60	176	356
6	13 59	60	174	14 59	60	174	15 59	60	174	16 59	60	174	17 59	60	174	354
8	13 58	60	172	14 58	60	172	15 58	60	172	16 58	60	172	17 58	60	172	352
10	13 56	+60	170	14 56	+60	170	15 56	+60	170	16 56	+60	170	17 56	+60	170	350
12	13 55	60	168	14 55	60	168	15 55	60	168	16 55	60	168	17 55	60	168	348
14	13 53	60	166	14 53	60	166	15 53	60	166	16 53	60	166	17 53	60	166	346
16	13 51	60	164	14 51	60	164	15 51	60	164	16 51	60	164	17 51	60	164	344
18	13 48	60	162	14 48	60	162	15 48	60	162	16 48	60	162	17 48	60	162	342
20	13 45	+60	160	14 45	+60	160	15 45	+60	160	16 45	+60	160	17 45	+60	160	340
22	13 42	60	158	14 42	60	158	15 42	60	158	16 42	60	158	17 42	60	158	338
24	13 39	60	156	14 39	60	156	15 39	60	156	16 39	60	156	17 39	60	156	336
26	13 35	60	154	14 35	60	154	15 35	60	154	16 35	60	154	17 35	60	154	334
28	13 32	60	152	14 32	60	152	15 32	59	152	16 31	60	152	17 31	60	152	332
30	13 27	+60	150	14 27	+60	150	15 27	+60	150	16 27	+60	150	17 27	+60	149	330
32	13 23	60	148	14 23	60	148	15 23	60	148	16 23	60	147	17 23	60	147	328
34	13 19	59	146	14 18	60	146	15 18	60	146	16 18	60	145	17 18	60	145	326
36	13 14	60	144	14 14	60	144	15 14	59	143	16 13	60	143	17 13	60	143	324
38	13 09	59	142	14 08	60	141	15 08	60	141	16 08	60	141	17 08	60	141	322
40	13 03	+60	140	14 03	+60	139	15 03	+60	139	16 03	+60	139	17 03	+60	139	320
42	12 58	60	138	13 58	60	137	14 58	59	137	15 57	60	137	16 57	60	137	318
44	12 52	60	135	13 52	60	135	14 52	60	135	15 52	60	135	16 52	60	135	316
46	12 46	60	133	13 46	60	133	14 46	60	133	15 46	60	133	16 46	60	133	314
48	12 40	60	131	13 40	60	131	14 40	59	131	15 39	60	131	16 39	60	131	312
50	12 33	+60	129	13 33	+60	129	14 33	+60	129	15 33	+60	129	16 33	+60	129	310
52	12 27	60	127	13 27	60	127	14 27	60	127	15 27	59	127	16 26	60	127	308
54	12 20	60	125	13 20	60	125	14 20	60	125	15 20	60	125	16 20	60	125	306
56	12 13	60	123	13 13	60	123	14 13	60	123	15 13	60	123	16 13	60	123	304
58	12 06	60	121	13 06	60	121	14 06	60	121	15 06	60	121	16 06	60	121	302
60	11 59	+60	119	12 59	+60	119	13 59	+60	119	14 59	+59	119	15 58	+60	119	300
62	11 51	60	117	12 51	60	117	13 51	60	117	14 51	60	117	15 51	60	117	298
64	11 44	60	115	12 44	60	115	13 44	60	115	14 44	59	115	15 43	60	115	296
66	11 36	60	113	12 36	60	113	13 36	60	113	14 36	60	113	15 36	60	113	294
68	11 29	59	111	12 28	60	111	13 28	60	111	14 28	60	111	15 28	60	111	292
70	11 21	+60	109	12 21	+59	109	13 20	+60	109	14 20	+60	109	15 20	+60	109	290
72	11 13	60	107	12 13	60	107	13 13	59	107	14 12	60	107	15 12	60	107	288
74	11 05	60	105	12 05	60	105	13 05	59	105	14 04	60	105	15 04	60	105	286
76	10 57	60	103	11 57	59	103	12 56	60	103	13 56	60	103	14 56	60	103	284
78	10 48	60	101	11 48	60	101	12 48	60	101	13 48	60	101	14 48	60	101	282
80	10 40	+60	99	11 40	+60	99	12 40	+60	99	13 40	+60	99	14 40	+60	99	280
82	10 32	60	97	11 32	60	97	12 32	60	97	13 32	59	97	14 31	60	97	278
84	10 24	60	95	11 24	59	95	12 23	60	95	13 23	60	95	14 23	60	95	276
86	10 15	60	93	11 15	60	93	12 15	60	93	13 15	60	93	14 15	60	93	274
88	10 07	60	91	11 07	60	91	12 07	59	91	13 06	60	91	14 06	60	91	272
90	09 59	+59	89	10 58	+60	89	11 58	+60	89	12 58	+60	89	13 58	+60	89	270
92	09 50	60	87	10 50	60	87	11 50	60	87	12 50	60	87	13 50	59	87	268
94	09 42	60	85	10 42	60	85	11 42	59	85	12 41	60	85	13 41	60	85	266
96	09 34	59	83	10 33	60	83	11 33	60	83	12 33	60	83	13 33	60	83	264
98	09 25	60	81	10 25	60	81	11 25	60	81	12 25	60	81	13 25	59	81	262
100	09 17	+60	79	10 17	+60	79	11 17	+60	79	12 17	+59	79	13 16	+60	79	260
102	09 09	60	77	10 09	59	77	11 08	60	77	12 08	60	77	13 08	60	77	258
104	09 01	60	75	10 01	59	75	11 00	60	75	12 00	60	75	13 00	60	75	256
106	08 53	59	73	09 52	60	73	10 52	60	73	11 52	60	73	12 52	60	73	254
108	08 45	59	71	09 44	60	71	10 44	60	71	11 44	60	71	12 44	60	71	252
110	08 37	+60	69	09 37	+59	69	10 36	+60	69	11 36	+60	69	12 36	+60	69	250
112	08 29	60	67	09 29	60	67	10 29	60	67	11 29	59	67	12 28	60	67	248
114	08 21	60	65	09 21	60	65	10 21	60	65	11 21	60	65	12 21	60	65	246
116	08 14	60	63	09 14	59	63	10 13	60	63	11 13	60	63	12 13	60	63	244
118	08 06	60	61	09 06	60	61	10 06	60	61	11 06	60	61	12 06	60	61	242
120	07 59	+60	60	08 59	+60	59	09 59	+60	59	10 59	+60	59	11 59	+59	59	240
122	07 52	60	58	08 52	60	57	09 52	60	57	10 52	59	57	11 51	60	57	238
124	07 45	60	56	08 45	60	55	09 45	60	55	10 45	59	55	11 44	60	55	236
126	07 38	60	54	08 38	60	53	09 38	60	53	10 38	60	53	11 38	60	53	234
128	07 31	60	52	08 31	60	52	09 31	60	51	10 31	60	51	11 31	60	51	232
130	07 25	+60	50	08 25	+60	50	09 25	+60	49	10 25	+60	49	11 25	+60	49	230
132	07 19	60	48	08 19	60	48	09 19	59	47	10 18	60	47	11 18	60	47	228
134	07 13	60	46	08 13	59	46	09 12	60	46	10 12	60	45	11 12	60	45	226
136	07 07	60	44	08 07	60	44	09 07	60	44	10 07	59	43	11 06	60	43	224
138	07 01	60	42	08 01	60	42	09 01	60	42	10 01	60	42	11 01	60	41	222

S. Lat. {LHA greater than 180°....... Zn=180−Z; LHA less than 180°........... Zn=180+Z}

DECLINATION (0°-14°) SAME NAME AS LATITUDE

LAT 86°

N. Lat. {LHA greater than 180°....... Zn=Z; LHA less than 180°........... Zn=360−Z}

DECLINATION (0°-14°) SAME NAME AS LATITUDE

LHA	0° Hc	d	Z	1° Hc	d	Z	2° Hc	d	Z	3° Hc	d	Z	4° Hc	d	Z	5° Hc	d	Z	6° Hc	d	Z	7° Hc	d	Z
	° ′	′	°	° ′	′	°	° ′	′	°	° ′	′	°	° ′	′	°	° ′	′	°	° ′	′	°	° ′	′	°
140	−3 04	+60	40	−2 04	+60	40	−1 04	+60	40	−0 04	+60	40	00 56	+60	40	01 56	+60	40	02 56	+60	40	03 56	+60	40
142	−3 09	60	38	−2 09	60	38	−1 09	60	38	−0 09	60	38	00 51	60	38	01 51	60	38	02 51	60	38	03 51	59	38
144	−3 14	60	36	−2 14	60	36	−1 14	60	36	−0 14	60	36	00 46	60	36	01 46	60	36	02 46	60	36	03 46	59	36
146	−3 19	60	34	−2 19	60	34	−1 19	60	34	−0 19	60	34	00 41	60	34	01 41	60	34	02 41	60	34	03 41	60	34
148	−3 23	59	32	−2 24	60	32	−1 24	60	32	−0 24	60	32	00 36	60	32	01 36	60	32	02 36	60	32	03 36	60	32
150	−3 28	+60	30	−2 28	+60	30	−1 28	+60	30	−0 28	+60	30	00 32	+60	30	01 32	+60	30	02 32	+60	30	03 32	+60	30
152	−3 32	60	28	−2 32	60	28	−1 32	60	28	−0 32	60	28	00 28	60	28	01 28	60	28	02 28	60	28	03 28	60	28
154	−3 36	60	26	−2 36	60	26	−1 36	60	26	−0 36	60	26	00 24	60	26	01 24	60	26	02 24	60	26	03 24	60	26
156	−3 39	60	24	−2 39	60	24	−1 39	60	24	−0 39	60	24	00 21	60	24	01 21	60	24	02 21	60	24	03 21	60	24
158	−3 43	60	22	−2 43	60	22	−1 43	60	22	−0 43	60	22	00 17	60	22	01 17	60	22	02 17	60	22	03 17	60	22
160	−3 46	+60	20	−2 46	+60	20	−1 46	+60	20	−0 46	+60	20	00 14	+60	20	01 14	+60	20	02 14	+60	20	03 14	+60	20
162	−3 48	60	18	−2 48	60	18	−1 48	60	18	−0 48	60	18	00 12	60	18	01 12	60	18	02 12	60	18	03 12	60	18
164	−3 51	60	16	−2 51	60	16	−1 51	60	16	−0 51	60	16	00 09	60	16	01 09	60	16	02 09	60	16	03 09	60	16
166	−3 53	60	14	−2 53	60	14	−1 53	60	14	−0 53	60	14	00 07	60	14	01 07	60	14	02 07	60	14	03 07	60	14
168	−3 55	60	12	−2 55	60	12	−1 55	60	12	−0 55	60	12	00 05	60	12	01 05	60	12	02 05	60	12	03 05	60	12
170	−3 56	+60	10	−2 56	+60	10	−1 56	+60	10	−0 56	+60	10	00 04	+60	10	01 04	+60	10	02 04	+60	10	03 04	+60	10
172	−3 58	60	8	−2 58	60	8	−1 58	60	8	−0 58	60	8	00 02	60	8	01 02	60	8	02 02	60	8	03 02	60	8
174	−3 59	60	6	−2 59	60	6	−1 59	60	6	−0 59	60	6	00 01	60	6	01 01	60	6	02 01	60	6	03 01	60	6
176	−3 59	60	4	−2 59	60	4	−1 59	60	4	−0 59	60	4	00 01	60	4	01 01	60	4	02 01	60	4	03 01	60	4
178	−4 00	60	2	−3 00	60	2	−2 00	60	2	−1 00	60	2	00 00	60	2	01 00	60	2	02 00	60	2	03 00	60	2
180	−4 00	+60	0	−3 00	+60	0	−2 00	+60	0	−1 00	+60	0	00 00	+60	0	01 00	+60	0	02 00	+60	0	03 00	+60	0

8° Hc	d	Z	9° Hc	d	Z	10° Hc	d	Z	11° Hc	d	Z	12° Hc	d	Z	13° Hc	d	Z	14° Hc	d	Z	LHA
° ′	′	°	° ′	′	°	° ′	′	°	° ′	′	°	° ′	′	°	° ′	′	°	° ′	′	°	
04 56	+60	40	05 56	+60	40	06 56	+60	40	07 56	+60	40	08 56	+59	40	09 55	+60	40	10 55	+60	39	220
04 50	60	38	05 50	60	38	06 50	60	38	07 50	60	38	08 50	60	38	09 50	60	38	10 50	60	38	218
04 45	60	36	05 45	60	36	06 45	60	36	07 45	60	36	08 45	60	36	09 45	60	36	10 45	60	36	216
04 41	60	34	05 41	60	34	06 41	60	34	07 41	60	34	08 41	60	34	09 41	59	34	10 40	60	34	214
04 36	60	32	05 36	60	32	06 36	60	32	07 36	60	32	08 36	60	32	09 36	60	32	10 36	60	32	212
04 32	+60	30	05 32	+60	30	06 32	+60	30	07 32	+60	30	08 32	+60	30	09 32	+60	30	10 32	+60	30	210
04 28	60	28	05 28	60	28	06 28	60	28	07 28	60	28	08 28	60	28	09 28	60	28	10 28	60	28	208
04 24	60	26	05 24	60	26	06 24	60	26	07 24	60	26	08 24	60	26	09 24	60	26	10 24	60	26	206
04 21	60	24	05 21	60	24	06 21	60	24	07 21	60	24	08 21	60	24	09 21	59	24	10 20	60	24	204
04 17	60	22	05 17	60	22	06 17	60	22	07 17	60	22	08 17	60	22	09 17	60	22	10 17	60	22	202
04 14	+60	20	05 14	+60	20	06 14	+60	20	07 14	+60	20	08 14	+60	20	09 14	+60	20	10 14	+60	20	200
04 12	60	18	05 12	60	18	06 12	60	18	07 12	60	18	08 12	60	18	09 12	60	18	10 12	60	18	198
04 09	60	16	05 09	60	16	06 09	60	16	07 09	60	16	08 09	60	16	09 09	60	16	10 09	60	16	196
04 07	60	14	05 07	60	14	06 07	60	14	07 07	60	14	08 07	60	14	09 07	60	14	10 07	60	14	194
04 05	60	12	05 05	60	12	06 05	60	12	07 05	60	12	08 05	60	12	09 05	60	12	10 05	60	12	192
04 04	+60	10	05 04	+60	10	06 04	+60	10	07 04	+60	10	08 04	+60	10	09 04	+60	10	10 04	+60	10	190
04 02	60	8	05 02	60	8	06 02	60	8	07 02	60	8	08 02	60	8	09 02	60	8	10 02	60	8	188
04 01	60	6	05 01	60	6	06 01	60	6	07 01	60	6	08 01	60	6	09 01	60	6	10 01	60	6	186
04 01	60	4	05 01	60	4	06 01	60	4	07 01	60	4	08 01	60	4	09 01	60	4	10 01	60	4	184
04 00	60	2	05 00	60	2	06 00	60	2	07 00	60	2	08 00	60	2	09 00	60	2	10 00	60	2	182
04 00	+60	0	05 00	+60	0	06 00	+60	0	07 00	+60	0	08 00	+60	0	09 00	+60	0	10 00	+60	0	180

LAT 86°

0°	1°	2°	3°	4°	5°	6°	7°	8°	9°	10°	11°	12°	13°	14°

S. Lat. {LHA greater than 180°....... Zn=180−Z; LHA less than 180°........... Zn=180+Z}

DECLINATION (0°-14°) SAME NAME AS LATITUDE

LAT 86°

N. Lat. {LHA greater than 180°....... Zn=Z; LHA less than 180°.......... Zn=360−Z}

DECLINATION (0°-14°) CONTRARY NAME TO LATITUDE

LHA	0° Hc d Z	1° Hc d Z	2° Hc d Z	3° Hc d Z	4° Hc d Z	5° Hc d Z	6° Hc d Z	7° Hc d Z	8° Hc d Z	9° Hc d Z	10° Hc d Z	11° Hc d Z	12° Hc d Z	13° Hc d Z	14° Hc d Z	LHA
	° ′ ′ °	° ′ ′ °	° ′ ′ °	° ′ ′ °	° ′ ′ °	° ′ ′ °	° ′ ′ °	° ′ ′ °	° ′ ′ °	° ′ ′ °	° ′ ′ °	° ′ ′ °	° ′ ′ °	° ′ ′ °	° ′ ′ °	
180	−4 00 −60 0	−5 00 −60 0	−6 00 −60 0	−7 00 −60 0												180
178	−4 00 60 2	−5 00 60 2	−6 00 60 2	−7 00 60 2												182
176	−3 59 60 4	−4 59 60 4	−5 59 60 4	−6 59 60 4												184
174	−3 59 60 6	−4 59 60 6	−5 59 60 6	−6 59 60 6												186
172	−3 58 60 8	−4 58 60 8	−5 58 60 8	−6 58 60 8												188
170	−3 56 −60 10	−4 56 −60 10	−5 56 −60 10	−6 56 −60 10												190
168	−3 55 60 12	−4 55 60 12	−5 55 60 12	−6 55 60 12												192
166	−3 53 60 14	−4 53 60 14	−5 53 60 14	−6 53 60 14												194
164	−3 51 60 16	−4 51 60 16	−5 51 60 16	−6 51 60 16												196
162	−3 48 60 18	−4 48 60 18	−5 48 60 18	−6 48 60 18												198
160	−3 46 −60 20	−4 46 −60 20	−5 46 −60 20	−6 46 −59 20												200
158	−3 43 60 22	−4 43 60 22	−5 43 59 22	−6 42 60 22												202
156	−3 39 60 24	−4 39 60 24	−5 39 60 24	−6 39 60 24												204
154	−3 36 60 26	−4 36 60 26	−5 36 60 26	−6 36 60 26												206
152	−3 32 60 28	−4 32 60 28	−5 32 60 28	−6 32 60 28												208
150	−3 28 −60 30	−4 28 −60 30	−5 28 −60 30	−6 28 −60 30												210
148	−3 23 60 32	−4 23 60 32	−5 23 60 32	−6 23 60 32												212
146	−3 19 60 34	−4 19 60 34	−5 19 60 34	−6 19 60 34												214
144	−3 14 60 36	−4 14 60 36	−5 14 60 36	−6 14 60 36												216
142	−3 09 60 38	−4 09 60 38	−5 09 60 38	−6 09 60 38	−7 09 60 38											218
140	−3 04 −60 40	−4 04 −60 40	−5 04 −60 40	−6 04 −60 40	−7 04 −60 40											220

S. Lat. {LHA greater than 180°....... Zn=180−Z; LHA less than 180°.......... Zn=180+Z}

DECLINATION (0°-14°) CONTRARY NAME TO LATITUDE

N. Lat. {LHA greater than 180°....... Zn=Z; LHA less than 180°........... Zn=360−Z}

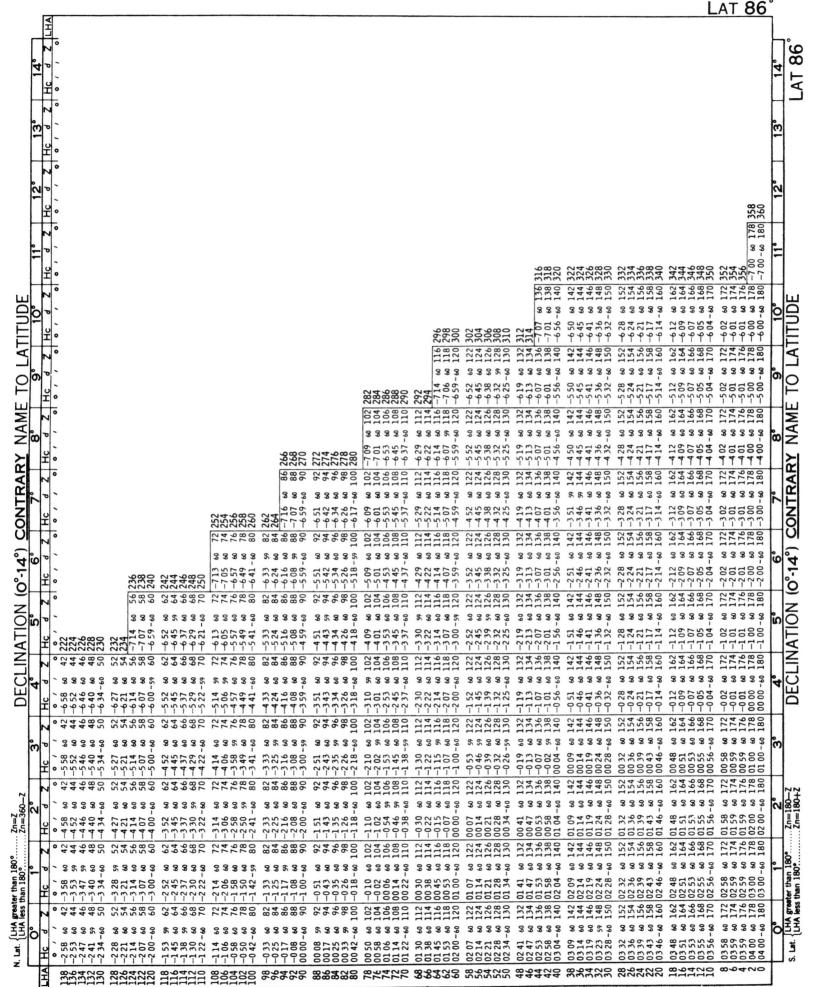

DECLINATION (0°-14°) CONTRARY NAME TO LATITUDE

LHA	0° Hc d Z	1° Hc d Z	2° Hc d Z	3° Hc d Z	4° Hc d Z	5° Hc d Z	6° Hc d Z	7° Hc d Z	8° Hc d Z	9° Hc d Z	10° Hc d Z	11° Hc d Z	12° Hc d Z	13° Hc d Z	14° Hc d Z	LHA
	° ′ ′ °	° ′ ′ °	° ′ ′ °	° ′ ′ °	° ′ ′ °	° ′ ′ °	° ′ ′ °	° ′ ′ °	° ′ ′ °	° ′ ′ °	° ′ ′ °	° ′ ′ °	° ′ ′ °	° ′ ′ °	° ′ ′ °	
138	-2 58 60 42	-3 58 60 42	-4 58 60 42	-5 58 60 42	-6 58 60 42											222
136	-2 53 60 44	-3 53 59 44	-4 52 60 44	-5 52 60 44	-6 52 60 44											224
134	-2 47 60 46	-3 47 59 46	-4 46 60 46	-5 46 60 46	-6 46 60 46											226
132	-2 41 59 48	-3 40 60 48	-4 40 60 48	-5 40 60 48	-6 40 60 48											228
130	-2 34 -60 50	-3 34 -60 50	-4 34 -60 50	-5 34 -60 50	-6 34 -60 50											230
128	-2 28 60 52	-3 28 59 52	-4 27 60 52	-5 27 60 52	-6 27 60 52											232
126	-2 21 60 54	-3 21 60 54	-4 21 60 54	-5 21 60 54	-6 21 60 54											234
124	-2 14 60 56	-3 14 60 56	-4 14 60 56	-5 14 60 56	-6 14 60 56	-7 14 60 56										236
122	-2 07 60 58	-3 07 60 58	-4 07 60 58	-5 07 60 58	-6 07 60 58	-7 07 60 58										238
120	-2 00 -60 60	-3 00 -60 60	-4 00 -60 60	-5 00 -60 60	-6 00 -59 60	-6 59 -60 60										240
118	-1 53 59 62	-2 52 60 62	-3 52 60 62	-4 52 60 62	-5 52 60 62	-6 52 60 62										242
116	-1 45 60 64	-2 45 60 64	-3 45 60 64	-4 45 60 64	-5 45 60 64	-6 45 59 64										244
114	-1 38 59 66	-2 37 60 66	-3 37 60 66	-4 37 60 66	-5 37 60 66	-6 37 60 66										246
112	-1 30 60 68	-2 30 60 68	-3 30 59 68	-4 29 60 68	-5 29 60 68	-6 29 60 68										248
110	-1 22 -60 70	-2 22 -60 70	-3 22 -60 70	-4 22 -60 70	-5 22 -59 70	-6 21 -60 70										250
108	-1 14 60 72	-2 14 60 72	-3 14 60 72	-4 14 60 72	-5 14 59 72	-6 13 60 72	-7 13 60 72									252
106	-1 06 60 74	-2 06 60 74	-3 06 60 74	-4 06 60 74	-5 06 59 74	-6 05 60 74	-7 05 60 74									254
104	-0 58 60 76	-1 58 60 76	-2 58 60 76	-3 58 59 76	-4 57 60 76	-5 57 60 76	-6 57 60 76									256
102	-0 50 60 78	-1 50 60 78	-2 50 59 78	-3 49 60 78	-4 49 60 78	-5 49 60 78	-6 49 60 78									258
100	-0 42 -60 80	-1 42 -59 80	-2 41 -60 80	-3 41 -60 80	-4 41 -60 80	-5 41 -60 80	-6 41 -60 80									260
98	-0 33 60 82	-1 33 60 82	-2 33 60 82	-3 33 60 82	-4 33 60 82	-5 33 60 82	-6 33 59 82									262
96	-0 25 60 84	-1 25 60 84	-2 25 60 84	-3 25 59 84	-4 24 60 84	-5 24 60 84	-6 24 60 84									264
94	-0 17 60 86	-1 17 59 86	-2 16 60 86	-3 16 60 86	-4 16 60 86	-5 16 60 86	-6 16 60 86	-7 16 60 86								266
92	-0 08 60 88	-1 08 60 88	-2 08 60 88	-3 08 60 88	-4 08 60 88	-5 08 60 88	-6 08 59 88	-7 07 60 88								268
90	00 00 -60 90	-1 00 -60 90	-2 00 -60 90	-3 00 -59 90	-3 59 -60 90	-4 59 -60 90	-5 59 -60 90	-6 59 -60 90								270
88	00 08 59 92	-0 51 60 92	-1 51 60 92	-2 51 60 92	-3 51 60 92	-4 51 60 92	-5 51 60 92	-6 51 60 92								272
86	00 17 60 94	-0 43 60 94	-1 43 60 94	-2 43 60 94	-3 43 60 94	-4 43 59 94	-5 42 60 94	-6 42 60 94								274
84	00 25 60 96	-0 35 60 96	-1 35 60 96	-2 35 59 96	-3 34 60 96	-4 34 60 96	-5 34 60 96	-6 34 60 96								276
82	00 33 59 98	-0 26 60 98	-1 26 60 98	-2 26 60 98	-3 26 60 98	-4 26 60 98	-5 26 60 98	-6 26 60 98								278
80	00 42 -60 100	-0 18 -60 100	-1 18 -60 100	-2 18 -60 100	-3 18 -60 100	-4 18 -60 100	-5 18 -59 100	-6 17 -60 100								280
78	00 50 60 102	-0 10 60 102	-1 10 60 102	-2 10 60 102	-3 10 59 102	-4 09 60 102	-5 09 60 102	-6 09 60 102	-7 09 60 102							282
76	00 58 60 104	-0 02 60 104	-1 02 60 104	-2 02 59 104	-3 01 60 104	-4 01 60 104	-5 01 60 104	-6 01 60 104	-7 01 60 104							284
74	01 06 60 106	00 06 60 106	-0 54 59 106	-1 53 60 106	-2 53 60 106	-3 53 60 106	-4 53 60 106	-5 53 60 106	-6 53 60 106							286
72	01 14 60 108	00 14 60 108	-0 46 59 108	-1 45 60 108	-2 45 60 108	-3 45 60 108	-4 45 60 108	-5 45 60 108	-6 45 60 108							288
70	01 22 -60 110	00 22 -60 110	-0 38 -60 110	-1 38 -59 110	-2 37 -60 110	-3 37 -60 110	-4 37 -60 110	-5 37 -60 110	-6 37 -60 110							290
68	01 30 60 112	00 30 60 112	-0 30 60 112	-1 30 60 112	-2 30 60 112	-3 30 59 112	-4 29 60 112	-5 29 60 112	-6 29 60 112							292
66	01 38 60 114	00 38 60 114	-0 22 60 114	-1 22 60 114	-2 22 60 114	-3 22 60 114	-4 22 60 114	-5 22 60 114	-6 22 60 114							294
64	01 45 60 116	00 45 60 116	-0 15 60 116	-1 15 59 116	-2 14 60 116	-3 14 60 116	-4 14 60 116	-5 14 60 116	-6 14 60 116	-7 14 60 116						296
62	01 53 60 118	00 53 60 118	-0 07 60 118	-1 07 60 118	-2 07 60 118	-3 07 60 118	-4 07 60 118	-5 07 60 118	-6 07 59 118	-7 06 60 118						298
60	02 00 -60 120	01 00 -60 120	00 00 -60 120	-1 00 -60 120	-2 00 -60 120	-3 00 -59 120	-3 59 -60 120	-4 59 -60 120	-5 59 -60 120	-6 59 -60 120						300
58	02 07 60 122	01 07 60 122	00 07 60 122	-0 53 59 122	-1 52 60 122	-2 52 60 122	-3 52 60 122	-4 52 60 122	-5 52 60 122	-6 52 60 122						302
56	02 14 60 124	01 14 60 124	00 14 60 124	-0 46 59 124	-1 45 60 124	-2 45 60 124	-3 45 60 124	-4 45 60 124	-5 45 60 124	-6 45 60 124						304
54	02 21 60 126	01 21 60 126	00 21 60 126	-0 39 60 126	-1 39 60 126	-2 39 59 126	-3 38 60 126	-4 38 60 126	-5 38 60 126	-6 38 60 126						306
52	02 28 60 128	01 28 60 128	00 28 60 128	-0 32 60 128	-1 32 60 128	-2 32 60 128	-3 32 60 128	-4 32 60 128	-5 32 60 128	-6 32 59 128						308
50	02 34 -60 130	01 34 -60 130	00 34 -60 130	-0 26 -59 130	-1 25 -60 130	-2 25 -60 130	-3 25 -60 130	-4 25 -60 130	-5 25 -60 130	-6 25 -60 130						310
48	02 41 60 132	01 41 60 132	00 41 60 132	-0 19 60 132	-1 19 60 132	-2 19 60 132	-3 19 60 132	-4 19 60 132	-5 19 60 132	-6 19 60 132						312
46	02 47 60 134	01 47 60 134	00 47 60 134	-0 13 60 134	-1 13 60 134	-2 13 60 134	-3 13 60 134	-4 13 60 134	-5 13 60 134	-6 13 60 134						314
44	02 53 60 136	01 53 60 136	00 53 60 136	-0 07 60 136	-1 07 60 136	-2 07 60 136	-3 07 60 136	-4 07 60 136	-5 07 60 136	-6 07 60 136	-7 07 60 136					316
42	02 58 60 138	01 58 60 138	00 58 60 138	-0 02 59 138	-1 01 60 138	-2 01 60 138	-3 01 60 138	-4 01 60 138	-5 01 60 138	-6 01 60 138	-7 01 60 138					318
40	03 04 -60 140	02 04 -60 140	01 04 -60 140	00 04 -60 140	-0 56 -60 140	-1 56 -60 140	-2 56 -60 140	-3 56 -60 140	-4 56 -60 140	-5 56 -60 140	-6 56 -60 140					320
38	03 09 60 142	02 09 60 142	01 09 60 142	00 09 60 142	-0 51 60 142	-1 51 60 142	-2 51 60 142	-3 51 59 142	-4 50 60 142	-5 50 60 142	-6 50 60 142					322
36	03 14 60 144	02 14 60 144	01 14 60 144	00 14 60 144	-0 46 60 144	-1 46 60 144	-2 46 60 144	-3 46 59 144	-4 45 60 144	-5 45 60 144	-6 45 60 144					324
34	03 19 60 146	02 19 60 146	01 19 60 146	00 19 60 146	-0 41 60 146	-1 41 60 146	-2 41 60 146	-3 41 60 146	-4 41 60 146	-5 41 60 146	-6 41 60 146					326
32	03 23 59 148	02 24 60 148	01 24 60 148	00 24 60 148	-0 36 60 148	-1 36 60 148	-2 36 60 148	-3 36 60 148	-4 36 60 148	-5 36 60 148	-6 36 60 148					328
30	03 28 -60 150	02 28 -60 150	01 28 -60 150	00 28 -60 150	-0 32 -60 150	-1 32 -60 150	-2 32 -60 150	-3 32 -60 150	-4 32 -60 150	-5 32 -60 150	-6 32 -60 150					330
28	03 32 60 152	02 32 60 152	01 32 60 152	00 32 60 152	-0 28 60 152	-1 28 60 152	-2 28 60 152	-3 28 60 152	-4 28 60 152	-5 28 60 152	-6 28 60 152					332
26	03 36 60 154	02 36 60 154	01 36 60 154	00 36 60 154	-0 24 60 154	-1 24 60 154	-2 24 60 154	-3 24 60 154	-4 24 60 154	-5 24 60 154	-6 24 60 154					334
24	03 39 60 156	02 39 60 156	01 39 60 156	00 39 60 156	-0 21 60 156	-1 21 60 156	-2 21 60 156	-3 21 60 156	-4 21 60 156	-5 21 60 156	-6 21 60 156					336
22	03 43 60 158	02 43 60 158	01 43 60 158	00 43 60 158	-0 17 60 158	-1 17 60 158	-2 17 60 158	-3 17 60 158	-4 17 60 158	-5 17 60 158	-6 17 60 158					338
20	03 46 -60 160	02 46 -60 160	01 46 -60 160	00 46 -60 160	-0 14 -60 160	-1 14 -60 160	-2 14 -60 160	-3 14 -60 160	-4 14 -60 160	-5 14 -60 160	-6 14 -60 160					340
18	03 48 60 162	02 48 60 162	01 48 60 162	00 48 60 162	-0 12 60 162	-1 12 60 162	-2 12 60 162	-3 12 60 162	-4 12 60 162	-5 12 60 162	-6 12 60 162					342
16	03 51 60 164	02 51 60 164	01 51 60 164	00 51 60 164	-0 09 60 164	-1 09 60 164	-2 09 60 164	-3 09 60 164	-4 09 60 164	-5 09 60 164	-6 09 60 164					344
14	03 53 60 166	02 53 60 166	01 53 60 166	00 53 60 166	-0 07 60 166	-1 07 60 166	-2 07 60 166	-3 07 60 166	-4 07 60 166	-5 07 60 166	-6 07 60 166					346
12	03 55 60 168	02 55 60 168	01 55 60 168	00 55 60 168	-0 05 60 168	-1 05 60 168	-2 05 60 168	-3 05 60 168	-4 05 60 168	-5 05 60 168	-6 05 60 168					348
10	03 56 -60 170	02 56 -60 170	01 56 -60 170	00 56 -60 170	-0 04 -60 170	-1 04 -60 170	-2 04 -60 170	-3 04 -60 170	-4 04 -60 170	-5 04 -60 170	-6 04 -60 170					350
8	03 58 60 172	02 58 60 172	01 58 60 172	00 58 60 172	-0 02 60 172	-1 02 60 172	-2 02 60 172	-3 02 60 172	-4 02 60 172	-5 02 60 172	-6 02 60 172					352
6	03 59 60 174	02 59 60 174	01 59 60 174	00 59 60 174	-0 01 60 174	-1 01 60 174	-2 01 60 174	-3 01 60 174	-4 01 60 174	-5 01 60 174	-6 01 60 174					354
4	03 59 60 176	02 59 60 176	01 59 60 176	00 59 60 176	-0 01 60 176	-1 01 60 176	-2 01 60 176	-3 01 60 176	-4 01 60 176	-5 01 60 176	-6 01 60 176					356
2	04 00 60 178	03 00 60 178	02 00 60 178	01 00 60 178	00 00 60 178	-1 00 60 178	-2 00 60 178	-3 00 60 178	-4 00 60 178	-5 00 60 178	-6 00 60 178	-7 00 60 178				358
0	04 00 -60 180	03 00 -60 180	02 00 -60 180	01 00 -60 180	00 00 -60 180	-1 00 -60 180	-2 00 -60 180	-3 00 -60 180	-4 00 -60 180	-5 00 -60 180	-6 00 -60 180	-7 00 -60 180				360
	0°	1°	2°	3°	4°	5°	6°	7°	8°	9°	10°	11°	12°	13°	14°	

S. Lat. {LHA greater than 180°....... Zn=180−Z; LHA less than 180°........... Zn=180+Z}

DECLINATION (0°-14°) CONTRARY NAME TO LATITUDE

N. Lat. {LHA greater than 180°....... Zn=Z; LHA less than 180°........... Zn=360−Z}

DECLINATION (15°-29°) SAME NAME AS LATITUDE

LAT 86°

LHA	15° Hc	d	Z	16° Hc	d	Z	17° Hc	d	Z	18° Hc	d	Z	19° Hc	d	Z
	° ′	′	°	° ′	′	°	° ′	′	°	° ′	′	°	° ′	′	°
0	19 00	+60	180	20 00	+60	180	21 00	+60	180	22 00	+60	180	23 00	+60	180
2	19 00	60	178	20 00	60	178	21 00	60	178	22 00	60	178	23 00	60	178
4	18 59	60	176	19 59	60	176	20 59	60	176	21 59	60	176	22 59	60	176
6	18 59	60	174	19 59	60	174	20 59	60	174	21 59	60	174	22 59	60	174
8	18 58	60	172	19 58	60	172	20 58	60	172	21 58	60	172	22 58	60	172
10	18 56	+60	170	19 56	+60	170	20 56	+60	170	21 56	+60	170	22 56	+60	170
12	18 55	60	168	19 55	60	168	20 55	60	168	21 55	60	168	22 55	60	168
14	18 53	60	166	19 53	60	166	20 53	60	166	21 53	60	166	22 53	60	166
16	18 51	60	164	19 51	60	164	20 51	60	164	21 51	60	164	22 51	60	164
18	18 48	60	162	19 48	60	162	20 48	60	162	21 48	60	162	22 48	60	162
20	18 45	+60	160	19 45	+60	160	20 45	+60	160	21 45	+60	160	22 45	+60	160
22	18 42	60	158	19 42	60	158	20 42	60	158	21 42	60	158	22 42	60	157
24	18 39	60	156	19 39	60	156	20 39	60	155	21 39	60	155	22 39	60	155
26	18 35	60	154	19 35	60	153	20 35	60	153	21 35	60	153	22 35	60	153
28	18 31	60	151	19 31	60	151	20 31	60	151	21 31	60	151	22 31	60	151
30	18 27	+60	149	19 27	+60	149	20 27	+60	149	21 27	+60	149	22 27	+60	149
32	18 23	60	147	19 23	60	147	20 23	60	147	21 23	60	147	22 23	60	147
34	18 18	60	145	19 18	60	145	20 18	60	145	21 18	60	145	22 18	60	145
36	18 13	60	143	19 13	60	143	20 13	60	143	21 13	60	143	22 13	60	143
38	18 08	60	141	19 08	60	141	20 08	60	141	21 08	60	141	22 08	60	141
40	18 03	+60	139	19 03	+60	139	20 03	+60	139	21 03	+60	139	22 03	+60	139
42	17 57	60	137	18 57	60	137	19 57	60	137	20 57	60	137	21 57	60	137
44	17 52	59	135	18 51	60	135	19 51	60	135	20 51	60	135	21 51	60	135
46	17 46	59	133	18 45	60	133	19 45	60	133	20 45	60	133	21 45	60	133
48	17 39	60	131	18 39	60	131	19 39	60	131	20 39	60	131	21 39	60	131
50	17 33	+60	129	18 33	+60	129	19 33	+60	129	20 33	+60	129	21 33	+59	129
52	17 26	60	127	18 26	60	127	19 26	60	127	20 26	60	127	21 26	60	127
54	17 20	59	125	18 19	60	125	19 19	60	125	20 19	60	125	21 19	60	125
56	17 13	60	123	18 13	59	123	19 12	60	123	20 12	60	123	21 12	60	123
58	17 06	59	121	18 05	60	121	19 05	60	121	20 05	60	121	21 05	60	121
60	16 58	+60	119	17 58	+60	119	18 58	+60	119	19 58	+60	119	20 58	+60	119
62	16 51	60	117	17 51	60	117	18 51	60	117	19 51	59	117	20 50	60	117
64	16 43	60	115	17 43	60	115	18 43	60	115	19 43	60	115	20 43	60	115
66	16 36	60	113	17 36	59	113	18 35	60	113	19 35	60	113	20 35	60	113
68	16 28	60	111	17 28	60	111	18 28	60	111	19 28	59	111	20 27	60	111
70	16 20	+60	109	17 20	+60	109	18 20	+60	109	19 20	+60	109	20 20	+59	109
72	16 12	60	107	17 12	60	107	18 12	60	107	19 12	60	107	20 12	59	107
74	16 04	60	105	17 04	60	105	18 04	60	105	19 04	59	105	20 03	60	105
76	15 56	60	103	16 56	60	103	17 56	59	103	18 55	60	103	19 55	60	103
78	15 48	60	101	16 48	59	101	17 47	60	101	18 47	60	101	19 47	60	101
80	15 40	+59	99	16 39	+60	99	17 39	+60	99	18 39	+60	99	19 39	+60	99
82	15 31	60	97	16 31	60	97	17 31	60	97	18 31	60	97	19 31	59	97
84	15 23	60	95	16 23	60	95	17 23	59	95	18 22	60	95	19 22	60	95
86	15 15	59	93	16 14	60	93	17 14	60	93	18 14	60	93	19 14	60	93
88	15 06	60	91	16 06	60	91	17 06	60	91	18 06	60	91	19 06	59	91
90	14 58	+60	89	15 58	+59	89	16 57	+60	89	17 57	+60	89	18 57	+60	89
92	14 49	60	87	15 49	60	87	16 49	60	87	17 49	60	87	18 49	60	87
94	14 41	60	85	15 41	60	85	16 41	60	85	17 41	59	85	18 40	60	85
96	14 33	60	83	15 33	59	83	16 32	60	83	17 32	60	83	18 32	60	83
98	14 24	60	81	15 24	60	81	16 24	60	81	17 24	60	81	18 24	60	81
100	14 16	+60	79	15 16	+60	79	16 16	+60	79	17 16	+60	79	18 16	+59	79
102	14 08	60	77	15 08	60	77	16 08	60	77	17 08	59	77	18 07	60	77
104	14 00	60	75	15 00	60	75	16 00	59	75	16 59	60	75	17 59	60	75
106	13 52	60	73	14 52	60	73	15 52	59	73	16 51	60	73	17 51	60	73
108	13 44	60	71	14 44	60	71	15 44	59	71	16 43	60	71	17 43	60	71
110	13 36	+60	69	14 36	+60	69	15 36	+60	69	16 36	+59	69	17 35	+60	69
112	13 28	60	67	14 28	60	67	15 28	60	67	16 28	60	67	17 28	60	67
114	13 21	60	65	14 21	59	65	15 20	60	65	16 20	60	65	17 20	60	65
116	13 13	60	63	14 13	60	63	15 13	60	63	16 13	60	63	17 13	59	63
118	13 06	60	61	14 06	59	61	15 05	60	61	16 05	60	61	17 05	60	61
120	12 58	+60	59	13 58	+60	59	14 58	+60	59	15 58	+60	59	16 58	+60	59
122	12 51	60	57	13 51	60	57	14 51	60	57	15 51	60	57	16 51	60	57
124	12 44	60	55	13 44	60	55	14 44	60	55	15 44	60	55	16 44	60	55
126	12 38	60	53	13 38	59	53	14 37	60	53	15 37	60	53	16 37	60	53
128	12 31	60	51	13 31	60	51	14 31	60	51	15 31	60	51	16 31	59	51
130	12 25	+59	49	13 24	+60	49	14 24	+60	49	15 24	+60	49	16 24	+60	49
132	12 18	60	47	13 18	60	47	14 18	60	47	15 18	60	47	16 18	60	47
134	12 12	60	45	13 12	60	45	14 12	60	45	15 12	60	45	16 12	60	45
136	12 06	60	43	13 06	60	43	14 06	60	43	15 06	60	43	16 06	60	43
138	12 01	60	41	13 01	60	41	14 01	60	41	15 01	59	41	16 00	60	41

LHA	20° Hc	d	Z	21° Hc	d	Z	22° Hc	d	Z	23° Hc	d	Z	24° Hc	d	Z
	° ′	′	°	° ′	′	°	° ′	′	°	° ′	′	°	° ′	′	°
0	24 00	+60	180	25 00	+60	180	26 00	+60	180	27 00	+60	180	28 00	+60	180
2	24 00	60	178	25 00	60	178	26 00	60	178	27 00	60	178	28 00	60	178
4	23 59	60	176	24 59	60	176	25 59	60	176	26 59	60	176	27 59	60	176
6	23 59	60	174	24 59	60	174	25 59	60	174	26 59	60	174	27 59	60	174
8	23 58	60	172	24 58	60	172	25 58	60	172	26 58	60	172	27 58	60	172
10	23 56	+60	170	24 56	+60	170	25 56	+60	170	26 56	+60	170	27 56	+60	170
12	23 55	60	168	24 55	60	168	25 55	60	168	26 55	60	168	27 55	60	168
14	23 53	60	166	24 53	60	166	25 53	60	166	26 53	60	166	27 53	60	166
16	23 51	59	164	24 50	60	164	25 50	60	164	26 50	60	164	27 50	60	164
18	23 48	60	162	24 48	60	162	25 48	60	161	26 48	60	161	27 48	60	161
20	23 45	+60	159	24 45	+60	159	25 45	+60	159	26 45	+60	159	27 45	+60	159
22	23 42	60	157	24 42	60	157	25 42	60	157	26 42	60	157	27 42	60	157
24	23 39	60	155	24 39	60	155	25 39	60	155	26 39	60	155	27 39	60	155
26	23 35	60	153	24 35	60	153	25 35	60	153	26 35	60	153	27 35	60	153
28	23 31	60	151	24 31	60	151	25 31	60	151	26 31	60	151	27 31	60	151
30	23 27	+60	149	24 27	+60	149	25 27	+60	149	26 27	+60	149	27 27	+60	149
32	23 23	60	147	24 23	60	147	25 23	60	147	26 23	59	147	27 22	60	147
34	23 18	60	145	24 18	60	145	25 18	60	145	26 18	60	145	27 18	60	145
36	23 13	60	143	24 13	60	143	25 13	60	143	26 13	60	143	27 13	60	143
38	23 08	60	141	24 08	60	141	25 08	60	141	26 08	60	141	27 08	60	141
40	23 03	+59	139	24 02	+60	139	25 02	+60	139	26 02	+60	139	27 02	+60	139
42	22 57	60	137	23 57	60	137	24 57	60	137	25 57	60	137	26 57	60	137
44	22 51	60	135	23 51	60	135	24 51	60	135	25 51	60	135	26 51	60	135
46	22 45	60	133	23 45	60	133	24 45	60	133	25 45	60	133	26 45	60	133
48	22 39	60	131	23 39	60	131	24 39	60	131	25 39	59	131	26 38	60	131
50	22 32	+60	129	23 32	+60	129	24 32	+60	129	25 32	+60	129	26 32	+60	129
52	22 26	60	127	23 26	60	127	24 26	59	127	25 25	60	127	26 25	60	127
54	22 19	60	125	23 19	60	125	24 19	60	125	25 19	60	125	26 19	59	125
56	22 12	60	123	23 12	60	123	24 12	60	123	25 12	60	123	26 12	59	122
58	22 05	60	121	23 05	60	121	24 05	60	121	25 05	59	121	26 04	60	120
60	21 58	+60	119	22 58	+59	119	23 57	+60	119	24 57	+60	118	25 57	+60	118
62	21 50	60	117	22 50	60	117	23 50	60	117	24 50	60	116	25 50	60	116
64	21 43	60	115	22 43	59	115	23 42	60	115	24 42	60	114	25 42	60	114
66	21 35	60	113	22 35	60	113	23 35	60	113	24 35	59	112	25 34	60	112
68	21 27	60	111	22 27	60	111	23 27	60	110	24 27	60	110	25 27	59	110
70	21 19	+60	109	22 19	+60	109	23 19	+60	108	24 19	+60	108	25 19	+60	108
72	21 11	60	107	22 11	60	107	23 11	60	106	24 11	60	106	25 11	60	106
74	21 03	60	105	22 03	60	105	23 03	60	104	24 03	60	104	25 03	60	104
76	20 55	60	103	21 55	60	103	22 55	60	102	23 55	60	102	24 55	59	102
78	20 47	60	101	21 47	60	101	22 47	59	100	23 46	60	100	24 46	60	100
80	20 39	+60	99	21 39	+59	99	22 38	+60	98	23 38	+60	98	24 38	+60	98
82	20 30	60	97	21 30	60	97	22 30	60	96	23 30	60	96	24 30	60	96
84	20 22	60	95	21 22	60	95	22 22	60	94	23 22	59	94	24 21	60	94
86	20 14	60	93	21 14	59	93	22 13	60	92	23 13	60	92	24 13	60	92
88	20 05	60	91	21 05	60	91	22 05	60	90	23 05	60	90	24 05	60	90
90	19 57	+60	89	20 57	+60	89	21 57	+59	88	22 56	+60	88	23 56	+60	88
92	19 49	59	87	20 48	60	87	21 48	60	86	22 48	60	86	23 48	60	86
94	19 40	60	85	20 40	60	85	21 40	60	84	22 40	60	84	23 40	59	84
96	19 32	60	83	20 32	60	83	21 32	59	82	22 31	60	82	23 31	60	82
98	19 24	60	81	20 24	59	81	21 23	60	80	22 23	60	80	23 23	60	80
100	19 15	+60	79	20 15	+60	79	21 15	+60	78	22 15	+60	78	23 15	+60	78
102	19 07	60	77	20 07	60	77	21 07	60	77	22 07	60	76	23 07	59	76
104	18 59	60	75	19 59	60	75	20 59	60	75	21 59	60	74	22 59	59	74
106	18 51	60	73	19 51	60	73	20 51	60	73	21 51	60	72	22 51	59	72
108	18 43	60	71	19 43	60	71	20 43	60	71	21 43	60	70	22 43	59	70
110	18 35	+60	69	19 35	+60	69	20 35	+60	69	21 35	+60	69	22 35	+60	68
112	18 28	59	67	19 27	60	67	20 27	60	67	21 27	60	67	22 27	60	66
114	18 20	60	65	19 20	60	65	20 20	60	65	21 20	59	65	22 19	60	64
116	18 12	60	63	19 12	60	63	20 12	60	63	21 12	60	63	22 12	60	63
118	18 05	60	61	19 05	60	61	20 05	60	61	21 05	60	61	22 05	59	61
120	17 58	+60	59	18 58	+60	59	19 58	+59	59	20 57	+60	59	21 57	+60	59
122	17 51	60	57	18 51	60	57	19 51	59	57	20 50	60	57	21 50	60	57
124	17 44	60	55	18 44	60	55	19 44	60	55	20 44	59	55	21 43	60	55
126	17 37	60	53	18 37	60	53	19 37	60	53	20 37	60	53	21 37	60	53
128	17 30	60	51	18 30	60	51	19 30	60	51	20 30	60	51	21 30	60	51
130	17 24	+60	49	18 24	+60	49	19 24	+60	49	20 24	+60	49	21 24	+60	49
132	17 18	60	47	18 18	60	47	19 18	60	47	20 18	60	47	21 18	59	47
134	17 12	60	45	18 12	60	45	19 12	60	45	20 12	60	45	21 12	59	45
136	17 06	60	43	18 06	60	43	19 06	60	43	20 06	60	43	21 06	60	43
138	17 00	60	41	18 00	60	41	19 00	60	41	20 00	60	41	21 00	60	41

LHA	25° Hc	d	Z	26° Hc	d	Z	27° Hc	d	Z	28° Hc	d	Z	29° Hc	d	Z	LHA
	° ′	′	°	° ′	′	°	° ′	′	°	° ′	′	°	° ′	′	°	
0	29 00	+60	180	30 00	+60	180	31 00	+60	180	32 00	+60	180	33 00	+60	180	360
2	29 00	60	178	30 00	60	178	31 00	60	178	32 00	60	178	33 00	60	178	358
4	28 59	60	176	29 59	60	176	30 59	60	176	31 59	60	176	32 59	60	176	356
6	28 59	60	174	29 59	60	174	30 59	60	174	31 59	60	174	32 59	60	174	354
8	28 58	60	172	29 58	60	172	30 58	60	172	31 58	60	172	32 58	60	172	352
10	28 56	+60	170	29 56	+60	170	30 56	+60	170	31 56	+60	170	32 56	+60	170	350
12	28 55	60	168	29 55	60	168	30 55	60	168	31 55	60	168	32 55	60	168	348
14	28 53	60	166	29 53	60	166	30 53	60	166	31 53	60	165	32 53	60	165	346
16	28 50	60	163	29 50	60	163	30 50	60	163	31 50	60	163	32 50	60	163	344
18	28 48	60	161	29 48	60	161	30 48	60	161	31 48	60	161	32 48	60	161	342
20	28 45	+60	159	29 45	+60	159	30 45	+60	159	31 45	+60	159	32 45	+60	159	340
22	28 42	60	157	29 42	60	157	30 42	60	157	31 42	60	157	32 42	60	157	338
24	28 39	60	155	29 39	60	155	30 39	60	155	31 39	59	155	32 38	60	155	336
26	28 35	60	153	29 35	60	153	30 35	60	153	31 35	60	153	32 35	60	153	334
28	28 31	60	151	29 31	60	151	30 31	60	151	31 31	60	151	32 31	60	151	332
30	28 27	+60	149	29 27	+60	149	30 27	+60	149	31 27	+60	149	32 27	+60	149	330
32	28 22	60	147	29 22	60	147	30 22	60	147	31 22	60	147	32 22	60	147	328
34	28 18	60	145	29 18	60	145	30 18	60	145	31 18	59	145	32 17	60	145	326
36	28 13	60	143	29 13	60	143	30 13	60	143	31 13	60	143	32 13	59	143	324
38	28 08	60	141	29 08	59	141	30 07	60	141	31 07	60	141	32 07	60	141	322
40	28 02	+60	139	29 02	+60	139	30 02	+60	139	31 02	+60	139	32 02	+60	139	320
42	27 57	59	137	28 56	60	137	29 56	60	137	30 56	60	137	31 56	60	136	318
44	27 51	60	135	28 51	60	135	29 51	59	135	30 50	60	134	31 50	60	134	316
46	27 45	60	133	28 45	59	133	29 44	60	132	30 44	60	132	31 44	60	132	314
48	27 38	60	131	28 38	60	130	29 38	60	130	30 38	60	130	31 38	60	130	312
50	27 32	+60	129	28 32	+60	128	29 32	+60	128	30 32	+59	128	31 31	+60	128	310
52	27 25	60	126	28 25	60	126	29 25	60	126	30 25	60	126	31 25	60	126	308
54	27 18	60	124	28 18	60	124	29 18	60	124	30 18	60	124	31 18	60	124	306
56	27 11	60	122	28 11	60	122	29 11	60	122	30 11	60	122	31 11	60	122	304
58	27 04	60	120	28 04	60	120	29 04	60	120	30 04	60	120	31 04	60	120	302
60	26 57	+60	118	27 57	+60	118	28 57	+60	118	29 57	+59	118	30 56	+60	118	300
62	26 50	59	116	27 49	60	116	28 49	60	116	29 49	60	116	30 49	60	116	298
64	26 42	60	114	27 42	60	114	28 42	60	114	29 42	59	114	30 41	60	114	296
66	26 34	60	112	27 34	60	112	28 34	60	112	29 34	60	112	30 34	59	112	294
68	26 26	60	110	27 26	60	110	28 26	60	110	29 26	60	110	30 26	60	110	292
70	26 19	+59	108	27 18	+60	108	28 18	+60	108	29 18	+60	108	30 18	+60	108	290
72	26 11	59	106	27 10	60	106	28 10	60	106	29 10	60	106	30 10	60	106	288
74	26 03	59	104	27 02	60	104	28 02	60	104	29 02	60	104	30 02	60	104	286
76	25 54	60	102	26 54	60	102	27 54	60	102	28 54	60	102	29 54	59	102	284
78	25 46	60	100	26 46	60	100	27 46	60	100	28 46	59	100	29 45	60	100	282
80	25 38	+60	98	26 38	+60	98	27 38	+59	98	28 37	+60	98	29 37	+60	98	280
82	25 30	59	96	26 29	60	96	27 29	60	96	28 29	60	96	29 29	60	96	278
84	25 21	60	94	26 21	60	94	27 21	60	94	28 21	60	94	29 21	59	94	276
86	25 13	60	92	26 13	60	92	27 13	59	92	28 12	60	92	29 12	60	92	274
88	25 05	59	90	26 04	60	90	27 04	60	90	28 04	60	90	29 04	60	90	272
90	24 56	+60	88	25 56	+60	88	26 56	+60	88	27 56	+59	88	28 55	+60	88	270
92	24 48	60	86	25 48	59	86	26 47	60	86	27 47	60	86	28 47	60	86	268
94	24 39	60	84	25 39	60	84	26 39	60	84	27 39	60	84	28 39	60	84	266
96	24 31	60	82	25 31	60	82	26 31	60	82	27 31	59	82	28 30	60	82	264
98	24 23	60	80	25 23	60	80	26 23	59	80	27 22	60	80	28 22	60	80	262
100	24 15	+59	78	25 14	+60	78	26 14	+60	78	27 14	+60	78	28 14	+60	78	260
102	24 06	60	76	25 06	60	76	26 06	60	76	27 06	60	76	28 06	60	76	258
104	23 58	60	74	24 58	60	74	25 58	60	74	26 58	60	74	27 58	60	74	256
106	23 50	60	72	24 50	60	72	25 50	60	72	26 50	60	72	27 50	60	72	254
108	23 42	60	70	24 42	60	70	25 42	60	70	26 42	60	70	27 42	60	70	252
110	23 35	+59	68	24 34	+60	68	25 34	+60	68	26 34	+60	68	27 34	+60	68	250
112	23 27	60	66	24 27	60	66	25 27	59	66	26 26	60	66	27 26	60	66	248
114	23 19	60	64	24 19	60	64	25 19	60	64	26 19	60	64	27 19	60	64	246
116	23 12	60	62	24 12	60	62	25 12	59	62	26 11	60	62	27 11	60	62	244
118	23 04	60	60	24 04	60	60	25 04	60	60	26 04	60	60	27 04	60	60	242
120	22 57	+60	59	23 57	+60	58	24 57	+60	58	25 57	+60	58	26 57	+60	58	240
122	22 50	60	57	23 50	60	56	24 50	60	56	25 50	60	56	26 50	60	56	238
124	22 43	60	55	23 43	60	55	24 43	60	54	25 43	60	54	26 43	60	54	236
126	22 37	59	53	23 36	60	53	24 36	60	53	25 36	60	52	26 36	60	52	234
128	22 30	60	51	23 30	60	51	24 30	60	51	25 30	60	50	26 30	59	50	232
130	22 24	+60	49	23 24	+59	49	24 23	+60	49	25 23	+60	49	26 23	+60	48	230
132	22 17	60	47	23 17	60	47	24 17	60	47	25 17	60	47	26 17	60	47	228
134	22 11	60	45	23 11	60	45	24 11	60	45	25 11	60	45	26 11	60	45	226
136	22 06	60	43	23 06	59	43	24 05	60	43	25 05	60	43	26 05	60	43	224
138	22 00	60	41	23 00	60	41	24 00	60	41	25 00	60	41	26 00	60	41	222

S. Lat. {LHA greater than 180°....... Zn=180−Z; LHA less than 180°........... Zn=180+Z}

DECLINATION (15°-29°) SAME NAME AS LATITUDE

LAT 86°

N. Lat. {LHA greater than 180°....... Zn=Z
{LHA less than 180°........... Zn=360−Z

DECLINATION (15°-29°) SAME NAME AS LATITUDE

LHA	15° Hc	15° d	15° Z	16° Hc	16° d	16° Z	17° Hc	17° d	17° Z	18° Hc	18° d	18° Z	19° Hc	19° d	19° Z
	° ′	′	°	° ′	′	°	° ′	′	°	° ′	′	°	° ′	′	°
140	11 55	+60	39	12 55	+60	39	13 55	+60	39	14 55	+60	39	15 55	+60	39
142	11 50	60	37	12 50	60	37	13 50	60	37	14 50	60	37	15 50	60	37
144	11 45	60	35	12 45	60	35	13 45	60	35	14 45	60	35	15 45	60	35
146	11 40	60	34	12 40	60	33	13 40	60	33	14 40	60	33	15 40	60	33
148	11 36	60	32	12 36	60	32	13 36	60	31	14 36	60	31	15 36	60	31
150	11 32	+60	30	12 32	+60	30	13 32	+60	30	14 32	+60	29	15 32	+59	29
152	11 28	60	28	12 28	60	28	13 28	60	28	14 28	60	28	15 28	60	27
154	11 24	60	26	12 24	60	26	13 24	60	26	14 24	60	26	15 24	60	26
156	11 20	60	24	12 20	60	24	13 20	60	24	14 20	60	24	15 20	60	24
158	11 17	60	22	12 17	60	22	13 17	60	22	14 17	60	22	15 17	60	22
160	11 14	+60	20	12 14	+60	20	13 14	+60	20	14 14	+60	20	15 14	+60	20
162	11 12	60	18	12 12	60	18	13 12	60	18	14 12	60	18	15 12	60	18
164	11 09	60	16	12 09	60	16	13 09	60	16	14 09	60	16	15 09	60	16
166	11 07	60	14	12 07	60	14	13 07	60	14	14 07	60	14	15 07	60	14
168	11 05	60	12	12 05	60	12	13 05	60	12	14 05	60	12	15 05	60	12
170	11 04	+60	10	12 04	+60	10	13 04	+60	10	14 04	+60	10	15 04	+60	10
172	11 02	60	8	12 02	60	8	13 02	60	8	14 02	60	8	15 02	60	8
174	11 01	60	6	12 01	60	6	13 01	60	6	14 01	60	6	15 01	60	6
176	11 01	60	4	12 01	60	4	13 01	60	4	14 01	60	4	15 01	60	4
178	11 00	60	2	12 00	60	2	13 00	60	2	14 00	60	2	15 00	60	2
180	11 00	+60	0	12 00	+60	0	13 00	+60	0	14 00	+60	0	15 00	+60	0

LHA	20° Hc	20° d	20° Z	21° Hc	21° d	21° Z	22° Hc	22° d	22° Z	23° Hc	23° d	23° Z	24° Hc	24° d	24° Z
	° ′	′	°	° ′	′	°	° ′	′	°	° ′	′	°	° ′	′	°
140	16 55	+60	39	17 55	+60	39	18 55	+60	39	19 55	+60	39	20 55	+60	39
142	16 50	60	37	17 50	60	37	18 50	60	37	19 50	60	37	20 50	60	37
144	16 45	60	35	17 45	60	35	18 45	60	35	19 45	60	35	20 45	60	35
146	16 40	60	33	17 40	60	33	18 40	60	33	19 40	60	33	20 40	60	33
148	16 36	60	31	17 36	60	31	18 36	60	31	19 36	60	31	20 36	59	31
150	16 31	+60	29	17 31	+60	29	18 31	+60	29	19 31	+60	29	20 31	+60	29
152	16 28	59	27	17 27	60	27	18 27	60	27	19 27	60	27	20 27	60	27
154	16 24	60	25	17 24	60	25	18 24	60	25	19 24	60	25	20 24	60	25
156	16 20	60	24	17 20	60	23	18 20	60	23	19 20	60	23	20 20	60	23
158	16 17	60	22	17 17	60	22	18 17	60	22	19 17	60	21	20 17	60	21
160	16 14	+60	20	17 14	+60	20	18 14	+60	20	19 14	+60	20	20 14	+60	20
162	16 12	60	18	17 12	59	18	18 11	60	18	19 11	60	18	20 11	60	18
164	16 09	60	16	17 09	60	16	18 09	60	16	19 09	60	16	20 09	60	16
166	16 07	60	14	17 07	60	14	18 07	60	14	19 07	60	14	20 07	60	14
168	16 05	60	12	17 05	60	12	18 05	60	12	19 05	60	12	20 05	60	12
170	16 04	+60	10	17 04	+60	10	18 04	+60	10	19 04	+60	10	20 04	+60	10
172	16 02	60	8	17 02	60	8	18 02	60	8	19 02	60	8	20 02	60	8
174	16 01	60	6	17 01	60	6	18 01	60	6	19 01	60	6	20 01	60	6
176	16 01	60	4	17 01	60	4	18 01	60	4	19 01	60	4	20 01	60	4
178	16 00	60	2	17 00	60	2	18 00	60	2	19 00	60	2	20 00	60	2
180	16 00	+60	0	17 00	+60	0	18 00	+60	0	19 00	+60	0	20 00	+60	0

LHA	25° Hc	25° d	25° Z	26° Hc	26° d	26° Z	27° Hc	27° d	27° Z	28° Hc	28° d	28° Z	29° Hc	29° d	29° Z	LHA
	° ′	′	°	° ′	′	°	° ′	′	°	° ′	′	°	° ′	′	°	
140	21 55	+60	39	22 55	+60	39	23 55	+59	39	24 54	+60	39	25 54	+60	39	220
142	21 50	59	37	22 49	60	37	23 49	60	37	24 49	60	37	25 49	60	37	218
144	21 45	60	35	22 45	60	35	23 45	59	35	24 44	60	35	25 44	60	35	216
146	21 40	60	33	22 40	60	33	23 40	60	33	24 40	60	33	25 40	60	33	214
148	21 35	60	31	22 35	60	31	23 35	60	31	24 35	60	31	25 35	60	31	212
150	21 31	+60	29	22 31	+60	29	23 31	+60	29	24 31	+60	29	25 31	+60	29	210
152	21 27	60	27	22 27	60	27	23 27	60	27	24 27	60	27	25 27	60	27	208
154	21 24	60	25	22 24	60	25	23 24	60	25	24 24	60	25	25 24	59	25	206
156	21 20	60	23	22 20	60	23	23 20	60	23	24 20	60	23	25 20	60	23	204
158	21 17	60	21	22 17	60	21	23 17	60	21	24 17	60	21	25 17	60	21	202
160	21 14	+60	19	22 14	+60	19	23 14	+60	19	24 14	+60	19	25 14	+60	19	200
162	21 11	60	18	22 11	60	18	23 11	60	17	24 11	60	17	25 11	60	17	198
164	21 09	60	16	22 09	60	16	23 09	60	16	24 09	60	16	25 09	60	15	196
166	21 07	60	14	22 07	60	14	23 07	60	14	24 07	60	14	25 07	60	14	194
168	21 05	60	12	22 05	60	12	23 05	60	12	24 05	60	12	25 05	60	12	192
170	21 04	+60	10	22 04	+60	10	23 04	+60	10	24 04	+60	10	25 04	+60	10	190
172	21 02	60	8	22 02	60	8	23 02	60	8	24 02	60	8	25 02	60	8	188
174	21 01	60	6	22 01	60	6	23 01	60	6	24 01	60	6	25 01	60	6	186
176	21 01	60	4	22 01	60	4	23 01	60	4	24 01	60	4	25 01	60	4	184
178	21 00	60	2	22 00	60	2	23 00	60	2	24 00	60	2	25 00	60	2	182
180	21 00	+60	0	22 00	+60	0	23 00	+60	0	24 00	+60	0	25 00	+60	0	180

LAT 86°

S. Lat. {LHA greater than 180°....... Zn=180−Z
{LHA less than 180°........... Zn=180+Z

N. Lat. {LHA greater than 180°....... Zn=Z; LHA less than 180°........... Zn=360−Z}

DECLINATION (0°-14°) SAME NAME AS LATITUDE

LAT 87°

LHA	0° Hc	0° d	0° Z	1° Hc	1° d	1° Z	2° Hc	2° d	2° Z	3° Hc	3° d	3° Z	4° Hc	4° d	4° Z
	° ′	′	°	° ′	′	°	° ′	′	°	° ′	′	°	° ′	′	°
0	03 00	+60	180	04 00	+60	180	05 00	+60	180	06 00	+60	180	07 00	+60	180
2	03 00	60	178	04 00	60	178	05 00	60	178	06 00	60	178	07 00	60	178
4	03 00	60	176	04 00	60	176	05 00	60	176	06 00	60	176	07 00	60	176
6	02 59	60	174	03 59	60	174	04 59	60	174	05 59	60	174	06 59	60	174
8	02 58	60	172	03 58	60	172	04 58	60	172	05 58	60	172	06 58	60	172
10	02 57	+60	170	03 57	+60	170	04 57	+60	170	05 57	+60	170	06 57	+60	170
12	02 56	60	168	03 56	60	168	04 56	60	168	05 56	60	168	06 56	60	168
14	02 55	60	166	03 55	60	166	04 55	60	166	05 55	60	166	06 55	60	166
16	02 53	60	164	03 53	60	164	04 53	60	164	05 53	60	164	06 53	60	164
18	02 51	60	162	03 51	60	162	04 51	60	162	05 51	60	162	06 51	60	162
20	02 49	+60	160	03 49	+60	160	04 49	+60	160	05 49	+60	160	06 49	+60	160
22	02 47	60	158	03 47	60	158	04 47	60	158	05 47	60	158	06 47	60	158
24	02 44	60	156	03 44	60	156	04 44	60	156	05 44	60	156	06 44	60	156
26	02 42	60	154	03 42	60	154	04 42	60	154	05 42	60	154	06 42	60	154
28	02 39	60	152	03 39	60	152	04 39	60	152	05 39	60	152	06 39	60	152
30	02 36	+60	150	03 36	+60	150	04 36	+60	150	05 36	+60	150	06 36	+60	150
32	02 33	60	148	03 33	60	148	04 33	60	148	05 33	60	148	06 33	60	148
34	02 29	60	146	03 29	60	146	04 29	60	146	05 29	60	146	06 29	60	146
36	02 26	60	144	03 26	60	144	04 26	60	144	05 26	60	144	06 26	60	144
38	02 22	60	142	03 22	60	142	04 22	60	142	05 22	60	142	06 22	60	142
40	02 18	+60	140	03 18	+60	140	04 18	+60	140	05 18	+60	140	06 18	+60	140
42	02 14	60	138	03 14	60	138	04 14	60	138	05 14	60	138	06 14	60	138
44	02 09	60	136	03 09	60	136	04 09	60	136	05 09	60	136	06 09	60	136
46	02 05	60	134	03 05	60	134	04 05	60	134	05 05	60	134	06 05	60	134
48	02 00	60	132	03 00	60	132	04 00	60	132	05 00	60	132	06 00	60	132
50	01 56	+60	130	02 56	+60	130	03 56	+60	130	04 56	+60	130	05 56	+59	130
52	01 51	60	128	02 51	60	128	03 51	60	128	04 51	60	128	05 51	60	128
54	01 46	60	126	02 46	60	126	03 46	60	126	04 46	60	126	05 46	60	126
56	01 41	60	124	02 41	60	124	03 41	59	124	04 40	60	124	05 40	60	124
58	01 35	60	122	02 35	60	122	03 35	60	122	04 35	60	122	05 35	60	122
60	01 30	+60	120	02 30	+60	120	03 30	+60	120	04 30	+60	120	05 30	+60	120
62	01 24	60	118	02 24	60	118	03 24	60	118	04 24	60	118	05 24	60	118
64	01 19	60	116	02 19	60	116	03 19	60	116	04 19	60	116	05 19	60	116
66	01 13	60	114	02 13	60	114	03 13	60	114	04 13	60	114	05 13	60	114
68	01 07	60	112	02 07	60	112	03 07	60	112	04 07	60	112	05 07	60	112
70	01 02	+59	110	02 01	+60	110	03 01	+60	110	04 01	+60	110	05 01	+60	110
72	00 56	60	108	01 56	59	108	02 55	60	108	03 55	60	108	04 55	60	108
74	00 50	60	106	01 50	59	106	02 49	60	106	03 49	60	106	04 49	60	106
76	00 44	59	104	01 43	60	104	02 43	60	104	03 43	60	104	04 43	60	104
78	00 37	60	102	01 37	60	102	02 37	60	102	03 37	60	102	04 37	60	102
80	00 31	+60	100	01 31	+60	100	02 31	+60	100	03 31	+60	100	04 31	+60	100
82	00 25	60	98	01 25	60	98	02 25	60	98	03 25	60	98	04 25	60	98
84	00 19	60	96	01 19	60	96	02 19	60	96	03 19	59	96	04 18	60	96
86	00 13	59	94	01 12	60	94	02 12	60	94	03 12	60	94	04 12	60	94
88	00 06	60	92	01 06	60	92	02 06	60	92	03 06	60	92	04 06	60	92
90	00 00	+60	90	01 00	+60	90	02 00	+60	90	03 00	+60	90	04 00	+60	90
92	−0 06	60	88	00 54	60	88	01 54	59	88	02 53	60	88	03 53	60	88
94	−0 13	60	86	00 47	60	86	01 47	60	86	02 47	60	86	03 47	60	86
96	−0 19	60	84	00 41	60	84	01 41	60	84	02 41	60	84	03 41	60	84
98	−0 25	60	82	00 35	60	82	01 35	60	82	02 35	60	82	03 35	60	82
100	−0 31	+60	80	00 29	+60	80	01 29	+60	80	02 29	+59	80	03 28	+60	80
102	−0 37	60	78	00 23	59	78	01 22	60	78	02 22	60	78	03 22	60	78
104	−0 44	60	76	00 16	60	76	01 16	60	76	02 16	60	76	03 16	60	76
106	−0 50	60	74	00 10	60	74	01 10	60	74	02 10	60	74	03 10	60	74
108	−0 56	60	72	00 04	60	72	01 04	60	72	02 04	60	72	03 04	60	72
110	−1 02	+60	70	−0 02	+60	70	00 58	+60	70	01 58	+60	70	02 58	+60	70
112	−1 07	60	68	−0 07	59	68	00 52	60	68	01 52	60	68	02 52	60	68
114	−1 13	60	66	−0 13	60	66	00 47	60	66	01 47	60	66	02 47	59	66
116	−1 19	60	64	−0 19	60	64	00 41	60	64	01 41	60	64	02 41	60	64
118	−1 24	59	62	−0 25	60	62	00 35	60	62	01 35	60	62	02 35	60	62
120	−1 30	+60	60	−0 30	+60	60	00 30	+60	60	01 30	+60	60	02 30	+60	60
122	−1 35	60	58	−0 35	60	58	00 25	59	58	01 24	60	58	02 24	60	58
124	−1 41	60	56	−0 41	60	56	00 19	60	56	01 19	60	56	02 19	60	56
126	−1 46	60	54	−0 46	60	54	00 14	60	54	01 14	60	54	02 14	60	54
128	−1 51	60	52	−0 51	60	52	00 09	60	52	01 09	60	52	02 09	60	52
130	−1 56	+60	50	−0 56	+60	50	00 04	+60	50	01 04	+60	50	02 04	+60	50
132	−2 00	60	48	−1 00	59	48	−0 01	60	48	00 59	60	48	01 59	60	48
134	−2 05	60	46	−1 05	60	46	−0 05	60	46	00 55	60	46	01 55	60	46
136	−2 09	60	44	−1 09	60	44	−0 09	59	44	00 50	60	44	01 50	60	44
138	−2 14	60	42	−1 14	60	42	−0 14	60	42	00 46	60	42	01 46	60	42

LHA	5° Hc	5° d	5° Z	6° Hc	6° d	6° Z	7° Hc	7° d	7° Z	8° Hc	8° d	8° Z	9° Hc	9° d	9° Z
	° ′	′	°	° ′	′	°	° ′	′	°	° ′	′	°	° ′	′	°
0	08 00	+60	180	09 00	+60	180	10 00	+60	180	11 00	+60	180	12 00	+60	180
2	08 00	60	178	09 00	60	178	10 00	60	178	11 00	60	178	12 00	60	178
4	08 00	60	176	09 00	60	176	10 00	60	176	11 00	60	176	12 00	60	176
6	07 59	60	174	08 59	60	174	09 59	60	174	10 59	60	174	11 59	60	174
8	07 58	60	172	08 58	60	172	09 58	60	172	10 58	60	172	11 58	60	172
10	07 57	+60	170	08 57	+60	170	09 57	+60	170	10 57	+60	170	11 57	+60	170
12	07 56	60	168	08 56	60	168	09 56	60	168	10 56	60	168	11 56	60	168
14	07 55	60	166	08 55	60	166	09 55	60	166	10 55	60	166	11 55	60	166
16	07 53	60	164	08 53	60	164	09 53	60	164	10 53	60	164	11 53	60	164
18	07 51	60	162	08 51	60	162	09 51	60	162	10 51	60	162	11 51	60	162
20	07 49	+60	160	08 49	+60	160	09 49	+60	160	10 49	+60	160	11 49	+60	160
22	07 47	60	158	08 47	60	158	09 47	60	158	10 47	60	158	11 47	60	158
24	07 44	60	156	08 44	60	156	09 44	60	156	10 44	60	156	11 44	60	156
26	07 42	60	154	08 42	60	154	09 42	60	154	10 42	60	154	11 42	60	154
28	07 39	60	152	08 39	60	152	09 39	60	152	10 39	60	152	11 39	60	152
30	07 36	+60	150	08 36	+60	150	09 36	+60	150	10 36	+60	150	11 36	+60	150
32	07 33	60	148	08 33	60	148	09 33	59	148	10 32	60	148	11 32	60	148
34	07 29	60	146	08 29	60	146	09 29	60	146	10 29	60	146	11 29	60	146
36	07 26	59	144	08 25	60	144	09 25	60	144	10 25	60	144	11 25	60	144
38	07 22	60	142	08 22	60	142	09 22	60	142	10 22	60	142	11 22	60	142
40	07 18	+60	140	08 18	+60	140	09 18	+60	140	10 18	+60	140	11 18	+60	140
42	07 14	60	138	08 14	60	138	09 14	59	138	10 13	60	138	11 13	60	138
44	07 09	60	136	08 09	60	136	09 09	60	136	10 09	60	136	11 09	60	136
46	07 05	60	134	08 05	60	134	09 05	60	134	10 05	60	134	11 05	60	134
48	07 00	60	132	08 00	60	132	09 00	60	132	10 00	60	132	11 00	60	132
50	06 55	+60	130	07 55	+60	130	08 55	+60	130	09 55	+60	130	10 55	+60	130
52	06 51	60	128	07 51	59	128	08 50	60	128	09 50	60	128	10 50	60	128
54	06 46	59	126	07 45	60	126	08 45	60	126	09 45	60	126	10 45	60	126
56	06 40	60	124	07 40	60	124	08 40	60	124	09 40	60	124	10 40	60	124
58	06 35	60	122	07 35	60	122	08 35	60	122	09 35	60	122	10 35	60	122
60	06 30	+60	120	07 30	+60	120	08 30	+60	120	09 30	+59	120	10 29	+60	120
62	06 24	60	118	07 24	60	118	08 24	60	118	09 24	60	118	10 24	60	118
64	06 19	60	116	07 19	59	116	08 18	60	116	09 18	60	116	10 18	60	116
66	06 13	60	114	07 13	60	114	08 13	60	114	09 13	60	114	10 13	60	114
68	06 07	60	112	07 07	60	112	08 07	60	112	09 07	60	112	10 07	60	112
70	06 01	+60	110	07 01	+60	110	08 01	+60	110	09 01	+60	110	10 01	+60	110
72	05 55	60	108	06 55	60	108	07 55	60	108	08 55	60	108	09 55	60	108
74	05 49	60	106	06 49	60	106	07 49	60	106	08 49	60	106	09 49	60	106
76	05 43	60	104	06 43	60	104	07 43	60	104	08 43	60	104	09 43	60	104
78	05 37	60	102	06 37	60	102	07 37	60	102	08 37	60	102	09 37	60	102
80	05 31	+60	100	06 31	+60	100	07 31	+60	100	08 31	+60	100	09 31	+59	100
82	05 25	60	98	06 25	60	98	07 25	59	98	08 24	60	98	09 24	60	98
84	05 18	60	96	06 18	60	96	07 18	60	96	08 18	60	96	09 18	60	96
86	05 12	60	94	06 12	60	94	07 12	60	94	08 12	60	94	09 12	60	94
88	05 06	60	92	06 06	60	92	07 06	60	92	08 06	60	92	09 06	59	92
90	05 00	+60	90	06 00	+59	90	06 59	+60	90	07 59	+60	90	08 59	+60	90
92	04 53	60	88	05 53	60	88	06 53	60	88	07 53	60	88	08 53	60	88
94	04 47	60	86	05 47	60	86	06 47	60	86	07 47	60	86	08 47	60	86
96	04 41	60	84	05 41	60	84	06 41	60	84	07 41	60	84	08 41	59	84
98	04 35	60	82	05 35	59	82	06 34	60	82	07 34	60	82	08 34	60	82
100	04 28	+60	80	05 28	+60	80	06 28	+60	80	07 28	+60	80	08 28	+60	80
102	04 22	60	78	05 22	60	78	06 22	60	78	07 22	60	78	08 22	60	78
104	04 16	60	76	05 16	60	76	06 16	60	76	07 16	60	76	08 16	60	76
106	04 10	60	74	05 10	60	74	06 10	60	74	07 10	60	74	08 10	60	74
108	04 04	60	72	05 04	60	72	06 04	60	72	07 04	60	72	08 04	60	72
110	03 58	+60	70	04 58	+60	70	05 58	+60	70	06 58	+60	70	07 58	+60	70
112	03 52	60	68	04 52	60	68	05 52	60	68	06 52	60	68	07 52	60	68
114	03 46	60	66	04 46	60	66	05 46	60	66	06 46	60	66	07 46	60	66
116	03 41	60	64	04 41	60	64	05 41	60	64	06 41	60	64	07 41	60	64
118	03 35	60	62	04 35	60	62	05 35	60	62	06 35	60	62	07 35	60	62
120	03 30	+60	60	04 30	+60	60	05 30	+60	60	06 30	+60	60	07 30	+59	60
122	03 24	60	58	04 24	60	58	05 24	60	58	06 24	60	58	07 24	60	58
124	03 19	60	56	04 19	60	56	05 19	60	56	06 19	60	56	07 19	60	56
126	03 14	60	54	04 14	60	54	05 14	60	54	06 14	60	54	07 14	60	54
128	03 09	60	52	04 09	60	52	05 09	60	52	06 09	60	52	07 09	60	52
130	03 04	+60	50	04 04	+60	50	05 04	+60	50	06 04	+60	50	07 04	+60	50
132	02 59	60	48	03 59	60	48	04 59	60	48	05 59	60	48	06 59	60	48
134	02 55	60	46	03 55	60	46	04 55	60	46	05 55	60	46	06 55	60	46
136	02 50	60	44	03 50	60	44	04 50	60	44	05 50	60	44	06 50	60	44
138	02 46	60	42	03 46	60	42	04 46	60	42	05 46	60	42	06 46	60	42

LHA	10° Hc	10° d	10° Z	11° Hc	11° d	11° Z	12° Hc	12° d	12° Z	13° Hc	13° d	13° Z	14° Hc	14° d	14° Z	LHA
	° ′	′	°	° ′	′	°	° ′	′	°	° ′	′	°	° ′	′	°	
0	13 00	+60	180	14 00	+60	180	15 00	+60	180	16 00	+60	180	17 00	+60	180	360
2	13 00	60	178	14 00	60	178	15 00	60	178	16 00	60	178	17 00	60	178	358
4	13 00	60	176	14 00	60	176	15 00	60	176	16 00	60	176	17 00	60	176	356
6	12 59	60	174	13 59	60	174	14 59	60	174	15 59	60	174	16 59	60	174	354
8	12 58	60	172	13 58	60	172	14 58	60	172	15 58	60	172	16 58	60	172	352
10	12 57	+60	170	13 57	+60	170	14 57	+60	170	15 57	+60	170	16 57	+60	170	350
12	12 56	60	168	13 56	60	168	14 56	60	168	15 56	60	168	16 56	60	168	348
14	12 55	60	166	13 55	60	166	14 55	60	166	15 55	60	166	16 55	60	166	346
16	12 53	60	164	13 53	60	164	14 53	60	164	15 53	60	164	16 53	60	164	344
18	12 51	60	162	13 51	60	162	14 51	60	162	15 51	60	162	16 51	60	162	342
20	12 49	+60	160	13 49	+60	160	14 49	+60	160	15 49	+60	160	16 49	+60	160	340
22	12 47	60	158	13 47	60	158	14 47	60	158	15 47	60	158	16 47	60	158	338
24	12 44	60	156	13 44	60	156	14 44	60	156	15 44	60	156	16 44	60	156	336
26	12 42	60	154	13 42	60	154	14 42	60	154	15 42	60	154	16 42	60	154	334
28	12 39	60	152	13 39	60	152	14 39	60	152	15 39	60	152	16 39	60	152	332
30	12 36	+60	150	13 36	+60	150	14 36	+60	150	15 36	+60	150	16 36	+60	150	330
32	12 32	60	148	13 32	60	148	14 32	60	148	15 32	60	148	16 32	60	148	328
34	12 29	60	146	13 29	60	146	14 29	60	146	15 29	60	146	16 29	60	146	326
36	12 25	60	144	13 25	60	144	14 25	60	144	15 25	60	144	16 25	60	144	324
38	12 22	60	142	13 22	59	142	14 21	60	142	15 21	60	142	16 21	60	142	322
40	12 18	+60	140	13 18	+59	140	14 17	+60	140	15 17	+60	140	16 17	+60	140	320
42	12 13	60	138	13 13	60	138	14 13	60	138	15 13	60	138	16 13	60	138	318
44	12 09	60	136	13 09	60	136	14 09	60	136	15 09	60	136	16 09	60	135	316
46	12 05	60	134	13 05	60	134	14 05	59	134	15 04	60	134	16 04	60	133	314
48	12 00	60	132	13 00	60	132	14 00	60	132	15 00	60	131	16 00	60	131	312
50	11 55	+60	130	12 55	+60	130	13 55	+60	130	14 55	+60	129	15 55	+60	129	310
52	11 50	60	128	12 50	60	128	13 50	60	128	14 50	60	127	15 50	60	127	308
54	11 45	60	126	12 45	60	126	13 45	60	125	14 45	60	125	15 45	60	125	306
56	11 40	60	124	12 40	60	124	13 40	60	123	14 40	60	123	15 40	60	123	304
58	11 35	60	122	12 35	60	122	13 35	60	121	14 35	60	121	15 35	59	121	302
60	11 29	+60	120	12 29	+60	120	13 29	+60	119	14 29	+60	119	15 29	+60	119	300
62	11 24	60	118	12 24	60	118	13 24	60	117	14 24	60	117	15 24	60	117	298
64	11 18	60	116	12 18	60	115	13 18	60	115	14 18	60	115	15 18	60	115	296
66	11 13	59	114	12 12	60	113	13 12	60	113	14 12	60	113	15 12	60	113	294
68	11 07	60	112	12 07	60	111	13 07	60	111	14 07	59	111	15 06	60	111	292
70	11 01	+60	110	12 01	+60	109	13 01	+60	109	14 01	+60	109	15 01	+59	109	290
72	10 55	60	108	11 55	60	107	12 55	60	107	13 55	60	107	14 55	60	107	288
74	10 49	60	106	11 49	60	105	12 49	60	105	13 49	59	105	14 49	59	105	286
76	10 43	60	104	11 43	60	103	12 43	60	103	13 43	59	103	14 42	60	103	284
78	10 37	60	102	11 37	59	101	12 36	60	101	13 36	60	101	14 36	60	101	282
80	10 30	+60	100	11 30	+60	99	12 30	+60	99	13 30	+60	99	14 30	+60	99	280
82	10 24	60	98	11 24	60	97	12 24	60	97	13 24	60	97	14 24	60	97	278
84	10 18	60	96	11 18	60	95	12 18	60	95	13 18	60	95	14 18	60	95	276
86	10 12	60	94	11 12	60	93	12 12	60	93	13 12	59	93	14 11	60	93	274
88	10 05	60	92	11 05	60	91	12 05	60	91	13 05	60	91	14 05	60	91	272
90	09 59	+60	90	10 59	+60	89	11 59	+60	89	12 59	+60	89	13 59	+60	89	270
92	09 53	60	88	10 53	60	87	11 53	60	87	12 53	60	87	13 53	60	87	268
94	09 47	60	86	10 47	60	85	11 47	59	85	12 46	60	85	13 46	60	85	266
96	09 40	60	84	10 40	60	83	11 40	60	83	12 40	60	83	13 40	60	83	264
98	09 34	60	82	10 34	60	81	11 34	60	81	12 34	60	81	13 34	60	81	262
100	09 28	+60	80	10 28	+60	79	11 28	+60	79	12 28	+60	79	13 28	+60	79	260
102	09 22	60	78	10 22	60	77	11 22	60	77	12 22	60	77	13 22	59	77	258
104	09 16	60	76	10 16	60	76	11 16	60	75	12 16	59	75	13 15	60	75	256
106	09 10	60	74	10 10	60	74	11 10	59	73	12 09	60	73	13 09	60	73	254
108	09 04	60	72	10 04	60	72	11 04	59	71	12 03	60	71	13 03	60	71	252
110	08 58	+60	70	09 58	+60	70	10 58	+60	69	11 58	+59	69	12 57	+60	69	250
112	08 52	60	68	09 52	60	68	10 52	60	67	11 52	60	67	12 52	60	67	248
114	08 46	60	66	09 46	60	66	10 46	60	65	11 46	60	65	12 46	60	65	246
116	08 41	59	64	09 40	60	64	10 40	60	64	11 40	60	63	12 40	60	63	244
118	08 35	60	62	09 35	60	62	10 35	60	62	11 35	60	61	12 35	60	61	242
120	08 29	+60	60	09 29	+60	60	10 29	+60	60	11 29	+60	59	12 29	+60	59	240
122	08 24	60	58	09 24	60	58	10 24	60	58	11 24	60	58	12 24	60	57	238
124	08 19	60	56	09 19	60	56	10 19	60	56	11 19	60	56	12 19	60	55	236
126	08 14	60	54	09 14	60	54	10 14	60	54	11 14	60	54	12 14	59	53	234
128	08 09	60	52	09 09	60	52	10 09	60	52	11 09	60	52	12 09	59	52	232
130	08 04	+60	50	09 04	+60	50	10 04	+60	50	11 04	+60	50	12 04	+60	50	230
132	07 59	60	48	08 59	60	48	09 59	60	48	10 59	60	48	11 59	60	48	228
134	07 55	60	46	08 55	60	46	09 55	59	46	10 54	60	46	11 54	60	46	226
136	07 50	60	44	08 50	60	44	09 50	60	44	10 50	60	44	11 50	60	44	224
138	07 46	60	42	08 46	60	42	09 46	60	42	10 46	60	42	11 46	60	42	222

S. Lat. {LHA greater than 180°....... Zn=180−Z; LHA less than 180°........... Zn=180+Z}

DECLINATION (0°-14°) SAME NAME AS LATITUDE

N. Lat. {LHA greater than 180°....... Zn=Z / LHA less than 180°........... Zn=360−Z}

DECLINATION (0°-14°) SAME NAME AS LATITUDE

LHA	0° Hc	0° d	0° Z	1° Hc	1° d	1° Z	2° Hc	2° d	2° Z	3° Hc	3° d	3° Z	4° Hc	4° d	4° Z
	° ′	′	°	° ′	′	°	° ′	′	°	° ′	′	°	° ′	′	°
140	−2 18	+60	40	−1 18	+60	40	−0 18	+60	40	00 42	+60	40	01 42	+60	40
142	−2 22	60	38	−1 22	60	38	−0 22	60	38	00 38	60	38	01 38	60	38
144	−2 26	60	36	−1 26	60	36	−0 26	60	36	00 34	60	36	01 34	60	36
146	−2 29	60	34	−1 29	60	34	−0 29	60	34	00 31	60	34	01 31	60	34
148	−2 33	60	32	−1 33	60	32	−0 33	60	32	00 27	60	32	01 27	60	32
150	−2 36	+60	30	−1 36	+60	30	−0 36	+60	30	00 24	+60	30	01 24	+60	30
152	−2 39	60	28	−1 39	60	28	−0 39	60	28	00 21	60	28	01 21	60	28
154	−2 42	60	26	−1 42	60	26	−0 42	60	26	00 18	60	26	01 18	60	26
156	−2 44	60	24	−1 44	60	24	−0 44	60	24	00 16	60	24	01 16	60	24
158	−2 47	60	22	−1 47	60	22	−0 47	60	22	00 13	60	22	01 13	60	22
160	−2 49	+60	20	−1 49	+60	20	−0 49	+60	20	00 11	+60	20	01 11	+60	20
162	−2 51	60	18	−1 51	60	18	−0 51	60	18	00 09	60	18	01 09	60	18
164	−2 53	60	16	−1 53	60	16	−0 53	60	16	00 07	60	16	01 07	60	16
166	−2 55	60	14	−1 55	60	14	−0 55	60	14	00 05	60	14	01 05	60	14
168	−2 56	60	12	−1 56	60	12	−0 56	60	12	00 04	60	12	01 04	60	12
170	−2 57	+60	10	−1 57	+60	10	−0 57	+60	10	00 03	+60	10	01 03	+60	10
172	−2 58	60	8	−1 58	60	8	−0 58	60	8	00 02	60	8	01 02	60	8
174	−2 59	60	6	−1 59	60	6	−0 59	60	6	00 01	60	6	01 01	60	6
176	−3 00	60	4	−2 00	60	4	−1 00	60	4	00 00	60	4	01 00	60	4
178	−3 00	60	2	−2 00	60	2	−1 00	60	2	00 00	60	2	01 00	60	2
180	−3 00	+60	0	−2 00	+60	0	−1 00	+60	0	00 00	+60	0	01 00	+60	0

LHA	5° Hc	5° d	5° Z	6° Hc	6° d	6° Z	7° Hc	7° d	7° Z	8° Hc	8° d	8° Z	9° Hc	9° d	9° Z
	° ′	′	°	° ′	′	°	° ′	′	°	° ′	′	°	° ′	′	°
140	02 42	+60	40	03 42	+60	40	04 42	+60	40	05 42	+60	40	06 42	+60	40
142	02 38	60	38	03 38	60	38	04 38	60	38	05 38	60	38	06 38	60	38
144	02 34	60	36	03 34	60	36	04 34	60	36	05 34	60	36	06 34	60	36
146	02 31	60	34	03 31	60	34	04 31	60	34	05 31	60	34	06 31	60	34
148	02 27	60	32	03 27	60	32	04 27	60	32	05 27	60	32	06 27	60	32
150	02 24	+60	30	03 24	+60	30	04 24	+60	30	05 24	+60	30	06 24	+60	30
152	02 21	60	28	03 21	60	28	04 21	60	28	05 21	60	28	06 21	60	28
154	02 18	60	26	03 18	60	26	04 18	60	26	05 18	60	26	06 18	60	26
156	02 16	60	24	03 16	60	24	04 16	60	24	05 16	60	24	06 16	59	24
158	02 13	60	22	03 13	60	22	04 13	60	22	05 13	60	22	06 13	60	22
160	02 11	+60	20	03 11	+60	20	04 11	+60	20	05 11	+60	20	06 11	+60	20
162	02 09	60	18	03 09	60	18	04 09	60	18	05 09	60	18	06 09	60	18
164	02 07	60	16	03 07	60	16	04 07	60	16	05 07	60	16	06 07	60	16
166	02 05	60	14	03 05	60	14	04 05	60	14	05 05	60	14	06 05	60	14
168	02 04	60	12	03 04	60	12	04 04	60	12	05 04	60	12	06 04	60	12
170	02 03	+60	10	03 03	+60	10	04 03	+60	10	05 03	+60	10	06 03	+60	10
172	02 02	60	8	03 02	60	8	04 02	60	8	05 02	60	8	06 02	60	8
174	02 01	60	6	03 01	60	6	04 01	60	6	05 01	60	6	06 01	60	6
176	02 00	60	4	03 00	60	4	04 00	60	4	05 00	60	4	06 00	60	4
178	02 00	60	2	03 00	60	2	04 00	60	2	05 00	60	2	06 00	60	2
180	02 00	+60	0	03 00	+60	0	04 00	+60	0	05 00	+60	0	06 00	+60	0

LHA	10° Hc	10° d	10° Z	11° Hc	11° d	11° Z	12° Hc	12° d	12° Z	13° Hc	13° d	13° Z	14° Hc	14° d	14° Z	LHA
	° ′	′	°	° ′	′	°	° ′	′	°	° ′	′	°	° ′	′	°	
140	07 42	+60	40	08 42	+60	40	09 42	+60	40	10 42	+60	40	11 42	+60	40	220
142	07 38	60	38	08 38	60	38	09 38	60	38	10 38	60	38	11 38	60	38	218
144	07 34	60	36	08 34	60	36	09 34	60	36	10 34	60	36	11 34	60	36	216
146	07 31	60	34	08 31	60	34	09 31	60	34	10 31	59	34	11 30	60	34	214
148	07 27	60	32	08 27	60	32	09 27	60	32	10 27	60	32	11 27	60	32	212
150	07 24	+60	30	08 24	+60	30	09 24	+60	30	10 24	+60	30	11 24	+60	30	210
152	07 21	60	28	08 21	60	28	09 21	60	28	10 21	60	28	11 21	60	28	208
154	07 18	60	26	08 18	60	26	09 18	60	26	10 18	60	26	11 18	60	26	206
156	07 15	60	24	08 15	60	24	09 15	60	24	10 15	60	24	11 15	60	24	204
158	07 13	60	22	08 13	60	22	09 13	60	22	10 13	60	22	11 13	60	22	202
160	07 11	+60	20	08 11	+60	20	09 11	+60	20	10 11	+60	20	11 11	+60	20	200
162	07 09	60	18	08 09	60	18	09 09	60	18	10 09	60	18	11 09	60	18	198
164	07 07	60	16	08 07	60	16	09 07	60	16	10 07	60	16	11 07	60	16	196
166	07 05	60	14	08 05	60	14	09 05	60	14	10 05	60	14	11 05	60	14	194
168	07 04	60	12	08 04	60	12	09 04	60	12	10 04	60	12	11 04	60	12	192
170	07 03	+60	10	08 03	+60	10	09 03	+60	10	10 03	+60	10	11 03	+60	10	190
172	07 02	60	8	08 02	60	8	09 02	60	8	10 02	60	8	11 02	60	8	188
174	07 01	60	6	08 01	60	6	09 01	60	6	10 01	60	6	11 01	60	6	186
176	07 00	60	4	08 00	60	4	09 00	60	4	10 00	60	4	11 00	60	4	184
178	07 00	60	2	08 00	60	2	09 00	60	2	10 00	60	2	11 00	60	2	182
180	07 00	+60	0	08 00	+60	0	09 00	+60	0	10 00	+60	0	11 00	+60	0	180

LAT 87°

0°	1°	2°	3°	4°	5°	6°	7°	8°	9°	10°	11°	12°	13°	14°

S. Lat. {LHA greater than 180°....... Zn=180−Z / LHA less than 180°........... Zn=180+Z}

DECLINATION (0°-14°) SAME NAME AS LATITUDE

LAT 87°

N. Lat. {LHA greater than 180°....... Zn=Z; LHA less than 180°........... Zn=360−Z}

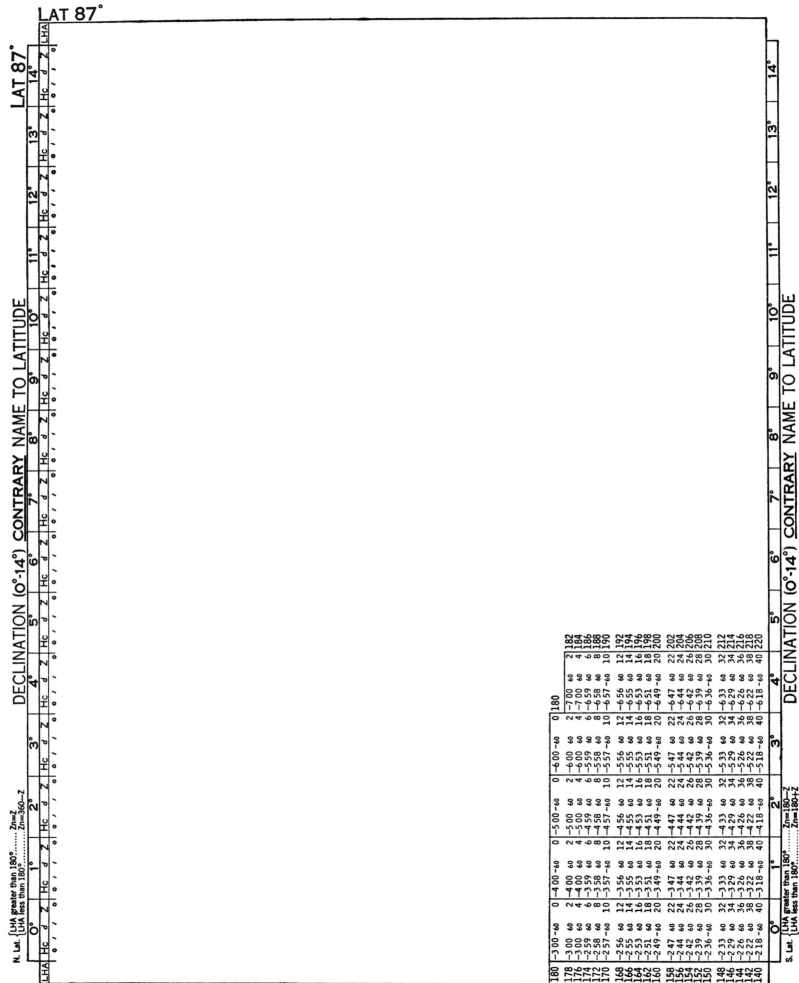

DECLINATION (0°-14°) CONTRARY NAME TO LATITUDE

LAT 87°

LHA	0° Hc	0° d	0° Z	1° Hc	1° d	1° Z	2° Hc	2° d	2° Z	3° Hc	3° d	3° Z	4° Hc	4° d	4° Z	LHA
	° ′	′	°	° ′	′	°	° ′	′	°	° ′	′	°	° ′	′	°	
180	−3 00	−60	0	−4 00	−60	0	−5 00	−60	0	−6 00	−60	0				180
178	−3 00	60	2	−4 00	60	2	−5 00	60	2	−6 00	60	2	−7 00	60	2	182
176	−3 00	60	4	−4 00	60	4	−5 00	60	4	−6 00	60	4	−7 00	60	4	184
174	−2 59	60	6	−3 59	60	6	−4 59	60	6	−5 59	60	6	−6 59	60	6	186
172	−2 58	60	8	−3 58	60	8	−4 58	60	8	−5 58	60	8	−6 58	60	8	188
170	−2 57	−60	10	−3 57	−60	10	−4 57	−60	10	−5 57	−60	10	−6 57	−60	10	190
168	−2 56	60	12	−3 56	60	12	−4 56	60	12	−5 56	60	12	−6 56	60	12	192
166	−2 55	60	14	−3 55	60	14	−4 55	60	14	−5 55	60	14	−6 55	60	14	194
164	−2 53	60	16	−3 53	60	16	−4 53	60	16	−5 53	60	16	−6 53	60	16	196
162	−2 51	60	18	−3 51	60	18	−4 51	60	18	−5 51	60	18	−6 51	60	18	198
160	−2 49	−60	20	−3 49	−60	20	−4 49	−60	20	−5 49	−60	20	−6 49	−60	20	200
158	−2 47	60	22	−3 47	60	22	−4 47	60	22	−5 47	60	22	−6 47	60	22	202
156	−2 44	60	24	−3 44	60	24	−4 44	60	24	−5 44	60	24	−6 44	60	24	204
154	−2 42	60	26	−3 42	60	26	−4 42	60	26	−5 42	60	26	−6 42	60	26	206
152	−2 39	60	28	−3 39	60	28	−4 39	60	28	−5 39	60	28	−6 39	60	28	208
150	−2 36	−60	30	−3 36	−60	30	−4 36	−60	30	−5 36	−60	30	−6 36	−60	30	210
148	−2 33	60	32	−3 33	60	32	−4 33	60	32	−5 33	60	32	−6 33	60	32	212
146	−2 29	60	34	−3 29	60	34	−4 29	60	34	−5 29	60	34	−6 29	60	34	214
144	−2 26	60	36	−3 26	60	36	−4 26	60	36	−5 26	60	36	−6 26	60	36	216
142	−2 22	60	38	−3 22	60	38	−4 22	60	38	−5 22	60	38	−6 22	60	38	218
140	−2 18	−60	40	−3 18	−60	40	−4 18	−60	40	−5 18	−60	40	−6 18	−60	40	220

S. Lat. {LHA greater than 180°....... Zn=180−Z; LHA less than 180°........... Zn=180+Z}

DECLINATION (0°-14°) CONTRARY NAME TO LATITUDE

N. Lat. {LHA greater than 180°....... Zn=Z; LHA less than 180°............ Zn=360−Z}

DECLINATION (0°-14°) CONTRARY NAME TO LATITUDE

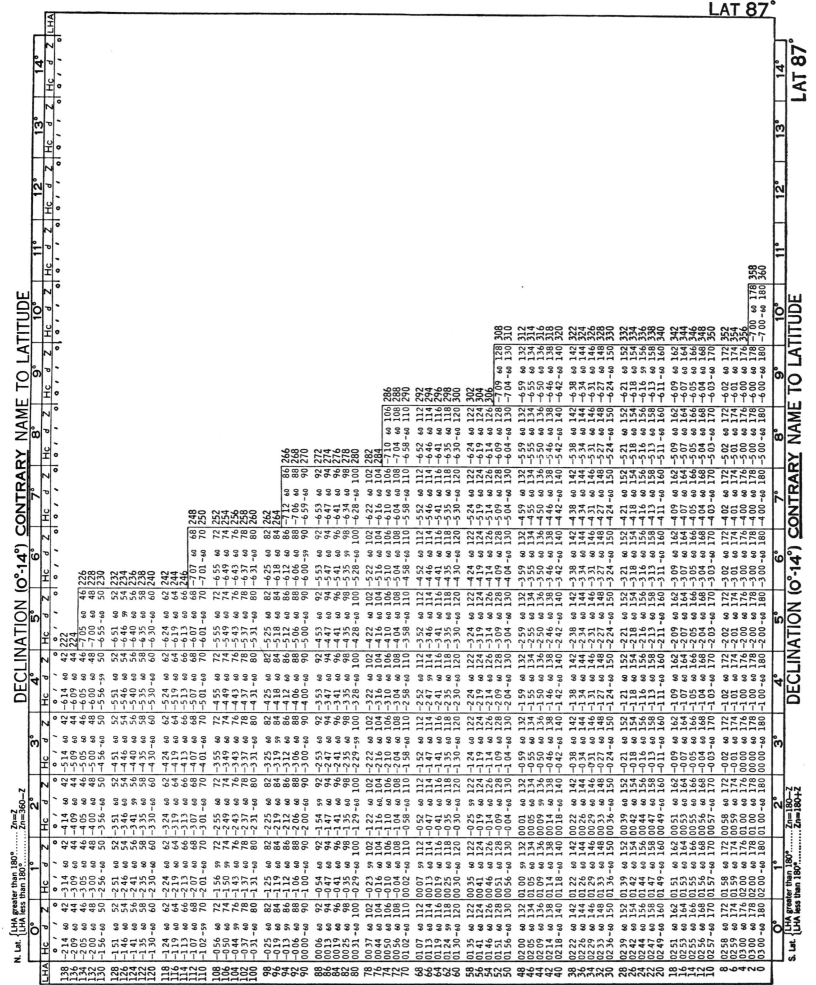

LHA	0°			1°			2°			3°			4°			5°			6°			7°			8°			9°			10°			11°	12°	13°	14°	LHA
	Hc	d	Z	Hc	d	Z	Hc	d	Z	Hc	d	Z	Hc	d	Z	Hc	d	Z	Hc	d	Z	Hc	d	Z	Hc	d	Z	Hc	d	Z	Hc	d	Z	Hc d Z	Hc d Z	Hc d Z	Hc d Z	
	° ′	′	°	° ′	′	°	° ′	′	°	° ′	′	°	° ′	′	°	° ′	′	°	° ′	′	°	° ′	′	°	° ′	′	°	° ′	′	°	° ′	′	°	° ′ ′ °	° ′ ′ °	° ′ ′ °	° ′ ′ °	
138	-2 14	60	42	-3 14	60	42	-4 14	60	42	-5 14	60	42	-6 14	60	42																							222
136	-2 09	60	44	-3 09	60	44	-4 09	60	44	-5 09	60	44	-6 09	60	44																							224
134	-2 05	60	46	-3 05	60	46	-4 05	60	46	-5 05	60	46	-6 05	60	46	-7 05	60	46																				226
132	-2 00	60	48	-3 00	60	48	-4 00	60	48	-5 00	60	48	-6 00	60	48	-7 00	60	48																				228
130	-1 56	-60	50	-2 56	-60	50	-3 56	-60	50	-4 56	-60	50	-5 56	-59	50	-6 55	-60	50																				230
128	-1 51	60	52	-2 51	60	52	-3 51	60	52	-4 51	60	52	-5 51	60	52	-6 51	60	52																				232
126	-1 46	60	54	-2 46	60	54	-3 46	60	54	-4 46	60	54	-5 46	60	54	-6 46	59	54																				234
124	-1 41	60	56	-2 41	60	56	-3 41	59	56	-4 40	60	56	-5 40	60	56	-6 40	60	56																				236
122	-1 35	60	58	-2 35	60	58	-3 35	60	58	-4 35	60	58	-5 35	60	58	-6 35	60	58																				238
120	-1 30	-60	60	-2 30	-60	60	-3 30	-60	60	-4 30	-60	60	-5 30	-60	60	-6 30	-60	60																				240
118	-1 24	60	62	-2 24	60	62	-3 24	60	62	-4 24	60	62	-5 24	60	62	-6 24	60	62																				242
116	-1 19	60	64	-2 19	60	64	-3 19	60	64	-4 19	60	64	-5 19	60	64	-6 19	60	64																				244
114	-1 13	60	66	-2 13	60	66	-3 13	60	66	-4 13	60	66	-5 13	60	66	-6 13	60	66																				246
112	-1 07	60	68	-2 07	60	68	-3 07	60	68	-4 07	60	68	-5 07	60	68	-6 07	60	68	-7 07	60	68																	248
110	-1 02	-59	70	-2 01	-60	70	-3 01	-60	70	-4 01	-60	70	-5 01	-60	70	-6 01	-60	70	-7 01	-60	70																	250
108	-0 56	60	72	-1 56	59	72	-2 55	60	72	-3 55	60	72	-4 55	60	72	-5 55	60	72	-6 55	60	72																	252
106	-0 50	60	74	-1 50	59	74	-2 49	60	74	-3 49	60	74	-4 49	60	74	-5 49	60	74	-6 49	60	74																	254
104	-0 44	59	76	-1 43	60	76	-2 43	60	76	-3 43	60	76	-4 43	60	76	-5 43	60	76	-6 43	60	76																	256
102	-0 37	60	78	-1 37	60	78	-2 37	60	78	-3 37	60	78	-4 37	60	78	-5 37	60	78	-6 37	60	78																	258
100	-0 31	-60	80	-1 31	-60	80	-2 31	-60	80	-3 31	-60	80	-4 31	-60	80	-5 31	-60	80	-6 31	-60	80																	260
98	-0 25	60	82	-1 25	60	82	-2 25	60	82	-3 25	60	82	-4 25	60	82	-5 25	60	82	-6 25	60	82																	262
96	-0 19	60	84	-1 19	60	84	-2 19	60	84	-3 19	59	84	-4 18	60	84	-5 18	60	84	-6 18	60	84																	264
94	-0 13	59	86	-1 12	60	86	-2 12	60	86	-3 12	60	86	-4 12	60	86	-5 12	60	86	-6 12	60	86	-7 12	60	86														266
92	-0 06	60	88	-1 06	60	88	-2 06	60	88	-3 06	60	88	-4 06	60	88	-5 06	60	88	-6 06	60	88	-7 06	60	88														268
90	00 00	-60	90	-1 00	-60	90	-2 00	-60	90	-3 00	-60	90	-4 00	-60	90	-5 00	-60	90	-6 00	-59	90	-6 59	-60	90														270
88	00 06	60	92	-0 54	60	92	-1 54	59	92	-2 53	60	92	-3 53	60	92	-4 53	60	92	-5 53	60	92	-6 53	60	92														272
86	00 13	60	94	-0 47	60	94	-1 47	60	94	-2 47	60	94	-3 47	60	94	-4 47	60	94	-5 47	60	94	-6 47	60	94														274
84	00 19	60	96	-0 41	60	96	-1 41	60	96	-2 41	60	96	-3 41	60	96	-4 41	60	96	-5 41	60	96	-6 41	60	96														276
82	00 25	60	98	-0 35	60	98	-1 35	60	98	-2 35	60	98	-3 35	60	98	-4 35	60	98	-5 35	59	98	-6 34	60	98														278
80	00 31	-60	100	-0 29	-60	100	-1 29	-60	100	-2 29	-59	100	-3 28	-60	100	-4 28	-60	100	-5 28	-60	100	-6 28	-60	100														280
78	00 37	60	102	-0 23	59	102	-1 22	60	102	-2 22	60	102	-3 22	60	102	-4 22	60	102	-5 22	60	102	-6 22	60	102														282
76	00 44	60	104	-0 16	60	104	-1 16	60	104	-2 16	60	104	-3 16	60	104	-4 16	60	104	-5 16	60	104	-6 16	60	104														284
74	00 50	60	106	-0 10	60	106	-1 10	60	106	-2 10	60	106	-3 10	60	106	-4 10	60	106	-5 10	60	106	-6 10	60	106	-7 10	60	106											286
72	00 56	60	108	-0 04	60	108	-1 04	60	108	-2 04	60	108	-3 04	60	108	-4 04	60	108	-5 04	60	108	-6 04	60	108	-7 04	60	108											288
70	01 02	-60	110	00 02	-60	110	-0 58	-60	110	-1 58	-60	110	-2 58	-60	110	-3 58	-60	110	-4 58	-60	110	-5 58	-60	110	-6 58	-60	110											290
68	01 07	60	112	00 07	59	112	-0 52	60	112	-1 52	60	112	-2 52	60	112	-3 52	60	112	-4 52	60	112	-5 52	60	112	-6 52	60	112											292
66	01 13	60	114	00 13	60	114	-0 47	60	114	-1 47	60	114	-2 47	59	114	-3 46	60	114	-4 46	60	114	-5 46	60	114	-6 46	60	114											294
64	01 19	60	116	00 19	60	116	-0 41	60	116	-1 41	60	116	-2 41	60	116	-3 41	60	116	-4 41	60	116	-5 41	60	116	-6 41	60	116											296
62	01 24	59	118	00 25	60	118	-0 35	60	118	-1 35	60	118	-2 35	60	118	-3 35	60	118	-4 35	60	118	-5 35	60	118	-6 35	60	118											298
60	01 30	-60	120	00 30	-60	120	-0 30	-60	120	-1 30	-60	120	-2 30	-60	120	-3 30	-60	120	-4 30	-60	120	-5 30	-60	120	-6 30	-60	120											300
58	01 35	60	122	00 35	60	122	-0 25	59	122	-1 24	60	122	-2 24	60	122	-3 24	60	122	-4 24	60	122	-5 24	60	122	-6 24	60	122											302
56	01 41	60	124	00 41	60	124	-0 19	60	124	-1 19	60	124	-2 19	60	124	-3 19	60	124	-4 19	60	124	-5 19	60	124	-6 19	60	124											304
54	01 46	60	126	00 46	60	126	-0 14	60	126	-1 14	60	126	-2 14	60	126	-3 14	60	126	-4 14	60	126	-5 14	60	126	-6 14	60	126											306
52	01 51	60	128	00 51	60	128	-0 09	60	128	-1 09	60	128	-2 09	60	128	-3 09	60	128	-4 09	60	128	-5 09	60	128	-6 09	60	128	-7 09	60	128								308
50	01 56	-60	130	00 56	-60	130	-0 04	-60	130	-1 04	-60	130	-2 04	-60	130	-3 04	-60	130	-4 04	-60	130	-5 04	-60	130	-6 04	-60	130	-7 04	-60	130								310
48	02 00	60	132	01 00	59	132	00 01	60	132	-0 59	60	132	-1 59	60	132	-2 59	60	132	-3 59	60	132	-4 59	60	132	-5 59	60	132	-6 59	60	132								312
46	02 05	60	134	01 05	60	134	00 05	60	134	-0 55	60	134	-1 55	60	134	-2 55	60	134	-3 55	60	134	-4 55	60	134	-5 55	60	134	-6 55	60	134								314
44	02 09	60	136	01 09	60	136	00 09	59	136	-0 50	60	136	-1 50	60	136	-2 50	60	136	-3 50	60	136	-4 50	60	136	-5 50	60	136	-6 50	60	136								316
42	02 14	60	138	01 14	60	138	00 14	60	138	-0 46	60	138	-1 46	60	138	-2 46	60	138	-3 46	60	138	-4 46	60	138	-5 46	60	138	-6 46	60	138								318
40	02 18	-60	140	01 18	-60	140	00 18	-60	140	-0 42	-60	140	-1 42	-60	140	-2 42	-60	140	-3 42	-60	140	-4 42	-60	140	-5 42	-60	140	-6 42	-60	140								320
38	02 22	60	142	01 22	60	142	00 22	60	142	-0 38	60	142	-1 38	60	142	-2 38	60	142	-3 38	60	142	-4 38	60	142	-5 38	60	142	-6 38	60	142								322
36	02 26	60	144	01 26	60	144	00 26	60	144	-0 34	60	144	-1 34	60	144	-2 34	60	144	-3 34	60	144	-4 34	60	144	-5 34	60	144	-6 34	60	144								324
34	02 29	60	146	01 29	60	146	00 29	60	146	-0 31	60	146	-1 31	60	146	-2 31	60	146	-3 31	60	146	-4 31	60	146	-5 31	60	146	-6 31	60	146								326
32	02 33	60	148	01 33	60	148	00 33	60	148	-0 27	60	148	-1 27	60	148	-2 27	60	148	-3 27	60	148	-4 27	60	148	-5 27	60	148	-6 27	60	148								328
30	02 36	-60	150	01 36	-60	150	00 36	-60	150	-0 24	-60	150	-1 24	-60	150	-2 24	-60	150	-3 24	-60	150	-4 24	-60	150	-5 24	-60	150	-6 24	-60	150								330
28	02 39	60	152	01 39	60	152	00 39	60	152	-0 21	60	152	-1 21	60	152	-2 21	60	152	-3 21	60	152	-4 21	60	152	-5 21	60	152	-6 21	60	152								332
26	02 42	60	154	01 42	60	154	00 42	60	154	-0 18	60	154	-1 18	60	154	-2 18	60	154	-3 18	60	154	-4 18	60	154	-5 18	60	154	-6 18	60	154								334
24	02 44	60	156	01 44	60	156	00 44	60	156	-0 16	60	156	-1 16	60	156	-2 16	60	156	-3 16	60	156	-4 16	60	156	-5 16	60	156	-6 16	59	156								336
22	02 47	60	158	01 47	60	158	00 47	60	158	-0 13	60	158	-1 13	60	158	-2 13	60	158	-3 13	60	158	-4 13	60	158	-5 13	60	158	-6 13	60	158								338
20	02 49	-60	160	01 49	-60	160	00 49	-60	160	-0 11	-60	160	-1 11	-60	160	-2 11	-60	160	-3 11	-60	160	-4 11	-60	160	-5 11	-60	160	-6 11	-60	160								340
18	02 51	60	162	01 51	60	162	00 51	60	162	-0 09	60	162	-1 09	60	162	-2 09	60	162	-3 09	60	162	-4 09	60	162	-5 09	60	162	-6 09	60	162								342
16	02 53	60	164	01 53	60	164	00 53	60	164	-0 07	60	164	-1 07	60	164	-2 07	60	164	-3 07	60	164	-4 07	60	164	-5 07	60	164	-6 07	60	164								344
14	02 55	60	166	01 55	60	166	00 55	60	166	-0 05	60	166	-1 05	60	166	-2 05	60	166	-3 05	60	166	-4 05	60	166	-5 05	60	166	-6 05	60	166								346
12	02 56	60	168	01 56	60	168	00 56	60	168	-0 04	60	168	-1 04	60	168	-2 04	60	168	-3 04	60	168	-4 04	60	168	-5 04	60	168	-6 04	60	168								348
10	02 57	-60	170	01 57	-60	170	00 57	-60	170	-0 03	-60	170	-1 03	-60	170	-2 03	-60	170	-3 03	-60	170	-4 03	-60	170	-5 03	-60	170	-6 03	-60	170								350
8	02 58	60	172	01 58	60	172	00 58	60	172	-0 02	60	172	-1 02	60	172	-2 02	60	172	-3 02	60	172	-4 02	60	172	-5 02	60	172	-6 02	60	172								352
6	02 59	60	174	01 59	60	174	00 59	60	174	-0 01	60	174	-1 01	60	174	-2 01	60	174	-3 01	60	174	-4 01	60	174	-5 01	60	174	-6 01	60	174								354
4	03 00	60	176	02 00	60	176	01 00	60	176	00 00	60	176	-1 00	60	176	-2 00	60	176	-3 00	60	176	-4 00	60	176	-5 00	60	176	-6 00	60	176								356
2	03 00	60	178	02 00	60	178	01 00	60	178	00 00	60	178	-1 00	60	178	-2 00	60	178	-3 00	60	178	-4 00	60	178	-5 00	60	178	-6 00	60	178	-7 00	60	178					358
0	03 00	-60	180	02 00	-60	180	01 00	-60	180	00 00	-60	180	-1 00	-60	180	-2 00	-60	180	-3 00	-60	180	-4 00	-60	180	-5 00	-60	180	-6 00	-60	180	-7 00	-60	180					360
	0°			1°			2°			3°			4°			5°			6°			7°			8°			9°			10°			11°	12°	13°	14°	

S. Lat. {LHA greater than 180°....... Zn=180−Z; LHA less than 180°............ Zn=180+Z}

DECLINATION (0°-14°) CONTRARY NAME TO LATITUDE

N. Lat. {LHA greater than 180°....... Zn=Z; LHA less than 180°........... Zn=360−Z}

DECLINATION (15°-29°) **SAME** NAME AS LATITUDE

LAT 87°

LHA	15° Hc	d	Z	16° Hc	d	Z	17° Hc	d	Z	18° Hc	d	Z	19° Hc	d	Z	20° Hc	d	Z	21° Hc	d	Z
	° ′	′	°	° ′	′	°	° ′	′	°	° ′	′	°	° ′	′	°	° ′	′	°	° ′	′	°
0	18 00	+60	180	19 00	+60	180	20 00	+60	180	21 00	+60	180	22 00	+60	180	23 00	+60	180	24 00	+60	180
2	18 00	60	178	19 00	60	178	20 00	60	178	21 00	60	178	22 00	60	178	23 00	60	178	24 00	60	178
4	18 00	60	176	19 00	60	176	20 00	60	176	21 00	60	176	22 00	60	176	23 00	60	176	24 00	60	176
6	17 59	60	174	18 59	60	174	19 59	60	174	20 59	60	174	21 59	60	174	22 59	60	174	23 59	60	174
8	17 58	60	172	18 58	60	172	19 58	60	172	20 58	60	172	21 58	60	172	22 58	60	172	23 58	60	172
10	17 57	+60	170	18 57	+60	170	19 57	+60	170	20 57	+60	170	21 57	+60	170	22 57	+60	170	23 57	+60	170
12	17 56	60	168	18 56	60	168	19 56	60	168	20 56	60	168	21 56	60	168	22 56	60	168	23 56	60	168
14	17 55	60	166	18 55	60	166	19 55	60	166	20 55	60	166	21 55	60	166	22 55	60	166	23 55	60	166
16	17 53	60	164	18 53	60	164	19 53	60	164	20 53	60	164	21 53	60	164	22 53	60	164	23 53	60	164
18	17 51	60	162	18 51	60	162	19 51	60	162	20 51	60	162	21 51	60	162	22 51	60	162	23 51	60	162
20	17 49	+60	160	18 49	+60	160	19 49	+60	160	20 49	+60	160	21 49	+60	160	22 49	+60	160	23 49	+60	160
22	17 47	60	158	18 47	60	158	19 47	60	158	20 47	60	158	21 47	60	158	22 47	60	158	23 47	60	158
24	17 44	60	156	18 44	60	156	19 44	60	156	20 44	60	156	21 44	60	156	22 44	60	156	23 44	60	156
26	17 42	60	154	18 42	60	154	19 42	60	154	20 42	60	154	21 42	59	154	22 41	60	154	23 41	60	154
28	17 39	60	152	18 39	60	152	19 39	60	152	20 39	60	152	21 39	60	152	22 39	60	151	23 39	60	151
30	17 36	+60	150	18 36	+60	150	19 36	+60	150	20 36	+60	150	21 36	+59	149	22 35	+60	149	23 35	+60	149
32	17 32	60	148	18 32	60	148	19 32	60	148	20 32	60	147	21 32	60	147	22 32	60	147	23 32	60	147
34	17 29	60	146	18 29	60	146	19 29	60	145	20 29	60	145	21 29	60	145	22 29	60	145	23 29	60	145
36	17 25	60	144	18 25	60	143	19 25	60	143	20 25	60	143	21 25	60	143	22 25	60	143	23 25	60	143
38	17 21	60	142	18 21	60	141	19 21	60	141	20 21	60	141	21 21	60	141	22 21	60	141	23 21	60	141
40	17 17	+60	139	18 17	+60	139	19 17	+60	139	20 17	+60	139	21 17	+60	139	22 17	+60	139	23 17	+60	139
42	17 13	60	137	18 13	60	137	19 13	60	137	20 13	60	137	21 13	60	137	22 13	60	137	23 13	60	137
44	17 09	60	135	18 09	60	135	19 09	60	135	20 09	60	135	21 09	60	135	22 09	60	135	23 09	60	135
46	17 04	60	133	18 04	60	133	19 04	60	133	20 04	60	133	21 04	60	133	22 04	60	133	23 04	60	133
48	17 00	60	131	18 00	60	131	19 00	60	131	20 00	60	131	21 00	60	131	22 00	59	131	22 59	60	131
50	16 55	+60	129	17 55	+60	129	18 55	+60	129	19 55	+60	129	20 55	+60	129	21 55	+60	129	22 55	+60	129
52	16 50	60	127	17 50	60	127	18 50	60	127	19 50	60	127	20 50	60	127	21 50	60	127	22 50	60	127
54	16 45	60	125	17 45	60	125	18 45	60	125	19 45	60	125	20 45	60	125	21 45	60	125	22 45	60	125
56	16 40	60	123	17 40	60	123	18 40	60	123	19 40	60	123	20 40	59	123	21 39	60	123	22 39	60	123
58	16 34	60	121	17 34	60	121	18 34	60	121	19 34	60	121	20 34	60	121	21 34	60	121	22 34	60	121
60	16 29	+60	119	17 29	+60	119	18 29	+60	119	19 29	+60	119	20 29	+60	119	21 29	+60	119	22 29	+60	119
62	16 24	59	117	17 23	60	117	18 23	60	117	19 23	60	117	20 23	60	117	21 23	60	117	22 23	60	117
64	16 18	60	115	17 18	60	115	18 18	60	115	19 18	60	115	20 18	60	115	21 18	59	115	22 17	60	115
66	16 12	60	113	17 12	60	113	18 12	60	113	19 12	60	113	20 12	60	113	21 12	60	113	22 12	60	113
68	16 06	60	111	17 06	60	111	18 06	60	111	19 06	60	111	20 06	60	111	21 06	60	111	22 06	60	111
70	16 00	+60	109	17 00	+60	109	18 00	+60	109	19 00	+60	109	20 00	+60	109	21 00	+60	109	22 00	+60	109
72	15 55	59	107	16 54	60	107	17 54	60	107	18 54	60	107	19 54	60	107	20 54	60	107	21 54	60	107
74	15 48	60	105	16 48	60	105	17 48	60	105	18 48	60	105	19 48	60	105	20 48	60	105	21 48	60	105
76	15 42	60	103	16 42	60	103	17 42	60	103	18 42	60	103	19 42	60	103	20 42	60	103	21 42	60	103
78	15 36	60	101	16 36	60	101	17 36	60	101	18 36	60	101	19 36	60	101	20 36	60	101	21 36	60	101
80	15 30	+60	99	16 30	+60	99	17 30	+60	99	18 30	+60	99	19 30	+60	99	20 30	+60	99	21 30	+59	99
82	15 24	60	97	16 24	60	97	17 24	60	97	18 24	59	97	19 23	60	97	20 23	60	97	21 23	60	97
84	15 18	60	95	16 18	59	95	17 17	60	95	18 17	60	95	19 17	60	95	20 17	60	95	21 17	60	95
86	15 11	60	93	16 11	60	93	17 11	60	93	18 11	60	93	19 11	60	93	20 11	60	93	21 11	60	93
88	15 05	60	91	16 05	60	91	17 05	60	91	18 05	60	91	19 05	60	91	20 05	60	91	21 05	59	91
90	14 59	+60	89	15 59	+60	89	16 59	+60	89	17 59	+59	89	18 58	+60	89	19 58	+60	89	20 58	+60	89
92	14 53	59	87	15 52	60	87	16 52	60	87	17 52	60	87	18 52	60	87	19 52	60	87	20 52	60	87
94	14 46	60	85	15 46	60	85	16 46	60	85	17 46	60	85	18 46	60	85	19 46	60	85	20 46	60	85
96	14 40	60	83	15 40	60	83	16 40	60	83	17 40	60	83	18 40	60	83	19 40	59	83	20 39	60	83
98	14 34	60	81	15 34	60	81	16 34	60	81	17 34	59	81	18 33	60	81	19 33	60	81	20 33	60	81
100	14 28	+59	79	15 27	+60	79	16 27	+60	79	17 27	+60	79	18 27	+60	79	19 27	+60	79	20 27	+60	79
102	14 21	60	77	15 21	60	77	16 21	60	77	17 21	60	77	18 21	60	77	19 21	60	77	20 21	60	77
104	14 15	60	75	15 15	60	75	16 15	60	75	17 15	60	75	18 15	60	75	19 15	60	75	20 15	60	75
106	14 09	60	73	15 09	60	73	16 09	60	73	17 09	60	73	18 09	60	73	19 09	60	73	20 09	60	73
108	14 03	60	71	15 03	60	71	16 03	60	71	17 03	60	71	18 03	60	71	19 03	60	71	20 03	60	71
110	13 57	+60	69	14 57	+60	69	15 57	+60	69	16 57	+60	69	17 57	+60	69	18 57	+60	69	19 57	+60	69
112	13 52	59	67	14 51	60	67	15 51	60	67	16 51	60	67	17 51	60	67	18 51	60	67	19 51	60	67
114	13 46	60	65	14 46	60	65	15 46	60	65	16 46	60	65	17 46	59	65	18 45	60	65	19 45	60	65
116	13 40	60	63	14 40	60	63	15 40	60	63	16 40	60	63	17 40	60	63	18 40	60	63	19 40	60	63
118	13 35	60	61	14 35	59	61	15 34	60	61	16 34	60	61	17 34	60	61	18 34	60	61	19 34	60	61
120	13 29	+60	59	14 29	+60	59	15 29	+60	59	16 29	+60	59	17 29	+60	59	18 29	+60	59	19 29	+60	59
122	13 24	60	57	14 24	60	57	15 24	60	57	16 24	60	57	17 24	59	57	18 23	60	57	19 23	60	57
124	13 19	60	55	14 19	59	55	15 18	60	55	16 18	60	55	17 18	60	55	18 18	60	55	19 18	60	55
126	13 13	60	53	14 13	60	53	15 13	60	53	16 13	60	53	17 13	60	53	18 13	60	53	19 13	60	53
128	13 08	60	51	14 08	60	51	15 08	60	51	16 08	60	51	17 08	60	51	18 08	60	51	19 08	60	51
130	13 04	+60	49	14 04	+60	49	15 04	+59	49	16 03	+60	49	17 03	+60	49	18 03	+60	49	19 03	+60	49
132	12 59	60	47	13 59	60	47	14 59	60	47	15 59	60	47	16 59	60	47	17 59	60	47	18 59	60	47
134	12 54	60	46	13 54	60	45	14 54	60	45	15 54	60	45	16 54	60	45	17 54	60	45	18 54	60	45
136	12 50	60	44	13 50	60	43	14 50	60	43	15 50	60	43	16 50	60	43	17 50	60	43	18 50	60	43
138	12 46	60	42	13 46	60	42	14 46	60	41	15 46	60	41	16 46	60	41	17 46	60	41	18 46	59	41

LHA	22° Hc	d	Z	23° Hc	d	Z	24° Hc	d	Z	25° Hc	d	Z	26° Hc	d	Z	27° Hc	d	Z	28° Hc	d	Z	29° Hc	d	Z	LHA
	° ′	′	°	° ′	′	°	° ′	′	°	° ′	′	°	° ′	′	°	° ′	′	°	° ′	′	°	° ′	′	°	
0	25 00	+60	180	26 00	+60	180	27 00	+60	180	28 00	+60	180	29 00	+60	180	30 00	+60	180	31 00	+60	180	32 00	+60	180	360
2	25 00	60	178	26 00	60	178	27 00	60	178	28 00	60	178	29 00	60	178	30 00	60	178	31 00	60	178	32 00	60	178	358
4	25 00	60	176	26 00	60	176	27 00	60	176	28 00	60	176	29 00	60	176	30 00	60	176	31 00	60	176	32 00	60	176	356
6	24 59	60	174	25 59	60	174	26 59	60	174	27 59	60	174	28 59	60	174	29 59	60	174	30 59	60	174	31 59	60	174	354
8	24 58	60	172	25 58	60	172	26 58	60	172	27 58	60	172	28 58	60	172	29 58	60	172	30 58	60	172	31 58	60	172	352
10	24 57	+60	170	25 57	+60	170	26 57	+60	170	27 57	+60	170	28 57	+60	170	29 57	+60	170	30 57	+60	170	31 57	+60	170	350
12	24 56	60	168	25 56	60	168	26 56	60	168	27 56	60	168	28 56	60	168	29 56	60	168	30 56	60	168	31 56	60	168	348
14	24 55	60	166	25 55	60	166	26 55	60	166	27 55	60	166	28 55	60	166	29 55	60	166	30 55	60	166	31 55	60	166	346
16	24 53	60	164	25 53	60	164	26 53	60	164	27 53	60	164	28 53	60	164	29 53	60	164	30 53	60	164	31 53	60	164	344
18	24 51	60	162	25 51	60	162	26 51	60	162	27 51	60	162	28 51	60	162	29 51	60	162	30 51	60	162	31 51	60	161	342
20	24 49	+60	160	25 49	+60	160	26 49	+60	160	27 49	+60	160	28 49	+60	160	29 49	+60	159	30 49	+60	159	31 49	+60	159	340
22	24 47	60	158	25 47	60	158	26 47	60	158	27 47	60	157	28 47	60	157	29 47	60	157	30 47	60	157	31 47	60	157	338
24	24 44	60	156	25 44	60	155	26 44	60	155	27 44	60	155	28 44	60	155	29 44	60	155	30 44	60	155	31 44	60	155	336
26	24 41	60	153	25 41	60	153	26 41	60	153	27 41	60	153	28 41	60	153	29 41	60	153	30 41	60	153	31 41	60	153	334
28	24 39	60	151	25 39	59	151	26 38	60	151	27 38	60	151	28 38	60	151	29 38	60	151	30 38	60	151	31 38	60	151	332
30	24 35	+60	149	25 35	+60	149	26 35	+60	149	27 35	+60	149	28 35	+60	149	29 35	+60	149	30 35	+60	149	31 35	+60	149	330
32	24 32	60	147	25 32	60	147	26 32	60	147	27 32	60	147	28 32	60	147	29 32	60	147	30 32	60	147	31 32	60	147	328
34	24 29	60	145	25 29	60	145	26 29	60	145	27 29	60	145	28 29	59	145	29 28	60	145	30 28	60	145	31 28	60	145	326
36	24 25	60	143	25 25	60	143	26 25	60	143	27 25	60	143	28 25	60	143	29 25	60	143	30 25	60	143	31 25	60	143	324
38	24 21	60	141	25 21	60	141	26 21	60	141	27 21	60	141	28 21	60	141	29 21	60	141	30 21	60	141	31 21	60	141	322
40	24 17	+60	139	25 17	+60	139	26 17	+60	139	27 17	+60	139	28 17	+60	139	29 17	+60	139	30 17	+60	139	31 17	+60	139	320
42	24 13	60	137	25 13	60	137	26 13	60	137	27 13	60	137	28 13	60	137	29 13	60	137	30 13	60	137	31 13	60	137	318
44	24 09	60	135	25 09	59	135	26 08	60	135	27 08	60	135	28 08	60	135	29 08	60	135	30 08	60	135	31 08	60	135	316
46	24 04	60	133	25 04	60	133	26 04	60	133	27 04	60	133	28 04	60	133	29 04	60	133	30 04	60	133	31 04	60	133	314
48	23 59	60	131	24 59	60	131	25 59	60	131	26 59	60	131	27 59	60	131	28 59	60	131	29 59	60	131	30 59	60	131	312
50	23 55	+60	129	24 55	+59	129	25 54	+60	129	26 54	+60	129	27 54	+60	129	28 54	+60	129	29 54	+60	129	30 54	+60	129	310
52	23 50	60	127	24 50	60	127	25 50	59	127	26 49	60	127	27 49	60	127	28 49	60	127	29 49	60	127	30 49	60	127	308
54	23 45	59	125	24 44	60	125	25 44	60	125	26 44	60	125	27 44	60	125	28 44	60	125	29 44	60	125	30 44	60	125	306
56	23 39	60	123	24 39	60	123	25 39	60	123	26 39	60	123	27 39	60	123	28 39	60	123	29 39	60	123	30 39	60	123	304
58	23 34	60	121	24 34	60	121	25 34	60	121	26 34	60	121	27 34	60	121	28 34	60	121	29 34	59	121	30 33	60	121	302
60	23 29	+60	119	24 29	+59	119	25 28	+60	119	26 28	+60	119	27 28	+60	119	28 28	+60	119	29 28	+60	119	30 28	+60	119	300
62	23 23	60	117	24 23	60	117	25 23	60	117	26 23	60	117	27 23	60	117	28 23	60	117	29 23	59	117	30 22	60	117	298
64	23 17	60	115	24 17	60	115	25 17	60	115	26 17	60	115	27 17	60	115	28 17	60	115	29 17	60	115	30 17	60	115	296
66	23 12	60	113	24 12	59	113	25 11	60	113	26 11	60	113	27 11	60	113	28 11	60	113	29 11	60	113	30 11	60	112	294
68	23 06	60	111	24 06	60	111	25 06	60	111	26 06	59	111	27 05	60	111	28 05	60	111	29 05	60	111	30 05	60	110	292
70	23 00	+60	109	24 00	+60	109	25 00	+60	109	26 00	+60	109	27 00	+59	109	27 59	+60	109	28 59	+60	109	29 59	+60	108	290
72	22 54	60	107	23 54	60	107	24 54	60	107	25 54	60	107	26 54	59	107	27 53	60	107	28 53	60	106	29 53	60	106	288
74	22 48	60	105	23 48	60	105	24 48	60	105	25 48	60	105	26 48	59	105	27 47	60	105	28 47	60	104	29 47	60	104	286
76	22 42	60	103	23 42	60	103	24 42	59	103	25 41	60	103	26 41	60	103	27 41	60	103	28 41	60	102	29 41	60	102	284
78	22 36	60	101	23 36	59	101	24 35	60	101	25 35	60	101	26 35	60	101	27 35	60	101	28 35	60	100	29 35	60	100	282
80	22 29	+60	99	23 29	+60	99	24 29	+60	99	25 29	+60	99	26 29	+60	99	27 29	+60	99	28 29	+60	98	29 29	+60	98	280
82	22 23	60	97	23 23	60	97	24 23	60	97	25 23	60	97	26 23	60	97	27 23	60	97	28 23	60	96	29 23	59	96	278
84	22 17	60	95	23 17	60	95	24 17	60	95	25 17	60	95	26 17	59	95	27 16	60	95	28 16	60	94	29 16	60	94	276
86	22 11	60	93	23 11	60	93	24 11	59	93	25 10	60	93	26 10	60	93	27 10	60	93	28 10	60	92	29 10	60	92	274
88	22 04	60	91	23 04	60	91	24 04	60	91	25 04	60	91	26 04	60	91	27 04	60	91	28 04	60	90	29 04	60	90	272
90	21 58	+60	89	22 58	+60	89	23 58	+60	89	24 58	+60	89	25 58	+60	89	26 58	+60	89	27 58	+59	88	28 57	+60	88	270
92	21 52	60	87	22 52	60	87	23 52	60	87	24 52	59	87	25 51	60	87	26 51	60	87	27 51	60	86	28 51	60	86	268
94	21 46	60	85	22 46	59	85	23 45	60	85	24 45	60	85	25 45	60	85	26 45	60	85	27 45	60	84	28 45	60	84	266
96	21 39	60	83	22 39	60	83	23 39	60	83	24 39	60	83	25 39	60	83	26 39	60	83	27 39	60	82	28 39	60	82	264
98	21 33	60	81	22 33	60	81	23 33	60	81	24 33	60	81	25 33	60	81	26 33	60	81	27 33	59	80	28 32	60	80	262
100	21 27	+60	79	22 27	+60	79	23 27	+60	79	24 27	+60	79	25 27	+59	79	26 26	+60	79	27 26	+60	79	28 26	+60	78	260
102	21 21	60	77	22 21	60	77	23 21	60	77	24 21	59	77	25 20	60	77	26 20	60	77	27 20	60	77	28 20	60	76	258
104	21 15	60	75	22 15	60	75	23 15	59	75	24 14	60	75	25 14	60	75	26 14	60	75	27 14	60	75	28 14	60	74	256
106	21 09	60	73	22 09	60	73	23 09	59	73	24 08	60	73	25 08	60	73	26 08	60	73	27 08	60	73	28 08	60	72	254
108	21 03	60	71	22 03	60	71	23 03	59	71	24 02	60	71	25 02	60	71	26 02	60	71	27 02	60	71	28 02	60	71	252
110	20 57	+60	69	21 57	+60	69	22 57	+60	69	23 57	+59	69	24 56	+60	69	25 56	+60	69	26 56	+60	69	27 56	+60	69	250
112	20 51	60	67	21 51	60	67	22 51	60	67	23 51	60	67	24 51	60	67	25 51	60	67	26 51	59	67	27 50	60	67	248
114	20 45	60	65	21 45	60	65	22 45	60	65	23 45	60	65	24 45	60	65	25 45	60	65	26 45	60	65	27 45	60	65	246
116	20 40	60	63	21 40	59	63	22 39	60	63	23 39	60	63	24 39	60	63	25 39	60	63	26 39	60	63	27 39	60	63	244
118	20 34	60	61	21 34	60	61	22 34	60	61	23 34	60	61	24 34	60	61	25 34	60	61	26 34	60	61	27 34	59	61	242
120	20 29	+60	59	21 29	+60	59	22 29	+59	59	23 28	+60	59	24 28	+60	59	25 28	+60	59	26 28	+60	59	27 28	+60	59	240
122	20 23	60	57	21 23	60	57	22 23	60	57	23 23	60	57	24 23	60	57	25 23	60	57	26 23	60	57	27 23	60	57	238
124	20 18	60	55	21 18	60	55	22 18	60	55	23 18	60	55	24 18	60	55	25 18	60	55	26 18	60	55	27 18	60	55	236
126	20 13	60	53	21 13	60	53	22 13	60	53	23 13	60	53	24 13	60	53	25 13	60	53	26 13	60	53	27 13	60	53	234
128	20 08	60	51	21 08	60	51	22 08	60	51	23 08	60	51	24 08	60	51	25 08	60	51	26 08	60	51	27 08	60	51	232
130	20 03	+60	49	21 03	+60	49	22 03	+60	49	23 03	+60	49	24 03	+60	49	25 03	+60	49	26 03	+60	49	27 03	+60	49	230
132	19 59	60	47	20 59	59	47	21 58	60	47	22 58	60	47	23 58	60	47	24 58	60	47	25 58	60	47	26 58	60	47	228
134	19 54	60	45	20 54	60	45	21 54	60	45	22 54	60	45	23 54	60	45	24 54	60	45	25 54	60	45	26 54	60	45	226
136	19 50	60	43	20 50	60	43	21 50	60	43	22 50	60	43	23 50	59	43	24 49	60	43	25 49	60	43	26 49	60	43	224
138	19 45	60	41	20 45	60	41	21 45	60	41	22 45	60	41	23 45	60	41	24 45	60	41	25 45	60	41	26 45	60	41	222

S. Lat. {LHA greater than 180°....... Zn=180−Z; LHA less than 180°........... Zn=180+Z}

DECLINATION (15°-29°) **SAME** NAME AS LATITUDE

N. Lat. {LHA greater than 180°....... Zn=Z; LHA less than 180°........... Zn=360−Z}

DECLINATION (15°-29°) SAME NAME AS LATITUDE

LHA	15° Hc	d	Z	16° Hc	d	Z	17° Hc	d	Z	18° Hc	d	Z	19° Hc	d	Z
	° ′	′	°	° ′	′	°	° ′	′	°	° ′	′	°	° ′	′	°
140	12 42	+60	40	13 42	+60	40	14 42	+60	40	15 42	+60	39	16 42	+59	39
142	12 38	60	38	13 38	60	38	14 38	60	38	15 38	60	37	16 38	60	37
144	12 34	60	36	13 34	60	36	14 34	60	36	15 34	60	36	16 34	60	35
146	12 30	60	34	13 30	60	34	14 30	60	34	15 30	60	34	16 30	60	34
148	12 27	60	32	13 27	60	32	14 27	60	32	15 27	60	32	16 27	60	32
150	12 24	+60	30	13 24	+60	30	14 24	+60	30	15 24	+60	30	16 24	+60	30
152	12 21	60	28	13 21	60	28	14 21	60	28	15 21	60	28	16 21	60	28
154	12 18	60	26	13 18	60	26	14 18	60	26	15 18	60	26	16 18	60	26
156	12 15	60	24	13 15	60	24	14 15	60	24	15 15	60	24	16 15	60	24
158	12 13	60	22	13 13	60	22	14 13	60	22	15 13	60	22	16 13	60	22
160	12 11	+60	20	13 11	+60	20	14 11	+60	20	15 11	+60	20	16 11	+60	20
162	12 09	60	18	13 09	60	18	14 09	60	18	15 09	60	18	16 09	60	18
164	12 07	60	16	13 07	60	16	14 07	60	16	15 07	60	16	16 07	60	16
166	12 05	60	14	13 05	60	14	14 05	60	14	15 05	60	14	16 05	60	14
168	12 04	60	12	13 04	60	12	14 04	60	12	15 04	60	12	16 04	60	12
170	12 03	+60	10	13 03	+60	10	14 03	+60	10	15 03	+60	10	16 03	+60	10
172	12 02	60	8	13 02	60	8	14 02	60	8	15 02	60	8	16 02	60	8
174	12 01	60	6	13 01	60	6	14 01	60	6	15 01	60	6	16 01	60	6
176	12 00	60	4	13 00	60	4	14 00	60	4	15 00	60	4	16 00	60	4
178	12 00	60	2	13 00	60	2	14 00	60	2	15 00	60	2	16 00	60	2
180	12 00	+60	0	13 00	+60	0	14 00	+60	0	15 00	+60	0	16 00	+60	0

LHA	20° Hc	d	Z	21° Hc	d	Z	22° Hc	d	Z	23° Hc	d	Z	24° Hc	d	Z
	° ′	′	°	° ′	′	°	° ′	′	°	° ′	′	°	° ′	′	°
140	17 41	+60	39	18 41	+60	39	19 41	+60	39	20 41	+60	39	21 41	+60	39
142	17 38	60	37	18 38	60	37	19 38	59	37	20 37	60	37	21 37	60	37
144	17 34	60	35	18 34	60	35	19 34	60	35	20 34	60	35	21 34	60	35
146	17 30	60	33	18 30	60	33	19 30	60	33	20 30	60	33	21 30	60	33
148	17 27	60	32	18 27	60	31	19 27	60	31	20 27	60	31	21 27	60	31
150	17 24	+60	30	18 24	+60	30	19 24	+60	29	20 24	+60	29	21 24	+60	29
152	17 21	60	28	18 21	60	28	19 21	60	28	20 21	60	27	21 21	60	27
154	17 18	60	26	18 18	60	26	19 18	60	26	20 18	60	26	21 18	60	26
156	17 15	60	24	18 15	60	24	19 15	60	24	20 15	60	24	21 15	60	24
158	17 13	60	22	18 13	60	22	19 13	60	22	20 13	60	22	21 13	60	22
160	17 11	+60	20	18 11	+60	20	19 11	+60	20	20 11	+60	20	21 11	+60	20
162	17 09	60	18	18 09	60	18	19 09	60	18	20 09	60	18	21 09	60	18
164	17 07	60	16	18 07	60	16	19 07	60	16	20 07	60	16	21 07	60	16
166	17 05	60	14	18 05	60	14	19 05	60	14	20 05	60	14	21 05	60	14
168	17 04	60	12	18 04	60	12	19 04	60	12	20 04	60	12	21 04	60	12
170	17 03	+60	10	18 03	+60	10	19 03	+60	10	20 03	+60	10	21 03	+60	10
172	17 02	60	8	18 02	60	8	19 02	60	8	20 02	60	8	21 02	60	8
174	17 01	60	6	18 01	60	6	19 01	60	6	20 01	60	6	21 01	60	6
176	17 00	60	4	18 00	60	4	19 00	60	4	20 00	60	4	21 00	60	4
178	17 00	60	2	18 00	60	2	19 00	60	2	20 00	60	2	21 00	60	2
180	17 00	+60	0	18 00	+60	0	19 00	+60	0	20 00	+60	0	21 00	+60	0

LHA	25° Hc	d	Z	26° Hc	d	Z	27° Hc	d	Z	28° Hc	d	Z	29° Hc	d	Z	LHA
	° ′	′	°	° ′	′	°	° ′	′	°	° ′	′	°	° ′	′	°	
140	22 41	+60	39	23 41	+60	39	24 41	+60	39	25 41	+60	39	26 41	+60	39	220
142	22 37	60	37	23 37	60	37	24 37	60	37	25 37	60	37	26 37	60	37	218
144	22 34	60	35	23 34	60	35	24 34	60	35	25 34	60	35	26 34	60	35	216
146	22 30	60	33	23 30	60	33	24 30	60	33	25 30	60	33	26 30	60	33	214
148	22 27	60	31	23 27	60	31	24 27	60	31	25 27	60	31	26 27	60	31	212
150	22 24	+60	29	23 24	+60	29	24 24	+60	29	25 24	+60	29	26 24	+60	29	210
152	22 21	60	27	23 21	60	27	24 21	60	27	25 21	60	27	26 21	60	27	208
154	22 18	60	25	23 18	60	25	24 18	60	25	25 18	60	25	26 18	60	25	206
156	22 15	60	24	23 15	60	23	24 15	60	23	25 15	60	23	26 15	60	23	204
158	22 13	60	22	23 13	60	22	24 13	60	22	25 13	60	21	26 13	60	21	202
160	22 11	+60	20	23 11	+60	20	24 11	+60	20	25 11	+60	20	26 11	+60	20	200
162	22 09	60	18	23 09	60	18	24 09	60	18	25 09	60	18	26 09	60	18	198
164	22 07	60	16	23 07	60	16	24 07	60	16	25 07	60	16	26 07	60	16	196
166	22 05	60	14	23 05	60	14	24 05	60	14	25 05	60	14	26 05	60	14	194
168	22 04	60	12	23 04	60	12	24 04	60	12	25 04	60	12	26 04	60	12	192
170	22 03	+60	10	23 03	+60	10	24 03	+60	10	25 03	+60	10	26 03	+60	10	190
172	22 02	60	8	23 02	60	8	24 02	60	8	25 02	60	8	26 02	60	8	188
174	22 01	60	6	23 01	60	6	24 01	60	6	25 01	60	6	26 01	60	6	186
176	22 00	60	4	23 00	60	4	24 00	60	4	25 00	60	4	26 00	60	4	184
178	22 00	60	2	23 00	60	2	24 00	60	2	25 00	60	2	26 00	60	2	182
180	22 00	+60	0	23 00	+60	0	24 00	+60	0	25 00	+60	0	26 00	+60	0	180

15°	16°	17°	18°	19°	20°	21°	22°	23°	24°	25°	26°	27°	28°	29°

S. Lat. {LHA greater than 180°....... Zn=180−Z; LHA less than 180°........... Zn=180+Z}

DECLINATION (15°-29°) SAME NAME AS LATITUDE

LAT 87°

N. Lat. {LHA greater than 180°....... Zn=Z; LHA less than 180°........... Zn=360−Z}

DECLINATION (0°-14°) SAME NAME AS LATITUDE

LAT 88°

LHA	0° Hc	0° d	0° Z	1° Hc	1° d	1° Z	2° Hc	2° d	2° Z	3° Hc	3° d	3° Z	4° Hc	4° d	4° Z
	° ′	′	°	° ′	′	°	° ′	′	°	° ′	′	°	° ′	′	°
0	02 00	+60	180	03 00	+60	180	04 00	+60	180	05 00	+60	180	06 00	+60	180
2	02 00	60	178	03 00	60	178	04 00	60	178	05 00	60	178	06 00	60	178
4	02 00	60	176	03 00	60	176	04 00	60	176	05 00	60	176	06 00	60	176
6	01 59	60	174	02 59	60	174	03 59	60	174	04 59	60	174	05 59	60	174
8	01 59	60	172	02 59	60	172	03 59	60	172	04 59	60	172	05 59	60	172
10	01 58	+60	170	02 58	+60	170	03 58	+60	170	04 58	+60	170	05 58	+60	170
12	01 57	60	168	02 57	60	168	03 57	60	168	04 57	60	168	05 57	60	168
14	01 56	60	166	02 56	60	166	03 56	60	166	04 56	60	166	05 56	60	166
16	01 55	60	164	02 55	60	164	03 55	60	164	04 55	60	164	05 55	60	164
18	01 54	60	162	02 54	60	162	03 54	60	162	04 54	60	162	05 54	60	162
20	01 53	+60	160	02 53	+60	160	03 53	+60	160	04 53	+60	160	05 53	+60	160
22	01 51	60	158	02 51	60	158	03 51	60	158	04 51	60	158	05 51	60	158
24	01 50	60	156	02 50	60	156	03 50	60	156	04 50	60	156	05 50	60	156
26	01 48	60	154	02 48	60	154	03 48	60	154	04 48	60	154	05 48	60	154
28	01 46	60	152	02 46	60	152	03 46	60	152	04 46	60	152	05 46	60	152
30	01 44	+60	150	02 44	+60	150	03 44	+60	150	04 44	+60	150	05 44	+60	150
32	01 42	60	148	02 42	60	148	03 42	60	148	04 42	60	148	05 42	60	148
34	01 39	60	146	02 39	60	146	03 39	60	146	04 39	60	146	05 39	60	146
36	01 37	60	144	02 37	60	144	03 37	60	144	04 37	60	144	05 37	60	144
38	01 35	60	142	02 35	60	142	03 35	60	142	04 35	60	142	05 35	60	142
40	01 32	+60	140	02 32	+60	140	03 32	+60	140	04 32	+60	140	05 32	+60	140
42	01 29	60	138	02 29	60	138	03 29	60	138	04 29	60	138	05 29	60	138
44	01 26	60	136	02 26	60	136	03 26	60	136	04 26	60	136	05 26	60	136
46	01 23	60	134	02 23	60	134	03 23	60	134	04 23	60	134	05 23	60	134
48	01 20	60	132	02 20	60	132	03 20	60	132	04 20	60	132	05 20	60	132
50	01 17	+60	130	02 17	+60	130	03 17	+60	130	04 17	+60	130	05 17	+60	130
52	01 14	60	128	02 14	60	128	03 14	60	128	04 14	60	128	05 14	60	128
54	01 11	59	126	02 10	60	126	03 10	60	126	04 10	60	126	05 10	60	126
56	01 07	60	124	02 07	60	124	03 07	60	124	04 07	60	124	05 07	60	124
58	01 04	60	122	02 04	60	122	03 04	60	122	04 04	60	122	05 04	59	122
60	01 00	+60	120	02 00	+60	120	03 00	+60	120	04 00	+60	120	05 00	+60	120
62	00 56	60	118	01 56	60	118	02 56	60	118	03 56	60	118	04 56	60	118
64	00 53	60	116	01 53	60	116	02 53	60	116	03 53	59	116	04 52	60	116
66	00 49	60	114	01 49	60	114	02 49	60	114	03 49	60	114	04 49	60	114
68	00 45	60	112	01 45	60	112	02 45	60	112	03 45	60	112	04 45	60	112
70	00 41	+60	110	01 41	+60	110	02 41	+60	110	03 41	+60	110	04 41	+60	110
72	00 37	60	108	01 37	60	108	02 37	60	108	03 37	60	108	04 37	60	108
74	00 33	60	106	01 33	60	106	02 33	60	106	03 33	60	106	04 33	60	106
76	00 29	60	104	01 29	60	104	02 29	60	104	03 29	60	104	04 29	60	104
78	00 25	60	102	01 25	60	102	02 25	60	102	03 25	60	102	04 25	60	102
80	00 21	+60	100	01 21	+60	100	02 21	+60	100	03 21	+60	100	04 21	+60	100
82	00 17	60	98	01 17	60	98	02 17	60	98	03 17	60	98	04 17	60	98
84	00 13	59	96	01 12	60	96	02 12	60	96	03 12	60	96	04 12	60	96
86	00 08	60	94	01 08	60	94	02 08	60	94	03 08	60	94	04 08	60	94
88	00 04	60	92	01 04	60	92	02 04	60	92	03 04	60	92	04 04	60	92
90	00 00	+60	90	01 00	+60	90	02 00	+60	90	03 00	+60	90	04 00	+60	90
92	-0 04	60	88	00 56	60	88	01 56	60	88	02 56	60	88	03 56	60	88
94	-0 08	60	86	00 52	60	86	01 52	60	86	02 52	60	86	03 52	60	86
96	-0 13	60	84	00 47	60	84	01 47	60	84	02 47	60	84	03 47	60	84
98	-0 17	60	82	00 43	60	82	01 43	60	82	02 43	60	82	03 43	60	82
100	-0 21	+60	80	00 39	+60	80	01 39	+60	80	02 39	+60	80	03 39	+60	80
102	-0 25	60	78	00 35	60	78	01 35	60	78	02 35	60	78	03 35	60	78
104	-0 29	60	76	00 31	60	76	01 31	60	76	02 31	60	76	03 31	60	76
106	-0 33	60	74	00 27	60	74	01 27	60	74	02 27	60	74	03 27	60	74
108	-0 37	60	72	00 23	60	72	01 23	60	72	02 23	60	72	03 23	60	72
110	-0 41	+60	70	00 19	+60	70	01 19	+60	70	02 19	+60	70	03 19	+60	70
112	-0 45	60	68	00 15	60	68	01 15	60	68	02 15	60	68	03 15	60	68
114	-0 49	60	66	00 11	60	66	01 11	60	66	02 11	60	66	03 11	60	66
116	-0 53	60	64	00 07	60	64	01 07	60	64	02 07	60	64	03 07	60	64
118	-0 56	60	62	00 04	60	62	01 04	60	62	02 04	60	62	03 04	60	62
120	-1 00	+60	60	00 00	+60	60	01 00	+60	60	02 00	+60	60	03 00	+60	60
122	-1 04	60	58	-0 04	60	58	00 56	60	58	01 56	60	58	02 56	60	58
124	-1 07	60	56	-0 07	60	56	00 53	60	56	01 53	60	56	02 53	60	56
126	-1 11	60	54	-0 11	60	54	00 49	60	54	01 49	60	54	02 49	60	54
128	-1 14	60	52	-0 14	60	52	00 46	60	52	01 46	60	52	02 46	60	52
130	-1 17	+60	50	-0 17	+60	50	00 43	+60	50	01 43	+60	50	02 43	+60	50
132	-1 20	60	48	-0 20	60	48	00 40	60	48	01 40	60	48	02 40	60	48
134	-1 23	60	46	-0 23	60	46	00 37	60	46	01 37	60	46	02 37	60	46
136	-1 26	60	44	-0 26	60	44	00 34	60	44	01 34	60	44	02 34	60	44
138	-1 29	60	42	-0 29	60	42	00 31	60	42	01 31	60	42	02 31	60	42

LHA	5° Hc	5° d	5° Z	6° Hc	6° d	6° Z	7° Hc	7° d	7° Z	8° Hc	8° d	8° Z	9° Hc	9° d	9° Z
	° ′	′	°	° ′	′	°	° ′	′	°	° ′	′	°	° ′	′	°
0	07 00	+60	180	08 00	+60	180	09 00	+60	180	10 00	+60	180	11 00	+60	180
2	07 00	60	178	08 00	60	178	09 00	60	178	10 00	60	178	11 00	60	178
4	07 00	60	176	08 00	60	176	09 00	60	176	10 00	60	176	11 00	60	176
6	06 59	60	174	07 59	60	174	08 59	60	174	09 59	60	174	10 59	60	174
8	06 59	60	172	07 59	60	172	08 59	60	172	09 59	60	172	10 59	60	172
10	06 58	+60	170	07 58	+60	170	08 58	+60	170	09 58	+60	170	10 58	+60	170
12	06 57	60	168	07 57	60	168	08 57	60	168	09 57	60	168	10 57	60	168
14	06 56	60	166	07 56	60	166	08 56	60	166	09 56	60	166	10 56	60	166
16	06 55	60	164	07 55	60	164	08 55	60	164	09 55	60	164	10 55	60	164
18	06 54	60	162	07 54	60	162	08 54	60	162	09 54	60	162	10 54	60	162
20	06 53	+60	160	07 53	+60	160	08 53	+60	160	09 53	+60	160	10 53	+60	160
22	06 51	60	158	07 51	60	158	08 51	60	158	09 51	60	158	10 51	60	158
24	06 50	60	156	07 50	60	156	08 50	60	156	09 50	60	156	10 50	60	156
26	06 48	60	154	07 48	60	154	08 48	60	154	09 48	60	154	10 48	60	154
28	06 46	60	152	07 46	60	152	08 46	60	152	09 46	60	152	10 46	60	152
30	06 44	+60	150	07 44	+60	150	08 44	+60	150	09 44	+60	150	10 44	+60	150
32	06 42	60	148	07 42	60	148	08 42	60	148	09 42	60	148	10 42	60	148
34	06 39	60	146	07 39	60	146	08 39	60	146	09 39	60	146	10 39	60	146
36	06 37	60	144	07 37	60	144	08 37	60	144	09 37	60	144	10 37	60	144
38	06 35	60	142	07 35	60	142	08 35	59	142	09 34	60	142	10 34	60	142
40	06 32	+60	140	07 32	+60	140	08 32	+60	140	09 32	+60	140	10 32	+60	140
42	06 29	60	138	07 29	60	138	08 29	60	138	09 29	60	138	10 29	60	138
44	06 26	60	136	07 26	60	136	08 26	60	136	09 26	60	136	10 26	60	136
46	06 23	60	134	07 23	60	134	08 23	60	134	09 23	60	134	10 23	60	134
48	06 20	60	132	07 20	60	132	08 20	60	132	09 20	60	132	10 20	60	132
50	06 17	+60	130	07 17	+60	130	08 17	+60	130	09 17	+60	130	10 17	+60	130
52	06 14	60	128	07 14	60	128	08 14	60	128	09 14	60	128	10 14	60	128
54	06 10	60	126	07 10	60	126	08 10	60	126	09 10	60	126	10 10	60	126
56	06 07	60	124	07 07	60	124	08 07	60	124	09 07	60	124	10 07	60	124
58	06 03	60	122	07 03	60	122	08 03	60	122	09 03	60	122	10 03	60	122
60	06 00	+60	120	07 00	+60	120	08 00	+60	120	09 00	+60	120	10 00	+60	120
62	05 56	60	118	06 56	60	118	07 56	60	118	08 56	60	118	09 56	60	118
64	05 52	60	116	06 52	60	116	07 52	60	116	08 52	60	116	09 52	60	116
66	05 49	60	114	06 49	60	114	07 49	60	114	08 49	60	114	09 49	60	114
68	05 45	60	112	06 45	60	112	07 45	60	112	08 45	60	112	09 45	60	112
70	05 41	+60	110	06 41	+60	110	07 41	+60	110	08 41	+60	110	09 41	+60	110
72	05 37	60	108	06 37	60	108	07 37	60	108	08 37	60	108	09 37	60	108
74	05 33	60	106	06 33	60	106	07 33	60	106	08 33	60	106	09 33	60	106
76	05 29	60	104	06 29	60	104	07 29	60	104	08 29	60	104	09 29	60	104
78	05 25	60	102	06 25	60	102	07 25	60	102	08 25	60	102	09 25	60	102
80	05 21	+60	100	06 21	+60	100	07 21	+60	100	08 21	+60	100	09 21	+60	100
82	05 17	60	98	06 17	59	98	07 16	60	98	08 16	60	98	09 16	60	98
84	05 12	60	96	06 12	60	96	07 12	60	96	08 12	60	96	09 12	60	96
86	05 08	60	94	06 08	60	94	07 08	60	94	08 08	60	94	09 08	60	94
88	05 04	60	92	06 04	60	92	07 04	60	92	08 04	60	92	09 04	60	92
90	05 00	+60	90	06 00	+60	90	07 00	+60	90	08 00	+60	90	09 00	+60	90
92	04 56	60	88	05 56	60	88	06 56	60	88	07 56	60	88	08 56	59	88
94	04 52	59	86	05 51	60	86	06 51	60	86	07 51	60	86	08 51	60	86
96	04 47	60	84	05 47	60	84	06 47	60	84	07 47	60	84	08 47	60	84
98	04 43	60	82	05 43	60	82	06 43	60	82	07 43	60	82	08 43	60	82
100	04 39	+60	80	05 39	+60	80	06 39	+60	80	07 39	+60	80	08 39	+60	80
102	04 35	60	78	05 35	60	78	06 35	60	78	07 35	60	78	08 35	60	78
104	04 31	60	76	05 31	60	76	06 31	60	76	07 31	60	76	08 31	60	76
106	04 27	60	74	05 27	60	74	06 27	60	74	07 27	60	74	08 27	60	74
108	04 23	60	72	05 23	60	72	06 23	60	72	07 23	60	72	08 23	60	72
110	04 19	+60	70	05 19	+60	70	06 19	+60	70	07 19	+60	70	08 19	+60	70
112	04 15	60	68	05 15	60	68	06 15	60	68	07 15	60	68	08 15	60	68
114	04 11	60	66	05 11	60	66	06 11	60	66	07 11	60	66	08 11	60	66
116	04 07	60	64	05 07	60	64	06 07	60	64	07 07	60	64	08 07	60	64
118	04 04	60	62	05 04	60	62	06 04	59	62	07 03	60	62	08 03	60	62
120	04 00	+60	60	05 00	+60	60	06 00	+60	60	07 00	+60	60	08 00	+60	60
122	03 56	60	58	04 56	60	58	05 56	60	58	06 56	60	58	07 56	60	58
124	03 53	60	56	04 53	60	56	05 53	60	56	06 53	60	56	07 53	60	56
126	03 49	60	54	04 49	60	54	05 49	60	54	06 49	60	54	07 49	60	54
128	03 46	60	52	04 46	60	52	05 46	60	52	06 46	60	52	07 46	60	52
130	03 43	+60	50	04 43	+60	50	05 43	+60	50	06 43	+60	50	07 43	+60	50
132	03 40	60	48	04 40	60	48	05 40	60	48	06 40	60	48	07 40	60	48
134	03 37	60	46	04 37	60	46	05 37	60	46	06 37	60	46	07 37	60	46
136	03 34	60	44	04 34	60	44	05 34	60	44	06 34	60	44	07 34	60	44
138	03 31	60	42	04 31	60	42	05 31	60	42	06 31	60	42	07 31	60	42

LHA	10° Hc	10° d	10° Z	11° Hc	11° d	11° Z	12° Hc	12° d	12° Z	13° Hc	13° d	13° Z	14° Hc	14° d	14° Z	LHA
	° ′	′	°	° ′	′	°	° ′	′	°	° ′	′	°	° ′	′	°	
0	12 00	+60	180	13 00	+60	180	14 00	+60	180	15 00	+60	180	16 00	+60	180	360
2	12 00	60	178	13 00	60	178	14 00	60	178	15 00	60	178	16 00	60	178	358
4	12 00	60	176	13 00	60	176	14 00	60	176	15 00	60	176	16 00	60	176	356
6	11 59	60	174	12 59	60	174	13 59	60	174	14 59	60	174	15 59	60	174	354
8	11 59	60	172	12 59	60	172	13 59	60	172	14 59	60	172	15 59	60	172	352
10	11 58	+60	170	12 58	+60	170	13 58	+60	170	14 58	+60	170	15 58	+60	170	350
12	11 57	60	168	12 57	60	168	13 57	60	168	14 57	60	168	15 57	60	168	348
14	11 56	60	166	12 56	60	166	13 56	60	166	14 56	60	166	15 56	60	166	346
16	11 55	60	164	12 55	60	164	13 55	60	164	14 55	60	164	15 55	60	164	344
18	11 54	60	162	12 54	60	162	13 54	60	162	14 54	60	162	15 54	60	162	342
20	11 53	+60	160	12 53	+60	160	13 53	+60	160	14 53	+60	160	15 53	+60	160	340
22	11 51	60	158	12 51	60	158	13 51	60	158	14 51	60	158	15 51	60	158	338
24	11 50	60	156	12 50	60	156	13 50	60	156	14 50	60	156	15 50	60	156	336
26	11 48	60	154	12 48	60	154	13 48	60	154	14 48	60	154	15 48	60	154	334
28	11 46	60	152	12 46	60	152	13 46	60	152	14 46	60	152	15 46	60	152	332
30	11 44	+60	150	12 44	+60	150	13 44	+60	150	14 44	+60	150	15 44	+60	150	330
32	11 42	60	148	12 42	60	148	13 42	60	148	14 42	60	148	15 42	60	148	328
34	11 39	60	146	12 39	60	146	13 39	60	146	14 39	60	146	15 39	60	146	326
36	11 37	60	144	12 37	60	144	13 37	60	144	14 37	60	144	15 37	60	144	324
38	11 34	60	142	12 34	60	142	13 34	60	142	14 34	60	142	15 34	60	142	322
40	11 32	+60	140	12 32	+60	140	13 32	+60	140	14 32	+60	140	15 32	+60	140	320
42	11 29	60	138	12 29	60	138	13 29	60	138	14 29	60	138	15 29	60	138	318
44	11 26	60	136	12 26	60	136	13 26	60	136	14 26	60	136	15 26	60	136	316
46	11 23	60	134	12 23	60	134	13 23	60	134	14 23	60	134	15 23	60	134	314
48	11 20	60	132	12 20	60	132	13 20	60	132	14 20	60	132	15 20	60	132	312
50	11 17	+60	130	12 17	+60	130	13 17	+60	130	14 17	+60	130	15 17	+60	130	310
52	11 14	60	128	12 14	60	128	13 14	60	128	14 14	60	128	15 14	60	128	308
54	11 10	60	126	12 10	60	126	13 10	60	126	14 10	60	126	15 10	60	126	306
56	11 07	60	124	12 07	60	124	13 07	60	124	14 07	60	124	15 07	60	124	304
58	11 03	60	122	12 03	60	122	13 03	60	122	14 03	60	122	15 03	60	122	302
60	11 00	+60	120	12 00	+60	120	13 00	+60	120	14 00	+60	120	15 00	+60	120	300
62	10 56	60	118	11 56	60	118	12 56	60	118	13 56	60	118	14 56	60	118	298
64	10 52	60	116	11 52	60	116	12 52	60	116	13 52	60	116	14 52	60	116	296
66	10 49	60	114	11 49	59	114	12 48	60	114	13 48	60	114	14 48	60	114	294
68	10 45	60	112	11 45	60	112	12 45	60	112	13 45	60	112	14 45	60	112	292
70	10 41	+60	110	11 41	+60	110	12 41	+60	110	13 41	+60	110	14 41	+60	110	290
72	10 37	60	108	11 37	60	108	12 37	60	108	13 37	60	108	14 37	60	108	288
74	10 33	60	106	11 33	60	106	12 33	60	106	13 33	60	106	14 33	60	106	286
76	10 29	60	104	11 29	60	104	12 29	60	104	13 29	60	104	14 29	60	104	284
78	10 25	60	102	11 25	60	102	12 25	60	102	13 25	59	102	14 24	60	102	282
80	10 21	+59	100	11 20	+60	100	12 20	+60	100	13 20	+60	100	14 20	+60	100	280
82	10 16	60	98	11 16	60	98	12 16	60	98	13 16	60	98	14 16	60	98	278
84	10 12	60	96	11 12	60	96	12 12	60	96	13 12	60	96	14 12	60	96	276
86	10 08	60	94	11 08	60	94	12 08	60	94	13 08	60	94	14 08	60	94	274
88	10 04	60	92	11 04	60	92	12 04	60	92	13 04	60	92	14 04	60	92	272
90	10 00	+60	90	11 00	+60	90	12 00	+60	90	13 00	+60	90	14 00	+59	90	270
92	09 55	60	88	10 55	60	88	11 55	60	88	12 55	60	88	13 55	60	88	268
94	09 51	60	86	10 51	60	86	11 51	60	86	12 51	60	86	13 51	60	86	266
96	09 47	60	84	10 47	60	84	11 47	60	84	12 47	60	84	13 47	60	84	264
98	09 43	60	82	10 43	60	82	11 43	60	82	12 43	60	82	13 43	60	82	262
100	09 39	+60	80	10 39	+60	80	11 39	+60	80	12 39	+60	80	13 39	+60	80	260
102	09 35	60	78	10 35	60	78	11 35	60	78	12 35	60	78	13 35	60	78	258
104	09 31	60	76	10 31	60	76	11 31	60	76	12 31	60	76	13 31	59	76	256
106	09 27	60	74	10 27	60	74	11 27	60	74	12 27	59	74	13 26	60	74	254
108	09 23	60	72	10 23	60	72	11 23	60	72	12 23	60	72	13 23	59	72	252
110	09 19	+60	70	10 19	+60	70	11 19	+60	70	12 19	+60	70	13 19	+60	70	250
112	09 15	60	68	10 15	60	68	11 15	60	68	12 15	60	68	13 15	60	68	248
114	09 11	60	66	10 11	60	66	11 11	60	66	12 11	60	66	13 11	60	66	246
116	09 07	60	64	10 07	60	64	11 07	60	64	12 07	60	64	13 07	60	64	244
118	09 03	60	62	10 03	60	62	11 03	60	62	12 03	60	62	13 03	60	62	242
120	09 00	+60	60	10 00	+60	60	11 00	+60	60	12 00	+60	60	13 00	+60	60	240
122	08 56	60	58	09 56	60	58	10 56	60	58	11 56	60	58	12 56	60	58	238
124	08 53	60	56	09 53	60	56	10 53	60	56	11 53	60	56	12 53	60	56	236
126	08 49	60	54	09 49	60	54	10 49	60	54	11 49	60	54	12 49	60	54	234
128	08 46	60	52	09 46	60	52	10 46	60	52	11 46	60	52	12 46	60	52	232
130	08 43	+60	50	09 43	+60	50	10 43	+60	50	11 43	+60	50	12 43	+60	50	230
132	08 40	60	48	09 40	60	48	10 40	59	48	11 39	60	48	12 39	60	48	228
134	08 37	59	46	09 36	60	46	10 36	60	46	11 36	60	46	12 36	60	46	226
136	08 34	60	44	09 34	60	44	10 34	60	44	11 34	59	44	12 33	60	44	224
138	08 31	60	42	09 31	60	42	10 31	60	42	11 31	60	42	12 31	60	42	222

0° 1° 2° 3° 4° 5° 6° 7° 8° 9° 10° 11° 12° 13° 14°

S. Lat. {LHA greater than 180°....... Zn=180−Z; LHA less than 180°........... Zn=180+Z}

DECLINATION (0°-14°) SAME NAME AS LATITUDE

LAT 88°

N. Lat. {LHA greater than 180°........ Zn=Z; LHA less than 180°........ Zn=360−Z}

DECLINATION (0°-14°) SAME NAME AS LATITUDE

LHA	0°			1°			2°			3°			4°			5°			6°			7°		
	Hc	d	Z	Hc	d	Z	Hc	d	Z	Hc	d	Z	Hc	d	Z	Hc	d	Z	Hc	d	Z	Hc	d	Z
	° ′	′	°	° ′	′	°	° ′	′	°	° ′	′	°	° ′	′	°	° ′	′	°	° ′	′	°	° ′	′	°
140	-1 32	+60	40	-0 32	+60	40	00 28	+60	40	01 28	+60	40	02 28	+60	40	03 28	+60	40	04 28	+60	40	05 28	+60	40
142	-1 35	60	38	-0 35	60	38	00 25	60	38	01 25	60	38	02 25	60	38	03 25	60	38	04 25	60	38	05 25	60	38
144	-1 37	60	36	-0 37	60	36	00 23	60	36	01 23	60	36	02 23	60	36	03 23	60	36	04 23	60	36	05 23	60	36
146	-1 39	60	34	-0 39	60	34	00 21	60	34	01 21	60	34	02 21	60	34	03 21	59	34	04 20	60	34	05 20	60	34
148	-1 42	60	32	-0 42	60	32	00 18	60	32	01 18	60	32	02 18	60	32	03 18	60	32	04 18	60	32	05 18	60	32
150	-1 44	+60	30	-0 44	+60	30	00 16	+60	30	01 16	+60	30	02 16	+60	30	03 16	+60	30	04 16	+60	30	05 16	+60	30
152	-1 46	60	28	-0 46	60	28	00 14	60	28	01 14	60	28	02 14	60	28	03 14	60	28	04 14	60	28	05 14	60	28
154	-1 48	60	26	-0 48	60	26	00 12	60	26	01 12	60	26	02 12	60	26	03 12	60	26	04 12	60	26	05 12	60	26
156	-1 50	60	24	-0 50	60	24	00 10	60	24	01 10	60	24	02 10	60	24	03 10	60	24	04 10	60	24	05 10	60	24
158	-1 51	60	22	-0 51	60	22	00 09	60	22	01 09	60	22	02 09	60	22	03 09	60	22	04 09	60	22	05 09	60	22
160	-1 53	+60	20	-0 53	+60	20	00 07	+60	20	01 07	+60	20	02 07	+60	20	03 07	+60	20	04 07	+60	20	05 07	+60	20
162	-1 54	60	18	-0 54	60	18	00 06	60	18	01 06	60	18	02 06	60	18	03 06	60	18	04 06	60	18	05 06	60	18
164	-1 55	60	16	-0 55	60	16	00 05	60	16	01 05	60	16	02 05	60	16	03 05	60	16	04 05	60	16	05 05	60	16
166	-1 56	60	14	-0 56	60	14	00 04	60	14	01 04	60	14	02 04	60	14	03 04	60	14	04 04	60	14	05 04	60	14
168	-1 57	60	12	-0 57	60	12	00 03	60	12	01 03	60	12	02 03	60	12	03 03	60	12	04 03	60	12	05 03	60	12
170	-1 58	+60	10	-0 58	+60	10	00 02	+60	10	01 02	+60	10	02 02	+60	10	03 02	+60	10	04 02	+60	10	05 02	+60	10
172	-1 59	60	8	-0 59	60	8	00 01	60	8	01 01	60	8	02 01	60	8	03 01	60	8	04 01	60	8	05 01	60	8
174	-1 59	60	6	-0 59	60	6	00 01	60	6	01 01	60	6	02 01	60	6	03 01	60	6	04 01	60	6	05 01	60	6
176	-2 00	60	4	-1 00	60	4	00 00	60	4	01 00	60	4	02 00	60	4	03 00	60	4	04 00	60	4	05 00	60	4
178	-2 00	60	2	-1 00	60	2	00 00	60	2	01 00	60	2	02 00	60	2	03 00	60	2	04 00	60	2	05 00	60	2
180	-2 00	+60	0	-1 00	+60	0	00 00	+60	0	01 00	+60	0	02 00	+60	0	03 00	+60	0	04 00	+60	0	05 00	+60	0

8°			9°			10°			11°			12°			13°			14°			LHA
Hc	d	Z	Hc	d	Z	Hc	d	Z	Hc	d	Z	Hc	d	Z	Hc	d	Z	Hc	d	Z	
° ′	′	°	° ′	′	°	° ′	′	°	° ′	′	°	° ′	′	°	° ′	′	°	° ′	′	°	
06 28	+60	40	07 28	+60	40	08 28	+60	40	09 28	+60	40	10 28	+60	40	11 28	+60	40	12 28	+60	40	220
06 25	60	38	07 25	60	38	08 25	60	38	09 25	60	38	10 25	60	38	11 25	60	38	12 25	60	38	218
06 23	60	36	07 23	60	36	08 23	60	36	09 23	60	36	10 23	60	36	11 23	60	36	12 23	60	36	216
06 20	60	34	07 20	60	34	08 20	60	34	09 20	60	34	10 20	60	34	11 20	60	34	12 20	60	34	214
06 18	60	32	07 18	60	32	08 18	60	32	09 18	60	32	10 18	60	32	11 18	60	32	12 18	60	32	212
06 16	+60	30	07 16	+60	30	08 16	+60	30	09 16	+60	30	10 16	+60	30	11 16	+60	30	12 16	+60	30	210
06 14	60	28	07 14	60	28	08 14	60	28	09 14	60	28	10 14	60	28	11 14	60	28	12 14	60	28	208
06 12	60	26	07 12	60	26	08 12	60	26	09 12	60	26	10 12	60	26	11 12	60	26	12 12	60	26	206
06 10	60	24	07 10	60	24	08 10	60	24	09 10	60	24	10 10	60	24	11 10	60	24	12 10	60	24	204
06 09	60	22	07 09	60	22	08 09	60	22	09 09	60	22	10 09	60	22	11 09	60	22	12 09	60	22	202
06 07	+60	20	07 07	+60	20	08 07	+60	20	09 07	+60	20	10 07	+60	20	11 07	+60	20	12 07	+60	20	200
06 06	60	18	07 06	60	18	08 06	60	18	09 06	60	18	10 06	60	18	11 06	60	18	12 06	60	18	198
06 05	60	16	07 05	60	16	08 05	60	16	09 05	60	16	10 05	60	16	11 05	60	16	12 05	60	16	196
06 04	60	14	07 04	60	14	08 04	60	14	09 04	60	14	10 04	60	14	11 04	60	14	12 04	60	14	194
06 03	60	12	07 03	60	12	08 03	60	12	09 03	60	12	10 03	60	12	11 03	60	12	12 03	60	12	192
06 02	+60	10	07 02	+60	10	08 02	+60	10	09 02	+60	10	10 02	+60	10	11 02	+60	10	12 02	+60	10	190
06 01	60	8	07 01	60	8	08 01	60	8	09 01	60	8	10 01	60	8	11 01	60	8	12 01	60	8	188
06 01	60	6	07 01	60	6	08 01	60	6	09 01	60	6	10 01	60	6	11 01	60	6	12 01	60	6	186
06 00	60	4	07 00	60	4	08 00	60	4	09 00	60	4	10 00	60	4	11 00	60	4	12 00	60	4	184
06 00	60	2	07 00	60	2	08 00	60	2	09 00	60	2	10 00	60	2	11 00	60	2	12 00	60	2	182
06 00	+60	0	07 00	+60	0	08 00	+60	0	09 00	+60	0	10 00	+60	0	11 00	+60	0	12 00	+60	0	180

0°	1°	2°	3°	4°	5°	6°	7°	8°	9°	10°	11°	12°	13°	14°

S. Lat. {LHA greater than 180°........ Zn=180−Z; LHA less than 180°........ Zn=180+Z}

DECLINATION (0°-14°) SAME NAME AS LATITUDE

N. Lat. {LHA greater than 180°....... Zn=Z; LHA less than 180°.......... Zn=360−Z}

DECLINATION (0°-14°) **CONTRARY** NAME TO LATITUDE

LHA	0° Hc	d	Z	1° Hc	d	Z	2° Hc	d	Z	3° Hc	d	Z	4° Hc	d	Z	5° Hc	d	Z	LHA
	° ′	′	°	° ′	′	°	° ′	′	°	° ′	′	°	° ′	′	°	° ′	′	°	
180	−2 00	−60	0	−3 00	−60	0	−4 00	−60	0	−5 00	−60	0	−6 00	−60	0				180
178	−2 00	60	2	−3 00	60	2	−4 00	60	2	−5 00	60	2	−6 00	60	2	−7 00	60	2	182
176	−2 00	60	4	−3 00	60	4	−4 00	60	4	−5 00	60	4	−6 00	60	4	−7 00	60	4	184
174	−1 59	60	6	−2 59	60	6	−3 59	60	6	−4 59	60	6	−5 59	60	6	−6 59	60	6	186
172	−1 59	60	8	−2 59	60	8	−3 59	60	8	−4 59	60	8	−5 59	60	8	−6 59	60	8	188
170	−1 58	−60	10	−2 58	−60	10	−3 58	−60	10	−4 58	−60	10	−5 58	−60	10	−6 58	−60	10	190
168	−1 57	60	12	−2 57	60	12	−3 57	60	12	−4 57	60	12	−5 57	60	12	−6 57	60	12	192
166	−1 56	60	14	−2 56	60	14	−3 56	60	14	−4 56	60	14	−5 56	60	14	−6 56	60	14	194
164	−1 55	60	16	−2 55	60	16	−3 55	60	16	−4 55	60	16	−5 55	60	16	−6 55	60	16	196
162	−1 54	60	18	−2 54	60	18	−3 54	60	18	−4 54	60	18	−5 54	60	18	−6 54	60	18	198
160	−1 53	−60	20	−2 53	−60	20	−3 53	−60	20	−4 53	−60	20	−5 53	−60	20	−6 53	−60	20	200
158	−1 51	60	22	−2 51	60	22	−3 51	60	22	−4 51	60	22	−5 51	60	22	−6 51	60	22	202
156	−1 50	60	24	−2 50	60	24	−3 50	60	24	−4 50	60	24	−5 50	60	24	−6 50	60	24	204
154	−1 48	60	26	−2 48	60	26	−3 48	60	26	−4 48	60	26	−5 48	60	26	−6 48	60	26	206
152	−1 46	60	28	−2 46	60	28	−3 46	60	28	−4 46	60	28	−5 46	60	28	−6 46	60	28	208
150	−1 44	−60	30	−2 44	−60	30	−3 44	−60	30	−4 44	−60	30	−5 44	−60	30	−6 44	−60	30	210
148	−1 42	60	32	−2 42	60	32	−3 42	60	32	−4 42	60	32	−5 42	60	32	−6 42	60	32	212
146	−1 39	60	34	−2 39	60	34	−3 39	60	34	−4 39	60	34	−5 39	60	34	−6 39	60	34	214
144	−1 37	60	36	−2 37	60	36	−3 37	60	36	−4 37	60	36	−5 37	60	36	−6 37	60	36	216
142	−1 35	60	38	−2 35	60	38	−3 35	60	38	−4 35	60	38	−5 35	60	38	−6 35	60	38	218
140	−1 32	−60	40	−2 32	−60	40	−3 32	−60	40	−4 32	−60	40	−5 32	−60	40	−6 32	−60	40	220

0° 1° 2° 3° 4° 5° 6° 7° 8° 9° 10° 11° 12° 13° 14°

S. Lat. {LHA greater than 180°........ Zn=180−Z; LHA less than 180°.......... Zn=180+Z}

DECLINATION (0°-14°) **CONTRARY** NAME TO LATITUDE

N. Lat. {LHA greater than 180°....... Zn=Z ; LHA less than 180°........... Zn=360−Z}

DECLINATION (0°-14°) CONTRARY NAME TO LATITUDE

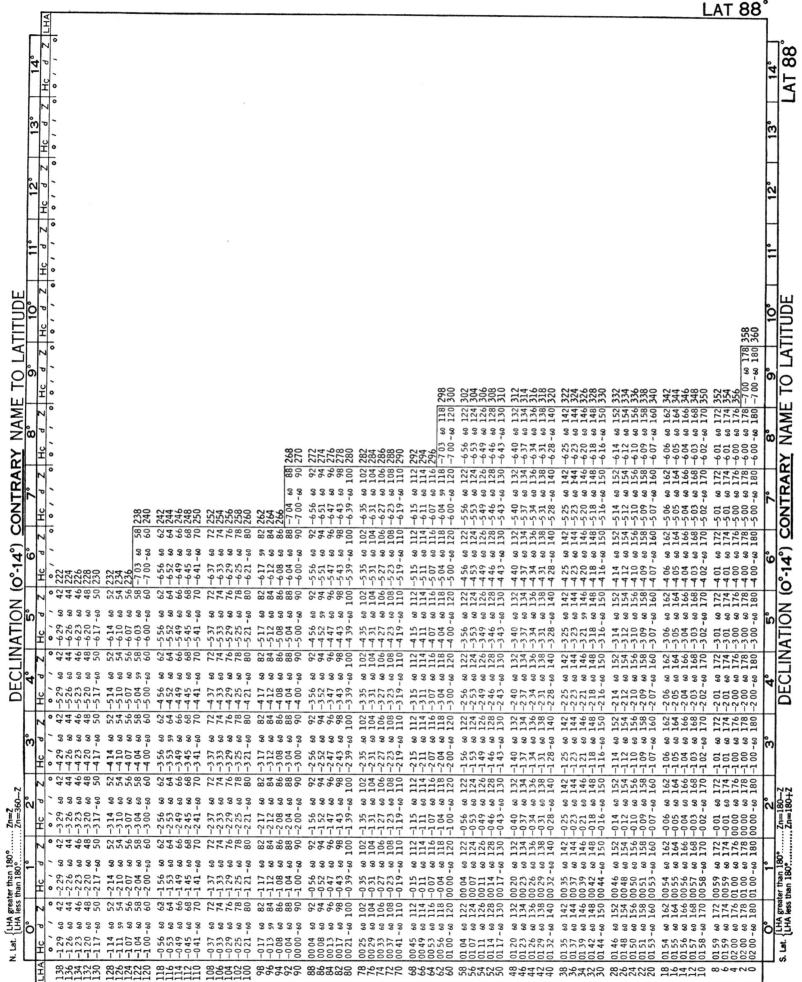

LHA	0°			1°			2°			3°			4°			5°			6°			7°			8°			9°			10°			11°			12°			13°			14°			LHA
	Hc	d	Z	Hc	d	Z	Hc	d	Z	Hc	d	Z	Hc	d	Z	Hc	d	Z	Hc	d	Z	Hc	d	Z	Hc	d	Z	Hc	d	Z	Hc	d	Z	Hc	d	Z	Hc	d	Z	Hc	d	Z	Hc	d	Z	
	° ′	′	°	° ′	′	°	° ′	′	°	° ′	′	°	° ′	′	°	° ′	′	°	° ′	′	°	° ′	′	°	° ′	′	°	° ′	′	°	° ′	′	°	° ′	′	°	° ′	′	°	° ′	′	°	° ′	′	°	
138	-1 29	60	42	-2 29	60	42	-3 29	60	42	-4 29	60	42	-5 29	60	42	-6 29	60	42																												222
136	-1 26	60	44	-2 26	60	44	-3 26	60	44	-4 26	60	44	-5 26	60	44	-6 26	60	44																												224
134	-1 23	60	46	-2 23	60	46	-3 23	60	46	-4 23	60	46	-5 23	60	46	-6 23	60	46																												226
132	-1 20	60	48	-2 20	60	48	-3 20	60	48	-4 20	60	48	-5 20	60	48	-6 20	60	48																												228
130	-1 17	-60	50	-2 17	-60	50	-3 17	-60	50	-4 17	-60	50	-5 17	-60	50	-6 17	-60	50																												230
128	-1 14	60	52	-2 14	60	52	-3 14	60	52	-4 14	60	52	-5 14	60	52	-6 14	60	52																												232
126	-1 11	59	54	-2 10	60	54	-3 10	60	54	-4 10	60	54	-5 10	60	54	-6 10	60	54																												234
124	-1 07	60	56	-2 07	60	56	-3 07	60	56	-4 07	60	56	-5 07	60	56	-6 07	60	56																												236
122	-1 04	60	58	-2 04	60	58	-3 04	60	58	-4 04	60	58	-5 04	59	58	-6 03	60	58	-7 03	60	58																									238
120	-1 00	-60	60	-2 00	-60	60	-3 00	-60	60	-4 00	-60	60	-5 00	-60	60	-6 00	-60	60	-7 00	-60	60																									240
118	-0 56	60	62	-1 56	60	62	-2 56	60	62	-3 56	60	62	-4 56	60	62	-5 56	60	62	-6 56	60	62																									242
116	-0 53	60	64	-1 53	60	64	-2 53	60	64	-3 53	59	64	-4 52	60	64	-5 52	60	64	-6 52	60	64																									244
114	-0 49	60	66	-1 49	60	66	-2 49	60	66	-3 49	60	66	-4 49	60	66	-5 49	60	66	-6 49	60	66																									246
112	-0 45	60	68	-1 45	60	68	-2 45	60	68	-3 45	60	68	-4 45	60	68	-5 45	60	68	-6 45	60	68																									248
110	-0 41	-60	70	-1 41	-60	70	-2 41	-60	70	-3 41	-60	70	-4 41	-60	70	-5 41	-60	70	-6 41	-60	70																									250
108	-0 37	60	72	-1 37	60	72	-2 37	60	72	-3 37	60	72	-4 37	60	72	-5 37	60	72	-6 37	60	72																									252
106	-0 33	60	74	-1 33	60	74	-2 33	60	74	-3 33	60	74	-4 33	60	74	-5 33	60	74	-6 33	60	74																									254
104	-0 29	60	76	-1 29	60	76	-2 29	60	76	-3 29	60	76	-4 29	60	76	-5 29	60	76	-6 29	60	76																									256
102	-0 25	60	78	-1 25	60	78	-2 25	60	78	-3 25	60	78	-4 25	60	78	-5 25	60	78	-6 25	60	78																									258
100	-0 21	-60	80	-1 21	-60	80	-2 21	-60	80	-3 21	-60	80	-4 21	-60	80	-5 21	-60	80	-6 21	-60	80																									260
98	-0 17	60	82	-1 17	60	82	-2 17	60	82	-3 17	60	82	-4 17	60	82	-5 17	60	82	-6 17	59	82																									262
96	-0 13	59	84	-1 12	60	84	-2 12	60	84	-3 12	60	84	-4 12	60	84	-5 12	60	84	-6 12	60	84																									264
94	-0 08	60	86	-1 08	60	86	-2 08	60	86	-3 08	60	86	-4 08	60	86	-5 08	60	86	-6 08	60	86																									266
92	-0 04	60	88	-1 04	60	88	-2 04	60	88	-3 04	60	88	-4 04	60	88	-5 04	60	88	-6 04	60	88	-7 04	60	88																						268
90	00 00	-60	90	-1 00	-60	90	-2 00	-60	90	-3 00	-60	90	-4 00	-60	90	-5 00	-60	90	-6 00	-60	90	-7 00	-60	90																						270
88	00 04	60	92	-0 56	60	92	-1 56	60	92	-2 56	60	92	-3 56	60	92	-4 56	60	92	-5 56	60	92	-6 56	60	92																						272
86	00 08	60	94	-0 52	60	94	-1 52	60	94	-2 52	60	94	-3 52	60	94	-4 52	59	94	-5 51	60	94	-6 51	60	94																						274
84	00 13	60	96	-0 47	60	96	-1 47	60	96	-2 47	60	96	-3 47	60	96	-4 47	60	96	-5 47	60	96	-6 47	60	96																						276
82	00 17	60	98	-0 43	60	98	-1 43	60	98	-2 43	60	98	-3 43	60	98	-4 43	60	98	-5 43	60	98	-6 43	60	98																						278
80	00 21	-60	100	-0 39	-60	100	-1 39	-60	100	-2 39	-60	100	-3 39	-60	100	-4 39	-60	100	-5 39	-60	100	-6 39	-60	100																						280
78	00 25	60	102	-0 35	60	102	-1 35	60	102	-2 35	60	102	-3 35	60	102	-4 35	60	102	-5 35	60	102	-6 35	60	102																						282
76	00 29	60	104	-0 31	60	104	-1 31	60	104	-2 31	60	104	-3 31	60	104	-4 31	60	104	-5 31	60	104	-6 31	60	104																						284
74	00 33	60	106	-0 27	60	106	-1 27	60	106	-2 27	60	106	-3 27	60	106	-4 27	60	106	-5 27	60	106	-6 27	60	106																						286
72	00 37	60	108	-0 23	60	108	-1 23	60	108	-2 23	60	108	-3 23	60	108	-4 23	60	108	-5 23	60	108	-6 23	60	108																						288
70	00 41	-60	110	-0 19	-60	110	-1 19	-60	110	-2 19	-60	110	-3 19	-60	110	-4 19	-60	110	-5 19	-60	110	-6 19	-60	110																						290
68	00 45	60	112	-0 15	60	112	-1 15	60	112	-2 15	60	112	-3 15	60	112	-4 15	60	112	-5 15	60	112	-6 15	60	112																						292
66	00 49	60	114	-0 11	60	114	-1 11	60	114	-2 11	60	114	-3 11	60	114	-4 11	60	114	-5 11	60	114	-6 11	60	114																						294
64	00 53	60	116	-0 07	60	116	-1 07	60	116	-2 07	60	116	-3 07	60	116	-4 07	60	116	-5 07	60	116	-6 07	60	116																						296
62	00 56	60	118	-0 04	60	118	-1 04	60	118	-2 04	60	118	-3 04	60	118	-4 04	60	118	-5 04	60	118	-6 04	59	118	-7 03	60	118																			298
60	01 00	-60	120	00 00	-60	120	-1 00	-60	120	-2 00	-60	120	-3 00	-60	120	-4 00	-60	120	-5 00	-60	120	-6 00	-60	120	-7 00	-60	120																			300
58	01 04	60	122	00 04	60	122	-0 56	60	122	-1 56	60	122	-2 56	60	122	-3 56	60	122	-4 56	60	122	-5 56	60	122	-6 56	60	122																			302
56	01 07	60	124	00 07	60	124	-0 53	60	124	-1 53	60	124	-2 53	60	124	-3 53	60	124	-4 53	60	124	-5 53	60	124	-6 53	60	124																			304
54	01 11	60	126	00 11	60	126	-0 49	60	126	-1 49	60	126	-2 49	60	126	-3 49	60	126	-4 49	60	126	-5 49	60	126	-6 49	60	126																			306
52	01 14	60	128	00 14	60	128	-0 46	60	128	-1 46	60	128	-2 46	60	128	-3 46	60	128	-4 46	60	128	-5 46	60	128	-6 46	60	128																			308
50	01 17	-60	130	00 17	-60	130	-0 43	-60	130	-1 43	-60	130	-2 43	-60	130	-3 43	-60	130	-4 43	-60	130	-5 43	-60	130	-6 43	-60	130																			310
48	01 20	60	132	00 20	60	132	-0 40	60	132	-1 40	60	132	-2 40	60	132	-3 40	60	132	-4 40	60	132	-5 40	60	132	-6 40	60	132																			312
46	01 23	60	134	00 23	60	134	-0 37	60	134	-1 37	60	134	-2 37	60	134	-3 37	60	134	-4 37	60	134	-5 37	60	134	-6 37	60	134																			314
44	01 26	60	136	00 26	60	136	-0 34	60	136	-1 34	60	136	-2 34	60	136	-3 34	60	136	-4 34	60	136	-5 34	60	136	-6 34	60	136																			316
42	01 29	60	138	00 29	60	138	-0 31	60	138	-1 31	60	138	-2 31	60	138	-3 31	60	138	-4 31	60	138	-5 31	60	138	-6 31	60	138																			318
40	01 32	-60	140	00 32	-60	140	-0 28	-60	140	-1 28	-60	140	-2 28	-60	140	-3 28	-60	140	-4 28	-60	140	-5 28	-60	140	-6 28	-60	140																			320
38	01 35	60	142	00 35	60	142	-0 25	60	142	-1 25	60	142	-2 25	60	142	-3 25	60	142	-4 25	60	142	-5 25	60	142	-6 25	60	142																			322
36	01 37	60	144	00 37	60	144	-0 23	60	144	-1 23	60	144	-2 23	60	144	-3 23	60	144	-4 23	60	144	-5 23	60	144	-6 23	60	144																			324
34	01 39	60	146	00 39	60	146	-0 21	60	146	-1 21	60	146	-2 21	60	146	-3 21	59	146	-4 20	60	146	-5 20	60	146	-6 20	60	146																			326
32	01 42	60	148	00 42	60	148	-0 18	60	148	-1 18	60	148	-2 18	60	148	-3 18	60	148	-4 18	60	148	-5 18	60	148	-6 18	60	148																			328
30	01 44	-60	150	00 44	-60	150	-0 16	-60	150	-1 16	-60	150	-2 16	-60	150	-3 16	-60	150	-4 16	-60	150	-5 16	-60	150	-6 16	-60	150																			330
28	01 46	60	152	00 46	60	152	-0 14	60	152	-1 14	60	152	-2 14	60	152	-3 14	60	152	-4 14	60	152	-5 14	60	152	-6 14	60	152																			332
26	01 48	60	154	00 48	60	154	-0 12	60	154	-1 12	60	154	-2 12	60	154	-3 12	60	154	-4 12	60	154	-5 12	60	154	-6 12	60	154																			334
24	01 50	60	156	00 50	60	156	-0 10	60	156	-1 10	60	156	-2 10	60	156	-3 10	60	156	-4 10	60	156	-5 10	60	156	-6 10	60	156																			336
22	01 51	60	158	00 51	60	158	-0 09	60	158	-1 09	60	158	-2 09	60	158	-3 09	60	158	-4 09	60	158	-5 09	60	158	-6 09	60	158																			338
20	01 53	-60	160	00 53	-60	160	-0 07	-60	160	-1 07	-60	160	-2 07	-60	160	-3 07	-60	160	-4 07	-60	160	-5 07	-60	160	-6 07	-60	160																			340
18	01 54	60	162	00 54	60	162	-0 06	60	162	-1 06	60	162	-2 06	60	162	-3 06	60	162	-4 06	60	162	-5 06	60	162	-6 06	60	162																			342
16	01 55	60	164	00 55	60	164	-0 05	60	164	-1 05	60	164	-2 05	60	164	-3 05	60	164	-4 05	60	164	-5 05	60	164	-6 05	60	164																			344
14	01 56	60	166	00 56	60	166	-0 04	60	166	-1 04	60	166	-2 04	60	166	-3 04	60	166	-4 04	60	166	-5 04	60	166	-6 04	60	166																			346
12	01 57	60	168	00 57	60	168	-0 03	60	168	-1 03	60	168	-2 03	60	168	-3 03	60	168	-4 03	60	168	-5 03	60	168	-6 03	60	168																			348
10	01 58	-60	170	00 58	-60	170	-0 02	-60	170	-1 02	-60	170	-2 02	-60	170	-3 02	-60	170	-4 02	-60	170	-5 02	-60	170	-6 02	-60	170																			350
8	01 59	60	172	00 59	60	172	-0 01	60	172	-1 01	60	172	-2 01	60	172	-3 01	60	172	-4 01	60	172	-5 01	60	172	-6 01	60	172																			352
6	01 59	60	174	00 59	60	174	-0 01	60	174	-1 01	60	174	-2 01	60	174	-3 01	60	174	-4 01	60	174	-5 01	60	174	-6 01	60	174																			354
4	02 00	60	176	01 00	60	176	00 00	60	176	-1 00	60	176	-2 00	60	176	-3 00	60	176	-4 00	60	176	-5 00	60	176	-6 00	60	176																			356
2	02 00	60	178	01 00	60	178	00 00	60	178	-1 00	60	178	-2 00	60	178	-3 00	60	178	-4 00	60	178	-5 00	60	178	-6 00	60	178	-7 00	60	178																358
0	02 00	-60	180	01 00	-60	180	00 00	-60	180	-1 00	-60	180	-2 00	-60	180	-3 00	-60	180	-4 00	-60	180	-5 00	-60	180	-6 00	-60	180	-7 00	-60	180																360
	0°			1°			2°			3°			4°			5°			6°			7°			8°			9°			10°			11°			12°			13°			14°			

S. Lat. {LHA greater than 180°....... Zn=180−Z ; LHA less than 180°........... Zn=180+Z}

DECLINATION (0°-14°) CONTRARY NAME TO LATITUDE

N. Lat. {LHA greater than 180°....... Zn=Z; LHA less than 180°........... Zn=360−Z}

DECLINATION (15°-29°) SAME NAME AS LATITUDE

LHA	15°			16°			17°			18°			19°		
	Hc	d	Z	Hc	d	Z	Hc	d	Z	Hc	d	Z	Hc	d	Z
	° ′	′	°	° ′	′	°	° ′	′	°	° ′	′	°	° ′	′	°
0	17 00	+60	180	18 00	+60	180	19 00	+60	180	20 00	+60	180	21 00	+60	180
2	17 00	60	178	18 00	60	178	19 00	60	178	20 00	60	178	21 00	60	178
4	17 00	60	176	18 00	60	176	19 00	60	176	20 00	60	176	21 00	60	176
6	16 59	60	174	17 59	60	174	18 59	60	174	19 59	60	174	20 59	60	174
8	16 59	60	172	17 59	60	172	18 59	60	172	19 59	60	172	20 59	60	172
10	16 58	+60	170	17 58	+60	170	18 58	+60	170	19 58	+60	170	20 58	+60	170
12	16 57	60	168	17 57	60	168	18 57	60	168	19 57	60	168	20 57	60	168
14	16 56	60	166	17 56	60	166	18 56	60	166	19 56	60	166	20 56	60	166
16	16 55	60	164	17 55	60	164	18 55	60	164	19 55	60	164	20 55	60	164
18	16 54	60	162	17 54	60	162	18 54	60	162	19 54	60	162	20 54	60	162
20	16 53	+60	160	17 53	+60	160	18 53	+60	160	19 53	+60	160	20 53	+60	160
22	16 51	60	158	17 51	60	158	18 51	60	158	19 51	60	158	20 51	60	158
24	16 50	60	156	17 50	60	156	18 50	60	156	19 50	60	156	20 50	60	156
26	16 48	60	154	17 48	60	154	18 48	60	154	19 48	60	154	20 48	60	154
28	16 46	60	152	17 46	60	152	18 46	60	152	19 46	60	152	20 46	60	152
30	16 44	+60	150	17 44	+60	150	18 44	+60	150	19 44	+60	150	20 44	+60	150
32	16 42	60	148	17 42	60	148	18 42	60	148	19 42	60	148	20 42	60	148
34	16 39	60	146	17 39	60	146	18 39	60	146	19 39	60	146	20 39	60	146
36	16 37	60	144	17 37	60	144	18 37	60	144	19 37	60	144	20 37	60	144
38	16 34	60	142	17 34	60	142	18 34	60	142	19 34	60	142	20 34	60	142
40	16 32	+60	140	17 32	+60	140	18 32	+60	140	19 32	+60	140	20 32	+60	140
42	16 29	60	138	17 29	60	138	18 29	60	138	19 29	60	138	20 29	60	138
44	16 26	60	136	17 26	60	136	18 26	60	136	19 26	60	136	20 26	60	136
46	16 23	60	134	17 23	60	134	18 23	60	134	19 23	60	134	20 23	60	134
48	16 20	60	132	17 20	60	132	18 20	60	132	19 20	60	132	20 20	60	132
50	16 17	+60	130	17 17	+60	130	18 17	+60	130	19 17	+60	130	20 17	+60	130
52	16 14	60	128	17 14	60	128	18 14	59	128	19 13	60	128	20 13	60	127
54	16 10	60	126	17 10	60	126	18 10	60	126	19 10	60	126	20 10	60	125
56	16 07	60	124	17 07	60	124	18 07	60	124	19 07	60	123	20 07	60	123
58	16 03	60	122	17 03	60	122	18 03	60	122	19 03	60	121	20 03	60	121
60	16 00	+60	120	17 00	+60	120	18 00	+60	120	19 00	+59	119	19 59	+60	119
62	15 56	60	118	16 56	60	118	17 56	60	117	18 56	60	117	19 56	60	117
64	15 52	60	116	16 52	60	116	17 52	60	115	18 52	60	115	19 52	60	115
66	15 48	60	114	16 48	60	114	17 48	60	113	18 48	60	113	19 48	60	113
68	15 45	59	112	16 44	60	112	17 44	60	111	18 44	60	111	19 44	60	111
70	15 41	+60	110	16 41	+60	109	17 41	+59	109	18 40	+60	109	19 40	+60	109
72	15 37	60	108	16 37	60	107	17 37	60	107	18 37	59	107	19 36	60	107
74	15 33	60	106	16 33	60	105	17 33	59	105	18 32	60	105	19 32	60	105
76	15 29	60	104	16 29	59	103	17 28	60	103	18 28	60	103	19 28	60	103
78	15 24	60	102	16 24	60	101	17 24	60	101	18 24	60	101	19 24	60	101
80	15 20	+60	100	16 20	+60	99	17 20	+60	99	18 20	+60	99	19 20	+60	99
82	15 16	60	98	16 16	60	97	17 16	60	97	18 16	60	97	19 16	60	97
84	15 12	60	96	16 12	60	95	17 12	60	95	18 12	60	95	19 12	60	95
86	15 08	60	94	16 08	60	93	17 08	60	93	18 08	60	93	19 08	60	93
88	15 04	60	92	16 04	60	91	17 04	60	91	18 04	60	91	19 04	59	91
90	14 59	+60	90	15 59	+60	89	16 59	+60	89	17 59	+60	89	18 59	+60	89
92	14 55	60	88	15 55	60	87	16 55	60	87	17 55	60	87	18 55	60	87
94	14 51	60	86	15 51	60	85	16 51	60	85	17 51	60	85	18 51	60	85
96	14 47	60	84	15 47	60	83	16 47	60	83	17 47	60	83	18 47	60	83
98	14 43	60	82	15 43	60	81	16 43	60	81	17 43	60	81	18 43	60	81
100	14 39	+60	80	15 39	+60	79	16 39	+60	79	17 39	+60	79	18 39	+59	79
102	14 35	60	78	15 35	59	77	16 34	60	77	17 34	60	77	18 34	60	77
104	14 30	60	76	15 30	60	76	16 30	60	75	17 30	60	75	18 30	60	75
106	14 26	60	74	15 26	60	74	16 26	60	73	17 26	60	73	18 26	60	73
108	14 22	60	72	15 22	60	72	16 22	60	71	17 22	60	71	18 22	60	71
110	14 19	+59	70	15 18	+60	70	16 18	+60	69	17 18	+60	69	18 18	+60	69
112	14 15	60	68	15 15	60	68	16 15	60	67	17 15	59	67	18 14	60	67
114	14 11	60	66	15 11	60	66	16 11	60	66	17 11	60	65	18 11	60	65
116	14 07	60	64	15 07	60	64	16 07	60	64	17 07	60	63	18 07	60	63
118	14 03	60	62	15 03	60	62	16 03	60	62	17 03	60	61	18 03	60	61
120	14 00	+60	60	15 00	+60	60	16 00	+60	60	17 00	+60	60	18 00	+59	59
122	13 56	60	58	14 56	60	58	15 56	60	58	16 56	60	58	17 56	60	57
124	13 53	60	56	14 53	60	56	15 53	59	56	16 52	60	56	17 52	60	55
126	13 49	60	54	14 49	60	54	15 49	60	54	16 49	60	54	17 49	60	54
128	13 46	60	52	14 46	60	52	15 46	60	52	16 46	60	52	17 46	60	52
130	13 43	+60	50	14 43	+60	50	15 43	+60	50	16 43	+60	50	17 43	+59	50
132	13 39	60	48	14 39	60	48	15 39	60	48	16 39	60	48	17 39	60	48
134	13 36	60	46	14 36	60	46	15 36	60	46	16 36	60	46	17 36	60	46
136	13 33	60	44	14 33	60	44	15 33	60	44	16 33	60	44	17 33	60	44
138	13 31	60	42	14 31	60	42	15 31	60	42	16 31	60	42	17 31	60	42

LHA	20°			21°			22°			23°			24°		
	Hc	d	Z	Hc	d	Z	Hc	d	Z	Hc	d	Z	Hc	d	Z
	° ′	′	°	° ′	′	°	° ′	′	°	° ′	′	°	° ′	′	°
0	22 00	+60	180	23 00	+60	180	24 00	+60	180	25 00	+60	180	26 00	+60	180
2	22 00	60	178	23 00	60	178	24 00	60	178	25 00	60	178	26 00	60	178
4	22 00	60	176	23 00	60	176	24 00	60	176	25 00	60	176	26 00	60	176
6	21 59	60	174	22 59	60	174	23 59	60	174	24 59	60	174	25 59	60	174
8	21 59	60	172	22 59	60	172	23 59	60	172	24 59	60	172	25 59	60	172
10	21 58	+60	170	22 58	+60	170	23 58	+60	170	24 58	+60	170	25 58	+60	170
12	21 57	60	168	22 57	60	168	23 57	60	168	24 57	60	168	25 57	60	168
14	21 56	60	166	22 56	60	166	23 56	60	166	24 56	60	166	25 56	60	166
16	21 55	60	164	22 55	60	164	23 55	60	164	24 55	60	164	25 55	60	164
18	21 54	60	162	22 54	60	162	23 54	60	162	24 54	60	162	25 54	60	162
20	21 53	+60	160	22 53	+60	160	23 53	+60	160	24 53	+60	160	25 53	+60	160
22	21 51	60	158	22 51	60	158	23 51	60	158	24 51	60	158	25 51	60	158
24	21 50	60	156	22 50	60	156	23 50	60	156	24 50	60	156	25 50	60	156
26	21 48	60	154	22 48	60	154	23 48	60	154	24 48	60	154	25 48	60	154
28	21 46	60	152	22 46	60	152	23 46	60	152	24 46	60	152	25 46	60	152
30	21 44	+60	150	22 44	+60	150	23 44	+60	150	24 44	+60	150	25 44	+60	150
32	21 42	60	148	22 42	60	148	23 42	60	148	24 42	60	148	25 42	60	148
34	21 39	60	146	22 39	60	146	23 39	60	146	24 39	60	146	25 39	60	146
36	21 37	60	144	22 37	60	144	23 37	60	144	24 37	60	144	25 37	60	144
38	21 34	60	142	22 34	60	142	23 34	60	142	24 34	60	142	25 34	60	141
40	21 32	+60	140	22 32	+60	140	23 32	+60	140	24 32	+60	139	25 32	+60	139
42	21 29	60	138	22 29	60	138	23 29	60	137	24 29	60	137	25 29	60	137
44	21 26	60	136	22 26	60	135	23 26	60	135	24 26	60	135	25 26	60	135
46	21 23	60	134	22 23	60	133	23 23	60	133	24 23	60	133	25 23	60	133
48	21 20	60	131	22 20	60	131	23 20	60	131	24 20	60	131	25 20	60	131
50	21 17	+60	129	22 17	+60	129	23 17	+60	129	24 17	+60	129	25 17	+60	129
52	21 13	60	127	22 13	60	127	23 13	60	127	24 13	60	127	25 13	60	127
54	21 10	60	125	22 10	60	125	23 10	60	125	24 10	60	125	25 10	60	125
56	21 07	60	123	22 07	60	123	23 07	60	123	24 07	59	123	25 06	60	123
58	21 03	60	121	22 03	60	121	23 03	60	121	24 03	60	121	25 03	60	121
60	20 59	+60	119	21 59	+60	119	22 59	+60	119	23 59	+60	119	24 59	+60	119
62	20 56	60	117	21 56	60	117	22 56	60	117	23 56	60	117	24 56	60	117
64	20 52	60	115	21 52	60	115	22 52	60	115	23 52	60	115	24 52	60	115
66	20 48	60	113	21 48	60	113	22 48	60	113	23 48	60	113	24 48	60	113
68	20 44	60	111	21 44	60	111	22 44	60	111	23 44	60	111	24 44	60	111
70	20 40	+60	109	21 40	+60	109	22 40	+60	109	23 40	+60	109	24 40	+60	109
72	20 36	60	107	21 36	60	107	22 36	60	107	23 36	60	107	24 36	60	107
74	20 32	60	105	21 32	60	105	22 32	60	105	23 32	60	105	24 32	60	105
76	20 28	60	103	21 28	60	103	22 28	60	103	23 28	60	103	24 28	60	103
78	20 24	60	101	21 24	60	101	22 24	60	101	23 24	60	101	24 24	60	101
80	20 20	+60	99	21 20	+60	99	22 20	+60	99	23 20	+60	99	24 20	+60	99
82	20 16	60	97	21 16	60	97	22 16	60	97	23 16	60	97	24 16	60	97
84	20 12	60	95	21 12	60	95	22 12	60	95	23 12	60	95	24 12	60	95
86	20 08	60	93	21 08	60	93	22 08	60	93	23 08	59	93	24 07	60	93
88	20 03	60	91	21 03	60	91	22 03	60	91	23 03	60	91	24 03	60	91
90	19 59	+60	89	20 59	+60	89	21 59	+60	89	22 59	+60	89	23 59	+60	89
92	19 55	60	87	20 55	60	87	21 55	60	87	22 55	60	87	23 55	60	87
94	19 51	60	85	20 51	60	85	21 51	60	85	22 51	60	85	23 51	60	85
96	19 47	60	83	20 47	60	83	21 47	60	83	22 47	60	83	23 47	60	83
98	19 43	60	81	20 43	60	81	21 43	59	81	22 42	60	81	23 42	60	81
100	19 38	+60	79	20 38	+60	79	21 38	+60	79	22 38	+60	79	23 38	+60	79
102	19 34	60	77	20 34	60	77	21 34	60	77	22 34	60	77	23 34	60	77
104	19 30	60	75	20 30	60	75	21 30	60	75	22 30	60	75	23 30	60	75
106	19 26	60	73	20 26	60	73	21 26	60	73	22 26	60	73	23 26	60	73
108	19 22	60	71	20 22	60	71	21 22	60	71	22 22	60	71	23 22	60	71
110	19 18	+60	69	20 18	+60	69	21 18	+60	69	22 18	+60	69	23 18	+60	69
112	19 14	60	67	20 14	60	67	21 14	60	67	22 14	60	67	23 14	60	67
114	19 11	60	65	20 11	60	65	21 11	60	65	22 11	59	65	23 10	60	65
116	19 07	60	63	20 07	60	63	21 07	60	63	22 07	60	63	23 07	60	63
118	19 03	60	61	20 03	60	61	21 03	60	61	22 03	60	61	23 03	60	61
120	18 59	+60	59	19 59	+60	59	20 59	+60	59	21 59	+60	59	22 59	+60	59
122	18 56	60	57	19 56	60	57	20 56	60	57	21 56	60	57	22 56	60	57
124	18 52	60	55	19 52	60	55	20 52	60	55	21 52	60	55	22 52	60	55
126	18 49	60	53	19 49	60	53	20 49	60	53	21 49	60	53	22 49	60	53
128	18 46	60	51	19 46	60	51	20 46	60	51	21 46	60	51	22 46	60	51
130	18 42	+60	50	19 42	+60	49	20 42	+60	49	21 42	+60	49	22 42	+60	49
132	18 39	60	48	19 39	60	48	20 39	60	47	21 39	60	47	22 39	60	47
134	18 36	60	46	19 36	60	46	20 36	60	45	21 36	60	45	22 36	60	45
136	18 33	60	44	19 33	60	44	20 33	60	44	21 33	60	44	22 33	60	43
138	18 31	60	42	19 31	60	42	20 31	59	42	21 30	60	42	22 30	60	41

25°			26°			27°			28°			29°			LHA
Hc	d	Z	Hc	d	Z	Hc	d	Z	Hc	d	Z	Hc	d	Z	
° ′	′	°	° ′	′	°	° ′	′	°	° ′	′	°	° ′	′	°	
27 00	+60	180	28 00	+60	180	29 00	+60	180	30 00	+60	180	31 00	+60	180	360
27 00	60	178	28 00	60	178	29 00	60	178	30 00	60	178	31 00	60	178	358
27 00	60	176	28 00	60	176	29 00	60	176	30 00	60	176	31 00	60	176	356
26 59	60	174	27 59	60	174	28 59	60	174	29 59	60	174	30 59	60	174	354
26 59	60	172	27 59	60	172	28 59	60	172	29 59	60	172	30 59	60	172	352
26 58	+60	170	27 58	+60	170	28 58	+60	170	29 58	+60	170	30 58	+60	170	350
26 57	60	168	27 57	60	168	28 57	60	168	29 57	60	168	30 57	60	168	348
26 56	60	166	27 56	60	166	28 56	60	166	29 56	60	166	30 56	60	166	346
26 55	60	164	27 55	60	164	28 55	60	164	29 55	60	164	30 55	60	164	344
26 54	60	162	27 54	60	162	28 54	60	162	29 54	60	162	30 54	60	162	342
26 53	+60	160	27 53	+60	160	28 53	+60	160	29 53	+60	160	30 53	+60	160	340
26 51	60	158	27 51	60	158	28 51	60	158	29 51	60	158	30 51	60	158	338
26 50	59	156	27 49	60	156	28 49	60	156	29 49	60	156	30 49	60	156	336
26 48	60	154	27 48	60	154	28 48	60	154	29 48	60	154	30 48	60	154	334
26 46	60	152	27 46	60	152	28 46	60	152	29 46	60	152	30 46	60	152	332
26 44	+60	150	27 44	+60	150	28 44	+60	150	29 44	+60	149	30 44	+60	149	330
26 42	60	148	27 42	60	148	28 42	59	147	29 41	60	147	30 41	60	147	328
26 39	60	146	27 39	60	145	28 39	60	145	29 39	60	145	30 39	60	145	326
26 37	60	143	27 37	60	143	28 37	60	143	29 37	60	143	30 37	60	143	324
26 34	60	141	27 34	60	141	28 34	60	141	29 34	60	141	30 34	60	141	322
26 32	+60	139	27 32	+60	139	28 32	+59	139	29 31	+60	139	30 31	+60	139	320
26 29	60	137	27 29	60	137	28 29	60	137	29 29	60	137	30 29	60	137	318
26 26	60	135	27 26	60	135	28 26	60	135	29 26	60	135	30 26	60	135	316
26 23	60	133	27 23	60	133	28 23	60	133	29 23	60	133	30 23	60	133	314
26 20	60	131	27 20	60	131	28 20	60	131	29 20	60	131	30 20	60	131	312
26 17	+60	129	27 17	+60	129	28 17	+60	129	29 17	+59	129	30 16	+60	129	310
26 13	60	127	27 13	60	127	28 13	60	127	29 13	60	127	30 13	60	127	308
26 10	60	125	27 10	60	125	28 10	60	125	29 10	60	125	30 10	60	125	306
26 06	60	123	27 06	60	123	28 06	60	123	29 06	60	123	30 06	60	123	304
26 03	60	121	27 03	60	121	28 03	60	121	29 03	60	121	30 03	60	121	302
25 59	+60	119	26 59	+60	119	27 59	+60	119	28 59	+60	119	29 59	+60	119	300
25 56	60	117	26 56	60	117	27 56	60	117	28 56	59	117	29 55	60	117	298
25 52	60	115	26 52	60	115	27 52	60	115	28 52	60	115	29 52	60	115	296
25 48	60	113	26 48	60	113	27 48	60	113	28 48	60	113	29 48	60	113	294
25 44	60	111	26 44	60	111	27 44	60	111	28 44	60	111	29 44	60	111	292
25 40	+60	109	26 40	+60	109	27 40	+60	109	28 40	+60	109	29 40	+60	109	290
25 36	60	107	26 36	60	107	27 36	60	107	28 36	60	107	29 36	60	107	288
25 32	60	105	26 32	60	105	27 32	60	105	28 32	60	105	29 32	60	105	286
25 28	60	103	26 28	60	103	27 28	60	103	28 28	60	103	29 28	60	103	284
25 24	60	101	26 24	60	101	27 24	60	101	28 24	60	101	29 24	60	101	282
25 20	+60	99	26 20	+60	99	27 20	+60	99	28 20	+60	99	29 20	+60	99	280
25 16	60	97	26 16	60	97	27 16	60	97	28 16	60	97	29 16	60	97	278
25 12	60	95	26 12	60	95	27 12	59	95	28 11	60	95	29 11	60	95	276
25 07	60	93	26 07	60	93	27 07	60	93	28 07	60	93	29 07	60	93	274
25 03	60	91	26 03	60	91	27 03	60	91	28 03	60	91	29 03	60	91	272
24 59	+60	89	25 59	+60	89	26 59	+60	89	27 59	+60	89	28 59	+60	89	270
24 55	60	87	25 55	60	87	26 55	60	87	27 55	60	87	28 55	60	87	268
24 51	60	85	25 51	60	85	26 51	60	85	27 51	60	85	28 51	59	85	266
24 47	60	83	25 47	59	83	26 46	60	83	27 46	60	83	28 46	60	83	264
24 42	60	81	25 42	60	81	26 42	60	81	27 42	60	81	28 42	60	81	262
24 38	+60	79	25 38	+60	79	26 38	+60	79	27 38	+60	79	28 38	+60	79	260
24 34	60	77	25 34	60	77	26 34	60	77	27 34	60	77	28 34	60	77	258
24 30	60	75	25 30	60	75	26 30	60	75	27 30	60	75	28 30	60	75	256
24 26	60	73	25 26	60	73	26 26	60	73	27 26	60	73	28 26	60	73	254
24 22	60	71	25 22	60	71	26 22	60	71	27 22	60	71	28 22	60	71	252
24 18	+60	69	25 18	+60	69	26 18	+60	69	27 18	+60	69	28 18	+60	69	250
24 14	60	67	25 14	60	67	26 14	60	67	27 14	60	67	28 14	60	67	248
24 10	60	65	25 10	60	65	26 10	60	65	27 10	60	65	28 10	60	65	246
24 07	60	63	25 07	60	63	26 07	60	63	27 07	60	63	28 07	59	63	244
24 03	60	61	25 03	60	61	26 03	60	61	27 03	60	61	28 03	60	61	242
23 59	+60	59	24 59	+60	59	25 59	+60	59	26 59	+60	59	27 59	+60	59	240
23 56	60	57	24 56	60	57	25 56	60	57	26 56	60	57	27 56	60	57	238
23 52	60	55	24 52	60	55	25 52	60	55	26 52	60	55	27 52	60	55	236
23 49	60	53	24 49	60	53	25 49	60	53	26 49	60	53	27 49	60	53	234
23 46	60	51	24 46	60	51	25 46	59	51	26 45	60	51	27 45	60	51	232
23 42	+60	49	24 42	+60	49	25 42	+60	49	26 42	+60	49	27 42	+60	49	230
23 39	60	47	24 39	60	47	25 39	60	47	26 39	60	47	27 39	60	47	228
23 36	60	45	24 36	60	45	25 36	60	45	26 36	60	45	27 36	60	45	226
23 33	60	43	24 33	60	43	25 33	60	43	26 33	60	43	27 33	60	43	224
23 30	60	41	24 30	60	41	25 30	60	41	26 30	60	41	27 30	60	41	222

S. Lat. {LHA greater than 180°....... Zn=180−Z; LHA less than 180°........... Zn=180+Z}

DECLINATION (15°-29°) SAME NAME AS LATITUDE

LAT 88°

N. Lat. {LHA greater than 180°....... Zn=Z; LHA less than 180°........... Zn=360−Z}

DECLINATION (15°-29°) SAME NAME AS LATITUDE

LHA	15°			16°			17°			18°			19°		
LHA	Hc	d	Z	Hc	d	Z	Hc	d	Z	Hc	d	Z	Hc	d	Z
	° ′	′	°	° ′	′	°	° ′	′	°	° ′	′	°	° ′	′	°
140	13 28	+60	40	14 28	+60	40	15 28	+60	40	16 28	+60	40	17 28	+60	40
142	13 25	60	38	14 25	60	38	15 25	60	38	16 25	60	38	17 25	60	38
144	13 23	60	36	14 23	60	36	15 23	60	36	16 23	60	36	17 23	60	36
146	13 20	60	34	14 20	60	34	15 20	60	34	16 20	60	34	17 20	60	34
148	13 18	60	32	14 18	60	32	15 18	60	32	16 18	60	32	17 18	60	32
150	13 16	+60	30	14 16	+60	30	15 16	+60	30	16 16	+60	30	17 16	+60	30
152	13 14	60	28	14 14	60	28	15 14	60	28	16 14	60	28	17 14	60	28
154	13 12	60	26	14 12	60	26	15 12	60	26	16 12	60	26	17 12	60	26
156	13 10	60	24	14 10	60	24	15 10	60	24	16 10	60	24	17 10	60	24
158	13 09	60	22	14 09	60	22	15 09	60	22	16 09	60	22	17 09	60	22
160	13 07	+60	20	14 07	+60	20	15 07	+60	20	16 07	+60	20	17 07	+60	20
162	13 06	60	18	14 06	60	18	15 06	60	18	16 06	60	18	17 06	60	18
164	13 05	60	16	14 05	60	16	15 05	60	16	16 05	60	16	17 05	60	16
166	13 04	60	14	14 04	60	14	15 04	60	14	16 04	60	14	17 04	60	14
168	13 03	60	12	14 03	60	12	15 03	60	12	16 03	60	12	17 03	60	12
170	13 02	+60	10	14 02	+60	10	15 02	+60	10	16 02	+60	10	17 02	+60	10
172	13 01	60	8	14 01	60	8	15 01	60	8	16 01	60	8	17 01	60	8
174	13 01	60	6	14 01	60	6	15 01	60	6	16 01	60	6	17 01	60	6
176	13 00	60	4	14 00	60	4	15 00	60	4	16 00	60	4	17 00	60	4
178	13 00	60	2	14 00	60	2	15 00	60	2	16 00	60	2	17 00	60	2
180	13 00	+60	0	14 00	+60	0	15 00	+60	0	16 00	+60	0	17 00	+60	0

LHA	20°			21°			22°			23°			24°		
LHA	Hc	d	Z	Hc	d	Z	Hc	d	Z	Hc	d	Z	Hc	d	Z
	° ′	′	°	° ′	′	°	° ′	′	°	° ′	′	°	° ′	′	°
140	18 28	+60	40	19 28	+60	40	20 28	+60	40	21 28	+60	40	22 28	+60	40
142	18 25	60	38	19 25	60	38	20 25	60	38	21 25	60	38	22 25	60	38
144	18 23	60	36	19 23	60	36	20 23	60	36	21 23	60	36	22 23	60	36
146	18 20	60	34	19 20	60	34	20 20	60	34	21 20	60	34	22 20	60	34
148	18 18	60	32	19 18	60	32	20 18	60	32	21 18	60	32	22 18	60	32
150	18 16	+60	30	19 16	+60	30	20 16	+60	30	21 16	+60	30	22 16	+60	30
152	18 14	60	28	19 14	60	28	20 14	60	28	21 14	60	28	22 14	60	28
154	18 12	60	26	19 12	60	26	20 12	60	26	21 12	60	26	22 12	60	26
156	18 10	60	24	19 10	60	24	20 10	60	24	21 10	60	24	22 10	60	24
158	18 09	60	22	19 09	60	22	20 09	60	22	21 09	60	22	22 09	60	22
160	18 07	+60	20	19 07	+60	20	20 07	+60	20	21 07	+60	20	22 07	+60	20
162	18 06	60	18	19 06	60	18	20 06	60	18	21 06	60	18	22 06	60	18
164	18 05	60	16	19 05	60	16	20 05	60	16	21 05	60	16	22 05	60	16
166	18 04	60	14	19 04	60	14	20 04	60	14	21 04	60	14	22 04	60	14
168	18 03	60	12	19 03	60	12	20 03	60	12	21 03	60	12	22 03	60	12
170	18 02	+60	10	19 02	+60	10	20 02	+60	10	21 02	+60	10	22 02	+60	10
172	18 01	60	8	19 01	60	8	20 01	60	8	21 01	60	8	22 01	60	8
174	18 01	60	6	19 01	60	6	20 01	60	6	21 01	60	6	22 01	60	6
176	18 00	60	4	19 00	60	4	20 00	60	4	21 00	60	4	22 00	60	4
178	18 00	60	2	19 00	60	2	20 00	60	2	21 00	60	2	22 00	60	2
180	18 00	+60	0	19 00	+60	0	20 00	+60	0	21 00	+60	0	22 00	+60	0

LHA	25°			26°			27°			28°			29°			LHA
LHA	Hc	d	Z	Hc	d	Z	Hc	d	Z	Hc	d	Z	Hc	d	Z	LHA
	° ′	′	°	° ′	′	°	° ′	′	°	° ′	′	°	° ′	′	°	
140	23 28	+60	39	24 28	+60	39	25 28	+60	39	26 28	+60	39	27 28	+60	39	220
142	23 25	60	37	24 25	60	37	25 25	60	37	26 25	60	37	27 25	60	37	218
144	23 23	60	36	24 23	60	36	25 23	60	35	26 23	60	35	27 23	60	35	216
146	23 20	60	34	24 20	60	34	25 20	60	34	26 20	60	33	27 20	60	33	214
148	23 18	60	32	24 18	60	32	25 18	60	32	26 18	60	32	27 18	60	31	212
150	23 16	+60	30	24 16	+60	30	25 16	+60	30	26 16	+60	30	27 16	+60	30	210
152	23 14	60	28	24 14	60	28	25 14	60	28	26 14	60	28	27 14	60	28	208
154	23 12	60	26	24 12	60	26	25 12	60	26	26 12	60	26	27 12	60	26	206
156	23 10	60	24	24 10	60	24	25 10	60	24	26 10	60	24	27 10	60	24	204
158	23 09	60	22	24 09	60	22	25 09	60	22	26 09	60	22	27 09	60	22	202
160	23 07	+60	20	24 07	+60	20	25 07	+60	20	26 07	+60	20	27 07	+60	20	200
162	23 06	60	18	24 06	60	18	25 06	60	18	26 06	60	18	27 06	60	18	198
164	23 05	60	16	24 05	60	16	25 05	60	16	26 05	60	16	27 05	60	16	196
166	23 04	60	14	24 04	60	14	25 04	60	14	26 04	60	14	27 04	60	14	194
168	23 03	60	12	24 03	60	12	25 03	60	12	26 03	60	12	27 03	60	12	192
170	23 02	+60	10	24 02	+60	10	25 02	+60	10	26 02	+60	10	27 02	+60	10	190
172	23 01	60	8	24 01	60	8	25 01	60	8	26 01	60	8	27 01	60	8	188
174	23 01	60	6	24 01	60	6	25 01	60	6	26 01	60	6	27 01	60	6	186
176	23 00	60	4	24 00	60	4	25 00	60	4	26 00	60	4	27 00	60	4	184
178	23 00	60	2	24 00	60	2	25 00	60	2	26 00	60	2	27 00	60	2	182
180	23 00	+60	0	24 00	+60	0	25 00	+60	0	26 00	+60	0	27 00	+60	0	180

LAT 88°

15° 16° 17° 18° 19° 20° 21° 22° 23° 24° 25° 26° 27° 28° 29°

S. Lat. {LHA greater than 180° ...... Zn=180−Z; LHA less than 180°........... Zn=180+Z}

DECLINATION (15°-29°) SAME NAME AS LATITUDE

LAT 88°

N. Lat. {LHA greater than 180°....... Zn=Z
{LHA less than 180°.......... Zn=360−Z

DECLINATION (0°-14°) SAME NAME AS LATITUDE

LHA	0° Hc	d	Z	1° Hc	d	Z	2° Hc	d	Z	3° Hc	d	Z	4° Hc	d	Z	LHA
	° '	'	°	° '	'	°	° '	'	°	° '	'	°	° '	'	°	
0	01 00	+60	180	02 00	+60	180	03 00	+60	180	04 00	+60	180	05 00	+60	180	360
2	01 00	60	178	02 00	60	178	03 00	60	178	04 00	60	178	05 00	60	178	358
4	01 00	60	176	02 00	60	176	03 00	60	176	04 00	60	176	05 00	60	176	356
6	01 00	60	174	02 00	60	174	03 00	60	174	04 00	60	174	05 00	60	174	354
8	00 59	60	172	01 59	60	172	02 59	60	172	03 59	60	172	04 59	60	172	352
10	00 59	+60	170	01 59	+60	170	02 59	+60	170	03 59	+60	170	04 59	+60	170	350
12	00 59	60	168	01 59	60	168	02 59	60	168	03 59	60	168	04 59	60	168	348
14	00 58	60	166	01 58	60	166	02 58	60	166	03 58	60	166	04 58	60	166	346
16	00 58	60	164	01 58	60	164	02 58	60	164	03 58	60	164	04 58	60	164	344
18	00 57	60	162	01 57	60	162	02 57	60	162	03 57	60	162	04 57	60	162	342
20	00 56	+60	160	01 56	+60	160	02 56	+60	160	03 56	+60	160	04 56	+60	160	340
22	00 56	60	158	01 56	60	158	02 56	60	158	03 56	60	158	04 56	60	158	338
24	00 55	60	156	01 55	60	156	02 55	60	156	03 55	60	156	04 55	60	156	336
26	00 54	60	154	01 54	60	154	02 54	60	154	03 54	60	154	04 54	60	154	334
28	00 53	60	152	01 53	60	152	02 53	60	152	03 53	60	152	04 53	60	152	332
30	00 52	+60	150	01 52	+60	150	02 52	+60	150	03 52	+60	150	04 52	+60	150	330
32	00 51	60	148	01 51	60	148	02 51	60	148	03 51	60	148	04 51	60	148	328
34	00 50	60	146	01 50	60	146	02 50	60	146	03 50	60	146	04 50	60	146	326
36	00 49	60	144	01 49	60	144	02 49	60	144	03 49	60	144	04 49	60	144	324
38	00 47	60	142	01 47	60	142	02 47	60	142	03 47	60	142	04 47	60	142	322
40	00 46	+60	140	01 46	+60	140	02 46	+60	140	03 46	+60	140	04 46	+60	140	320
42	00 45	60	138	01 45	60	138	02 45	60	138	03 45	60	138	04 45	60	138	318
44	00 43	60	136	01 43	60	136	02 43	60	136	03 43	60	136	04 43	60	136	316
46	00 42	60	134	01 42	60	134	02 42	60	134	03 42	60	134	04 42	60	134	314
48	00 40	60	132	01 40	60	132	02 40	60	132	03 40	60	132	04 40	60	132	312
50	00 39	+60	130	01 39	+60	130	02 39	+60	130	03 39	+60	130	04 39	+60	130	310
52	00 37	60	128	01 37	60	128	02 37	60	128	03 37	60	128	04 37	60	128	308
54	00 35	60	126	01 35	60	126	02 35	60	126	03 35	60	126	04 35	60	126	306
56	00 34	60	124	01 34	60	124	02 34	60	124	03 34	60	124	04 34	60	124	304
58	00 32	60	122	01 32	60	122	02 32	60	122	03 32	60	122	04 32	60	122	302
60	00 30	+60	120	01 30	+60	120	02 30	+60	120	03 30	+60	120	04 30	+60	120	300
62	00 28	60	118	01 28	60	118	02 28	60	118	03 28	60	118	04 28	60	118	298
64	00 26	60	116	01 26	60	116	02 26	60	116	03 26	60	116	04 26	60	116	296
66	00 24	60	114	01 24	60	114	02 24	60	114	03 24	60	114	04 24	60	114	294
68	00 22	60	112	01 22	60	112	02 22	60	112	03 22	60	112	04 22	60	112	292
70	00 21	+60	110	01 21	+60	110	02 21	+60	110	03 21	+60	110	04 21	+60	110	290
72	00 19	60	108	01 19	60	108	02 19	60	108	03 19	60	108	04 19	60	108	288
74	00 17	60	106	01 17	60	106	02 17	60	106	03 17	60	106	04 17	60	106	286
76	00 15	60	104	01 15	59	104	02 14	60	104	03 14	60	104	04 14	60	104	284
78	00 12	60	102	01 12	60	102	02 12	60	102	03 12	60	102	04 12	60	102	282
80	00 10	+60	100	01 10	+60	100	02 10	+60	100	03 10	+60	100	04 10	+60	100	280
82	00 08	60	98	01 08	60	98	02 08	60	98	03 08	60	98	04 08	60	98	278
84	00 06	60	96	01 06	60	96	02 06	60	96	03 06	60	96	04 06	60	96	276
86	00 04	60	94	01 04	60	94	02 04	60	94	03 04	60	94	04 04	60	94	274
88	00 02	60	92	01 02	60	92	02 02	60	92	03 02	60	92	04 02	60	92	272
90	00 00	+60	90	01 00	+60	90	02 00	+60	90	03 00	+60	90	04 00	+60	90	270
92	-0 02	60	88	00 58	60	88	01 58	60	88	02 58	60	88	03 58	60	88	268
94	-0 04	60	86	00 56	60	86	01 56	60	86	02 56	60	86	03 56	60	86	266
96	-0 06	60	84	00 54	60	84	01 54	60	84	02 54	60	84	03 54	60	84	264
98	-0 08	60	82	00 52	60	82	01 52	60	82	02 52	60	82	03 52	60	82	262
100	-0 10	+60	80	00 50	+60	80	01 50	+60	80	02 50	+60	80	03 50	+60	80	260
102	-0 12	60	78	00 48	60	78	01 48	60	78	02 48	60	78	03 48	60	78	258
104	-0 15	60	76	00 45	60	76	01 45	60	76	02 45	60	76	03 45	60	76	256
106	-0 17	60	74	00 43	60	74	01 43	60	74	02 43	60	74	03 43	60	74	254
108	-0 19	60	72	00 41	60	72	01 41	60	72	02 41	60	72	03 41	60	72	252
110	-0 21	+60	70	00 39	+60	70	01 39	+60	70	02 39	+60	70	03 39	+60	70	250
112	-0 22	60	68	00 38	60	68	01 38	60	68	02 38	60	68	03 38	60	68	248
114	-0 24	60	66	00 36	60	66	01 36	60	66	02 36	60	66	03 36	60	66	246
116	-0 26	60	64	00 34	60	64	01 34	60	64	02 34	60	64	03 34	60	64	244
118	-0 28	60	62	00 32	60	62	01 32	60	62	02 32	60	62	03 32	60	62	242
120	-0 30	+60	60	00 30	+60	60	01 30	+60	60	02 30	+60	60	03 30	+60	60	240
122	-0 32	60	58	00 28	60	58	01 28	60	58	02 28	60	58	03 28	60	58	238
124	-0 34	60	56	00 26	60	56	01 26	60	56	02 26	60	56	03 26	60	56	236
126	-0 35	60	54	00 25	60	54	01 25	60	54	02 25	60	54	03 25	60	54	234
128	-0 37	60	52	00 23	60	52	01 23	60	52	02 23	60	52	03 23	60	52	232
130	-0 39	+60	50	00 21	+60	50	01 21	+60	50	02 21	+60	50	03 21	+60	50	230
132	-0 40	60	48	00 20	60	48	01 20	60	48	02 20	60	48	03 20	60	48	228
134	-0 42	60	46	00 18	60	46	01 18	60	46	02 18	60	46	03 18	60	46	226
136	-0 43	60	44	00 17	60	44	01 17	60	44	02 17	60	44	03 17	60	44	224
138	-0 45	60	42	00 15	60	42	01 15	60	42	02 15	60	42	03 15	60	42	222

LHA	5° Hc	d	Z	6° Hc	d	Z	7° Hc	d	Z	8° Hc	d	Z	9° Hc	d	Z	LHA
	° '	'	°	° '	'	°	° '	'	°	° '	'	°	° '	'	°	
0	06 00	+60	180	07 00	+60	180	08 00	+60	180	09 00	+60	180	10 00	+60	180	360
2	06 00	60	178	07 00	60	178	08 00	60	178	09 00	60	178	10 00	60	178	358
4	06 00	60	176	07 00	60	176	08 00	60	176	09 00	60	176	10 00	60	176	356
6	06 00	60	174	07 00	60	174	08 00	60	174	09 00	60	174	10 00	60	174	354
8	05 59	60	172	06 59	60	172	07 59	60	172	08 59	60	172	09 59	60	172	352
10	05 59	+60	170	06 59	+60	170	07 59	+60	170	08 59	+60	170	09 59	+60	170	350
12	05 59	60	168	06 59	60	168	07 59	60	168	08 59	60	168	09 59	60	168	348
14	05 58	60	166	06 58	60	166	07 58	60	166	08 58	60	166	09 58	60	166	346
16	05 58	60	164	06 58	60	164	07 58	60	164	08 58	60	164	09 58	60	164	344
18	05 57	60	162	06 57	60	162	07 57	60	162	08 57	60	162	09 57	60	162	342
20	05 56	+60	160	06 56	+60	160	07 56	+60	160	08 56	+60	160	09 56	+60	160	340
22	05 56	60	158	06 56	60	158	07 56	60	158	08 56	60	158	09 56	60	158	338
24	05 55	60	156	06 55	60	156	07 55	60	156	08 55	60	156	09 55	60	156	336
26	05 54	60	154	06 54	60	154	07 54	60	154	08 54	60	154	09 54	60	154	334
28	05 53	60	152	06 53	60	152	07 53	60	152	08 53	60	152	09 53	60	152	332
30	05 52	+60	150	06 52	+60	150	07 52	+60	150	08 52	+60	150	09 52	+60	150	330
32	05 51	60	148	06 51	60	148	07 51	60	148	08 51	60	148	09 51	60	148	328
34	05 50	60	146	06 50	60	146	07 50	60	146	08 50	60	146	09 50	60	146	326
36	05 49	60	144	06 49	60	144	07 49	60	144	08 49	60	144	09 49	60	144	324
38	05 47	60	142	06 47	60	142	07 47	60	142	08 47	60	142	09 47	60	142	322
40	05 46	+60	140	06 46	+60	140	07 46	+60	140	08 46	+60	140	09 46	+60	140	320
42	05 45	60	138	06 45	60	138	07 45	60	138	08 45	60	138	09 45	60	138	318
44	05 43	60	136	06 43	60	136	07 43	60	136	08 43	60	136	09 43	60	136	316
46	05 42	60	134	06 42	60	134	07 42	60	134	08 42	60	134	09 42	60	134	314
48	05 40	60	132	06 40	60	132	07 40	60	132	08 40	60	132	09 40	60	132	312
50	05 39	+60	130	06 39	+60	130	07 39	+60	130	08 39	+60	130	09 39	+60	130	310
52	05 37	60	128	06 37	60	128	07 37	60	128	08 37	60	128	09 37	60	128	308
54	05 35	60	126	06 35	60	126	07 35	60	126	08 35	60	126	09 35	60	126	306
56	05 34	60	124	06 34	60	124	07 34	60	124	08 34	60	124	09 34	60	124	304
58	05 32	60	122	06 32	60	122	07 32	60	122	08 32	60	122	09 32	60	122	302
60	05 30	+60	120	06 30	+60	120	07 30	+60	120	08 30	+60	120	09 30	+60	120	300
62	05 28	60	118	06 28	60	118	07 28	60	118	08 28	60	118	09 28	60	118	298
64	05 26	60	116	06 26	60	116	07 26	60	116	08 26	60	116	09 26	60	116	296
66	05 24	60	114	06 24	60	114	07 24	60	114	08 24	60	114	09 24	60	114	294
68	05 22	60	112	06 22	60	112	07 22	60	112	08 22	60	112	09 22	60	112	292
70	05 21	+60	110	06 21	+60	110	07 21	+60	110	08 21	+59	110	09 20	+60	110	290
72	05 19	60	108	06 19	60	108	07 19	60	108	08 19	60	108	09 19	60	108	288
74	05 17	60	106	06 17	60	106	07 17	60	106	08 17	60	106	09 17	60	106	286
76	05 14	60	104	06 14	60	104	07 14	60	104	08 14	60	104	09 14	60	104	284
78	05 12	60	102	06 12	60	102	07 12	60	102	08 12	60	102	09 12	60	102	282
80	05 10	+60	100	06 10	+60	100	07 10	+60	100	08 10	+60	100	09 10	+60	100	280
82	05 08	60	98	06 08	60	98	07 08	60	98	08 08	60	98	09 08	60	98	278
84	05 06	60	96	06 06	60	96	07 06	60	96	08 06	60	96	09 06	60	96	276
86	05 04	60	94	06 04	60	94	07 04	60	94	08 04	60	94	09 04	60	94	274
88	05 02	60	92	06 02	60	92	07 02	60	92	08 02	60	92	09 02	60	92	272
90	05 00	+60	90	06 00	+60	90	07 00	+60	90	08 00	+60	90	09 00	+60	90	270
92	04 58	60	88	05 58	60	88	06 58	60	88	07 58	60	88	08 58	60	88	268
94	04 56	60	86	05 56	60	86	06 56	60	86	07 56	60	86	08 56	60	86	266
96	04 54	60	84	05 54	60	84	06 54	60	84	07 54	60	84	08 54	60	84	264
98	04 52	60	82	05 52	60	82	06 52	60	82	07 52	60	82	08 52	60	82	262
100	04 50	+60	80	05 50	+60	80	06 50	+60	80	07 50	+60	80	08 50	+60	80	260
102	04 48	60	78	05 48	60	78	06 48	60	78	07 48	59	78	08 47	60	78	258
104	04 45	60	76	05 45	60	76	06 45	60	76	07 45	60	76	08 45	60	76	256
106	04 43	60	74	05 43	60	74	06 43	60	74	07 43	60	74	08 43	60	74	254
108	04 41	60	72	05 41	60	72	06 41	60	72	07 41	60	72	08 41	60	72	252
110	04 39	+60	70	05 39	+60	70	06 39	+60	70	07 39	+60	70	08 39	+60	70	250
112	04 38	60	68	05 38	60	68	06 38	60	68	07 38	60	68	08 38	59	68	248
114	04 36	60	66	05 36	60	66	06 36	60	66	07 36	60	66	08 36	60	66	246
116	04 34	60	64	05 34	60	64	06 34	60	64	07 34	60	64	08 34	60	64	244
118	04 32	60	62	05 32	60	62	06 32	60	62	07 32	60	62	08 32	60	62	242
120	04 30	+60	60	05 30	+60	60	06 30	+60	60	07 30	+60	60	08 30	+60	60	240
122	04 28	60	58	05 28	60	58	06 28	60	58	07 28	60	58	08 28	60	58	238
124	04 26	60	56	05 26	60	56	06 26	60	56	07 26	60	56	08 26	60	56	236
126	04 25	60	54	05 25	60	54	06 25	60	54	07 25	60	54	08 25	60	54	234
128	04 23	60	52	05 23	60	52	06 23	60	52	07 23	60	52	08 23	60	52	232
130	04 21	+60	50	05 21	+60	50	06 21	+60	50	07 21	+60	50	08 21	+60	50	230
132	04 20	60	48	05 20	60	48	06 20	60	48	07 20	60	48	08 20	60	48	228
134	04 18	60	46	05 18	60	46	06 18	60	46	07 18	60	46	08 18	60	46	226
136	04 17	60	44	05 17	60	44	06 17	60	44	07 17	60	44	08 17	60	44	224
138	04 15	60	42	05 15	60	42	06 15	60	42	07 15	60	42	08 15	60	42	222

LHA	10° Hc	d	Z	11° Hc	d	Z	12° Hc	d	Z	13° Hc	d	Z	14° Hc	d	Z	LHA
	° '	'	°	° '	'	°	° '	'	°	° '	'	°	° '	'	°	
0	11 00	+60	180	12 00	+60	180	13 00	+60	180	14 00	+60	180	15 00	+60	180	360
2	11 00	60	178	12 00	60	178	13 00	60	178	14 00	60	178	15 00	60	178	358
4	11 00	60	176	12 00	60	176	13 00	60	176	14 00	60	176	15 00	60	176	356
6	11 00	60	174	12 00	60	174	13 00	60	174	14 00	60	174	15 00	60	174	354
8	10 59	60	172	11 59	60	172	12 59	60	172	13 59	60	172	14 59	60	172	352
10	10 59	+60	170	11 59	+60	170	12 59	+60	170	13 59	+60	170	14 59	+60	170	350
12	10 59	60	168	11 59	60	168	12 59	60	168	13 59	60	168	14 59	60	168	348
14	10 58	60	166	11 58	60	166	12 58	60	166	13 58	60	166	14 58	60	166	346
16	10 58	60	164	11 58	60	164	12 58	60	164	13 58	60	164	14 58	60	164	344
18	10 57	60	162	11 57	60	162	12 57	60	162	13 57	60	162	14 57	60	162	342
20	10 56	+60	160	11 56	+60	160	12 56	+60	160	13 56	+60	160	14 56	+60	160	340
22	10 56	60	158	11 56	60	158	12 56	60	158	13 56	60	158	14 56	60	158	338
24	10 55	60	156	11 55	60	156	12 55	60	156	13 55	60	156	14 55	60	156	336
26	10 54	60	154	11 54	60	154	12 54	60	154	13 54	60	154	14 54	60	154	334
28	10 53	60	152	11 53	60	152	12 53	60	152	13 53	60	152	14 53	60	152	332
30	10 52	+60	150	11 52	+60	150	12 52	+60	150	13 52	+60	150	14 52	+60	150	330
32	10 51	60	148	11 51	60	148	12 51	60	148	13 51	60	148	14 51	60	148	328
34	10 50	60	146	11 50	60	146	12 50	60	146	13 50	60	146	14 50	60	146	326
36	10 49	60	144	11 49	60	144	12 49	60	144	13 49	60	144	14 49	60	144	324
38	10 47	60	142	11 47	60	142	12 47	60	142	13 47	60	142	14 47	60	142	322
40	10 46	+60	140	11 46	+60	140	12 46	+60	140	13 46	+60	140	14 46	+60	140	320
42	10 45	60	138	11 45	60	138	12 45	60	138	13 45	60	138	14 45	60	138	318
44	10 43	60	136	11 43	60	136	12 43	60	136	13 43	60	136	14 43	60	136	316
46	10 42	60	134	11 42	60	134	12 42	60	134	13 42	60	134	14 42	60	134	314
48	10 40	60	132	11 40	60	132	12 40	60	132	13 40	60	132	14 40	60	132	312
50	10 39	+60	130	11 39	+60	130	12 39	+60	130	13 39	+60	130	14 39	+60	130	310
52	10 37	60	128	11 37	60	128	12 37	60	128	13 37	60	128	14 37	60	128	308
54	10 35	60	126	11 35	60	126	12 35	60	126	13 35	60	126	14 35	60	126	306
56	10 34	60	124	11 34	60	124	12 34	60	124	13 34	60	124	14 34	60	124	304
58	10 32	60	122	11 32	60	122	12 32	60	122	13 32	60	122	14 32	60	122	302
60	10 30	+60	120	11 30	+60	120	12 30	+60	120	13 30	+60	120	14 30	+60	120	300
62	10 28	60	118	11 28	60	118	12 28	60	118	13 28	60	118	14 28	60	118	298
64	10 26	60	116	11 26	60	116	12 26	60	116	13 26	60	116	14 26	60	116	296
66	10 24	60	114	11 24	60	114	12 24	60	114	13 24	60	114	14 24	60	114	294
68	10 22	60	112	11 22	60	112	12 22	60	112	13 22	60	112	14 22	60	112	292
70	10 20	+60	110	11 20	+60	110	12 20	+60	110	13 20	+60	110	14 20	+60	110	290
72	10 19	59	108	11 18	60	108	12 18	60	108	13 18	60	108	14 18	60	108	288
74	10 17	59	106	11 16	60	106	12 16	60	106	13 16	60	106	14 16	60	106	286
76	10 14	60	104	11 14	60	104	12 14	60	104	13 14	60	104	14 14	60	104	284
78	10 12	60	102	11 12	60	102	12 12	60	102	13 12	60	102	14 12	60	102	282
80	10 10	+60	100	11 10	+60	100	12 10	+60	100	13 10	+60	100	14 10	+60	100	280
82	10 08	60	98	11 08	60	98	12 08	60	98	13 08	60	98	14 08	60	98	278
84	10 06	60	96	11 06	60	96	12 06	60	96	13 06	60	96	14 06	60	96	276
86	10 04	60	94	11 04	60	94	12 04	60	94	13 04	60	94	14 04	60	94	274
88	10 02	60	92	11 02	60	92	12 02	60	92	13 02	60	92	14 02	60	92	272
90	10 00	+60	90	11 00	+60	90	12 00	+60	90	13 00	+60	90	14 00	+60	90	270
92	09 58	60	88	10 58	60	88	11 58	60	88	12 58	60	88	13 58	60	88	268
94	09 56	60	86	10 56	60	86	11 56	60	86	12 56	60	86	13 56	60	86	266
96	09 54	60	84	10 54	60	84	11 54	60	84	12 54	60	84	13 54	60	84	264
98	09 52	60	82	10 52	60	82	11 52	60	82	12 52	60	82	13 52	60	82	262
100	09 50	+60	80	10 50	+60	80	11 50	+60	80	12 50	+60	80	13 50	+59	80	260
102	09 47	60	78	10 47	60	78	11 47	60	78	12 47	60	78	13 47	60	78	258
104	09 45	60	76	10 45	60	76	11 45	60	76	12 45	60	76	13 45	60	76	256
106	09 43	60	74	10 43	60	74	11 43	60	74	12 43	60	74	13 43	60	74	254
108	09 41	60	72	10 41	60	72	11 41	60	72	12 41	60	72	13 41	60	72	252
110	09 39	+60	70	10 39	+60	70	11 39	+60	70	12 39	+60	70	13 39	+60	70	250
112	09 37	60	68	10 37	60	68	11 37	60	68	12 37	60	68	13 37	60	68	248
114	09 36	60	66	10 36	60	66	11 36	60	66	12 36	60	66	13 36	60	66	246
116	09 34	60	64	10 34	60	64	11 34	60	64	12 34	60	64	13 34	60	64	244
118	09 32	60	62	10 32	60	62	11 32	60	62	12 32	60	62	13 32	60	62	242
120	09 30	+60	60	10 30	+60	60	11 30	+60	60	12 30	+60	60	13 30	+60	60	240
122	09 28	60	58	10 28	60	58	11 28	60	58	12 28	60	58	13 28	60	58	238
124	09 26	60	56	10 26	60	56	11 26	60	56	12 26	60	56	13 26	60	56	236
126	09 25	60	54	10 25	60	54	11 25	60	54	12 25	60	54	13 25	60	54	234
128	09 23	60	52	10 23	60	52	11 23	60	52	12 23	60	52	13 23	60	52	232
130	09 21	+60	50	10 21	+60	50	11 21	+60	50	12 21	+60	50	13 21	+60	50	230
132	09 20	60	48	10 20	60	48	11 20	60	48	12 20	60	48	13 20	60	48	228
134	09 18	60	46	10 18	60	46	11 18	60	46	12 18	60	46	13 18	60	46	226
136	09 17	60	44	10 17	60	44	11 17	60	44	12 17	60	44	13 17	60	44	224
138	09 15	60	42	10 15	60	42	11 15	60	42	12 15	60	42	13 15	60	42	222

S. Lat. {LHA greater than 180°....... Zn=180−Z
{LHA less than 180°.......... Zn=180+Z

DECLINATION (0°-14°) SAME NAME AS LATITUDE

LAT 89°

N. Lat. {LHA greater than 180°....... Zn=Z; LHA less than 180°........... Zn=360−Z}

DECLINATION (0°-14°) SAME NAME AS LATITUDE

LHA	0° Hc	0° d	0° Z	1° Hc	1° d	1° Z	2° Hc	2° d	2° Z	3° Hc	3° d	3° Z	4° Hc	4° d	4° Z	5° Hc	5° d	5° Z	6° Hc	6° d	6° Z	7° Hc	7° d	7° Z
	° ′	′	°	° ′	′	°	° ′	′	°	° ′	′	°	° ′	′	°	° ′	′	°	° ′	′	°	° ′	′	°
140	−0 46	+60	40	00 14	+60	40	01 14	+60	40	02 14	+60	40	03 14	+60	40	04 14	+60	40	05 14	+60	40	06 14	+60	40
142	−0 47	60	38	00 13	60	38	01 13	60	38	02 13	60	38	03 13	60	38	04 13	60	38	05 13	60	38	06 13	60	38
144	−0 49	60	36	00 11	60	36	01 11	60	36	02 11	60	36	03 11	60	36	04 11	60	36	05 11	60	36	06 11	60	36
146	−0 50	60	34	00 10	60	34	01 10	60	34	02 10	60	34	03 10	60	34	04 10	60	34	05 10	60	34	06 10	60	34
148	−0 51	60	32	00 09	60	32	01 09	60	32	02 09	60	32	03 09	60	32	04 09	60	32	05 09	60	32	06 09	60	32
150	−0 52	+60	30	00 08	+60	30	01 08	+60	30	02 08	+60	30	03 08	+60	30	04 08	+60	30	05 08	+60	30	06 08	+60	30
152	−0 53	60	28	00 07	60	28	01 07	60	28	02 07	60	28	03 07	60	28	04 07	60	28	05 07	60	28	06 07	60	28
154	−0 54	60	26	00 06	60	26	01 06	60	26	02 06	60	26	03 06	60	26	04 06	60	26	05 06	60	26	06 06	60	26
156	−0 55	60	24	00 05	60	24	01 05	60	24	02 05	60	24	03 05	60	24	04 05	60	24	05 05	60	24	06 05	60	24
158	−0 56	60	22	00 04	60	22	01 04	60	22	02 04	60	22	03 04	60	22	04 04	60	22	05 04	60	22	06 04	60	22
160	−0 56	+60	20	00 04	+60	20	01 04	+60	20	02 04	+60	20	03 04	+60	20	04 04	+60	20	05 04	+60	20	06 04	+60	20
162	−0 57	60	18	00 03	60	18	01 03	60	18	02 03	60	18	03 03	60	18	04 03	60	18	05 03	60	18	06 03	60	18
164	−0 58	60	16	00 02	60	16	01 02	60	16	02 02	60	16	03 02	60	16	04 02	60	16	05 02	60	16	06 02	60	16
166	−0 58	60	14	00 02	60	14	01 02	60	14	02 02	60	14	03 02	60	14	04 02	60	14	05 02	60	14	06 02	60	14
168	−0 59	60	12	00 01	60	12	01 01	60	12	02 01	60	12	03 01	60	12	04 01	60	12	05 01	60	12	06 01	60	12
170	−0 59	+60	10	00 01	+60	10	01 01	+60	10	02 01	+60	10	03 01	+60	10	04 01	+60	10	05 01	+60	10	06 01	+60	10
172	−0 59	60	8	00 01	60	8	01 01	60	8	02 01	60	8	03 01	60	8	04 01	60	8	05 01	60	8	06 01	60	8
174	−1 00	60	6	00 00	60	6	01 00	60	6	02 00	60	6	03 00	60	6	04 00	60	6	05 00	60	6	06 00	60	6
176	−1 00	60	4	00 00	60	4	01 00	60	4	02 00	60	4	03 00	60	4	04 00	60	4	05 00	60	4	06 00	60	4
178	−1 00	60	2	00 00	60	2	01 00	60	2	02 00	60	2	03 00	60	2	04 00	60	2	05 00	60	2	06 00	60	2
180	−1 00	+60	0	00 00	+60	0	01 00	+60	0	02 00	+60	0	03 00	+60	0	04 00	+60	0	05 00	+60	0	06 00	+60	0

LHA	8° Hc	8° d	8° Z	9° Hc	9° d	9° Z	10° Hc	10° d	10° Z	11° Hc	11° d	11° Z	12° Hc	12° d	12° Z	13° Hc	13° d	13° Z	14° Hc	14° d	14° Z	LHA
	° ′	′	°	° ′	′	°	° ′	′	°	° ′	′	°	° ′	′	°	° ′	′	°	° ′	′	°	
140	07 14	+60	40	08 14	+60	40	09 14	+60	40	10 14	+60	40	11 14	+60	40	12 14	+60	40	13 14	+60	40	220
142	07 13	60	38	08 13	60	38	09 13	60	38	10 13	60	38	11 13	60	38	12 13	60	38	13 13	60	38	218
144	07 11	60	36	08 11	60	36	09 11	60	36	10 11	60	36	11 11	60	36	12 11	60	36	13 11	60	36	216
146	07 10	60	34	08 10	60	34	09 10	60	34	10 10	60	34	11 10	60	34	12 10	60	34	13 10	60	34	214
148	07 09	60	32	08 09	60	32	09 09	60	32	10 09	60	32	11 09	60	32	12 09	60	32	13 09	60	32	212
150	07 08	+60	30	08 08	+60	30	09 08	+60	30	10 08	+60	30	11 08	+60	30	12 08	+60	30	13 08	+60	30	210
152	07 07	60	28	08 07	60	28	09 07	60	28	10 07	60	28	11 07	60	28	12 07	60	28	13 07	60	28	208
154	07 06	60	26	08 06	60	26	09 06	60	26	10 06	60	26	11 06	60	26	12 06	60	26	13 06	60	26	206
156	07 05	60	24	08 05	60	24	09 05	60	24	10 05	60	24	11 05	60	24	12 05	60	24	13 05	60	24	204
158	07 04	60	22	08 04	60	22	09 04	60	22	10 04	60	22	11 04	60	22	12 04	60	22	13 04	60	22	202
160	07 04	+60	20	08 04	+60	20	09 04	+60	20	10 04	+60	20	11 04	+60	20	12 04	+60	20	13 04	+60	20	200
162	07 03	60	18	08 03	60	18	09 03	60	18	10 03	60	18	11 03	60	18	12 03	60	18	13 03	60	18	198
164	07 02	60	16	08 02	60	16	09 02	60	16	10 02	60	16	11 02	60	16	12 02	60	16	13 02	60	16	196
166	07 02	60	14	08 02	60	14	09 02	60	14	10 02	60	14	11 02	60	14	12 02	60	14	13 02	60	14	194
168	07 01	60	12	08 01	60	12	09 01	60	12	10 01	60	12	11 01	60	12	12 01	60	12	13 01	60	12	192
170	07 01	+60	10	08 01	+60	10	09 01	+60	10	10 01	+60	10	11 01	+60	10	12 01	+60	10	13 01	+60	10	190
172	07 01	60	8	08 01	60	8	09 01	60	8	10 01	60	8	11 01	60	8	12 01	60	8	13 01	60	8	188
174	07 00	60	6	08 00	60	6	09 00	60	6	10 00	60	6	11 00	60	6	12 00	60	6	13 00	60	6	186
176	07 00	60	4	08 00	60	4	09 00	60	4	10 00	60	4	11 00	60	4	12 00	60	4	13 00	60	4	184
178	07 00	60	2	08 00	60	2	09 00	60	2	10 00	60	2	11 00	60	2	12 00	60	2	13 00	60	2	182
180	07 00	+60	0	08 00	+60	0	09 00	+60	0	10 00	+60	0	11 00	+60	0	12 00	+60	0	13 00	+60	0	180

0°	1°	2°	3°	4°	5°	6°	7°	8°	9°	10°	11°	12°	13°	14°

S. Lat. {LHA greater than 180°....... Zn=180−Z; LHA less than 180°........... Zn=180+Z}

DECLINATION (0°-14°) SAME NAME AS LATITUDE

LAT 89°

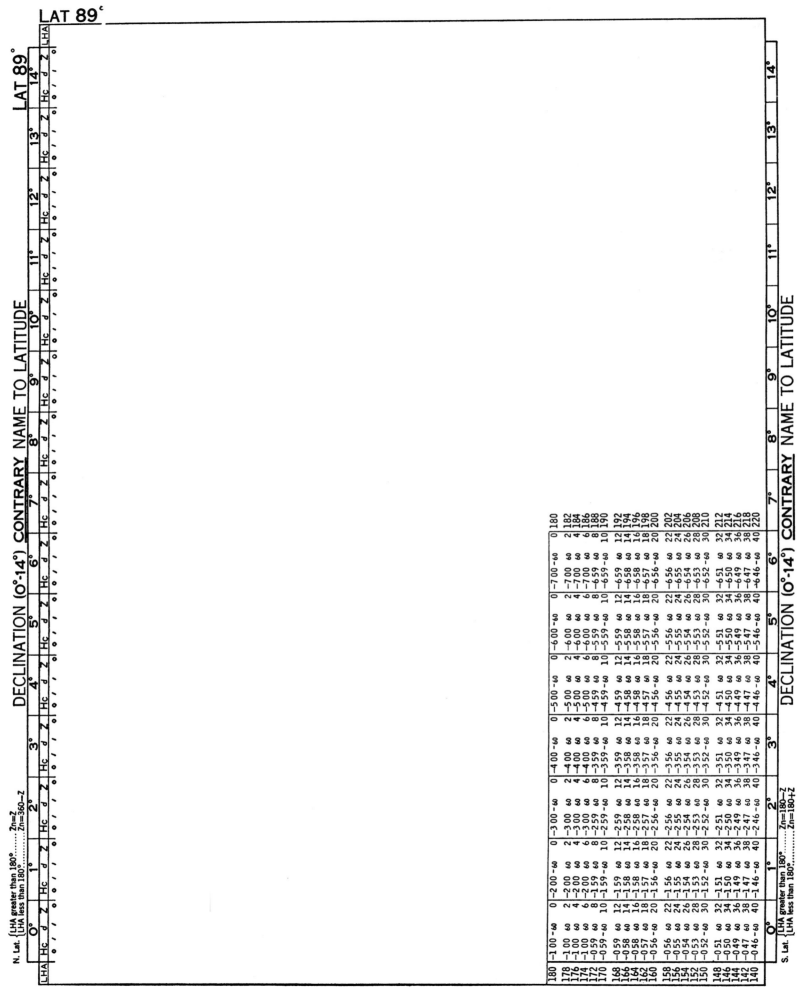

LHA	0° Hc	0° d	0° Z	1° Hc	1° d	1° Z	2° Hc	2° d	2° Z	3° Hc	3° d	3° Z	4° Hc	4° d	4° Z	5° Hc	5° d	5° Z	6° Hc	6° d	6° Z	LHA
	° ′	′	°	° ′	′	°	° ′	′	°	° ′	′	°	° ′	′	°	° ′	′	°	° ′	′	°	
180	−1 00	−60	0	−2 00	−60	0	−3 00	−60	0	−4 00	−60	0	−5 00	−60	0	−6 00	−60	0	−7 00	−60	0	180
178	−1 00	60	2	−2 00	60	2	−3 00	60	2	−4 00	60	2	−5 00	60	2	−6 00	60	2	−7 00	60	2	182
176	−1 00	60	4	−2 00	60	4	−3 00	60	4	−4 00	60	4	−5 00	60	4	−6 00	60	4	−7 00	60	4	184
174	−1 00	60	6	−2 00	60	6	−3 00	60	6	−4 00	60	6	−5 00	60	6	−6 00	60	6	−7 00	60	6	186
172	−0 59	60	8	−1 59	60	8	−2 59	60	8	−3 59	60	8	−4 59	60	8	−5 59	60	8	−6 59	60	8	188
170	−0 59	−60	10	−1 59	−60	10	−2 59	−60	10	−3 59	−60	10	−4 59	−60	10	−5 59	−60	10	−6 59	−60	10	190
168	−0 59	60	12	−1 59	60	12	−2 59	60	12	−3 59	60	12	−4 59	60	12	−5 59	60	12	−6 59	60	12	192
166	−0 58	60	14	−1 58	60	14	−2 58	60	14	−3 58	60	14	−4 58	60	14	−5 58	60	14	−6 58	60	14	194
164	−0 58	60	16	−1 58	60	16	−2 58	60	16	−3 58	60	16	−4 58	60	16	−5 58	60	16	−6 58	60	16	196
162	−0 57	60	18	−1 57	60	18	−2 57	60	18	−3 57	60	18	−4 57	60	18	−5 57	60	18	−6 57	60	18	198
160	−0 56	−60	20	−1 56	−60	20	−2 56	−60	20	−3 56	−60	20	−4 56	−60	20	−5 56	−60	20	−6 56	−60	20	200
158	−0 56	60	22	−1 56	60	22	−2 56	60	22	−3 56	60	22	−4 56	60	22	−5 56	60	22	−6 56	60	22	202
156	−0 55	60	24	−1 55	60	24	−2 55	60	24	−3 55	60	24	−4 55	60	24	−5 55	60	24	−6 55	60	24	204
154	−0 54	60	26	−1 54	60	26	−2 54	60	26	−3 54	60	26	−4 54	60	26	−5 54	60	26	−6 54	60	26	206
152	−0 53	60	28	−1 53	60	28	−2 53	60	28	−3 53	60	28	−4 53	60	28	−5 53	60	28	−6 53	60	28	208
150	−0 52	−60	30	−1 52	−60	30	−2 52	−60	30	−3 52	−60	30	−4 52	−60	30	−5 52	−60	30	−6 52	−60	30	210
148	−0 51	60	32	−1 51	60	32	−2 51	60	32	−3 51	60	32	−4 51	60	32	−5 51	60	32	−6 51	60	32	212
146	−0 50	60	34	−1 50	60	34	−2 50	60	34	−3 50	60	34	−4 50	60	34	−5 50	60	34	−6 50	60	34	214
144	−0 49	60	36	−1 49	60	36	−2 49	60	36	−3 49	60	36	−4 49	60	36	−5 49	60	36	−6 49	60	36	216
142	−0 47	60	38	−1 47	60	38	−2 47	60	38	−3 47	60	38	−4 47	60	38	−5 47	60	38	−6 47	60	38	218
140	−0 46	−60	40	−1 46	−60	40	−2 46	−60	40	−3 46	−60	40	−4 46	−60	40	−5 46	−60	40	−6 46	−60	40	220

S. Lat. {LHA greater than 180°....... Zn=180−Z / LHA less than 180°........... Zn=180+Z

N. Lat. {LHA greater than 180°……Zn=Z; LHA less than 180°……Zn=360−Z

DECLINATION (0°-14°) CONTRARY NAME TO LATITUDE

LHA	0°			1°			2°			3°			4°			5°			6°			7°			8°			9°			10°			11°			12°			13°			14°			LHA
	Hc	d	Z	Hc	d	Z	Hc	d	Z	Hc	d	Z	Hc	d	Z	Hc	d	Z	Hc	d	Z	Hc	d	Z	Hc	d	Z	Hc	d	Z	Hc	d	Z	Hc	d	Z	Hc	d	Z	Hc	d	Z	Hc	d	Z	
	° ′	′	°	° ′	′	°	° ′	′	°	° ′	′	°	° ′	′	°	° ′	′	°	° ′	′	°	° ′	′	°	° ′	′	°	° ′	′	°	° ′	′	°	° ′	′	°	° ′	′	°	° ′	′	°	° ′	′	°	
138	-0 45	60	42	-1 45	60	42	-2 45	60	42	-3 45	60	42	-4 45	60	42	-5 45	60	42	-6 45	60	42																									222
136	-0 43	60	44	-1 43	60	44	-2 43	60	44	-3 43	60	44	-4 43	60	44	-5 43	60	44	-6 43	60	44																									224
134	-0 42	60	46	-1 42	60	46	-2 42	60	46	-3 42	60	46	-4 42	60	46	-5 42	60	46	-6 42	60	46																									226
132	-0 40	60	48	-1 40	60	48	-2 40	60	48	-3 40	60	48	-4 40	60	48	-5 40	60	48	-6 40	60	48																									228
130	-0 39	-60	50	-1 39	-60	50	-2 39	-60	50	-3 39	-60	50	-4 39	-60	50	-5 39	-60	50	-6 39	-60	50																									230
128	-0 37	60	52	-1 37	60	52	-2 37	60	52	-3 37	60	52	-4 37	60	52	-5 37	60	52	-6 37	60	52																									232
126	-0 35	60	54	-1 35	60	54	-2 35	60	54	-3 35	60	54	-4 35	60	54	-5 35	60	54	-6 35	60	54																									234
124	-0 34	60	56	-1 34	60	56	-2 34	60	56	-3 34	60	56	-4 34	60	56	-5 34	60	56	-6 34	60	56																									236
122	-0 32	60	58	-1 32	60	58	-2 32	60	58	-3 32	60	58	-4 32	60	58	-5 32	60	58	-6 32	60	58																									238
120	-0 30	-60	60	-1 30	-60	60	-2 30	-60	60	-3 30	-60	60	-4 30	-60	60	-5 30	-60	60	-6 30	-60	60																									240
118	-0 28	60	62	-1 28	60	62	-2 28	60	62	-3 28	60	62	-4 28	60	62	-5 28	60	62	-6 28	60	62																									242
116	-0 26	60	64	-1 26	60	64	-2 26	60	64	-3 26	60	64	-4 26	60	64	-5 26	60	64	-6 26	60	64																									244
114	-0 24	60	66	-1 24	60	66	-2 24	60	66	-3 24	60	66	-4 24	60	66	-5 24	60	66	-6 24	60	66																									246
112	-0 22	60	68	-1 22	60	68	-2 22	60	68	-3 22	60	68	-4 22	60	68	-5 22	60	68	-6 22	60	68																									248
110	-0 21	-60	70	-1 21	-60	70	-2 21	-60	70	-3 21	-60	70	-4 21	-60	70	-5 21	-60	70	-6 21	-60	70																									250
108	-0 19	60	72	-1 19	60	72	-2 19	60	72	-3 19	60	72	-4 19	60	72	-5 19	60	72	-6 19	60	72																									252
106	-0 17	60	74	-1 17	60	74	-2 17	60	74	-3 17	60	74	-4 17	60	74	-5 17	60	74	-6 17	60	74																									254
104	-0 15	60	76	-1 15	59	76	-2 14	60	76	-3 14	60	76	-4 14	60	76	-5 14	60	76	-6 14	60	76																									256
102	-0 12	60	78	-1 12	60	78	-2 12	60	78	-3 12	60	78	-4 12	60	78	-5 12	60	78	-6 12	60	78																									258
100	-0 10	-60	80	-1 10	-60	80	-2 10	-60	80	-3 10	-60	80	-4 10	-60	80	-5 10	-60	80	-6 10	-60	80																									260
98	-0 08	60	82	-1 08	60	82	-2 08	60	82	-3 08	60	82	-4 08	60	82	-5 08	60	82	-6 08	60	82																									262
96	-0 06	60	84	-1 06	60	84	-2 06	60	84	-3 06	60	84	-4 06	60	84	-5 06	60	84	-6 06	60	84																									264
94	-0 04	60	86	-1 04	60	86	-2 04	60	86	-3 04	60	86	-4 04	60	86	-5 04	60	86	-6 04	60	86																									266
92	-0 02	60	88	-1 02	60	88	-2 02	60	88	-3 02	60	88	-4 02	60	88	-5 02	60	88	-6 02	60	88	-7 02	60	88																						268
90	00 00	-60	90	-1 00	-60	90	-2 00	-60	90	-3 00	-60	90	-4 00	-60	90	-5 00	-60	90	-6 00	-60	90	-7 00	-60	90																						270
88	00 02	60	92	-0 58	60	92	-1 58	60	92	-2 58	60	92	-3 58	60	92	-4 58	60	92	-5 58	60	92	-6 58	60	92																						272
86	00 04	60	94	-0 56	60	94	-1 56	60	94	-2 56	60	94	-3 56	60	94	-4 56	60	94	-5 56	60	94	-6 56	60	94																						274
84	00 06	60	96	-0 54	60	96	-1 54	60	96	-2 54	60	96	-3 54	60	96	-4 54	60	96	-5 54	60	96	-6 54	60	96																						276
82	00 08	60	98	-0 52	60	98	-1 52	60	98	-2 52	60	98	-3 52	60	98	-4 52	60	98	-5 52	60	98	-6 52	60	98																						278
80	00 10	-60	100	-0 50	-60	100	-1 50	-60	100	-2 50	-60	100	-3 50	-60	100	-4 50	-60	100	-5 50	-60	100	-6 50	-60	100																						280
78	00 12	60	102	-0 48	60	102	-1 48	60	102	-2 48	60	102	-3 48	60	102	-4 48	60	102	-5 48	60	102	-6 48	60	102																						282
76	00 15	60	104	-0 45	60	104	-1 45	60	104	-2 45	60	104	-3 45	60	104	-4 45	60	104	-5 45	60	104	-6 45	60	104																						284
74	00 17	60	106	-0 43	60	106	-1 43	60	106	-2 43	60	106	-3 43	60	106	-4 43	60	106	-5 43	60	106	-6 43	60	106																						286
72	00 19	60	108	-0 41	60	108	-1 41	60	108	-2 41	60	108	-3 41	60	108	-4 41	60	108	-5 41	60	108	-6 41	60	108																						288
70	00 21	-60	110	-0 39	-60	110	-1 39	-60	110	-2 39	-60	110	-3 39	-60	110	-4 39	-60	110	-5 39	-60	110	-6 39	-60	110																						290
68	00 22	60	112	-0 38	60	112	-1 38	60	112	-2 38	60	112	-3 38	60	112	-4 38	60	112	-5 38	60	112	-6 38	60	112																						292
66	00 24	60	114	-0 36	60	114	-1 36	60	114	-2 36	60	114	-3 36	60	114	-4 36	60	114	-5 36	60	114	-6 36	60	114																						294
64	00 26	60	116	-0 34	60	116	-1 34	60	116	-2 34	60	116	-3 34	60	116	-4 34	60	116	-5 34	60	116	-6 34	60	116																						296
62	00 28	60	118	-0 32	60	118	-1 32	60	118	-2 32	60	118	-3 32	60	118	-4 32	60	118	-5 32	60	118	-6 32	60	118																						298
60	00 30	-60	120	-0 30	-60	120	-1 30	-60	120	-2 30	-60	120	-3 30	-60	120	-4 30	-60	120	-5 30	-60	120	-6 30	-60	120																						300
58	00 32	60	122	-0 28	60	122	-1 28	60	122	-2 28	60	122	-3 28	60	122	-4 28	60	122	-5 28	60	122	-6 28	60	122																						302
56	00 34	60	124	-0 26	60	124	-1 26	60	124	-2 26	60	124	-3 26	60	124	-4 26	60	124	-5 26	60	124	-6 26	60	124																						304
54	00 35	60	126	-0 25	60	126	-1 25	60	126	-2 25	60	126	-3 25	60	126	-4 25	60	126	-5 25	60	126	-6 25	60	126																						306
52	00 37	60	128	-0 23	60	128	-1 23	60	128	-2 23	60	128	-3 23	60	128	-4 23	60	128	-5 23	60	128	-6 23	60	128																						308
50	00 39	-60	130	-0 21	-60	130	-1 21	-60	130	-2 21	-60	130	-3 21	-60	130	-4 21	-60	130	-5 21	-60	130	-6 21	-60	130																						310
48	00 40	60	132	-0 20	60	132	-1 20	60	132	-2 20	60	132	-3 20	60	132	-4 20	60	132	-5 20	60	132	-6 20	60	132																						312
46	00 42	60	134	-0 18	60	134	-1 18	60	134	-2 18	60	134	-3 18	60	134	-4 18	60	134	-5 18	60	134	-6 18	60	134																						314
44	00 43	60	136	-0 17	60	136	-1 17	60	136	-2 17	60	136	-3 17	60	136	-4 17	60	136	-5 17	60	136	-6 17	60	136																						316
42	00 45	60	138	-0 15	60	138	-1 15	60	138	-2 15	60	138	-3 15	60	138	-4 15	60	138	-5 15	60	138	-6 15	60	138																						318
40	00 46	-60	140	-0 14	-60	140	-1 14	-60	140	-2 14	-60	140	-3 14	-60	140	-4 14	-60	140	-5 14	-60	140	-6 14	-60	140																						320
38	00 47	60	142	-0 13	60	142	-1 13	60	142	-2 13	60	142	-3 13	60	142	-4 13	60	142	-5 13	60	142	-6 13	60	142																						322
36	00 49	60	144	-0 11	60	144	-1 11	60	144	-2 11	60	144	-3 11	60	144	-4 11	60	144	-5 11	60	144	-6 11	60	144																						324
34	00 50	60	146	-0 10	60	146	-1 10	60	146	-2 10	60	146	-3 10	60	146	-4 10	60	146	-5 10	60	146	-6 10	60	146																						326
32	00 51	60	148	-0 09	60	148	-1 09	60	148	-2 09	60	148	-3 09	60	148	-4 09	60	148	-5 09	60	148	-6 09	60	148																						328
30	00 52	-60	150	-0 08	-60	150	-1 08	-60	150	-2 08	-60	150	-3 08	-60	150	-4 08	-60	150	-5 08	-60	150	-6 08	-60	150																						330
28	00 53	60	152	-0 07	60	152	-1 07	60	152	-2 07	60	152	-3 07	60	152	-4 07	60	152	-5 07	60	152	-6 07	60	152																						332
26	00 54	60	154	-0 06	60	154	-1 06	60	154	-2 06	60	154	-3 06	60	154	-4 06	60	154	-5 06	60	154	-6 06	60	154																						334
24	00 55	60	156	-0 05	60	156	-1 05	60	156	-2 05	60	156	-3 05	60	156	-4 05	60	156	-5 05	60	156	-6 05	60	156																						336
22	00 56	60	158	-0 04	60	158	-1 04	60	158	-2 04	60	158	-3 04	60	158	-4 04	60	158	-5 04	60	158	-6 04	60	158																						338
20	00 56	-60	160	-0 04	-60	160	-1 04	-60	160	-2 04	-60	160	-3 04	-60	160	-4 04	-60	160	-5 04	-60	160	-6 04	-60	160																						340
18	00 57	60	162	-0 03	60	162	-1 03	60	162	-2 03	60	162	-3 03	60	162	-4 03	60	162	-5 03	60	162	-6 03	60	162																						342
16	00 58	60	164	-0 02	60	164	-1 02	60	164	-2 02	60	164	-3 02	60	164	-4 02	60	164	-5 02	60	164	-6 02	60	164																						344
14	00 58	60	166	-0 02	60	166	-1 02	60	166	-2 02	60	166	-3 02	60	166	-4 02	60	166	-5 02	60	166	-6 02	60	166																						346
12	00 59	60	168	-0 01	60	168	-1 01	60	168	-2 01	60	168	-3 01	60	168	-4 01	60	168	-5 01	60	168	-6 01	60	168																						348
10	00 59	-60	170	-0 01	-60	170	-1 01	-60	170	-2 01	-60	170	-3 01	-60	170	-4 01	-60	170	-5 01	-60	170	-6 01	-60	170																						350
8	00 59	60	172	-0 01	60	172	-1 01	60	172	-2 01	60	172	-3 01	60	172	-4 01	60	172	-5 01	60	172	-6 01	60	172																						352
6	01 00	60	174	00 00	60	174	-1 00	60	174	-2 00	60	174	-3 00	60	174	-4 00	60	174	-5 00	60	174	-6 00	60	174																						354
4	01 00	60	176	00 00	60	176	-1 00	60	176	-2 00	60	176	-3 00	60	176	-4 00	60	176	-5 00	60	176	-6 00	60	176																						356
2	01 00	60	178	00 00	60	178	-1 00	60	178	-2 00	60	178	-3 00	60	178	-4 00	60	178	-5 00	60	178	-6 00	60	178	-7 00	60	178																			358
0	01 00	-60	180	00 00	-60	180	-1 00	-60	180	-2 00	-60	180	-3 00	-60	180	-4 00	-60	180	-5 00	-60	180	-6 00	-60	180	-7 00	-60	180																			360
	0°			1°			2°			3°			4°			5°			6°			7°			8°			9°			10°			11°			12°			13°			14°			

S. Lat. {LHA greater than 180°……Zn=180−Z; LHA less than 180°……Zn=180+Z

DECLINATION (0°-14°) CONTRARY NAME TO LATITUDE

N. Lat. {LHA greater than 180°....... Zn=Z; LHA less than 180°........... Zn=360−Z}

DECLINATION (15°-29°) SAME NAME AS LATITUDE

LHA	15°			16°			17°			18°			19°		
	Hc	d	Z	Hc	d	Z	Hc	d	Z	Hc	d	Z	Hc	d	Z
	° ′	′	°	° ′	′	°	° ′	′	°	° ′	′	°	° ′	′	°
0	16 00	+60	180	17 00	+60	180	18 00	+60	180	19 00	+60	180	20 00	+60	180
2	16 00	60	178	17 00	60	178	18 00	60	178	19 00	60	178	20 00	60	178
4	16 00	60	176	17 00	60	176	18 00	60	176	19 00	60	176	20 00	60	176
6	16 00	60	174	17 00	60	174	18 00	60	174	19 00	60	174	20 00	60	174
8	15 59	60	172	16 59	60	172	17 59	60	172	18 59	60	172	19 59	60	172
10	15 59	+60	170	16 59	+60	170	17 59	+60	170	18 59	+60	170	19 59	+60	170
12	15 59	60	168	16 59	60	168	17 59	60	168	18 59	60	168	19 59	60	168
14	15 58	60	166	16 58	60	166	17 58	60	166	18 58	60	166	19 58	60	166
16	15 58	60	164	16 58	60	164	17 58	60	164	18 58	60	164	19 58	60	164
18	15 57	60	162	16 57	60	162	17 57	60	162	18 57	60	162	19 57	60	162
20	15 56	+60	160	16 56	+60	160	17 56	+60	160	18 56	+60	160	19 56	+60	160
22	15 56	60	158	16 56	60	158	17 56	60	158	18 56	60	158	19 56	60	158
24	15 55	60	156	16 55	60	156	17 55	60	156	18 55	60	156	19 55	60	156
26	15 54	60	154	16 54	60	154	17 54	60	154	18 54	60	154	19 54	60	154
28	15 53	60	152	16 53	60	152	17 53	60	152	18 53	60	152	19 53	60	152
30	15 52	+60	150	16 52	+60	150	17 52	+60	150	18 52	+60	150	19 52	+60	150
32	15 51	60	148	16 51	60	148	17 51	60	148	18 51	60	148	19 51	60	148
34	15 50	60	146	16 50	60	146	17 50	60	146	18 50	60	146	19 50	60	146
36	15 49	60	144	16 49	60	144	17 49	60	144	18 49	60	144	19 49	60	144
38	15 47	60	142	16 47	60	142	17 47	60	142	18 47	60	142	19 47	60	142
40	15 46	+60	140	16 46	+60	140	17 46	+60	140	18 46	+60	140	19 46	+60	140
42	15 45	60	138	16 45	60	138	17 45	60	138	18 45	60	138	19 45	60	138
44	15 43	60	136	16 43	60	136	17 43	60	136	18 43	60	136	19 43	60	136
46	15 42	60	134	16 42	60	134	17 42	60	134	18 42	60	134	19 42	60	134
48	15 40	60	132	16 40	60	132	17 40	60	132	18 40	60	132	19 40	60	132
50	15 39	+60	130	16 39	+60	130	17 39	+60	130	18 39	+60	130	19 39	+60	130
52	15 37	60	128	16 37	60	128	17 37	60	128	18 37	60	128	19 37	60	128
54	15 35	60	126	16 35	60	126	17 35	60	126	18 35	60	126	19 35	60	126
56	15 34	59	124	16 33	60	124	17 33	60	124	18 33	60	124	19 33	60	124
58	15 32	60	122	16 32	60	122	17 32	60	122	18 32	60	122	19 32	60	122
60	15 30	+60	120	16 30	+60	120	17 30	+60	120	18 30	+60	120	19 30	+60	120
62	15 28	60	118	16 28	60	118	17 28	60	118	18 28	60	118	19 28	60	118
64	15 26	60	116	16 26	60	116	17 26	60	116	18 26	60	116	19 26	60	116
66	15 24	60	114	16 24	60	114	17 24	60	114	18 24	60	114	19 24	60	114
68	15 22	60	112	16 22	60	112	17 22	60	112	18 22	60	112	19 22	60	112
70	15 20	+60	110	16 20	+60	110	17 20	+60	110	18 20	+60	110	19 20	+60	110
72	15 18	60	108	16 18	60	108	17 18	60	108	18 18	60	108	19 18	60	108
74	15 16	60	106	16 16	60	106	17 16	60	106	18 16	60	106	19 16	60	106
76	15 14	60	104	16 14	60	104	17 14	60	104	18 14	60	104	19 14	60	104
78	15 12	60	102	16 12	60	102	17 12	60	102	18 12	60	102	19 12	60	102
80	15 10	+60	100	16 10	+60	100	17 10	+60	100	18 10	+60	100	19 10	+60	100
82	15 08	60	98	16 08	60	98	17 08	60	98	18 08	60	98	19 08	60	98
84	15 06	60	96	16 06	60	96	17 06	60	96	18 06	60	96	19 06	60	96
86	15 04	60	94	16 04	60	94	17 04	60	94	18 04	60	94	19 04	60	94
88	15 02	60	92	16 02	60	92	17 02	60	92	18 02	60	92	19 02	60	92
90	15 00	+60	90	16 00	+60	90	17 00	+60	90	18 00	+60	90	19 00	+60	90
92	14 58	60	88	15 58	60	88	16 58	60	88	17 58	60	88	18 58	60	88
94	14 56	60	86	15 56	60	86	16 56	60	86	17 56	60	86	18 56	60	86
96	14 54	60	84	15 54	60	84	16 54	60	84	17 54	60	84	18 54	60	84
98	14 52	60	82	15 52	60	82	16 52	60	82	17 52	60	82	18 52	60	82
100	14 49	+60	80	15 49	+60	80	16 49	+60	80	17 49	+60	80	18 49	+60	80
102	14 47	60	78	15 47	60	78	16 47	60	78	17 47	60	78	18 47	60	78
104	14 45	60	76	15 45	60	76	16 45	60	76	17 45	60	76	18 45	60	76
106	14 43	60	74	15 43	60	74	16 43	60	74	17 43	60	74	18 43	60	74
108	14 41	60	72	15 41	60	72	16 41	60	72	17 41	60	72	18 41	60	72
110	14 39	+60	70	15 39	+60	70	16 39	+60	70	17 39	+60	70	18 39	+60	70
112	14 37	60	68	15 37	60	68	16 37	60	68	17 37	60	68	18 37	60	68
114	14 36	60	66	15 36	60	66	16 36	60	66	17 36	59	66	18 35	60	66
116	14 34	60	64	15 34	60	64	16 34	60	64	17 34	60	64	18 34	60	64
118	14 32	60	62	15 32	60	62	16 32	60	62	17 32	60	62	18 32	60	62
120	14 30	+60	60	15 30	+60	60	16 30	+60	60	17 30	+60	60	18 30	+60	60
122	14 28	60	58	15 28	60	58	16 28	60	58	17 28	60	58	18 28	60	58
124	14 26	60	56	15 26	60	56	16 26	60	56	17 26	60	56	18 26	60	56
126	14 25	60	54	15 25	60	54	16 25	60	54	17 25	60	54	18 25	60	54
128	14 23	60	52	15 23	60	52	16 23	60	52	17 23	60	52	18 23	60	52
130	14 21	+60	50	15 21	+60	50	16 21	+60	50	17 21	+60	50	18 21	+60	50
132	14 20	60	48	15 20	60	48	16 20	60	48	17 20	60	48	18 20	60	48
134	14 18	60	46	15 18	60	46	16 18	60	46	17 18	60	46	18 18	60	46
136	14 17	60	44	15 17	60	44	16 17	60	44	17 17	60	44	18 17	60	44
138	14 15	60	42	15 15	60	42	16 15	60	42	17 15	60	42	18 15	60	42

LHA	20°			21°			22°			23°			24°		
	Hc	d	Z	Hc	d	Z	Hc	d	Z	Hc	d	Z	Hc	d	Z
	° ′	′	°	° ′	′	°	° ′	′	°	° ′	′	°	° ′	′	°
0	21 00	+60	180	22 00	+60	180	23 00	+60	180	24 00	+60	180	25 00	+60	180
2	21 00	60	178	22 00	60	178	23 00	60	178	24 00	60	178	25 00	60	178
4	21 00	60	176	22 00	60	176	23 00	60	176	24 00	60	176	25 00	60	176
6	21 00	60	174	22 00	60	174	23 00	60	174	24 00	60	174	25 00	60	174
8	20 59	60	172	21 59	60	172	22 59	60	172	23 59	60	172	24 59	60	172
10	20 59	+60	170	21 59	+60	170	22 59	+60	170	23 59	+60	170	24 59	+60	170
12	20 59	60	168	21 59	60	168	22 59	60	168	23 59	60	168	24 59	60	168
14	20 58	60	166	21 58	60	166	22 58	60	166	23 58	60	166	24 58	60	166
16	20 58	60	164	21 58	60	164	22 58	60	164	23 58	60	164	24 58	60	164
18	20 57	60	162	21 57	60	162	22 57	60	162	23 57	60	162	24 57	60	162
20	20 56	+60	160	21 56	+60	160	22 56	+60	160	23 56	+60	160	24 56	+60	160
22	20 56	60	158	21 56	60	158	22 56	60	158	23 56	60	158	24 56	60	158
24	20 55	60	156	21 55	60	156	22 55	60	156	23 55	60	156	24 55	60	156
26	20 54	60	154	21 54	60	154	22 54	60	154	23 54	60	154	24 54	60	154
28	20 53	60	152	21 53	60	152	22 53	60	152	23 53	60	152	24 53	60	152
30	20 52	+60	150	21 52	+60	150	22 52	+60	150	23 52	+60	150	24 52	+60	150
32	20 51	60	148	21 51	60	148	22 51	60	148	23 51	60	148	24 51	60	148
34	20 50	60	146	21 50	60	146	22 50	60	146	23 50	60	146	24 50	60	146
36	20 49	60	144	21 49	60	144	22 49	60	144	23 49	60	144	24 49	60	144
38	20 47	60	142	21 47	60	142	22 47	60	142	23 47	60	142	24 47	60	142
40	20 46	+60	140	21 46	+60	140	22 46	+60	140	23 46	+60	140	24 46	+60	140
42	20 45	60	138	21 45	60	138	22 45	60	138	23 45	60	138	24 45	60	138
44	20 43	60	136	21 43	60	136	22 43	60	136	23 43	60	136	24 43	60	136
46	20 42	60	134	21 42	60	134	22 42	60	134	23 42	60	134	24 42	60	134
48	20 40	60	132	21 40	60	132	22 40	60	132	23 40	60	132	24 40	60	132
50	20 39	+59	130	21 38	+60	130	22 38	+60	130	23 38	+60	130	24 38	+60	130
52	20 37	60	128	21 37	60	128	22 37	60	128	23 37	60	128	24 37	60	128
54	20 35	60	126	21 35	60	126	22 35	60	126	23 35	60	126	24 35	60	126
56	20 33	60	124	21 33	60	124	22 33	60	124	23 33	60	124	24 33	60	124
58	20 32	60	122	21 32	60	122	22 32	60	122	23 32	60	122	24 32	60	122
60	20 30	+60	120	21 30	+60	120	22 30	+60	120	23 30	+60	120	24 30	+60	120
62	20 28	60	118	21 28	60	118	22 28	60	118	23 28	60	118	24 28	60	118
64	20 26	60	116	21 26	60	116	22 26	60	116	23 26	60	116	24 26	60	116
66	20 24	60	114	21 24	60	114	22 24	60	114	23 24	60	114	24 24	60	114
68	20 22	60	112	21 22	60	112	22 22	60	112	23 22	60	112	24 22	60	112
70	20 20	+60	110	21 20	+60	110	22 20	+60	110	23 20	+60	110	24 20	+60	110
72	20 18	60	108	21 18	60	108	22 18	60	108	23 18	60	108	24 18	60	108
74	20 16	60	106	21 16	60	106	22 16	60	106	23 16	60	106	24 16	60	106
76	20 14	60	104	21 14	60	104	22 14	60	104	23 14	60	104	24 14	60	104
78	20 12	60	102	21 12	60	102	22 12	60	102	23 12	60	102	24 12	60	102
80	20 10	+60	100	21 10	+60	100	22 10	+60	100	23 10	+60	100	24 10	+60	100
82	20 08	60	98	21 08	60	98	22 08	60	98	23 08	60	98	24 08	60	98
84	20 06	60	96	21 06	60	96	22 06	60	96	23 06	60	96	24 06	60	96
86	20 04	60	94	21 04	60	94	22 04	60	94	23 04	60	94	24 04	60	94
88	20 02	60	92	21 02	60	92	22 02	60	92	23 02	60	92	24 02	60	92
90	20 00	+60	90	21 00	+60	90	22 00	+60	90	23 00	+60	90	24 00	+60	90
92	19 58	60	88	20 58	60	88	21 58	60	88	22 58	60	88	23 58	60	88
94	19 56	60	86	20 56	60	86	21 56	60	86	22 56	60	86	23 56	60	86
96	19 54	60	84	20 54	60	84	21 54	60	84	22 54	60	84	23 54	60	84
98	19 52	60	82	20 52	59	82	21 51	60	82	22 51	60	82	23 51	60	82
100	19 49	+60	80	20 49	+60	80	21 49	+60	80	22 49	+60	80	23 49	+60	80
102	19 47	60	78	20 47	60	78	21 47	60	78	22 47	60	78	23 47	60	78
104	19 45	60	76	20 45	60	76	21 45	60	76	22 45	60	76	23 45	60	76
106	19 43	60	74	20 43	60	74	21 43	60	74	22 43	60	74	23 43	60	74
108	19 41	60	72	20 41	60	72	21 41	60	72	22 41	60	72	23 41	60	72
110	19 39	+60	70	20 39	+60	70	21 39	+60	70	22 39	+60	70	23 39	+60	70
112	19 37	60	68	20 37	60	68	21 37	60	68	22 37	60	68	23 37	60	68
114	19 35	60	66	20 35	60	66	21 35	60	66	22 35	60	66	23 35	60	66
116	19 34	60	64	20 34	60	64	21 34	60	64	22 34	60	64	23 34	60	64
118	19 32	60	62	20 32	60	62	21 32	60	62	22 32	60	62	23 32	60	62
120	19 30	+60	60	20 30	+60	60	21 30	+60	60	22 30	+60	60	23 30	+60	60
122	19 28	60	58	20 28	60	58	21 28	60	58	22 28	60	58	23 28	60	58
124	19 26	60	56	20 26	60	56	21 26	60	56	22 26	60	56	23 26	60	56
126	19 25	60	54	20 25	60	54	21 25	60	54	22 25	60	54	23 25	60	54
128	19 23	60	52	20 23	60	52	21 23	60	52	22 23	60	52	23 23	60	52
130	19 21	+60	50	20 21	+60	50	21 21	+60	50	22 21	+60	50	23 21	+60	50
132	19 20	60	48	20 20	60	48	21 20	60	48	22 20	60	48	23 20	60	48
134	19 18	60	46	20 18	60	46	21 18	60	46	22 18	60	46	23 18	60	46
136	19 17	60	44	20 17	60	44	21 17	60	44	22 17	60	44	23 17	60	44
138	19 15	60	42	20 15	60	42	21 15	60	42	22 15	60	42	23 15	60	42

LHA	25°			26°			27°			28°			29°			LHA
	Hc	d	Z	Hc	d	Z	Hc	d	Z	Hc	d	Z	Hc	d	Z	
	° ′	′	°	° ′	′	°	° ′	′	°	° ′	′	°	° ′	′	°	
0	26 00	+60	180	27 00	+60	180	28 00	+60	180	29 00	+60	180	30 00	+60	180	360
2	26 00	60	178	27 00	60	178	28 00	60	178	29 00	60	178	30 00	60	178	358
4	26 00	60	176	27 00	60	176	28 00	60	176	29 00	60	176	30 00	60	176	356
6	26 00	60	174	27 00	60	174	28 00	60	174	29 00	60	174	30 00	60	174	354
8	25 59	60	172	26 59	60	172	27 59	60	172	28 59	60	172	29 59	60	172	352
10	25 59	+60	170	26 59	+60	170	27 59	+60	170	28 59	+60	170	29 59	+60	170	350
12	25 59	60	168	26 59	60	168	27 59	60	168	28 59	60	168	29 59	60	168	348
14	25 58	60	166	26 58	60	166	27 58	60	166	28 58	60	166	29 58	60	166	346
16	25 58	60	164	26 58	60	164	27 58	60	164	28 58	60	164	29 58	60	164	344
18	25 57	60	162	26 57	60	162	27 57	60	162	28 57	60	162	29 57	60	162	342
20	25 56	+60	160	26 56	+60	160	27 56	+60	160	28 56	+60	160	29 56	+60	160	340
22	25 56	60	158	26 56	60	158	27 56	60	158	28 56	60	158	29 56	60	158	338
24	25 55	60	156	26 55	60	156	27 55	60	156	28 55	60	156	29 55	60	156	336
26	25 54	60	154	26 54	60	154	27 54	60	154	28 54	60	154	29 54	60	154	334
28	25 53	60	152	26 53	60	152	27 53	60	152	28 53	60	152	29 53	60	152	332
30	25 52	+60	150	26 52	+60	150	27 52	+60	150	28 52	+60	150	29 52	+60	150	330
32	25 51	60	148	26 51	60	148	27 51	60	148	28 51	60	148	29 51	60	148	328
34	25 50	60	146	26 50	60	146	27 50	60	146	28 50	60	146	29 50	60	146	326
36	25 49	60	144	26 49	59	144	27 48	60	144	28 48	60	144	29 48	60	144	324
38	25 47	60	142	26 47	60	142	27 47	60	142	28 47	60	142	29 47	60	142	322
40	25 46	+60	140	26 46	+60	140	27 46	+60	140	28 46	+60	140	29 46	+60	140	320
42	25 45	60	138	26 45	60	138	27 45	60	138	28 45	60	138	29 45	60	138	318
44	25 43	60	136	26 43	60	136	27 43	60	136	28 43	60	136	29 43	60	136	316
46	25 42	60	134	26 42	60	134	27 42	60	134	28 42	60	134	29 42	60	134	314
48	25 40	60	132	26 40	60	132	27 40	60	132	28 40	60	132	29 40	60	132	312
50	25 38	+60	130	26 38	+60	130	27 38	+60	130	28 38	+60	130	29 38	+60	130	310
52	25 37	60	128	26 37	60	128	27 37	60	128	28 37	60	128	29 37	60	128	308
54	25 35	60	126	26 35	60	126	27 35	60	126	28 35	60	126	29 35	60	126	306
56	25 33	60	124	26 33	60	124	27 33	60	124	28 33	60	124	29 33	60	124	304
58	25 32	60	122	26 32	60	122	27 32	60	122	28 32	60	122	29 32	60	122	302
60	25 30	+60	120	26 30	+60	120	27 30	+60	120	28 30	+60	120	29 30	+60	120	300
62	25 28	60	118	26 28	60	118	27 28	60	118	28 28	60	118	29 28	60	118	298
64	25 26	60	116	26 26	60	116	27 26	60	116	28 26	60	116	29 26	60	116	296
66	25 24	60	114	26 24	60	114	27 24	60	114	28 24	60	114	29 24	60	114	294
68	25 22	60	112	26 22	60	112	27 22	60	112	28 22	60	112	29 22	60	112	292
70	25 20	+60	110	26 20	+60	110	27 20	+60	110	28 20	+60	110	29 20	+60	110	290
72	25 18	60	108	26 18	60	108	27 18	60	108	28 18	60	108	29 18	60	108	288
74	25 16	60	106	26 16	60	106	27 16	60	106	28 16	60	106	29 16	60	106	286
76	25 14	60	104	26 14	60	104	27 14	60	104	28 14	60	104	29 14	60	104	284
78	25 12	60	102	26 12	60	102	27 12	60	102	28 12	60	102	29 12	60	102	282
80	25 10	+60	100	26 10	+60	100	27 10	+60	100	28 10	+60	100	29 10	+60	100	280
82	25 08	60	98	26 08	60	98	27 08	60	98	28 08	60	98	29 08	60	97	278
84	25 06	60	96	26 06	60	96	27 06	60	96	28 06	60	96	29 06	60	95	276
86	25 04	60	94	26 04	60	94	27 04	60	94	28 04	60	94	29 04	60	93	274
88	25 02	60	92	26 02	60	92	27 02	60	92	28 02	60	92	29 02	60	91	272
90	25 00	+60	90	26 00	+60	90	27 00	+60	90	28 00	+60	90	29 00	+60	89	270
92	24 58	60	88	25 58	60	88	26 58	60	88	27 58	60	88	28 58	60	87	268
94	24 56	60	86	25 56	60	86	26 56	60	86	27 56	60	86	28 56	60	85	266
96	24 54	60	84	25 54	60	84	26 54	60	84	27 54	59	84	28 53	60	83	264
98	24 51	60	82	25 51	60	82	26 51	60	82	27 51	60	82	28 51	60	82	262
100	24 49	+60	80	25 49	+60	80	26 49	+60	80	27 49	+60	80	28 49	+60	80	260
102	24 47	60	78	25 47	60	78	26 47	60	78	27 47	60	78	28 47	60	78	258
104	24 45	60	76	25 45	60	76	26 45	60	76	27 45	60	76	28 45	60	76	256
106	24 43	60	74	25 43	60	74	26 43	60	74	27 43	60	74	28 43	60	74	254
108	24 41	60	72	25 41	60	72	26 41	60	72	27 41	60	72	28 41	60	72	252
110	24 39	+60	70	25 39	+60	70	26 39	+60	70	27 39	+60	70	28 39	+60	70	250
112	24 37	60	68	25 37	60	68	26 37	60	68	27 37	60	68	28 37	60	68	248
114	24 35	60	66	25 35	60	66	26 35	60	66	27 35	60	66	28 35	60	66	246
116	24 34	60	64	25 34	60	64	26 34	60	64	27 34	60	64	28 34	60	64	244
118	24 32	60	62	25 32	60	62	26 32	60	62	27 32	60	62	28 32	60	62	242
120	24 30	+60	60	25 30	+60	60	26 30	+60	60	27 30	+60	60	28 30	+60	60	240
122	24 28	60	58	25 28	60	58	26 28	60	58	27 28	60	58	28 28	60	58	238
124	24 26	60	56	25 26	60	56	26 26	60	56	27 26	60	56	28 26	60	56	236
126	24 25	60	54	25 25	60	54	26 25	60	54	27 25	60	54	28 25	60	54	234
128	24 23	60	52	25 23	60	52	26 23	60	52	27 23	60	52	28 23	60	52	232
130	24 21	+60	50	25 21	+60	50	26 21	+60	50	27 21	+60	50	28 21	+60	50	230
132	24 20	60	48	25 20	60	48	26 20	60	48	27 20	60	48	28 20	60	48	228
134	24 18	60	46	25 18	60	46	26 18	60	46	27 18	60	46	28 18	60	46	226
136	24 17	60	44	25 17	60	44	26 17	60	44	27 17	60	44	28 17	60	44	224
138	24 15	60	42	25 15	60	42	26 15	60	42	27 15	60	42	28 15	60	42	222

15° 16° 17° 18° 19° 20° 21° 22° 23° 24° 25° 26° 27° 28° 29°

S. Lat. {LHA greater than 180°....... Zn=180−Z; LHA less than 180°........... Zn=180+Z}

DECLINATION (15°-29°) SAME NAME AS LATITUDE

LAT 89°

N. Lat. {LHA greater than 180°....... Zn=Z; LHA less than 180°........... Zn=360−Z}

DECLINATION (15°-29°) SAME NAME AS LATITUDE

LHA	15° Hc	d	Z	16° Hc	d	Z	17° Hc	d	Z	18° Hc	d	Z	19° Hc	d	Z
	° ′	′	°	° ′	′	°	° ′	′	°	° ′	′	°	° ′	′	°
140	14 14	+60	40	15 14	+60	40	16 14	+60	40	17 14	+60	40	18 14	+60	40
142	14 13	60	38	15 13	60	38	16 13	60	38	17 13	60	38	18 13	60	38
144	14 11	60	36	15 11	60	36	16 11	60	36	17 11	60	36	18 11	60	36
146	14 10	60	34	15 10	60	34	16 10	60	34	17 10	60	34	18 10	60	34
148	14 09	60	32	15 09	60	32	16 09	60	32	17 09	60	32	18 09	60	32
150	14 08	+60	30	15 08	+60	30	16 08	+60	30	17 08	+60	30	18 08	+60	30
152	14 07	60	28	15 07	60	28	16 07	60	28	17 07	60	28	18 07	60	28
154	14 06	60	26	15 06	60	26	16 06	60	26	17 06	60	26	18 06	60	26
156	14 05	60	24	15 05	60	24	16 05	60	24	17 05	60	24	18 05	60	24
158	14 04	60	22	15 04	60	22	16 04	60	22	17 04	60	22	18 04	60	22
160	14 04	+60	20	15 04	+60	20	16 04	+60	20	17 04	+60	20	18 04	+60	20
162	14 03	60	18	15 03	60	18	16 03	60	18	17 03	60	18	18 03	60	18
164	14 02	60	16	15 02	60	16	16 02	60	16	17 02	60	16	18 02	60	16
166	14 02	60	14	15 02	60	14	16 02	60	14	17 02	60	14	18 02	60	14
168	14 01	60	12	15 01	60	12	16 01	60	12	17 01	60	12	18 01	60	12
170	14 01	+60	10	15 01	+60	10	16 01	+60	10	17 01	+60	10	18 01	+60	10
172	14 01	60	8	15 01	60	8	16 01	60	8	17 01	60	8	18 01	60	8
174	14 00	60	6	15 00	60	6	16 00	60	6	17 00	60	6	18 00	60	6
176	14 00	60	4	15 00	60	4	16 00	60	4	17 00	60	4	18 00	60	4
178	14 00	60	2	15 00	60	2	16 00	60	2	17 00	60	2	18 00	60	2
180	14 00	+60	0	15 00	+60	0	16 00	+60	0	17 00	+60	0	18 00	+60	0

LHA	20° Hc	d	Z	21° Hc	d	Z	22° Hc	d	Z	23° Hc	d	Z	24° Hc	d	Z
	° ′	′	°	° ′	′	°	° ′	′	°	° ′	′	°	° ′	′	°
140	19 14	+60	40	20 14	+60	40	21 14	+60	40	22 14	+60	40	23 14	+60	40
142	19 13	60	38	20 13	60	38	21 13	60	38	22 13	60	38	23 13	60	38
144	19 11	60	36	20 11	60	36	21 11	60	36	22 11	60	36	23 11	60	36
146	19 10	60	34	20 10	60	34	21 10	60	34	22 10	60	34	23 10	60	34
148	19 09	60	32	20 09	60	32	21 09	60	32	22 09	60	32	23 09	60	32
150	19 08	+60	30	20 08	+60	30	21 08	+60	30	22 08	+60	30	23 08	+60	30
152	19 07	60	28	20 07	60	28	21 07	60	28	22 07	60	28	23 07	60	28
154	19 06	60	26	20 06	60	26	21 06	60	26	22 06	60	26	23 06	60	26
156	19 05	60	24	20 05	60	24	21 05	60	24	22 05	60	24	23 05	60	24
158	19 04	60	22	20 04	60	22	21 04	60	22	22 04	60	22	23 04	60	22
160	19 04	+60	20	20 04	+60	20	21 04	+60	20	22 04	+60	20	23 04	+60	20
162	19 03	60	18	20 03	60	18	21 03	60	18	22 03	60	18	23 03	60	18
164	19 02	60	16	20 02	60	16	21 02	60	16	22 02	60	16	23 02	60	16
166	19 02	60	14	20 02	60	14	21 02	60	14	22 02	60	14	23 02	60	14
168	19 01	60	12	20 01	60	12	21 01	60	12	22 01	60	12	23 01	60	12
170	19 01	+60	10	20 01	+60	10	21 01	+60	10	22 01	+60	10	23 01	+60	10
172	19 01	60	8	20 01	60	8	21 01	60	8	22 01	60	8	23 01	60	8
174	19 00	60	6	20 00	60	6	21 00	60	6	22 00	60	6	23 00	60	6
176	19 00	60	4	20 00	60	4	21 00	60	4	22 00	60	4	23 00	60	4
178	19 00	60	2	20 00	60	2	21 00	60	2	22 00	60	2	23 00	60	2
180	19 00	+60	0	20 00	+60	0	21 00	+60	0	22 00	+60	0	23 00	+60	0

LHA	25° Hc	d	Z	26° Hc	d	Z	27° Hc	d	Z	28° Hc	d	Z	29° Hc	d	Z	LHA
	° ′	′	°	° ′	′	°	° ′	′	°	° ′	′	°	° ′	′	°	
140	24 14	+60	40	25 14	+60	40	26 14	+60	40	27 14	+60	40	28 14	+60	40	220
142	24 13	60	38	25 13	60	38	26 13	60	38	27 13	60	38	28 13	60	38	218
144	24 11	60	36	25 11	60	36	26 11	60	36	27 11	60	36	28 11	60	36	216
146	24 10	60	34	25 10	60	34	26 10	60	34	27 10	60	34	28 10	60	34	214
148	24 09	60	32	25 09	60	32	26 09	60	32	27 09	60	32	28 09	60	32	212
150	24 08	+60	30	25 08	+60	30	26 08	+60	30	27 08	+60	30	28 08	+60	30	210
152	24 07	60	28	25 07	60	28	26 07	60	28	27 07	60	28	28 07	60	28	208
154	24 06	60	26	25 06	60	26	26 06	60	26	27 06	60	26	28 06	60	26	206
156	24 05	60	24	25 05	60	24	26 05	60	24	27 05	60	24	28 05	60	24	204
158	24 04	60	22	25 04	60	22	26 04	60	22	27 04	60	22	28 04	60	22	202
160	24 04	+60	20	25 04	+60	20	26 04	+60	20	27 04	+60	20	28 04	+60	20	200
162	24 03	60	18	25 03	60	18	26 03	60	18	27 03	60	18	28 03	60	18	198
164	24 02	60	16	25 02	60	16	26 02	60	16	27 02	60	16	28 02	60	16	196
166	24 02	60	14	25 02	60	14	26 02	60	14	27 02	60	14	28 02	60	14	194
168	24 01	60	12	25 01	60	12	26 01	60	12	27 01	60	12	28 01	60	12	192
170	24 01	+60	10	25 01	+60	10	26 01	+60	10	27 01	+60	10	28 01	+60	10	190
172	24 01	60	8	25 01	60	8	26 01	60	8	27 01	60	8	28 01	60	8	188
174	24 00	60	6	25 00	60	6	26 00	60	6	27 00	60	6	28 00	60	6	186
176	24 00	60	4	25 00	60	4	26 00	60	4	27 00	60	4	28 00	60	4	184
178	24 00	60	2	25 00	60	2	26 00	60	2	27 00	60	2	28 00	60	2	182
180	24 00	+60	0	25 00	+60	0	26 00	+60	0	27 00	+60	0	28 00	+60	0	180

LAT 89°

15° 16° 17° 18° 19° 20° 21° 22° 23° 24° 25° 26° 27° 28° 29°

S. Lat. {LHA greater than 180°....... Zn=180−Z; LHA less than 180°........... Zn=180+Z}

DECLINATION (15°-29°) SAME NAME AS LATITUDE

LAT 89°

TABLE 1 — ALTITUDE CORRECTION FOR CHANGE IN POSITION OF OBSERVER

Rel. Zn	Distance Made Good — nautical miles																				Rel. Zn
	1	2	3	4	5	6	7	8	10	15	20	25	30	35	40	45	50	75	100	150	
°	′	′	′	′	′	′	′	′	′	′	′	′	′	′	′	′	′	′	′	′	°
000	+1·0	+2·0	+3·0	+4·0	+5·0	+6·0	+7·0	+8·0	+10·0	+15·0	+20·0	+25·0	+30·0	+35·0	+40·0	+45·0	+50·0	+75·0	+100·0	+150·0	**000**
002	1·0	2·0	3·0	4·0	5·0	6·0	7·0	8·0	10·0	15·0	20·0	25·0	30·0	35·0	40·0	45·0	50·0	75·0	99·9	149·9	**358**
004	1·0	2·0	3·0	4·0	5·0	6·0	7·0	8·0	10·0	15·0	20·0	24·9	29·9	34·9	39·9	44·9	49·9	74·8	99·8	149·6	**356**
006	1·0	2·0	3·0	4·0	5·0	6·0	7·0	8·0	9·9	14·9	19·9	24·9	29·8	34·8	39·8	44·8	49·7	74·6	99·5	149·2	**354**
008	1·0	2·0	3·0	4·0	5·0	5·9	6·9	7·9	9·9	14·9	19·8	24·8	29·7	34·7	39·6	44·6	49·5	74·3	99·0	148·5	**352**
010	+1·0	+2·0	+3·0	+3·9	+4·9	+5·9	+6·9	+7·9	+9·8	+14·8	+19·7	+24·6	+29·5	+34·5	+39·4	+44·3	+49·2	+73·9	+98·5	+147·7	**350**
012	1·0	2·0	2·9	3·9	4·9	5·9	6·8	7·8	9·8	14·7	19·6	24·5	29·3	34·2	39·1	44·0	48·9	73·4	97·8	146·7	**348**
014	1·0	1·9	2·9	3·9	4·9	5·8	6·8	7·8	9·7	14·6	19·4	24·3	29·1	34·0	38·8	43·7	48·5	72·8	97·0	145·5	**346**
016	1·0	1·9	2·9	3·8	4·8	5·8	6·7	7·7	9·6	14·4	19·2	24·0	28·8	33·6	38·5	43·3	48·1	72·1	96·1	144·2	**344**
018	1·0	1·9	2·9	3·8	4·8	5·7	6·7	7·6	9·5	14·3	19·0	23·8	28·5	33·3	38·0	42·8	47·6	71·3	95·1	142·7	**342**
020	+0·9	+1·9	+2·8	+3·8	+4·7	+5·6	+6·6	+7·5	+9·4	+14·1	+18·8	+23·5	+28·2	+32·9	+37·6	+42·3	+47·0	+70·5	+94·0	+141·0	**340**
022	0·9	1·9	2·8	3·7	4·6	5·6	6·5	7·4	9·3	13·9	18·5	23·2	27·8	32·5	37·1	41·7	46·4	69·5	92·7	139·1	**338**
024	0·9	1·8	2·7	3·7	4·6	5·5	6·4	7·3	9·1	13·7	18·3	22·8	27·4	32·0	36·5	41·1	45·7	68·5	91·4	137·0	**336**
026	0·9	1·8	2·7	3·6	4·5	5·4	6·3	7·2	9·0	13·5	18·0	22·5	27·0	31·5	36·0	40·4	44·9	67·4	89·9	134·8	**334**
028	0·9	1·8	2·6	3·5	4·4	5·3	6·2	7·1	8·8	13·2	17·7	22·1	26·5	30·9	35·3	39·7	44·1	66·2	88·3	132·4	**332**
030	+0·9	+1·7	+2·6	+3·5	+4·3	+5·2	+6·1	+6·9	+8·7	+13·0	+17·3	+21·7	+26·0	+30·3	+34·6	+39·0	+43·3	+65·0	+86·6	+129·9	**330**
032	0·8	1·7	2·5	3·4	4·2	5·1	5·9	6·8	8·5	12·7	17·0	21·2	25·4	29·7	33·9	38·2	42·4	63·6	84·8	127·2	**328**
034	0·8	1·7	2·5	3·3	4·1	5·0	5·8	6·6	8·3	12·4	16·6	20·7	24·9	29·0	33·2	37·3	41·5	62·2	82·9	124·4	**326**
036	0·8	1·6	2·4	3·2	4·0	4·9	5·7	6·5	8·1	12·1	16·2	20·2	24·3	28·3	32·4	36·4	40·5	60·7	80·9	121·4	**324**
038	0·8	1·6	2·4	3·2	3·9	4·7	5·5	6·3	7·9	11·8	15·8	19·7	23·6	27·6	31·5	35·5	39·4	59·1	78·8	118·2	**322**
040	+0·8	+1·5	+2·3	+3·1	+3·8	+4·6	+5·4	+6·1	+7·7	+11·5	+15·3	+19·2	+23·0	+26·8	+30·6	+34·5	+38·3	+57·5	+76·6	+114·9	**320**
042	0·7	1·5	2·2	3·0	3·7	4·5	5·2	5·9	7·4	11·1	14·9	18·6	22·3	26·0	29·7	33·4	37·2	55·7	74·3	111·5	**318**
044	0·7	1·4	2·2	2·9	3·6	4·3	5·0	5·8	7·2	10·8	14·4	18·0	21·6	25·2	28·8	32·4	36·0	54·0	71·9	107·9	**316**
046	0·7	1·4	2·1	2·8	3·5	4·2	4·9	5·6	6·9	10·4	13·9	17·4	20·8	24·3	27·8	31·3	34·7	52·1	69·5	104·2	**314**
048	0·7	1·3	2·0	2·7	3·3	4·0	4·7	5·4	6·7	10·0	13·4	16·7	20·1	23·4	26·8	30·1	33·5	50·2	66·9	100·4	**312**
050	+0·6	+1·3	+1·9	+2·6	+3·2	+3·9	+4·5	+5·1	+6·4	+9·6	+12·9	+16·1	+19·3	+22·5	+25·7	+28·9	+32·1	+48·2	+64·3	+96·4	**310**
052	0·6	1·2	1·8	2·5	3·1	3·7	4·3	4·9	6·2	9·2	12·3	15·4	18·5	21·5	24·6	27·7	30·8	46·2	61·6	92·3	**308**
054	0·6	1·2	1·8	2·4	2·9	3·5	4·1	4·7	5·9	8·8	11·8	14·7	17·6	20·6	23·5	26·5	29·4	44·1	58·8	88·2	**306**
056	0·6	1·1	1·7	2·2	2·8	3·4	3·9	4·5	5·6	8·4	11·2	14·0	16·8	19·6	22·4	25·2	28·0	41·9	55·9	83·9	**304**
058	0·5	1·1	1·6	2·1	2·6	3·2	3·7	4·2	5·3	7·9	10·6	13·2	15·9	18·5	21·2	23·8	26·5	39·7	53·0	79·5	**302**
060	+0·5	+1·0	+1·5	+2·0	+2·5	+3·0	+3·5	+4·0	+5·0	+7·5	+10·0	+12·5	+15·0	+17·5	+20·0	+22·5	+25·0	+37·5	+50·0	+75·0	**300**
062	0·5	0·9	1·4	1·9	2·3	2·8	3·3	3·8	4·7	7·0	9·4	11·7	14·1	16·4	18·8	21·1	23·5	35·2	46·9	70·4	**298**
064	0·4	0·9	1·3	1·8	2·2	2·6	3·1	3·5	4·4	6·6	8·8	11·0	13·2	15·3	17·5	19·7	21·9	32·9	43·8	65·8	**296**
066	0·4	0·8	1·2	1·6	2·0	2·4	2·8	3·3	4·1	6·1	8·1	10·2	12·2	14·2	16·3	18·3	20·3	30·5	40·7	61·0	**294**
068	0·4	0·7	1·1	1·5	1·9	2·2	2·6	3·0	3·7	5·6	7·5	9·4	11·2	13·1	15·0	16·9	18·7	28·1	37·5	56·2	**292**
070	+0·3	+0·7	+1·0	+1·4	+1·7	+2·1	+2·4	+2·7	+3·4	+5·1	+6·8	+8·6	+10·3	+12·0	+13·7	+15·4	+17·1	+25·7	+34·2	+51·3	**290**
072	0·3	0·6	0·9	1·2	1·5	1·9	2·2	2·5	3·1	4·6	6·2	7·7	9·3	10·8	12·4	13·9	15·5	23·2	30·9	46·4	**288**
074	0·3	0·6	0·8	1·1	1·4	1·7	1·9	2·2	2·8	4·1	5·5	6·9	8·3	9·6	11·0	12·4	13·8	20·7	27·6	41·3	**286**
076	0·2	0·5	0·7	1·0	1·2	1·5	1·7	1·9	2·4	3·6	4·8	6·0	7·3	8·5	9·7	10·9	12·1	18·1	24·2	36·3	**284**
078	0·2	0·4	0·6	0·8	1·0	1·2	1·5	1·7	2·1	3·1	4·2	5·2	6·2	7·3	8·3	9·4	10·4	15·6	20·8	31·2	**282**
080	+0·2	+0·3	+0·5	+0·7	+0·9	+1·0	+1·2	+1·4	+1·7	+2·6	+3·5	+4·3	+5·2	+6·1	+6·9	+7·8	+8·7	+13·0	+17·4	+26·0	**280**
082	0·1	0·3	0·4	0·6	0·7	0·8	1·0	1·1	1·4	2·1	2·8	3·5	4·2	4·9	5·6	6·3	7·0	10·4	13·9	20·9	**278**
084	0·1	0·2	0·3	0·4	0·5	0·6	0·7	0·8	1·0	1·6	2·1	2·6	3·1	3·7	4·2	4·7	5·2	7·8	10·5	15·7	**276**
086	0·1	0·1	0·2	0·3	0·3	0·4	0·5	0·6	0·7	1·0	1·4	1·7	2·1	2·4	2·8	3·1	3·5	5·2	7·0	10·5	**274**
088	0·0	0·1	0·1	0·1	0·2	0·2	0·2	0·3	0·3	0·5	0·7	0·9	1·0	1·2	1·4	1·6	1·7	2·6	3·5	5·2	**272**
090	0·0	0·0	0·0	0·0	0·0	0·0	0·0	0·0	0·0	0·0	0·0	0·0	0·0	0·0	0·0	0·0	0·0	0·0	0·0	0·0	**270**
092	0·0	−0·1	−0·1	−0·1	−0·2	−0·2	−0·2	−0·3	−0·3	−0·5	−0·7	−0·9	−1·0	−1·2	−1·4	−1·6	−1·7	−2·6	−3·5	−5·2	**268**
094	0·1	0·1	0·2	0·3	0·3	0·4	0·5	0·6	0·7	1·0	1·4	1·7	2·1	2·4	2·8	3·1	3·5	5·2	7·0	10·5	**266**
096	0·1	0·2	0·3	0·4	0·5	0·6	0·7	0·8	1·0	1·6	2·1	2·6	3·1	3·7	4·2	4·7	5·2	7·8	10·5	15·7	**264**
098	0·1	0·3	0·4	0·6	0·7	0·8	1·0	1·1	1·4	2·1	2·8	3·5	4·2	4·9	5·6	6·3	7·0	10·4	13·9	20·9	**262**
100	0·2	0·3	0·5	0·7	0·9	1·0	1·2	1·4	1·7	2·6	3·5	4·3	5·2	6·1	6·9	7·8	8·7	13·0	17·4	26·0	**260**
102	−0·2	−0·4	−0·6	−0·8	−1·0	−1·2	−1·5	−1·7	−2·1	−3·1	−4·2	−5·2	−6·2	−7·3	−8·3	−9·4	−10·4	−15·6	−20·8	−31·2	**258**
104	0·2	0·5	0·7	1·0	1·2	1·5	1·7	1·9	2·4	3·6	4·8	6·0	7·3	8·5	9·7	10·9	12·1	18·1	24·2	36·3	**256**
106	0·3	0·6	0·8	1·1	1·4	1·7	1·9	2·2	2·8	4·1	5·5	6·9	8·3	9·6	11·0	12·4	13·8	20·7	27·6	41·3	**254**
108	0·3	0·6	0·9	1·2	1·5	1·9	2·2	2·5	3·1	4·6	6·2	7·7	9·3	10·8	12·4	13·9	15·5	23·2	30·9	46·4	**252**
110	0·3	0·7	1·0	1·4	1·7	2·1	2·4	2·7	3·4	5·1	6·8	8·6	10·3	12·0	13·7	15·4	17·1	25·7	34·2	51·3	**250**
112	−0·4	−0·7	−1·1	−1·5	−1·9	−2·2	−2·6	−3·0	−3·7	−5·6	−7·5	−9·4	−11·2	−13·1	−15·0	−16·9	−18·7	−28·1	−37·5	−56·2	**248**
114	0·4	0·8	1·2	1·6	2·0	2·4	2·8	3·3	4·1	6·1	8·1	10·2	12·2	14·2	16·3	18·3	20·3	30·5	40·7	61·0	**246**
116	0·4	0·9	1·3	1·8	2·2	2·6	3·1	3·5	4·4	6·6	8·8	11·0	13·2	15·3	17·5	19·7	21·9	32·9	43·8	65·8	**244**
118	0·5	0·9	1·4	1·9	2·3	2·8	3·3	3·8	4·7	7·0	9·4	11·7	14·1	16·4	18·8	21·1	23·5	35·2	46·9	70·4	**242**
120	0·5	1·0	1·5	2·0	2·5	3·0	3·5	4·0	5·0	7·5	10·0	12·5	15·0	17·5	20·0	22·5	25·0	37·5	50·0	75·0	**240**
122	−0·5	−1·1	−1·6	−2·1	−2·6	−3·2	−3·7	−4·2	−5·3	−7·9	−10·6	−13·2	−15·9	−18·5	−21·2	−23·8	−26·5	−39·7	−53·0	−79·5	**238**
124	0·6	1·1	1·7	2·2	2·8	3·4	3·9	4·5	5·6	8·4	11·2	14·0	16·8	19·6	22·4	25·2	28·0	41·9	55·9	83·9	**236**
126	0·6	1·2	1·8	2·4	2·9	3·5	4·1	4·7	5·9	8·8	11·8	14·7	17·6	20·6	23·5	26·5	29·4	44·1	58·8	88·2	**234**
128	0·6	1·2	1·8	2·5	3·1	3·7	4·3	4·9	6·2	9·2	12·3	15·4	18·5	21·5	24·6	27·7	30·8	46·2	61·6	92·3	**232**
130	0·6	1·3	1·9	2·6	3·2	3·9	4·5	5·1	6·4	9·6	12·9	16·1	19·3	22·5	25·7	28·9	32·1	48·2	64·3	96·4	**230**
132	−0·7	−1·3	−2·0	−2·7	−3·3	−4·0	−4·7	−5·4	−6·7	−10·0	−13·4	−16·7	−20·1	−23·4	−26·8	−30·1	−33·5	−50·2	−66·9	−100·4	**228**
134	0·7	1·4	2·1	2·8	3·5	4·2	4·9	5·6	6·9	10·4	13·9	17·4	20·8	24·3	27·8	31·3	34·7	52·1	69·5	104·2	**226**
136	0·7	1·4	2·2	2·9	3·6	4·3	5·0	5·8	7·2	10·8	14·4	18·0	21·6	25·2	28·8	32·4	36·0	54·0	71·9	107·9	**224**
138	0·7	1·5	2·2	3·0	3·7	4·5	5·2	5·9	7·4	11·1	14·9	18·6	22·3	26·0	29·7	33·4	37·2	55·7	74·3	111·5	**222**
140	0·8	1·5	2·3	3·1	3·8	4·6	5·4	6·1	7·7	11·5	15·3	19·2	23·0	26·8	30·6	34·5	38·3	57·5	76·6	114·9	**220**
142	−0·8	−1·6	−2·4	−3·2	−3·9	−4·7	−5·5	−6·3	−7·9	−11·8	−15·8	−19·7	−23·6	−27·6	−31·5	−35·5	−39·4	−59·1	−78·8	−118·2	**218**
144	0·8	1·6	2·4	3·2	4·0	4·9	5·7	6·5	8·1	12·1	16·2	20·2	24·3	28·3	32·4	36·4	40·5	60·7	80·9	121·4	**216**
146	0·8	1·7	2·5	3·3	4·1	5·0	5·8	6·6	8·3	12·4	16·6	20·7	24·9	29·0	33·2	37·3	41·5	62·2	82·9	124·4	**214**
148	0·8	1·7	2·5	3·4	4·2	5·1	5·9	6·8	8·5	12·7	17·0	21·2	25·4	29·7	33·9	38·2	42·4	63·6	84·8	127·2	**212**
150	0·9	1·7	2·6	3·5	4·3	5·2	6·1	6·9	8·7	13·0	17·3	21·7	26·0	30·3	34·6	39·0	43·3	65·0	86·6	129·9	**210**
152	−0·9	−1·8	−2·6	−3·5	−4·4	−5·3	−6·2	−7·1	−8·8	−13·2	−17·7	−22·1	−26·5	−30·9	−35·3	−39·7	−44·1	−66·2	−88·3	−132·4	**208**
154	0·9	1·8	2·7	3·6	4·5	5·4	6·3	7·2	9·0	13·5	18·0	22·5	27·0	31·5	36·0	40·4	44·9	67·4	89·9	134·8	**206**
156	0·9	1·8	2·7	3·7	4·6	5·5	6·4	7·3	9·1	13·7	18·3	22·8	27·4	32·0	36·5	41·1	45·7	68·5	91·4	137·0	**204**
158	0·9	1·9	2·8	3·7	4·6	5·6	6·5	7·4	9·3	13·9	18·5	23·2	27·8	32·5	37·1	41·7	46·4	69·5	92·7	139·1	**202**
160	0·9	1·9	2·8	3·8	4·7	5·6	6·6	7·5	9·4	14·1	18·8	23·5	28·2	32·9	37·6	42·3	47·0	70·5	94·0	141·0	**200**
162	−1·0	−1·9	−2·9	−3·8	−4·8	−5·7	−6·7	−7·6	−9·5	−14·3	−19·0	−23·8	−28·5	−33·3	−38·0	−42·8	−47·6	−71·3	−95·1	−142·7	**198**
164	1·0	1·9	2·9	3·8	4·8	5·8	6·7	7·7	9·6	14·4	19·2	24·0	28·8	33·6	38·5	43·3	48·1	72·1	96·1	144·2	**196**
166	1·0	1·9	2·9	3·9	4·9	5·8	6·8	7·8	9·7	14·6	19·4	24·3	29·1	34·0	38·8	43·7	48·5	72·8	97·0	145·5	**194**
168	1·0	2·0	2·9	3·9	4·9	5·9	6·8	7·8	9·8	14·7	19·6	24·5	29·3	34·2	39·1	44·0	48·9	73·4	97·8	146·7	**192**
170	1·0	2·0	3·0	3·9	4·9	5·9	6·9	7·9	9·8	14·8	19·7	24·6	29·5	34·5	39·4	44·3	49·2	73·9	98·5	147·7	**190**
172	−1·0	−2·0	−3·0	−4·0	−5·0	−5·9	−6·9	−7·9	−9·9	−14·9	−19·8	−24·8	−29·7	−34·7	−39·6	−44·6	−49·5	−74·3	−99·0	−148·5	**188**
174	1·0	2·0	3·0	4·0	5·0	6·0	7·0	8·0	9·9	14·9	19·9	24·9	29·8	34·8	39·8	44·8	49·7	74·6	99·5	149·2	**186**
176	1·0	2·0	3·0	4·0	5·0	6·0	7·0	8·0	10·0	15·0	20·0	24·9	29·9	34·9	39·9	44·9	49·9	74·8	99·8	149·6	**184**
178	1·0	2·0	3·0	4·0	5·0	6·0	7·0	8·0	10·0	15·0	20·0	25·0	30·0	35·0	40·0	45·0	50·0	75·0	99·9	149·9	**182**
180	1·0	2·0	3·0	4·0	5·0	6·0	7·0	8·0	10·0	15·0	20·0	25·0	30·0	35·0	40·0	45·0	50·0	75·0	100·0	150·0	**180**

Time of fix or computation	Sign from Table	To observed altitude	To tabulated altitude	To intercept	Time of fix or computation	Sign from Table	To observed altitude	To tabulated altitude	To intercept
Later than observation	+ −	Add Subtract	Subtract Add	Add Subtract	**Earlier than observation**	+ −	Subtract Add	Add Subtract	Subtract Add

Rel. Z_n = Relative Azimuth = $Z_n - C$ = True Azimuth − True Track

TABLE 2 — ALTITUDE CORRECTION FOR CHANGE IN POSITION OF BODY

Correction for 1 Minute of Time

True Zn	Latitude 0°	5°	10°	15°	20°	25°	30°	35°	40°	45°	50°	55°	60°	65°	70°	75°	80°	85°	True Zn
°	′	′	′	′	′	′	′	′	′	′	′	′	′	′	′	′	′	′	°
090	+15·0	+15·0	+14·8	+14·5	+14·1	+13·6	+13·0	+12·3	+11·5	+10·6	+9·7	+8·6	+7·5	+6·4	+5·1	+3·9	+2·6	+1·3	090
093	15·0	15·0	14·8	14·5	14·1	13·6	13·0	12·3	11·5	10·6	9·7	8·6	7·5	6·3	5·1	3·9	2·6	1·3	087
096	15·0	14·9	14·7	14·4	14·1	13·6	13·0	12·3	11·5	10·6	9·6	8·6	7·5	6·3	5·1	3·9	2·6	1·3	084
099	14·9	14·8	14·6	14·3	14·0	13·5	12·9	12·2	11·4	10·5	9·5	8·5	7·4	6·3	5·1	3·8	2·6	1·3	081
102	14·7	14·7	14·5	14·2	13·8	13·3	12·7	12·1	11·3	10·4	9·5	8·4	7·4	6·2	5·0	3·8	2·6	1·3	078
105	+14·5	+14·5	+14·3	+14·0	+13·7	+13·2	+12·6	+11·9	+11·1	+10·3	+9·3	+8·3	+7·3	+6·1	+5·0	+3·8	+2·5	+1·3	075
108	14·3	14·3	14·1	13·8	13·4	13·0	12·4	11·7	11·0	10·1	9·2	8·2	7·2	6·0	4·9	3·7	2·5	1·2	072
111	14·0	14·0	13·8	13·6	13·2	12·7	12·2	11·5	10·8	9·9	9·0	8·1	7·0	5·9	4·8	3·6	2·4	1·2	069
114	13·7	13·7	13·5	13·3	12·9	12·5	11·9	11·3	10·5	9·7	8·8	7·9	6·9	5·8	4·7	3·6	2·4	1·2	066
117	13·4	13·4	13·2	12·9	12·6	12·1	11·6	11·0	10·3	9·5	8·6	7·7	6·7	5·7	4·6	3·5	2·3	1·2	063
120	+13·0	+13·0	+12·8	+12·6	+12·2	+11·8	+11·3	+10·7	+10·0	+9·2	+8·4	+7·5	+6·5	+5·5	+4·5	+3·4	+2·3	+1·1	060
123	12·6	12·6	12·4	12·2	11·9	11·4	10·9	10·3	9·7	8·9	8·1	7·2	6·3	5·3	4·3	3·3	2·2	1·1	057
126	12·2	12·1	12·0	11·8	11·4	11·0	10·5	10·0	9·3	8·6	7·8	7·0	6·1	5·1	4·2	3·1	2·1	1·1	054
129	11·7	11·6	11·5	11·3	11·0	10·6	10·1	9·6	9·0	8·3	7·5	6·7	5·8	4·9	4·0	3·0	2·0	1·0	051
132	11·2	11·1	11·0	10·8	10·5	10·1	9·7	9·2	8·6	7·9	7·2	6·4	5·6	4·7	3·8	2·9	1·9	1·0	048
135	+10·6	+10·6	+10·5	+10·3	+10·0	+9·6	+9·2	+8·7	+8·1	+7·5	+6·8	+6·1	+5·3	+4·5	+3·6	+2·8	+1·8	+0·9	045
138	10·1	10·0	9·9	9·7	9·5	9·1	8·7	8·2	7·7	7·1	6·5	5·8	5·0	4·3	3·4	2·6	1·7	0·9	042
141	9·5	9·4	9·3	9·1	8·9	8·6	8·2	7·8	7·3	6·7	6·1	5·4	4·7	4·0	3·2	2·4	1·6	0·8	039
144	8·8	8·8	8·7	8·5	8·3	8·0	7·7	7·2	6·8	6·3	5·7	5·1	4·4	3·7	3·0	2·3	1·5	0·8	036
147	8·2	8·2	8·1	7·9	7·7	7·4	7·1	6·7	6·3	5·8	5·3	4·7	4·1	3·5	2·8	2·1	1·4	0·7	033
150	+7·5	+7·5	+7·4	+7·3	+7·1	+6·8	+6·5	+6·2	+5·8	+5·3	+4·8	+4·3	+3·8	+3·2	+2·6	+1·9	+1·3	+0·7	030
153	6·8	6·8	6·7	6·6	6·4	6·2	5·9	5·6	5·2	4·8	4·4	3·9	3·4	2·9	2·3	1·8	1·2	0·6	027
156	6·1	6·1	6·0	5·9	5·7	5·5	5·3	5·0	4·7	4·3	3·9	3·5	3·1	2·6	2·1	1·6	1·1	0·5	024
159	5·4	5·4	5·3	5·2	5·1	4·9	4·7	4·4	4·1	3·8	3·5	3·1	2·7	2·3	1·8	1·4	0·9	0·5	021
162	4·6	4·6	4·6	4·5	4·4	4·2	4·0	3·8	3·6	3·3	3·0	2·7	2·3	2·0	1·6	1·2	0·8	0·4	018
165	+3·9	+3·9	+3·8	+3·8	+3·7	+3·5	+3·4	+3·2	+3·0	+2·8	+2·5	+2·2	+1·9	+1·6	+1·3	+1·0	+0·7	+0·3	015
168	3·1	3·1	3·1	3·0	2·9	2·8	2·7	2·6	2·4	2·2	2·0	1·8	1·6	1·3	1·1	0·8	0·5	0·3	012
171	2·4	2·3	2·3	2·3	2·2	2·1	2·0	1·9	1·8	1·7	1·5	1·3	1·2	1·0	0·8	0·6	0·4	0·2	009
174	1·6	1·6	1·5	1·5	1·5	1·4	1·4	1·3	1·2	1·1	1·0	0·9	0·8	0·7	0·5	0·4	0·3	0·1	006
177	0·8	0·8	0·8	0·8	0·7	0·7	0·7	0·6	0·6	0·6	0·5	0·5	0·4	0·3	0·3	0·2	0·1	0·1	003
180	0·0	0·0	0·0	0·0	0·0	0·0	0·0	0·0	0·0	0·0	0·0	0·0	0·0	0·0	0·0	0·0	0·0	0·0	000
183	−0·8	−0·8	−0·8	−0·8	−0·7	−0·7	−0·7	−0·6	−0·6	−0·6	−0·5	−0·5	−0·4	−0·3	−0·3	−0·2	−0·1	−0·1	357
186	1·6	1·6	1·5	1·5	1·5	1·4	1·4	1·3	1·2	1·1	1·0	0·9	0·8	0·7	0·5	0·4	0·3	0·1	354
189	2·4	2·3	2·3	2·3	2·2	2·1	2·0	1·9	1·8	1·7	1·5	1·3	1·2	1·0	0·8	0·6	0·4	0·2	351
192	3·1	3·1	3·1	3·0	2·9	2·8	2·7	2·6	2·4	2·2	2·0	1·8	1·6	1·3	1·1	0·8	0·5	0·3	348
195	3·9	3·9	3·8	3·8	3·7	3·5	3·4	3·2	3·0	2·8	2·5	2·2	1·9	1·6	1·3	1·0	0·7	0·3	345
198	−4·6	−4·6	−4·6	−4·5	−4·4	−4·2	−4·0	−3·8	−3·6	−3·3	−3·0	−2·7	−2·3	−2·0	−1·6	−1·2	−0·8	−0·4	342
201	5·4	5·4	5·3	5·2	5·1	4·9	4·7	4·4	4·1	3·8	3·5	3·1	2·7	2·3	1·8	1·4	0·9	0·5	339
204	6·1	6·1	6·0	5·9	5·7	5·5	5·3	5·0	4·7	4·3	3·9	3·5	3·1	2·6	2·1	1·6	1·1	0·5	336
207	6·8	6·8	6·7	6·6	6·4	6·2	5·9	5·6	5·2	4·8	4·4	3·9	3·4	2·9	2·3	1·8	1·2	0·6	333
210	7·5	7·5	7·4	7·3	7·1	6·8	6·5	6·2	5·8	5·3	4·8	4·3	3·8	3·2	2·6	1·9	1·3	0·7	330
213	−8·2	−8·2	−8·1	−7·9	−7·7	−7·4	−7·1	−6·7	−6·3	−5·8	−5·3	−4·7	−4·1	−3·5	−2·8	−2·1	−1·4	−0·7	327
216	8·8	8·8	8·7	8·5	8·3	8·0	7·7	7·2	6·8	6·3	5·7	5·1	4·4	3·7	3·0	2·3	1·5	0·8	324
219	9·5	9·4	9·3	9·1	8·9	8·6	8·2	7·8	7·3	6·7	6·1	5·4	4·7	4·0	3·2	2·4	1·6	0·8	321
222	10·1	10·0	9·9	9·7	9·5	9·1	8·7	8·2	7·7	7·1	6·5	5·8	5·0	4·3	3·4	2·6	1·7	0·9	318
225	10·6	10·6	10·5	10·3	10·0	9·6	9·2	8·7	8·1	7·5	6·8	6·1	5·3	4·5	3·6	2·8	1·8	0·9	315
228	−11·2	−11·1	−11·0	−10·8	−10·5	−10·1	−9·7	−9·2	−8·6	−7·9	−7·2	−6·4	−5·6	−4·7	−3·8	−2·9	−1·9	−1·0	312
231	11·7	11·6	11·5	11·3	11·0	10·6	10·1	9·6	9·0	8·3	7·5	6·7	5·8	4·9	4·0	3·0	2·0	1·0	309
234	12·2	12·1	12·0	11·8	11·4	11·0	10·5	10·0	9·3	8·6	7·8	7·0	6·1	5·1	4·2	3·1	2·1	1·1	306
237	12·6	12·6	12·4	12·2	11·9	11·4	10·9	10·3	9·7	8·9	8·1	7·2	6·3	5·3	4·3	3·3	2·2	1·1	303
240	13·0	13·0	12·8	12·6	12·2	11·8	11·3	10·7	10·0	9·2	8·4	7·5	6·5	5·5	4·5	3·4	2·3	1·1	300
243	−13·4	−13·4	−13·2	−12·9	−12·6	−12·1	−11·6	−11·0	−10·3	−9·5	−8·6	−7·7	−6·7	−5·7	−4·6	−3·5	−2·3	−1·2	297
246	13·7	13·7	13·5	13·3	12·9	12·5	11·9	11·3	10·5	9·7	8·8	7·9	6·9	5·8	4·7	3·6	2·4	1·2	294
249	14·0	14·0	13·8	13·6	13·2	12·7	12·2	11·5	10·8	9·9	9·0	8·1	7·0	5·9	4·8	3·6	2·4	1·2	291
252	14·3	14·3	14·1	13·8	13·4	13·0	12·4	11·7	11·0	10·1	9·2	8·2	7·2	6·0	4·9	3·7	2·5	1·2	288
255	14·5	14·5	14·3	14·0	13·7	13·2	12·6	11·9	11·1	10·3	9·3	8·3	7·3	6·1	5·0	3·8	2·5	1·3	285
258	−14·7	−14·7	−14·5	−14·2	−13·8	−13·3	−12·7	−12·1	−11·3	−10·4	−9·5	−8·4	−7·4	−6·2	−5·0	−3·8	−2·6	−1·3	282
261	14·9	14·8	14·6	14·3	14·0	13·5	12·9	12·2	11·4	10·5	9·5	8·5	7·4	6·3	5·1	3·8	2·6	1·3	279
264	15·0	14·9	14·7	14·4	14·1	13·6	13·0	12·3	11·5	10·6	9·6	8·6	7·5	6·3	5·1	3·9	2·6	1·3	276
267	15·0	15·0	14·8	14·5	14·1	13·6	13·0	12·3	11·5	10·6	9·7	8·6	7·5	6·3	5·1	3·9	2·6	1·3	273
270	15·0	15·0	14·8	14·5	14·1	13·6	13·0	12·3	11·5	10·6	9·7	8·6	7·5	6·4	5·1	3·9	2·6	1·3	270

Interpolation for Altitude Correction for less than 1ᵐ of Time

δt	Value from Table 2: 1′	2′	3′	4′	5′	6′	7′	8′	9′	10′	11′	12′	13′	14′	15′
s	′	′	′	′	′	′	′	′	′	′	′	′	′	′	′
00	0·0	0·0	0·0	0·0	0·0	0·0	0·0	0·0	0·0	0·0	0·0	0·0	0·0	0·0	0·0
10	0·2	0·3	0·5	0·7	0·8	1·0	1·2	1·3	1·5	1·7	1·8	2·0	2·2	2·3	2·5
20	0·3	0·7	1·0	1·3	1·7	2·0	2·3	2·7	3·0	3·3	3·7	4·0	4·3	4·7	5·0
30	0·5	1·0	1·5	2·0	2·5	3·0	3·5	4·0	4·5	5·0	5·5	6·0	6·5	7·0	7·5
40	0·7	1·3	2·0	2·7	3·3	4·0	4·7	5·3	6·0	6·7	7·3	8·0	8·7	9·3	10·0
50	0·8	1·7	2·5	3·3	4·2	5·0	5·8	6·7	7·5	8·3	9·2	10·0	10·8	11·7	12·5
60	1·0	2·0	3·0	4·0	5·0	6·0	7·0	8·0	9·0	10·0	11·0	12·0	13·0	14·0	15·0

Rules of How to Apply the Sign of Tables 1 and 2

Time of fix or computation	Sign from Table	To observed Altitude	To tabulated Altitude	To Intercept
Later than observation	+	Add	Subtract	Add
	−	Subtract	Add	Subtract
Earlier than observation	+	Subtract	Add	Subtract
	−	Add	Subtract	Add

TABLE 3 — CONVERSION OF ARC TO TIME

0°–60°		60°–120°		120°–180°		180°–240°		240°–300°		300°–360°		0′–60′		0″–60″	
°	h m	°	h m	°	h m	°	h m	°	h m	°	h m	′	m s	″	s
0	0 00	60	4 00	120	8 00	180	12 00	240	16 00	300	20 00	0	0 00	0	0·00
1	0 04	61	4 04	121	8 04	181	12 04	241	16 04	301	20 04	1	0 04	1	0·07
2	0 08	62	4 08	122	8 08	182	12 08	242	16 08	302	20 08	2	0 08	2	0·13
3	0 12	63	4 12	123	8 12	183	12 12	243	16 12	303	20 12	3	0 12	3	0·20
4	0 16	64	4 16	124	8 16	184	12 16	244	16 16	304	20 16	4	0 16	4	0·27
5	0 20	65	4 20	125	8 20	185	12 20	245	16 20	305	20 20	5	0 20	5	0·33
6	0 24	66	4 24	126	8 24	186	12 24	246	16 24	306	20 24	6	0 24	6	0·40
7	0 28	67	4 28	127	8 28	187	12 28	247	16 28	307	20 28	7	0 28	7	0·47
8	0 32	68	4 32	128	8 32	188	12 32	248	16 32	308	20 32	8	0 32	8	0·53
9	0 36	69	4 36	129	8 36	189	12 36	249	16 36	309	20 36	9	0 36	9	0·60
10	0 40	70	4 40	130	8 40	190	12 40	250	16 40	310	20 40	10	0 40	10	0·67
11	0 44	71	4 44	131	8 44	191	12 44	251	16 44	311	20 44	11	0 44	11	0·73
12	0 48	72	4 48	132	8 48	192	12 48	252	16 48	312	20 48	12	0 48	12	0·80
13	0 52	73	4 52	133	8 52	193	12 52	253	16 52	313	20 52	13	0 52	13	0·87
14	0 56	74	4 56	134	8 56	194	12 56	254	16 56	314	20 56	14	0 56	14	0·93
15	1 00	75	5 00	135	9 00	195	13 00	255	17 00	315	21 00	15	1 00	15	1·00
16	1 04	76	5 04	136	9 04	196	13 04	256	17 04	316	21 04	16	1 04	16	1·07
17	1 08	77	5 08	137	9 08	197	13 08	257	17 08	317	21 08	17	1 08	17	1·13
18	1 12	78	5 12	138	9 12	198	13 12	258	17 12	318	21 12	18	1 12	18	1·20
19	1 16	79	5 16	139	9 16	199	13 16	259	17 16	319	21 16	19	1 16	19	1·27
20	1 20	80	5 20	140	9 20	200	13 20	260	17 20	320	21 20	20	1 20	20	1·33
21	1 24	81	5 24	141	9 24	201	13 24	261	17 24	321	21 24	21	1 24	21	1·40
22	1 28	82	5 28	142	9 28	202	13 28	262	17 28	322	21 28	22	1 28	22	1·47
23	1 32	83	5 32	143	9 32	203	13 32	263	17 32	323	21 32	23	1 32	23	1·53
24	1 36	84	5 36	144	9 36	204	13 36	264	17 36	324	21 36	24	1 36	24	1·60
25	1 40	85	5 40	145	9 40	205	13 40	265	17 40	325	21 40	25	1 40	25	1·67
26	1 44	86	5 44	146	9 44	206	13 44	266	17 44	326	21 44	26	1 44	26	1·73
27	1 48	87	5 48	147	9 48	207	13 48	267	17 48	327	21 48	27	1 48	27	1·80
28	1 52	88	5 52	148	9 52	208	13 52	268	17 52	328	21 52	28	1 52	28	1·87
29	1 56	89	5 56	149	9 56	209	13 56	269	17 56	329	21 56	29	1 56	29	1·93
30	2 00	90	6 00	150	10 00	210	14 00	270	18 00	330	22 00	30	2 00	30	2·00
31	2 04	91	6 04	151	10 04	211	14 04	271	18 04	331	22 04	31	2 04	31	2·07
32	2 08	92	6 08	152	10 08	212	14 08	272	18 08	332	22 08	32	2 08	32	2·13
33	2 12	93	6 12	153	10 12	213	14 12	273	18 12	333	22 12	33	2 12	33	2·20
34	2 16	94	6 16	154	10 16	214	14 16	274	18 16	334	22 16	34	2 16	34	2·27
35	2 20	95	6 20	155	10 20	215	14 20	275	18 20	335	22 20	35	2 20	35	2·33
36	2 24	96	6 24	156	10 24	216	14 24	276	18 24	336	22 24	36	2 24	36	2·40
37	2 28	97	6 28	157	10 28	217	14 28	277	18 28	337	22 28	37	2 28	37	2·47
38	2 32	98	6 32	158	10 32	218	14 32	278	18 32	338	22 32	38	2 32	38	2·53
39	2 36	99	6 36	159	10 36	219	14 36	279	18 36	339	22 36	39	2 36	39	2·60
40	2 40	100	6 40	160	10 40	220	14 40	280	18 40	340	22 40	40	2 40	40	2·67
41	2 44	101	6 44	161	10 44	221	14 44	281	18 44	341	22 44	41	2 44	41	2·73
42	2 48	102	6 48	162	10 48	222	14 48	282	18 48	342	22 48	42	2 48	42	2·80
43	2 52	103	6 52	163	10 52	223	14 52	283	18 52	343	22 52	43	2 52	43	2·87
44	2 56	104	6 56	164	10 56	224	14 56	284	18 56	344	22 56	44	2 56	44	2·93
45	3 00	105	7 00	165	11 00	225	15 00	285	19 00	345	23 00	45	3 00	45	3·00
46	3 04	106	7 04	166	11 04	226	15 04	286	19 04	346	23 04	46	3 04	46	3·07
47	3 08	107	7 08	167	11 08	227	15 08	287	19 08	347	23 08	47	3 08	47	3·13
48	3 12	108	7 12	168	11 12	228	15 12	288	19 12	348	23 12	48	3 12	48	3·20
49	3 16	109	7 16	169	11 16	229	15 16	289	19 16	349	23 16	49	3 16	49	3·27
50	3 20	110	7 20	170	11 20	230	15 20	290	19 20	350	23 20	50	3 20	50	3·33
51	3 24	111	7 24	171	11 24	231	15 24	291	19 24	351	23 24	51	3 24	51	3·40
52	3 28	112	7 28	172	11 28	232	15 28	292	19 28	352	23 28	52	3 28	52	3·47
53	3 32	113	7 32	173	11 32	233	15 32	293	19 32	353	23 32	53	3 32	53	3·53
54	3 36	114	7 36	174	11 36	234	15 36	294	19 36	354	23 36	54	3 36	54	3·60
55	3 40	115	7 40	175	11 40	235	15 40	295	19 40	355	23 40	55	3 40	55	3·67
56	3 44	116	7 44	176	11 44	236	15 44	296	19 44	356	23 44	56	3 44	56	3·73
57	3 48	117	7 48	177	11 48	237	15 48	297	19 48	357	23 48	57	3 48	57	3·80
58	3 52	118	7 52	178	11 52	238	15 52	298	19 52	358	23 52	58	3 52	58	3·87
59	3 56	119	7 56	179	11 56	239	15 56	299	19 56	359	23 56	59	3 56	59	3·93
60	4 00	120	8 00	180	12 00	240	16 00	300	20 00	360	24 00	60	4 00	60	4·00

TABLE 4 — GHA and Declination of the Sun for the Years 2001 – 2036 — Argument "Orbit Time"

OT 00ʰ	JAN E	JAN Dec		FEB E	FEB Dec		MAR E	MAR Dec		APR E	APR Dec	
d	° ′	° ′		° ′	° ′		° ′	° ′		° ′	° ′	
1	4 12	S23 03	5	1 38	S17 16	17	1 53	S7 49	23	3 58	N 4 19	23
2	4 05	22 58	6	1 36	16 59	18	1 56	7 26	23	4 03	4 42	23
3	3 58	22 52	5	1 35	16 41	17	1 59	7 03	23	4 07	5 05	23
4	3 52	22 47	7	1 33	16 24	18	2 02	6 40	23	4 12	5 28	23
5	3 45	22 40	6	1 32	16 06	18	2 05	6 17	23	4 16	5 51	23
6	3 38	S22 34	8	1 30	S15 48	19	2 09	S5 54	23	4 20	N 6 14	22
7	3 31	22 26	7	1 29	15 29	18	2 12	5 31	24	4 25	6 36	23
8	3 25	22 19	8	1 28	15 11	19	2 16	5 07	23	4 29	6 59	22
9	3 19	22 11	9	1 28	14 52	20	2 19	4 44	24	4 33	7 21	23
10	3 12	22 02	9	1 27	14 32	19	2 23	4 20	23	4 37	7 44	22
11	3 06	S21 53	9	1 27	S14 13	20	2 27	S3 57	24	4 41	N 8 06	22
12	3 00	21 44	10	1 27	13 53	20	2 31	3 33	23	4 45	8 28	22
13	2 55	21 34	10	1 27	13 33	20	2 35	3 10	24	4 49	8 50	21
14	2 49	21 24	10	1 28	13 13	20	2 39	2 46	24	4 53	9 11	22
15	2 43	21 14	11	1 28	12 53	21	2 43	2 22	23	4 57	9 33	22
16	2 38	S21 03	12	1 29	S12 32	21	2 47	S1 59	24	5 00	N 9 55	21
17	2 33	20 51	12	1 30	12 11	21	2 51	1 35	24	5 04	10 16	21
18	2 28	20 39	12	1 31	11 50	21	2 56	1 11	24	5 07	10 37	21
19	2 23	20 27	12	1 32	11 29	21	3 00	0 47	23	5 11	10 58	21
20	2 19	20 15	13	1 33	11 08	22	3 04	0 24	24	5 14	11 19	20
21	2 14	S20 02	14	1 35	S10 46	21	3 09	0 00	24	5 17	N11 39	21
22	2 10	19 48	13	1 36	10 25	22	3 13	N0 24	23	5 20	12 00	20
23	2 06	19 35	14	1 38	10 03	22	3 18	0 47	24	5 23	12 20	20
24	2 02	19 21	15	1 40	9 41	22	3 22	1 11	24	5 26	12 40	20
25	1 58	19 06	15	1 43	9 19	23	3 27	1 35	23	5 28	13 00	19
26	1 55	S18 51	15	1 45	S 8 56	22	3 31	N1 58	24	5 31	N13 19	20
27	1 52	18 36	15	1 47	8 34	23	3 36	2 22	23	5 34	13 39	19
28	1 48	18 21	16	1 50	8 11	22	3 40	2 45	24	5 36	13 58	19
29	1 46	18 05	16	1 53	7 49		3 45	3 09	23	5 38	14 17	18
30	1 43	17 49	16			23	3 49	3 32	23	5 40	14 35	19
31	1 41	S17 33	17				3 54	N3 55	24	5 42	N14 54	

OT 00ʰ	MAY E	MAY Dec		JUN E	JUN Dec		JUL E	JUL Dec		AUG E	AUG Dec	
d	° ′	° ′		° ′	° ′		° ′	° ′		° ′	° ′	
1	5 42	N14 54	18	5 35	N21 58	8	4 05	N23 08	4	3 24	N18 10	16
2	5 44	15 12	18	5 32	22 06	8	4 02	23 04	4	3 25	17 54	15
3	5 46	15 30	17	5 30	22 14	8	3 59	23 00	5	3 26	17 39	16
4	5 47	15 47	18	5 28	22 22	7	3 56	22 55	5	3 28	17 23	15
5	5 49	16 05	17	5 25	22 29	6	3 53	22 50	6	3 29	17 08	17
6	5 50	N16 22	17	5 22	N22 35	6	3 51	N22 44	6	3 30	N16 51	16
7	5 51	16 39	16	5 20	22 41	6	3 48	22 38	6	3 32	16 35	17
8	5 52	16 55	17	5 17	22 47	6	3 46	22 32	7	3 34	16 18	17
9	5 53	17 12	16	5 14	22 53	5	3 44	22 25	7	3 36	16 01	17
10	5 54	17 28	15	5 11	22 58	4	3 41	22 18	7	3 38	15 44	18
11	5 54	N17 43	16	5 08	N23 02	4	3 39	N22 11	8	3 40	N15 26	17
12	5 55	17 59	15	5 05	23 06	4	3 37	22 03	9	3 42	15 09	19
13	5 55	18 14	15	5 02	23 10	4	3 35	21 54	8	3 45	14 50	18
14	5 55	18 29	14	4 59	23 14	3	3 33	21 46	9	3 48	14 32	18
15	5 55	18 43	15	4 56	23 17	2	3 32	21 37	10	3 50	14 14	19
16	5 55	N18 58	13	4 52	N23 19	2	3 30	N21 27	10	3 53	N13 55	19
17	5 55	19 11	14	4 49	23 21	2	3 29	21 17	10	3 56	13 36	19
18	5 54	19 25	13	4 46	23 23	2	3 27	21 07	10	3 59	13 17	19
19	5 54	19 38	13	4 43	23 25	0	3 26	20 57	11	4 03	12 58	20
20	5 53	19 51	13	4 39	23 25	1	3 25	20 46	11	4 06	12 38	20
21	5 52	N20 04	12	4 36	N23 26	0	3 24	N20 35	12	4 10	N12 18	20
22	5 51	20 16	12	4 33	23 26	0	3 24	20 23	12	4 13	11 58	20
23	5 50	20 28	11	4 29	23 26	1	3 23	20 11	12	4 17	11 38	20
24	5 49	20 39	11	4 26	23 25	1	3 23	19 59	13	4 21	11 18	21
25	5 47	20 50	11	4 23	23 24	2	3 22	19 46	12	4 25	10 57	20
26	5 46	N21 01	11	4 20	N23 22	2	3 22	N19 34	14	4 29	N10 37	21
27	5 44	21 12	10	4 17	23 20	2	3 22	19 20	13	4 34	10 16	21
28	5 43	21 22	9	4 14	23 18	3	3 22	19 07	14	4 38	9 55	21
29	5 41	21 31	10	4 11	23 15	3	3 23	18 53	14	4 42	9 34	21
30	5 39	21 41	9	4 08	23 12	4	3 23	18 39	15	4 47	9 13	22
31	5 37	N21 50	8	4 05	N23 08		3 24	N18 24	14	4 52	N 8 51	22

OT 00ʰ	SEP E	SEP Dec		OCT E	OCT Dec		NOV E	NOV Dec		DEC E	DEC Dec		OT 00ʰ
d	° ′	° ′		° ′	° ′		° ′	° ′		° ′	° ′		d
1	4 56	N8 29	21	7 31	S 2 57	24	9 06	S14 14	19	7 50	S21 42	9	**1**
2	5 01	8 08	22	7 36	3 21	23	9 07	14 33	19	7 44	21 51	9	**2**
3	5 06	7 46	22	7 41	3 44	23	9 07	14 52	19	7 38	22 00	9	**3**
4	5 11	7 24	22	7 46	4 07	23	9 07	15 11	18	7 33	22 09	8	**4**
5	5 16	7 02	22	7 50	4 30	23	9 07	15 29	19	7 27	22 17	8	**5**
6	5 21	N6 40	23	7 55	S 4 53	23	9 06	S15 48	18	7 20	S22 25	7	**6**
7	5 26	6 17	22	7 59	5 16	23	9 06	16 06	17	7 14	22 32	7	**7**
8	5 31	5 55	23	8 03	5 39	23	9 05	16 23	18	7 08	22 39	6	**8**
9	5 36	5 32	22	8 08	6 02	23	9 04	16 41	17	7 01	22 45	6	**9**
10	5 41	5 10	23	8 12	6 25	23	9 03	16 58	17	6 54	22 51	6	**10**
11	5 46	N4 47	23	8 16	S 6 48	22	9 01	S17 15	17	6 47	S22 57	5	**11**
12	5 52	4 24	23	8 20	7 10	23	9 00	17 32	16	6 41	23 02	4	**12**
13	5 57	4 01	23	8 23	7 33	22	8 58	17 48	16	6 34	23 06	4	**13**
14	6 02	3 38	23	8 27	7 55	23	8 56	18 04	16	6 27	23 10	4	**14**
15	6 07	3 15	23	8 31	8 18	22	8 53	18 20	15	6 19	23 14	3	**15**
16	6 13	N2 52	23	8 34	S 8 40	22	8 51	S18 35	15	6 12	S23 17	3	**16**
17	6 18	2 29	23	8 37	9 02	22	8 48	18 50	15	6 05	23 20	2	**17**
18	6 23	2 06	23	8 40	9 24	22	8 45	19 05	14	5 58	23 22	2	**18**
19	6 29	1 43	24	8 43	9 46	21	8 42	19 19	14	5 50	23 24	1	**19**
20	6 34	1 19	23	8 46	10 07	22	8 39	19 33	13	5 43	23 25	1	**20**
21	6 40	N0 56	23	8 49	S10 29	21	8 35	S19 46	14	5 35	S23 26	0	**21**
22	6 45	0 33	24	8 51	10 50	21	8 32	20 00	13	5 28	23 26	0	**22**
23	6 50	0 09	23	8 53	11 11	21	8 28	20 13	12	5 21	23 26	1	**23**
24	6 55	S0 14	23	8 56	11 32	21	8 24	20 25	12	5 13	23 25	1	**24**
25	7 01	0 37	24	8 58	11 53	21	8 19	20 37	12	5 06	23 24	1	**25**
26	7 06	S1 01	23	8 59	S12 14	21	8 15	S20 49	12	4 58	S23 23	2	**26**
27	7 11	1 24	23	9 01	12 35	20	8 10	21 01	11	4 51	23 21	3	**27**
28	7 16	1 47	24	9 02	12 55	20	8 05	21 12	10	4 44	23 18	3	**28**
29	7 21	2 11	23	9 04	13 15	20	8 00	21 22	10	4 36	23 15	3	**29**
30	7 26	2 34	23	9 05	13 35	19	7 55	21 32	10	4 29	23 12	4	**30**
31	7 31	S2 57		9 05	S13 54	20	7 50	S21 42		4 22	S23 08	4	**31**

a — Correction from UT to OT

Year	Corr.	Year	Corr.	Year	Corr.
	h		h		h
2001	+ 10	**2013**	+ 13	**2025**	+ 15
2002	+ 5	**2014**	+ 7	**2026**	+ 9
2003	− 1	**2015**	+ 1	**2027**	+ 4
2004	− 7	**2016**	− 5	**2028**	− 2
...	+ 17*	...	+ 19*	...	+ 22*
2005	+ 11	**2017**	+ 14	**2029**	+ 16
2006	+ 6	**2018**	+ 8	**2030**	+ 10
2007	0	**2019**	+ 2	**2031**	+ 4
2008	− 6	**2020**	− 4	**2032**	− 1
...	+ 18*	...	+ 20*	...	+ 23*
2009	+ 12	**2021**	+ 14	**2033**	+ 17
2010	+ 6	**2022**	+ 8	**2034**	+ 11
2011	+ 1	**2023**	+ 3	**2035**	+ 5
2012	− 5	**2024**	− 3	**2036**	− 1
...	+ 19*	...	+ 21*	...	+ 23*

* After Feb. 29

b — Interpolation for Hours of OT

Diff.	1	2	3	4	5	6	7	8	9	10	11	12	13	14	15	16	17	18	19	20	21	22	23	24
h	′	′	′	′	′	′	′	′	′	′	′	′	′	′	′	′	′	′	′	′	′	′	′	′
0	0	0	0	0	0	0	0	0	0	0	0	0	0	0	0	0	0	0	0	0	0	0	0	0
1	0	0	0	0	0	0	0	0	0	0	0	1	1	1	1	1	1	1	1	1	1	1	1	1
2	0	0	0	0	0	1	1	1	1	1	1	1	1	1	1	1	1	2	2	2	2	2	2	2
3	0	0	0	1	1	1	1	1	1	1	1	2	2	2	2	2	2	2	2	3	3	3	3	3
4	0	0	1	1	1	1	1	1	2	2	2	2	2	2	3	3	3	3	3	3	4	4	4	4
5	0	0	1	1	1	1	1	2	2	2	2	3	3	3	3	3	4	4	4	4	4	5	5	5
6	0	1	1	1	1	2	2	2	2	3	3	3	3	4	4	4	4	5	5	5	5	6	6	6
7	0	1	1	1	1	2	2	2	3	3	3	4	4	4	4	5	5	5	6	6	6	6	7	7
8	0	1	1	1	2	2	2	3	3	3	4	4	4	5	5	5	6	6	6	7	7	7	8	8
9	0	1	1	2	2	2	3	3	3	4	4	5	5	5	6	6	6	7	7	8	8	8	9	9
10	0	1	1	2	2	3	3	3	4	4	5	5	5	6	6	7	7	8	8	8	9	9	10	10
11	0	1	1	2	2	3	3	4	4	5	5	6	6	6	7	7	8	8	9	9	10	10	11	11

Diff.	1	2	3	4	5	6	7	8	9	10	11	12	13	14	15	16	17	18	19	20	21	22	23	24
h	′	′	′	′	′	′	′	′	′	′	′	′	′	′	′	′	′	′	′	′	′	′	′	′
12	1	1	2	2	3	3	4	4	5	5	6	6	7	7	8	8	9	9	10	10	11	11	12	12
13	1	1	2	2	3	3	4	4	5	5	6	7	7	8	8	9	9	10	10	11	11	12	12	13
14	1	1	2	2	3	4	4	5	5	6	6	7	8	8	9	9	10	11	11	12	12	13	13	14
15	1	1	2	3	3	4	4	5	6	6	7	8	8	9	9	10	11	11	12	13	13	14	14	15
16	1	1	2	3	3	4	5	5	6	7	7	8	9	9	10	11	11	12	13	13	14	15	15	16
17	1	1	2	3	4	4	5	6	6	7	8	9	9	10	11	11	12	13	13	14	15	16	16	17
18	1	2	2	3	4	5	5	6	7	8	8	9	10	11	11	12	13	14	14	15	16	17	17	18
19	1	2	2	3	4	5	6	6	7	8	9	10	10	11	12	13	13	14	15	16	17	17	18	19
20	1	2	3	3	4	5	6	7	8	8	9	10	11	12	13	13	14	15	16	17	18	18	19	20
21	1	2	3	4	4	5	6	7	8	9	10	11	11	12	13	14	15	16	17	18	18	19	20	21
22	1	2	3	4	5	6	6	7	8	9	10	11	12	13	14	15	16	17	17	18	19	20	21	22
23	1	2	3	4	5	6	7	8	9	10	11	12	12	13	14	15	16	17	18	19	20	21	22	23

c: — Hours and Tens of Minutes of UT

h	**00**^{m} ° ′	**10**^{m} ° ′	**20**^{m} ° ′	**30**^{m} ° ′	**40**^{m} ° ′	**50**^{m} ° ′
0	175 00	177 30	180 00	182 30	185 00	187 30
1	190 00	192 30	195 00	197 30	200 00	202 30
2	205 00	207 30	210 00	212 30	215 00	217 30
3	220 00	222 30	225 00	227 30	230 00	232 30
4	235 00	237 30	240 00	242 30	245 00	247 30
5	250 00	252 30	255 00	257 30	260 00	262 30
6	265 00	267 30	270 00	272 30	275 00	277 30
7	280 00	282 30	285 00	287 30	290 00	292 30
8	295 00	297 30	300 00	302 30	305 00	307 30
9	310 00	312 30	315 00	317 30	320 00	322 30
10	325 00	327 30	330 00	332 30	335 00	337 30
11	340 00	342 30	345 00	347 30	350 00	352 30
12	355 00	357 30	0 00	2 30	5 00	7 30
13	10 00	12 30	15 00	17 30	20 00	22 30
14	25 00	27 30	30 00	32 30	35 00	37 30
15	40 00	42 30	45 00	47 30	50 00	52 30
16	55 00	57 30	60 00	62 30	65 00	67 30
17	70 00	72 30	75 00	77 30	80 00	82 30
18	85 00	87 30	90 00	92 30	95 00	97 30
19	100 00	102 30	105 00	107 30	110 00	112 30
20	115 00	117 30	120 00	122 30	125 00	127 30
21	130 00	132 30	135 00	137 30	140 00	142 30
22	145 00	147 30	150 00	152 30	155 00	157 30
23	160 00	162 30	165 00	167 30	170 00	172 30

d Minutes and Seconds of UT (in critical cases ascend)

m s	° ′	m s	° ′	m s	° ′	m s	° ′	m s	° ′	m s	° ′
00 00		**01 37**		**03 17**		**04 57**		**06 37**		**08 17**	
	0 00		0 25		0 50		1 15		1 40		2 05
01		**41**		**21**		**05 01**		**41**		**21**	
	0 01		0 26		0 51		1 16		1 41		2 06
05		**45**		**25**		**05**		**45**		**25**	
	0 02		0 27		0 52		1 17		1 42		2 07
09		**49**		**29**		**09**		**49**		**29**	
	0 03		0 28		0 53		1 18		1 43		2 08
13		**53**		**33**		**13**		**53**		**33**	
	0 04		0 29		0 54		1 19		1 44		2 09
17		**01 57**		**37**		**17**		**06 57**		**37**	
	0 05		0 30		0 55		1 20		1 45		2 10
21		**02 01**		**41**		**21**		**07 01**		**41**	
	0 06		0 31		0 56		1 21		1 46		2 11
25		**05**		**45**		**25**		**05**		**45**	
	0 07		0 32		0 57		1 22		1 47		2 12
29		**09**		**49**		**29**		**09**		**49**	
	0 08		0 33		0 58		1 23		1 48		2 13
33		**13**		**53**		**33**		**13**		**53**	
	0 09		0 34		0 59		1 24		1 49		2 14
37		**17**		**03 57**		**37**		**17**		**08 57**	
	0 10		0 35		1 00		1 25		1 50		2 15
41		**21**		**04 01**		**41**		**21**		**09 01**	
	0 11		0 36		1 01		1 26		1 51		2 16
45		**25**		**05**		**45**		**25**		**05**	
	0 12		0 37		1 02		1 27		1 52		2 17
49		**29**		**09**		**49**		**29**		**09**	
	0 13		0 38		1 03		1 28		1 53		2 18
53		**33**		**13**		**53**		**33**		**13**	
	0 14		0 39		1 04		1 29		1 54		2 19
00 57		**37**		**17**		**05 57**		**37**		**17**	
	0 15		0 40		1 05		1 30		1 55		2 20
01 01		**41**		**21**		**06 01**		**41**		**21**	
	0 16		0 41		1 06		1 31		1 56		2 21
05		**45**		**25**		**05**		**45**		**25**	
	0 17		0 42		1 07		1 32		1 57		2 22
09		**49**		**29**		**09**		**49**		**29**	
	0 18		0 43		1 08		1 33		1 58		2 23
13		**53**		**33**		**13**		**53**		**33**	
	0 19		0 44		1 09		1 34		1 59		2 24
17		**02 57**		**37**		**17**		**07 57**		**37**	
	0 20		0 45		1 10		1 35		2 00		2 25
21		**03 01**		**41**		**21**		**08 01**		**41**	
	0 21		0 46		1 11		1 36		2 01		2 26
25		**05**		**45**		**25**		**05**		**45**	
	0 22		0 47		1 12		1 37		2 02		2 27
29		**09**		**49**		**29**		**09**		**49**	
	0 23		0 48		1 13		1 38		2 03		2 28
33		**13**		**53**		**33**		**13**		**53**	
	0 24		0 49		1 14		1 39		2 04		2 29
37		**17**		**04 57**		**37**		**17**		**09 57**	
	0 25		0 50		1 15		1 40		2 05		2 30
01 41		**03 21**		**05 01**		**06 41**		**08 21**		**10 00**	

EXPLANATION

Table 4 and supplementary tables **a**, **b**, **c**, **d**, make possible the determination of the GHA and declination of the Sun for any time during the years 2001-2036. The main table gives E (5°+ Equation of Time) and declination of the Sun for the argument "Orbit Time" OT, the latter is formed by applying the h correction from Table **a** to the nearest integral hour of UT. In leap years the upper value of the correction is to be used for January and February and the lower value for the rest of the year. Thus, OT's corresponding to 2004 February 29^d 16^h 31^m UT and 2004 March 1^d 05^h 29^m UT are February 29^d 10^h 00^m and March 1^d 22^h 00^m, respectively.

Corrections to E and declination for OT are determined by entering Table **b** with the differences between consecutive values of E and of declination, respectively, as the horizontal argument, and with the number of hours of OT as the vertical argument. The declination differences are given in the main table.

The GHA is obtained by adding to the corrected E the value of the diurnal arc obtained from Tables **c** and **d**. The latter two tables must be entered with argument UT.

Example. To find the GHA and declination of the Sun on 2004 January 18^d at 03^h 30^m 35^s UT.

OT = UT nearest integral hour + Corr. (Table **a**).
= Jan. 18^d 04^h $- 7^h$ = Jan. 17^d 21^h

	° ′	Diff.		° ′	Diff.
Main Table, Jan 17^d OT, E	2 33	(−5)	Dec.	S 20 51	(−12)
Table **b** for 21^h OT	−4			−11	
Jan 17^d 21^h OT, corrected E	2 29		Dec.	S 20 40	
Table **c** for 03^h 30^m UT	227 30				
Table **d** for 00^m 35^s UT	0 09				
Sum GHA Sun =	230 08				

Table 5 — Correction to Tabulated Altitude for Minutes of Declination

d	1	2	3	4	5	6	7	8	9	10	11	12	13	14	15	16	17	18	19	20	21	22	23	24	25	26	27	28	29	30	31	32	33	34	35	36	37	38	39	40	41	42	43	44	45	46	47	48	49	50	51	52	53	54	55	56	57	58	59	60	d
′	′	′	′	′	′	′	′	′	′	′	′	′	′	′	′	′	′	′	′	′	′	′	′	′	′	′	′	′	′	′	′	′	′	′	′	′	′	′	′	′	′	′	′	′	′	′	′	′	′	′	′	′	′	′	′	′	′	′	′	′	′
0	0	0	0	0	0	0	0	0	0	0	0	0	0	0	0	0	0	0	0	0	0	0	0	0	0	0	0	0	0	0	0	0	0	0	0	0	0	0	0	0	0	0	0	0	0	0	0	0	0	0	0	0	0	0	0	0	0	0	0	0	**0**
1	0	0	0	0	0	0	0	0	0	0	0	0	0	0	0	0	0	0	0	0	0	0	0	0	0	0	0	0	0	0	1	1	1	1	1	1	1	1	1	1	1	1	1	1	1	1	1	1	1	1	1	1	1	1	1	1	1	1	1	1	**1**
2	0	0	0	0	0	0	0	0	0	0	0	0	0	0	0	1	1	1	1	1	1	1	1	1	1	1	1	1	1	1	1	1	1	1	1	1	1	1	1	1	1	1	1	1	2	2	2	2	2	2	2	2	2	2	2	2	2	2	2	2	**2**
3	0	0	0	0	0	0	0	0	0	0	1	1	1	1	1	1	1	1	1	1	1	1	1	1	1	1	1	1	1	2	2	2	2	2	2	2	2	2	2	2	2	2	2	2	2	2	2	2	2	2	3	3	3	3	3	3	3	3	3	3	**3**
4	0	0	0	0	0	0	0	1	1	1	1	1	1	1	1	1	1	1	1	1	1	1	2	2	2	2	2	2	2	2	2	2	2	2	2	2	2	3	3	3	3	3	3	3	3	3	3	3	3	3	3	3	4	4	4	4	4	4	4	4	**4**
5	0	0	0	0	0	0	1	1	1	1	1	1	1	1	1	1	1	2	2	2	2	2	2	2	2	2	2	2	2	2	3	3	3	3	3	3	3	3	3	3	3	4	4	4	4	4	4	4	4	4	4	4	4	4	5	5	5	5	5	5	**5**
6	0	0	0	0	0	1	1	1	1	1	1	1	1	1	2	2	2	2	2	2	2	2	2	2	2	3	3	3	3	3	3	3	3	3	4	4	4	4	4	4	4	4	4	4	4	5	5	5	5	5	5	5	5	5	6	6	6	6	6	6	**6**
7	0	0	0	0	1	1	1	1	1	1	1	1	2	2	2	2	2	2	2	2	2	3	3	3	3	3	3	3	3	4	4	4	4	4	4	4	4	4	5	5	5	5	5	5	5	5	5	6	6	6	6	6	6	6	6	7	7	7	7	7	**7**
8	0	0	0	1	1	1	1	1	1	1	1	2	2	2	2	2	2	2	3	3	3	3	3	3	3	3	4	4	4	4	4	4	4	5	5	5	5	5	5	5	5	6	6	6	6	6	6	6	7	7	7	7	7	7	7	7	8	8	8	8	**8**
9	0	0	0	1	1	1	1	1	1	2	2	2	2	2	2	2	3	3	3	3	3	3	3	4	4	4	4	4	4	4	5	5	5	5	5	5	6	6	6	6	6	6	6	7	7	7	7	7	7	8	8	8	8	8	8	8	9	9	9	9	**9**
10	0	0	0	1	1	1	1	1	2	2	2	2	2	2	2	3	3	3	3	3	4	4	4	4	4	4	4	5	5	5	5	5	6	6	6	6	6	6	6	7	7	7	7	7	8	8	8	8	8	8	8	9	9	9	9	9	10	10	10	10	**10**
11	0	0	1	1	1	1	1	1	2	2	2	2	2	3	3	3	3	3	3	4	4	4	4	4	5	5	5	5	5	6	6	6	6	6	6	7	7	7	7	7	8	8	8	8	8	8	9	9	9	9	9	10	10	10	10	10	10	11	11	11	**11**
12	0	0	1	1	1	1	1	2	2	2	2	2	3	3	3	3	3	4	4	4	4	4	5	5	5	5	5	6	6	6	6	6	7	7	7	7	7	8	8	8	8	8	9	9	9	9	9	10	10	10	10	10	11	11	11	11	11	12	12	12	**12**
13	0	0	1	1	1	1	2	2	2	2	2	3	3	3	3	3	4	4	4	4	5	5	5	5	5	6	6	6	6	6	7	7	7	7	8	8	8	8	8	9	9	9	9	10	10	10	10	10	11	11	11	11	11	12	12	12	12	13	13	13	**13**
14	0	0	1	1	1	1	2	2	2	2	3	3	3	3	4	4	4	4	4	5	5	5	5	6	6	6	6	7	7	7	7	7	8	8	8	8	9	9	9	9	10	10	10	10	10	11	11	11	11	12	12	12	12	13	13	13	13	14	14	14	**14**
15	0	0	1	1	1	2	2	2	2	2	3	3	3	4	4	4	4	4	5	5	5	6	6	6	6	6	7	7	7	8	8	8	8	8	9	9	9	10	10	10	10	10	11	11	11	12	12	12	12	12	13	13	13	14	14	14	14	14	15	15	**15**
16	0	1	1	1	1	2	2	2	2	3	3	3	3	4	4	4	5	5	5	5	6	6	6	6	7	7	7	7	8	8	8	9	9	9	9	10	10	10	10	11	11	11	11	12	12	12	13	13	13	13	14	14	14	14	15	15	15	15	16	16	**16**
17	0	1	1	1	1	2	2	2	3	3	3	3	4	4	4	5	5	5	5	6	6	6	7	7	7	7	8	8	8	8	9	9	9	10	10	10	10	11	11	11	12	12	12	12	13	13	13	14	14	14	14	15	15	15	16	16	16	16	17	17	**17**
18	0	1	1	1	2	2	2	2	3	3	3	4	4	4	4	5	5	5	6	6	6	7	7	7	8	8	8	8	9	9	9	10	10	10	10	11	11	11	12	12	12	13	13	13	14	14	14	14	15	15	15	16	16	16	16	17	17	17	18	18	**18**
19	0	1	1	1	2	2	2	3	3	3	3	4	4	4	5	5	5	6	6	6	7	7	7	8	8	8	9	9	9	10	10	10	10	11	11	11	12	12	12	13	13	13	14	14	14	15	15	15	16	16	16	16	17	17	17	18	18	18	19	19	**19**
20	0	1	1	1	2	2	2	3	3	3	4	4	4	5	5	5	6	6	6	7	7	7	8	8	8	9	9	9	10	10	10	11	11	11	12	12	12	13	13	13	14	14	14	15	15	15	16	16	16	17	17	17	18	18	18	19	19	19	20	20	**20**
21	0	1	1	1	2	2	2	3	3	4	4	4	5	5	5	6	6	6	7	7	7	8	8	8	9	9	9	10	10	10	11	11	12	12	12	13	13	13	14	14	14	15	15	15	16	16	16	17	17	18	18	18	19	19	19	20	20	20	21	21	**21**
22	0	1	1	1	2	2	3	3	3	4	4	4	5	5	6	6	6	7	7	7	8	8	8	9	9	10	10	10	11	11	11	12	12	12	13	13	14	14	14	15	15	15	16	16	16	17	17	18	18	18	19	19	19	20	20	21	21	21	22	22	**22**
23	0	1	1	2	2	2	3	3	3	4	4	5	5	5	6	6	7	7	7	8	8	8	9	9	10	10	10	11	11	12	12	12	13	13	13	14	14	15	15	15	16	16	16	17	17	18	18	18	19	19	20	20	20	21	21	21	22	22	23	23	**23**
24	0	1	1	2	2	2	3	3	4	4	4	5	5	6	6	6	7	7	8	8	8	9	9	10	10	10	11	11	12	12	12	13	13	14	14	14	15	15	16	16	16	17	17	18	18	18	19	19	20	20	20	21	21	22	22	22	23	23	24	24	**24**
25	0	1	1	2	2	2	3	3	4	4	5	5	5	6	6	7	7	8	8	8	9	9	10	10	10	11	11	12	12	12	13	13	14	14	15	15	15	16	16	17	17	18	18	18	19	19	20	20	20	21	21	22	22	22	23	23	24	24	25	25	**25**
26	0	1	1	2	2	3	3	3	4	4	5	5	6	6	6	7	7	8	8	9	9	10	10	10	11	11	12	12	13	13	13	14	14	15	15	16	16	16	17	17	18	18	19	19	20	20	20	21	21	22	22	23	23	23	24	24	25	25	26	26	**26**
27	0	1	1	2	2	3	3	4	4	4	5	5	6	6	7	7	8	8	9	9	9	10	10	11	11	12	12	13	13	14	14	14	15	15	16	16	17	17	18	18	18	19	19	20	20	21	21	22	22	22	23	23	24	24	25	25	26	26	27	27	**27**
28	0	1	1	2	2	3	3	4	4	5	5	6	6	7	7	7	8	8	9	9	10	10	11	11	12	12	13	13	14	14	14	15	15	16	16	17	17	18	18	19	19	20	20	21	21	21	22	22	23	23	24	24	25	25	26	26	27	27	28	28	**28**
29	0	1	1	2	2	3	3	4	4	5	5	6	6	7	7	8	8	9	9	10	10	11	11	12	12	13	13	14	14	14	15	15	16	16	17	17	18	18	19	19	20	20	21	21	22	22	23	23	24	24	25	25	26	26	27	27	28	28	29	29	**29**
30	0	1	2	2	2	3	4	4	4	5	6	6	6	7	8	8	8	9	10	10	10	11	12	12	12	13	14	14	14	15	16	16	16	17	18	18	18	19	20	20	20	21	22	22	22	23	24	24	24	25	26	26	26	27	28	28	28	29	30	30	**30**
31	1	1	2	2	3	3	4	4	5	5	6	6	7	7	8	8	9	9	10	10	11	11	12	12	13	13	14	14	15	16	16	17	17	18	18	19	19	20	20	21	21	22	22	23	23	24	24	25	25	26	26	27	27	28	28	29	29	30	30	31	**31**
32	1	1	2	2	3	3	4	4	5	5	6	6	7	7	8	9	9	10	10	11	11	12	12	13	13	14	14	15	15	16	16	17	18	18	19	19	20	20	21	21	22	22	23	23	24	25	25	26	26	27	27	28	28	29	29	30	30	31	31	32	**32**
33	1	1	2	2	3	3	4	4	5	6	6	7	7	8	8	9	9	10	10	11	12	12	13	13	14	14	15	15	16	16	17	18	18	19	19	20	20	21	21	22	23	23	24	24	25	25	26	26	27	28	28	29	29	30	30	31	31	32	32	33	**33**
34	1	1	2	2	3	3	4	5	5	6	6	7	7	8	8	9	10	10	11	11	12	12	13	14	14	15	15	16	16	17	18	18	19	19	20	20	21	22	22	23	23	24	24	25	26	26	27	27	28	28	29	29	30	31	31	32	32	33	33	34	**34**
35	1	1	2	2	3	4	4	5	5	6	6	7	8	8	9	9	10	10	11	12	12	13	13	14	15	15	16	16	17	18	18	19	19	20	20	21	22	22	23	23	24	24	25	26	26	27	27	28	29	29	30	30	31	32	32	33	33	34	34	35	**35**
36	1	1	2	2	3	4	4	5	5	6	7	7	8	8	9	10	10	11	11	12	13	13	14	14	15	16	16	17	17	18	19	19	20	20	21	22	22	23	23	24	25	25	26	26	27	28	28	29	29	30	31	31	32	32	33	34	34	35	35	36	**36**
37	1	1	2	2	3	4	4	5	6	6	7	7	8	9	9	10	10	11	12	12	13	14	14	15	15	16	17	17	18	18	19	20	20	21	22	22	23	23	24	25	25	26	27	27	28	28	29	30	30	31	31	32	33	33	34	35	35	36	36	37	**37**
38	1	1	2	3	3	4	4	5	6	6	7	8	8	9	10	10	11	11	12	13	13	14	15	15	16	16	17	18	18	19	20	20	21	22	22	23	23	24	25	25	26	27	27	28	28	29	30	30	31	32	32	33	34	34	35	35	36	37	37	38	**38**
39	1	1	2	3	3	4	5	5	6	6	7	8	8	9	10	10	11	12	12	13	14	14	15	16	16	17	18	18	19	20	20	21	21	22	23	23	24	25	25	26	27	27	28	29	29	30	31	31	32	32	33	34	34	35	36	36	37	38	38	39	**39**
40	1	1	2	3	3	4	5	5	6	7	7	8	9	9	10	11	11	12	13	13	14	15	15	16	17	17	18	19	19	20	21	21	22	23	23	24	25	25	26	27	27	28	29	29	30	31	31	32	33	33	34	35	35	36	37	37	38	39	39	40	**40**
41	1	1	2	3	3	4	5	5	6	7	8	8	9	10	10	11	12	12	13	14	14	15	16	16	17	18	18	19	20	20	21	22	23	23	24	25	25	26	27	27	28	29	29	30	31	31	32	33	33	34	35	36	36	37	38	38	39	40	40	41	**41**
42	1	1	2	3	4	4	5	6	6	7	8	8	9	10	10	11	12	13	13	14	15	15	16	17	18	18	19	20	20	21	22	22	23	24	24	25	26	27	27	28	29	29	30	31	32	32	33	34	34	35	36	36	37	38	38	39	40	41	41	42	**42**
43	1	1	2	3	4	4	5	6	6	7	8	9	9	10	11	11	12	13	14	14	15	16	16	17	18	19	19	20	21	22	22	23	24	24	25	26	27	27	28	29	29	30	31	32	32	33	34	34	35	36	37	37	38	39	39	40	41	42	42	43	**43**
44	1	1	2	3	4	4	5	6	7	7	8	9	10	10	11	12	12	13	14	15	15	16	17	18	18	19	20	21	21	22	23	23	24	25	26	26	27	28	29	29	30	31	32	32	33	34	34	35	36	37	37	38	39	40	40	41	42	43	43	44	**44**
45	1	2	2	3	4	4	5	6	7	8	8	9	10	10	11	12	13	14	14	15	16	16	17	18	19	20	20	21	22	22	23	24	25	26	26	27	28	28	29	30	31	32	32	33	34	34	35	36	37	38	38	39	40	40	41	42	43	44	44	45	**45**
46	1	2	2	3	4	5	5	6	7	8	8	9	10	11	12	12	13	14	15	15	16	17	18	18	19	20	21	21	22	23	24	25	25	26	27	28	28	29	30	31	31	32	33	34	34	35	36	37	38	38	39	40	41	41	42	43	44	44	45	46	**46**
47	1	2	2	3	4	5	5	6	7	8	9	9	10	11	12	13	13	14	15	16	16	17	18	19	20	20	21	22	23	24	24	25	26	27	27	28	29	30	31	31	32	33	34	34	35	36	37	38	38	39	40	41	42	42	43	44	45	45	46	47	**47**
48	1	2	2	3	4	5	6	6	7	8	9	10	10	11	12	13	14	14	15	16	17	18	18	19	20	21	22	22	23	24	25	26	26	27	28	29	30	30	31	32	33	34	34	35	36	37	38	38	39	40	41	42	42	43	44	45	46	46	47	48	**48**
49	1	2	2	3	4	5	6	7	7	8	9	10	11	11	12	13	14	15	16	16	17	18	19	20	20	21	22	23	24	24	25	26	27	28	29	29	30	31	32	33	33	34	35	36	37	38	38	39	40	41	42	42	43	44	45	46	47	47	48	49	**49**
50	1	2	2	3	4	5	6	7	8	8	9	10	11	12	12	13	14	15	16	17	18	18	19	20	21	22	22	23	24	25	26	27	28	28	29	30	31	32	32	33	34	35	36	37	38	38	39	40	41	42	42	43	44	45	46	47	48	48	49	50	**50**
51	1	2	3	3	4	5	6	7	8	8	9	10	11	12	13	14	14	15	16	17	18	19	20	20	21	22	23	24	25	26	26	27	28	29	30	31	31	32	33	34	35	36	37	37	38	39	40	41	42	42	43	44	45	46	47	48	48	49	50	51	**51**
52	1	2	3	3	4	5	6	7	8	9	10	10	11	12	13	14	15	16	16	17	18	19	20	21	22	23	23	24	25	26	27	28	29	29	30	31	32	33	34	35	36	36	37	38	39	40	41	42	42	43	44	45	46	47	48	49	49	50	51	52	**52**
53	1	2	3	4	4	5	6	7	8	9	10	11	11	12	13	14	15	16	17	18	19	19	20	21	22	23	24	25	26	26	27	28	29	30	31	32	33	34	34	35	36	37	38	39	40	41	42	42	43	44	45	46	47	48	49	49	50	51	52	53	**53**
54	1	2	3	4	4	5	6	7	8	9	10	11	12	13	14	14	15	16	17	18	19	20	21	22	22	23	24	25	26	27	28	29	30	31	32	32	33	34	35	36	37	38	39	40	40	41	42	43	44	45	46	47	48	49	50	50	51	52	53	54	**54**
55	1	2	3	4	5	6	6	7	8	9	10	11	12	13	14	15	16	16	17	18	19	20	21	22	23	24	25	26	27	28	28	29	30	31	32	33	34	35	36	37	38	38	39	40	41	42	43	44	45	46	47	48	49	50	50	51	52	53	54	55	**55**
56	1	2	3	4	5	6	7	7	8	9	10	11	12	13	14	15	16	17	18	19	20	21	21	22	23	24	25	26	27	28	29	30	31	32	33	34	35	35	36	37	38	39	40	41	42	43	44	45	46	47	48	49	49	50	51	52	53	54	55	56	**56**
57	1	2	3	4	5	6	7	8	9	10	10	11	12	13	14	15	16	17	18	19	20	21	22	23	24	25	26	27	28	28	29	30	31	32	33	34	35	36	37	38	39	40	41	42	43	44	45	46	47	48	48	49	50	51	52	53	54	55	56	57	**57**
58	1	2	3	4	5	6	7	8	9	10	11	12	13	14	14	15	16	17	18	19	20	21	22	23	24	25	26	27	28	29	30	31	32	33	34	35	36	37	38	39	40	41	42	43	44	44	45	46	47	48	49	50	51	52	53	54	55	56	57	58	**58**
59	1	2	3	4	5	6	7	8	9	10	11	12	13	14	15	16	17	18	19	20	21	22	23	24	25	26	27	28	29	30	30	31	32	33	34	35	36	37	38	39	40	41	42	43	44	45	46	47	48	49	50	51	52	53	54	55	56	57	58	59	**59**

a. Dip of the Horizon

Ht. of Eye (m)	Corrⁿ D (′)	Ht. of Eye (ft.)
0·00		0·0
	−0·3	
0·03		0·1
	−0·4	
0·06		0·2
	−0·5	
0·09		0·3
	−0·6	
0·13		0·4
	−0·7	
0·18		0·5
	−0·8	
0·23		0·7
	−0·9	
0·29		0·9
	−1·0	
0·35		1·1
	−1·1	
0·42		1·4
	−1·2	
0·45		1·6
	−1·3	
0·5		1·9
	−1·4	
0·6		2·2
	−1·5	
0·7		2·5
	−1·6	
0·8		2·8
	−1·7	
0·9		3·2
	−1·8	
1·1		3·6
	−1·9	
1·2		4·0
	−2·0	
1·3		4·4
	−2·1	
1·4		4·9
	−2·2	
1·6		5·3
	−2·3	
1·7		5·8
	−2·4	
1·9		6·3
	−2·5	
2·0		6·9
	−2·6	
2·2		7·4
	−2·7	
2·4		8·0
	−2·8	
2·6		8·6
	−2·9	
2·8		9·2
	−3·0	
3·0		9·8
	−3·1	
3·2		10·5
	−3·2	
3·4		11·2
	−3·3	
3·6		11·9
	−3·4	
3·8		12·6
	−3·5	
4·0		13·3
	−3·6	
4·3		14·1
	−3·7	
4·5		14·9
	−3·8	
4·7		15·7
	−3·9	
5·0		16·5
	−4·0	
5·2		17·4
	−4·1	
5·5		18·3
	−4·2	
5·8		19·1
	−4·3	
6·1		20·1
	−4·4	
6·3		21·0
	−4·5	
6·6		22·0
	−4·6	
6·9		22·9
	−4·7	
7·2		23·9
	−4·8	
7·5		25·0
	−4·9	
7·9		26·0
	−5·0	
8·2		27·1
	−5·1	
8·5		28·1
	−5·2	
8·8		29·2
	−5·3	
9·2		30·4
	−5·4	
9·5		31·5
	−5·5	
9·9		32·7
	−5·6	
10·3		33·9
	−5·7	
10·6		35·1
	−5·8	
11·0		36·3
	−5·9	
11·4		37·6
	−6·0	
11·8		38·9
	−6·1	
12·2		40·1
	−6·2	
12·6		41·5
	−6·3	
13·0		42·8

Ht. of Eye (m)	Corrⁿ D (′)	Ht. of Eye (ft.)
13·0		42·8
	−6·4	
13·4		44·2
	−6·5	
13·8		45·5
	−6·6	
14·2		47·0
	−6·7	
14·7		48·4
	−6·8	
15·1		49·8
	−6·9	
15·5		51·3
	−7·0	
16·0		52·8
	−7·1	
16·5		54·3
	−7·2	
16·9		55·8
	−7·3	
17·4		57·4
	−7·4	
17·9		58·9
	−7·5	
18·4		60·5
	−7·6	
18·8		62·1
	−7·7	
19·3		63·8
	−7·8	
19·8		65·4
	−7·9	
20·4		67·1
	−8·0	
20·9		68·8
	−8·1	
21·4		70·5
	−8·2	
21·9		72·3
	−8·3	
22·5		74·1
	−8·4	
23·0		75·8
	−8·5	
23·5		77·6
	−8·6	
24·1		79·5
	−8·7	
24·7		81·3
	−8·8	
25·2		83·2
	−8·9	
25·8		85·1
	−9·0	
26·4		87·0
	−9·1	
27·0		88·9
	−9·2	
27·6		90·9
	−9·3	
28·2		92·9
	−9·4	
28·8		94·9
	−9·5	
29·4		96·9
	−9·6	
30·0		98·9
	−9·7	
30·6		101·0
	−9·8	
31·3		103·1
	−9·9	
31·9		105·2
	−10·0	
32·6		107·3
	−10·1	
33·2		109·4
	−10·2	
33·9		111·6
	−10·3	
34·5		113·8
	−10·4	
35·2		116·0
	−10·5	
35·9		118·2
	−10·6	
36·6		120·5
	−10·7	
37·3		122·8
	−10·8	
38·0		125·1
	−10·9	
38·7		127·4
	−11·0	
39·4		129·7
	−11·1	
40·1		132·1
	−11·2	
40·8		134·5
	−11·3	
41·5		136·9
	−11·4	
42·3		139·3
	−11·5	
43·0		141·7
	−11·6	
43·8		144·2
	−11·7	
44·5		146·7
	−11·8	
45·3		149·2
	−11·9	
46·1		151·7
	−12·0	
46·8		154·3
	−12·1	
47·6		156·8
	−12·2	
48·4		159·4
	−12·3	
49·2		162·1
	−12·4	
50·0		164·7

b. Refraction for Stars & Planets

App. Alt. Ha (° ′)	Corrⁿ R (′)
0 00	−33·8
0 03	33·2
0 06	32·6
0 09	32·0
0 12	31·5
0 15	30·9
0 18	−30·4
0 21	29·8
0 24	29·3
0 27	28·8
0 30	28·3
0 33	27·9
0 36	−27·4
0 39	26·9
0 42	26·5
0 45	26·1
0 48	25·7
0 51	25·3
0 54	−24·9
0 57	24·5
1 00	24·1
1 03	23·7
1 06	23·4
1 09	23·0
1 12	−22·7
1 15	22·3
1 18	22·0
1 21	21·7
1 24	21·4
1 27	21·1
1 30	−20·8
1 35	20·3
1 40	19·9
1 45	19·4
1 50	19·0
1 55	18·6
2 00	−18·2
2 05	17·8
2 10	17·4
2 15	17·1
2 20	16·7
2 25	16·4
2 30	−16·1
2 35	15·8
2 40	15·4
2 45	15·2
2 50	14·9
2 55	14·6
3 00	−14·3
3 05	14·1
3 10	13·8
3 15	13·6
3 20	13·4
3 25	13·1
3 30	−12·9

App. Alt. Ha (° ′)	Corrⁿ R (′)
3 30	−12·9
3 35	12·7
3 40	12·5
3 45	12·3
3 50	12·1
3 55	11·9
4 00	−11·7
4 05	11·5
4 10	11·4
4 15	11·2
4 20	11·0
4 25	10·9
4 30	−10·7
4 35	10·6
4 40	10·4
4 45	10·3
4 50	10·1
4 55	10·0
5 00	− 9·8
5 05	9·7
5 10	9·6
5 15	9·5
5 20	9·3
5 25	9·2
5 30	− 9·1
5 35	9·0
5 40	8·9
5 45	8·8
5 50	8·7
5 55	8·6
6 00	− 8·5
6 10	8·3
6 20	8·1
6 30	7·9
6 40	7·7
6 50	7·6
7 00	− 7·4
7 10	7·2
7 20	7·1
7 30	6·9
7 40	6·8
7 50	6·7
8 00	− 6·6
8 10	6·4
8 20	6·3
8 30	6·2
8 40	6·1
8 50	6·0
9 00	− 5·9
9 10	5·8
9 20	5·7
9 30	5·6
9 40	5·5
9 50	5·4
10 00	− 5·3

App. Alt. Ha (° ′)	Corrⁿ R (′)
9 55	
	−5·3
10 07	
	−5·2
10 20	
	−5·1
10 32	
	−5·0
10 46	
	−4·9
10 59	
	−4·8
11 14	
	−4·7
11 29	
	−4·6
11 44	
	−4·5
12 00	
	−4·4
12 17	
	−4·3
12 35	
	−4·2
12 53	
	−4·1
13 12	
	−4·0
13 32	
	−3·9
13 53	
	−3·8
14 16	
	−3·7
14 39	
	−3·6
15 03	
	−3·5
15 29	
	−3·4
15 56	
	−3·3
16 25	
	−3·2
16 55	
	−3·1
17 27	
	−3·0
18 01	
	−2·9
18 37	
	−2·8
19 16	
	−2·7
19 56	
	−2·6
20 40	
	−2·5
21 27	
	−2·4
22 17	
	−2·3
23 11	
	−2·2
24 09	
	−2·1
25 12	
	−2·0
26 20	
	−1·9
27 34	
	−1·8
28 54	
	−1·7
30 22	
	−1·6
31 58	
	−1·5
33 43	
	−1·4
35 38	
	−1·3
37 45	
	−1·2
40 06	
	−1·1
42 42	
	−1·0
45 34	
	−0·9
48 45	
	−0·8
52 16	
	−0·7
56 09	
	−0·6
60 26	
	−0·5
65 06	
	−0·4
70 09	
	−0·3
75 32	
	−0·2
81 12	
	−0·1
87 03	
	0·0
90 00	

H_a = App. Alt. = Apparent Altitude
= Sextant altitude corrected for index error (IE) and dip (*D*)
= H_s + IE + *D*

In critical cases ascend.

TABLE 6 — ALTITUDE CORRECTION TABLES

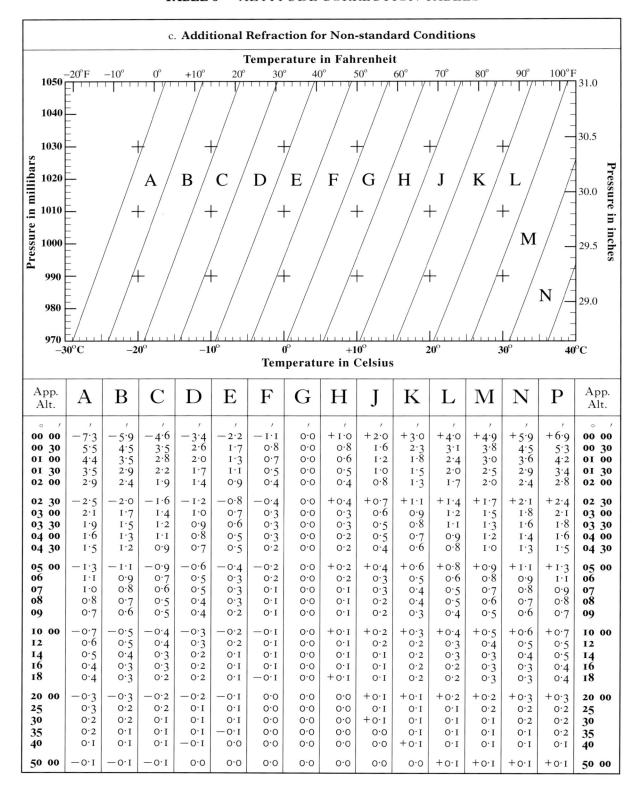

c. **Additional Refraction for Non-standard Conditions**

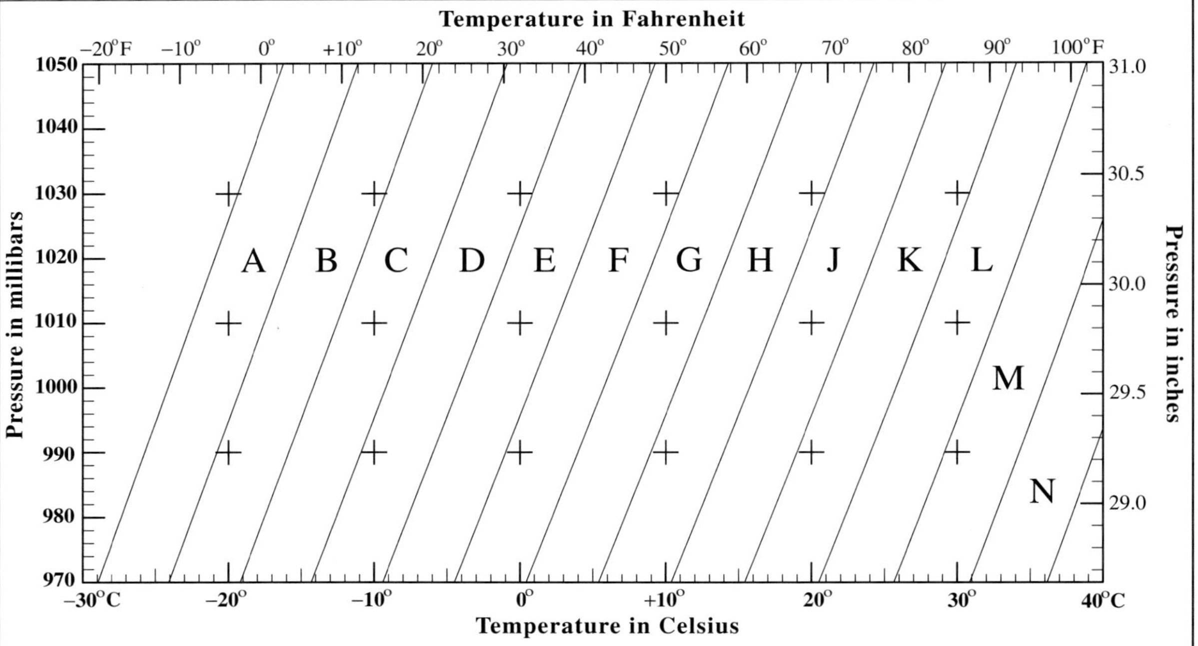

App. Alt.	A	B	C	D	E	F	G	H	J	K	L	M	N	P	App. Alt.
° ′	′	′	′	′	′	′	′	′	′	′	′	′	′	′	° ′
00 00	−7·3	−5·9	−4·6	−3·4	−2·2	−1·1	0·0	+1·0	+2·0	+3·0	+4·0	+4·9	+5·9	+6·9	**00 00**
00 30	5·5	4·5	3·5	2·6	1·7	0·8	0·0	0·8	1·6	2·3	3·1	3·8	4·5	5·3	**00 30**
01 00	4·4	3·5	2·8	2·0	1·3	0·7	0·0	0·6	1·2	1·8	2·4	3·0	3·6	4·2	**01 00**
01 30	3·5	2·9	2·2	1·7	1·1	0·5	0·0	0·5	1·0	1·5	2·0	2·5	2·9	3·4	**01 30**
02 00	2·9	2·4	1·9	1·4	0·9	0·4	0·0	0·4	0·8	1·3	1·7	2·0	2·4	2·8	**02 00**
02 30	−2·5	−2·0	−1·6	−1·2	−0·8	−0·4	0·0	+0·4	+0·7	+1·1	+1·4	+1·7	+2·1	+2·4	**02 30**
03 00	2·1	1·7	1·4	1·0	0·7	0·3	0·0	0·3	0·6	0·9	1·2	1·5	1·8	2·1	**03 00**
03 30	1·9	1·5	1·2	0·9	0·6	0·3	0·0	0·3	0·5	0·8	1·1	1·3	1·6	1·8	**03 30**
04 00	1·6	1·3	1·1	0·8	0·5	0·3	0·0	0·2	0·5	0·7	0·9	1·2	1·4	1·6	**04 00**
04 30	1·5	1·2	0·9	0·7	0·5	0·2	0·0	0·2	0·4	0·6	0·8	1·0	1·3	1·5	**04 30**
05 00	−1·3	−1·1	−0·9	−0·6	−0·4	−0·2	0·0	+0·2	+0·4	+0·6	+0·8	+0·9	+1·1	+1·3	**05 00**
06	1·1	0·9	0·7	0·5	0·3	0·2	0·0	0·2	0·3	0·5	0·6	0·8	0·9	1·1	**06**
07	1·0	0·8	0·6	0·5	0·3	0·1	0·0	0·1	0·3	0·4	0·5	0·7	0·8	0·9	**07**
08	0·8	0·7	0·5	0·4	0·3	0·1	0·0	0·1	0·2	0·4	0·5	0·6	0·7	0·8	**08**
09	0·7	0·6	0·5	0·4	0·2	0·1	0·0	0·1	0·2	0·3	0·4	0·5	0·6	0·7	**09**
10 00	−0·7	−0·5	−0·4	−0·3	−0·2	−0·1	0·0	+0·1	+0·2	+0·3	+0·4	+0·5	+0·6	+0·7	**10 00**
12	0·6	0·5	0·4	0·3	0·2	0·1	0·0	0·1	0·2	0·2	0·3	0·4	0·5	0·5	**12**
14	0·5	0·4	0·3	0·2	0·1	0·1	0·0	0·1	0·1	0·2	0·3	0·3	0·4	0·5	**14**
16	0·4	0·3	0·3	0·2	0·1	0·1	0·0	0·1	0·1	0·2	0·2	0·3	0·3	0·4	**16**
18	0·4	0·3	0·2	0·2	0·1	−0·1	0·0	+0·1	0·1	0·2	0·2	0·3	0·3	0·4	**18**
20 00	−0·3	−0·3	−0·2	−0·2	−0·1	0·0	0·0	0·0	+0·1	+0·1	+0·2	+0·2	+0·3	+0·3	**20 00**
25	0·3	0·2	0·2	0·1	0·1	0·0	0·0	0·0	0·1	0·1	0·1	0·2	0·2	0·2	**25**
30	0·2	0·2	0·1	0·1	0·1	0·0	0·0	0·0	+0·1	0·1	0·1	0·1	0·2	0·2	**30**
35	0·2	0·1	0·1	0·1	−0·1	0·0	0·0	0·0	0·0	0·1	0·1	0·1	0·1	0·2	**35**
40	0·1	0·1	0·1	−0·1	0·0	0·0	0·0	0·0	0·0	+0·1	0·1	0·1	0·1	0·1	**40**
50 00	−0·1	−0·1	−0·1	0·0	0·0	0·0	0·0	0·0	0·0	0·0	+0·1	+0·1	+0·1	+0·1	**50 00**

The graph is entered with arguments temperature and pressure to find a zone letter; using as arguments this zone letter and apparent altitude (sextant altitude corrected for index error and dip), a correction is taken from the table. This correction is to be applied to the sextant altitude in addition to the corrections for standard conditions (Table **6**b).

TABLE 6d — ALTITUDE CORRECTION TABLES FOR THE SUN

App. Alt. H_a	OCT.—MAR. Lower Limb *R*	OCT.—MAR. Upper Limb *R*	APR.—SEPT. Lower Limb *R*	APR.—SEPT. Upper Limb *R*
° ′	′	′	′	′
0 00	−17·5	−49·8	−17·8	−49·6
0 03	16·9	49·2	17·2	49·0
0 06	16·3	48·6	16·6	48·4
0 09	15·7	48·0	16·0	47·8
0 12	15·2	47·5	15·4	47·2
0 15	14·6	46·9	14·8	46·6
0 18	−14·1	−46·4	−14·3	−46·1
0 21	13·5	45·8	13·8	45·6
0 24	13·0	45·3	13·3	45·1
0 27	12·5	44·8	12·8	44·6
0 30	12·0	44·3	12·3	44·1
0 33	11·6	43·9	11·8	43·6
0 36	−11·1	−43·4	−11·3	−43·1
0 39	10·6	42·9	10·9	42·7
0 42	10·2	42·5	10·5	42·3
0 45	9·8	42·1	10·0	41·8
0 48	9·4	41·7	9·6	41·4
0 51	9·0	41·3	9·2	41·0
0 54	− 8·6	−40·9	− 8·8	−40·6
0 57	8·2	40·5	8·4	40·2
1 00	7·8	40·1	8·0	39·8
1 03	7·4	39·7	7·7	39·5
1 06	7·1	39·4	7·3	39·1
1 09	6·7	39·0	7·0	38·8
1 12	− 6·4	−38·7	− 6·6	−38·4
1 15	6·0	38·3	6·3	38·1
1 18	5·7	38·0	6·0	37·8
1 21	5·4	37·7	5·7	37·5
1 24	5·1	37·4	5·3	37·1
1 27	4·8	37·1	5·0	36·8
1 30	− 4·5	−36·8	− 4·7	−36·5
1 35	4·0	36·3	4·3	36·1
1 40	3·6	35·9	3·8	35·6
1 45	3·1	35·4	3·4	35·2
1 50	2·7	35·0	2·9	34·7
1 55	2·3	34·6	2·5	34·3
2 00	− 1·9	−34·2	− 2·1	−33·9
2 05	1·5	33·8	1·7	33·5
2 10	1·1	33·4	1·4	33·2
2 15	0·8	33·1	1·0	32·8
2 20	0·4	32·7	0·7	32·5
2 25	− 0·1	32·4	− 0·3	32·1
2 30	+ 0·2	−32·1	0·0	−31·8
2 35	0·5	31·8	+ 0·3	31·5
2 40	0·8	31·5	0·6	31·2
2 45	1·1	31·2	0·9	30·9
2 50	1·4	30·9	1·2	30·6
2 55	1·7	30·6	1·4	30·4
3 00	+ 2·0	−30·3	+ 1·7	−30·1
3 05	2·2	30·1	2·0	29·8
3 10	2·5	29·8	2·2	29·6
3 15	2·7	29·6	2·5	29·3
3 20	2·9	29·4	2·7	29·1
3 25	3·2	29·1	2·9	28·9
3 30	+ 3·4	−28·9	+ 3·1	−28·7

App. Alt. H_a	OCT.—MAR. Lower Limb *R*	OCT.—MAR. Upper Limb *R*	APR.—SEPT. Lower Limb *R*	APR.—SEPT. Upper Limb *R*
° ′	′	′	′	′
3 30	+ 3·4	−28·9	+ 3·1	−28·7
3 35	3·6	28·7	3·3	28·5
3 40	3·8	28·5	3·6	28·2
3 45	4·0	28·3	3·8	28·0
3 50	4·2	28·1	4·0	27·8
3 55	4·4	27·9	4·1	27·7
4 00	+ 4·6	−27·7	+ 4·3	−27·5
4 05	4·8	27·5	4·5	27·3
4 10	4·9	27·4	4·7	27·1
4 15	5·1	27·2	4·9	26·9
4 20	5·3	27·0	5·0	26·8
4 25	5·4	26·9	5·2	26·6
4 30	+ 5·6	−26·7	+ 5·3	−26·5
4 35	5·7	26·6	5·5	26·3
4 40	5·9	26·4	5·6	26·2
4 45	6·0	26·3	5·8	26·0
4 50	6·2	26·1	5·9	25·9
4 55	6·3	26·0	6·1	25·7
5 00	+ 6·4	−25·9	+ 6·2	−25·6
5 05	6·6	25·7	6·3	25·5
5 10	6·7	25·6	6·5	25·3
5 15	6·8	25·5	6·6	25·2
5 20	7·0	25·3	6·7	25·1
5 25	7·1	25·2	6·8	25·0
5 30	+ 7·2	−25·1	+ 6·9	−24·9
5 35	7·3	25·0	7·1	24·7
5 40	7·4	24·9	7·2	24·6
5 45	7·5	24·8	7·3	24·5
5 50	7·6	24·7	7·4	24·4
5 55	7·7	24·6	7·5	24·3
6 00	+ 7·8	−24·5	+ 7·6	−24·2
6 10	8·0	24·3	7·8	24·0
6 20	8·2	24·1	8·0	23·8
6 30	8·4	23·9	8·2	23·6
6 40	8·6	23·7	8·3	23·5
6 50	8·7	23·6	8·5	23·3
7 00	+ 8·9	−23·4	+ 8·7	−23·1
7 10	9·1	23·2	8·8	23·0
7 20	9·2	23·1	9·0	22·8
7 30	9·3	23·0	9·1	22·7
7 40	9·5	22·8	9·2	22·6
7 50	9·6	22·7	9·4	22·4
8 00	+ 9·7	−22·6	+ 9·5	−22·3
8 10	9·9	22·4	9·6	22·2
8 20	10·0	22·3	9·7	22·1
8 30	10·1	22·2	9·9	21·9
8 40	10·2	22·1	10·0	21·8
8 50	10·3	22·0	10·1	21·7
9 00	+10·4	−21·9	+10·2	−21·6
9 10	10·5	21·8	10·3	21·5
9 20	10·6	21·7	10·4	21·4
9 30	10·7	21·6	10·5	21·3
9 40	10·8	21·5	10·6	21·2
9 50	10·9	21·4	10·6	21·2
10 00	+11·0	−21·3	+10·7	−21·1

OCT.—MAR. App. Alt. H_a	OCT.—MAR. Lower Limb *R*	OCT.—MAR. Upper Limb *R*	APR.—SEPT. App. Alt. H_a	APR.—SEPT. Lower Limb *R*	APR.—SEPT. Upper Limb *R*
° ′	′	′	° ′	′	′
9 33			9 39		
	+10·8	−21·5		+10·6	−21·2
9 45			9 50		
	+10·9	−21·4		+10·7	−21·1
9 56			10 02		
	+11·0	−21·3		+10·8	−21·0
10 08			10 14		
	+11·1	−21·2		+10·9	−20·9
10 20			10 27		
	+11·2	−21·1		+11·0	−20·8
10 33			10 40		
	+11·3	−21·0		+11·1	−20·7
10 46			10 53		
	+11·4	−20·9		+11·2	−20·6
11 00			11 07		
	+11·5	−20·8		+11·3	−20·5
11 15			11 22		
	+11·6	−20·7		+11·4	−20·4
11 30			11 37		
	+11·7	−20·6		+11·5	−20·3
11 45			11 53		
	+11·8	−20·5		+11·6	−20·2
12 01			12 10		
	+11·9	−20·4		+11·7	−20·1
12 18			12 27		
	+12·0	−20·3		+11·8	−20·0
12 36			12 45		
	+12·1	−20·2		+11·9	−19·9
12 54			13 04		
	+12·2	−20·1		+12·0	−19·8
13 14			13 24		
	+12·3	−20·0		+12·1	−19·7
13 34			13 44		
	+12·4	−19·9		+12·2	−19·6
13 55			14 06		
	+12·5	−19·8		+12·3	−19·5
14 17			14 29		
	+12·6	−19·7		+12·4	−19·4
14 41			14 53		
	+12·7	−19·6		+12·5	−19·3
15 05			15 18		
	+12·8	−19·5		+12·6	−19·2
15 31			15 45		
	+12·9	−19·4		+12·7	−19·1
15 59			16 13		
	+13·0	−19·3		+12·8	−19·0
16 27			16 43		
	+13·1	−19·2		+12·9	−18·9
16 58			17 14		
	+13·2	−19·1		+13·0	−18·8
17 30			17 47		
	+13·3	−19·0		+13·1	−18·7
18 05			18 23		
	+13·4	−18·9		+13·2	−18·6
18 41			19 00		
	+13·5	−18·8		+13·3	−18·5
19 20			19 41		
	+13·6	−18·7		+13·4	−18·4
20 02			20 24		
	+13·7	−18·6		+13·5	−18·3
20 46			21 10		
	+13·8	−18·5		+13·6	−18·2
21 34			21 59		
	+13·9	−18·4		+13·7	−18·1
22 25			22 52		
	+14·0	−18·3		+13·8	−18·0
23 20			23 49		
	+14·1	−18·2		+13·9	−17·9
24 20			24 51		
	+14·2	−18·1		+14·0	−17·8
25 24			25 58		
	+14·3	−18·0		+14·1	−17·7
26 34			27 11		
	+14·4	−17·9		+14·2	−17·6
27 50			28 31		
	+14·5	−17·8		+14·3	−17·5
29 13			29 58		
	+14·6	−17·7		+14·4	−17·4
30 44			31 33		
	+14·7	−17·6		+14·5	−17·3
32 24			33 18		
	+14·8	−17·5		+14·6	−17·2
34 15			35 15		
	+14·9	−17·4		+14·7	−17·1
36 17			37 24		
	+15·0	−17·3		+14·8	−17·0
38 34			39 48		
	+15·1	−17·2		+14·9	−16·9
41 06			42 28		
	+15·2	−17·1		+15·0	−16·8
43 56			45 29		
	+15·3	−17·0		+15·1	−16·7
47 07			48 52		
	+15·4	−16·9		+15·2	−16·6
50 43			52 41		
	+15·5	−16·8		+15·3	−16·5
54 46			56 59		
	+15·6	−16·7		+15·4	−16·4
59 21			61 50		
	+15·7	−16·6		+15·5	−16·3
64 28			67 15		
	+15·8	−16·5		+15·6	−16·2
70 10			73 14		
	+15·9	−16·4		+15·7	−16·1
76 24			79 42		
	+16·0	−16·3		+15·8	−16·0
83 05			86 31		
	+16·1	−16·2		+15·9	−15·9
90 00			90 00		

App. Alt. = Apparent altitude = Sextant altitude corrected for index error and dip = $H_a = H_s + IE + D$

In critical cases ascend. Additional corrections for temperature and pressure are given on the previous page.

AP3270 VOLUME 3 — RAPID SIGHT REDUCTION FORM — EXAMPLE

1 Estimated position at the time of fix:	(See 5.2.4 page xxvi)	Navigator			
DR/EP:	Lat. S 49° 12′, Long. E 56° 20′	Height of eye	6·0 m/ft		
2 Convert Date/Times:	Year month d h m s	Index Error	−1′·3 on arc − off arc +		
Fix, local date & time	2003 October 26 12 00 00	Course	345 °T	Temp.	9/17/15 °C/F
Zone Correction W + E − ZT	−4	Speed	8/10 kn	Pressure	990 mb/in
Greenwich date & UT UT_f	2003 October 26 08 00 00	Depart		To	

Observations of	**Sun am (lower limb)**	**Sun (lower limb)**	**Sun pm (lower limb)**
Local date & watch time DWT	Year month d h m s 2003 October 26 07 38 47	Year month d h m s 2003 October 26 11 58 59	Year month d h m s 2003 October 26 16 39 40
Watch error fast − slow + DWE	0	0	0
Local time	07 38 47	11 58 59	16 39 40
Zone correction W + E − ZT	−4	−4	−4
Greenwich date & UT UT	2003 October 26 03 38 47	2003 October 26 07 58 59	2003 October 26 12 39 40
UT of Fix UT_f	08 00 00	08 00 00	08 00 00
Fix later + earlier − $UT_f - UT$	+4 21 13	+1 01	−4 39 40
3 Body's position: GHA & Dec or GHA♈	h m s ° ′ ° ′ 03 228 59·2 S 12 15·9	h m s ° ′ ° ′ 07 288 59·5 S 12 19·3	h m s ° ′ ° ′ 12 3 59·8 S 12 23·6
Increment for mins and secs	38 47 9 41·8	58 59 14 44·8	39 40 9 55·0
Correction (*v*, *d*)/* SHA & Dec	(*d*=+0′·9) +0·6	(*d*=+0′·9) +0·9	(*d*=+0′·9) +0·6
Sum = GHA & Dec for UT	03 38 47 238 41·0 S 12 16·5	07 58 59 303 44·3 S 12 20·2	12 39 40 13 54·8 S 12 24·2
4 Calculate LHA: ±360°			
Assumed longitude, E + W −	+56 19·0	+56 15·7	+56 05·2
Sum	295	360	70
±360° if required		360	
LHA body = Sum	295	000	70
5 Main tables (Lat, Dec, LHA)	S 49°, S 12°16′, Same, 295°	S 49°, S 12°20′, Same, 000°	S 49°, S 12°24′, Same, 70°
Extracted H_c, *d*, Z	25° 21′ +45′ 101°	53° 00′ +60′ 180°	22° 07′ +44′ 97°
Table **5** (Dec′, *d*)	+12	+20	+18
Calculated altitude H_c	25 33	53 20	22 25
6 Correct sextant altitudes: H_s	25° 32′·5	52° 54′·5	22° 17′·7
Index error on arc − off arc + IE	−1·3		
Dip, Table **6**a, ht 6·0 m *D*	−4·3		
Sum IE+*D*	−5·6 −5·6	−5·6	−5·6
Apparent altitude H_a	25 26·9	52 48·9	22 12·1
Alt. corrn. Table **6** /Moon (NA)	+14·3	+15·5	+13·9
Addn. alt. corrns (see NA)			
Additional ref Table **6**c	0·0	0·0	+0·1
Observed altitude H_o	25 41·2	53 04·4	22 26·1
7 Calculate intercept: (Step 5) H_c	25 33·0	53 20·0	22 25·0
Intercept = $H_o - H_c$ *p*	+8·2	−15·6	+1·1
Z_n=Z, Z_n=180°−Z, LHA>180° Z_n=360−Z, Z_n=180°+Z, LHA<180°	180°	180°	180°
North Lat South Lat. ±Z	−101°	−180°	+97°
True azimuth Z_n	079°	000°	277°
8 (a) Motion of vessel:	360°	360°	360°
±360° if required	439°	360°	637°
True track of vessel *C*	345°	345°	345°
$Z_n - C$ Rel.Z_n	94°	15°	292°
Table **1** (DMG, Rel.Z_n) MOO	−2·1	0·0	−18·7
(b) Motion of body, Tbl **2** MOB	0·0	0·0	0·0
9 Intercept, corrected + towards − away *p*	+6·1	−15·6	−17·6

1 Estimated position at the time of fix:		Navigator		
DR/EP:	Lat. ° ′, Long. W ° ′	Height of eye	m/ft	
2 Convert Date/Times:	Year month d h m s	Index Error	on arc − off arc +	
Fix, local date & time	20	Course °T	Temp. °C/F	
Zone Correction W + E − ZT		Speed kn	Pressure mb/in	
Greenwich date & UT UT_f	20	Depart	To	

Observations of			
Local date & watch time DWT	Year month d h m s 20	Year month d h m s 20	Year month d h m s 20
Watch error fast − slow + DWE			
Local time			
Zone correction W + E − ZT			
Greenwich date & UT UT	20	20	20
UT of Fix UT_f			
Fix later + earlier − $UT_f - UT$			
3 Body's position: GHA & Dec or GHAϒ	h m s ° ′ ° ′	h m s ° ′ ° ′	h m s ° ′ ° ′
Increment for mins and secs			
Correction (v, d)/* SHA & Dec		(′ ′)	(′ , ′)
Sum = GHA & Dec for UT			
4 Calculate LHA: ±360°			
Assumed longitude, E + W −			
Sum			
±360° if required			
LHA body = Sum			
5 Main tables: (Lat,Dec,LHA)	Same Contrary °	Same Contrary °	Same Contrary °
Extracted H_c, d, Z	° ′ ′ °	° ′ ′ °	° ′ ′ °
Table **5** (Dec′, d)			
Calculated altitude H_c			
6 Correct sextant altitudes: H_s	′ ° ′	′ ° ′	′ ° ′
Index error on arc − off arc + IE			
Dip, Table **6**a, ht m D			
Sum IE+D			
Apparent altitude H_a			
Alt. corrn. Table **6**/Moon (NA)			
Addn. alt. corrns (see NA)			
Additional ref Table **6**c			
Observed altitude H_o			
7 Calculate intercept: (Step 5) H_c			
Intercept = $H_o - H_c$ p			
Z_n=Z, Z_n=180°−Z, LHA > 180° Z_n=360°−Z, Z_n=180°+Z, LHA < 180° North Lat South Lat. ±Z	°	°	°
True azimuth Z_n	°	°	°
8 (a) Motion of vessel:			
±360° if required			
True track of vessel C			
$Z_n - C$ Rel.Z_n			
Table **1** (DMG, Rel.Z_n) MOO			
(b) Motion of body, Tbl **2** MOB			
9 Intercept, corrected + towards − away p			

RELATED PUBLICATIONS

1. *The Astronomical Almanac* contains ephemerides of the Sun, Moon, planets and their natural satellites, as well as data on eclipses and other astronomical phenomena.

2. *Astronomical Phenomena* contains data on the principal astronomical phenomena of the Sun, Moon and planets (including eclipses), the times of rising and setting of the Sun and Moon at latitudes between S 55° and N 66°, and data on the calendar.

3. *The Nautical Almanac* contains ephemerides at an interval of one hour and auxiliary astronomical data for marine navigation.

4. *Planetary and Lunar Coordinates, 2001–2020* provides low-precision astronomical data for use in advance of the annual ephemerides and for other purposes. It contains heliocentric, geocentric, spherical and rectangular coordinates of the Sun, Moon and planets, eclipse maps, and auxiliary data, such as orbital elements and precessional constants. All the tabular planetary ephemerides are only supplied as ASCII and Adobe's portable document format (pdf) files on an accompanying CD-ROM. The US edition, published by Willmann-Bell Inc., provides all the tabular material in printed form. The CD-ROM only contains the ASCII files.

5. *Rapid Sight Reduction Tables for Navigation* (AP3270/NP303), 3 volumes. Volume 1, selected stars for epoch 2005·0, containing the altitude to 1′ and true azimuth to 1° for the seven stars most suitable for navigation, for the complete range of latitudes and hour angles of Aries. Volumes 2 and 3 contain values of the altitude to 1′ and azimuth to 1° for integral degrees of declination from N 29° to S 29°, for the complete range of latitudes and for all hour angles at which the zenith distance is less than 95° providing for sights of the Sun, Moon and planets. Formally *Sight Reduction Tables for Air Navigation*.

6. *The Star Almanac for Land Surveyors* contains the Greenwich hour angle of Aries and the position of the Sun, tabulated for every six hours, and represented by monthly polynomial coefficients. Positions of all stars brighter than magnitude 4·0 are tabulated monthly to a precision of $0^{s}.1$ in right ascension and 1″ in declination. A CD-ROM accompanies the book which contains the data represented compactly in ASCII files and a portable document format (pdf) version of the almanac.

7. *NavPac and Compact Data for 2001–2005* contains ready-to-use software, algorithms and data, which are mainly in the form of polynomial coefficients, for use by astronomers and others to calculate the positions of the Sun, Moon, navigational planets and bright stars. NavPac is supplied on a CD-ROM and enables navigators to compute their position at sea from observations made with a marine sextant using an IBM PC or compatible for the period 1986–2005. In addition times of rising and setting, distance and course between locations, may be calculated. The tabular data is also supplied as ASCII files. It is published in the United States by, Willmann-Bell Inc., where it is entitled *AstroNavPC and Compact Data 2001-2005*.

Publications 1–5 are prepared jointly by HM Nautical Almanac Office, Rutherford Appleton Laboratory, and the Nautical Almanac Office of the United States Naval Observatory. Items 1 and 3 are published jointly by The Stationery Office (see back cover) and the United States Government Printing Office. *Astronomical Phenomena* (item 2), is published by the USGPO, and is available in the UK from Earth and Sky. TSO also publishes *The Star Almanac* (6) and *NavPac and Compact Data* (7).

Further details about our publications and services may be obtained by writing to H.M. Nautical Almanac Office, or from

http://www.nao.rl.ac.uk/

Please refer to the relevant World Wide Web address for further details about the publications and services provided by the following organisations.

- U.S. Naval Observatory at http://aa.usno.navy.mil/AA/
- The Stationery Office (UK) at http://www.thestationeryoffice.com/
- U.S. Government Printing Office at http://www.access.gpo.gov/
- Willmann-Bell, PO Box 35025, Richmond VA 23235, http://www.willbell.com/
- Earth and Sky, Fieldview Astronomy Centre, East Barsham, North Norfolk NR21 0AR, UK, telephone +44 (0)1328 820083, http://www.earthandsky.co.uk/

2002 July